The Pegans of Martic Township, Lancaster County, Pennsylvania, and Their Descendants in America

Vol. I Direct Lines

By Ann (PeGan) Miller Carr

Pegan Family History

Vol. I Direct Lines

Ann "PeGan" Miller Carr

© Copyright 2020, Ann Miller Carr

All Rights Reserved.

In accordance with the U.S. Copyright Act of 1976, the scanning, uploading, and electronic sharing of any part of this book without the permission of the publisher constitute unlawful privacy and theft of the author's intellectual property. If you would like to use material from the book (other than for preview purposes), prior written permission must be obtained by contacting the publisher at the address below. Thank you for your support of the author's rights.

ISBN: 978-1-948638-01-2

Published by
Fideli Publishing, Inc.
www.FideliPublishing.com

Dedication

For my wonderful husband, David Allen Carr, who encouraged and supported me every step of the way; and my grandsons, Reuben Anthony Miller and Sidney Grayson Miller (and any siblings who may join them).

TABLE OF CONTENTS

Credits .... *ix*

Forward .... *xiii*
    Our Pagan/Pegan Homelands .... *xiv*
    Immigration .... *xvii*
    Spelling and Pronunciation .... *xviii*

Preface .... *xxi*

Introduction .... *xxv*

James Pagan, The Immigrant 1

Andrew Pagan I 5

Andrew Pegan II 11

Robert A. Pegan 19

Andrew Pegan, Son of Robert 27
    6th Generation 30
    7th Generation 47
    8th Generation 76
    9th Generation 102
    10th Generation 119
    11th Generation 124

John Pegan, Son of Robert 153
    6th Generation 156
    7th Generation 168
    8th Generation 193
    9th Generation 211
    10th Generation 221
    11th Generation 225

Henry Pegan 245
    6th Generation 247
    7th Generation 255
    8th Generation 275
    9th Generation 311
    10th Generation 339
    11th Generation 352
    12th Generation 354
    13th Generation 355

Harrison James Pegan 391
    6th Generation 394
    7th Generation 406
    8th Generation 431
    9th Generation 464
    10th Generation 487
    11th Generation 498
    12th Generation 502

Mary Ann Pegan 539
    6th Generation 541
    7th Generation 544
    8th Generation 555
    9th Generation 570
    10th Generation 580
    11th Generation 585
    12th Generation 586

Elsey Pegan 602
    6th Generation 604
    7th Generation 611
    8th Generation 622
    9th Generation 636
    10th Generation 645
    11th Generation 647

William Louis/Lewis Pegan 662
    6th Generation 666
    7th Generation 671
    8th Generation 679
    9th Generation 681

Isaiah Ira Pegan 686
    6th Generation 690

Addendum 693

Appendix 695

Index 719

Credits

I couldn't have written this book without help. I owe so much to my wonderful uncle, Hugh Frederick "Fritz" PeGan, who, at age 90, finally divulged what he knew to me when I asked because, as he said, "Well, Ann Marie, I guess it won't hurt anyone because they're all dead." As my research progressed, I was so gratified that he seemed enthralled with everything I sent him. Bless you, Uncle Fritz, I couldn't have done this without you.

To Jim and Pat Hildreth and their daughter Ginny Ashonosheni, who broke down my biggest brick wall. In early October 2008, I was astonished to see a recent posting on a genealogical website looking for descendants of "Robert and Christina 'Engle' Pagan". For seven years, Robert had been my stumbling block, and I had never been able to find any clues to Christina's maiden name either! I immediately e-mailed the poster, Ginny, and included some information to prove that I was descended from this couple.

Ginny's great-aunt, Virginia Engle, had written a book on their Engle line, published about 1940. After Virginia Engle had sent the manuscript to the publisher, an unknown descendant from the Robert Pegan line found out somehow about her Engle research and sent Virginia the "Robert and Christina 'Engle' Pagan's" bible. Virginia always thought Christina may be a daughter of a Michael Engle, who had children, but their names were either unknown or undocumented. Virginia kept the bible in her closet until she died about 60 years later, but she was never able to connect Christina to any of her Engle lines. Virginia left the bible to her nephew and his wife, Jim and Pat Hildreth. They didn't quite know what to do with it, as it seemed to have little to do with their family. As they were unfamiliar with computers, Jim and Pat asked Ginny, their daughter to help them. So, Ginny posted a query hoping to find a descendant of Robert and Christina's to give the bible to.

When she read my e-mail, she recognized some of the names in the bible and was convinced that I was descended from Robert and Christina. She replied and offered the bible to me. I was amazed and excited. Several days later, I drove to Jim and Pat's to get the bible. I couldn't believe it. It was a treasure trove of information. Without the bible, this book would not have been written. It verified many of my assumptions and revealed so much more. I am forever in debt to the Hildreth family for their generosity.

The first thing I noticed about Robert and Christina's bible was that the surname was spelled "Pegan", not "Pagan".

I am deeply indebted to those Pegan family members from all over the United States who spoke with me about the family. Their facts, reminisces, and anecdotes illustrated the family line, and gave me clues on the family's history and background. Among them are Tamara Brush of Albuquerque, New Mexico and Frances Stanley of Ashland, Virginia, who were particularly generous with information and assistance. Christy Ann Wallace Gall of Columbus, Ohio, great-great granddaughter of Margaret Pegan Roush Warren, gave me information on her grandmother Lora Belle Roush Bussey Brust's line which I couldn't find anywhere else!

As stated above, a special thank you goes to my uncle, Hugh Frederick PeGan, and to (Mattie) Leona Pearson Hatfield, daughter of Sarah PeGan Pearson. Sadly, neither Uncle Fritz nor Leona lived to see this book.

I am especially indebted to the late Connie Abbott Hamilton, Niles, Michigan, granddaughter of Phillip Garl Pegan, who provided all the data on Philip Garl Pegan family in Niles and much encouragement; her aunt, Darlene Pegan Stanley, helped also helped keep the Philip G. Pegan family history and notes; Betty Pegan Corn (Mrs. Harvey) of Kokomo, Indiana, and Florence Marie Flowers Koesters (Mrs. Darin), Toledo, Ohio, granddaughter and great-granddaughter, respectively, of Jesse Pegan informed me about Jesse's line, as did Jim Hastings, Ann Arbor, Michigan, who is married to Liza

Pegan Hastings, another granddaughter of Jesse's. Both Jesse and Philip were brothers of my paternal grandfather, Clanzie PeGan.

I was elated to find Robert Pegan, of New York, a descendant of James Pegan, the son of Andrew Pagan/Pegan II. Bob and his sons are the only Pegans from that line, which I could find, who bear the Pegan surname. Bob sent me maps and information on the Pegan homestead, now underwater at Muddy Run Park near Bethesda, Pennsylvania, in Martic Township, Lancaster County. Bob noted that, when it was flooded in building the Susquehanna Dam, there were still remnants of a sawmill and a foundation on the property—once claimed, but never owned legally, by Andrew Pegan I, and perhaps his father James I, the immigrant, and Archibald, his brother who died young. As Archibald's only child, James "The Miller" Pagan/Pegan, was listed in the Martic Township tax lists in the late 18th century, this James may have operated the sawmill for his uncle. According to the late Roy Pegan of Lancaster, Pennsylvania, a family historian of James, son of Andrew Sr.'s line, the Pegans held family reunions at a large house on the homestead at least until the late 1940s. Roy donated his extensive research on this James' branch to the Lancaster County, Pennsylvania Library and Archives.

I also thank the staffs of innumerable genealogy/local history/research services departments at libraries both university and public, for their patience and assistance, including the staff of the Huntington Room at the Huntington City-Township Public Library, Huntington, Indiana, the Wells County, Public Library, Bluffton, Indiana, the St. Joseph County, Indiana Public Library, South Bend, Indiana (especially Greta Fisher), the Genealogy Center at the Allen County Public Library, Fort Wayne Indiana; the Marion Public Library, Marion, Indiana (Betty Reynolds), the Fayette County Public Library, Connersville, Indiana, the Wabash Carnegie Library, Wabash, Indiana, the Cincinnati Public Library, Cincinnati, Ohio, the Greene County Public Library, Xenia, Ohio, the Lane Library, Hamilton, Ohio and Oxford, Ohio, the Highland County District Library, Hillsboro, Ohio, the Logan County, Ohio Public Library, Bellefontaine, Ohio, the Fairfield County District Library, Lancaster, Ohio, the Wilmington Public Library, Wilmington, Ohio, the Dayton Metro Library, Dayton, Ohio, the Champaign County Library, Urbana, Ohio, the Columbus Metropolitan Library, Columbus, Ohio, the Springfield Public Library, Springfield, Ohio, the Mercer County District Library, Celina, Ohio, the Niles Public Library, Niles, Michigan, the Holbrook History Room at the Coldwater-Branch District Library, Coldwater, Michigan (Dave Renshaw), the Lincoln Library, Springfield, Illinois. the Saint Louis County Library, St. Louis, Missouri, the St. Joseph Public Library, St. Joseph, Missouri, the Minneapolis Public Library, Minneapolis, Minnesota, the Musser Library, Muscatine, Iowa, the Belleville Public Library, Belleville, Kansas, the Harper County Library, Harper, Kansas, the Fort Worth Public Library, Fort Worth, Texas, the Brooke County Public Library, Wellsburg, West Virginia, The Citizens Library, Washington County, Pennsylvania (Ellen Hatfield), the Richmond Public Library, Richmond Virginia (David Kilmon), the Massanutten Regional Library, Harrisonburg, Virginia branch, the Palm Beach County Library, Palm Beach, Florida, the Flower Memorial Library, Watertown, New York (Terry Mandigo), the New York Public Library, New York, New York, the Denver Public Library, Denver, Colorado, the Oakland Public Library, Oakland, California, the Park City Library, Park City, Utah, the Multnomah County Library, Portland, Oregon, the Ontario Community Library, Ontario, Oregon, the Boise Public Library, Boise, Idaho, and the Indiana State Library, Indianapolis, Indiana,

Also, I wish to acknowledge the staffs at these university libraries and historical and genealogical societies: the St. Mary's College Archive Department at the Cushwa-Leighton Library, St. Mary's College, Notre Dame, Indiana (John Kovach); Hesburgh Library, the University of Notre Dame, Notre Dame, Indiana, the University of Florida Library (Melissa Espino), Gainesville, Florida and Florida State University Library, the Southern State Community College, Hillsboro, Ohio. Also, the volunteers and staffs at the Logan County, Ohio Historical Society and Genealogical Society, Bellefontaine, Ohio, the Clinton County Historical Society Library, Wilmington, Ohio, The Ohio Historical Society, Columbus, Ohio, the Ohio Genealogical Society Library, Marion, Ohio, the Fairfield County Historical Society, Lancaster, Ohio, the Erie County Genealogical Society, Sandusky, Ohio (Janis Burke), the Warren

County Genealogical Society, Lebanon, Ohio, the Shelby County Historical and Genealogical Society, Shelbyville, Illinois, the Rock Island County Historical Society, Moline, Illinois, the Pike County Genealogical Society and Museum, Bowling Green, Missouri (especially Harriet Worrell), The Minnesota Historical Society, Minneapolis, Minnesota, the Midwest Historical and Genealogical Society, Wichita, Kansas, The Brown County Genealogical Society, Hiawatha, Kansas, The Harper County Genealogical Society, Harper, Kansas (Gail Bellar), The Historical Society of Missouri, Springfield, Missouri, the Bergen County Historical Society, River Edge, New Jersey, the Giles County Historical Society & Museum, Pulaski, Tennessee, the Natchitoches Genealogical and Historical Association Library, Natchitoches, Louisiana, the Brazoria County Historical Society, Brazoria, Texas, the Wilson-Cobb History and Genealogy Research Library, Roswell, New Mexico, the Marion County Historical Society, Ocala, Florida (Marcia Winne), the Brooke County Historical Society, Wellsburg, West Virginia, The Carnegie Library of Pittsburgh, Pittsburgh, Pennsylvania, the Huntingdon County Historical Society, Huntingdon, Pennsylvania, the Lancaster County Historical Society, Lancaster, Pennsylvania, the Conestoga Historical Society, Conestoga, Pennsylvania, the Pennsylvania State Archives, Harrisburg, Pennsylvania, the Genealogical Society of Siskiyou County, California, Yreka, California, the California State Historical Society, Sacramento, California the Kitsap Historical Society & Museum, Bremerton, Washington, The Family History Library, Salt Lake City, Utah, the Idaho State Archives and Records Center at the Idaho State Historical Society (Peg Schroll), Boise, Idaho, and the Rutherford B. Hayes Presidential Center Library, Fremont, Ohio, along with many other libraries across the United States.

Several staff members at cemeteries and funeral homes were also instrumental, including the Green-Wood Cemetery archivist, Jahongir Usmanov, in Brooklyn, New York and Pieter Visser at the Manasota Memorial Cemetery, Bradenton, Florida, Josh Osborne at the Greenwood Cemetery, DeGraff, Ohio, and Krista Werner from Woodlawn Cemetery in Toledo, Ohio. The staffs at the Glenwood Cemetery, Shelbyville, Illinois, the Fairbury Cemetery, Fairbury, Nebraska, Olinger Crown Hill Mortuary & Cemetery, Wheat Ridge, Colorado, the Flower Memorial Gardens Cemetery, Rockledge, Florida, the Rexburg Funeral Home, Rexburg, Idaho, and the Angeles Abbey Memorial Park Cemetery in Compton, California also provided facts.

I received information from several helpful church secretaries, especially the one at St. Robert Bellarmine Catholic Church in Detroit, Michigan, who asked that her name not be mentioned.

I am also grateful for the help I received at many governmental offices, such as those clerk's and recorder's offices in Huntington County, Indiana (Huntington, Indiana), Grant County, Indiana (Marion, Indiana [Joyce Shaffer]), Miami Co., Indiana (Peru, Indiana), Wabash Co., Indiana (Wabash, Indiana), Highland Co., Ohio (Hillsboro, Ohio), Logan County, Ohio (Bellefontaine, Ohio), Champaign Co., Ohio (Urbana, Ohio), Fairfield County, Ohio (Lancaster, Ohio), Clark Co., Ohio (Springfield, Ohio), Clinton County, Ohio (Wilmington, Ohio), Hamilton County, Ohio (Cincinnati, Ohio), Pike County, Missouri (Bowling Green, Missouri), LaSalle County, Illinois in Streator, Illinois, Cook County, Illinois, Manatee County, Florida (especially their historical records librarian Cincy Russell), Allegheny Co., Pennsylvania (Pittsburgh, Pennsylvania), Lancaster Co., Pennsylvania (Lancaster, Pennsylvania), the Town Clerk in Westerly, Rhode Island and the City Clerk's Office in Clarksville, Missouri. Daniel Bluford at the California State Department of Health was more than generous with his assistance, as was the staff at the Clinton County, Ohio Records and Archives in Wilmington, Ohio.

Several individuals also helped me, such as Rosemary Chandler of Wilmington, Ohio, Norma Karter of Coshocton, Ohio, Mary Ann Rogers of Jersey County, Illinois, and Rebecca Ewing Peterson in Houston, Texas.

Forward

Origin of the Surname Pegan/PeGan

Forebearers.co.uk, an authoritative website dedicated to defining the origins of surnames, has much information on the Pagan name, of which "Pegan" is a derivative: [1]

Forebearers states that, according to the *Dictionary of American Family Names*, edited by Patrick Hanks, the surname "Pagan" is found in two languages, Castilian-dialect Spanish and Northern English/Scottish. However, the name is derived in both languages from the late Latin medieval personal name *Paganus* meaning *"dweller in an outlying village"*.[2] (My beloved husband teases, "Then it really does mean "hick from the sticks.")

In the *Surnames of Scotland,* George Fraser Black notes that Paganus was a common given name among the Normans, with records of such dating back to the early 12th century, even though he admits the surname appeared earlier than 1066:

> "Paganus was a favorite personal name among the Normans (e.g. Paganus de Brausa, 1124, REG., I), and in French was reduced to Payen and Pain and Paine. It is also a pre-Conquest name in (Yorkshire) England, Ralph Pagan occurring in a document of 1055. The word "originally denoted the inhabitant of a pagus or country district. As such people were late in receiving new ideas, the modern notion of pagan developed out of the word" (Giles, A Short manual of comparative philology, 1901, p. 67). "Either in the sense of habitation or patriotism, Pagano was erected into a Christian name in Italy, and Payen in France; whence England took Payne or Pain, still one of the most frequent surnames" (Yonge, p. 202). Paganus was chaplain Glasgow, c. 1180 (Kelso, 338), Uctred filius Pagani gifted the lands of Carnebro to Paisley before 1265 (RMP., p. 310; Pap. Lett., I, p. 107). The surname is found in the west and southwest of Scotland records for more than three centuries back."[3]

Charles Wareing Endell Bardsley in his *A Dictionary of English and Welsh Surnames* states that the name evolved from a given name into a surname, as many surnames did, and cites the *Doomsday Book* and *Gibbon's Decline and Fall of the Roman Empire* among other sources:

> *"This surname is derived from the name of an ancestor. 'the son of Pagan.' A very familiar font-name in the 13th century, and earlier, leaving a large legacy to our directories in the shape of Paine, Payn, Payne, and their other forms (q.v.). Edmundus filing Pagani (Domesday). For a history of this word, v. Gibbon's Decline and Fall. For diminutives, v. Paynel and Pannett.*
>
> Paganus de Vilers, temp. 1109: Lincolnshire Survey.
>
> Geoffrey, s. Paganus: ibid.
>
> Pagan de Shenefeld: Pipe Roll, 11 Henry.
>
> Pagan de Staning: ibid.
>
> Pagan a la Legh, Wiltshire, 1273. Hundred Rolls.
>
> Pagan de la Hale, Kent, ibid.
>
> Roger fil. Pagan, Devon, ibid.
>
> This surname has been gradually shuffled off or changed into Paine, Payne, &c, the bearers not caring to be so entitled. Yet it is one of the most interesting names in our directories."[4]

David Dobson in *The Scottish Surnames of Colonial America* agrees with the authors above that the Pagan surname was introduced into Scotland by the Normans, first as a given name which eventually became a surname. Dobson states the *Ludus Patronymicus (1868) by Richard Stephen Charnock lists the surnames* Pain, Paine, Pane, Pen, Paganellus, Pagnel, Paganel, Paynel; Fitz-Payne or Fitz-Pen, by corruption Phippen, as derivative surnames.[5]

Our Pagan/Pegan Homelands

Our Pagan/Pegan line is "Scots-Irish". They arrived in America around 1737, arriving with other Scots-Irish Covenanters to Drumore and Martic townships in Lancaster Co., Pennsylvania.[6]

Although we can't be 100 percent sure, our Pagan/Pegan line, if not also the name, seems to have originated Dumfries and Galloway region in southwest Scotland (not to be confused with the County Galway in Ireland). The modern Dumfries and Galloway Council Administration district, and area of 2,481 square miles, is comprised of the counties of Dumfriesshire and the two counties which comprise Galloway proper: the county of Wigtown (West Galloway) and the stewartry, sort of a sub-county, of Kirkcudbright (East Galloway).[7] All three of these counties date back centuries. Historically, a concentration of families with the surname Pagan have been found in this region and, later, the county just north of Dumfriesshire in Peebleshire.[8]

Glenda Pagan Hibdon in her *The Pagan, Hunt and Sanderson genealogies*, outlines the family of David Pagan of Virginia (discussed later in the section on Robert Pegan). Hibdon quotes a Scottish history book, *The Birthplace and Parentage of William Patterson,* written by William Pagan of Clayton, near St. Andrew's, in 1865:

> "According to the Compe De Pagan (Paris, 1655), the name Pagan was given to Albertin de Pagan about 980a.d.[sic] by the Italians for having driven the Pagans, or infidel Saracens, from the county there…I do not know in what era or by whom the name was carried to the British Isles (possibly at the time of the Norman Conquest, 1066a.d.[sic] The oldest Scottish record noticed by me where the name appears is a charter by David II to the abbacy of Coldingham in Berwickshire dated at Peebles in 1126, where "Paganus de Braiosa" was one of the witnesses. The same volume also mentions a charter granted by the same Scottish monarch in favor of Malcolm Pagainson, keeper of the king's garden in Edinburgh. The name is to be found in the west of Scotland for nearly three centuries back. At least seven generations of my direct ancestors are buried in Terragles Churchyard near Dumfries."[9]

Sources, like Black's *Surnames of Scotland*, note that the name Ralph Pagan is found on a pre-Norman conquest document in 1055. This could mean the name may have date back into the Middle Ages or even before, into the Dalraidan kingdom in the 5th century.[3]

A second-century map by the Greco-Roman geographer and map-maker Ptolomy shows landmarks in Galloway. According to Ptolemy, the Romans termed the aboriginal residents of Dumfries, the "Selgovae", which may have meant "The Hunters", and the natives of Galloway, "the Novantae", which Sir Herbert Maxwell, writer of *A History of Dumfriesshire and Galloway*, believed was derived from "the people of the river Novios".[10] Although Ptolomy labeled them as Britons, Maxwell described these two aboriginal groups as different from others in Ireland, Scotland and Wales, because they "spoke neither the Welsh form of Celtic" or the Cymric tongue the Britons spoke, "nor the Pictish dialect of Gaelic". He states that they were Picts, yet not the same as other Picts as those that dwelled in the north, and Gaels, but not "in the brotherhood with other Gaels" and thus their land was called that of the stranger Gaels. This suggested earlier contact with Gaelic groups even before the Dal Raitans.[11, 12]

The Dal Raitans, now more commonly referred to as Scoti/Gaels, migrated from central Ireland and established a small kingdom in present-day County Antrim by the 2nd century. Even before the Romans left, they were raiding into Galloway and perhaps Dumfriesshire, although they did not stay there. They did settle permanently north, removing from Ireland to Argyll just after the Romans left the British Isles in 407 A.D. and lent their name to Scotland.[13] But there is evidence that they did trade and intermarry with the native groups in Dumfrieshire and Galloway. The Scoti/Gaels were influenced by the Romans and were Christian, and they may have brought Christianity to the area. The Romans had a sizeable camp in Dumfriesshire, and governed there and to the east, but left Galloway to the native chieftains.[14, 15]

Our surname origin leans toward Dumfriesshire rather than the two Gallowegian counties, as Pagan/Pegan families are registered there in more significant numbers from early censuses up to the present day. The 1881 Census in England lists 159 people with the Pagan surname living in Dumfriesshire, 23 in Kirkcudbright, but none in Wigtownshire. The name appears in other counties in England in 1881, particularly in Lancashire, England, where there are 59, and Larnackshire, Scotland (Glasgow), just north of Dumfriesshire, with 51, and 29 found in Cumberland, England. The name is found in southern English counties, but none has more than 10 Pagan/Pegan residents. It is also present in Irish counties in that country's 1901 census, But the incidence is miniscule, as the county with the most inhabitants with the name Pagan is County Down, Ireland, which only had five.[1]

However, it can't be assumed that our Pagan line was still living in Dumfries and Galloway when they emigrated with other Covenanters to Ireland. Our specific line may have already removed to other parts of the Scottish Lowlands, especially north to the larger cities of Glasgow and Edinburgh. Online sources, such as Scottish marriage records on *FamilySearch.org* lists marriages in the 1700s in Ayrshire, and there are Pagan gravesites on *FindaGrave.com* as far north as Perth and Kinrose and Fife counties in Scotland, in addition to those in Dumfriesshire, that date back into the 1700s.[16, 17]

The Pagans were not members of any Scottish clan. "Clan", taken from the Gaelic "Clann", means children or progeny.[18] Traditionally, a clan meant everyone who lived in a chieftain's territory, or in the territory of someone else, often a minor leader, who had pledged allegiance to a more powerful one. In the beginning, the majority in a clan were related by blood or marriage. In addition, there were septs, families who, for some reason, were not members of a clan but were associated with it, perhaps by marriage or the pledge of allegiance. So, as years passed and with clan boundary changes and population dispersion, clans grew in number—but were times comprised of members who were often unrelated, with many different surnames. Loyalty was owed to the clan first and the kingdom, second.[19]

Genealogists and others separate Scotland into two distinct general groups, Highland Scots and Lowland Scots because of their differences in origins, religion and culture. Historically, until modern times (but some would argue even today), each had disdain for the other, as neither considered the other to be a true Scotsman. Highland Scots were Celtic and Gaelic. Highlanders viewed the Lowlanders, as *English*, not Scottish, because, unlike the Highlanders, Lowlanders were a mix of many peoples and cultures, as explained below. The Lowland Scots considered their kilt-wearing Highland counterparts as untamed, backward barbarians who viewed outsiders as suspicious.[20]

Clans were prevalent and powerful among the Highland Scots, who lived in the north above the Antonine Wall (a Roman fortification marking their northernmost advance into Scotland) or a line from the Firth of Clyde to the Firth of Forth. Two main cultural groups lived in the Highlands: Picts, Dalraidans, or Scoti/Gaels, The Picts, whom most consider Celtic in origin, were the aboriginal inhabitants of the north and east.[21]

Following more than two centuries of raiding (and perhaps non-permanent settlements) in southwestern Scotland, Gaelic Dalraidans, or Scoti/Gaels, had migrated from the area of modern-day County Antrim in Northern Ireland and settled in Argyll and environs, some say beginning as early as the 3rd century, but certainly by the 5th.[22]

The Picts resisted the Romans and all other conquerors until the Vikings, whose inroads in the 9th century forced them to unite with the Kingdom of Dalraida to defeat these invaders. Under a Pict and Scoti/Gael descendant, Kenneth of the Clan MacAlpin, the joint forces stalled the Viking advance. Kenneth MacAlpin, as he is now known, became first king of Alba over both the Highland Picts and the Scoti/Gaels in 844 A.D.[23] However, intermarriage between these groups started hundreds of years before the Alba was established. Both groups had clans, which arose from their tribal aboriginal settlers. So even after these cultures blended, the strength of the clan system continued.

The clans actually grew in power in the 12th century, when Alba absorbed two small kingdoms of Strathclyde, to the east and Lothian (Bernicia) to the southeast, below the old Highlands border, forming the Kingdom of Scotland. (Strathclyde was Brythonic, referring to the Britons, a Celtic people related to the Picts with similar ways and language. Lothian, or Bernicia, was originally a Brythonic area that was invaded and settled by the Angles, a Germanic/Teutonic group, in the 600s.) A century later, King David I of Scotland began introducing the feudal system to the country, a process that took decades to complete, and clan chieftains became earls.[24]

But the clan bonding was still based more on relationships than on land ownership/tenancy. The Highlanders defiant stance and their extremely rugged, mountainous country isolated them, preventing their exposure to the scientific and other advances of the Renaissance through the latter half of the 18th century until George II of England finally gained control of Scotland after the Jacobite uprising. He essentially ended clan domination by sending his son, William, Duke of Cumberland, to kill all clan leaders who opposed him during the ebellion.[25]

Conversely, the Scottish Lowlands in the south and east from the border with England to the Antonine Wall—including Dumfriesshire and Galloway, where our Pagan/Pegan ancestors originated—had no such geographical barriers. The Lowland Scots shared more in common with the English than they did with the Highlanders, as they were a patchwork quilt of many cultural groups—Celtic Britons and Picts, Romans, Scoti/Gaels, Teutons/Norse-Gaels, Angles (also Teutonic), Saxons, Frisians (Flemish), Scandinavian Vikings— through the centuries even before the Normans came in 1066., This is especially true of the border shires, including Dumfries and, to a lesser extent, Galloway.[26] As described, Lowlanders supported the Normans against Saxons in England, and some, including those with the Pagan surname, were rewarded with land, not in Lowland Scotland, but in what is now northern England.[4]

Lowland Scots, like their Highland counterparts, did have a clan system early on, as a remnant of their Brythonic (Briton) aboriginal groups and, in Galloway, early contact with the Scoti-Gaels. This ancient tradition lasted longer Galloway than it did in the rest of the Lowlands, but not nearly as long as it did in the Highlands. Galloway remained in the hands of native chieftains even when the Romans were there and through the ascent of the Scottish kings to the north—until 1234, when the Scottish king Alexander II defeated the Gallowegian chieftains and forced feudalism into the shire. By then the chieftains had become more like English nobles but who paid no fealty to any king.[27] However, the clan system had been replaced by feudalism at least two centuries earlier in Dumfriesshire. After 1066, the land there was divided up and given to Norman barons.[28]

Although the complete history of Dumfries and Galloway is very complicated and too long to discuss in depth here, but a little background will help define the term "Scots-Irish". It will also explain why our Pagan line may have left their homeland for America.

When the Pagans/Pegans left the area of Dumfries and Galloway is uncertain. As mentioned, they may even have migrated to another area in the Lowlands. But chances are they moved from Scotland itself years before boarding a ship to the New World. They were probably among the Scottish citizens who were recruited to live and work in Ulster, or Northern Ireland, in the 1600s.

Dumfriesshire and Galloway throughout time has remained pastoral—horses and cattle, especially dairy cattle, in earlier times (but sheep were never in abundance until the 1800s). The area traditionally does have some agriculture, primarily oats, and fishing, particularly salmon. Insufficient coal and a dearth of lime, and good stone for carving and masonry made it unsuitable for the establishment of a manufacturing base. (The mining of lead and other minerals in Dumfriesshire starting in the late 18th century did boost the local economy somewhat, but mining was never as prosperous as in other areas of Scotland and England.) But the area prior to that was never prosperous. As generations passed, the area's soil tapped out and economic conditions worsened in the late 1600s.[29] The economic hardship and Crown offers of land in Ireland prompted many Lowlanders to leave for Ulster.

Scots-Irish is a term especially associated with "The Plantation of Ulster". Ulster is a province in Ireland. It is historically Northern Ireland, consisting of present counties Antrim, Armagh, Cavan, Coleraine, Donegal, Down, Fermanagh, Monaghan, and Tyrone. Historically this area was sparsely populated and the English, who already ruled the rest of Eire, thought Ulster underused and underproductive.[30] The Gaelic and Catholic clan chieftains/earls controlled the area and resisted English advances until the Nine Years War (1594-1603), where Queen Elizabeth I defeated them and England completed England's total domination of Ireland—a process started decades earlier by her father, King Henry VIII.[31]

Almost immediately after the war, rich businessmen bought huge tracts of land in counties Antrim and Down from the Crown and hired hundreds of Lowland Scots, most of the Presbyterian, to colonize them.[32] King James I, Elizabeth's successor, approved their efforts, knowing that populating Ulster with Presbyterian Scotsman loyal to the Crown would prevent more revolt in the region. Although a few Irish landowners who had supported the English remained, some rebellious native chieftains/earls were also still in the area, especially in west Ulster. In 1607, these earls escaped south, intending to solicit Spain's help in regaining their territory—an effort that failed. James I promptly claimed all their land, and immediately established the "Ulster Plantation", a Crown endeavor to settle the rest of Ulster. Wealthy English and Lowland Scottish landowners were encouraged to buy land and bring their own tenants to Ulster. These Colonists were required to be loyal British (English and Scottish) citizens, English-speaking and Protestant.[33]

Our Pagan/Pegan ancestors may have been among these settlers, who were colonizing Ulster about the same time as the English established the Virginia Colony in Jamestown. However, even more Gallwegians and Dumfriesians flooded Ulster in 1690s, when a dire famine, caused by several years of extremely cold weather, struck far southern Scotland.[34]

Another factor also caused a mass migration from Scotland to Ulster in the late 1600s. Despite their other similarities to England, the citizens of Dumfries and Galloway were mostly loyal to their own Church of Scotland (Presbyterian), founded in the latter half of the 16th century, rather than the Church of England. One of the primary differences between the two were the Presbyterians believed that God was the head of their church, while the Church of England (Episcopalian or Anglican) maintained that the King of England was their church leader. Many Galwegians became Covenanters, Presbyterians who dedicated themselves to keeping Presbyterianism as the only religion in Scotland. But English kings, starting in 1637, were determined to change that, and to force a new, more Episcopalian liturgy in Scottish churches—a "Book of Common Prayer" that the Scotsman considered too Roman Catholic in nature. Through more than a century of religious and civil wars in England and Scotland, Convenanters were eventually defeated, first by Oliver Cromwell in 1650-52, and later, after a rebellion which started in Galloway in 1666, again by 1680. Covenanters were oppressed—and many martyred, by the English until Charles II died and William of Orange assumed the throne (1689) and restored Presbyterianism in Scotland in 1691.[35]

But by 1700 after generations of turmoil, tens of thousands of Covenanters in Galloway, Dumfriesshire, and the rest of the Scottish Lowlands had fled to Northern Ireland to escape the economic conditions, religious persecution and political repression. But the Covenanters found the conditions in Northern Ireland no better. In 1703, the English government passed a law to prevent Catholics from being elected to public office or appointed to civil posts, but the law unintentionally worked against Presbyterians as well. Also, the "plantations" in Ireland had become so successful that they goods they were producing were better than those from England. So the English parliament imposed costly tariffs on goods shipped from Ireland and other laws to protect English trade at the expense of the Scots-Irish in Ulster.[36] By 1717-1740, legions of Covenantors removed from Northern Ireland for America for the same reasons they'd left Scotland.[37] Our Pagans/Pegans were among them.

Immigration

Our Pegan ancestors left the Belfast, Ireland area and arrived in America, along with about a dozen other Convenanter Scots-Irish families, settling first in Drumore and Martic townships in the southwestern part of Lancaster Co., Pennsylvania, according to the section on Martic Township in *History of Lancaster County, Pennsylvania, with Biographical Sketches of Many of Its Pioneers and Prominent Men*: "The southern part of the township was settled by the Scotch-Irish Covenanters about the year 1740 or 1742..."Among the earliest settlers were the following: David Jones, John Marshall, William Andrews, James Stewart, the Duncans, Grays, Dixons, Boyds, Steeles, McCaughlins, Robinsons, Whorrys, Whites, Pegans, and Soskes. None of their descendants, as far as known, now live in the township, except the Pegans..."[38] However, but records in the Lancaster County, Pennsylvania Historical Society Library and Archives indicate the date was earlier, possibly 1737-1739.[39]

According to the section on Martic Township in Ellis and Evan's *History of Lancaster County, Pennsylvania...*, the township is named for a Native American tribe who lived on Pequa Creek, the townships northern border. Martic Township is also bordered by Providence township to the northeast and east (partially), and Drumore township to the east (partially) southeast and south, and the Susquehanna River to the west. The land in the eastern portion of Martic Township is even, but the rest is gently rolling, becoming especially hilly in the center of the township and sloping in the west towards the river. Extensive lime deposits make most of the township very fertile for both the abundant natural flora and agriculture.[40]

Exactly how many Pagans/Pegans immigrated is not certain. But early records indicated males were an older James, a younger James, an Andrew, and an Archibald. The latter three seem to be the elder James' sons. All are found in Martic township records. Another brother, or possibly a nephew, Alexander, either came with them or shortly afterwards, but by 1763 he left Martic Twp. for Fishing Creek, Chester Co., South Carolina.[9] In this book, Alexander Pagan is considered a son of the immigrant James Pagan I.

Spelling and Pronunciation

The original spelling of the surname in Scotland was Piggon. (*Pig*-gon). Later, the surname evolved into the spelling Pagan, pronounced Pah-*gawn*.

After our Pagan/Pegan line arrived in the Pennsylvania Colony, there are innumerable spellings of the surname found on documents, including Pagan, Pegan, Pigon, Pegon, Pagon, Pigan, and more— with one or two "g"s. The primary spelling, however, was Pagan for the most part, until about the Revolutionary War, when "Pegan" began to emerge as the preferred spelling in some lines. Andrew Pegan II/Jr. used this spelling, but his brother, John, continued to use Pagan. Andrew Jr.'s son Robert spelled it both ways, while his brother Alexander, like his uncle John, kept the original spelling. But by 1850, every male in the line was using "Pegan". It can be surmised that the spelling change happened because of the connotation associated with the "Pagan" spelling as literacy became more common.

Lines throughout America also pronounce the surname differently. Some emphasize the first syllable, others the second. My line pronounces it "*Pee*-gan", with a short "a". The lines in the Highland County, Ohio region say it like the word "pagan". Descendants around Clarksville, Missouri put the emphasis on the second syllable, "Pug-*gan*".

My great-grandfather Harrison PeGan Jr. was the first to capitalize the "G". It appears on his marriage license to Angeline Stout. No one knows why he did this. Perhaps he just wanted to give his name a "flourish" or distinction to show his separation from other Pegan lines. However, at least one other line also capitalizes the "G".

Endnotes

1. "Pagan Surname Meaning & Statistics", *Forebearers, 2012-2017*. Website: *http://forebears.co.uk/surnames/pagan*

2. *Dictionary of American Family Names*, Patrick Hanks, ed. Vol. 3, New York: Oxford University Press; 2003, pg. 38.2013. Genealogy Center, Allen County Public Library, 900 Library Plaza, Fort Wayne, IN.

3. Black, George F. *The Surnames of Scotland: their origin, meaning and history*. Edinburgh: Birlinn; 1999, Reprinted 2004, p. 644 (first published by the New York Public Library, 1946). Genealogy Center, Allen County Public Library, 900 Library Plaza, Fort Wayne, IN.

4. Bardsley, Charles Wareing Endell, *A Dictionary of English and Welsh Surnames, With Special American Instances*. Baltimore: Clearfield Co.; 1967, p. 579. Genealogy Center, Allen County Public Library, 900 Library Plaza, Fort Wayne, IN.

5. Dobson, David. *The Scottish Surnames of Colonial America*. Baltimore: Genealogical Publishing Co.; 2003, pg. 115. Genealogy Center, Allen County Public Library, 900 Library Plaza, Fort Wayne, IN.

6. "from days long past…Martic Township, 275 Years of History 1705-1980", by Larry E. Hess, Southern Lancaster Historical Society Newsletter, July-September 2013, pg. 6; Southern Lancaster, Pennsylvania Historical Society, Quarryville, Pennsylvania. Copy at the Conestoga Historical Society, 51 Kendig Road, Conestoga, PA.

7. "Dumfries and Galloway", Wikipedia, retrieved July 25, 2018; https://en.wikipedia.org/wiki/Dumfries_and_Galloway

8. Lewis, Penny and Fergus Smith, "Surnames Beginning with 'P'", Old Scottish Genealogy & Family History, Greylags, Mayfied, Findo Gask, Tibbermore, Perthshire. Webiste, https//www.oldscottish.com/surnames-p.html

9. Hibdon, Glenda Pagan, Pagan, Hunt and Sanderson Genealogies, Knoxville, Tennessee: Tennessee Valley Publishing; 1994, frontspiece/introduction; quoting Pagan, William, *The Birthplace and Parentage of William Patterson, Founder of the Bank of England, and Projector of the Darien Scheme: With Suggestions for Improvement in the Scottish Registers*, Edinburgh: W.P. Nimmo; 1865. Genealogy Center, Allen County Public Library, 900 Library Plaza, Fort Wayne, IN.

10. Maxwell, Sir Herbert, *A History of Dumfriesshire and Galloway*. Second edition. Edinburgh and London: William Blackwood & Sons; 1900, pg. 3. Genealogy Center, Allen County Public Library, 900 Library Plaza, Fort Wayne, IN.

11. *Ptolemy, Bk. II, Ch. 2. Trans. Albion island of Britannia- First Map of Europe from Stevenson*, Edward Luther and Fischer, Joseph; Ptolemy, *The Geography*, New York Public Library, New York; 1991 (limited edition) Ptolemy (c. 140), Thayer, Bill, ed., Geographia, LacusCurtius website at the University of Chicago, published 2008; http://penelope.uchicago.edu/Thayer/E/Gazetteer/Periods/ Roman/_Texts/Ptolemy/home.html#Text

12. Maxwell, A History of Dumfriesshire and Galloway, pg. 5. Ptolemy, Bk. II, Ch. 2. Trans. Albion island of Britannia- First Map of Europe from Stevenson, Edward Luther and Fischer, Joseph, The Geography, Ptolemy, New York Public Library, New York; 1991 (limited edition) *Ptolemy* (c. 140), Thayer, Bill, ed., *Geographia*, LacusCurtius website at the University of Chicago, published 2008, retrieved 2008-04.

13. Maxwell, *A History of Dumfriesshire and Galloway*, pg. 31.

14. Maxwell, *A History of Dumfriesshire and Galloway*, pg. 10.

15. Maxwell, *A History of Dumfriesshire and Galloway*, pg. 22.

16. "Scotland Marriages, 1561-1910", Pagan surname, FamilySearch.org, Website, https://www.familysearch.org/search/collection/results?count=20&query=%2Bsurname%3Apagan~&collection_id=1771074

17. Find A Grave, findagrave.com, search for Pagan burial sites, Website, https://www.findagrave.com/memorial/search?firstname=&middlename=&lastname=pagan&birthyear=&birthyearfilter=&deathyear=&deathyearfilter=&location=Scotland&locationId=country_50&memorialid=&datefilter=&orderby=&page=1#sr-186134103

18. Way of Plean, George; Squire, Romilly; *Squire Clans & Tartans*. Glasgow: Harper Collins; 2000, pg. 21. Genealogy Center, Allen County Public Library, 900 Library Plaza, Fort Wayne, IN.

19. Way of Plean, *Squire Clans & Tartans*, pg. 28-29.

20. McDonald Tate, Shannon, "Scotland: Differences Between Highlanders and Lowlanders", Scottish Dream Tours, 21 Jan 2010, http://scottishdreamtours.blogspot.com/2010/01/scotland-difference-between-highlanders.html

21. Foster, Sally M., *Picts, Gaels and Scots*. London: B.T. Batsford/Historic Scotland; 2004; pg. 11-13. Theodore M. Hesburgh Library, 221 Hesburgh Library, University of Notre Dame, Notre Dame, IN.

22. Sharpe, Richard, "The thriving of Dalriada" in Simon Taylor (ed.), *Kings, Clerics and Chronicles in Scotland 500–1297*. Dublin: Fourt Courts; 2000, pg. 47-50. Theodore M. Hesburgh Library, 221 Hesburgh Library, University of Notre Dame, Notre Dame, IN.

23. Maxwell, *A History of Dumfriesshire and Galloway*, pg. 40.

24. "Balance of New and Old", G. W. S. Barrow, ed., *The Charters of King David I: The Written acts of David I King of Scots, 1124–1153 and of His Son Henry Earl of Northumberland, 1139–1152*. Woodbridge, England: Boyton & Brewer; 1999, pg. 9-11. Theodore M. Hesburgh Library, 221 Hesburgh Library, University of Notre Dame, Notre Dame, IN.

25. Clee. Nicholas, Eclipse. London: Black Swan; 2011, pg. 42.

26. Maxwell, *A History of Dumfriesshire and Galloway*, pg. 31-33.

27 Maxwell, *A History of Dumfriesshire and Galloway*, pg. 62.

28 Maxwell, *A History of Dumfriesshire and Galloway*, pg. 59.

29 Pryde, George S., *Scotland from 1603 to the present day*. London: Nelson; 1982. Indiana University-Purdue University Library, 755 West Michigan Street, Indianapolis, IN.

30 Bardon, Jonathan, *A History of Ulster*. Belfast: Blackstaff Press; 2001, Pg. 75. Genealogy Center, Allen County Public Library, 900 Library Plaza, Fort Wayne, IN.

31 Lecky, William Edward Hartpole, *History of Ireland in the Eighteenth Century, Vol. 1*. London: Longmans, Greens and Co., 1913, pg. 4-6. Theodore M. Hesburgh Library, 221 Hesburgh Library, University of Notre Dame, Notre Dame, IN.

32 Perceval-Maxwell, M., *The Scottish Migration to Ulster in the Reign of James I*. Belfast: Ulster Historical Foundation; 1999, pg. 55. Theodore M. Hesburgh Library, 221 Hesburgh Library, University of Notre Dame, Notre Dame, IN.

33 Canny, Nicholas, *Making Ireland British, 1580-1650*. London: Oxford University Press; 2003, pg. 200-201, 208-209. Theodore M. Hesburgh Library, 221 Hesburgh Library, University of Notre Dame, Notre Dame, IN.

34 Cullen, Karen J., *Famine in Scotland: The 'Ill years' of the 1690s*. Edinburgh: Edinburgh University Press; 2010, pg. 176. Theodore M. Hesburgh Library, 221 Hesburgh Library, University of Notre Dame, Notre Dame, IN.

35 Maxwell, *A History of Dumfriesshire and Galloway*, pg. 261-286.

36 Leyburn, James G., *The Scotch-Irish: a social history*, Chapel Hill, N. Car.: University of North Carolina Press; 1989, pg. 90-94. Genealogy Center, Allen County Public Library, 900 Library Plaza, Fort Wayne, IN.

37 Fischer, David Hackett, *Albion's Seed: four British Folkways in America*. New York: Oxford University Press; 1989, pg. 608-11. Genealogy Center, Allen County Public Library, 900 Library Plaza, Fort Wayne, IN.

38 Ellis, Franklin and Evans, Samuel, *History of Lancaster County, Pennsylvania, with Biographical Sketches of Many of Its Pioneers and Prominent Men*, Philadelphia: Everts & Peck, 1883; pg. 968. Mishawaka Heritage Center, Mishawaka Penn-Harris Public Library, 209 Lincolnway East, Mishawaka, IN.

39 Interviews with the staff at the Lancaster Historical Society Library and Archives, 11 & 12 July 2013, 230 North President Avenus, Lancaster, PA.

40 Ellis, Franklin and Evans, Samuel, *History of Lancaster County, Pennsylvania…*, pg. 967-8.

Preface

Our line of Pegans came from Scotland about 1737 to Lancaster County, Pennsylvania, settling in Martic Township. This book will concentrate on the lines of Andrew Pagan/Pegan Sr., his son, Andrew Jr., and Andrew Jr.'s son Robert. But in colonial America there were a handful of other families with the Pagan/Pegan surname:

1. The Nipmuc tribal members, who may have been mixed Scottish and Native American descendants of a Scottish immigrant, Alexander Piggon, who is recorded in New London, Connecticut in 1695.[1] Men with the Pagan surname, most likely from this line, were Revolutionary War soldiers from New England colonies. Eleazer and Thomas from Connecticut, Darias (Darius?) and Thomas of Rhode Island, Samuel of Massachusetts.[2] They had progeny in those states, some of whom, according to census records, may have later migrated to New Jersey.

2. An Isaac "Pigon", an unmarried Quaker, is found in the Quaker records in 1736-7, gets a transfer certificate on June 27, 1738 from "Meeting near Grange at Charlemont" to return to Ireland at the request of his father. He never seems to return to the colonies. He seemed to be the only Pegan in his family to have immigrated.[3]

3. Harbott, Pagan, and sons William and John Pagan, Scots-Irish immigrants in the 1600s to Dorchester County, Maryland. Later, most of their descendants changed the surname spelling to "Pagon". Harbott died on Taylor's Island in 1744.[4] William was a lawyer.[5, 6] John was on the tax list in Dorchester County in 1783.[7] These marriages were recorded in that county:

    a. A widow, Elizabeth, who married John Wollen in 1747,
    b. A daughter, Priscilla, who married Aaron Jones on September 13, 1785,
    c. A son, Henry Jr., who married Keziah Travers on December 28, 1790,
    d. A daughter, Elizabeth, who married Philamon Simmons on November 20, 1794,
    e. A Jane Pegan who married Jacob Travers on July 19, 1781.[8]

4. The Canadian Pagans: Loyalists William Pagan, Jr. and his brothers Robert and Thomas the sons of William and Margaret Maxwell Sr. of Glasgow, Scotland. William Jr. immigrated to New York State in 1769. He and his son John were Loyalists who fled to Canada during the Revolutionary War. William, a "merchant skipper" lived in New Brunswick and died on March 12, 1819 in Fredericton. John, a merchant, went to Quebec and died on October 8, 1799.[9] William's brother Robert came to America about the same time as William Jr., but settled in Portland, Maine, which was then still in the Massachusetts colony. Thomas joined him shortly afterwards. They were involved in the timber trade and in shipbuilding. When the Revolutionary War broke out, Robert and Thomas fled to the West Indies. After the war, they returned to the Northeast, this time in New Brunswick. They continued in the timber trade, founded a prosperous shipping company, and also had retail interests in New Brunswick and Nova Scotia. Robert became politically influential and one of the richest men in Canada at the time; he died in St. Andrews in 1821.[10] These Pegans/Pagans also seem unrelated to our line, at least in America. Their line may join with our Pagan/Pegan line in Scotland or in Ireland/Ulster, however.

5. An Abraham Pagan, who was ordered on January 13, 1779 in Surry Co., North Carolina to report for jury duty on February 2nd of that year.[11] However, Abraham may not be a Pagan; the surname may be a misspelled.

6. A Lucy Pagan, who appears in the 1790 census in Clarendon, South Carolina, with two males under age 16 and one female.[12] Lucy may somehow related

to Alexander Pagan, the son (or possibly a nephew) to James Pagan I and a brother to James II, Archibald and Andrew Sr. of Lancaster County, Pennsylvania. Alexander Pagan and his sons left Lancaster County for Fishing Creek, Chester Co., South Carolina in 1763.[13] But Chester County is quite a distance from Clarendon, and the sons' spouses and children are all accounted for.

7. There is a Pagan River (sometimes seen as Pagan Creek or, lesser, as Pagan Bay or Point) in Isle of Wight County, Virginia near Smithfield and Jamestown and flows into the James River. records. The river was first called the New Haven River, but between 1737 and 1743 it was changed to the Pagan River. Why this name, and why the name was changed, is not certain.[14] However, the word may have been a derived from the Algonquin word for "nut", "pakan", and the pecan trees are numerous in Virginia and the southern United States.[15]

8. A Quaker Monthly Meeting house, called Pagan Creek, in Isle of Wight County founded prior to 1702 and disbanded in 1752.[16]

9. The name is found early in Virginia. A James Pagan arrived in colonial Virginia in 1688, one of 52 Englanders brought there as "headrights" (men who were promised 50 acres of land after seven years of indentured servitude) by Lemuel Mason, Thomas Jarves and Thomas Willoughby, who on April 28 of that year received a 2600-acre patent for land near Currituck, in what was then the county of Lower Norfolk, Virginia (now in North Carolina), from Francis Lord Howard, the crown governor of the Virginia Colony.[17] A John James Pagan came to the colony in 1709.[18] Either he or another John Pagan witnesses a deed between the Trustees of Fredericksburg, Virginia to Lawrence Washington of Prince William Co., Virginia on August 7, 1739 and September 4th of the same year between the same trustees and John Waller of Spotsylvania County, Virginia?[19, 20] He is undoubtedly the same John Pagan, who, with two others, sailed up the James River from Dumfries, Virginia, to establish Alexandria, Virginia in November 1748 is listed as a colonial soldier in that state. He may or may not have been the ancestor of a Joseph Pagan who is found on the 1782 tax list in Bedford County, Pennsylvania.[21] Joseph, in turn, may be related to David Pagan of Pagan's Creek, Franklin County, Virginia a Revolutionary War soldier.[22] Bedford County and Franklin County are adjacent. Also, David Pagan named one of his sons "Joseph". David Pagan received bounty land in Randolph County, Illinois on Nine-Mile Creek near Kaskaskia.[23] David's first wife, said to be Elizabeth Farrell, died before the Revolutionary War. He left his young son, Joseph, with neighbors while he was away fighting under Gen. George Rogers Clark. David Pagan returned to Virginia after the war and married Mary Harmon on October 8, 1795 in Franklin County, Virginia. He then left again for Kaskaskia. Joseph stayed in Virginia, residing in Bedford and Franklin counties, before removing to Preble County, Ohio before 1820. By 1835, he had settled in LaPorte County, Indiana. This Joseph Pagan/Pagin, was the master carpenter of Preble and Montgomery counties, Ohio, who trained several sons of Robert Pagan/Pegan of the Lancaster County, Pennsylvania line.[24, 25] Moreover, one of Robert's sons, William Louis, married Joseph's daughter Drusilla. These Pagan lines seem to be related, but how is not yet known.

According to census records, after the American Revolution, these Pegans/Pagans were joined by:

1. A George Pegan, who is found in Ripley Co., Indiana in 1820.[26] He is not found in any other records, and his surname may have been misspelled.

2. Patrick Pagan, who immigrated from Ireland or Scotland to western New York by 1830.[27]

Both of these seem to have no connection to our Pagans/Pegans from Lancaster County, Pennsylvania. After 1850, there were many more with the surname Pagan or Pegan or a spelling variation immigrating from Scotland, Ireland, France, Germany, Czechoslovakia and even Hungary. Of course, there are legions of Pagans in the U.S. who have Hispanic backgrounds. There were Pegans who settled in Cochranton, Crawford Co., Pennsylvania, who are not related to the Lancaster County line.

Endnotes

1. Dobson, David, *Scottish Surnames of Colonial America*. Baltimore: Genealogical Publishing Co: Clearfield Co.; 2003, pg. 115. Genealogy Center, Allen County Public Library, 900 Library Plaza, Fort Wayne, IN.

2. Compiled Service Records of Soldiers Who Served in the American Army During the Revolutionary War, 1775-1783, Ancestry.com.

3. Myers, Albert Cook, *Immigration of the Irish Quakers into Pennsylvania, 1682-1750: with their early history in Ireland*. Baltimore: Genealogical Publishing Co.; 1969, pg. 364. Genealogy Center, Allen County Public Library, 900 Library Plaza, Fort Wayne, IN.

4. Family Data: Madeleine K. Pagon Brownell, Philadelphia, Pennsylvania, 2005. Ms. Brownell was a frequent poster on Genealogy.com on this family line. (Genealogy.com, Online database: https://www.genealogy.com/forum/surnames/topics/pagan/258/

5. Skinner Jr., V.L., "Thomas Skinner", 110.285; TA/ L13.0.6; 1772. *Abstracts of the testamentary proceedings of the Perogative Court of Maryland*, Westminster, Maryland: Family Line Publications, 1988. Genealogy Center, Allen County Public Library, 900 Library Plaza, Fort Wayne, IN.

6. Calvert County, Maryland, Will of John Bowling (09 Jul 1686), 9:32 A L 103.14.2; Maryland State Archives, 350 Rose Boulevard, Annapolis, MD.

7. Maryland Indexes, Tax Assessment of 1783, Index, 1783, Dorchester County, MSA S 437, entry for John Pagan. Maryland Archives, Online database: https://msa.maryland.gov/msa/stagser/s1400/s1437/html/1437do.html

8. "All Maryland, Compiled Marriages, 1655-1850, Ancestry.com, entries for Pagan (all in Dorchester County).

9. David S. Macmillan and Roger Nason, "Pagan, William", in *Dictionary of Canadian Biography*, vol. 5, University of Toronto/Université Laval: 2003–, accessed July 26, 2018, http://www.biographi.ca/en/bio/pagan_william_5E.html.

10. David S. Macmillan and Roger Nason, "Pagan, Robert", in *Dictionary of Canadian Biography*, vol. 5, University of Toronto/Université Laval: 2003–, accessed July 26, 2018, http://www.biographi.ca/en/bio/pagan_robert_6E.html.

11. Surry County, North Carolina, Court Minutes, Volume 1. North Carolina State Archives, 109 East Jones Street, Raleigh, NC.

12. 1790 U.S. Federal Census, Ancestry.com, Year: 1790; Census Place: Clarendon, South Carolina; Series: M637; Roll 11; Page 211; Image: 136, entry for Pagan, Lucy.

13. Ellis, Frank and Samuel Evans, *History of Lancaster County, Pennsylvania: with biographical sketches of its pioneers and prominent men*. Philadelphia: Everts & Peck; 1883, pg. 974. Mishawaka Heritage Center, Mishawaka Penn-Harris Public Library, 209 Lincolnway East, Mishawaka, IN.

14. Boddie, John Bennet, *Seventeenth Century Isle of Wight County, Virginia*. Baltimore: Genealogical Publishing Co; 1938, pg. 510. Genealogy Center, Allen County Public Library, 900 Library Plaza, Fort Wayne, IN.

15. "It's 'PEE-kan' not pick-AHN'", The Science of the South.com (website), 24 Nov 2014, Craig McLain, The Science of the South, http://www.scienceofthesouth.com/its-pee-can-not-pick-ahn/

16. Hinshaw, William Wade, *The Encyclopedia of Quaker Genealogy, 1750-1930, Vol. VI*. Ann Arbor: Edwards Bros.; 1938-, pg. 39. Genealogy Center, Allen County Public Library, 900 Library Plaza, Fort Wayne, IN.

17. "Currituck Co., NC Land & Deeds", Currituck County, USGENWEB, sources: Jones, Gary and Gordon C., *Abstracts of Wills and Other Records, Currituck and Dare County, North Carolina, 1663-1850*, Baltimore: Genealogical Publishing Co.; 1958, reprinted 1991, pg. Lower Norfolk, Virginia and Land Office Patents, No. 7 (microfilm reel 7), pg. 655, Thomas Jarvis, et. al., Library of Virginia, 800 East Broad Street, Richmond, VA. USGENWEB, Online database: http://www.ncgenweb.us/currituck/deeds/miscearly.html

18. Filby, P. William, Meyer, Mary K., *Passenger and immigration lists index: a guide to published arrival records of about 500,000 passengers who came to the United States and Canada in the seventeenth, eighteenth, and nineteenth centuries. 1982-1985 Cumulated Supplements in Four Volumes*. Detroit, Mich: Gale Research Co., 1985; pg. 580, 590.

19. Spotsylvania County, Virginia, Deeds, Deed Book C-1734-1742, pg. 147, Trustees of Fredericksburg, Virginia to Lawrence Washington, 07 Aug 1739. Spotsylvania County, Clerk of the Circuit Court, 9107 Judicial Center Lane, Spotsylvania, VA.

20. Spotsylvania County, Virginia, Deeds, Deed Book C-1734-1742, pg. 148, Trustees of Fredericksburg, Virginia to John Waller, 04 Sep 1739. Spotsylvania County, Clerk of the Circuit Court, 9107 Judicial Center Lane, Spotsylvania, VA.

21. "1782 Bedford County Tax Lists", Virginia Appalachian Notes, Vol. 5, No. 1 (Feb 1981); Vol. 5 No. 2 (May 1981).

22. U.S., Compiled Revolutionary War Service Records, 1775-1783, Ancestry.com; Pagan, David, Clark's Illinois Regiment, Virginia State Troops, card #39190357.

23. Walker, Harriet J., *Revolutionary Soldiers Buried in Illinois*. Los Angeles: Standard Printing Co., 1918. Reprinted by Genealogical Publishing Co., Baltimore, 1967, pg. 126. Genealogy Center, Allen County Public Library, 900 Library Plaza, Fort Wayne, IN.

24. "James R. Pagin", *History of Porter County, Indiana: A Narrative History of its Progress, its People and Principal Interests*. Chicago: Lewis Publishing Co.; 1912, pg. 692. Genealogy Center, Allen County Public Library, 900 Library Plaza, Fort Wayne, IN.

25 Gilbert, Audrey, *Twin Valley Tidbits, 1888-1897, Vol. III*. West Alexandria, Ohio: A. Gilbert; 1999, pg. 72. Lynchburg Public Library, 102 Main Street, Lynchburg, OH.

26 1820 U.S. Federal Census, Ancestry.com, Year: 1820; Census Place: *Ripley, Indiana*; Page: *77;* NARA Roll: *M33_15;* Image: 51; entry for Pagan, George.

27 1830 U.S. Federal Census, Ancestry.com, Year: 1830; Census Place: *Salina, Onondaga, New York*; Series: *M19;* Roll: *100;* Page: *32;* entry for Pagan, Patrick.

Introduction

Growing up with a name like "P-e-G-a-n" wasn't easy. Few pronounced it correctly the first time. Often, I was asked, "What kind of a name is *that*?" or "Where did *that* name come from?" And, in particular, "Why is the G capitalized?" and "Are you an (American) Indian?"

These were questions I couldn't answer. My father, Kenneth PeGan, never talked about the family history. Twice, when I was about 10 or 12, I asked him where our PeGan family was from. The first time he answered, "French Canada"; the second, "Alsace-Lorraine." I've found no evidence that the PeGans were Canadian. (However, my father was correct—but it was about his mother's family. I've discovered the Schetzszle ancestors of my paternal grandmother, Josephine Schetzszle PeGan, *were* from Alsace-Lorraine. Also, Josephine Schetzszle's maternal grandparents, Hugh and Anna Ferrin McNarney, emigrated from Northern Ireland to Ontario, Canada in 1836 and two years later settled in Niagara Co., New York.)

Also, about the same time, I asked my paternal grandfather, Clanzie PeGan, what his parents' names were. He told me "Harrison and Angeline." But he would say no more about his background. In fact, he and my father were as stone-faced as the presidents on Mount Rushmore regarding our family history.

This only made me wonder more about my maiden name, and about my ancestors. I told myself when I was just a young girl that someday I was going to find out. And I was going to find out why my grandfather and father were so reluctant to talk.

When I was 15, I saw the name "Pegan" for the first time—that is, outside of the Huntington, Indiana phone book. I'd found a book on the American Revolution in the Huntington library, and it talked about Native-Americans who fought in the Colonial army. These Pegans were from New England. I was convinced that this was the reason why my father and grandfather weren't talking about the family background—that we were American Indian, and they were embarrassed and ashamed of it. In the first half and more of the 20th century, being Native American or mixed Indian-white wasn't considered socially acceptable.

A year or so later in one of my high school classes, I discovered that Algonquin-speaking tribal units did have a word "pegan" in their language. In a college anthropology college course, I learned the Piegan are one of the major tribal units of the Blackfoot nation, who also have an Algonquin language. I explored deeper into the possibility that my family was Native American. My curiosity was especially piqued when I found that the one of the most noted civil chieftains of the Miami nation was Pacanne. As the Miami, an Algonquin-speaking tribe which migrated into Indiana from Pennsylvania, resided in northeastern Indiana area where I was born, this only made me more convinced that maybe the PeGans were American Indians. By then, I was almost positive that when I finally had time to research my family background, I would discover we were Native American.

When I finally started my Pegan surname research in earnest in 1999, I quickly found references to those Native American's who'd fought in the American Revolution—a Pegan/Pagan family who were Nipmuc, a Massachusetts tribe whose language wasn't an Algonquin language. I traced what I could about this Pagan/Pegan surname in Massachusetts and Connecticut, but it didn't connect with my family.

But I still persisted in my thinking that my family was Native American in some way. To my surprise, I found out I was wrong all those years, and that *our* PeGans weren't American Indians after all.

I can't claim that in my 20 years of research that I've found all the answers, but I've discovered much about the Pegan/Pagan families who came to America. This book outlines what I've learned.

James Pagan, The Immigrant

1. **James[1] Pagan** was born about 1690 in Dumfries or Gallaway, Scotland or Ulster, Ireland. James immigrated to Port of Philadelphia, Philadelphia Co., Pennsylvania, or the Port of Baltimore, Baltimore, Maryland, about 1736. He seems to have died in Martic Twp., Lancaster Co., Pennsylvania, between April 1747 and November 1749. James Pagan I, the eldest immigrant ancestor, was probably born in either Dumfries or Galloway, Scotland or in Ulster, Ireland. (Ulster is a general term for Northern Ireland counties.)

James Pagan I arrived with his sons Archibald, Andrew and James II, amongst a group of other Scots-Irish to Drumore and Martic townships in southwestern Lancaster Co., Pennsylvania between 1736-1738. The exact date of their arrival is not known. Although they probably arrived at the port of Philadelphia, they could have immigrated through the port of Baltimore.[1]

These Scots-Irish were from Ulster. According to the chapter on Martic Township in Ellis and Evans' *History of Lancaster County, Pennsylvania...*:

> "The southern part of the township was settled by the Scotch-Irish Covenanters about the year 1740 or 1742...Among the earliest settlers were the following: David Jones, John Marshall, William Andrews, James Stewart, the Duncans, Grays, Dixons, Boyds, Steeles, McLaughlins, Robinsons, Whorrys, Whites, Pegans and Soskes."[1]

(Note: The 1740-1742 date is considered too late now, as two historians at the Lancaster County Historical Society in Lancaster, Pennsylvania told this author in July 2013).

The family legend as told by the descendants of Alexander Pagan, the son of James Pagan I, claims that Alexander and his sons emigrated from County Antrim, Ireland to Lancaster Co., Pennsylvania.[2] It is unknown if Alexander and his sons immigrated to Martic Township with James I and his other sons, Archibald, Andrew and James II, or whether they came later, perhaps in the 1750s. However, some of the Scots-Irish Covenanters in this immigrant group are known to have originated in County Derry.[3]

Deed records show James Pagan I never owned land in either township, or anywhere else. (The tax records for Lancaster Co. prior to 1751 are not extent.) This implies that he was a tradesman who rented his living and working space, or perhaps he was a farmworker. However, as he served on a jury and was the executor of an estate (see below), he was probably a tradesman.

James Pagan I served as a juror in a Lancaster Co., Pennsylvania court case on August 4, 1741. The court case involves William Steele, who was charged with fornication with Elizabeth Miller. Steele was found not guilty.[4] This is the first mention of the Pagan family in the United States. His surname is spelled "Pagan" in the reference.

James Pagan I was the executor of Charles Wallace's estate on April 2, 1747.[5] Charles Wallace lived in Bethlehem Twp., Lancaster Co., Pennsylvania; his children were Mary, Jean, Elizabeth, Margaret and Robert. (There is an outside possibility that this was James Pagan Jr., son of James I, the immigrant father. But as the younger James would be barely of age, if that, this is highly unlikely.) The relationship between the Wallaces and the Pagans is unknown.

As James Pagan I is not mentioned in his son Archibald's will, dated November 17, 1749, there is a good chance that James I was deceased by then.[6] There are no other references found for James Pagan I after the Charles Wallace will in 1747.

From "from days long past...Martic Township, 275 years of History, 1705-1980", by Larry E. Hess:

"Bethesda

One of the earliest settlers in this area was James Pagan who came here in 1736, and following him, were familiar names such as David Jones, John Marshall, William Andrews, Jacob Clark, Thomas McLaughlin, Aaron Dunkle, James Stewart, Divans, Boyds, Steeles and Robinsons.

It is uncertain as to the origin of the name Bethesda; but early writing list the name of the area as "Pagan's Fancy." A patent for this land was issued to Andrew Pagan (1810).

In 1883, Bethesda contained 100 inhabitants, two stores, a Methodist Church, one resident physician, one public school, and post office."

In 2013, the post office and stores were long gone, but there is still a small, unincorporated settlement which appears on some Lancaster County maps. The Methodist Church is still active but is now located about a mile from Bethesda. There is, however, a church of another denomination in the settlement.[7]

(Note: Mr. Hess appears to contradict himself in "The History of Martic Township" a chapter in the *Millersville-Penn Manor Community History*, published by that area's Bicentennial Committee in 1976. In this article, Hess says that the Pagans/Pegans arrived in Martic Township in 1746. Perhaps, as he said in his earlier writings that the Pagans/Pegans immigrated in 1736 and known to have been in Lancaster County in 1741, Hess' "1746" in this article was a typographical error.[8])

James married **Unknown Unknown** before 1714 in Scotland?. They had four sons. Unknown Unknown was born in Dumfries or Gallaway, Scotland or Ulster, Ireland. Unknown died in Scotland, Ulster, Ireland or Martic Twp., Lancaster Co., Pennsylvania?. Nothing is known of the wife of James Pagan/Pagan I. She may have died in Ireland before her husband and sons left for America, or died, most likely before James I did, in Martic Twp., Lancaster Co., Pennsylvania.

Sons of James Pagan and Unknown Unknown:

m I. **Alexander[1] Pagan** was born in Dumfries or Gallaway, Scotland or Ulster, Ireland, about 1714. He died in Fishing Creek, Chester Co., South Carolina?, after 1763.

m II. **Archibald Pagan** was born in Dumfries or Gallaway, Scotland or Ulster, Ireland, in 1717.[9] He died in Martic Twp., Lancaster Co., Pennsylvania, on November 20, 1749, at the age of 32.[9] Archibald was buried in Old Chestnut Level Presbyterian Lower Cemetery, Drumore Twp., Lancaster Co., Pennsylvania.[9]

m III. **Andrew Pagan** was born in Dumfries or Gallaway, Scotland or Ulster, Ireland, about 1724. He immigrated to Port of Philadelphia, Philadelphia Co., Pennsylvania, in 1745. He died in Martic Twp., Lancaster Co., Pennsylvania, between September 9, 1788 and January 13, 1789.[10]

m IV. **James Pagan II** was born in Dumfries or Gallaway, Scotland or Ulster, Ireland, about 1726. He died in Mifflin Twp., Allegheny Co., Pennsylvania?, after 1787.

Endnotes

1. Ellis, Frank and Samuel Evans, *History of Lancaster County, Pennsylvania: with biographical sketches of its pioneers and prominent men*, Philadelphia: Everts & Peck; 1883, pg. 680. Mishawaka Heritage Center, Mishawaka Penn-Harris Public Library, 209 Lincolnway East, Mishawaka, IN.

2. Collins, Anne Pickens, *Heritage History of Chester County, South Carolina, Vol. 1*; ed. by Louise Gill Knox, Chester, South Carolina: Chester County Historical Society, 1982, pg. 199. The Genealogy Center, Allen County Public Library, 900 Library Plaza, Fort Wayne, IN.

3. Interview with volunteers at the SOLANCO Historical Society, 1932 Robert Fulton Highway, Quarryville, PA, Ann Miller Carr, author, July 2013.

4. *Lancaster County., Pennsylvania, Quarter Sessions Abstracts (1729-1742), Book 1*, ed. by Gary T. Hawbaker. Hershey, Pennsylvania: Gary T Hawbaker; 1986, pg. 104. Originals at the Lancaster County, Pennsylvania Archives, 230 North President Avenue, Lancaster, PA. Greene County Room, Greene County Public Library-Xenia Community Library, 76 East Market Street, Xenia, OH.

5. Charles Wallace will (1747), Lancaster County, Pennsylvania Will Book A: Vol. 1: 128. Lancaster County, Pennsylvania Archives, 150 North Queen Street, Lancaster, PA.

6. Archibald Pagan will (1749), Lancaster County, Pennsylvania Will book J: Vol. 1: p.163. Lancaster Co., Archives, 150 North Queen Street, Lancaster, PA.

7. "from days long past…Martic Township, 275 Years of History 1705-1980", by Larry E. Hess, Southern Lancaster Historical Society Newsletter, July-September 2013, pg. 6; Southern Lancaster, Pennsylvania Historical Society (SOLANCO), 1932 Robert Fulton Highway, Quarryville, PA. Copy at the Conestoga Historical Society, 51 Kendig Road, Conestoga, PA.

8. Larry E. Hess, "History of Martic Township", *Millersville-Penn Manor Community History*; ed. By Robert E. Coley, James A. Jolly and Carole L. Slotter. Millersville, Pennsylvania: Produced by the Research Committee of the Millersville-Penn Manor Bicentennial Committee, 1976, pg. 80. Conestoga Historical Society, 51 Kendig Road, Conestoga, PA.

9. Find A Grave—Old Chestnut Level Presbyterian Cemetery, Find A Grave.com, Archibald Pagan, Find A Grave Memorial #159014964.

10. Andrew Pegan will (1787), Lancaster County, Pennsylvania Will Book F: Vol. 1: 84-86. Lancaster County, Pennsylvania Archives, 150 North Queen Street, Lancaster, PA.

Andrew Pagan or Pegan I

1. **Andrew[2] Pagan or Pegan** (*James[1]*) was born about 1721 in Dumfries or Galloway, Scotland or Ulster, Ireland. He was the son of James Pagan and **Unknown Unknown.** Andrew I died in Martic Twp., Lancaster Co., Pennsylvania, between September 9, 1788 and January 13, 1789.[3]

Andrew immigrated either through the Port of Philadelphia or the Port of Baltimore around 1736-7, with his father James and brothers Archibald and James II, and other Scots-Irish Covenanters from Northern Ireland.[1, 2] His brother Alexander came later.

His surname is Pagan in most documents, but, like on his will, the surname is Pegan.

Andrew I worked as a sawmill owner and yeoman (a farmer who owns a small farm).

Andrew married **Ann(?) Unknown** (perhaps McDowell)? about 1742 in Lancaster County, Pennsylvania? They had seven known children. Ann Unknown was born in Dumfries or Gallaway, Scotland or Ulster, Ireland. Ann died in Martic Twp., Lancaster Co., Pennsylvania, before September 9, 1788, as she is not mentioned in her hus-band's will.[3]

Although her given name is not proven, her husband, Andrew Pegan I mentioned two granddaughters named Ann in his will: Ann, the daughter of their son James Pegan and Ann Herran, daughter of Margaret Pegan Herran. In addition, Jane/Jean Pegan Lusk also named a daughter Ann. Since it was customary among British families to name a daughter after a grandmother, and Ann is the only name known to be common in Andrew I's daughter's families, it is highly likely his wife was named Ann.

Of their seven known children, one, their eldest son Alexander, died as an unmarried man at age 22-23 years old. Two daughters, Jane/Jean Pagan Lusk and Mary Pagan Downing, moved from Martic Twp., Lancaster Co., Pennsylvania with their husbands and families, along with some other families belonging to Muddy Run Presbyterian Church, to Fishing Creek, Chester Co., South Carolina in the early 1760s after raids by Native Americans during the French and Indian War. Their remaining daughter, Margaret Pegan/Pagan Herron, and youngest son Andrew Pegan II removed to Washington Co., Pennsylvania after Andrew I's death. Andrew II later moved to Brooke Co., (West) Virginia and Highland Co., Ohio. Son John Pagan lived in Philadelphia, Pennsylvania and Gallipolis, Gallipolis Twp., Gallia Co., Ohio. Only their son James Pegan would remain in Martic Township.

The earliest record of Andrew I appears in 1749, when his brother Archibald's will was proved. In his will, Archibald entrusts his only child, James, to his brother Andrew to raise and educate.[4]

Andrew and his brother James appear on the earliest extent tax record for Martic Twp., Lancaster Co., Pennsylvania, in 1751. Andrew Pagan/Pegan is listed on the 1751 Lancaster County tax list as "Andrew Peagon" and on the 1754 tax list as "Andrew Pagon". Subsequent tax lists have him as "Andrew Pagan".[5]

Andrew Pegan/Pagan was the tax collector for Martic Township, Lancaster Co., Pennsylvania in 1776:

> January 26, Friday
> Today's Officer of the Day is Ensign Fortine and his Sergeant is Henry Geiger.

Adam Reigart, County Treasurer, in his settlement with the Commissioners, today listed the following tax collectors: Jacob Krugh, Lancaster Borough; MichaelShank, Lancaster Township; Christian Swarr, Hempfield; John Kreamer, Manor; Abraham Kendig, Conestoga; Andrew Pegan, Martick; James Moore, Drumore;...[5]

Andrew Pagan was named as overseer to the will of John McDowell in York Co., Pennsylvania. John McDowell bequeaths to his daughter Mary, wife of Isaac Williams, his daughters Elizabeth and Agnes and sons William and John. The relationship between the McDowells and the Pagans/Pegans is unknown.[6]

In 1779, Andrew Pagan Sr. signs a petition from Martick Twp., Lancaster Co., Pennsylvania to the governing body of the Commonwealth of Pennsylvania endorsing the new Pennsylvania constitution and asserting that there was no need to call a new state convention to revise it. His son Andrew "Andy" Pegan/Pagan II signs below his father's signature. Andrew Sr.'s son James and James' sons, and his brother James and his sons also sign this document.[7]

When Andrew Sr. died in 1789, he willed the property to his son James. The following is the will of Andrew Pegan I, as written:

> Andrew Pegan, decd.}} In The Name of God Amen
>
> I, Andrew Pegan, Sr, of Martick Township, Lancaster County and state of Pennsylvania, yeoman, being mindfull of Mortality and knowing that it is appointed for all men once to die, do make this my last Will and Testament in the manner following that is to say, recommending my soul to the Hands of God that gave it, nothing doubting, but that I will have the same again by the mighty power of God at the day of the Great Resurrection and for my Body I recommend the same to the Earth to be buried in a Christian and decent like manner at the direction of my Executors, and I do order that all my just debts and other my funeral charges be duly paid and for all my worldly Estate wherewith it hath pleased God to Bless me in this life I give and dispose of the same in the following manner. I give and bequeath to my well beloved Son, John Pegan the one half of my part of the Stock, such as Cows sheep and hogs, likewise eight pounds lawfull Money to be paid of the Land one year and half after my decease, likewise my large Poot [Pot] and little Walnut table. I give and bequeath to my well beloved son James Pegan, the whole land I now live on with all the Horses and his half of the moveable stock such as cows, sheep, and hogs now in his Possession. I give and bequeath to my well beloved son Andrew Pegan, the other half of my part of cows, sheep and hogs with all my wearing or Body cloths [clothes]. I give and bequeath to my well beloved daughter Jean Lusk, the sum of seven shilling and six pence. I give and bequeath to my well beloved Daughter Margaret Herran, the one half of my Puter [Pewter] and to my Granddaughter Ann Herran, the other half of the Puter [Pewter]; to wit, four dishes and twelve plates to be equally divided between them both. I give and bequeath to my well beloved Daughter Mary Downing, the sum of seven shilling and six pence. I give and bequeath to my Granddaughter Ann Pegan, daughter to son James Pegan, my Father [feather] Bed and Bed Cloths such as Rugs and Blankets. And do hereby nominate and appoint my two trusty Friends, John Caldwell and James Pegan, my son, to be my Executors of this my last Will and Testament ratifying and confirming this and no other to be my last Will and Testament. In Witness whereof I have hereto set my hand and seal this ninth day of September, Anno Domini 1788.
>
> his
> Andrew A Pegan <seal>
> mark
>
> Signed sealed published pronounced and declared by the said Andrew Pegan the Testator as his last Will and Testament in the presence of us, the Subscribers.
>
> s/ Hugh Penny; s/ John Maffet

Lancaster County ss: On the thirteenth day of January Anno Domini 1789, before me personally appeared Hugh Penny and John Maffet, the two subscribing Witnesses to the above and foregoing Will and on their Solemn Oath by uplifted hand respectively did depose and say that they were present and saw and heard Andrew Pegan the Testator therein named, sign, seal, publish, pronounce, and declare the said above writing as and for his last Will and Testament, and that at the doing thereof, he was of sound and well deposing Mind, Memory, and Understanding, to the best of their Knowledge, Observation, and Belief.s/ James Jacks, Regr.

Be It Remembered that on the thirteenth day of January Anno Domini 1789, the last Will and Testament of Andrew Pegan, late of Martick Township has been approved in due form of Law and Letters of Testamentary therein were granted to John Caldwell and James Pegan, the Executors therein named, they being fit and truly qualified well and truly to administer the Estate of the Decd. and especially to Exhibit a true and perfect Inventory thereof into the Registrars Office at Lancaster within one Month from this date and to render a just and true account of their Administration on the said Estate within one year or when thereunto lawfully required. Given under the Seal of said Office.

Recorded James Jacks, Regr.s/ James Jacks, Regr.[3]

However, although Andrew Sr. bequeathed his property to his son James, there is a problem. Extensive searches performed by this author for land warrants or patents issued, as mandated by Pennsylvania colonial and subsequently state law, to Andrew Pegan/Pagan I, or deeds or legal titles to any land, yielded nothing in Lancaster County.

A letter from Aaron McWilliams, a historian at the Pennsylvania State Archives, states:

"We did not find a record for Andrew or James Pagan/Pegan (Note: Andrew's father) for the periods specified in your request (Note: 1735-1790) in the state land records. However, the records noted above and attached pertain to the land claimed by Andrew Pagan at least as early as the 1760s. Based on the information in your request and our findings, Andrew Pagan either squatted on the land or purchased the land from someone with no claim to the land besides physical possession and improvements. If such transaction occurred, it doesn't appear to have been recorded."[8]

Several deeds and warrants/patent surveys do mention that lands others buy are adjacent to "Andrew Pagan" or "Andrew Pagan's claim" as early as 1763. On January 15, 1763, Andrew's own brother, James Pagan II, buys 203 acres from Benjamin Arnold mentioned as adjacent to Andrew Pagan's:

"All that Tract of Land Situate in Martock (sic) Township in the said County joyning (sic) Widow Steels Plantation on the East side & Thomas Whites on the North Side and Andrew Pagans on the West and South Sides..."[9]

McWilliams also notes that the warrant survey map for Elizabeth "Luske" (Lusk), in 1763 *(Warrant B-20-19)*, and the one for Robert Gill in 1769 *(Warrant B-4-29)* show "Andrew Pagan's Claim". Robert Gill's warrant survey map *(Warrant B-4-29)* cites "Andrew Pagon" lives on the land on the east and southeast of the warranted land. John McLaughlin's warrant survey map in 1790 *(Warrant C-142-188)* misspells his name as "Andrew Regan's Claim", although it is clearly the same land as it appears in the other two survey maps and Andrew Pagan/Pegan Sr. was deceased by that time. But according to Aaron McWilliams, a research historian at the Pennsylvania State Archives in Harrisburg, Pennsylvania, Andrew Pagan/Pegan never had legal title to this land and no legal patent or warrant papers were ever filed.[8]

McWilliams and this author believe Andrew Pegan I may have acquired this land by squatting on it himself, or he bought it from another man who did not have legal title to the property. There is a possibility that Andrew I's father James I, or perhaps Andrew's brother Archibald, squatted on it first and then either sold it or gave it to Andrew I. Interestingly, Archibald Pagan, who died in 1749, mentions that he has land in his will, but, again, no deed is recorded for it and no warrant or patent was applied for in Archibald's name either.[4, 8]

It wasn't until November 11, 1795 that Andrew I's son, James Pegan, applies for a warrant and pays 10 pounds Pennsylvania currency to purchase the property his father, and perhaps his grandfather James I. and his uncle Archibald, squatted on for years. The warrant was for 100 acres in Martic Township, Lancaster Co., Pennsylvania and is named as "Pegan's Fancy". On the warrant application, James Pegan states he has lived on this land "for about 10 years".[10]

The land was surveyed on February 22, 1797 *(Survey Book B4, pg. 29, #185As122Ps)*. The land, according to the survey, was adjoining the lands of George McGlaughlin (sic, McLaughlin), Samuel Ankrim, John Long (deceased) and Patrick "Cample" (sic, Campbell) and others".[11] James Pegan received a patent for this land on February 6, 1810.[12, 13]

James Pegan's warrant and survey and the other aforementioned surveys clearly show that the James Pegan who took out the warrant and patent was the son of Andrew Pagan/Pegan Sr., although he is referred to on the 1790 census as "James Pagan Jr." He may have been cited as this because his much older cousin, James Pagan, the miller and son of Archibald Pagan, Andrew Pegan/Pagan Sr.'s brother, was still a resident of Martic Twp., Lancaster County. Although he is not enumerated in the census, James, the son of Archibald, still appears on the Martic Twp. tax lists. (Often on colonial and early American tax lists, if there were two men with the same name on the tax lists, the elder was referred to as "Sr." and the younger as "Jr.", even though they were not father and son.)[5, 10, 11, 12, 13]

That Andrew Pagan/Pegan's land, even without legal title in 1788, was inherited by his son James Pagan/Pegan is evident in a deed for land belonging to the late John Long of Drumore Township, Lancaster Co., Pennsylvania. The deed, drawn up on April 2, 1800 and recorded on May 17, 1803 to settle John Long's will, was between the grantors "Hugh Long and Others", the children of John Long, and grantee Peter Baughman. The deed mentions the land is in Martic Township adjacent to "the land of Andrew Pagan" which was now in the hands of "James Pagan":

> "Whereas, Thomas and Richard Penn, Proprietaries and Governors of Pennsylvania, Patent dated September 8, 1769, granted unto John Long, of Drumore township, Lancaster County, aforesaid. All that certain tract of land in Martick township, Coxanty of Lancaster, in the then Province of Pennsylvania, bounded and described as follows, Beginning at a marked maple tree, thence by lands of Andrew Pagan, now James Pagan...Said Patent recorded in Patent Book AA, Vol, II, page 118..."[14]

According to an article, "The History of Martic Township" by Lancaster County, Pennsylvania historian Larry E. Hess, Andrew Sr.'s land, which was near the village of Bethesda, also contained a sawmill.[15]

Mr. Hess, however, mistakenly cites Andrew Pagan's name as "Adam" Pagan in the article. However, James Pegan, the son of Andrew Sr., may not have operated it. The operator of the sawmill is always listed in the Martic Township, tax lists as "James Pegan, the miller" and he is always found on the freeman's list, which means he was not married. This James seems to be the son of Archibald Pagan, who became the ward of his uncle, Andrew Pegan/Pagan Sr. This James Pagan, the miller is found on Martic Twp. tax lists from 1773-1800.[5]

James Pegan's descendants held this land for many generations afterwards. Roy D. Pegan, a descendant of James and Pegan family historian who lived in Lancaster, Pennsylvania, says James Pegan's descendants held reunions until the early 1950s at a house built by James' son Andrew on "Pegan's Fancy" in 1851.[16]

The land was acquired, either by purchase of by public domain, by the Susquehanna Electric Company to build the Coniwingo Dame and two reservoirs, the Coniwingo and the Muddy Run. The project was completed in 1968. The Pegan land is underwater at the 1000-acre Muddy Run Reservoir, the upper reservoir. The electric company, now called Excelon Generation, created a 500-acre recreational facility, Muddy Run Park, on the north edge of this reservoir several years later. According to Robert Pegan, another descendant of James Pegan's and one of the few in his line with the surname, says the entire land tract, including a large home which descendants built in the early 1900s, is now underwater in the park about 100 feet from the water's edge. Robert Pegan believes that part of the foundation from Andrew Pagan/Pegan Sr.'s sawmill still existed when the land was flooded.[17]

Children of Andrew Pagan or Pegan I and Ann(?) Unknown:

+ 2 f I. **Jane**[3] **Pagan** was born in Martic Twp., Lancaster Co., Pennsylvania, about 1743. She died in York, York Co, South Carolina, about January 1821. Married **Robert Lusk.**

+ 3 f II. **Mary**[3] **Pagan** was born in Martic Twp., Lancaster Co., Pennsylvania, about 1746. She died in Fishing Creek, Chester Co. South Carolina, on March 19, 1832. Mary was buried in Fising Creek Presbyterian Cemetery, Chester, Chester Co., South Carolina.[18] Married **John Downing.**

+ 4 m III. **Alexander**[3] **Pagan** was born in Martic Twp., Lancaster Co., Pennsylvania, about 1749. He died in Martic Twp., Lancaster Co., Pennsylvania, between about 1773 Alexander, Andrew Sr.'s eldest son, is found on the 1761-1763 Martic Township, Lancaster County, Pennsylvania "freeman's" tax lists for single men of age as "Alexander Pagan, son of Andrew". But he does not appear in subsequent tax lists. As he is not mentioned in his father's will, it seems he died about 1763.[3,5]

+ 5 m IV. **James**[3] **Pegan** was born in Martic Twp., Lancaster Co., Pennsylvania, in 1752. He died in Martic Twp., Lancaster Co., Pennsylvania, on January 20, 1834. James was buried in Old Chestnut Level Presbyterian Lower Cemetery, Drumore Twp., Lancaster Co., Pennsylvania.[19] Married **Sarah Brannon.**

+ 6 f V. **Margaret**[3] **Pagan** was born in Martic Twp., Lancaster Co., Pennsylvania, before 1754. She died after 1790. Married **John Herron/ Herran.**

+ 7 m VI. **John**[3] **Pagan** was born in Martic Twp., Lancaster Co., Pennsylvania, about 1754. He died in Gallipolis, Gallipolis Twp., Gallia Co., Ohio, between 1819 and 1820. Married first **Ann Chorry/Cherry,** married second **Mary Margaret Russell.**

+ 8 m VII. **Andrew**[3] **Pegan II** was born in Martic Twp., Lancaster Co., Pennsylvania, between September 16, 1756 and December 31, 1756.[20] He died in Union Twp., Highland Co., Ohio, on September 16, 1825.[20] Married **Mary Unknown.**

Endnotes

1. Drumore and Martic Township histories, Southern Lancaster County, Pennsylvania Historical Society (SOLANCO), 1932 Robert Fulton Highway, Quarryville PA.

2. Ellis, Franklin and Samuel Evans, *History of Lancaster County, Pennsylvania with biographical sketches of many of the pioneers and prominent men.* Philadelphia: Everts & Peck; 1883, pg. 969. Mishawaka Heritage Center, Mishawaka Penn-Harris Library, 209 Lincolnway East, Mishawaka, IN. Note: Although the book cites the date as 1745, volunteers at the Southern Lancaster Historical Society told the author that this date is too late. The Scots-Irish came to southwestern Lancaster County around 1737-8. As James Pegan I, the father of Andrew I, serves on a jury in 1741, the 1745 date has to be incorrect.

3. Andrew Pegan will (1788), Lancaster County, Pennsylvania Will Book F: Vol. 1: 84-86. Lancaster County, Pennsylvania Archives, 150 North Queen Street, Lancaster, PA.

4. Archibald Pagan will (1749), Lancaster County, Pennsylvania Will Book J: Vol. I: 163. Lancaster County, Pennsylvania Archives, 150 North Queen Street, Lancaster, PA.

5. Pagan/Pegan entries, Lancaster County, Pennsylvania Tax Lists, 1751-1800, Microfilm, Roll #23, Genealogy Center, Allen County Public Library, Fort Wayne, IN.

6. John McDowell will (1770), York County, Pennsylvania Will Book D: 217. York County, Pennsylvania Archives, 150 Pleasant Acres Road, York, PA.

7. "Memorials Against Calling a Convention, 1779", *Pennsylvania Archive Series: Series 2, Vol. III*; ed. by Samuel Hazard, et. al. Harrisburg, Pennsylvania: C.M. Busch; 1875, pg. 359. Family History Library, 35 North West Temple, Salt Lake City, UT.

8. Letter, along with warrant survey documents and maps, from Aaron McWilliams, research historian at the Pennsylvania State Archives, Harrisburg, Pennsylvania, to author Ann Miller Carr on July 24, 2015.

9. Lancaster County, Pennsylvania Deeds, Benjamin Arnold to James Pegan, Lancaster County, Pennsylvania Deed Book C: 436-438 (15 Jan 1763). Lancaster County, 150 North Queen Street, Lancaster, PA.

10. "Warrant Registers, 1733-1957." {series #17.88, RG-17, Records of the Land Office, Lancaster County, Pennsylvania, pg. 175, James Pegan, #323. Pennsylvania Historical and Museum Commission, Bureau of Archives and History, Pennsylvania State Archives, 350 North Street, Harrisburg, PA; Online database: http://www.phmc.state.pa.us/bah/dam/rg/di/r17-88WarrantRegisters/Lancaster/175.pdf.

11. Letter, along with warrant survey documents and maps, from Aaron McWilliams, research historian at the Pennsylvania State Archives, Harrisburg, Pennsylvania, to author Ann Miller Carr on July 24, 2015. Commonwealth of Pennsylvania, Lancaster County, Survey Book B4, pg. 29, James Pegan, #185As122Ps. Original document at the Pennsylvania State Archives, 350 North Street, Harrisburg, PA.

12. Letter, along with warrant survey documents and maps, from Aaron McWilliams, research historian at the Pennsylvania State Archives, Harrisburg, Pennsylvania, to author Ann Miller Carr on July 24, 2015. Commonwealth of Pennsylvania, Lancaster County, Patent Book H, No. 3, pg. 135, James Pegan, #323. Original document at the Pennsylvania State Archives, 350 North St., Harrisburg, PA.

13. "Patent Indexes, 1684- {ca 1957} {series #17.147, 154 & 155}. RG-17, Records of the Land Office, Lancaster County, Pennsylvania, H series, Vol. 1, 1809-1823, pg. 270/273, James Pegan. Pennsylvania Historical and Museum Commission, Bureau of Archives and History, Pennsylvania State Archives, 350 North Street, Harrisburg, PA; Online database: http://www.phmc.state.pa.us/bah/dam/rg/di/r17PatentIndexes/H1809-23PatentIndex273.pdf.

14. Lancaster County, Pennsylvania Deeds, Hugh Long and others to Peter Baughman, Lancaster County Deed Book N: Vol. 3: 305 (02 Apr 1800). Lancaster County, Pennsylvania Archives, 150 North Queen Street, Lancaster, PA.

15. Hess, Larry E., "The History of Martic Township", *Millersville-Penn Manor Community History;* ed. by Robert E. Coley, James A. Jolly and Carole L. Slotter. Millersville, Pennsylvania: Produced by the Millersville-Penn Bicentennial Committee, 1976, pg. 80. Conestoga Area Historical Society, 51 Kendig Road, Conestoga, PA.

16. Roy D. Pegan file, Archives, Lancaster County Historical Society, 230 North President Avenue, Lancaster, PA.

17. "Muddy Run Pumped Storage Facility" in Wikipedia. n.d. https://en.wikipedia.org/wiki/Muddy_Run_Pumped_Storage_Facility. Also phone interview with Robert Pegan, Rochester, NY, Ann Miller Carr, author, 19 Mar 2017.

18. Find-A-Grave--Fishing Creek Presbyterian Cemetery, Chester, Chester Co., South Carolina, Find A Grave.com.

19. Find-A-Grave—Lower Chanceford Presbyterian Cemetery, Drumore Twp., Lancaster Co., Pennsylvania, Find A Grave.com.

20. Family Data: Robert and Christina "Engle" Pegan family bible, American Bible Society, Brattleboro(ugh), Vermont: Holbrook & Fessenden, 1828. In possession of the author, Ann Miller Carr.

Andrew Pegan II

1. **Andrew**[3] **Pegan II** (*Andrew*[2] *Pagan, James*[1] was born between September 16, 1756 and December 31, 1756 in Martic Township, Lancaster County, Pennsylvania.[1, 2] He was the son of Andrew Pagan and Ann Unknown. Andrew died in Union Twp., Highland Co., Ohio, on September 16, 1825.[2] He was buried in Highland Co., Ohio.[3, 4, 5]

In contrast to his father, Andrew Pagan Sr., his surname is Pegan in most documents, but sometimes the name is Pagan.

Andrew served in the military in 1776 as a marine on the Pennsylvania Navy's ship *Montgomery* during the Revolutionary War.[1]

He was a weaver by trade.[1, 6, A]

Andrew Pagan/Pegan II first appears as a "freeman" on the Martic Twp., Lancaster Co., Pennsylvania tax records in 1777, also indicating he has reached his majority age but had not yet married. In 1779, he is listed on the freeman tax list in Martic Twp. as a weaver. As he appears on the Martic Twp. tax list with his father and other heads of families in 1780, Andrew Jr. may have married in late 1879 or early 1780. He is also listed with the heads of families in 1781 in Martic Twp., but he is not assessed with any land.[6]

Andrew II married **Mary Unknown** in Lancaster Co., Pennsylvania around 1780.[2] They had five known children. Mary Unknown was born in Lancaster Co., Pennsylvania?, between January 1, 1750 and September 13, 1750.[1, 7, 8, 9] Mary died in Union Twp., Highland Co., Ohio, on September 13, 1825.[2]

Mary's maiden surname is unknown. According to Andrew II's Revolutionary War pension application and census records, Mary was about five to six years older than Andrew II.[1] She may have been a widow prior to her marriage to Andrew II, as this was often seen in this era if a wife was several years her husband's senior. Perhaps her first husband died in the Revolutionary War.

Andrew and Mary had two sons and three daughters, but only four are traceable; one daughter is not found. Eldest daughter Elizabeth Pegan Goudy and her family lived in Wheeling, Ohio Co., (West) Virginia. Sons Alexander and Robert followed their parents to Ohio, Robert to Highland County like his parents then to Montgomery County. Alexander went to Brown County, adjacent to Highland County. Youngest daughter Mary Pegan VanAusdall also removed to Ohio, but eventually settled in Jersey Twp., Jersey Co., Illinois.

In 1779, Andrew Pegan II signs a petition from the men of Martic Twp., Lancaster Co., Pennsylvania to the governing body of the Commonwealth of Pennsylvania endorsing the new Pennsylvania constitution and asserting that there was no need to call a new state convention to revise it. He signs as "Andy Pagan" below his father Andrew Sr.'s signature. Andrew II's uncle James and James' sons, and his brother James also sign this document.[10]

Andrew Pegan II served in the Pennsylvania Navy during the Revolutionary War on the ship *Montgomery*, according to *The Officers and Men of the Pennsylvania Navy, 1775-1781*. Although he states in his pension application that he served 21 months in the Navy, he is registered in Pennsylvania Navy records as enlisting on March 20, 1776 but "ran away" on June 25th of that year.[11]

He left the *Montgomery* with four other young marines. According to a Philadelphia, Pennsylvania newspaper (which may be the *Pennsylvania Gazette*) the ship's captain, William Brown, advertised a $20 reward for the capture of all the deserters, four dollars for each. The article describes Andrew II as:

> "ANDREW PEGAN, country born, about 19 years of age, 5 feet 8 or 9 inches high, straight and well made, a weaver by trade, supposed to have gone to his father's in

Martick township, Lancaster county… Whoever takes up said Deserters and brings them on board said ship, or confines them in jail, shall have the above reward…"[A]

It is unknown whether anyone collected the reward.

It is not recorded in the Navy records if he returned, but his pension was approved, indicating that he most likely did—either by choice or by force. When he returned to his ship, he could have faced punishment (probably a heavy flogging, the usual punishment for such desertion) and served the rest of his stated time. If he did return to the *Montgomery*, as believed, he was on the ship when the British frigate *Levant* defeated the *Montgomery* on March 8, 1777 on the Atlantic Ocean. The *Montgomery* eluded capture, however.[12]

Confusingly, there was another ship named *Montgomery*, built in New York, in the fledgling Continental Navy. On its maiden voyage, This *Montgomery* ran aground on a sandbar in the Hudson River on the way to New York's Fort Saratoga in October 1777. The crew scuttled the vessel attempting to block the British Navy on the way to attack the fort. This was not the ship *Montgomery* on which Andrew Pegan II served..[13]

Although *The Officers and Men of the Pennsylvania Navy, 1776-1881* and his pension clearly state he served in the Pennsylvania Navy or "Pennsylvania Sea Service", it seems he may have actually served in the Virginia Navy.[1, 11] Andrew Pegan II is not listed in *The Revolutionary Patriots of Lancaster County, Pennsylvania*, by Henry Peden, Jr.[14] But least two sources, Brumbaugh's *Revolutionary War Records, Virginia, Virginia Navy, Vol. 1*, Gusathmey's, *John H., Historical Register of Virginians in the Revolution*, cite Andrew Pegan II as serving in the Virginia Navy.[15, 16]

There is no confusion, however, as to his role on the ship, *Montgomery*. Andrew II was a marine. According to C.R. Smith's *Marines the Revolution: A History of the Continental Marines in the American Revolution*, a marine's duty is to be the first to disembark to attack the enemy on land. Marines also performed reconnaissance and conducted raids. They were also charged with boarding an enemy ship in the open sea and fighting to subdue its crew. If their own ship was boarded by foes, they protected the captain and reloaded the guns used by the other seamen. When not engaging a foe, marines acted as the "military patrol" onboard, ensuring that the crew adhered to the captain's orders. They also maintained the guns and other weaponry, making sure they were in battle-ready condition.[17]

After his naval service, he also served in the Pennsylvania state militia. Andrew Pegan II, listed as "Andrew Pagon", is among the soldiers in the Lancaster County Militia in 1781, assigned to guard prisoners of war at the Lancaster prison and several stockades outside the city. He is in Martic Township's 7th Company, 6th Battalion as a private, 7th Class, under the command of Col. James Taylor.[18] The Lancaster, Pennsylvania prison stockade housed thousands of captured British and Hessian soldiers during the Revolution. The Lancaster stockades may have been the main guarded enclave for Hessians, as a great many of Lancaster County's residents were of German origin and spoke German.[19]

Andrew Pegan II is mentioned in his father Andrew Pegan/Pagan's will, written in 1788 and proven in 1789. His father wills to Andrew II half of his cows, sheep, and hogs and all of his (Andrew Sr.'s) clothes.[20]

Andrew II may have moved to Strabane Twp., Washington Co., Pennsylvania, before his father died. His name no longer appears on the Martic Twp., Lancaster Co., Pennsylvania tax list after 1787.[6] But his name doesn't appear on the Strabane Twp., Washington Co., tax lists until 1791.[21]

When researching in Brooke County, West Virginia, a member of the Brooke County Historical Society, told this writer that the hilly Washington County, Pennsylvania-Brooke County, West Virginia area, was considered part of the American frontier just after the American Revolutionary War. At this time, the area was known for its stock-raising and particularly for sheep raising. Weavers were needed there to process wool into thread and then into fabric. The goods were shipped to overland to the East and down the Ohio River from Wellsburg, the Brooke County seat, to the South and West.

Andrew Pegan II is not enumerated in the 1790 U.S. census.

In 1800, Andrew Pegan II is named as "Andrew Pagan" in "Straban" Twp., Washington Co., Pennsylvania *(Census Place: "Straban", Washington, Pennsylvania; Series: M32; Roll: 44; Page: 898,899; Image: 116)*. On the census form, there is a one in col. 2, a one in col. 3 and a one in col. 4; a one in col. 6, a one in col. 7 and a one in col. 9. This computes as one male age 10-15 (Robert, about 15 years old), 1 male 16-24 (Alexander, about 18) and one male 25-44 (Andrew would have been about 43 years old); one female under age 10 (daughter Mary), one female 10-15 (name not known), one female 16-25 (Elizabeth Jane, about 16), and one female age 45 and up (Mary, about 49 years old). He is the only "Andrew Pagan" enumerated in this United States census.

Andrew Pegan II is in Brooke County, Virginia (now West Virginia) in 1810 *(Year: 1810; Census Place: Brooke, Virginia; Roll 66; Page: 680; Image: 00670)*. Brooke County, West Virginia is adjacent to Washington County, Pennsylvania, where Andrew was in the 1800 census. There is a 1 in col. 5; a 1 in col. 7 and a 1 in col. 10. This computes to one male age 44 and over; one female 10-15 and one female 44 and over. Son Alexander Pegan is nearby. His other son Robert Pegan is in Strabane Twp., Washington Co., Pennsylvania. His cousin Archibald Pegan, son of Andrew II's uncle James Pegan II, is in nearby Allegheny Co., Pennsylvania. There is also an older "Alexander Pagan" listed in Strabane Twp., but his name in seen in subsequent censuses and Washington Co. records as Alexander Fagan.

Andrew Pegan II is listed on the Brooke County, (West) Virginia personal property tax lists from 1811-1819. His name does not appear on any property tax lists, so he owned no property there, just as he hadn't in Lancaster or Washington counties, Pennsylvania.[22]

Andrew Pegan II was living in Brooke County, (West) Virginia when he filed a for a military pension from his Revolutionary War service. On his pension application, dated April 27, 1818 in the Brooke County court, Andrew says he enlisted in the Pennsylvania Navy at Philadelphia in 1776 to serve one year He says he spent that year as a marine on the ship *Montgomery*, under Captain John Brown. In addition, he served two months in Pennsylvania militia in Lancaster, Lancaster Co., Pennsylvania guarding British prisoners of war taken at the surrender of General Burgoyne. In this application, Andrew states that he is more than 61 years old and is a weaver.[1]

He was declared eligible for a pension in Virginia State Papers, 16th Congress, 1st session, Act of March 18, 1818 to December 20, 1819.[15]

But apparently before his first pension check was sent, Andrew Pegan II moved in September 1819 from Brooke County, (West) Virginia to Highland County, Ohio, as his pension is transferred retroactively in 1820 from the Virginia agency to Ohio. On July 21, 1821, for some reason, he had to start his pension application process all over again the Highland County court.[1, 23]

In this court hearing, Andrew II tells the court that his original declaration for a pension was made on April 27, 1818, and that his pension was granted, but on September 12, 1819, he was transferred from the Virginia (pension) agency to the one in Ohio, retroactive to September 4th. He states to the court that he is 64 years old and his wife is 70. Andrew II also says that, although he is not yet quite destitute enough to be pension eligible, he is infirm and cannot work, is of limited finances and that his wife cannot work either. He says he has no other residents in his home, other than his wife, who could help support him. This time, Andrew II testifies that he served on board the "United Ship of War Montgomery Commanded by Capt. John Brown", and that he enlisted for one year but served 21 months. But he does not mention his prisoner-of-war guard under General Burgoyne.[23]

On July 26, 1821, Andrew II, as part of the pension process, filed an appraisal, or schedule, of his property, with the Highland County court. His property "was proved to be worth forty three dollars by the oath of William Smith Senior." The appraisal:

One Cow...$10.00
Two calves $7.00
One pinchback watch.......................$5.00
One shotgun $9.00

One chest	$3.00
One spinning wheel	$2.00
Two chairs	$1.00
Two flour barrels	$.50
One table	$1.50
Dresser furniture and looking glass	$4.00
Total	**$43.00**[23]

Andrew II's pension was granted in September 1821.[1]

According to several Highland County, Ohio, history books, Andrew Pagan/ Pegan II was one of the earliest settlers of the county and his first residence may have been near Webertown in Salem Township (now in Dodson Township).[24]

On May 15, 1820, Andrew Pegan II and other residents of the newly-formed Salem Township in Highland County, Ohio, petitioned in the Highland County Court of Common Pleas to have the court grant them the liberty to elect an additional justice of the peace. Signing below him is son-in-law John VanAusdall ("Vannossale?").[25]

Andrew II's son Alexander also migrates to the area, settling in Brown County, Ohio. Andrew II's other son, Robert Pegan, seems to have been in Ohio by November 1815, as the Robert and Christina "Engle" Pegan family bible says their only daughter, Mary Ann, was born in Ohio. But Robert Pegan is not found on any tax list in Ohio before 1820. Indeed, according to all tax records, Andrew Pegan and his two sons never owned land/property in Pennsylvania, (West) Virginia or Ohio. No deeds are found in any deed books in the counties where they resided.

Both Andrew II and Robert Pegan are mentioned in Elsie Johnson Ayres' *Highland County, Ohio Pioneer Sketches and Family Genealogies*. Ayres notes that Andrew II, "Marine during the Revolution", migrated to Highland County and was buried there. She also mentions that Andrew's son Robert "lived in the area of Fairview" and that he was descended from Andrew II.[26]

Andrew Pegan is enumerated as "Andrew Pegans" in the 1820 census, in "Salem" Twp., Highland Co., Ohio *(Census Place: Salem, Highland, Ohio; Roll: M33_92; Page: 37; Image: 44.)* In the household are one male under age 10, one male 26-45, one male more than age 45 (Andrew II); one female under age 10, one female 16-26 and one female 26-45 (this is probably an error, as in Andrew's July 1821 court appearance for his pension hearing, he says his wife is 70 years old, and bible records prove that Mary Unknown Pegan is still alive). (Note: The census source, Ancestry.com, claims that Andrew is living in Salem Twp., Fayette Co., Ohio in 1820. However, he was in Salem Township in Highland County. There has never been a Salem Township in Fayette County.)

Andrew II and Mary's daughter, Mary VanAusdall, and her son and daughter, seem to be living with Andrew and Mary Unknown Pagan. Her husband, John VanAusdall, may have been in Butler County, Ohio preparing for their move there, as John and Mary were known to have been residing in Butler Co. in 1827.

The Robert and Christina Pegan family bible says Andrew Pegan Jr. died on September 16, 1825, just three days after his wife Mary.[2] According to pension payout records, Andrew II's pension checks stop in 1825.[27]

The Waw-wil-a-way Chapter of the of the Daughters of the American Revolution, Highland County, Ohio, lists Andrew Pegan II among the county's Revolutionary War veterans. He buried in Highland County, but the location of his grave is unknown.[3, 4, 5]

Andrew "Pagan" is on a list of unclaimed letters at the Hillsboro, Highland Co., Ohio post office on March 1, 1827, when Andrew II had been deceased for 17 months. But it is unclear if the letter is for Andrew Pegan II, or Andrew Pegan, Andrew II's grandson by his son Robert.[28]

Children of Andrew Pegan II and Mary Unknown:

+   2   m   I.   **Alexander**[4] **Pagan** was born in Martic Twp., Lancaster Co., Pennsylvania, about 1782. He died in Pleasant Twp., Brown Co., Ohio, between 1820 and 1830. Married **Elizabeth McGrath?** Hamen (later Sloane).

+ 3 f II. **Elizabeth Jane**[4] **Pegan** was born in Martic Twp., Lancaster Co., Pennsylvania, in 1784. She was also known as **Jane**. Elizabeth Jane died in Wheeling, Ohio Co., West Virginia, on March 8, 1864. Married **Isaac Goudy.**

+ 4 m III. **Robert A.**[4] **Pegan** was born in Martic Twp., Lancaster Co., Pennsylvania, on May 14, 1785.[2] He died in Dayton, Montgomery Co., Ohio, on September 12, 1835.[2] Married **Christina** or **Christiana Ingle.**

+ 5 f IV. **Daughter or Ann**[4] **Pegan** was born in Pennsylvania between 1785 and 1790. She died after 1800.

+ 6 f V. **Mary**[4] **Pegan** was born in Strabane Twp., Washington Co., Pennsylvania on June 3, 1795. She died in Otter Creek Twp., Jersey Co., Illinois, on April 17, 1872. Married **John VanAusdall.**

Endnotes

1. Andrew Pegan, Revolutionary War Pension Application, National Archives, Virginia, Series M805, Roll 642, Image 432, Penn. Sea Service S40249. National Archives, Washington, DC.

2. Family Data: Robert and Christina "Engle" Pegan family bible, American Bible Society, Brattleboro(ugh), Vermont: Holbrook & Fessenden, 1828. In possession of the author, Ann Miller Carr.

3. Andrew Pegan's (II) name appears on a bronze plaque on the Highland County, Ohio courthouse's south wall, an effort by the Waw-Wili-Way Chapter of the Daughters of the American Revolution, Highland County, Ohio.

4. "To Locate Soldier's Graves", (Hillsboro, Ohio, Hillsboro News Herald, 09 Nov 1919), Highland County District Library, 10 Willettsville Pike, Hillsboro, OH.

5. *The Official Roster of the Soldiers of the American Revolution buried in the State of Ohio*, Ohio Adjutant General's Department, Columbus, Ohio, 1929-1959, Vol. 2; Compiled Under the Direction of Frank D. Henderson, The Adjutant General, John R. Rea, Military Registrar, and Daughters of the American Revolution, Jane Dowd Dailey (Mrs. O.D.), State Chairman. Columbus, Ohio: The F.J. Heer Printing Co.; 1929, pg. r19 and 275. Genealogy Center, Allen County Public Library, 900 Library Plaza, Fort Wayne, IN.

6. Pagan/Pegan entries, Lancaster County, Pennsylvania, Tax Records, 1751-1831, Microfilm, Lancaster County, Roll #23. Genealogy Center, Allen County Public Library, Fort Wayne, IN.

7. U.S. Federal Census, Ancestry.com, Year: 1800; Census Place: "Straban", Washington, Pennsylvania; Roll: 44; Page: 899; Image: 110.

8. U.S. Federal Census, Ancestry.com, Year: 1810; Census Place: Brooke, Virginia; Roll: 66; Page: 680; Image: 665.00.

9. 1820 U.S. Census Year: 1820; Census Place: Salem, Fayette (Incorrect—it is Union, Highland), Ohio; Roll: M33_92; Page: 37; Image: 44.

10. "Memorials Against Calling a Convention", 1779. *Pennsylvania Archives, Second Series, Vol. III*, ed. By Samuel Hazard, et. al., C.M. Busch, Harrisburg, Penn: Pennsylvania State Archives; 1875, pg. 359. Family History Library, 35 North Temple, Salt Lake City, UT.

11. *The Officers and Men of the Pennsylvania Navy, 1775-1781*, Pennsylvania Navy Board (1874). Princeton, New Jersey: Banner Press; 1982, pg. 318-326; Taken from the *Pennsylvania Archives, Second Series, Vol. 1*. Harrisburg, Pennsylvania, 1879, pg. 325. The Newberry Library, 60 West Walton Street, Chicago, IL.

12. Hoffman, Jon T., *USMC: A Complete History*. New York, New York: Universe Publishing, 2002, pg. 19. Genealogy Center, Allen County Public Library, 900 Library Plaza, Fort Wayne, IN.

13. Continental Navy. Wikipedia. https://en.wikipedia.org/wiki/Continental_Navy.

14. Peden, Henry Jr., *Revolutionary Patriots of Lancaster Co., Pennsylvania*. Westminster, Maryland: Willow Bend Books; 2000. Genealogy Center, Allen County Public Library, 900 Library Plaza, Fort Wayne, IN.

15. Brumbaugh, Gaius Marcus, *Revolutionary War Records: Virginia, Virginia Army and Navy Forces with Bounty Land Warrants for Virginia Military District of Ohio and Virginia Military Scrip from Federal and State Archives, Vol. 1*. Washington, DC (s.n.) Lancaster, Pennsylvania: Lancaster Publishing; 1936, pg. 82. Theodore M. Hesburgh Library, 221 Hesburgh Library, University of Notre Dame, Notre Dame, IN.

16. Gusathmey, John H., *Historical Register of Virginians in the Revolution*. Baltimore, Genealogical Publishing Co.; 1966, pg. 614. Genealogy Center, Allen County Public Library, 900 Library Plaza, Fort Wayne, IN.

17. Smith, C.R., *Marines in the Revolution: A History of the Continental Marines in the American Revolution*. Honolulu, Hawaii, University Press of the Pacific.; 2005. Genealogy Center, Allen County Public Library, 900 Library Plaza, Fort Wayne, IN.

18. *Pennsylvania Archives, Fifth Series, Vol. VII*, Harrisburg, Penn: Pennsylvania State Archives, Pennsylvania. pg. 581. Family History Library, 35 North Temple, Salt Lake City, UT.

19. "Lancaster's Role in the Revolution", LancasterHistory.org. [online] lancasterhistory.org/county-commonwealth-country/turmoil-transitions/3021-lancaster-s-role-in-the-american-revolution.

20. Andrew Pegan Sr. will (1788), Lancaster County, Pennsylvania Will Book F: Vol. 1: 84-86. Lancaster County, Pennsylvania Archives, 150 North Queen Street, Lancaster, PA.

21. Andrew Pegan, Washington County, Pennsylvania. Tax Records. Somerset Township through 1821; Strabane Township through 1811. Microfilm, Washington County, Roll #29. Genealogy Center, Allen County Public Library, Fort Wayne, IN.

22. Hubbard, Gwendolyn Mackey. Elliott, Bobbie Britt. Craft, Kenneth Fischer. *Brooke County (WV) index: "Personal Time Line" Index to Vols. 1-63 with over 346, 000 entries!; master cumulative index to pages 1-5662*. Beach Bottom, WV, Brooke County Genealogical Society; c2008, pg. 1942. Genealogy Center, Allen County Public Library, 900 Library Plaza, Fort Wayne, IN.

23. Highland County, Ohio Order Book 1820-1824, pg. 86; Highland County Courthouse, 105 North High Street, Hillsboro, OH.

24. Ayers, Elsie Johnson, *Highland County, Ohio Pioneer Sketches and Family Genealogies*. Springfield, Ohio: H.K. Skinner; pg.

592. Highland County District Library, 10 Willettsville Pike, Hillsboro, OH.

25 McBride, David N. and Jane N., *Highland County, Ohio Common Pleas Court Records, 1805-1860*. Hillsboro, Ohio: The Southern Ohio Genealogical Society; reprint ed. 1984, pg. 270-1. Highland County District Library, 10 Willettsville Pike, Hillsboro, OH.

26 Ayers, Elsie Johnson, *Highland County, Ohio Pioneer Sketches and Family Genealogies*, pg. 604.

27 The National Archives; Washington, D.C.; Ledgers of Payments, 1818-1872, to U.S. Pensioners Under Acts of 1818 Through 1858, Ancestry.com; From Records of the Office of the Third Auditor of the Treasury; Record Group Title: Records of the Accounting Officers of the Department of the Treasury; Record Group Number: 217; Series Number: T718; Roll Number: 1, pg. 500,

28 "List of Letters Left at the Hillsboro, Ohio Post Office, September 30, 1826", Abstracts From Before 1850, Southwestern Ohio Newspapers, Hillsborough Gazette and Highland Advertiser, Highland County; taken from original, (Hillsboro, Ohio, Hillsborough Gazette and Highland Advertiser, 09 Oct 1826) Microfilm #21714. Highland County District Library, 10 Willettsville Pike, Hillsboro, OH. Online database: http://marsharising.com/newspapers/Ohio%20Newspapers/hillsborough_gazette and highlan.htm.

[A] Article from a Philadelphia, Pennsylvania newspaper (the *Pennsylvania Gazette*?) in late June or early July 1776. Given to the author, Ann Miller Carr, by Vikki Sorel, Ankenny, IA, 04 Apr 2019.

Robert A. Pegan

1. **Robert A.**[4] **Pegan** (*Andrew*[3], *Andrew*[2] *Pagan, James*[1]) was born on Saturday, May 14, 1785, in Martic Twp., Lancaster Co., Pennsylvania.[1] He was the son of Andrew Pegan II and Mary Unknown. Robert A. died in Dayton, Montgomery Co., Ohio, on September 12, 1835, at age 50.[1, A]

His surname is seen as Pegan and Pagan, but in his own family bible it is Pegan.[1] In the censuses, it is Pagan. His middle name may have been Andrew, as he is listed by that given name in the 1834 Montgomery County, Ohio tax records. But in all the other tax records he is listed as Robert.[A]

Robert Pegan was a farmer, yet his father was a weaver and most of his sons were carpenters. Robert never owned land—there have been no deeds found registered to him. He seemed to be an itinerant or tenant farm laborer.

Robert married **Christina or Christiana Ingle** on January 16, 1806, in Washington Co., Pennsylvania.[1] She was also known as **Tina or Tiney.** They had eleven children. Christina or Christiana Ingle was born in Strabane Twp., Washington Co., Pennsylvania, on March 26, 1786.[1] Christina or Christiana Ingle reached age 71 and died in Logansville, Pleasant Twp., Logan Co., Ohio, on January 16, 1858.[1]

Her name may have been Christiana, as her daughter, Mary Ann Pegan Coover Wagoner, named her only daughter "Chrystiana". But most often her given name was seen as Christina, which will be used in this book.

According to their own family bible, Robert and Christina "Engle" Pegan were married by Andrew "Swenengen".[1] Andrew Swearingen was a justice of the peace in Chartiers Township in Washington County.[2]

Robert Pagan is listed in the 1810-1811 Strabane Twp., Washington Co., Pennsylvania tax list.[3] However, he never appears on any tax list in Brooke County, (West) Virginia, where his father Andrew II and his brother Alexander lived in 1810.

From 1810 through 1830, our Robert "Pagan" is the only person with that name enumerated in the U.S. Federal Census.

Robert "Pagan" is enumerated in the 1810 census in Strabane Twp., Washington Co., Pennsylvania *(Year: 1810; Census Place: Strabane, Washington, Pennsylvania; Roll 57; Page: 12;& nbsp; Image: 00017)*. with a 4 in col. 1, a 1 in col. 3; and a 1 in col. 8. This would be four males under age 10, a male age 16-25 and a female 16-25.

Robert seems to have removed from Washington County, Pennsylvania to Ohio by November 1815, according to the registry of his only daughter Mary Ann Pegan Coover Wagoner's birth in the family bible. Also, Mary Ann consistently says in U.S. Federal Censuses that she was born in Ohio, while her brothers born before her consistently say they were born in Pennsylvania.[1]

Robert's brother, Alexander "Pagen" (along with a Walter Cain, whose relationship to the Pegans is unknown) had two lawsuits filed for debts owed in Brooke County, (West) Virginia, the second on April 27, 1818. In a compilation index, *Brooke County (WV) Index, Vol.16, Complete Transcription of the First Third of County Court Order Book #8, December 1817-June 1819*, Alexander is named as "Robert" for that case, although a check of the actual court documents in Brooke County only mention Alexander and don't mention Robert at all.[B] However, Robert's name is not found on the voter's list in Highland County for that year, or any other year until 1820. Mary Ann's descendants disagree as to where she was born. Online sources from descendants claim she was born in Auglaize County which was then a part of Miami County. Others say she was born in Gallia County. Gallia is a good possibility, as Robert's uncle John Pagan may have been living there at that time and is believed to have died in Gallia County in 1819.

Robert Pegan is enumerated as Robert "Pagan" in the 1820 Union Twp., Highland Co., Ohio census *(Census Place: Union, Highland, Ohio; Roll M33_92; Page: 37; Image: 74)*. He is living near his father, Andrew, who is in Salem Township. (At the time of publication, the census source, Ancestry.com, has both Andrew Pegan II and Robert Pegan residing in Fayette County, Ohio. Andrew in Salem Township and Robert in Union. This seems to be an error. A check on Robert's 1820 neighbors in the 1830 census has most living in Union Twp. Highland Co., Ohio. As for Andrew II, there was never a township called Salem in Fayette County. Both were living in Highland County, not Fayette.) In the household are four males under age 10 (Henry, Elsey, Harrison and William), three males 10-16 (Andrew, John and Alexander), one male 26-45 years old (Robert); one female under age 10 (Mary Ann), and one female 26-45 years old (Christina). Alexander Pegan/Pagan is in adjacent Brown County, Ohio.

Elsie Johnson Ayres, in her *Highland County, Ohio Pioneer Sketches and Genealogies*, mentions that Robert Pegan "lived in the area of Fairview" which is in Union Township. Ayres also says he was descended from Andrew Pegan, who served as a Marine during the Revolution".[4]

Robert "Pagan" is on a list of unclaimed letters at the Hillsboro, Highland Co., Ohio post office on September 30, 1826, after he and his family removed to Clark Twp., Clinton Co., Ohio shortly after his father Andrew Pegan II died.[5]

"Robert Pagan" is found in the Clark Twp., Clinton Co., Ohio tax rolls in 1826 and 1827.[A] He owns no land, only two cows.

But Robert didn't remain in Clinton County long. In 1828, he removed to Wayne Twp., Montgomery Co., Ohio.[A] Robert and Christina's son Andrew, however, stayed behind in Clinton County, perhaps because he was already courting Mary Jane McKibben, whom he married in 1828. Andrew stayed in Clinton County until he removed to Missouri around 1856.

Another of Robert's sons, Henry, who would have been 14 years old in 1826, moved with Robert and Christina Pegan. Later, he returned to his home area for good, first to Clinton County and then to Highland County, when he was older.

Robert Pegan is enumerated again as Robert Pagan in the 1830 census, Wayne Twp., Montgomery Co., Ohio 1830 *(Census Place: Wayne, Montgomery, Ohio, Roll: M19-136, Page 245.)* Robert and his wife, Christina Ingle Pegan, were both age 40-50. Also in the household were one male 15-20 (Henry), two males 10-15 (Harrison and Elsey), two males age five-10 (William and Pleasant), and one male under age five (Isaiah); and one female 10-15 (Mary). Robert is a farmer or farm worker. Son John Pagan/Pegan is nearby and newly married. Oldest son Andrew, who is not enumerated in this census, is married and living in Clark Twp., Clinton Co., Ohio.

Robert Pegan, again named as "Pagan", continues to reside in Wayne Twp., Montgomery Co., Ohio and is on the tax list in 1931 and 1832. He still owns only two cows.[A]

According to his family bible, Robert died on September 12, 1835, but the bible does not say where. However, the Ohio personal property tax records for 1834, the last year he would have been taxed, show he had moved from Wayne Township in Montgomery County into the town of Dayton.[A] That tax record oddly lists him as "Andrew Pagun", but this has to be Robert, as his son Andrew is in Clinton County. As Robert had owned no land, he had no will or estate.

A few years after Robert's death, his widow Christina Pegan buys Lot 48 in Logansville, Pleasant Twp., Logan Co., Ohio in March of 1838. The deed indicates she is living in Logan County when she buys the property.[6]

She lives there until April 1846, when she sells it.[7] Exactly a week later, she buys the same property back! On the deed, it says she was living in Miami County, Ohio when she re-purchased the lot.[8]

Their son William Louis/Lewis Pegan was involved in a scandalous court case in Montgomery County, Ohio, in 1839. He was undoubtedly the "Lewis Pegan" who sued Rev. David Winters for slander and defamation of character in Montgomery Co., Ohio on September 24, 1839. claiming damages of $1000. Lewis Pegan said Winters slandered him by saying that Lewis committed sodomy with a man, alleged to be a minister and teacher, who, when in Dayton, Montgomery Co., Ohio, called himself Francis Frederick Langhoff. Lewis Pegan was a pupil of Langhoff's and was living in his house.[9]

Rev. Winters, a well-known German Reformed Church "circuit rider" minister in Montgomery and Greene counties, Ohio, was highly respected and popular. He helped found two German Reformed Churches in the Xenia, Greene Co., Ohio area before becoming the minister of the First Reformed Church in Xenia. Later, he established David's Church in Kettering, Montgomery Co., Ohio, which still is active. Rev. Winters knew the Pegan family; he solemnized the marriages of several of Robert and Christiana/Christina Ingle Pegan's children and their spouses.[10]

"Lewis" Pegan, was only 18 years old at the time of the suit. As he was a minor (under 21), he was represented in court by his "next friend", John Jacob Pegan. This "next friend" could have been one of two men.

"John Jacob Pagan/Pegan" was a distant cousin who lived in Knox Twp., Columbiana County, Ohio from 1829-1833.[11] He is later found in Wheeling, West Virginia in 1840 (*Census Place: Wheeling Ward 1, Ohio, Virginia; Roll: 571; Page: 50*). This John J. Pegan/Pagan is believed to be the son of James Pagan III, son of James Pagan II, a brother to Andrew Pagan Sr., William Louis/Lewis' great-grandfather.

It seems this "next friend" could have also been John Pegan, William Louis/Louis' eldest brother. But this John Pegan never used a middle- initial on any document. Nor was ever referred to with a middle initial in censuses or any other source. Conversely, the John Jacob Pegan always signed documents as "John J." or "John Jacob", and is enumerated with this initial in censuses, etc.

Also, Joseph Pagan/Pagin, the master carpenter of Preble and Montgomery counties, Ohio and later LaPorte County, Indiana (who became William Louis/Lewis Pegan's father-in-law), had son named Lewis. However, this Lewis Pagan/Pagin was born August 24, 1818, so he would have reached the majority age of 21 by the time of the trial. (Note: Joseph Pagan/Pagin is believed to have trained William Louis/Louis' older brothers John, Harrison and Elsey in the carpentry trade. But a blood relationship between the families has not been identified.)[12]

The case, heard in Montgomery County, Ohio Court of Common Pleas on September 24, 1839 before Judge William L. Helfenstein. The attorneys for the Plaintiffs, Lewis Pegan and his representative John Jacob Pegan, were "Crane and Henderson". The court document language is stilted and hard to decipher, and some of the evidence is in German.

The Pegans testified that Rev. David Winters told a church congregation in Lancaster, Ohio on July 1, 1839 that Langhoff had committed sodomy with a boy who was living with him in Dayton, Montgomery Co., Ohio. In addition, on July 3, the Pegans claimed Rev. Winters repeated this same accusation in Dayton to another man, Simon Snyder, but this time naming Lewis Pegan as the boy Langhoff was involved with.

The Pegans testified that Winters assumed there was a carnal relationship between Langhoff and Lewis Pegan because of a letter, in German, from a Wheeling, West Virginia church Winters received on May 29, 1839. The Wheeling church wrote that Langhoff, under another name, had been their minister prior to his move to Dayton. But the Wheeling church discovered that Langhoff had falsified his clerical credentials and had never been ordained. The letter from the Wheeling church went on to say that Langhoff "had attached a certain party to himself" and "his immoral sinful course of life came more and more into light." The Wheeling church had also found out that Langhoff, under yet another name, had also been a clergyman in Pittsburgh, Pennsylvania before he was in Wheeling and had committed the same act.

Lewis Pegan, through John Jacob Pegan, told the court that, although he was still living in Langhoff's house, had always been "a good citizen of this State and as such hath always conducted and until the speaking of the false and defamatory words heriein (sic) after mentioned hath not been suspected of that horrid and detestable crime not fit to be named among Christians called sodomy". The Pegans said that Rev. Winters intended to "injure the said Lewis Pegan in his good name and reputation."

Rev. Winters, through his lawyers "Odlin and Schenk", disputed that he ever told anyone that Lewis Pegan had committed sodomy. Winters said that, regarding the first charge (telling the Lancaster congregation), he was not guilty of "the said supposed grievances laid to his charge in manner and form". Winters also said that, as to the second count (recounting his accusation to Simon Snyder), he contested that the evidence the Pegans presented was insufficient to support their claim against him. that "the matters therein contained are not sufficient in law to maintain the action."

The case ended shortly thereafter, although no date is given, when the Pegans discontinued their suit. The court assessed the Pegans $9.53 and Rev. Winters $3.53 in court costs.[9]

Christiana/Christina Pegan is enumerated as "Christina Peggan" in the 1840 census in Miami Twp., Logan County, Ohio *(Census Place: Miami, Logan, Ohio; Roll 409; Page: 34; Image: 76)*. In the household are Christina, age 50-60 years old, and a male age 10-15 (Isaiah). Next door are son-in-law and daughter, Abraham and Mary Pegan Coover, who are childless at the time.[13] The census was taken not too long after the death of (Robert and) Christina's son Pleasant, who died in 1840.

By 1849, however, she is residing with the Abraham Coovers, despite seemingly still owning her house she bought back from the Vials.[8] Abraham Coover says on a deed that Christina Pegan has built "a tenement" (perhaps an addition) to his house and the two agree that she can stay there permanently unless he sells the property. If he sells the house, he has to give her $50.[14] Abraham Coover does sell the house less than six months later, on February 28, 1850, and he and Mary Ann move to his home area, Upper Dickinson Twp., Cumberland Co., Pennsylvania.[15]

In 1850, Christina ("Christena") Pegan, age 64, is enumerated as Christina Pagan in Logansville, Pleasant Twp., Logan Co., Ohio as the head of household *(Census Place: Logansville, Logan, Ohio; Roll: M432_704; Page: 72; Image: 150*. Also in the house are William Black, age 60, born Ireland, Mary Black, age 22, Isabel Black, age 16, and William Black II, 14, all born in Pennsylvania. The Black family is unrelated and may have rented Christiana's home in Logansville when she moved in with the Coovers. Samuel Black, a widower, and his family were in transition between a farm in he sold in Harrison Twp., Logan Co., Ohio to a new farm he'd bought near Logansville.[16] When the Coovers left, Christina may have moved back into her own home, which she bought back from the Vials in 1846, and shared it with the Blacks for a while. However, there is no deed registered in Logan County, Ohio for her home's sale, even after Christina dies.

Robert and Christina/Christiana Ingle Pegan's only daughter, Mary Ann Pegan Coover and her two children moved back to Logan County, Ohio following the death of Mary Ann's first husband, Abraham Coover, in Cumberland County, Pennsylvania in May 1851. Mary Ann Pegan Coover and family probably lived with her mother Christina/Christiana until she married her second husband, John Waggoner, in Logan County, Ohio in February 1852.

According to the family bible, Christina Ingle Pegan died on January 16, 1858, presumably in Logansville, Pleasant Twp., Logan Co., Ohio.[1] She has no estate in Logan County, even though there is no record of her selling her property. Her burial place is unknown, but she may be buried in Greenwood Cemetery, DeGraff, Miami Twp., Logan Co., Ohio, as many Pegan descendants, including her sons John and Elsey, are buried there.

The family bible also reveals three more sons born to Robert and Christina who died before reaching maturity. They are: Alexander, the third eldest, who died at age 17; Perry, their ninth child, who died when he was 18 months old; and Pleasant, the second youngest, who succumbed at age 15. Other than the following information at the end of this chapter, they are not delineated—unlike their siblings, as nothing more is known about them.

So, in total, Robert and Christina had 10 sons and one daughter.

Christina's given name is sometimes seen as "Christiana". Her surname in the Pegan family bible is "Engle". But this is incorrect, as Washington County, Pennsylvania deeds, most census enumerations, and tax records state her presumed father's name as "John Ingle Sr." Although John Ingle Sr. died intestate and there is no Ingle family bible, there is very strong circumstantial evidence that he was Christina's father. The census data say John Ingle's youngest daughter was Christina's age group. Strabane Township is where Robert's father Andrew Pegan II was the 1800 U.S. Federal Census (*Census Place: Straban, Washington, Pennsylvania; Series M32, Roll: 44; Page: 898-899; Image: 116*) and Robert was in his household.

John Ingle Sr. was the only "Engle" or "Ingle" in Washington County, Pennsylvania in 1790 and/or 1800, and census data confirms he was living in Strabane Township in those years (*Year: 1790; Census Place: Washington, Pennsylvania; Roll: M637_9; Page: 150/151; Image: 90 and Year: 1800; Census Place: Straban, Washington, Pennsylvania; Roll: 44; Page: 892,893; Image: 113.*).

While there are no "Engle" deeds in Washington County, Pennsylvania before 1800, there were several deeds involving John Ingle including one where he and his wife Lenora sell land to a Robert Hutchinson in 1796.[17] In addition, his surname is seen as "Ingle" in all Washington County tax records.[C]

John Ingle Sr.'s wife's given name was Lenora, as seen on the Ingle deeds.[17] Lenora may not have been Christina's mother; Lenora may have been a second/subsequent wife, as there are no deeds or other documentation to dating back to the 1786, the year Christina was born, to confirm that Lenora was her mother. Lenora/Christina's mother's maiden name may have been Elsey/Elzey. Robert and Christina/Christiana Ingle Pegan named a son Elsey, who, in turn, had a son named Elsey who died in infancy. Robert and Christina's eldest son, John, and his second wife Phoebe Moore Pegan also named a son Elsey, who also died as an infant. "Elsey", as a male name and with this spelling, is not found in any other Pegan line.

Children of Robert Pegan and Christina or Christiana Ingle:

+ 2 m I. **Andrew[5] Pegan** was born in Strabane Twp., Washington Co., Pennsylvania, on November 22, 1806.[1] He died in Clarksville, Calumet Twp., Pike Co., Missouri, on August 28, 1894.[18] Andrew was buried in Greenwood Cemetery, Clarksville, Calumet Twp., Pike Co., Missouri.[19]

+ 3 m II. **John[5] Pegan** was born in Strabane Twp., Washington Co., Pennsylvania, on September 14, 1808.[1] He died in Quincy, Miami Twp., Logan Co., Ohio, on March 20, 1874.[20] John was buried in Greenwood Cemetery, Pleasant Twp., Logan Co., Ohio.[21]

+ 4 m III. **Alexander[5] Pegan** was born in Strabane Twp., Washington Co., Pennsylvania, on May 5, 1810.[1] He died in Wayne Twp., Montgomery Co., Ohio, on December 16, 1827.[1]

+ 5 m IV. **Henry[5] Pegan** was born in Strabane Twp., Washington Co., Pennsylvania, on April 7, 1812.[1] He died in Dodson Twp., Highland Co., Ohio, on March 29, 1880.[22, 23] Henry was buried in Lynchburg Masonic Cemetery, Lynchburg, Dodson Twp., Highland Co., Ohio.[23]

+ 6 m V. **Harrison James[5] Pegan** was born in Strabane Twp., Washington Co., Pennsylvania, on September 30, 1813.[1, 24] He died in Lynchburg, Dodson Twp., Highland

Co., Ohio, on April 27, 1854.[1, 24] Harrison James was buried in Lynchburg Masonic Cemetery, Lynchburg, Dodson Twp., Highland Co., Ohio.[24]

+ 7 f VI. **Mary Ann[5] Pegan** was born in Gallia Co., Ohio or Fairview, Union Twp., Highland Co., Ohio?, on November 7, 1815.[1] She died in Bloomfield Twp., Logan Co., Ohio, on May 2, 1896.[25] Mary Ann was buried in Rea Cemetery, Bloomfield Twp., Logan Co., Ohio.[25]

+ 8 m VII. **Elsey[5] Pegan** was born in Fairview, Union Twp., Highland Co., Ohio, on April 27, 1818.[1] He died in DeGraff, Miami Twp., Logan Co., Ohio, on June 13, 1857.[26, 27] Elsey was buried in Greenwood Cemetery, Pleasant Twp., Logan Co., Ohio.[27]

+ 9 m VIII. **William Louis or Lewis[5] Pegan** was born in Fairview, Union Twp., Highland Co., Ohio, on June 7, 1820.[1] He died in Marysville, Marysville Twp., Sutter Co., California, on November 8, 1849.[1] William Louis or Lewis was buried in Marysville, Marysville Twp., Sutter Co., California.[1]

+ 10 m IX. **Perry[5] Pegan** was born in Fairview, Union Twp., Highland Co., Ohio, on April 6, 1822.[1] He died in Fairview, Union Twp., Highland Co., Ohio, on October 25, 1823.[1]

+ 11 m X. **Pleasant[5] Pegan** was born in Fairview, Union Twp., Highland Co., Ohio, on February 25, 1825.[1] He died in Logansville, Pleasant Twp., Logan Co., Ohio, on June 13, 1840.[1]

+ 12 m XI. **Isaiah Ira[5] Pegan** was born in Wayne Twp., Montgomery Co., Ohio, on May 19, 1829.[1, 28, 29] He was also known as **Ira**. Isaiah Ira died in Shelbyville, Shelby Twp., Shelby Co., Illinois, on February 1, 1911.[28, 30, 31, 32] He was buried in Glenwood Cemetery, Shelbyville, Shelby Twp., Shelby Co., Illinois.[32, 33]

Endnotes

1. Family Data: Robert and Christina "Engle" Pegan family bible, American Bible Society, Brattleboro(ugh), Vermont: Holbrook & Fessenden, 1828. In possession of the author, Ann Miller Carr.

2. Boyd, Crumine, *History of Washington County, Pennsylvania with Biographical Sketches of Many of Its Pioneers and Prominent Men*. Philadelphia: L.H. Levers & Co.; 1982, pg. 707. Genealogy Center, Allen County Public Library, 900 Library Plaza, Fort Wayne, IN.

3. Robert "Pagan" entry, Washington County, Pennsylvania. Tax Records. Somerset Township through 1821; Strabane Township through 1811. Washington County, roll #29. Genealogy Center, Allen County Public Library, 900 Library Plaza, Fort Wayne, IN.

4. Ayers, Elsie Johnson, *Highland County, Ohio Pioneer Sketches and Family Genealogies*. Springfield, Ohio: H.K. Skinner; 1971, pg. 604. Highland County District Library, 10 Willettsville Pike, Hillsboro, OH.

5. "List of Letters Left at the Hillsboro, Ohio Post Office, September 30, 1826", Abstracts From Before 1850, Southwestern Ohio Newspapers, Hillsborough Gazette and Highland Advertiser, Highland County; Online database: http://marsharising.com/newspapers/Ohio%20Newspapers/hillsborough_gazette_and_highlan.htm. Originals from (Hillsboro, Ohio, Hillsborough Gazette and Highland Advertiser, 09 Oct 1826) Microfilm #21714. Highland County District Library, 10 Willettsville Pike, Hillsboro, OH.

6. Logan County, Ohio Deeds, Squire and Letitia Knight to Christina Pegan, Logan County, Ohio Deed Book J: 157-58 (10 Mar 1838). Logan County, Ohio Recorder's Office, 100 South Mad River Street, Bellefontaine, OH.

7. Logan County, Ohio Deeds, Christina Pegan to James Madison and Sarah Vial, Logan County, Ohio Deed Book Q: 428 (10 Apr 1846). Logan County, Ohio Recorder's Office, 100 South Mad River Street, Bellefontaine, OH.

8. Logan County, Ohio Deeds, James Madison and Sarah Vial to Christina Pegan, Logan County, Ohio Deed Book Q: 258 (17 Apr 1846). Logan County, Ohio Recorder's Office, 100 South Mad River Street, Bellefontaine, OH. (Recorded before the initial sale was.)

9. Lewis Pegan by his Next Friend John Jacob Pegan vs. David Winters, Montgomery County, Ohio Common Pleas Court Records, September Term 1839, Book N, pg. 515. Montgomery County, Ohio Records Center and Archives, 117 South Main Street, 6th Floor, Dayton, OH.

10. David's United Church of Christ, History of David's Church, 1826-1976; Website: http://davidsucc.org/pages/history/html

11. All Ohio, Tax Lists, 1800-1850, Ancestry.com, entry for John J. or John Jacob Pagan, Knox Twp., Columbiana County, Ohio, 1829-1833.

12. Gilbert, Audrey, *Twin Valley Tidbits, 1888-1897, Vol. 3*. New Alexandria, Ohio: A. Gilbert; 1999, pg. 72. Lynchburg Public Library, 120 Main Street, Lynchburg, OH.

13. 1840 U.S. Federal Census: Abraham Coover, Year 1840, Census Place: Logan, Ohio; Roll: 409; Page: 34. Ancestry.com.

14. Logan County, Ohio Deeds, Logan County, Ohio Deeds, Abraham Coover to Christina Pegan, Agreement, Logan County, Ohio Deed Book T:334 (07 Aug 1849). Logan County, Ohio Recorder's Office, 100 South Mad River Street, Bellefontaine, OH.

15. Logan County, Ohio Deeds, Abraham Coover to Dennis Warner, Logan County, Ohio Deed Book U: 130 (08 Feb 1850). Logan County, Ohio Recorder's Office, 100 South Mad River Street, Bellefontaine, OH.

16. *Portrait and Biographical Record of Auglaize, Logan and Shelby Counties, Ohio, containing Biographical Sketches of Prominent and Representative Citizens Together with Biographies and Portraits of the Presidents of the United States*. Chicago: Chapman Bros; 1892, pg. 659. Genealogy Center, Allen County Public Library, 900 Library Plaza, Fort Wayne, IN.

17. Washington County, Pennsylvania Deeds, John Ingle Sr.and wife Lenora to Robert Hutchinson, Washington County, Pennsylvania Deed Book 1P (15): 59- 61 (08 Jun 1796). Washington County Recorder—Deeds, 100 West Beau Street, Washington, PA. (Note: There are several more deeds where John Ingle Sr. and Lenora sell land in Washington County, but, for the sake of brevity, the author has decided to include only one in the citations.)

18. Greenwood Cemetery Records, Andrew Pegan, Clarksville, Calumet Twp., Pike Co., Missouri; Clarksville City Hall, 111 Howard Street, Clarksville, MO.

19. Ohio, County Death Records, 1840-2001, FamilySearch.org, John Pegan, Logan Co., Ohio Death Record, Vol. 1, pg. 122.

20. Find A Grave--Greenwood Cemetery, DeGraff, Pleasant Twp., Logan Co., Ohio, Find A Grave.com, John Pegan, Find A Grave Memorial #18416902.

21. Find A Grave--Lynchburg Masonic Cemetery, Lynchburg, Dodson Twp., Highland Co., Ohio, Find A Grave.com, Henry Pegan, Find A Grave Memorial #93717200.

22. Ohio, County Death Records, 1840-2001, FamilySearch.org, Henry Pegan, Highland Co., Ohio Death Record, Vol. 1, pg. 156.

23. Find A Grave--Lynchburg Masonic Cemetery, Lynchburg, Dodson Twp., Highland Co., Ohio, Find A Grave.com, Henry Pegan, Find A Grave Memorial #93717200.

24. Find A Grave--Lynchburg Masonic Cemetery, Lynchburg, Dodson Twp., Highland Co., Ohio, Find A Grave.com, Harrison Pegan, Find A Grave Memorial # #93957435.

25 Find A Grave--Rea Cemetery, Bloomfield Twp., Logan Co., Ohio, Find A Grave.com, Mary A. Wagoner, Find A Grave Memorial #20326312.

26 Obituary of Elsey Pegan (Bellefontaine, Ohio, Bellefontaine Republican, 26 Jun 26, 1857), Logan Co., Ohio Genealogical Library, Bellefontaine, OH.

27 Find A Grave--Greenwood Cemetery, DeGraff, Pleasant Twp., Logan Co., Ohio, Find A Grave.com, Elsey Pegan, Find A Grave Memorial #18416894.

28 Obituary of Isaiah "Ira" Pegan (Decatur, Illinois, The Daily Review, 02 Feb 1911), Decatur Public Library, 130 North Franklin Street, Decatur, IL.

29 Isaiah Pegan, Civil War Pension Application (1904), NARA—National Archives and Records Administration, 8601 Adelphi Road, College Park, MD, Application #7322096, 1904; Jennie A. Pegan, widow's pension application (1911) #928323.

30 Illinois Statewide Death Index, Pre-1916, Office of the Illinois Secretary of State, 213 State Capitol, Springfield, IL. An Ongoing Project of the Illinois State Archives and the Illinois State Genealogical Society, Springfield, IL.; Online database: http://www.cyberdriveillinois.com/departments/archives/databses/death.html

31 Death record of Isaiah Pegan, Shelby County, Illinois Death Records, Vol. 5, pg. 110. Shelby County Clerk, Shelby County Courthouse, 301 East Main Street, Shelbyville, IL.

32 Glenwood Cemetery Records (Illinois), Isaiah Pegan, Glenwood Cemetery (Illinois), 306 North 6th Street, Shelbyville, IL.

33 Find A Grave—Glenwood Cemetery, Shelbyville, Shelby Twp., Shelby Co., Illinois, Find A Grave.com, Isaiah Pegan, Find A Grave Memorial #84740920.

[A] Ohio, Tax Records, 1800-1850, FamilySearch.com, "Robert Pagan", Clark Township, Clinton County Ohio, 1826; Green Township, Clinton County, Ohio, 1827-1829; Wayne Twp., Montgomery Co., Ohio, 1830-1833; City of Dayton, Montgomery Co. Ohio in 1834 (Andrew"Pagun").

[B] Brooke County (WV) Index, Vol.16, Complete Transcription of the First Third of County Court Order Book #8, December 1817- June 1819. Compiled by Gwendolyn Mackey Hubbard and Bobbie Britt Elliott, Beach Bottom, West Virginia: Brooke County Genealogical Society; 2002, pg. 1597. Genealogy Center, Allen County Public Library, 900 Library Plaza, Fort Wayne, IN.

[C] John Ingle entry, Washington County, Pennsylvania. Tax Records. Amwell Twp., 1781-1782, 1787-1789; Rostraver Township, Westmoreland County, 1783; Strabane Township 1789-1802. Microfilm, Washington County, roll #29. Genealogy Center, Allen County Public Library, 900 Library Plaza, Fort Wayne, IN. (Note: Amwell Township became a part of Westmoreland County in 1783 but was reclaimed by Washington County by 1787. Part of Amwell Township became Strabane Township in 1789.)

Andrew Pegan, Son of Robert

1. **Andrew**[5] **Pegan** (*Robert A.*[4], *Andrew*[3], *Andrew*[2] *Pagan, James*[1]) was born on November 22, 1806, in Strabane Twp., Washington Co., Pennsylvania.[1, 2] He was the son of Robert A. Pegan and Christina or Christiana Ingle. Andrew died in Clarksville, Calumet Twp., Pike Co., Missouri, on August 28, 1894, at age 87.[3] He was buried in Greenwood Cemetery, Clarksville, Calumet Twp., Pike Co., Missouri.[4]

Andrew Pegan moved with his parents, Robert and Christina Ingle Pegan, from Union Twp., Highland Co., Ohio to Clark Twp., Clinton Co., Ohio shortly after his namesake and grandfather, Andrew Pegan II, dies in September 1825.[A] Robert "Pagan" is on a list of unclaimed letters at the Hillsboro, Highland Co., Ohio post office on September 30, 1826, but it is unclear whether this is Andrew II or Andrew, the son of Robert.

Andrew Pegan remains in Clark Twp., Clinton Co., Ohio when his family leaves for Wayne Twp., Montgomery Co., Ohio about 1827. Perhaps he was already courting his future wife, Mary Jane McKibben.

Andrew married **Mary Jane McKibben** on December 21, 1828, in Clinton Co., Ohio.[3, 5, 6] They had eight children. Mary Jane McKibben was born in Green Twp., Clinton Co., Ohio, on February 12, 1811.[6, 7] Mary Jane reached age 84 and died in Clarksville, Calumet Twp., Pike Co., Missouri, on December 7, 1895.[6, 7] She was buried in Greenwood Cemetery, Clarksville, Calumet Twp., Pike Co., Missouri.[8]

On her Pike County, Missouri death certificate, Mary Jane McKibben is listed as "Mrs. Pegan".[7]

Andrew Pegan is not found in the 1830 census. However, he is found as "Andrew Pagan" on the 1829-1831 Ohio tax lists in Clark Twp., Clinton Co., Ohio. The original proprietor of his land was "R. Throgmorton". From from 1832-1835 the tax list indicates he is in Green Twp., Clinton Co., Ohio, formed from Clark Township. As the size of the property is the same as before and the original owner still Mr. Throgmorton, he seems to be residing on the same property.[A] Andrew Pegan II is enumerated in the 1840 census, Highland Co., Ohio, Dodson Twp. *(Census Place: Highland, Ohio; Roll: 403; Page: 102)*. Andrew is enumerated with two sons under five years of age, one son 5-10, one son 10-15, a son 15-20, himself, 30-40, a daughter 5-10, and his wife, 20-30 (a mistake by the census taker). Nearby are brothers Elsey and Henry.

In 1850, he is enumerated as "Andrew Piggin" in Washington Twp., Clinton Co., Ohio *(Census Place: Washington, Clinton, Ohio; Roll: M432_668; Page: 278; Image: 229)*. In the home are Andrew, 44, a carpenter; Jane (Mary Jane), 39; Leonidas, 20, Joseph, 18, Mary J., 16, James, 12, William H., 10, John, seven, Samuel, three and Robert, one. Everyone in the household is listed as born in Ohio, but this is incorrect, as proven in later censuses. Andrew was born in Pennsylvania.

Andrew and Mary Jane McKibben left Highland County, Ohio around 1856 with some McKibben relatives and moved to Audrain County, Missouri.

In 1860, Andrew and "Jane" McKibben Pegan are found in the town of Mexico, Salt River Twp., Audrain Co., Missouri *(Census Place: Mexico, Audrain, Missouri; Roll: M653_606; Page: 0; Image: 225)*. In the home are Andrew, 53, born Pennsylvania; Mary, 49, born Ohio; and children James, 30 (Incorrect—he was 20), John 16, Samuel, 14 and Robert, 13, all born in Ohio. Living next door to Andrew and Mary Jane McKibben in 1860 in Mexico, Audrain Twp., Missouri were their daughter, Mary J. Pegan Kelley and her husband, John, and their family.

Andrew buys land in Clarksville, Calumet Twp., Pike Co., Missouri on May 2, 1864. According to the Pike County, Missouri Recorder of Deeds office, the plot is located at the modern-day corner of Smith and Second streets in Clarksville. There he established his home and carpentry shop.[9]

In 1870, Andrew and Mary Jane McKibben Pegan are found in Clarksville, Pike Co., Missouri *(Census Place: Clarksville, Pike, Missouri; Roll: M593_798; Page: 111; Image: 226)*. In the home are Andrew, age 63 and Mary Jane, 58, both born in Ohio. Also in the household are son Robert, 21, born Ohio, and their son John Pegan's two children Flora, age three and Andrew, age one, both born in Missouri. The children's ages may be switched, as later Andrew is age 13 in 1880. Andrew (the father) lists his occupation as cabinet maker and Robert says he is a carpenter. In addition, there is a female "house servant", Nanny Williams, 15, born in Iowa. Son John, the father of Andrew and Flora, is listed as a farmhand and living with James and Carrie Mulherin Calumet Twp., Pike Co., Missouri. But John may have been living with his parents and just working at the Mulherin farm, as the Mulherins, ages 29 and 23 and both born in Missouri, do not seem to be related.

In 1880, Andrew and Mary Jane McKibben are again enumerated in Clarksville, Pike Co., Missouri *(Census Place: Clarksville, Pike, Missouri; Roll: T9_709; Page: 551.3000; Enumeration District: 135; Image: 0473)*. In the household are Andrew, age 75, who says he and his parents were born in Pennsylvania; "Jane" (Mary Jane), 70, who says she was born in Ohio and her parents in Kentucky. Living with them are two sons, John, 37, born Ohio, a carpenter and a widower and "Rob" (Robert), 31, born Ohio, single, who now says he is a fireman on the railroad. Also in the home in a grandson, Andrew, age 13, born Missouri, son of John Pegan and his late wife, Margaret Duncan Pegan.

Andrew Pegan sued his son John, and several other men, on March 14, 1873, over a $333.06 debt Andrew said John had owed him since December 22, 1870. According to the Pike County, Missouri court records, John offered as collateral his share of a tobacco crop, harvested but not yet cured, which he owned with a business partner, the James Mulherin who John was enumerated with in the 1870 census. The tobacco cured, but John had not paid his debt to Andrew. Andrew claimed John's share of the tobacco crop, and Andrew and John's business partner gave the crop to two other men, merchant brokers, to sell. The merchant brokers sold the crop, and made a partial payment to Mulherin, but Andrew had not been paid a cent. Andrew sued John, James Mulherin, and the two merchant brokers. The merchant brokers testified that John's share was only worth $256.50. The court ruled that the merchant brokers pay Andrew this sum at once; also, the brokers were to pay the rest of what they owed to Mr. Mulherin. The court said John still owed his father the rest of the debt, $79.56, plus 10 percent interest per annum. It is unknown whether John ever paid Andrew the remainder, plus interest. The merchant brokers, John and his business partner were also ordered to pay Andrew's court costs.[10]

Children of Andrew Pegan and Mary Jane McKibben:

+ 2 m I. **Leonidas Alonzo[6] Pegan** was born in Clark Twp., Clinton Co., Ohio, on December 9, 1829.[11, A] He died in Perry's Landing, Brazoria Co., Texas, on April 3, 1883.[11,12]

+ 3 m II. **Joseph[6] Pegan** was born in Green Twp., Clark Co., Co, Ohio, on March 17, 1832.[13, A] He died in Clarksville, Calumet Twp., Pike Co., Missouri, on August 4, 1901.[13]

+ 4 f III. **Mary Jane[6] Pegan** was born in Dodson Twp., Highland Co., Ohio or Montgomery Co., Ohio, on April 28, 1834.[14] She died in Clarksville, Calumet Twp., Pike Co., Missouri, on June 3, 1901.[14]

+ 5 m IV. **William Henry[6] Pegan** was born in Clark Twp., Clinton Co., Ohio, on January 18, 1837.[15] He died in Jamestown, Silvercreek Twp., Greene Co., Ohio, on October 12, 1914.[15, 16]

+ 6 m V. **James Robert**[6] **Pegan** was born in Dodson Twp., Highland Co., Ohio, on October 5, 1839.[17] He died in French Camp, Stockton Twp., San Joaquin Co., California, on June 21, 1913.[17, 18]

+ 7 m VI. **John S.**[6] **Pegan** was born in Dodson Twp., Highland Co., Ohio, on November 22, 1843.[19] He died in Clarksville, Calumet Twp., Pike Co., Missouri, on April 9, 1939.[19]

+ 8 m VII. **Samuel Alexander**[6] **Pegan** was born in Washington Twp., Clinton Co., Ohio or Dodson Twp., Highland Co., Ohio, on August 2, 1846.[20] He died in St. Louis, Missouri, on April 5, 1906.[20, 21]

+ 9 m VIII. **Robert Andrew**[6] **Pegan** was born in Washington Twp., Clinton Co., Ohio, on March 3, 1848.[22] He was also known as **Rob**. Robert Andrew died in Kansas City, Jackson Co., Missouri, on July 13, 1929.[22]

6th Generation

2. Leonidas Alonzo[6] Pegan (*Andrew[5], Robert A.[4], Andrew[3], Andrew[2] Pagan, James[1]*) was born on December 9, 1829, in Clark Twp., Clinton Co., Ohio.[11, A] He was the son of Andrew Pegan (1) and Mary Jane McKibben. Leonidas Alonzo died in Perry's Landing, Brazoria Co., Texas, on April 3, 1883, at age 53.[11, 12] He was buried in Gulf Prairie Cemetery (also Peach Point Cemetery), Jones Creek, Brazoria Co., Texas.[11]

The only record of Leonidas Pegan's birthdate is on his tombstone in Gulf Prairie (Peach Point) Cemetery, Jones Creek, Brazoria Co., Texas.[11]

Leonidas Alonzo married **Martha Jane Pegan** on July 25, 1854, in Clinton Co., Ohio.[23] They had two children. Martha Jane Pegan was born in Piqua, Washington Twp., Miami Co., Ohio, on August 19, 1839.[24] She was also known as **Mattie or Jane**. Martha Jane reached age 76 and died in Houston, Harris Co., Texas, on June 22, 1916.[24, 25] She was buried in Glenwood Cemetery, Houston, Harris Co., Texas.[24, 25, 26] She was the daughter of Harrison James Pegan and Sarah Ann Mentzer.

The only record of Martha Jane Pegan Pegan Brown's birthdate is on her tombstone in Glenwood Cemetery, Houston, Harris Co., Texas.[24]

Leonidas and his wife Martha Pegan were first cousins. Harrison Pegan Sr., Martha's father, was a brother to Leonidas' father Andrew. Leonidas was 24 years old and Martha only 14 when they wed in July 1854. Permission for the union was given by Sarah Mentzer Pegan, Martha's mother. Harrison Pegan Sr. had died that March.[1, 23] Soon after their marriage, Leonidas and Martha Jane left the Highland/Clinton counties, Ohio area for Poweshiek County, Iowa.

Leonidas and Martha Pegan Pegan had no children listed in any census and, in the 1900 U.S. Census, Martha Jane Pegan Pegan Brown says she has borne no children (*Census Place: Justice Precinct 6, Brazoria, Texas; Roll: T623_1614; Page: 14A; Enumeration District: 7*). But according to Martha Pegan Brown's 1905 Civil War widow's pension application through Leonidas's service, the couple had two children who died in infancy.[27] These infants probably were born and died while Leonidas and Martha were residing in Montezuma Twp., Poweshiek Co., Iowa.

Leonidas and Martha Jane Pegan Pegan are listed in the 1856 Iowa State Census in Jackson Twp., Poweshiek Co., Iowa (*Iowa State Census, Roll IA-64, p. 60, line 30*). Leonidas is a carpenter and a member of the militia.[28]

Leonidas Pegan is enumerated in the 1860 Census in Montezuma Twp., Poweshiek Co., Iowa as a carpenter (*Montezuma, Poweshiek, Iowa; Roll: M653_339; Page: 575; Image: 137*). In the household are Leonidas Pegan, age 30, a journeyman carpenter, and Martha Pegan, 21. Both were born in Ohio.

Living in Poweshiek County, Iowa at this same time is Joel Pagin, son of Joseph Pagan/Pagin, the master carpenter of western Ohio and then northern Indiana. (*See Joseph Pegan [3] below*)

Leonidas served in the Civil War in Company B, 40th Iowa Infantry as a hospital steward and was discharged because of "disability". He had contracted lung disease while encamped in Kentucky.[29]

Leonidas filed for a Civil War pension on April 16, 1878 and Martha for a widow's Civil War widow's pension in 1905. Both were refused, as the U.S. government pension office contended that neither Leonidas' lung problems nor his death could be directly attributed to his war service. According to an 1884 letter in Leonidas' file, Martha Jane Pegan Brown writes that her late husband Leonidas was never the same man physically after his discharge from the army. His lung illness prevented him from resuming the carpenter's trade. In 1865, they moved from Montezuma Twp., Poweshiek Co., Iowa to Burlington, Burlington Twp., Des Moines Co., Iowa, where he "engaged in any light employment he could obtain."[29]

In 1870, Leonidas is enumerated as "L. Pegan" in the 6th Ward, Burlington, Burlington Twp., Des Moines Co., Iowa (*Census Place: Burlington Ward 6, Des Moines, Iowa; Roll: M593_388; Page: 418A; Image: 379*). Leonidas, 40, is a railroad baggageman (railroad); Martha Jane, listed as "M.J.", is 30 years old. Both were born in Ohio. Leonidas' brother Samuel Pegan is living in Ward 3 in Burlington.

But, according to Martha's 1884 letter in his pension application file, Leonidas' frequent sickness prevented him from working and he lost his railroad job and others because of it. He traveled Minnesota and sometime in the 1870s for health reasons and found work found work as a liveryman. But the move did not improve his health, and he only stayed in Minnesota for a short time before returning to Burlington. His health improved somewhat after he relocated to Colorado in late 1878, but then an attack of lung inflammation weakened him further and he returned to Burlington in early 1879. Meanwhile, Martha stayed in Burlington during her husband's absences and tried to find occasional work herself.[29]

Leonidas and Martha Jane Pegan Pegan are still living in Burlington, Burlington Twp., Des Moines Co., Iowa in 1880 *(Census Place: Burlington, Des Moines, Iowa; Roll: 337; Page: 284C; Enumeration District: 116; Image: 0568)* in the 5th Ward. Leonidas, 51, is a painter and Martha Jane is age 40. There is no other information on the census entry.

Leonidas' death notice in the *Burlington (IA) Weekly Hawk Eye And Telegraph* on April 12, 1883 says Leonidas and Martha Jane Pegan Pegan removed to Perry's Landing, Texas in the spring of 1882 and Leonidas was working on a cattle ranch in Jones Creek, Brazoria Co., Texas, when he died.[12]

At his gravesite in Gulf Prairie Cemetery, Jones Creek, Brazoria Co., Texas (a famous historic cemetery associated with "The Father of Texas" Stephen F. Austin and his family), there are two very elaborate tombstones for him, which is highly unusual. The cemetery director says there are two graves at the site, but both tombstones are for Leonidas. The director thinks that one gravestone was ordered but thought lost in shipment (by sea) and another was ordered before the first finally arrived. Both stones have two hands clasped together, meaning one spouse (Martha Jane) was saying goodbye to the other (Leonidas).[11, 30]

Leonidas Pegan's brother Joseph named a son Leonidas, and Harrison and Angeline Stout PeGan Jr. probably named their son Leonidas after Harrison's brother-in-law/cousin.

About four months after Leonidas' death, Martha Jane Pegan Pegan married again to Reuben R. Brown Sr. on August 11, 1883, according to Brazoria County marriage records.[31]

Recently widowed with grown children, Reuben R. Brown Sr, was the wealthy and prominent owner of the farm and ranch where Leonidas Pegan had worked. According to his obituary, Reuben Brown Sr. was born in Georgia on February 2, 1810, but moved to Brazoria County, Texas around 1845. He fought in the Texas War of Independence and in the Civil War was a Confederate colonel. Reuben Brown knew both Sam Houston and Stephen F. Austin; Reuben Brown Sr.'s first wife was Austin's niece. Reuben Robinson Brown Sr. died on March 2, 1894 in Jones Creek, Brazoria Co., Texas. His obituary also says Martha Jane Pegan Pegan Brown "made (Brown) a devoted and affectionate companion. She was an excellent nurse and contributed to his happiness of his last few years."[32]

In 1900, Martha J. (Pegan Pegan) Brown, age 60, a widow, born in Sep 1839 in Ohio, is living in Justice Precinct 6 (Quintana), Brazoria Co., Texas *(Census Place: Justice Precinct 6, Brazoria, Texas; Roll: T623_1614; Page: 14A; Enumeration District: 7)*. She is boarding in the home of S.W. Jarvis, along with a couple of other lodgers and two servants. On the census form, Martha states has borne no children; she does not list a birthplace for her father, but says her mother was born in Pennsylvania.

Quintana was hard hit during the September 8, 1900 hurricane which virtually destroyed the greater Galveston area. It is estimated that 6-8000 people lost their lives during this vicious storm (estimated to be at least a level 4 on the Saffir-Simpson Hurricane Wind Scale and some scientists believe a level 5), which left many places in Brazoria County in ruins. In fact, most families who survived in Quintana left afterwards and moved inland, and (especially after it was struck again by a hurricane in 1915) the town never recovered its population. The 1900 hurricane still stands as the worst natural disaster ever to hit the United States. Martha Jane Pegan Pegan Brown survived this calamity![33]

By early August 1905, Martha J. Pegan Pegan Brown was back living in Poweshiek County, Iowa, according to a Brazoria County deed where she sells property in Brazoria County.[34] That same month, Martha Jane Pegan Brown "then of Poweshiek County, Iowa and formerly of Brazoria County, Texas, executes another deed to sell more land in Brazoria County. But the sale does not conclude until July 21, 1906, after Martha has moved to either Wabash County or Grant County, Indiana. The deed is transcribed in Grant County, Indiana and in Brazoria County, Texas.[35]

On November 4, 1905, when Martha J. Pegan Pegan Brown applied for a Civil War widow's pension, she was living in Wabash County, Indiana. Her nephew, Alvah PeGan, son of Harrison James PeGan Jr., was the witness on her application. Undoubtedly, she was living with her brother Harrison at the time. In that pension application, she says she and Leonidas had two children who died in infancy. Her request was rejected on February 3, 1907, and the denial letter was sent to Angleton, Texas (Brazoria County)—so she seemed to be living back in Texas then. The reason given for the pension denial was that Leonidas' cause of death, a stroke, was not related to his war injury (lung disease). But was she turned down because her second husband, Reuben Robinson Brown, was a Confederate Army colonel?[27]

In 1908, a Brazoria County deed indicates that Martha J. Pegan Pegan Brown had removed back to Texas and was living in Houston, Harris Co., Texas.[36]

In 1910, Martha Jane Pegan Pegan Brown is found in Ward 4, Houston, Harris Co., Texas *(Census Place: Houston Ward 4, Harris, Texas; Roll: T624_1559; Page: 1A; Enumeration District: 0076)*. Martha Brown, age 50 (Incorrect—she is 60), lists herself as a lodger, but she is the only one living at the address 615 Elgin Avenue. Perhaps it was a double residence and the other side, inhabited by John and Emma Whitted, faced the other street. Martha, a widow, lists her occupation as "capitalist". She says she and her father were born in Ohio and her mother in Pennsylvania, and that she bore two children, with none surviving.

A year later, Martha Jane Pegan Brown sells more property in Brazoria County, Texas through the Wabash County, Indiana recorder's office, stating she is a resident of the latter county.[37] She may have lived in Lagro, Lagro Twp., Wabash Co., Indiana with or near her brother, Harrison PeGan Jr. Perhaps she was a "snowbird" who lived in Houston, Texas during the winter and Wabash County, Indiana in the summer. But it seems she moved back to Houston permanently before her death, maybe when Harrison Jr. left Lagro to reside in Huntington, Huntington Twp., Huntington Co., Indiana in 1913.

Her death certificate is under "Mattie Brown". Her Glenwood Cemetery burial record, will and probate are under the name "Mrs. Reuben R. Brown".[25, 38, 39] However, one of the claimants on the probate, Ed S. Phleps, her stepson-in-law, is the informant on the death certificate, so there is little doubt that this is Martha Jane Pegan Pegan Brown.[25, 39] She was buried the same day she died in Glenwood Cemetery in Houston, in a plot owned by her stepson-in-law lawyer and his wife, Ed and Olive Brown Phelps.[24, 26] Her stepchildren didn't even ship her body back to Peach Point/Gulf Prairie Cemetery to be buried next to her first husband and first cousin, Leonidas Pegan (her second husband, Col. Reuben R. Brown, is also buried there).[11, 40]

Her lawyer/stepson-in-law, Ed S. Phelps, filed her probate two days after her death, claiming an estate worth $7000 in monies, possessions and properties. But it seems that her property, two lots in Quintana, Brazoria Co., Texas, were sold for the mysterious price of $25 each, instead of the thousands they were worth. The appraisal listed assets of only about $3000, while claims against the estate were more than $5000. It is unknown if her legatees named in her will, her brother Harrison PeGan (Jr.), (bequeathed $500), her niece Sarah PeGan Pearson ($600), and nephews Jesse, Clanzie, Alvah/Alvin and Philip (each $600) received any money from her estate.[38, 39]

Children of Leonidas Alonzo Pegan and Martha Jane Pegan:

+ 10   I.   **Child One**[7] **Pegan** was born in Montezuma Twp., Poweshiek Co., Iowa, between 1855 and 1862. He

+ 11   II. **Child Two⁷ Pegan** was born in Montezuma Twp., Poweshiek Co., Iowa, between 1855 and 1862. He or she died in Montezuma Twp., Poweshiek Co., Iowa, between 1855 and 1862.

3. **Joseph⁶ Pegan** (*Andrew⁵, Robert A.⁴, Andrew³, Andrew² Pagan, James¹*) was born on March 17, 1832, in Green Twp., Clinton Co., Ohio.[13, A] He was the son of Andrew Pegan (1) and Mary Jane McKibben. Joseph died in Clarksville, Calumet Twp., Pike Co., Missouri, on August 4, 1901, at age 69.[13] He was buried in Greenwood Cemetery, Clarksville, Calumet Twp., Pike Co., Missouri.[13, 41]

Joseph may have been named for Joseph Pagan/Pagin, the master carpenter of western Ohio and then northern Indiana.[42, 43] Joseph Pagan/Pagin is thought to have trained this Joseph's uncles John, Harrison Sr. and Elsey Pegan in the carpentry trade. It is quite possible that Joseph Pegan's father Andrew removed to the Montgomery and Preble counties, Ohio area after marrying Mary Jane McKibben, and Andrew was also trained by Joseph Pagan/Pagin. In addition, Joseph Pagan/Pagin's daughter Drusilla married William Louis Pegan, another of this Joseph's uncles and a brother to Andrew, John, Harrison Sr. and Elsey. A kinship between Joseph Pagan/Pagin and the Pegans is suspected, but not yet proven.

Joseph married **Mary Elizabeth Curry** on December 23, 1859, in Audrain Co., Missouri.[44, 45] They had seven children. Mary Elizabeth Curry was born in Lexington, Fayette Co., Kentucky, on October 17, 1839.[45, 46, 47, 48] Mary Elizabeth reached age 97 and died in Clarksville, Calumet Twp., Pike Co., Missouri, on February 28, 1937.[45, 46, 47, 48] She was buried in Greenwood Cemetery, Clarksville, Calumet Twp., Pike Co., Missouri.[45, 46, 47, 48]

In 1860, Joseph Pegan is enumerated in Mexico, Salt River Twp., Audrain Co., Missouri (*Census Place: Mexico, Audrain, Missouri; Roll: M653_606; Page: 0; Image: 221*). Joseph, age 25, born Ohio is a plasterer and Mary Elizabeth Curry Pegan, born Kentucky, is age 20. Mary Elizabeth is listed as "M.J."

Joseph Pegan fought for the Union Army in the Civil War in Company H, 49th Missouri Infantry, leaving with the rank of corporal. He applies for a pension on April 19, 1880 as an invalid. His wife, Mary Elizabeth Curry Pegan, files for a widow's pension on August 14, 1901.[49]

Joseph Pegan is found in Calumet Twp., Pike Co., Missouri in 1870 (*Census Place: Calumet, Pike, Missouri; Roll: M593_798; Page: 57; Image: 119*). In the household are Joseph, 34, a plasterer, born Ohio; Mary, 26 (?), born Kentucky, and children Leonidas, 10, Alexander, seven, Charles, four (?), and Josephine, seven months. The children were born in Missouri.

In 1880, Joseph Pegan is enumerated in Calumet Twp., Pike Co., Missouri (*Census Place: Calumet, Pike, Missouri; Roll: T9_709; Page: 524.3000; Enumeration District: 133; Image: 0419*). In the home are Joseph, age 48, born Ohio, a plasterer; Mary, age 42, born Kentucky; and children Leonidas, age 20, and Charles, 18, both farm workers; Josephine, 11, Lenora, eight, and Edwin, five.

Charles' age is incorrect; he should be 12. (Did the census taker accidentally leave out Alexander, who would have been 18, and substitute Charles instead?) All the children were born in Missouri. Joseph says his father was born in Pennsylvania and his mother in Ohio; Mary Elizabeth Curry Pegan says her father was born in Virginia and her mother in Kentucky.

Living with Joseph and Mary Elizabeth Curry Pegan in 1900 in Clarksville, Calumet Twp., Pike Co., Missouri are unmarried sons Leonidas and Edwin and their divorced daughter, Lenora Pegan Reneau and her daughter Hazel Reneau (*Census Place: Calumet, Pike, Missouri; Roll: T623_882; Page: 2B; Enumeration District: 86*). Joseph Pegan, age 68, born Mar 1932, is a plasterer who says he and his mother were born in Ohio and his father in Pennsylvania. Mary E. Curry Pegan, 54, born Oct 1835, says she and her mother were born in Kentucky and her father in Virginia. Joseph and Mary Elizabeth say they have been married 42 years and Mary Elizabeth has borne seven children, six still alive. Leonidas Pegan, listed as "Lonnie", is 39, born Oct 1860, and a plasterer like his father. Edwin Pegan, listed as "Eddie", is 24, a blacksmith, born Sep 1875. Lenora Pegan Reneau, age 27, born Sep 1872, lists no occupation. Hazel Reneau is five years old, born Aug 1895. All of the grown children and Hazel were born in Missouri.

Mary Elizabeth Curry Pegan, 70, a widow, is living in Ward 1, Clarksville, Calumet Twp., Pike Co., Missouri in 1910 *(Census Place: Clarksville Ward 1, Pike, Missouri; Roll: T624_805; Page: 2B; Enumeration District: 0123; Image: 234).* In the home with her are unmarried sons Leonidas, 49, a railroad worker; and "Edward", 34, a blacksmith. Mary Elizabeth Curry Pegan says she has borne seven children with six still surviving. Mary states she and her mother were born in Kentucky and her father in Virginia. Both her sons say they were born in Missouri, their father in Ohio and their mother in Kentucky.

Mary Elizabeth Curry Pegan, age 80, and her son "Edward" (Edwin), 44, a blacksmith, are still in Clarksville, Calumet Twp., Pike Co., Missouri in 1920 *(Census Place: Calumet, Pike, Missouri; Roll: T625_941; Page: 2B; Enumeration District: 137; Image: 771).* Again, Mary says she and her mother were Kentucky natives and her father was from Virginia. "Edward" was born in Missouri.

In 1930, Mary Elizabeth Curry Pegan, listed as "Mary L.", continues to reside in Clarksville, Calumet Twp., Pike Co., Missouri *(Census Place: Calumet, Pike, Missouri; Roll: 1218; Page: 3A; Enumeration District: 9; Image: 653.0).* She is 90 years old and a Kentucky native, like her mother. Her father was born in Virginia. Still living with her is unmarried son "Edward", 54, a blacksmith, born Missouri.

Children of Joseph Pegan and Mary Elizabeth Curry:

+ 12   m   I.   **Leonidas Alonzo**[7] **Pegan** was born in Mexico, Salt River Twp., Audrain Co., Missouri, on October 24, 1860.[50] He was also known as **Alonzo** and **Lon or Lonnie**. Leonidas Alonzo died in Clarksville, Calumet Twp., Pike Co., Missouri, on November 30, 1918.[50]

+ 13   m   II. **Alexander Campbell**[7] **Pegan** was born in Slemmensburg, Calumet Twp., Pike Co., Missouri, on May 11, 1864.[51, 52] He was also known as **Aleck**. Alexander Campbell died in Quincy, Quincy Twp., Adams Co., Illinois, on August 28, 1936.[51, 52, 53]

+ 14   m   III. **Charles H.**[7] **Pegan** was born in Slemmensburg, Calumet Twp., Pike Co., Missouri, on February 3, 1867.[54] He died in Bowling Green, Cuivre Twp., Pike Co., Missouri, on December 15, 1950.[54]

+ 15   f   IV. **Josephine**[7] **Pegan** was born in Calumet Twp., Pike Co., Missouri, on October 10, 1869.[55] She died in Louisiana, Buffalo Twp., Pike Co., Missouri, on December 15, 1948.[55]

+ 16   f   V.   **Lenora or Nora Lee**[7] **Pegan** was born in Calumet Twp., Pike Co., Missouri, on September 13, 1872.[56] She was also known as **Nora Lee**. Lenora or Nora Lee died in Clayton, Clayton Twp., St. Louis Co., Missouri, on March 3, 1948.[56]

+ 17   m   VI. **Edwin**[7] **Pegan** was born in Calumet Twp., Pike Co., Missouri, on September 21, 1875.[57] He died in Clarksville, Calumet Twp., Pike Co., Missouri, on October 7, 1955.[57]

+ 18   VII. **Child**[7] **Pegan** was born in Calumet Twp., Pike Co., Missouri, between 1861 and 1900. He or she died in Calumet Twp., Pike Co., Missouri, between 1861 and 1900.

4. **Mary Jane**[6] **Pegan** *(Andrew*[5]*, Robert A.*[4]*, Andrew*[3]*, Andrew*[2] *Pagan, James*[1]*)* was born on April 28, 1834, in Dodson Twp., Highland Co., Ohio or Montgomery Co., Ohio.[14] She was the daughter of Andrew Pegan (1) and Mary Jane McKibben.

Mary Jane died in Clarksville, Calumet Twp., Pike Co., Missouri, on June 3, 1901, at age 67.[14] She was buried in Greenwood Cemetery, Clarksville, Calumet Twp., Pike Co., Missouri.[14, 58]

Mary's middle name was Jane, according to her son Lorenzo "Louie" Kelley's ("Kelly") death certificate and obituary.[59, 60]

Mary Jane married **John A. Kelley** on December 5, 1855, in Clinton Co., Ohio.[61] They had seven children. John A. Kelley was born in Clark Twp., Clinton Co., Ohio, on September 4, 1833.[62, 63, 64] John A. Kelley reached age 78 and died in Clarksville, Calumet Twp., Pike Co., Missouri, on December 25, 1911.[62, 63, 64] He was buried in Greenwood Cemetery, Clarksville, Calumet Twp., Pike Co., Missouri.[64, 65]

According to John Kelley's obituary, John A. and Mary Jane Pegan Kelley removed first to Pittsfield, Pittsfield Twp., Pike Co., Illinois before joining Mary Jane's parents, Andrew and Mary Jane McKibben Pegan, in Mexico, Audrain Co., Missouri around 1860. He was a plasterer who taught his sons the trade.[63]

In 1860, John A. and Mary J. Pegan "Kelly" are found in Mexico Twp., Audrain Co., Missouri (*Census Place: Mexico, Audrain, Missouri; Roll: M653_606; Page: 0; Image: 225*). In the household are John Kelley and Mary J. Pegan Kelley, both age 47 and born in Ohio. Their children are: Lorenzo, 24, a plasterer, born Ohio; and John A. II, 23, a shoemaker, Harrison, 19, a plasterer; "Allie" (this time listed as female), 17, Laura, 15, Joshua, 12, and "Annie" (Fannie), nine, all born in Missouri.

By 1870, John A. and Mary J. Pegan Kelley are in Clarksville, Calumet Twp., Pike Co., Missouri (*Census Place: Clarksville, Pike, Missouri; Roll: M593_798; Page: 120B; Image: 248*). John A. Kelley is age 37, born Ohio, a plasterer. With him is wife Mary J., 36, born Ohio. In the home are children Lorenzo, 14, born Ohio; and John II, 12, Harrison, nine, "Louis A.", (listed as male) seven, Laura, six, and Joshua, two, all born in Missouri.

John A. and Mary J. Pegan Kelley are still in Clarksville, Calumet Twp., Pike Co., Missouri in 1880 (*Census Place: Clarksville, Pike, Missouri;* *Roll: 709; Page: 560B; Enumeration District: 135; Image: 0492*). The surname is again spelled "Kelly" on the census form. In the home are John Kelley and Mary J. Pegan Kelley, both age 47 and born in Ohio. Children are: Lorenzo, 24, a plasterer, born Ohio; and John A. II, 23, a shoemaker, Harrison, 19, a plasterer; "Allie" (this time listed as female), 17, Laura, 15, Joshua, 12 and "Annie" (Fannie), nine, all born in Missouri.

In 1900, John A. and Mary J. Pegan Kelley are enumerated Clarksville, Calumet Twp., Pike Co., Missouri (*Census Place: Calumet, Pike, Missouri; Roll: T623_882; Page: 5A; Enumeration District: 86*). In the home are John Kelley, age 66, born Sep 1833 in Ohio, with his father born in Virginia and his mother in Ohio; and wife Mary J. Pegan Kelley, also 66, born May 1834, also in Ohio, with her father born in Pennsylvania and her mother in Ohio. The couple says they have been married 44 years. But Mary is listed as saying she has borne only one child, who is still living. This is incorrect as their children are all still alive, and were still so when John Kelley died in 1911, according to his will and probate. Perhaps the Kelleys misunderstood the question and thought the census taker meant, "children living with you". Son Lorenzo Kelley, 43, single and a plasterer born in Ohio, is in the household with them.

John A. Kelley is still living in Clarksville, Calumet Twp., Pike Co., Missouri in 1910 (*Census Place: Clarksville Ward 2, Pike, Missouri; Roll: T624_805; Page: 8A; Enumeration District: 0123; Image: 245*). In the home are John, age 76 and born Ohio, a widower who says he is still a plasterer; and son "Lou" (Lorenzo), 54, single, also a plasterer also born in Ohio. Close by is his brother-in-law John Pegan and his family.

Children of Mary Jane Pegan and John A. Kelley:

+ 19 m I. **Lorenzo Kelley or[7] Kelly** was born in Clark Twp., Clinton Co., Ohio, on March 5, 1857.[59] He was also known as **Louie**. Lorenzo Kelley or died in

				Clarksville, Calumet Twp., Pike Co., Missouri, on August 14, 1924.[59]
+	20	m	II.	**John A.[7] Kelley II** was born in Mexico Twp., Audrain Co., Missouri, on November 19, 1858.[66] He died in Warm Springs, Warm Springs Twp, Deer Lodge Co., Montana, on April 13, 1947.[66]
+	21	m	III.	**Harrison[7] Kelley** was born in Mexico Twp., Audrain Co., Missouri, on December 25, 1860.[67] He died in Havre, Hill Co., Montana, on June 12, 1932.[67]
+	22	m	IV.	**Lewis Albert[7] Kelley** was born in Mexico Twp., Audrain Co., Missouri, on May 2, 1862.[68] He was also known as **Allie**. Lewis Albert died in Palmyra, Liberty Twp., Marion Co., Missouri, on April 27, 1944.[68]
+	23	f	V.	**Laura Belle[7] Kelley** was born in Mexico Twp., Audrain Co., Missouri?, in 1864. She was also known as **Lollie**. Laura Belle died in Oklahoma? between 1936 and 1944. was also known as **Allie**. Lewis Albert died in Palmyra, Liberty Twp., Marion Co., Missouri, on April 27, 1944.[68]
+	24	m	VI.	**Joshua[7] Kelley** was born in Clarksville, Calumet Twp., Pike Co., Missouri, on February 11, 1868.[69] He died in Winfield, Monroe Twp., Lincoln Co., Missouri, on December 13, 1953.[69]
+	25	f	VII.	**Fannie Anna[7] Kelley** was born in Clarksville, Calumet Twp., Pike Co., Missouri, on June 24, 1871.[70] She was also known as **Fannie**. Fannie Anna died in a hospital in Fulton, Callaway Co., Missouri, on June 7, 1952.[70]

5. **William Henry[6] Pegan** (*Andrew[5], Robert A.[4], Andrew[3], Andrew[2] Pagan, James[1]*) was born on January 18, 1837, in Clark Twp., Clinton Co., Ohio.[14] He was the son of Andrew Pegan (1) and Mary Jane McKibben. William Henry died in Jamestown, Silvercreek Twp., Greene Co., Ohio, on October 12, 1914, at age 77.[14, 15] He was buried in Old Silvercreek Cemetery, Jamestown, Silvercreek Twp., Greene Co., Ohio.[71]

William Henry married **Mary Ann Liggett** on November 27, 1859, in Highland Co., Ohio.[72] They divorced. They had two children. Mary Ann Liggett was born in Dodson Twp., Highland Co., Ohio, on June 29, 1842.[73] She reached age 75 and died in Watertown, Watertown Town, Jefferson Co., New York, on April 17, 1918.[73, 74] Mary Ann Liggett Pegan McIlhenny was buried in Troutwine Cemetery, Dodson Twp., Highland Co., Ohio and Clark Twp., Clinton Co., Ohio.[75, 76]

William and Mary Liggett Pegan are living with Mary's parents, Sinclair and Mary Liggett, in Dodson Twp., Highland Co., Ohio in 1860 *(Census Place: Dodson, Highland, Ohio; Roll: M653_986; Page: 72; Image: 148)*. In the home are William Pegan, listed as "Wm. Peagon", age 23, a farm laborer born in Ohio and Mary Ann Liggett Pegan, 17, also born Ohio. Sinclair Liggett is 53 and a farmer and his wife Rebecca is 47; both were born in Virginia. Also in the home is Sinclair and Rebecca's son and Mary's brother John Liggett, 20, born Ohio.

William Henry Pegan was drafted into Company I, 79th Ohio regiment during the Civil War. He was a fifer.[77, 78]

William Henry Pegan was the only one of Andrew and Mary Jane McKibben Pegan's children to stay in southwestern Ohio when his parents and siblings moved to Missouri in the mid-1860s

William Henry Pegan is enumerated in that county in 1870 *(Census Place: Dodson, Highland, Ohio; Roll: M593_1222; Page: 348; Image: 698)*. In the home are William, 33, a plasterer, Mary, 28, and children "Edmund" (Edwin), nine, and "Jane", two. They were all born in Ohio. A farm laborer, Frank

Thompson, 17, born Ohio, is also a member of the household.

William Henry Pegan and his first wife, Mary Liggett Pegan, seem to have divorced before 1872. After the divorce, he seems to have had little contact with his two children by his first marriage, Edwin Sinclair Pegan and Elizabeth Jane "Libbie" Pegan Gregor. A biography of Libbie's husband, Dr. Gilbert David Gregor, of Watertown, Jefferson Co., New York says that Elizabeth Jane Pegan was the daughter of "John and Mary McElhaney Pegan".[79] Many articles appear later about his ex-wife, son and daughter in the Park City, Utah newspapers, but William H. Pegan is never mentioned.

William Henry Pegan is found in Sabina Twp., Clinton Co., Ohio in 1880, listed as William "Pagan" *(Census Place: Sabina, Clinton, Ohio; Roll: 1001; Page: 132C; Enumeration District: 061; Image: 0267)*. He says he is age 43, divorced, and is a hired man/servant in the household of Albert Haines, a farmer. William also says he was born in Ohio and his parents in Virginia. (His ex-wife is in Montana, his son in Utah, and his 12-year-old daughter is boarding as a "music teacher" in Clinton County, Ohio.)

William Henry Pegan married **Hattie Ann Griffith** on December 28, 1883, in Greene Co., Ohio.[80] They had one daughter. Hattie Ann Griffith was born in Winchester, Frederick Co., Virginia, on May 13, 1842.[81, 82] Hattie Ann reached age 96 and died in Xenia, Xenia Twp., Greene Co., Ohio, on May 19, 1938.[80, 81] She was buried in Old Silvercreek Cemetery, Jamestown, Silvercreek Twp., Greene Co., Ohio.[83]

In 1900, William H. Pegan is enumerated in Jamestown, Silvercreek Twp., Greene Co., Ohio. *(Census Place: Jamestown, Greene, Ohio; Roll: T623_1272; Page: 6A; Enumeration District: 90)*. William H., age 62, born Ohio, is once again a plasterer; he says his parents were also born in Ohio. His wife, Hattie Griffith Pegan, 58, was also born in Ohio; she says her father was born in Virginia and her mother in Maryland. The pair say they have been married 16 years and Hattie has borne one child, who is still alive. This is daughter Inez, age 10, who is also in the home.

William H. Pegan and wife Hattie are still in Silvercreek Twp., Greene Co., Ohio in 1910 *(Census Place: Silver Creek, Greene, Ohio; Roll: T624_1185; Page: 7A; Enumeration District: 0095; Image: 676)*. William H. is listed as 69 years old (?) and Hattie is 67. William again says he and his parents were born in Ohio, and Hattie also gives the same birth information she gave in 1900. Still living with them is daughter Inez, 20, born Ohio.

Hattie Griffith Pegan, a widow, is living with her son-in-law and and daughter, Harold and Inez Pegan Owens, in 1920 in Xenia, Xenia Twp., Greene Co., Ohio *(Census Place: Xenia Ward 3, Greene, Ohio; Roll: T625_1386; Page: 1A; Enumeration District: 178; Image: 1088)*. Hattie is age 77 and says she and her parents were born in Ohio (Incorrect—she was born in Virginia and her parents were not born in Ohio). Harold Owens, age 29, born Ohio, with his father born in Ohio and his mother in Virginia, is a manager of a clothing store. Inez is 30 years old; she and her parents were Ohio natives.

Hattie Griffith Pegan, age 88, is still living with Harold and Inez Pegan Owens in Xenia, Xenia Twp., Greene Co., Ohio in 1930 *(Census Place: Xenia, Greene, Ohio; Roll: 1804; Page: 15A; Enumeration District: 24; Image: 347.0)*. This time, Hattie says she and her mother were Virginia natives and her father was born in Maryland. Harold Owens, 39, is still the manager of the clothing store. He says he and his parents were born in Ohio. Inez is age 40, born Ohio, as was her father; her mother born in Virginia.

om William Henry Pegan, Mary Ann Liggett Pegan married Scipio McIlhenny on 12 September 12, 1877 in Ogden, Weber Co., Utah.[84]

In 1880, Mary Ann Liggett Pegan McIlhenny is found with her second husband, Dr. Scipio McIlheney, a physician, in Helena, Lewis and Clark Co., Montana *(Census Place: Helena, Lewis and Clark, Montana; Roll: 742; Page: 305C; Enumeration District: 018; Image: 0622)*. Scipio McIlhenny is age 40, and a physician, born Ohio as were his parents. Mary A. Liggett Pegan McIlhaney is 37, and she and her father were born in Ohio and her mother in Virginia. They are operating a boarding house filled with miners.

Dr. Scipio McIlhenny sued Mary Ann Pegan McIlhenny for divorce in Salt Lake City, Salt Lake Co., Utah in 1883. Dr. McIlhenny died not long after the divorce, on August 9, 1884, in Salt Lake City. According to a newspaper article about his death, McIlhenny, who was born in Fairfield, Fairfield Twp., Butler Co., Ohio in 1840, died from alcohol (whiskey) addiction and "excessive use of narcotics", specifically morphine and "chlorol" (chlorol hydrate).[85]

By 1883, Mary Ann Liggett Pegan McIlhenny is living in Park City, Summit Co., Utah, along with her daughter Elizabeth "Libbie" Pegan, according to newspaper articles in the *Park Record (Park City, UT)*.[86] Later, according to her obituary, Mary Ann becomes a missionary in the "Home Service Missionary", working in Louisville, Kentucky and Indianapolis, Indiana.[73]

By 1900, Mary Ann Liggett Pegan McIlhenny is divorced for the second time and living in Indianapolis, Center Twp., Marion Co., Indiana (*Census Place: Indianapolis, Marion, Indiana; Roll: 388; Page: 2A; Enumeration District: 55*). She is a boarder in the household of Rena Dowler. She is enumerated as Mary Ann "McIllheney", born June 27, 1842 according to the census form, says she and her father were born in Ohio and her mother in Virginia. Mary Ann lists her occupation as missionary, and says she is a widow who bore two children, both still alive.

By September 15, 1901, Mary Liggett Pegan McIlhenny is residing in Watertown, Watertown Town, New York, most likely with her son-in-law and daughter, Gilbert D. and Elizabeth "Libbie" Pegan Gregor. The *Park Herald (Park City, UT)* mentions on that date that "Mrs. Mary McElhaney" had ended a two-month visit with her son Edwin Pegan and was returning to Watertown.[87]

Although she was residing in Watertown with her the Gregors, Mary Ann is not found in the 1910 census in their household. Perhaps she was traveling between Watertown and Park City. She continued to live in Watertown until she died.

Children of William Henry Pegan and Mary Ann Liggett:

+ 26 m I. **Sinclair Edwin**[7] **Pegan** was born in Dodson Twp., Highland Co., Ohio, on September 11, 1860.[88] He was also known as **Edwin Sinclair Pegan; S.E. Pegan** and **Ed**. Sinclair Edwin died in Spokane, Diana Precinct, Spokane Co., Washington, on November 9, 1922.[88]

+ 27 f II. **Elizabeth Jane**[7] **Pegan** was born in Marathon, Jackson Twp., Clermont Co., Ohio, on July 2, 1867.[89, 90] She was also known as **Libbie** (**Jennie** in 1870). Elizabeth Jane died in Watertown, Watertown Town, Jefferson Co., New York, on September 16, 1926.[89, 90, 91, 92]

Daughter of William Henry Pegan and Hattie Ann Griffith:

+ 28 f I. **Inez Mae**[7] **Pegan** was born in Silver Creek Twp., Greene Co., Ohio, on September 5, 1889.[93] She died in South Pasadena, Pinellas Co., Florida, on November 3, 1983.[93, 94]

6. **James Robert**[6] **Pegan** (*Andrew*[5], *Robert A.*[4], *Andrew*[3], *Andrew*[2] *Pagan, James*[1]) was born on October 5, 1839, in Dodson Twp., Highland Co., Ohio.[17] He was the son of Andrew Pegan (1) and Mary Jane McKibben. James Robert died in French Camp, Stockton Twp., San Joaquin Co., California, on June 21, 1913, at age 73.[17, 18] He was buried in Yuba City Cemetery, Yuba City, Sutter Co., California.[95]

James Pegan, age 24, an unmarried farmer, registers for the Civil War draft in Northern California in "Slough", probably Sloughhouse, Sacramento Co., California in 1863.[96]

James Robert seems to have married **Catherine Unknown** between 1863-1868. Catherine died in Sutter Co., California?, before 1868.

James Robert Pegan married Mrs. **Queen Isabella Coates** Galbraith on October 1, 1868, in Sutter Co., California.[97, 98] They were legally separated before 1910. They had four children. Queen Isabella Coates was born in Perche Twp., Boone Co., Missouri, on August 29, 1846.[99] She was also known as **Isabella** or **Belle**. She reached age 74 and died in San Francisco, San Francisco Co., California, on April 16, 1921.[99, 100] Queen Isabella was buried in Yuba City Cemetery, Yuba City, Sutter Co., California.[101]

Queen Isabella Coates Galbraith Pegan was born in District 8, Boone Co., Missouri, which later became Perche Township. She rarely used "Queen" as her given name and usually used her middle name, Isabella, as her preferred name. On her marriage license to James Pegan, however, Isabelle's name is "Mrs. Queen Galbraith".[97]

James Pagan, age 29, born Ohio, a farmer, is first found in Sutter Twp., Sutter Co., California in 1870 *(Census Place: Sutter, Sutter, California; Roll: M593_92; Page: 117A; Image: 235)*. He is enumerated as "Pegin". With him is wife (Queen) Isabelle "Belle" Coates Galbreath Pegan, 24, born Missouri. James is working on a farm owned by Solomon Turpinseed. Also living with them but listed with the surname Pegan ("Pegin") are Isabelle's two children by her first marriage John Alexander ("Alexander") and Mary T. Galbreath, ages six and four respectively and both born in California.

In 1880, James Pegan, 40, farmer, is enumerated in Butte Twp., Sutter Co., California *(Census Place: Butte, Sutter, California; Roll: 84; Page: 380C; Enumeration District: 134; Image: 0764)*. He says he was born in Ohio and his parents were born in Pennsylvania. In the home with him are wife (Queen) Isabelle Coates Galbreath Pegan, 34, born Missouri, with her parents born in Kentucky; his stepson John Galbreath, 16, and stepdaughter May (Mary) Galbreath, 14; and daughter Carrie, seven, and son Frank, three. All the children were born in California.

In 1884, James Robert Pegan is living in Cottonwood Twp., Shasta Co., California, according to the county's voter registration rolls.[102] In 1891, James Robert Pegan obtains a U.S. government land grant for land on the Mount Diablo meridian in Anderson Twp. in Shasta Co. in 1891.[103]

Queen Isabella Coates Galbraith Pegan suffered from mental illness and often behaved erratically. In December 1897, according to the Los Angeles (CA) Herald on December 31st of that year, Isabella was arrested on a charge of "insanity" in Los Angeles for assaulting a railway conductor. She pulled his hair and scratched his face. The article also says she suffered from hallucinations and thought that people were calling her a thief. In addition, the newspaper reports that she had once been an inmate in a Stockton, California asylum, but recently had been living with her brother in Pasadena before he left for the Klondike gold rush.[104] But by the 1900 census, Queen Isabella Coates Galbreath Pegan is back living with her husband and family in Anderson Twp., Shasta Co., California.

In 1900, James Pegan, age 63 (incorrect) is residing in Anderson Twp., Shasta Co., California *(Census Place: Anderson, Shasta, California; Roll: T623_112; Page: 15A; Enumeration District: 111)*. James' birthdate is listed as Oct 1836, but as his brother William Henry Pegan was born in Jan 1837, this is impossible. His age the past two censuses are consistent with a birthdate in 1839 or 1840. This time James says he was born in Ohio, his father in Pennsylvania and his mother in Kentucky. His occupation is listed as stock raiser. Also living in the home are his wife (Queen) Isabelle Coates Galbreath Pegan, 53, born Missouri. The couple says they have been married 30 years and Isabelle has born six children, with five of them still living. Children in the home are daughters Ruby Z., 16, born Jul 1883; and Zoa, 14, born Jun 1886; both born in California with their father born in Ohio and their mother in Missouri. Also in the household is unmarried stepson John Galbreath, 35, born Jul 1864 in California, with his parents born in Missouri.

James Robert Pegan, age 70, is still living in Anderson Twp., Shasta Co., California in 1910 *(Census Place: Anderson, Shasta, California; Roll: T624_107; Page:*

10A; Enumeration District: 0089; Image: 738). This time, he says he was born in Ohio, with his father born in Pennsylvania and his mother in Ohio. James and (Queen) Isabelle Coats Galbreath Pegan seem to be separated. He says he has been married 40 years and is still married to his wife, but Isabelle is not in the home with him nor are any of the children. He says he is a laborer doing odd jobs and is renting his residence.

In 1910, Queen Isabelle Coates Galbreath Pegan is separated from her husband, James Robert Pegan, although both list themselves as married. James is in Anderson Twp., Shasta Co., California, while Isabelle is running a boarding house in Stockton, Stockton Twp., San Joaquin Co., California *(Census Place: Stockton Ward 2, San Joaquin, California; Roll: T624_103; Page: 1B; Enumeration District: 0135; Image: 356).* Daughters Ruby Z., 24, a schoolteacher, and Zoa, 22, a stenographer, are living with their mother. There are four lodgers in the boarding house, and one is Ernest Camp, age 30, born Nebraska (Incorrect—he was born in Iowa), who would soon be Zoa's husband. Ernest says his father was born in Pennsylvania and his mother in New York, and his occupation is musician in a dance hall. Perhaps James was just tending to the sale of the farm, or the separation was short-lived, as James Pegan dies in Stockton, Stockton Twp., San Joaquin Co., California in 1913.

There seems to be some discrepancy in James Robert Pegan's age. He is enumerated as born in 1830 (1860), 1840 (1870, 1910), Oct 1836 (1900—impossible, as another sibling is born in Jan 1837). However, his death certificate says he was born on October 5, 1839. He died in the Stockton County Hospital on June 21, 1913. His daughter (Ruby) Zella Pegan (later Paganetti) was the informant and says her father had lived in Stockton Co. five months at the time of his death.[17] His death certificate says he was buried in "Marysville", Sutter Co., California; his wife's, Queen Isabella Coates Galbraith Pegan's says she was also buried there.[17, 99] But both James' and "Belle" Pegan's obituaries say their burials were in the Yuba City Cemetery. Yuba City is across the Feather River from Maryville.[101, 105]

Children of James Robert Pegan and Queen Isabella Coates:

+ 29 f I. **Carrie Etta**[7] **Pegan** was born in Sutter Twp., Sutter Co., California, on June 28, 1872.[106] She died in Vernon Twp., Sutter Co., California, on September 28, 1947.[106]

+ 30 m II. **Franklin Andrew**[7] **Pegan** was born in Butte Twp., Sutter Co., California, on September 28, 1876.[107] He died in Butte Twp., Sutter Co., California, on November 12, 1880.[107]

+ 31 f III. **Ruby Zetta**[7] **Pegan** was born in Butte Twp., Sutter Co., California, on July 27, 1883.[108, 109] She died in Pescadero, Washington Twp., San Mateo Co., California, on February 21, 1978.[108, 110]

+ 32 f IV. **Zoa Faretta**[7] **Pegan** was born in Butte Twp., Sutter Co., California, on June 13, 1886.[111, 112] She died in a hospital in San Jose, Santa Clara Co., California, on February 22, 1961.[111, 112]

7. **John S.**[6] **Pegan** (*Andrew*[5], *Robert A.*[4], *Andrew*[3], *Andrew*[2] *Pagan, James*[1]) was born on November 22, 1843, in Dodson Twp., Highland Co., Ohio.[19] He was the son of Andrew Pegan (1) and Mary Jane McKibben. John S. died in Clarksville, Calumet Twp., Pike Co., Missouri, on April 9, 1939, at age 95.[19] He was buried in Greenwood Cemetery, Clarksville, Calumet Twp., Pike Co., Missouri.[19, 113]

John S. married **Margaret N. Duncan** on December 28, 1865, in Pike Co., Missouri.[114, 115] They had two children. Margaret N. Duncan was born in Warren Twp., Marion Co., Missouri, on August 23, 1847.[116, 117] Margaret N. reached age 21 and died in Clarksville, Calumet Twp., Pike Co., Missouri, on May 23, 1869.[116, 117] She was buried in Greenwood Cemetery, Clarksville, Calumet Twp., Pike Co., Missouri.[116, 117]

Margaret N. Duncan, age four, is found with her parents in 1850 in Warren Twp., Marion Co., Missouri *(Census Place: Warren, Marion, Missouri; Roll: M432_406; Page: 339A; Image: 166; entry for Margaret Duncan, Robert Duncan, head of household)*. By 1860, her family is in Clarksville, Calumet Twp., Pike Co., Missouri *(Census Place: Calumet, Pike, Missouri; Roll: M653_639; Page: 345; Image: 349; Robert Duncan, head of household)*. Both times, she is listed as born in Missouri.

Widower John Pegan is enumerated as "John Pagans" in Calumet Twp., Pike Co., Missouri in 1870 *(Census Place: Calumet, Pike, Missouri; Roll: M593_798; Page: 100B; Image: 208)*. He is 27 years old, born Ohio, and is a farm hand working for James and Carrie Mulherin, ages 29 and 23 respectively and both born in Missouri. It is quite possible that John was not living with the Mulherins, but living in his parent's, Andrew and Mary Jane McKibben Pegan's home. (Sometimes a census taker reported who was at a household when he arrived, not necessarily who was living in the house.) His two children, listed as Flora, age three, and Andrew, age one, are living with their paternal grandparents Andrew and Mary Jane McKibben Pegan in Clarksville, Calumet Twp., Pike Co., Missouri. However, on the census form the children's ages were switched.

The relationship between John S. Pegan and his father Andrew may have been strained after 1870. On March 14, 1873, Andrew sues John, and several other men, over a $333.06 debt Andrew said John had owed him since December 22, 1870. According to the court records, John offered as collateral his share of a tobacco crop, harvested but not yet cured, which he owned with a business partner, the James Mulherin who John was enumerated with in the 1870 census. The tobacco cured, but John had not paid his debt to Andrew. Andrew claimed John's share of the tobacco crop, and Andrew and John's business partner gave the crop to two other men, merchant brokers, to sell. The merchant brokers sold the crop, and made a partial payment to Mulherin, but Andrew had not been paid a cent. Andrew sued John, James Mulherin, and the two merchant brokers. The merchant brokers testified that John's share was only worth $256.50. The court ruled that the merchant brokers pay Andrew this sum at once; also, the brokers were to pay the rest of what they owed to Mr. Mulherin. The court said John still owed his father the rest of the debt, $79.56, plus 10 percent interest per annum. It is unknown whether John ever paid Andrew the remainder, plus interest. The merchant brokers, John and his business partner were also ordered to pay Andrew's court costs.[10]

In 1880, John Pegan, age 37, a widower born in Ohio, is living with his parents, Andrew and Mary Jane McKibben in Clarksville, Calumet Twp., Pike Co., Missouri *(Census Place: Clarksville, Pike, Missouri; Roll: T9_709; Page: 551.3000; Enumeration District: 135; Image: 0473)*. John says he is a carpenter. Also in the home is John Pegan's son by his first wife Margaret Duncan Pegan, Andrew Pegan, age 13, born Missouri. John Pegan's father, Andrew Pegan, age 75 and the head of the household, says he and his parents were born in Pennsylvania. John's mother, "Jane" (Mary Jane) Pegan, 70, says she was born in Ohio and her parents in Kentucky. The final member of the household is John's brother "Rob" (Robert) Pegan, 31, born Ohio, single, who now says he is a fireman on the railroad.

John S. Pegan married **Dulcinea Nannie Vaughn Jeans** on March 17, 1881, in Pike Co., Missouri.[118, 119] They had one son. Dulcinea Nannie Vaughn Jeans was born in Calumet Twp., Pike Co., Missouri, on May 11, 1860.[119] She was also known as **Nannie**. Dulcinea Nannie Vaughn reached age 78 and died in Clarksville, Calumet Twp., Pike Co., Missouri, on February 17, 1939.[119] She was buried in Greenwood Cemetery, Clarksville, Calumet Twp., Pike Co., Missouri.[119, 120]

Dulcinea Nannie Vaughn Jeans always was called Nannie.

John Pegan is enumerated in Clarksville, Calumet Twp., Pike Co., Missouri in 1900 *(Census Place: Calumet, Pike, Missouri; Roll: T623_882; Page: 5A; Enumeration District: 86)*. John, 56, is a carpenter who says he was born in Ohio, his father in Pennsylvania, and his mother in Ohio. With him is second wife Nannie Vaughn Jeans Pegan, listed as "Jammie", age 40, who says she and her mother are Missouri natives; her father was born in Kentucky. The couple states they have been married 19 years and Nannie has born one child who is still alive.

Their son Morrow W., listed as "Morya W.", is age six and born in Missouri. Living close by is his cousin Mary J. Pegan Kelley, her husband John, and son Lorenzo ("Louis").

In 1910, John Pegan, 62, a carpenter, is still in Clarksville, Calumet Twp., Pike Co., Missouri *(Census Place: Clarksville Ward 2, Pike, Missouri; Roll: T624_805; Page: 8A; Enumeration District: 0123; Image: 245)*. John says he and his mother are Ohio natives, with his father born in Pennsylvania. Also in the home is wife Nannie, 47, and son Morrow W., 15, born Missouri. Nannie repeats that she and her mother were born in Missouri and her father in Kentucky. This time, John and Nannie Vaughn Jeans Pegan say they have been married 26 years (?) and Nannie has had one child, still living. (John Kelley and son Lorenzo "Lou" Kelley are still neighbors, but Mary J. Pegan Kelley is deceased.)

John Pegan, age 72, and his wife Nannie Vaughn Jeans Pegan, continue to reside in Clarksville, Calumet Twp., Pike Co., Missouri in 1920 *(Census Place: Calumet, Pike, Missouri; Roll: T625_941; Page: 6A; Enumeration District: 137; Image: 778)*. He still lists his occupation as a carpenter. John says his father was born in Pennsylvania and his mother in Ohio, while Nannie states her father was a Kentucky native and her mother was from Missouri.

John and Nannie Vaughn Jeans Pegan, ages 83 and 62 respectively, are again found in Clarksville, Calumet Twp., Pike Co., Missouri in 1930 *(Census Place: Calumet, Pike, Missouri; Roll: 1218; Page: 5A; Enumeration District: 9; Image: 657.0.)*. John says once again he was born in Ohio, with his father born in Pennsylvania and his mother in Ohio. Nannie, like her mother, was born in Missouri; but this time she says her father was a born in Virginia. John errs in stating that he was first married at age 43—he gave his age at his second marriage. Nannie correctly says she was 22 years old when she first wed.

Children of John S. Pegan and Margaret N. Duncan:

+ 33 f I. **Flora**[7] **Pegan** was born in Clarksville, Calumet Twp., Pike Co., Missouri, on November 21, 1866.[121, 122] She died in Clarksville, Calumet Twp., Pike Co., Missouri, on August 21, 1875.[121, 122, 123]

+ 34 m II. **Andrew M.**[7] **Pegan** was born in Iowa or Missouri on November 14, 1868.[124] He died in Spokane, Diana Precinct, Spokane Co., Washington, on December 10, 1910.[124, 125]

Son of John S. Pegan and Dulcinea Nannie Vaughn Jeans:

+ 35 m I. **Morrow Walton**[7] **Pegan** was born in Clarksville, Calumet Twp., Pike Co., Missouri, on May 16, 1894.[126, 127] He died in St. Louis, Missouri, on April 3, 1970.[128, 129]

8. Samuel Alexander[6] **Pegan** (*Andrew*[5], *Robert A.*[4], *Andrew*[3], *Andrew*[2] *Pagan, James*[1]) was born on August 2, 1846, in Washington Twp., Clinton Co., Ohio or Dodson Twp., Highland Co., Ohio.[20] He was the son of Andrew Pegan (1) and Mary Jane McKibben. Samuel Alexander died in St. Louis, Missouri, on April 5, 1906, at age 59.[20, 21] He was buried in St. Louis Potter's Field Cemetery/Mt. Lebanon Cemetery, St. Louis, Missouri.[21]

There is a Samuel A. Pegan, born Ohio, allegedly age 38?, listed on the Yuba City, Sutter Twp., Sutter Co., California voters list in 1866.[130] Samuel seems to have traveled to California with his brother James Robert Pegan, but wandered back east to Iowa by 1870.

In 1870, Samuel Pegan, 24, born in Missouri, is found in Ward 3, Burlington, Burlington Twp., Des Moines Co., Iowa *(Census Place: Burlington Ward 3, Des Moines, Iowa; Roll: M593_388; Page: 336B; Image: 214)*. He is single and living in a boarding house run by John and Ada Woods. He lists his occupation as "working in a sash factory". His brother and sister-in-law, Leonidas and Martha Jane Pegan Pegan are also living in Burlington.

In 1876, there is a Samuel Pegan, a machinist, listed in the Denver, Arapahoe Co., Colorado city directory.[131] But he may not have lived in Denver long, as Samuel A. Pegan is again found on the voter's list in Yuba City, Sutter Co., California that same year.[132] He is still there in 1879.[133] However, the latter may be a mistake, or a failure to purge the voters list.

Samuel Alexander married **Flora Johnston** on November 20, 1877, in Pike Co., Missouri.[134, 135] They divorced in Missouri before 1896. They had one son. Flora Johnston was born in Pittsfield, Pittsfield Twp., Pike Co., Illinois, on June 6, 1849.[136] She reached age 79 and died in Clarksville, Calumet Twp., Pike Co., Missouri, on March 1, 1929.[136] Flora was buried in Greenwood Cemetery, Clarksville, Calumet Twp., Pike Co., Missouri.[136, 137]

Samuel Pegan is enumerated as "Samuel Pegans" in 1880 in Clarksville, Calumet Twp., Pike Co., Missouri *(Census Place: Clarksville, Pike, Missouri; Roll: 709; Page: 563D; Enumeration District: 135; Image: 0498).* Samuel, age 34, born Ohio, as were his parents, is a stone cutter. He now has a wife, Flora Johnston Pegan, 21, born in Illinois, with her father born in Missouri and her mother in Ohio. Also in the home is their son Harry Clark Pegan, age two, born Missouri.

In 1890, Samuel A. Pegan, now a carpenter, is found in the St. Louis, Missouri city directory.[138]

Samuel Alexander Pegan married **Jessie Unknown Taylor** on October 6, 1896, in Pike Co., Missouri.[139] They divorced before 1900.

Nothing is known of Jessie Taylor. Taylor seems not to have been her maiden name.

In 1900, Samuel Pegan, 54, born Missouri, is divorced again. He is a lodger who lists himself as single in the household of Thomas D. Richardson in West Twp., New Madrid Co., Missouri *(Census Place: West, New Madrid, Missouri; Roll: T623_877; Page: 6A; Enumeration District: 78).* He is a day laborer. For some reason, he says his father was born in Tennessee and his mother in Kentucky, but perhaps someone else gave his information to the census taker.

Inexplicably, Samuel A. Pegan is listed as "Pete" Pegan on his death certificate in St. Louis, Missouri.[20] Samuel's obituary in the *Clarksville (MO) Banner* on April 13, 1906 confirms his death date and place, age, reason for death and parents' birthplaces (Ohio) as this "Pete" Pegan.[21] His death record says Samuel was living in the Windsor Hotel in St. Louis when he died, and was buried in St. Louis' Potter's Field Cemetery.[20] According to the online *St. Louis Magazine,* this Potter's Field Cemetery was a property bordered by Hampton, Fyler, Scanlon and Sublette streets, which is currently the site of an apartment complex. The bodies buried there were disinterred when the apartment complex was built in 1952 and taken to the Mt. Lebanon Cemetery, Lindbergh Avenue at St. Charles Rock Road, in St. Louis.[140]

In 1910, Samuel's first wife, Flora Johnston Pegan, age 60, who claims she is a widow, is living with her mother Elizabeth Johnston and unmarried sister Ada in Clarksville, Calumet Twp., Pike Co., Missouri *(Census Place: Clarksville Ward 1, Pike, Missouri; Roll: T624_805; Page: 4A; Enumeration District: 0123; Image: 237).* Flora, born Illinois, says she is a self-employed dressmaker, and states her father was born in Missouri and her mother in Ohio. Her mother Elizabeth, 87, born Ohio, is the head of the household. Flora's unmarried sister, Ada, 40, a milliner who owns her own store, is also in the home.

Flora Johnston Pegan, 70, continues to live in Clarksville, Calumet Twp., Pike Co., Missouri in 1920 *(Census Place: Calumet, Pike, Missouri; Roll: T625_941; Page: 4B; Enumeration District: 137).* Again, she says she is a widow, but this time with no occupation. Listed as the head of household is her sister Ada Johnston, 50, a milliner who owns her own store. A servant, Beulah Ayston or Austin, 34, is also in the home.

Son of Samuel Alexander Pegan and Flora Johnston:

+ 36 m I. **Harry Clark[7] Pegan** was born in Clarksville, Calumet Twp., Pike Co., Missouri, on April 14, 1878.[141] He died in Hannibal, Mason Twp., Marion Co., Missouri, on October 3, 1916.[141]

9. **Robert Andrew**[6] **Pegan** (*Andrew*[5], *Robert A.*[4], *Andrew*[3], *Andrew*[2] *Pagan*, *James*[1]) was born on March 3, 1848, in Washington Twp., Clinton Co., Ohio.[22] He was also known as **Rob**. He was the son of Andrew Pegan (1) and Mary Jane McKibben. Robert Andrew died in Kansas City, Jackson Co., Missouri, on July 13, 1929, at age 81.[22] He was buried in Mt. Washington Cemetery, Independence, Jackson Co., Missouri.[22, 142]

In 1870, Robert Pegan, age 21, a carpenter, born Ohio, is living with his parents Andrew and Mary Jane McKibben in Clarksville, Calumet Twp., Pike Co., Missouri *(Census Place: Clarksville, Pike, Missouri; Roll: M593_798; Page: 111; Image: 226)*. There are two children in the home who are his brother John's: Flora, age three and Andrew, age one, both born in Missouri.

In 1880, Robert A. Pegan, enumerated as "Rob Pegan", is still residing in Clarksville, Calumet Twp., Pike Co., Missouri in his parent's home *(Census Place: Clarksville, Pike, Missouri; Roll: T9_709; Page: 551.3000; Enumeration District: 135; Image: 0473)*. Robert is age 31, single, born Missouri with his father born in Pennsylvania and his mother in Ohio. He lists his occupation as a fireman on the railroad.

Robert Andrew married **Jessie Farrington** on September 3, 1890, in Carroll Co., Missouri.[143] They had one son. Jessie Farrington was born in Waterville Twp., Lucas Co., Ohio, on March 1, 1868.[144] Jessie lived in 1940 in Kansas City, Jackson Co., Missouri. She reached age 72 and died in Kansas City, Jackson Co., Missouri, on September 5, 1940.[144] Jessie was buried in Mt. Washington Cemetery, Independence, Jackson Co., Missouri.[144, 145]

Jessie Farrington Pegan's father, Josiah "Ferrington", is found in the 1860 census in Waterville Twp., Lucas Co., Ohio *(Census Place: Waterville, Lucas, Ohio; Roll: M653_1003; Page: 311; entry for Josiah "Ferrington")*. In the Civil War Draft Registration Records, he is still a resident of Waterville.[146] Jessie was only a few months old in 1869 when her family moved to Sugartree Twp., Carroll Company, Missouri, and they are found there in the 1870 census, with Jessie listed as born in Ohio *(Census Place: Sugartree, Carroll, Missouri; Roll: M593_766; Page: 378A; entry for Jessie Farrington; Josiah Ferrington, head of household)*. All indications are Jessie, whose real name may have been Justina, was born in Waterville Twp., Lucas Co., Ohio.

By 1893, Robert A. Pegan was living in St. Joseph, Buchanan Co., Missouri, per the St. Joseph city directory. He is listed as a partner in Thornton and Pegan Undertakers.[147] His nephew, Andrew M. Pegan, son of Robert's brother John, is also a resident there.

The October 23, 1894 edition of the *Quincy (IL) Daily Journal*, reprinted an article from a paper in St. Joseph, Missouri which mentions an "Undertaker Pegan", undoubtedly Robert A. Pegan, in a story about the mysterious disappearance of a corpse. The widow of Thomas J. Tinsley was exhuming the body of her late husband, who died three weeks earlier, from his Ashland Cemetery grave in St. Joseph to bury him in another cemetery. When Mr. Tinsley's coffin was disinterred, it was discovered that his body was missing. The paper reported that "Undertaker Pegan, who had charge of the funeral, advised Mrs. Tinsley not to have the coffin opened when the body was removed." The article said that the sheriff's department had not yet found the body, but believed it was concealed in the city and had obtained search warrants for all the "medical colleges" and funeral parlors in St. Joseph.[148]

In 1900, Robert A. Pegan is enumerated in St. Joseph, Washington Twp., Buchanan Co., Missouri *(Census Place: St Joseph Ward 3, Buchanan, Missouri; Roll: 841; Page: 8B; Enumeration District: 51)*. But the information on Robert's age is incorrect. It is apparent either the census taker erred, or someone else besides Robert or his wife Jessie gave the census taker the information. Robert is listed as Robert "N." or "H." Pegan, age 35, a merchant, born Sep 1866 in Missouri, where his parents were also born. His wife is listed as "Mary", age 33, born Oct 1866 in Missouri, where her parents were born. The couple is said to have been married seven years, with "Mary" having borne no children.

Robert Pegan, listed as "R.A. Peagan", is found in the 1910 census in Laramie, Precinct 6, Albany Co., Wyoming *(Census Place: Laramie, Albany, Wyoming; Roll: T624_1745; Page: 2B; Enumeration District:*

13; Image: 246). He is a bartender in a saloon. He and his family are residing in the household of John Sieverts, age 45, born in Germany. Robert's relationship to Mr. Sieverts is a "hired hand", as Sieverts owns the saloon where Robert is employed. Robert is 57 years old (?) and married to 38-year-old wife, Jesse Farrington Pegan (Incorrect—Jessie was 42). They have a son, Robert D., age three. Robert Pegan says he was born in Ohio, his father in Pennsylvania and his mother in Ohio. He lists his occupation as a bartender in a saloon. Jesse says she and her mother were born in Ohio and her father in Massachusetts. Robert and Jessie say they have been married 20 years and Jessie has borne one child, still living. The census taker says little Robert D. Pegan II was born in Missouri, his father in Ohio and his mother in Missouri. This is an error, as both Robert Donald's parents were born in Ohio. Also living in the household is another "hired hand", E. Meyer, also age 57, born in Germany. However, there is a cryptic "N.H." by Robert Pegan's name, which may indicate that the census taker made a mistake and Robert should have been listed as a "new house". Or does the "N.H." mean "not home"? This census was taken on April 18, 1910, and perhaps Robert was traveling between Laramie and Kansas City.

However, Jessie Farrington Pegan and little Robert Donald Pegan are also enumerated in 1910 in Ward 10, Kansas City, Jackson Co., Missouri, with Jessie's father and some of her siblings *(Census Place: Kansas Ward 10, Jackson, Missouri; Roll: T624_787; Page: 5B; Enumeration District: 0134; Image: 1088).* This census was taken on April 10th, This time, Jessie Farrington Pegan shaves even more years off her age and says she is 35, born in Ohio, like her mother, with her father born in New Jersey. Jessie, who is listed as a daughter of the head of the household, says she is on her first marriage and had born one child, who is still living. This would be son Robert D., age three, born Missouri with his parents born in Ohio, who is also living in the home. The head of the household is "Gerald" Farrington (really Josiah), age 68, who is mistakenly listed as born in Ohio with his parents born in New Jersey. But the other adults living in the home are also Josiah's children, who, like Jessie, say their father was born in New Jersey and their mother in Ohio. They are Electa Farrington, age 43, single, a milliner; and John Farrington, 34, a salesman, both born in Ohio. Jessie seems to be visiting and functioning as the main housekeeper in the home, as her mother is not there.

In 1920, Robert A. Pegan, wife Jessie and son Robert D. II are living in Kansas City, Jackson Co., Missouri *(Census Place: Kansas City Ward 10, Jackson, Missouri; Roll: T625_926; Page: 13A; Enumeration District: 152; Image: 776).* Robert Sr. says he is 67, born in Ohio and is a merchant. He lists his parents as born in the U.S. Jessie Farrington Pegan, is enumerated as age 50, born in Missouri, her father in Vermont and her mother in New Jersey (Incorrect—she is 52 years old and she and her mother were born in Ohio and her father in New Jersey). Robert, age 12, was born in Missouri, his father in Ohio and mother in Missouri (incorrect).

Robert A. Pegan's death certificate was indexed under the name "Robert A. Regan", but the information on the certificate confirms he is Robert A. Pegan. Jessie Farrington Pegan, the informant on her husband's Robert's death certificate, gave his paternal grandparents' names, R.A. and Christina "Engle" Pegan, as the parent's' names instead of Andrew and Mary Jane McKibben! Also, for some reason, Robert's birth year is listed as 1849 instead of 1848, which is the year on his gravestone.[22, 142]

In 1930, Jessie Farrington Pegan, age 62 and a widow, is living with her mother Sarah L. Farrington in Kansas City, Jackson Co., Missouri *(Census Place: Kansas City, Jackson, Missouri; Roll: 1200; Page: 7A; Enumeration District: 182; Image: 384.0).* Also in the home is Jessie's sister Electa Farrington. Jessie says she was born in Ohio, with her father born in Vermont and her mother in New Jersey.

Jessie Farrington Pegan is residing with her sister Electa Farrington in Kansas City, Jackson Co., Missouri in 1940 *(Census Place: Kansas City, Jackson, Missouri; Roll: T627_2176; Page: 1B; Enumeration District: 116-258).* Jessie Farrington Pegan, a widow, is age 72. The head of the household is Electa Farrington, who is 74 and unmarried. Neither lists an occupation. Both were born in Ohio and say they were living at the same address, 1430 Cleveland Avenue in 1935.

Son of Robert Andrew Pegan and Jessie Farrington:

+ 37 m I. **Robert Donald[7] Pegan II** was born in Kansas City, Jackson Co., Missouri, on February 23, 1907.[149, 150, 151] He was also known as **Don** and **R. Don**. Robert Donald died in West Los Angeles, Los Angeles Co., California, on October 1, 1976.[150, 151]

7th Generation

10. Child One[7] Pegan (*Leonidas Alonzo[6], Andrew[5], Robert A.[4], Andrew[3], Andrew[2] Pagan, James[1]*) was born between 1855 and 1862 in Montezuma Twp., Poweshiek Co., Iowa. He or she was a child of Leonidas Alonzo Pegan (2) and Martha Jane Pegan. Child One died in Montezuma Twp., Poweshiek Co., Iowa, between 1855 and 1862.

11. Child Two[7] Pegan (*Leonidas Alonzo[6], Andrew[5], Robert A.[4], Andrew[3], Andrew[2] Pagan, James[1]*) was born between 1855 and 1862 in Montezuma Twp., Poweshiek Co., Iowa. He or she was a child of Leonidas Alonzo Pegan (2) and Martha Jane Pegan. Child Two died in Montezuma Twp., Poweshiek Co., Iowa, between 1855 and 1862.

12. Leonidas Alonzo[7] Pegan (*Joseph[6], Andrew[5], Robert A.[4], Andrew[3], Andrew[2] Pagan, James[1]*) was born on October 24, 1860, in Mexico, Salt River Twp., Audrain Co., Missouri.[50] He was also known as **Alonzo**, **Lon or Lonnie**. He was the son of Joseph Pegan (3) and Mary Elizabeth Curry. Leonidas Alonzo died in Clarksville, Calumet Twp., Pike Co., Missouri, on November 30, 1918, at age 58.[50] He was buried in Greenwood Cemetery, Clarksville, Calumet Twp., Pike Co., Missouri.[50]

Never married.

Leonidas Pegan, listed as "Lonnie", is found with his parents Joseph and Mary Elizabeth Curry Pegan in 1900 1900 in Clarksville, Calumet Twp., Pike Co., Missouri *(Census Place: Calumet, Pike, Missouri; Roll: T623_882; Page: 2B; Enumeration District: 86)*. Leonidas Pegan, listed as Lonnie, is 39, single, born Oct 1860 in Missouri, and a plasterer (probably working for his uncle, John Kelley). The head of the household is Joseph Pegan, age 68, born Mar 1932, a plasterer who says he and his mother were born in Ohio and his father in Pennsylvania. Mary E. Curry Pegan, 54, born Oct 1835, says she and her mother were born in Kentucky and her father in Virginia. Joseph and Mary Elizabeth say they have been married 42 years and Mary Elizabeth has borne seven children, six still alive. Two of Leonidas' siblings are also in the household: brother Edwin and sister Nora Lee Pegan Reneau. Edwin Pegan, listed as "Eddie", is 24, born Sep 1875 in Missouri, and a blacksmith. Nora Lee Pegan Reneau, listed as "Lenora", is 27, born Sep 1872, divorced, and lists no occupation. Also in the home is Nora Lee's daughter, Hazel Reneau, five years old, born Aug 1895. Nora Lee and Hazel were also born in Missouri.

Leonidas Pegan, 49, single and a railroad worker, is residing with his widowed mother Mary Elizabeth Curry Pegan, 70, in Ward 1, Clarksville, Calumet Twp., Pike Co., Missouri in 1910 *(Census Place: Clarksville Ward 1, Pike, Missouri; Roll: T624_805; Page: 2B; Enumeration District: 0123; Image: 234)*. Also in the home is Leonidas' brother Edwin ("Edward") Pegan, 34, single, a blacksmith.

According to his obituary, Leonidas Alonzo "Lon" Pegan died when, inebriated, he apparently fell asleep on the railroad tracks and a train ran over him.[152]

13. Alexander Campbell[7] Pegan (*Joseph[6], Andrew[5], Robert A.[4], Andrew[3], Andrew[2] Pagan, James[1]*) was born on May 11, 1864, in Slemmensburg, Calumet Twp., Pike Co., Missouri.[51, 52] He was also known as **Aleck**. He was the son of Joseph Pegan (3) and Mary Elizabeth Curry. Alexander Campbell died in Quincy, Quincy Twp., Adams Co., Illinois, on August 28, 1936, at age 72.[51, 52, 53] He was buried in Graceland Quincy Cemetery, Quincy, Melrose Twp., Adams Co., Illinois.[52]

Alexander Campbell Pegan married **Dempsey Summers Bass** on December 19, 1889, in Pike Co., Missouri.[153] They divorced. They had three children. Dempsey Summers Bass was born in Clarksville, Calumet Twp., Pike Co., Missouri, on July 3, 1869. Dempsey Summers Pegan was living in 1936 in Huntington Park, San Antonio Twp., Los Angeles Co., California. She reached age 67 and died in a hospital in Hollywood, Los Angeles Co., California, on August 22, 1936.[154] She was cremated and her cremains buried in Angeles Abbey Memorial Park Mausoleum, Compton, Los Angeles Co., California.[154, 155]

On her death certificate, Dempsey Pegan's date of birth and birthplace are listed as July 3, 1871 in Louisiana, Buffalo Twp., Pike Co., Missouri by her informant, her daughter Frances Pegan Gough. But census data and all other records indicate her birth year was 1869 in Clarksville, Calumet Twp., Pike Co., Missouri, as Dempsey ("Dempty"), age 11 months, and her parents are enumerated there in the 1870 census *(Census Place: Clarksville, Pike, Missouri; Roll: M593_798; Page: 113B; entry for "Dempty" Bass, James M. Bass, head of household)*. In addition, her burial place is noted as Westwood Memorial Cemetery, but Angeles Abbey Memorial Park Mausoleum records state that Dempsey's ashes are buried there, along with those of her children and lone grandchild. It is possible she was interred first at Westwood, then moved to Angeles Abbey.[154, 155]

In 1900, Alexander C. and Dempsey Bass Pegan are listed in Clarksville, Calumet Twp., Pike Co., Missouri *(Census Place: Calumet, Pike, Missouri; Roll: T623_882; Page: 2B; Enumeration District: 86)*. Alexander Pegan, age 36, a wallpaper hanger, says he was born in May 1864 in Missouri and his parents in Kentucky (incorrect). Dempsey Pegan, age 30, born July 1869, says she and her mother were born in Missouri and her father in Virginia. Alexander and Dempsey say they have been wed 10 years. Oddly, Dempsey Bass Pegan is enumerated as having borne one child, but the child is not living. The census taker erred. They are living either in a double or next door to Dempsey's parents, James Michael and Stella Frances Bass. Little Stella Frances Pegan, Alexander and Dempsey's daughter, listed as Stella May Bass, age three, is at her grandparents' Bass' home that day but is incorrectly listed as a daughter of Eliza Bass, James Michael and Stella's widowed daughter-in-law *(Census Place: Calumet, Pike, Missouri; Page: 2; Enumeration District: 0086; entry for Stella May Bass, Michael Bass, head of household)*. Again, an error made by the census taker. Living close to Alexander and his family are his brother Charles H. Pegan and his family and his parents Joseph and Mary Elizabeth Curry Pegan and his brother Leonidas.

Alexander Pegan is again enumerated in Clarksville, Calumet Twp., Pike Co., Missouri in 1910 *(Census Place: Clarksville Ward 1, Pike, Missouri; Roll: T624_805; Page: 2A; Enumeration District: 0123; Image: 233)*. "Alex", age 45, is a house painter while his wife Dempsey Bass Pegan is 40 years old. They say they have been married 20 years and Dempsey has borne three children, all still alive. Children in the home are Stella F., 12, Otho W., seven, and Luther C., five. All in the house were born in Missouri.

According to his brother Leonidas Alonzo "Lon" Pegan's obituary in December 1918, Alexander Campbell "Aleck" Pegan was a resident of Chicago, Cook Co., Illinois at that time.[152]

Alex Pegan is listed as "Aleck" Pegan in 1920 as a roomer in the home of J.A Richardson and his wife Clara in Quincy, Adams Co., Illinois *(Census Place: Quincy Ward 2, Adams, Illinois; Roll: T625_296; Page: 2B; Enumeration District: 35; Image: 742)*. Alexander, 56, a house painter, says he is still married—but he is not living with his wife, Dempsey Bass Pegan.

In 1930, Andrew Pegan, is a roomer in the home of Henry Herrin and his family in Quincy, Adams Co., *Illinois (Census Place: Quincy, Adams, Illinois; Roll: 405; Page: 2B; Enumeration District: 38; Image: 690.0)*. He says he is a widower, but wife Dempsey is still alive and living in Los Angeles, California.

By his death on August 28, 1936, Alexander Campbell Pegan had remarried **Laura Unknown**, as she is mentioned on his death certificate and is the informant. The certificate is under "Alex" Pegan, and says Alexander's father, Joseph Pegan, was born in Jamestown, Greene Co., Ohio, an error.[52]

In 1920, Dempsey Summers Bass Pegan, 50, who, unlike her former husband, says she is divorced, is living in Clarksville, Calumet Twp., Pike Co., Missouri *(Census Place: Calumet, Pike, Missouri; Roll: T625_941; Page: 3A; Enumeration District: 137; Image: 772)*. She and her two sons Otho Pegan,16, and Luther Carlisle Pegan, 14, are living with her son-in-law and daughter, Miles and (Stella) Frances Gough and granddaughter Dempsey Gough, age 21 months. Miles Gough, 31, is a telegrapher with the railroad and Stella Frances is age 22. All in the home were born in Missouri except for Miles Gough, who was Iowa-born.

Dempsey Summers Bass, her two unmarried sons Otho and Luther, and widowed daughter (Stella)

Frances Pegan Gough are all listed in the 1925 Hannibal, Marion Co., Missouri city directory. All are living at 721 Center Street, and undoubtedly, although not mentioned, Frances' daughter Dempsey Gough is there also. Luther is a mechanic, and Otho is an "inspector." Frances is a clerk at Sonnenberg & Sons.[156]

In 1930, Dempsey Bass Pegan, 60, a saleslady in a dry goods store, is living in Huntington Park, San Antonio Twp., Los Angeles Co., California *(Census Place: Huntington Park, Los Angeles, California; Roll: 171; Page: 1B; Enumeration District: 1315; Image: 582.0)*. Living with her are her widowed daughter (Stella) Frances Pegan Gough, 32, and Frances' daughter Dempsey Gough, 12; her unmarried son Otho Pegan, 27; and newlywed son Luther C. Pegan, 25, and his wife Alice Unknown Pegan, 19. Otho Pegan is a cost estimator at a dynamite works and Luther Pegan a battery maker at a radio factory. Dempsey Bass Pegan lists herself as a "widow" this time, but her husband Alexander Pegan is alive and residing in Quincy, Quincy Twp., Adams Co., Illinois. All were born in Missouri except Alice, who was born in Oklahoma.

Children of Alexander Campbell Pegan and Dempsey Summers Bass:

+ 38 f I. **Stella Frances**[8] **Pegan** was born in Clarksville, Calumet Twp., Pike Co., Missouri, on October 19, 1897.[109, 157, 158] She was also known as **Frances**. Stella Frances died in Los Angeles, Los Angeles Co., California, on November 14, 1984.[109, 157, 158]

+ 39 m II. **Otho M.**[8] **Pegan** was born in Clarksville, Calumet Twp., Pike Co., Missouri, on February 21, 1903.[159] He died in Portland, Multnomah Co., Oregon, on January 16, 1959.[159, 160]

+ 40 m III. **Luther Carlisle**[8] **Pegan** was born in Clarksville, Calumet Twp., Pike Co., Missouri, on June 1, 1905.[109, 161] He was also known as **Carl**. Luther Carlisle died in Fort Worth, Tarrant Co., Texas, on July 14, 1964.[109, 161, 162]

14. **Charles H.**[7] **Pegan** (*Joseph*[6], *Andrew*[5], *Robert A.*[4], *Andrew*[3], *Andrew*[2] *Pagan*, *James*[1]) was born on February 3, 1867, in Slemmensburg, Calumet Twp., Pike Co., Missouri.[54] He was the son of Joseph Pegan (3) and Mary Elizabeth Curry. He died in Bowling Green, Cuivre Twp., Pike Co., Missouri, on December 15, 1950, at age 83.[54] Charles H. was buried in Greenwood Cemetery, Clarksville, Calumet Twp., Pike Co., Missouri.[54, 163]

Charles H. married **Lilly Belle Knowles** on May 25, 1889, in Pike Co., Missouri.[164] They divorced. They had two daughters. Lilly Belle Knowles was born in Prairie Twp., Hancock Co., Illinois, on March 23, 1870.[165, 166, 167] She reached age 75 and died in Dallas City, Dallas City Twp., Hancock Co., Illinois, on March 26, 1945.[165, 166, 167] Lilly Belle Knowles Pegan Bracken was buried in Dallas City Cemetery, Lomax Twp., Henderson Co., Illinois.[166, 168]

Charles H. Pegan and his first wife Lillie Belle Knowles Pegan are enumerated in Clarksville, Calumet Twp., Pike Co., Missouri in 1900 *(Census Place: Calumet, Pike, Missouri; Roll: T623_882; Page: 2B; Enumeration District: 86)*. Charles H., 33, born in Feb 1867 in Missouri, is a plasterer while Lille Belle Knowles Pegan, 30 was born in Mar 1870 in Illinois. The couple says they have been married 11 years and Lillie Belle has born two children, both still living. They are daughters "May", 10, born Oct 1889, and Alta, nine, born Dec 1890, both born in Missouri.

Charles H. and Lillie Belle Knowles Pegan divorced before October 1908.

Charles H. Pegan married Mrs. **Minerva Alida Goewey** McLaughlin Blackstun on October 23, 1908, in Adams Co., Illinois.[169] Minerva Alida Goewey was born in Belleview Twp., Calhoun Co., Illinois, on September 9, 1857.[170] She was also known as **Alida**. Minerva Alida reached age 70 and died in Clarksville, Calumet Twp., Pike Co.,

Missouri, on April 2, 1928.[170] She was buried in Long Cemetery, Belleview Twp., Calhoun Co., Illinois.[170, 171]

Minerva Alida Goeway McLaughlin Blackstun Pegan always used her middle name, Alida, as her preferred name. Minerva Alida Goeway was eight months old in 1860 in Hamburg Twp., Calhoun Co., IL and is mentioned in the *Portrait and Biographical Album of Pike and Calhoun Counties, Illinois* as the daughter of Abram Goewey, and (she was) the wife of Thomas Blackstun.[172]

Charles and his second wife, (Minerva) Alida Goewey McLaughlin Blackstun Pegan, apply for a marriage license in Adams Co., Illinois on October 23, 1908. The marriage record says that a J.U. Milk, clergyman, married Charles and Alida on that same day, October 23, 1908.[169] The *Quincy (IL) Daily Herald* printed an article about wedding on October 23, 1908 However, the minister's name in the article is J.W. Miller.[173]

The Adams County clerk's office thinks Rev. Milk may not have recorded the marriage at the clerk's office within 30 days, thus invalidating the marriage according to Illinois state law at the time—there seems to be no record of exactly when Milk notified the clerk's office of the marriage. Or, perhaps, since Rev. Milk did not perform the marriage, yet recorded it, this would still invalidate the marriage.

On the license, Charles lists his residence as Clarksville, Missouri and Alida says she is residing in Belleville, Illinois, but there is no other information, required by law, on the back of license, which is also odd. The back of the license is blank.[169]

In 1910, Charles H. Pegan is now residing in Belleview Twp., Calhoun Co., Illinois *(Census Place: Belleview, Calhoun, Illinois; Roll: T624_232; Page: 6A; Enumeration District: 0010; Image: 428)*. In the home are Charles, 43, born Missouri, a plasterer, and his second wife "Alida", 46. (Alida has shaved some years off her age.) The pair say they have been married two years, and that Alida has born five children, four still living. Two of her children by Alida's first marriage are in the household: her son Floyd Blackstun, 21, and daughter Stella Blackstun, 19. Charles H. Pegan says his father was an Ohio native and his mother was born in Kentucky. Alida Goewey McLaughlin Blackston Pegan says she and her father were born in Illinois and her mother was Missouri-born. Alida's two children say they and their parents were born in Missouri.

"C. H." Pegan and "Alida Blackston" apply for a marriage license and marry in Pike Co., Missouri on January 17, 1916. Did they somehow suspect, or discover, that their Illinois marriage was invalid? Did they divorce and remarry? [174]

In 1920, Charles H. Pegan is found in Clarksville, Calumet Twp., Pike Co., Missouri *(Census Place: Calumet, Pike, Missouri; Roll: T625_941; Page: 1B; Enumeration District: 137; Image: 769)*. Charles Pegan, age 52, a house plasterer, says he was born in Missouri, his father in Ohio and his mother in Kentucky. With him is his second wife, Alida Gowey McLaughlin Blackstun Pegan, who says she is 57, born Illinois, with her father born in New York and her mother in Missouri.

Charles H. Pegan married Mrs. **Ona S. Williams** Rice Jones on March 19, 1930, in Pike Co., Missouri.[175, 176] Ona S. Williams was born in Spencer Twp., Pike Co., Missouri, on August 3, 1892.[176] Ona S. lived in 1939 in Clarksville, Calumet Twp., Pike Co., Missouri. She reached age 46 and died in a hospital in Hannibal, Mason Twp., Marion Co., Missouri, on January 7, 1939.[176] Ona S. was buried in Greenwood Cemetery, Clarksville, Calumet Twp., Pike Co., Missouri.[176, 177]

In 1930, Charles H. Pegan, 52, and his third wife, Ona Williams Rice Jones Pegan, are enumerated in Clarksville, Calumet Twp., Pike Co., Missouri *(Census Place: Calumet, Pike, Missouri; Roll: 1218; Page: 2B; Enumeration District: 9; Image: 652.0)*. Charles, 63, is a plasterer. Ona, 37, was born in Missouri. Charles says his first marriage was at age 18 and Ona says she was 17 when she was first married. Charles says he was born in Missouri, his father in Ohio and his mother in Kentucky. Ona says she and her mother were Missouri natives and her father was born in the United States.

Widower Charles Pegan, age 73, born Missouri, is living alone in Clarksville, Calumet Twp., Pike Co., Missouri in 1940 *(Census Place: Clarksville, Pike,*

Missouri; Roll: T627_2140; Page: 9A; Enumeration District: 82-9). He is a house painter who says he was residing in the same house on Fourth Street (no numerical address listed) in 1935.

In 1910, Charles first wife, Lilly B. Knowles Pegan, age 40, and her daughter Alta L. Pegan, 19, are servants in the home of Napoleon Lamb, age 38, in Pontoosuc Twp., Hancock, Illinois *(Census Place: Pontoosuc, Hancock, Illinois; Roll: T624_290; Page: 5A; Enumeration District: 0019; Image: 416).* Lilly Belle Knowles Pegan says she was born in Illinois, her father in Ohio and her mother in the United States. Alta Pegan says she and her father were born in Missouri and her mother in Illinois.

Lilly Belle Knowles Pegan marries William Bracken on September 5, 1919 in Randolph Co., Missouri.[178]

William Thomas and Lilly Belle Knowles Pegan Bracken are enumerated in Dallas City Twp., Hancock Co., Illinois in 1920 *(Census Place: Dallas, Hancock, Illinois; Roll: T625_370; Page: 4A; Enumeration District: 10; Image: 744).* William Bracken, listed as "W.T. Brachen", is age 40, a farmer, and he and his parents were born in Kentucky. Lilly Belle Knowles Pegan Bracken says she is 48 years old. With them are William's nine children by his late first wife.

By 1930, William Thomas and Lilly Belle Knowles Pegan Bracken have removed to Prairie Twp., Howard Co., Missouri *(Census Place: Prairie, Howard, Missouri; Roll: 1191; Page: 2B; Image: 510.0).* William Brachen says he is age 51 and a farmer; he and is parents were born in Kentucky. He says he was first married at age 22. Lilly Belle Knowles Pegan Brachen is 58, but this time she says she and her mother were born in Missouri and her father in Tennessee. Lilly states her first marriage occurred at age 15. William still has four children by his first wife living in the home.

William Thomas and Lilly Belle Knowles Pegan Bracken are located in Dallas City, Dallas City Twp., Hancock Co., Illinois in 1940 *(Census Place: Dallas City, Hancock, Illinois; Roll: T627_810; Page: 7A; Enumeration District: 34-10).* William Thomas Bracken, enumerated as W.T. Bracken, is age 60, a farmer, born in Kentucky. Lilly Belle Knowles Pegan Bracken, 68, was born in Illinois. They state they were living in the same house, on County Line Road, in 1935.

Lilly Belle Knowles Pegan Bracken died in Dallas City, Illinois, part of which is in Lomax Twp., Hancock Co., Illinois and part in Dallas Twp., Henderson Co., Illinois. Her death certificate says she died in Dallas City, Hancock Co., Illinois, but was buried in Dallas City Cemetery, Lomax Twp., Illinois.[166] Her obituary says she was born near Terre Haute, Illinois, in Hancock Co., and spent her childhood in Clarksville, Calumet Twp., Pike Co., Missouri.[167]

Daughters of Charles H. Pegan and Lilly Belle Knowles:

+ 41 f I. **Grace May**[8] **Pegan** was born in Nebo, Spring Creek Twp., Pike Co., Illinois, on November 21, 1889.[179] She was also known as **May**. Grace May died in Buffalo Twp., Pike Co., Missouri, on August 21, 1947.[179]

+ 42 f II. **Alta Lee**[8] **Pegan** was born in Clarksville, Calumet Twp., Pike Co., Missouri, on December 7, 1891.[180] She died in Chicago, Cook Co., Illinois, on November 15, 1958.[180]

15. Josephine[7] **Pegan** (*Joseph*[6], *Andrew*[5], *Robert A.*[4], *Andrew*[3], *Andrew*[2] *Pagan, James*[1]) was born on October 10, 1869, in Calumet Twp., Pike Co., Missouri.[55] She was the daughter of Joseph Pegan (3) and Mary Elizabeth Curry. Josephine died in Louisiana, Buffalo Twp., Pike Co., Missouri, on December 15, 1948, at age 79.[55] She was buried in Oak Grove Cemetery, Bel-Nor, St. Louis Co., Missouri.[55, 181]

Josephine married **Major Oury Martin** on June 24, 1890, in Pike Co., Missouri.[182] They had one daughter. Major Oury Martin was born in Louisiana, Buffalo Twp., Pike Co., Missouri, on February 10, 1865.[183] He reached age 62 and died in Maplewood, Jefferson Twp., St. Louis Co.,

Missouri, on August 16, 1927.[183] Major Oury was buried in Oak Grove Cemetery, Bel-Nor, St. Louis Co., Missouri.[183, 184]

Major and Josephine Pegan Martin are enumerated in 1900 in Ward 24, St. Louis, Missouri *(Census Place: St Louis Ward 24, St Louis (Independent City), Missouri; Roll: T623_899; Page: 11A; Enumeration District: 356)*. In the home is "M.O." Martin, age 35, born Missouri, with his parents born in Kentucky. His occupation is listed as "tobacconist". With him is wife Josephine Pegan Martin, 30, born Missouri. Her parents are also listed as born in Missouri (Incorrect— her father was born in Ohio and her mother in Kentucky). Their daughter "Lorene" is age 10, is a Kentucky native.

In 1910, Major O. and Josephine Pegan Martin are living in Ward 3, Maplewood, Jefferson Twp., St. Louis Co., Missouri *(Maplewood Ward 3, Saint Louis, Missouri; Roll: T624_810; Page: 36A; Enumeration District: 0112; Image: 76)*. Major Martin is listed as "Oury", age 45, a tobacco worker; he says he was born in Missouri, his father in Kentucky and his mother in Germany. Josephine Pegan Martin is listed as "Jossie," age 40, born Missouri, with her father born in Ohio and her mother in Kentucky (correct). Daughter Lorraine, 19, born Kentucky, is a stenographer at a rattan company. They say they have been married 20 years and Josephine has borne one child, still living.

In 1920, Major O. and Josephine Pegan Martin are found in Maplewood, Jefferson Twp., St. Louis Co., Missouri *(Census Place: Maplewood, St Louis, Missouri; Roll: T625_946; Page: 27B; Enumeration District: 124; Image: 58)*. Marion O., age 54, is a twistmaker in a tobacco factory. This time, he says he was born in Pennsylvania, his father in Scotland and his mother in Alsace! Wife Josephine Pegan Martin, 50, again she was born in Missouri, her father in Ohio and her mother in Kentucky, which is correct. Living with them are their son-in-law and daughter, Clifford and Lorraine Martin Lucas and daughter Jean. Clifford, 26, a plumber, says he was born in Alabama, his father in Pennsylvania and his mother in Missouri. Lorraine Martin Lucas is 28, born in Kentucky, her father in Pennsylvania and her mother in Missouri. Jean Lucas is 11 months, born Missouri, while her father is an Alabama native and her mother was Kentucky-born.

In 1930, widow Josephine Pegan Martin is residing in Webster Groves, Carondelet Twp., St. Louis Co., Missouri with her son-in-law and daughter, Clifford Y. and Lorraine Martin Lucas *(Census Place: Carondelet, St Louis, Missouri; Roll: 1225; Page: 24A; Enumeration District: 16; Image: 234.0)*. Josephine, age 60. a Missouri native, says her father was born in Ohio and her mother in Kentucky. Clifford Lucas, 36, a plumber, states he was born in Alabama, his father in England and his mother in Missouri. Lorraine Martin Lucas states she is 38 years old, born in Kentucky, with her father born in Pennsylvania and her mother in Missouri. Clifford and Lorraine Martin Lucas' daughter, Jean F., is 11 years old and a Missouri native; her father was born in Alabama and her mother was Kentucky-born.

Josephine Pegan Martin, age 70, is living with her youngest brother Edwin Pegan in 1940 in Clarksville, Calumet Twp., Pike Co., Missouri *(Census Place: Calumet, Pike, Missouri; Roll: T627_2140; Page: 7B; Enumeration District: 82-9)*. Josephine is incorrectly listed as married, but the "M" is crossed out. The head of the household, Edwin Pegan, listed as "Edward", is 64, single, and a blacksmith. Both say they were born in Missouri and in 1935 were residing in the same house, but no street or address is designated.

Josephine Pegan Martin married **Angus Frederick Reed** on May 4, 1948, in Pike Co., Missouri.[185] Angus Frederick Reed was born in Louisiana, Buffalo Twp., Pike Co., Missouri, on November 15, 1869.[186] Angus Frederick lived in 1957 in Louisiana, Buffalo Twp., Pike Co., Missouri. Angus Frederick reached age 87 and died in Lincoln, Troy Twp., Pemiscot Co., Missouri, on August 10, 1957.[186] He was buried in Riverview Cemetery, Louisiana, Buffalo Twp., Pike Co., Missouri.[186, 187]

Angus Reed, a building contractor, died in a nursing home facility in Lincoln, Troy Twp., Pemiscot Co., Missouri, but his death certificate says his residence was Louisiana, Buffalo Twp., Pike Co., Missouri.[186]

According to her death certificate, Josephine Pegan Martin Reed had only lived in Louisiana, Buffalo

Twp., Pike Co., Missouri for seven months when she died.[55]

Daughter of Josephine Pegan and Major Oury Martin:

+ 43 f I. **Lorraine Ruth**[8] **Martin** was born in Henderson, Henderson Co., Kentucky, on August 21, 1892.[109, 188] She died in Sappington, St. Louis Co., Missouri, on February 27, 1976.[109, 189]

16. **Lenora or Nora Lee**[7] **Pegan** (*Joseph*[6], *Andrew*[5], *Robert A.*[4], *Andrew*[3], *Andrew*[2] *Pagan, James*[1]) was born on September 13, 1872, in Calumet Twp., Pike Co., Missouri.[56] She was also known as **Nora Lee**. She was the daughter of Joseph Pegan (3) and Mary Elizabeth Curry. She was living in 1948 in Maplewood, Jefferson Twp., St. Louis Co., Missouri. Lenora/ Nora Lee died in Clayton, Clayton Twp., St. Louis Co., Missouri, on March 3, 1948, at age 75.[56] She was buried in Oak Hill Cemetery, Kirkwood, St. Louis Co., Missouri.[56, 190]

Although her real name seems to be Lenora, as this is how her parents Joseph and Mary Elizabeth Curry Pegan enumerate her in censuses, she always used Nora Lee as her given name.

Lenora or Nora Lee married **Samuel Houston Reneau** on July 27, 1893, in Pike Co., Missouri.[191] They were divorced in Pike Co., Missouri, before 1900. They had one daughter. Samuel Houston Reneau was born in Calumet Twp., Pike Co., Missouri, in August 1871. He reached age 93 and died in Rochester, Alberta, Canada, on September 23, 1964.[192, 193] Samuel Houston was buried in Peaceful Pines Cemetery, White Court Census Division, Rochester, Alberta, Canada.[193]

In 1900, Lenora Pegan Reneau, age 27, divorced, and her five-year-old daughter Hazel Reneau are living with Lenora's parents, Joseph and Mary Elizabeth Curry Pegan, in Clarksville, Calumet Twp., Pike Co., Missouri (*Census Place: Calumet, Pike, Missouri; Roll: T623_882; Page: 2B; Enumeration District: 86)*. Also in the home are Joseph and Mary Curry Pegan's unmarried sons Leonidas ("Lonnie"), 39, a plasterer, and Edwin ("Edward"), 24, a blacksmith. Lenora says she has borne one child, who is still alive. Joseph and Mary Elizabeth say they have been married 42 years and Mary Elizabeth has borne seven children, six still alive.

Her ex-husband, Samuel H. Reneau is living with his parents, Robert and Chalon Reneau, in 1900 in Calumet Twp., Pike Co., Missouri *(Census Place: Calumet, Pike, Missouri; Roll: 882; Page: 8B; Enumeration District: 84)*, Samuel H. Reneau is age 25, a teamster, born Aug 1871 in Missouri, with his father born in Tennessee and his mother in Virginia. He lists himself as a widower, but his ex-wife, Lenora "Nora Lee" Pegan Reneau, is still alive.

Samuel H. Reneau is not found in any other U.S. Federal Censuses, as he moved to Canada between 1900-1910. He is buried in Peaceful Pines Cemetery, Rochester, Alberta, Canada, with his second wife (name unknown), his third wife Agnes C. Unknown, and two sons.[193]

Lenora "Nora Lee" Pegan Reneau married **Archibald Crosson** on March 30, 1916, in St. Louis, Missouri.[194] Archibald Crosson was born in Elgin West, Southwold, Ontario, Canada, on December 25, 1865.[195] Archibald reached age 73 and died in Maplewood, Jefferson Twp., St. Louis Co., Missouri, on May 13, 1939.[195] He was buried in Oak Hill Cemetery, Kirkwood, St. Louis Co., Missouri.[195, 196]

Archibald is listed as "Archie Crosson" on his death certificate and, for some reason, his birthdate is given as December 25, 1875 (it was 1865). But the age on the certificate, 63, clearly indicates the 1875 birth year was a clerical error.[195]

Archibald Crosson was married to two Pegan descendants. His first wife was Laura Belle Kelley (Crosson Baldwin [LNU]), daughter of John and Mary Jane Pegan Kelley and granddaughter of Andrew and Mary Jane McKibben Pegan. His second wife was Lenora "Nora Lee" Pegan Reneau, the first cousin of his first wife Laura, daughter of Joseph and Mary Elizabeth Curry Pegan. Joseph Pegan and Mary Jane Pegan Kelley were siblings. (See Laura Belle Kelley's (#23) entry for further information on Archibald Crosson.) In 1920, Archibald and his second wife, Lenora "Nora Lee" Pegan Reneau Crosson are found in Maplewood, Central Twp., St. Louis

Co., Missouri *(Census Place: Maplewood, St Louis, Missouri; Roll: T625_946; Page: 10B; Enumeration District: 124)*. Archibald Crosson is age 55, born Canada, and is a concrete maker at Erie Bricks Company. "Norah" Pegan Crosson is 47 years old, born Missouri, with her father born in Ohio and her mother in Kentucky. Archibald says he entered the United States in 1890 and was naturalized in 1902.

Archibald and Nora Lee Pegan Reneau Crossen are again found in Maplewood, Central Twp., St. Louis Co., Missouri in 1930 *(Census Place: Maplewood, St Louis, Missouri; Roll: 1224; Page: 13B; Enumeration District: 42; Image: 120.0)*. Archibald Crossen is age 65, born Canada, and "Nora" is 57. They repeat the birthplace information for their parents. Archibald says he is the night watchman at a can factory. The couple says they were first married at ages 29 and 19 respectively.

"Nora Lee" Pegan Reneau Crosson and her daughter, Hazel Reneau Brockman, are living together in 1940 in Maplewood, Jefferson Twp., St. Louis Co., Missouri *(Census Place: Maplewood, St Louis, Missouri; Roll: T627_2150; Page: 8A; Enumeration District: 95-147)*. The head of the household, Nora Lee Pegan Reneau Crossen, is age 67 and a widow. Hazel Reneau Brockman, 45, first lists herself as divorced, but an "S" for single is written on top of the "D". Neither lists an occupation. Both say they were born in Missouri and were residing in the same home at 2617 Sutton Avenue in 1935. Also in the household is a lodger, Charlotte Bemont, 77, a widow with no occupation.

Daughter of Lenora or Nora Lee Pegan and Samuel Houston Reneau:

+ 44 f I. **Hazel**[8] **Reneau** was born in Clarksville, Calumet Twp., Pike Co., Missouri, on August 26, 1894.[197] She died in Emmaus, St. Charles Co., Missouri, on October 18, 1957.[197]

17. **Edwin**[7] **Pegan** *(Joseph*[6]*, Andrew*[5]*, Robert A.*[4]*, Andrew*[3]*, Andrew*[2] *Pagan, James*[1]*)* was born on September 21, 1875, in Calumet Twp., Pike Co., Missouri.[57] He was the son of Joseph Pegan (3) and Mary Elizabeth Curry. He was also known as **Edward**. Edwin died in Clarksville, Calumet Twp., Pike Co., Missouri, on October 7, 1955, at age 80.[57] He was buried in Greenwood Cemetery, Clarksville, Calumet Twp., Pike Co., Missouri.[57, 198]

Edwin Pegan is sometimes seen as "Edward" Pegan, but his death certificate confirms his name as Edwin.[57]

Childless.

Edwin ("Edward") Pegan, single, a blacksmith, is living with his mother Mary Elizabeth Curry Pegan, 70, a widow, in Ward 1, Clarksville, Calumet Twp., Pike Co., Missouri in 1910 *(Census Place: Clarksville Ward 1, Pike, Missouri; Roll: T624_805; Page: 2B; Enumeration District: 0123; Image: 234)*. Also in the home is Edwin's brother Leonidas Pegan, 49, a railroad worker and also unmarried.

Edwin Pegan, again enumerated as "Edward", age 44, an unmarried blacksmith, and his mother Mary Elizabeth Curry Pegan, 80, are still in Clarksville, Calumet Twp., Pike Co., Missouri in 1920 *(Census Place: Calumet, Pike, Missouri; Roll: T625_941; Page: 2B; Enumeration District: 137; Image: 771)*.

In 1930, "Edward" Pegan, and his mother Mary Elizabeth Curry Pegan, listed as "Mary L.", continue to reside in Clarksville, Calumet Twp., Pike Co., Missouri *(Census Place: Calumet, Pike, Missouri; Roll: 1218; Page: 3A; Enumeration District: 9; Image: 653.0)*. Edwin, 54, a blacksmith, is still single. Mary Elizabeth is age 90.

Edwin Pegan, again named as "Edward", is found in 1940 in Clarksville, Calumet Twp., Pike Co., Missouri *(Census Place: Calumet, Pike, Missouri; Roll: T627_2140; Page: 7B; Enumeration District: 82-9)*. Edwin, age 64 and single, is a blacksmith. Living with him is his widowed sister, Josephine Pegan Martin, age 70. Josephine is incorrectly listed as married, but the "M" is crossed out. Both say they were born in Missouri and in 1935 were residing in the same house, but no street or address is designated.

Edwin married Mrs. **Emma Lou Higgens** Oliver on April 26, 1945, in Pike Co., Missouri.[199] Emma Lou Higgens was born in Calumet Twp., Pike Co., Missouri, on September 8, 1878.[200] Emma Lou reached age 83 and died in Clarksville, Calumet Twp., Pike Co., Missouri, on January 8, 1962.[200] She was buried in Greenwood Cemetery, Clarksville, Calumet Twp., Pike Co., Missouri.[200, 201]

18. **Child[7] Pegan** (*Joseph[6], Andrew[5], Robert A.[4], Andrew[3], Andrew[2] Pagan, James[1]*) was born between 1861 and 1900 in Calumet Twp., Pike Co., Missouri. He or she was a child of Joseph Pegan (3) and Mary Elizabeth Curry. Child died in Calumet Twp., Pike Co., Missouri, between 1861 and 1900.

19. **Lorenzo Kelley or[7] Kelly** (*Mary Jane[6] Pegan, Andrew[5], Robert A.[4], Andrew[3], Andrew[2] Pagan, James[1]*) was born on March 5, 1857, in Clark Twp., Clinton Co., Ohio.[59] He was also known as **Lou** or **Louie**. He was the son of John A. Kelley and Mary Jane Pegan (4). He died in Clarksville, Calumet Twp., Pike Co., Missouri, on August 14, 1924, at age 67.[59] Lorenzo Kelley or was buried in Greenwood Cemetery, Clarksville, Calumet Twp., Pike Co., Missouri.[59, 202]

Never married.

Lorenzo "Lou" Kelly/Kelly was unmarried in 1900 and living with his parents, John A. and Mary J. Pegan Kelley in Clarksville, Calumet Twp., Pike Co., Missouri *(Census Place: Calumet, Pike, Missouri; Roll: T623_882; Page: 5A; Enumeration District: 86)*. Lorenzo Kelley, listed as Louis Kelley is age 43, single, born Ohio, and a plasterer.

Lorenzo "Lou" Kelley is still living in Clarksville, Calumet Twp., Pike Co., Missouri with his parents in 1910 *(Census Place: Clarksville Ward 2, Pike, Missouri; Roll: T624_805; Page: 8A; Enumeration District: 0123; Image: 245)*. "Lou" (Lorenzo), 54, single, is plasterer born in Ohio. The head of the household is John Kelley, age 76, born Ohio, a widower who also says he is a plasterer.

Lorenzo Kelley/Kelly is not found in the 1920 census, but he was most likely living in Clarksville, Calumet Twp., Pike Co., Missouri, as he dies there in 1924.

The informant on Lorenzo's death certificate was his brother Joshua. However, Joshua Kelley/Kelly incorrectly lists his brother Lorenzo's birthplace as "Mexico, Missouri". On his tombstone, Lorenzo's name is misspelled as "Lorenza".[202] "Louie" Kelley left a probate naming his then-widowed sister Laura Belle "Lollie" Kelley Crosson Baldwin (she later remarried but her surname is not known), as his administrator. Much information about his siblings' whereabouts were in this probate.[203]

20. **John A.[7] Kelley II** (*Mary Jane[6] Pegan, Andrew[5], Robert A.[4], Andrew[3], Andrew[2] Pagan, James[1]*) was born on November 19, 1858, in Mexico Twp., Audrain Co., Missouri.[66] He was the son of John A. Kelley and Mary Jane Pegan (4).

John A. died in Warm Springs, Warm Springs Twp., Deer Lodge Co., Montana, on April 13, 1947, at age 88.[66] He was buried in Warm Spring Institutional Cemetery, Warm Springs, Warm Springs Twp., Deer Lodge Co. Montana.[66]

Never married.

In 1880, John A. Kelley II, 23, a plasterer, is living with his parents, John and Mary Jane Pegan Kelley, and siblings in Clarksville, Calumet Twp., Pike Co., Missouri *(Census Place: Clarksville, Pike, Missouri; Roll: 709; Page: 560B; Enumeration District: 135; Image: 0492)*.

John A. Kelley II is not found in the 1900 or 1910 U.S. Federal Censuses.

John A. Kelley is enumerated in Simpson, Sprin Coulee Twp., Hill Co., Montana in 1920 *(Census Place: Sprin Coulee, Hill, Montana; Roll: T625_971; Page: 2B; Enumeration District: 141; Image: 1129)*. John A. Kelley, age 62, single, says he was born in Missouri and his parents in Ohio. He is a farmer and herder on his own farm.

In November 1925, as one of the heirs to his brother's, Lorenzo "Louis" Kelley's, estate in Pike Co., Missouri, John is listed as a resident of Chinook, Blaine Co., Montana.[203]

In 1930, John Kelley is residing in Sabra Twp., Rosebud Co., Montana *(Census Place: Sabra, Rosebud, Montana; Roll: 1260; Page: 1B; Enumeration District: 8; Image: 459.0)*. John Kelley is listed as age 48, single born in Ohio, with his parents born in Kentucky. He is a hired hand on the farm owned by Sirrit and Ella Sands.

By 1932, he seems to be back in Chinook, Blaine Co., Montana, as stated on his death certificate.[66] Also, his brother Harrison's body was shipped for burial to Chinook that year.[67]

Although he is not found in the 1940 census, John A. Kelley II was an inmate in the Montana State Mental Hospital in Warm Springs Twp., Deer Lodge Co., Montana, where his death certificate claimed he'd been "for more than 16 years".[66] This may not be quite right, but he may have entered the institution right after Harrison Kelley's death.

John A. Kelley consistently gives the wrong age and birthplace in the censuses as an adult. Also, his age may have been wrong on his death certificate. His brother Lorenzo Kelley's death certificate lists Lorenzo's birthdate as March 5, 1857 which is a year and four months after their parents' marriage, and Harrison, who was John's immediate junior, was most likely born in 1860.[59, 67] But John A. Kelley II's age on his death certificate is 89 years, 4 months and 25 days, making his birthdate to be November 19, 1857. This is not possible. Most likely, he was born on November 19, 1858. His occupation on his death certificate is sheepherder.[66]

21. **Harrison**[7] **Kelley** (*Mary Jane*[6] *Pegan, Andrew*[5], *Robert A.*[4], *Andrew*[3], *Andrew*[2] *Pagan, James*[1]) was born on December 25, 1860, in Mexico Twp., Audrain Co., Missouri.[67] He was the son of John A. Kelley and Mary Jane Pegan (4). He died in Havre, Hill Co., Montana, on June 12, 1932, at age 71.[67] Harrison was buried in Chinook Cemetery, Chinook, Blaine Co., Montana.[67]

Never married.

Harrison Kelley, 19, a plasterer, is residing with his parents, John and Mary Jane Pegan Kelley, in Clarksville, Calumet Twp., Pike Co., Missouri *(Census Place: Clarksville, Pike, Missouri; Roll: 709; Page: 560B; Enumeration District: 135; Image: 0492).* He is unmarried.

Little is known of Harrison Kelley. He is not found in any census as an adult, but he signs an inheritance check as one of his father's, John Kelley's heirs.[204] He is listed as Montana resident in his brother, Lorenzo "Louie" Kelley's probate in 1924. But no specific place is mentioned and there is no signed receipt in Lorenzo's probate packet indicating that Harrison ever received his inheritance.[203] It seems he family, except for John, never found him and didn't know if he was still alive. Even John A. Kelley may not have known where Harrison was in 1924, but he did in 1932. When Harrison died in Havre, Hill Co., Montana in 1932, his body was shipped to Chinook Cemetery in Chinook, Montana for burial.[67] John A. Kelley was living in Chinook at the time.[66]

On his death certificate, Harrison's occupation was listed as plasterer. Like his brother John, Harrison's birthdate on his death certificate, December 25, 1861, is incorrect. But, as his brother immediately his junior, Lewis A. Kelley, has a date of birth on his death certificate as May 2, 1862, Harrison's cannot be correct. Harrison was most likely born on December 25, 1860.[67, 68]

22. **Lewis Albert**[7] **Kelley** (*Mary Jane*[6] *Pegan, Andrew*[5], *Robert A.*[4], *Andrew*[3], *Andrew*[2] *Pagan, James*[1]) was born on May 2, 1862, in Mexico Twp., Audrain Co., Missouri.[68] He was also known as **Allie**. He was the son of John A. Kelley and Mary Jane Pegan (4). He died in Palmyra, Liberty Twp., Marion Co., Missouri, on April 27, 1944, at age 81.[68] Lewis Albert was buried in Greenwood Cemetery, Clarksville, Calumet Twp., Pike Co., Missouri.[68, 205]

Was "Albert" his middle name? His middle name is also seen as "Album", and in his obituary it is "Alumum".[205]

Lewis A. married **Sarah Carlisle** on December 13, 1893, in Monroe Co., Missouri.[206] They divorced. They had three children. Sarah Carlisle was born in Denton, Caroline Co., Maryland, on October 23, 1867.[207, 208] She was also known as **Sallie**. She reached age 95 and died in Monroe City, Monroe Twp., Monroe Co., Missouri, on July 1, 1963.[207,208] Sarah was buried in St. Jude Cemetery, Monroe City, Monroe Co., Missouri.[207, 208, 209]

Sarah Carlisle Kelley always used her nickname, Sallie, as her given name.

In 1900, Lewis A. Kelley, enumerated as Louis Kelley, is enumerated in Monroe City, Monroe Twp., Monroe Co., Missouri *(Census Place: Monroe, Monroe, Missouri; Roll: 876; Page: 1A; Enumeration*

District: 119). Lewis A. Kelley, age 37, born May 1863 in Missouri, a plasterer, says his parents were both born in Ohio. His wife, Sallie C. Carlisle Kelley, 32, born Oct 1867, says she and her mother were born in Maryland and her father was a Delaware native. They say they have been married six years and Sallie has borne two children, both still alive. With them are their two daughters, Mary E., five, born Feb 1895, and "A. Lucile", three, born Jan 1897; both daughters were born in Missouri.

Lewis A. Kelley, again listed as Louis A. Kelley, is still living in Monroe City, Monroe Twp., Monroe Co., Missouri, in 1910 *(Census Place: Monroe Ward 3, Monroe, Missouri; Roll: T624_800; Page: 11A; Enumeration District: 0126; Image: 94)*. Lewis A. Kelley, age 46, born Missouri, is a plasterer who says his father was born in Ohio and his mother in Pennsylvania (Incorrect—she was born in Ohio). This time, Sallie Carlisle Pegan, 42, says she was born in Missouri, her father in Delaware and her mother in Maryland. The couple says they are on their first marriage, they have been wed 16 years, and Sallie has born three children, all surviving. They are Mary, 15, "Lucile", 13, and John, three, all born in Missouri.

In 1920, Lewis A. Kelley is found in Monroe City, Monroe Twp., Monroe Co., Missouri *(Census Place: Monroe, Monroe, Missouri; Roll: T625_936; Page: 11B; Enumeration District: 127; Image: 245)*. Lewis A. Kelley, age 56, says he was born in Missouri and his parents in Ohio; he is a house plasterer. With him is wife Sallie C. Carlisle Kelley, 52, who again says she born Maryland, with her father born in Delaware and her mother in Maryland. Sallie says she is a seamstress with private clients. With them are children Mary Etta, 24, and John, 12, both born in Missouri. Mary Etta does "fancy work", most likely embroidery, lacework, etc., on items her mother sews.

By 1930, Lewis A. Kelley may have been separated from his wife Sallie Carlisle Kelley—or he is away on a construction job. He is residing in a boarding house, along with his son, in Hannibal, Mason Twp., Marion Co., Missouri *(Census Place: Hannibal, Marion, Missouri; Roll: 1211; Page: 19A; Enumeration District: 6; Image: 777.0)*. Lewis A. Kelley, age 67, born Missouri with his parents born in Ohio, is still a plasterer. Lewis says he is still married and was first married at age 23, but his wife Sallie is not with him. His son, John C. Kelley, age 28, single was born Missouri as was his father while his mother born in Maryland. John says he is salesman at a radio and electrical factory.

His wife, Sallie C. Kelley, is enumerated as Sallie Kelly in Monroe City, Monroe Twp., Monroe Co., Missouri in 1930 *(Census Place: Monroe, Monroe, Missouri; Roll: 1213; Page: 16A; Enumeration District: 11; Image: 764.0)*. Sallie Carlisle Kelley is age 58, says she is married and was first wed at age 18. Oddly she and her parents are listed as born in Missouri (incorrect). Sallie lists no occupation. With her is daughter Mary (Mary Etta), age 35, single, born Missouri, is a typesetter at a newspaper.

In 1940, Sallie Carlisle Kelley and unmarried daughter Mary Etta continue to reside in Monroe City, Monroe Twp., Monroe Co., Missouri *(Census Place: Monroe City, Monroe, Missouri; Roll: T627_2130; Page: 61A; Enumeration District: 69-14)*. Sallie Carlisle Kelley, age 72 and divorced, born Maryland, lists her occupation as washing and janitor work at church and home. "Maryetta" Kelley, 45, born Missouri, has no occupation. Both say they were living in the same home at 415 Catherine Street in 1935.

Children of Lewis Albert Kelley and Sarah Carlisle:

+ 45   f   I.   **Mary Etta[8] Kelley** was born in Monroe City, Monroe Twp., Monroe Co., Missouri, on February 12, 1895.[109, 210] She died in a hospital in Fulton, Calloway Co., Missouri, on September 4, 1971.[109, 210]

+ 46   f   II.   **Alice Lucille[8] Kelley** was born in Monroe City, Monroe Twp., Monroe Co., Missouri, on January 16, 1897.[211] She died in Port Huron, Port Huron Twp., St. Clair Co., Michigan, on November 16, 1997.[211]

+ 47   m   III. **John Carlisle**[8] **Kelley** was born in Monroe City, Monroe Twp., Monroe Co., Missouri, on March 23, 1907.[212] He died in St. Louis, Missouri, on January 6, 1967.[213]

23. Laura Belle[7] **Kelley** (*Mary Jane*[6] *Pegan, Andrew*[5], *Robert A.*[4], *Andrew*[3], *Andrew*[2] *Pagan, James*[1]) was born in 1864 in Mexico Twp., Audrain Co., Missouri? She was also known as **Lollie**. She was the daughter of John A. Kelley and Mary Jane Pegan (4). Laura Belle died in Oklahoma? between 1936 and 1944.

Laura Belle married **Archibald Crosson** on September 27, 1894, in Pike Co., Missouri.[214] They had at least one daughter. Archibald Crosson was born in Elgin West, Southwold, Ontario, Canada, on December 25, 1865.[195] He was also known as **Archie**. Archibald reached age 73 and died in Maplewood, Jefferson Twp., St. Louis Co., Missouri, on May 13, 1939.[195] He was buried in Oak Hill Cemetery, Kirkwood, St. Louis Co., Missouri.[195, 196]

Archibald Crosson was married to two Pegan descendants who were first cousins. His first wife was Laura Belle Kelley (Crosson Baldwin [LNU]), daughter of John and Mary Jane Pegan Kelley and granddaughter of Andrew Pegan (born 1806). His second wife was Laura Belle Kelley Lenora "Nora Lee" Pegan Reneau, daughter of Joseph and Mary Elizabeth Curry Pegan.[194] Joseph Pegan and Mary Jane Pegan Kelley were siblings.

Archibald Crosson was born in Elgin West, Southwold, Ontario, Canada, and is found there in his father David Crosson's in the Canadian censuses of 1871 (*Census Place: Southwold, Elgin West, Ontario; Roll: C-9898; Page: 55; Family No: 185*) and 1881 (*Census Place: Southwold, Elgin West, Ontario; Roll: C_13266; Page: 24; Family No: 112*). He immigrated to the United States around 1890, and by 1894 had lived in Clarksville, Calumet Twp., Pike Co., Missouri, where he married his first wife, Laura B. Kelley. But on their marriage license in September 1894, Archibald Crosson lists his residence as Chouteau County, Montana.[214]

Laura Belle Kelley Crosson Baldwin (LNU) led a peripatetic life. According to their great-granddaughter, Frances Stanley, Laura B. Kelley Crosson Baldwin and her first husband Archibald Crosson lived in many places before their divorce, including Missouri, Montana, California, Oklahoma, Texas, Georgia, and and Virginia.[215]

In 1900, Archie and Laura are found in Havre Twp., Chouteau Co., Montana (*Census Place: Havre, Chouteau, Montana; Roll: 910; Page: 13; Enumeration District: 0190*). "Archie Crassie", age 35, a farmer, is enumerated as born Dec 1864 in English Canada, where both is parents were born. With him is wife Laura, 33, born Oct 1866(?) in Missouri, with her parents born in Ohio. They say they have been married six years and Laura had borne one child, who is still alive. They have a daughter, "Maurine", 2, born Oct 1897 in Missouri. Also in the home is a sister-in-law to the head of the household, Fannie Kelley, age 29, born Jun 1870 in Missouri, who, like her sister Laura, says her parents were Ohio natives. This enumeration seems to be correct, except for the surname misspelling and Laura shaving about two years off her age.

But Archie and Laura seem to be doubly enumerated in this census, but the information on the second entry is confusing, error-ridden, and seems to have been given by a neighbor (which, in this era, happened, especially in remote areas). Again, they are found in Havre Twp., Chouteau Co., Montana, on a different census page (*Census Place: Havre, Chouteau, Montana; Roll: 910; Page: 23A; Enumeration District: 190*). But the names, except for Archie's are incorrect. This time, Archie Crosson, age 36, a "wool grower" (sheep farmer) is enumerated as born Jan 1864 in Illinois, where his father was born, with his mother born in Kentucky. His wife "Ella S.", 31, was born Oct 1868 in Minnesota, with her parents born in Illinois. In this entry, Archie and "Ella" have been wed five years and "Ella" has borne two children, both surviving. Here they have two daughters, Alma, six, born May 1894 and Josie, three, born May 1897, both born in Montana. With them, listed as a sister-in-law to the head of the household, is an "Alma Kelly," age 19, born Jul 1880 in Minnesota. "Alma" is a seamstress.

There are no dates on either census page. The first enumeration given is the correct one. The second one has to be considered, because Archie's brother Abraham Crosson is living next door on this census page. Did Abraham or his wife Amanda give the census taker the erroneous information? Did Archie and Laura actually have two daughters? In the 1910 census, the Crossens are still in Chouteau County and continue to be sheep farmers/wool growers. But the two Almas are gone from Archie's house, and the names and birthplaces for Archie, Laura and (Frances) Maurene and their parents are correct. Abe Crossen, Archibald's brother, and his family are also found on the same census page.

In 1910, Archibald and Laura B. Kelley Crosson are enumerated in Cypress Twp., Chouteau Co., Montana *(Census Place: Cypress, Chouteau, Montana; Roll: T624_830; Page: 6A; Enumeration District: 0067; Image: 1052)*. In the household are "Archie" Crossen, age 45, born Canada, as was his father, with his mother born in Scotland. He is sheep farming, as are several of his siblings, who are neighbors. His wife, Laura B. Crosson, is 43, born Missouri, with her parents born in Ohio. They have a daughter, "Maureen F.", 12, born Missouri. Archibald and Laura say they have been married 15 years, and this time Laura states she has borne one child, who is still alive.

In 1911, when Laura's father, John Kelley, dies, the Crossons are in Fort Mitchell, Lunenburg Co., Virginia. About two years later, when their daughter, Frances Maurene Crosson, was about 16, Archie and Laura announced they were moving again, perhaps back to Missouri. Young "Maurene" was tired of moving all over the country and may have already met "the boy down the road", Sam Mason Eudailey. She emphatically told her parents she was not moving with them and would not be swayed. Her parents relented, and left Frances Maurene with two women, sisters, who had been good neighbors of theirs in Ft. Mitchell. After they returned to Missouri, Archibald and Laura B. Kelley Crosson promptly divorced. Laura seems to have gone directly back to Lunenberg County, Virginia.[215]

Laura Belle Kelley Crosson married **Robert Newell Baldwin**, a Canadian like her first husband Archibald Crosson, on February 16, 1916, in Lunenburg Co., Virginia.[216] Robert Newall Baldwin was born in Pouch Cove, Newfoundland, Canada, on May 6, 1865.[217] He was also known as **Roy**. Robert Newell reached age 55 and died in Rehoboth Precinct, Lunenburg Co., Virginia, on August 21, 1920.[218, 219] He was buried in Cool Spring Cemetery, Chickahominy, Lunenburg Co., Virginia.[220] He was the son of Thomas Baldwin and Elizabeth Newell?

Robert Newell Baldwin states on the 1910 U.S. Census form that he immigrated to America in 1906 *(Census Place: Lynn Ward 7, Essex, Massachusetts; Roll: T624_585; Page: 7A; Enumeration District: 0413)*.

When he marries Laura in 1916 Robert states that he is only 39 years old, was born in Newfoundland, and his parents were Edward A. and Grace (Note: her maiden name was Wells).[214] But baptismal records in Pouch Cove, Newfoundland attest that Robert Baldwin, of Pouch Cove, Newfoundland was born on May 6, 1865, and was the son of Thomas and Elizabeth Unknown (Newell?) Baldwin.[215] There are no births recorded for a Robert Baldwin 1877, and Grace Wells Baldwin, the wife of Edward Baldwin II, was, according to other records, born in 1824, which would have made her too old to have a child in 1877. (Robert and Grace Wells Baldwin may have been his grandparents.) In turn, Laura B. Kelley Crosson says she is only 40 years of age when she marries Robert. Robert, if Robert's birth record and earlier census records for Laura are correct, was 51 years old and Laura about 52.[214]

(Archie Crosson would marry Laura's cousin, Nora Lee Pegan Reneau, that same year, 1916, in St. Louis, Missouri.[194] See Lenora or Nora Lee Pegan, #16, for information on Archibald Crosson's remaining years.)

On April 20, 1916, Robert N. and Laura B. Kelley Crosson Baldwin would emigrate to Canada. When they cross the border at Windsor, both Robert and Laura would claim British citizenship (Canada was still a British domain at that time). They said they had been living in Massachusetts, perhaps in Lynn, Essex Co., Massachusetts where Robert Baldwin had lived at the time of the 1910 census. Once again, they "fudge" on their ages, with Robert stating he is 43 and Laura declaring she is 41.[221]

On April 1, 1919, the Baldwins return to America, crossing the Canadian border at Niagara Falls, New York. This time, Robert claims he is 48 years old and Laura says she is 42 (they are actually about 54 and 55 respectively). Their last place of residence was Bracebridge, Ontario, and they are traveling to visit a friend, Thomas Flanagan, in Mexico Station, New York. This may be the town/village of Mexico in Oswego Co., New York.[222]

From there, Robert N. and Laura Belle Kelley Crosson Baldwin (later LNU) removed back to Rehoboth, Lunenburg Co., Virginia, where Robert N. Baldwin died.

Laura Kelley Crosson Baldwin was the administrator of her brother Lorenzo "Lon" Kelley's estate in 1924 in Clarksville, Calumet Twp., Pike Co., Missouri. She refers to herself "Mrs. Roy Baldwin" on the probate papers. Lorenzo's obituary states, Laura was "of Virginia" but had been living with Lorenzo before he died.[59, 203]

Laura Belle Kelley Crosson Baldwin married **Unknown Unknown** in 1936. Her descendants know that she married for a third time that year, because, according to Laura's great-great-granddaughter, Frances Stanley, the family has a letter that Laura wrote to (Frances) Maurene Crosson Eudailey. But the letter does not say whom she is marrying or where she is residing. The envelope for this letter is no longer extent. A picture of Laura accompanied the letter, but the black-and-white photo bears no photographer's mark or other information. There is no marriage record has been found online or in repositories for this marriage yet.[215]

The 1940 census entry for Sam Mason and (Frances) Maurene Crosson Eudailey states that, while Sam and the children were living in Lunenburg County, Virginia in 1935, Maurene was said to be living in "Clarkston, North Carolina" in Bladen County *(Census Place: Rehoboth, Lunenburg, Virginia; Roll: T627_4275; Page: 3B; Enumeration District: 56-14)*. However, this notation was written above the census form by someone other than the census taker, as the handwriting is different. Was this a mistake—could Maurene have been in Clarksville, Calumet Twp., Pike Co., Missouri? Another possibility is Clarksville, Mecklenburg Co., Virginia, which would have been very near the Eudailey's home in Lunenburg County. If Laura were living in either Clarksville, Virginia or Clarksville, Missouri in 1935, she apparently left before she died, as no Virginia or Missouri death certificate is found for her.

Laura was deceased by 1944, as she is not listed as a survivor in her brother Lewis A. Kelley's obituary, which says he was predeceased by two brothers and a sister. As Frances Anna Kelley Shaw is mentioned, the deceased sister is Laura.[205]

Frances Stanley says her great aunt, Laura's granddaughter, claimed Laura died in Oklahoma at the home of a stepdaughter, the daughter of her third husband.[215]

Daughters of Laura Belle Kelley and Archibald Crosson:

+ 48 f I. **Alma**[8] **Crosson?** was born in Clarksville, Calumet Twp., Pike Co., Missouri, in May 1895. She died in Cypress Twp., Chouteau Co., Montana?, before 1910. This child may have never existed.

+ 49 f II. **Frances Maurene**[8] **Crosson** was born in Clarksville, Calumet Twp., Pike Co., Missouri, on October 7, 1897.[109, 223, 224] She was also known as **Maurene**. Frances Maurene died in Palmyra, Fluvanna Co., Virginia, on December 22, 1987.[109, 223, 224]

24. Joshua[7] **Kelley** (*Mary Jane*[6] *Pegan, Andrew*[5]*, Robert A.*[4]*, Andrew*[3]*, Andrew*[2] *Pagan, James*[1]) was born on February 11, 1868, in Clarksville, Calumet Twp., Pike Co., Missouri.[69] He was the son of John A. Kelley and Mary Jane Pegan (4). He died in Winfield, Monroe Twp., Lincoln Co., Missouri, on December 13, 1953, at age 85.[69] Joshua was buried in Bethany Cemetery, Foley, Burr Oak Twp., Lincoln Co., Missouri.[69, 225]

Childless.

Joshua Kelley, with the surname enumerated as "Kellie", is found in Palmyra, Liberty Twp., Marion Co., Missouri in 1900 *(Census Place: Palmyra, Marion, Missouri; Roll: T623_874; Page:*

14A; Enumeration District: 94). He is single and a plasterer.

Joshua Kelley is not found in the 1910 census.

Joshua married **May Missouri Dixon** on November 15, 1910, in Lincoln Co., Missouri.[226] May Missouri Dixon was born in Monroe Twp., Lincoln Co., Missouri, on May 1, 1879.[227] She was also known as **May**. May Missouri lived in 1962 in Winfield, Monroe Twp., Lincoln Co., Missouri. She reached age 84 and died in a facility in Union Twp. Lincoln Co., Missouri, on July 20, 1963.[227] May Missouri was buried in Bethany Cemetery, Foley, Burr Oak Twp., Lincoln Co., Missouri.[227, 228]

Joshua Kelley is residing in 1920 in Monroe Twp., Lincoln Co., Missouri *(Census Place: Monroe, Lincoln, Missouri; Roll: T625_933; Page: 10B; Enumeration District: 104; Image: 234)*. Joshua Kelley, listed as Kelly, is 51 years old, born Missouri with his parents born in Ohio. With him is wife Mary, 39, born Missouri, with her father born in England and her mother in Missouri.

In 1930, Joshua Kelley, enumerated as "Joshia Kelly" is again located in Winfield, Monroe Twp., Lincoln Co., Missouri *(Census Place: Winfield, Lincoln, Missouri; Roll: 1209; Page: 1A; Enumeration District: 14; Image: 468.0)*. Joshua, age 62, born Missouri, is still a plasterer; wife "May M." is 50.

Joshua Kelley continues to live in Winfield, Monroe Twp., Lincoln Co., Missori in 1940 *(Census Place: Winfield, Lincoln, Missouri; Roll: T627_2124; Page: 2A; Enumeration District: 57-14)*. "Josh" Kelley, age 72, is still a plasterer. Mary May Dixon Kelley, listed as "M. May", is 60. Both were born in Missouri and state they were living in the same home on Hewitt Street. (no numerical address designated) in 1935.

25. Fannie Anna⁷ Kelley (*Mary Jane⁶ Pegan, Andrew⁵, Robert A.⁴, Andrew³, Andrew² Pagan, James¹*) was born on June 24, 1871, in Clarksville, Calumet Twp., Pike Co., Missouri.[70] She was also known as **Fannie**. She was the daughter of John A. Kelley and Mary Jane Pegan (4). Fannie Anna lived between 1910 and 1941 in Hannibal, Mason Twp., Marion Co., Missouri. She died in a hospital in Fulton, Callaway Co., Missouri, on June 7, 1952, at age 80.[70] Fannie Anna was buried in Greenwood Cemetery, Clarksville, Calumet Twp., Pike Co., Missouri.[229, 230]

Childless.

Is Anna Kelley the "Alma Kelley" found with her brother-in-law and sister, Archie and Laura Kelley Crosson, in Havre Twp., Chouteau Co., Montana?

In 1900, Fannie Kelley, age 29, born Jun 1870 in Missouri, is residing with her brother-in-law and sister, Archie and Laura Belle Kelley Crosson, in Havre Twp., Chouteau Co., Montana *(Census Place: Havre, Chouteau, Montana; Roll: 910; Page: 13; Enumeration District: 0190)*. She is listed as a sister-in-law to the head of the household, "Archie Crassie", age 35. Archie, a farmer, is enumerated as born Dec 1864 in English Canada, where both is parents were born. With him is wife Laura, 33, born Oct 1866(?) in Missouri. The pair say they have been married six years and Laura had borne one child, who is still alive. They have a daughter, "Maurine", 2, born Oct 1897 in Missouri. Fannie and Laura say their parents were Ohio natives. This enumeration seems to be correct, except for the surname misspelling and Laura shaving about two years off her age.

Fannie returns to Missouri by 1903.

Fannie Anna married **George Henry Shaw** on July 30, 1903, in Pike Co., Missouri.[231] George Henry Shaw was born in Calumet Twp., Pike Co., Missouri, on November 6, 1875.[232] George Henry reached age 83 and died in a hospital in Fulton, Callaway Co., Missouri, on April 19, 1959.[232] He was buried in Greenwood Cemetery, Clarksville, Calumet Twp., Pike Co., Missouri.[232, 233]

George Henry and Anna Frances "Fannie" Shaw are not found in the 1910 census.

George Henry and Fannie Anna Kelley Shaw are enumerated in Hannibal, Mason Twp., Marion Co., Missouri in 1920 *(Census Place: Hannibal Ward 2, Marion, Missouri; Roll: T625_934; Page: 13B; Enumeration District: 104; Image: 840)*. George Shaw is listed as "G.H." Shaw, age 44, born Missouri with is parents both born in Virginia, a railroad fireman. Oddly, Fannie Shaw is listed with no given name, but her age is listed as 40, born Missouri, with both parents born in Ohio.

In 1930, George Henry and Fannie Anna Shaw are found in Mason Twp., Marion Co., Missouri (*Census Place: Mason, Marion, Missouri; Roll: 1212; Page: 22A; Enumeration District: 14; Image: 45.0*). In the household are George H. Shaw, age 52, born Missouri with his parents born in Virginia, a railroad engineer. "Fannie B." Shaw is listed as age 50, born Missouri with her parents born in Ohio. The couple says they were first married at ages 28 and 25 respectively. Fannie apparently is stating a wrong age to be younger than her husband.

George and Fannie Anna Kelley Shaw continue to reside in Mason Twp., Marion Co., Missouri, in 1940 (*Census Place: Mason, Marion, Missouri; Roll: T627_2128; Page: 15A; Enumeration District: 64-19*). George H. Shaw, age 64, lists no occupation. Fannie Kelley Shaw is 60 years old. Both were born in Missouri and say they were living in the same house on Rural Route #1 in 1935 (no numerical address designated).

By 1941, George Henry and Anna Frances Kelley Shaw are living in the Missouri State Hospital in Fulton, Callaway Co., Missouri, and they both die there.

Although her death certificate says she was buried in Riverview Cemetery in Louisiana, Buffalo Twp., Missouri, that cemetery has no record of her burial. It is a mistake. She is buried in Greenwood Cemetery, Calumet Twp., Pike Co., Missouri, according to the Greenwood Cemetery records.[229, 230]

26. Sinclair Edwin[7] Pegan (*William Henry[6], Andrew[5], Robert A.[4], Andrew[3], Andrew[2] Pagan, James[1]*) was born on September 11, 1860, in Dodson Twp., Highland Co., Ohio.[88] He was also known as **Edwin Sinclair Pegan; S.E. Pegan** and **Ed**. He was the son of William Henry Pegan (5) and Mary Ann Liggett. Sinclair Edwin died in Spokane, Diana Precinct, Spokane Co., Washington, on November 9, 1922, at age 62.[88] He was buried in Fairmount Memorial Park Cemetery, Spokane, Spokane Co., Washington.[234]

His birth name may have been Sinclair Edwin Pegan, and in newspaper articles and documents he is sometimes listed as S.E. Pegan. But he nearly always used Edwin Sinclair Pegan as his name.

Edwin Sinclair Pegan and his sister, Elizabeth "Libbie" Pegan Gregor and their families are mentioned frequently in *Park Record (Park City, Utah)* newspaper articles.

In 1880, Sinclair Edwin Pegan ("Edward Peagan"), age 19, was living in a mining camp in Park City, Summit Co., Utah (*Census Place: Park City, Summit, Utah; Roll: 1338; Page: 47C; Enumeration District: 074*). Edwin, single, a quartz miner, says he and his parents were born in Ohio.

By late 1884, his sister, Elizabeth "Libby" Pegan had joined him in Park City. according to an article in the December 20, 1884 *Park Record* newspaper, Libby Pegan sang in a musical recital.[235] His mother, twice-divorced Mary A. Liggett Pegan McIlhenny, was also residing in Park City by 1885.[236]

Sinclair Edwin married **Emma May Kelso** on September 22, 1886, in Summit Co., Utah.[237] They divorced. They had two children. Emma May Kelso was born in Pipe Creek, Madison Co., Indiana, on September 27, 1865.[238] She was also known as **May** and **Emily**. Emma May reached age 62 and died in Oakland, Alameda Co., California, on June 29, 1928.[238, 239] She was buried in California Crematory (now Chapel of the Chimes Columbarium and Mausoleum), Oakland, Alameda Co., California.[238, 240]

In the 1880 census, Emma "Emily" Kelso was living in an orphanage in Grass Valley, Nevada Co., California (*Census Place: Grass Valley, Nevada, California; Roll: 70; Page: 80A; Enumeration District: 061; Image: 0161*).

In Park City, Emma was active in the Women's Athenaeum and participated in musicales, as she played piano well.[241] Before her divorce, she often accompanied her future sister-in-law, Elizabeth "Libbie" Pegan Gregor, when the latter sang.[235]

Edwin and Emma Kelso Pegan divorced in June 1897 in Summit County, Utah according to the *Coalville (UT) Times* on June 11, 1897. Edwin Sinclair Pegan was granted a divorce on grounds of the desertion of his wife; he retained custody of their two children, Eleanor and Lewis.[242]

Emma Kelso Pegan left Park City, Park City Twp., Summit Co., Utah, om Sinclair Edwin Pegan. According to articles in the *Park Record* newspaper, she stayed in New York City with her dying father in April 1899.[243] In this item, she is referred to as "Mrs. Emma Pegan". A later mention in the *Park Record* says she returned to Park City in August 1900 after spending some time in Grand Rapids, Grand Rapids Twp., Kent Co., Michigan.[244] This time, and in future mentions, she is named as "Mrs. Emma Kelso".

Emma Kelso (Pegan) is not found in the 1900 census.

Sinclair Edwin Pegan married **Kate or Katherine Ann Martin** on May 24, 1899, in Summit Co., Utah.[245] They had three children. Kate or Katherine Ann Martin may have been born in Daly City, San Mateo Co., California?, on May 2, 1872. She was also known as **Kate**. Kate or Katherine Ann reached age 47 and died in Spokane, Diana Precinct, Spokane Co., Washington, on August 31, 1921.[246] She was buried in Fairmount Memorial Park Cemetery, Spokane, Spokane Co., Washington.[247]

Kate or Katherine Ann Martin Pegan always used Kate as her preferred name. Although she consistently uses 1874 as a birth year in census records, she seems to have been born in late 1871-1872.

Kate Martin, age eight, born California, is living with her parents, Timothy S. and Catherine Martin, and siblings in Virginia City, Storey Co., Nevada in 1880 *(Census Place: Virginia City, Storey, Nevada: Roll 759; Page: 227D; Enumeration District: 048)*.

Sinclair Edwin Pegan, enumerated as Sinclair Pegan, is living in Park City, Park City Twp., Summit Co., Utah in 1900 *(Census Place: Park City, Summit, Utah; Roll: 1686; Page: 1B; Enumeration District: 142)*. The head of the household is Sinclair Pegan, age 39, born Sep 1860 in Ohio, where his parents were also born, a quartz miner. With him is his second wife, Kate M. Martin Pegan, 26, born California, with her parents born in Maine. The couple says they have been married two years and Kate has borne one child, still alive. Children living with them are: "Elinore", 12, born June 1887, and Lewis, eight, born Jul 1891, Edwin's two children by his first wife Emma Kelso Pegan; and Mary E., eight months, born Sep 1899, the child of Edwin and Kate. All the children were born in Utah.

In April 1900, Sinclair Edwin "Ed" Pegan, a mining manager and engineer and land surveyor who scouted coal and silver mining sites, was severely injured in a mine accident. According to the Park Record account on April 14, 1900, he fractured his skull and had other internal injuries. He was not expected to recover, but he did, and went back to work in mining.[248]

In 1903, Kate Martin Pegan opened a kindergarten in Park City, Summit Co., Utah, but it closed in a few months, as mentioned in the August 20, 1904 *Park Record*.[249] Another article in the same paper mentions that Kate is leaving Park City to find a teaching position Spokane, Spokane Co., Washington, where her mother and other family members had moved when they left Park City.[250] The Salt Lake City (UT) Tribune reported on October 23, 1904 that Kate Martin Pegan did leave that day to be a teacher in Spokane, and she took her two small daughters with her.[251]

Kate and her daughters have returned to Park City by May 28, 1905, as a *Park Record* article mentions Mary and Grace Pegan attended a party there.[252] Did Edwin and Kate's separate, but eventually reconcile?

In 1904, Sinclair Edwin Pegan was on a board to erect new hospital, named Miner's Hospital, in Park City.[253]

Sinclair Edwin/Edwin Sinclair Pegan is still residing in Park City, Summit Co., Utah in 1910 *(Census Place: Park City, Summit, Utah; Roll: T624_1608; Page: 3B; Enumeration District: 0171; Image: 745)*. Edwin, 48, is a miner in a silver mine. The census taker writes that Edwin was born in California and his parents in Ireland. Also in the home is wife Kate Martin Pegan, age 35, who is listed as saying she and her parents were born in Ohio. The census taker switched their parental information. Edwin states he is on his second marriage and Kate her first. They have been married 15 years (incorrect) and Kate has borne two children, both surviving. Also in the home are their daughters Mary E., and Grace, born in Utah. Next door is Edwin's son-in-law and daughter, William and Eleanor Pegan McLaughlin and their daughter Eleanor.

Sinclair Edwin's son by his first marriage, Lewis Pegan, is living with his mother Emma May Kelso (Pegan) in 1910 in Evanston, Uinta Co., Wyoming *(Census Place: Evanston, Uinta, Wyoming; Roll: T624_1747; Page: 4A; Enumeration District: 0124; Image: 715)*. But he has changed his name permanently to Lewis Kelso. Emma Kelso (Pegan) says she is 39 years old, a widow (incorrect), and that she and her father were born in Indiana and her mother in Louisiana. She lists her occupation as music teacher. With her is son Lewis Pegan, enumerated as Lewis Kelso, age 18, born in Utah, whose father was born in Ohio and his mother in Indiana. He is a laborer at a railroad shop/yard.

After living in Park City for seven years, Emma May Kelso (Pegan) had moved to Evanston, Uinta Co., Wyoming by 1908. According to an article in the *Park Record* on October 24, 1908, she and her son-in-law, William F. "Billy" McLaughlin, husband of her daughter Eleanor Pegan McLaughlin (Ridge), started "moving picture" theaters for silent movies in Evanston and the nearby town of Kemmerer that year, where she was the pianist for the silent films.[254] The venture may have failed, as the McLaughlins move back to Park City by 1910.

While living in Park City, Edwin Pegan was politically active. He ran for Summit County, Utah assessor on the Socialist Party ticket in November 1903.[255] In 1907, someone apparently put Kate Martin Pegan's name on the ticket, and in a newspaper article the next week she objected strongly to this, emphatically denying she belonged to the party.[256, 257] But by 1915, according to articles in the *Park Record* newspaper, he was a Democrat and that party appointed him to a city committee.[258]

However, that year, 1915, Sinclair Edwin Pegan was in financial trouble. He was cited for delinquent taxes of $22.20 on Lot 8 Block 2 in Park City, and this property was included in a long list of properties to be sold at a tax sale on December 20, 1915.[259] He must have paid his late tax, because he was cited the next year for delinquent tax of $10.39 on the same property.[260] Again, he seems to have paid the tax in time, because in December 1917 the property appeared once more on the delinquent tax sale list; this time Sinclair Edward owed $15.97.[261] It is unknown if the property was sold. But the Pegans may have left Park City by 1917. A *Park Record* notation on August 25, 1916 mentioned that "Mrs. Ed Pegan" and her children had left Park City with Mrs. Cutts, Kate Martin Pegan's sister, a Spokane, Washington resident, for that city and would be living there.[262]

Sinclair Edwin Pegan is enumerated as Edwin Pegan in 1920 *(Census Place: Spokane, Spokane, Washington; Roll: T625_1941; Page: 4B; Enumeration District: 227; Image: 1012)*. In the home are "Ed. S.", 59, a stationary engineer in a mill, born Ohio as were his parents. This time, wife Kate Martin Pegan, 46, says she was born in California and her parents in Maine. Also in the home are children Mary, 20, Grace, 18, and John, 10, all born in Utah.

Sinclair Edwin's first wife, Emma Kelso (Pegan), is enumerated in 1920 in Oakland, Alameda Co., California *(Census Place: Oakland, Alameda, California; Roll: T625_87; Page: 21A; Enumeration District: 23; Image: 754)*. An Indiana native, Emma is listed as 45 years old and says she is a widow (Incorrect—she is 55 and divorced). With her is her son Lewis ("Louis") (Pegan) Kelso, 26, a railroad conductor, and her granddaughter Eleanor McLaughlin, 12, daughter of Emma's late daughter Eleanor and her first husband William McLaughlin.

Children of Sinclair Edwin Pegan and Emma May Kelso:

+ 50 f I. **Eleanor Margaret[8] Pegan** was born in Park City Twp., Summit Co., Utah, on June 8, 1887.[263] She died in Salt Lake City, Salt Lake Co., Utah, on October 31, 1913.[264, 265]

+ 51 m II. **Lewis Sinclair[8] (Pegan) Kelso** was born in Park City Twp., Summit Co., Utah, on July 6,1891.[266, 267] He died in Oakland, Alameda Co., California, on February 11, 1954.[266, 267, 268]

Children of Sinclair Edwin Pegan and Kate or Katherine Ann Martin:

+ 52 f I. **Mary Elizabeth**[8] **Pegan** was born in Park City, Park City Twp., Summit Co., Utah, on October 28, 1899.[109] She died in a hospital in Tacoma, Pierce Co., Washington, on January 2, 1973.[269, 270, 271]

+ 53 f II. **Grace**[8] **Pegan** was born in Park City, Park City Twp., Summit Co., Utah, on July 8, 1901.[109, 272] She died in Issaquah, King Co., Washington, on October 12, 1998.[109, 272]

+ 54 m III. **John Edwin**[8] **Pegan** was born in Park City, Park City Twp., Summit Co., Utah, on June 1, 1908.[109, 273, 274, 275] He died in a facility in Killeen, Bell Co., Texas, on February 6, 1980.[273, 274, 275, 276]

27. Elizabeth Jane[7] **Pegan** (*William Henry*[6], *Andrew*[5], *Robert A.*[4], *Andrew*[3], *Andrew*[2] *Pagan*, *James*[1]) was born on July 2, 1867, in Marathon, Jackson Twp., Clermont Co., Ohio.[89, 90] She was also known as **Libbie** (**Jennie** in 1870). She was the daughter of William Henry Pegan (5) and Mary Ann Liggett. She died in Watertown, Watertown Town, Jefferson Co., New York, on September 16, 1926, at age 59.[89, 90, 91, 92] Elizabeth Jane was buried in Brookside Cemetery, Watertown, Water Town, Jefferson Co., New York.[90]

"Libbie" Pegan was gifted with a lovely soprano voice and played piano and organ.

Twelve-year-old Elizabeth Pegan in is found in Clarke Twp., Clinton Co., Ohio living in the Salathial J. Haines household (*Census Place: Clarke, Clinton, Ohio*; *Roll: 1001*; *Page: 30C*; *Enumeration District: 056*). Elizabeth Jane Pegan, enumerated as "Libbie", is listed as a boarder and her occupation is music teacher! Salathial J. Haines, is age 36, his wife Mary, 29, and their son, Clarence, is seven. Libbie's obituary in the *Wilmington (OH) Journal,* says the Haines' reared her.[91]

Elizabeth Jane "Libbie" Pegan graduated from the Martinsville, Ohio high school in Clinton County, according to her obituary in the *Watertown (NY) Daily Times.*

Elizabeth Jane "Libbie" Pegan Gregor and her brother, Edwin Sinclair Pegan, and their families are mentioned frequently in *Park Record (Park City, UT)* newspaper articles.

By 1884, "Libbie" Pegan was singing in Park City, Utah musical recitals, sometimes accompanied on piano by her future sister-in-law, Emma Kelso Pegan, first wife of Sinclair Edwin Pegan.[235, 277]

The August 27, 1885 edition of the *Park Record* mentions that "Libbie" Pegan left Park City for Boston to study at the New England Conservatory of Music; she was accompanied by her brother, Edwin, Miss Emma Kelso (later Mrs. Edwin S. Pegan) and Dr. G.D. Gregor, Libbie's future husband.[278] She graduated from the prestigious music college and by April 1890 was teaching music at Millersburg College in Millersburg, Bourbon Co., Kentucky.[279]

She sang at several recitals in nearby Stanford, Lincoln Co., Kentucky while teaching at Millersburg College:

From the *Stanford (KY) Semi-Weekly Interior Journal,* April 7, 1891

> "Hearty Thanks—In response to a telegram to come over and assist in the Woody Bros. concert, Misses Libbie Pegan and Nodie Andrews, of Millersburg College…Miss Pegan is the teacher of music, while Miss Andrews is an apt pupil who has graduated in instrumental and is fast becoming an adept in vocal. Hers is a rich contralto, while Miss Pegan's voice is the sweetest soprano imaginable. Both are as lovely in form and feature as they are musically gifted, and by their accommodating spirit in assisting at every entertainment, both public and in the home circle, they added hundreds to their already large circle of admirers. Being very dear friends of the editor, they called with Miss Myers and Mr. S.S. Myers twice in his sick room and treated him both times to the sweetest songs, which will ring in his ears till he hears them repeated in Heaven, where all good editors expect to go, and will fill his

heart with thankfulness till death shall still it. God bless them both and make them to know how truly grateful to them the writer is and how sincerely he appreciates so strong an evidence of their esteem."

In column three on the same page:

"... prospects were that a good crowd would witness the entertainment at Walton's Opera House given by the Stanford Musical Association. The programme was a lengthy one and as it embraced solos, duets, etc. by such singers as Misses Pegan and Andrews, ..."

In column four under the heading "Church Affairs":

"—the union song service at the Presbyterian church Sunday night was well attended ... Miss Pegan very sweetly sang, "Some Sweet Day.""[280]

From the *Stanford (KY) Semi-Weekly Interior Journal*, April 10, 1891:

"The entertainment given by the Stanford Musical Association Monday evening was a rare vocal treat as those who braved the severe snow storm will attest...there were solos by Misses Pegan...Miss Pegan first sang "Flower of the Alps" and so delighted the audience that they encored until she again appeared when she very sweetly sang, "I'll be the Mother, You be the Child."(sic) ...After an anthem by the chorus Misses Pegan and Andrews together sang, "In the Cold Blast" with great credit, and later the former beautifully sang 'Jamie Dear'..."[281]

Elizabeth Jane Pegan married **Gilbert David Gregor** on June 24, 1891, in Jefferson Co., Kentucky.[282] They had three children. Gilbert David Gregor was born in Hammond, Hammond Town, St. Lawrence Co., New York, on January 23, 1859.[283, 284, 285] Gilbert David reached age 72 and died in Watertown, Watertown Town, Jefferson Co., New York, on March 13, 1931.[283, 284, 286] He was buried in Brookside Cemetery, Watertown, Water Town, Jefferson Co., New York.[283, 284]

On June 30, 1891, Dr. Gilbert D. Gregor and Elizabeth "Libbie" Pegan, sweethearts since before August 1885, were married in the home of Mr. William Liggett, Libbie's uncle, in Louisville, Jefferson Co., Kentucky. The couple took a three-month long honeymoon before returning to Park City, Summit Co., Utah, to live. Strange, as Dr. Gregor was also mayor of Park City at the time![287]

On January 12, 1892, Elizabeth Pegan Gregor had a miscarriage that threatened her life. But she recovered, thanks to the efforts of her husband and also her brother-in-law Dr. C.W. Wilson, who was married to Gilbert Gregor's older sister and was her husband's partner in a medical practice in Park City.[288]

Elizabeth "Libbie" Pegan Gregor continued to sing and play piano and organ for many church and civic functions in Park City (and later in Watertown, New York). By all accounts, she was an amazing talent.

In addition to his medical practice and serving as mayor of Park City, Summit Co., Utah from 1891-1893, Dr. Gilbert David Gregor was an investor in and served as an officer of several business ventures in Park City, including a gold mining company and a bank. In 1898, the bank formed in 1893 by Dr. Gilbert Gregor and partners failed. As one of the primary stockholders in the bank's incorporation, he was a defendant in a suit for recovery of funds. A Summit County, Utah judge held him liable for $5000, according to the July 9, 1898 *Park Record*.[289] Before the verdict, the Dr. Gilbert D. Gregor and his family left Park City and moved back to his home area in upstate New York, settling in Watertown, Town of Watertown, Jefferson Co., New York. Libbie gave a "farewell concert" to the town in early May 1898.[290]

In 1900, Gilbert D. and Elizabeth J. Pegan Gregor are enumerated in Watertown, Watertown Town, Jefferson Co., New York *(Census Place: Watertown Ward 3, Jefferson, New York; Roll: T623_1042; Page: 8B; Enumeration District: 39)*. In the home are Gilbert D. Gregor, age 41, a surgeon, born Jan 1859 in New York, with his parents born in Scotland. His wife, Elizabeth J. Pegan Gregor, 32, born July 1867 in Ohio, where her parents were born. The pair say they have been married eight years and Elizabeth has borne two children, both still alive. (This is incorrect, as Utah birth records document they had a stillborn daughter in 1892). Their two living children are David G., seven, born Apr 1893, and Mary M., five, born Feb 1895, both born in Utah. Also in the residence is a servant, Nissa Staulon.

Gilbert D. and Elizabeth Jane Pegan Gregor are still found in Watertown, Watertown Town, Jefferson Co., New York in 1910 *(Census Place: Watertown Ward 3, Jefferson, New York; Roll: T624_954; Page: 6B; Enumeration District: 0052; Image: 893)*. Gilbert D. Gregor, 51, is a surgeon; born New York with his parents born in Scotland. Elizabeth J. Pegan Gregor, is 42, born Ohio, as were her parents. They state they are on their first marriage, have been married 18 years, and Elizabeth has born two children, both surviving (again, incorrect). They are David G., 17, and "Margaret", 15, both born in Utah. Sarah Gleason, a servant, is also in the household.

In 1920, Gilbert D. and Elizabeth J. Pegan Gregor are again located in Watertown, Watertown Town, Jefferson Co., New York *(Census Place: Watertown Ward 5, Jefferson, New York; Roll: T625_1117; Page: 1A; Enumeration District: 51; Image: 5)*. In the home are Gilbert D. Gregor, 60, a surgeon, born New York, but this time he says his father was born in New York and his mother in Scotland. Elizabeth J. Pegan Gregor is age 52, born Ohio as were her parents. Their son, David G. Gregor, 26, single, born Utah, also a surgeon, is still residing with them.

Gilbert D. Gregor, 71, a widower, is living with his son David G. Gregor and his family in 1930 *(Census Place: Watertown, Jefferson, New York; Roll: 4661113; Page: 4B; Image: 1083.0)*. Gilbert, who lists no occupation, says he and his father were born in New York while his mother was born in Scotland. David G. Gregor, 36, is listed as the head of household. He is a surgeon who says he was born in Utah, his father in New York and his mother in Kentucky (Incorrect—Elizabeth J. Pegan Gregor was born in Ohio). David G. Gregor says his first marriage occurred at age 33. David's wife, Elizabeth Q. Stebbins Gregor, 22, was born in New York as were her parents; she says she was first married at age 19. David and Elizabeth Stebbins Gregor have a son, David G. Jr., age 11 months.

He was an esteemed physician in Park City, Utah, where he was a partner with his brother-in-law, Dr. C.W. Wilson. After moving back to New York, he focused on surgery and became a leading surgeon in his home state.[283, 288]

Children of Elizabeth Jane Pegan and Gilbert David Gregor:

+ 55 f I. **Daughter⁸ Gregor** was born in Park City, Park City Twp., Summit Co., Utah, on January 12, 1892.[291] She died in Park City, Park City Twp., Summit Co., Utah, on January 12, 1892.[291]

+ 56 m II. **David Gilbert⁸ Gregor** was born in Park City, Park City Twp., Summit Co., Utah, on April 28, 1893.[292] He died in Watertown, Watertown Town, Jefferson Co., New York, on October 16, 1954.[293, 294]

+ 57 f III. **Mary Margaret⁸ Gregor** was born in Park City, Park City Twp., Summit Co., Utah, on February 4, 1895.[295] She died in Watertown, Watertown Town, Jefferson Co., New York, on May 8, 1975.[296]

28. Inez Mae⁷ Pegan (*William Henry⁶, Andrew⁵, Robert A.⁴, Andrew³, Andrew² Pagan, James¹*) was born on September 5, 1889, in Silver Creek Twp., Greene Co., Ohio.[93] She was the daughter of William Henry Pegan (5) and Hattie Ann Griffith. Inez Mae died in South Pasadena, Pinellas Co., Florida, on November 3, 1983, at age 94.[93, 94] She was cremated.[94]

Childless.

Inez Mae married **Harold Munger Owens** on August 23, 1909, in Newport, Campbell Co., Kentucky.[297] Harold Munger Owens was born in Xenia, Xenia Twp., Greene Co., Ohio, on November 19, 1890.[109, 298] He lived in 1945 in St. Petersburg, Pinellas Co., Florida.[299] Harold Munger reached age 74 and died in St. Petersburg, Pinellas Co., Florida, on March 29, 1965.[299, 300] He was buried in Vale Road Cemetery, Springfield, Springfield Twp., Clark Co., Ohio.[299, 301]

Although they were married in 1909, Harold M. Owens and Inez Pegan Owens were both listed in their parents' households in the 1910 census (see #5 William Henry Pegan for Inez; Harold's: (Harold's: *Census Place: Xenia Ward 2, Greene, Ohio; Roll: T624_1185; Page: 6A; Enumeration District: 0104; entry for Harold M. Owens, Harley Owens, head of household*). They'd eloped and didn't announce their union until several months after the census was taken, a year after they wed, according to an article in the July 19, 1910 *Xenia (OH) Daily Gazette*. Only a few, including Hattie Griffith Pegan, Inez' mother, knew their secret. They probably eloped to Kentucky, as Harold, who was only 19, could marry at that age without a parent's permission in that state.[302]

In 1920, Harold and Inez Pegan Owens are living in Xenia, Xenia Twp., Greene Co., Ohio *(Census Place: Xenia Ward 3, Greene, Ohio; Roll: T625_1386; Page: 1A; Enumeration District: 178; Image: 1088)*. Harold Owens, age 29, born Ohio, with his father born in Ohio and his mother in Virginia, is a manager of a clothing store. Inez is 30 years old and says she and her parents were born in Ohio. Living with them is Inez' mother, Hattie Griffith Pegan, 77, a widow, who also says she and her parents were born in Ohio.

Harold and Inez Pegan Owens are again residing in Xenia, Xenia Twp., Greene Co., Ohio in 1930 *(Census Place: Xenia, Greene, Ohio; Roll: 1804; Page: 15A; Enumeration District: 24; Image: 347.0)*. Harold, 39, is still the manager of the clothing store. Inez Pegan Owens is 40 years old. This time, both say that they and their parents were born in Ohio (Incorrect—Inez' mother was born in Virginia). The couple says they were first married at ages 19 and 20 respectively. Inez' mother, Hattie Griffith Pegan, is still with them; she is now 88 years old and says she and her mother was born in Virginia and her father in Maryland (Incorrect—Hattie was born in Ohio).

In 1940, Harold and Inez Pegan Owens are still located in Xenia, Xenia Twp., Greene Co., Ohio *(Census Place: Xenia, Greene, Ohio; Roll: T627_3074; Page: 12B; Enumeration District: 29-27)*. In the household are Harold Owens, age 49, the manager of a clothing store. Inez Pegan Owens is 50 years old. Both say they were born in Ohio and were living in their home at 843 King Street in 1935.

Harold Owen's obituary mistakenly says he was born in 1889; he was born in 1890.[299]

29. Carrie Etta[7] Pegan (*James Robert[6], Andrew[5], Robert A.[4], Andrew[3], Andrew[2] Pagan, James[1]*) was born on June 28, 1872, in Sutter Twp., Sutter Co., California.[106] She was the daughter of James Robert Pegan (6) and Queen Isabella Coates. She died in Vernon Twp., Sutter Co., California, on September 28, 1947, at age 75.[106] Carrie Etta was buried in Sutter Cemetery, Sutter, Sutter Co., California.[303]

Childless.

Carrie Etta married **Augustus Saxton VanBlarcom** on May 19, 1889, in Sutter Co., California.[304] Augustus Saxton VanBlarcom was born in Brooklyn, Kings Co., New York, on June 25, 1868.[305] He reached age 54 and died in Normal Heights, San Diego Co., California, on December 5, 1922.[305, 306,] Augustus Saxton was buried in Oakland, Alameda Co., California.[305]

In 1900, Augustus and Carrie Etta Pegan VanBlarcom are found in Anderson Twp., Shasta Co., California, where Augustus is a farmer *(Census Place: Anderson, Shasta, California; Roll: T623_112; Page: 15B; Enumeration District: 111)*. Augustus is 33 years old, born New York with his parents born in New Jersey; Carrie is 28, born California, with her father born in Ohio and her mother in Missouri. The couple have been married 11 years and Carrie has borne no children.

Augustus and Carrie Etta Pegan Vanblarcom are not found in the 1910 census.

Augustus "Van Blarcom" is listed in the 1916 Oakland, Alameda Co., California city directory.[307]

In 1920, Augustus and Carrie Etta Pegan VanBlarcom are living in Coronado Twp., San Diego Co., California *(Census Place: Coronado, San Diego, California; Roll: T625_130; Page: 3B; Enumeration District: 238; Image: 685)*. In the household are Augustus VanBlarcom, 56, born New York with his parents born in New Jersey, who is an engineer in a hotel; and his wife, Carrie Etta Pegan VanBlarcom, 48, a "pantry girl" in the hotel, who says she was born in California, her father in Ohio and her mother in Missouri.

Augustus VanBlarcom's death certificate and obituary say he was to be buried in Oakland, Alameda Co., California, but no cemetery was specified in either.[305, 308]

Carrie Etta Pegan VanBlarcom married **Daniel McKenzie Stevenson** on June 12, 1926, in Sutter Co., California.[309, 310] Daniel McKenzie Stevenson was born in Butte Twp., Sutter Co., California, on January 13, 1873.[311] He reached age 78 and died in Vernon Twp., Sutter Co., California, on May 19, 1951.[311] Daniel McKenzie was buried in Sutter Cemetery, Sutter, Sutter Co., California.[312]

Daniel M. and Carrie Etta Pegan VanBlarcom Stevenson are enumerated in Slough Precinct, Vernon Twp., Sutter Co., California in 1930 *(Census Place: Vernon, Sutter, California; Roll: 224; Page: 1A; Enumeration District: 0008; Image: 406.0)*. In the household are Daniel M. Stevenson, age 56, a fruit farmer, who says he was born in California and his parents in Missouri. His wife, Carrie Etta Pegan VanBlarcom Pegan is 55 and says she was born in California, her father in Ohio and her mother in Missouri. Daniel says he was first married at age 25, while Carrie Etta says her first marriage occurred at age 18. With them Daniel's son by his first marriage, Claire, 15, born California.

In 1940, Daniel M. and Carrie Etta Pegan VanBlarcum Stevenson are found in Yuba City, Sutter Co., California *(Census Place: Yuba City, Sutter, California; Roll: T627_354; Page: 13A; Enumeration District: 51-14A)*. Both are age 67, born in California, and state they were living in Sutter Co., California in 1935. Daniel Stevenson lists no occupation. They are living at 235 C Street.

30. **Franklin Andrew⁷ Pegan** (*James Robert⁶, Andrew⁵, Robert A.⁴, Andrew³, Andrew² Pagan, James¹*) was born on September 28, 1876, in Butte Twp., Sutter Co., California.[107] He was the son of James Robert Pegan (6) and Queen Isabella Coates. Franklin Andrew died in Butte Twp., Sutter Co., California, on November 12, 1880, at age four.[107] He was buried in Yuba City Cemetery, Yuba City, Sutter Co., California.[107]

31. **Ruby Zetta⁷ Pegan** (*James Robert⁶, Andrew⁵, Robert A.⁴, Andrew³, Andrew² Pagan, James¹*) was born on July 27, 1883, in Butte Twp., Sutter Co., California.[108,109] She was the daughter of James Robert Pegan (6) and Queen Isabella Coates. Ruby Zetta died in Pescadero, Washington Twp., San Mateo Co., California, on February 21, 1978, at age 94.[108, 110] She was buried in Skylawn Memorial Park Cemetery, San Mateo, San Mateo Co., California.[313, 314]

Childless.

Ruby Zetta Pegan was a noted schoolteacher in Stockton and San Francisco, California who was mentioned in "Who's Who Among Women in California" in 1922.[315]

Ruby Zetta Pegan is enumerated in Stockton, Stockton Twp., San Joaquin Co., California in 1910. *(Census Place: Stockton Ward 2, San Joaquin, California; Roll: T624_103; Page: 1B; Enumeration District: 0135; Image: 356)*. Ruby Z., 24, single is a schoolteacher. She is living with her mother, Queen Isabella Coates Galbreath Pegan, a boarding house owner, and her sister Zoa, 22, a stenographer. There are four lodgers also in the household, including Ernest Camp, 30, a musician in a dance hall, Zoa's future husband.

In 1920, Ruby Zetta Pegan, 36, single, a schoolteacher, is living in San Francisco, San Francisco Co., California *(Census Place: San Francisco Assembly District 30, San Francisco, California; Roll: T625_139; Page: 8A; Enumeration District: 236; Image: 467)*. She has a 22-year-old boarder, Louis Spiegelman, born Russia, an upholsterer, lodging in her home.

Although she is not found in the 1930 census, California Voter Registrations list her in San Francisco under "Ruby Pegan".[316]

Ruby Zetta married **Angelo Anthony Paganetti** about 1931 in San Francisco Co., California. Angelo Anthony Paganetti was born in San Francisco, San Francisco Co., California, on November 21, 1896.[317, 318, 319] He reached age 69 and died in Pescadero, Washington Twp., San Mateo Co., California, on August 21, 1966.[317, 318] Angelo Anthony was buried in Skylawn Memorial Park Cemetery, San Mateo, San Mateo Co., California.[320]

Angelo Anthony Paganetti and Ruby Zetta Pegan were probably married in late 1930 or in 1931, as he is a 33-year-old single shipfitter (ironworker) for a ship builder and still living with his parents in the 1930 census *(Census Place: San Francisco, San Francisco, California; Roll: 198; Page: 17A; Enumeration District: 0109)*. But they are married in the 1932 San Francisco city directory, living at 3032 Fulton Street in San Francisco. (Angelo Paganetti is erroneously listed as "Angelo Pagenelli", but Zetta has the correct surname.)[321]

In 1940, Angelo and Ruby Zetta Pegan Paganetti are found in San Francisco, San Francisco Co., California *(Census Place: San Francisco, San Francisco, California; Roll: T627_301; Page: 11B; Enumeration District: 38-81)*. In the household are Angelo Paganetti, mistakenly listed as age 43, an ironworker/shipfitter in a shipyard, and Ruby Zetta Pegan Paganetti, also 43, a grammar school teacher. Both were born in California and living in the same place in 1935. Their address is 783 Ingerson Avenue.

By 1942, Angelo Anthony Paganetti is working at Bethlehem Steel, according to his WWII draft registration in San Francisco, San Francisco Co., California.[319]

The Angelo and Ruby Zetta Pegan Paganetti ranch home, the Lone Cypress Ranch, in Pescadero, San Mateo Co., California was destroyed by fire on the night of August 21, 1966. Angelo Paganetti died trying to save his wife Ruby Pegan Paganetti, whom he mistakenly believed was trapped in their bedroom. Ruby had already escaped and had phoned the fire department before she fled outside. However, "Zetta" may have been flustered, and she gave an incorrect address to the fire department. By the time the firefighters were notified of the correct address, the entire house was engulfed. According to the newspaper article in the San Mateo Times (22 Aug 1966), the house was "filled with valuable antiques and many family heirlooms", all of which were burned.[318]

32. Zoa Faretta[7] Pegan (*James Robert[6], Andrew[5], Robert A.[4], Andrew[3], Andrew[2] Pagan, James[1]*) was born on June 13, 1886, in Butte Twp., Sutter Co., California.[111, 112] She was the daughter of James Robert Pegan (6) and Queen Isabella Coates. Zoa Faretta died in a hospital in San Jose, Santa Clara Co, California, on February 22, 1961, at age 74.[111, 112] She was buried in Santa Clara Mission Cemetery (Santa Clara Catholic Cemetery), Santa Clara, Santa Clara Co., California.[112, 322]

Zoa F. Pegan is enumerated in Stockton, Stockton Twp., San Joaquin Co., California in 1910 *(Census Place: Stockton Ward 2, San Joaquin, California; Roll: T624_103; Page: 1B; Enumeration District: 0135; Image: 356)*. Zoa, 22, a stenographer, is living with her mother Queen Isabella Coates Galbreath Pegan, who owns a boardinghouse, and her sister Ruby Z., 24, a schoolteacher. There are four lodgers in the boarding house, and one is Ernest Camp, age 30, born Nebraska (Incorrect—he was born in Iowa), who would soon marry Zoa Pegan. Ernest says his father was born in Pennsylvania and his mother in New York, and his occupation is musician in a dance hall.

Zoa Faretta married **Ernest Franklin Camp** on May 15, 1910, in San Joaquin Co., California.[323] They divorced. They had one son. Ernest Franklin Camp was born in Geneva, Geneva Twp., Fillmore Co., Nebraska, on January 20, 1880.[324] He reached age 57 and died in Los Angeles, Los Angeles Co., California, on February 5, 1937.[325, 326] Ernest Franklin was buried in Inglewood Park Cemetery, Inglewood, Los Angeles Co., California.[326, 327]

Ernest is enumerated as "Earnest O. Camp" in the 1880 census in Geneva, Geneva Twp., Fillmore Co., Nebraska with his parents, Silas ("S.B.") and Ida Purdy Camp *(Census Place: Geneva, Fillmore, Nebraska; Roll: 748; Page: 489B; Enumeration District: 327; Image: 0561)*.

By 1917, Ernest Camp, born Nebraska, was working as a musician at the Hippodrome Theater in San Diego in 1917.[324]

In 1920, Ernest Franklin and Zoa F. Pegan Camp are living in San Diego, San Diego Twp., San Diego Co., California *(Census Place: San Diego, San Diego, California; Roll: T625_131; Page: 2B; Enumeration District: 306; Image: 754)*. Ernest Camp, 39, is a theater musician, who says he was born in Nebraska, his father in Pennsylvania and his mother in New York. Zoa F. Pegan Camp. listed as "Zoan", is listed as age 36(?), born California, with her father born in Ohio and her mother in Missouri. Zoa lists her occupation as a saleslady in a retail store. With them is son Richard, eight, born in California.

In 1930, Zoa F. Pegan Camp, 43, born California, with her father born in Ohio and her mother in Missouri, is residing in a hotel in San Francisco, San Francisco Co., California *(Census Place: San Francisco, San Francisco, California; Roll: 210; Page: 10A; Enumeration District: 405; Image: 362.0.)* She lists herself as married, with her first marriage occuring at age 24, and says her occupation as a hair and scalp specialist at a hotel beauty shop. With her is son "Ralph" (Richard), 18, also born in California, with his father born in Nebraska and his mother in California.

Zoa F. Pegan Camp is not found in the 1940 U.S. Census. However, she continued to live in San Francisco, San Francisco Co., California until 1958, according to her death certificate. She died in Agnews State Hospital in San Jose, Santa Clara Co., California.

In 1930, Ernest Camp, Zoa's estranged husband, is a musician and merchant seaman on the ship *Yale*, harbored at the port of Los Angeles in Wilmington, Los Angeles Co., California *(Census Place: Wilmington, Los Angeles, California; Roll: 1932_1; Page: 97A; Enumeration District: 19-1599)*. Ernest Camp is age 50, a musician, born Nebraska, who says he is married and lists his permanent address as San Diego, California.

On his death certificate, Ernest Camp's birthdate and place are listed as January 20, 1881 in Geneva, Geneva Twp., Fillmore Co., Nebraska by his informant, his second wife Hilah Norine Buchanan Marshall Camp.[326] But on his WWI draft application, Ernest gives his own birth information as 20 January 20, 1880, and census data support this date.[324]

Son of Zoa Faretta Pegan and Ernest Franklin Camp:

+ 58 m I. **Richard Ernie**[8] **Camp** was born in Stockton, San Joaquin Co., California, on June 1, 1911.[328, 329, 330]

He died in San Francisco, San Francisco Co., California, on November 30, 1963.[329, 330]

33. Flora[7] **Pegan** (*John S.*[6], *Andrew*[5], *Robert A.*[4], *Andrew*[3], *Andrew*[2] *Pagan, James*[1]) was born on November 21, 1866, in Clarksville, Calumet Twp., Pike Co., Missouri.[121, 122] She was the daughter of John S. Pegan (7) and Margaret N. Duncan. Flora died in Clarksville, Calumet Twp., Pike Co., Missouri, on August 21, 1875, at age eight.[121, 122, 123] She was buried in Greenwood Cemetery, Clarksville, Calumet Twp., Pike Co., Missouri.[121, 122]

34. Andrew M.[7] **Pegan** (*John S.*[6], *Andrew*[5], *Robert A.*[4], *Andrew*[3], *Andrew*[2] *Pagan, James*[1]) was born on November 14, 1868, in Iowa or Missouri.[124] He was the son of John S. Pegan (7) and Margaret N. Duncan. Andrew M. died in Spokane, Diana Precinct, Spokane Co., Washington, on December 10, 1910, at age 42.[124, 125] He was buried in Mount Mora Cemetery, St. Joseph, Washington Twp., Buchanan Co., Missouri.[124, 331]

In 1880, Andrew M. Pegan is listed as born in Missouri *(Census Place: Clarksville, Pike, Missouri; Roll: T9_709; Page: 551.3000; Enumeration District: 135; Image: 0473; Andrew Pegan, Andrew Pegan [his grandfather], head of household)*. In later censuses, however, Andrew says he was born in Iowa.

Andrew Pegan, an employee of Sam Reid Tobacco Company, is listed in the St. Joseph, Washington Twp., Buchanan Co., Missouri city directory in 1888.[332]

Andrew M. married **Ella M. Young** on April 5, 1893, in Buchanan Co., Missouri.[333, 334] They had one son. Ella M. Young was born in St. Joseph, Washington Twp., Buchanan Co., Missouri, on May 17, 1868.[335, 336] She reached age 86 and died in St. Joseph, Washington Twp., Buchanan Co., Missouri, on August 24, 1954.[335,336] Ella M. was buried in Mount Mora Cemetery, St. Joseph, Washington Twp., Buchanan Co., Missouri.[335,336, 337]

Andrew and Ella Young Pegan remain St. Joseph through 1895, when he is in the city directory again as a clerk at Martin and Sheridan Bros.[338] His uncle, Robert A. Pegan, is also residing there.

According to the Albuquerque (NM) Daily Citizen on May 3, 1899, Andrew M. Pegan arrived in Albuquerque with his son (James).[339] Ella may have followed shortly thereafter. While in Albuquerque, Andrew Pegan was active in the Federal Labor Union there, and was elected an officer in 1903.[340]

Andrew Pegan is enumerated in the 1900 census in Albuquerque, Bernalillo Co., New Mexico (*Census Place: Albuquerque, Bernalillo, New Mexico; Roll: T623_999; Page: 6B; Enumeration District: 18*). Andrew, 31, is a chemical compounder. He says he was born in Nov 1868 in Iowa, his father in Missouri and his mother in New York (Incorrect—his mother was born in Missouri). His wife, Ella Young Pegan is 31, born in May 1869 in Missouri, with her father born in Virginia and her mother in Kentucky. The pair say they have been married seven years and Ella has borne one child, who survives. This is son James, age five, born Oct 1894 in Missouri. (Ella may have taken a year off her age to be younger than Andrew.)

In 1910, Andrew Pegan, 41, is found in Spokane, Spokane Co., Washington (*Census Place: Spokane Ward 4, Spokane, Washington; Roll: T624_1671; Page: 12A; Enumeration District: 0185; Image: 334*). He again says he was born in Iowa and lists his occupation as a compounder of wines and liquors. Wife Ella Young Pegan is age 40 and son James A. is 15. Ella has borne no more children.

After her husband Andrew Pegan dies in 1910, Ella Young Pegan and her son leave Spokane, Spokane Co., Washington and move back to St. Joseph, Washington Twp., Buchanan Co., Missouri.

Ella Young Pegan and her son James A. Pegan are living with her widowed mother Rebecca Young, age 75, in St. Joseph, Washington Twp., Buchanan Co., Missouri in 1920 (*Census Place: St Joseph Ward 7, Buchanan, Missouri; Roll: T625_908; Page: 6A; Enumeration District: 111; Image: 498*). Their surname, however, is listed as "Began". Ella, now a widow, is age 50 and James, 25, still single, is a postal clerk.

In 1930, Ella Young Pegan is again found in St. Joseph, Washington Twp., Buchanan Co., Missouri (*Census Place: St Joseph, Buchanan, Missouri; Roll: 1178; Page: 2A; Enumeration District: 42; Image: 762.0*). Ella Young Pegan, 61, is listed as the head of the household. Ella was born in Missouri, her father in Virginia and her mother in Kentucky, and she lists her occupation as a clerk in a retail dry goods store. Living with her is her mother Rebecca Young, 85, born Kentucky with her parents born in Virginia. Both women are widows.

Ella Young Pegan continues to reside in St. Joseph, Washington Twp., Buchanan Co., Missouri in 1940 (*Census Place: St Joseph, Buchanan, Missouri; Roll: T627_2088; Page: 5A; Enumeration District: 11-54*). Ella Young Pegan, age 70, born Missouri, a widow, is living alone. She lists no occupation and says she was at the same address, 2110 Eleventh Street, an apartment building, in 1935.

Son of Andrew M. Pegan and Ella M. Young:

+ 59 m I. **James Andrew**[8] **Pegan** was born in St. Joseph, Washington Twp., Buchanan Co., Missouri, on October 29, 1894.[109] He died in St. Joseph, Washington Twp., Buchanan Co., Missouri, on February 16, 1981.[109, 341]

35. Morrow Walton[7] **Pegan** (*John S.*[6], *Andrew*[5], *Robert A.*[4], *Andrew*[3], *Andrew*[2] *Pagan, James*[1]) was born on May 16, 1894, in Clarksville, Calumet Twp., Pike Co., Missouri.[126, 127] He was the son of John S. Pegan (7) and Dulcinea Nannie Vaughn Jeans. Morrow Walton Pegan died in St. Louis, Missouri, on April 3, 1970 at age 75.[128, 129] He was buried in Greenwood Cemetery, Clarksville, Calumet Twp., Pike Co., Missouri.[129, 342]

Morrow Walton married **Julia Meloan** on October 2, 1915, in Randolph Co., Missouri.[343, 344] They had two children. Julia Meloan was born in Elsberry, Hurricane Twp., Lincoln Co., Missouri, on December 29, 1893.[345, 346] Julia reached age 34 and died in a hospital in St. Louis, Missouri, on May 2, 1928.[345, 346] She was buried in Greenwood

Cemetery, Clarksville, Calumet Twp., Pike Co., Missouri.[346, 347]

In 1917, on his WWI draft registration form, Morrow W. Pegan is living in Moberly, Randolph Co., Missouri. He is married, and says he was born on 16 May 1894 in Clarksville, Calumet Twp., Pike Co., Missouri. He lists his occupation as time keeper at the Wabash Regulator plant.[126] Shortly afterwards, Morrow moves his family to Elsberry, Hurricane Twp., Lincoln Co., Missouri, as daughter Jane Temple Pegan was born there in Dec 1917, according to Jane's 1922 death certificate.[348] Later, Morrow and Julia move to St. Louis, Missouri.

Morrow Walton Pegan is found in Ward 21, St Louis, St. Louis Co., Missouri in 1920 *(Census Place: St Louis Ward 21, St Louis (Independent City), Missouri; Roll: T625_957; Page: 5B; Enumeration District: 409; Image: 628)*. He is enumerated as "M.W. Pegan". Morrow, age age 25, a railroad clerk, and is wife, Julia Meloan Pegan, 26, both say they were born in Missouri, as were their parents. Also in the home is their daughter Jane Pegan, age two, born in Missouri.

About two years after their four-year-old daughter, Jane Temple Pegan, died, Morrow and Julia Meloan Pegan moved from St. Louis, Missouri back to Morrow's hometown of Clarksville, Calumet Twp., Pike Co., Missouri. In 1928, Julia Meloan Pegan, sick with tuberculosis, was taken to a sanitarium in St. Louis, where she died.[345]

In 1930, Morrow W. Pegan is enumerated as Morrow W. "Peggan" in St. Louis, Missouri *(Census Place: St Louis, St Louis (Independent City), Missouri; Roll: 1236; Page: 19A; Enumeration District: 28; Image: 1040.0)*. Morrow W. Pegan, age 35, a widower, lists his occupation as chief clerk in a freight office. Morrow says he and his mother were born in Missouri, his father in Pennsylvania (?), and that he was first married at age 19. He is a roomer in the home of Harry and Frances Sanford. His son, Morrow Pegan, is not with him, and is residing with his grandparents Meloan in Lincoln Co., Missouri. There is another boarder in the home: Leona Newhous, 26, a teacher, born Illinois as were her parents.

Morrow Walton Pegan married **Mary Bragg Minor** on September 13, 1933.[128] They had no children. Mary Bragg Minor was born in Calumet Twp., Pike Co., Missouri, on January 1, 1894.[109] She reached age 83 and died in St Louis, St. Louis Co., Missouri, on April 25, 1977.[109] Mary Bragg was buried in Greenwood Cemetery, Clarksville, Calumet Twp., Pike Co., Missouri.[349]

Morrow Pegan is still a resident of St. Louis, Missouri in 1940 *(Census Place: St Louis, St Louis City, Missouri; Roll: T627_2194; Page: 5A; Enumeration District: 96-325)*. Morrow Pegan, age 45, is a cost (?) accountant for a railroad. His wife, Mary B. Minor Pegan is 47 years old and a millinery designer. With them is Morrow's son John Pegan, 15. Also in the household is Mary's unmarried sister, Edith Minor, 42. Their home address is 116 Arsenal Street.

Morrow Pegan worked for the Wabash Railroad for 45 years, starting in Moberly, Missouri before his transfer to St. Louis.

Children of Morrow Walton Pegan and Julia Meloan:

+ 60 f I. **Jane Temple⁸ Pegan** was born in Elsberry, Hurricane Twp., Lincoln Co., Missouri, on December 30, 1917.[348] She died in Elsberry, Hurricane Twp., Lincoln Co., Missouri, on April 21, 1922.[348]

+ 61 m II. **John Robert⁸ Pegan** was born in Elsberry, Hurricane Twp., Lincoln Co., Missouri, on July 13, 1924.[109, 350] He died in Boise, Ada Co., Idaho, on January 24, 2004.[109, 350, 351]

36. Harry Clark⁷ Pegan (*Samuel Alexander⁶, Andrew⁵, Robert A.⁴, Andrew³, Andrew² Pagan, James¹*) was born on April 14, 1878, in Clarksville, Calumet Twp., Pike Co., Missouri.[141] He was the son of Samuel Alexander Pegan (8) and Flora Johnston. He died in Hannibal, Mason Twp., Marion Co., Missouri, on October 3, 1916, at age 38.[141] Harry Clark was buried in Nebo Cemetery, Spring Creek Twp., Pike Co., Illinois.[352]

According to the November 15, 1893 *Quincy (IL) Morning Whig*, 16-year-old Harry Clark Pegan and Charles Adkins, age not mentioned, were arguing "over a trivial matter" when Harry Pegan struck Adkins in the head with a rock. Adkins died that night. The article, reprinted from a Clarksville, Missouri newspaper, says that a coroner's jury deemed Harry Pegan responsible for his actions, and that both boys "were well connected and the sympathy of the entire community extends to both families."[353]

Harry Clark married **Vinnie Mary Main** on December 28, 1898, in Pike Co., Illinois.[354, 355] They had three children. Vinnie Mary Main was born in Time Twp., Pike Co., Illinois, on August 16, 1877.[356, 357] Vinnie Mary reached age 48 and died in Hannibal, Mason Twp., Marion Co., Missouri, on August 10, 1926.[356, 357] She was buried in Nebo Cemetery, Spring Creek Twp., Pike Co., Illinois.[356, 357]

Their marriage entry on the Illinois Statewide Marriage Index says Vinnie Main's surname was "Abair" when she married Harry Clark Pegan in Pike Co., Illinois. But there is no entry for a marriage in that index between a Vinnie Main and an Abair.[354, 355]

Harry Clark Pegan is enumerated in the 1900 census in Nebo, Spring Creek Twp., Pike Co., Illinois *(Census Place: Spring Creek, Pike, Illinois; Roll: T623_337; Page: 4B; Enumeration District: 130)*. In the household is Harry, 22, a laborer, born Missouri, with his father in Ohio and his mother in Illinois. His wife, Vinnie Main Pegan, is 21, born in Illinois, her father in Pennsylvania and her mother in Ohio. The couple have been married three years and Vinnie has borne no children.

In 1910, Harry C. Pegan is again found in Nebo, Spring Creek Twp., Pike Co., *Illinois (Census Place: Spring Creek, Pike, Illinois; Roll: T624_318; Page: 1A; Enumeration District: 0144; Image: 641)*. Harry, 32, is now a barber, Vinnie Main Pegan is also age 32. They say they have been married for 11 years(?) and Vinnie has borne three children, all still living: Dorothy, nine, Henry, eight, and Flora, four; all were born in Illinois.

Harry Clark Pegan was a shoe cutter in a St. Louis shoe factory when he died, according to his death certificate.[141]

Following the death of Harry Clark Pegan, Vinnie Main Abair Pegan remarried to Albert John Niemann (July 4, 1881, Burlington, Burlington Twp., Des Moines Co., Iowa-December 28, 1957?).[358]

In 1920, Al and Vinnie Main Abair Pegan Niemann are living in Hannibal, Mason Twp., Marion Co., Missouri *(Census Place: Hannibal Ward 1, Marion, Missouri; Roll: T625_934; Page: 5A; Enumeration District: 103; Image: 786)*. Al Niemann, 38, born Illinois, is a pipe fitter at a railroad yard. Vinnie Main Abair Pegan Niemann 38 years old. With them are Vinnie's children by her first marriage to Harry Clark Pegan: Dorothy, 19, is a toe stitcher in a shoe factory; Ermann Henry, 17, is a machinist in a factory; and "Josephine" (Flora), 14, is a heel stayer in a shoe factory, probably the same one where her older sister Dorothy is employed.

Children of Harry Clark Pegan and Vinnie Mary Main:

+ 62 f I. **Dorothy Geneva[8] Pegan** was born in Nebo, Spring Creek Twp., Pike Co., Illinois, on January 15, 1901.[109] She died in Phoenix, Maricopa Co., Arizona, on July 1, 1987.[109, 359]

+ 63 m II. **Erman Henry[8] Pegan** was born in Nebo, Spring Creek Twp., Pike Co., Illinois, on July 25, 1902.[109, 360, 361] He was also known as **Pete** and **Bud**. Erman Henry died in San Pedro, Los Angeles Co., California, on May 6, 1982.[109, 360, 361]

+ 64 f III. **Flora Josephine[8] Pegan** was born in Nebo, Spring Creek Twp., Pike Co., Illinois, on June 7, 1905.[109, 362, 363, 364] She died in a hospital in Joshua Tree, San Bernardino Co., California, on June 5, 1979.[109, 362, 364]

37. Robert Donald⁷ Pegan II (*Robert Andrew⁶, Andrew⁵, Robert A.⁴, Andrew³, Andrew² Pagan, James¹*) was born on February 23, 1907, in Kansas City, Jackson Co., Missouri.[149, 150, 151] He was also known as **Don** and **R. Don**. He was the son of Robert Andrew Pegan (9) and Jessie Farrington. Robert Donald died in West Los Angeles, Los Angeles Co., California, on October 1, 1976, at age 69.[150, 151] He was buried in Willamette National Cemetery, Portland, Multnomah Co., Oregon, on October 15, 1976.[151, 365, 366]

Childless.

Robert D. Pegan II is not found in the 1930 census.

Robert Donald married **Helen Pauline Stults** on December 24, 1936, in Jackson Co., Missouri.[367] Helen Pauline Stults was born in Joplin, Joplin Twp., Jasper Co., Missouri, on December 17, 1900.[368, 369] Helen Pauline reached age 63 and died in North Hollywood, Los Angeles, Los Angeles Co., California, on January 13, 1964.[368, 369] She was buried in Valhalla Memorial Park Cemetery, North Hollywood, Los Angeles Co., California.[369, 370]

Robert D. and Helen Stults Pegan II are listed in the 1938 Joplin, Joplin Twp., Jackson Co., Missouri city directory.[371]

In 1940, Robert Donald Pegan II, enumerated as "Robert D. Regan", is living in Joplin, Joplin Twp., Jackson Co., Missouri *(Census Place: Joplin, Jasper, Missouri; Roll: T627_2117; Page: 17A; Enumeration District: 49-12)*. Robert D. Pegan, age 43, is a salesman for a retail liquor store. His wife, Helen Stults Pegan, is 49 and an information clerk and cashier in a theater. Both were born in Missouri and were living in Joplin in 1935. Their residence address is 5 West Sixth Street.

By 1943, Robert Donald and Helen Stults Pegan II relocated to Los Angeles, Los Angeles Co., California.[372]

Before she married Robert Donald Pegan, Helen Stults and a Eugene B. O'Reilly completed a marriage application in Jackson Co., Missouri on April 16, 1924. But there is no license for the marriage, which apparently didn't occur.[373]

8th Generation

38. Stella Frances[8] Pegan (*Alexander Campbell[7], Joseph[6], Andrew[5], Robert A.[4], Andrew[3], Andrew[2] Pagan, James[1]*) was born on October 19, 1897, in Clarksville, Calumet Twp., Pike Co., Missouri.[109, 157, 158] She was also known as **Frances**. She was the daughter of Alexander Campbell Pegan (13) and Dempsey Summers Bass. Stella Frances died in Los Angeles, Los Angeles Co., California, on November 14, 1984, at age 87.[109, 157, 158] She was buried in Angeles Abbey Memorial Park Mausoleum, Compton, Los Angeles Co., California.[374]

Stella Frances married **Miles Prudie Gough** on June 5, 1917, in Marion Co., Missouri.[375] They had one daughter. Miles Prudie Gough was born in Salem Twp., Henry Co., Iowa, on January 18, 1888.[376] He reached age 34 and died in Clarksville, Calumet Twp., Pike Co., Missouri, on August 12, 1922.[377, 378] Miles Prudie was buried in Greenwood Cemetery, Clarksville, Calumet Twp., Pike Co., Missouri.[378, 379]

When he registered for the WWI draft in 1917, Miles Gough was living in Ashburn, Salt River Twp., Pike Co., Missouri and working as an agent and operator for the Chicago, Burlington and Quincy Railroad.[376]

In 1920, Miles and Stella Frances Pegan Gough are living in Clarksville, Calumet Twp., Pike Co., Missouri *(Census Place: Calumet, Pike, Missouri; Roll: T625_941; Page: 3A; Enumeration District: 137; Image: 772)*. Miles Gough, 31, born Iowa, is a telegrapher with the railroad and Stella Frances is age 22. Also in the household is their daughter Dempsey Gough, 21 months, and Stella's mother, Dempsey Summers Bass Pegan, 50, divorced; and Stella's two brothers Otho Pegan, 16, and Luther Carlisle Pegan, 14. All in the home were born in Missouri except for Miles.

On the morning of August 12, 1922, Miles Prudie Gough bid his wife Stella Frances and daughter Dempsey goodbye when they boarded a train to Hannibal to attend a funeral. After visiting some friends until about 2 p.m., he went home, spread kerosene around his shed, lit it on fire, locked himself inside the shed hanged himself. He was allegedly despondent over a threatened railroad strike, according to his obituary.[377]

Stella Frances lived in 1925 in Hannibal, Mason Twp., Marion Co., Missouri, according to the Hannibal city directory. She is living with her mother, Dempsey Pegan, her two unmarried brothers Otho and Luther Pegan. Undoubtedly, although not mentioned, Frances' daughter Dempsey Gough is there also. Frances is a clerk at Sonnenberg & Sons department store. Luther's a mechanic, and Otho is an inspector.[156]

In 1930, Stella Frances Pegan Gough, 32, a widow, and her daughter Dempsey Gough, 12, are still residing with Stella's mother Dempsey Bass Pegan, but they have removed to Huntington Park, San Antonio Twp., Los Angeles Co., California *(Census Place: Huntington Park, Los Angeles, California; Roll: 171; Page: 1B; Enumeration District: 1315; Image: 582.0)*. Dempsey Bass Pegan, 60, now says she is a widow, even though her husband Alexander Pegan is alive and living in Quincy, Quincy Twp., Adams Co., Illinois. Living with them are Dempsey Bass Pegan's sons and Stella Frances Pegan Gough's brothers, Otho Pegan, 27 and unmarried; and newlyweds Luther C. Pegan, 25, and his wife Alice Unknown Pegan, 19. Stella Frances Gough says she has no occupation, but her mother Dempsey Bass Pegan is a saleslady in a dry goods store, her brother Otho Pegan is a cost estimator at a dynamite works, and brother Luther Pegan is a battery maker at a radio factory. All were born in Missouri except Alice, who was born in Oklahoma.

Stella Frances Pegan Gough is enumerated as Frances Gough and is living with her daughter Dempsey Gough and her brother Otho Pegan in Long Beach, Los Angeles Co., California in 1940 *(Census Place: Long Beach, Los Angeles, California; Roll: T627_369; Page: 8A; Enumeration District: 59-39)*. (Stella) Frances Pegan Gough, listed as head of the household, is a saleslady at a retail store. Dempsey Gough, 22, is listed as a "new worker" (WPA), but her occupation is not identified. Otho Pegan, age 37, single, is a public accountant at an accounting/auditing firm. All in the home say they were born in Missouri and were living in California in 1935. The house address is 833 Belmont Avenue.

She and her daughter lived between 1952 and 1959 in Dallas and Fort Worth, Texas, where France's brother Luther Carlisle Pegan also was at the time, before returning to Los Angeles County, California.[380, 381]

Daughter of Stella Frances Pegan and Miles Prudie Gough:

+ 65 f I. **Dempsey Rachel**[9] **Gough** was born in Clarksville, Calumet Twp., Pike Co., Missouri, on March 24, 1918.[109, 382] She died in Long Beach, Los Angeles Co., California, on August 19, 1981.[382]

39. Otho M.[8] **Pegan** (*Alexander Campbell*[7], *Joseph*[6], *Andrew*[5], *Robert A.*[4], *Andrew*[3], *Andrew*[2] *Pagan, James*[1]) was born on February 21, 1903, in Clarksville, Calumet Twp., Pike Co., Missouri.[159] He was the son of Alexander Campbell Pegan (13) and Dempsey Summers Bass. Otho M. died in Portland, Multnomah Co., Oregon, on January 16, 1959, at age 55.[159, 160] He was buried in Angeles Abbey Memorial Park Mausoleum, Compton, Los Angeles Co., California.[383, 384, 385]

Childless.

Otho Pegan, along with his mother Dempsey and siblings Luther Carlisle and Frances, lived in Hannibal, Mason Twp., Marion Co., Missouri, in 1925, according to the Hannibal city directory. Otho's niece, Dempsey Gough, the daughter of his sister Stella Frances, was most likely in the home as well. His brother Luther is a mechanic and Otho an "inspector". Frances is a clerk at Sonnenberg & Sons.[156]

In 1930, Otho Pegan, 27 and single, is living with his mother Dempsey Bass Pegan, 60, in Huntington Park, San Antonio Twp., Los Angeles Co., California (*Census Place: Huntington Park, Los Angeles, California; Roll: 171; Page: 1B; Enumeration District: 1315; Image: 582.0*). Also in the home are Dempsey's daughter and Otho's sister (Stella) Frances Pegan Gough, 32, a widow, and Frances' daughter Dempsey Gough, 12; and newlyweded son Luther C. Pegan, 25, and his wife Alice Unknown Pegan, 19. Dempsey Bass Pegan lists herself as "widowed," but her husband Alexander Pegan is alive and residing in Quincy, Quincy Twp., Adams Co., Illinois. Ortho's occupation is a cost estimator at a dynamite works, while his mother, Dempsey Bass Pegan, is a saleslady in a dry goods store and his brother, Luther Pegan, is a battery maker at a radio factory. All were born in Missouri except Alice, who was born in Oklahoma.

In the 1940 census, Otho Pegan is living with his widowed sister, Stella Frances Pegan Gough, and her daughter Dempsey Gough in Long Beach, Los Angeles Co., California (*Census Place: Long Beach, Los Angeles, California; Roll: T627_369; Page: 8A; Enumeration District: 59-39*). Otho Pegan, age 37, single, is a public accountant at an accounting/auditing firm. Frances Pegan Gough, listed as "Frances" and as the head of the household, is a saleslady at a retail store. Dempsey Gough, 22, is listed as a "new worker (WPA)," but her occupation is not identified. All in the home say they were born in Missouri and were living in California in 1935. The house address is 833 Belmont Avenue.

Otho M. married Mrs. **Ruby C. Slagle** (Davis) Tobin on September 17, 1947, in Kootenai Co., Idaho.[386, 387] Ruby C. Slagle was born in Waldo Precinct, Josephine Co., Oregon, on April 4, 1899.[388, 389] Ruby C. reached age 98 and died in Bellevue, King Co., Washington, on July 9, 1997.[109, 389, 390]

Ruby C. Slagle Davis Tobin Pegan's date of birth on the Social Security Death Index, April 5, 1899, is incorrect. On her Social Security Application (SS-5), she states she was born on April 4, 1899 in Grants Pass, Oregon (her parents were living in Waldo Precinct, Josephine Co. Oregon, near Grants Pass, at the time of the 1900 census (*Census Place: Waldo, Josephine, Oregon; Roll: 1347; Page: 7A; Enumeration District: 0017; entry for "Ruba Slagde", David "Slagde" head of household*).

Otho and Ruby Pegan may have been living in Richland, Benton Co., Washington in 1957.

Otho Pegan's occupation is listed on his death certificate as "retired accountant" at "General Electric Corp." Although his death certificate says he was buried in Riverview Abbey & Mausoleum in Portland, Multnomah Co., Oregon, Riverview Abbey & Mausoleum records say Otho was cremated and his ashes sent to Angeles Abbey Memorial Park Mausoleum in Compton, Los Angeles Co., California.[159, 383, 384, 385]

40. Luther Carlisle[8] Pegan (*Alexander Campbell[7], Joseph[6], Andrew[5], Robert A.[4], Andrew[3], Andrew[2] Pagan, James[1]*) was born on June 1, 1905, in Clarksville, Calumet Twp., Pike Co., Missouri.[109, 161] He was also known as **Carl**. He was the son of Alexander Campbell Pegan (13) and Dempsey Summers Bass. He died in Fort Worth, Tarrant Co., Texas, on July 14, 1964, at age 59.[109, 161, 162] Luther Carlisle was cremated and his ashes buried in Laurel Land Memorial Park Cemetery, Dallas, Dallas Co., Texas, about July 17, 1974, but later his niece and informant on his death certificate, Dempsey Rachel Gough, had them disinterred and redeposited in Angeles Abbey Memorial Park Mausoleum, Compton, Los Angeles Co., California.[161, 391, 392]

Luther Carlisle "Carl" Pegan was married at least 10 times but seems to have been childless.

Luther Carlisle lived in 1925 in Hannibal, Mason Twp., Marion Co., Missouri, with his mother Dempsey Pegan, his sister Stella Frances Pegan Gough and brother Otho Pegan. Luther's niece and Frances' daughter, Dempsey Gough, is most certainly with them. Luther is a mechanic, and Otho is an inspector. Frances is a clerk at Sonnenberg & Sons department store.[156]

Luther Carlisle married **Oreta I. Robb** on December 10, 1926, in Marion Co., Missouri.[393] They divorced. Oreta I. Robb was born in Chariton Twp., Randolph Co., Missouri, on September 17, 1910.[109, 394] She reached age 87 and died in Portage, Kalamazoo Co., Michigan, on October 11, 1997.[109] Oreta I. Robb Pegan Cheney Potts was buried in Mt. Hope Cemetery, Middleville, Thornapple Twp., Barry Co., Michigan.[395]

Luther Carlisle Pegan married **Alice Unknown** in 1930 in Los Angeles Co., California. They divorced. Alice Unknown was born in Oklahoma in 1910.

In 1930, newlyweds Luther Carlisle Pegan, age 25, a battery maker at a radio factory, and his wife, Alice Unknown Pegan, 19, are living with Luther's mother Dempsey Bass Pegan, 60, in Huntington Park, San Antonio Twp., Los Angeles Co., California (*Census Place: Huntington Park, Los Angeles, California; Roll: 171; Page: 1B; Enumeration District: 1315; Image: 582.0*). Also in the home are Dempsey's daughter and Luther's sister, (Stella) Frances Pegan Gough, 32, a widow, and Frances' daughter Dempsey Gough, 12; and Dempsey's son and Luther's brother Otho Pegan, 27; single. Dempsey lists herself as a "widow, but her husband Alexander Pegan is alive and residing in Quincy, Quincy Twp., Adams Co., Illinois. Luther Pegan is a battery maker in a radio factory, while his mother Dempsey Bass Pegan is a saleslady in a dry goods store and his brother Otho Pegan is a cost estimator at a dynamite works. All were born in Missouri except Alice, who was born in Oklahoma.

Luther Carlisle Pegan married **Evelyn Unknown** before 1940 in Los Angeles Co., California? They divorced.

Luther Carlisle Pegan is not found in the 1940 census. However, according to the 1940 Long Beach, Los Angeles Co., California city directory, "Carl L. Pegan" and a wife, Evelyn, are living at 2701 Alamitos Avenue. He lists no occupation. Since his brother Otho and sister Stella Frances Pegan Gough are both living in Long Beach then, this is the correct Luther Carlisle Pegan.[396]

Luther Carlisle Pegan married **Grace O'Brien** on November 3, 1940, in Yuma Co., Arizona.[397] Grace O'Brien was born in Colorado in 1896.

"Carl Pagen" of El Paso, Texas, born Clarksville, Missouri, married **Jackie Bliss?,** a Killeen, Texas native and also an El Paso resident, on January 1, 1942, in Juarez, Chihauhua, Mexico.[398]

In 1942, "Carl" Pegan is a service manager in San Bernardino, San Bernardino Co., California.[399]

But by early 1943, his WWII draft card states he had moved to Eugene, Lane Co., Oregon and was employed by Smith and Crook Chevrolet Dealers.[400]

Luther Carlisle Pegan married **Lora M. Clayton** on July 27, 1943, in Lane Co., Oregon.[401] Luther and Lora divorced before March 1944.

Luther Carlisle Pegan married **Ethel Snellstrom** on March 6, 1944, in Spokane Co., Washington.[402] They were divorced in Reno, Washoe Co., Nevada, about April 14, 1944.[403] Ethel Snellstrom was born in Eugene, Lane Co., Oregon?

"L. Carl Pegan" and **W. Kathryn Lynch**, both of Sparks, Nevada, married about July 15, 1944 in Reno, Washoe Co., Nevada.[404] They were divorced in Reno, Washoe Co., Nevada, about September 25, 1946.[405]

Carl Pegan, no occupation, is in San Francisco, San Francisco Co., California in 1948.[406]

Luther Carlisle Pegan married **Beatrice Florence Guilbault** on November 16, 1951, in San Francisco Co., California.[407] They divorced. Beatrice Florence Guilbault was born in Anaconda, Deer Lodge Co., Montana, on October 25, 1893.[408, 409] She reached age 61 and died in San Francisco, San Francisco Co., California, on September 18, 1955.[409] Beatrice Florence Guilbault Pegan Brennan was buried in Colma Cemetery, San Francisco, San Francisco Co., California.[410]

Luther Carlisle Pegan married **Willie Assiter?** on March 3, 1960, in Tarrant Co., Texas.[411] She may have died?

The informant on Luther Carlisle Pegan's death certificate was his niece, Dempsey Gough. He was a widower and a retired auto salesman when he died. He was cremated, with his ashes buried in Laurel Land Memorial Park.[161] However, after Luther Carlisle Pegan's ashes were buried, his niece Dempsey Gough, apparently his next of kin, changed her mind. His ashes were transferred to Angeles Abbey Memorial Park Mausoleum in Compton, California, where his mother, sister Stella Frances, and niece Dempsey, who never married, are buried.[391, 392]

On the Social Security Death Index, he is listed as Carl Pegan.[109]

41. Grace May^8 Pegan (*Charles H.^{7}, Joseph^6, Andrew^5, Robert A.^{4}, Andrew^3, Andrew^2 Pagan, James^1*) was born on November 21, 1889, in Nebo, Spring Creek Twp., Pike Co., Illinois.[179] She was also known as **May**. She was the daughter of Charles H. Pegan (14) and Lilly Belle Knowles. Grace May died in Buffalo Twp., Pike Co., Missouri, on August 21, 1947, at age 57.[179] She was buried in Greenwood Cemetery, Clarksville, Calumet Twp., Pike Co., Missouri.[179, 412]

Grace May married **Arthur Jerome Ewing** on November 23, 1905, in (North) Lee County, Iowa.[413, 414] They divorced. They had six children. Arthur Jerome Ewing was born in Belliot, Belliot Twp., Mitchell Co., Kansas, on May 10, 1882.[415, 416] He reached age 91 and died in Muscatine, Muscatine Co., Iowa, on January 1, 1974.[416] Arthur Jerome was buried in Columbus City Cemetery, Columbus City, Columbus City Twp., Louisa Co., Iowa.[416, 417]

In 1910, Arthur and "May G." Pegan Ewing are enumerated in Stronghurst Twp., Henderson Co., Illinois (*Census Place: Stronghurst, Henderson, Illinois; Roll: T624_289; Page: 4B; Enumeration District: 0039; Image: 560*). Arthur Ewing, 27, born Kansas, with his parents born in Ohio, is a farm laborer and "May" is 20 years old, born Missouri, as were her parents. They are daughter "Gladis" (Gladys), three, and Harold, 18 months, both born in Illinois.

In 1920, Arthur J. and "May G." Pegan Ewing are found in Cairo Twp., Randolph Co., Missouri (*Census Place: Cairo, Randolph, Missouri; Roll: T625_944; Page: 4B; Enumeration District: 134; Image: 15*). Arthur, age 35, is a farmer and "May" is 30 years old. Children in the home are Gladys, 12, Howard, 11, Arthur II, nine, Clara B., six, all born in Illinois; and Thomas, 4 years and six months, born in Missouri.

In the Iowa State Census in 1925, Arthur Ewing, age 43, is residing in Dutch Creek Twp., Washington Co., Iowa, along with wife May G. Pegan Ewing, 35, who states she was born in Illinois and was the daughter of "Charlie" Pegan, born Missouri, and "Lillie" Knowles, born Illinois. Children in the home were Gladys, 18, Howard, 16, "Waren", 15, "Clara B.", 11, Thomas, nine, and "Charolin", one.[418]

"May G." Ewing Ewing and her children are found in Chicago, Cook Co., Illinois in 1930, *(Census Place: Chicago, Cook, Illinois; Roll: 447; Page: 4A; Enumeration District: 716; Image: 112.0).* They are living with her eventual second husband, Claude Ewing, her first husband Arthur Ewing's, brother. "May G." Ewing, 38, born Missouri, says she was first married at age 14. "May" Ewing claims she is a widow, though her husband, Arthur, is incarcerated as a prisoner in an asylum for epileptics and the feeble-minded in Cass Twp., Boone Co., Iowa. Claude Ewing, 36, an Illinois native who is a stationary engineer at a food products company, says he was first married at age 27. Children in the home are Gladys, 23, a drug store clerk; Howard, 21, an oiler in a packing company; Clarabelle, 16, a furniture store clerk; Thomas, 14, and Charlene, five. All the children are listed as born in Illinois except for Charlene, who was born in Iowa. (However, Thomas may have been born in Randolph Co., Missouri.) May's 20-year-old son Arthur Warren Ewing II is a servant in the home of Alex and Georgiana Smith in Lime Creek Twp., Washington Co., Iowa.

Grace May Pegan Ewing married **Claud Richard Ewing** on November 9, 1933, in Cook Co., Illinois.[419] Claud Richard Ewing was born in Hamilton, Montebello Twp., Hancock Co., Illinois, on June 27, 1894.[420, 421, 422] He reached age 71 and died in Wadsworth, Leavenworth Twp., Leavenworth Co., Kansas, on September 29, 1965.[420, 423] Claud Richard was buried in Ft. Leavenworth National Military Cemetery, Leavenworth, Leavenworth Twp., Leavenworth Co., Kansas.[420, 424]

In 1940, Claud and Grace "Mae" Pegan Ewing are still residing in Chicago, Cook Co., Illinois *(Census Place: Chicago, Cook, Illinois; Roll: T627_955; Page: 7A; Enumeration District: 103-1125).* "Claude" Ewing, age 44, is an engineer in a meat packing plant. Grace May Pegan Ewing, listed as "Mae", is 50 years old. With them is Grace May's daughter by Arthur J. Ewing, Charlene, 15, born Iowa. Also in the household are Grace May's son-in-law and daughter, Harm "Jack" Fischer, the manager of a radio store, Gladys Ewing Fischer, 33, an office worker at a textile company. They have a daughter Marie, two. All were born in Illinois except for Charlene. Their home address is 6926 Lafayette Avenue. All, but little Marie Fischer, say they were Chicago residents in 1935.

Claud and Grace May Pegan Ewing Ewing removed to Buffalo Twp., Pike Co., Missouri around 1945, according to her obituary.[425] Grace May dies there two years later. On her death certificate and several other family records, Grace May Pegan Ewing's birthdate is listed as November 21, 1891. But the 1900 census says Oct 1889, and her chronological age in the 1910 and 1920 censuses match with this birthdate. In 1930, she states she is only 38—perhaps shaving a few years off her age because her second husband Claud Ewing, her first husband Arthur Ewing's brother, was younger than she.

After Grace died, Claud relocated to Kansas City, Wyandotte Co., Kansas and married again to a Dora McNickle.[426, 427]

In 1930, Grace's first husband, Arthur Ewing, listed as a prisoner, is institutionalized in a home for epileptics and the feeble-minded in Cass Twp., Boone Co., Iowa *(Census Place: Cass, Boone, Iowa; Roll: 643; Page: 10A; Enumeration District: 6; Image: 530.0).*

On July 24, 1934, Arthur Jerome Ewing Sr. married his second wife, Anna Belle Bliven Wagner, a divorcee with three children, in Randolph Co., Missouri.[428] They soon move to Muscatine County, Iowa. But by 1940, they are living in Anna's birthplace, Louisa County, Iowa.

Arthur Jerome Ewing Sr. is located in Grandview Twp., Louisa Co., Iowa in 1940 *(Census Place: Grandview, Louisa, Iowa; Roll: T627_1178; Page: 4A; Enumeration District: 58-14).* In the household are Arthur Ewing, age 57, a farm laborer, born Kansas; his second wife Anna Blivins Ewing, 52, born Iowa, and Anna's granddaughter Betty Wagner, 11, also born in Iowa. All say they were living in Muscatine County, Iowa in 1935, perhaps with or near Arthur's son, Thomas Butler Ewing, who is still in Muscatine County in the 1940 census. There is no road or address listed.

In his obituary, Arthur J. Ewing is said to have been born in Loveland, Larimer Co., Colorado.[416] But all census and other records indicate he was born in Belliot, Belloit Twp., Mitchell Co., Kansas.

Children of Grace May Pegan and Arthur Jerome Ewing:

+ 66 f I. **Gladys Wynne**[9] **Ewing** was born in Stronghurst Twp., Henderson Co., Illinois, on January 28, 1907.[429, 430] She died in a facility in Sylmar, Los Angeles Co., California, on February 10, 1997.[429, 430]

+ 67 m II. **Lawrence Howard**[9] **Ewing** was born in Stronghurst Twp., Henderson Co., Illinois, on October 13, 1908.[431, 432] He was also known as **Howard**. Lawrence Howard died in Chicago, Cook Co., Illinois, on November 3, 1938.[431, 432]

+ 68 m III. **Arthur Warren**[9] **Ewing II** was born in Lomax Twp., Hancock Co., Illinois, on August 13, 1911.[433, 434] He died in Roswell, Chaves Co., New Mexico, on September 24, 1991.[434]

+ 69 f IV. **Claribel**[9] **Ewing** was born in Dallas City Twp., Henderson Co., Illinois, on October 12, 1913.[109, 435] She died in Belleville, Belleville Twp., Republic Co., Kansas, on January 28, 1986.[109, 435]

+ 70 m V. **Thomas Butler**[9] **Ewing** was born in Cairo Twp., Randolph Co., Missouri, on January 6, 1915.[109, 436] He died in a hospital in Pineville, Rapides Parish, Louisiana, on May 25, 1987.[436, 437]

+ 71 f VI. **Charlene Effie Lilliebelle**[9] **Ewing** was born in Dutch Creek Twp., Washington Co., Iowa, on September 29, 1924.[109, 438, 439] She died in a facility in Belleville, Belleville Twp., Republic Co., Kansas, on August 15, 1996.[109, 438]

42. Alta Lee[8] **Pegan** (*Charles H.*[7], *Joseph*[6], *Andrew*[5], *Robert A.*[4], *Andrew*[3], *Andrew*[2] *Pagan*, *James*[1]) was born on December 7, 1891, in Clarksville, Calumet Twp., Pike Co., Missouri.[180] She was the daughter of Charles H. Pegan (14) and Lilly Belle Knowles. Alta Lee died in Chicago, Cook Co., Illinois, on November 15, 1958, at age 66.[180] She was buried in Ridgewood Cemetery, Des Plaines, Cook Co., Illinois.[180]

In 1910, Alta L. Pegan, 19, is a servant in the home of Napoleon Lamb in Pontoosuc Twp., Hancock, Illinois, along with her mother, Lilly B. Pegan, age 40 (*Census Place: Pontoosuc, Hancock, Illinois; Roll: T624_290; Page: 5A; Enumeration District: 0019; Image: 416*). Lilly Belle Knowles Pegan says she was born in Illinois, her father in Ohio and her mother in the United States. Alta Pegan says she and her father were born in Missouri and her mother in Illinois.

Alta Lee married **James Walter Jacobs** on January 26, 1912, in LaSalle Co., Illinois.[440] They had one daughter. James Walter Jacobs was born in Colusa, Dallas City Twp., Hancock Co., Illinois, on May 20, 1893.[441, 442] He reached age 25 and died in Streator, Bruce Twp., LaSalle Co., Illinois, on April 23, 1919.[442] James Walter was buried in Phillips Cemetery, Streator, (part) Newtown Twp., Livingston Co., Illinois.[443, 444]

In 1920, Alta Pegan Jacobs, a widow, is living with Clark and Melinda Jane Jacobs, the grandfather and grandmother of her late husband, James Walter Jacobs, in Reading Twp., Livingston Co., Illinois (*Census Place: Reading, Livingston, Illinois; Roll: T625_383; Page: 17B; Enumeration District: 45; Image: 535*). Alta Pegan Jacobs, age 27, says she was born in Illinois and her parents in Missouri (Incorrect—her mother was born in Illinois). She lists no occupation. She has her daughter, Lois, age four, born Illinois, with her. The head of the household is Clark Jacobs, 73, born Ohio as were his parents, is a laborer at the water works. Melinda Jane is listed as "Jane", 67, born Indiana as was her mother; her father was born in Virginia.

Alta Lee Pegan Jacobs married **John Henry Bader** on June 9, 1920, in LaSalle Co., Illinois.[445] They divorced. John Henry Bader was born in Lexington Twp., Cleveland Co., Oklahoma, on April 28, 1893.[446] He lived in 1949 in Edgar Springs, Phelps Co., Missouri. John Henry reached age 56 and died in a hospital in Jefferson Barracks, St. Louis Co., Missouri, on September 3, 1949.[447] He was buried in Jefferson Barracks National Cemetery, Lemay Twp., St. Louis Co., Missouri.[447, 448]

Alta Lee Pegan Jacobs Bader married her third husband, **James Brown,** on November 6, 1924, in LaSalle Co., Illinois.[449] They had three children. James Brown was born in Streator, Bruce Twp., LaSalle Co., Illinois, on July 29, 1890.[450, 451] James reached age 68 and died in Chicago, Cook Co., Illinois, on November 2, 1958.[452] He was buried in Ridgewood Cemetery, Des Plaines, Cook Co., Illinois.[452]

Alta L. Pegan Brown is enumerated as the head of her household in Joliet, Will Co., Illinois in 1930 *(Census Place: Joliet, Will, Illinois; Roll: 568; Page: 19A; Image: 38.0)*. Alta, age 39, says she is married, but her husband James Brown is not living with her. Alta, who lists no occupation, says she and her father were born in Missouri and her mother in Illinois and that her first marriage occurred at age 21. She has a son, Walter, age three years and 11 months old, with her. Walter was born in Illinois, as was his father.

Lois Jacobs, Alta's daughter by her first husband, is not living with her mother in 1930; she is residing in Bellwood, Proviso Twp., Cook Co., Illinois with her paternal aunt, Jeanette Jacobs Cochran, Jeanette's husband Dale Cochran and their one-year-old daughter Marilyn *(Census Place: Proviso, Cook, Illinois; Roll: 506; Page: 2B; Enumeration District: 2297; Image: 121.0)*. The Cochrans may have legally adopted Lois later.

James and Alta L. Pegan Brown may have been separated by 1930. However, as James is an engineer, he may have been away on an assignment at the time of the census. In any case, they reconcile the next year, as their daughter Pauline was born in 1932.

In 1940, James and Alta Pegan Brown are again residing together and are enumerated in Chicago, Cook Co., Illinois *(Census Place: Chicago, Cook, Illinois; Roll: T627_974; Page: 9A; Enumeration District: 103-1660)*. James Brown, age, 50, born Illinois, is an engineer at a steel company. Alta Pegan Jacobs is 48 years old, born in Illinois. With them are children Walter, 13, and Pauline, seven, both born in Illinois. All say they were living in Chicago in 1935. Their home address is 616 Noble Street.

When he registers for the WWII draft in 1942, James Brown is single and living alone in Chicago, Cook Co., Illinois.[451] But James and Alta Pegan Jacobs Bader Brown must have reconciled (again?), as they are living together at the time of James Brown's death.[453] Alta dies just short of two weeks later.

Daughter of Alta Lee Pegan and James Walter Jacobs:

+ 72 f I. **Lois Lorraine**[9] **Jacobs (Cochran)** was born in Streator, Bruce Twp., LaSalle Co., Illinois, on February 4, 1915.[454] She died in Bellwood, Cook Co., Illinois, on October 5, 2012.[455]

Children of Alta Lee Pegan and James Brown:

+ 73 m I. **James**[9] **Brown II** was born in Streator, Bruce Twp., LaSalle Co., Illinois, on June 2, 1925.[456, 457] He died in Streator, Bruce Twp., LaSalle Co., Illinois, on July 18, 1928.[456, 457]

+ 74 m II. **Walter David**[9] **Brown** was born in Streator, Bruce Twp., LaSalle Co., Illinois, on May 10, 1926.[109, 458, 459] He died in a hospital in Hudson, Pasco Co., Florida, on November 3, 1992.[109, 458, 459]

+ 75 f III. **Pauline Theresa**[9] **Brown** was born in Joliet, Will Co., Illinois, on April 15, 1932.[109, 460, 461] She was also known as **Paula**. Pauline Theresa died in River Grove, Cook Co., Illinois, on September 15, 2007.[109, 461]

43. Lorraine Ruth[8] **Martin** (*Josephine*[7] *Pegan, Joseph*[6]*, Andrew*[5]*, Robert A.*[4]*, Andrew*[3]*, Andrew*[2] *Pagan, James*[1]) was born on August 21, 1892, in Henderson, Henderson Co., Kentucky.[109, 188] She was the daughter of Major Oury Martin and Josephine Pegan (15). Lorraine Ruth worked as a

Stenographer at a rattan company in 1910. She died in Sappington, St. Louis Co., Missouri, on February 27, 1976, at age 83.[109, 189] Lorraine Ruth was buried in Oak Grove Cemetery, Bel-Nor, St. Louis Co., Missouri.[189, 462, 463]

Lorraine Ruth married **Clifford Young Lucas** on November 29, 1916, in St. Louis, Missouri.[188] They had one daughter. Clifford Young Lucas was born in Gadson, Etowah Co., Alabama, on May 2, 1893.[109, 464] He reached age 98 and died in St. Louis, Missouri, on May 16, 1991.[109] Clifford Young was buried in Oak Grove Cemetery, Bel-Nor, St. Louis Co., Missouri.[351, 465, 466]

In 1920, Clifford and Lorraine Martin Lucas are living with Lorraine's parents, Marion O. and Josephine Pegan Martin, in Ward 124, Maplewood, Jefferson Twp., St. Louis Co., Missouri *(Census Place: Maplewood, St Louis, Missouri; Roll: T625_946; Page: 27B; Enumeration District: 124; Image: 58)*. Clifford, 26, a plumber, says he was born in Alabama, his father in Pennsylvania and his mother in Missouri. Lorraine is 28, and says she was born in Kentucky, her father in Pennsylvania and her mother in Missouri. Jean is 11 months, born in Missouri. Marion O. Martin, 54, is a "twistmaker" in a tobacco factory. This time, he says he was born in Pennsylvania, his father in Scotland and his mother in Alsace (France). Wife Josephine Pegan Martin, 50, says she was born in Missouri, her father in Ohio and her mother in Kentucky.

In 1930, Clifford Y. and Lorraine Martin Lucas are residing in Webster Groves, Carondelet Twp., St. Louis Co., Missouri *(Census Place: Carondelet, St Louis, Missouri; Roll: 1225; Page: 24A; Enumeration District: 16; Image: 234.0)*. Clifford Lucas is 36 years old and still a plumber. This time, he says he was born in Alabama, his father in England and his mother in Missouri. Lorraine Martin Lucas is 38 and born in Kentucky, with her father born in Pennsylvania and her mother in Missouri. Clifford was 23 years old when he first married, and Lorraine was 25. Their daughter, 11-year-old Jean F. Lucas was born in Missouri, while her father was an Alabama native and her mother was Kentucky-born. Living with them is Lorraine's widowed mother, Josephine Pegan Martin, age 60, is also a Missouri native, with her father born in Ohio and her mother in Kentucky.

Clifford and Lorraine Martin Lucas are found once more in Webster Groves, Carondelet Twp., St. Louis Co., Missouri by 1940 *(Census Place: Webster Groves, St Louis, Missouri; Roll: T627_2149; Page: 5A; Enumeration District: 95-112)*. Clifford Lucas, age 46, born Alabama, is the owner of a plumbing and heating company. Lorraine Martin Lucas is 48 years old and born in Kentucky. Their daughter Jean, 21, was born in Missouri. All say they were residing at the same address, 412 Sherwood, in 1935.

In 1948, Clifford Y. and Lorraine Martin Lucas are living in Sappington, St. Louis Co., Missouri, as that is the address Lorraine Martin Lucas, the informant, puts on her mother's, Josephine Pegan Martin Reed's, death certificate.[55]

Daughter of Lorraine Ruth Martin and Clifford Young Lucas:

+ 76 f I. **Jean[9] Lucas** was born in Maplewood, Jefferson Twp., St. Louis Co., Missouri, on January 3, 1919.[109] She died in St. Louis, Missouri, on March 24, 2011.[109, 467]

44. Hazel[8] Reneau *(Lenora or Nora Lee[7] Pegan, Joseph[6], Andrew[5], Robert A.[4], Andrew[3], Andrew[2] Pagan, James[1])* was born on August 26, 1894, in Clarksville, Calumet Twp., Pike Co., Missouri.[197] She was the daughter of Samuel Houston Reneau and Lenora or Nora Lee Pegan (16). Hazel died in Emmaus, St. Charles Co., Missouri, on October 18, 1957, at age 63.[160] She was buried in Emmaus Cemetery, Emmaus, St. Charles Co., Missouri.[197, 468]

Hazel married **Harry Gus Brockman** on November 12, 1913, in St. Charles Co., Missouri.[469] They divorced. They had two children. Harry Gus Brockman was born in St. Louis, Missouri, on April 25, 1892.[470] He reached age 44 and died in a hospital in Clayton, St. Louis Co., Missouri, on April 27, 1936.[470] Harry Gus was buried in Oak Hill Cemetery, Kirkwood, St. Louis Co., Missouri.[470, 471]

Harry G. and Hazel Reneau Brockman are enumerated in 1920 in Maplewood, Jefferson Twp., St. Louis Co., Missouri *(Census Place: Maplewood, St Louis, Missouri; Roll: T625_946; Page: 62B; Enumeration District: 124; Image: 128).* Harry G. Brockman, age 27, a master mechanic, says he and his mother were born in Missouri, and his father in Germany. Hazel Reneau Brockman, 25, says she and her parents were born in Missouri. They have two children, Martha, five, and Raymond, one year and three months, both born in Missouri.

In 1930, Harry G. and Hazel Reneau Brockman are again found in Maplewood, Jefferson Twp., St. Louis Co., Missouri *(Census Place: Maplewood, St Louis, Missouri; Roll: 1224; Page: 7B; Enumeration District: 48; Image: 301.0).* Harry G. Brockman, 38, is a lather, born in Missouri, like his mother, with his father born in Germany. With him are wife Hazel Reneau Brockman is 35, born Missouri as were her parents; and their two children, Martha, 15, and Raymond, 11, both born Missouri. Harry and Hazel say they were first married at ages 21 and 18 respectively. They are living with Harry's parents, Henry and Louise Brockman.

Harry G. Brockman and Hazel Reneau Brockman divorced around 1931. Harry G. Brockman may have lived briefly in Imperial Valley, California in 1932 before moving back to Maplewood, Jefferson Twp., St. Louis Co., Missouri. The informant on Harry Brockman's death certificate is listed as his second wife, Teresa Nowack Brockman, who says Harry was a carpenter at the time of his death.[470]

Hazel Reneau Brockman and her mother, Lenora "Nora Lee" Pegan Reneau Crosson, are living together in 1940 in Maplewood, Jefferson Twp., St. Louis Co., Missouri *(Census Place: Maplewood, St Louis, Missouri; Roll: T627_2150; Page: 8A; Enumeration District: 95-147).* Hazel Reneau Brockman, 45, first lists herself as divorced, but an "S" for single is written on top of the "D". The head of the household, "Nora Lee" Pegan Reneau Crosson, is age 67 and a widow. Neither lists an occupation. Both say they were born in Missouri and were residing in the same home at 2617 Sutton Avenue in 1935. Also in the household is a lodger, Charlotte Bemont, 77, a widow with no occupation, who says she was living in St. Louis in 1935.

Hazel Reneau Brockman fell into the Missouri River on an outing and drowned. Her death certificate states that the incident happened on or about October 18, 1957, but the body wasn't recovered for nearly a week. She was pronounced dead on October 25, 1957, which is the date of her death certificate. She had been a resident at the Emmaus Home in Emmaus, St. Charles Co., Missouri, an institution for cognitively-challenged adults, for nine years at the time of her death. Oddly, on October 28, 1957, three days after her body was recovered and her death certificate was issued, an article on the front page of the *St. Charles (MO) Daily Cosmos Monitor* says the St. Charles county sheriff reported her missing. The sheriff, as reported in the article, gave Hazel's description and was asking county residents to look for her. The *Daily Cosmos Monitor*, the only newspaper in St. Charles, Missouri at that time, never printed a follow-up article or an obituary.[472]

Children of Hazel Reneau and Harry Gus Brockman:

+ 77 f I. **Martha Lee**[9] **Brockman** was born in Maplewood, Jefferson Twp., St. Louis Co., Missouri, on October 31, 1914.[109, 473] She died in Waukesha, Waukesha Twp., Waukesha Co., Wisconsin, on January 13, 2009.[109, 473]

+ 78 m II. **Raymond Harry**[9] **Brockman** was born in Maplewood, Jefferson Twp., St. Louis Co., Missouri, on September 14, 1918.[109, 474, 475, 476, 477] He was also known as **Ray Harry**. Raymond Harry died in Milwaukee, Milwaukee Co., Wisconsin, on July 25, 1989.[109, 474, 475, 476]

45. Mary Etta[8] **Kelley** (*Lewis Albert*[7], *Mary Jane*[6] *Pegan, Andrew*[5], *Robert A.*[4], *Andrew*[3], *Andrew*[2] *Pagan, James*[1]) was born on February 12, 1895, in Monroe City, Monroe Twp., Monroe Co., Missouri.[109, 210] She was the daughter of Lewis

Albert Kelley (22) and Sarah Carlisle. Mary Etta died in Fulton, Calloway Co., Missouri, on September 4, 1971, at age 76.[109, 210] She was buried in St. Jude Cemetery, Monroe City, Monroe Co., Missouri.[210, 478]

Never married.

In 1920, Mary Etta Kelley, age 24, is found in Monroe City, Monroe Twp., Monroe Co., Missouri *(Census Place: Monroe, Monroe, Missouri; Roll: T625_936; Page: 11B; Enumeration District: 127; Image: 245)*. Mary Etta is single, born in Missouri like her father; her mother was born in Maryland. She does "fancy work", most likely embroidery, lacework, etc., on items her mother sews. The head of the household, her father Lewis A. Kelley, age 56, says he was born in Missouri and his parents in Ohio; he is a house plasterer. Her mother, Sallie C. Carlisle Kelley, 52, is a seamstress with private clients. She says she born Maryland, with her father born in Delaware and her mother in Maryland. Also in the home is Mary Etta's brother, John, 12, born in Missouri.

Mary Kelley, age 35, unmarried, is enumerated in born Missouri, Monroe City, Monroe Twp., Monroe Co., Missouri in 1930 *(Census Place: Monroe, Monroe, Missouri; Roll: 1213; Page: 16A; Enumeration District: 11; Image: 764.0)*. She is a typesetter at a newspaper. Her parents are listed as born in Missouri (Incorrect—her mother was born in Maryland). She is living with her mother, Sallie C. Kelley, age 58, who lists no occupation. Sallie says she is married and was first married at age 18. Oddly she and her parents are listed as born in Missouri (incorrect). Sallie lists no occupation. However, Lewis A. Kelley, Mary Etta's father and Sallie's husband, is not in the home. He and son John Kelley are in a boarding house in Hannibal, Mason Twp., Marion Co., Missouri.

In 1940, Mary Etta Kelley, unmarried, is residing with her mother, Sallie Carlisle Kelley, in Monroe City, Monroe Twp., Monroe Co., Missouri *(Census Place: Monroe City, Monroe, Missouri; Roll: T627_2130; Page: 61A; Enumeration District: 69-14)*. "Maryetta" Kelley, 45, born Missouri, has no occupation. The head of the household, Sallie Carlisle Kelley, age 72 and divorced and born in Maryland, lists her occupation as washing and janitor work at church and home. Both say they were living in the same home at 415 Catherine Street in 1935.

Mary Etta Kelley died in the Missouri State Mental Hospital, as did her aunt, Frances "Fannie" Kelley Shaw.[210] Mary Etta Kelley's surname is listed as Kelly on the Social Security Death Index.[109]

46. Alice Lucille[8] Kelley (*Lewis Albert[7], Mary Jane[6] Pegan, Andrew[5], Robert A.[4], Andrew[3], Andrew[2] Pagan, James[1]*) was born on January 16, 1897, in Monroe City, Monroe Twp., Monroe Co., Missouri.[211] She was the daughter of Lewis Albert Kelley (22) and Sarah Carlisle. She died in Port Huron, Port Huron Twp., St. Clair Co., Michigan, on November 16, 1997, at age 100.[211] She was cremated.[211]

Alice Lucille married **Albert Lawrence Green** on June 12, 1923, in Pettis Co., Missouri.[479, 480, 481] They had one son. Albert Lawrence Green was born in Sedalia, Sedalia Twp., Pettis Co., Missouri, on September 25, 1895.[109, 482] Albert Lawrence reached age 80 and died in Port Huron, Port Huron Twp., St. Clair Co., Michigan, on December 13, 1975.[482] He was buried in Riverlawn Cemetery; Marysville, St. Clair Twp., St. Clair Co., Michigan.[482, 483]

Albert Lawrence and Alice Lucille Kelley Green are enumerated in Port Huron, Port Huron Twp., St. Clair Co., Michigan in 1930 *(Census Place: Port Huron, St Clair, Michigan; Roll: 1025; Page: 4A; Enumeration District: 34; Image: 301.0)*. Albert L. Green, age 33, says he was born in Missouri, his father in Illinois and his mother in Tennessee; he is a salesman in a retail clothing store. "A. Lucille" Kelley Green is 32, born in Missouri as were her parents. The couple says they were first married at ages 26 and 25 respectively. They have one child, Albert L. Jr., age four years and 10 months, born in Michigan.

In 1940, Albert and Alice Lucille Kelley Green are still residents of Port Huron, Port Huron Twp., St. Clair Co., Michigan *(Census Place: Port Huron, St Clair, Michigan; Roll: T627_1816; Page: 8B; Enumeration District: 74-36)*. In the household are Albert L. Green, age 44, born Missouri, a manager for the Sperry Company; his wife, "Lucille" Kelley Green, 43, born Missouri, and their son, Albert J.,

14, who is listed as also born in Missouri (he was born in Michigan). They state they were living in the same house at 1304 10th Avenue in 1935.

Son of Alice Lucille Kelley and Albert Lawrence Green:

+ 79 m I. **Albert Lawrence**[9] **Green II** was born in Lansing, Lansing Twp., Ingham Co., Michigan, on May 9, 1925.[109, 484, 485] He died in Cheyenne, Laramie Co., Wyoming, on November 30, 1991.[109, 484, 485]

47. John Carlisle[8] **Kelley** (*Lewis Albert*[7], *Mary Jane*[6] *Pegan, Andrew*[5], *Robert A.*[4], *Andrew*[3], *Andrew*[2] *Pagan, James*[1]) was born on September 23, 1907, in Monroe City, Monroe Twp., Monroe Co., Missouri?[212] He was the son of Lewis Albert Kelley (22) and Sarah Carlisle. John Carlisle Kelley died on January 6, 1967 in St. Louis, Missouri.[213] He was buried in Sunset Memorial Park Cemetery and Mausoleum, Affton, St. Louis Co., Missouri.[213, 486]

Childless.

In 1930, John C. Kelley is residing in a boarding house, along with his father, Lewis A. Kelley, in Hannibal, Mason Twp., Marion Co., Missouri (*Census Place: Hannibal, Marion, Missouri; Roll: 1211; Page: 19A; Enumeration District: 6; Image: 777.0*). John C. Kelley, age 28, single was born Missouri as was his father while his mother born in Maryland. John says he is salesman at a radio and electrical factory. Lewis A. Kelley, age 67, born Missouri with his parents born in Ohio, is still a plasterer. Lewis says he is still married and was first married at age 23, but his wife Sallie is not with him. He may have been separated from his wife Sallie Carlisle Kelley—or he is away on a construction job.

John Carlisle married Mrs. **Thelma Rita Illene Berry (Leitschuh)** Sabourin before 1935. Thelma was born on August 17, 1911 in Mattoon, Mattoon Twp., Coles Co., Illinois.[487] She died on February 15, 1980 in St. Louis, Missouri.[488] Thelma Rita was buried in Sunset Memorial Park Cemetery and Mausoleum, Affton, St. Louis Co., Missouri.[489]

Thelma Rita Illene Berry may have been adopted by her stepfather, George Leitschuh. She often used his surname. Also, she preferred to use Illene as her middle name and "I" as her middle initial.

John Carlisle and Thelma Rita Illene Berry Kelley are living with Thelma's stepfather and mother, George and Loretta Leitschuh, in St. Louis, Missouri in 1940 (*Census Place: St Louis, St Louis City, Missouri; Roll: m-t0627-02207; Page: 7A; Enumeration District: 96-641*). The census taker made numerous mistakes on the form. John C. "Kelly" is 32 years old, born Illinois (incorrect) is a railroad clerk. Thelma is listed as "Selma I. Kelly", age 26 (Incorrect—she is 28), born in Illinois. With them is Patsy Sabourin, nine, Thelma's daughter by her first marriage. However, Patsy is listed as a Kelly. John relationship to the the head of household, George Leitschuh, is "nephew", and Thelma's is "niece", both wrong. John C. Kelley is George Leitschuh's stepson-in-law and Thelma is George's stepdaughter. All say they were living in the St. Louis in 1935. There are numerous lodgers in the household as well. The home is at 5109 Washington Avenue.

Although John Carlisle Kelley was childless, he was a loving stepfather to Patsy Lee Sabourin, later Mrs. Arthur J. Raymond.[213]

48. Alma[8] **Crosson?** (*Laura Belle*[7] *Kelley, Mary Jane*[6] *Pegan, Andrew*[5], *Robert A.*[4], *Andrew*[3], *Andrew*[2] *Pagan, James*[1]) was born in May 1894 in Clarksville, Calumet Twp., Pike Co., Missouri? She was the daughter of Archibald Crosson and Laura Belle Kelley (23). Alma died in Cypress Twp., Chouteau Co., Montana?, before 1910.

Did Alma Crosson exist? Descendants of Frances Maurene "Maureen" Crosson Eudailey, who was the daughter of Archibald and Laura Belle Kelley Crosson, maintain that Frances Maurene thought she was an only child. She never mentioned having a sibling. Birth and death records in Montana in that era are spotty.

Archibald and Laura Belle Kelley Crosson are doubly enumerated in the 1900 U. S. Census in Havre Twp., Chouteau Co., Montana. In their second entry, "Archie" Crosson and his wife, who is listed as "Elma," say that "Elma" has borne two children, both of whom were still living (*Census Place: Havre, Chouteau, Montana; Roll: 910; Page: 23A;*

Enumeration District: 190). Other information on this entry for Archibald Crosson and family is also wrong. But some credence may be given to this entry, as Archie's brother Abraham and his wife Amanda are living next door, and the census taker may have actually spoken to them instead of Archie or Laura. (Sometimes census takers in this era, and in remote areas, did take information from neighbors.)

However, Archie and Laura's other entry in the 1900 census *(Census Place: Havre, Chouteau, Montana; Roll: 910; Page: 13; Enumeration District: 0190)*, and data from their 1910 census *(Census Place: Cypress, Chouteau, Montana; Roll: T624_830; Page: 6A; Enumeration District: 0067; Image: 1052)* indicate Frances Maurene was an only child. On the 1910 U.S. Census form, the information on the Crosson family is correct, and this time Laura is enumerated as having only one child (Frances Maurene Crosson Eudailey), and the child still alive *(Census Place: Cypress, Chouteau, Montana; Roll: T624_830; Page: 6A; Enumeration District: 0067; Image: 1052)*.

So, given all the erroneous information on the 1900 census form, it is possible that "Alma Crosson" never existed.

49. Frances Maurene[8] Crosson (*Laura Belle[7] Kelley, Mary Jane[6] Pegan, Andrew[5], Robert A.[4], Andrew[3], Andrew[2] Pagan, James[1]*) was born on October 7, 1897, in Clarksville, Calumet Twp., Pike Co., Missouri.[109, 223, 224] She was also known as **Maurene**. She was the daughter of Archibald Crosson and Laura Belle Kelley (23). Frances Maurene lived in 1935 in Clarkston, Bladen Co., North Carolina. She died in Palmyra, Fluvanna Co., Virginia, on December 22, 1987, at age 90.[109, 223, 224] Frances Maurene was buried in Cool Spring Christian Church Cemetery, Chickahominy, Lunenburg Co., Virginia.[223]

Frances Maurene Crosson never liked her first given name and always used her middle name, Maurene (spelling is correct).

Frances Maurene Crosson Eudailey spent her childhood roaming from place to place with her parents, Archibald and Laura Belle Kelley Crosson. Archie and Laura never liked to in one place too long, and criss-crossed the country. The family made their way to Lunenburg Co., Virginia in 1911, when "Maurene" was about 13 years old. About four years later, Archibald and Laura were ready to move on again, but Frances Maurene adamantly refused to go. She was tired of the gypsy-like life, and she'd probably already met a neighbor boy, Sam Mason Eudailey, who was six years her senior. Two neighbors who were sisters offered to care for Maurene, so her parents left her in Virginia and moved on. According to her great-great-granddaughter, Frances Stanley, Frances Maurene never saw her father again and only saw her mother occasionally after they left. She did communicate with her mother by letter.[215]

Frances Maurene married **Sam Mason Eudailey** on November 7, 1915, in Lunenburg Co., Virginia.[490] They had four children. Samuel Mason Eudailey was born in Charlotte Court House, Charlotte Co., Virginia, on September 27, 1891.[491, 492, 493] Samuel Mason resided in 1946 in Keysville, Charlotte Co., Virginia. He reached age 55 and died in a hospital in Farmville, Prince Edward Co., Virginia, on October 13, 1946.[494] Samuel Mason was buried in Cool Spring Christian Church Cemetery, Chickahominy, Lunenburg Co., Virginia.[490, 495]

Although his name on his marriage record to Frances Maurene Crosson is Samuel M. Eudailey, his actual name seems to have been Sam Mason Eudailey. He used this name on his WWI and WWII U.S. draft registrations and his Social Security information, and this name appears on his death certificate and gravestone..[491, 492, 493, 494, 495]

In 1920, Sam Mason and Frances Maurene Crosson Eudailey are enumerated in Rehoboth District, Lunenburg Co., Virginia *(Census Place: Rehoboth, Lunenburg, Virginia; Roll: T625_1893; Page: 11B; Enumeration District: 42; Image: 1132)*. In the home are Sam Mason Eudailey, age 28, born Virginia as were his parents, a farmer. His wife, Frances Maurene Crosson Eudailey is 22, but she and her parents are mistakenly listed as born in Virginia. They have two children, daughter Frances L., age three, and son Samuel P., age one, both born in Virginia.

Sam Mason and Frances Maurene Crosson Eudailey are still living in Rehoboth District, Lunenburg Co., Virginia in 1930 *(Census Place: Rehoboth, Lunenburg, Virginia; Roll: 2449; Page: 2A; Enumeration District: 12; Image: 1206.0)*. Sam Mason Eudailey, age 38, born Virginia as were his parents, is a farmer. His wife, Frances "Maurene" Crosson Eudailey, 32, says she and her parents were born in Missouri. The couple states they were first married at ages 24 and 18 respectively. With them are their children: "Lucille", 14, Samuel Jr., 12, Richard, nine, and Edith, six, all born in Virginia.

In 1940, Sam and Frances Maurene Crosson Eudailey continue to reside in Rehoboth District, Lunenburg Co., Virginia (*Census Place: Rehoboth, Lunenburg, Virginia; Roll: T627_4275; Page: 3B; Enumeration District: 56-14*). In the household are Sam Eudailey, age 48, who says he was living in Lunenburg Co. in 1935; and his wife, Frances Maurene Crosson Eudailey, 42, who says she was residing in Clarkston, Bladen Co., North Carolina in 1935. Children in the home include "F. Lucille", 23, Samuel P., 21, Richard, 18, and Edith V., 16, all of whom say they were living in Lunenberg Co. in 1935. All in the home were born in Virginia except for Frances Maurene, who was born in Missouri. The three men, Sam, Samuel P. and Richard, all list their occupations as farmers. They are living on a farm in a rural area, and no road or house address is listed.

Note: The family does not believe that Frances Maurene Crosson Eudailey was living in Clarkston, Bladen Co., North Carolina in 1935. They believe that Sam Eudailey, who talked to the census taker, said his wife Frances Maurene was living in "Clarksville". The census taker either heard, or thought Sam meant, Clarkston, a town in Bladen County, North Carolina ("Clarkston, North Carolina" is written on the census form), or maybe Clarksville, Mecklenburg Co., Virginia, which is a short distance from their home. Perhaps Frances Maurene was in Clarksville, Calumet Twp., Pike Co., Missouri, visiting her mother, Laura B. Kelley Baldwin (LNU)?

Children of Frances Maurene Crosson and Sam Mason Eudailey:

+ 80 f I. **Frances Lucille**[9] **Eudailey** was born in Rehoboth Precinct, Lunenburg Co., Virginia, on July 31, 1916.[496] She was also known as **Lucille**. Frances Lucille died in Keysville, Charlotte Co., Virginia, on October 5, 2014.[497]

+ 81 m II. **Samuel Purnell**[9] **Eudailey** was born in Rehoboth Precinct, Lunenburg Co., Virginia, on June 28, 1918.[109, 498] He died in Keysville, Charlotte Co., Virginia, on October 4, 1993.[109, 499]

+ 82 m III. **Richard Louis**[9] **Eudailey** was born in Rehoboth Precinct, Lunenburg Co., Virginia, on November 20, 1921.[109, 500] He died in Richmond, Henrico Co., Virginia, on November 15, 2011.[109, 501, 502]

+ 83 f IV. **Edith Virginia**[9] **Eudailey** was born in Rehoboth Precinct, Lunenburg Co., Virginia, on November 29, 1923.[109, 503] She died in Keysville, Charlotte Co., Virginia, on November 20, 2010.[504, 505, 506]

50. Eleanor Margaret[8] **Pegan** (*Sinclair Edwin*[7], *William Henry*[6], *Andrew*[5], *Robert A.*[4], *Andrew*[3], *Andrew*[2] *Pagan, James*[1]) was born on June 8, 1887, in Park City Twp., Summit Co., Utah.[263] She was the daughter of Sinclair Edwin Pegan (26) and Emma May Kelso. Eleanor Margaret died in Salt Lake City, Salt Lake Co., Utah, on October 31, 1913, at age 26.[264, 265] She was buried in Mt. Olivet Cemetery, Salt Lake City, Salt Lake Co., Utah.[265, 507]

Eleanor Margaret married **William Francis McLaughlin** on November 14, 1904, in Wasatch Co., Utah.[508, 509] They divorced. They had one daughter. William F. McLaughlin was born in Ontario, Canada, on October 26, 1879.[510, 511] He reached age 52 and died in Salt Lake City, Salt Lake Co., Utah, on July 20, 1932.[510, 511] William Francis was buried in Park City Cemetery, Park City, Park City Twp., Summit Co., Utah.[511, 512]

William F. and Eleanor M. McLaughlin removed to Evanston, Uinta Co., Wyoming in 1908, as an article in the *Park City (UT) Record* newspaper notes that in early February that year says Mrs.

W.L. McLaughlin and her brother "Lew" Pegan left Park City, Utah for Evanston, Wyoming, where "they would make their home".[513] It seems that William and Eleanor's mother, Emma Kelso (Pegan) were already there. Another article in the Park City Record reports that William and Emma bought a movie theater in Evanston, and Emma was playing piano for the silent movies.[254] The business venture apparently failed, as William and Eleanor are back in Park City by 1910.

In 1910, William and Eleanor Pegan McLaughlin are enumerated in Park City, Summit Co., Utah *(Census Place: Park City, Summit, Utah; Roll: T624_1608; Page: 3B; Enumeration District: 0171; Image: 745)*. In the home are William, age 33, born Kansas (?); he is a barber. Wife Eleanor Pegan is 22 years old, and says she was born in Utah, her father in Ohio and her mother in Indiana. They say have been married three years and Eleanor has borne one child, still living. Also in the home is daughter Eleanor, age two. Next door are Eleanor's father, Sinclair Edwin Pegan, her stepmother Kate Martin Pegan, and Eleanor's half-sisters Mary and Grace.

William F. and Eleanor M. McLaughlin divorce by September 1913.

Eleanor Margaret Pegan McLaughlin married **Victor Emmanuel Ridge** on September 13, 1913, in Salt Lake Co., Utah.[263] Victor Emmanuel Ridge was born in Aspen, Pitkin Co., Colorado, on July 1, 1891.[514] He reached age 47 and died in Tacoma, Pierce Co., Washington, on March 22, 1939.[515] Victor Emmanuel was buried in Bayview Cemetery, Bellingham, Whatcom Co., Washington.[516]

According to his WWI draft registration, Victor Emmanuel Ridge was born in Aspen, Pitkin Co., Colorado, although, on his marriage license, he says he is from Denver, Colorado.[263, 514] In 1910, he is 18 years old and living with younger brothers and sisters in Cripple Creek, Teller Co., Colorado *(Census Place: Cripple Creek Ward 1, Teller, Colorado; Roll: T624_125; Page: 14A; Enumeration District: 0193; Image: 1171)*. He is a fireman in a laundry.

Victor and Eleanor Pegan McLaughlin Ridge lived in the Stafford Hotel, where Eleanor was a cashier and Victor a porter. Tragically, only a month and a half after Victor Ridge and Eleanor Pegan McLaughlin marry, Eleanor dies of endocarditis. The birth date on Eleanor Margaret Pegan McLaughlin Ridge's death certificate (June 8, 1890) is incorrect.[264]

After Eleanor died, Victor eventually moved back to Cripple Creek, Teller Co., Colorado, where he is still single and a shoe salesman when he registers for the WWI draft in 1917.[514]

By 1920, Victor, age 29, has moved to Seattle, King Co., Washington *(Census Place: Seattle, King, Washington; Roll: T625_1926; Page: 4B; Enumeration District: 97; Image: 165)* and is remarried to a woman named Lena, who has two children from a prior relationship, ages 10 and five.

He is still living in Seattle in 1930 with Lena and her children *(Census Place: Seattle, King, Washington; Roll: 2493; Page: 15A; Enumeration District: 34; Image: 633.0)*. Victor, age 39, who is now a buyer at a department store, says he was first married at age 21.

Eleanor Margaret's first husband, William F. McLaughlin is not found in the 1920 census.

In 1930, William McLaughlin, age 50, a widower, a barber, is found in Salt Lake City, Salt Lake Co., Utah *(Census Place: Salt Lake City, Salt Lake, Utah; Roll: 4547816; Page: 8A; Image: 1406.0)*. He says he was born in Canada, but that is crossed out with "am" written above it. He also says his father was born in New York and his mother in Canada. Living with him are his son-in-law and daughter, Randolph John and Eleanor McLaughlin Nittler. Randolph Nittler is mistakenly enumerated as "William Nutter". Randolph Nittler, age 27, born California, is a shipping clerk in an automobile factory who says his father was born in Germany and his mother in Wisconsin. Eleanor McLaughlin, 22, says she was born in Utah, her father in Canada (which is crossed out and "Am" written above it) and her mother in Utah. Randolph and Eleanor McLaughlin Nittler say their first marriages occurred at ages 25 and 19 respectively.

On his death certificate in Salt Lake Co., Utah, William Francis McLaughlin's middle name is spelled Frances, and his informant, R.J. Nittler, says William F. McLaughlin was born in Ontario,

Canada. The informant was Randolph John Nittler, William's son-in-law.[510]

Daughter of Eleanor Margaret Pegan and William Francis McLaughlin:

+ 84 f I. **Eleanor Margaret**[9] **McLaughlin** was born in Park City, Park City Twp., Summit Co., Utah, on February 15, 1907.[517, 518] She died in Imola, Napa Co., California, on April 25, 1958.[517, 518, 519]

51. Lewis Sinclair (Pegan)[8] **Kelso** (*Sinclair Edwin*[7] *Pegan, William Henry*[6]*, Andrew*[5]*, Robert A.*[4]*, Andrew*[3]*, Andrew*[2] *Pagan, James*[1]) was born on July 6, 1891, in Park City Twp., Summit Co., Utah.[266, 267] He was the son of Sinclair Edwin Pegan (26) and Emma May Kelso. Lewis Sinclair (Pegan) died in Oakland, Alameda Co., California, on February 11, 1954, at age 62.[266, 267, 268] He was buried in Mountain View Cemetery, Oakland, Alameda Co., California.[268, 520, 521]

Lewis Sinclair Pegan Kelso leaves his hometown, Park City, Summit Co., Utah, in 1908 with his sister, Eleanor Margaret Pegan McLaughlin (Ridge), as an article in the *Park City (UT) Record* newspaper notes that in early February that year says Mrs. W.L. McLaughlin and her brother "Lew" Pegan had moved to Evanston, Wyoming, where "they would make their home".[513] It seems that their mother, Emma Kelso (Pegan) and William F. McLaughlin, Eleanor's first husband, were already there. William and Emma had bought a movie theater, where Emma was playing piano for the silent movies.[254] But the business venture apparently failed before 1910, and the McLaughlins returned to Park City.

In 1910, Lewis Pegan is living with his mother, Emma Kelso (Pegan) in Evanston, Uinta Co., Wyoming (*Census Place: Evanston, Uinta, Wyoming; Roll: T624_1747; Page: 4A; Enumeration District: 0124; Image: 715*). Lewis Pegan is enumerated as Lewis Kelso, age 18, born in Utah, whose father was born in Ohio and his mother in Indiana. He is a laborer at a railroad shop/yard. Emma says she is 39 years old, a widow, and that she and her father were born in Indiana and her mother in Louisiana. She lists her occupation as music teacher.

Lewis never uses the Pegan surname again.

According to his WWI draft registration in 1917, Lewis Sinclair (Pegan) Kelso is living in Oakland, Alameda Co., California, where he is a railroad conductor. He lists himself as the sole support of his mother, Emma, and niece (Eleanor Kelso McLaughlin), the daughter of his late sister, Eleanor Margaret Pegan McLauglin Ridge.[522]

In 1920, Lewis Pegan, 26 (?), is enumerated as Louis Kelso and living with his mother Emma Kelso (Pegan) in Oakland, Alameda Co., California (*Census Place: Oakland, Alameda, California; Roll: T625_87; Page: 21A; Enumeration District: 23; Image: 754*). Louis, who is a railroad conductor, says he was born in Utah, his father in the United States and his mother in Indiana. Also in the home is Eleanor McLaughlin, 12, born Utah, Lewis' niece.

Lewis Sinclair (Pegan) married **Cora A. Tripplett** before 1926.[523] They had three children. Cora A. Tripplett was born in Oakland, Alameda Co., California, on May 29, 1899.[523, 524] Cora A. reached age 52 and died in Oakland, Alameda Co., California, on March 24, 1952.[523, 525] She was buried in Mountain View Cemetery, Oakland, Alameda Co., California.[524, 526]

Lewis (Pegan) Kelso is still living in Oakland, Alameda Co., California in 1930, and is enumerated as "Lundo S. Kelso" (*Census Place: Oakland, Alameda, California; Roll: 106; Page: 23B; Enumeration District: 136; Image: 46.0*). Lewis Kelso is age 38, born Utah, with his father born in Kentucky (Incorrect—he was born in Ohio) and his mother born in Indiana. He says he was first married at age 32 and lists his occupation as a carpenter for a railroad. His wife, Cora Tripplett Kelso, is 24, born California, with her father born in Ohio and her mother in Northern Ireland. They have two children, Eleanor L., age three years and nine months, and George R., one year and 10 months, both born in California.

In 1940, Lewis (Pegan) Kelso is again residing in Oakland, Alameda Co., California (*Census Place: Oakland, Alameda, California; Roll: T627_435; Page:*

2A; Enumeration District: 61-210). Lewis (Pegan) Kelso, age 48, a railroad conductor, says he was born in Utah. His wife, Cora Tripplett Kelso is 40 years old. With them are children Eleanor ("Elanore"), 13, George, 11, and Josiah (Joseph), five. Cora and the children were all born in California. The family says they were living in Oakland in 1935. The home is at 1305 50th Avenue.

On his death certificate, Lewis Pegan's name is "Lewis Sinclair Kelso" and his birthplace is listed as Wyoming. Both his parents are listed as having the surname Kelso. Although Edward Sinclair Pegan is undoubtedly his father, Lewis apparently uses the name Kelso throughout his adult life. His obituary states he was a native of Wyoming, but he was born in Park City, Summit Co., Utah.[267, 268]

Children of Lewis Sinclair (Pegan) Kelso and Cora A. Tripplett:

+ 85 f I. **Eleanor Lois**[9] **Kelso** was born in Alameda, Alameda Co., California, on July 6, 1926.[109, 527, 528] She was also known as **Lois**. Eleanor Lois died in Milpitas, Santa Clara Co., California, on April 24, 1995.[109, 528, 529]

+ 86 m II. **George Lewis**[9] **Kelso** was rn in Oakland, Alameda Co., California, on December 11, 1928.[109, 530] He died in San Jose, Santa Clara Co., California, on January 11, 2001.[109]

+ 87 m III. **Joseph Sinclair**[9] **Kelso** was born in Oakland, Alameda Co., California, on April 29, 1934.[109, 531] He died in Concord, Contra Costa Co., California, on October 9, 2003.[109]

52. Mary Elizabeth[8] **Pegan** (*Sinclair Edwin*[7], *William Henry*[6], *Andrew*[5], *Robert A.*[4], *Andrew*[3], *Andrew*[2] *Pagan, James*[1]) was born on October 28, 1899, in Park City, Park City Twp., Summit Co., Utah.[109] She was the daughter of Sinclair Edwin Pegan (26) and Kate or Katherine Ann Martin. Mary Elizabeth lived in 1972 in Bremerton, Kitsap Co., Washington. She died in a hospital in Tacoma, Pierce Co., Washington, on January 2, 1973, at age 73.[269, 270, 271] Mary Elizabeth was buried in Miller-Woodlawn Memorial Park Cemetery), Bremerton, Kitsap Co., Washington.[270, 532]

Mary Elizabeth married **Kenneth Whitford Johnson** on November 20, 1920, in Spokane Co., Washington.[533] They were divorced about 1929. Kenneth Whitford Johnson was born in Kearney, Buffalo Co., Nebraska, on September 10, 1899.[534] He reached age 74 and died in Roseburg, Douglas Co., Oregon, on December 27, 1973.[535] Kenneth Whitford was buried in Cypress Lawn Memorial Park Cemetery, Everett, Snohomish Co., Washington.[536]

Kenneth Johnson, age eight months and born in Nebraska, is enumerated with his parents, John H. and Lou Johnson, in Kearney, Buffalo Co., Nebraska in the 1900 census (*Census Place: Kearney Ward 4, Buffalo, Nebraska; Page: 5; Enumeration District: 0035; Kenneth Johnson, John H. Johnson, head of household*).

After his divorce from Mary Elizabeth Pegan Johnson (Boggs), Kenneth Whitford Johnson, a railway clerk, lives with his parents in Spokane, Spokane Co., Washington in 1930 (*Census Place: Spokane, Spokane, Washington; Roll: 2516; Page: 19B; Enumeration District: 49; Image: 804.0; Kenneth W. Johnson, John H. Johnson, head of household*).

In 1940, Kenneth W. Johnson is remarried to Beatrice E. Spores Johnson; they are residing with his father-in-law, William F. Spores in Spokane, Spokane Co., Washington (*Washington (Census Place: Spokane, Spokane, Washington; Roll: m-t0627-04384; Page: 12A; Enumeration District: 41-17; Kenneth W. Johnson, Willam F. Spores, head of household*). He is listed as born in Utah, which is incorrect. He is the proprietor of a grocery.

Mary Elizabeth Pegan Johnson is found in Ferndale Twp., Whatcom Co., Washington in 1930 living with her brother-in-law and sister, Loraine C. and Grace Pegan Boggs and their family (*Census Place: Ferndale, Whatcom, Washington; Roll: 2522; Page: 1B; Enumeration District: 33; Image: 575.0*). She and her first husband, Kenneth Whitford Johnson, are newly divorced. Mary Elizabeth Johnson, age 29, born Utah, with her father born in Kentucky (Incorrect—he was born in Ohio) and her mother in California, says she was first married at age 21 and lists no occupation.

Mary Elizabeth Pegan Johnson married **Francis Llewellyn Boggs** on April 19, 1930, in Whatcom Co., Washington.[537] They had one daughter. Francis Llewellyn Boggs was born in Kirkland Twp., King Co., Washington, on September 19, 1891.[538, 539]

Francis Llewellyn reached age 79 and died in Bremerton, Kitsap Co., Washington, on July 29, 1971.[540, 81] He was buried in Miller-Woodlawn Memorial Park Cemetery), Bremerton, Kitsap Co., Washington.[541, 542] He was the son of William Boggs and Abbie Hastings.

Francis Llewllyn Boggs married Mary Elizabeth Pegan Johnson, whose sister, Grace, was the wife of Francis' brother Lorraine Cornelius Boggs.

Even though he was an American citizen living in North Bend, King Co., Washington, Francis L. Boggs, a mechanical engineer with gas and steam powered machines, joined the Canadian Overseas Expeditionary Forces in September 1918.[538] It is unknown if he ever saw action, as the war ended that November.

In the 1930 census, just before he marries Mary Elizabeth Pegan Johnson, Francis L. Boggs, 38, is living in Stanwood Twp., Snohomish Co., Washington, working as a kiln operator and living in a boarding house *(Census Place: Stanwood, Snohomish, Washington; Roll: 2520; Page: 5B; Enumeration District: 125; Image: 439.0)*.

Francis and Mary Elizabeth Pegan Johnson Boggs are enumerated in Bellingham, Whatcom Co., Washington in 1940 *(Census Place: Bellingham, Whatcom, Washington; Roll: T627_4368; Page: 3B; Enumeration District: 37-4)*. Francis Boggs, age 48, a manager of a lumber yard, says he was born in Washington. His wife, Mary Elizabeth Pegan Johnson Boggs, 40, says she was born in Utah. They have a daughter, Katherine, age five, born in Washington. They are living in a home at 2712 Russel Street, and say they were living in Bellingham in 1935.

Francis Llewellyn Boggs, now a pipefitter, had relocated to Bremerton, Kitsap Co., Washington by 1942.[543]

On her Washington state death certificate, Mary Elizabeth Pegan Johnson Bogg's birthdate was given by her daughter, Katherine Boggs Davie, as October 28, 1900.[271] This date is repeated in her obituary in the *Bremerton (WA) Sun* on January 5, 1973.[270] However, she was listed as born in Oct 1899 and was eight months old by her parents, Sinclair Edwin and Kate Martin Pegan, in the 1900 census *(Census Place: Park City, Summit, Utah; Roll: 1686; Page: 1B; Enumeration District: 142)*. The birth date on her death certificate seems to be wrong, and the correct date is October 28, 1899.

Daughter of Mary Elizabeth Pegan and Francis Llewellyn Boggs:

+ 88 f I. **Katherine Anne**^{9} **Boggs** was born in Bellingham, Whatcom Co., Washington, on April 5, 1935. She is also known as **Kathie**.

53. Grace^8 **Pegan** (*Sinclair Edwin*^{7}, *William Henry*^{6}, *Andrew*^{5}, *Robert A.*^{4}, *Andrew*^{3}, *Andrew*^{2} *Pagan*, *James*^{1}) was born on July 8, 1901, in Park City, Park City Twp., Summit Co., Utah.[109, 272] She was the daughter of Sinclair Edwin Pegan (26) and Kate or Katherine Ann Martin. Grace lived in 1998 in Galvan, Lewis Co., Washington. She died in Issaquah, King Co., Washington, on October 12, 1998, at age 97.[109, 272] Grace was buried in Mount Si Memorial Cemetery, North Bend, King Co., Washington.[544]

Grace Pegan may have inherited her aunt's, Elizabeth Jane "Libbie" Pegan's love for music. According to an article in the Pullman (WA) Herald on September 22, 1922, Grace Pegan joined the staff of Washington State University as a clerk in the music department.[545]

Grace married **Lorraine Cornelius Boggs** about June 18, 1925 in Los Angeles Co., California.[546] They had two children. Lorraine Cornelius Boggs was born in Kirkland Twp., King Co., Washington, on March 24, 1897.[109, 547, 548] He was also known as **Shorty**. He resided in 1971 in Centralia, Lewis Co., Washington. Lorraine Cornelius reached age 73 and died in North Bend, King Co., Washington, on February 6, 1971.[547, 548] He was cremated and his ashes buried in Mount Si Memorial Cemetery, North Bend, King Co., Washington.[549] He was the son of William Boggs and Abbie Hastings.

The late John Francis Boggs said his father Lorraine Cornelius Boggs was a county extension agent in Arizona in the 1920s before marrying Grace Pegan.[550]

Lorraine Cornelius and Grace Pegan Boggs are enumerated in Ferndale Twp., Whatcom Co.., Washington in 1930 *(Census Place: Ferndale, Whatcom, Washington; Roll: 4547540; Page: 1B; Image: 575.0)*. The head of the household is Lorraine Boggs, listed as "Loriane C.", 33, a farm manager of a chicken farm, who says he was born in Washington and his parents in Kansas (Note: On the 1900 census, his father says he was born in Indiana and his mother says she was born in Illinois). His wife, Grace Pegan Boggs (spelled "Garace" on the census form) 28, says she was born in Utah, her father in Kentucky and her mother in California (Incorrect—her father was born in Ohio). The pair say they were first married at ages 28 and 23 respectively. They have two children, John F., two, and Mary L., nine months, both born in Washington. Living with them is Grace Pegan Bogg's sister, Mary Elizabeth Pegan Johnson, age 29 and divorced, and several male boarders/workers.

In 1940 Lorraine Cornelilus and Grace Pegan Boggs are still found in Ferndale Twp., Whatcom Co., Washington *(Census Place: Ferndale, Whatcom, Washington; Roll: T627_4369; Page: 2B; Enumeration District: 37-46)*. Lorraine C. Boggs, age 43, born Washington, is the manager of a chicken cooperative (co-op association?). Grace Pegan Boggs is 38 years old and was born in Utah. With them are their two children, John, 12, and Mary Lee, 10, both born in Washington. They are living on a farm, but no road address is listed.

Children of Grace Pegan and Lorraine Cornelius Boggs:

+ 89 m I. **John Francis**[9] **Boggs** was born in Ferndale Twp., Whatcom Co., Washington, on September 7, 1927.[C] He died in Forks, Clallam Co., Washington, on April 29, 2018.[C]

+ 90 f II. **Mary Lee**[9] **Boggs** was born in Bellingham, Whatcom Co., Washington, on July 13, 1929.[D] She died in Issaquah, King Co., Washington on May 29, 2018.[D]

54. John Edwin[8] **Pegan** *(Sinclair Edwin*[7]*, William Henry*[6]*, Andrew*[5]*, Robert A.*[4]*, Andrew*[3]*, Andrew*[2] *Pagan, James*[1]*)* was born on June 1, 1908, in Park City, Park City Twp., Summit Co., Utah.[109, 273, 274, 275] He was the son of Sinclair Edwin Pegan (26) and Kate or Katherine Ann Martin. He died in a facility in Killeen, Bell Co., Texas, on February 6, 1980, at age 71.[273, 274, 275, 276] John Edwin was buried in Fort Sam Houston National Cemetery, San Antonio, Bexar Co., Texas.[273, 274, 551]

In 1930, John E. Pegan, age 21 (?), still unmarried, a bank clerk, was a boarder, with others, in the home of Alice Rhodes in Spokane, Spokane Co., Washington *(Census Place: Spokane, Spokane, Washington; Roll: 2516; Page: 3A; Enumeration District: 56; Image: 1123.0)*. For some reason, John E. is listed as born in Ethiopia! (He was born in Utah.)

John Edwin married **Elizabeth Marie Maletzki** on May 31, 1934, in Whatcom Co., Washington.[552] They divorced. They had three children. Elizabeth Marie Maletzki was born in Houston, Harris Co., Texas, on April 28, 1914.[109, 553] Elizabeth Marie reached age 88 and died in San Pedro, Los Angeles Co., California, on May 22, 2002.[109, 553, 554] She was cremated.[554]

She died under the name Elizabeth Lammon.

John Edwin Pegan is enumerated in Houston, Harris Co., Texas in 1940 *(Census Place: Houston, Harris, Texas; Roll: T627_4199; Page: 13B; Enumeration District: 258-268)*. John E. Pegan, age 31, born Utah, is a machine operator at an oil well tools manufacturer. With him are wife Elizabeth Maletzki Pegan, 25, born Texas, and sons Robert E., five, born Washington, and John E. Jr., two, born Texas. Their address is 7646 1/2 Avenue D.

Elizabeth Maletzki Pegan Lammon met and seriously dated Daniel C. Lammon when the latter was stationed in Bellingham, Whatcom Co., Washington. They planned to marry, but Elizabeth's mother was against the match because he was a Navy man and a non-Catholic. So they parted. Elizabeth then met and married John Edwin Pegan, who was, according to their daughter, considered "quite a catch" in Bellingham. But the marriage, which produced three children ended in divorce. After John Edwin Pegan left for WWII, Elizabeth Maletzki wrote to Daniel Lammon, and they reconnected and eventually married.[555]

John Edwin Pegan married **Dorothy Inez Unknown** before 1948. They divorced.

John Edwin Pegan, a machinist and tool maker, was residing in Galveston, Galveston Co., Texas in 1949.

Children of John Edwin Pegan and Elizabeth Marie Maletzki:

+ 91 m I. **Robert Edwin**[9] **Pegan** was born in Bellingham, Whatcom Co., Washington, on March 2, 1935.[109, 556, 557, 558, 559] He died in San Diego, San Diego Co., California, on March 13, 1981.[556, 557, 558, 559]

+ 92 m II. **John Edward**[9] **Pegan II** was born in Houston, Harris Co., Texas, on September 27, 1937.[109] He died in Spring, Harris Co., Texas, on February 21, 2003.[109]

+ 93 f III. **Anna Marie**[9] **Pegan** was born in Houston, Harris Co., Texas, on September 25, 1940.

55. Daughter[8] **Gregor** (*Elizabeth Jane*[7] *Pegan, William Henry*[6], *Andrew*[5], *Robert A.*[4], *Andrew*[3], *Andrew*[2] *Pagan, James*[1]) was born on January 12, 1892, in Park City, Park City Twp., Summit Co., Utah.[291] She was the daughter of Gilbert David Gregor and Elizabeth Jane Pegan (27). Daughter died in Park City, Park City Twp., Summit Co., Utah, on January 12, 1892.[291]

56. David Gilbert[8] **Gregor** (*Elizabeth Jane*[7] *Pegan, William Henry*[6], *Andrew*[5], *Robert A.*[4], *Andrew*[3], *Andrew*[2] *Pagan, James*[1]) was born on April 28, 1893, in Park City, Park City Twp., Summit Co., Utah.[292] He was the son of Gilbert David Gregor and Elizabeth Jane Pegan (27). David Gilbert died in Watertown, Watertown Town, Jefferson Co., New York, on October 16, 1954, at age 61.[293, 294] He was buried in Brookside Cemetery, Watertown, Water Town, Jefferson Co., New York.[293, 560]

David Gilbert married **Elisabeth Quincy Stebbins** on March 1, 1927, in Watertown, Watertown Town, Jefferson Co., New York.[293] They had two children. Elisabeth Quincy Stebbins was born in Watertown, Watertown Town, Jefferson Co., New York, on April 7, 1907.[561] Elisabeth Quincy reached age 85 and died in Watertown, Watertown Town, Jefferson Co., New York, on November 21, 1992.[561]

She died under the name Elisabeth Q. Taylor.

David G. Gregor is enumerated in 1930 in Watertown, Water Town, Jefferson Co., New York (*Census Place: Watertown, Jefferson, New York; Roll: 4661113; Page: 4B; Image: 1083.0*). David G. Gregor, age 36, is a surgeon who says he was born in Utah, his father in New York and his mother in Kentucky (Incorrect—Elizabeth J. Pegan Gregor was born in Ohio). He says his first marriage occurred at age 33. His wife, Elizabeth Q. Stebbins, Gregor, 22, was born in New York as were her parents; she says she was first married at age 19. David and Elizabeth Stebbins Gregor have a son, David G. Jr., age 11 months, born in New York. Living with them is David's father, Gilbert D. Gregor, 71, a widower who lists no occupation (probably retired), says he and his father were born in New York while his mother was born in Scotland.

In 1940, David Gilbert Gregor is still living in Watertown, Watertown Town, Jefferson Co., New York in 1940 (*Census Place: Watertown, Jefferson, New York; Roll: T627_2545; Page: 11A; Enumeration District: 23-77*). In the home are David G. Gregor, age 46, born Utah, a physician; his wife, Elizabeth Q. Stebbins Gilbert, 33, and children David G. Jr., 10, and Ann S., seven. Elizabeth and the children were born in New York. The family says they were living in the same place in 1935. Also living with them are a cook, Doris Doane, 36, married, and Anna Wilson, 32, a widow, who is a nurse for the children; both were born in New York. Their home address is 229 Clinton Street.

After Dr. David G. Gregor's death, Elizabeth Q. Stebbins Gregor married Roswell Flower Taylor.[561]

Children of David Gilbert Gregor and Elisabeth Quincy Stebbins:

+ 94 m I. **David Gilbert⁹ Gregor II** was born in Watertown, Watertown Town, Jefferson Co., New York, on May 22, 1929.[109, 562] He died in Watertown, Watertown Town, Jefferson Co., New York, on August 18, 2013.[109, 562]

+ 95 f II. **Ann Sewall⁹ Gregor** was born in New York, Kings Co., New York, on July 8, 1932.[563] She was also known as **Ann MacGregor Sewall**. Ann Sewall died in Bar Harbor, Hancock Co., Maine, on June 18, 2015.[563]

57. Mary Margaret⁸ Gregor (*Elizabeth Jane⁷ Pegan, William Henry⁶, Andrew⁵, Robert A.⁴, Andrew³, Andrew² Pagan, James¹*) was born on February 4, 1895, in Park City, Park City Twp., Summit Co., Utah.[295] She was the daughter of Gilbert David Gregor and Elizabeth Jane Pegan (27). She died in Watertown, Watertown Town, Jefferson Co., New York, on May 8, 1975, at age 80.[296] Mary Margaret was buried in Brookside Cemetery, Watertown, Water Town, Jefferson Co., New York.[296, 564]

Mary Margaret married **Roderick Pirnie** on June 23, 1917, in Jefferson Co., New York.[285] They had two children. Roderick Pirnie was born in Springfield, Hampden Co., Massachusetts, on February 12, 1894.[109, 565] He was also known as **Roderick or Rod**. Roderick was living in 1975 in Palm Beach, Palm Beach Co., Florida. Roderick reached age 81 and died in Broward Co., Florida, on June 26, 1975.[109, 566]

In 1920, Roderick and Mary Margaret Gregor Pirnie are living in Detroit, Wayne Co., Michigan (*Census Place: Detroit Ward 10, Wayne, Michigan; Roll: T625_809; Page: 6B; Enumeration District: 324; Image: 1134*). In the household are Roderick PIrnie, age 25, a salesman, born Massachusetts, with his father born in New York and his mother in Connecticut, and his wife, Mary Margaret Gregor Pirnie, 24, born Utah, with her father born in New York and her mother in Ohio.

Roderick and Mary Margaret Gregor Pirnie are enumerated in 1930 in Springfield, Hampden Co., Massachusetts (*Census Place: Springfield, Hampden, Massachusetts; Roll: 4607006; Page: 7B; Image: 251.0*). In the home are Roderick Pirnie, 36, and insurance agent, born Massachusetts, with his father born in New York and his mother in Connecticut. Mary Margaret Gregor Pirnie, 35, says she was born in Utah, her father in New York and her mother in Kentucky (Incorrect—Elizabeth Jane Pegan Gregor was born in Ohio). They have a daughter, Elisabeth, age eight, born Michigan. Residing with them is a servant, Sarah Long.

Roderick and Mary Margaret Gregor Pirnie divorce in 1931.

In 1940, Roderick Pirnie and his daughter Elisabeth are found in Providence, Providence Co., Rhode Island (*Census Place: Providence, Providence, Rhode Island; Roll: T627_3773; Page: 1A; Enumeration District: 6-23*). Roderick Pirnie, an insurance agent born in Massachusetts, is age 46. He has a second wife, Virginia Billings Pirnie, 38, born in New York. Elisabeth Pirnie, Roderick's daughter by Mary Margaret Gregor Pirnie, is 21 years old, born in Michigan. The women list no occupation. All say they were living in Suffield, Hartford Co., Connecticut in 1935. Their residence address is 56 Alumni Avenue.

Roderick Pirnie Sr. was politically active when he lived in Rhode Island; he was appointed the director of Rhode Island's War Finance Department during WWII This department was the official office for selling war bonds in the state. Under his direction, Rhode Island was the first state to exceed its war bond sales goals.[567, 568]

An insurance agent, Roderick L. Pirnie wrote a book on life insurance, entitled *Planning and Selling the Basic Estate*, published in 1939 by the National Underwriting Company in Cincinnati. "Roderick" Pirnie also lectured in cities on the East Coast about the subject.[569]

According to an article in the Newport (RI) *Daily News* on September 3, 1954, Hurricane Carol destroyed Roderick Pirnie's house, including his guest quarters, and power boat and damaged his wharf. According to the article, "police…said Pirnie warned that he would 'meet all looters with bullets.'" Looters had torn wood from his wharf.[570]

Mary Margaret Gregor Pirnie married **James Raymond Sexsmith** on December 21, 1933, in New York, New York.[296, 571] James Raymond Sexsmith was born in Watertown, Watertown Town, Jefferson Co., New York, on April 5, 1897.[109, 571] He was living in 1963 in Watertown, Watertown Town, Jefferson Co., New York.[296] James Raymond reached age 85 and died in Watertown, Watertown Town, Jefferson Co., New York, on August 3, 1982.[571, 572] He was buried in Brookside Cemetery, Watertown, Water Town, Jefferson Co., New York.[572]

In 1940 Mary Margaret Gregor Pirnie Sexsmith is found with her second husband, J. Raymond Sexsmith, in Malone, Malone Town, Franklin Co., New York *(Census Place: Malone, Franklin, New York; Roll: T627_2535; Page: 5B; Enumeration District: 17-43)*. J. Raymond Sexsmith, age 43, born New York, is a trust officer in a bank. Mary Margaret Gregor Pirnie Sexsmith, 45, was born in Utah. Both say they were living in Malone in 1935. They are residing at 10 First Street.

James R. Sexsmith's obituary says he became a successful bank officer first at the Northern New York Bank in Malone, Franklin Co., New York and before 1950 at the Union State Bank and Trust of Jamestown, Chautauqua Co., New York. After retiring, he and Mary Margaret returned to Watertown, New York. Also, he was an excellent musician.[571]

Her marriage announcement to James Sexsmith and her obituary note that Mary Margaret Gregor Pirnie Sexsmith acted in regional play productions and was an outstanding golfer, winning many local and regional tournaments.[296, 573]

Children of Mary Margaret Gregor and Roderick Pirnie:

+ 96 m I. **Roderick**[9] **Pirnie II** was born in Watertown, Watertown Town, Jefferson Co., New York, on April 10, 1918.[574, 575] He died in Watertown, Watertown Town, Jefferson Co., New York, on March 23, 1919.[576, 577]

+ 97 f II. **Elisabeth**[9] **Pirnie** was born in Detroit, Wayne Co., Michigan, on December 15, 1921.[109] She was also known as **Betsy**. Elisabeth died in Tucson, Pima Co., Arizona, on April 6, 2013.[109, 578]

58. Richard Ernie[8] **Camp** (*Zoa Faretta*[7] *Pegan, James Robert*[6]*, Andrew*[5]*, Robert A.*[4]*, Andrew*[3]*, Andrew*[2] *Pagan, James*[1]) was born on June 1, 1911, in Stockton, San Joaquin Co., California.[328, 329, 330] He was the son of Ernest Franklin Camp and Zoa Faretta Pegan (32). Richard Ernie worked as a Recording engineer. He died in San Francisco, San Francisco Co., California, on November 30, 1963, at age 52.[329, 330] Richard Ernie was buried in Skylawn Memorial Park Cemetery, San Mateo, San Mateo Co., California.[330, 579]

Never married.

Richard Ernie Camp is not found in the 1940 U.S. Census.

According to his death certificate, he had lived in San Francisco, San Francisco Co., California for 30 years and was a recording engineer in the music industry.

59. James Andrew[8] **Pegan** (*Andrew M.*[7]*, John S.*[6]*, Andrew*[5]*, Robert A.*[4]*, Andrew*[3]*, Andrew*[2] *Pagan, James*[1]) was born on October 29, 1894, in St. Joseph, Washington Twp., Buchanan Co., Missouri.[109] He was the son of Andrew M. Pegan (34) and Ella M. Young. James Andrew died in St. Joseph, Washington Twp., Buchanan Co., Missouri, on February 16, 1981, at age 86.[109, 341] He was buried in Memorial Park Cemetery, St. Joseph, Washington Twp., Buchanan Co., Missouri.[341, 580]

Childless.

James A. Pegan is found living with his mother Ella Pegan and his grandmother Rebecca Young in St. Joseph, Washington Twp., Buchanan Co., Missouri in *1920 (Census Place: St Joseph Ward 7, Buchanan, Missouri; Roll: T625_908; Page: 6A; Enumeration District: 111; Image: 498)*. The surname, however, is listed as "Began". Ella, now a widow, is age 50 and James, still single, is 25 and a postal clerk.

James Andrew married **Opal E. Sample** on February 5, 1921, in Buchanan Co., Missouri.[581, 582] Opal E. Sample was born in St. Joseph, Washington Twp., Buchanan Co., Missouri, on October 4, 1898.[109, 582] She reached age 79 and died in St. Joseph, Washington Twp., Buchanan Co., Missouri, on February 20, 1978.[81, 582] Opal E. was buried in Memorial Park Cemetery, St. Joseph, Washington Twp., Buchanan Co., Missouri.[582, 583]

James Andrew Pegan is enumerated in St. Joseph, Washington Twp., Buchanan Co., Missouri in 1930 *(Census Place: St Joseph, Buchanan, Missouri; Roll: 1178; Page: 12B; Enumeration District: 40; Image: 686.0)*. James A., 35, is a stamp clerk in the post office and wife Opal Sample Pegan is age 30. Both were born in Missouri. James and Opal say they married when James was 26 and Opal 22, so they have been married nine years. James says he and his parents were Missouri natives. Opal states she was born in Missouri, her father in Indiana and her mother in Iowa.

In 1940, James Andrew Pegan is still a resident of St. Joseph, Washington Twp., Buchanan Co., Missouri *(Census Place: St Joseph, Buchanan, Missouri; Roll: T627_2088; Page: 63A; Enumeration District: 11-44)*. In the home are James Pegan, age 45, a postal clerk, and Opal Sample Pegan, 31. Both were born in Missouri and say they were living in the same house at 3130 Felix Street in 1935.

After retiring from the U.S. Postal Service, James Andrew Pegan worked in the laboratory at Noma Lites, the leading manufacturer of Christmas lights and bulbs.[584] Opal E. Sample Pegan was the long-time secretary of the St. Joseph, Missouri Chamber of Commerce.[582]

60. Jane Temple[8] **Pegan** (*Morrow Walton*[7], *John S.*[6], *Andrew*[5], *Robert A.*[4], *Andrew*[3], *Andrew*[2] *Pagan*, *James*[1]) was born on December 30, 1917, in Elsberry, Hurricane Twp., Lincoln Co., Missouri.[348] She was the daughter of Morrow Walton Pegan (35) and Julia Meloan. Jane Temple died in Elsberry, Hurricane Twp., Lincoln Co., Missouri, on April 21, 1922, at age four.[348] She was buried in Greenwood Cemetery, Clarksville, Calumet Twp., Pike Co., Missouri.[348, 585, 586]

61. John Robert[8] **Pegan** (*Morrow Walton*[7], *John S.*[6], *Andrew*[5], *Robert A.*[4], *Andrew*[3], *Andrew*[2] *Pagan*, *James*[1]) was born on July 13, 1924, in Elsberry, Hurricane Twp., Lincoln Co., Missouri.[109, 350] He was the son of Morrow Walton Pegan (35) and Julia Meloan. John Robert died in Boise, Ada Co., Idaho, on January 24, 2004, at age 79.[109, 350, 351] He was buried in Mount Lebanon Cemetery, Mount Lebanon, Allegheny Co., Pennsylvania.[351, 587, 588]

In 1930, John Robert Pegan is enumerated as "John R.P." in the home of his maternal grandparents, Robert and Mary Meloan, in Elsberry, Hurricane Twp., Lincoln Co., Missouri *(Census Place: Elsberry, Lincoln, Missouri; Roll: 1209; Page: 11B; Enumeration District: 9; Image: 408.0)*. John Robert Pegan is listed as age five and eight months, born Missouri. Robert Meloan, 65, a grain farmer, born Missouri as were his parents, is the head of the household. His wife Mary is 58, born Missouri, with her father born in Vermont and her mother in Kentucky. Robert and Mary's son Robert Jr., 28, born Missouri, is also in the home.

By 1940, however, John Robert Pegan, age 15, is living with his father, Morrow W. Pegan and stepmother Mary B. Minor Pegan in St. Louis, Missouri *(Census Place: St Louis, St Louis City, Missouri; Roll: T627_2194; Page: 5A; Enumeration District: 96-325)*.

John Robert married **Juanita Malissa Blumenauer** on November 25, 1950, in Frederick Co., Maryland.[589] They had four children. Juanita Malissa Blumenauer was born in Frederick, Frederick Co., Maryland, on August 24,

1923.[109, 590, 591] Juanita Malissa lived in 1979 in Lebanon, North Lebanon Twp., Lebanon Co., Pennsylvania. She reached age 55 and died in a hospital in Pittsburgh, Allegheny Co., Pennsylvania, on July 5, 1979.[590] Juanita Malissa was buried in Mount Lebanon Cemetery, Mount Lebanon, Allegheny Co., Pennsylvania.[590, 592, 593]

John Robert Pegan married **Teresa Yoon?** They divorced. Teresa Yoon? was born in Pittsburgh, Allegheny Co., Pennsylvania?, on September 1, 1935.

According to his obituary in the *Idaho Stateman (Boise, ID)*, on January 27, 2004, John Robert Pegan was reared by his maternal grandparents after his mother died.. During his adulthood, John Robert Pegan lived in Dugway, Tooele Co., Utah, Lewiston, Frederick Co., Maryland, Long Island, New York, and Lebanon, Lebanon Co., Pennsylvania before retiring to Boise, Ada Co., Idaho. He worked as a chemical engineer for the Army Corps of Engineers before completing a law degree and becoming a corporate lawyer for Bristol-Myers and U.S. Steel.[351]

John Robert Pegan and Juanita Malissa Blumenauer had four children, including:

+ 98 m IV. **Leslie Meloan⁹ Pegan** was born in Frederick, Frederick Co., Maryland, on January 16, 1957.[109, 594, 595, 596] He died in Bakersfield, Kern Co., California, on December 21, 1978.[109, 594]

62. Dorothy Geneva⁸ Pegan (*Harry Clark⁷, Samuel Alexander⁶, Andrew⁵, Robert A.⁴, Andrew³, Andrew² Pagan, James¹*) was born on January 15, 1901, in Nebo, Spring Creek Twp., Pike Co., Illinois.[109] She was the daughter of Harry Clark Pegan (36) and Vinnie Mary Main. Dorothy Geneva died in Phoenix, Maricopa Co., Arizona, on July 1, 1987, at age 86.[109, 359]

Dorothy, Erman, and Josephine Pegan are living with their mother, Vinnie Main Pegan Niemann, and their stepfather Al Niemann in 1920 in Hannibal, Mason Twp., Marion Co., Missouri (*Census Place: Hannibal Ward 1, Marion, Missouri; Roll: T625_934; Page: 5A; Enumeration District: 103; Image: 786*). Her siblings Erman Henry and Flora Josephine are also in the home. Dorothy, 19, is a toe stitcher at a shoe factory. Her sister "Josephine" (Flora) is also working at the same factory at age 14.

Dorothy Geneva married **Stephen Albert Paul Reher** on June 28, 1921, in Marion Co., Missouri.[597] They had one daughter. Stephen Albert Paul Reher was born in Jerseyville, Jersey Twp., Jersey Co., Illinois, on April 24, 1895.[598] He was also known as **Paul**. He reached age 54 and died in Hannibal, Mason Twp., Marion Co., Missouri, on December 1, 1949.[598] Stephen Albert Paul was buried in St. Mary's/Holy Family Cemetery, Hannibal, Mason Twp., Marion Co., Missouri.[598, 599]

Stephen Albert Paul and Dorothy Pegan Reher are enumerated in Hannibal, Mason Twp., Marion Co., Missouri in 1930 (*Census Place: Hannibal, Marion, Missouri; Roll: 1211; Page: 3B; Enumeration District: 4; Image: 642.0*). Stephen is enumerated as "Paul", his preferred name. "Paul" is age 35, born Illinois, with his parents born in Germany, works at a shoe factory. Dorothy is 29 years old and says she and her mother were born in Illinois and her father in Missouri. With them is their daughter Rosena, seven, born Missouri. Also in the home is Dorothy's widower stepfather, Al Niemann, 49, born Iowa, with his parents born in Germany. He is unemployed.

In 1940, Stephen and Dorothy Pegan Reher are still residing in Hannibal, Mason Twp., Marion Co., Missouri (*Census Place: Hannibal, Marion, Missouri; Roll: T627_2128; Page: 20A; Enumeration District: 64-6*). Stephen Reher, age 45, born Illinois, lists no occupation. Dorothy Pegan Reher is 39 years old, also born in Illinois, and their daughter "Rosina", 15, was born in Missouri. No one in the home lists an occupation. The family says they were living in Hannibal in 1935. Their home address is 618 Rock Street.

After Stephen died, Dorothy Geneva Pegan Reher married **Fred Dee Gaines** between 1956 and 1960. Fred Dee Gaines was born in Blair or Warren, Jackson Co., Oklahoma, on October 22, 1912.[109, 600, 601, 602, 603] He reached age 61 and died in Baldwin Park, Los Angeles Co., California?, on February 24, 1974.[601, 603] Fred D. is buried in

Inglewood Park Cemetery, Inglewood, Los Angeles Co., California.[603]

Fred Dee Gaines is not found in any census except for 1940, when he is incarcerated in Leavenworth Federal Prison in Kansas *(Census Place: Kickapoo, Leavenworth, Kansas; Roll: T627_1240; Page: 12B; Enumeration District: 52-16A)*. Fred D. Gaines says he is 28 years old, divorced, born in Oklahoma, and was living in California in 1935.

Three years later, he is living with an aunt in Oklahoma City, Oklahoma, according to his WWII draft card. He states on his draft card that he was born in Blair, Jackson Co., Oklahoma.[600] By 1947, he is in Los Angeles County, California, debarking from a Pacific Overseas Airways plane in San Pedro on 02 Jun 1947. This time, he says he was born in Warren, Jackson Co., Oklahoma.[602]

Fred Dee Gaines and Dorothy Geneva Pegan Reher marry between 1956, when Fred is single and living in Alhambra, Los Angeles Co., California, according to the city directory, and 1960, when they are found living at 3151 Feather Avenue in Baldwin Park, Los Angeles, Los Angeles, California on the California Voter Registrations.[604, 605]

Daughter of Dorothy Geneva Pegan and Stephen Albert Paul Reher:

+ 99 f I. **Rosena Cecilia**[9] **Reher** was born in Hannibal, Mason Twp., Marion Co., Missouri, on July 18, 1922.[109, 606, 607] She died in Glendale, Maricopa Co., Arizona, on July 31, 2002.[109, 606, 607]

63. Erman Henry[8] **Pegan** (*Harry Clark*[7], *Samuel Alexander*[6], *Andrew*[5], *Robert A.*[4], *Andrew*[3], *Andrew*[2] *Pagan, James*[1]) was born on July 25, 1902, in Nebo, Spring Creek Twp., Pike Co., Illinois.[109, 360, 361] He was also known as **Pete** and **Bud**. He was the son of Harry Clark Pegan (36) and Vinnie Mary Main. He died in San Pedro, Los Angeles Co., California, on May 6, 1982, at age 79.[109, 360, 361] Erman Henry was buried in Green Hills Memorial Park Cemetery, Rancho Pales Verdes, Los Angeles Co., California.[361, 608]

Ermann Henry Pegan is living with his mother Vinnie Main Abair Pegan Niemann and his stepfather Al Niemann in 1920 in Hannibal, Mason Twp., Marion Co., Missouri *(Census Place: Hannibal Ward 1, Marion, Missouri; Roll: T625_934; Page: 5A; Enumeration District: 103; Image: 786)*. His two sisters Dorothy and Flora Josephine are also living in the home. Ermann, 17, is a machinist at a factory.

Ermann Henry Pegan is enumerated as "Erman Began" in 1930 in St. Louis, Missouri *(Census Place: St Louis, St Louis [Independent City], Missouri; Roll: 1242; Page: 11A; Enumeration District: 509; Image: 666.0)*. Erman Pegan, age 27, born Missouri as were his parents, is a machinist with a piston ring company. He is a lodger in the home of his future wife, Helen Thornton and her family. Helen Thornton, 21, born Missouri with her father born in Scotland and her mother in Missouri, is a presser in a laundry. The head of the household is "Kate" Thornton, age 44, born Missouri, with her father born in Germany and her mother in Missouri. With her are her children Oliver, 14, George Jr., 12 and Delores, 10. Helen Thornton marries Ermann Pegan two months later.

Erman Henry married **Helen Kathryn Thornton** on June 28, 1930, in St. Louis, Missouri.[609] They had three children. Helen Kathryn Thornton was born in St. Louis, Missouri, on April 30, 1908.[610] She was also known as **Gigi**. Helen Kathryn reached age 108 and died in San Pedro, Los Angeles Co., California, on June 18, 2016.[611, 612] She was buried in Green Hills Memorial Park Cemetery, Rancho Palos Verdes, Los Angeles Co., California.[611, 612]

In 1940, Erman Henry Pegan is again found in St. Louis, Missouri *(Census Place: St Louis, St Louis City, Missouri; Roll: T627_2201; Page: 14A; Enumeration District: 96-477)*. In the household are Erman Pegan, age 37, a "chauffeur or driver for a box truck", his wife, Helen Thornton Pegan, 28, and their children Joan, eight, James, five, and Jacquelin, one. Erman was born in Illinois and the rest of the family in Missouri. The family was living in St. Louis in 1935. Their address is 3801 Kinnesley Avenue.

By 1942, Erman Henry and Helen K. Thornton Pegan moved to San Pedro, Los Angeles, California, where Erman Henry worked as a supervisor at the Long Beach Naval Shipyard for 40 years.[361]

He is listed as "E. Pegan" on the Social Security Death Index.

According to an email to the author from Helen's granddaughter, Helen K. Thornton Pegan died peacefully on June 18, 2016, at age 108. She was buried beside her husband, Erman Henry "Pete" Pegan, whom she called "Bud," in Green Hills Memorial Park Cemetery, Rancho Palos Verdes, Los Angeles Co., California.[612]

Children of Erman Henry Pegan and Helen Kathryn Thornton:

+ 100 f I. **Joan Kathryn**[9] **Pegan** was born in St. Louis, Missouri, on December 1, 1932.

+ 101 m II. **James Kenneth**[9] **Pegan** was born in St. Louis, Missouri, on December 15, 1934.

+ 102 f III. **Jacquelin K.**[9] **Pegan** was born in St. Louis, Missouri, on March 13, 1939.

64. **Flora Josephine**[8] **Pegan** (*Harry Clark*[7], *Samuel Alexander*[6], *Andrew*[5], *Robert A.*[4], *Andrew*[3], *Andrew*[2] *Pagan*, *James*[1]) was born on June 7, 1905, in Nebo, Spring Creek Twp., Pike Co., Illinois.[81, 362, 363, 364] She was the daughter of Harry Clark Pegan (36) and Vinnie Mary Main. She was also known as **Josephine**. Flora Josephine also resided in 1979 in Yucca Valley, San Bernardino Co., California Flora Josephine died in a hospital in Joshua Tree, San Bernardino Co., California, on June 5, 1979, at age 73.[81, 362, 364] She was cremated and her ashes buried in Montecito Memorial Park Cemetery, Colton, San Bernardino Co., California.[364, 613]

Flora Josephine Pegan used both Flora and Josephine as a given name. Her birthplace is documented on her infant son's Michigan death certificate; he died at age two days and was unnamed.[363]

In 1920, Flora Josephine Pegan is living with her stepfather and mother, Al and Vinnie Main Abair Pegan Niemann, in Hannibal, Mason Twp., Marion Co., Missouri (*Census Place: Hannibal Ward 1, Marion, Missouri; Roll: T625_934; Page: 5A; Enumeration District: 103; Image: 786*). Her siblings Dorothy and Ermann Henry are also in the home. Flora, enumerated as "Josephine", is age 14 and working as a heel stayer in a shoe factory. Her sister Dorothy and her stepfather Albert Niemann are also working at the same factory.

Flora Josephine married **Herbert Eugene McCann** on February 3, 1923, in Marion Co., Missouri.[614] They were divorced before 1951. They had five children. Herbert Eugene McCann was born in Hannibal, Mason Twp., Marion Co., Missouri, on August 14, 1902.[363, 615, 616] Herbert Eugene reached age 62 and died in Osseo, Jefferson Twp., Hillsdale Co., Michigan, on May 10, 1965.[109, 615, 616] He was buried in East Hill Cemetery, Osseo, Jefferson Twp., Hillsdale Co., Michigan.[615, 616]

Herbert McCann's birthplace is documented on his infant son's Michigan death certificate.[363]

Herbert and Flora Josephine Pegan McCann are enumerated in the 1930 census in Detroit, Wayne Co., Michigan (*Census Place: Detroit, Wayne, Michigan; Roll: 1058; Page: 12B; Enumeration District: 637; Image: 444.0*). Herbert, age 28, born Missouri, is a toolmaker in an auto factory. Flora Josephine Pegan McCann is 24 years old. Herbert says he was first married at age 24 and Flora Josephine states she was 19, so they have been married at least six years. Children in the home include Herbert Jr., six, born Missouri, "A. Frances", five, and Shirley, three years and 11 months. The daughters were born in Michigan. The family is living on Herbert Street!

In 1940, Herbert and Flora Josephine Pegan McCann are still living in Detroit, Wayne Co., Michigan (*Census Place: Detroit, Wayne, Michigan; Roll: T627_1851; Page: 14A; Enumeration District: 84-359*). Their home is at 439 Seward Street. Herbert McCann, age 37, born Missouri, is a tool and die maker at an automobile factory. Flora Josephine Pegan McCann, listed as Josephine, is 34 years old and born in Illinois. Their son Herbert

Jr., 19, a grocery clerk, was born in Missouri. The other children, Ada, 15, Shirley, 13, and David, nine were born in Michigan. The family says they were living in Marion Co., Missouri in 1935.

At the time of his death, Herbert had lived in Osseo, Hillsdale Co., Michigan, with his sister Geraldine McCann Persinger for four years.[616]

Flora Josephine Pegan McCann married **Unknown Bogardus** before 1951.

Flora Josephine Pegan McCann Bogardus married **William Burt or Bird Shields** on February 19, 1958, in Riverside Co., California.[617] William Burt Shields was born in Turner, McIntosh Co., Oklahoma, on October 20, 1904.[109, 618, 619] He was also known as **Burt or Bert**. He reached age 75 and died in Yucca Valley, San Bernardino Co., California, on October 1, 1980.[109, 618, 619] He was cremated.[619]

William B. Shields was a bartender.

On her death certificate, Flora Josephine Pegan McCann Bogardus Shields' father is listed as Harry "Regan". She worked as a store detective at Buffims Department Store.[364]

Children of Flora Josephine Pegan and Herbert Eugene McCann:

+ 103 m I. **Herbert Eugene**[9] **McCann II** was born in Hannibal, Mason Twp., Marion Co., Missouri, on May 18, 1923.[109, 620, 621, 622] He was also known as **Mac**. Herbert Eugene died in a hospital in Upland, San Bernardino Co., California, on January 16, 2002.[109, 620, 621]

+ 104 f II. **Ada Frances**[9] **McCann** was born in Detroit, Wayne Co., Michigan, on January 31, 1925.[109, 623] She died in Dearborn Heights, Wayne Co., Michigan, on March 23, 1998.[109, 623]

+ 105 f III. **Shirley Theresa**[9] **McCann** was born in Detroit, Wayne Co., Michigan, on May 5, 1926.[109, 624] She died in Dearborn Heights, Wayne Co., Michigan, on August 2, 1989.[109, 624]

+ 106 m IV. **Infant Son**[9] **McCann** was born in Detroit, Wayne Co., Michigan, on September 26, 1927.[363] He died in Detroit, Wayne Co., Michigan, on September 28, 1927.[363]

+ 107 m V. **David Donald**[9] **McCann** was born in Detroit, Wayne Co., Michigan, on October 20, 1930.[625, 626] He died in Tustin, Orange Co., California, on September 5, 1951.[625, 627]

9th Generation

65. Dempsey Rachel[9] **Gough** (*Stella Frances*[8] *Pegan, Alexander Campbell*[7]*, Joseph*[6]*, Andrew*[5]*, Robert A.*[4]*, Andrew*[3]*, Andrew*[2] *Pagan, James*[1]) was born on March 24, 1918, in Clarksville, Calumet Twp., Pike Co., Missouri.[81,382] She was the daughter of Miles Prudie Gough and Stella Frances Pegan (38). She died in Long Beach, Los Angeles Co., California, on August 19, 1981, at age 63.[382] Dempsey Rachel was buried in Angeles Abbey Memorial Park Mausoleum, Compton, Los Angeles Co., California.[628]

Never married.

Dempsey Rachel Gough is enumerated with her mother Stella Frances Pegan Gough and her uncle Otho Pegan in Long Beach, Los Angeles Co., California in 1940 *(Census Place: Long Beach, Los Angeles, California; Roll: T627_369; Page: 8A; Enumeration District: 59-39)*. Dempsey Gough, 22, is listed as a "new worker" (WPA), but her occupation is not identified. (Stella) Frances Pegan Gough, listed as head of the household, is a saleslady at a retail store. Otho Pegan, age 37, single, is a public accountant at an accounting/auditing firm. All in the home say they were born in Missouri and were living in California in 1935. The house address is 833 Belmont Avenue.

Dempsey Rachel Gough and her mother, Stella Frances Pegan Gough, were residents of Los Angeles, Los Angeles Co., California in the 1930s and 1940s before relocating to Texas, where they lived between 1952 and 1959 in Dallas and Fort Worth, Texas. There Dempsey, an office clerk, was the informant on her uncle Luther Carlisle Pegan's death certificate. [161] After Luther's death, Dempsey and her mother returned to Los Angeles.

66. Gladys Wynne[9] **Ewing** (*Grace May*[8] *Pegan, Charles H.*[7]*, Joseph*[6]*, Andrew*[5]*, Robert A.*[4]*, Andrew*[3]*, Andrew*[2] *Pagan, James*[1]) was born on January 28, 1907, in Stronghurst Twp., Henderson Co., Illinois.[429, 430] She was the daughter of Arthur Jerome Ewing and Grace May Pegan (41). Gladys Wynne also resided in Sylmar, Los Angeles Co., California. She died in a facility in Sylmar, Los Angeles Co., California, on February 10, 1997, at age 90.[429, 430] She was cremated and her ashes buried in Holy Cross Cemetery, Colma, San Mateo Co., California.[430, 629]

Gladys Wynne married **Harm Meint Fischer** before 1938 in Illinois? They had five children. Harm Meint Fischer was born in Benson, Clayton Twp., Woodford Co., Illinois, on March 13, 1898.[109, 630, 631] He was also known as **Hiram** and **Jack**. Harm Meint reached age 79 and died in Roswell, Chaves Co., New Mexico, on February 27, 1978.[632, 632] He was buried in South Park Cemetery, Roswell, Chaves Co., New Mexico.[633]

Harm Meint Fischer may have eventually used Hiram as his given name; his nickname was Jack. His Social Security Death Index entry, however, is under Harm M. Fischer.

In 1940, Harm "Jack" and Gladys Ewing Fischer are living with Glady's stepfather and mother, Claud and Grace "Mae" Pegan Ewing, in Chicago, Cook Co., Illinois *(Census Place: Chicago, Cook, Illinois; Roll: T627_955; Page: 7A; Enumeration District: 103-1125)*. Harm "Jack" Fischer, enumerated as "Jack", manages a radio store, Gladys Ewing Fischer, 33, is an office worker at a textile company. They have a daughter Marie, two. The head of the household, "Claude" Ewing, age 44, is an engineer in a meat packing plant. Grace May Pegan Ewing, listed as "Mae," is 50 years old. Also with them is Grace May's daughter by Arthur J. Ewing, Charlene, 15, born Iowa. All were born in Illinois except for Charlene. Their home address is 6926 Lafayette Avenue. Save for little Marie Fischer, all were Chicago residents in 1935.

A descendant says the family moved around. Among the places they lived were in Peoria, Peoria Twp., Peoria Co., Illinois in 1941, Bloomington, McLean Co., Illinois in 1942, back in Chicago by 1947, but on to Dubuque, Dubuque Twp., Dubuque Co., Iowa. Later, Harm/Hiram settled in Roswell, Chaves Co., New Mexico. He is buried under the name Hiram M. Fischer in South Park Cemetery, Roswell, Chaves Co., New Mexico. Gladys Wynne Ewing Fischer lived in 1991 in Las Vegas, Clark Co., Nevada.[633] before removing to Sylmar, Los

Angeles Co., California. She was a self-employed dressmaker.[430]

Children of Gladys Wynne Ewing and Harm Meint Fischer:

+ 108 f I. **Marie Wynne**[10] **Fischer** was born in Chicago, Cook Co., Illinois, on March 1, 1938.[634] She died in Las Vegas, Clark Co., Nevada, on April 7, 1978.[635]

+ 109 m II. **Charles**[10] **Fischer** was born in either Chicago, Cook Co., Illinois or Peoria, Peoria Twp., Peoria Co., Illinois?, in 1940.

+ 110 m III. **Jay Jackson**[10] **Fischer** was born in Peoria, Peoria Twp., Peoria Co., Illinois, on July 31, 1941.[109, 636] He died in Deltona, Volusia Co., Florida, on June 9, 2007.[109, 636]

+ 111 m IV. **BillyJo**[10] **Fischer** was born in Chicago, Cook Co., Illinois, on August 4, 1942.[637] He died in Chicago, Cook Co., Illinois, on October 22, 1943.[637]

+ 112 f V. **Daughter Fischer** was born in Dubuque, Dubuque Twp., Dubuque Co., Iowa.

67. Lawrence Howard[9] **Ewing** (*Grace May*[8] *Pegan, Charles H.*[7]*, Joseph*[6]*, Andrew*[5]*, Robert A.*[4]*, Andrew*[3]*, Andrew*[2] *Pagan, James*[1]) was born on October 13, 1908, in Stronghurst Twp., Henderson Co., Illinois.[431, 432] He was also known as **Howard**. He was the son of Arthur Jerome Ewing and Grace May Pegan (41). He died in Chicago, Cook Co., Illinois, on November 3, 1938, at age 30.[431, 432] Lawrence Howard was buried in Mt. Hope Cemetery, Worth Twp., Cook Co., Illinois.[432, 638]

Howard Harold Ewing committed suicide.

Lawrence Howard married **Anna May Mathis** on August 22, 1932, in Cook Co., Illinois.[639, 640] They had two sons. Anna May Mathis was born in Philadelphia, Philadelphia Co., Pennsylvania, on May 7, 1912.[109, 641] Anna May reached age 88 and died in St. Petersburg, Pinellas Co., Florida, on February 21, 2001.[109, 642]

Anna May Mathis Ewing's birthplace is documented on her stillborn son's death certificate.[641]

After Lawrence Howard Ewing Sr.'s death, Anna May Hirsch Ewing married Lubert Hirsch on July 31, 1933 in Chicago, Cook Co., Illinois.[643] She died with that surname.

Sons of Lawrence Howard Ewing and Anna May Mathis:

+ 113 m I. **Infant Son**[10] **Ewing** was born in Chicago, Cook Co., Illinois, on May 1, 1937.[641] He died in Chicago, Cook Co., Illinois, on May 1, 1937.[641]

+ 114 m II. **Lawrence Howard**[10] **Ewing II** was born in Chicago, Cook Co., Illinois, on February 2, 1934.[109, 644, 645, 646, 647] He died in a hospital in Indianapolis, Marion Co., Indiana, on November 5, 2006.[109, 645, 646, 647]

68. Arthur Warren[9] **Ewing II** (*Grace May*[8] *Pegan, Charles H.*[7]*, Joseph*[6]*, Andrew*[5]*, Robert A.*[4]*, Andrew*[3]*, Andrew*[2] *Pagan, James*[1]) was born on August 13, 1911, in Lomax Twp., Hancock Co., Illinois.[433, 434] He was the son of Arthur Jerome Ewing and Grace May Pegan (41). He died in Roswell, Chaves Co., New Mexico, on September 24, 1991, at age 80.[434] Arthur Warren was buried in South Park Cemetery, Roswell, Chaves Co., New Mexico.[648]

In 1930, Arthur Warren Ewing is a servant in the home of Alex and Georgiana Schmidt in Lime Creek Twp. Washington Co., Iowa *(Census Place: Lime Creek, Washington, Iowa; Roll: 687; Page: 1B; Enumeration District: 17; Image: 220.0)*. Arthur Ewing, age 19, single, says he was born in Illinois, his father in Iowa and his mother in Illinois.

Arthur Warren married **Iva Jane Ballard** on April 13, 1932, in Washington Co., Iowa.[433] They had one son. Iva Jane Ballard was born in Troy Twp., Iowa Co., Iowa, on January 21, 1912.[433, 649, 650] Iva Jane lived in Marengo, Marengo Twp., Iowa Co.,

Iowa in 1935. She reached age 23 and died in a hospital in Iowa City, Johnson Co., Iowa, on July 14, 1935.[649, 650] Iva Jane was buried in North English Cemetery, North English, English Twp., Iowa Co., Iowa.[649, 650, 651]

Arthur Warren Ewing II married **Gayle Aileen Long** on September 1, 1937, in Scott Co., Iowa.[434, 652, 653] They had two daughters. Gayle Aileen Long was born in Wellman, Lime Creek Twp., Washington Co., Iowa, on May 20, 1916.[652, 654] Gayle Aileen reached age 81 and died in Roswell, Chaves Co., New Mexico, on September 6, 1997.[653, 654] She was buried in South Park Cemetery, Roswell, Chaves Co., New Mexico.[653, 655]

Arthur Ewing II and his second wife Gayle Long Ewing are not found in the 1940 U.S. census.

Military records have Arthur Warren Ewing, as a resident Des Moines, Polk Co., Iowa in 1944 and of North English, English Twp., Iowa Co., Iowa in 1949.[656, 657] Arthur Warren Ewing lived in 1973 in Goodland, Sherman Co., Kansas, where he was a railroad brakeman.[658]

Son of Arthur Warren Ewing II and Iva Jane Ballard:

+ 115 m I.   **Son**[10] Ewing was born between 1932 and 1935. He died between 1932 and 1935.

Daughters of Arthur Warren Ewing II and Gayle Aileen Long had two children, including:

+ 116 f I.   **Janet Carolyn**[10] Ewing was born in Wellman, Lime Creek Twp., Washington Co., Iowa, on March 6, 1939.[109, 659, 660] She died in Roswell, Chaves Co., New Mexico, on December 11, 2000.[109, 659, 660]

+ 117 f II. **Daughter**[10] Ewing was born in Iowa.

69. Claribel[9] **Ewing** (*Grace May*[8] *Pegan, Charles H.*[7]*, Joseph*[6]*, Andrew*[5]*, Robert A.*[4]*, Andrew*[3]*, Andrew*[2] *Pagan, James*[1]) was born on October 12, 1913, in Dallas City Twp., Henderson Co., Illinois.[109, 435] She was the daughter of Arthur Jerome Ewing and Grace May Pegan (41). She died in Belleville, Belleville Twp., Republic Co., Kansas, on January 28, 1986, at age 72.[109, 435] Claribel was buried in Fairbury Cemetery, Fairbury, Washington Twp., Jefferson Co., Nebraska.[435, 661]

Claribel married **Roy Emil Williams** on May 30, 1937, in Chicago, Cook Co., Illinois.[435, 662] They had three children. Roy Emil Williams was born in Wilsey, Washington Twp., Morris Co., Kansas, on August 3, 1906.[662]

Roy Emil reached age 66 and died in Belleville, Belleville Twp., Republic Co., Kansas, on September 5, 1972.[662] He was buried in Fairbury Cemetery, Fairbury, Washington Twp., Jefferson Co., Nebraska.[663]

In 1940, Roy and Claribel Ewing Williams are enumerated in Kansas City, Jackson Co., Missouri *(Census Place: Kansas City, Jackson, Missouri; Roll: T627_2170; Page: 2B; Enumeration District: 116-123)*. Roy Williams, age 34, born "K" (Kansas), is a "TEL" (telegraph operator?) for a railroad. Claribel Ewing Williams, born Illinois, is 27 years old. Their son Robert is four months old and was born in Illinois. Roy and Claribel say that they were residents of Cook Co., Illinois in 1935. Their address is 512 East 44th Street.

According to his obituary and family records, Roy Emil Williams worked for the Rock Island Railroad for 49 years, with assignments in Herington, Kansas; Rock Island and Chicago, Illinois; Cheyenne, Wyoming; Goodland, Kansas; Aurora, Colorado; and St. Louis, Missouri. Roy and his wife, Claribel Ewing Williams, moved to Belleville, Belleville Twp., Republic Co., Kansas, where some of Claribel's relatives lived, shortly before his death.

Children of Claribel Ewing and Roy Emil Williams:

+ 118 m I.   **Robert Karl**[10] **Williams** was born in Chicago, Cook Co., Illinois, on November 25, 1939.[664] He died in Clinton, Clinton Co., Iowa, on July 28, 1951.[664]

+ 119 f II. **Dolores M.**[10] **Williams** was born in Chicago, Cook Co., Illinois, on December 12, 1940.[665, 666] She was also known as **Dee**. Dolores M. died in Scandia, Scandia Twp., Republic Co., Kansas, on April 10, 2015.[665, 666]

+ 120 m III. **Richard Emil**[10] **Williams** was born in Chicago, Cook Co., Illinois, on November 14, 1941.[109, 667] He died in Los Angeles, Los Angeles Co., California, on September 27, 1992.[109, 667]

70. Thomas Butler[9] **Ewing** (*Grace May*[8] *Pegan, Charles H.*[7]*, Joseph*[6]*, Andrew*[5]*, Robert A.*[4]*, Andrew*[3]*, Andrew*[2] *Pagan, James*[1]) was born on January 6, 1915, in Cairo Twp., Randolph Co., Missouri.[109, 436] He was the son of Arthur Jerome Ewing and Grace May Pegan (41). Thomas Butler lived in 1987 in Provencal Twp., Natchitoches Parish, Louisiana. He died in a hospital in Pineville, Rapides Parish, Louisiana, on May 25, 1987, at age 72.[436, 437] Thomas Butler was buried in Lambertown Cemetery, Robeline, Robeline Twp., Natchitoches Parish, Louisiana.[437, 668]

Thomas Butler married **Alta Grace Westaway** on January 15, 1938, in Scott Co., Iowa.[669, 670] They divorced. They had three children. Alta Grace Westaway was born in Ensley, Jefferson Co., Alabama, on August 18, 1919.[671, 672] She was also known as **Grace**. Alta Grace lived in 2012 in Davenport, Davenport Twp., Scott Co., Iowa. She reached age 94 and died in Lincoln, Talladega Co., Alabama, on August 17, 2014.[673] Alta Grace was buried in Conesville Cemetery, Conesville. Orono Twp., Muscatine Co., Iowa.[671]

In 1940, Thomas Butler Ewing is enumerated in Orono Twp., Muscatine Co., Iowa (*Census Place: Orono, Muscatine, Iowa; Roll: T627_1186; Page: 3B; Enumeration District: 70-21*). In the household are "Tom" Ewing, age 24, born Missouri, a farmer; his wife, (Alta) Grace Westaway Ewing, 20, born Alabama, and their son Marvin, one, born Iowa. Both Thomas and (Alta) Grace Westaway Ewing say they were living in Muscatine Co. in 1935. They live in a rural area with no numerical street or road designated.

Alta Grace Westaway always used her middle name, Grace, as her given name. Her true first name is confirmed on her son Marvin's death certificate.[670] om Thomas Butler Ewing, she married Robert E. Armstrong on August 31, 1950 in Aledo, Mercer County, Illinois.[674] Alta Grace Westaway Ewing Armstrong passed away at her daughter's home in Alabama.

Thomas Butler Ewing married **Ellie Faye Brown** after 1945. Ellie Faye Brown was born in Robeline, Robeline Twp., Natchitoches Parish, Louisiana, on July 19, 1921.[109, 675] Ellie Faye reached age 85 and died in Robeline, Robeline Twp., Natchitoches Parish, Louisiana, on October 31, 2006.[109, 675] She was buried in Lambertown Cemetery, Robeline, Robeline Twp., Natchitoches Parish, Louisiana.[675, 676]

Before her marriage to Thomas B. Ewing, Ellie Faye worked as a retail buyer at Cohen Department Store in Galveston, Texas.[675]

Children of Thomas Butler Ewing and Alta Grace Westaway:

+ 121 m I. **Marvin Kenneth**[10] **Ewing** was born in Orono Twp., Muscatine Co., Iowa, on January 9, 1939.[109, 670] He died in Austin, Travis Co., Texas, on September 29, 1978.[670]

+ 122 m II. **Charles**[10] **Ewing** was born in Orono Twp., Muscatine Co., Iowa, on March 10, 1941.[677] He died in Orono Twp., Muscatine Co., Iowa, on March 10, 1941.[677]

+ 123 f III. **Daughter**[10] **Ewing** was born in Orono Twp., Muscatine Co., Iowa.

71. Charlene Effie Lilliebelle[9] **Ewing** (*Grace May*[8] *Pegan, Charles H.*[7]*, Joseph*[6]*, Andrew*[5]*, Robert A.*[4]*, Andrew*[3]*, Andrew*[2] *Pagan, James*[1]) was born on September 29, 1924, in Dutch Creek Twp., Washington Co., Iowa.[81, 438, 439] She was the daughter of Arthur Jerome Ewing and Grace May Pegan (41).

Charlene Effie Lilliebelle lived in 1989 in Scandia, Scandia Twp., Republic Co., Kansas. She died in a facility in Belleville, Belleville Twp., Republic Co., Kansas, on August 15, 1996, at age 71.[81, 438] She was cremated and her ashes buried in Fairbury Cemetery, Fairbury, Washington Twp., Jefferson Co., Nebraska.[438, 678]

Childless.

Charlene Effie Lilliebelle married **Deryl Richard Heathco** on November 20, 1969, in Las Vegas, Clark County, Nevada.[679] Deryl Richard Heathco was born in Rushville, Rushville Twp., Rush Co., Indiana, on October 15, 1899.[680, 681, 682] He was also known as **Richard D**. Deryl Richard reached age 88 and died in Roswell, Chaves Co., New Mexico, on August 15, 1988.[682, 683, 684] He was buried in Fairbury Cemetery, Fairbury, Washington Twp., Jefferson Co., Nebraska.[683, 684]

According to their marriage certificate in Las Vegas, Clark Co., Nevada, Charlene Effie Lilliebelle Ewing was living in Idaho and her husband, Deryl Richard Heathco was living in Illinois at the time of their marriage.[679]

There seems to be a typographical error in the indexing of Deryl Richard Heathco's entry on the U.S., Social Security Applications and Claims Index, which says he was born in 1894. This is incorrect, and all other sources, including census enumerations, register his birth year as 1899.[680]

72. Lois Lorraine[9] **Jacobs (Cochran)** (*Alta Lee*[8] *Pegan, Charles H.*[7]*, Joseph*[6]*, Andrew*[5]*, Robert A.*[4]*, Andrew*[3]*, Andrew*[2] *Pagan, James*[1]) was born on February 4, 1915, in Streator, Bruce Twp., LaSalle Co., Illinois.[454] She was the daughter of James Walter Jacobs and Alta Lee Pegan (42). Lois Lorraine died in Bellwood, Cook Co., Illinois, on October 5, 2012, at age 97.[455] She was buried in Arlington Cemetery, Elmhurst, DuPage Co., Illinois.[685, 686]

After her mother, Alta Lee Pegan Jacobs Bader Brown, remarried to John Henry Bader, Lois Lorraine Jacobs was reared by her paternal uncle and aunt, Dale and Jeanette Jacobs Cochran. The Cochrans may have legally adopted Lois. She is known to have used their surname, as her maiden name on her son Donald Fred Bonacker's birth certificate is "Lois Lorraine Cochrane" (sic).[LL]

Lois L. Jacobs is listed as a niece in the home of her uncle and aunt, Dale and Jeanette Jacobs Cochran in Bellwood, Proviso Twp., Cook Co., Illinois in 1930 *(Census Place: Proviso, Cook, Illinois; Roll: 506; Page: 2B; Enumeration District: 2297; Image: 121.0)*. Lois L. Jacobs, age 15, says she was born in Illinois as were her parents. Jeanette Jacobs Cochran, known "Nettie May" in childhood and later as Jeanne/Jean, was the sister of Lois' father, James Walter Jacobs.

The Cochrans also had a daughter, Loretta "Marilyn" Cochran Malek (Mrs. Joseph Malek); she died in Danbury, Connecticut in 2007. In Loretta Marilyn Malek's obituary, Lois Bonacker is named as her sister, but, according to Fred John Bonacker's Cook County, Illinois death certificate, his wife's maiden name was Lois Jacobs.[687, 688]

Lois Lorraine married **Fred John Bonacker** before 1932. They had one son. Fred John Bonacker was born in Germany on September 9, 1911.[687] Fred John reached age 66 and died in Bellwood, Cook Co., Illinois, on February 17, 1978.[688] He was buried in Arlington Cemetery, Elmhurst, DuPage Co., Illinois.[688, 689]

Frederick "Fred" and Lois Jacobs (Cochran) Bonacker are enumerated in Melrose Park, Cook Co., Illinois in 1940 *(Census Place: Melrose Park, Cook, Illinois; Roll: T627_788; Page: 6B; Enumeration District: 16-447)*. Fred Bonacker, age 28, born Germany, is a repairman for a steam railroad. Lois L. Jacobs (Cochran) Bonacker, 24, an Illinois native, lists her occupation as a packer in an electrical appliances plant. With them is son Donald, six, born Illinois. Their residence is 118 15th Avenue..

Son of Lois Lorraine Jacobs and Fred John Bonacker:

+ 124 m I. **Donald Fred**[10] **Bonacker** was born in Melrose Park, Cook Co., Illinois, on September 30, 1933.[LL] He died in Bellwood, Proviso Twp., Cook Co., Illinois, on March 5, 2019.[MM, NN]

73. James[9] **Brown II** (*Alta Lee*[8] *Pegan, Charles H.*[7]*, Joseph*[6]*, Andrew*[5]*, Robert A.*[4]*, Andrew*[3]*,*

Andrew² Pagan, James¹) was born on June 2, 1925, in Streator, Bruce Twp., LaSalle Co., Illinois.[456, 457] He was the son of James Brown and Alta Lee Pegan (42). James died in Streator, Bruce Twp., LaSalle Co., Illinois, on July 18, 1928, at age three.[456, 457] He was buried in Phillips Cemetery, Streator, (part), Newtown Twp., Livingston Co., Illinois.[457]

74. Walter David⁹ Brown (*Alta Lee⁸ Pegan, Charles H.⁷, Joseph⁶, Andrew⁵, Robert A.⁴, Andrew³, Andrew² Pagan, James¹*) was born on May 10, 1926, in Streator, Bruce Twp., LaSalle Co., Illinois.[109, 458, 459] He was the son of James Brown and Alta Lee Pegan (42). Walter David lived in 1992 in Brooksville, Hernando Co., Florida. He died in a hospital in Hudson, Pasco Co., Florida, on November 3, 1992, at age 66.[109, 458, 459] Walter David was buried in Curlew Hills Memory Gardens Cemetery, Palm Harbor, Pinellas Co., Florida.[690]

Walter David married **Minerva DiMichele** on April 30, 1949, in Cook Co., Illinois.[691] They had two daughters. Minerva DiMichele was born in Chicago, Cook Co., Illinois, on November 20, 1922.[109, 692, 693] Minerva reached age 62 and died in Palm Harbor, Pinellas Co., Florida, on June 8, 1985.[692, 693] She was buried in Curlew Hills Memory Gardens Cemetery, Palm Harbor, Pinellas Co., Florida.[694]

Walter David Brown married **Joan Marie Myers?** on July 29, 1990, in Pinellas Co., Florida.[695]

75. Pauline Theresa⁹ Brown (*Alta Lee⁸ Pegan, Charles H.⁷, Joseph⁶, Andrew⁵, Robert A.⁴, Andrew³, Andrew² Pagan, James¹*) was born on April 15, 1932, in Joliet, Will Co., Illinois.[109, 350] She was also known as **Paula**. She was the daughter of James Brown and Alta Lee Pegan (42). Pauline died in River Grove, Cook Co., Illinois, on September 15, 2007, at age 75.[109]

Pauline Theresa married **Unknown Buchanan** before 1952. They probably divorced.

Pauline Theresa Brown Buchanan married **Frank J. Fabian** on October 11, 1952, in Cook Co., Illinois.[696] They had four sons. Frank J. Fabian was born in Niles, Niles Twp., Cook Co., Illinois?, on December 3, 1926.109] Frank J. reached age 67 and died in Chicago, Cook Co., Illinois, on December 29, 1993.[109] He was buried in St. Adalbert Catholic Cemetery, Niles, Niles Twp., Cook Co., Illinois.[697]

Pauline Theresa Brown Buchanan Fabian married **Walter? Slusarz** about 1995. They divorced, and Pauline restored her Fabian surname.

Pauline Theresa Brown and Frank J. Fabian had four sons, including:

+ 125 m I. **James W.¹⁰ Fabian** was born in Chicago, Cook Co., Illinois, on August 18, 1949.[698] He died in Chicago, Cook Co., Illinois, on October 30, 1972.[698]

+ 126 m III. **Bradley Fred¹⁰ Fabian** was born in Chicago, Cook Co., Illinois, on August 13, 1954.[699] He died in Chicago, Cook Co., Illinois, on December 8, 2014.[699]

76. Jean⁹ Lucas (*Lorraine Ruth⁸ Martin, Josephine⁷ Pegan, Joseph⁶, Andrew⁵, Robert A.⁴, Andrew³, Andrew² Pagan, James¹*) was born on January 3, 1919, in Maplewood, Jefferson Twp., St. Louis Co., Missouri.[109] She was the daughter of Clifford Young Lucas and Lorraine Ruth Martin (43). Jean died in St. Louis, Missouri, on March 24, 2011, at age 92.[109, 467] She was buried in Jefferson Barracks National Cemetery, Lemay Twp., St. Louis Co., Missouri.[700]

Jean married **George Farrell Rush** on June 6, 1944, in St. Louis Co., Missouri.[701] They had three sons. George Farrell Rush was born in Louisville, Jefferson Co., Kentucky, on March 1, 1918.[109, 702] George Farrell Rush reached 81 and died in Sunset Hills, St. Louis Co., Missouri, on June 14, 1999.[109, 703] He was buried in Jefferson Barracks National Cemetery, Lemay Twp., St. Louis Co., Missouri.[703, 704]

George F. Rush was a U.S. Navy Commander in WWII.

77. Martha Lee⁹ Brockman (*Hazel⁸ Reneau, Lenora or Nora Lee⁷ Pegan, Joseph⁶, Andrew⁵, Robert A.⁴, Andrew³, Andrew² Pagan, James¹*) was born on October 31, 1914, in Maplewood, Jefferson Twp.,

St. Louis Co., Missouri.[109, 473] She was the daughter of Harry Gus Brockman and Hazel Reneau (44). Martha Lee was living in 2009 in Hartford, Hartford Twp., Washington Co., Wisconsin. She died in a facility in Waukesha, Waukesha Twp., Waukesha Co., Wisconsin, on January 13, 2009, at age 94.[109, 473] Martha Lee was buried in Wisconsin Memorial Park Cemetery, Brookfield, Waukesha Co., Wisconsin.[705, 706]

Martha Lee married **Robert George Krueger** on June 5, 1937, in Milwaukee Co., Wisconsin.[707] They had two sons. Robert George Krueger was born in Milwaukee, Milwaukee Co., Wisconsin, on February 22, 1906.[708] Robert George reached age 73 and died in West Bend, Washington Co., Wisconsin, on June 5, 1979.[708] He was cremated and his cremains buried in Wisconsin Memorial Park Cemetery, Brookfield, Waukesha Co., Wisconsin.[707, 709]

In 1940, Robert George and Martha Lee Brockman Krueger are residing in Milwaukee, Milwaukee Co., Wisconsin (*Census Place: Milwaukee, Milwaukee, Wisconsin; Roll: T627_4555; Page: 2B; Enumeration District: 72-335*). In the home are Robert Krueger, 44, a designer of outboard motors; his wife Martha Brockman Krueger, 25, and their son William, 11 months old. Also with them is Robert's mother, Elizabeth Krueger, 73. All in the home were born in Wisconsin except Martha, who is a Missouri native The three adults were living in the same home at 1635 Fifty Third Street in 1935.

Robert G. and Martha L. Brockman Krueger resided in Milwaukee, Milwaukee Co., Wisconsin and West Bend, Washington Co., Wisconsin. They seemed to have been residents of Grafton, Ozaukee Co., Wisconsin for a while, as Robert was the co-founder of Power Products Corporation, there in 1947. He earned both an electrical engineering bachelor's and master's and a master's in psychology. They may have spent time in Hartford, Connecticut and Delaware, Ohio, as Robert taught psychology at Yale and Ohio Wesleyan universities. He did research in and wrote books on hypnosis and related topics.[707]

After Robert's death, Martha resided in Hartford Twp., Washington Co., Wisconsin.

Martha Lee Brockman and Robert George Krueger had two sons, including:

+ 127 m I. **William Robert**[10] **Krueger** was born in Milwaukee, Milwaukee Co., Wisconsin, in 1939.

78. Raymond Harry[9] **Brockman** (*Hazel*[8] *Reneau, Lenora or Nora Lee*[7] *Pegan, Joseph*[6]*, Andrew*[5]*, Robert A.*[4]*, Andrew*[3]*, Andrew*[2] *Pagan, James*[1]) was born on September 14, 1918, in Maplewood, Jefferson Twp., St. Louis Co., Missouri.[109, 474, 475, 476, 477] He was also known as **Ray Harry**. He was the son of Harry Gus Brockman and Hazel Reneau (44). Raymond Harry died in Milwaukee, Milwaukee Co., Wisconsin, on July 25, 1989, at age 70.[109, 474, 475, 476] He was buried in Wisconsin Memorial Park Cemetery, Brookfield, Waukesha Co., Wisconsin.[710, 711]

Raymond H. Brockman is found in Maplewood, Jefferson Twp., St. Louis Co., Missouri in 1940 (*Census Place: Maplewood, St Louis, Missouri; Roll: T627_2150; Page: 6A; Enumeration District: 95-154*). "Ray" Brockman, 21, single, a stock boy at an electrical supply company, is living with his paternal grandmother, Louise Wahl, 71, and her second husband Henry B. Wahl, 77, who has no occupation. All were born in Missouri and were living in the same place, the rear half of a double at 3714 Cambridge Street, in 1935.

Later, he worked at Schlitz Brewing Company for 33 years.[710]

Raymond Harry married **Marcella B. Schwartz** before 1949. They had three sons. Marcella B. Schwartz was born in Chilton, Calumet Co., Wisconsin, on July 27, 1911.[109, 712, 713] Marcella B. reached age 89 and died in New Berlin, Waukesha Co., Wisconsin, on June 20, 2001.[109, 712,713] She was buried in Wisconsin Memorial Park Cemetery, Brookfield, Waukesha Co., Wisconsin.[712, 714]

Raymond Harry Brockman and Marcella B. Schwartz had three sons, including:

+ 128 m III. **Son**[10] **Brockman** was born in Milwaukee, Milwaukee Co., Wisconsin.

79. Albert Lawrence[9] **Green II** (*Alice Lucille*[8] *Kelley, Lewis Albert*[7]*, Mary Jane*[6] *Pegan, Andrew*[5]*, Robert A.*[4]*, Andrew*[3]*, Andrew*[2] *Pagan, James*[1]) was born on May 9, 1925, in Lansing, Lansing Twp., Ingham Co., Michigan.[109, 484, 485] He was the son of Albert Lawrence Green and Alice Lucille Kelley (46). He died in Cheyenne, Laramie Co., Wyoming, on November 30, 1991, at age 66.[109, 484, 485] He was cremated and his ashes buried in Mountain View Memorial Park Cemetery, Cheyenne, Laramie Co., Wyoming.[484, 485]

Albert Lawrence II married **Barbara Anne Stickney** on June 14, 1952, in Detroit, Wayne Co., Michigan.[485] They had five daughters. Barbara Anne Stickney was born in Detroit, Wayne Co., Michigan, on March 21, 1927.

Albert Lawrence Green Jr., a sales representative for IBM Corporation, moved to Cheyenne, Laramie Co., Wyoming in 1973.[485]

Albert Lawrence Green II and Barbara Anne Stickney had four daughters, including:

+ 128 f III. **Daughter**[10] **Green** was born in Detroit, Wayne Co., Michigan.

80. Frances Lucille[9] **Eudailey** (*Frances Maurene*[8] *Crosson, Laura Belle*[7] *Kelley, Mary Jane*[6] *Pegan, Andrew*[5]*, Robert A.*[4]*, Andrew*[3]*, Andrew*[2] *Pagan, James*[1]) was born on July 31, 1916, in Rehoboth Precinct, Lunenburg Co., Virginia.[496] She was also known as **Lucille**. She was the daughter of Samuel Mason Eudailey and Frances Maurene Crosson (49). Frances Lucille died in Keysville, Charlotte Co., Virginia, on October 5, 2014, at age 98.[497] She was buried in Tussekiah Baptist Church Cemetery, Meherrin, Lunenburg Co., Virginia.[497, 715]

Frances Lucille married **Earl Carlyle Currin** on September 23, 1942, in Lunenburg Co., Virginia.[716] They had four sons. Earl Carlyle Currin was born in Rehoboth Precinct, Lunenburg Co., Virginia, on July 20, 1922.[109, 717] Earl Carlyle reached age 66 and died in Chesterfield Co., Virginia, on October 27, 1988.[109, 718, 719] He was buried in Tussekiah Baptist Church Cemetery, Meherrin, Lunenburg Co., Virginia.[719, 720]

Frances Lucille Eudailey and Earl Carlyle Currin had four sons, including:

+ 129 m III. **Infant Son**[10] **Currin** was born in Farmville, Prince Edward Co., Virginia, on April 7, 1949.[721] He died in a hospital in Farmville, Prince Edward Co., Virginia, on April 7, 1949.[721]

81. Samuel Purnell[9] **Eudailey** (*Frances Maurene*[8] *Crosson, Laura Belle*[7] *Kelley, Mary Jane*[6] *Pegan, Andrew*[5]*, Robert A.*[4]*, Andrew*[3]*, Andrew*[2] *Pagan, James*[1]) was born on June 28, 1918, in Rehoboth Precinct, Lunenburg Co., Virginia.[109, 498] He was the son of Samuel Mason Eudailey and Frances Maurene Crosson (49). Samuel Purnell died in Keysville, Charlotte Co., Virginia, on October 4, 1993, at age 75.[109, 499] He was buried in Cool Spring Christian Church Cemetery, Chickahominy, Lunenburg Co., Virginia.[722]

Samuel Purnell married **Edna Earl Reed** on October 1, 1946, in Nottaway Co., Virginia.[723] They had two sons. Edna Earl Reed was born in Walton, Charlotte Co., Virginia, on July 6, 1924.[723, 724, 725] Edna Earl reached age 75 and died in Midlothian, Chesterfield Co., Virginia, on August 6, 1999.[109, 725, 726] She was buried in Cool Spring Christian Church Cemetery, Chickahominy, Lunenburg Co., Virginia.[725]

82. Richard Louis[9] **Eudailey** (*Frances Maurene*[8] *Crosson, Laura Belle*[7] *Kelley, Mary Jane*[6] *Pegan, Andrew*[5]*, Robert A.*[4]*, Andrew*[3]*, Andrew*[2] *Pagan, James*[1]) was born on November 20, 1921, in Rehoboth Precinct, Lunenburg Co., Virginia.[109, 500] He was the son of Samuel Mason Eudailey and Frances Maurene Crosson (49). Richard Louis died in Richmond, Henrico Co., Virginia, on November 15, 2011, at age 89.[109, 501, 502] He was buried in Greenwood Memorial Gardens, Richmond, Henrico Co., Virginia.[501, 727]

Widower Richard Louis married **Mabel Lucy Procise** on March 20, 1942, in Lunenburg Co., Virginia.[728] They had two daughters. Mabel Lucy Procise was born in Mecklenburg Co., Virginia, on January 27, 1920.[109, 729] She was also known as **Mabel**. Mabel Lucy lived in 1999 in Ashland,

Hanover Co., Virginia. She reached age 79 and died in Richmond, Henrico Co., Virginia, on February 10, 1999.[109, 730, 731] Mabel Lucy was buried in Greenwood Memorial Gardens, Richmond, Henrico Co., Virginia.[730, 732]

Although her name on her marriage record to Richard Louis Eudailey is Lucy Mabel Procise, her birth and death records and other documents have her given name as Mabel.[728, 729, 731]

Richard Louis Eudailey married Mrs. **Frances Via** Franklin on November 19, 2000, in Hampton, Elizabeth Co., Virginia.[733] Frances Via was born in Samuel Miller Twp., Albemarle Co., Virginia, on April 13, 1929.[109, 734] Frances reached age 77 and died in Victoria, Rehoboth Precinct, Lunenburg Co., Virginia, on January 14, 2007.[109, 735, 736] She was buried in Cunningham United Methodist Church Cemetery, Cunningham, Fluvanna Co., Virginia.[737]

83. **Edith Virginia**[9] **Eudailey** (*Frances Maurene*[8] *Crosson, Laura Belle*[7] *Kelley, Mary Jane*[6] *Pegan, Andrew*[5], *Robert A.*[4], *Andrew*[3], *Andrew*[2] *Pagan, James*[1]) was born on November 29, 1923, in Rehoboth Precinct, Lunenburg Co., Virginia.[109, 388] She was the daughter of Samuel Mason Eudailey and Frances Maurene Crosson (49). Edith Virginia died in Keysville, Charlotte Co., Virginia, on November 20, 2010, at age 86.[504,505,506] She was buried in Tussekiah Baptist Church Cemetery, Meherrin, Lunenburg Co., Virginia.[504]

Edith Virginia married **Aubrey Bailey Chaney** on November 12, 1941, in Lunenburg Co., Virginia.[738] They divorced. They had one son. Aubrey Bailey Chaney was born in Central District, Charlotte Co., Virginia, on November 13, 1920.[739, 740] He reached age 51 and died in Wylliesburg, Charlotte Co., Virginia, on March 22, 1972.[739,740] Aubrey Bailey was buried in Wylliesburg Baptist Cemetery, Wylliesburg, Charlotte Co., Virginia.[739]

Edith Virginia Eudailey married **Claude Lee Tomlinson** on April 13, 1962, in Brunswick Co., Virginia.[741] They had one son. Claude Lee Tomlinson was born in Plymouth District, Lunenburg Co., Virginia, on October 9, 1911.[109, 742, 743] Claude Lee reached age 89 and died in Keysville, Charlotte Co., Virginia, on March 31, 2001.[109, 742, 744, 745] He was buried in Tussekiah Baptist Church Cemetery, Meherrin, Lunenburg Co., Virginia.[742, 745]

Son of Edith Virginia Eudailey and Claude Lee Tomlinson:

+ 130 m I. **Robert Victor**[10] **Tomlinson** was born in Keysville, Charlotte Co., Virginia, on July 31, 1962.[746, 747] He died in Kenbridge, Lunenburg Co., Virginia, on November 4, 1987.[746]

84. **Eleanor Margaret**[9] **McLaughlin** (*Eleanor Margaret*[8] *Pegan, Sinclair Edwin*[7], *William Henry*[6], *Andrew*[5], *Robert A.*[4], *Andrew*[3], *Andrew*[2] *Pagan, James*[1]) was born on February 15, 1907, in Park City, Park City Twp., Summit Co., Utah.[517, 518] She was the daughter of William Francis McLaughlin and Eleanor Margaret Pegan (50). She died in Imola, Napa Co., California, on April 25, 1958, at age 51.[517, 518, 519] Eleanor Margaret was buried in Suison-Fairfield Cemetery, Fairfield, Solano Co., California.[518, 519]

Childless.

After her mother, Eleanor Pegan McLaughlin, died, Eleanor McLaughlin lived with her maternal grandmother, Emma Kelso (Pegan) in Oakland, Alameda Co., California.

In 1920, Eleanor McLaughlin, age 12, born Utah, is living with her maternal grandmother, Emma Kelso (Pegan), in Oakland, Alameda Co., California *(Census Place: Oakland, Alameda, California; Roll: T625_87; Page: 21A; Enumeration District: 23; Image: 754)*. Also in the home is Eleanor's uncle, Louis Pegan, listed as Louis Kelso, age 26, a railroad conductor.

Eleanor Nittler was an inpatient at the Napa State Mental Hospital in Imola, Napa Co., California when she died.[518]

Eleanor Margaret married **Rudolph John Nittler** in 1926. Rudolph John Nittler was born in Alameda, Alameda Co., California, on June 20, 1902.[109, 748, 749, 750] They divorced after 1948. Rudolph John reached age 77 and died in Stockton,

Stockton Twp., San Joaquin Co., California, on November 1, 1979.[109, 748]

Rudolph Nittler signed up for the WWI draft, and listed his birthdate as June 20, 1899—perhaps he was doing so to be old enough to go to war. But other records confirm a 1902 birth.[109, 748, 750]

In 1930, Rudolph John and Eleanor McLaughlin Nittler are living with Eleanor's father, William F. McLaughlin, in Salt Lake City, Salt Lake Co., Utah (*Census Place: Salt Lake City, Salt Lake, Utah; Roll: 4547816; Page: 8A; Image: 1406.0*). Listed as head of the household, William McLaughlin, age 50, a barber. is a widower who says he was born in Canada (which is crossed out and "am" written above it), his father in New York and his mother in Canada. Rudolph Nittler, mistakenly listed as "William Nutter". Rudolph Nittler is age 27, born California, is a shipping clerk in an automobile factory who says his father was born in Germany and his mother in Wisconsin. Eleanor McLaughlin Nittler, 22, says she was born in Utah, her father in Canada and her mother in Utah. Rudolph and Eleanor McLaughlin Nittler say their first marriages occurred at ages 25 and 19 respectively.

Rudolph J. and Eleanor McLaughlin Nittler are found in Oakland, Alameda Co., California in 1940 (*Census Place: Oakland, Alameda, California; Roll: T627_438; Page: 7B; Enumeration District: 61-237*). Rudolph "Nitlerr", age 37, born California, is an auto loader at an auto plant. His wife, Eleanor McLaughlin Nittler, is 33, born Utah, and a hospital nurse working in an institution. Both say they were living in Oakland in 1935. Their home address is 5327 Trask Street.

Rudolph John Nittler became a partner in a real estate and insurance agency by 1948 in Napa, Napa Co., California. He and Eleanor were still married at that time.[751]

After he and Eleanor divorced, Rudolph Nittler married Mrs. Iola Mae Chittim in Carson City, Nevada on June 12 1958.[752] Although his obituary lists his second wife Iola and a "daughter" Naomi, Naomi was his second wife's daughter by her first marriage.[753]

85. **Eleanor Lois**[9] **Kelso** (*Lewis Sinclair (Pegan)*[8], *Sinclair Edwin*[7] *Pegan, William Henry*[6], *Andrew*[5], *Robert A.*[4], *Andrew*[3], *Andrew*[2] *Pagan, James*[1]) was born on July 6, 1926, in Alameda, Alameda Co., California.[109, 527, 528] She was also known as **Lois**. She was the daughter of Lewis Sinclair (Pegan) Kelso (51) and Cora A. Tripplett. Eleanor Lois died in Milpitas, Santa Clara Co., California, on April 24, 1995, at age 68.[109, 528, 529] She was buried in Cedar Lawn Memorial Park Cemetery, Fremont, Alamada Co., California.[754, 755]

Eleanor Lois married **Unknown Theriault** before 1944.[756] They have one daughter.

Eleanor Lois Kelso Theriault married **Unknown Kapp** in 1949.[756]

Eleanor Lois Kelso Theriault Kapp married **Walter C. Seed** in 1961.[756] They divorced.[757] Walter C. Seed was born in Oakland, Alameda Co., California, on October 23, 1919.[109, 758] He reached age 90 and died in Oakland, Alameda Co., California, on March 29, 2010.[109]

Eleanor Lois Kelso Theriault Kapp Seed married **Joseph James Dibello** on March 11, 1972, in Washoe Co., Nevada.[759] They divorced in December 1973.[760] They remarried in Douglas Co., Nevada on September 27, 1987.[761] Joseph James Dibello was born in Philadelphia, Delaware Co., Pennsylvania, on March 19, 1924.[109, 762] He lived in 2005 in Mountain View, Santa Clara Co., California. He reached age 81 and died in a hospital in Fremont, Alameda Co., California, on December 22, 2005.[109,762] Joseph James was buried in San Joaquin Valley National Cemetery, Santa Nella, Merced Co., California.[762, 763, 764]

Joseph James Dibello was a bartender.[762]

86. **George Lewis**[9] **Kelso** (*Lewis Sinclair (Pegan)*[8], *Sinclair Edwin*[7] *Pegan, William Henry*[6], *Andrew*[5], *Robert A.*[4], *Andrew*[3], *Andrew*[2] *Pagan, James*[1]) was born on December 11, 1928, in Oakland, Alameda Co., California.[109, 530] He was the son of Lewis Sinclair (Pegan) Kelso (51) and Cora A. Tripplett. George Lewis died in San Jose, Santa Clara Co., California, on January 11, 2001, at age 72.[109]

George Lewis married Mrs. **Frances E. Barker** Cortinas? before 1966. They divorced. They had one son. Frances E. Barker Cortinas? was born in 1918.

George Lewis Kelso and his wife, Frances Cortinas Kelso may have married and divorced three times. Divorces are recorded in the California, Divorce Index as occurring in December 1966, November 1968 and April 1973, all in Santa Clara County.[765] But no marriages in California or Nevada are recorded.

Son of George Lewis Kelso and Frances E. Barker Cortinas?:

+ 131 m I. **Son**[10] **Kelso** was born in Alameda Co., California.

87. Joseph Sinclair[9] **Kelso** (*Lewis Sinclair (Pegan)*[8], *Sinclair Edwin*[7] *Pegan, William Henry*[6], *Andrew*[5], *Robert A.*[4], *Andrew*[3], *Andrew*[2] *Pagan, James*[1]) was born on April 29, 1934, in Oakland, Alameda Co., California.[109, 531] He was the son of Lewis Sinclair (Pegan) Kelso (51) and Cora A. Tripplett. Joseph Sinclair died in Concord, Contra Costa Co., California, on October 9, 2003, at age 69.[109]

Joseph Sinclair married **Sang Soon Yung** before 1962 in South Korea. They had one son. Sang Soon Yung was born in Inchon, Korea (now South Korea), on November 19, 1937.[109, 766, 767] She was also known as **Haja**. Sang Soon reached age 59 and died in Pleasant Hill, Contra Costa Co., California, on July 26, 1997.[109, 766, 767]

Son of Joseph Sinclair Kelso and Sang Soon Yung:

+ 132 m I. **Tony Son**[10] **Kelso** was born in Inchon, South Korea, on January 18, 1962.[109, 768] He died in Concord, Contra Costa Co., California, on June 10, 2009.[109, 768]

88. Katherine Anne[9] **Boggs** (*Mary Elizabeth*[8] *Pegan, Sinclair Edwin*[7], *William Henry*[6], *Andrew*[5], *Robert A.*[4], *Andrew*[3], *Andrew*[2] *Pagan, James*[1]) was born on April 5, 1935, in Bellingham, Whatcom Co., Washington. She is the daughter of Francis Llewellyn Boggs and Mary Elizabeth Pegan (52).

Katherine Anne married **Thomas W. Davie** about May 3, 1956 in Kitsap Co., Washington.[769] They divorced. They had two children. Thomas W. Davie was born in American Falls, Power Co., Idaho, on July 22, 1931.[770] He reached age 59 and died in Seattle, King Co., Washington, on April 13, 1991.[770, 771] Thomas W. was buried in Falls View Cemetery, American Falls, Power Co., Idaho.[772]

A noted newspaper cartoonist and artist, Thomas W. Davie also worked for seven years as a "cartooning weatherman" at KING-TV in Seattle, Washington.[770]

Katherine Anne Boggs Davie married **Richard Edward Strep** about 1980. Richard Edward Strep was born in Buffalo, Erie Co., New York, on September 26, 1933.[109, 773] Richard Edward reached age 70 and died in Tacoma, Pierce Co., Washington, on June 7, 2004.[109, 773, 774, 775] He was buried in Mountain View Memorial Park Cemetery & Crematorium, Lakewood, Pierce Co., Washington.[774]

Richard Edward Strep was a sign painter and talented wood carver.[774]

89. John Francis[9] **Boggs** (*Grace*[8] *Pegan, Sinclair Edwin*[7], *William Henry*[6], *Andrew*[5], *Robert A.*[4], *Andrew*[3], *Andrew*[2] *Pagan, James*[1]) was born on September 7, 1927, in Ferndale Twp., Whatcom Co., Washington.[C] He was the son of Lorraine Cornelius Boggs and Grace Pegan (53). He died in Forks, Clallam Co., Washington, on April 29, 2018.[C]

John Francis married Mrs. **Janice Orilla Wasson (Klahn)** Fisch on September 7, 1963, in Lewis Co., Washington.[776, 777] They divorced. They had two daughters. Janice Orrilla Wasson (Klahn) was born in Sedro-Wolley, Skagit Co., Washington, on April 29, 1937.[109, 778, 779] She reached age 56 and died in Port Angeles, Clallam Co., Washington, on November 23, 1993.[109, 778, 779, 780] She was cremated and her cremains buried in Mount Angeles Memorial Park Cemetery, Port Angeles, Clallam Co., Washington.[779, 781]

May have used her stepfather's surname, Klahn. Although she married twice after divorcing John F. Boggs, Janice Orilla Klahn Wasson Fisch Chaussee Boggs Huston Conerly was buried under the name Janice O. Boggs.[778, 780, 781]

90. Mary Lee[9] **Boggs** (*Grace*[8] *Pegan, Sinclair Edwin*[7]*, William Henry*[6]*, Andrew*[5]*, Robert A.*[4]*, Andrew*[3]*, Andrew*[2] *Pagan, James*[1]) was born in Bellingham, Whatcom Co., Washington, on July 13, 1929.[D] She was the daughter of Lorraine Cornelius Boggs and Grace Pegan (53). She died in Issaquah, King Co., Washington on May 29, 2018.[D]

Mary Lee married **Merle Edwin Landerholm** on June 9, 1951, in Whitman Co., Washington.[782] They had four children. Merle Edwin Landerholm was born in La Center, Clark Co., Washington, on September 9, 1927.[109, 782] Merle Edwin lived in 1976 in Bellevue, King Co., Washington. He reached age 48 and died in Victoria, British Columbia, Canada, on August 29, 1976.[783, 784]

Dr. Merle Edwin Landerholm earned a doctorate in education and was the first president of Bellevue Community College in Bellevue, King Co., Washington at the time of his death. He died while on vacation in British Columbia.[784]

91. Robert Edwin[9] **Pegan** (*John Edwin*[8]*, Sinclair Edwin*[7]*, William Henry*[6]*, Andrew*[5]*, Robert A.*[4]*, Andrew*[3]*, Andrew*[2] *Pagan, James*[1]) was born on March 2, 1935, in Bellingham, Whatcom Co., Washington.[109, 556, 557, 558, 559] He was the son of John Edwin Pegan (54) and Elizabeth Marie Maletzki. He died in San Diego, San Diego Co., California, on March 13, 1981, at age 46.[556, 557, 558, 559] Robert Edwin was buried in Eternal Hills Memorial Park Cemetery, Oceanside, San Diego Co., California.[558, 785]

Robert Edwin married **Gloria Louise Donovan** on April 13, 1956, in Los Angeles Co., California.[786] They had four children. Gloria Louise Donovan was born in Bell, Los Angeles Co., California, on June 11, 1936.[109, 787, 788] Gloria Louise reached age 68 and died in Carlsbad, San Diego Co., California, on July 30, 2004.[109, 787]

Robert Edwin Pegan was a salesman for the Lipton Tea Company.

92. John Edward[9] **Pegan II** (*John Edwin*[8]*, Sinclair Edwin*[7]*, William Henry*[6]*, Andrew*[5]*, Robert A.*[4]*, Andrew*[3]*, Andrew*[2] *Pagan, James*[1]) was born on September 27, 1937, in Houston, Harris Co., Texas.[109] He was the son of John Edwin Pegan (54) and Elizabeth Marie Maletzki. He died in Spring, Harris Co., Texas, on February 21, 2003, at age 65.[109]

According to his son, John Edward Pegan II was born in Houston, Harris Co., Texas, but grew up in Galveston, Galveston Co., Texas.[789]

He married **Ms. Jacobs**. They divorced. They had three children.

John Edward Pegan II married **Virginia Marie Unknown**. They divorced.

93. Anna Marie[9] **Pegan** (*John Edwin*[8]*, Sinclair Edwin*[7]*, William Henry*[6]*, Andrew*[5]*, Robert A.*[4]*, Andrew*[3]*, Andrew*[2] *Pagan, James*[1]) was born on September 25, 1940, in Houston, Harris Co., Texas. She is the daughter of John Edwin Pegan (54) and Elizabeth Marie Maletzki.

She married **Unknown Unknown**. They have one daughter.

Anna Marie Pegan Unknown married **John Charles Mills** on September 3, 1963, in Los Angeles Co., California.[790] They divorced. They had one daughter. John Charles Mills was born in North Hollywood, Los Angeles Co., California, on August 13, 1932.[791] John Charles lived in Hermosa Beach, Los Angeles Co., California. He reached age 66 and died in a facility in Torrance, Los Angeles Co., California, on May 26, 1999.[791, 792] He was cremated and his ashes buried in Forest Lawn Memorial Park Cemetery, Glendale, Los Angeles Co., California.[791, 792]

John Charles Mills was a salesman for PDQ Electronics. He seems to have adopted his wife's elder daughter.[792]

94. David Gilbert[9] **Gregor II** (*David Gilbert*[8]*, Elizabeth Jane*[7] *Pegan, William Henry*[6]*, Andrew*[5]*, Robert A.*[4]*, Andrew*[3]*, Andrew*[2] *Pagan, James*[1]) was born on May 22, 1929, in Watertown, Watertown Town, Jefferson Co., New York.[109, 562] He was the son of David Gilbert Gregor (56) and Elisabeth Quincy Stebbins. He died in Watertown, Watertown Town, Jefferson Co., New York, on August 18, 2013, at age 84.[109, 562]

Never married.

David Gilbert Gregor Jr. was a third-generation physician and surgeon.

95. **Ann Sewall**[9] **Gregor** (*David Gilbert*[8], *Elizabeth Jane*[7] *Pegan, William Henry*[6], *Andrew*[5], *Robert A.*[4], *Andrew*[3], *Andrew*[2] *Pagan, James*[1]) was born on July 8, 1932, in New York, Kings Co., New York.[563] She was also known as **Ann MacGregor Sewall**. She was the daughter of David Gilbert Gregor (56) and Elisabeth Quincy Stebbins. Ann Sewall died in Bar Harbor, Hancock Co., Maine, on June 18, 2015, at age 82.[563] She was cremated and her ashes buried in Brookside Cemetery, Watertown, Water Town, Jefferson Co., New York.[563, 564]

Ann Sewall married **William A. Cauldwell III** on June 26, 1954, in Jefferson Co., New York.[793] They divorced. They had two children. William A. Cauldwell III was born in New York, King's Co., New York, on June 2, 1926.[109, 794] He reached age 82 and died in Jacksonville, Duval Co., Florida, on January 9, 2009.[109, 794]

Ann Sewall Gregor Cauldwell married **Abner Graboff** in 1982 in New York, Kings Co., New York.[795] Abner Graboff was born in New York, King's Co., New York, on June 28, 1919.[109, 796] He reached age 67 and died in New York, King's Co., New York, on October 15, 1986.[796]

Abner Graboff, the son of Russian immigrants, was a noted book illustrator, specializing in children's books, but he also illustrated for non-fiction. His work graced many books written from the 1940s-1980s, including *Mrs. McGarrity's Peppermint Sweater*, by Adelaide Holl; *Mr. Angelo*, by Marjory Schwalje; *The Sun Looks Down*, by Miriam Schlein; *The Abelard Folk Song Book, Edited and Arranged for Piano and Guitar*, by Norman Carden; *Do You Want To See Something?*, by Eve Merriam, *10 Little Indians*, Illustrated by Abner Graboff, *The Hamburger Cookbook*, by Esther K. Schwartz, and *It's A Picnic!*, by Nancy Fair McIntyre, among others.[797, 798]

Ann Sewall Gregor Caldwell Graboff married **Edward Graham Kaelber** after 1986. Edward Graham Kaelber was born in Philadelphia, Philadelphia Co., Pennsylvania, on May 11, 1924.

Edward Graham Kaelber, former lumber magnate and assistant dean of Harvard's Graduate School of Business, became the first president of the College of the Atlantic, a "human ecology" college, in Bar Harbor, Maine in January 1970.[799]

96. **Roderick**[9] **Pirnie II** (*Mary Margaret*[8] *Gregor, Elizabeth Jane*[7] *Pegan, William Henry*[6], *Andrew*[5], *Robert A.*[4], *Andrew*[3], *Andrew*[2] *Pagan, James*[1]) was born on April 10, 1918, in Watertown, Watertown Town, Jefferson Co., New York.[574, 575] He was the son of Roderick Pirnie and Mary Margaret Gregor (57). Roderick died in Watertown, Watertown Town, Jefferson Co., New York, on March 23, 1919.[576, 577] He was buried in Brookside Cemetery, Watertown, Water Town, Jefferson Co., New York.[800]

97. **Elisabeth**[9] **Pirnie** (*Mary Margaret*[8] *Gregor, Elizabeth Jane*[7] *Pegan, William Henry*[6], *Andrew*[5], *Robert A.*[4], *Andrew*[3], *Andrew*[2] *Pagan, James*[1]) was born on December 15, 1921, in Detroit, Wayne Co., Michigan.[109] She was also known as **Betsy**. She was the daughter of Roderick Pirnie and Mary Margaret Gregor (57). She died in Tucson, Pima Co., Arizona, on April 6, 2013, at age 91.[109, 578]

There is compelling evidence that Elisabeth Pirnie was born in Detroit, Wayne Co., Michigan. A newspaper item in the September 4, 1919 Watertown Daily News, Watertown, New York, mentioned that Elisabeth Pirnie McKay Carroll Gruet's parents, Roderick "Roderick" and Mary Margaret Gregor Pirnie, were moving from Watertown to Detroit and that city would be their home for some time.[801] Roderick and May Margaret Pirnie are enumerated in the 1920 census in Detroit, Wayne Co., Michigan. In the 1930 and 1940 census records, Elisabeth's birthplace is listed as Michigan. (see #57)

Elisabeth married **Robert Hamilton McKay** in 1944 in Providence, Providence Co., Rhode Island. They divorced. They had one daughter. Robert Hamilton McKay was born in Woodhaven, Queens Co., New York, on February 8, 1915.[802, 803, 804, 805] Robert Hamilton McKay

Robert Hamilton reached age 86 and died in Jacksonville, Duval Co., Florida, on December 4, 2001.[109, 803, 804, 805]

Elisabeth Pirnie McKay married **Wendell Eugene Carroll** before 1973. They divorced. Wendell Eugene Carroll was born in Terre Haute, Harrison

Twp., Vigo Co., Indiana, on November 22, 1916.[806, 807] Wendell Eugene reached age 86 and died in Seattle, King Co., Washington, on January 27, 2003.[807, 808] He was buried in Arlington National Cemetery, Arlington, Virginia.[807, 809]

A graduate of Rose Polytechnic Institute (now Rose-Hulman Institute of Technology) near hometown of Terre Haute, Indiana, Wendell E. Carroll was an electrical engineer who designed one of the first solid-state industrial timers and founded Regent Controls, a manufacturer of these timers and automatic control panels, in Ansonia, Connecticut in 1947. Wendell Eugene and Elisabeth Pirnie McKay Carroll resided in Stamford, Fairfield Co., Connecticut while married. Wendell Carroll retired to California, living in 1989 in Santa Rosa, Sonoma Co., California, in 1993 in Sebastopol, Sonoma Co., California, and in San Diego, San Diego Co., California in 1998 before relocating to Seattle to be near his son by his first marriage.

Elisabeth Pirnie McKay Carroll married **Charles Peter Gruet** on February 16, 1973, in Fairfield Co., Connecticut.[810] They divorced. Charles Peter Gruet was born in Lenox, Berkshire Co., Massachusetts, on June 29, 1906.[109, 811, 812, 813, 814] He was also known as **The Silver Fox**. Charles Peter reached age 81 and died in Westfield, Hampden Co., Massachusetts, on August 1, 1987.[811, 812, 813] He was buried in Willowbrook Cemetery, Weston, Fairfield Co., Connecticut.[811]

Charles P. Gruet, a Pan American Airways employee from New Jersey, immigrated to Rio De Janiero, Brazil in 1942 as a permanent resident.[814] He later returned to the United States, where he became the manager of a heavy equipment manufacturing company, according to his Connecticut death file.[812] He died in Massachusetts, but lived and was buried in Weston, Fairfield Co., Connecticut, so he has a death file on record both states. While his official Massachusetts death certificate says Charles died in Westfield, Hampden Co., Massachusetts, his Connecticut file says he died in Montville, Berkshire Co., Massachusetts. The Massachusetts death entry is more likely correct.[812, 813]

Elisabeth Pirnie McKay Carroll Gruet, known as Betsy Gruett, lived in 1975 in South Dartmouth, Bristol Co., Massachusetts before relocating to West Barnstable, Barnstable Co., Massachusetts in 1980. Elisabeth was employed in Hyannis Whale Watching Company and the *Barnstable (MA) Register* newspaper.[578]

98. Leslie Meloan[9] **Pegan** (*John Robert*[8], *Morrow Walton*[7], *John S.*[6], *Andrew*[5], *Robert A.*[4], *Andrew*[3], *Andrew*[2] *Pagan*, *James*[1]) was born on January 16, 1957, in Frederick, Frederick Co., Maryland.[109, 594, 595, 596] He was the son of John Robert Pegan (61) and Juanita Malissa Blumenauer. Leslie Meloan died in Bakersfield, Kern Co., California, on December 21, 1978, at age 21.[109, 594] He was buried in Mount Lebanon Cemetery, Mount Lebanon, Allegheny Co., Pennsylvania.[815]

Although his military record says he was born in Maryland, a birth mention in *The Post (Frederick, MD)* on January 21, 1957 says Leslie Meloan Pegan was born in Huntington, Suffolk Co., New York.[594, 596]

99. Rosena Cecilia[9] **Reher** (*Dorothy Geneva*[8] *Pegan*, *Harry Clark*[7], *Samuel Alexander*[6], *Andrew*[5], *Robert A.*[4], *Andrew*[3], *Andrew*[2] *Pagan*, *James*[1]) was born on July 18, 1922, in Hannibal, Mason Twp., Marion Co., Missouri.[109, 606, 607] She was the daughter of Stephen Albert Paul Reher and Dorothy Geneva Pegan (62). Rosena Cecilia died in Glendale, Maricopa Co., Arizona, on July 31, 2002, at age 80.[109, 606, 607] She was buried in Greenwood Memory Lawn Cemetery, Phoenix, Maricopa Co., Arizona.[606, 816]

Rosena Cecilia married **Mason Avery Leake** on July 6, 1944, in Marion Co., Missouri.[817] They had one daughter. Mason Avery Leake was born in Perry, Salt River Twp., Ralls Co., Missouri, on January 20, 1918.[818, 819] Mason Avery reached age 27 and died in Levee Twp., Pike Co., Illinois, on August 9, 1945.[818, 819] He was buried in St. Mary's/Holy Family Cemetery, Hannibal, Mason Twp., Marion Co., Missouri.[820]

Lieutenant Mason Leake, U.S. Army, drowned in the Mississippi River while on an outing with friends when he was on leave. Previously stationed in Ipswich, England, he had turned down a post as special navigator to famed pilot General Jimmy

Doolittle to return to the U.S. and his next assignment at Jefferson Barracks near St. Louis, Missouri. He had received the Distinguished Flying Cross and other medals.[819]

Rosena Cecilia Reher Leake married **James Gary Kondos** on December 23, 1947, in Marion Co., Missouri.[821] They had seven children. James Gary Kondos was born in Mansfield, Madison Twp., Richland Co., Ohio, on May 15, 1919.[822, 823] James Gary reached age 59 and died in Phoenix, Maricopa Co., Arizona, on August 1, 1978.[109, 823, 824] He was buried in Greenwood Memory Lawn Cemetery, Phoenix, Maricopa Co., Arizona.[824, 825]

The Social Security Death Index lists James Gary Kondos' birth as May 15, 1918, but his Ohio birth certificate and his military record says he was born May 15, 1919.

Rosena Cecilia Reher and James Gary Kondos had seven children, including:

+ 133 f I. **Emily S.**^{10} **Kondos** was born in Cleveland, Cuyahoga Co., Ohio, on July 31, 1948.[826] She died in Cleveland, Cuyahoga Co., Ohio, on February 4, 1957.[827, 828]

+ 134 m IV. **Thomas George**^{10} **Kondos** was born in Hannibal, Mason Twp., Marion Co., Missouri?, on November 16, 1955.[109] He died in Hazelwood, St. Louis Co., Missouri, on January 13, 2009.[109, 829]

+ 135 m V. **Stephen Mark**^{10} **Kondos** was born in Euclid, Cuyahoga Co., Ohio, on May 10, 1959.[109, 830] He died in Hazelwood, St. Louis Co., Missouri, on September 13, 2013.[109]

100. Joan Kathryn^9 **Pegan** (*Erman Henry*^{8}, *Harry Clark*^{7}, *Samuel Alexander*^{6}, *Andrew*^{5}, *Robert A.*^{4}, *Andrew*^{3}, *Andrew*^{2} *Pagan*, *James*^{1}) was born on December 1, 1932, in St. Louis, Missouri. She is the daughter of Erman Henry Pegan (63) and Helen Kathryn Thornton.

Joan Kathryn married **Frank Vincent Bakulich** on June 27, 1953, in San Pedro, Los Angeles Co., California.[831] They had four children. Frank Vincent Bakulich was born in San Pedro, Los Angeles Co., California, on May 14, 1932.[832, 833, 834] He reached age 66 and died in San Pedro, Los Angeles Co., California, on May 14, 1998.[109, 832, 833] Frank Vincent was buried in Green Hills Memorial Park Cemetery, Rancho Pales Verdes, Los Angeles Co., California.[832, 835]

Frank Vincent Bakulich was s a real estate agent at All American Realty.

101. James Kenneth^9 **Pegan** (*Erman Henry*^{8}, *Harry Clark*^{7}, *Samuel Alexander*^{6}, *Andrew*^{5}, *Robert A.*^{4}, *Andrew*^{3}, *Andrew*^{2} *Pagan*, *James*^{1}) was born on December 15, 1934, in St. Louis, Missouri. He is the son of Erman Henry Pegan (63) and Helen Kathryn Thornton.

James Kenneth Pegan married and had three children.

102. Jacquelin K.^{9} **Pegan** (*Erman Henry*^{8}, *Harry Clark*^{7}, *Samuel Alexander*^{6}, *Andrew*^{5}, *Robert A.*^{4}, *Andrew*^{3}, *Andrew*^{2} *Pagan*, *James*^{1}) was born on March 13, 1939, in St. Louis, Missouri. She is the daughter of Erman Henry Pegan (63) and Helen Kathryn Thornton.

Jacquelin K. married **Leonard Robert Risler** on September 15, 1962, in Los Angeles Co., California.[836] They divorced. They had one daughter. Leonard Robert Risler was born in Inglewood, Los Angeles Co., California, on April 1, 1935.

Jacquelin K. Pegan Risler married **Leonardo Bologna** on January 26, 1975, in Los Angeles Co., California.[837] Leonardo Bologna was born in Trapani, Trapani Province, Sicily, Italy, on September 16, 1933.[109, 838, 839] He was also known as **Leo**. He reached age 80 and died in Los Angeles, Los Angeles Co., California, on September 21, 2013.[109, 838, 839] Leonardo was buried in Green Hills Memorial Park Cemetery, Rancho Pales Verdes, Los Angeles Co., California.[838]

Leonardo Bologna was a general contractor.

103. Herbert Eugene^9 **McCann II** (*Flora Josephine*^{8} *Pegan*, *Harry Clark*^{7}, *Samuel Alexander*^{6}, *Andrew*^{5}, *Robert A.*^{4}, *Andrew*^{3}, *Andrew*^{2} *Pagan*, *James*^{1}) was born on May 18, 1923, in Hannibal, Mason

Twp., Marion Co., Missouri.[109, 620, 621, 622] He was also known as **Mac**. He was the son of Herbert Eugene McCann and Flora Josephine Pegan (64). He resided in 2002 in Pomona, Los Angeles Co., California. He died in a hospital in Upland, San Bernardino Co., California, on January 16, 2002, at age 78.[109, 620, 621] Herbert Eugene was buried in Bellevue Memorial Park Cemetery, Ontario, San Bernardino Co., California.[620, 840]

Herbert Eugene married **LaVerne Marie Gallagher** on April 21, 1945, in Stafford Co., Virginia.[622] They had six children. LaVerne Marie Gallagher was born in Pittsburgh, Allegheny Co., Pennsylvania, on July 23, 1925.[622, 841, 842, 843] She was also known as **Marie**. LaVerne Marie lived in 1979 in Chino, San Bernardino Co., California. She reached age 53 and died in a hospital in Upland, San Bernardino Co., California, on April 2, 1979.[841, 842, 843] She was cremated, and her cremains buried in Bellevue Memorial Park Cemetery, Ontario, San Bernardino Co., California.[842, 844]

She used both LaVerne (Laverne) and Marie as given names. Her Social Security application and her marriage license have the given and middle name Laverne Marie; her death certificate says Marie LaVerne.[622, 842, 843]

Herbert Eugene McCann Jr. and LaVerne Marie Gallagher met at Quantico, Virginia while he was in the Marines and she was a secretary at the Coast Guard headquarters. They married in Stafford, Virginia.[622]

Widower Herbert Eugene McCann II married Mrs. **Norma Eleanor Dillon** Miracle on September 1, 1979, in San Bernardino Co., California.[845] Norma Eleanor Dillon was born in Pittsburgh, Allegheny Co., Pennsylvania, on June 20, 1931.[846] She was also known as **Ellie**. Norma Eleanor reached age 82 and died in Pomona, Los Angeles Co., California, on March 7, 2014.[846] She was buried in Bellevue Memorial Park Cemetery, Ontario, San Bernardino Co., California.[846]

Herbert Eugene McCann II's mother is listed as "Josephine Pigan" on his death certificate. Before moving to Pomona, Herbert was a resident of Chino, San Bernardino Co., California and was employed as a lithographer at a printing company.[620]

Herbert Eugene McCann II and LaVerne Marie Gallagher had six children, including:

+ 136 m I. **Michael Kevin**[10] **McCann** was born in New York, New York, on April 5, 1953.[109, 847] He died in Madison, Davidson Co., Tennessee, on May 19, 2004.[109, 847]

104. Ada Frances[9] **McCann** (*Flora Josephine*[8] *Pegan, Harry Clark*[7]*, Samuel Alexander*[6]*, Andrew*[5]*, Robert A.*[4]*, Andrew*[3]*, Andrew*[2] *Pagan, James*[1]) was born on January 31, 1925, in Detroit, Wayne Co., Michigan.[81, 623] She was the daughter of Herbert Eugene McCann and Flora Josephine Pegan (64). Ada Frances died in Dearborn Heights, Wayne Co., Michigan, on March 23, 1998, at age 73.[109, 623]

Ada Frances married **Leslie E. MacQueen** on August 26, 1944, in Wayne Co., Michigan.[848] They had four children. Leslie E. MacQueen was born in Detroit, Wayne Co., Michigan, on August 19, 1923.[109, 849] Leslie E. reached age 75 and died in Wayne, Wayne Co., Michigan, on January 3, 1999.[109, 849]

Ada Frances McCann and Leslie E. MacQueen had four children, including:

+ 137 f I. **Sharon L.**[10] **MacQueen** was born in Dearborn Heights, Wayne Co., Michigan, on May 25, 1945.[109] She died in Gaylord, Bagley Twp., Otsego Co., Michigan, on October 12, 2012, at age 67.[109, 850]

105. Shirley Theresa[9] **McCann** (*Flora Josephine*[8] *Pegan, Harry Clark*[7]*, Samuel Alexander*[6]*, Andrew*[5]*, Robert A.*[4]*, Andrew*[3]*, Andrew*[2] *Pagan, James*[1]) was born on May 5, 1926, in Detroit, Wayne Co., Michigan.[109, 624] She was the daughter of Herbert Eugene McCann and Flora Josephine Pegan (64). Shirley Theresa died in Dearborn Heights, Wayne Co., Michigan, on August 2, 1989, at age 63.[109, 624] She was cremated and her ashes buried in Holy Sepulchre Cemetery, Southfield, Oakland Co., Michigan.[851]

Shirley Theresa married **Albert Dominic Pratto** on May 6, 1944? They had four children. Albert Dominic Pratto was born in Homer City, Indiana Co., Pennsylvania, on March 15, 1924.[109, 852] Albert Dominic reached age 41 and died in Livonia, Wayne Co., Michigan, on March 8, 1966.[109, 852, 853] He was buried in Holy Sepulchre Cemetery, Southfield, Oakland Co., Michigan.[852]

Shirley Theresa McCann Pratto married **William Raymond Farwell** after 1966. William Raymond Farwell was born in Detroit, Wayne Co., Michigan, on May 12, 1927.[109, 854] William Raymond lived in 1982 in Livonia, Wayne Co., Michigan. He reached age 55 and died in Westland, Wayne Co., Michigan, on August 3, 1982.[854]

Shirley Theresa McCann and Albert Dominic Pratto had four children, including:

+ 138 m II.   **Patrick Dominic**[10] **Pratto** was born in Detroit, Wayne Co., Michigan, on November 4, 1947.[855] He died in Gilbert, Maricopa Co., Arizona, on December 8, 2011.[855]

+ 139 f III. **Jeanine Marie**[10] **Pratto** was born in Detroit, Wayne Co., Michigan, on December 3, 1952.[856, 857] She died in a hospital in Detroit, Wayne Co., Michigan, on March 11, 1964.[856, 857, 858]

106. Infant Son[9] **McCann** (*Flora Josephine*[8] *Pegan, Harry Clark*[7]*, Samuel Alexander*[6]*, Andrew*[5]*, Robert A.*[4]*, Andrew*[3]*, Andrew*[2] *Pagan, James*[1]) was born on September 26, 1927, in Detroit, Wayne Co., Michigan.[363] He was the son of Herbert Eugene McCann and Flora Josephine Pegan (64). Infant Son died in Detroit, Wayne Co., Michigan, on September 28, 1927.[363] He was buried in Holy Cross Cemetery, Detroit, Wayne Co., Michigan.[363]

107. David Donald[9] **McCann** (*Flora Josephine*[8] *Pegan, Harry Clark*[7]*, Samuel Alexander*[6]*, Andrew*[5]*, Robert A.*[4]*, Andrew*[3]*, Andrew*[2] *Pagan, James*[1]) was born on October 20, 1930, in Detroit, Wayne Co., Michigan.[625, 627] He was the son of Herbert Eugene McCann and Flora Josephine Pegan (64). David Donald died in Tustin, Orange Co., California, on September 5, 1951, at age 20.[625, 626, 627] He was buried in Holy Cross Cemetery, Detroit, Wayne Co., Michigan.[625, 627]

David Donald McCann's birthdate on his California Death Index entry is incorrect. The California Death Index says his birthdate was November 11, 1928 and that he was born in Missouri, but David is not found in the 1930 census with his parents, and his age on the 1940 census form indicates a birth year of either 1930 or 1931. His birthplace on that census form is Michigan. (*Year: 1940; Census Place: Detroit, Wayne, Michigan; Roll: T627_1851; Page: 14A; Enumeration District: 84-359*). David Donald McCann's date of birth on the application for his U.S. military headstone is October 30, 1930, which is consistent with his birth information on the 1940 census form. The application for the military headstone also states he died on September 5, 1951 in Tustin, California in a motorcycle accident, and that the headstone should be shipped to Holy Cross Cemetery in Detroit, Michigan. His mother, Flora Josephine Pegan McCann Bogardus Shields requested the headstone under the name Flora Josephine Bogardus.[625]

David Donald married **Phyllis Jean Lachmeyer** on July 8, 1950, in Orange Co., California.[859] They had one son. Phyllis Jean Lachmeyer was born in Dayton, Montgomery Co., Ohio, on July 16, 1930.[860, 861, 862] Phyllis Jean reached age 82 and died in San Diego, San Diego Co., California, on March 18, 2013?

After David Donald McCann's death, Phyllis Jean Lachmeyer McCann married **Albert W. Lord** on October 19, 1954 in San Diego Co., California.[863]

10th Generation

108. Marie Wynne¹⁰ Fischer (*Gladys Wynne⁹ Ewing, Grace May⁸ Pegan, Charles H.⁷, Joseph⁶, Andrew⁵, Robert A.⁴, Andrew³, Andrew² Pagan, James¹*) was born on March 1, 1938, in Chicago, Cook Co., Illinois.[634] She was the daughter of Harm Meint Fischer and Gladys Wynne Ewing (66). Marie Wynne died in Las Vegas, Clark Co., Nevada, on April 7, 1978, at age 40.[635]

Marie Wynne married **Jack Morris III** in November 1958 in Dade Co., Florida.[864] They had three children. Jack Morris III was born in Manhattan, New York Co., New York, on January 23, 1937.[109, 865] Jack reached age 68 and died in Redondo Beach, Los Angeles Co., California, on March 2, 2005.[109]

Marie Wynne Fischer married **Unknown Cappelina** after 1959.

Marie Wynne Fischer married **Charles Henry Keller** on June 1, 1973, in Clark Co., Nevada.[866]

109. Charles¹⁰ Fischer (*Gladys Wynne⁹ Ewing, Grace May⁸ Pegan, Charles H.⁷, Joseph⁶, Andrew⁵, Robert A.⁴, Andrew³, Andrew² Pagan, James¹*) was born in 1940 in Peoria, Peoria Twp., Peoria Co., Illinois? He is the son of Harm Meint Fischer and Gladys Wynne Ewing (66).

110. Jay Jackson¹⁰ Fischer (*Gladys Wynne⁹ Ewing, Grace May⁸ Pegan, Charles H.⁷, Joseph⁶, Andrew⁵, Robert A.⁴, Andrew³, Andrew² Pagan, James¹*) was born on July 31, 1941, in Peoria, Peoria Twp., Peoria Co., Illinois.[109,636] He was the son of Harm Meint Fischer and Gladys Wynne Ewing (66). Jay Jackson lived before 1985 in Herndon, Fairfax Co., Virginia. He also resided in 1985 in Deltona, Volusia Co., Florida. Jay Jackson died in Deltona, Volusia Co., Florida, on June 9, 2007, at age 65.[109, 636]

Jay Jackson Fischer married twice and had two children by his first wife.

111. BillyJo¹⁰ Fischer (*Gladys Wynne⁹ Ewing, Grace May⁸ Pegan, Charles H.⁷, Joseph⁶, Andrew⁵, Robert A.⁴, Andrew³, Andrew² Pagan, James¹*) was born on August 4, 1942, in Chicago, Cook Co., Illinois.[637] He was the son of Harm Meint Fischer and Gladys Wynne Ewing (66). BillyJo died in Chicago, Cook Co., Illinois, on October 22, 1943, at age one.[637] He was buried in Oak Hill Cemetery, Wirth, Cook Co., Illinois.[637, 867]

112. Daughter¹⁰ Fischer (*Gladys Wynne⁹ Ewing, Grace May⁸ Pegan, Charles H.⁷, Joseph⁶, Andrew⁵, Robert A.⁴, Andrew³, Andrew² Pagan, James¹*) was born on April 4, 1949, in Dubuque, Dubuque Twp., Dubuque Co., Iowa.[513] She is the daughter of Harm Meint Fischer and Gladys Wynne Ewing (66).

Daughter Fischer married **Ray Matthew Devlin**. Ray Matthew Devlin was born in Los Angeles, Los Angeles Co., California, on June 20, 1950.[868, 869] Ray Matthew lived in 1979 in Sylmar, Los Angeles Co., California. Ray Matthew reached age 61 and died in Sylmar, Los Angeles, Co., California, on September 6, 2011.[109, 869] He was cremated.[869]

Ray was a computer technician.[869]

113. Infant Son¹⁰ Ewing (*Lawrence Howard⁹, Grace May⁸ Pegan, Charles H.⁷, Joseph⁶, Andrew⁵, Robert A.⁴, Andrew³, Andrew² Pagan, James¹*) was born on May 1, 1937, in Chicago, Cook Co., Illinois.[641] He was the son of Lawrence Howard Ewing (67) and Anna May Mathis. Infant Son died in Chicago, Cook Co., Illinois, on May 1, 1937.[641]

114. Lawrence Howard¹⁰ Ewing II (*Lawrence Howard⁹, Grace May⁸ Pegan, Charles H.⁷, Joseph⁶, Andrew⁵, Robert A.⁴, Andrew³, Andrew² Pagan, James¹*) was born on February 2, 1934, in Chicago, Cook Co. Illinois.[109, 644, 645, 646, 647] He was the son of Lawrence Howard Ewing (67) and Anna May Mathis. Lawrence Howard lived in 2006 in Bringhurst, Monroe Twp., Carroll Co., Indiana. He died in a hospital in Indianapolis, Marion Co., Indiana, on November 5, 2006, at age 72.[109, 522, 523, 647] He was cremated.[647]

Lawrence Howard married **Shirley Jean Miller** on January 2, 1972, in Avon, Hendricks Co.,

Indiana.[645, 870] Shirley Jean Miller was born in 1935.

Lawrence Howard Ewing II was married at least twice before he married Shirley Jean Miller. But his other wives' names and information are not known. Lawrence Howard Ewing II had one son.

115. Son[10] Ewing (*Arthur Warren[9], Grace May[8] Pegan, Charles H.[7], Joseph[6], Andrew[5], Robert A.[4], Andrew[3], Andrew[2] Pagan, James[1]*) was born between 1932 and 1935. He was the son of Arthur Warren Ewing II (68) and Iva Jane Ballard. Son died between 1932 and 1935.

116. Janet Carolyn[10] Ewing (*Arthur Warren[9], Grace May[8] Pegan, Charles H.[7], Joseph[6], Andrew[5], Robert A.[4], Andrew[3], Andrew[2] Pagan, James[1]*) was born on March 6, 1939, in Wellman, Lime Creek Twp., Washington Co., Iowa.[109,659,660] She was the daughter of Arthur Warren Ewing II (68) and Gayle Aileen Long. Janet Carolyn died in Roswell, Chaves Co., New Mexico, on December 11, 2000, at age 61.[109,659,660] She was buried in South Park Cemetery, Roswell, Chaves Co., New Mexico.[871]

Childless.

Janet Carolyn married **Unknown Butcher**. They divorced. They had no children. om Mr. Butcher, Janet Ewing Butcher resumed using her maiden name.

117. Daughter[10] Ewing (*Arthur Warren[9], Grace May[8] Pegan, Charles H.[7], Joseph[6], Andrew[5], Robert A.[4], Andrew[3], Andrew[2] Pagan, James[1]*) was born on September 1, 1943. She is the daughter of Arthur Warren Ewing II (68) and Gayle Aileen Long.

Daughter Ewing married **Richard G. Moore** on November 18, 1972, in Aurora, Colorado.[872] They had three sons. Richard G. Moore was born in Chattanooga, Hamilton Co., Tennessee, on May 1, 1933.[872] Richard G. reached age 80 and died in Roswell, Chaves Co., New Mexico, on June 18, 2013.[872] He was buried in South Park Cemetery, Roswell, Chaves Co., New Mexico.[872, 873]

118. Robert Karl[10] Williams (*Claribel[9] Ewing, Grace May[8] Pegan, Charles H.[7], Joseph[6], Andrew[5], Robert A.[4], Andrew[3], Andrew[2] Pagan, James[1]*) was born on November 25, 1939, in Chicago, Cook Co., Illinois.[664] He was the son of Roy Emil Williams and Claribel Ewing (69). Robert Karl died in Clinton, Clinton Co., Iowa, on July 28, 1951, at age 11.[664] He was buried in Fairbury Cemetery, Fairbury, Washington Twp., Jefferson Co., Nebraska.[874]

Robert Williams drowned on a Boy Scout camping trip when he was 11 years old. His scout troop from Rock Island, Illinois was rafting on the Mississippi River near the Clinton, Clinton Co., Iowa business district and wading on a sandbar when Robert slipped and fell into deeper water with a strong current. His parents, Roy and Claribel Ewing Williams and the family were living in Rock Island, Illinois, across the river from Clinton Co., Iowa, at the time.

119. Dolores M.[10] Williams (*Claribel[9] Ewing, Grace May[8] Pegan, Charles H.[7], Joseph[6], Andrew[5], Robert A.[4], Andrew[3], Andrew[2] Pagan, James[1]*) was born on December 12, 1940, in Chicago, Cook Co., Illinois.[665, 666] She was also known as **Dee**. She was the daughter of Roy Emil Williams and Claribel Ewing (69). Dolores M. died in Scandia, Scandia Twp., Republic Co., Kansas, on April 10, 2015, at age 74.[665, 666] She was buried in Riverview Cemetery, Scandia, Scandia Twp., Republic Co., Kansas.[665, 666]

Dolores married **Mr. Erickson**. They had two children.

She was an English teacher.[665]

120. Richard Emil[10] Williams (*Claribel[9] Ewing, Grace May[8] Pegan, Charles H.[7], Joseph[6], Andrew[5], Robert A.[4], Andrew[3], Andrew[2] Pagan, James[1]*) was born on November 14, 1941, in Chicago, Cook Co., Illinois.[109, 667] He was the son of Roy Emil Williams and Claribel Ewing (69). Richard Emil lived in 1986 in Fullerton, California. He died in Los Angeles, Los Angeles Co., California, on September 27, 1992, at age 50.[109, 667] Richard Emil was buried in Fairbury Cemetery, Fairbury, Washington Twp., Jefferson Co., Nebraska.[875]

Never married.

121. Marvin Kenneth[10] Ewing (*Thomas Butler[9], Grace May[8] Pegan, Charles H.[7], Joseph[6], Andrew[5], Robert*

A.⁴, *Andrew³, Andrew² Pagan, James¹*) was born on January 9, 1939, in Orono Twp., Muscatine Co., Iowa.[109, 670] He was the son of Thomas Butler Ewing (70) and Alta Grace Westaway. Marvin Kenneth died in Austin, Travis Co., Texas, on September 29, 1978, at age 39.[670] He was buried in Conesville Cemetery, Conesville. Orono Twp., Muscatine Co., Iowa.[670, 876]

Marvin Kenneth married **Karen Kay Heritage** on June 23, 1959, in Scott Co., Iowa.[877] They had three children. Karen Kay Heritage was born in Davenport, Davenport Twp., Scott Co., Iowa, in 1940.[878] Karen Kay reached age 48 and died in Davenport, Davenport Twp., Scott Co., Iowa, on December 7, 1988.[879] She was cremated and her cremains buried in Oakdale Memorial Gardens Cemetery, Davenport, Davenport Twp., Scott Co., Iowa.[879, 880]

122. Charles¹⁰ Ewing (*Thomas Butler⁹, Grace May⁸ Pegan, Charles H.⁷, Joseph⁶, Andrew⁵, Robert A.⁴, Andrew³, Andrew² Pagan, James¹*) was born on March 10, 1941, in Orono Twp., Muscatine Co., Iowa.[677] He was the son of Thomas Butler Ewing (70) and Alta Grace Westaway. Charles died in Orono Twp., Muscatine Co., Iowa, on March 10, 1941.[677] He was buried in Conesville Cemetery, Conesville. Orono Twp., Muscatine Co., Iowa.[677, 881]

123. Daughter¹⁰ Ewing (*Thomas Butler⁹, Grace May⁸ Pegan, Charles H.⁷, Joseph⁶, Andrew⁵, Robert A.⁴, Andrew³, Andrew² Pagan, James¹*) was born on January 28, 1943, in Orono Twp., Muscatine Co., Iowa. She is the daughter of Thomas Butler Ewing (70) and Alta Grace Westaway.

Daughter Ewing married **Donald Wallace Bach** on June 13, 1965, in Clark Co., Nevada.[882] They had four children. Donald Wallace Bach was born in Queens, Queens Co., New York, on May 26, 1941.[109, 883] He reached age 72 and died in Lincoln, Talladega Co., or Pell City, St. Clair Co., Alabama, on October 23, 2013.[109, 884]

Donald Wallace Back lived in Downey, Los Angeles Co., California and in 1968 and in 1983 in Huntington Beach, Orange Co., California. He was a chiropractor.[884]

124. Donald Fred¹⁰ Bonacker (*Lois Lorraine⁹ Jacobs [Cochran], Alta Lee⁸ Pegan, Charles H.⁷, Joseph⁶, Andrew⁵, Robert A.⁴, Andrew³, Andrew² Pagan, James¹*) was born on September 30, 1933, in Melrose Park, Cook Co., Illinois.[LL] He was the son of Fred John Bonacker and Lois Lorraine Jacobs (72). He died in Bellwood, Proviso Twp., Cook Co., Illinois, on March 5, 2019.[MM,NN] He was buried in Arlington Cemetery, Elmhurst, DuPage Co., Illinois.[MM,NN]

Childless.

Donald F. married **Peggy H. Budek** on July 23, 1958, in Cook Co., Illinois.[885, 886] They divorced. Peggy H. Budek was born about 1940.

Donald F. Bonacker married **Juanita C. Snyder** before 1978. Juanita C. Snyder was born in Chicago, Cook Co., Illinois, on February 2, 1931.[109] Juanita C. reached age 76 and died in Bradenton, Manatee Co., Florida, on June 26, 2007.[109, 887] She was buried in Elm Lawn Memorial Park Cemetery, Elmhurst, DuPage Co., Illinois.[887, 888]

125. James W.¹⁰ Fabian (*Pauline⁹ Brown, Alta Lee⁸ Pegan, Charles H.⁷, Joseph⁶, Andrew⁵, Robert A.⁴, Andrew³, Andrew² Pagan, James¹*) was born on August 18, 1949, in Chicago, Cook Co., Illinois.[698] He was the son of Frank J. Fabian and Pauline Theresa Brown (75). James W. worked as an Airplane refueler (Lockheed Martin). He died in Chicago, Cook Co., Illinois, on October 30, 1972, at age 23.[698] James W. was buried in Maryhill Catholic Cemetery and Mausoleum, Niles, Niles Twp., Cook Co., Illinois.[889]

James W. Fabian, an airplane refueler for the Lockheed Martin Co., was killed when he was crushed between two refueling trucks at Chicago's O'Hare Airport.[698]

He married **Ms. Johnson**. They had one son.

126. Bradley Fred¹⁰ Fabian (*Pauline⁹ Brown, Alta Lee⁸ Pegan, Charles H.⁷, Joseph⁶, Andrew⁵, Robert A.⁴, Andrew³, Andrew² Pagan, James¹*) was born on August 13, 1954, in Chicago, Cook Co., Illinois.[699] He was the son of Frank J. Fabian and Pauline Theresa Brown (75). Bradley Fred died in Chicago, Cook Co., Illinois, on December 8, 2014, at age 60.[699] He was cremated.[699]

He married and had two sons.

127. William Robert[10] Krueger (*Martha Lee[9] Brockman, Hazel[8] Reneau, Lenora or Nora Lee[7] Pegan, Joseph[6], Andrew[5], Robert A.[4], Andrew[3], Andrew[2] Pagan, James[1]*) was born in 1939 in Milwaukee, Milwaukee Co., Wisconsin. He was the son of Robert George Krueger and Martha Lee Brockman (77). William Robert lived in 1979 in West Allis, Milwaukee Co., Wisconsin.

He married **Karen J. Unknown**.

128. Son[10] Brockman (*Raymond Harry[9], Hazel[8] Reneau, Lenora or Nora Lee[7] Pegan, Joseph[6], Andrew[5], Robert A.[4], Andrew[3], Andrew[2] Pagan, James[1]*) was born in Milwaukee, Milwaukee Co., Wisconsin. He is the son of Raymond Harry Brockman (78) and Marcella B. Schwartz.

Son Brockman married **Kathleen Mary Young** before 1973 in Milwaukee Co., Wisconsin? They had two daughters. Kathleen Mary Young was born in Milwaukee, Milwaukee Co., Wisconsin, on April 7, 1955.[109] Kathleen Mary reached age 54 and died in Waukesha, Waukesha Twp., Waukesha Co., Wisconsin, on August 16, 2009.[109, 890]

128. Daughter[10] Green (*Albert Lawrence[9], Alice Lucille[8] Kelley, Lewis Albert[7], Mary Jane[6] Pegan, Andrew[5], Robert A.[4], Andrew[3], Andrew[2] Pagan, James[1]*) was born on November 15, 1955, in Detroit, Wayne Co., Michigan. She is the daughter of Albert Lawrence Green II (79) and Barbara Anne Stickney.

She married **Mr. Kirby**. They divorced. They had two children.

Daughter Green Kirby married **Harold Lawrence Olbekson**. Harold Lawrence Olbekson was born in Libby, Lincoln Co., Montana, on March 25, 1955.[109, 891] He was also known as **O.B.** Harold Lawrence reached age 52 and died in Summerfield, Marion Co., Florida, on December 3, 2007.[109, 891] He was buried in Florida National Cemetery, Bushnell, Sumter Co., Florida.[892]

129. Infant Son[10] Currin (*Frances Lucille[9] Eudailey, Frances Maurene[8] Crosson, Laura Belle[7] Kelley, Mary Jane[6] Pegan, Andrew[5], Robert A.[4], Andrew[3], Andrew[2] Pagan, James[1]*) was born on April 7, 1949, in Farmville, Prince Edward Co., Virginia.[721] He was the son of Earl Carlyle Currin and Frances Lucille Eudailey (80). Infant Son died in a hospital in Farmville, Prince Edward Co., Virginia, on April 7, 1949.[721] He was buried in Cool Spring Christian Church Cemetery, Chickahominy, Lunenburg Co., Virginia.[721]

130. Robert Victor[10] Tomlinson (*Edith Virginia[9] Eudailey, Frances Maurene[8] Crosson, Laura Belle[7] Kelley, Mary Jane[6] Pegan, Andrew[5], Robert A.[4], Andrew[3], Andrew[2] Pagan, James[1]*) was born on July 31, 1962, in Keysville, Charlotte Co., Virginia.[746,747] He was the son of Claude Lee Tomlinson and Edith Virginia Eudailey (83). Robert Victor lived in 1987 in Keysville, Charlotte Co., Virginia. He died in Kenbridge, Lunenburg Co., Virginia, on November 4, 1987, at age 25.[746] Robert Victor was buried in Tussekiah Baptist Church Cemetery, Meherrin, Lunenburg Co., Virginia.[893]

131. Son[10] Kelso (*George Lewis[9], Lewis Sinclair (Pegan)[8], Sinclair Edwin[7] Pegan, William Henry[6], Andrew[5], Robert A.[4], Andrew[3], Andrew[2] Pagan, James[1]*) was born in Alameda Co., California. He is the son of George Lewis Kelso (86) and Frances E. Barker Cortinas?

Son Kelso and his wife had three children, including:

+ 140 m I. **Thomas Lewis[11] Kelso** was born in Fremont, Alameda Co., California, on June 19, 1972.[894, 895] He died in Fremont, Alameda Co., California, on June 20, 1972.[894]

132. Tony Son[10] Kelso (*Joseph Sinclair[9], Lewis Sinclair (Pegan)[8], Sinclair Edwin[7] Pegan, William Henry[6], Andrew[5], Robert A.[4], Andrew[3], Andrew[2] Pagan, James[1]*) was born on January 18, 1962, in Inchon, South Korea.[109, 768] He was the son of Joseph Sinclair Kelso (87) and Sang Soon Yung. Tony Son died in Concord, Contra Costa Co., California, on June 10, 2009, at age 47.[109, 768]

Tony Son married and had two sons.

133. Emily S.[10] Kondos (*Rosena Cecilia[9] Reher, Dorothy Geneva[8] Pegan, Harry Clark[7], Samuel*

Alexander⁶, Andrew⁵, Robert A.⁴, Andrew³, Andrew² Pagan, James¹) was born on July 31, 1948, in Cleveland, Cuyahoga Co., Ohio.[826] She was the daughter of James Gary Kondos and Rosena Cecilia Reher (99). Emily S. died in Cleveland, Cuyahoga Co., Ohio, on February 4, 1957, at age eight.[826, 827] She was buried in St. Mary's/Holy Family Cemetery, Hannibal, Mason Twp., Marion Co., Missouri.[826, 896]

134. **Thomas George¹⁰ Kondos** (*Rosena Cecilia⁹ Reher, Dorothy Geneva⁸ Pegan, Harry Clark⁷, Samuel Alexander⁶, Andrew⁵, Robert A.⁴, Andrew³, Andrew² Pagan, James¹*) was born on November 16, 1955, in Euclid, Cuyahoga Co., Ohio.[109] He was the son of James Gary Kondos and Rosena Cecilia Reher (99). Thomas George Kondos died in Hazelwood, St. Louis Co., Missouri, on January 13, 2009, at age 53.[109, 829]

Stephen Mark Kondos married and had one daughter.

135. **Stephen Mark¹⁰ Kondos** (*Rosena Cecilia⁹ Reher, Dorothy Geneva⁸ Pegan, Harry Clark⁷, Samuel Alexander⁶, Andrew⁵, Robert A.⁴, Andrew³, Andrew² Pagan, James¹*) was born on May 10, 1959, in Euclid, Cuyahoga Co., Ohio.[109, 830] He was the son of James Gary Kondos and Rosena Cecilia Reher (99). Stephen Mark Kondos died in Hazelwood, St. Louis Co., Missouri, on September 13, 2013, at age 54.[109]

136. **Michael Kevin¹⁰ McCann** (*Herbert Eugene⁹, Flora Josephine⁸ Pegan, Harry Clark⁷, Samuel Alexander⁶, Andrew⁵, Robert A.⁴, Andrew³, Andrew² Pagan, James¹*) was born on April 5, 1953, in New York, New York.[109, 847] He was the son of Herbert Eugene McCann II (103) and LaVerne Marie Gallagher. Michael Kevin died in Madison, Davidson Co., Tennessee, on May 19, 2004, at age 51.[109, 847]

He married **Cheryl L. Unknown**. They divorced.

137. **Sharon L.¹⁰ MacQueen** (*Ada Frances⁹ McCann, Flora Josephine⁸ Pegan, Harry Clark⁷, Samuel Alexander⁶, Andrew⁵, Robert A.⁴, Andrew³, Andrew² Pagan, James¹*) was born on May 25, 1945, in Dearborn Heights, Wayne Co., Michigan.[109] She was the daughter of Leslie E. MacQueen and Ada Frances McCann (104). Sharon L. lived in 1989 in Westland, Wayne Co., Michigan. Sharon L. died in Gaylord, Bagley Twp., Otsego Co., Michigan, on October 12, 2012, at age 67.[109, 850]

Sharon L. married **Donald Benjamin Rainey** before 1967. They had two sons. Donald Benjamin Rainey was born in Arkansas? on May 13, 1942.[109] Donald Benjamin reached age 71 and died in Gaylord, Bagley Twp., Otsego Co., Michigan, on December 21, 2013.[109]

138. **Patrick Dominic¹⁰ Pratto** (*Shirley Theresa⁹ McCann, Flora Josephine⁸ Pegan, Harry Clark⁷, Samuel Alexander⁶, Andrew⁵, Robert A.⁴, Andrew³, Andrew² Pagan, James¹*) was born on November 4, 1947, in Detroit, Wayne Co., Michigan.[855] He was the son of Albert Dominic Pratto and Shirley Theresa McCann (105). Patrick Dominic died in Gilbert, Maricopa Co., Arizona, on December 8, 2011, at age 64.[855]

Patrick Dominic married and had two children.

139. **Jeanine Marie¹⁰ Pratto** (*Shirley Theresa⁹ McCann, Flora Josephine⁸ Pegan, Harry Clark⁷, Samuel Alexander⁶, Andrew⁵, Robert A.⁴, Andrew³, Andrew² Pagan, James¹*) was born on December 3, 1952, in Detroit, Wayne Co., Michigan.[856, 857] She was the daughter of Albert Dominic Pratto and Shirley Theresa McCann (105). Jeanine Marie lived in Livonia, Wayne Co., Michigan. She died in a hospital in Detroit, Wayne Co., Michigan, on March 11, 1964, at age 11.[856, 857, 858] Jeanine Marie was buried in Holy Sepulchre Cemetery, Southfield, Oakland Co., Michigan.[857, 897]

11th Generation

140. Thomas Lewis[11] Kelso (*Son[10], George Lewis[9], Lewis Sinclair (Pegan)[8], Sinclair Edwin[7] Pegan, William Henry[6], Andrew[5], Robert A.[4], Andrew[3], Andrew[2] Pagan, James[1]*) was born on June 19, 1972, in Fremont, Alameda Co., California.[894, 895] He was the son of Son Kelso (131) and his wife. Thomas Lewis died in Fremont, Alameda Co., California, on June 20, 1972.[894] He was buried in Irvington Memorial Cemetery, Fremont, Alameda Co., California.[898]

Endnotes

1. Family Data: Robert and Christina "Engle" Pegan family bible, American Bible Society, Brattleboro(ugh), Vermont: Holbrook & Fessenden, 1828. In possession of the author, Ann Miller Carr.

2. Obituary of Andrew Pegan (Clarksville, Missouri, Calumet Banner, 31 Aug 1894), Pike County, Missouri Genealogical Society Library, 100 West Church Street, Bowling Green, MO.

3. Pike County, Missouri Death Records, 1878-1917, Ancestry.com, Andrew Pegan.

4. Greenwood Cemetery Records, Clarksville, Calumet Twp., Pike Co., Missouri, Andrew Pegan. Clarksville City Hall, 111 Howard Street, Clarksville, MO.

5. Ohio, County Marriages, 1789-2013, FamilySearch.org, Andrew Pegan and Jane McKibben, Clinton County, Ohio Marriage Records, Vol. 2, pg. 223.

6. Obituary of Mary Pegan (Clarksville, Missouri, Clarksville Sentinel, 17 Dec 1895), Pike County, Missouri Genealogical Society Library, 100 West Church Street, Bowling Green, MO.

7. Pike County, Missouri Death Records, 1878-1917, Ancestry.com, Mrs. Mary Pegan.

8. Greenwood Cemetery Records, Clarksville, Calumet Twp., Pike Co., Missouri, Mary Pegan. Clarksville City Hall, 111 Howard Street, Clarksville, MO.

9. Thomas C. and Aurelia Kelsey to Andrew Pegan, Pike County, Missouri Deed Records, Vol. 27, pgs. 130-131. Pike County, Missouri Recorder of Deeds, 115 West Main Street #2, Bowling Green, MO.

10. Andrew Pegan v. John Pegan, James Mulherin, Pike County, Missouri Common Pleas Court, Pike County, Missouri Circuit Clerk, Civil & Probate Division, 115 West Main Street #24, Bowling Green, MO.

11. Find A Grave—Gulf Prairie Cemetery (also Peach Point Cemetery), Jones Creek, Brazoria Co., Texas, Find A Grave.com, Leonidas Pegan, Find A Grave Memorial #66561018.

12. Obituary of Leonidas ("L.") Pegan (Burlington, Iowa, Weekly Hawk Eye and Telegraph, 12 Apr 1883), Newspapers and Periodicals, Ancestry.com.

13. Pike County Chapter of the DAR, *Cemetery Inscriptions. Pike County, Missouri, Vol. II*, Pike County Chapter of the DAR: Louisiana, Missouri; 1984, pg. 69, Calumet Township., Greenwood Cemetery: Pegan, Joseph. Genealogy Center, Allen County Public Library, 900 Library Plaza, Fort Wayne, IN.

14. Pike County Chapter of the DAR, *Cemetery Inscriptions. Pike County, Missouri, Vol. II*, pg. 128, Calumet Township, Greenwood Cemetery, Kelley, Mrs. John.

15. Obituary of William Pegan (Xenia, Ohio, Xenia Republican, 12 Oct 1914), Greene County Public Library-Xenia Community Library, Greene County Room, 76 East Market Street, Xenia, OH.

16. Ohio Death Certificate, Ohio Department of Health, Center for Vital and Health Statistics, 246 North High Street, Columbus, OH, William H. Pegan, death cert. #55192.

17. California Death Certificate, California Health and Strategic Planning, Vital Records, M.S. 5103, P.O. Box 997410, Sacramento, CA, James Pegan, death cert. #13-020640.

18. California Death Index, 1905-1940, FamilySearch.org, James Pegan, Index Book A, pg. 8448, California Death Record Book 1913, cert. #20640.

19. Missouri Death Certificates, 1910-1966, Missouri Secretary of State, 600 West Main Street, Jefferson City, MO; Online database: http://s1.sos.mo.gov/records/archives/archivesmvc/deathcertificates, John Pegan, death certificate #15814.

20. Missouri, Death Records 1834-1910, Ancestry.com, "Pete" Pegan, St. Louis City, Missouri death cert. #978-2237. Although the death certificate does not say "Samuel", Samuel A. Pegan's obituary (Clarksville, Missouri, Clarksville Banner, 13 Apr 1906) confirms the same age, death date and place and reason for death for Samuel as this "Pete". Also, both parents are listed as born in Ohio, which matches with Samuel A. Pegan.

21. Obituary of Samuel A. Pegan (Clarksville, Missouri, Clarksville Banner, 13 Apr 1906), Pike County, Missouri Genealogical Society Library, 100 West Church Street, Bowling Green, MO.

22. Missouri Death Certificates, 1910-1966, Missouri Secretary of State, 600 West Main Street, Jefferson City, MO; Online database: http://s1.sos.mo.gov/records/archives/archivesmvc/deathcertificates, Robert A. Pegan, death cert. #24679.

23. Ohio, County Marriages, 1789-2013, FamilySearch.org, Leonidas "Pagan" and Martha J. "Pagan", Clinton County, Ohio Marriage Records, Vol. 1, pg. 105.

24. Find A Grave—Glenwood Cemetery, Houston, Harris Co., Texas, Find A Grave.com, Martha Jane (Mrs. Reuben R.) "Mattie" Brown, Find A Grave Memorial #108603016.

25. Texas Death Certificate, Texas Department of State Health Services, Vital Statistics Unit, 1100 West 49th Street, Austin, TX, Mattie Brown, death cert. #14453.

26. Glenwood Cemetery Records (Texas), Glenwood Cemetery (Texas), 2525 Washington Avenue, Houston, TX, Buried in section H-3, lot #024 with a gravestone.

27. Martha J. Brown, denied U.S. Civil War Widow's Pension Application, #837545, NARA: Washington, DC.

28. Iowa State Census Collection, 1836-1925, Ancestry.com, 1865: Leonidas Pegan, Roll IA-64, pg. 60, line 30.

29. Leonidas Pegan, denied U.S. Civil War Pension Application, #252858, NARA: Washington, DC.

30 Email from the Gulf Prairie Cemetery Association, PO Box 98, Brazoria, TX to Ann Miller Carr, author, 22 Aug 2015.

31 Texas, County Marriage Index, 1837-1973, Reuben R. Brown and Martha J. Pegan, FamilySearch.org; Online database: https://familysearch.org/ark:/61903/1:1:XLQ6-VHM.

32 Obituary of Colonel Reuben Brown (Velasco, Texas, Velasco Times, 09 Mar 1894), Brazoria, Texas Historical Museum, Brazoria County Courthouse, 111 East Locust Street, Brazoria, TX.

33 "The Galveston Hurricane of 1900", National Oceanic and Atmospheric Administration, U.S. Department of Commerce, NOAA, Silver Spring, MD; Website: Online database: https://oceanservice.noaa.gov/news/features/sep13/galveston.html

34 Brazoria County, Texas Deeds, Mrs. Reuben R. Brown to Sam Lazarus and the City of St. Louis, Missouri, Book D, Vol. 66, pg. 580, (14 Aug 1905). Brazoria County, Texas Clerk's Office, Real Property Records Office, East Annex, 1524 East Mulberry Street, Angleton, TX.

35 Brazoria County, Texas Deeds, Mrs. Reuben R. Brown to St. Louis and Brownsville Railway, Deed Book D., Vol. 71, pg.182 (21 Aug 1905). Brazoria County, Texas Clerk's Office, Real Property Records Office, East Annex, 1524 East Mulberry Street, Angleton, TX.

36 Brazoria County, Texas Deeds, Martha Jane Brown to J.A. Hollingsworth, Book D, Vol. 82, pg. 499 (23 Nov 1908). Brazoria County, Texas Clerk's Office, Real Property Records Office, East Annex, 1524 East Mulberry Street, Angleton, TX.

37 Brazoria County, Texas Deeds, Mrs. R.R. Brown to T.J. McMillan, Book D, Vol. 102, pg. 462 (12 Jan 1911). Brazoria County, Texas Clerk's Office, Real Property Records Office, East Annex, 1524 East Mulberry Street, Angleton, TX.

38 Brazoria County, Texas Deeds, Estate of R.R. Brown, Mrs. Reuben R. Brown, Will (14 Jan 1915). Brazoria County, Texas Clerk's Office, Real Property Records Office, East Annex, 1524 East Mulberry Street, Angleton, TX.

39 Mrs. Reuben R. Brown probate, Harris County, Texas #007293 (filed 24 Jun 1916, closed 06 Sep 1916). Harris County Clerk, Probate Department, Civil Courthouse, 201 Caroline Street, Suite 100, Houston, TX.

40 Find-A-Grave—Gulf Prairie Cemetery (also Peach Point Cemetery), Jones Creek, Brazoria Co., Texas, Findagrave.com, Maj. Reuben Rodolphus Brown, Find A Grave Memorial #13971209.

41 Find A Grave—Greenwood Cemetery, Clarksville, Calumet Twp., Pike Co., Missouri, Find A Grave.com, Joseph Pegan, Find A Grave Memorial #100362035.

42 "James R. Pagin", *History of Porter County, Indiana: A Narrative History of its Progress, its People and Principal Interests*. Chicago: Lewis Publishing Co.; 1912, pg. 692. Genealogy Center, Allen County Public Library, 900 Library Plaza, Fort Wayne, IN.

43 Gilbert, Audrey, *Twin Valley Tidbits, 1888-1897, Vol. 3*. New Alexandria, Ohio: A. Gilbert; 1999, pg. 72. Lynchburg Public Library, 120 Main Street, Lynchburg, OH.

44 Missouri Marriages, 1750-1920, FamilySearch.org, Joseph "Pogan" and M.E. Curry, Audrain County, Missouri Marriage Records, Vol. A, pg. 358.

45 Obituary of Mrs. Mary Elizabeth Curry Pegan (Clarksville, Missouri, Clarksville Sentinel, 05 Mar 1937), Pike County, Missouri Genealogical Society Library, 100 West Church Street, Bowling Green, MO.

46 Missouri Death Certificates, 1910-1966, Missouri Secretary of State, 600 West Main Street, Jefferson City, MO; Online database: http://s1.sos.mo.gov/records/archives/archivesmvc/deathcertificates, Mary Elizabeth Curry Pegan death cert. #7658.

47 Find A Grave—Greenwood Cemetery, Clarksville, Calumet Twp., Pike Co., Missouri, Find A Grave.com, Mary E. Curry Pegan, Find A Grave Memorial# 100362037.

48 Pike County Chapter of the DAR, *Cemetery Inscriptions. Pike County, Missouri, Vol. II*, pg. 69, Calumet Township Greenwood Cemetery, Pegan, Mary E.

49 U.S., Civil War Pension Index: General Index to Pension Files, 1861-1934, Ancestry.com, Joseph Pegan, application #358875; Mary Pegan, widow's application #746946. Original file at NARA, Washington, DC.

50 Missouri Death Certificates, 1910-1966, Missouri Secretary of State, 600 West Main Street, Jefferson City, MO; Online database: http://s1.sos.mo.gov/records/archives/archivesmvc/deathcertificates, Leonidas Pegan "Tegan", death cert. #41436.

51 Illinois, Deaths and Stillbirths Index, 1916-1947, Ancestry.com, Alex Pegan, death cert. #0034116.

52 Illinois Death Certificate, Illinois Department of Public Health, Division of Vital Records, 605 West Jefferson Street, Springfield, IL, Alex Pegan, death cert. #34116.

53 Illinois Statewide Death Index, 1916-1950, Illinois State Archives, Margaret Cross Norton Building, Capitol Complex, Springfield, IL, http://www.ilsos.gov/isavital/idphdeathsrch.jsp.

54 Missouri Death Certificates, 1910-1966, Missouri Secretary of State, 600 West Main Street, Jefferson City, MO; Online database: http://s1.sos.mo.gov/records/archives/archivesmvc/deathcertificates, Charles H. Pegan, death cert. #41774.

55 Missouri Death Certificates, 1910-1966, Missouri Secretary of State, 600 West Main Street, Jefferson City, MO; Online database: http://s1.sos.mo.gov/records/archives/archivesmvc/deathcertificates, Josephine Reed, death cert. #41063.

56 Missouri Death Certificates, 1910-1966, Missouri Secretary of State, 600 West Main Street, Jefferson City, MO; Online database: http://s1.sos.mo.gov/records/archives/archivesmvc/deathcertificates, Nora Lee Crossen, death cert. #1948-10887.

57 Missouri Death Certificates, 1910-1966, Missouri Secretary of State, 600 West Main Street, Jefferson City, MO; Online database: http://s1.sos.mo.gov/records/archives/archivesmvc/deathcertificates, Edwin Pegan, death certificate #30410.

58 Find A Grave—Greenwood Cemetery, Clarksville, Calumet Twp., Pike Co., Missouri, Find A Grave.com, Mary J. Kelley, Find A Grave Memorial #100125260.

59 Missouri Death Certificates, 1910-1966, Missouri Secretary of State, 600 West Main Street, Jefferson City, MO; Online database: http://s1.sos.mo.gov/records/archives/archivesmvc/deathcertificates, Lorenzo Kelley, death cert. #2409

60 "'Louie Kelly' Passes Away" (Clarksville, Missouri, Clarksville Banner, 04 Dec 1918), Pike County, Missouri Genealogical Society Library, 100 West Church Street, Bowling Green, MO.

61 Ohio, County Marriages, 1789-2013, FamilySearch.org, John "Kelly" and Mary J. "Pagan", Clinton County, Ohio Marriage Records, Vol. 1, pg. 170.

62 Missouri Death Certificates, 1910-1966, Missouri Secretary of State, 600 West Main Street, Jefferson City, MO; Online database: http://s1.sos.mo.gov/records/archives/archivesmvc/deathcertificates, John Kelley, death cert. #42330.

63 Obituary of John "Kelly" (Clarksville, Missouri, Clarksville Banner, 29 Dec 1910), Pike County, Missouri Genealogical Society Library, 100 West Church Street, Bowling Green, MO.

64 Pike County Chapter of the DAR, *Cemetery Inscriptions. Pike County, Missouri, Vol. II*, pg. 128, Calumet Township, Greenwood Cemetery, Kelley, John.

65 Find A Grave—Greenwood Cemetery, Clarksville, Calumet Twp., Pike Co., Missouri, Find A Grave.com, John Kelley, Find A Grave Memorial #100125240.

66 Montana Death Certificate, State of Montana, Department of Health and Human Services, Office of Vital Statistics, 111 North Sanders, Room 6, Helena, MT, John A. Kelley, death cert. #DL5961.

67 Montana Death Certificate, State of Montana, Department of Health and Human Services, Office of Vital Statistics, 111 North Sanders, Room 6, Helena, MT, Harrison Kelley, cert. # HAV 1334.

68 Missouri Death Certificates, 1910-1966, Missouri Secretary of State, 600 West Main Street, Jefferson City, MO; Online database: http://s1.sos.mo.gov/records/archives/archivesmvc/deathcertificates, Lewis Album Kelley, death cert. #22035.

69 Missouri Death Certificates, 1910-1966, Missouri Secretary of State, 600 West Main Street, Jefferson City, MO; Online database: http://s1.sos.mo.gov/records/archives/archivesmvc/deathcertificates, Joshua Kelley, death cert. #43533.

70 Missouri Death Certificates, 1910-1966, Missouri Secretary of State, 600 West Main Street, Jefferson City, MO; Online database: http://s1.sos.mo.gov/records/archives/archivesmvc/deathcertificates, Fannie Kelley Shaw, death cert. #15766.

71 Find A Grave—Old Silvercreek Cemetery, Jamestown, Silvercreek Twp., Greene Co., Ohio, Find A Grave.com, William H. Pegan, Find A Grave Memorial #84193076.

72 Ohio, County Marriages, 1789-2013, FamilySearch.org, William Henry Pegan and Mary Liggett, Highland County, Ohio Marriage Records, Vol. 7, pg. 283, lic. #408.

73 Obituary of Mary McIllheney (Watertown, New York, Watertown Daily Times, 18 Apr 1918), Flower Memorial Library, 229 Washington Street, Watertown, NY.

74 Watertown, New York, city directory, 1919, pg. 331, entry for Mary McIlhenny. Flower Memorial Library, 229 Washington Street, Watertown, NY.

75 Find A Grave—Troutwine Cemetery, Dodson Twp., Highland Co., Ohio, Find A Grave.com, Mary Liggett McIllhenny, Find A Grave Memorial #128710650.

76 The Genealogical Committee of The Clinton County Historical Society, Cemetery Records of Clinton Co., Ohio, 1798-1998, Troutwine Cemetery: Mary Liggett McIlhenny. Clinton County, Ohio Records Center and Archives, 111 South Nelson Avenue, Suite 3, Wilmington, OH.

77 All U.S., Civil War Draft Registration Records, 1863-1865, Ancestry.com, William H. Pegan, Dodson, Ohio.

78 U.S., Civil War Soldiers, 1961-1865, Ancestry.com, William H. Pegan, Company I, 79th Ohio Infantry.

79 Landon, Harry, *The North Country: A History, Embracing Jefferson, St. Lawrence, Oswego, Lewis and Franklin Counties, New York, Vol. II*. Indianapolis, Indiana: Historical Publishing Company, 1932, "Gilbert David Gregor, M.D.", pg. 553.

80 Ohio, County Marriages, 1789-2013, FamilySearch.org, William H. Pegan and Hattie Griffith, Greene County, Ohio Marriage Records, Vol. 8, pg. 261.

81 Ohio Death Certificate, Ohio Department of Health, Center for Vital and Health Statistics, 246 North High Street, Columbus, OH, Hattie Pegan certificate #28756.

82 Obituary of Hattie Pegan (Xenia, Ohio, Xenia Evening Gazette, 20 May 1938), Greene County Public Library-Xenia Community Library, Greene County Room, 76 East Market Street, Xenia, OH.

83 Find A Grave—Old Silvercreek Cemetery, Jamestown, Silvercreek Twp., Greene Co., Ohio, Find A Grave.com, Harriet A. Pegan, Find A Grave Memorial #84193064.

84 Utah Digital Newspapers, "Married" (Salt Lake City, Utah, Salt Lake Tribune, 15 Sep 1877), hosted by the University of Utah, J. W. Marriott Library, 295 South 1500 East, Salt Lake City, UT; https://newspapers.lib.utah.edu/details?id=12993973

85 Utah Digital Newspapers, "Found Dead" (Salt Lake City, Utah, Deseret News, 13 Aug 1884); https://newspapers.lib.utah.edu/details?id=2654385

86 Utah Digital Newspapers, "Progressive Euchre" (Park City, Utah, Park Record, 15 Aug 1885); https://newspapers.lib.utah.edu/details?id=8299557

87 Utah Digital Newspapers, "Park City" (Salt Lake City, Utah, Salt Lake Herald, 15 Sep 1901); https://newspapers.lib.utah.edu/details?id=10367487

88 Washington Death Certificates, 1907-1960, FamilySearch.org, Ed. S. Pegan, b. 11 Sep 1860, d. 09 Nov 1922, cert. #392.

89 Obituary of Elizabeth "Libbie" Pegan Gregor (Watertown, New York, Watertown Daily Times, 18 Sep 1926), Flower Memorial Library, 229 Washington Street, Watertown, NY.

90 Find A Grave—Brookside Cemetery, Watertown, Jefferson Co., New York, Find A Grave.com, Elizabeth Pegan Gregor, Find A Grave Memorial #115018920.

91 Obituary of Mrs. Elizabeth Pegan Gregor (Wilmington, Ohio, Wilmington News, 20 Sep 1926), The Clinton County History Center, 149 East Locust Street, Wilmington, OH.

92 New York, Death Index, 1880-1956, Ancestry.com, "Elizabeth P. Gregory", death cert. #56312.

93 Florida Death Index 1877-1998, Ancestry.com, Inez Owens, death cert. #102044.

94 Obituary of Inez Mae Owens (St. Petersburg, Fl, St. Petersburg Times, 05 Nov 1983), Largo Library, 201 Highland Avenue NE, Largo, FL.

95 Obituary of James Pegan (Yuba City, Sutter Co., California, Sutter County Farmer, 27 Jun 1913), Marysville Public Library, 231 South Plum Street, Marysville, OH.

96 U.S., Civil War Draft Registration Records, 1863-1865, Ancestry.com: James Pegan, Slough, California.

97 Western States Marriage Index, Brigham Young University, BYU-Idaho Special Collections: McKay Library 240A, Rexburg, ID familyhistory@byui.edu, James Robert Pegan and Mrs. Queen Galbraith, Sutter County, Marriage Vol. B, pg. 77, ID#244324 http://abish.byui.edu/specialCollections/westernStates/westernStatesRecordDetail.cfm?recordID=244324.

98 "Married" (Yuba City, California, Weekly Sutter Banner, 03 Oct 1868), Marysville Public Library, 231 South Plum Street, Marysville, CA. http://abish.byui.edu specialCollections/westernStates/westernStatesRecordDetail.cfm?recordID=244324.

99 California Death Certificate, California Health and Strategic Planning, Vital Records, M.S. 5103, P.O. Box 997410, Sacramento, CA, Queen Isabella Pegan, death cert. #21-016556.

100 California Death Index, 1905-1940, FamilySearch.org, Queen Pegan, Index Book A., pg. 8448, California Death Record Book 1921, cert. #16556.

101 Obituary of "Belle" Pegan (Marysville, California, Marysville Democrat, 18 Apr 1921), Marysville Public Library, 231 South Plum Street, Marysville, CA.

102 "1866 - 1884 Voters Register For Shasta County, P – RO", Transcribed and Donated to Rootsweb by Madge Richardson Walsh, Copyright ©1993, Rootsweb.com, http://freepages.genealogy.rootsweb.ancestry.com/~shastaca/1866p-ro.html

103 James Pegan (California, Shasta) patent #1072, U.S. Bureau of Land Management, "Patent Search", digital images, General Land Office Records, http://www.glorecords.blm.gove/PatentSearch

104 "Insane Woman" (Los Angeles, California, Los Angeles Herald, 31 Dec 1897), Chronicling America, Library of Congress, 101 Independence Avenue SE, Washington, DC. Online database: http://chroniclingamerica.loc.gov/lccn/sn85042461/1897-12-31/ed-1/seq-10/#

105 "Was Old Time Resident Of This County; Death of James Pegan at Stockton Last Monday—Funeral Here Tuesday" (Yuba City, California, Yuba City Farmer, 27 Jun 1913), Marysville Public Library, 231 South Plum Street, Marysville, CA.

106 California, Death Index, 1940-1997, Ancestry.com, Carrie Etta Stevenson.

107 Sutter County, California Burial Records, Sutter County, California Historical Society, Community Memorial Museum of Sutter County, 1333 Butte House Road, Yuba City, CA, Franklin Andrew Pegan.

108 California, Death Index, 1940-1997, Ancestry.com, Ruby Zetta Paganetti.

109 Social Security Death Index, Ancestry.com.

110 Obituary of Ruby Z. Paganetti (Redwood City, California, Redwood City Tribune, 23 Feb 1976), California State Library, California History Room, 900 N Street, Sacramento, CA.

111 California, Death Index, 1940-1997, Ancestry.com, Zoa Faretta Camp

112 California Death Certificate, California Health and Strategic Planning, Vital Records, M.S. 5103, P.O. Box 997410, Sacramento, CA, Zoa Camp, death cert. #61-032397.

113 Find A Grave—Greenwood Cemetery, Clarksville, Calumet Twp., Pike Co., Missouri, Find A Grave.com, John S. Pegan, Find A Grave Memorial #150200883.

114 Pike County, Missouri Marriage Records, Pike County Clerk's Office, Pike County Courthouse 115 West Main Street, #24 Bowling Green, MO 63334, Pike County, Missouri Marriage Records, Vol. 4, pg. 36.

115 Missouri Marriage Records, 1805-2002, Ancestry.com, Pike County, Missouri Marriage Records, Vol. 4, pg. 36.

116 Find A Grave—Greenwood Cemetery, Clarksville, Calumet Twp., Pike Co., Missouri, Find A Grave.com, Margaret Pegan, Find A Grave Memorial #100361435.

117 Pike County Chapter of the DAR, *Cemetery Inscriptions. Pike County, Missouri, Vol. II*, pg. 69, Calumet Township, Greenwood Cemetery, Margaret, wife of John Pegan, died May 23, 1869, Aged 21 yrs., 9 mos., 28 da.

118 Missouri Marriages, 1750-1920, FamilySearch.org, John "Pagans" and Nannie Jeans, Pike County, Missouri Marriage Records, Vol. 5, pg. 71.

119 Missouri Death Certificates, 1910-1966, Missouri Secretary of State, 600 West Main Street, Jefferson City, MO; Online database: http://s1.sos.mo.gov/records/archives/archivesmvc/deathcertificates, Nannie Vaughn Pegan, death cert. #7497.

120 Find A Grave—Greenwood Cemetery, Clarksville, Calumet Twp., Pike Co., Missouri, Find A Grave.com, Nannie V. Pegan, Find A Grave Memorial #150200912.

121 Find A Grave—Greenwood Cemetery, Clarksville, Calumet Twp., Pike Co., Missouri, Find A Grave.com, Flora Pegan, Find A Grave Memorial #100361439.

122 Pike County Chapter of the DAR, *Cemetery Inscriptions. Pike County, Missouri, Vol. II*, pg. 69, Calumet Township, Greenwood Cemetery, Flora Pegan, died Aug. 21, 1875, Aged 8 yrs., 9 mos.

123 Obituary of Flora Pegan (Louisiana, Missouri, Riverside Press, 02 Sep 1875), Pike County, Missouri Genealogical Society Library, 100 West Church Street, Bowling Green, MO.

124 Mount Mora Cemetery Records, Andrew M. Pegan, Mount Mora Cemetery, 824 Mount Mora Road, St. Joseph, MO.

125 Washington Death Certificates, 1907-1960, FamilySearch.org, Andrew Pegan, d. 10 Dec 1910 in Spokane, cert. #1423.

126 U.S., WWI Draft Registration Cards, 1917-1918, Ancestry.com, Morrow W. "Pagan" in Moberly, Randolph Co., Missouri.

127 U.S., Social Security Applications and Claims Index, 1936-2007, Ancestry.com, Morrow Walton Pegan.

128 Obituary of Morrow W. Pegan (Bowling Green, Missouri, Bowling Green Times, 06 Apr 1970), The State Historical Society of Missouri, 1020 Lowry Street, Columbia, MO.

129 Greenwood Cemetery Records, Clarksville, Calumet Twp., Pike Co., Missouri, Morrow W. Pegan. Clarksville City Hall, 111 Howard Street, Clarksville, MO.

130 California, Voter Registers, 1866-1898, Ancestry.com, Samuel A. Pegan, 1866, Yuba City, California.

131 U.S. City Directories, 1822-1995, Ancestry.com, Corbett, Hoye and Co.'s Fourth Annual City Directory City of Denver 1876, pg. 191. Ancestry.com, entry for Pegan, Samuel, machinist.

132 California, Voter Registers, 1866-1898, Ancestry.com, Samuel A. Pegan, 1876, Yuba City, California.

133 California, Voter Registers, 1866-1898, Ancestry.com, Samuel A. Pegan, 1879, Yuba City, California.

134 Missouri Marriages, 1750-1920, FamilySearch.org, Samuel Pegan and Flora Johnson, Pike County, Missouri Marriage Records, Vol. 4, pg. 36.

135 Pike County, Missouri Marriage Records, Pike County Clerk's Office, Pike County Courthouse, 115 West Main Street, #24, Bowling Green, MO 63334, Samuel Pegan and Flora Johnston, Pike County, Missouri Marriage Records, Vol. 4, pg. 36.

136 Missouri Death Certificates, 1910-1966, Missouri Secretary of State, 600 West Main Street, Jefferson City, MO; Online database: http://s1.sos.mo.gov/records/archives/archivesmvc/deathcertificates, Flora Pegan, death certificate #11875.

137 Find A Grave—Greenwood Cemetery, Clarksville, Calumet Twp., Pike Co., Missouri, Find A Grave.com, Flora Pegan, Find A Grave Memorial #182442973.

138 U.S. City Directories, Ancestry.com, St. Louis, Missouri, 1890, pg. 1074, entry for Pegan, Samuel A., carpenter.

139 Pike County, Missouri Marriage Records, Pike County Clerk's Office, Pike County Courthouse, 115 West Main Street, #24, Bowling Green, MO 63334, S.A. Pegan and Jessie Taylor, Pike County, Missouri Marriage Records, Vol. 10, pg. 150.

140 "Ask St. Louis Magazine: Was There Once a Potter's Field in South St. Louis?", *St. Louis Magazine* online, 10 Jul 2007, https://www.stlmag.com/Ask-STLMag-Was-there-once-a-potters-field-in-South-St-Louis/

141 Missouri Death Certificates, 1910-1966, Missouri Secretary of State, 600 West Main Street, Jefferson City, MO; Online database: http://s1.sos.mo.gov/records/archives/archivesmvc/deathcertificates, Harry C. Pegan death certificate #34950.

142 Find A Grave—Mt. Washington Cemetery, Independence, Jackson Co., Missouri, Find A Grave.com, Robert A. Pegan, Find A Grave Memorial #79821258.

143 Missouri Marriage Records, 1805-2002, Ancestry.com, Robert A. Pegan and Jessie Farrington, Carroll County, Missouri Marriage Records, pg. 218, lic. #804.

144 Missouri Death Certificates, 1910-1966, Missouri Secretary of State, 600 West Main Street, Jefferson City, MO; Online database: http://s1.sos.mo.gov/records/archives/archivesmvc/deathcertificates, Jessie Pegan, death certificate #30943.

145 Find A Grave—Mt. Washington Cemetery, Independence, Jackson Co., Missouri, Find A Grave.com, Jessie Pegan, Find A Grave Memorial #79821278.

146 U.S., Civil War Draft Registration Records, 1863-1865, Ancestry.com, entry for Josiah Farrington, Waterville, Ohio.

147 U.S. City Directories, 1822-1995, Ancestry.com, St. Joseph, Missouri, 1893, pg. 391, entry for Pegan, Robert A.

148 Hunting a Dead Man's Body" (Quincy, Illinois, Quincy Daily Journal, 23 Oct 1894), Quincy Public Library, 526 Jersey Street, Quincy, IL; Online database; http://archive.quincylibrary.org/Olive/APA/QPL/default.aspx#panel=document

149 All Missouri, Birth Registers, 1847-1910, Ancestry.com, "Pegan", Kansas City, Jackson Co., fa: R.A., mo: "Jennie".

150 California, Death Index, 1940-1997, Ancestry.com, Robert D. Pegan.

151 California Death Certificate, California Health and Strategic Planning, Vital Records, M.S. 5103, P.O. Box 997410, Sacramento, CA, Robert D. Pegan, death cert. #76-128852.

152 Obituary of "Alonzo" Pegan (Louisiana, Missouri, Louisiana Press Journal, 12 Dec 1918), Pike County, Missouri Genealogical Society Library, 100 West Church Street, Bowling Green, MO.

153 Missouri Marriage Records, 1805-2002, Ancestry.com, Alexander Pegan and Dempsey Bass, Pike County, Missouri Marriage Records, Book 8, pg. 185.

154 California Death Certificate, California Health and Strategic Planning, Vital Records, M.S. 5103, P.O. Box 997410, Sacramento, CA, Dempsey Pegan, death cert. #36-047762.

155 Find A Grave—Angeles Abbey Memorial Park Cemetery, Compton, Los Angeles Co., California, Find A Grave.com, Dempsey Bass Pegan, Find A Grave Memorial #181631226.

156 U.S. City Directories, 1822-1995, Ancestry.com, Hannibal, Missouri city directory, 1925, pg. 139, entry for Gough, Frances P.; pg. 228, entry for Pegan, Dempsey S., Pegan, Luther and Pegan, Carl.

157 U.S., Social Security Applications and Claims Index, 1936-2007, Ancestry.com, Frances Pegan Gough.

158 California, Death Index, 1940-1997, Ancestry.com, Frances P. Gough.

159 Oregon Death Certificate, Oregon Public Health Division, Center for Health Statistics & Vital Records, 800 NE Oregon Street, Suite 205, Portland, OR, Otho M. Pegan, death cert. #1216.

160 Oregon, Death Index, 1898-2008, Ancestry.com, Otho M. Pegan, Multnomah Co., death cert. #1216.

161 Texas, Deaths, 1890-1976, FamilySearch.org, Luther C. Pegan, death cert. #46363.

162 Texas Death Index, 1903-2000, Ancestry.com, Luther Pegan.

163 Find A Grave—Greenwood Cemetery, Clarksville, Calumet Twp., Pike Co., Missouri, Find A Grave.com, Charles H. Pegan, Find A Grave Memorial #97438995.

164 Pike County, Missouri Marriage Records, Pike County Clerk's Office, Pike County Courthouse 115 West Main Street, #24, Bowling Green, MO 63334, Charles H. "Pegam" and Lilly Belle Knowles, Pike County, Missouri Marriage Records, Book 8, pg. 117.

165 Illinois, Deaths and Stillbirths Index, 1916-1947, Ancestry.com, Lilly Bracken.

166 Illinois Death Certificate, Illinois Department of Public Health, Division of Vital Records, 605 West Jefferson Street, Springfield, IL, Lilly Bracken, death cert. #13419 (1945).

167 Obituary of Lilly Bracken (Carthage, IL, Antioch Journal, 05 Apr 1945), Hancock County Historical Society, 306 Walnut Street, Carthage, IL.

168 Find A Grave—Dallas City Cemetery, Lomax Twp., Henderson Co., Illinois, Find A Grave.com, Lilly Bell Knowles Bracken, Find A Grave Memorial #84799908.

169 Adams County, Illinois Marriage Records, Adams County, Illinois Clerk's Office, 507 Vermont Street, Quincy, IL, C.H. Pegan and Alida Blackstun, Adams County, Illinois Marriage Records, Book 1908, cert. #17842.

170 Missouri Death Certificates, 1910-1966, Missouri Secretary of State, 600 West Main Street, Jefferson City, MO; Online database: http://s1.sos.mo.gov/records/archives/archivesmvc/deathcertificates, Minerva A. Pegan, death cert. #14374.

171 Find A Grave—Long Cemetery, Belleview Twp., Calhoun Co., Illinois, Find A Grave.com, Alida Minerva Goeway Pegan, Find A Grave Memorial #122048974.

172 "Abram Goeway", *Portrait and Biographical Album of Pike and Calhoun Counties, Illinois*. Chicago: Biographical Publishing Co., 1891, pg. 445.

173 "Clarksville Couple Weds" (Quincy, Illinois, Quincy Daily Journal, 23 Oct 1908), Quincy Public Library, 526 Jersey Street, Quincy, IL; Online database: http://archive.quincylibrary.org/Olive/APA/QPL/default.aspx#panel / pegan"

174 Missouri Marriage Records, 1805-2002, Ancestry.com, C.H. Pegan and Alida Blackstun, Pike County, Missouri Marriage Records, Vol. 15, pg. 627.

175 Pike County, Missouri Marriage Records, Pike County Clerk's Office, Pike County Courthouse, 115 West Main Street, #24, Bowling Green, MO 63334, C. H. Pegan and Ona Jones, Pike County, Missouri Marriage Records, Book 18, pg. 256.

176 Missouri Death Certificates, 1910-1966, Missouri Secretary of State, 600 West Main Street, Jefferson City, MO; Online database: http://s1.sos.mo.gov/records/archives/archivesmvc/deathcertificates, Ona E. Pegan, death certificate #3031.

177 Find A Grave—Greenwood Cemetery, Clarksville, Calumet Twp., Pike Co., Missouri, Find A Grave.com, Ona S. Pegan, Find A Grave Memorial #97438992.

178 Missouri Marriage Records, 1805-2002, Ancestry.com, William Bracken and Mrs. Lilly Pegan, Randolph County, Missouri Marriage Records, Vol. 12, pg. 294.

179 Missouri Death Certificates, 1910-1966, Missouri Secretary of State, 600 West Main Street, Jefferson City, MO; Online database: http://s1.sos.mo.gov/records/archives/archivesmvc/deathcertificates, Grace M. Ewing, death cert. #28610.

180 Illinois Death Certificate, Illinois Department of Public Health, Division of Vital Records, 605 West Jefferson Street, Springfield, IL, Alta Lee Brown, death cert. #81361.

181 Find A Grave—Oak Grove Cemetery, Bel-Nor, St. Louis Co., Missouri, Find A Grave.com, Josephine Reed, Find A-Grave Memorial #175641888.

182 Missouri Marriage Records, 1805-2002, Ancestry.com, Major O. Martin and Josephine Pegan, Pike County, Missouri Marriage Records, Book 8, pg. 263.

183 Missouri Death Certificates, 1910-1966, Missouri Secretary of State, 600 West Main Street, Jefferson City, MO; Online database: http://s1.sos.mo.gov/records/archives/archivesmvc/deathcertificates, Major O. Martin, death cert. #25801.

184 Find A Grave—Oak Grove Cemetery, Bel-Nor, St. Louis Co., Missouri, Find A Grave.com, Major O. Martin, Find A Grave Memorial #175641785.

185 Pike County, Missouri Marriage Records, Pike County Clerk's Office, Pike County Courthouse, 115 West Main Street, #24, Bowling Green, MO 63334, Angus Reed and Josephine Martin, Pike County, Missouri Marriage Records, Book 24, pg. 617.

186 Missouri Death Certificates, 1910-1966, Missouri Secretary of State, 600 West Main Street, Jefferson City, MO; Online database: http://s1.sos.mo.gov/records/archives/archivesmvc/deathcertificates, Angus Reed, death cert. #32568.

187 Find A Grave—Riverview Cemetery, Buffalo Twp., Pike Co., Missouri, Find A Grave.com, Angus Frederick Reed, Find A Grave Memorial # 65568385.

188 St. Louis County, Missouri Marriage Records, St. Louis County Public Library, 1640 South Lindbergh Boulevard, St.

Louis, MO, Clifford Y. Lucas and Lorraine Martin, St. Louis County Marriage Records, Vol. 86, pg. 23.

189 Obituary of Lorraine Lucas (St. Louis, Missouri, St. Louis Post-Dispatch, 29 Feb 1976, pg. 40), St. Louis County Public Library, 1640 South Lindbergh Boulevard, St. Louis, MO.

190 Find A Grave—Oak Hill Cemetery, Kirkwood, St. Louis Co., Missouri, Find A Grave.com, Nora Lee Crossen, Find A Grave Memorial #73319646.

191 Missouri Marriage Records, 1805-2002, Ancestry.com, Samuel "Rulan" (Reneau) and Nora Lee Pegan, Pike County, Missouri Marriage Records, Book 9, pg. 189.

192 Find A Grave—Peaceful Pines Cemetery, Rochester, White Court Census Division, Alberta, Canada, Find A Grave.com, Samuel Houston Reneau, Find A Grave Memorial # 86207770.

193 Find A Grave—Peaceful Pines Cemetery, Rochester, White Court Census Division, Alberta, Canada, Find A Grave.com, Agnes C. Reneau, Find A Grave Memorial #86207767; James Reneau, #86207768; Robert Mathew Reneau, #86207769, Mildred Reneau, #86207771.

194 St. Louis County, Missouri Marriage Records, St. Louis County Public Library, 1640 South Lindbergh Boulevard, St. Louis, MO, Archibald Crosson and Nora Lee Reneau, St. Louis County, Missouri Marriage Records, Vol. 84, pg. 398, cert. #201875.

195 Missouri Death Certificates, 1910-1966, Missouri Secretary of State, 600 West Main Street, Jefferson City, MO; Online database: http://s1.sos.mo.gov/records/archives/archivesmvc/deathcertificates, Archie Crosson, death cert. #19694.

196 Find A Grave—Oak Hill Cemetery, Kirkwood, St. Louis Co., Missouri, Find A Grave.com, Archie Crossen, Find A Grave Memorial #73319645.

197 Missouri Death Certificates, 1910-1966, Missouri Secretary of State, 600 West Main Street, Jefferson City, MO; Online database: http://s1.sos.mo.gov/records/archives/archivesmvc/deathcertificates, Hazel Brockman, death cert. #41622.

198 Find A Grave—Greenwood Cemetery, Clarksville, Calumet Twp., Pike Co., Missouri, Find A Grave.com, Edwin Pegan, Find A Grave Memorial #100362050.

199 Pike County, Missouri Marriage Records, Pike County Clerk's Office, Pike County Courthouse, 115 West Main Street, #24 Bowling Green, MO 63334, Edwin Pegan and Emma Oliver, Pike County, Missouri Marriage Records, Book 24, pg. 273.

200 Missouri Death Certificates, 1910-1966, Missouri Secretary of State, 600 West Main Street, Jefferson City, MO; Online database: http://s1.sos.mo.gov/records/archives/archivesmvc/deathcertificates, Emma Lou Pegan, death cert. #62-003138.

201 Find A Grave—Greenwood Cemetery, Clarksville, Calumet Twp., Pike Co., Missouri, Find A Grave.com, Emma Lou Higgens Pegan, Find A Grave Memorial #105583493.

202 Find A Grave—Greenwood Cemetery, Clarksville, Calumet Twp., Pike Co., Missouri, Find A Grave.com, Lorenzo Kelley, Find A Grave Memorial #100125228.

203 Pike County, Missouri Probate Records, Pike County Circuit Clerk, Civil & Probate Division, Pike County Courthouse, 115 West Main Street, #24, Bowling Green, MO. "Louie" Kelley, Vol. Y, pg. 479.

204 Pike County, Missouri Probate Records, Pike County Circuit Clerk, Civil & Probate Division, Pike County Courthouse, 115 West Main Street, #24, Bowling Green, MO. John Kelley, Vol. Z, pg. 210.

205 Obituary of Louis Kelly (sic) (Clarksville, Missouri, Clarksville Banner, 04 May 1944), Pike County, Missouri Genealogical Society Library, 100 West Church Street, Bowling Green, MO. This was really Lewis A. Kelley, whose nickname was "Allie". His brother Lorenzo was commonly called, "Louie".

206 Missouri Marriage Records, 1805-2002, Ancestry.com, Lewis A. Kelley and Sallie Carlisle.

207 Missouri Death Certificates, 1910-1966, Missouri Secretary of State, 600 West Main Street, Jefferson City, MO; Online database: http://s1.sos.mo.gov/records/archives/archivesmvc/deathcertificates, Sarah C. Kelley, death cert. #63-025128.

208 Obituary of Sarah "Sallie" Kelley (Monroe, Missouri, Monroe City News, 04 Jul 1963), The State Historical Society of Missouri, 1020 Lowry Street, Columbia, MO.

209 Find A Grave—Saint Jude Cemetery, Monroe, Monroe Twp., Monroe Co., Missouri, Find A Grave.com, Sarah C. Kelley, Find A Grave Memorial #182411761.

210 Obituary of Mary Etta Kelley (Monroe, Missouri, Monroe City News, 04 Jul 1963), The State Historical Society of Missouri, 1020 Lowry Street, Columbia, MO.

211 Michigan Death Certificate, State of Michigan Vital Records Office, Office of Vital Records, Michigan Department of Community Health, Capitol View Building 3rd Floor, 201 Townsend Street, Lansing, MI, Alice Lucille Green, death cert. #97-1382526.

212 U.S. WWII Draft Cards Young Men, 1940-1947, Ancestry.com, John Carlisle Kelley, St. Louis, Missouri.

213 Obituary of John Carlisle Kelley (St. Louis, Missouri, St. Louis Post Dispatch, 07 Jan 1967), St. Louis County Public Library, 1640 South Lindbergh Boulevard, St. Louis, MO.

214 Missouri Marriage Records, 1805-2002, Ancestry.com, "Archbald Crosson" and Laura Kelley, Pike County, Missouri Marriage Records, Book 9, pg. 313.

215 Phone conversations with and emails from Ms. Frances Stanley of Virginia, who soon will be the Rev. Frances Stanley. Frances is a Eudailey-Crosson family historian. She and the author, Ann Miller Carr, have become friends through genealogy, and have collaborated in researching Laura Belle "Lollie" Kelley Crosson Baldwin Unknown, Frances' great-great-grandmother. But, despite years of searching, Laura remains a "brick wall" as of this book's publication. We have not been able to find out what happened to her, or her correct birth date, her death information, or any information about her third husband and where or exactly when they married.

216 Virginia, Marriages, 1785-1940, FamilySearch.org, Robt. N. Baldwin and Mrs. Laura B. Crosson, 16 Feb 1916; citing Lunenburg, Virginia, pg. 116, #13.

217 Pre-1891 Registration Records, St. John's East District, Vol. 32, Church of England Baptisms, Pouch Cove, pg. 19 (2013), Newfoundland Grand Banks: Historical and Genealogical Data, Transcribed by Bonnie Clark. http://ngb.chebucto.org/Vstats/pre-1891-pouch-cove-ce-bap-1841-1891-p-1-41-sje.shtml Captured March 12, 2015,

218 Virginia Death Certificate, Commonwealth of Virginia State Board of Health, Vital Records/Health Statistics, 2001 Maywill Street, Richmond, VA, Robert Newell Baldwin, death cert. #1920-20165.

219 Virginia, Death Records, 1912-2014, Ancestry.com, Robert Newell Baldwin, state file #20165.

220 Find A Grave—Cool Spring Cemetery, Chickahominy, Lunenburg Co., Virginia, Find A Grave.com, Robert N. "Roy" Baldwin, Find A Grave Memorial #161439614.

221 Border Crossings: From U.S. to Canada, 1908-1935, Ancestry.com, Library and Archives Canada; *Border Entries;* Roll: *T-5461: R.M. Baldwin and Laura Baldwin.*

222 U.S., Border Crossings from Canada to U.S., 1895-1960, Ancestry.com, The National Archives at Washington, D.C.; Washington, D.C.; *Manifests of Alien Arrivals at Buffalo, Lewiston, Niagara Falls, and Rochester, New York, 1902-1954;* Record Group Title: *Records of the Immigration and Naturalization Service, 1787 - 2004;* Record Group Number: *85;* Series Number: *M1480;* Roll Number: *012: Robert Baldwin and Laura Baldwin.*

223 Find A Grave—Cool Spring Christian Church Cemetery, Chickahominy, Lunenburg Co., Virginia, Find A Grave.com, Maurene C. Eudailey, Find A Grave Memorial #84552636.

224 Virginia, Death Records, 1912-2014, Ancestry.com, "Maurene Crossing Eudailey", state file #87-045202.

225 Find A Grave—Bethany Cemetery, Foley, Burr Oak Twp., Lincoln Co., Missouri, Find A Grave.com, Joshua Kelley, Find A Grave Memorial #93985270.

226 Lincoln County, Missouri Marriage Records, Lincoln County Recorder of Deeds, 201 Main Street, Suite 203, Troy, MO, Joshua Kelley and May Dixon, Lincoln County, Missouri Marriage Records, Vol. 10, pg. 113.

227 Missouri Death Certificates, 1910-1966, Missouri Secretary of State, 600 West Main Street, Jefferson City, MO; Online database: http://s1.sos.mo.gov/records/archives/archivesmvc/deathcertificates, May Missouri Kelley, death cert. #63-029095.

228 Find A Grave—Bethany Cemetery, Foley, Burr Oak Twp., Lincoln Co., Missouri, Find A Grave.com, May Missouri Dixon Kelley, Find A Grave Memorial #93985382.

229 Find A Grave—Greenwood Cemetery, Clarksville, Calumet Twp., Pike Co., Missouri, Find A Grave.com, Fannie Kelley Shaw, Find A Grave Memorial #126131747.

230 Greenwood Cemetery Records, Clarksville, Calumet Twp., Pike Co., Missouri, Fannie A. Shaw. Clarksville City Hall, 111 Howard Street, Clarksville, MO.

231 Pike County, Missouri Marriage Records, Pike County Clerk's Office, Pike County Courthouse, 115 West Main Street, #24 Bowling Green, MO 63334, George H. Shaw and Fannie A. Kelley, Pike County, Missouri Marriage Records, Vol.12, pg. 274.

232 Missouri Death Certificates, 1910-1966, Missouri Secretary of State, 600 West Main Street, Jefferson City, MO; Online database: http://s1.sos.mo.gov/records/archives/archivesmvc/deathcertificates, George Henry Shaw, death cert. #59-012543.

233 Find A Grave—Greenwood Cemetery, Clarksville, Calumet Twp., Pike Co., Missouri, Find A Grave.com, George H. Shaw, Find A Grave Memorial #100361831.

234 Find A Grave—Fairmount Memorial Park Cemetery, Spokane, Spokane Co., Washington, Findagrave.com, Edwin S. Pegan, Find A Grave Memorial #150197745.

235 Utah Digital Newspapers, "The Musical and Literary Soiree" (Park City, Utah, Park Record, 20 Dec 1884); https://newspapers.lib.utah.edu/details?id=8294634

236 Utah Digital Newspapers "Progressive Euchre" (Park City, Utah, Park Record, 15 Aug 1885); https://newspapers.lib.utah.edu/details?id=8299557

237 Marriage Announcement of Edwin S. Pegan and Emma Kelso (Park City, Utah, Park City Recorder, 25 Sep 1886), Park City Library, 1354 Park Avenue, Park City, UT

238 California Death Certificate, California Health and Strategic Planning, Vital Records, M.S. 5103, P.O. Box 997410, Sacramento, CA, Emma Kelso, death cert. #28-028978.

239 California Death Index, 1905-1940, FamilySearch.org, Emma Kelso, California Death Index A, pg. 710, California Deaths Volume 1928, cert. #28978.

240 Find A Grave—Chapel of the Chimes Columbarium and Mausoleum, Oakland, Alameda Co., California, Find A Grave.com, Emma May Kelso, Find A Grave Memorial #181627380.

241 Utah Digital Newspapers, "Women's Athenaeum" (Park City, Utah, Park Record, 27 Feb 1904); https://newspapers.lib.utah.edu/details?id=8343218

242 Utah Digital Newspapers, "Third District Court" (Coalville, Utah, Coalville Times, 11 Jun 1897); https://newspapers.lib.utah.edu/details?id=647287&q=pegan&rows=50&facet_paper=%22Coalville+Times%22&year_t=1897

243 Utah Digital Newspapers, "Park Record…Mrs. C.H. Witley…" (Park City, Utah, Park Record, 15 Apr 1899); https://newspapers.lib.utah.edu/details?id=8326982

244 Utah Digital Newspapers, "Park City Society" (Park City, Utah, Park Record, 11 Aug 1900); https://newspapers.lib.utah.edu/details?id=8331461

245 Utah, County Marriages, 1887-1940, FamilySearch.org, S.E. Pegan and Kate Martin, Summit Co., Utah Marriage Records, pg. 308.

246 Washington Death Certificates, 1907-1960, FamilySearch.org, Kate Martin Pegan, d. 31 Aug 1921, cert. #849 (age wrong on death cert.as she had to be born on 02 May 1874).

247 Find A Grave—Fairmount Memorial Park Cemetery, Spokane, Spokane Co., Washington, Find A Grave.com, Kate M. Martin Pegan, Find A Grave Memorial #150197780.

248 Utah Digital Newspapers, "Ed Pegan Hurt" (Park City, Utah, Park Record, 14 Apr 1900); https://newspapers.lib.utah.edu/details?id=8330346

249 Utah Digital Newspapers, "Park Float…Mrs. S.E. Pegan…" (Park City, Utah, Park Record, 20 Aug 1904); https://newspapers.lib.utah.edu/details?id=8343083

250 Utah Digital Newspapers, "Society Notes…Mrs. S.E. Pegan…" (Park City, Utah, Park Record, 20 Aug 1904); https://newspapers.lib.utah.edu/details?id=8343083

251 Utah Digital Newspapers, "Park City Society…Mrs. Ed Pegan…" (Salt Lake City, Utah, Salt Lake Tribune, 23 Oct 1904); https://newspapers.lib.utah.edu/details?id=13685406

252 Utah Digital Newspapers, "Park City Society" (Park City, Utah, Park Record, 28 May 1905); https://newspapers.lib.utah.edu/details?id=13754447

253 Utah Digital Newspapers, "History of Park City Miner's Hospital" (Park City, Utah, Park Record, 22 May 1925); https://newspapers.lib.utah.edu/details?id=7976998

254 Utah Digital Newspapers, "Personal Mention…Chas. T. Frisk…" (Park City, Utah, Park Record, 24 Oct 1908); https://newspapers.lib.utah.edu/details?id=7932315

255 Utah Digital Newspapers, "Political Points" (Park City, Utah, Park Record, 10 Oct 1903); https://newspapers.lib.utah.edu/details?id=8340688

256 Utah Digital Newspapers, "Socialists Take Lead" (Park City, Utah, Park Record, 05 Oct 1907); https://newspapers.lib.utah.edu/details?id=7928876

257 Utah Digital Newspapers, "Things Political" (Park City, Utah, Park Record, 12 Oct 1907); https://newspapers.lib.utah.edu/details?id=7928924

258 Utah Digital Newspapers, "Democratic Convention" (Park City, Utah, Park Record, 22 Oct 1915); https://newspapers.lib.utah.edu/details?id=7952223

259 Utah Digital Newspapers, "Delinquent Tax List for Summit County" (Park City, Utah, Park Record, 10 Dec 1915); https://newspapers.lib.utah.edu/details?id=7952714

260 Utah Digital Newspapers, "Delinquent Tax List for Summit County" (Park City, Utah, Park Record, 08 Dec 1916); https://newspapers.lib.utah.edu/details?id=7955522

261 Utah Digital Newspapers, "Delinquent Tax List" (Park City, Utah, Park Record, 12 Dec 1917); https://newspapers.lib.utah.edu/details?id=7958487

262 Utah Digital Newspapers, "Society and Personal" (Park City, Utah, Park Record, 25 Aug 1916); https://newspapers.lib.utah.edu/details?id=7954641

263 Utah, County Marriages, 1887-1940, FamilySearch.org, Victor E. Ridge and Eleanor McLaughlin, Salt Lake County Marriage Records, Book 45, cert. #17687.

264 Utah, Salt Lake County Death Records, 1908-1949, FamilySearch.org, Eleanor McLaughlin Ridge, cert. #I-4II.

265 Utah Death Certificates, 1904-1964, FamilySearch.org, Eleanor Mclaughlin Ridge, state file #1456320.

266 California, Death Index, 1940-1997, Ancestry.com, Lewis Sinclair Kelso.

267 U.S., Social Security Applications and Claims Index, 1936-2007, Ancestry.com, Lewis S. Kelso.

268 Obituary of Lewis (Pegan) Kelso (Oakland, California, Oakland Tribune, 14 Feb 1954), San Francisco Public Library, Main Branch, 100 Larkin Street, San Francisco, CA.

269 Washington, Death Index, 1940-2014, Ancestry.com, Mary E. Boggs, death cert. #001524.

270 Obituary of Mary Boggs (Bremerton, Washington, Bremerton Sun, 05 Jan 1973), Kitsap Regional Library, 1301 Sylvan Way, Bremerton, WA.

271 State of Washington, Washington Death Certificate (Olympia, Washington, Washington State Department of Health), Washington State Department of Health, Center for Health Statistics, Town Center 1, 101 Israel Road SE, Tumwater, WA, Mary Elizabeth Boggs, death cert. #1524.

272 Obituary of Grace Pegan Boggs (Seattle, Washington, Seattle Times, 08 Nov 1998), Washington State Library, Reference Section, Point Plaza East, 6880 Capitol Boulevard SE, Tumwater, WA.

273 Find A Grave—Fort Sam Houston Cemetery, San Antonio, Bexar Co., Texas, Find A Grave.com, John E. Pegan Sr., Find A Grave Memorial #3040824.

274 Texas Death Certificate, Texas Department of State Health Services, Vital Statistics Unit, 1100 West 49th Street, Austin, TX, John E. Pegan Sr., death cert. #04522.

275 U.S., Department of Veterans Affairs BIRLS Death File, 1850-2010, Ancestry.com, John Pegan.

276 Texas Death Index, 1903-2000, Ancestry.com, John Pegan Sr.

277 Utah Digital Newspapers, "Park City Pickings" (Salt Lake City, Utah, Salt Lake Herald, 08 Aug 1885); https://newspapers.lib.utah.edu/details?id=10862776.

278 Utah Digital Newspapers, "Personal Mention" (Park City, Utah, Park Record, 29 Aug 1885); https://newspapers.lib.utah.edu/details?id=8299797.

279 Kentucky Digital Library, hosted by the University of Kentucky, William T. Young University Library, 401 Hilltop Avenue, Lexington, KY; "Church Affairs" (Stanford, Kentucky, Semi Weekly Interior Journal, 04 Nov 1890); http://kdl.kyvl.org/catalog/xt7wd3pxk5x_2/viewer

280 Kentucky Digital Library, "Column" (Stanford, Kentucky, Semi Weekly Interior Journal, 07 Apr 1891); http://kdl.kyvl.org/catalog/xt7wm32n7r7g_3

281 Kentucky Digital Library, "The entertainment given…" (Stanford, Kentucky, Semi Weekly Interior Journal, 10 Apr 1891); http://kdl.kyvl.org/catalog/xt7kh12v5s0q_5

282 Kentucky, County Marriages, 1785-1979, FamilySearch.org, Gilbert D. Gregor and Elizabeth J. Pegan. Jefferson County, Kentucky Marriage Records. They married in Louisville. "Libbie" Pegan was teaching at Millersburg women's college in the area, and also had uncles on her Liggett side living in Louisville.

283 Obituary of Gilbert D. Gregor (Dr.) (Watertown, New York, Watertown Daily Times, 19 Mar 1931), Flower Memorial Library, 229 Washington Street, Watertown, NY.

284 Find A Grave—Brookside Cemetery, Watertown, Jefferson Co., New York, Find A Grave.com, Gilbert David Gregor, Find A Grave Memorial #115018860.

285 New York, County Marriages, 1847-1849, 1907-1936, FamilySearch.org, Roderick Pirnie and Mary Margaret Gregor, Jefferson County, New York Marriage Records, 1914-1922, pg. 250, lic. #6246. Lists Mary's father's birthplace.

286 New York, Death Index, 1880-1956, Ancestry.com, Gilbert D. Gregor, death cert. #15530.

287 Utah Digital Newspapers, "Returned" (Park City, Utah, Park Record, 01 Aug 1891); https://newspapers.lib.utah.edu/details?id=8314570

288 Utah Digital Newspapers, "Park Float" (Park City, Utah, Park Record, 16 Jan 1892); https://newspapers.lib.utah.edu/details?id=8312546

289 Utah Digital Newspapers, "Stockholders Are Liable" (Park City, Utah, Park Record, 09 Jul 1898); https://newspapers.lib.utah.edu/details?id=8325728

290 Utah Digital Newspapers, "Mrs. Gregor's Farewell" (Park City, Utah, Park Record, 30 Apr 1898); https://newspapers.lib.utah.edu/details?id=8324872

291 Utah Deaths and Burials, 1888-1946, FamilySearch.org, Infant Gregor, Infant Gregor, source film #1654374, batch number, B54990-8, reference # p 1 rn 4.

292 Utah Births and Christenings, 1892-1941, FamilySearch.org, David G. Gregor, source film #1654376, batch #C74658-8, reference #p6 n43.

293 Obituary of David G. Gregor (Watertown, New York, Watertown Daily Times, 18 Oct 1954), Flower Memorial Library, 229 Washington Street, Watertown, NY, (Watertown, New York) Watertown Daily Times, pub. 18 Oct 1954.

294 New York, Death Index, 1880-1956, Ancestry.com, David G. Gregor, death cert. #61977.

295 Utah Births and Christenings, 1892-1941, FamilySearch.org, Mary Margaret Gregor, source film #1654376, batch #C74658-8, reference #p12 n11.

296 Obituary of Mary Margaret Sexsmith (Mrs. J.R. Sexsmith) (Watertown, New York, Watertown Daily Times, 08 May 1975), Flower Memorial Library, 229 Washington Street, Watertown, NY.

297 Kentucky, County Marriages, 1785-1979, FamilySearch.org, H.M. Owens and Inez Pegan.

298 U.S., WWI Draft Registration Cards, 1917-1918, Ancestry.com, Harold Munger Owens, Xenia, Ohio.

299 Obituary of Harold M. Owens (Xenia, Ohio, Xenia Daily Gazette, 30 Mar 1965), Greene County Public Library-Xenia Community Library, Greene County Room, 76 East Market Street, Xenia, OH.

300 Florida Death Index 1877-1998, Ancestry.com, Harold M. Owens, death cert. #16301.

301 Find A Grave—Vale Road Cemetery, Springfield, Springfield Twp., Clark Co., Ohio, Find A Grave.com, Harold M. Owens, Find A Grave Memorial #182415434.

302 "Kept Marriage a Secret for a Year (Xenia, Ohio, Xenia Daily Gazette, 19 Jul 1910), Newspaper Archive, Online database: https://access.newspaperarchive.com/us/ohio/xenia/xenia-daily-gazette/1910/07-19/page-8?tag=Inez

303 Find A Grave—Sutter Cemetery, Sutter, Sutter Co., California, Find A Grave.com, Carrie Etta Stevenson, Find A Grave Memorial #126181004.

304 California, County Marriages, 1850-1952, FamilySearch.org, Augustus VanBlarcum and Carietta Pegan, Sutter County, California Marriage Records, Vol. J, pg. 209.

305 California Death Certificate, California Health and Strategic Planning, Vital Records, M.S. 5103, P.O. Box 997410, Sacramento, CA, Augustus Saxton VanBlarcom, death cert. #22-052989.

306 California Death Index, 1905-1940, FamilySearch.org, Augustus Vanblarcum, Index Book A, pg. 11138, California Death Record Book 1922, cert. #52989.

307 U.S. City Directories, 1822-1995, Ancestry.com, Polk-Husted Co., Oakland, California, 1916, pg. 850: entry for VanBlarcom, Augustus S.

308 Obituary of Augustus A. Van Blarcom (San Diego, California, San Diego Union, 07 Dec 1922), San Diego Public Library, 330 Park Boulevard, San Diego, CA.

309 California, County Marriages, 1850-1952, FamilySearch.org, Daniel McKenzie Stevenson and Carrie E. Vanblarcom, Sutter County, California Marriage Records.

310 U.S., WWI Draft Registration Cards, 1917-1918, Ancestry.com, Daniel McKenzie Stevenson.

311 California, Death Index, 1940-1997, Ancestry.com, Daniel M. Stevenson.

312 Find A Grave—Sutter Cemetery, Sutter, Sutter Co., California, Find A Grave.com, Daniel M. Stevenson, Find A Grave Memorial #126181038.

313 Obituary of Zetta Paganetti (San Mateo, California, San Mateo Times, 23 Feb 1978), San Francisco Public Library, Main Branch, 100 Larkin Street, San Francisco, CA.

314 Find A Grave—Skylawn Memorial Park Cemetery, San Mateo, San Mateo Co., California, Find A Grave.com, Ruby Zetta Paganetti, Find A Grave Memorial #164487850.

315 Who's Who Among the Women of California, ed. by Louis S. Lyons, acting ed. Josephine Wilson, San Francisco: Security Publishing Co., 1922, pg. 527: Pegan, Miss Z.

316 California, Voter Registrations, 1900-1968, Ancestry.com, 1930, entry for Pegan, Miss Ruby Z.

317 California, Death Index, 1940-1997, Ancestry.com, Angelo Anthony Paganetti.

318 "Farmer Seeks Wife in Fire, Perishes" (San Mateo, California, San Mateo Times, 22 Aug 1966), San Mateo Public Library, 55 West 3rd Avenue, San Mateo, CA.

319 U.S., WWII Draft Registration Cards, 1942, Ancestry.com, Angelo Paganetti, San Francisco, California.

320 Find A Grave—Skylawn Memorial Park Cemetery, San Mateo, San Mateo Co., California, Find A Grave.com, Angelo A. Paganetti, Find A Grave Memorial #164487851.

321 U.S. City Directories, 1822-1995, Ancestry.com, San Francisco, California, 1932, pg. 931: entries for "Paganelli", Angleo "Paganelli, Zetta".

322 Find A Grave—Santa Clara Mission Cemetery, Santa Clara, Santa Clara Co., California, Find A Grave.com, Zoa Camp, Find A Grave Memorial #182440261.

323 California, County Marriages, 1850-1952, FamilySearch.org, Ernest F. Camp and Zoa F. Pegan, San Joaquin County, California Marriage Records, Book M, Vol. 15, pg. 265, lic. #5551.

324 U.S., WWI Draft Registration Cards, 1917-1918, Ancestry.com, Ernest Camp in San Diego, San Diego Co., California.

325 California Death Index, 1905-1940, FamilySearch.org, Ernest Camp, Index Book B., pg. 993, California Death Record Book 1937, cert. #11550.

326 California Death Certificate, California Health and Strategic Planning, Vital Records, M.S. 5103, P.O. Box 997410, Sacramento, CA, Ernest Camp, death cert. #37-011550.

327 Find A Grave—Inglewood Park Cemetery, Inglewood, Los Angeles Co., California, Find A Grave.com, Ernest Camp, Find A Grave Memorial #182440356.

328 California Birth Index, 1905-1995, Ancestry.com, Richard E. Camp.

329 California, Death Index, 1940-1997, Ancestry.com, Richard E. Camp.

330 California Death Certificate, California Health and Strategic Planning, Vital Records, M.S. 5103, P.O. Box 997410, Sacramento, CA, Richard Ernie Camp, death cert. #63-134546.

331 Find A Grave—Mount Mora Cemetery, St. Joseph, Washington Twp. Buchanan Co., Missouri, Find A Grave.com, Andrew Pegan, Find A Grave Memoria l#83440104.

332 U.S. City Directories, 1822-1995, Ancestry.com, St. Joseph, Missouri, 1888, pg. 381: entry for Pegan, Andrew, clerk at Martin and Sheridan Bros.

333 Missouri Marriage Records, 1805-2002, Ancestry.com, Andrew M. Pegan and Ella Young, Buchanan County, Missouri Marriage Records, Vol. K, pg. 48, lic. #175.

334 Buchanan County, Missouri Recorder of Deeds, Buchanan County, Missouri Recorder of Deeds, 411 Jules Street, Room 103, St. Joseph, MO, Buchanan County Marriage Records, Andrew M. Pegan and Ella Young, Vol. K, pg. 48, lic. #175.

335 Missouri Death Certificates, 1910-1966, Missouri Secretary of State, 600 West Main Street, Jefferson City, MO; Online database: http://s1.sos.mo.gov/records/archives/archivesmvc/deathcertificates, Ella M. Pegan, death certificate #26349.

336 Mount Mora Cemetery Records, Ella M. Pegan, Mount Mora Cemetery, 824 Mount Mora Road, St. Joseph, MO.

337 Find A Grave—Mount Mora Cemetery, St. Joseph, Washington Twp. Buchanan Co., Missouri, Find A Grave.com, Ella Pegan, Find A Grave Memorial #182440848.

338 U.S. City Directories, 1822-1995, Ancestry.com, St. Joseph, Missouri, 1895, pg. 397: entry for Pegan, Andrew, clerk (probably at Martin and Sheridan Bros, as listed the two prior years).

339 "Hotel Arrivals: Grand Central: A.M. Pegan and son" (Albuquerque New Mexico, Albuquerque Daily Citizen, 03 May 1899), Chronicling America: Historic American Newspapers, Library of Congress, 101 Independence Avenue SE, Washington, D.C.; Online database: Image provided by the University of New Mexico; http://chroniclingamerica.loc.gov/lccn/sn84020613/1899-05-03/ed-1/seq-2/#date1=1836&index=3&date2=1922&searchType=advanced&language=&sequence=0&lccn=sn84020613&words=Pegan&proxdistance=5&state=New+Mexico&rows=20&ortext=&proxtext=&phrasetext=pegan&andtext=&dateFilterType=yearRange&page=1

340 "Officers Elected" (Albuquerque New Mexico, Albuquerque Daily Citizen, 20 Apr 1903), Chronicling America: Historic American Newspapers, Library of Congress, 101 Independence Avenue SE, Washington, D.C.; Online database: http://chroniclingamerica.loc.gov/lccn/sn84020613/1903-04-20/ed-1/seq-4/#date1=1836&index=1&date2=1922&searchType=advanced&language=&sequence=0&lccn=sn84020613&words=Pegan&proxdistance=5&state=New+Mexico&rows=20-&ortext=&proxtext).

341 Obituary of James A. Pegan (St. Joseph, Missouri, St. Joseph Gazette, 17 Feb 1981), St. Joseph Public LIbrary, 927 Felix Street, St. Joseph, MO.

342 Find A Grave—Greenwood Cemetery, Clarksville, Calumet Twp., Pike Co., Missouri, Find A Grave.com, Morrow W. Pegan, Find A Grave Memorial #104714664.

343 Missouri Marriage Records, 1805-2002, Ancestry.com, M.W. Pegan and Julia Meloan, Randolph County, Missouri Marriage Records, Vol. 11, pg. 159.

344 Randolph County, Missouri Marriage Records, Randolph County, Missouri Recorder's Office, 110 South Main Street, Huntsville, MO, M.W. Pegan and Julia Meloan, Randolph County, Missouri Marriage Records, Vol., 11, pg. 159.

345 Missouri Death Certificates, 1910-1966, Missouri Secretary of State, 600 West Main Street, Jefferson City, MO; Online database: http://s1.sos.mo.gov/records/archives/archivesmvc/deathcertificates, Julia Meloan Pegan, death certificate #18472.

346 Greenwood Cemetery Records, Clarksville, Calumet Twp., Pike Co., Missouri, Juia Meloan Pegan. Clarksville City Hall, 111 Howard Street, Clarksville, MO.

347 Missouri Death Certificates, 1910-1966, Missouri Secretary of State, 600 West Main Street, Jefferson City, MO; Online database: http://s1.sos.mo.gov/records/archives/archivesmvc/deathcertificates, Julia Meloan Pegan, death certificate #18472.

348 Missouri Death Certificates, 1910-1966, Missouri Secretary of State, 600 West Main Street, Jefferson City, MO; Online database: http://s1.sos.mo.gov/records/archives/archivesmvc/deathcertificates, Jane Temple "Pigan", death cert. #13076.

349 Find A Grave—Greenwood Cemetery, Clarksville, Calumet Twp., Pike Co., Missouri, Find A Grave.com, Mary B. Pegan, Find A Grave Memorial #104714657.

350 U.S., Social Security Applications and Claims Index, 1936-2007, Ancestry.com, John Robert Pegan.

351 Obituary of John Robert Pegan (Boise, Idaho, The Idaho Statesman, 27 Jan 2004), Boise Public Library, 715 South Capitol Avenue, Boise, ID.

352 Find A Grave—Nebo Cemetery, Nebo, Spring Creek Twp., Pike Co., Illinois, Find A Grave.com, Harry Pegan, Find A Grave Memorial #85296073.

353 Quincy, Illinois Public Library Newspaper Archive, ("Brevities', Quincy, Illinois, Quincy Morning Whig, 15 Nov 1893); Online database: http://archive.quincylibrary.org/Olive/APA/QPL/default.aspx#panel=document

354 Illinois Statewide Marriage Index 1763-1900, Illinois State Archives, Margaret Cross Norton Building, Capitol Complex, Springfield, IL, Harry Clark Pegan and Vinnie Mary Abair.

355 Pike County, Illinois Marriage Records, Pike County, Illinois Clerk, Pike County Government Building, 121 East Washington Street, Pittsfield, IL, Harry C. Pegan and Vinnie Abair, Pike County, Illinois Marriage Records, Book 4, pg. 27, lic. #00000019.

356 Missouri Death Certificates, 1910-1966, Missouri Secretary of State, 600 West Main Street, Jefferson City, MO; Online database: http://s1.sos.mo.gov/records/archives/archivesmvc/deathcertificates, Vinnie Mary Niemann, death cert. #26233.

357 Find A Grave—Nebo Cemetery, Nebo, Spring Creek Twp., Pike Co., Illinois, Find A Grave.com, Vinnie Mary Main Niemann, Find A Grave Memorial #131178236.

358 Marion County, Missouri Marriage Records, Marion County, Missouri Clerk's Office, 101 South Main Street, #107, Palmyra, MO, Albert J. Niemann and Vinnie Pegan, Marion County, Missouri Marriage Records, Book 19, pg. 162.

359 Family records: Email from Dorothy Geneva Pegan Reher Gaines' niece in Phoenix, AZ to the author, Ann Miller Carr, on 04 Feb 2012.

360 California, Death Index, 1940-1997, Ancestry.com, Erman Henry Pegan.

361 California Death Certificate, California Health and Strategic Planning, Vital Records, M.S. 5103, P.O. Box 997410, Sacramento, CA, Erman Henry Pegan, death cert. #0190-021693.

362 California, Death Index, 1940-1997, Ancestry.com, Flora Josephine Shields.

363 Michigan Death Certificate, State of Michigan Vital Records Office, Office of Vital Records, Michigan Department of Community Health, Capitol View Building 3rd Floor, 201 Townsend Street, Lansing, MI, Baby McCann, death certificate #58288204.

364 California Death Certificate, California Health and Strategic Planning, Vital Records, M.S. 5103, P.O. Box 997410, Sacramento, CA, Flora Josephine Shields, death cert. #79-075512.

365 Find A Grave—Willamette National Cemetery, Portland, Multnomah Co., Oregon, Find A Grave.com, Robert D. Pegan, Find A Grave Memorial # 36328184.

366 U.S. Veterans' Gravesites, ca. 1775-2006, Ancestry.com, Robert D. Pegan.

367 Missouri Marriage Records, 1805-2002, Ancestry.com, R. Donald Pegan and Helen P. Stults, Jackson County, Missouri Marriage Records, cert. #A65459.

368 California, Death Index, 1940-1997, Ancestry.com, Helen P. Pegan.

369 California Death Certificate, California Health and Strategic Planning, Vital Records, M.S. 5103, P.O. Box 997410, Sacramento, CA, Helen Pauline Pegan, death cert. #64-011803.

370 Find A Grave—Valhalla Memorial Park Cemetery, North Hollywood, Los Angeles Co., California, Find A Grave.com, Helen Pegan, Find A Grave Memorial #182442829.

371 U.S. City Directories, 1822-1995, Ancestry.com, Joplin, Missouri, 1937, pg. 268: entry for Pegan, R. Donald.

372 U.S., WWII Army Enlistment Records, 1938-1946, Ancestry.com, Robert D. Pegan, Los Angeles, California.

373 Missouri Marriage Records, 1805-2002, Ancestry.com, Eugene B. O'Reilly and Helen P. Stults, lic. #12614.

374 Find A Grave—Angeles Abbey Memorial Park Cemetery, Compton, Los Angeles Co., California, Find A Grave.com, Stella Gough, Find A Grave Memorial #181631312.

375 Marion County, Missouri Marriage Records, Marion County, Missouri Clerk's Office, 101 South Main Street, #107, Palmyra, MO, Miles Gough and Stella Pegan, Marion County, Missouri Marriage Records, Book 19, pg. 226.

376 U.S., WWI Draft Registration Cards, 1917-1918, Ancestry.com, Miles Prudie Gough.

377 Obituary of M. P. Gough (Louisiana, Missouri, Louisiana Press Journal, 08 Aug 1922), Pike County, Missouri Genealogical Society Library, 100 West Church Street, Bowling Green, MO.

378 Missouri Death Certificates, 1910-1966, Missouri Secretary of State, 600 West Main Street, Jefferson City, MO; Online database: http://s1.sos.mo.gov/records/archives/archivesmvc/deathcertificates, Miles Prudie Gough, death cert. #24447.

379 Find A Grave—Greenwood Cemetery, Clarksville, Calumet Twp., Pike Co., Missouri, Find A Grave.com, Miles P. Gough, Find A Grave Memorial# 104714581.

380 U.S. City Directories, 1822-1995, Ancestry.com, Fort Worth, Texas, 1952, pg. 393; entry for Gough, Frances P.

381 U.S. City Directories, 1822-1995, Ancestry.com, Dallas, Texas, 1959, pg. 423, entry for Gough, Frances P.

382 California, Death Index, 1940-1997, Ancestry.com, Dempsey Rachel Gough.

383 Riverview Abbey & Mausoleum Records, Otho Pegan, Riverview Abbey & Mausoleum, 319 Southwest Taylors Ferry Road, Portland, OR.

384 Find A Grave—Angeles Abbey Memorial Park Cemetery, Compton, Los Angeles Co., California, Find A Grave.com, Otho M. Pegan, Find A Grave Memorial #181631416.

385 Angeles Abbey Memorial Park Mausoleum Records, Otho M. Pegan, Angeles Abbey Cemetery and Mausoleum, 1515 East Compton Boulevard, Compton, CA.

386 Idaho, Marriage Index, 1842-1964, 1975-1996, Ancestry.com, Otho M. "Pagan" and Ruby Tobin.

387 Idaho Marriage Index, 1947-1961, FamilySearch.org, Otho M. "Pagan" and Ruby Tobin, Kootenai County, Idaho, cert. #03528.

388 Social Security Application (SS-5), Ruby Slagle Tobin, Social Security Administration, OEO FOIA Workgroup, 300 N. Greene Street, Baltimore, MD.

389 U.S., Social Security Applications and Claims Index, 1936-2007, Ancestry.com, Ruby Slagle Tobin Pegan.

390 Washington, Death Index, 1940-2014, Ancestry.com, Ruby C. Pegan.

391 Angeles Abbey Memorial Park Mausoleum Records, Luther Carlisle Pegan, Angeles Abbey Memorial Park Mausoleum, 1515 East Compton Boulevard, Compton, CA, Niche: E-53 Columbarium: West Building.

392 Find A Grave—Angeles Abbey Memorial Park Cemetery, Compton, Los Angeles Co., California, Find A Grave.com, Luther C. Pegan, Find A Grave Memorial #181631484.

393 Marion County, Missouri Marriage Records, Marion County, Missouri Clerk's Office, 101 South Main Street, #107, Palmyra, MO, Carlisle Pegan and Oreta Robb, Marion County, Missouri Marriage Records, Book 25, pg. 241.

394 Michigan, Marriage Records, 1867-1952, Ancestry.com, Gerald R. Potts and Oreta I. Cheney, Barry County, Michigan Marriage Records, 1939-41-23006, #441.

395 Find A Grave—Mt. Hope Cemetery, Middleville, Thornapple Twp., Barry Co., Michigan, Find A Grave.com, Oreta Potts, Find A Grave Memorial #5627527.

396 U.S. City Directories, 1822-1995, Ancestry.com, Long Beach, California, 1940, pg. 434: entry for Pegan, Carl L.

397 Arizona, County Marriage Records, 1865-1972, Ancestry.com, "Carl" Pegan and Grace O'Brien, Yuma County, Arizona Marriage Records.

398 Chihuahua, Mexico, Civil Registration Marriages, 1861-1967, FamilySearch.org, "Carl Pagen" and Jackie Bliss.

399 U.S. City Directories, 1822-1995, Ancestry.com, San Bernardino, California, 1942, pg. 309: entry for Pegan, Carl.

400 U.S. WWII Draft Cards Young Men, 1940-1947, Ancestry.com, Luther Carlisle Pegan, Eugene, Oregon.

401 Oregon, Marriage Index, 1906-2009, Ancestry.com, Luther Carlisle Pegan and Lora M. Clayton.

402 Washington, Marriage Records, 1854-2013, Ancestry.com, Carl Pegan and Ethel S. Snellstrom, cert. easpmca64929.

403 "Decrees Granted", Ethel Pegan from "Carl" Pegan (Reno, Nevada, Nevada State Journal, 13 Apr 1944), Newspapers and Periodicals, Ancestry.com.

404 "Marriage Licenses" L. Carl Pegan and W. Kathryn Lynch, (Reno, Nevada, Nevada State Journal, 16 Jul 1944), Newspapers and Periodicals, Ancestry.com.

405 "Decrees Granted", Kathryn Pegan from "Carl" Pegan (Reno, Nevada, Nevada State Journal, 25 Sep 1946), Newspapers and Periodicals, Ancestry.com.

406 U.S. City Directories, 1822-1995, Ancestry.com, San Francisco, California, 1948, pg. 1490: entry for Pegan, Carl.

407 California, Marriage Index, 1949-1959, Ancestry.com, Carl Pegan and Beatrice Guilbault, California state lic. #67729.

408 Montana, County Marriages, 1865-1950, FamilySearch.org, Patrick Brennan and Beatrice Guilbault.

409 California, Death Index, 1940-1997, Ancestry.com, Beatrice F. Brennan.

410 Find A Grave—Colma Cemetery, San Francisco, San Francisco Co., California, Find A Grave.com, Beatrice F. Brennan, Find A Grave Memorial #180786105.

411 Texas, Marriage Index, 1824-2014, Ancestry.com, "Carl" Pegan and Willie Assiter, Tarrant County, Texas Marriage Records, lic. #M160042048.

412 Find A Grave—Greenwood Cemetery, Clarksville, Calumet Twp., Pike Co., Missouri, Find A Grave.com, Grace May Ewing, Find A Grave Memorial #97438778.

413 LaHarpe Historical & Genealogical Society, *Deaths, Marriages & Excerpts from the Dallas City Review, Dallas City, Hancock County, Illinois, 1887-1937*. LeHarpe, Illinois: LaHarpe Historical & Genealogical Society; 1999. Genealogy Center, Allen County Public Library, 900 Library Plaza, Fort Wayne, IN.

414 Iowa, County Marriages, 1838-1934, FamilySearch.org, Arthur Ewing and May Pegan, (North) Lee County, Iowa Marriage Records, pg. 362.

415 U.S., WWII Draft Registration Cards, 1942, Ancestry.com, Arthur Jerome Ewing, Muscatine, Iowa.

416 Obituary of Arthur Jerome Ewing (Muscatine, Iowa, Muscatine Journal, 02 Jan 1974), Musser Public Library, 304 Iowa Avenue, Muscatine, IA.

417 Find A Grave—Columbus City Cemetery, Columbus City, Columbus City Twp., Louisa Co., Iowa, Find A Grave.com, Arthur Ewing, Find A Grave Memorial #103238980.

418 Iowa, State Census Collection, 1836-1925, Ancestry.com; entry for Arthur J. Ewing.

419 Cook County, Illinois Clerk's Office Records, Cook County Clerk's Office—Bureau of Vital Records, 50 West Washington Street, East Concourse Level-25, Chicago, IL, Claude R. Ewing and "Mary" (May) Ewing, Cook County, Illinois Marriage lic. #1388651.

420 U.S. Veterans' Gravesites, ca. 1775-2006, Ancestry.com, Claud Richard Ewing.

421 U.S., WWI Draft Registration Cards, 1917-1918, Ancestry.com, Claud Richard Ewing.

422 U.S., WWII Draft Registration Cards, 1942, Ancestry.com, Claud Richard Ewing.

423 Leavenworth County, Kansas Burials, 1954-58, 1963-70, Ancestry.com, Claud R. Ewing.

424 Find A Grave—Ft. Leavenworth National Military Cemetery, Leavenworth, Leavenworth Twp., Leavenworth Co., Kansas, Find A Grave.com, Claud R. Ewing, Find A Grave Memorial #634085.

425 "Services Held For Mrs. Ewing Sunday Afternoon" (Clarksville, Missouri, Clarksville Sentinel, 28 Aug 1947), Pike County, Missouri Genealogical Society Library, 100 West Church Street, Bowling Green, MO.

426 "Claud R. Ewing's Rites Wadsworth" (Leavenworth, Kansas, Leavenworth Times, 30 Sep 1965), Leavenworth Public Library, 417 Spruce Street, Leavenworth, KS.

427 Missouri Marriage Records, 1805-2002, Ancestry.com, Claud R. Ewing and Dora McNickle.

428 Missouri Marriage Records, 1805-2002, Ancestry.com, Claud R. Ewing and Dora McNickle.

429 California, Death Index, 1940-1997, Ancestry.com, Gladys Wynne Fischer.

430 California Death Certificate, California Health and Strategic Planning, Vital Records, M.S. 5103, P.O. Box 997410, Sacramento, CA, Gladys Wynne Fischer, death cert. #3051997065829.

431 Illinois, Deaths and Stillbirths Index, 1916-1947, Ancestry.com, Lawrence Howard Ewing, death cert. #29200.

432 Cook County, Illinois Clerk's Office Records, Cook County Clerk's Office—Bureau of Vital Records, 50 West Washington Street, East Concourse Level-25, Chicago, IL, Lawrence Howard Ewing, death cert #29200.

433 Iowa, Marriages, 1809-1992, FamilySearch.org, Arthur Ewing Jr. and Iva Jane Ballard, Washington County, Iowa Marriage Records, Book 11, pg. 630.

434 Obituary of Arthur Warren Ewing (Roswell, New Mexico, Roswell Daily Record, 26 Sep 1991), Roswell Public Library, 301 North Pennsylvania Street, Roswell, NM.

435 Obituary of Claribel Williams (Belleville, Kansas, Belleville Telescope, 06 Feb 1986), Belleville Public Library, 1327 19th Street, Belleville, Kansas.

436 U.S., Department of Veterans Affairs BIRLS Death File, 1850-2010, Ancestry.com, Thomas Ewing.

437 Obituary of Thomas B. Ewing, Natchitoches Historical and Genealogical Society Library, 600 Second Street, Natchitoches, LA, Natchitoches Times, Natchitoches, LA, pub. 28 May 1987.

438 Obituary of Charlene Effie Heathco, (Scandia, Kansas Scandia Journal, 22 Aug 1996), Belleville Public Library, 1327 19th Street, Belleville, KS.

439 Iowa, County Births, 1880-1935, FamilySearch.org, Charlene Effie Ewing, birth cert. #51.

440 Illinois Marriages, 1815-1935, FamilySearch.org, James Walter Jacobs and Alta Pegan, lic. #4691, 26 Jan 1912; citing Streator, La Salle, Illinois; (https://familysearch.org/ark:/61903/1:1:V2PX-44W: 29 December 2014).

441 U.S., WWI Draft Registration Cards, 1917-1918, Ancestry.com, James Walter Jacobs, Streator, Illinois.

442 Illinois, Deaths and Stillbirths Index, 1916-1947, Ancestry.com, Walter Jacobs.

443 Find A Grave—Phillips Cemetery, Cornell, Amity Twp., Livingston Co., Illinois, Findagrave.com, James Walter Jacobs, Find A Grave Memorial #155452714

444 The Honor Roll of Veterans Buried in Illinois (Illinois Department of Veterans Affairs, 1956), Illinois Department of Veterans Affairs, 33 S. Spring Street, Springfield, IL.

445 LaSalle County Genealogical Guild website (http://www.lscgg.org/htdocs/retrievelicensebride_nu.php,), LaSalle County Genealogical Guild, 115 West Glover Street, Ottawa, IL, John Bader and Alta Jacobs, LaSalle County, Illinois Marriage lic. #1378.

446 U.S., WWI Draft Registration Cards, 1917-1918, Ancestry.com, John Henry Bader.

447 Missouri Death Certificates, 1910-1966, Missouri Secretary of State, 600 West Main Street, Jefferson City, MO; Online database: http://s1.sos.mo.gov/records/archives/archivesmvc/deathcertificates, John Bader, death cert. #32493.

448 Find A Grave—Jefferson Barracks National Cemetery, Lemay Twp., St. Louis Co., Missouri, Find A Grave.com, John H. Bader, Find A Grave Memorial # 81259298.

449 LaSalle County, Illinois Marriage Records, LaSalle County, Illinois Clerk's Office, 707 East Etna Road, Ottawa, IL, James Brown and Alta Jacobs, LaSalle County, Illinois Marriage Records, Book 10, pg. 92, cert. #5093.

450 U.S., WWI Draft Registration Cards, 1917-1918, Ancestry.com, James Brown.

451 U.S., WWII Draft Registration Cards, 1942, Ancestry.com, James Brown.

452 Illinois Death Certificate, Illinois Department of Public Health, Division of Vital Records, 605 West Jefferson Street, Springfield, IL, James Brown, death cert. #80148.

453 Obituary of James Brown (Chicago, Illinois, Chicago Tribune, 04 Nov 1958), St. Joseph County Public Library, 304 South Main Street, South Bend, IN.

454 LaSalle County, Illinois Birth Records, LaSalle County, Illinois Clerk's Office, 707 East Etna Road, Ottawa, IL. Lois Jacobs, Birth cert. #1915-746.

455 Hurson Funeral Home Records, Lois L. Bonacker, Hurson Funeral Home, 4001 Roosevelt Road, Hillside, IL.

456 Illinois, Deaths and Stillbirths Index, 1916-1947, Ancestry.com, James Brown Jr.

457 Illinois Death Certificate, Illinois Department of Public Health, Division of Vital Records, 605 West Jefferson Street, Springfield, IL, James Brown Jr., death cert. #27305 (1928).

458 U.S., Social Security Applications and Claims Index, 1936-2007, Ancestry.com, Walter David Brown.

459 Florida Death Index 1877-1998, Ancestry.com, Walter David Brown.

460 Social Security Application (SS-5), Social Security Administration, OEO FOIA Workgroup, 300 N. Greene Street, Baltimore, MD, Pauline T. Brown.

461 U.S., Social Security Applications and Claims Index, 1936-2007, Ancestry.com, Pauline Theresa Brown Buchanan Fabian Slusarz (Fabian).

462 Oak Grove Cemetery Records, Oak Grove Cemetery, 7800 Saint Charles Rock Road, St. Louis, MO.

463 Find A Grave—Oak Grove Cemetery, Bel-Nor, St. Louis Co., Missouri, Find A Grave.com, Lorraine Lucas, Find A Grave Memorial #175642397.

464 U.S., WWI Draft Registration Cards, 1917-1918, Ancestry.com, Clifford Young Lucas, St. Louis, Missouri.

465 Obituary of Clifford Y. Lucas (St. Louis, Missouri, St. Louis Post-Dispatch, 18 May 1991, pg. 4B), St. Louis County Public Library, 1640 South Lindbergh Boulevard, St. Louis, MO.

466 Find A Grave—Oak Grove Cemetery, Bel-Nor, St. Louis Co., Missouri, Find A Grave.com, Clifford Lucas, Find A Grave Memorial, #175642340.

467 Obituary of Jean Lucas Rush (St. Louis, MO, St. Louis Post-Dispatch, 27 Mar 2011), St. Louis County Public Library, 1640 South Lindbergh Boulevard, St. Louis, MO.

468 Find A Grave—Emmaus Cemetery, Emmaus, St. Charles Co., Missouri, Find A Grave.com, Hazel Reneau Brockman, Find A Grave Memorial #149324752.

469 Missouri Marriage Records, 1805-2002, Ancestry.com, Harry G. Brockman and Hazel Reneau, pg. 62.

470 Missouri Death Certificates, 1910-1966, Missouri Secretary of State, 600 West Main Street, Jefferson City, MO; Online database: http://s1.sos.mo.gov/records/archives/archivesmvc/deathcertificates, Harry Brockman, cert. #12365.

471 Find A Grave—Oak Hill Cemetery, Kirkwood, St. Louis Co., Missouri, Find A Grave.com, Harry Brockman, Find A Grave Memorial #71142647.

472 "Woman Missing From Emmaus Home 10 Days" (St. Charles, Missouri, St. Charles Daily Cosmos Monitor, 28 Oct 1957), St. Charles City-County Library, 77 Boone Hills Dr., Peters, MO.

473 Jelacic Funeral Home Records, Martha Lee Brockman Krueger; Jelacic Funeral Home, 5639 West Hampton Avenue, Milwaukee, WI.

474 Wisconsin Death Index- 1959-1997, Ancestry.com, Ray Harry Brockman, death cert. #203897.

475 U.S., Social Security Applications and Claims Index, 1936-2007, Ancestry.com, Ray Henry Brockman.

476 U.S., Department of Veterans Affairs BIRLS Death File, 1850-2010, Ancestry.com, Ray Brockman.

477 U.S., WWII Draft Registration Cards, 1942, Ancestry.com, Ray Harry Brockman.

478 Find A Grave—Saint Jude Cemetery, Monroe, Monroe Twp., Monroe Co., Missouri, Find A Grave.com, Mary E. Kelley, Find A Grave Memorial #182411836.

479 Obituary of Albert L. Green Sr., St. Clair County Public Library, 210 McMorran Boulevard, Port Huron, MI, Albert L. Green Sr., pub. 14 Sep 1975.

480 Missouri Marriage Records, 1805-2002, Ancestry.com, Albert Green and Lucille Kelley.

481 Pettis County, Missouri Marriage Records, Pettis Co., Missouri Recorder's Office, Pettis Co. Courthouse, Suite 106, 415 South Ohio Avenue, Sedalia, MO, Albert Green and Lucille Kelley, Pettis County, Missouri Marriage Records, Book 54, pg. 399, lic. # #CC 2-16-62.

482 Michigan Death Certificate, State of Michigan Vital Records Office, Office of Vital Records, Michigan Department of Community Health, Capitol View Building 3rd Floor, 201 Townsend Street, Lansing, MI, Albert Lawrence Green Sr., death cert. # 75-882.

483 Find A Grave—Riverlawn Cemetery, Marysville, St. Clair Twp, St. Clair Co., Michigan, Find A Grave.com, Albert L. Green, Find A Grave Memorial #182411950.

484 Find A Grave—Mountain View Memorial Park Cemetery, Cheyenne, Laramie Co., Wyoming, Find A Grave.com, Albert Lawrence Green Jr., Find A Grave Memorial #39771265.

485 Obituary of Albert L. Green Jr. (Cheyenne, Wyoming, Wyoming State Tribune, 02 Dec 1991), Wyoming State Archives, Barrett Building, 2301 Central Avenue, Cheyenne, WY.

486 Find A Grave—Sunset Memorial Park Cemetery & Mausoleum, Affton, St. Louis Co., Missouri, Find A Grave.com, John C. Kelley, Find A Grave Memorial #140071622.

487 U.S., Social Security Applications and Claims Index, 1936-2007, Ancestry.com, Thelma Rita Berry Leitschuh Kelley.

488 Obituary of Thelma I. Kelley (St. Louis, Missouri, St. Louis Post-Dispatch, 17 Feb 1980), St. Louis County Public Library, 1640 South Lindbergh Boulevard, St. Louis, MO.

489 Sunset Memorial Park Cemetery Records, Thelma I. Kelley, Sunset Memorial Park Cemetery & Mausoleum, 10180 Gravois Road, Affton, MO.

490 Virginia, Marriages, 1785-1940, FamilySearch.org, Samuel M. Eudailey and Frances M. Crosson, 07 Nov 1915, citing Lunenburg, Virginia, reference p 1141 80.

491 U.S., WWI Draft Registration Cards, 1917-1918, Ancestry.com, Sam Mason Eudailey, Lunenburg Co., Virginia.

492 U.S., WWII Draft Registration Cards, 1942, Ancestry.com, Sam Mason Eudailey, Keysville, Lunenburg Co., Virginia.

493 U.S., Social Security Applications and Claims Index, 1936-2007, Ancestry.com, Sam Mason Eudailey.

494 Virginia, Death Records, 1912-2014, Ancestry.com, Samuel Mason Eudailey, state file #46-22593.

495 Find A Grave—Cool Spring Christian Church Cemetery, Chickahominy, Lunenburg Co., Virginia, Find A Grave.com, Sam M. Eudailey, Find A Grave Memorial #84552604.

496 Virginia, Birth Records, 1864-2014, Ancestry.com, "Francis" Lucille Eudailey.

497 Obituary of Frances Currin (Richmond, Virginia, Richmond Times-Union, 07 Oct 2014), Richmond Public Library, 101 East Franklin Street, Richmond, VA.

498 Virginia, Birth Records, 1864-2014, Ancestry.com, Samuel Purnell Eudailey.

499 Virginia, Death Records, 1912-2014, Ancestry.com, Samuel Purnell Eudailey.

500 Virginia, Birth Records, 1864-2014, Ancestry.com, Richard Louis "Endailey" (Eudailey).

501 Obituary of Richard Louis Eudailey (Richmond, Virginia, Richmond Times Dispatch, 17 Nov 2011), Richmond Public Library, 101 East Franklin Street, Richmond, VA.

502 Virginia, Death Records, 1912-2014, Ancestry.com, Richard Louis Eudailey.

503 Virginia, Birth Records, 1864-2014, Ancestry.com, Edith Virginia Eudailey.

504 Find A Grave—Tussekiah Baptist Church Cemetery, Meherrin Lunenburg Co., Virginia, Find A Grave.com, Edith Virginia Eudailey Tomlinson, Find A Grave Memorial #62145790.

505 Obituary of Edith Virginia Eudailey Tomlinson (Richmond, Virginia, Richmond (VA) Times Dispatch (online), 21 Nov 1910).

506 Virginia, Death Records, 1912-2014, Ancestry.com, Edith Eudailey Tomlinson.

507 Find A Grave—Mt. Olivet Cemetery, Salt Lake City, Salt Lake Co., Utah, Find A Grave.com, Eleanor McLaughlin Ridge, Find A Grave Memorial #174054.

508 Western States Marriage Index, Brigham Young University, BYU-Idaho Special Collections: McKay Library 240A, Rexburg, ID familyhistory@byui.edu, William F. McLaughlin and Eleanor Pegan, Vol. A., pg. 394, ID http://abish.byui.edu/specialCollections/westernStates/westernStatesRecordDetail.cfm?recordID=247691Detail.cfm?recordID=247691.

509 Utah, County Marriages, 1887-1940, FamilySearch.org, William F. McLaughlin and Eleanor Pegan, Wasatch County Marriage Records, Vol. A., Pg. 394.

510 Utah, Salt Lake County Death Records, 1908-1949, FamilySearch.org, William Francis McLaughlin, Death Record 1932, #1046.

511 Obituary of William McLaughlin (Park City, Utah, Park City Record, First obituary 22 Jul 1932; second obituary 29 Jul 1932), Park City Library, 1354 Park Avenue, Park City, UT.

512 Find A Grave—Glenwood Cemetery, Park City, Summit Co., Utah, Find A Grave.com, William Francis McLaughlin, Find A Grave Memorial # 71887.

513 Utah Digital Newspapers, "Society Notes and Personal" (Park City, Utah, Park Record, 15 Feb 1908); https://newspapers.lib.utah.edu/details?id=7932401

514 U.S., WWI Draft Registration Cards, 1917-1918, Ancestry.com, Victor Emmanuel Ridge.

515 Tacoma, Washington Obituary Index, 1939-2010, Ancestry.com, Victor Ridge, d. 22 Mar 1939 from the files of the Tacoma, Washington Public Library.

516 Find A Grave—Bayview Cemetery, Bellingham, Whatcom Co., Washington, Find A Grave.com, Victor E. Ridge, Find A Grave Memorial #7823649.

517 California, Death Index, 1940-1997, Ancestry.com, Eleanor Nittler.

518 California Death Certificate, California Health and Strategic Planning, Vital Records, M.S. 5103, P.O. Box 997410, Sacramento, CA, Eleanor Margaret Nittler, death cert. #58-032607.

519 Find A Grave—Suison-Fairfield Cemetery, Fairfield, Solano Co., California, Find A Grave.com, Eleanor M. Nittler, Find A Grave Memorial #31104718.

520 Find A Grave—Mountain View Cemetery, Oakland, Alameda Co., California, Find A Grave.com, Lewis S. Kelso, Find A Grave Memorial #166772821.

521 Mountain View Cemetery Records, (Alameda Co., California), Lewis S. Kelso; Mountain View Cemetery, 5000 Piedmont Avenue, Oakland, CA.

522 U.S., WWI Draft Registration Cards, 1917-1918, Ancestry.com, Lewis Sinclair Kelso in Oakland, Alameda Co., California.

523 California, Death Index, 1940-1997, Ancestry.com, Cora A. Kelso.

524 Mountain View Cemetery Records, (Alameda Co., California), Cora A. Kelso; Mountain View Cemetery, 5000 Piedmont Avenue, Oakland, CA.

525 Obituary of Cora Kelso (Oakland, California, Oakland Tribune, 25 Mar 1952), San Francisco Public Library, Main Branch, 100 Larkin Street, San Francisco, CA, Oakland (CA) Tribune, 25 Mar 1952, pg. E39.

526 Find A Grave—Mountain View Cemetery, Oakland, Alameda Co., California, Find A Grave.com, Cora A. Kelso, Find A Grave Memorial #166772820.

527 California Birth Index, 1905-1995, Ancestry.com, Eleanor Lois Kelso.

528 California, Death Index, 1940-1997, Ancestry.com, Eleanor Lois Dibello.

529 Obituary of Eleanor Lois Dibello (San Jose, California, San Jose Mercury News, 26 Apr 1995), Martin Luther King, Jr. Library, California Room, 150 East San Fernando Street, San Jose, CA.

530 California Birth Index, 1905-1995, Ancestry.com, George Kelso.

531 California Birth Index, 1905-1995, Ancestry.com, Joseph "St. Clair" Kelso.

532 Miller-Woodlawn Memorial Park Cemetery Records, Mary E. Boggs, Miller-Woodlawn Memorial Park Cemetery, 5505 Kitsap Way, Bremerton, WA.

533 Washington, Marriage Records, 1854-2013, Ancestry.com, Kenneth W. Johnson and Mary Elizabeth Pegan, Sokane County, Washington, cert. easpmca28932.

534 U.S., WWI Draft Registration Cards, 1917-1918, Ancestry.com, Kenneth Whitford Johnson.

535 Oregon, Death Index, 1898-2008, Ancestry.com, Kenneth Whitford Johnson, death cert. #73-19321.

536 Find A Grave—Cypress Lawn Memorial Park Cemetery, Everett, Snohomish Co., Washington, Find A Grave.com, Kenneth W. Johnson, Find A Grave Memorial # 94337027.

537 Washington, Marriage Records, 1854-2013, Ancestry.com, F.L. Boggs and Mary E. Johnson, Whatcom County, Washington, cert. nwwtcmcv15_1471.

538 Canadian Soldiers of the First World War, 1914-1918, Ancestry.com, Francis Llewellyn Boggs of North Bend, Washington, USA.

539 Washington, Births, 1883-1935, Ancestry.com, Male child Boggs, born 19 Sep 1891 to William and Abbie Hastings Boggs in Kirkland, King Co., Washington.

540 Washington, Death Index, 1940-2014, Ancestry.com, Francis L. Boggs, death cert. #018942.

541 Obituary of Francis L. Boggs (Bremerton, Washington, Bremerton Sun, 31 Jul 1971), Kitsap Regional Library, 1301 Sylvan Way, Bremerton, WA.

542 Miller-Woodlawn Memorial Park Cemetery Records, Francis L. Boggs, Miller-Woodlawn Memorial Park Cemetery, 5505 Kitsap Way, Bremerton, WA.

543 U.S., WWII Draft Registration Cards, 1942, Ancestry.com, Francis Lleywellyn Boggs.

544 Find A Grave—Mount Si Memorial Cemetery, North Bend, King Co., Washington, Find A Grave.com, Grace Boggs, Find A Grave Memorial #71693397.

545 "New Faculty Members At State College" (Pullman, Washington, Pullman Herald, 22 Sep 1922), Washington State Library, 6880 Capitol Boulevard SE, Tumwater, WA.

546 Historical Newspapers, Birth, Marriage and Death Announcements—1851-2003, Ancestry.com, Marriage license application, L.C. Boggs and Grace Pegan, (Los Angeles, California, Los Angeles Times, 18 Jun 1925).

547 Washington, Death Index, 1940-2014, Ancestry.com, Lorraine C. Boggs, cert. #003424.

548 U.S., Department of Veterans Affairs BIRLS Death File, 1850-2010, Ancestry.com, Lorraine Boggs.

549 Find A Grave—Mount Si Memorial Cemetery, North Bend, King Co., Washington, Find A Grave.com, L.C. Boggs, Find A Grave Memorial #71693313.

550 Phone interview with John Francis Boggs, Forks, WA, Ann Miller Carr, author, 08 Feb 2012.

551 U.S. Veterans' Gravesites, ca. 1775-2006, Ancestry.com, John E. Pegan Sr.

552 Washington, Marriage Records, 1854-2013, Ancestry.com, John E. Pegan and Elizabeth Marie Maletzski, Whatcom County, Washington, cert. #nwwtcmcv19a_5344, No. 2856.

553 U.S., Social Security Applications and Claims Index, 1936-2007, Ancestry.com, Elizabeth Maletzki Pegan Lammon.

554 California Death Certificate, California Health and Strategic Planning, Vital Records, M.S. 5103, P.O. Box 997410, Sacramento, CA, Elizabeth Marie Lammon, death cert. #3052002113609.

555 Source is the spouse of one of John Edwin and Mary Maletzski Pegan's children who wishes to remain anonymous.

556 U.S., Social Security Applications and Claims Index, 1936-2007, Ancestry.com, Robert Edwin Pegan.

557 California, Death Index, 1940-1997, Ancestry.com, Robert Edwin Pegan.

558 California Death Certificate, California Health and Strategic Planning, Vital Records, M.S. 5103, P.O. Box 997410, Sacramento, CA, Robert Edwin Pegan, death cert. ##81-052614.

559 U.S., Department of Veterans Affairs BIRLS Death File, 1850-2010, Ancestry.com, Robert Pegan.

560 Find A Grave—Brookside Cemetery, Watertown, Jefferson Co., New York, Find A Grave.com, David Gilbert Gregor, Find A Grave Memorial #115018860.

561 Obituary of Elisabeth Taylor (Watertown, New York, Watertown Daily News, 22 Nov 1992), Flower Memorial Library, 229 Washington Street, Watertown, NY.

562 Obituary of David G. Gregor Jr. (Watertown, New York, Watertown Daily Times, 21 Aug 2013), Flower Memorial Library, 229 Washington Street, Watertown, NY.

563 Obituary of Ann MacGregor Sewall (Watertown, New York, Watertown Times, 03 Jul 2015), Flower Memorial Library, 229 Washington Street, Watertown, NY.

564 Find A Grave—Brookside Cemetery, Watertown, Jefferson Co., New York, Find A Grave.com, Mary Margaret Sexsmith, Find A Grave Memorial #107450781.

565 Massachusetts, Birth Records, 1840-1915, Ancestry.com, Roderick Pirnie, Springfield Town Birth Records.

566 Florida Death Index 1877-1998, Ancestry.com, Roderick Pirnie.

567 War Industry Coordination, William E. Spragg Corespondence, 1942-1943, letter to Mr. David Levin from Roderick Pirnie, 02 Sep 1943, University of Iowa Archives, http://digital.lib.uiowa.edu/cdm/ref/collection/keithalbee/id/32848

568 "Rhode Island Is First Over Top In War Bonds" (Indianapolis, Indiana, *Indianapolis Star,* 05 Feb 1944, pg. 15), Indiana State Library, 315 West Ohio Street, Indianapolis, IN.

569 Pirnie, Roderick, *Planning and Selling the Basic Estate.* Cincinnati, National Underwriter Co., 1939.

570 "Hurricane Carol" (Newport, Rhode Island, Newport Daily News, 03 Sep 1954), Newspapers.com; Online database: https://www.newspapers.com/newspage/59294375/

571 Obituary of J.R. Sexsmith (Watertown, New York, Watertown Daily Times, 05 Aug 1984), Flower Memorial Library, 229 Washington Street, Watertown, NY.

572 Find A Grave—Brookside Cemetery, Watertown, Jefferson Co., New York, Find A Grave.com, James R. Sexsmith, Find A Grave Memorial #107450780.

573 "J.R. Sexsmith Takes Bride During Yuletide Season" (Malone, New York, The Malone Farmer, 27 Dec 1933), New York State Newspapers; Online database: http://nyshistoricnewspapers.org/lccn/sn84031968/1933-12-27/ed-1/seq-1.pdf

574 Birth Announcement of Roderick Pirnie Jr. (Watertown, New York, Watertown Daily Times, 10 Apr 1918), Flower Memorial Library, 229 Washington Street, Watertown, NY.

575 New York State Vital Statistics—Births (microfisch), Flower Memorial Library, 229 Washington Street, Watertown, NY, Birth cert. #30698.

576 Obituary of Roderick Pirnie Jr. (Watertown, NY, Watertown Daily Times, 24 Mar 1919), Flower Memorial Library, 229 Washington Street, Watertown, NY.

577 New York, Death Index, 1880-1956, Ancestry.com, Roderick Pirnie, Jr., death cert. #17065.

578 Obituary of Elisabeth (Betsy) P. Gruet (Barnstable, Massachusetts, Barnstable Register, 08 Apr 2013), Sturgis Library, 3090 Main Street, Barnstable, MA.

579 Find A Grave—Skylawn Memorial Park Cemetery, San Mateo, San Mateo Co., California, Find A Grave.com, Richard E. Camp, Find A Grave Memorial #164487852.

580 Find A Grave—Memorial Park Cemetery, St. Joseph, Washington Twp., Buchanan Co., Missouri, Find A Grave.com, James A. Pegan, Find A Grave Memorial #103736024.

581 Buchanan County, Missouri Recorder of Deeds, Buchanan County, Missouri Recorder of Deeds, 411 Jules Street, Room 103, St. Joseph, MO, James A. Pegan and Opal Sample, Buchanan County, Missouri Marriage Records, Vol. 40, pg. 198.

582 Obituary of Opal Pegan (St. Joseph, Missouri, St. Joseph News-Press, 20 Feb 1978), St. Joseph Public Library, 927 Felix Street, St. Joseph, MO.

583 Find A Grave—Memorial Park Cemetery, St. Joseph, Washington Twp., Buchanan Co., Missouri, Find A Grave.com, Opal Sample Pegan, Find A Grave Memorial #103736051.

584 U.S. City Directories, 1822-1995, Ancestry.com, St. Joseph, Missouri, pg. 352, entry for Pegan, James A.

585 *Pike County Chapter of the DAR, Cemetery Inscriptions. Pike County, Missouri, Vol. II,* pg. 21, Calumet Township, Greenwood Cemetery, Jane Temple Pegan.

586 Find A Grave—Greenwood Cemetery, Clarksville, Calumet Twp., Pike Co., Missouri, Find A Grave.com, Jane Temple Pegan, Find A Grave Memorial #182441253.

587 Mount Lebanon Cemetery Records, Mt. Lebanon Cemetery Company, 509 Washington Road, Pittsburgh, PA.

588 Find A Grave—Mount Lebanon Cemetery, Mount Lebanon, Allegheny Co., Pennsylvania, Find A Grave.com, John R. Pegan, Find A Grave Memorial #18162544.

589 Marriage Announcement of John Robert Pegan and Juanita Blumenthal (Frederick, Maryland, Frederick Post, December 20, 1950), Frederick County Public Library, C. Burr Artz Branch—Maryland Room, 110 East Patrick Street, Frederick, MD.

590 Obituary of Juanita "Pagan" (Frederick, Maryland, The Post, 07 Jul 1979), Frederick County Public Library, C. Burr Artz Branch—Maryland Room, 110 East Patrick Street, Frederick, MD.

591 U.S., Social Security Applications and Claims Index, 1936-2007, Ancestry.com, Juanita Malissa Blumenauer Pegan.

592 Obituary of Juanita Pegan (Pittsburgh, Pennsylvania, Pittsburgh Press, 06 Jul 1979), Carnegie Library of Pittsburgh, 4400 Forbes Avenue, Pittsburgh, PA.

593 Find A Grave—Mount Lebanon Cemetery, Mount Lebanon, Allegheny Co., Pennsylvania, Find A Grave.com, Juanita Pegan, Find A Grave Memorial #181625337.

594 U.S., Department of Veterans Affairs BIRLS Death File, 1850-2010, Ancestry.com, Leslie Pegan.

595 California, Death Index, 1940-1997, Ancestry.com, Leslie Pegan.

596 Birth Announcement of Leslie Meloan Pegan (Frederick, Maryland, The Post, 21 Jan 1957), Frederick County Public Library, C. Burr Artz Branch—Maryland Room, 110 East Patrick Street, Frederick, MD.

597 Marion County, Missouri Marriage Records, Marion County, Missouri Clerk's Office, 101 South Main Street, #107, Palmyra, MO, Stephen A. Reher and Dorothy G. Pegan, Marion County, Missouri Marriage Records, Vol. 22, pg. 73.

598 Missouri Death Certificates, 1910-1966, Missouri Secretary of State, 600 West Main Street, Jefferson City, MO; Online

database: http://s1.sos.mo.gov/records/archives/archivesmvc/deathcertificates, Stephen A. Reher, death cert. #41742.

599 Holy Family Cemetery Records, Holy Name Catholic Church, 2103 Broadway Street, Hannibal, MO, Stephen A. Reher.

600 WWII Draft Cards Young Men, 1940-1947, Ancestry.com, Fred Dee Gaines, Oklahoma City, Oklahoma, says he was born in Blair, Oklahoma.

601 California, Death Index, 1940-1997, Ancestry.com, Fred D. Gaines

602 California, Passengers and Crew List, 1882-1959, Ancestry.com, Fred Gaines, b. abt. 1913, 02 Jun 1947, debarking in San Pedro, California from Pacific Overseas Airways, says he was born in Warren, Oklahoma.

603 Find A Grave—Inglewood Park Cemetery, Inglewood, Los Angeles Co., California, Find A Grave.com, Fred D. Gaines, Find A Grave Memorial #131731957.

604 U.S. City Directories, 1822-1995, Ancestry.com, Alhambra, California, 1956, pg. 236, entry for Gaines, Fred D.

605 California, Voter Registrations, 1900-1968, Ancestry.com, Baldwin Park, California, 1960, Roll 134, entries for Gaines, Fred D. and Gaines, Mrs. Dorothy G.

606 Obituary of Rosena Kondos (Phoenix, Arizona, Arizona Republic, 03 Aug 2002), Arizona State Library, Archives and Public Records, Archives and Records Management Branch, 1901 West Madison Street, Phoenix, AZ.

607 U.S., Social Security Applications and Claims Index, 1936-2007, Ancestry.com, Rosena Cecilia Reher Leake Kondos.

608 Find A Grave—Green Hills Memorial Park Cemetery, Rancho Palos Verdes, Los Angeles Co., California, Find A Grave.com, Erman Henry Pegan, Find A Grave Memorial #72135095.

609 St. Louis County, Missouri Marriage Records, St. Louis County Public Library, 1640 South Lindbergh Boulevard, St. Louis, MO, Erman Henry Pegan and Helen Kathryn Thornton, St. Louis County, Missouri Marriage Records, Vol. 118, pg. 85.

610 Missouri Birth Records 1851-1910, Ancestry.com, Helen Catherine Thornton, St. Louis, Missouri, 1908, pg. 585.

611 Find A Grave—Green Hills Memorial Park Cemetery, Rancho Palos Verdes, Los Angeles Co., California, Find A Grave.com, Helen K. Pegan, Find A Grave Memorial #172456674.

612 Family records: Email from Helen K. Thornton's granddaughter in Los Angeles, CA to the author, Ann Miller Carr, on 25 Jun 2016.

613 Find A Grave—Montecito Memorial Park Cemetery, Colton, San Bernardino Co., California, Find A Grave.com, Flora Josephine Shields, Find A Grave Memorial #171240434.

614 Marion County, Missouri Marriage Records, Marion County, Missouri Clerk's Office, 101 South Main Street, #107, Palmyra, MO, Herbert E. McCann and Flora J. Pegan, Marion County, Missouri Marriage Records, Book 23, pg. 111.

615 Find A Grave—East Hill Cemetery, Osseo, Jefferson Twp., Hillsdale Co., Michigan, Find A Grave.com.

616 Obituary of Herbert E. McCann (Hilldale, Michigan, Hillsdale Daily News, 13 May 1965), Michigan Historical Museum, 702 West Kalamazoo Street, Lansing, MI.

617 California, Marriage Index, 1949-1959, Ancestry.com, William B. Shields and Josephine F. Bogardus, Riverside County, California Marriage Records, California state lic. #9833.

618 California, Death Index, 1940-1997, Ancestry.com, William Burt Shields.

619 California Death Certificate, California Health and Strategic Planning, Vital Records, M.S. 5103, P.O. Box 997410, Sacramento, CA, William Bird (A.K.A. Burt) Shields, death cert. #80-138469.

620 California Death Certificate, California Health and Strategic Planning, Vital Records, M.S. 5103, P.O. Box 997410, Sacramento, CA, Herbert Eugene McCann, death cert. #3052002013822.

621 U.S., Social Security Applications and Claims Index, 1936-2007, Ancestry.com, Herbert Eugene McCann Jr.

622 Virginia, Marriage Records, 1936-2014, Ancestry.com, Herbert E. McCann Jr. and LaVerne M. Gallagher, Prince William County, Virginia Marriage Records, lic. #9412.

623 U.S., Social Security Applications and Claims Index, 1936-2007, Ancestry.com, Ada Frances McCann MacQueen.

624 Michigan, Death Index, 1971-1996, Ancestry.com, Shirley Farwell.

625 U.S., Headstone Applications for Military Veterans, 1925-1963, Ancestry.com, David Donlad McCann, serial #1049674, Order #WM2219393.

626 California, Death Index, 1940-1997, Ancestry.com, David Donald McCann.

627 David Donald McCann. Find A Grave—Holy Cross Catholic Cemetery, Detroit, Wayne Co., Michigan, Find A Grave.com, David D. McCann, Find A Grave Memorial #182500504.

628 Find A Grave—Angeles Abbey Memorial Park Cemetery, Compton, Los Angeles Co., California, Find A Grave.com, Dempsey Gough, Find A Grave Memorial #181631359.

629 Find A Grave—Holy Cross Cemetery, Colma, San Mateo Co., California, Find A Grave.com, Gladys Ewing, Find A Grave Memorial #106527487.

630 All U.S., Evangelical Lutheran Church of America Records, 1826-1940, Ancestry.com, Harm M. Fischer, born 13 Mar 1898 in Benson, Illinois.

631 U.S., Department of Veterans Affairs BIRLS Death File, 1850-2010, Ancestry.com, Harm Fischer.

632 Find A Grave—South Park Cemetery, Roswell, Chaves Co., New Mexico, Find A Grave.com, Hiram M. Fischer, Find A Grave Memorial #102672124.

633 Obituary of Arthur Ewing Jr., Roswell Public Library, 301 North Pennsylvania Street, Roswell, NM, Roswell Daily Record, Roswell, New Mexico, pub. 26 Sep 1991.

634 U.S., Social Security Applications and Claims Index, 1936-2007, Ancestry.com, Marie Wynne Fischer Morris Cappelini Keller.

635 Phone interview with "Daughter" Devlin, Meidmeier, AZ, author Ann Miller Carr, 20 Mar 2015.

636 U.S., Social Security Applications and Claims Index, 1936-2007, Ancestry.com, Jay Jackson Fischer.

637 Cook County, Illinois Clerk's Office Records, Cook County Clerk's Office—Bureau of Vital Records, 50 West Washington Street, East Concourse Level-25, Chicago, IL, BillyJo Fischer, death cert. #29806.

638 Lawrence Howard Ewing Sr. death certificate, Cook County Clerk's Office—Bureau of Vital Records, 50 West Washington Street, East Concourse Level-25, Chicago, IL, Lawrence Howard Ewing Sr., death cert. #29200.

639 Cook County, Illinois Clerk's Office Records, Cook County Clerk's Office—Bureau of Vital Records, 50 West Washington Street, East Concourse Level-25, Chicago, IL, Lawrence Ewing and Anna M. Mathis, Cook County Marriage Records, File #1350275, {1C614F43-7BEE-4C74-914F-CFF319847A64}.

640 Cook County, Illinois Marriage Index, 1930-1960, Ancestry.com, Howard Ewing and Anna May Mathis.

641 Illinois, Deaths and Stillbirths Index, 1916-1947, Ancestry.com, Infant male Ewing, death cert. #cn446.

642 Obituary of Anna Hirsch (St. Petersburg, Florida, St. Petersburg Times, 24 Feb 2001), Largo Library, 201 Highland Avenue NE, Largo, FL.

643 Cook County, Illinois Clerk's Office Records, Cook County Clerk's Office—Bureau of Vital Records, 50 West Washington Street, East Concourse Level-25, Chicago, IL, Lubert Hirsch and Anna M. Ewing, Cook County Marriage Records, File #2281388.

644 Cook County, Illinois Birth Index, 1916-1935, Ancestry.com, Lawrence Ewing, birth cert. #6006100 (file number).

645 Obituary of Lawrence H. Ewing Jr. (Lafayette, Indiana, Lafayette Journal-Courier, 08 Nov 2006), Tippecanoe County Public Library, 627 South Street, Lafayette, IN.

646 U.S., Social Security Applications and Claims Index, 1936-2007, Ancestry.com, Larry Howard Ewing.

647 Indiana, Death Certificates, 1899-2011, Ancestry.com, Lawrence H. Ewing Jr., death cert. #107979.

648 Find A Grave—South Park Cemetery, Roswell, Chaves Co., New Mexico, Find A Grave.com, Arthur W. Ewing, Find A Grave Memorial #26863454.

649 Obituary of Mrs. Iva Jane Ewing (nee Ballard) (North English, Iowa, North English Record, 18 Jul 1935), Iowa County Genealogical Society Library, 121 Main Street, North English, IA.

650 Iowa, Death Records, 1920-1940, Ancestry.com, Iva Jane Ewing, death cert. #255.

651 Find A Grave—North English Cemetery, North English, English Twp., Iowa Co., Iowa, Find A Grave.com, Iva Ballard Ewing, Find A Grave Memorial #65574433.

652 Iowa, County Marriages, 1838-1934, FamilySearch.org, Arthur W. Ewing and Gayle Long.

653 Obituary of Gayle A. Ewing (Roswell, New Mexico, Roswell Daily Record, 09 Nov 1997), Roswell Public Library, 301 North Pennsylvania Street, Roswell, NM.

654 U.S., Social Security Applications and Claims Index, 1936-2007, Ancestry.com, Gayle Aileen "Lang" Ewing.

655 Find A Grave—South Park Cemetery, Roswell, Chaves Co., New Mexico, Find A Grave.com, Gayle Aileen Long Ewing, Find A Grave Memorial #26863455.

656 U.S. Navy Muster Rolls, 1938-1949, Arthur Warren Ewing, Des Moines, Iowa, Ship LST 925.

657 Iowa, WWII Bonus Case Files, 1947-1954, Ancestry.com, Arthur Warren Ewing.

658 U.S. City Directories, 1822-1995, Ancestry.com, Goodland, Kansas, 1963, pg. 112, entry for Ewing, Arthur W.

659 U.S., Social Security Applications and Claims Index, 1936-2007, Ancestry.com, Janet Carolyn Ewing.

660 Obituary of Janet C. Ewing (Roswell, New Mexico, Roswell Daily Record, 12 Dec 2000), Roswell Public Library, 301 North Pennsylvania Street, Roswell, NM.

661 Find A Grave—Fairbury Cemetery, Fairbury, Washington Twp., Jefferson Co., Nebraska, Find A Grave.com, Claribel Ewing Williams, Find A Grave Memorial #21434361.

662 Obituary of Roy Emil Williams (Belleville, Kansas, Belleville Telescope, 14 Sep 1972), Belleville Public Library, 1327 19th Street, Belleville, Kansas.

663 Find A Grave—Fairbury Cemetery, Fairbury, Washington Twp., Jefferson Co., Nebraska, Find A Grave.com, Roy Emil Williams, Find A Grave Memorial #21434357.

664 "Drag River at Clinton for Rock Island Lad; Youth, 16, Drowns Near Taylor Ridge" (Rock Island, Illinois, The Rock Island Argus, 30 Jul 1951), Rock Island Library, 401 19th Street, Rock Island, IL.

665 Obituary of Delores Erickson (Belleville, Kansas, Belleville Telescope, 15 Apr 2015), Belleville Public Library, 1327 19th Street, Belleville, Kansas.

666 Find A Grave—Riverview Cemetery, Scandia, Scandia Twp., Republic Co., Kansas, Find A Grave.com, Delores May "Dee" Williams Erickson, Find A Grave Memorial #144862504.

667 California, Death Index, 1940-1997, Ancestry.com, Richard Emil Williams.

668 Find A Grave—Lambertown Cemetery, Robeline, Robeline Twp., Natchitoches Parish, Lousiana, Find A Grave.com, Thomas B. Ewing, Find A Grave Memorial #15034597.

669 Iowa, County Marriages, 1838-1934, FamilySearch.org, Tommy Butler Ewing and Grace Westaway.

670 Texas Deaths, 1977-1986, FamilySearch.org, Marvin Kenneth Ewing, death cert. #97637.

671 Find A Grave—Conesville Cemetery, Conesville. Orono Twp., Muscatine Co., Iowa, Find A Grave.com, Grace Westaway Armstrong, Find A Grave Memorial #134588050.

672 U.S. Public Records Index, 1950-1993, Vol. 2, Ancestry.com, Grace W. Armstrong, b. 18 Aug 1919, 3229 West Rusholme St, Davenport, IA, 52804-2609.

673 Obituary of Grace W. Armstrong (Davenport, IA, Quad City Times, 20 Aug 2014), Davenport Public Library, 321 Main Street, Davenport, IA.

674 Obituary of Robert. Armstrong (Davenport, IA, Quad City Times, 19 Jul 2013), Davenport Public Library, 321 Main Street, Davenport, IA.

675 Obituary of Ellie Fay Brown Ewing (Nachitoches, Louisiana, Nachitoches Times, 01 Nov 2006), Natchitoches Historical and Genealogical Society Library, 600 Second Street, Natchitoches, LA.

676 Find A Grave—Lambertown Cemetery, Robeline, Robeline Twp., Natchitoches Parish, Lousiana, Find A Grave.com, Ellie Fay Brown Ewing, Find A Grave Memorial #16417184.

677 Conesville Cemetery Records, Charles Ewing, Conesville, Orono Twp., Muscatine Co., Iowa, Musser Public Library, 304 Iowa Avenue, Muscatine, IA, Muscatine County, Iowa Genealogical Society.

678 Find A Grave—Fairbury Cemetery, Fairbury, Washington Twp., Jefferson Co., Nebraska, Find A Grave.com, Effie Lilliebelle "Charlene" Ewing Heathco, Find A Grave Memorial #21434392.

679 Nevada, Marriage Index, 1956-2005, Ancestry.com, Deryl Richard Heathco and Charlene Ewing.

680 U.S., Social Security Applications and Claims Index, 1936-2007, Ancestry.com, Deryl Richard Heathco.

681 U.S., WWI Draft Registration Cards, 1917-1918, Ancestry.com, Deryl Richard Heathco.

682 U.S., Railroad Retirement Pension Index, 1934-1997, Ancestry.com, D. Heathco, born Oct 1899, died Aug 1988.

683 Find A Grave—Fairbury Cemetery, Fairbury, Washington Twp., Jefferson Co., Nebraska, Find A Grave.com, Deryl Richard "Richard D." Heathco, Find A Grave Memorial #21434380.

684 Find A Grave—Fairbury Cemetery Records, "Richard D." Heathco, Fairbury Cemetery Association, 56924 PWF Road, Fairbury, NE.

685 Obituary of Lois Bonacker (Chicago, Illinois, Chicago Tribune, 07 Oct 2012), Chicago Public Library, 400 South State Street, Chicago, IL.

686 Find A Grave—Arlington Cemetery, Elmhurst, DuPage Co., Illinois, Find A Grave.com, Lois L. Bonacker, Find A Grave Memorial #182339797.

687 Obituary of Loretta Marilyn Malek (Danbury, Connecticut, The News Times, 23 Feb 2007), Danbury Public Library, 170 Main Street, Danbury, CT.

688 Cook County, Illinois Death Certificates, Cook County Clerk's Office—Bureau of Vital Records, 50 West Washington Street, East Concourse Level-25, Chicago, IL, Fred John Bonacker, death cert. file #012690.

689 Find A Grave—Arlington Cemetery, Elmhurst, DuPage Co., Illinois, Find A Grave.com, Frederick J. Bonacker, Find A Grave Memorial #182339554.

690 Find A Grave—Curlew Hills Memory Gardens Cemetery, Palm Harbor, Pinellas Co., Florida, Find A Grave.com, Walter D. Brown, Find A Grave Memorial #144629220.

691 Cook County, Illinois Clerk's Office Records, Cook County Clerk's Office—Bureau of Vital Records, 50 West Washington Street, East Concourse Level-25, Chicago, IL, Walter J. Brown and Minerva D. Brown, Cook County, Illinois Marriage file #2079882.

692 Florida Death Index 1877-1998, Ancestry.com, Minerva D. Brown.

693 Obituary of Minerva D. Brown (St. Petersburg, Florida, St. Petersburg Times, 10 Jun 1985), Largo Library, 201 Highland Avenue NE, Largo, FL.

694 Find A Grave—Curlew Hills Memory Gardens Cemetery, Palm Harbor, Pinellas Co., Florida, Find A Grave.com, Minerva D. Brown, Find A Grave Memorial #144629341.

695 Florida Marriage Indexes, 1822-1875, 1927-2001, Ancestry.com, Walter D. Brown and Joan Marie Myers, Florida Dept. of Health cert. #089407.

696 Cook County, Illinois Marriage Index, 1930-1960, Ancestry.com, Frank J. Fabian and Pauline Buchanan, Cook County, Illinois Marriage file #2247096, marriage license D5E0F919-ADAA-4BDA-92EC-31E3A59DAFF4.

697 Find A Grave—St. Adalbert Catholic Cemetery, Niles, Niles Twp., Cook Co., Illinois, Find A Grave.com, Frank J. Fabian, Find A Grave Memorial #50821094.

698 Obituary of James W. Fabian (Chicago, Illinois, Chicago Tribune, 02 Nov 1972), Chicago Public Library, 400 South State Street, Chicago, IL.

699 Obituary of Bradley Fabian (Chicago, Illinois, Chicago Tribune, 21 Dec 2014), Chicago Public Library, 400 South State Street, Chicago, IL.

700 Find A Grave—Jefferson Barracks National Cemetery, Lemay Twp., St. Louis Co., Missouri, Find A Grave.com, Jean L. Rush, Find A Grave Memorial #81372118.

701 St. Louis County, Missouri Marriage Records, St. Louis County Public Library, 1640 South Lindbergh Boulevard, St. Louis, MO, George F. Rush and Jean Lucas, St. Louis County Marriage Records, Vol. 50, pg. 132.

702 Kentucky, Birth Index, 1911-1999, Ancestry.com, George F. Rush, Birth Vol. 1918, cert #11858.

703 Obituary of George F. Rush (St. Louis, Missouri, St. Louis Post-Dispatch, 15 Jun 1999), St. Louis County Public Library, 1640 South Lindbergh Boulevard, St. Louis, MO.

704 Find A Grave—Jefferson Barracks National Cemetery, Lemay Twp., St. Louis Co., Missouri, Find A Grave.com, George F. Rush, Find A Grave Memorial #81372112.

705 Wisconsin Memorial Park Cemetery Records, Martha L. Krueger, Wisconsin Memorial Park Cemetery, 13235 West Capitol Drive, Brookfield, WI.

706 Find A Grave—Wisconsin Memorial Park Cemetery, Brookfield, Waukesha Co., Wisconsin, Find A Grave.com, Martha L. Krueger, Find A Grave Memorial #182409262.

707 Obituary of Robert G. Krueger (West Bend, Wisconsin, West Bend Daily News, 27 Jul 1989), West Bend Community Memorial Library, 630 Poplar Street, West Bend, WI.

708 Wisconsin Death Index- 1959-1997, Ancestry.com, Robert George Krueger, death cert. #011799.

709 Find A Grave—Wisconsin Memorial Park Cemetery, Brookfield, Waukesha Co., Wisconsin, Find A Grave.com, Robert G. Krueger, Find A Grave Memorial #129867315.

710 Obituary of Raymond H. Brockman (Milwaukee, Wisconsin, Milwaukee Journal-Sentinel, 27 Jun 1989), Milwaukee Public Library, 814 West Wisconsin Avenue, Milwaukee, WI.

711 Find A Grave—Wisconsin Memorial Park Cemetery, Brookfield, Waukesha Co., Wisconsin, Find A Grave.com, Raymond H. Brockman, Find A Grave Memorial #182409687.

712 Obituary of Marcella B. Brockman (Milwaukee, Wisconsin, Milwaukee Journal Sentinel, 22 Jun 2001), Milwaukee Public Library, 814 West Wisconsin Avenue, Milwaukee, WI.

713 U.S., Social Security Applications and Claims Index, 1936-2007, Ancestry.com, Marcella B. Brockman.

714 Find A Grave—Wisconsin Memorial Park Cemetery, Brookfield, Waukesha Co., Wisconsin, Find A Grave.com, Marcella Brockman, Find A Grave Memorial #182409789.

715 Find A Grave—Tussekiah Baptist Church Cemetery, Meherrin Lunenburg Co., Virginia, Find A Grave.com, Frances Lucille Currin, Find A Grave Memorial #136968114.

716 Virginia, Marriage Records, 1936-2014, Ancestry.com, Earl Carlyle Currin and Frances Lucille Eudailey, Lunenburg County Marriage cert. #39825.

717 Virginia, Birth Records, 1864-2014, Ancestry.com, Earl Carlyle "Curran".

718 Virginia, Death Records, 1912-2014, Ancestry.com, Earl Carlyle Currin.

719 Obituary of Earl Carlyle Currin (Richmond, Virginia, Richmond Times, 28 Oct 1988), Richmond Public Library, 101 East Franklin Street, Richmond, VA.

720 Find A Grave—Tussekiah Baptist Church Cemetery, Meherrin Lunenburg Co., Virginia, Find A Grave.com, Earl Carlyle Currin, Find A Grave Memorial #90761550.

721 Virginia, Death Records, 1912-2014, Ancestry.com, Currin, state file #49-9221.

722 Find A Grave—Cool Spring Christian Church Cemetery, Chickahominy, Lunenburg Co., Virginia, Find A Grave.com, Samuel P. Eudailey, Find A Grave Memorial #84043048.

723 Virginia, Marriage Records, 1936-2014, Ancestry.com, Samuel Purnell Eudailey and Edna Earl Reed, Nottaway County, Virginia Marriage cert. #37549.

724 Virginia, Birth Records, 1864-2014, Ancestry.com, Edna Earl Reed.

725 Find A Grave—Cool Spring Christian Church Cemetery, Chickahominy, Lunenburg Co., Virginia, Find A Grave.com, Edna R. Eudailey, Find A Grave Memorial #84043243.

726 Virginia, Death Records, 1912-2014, Ancestry.com, Edna Reed Eudailey.

727 Find A Grave—Greenwood Memorial Gardens Cemetery, Richmond, Henrico Co., Virginia, Find A Grave.com, Richard Louis Eudailey, Find A Grave Memorial #82754784.

728 Virginia, Marriage Records, 1936-2014, Ancestry.com, Richard Louis Eudailey and Lucy Mabel Procise, Lunenburg County, Virginia Marriage cert. #8611.

729 Virginia, Birth Records, 1864-2014, Ancestry.com, Mabel Procise.

730 Obituary of Mabel Procise Eudailey (Richmond, Virginia, Richmond Times Dispatch, 12 Feb 1999), Richmond Public Library, 101 East Franklin Street, Richmond, VA.

731 Virginia, Death Records, 1912-2014, Ancestry.com, Mabel Procise Eudailey.

732 Find A Grave—Greenwood Memorial Gardens Cemetery, Richmond, Henrico Co., Virginia, Find A Grave.com, Mabel Procise Eudailey, Find A Grave Memorial #82754664.

733 Virginia, Marriage Records, 1936-2014, Ancestry.com, Richard Louis Eudailey and Frances Via Franklin.

734 Virginia, Birth Records, 1864-2014, Ancestry.com, Frances May "Viar".

735 Obituary of Frances Franklin Eudailey (Newport News, Virginia, Hampton Roads Daily Press), Main Street Library, 110 Main Street, Newport News, VA, Hampton Roads (VA) Daily Press, pub. 17 Jan 2007.

736 Virginia, Death Records, 1912-2014, Ancestry.com, Frances Via Eudailey.

737 Find A Grave—Cunningham United Methodist Cemetery, Cunningham, Fluvanna Co., Virginia, Find A Grave.com, Frances Mae Via Franklin-Eudailey, Find A Grave Memorial #83715502.

738 Virginia, Marriage Records, 1936-2014, Ancestry.com, Aubrey Bailey Chaney and Edith Virginia Eudailey, Lunenburg County, Virginia Marriage cert. #30187.

739 Find A Grave—Wylliesburg Baptist Cemetery, Wyllieisburg, Charlotte Co., Virginia, Find A Grave.com, Aubrey B. Chaney, Find A Grave Memorial #27569378.

740 Virginia, Death Records, 1912-2014, Ancestry.com, Aubrey Bailey Chaney, state file #72-009967.

741 Virginia, Marriage Records, 1936-2014, Ancestry.com, Claude Lee Tomlinson and Edith Virginia Eudailey Chaney, Lunenburg County, Virginia Marriage cert. #9528.

742 U.S. Veterans' Gravesites, ca. 1775-2006, Ancestry.com, Claude Tomlinson Sr.

743 Virginia, Birth Records, 1864-2014, Ancestry.com, Claude Lee Tomlinson.

744 Virginia, Death Records, 1912-2014, Ancestry.com, Claude Lee Tomlinson.

745 Find A Grave—Tussekiah Baptist Church Cemetery, Meherrin Lunenburg Co., Virginia, Find A Grave.com, Claude L. Tomlinson, Find A Grave Memorial #23928074.

746 Virginia, Death Records, 1912-2014, Ancestry.com, Robert Victor Tomlinson, state file #87-039815.

747 Virginia, Birth Records, 1864-2014, Ancestry.com, Robert Victor Tomlinson.

748 California, Death Index, 1940-1997, Ancestry.com, Rudolph John Nittler.

749 California, San Joaquin, County Public Library Obituary Index, 1850-1991, Obituary of Rudolph Nittler (Stockton, California, The Record, 02 Nov 1979), FamilySearch.org.

750 U.S., WWI Draft Registration Cards, 1917-1918, Ancestry.com, Rudolph John Nittler.

751 U.S. City Directories, 1822-1995, Ancestry.com, Napa, California, 1948, pg. 681, entry for Nittler, Rudolph J.; wife Eleanor.

752 Carson City, Nevada Marriage Index, 1855-1985, Ancestry.com, Rudolph J. Nittler and Iola Mae Chittim, lic. #39758647.

753 Obituary of Rudolph "Rudy" Nittler (Stockton, California, The Record, 02 Nov 1979), Cesar Chavez Central Library, 604 North El Dorado Street, Stockton, CA.

754 Obituary of Eleanor Lois Dibello (San Jose, CA, San Jose Mercury News, 26 Apr 1995), Martin Luther King, Jr. Library, California Room, 150 East San Fernando Street, San Jose, CA.

755 Find A Grave—Cedar Lawn Memorial Park Cemetery, Fremont, Alameda Co., California, Find A Grave.com, Eleanor L. Dibello, Find A Grave Memorial #182431093.

756 U.S., Social Security Applications and Claims Index, 1936-2007, Ancestry.com, Eleanor Kelso Theriault Kapp Seed DiBello.

757 California Divorce Index, 1940-1997, Ancestry.com, Walter Seed and Eleanor Lois Kelso Seed.

758 California Birth Index, 1905-1995, Ancestry.com, Walter C. Seed.

759 Nevada, Marriage Index, 1956-2005, Ancestry.com, Joseph James Dibello and Eleanor Lois Seed, Washoe County, Nevada Marriage Records.

760 California Divorce Index, 1940-1997, Ancestry.com, Joseph J. Dibello and Eleanor Kelso Dibello.

761 Nevada, Marriage Index, 1956-2005, Ancestry.com, Joseph James Dibello and Eleanor Lois Dibello, Douglas County, Nevada Marriage Records.

762 California Death Certificate, California Health and Strategic Planning, Vital Records, M.S. 5103, P.O. Box 997410, Sacramento, CA, Joseph Dibello, death cert. #3052005198424.

763 U.S. Veterans' Gravesites, ca. 1775-2006, Ancestry.com, Joseph J. Dibello.

764 Find A Grave—San Joaquin Valley National Cemetery, Santa Nella, Merced Co., California, Find A Grave.com, Joseph J. Dibello, Find A Grave Memorial #72886937.

765 All California, Divorce Index, 1966-1984, Ancestry.com, George L. Kelso and Frances E. Cortinas, three divorces, Dec 1966, Nov 1968, Apr 1973.

766 California, Death Index, 1940-1997, Ancestry.com, Sang Soon Kelso.

767 Obituary of Sang Soon "Haja" Kelso (Walnut Creek, CA, Contra Costa Times, 30 Jul 1997), Contra Costa County Library-Walnut Creek Branch, 1644 North Broadway Walnut Creek, CA.

768 Obituary of Tony Kelso (Walnut Creek, CA, Contra Costa Times, 12 Jun 2009), Contra Costa County Library-Walnut Creek Branch, 1644 North Broadway, Walnut Creek, CA.

769 Marriage Announcement of Thomas W. Davie and Katherine Anne Boggs (Moulton, IA, Moulton Times, 03 May 1956), Newspaper Archive online, https://access.newspaperarchive.com/us/iowa/moulton/moulton-weekly-tribune/1956/05-03?tag=Thomas+Davie&rtserp=tags/?psi=39&pci=7&pf=thomas&pl=davie&pc=19389.

770 Obituary of Thomas W. Davie (Tacoma, Washington, Tacoma News Tribune, 19 Apr 1991), Tacoma Public Library, 1102 Tacoma Avenue South, Tacoma, WA.

771 Washington, Death Index, 1940-2014, Ancestry.com, Thomas W. Davie, deat cdert. #011140.

772 Find A Grave—Falls View Cemetery, American Falls, Power Co., Idaho, Find A Grave.com, Thomas W. Davie, Find A Grave Memorial #75968732.

773 U.S., Social Security Applications and Claims Index, 1936-2007, Ancestry.com, Richard Edward Strep.

774 Obituary of Richard E. Strep (Tacoma, Washington, Tacoma News Tribune, June 9, 2004), Pierce County Public Library Main Branch, 5107 West 112th Street, Tacoma, WA.

775 Washington, Death Index, 1940-2014, Ancestry.com, Richard E. Strep.

776 Marriage Announcement of John F. Boggs and Janice Chaussee (Centralia, Washington, The Daily Chronicle), Washington State Library, Reference Section, Point Plaza East, 6880 Capitol Boulevard SE, Tumwater, WA.

777 Washington, Marriage Records, 1854-2013, Ancestry.com, John F. Boggs and Janice O. Chaussee, Lewis County, Washington Marriage Records, lic. #25913-19288.

778 U.S., Social Security Applications and Claims Index, 1936-2007, Ancestry.com, Janice Orella Wasson Fisch Chaussee Boggs Houston Conerly.

779 Obituary of Janice Orilla Boggs (Port Angeles, Washington, Peninsula Daily News, 30 Nov 1993), North Olympic Library System—Port Angeles Main Library, 2210 South Peabody Street, Port Angeles, WA.

780 Washington, Death Index, 1940-2014, Ancestry.com, Janice O. Boggs.

781 Find A Grave—Mount Angeles Memorial Park Cemetery, Port Angeles, Clallam Co., Washington, Find A Grave.com, Janice O. Boggs, Find A Grave Memorial #19698839.

782 Washington, Marriage Records, 1865-2004, Ancestry.com, Merle Edwin Landerholm and Mary Lee Boggs, Whitman County, Washington, Ref. #eawhmc3794.

783 British Columbia, Canada, Death Index, 1872-1990, Ancestry.com, Merle Edwin Landerholm, death registration #1976-09-012980; BCA #B13354; GSU #2050567.

784 Obituary of Dr. Merle Landerholm (Bellevue, Washington, Bellevue Times, 31 Aug 1976), Washington State Library, Reference Section, Point Plaza East, 6880 Capitol Boulevard SE, Tumwater, WA.

785 Find A Grave—Eternal Hills Memorial Park Cemetery, Oceanside, San Diego Co., California, Find A Grave.com, Robert E. Pegan, Find A Grave Memorial# 162396689.

786 Los Angeles County, California Marriage Records, California Health and Strategic Planning, Vital Records, M.S. 5103, P.O. Box 997410, Sacramento, CA, Robert E. Pegan and Gloria L. Donovan, Los Angeles County Marriage Records, Vol. 3894. pg. 353, lic. #8551.

787 U.S., Social Security Applications and Claims Index, 1936-2007, Ancestry.com, Gloria Donovan Pegan.

788 California Birth Index, 1905-1995, Ancestry.com, Gloria Louise Donovan.

789 Phone interview with John E. Pegan II's son in Texas, Ann Miller Carr, author, 10 Oct 2015.

790 California, Marriage Index, 1960-1985, Ancestry.com, John C. Mills and Anna Marie Pegan, Los Angeles County, California Marriage Records, California state Vol. 31535, lic. #84022.

791 California Death Certificate, California Health and Strategic Planning, Vital Records, M.S. 5103, P.O. Box 997410, Sacramento, CA, John Charles Mills, death cert. #3051999115666.

792 Obituary of John Charles Mills (Torrance, California, Daily Breeze, 19 Jun 1999), Katie Geissert Civic Center Library, 3301 Torrance Boulevard, Torrance, CA.

793 Marriage Announcement of William A. Cauldwell III and Ann Sewall Gregor (Syracuse, NY, Syracuse Herald Journal, 28 Jun 1954), Newspaper Archive online, https://access.newspaperarchive.com/us/new-york/syracuse/syracuse-herald-journal/1954/06-28/page-36?tag=William+Cauldwell&rtserp=tags/?pf=william&pl=cauldwell&psb=relavance&ndt=by&py=1950&pey=1959.

794 Obituary of William A. Cauldwell (Jacksonville, Florida, Florida Times-Union, 18 Jan 2009), Jacksonville Public Library, 303 North Laura Street, Jacksonville, FL.

795 New York, New York City Marriage Licenses Index, 1950-1995, FamilySearch.org, Abner Graboff and Ann G. Cauldwell.

796 U.S., Department of Veterans Affairs BIRLS Death File, 1850-2010, Ancestry.com, Abner Graboff.

797 "Who Was Abner Graboff?", The Ward-O-Matic, wardomaticblogspot.com/2009/06/who-was-abner-graboff.html

798 "Craig", "Abner Graboff. Quirky Children's Illustrator", Manchester, England, 28 May 2012; Online blog: Fishink, fishinkblog.com/2012/05/28/abner-graboff-quirky-children's-illustrator/

799 "Mission & History", College of the Atlantic, Bar Harbor, Maine; College of the Atlantic website: www.coa.edu/about/mission-history

800 Find A Grave—Brookside Cemetery, Watertown, Jefferson Co., New York, Find A Grave.com, Roderick Pirnie Jr., Find A Grave Memorial #150195031.

801 "Personals" (Watertown, New York, Watertown Daily Times, 04 Sep 1919). Flower Memorial Library, 229 Washington Street, Watertown, NY.

802 New York, WWII Enlistment Men's Cards, 1940-1945, Ancestry.com, Robert H. McKay.

803 Obituary of Robert Hamilton McKay (Jacksonville, Florida, Florida Times Union, 07 Dec 2001), State Library and Archives of Florida, R.A. Gray Building, 500 South Bronaugh Street, Tallahassee, FL.

804 U.S., Department of Veterans Affairs BIRLS Death File, 1850-2010, Ancestry.com, Robert McKay.

805 U.S., Social Security Applications and Claims Index, 1936-2007, Ancestry.com, Robert Hamilton McKay.

806 Indiana, Birth Certificates, 1907-1940, Ancestry.com, Wendell Eugene Carroll, Vigo Co., #1143.

807 Obituary of Wendell E. Carroll (Santa Rosa, California, Press Democrat, 23 Mar 2003), Sonoma County Library, 211 E Street, Santa Rosa, CA.

808 Washington, Death Index, 1940-2014, Ancestry.com, Wendell Carroll.

809 Find A Grave—Arlington National Cemetery, Arlington, Virginia, Find A Grave.com, Wendell E. Carroll, Find A Grave Memorial #152703268.

810 Connecticut Marriage Index, 1959-2001, FamilySearch.org, Charl P. Gruet and Elisa P. Carroll

811 Find A Grave—Willowbrook Cemetery, Westport, Fairfield Co., Connecticut, Find A Grave.com, Charles P. Gruet, Find A Grave Memorial# 166305218.

812 Connecticut Death Index, 1949-2012, Ancestry.com, Charles P. Gruet, state file #90351.

813 Massachusetts Death Index, 1970-2003, Ancestry.com, Charles P. Gruet, death cert. #041674.

814 Rio De Janiero, Brazil, Immigration Cards, 1900-1965, Ancestry.com, Charles Peter Gruet, born Lenox, Massachusetts.

815 Find A Grave—Mount Lebanon Cemetery, Mount Lebanon, Allegheny Co., Pennsylvania, Find A Grave.com, Leslie M. Pegan, Find A Grave Memorial #181625487.

816 Greenwood Memory Lawn Cemetery Records, Rosena Kondos, Greenwood Memory Lawn Cemetery, 2300 West Van Buren Street, Phoenix, AZ.

817 Marion County, Missouri Marriage Records, Marion County, Missouri Clerk's Office, 101 South Main Street, #107,

818 Illinois, Deaths and Stillbirths Index, 1916-1947, Ancestry.com, Mason Avery Leake.

Palmyra, MO, Mason A. Leake and Rosena C. Reher, Marion County, Missouri Marriage Records, Book 40, pg. 124.

819 "Inquest On Drowning Of Lieut. Leake" (Hannibal, Missouri, Hannibal Courier-Post, 10 Aug 1945), Hannibal Free Public Library, 200 South 5th Street, Hannibal, MO.

820 Find A Grave—Holy Family Cemetery, Hannibal, Mason Twp., Marion Co., Missouri, Find A Grave.com, Mason Avery Leake, Find A Grave Memorial #5478747.

821 Marion County, Missouri Marriage Records, Marion County, Missouri Clerk's Office, 101 South Main Street, #107, Palmyra, MO, James G. Kondos and Rosena C. Leake, Marion County, Missouri Marriage Records, Vol. 42, pg. 66.

822 Ohio, Births and Christenings Index, 1800-1962, Ancestry.com, James Gary Kondos, Richland Co., Ohio Birth Record Vol. 4, pg. 219.

823 U.S., Department of Veterans Affairs BIRLS Death File, 1850-2010, Ancestry.com, James Kondos.

824 Obituary of James G. Kondos (Phoenix, Arizona, Arizona Republic, 28 Aug 1978), Arizona State Library, Archives and Public Records, Archives and Records Management Branch, 1901 West Madison Street, Phoenix, AZ.

825 Greenwood Memory Lawn Cemetery Records, James Gary Kondos, Greenwood Memory Lawn Cemetery, 2300 West Van Buren Street, Phoenix, AZ.

826 Ohio Death Certificate, Ohio Department of Health, Center for Vital and Health Statistics, 246 North High Street, Columbus, OH, Emily D. Kondos, death cert. #08347.

827 Obituary of Emily Kondos (Cleveland, Ohio, Cleveland News, 04 Feb 1957), Cleveland Public Library, Rhodes Tower, 1212 Euclid Avenue, Cleveland, OH.

828 Ohio Death Certificate, Ohio Department of Health, Center for Vital and Health Statistics, 246 North High Street, Columbus, OH, Emily S. Kondos, death cert. #08347.

829 Obituary of Thomas George Kondos (St. Louis, Missouri, St. Louis Post-Dispatch, 16 Jan 2009), St. Louis County Public Library, 1640 South Lindbergh Boulevard, St. Louis, MO.

830 Ohio, Birth Index, 1908-1964, Ancestry.com, Stephen M. Kondos, state file #1959095203.

831 California, Marriage Index, 1949-1959, Ancestry.com, Frank V. Bakulich and Joan K. Pegan, Los Angeles County, California Marriage Records, Vol. 3669, pg. 244, lic. #14989.

832 California Death Certificate, California Health and Strategic Planning, Vital Records, M.S. 5103, P.O. Box 997410, Sacramento, CA, Frank Vincent Bakulich Sr., death cert. #3051998101156.

833 U.S., Social Security Applications and Claims Index, 1936-2007, Ancestry.com, Frank Vincent Bakulich.

834 California Birth Index, 1905-1995, Ancestry.com, Frank Vincent Bakulich.

835 Find A Grave—Green Hills Memorial Park Cemetery, Rancho Palos Verdes, Los Angeles Co., California, Find A Grave.com, Frank Bakulich, Find A Grave Memorial #5252339.

836 California, Marriage Index, 1960-1985, Leonard R. Jones and Jacquelin Pegan, Los Angeles County, California Marriage Records, California state file #79214.

837 California, Marriage Index, 1960-1985, Ancestry.com, Leo Bologna and Jacquelin K. Risler, Los Angeles County, California Marriage Records, California state file #8263.

838 Find A Grave—Green Hills Memorial Park Cemetery, Rancho Palos Verdes, Los Angeles Co., California, Find A Grave.com, Leonardo Bologna, Find A Grave Memorial #117766194.

839 Obituary of Leonardo Bologna (Torrance, California, The Daily Breeze, 01 Oct 2013), Katie Geissert Civic Center Library, 3301 Torrance Boulevard, Torrance, CA.

840 Find A Grave—Bellevue Memorial Park Cemetery, Ontario, San Bernardino Co., California, Find A Grave.com, Herbert E. McCann, Find A Grave Memorial #150939539.

841 California, Death Index, 1940-1997, Ancestry.com, Marie Laverne McCann.

842 California Death Certificate, California Health and Strategic Planning, Vital Records, M.S. 5103, P.O. Box 997410, Sacramento, CA, Marie LaVerne McCann, death cert. #79-045746.

843 U.S., Social Security Applications and Claims Index, 1936-2007, Ancestry.com, Marie LaVerne Gallagher McCann.

844 Find A Grave—Bellevue Memorial Park Cemetery, Ontario, San Bernardino Co., California, Find A Grave.com, Marie LaVerne McCann, Find A Grave Memorial #156990275.

845 California, Marriage Index, 1960-1985, Ancestry.com, Herbert E. McCann and Norma E. Miracle, San Bernardino County, California Marriage Records, California state lic. #102804.

846 Find A Grave—Bellevue Memorial Park Cemetery, Ontario, San Bernardino Co., California, Find A Grave.com, Norma "Ellie" McCann, Find A Grave Memorial #126671043.

847 U.S., Social Security Applications and Claims Index, 1936-2007, Ancestry.com, Michael Kevin McCann.

848 Michigan, Marriage Records, 1867-1952, Ancestry.com, Leslie Mc Queen and Ada Mc Cann, Wayne County, Michigan Marriage Records, Michigan state file #316186, Wayne County file #634549.

849 Obituary of Leslie E. MacQueen (Westland, Michigan, Westland Observer, 07 Jan 1999), William P. Faust Public Library of Westland, 6123 Central City Parkway, Westland, MI.

850 Obituary of Sharon Rainey (Traverse City, Michigan, Traverse City Record-Eagle, 14 Oct 2012), Traverse City District Library, Woodmere Main Library, 610 Woodmere Avenue, Traverse City, MI.

851 Howe-Peterson Funeral Home Records, Lois Bonacker, Howe-Peterson Funeral Home, 9800 South Telegraph Road, Taylor, MI.

852 Holy Sepulchre Cemetery Records, Albert D. Pratto, Holy Sepulchre Cemetery, The Archdiocesan Catholic Cemeteries, 25800 West 10 Mile Road, Southfield, MI.

853 Obituary of Albert Pratto (Detroit, Michigan, Detroit Free Press, 11 Mar 1966), Library of Michigan, 702 West Kalamazoo Street, Lansing, MI.

854 Michigan, Death Index, 1971-1996, Ancestry.com, William R. Farwell.

855 Obituary of Patrick D. Pratto (Phoenix, Arizona, The Arizona Republic, 13 Dec 2011), Arizona State Library, Archives and Public Records, Archives and Records Management Branch, 1901 West Madison Street, Phoenix, AZ.

856 St. Robert Bellarmine Church Records, Baptisms, Jeanine M. Pratto, St. Robert Bellermine Catholic Church, 27101 West Chicago Street, Redford, MI.

857 Holy Sepulchre Cemetery Records, Jeanine M. Pratto, Holy Sepulchre Cemetery, The Archdiocesan Catholic Cemeteries, 25800 West 10 Mile Road, Southfield, M.

858 Obituary of Jeanine Marie Pratto (Detroit, Michigan, Detroit Free Press, 13 Mar 1964), Library of Michigan, 702 West Kalamazoo Street, Lansing, MI.

859 California, Marriage Index, 1949-1959, Ancestry.com, David D. McCann and Phyllis J. Lachmeyer, Orange County, California Marriage Records, California state file #38713.

860 U.S. Public Records Index, 1950-1993, Vol. 1, Ancestry.com, Phyllis J. Lord, Costa Mesa and San Clemente, California.

861 U.S. Public Records Index, 1950-1993, Vol. 2, Ancestry.com, Phyllis J. Lord, San Clemente and Torrance, California.

862 Ohio, Birth Index, 1908-1964, Ancestry.com, Lachmeyer, fa. Albert, state file #1930067580.

863 California, Marriage Index, 1949-1959, Ancestry.com, Alfred W. Lord and Phyllis J. McCann, San Diego County, California Marriage Records, California state file #61886

864 Florida Marriage Indexes, 1822-1875, 1927-2001, Ancestry.com, Jack Morris and Marie Fischer.

865 New York, New York Births, 1910-1965, Ancestry.com, Jack Morris, Jr., Manhattan, 23 Jan 1937, cert. #2456.

866 Nevada, Marriage Index, 1956-2005, Ancestry.com, Charles Henry Keller and Marie Morris.

867 Find A Grave—Oak Hill Cemetery, Blue Island, Illinois, Find A Grave.com, BillyJo Fischer, Find A Grave Memorial #182290774.

868 California Birth Index, 1905-1995, Ancestry.com, Ray Matthew Devlin.

869 California Death Certificate, California Health and Strategic Planning, Vital Records, M.S. 5103, P.O. Box 997410, Sacramento, CA, Ray Matthew Devlin, death cert. #305201162695.

870 Indiana, Marriage Certificates, 1917-2005, Ancestry.com, Lawrence Howard Ewing and Shirley Jean Howe, Clinton County, Indiana Marriage Records, #72-000281.

871 Find A Grave—South Park Cemetery, Roswell, Chaves Co., New Mexico, Find A Grave.com, Janet C. Ewing, Find A Grave Memorial #26863456.

872 Obituary of Richard Moore (Roswell, New Mexico, Roswell Daily Record, 20 Jun 2013), Wilson-Cobb History and Genealogy Research Library, 301 South Richardson Street, Roswell, NM.

873 Find A Grave—South Park Cemetery, Roswell, Chaves Co., New Mexico, Find A Grave.com, Richard G. "Dick" Moore, Find A Grave Memorial # 112586044.

874 Find A Grave—Fairbury Cemetery, Fairbury, Washington Twp., Jefferson Co., Nebraska, Find A Grave.com, Robert Karl Williams, Find A Grave Memorial #21434351.

875 Find A Grave—Fairbury Cemetery, Fairbury, Washington Twp., Jefferson Co., Nebraska, Find A Grave.com, Richard Emil Williams, Find A Grave Memorial #21434371.

876 Find A Grave—Conesville Cemetery, Conesville. Orono Twp., Muscatine Co., Iowa, Find A Grave.com, Capt. Marvin K. Ewing, Find A Grave Memorial #108893254.

877 Marriage Announcement of Marvin K. Ewing and Karen Heritage (Davenport, Iowa, Davenport Democrat, 29 jun 1959), Davenport Public Library, 321 Main Street, Davenport, IA.

878 U.S. Public Records Index, 1950-1993, Vol. 2, Ancestry.com, Karen K. Ewing, 21 Feb 1941, Lansing, IA.

879 Obituary of Karen Ewing (Davenport, Iowa, Quad City Times, 08 Dec 1988), Davenport Public Library, 321 Main Street, Davenport, IA.

880 Find A Grave—Oakdale Memorial Gardens Cemetery, Davenport, Davenport Twp., Scott Co., Iowa, Find A Grave.com, Karen K. Ewing, Find A Grave Memorial #132966713.

881 Find A Grave—Conesville Cemetery, Conesville. Orono Twp., Muscatine Co., Iowa, Find A Grave.com, Charles Ewing, Find A Grave Memorial #108893237.

882 Nevada, Marriage Index, 1956-2005, Ancestry.com, Donald W. Bach and Linda Eileen Ewing, Clark County, Nevada Marriage Records, pg. B11.

883 New York, New York Births, 1910-1965, Ancestry.com, Donald W. Bach, Queens, birth cert. #5354.

884 Obituary of Donald W. Bach (Talladega, Alabama, The Daily Home, 25 Oct 2013), Talladega Armstrong-Osborne Library, 202 South Street E, Talladega, AL.

885 Marriage Announcement of Donald F. Bonacker and Peggy H. Budek (Suburban Economist, Chicago, Illinois, 23 Jul 1958) Newspaper Archive, online, newspaperarchive.com: https://www. Newspapers.com/image/54192574/

886 Marriage Announcement of Donald F. Bonacker and Peggy H. Budek (Chicago, IL, Chicago Austin News, 23 Jul 1958), Newspaper Archive online.

887 Find A Grave—Elm Lawn Cemetery, Elmhurst, DuPage Co., Illinois, Find A Grave.com, Juanita C. Bonacker, Find A Grave Memorial #182339439.

888 Obituary of Juanita Pitts Maka Bonacker (Chicago, Illinois, Chicago Tribune, 28 Jun 2007), Chicago Public Library, 400 South State Street, Chicago, IL.

889 Obituary of James W. Fabian (Chicago, IL, Chicago Tribune, 02 Nov 1972), St. Joseph County Public Library, 304 South Main Street, South Bend, IN.

890 Obituary of Katie Brockman (Milwaukee, Wisconsin, Milwaukee Journal, 18 Aug 2009), Milwaukee Public Library, 814 West Wisconsin Avenue, Milwaukee, WI.

891 Obituary of Harold Olbekson (Cheyenne, Wyoming, Wyoming Tribune Eagle, 09 Dec 2007), Laramie County Library in Cheyenne, 2200 Pioneer Avenue, Cheyenne, WY.

892 Find A Grave—Florida National Cemetery, Bushnell, Sumter Co., Florida, Find A Grave.com, Harold L "O.B." Olbekson, Find A Grave Memorial #23323453.

893 Find A Grave—Tussekiah Baptist Church Cemetery, Meherrin Lunenburg Co., Virginia, Find A Grave.com, Robert Victor Tomlinson, Find A Grave Memorial #96598425.

894 California, Death Index, 1940-1997, Ancestry.com, Thomas L. Kelso.

895 California Birth Index, 1905-1995, Ancestry.com, Thomas L. Kelso.

896 Holy Family Cemetery Records, Emily S. Kondos, Holy Name Catholic Church, 2103 Broadway Street, Hannibal, MO.

897 Holy Sepulchre Cemetery Records, Jeanine M. Pratto, Holy Sepulchre Cemetery, The Archdiocesan Catholic Cemeteries, 25800 West 10 Mile Road, Southfield, MI.

898 Find A Grave—Irvington Memorial Cemetery, Fremont, Alameda Co., California, Find A Grave.com, Thomas L. Kelso, Jr., Find A Grave Memorial #52789157.

[A] Ohio, Tax Records, 1800-1850, FamilySearch.com, "Andrew Pagan", Clark Township, Clinton County Ohio, 1829-1831; Green Township, Clinton County Ohio, 1832-1835 (Andrew "Pagun" in 1834).

[B] "List of Letters Left at the Hillsboro, Ohio Post Office, September 30, 1826", Abstracts From Before 1850, Southwestern Ohio Newspapers, Hillsborough Gazette and Highland Advertiser, Highland County; Online database: http://marsharising.com/newspapers/Ohio%20Newspapers/hillsborough_gazette_and_highlan.htm. Originals from (Hillsboro, Ohio, Hillsborough Gazette and Highland Advertiser, 09 Oct 1826) Microfilm #21714. Highland County District Library, 10 Willettsville Pike, Hillsboro, OH.

[C] Obituary of John F. Boggs (Port Angeles, WA, Peninsula Daily News, 21 May 2018), North Olympic Library System, Port Angeles Main Library, 2210 South Peabody Street, Port Angeles, WA.

[D] Obituary of Mary Lee Landerholm, (Seattle, Washington, Seattle Times, 08 Jul 2018), The Seattle Public Library-Central Library, 1000 Fourth Avenue, Seattle, WA.

John Pegan, Son of Robert

1. **John**[5] **Pegan** (*Robert A.*[4], *Andrew*[3], *Andrew*[2] *Pagan, James*[1]) was born on September 14, 1808, in Strabane Twp., Washington Co., Pennsylvania.[1] He was the son of Robert A. Pegan and Christina or Christiana Ingle. John died in Quincy, Miami Twp., Logan Co., Ohio, on March 20, 1874, at age 65.[2] He was buried in Greenwood Cemetery, Pleasant Twp., Logan Co., Ohio.[3]

John Pegan was a carpenter; he was probably trained by master carpenter Joseph Pagan/Pagin who may have been related.[4, 5]

John married **Rebecca Shearer** on June 3, 1830, in Montgomery Co., Ohio.[1, 6] They had six children. Rebecca Shearer was born in Belmont Co., Ohio, on June 6, 1810.[7] Rebecca reached age 33 and died in Piqua, Washington Twp., Miami Co., Ohio, about September 18, 1843.

Rebecca Shearer Pegan seems to have died in childbirth with daughter Margaret or shortly thereafter.

John Pegan is enumerated as John "Pagan" in the 1830 census in Wayne Twp., Montgomery Co., Ohio (*Census Place: Wayne, Montgomery, Ohio; Page: 245; NARA Series: M19; Roll Number: 136*). There is a one in col. 5 and a one in col. 18, so there is one male (John) and one female (his new bride, Rebecca Shearer Pegan) between the ages of 20-30 years old. Both sets of their parents are close neighbors.

A "John Jacob Pagan" represents John Pegan's younger brother, William Louis ("Lewis") Pagan, the plaintiff in a scandalous slander suit in Montgomery Co., Ohio on September 4, 1839. The suit claimed that Rev. David Winters, a well-known pastor and founder of a church on the Montgomery/Greene county line, defamed young "William Lewis Pagan", who, from 1830 to July 1, 1839 was "living with and under the tutelage of" Rev. Francis Frederick Langoff. Winters allegedly had told others that William Lewis, then a minor, had committed sodomy with Langhoff, who had earlier been dismissed from a church in Pittsburgh, Pennsylvania for unspecified and mysterious reasons.[8] A few months later, the Pagans/Pegans withdrew the charges. This probable legal representative specifically states his name as "John Jacob Pagan", and is likely the "John J. Pagan" found on the Knox Twp., Columbiana Co., Ohio tax lists from 1829-1832 and as John Jacob Pagan in the same township in 1833.[9] He is also enumerated as a 60-69-year-old male in the 1840 census in Wheeling, Ohio Co., West Virginia (*Census Place: Wheeling Ward 1, Ohio, Virginia; Roll: 571; Page: 50*). As John Pegan, the carpenter and older brother of William Louis Pegan, never writes his name or is referred to as "John Jacob", this John Pegan probably did not represent his brother. Also, this John Pegan is not known to have used a middle initial.

In 1840, John Pegan may be the "John Reagan" in Olney, Washington Twp., Miami Co., Ohio (*Census Place: Washington, Miami, Ohio; Roll: 415; Page: 349; Image: 712*). There is a one in col. 1, a one in col. 2, a one in col. 4, a two in col. 5, and a one in col. 6; a two in col. 14, a one in col. 17, and a one in col. 19 (one male under age five, one male age five-10, one male age 15-19, two males age 20-30 and one male age 30-40 (John); two females under age five, one female 15-20 and one female 30-40 (Rebecca). The male 15-19 may be Perry Pegan, who would die shortly after the census, and William Lewis Pegan is one of the males 20-30. The other may be a carpenter who is apprenticing under John. The female 15-19 is most likely a servant.

John Pegan married **Phoebe Moore** on July 14, 1845, in Miami Co., Ohio.[10] They had four children. Phoebe Moore was born in Ohio on June 21, 1820.[11] Phoebe reached age 91 and died in Montclair Twp., Essex Co., New Jersey, on June 22, 1911.[12] She was buried in Greenwood Cemetery,

Pleasant Twp., Logan Co., Ohio.[12, 13] She was the daughter of Robert Moore and Martha Preifix. Her given name is sometimes seen as Phebe.

John Pegan is enumerated in the 1850 census in Piqua, Washington Twp., Miami Co., Ohio *(Census Place: Washington, Miami, Ohio; Roll: M432_711; Page: 377; Image: 131)*. In the home are John, age 42, a carpenter, born in Pennsylvania and his second wife Phoebe Moore Pegan, 30, born Ohio. With them are John's children by his late first wife Rebecca Shearer Pegan: Emmanuel, 19, then a carpenter (later a physician), David, 17, Mary, 15, Catherine, 13, James M., nine, and Margaret, seven; plus his children by Phoebe: Martha, five, and John Jr., two. All of these children were born in Ohio. Two young carpenters are living with the family, Abner Bean, 22 and John Yaney, 20. John's brothers Elsey and Harrison are neighbors.

In 1860, John Pegan is found in DeGraff Twp., Logan Co., Ohio *(Census Place: Miami, Logan, Ohio; Roll: M653_1000; Page: 82; Image: 164)*. In the household are John, age 52, a carpenter, born Pennsylvania; Phoebe, 39, born Ohio; and children Martha, 14, John Jr., 11, Laura, seven, and son "Elsie" (Elsey), two. Elsey, named for his late uncle Elsey Pegan and, perhaps, an as yet unknown ancestor, would succumb later that year.

John Pegan Sr. is found in Miami Twp., Logan Co., Ohio in 1870 *(Census Place: Miami, Logan, Ohio; Roll: M593_1234; Page: 158; Image: 316)*. In the household are John, age 61, born Pennsylvania; Phoebe, 49, born Ohio; and their children Martha, 23, John Jr. 21, and "Lucy", (Laura Louise) 16. Living with them is a Frank Dills, 29, who works in a carpenter's shop and was born in Ohio.

John Pegan left a will in Logan County, Ohio, bequeathing his property and personal items to his widow, Phebe. He willed his silver watch engraved with his name to his son John II, and specified that son James be allowed to occupy the house in which James was living as long as he paid $3 a month to Phebe.[14]

In 1880, "Phoeba" Moore PeGan, age 59, a widow, was living with children Martha (Mattie), 32, and John Jr., 30, and John's wife Anna Armstrong Pegan, 28, in DeGraff Twp., Logan Co., Ohio *(Census Place: De Graff, Logan, Ohio; Roll: 1041; Page: 144B; Enumeration District: 119; Image: 0291)*. Phoebe Moore Pegan says she was born in Ohio, her father in Pennsylvania and her mother in Virginia. "Mattie" says she is a dressmaker, while John Jr. is a carpenter. All but Phoebe say they were born in Ohio, as were their parents. This is incorrect, as John Pegan Sr., the father of Martha and John Jr., was born in Pennsylvania.

Phebe Moore Pegan is enumerated as "Phoebe Strayer" and was living with son-in-law and daughter, James and Martha "Mattie" Pegan Strayer in De Graff, Miami Twp., Logan Co., Ohio in 1900 *(Census Place: Miami, Logan, Ohio; Roll: T623_1294; Page: 6A; Enumeration District: 117)*. Phoebe is listed as age 77, born Jun 1822. (This is incorrect, according to her death certificate and information in other censuses, she was born earlier.) Phoebe says she bore four children, three still living. This time, she says she was born in Ohio and both her parents in Virginia. James Strayer, 42, born March 1858 in Ohio, is a farmer and stock raiser. He says his father was born in Virginia and his mother in Ohio. Martha "Mattie" Pegan Strayer, 54, born Apr 1846, says she was born in Ohio, her father in Pennsylvania and her mother in Ohio. The couple says they have been married seven years and Martha has borne no children.

Phoebe Moore Pegan continues to reside with James and Martha "Mattie" Pegan Strayer in De Graff, Miami Twp., Logan Co., Ohio in 1910 *(Census Place: Miami, Logan, Ohio; Roll: T624_1204; Page: 8B; Enumeration District: 0138; Image: 997)*. Phoebe, 89 years old and a widow was born Ohio, with her parents born in Virginia. James Strayer is listed as age 52, a wool buyer. Martha Pegan Strayer, enumerated as "Mattie", is listed as age 53—this is incorrect, as she is 63. Both say they and their parents were born in Ohio (again, incorrect).

After living in Miami Twp., Logan Co., Ohio for perhaps all of her life, Phoebe Moore Pegan died at the home of her son-in-law and daughter, Edward and Laura Pegan Hill III, who were living in Montclair Twp., Essex Co., New Jersey in 1911

There is considerable confusion on Phoebe Moore Pegan's exact date and place of birth. Phoebe's obituary in the Indianapolis Star says Phebe was proud of being "born on the day of the birth of Queen Victoria. Queen Victoria was born May 24, 1819. Phoebe Moore Pegan could not have been born on the same day as Queen Victoria. Phebe's tombstone says she was born on June 20, 1820.[11] Her New Jersey death certificate says she was born on June 22, 1821. On her death certificate, her date of death is June 21, 1911 and her age is given as exactly 90 years old.[12] According to her obituary in the Indianapolis (IN) Star, she was 92.[15] Yet her obituary in the Bellefontaine, Ohio Examiner says she died on her 91st birthday![16] Her birth date seems to have been May 24, 1819 or June 21, 1820. Also, although her New Jersey death certificate states that Phoebe was born in Virginia, in the censuses she consistently says she was born in Ohio.[12]

Children of John Pegan and Rebecca Shearer:

+ 2 m I. **Emmanuel**[6] **Pegan** was born in Wayne Twp., Montgomery Co., Ohio, on April 22, 1831.[17] He died in Camden, Kent Co., Delaware, on May 16, 1865.[17]

+ 3 m II. **David Shearer**[6] **Pegan** was born in Wayne Twp., Montgomery Co., Ohio, in 1833. He died in Hamilton, Butler Co., Ohio, on November 15, 1865.[18]

+ 4 f III. **Mary Elizabeth**[6] **Pegan** was born in Rossville, Springcreek Twp., Miami Co., Ohio, on June 25, 1835.[19] She died in Miami Twp., Logan Co., Ohio, on October 10, 1896.[20, 21]

+ 5 f IV. **Catherine**[6] **Pegan** was born in Rossville, Springcreek Twp., Miami Co., Ohio, about 1837. She was also known as **Kate**. Catherine died in Miami Twp., Logan Co., Ohio, on September 27, 1886.[22]

+ 6 m V. **James Milton**[6] **Pegan** was born in Piqua, Washington Twp., Miami Co., Ohio, on June 6, 1842.[23] He died in DeGraff, Miami Twp., Logan Co., Ohio, on August 4, 1894.[23]

+ 7 f VI. **Margaret**[6] **Pegan** was born in Piqua, Washington Twp., Miami Co., Ohio, on September 18, 1843.[24] She was also known as **Mattie or Maggie**. Margaret died in Los Angeles, Los Angeles Co., California, on October 6, 1929.[24, 25]

Children of John Pegan and Phoebe Moore:

+ 8 f I. **Martha Ann**[6] **Pegan** was born in Piqua, Washington Twp., Miami Co., Ohio, on April 13, 1846.[26] She was also known as **Mattie**. Martha Ann died in DeGraff, Miami Twp., Logan Co., Ohio, on July 27, 1923.[26]

+ 9 m II. **John Andrew**[6] **Pegan II** was born in Piqua, Washington Twp., Miami Co., Ohio, on December 25, 1849.[27] He died in Indianapolis, Marion Co., Indiana, on May 11, 1918.[27, 28]

+ 10 f III. **Laura Louisa**[6] **Pegan** was born in Miami Twp., Logan Co., Ohio, on March 21, 1854.[29] She died in Los Angeles, Los Angeles Co., California, on May 5, 1944.[29]

+ 11 m IV. **Elsey**[6] **Pegan** was born in Miami Twp., Logan Co., Ohio, on August 31, 1858.[30] He died in Miami Twp., Logan Co., Ohio, on November 15, 1860.[30]

6th Generation

2. **Emmanuel**[6] Pegan (*John*[5], *Robert A.*[4], *Andrew*[3], *Andrew*[2] *Pagan, James*[1]) was born on April 22, 1831, in Wayne Twp., Montgomery Co., Ohio.[17] He was the son of John Pegan (1) and Rebecca Shearer. Emmanuel lived in 1855 in Mexico, Miami Co., Indiana. Emmanuel died in Camden, Kent Co., Delaware, on May 16, 1865, at age 34.[17] He was buried in Old Mexico Cemetery, Mexico, Jefferson Twp., Miami Co., Indiana.[31]

Emmanuel married **Sarah Strouse** on February 17, 1855, in Miami Co., Indiana.[32, 33] They had two children. Sarah Strouse was born in Congress Twp., Wayne Co., Ohio, on October 4, 1837.[34] Sarah reached age 87 and died in Anthony, Anthony Twp., Harper Co., Kansas, on June 17, 1925.[34] She was buried in Forest Park Cemetery, Anthony, Anthony Twp., Harper Co., Kansas.[34, 35]

In 1860, Emmanuel Pegan, a physician, is enumerated in Sidney, Turtle Creek Twp., Shelby Co., Ohio as "E. Pegan" (*Census Place: Turtle Creek, Shelby, Ohio; Roll: M653_1036; Page: 287; Image: 18*). In the home are Emmanuel, 28, a physician; Sarah Strause Pegan, 21, "'O/P'.M.C." (Pliny Moses Crume), four, and Florence, two. All were born in Ohio.

Emmanuel Pegan, M.D. undoubtedly trained under the famous regional physician, Dr. Pliny Moses Crume, son of the Rev. Moses Crume, in the Butler—Preble counties, Ohio area.[36] Emmanuel named his only son, Pliny Moses Crume Pegan, after his mentor. Dr. Emmanuel Pegan practiced for a short time in Miami Co., Indiana, where he met and married his wife, Sarah Strouse Pegan (Shields). After their marriage, however, they moved to Turtle Creek Twp., Shelby Co., Ohio, nearer to Emmanuel's family, and both their children were born there. In 1864, following his first stint in the Civil War, Dr. Emmanuel Pegan moved his family back to Indiana, this time to Rochester, Rochester Twp., Fulton Co., Indiana. Shortly after this relocation, Emmanual Pegan, M.D. either enlisted or was asked to return to the Union Army to be the federal examining surgeon. He was at an Army medical camp in Camden, Delaware, when he died of sickness.[17]

After Emmanuel Pegan's death, Sarah Strouse Pegan married Robert McBain Shields on January 12, 1866 in Miami Co., Indiana.[37] They had two children, one of whom died in infancy. Robert M. Shields, was born on March 17, 1835 in Vincennes, Vincennes Twp., Knox Co., Indiana.[38] He died on March 23, 1903 in Mexico, Jefferson Twp., Miami Co., Indiana.[38, 39]

In 1870 Sarah Strouse Pegan Shields is enumerated with her second husband Robert McBain Shields, listed as "R.M. Shields", in Henry Twp., Fulton Co., Indiana (*Census Place: Henry, Fulton, Indiana; Roll: M593_316; Page: 25A; Image: 53*). In the home are Robert Shields, 35, born Indiana, a saddler; Sarah Strouse Pegan Shields, 30, Pliny Crume Pegan (listed as "C.P.M. Peyan"), 14, and Florence G. "Peyan", 11. Sarah, Pliny Crume and Florence were all born in Ohio. Also in the home is Mary Shields, age two, born Indiana, Robert and Sarah's first child together.

By 1880, Robert M. and Sarah Strouse Pegan Shields have moved to Liberty Twp., Barton Co., Kansas (*Census Place: Liberty, Barton, Kansas; Roll: 373; Page: 150A; Enumeration District: 352; Image: 0305*). In the home are Robert M. Shields, 45, a farmer, born Indiana, with his father born in Virginia and his mother, Kentucky. With him are his wife, Sarah Strouse Pegan Shields, 40, born Ohio, with her parents both born in Kentucky, and their son Frank, nine, born Indiana. Daughter Mary seems to be deceased.

Robert M. and Sarah Strouse Shields are found in Jefferson Twp., Miami Co., Indiana in 1900, living in or near the town of Denver (*Census Place: Jefferson, Miami, Indiana; Roll: T623_393; Page: 19A; Enumeration District: 101*). Robert Shields is 65 years old, born in March 1835 in Indiana, with his parents born in Virginia, says he is a harness maker. Sarah Strouse Pegan Shields is 62, born in Indiana, with her father born in New Jersey and her mother in Kentucky. The couple says they have been married 34 years and that Sarah has borne three children, all of them still alive (Incorrect—she bore four children, and one died).

In 1910, Sarah Strouse Pegan Shields is living in Anthony, Anthony Twp., Harper Co., Kansas

(Census Place: Anthony Ward 1, Harper, Kansas; Roll: T624_441; Page: 5B; Enumeration District: 0073; Image: 713). She is a widow, age 72, and listed as the head of household. She says she was born in Ohio, her father in Germany and her mother in Kentucky; and that she had borne three children, all still surviving (Again, incorrect). Living with her are her son-in-law and daughter, Mervin O. and Florence G. Pegan Cissel and their son Benjamin. Mervin Cisell, 58, was born in Indiana, his father in Maryland and his mother in Pennsylvania. He says he is the editor of the Argonia Clipper (in Argonia, Dixon Twp., Sumner Co., Kansas, adjacent to Harper Co.). Florence G., 51, says she and her father were born in Ohio and but, oddly, says her mother in Indiana. This is incorrect. Mervin and Florence say they have been married 32 years and Florence has borne three children, all still alive. Their son Benjamin Z., age 26, born Indiana, is also in the home; he says he is silversmith at a jewelry store. Again, the census taker erred, as he says Benjamin was born in Indiana, but his father was born in Maryland and his mother in Ohio. The census taker was most likely wrong about the head of household as well—it was probably Mervin Cissel.

In 1920, Sarah Strouse Pegan Shields is still living with her son-in-law and daughter, Mervin O. and Florence G. Pegan Cissel in Anthony, Anthony Twp., Harper Co., Kansas *(Census Place: Anthony, Harper, Kansas; Roll: T625_533; Page: 8B; Enumeration District: 75; Image: 923).* This time, Mervin Cissel is listed as head of the household. Sarah is age 82, born Ohio, with her father born in Pennsylvania and her mother in Kentucky. Mervin O. Cissel, 58, was born in Indiana, his father in Maryland and his mother in Pennsylvania. This time, he lists his occupation as a bookkeeper at a plumbing company. Florence G. Pegan Cissel, age 51, still says she and her father were born in Ohio and her mother in Indiana.

Children of Emmanuel Pegan and Sarah Strouse:

+ 12 m I. **Pliny Moses Crume**[7] **Pegan** was born in Hardin, Turtle Creek Twp., Shelby Co., Ohio, on May 15, 1856.[40] He died in Denver, Denver Co., Colorado, on December 18, 1947.[40]

+ 13 f II. **Florence Genevieve**[7] **Pegan** was born in Hardin, Turtle Creek Twp., Shelby Co., Ohio, on December 9, 1858.[41, 42] She was also known as **Jennie**. Florence Genevieve died in Anthony, Anthony Twp., Harper Co., Kansas, on April 15, 1929.[41, 42]

3. **David Shearer**[6] **Pegan** (*John*[5], *Robert A.*[4], *Andrew*[3], *Andrew*[2] *Pagan, James*[1]) was born in 1833 in Wayne Twp., Montgomery Co., Ohio. He was the son of John Pegan (1) and Rebecca Shearer. David Shearer lived in 1860 in Hamilton Twp., Butler Co., Ohio. He served in the military. Civil War, Company D 35th Ohio Infantry. Private. David Shearer died in Hamilton, Butler Co., Ohio, on November 15, 1865, at age 32.[18] He was buried in Greenwood Cemetery, Hamilton, Butler Co., Ohio.[18]

Never married.

In 1860, David Pegan, spelled "Pagin", is enumerated in Hamiton, Butler Co., Ohio *(Census Place: Hamilton, Butler, Ohio; Roll: M653_941; Page: 435; Image: 436).* David Pegan is age 26, single, a carpenter, born Ohio. He seems to be living in a large boarding house or hotel.

David S. Pegan was a casualty of the Civil War. He enlisted in Company D, Ohio 35th Infantry on August 26, 1861[43] According to military records, David S. was wounded in the Battle of Chickamauga on September 19, 1863 and was registered as dying of his wounds on May 7, 1864 at Ringgold, Catoosa Co., Georgia on the Georgia-Tennessee border.[44] This conflicts with the official death record from the military gravestone purchase record for David S. Pegan, which says he died on November 15, 1865.[18]

4. **Mary Elizabeth**[6] **Pegan** (*John*[5], *Robert A.*[4], *Andrew*[3], *Andrew*[2] *Pagan, James*[1]) was born on June 25, 1835, in Rossville, Springcreek Twp., Miami Co., Ohio.[19] She was the daughter of John Pegan (1) and Rebecca Shearer. Mary Elizabeth died in Miami Twp., Logan Co., Ohio, on October 10, 1896, at age 61.[20, 21]

She was buried in Greenwood Cemetery, DeGraff, Pleasant Twp., Logan Co., Ohio.[19, 20]

Mary Elizabeth married **Samuel Myer or Meyers Mason II** on May 13, 1855, in Logan Co., Ohio.[45] They had nine children. Samuel Myer or Meyers Mason II was born in Lake Twp., Logan Co., Ohio, on March 17, 1833.[46, 47] Samuel Myer or Meyers reached age 73 and died in Indianapolis, Marion Co., Indiana, on June 14, 1906.[46, 47] He was buried in Greenwood Cemetery, DeGraff, Pleasant Twp., Logan Co., Ohio.[46, 48]

Samuel M. Mason worked as a carpenter and architect.

Samuel and Mary E. Pegan Mason II are enumerated in Rushylvania, Rush Creek Twp., Logan Co., Ohio in 1860 *(Census Place: Rushsylvania, Logan, Ohio; Roll: M653_1000; Page: 213; Image: 429)*. In the home are Samuel Mason, age 27, a carpenter; his wife, Mary E. Pegan Mason, 25, and their children, Ida, four and Charles, six months. Living with them is Mary's 17-year-old cousin, Margaret Pegan, daughter of John and Rebecca Shearer Pegan. Margaret is listed as a housekeeper. (Margaret later marries William C. Miller.) Also in the abode is James Mason, 16, probably a relative of Samuel's. All were born in Ohio.

In 1870, Samuel M. and Mary E. Pegan Mason II still reside in Rushylvania, Rush Creek Twp., Logan Co., Ohio *(Census Place: Rushcreek, Logan, Ohio; Roll: M593_1234; Page: 251B; Image: 515)*. Samuel Mason, 35, is still a carpenter; Mary E. Pegan Mason is 25. With them are children Ida, 14, "Edwin" (Charles Edwin), 10, "Katie" (Katherine), eight, and "Allie" (Alta Dell), five. All were born in Ohio.

Samuel and Mary E. Pegan Mason II are found in Rush Twp., Champaign Co., Ohio in 1880 *(Census Place: Rush, Champaign, Ohio; Roll: 998; Page: 347C; Enumeration District: 27; Image: 0380)*. Samuel is 47, a carpenter, born Ohio, with his father born in Virginia and his mother in Germany. Mary E. Pegan Mason is 35 and says she and her parents were born in Ohio (Incorrect—her father was born in Pennsylvania). Children in the home include: Ida, 24, Charles E., 20, who works on a farm; "Katie", 18, "Della", 14, Cora, eight, John, six, and Minnie, four. All the children were born in Ohio.

Samuel Mason II, who would have been a widower, is not found in the 1900 census in Logan County, Ohio. He may have removed to Indianapolis by then, as stated in his obituary in the Bellefontaine Examiner, published the day after he died.[49] But he is not found in the census there either. His gravestone erroneously says he died in 1905.[48] All references the author found mentioned this date, but this author could not find any verification. His death certificate was finally found in Indianapolis, Marion Co., Indiana, and he died on June 14, 1906.[46]

Children of Mary Elizabeth Pegan and Samuel Myer or Meyers Mason II:

+ 14 f I. **Ada**[7] **Mason** was born in Rushylvania, Rush Creek Twp., Logan Co., Ohio, on March 10, 1856.[50] She died in Rushylvania, Rush Creek Twp., Logan Co., Ohio, on July 28, 1856.[51]

+ 15 f II. **Ida May**[7] **Mason** was born in Rushylvania, Rush Creek Twp., Logan Co., Ohio, on March 10, 1856.[50] She died in Clay Twp., Hamilton Co., Indiana, on August 17, 1927.[50]

+ 16 m III. **Charles Edwin**[7] **Mason** was born in Rushylvania, Rush Creek Twp., Logan Co., Ohio, on November 6, 1859.[52] He died in Bellefontaine, Lake Twp., Logan Co., Ohio, on March 3, 1950.[52]

+ 17 f IV. **Katherine**[7] **Mason** was born in Rushylvania, Rush Creek Twp., Logan Co., Ohio, on May 9, 1862.[53] She was also known as **Kate**. Katherine died in Indianapolis, Center Twp., Marion Co., Indiana, on December 15, 1929.[53]

+ 18 f V. **Alta Dell**[7] **Mason** was born in Rushylvania, Rush Creek Twp.,

Logan Co., Ohio, on January 29, 1865.[54] She was also known as **Allie or Della**. Alta Dell died in on a journey to Rangoon, Burma, on October 27, 1921, at age 56.[55, 56]

+ 19 m VI. **Samuel⁷ Mason III** was born in Rushylvania, Rush Creek Twp., Logan Co., Ohio, about 1868. He died in Rushylvania, Rush Creek Twp., Logan Co., Ohio, between 1868 and 1870.

+ 20 f VII. **Cora⁷ Mason** was born in Rushylvania, Rush Creek Twp., Logan Co., Ohio, on June 9, 1871.[57] She died in Indianapolis, Marion Co., Indiana, on March 26, 1949.[58, 59]

+ 21 m VIII. **John Pegan⁷ Mason** was born in Rushylvania, Rush Creek Twp., Logan Co., Ohio, on February 26, 1873.[60, 61, 62] He died in Indianapolis, Center Twp., Marion Co., Indiana, on June 2, 1924.[62]

+ 22 f IX. **Minnie or Mary Elizabeth⁷ Mason** was born in North Lewisburg, Rush Twp., Champaign Co., Ohio, on January 13, 1876.[63] She was also known as **Elizabeth**. Minnie or Mary Elizabeth died in Indianapolis, Center Twp., Marion Co., Indiana, on May 17, 1956.[63]

5. Catherine⁶ Pegan (*John⁵, Robert A.⁴, Andrew³, Andrew² Pagan, James¹*) was born about 1837 in Rossville, Springcreek Twp., Miami Co., Ohio. She was also known as **Kate**. She was the daughter of John Pegan (1) and Rebecca Shearer. Catherine died in Miami Twp., Logan Co., Ohio, on September 27, 1886?, at age 49.[22] She was buried in Fairview Cemetery, Quincy, Miami Twp., Logan Co., Ohio.[64] Catherine Pegan Baughman's exact birth date is unknown, and her death date is not definitively documented.

Catherine married **Joshua B. Baughman** on September 28, 1856, in Logan Co., Ohio.[65] They had two sons. Joshua B. Baughman was born in Pleasant Twp., Franklin Co., Ohio, on January 18, 1831.[22, 66] He lived in 1894 in Quincy, Miami Twp., Logan Co., Ohio. He reached age 90 and died in Marion, Marion Twp., Marion Co., Ohio, on October 6, 1921.[66, 67] Joshua B. was buried in Greenwood Cemetery, DeGraff, Pleasant Twp., Logan Co., Ohio.[66, 68]

Joshua and Catherine Pegan Baughman are enumerated in De Graff, Miami Twp., Logan Co., Ohio in 1860 *(Census Place: De Graff, Logan, Ohio; Roll: M653_1000; Page: 86; Image: 175)*. In the household are Joshua Baughman, age 29, a master carpenter; Catherine Pegan Baughman, 23, and son John B. Baughman, age two. All were born in Ohio.

In 1870, Joshua and Catherine Pegan Baughman are still living in De Graff, Miami Twp., Logan Co., Ohio *(Census Place: De Graff, Logan, Ohio; Roll: M593_1234; Page: 170B; Image: 349)*. They are listed as "Josh" and "Kate" Baughman. Joshua is 38, a carpenter and Catherine is 33. The only child in the home is son Otto, age two. All were born in Ohio.

By 1880, Joshua and Catherine Pegan Baughman have moved to Piqua, Washington Twp., Miami Co., Ohio, where her father, two uncles, and her grandparents once lived *(Census Place: Piqua, Miami, Ohio; Roll: 1049; Page: 287C; Enumeration District: 142; Image: 0624)*. Joshua Baughman, age 49, works in a carpentry shop and says he was born in Ohio and his parents in Pennsylvania. Catherine Pegan Baughman is 44 and states she and her parents were born in Ohio (Incorrect—her father was born in Pennsylvania). Son Otto G, 12, was born in Ohio.

Catherine "Kate" Pegan Baughman seems to have died around 1886. Her husband Joshua Baughman's obituary *(Bellefontaine [OH] Daily Examiner, October 6, 1921, reprinted from the Marion (OH) Tribune)* says she died on September 27, 1856. This is incorrect—the paper somehow confused her death date with a date close to their documented marriage date September 28, 1856.[22]

Joshua Baughman is found back in De Graff, Miami Twp., Logan Co., Ohio in 1900 *(Census Place: Miami,*

Logan, Ohio; Roll: T623_1294; Page: 5B; Enumeration District: 117). Joshua B. Baughman, a widower, is 69, born Jan 1831 in Ohio, with his father born in Pennsylvania and his mother in Ohio. Son Otto G., now 32 and also a carpenter, was born in May 1868; he was born in Ohio as were his parents.

Joshua Baughman is enumerated as "Josh Baufman" in 1910 in Marion, Marion Twp., Marion Co., Ohio *(Census Place: Marion Ward 2, Marion, Ohio; Roll: T624_1213; Page: 3B; Enumeration District: 0085; Image: 735).* He is living in his son Otto G. "Baufman's" household. Joshua is listed as age 80, a widower who is still a house carpenter. He says he was born in Ohio and his parents in Pennsylvania. Otto Baughman, 41, now a lamp inspector (probably a streetlight inspector), says he was born in Ohio as were his parents. Wife Tina Stahler Stedlinger Baughman ("Baufman") is 26, also born in Ohio as were her parents. The couple have been married four years and Tina has borne no children. Tina Stahler Stedlinger Baughman does say this is her second marriage.

In 1920, Joshua Baughman is again living with his son Otto G. Baughman and Otto's wife Tina in Marion, Marion Co., Ohio *(Census Place: Marion Ward 2, Marion, Ohio; Roll: T625_1416; Page: 5A; Enumeration District: 122; Image: 182).* Otto is still listed as head of household. Joshua Baughman is 88 and retired. Otto G., who says he is only 48, is a railroad car repairer while wife Tina Stahler Stedlinger Baughman, 35, is a saleslady at a dry good store. All in the home say they and their parents were born in Ohio.

Sons of Catherine Pegan and Joshua B. Baughman:

+ 23 m I. **John B.⁷ Baughman** was born in DeGraff, Miami Twp., Logan Co., Ohio, on June 5, 1858.[69] He died in DeGraff, Miami Twp., Logan Co., Ohio, on September 7, 1863.[69]

+ 24 m II. **Otto G.⁷ Baughman** was born in Logansville, Pleasant Twp., Logan Co., Ohio, on May 16, 1868.[70] He died in Marion, Marion Twp., Marion Co., Ohio, on April 19, 1925.[70]

6. **James Milton⁶ Pegan** (*John⁵, Robert A.⁴, Andrew³, Andrew² Pagan, James¹*) was born on June 6, 1842, in Piqua, Washington Twp., Miami Co., Ohio.[23] He was the son of John Pegan (1) and Rebecca Shearer. James Milton died in DeGraff, Miami Twp., Logan Co., Ohio, on August 4, 1894, at age 52.[23] He was buried in Greenwood Cemetery, DeGraff, Pleasant Twp., Logan Co., Ohio.[71]

James Milton Pegan served in Company F, 132th Ohio Infantry as a musician in Company F 132nd Ohio Infantry during the Civil War.[23]

After he was discharged from the military, James Milton Pegan moved to Marion County, Indiana, according to his Civil War pension records.[23] He is listed as a resident there in the 1867 Indianapolis City Directory.[72]

James Milton married **Catherine Hendrickson** on December 25, 1867, in Indianapolis, Marion Co., Indiana.[73] They had five children. Catherine Hendrickson was born in Bridgeport, Wayne Twp., Marion Co., Indiana, on October 26, 1849.[23] She was also known as **Kate**. Catherine reached age 76 and died in Cleveland, Cuyahoga Co., Ohio, on January 17, 1926.[74] She was buried in Greenwood Cemetery, DeGraff, Pleasant Twp., Logan Co., Ohio.[75]

After their marriage, James and Kate move back to James' hometown of DeGraff, Miami Twp., Logan Co., Ohio before their first child, daughter Orpha Estella was born in 1868.

James Pegan is enumerated in the 1870 census in Miami Twp., Logan Co., Ohio *(Census Place: Miami, Logan, Ohio; Roll: M593_1234; Page: 158; Image: 316).* In the home are James, 27, who "works in a carpenter's shop", born Ohio; Catherine, 21, born Indiana, and daughter Estella, two, born Ohio.

In 1880, James Pegan is living in DeGraff, Miami Twp., Logan Co., Ohio *(Census Place: De Graff, Logan, Ohio; Roll: 1041; Page: 151D; Enumeration District: 119; Image: 0305).* James Pegan, 40, is a carpenter, born Ohio as were his parents.

(Incorrect—his father was born in Pennsylvania.) It looks like he says his father was born in New Jersey, but the census taker, when correcting mistakes in the household above, accidentally changes James' entry for his father.) Catherine Hendrickson Pegan is listed as "Kate". She says she was born in Indiana, but does not list birthplaces for her parents. Children in the home include: "Estella", 12, Gertrude, eight, and twins Elgie and Arthur, five. All the children were born in Ohio.

On December 18, 1880, James files for and receives a Civil War (invalid's) pension from the federal government. After he dies, Catherine files for a widow's pension in 1893. James Milton Pegan's birth date is recorded in a letter from his daughter, Orpha Estella "Stella" Pegan, in her mother Catherine's Civil War widow's pension papers. His death date is also recorded in the same pension papers on a physician's affidavit.[23]

After her husband, James Milton Pegan's death, Catherine "Kate" Hendrickson Pegan and her unmarried children leave DeGraff, Miami Twp, Logan Co., Ohio and move to Catherine's hometown, Indianapolis, Marion Co., Indiana. "Kate" and her son Arthur are listed in the 1895 Indianapolis City Directory, living at 47 Vinton Street.[76]

Catherine Hendrickson Pegan is found in Center Twp., Marion Co., Indiana in 1900, but daughter Orpha Estella "Stella" Pegan is listed as the head of household *(Census Place: Center, Marion, Indiana; Roll: T623_389; Page: 4A; Enumeration District: 137)*. The surname is spelled "Peggan" on the census form. In the household are Catherine Hendrickson Pegan, age 49, born Indiana as were her parents, Catherine says she is a widow who bore five children, four still alive. Orpha Estella is listed as age 22, but, as she was born in March 1868, she is 32. Orpha Estella is single, and her occupation is working as a saleslady. Twins Arthur and Elgie, age 24 (November 1875) are also in the home. Arthur is a bookkeeper and Elgie is an assistant to a dentist. All three children were born in Ohio.

Catherine Hendrickson Pegan was living with her son Arthur and daughter "Estella" in Ward 1, Indianapolis, Marion Co., Indiana in 1910 *(Census Place: Indianapolis Ward 1, Marion, Indiana; Roll: T624_366; Page: 13B; Enumeration District: 0045; Image: 722)*. Catherine, listed as "Kathryn", is age 60, a widow, born in Indiana, says her father was born in Indiana and her mother in Pennsylvania. This time she says she has borne four children, all still living. Son Arthur, 35, is listed as the head of the household. Arthur's occupation is a veterinary surgeon who owns his own practice. (He probably wasn't a "veterinary surgeon", as his real vocation was carpentry. He was most likely employed his twin sister Elgie's husband, August Albershardt, a noted veterinary surgeon, in the latter's practice.) Orpha Estella Pegan, 41, is listed as having no occupation; she may have been studying to be an orthopedist at the time. Both Arthur and Orpha Estella are unmarried and born in Ohio.

In 1920, Katherine Hendrickson Pegan, 73, is still in Indianapolis, Center Twp., Marion Co., Indiana *(Census Place: Indianapolis Ward 2, Marion, Indiana; Roll: T625_450; Page: 5B; Enumeration District: 50; Image: 815)*. Her son Arthur, 48 years old, single, an overseer at an automobile company, is living with her. Catherine was born in Ohio, Arthur in Indiana.

Early in the 1920s, Catherine Hendrickson Pegan and son Arthur Pegan move to Cleveland, Cuyahoga Co., Ohio, where Orpha Estella Pegan may have been living, although she is not found anywhere in the 1920 census.

Orpha Estella Pegan's death certificate in Cleveland, Cuyahoga Co., Ohio lists her mother Catherine Hendrickson Pegan's birthplace as Bridgeport, England, but it was Bridgeport, Wayne Twp., Marion Co., Indiana.[23]

Children of James Milton Pegan and Catherine Hendrickson:

+ 25 f I. **Orpha Estella[7] Pegan** was born in DeGraff, Miami Twp., Logan Co., Ohio, on March 10, 1868.[77] She died in Parma, Parma Twp., Cuyahoga Co., Ohio, on December 10, 1939.[77]

+ 26 f II. **Daughter**[7] **Pegan** was born in DeGraff, Miami Twp., Logan Co., Ohio, on February 6, 1870.[78] She died in DeGraff, Miami Twp., Logan Co., Ohio, on February 9, 1870.[78]

+ 27 f III. **Gertrude P.**[7] **Pegan** was born in DeGraff, Miami Twp., Logan Co., Ohio, on July 29, 1871.[79] She died in Pittsfield Twp., Washtenaw Co., Michigan, on April 12, 1959.[80, 81]

+ 28 m IV. **Arthur**[7] **Pegan** was born in DeGraff, Miami Twp., Logan Co., Ohio, on September 20, 1874.[82, 83] He died in Cleveland, Cuyahoga Co., Ohio, on February 28, 1946.[82]

+ 29 f V. **Elgie Elenor**[7] **Pegan** was born in DeGraff, Miami Twp., Logan Co., Ohio, on September 20, 1874.[83, 84, 85] She died in Indianapolis, Marion Co., Indiana, on July 24, 1960.[85, 86]

7. **Margaret**[6] **Pegan** (*John*[5], *Robert A.*[4], *Andrew*[3], *Andrew*[2] *Pagan, James*[1]) was born on September 18, 1843, in Piqua, Washington Twp., Miami Co., Ohio.[24] She was also known as **Mattie or Maggie**. She was the daughter of John Pegan (1) and Rebecca Shearer. Margaret died in Los Angeles, Los Angeles Co., California, on October 6, 1929, at age 86.[24, 25] She was buried in Angeles Abbey Memorial Park Mausoleum, Compton, Los Angeles Co., California.[24, 87]

In 1860, 17-year-old Margaret Pegan is residing with her brother-in-law and sister, Samuel and Mary E. Pegan Mason in Rushylvania, Rush Creek Twp., Logan Co., Ohio (*Census Place: Rushsylvania, Logan, Ohio; Roll: M653_1000; Page: 213; Image: 429*). Margaret is listed as a "domestic". Samuel Mason, 27, is a carpenter and Mary E. Pegan Mason, 25, is Mary is Margaret's sister.

Margaret married **Adam Addison Brunner or Bruner** on January 26, 1863, in Logan Co., Ohio.[88] They had at least one child, perhaps two. Adam Addison Bruner was born in German Twp., Clark Co., Ohio, on November 15, 1836.[89, 90] Adam Addison reached age 32 and died in either DeGraff, Miami Twp., Logan Co., Ohio or Indianapolis, Center Twp., Marion Co., Indiana, on September 30, 1869.[90] He was buried in Greenwood Cemetery, DeGraff, Pleasant Twp., Logan Co., Ohio.[90]

In the Logan County marriage records, his name is listed as Addison Brunner.[88] According to Civil War draft registration records, he used the name Adam Brunner. He was living in Miami Twp., Logan Co., Ohio on July 1, 1863, was age 26 and a carpenter.[89] The surname on his gravestone is "Bruner".[90] His only surviving daughter, Marcia Pet, also preferred "Bruner".[89]

In 1870, the widowed Margaret "Maggie" Pegan Bruner, 26, born Ohio and a milliner, is enumerated in De Graff, Miami Twp., Logan Co., Ohio (*Census Place: De Graff, Logan, Ohio; Roll: M593_1234; Page: 169A; Image: 346*). Living with her is daughter "Pet", (Marcia) age two, born in Indiana, with her parents born in Ohio.

Margaret Pegan married **William C. Miller** on April 29, 1873, in Hardin Co., Ohio.[91] They had at least three children, maybe four. William C. Miller was born in Liberty Twp., Logan Co., Ohio?, on January 8, 1841.[92] He reached age 73 and died in Perkins Twp., Erie Co., Ohio, on April 7, 1914.[92] William C. was buried in Old Soldiers Home Cemetery, Perkins Twp., Erie Co., Ohio.[92, 93]

In 1880, William C. and Margaret Pegan Miller are found in Bellefontaine, Lake Twp., Logan Co., Ohio (*Census Place: Bellefontaine, Logan, Ohio; Roll: 1041; Page: 67D; Enumeration District: 115; Image: 0137*). In the household are William C. Miller, listed as Wm. C. Miller, age 38, a life insurance agent. Margaret Pegan Bruner Miller is age 34. Their children in the home include Willette, five, Fred, four, and Blanch, one. Also living in the home is Marcia Pet ("Petty") Bruner, Margaret's daughter by her first marriage to Adam Bruner, age 11, born Indiana, with her parents born in Ohio. However, Pet is enumerated as a Miller and listed as a daughter to the head of household. All (except for Marcia Pet Bruner) and their parents were Ohio natives.

William C. and Margaret Pegan Bruner Miller are enumerated in Toledo, Lucas Co., Ohio in 1900 *(Census Place: Toledo Ward 8, Lucas, Ohio; Roll: T623_1298; Page: 2A; Enumeration District: 71)*. William C. Miller, 59, born Jan 1841 in Ohio is a real estate agent; he says his father was born in Pennsylvania and her mother in Ohio. Margaret Pegan Miller, 54, was born Sep 1845 in Ohio, where her parents were also born. The pair say they have been married 26 years and Margaret has borne five children, four still alive. They have (Marcia) "Pet" ("P.M") Bruner, age 29, Margaret's daughter by Adam Bruner, and their own daughter Willette ("W.E.") Miller, 24, in the household with them. "Pet" Bruner, 29, single, born Mar 1871 in Indiana, with her parents born in Ohio, lists her occupation as traveling saleswoman. Willette Miller, age 24, born Dec 1875, lists no occupation.

With Margaret Pegan Bruner Miller stating she has borne five children with four surviving, one of her children is deceased. No birth or death records are found for this child. It's likely he or she died at birth. But it is not known which of her husbands was the father of this child.

In 1910, the William Millers are still residing in Toledo, Lucas Co., Ohio *(Census Place: Toledo Ward 8, Lucas, Ohio; Roll: T624_1209; Page: 27A; Enumeration District: 0110; Image: 490)*. William C. Miller, 67, was born in Ohio, but this time he says both of his parents were born in Kentucky. He is still a real estate agent. Margaret Pegan Bruner Miller, listed as "Margret", is 61 and says she and her parents were Ohio natives. William C. and Margaret say they have been married 30 years and Margaret has borne five children, with four surviving. Living with them is their daughter Blanche H. Miller Humason, 26, a "widow" (she was divorced), born Ohio as were her parents, who lists her occupation as sewing. Margaret's daughter by her first marriage, Marcia, has married, and she and her husband Gustavas Adolphus Reiling are also in the household. "Adolph" Reiling, 41, born Indiana with his parents born in Germany, is a machinist in a factory. Marcia Brunner Reiling, 36, states she was born in Indiana and her parents in Ohio.[161] Adolphus and Marcia have been married two years and both say this is their first marriage. Neither Marcia nor Blanche has borne children.

A Civil War veteran, William C. Miller, a married real estate agent from Toledo, was admitted to the Old Soldiers Home in Perkins Twp., Erie Co., Ohio around March 14, 1914. He dies there on April 7th of that year.[92]

After her second husband William C. Miller dies in 1914, Margaret, her son Fred Miller, her sons-in-law and daughters Gustave Adolph and Marcia P. Bruner Reiling, Perry and Willette Miller Sawyer, and Margaret's divorced daughter Blanche Miller Humason all relocate to Los Angeles, Los Angeles Co., California.

In 1920, Margaret Pegan Bruner Miller is living with her son-in-law and daughter, Perry and Willette Miller Sawyer, in Los Angeles, Los Angeles Co., California *(Census Place: Los Angeles Assembly District 64, Los Angeles, California; Roll: T625_108; Page: 20B; Enumeration District: 206; Image: 80)*. Margaret is listed as Margaret J. Miller, age 76, a widow, born Ohio, her father in Ohio and her mother in the United States. She is enumerated as Perry Sawyer's mother-in-law. Perry Sawyer, 41, born Ohio as were his parents, is the secretary-treasurer at a lime company. Willette Miller Sawyer, 40, was born in Ohio as were her parents, lists her occupation as "manager of a bungalow court". Also in the home is Margaret's daughter and Willette's sister, Blanche Miller Humason, who says she is age 31, a widow, born Ohio as were her parents, a milliner. Also in the household with them are five lodgers.

Daughters of Margaret Pegan and Adam Addison Bruner or Brunner:

+ 30 f I. **Child**[7] **Bruner**? was born bet. 1864-1868 in DeGraff, Miami, Twp., Logan Co., Ohio or Indianapolis, Center Twp., Marion Co., Indiana. He or she died in DeGraff, Miami Twp., Logan Co., Ohio, or Indianapolis, Center Twp., Marion Co., Indiana bet. 1864-1868. This Child was either Child Bruner or Child Miller (below).

+ 31 f II. **Marcia Pet⁷ Bruner** was born in Indianapolis, Center Twp., Marion Co., Indiana, on March 21, 1868.[94] She died in Florence, San Antonio Twp., Los Angeles Co., California, on April 27, 1931.[95]

Children of Margaret Pegan and William C. Miller:

+ 32 f I. **Willette⁷ Miller** was born in Bellefontaine, Lake Twp., Logan Co., Ohio, on December 20, 1874.[96] She died in Redondo Beach, Los Angeles Co., California, on December 27, 1935.[97, 98]

+ 33 m II. **Fred Pegan⁷ Miller** was born in Toledo, Lucas Co., Ohio, on June 2, 1876.[99, 100, 101] He died in a hospital in Los Angeles Co., California, on January 6, 1948.[99, 100, 101]

+ 34 f III. **Blanche H.⁷ Miller** was born in Bellefontaine, Lake Twp., Logan Co., Ohio, on June 29, 1878.[102, 103] She died in Los Angeles, Los Angeles Co., California, on June 19, 1944.[103, 104]

+ 35 IV. **Child⁷ Miller?** was born in Bellefontaine, Lake Twp., Logan Co., Ohio?, between 1873 and 1900. He or she died in Bellefontaine, Lake Twp., Logan Co., Ohio, before 1900. This child was either Child Bruner or Child Miller (above).

8. **Martha Ann⁶ Pegan** (*John⁵, Robert A.⁴, Andrew³, Andrew² Pagan, James¹*) was born on April 13, 1846, in Piqua, Washington Twp., Miami Co., Ohio.[26] She was also known as **Mattie**. She was the daughter of John Pegan (1) and Phoebe Moore. Martha Ann died in DeGraff, Miami Twp., Logan Co., Ohio, on July 27, 1923, at age 77.[26] She was buried in Greenwood Cemetery, DeGraff, Pleasant Twp., Logan Co., Ohio.[26, 105]

Childless.

In 1880, Martha "Mattie" Pegan, 32, was single and living with her widowed mother"Phoeba" Moore PeGan, age 59, a widow, in DeGraff Twp. Logan Co., Ohio (*Census Place: De Graff, Logan, Ohio; Roll: 1041; Page: 144B; Enumeration District: 119; Image: 0291*). Phoebe Moore Pegan says she was born in Ohio, her father in Pennsylvania and her mother in Virginia. "Mattie" says she is a dressmaker, Also in the home is Mattie's brother and Phoebe's son, John Pegan Jr., 30 and John's wife Anna Armstrong Pegan, 28, John Pegan II is a carpenter. All but Phoebe say they were born in Ohio, as were their parents. This is incorrect, as John Pegan Sr., the father of Martha and John Jr., was born in Pennsylvania.

Martha Ann married **James Monroe Strayer** on November 29, 1892, in Logan Co., Ohio.[106, 107] James Monroe Strayer was born in Logan Co., Ohio, on March 23, 1858.[107] James Monroe Strayer reached age 65 and died in DeGraff, Miami Twp., Logan Co., Ohio, on September 20, 1923.[107] He was buried in Greenwood Cemetery, DeGraff, Pleasant Twp., Logan Co., Ohio.[107, 108]

James and Martha "Mattie" Pegan Stayer lived all their lives in De Graff, Miami Twp., Logan Co., Ohio. They took care of Mattie's mother, Phoebe Moore Pegan, for about 30 years.

James and Martha "Mattie" Pegan Stayer are enumerated in De Graff, Miami Twp., Logan Co., Ohio in 1900 (*Census Place: Miami, Logan, Ohio; Roll: T623_1294; Page: 6A; Enumeration District: 117*). James Strayer, 42, born March 1858 in Ohio, is a farmer and stock raiser. He says his father was born in Virginia and his mother in Ohio. Martha "Mattie" Pegan Strayer, 54, born Apr 1846, says she was born in Ohio, her father in Pennsylvania and her mother in Ohio. The couple states they have been married seven years and Martha has borne no children. Also in the home is Phoebe Moore Pegan, Martha's widowed mother, who is listed as "Phoebe Strayer". Phoebe Moore Pegan is listed as age 77, born Jun 1822, but in other censuses she is listed as born in 1818. Phoebe says she bore four children, three still living. This time, she says she was born in Ohio and both her parents in Virginia.

In 1910, James and Martha Pegan Strayer are again residing in De Graff, Miami Twp., Logan Co., Ohio *(Census Place: Miami, Logan, Ohio; Roll: T624_1204; Page: 8B; Enumeration District: 0138; Image: 997)*. James Strayer is listed as age 52, a wool buyer. Martha Pegan Strayer, enumerated as "Mattie", is listed as age 53 (Incorrect—she is 63). Both say they and their parents were born in Ohio (also incorrect). Still living with them is Martha's mother, Phoebe Moore Pegan, 89, a widow, born Ohio with her parents born in Virginia.

James and Martha Pegan Strayer continue to live in De Graff, Miami Twp., Logan Co., Ohio in 1920 *(Census Place: Miami, Logan, Ohio; Roll: T625_1405; Page: 9A; Enumeration District: 198; Image: 401)*. James M. Strayer, age 61, is a farmer who says he was born in Ohio, his father in Virginia and his mother in Ohio. Martha A. Pegan Strayer says she is 68 and she and her parents were born in Ohio (Incorrect—she is 73 years old and her father was born in Pennsylvania).

9. **John Andrew**[6] **Pegan II** (*John*[5], *Robert A.*[4], *Andrew*[3], *Andrew*[2] *Pagan, James*[1]) was born on December 25, 1849, in Piqua, Washington Twp., Miami Co., Ohio.[27] He was the son of John Pegan (1) and Phoebe Moore. John Andrew died in Indianapolis, Marion Co., Indiana, on May 11, 1918, at age 68.[27, 28] He was buried in Greenwood Cemetery, DeGraff, Pleasant Twp., Logan Co., Ohio.[28, 109]

John Andrew married **Anna Belle Armstrong** on December 23, 1879, in Logan Co., Ohio.[110] They had two children. Anna Belle Armstrong was born in DeGraff, Miami Twp., Logan Co., Ohio, on April 5, 1860.[111] Anna Belle reached age 82 and died in Columbus, Franklin Co., Ohio, on January 17, 1943.[111] She was buried in Eastlawn Cemetery, Columbus, Franklin Co., Ohio.[112]

In 1880, John Andrew Pegan II and his wife Anna Armstrong Pegan are living with John's widowed mother, "Phoeba" Moore Pegan, in De Graff, Miami Twp., Logan Co., Ohio *(Census Place: De Graff, Logan, Ohio; Roll: 1041; Page: 144B; Enumeration District: 119; Image: 0291)*. John Pegan Jr. is age 30, a carpenter and Anna Armstrong Pegan is 28. Both say they and their parents were born in Ohio. Phoebe Moore Pegan, listed as head of the household, is 59, born Ohio, with her father born in Pennsylvania and her mother in Virginia. Also in the home is John Jr.'s sister and Phoebe's daughter, Martha "Mattie" Pegan, 32, single, born Ohio as were her parents, who is a dressmaker.

John Andrew and Anna Belle Armstrong Pegan II have two children by 1880, only one of whom, son Edward E., survives. The other is a female child born July 18, 1884, and on the Logan County, Ohio birth record her name is "Anna M." This little girl expired on February 5, 1886 according to the Logan County, Ohio death records. However, on her death record, her name is "Lena M." It is not known which name is correct, or, perhaps, her parents changed her name after her birth.

John A. Pegan II and his family are enumerated in DeGraff, Miami Twp., Logan Co., Ohio in 1900 *(Census Place: Miami, Logan, Ohio; Roll: T623 1294; Page: 1A)*. In the home are John, age 50, Anna B., 40, and son Edward, 19. John and Anna Belle Armstrong say they have been married 20 years and Anna has borne two children, with one surviving. John Jr. and Edward work in a livery stable. All and their parents were Ohio natives.

By 1910, John A. Pegan II and his family have moved to Marion, Marion Twp., Marion Co., Ohio *(Census Place: Marion Ward 1, Marion, Ohio; Roll: T624_1213; Page: 2B; Enumeration District: 0080; Image: 635)*. John A. Pegan (II) is age 60 and a restaurant manager. Anna Belle Armstrong Pegan is 50. The couple states they have been married 30 years and Anna has borne two children, one (Edward) still living. Son Edward E., 28, is in the home with them. He says he has been married for three years, but his wife is not with him. He is a clerk in a restaurant, most likely his father's. All in the home say they and their parents were born in Ohio.

Anna Belle Armstrong Pegan is listed as the head of the household in 1920 in Springfield, Springfield Twp., Clark Co., Ohio *(Census Place: Springfield Ward 6, Clark, Ohio; Roll: T625_1354; Page: 3B; Enumeration District: 95; Image: 878)*. Anna Pegan is age 59 and a widow. Her son, Edward Pegan is still living with her. Edward is listed as married, but his wife again is not in the household. He is 38, a salesman in a piano store. Both say they and their parents were born in Ohio.

In 1930, Anna Belle Armstrong Pegan is found in Akron, Summit Co., Ohio *(Census Place: Akron, Summit, Ohio; Roll: 1875; Page: 18A; Enumeration District: 42; Image: 596.0)*. This time her son, Edward Pegan, is listed as the head of household. Anna B. Armstrong Pegan, a widow, is 70. Edward Pegan, 49, a barber, is divorced. Again, both say they and their parents were born in Ohio.

Anna Belle Armstrong Pegan and her son Edward Pegan are enumerated in Columbus, Franklin Co., Ohio in 1940 *(Census Place: Columbus, Franklin, Ohio; Roll: T627_3247; Page: 5A; Enumeration District: 93-211)*. Anna Pegan, age 79, born Ohio, is divorced. The head of the household is listed as Edward Pegan, 48, born Ohio, a self-employed barber. Edward says he was living in the same place, Columbus, Ohio, in 1935, while Anna Pegan says she was living in the same house at 501 Buckingham Street in 1935.

Children of John Andrew Pegan II and Anna Belle Armstrong:

+ 36 m I. **Edward Ephraim[7] Pegan** was born in DeGraff, Miami Twp., Logan Co., Ohio, on March 18, 1881.[113] He died in Columbus, Franklin Co., Ohio, on February 15, 1942.[113]

+ 37 f II. **Anna or Lena M.[7] Pegan** was born in DeGraff, Miami Twp., Logan Co., Ohio, on July 18, 1884.[114] She died in DeGraff, Miami Twp., Logan Co., Ohio, on February 5, 1886.[115]

10. Laura Louisa[6] Pegan (*John[5], Robert A.[4], Andrew[3], Andrew[2] Pagan, James[1]*) was born on March 21, 1854, in Miami Twp., Logan Co., Ohio.[29] She was the daughter of John Pegan (1) and Phoebe Moore. Laura Louisa died in Los Angeles, Los Angeles Co., California, on May 5, 1944, at age 90.[29] She was buried in Hollywood Forever Cemetery, Hollywood, Los Angeles Co., California.[116]

Laura Louisa married **Edward Henry Hill II** on June 27, 1876, in Logan Co., Ohio.[117] They had one son. Edward Henry Hill II was born in Cincinnati, Hamilton Co., Ohio, on May 7, 1853.[118] Edward Henry reached age 78 and died in Los Angeles, Los Angeles Co., California, on July 25, 1931.[119, 120] He was buried in Hollywood Forever Cemetery, Hollywood, Los Angeles Co., California.[121]

Edward H. and Laura Louisa Pegan Hill are enumerated as E.H. and Laura Hill in Lynchburg, Dodson Twp., Highland Co., Ohio in 1880 *(Census Place: Lynchburg, Highland, Ohio; Roll: 1032; Page: 273B; Enumeration District: 41; Image: 0550)*. In the household are Edward H. Hill, 27, born Ohio, with his father born in Pennsylvania and his mother in Virginia. He lists his occupation as "drugs and hardware". With him is his wife Laura Pegan Hill, 26, born Ohio, with her father born in Pennsylvania and her mother in Ohio. They have a son, Fred, three, born Ohio. Also there is a boarder, D.H. Severn, a clerk in a store, born Pennsylvania; and a servant, Maggie Moon, 20, born Ohio.

In 1900, Edward and Laura Pegan Hill are found in Manhattan, New York Co., New York *(Census Place: Manhattan, New York, New York; Roll: T623_1105; Page: 17A; Enumeration District: 545)*. Edward Hill is age 47, born May 1853 in Ohio, a bookkeeper. Laura Pegan Hill is 46 and was born Mar 1854. The couple says they have been married 24 years and Laura has borne one child who is still alive. Son Fred, 23, born Mar 1877 is with them. Fred says he is divorced. On the form, it says everyone in the home was born in Ohio, as were their parents (Incorrect—although all three were born in Ohio, their parents were born elsewhere, as outlined below).

Edward and Laura L. Pegan Hill are listed in Montclair, Essex Co., New Jersey in 1910 *(Census Place: Montclair Ward 3, Essex, New Jersey; Roll: T624_883; Page: 5A; Enumeration District: 0198; Image: 1057)*. Edward Hill, 57, says he is a chemist. This time, he says he was born in Ohio, his father in Virginia and his mother in Indiana. Laura L. Pegan Hill is 56, born Ohio, with her father born in Ohio and her mother in Virginia (Incorrect—her father was born in Pennsylvania and her mother in Ohio). There is also a servant in the household, Jane Bargeson, 18, born in Norway.

In 1920, Edward and Laura L. Pegan Hill are still residing in Montclair, Essex Co., New Jersey *(Census Place: Montclair Ward 3, Essex, New Jersey; Roll: T625_1030; Page: 6B; Enumeration District: 83; Image: 869)*. The head of the household, Edward Hill, is enumerated as "Ed H. Hill". Edward Hill is 65 born in Ohio, with his father born in Virginia and his mother in France(?). He is a chemist. Laura Louisa Pegan Hill is also 65, and she says she and her parents were born in Ohio. Living with them is son Fred R., 43, born Ohio, who has no occupation. Also in the home is Ardonis Harkins (?) who is listed as Edward's cousin, age 70, born in "Montclair" (?) with his parents born in Ohio.

Edward and Laura L. Pegan Hill are living in 1930 in Los Angeles, Los Angeles Co., California *(Census Place: Los Angeles, Los Angeles, California; Roll: 132; Page: 4A; Enumeration District: 20; Image: 974.0)*. Edward H. Hill is 76, born Ohio with his father born in Virginia and his mother in Illinois (?). He lists no occupation. Laura L. Hill is 75, born Ohio, with her father born in Ohio and her mother in Virginia (again both parental birthplaces are erroneous). The couple states their first marriage occurred at ages 24 and 23 respectively.

Laura L. Hill, a widow, is found in the 1940 census in Los Angeles, Los Angeles Co., Cailfornia *(Census Place: Los Angeles, Los Angeles, California; Roll: T627_394; Page: 7B; Enumeration District: 60-98)*. She is 86 years old, says she was born in Ohio, and that she was living in Los Angeles in 1935. Her home is at 1815 New Hampshire Avenue.

Son of Laura Louisa Pegan and Edward Henry Hill II:

+ 38 m I. **Fred Roland**[7] **Hill** was born in DeGraff, Miami Twp., Logan Co., Ohio, on May 16, 1877.[122, 123, 124] He died in Los Angeles, Los Angeles Co., California, on October 31, 1941.[125

11. Elsey[6] **Pegan** (*John*[5], *Robert A.*[4], *Andrew*[3], *Andrew*[2] *Pagan, James*[1]) was born on August 31, 1858, in Miami Twp., Logan Co., Ohio.[30] He was the son of John Pegan (1) and Phoebe Moore. Elsey died in Miami Twp., Logan Co., Ohio, on November 15, 1860, at age two.[30] He was buried in Greenwood Cemetery, DeGraff, Pleasant Twp., Logan Co., Ohio.[30] According to his tombstone, Elsey Pegan was two years, two months and 15 days old when he died.[30]

7th Generation

12. Pliny Moses Crume[7] Pegan (*Emmanuel[6], John[5], Robert A.[4], Andrew[3], Andrew[2] Pagan, James[1]*) was born on May 15, 1856, in Hardin, Turtle Creek Twp., Shelby Co., Ohio.[40] He was the son of Emmanuel Pegan (2) and Sarah Strouse. He died in Denver, Denver Co., Colorado, on December 18, 1947, at age 91.[40] Pliny Moses Crume was buried in Crown Hill Cemetery, Wheat Ridge, Jefferson Co., Colorado.[40, 126]

Pliny Moses Crume Pegan, like many boys in east central Ohio, was named for Dr. Pliny Moses Crume, a noted physician in that area who trained his father, Dr. Emmanuel Pegan.[36] Later in life, Pliny Moses Crume Pegan seems to have dropped use of the middle name, "Moses", and just used Pliny Crume Pegan as his name.

In 1877, Pliny "Crume" Pegan was a student at the Kansas State Agricultural College in Gatesburg, Barton Co., Kansas.[127]

Pliny Moses Crume married **Francina Caroline Gwinn** on May 15, 1879, in Barton Co., Kansas.[128] They had two daughters. Francina Caroline Gwinn was born in Burlington Twp., Carroll Co., Indiana, on May 5, 1859.[129] Francina Caroline reached age 72 and died in Denver, Denver Co., Colorado, on July 28, 1931.[129] She was buried in Crown Hill Cemetery, Wheat Ridge, Jefferson Co., Colorado.[130]

Pliny Crume Pegan, enumerated as Crume Pegan, is found in Great Bend, Liberty Twp., Barton Co., Kansas in 1880 (*Census Place: Great Bend, Barton, Kansas; Roll: 373; Page: 37D; Enumeration District: 331; Image: 0077*). "Crume" Pegan, age 24, is a clerk. He says he was born in Ohio, as was his father, and his mother was born in Iowa (Incorrect—she was also born in Ohio). His wife, Francina Gwinn Pegan, 21, says she was born in Indiana and her parents in Virginia. They have a daughter, Mamie, two months old, born in Kansas.

He may have also had a small farm in Liberty Twp., Barton Co., Kansas, that same year, according to a Federal non-population schedule (*Census Year: 1880; Census Place: Liberty, Barton, Kansas; Archive Collection Number: T1130; Roll: 14; Page: 2; Line: 1; Schedule Type: Agriculture*).[131]

From 1882-1883, Pliny Crume Pegan was the proprietor of a hotel in Garden City, Garden City Twp., Finney Co., Kansas. "P.C. Pegan" is included among the first voters in the county. According to a newspaper account of the first fatal shooting in that town.

From *The History of Garden City, Kansas*:

> The first death resulting from a shooting affair occurred here on Easter in April, 1882. The following account was gathered from talking to P. C. Pegan, A. H. Burtis, and others who were living here at that time, and this is the way it happened:
>
> In the early eighties, the Santa Fe had what they called "emigrant cars". These were old passenger coaches attached to freight trains. It was a slow way to travel, but the fare was very low, and the people could sleep, cook and eat in the cars.
>
> Many of these passengers were honest, hard working people, going to new locations to build homes, or to find work. But there was always a rough element, taking advantage of this low rate to travel over the country, just to have a good time, and out looking for adventures in the "wild west". This latter class considered it great sport to look and act like "regular two-gun men" whose country they imagined they were invading. They carried firearms and used them pretty reckless, partly for devilment, shooting out of the car windows at rabbits, coyotes, antelope and birds, but some of them went farther and would see how close they would come to cattle, and even people travelling along the road, without quite hitting them. Sometimes when several were travelling together they would slip out when the train stopped at a station and make a raid on a store. For this reason, Levi Wilkinson, manager of the Landis and Hollinger store, was always on guard against these emigrant ruffians. Capt. J. R. Fulton was assisting in the store, and he always kept his Winchester loaded, ready for use when the emigrant train was due.

In April 1882, Robert Cartney, a young Scotchman from Pleasant Valley, Pa., was a passenger on the western bound emigrant train. He was on his way to Arizona to get the body of his father, who had been killed by a cave-in while working in the copper mines. The undertaker at Pleasant Valley, who was an old friend of the Cartney family, and expected to take charge of the father's body upon its arrival at the home town, accompanied Robert to the train. He noticed that the young man was armed, and he cautioned him:

"Bobby, I lived in Leadville, Colorado, for a few years, and let me tell you something. You are going into a country where, if you take out a gun, you've got to use it. You are a hot-headed young scamp, and you better just leave those guns with me." But Bobby took the guns.

It was about noon on Easter Sunday when his train reached age Garden City. Times were extremely dull here and there was no money in the country. There were several ambitious boys and girls from the best families in Garden City who desired to make a little money, and they had a habit of meeting these trains with baskets containing coffee, milk, pies, boiled eggs, etc., which they sold to the emigrants.

On this Sunday George Finnup, Eugene Stotts and Willie Jones, son of C. J., all about fifteen years of age, and some young girls, were on hand to meet the train with their baskets of food. There was a good crowd and by the time the train was ready to leave, they had about sold out, but Robert Cartney had got off the train and was scuffling with the boys, trying to get their baskets. He grabbed a pan of something belonging to George Finnup, and started for the train which was slowly moving out, and had reached age the rear platform, when George picked up a hard-boiled egg and threw it after him. The egg missed its mark and struck a car wheel, but Cartney leaped to the ground and a race started. George reached age Main Street about the time the train was on the west side of the present freight depot, but Cartney was a well-built athlete, and soon overtook him, and started shaking and kicking him.

Pliney C. Pegan, who operated the Metropolitan Hotel, had been watching the fracas, ran out and took hold of Cartney, saying:

"Here, fellow, we don't allow that kind of business here." He tried to hold him, but Cartney was strong, and swung around, and got loose. He started back toward the train which was still moving west, but as he ran, he began shooting back, firing three shots at Pegan, who was following. But they all missed, although the two men were not more than ten or fifteen feet apart. At this time a friend of Cartney's began shooting at Pegan from the rear platform of the train, and Pegan started for the depot to get a gun from B. B. Black, who was agent.

By this time the whole crowd was excited. Squire Worrell had just driven into town, and was standing on the opposite side of the street. He had in his pocket a new 38 Colt's revolver, which belonged to A. H. Burtis, who had just received the gun as a gift from Major Falls of the XY ranch. H. M. deCordova, a cattleman who had spent his life in the west and knew no fear, stepped up to Worrell, knowing he usually carried a gun, and said excitedly, "Give me your gun, Squire". Just as he took the gun, Cartney raised his arm to shoot again, but deCordova fired first and it struck Cartney under his uplifted arm, wounding him fatally. He was taken down to the depot and laid on the plank platform. An old French doctor, by the name of Ballou was over him examining his wound when Cartney asked:

"How am I getting along, Doc?"

"You are getting along pretty fast; you'll be in hell in about fifteen minutes," the doctor answered. And in a little while the man was dead.

While all this was taking place the passengers on the train had set the brakes and stopped the train, and a number of men got off in a rage, vowing they would burn the whole damn town, and their guns and rifles glistened in the noonday sun, as they started down the track. The townspeople scattered, and directly the barrels of Winchesters and carbines were protruding from doorways and around corners. These had been furnished to the town by the state to be used in case of Indian raids, and were kept stored in a blacksmith shop. It looked like a civil war was imminent. N. C. Jones fired some shots over the heads of the passengers to let them know they had opposition. This apparently calmed the emigrants, for they turned and went back to the train, and it im- mediately pulled out…

An inquest was held over Robert Cartney, and he was buried that evening. Mr. deCordova was cleared of any charges, the law holding that the shooting was justifiable, as it was done in self defense…

After the emigrant train left Garden City officers telegraphed to Lakin and had Cartney's partner, who had kept shooting from the rear platform, arrested. He was brought back and taken before Justice of Peace H. M. Wheeler. He was told that he had committed a terrible outrage, and that he was probably the cause of the death of his friend. A sort of trial was held, and the jury was then sent out to deliberate on what they had better do with him. They returned directly, and one of the men had a saddle rope. Their faces looked very grave, as they announced they had decided on a "necktie party". The man was almost scared to death, but they showed no mercy, and started to take him out. At that moment a train whistled. The Justice of Peace cleared his throat. "Men," he said, "let's give him a chance. If he can catch that train he is a free man. What do you say?" There was a shout of assent, and the man was turned loose. He bolted like a flash of lightning. Probably the foot race he made to catch the train broke the record for all time in Garden City, but he made it and got away. No doubt he thought he had narrowly escaped being the victim of real "Western justice", but the fact was that the trial and the whole proceeding was all a bluff to teach him and others like him a lesson." [132]

Perhaps this incident compelled Pliny Crume Pegan to relocate his family. By 1885, he has moved to Pueblo, Pueblo Co., Colorado.

Pliny Crume Pegan is enumerated as "Patrick C. Pegan" in the 1885 Colorado State Census in Pueblo, Pueblo Co., Colorado. Pliny C. Pegan is 28 and a railroad section head. Pliny and his parents are listed as born in Indiana (Incorrect—they were all born in Ohio). Francina Gwynn Pegan is listed as "Sarah". She is 26, born in Indiana with her parents born in Virginia. With them is daughter Mamie, age five, born in Kansas.[133]

Francina Pegan, listed as "Sina", is listed in the 1895 Kansas State Census in Great Bend, Barton Co., Kansas, along with daughters Patience and Mamie. "Sina" is listed as born in Indiana, with her daughters listed as born in Colorado (wrong, Mamie was born in Kansas). They are residing with Thomas and M.E. Kincaid, who are 42 and 43 respectively and both born in Virginia. M.E. Kincaid is Mary Elizabeth Gwinn Kincaid, Francina's sister, whom Francina and her daughters were apparently visiting.[134]

Pliny Crume Pegan is found in Denver, Arapahoe Co., Colorado in 1900 *(Census Place: Denver, Arapahoe, Colorado; Roll: T623_120; Page: 5B; Enumeration District: 123)*. He is enumerated as "Plenie B". In the home are Pliny C. Pegan, 44(?) born May 1862(?) in Ohio, a railroad conductor; Francina, 41, b. May 1869, in Indiana; and daughters Mamie, 20, in Kansas, and Patience, 16, born Colorado. Pliny C. and Francina say they have been married 21 years and Francina has borne two children, who survive. The census taker erred with some of the ages.

Pliny Crume Pegan is doubly enumerated in the 1910 census. He may have changed residences during census time. Both entries are erroneous, but one is especially wrong:

Pliny C. Crume is found in Ward 10, Denver, Denver Co., Colorado on Panacea Street *(Census Place: Denver Ward 10, Denver, Colorado; Roll: T624_116; Page: 14B; Enumeration District: 0138)*. Pliny is age 50 and a railroad conductor. His wife, "Suna S." Pegan is 48. Both were born in Missouri and their parents' birthplaces are all "Unknown". The pair has been married 30 years and "Suna" has borne three children with two still alive. They have two daughters: Ruby P., 25, who works at a public library, and Nona, 20. This enumeration seems to have been furnished by a neighbor, which was sometimes done. Pliny and Francina never had a third daughter named Nona.

The second entry, even with mistakes, is more correct:

Pliny Crume Pegan is a resident of Denver, Denver Co., Colorado, living on Bannock Street, in 1910 *(Census Place: Denver Ward 10, Denver, Colorado; Roll: T624_116; Page: 16A; Enumeration District: 0138; Image: 982)*. Pliny C. Pegan is age 52, born in Ohio, with his father born in Ohio and his mother born in Iowa (Incorrect—he was 53 years old and his mother was born in Ohio). He is a railroad conductor. With him is wife Francina Gwinn Pegan, listed as "Lina", age 50, born in Indiana with her parents born in Vermont. The couple says they have been married 31 years and Francina has borne two children, both still alive. With them is daughter "Minnie" (Mamie) Gage, 29, born in Kansas, who has been married five years and has borne two children, both surviving. (Was she just visiting?) Also listed as a "Gage" is their daughter "Patricia" (Patience) Pegan, 26, single and born in Colorado, a library clerk.

In 1920, Pliny Crume Pegan is still living in Denver, Denver Co. Colorado *(Census Place: Denver, Denver, Colorado; Roll: T625_158; Page: 2A; Enumeration District: 79; Image: 1120)*. In the household are Pliny C. Pegan, age 63; who is still a railroad conductor; Francina Gwinn Pegan, listed as "Sima", age 60, and daughter Patience, age 35, still unmarried, a school librarian. Pliny C. Pegan says he and his father were born in Ohio and his mother in Indiana (wrong; she was born in Ohio). Francina says she was born in Indiana and her parents in Virginia. Patience Pegan's birthplace is listed as Colorado.

Pliny Crume Pegan is again found in Denver, Denver Co., Colorado in 1930 *(Census Place: Denver, Denver, Colorado; Roll: 236; Page: 5B; Enumeration District: 82; Image: 47.0)*. Pliny C. Crume, age 73, a railroad conductor, says his father were born in Ohio and his mother in Iowa (again, not correct; she was born in Ohio). Francina Gwinn Pegan is 70 years old and says she was born in Illinois (Incorrect— she was born in Indiana) and her parents were born in Virginia. Pliny states his first marriage occurred at age 23 and Francina says she was first married at age 20. Daughter Patience Ruby Pegan, listed as "Ruby P.", 35, is single and a school librarian. She says she was born in Illinois, her father in Ohio and her mother in Illinois (wrong—she was born in Colorado and her mother in Indiana).

In 1940, Pliny Crume Pegan, a widower, is still residing in Denver, Denver Co., Colorado in 1940 *(Census Place: Denver, Denver, Colorado; Roll: T627_487; Page: 4B; Enumeration District: 16-111)*. In the home are Pliny C. Pegan, age 83, born Ohio, who lists no occupation and is probably retired. His unmarried daughter Patience, 50 (she is actually 45), is a librarian at a public library who was born in Colorado. Father and daughter say they were living in the same house at 165 South Clarkson Street in 1935. With them is a servant and housekeeper, Anna Atwood, 58, born in Iowa.

Daughters of Pliny Moses Crume Pegan and Francina Caroline Gwinn:

+ 39 f I. **Mamie Edna[8] Pegan** was born in Great Bend, Liberty Twp., Barton Co., Kansas, on March 26, 1880.[135] She died in Denver, Denver Co., Colorado, on July 12, 1968.[136]

+ 40 f II. **Patience Ruby[8] Pegan** was born in Pueblo, Pueblo Co., Colorado, on January 18, 1884.[137] She died in Denver, Denver Co., Colorado, on September 7, 1949.[137]

13. Florence Genevieve[7] Pegan (*Emmanuel[6], John[5], Robert A.[4], Andrew[3], Andrew[2] Pagan, James[1]*) was born on December 9, 1858, in Hardin, Turtle Creek Twp., Shelby Co., Ohio.[41, 42] She was also known as **Jennie**. She was the daughter of Emmanuel Pegan (2) and Sarah Strouse. Florence Genevieve died in Anthony, Anthony Twp., Harper Co., Kansas, on April 15, 1929, at age 70.[41, 42] She was buried in

Forest Park Cemetery, Anthony, Anthony Twp., Harper Co., Kansas.[41, 42, 138]

When she was a young woman, Florence Genevieve Pegan left Kansas, where she grew up, and returned to her birthplace, Miami County, Indiana, apparently to claim an inheritance:

From the *Rochester (IN) Sentinel* on August 5, 1876:

> "Miss Jennie Pegan, formerly of Akron, but recently of Great Bend, Kan., has returned to live in Mexico, Miami county, where there is a large legacy to which Jennie has the good fortune of being an heiress." [139]

Florence Genevieve married **Mervin Osborne Cissel** on March 13, 1878, in Miami Co., Indiana.[140, 141] They had three children. Mervin Osborne Cissel was born in Rensselaer, Marion Twp., Jasper Co., Indiana, on March 13, 1851.[142, 143] He reached age 71 and died in Anthony, Anthony Twp., Harper Co., Kansas, on May 30, 1922.[142] Mervin Osborne was buried in Forest Park Cemetery, Anthony, Anthony Twp., Harper Co., Kansas.[142, 143, 144]

In 1880, Mervin O. and Florence "Jenny" Cisell are found in Rensselaer, Marion Twp., Jasper Co., Indiana *(Census Place: Rensselaer, Jasper, Indiana; Roll: 286; Page: 293D; Enumeration District: 63; Image: 0590)*. In the home are Mervin O. Cissel, 24, born Indiana, with his father born in Maryland and his mother in Pennsylvania. Mervin is a printer. Florence G. Pegan Cissel, listed as "Jenny F.", 21, born Ohio, with her father born in Ohio and her mother in Indiana; and daughter Allie B., one, born Indiana.

Mervin O. Cissel and family are living in Ryan Twp., Sumner Co., Kansas in 1895, according to the 1895 Kansas State Census.[145]

Mervin and Florence Genevieve Pegan Cissel are enumerated in Argonia, Dixon Twp., Sumner Co., Kansas in 1900 *(Census Place: Dixon, Sumner, Kansas; Roll: T623_502; Page: 3A; Enumeration District: 325)*. Mervin Cissel, listed as "Marvin" Cissel, is age 49, born March 1851 in Indiana, with his father born in Maryland and his mother in Pennsylvania; he is an editor and publisher (newspaper). Florence G. Pegan Cissel, born December 1859, says she and her parents were Ohio natives. The couple says they have been married 22 years and Florence has borne three children, all still living. Children residing with them are Benjamin, 16, born November 1883 in Indiana, and Charles, 12, born June 1887 in Kansas.

In 1910, Mervin O. and Florence G. Pegan Cissel are located in Anthony, Harper Co., Kansas *(Census Place: Anthony Ward 1, Harper, Kansas; Roll: T624_441; Page: 5B; Enumeration District: 0073; Image: 713)*. Mervin Cisell, 58, was born in Indiana, his father in Maryland and his mother in Pennsylvania. He says he is the editor of the *Argonia (KS) Clipper* (in Argonia, Dixon Twp., Sumner Co., Kansas, adjacent to Harper County). Florence G. Pegan Cissel, 51, says she and her father were born in Ohio and (incorrectly) her mother in Indiana. Their son Benjamin Z, age 26, born Indiana, is also in the home; he says he is sliversmith at a jewelry store. However, Florence's mother, Sarah Strouse Pegan Shields, age 73, is listed as the head of the household. Sarah says she was born in Ohio, but this time she says her father was born in Germany and her mother in Kentucky.

Mervin Cissel's career as a newspaperman started his hometown, Rennsalear, Indiana, when he was 12 years old. When he was 30, he started *The Standard* in Rennsalear in 1880, but sold it three years later. Moving to Kansas, he founded the *Freeport Leader* in Freeport in 1885 before moving the paper to Argonia for a few months in 1991 and renamed it *The Peoples Press*. Before the end of that year, he transferred the paper to Milan, Kansas as *The Milan Press*. When his venture in Milan failed, he established a church newspaper in Winfield, Kansas. Mervin became the owner and editor of the *The Argonia Clipper*, between 1898 and 1915, when the paper dissolved.[146]

In 1920, Mervin O. and Florence G. Pegan Cissel are still residing in Anthony, Anthony Twp., Harper Co., Kansas *(Census Place: Anthony, Harper, Kansas; Roll: T625_533; Page: 8B; Enumeration District: 75; Image: 923)*. This time, Mervin Cissel is listed as head of the household. Mervin O. Cissel, 58, was born in Indiana, his father in Maryland and his mother in Pennsylvania. He is a bookkeeper at a plumbing company. Florence G. Pegan Cissel, age 51, still says she and her father were born in Ohio and her mother in Indiana! Sarah Strouse Pegan Shields is still living with her son-in-law and daughter. Sarah is age 82, born Ohio, with her father born in Pennsylvania and her mother in Kentucky.

Children of Florence Genevieve Pegan and Mervin Osborne Cissel:

+ 41 f I. **Allie Belle**[8] **Cissel** was born in Rensselaer, Marion Twp., Jasper Co., Indiana, on December 11, 1878.[147, 148] She died in Anthony, Anthony Twp., Harper Co., Kansas, on November 3, 1939.[147, 148]

+ 42 m II. **Benjamin Franklin**[8] **Cissel** was born in Rensselaer, Marion Twp., Jasper Co., Indiana, on November 8, 1883.[149] He died in St. Louis, Missouri, on June 27, 1913.[149]

+ 43 m III. **Charles Mervin**[8] **Cissel** was born in Freeport, Silver Creek Twp., Harper Co., Kansas, on June 2, 1887.[135, 150, 151] He died in Wichita, Sedgwick Co., Kansas, on June 8, 1969.[135, 150]

14. Ada[7] **Mason** (*Mary Elizabeth*[6] *Pegan, John*[5], *Robert A.*[4], *Andrew*[3], *Andrew*[2] *Pagan, James*[1]) was born on March 10, 1856, in Rushylvania, Rush Creek Twp., Logan Co., Ohio.[50] She was the daughter of Samuel Myer or Meyers Mason II and Mary Elizabeth Pegan (4). Ada died in Rushylvania, Rush Creek Twp., Logan Co., Ohio, on July 28, 1856.[51] She was buried in Miami Cemetery, Rush Creek Twp., Logan Co., Ohio.[51] Although her gravestone says she was age five months, 16 days, which would make her birth date February 12, 1856, Ada Mason birthdate, March 10, 1856, is confirmed by her twin Ida May Mason's Indiana death certificate.[50]

15. Ida May[7] **Mason** (*Mary Elizabeth*[6] *Pegan, John*[5], *Robert A.*[4], *Andrew*[3], *Andrew*[2] *Pagan, James*[1]) was born on March 10, 1856, in Rushylvania, Rush Creek Twp., Logan Co., Ohio.[50] She was the daughter of Samuel Myer or Meyers Mason II and Mary Elizabeth Pegan (4). She died in Clay Twp., Hamilton Co., Indiana, on August 17, 1927.[50] Ida May was buried in Greenwood Cemetery, DeGraff, Pleasant Twp., Logan Co., Ohio.[50, 152]

Never married.

In 1900, Ida May Mason, 44, a seamstress, is living in Cincinnati, Hamilton Co., Ohio (*Census Place: Cincinnati Ward 22, Hamilton, Ohio; Roll: T623_1278; Page: 3B; Enumeration District: 184*). She is listed as the head of the household, and says she and her parents were born in Ohio. Ida has another seamstress as a boarder, Helen Gilchrest, a widow, age 51, born in New York

By 1910, Ida May Mason, 54, and M. Elizabeth "Minnie" Mason have joined their sisters Kate, Cora and Minnie in Indianapolis, Marion Co., Indiana (*Census Place: Indianapolis Ward 9, Marion, Indiana; Roll: T624_368; Page: 9A; Enumeration District: 0169; Image: 995*). The sisters are living in Indianapolis in Warren Township, somewhere near the area of South Hawthorne Lane and University Avenue. Ida May, 50, lists no occupation. Kate, 47, and Minnie, 34, are school teachers and Cora, 39, is a bookkeeper. All were born in Ohio, as were their parents.

In 1920, Ida May Mason, 64, has moved to Newark, Licking Co., Ohio (*Census Place: Newark Ward 5, Licking, Ohio; Roll: T625_1404; Page: 4A; Enumeration District: 167; Image: 1123*). She is listed as a niece in the household of her widowed paternal aunt, Sarah Mason Buck, 74. Neither woman lists an occupation. Ida says she and her parents were born in Ohio, while Sarah says she was born in Ohio, her father in Virginia and her mother in Germany.

By 1924, Ida May Mason is back in Indianapolis, according to her brother John Pegan Mason's, obituary.[153] She dies at her sister Katherine "Kate" Mason's home, then just south of Carmel, Clay Twp., Hamilton Co., Indiana.[154]

16. Charles Edwin[7] **Mason** (*Mary Elizabeth*[6] *Pegan, John*[5], *Robert A.*[4], *Andrew*[3], *Andrew*[2] *Pagan, James*[1]) was born\ on November 6, 1859, in Rushylvania, Rush Creek Twp., Logan Co., Ohio.[52] He was the son of Samuel Myer or Meyers Mason II and Mary Elizabeth Pegan (4). He died in Bellefontaine, Lake Twp., Logan Co., Ohio, on March 3, 1950, at age 90.[52] Charles Edwin was buried in Bellefontaine City Cemetery, Bellefontaine, Lake Twp., Logan Co., Ohio.[52, 155]

Charles Edwin married **Mary Ellen Pickerell** around 1881.[156] They had five children. Mary Ellen Pickerell was born in Hopewell Twp., Muskingum Co., Ohio, on June 10, 1858.[156] Mary Ellen reached age 69 and died in Bellefontaine, Lake Twp., Logan Co., Ohio, on November 11, 1927.[156] She was buried in Bellefontaine City Cemetery, Bellefontaine, Lake Twp., Logan Co., Ohio.[156, 157]

Mary Ellen Pickerelll Mason's obituary states that she was born on January 10, 1849 and died at age 78.[158] This conflicts with her death certificate, which says she was born on June 10, 1859.[156] However, her gravestone says she was born in 1858.[157]

In 1900, Charles E. Mason, 40, a carpenter, is enumerated in Bellefontaine, Lake Twp., Logan Co., Ohio *(Census Place: Bellefontaine Ward 4, Logan, Ohio; Roll: T623_1294; Page: 2A; Enumeration District: 113)*. With him is wife Mary Pickerell Mason, 41. The couple have been married 19 years and Mary has borne four children, three still alive. They are Lawrence, 16, Margaret, nine, and Paul, five. All in the household were born in Ohio, as were their parents. Charles' unmarried sister, Minnie Mason, 24, is a boarder in a neighboring home.

In 1910, Charles Mason is found in Bellefontaine, Lake Twp., Logan Co., Ohio *(Census Place: Bellefontaine Ward 1, Logan, Ohio; Roll: T624_1204; Page: 6B; Enumeration District: 0127; Image: 749)*. Charles E. Mason, 51, is a carpenter who says he and his parents were born in Ohio. His wife Mary Pickerell Mason is 51. Mary has borne another child, which did not live. This time, Mary says her father was born in Virginia and her mother in Pennsylvania. Residing with them are children Margaret, 18, and Paul, 15, both born in Ohio.

In 1920, Charles E. Mason, 61, and his wife Mary Pickerell Mason, 61, are still in Bellefontaine, Lake Twp., Logan Co., Ohio *(Census Place: Bellefontaine Ward 1, Logan, Ohio; Roll: T625_1405; Page: 7B; Enumeration District: 188; Image: 155)*. They say they and their parents were Ohio natives. Charles is still a carpenter.

After his first wife died, Charles Edwin Mason married Mrs. **Mary Jane Taylor** Saum on November 25, 1928, in Logan Co., Ohio.[159] Mary Jane Taylor was born in Bellefontaine, Lake Twp., Logan Co., Ohio, on April 8, 1867.[160] She reached age 75 and died in Bellefontaine, Lake Twp., Logan Co., Ohio, on August 6, 1942.[160] Mary Jane was buried in Huntsville Cemetery, McArthur Twp., Logan Co., Ohio.[160]

In 1930, Charles E. Mason, 71, and his second wife, Mary Jane Taylor Saum Mason, 62, are living in Bellefontaine, Lake Twp., Logan Co., Ohio *(Census Place: Bellefontaine, Logan, Ohio; Roll: 1829; Page: 17A; Enumeration District: 5; Image: 803.0)*. Charles Mason says he and his mother were born in Ohio, and his father was born at sea! (Incorrect—he was born in Ohio.) Charles lists no occupation (retired?). Mary Jane Taylor Saum Mason says she and her father were born in Ohio and her mother in England. Charles Mason says he was first married at age 29 (incorrect), and Mary J. says she was 20 when she was first wed.

Charles Mason is not found in the 1940 census.

Children of Charles Edwin Mason and Mary Ellen Pickerell:

+ 44 m I. **Laurence Victor**[8] **Mason** was born in Bellefontaine, Lake Twp., Logan Co., Ohio, on December 20, 1883.[161] He died in Bradenton, Manatee Co., Florida, on October 28, 1954.[162]

+ 45 f II. **Laura Marguerite**[8] **Mason** was born in Bellefontaine, Lake Twp., Logan Co., Ohio, on January 22, 1891.[163, 164] She was also known as **Marguerite**. Laura Marguerite died in Orlando, Orange Co., Florida, on February 29, 1948.[164, 165, 166]

+ 46 m III. **Paul Edwin**[8] **Mason** was born in Bellefontaine, Lake Twp., Logan Co., Ohio, on July 13, 1893.[167, 168] He died in Ontario, San Bernardino Co., California, on January 2, 1955.[168, 169]

+ 47   IV. **Child One**[8] **Mason** was born in Bellefontaine, Lake Twp., Logan Co., Ohio, between 1882 and 1900. He or she died in Bellefontaine, Lake Twp., Logan Co., Ohio, before 1900.

+ 48   V. **Child Two**[8] **Mason** was born in Bellefontaine, Lake Twp., Logan Co., Ohio, between 1900 and 1910. He or she died in Bellefontaine, Lake Twp., Logan Co., Ohio, before 1910.

17. Katherine[7] **Mason** (*Mary Elizabeth*[6] *Pegan, John*[5], *Robert A.*[4], *Andrew*[3], *Andrew*[2] *Pagan, James*[1]) was born on May 9, 1862, in Rushylvania, Rush Creek Twp., Logan Co., Ohio.[53] She was also known as **Kate**. She was the daughter of Samuel Myer or Meyers Mason II and Mary Elizabeth Pegan (4). Katherine died in Indianapolis, Center Twp., Marion Co., Indiana, on December 15, 1929, at age 67.[53] She was buried in Greenwood Cemetery, DeGraff, Pleasant Twp., Logan Co., Ohio.[170]

Never married.

In 1900, sisters "Kate" Mason, 32(?), A. Della Mason, 30(?), and Cora, 26(?), are living on Fletcher Avenue in Center Twp., Marion Co., Indiana *(Census Place: Center, Marion, Indiana; Roll: T623_389; Page: 2B; Enumeration District: 123)*. All have shaved some years off their ages to appear younger, as many unmarried women did in that era. Katherine "Kate" Mason and Allie Della Mason are school teachers, while Cora Mason is an artist. All say they were born in Ohio, as were their parents.

By 1910, Ida May Mason and Minnie Mason have joined their sisters Kate and Cora in Indianapolis, Marion Co., Indiana *(Census Place: Indianapolis Ward 9, Marion, Indiana; Roll: T624_368; Page: 9A; Enumeration District: 0169; Image: 995)*. The sisters are living in Indianapolis in Warren Township, somewhere near the area of South Hawthorne Lane and University Avenue. Ida May, 50, lists no occupation. Kate, 47, and Minnie, 34, are school teachers and Cora, 39, is a bookkeeper. All were born in Ohio, as were their parents.

Katherine Mason is still living in Indianapolis, Warren Twp., Marion Co., Indiana in 1920 *(Census Place: Indianapolis Ward 9, Marion, Indiana; Roll: T625_454; Page: 6A; Enumeration District: 173; Image: 456)*. She is a lodger in the home of Morencie Wells, 80 and his granddaughter, Bessie Hereth, 25. Katherine Mason says she is only 40 years old(!) and lists her occupation as a teacher. She says she and her parents were born in Ohio. There is another lodger in the house, Edith Marie Eldridge, 42, born Maine, also a schooteacher.

Katherine "Kate" Mason was very respected Indianapolis citizen. After attaining degrees at the University of Chicago and Harvard, Katherine Mason devoted her life to teaching. When she died, she had been principal of Indianapolis Public School No. 9 for seven years and, before that, had held the same post at School No. 58 for twenty. In addition, "Kate" organized the first parent-teacher organization in the city as well as an "Opportunity" school for challenged pupils. Her obituary was printed on the front page of the Indianapolis Star on December 16, 1929, with her picture.[171]

18. Alta Dell[7] **Mason** (*Mary Elizabeth*[6] *Pegan, John*[5], *Robert A.*[4], *Andrew*[3], *Andrew*[2] *Pagan, James*[1]) was born on January 29, 1865, in Rushylvania, Rush Creek Twp., Logan Co., Ohio.[54] She was also known as **Allie or Della**. She was the daughter of Samuel Myer or Meyers Mason II and Mary Elizabeth Pegan (4). Alta Dell died in on a journey to Rangoon, Burma, on October 27, 1921, at age 56.[55, 56] She was buried in American Baptist Cemetery, Rangoon, Burma.[55]

Alta Dell Mason Young's real middle name may have been Della. But in adulthood she shortened it to Dell.

In 1900, sisters "Kate" Mason, 32(?), A. Della Mason, 30(?), and Cora, 26(?), are living on Fletcher Avenue in Center Twp., Marion Co., Indiana *(Census Place: Center, Marion, Indiana; Roll: T623_389; Page: 2B;*

Enumeration District: 123). All have shaved some years off their ages to appear younger, as many unmarried women did in that era. Katherine "Kate" Mason and Alta Dell Mason are school teachers, while Cora Mason is an artist. All say they were born in Ohio, as were their parents.

Shortly after the 1900 census, Alta Dell Mason decided to become a missionary to Burma (now Myanmar). Upon her departure to Burma to start her missionary endeavors, Alta Dell Mason was profiled in the Woman's Baptist Foreign Missionary Society's magazine, *Helping Hand*:

> "Miss ALTA DELL MASON was born in Rushsylvania, Ohio, in 1865, Jan. 29. She graduated from the High School in Bellefontaine, Ohio…She had attended a Methodist church, but when she first came into contact with the Baptist church felt that she came into fuller light and was baptized in 1890. When she was older and had consecrated her life to Christ, she never made a plan to teach that she did not ask herself the question, "Have I any right?" There had been obstacles to her leaving home, but God seemed to be opening the door and she was willing to go anywhere."[172]

On the ship to Burma in October 1900, Alta Dell met a minister and missionary, William Marcus Young, a widower with a daughter.

Alta Dell Mason married **William Marcus Young** on December 25, 1900, in Rangoon, Burma.[173] They had three sons. William Marcus Young was born in St. Augustine, Indian Point Twp., Knox Co., Illinois, on August 20, 1861.[174, 175] He reached age 74 and died in Los Angeles, Los Angeles Co., California, on April 8, 1936.[176, 177, 178] William Marcus was buried in Tulare Cemetery, Tulare, Tulare Co., California.[178, 179, 180]

From *Baptist Missionary Magazine* in March 1901:

> "REV. W. M. YOUNG and Miss ALTA DELL MASON were married December 25 in Rangoon, Burma. THE MAGAZINE extends congratulations and wishes them success in their new frontier station, Keng Tung, Burma."[173]

William Marcus Young is a noted American Baptist missionary who spent most of his life from 1894-1934 in Southeast Asia. He founded several missions in Burma (now Myanmar), Thailand and China. His primary base was a mission in Kengtung, Shan Province, Burma, but he also spent time in the capital of Shan Province, Taunggyi, and the Burmese village of Bana, all among the Lahu people. He also founded missions in the northeastern region of Shan Province, among the Wa tribes, then head-hunters. Rev. Young over the years persuaded the Wa to end this practice.[C]

On sabbaticals, William Marcus also had brief stints as a church minister in Gibson City, Drummer Twp., Ford Co., Illinois; Indianapolis, Marion Co., Indiana; and Granville, Granville Twp., Licking Co., Ohio.[178]

When he married Alta Dell Mason, William Marcus Young was a widower with a daughter, Ethel, who was left with her late mother's relatives.[178]

William Marcus and Alta Dell Mason Young made several trips to and from Asia and the United States before Alta died in 1921. In 1919, for a brief time, William Marcus was a minister in Granville, Granville Twp., Licking Co., Ohio; but, according to a passport application, they leave Granville and go back to Asia—this time to China—for missionary work.[175]

Alta Dell Mason Young fell ill in the village of Bana and was transported through the Burmese jungle to a British hospital in Rangoon, Burma's capital. Her malady, a neuromuscular condition, confounded physicians and was never diagnosed. She suffered for months before she died.[55, 181]

According to American Baptist church sources and other published material, the Burmese people in the area, the Lahu, practiced Buddhism mixed with tribal rituals, but there is evidence that the traditional tribal religion was monotheistic. Centuries earlier, a tribal oracle or shaman in the Shan Province foretold the coming of a white man who would have a whilte book, and he would confirm their monotheistic beliefs of one Supreme Being and bring salvation to the Lahu. Other Christian missionaries had come to the area and founded a small mission, with mixed success. But then Rev. Young arrived, a white man carrying a white bible, and the Shan Province people believed he was the fulfillment of the old prophecy. From then on, the mission had more success. Young's legend grew as several attempts on his life and that of his followers, by local gangs ended suddenly, seemingly by divine intervention. According to the "Grand Old Man of Chaing Mai: The Life of Harold Young", by David Lawitts, in Chaing Mai, Thailand's Citylife Magazine, April 2015: "Everytime a group of assassins leapt out of a jungle ambush, they claimed to see angelic figures and halos surrounding the missionaries, and they'd drop to their knees and beg forgiveness." The Lahu dubbed William M. Young, the "Jaw-Maw", meaning "Man-God", and he was considered a holy prophet.[182]

William Marcus Young retired in 1934, leaving Burma for California.[178] His son, Harold Mason Young, writes in his book, *To The Mountain Tops: A Sojourn Among the Lahu of Asia* that his father died on April 8, 1936 in Los Angeles, California.[178]

William Marcus and Alta Dell Mason Young's two sons continued their missionary work in Southeast Asia. At least one of their descendants is a missionary today in the Phillipines.

Sons of Alta Dell Mason and William Marcus Young:

+ 49 m I. **Harold Mason**[8] **Young** was born in Kengtung Ess, Shan State, Burma (now Myanmar), on September 25, 1901.[135, 183] He died in Chaing Mai, Thailand, on February 6, 1975.[135, 174, 184, 185]

+ 50 m II. **Marcus Vincent**[8] **Young** was was born in Kengtung Ess, Shan State, Burma (now Myanmar), on August 22, 1903.[135, 186] He died in a hospital in Redlands, San Bernardino Co., California, on December 2, 1990.[135, 187, D]

+ 51 m III. **Clarence Edwin**[8] **Young** was was born in Kengtung Ess, Shan State, Burma (now Myanmar), on November 13, 1906.[188] He died in Taunggyi, Shan State, Burma (now Myanmar), on May 30, 1908.[189]

19. **Samuel**[7] **Mason III** (*Mary Elizabeth*[6] *Pegan, John*[5]*, Robert A.*[4]*, Andrew*[3]*, Andrew*[2] *Pagan, James*[1]) was born about 1868 in Rushylvania, Rush Creek Twp., Logan Co., Ohio. He was the son of Samuel Myer or Meyers Mason II and Mary Elizabeth Pegan (4). Samuel died in Rushylvania, Rush Creek Twp., Logan Co., Ohio, between 1868 and 1870. He was buried in Miami Cemetery, Rush Creek Twp., Logan Co., Ohio.[190]

20. **Cora**[7] **Mason** (*Mary Elizabeth*[6] *Pegan, John*[5]*, Robert A.*[4]*, Andrew*[3]*, Andrew*[2] *Pagan, James*[1]) was born on June 9, 1871, in Rushylvania, Rush Creek Twp., Logan Co., Ohio.[57] She was the daughter of Samuel Myer or Meyers Mason II and Mary Elizabeth Pegan (4). She died in Indianapolis, Marion Co., Indiana, on March 26, 1949, at age 77.[58, 59] Cora was buried in Greenwood Cemetery, DeGraff, Pleasant Twp., Logan Co., Ohio.[191]

Never married.

In 1900, sisters "Kate" Mason, 32(?), A. Della Mason, 30(?), and Cora, 26(?), are living on Fletcher Avenue in Center Twp., Marion Co., Indiana *(Census Place: Center, Marion, Indiana; Roll: T623_389; Page: 2B; Enumeration District: 123)*. All have shaved some years off their ages to appear younger, as many single women did in that era. Katherine "Kate" Mason and Allie Della Mason are school teachers, while Cora Mason is an artist. All say they were born in Ohio, as were their parents.

By 1910, Ida and Minnie Mason, ages 50 and 34 respectively, have joined their sisters Katherine, 47, and Cora, 39, in Marion Co., Indiana *(Census Place: Indianapolis Ward 9, Marion, Indiana; Roll: T624_368; Page: 9A; Enumeration District: 0169; Image: 995)*. The sisters are living in Indianapolis in Warren Township, somewhere near the area of South Hawthorne Lane and University Avenue. Ida May, 50, lists no occupation. Kate and Minnie are school teachers and Cora is a bookkeeper. All were born in Ohio, as were their parents.

Cora Mason is not found in the 1920 census.

In 1930, Minnie Mason, 54, and sister Cora Mason, 58, are found in Clay Twp., Hamilton Co., Indiana *(Census Place: Clay, Hamilton, Indiana; Roll: 590; Page: 4A; Enumeration District: 5; Image: 758.0)*. Minnie is now a lawyer—a partner in a law firm. Cora lists no occupation. Both say they were born in Ohio, as were their parents. Also in the household is a boarder, Edith Eldridge, 52, a teacher born in Maine. This is the same Edith Eldridge who was a lodger with Minnie in 1920.

Cora Mason's birth date is erroneously stated as June 10, 1871 on her death certificate; the informant was her sister, Mary/Minnie ("M. Elizabeth Mason").[58] This conflicts with her birth record in the Logan County, Ohio birth registrations, which says she was born on June 9.[57]

21. **John Pegan[7] Mason** (*Mary Elizabeth[6] Pegan, John[5], Robert A.[4], Andrew[3], Andrew[2] Pagan, James[1]*) was born on February 26, 1873, in Rushylvania, Rush Creek Twp., Logan Co., Ohio.[61, 62] He was the son of Samuel Myer or Meyers Mason II and Mary Elizabeth Pegan (4). John Pegan Mason died in Indianapolis, Center Twp., Marion Co., Indiana, on June 2, 1924, at age 51.[62] He was buried in Greenwood Cemetery, DeGraff, Pleasant Twp., Logan Co., Ohio.[192]

John Pegan married **Anna Louisa Slusser** on December 24, 1899, in Logan Co., Ohio.[193] They had two daughters. Anna Louisa Slusser was born in Adams Twp., Champaign Co., Ohio, on July 5, 1875.[193] She was also known as **Lanna**. She reached age 65 and died in Vincennes, Vincennes Twp., Knox Co., Indiana, on December 25, 1940.[194] Anna Louisa was buried in Greenwood Cemetery, DeGraff, Pleasant Twp., Logan Co., Ohio.[195, 196]

John P. Mason, age 27, a carpenter, is residing on Lexington Avenue in Indianapolis, Center Twp., Marion Co., Indiana in 1900 *(Census Place: Center, Marion, Indiana; Roll: T623_389; Page: 5B; Enumeration District: 124)*. John has a wife "Louisa Anna" Slusser Mason, 25. John was born in Ohio, as were his parents; Louisa Anna (actually Anna Louisa) Slusser Mason was born in Ohio, as was her father, while her mother was born in Indiana. They have been married less than a year.

In 1910, John P. Mason, 38, a contractor, born Ohio as were his parents, is still living in Indianapolis, Center Twp., Marion Co., Indiana *(Census Place: Indianapolis Ward 10, Marion, Indiana; Roll: T624_368; Page: 8B; Enumeration District: 0180; Image: 1265)*. They family is living on Hoyt Avenue. With him are wife Anna, 35, born Ohio, who this time says her parents were both born in Indiana. The couple has been married 10 years and Anna Louisa Slusser Mason says she has borne two children, both surviving. The children are daughters Mildred, nine, and Alice, three, both Indiana natives.

In 1920, John P. Mason, 46, a carpenter/builder, is living on Southern Avenue in Center Twp., Indianapolis, Marion Co., Indiana *(Census Place: Indianapolis Ward 10, Marion, Indiana; Roll: T625_454; Page: 2A; Enumeration District: 197; Image: 1130)*. With him are wife "Lanna", 45, and daughters Mildred, 19, and Alice, 12. This time, both John and Anna Louisa Slusser Mason say they were born in Ohio. Both children were born in Indiana.

After her husband John Pegan Mason dies, Anna lives with her children.

In 1930, Anna Louisa "Lanna" Slusser Mason is living with her son-in-law and daughter, Horace and Alice Mason Honeycutt on Hoefgen Street in Indianapolis, Center Twp., Marion Co., Indiana. *(Census Place: Indianapolis, Marion, Indiana; Roll: 614; Page: 17A; Enumeration District: 161; Image: 35.0)*. Anna Louisa "Lanna" Slusser Mason, 55, a widow, born Ohio as were her parents, says her first marriage was at age 25. Horace Honeycutt is 25, born Tennessee as were his parents, a clerk in an auto factory; and Alice Mason Honeycutt is 23, born Indiana with her parents born in Ohio. Horace and Anna Mason Honeycutt have been married two years, as they say their first marriages occurred at ages 25 and 23 respectively. They have a son, Robert, 10 months old, born Indiana. Also in the home is Horace's widowed father, James Honeycutt, 56, born Tennessee as were his parents, a widower.

Anna Louisa Slusser Mason continues to reside with Horace and Alice Mason Honeycutt, her son-in-law and daughter, in Indianapolis in 1940 *(Census Place: Indianapolis, Marion, Indiana; Roll: T627_1129; Page: 2B; Enumeration District: 96-288)*. Anna Louisa Slusser Mason, 65, a widow, was born in Ohio. Horace Honeycutt, age 35, born Tennessee is an auditor for the State of Indiana. His wife, Alice Mason Honeycutt, 33, is a clerk for the Indiana State Department of Welfare. With them are sons Robert, 10, and Donald, seven. Alice and the children were born in Indiana. All state they were in Indianapolis in 1935. Their house address is 1542 Hoefgen Street.

After the Honeycutts move to Florida, Anna Louisa Slusser Mason lives with her elder son-in-law and daughter, Lance Alfred and MIldred Elizabeth Mason Mantle, in Vincennes, Knox Co., Indiana, where Lance was a minister.[195]

Anna Louisa Slusser Mason's birth date on her Indiana death certificate is wrong. On her death certificate, her informant, Rev. Lance Mantle, states her date of birth as October 27, 1874. But Anna Louisa says on her marriage license that her birth date is July 5, 1875.[193, 194]

Daughters of John Pegan Mason and Anna Louisa Slusser:

+ 52 f I. **Mildred Elizabeth**[8] **Mason** was born in Indianapolis, Center Twp., Marion Co., Indiana, on September 27, 1901.[197, 198, 199] She died in San Diego, San Diego Co., California, on November 19, 1957.[197]

+ 53 f II. **Alice Irene**[8] **Mason** was born in Indianapolis, Center Twp., Marion Co., Indiana, on February 4, 1907.[200, 201] She died in Satellite Beach, Brevard Co., Florida, on August 30, 1984.[135, 200, 201, 202]

22. Minnie or Mary Elizabeth[7] **Mason** (*Mary Elizabeth*[6] *Pegan, John*[5]*, Robert A.*[4]*, Andrew*[3]*, Andrew*[2] *Pagan, James*[1]) was born on January 13, 1876, in North Lewisburg, Rush Twp., Champaign Co., Ohio.[63] She was also known as **Elizabeth**. She was the daughter of Samuel Myer or Meyers Mason II and Mary Elizabeth Pegan (4). She died in Indianapolis, Center Twp., Marion Co., Indiana, on May 17, 1956, at age 80.[63]

Minnie or Mary Elizabeth was buried in Greenwood Cemetery, DeGraff, Pleasant Twp., Logan Co., Ohio.[203] It is unclear whether her given name was Minnie or Mary Elizabeth; even her death certificate identifies her as "M. Elizabeth Mason." She seems to have used Minnie almost exclusively as her preferred name.

Never married.

In 1900, Minnie Mason, 24, a schoolteacher, born in Ohio as were her parents, was a roomer in the home of Arnold and Margaret Miller in Bellefontaine, Lake Twp., Logan Co., Ohio *(Census Place: Bellefontaine Ward 4, Logan, Ohio; Roll: T623_1294; Page: 2A; Enumeration District: 113)*. Nearby was brother Charles Mason and his family.

By 1910, Minnie Mason and Ida May Mason have joined their sisters Kate and Cora in Marion Co., Indiana *(Census Place: Indianapolis Ward 9, Marion, Indiana; Roll: T624_368; Page: 9A; Enumeration District: 0169; Image: 995)*. The sisters are living in Indianapolis in Warren Township, somewhere near the area of South Hawthorne Lane and University Avenue. Ida May, 50, lists no occupation. Kate, 47, and Minnie, 34, are school teachers and Cora, 39, is a bookkeeper. All were born in Ohio, as were their parents.

In 1920, Minnie Mason, 44, is a boarder in the household of James and Bessie Cooley in Indianapolis, Center Twp., Marion Co., Indiana *(Census Place: Indianapolis Ward 2, Marion, Indiana; Roll: T625_450; Page: 22B; Enumeration District: 50; Image: 853)*. She is a schoolteacher who says she and her parents were born in Ohio. There are several other lodgers in the house.

In 1930, Minnie Mason, 54, and sister Cora Mason, 58, are found in Clay Twp., Hamilton Co., Indiana *(Census Place: Clay, Hamilton, Indiana; Roll: 590; Page: 4A; Enumeration District: 5; Image: 758.0)*. Minnie is now a lawyer—a partner in a law firm. Cora lists no occupation. Both say they were born in Ohio, as were their parents. Also in the household is a boarder, Edith Eldridge, 52, a teacher who was born in Maine. Edith was also others in the same home as "Minnie" in 1920.

23. **John B.**[7] **Baughman** (*Catherine*[6] *Pegan, John*[5]*, Robert A.*[4]*, Andrew*[3]*, Andrew*[2] *Pagan, James*[1]) was born on June 5, 1858, in DeGraff, Miami Twp., Logan Co., Ohio.[69] He was the son of Joshua B. Baughman and Catherine Pegan (5). John B. died in DeGraff, Miami Twp., Logan Co., Ohio, on September 7, 1863, at age five.[69]

24. **Otto G.**[7] **Baughman** (*Catherine*[6] *Pegan, John*[5]*, Robert A.*[4]*, Andrew*[3]*, Andrew*[2] *Pagan, James*[1]) was born on May 16, 1868, in Logansville, Pleasant Twp., Logan Co., Ohio.[70] He was the son of Joshua B. Baughman and Catherine Pegan (5). He died in Marion, Marion Twp., Marion Co., Ohio, on April 19, 1925, at age 56.[70] Otto G. was buried in Greenwood Cemetery, DeGraff, Pleasant Twp., Logan Co., Ohio.[70, 204]

Childless.

Otto Baughman is living with his widower father Joshua in De Graff, Miami Twp., Logan Co., Ohio in 1900 *(Census Place: Miami, Logan, Ohio; Roll: T623_1294; Page: 5B; Enumeration District: 117)*. Joshua B. Baughman, a widower, is 69 years old, born Jan 1831 in Ohio, with his father born in Pennsylvania and his mother in Ohio. Son Otto G. Baughman, now 32 and, like his father, a carpenter, was born in May 1868; he was born in Ohio as were his parents.

Otto G. married Mrs. **Tina D. Stahler** Bedlinger about 1906. Tina Stahler was born in Logansville, Pleasant Twp., Logan Co., Ohio, on June 21, 1882.[205] Tina reached age 54 and died in Marion, Marion Twp., Marion Co., Ohio, on July 14, 1936.[202] She was buried in Greenwood Cemetery, DeGraff, Pleasant Twp., Logan Co., Ohio as Tina Stahler Dreher.[202, 206]

Otto Baughman is enumerated as "Otto G. Baufman" in 1910 in Marion, Marion Twp., Marion Co., Ohio *(Census Place: Marion Ward 2, Marion, Ohio; Roll: T624_1213; Page: 3B; Enumeration District: 0085; Image: 735)*. Otto Baughman, 41, now a lamp inspector (probably a streetlight inspec- tor), says he was born in Ohio as were his parents. Wife Tina Baughman is 26, also born in Ohio as were her parents. The couple have been married four years and Tina has borne no children. Tina Stahler Bedlinger Baughman does say this is her second marriage. Living with them is Otto's father Joshua Baughman ("Baufman") is listed as age 80, a wid- ower who is still a house carpenter. He says he was born in Ohio and his parents in Pennsylvania.

In 1920, Otto G. Baughman is still in Marion, Marion Co., Ohio *(Census Place: Marion Ward 2, Marion, Ohio; Roll: T625_1416; Page: 5A; Enumeration District: 122; Image: 182)*. Otto G. Baughman, who says he is only 48, is a railroad car repairer while wife Tina Baughman, 35, is a saleslady at a dry good store. Joshua Baughman is 88 and retired. All in the home say they and their parents were born in Ohio.

In 1930, Otto's widow, Tina Stahler Bedlinger Baughman, age 47, is listed as the head of house- hold in Marion, Marion Twp., Marion Co., Ohio *(Census Place: Marion, Marion, Ohio; Roll: 1847; Page: 16A; Enumeration District: 17; Image: 889.0)*. Tina is 47, born Ohio as were her parents, and lists her assets as $4000. Living with her is her mother, Mary Stahler, 82, born Ohio, with her parents born in Pennsylvania. There is also a boarder in the home, Emery Dreher, male, single, born Ohio as were his parents. No one in the household lists an occupa- tion. On October 11 of that year, Tina D. Stahler Bedlinger Baughman marries Emery Dreher.[207]

25. **Orpha Estella**[7] **Pegan** (*James Milton*[6]*, John*[5]*, Robert A.*[4]*, Andrew*[3]*, Andrew*[2] *Pagan, James*[1]) was born on March 10, 1868, in DeGraff, Miami Twp., Logan Co., Ohio.[77] She was the daughter of James Milton Pegan (6) and Catherine Hendrickson. She died in Parma, Parma Twp., Cuyahoga Co., Ohio, on December 10, 1939, at age 71.[77] She was cremated.[77]

Never married.

Orpha Estella Pegan is listed as head of household, but is living with her mother Catherine Hendrickson Pegan in Center Twp., Marion Co., Indiana in 1900 *(Census Place: Center, Marion, Indiana; Roll: T623_389; Page: 4A; Enumeration District: 137)*.

The surname is spelled "Peggan". Orpha Estella ("Stella"), is listed as age 22, but, as she was born March 1868, she is 32. Orpha Estella is single, and her occupation is working as a saleslady. Catherine Hendrickson Pegan age 49, was born Indiana as were her parents, Catherine says she is a widow who bore five children, four still alive. Twins Arthur and Elgie, age 24, born November 1875, are also in the home. Arthur is a bookkeeper and Elgie is an assistant to a dentist. All three children were born in Ohio.

A mention in the *Indianapolis (IN) Star* on December 1, 1904 says that "Estelle Pegan" had just published a volume of short stories.[208]

Orpha Estella Pegan, listed as "Estella", was living with her mother Catherine Hendrickson Pegan and her brother Arthur in 1910 in Ward 1, Indianapolis, Marion Co., Indiana (*Census Place: Indianapolis Ward 1, Marion, Indiana; Roll: T624_366; Page: 13B; Enumeration District: 0045; Image: 722*). Orpha Estella Pegan, 41, born Ohio, is listed as having no occupation; she may have been studying to be an orthopedist at the time. Catherine, listed as "Kathryn", is age 60, a widow, born in Indiana, says her father was born in Indiana and her mother in Pennsylvania. This time she says she has borne four children, all still living. Son Arthur, 35, born Ohio, is listed as the head of the household. Arthur's occupation is a veterinary surgeon who owns his own practice. This is most likely an error—he was probably working at his brother-in-law August Albershardt's veterinary surgery practice. August Albershardt was the husband of Elgie Pegan Albershardt, Arthur's twin sister.

Orpha is not mentioned in the Indianapolis, Indiana city directories from 1913-1920. It seems for at least part of that time, she was living in Falls Church, Virginia, where her cousin and her cousin's second husband, Orpha Marie Pegan Andrews Conklin, daughter of William Louis Pegan, and Isaac Albert Conklin, resided. Orpha Estella "Stella" Pegan is listed as the informant on Orpha M. Pegan Andrews Conklin's death certificate in April 1918, and "Stella's" residence is listed on the certificate as Falls Church, Virginia.[209]

Orpha Estella Pegan is not found in the 1920 census.

Orpha Estella Pegan, still single, and her brother, Arthur, also still unmarried, are living in Cleveland, Cuyahoga Co., Ohio (*Census Place: Cleveland, Cuyahoga, Ohio; Roll: 1781; Page: 2B; Enumeration District: 255; Image: 297.0*). Arthur is listed as head of the household. Orpha is age 52 and an orthopedist who has her own practice. Arthur, 50, is a cabinetmaker at a furniture factory. Both say they and their father were born in Ohio and their mother in Indiana.

Orpha's death was mentioned in the *Coshocton (OH) Tribune* on December 11, 1939, in an article on automobile deaths in Ohio the previous weekend. The article says that Dr. Orpha E. Pegan, a chiropodist, was hit and killed by an automobile in Parma, Ohio.[210]

26. Daughter[7] **Pegan** (*James Milton*[6], *John*[5], *Robert A.*[4], *Andrew*[3], *Andrew*[2] *Pagan, James*[1]) was born on February 6, 1870, in DeGraff, Miami Twp., Logan Co., Ohio.[78] She was the daughter of James Milton Pegan (6) and Catherine Hendrickson. Daughter died in DeGraff, Miami Twp., Logan Co., Ohio, on February 9, 1870.[78] She is probably buried in DeGraff Cemetery, DeGraff, Pleasant Twp., Logan Co., Ohio.

27. Gertrude P.[7] **Pegan** (*James Milton*[6], *John*[5], *Robert A.*[4], *Andrew*[3], *Andrew*[2] *Pagan, James*[1]) was born on July 29, 1871, in DeGraff, Miami Twp., Logan Co., Ohio.[79] She was the daughter of James Milton Pegan (6) and Catherine Hendrickson. She died in Pittsfield Twp., Washtenaw Co., Michigan, on April 12, 1959, at age 87.[80, 81] Gertrude P. was buried in Greenwood Cemetery, DeGraff, Pleasant Twp., Logan Co., Ohio.[81]

Gertrude P. married **Otto H. Russell** on December 20, 1892, in Logan Co., Ohio.[211] They had one daughter. Otto H. Russell was born in Kickapoo Twp., Leavenworth Co., Kansas, on November 6, 1869.[212] Otto H. reached age 67 and died in DeGraff, Miami Twp., Logan Co., Ohio, on December 11, 1936.[212] He was buried in Greenwood Cemetery, DeGraff, Pleasant Twp., Logan Co., Ohio.[212, 213]

In 1900, Otto H. and Gertrude Pegan Russell are living in DeGraff, Miami Twp., Logan Co., Ohio (*Census Place: Miami, Logan, Ohio; Roll:*

T623_1294; Page: 10A; Enumeration District: 117). Some of Otto's information is missing—his age and his year of birth, although the month, November, is listed. Otto says he was born in Kansas and his parents in Ohio. Gertrude, 28, born July 1871, says she and her father were born in Ohio and her mother in Indiana. The couple states they have been married seven years and Gertrude has borne no children.

Otto H. and Gertrude Pegan Russell are still in DeGraff, Miami Twp., Logan Co., Ohio in 1910 *(Census Place: Miami, Logan, Ohio; Roll: T624_1204; Page: 6A; Enumeration District: 0138; Image: 992).* The surname is spelled "Russel" on the census form. Otto H. Russell is age 40, an Rural Free Delivery mail carrier, born Kansas with his parents born in Ohio. Gertrude, 38, was born in Ohio, as was her father. Her mother was born in Indiana. Otto and Gertrude state this is their first marriage, and they have been married 17 years. Gertrude has borne one child, still living. This is daughter, Pauline, 19 months, born Ohio.

In 1920, Otto H. and Gertrude Pegan Russell continue to reside in DeGraff, Miami Twp., Logan Co., Ohio *(Census Place: Miami, Logan, Ohio; Roll: T625_1405; Page: 6B; Enumeration District: 198; Image: 396).* Otto H., 50, is still a rural free delivery mail carrier. He was born in Kansas and his parents in Ohio. Gertrude Pegan Russell, 48, was born in Ohio, her father in Ohio and her mother in Indiana. With them is their daughter, Pauline, 11, an Ohio native, with her father born in Kansas and her mother in Ohio.

Otto H. and Gertrude Pegan Russell are enumerated in DeGraff, Miami Twp., Logan Co., Ohio in 1930 *(Census Place: Miami, Logan, Ohio; Roll: T625_1405; Page: 6B; Enumeration District: 198; Image: 396).* Otto H., 60, says he was born in Kansas, his father in Ohio, but this time he says his mother was born in Pennsylvania. He continues to be a U.S. mail carrier, R.F.D. Gertrude Pegan Russell, 58, still says she and her father were born in Ohio and her mother in Indiana. The couple states they were first married at ages 22 and 20 respectively. Living with them is their newly-wedded son-in-law and daughter, Donald O. and Pauline Russell Brown. Donald O. Brown is age 26, born Pennsylvania, as were his parents, is a pharmacist working in a drug store. Pauline Russell Brown, 21, was born in Ohio as was her mother; her father was born in Kansas.

In 1940, Gertrude Pegan Brown is residing with her son-in-law and daughter, Donald and Pauline Russell Brown, in Ann Arbor, Ann Arbor Twp., Washtenaw Co., Michigan *(Census Place: Ann Arbor, Washtenaw, Michigan; Roll: T627_1823; Page: 7B; Enumeration District: 81-23).* Gertrude Pegan Russell, 68, a widow, was born Ohio. The head of the household, Donald Brown, age 36, born Pennsylvania, is an assistant manager of a bookstore. His wife, Pauline Russell Brown, 31, and sons Robert, eight, and James, six were born in Ohio. All state they were living in Ann Arbor in 1935; however, as Otto Russell's death was in 1936, Gertrude, at least, was still a resident of DeGraff, Miami Twp., Logan Co., Ohio at that time. Their home address is 706 Arch Street.

Daughter of Gertrude P. Pegan and Otto H. Russell:

+ 54 f I. **Pauline Elizabeth**[8] **Russell** was born in DeGraff, Miami Twp., Logan Co., Ohio, on September 9, 1909.[214] She died in Venice, Sarasota Co., Florida, on June 1, 1999.[135, 215]

28. Arthur[7] **Pegan** (*James Milton*[6], *John*[5], *Robert A.*[4], *Andrew*[3], *Andrew*[2] *Pagan, James*[1]) was born on September 20, 1874, in DeGraff, Miami Twp., Logan Co., Ohio.[82, 83] He was the son of James Milton Pegan (6) and Catherine Hendrickson. Arthur died in Cleveland, Cuyahoga Co., Ohio, on February 28, 1946, at age 71.[82] He was buried in Whitehaven Memorial Park Cemetery, Cleveland, Cuyahoga Co., Ohio.[82]

Never married.

An article in the *Bellefontaine (OH) Republican* on April 26, 1904 indicates that "Dr. Arthur Pegan, veterinary surgeon" was one of 70 patients rescued from St. Vincent's Hospital in Indianapolis when the building caught fire on April 17. Arthur had to be carried out of the hospital.[216]

According to the U.S. Patent Office, Arthur C. Pegan of Indianapolis, Indiana, held United States

Patent Office Patent #840, 800 for a "Locked Coat Hook", patented on January 8, 1907.[217]

Arthur C. Pegan, age 24, born Ohio, is living with his mother, Catherine Hendrickson Pegan, twin sister Elgie, and older sister Orpha Estella in Center Twp., Marion Co., Indiana in 1900 *(Census Place: Center, Marion, Indiana; Roll: T623_389; Page: 4A; Enumeration District: 137)*. The surname is spelled "Peggan". In the household are Catherine Hendrickson Pegan, age 49, born Indiana as were her parents, Catherine says she is a widow who bore five children, four still alive. The head of the household, Orpha Estella ("Stella") Pegan is listed as age 22, but she was born in March 1868, so she is 32. Orpha Estella is single and is working as a saleslady. Arthur is a bookkeeper and Elgie is an assistant to a dentist. All three children were born in Ohio.

Arthur C. Pegan is again residing with his mother, Catherine Hendrickson Pegan and sister Orpha Estella Pegan in Ward 1, Indianapolis, Marion Co., Indiana in 1910 *(Census Place: Indianapolis Ward 1, Marion, Indiana; Roll: T624_366; Page: 13B; Enumeration District: 0045; Image: 722)*. Arthur, age 35, born Ohio, is the head of the household and he is still single. Arthur's occupation is a veterinary surgeon who owns his own practice. This is incorrect. As he was a carpenter by trade, he was probably working in some capacity for his twin sister Elgie Pegan Albershardt's husband, August Albershardt, in the latter's veterinary surgery office. Catherine Hendrickson Pegan, listed as "Kathryn," is age 60, a widow, born in Indiana, who says her father was born in Indiana and her mother in Pennsylvania. This time Catherine says she has borne four children, all still living. Orpha Estella Pegan, 41, born Ohio, is listed as having no occupation; she may have been studying to be an orthopedist at the time. Like her brother, she is unmarried.

Arthur Pegan lists his occupation as cabinetmaker on his WWI draft application in 1918, and says his date of birth was October 20, 1874 (his birth record in Logan County, Ohio says September 20, 1874 and the 1900 census says November 1875!).[83] The draft application also says Arthur, who was living at 715 East 25th Street in Indianapolis, Indiana, has a permanent injury to his right leg and his kneecap was gone.[218]

In 1920, Arthur Pegan, 48, is still a member of his mother Catherine Hendrickson Pegan's household in Indianapolis *(Census Place: Indianapolis Ward 2, Marion, Indiana; Roll: T625_450; Page: 5B; Enumeration District: 50; Image: 815)*. Arthur is single and an overseer at an automobile company. Catherine Hendrickson Pegan is 73 years old and has no occupation.

On May 5, 1920, the *Indianapolis (IN) Star* newspaper printed a short article about an incident where Arthur Pegan claimed he was robbed by two men, James C. Hollywood and Dru Hill, at the Colonial Hotel. Police, who were were called after Hollywood tried to force his way into another room at the hotel, said all three men were drinking. Hollywood was arrested for drunkenness and Arthur Pegan and Dru Hill were arrested for vagrancy. Prohibition had begun on January 1 of that year, and the police noted the three had been drinking "toilet water", meaning eau de toilet.[219]

In the early 1920s, Catherine Hendrickson Pegan and her son Arthur Pegan move to Cleveland, Cuyahoga Co., Ohio, where Catherine's daughter and Arthur's sister Orpha Estella Pegan had relocated.

Arthur Pegan and his sister, Orpha Estella Pegan, both still unwed, are living in Cleveland, Cuyahoga Co., Ohio *(Census Place: Cleveland, Cuyahoga, Ohio; Roll: 1781; Page: 2B; Enumeration District: 255; Image: 297.0)*. Arthur, listed as head of the household, is age 50, and a cabinetmaker at a furniture factory. Both say they are Ohio natives, like their father, and their mother was born in Indiana. Orpha is age 52 and an orthopedist who has her own practice.

In 1940, Arthur C. Pegan, single and living alone, is again found in Cleveland, Cuyahoga Co., Ohio *(Census Place: Cleveland, Cuyahoga, Ohio; Roll: T627_3214; Page: 4A; Enumeration District: 92-275)*. Arthur Pegan is 65 years old and lists no occupation. He was born in Ohio and says he was living in the same apartment at 3214 Prospect Avenue, #110, in 1935.

Arthur Pegan is listed as a "retired veterinarian" on his death certificate, and the source given was the records of the Ohio Division of Aid for the Aging. He is listed as a resident of the Cain Nursing Home in Cleveland at the time of his death.[82]

29. **Elgie Elenor**[7] **Pegan** (*James Milton*[6], *John*[5], *Robert A.*[4], *Andrew*[3], *Andrew*[2] *Pagan, James*[1]) was born on September 20, 1874, in DeGraff, Miami Twp., Logan Co., Ohio.[83, 84, 85] She was the daughter of James Milton Pegan (6) and Catherine Hendrickson. Elgie Elenor died in Indianapolis, Marion Co., Indiana, on July 24, 1960, at age 85.[84, 85, 86] She was buried in Crown Hill Cemetery, Indianapolis, Marion Co., Indiana.[84, 85, 220]

Elgie Pegan, age 24, born November 1875 in Ohio, is living with her mother Katherine Hendrickson Pegan, her twin brother Arthur Pegan, and older sister Orpha Estella Pegan in 1900 in Center Twp., Marion Co., Indiana (*Census Place: Center, Marion, Indiana; Roll: T623_389; Page: 4A; Enumeration District: 137*). The surname is spelled "Peggan". Elgie, 24, born Ohio, is an assistant to a dentist. Katherine, age 49, was born Indiana as were her parents, Katherine says she is a widow who bore five children, four still alive. Orpha Estella ("Stella"), is listed as age 22, but she was born in March 1868 so she is 32. Orpha Estella. listed as the head of the household, is single and working as a saleslady. Arthur Pegan is a bookkeeper. All three children were born in Ohio.

Elgie Elenor married **August H. Albershardt** on October 25, 1906, in Marion Co., Indiana.[221] They divorced. They had three children. August H. Albershardt was born in Indianapolis, Marion Co., Indiana, on June 11, 1870.[222, 223] August H. reached age 90 and died in Indianapolis, Marion Co., Indiana, on March 12, 1961.[223, 224] He was buried in Crown Hill Cemetery, Indianapolis, Marion Co., Indiana.[220, 225]

In 1910, August and Elgie Pegan Albershardt are found in Indianapolis, Center Twp., Marion Co., Indiana (*Census Place: Indianapolis Ward 10, Marion, Indiana; Roll: T624_368; Page: 1B; Enumeration District: 0185; Image: 1351*). In the home are August Albershardt, age 36, born Ohio with his parents born in Germany, who lists his occupation as a veterinary doctor. His wife, Elgie Pegan Albershardt is 34, and says she was born in Ohio and her parents in Indiana (Incorrect—her father James Milton Pegan was born in Ohio). The pair say they have been married three years and Elgie has borne two children, both surviving. They are son Milton, two, and daughter "Catherine", one month old.

August and Elgie Pegan Albershardt are still living in Indianapolis, Center Twp., Marion Co., Indiana in 1920 (*Census Place: Indianapolis Ward 10, Marion, Indiana; Roll: T625_454; Page: 14A; Enumeration District: 184; Image: 822*). "Augest Alerschardt", 49, a veterinary surgeon, says he was born in Indiana, his father in Germany and his mother in Ohio. Elgie Pegan Albershardt, 46, says she and her father were born in Ohio and her mother in Indiana. Children in the home include: Milton, 12, "Catherine", nine, and Arlton, five. All the children are Indiana natives. There is also a roomer in the house, Anna Woeniker, 25.

Between 1920-1930, August H. and Elgie Pegan Alberschardt divorce. According to Donald M. Albershardt, their grandson, August Albershardt, as a noted veterinary surgeon, was asked to judge dog shows. Their grandson says some women who owned the dogs would flirt with him, and rumors swelled that August was unfaithful. Although August declared his innocence, Elgie thought otherwise and divorced him.[226]

In 1930, Elgie Pegan Albershardt was living with her sons, Milton and Arlton, in Indianapolis, Washington Twp., Marion Co., Indiana (*Census Place: Indianapolis, Marion, Indiana; Roll: 610; Page: 14A; Enumeration District: 82; Image: 652.0*). Her home is between 52nd and 53rd Street on Winthrop Avenue. Elgie, 57, says she was born in Ohio as were both her parents (Incorrect—her mother was born in Indiana). She lists her occupation as laundress. Oddly, Elgie lists herself as married and was first married at age 29. (But her husband August Albershardt is enumerated as divorced in the same census.) Son Milton Albershardt, 21, single, born Indiana with his parents born in Ohio, says he is a proprietor of a radio shop. Son Arlton is 16. Both were born in Indiana.

That same census, Elgie's daughter Cathern Albershardt is living with her father, August Albershardt, in Washington Twp., Indianapolis, Marion Co., Indiana *(Census Place: Indianapolis, Marion, Indiana; Roll: 610; Page: 10B; Enumeration District: 447; Image: 50.0)*. "Catherine" is 19 years old, single, born Indiana, with her parents born in Ohio. She lists her occupation as a stenographer at a radio station. Her father August Albershardt, 59, lists himself as divorced and his occupation as veterinary surgeon. He says he was born in Ohio and his parents in Germany.

In 1940, Elgie Pegan Albershardt continues to reside in Indianapolis, Marion Co., Indiana *(Census Place: Indianapolis, Marion, Indiana; Roll: T627_1131; Page: 7B; Enumeration District: 96-362)*. Elgie Pegan Albershardt, age 65, born Ohio, is living alone at what seems to be an apartment building at 52nd Street and College Avenue. She lists her occupation as clerical worker and says she was living in Indianapolis in 1935.

August Albershardt is listed as "Albert Albershardt" in 1940 in Indianapolis, Washington Twp., Marion Co., Indiana *(Census Place: Indianapolis, Marion, Indiana; Roll: T627_1131; Page: 3B; Enumeration District: 96-351)*. In the household are August Albershardt, age 70, a veterinary surgeon who says he is a widower; and his son Arlton, 26, single, a radio repairman and proprietor of a radio shop. Both were born in Indiana and say they were living in Indianapolis in 1935. Their address is 4157 College Avenue.

Children of Elgie Elenor Pegan and August H. Albershardt:

+ 55 m I. **Milton James**[8] **Albershardt** was born in Indianapolis, Marion Co., Indiana, on August 15, 1907.[227, 228] He died in Indianapolis, Marion Co., Indiana, on June 25, 1937.[227, 228]

+ 56 f II. **Cathern**[8] **Albershardt** was born in Indianapolis, Marion Co., Indiana, on March 5, 1910.[135, 229, 230] She died in Hartwell, Hart Co., Georgia, on July 6, 1997.[229, 231]

+ 57 m III. **Arlton Henry**[8] **Albershardt** was born in Indianapolis, Marion Co., Indiana, on May 7, 1914.[135, 232, 233, 234] He died in Indianapolis, Marion Co., Indiana, on September 20, 1987.[135, 232, 234, 235, 236]

30. Child[7] **Bruner** (*Margaret*[6] *Pegan, John*[5]*, Robert A.*[4]*, Andrew*[3]*, Andrew*[2] *Pagan, James*[1]) was born between 1863-1868 in either DeGraff, Miami Twp., Logan Co., Ohio or Indianapolis, Center Twp., Marion Co., Indiana. He or she may have been the child of Adam Addison Bruner and Margaret Pegan (7). This child died in either DeGraff, Miami Twp., Logan Co., Ohio or Indianapolis, Center Twp., Marion Co., Indiana between 1863-1868. In 1900 and 1910 Margaret Pegan Bruner Miller says she bore five children with four surviving. She had a child, who died, by one of her husbands—but which one, Adam Bruner or William C. Miller, is not known. If the father was Adam Bruner, the child's placement would be here (30). Therefore, either (30) or (35) never existed.

31. Marcia Pet[7] **Bruner** (*Margaret*[6] *Pegan, John*[5]*, Robert A.*[4]*, Andrew*[3]*, Andrew*[2] *Pagan, James*[1]) was born on March 21, 1868, in Indianapolis, Center Twp., Marion Co., Indiana.[94] She was the daughter of Adam Addison Bruner and Margaret Pegan (7). Marcia Pet died in Florence, San Antonio Twp., Los Angeles Co., California, on April 27, 1931, at age 63.[95] She was buried in Angeles Abbey Memorial Park Mausoleum, Compton, Los Angeles Co., California.[237, 238]

Childless.

Marcia Pet Bruner Reiling seems to have been called "Pet" or "Petty" as a child, but as an adult, she preferred Marcia as her given name. She also preferred the surname spelling, "Bruner". Her birth year varies in documents, even when she gives the information herself. It seems she, like many women in her day, shaved a few years off her actual age to be younger than her husband.

In 1900, "Pet" Bruner, age 29, is still single and living with her stepfather and mother, William C. and Margaret Pegan Bruner Miller, in Toledo, Lucas Co., Ohio *(Census Place: Toledo Ward 8, Lucas, Ohio; Roll: T623_1298; Page: 2A; Enumeration District: 71)*. She shaves a few years off her age, saying she was born in March 1871 (instead of March 1868, her real birth year.) "Pet's" occupation is traveling saleswoman; she is an Indiana native and her parents were born in Ohio. Her stepfather, William C. Miller, 59, born Jan 1841 in Ohio is a real estate agent; he says his father was born in Pennsylvania and her mother in Ohio. Margaret Pegan Bruner Miller is 54, born Sep 1845. She is an Ohio native like her parents. The couple says they have been married 26 years and Margaret has borne five children, four still alive. Marcia Pet's half-sister, Willette ("W.E.") Miller, 24 is also in the household; she lists no occupation.

Marcia Pet married **Gustave Adolph Reiling** on November 23, 1908 in Lucas Co., Ohio.[94] Gustave Adolph Reiling was born in Fort Wayne, Allen Co., Indiana, on January 6, 1869.[94, 239] He was living in 1944 in San Antonio, Los Angeles Co., California. Gustave Adolph reached age 75 and died in a hospital in Los Angeles, Los Angeles Co., California, on June 15, 1944.[239, 240] He was buried in Angeles Abbey Memorial Park Mausoleum, Compton, Los Angeles Co., California.[239, 241, 242]

Gustave Adolph Reiling, was member of the notorious Dolan gang, who robbed numerous stores and homes in the Fort Wayne, Indiana area starting in 1893. The seven-member gang, including the wife of ringleader Dolan, employed several tactics in their countless raids; Reiling, whose gang name was "Hoots", specialized in blowing safes. The bandits terrorized storekeepers and homeowners until their capture on August 23, 1895. The police found a house loaded with their stolen goods, said to have made a well-stocked dry goods store--everything from silks and satins to firearms. The next day he posted a $200 bond but fled immediately. He was spied by former Fort Wayne residents again on March 26 in St. Louis, when he applied for a job in a washing machine factory. But he left that city, said to be moving west, when he realized he was spotted.[A, B] Mysteriously, it seems Adolph Reiling seems to have never been captured or jailed for his crimes. By 1897, he was living in Toledo, Ohio, where he was an engineer/machinist in a factory.[243] Did he turn "informant" for the police, in exchange for no prosecution, and aid the police in the gang's apprehension?

After he reached Toledo, Gustave Adolph used Adolph as his given name, and seems to have never crossed paths with the law again.

Gustave Adolph and Marcia Pet Bruner Reiling are living with Marcia's parents, William C. and Margaret Pegan Bruner Miller, in Toledo, Lucas Co., Ohio in 1910 *(Census Place: Toledo Ward 8, Lucas, Ohio; Roll: T624_1209; Page: 27A; Enumeration District: 0110; Image: 490)*. "Adolph" Reiling, 41, born Indiana with his parents born in Germany, is a machinist in a factory. Marcia Pet Bruner Reiling, 36, is an Indiana native whose parents were born in Ohio. Adolphus and Marcia have been married two years and both say this is their first marriage. Marcia has borne no children. William C. Miller, 67, was born in Ohio, but this time he says both of his parents were born in Kentucky. He is still a real estate agent. Margaret Pegan Bruner Miller, listed as "Margret", is 61 and says she and her parents were Ohio-born. Also in household was Marcia Pet Brunner Reiling's half-sister, Blanche Miller Humason, 26, born Ohio like her parents, who lists her occupation as sewing. Blanche, really a divorcee, has no children.

In 1920, Gustavas Adolph and Marcia Pet Bruner Reiling are again enumerated in Toledo, Lucas Co., Ohio *(Census Place: Toledo Ward 16, Lucas, Ohio; Roll: T625_1410; Page: 4B; Enumeration District: 162; Image: 377)*. Gustavas A. Reiling, age 50, born Indiana with his parents born in Germany, is a machinist at a "raillight" factory. Marcia Pet Bruner Reiling, 45, is listed as born in Indiana with her parents born in Ohio.

By 1921, according to the Redondo, Hermosa and Manhattan Beach, California City Directory, Gustavas Adolph and Marcia Pet Bruner Reiling are living at 1000 Strand in Redondo Beach.[244] By 1922, they are living at 7407

Walnut Drive in Florence, Los Angeles Co., California.[245]

Gustavas and Marcia Pet Bruner Reiling are found in Florence, San Antonio Twp., Los Angeles Co., California in 1930 *(Census Place: San Antonio, Los Angeles, California; Roll: 172; Page: 4A; Image: 244.0)*. Gustavas Adolph Reiling is listed as "Gustavious A. Reiling" is age 61, born Indiana with his parents born in Germany, is a machinist in an electric manufacturing company. Marcia Pet Bruner Reiling is 55, born in Indiana with her parents born in Ohio.

In 1940, widower Gustavas Reiling, enumerated as "Gustabe Religine", is residing in San Antonio, Los Angeles Co., California *(Census Place: San Antonio, Los Angeles, California; Roll: T627_249; Page: 61B; Enumeration District: 19-626)*. He is a lodger, who lists no occupation, in the home of Catherine Von Eick, age 52, born Indiana. Both say they were living in San Antonio, Los Angeles Co., California in 1935. Their home address is 7406 ½ Walnut Avenue.

32. Willette[7] Miller *(Margaret[6] Pegan, John[5], Robert A.[4], Andrew[3], Andrew[2] Pagan, James[1])* was born on December 20, 1874, in Bellefontaine, Lake Twp., Logan Co., Ohio.[96] She was the daughter of William C. Miller and Margaret Pegan (7). Willette died in Redondo Beach, Los Angeles Co., California, on December 27, 1935, at age 61.[97, 98] She was buried in Angeles Abbey Memorial Park Mausoleum, Compton, Los Angeles Co., California.[98, 246]

Childless.

Willette Miller Sawyer shaved a few years off her age to be younger than her husband, Perry Sawyer. In the 1920 census, she says she is 40 years old, when she was really 46.

Willette married **Perry Elsworth Sawyer** on February 20, 1905, in Hillsdale Co., Michigan.[247] They divorced in Los Angeles Co., California, between 1920 and 1930. Perry Elsworth Sawyer was born in Galion, Polk Twp., Crawford Co., Ohio on May 13, 1877.[248, 249] He reached age 88 and died in Los Angeles, Los Angeles Co., California, on September 24, 1965.[249] Perry Elsworth was buried in Forest Lawn Memorial Park Cemetery, Glendale, Los Angeles Co., California.[250]

Although he says he was born in Toledo, Lucas Co., Ohio on his marriage application to Willette Miller, Perry Sawyer states on his WWII draft registration that he was born in Galion, Polk Twp., Crawford Co., Ohio.[244, 245] He is enumerated in the 1880 census in Nevada Twp., Wyandot Co., Ohio with his mother Belle *(Census Place: Nevada, Wyandot, Ohio; Roll: 1079; Page: 602A; Enumeration District: 170)*.

Perry E. and Willette Miller Sawyer are not found in the 1910 U.S. Federal Census.

Perry E. Sawyer worked as a sales manager at a lime in Los Angeles, Los Angeles Co., California in 1917.[248]

In 1920, Perry and Willette Miller Sawyer are enumerated in Los Angeles, Los Angeles Co., California *(Census Place: Los Angeles Assembly District 64, Los Angeles, California; Roll: T625_108; Page: 20B; Enumeration District: 206; Image: 80)*. Perry Sawyer, 41, born Ohio as were his parents, is the secretary-treasurer at a lime company. Willette Miller Sawyer, 40, was born in Ohio as were her parents, lists her occupation as manager of a bungalow court. Living with them is Willette's mother, Margaret Pegan Bruner Miller, is listed as Margaret J. Miller, age 76, a widow, born Ohio, her father in Ohio and her mother in the United States. She is enumerated as Perry Sawyer's mother-in-law. Also in the home is Margaret's daughter and Willette's sister, Blanche Miller Humason, who says she is age 31 and a "widow" (she was divorced). Blanche, a milliner, says she and her parents were Ohio natives. Also in the household are five lodgers.

Perry and Willette Miller Sawyer divorce between 1920-1930 in Los Angeles.

In 1930, Willette Miller Sawyer is living with her sister, Blanche Humason, in Los Angeles, Los Angeles Co., California, with Blanche listed as head of household *(Census Place: Los Angeles, Los Angeles, California; Roll: 148; Page: 12B; Enumeration District: 410; Image: 408.0)*. Willette Miller Sawyer is 55, divorced, and she lists no occupation. Blanche H. Miller Humason lists her age as 41, her marital status as widowed, and her occupation as a housekeeper at a private house. Both say they and their parents were Ohio natives. Three lodgers are residing with them.

On her death certificate, Willette Sawyer's birthday is listed as December 1, 1873 by her informant, her younger sister Blanche H. Miller Humason. However, official county birth records in Logan Co., Ohio have her birth recorded as December 20, 1874.[96, 98]

In 1930, Perry Sawyer, listed as "Pery" Sawyer, is a lodger in the home of Adolph and Lottie Rickenbacker in Los Angeles, Los Angeles Co., California *(Census Place: Los Angeles, Los Angeles, California; Roll: 152; Page: 11B; Image: 950.0)*. He says he is single, age 52, and born Ohio as were his parents. He is a manager of a building materials company.

Perry E. Sawyer is married to his second wife, Florence Unknown, and still residing in Los Angeles, Los Angeles Co., California in 1940 *(Census Place: Los Angeles, Los Angeles, California; Roll: T627_397; Page: 8A; Enumeration District: 60-1192)*. Perry E. Sawyer, 61, born Ohio, is the owner of a building materials company. Florence Smith Irwin Sawyer is 45, born Illinois. With them is Florence's mother, Mary Smith, 71, born Germany. All say they were living in Los Angeles in 1935. Their home address is 3148 Atwater Street.

33. **Fred Pegan**[7] **Miller** (*Margaret*[6] *Pegan, John*[5]*, Robert A.*[4]*, Andrew*[3]*, Andrew*[2] *Pagan, James*[1]) was born on June 2, 1876, in Toledo, Lucas Co., Ohio.[99, 100, 101] He was the son of William C. Miller and Margaret Pegan (7). Fred P. worked as a salesman in 1948 living in Hondo, Los Angeles Co., California. Fred P. died in a hospital in Los Angeles Co., California, on January 6, 1948, at age 71.[99, 100, 101] He was cremated.[101]

Never married.

Fred Pegan Miller is not found in the 1920, 1930 or 1940 U.S. Federal Censuses.

34. **Blanche H.**[7] **Miller** (*Margaret*[6] *Pegan, John*[5]*, Robert A.*[4]*, Andrew*[3]*, Andrew*[2] *Pagan, James*[1]) was born on June 29, 1878, in Bellefontaine, Lake Twp., Logan Co., Ohio.[102, 103] She was the daughter of William C. Miller and Margaret Pegan (7). She died in Los Angeles, Los Angeles Co., California, on June 19, 1944, at age 65.[103, 104] Blanche was buried in Inglewood Park Cemetery, Inglewood, Los Angeles Co., California.[103]

Childless.

Blanche married **Charles Martin Humason** on June 30, 1897, in Lucas Co., Ohio.[251] They divorced before 1910. Charles Martin Humason was born in Harrisville, Butler Co., Pennsylvania, on December 23, 1874.[252, 253] He reached age 49 and died in Woodlawn Twp., Beaver Co., Pennsylvania, on March 12, 1924.[254] Charles Martin was buried in Woodlawn Cemetery, Woodlawn Twp., Beaver Co., Pennsylvania.[255]

In 1900, Charles and Blanche Miller Humason are enumerated in Toledo, Lucas Co., Ohio *(Census Place: Toledo Ward 6, Lucas, Ohio; Roll: T623; Page: 15A; Enumeration District: 55)*. Charles Humason, age 24, born Dec 1875, says he was born in Pennsylvania and his parents in Ohio; he lists his occupation as an oil teamster. Blanche Miller Humason is age 21, born Jun 1878, and says she and her parents were born in Ohio. The couple has been married three years and Blanche has borne no children.

Charles and Blanche Miller Humason are separated by 1909, as she is a single woman living in Toledo, Lucas Co., Ohio in that year's city directory.[256] They divorce in March 1916, according to. Charles M. Humason's marriage license for his second marriage.[253]

Charles Humason is not found in the 1910 census. On April 5, 1916, Charles M. Humason married Hazel Hendricks in Beaver Co., Pennsylvania. On this marriage license, Charles Humason says he was born in Harrisville, Butler Co., Pennsylvania.[253] Charles Martin Humason registered for the WWI draft in 1917, saying he was living in Woodlawn Twp., Beaver Co., Pennsylvania. He states he was born December 23, 1874 and listed himself as married on the draft registration.[252]

In 1920 he is found in Woodlawn Twp., Beaver Co., Pennsylvania *(Census Place: Woodlawn, Beaver, Pennsylvania; Roll: T625_1532; Page: 8A; Enumeration District: 72)*. He is living with his second wife Hazel Hendricks Humason and they have a son Jack, who was born in 1918 in West Virginia. Charles lists his occupation as heater helper in a rod mill

In 1910, Blanche Miller Humason, 26, was living with her parents, William C. and Margaret Pegan Bruner Miller in Toledo, Lucas Co., Ohio *(Census Place: Toledo Ward 8, Lucas, Ohio; Roll: T624_1209; Page: 27A; Enumeration District: 0110; Image: 490).* Blanche lists her occupation as sewing and says she has borne no children. Blanche states she is a widow, but she is actually divorced from Charles Martin Humason. William C. Miller, 67, was born in Ohio, but this time he says both of his parents were born in Kentucky. He is still a real estate agent. Margaret Pegan Bruner Miller, listed as "Margret", is 61 and says she and her parents were Ohio natives. Also in the household are Gustavas Adolph and Marcia Pet Bruner Reiling, Margaret's daughter with Adam Addison Bruner. "Adolph" Reiling, 41, born Indiana with his parents born in Germany, is a machinist in a factory. Marcia Bruner Reiling is 36 years old. Adolphus and Marcia have been married two years and both say this is their first marriage. Marcia has not borne a child.

Blanche Miller Humason, who again says she is a widow, is residing with her brother-in-law and sister, Perry and Willette Miller Sawyer, in Los Angeles, Los Angeles Co., California in 1920 *(Census Place: Los Angeles Assembly District 64, Los Angeles, California; Roll: T625_108; Page: 20B; Enumeration District: 206; Image: 80).* Blanche Miller Humason, who says she is age 31, a widow, born Ohio as were her parents, a milliner. Perry Sawyer, 41, born Ohio as were his parents, is the secretary-treasurer at a lime company. Willette Miller Sawyer, 40, was born in Ohio as were her parents, lists her occupation as manager of a bungalow court. Also in the home is Margaret Pegan Bruner Miller, Blanche and Willette's mother. Margaret, 76, a widow, born Ohio, with her father also born in Ohio and her mother in the United States, is listed as Perry Sawyer's mother-in-law. Living with them are five lodgers.

In 1930, Blanche Miller Humason and her sister Willette Miller Sawyer, now divorced from Perry E. Sawyer, are still in the same household. This time, Blanche listed as the head of household *(Census Place: Los Angeles, Los Angeles, California; Roll: 148; Page: 12B; Enumeration District: 410; Image: 408.0).* Blanche Miller Humason lists her age as 41 and her occupation as a housekeeper at a private house. She says she is a widow, but she was a divorcee (however, her former husband, Charles Martin Humason, had died in 1924). Willette Miller Sawyer is 55, divorced, and she lists no occupation. Both say they were born in Ohio as were their parents. They also have three lodgers with them.

Blanche Miller Humason is living by herself in 1940 in Los Angeles, Los Angeles Co., California *(Census Place: Los Angeles, Los Angeles, California; Roll: T627_392; Page: 14B; Enumeration District: 60-952).* Blanche Miller Humason, age 61, born Ohio, a widow (incorrect) lists no occupation. She says she was a Los Angeles resident in 1935. Her home address is 827 11th Street.

35. Child[7] Miller (*Margaret[6] Pegan, John[5], Robert A.[4], Andrew[3], Andrew[2] Pagan, James[1]*) was born between 1873 and 1900 in Bellefontaine, Lake Twp., Logan Co., Ohio? He or she was a child of William C. Miller and Margaret Pegan (7). Child died in Bellefontaine, Lake Twp., Logan Co., Ohio, before 1900.

In 1900 and 1910 Margaret Pegan Bruner Miller says she bore five children with four surviving. She had a child, who died, by one of her husbands—but which one, Adam Brunner or William C. Miller, is not known. If the father was William C. Miller, the placement would be here (35). If the father was Adam Brunner, the child's placement would be (30). Therefore, either (30) or (35) never existed.

36. Edward Ephraim[7] Pegan (*John Andrew[6], John[5], Robert A.[4], Andrew[3], Andrew[2] Pagan, James[1]*) was born on March 18, 1881, in DeGraff, Miami Twp., Logan Co., Ohio.[113, 257] He was the son of John Andrew Pegan II (9) and Anna Belle Armstrong. Edward Ephraim died in Columbus, Franklin Co., Ohio, on February 15, 1942, at age 60.[113] Although his death certificate says he was buried in Greenwood Cemetery, DeGraff, Pleasant Twp., Logan Co., Ohio, Tamara Brush, one of his descendants, has a letter that says he wasn't. His gravesite is unknown.[258]

Edward Ephraim married **Maud Lillian Abbott** on June 19, 1907, in Chicago, Cook Co., Illinois.[259, 260] They divorced between 1920-1930. They had one son. Maud Lillian Abbott was born in Cambridge City, Jackson Twp., Wayne Co., Indiana on April 27, 1882.[261 262] She reached age 83 and died in San Diego, San Diego Co., California, on May 6, 1965.[261, 263] Maud Lillian was buried in Mt. Hope Cemetery, San Diego, San Diego Co., California.[263, 264]

Edward Ephraim Pegan sometimes capitalized the "G" in his surname, as found in other Pegan lines. His wife, Maud, continued this practice.

In the 1910 census, Edward Pegan is enumerated twice.

In his first enumeration on April 16, 1910, he is found living with his parents, John A. and Anna Armstrong Pegan, in Marion, Marion Co., Ohio *(Census Place: Marion Ward 1, Marion, Ohio; Roll: T624_1213; Page: 2B; Enumeration District: 0080; Image: 635)*. This time, he says he is 28 and has been married for three years, but again his wife is not with him. He lists his occupation as clerk in a restaurant (probably the one managed by his father.) John A. Pegan is age 60 and a restaurant manager. Anna Belle Armstrong Pegan is 50. They have been married 30 years and Anna has borne two children, one still living.

In the second census listing, taken April 26, he is in Columbus, Franklin Co., Ohio *(Census Place: Columbus Ward 6, Franklin, Ohio; Roll: T624_1181; Page: 6B; Enumeration District: 0101; Image: 919)*. Edward E. Pegan is age 29, and lists his occupation as a barber in a hotel. Edward says he has been married for two years, but his wife is not living with him. (His wife, Maude Lillian Abbott Pegan and their son, Donald, are probably also living in Columbus and are found there again 1920). Edward says he and his parents were born in Ohio.

Edward Ephraim "PeGan" was a barber living between 1914 and 1917 in Indianapolis, Center Twp., Marion Co., Indiana.[265] However, by the time he registers for the WWI draft on September 12, 1918, he was a resident of Springfield, Springfield Twp., Clark Co., Ohio.[257]

In 1920, Edward is found in Springfield, Springfield Twp., Clark Co., Ohio *(Census Place: Springfield Ward 6, Clark, Ohio; Roll: T625_1354; Page: 3B; Enumeration District: 95; Image: 878)*. Edward Pegan is still listed as married, but his wife is not in the household. He is 38, a salesman in a piano store, and living with his widowed mother, Anna Armstrong Pegan, 59. Both say they and their parents were born in Ohio.

In the 1930 census, Edward Pegan and his mother, Anna Armstrong Pegan, are in Akron, Summit Co., Ohio *(Census Place: Akron, Summit, Ohio; Roll: 1875; Page: 18A; Enumeration District: 42; Image: 596.0)*. Edward Pegan, this time listed as head of household, is 49, a barber and divorced. Anna B. Armstrong Pegan, 70, is a widow. Once again, they both say they and their parents were born in Ohio.

His mother, Anna Belle Armstrong, outlives him and was the informant on his death certificate. On this certificate, she lists her husband, John Pegan Jr.'s birthplace as Piqua, Washington Twp., Miami Co., Ohio.[113]

According to Edward E. Pegan's great-granddaughter, Tamara Brush of Albuquerque, New Mexico, her maternal grandfather Donald Pegan "didn't have one good thing to say about his father". About the only things he would say were that his father was a "mama's boy" who struggled with alcoholism.[100]

Maud Lillian Abbott Pegan is not found in the 1910 or 1930 census. In 1910, she may have still been living in Chicago, Cook Co., Illinois, where her son, Donald Pegan, was born in 1908.

Maud Lillian Abbott Pegan is enumerated as "Maud" Pegan in 1920 in Columbus, Franklin Co., Ohio *(Census Place: Columbus Ward 14, Franklin, Ohio; Roll: T625_1384; Page: 2A; Enumeration District: 238; Image: 446)*. Maud Pegan is age 33, born Ohio as were her parents, and lists her occupation as a clerk in a drug store. She says she is divorced. With her is her son, Donald, 11, born Illinois with his parents born in Ohio. They are boarders in the home of widow, Nellie Ball, 55. There is also another boarder in the home, Felix Piasky, 23.

In 1930, Maud Lillian Abbott Pegan may have returned to Chicago, Cook Co., Illinois, Tamara

Brush says. Maud's son Donald Pegan was living there in 1930.[100]

Maud Lillian Abbott Pegan lived with her son and his wife, Donald and Elizabeth Steinbrenner Pegan, in San Diego, San Diego Co., California from at least 1946 until she died in 1965, according to that city's directories.[266]

Son of Edward Ephraim Pegan and Maude Lillian Abbott:

+ 58 m I. **Donald Abbott**[8] **Pegan** was born in Chicago, Cook Co., Illinois, on May 11, 1908.[135, 267] He died in San Diego, San Diego Co., California, on April 9, 1987.[267]

37. Anna M. or Lena M.[7] **Pegan** (*John Andrew*[6], *John*[5], *Robert A.*[4], *Andrew*[3], *Andrew*[2] *Pagan, James*[1]) was born on July 18, 1884, in DeGraff, Miami Twp., Logan Co., Ohio.[114] She was the daughter of John Andrew Pegan II (9) and Anna Belle Armstrong. Anna or Lena M. died in DeGraff, Miami Twp., Logan Co., Ohio, on February 5, 1886, at age one.[115] Anna or Lena M. Pegan is probably buried in Greenwood Cemetery, DeGraff, Miami Twp., Logan Co., Ohio, but no documentation for her burial can be found. She is registered as "Anna M." in the Logan County birth records and "Lena M." in the death register.

38. Fred Roland[7] **Hill** (*Laura Louisa*[6] *Pegan, John*[5], *Robert A.*[4], *Andrew*[3], *Andrew*[2] *Pagan, James*[1]) was born on May 16, 1877, in DeGraff, Miami Twp., Logan Co., Ohio.[121, 122, 123] He was the son of Edward Henry Hill II and Laura Louisa Pegan (10). He died in Los Angeles, Los Angeles Co., California, on October 31, 1941, at age 64.[124] Fred Roland was buried in Hollywood Forever Cemetery, Hollywood, Los Angeles Co., California.[268]

Childless.

Fred Roland married **Eugenia Adelaide Edwards** on December 31, 1907, in Manhattan, New York, New York Co., New York.[269, 270] Eugenia Adelaide Edwards was born in Saddle River, Bergen Co., New Jersey, in May 1878.[270]

On July 26, 1909 Fred Roland Hill obtains an annulment in the New York City court from his wife Eugenia. According to an article in the July 26, 1909 *Trenton (NJ) Evening Times,* Fred was unaware that Eugenia had been previously married to a Simon Harold Baker. The article says Eugenia had been "infatuated" with Baker before she married him, and had also forged checks to get money from Baker even before they were wed. She was caught, tried in 1901 and served three years in the Bedford Reformatory in Westchester Co., New York. Upon her release from prison, she resumed the use of her maiden name to hide her past history. Fred Hill stated he had known Eugenia for 15 months before their nuptials. She belonged to an upstanding upper middle-class family, and she was heavily involved in church activities at that time. So he believed her character to be above reproach. But shortly after their marriage, Fred noticed checks with his name on it, which he did not sign, arriving in the mail. He confronted his wife about it, and found she had forged them. Hill then investigated her background and found out about her prior arrest and prison term for forgery. He petitioned the New York City court to annul the marriage, and won his suit.[271]

Fred R. Hill is not found in the 1910 census.

Fred Roland Hill married Mrs. **Catherine Adeline Unknown** Wilt on December 3, 1911, in Philadelphia Co., Pennsylvania.[123] They divorced before 1936. Catherine Adeline Unknown was born in Dauphin Co., Pennsylvania, on April 2, 1876.[123] She died after 1930.

On his WWI draft application in 1917, Fred Roland Hill is living in Philadelphia, Philadelphia Co., Pennsylvania, and lists his occupation as automobile tire (sales?). He lists his next of kin as his wife, Catherine.[121]

In 1920 Fred is found living with his parents, Edward H. and Laura L. Pegan Hill, in Montclair Twp., Essex Twp., New Jersey *(Census Place: Montclair Ward 3, Essex, New Jersey; Roll: T625_1030; Page: 6B; Enumeration District: 83; Image: 869)*. Fred R. Hill is age 43, born Ohio as were his parents. Fred Hill says he is married, but his wife Catherine Unknown Wilt Hill is not in the household. He lists his occupation as none. Edward, enumerated as "Ed H. Hill", is listed as the head of the household. Edward Hill is 65 born in Ohio, with his father born in Virginia and his mother in France (?) He is a chemist. Laura Louisa Pegan Hill is also 65, and she says she and her parents were born in Ohio. Also in the home is Ardonis Harkins (?) who is listed as Edward's cousin, age 70, born in Montana (?) with his parents born in Ohio.

Fred R. Hill is enumerated in Los Angeles, Los Angeles Co., California in 1930 *(Census Place: Los Angeles, Los Angeles, California; Roll: 134; Page: 19B; Enumeration District: 71; Image: 794.00)*. Fred R. Hill is age 53, born Ohio as were his parents. Again, he lists his occupation as "none". With him is a wife, Catherine, age 50, born in Pennsylvania as were her parents. TThe couple says their first marriages were at ages 33 and 30 respectively. This is incorrect, as Catherine Unknown Wilt Hill was previously married.

Fred R. Hill either was divorced from Catherine Unknown Wilt Hill or Catherine died before January 1, 1936.

Fred Roland Hill and Mrs. **Helen Helma Bye** Gibson wed on January 1, 1936, in Los Angeles Co., California.[272] They divorced before Fred's death in 1941. Helen Helma Bye was born in Beaver Creek, Steele Co., North Dakota, on November 28, 1906.[135, 273] She reached age 85 and died in Los Angeles, Los Angeles Co., California, on September 19, 1992.[135] Helen Helma was buried in Forest Lawn Cemetery Hollywood Hills, Los Angeles Co., California.[274] She later remarried and died under the name Helen Baker.

Fred R. Hill is not found in the 1940 census.

8th Generation

39. Mamie Edna⁸ Pegan (*Pliny Moses Crume⁷, Emmanuel⁶, John⁵, Robert A.⁴, Andrew³, Andrew² Pagan, James¹*) was born on March 26, 1880, in Great Bend, Liberty Twp., Barton Co., Kansas.[135, 136] She was the daughter of Pliny Moses Crume Pegan (12) and Francina Caroline Gwinn. She died in Denver, Denver Co., Colorado, on July 12, 1968, at age 88.[136]

Mamie Edna married **Edward Ballard Gage** on December 16, 1903, in Denver Co., Colorado.[275] They had two sons. Edward Ballard Gage was born in Chicago, Cook Co., Illinois, on March 29, 1873.[276] Edward Ballard lived in 1907 in Chicago, Cook Co., Illinois. He lived in 1959 in Wilmette, New Trier Twp., Cook Co., Illinois. He reached age 85 and died in a hospital in Evanston, Evanston Twp., Cook Co., Illinois, on January 18, 1959.[135, 277]

In 1910 Mamie Edna Pegan Gage is doubly enumerated in the census.

In 1910, Edward Ballard and Mamie Edna Pegan Gage are found in Ward 4, Burlington, Racine Co., Wisconsin (*Census Place: Burlington Ward 4, Racine, Wisconsin; Roll: T624_1734; Page: 10B; Enumeration District: 0059; Image: 85*). In the household are "E.B." Gage, 36, born Illinois as were his parents, a condenser at a condensed milk company; and Mamie, age 30. born Kansas, with her father born in Ohio and her mother in Indiana. The pair say they have been married six years and Mamie has borne two children, both still alive. They are sons Henry "K.", age two, born Illinois; and Gwynn B., one, born in Wisconsin.

Mamie is also enumerated in 1910 at her parent's, Pliny Crume and Francina Gwynn Pegan's, home in Denver, Denver Co., Colorado during a visit (*Census Place: Denver Ward 10, Denver, Colorado; Roll: T624_116; Page: 16A; Enumeration District: 0138; Image: 982*). Mamie Pegan Gage is 29, born Kansas, with her father born in Ohio and her mother in Indiana. She says she has been married for five years and has borne two children, both living, but she is not with her husband or children.

Pliny Crume Pegan's age is indecipherable, but he was born in Ohio, like his father. On the census form, his mother's birthplace is not written clearly, but it seems to be "IA" (Iowa) or "IN" (Indiana). However, his mother was also born in Ohio. He says he is a railroad conductor. Francina Gwinn Gage is listed as "Lina", 50, born in Indiana with her parents born in Vermont. Also in the home is Pliny and Francina's daughter and Mamie's sister, Patience Pegan, 26, born in Colorado, a library clerk.

Edward Ballard Gage is a resident of Oostburg, Sheboygan Co., Wisconsin 1916 when he applies for a U.S. passport to work in Canada. He states he has accepted a position there as a condensed milk manufacturer.[278]

In 1920, Edward Ballard and Mamie Pegan Gage are found in Thompson Falls, Thompson Twp., Sanders Co., Montana (*Census Place: Thompson, Sanders, Montana; Roll: T625_975; Page: 14A; Enumeration District: 192; Image: 576*). Edward is age 46, a farmer, born in Illinois, while "Mamie P." is 40, born Kansas. This time, Mamie says her father was born in Indiana and her mother in Illinois. Also in the home are sons Henry C., 12, born Illinois, and Gwynn, 10, born Wisconsin.

Edward Ballard and Mamie Pegan Gage are found in Thompson Falls, Thompson Twp., (School District #4), Sanders Co., Montana in 1930 (*Census Place: School District 4, Sanders, Montana; Roll: 1261; Page: 3A; Enumeration District: 6; Image: 600.0*). The head of the household is Edward Gage, age 57, a stockman on a ranch, who says he and his parents were born in Illinois. His wife, Mamie Pegan Gage, 50, says she was born in Kansas, her father in Ohio and her mother in Illinois (Incorrect—she was born in Indiana). The only child in the home is son Gwynn, 20, who lists no occupation.

In 1940, Edward B. and Mamie Pegan Gage have moved to Chicago, Cook Co., Illinois (*Census Place: Chicago, Cook, Illinois; Roll: T627_935; Page: 7B; Enumeration District: 103-460*). Edward B. Gage, age 67, was born in Illinois; he lists no occupation (probably retired). His wife, Mamie Pegan Gage, born Kansas, is 60 years old. Both say they were living in Chicago in 1935. Their home address is 2650 East 75th Street.

According to their great-grandson, Edward D. Gage of Salem, Oregon, Edward Ballard and Mamie Edna Pegan Gage moved to Thompson Falls, Thompson Twp., Sanders Co., Montana around 1917 for the health of their eldest son, Henry Crume Gage, who was frail as a child. They bought a ranch/farm there and stayed in Thompson Falls until their sons were grown. Then moved back to Willmette, Frier Twp., Cook Co., Illinois, where Edward had inherited land from his family. After Edward died, Mamie relocated to Denver, where her son Henry and his family lived.[135] A short death notice for her was published in the *Denver (CO) Post* on July 14, 1968, but no birth or death dates were mentioned.[279]

Sons of Mamie Edna Pegan and Edward Ballard Gage:

+ 59   m   I.   **Henry Crume[9] Gage** was born in Chicago, Cook Co., Illinois, on May 14, 1907.[135, 280, 281, 282] He died in Denver, Denver Co., Colorado, on February 10, 1980.[282]

+ 60   m   II. **Gwynn Ballard[9] Gage** was born in Burlington Twp., Racine Co., Wisconsin, on April 7, 1909.[135, 283] He died in Portland, Multnomah Co., Oregon, on June 12, 1958.[135, 284]

40. Patience Ruby[8] Pegan (*Pliny Moses Crume[7], Emmanuel[6], John[5], Robert A.[4], Andrew[3], Andrew[2] Pagan, James[1]*) was born on January 18, 1884, in Pueblo, Pueblo Co., Colorado.[136] She was the daughter of Pliny Moses Crume Pegan (12) and Francina Caroline Gwinn. Patience Ruby died in Denver, Denver Co., Colorado, on September 7, 1949, at age 65.[136, 285] She was buried in Crown Hill Cemetery, Wheat Ridge, Jefferson Co., Colorado.[136, 286]

Childless.

A noted librarian, Patience R. Pegan was among the first generation of librarians trained in library science, or "library economy" as it was first known. Patience graduated from the library science school at Drexel Institute, now Drexel University, in Philadelphia, Pennsylvania in 1906.[287] She received master's from the University of Denver, as the Drexel Institute Library School report in the Library Journal, 1915, says Patience is studying there: "Ruby Patience Pegan is studying in the University of Denver."[287, 288] Patience continued to advance in her field and was active in her profession's professional organizations.

In 1910, Patience Ruby Pegan is living with her parents, Pliny Crume and Francina Gwinn Pegan, in Denver, Denver Co., Colorado *(Census Place: Denver Ward 10, Denver, Colorado; Roll: T624_116; Page: 16A; Enumeration District: 0138; Image: 982)*. Patience, 26, single and born in Colorado, works as a library clerk. However, the census clerk erred and entered her name as "Patricia Gage". Patience is listed below her elder sister, Mamie Pegan Gage, enumerated as "Minnie", age 29 and Kansas-born, who is visiting her parents and sister. Pliny C. Pegan is age 52, born in Ohio, with his father born in Ohio and his mother born in Iowa (Incorrect—he is 53 years old and his mother was born in Ohio). He is a railroad conductor. With him are wife Francina Gwinn Pegan, listed as "Lina", age 50, born in Indiana with her parents born in Vermont. They say they have been married 31 years and Francina has borne two children, both still alive.

Patience Pegan was listed among the faculty of North Side High School in 1914-15, also in Denver.[289] In 1918, Patience Pegan served as a clerk in the U.S. Ordnance Office in Washington, D.C duing WWI.[288, 290]

But apparently Patience didn't work there long, as she is back living with her parents at age 35 in Denver, Denver Co., Colorado in 1920 *(Census Place: Denver, Denver, Colorado; Roll: T625_158; Page: 2A; Enumeration District: 79; Image: 1120)*. Patience Pegan, age 35, unmarried, says she is a school librarian. She says she was born in Colorado, her father in Ohio and her mother in Indiana. The head of the household, Pliny C. Pegan, age 63, is still a railroad conductor. He says he and his father were Ohio natives while his mother was born in Indiana (wrong: she was also born in Ohio).

Francina Gwinn Pegan, listed as "Sima", age 60, says she was born in Indiana and her parents in Virginia.

Sometime in the 1920s, Patience Ruby Pegan was in Chicago, Cook Co., Illinois working for the International Harvester Company. But before 1930 she has returned to Denver and resumed working in the Denver Public Schools as a librarian.[286]

In 1930, Patience Ruby Pegan is once again residing with her parents, Pliny (Moses) Crume and Francina Gwinn Pegan, in Denver, Denver Co., Colorado *(Census Place: Denver, Denver, Colorado; Roll: 236; Page: 5B; Enumeration District: 82; Image: 47.0)*. Patience Pegan, listed as Ruby P., is age 35, single, and a school librarian; says she was born in Illinois, her father in Ohio and her mother in Illinois (wrong—she was born in Colorado and her mother in Indiana). Pliny C. Crume, age 73, a railroad conductor, says he and his father were born in Ohio and his mother in Iowa (again, not correct; she was born in Ohio). Francina Gwinn Pegan is 70 years old and says she was born in Illinois (Incorrect—she was born in Indiana) and her parents were born in Virginia. Perhaps the census taker misunderstood their birthplaces.

Patience Ruby Pegan is again found in Denver, Denver Co., Colorado in her father's household in 1940 *(Census Place: Denver, Denver, Colorado; Roll: T627_487; Page: 4B; Enumeration District: 16-111)*. Patience Pegan is enumerated as age 50 (she is 45); she is an unmarried Colorado native who is a librarian in a public library. Widower Pliny C. Pegan, age 83, born Ohio, lists no occupation and is probably retired. The Pegans say they were living in the same house at 165 South Clarkson Street in 1935. With them is a servant and housekeeper, Anna Atwood, 58, born in Iowa.

Patience Ruby Pegan became the second wife of **Charles Edgar Rosecrans (Ross Crane)** on May 14, 1947, in Denver Co., Colorado.[136, 286, 291] Charles Edgar Rosecrans (Ross Crane) was born in Owatonna, Steele Co., Minnesota, on August 6, 1868.[292, 293] He reached age 83 and died, possibly in Hawaii, on December 17, 1951.[294] Charles Edgar Rosecrans was buried in Pine Lake Cemetery, LaPorte, Center Twp., LaPorte Co., Indiana.[294]

Charles Edgar Rosecrans was a Rennaissance man. Born in Owatonna, Steele Co., Illinois, in 1868 he received extensive education at Oberlin College, the Newton Theological Institute in Newton Centre, Massachusetts; the Boston Museum of Art School and Cowles Art School in Boston, the Chicago Art Institute, and the Sorbonne in Paris, France. He first became a minister and teacher, employed in the Boston and Lynn, Massachusetts area. After marrying his first wife, Grace Gannon, in 1892 in Boston, he worked as a teacher in Lynn Massachusetts and then in Honolulu, Hawaii (where his brother lived) for some years.

But around 1904, he moved to Chicago, Cook Co., Illinois, took a stage name "Ross Crane" and became a regular on the Chatauqua/Lyceum circuit, an educational series which promoted improvement of oneself through knowledge gained from scientific, literary and artistic lectures. This movement was popular from the late 19th century until the Great Depression, and was considered a higher form of vaudeville. He became well-known, and traveled extensively on this circuit—all over the United States and to Europe and South America.

For his Lyceum lectures, Ross Crane was a cartoonist and sculptor/clay modeler, performing extemporaneously onstage. He was known for asking an audience member for his or her name, then writing the name on a large easel. He would then draw a portrait of that person incorporating the name he'd written on the easel. Crane would also pick up a large amount of clay, throw it on a table, and create a bust of someone famous, such as the then current or a former U.S. president. Later, as he developed his interior design skills, he would borrow home furnishings and fabrics from a local dealer and create various room designs on stage.

In 1912, he was elected president of the International Lyceum Association. His biographical sketch in the *Lyceumite and Talent Committeemen's Year Book For 1913*, it says of Crane, "He gives entertainment to the Nth degree. For artistic finish, rare versatility, and universal flavor with audiences, he stands at the top." At the time, he and his wife Grace were living in a houseboat on Pine Lake in LaPorte, Center Twp., LaPorte Co., Indiana.

As time went on, he rarely used his real name and used "Ross Crane" on almost all documents.

Charles Edgar Rosecrans/Ross Crane also became and interior designer of note, and from about 1914-1923 served as the director of the design extension department at the Chicago Institute of Art. While affiliated at the Chicago Institute of Art, he wrote a book that is still in print today, "The Ross Crane Book of Home Furnishing and Decoration; a Practical, Authoritative and Sympathetic Guide for the Amateur Home Decorator (1925 and an updated version in 1933). Other interior design books authored by Ross Crane, which can be found in libraries today, include: Interior Decoration: A Comprehensive Study Course for Furniture Men (1928), The Ross Crane Guide and Stylist (1929), The Joy of Color (1932) and Learn Interior Decoration by Looking (1940). Crane was considered one of the most influential interior designers of his day and of the early days of the design movement. His books were best sellers and can still be found in libraries today; some are used as historical references in university libraries and art libraries for current design students. He also founded the Better Homes Movement in the United States. He continued his performances on the Lyceum circuit throughout his employment at the Chicago Institute of Art and while lecturing around the country on home decorating and furniture design.

By 1924, he and Grace had moved to St. Louis, Missouri, where he became a magazine editor and the educational director of the American Homes Bureau. But he returned to Chicago by the time of the 1930 census, when Charles is enumerated under his real name and lists his occupation as writer and Lyceum lecturer. Grace Gannon Rosecrans died in Chicago in 1938.

After the Lyceum series waned, he still gave lectures and performances.

According to Pine Lake Cemetery records in LaPorte, Center Twp., LaPorte Co., Indiana, Charles Edgar Rosecrans/Ross Crane died on December 17, 1951 and was cremated. On August 16, 1952, his cremains were buried in Pine Lake Cemetery, where his first wife Grace Ellen Gannon Rosecrans is also buried. But his burial record lists no place of death, just that his ashes were shipped there for burial. No other death certificate or obituary has been found for him. He traveled all over the world and lectured to hundreds of thousands of people, was a well-known cartoonist, artist and interior designer—but died in obscurity. After his second wife, Patience Ruby Pegan Crane/Rosecrans died in Denver, Colorado in 1949, he may have returned to Honolulu, Oahu Island, Hawaii, where many of his family members still lived, and died there.[295, 296, 297, 298, 299, 300, 301, 302]

41. **Allie Belle**[8] **Cissel** (*Florence Genevieve*[7] *Pegan, Dr. Emmanuel*[6], *John*[5], *Robert A.*[4], *Andrew*[3], *Andrew*[2] *Pagan, James*[1]) was born on December 11, 1878, in Rensselaer, Marion Twp., Jasper Co., Indiana.[146, 147] She was the daughter of Mervin Osborne Cissel and Florence Genevieve Pegan (13). She died in Anthony, Anthony Twp., Harper Co., Kansas, on November 3, 1939, at age 60.[147, 148] Allie Belle was buried in Forest Park Cemetery, Anthony, Anthony Twp., Harper Co., Kansas.[147, 148, 303]

Allie Belle married **Bennett Franklin Michael** on August 30, 1898, in Cowley Co., Kansas.[146, 304] They had one daughter. Bennett Franklin Michael was born in Urbana, Urbana Twp., Champaign Co., Illinois, on December 26, 1875.[135, 305] He reached age 91 and died in Wichita, Sedgwick Co., Kansas, on March 24, 1966.[306, 307] Bennett Franklin was buried in Forest Park Cemetery, Anthony, Anthony Twp., Harper Co., Kansas.[307]

Bennett Franklin and Allie Cissel Belle Michael are found in Winfield, Pleasant Valley Twp., Cowley Co., Kansas in 1900 *(Census Place: Winfield Ward 1, Cowley, Kansas; Roll: T623_476; Page: 9A; Enumeration District: 67)*. Bennett Michael (listed as "B.F. Michael) is 25 years old, a dentist, born Dec 1874 in Illinois with his mother born in Ohio, but he doesn't know where his father was born. Allie B. is 21 and a music teacher, born Dec 1878 in Indiana, with her father born in Indiana and her mother in Ohio. The couple says they have been married two years and have no children.

In 1910, Bennett F. and Allie Belle Cissel Michael are enumerated in Anthony, Anthony Twp., Harper Co., Kansas *(Census Place: Anthony Ward 1, Harper, Kansas; Roll: T624_441; Page: 4A; Enumeration District: 0073; Image: 710)*. Bennett Michael, 35, born in Illinois with his parents born in Ohio, is still a dentist. Allie B., 31, says she was born in Indiana, as were her parents. The couple have been married 12 years with no children borne to Allie. This time, Allie lists no occupation.

Bennett F. and Allie Belle Cissel Michael have moved to Wichita, Sedgwick Co., Kansas by 1920 *(Census Place: Wichita Ward 3, Sedgwick, Kansas; Roll: T625_549; Page: 5B; Enumeration District: 197; Image: 483)*. In the home are Bennett F. Michael, again listed as "B.F.", 44, born Illinois with his parents born in Ohio, a dentist; Allie B. Cissel Michael, 40, born Indiana as were her parents; and their daughter, Frances ("Francis") G., age two years and two months, born in Kansas, with her father born in Illinois and her mother in Indiana.

But by 1930, Bennett Franklin and Allie Bell Cissel Michael are back in Anthony, Anthony Twp., Harper Co., Kansas *(Census Place: Anthony, Harper, Kansas; Roll: 704; Page: 2A; Enumeration District: 1; Image: 594.0)*. Bennett F. Michael is 54, born Illinois, with his parents born in the United States. He is a dentist. Allie B. Cissel Michael is 51, born Indiana, with her father born in Indiana and her mother in Ohio. The couple states that they were first married at ages 21 and 19 respectively (Incorrect—Bennett was 22). Daughter Francis G. (the name is again spelled like the masculine form) is 13, born in Kansas, with her father born in Illinois and her mother in Indiana.

Bennett Franklin Michael is still living in Anthony, Anthony Twp., Harper Co., Kansas in 1940 *(Census Place: Anthony, Harper, Kansas; Roll: T627_1234; Page: 8B; Enumeration District: 39-1B)*. Bennett F. Michael, age 64, born Illinois, a widower and a dentist, says he was living in the same house at 621 North Springfield Street in 1935. Residing with him is his brother John, 74.

According to his obituary, he was very active in many organizations, especially the Masonic order and related groups, and he formed the "Shrine Million Dollar Band" in Wichita in 1915.[306]

Daughter of Allie Belle Cissel and Bennett Franklin Michael:

+ 61 f I. **Frances Genevieve**[9] **Michael** was born in Harper or Sedgwick Co., Kansas, on February 9, 1917.[135, 308, 309] She was also known as **Genevieve**. Frances Genevieve died in Wichita, Sedgwick Co., Kansas, on March 30, 1996.[308, 310]

42. Benjamin Franklin[8] **Cissel** (*Florence Genevieve*[7] *Pegan, Emmanuel*[6]*, John*[5]*, Robert A.*[4]*, Andrew*[3]*, Andrew*[2] *Pagan, James*[1]) was born on November 8, 1883, in Rensselaer, Marion Twp., Jasper Co., Indiana.[148] He was the son of Mervin Osborne Cissel and Florence Genevieve Pegan (13). Benjamin Franklin died in St. Louis, Missouri, on June 27, 1913, at age 29.[149] He was buried in Forest Park Cemetery, Anthony, Anthony Twp., Harper Co., Kansas.[149, 311, 312]

Never married.

In 1910, Benjamin Franklin Cissel is living in Anthony, Anthony Twp., Harper Co., Kansas with is parents, Mervin and Florence G. Pegan Cissel *(Census Place: Anthony Ward 1, Harper, Kansas; Roll: T624_441; Page: 5B; Enumeration District: 0073; Image: 713)*. Benjamin Z. Cissel is age 26, born Indiana, and he says he is silversmith at a jewelry store. His father is listed as born in Maryland and his mother in Ohio, but this is incorrect. Mervin Cisell, 58, states he was born in Indiana, his father in Maryland and his mother in Pennsylvania. He says he is the editor of the *Argonia (KS) Clipper*. Florence G. Cissel, 51, says she and her father were born in Ohio and oddly, says her mother in Indiana. This is also incorrect. Mervin and Florence say they have been married 32 years and Florence has borne three children, all still alive. Also in the home is Benjamin's maternal grandmother, Sarah Strouse Pegan Shields, a widow, age 72, who is listed as the head of household. Sarah says she was born in Ohio, her father in Germany and her mother in Kentucky, and that she had borne three children, all still surviving (Incorrect—she had four children and one died). The census taker was most likely wrong about the head of household as well—it was probably Mervin Cissel.

His obituary says Benjamin Franklin Cissel, a printer in St. Louis at the time of his death, injured his hip in a fall when he was three years old, and it hampered his gait. He also contracted extrapulmonary tuberculosis of the lymph nodes, from which he suffered for 25 years.[309] His tombstone in Forest Park Cemetery in Anthony, Anthony Twp., Harper Co., Kansas reads "Bennie F. Cissel".[312]

43. Charles Mervin[8] Cissel (*Florence Genevieve[7] Pegan, Emmanuel[6], John[5], Robert A.[4], Andrew[3], Andrew[2] Pagan, James[1]*) was born on June 2, 1887, in Freeport, Silver Creek Twp., Harper Co., Kansas.[135, 150, 151] He was the son of Mervin Osborne Cissel and Florence Genevieve Pegan (13). Charles Mervin died in Wichita, Sedgwick Co., Kansas, on June 8, 1969, at age 82.[135, 150, 151] He was buried in Old Mission Cemetery, Wichita, Sedgwick Co., Kansas.[150]

Childless, but he adopted his two step-children from his second marriage, Aileen and Walter (Levett), who used the surname Cissel.

Charles M. Cissel is not found in the 1910 census.

Charles Mervin married **Louise Krouscup** on December 2, 1918, in Polk Co., Iowa.[313] They divorced. Louise Krouscup was born in Bevier, Macon Co., Missouri, in December 1897, and was living there with her parents Louis and Ollie Krouscup in 1900 (*Census Place: Bevier, Macon, Missouri; Roll: 873; Page: 14A; Enumeration District: 0063*). She was also known as **Lottie**. Louise died after 1930.

Charles Cissel is enumerated in Des Moines, Polk Co., Iowa in 1920 (*Census Place: Des Moines Ward 4, Polk, Iowa; Roll: T625_509; Page: 2A; Enumeration District: 135; Image: 266*). In the household are Charles Cissel, 33, born Kansas, a printer in a print shop, who says his parents were also born in Kansas (Incorrect—his father was born in Indiana and his mother in Ohio); his wife, Louise Crosco Cissel, 23, born Missouri as were her parents; and Marie Crosco, 19, born Missouri, who is Louise's sister, a worker in a lunch room. There are no children in the home.

Charles and Louise divorce before July 1928.

Charles Mervin Cissel married Mrs. **Lottie Hertha Irvine** Levett on July 5, 1928, in Caldwell Co., Missouri.[314] Lottie H. Irvine was born in Eagle Twp., Mason Co., Missouri, on February 22, 1900.[315, 316] Lottie H. reached age 62 and died in Wichita, Sedgwick Co., Kansas, on April 25, 1962.[315, 316] She was buried in Old Mission Cemetery, Wichita, Sedgwick Co., Kansas.[315, 317]

In 1930, Charles M. and Lottie H. Cissel are in Kansas City, Jackson Co., Missouri (*Census Place: Kansas City, Jackson, Missouri; Roll: 1201; Page: 2A; Enumeration District: 216; Image: 975.0*). Charles Cissel is 42, born Kansas, with his parents born in Indiana; he is a printer at a newspaper. Lottie Irvine Levett Cissel is 30, born Missouri, with her parents born in Virginia. Charles incorrectly says he was first married at age 40; Lottie say she was 28 when she first married—but she was also married before. Perhaps they misunderstood the census question. There are two children in the home, Aileen, 12, and Walter, 10, both born in Missouri as were their parents. The name "Levett" is partially erased in front of their names, but they are listed as a "daughter" and "son" respectively. Perhaps the children were, or in the process of being adopted by Charles Cissel?

Mervin's first wife, Louise Crouscup Cissel, is enumerated in 1930 in Kansas City, Jackson Co., Missouri (*Census Place: Kansas City, Jackson, Missouri; Roll: 1195; Page: 17A; Enumeration District: 0083; Image: 772.0*). Louise is a waitress in a sanatarium and a lodger in the home of Guy and Velma Russell. She says she was born in Missouri and her parents in the United States. She is not found in the 1940 census and may have remarried.

Charles Cissel is living in Wichita, Sedgwick Co., Kansas in 1940 (*Census Place: Wichita, Sedgwick, Kansas; Roll: T627_1273; Page: 11A; Enumeration District: 107-69A*). In the home are Charles M. Cisell, 52, born Kansas, a printer at a newspaper; his wife, Lottie Irvine Levett Cissel, 40, and children Aileen, 22, a packer in a factory, and Charles (listed as female and a daughter), who works at a newspaper. Lottie and the children were born in Missouri. The family's house is at 2620 Central East, and they say they were living in Wichita in 1935.

Charles and Lottie's grave stone says they were married on July 15, 1916; but this is not possible, as Lottie's marriage date to her former husband, Walter J. Levett, was August 27, 1916 in Macon Co., Missouri, (but recorded in Shelby Co., Missouri).[318] As Charles may have adopted Lottie's two children by her previous marriage, they may have had the 1916 date inscribed on their tombstone to accommodate for the birth of her first child, which was in 1917.

44. **Laurence Victor**[8] **Mason** (*Charles Edwin*[7], *Mary Elizabeth*[6] *Pegan, John*[5], *Robert A.*[4], *Andrew*[3], *Andrew*[2] *Pagan, James*[1]) was born on December 20, 1883, in Bellefontaine, Lake Twp., Logan Co., Ohio.[161] He was the son of Charles Edwin Mason (16) and Mary Ellen Pickerell. He died in Bradenton, Manatee Co., Florida, on October 28, 1954, at age 70.[162] Laurence Victor was buried in Manasota Memorial Park Cemetery, Bradenton, Manatee Co., Florida.[319, 320]

Laurence Victor Mason married **Anna Mae Evans** on February 3, 1904, in Logan Co., Ohio.[60] They had two children. Anna Mae Evans was born in Bellefontaine, Lake Twp., Logan Co., Ohio, on October 19, 1885.[60] Anna Mae reached age 67 and died in Bradenton, Manatee Co., Florida, on November 23, 1952.[321] She was buried in Manasota Memorial Park Cemetery, Bradenton, Manatee Co., Florida.[321, 322]

In 1910, Lawrence V. Mason, 27, a steel worker, is enumerated in Lake Twp., Logan Co., Ohio *(Census Place: Lake, Logan, Ohio; Roll: T624_1204; Page: 1B; Enumeration District: 0125; Image: 705)*. With him are wife Anna Mae Evans Mason, listed as Anna, 24, and children Katherine, five, and Donald, two. All were born in Ohio, as were their parents. Lawrence and Anna have been married six years, and Anna has borne just those two children.

By 1917, Laurence Victor Mason has moved to Alliance, Lexington Twp., Stark Co., Ohio, and is an engineer with an engineering firm, according to his WWI draft registration. The draft card says he was born on December 20, 1882, which is incorrect.[323]

In 1920, Laurence V. Mason, 37, is found in Alliance, Lexington Twp., Stark Co., Ohio *(Census Place: Alliance Ward 4, Stark, Ohio; Roll: T625_1436; Page: 4B; Enumeration District: 94; Image: 406)*. He is now a mechanical engineer. Anna May Evans Mason ("May Anna"), is 34 years old. Children Katherine, 15, and Donald, 12, are also in the home. All were born in Ohio, as were their parents.

Laurence V. Mason, 46, and wife Anna May Evans Mason, 44, are still living in Alliance, Lexington Twp., Stark Co., Ohio in 1930 *(Census Place: Alliance, Stark, Ohio; Roll: 1871; Page: 9A; Enumeration District: 78; Image: 986.0)*. Both say they and their parents were born in Ohio. Laurence V. Mason says he is still a mechanical engineer. They say they were first married at ages 21 and 18 respectively.

Laurence V. Mason is located in South Greensboro, Guilford Co., North Carolina in 1940 *(Census Place: South Greensboro, Guilford, North Carolina; Roll: T627_2922; Page: 29A; Enumeration District: 41-115)*. Laurence Mason, listed as "L." Mason, age 56, is a mechanical engineer for Guilford County. Anna "Mae" Evans Mason is 54 years old. Both say they were born in Ohio, and were living in Stark Co., Ohio in 1935. Their home is on High Point Road.

Laurence V. Mason was again residing again Alliance, Lexington Twp., Stark Co., Ohio by 1942, when he registered for the WWII draft. He lists his birthdate on this draft registration as December 20, 1883.[161] Later, Laurence and Anna Mae removed to Bradenton, Manatee Co., Florida.

Children of Laurence Victor Mason and Anna Mae Evans:

+ 62 f I. **Kathryn Louise**[9] **Mason** was born in Lake Twp., Logan Co., Ohio, on January 1, 1905.[135, 324, 325] She died in Bradenton, Manatee Co., Florida, on February 19, 1986.[325]

+ 63 m II. **Donald Earl**[9] **Mason** was born in Lake Twp., Logan Co., Ohio, on September 9, 1907.[135, 326] He died in West Plains, Howell Twp., Howell Co., Missouri, on August 22, 1994.[134, 327]

45. Laura Marguerite⁸ Mason (*Charles Edwin⁷, Mary Elizabeth⁶ Pegan, John⁵, Robert A.⁴, Andrew³, Andrew² Pagan, James¹*) was born on January 22, 1891, in Bellefontaine, Lake Twp., Logan Co., Ohio.[163, 164] She was also known as **Marguerite**. She was the daughter of Charles Edwin Mason (16) and Mary Ellen Pickerell. She lived in Winter Park, Orange Co., Florida. Laura Marguerite died in Orlando, Orange Co., Florida, on February 29, 1948, at age 57.[163, 165, 166] She was buried in Lone Oak Cemetery, Leesburg, Lake Co., Florida.[328]

Childless.

Laura Marguerite Mason Voorhees lists her birthdate as January 22, 1892 on her marriage license so she would be younger than her husband, Elsworth Charles Voorhees.

Laura's date and place of death is mentioned in her father, Charles E. Mason's, obituary.[164]

Laura Marguerite married **Elsworth Charles Voorhees** on June 15, 1918, in Marion Co., Ohio.[163] Elsworth Charles Voorhees was born in Sidney, Clinton Twp., Shelby Co., Ohio, on February 3, 1891.[163, 329] Elsworth Charles also resided in 1967 in Forest City, Seminole Co., Florida. Elsworth Charles reached age 76 and died in a facility in Orlando, Orange Co., Florida, on February 19, 1967.[135, 329] He was buried in Lone Oak Cemetery, Leesburg, Lake Co., Florida.[330]

In 1920, Elsworth C. and Laura "Marguerite" Mason Voorhees are enumerated in Marion, Marion Twp., Marion Co., Ohio (*Census Place: Marion Ward 2, Marion, Ohio; Roll: T625_1416; Page: 9A; Enumeration District: 123; Image: 210*). Elsworth, age 28, a baker, says he and his father were born in Ohio and his mother was born in Scotland. (Laura) Marguerite Mason Voorhees, 27, says she and her parents were born in Ohio.

Elsworth and Laura Marguerite Mason Voorhees are again living in Marion, Marion Twp., Marion Co., Ohio (*Census Place: Marion, Marion, Ohio; Roll: 1848; Page: 14A; Enumeration District: 26; Image: 168.0*). Elsworth is listed as E.C. Voorhees". Elsworth, age 39, is still a baker. Laura Marguerite Mason Voorhees is listed as L. Marguerite Voorhees, age 38. The couple says they were first married at ages 27 and 26 respectively.

Elsworth C. and Laura Marguerite Mason Voorhees are found in Leesburg, Lake Co., Florida in 1940 (*Census Place: Leesburg, Lake, Florida; Roll: T627_595; Page: 2A; Enumeration District: 35-15*). Elsworth C. Voorhees, incorrectly listed as "D.C." Voorhees, age 48, born Ohio, is a baker. Laura Marguerite Mason Voorhees, listed as Marguerite, is also 48. Both say they were born in Ohio and were residents of Marion, Marion Twp., Marion Co., Ohio in 1935. They are roomers in the home of May Laws at 120 Meadow Street.

After Laura Marguerite Mason Voorhees died, Elsworth remarried to a widow, Mrs. Millie Anna Presley Bowen.[331]

46. Paul Edwin⁸ Mason (*Charles Edwin⁷, Mary Elizabeth⁶ Pegan, John⁵, Robert A.⁴, Andrew³, Andrew² Pagan, James¹*) was born on July 13, 1893, in Bellefontaine, Lake Twp., Logan Co., Ohio.[167, 168] He was the son of Charles Edwin Mason (16) and Mary Ellen Pickerell. He died in Ontario, San Bernardino Co., California, on January 2, 1955, at age 61.[168, 169] Paul Edwin was buried in Bellefontaine City Cemetery, Bellefontaine, Lake Twp., Logan Co., Ohio.[332]

When Paul Mason registers for the WWI draft in 1917, he is residing in Akron, Summit Co., Ohio and is working for the Firestone Rubber Company.[167]

In 1920, Paul Mason, 26, single, is living in Cleveland, Cuyahoga Co., Ohio (*Census Place: Cleveland Ward 8, Cuyahoga, Ohio; Roll: T625_1363; Page: 4A; Enumeration District: 136; Image: 244*). He is a boarder in the home of Moses Mcgill, as are seven other people. Paul Mason says he was born in Ohio, as were his parents, and he is a carpenter in an auto body factory.

Paul Edwin married **Frances Louise Moore** on May 5, 1920, in Cuyahoga Co., Ohio.[333] They had three children. Frances Louise Moore was born in Bellefontaine, Lake Twp., Logan Co., Ohio, on May 7, 1894.[333] She reached age 76 and died in Bellefontaine, Lake Twp., Logan Co., Ohio, on February 26, 1971.[334] Frances Louise was buried in Bellefontaine City Cemetery, Bellefontaine, Lake Twp., Logan Co., Ohio.[335, 336]

By 1930, Paul Mason is back in Lake Twp., Logan Co., Ohio *(Census Place: Lake, Logan, Ohio; Roll: 1829; Page: 2A; Enumeration District: 14; Image: 1021.0).* In the household are Paul E. Mason, 37, a bakery truck driver; and his wife, Francis Louise Moore Mason, 35. The couple have been married 10 years, as they say they were first married at ages 27 and 25 respectively. They have three children: Mary J., eight, Robert E., six, and C. Stephen, three. All say they and their parents were born in Ohio.

Paul Mason is again found in Lake Twp., Logan Co., Ohio in 1940 *(Census Place: Lake, Logan, Ohio; Roll: T627_3100; Page: 5A; Enumeration District: 46-19).* Paul Mason, 46, is a farmer who has a hatchery. Frances Moore Mason is 45 years old. With them are their children Mary Jane, 18, Robert, 15, and Stephen, 13. All were born in Ohio, and say they were living in their home on Route 8 south of Iron City in 1935.

Although his death certificate says he died in San Bernardino, San Bernardino Co., California, Paul E. Mason died in Ontario, San Bernardino Co., California at the home of family friends according to his obituary. He and his wife, Frances Louise Moore Mason, had gone to California to visit his son Robert and his family, to attend the Tournament of Roses Parade and the Rose Bowl football game, and then stopped in to visit these family friends before they intended to return to Ohio.[169] His California death index entry says San Bernardino, perhaps because that is where the hospital for Ontario was at the time.[168]

Children of Paul Edwin Mason and Frances Louise Moore:

+ 64 f I. **Mary Jane**[9] **Mason** was born in Lake Twp., Logan Co., Ohio, on January 26, 1922.[337, 338] She died in Bellefontaine, Lake Twp., Logan Co., Ohio, on November 20, 1993.[338]

+ 65 m II. **Robert Edwin**[9] **Mason** was born in Lake Twp., Logan Co., Ohio, on March 7, 1924.[135, 339, 340] He died in Granville, Granville Twp., Licking Co., Ohio, on September 4, 2005.[135, 340, 341]

+ 66 m III. **Charles Stephen**[9] **Mason** was born in Bellefontaine, Lake Twp., Logan Co., Ohio, on October 17, 1926.[342]

47. **Child One**[8] **Mason** (*Charles Edwin*[7], *Mary Elizabeth*[6] *Pegan, John*[5], *Robert A.*[4], *Andrew*[3], *Andrew*[2] *Pagan, James*[1]) was born between 1882 and 1900 in Bellefontaine, Lake Twp., Logan Co., Ohio. He or she was a child of Charles Edwin Mason (16) and Mary Ellen Pickerell. Child One died in Bellefontaine, Lake Twp., Logan Co., Ohio, before 1900.

48. **Child Two**[8] **Mason** (*Charles Edwin*[7], *Mary Elizabeth*[6] *Pegan, John*[5], *Robert A.*[4], *Andrew*[3], *Andrew*[2] *Pagan, James*[1]) was born between 1900 and 1910 in Bellefontaine, Lake Twp., Logan Co., Ohio. He or she was a child of Charles Edwin Mason (16) and Mary Ellen Pickerell. Child Two died in Bellefontaine, Lake Twp., Logan Co., Ohio, before 1910.

49. **Harold Mason**[8] **Young** (*Alta Dell*[7] *Mason, Mary Elizabeth*[6] *Pegan, John*[5], *Robert A.*[4], *Andrew*[3], *Andrew*[2] *Pagan, James*[1]) was born on September 25, 1901, in Kengtung Ess, Shan State, Burma (now Myanmar).[135, 183] He was the son of William Marcus Young and Alta Dell Mason (18). Harold Mason lived in 1950 in Mariposa, Mariposa Co., California. Harold Mason died in Chaing Mai, Thailand, on February 6, 1975, at age 73.[135, 177, 184, 185] He was cremated in Wat Pa Paeng, Temple in Chiang Mai, Thailand.[184, 343]

Harold Mason married **Ruth Saada Pinkerton** on May 21, 1926, in Los Angeles Co., California.[177, 344] They had three children. Ruth Saada Pinkerton was born in Los Angeles, Los Angeles Co., California, on May 6, 1906.[135, 345, 346, 347] Ruth Saada reached age 75 and died in Oxnard, Ventura Co., California, on December 6, 1981.[344, 346, 347, 348, 349] She was cremated.[347]

At first, Harold Mason Young followed in his father William Marcus Young's footsteps as a Baptist minister in Southeast Asia. He and his wife Ruth were sent to the Baptist mission in Banna, China immediately after their marriage in 1926. By 1929, they were at the mission in Kengtung, Burma (now Myanmar), where Harold's parents served and where Harold was born. Later they were at new stations in Taunggyi and Lashio, Shan State. Ruth Saada Pinkerton Young, a teacher, worked alongside her husband in missionary work among the Lahu and for a time taught music at the American School in Taunggyi. In 1936, they were directed to establish a new mission in Pang-Yang, Manglun State, Burma, adjacent to the border with China.[350]

When WWII broke out, Ruth and their three children were evacuated to India to avoid the fighting in Burma. Despite his American citizenship, Harold Mason Young joined the British Army as an officer, and was ordered to recruit a Burmese labor force. After the Japanese invaded Burma in 1942, Harold Young, ill with malaria, escaped to Myitkyina, Kachin State, Burma, and American troops transported him to a military hospital in India. However, he was listed as "Missing in Action", and his family thought him dead until his eldest child, Gordon, traced him to that Indian hospital. After his recovery, Harold continued to serve in the British Army in India until 1943, when he finally was transferred to a U.S. Army Office of War Information in Assam, India.[177, 351]

But by 1944, the U.S. Army sent him back to Burma, where he enlisted the Wa warriors to fight the invading Japanese in their traditional way—by lopping off their heads with their usual weapon, a large knife called a "dah". The Wa were once known throughout the Southeast Asia as fierce fighters and head-hunters until the Young missionaries ended the practice, the news that the Wa were once again aiming to head-hunt kept the Japanese away from the Burmese northeastern highlands.[C]

According to Gordon Young, Harold then became an agent for the Central Intelligence Agency (CIA), pressed into service by that agency, in Southeast Asia during the rest of WWII, the Korean War and the Communist revolution in China in the late 1940s-early 1950s.[177] The Youngs returned to Pang-Yang following war's end, with Harold working for the British government. He never resumed his Baptist missionary work, but Ruth did continue hers while they lived in Pang-Yang. Harold, Ruth and their youngest son left in 1950 to California, intending to retire. But the CIA again called him into service, and in December 1952 Harold and Ruth were sent to Chaing Mai, Thailand. The CIA had Harold and others train a native police force to guard Thailand's borders. He and his family had several narrow escapes from the Chinese Communists.[177, 185]

During this time, Harold started rescuing injured animals, nursing them back to health and caring for them in a compound in Chaing Mai. Harold's animal collection gained attention, and soon people were coming to see them. After the revolution ended, Harold continued his zoological and entomological work, gathering many animal and insect species native to Thailand and the surrounding region. Although he was a dedicated naturalist, this work also served as his cover, for he was still a CIA agent.[182]

The Thai government took notice and endorsed his work. In 1957, Harold established the Chaing Mai Zoo, when the Thai government dedicated 24 acres at the base of Doi Suthep mountain near the city. After Harold's death, the King of Thailand became the zoo's patron, and the facility expanded to more than 200 acres. The Chaing Mai Zoo and Aquarium, thrives today, and Harold Mason is revered for his efforts.[352]

Harold's brother, Marcus Vincent Young, was also a missionary in Southeast Asia.[177, 185]

Harold Mason Young was the author of several books on the natives of Indochina, including *Burma Headhunters*, a study of the Wa people of Burma with whom he grew up, *To The Mountain Tops: A Sojourn Among the Lahu of Asia*, a treatise on the Lahu tribal groups in Thailand and China's Yunnan province.[177, 353, 354]

Children of Harold Mason Young and Ruth Saada Pinkerton:

+ 67 m I. **Oliver Gordon⁹ Young** was born in Banna, Yunnan Province, China, on August 16, 1927.[344, 355, 356] He was also known as **Gordon or O. Gordon**. Oliver Gordon died in Bella Vista, Shasta Co., California, on August 8, 2016.[357]

+ 68 f II. **Helen Elizabeth⁹ Young** was born in Kengtung Ess, Shan State, Burma (now Myanmar), on January 3, 1929.[344, 358]

+ 69 m III. **William Marcus⁹ Young II** was born in Berkeley, Alameda Co., California, on October 28, 1934.[135, 344, 359] He died in Chaing Mai, Thailand, on April 1, 2011.[135, 185, 187, 360, 361]

50. **Marcus Vincent⁸ Young** (*Alta Dell⁷ Mason, Mary Elizabeth⁶ Pegan, John⁵, Robert A.⁴, Andrew³, Andrew² Pagan, James¹*) was born on August 22, 1903, in Kengtung Ess, Shan State, Burma (now Myanmar).[135, 186] He was the son of William Marcus Young and Alta Dell Mason (18). He lived in 1990 in Mentone, San Bernardino, California. Marcus Vincent died in a hospital in Redlands, San Bernardino Co., California, on December 2, 1990, at age 87.[135, 187, D] Marcus Vincent was buried in Montecito Memorial Park Cemetery, Colton, San Bernardino Co., California.[362, 363]

Marcus Vincent Young spent his early life in Burma (now Myanmar) and China before going to America to study at the Berkeley Divinity School in California to become a missionary in Southeast Asia like his brother, Harold Mason Young, and their father, William Marcus Young.

In 1930, William Vincent Young, listed as M. Vincent Young, age 26 and single, was a student at the Berkeley Divinity School in Berkeley, Alameda Co., California (*Census Place: Berkeley, Alameda, California; Roll: 111; Page: 5A; Enumeration District: 294; Image: 51.0*). He seems to be living in a dormitory or rooming house for students at the college.

He says he is an American citizen born in Burma, is an American Baptist missionary, and that his father was born in Illinois and his mother in Ohio.

Marcus Vincent married **Vera Gibbs** on July 22, 1930, in San Bernardino Co., California.[364] They had three children. Vera Gibbs was born in San Bernardino, San Bernardino Co., California, on March 10, 1907.[135, 365, 366] She reached age 66 and died in San Bernardino, San Bernardino Co., California, on March 18, 1973.[135, 365, 366] Vera was buried in Montecito Memorial Park Cemetery, Colton, San Bernardino Co., California.[366, 367, 368]

After he completed his studies at Berkeley, Marcus Vincent Young and his family returned to Burma/Myanmar and are not found in the 1940 census.[364]

He was a minister and missionary in both the Kengtung, Shan State, Burma and the Yunnan province in China, as was his father, William Marcus Young. He directed the Lahu and Wa missions in Yunnan, and, along with his wife Vera Gibbs Young, translated the New Testament into the Lahu and Wa languages.[364, 369, 370]

When WWII broke out in British-held Burma, the Marcus Young family escaped the Japanese invasion of that country—on foot over the mountains into India.[177] Then Vera and their children boarded a ship to New York, traveling around Africa's Cape of Good Hope and across the Atlantic Ocean, somehow evading the German submarine activity during WWII. On July 13, 1942, Vera Gibbs Young and her three children arrived in New York City on the ship "Brazil".[371]

After the war, his family returned to Shan State, Burma, and remained there for nearly a year after the Communists took control of China in 1949. A year later, the family again had to flee and go to America, this time from internal strife in Burma among three groups trying to wrest control: the Chinese Communists under Mao Tse-Tung, and the Peoples Volunteer Organization (PVO or White Band), the Karen tribesmen.[174, 369]

There he remained until 1953, when, upon re-entering Burma/Myanmar after traveling elsewhere, he was denied an entrance visa—perhaps because of Chinese pressure on the Burmese government.

He then returned to the U.S., eventually settling in Mentone, San Bernardino, California.[177]

Children of Marcus Vincent Young and Vera Gibbs:

+ 70 m I. **Lael Marcus⁹ Young** was born in Kengtung Ess, Shan State, Burma (now Myanmar), on March 12, 1936.[135, 372, 373, 374] He died in a hospital in San Bernardino, San Bernardino Co., California, on May 28, 1996, at age 60.[135, 372, 374, 375]

+ 71 m II. **Philip Gibbs⁹ Young** was born in Kengtung Ess, Shan State, Burma (now Myanmar), on February 3, 1938.[376]

+ 72 f III. **Daughter⁹ Young** was born in Taunggyi, Shan State, Burma (now Myanmar).[377]

51. **Clarence Edwin⁸ Young** (*Alta Dell⁷ Mason, Mary Elizabeth⁶ Pegan, John⁵, Robert A.⁴, Andrew³, Andrew² Pagan, James¹*) was born on November 13, 1906, in Kengtung Ess, Shan State, Burma (now Myanmar).[188] He was the son of William Marcus Young and Alta Dell Mason (18). Clarence Edwin died in Taunggyi, Shan State, Burma (now Myanmar), on May 30, 1908, at age one.[189] He was buried in Taunggyi, Shan State, Burma (now Myanmar)?

52. **Mildred Elizabeth⁸ Mason** (*John Pegan⁷, Mary Elizabeth⁶ Pegan, John⁵, Robert A.⁴, Andrew³, Andrew² Pagan, James¹*) was born on September 27, 1901, in Indianapolis, Center Twp., Marion Co., Indiana.[197, 198, 199] She was the daughter of John Pegan Mason (21) and Anna Louisa Slusser. Mildred Elizabeth died in San Diego, San Diego Co., California, on November 19, 1957, at age 56.[197]

Mildred Elizabeth married **Launcelot Alfred Mantle** on June 12, 1920, in Marion Co., Indiana.[199] They divorced before 1955. They had three children. Launcelot Alfred Mantle was born in Bristol, Southampton, England, on June 15, 1895.[135, 199, 378, 379] He was also known as **Lance**. Launcelot Alfred reached age 95 and died in Pasadena, Los Angeles Co., California, on May 20, 1991.[135, 379, 380] He was cremated and his ashes scattered in the Pacific Ocean at Pt. Fermin, Los Angeles Co., California.[379]

Lance Alfred Mantle says on his U.S. Passport Application and his WWII draft registration that he was born in Bristol, England; his birth registration was under the name Launcelot Alfred Mantle in Barton Regis, Gloucestershire.[381, 382, 383] The 1901 England census indicates he was "Alfred" Mantle, age six, born in Bristol, Gloucester, England, living with his mother Mary and five siblings in West Brighton, Sussex, England (*1901 England Census, Launcelot A. Mantle; Mary Mantle, head of household; West Brighton, Sussex; Class: RG13; Piece: 932; Folio: 19; Page: 30. Census Returns of England and Wales, 1901. Kew, Surrey, England: The National Archives, 1901. Data imaged from the National Archives, London, England*).

Although he states on the 1930 census form that he was naturalized in 1912, ship's records indicate he immigrated to America on the ship "Oceanic" on September 24, 1913, which is the date he states on his 1920 passport application.[381, 384]

When Launcelot Alfred Mantle registered for the WWI draft in 1917, he was a resident of in 1917 in Louisville, Jefferson Co., Kentucky.[378] He served in the U.S. Army, and his daughter, Peg Mantle, says her father was an ambulance driver in that war. He became a naturalized American citizen on June 10, 1918 at Camp Greenleaf, Georgia.[385, 386, 387]

After their marriage in Indianapolis in 1920, Lance A. and Mildred Elizabeth Mason Mantle led a peripatetic life.

According to a U.S. consular registration dated November 29, 1920, Lance Alfred and Mildred Elizabeth Mason Mantle traveled to Tegucigalpa, Guatamala in June 1920, just a month after their marriage, to do missionary work for the American Baptist Home Missionary Society. According to the passenger list of the ship *Saramacca*, they arrived back from Puerto Barrios, Guatamala through the port of New Orleans on June 20, 1921. On this consular registration, Lance states his naturalization date and says he was in the U.S. Army ambulance corps in from July 1918-June 1919.[387]

They were back in Indianapolis by October 1921 when their son John G. Mantle was born. By 1923, they were in Obert, Cedar Co., Nebraska, where their daughter Norma was born, and Lance was a Baptist minister. As mentioned in Mildred's father's, John Pegan Mason's, June 1924 obituary, they were living in Dayton, Wayne Twp., Armstrong Co., Pennsylvania.[150] By 1925, they had returned to Indiananapolis, where they had their youngest child, daughter Margaret. Lance Mantle and his family relocated to Grand Rapids, Grand Rapids Township, Kent Co., Michigan by 1928, where Lance is listed as a printer.[388]

Lance A. and Mildred Elizabeth Mason Mantle are enumerated in 1930 in Tulsa, Tulsa Co., Oklahoma (*Census Place: Tulsa, Tulsa, Oklahoma; Roll: 1934; Page: 10B; Image: 459.0*). The head of the household is Lance A. Mantle, age 34, born in England as were his parents, a manager of an advertising company. Lance says he became a naturalized U.S. citizen in 1912 (incorrect). With him is his wife, Mildred E. Mason Mantle, 29, born Indiana, with her parents born in Ohio. They say they were first marriage at ages 24 and 20 respectively. They have three children, John G., eight, born in Indiana, Norma, six, born in Nebraska, and Margaret J., five, born in Indiana.

They were residing in Dallas, Tarrant Co., Texas by 1931, according to the 1931 and 1932 Dallas city directories, where Lance was the department manager of Commercial Printing & Letter Service.[389] The family spends a year in Atlanta, Fulton Co., Georgia in 1933; this time, Lance is a salesman for A.B. Dick office equipment company.[390]

Lance Mantle is listed in the 1935 and 1936 Indiananapolis, Indiana city directories. In 1935, he is a publisher, but by 1936, his occupation is Presbyterian minister.[391, 392]

In 1940, Lance and Mildred Mason Mantle are enumerated in Vincennes, Vincennes Twp., Knox Co., Indiana (*Census Place: Vincennes, Knox, Indiana; Roll: T627_1061; Page: 5A; Enumeration District: 42-24*). Lance Mantle, age 45, born England, is a clergyman. His wife, Mildred Mason Mantle, is 39 years old. Children in the home are: John, 18, Norma, 17, and Margaret, 15. Mildred, John and Margaret were born in Indiana; Norma was born in Nebraska. All say there were living in Indianapolis, Marion Co., Indiana in 1935. Also in the house is a maid, Betty Flory, 17. Their home address is 315 North 5th Street. The Mantles were still living in Vincennes in 1942, when Lance, still a minister, registers for the WWII draft.[382]

Captain Lance Mantle, a chaplain the Army-Air Force, was based in Goldsboro, Wayne Co., North Carolina in 1943, Greensboro, Guilford Co., North Carolina the next year, and in Denver, Denver Co., Colorado by 1945.[386, 393]

Lance was out of the service and living in 1950 in Golden, Jefferson Co., Colorado, but moved by 1952 to Van Nuys, Los Angeles Co., California.[386] Launcelot Alfred also resided in 1955 in La Jolla, San Diego Co., California, working as a salesman at the Bird Rock General Store by 1955. But Mildred is not mentioned in the directory with him.[394]

Mildred Elizabeth Mason Mantle died in San Diego, San Diego California in 1957. In 1958, Lance remarried to Mrs. Ella Wait Parente in San Diego Co., California.[395] They divorce before 1961.[396] From there, Lance Mantle moves back to Denver, Colorado, where he is found from 1964-1967, working first as a writer for a church extension service, then as a printer.[397] But he returns to California before 1991, when he died in Pasadena, Los Angeles Co., California.[379]

Children of Mildred Elizabeth Mason and Launcelot Alfred Mantle:

+ 73 m I. **John Gregory⁹ Mantle** was born in Indianapolis, Center Twp., Marion Co., Indiana, on October 3, 1921.[135, 398, 399, 400] He died in Thousand Oaks, Ventura Co., California, on December 15, 1988.[134, 398, 399, 401]

+ 74 f II. **Norma Louise⁹ Mantle** was born in Obert, Cedar Co., Nebraska, on May 19, 1923.[135, 402, 403, 404] She died in Harrisonburg, Rockingham Co., Virginia, on May 27, 2005.[135, 403, 404]

+ 75   f   III.   **Margaret Jean**[9] **Mantle** was born in Indiana, Indiana Twp., Allegheny Co., Pennsylvania? on November 29, 1924. She is also known as **Peg**.

53. Alice Irene[8] **Mason** (*John Pegan*[7], *Mary Elizabeth*[6] *Pegan, John*[5], *Robert A.*[4], *Andrew*[3], *Andrew*[2] *Pagan, James*[1]) was born on February 4, 1907, in Indianapolis, Center Twp., Marion Co., Indiana.[135, 200, 201] She was the daughter of John Pegan Mason (21) and Anna Louisa Slusser. She died in Satellite Beach, Brevard Co., Florida, on August 30, 1984, at age 77.[200, 201, 202] Alice Irene was buried in Florida Memorial Gardens Cemetery, Rockledge, Brevard Co., Florida.[201, 202]

Alice Irene married **Horace Russell Honeycutt** on November 5, 1927, in Marion Co., Indiana.[405, 406] They had two sons. Horace Russell Honeycutt was born in Hendersonville, Sumner Co., Tennessee, on February 13, 1905.[407, 408] He lived in Eue Gallie, Brevard Co., Florida in 1959. He reached age 53 and died in a hospital in Melbourne, Brevard Co., Florida, on February 12, 1959.[408, 409, 410] Horace Russell was buried in Florida Memorial Gardens Cemetery, Rockledge, Brevard Co., Florida.[408, 410, 411]

Horace and Alice Mason Honeycutt are enumerated in Indianapolis, Center Twp., Marion Co., Indiana in 1930 *(Census Place: Indianapolis, Marion, Indiana; Roll: 614; Page: 17A; Enumeration District: 161; Image: 35.0)*. In the home are Horace Honeycutt, 25, born Tennessee as were his parents, a clerk in an auto factory; and Alice Mason Honeycutt, 23, born Indiana with her parents born in Ohio. The couple have been married two years, as they say their first marriages occurred at ages 25 and 23 respectively. They have a son, Robert, 10 months old, born Indiana. Also in the home is Alice's mother, Anna Louisa Slusser Mason, 55, a widow. An Ohio native, as were her parents, she says she was first marriage at age 25. Horace's father James Honeycutt, 56, born Tennessee as were his parents, a widower, is also living in the home.

In 1940, Horace and Alice Mason Honeycutt are still residents of Indianapolis, Center Twp., Marion Co., Indiana *(Census Place: Indianapolis, Marion, Indiana; Roll: T627_1129; Page: 2B; Enumeration District: 96-288)*. Horace Honeycutt, age 35, born Tennessee is an auditor for the State of Indiana. His wife, Alice Mason Honeycutt, 33, is a clerk for the Indiana State Department of Welfare. With them are sons Robert, 10, and Donald, seven. Alice and the children were born in Indiana. Living with them is Alice's widowed mother, Anna Louisa Slusser Mason, 65, born Ohio. All state they were in Indianapolis, Marion Co., Indiana in 1935. Their house address is 1542 Hoefgen Street.

By 1944, Horace and Alice and their family were residents of Evansville, Vanderburgh Co., Indiana. Horace is an inspector for a federal government agency.[412] The next year, Horace and Alice Mason Honeycutt are found in the Florida State Census in Jacksonville, Duvall Co., Florida.[413] Horace is age 40, born Tennessee and Alice Mason Honeycutt is age 38. They have two sons, Robert, 15 and Donald, 12. Alice and the sons were all born in Indiana. Horace Honeycutt also appeared in the 1947-48 Jacksonville, Duval Co., Florida City Directory, where Horace is an enforcement supervisor for the federal government.[414]

According to his obituary, Horace R. Honeycutt resided between 1948-1952 in Bainbridge, Decatur Co., Georgia and in Eau Gallie, Brevard Co., Florida from 1953-1959. He worked for U.S. government as a civilian auditor for the military before his retirement in 1957.[415]

Sons of Alice Irene Mason and Horace Russell Honeycutt:

+ 76   m   I.   **Robert Lee**[9] **Honeycutt** was born in Indianapolis, Center Twp., Marion Co., Indiana, on June 3, 1929.[416, 417] He died in Gainesville, Alachua Co., Florida, on November 26, 1966.[417, 418]

+ 77   m   II.   **Donald James**[9] **Honeycutt** was born in Indianapolis, Center Twp., Marion Co., Indiana, on July 31, 1932.[419]

54. Pauline Elizabeth[8] **Russell** (*Gertrude P.*[7] *Pegan, James Milton*[6], *John*[5], *Robert A.*[4], *Andrew*[3], *Andrew*[2]

Pagan, James[1]) was born on September 9, 1909, in DeGraff, Miami Twp., Logan Co., Ohio.[214] She was the daughter of Otto H. Russell and Gertrude P. Pegan (27). Pauline Elizabeth died in Venice, Sarasota Co., Florida, on June 1, 1999, at age 89.[135, 215] She was buried in Greenwood Cemetery, DeGraff, Pleasant Twp., Logan Co., Ohio.[420]

Pauline Elizabeth married **Donald Otho Brown** on March 16, 1930, in Logan Co., Ohio.[421] They had two sons. Donald Otho Brown was born in Scottdale, Westmoreland Co., Pennsylvania, on November 6, 1903.[135] Donald Otho reached age 89 and died in Venice, Sarasota Co., Florida, on September 28, 1993.[135, 422] He was buried in Greenwood Cemetery, DeGraff, Pleasant Twp., Logan Co., Ohio.[423]

In 1930, newlyweds Donald O. and Pauline Russell Brown were newlyweds and living with Pauline's parents, Otto H. and Gertrude Pegan Russell, in DeGraff, Miami Twp., Logan Co., Ohio then. *(Census Place: Miami, Logan, Ohio; Roll: T625_1405; Page: 6B; Enumeration District: 198; Image: 396)*. Donald O. Brown is age 26, born Pennsylvania as were his parents, is a pharmacist working in a drug store. Pauline Russell Brown, 21, was born in Ohio as was her mother; her father was born in Kansas. Otto H. Russell, 60, says he was born in Kansas, his father in Ohio, but this time he says his mother was born in Pennsylvania. He is a U.S. mail carrier, R.F.D. Gertrude Pegan Russell, 58, still says she and her father were born in Ohio and her mother in Indiana. Otto and Gertrude say they were first married at ages 22 and 20 respectively.

Donald O. Brown was the informant on his father-in-law Otto H. Russell's death certificate, and at the time, December 1936, Donald O. and Pauline Russell Brown were living in Ada, Liberty Twp., Hardin Co., Ohio.[424]

By 1938, Donoald O. and Pauline E. Russell Brown had moved to Ann Arbor, Washetenaw Co., Michigan, according to the Ann Arbor City Directory. Donald was the assistant manager at Ulrich's Bookstore.[425]

Donald O. and Pauline Russell Brown are residing in Ann Arbor, Ann Arbor Twp., Washtenaw Co., Michigan in 1940 *(Census Place: Ann Arbor, Washtenaw, Michigan; Roll: T627_1823; Page: 7B; Enumeration District: 81-23)*. Donald Brown, age 36, born Pennsylvania, is an asst. manager of a bookstore. His wife, Pauline Russell Brown, 31, and sons Robert, eight, and James, six were born in Ohio. Also in the home is Pauline's widowed mother, Gertrude Pegan Russell, 68, born Ohio. All state they were living in Ann Arbor in 1935; however, as Otto Russell's death was in 1936, Gertrude, at least, was still a resident of DeGraff, Miami Twp., Logan Co., Ohio. Their home address is 706 Arch Street.

Donald and Pauline were still residents of Ann Arbor in 1951, and Donald was now the store manager at Ulrich's.[426]

According to one of her sons, Pauline Elizabeth Russell Brown was a family historian, but he didn't know what happened to her research/notes.[427]

Sons of Pauline E. Russell and Donald Otho Brown:

+ 78 m I. **Robert Rodney[9] Brown** was born in DeGraff, Miami Twp., Logan Co., Ohio, on December 12, 1931.

+ 79 m II. **James Russell[9] Brown** was born in DeGraff, Miami Twp., Logan Co., Ohio, on June 12, 1934.

55. Milton James[8] Albershardt (*Elgie Elenor[7] Pegan, James Milton[6], John[5], Robert A.[4], Andrew[3], Andrew[2] Pagan, James[1]*) was born on August 15, 1907, in Indianapolis, Marion Co., Indiana.[227, 228] He was the son of August H. Albershardt and Elgie Elenor Pegan (29). Milton James died in Indianapolis, Marion Co., Indiana, on June 25, 1937, at age 29.[227, 228] He was buried in Crown Hill Cemetery, Indianapolis, Marion Co., Indiana.[227, 228, 428]

In 1930, Milton James Albershardt was living with his mother, Elgie Pegan Albershardt and brother Carlton, in Indianapolis, Marion Co., Indiana *(Census Place: Indianapolis, Marion, Indiana; Roll: 610; Page: 14A; Enumeration District: 82; Image: 652.0)*. Milton Albershardt, 21, single, born Indiana with his parents born in Ohio, says he is a proprietor of a radio shop. Elgie Pegan Albershardt, 57, says she was born in Ohio as were both her parents (this in incorrect; her mother, Katherine Hendrickson Pegan, was born in Indiana). She lists her occupation as laundress. Oddly, Elgie lists herself as married and was first married at age 29, but August Albershardt is enumerated as divorced. Milton's brother Arlton Albershardt is 16 years old.

Milton James married **Frances L. Keaton** on June 11, 1930, in Marion Co., Indiana.[429] They had two sons. Frances Keaton was born in French Lick, French Lick Twp., Orange Co., Indiana, on May 2, 1911.[134] Frances reached age 91 and died in Indianapolis, Marion Co., Indiana, on October 21, 2002.[135, 430] She was buried as Frances Poisel in Washington Park East Cemetery, Indianapolis, Warren Twp., Marion Co., Indiana.[430, 431]

Milton Albershardt's widow, Frances L. Keaton Albershardt, and their sons Donald and Norman are not found in the 1940 census, but they were living in Indianapolis, Marion Co., Indiana, according to one of the sons.[226] After the death of her first husband, Milton James Albershardt, Frances Keaton Albershardt married Arthur Kenneth Poisel II; she may have married him before the 1940 census.[226] She died with the name Frances Poisel.

Sons of Milton James Albershardt and Frances Keaton:

+ 80 m I. **Donald Milton**[9] **Albershardt** was born in Indianapolis, Marion Co., Indiana, on November 8, 1932.

+ 81 m II. **Norman Ray**[9] **Albershardt** was born in Indianapolis, Marion Co., Indiana, on April 3, 1934.[135, 432] He died in a facility in Zionsville, Eagle Twp., Boone Co., Indiana, on March 3, 2013.[135, 432]

56. Cathern[8] **Albershardt** (*Elgie Elenor*[7] *Pegan, James Milton*[6], *John*[5], *Robert A.*[4], *Andrew*[3], *Andrew*[2] *Pagan, James*[1]) was born on March 5, 1910, in Indianapolis, Marion Co., Indiana.[135, 229, 230] She was the daughter of August H. Albershardt and Elgie Elenor Pegan (29). She died in Hartwell, Hart Co., Georgia, on July 6, 1997, at age 87.[229, 231] Cathern was buried in Floral Hills Memory Gardens Cemetery, Tucker, DeKalb Co., Georgia.[229, 433]

Her obituary in the Atlanta Constitution on July 8, 1997 says she was born in Martinsville, Morgan County, Indiana, but her Indiana birth certificate says she was born in Indianapolis, Marion Co., Indiana. Although her birth certificate says "Catherine, she always used "Cathern" is the correct spelling of her given name.[229, 230]

In 1930, Cathern Albershardt (Secrest) is living with her father, August Albershardt, in Washington Twp., Indianapolis, Marion Co., Indiana (*Census Place: Indianapolis, Marion, Indiana; Roll: 610; Page: 10B; Enumeration District: 447; Image: 50.0*). "Catherine" is 19 years old, single, born Indiana, with her parents born in Ohio. She lists her occupation as a stenographer at a radio station. Her father August Albershardt, 59, lists himself as divorced and his occupation as veterinary surgeon. He says he was born in Ohio and his parents in Germany.

Cathern married **Wayne D. Secrest** on November 25, 1936, in Marion Co., Indiana.[434] They had one son. Wayne D. Secrest was born in Liberty Twp., Hendricks Co., Indiana, on July 9, 1909.[135, 435] Wayne D. also resided in 1984 in Stone Mountain, De Kalb Co., Georgia. He reached age 74 and died in a hospital in Atlanta, Fulton Co., Georgia, on May 27, 1984.[436] Wayne D. was buried in Floral Hills Memory Gardens Cemetery, Tucker, DeKalb Co., Georgia.[437, 438]

Wayne and Catherine Albershardt Secrest are enumerated in Indianapolis, Washington Twp., Marion Co., Indiana in 1940 (*Census Place: Indianapolis, Marion, Indiana; Roll: T627_1130; Page: 1B; Enumeration District: 96-335*). Wayne Secrest, 30, is a core maker and assembler at American Car and Foundry Co. Cathern Albershardt Secrest, listed as Catherine, is also 30 years old. Both say they were Indiana natives and were residents of Indianapolis in 1935. Their home address is 4509 Caroline Avenue.

Son of Cathern Albershardt and Wayne D. Secrest:

+ 82 m I. **Wayne Donovan**[9] **Secrest II** was born in Indianapolis, Marion Co., Indiana, on October 12, 1940.[135, 439] He was also known as

W. Donovan Secrest. Wayne Donovan died in Hartwell, Hart Co., Georgia, on April 23, 2001.[135, 439]

57. Arlton Henry[8] **Albershardt** (*Elgie Elenor*[7] *Pegan, James Milton*[6]*, John*[5]*, Robert A.*[4]*, Andrew*[3]*, Andrew*[2] *Pagan, James*[1]) was born on May 7, 1914, in Indianapolis, Marion Co., Indiana.[135, 232, 233, 234, 236] He was the son of August H. Albershardt and Elgie Elenor Pegan (29). Arlton Henry died in Indianapolis, Marion Co., Indiana, on September 20, 1987, at age 73.[135, 234, 235, 236] He was buried in Oaklawn Memorial Gardens, Fishers, Delaware Twp., Hamilton Co., Indiana.[234, 236]

Childless.

Arlton Henry married **Verna Mae Hynes** on January 1, 1937, in Marion Co., Indiana.[440] Verna Mae Hynes was born in Indianapolis, Marion Co., Indiana, on September 28, 1921.[441] Verna Mae reached age 16 and died in Indianapolis, Marion Co., Indiana, on April 3, 1938.[441] She was buried in Crown Hill Cemetery, Indianapolis, Marion Co., Indiana.[441, 442]

Verna Hynes Albershardt, only 16 years old, died of pneumonia and a bladder bacterial infection which complicated her pregnancy.[439]

Arlton Albershardt is residing with his father, August Albershardt, in 1940 in Indianapolis, Washington Twp., Marion Co., Indiana *(Census Place: Indianapolis, Marion, Indiana; Roll: T627_1131; Page: 3B; Enumeration District: 96-351)*. Arlton Albershardt, 26, who says he is single (he is a widower), is a radio repairman and proprietor of a radio shop. The head of the household is August Albershardt, age 70, a veterinary surgeon who says he is a widower. Both were born in Indiana and say they were living in Indianapolis in 1935. Their address is 4157 College Avenue.

Arlton Henry Albershardt married **Helen Mary McAllister** on August 31, 1940, in Marion Co., Indiana.[443] Helen Mary McAllister was born in Indianapolis, Marion Co., Indiana, on February 12, 1916.[135] Helen Mary reached age 95 and died in Indianapolis, Marion Co., Indiana, on February 21, 2011.[135] She was buried in Oaklawn Memorial Gardens, Fishers, Delaware Twp., Hamilton Co., Indiana.[444]

58. Donald Abbott[8] **Pegan** (*Edward Ephraim*[7]*, John Andrew*[6]*, John*[5]*, Robert A.*[4]*, Andrew*[3]*, Andrew*[2] *Pagan, James*[1]) was born on May 11, 1908, in Chicago, Cook Co., Illinois?[135, 267] He was the son of Edward Ephraim Pegan (36) and Maud Lillian Abbott. Donald Abbott died in San Diego, San Diego Co., California, on April 9, 1987, at age 78.[267] He was cremated.[100, 445]

Although other documentation and famly records indicate that Donald Abbott Pegan was born in Chicago, Cook Co., Illinois, his birth record is not listed in the Cook County, Illinois Genealogy database, which has birth records from 1875 to 1942.

Donald Abbott Pegan is not found in the 1930 census, but his great-granddaughter, Tamera Brush of Albuquerque, New Mexico, says Donald was living in Chicago, Cook Co., Illinois.[100]

Donald Abbott married **Elizabeth Bertha Steinbrenner** on February 25, 1937, in Chicago, Cook Co., Illinois.[100] They had two daughters. Elizabeth Bertha Steinbrenner was born in Milwaukee, Milwaukee Co., Wisconsin, on July 25, 1918.[135, 446, 447] She was also known as **Betty**. Elizabeth Bertha reached age 74 and died in El Cajon, San Diego Co., California, on July 1, 1993.[443, 447] She was cremated.[100, 447]

However, like his Donald A. Pegan's birth record, no listing for Donald and Elizabeth's marriage is found in the Cook County, Illinois Genealogy database, which has marriage records from 1872-1967.

In 1940, Donald A. Pegan is enumerated in Chicago, Cook Co., Illinois *(Census Place: Chicago, Cook, Illinois; Roll: T627_1014; Page: 5B; Enumeration District: 103-2956)*. Donald A. Pegan, age 32, born Illinois, lists his occupation as cab driver. His wife, Elizabeth Steinbrenner Pegan, 21, born Wisconsin, says she is a waitress. They have a daughter, Gail, who is one year old and born in Illinois. Living with them is Donald's mother, Maud Abbott Pegan, 58, born Indiana, who also says she is a cab driver. All in the home, which is at 860 Fletcher Street, say they were living in Chicago in 1935.

By 1947 Donald Abbott Pegan and his family, along with his mother, Maud Lilian Abbott Pegan, are residing in San Diego, San Diego Co., California.[264]

Daughters of Donald Abbott Pegan and Elizabeth Bertha Steinbrenner:

+ 83 f I. **Gail Elizabeth[9] Pegan** was born in Chicago, Cook Co., Illinois, on July 6, 1938.[100]

+ 84 f II. **Roberta Jean[9] Pegan** was born in Chicago, Cook Co., Illinois, on June 24, 1940.[100, 135, 448, 449] She was also known as **Berta**. Roberta Jean died in Golden Valley, Mohave Co., Arizona, on August 2, 2002.[100, 135, 448, 449]

9th Generation

59. Henry Crume[9] **Gage** (*Mamie Edna*[8] *Pegan, Pliny Moses Crume*[7]*, Emmanuel*[6]*, John*[5]*, Robert A.*[4]*, Andrew*[3]*, Andrew*[2] *Pagan, James*[1]) was born on May 14, 1907, in Chicago, Cook Co., Illinois.[135, 280, 281, 282] He was the son of Edward Ballard Gage and Mamie Edna Pegan (39). He died in Denver, Denver Co., Colorado, on February 10, 1980, at age 72.[282]

Henry Crume Gage's parents, Edward Ballard and Mamie Edna Pegan Gage, moved from Racine, Wisconsin to Thompson Falls, Thompson Twp., Sanders Co., Montana around 1917 because of Henry's health, said to have been frail when he was a child.[136]

Henry Crume married **Floretta May Gentry** on August 9, 1931, in Denver Co., Colorado.[450] They had two children. Floretta May Gentry was born in Evansville, Vanderburgh Co., Indiana, on November 12, 1907.[135, 451] Floretta May reached age 84 and died in Denver, Denver Co., Colorado, on December 19, 1991.[135, 451]

Henry Crume Gage is enumerated in 1940 in Denver, Denver Co., Colorado *(Census Place: Denver, Denver, Colorado; Roll: T627_487; Page: 7B; Enumeration District: 16-113)*. In the home at 801 South Emerson are Henry Gage, age 32, born Illinois, who is a dentist; his wife, Floretta Gentry Gage, also 32, born Indiana, and their children Henrietta, three, and Ronald, five months, both born in Colorado. Henry and Floretta say they were both living in Callahan, El Paso Co., Colorado in 1935. Also in the home is a lodger, Virginia Gaddy, 25, single, born Missouri, who is a dental secretary, perhaps working for Henry Crume Gage. Their home address is 801 South Emerson.

After Henry C. Gage died, Floretta Gentry Gage married a Mr. King abaout 1982.[136, 451]

Children of Henry Crume Gage and Floretta May Gentry:

+ 85 f I. **Henrietta June**[10] **Gage** was born in Callahan, El Paso Co., Colorado, on October 2, 1936.

+ 86 m II. **Ronald Henry**[10] **Gage** was born in Denver, Denver Co., Colorado, on November 2, 1939.

60. Gwynn Ballard[9] **Gage** (*Mamie Edna*[8] *Pegan, Pliny Moses Crume*[7]*, Emmanuel*[6]*, John*[5]*, Robert A.*[4]*, Andrew*[3]*, Andrew*[2] *Pagan, James*[1]) was born on April 7, 1909, in Burlington Twp., Racine Co., Wisconsin.[136, 283] He was the son of Edward Ballard Gage and Mamie Edna Pegan (39). Gwynn Ballard died in Portland, Multnomah Co., Oregon, on June 12, 1958, at age 49.[136, 284] He was buried in Skyline Memorial Gardens, Portland, Multnomah Co., Oregon.[136, 283]

Gwynn Gage is not found in the 1940 census.

Gwynn Ballard Gage married a divorcee with two sons by her first marriage, **Inez Beatrice Lindseth** Odegard before 1943. Gwynn and Inez had two sons. Inez Beatrice Lindseth was born in Farmington, Teton Co., Montana, on May 22, 1907.[452, 453, 454] Inez Beatrice reached age 88 and died in Forest Grove, Washington Co., Oregon, on April 13, 1996.[452, 453, 454] She was buried in Skyline Memorial Gardens, Portland, Multnomah Co., Oregon.[452, 453] Inez remarried to a Glenn Harold Olson after Gwynn Gage died and is buried as Inez Beatrice Olson.[136, 452, 454, 455]

Gwynn Ballard Gage and Inez Beatrice Lindseth had two sons, including:

+ 87 m I. **Robert R.**[10] **Gage** was born in St. Helens, Columbia Co., Oregon, on June 16, 1943.[456, 457] He died in Woodburn, Marion Co., Oregon, on December 20, 2005.[456, 457]

61. Frances Genevieve[9] **Michael** (*Allie Belle*[8] *Cissel, Florence Genevieve*[7] *Pegan, Emmanuel*[6]*, John*[5]*, Robert A.*[4]*, Andrew*[3]*, Andrew*[2] *Pagan, James*[1]) was born on February 9, 1917, in Harper or Sedgwick Co., Kansas.[135, 308, 309] She was also known as **Genevieve**. She was the daughter of Bennett Franklin Michael and Allie Belle Cissel (41). She died in Wichita, Sedgwick Co., Kansas, on March 30, 1996, at age

79.[308, 309] Frances Genevieve was buried in Wichita Park Cemetery & Mausoleum, Wichita, Sedgwick Co., Kansas.[308]

Frances Genevieve Michael LeBlond often used her middle name as her preferred given name.

Frances Genevieve Michael is found in 1940 in Wichita, Sedgwick Co., Kansas *(Census Place: Wichita, Sedgwick, Kansas; Roll: T627_1273; Page: 8B; Enumeration District: 107-57A)*. Frances G. Michael is a lodger in the home of Ivy Myrtle Burditt at 924 North Broadway. Frances G. Michael, age 23, single, is a secretary at a fire insurance company. She says she was born in Kansas and living in Wichita in 1935.

Frances Genevieve married **Jack Donald LeBlond** on April 11, 1941, in Sedgwick Co., Kansas.[458] They had three children. Jack Donald LeBlond was born in Wichita, Sedgwick Co., Kansas, on February 26, 1919.[135, 459] Jack Donald reached age 61 and died in Wichita, Sedgwick Co., Kansas, on October 13, 1980.[459, 460] He was buried in Wichita Park Cemetery & Mausoleum, Wichita, Sedgwick Co., Kansas.[459]

After working in a Wichita lamp factory for several years, Jack Donald Leblond became the manager of the Old Heidelberg Inn in that city in 1947. Two years later, he opened a liquor store in Wichita, which he owned for the rest of his life. He was an expert golfer who participated in and won many amateur tournaments. He was elected president of the Wichita Golf Association in 1954.[460]

Frances Genevieve Michael LeBlond worked as a real estate agent after 1940.[310]

Frances Genevieve Michael and Jack Donald LeBlond had three children, including:

+ 88   f   III.   **Daughter LeBlond** was born in Wichita, Sedgwick Co., Kansas.

62. Kathryn Louise⁹ Mason (*Laurence Victor⁸, Charles Edwin⁷, Mary Elizabeth⁶ Pegan, John⁵, Robert A.⁴, Andrew³, Andrew² Pagan, James¹*) was born on January 1, 1905, in Lake Twp., Logan Co., Ohio.[135, 322, 323] She was the daughter of Laurence Victor Mason (44) and Anna Mae Evans. Kathryn Louise died in Bradenton, Manatee Co., Florida, on February 19, 1986, at age 81.[323] She was buried in Manasota Memorial Park Cemetery, Bradenton, Manatee Co., Florida.[461]

Kathryn Louise married **William Pascale Aldrich** on September 5, 1925, in Manatee Co., Florida.[462] They had one son. William Pascale Aldrich was born in Centralia, Illinois, on November 7, 1903.[463, 464] William Pascale reached age 82 and died in Bradenton, Manatee Co., Florida, on February 19, 1986.[463, 464] He was buried in Manasota Memorial Park Cemetery, Bradenton, Manatee Co., Florida.[465] He was the son of William Aldrich and Myrtle Morseman.

William P. and Kathryn Mason Aldrich are enumberated in Marion, Marion Twp., Marion Co., Ohio in 1930 *(Census Place: Marion, Marion, Ohio; Roll: 1848; Page: 2B; Enumeration District: 22; Image: 6.0)*. In the household are William P. Aldrich, age 26, born Illinois as were his parents, a presser at a dry cleaners; his wife, Kathryn Mason Aldrich, 25, born Ohio as were her parents, and their son William II, age two years and six months, born in Ohio.

In 1940, William and Kathryn Mason Aldrich are found in Bradenton, Manatee Co., Florida *(Census Place: Bradenton, Manatee, Florida; Roll: T627_599; Page: 1B; Enumeration District: 41-17)*. William P. Aldrich, age 36, born Illinois, a is still a presser at a dry cleaners. With him are Kathryn Mason Aldrich, 35, and son William L. Aldrich II, 12, both born in Ohio. The family states that they were living in Marion, Ohio in 1935. Their home address in Bradenton is 1405 12th Avenue.

Kathryn Mason Aldrich's brother, Donald Earl Mason, married Doris Martha Aldrich Mason, the sister of Kathryn's husband, William Pascale Aldrich.

(Centralia, Illinois is located at the junction of four Illinois counties.)

Son of Kathryn Louise Mason and William Pascale Aldrich:

+ 89   m   I.   **William Lawrence¹⁰ Aldrich II** was born in Marion, Marion Twp., Marion Co., Ohio, on February 10,

1928.[135, 466 467] He died in Bradenton, Manatee Co., Florida, on June 7, 2005.[135, 466, 467]

63. Donald Earl[9] Mason (*Laurence Victor[8], Charles Edwin[7], Mary Elizabeth[6] Pegan, John[5], Robert A.[4], Andrew[3], Andrew[2] Pagan, James[1]*) was born on September 9, 1907, in Lake Twp., Logan Co., Ohio. [135, 326] He was the son of Laurence Victor Mason (44) and Anna Mae Evans. Donald Earl was living in August 1994 in Bradenton, Manatee Co., Florida. He died in West Plains, Howell Twp., Howell Co., Missouri, on August 22, 1994, at age 86.[135, 327] Donald Earl was buried in Manasota Memorial Park Cemetery, Bradenton, Manatee Co., Florida.[468, 469]

Donald Earl married **Doris Martha Aldrich** about 1929. They had one daughter. Doris Martha Aldrich was born in Centralia, Illinois, on April 10, 1908.[135, 470] Doris Martha reached age 83 and died in Bradenton, Manatee Co., Florida, on January 6, 1992.[470, 471] She was buried in Manasota Memorial Park Cemetery, Bradenton, Manatee Co., Florida. [471, 472] She was the daughter of William Aldrich and Myrtle Morseman.

Donald E. Mason is enumerated in Alliance, Lexington Twp., Stark Co., Ohio in 1930 *(Census Place: Alliance, Stark, Ohio; Roll: 1871; Page: 17B; Enumeration District: 77; Image: 963.0)*. In the home are Donald E. Mason, 22, born Ohio as were his parents, and his wife, Doris Aldrich Mason, also 22, born Illinois as were her parents. The couple have been married one year, as they both say their first marriage was at age 21.

In 1940, Donald E. Mason, listed as "D.E." Mason, is living in Greensboro, Guilford Co., North Carolina *(Census Place: Greensboro, Guilford, North Carolina; Roll: T627_2920; Page: 1A; Enumeration District: 41-53)*. Donald Mason, age 32, born Ohio, is an accountant at a hosiery manufacturer. His wife, Doris Aldrich Mason, 31, born Illinois, is a bookkeeper at a retail jewelry store. They say they were living in Greensboro in 1935, and their house address is 512 Ashland Avenue.

Donald Earl Mason died while visiting friends in West Plains, Howell Co., Missouri.[327]

Donald Earl Mason's sister Kathryn Mason Aldrich married William Pascale Aldrich, the brother of Donald's wife Doris Martha Aldrich Mason.

Daughter of Donald Earl Mason and Doris Martha Aldrich:

+ 90 f I. **Dorothy Ann[10] Mason** was born in Alliance, Lexington Twp., Stark Co., Ohio, on April 25, 1930.[473] She died in Alliance, Lexington Twp., Stark Co., Ohio, on April 25, 1930.[473]

64. Mary Jane[9] Mason (*Paul Edwin[8], Charles Edwin[7], Mary Elizabeth[6] Pegan, John[5], Robert A.[4], Andrew[3], Andrew[2] Pagan, James[1]*) was born on January 26, 1922, in Lake Twp., Logan Co., Ohio.[337, 338] She was the daughter of Paul Edwin Mason (46) and Frances Louise Moore. Mary Jane died in Bellefontaine, Lake Twp., Logan Co., Ohio, on November 20, 1993, at age 71.[338] She was buried in Huntsville Cemetery, McArthur Twp., Logan Co., Ohio.[474]

Mary Jane married **Thomas J. Ewing** on August 31, 1942, in Monroe Co., Michigan.[475] They had four children. Thomas J. Ewing was born in Harrison Twp., Logan Co., Ohio, on June 11, 1922.[135, 476, 477] Thomas J. reached age 82 and died in Lakeview, Stokes Twp., Logan Co., Ohio, on April 6, 2005.[135, 476, 477, 478] He was buried in Huntsville Cemetery, McArthur Twp., Logan Co., Ohio.[478, 479]

Mary Jane Mason and Thomas J. Ewing had four children, including:

+ 91 m III. **Michael Leslie Ewing** was born in Bellefontaine, Lake Twp., Logan Co., Ohio, on February 5, 1949.[480] He died in Bellefontaine, Lake Twp., Logan Co., Ohio, on February 6, 1949.[480]

65. Robert Edwin[9] Mason (*Paul Edwin[8], Charles Edwin[7], Mary Elizabeth[6] Pegan, John[5], Robert A.[4], Andrew[3], Andrew[2] Pagan, James[1]*) was born on March 7, 1924, in Lake Twp., Logan Co., Ohio.[134, 339, 340] He was the son of Paul Edwin

Mason (46) and Frances Louise Moore. Robert Edwin died in Granville, Granville Twp., Licking Co., Ohio, on September 4, 2005, at age 81.[135, 340, 341] He was buried in Fairview Memorial Park, Delaware, Delaware Twp., Delaware Co., Ohio.[481, 482]

Robert Edwin married **Nancy Elisabeth Tarr** on December 26, 1950, in Allen Co., Ohio.[483] They divorced in El Dorado Co., California about 1971.[484] They had four children. Nancy Elisabeth Tarr was born in Toledo, Lucas Co., Ohio, on March 16, 1928.[485]

Robert Edwin Mason married **Jean L. Neill** Newschulz in 1992.[482] Jean L. Neill was born on September 3, 1924.

Robert E. Mason worked as a teacher and coach in Ohio and California before becoming a guidance counselor in 1970 in Granville, Ohio.[482]

66. **Charles Stephen**[9] **Mason** (*Paul Edwin*[8], *Charles Edwin*[7], *Mary Elizabeth*[6] *Pegan, John*[5], *Robert A.*[4], *Andrew*[3], *Andrew*[2] *Pagan, James*[1]) was born on October 17, 1926, in Bellefontaine, Lake Twp., Logan Co., Ohio.[342] He was the son of Paul Edwin Mason (46) and Frances Louise Moore.

Charles Stephen married **Mary Catherine Vanica** on October 16, 1950, in Logan Co., Ohio.[486] They had one daughter. Mary Catherine Vanica was born in Bellefontaine, Lake Twp., Logan Co., Ohio, on October 20, 1930.[487] She is also known as **Mary Kay**.

67. **Oliver Gordon**[9] **Young** (*Harold Mason*[8], *Alta Dell*[7] *Mason, Mary Elizabeth*[6] *Pegan, John*[5], *Robert A.*[4], *Andrew*[3], *Andrew*[2] *Pagan, James*[1]) was born on August 16, 1927, in Banna, Yunnan Province, China.[344, 355, 356] He was also known as **Gordon or O. Gordon**. He was the son of Harold Mason Young (49) and Ruth Saada Pinkerton. He also resided in 1953 in Thailand. Oliver Gordon was living in 2011 in San Luis Obispo, San Luis Obispo Co., California. He died in Bella Vista, Shasta Co., California, on August 8, 2016, at age 88.[357]

Oliver Gordon married **Margueriete Francia Karoleski** on June 2, 1950, in Los Angeles Co., California.[488] They had four daughters. Margueriete Francia Karoleski was born in Chicago, Cook Co., Illinois, on August 4, 1930.[135, 489] She was also known as **Peggy**. Margueriete Francia reached age 79 and died in San Luis Obispo, San Luis Obispo Co., California, on March 7, 2010.[135, 489] She was buried in Los Osos Memorial Park Cemetery, Los Osos, San Luis Obispo Co., California.[490]

After he graduated from college in 1953, Oliver Gordon Young, like his Young grandparents and parents, lived in Southeast Asia. From 1953 until the end of the Vietnam War, he worked for the CIA, U.S. Foreign Service as an aid worker and wildlife hunter, primarily in Thailand and Laos. "Gordon" also helped his father, Harold Mason Young, at the Chaing Mai Zoo in Chaing Mai, Thailand. He was fluent in many languages of the region. Like other Youngs, has also authored books on the region, including *The Hill Tribes of Northern Thailand*, an ethnological study, *Journey from Banna: My Life and Times*, an autobiography, and other tomes on Southeast Asian culture and peoples. Born in Chicago and raised in Vermont and California, Margueriete "Peggy" Karoleski Young, learned Thai and taught English at Thai schools and American schools in Southeast Asia.[177, 357, 489, 491, 492]

Oliver Gordon Young and Margueriete Francia Karoleski had four daughters, including:

+ 92 f II. **Daughter Young** was born in Chaing Mai, Thailand.

68. **Helen Elizabeth**[9] **Young** (*Harold Mason*[8], *Alta Dell*[7] *Mason, Mary Elizabeth*[6] *Pegan, John*[5], *Robert A.*[4], *Andrew*[3], *Andrew*[2] *Pagan, James*[1]) was born on January 3, 1929, in Kengtung Ess, Shan State, Burma (now Myanmar).[344, 358] She was the daughter of Harold Mason Young (49) and Ruth Saada Pinkerton.

Helen Elizabeth married **James Jacob Suter** on June 18, 1953, in Ventura Co., California.[493] They had three children. James Jacob Suter was born in Globe, Gila Co., Arizona, on January 13, 1926.[135, 494] James Jacob reached age 81 and died in Walnut Creek, Contra Costa Co., California, on May 3, 2007.[135, 494]

Helen Elizabeth Young and James Jacob Suter had three children, including:

+ 93 f I. **Kathleen Helen**[10] **Suter** was born in Oxnard, Ventura Co., California, on November 2, 1954.[135, 495, 496] She died in Sacramento, Sacramento Co., California, on May 22, 2011.[135, 496]

+ 94 m II. **Michael James Suter** was born in Oxnard, Ventura Co., California, on August 27, 1956.[497, 498] He died in Coral Gables, Dade Co., Florida, on August 14, 2012.[498]

69. William Marcus[9] **Young II** (*Harold Mason*[8], *Alta Dell*[7] *Mason, Mary Elizabeth*[6] *Pegan, John*[5], *Robert A.*[4], *Andrew*[3], *Andrew*[2] *Pagan, James*[1]) was born on October 28, 1934, in Berkeley, Alameda Co., California.[135, 344, 359] He was the son of Harold Mason Young (49) and Ruth Saada Pinkerton. William Marcus died in Chaing Mai, Thailand, on April 1, 2011, at age 76.[135, 185, 187, 360, 361] He was buried in Ban Den Chaing Mai Foreign Cemetery, Chaing Mai, Thailand.[341]

According to California birth records, William Marcus Young was born in Berkeley, Alameda Co., California, not in Burma as often stated, even in some of his obituaries.[360]

William Marcus Young II, like so many of his family members, lived and labored in Southeast Asia. He was named for his grandfather, William Marcus Young, a noted Baptist missionary in Burma (now Myanmar). William Marcus Young II's father, Harold Mason Young, continued his own father's work in the region; he also became a noted naturalist, founding Thailand's leading zoo, the Chaing Mai Zoo in Chaing Mai, the country's second-largest city. Harold Mason Young also worked for the CIA in China and Thailand during the Communist revolution in China in the late 1940s-early 1950s. William Marcus Young II's long family history and religious, zoologic, and other activities in the region built trust among both the native peoples and the American and British governments alike. His family's reputation, and his own vast knowledge and understanding of the tribal cultures and languages of the area, enabled him to form relationships and move fluidly throughout Southeast Asia. He was the ideal spy, and, from the references to him in books and other articles about his life, he was quite good at his job.

According to his obituary in *The Guardian,* one of England's major newspapers, William Marcus Young II spent most of his childhood and early adulthood in Burma and Thailand, and became fluent in various Southeast Asian and Chinese dialects. He was living in Chaing Mai, Thailand when he was approached by the the CIA in the late 1950s, before the Vietnam War. From then on, William Marcus Young II actively recruited Vietnamese and Laotian contacts to fight the nationalist movements and communist activity in those countries. In one of his obituaries, William Marcus Young was described by the noted historian Alfred McCoy, an expert on the CIA in Southeast Asia, as "one of the most effective agents ever". In addition, Young's biographer, David Lawitts, says in the obituary that Young was the CIA's "greatest asset" because he could speak all the local tongues—"Shan, Lahu, Lao, Thai and even a smattering of Yunnan Chinese."[360, 499]

In Luang Nam Tha in northern Laos in 1962, William Marcus Young II managed the construction of airstrips for Air America, the CIA airline that flew in supplies to support native Laotians against the Pathet Lao, the communist forces waging a civil war against the U.S-backed Royal Lao regime. The Laotians were attempting to stop supplies on the Ho Chi Mnh trail headed for the communist rebels. The head of the mercenary army in Laos, Vang Pao, a notorious opium warlord, and his Hmong troops were trained by W.M. Young, along with soldiers from the Lahu and Yao tribes. This CIA effort, through Young, was to offset the need for American troop involvement in Laos, technically a neutral country, yet still conduct a U.S.-guided undercover war against the Pathet Lao, the country's Communist forces.[499] By 1964, McCoy, in another obituary, states that William Young was in "command of all paramilitary operations" in northern Laos.[361]

In particular, William M. Young II is credited with recommending a Laotian village, Long Cheng, as the ideal place to build a small airstrip to conduct the CIA's clandestine operations in that country. Long Cheng grew from that one airstrip into what has been described as one of the largest U.S. military bases in any foreign country—one that was known, however, to only the CIA and the Pentagon. As one of the leaders at this base, Young has also been implicated in the CIA's alleged controversial involvement in the opium trade. One of his obituaries implies that Young may have been instrumental in shipping drugs out of Long Cheng for the Laotian drug lords, and using the money they paid him for this to purchase weapons to arm the Laotian tribes against Communist incursion.[361]

W.M. Young II also ran spy missions into China from Burma. He established three critical radio outposts within the Burmese Shan states. Most importantly, he operated a training camp there from which thousands of Burmese and other soldiers were sent into the Yunnan province of China to ward off Chinese incursion into Vietnam. Throughout the war, Young II was involved in numerous clashes and ambushes.

However, during the latter years of the Vietnam War, Young II became increasingly upset by CIA aerial bombings in Vietnam, and saw them as only hurting the poor and struggling Vietnamese and not Ho Chi Minh's army. After heated arguments with his CIA superiors, the agency fired him.

William Marcus Young II went back to Chaing Mai, Thailand and owned several businesses, including a guesthouse/inn, an orchard and a small jewelry/gem-trading outlet. He did occasional work for the CIA and the U.S. government, such as serving as a security advisor in Sudan for an oil company and as an advisor on the northern Burmese drug trade for the U.S. Drug Enforcement Administration. But, for the most part, his years of spying and intrigue were over.[360, 361, 499, 500]

William Marcus Young II married and divorced once, with one daughter. However, he had liaisons with at least two Thai women that produced five other children. William Marcus Young, sick with emphysema and other illnesses, took his own life on April 1, 2011 in Chaing Mai. According to his son, Jerrick Young, William is buried in the Ban Den Chaing Mai Foreign Cemetery there.[341 500]

His obituaries say William was despondent because, although he was paid $100,000 by a major film studio for the rights to his life story, the movie project never materialized. He was survived by five children.[360, 361, 499, 500]

William Marcus Young II married **Emilee Star Dailey**.[343] They had one daughter. Emilee Star Dailey was born in Missouri? in 1935.

William Marcus Young II had a relationship with **Thai Woman One**.[343]

William Marcus Young II had a relationship with **Thai Woman Two**.[343]

William Marcus Young II and Thai Woman Two had children, including:

+ 95 f I. **Daughter Young** was born in 1978. She died in 1983.[501]

70. Lael Marcus[9] **Young** (*Marcus Vincent*[8], *Alta Dell*[7] *Mason, Mary Elizabeth*[6] *Pegan, John*[5], *Robert A.*[4], *Andrew*[3], *Andrew*[2] *Pagan, James*[1]) was born on March 12, 1936, in Kengtung Ess, Shan State, Burma (now Myanmar).[135, 372, 373, 374] He was the son of Marcus Vincent Young (50) and Vera Gibbs. Lael Marcus died in Mentone, San Bernardino Co., California, on May 28, 1996, at age 60.[135, 372, 374, 375] He was buried in Montecito Memorial Park Cemetery, Colton, San Bernardino Co., California.[502, 503]

Never married.

Lael Marcus Young was a mathematics prodigy. He graduated from University of Redlands summa cum laude, and earned a PhD in mathematics from Stanford University in 1961 when he was 25 years old. He then joined the faculty at Harvard University before becoming a professor at Cal State Northridge.[375, 504, 505]

71. Philip Gibbs[9] **Young** (*Marcus Vincent*[8], *Alta Dell*[7] *Mason, Mary Elizabeth*[6] *Pegan, John*[5], *Robert A.*[4], *Andrew*[3], *Andrew*[2] *Pagan, James*[1]) was born on February 3, 1938, in Kengtung Ess, Shan State, Burma (now Myanmar).[376] He was the son of Marcus Vincent Young (50) and Vera Gibbs.

Philip Gibbs Young, M.D. was born in Kengung, Shan State, Burma, near the border with China.

When he was four years old, he and his mother and siblings escaped the Japanese invasion of Burma. Then the Marcus Young family boarded a ship to New York, traveling around Africa's Cape of Good Hope and across the Atlantic Ocean despite German submarine activity during WWII. After the war, his family returned to Shan State, Burma, and remained there for nearly a year after the Communists took control of China in 1949. Once again, the family had to flee and go to America, this time from internal strife in Burma among three groups trying to wrest control: the Communists and the Peoples Volunteer Organization (PVO or White Band), the Karen tribesmen, and the Burmese army.[177, 366, 369]

After graduating from the University of Nebraska School of Medicine, graduating in 1963, Philip joined the Navy. He served as a physician on a ship off the coast of Vietnam during the Vietnam War's early years. After his discharge from the Navy and a subsequent surgical residency, he went to the island of Palawn in the Phillipines to establish a mission hospital. In 1977, he returned to the U.S, to began studying and researching the thyroid gland, and he has published a book on his findings.[177, 506]

He married **Ruth Udy**. They have one son. Ruth Udy was born on November 25, 1938.

72. **Daughter⁹ Young** (*Marcus Vincent⁸, Alta Dell⁷ Mason, Mary Elizabeth⁶ Pegan, John⁵, Robert A.⁴, Andrew³, Andrew² Pagan, James¹*) was born in Taunggyi, Shan State, Burma (now Myanmar).[377] She is the daughter of Marcus Vincent Young (50) and Vera Gibbs.

She married **Fred Allen Widlund**. They had three daughters. Fred Allen Widlund was born in Los Angeles, Los Angeles Co., California, on April 15, 1940.[507, 508] He reached age 72 and died in Baker City, Baker Co., Oregon, on June 21, 2012.[508]

Fred Allen Widlund spent 35 years in law enforcement, first as a policeman for the Redlands, San Bernardino Co., California police department, and then as a fraud investigator for San Bernardino County, California.[503]

73. **John Gregory⁹ Mantle** (*Mildred Elizabeth⁸ Mason, John Pegan⁷, Mary Elizabeth⁶ Pegan, John⁵, Robert A.⁴, Andrew³, Andrew² Pagan, James¹*) was born on October 3, 1921, in Indianapolis, Center Twp., Marion Co., Indiana.[135, 398, 399, 400] He was the son of Launcelot Alfred Mantle and Mildred Elizabeth Mason (52). John Gregory lived in 1950 in Santa Rosa, Sonoma Co., California. He died in Thousand Oaks, Ventura Co., California, on December 15, 1988, at age 67.[135, 398, 399, 401] Like his father Lance, John Gregory was cremated and his ashes scattered in the Pacific Ocean at Pt. Fermin, Los Angeles Co., California.[509]

He married **Kay Joanne Storm** in 1947.[510] They had five children. Kay Joanne Storm was born in Loveland, Denver Co., Colorado, on July 31, 1929.[510] She reached age 86 and died in Thousand Oaks, Ventura Co., California, on December 15, 2015.[510] After John graduated from Purdue University in West Lafayette, Indiana, John and Kay Storm Mantle moved to California, eventually settling in Thousand Oaks, Ventura Co., California. John was an engineer at Rockwell International. Kay was a quilter, winning a blue ribbon at the Ventura County Fair.[509, 510]

John Gregory Mantle and Kay Joanne Storm had five children, including:

+ 96 f I. **Catherine Louise¹⁰ Mantle** was born in Lafayette, Fairfield Twp., Tippecanoe Co., Indiana, on April 1, 1948.[135, 511, 512, 513] She died in West Linn, Clackamas Co., Oregon, on October 6, 2000.[135, 511, 512, 513]

+ 97 f III. **Sandra Kay Mantle** was born in Livermore, Alameda Co., California, on December 13, 1953.[514, 515] She died in Grants Pass, Josephine Co., Oregon, on November 21, 1995.[514, 515]

74. **Norma Louise⁹ Mantle** (*Mildred Elizabeth⁸ Mason, John Pegan⁷, Mary Elizabeth⁶ Pegan, John⁵, Robert A.⁴, Andrew³, Andrew² Pagan, James¹*) was born on May 19, 1923, in Obert, Cedar Co., Nebraska.[135, 402, 403, 404] She is the daughter of Launcelot Alfred Mantle and Mildred Elizabeth Mason (52). Norma Louise died in Harrisonburg, Rockingham

Co., Virginia, on May 27, 2005, at age 82.[135, 403, 404] She was cremated and her cremains buried in Arlington National Cemetery, Arlington, Virginia.[516]

Norma Louise married **William Gray Park** on August 30, 1946.[517] They had four children. William Gray Park was born in Abbott, Hill Co., Texas, on October 30, 1923.[135, 517] William Gray reached age 89 and died in Harrisonburg, Rockingham Co., Virginia, on November 28, 2012.[135, 517] He was cremated and his cremains buried in Arlington National Cemetery, Arlington, Virginia.[517, 518]

Norma Louise Mantle and William Gray Park had four children, including:

+ 98 m II.   **Richard Dawson Park** was born in Golden, Jefferson Co., Colorado, on June 25, 1949.[519] He was also known as **Dick**. Richard Dawson died in a hospital in Boise, Ada Co., Idaho, on July 31, 2015.[519]

+ 99 f III. **Patricia Louise Park** was born in Fort Sill, Lawton, Commanche Co., Oklahoma, on October 31, 1951.[135, 520] She died in a hospital in Neptune, Neptune Twp., Monmouth Co., New Jersey, on June 15, 1999.[135, 520]

75. Margaret Jean[9] **Mantle** (*Mildred Elizabeth*[8] *Mason, John Pegan*[7]*, Mary Elizabeth*[6] *Pegan, John*[5]*, Robert A.*[4]*, Andrew*[3]*, Andrew*[2] *Pagan, James*[1]) was born on November 29, 1924 in Indiana, Indiana Twp., Allegheny Co., Pennsylvania? She is also known as **Peg**. She was the daughter of Launcelot Alfred Mantle and Mildred Elizabeth Mason (52).

Margaret Jean Mantle married **Joe L. Vongundy** about 1949. They divorced. They had three children. Joe L. Vongundy was born in Pueblo, Pueblo Co., Colorado, on August 16, 1922.[521] He resided in 2014 in Green Valley, Pima Co., Arizona. Joe L. reached age 92 and died in Tuscon, Pima Co., Arizona, on January 10, 2015.[522]

Margaret Jean Mantle Vongundy married **Meredith Ray Hodges** before 1974. They divorced. They had one son. Meredith Ray Hodges was born in Precinct 4, Hardeman Co., Texas, on October 9, 1921.[135] He was also known as **Jack**. Meredith Ray reached age 86 and died in Kingsland, Llano Co., Texas, on February 21, 2008.[135, 523]

Margaret Jean Mantle Vongundy Hodges married **Carl Lee Ingraham** on October 24, 1975, in Ventura Co., California.[524] They divorced. Carl Lee Ingraham was born in Orange Co., California, on September 21, 1921.[525] Carl Lee reached age 73 and died in Ojai, Ventura Co., California, on June 14, 1995.[135]

Margaret Jean Mantle Vongundy Hodges Ingraham married **Kenwood Moore Jackson** on July 20, 1984, in Las Vegas, Clark Co., Nevada. They divorced. Kenwood Moore Jackson was born in Arlington, Alexandria Co., Virginia, on September 10, 1919.[135, 526, 527] They divorced. Kenwood Moore reached age 80 and died in Albuquerque, Bernalillo Co., New Mexico, on March 24, 2000.[135] He was cremated and his cremains buried in Cathedral Church of Saint John Columbarium.[528]

Margaret Jean Mantle and Joe L. Vongundy had three children, including:

+ 100 m I.   **Mark Lane**[10] **Vongundy** was born in Denver, Denver Co., Colorado, on October 29, 1950.[135, 529] He died in Albuquerque, Bernalillo Co., New Mexico, on July 5, 1995.[135, 529]

76. Robert Lee[9] **Honeycutt** (*Alice Irene*[8] *Mason, John Pegan*[7]*, Mary Elizabeth*[6] *Pegan, John*[5]*, Robert A.*[4]*, Andrew*[3]*, Andrew*[2] *Pagan, James*[1]) was born on June 3, 1929, in Indianapolis, Center Twp., Marion Co., Indiana.[416, 417] He was the son of Horace Russell Honeycutt and Alice Irene Mason (53). He died in Gainesville, Alachua Co., Florida, on November 26, 1966, at age 37.[417, 418] Robert Lee was buried in Hillcrest Cemetery, Gainesville, Alachua Co., Florida.[418, 530]

Robert Lee Honeycutt married **Florida Arnetta Bronson** in Georgia? They divorced. They had three children. Florida Arnetta Bronson was born in Ocala, Marion Co., Florida, on April 16, 1934. She is also known as **Arnetta**.

Robert Lee married **Joan Kartzmark** on September 2, 1961, in Alachua Co., Florida.[531, 532] They had two sons. Joan Kartzmark was born in Atlantic City, Atlantic Co., New Jersey, on December 7, 1935.

According to his obituary, Robert Lee Honeycutt was an accountant who worked in the Power, Bower & Co. accounting firm in Orlando, Orange Co., Florida in 1957.[533] before owning his own firm in Holly Hill, Volusia Co., Florida by 1960. He removed to Gainesville, Alachua Co., Florida in 1961 to work for the Florida College of Engineering before becoming comptroller for the city of Gainesville in January 1964.[418]

77. **Donald James^9 Honeycutt** (*Alice Irene^8 Mason, John Pegan^7, Mary Elizabeth^6 Pegan, John^5, Robert A.^{4}, Andrew^3, Andrew^2 Pagan, James^1*) was born on July 31, 1932, in Indianapolis, Center Twp., Marion Co., Indiana.[416] He is the son of Horace Russell Honeycutt and Alice Irene Mason (53).

He married **Lois M. Unknown**. They had one son. Lois M. Unknown was born on July 9, 1930.

78. **Robert Rodney^9 Brown** (*Pauline Elizabeth^8 Russell, Gertrude P.^{7} Pegan, James Milton^6, John^5, Robert A.^{4}, Andrew^3, Andrew^2 Pagan, James^1*) was born on December 12, 1931, in DeGraff, Miami Twp., Logan Co., Ohio. He was the son of Donald Otho Brown and Pauline E. Russell (54).

Robert Rodney Brown is married.

79. **James Russell^9 Brown** (*Pauline Elizabeth^8 Russell, Gertrude P.^{7} Pegan, James Milton^6, John^5, Robert A.^{4}, Andrew^3, Andrew^2 Pagan, James^1*) was born on June 12, 1934, in DeGraff, Miami Twp., Logan Co., Ohio. He was the son of Donald Otho Brown and Pauline E. Russell (54). James Russell lived in 2012 in Venice, Sarasota Co., Florida.

James Russell married and had at least one son.

80. **Donald Milton^9 Albershardt** (*Milton James^8, Elgie Elenor^7 Pegan, James Milton^6, John^5, Robert A.^{4}, Andrew^3, Andrew^2 Pagan, James^1*) was born on November 8, 1932, in Indianapolis, Marion Co., Indiana. He was the son of Milton James Albershardt (55) and Frances Keaton.

Donald Milton married **Nancy Rogers** on June 5, 1954, in Marion Co., Indiana.[534] They had two sons. Nancy Rogers was born on July 1, 1933.

81. **Norman Ray^9 Albershardt** (*Milton James^8, Elgie Elenor^7 Pegan, James Milton^6, John^5, Robert A.^{4}, Andrew^3, Andrew^2 Pagan, James^1*) was born on April 3, 1934, in Indianapolis, Marion Co., Indiana.[134, 432] He was the son of Milton James Albershardt (55) and Frances Keaton. Norman Ray lived in 2013 in Plainfield, Guilford Twp., Hendricks Co., Indiana. He died in a facility in Zionsville, Eagle Twp., Boone Co., Indiana, on March 3, 2013, at age 78.[134, 432] Norman Ray was buried in Oaklawn Memorial Gardens, Fishers, Delaware Twp., Hamilton Co., Indiana.[535]

Childless.

Norman Ray married **Lila Jean Ziglar?** in January 1962 in Pinellas Co., Florida.[536] They divorced.

Norman Ray Albershardt married **Carollee Angela Potts** on November 17, 1971, in Hillsborough Co., Florida.[537] They divorced in Hillsborough Co., Florida, on October 24, 1974.[538]

Norman Ray Albershardt married **Alta J. Howell** on October 25, 1980, in Bartholomew Co., Indiana.[539] Alta J. Howell was born in French Lick, French Lick Twp., Orange Co., Indiana, on October 28, 1935.[135, 540] Alta J. reached age 75 and died in Plainfield, Guilford Twp., Hendricks Co., Indiana, on April 29, 2011.[135, 540] She was buried in Oaklawn Memorial Gardens, Fishers, Delaware Twp., Hamilton Co., Indiana.[540, 541]

82. **Wayne Donovan^9 Secrest II** (*Cathern^8 Albershardt, Elgie Elenor^7 Pegan, James Milton^6, John^5, Robert A.^{4}, Andrew^3, Andrew^2 Pagan, James^1*) was born on October 12, 1940, in Indianapolis, Marion Co., Indiana.[135, 439] He was also known as **W. Donovan Secrest**. He was the son of Wayne D. Secrest and Cathern Albershardt (56). He died in Hartwell, Hart Co., Georgia, on April 23, 2001, at age

60.[135, 439] Wayne Donovan was buried in Floral Hills Memory Gardens Cemetery, Tucker, DeKalb Co., Georgia.[439, 542]

Dr. Wayne Donovan Secrest, D.O. was an osteopath. He graduated from Indiana University and the Kirksville College of Osteopathic Medicine in Kirksville, Missouri.

Wayne Donovan married and legally adopted his wife's three children by her first marriage.

Wayne Donovan Secrest adopted three children, including:

+ 101 f I. **Wendy Renee (Jenich)**[10] **Secrest** was born in Ypsilanti, Washtenaw, Michigan, on March 28, 1967.[543] Wendy Renee (Jenich) died in Stone Mountain, De Kalb Co., Georgia, on May 11, 1986.[544]

83. Gail Elizabeth[9] **Pegan** (*Donald Abbott*[8], *Edward Ephraim*[7], *John Andrew*[6], *John*[5], *Robert A.*[4], *Andrew*[3], *Andrew*[2] *Pagan*, *James*[1]) was born on July 6, 1938, in Chicago, Cook Co., Illinois.[100] She is the daughter of Donald Abbott Pegan (58) and Elizabeth Bertha Steinbrenner.

Gail Elizabeth married **Jack Lee Marotte** on October 5, 1956, in San Diego, San Diego Co., California.[545] They divorced. They had two children. Jack Lee Marotte was born in Denver, Denver Co., Colorado, on February 13, 1938.[100]

Gail Elizabeth Pegan Marotte married **Ralph Philip Costain** on March 17, 1963, in San Diego Co., California.[546] They had two sons. Ralph Phillip Costain was born in Seattle, King Co., Washington, on July 5, 1938.[100, 135] Ralph Philip reached age 69 and died in Albuquerque, Bernalillo Co., New Mexico, on February 22, 2008.[100, 135]

Gail Elizabeth Pegan and Jack Lee Marotte had two children, including:

+ 102 m II. **Dale Allen**[10] **Marotte** was born in San Diego, San Diego Co., California, on January 10, 1960.[547, 548] He died in a hospital in La Mesa, San Diego Co., California, on September 13, 1977.[548, 549]

Gail Elizabeth Pegan and Ralph Phillip Costain had two children, including:

+ 103 m I. **Phillip Gregory**[10] **Costain** was born in San Diego, San Diego Co., California, on April 28, 1961.[100, 550, 551] He died in Boynton Beach, Palm Beach Co., Florida, on September 2, 2015.[100, 550]

84. Roberta Jean[9] **Pegan** (*Donald Abbott*[8], *Edward Ephraim*[7], *John Andrew*[6], *John*[5], *Robert A.*[4], *Andrew*[3], *Andrew*[2] *Pagan*, *James*[1]) was born on June 24, 1940, in Chicago, Cook Co., Illinois.[100, 135, 448, 449] She was also known as **Berta**. She was the daughter of Donald Abbott Pegan (58) and Elizabeth Bertha Steinbrenner. Roberta Jean died in Golden Valley, Mohave Co., Arizona, on August 2, 2002, at age 62.[100, 135, 448, 449] She was cremated.[100, 449]

Roberta Jean married **William Alexander Murdoch** on February 22, 1958, in San Diego Co., California.[552] They had two children. William Alexander Murdoch was born in San Diego, San Diego Co., California, on April 13, 1936.[100, 553, 554] William Alexander reached age 67 and died in Golden Valley, Mohave Co., Arizona, on February 16, 2004.[100, 135, 553] He was cremated.[100, 553]

Children of Roberta Jean Pegan and William Alexander Murdoch:

+ 104 m I. **Stephen Blaine**[10] **Murdoch** was born in San Diego, San Diego Co., California, on May 19, 1960.[100, 135, 555] He died in Golden Valley, Mohave Co., Arizona, on March 11, 2000.[100, 135, 556]

+ 105 f II. **Donna Ruth**[10] **Murdoch** was born in San Diego, San Diego Co., California, on August 19, 1961.[557] She died in San Diego, San Diego Co., California, on August 19, 1961.[558]

10th Generation

85. Henrietta June[10] **Gage** (*Henry Crume*[9], *Mamie Edna*[8] *Pegan, Pliny Moses Crume*[7], *Emmanuel*[6], *John*[5], *Robert A.*[4], *Andrew*[3], *Andrew*[2] *Pagan, James*[1]) was born on October 2, 1936, in Callahan, El Paso Co., Colorado. She is the daughter of Henry Crume Gage (59) and Floretta May Gentry.

Henrietta June married **George E. Rollert II** on December 3, 1955, in Denver Co., Colorado.[559] They had two daughters. Geo0rge E. Rollert II was born in Denver, Denver Co., Colorado, on November 12, 1932.[135] George E. reached age 72 and died in Denver, Denver Co., Colorado, on October 13, 2005.[135]

86. Ronald Henry[10] **Gage** (*Henry Crume*[9], *Mamie Edna*[8] *Pegan, Pliny Moses Crume*[7], *Emmanuel*[6], *John*[5], *Robert A.*[4], *Andrew*[3], *Andrew*[2] *Pagan, James*[1]) was born on November 2, 1939, in Denver, Denver Co., Colorado. He is the son of Henry Crume Gage (59) and Floretta May Gentry.

Ronald Henry married **Barbara Downs** on August 27, 1962, in Denver Co., Colorado.[560] They had two children. Barbara Downs was born in Denver, Denver Co., Colorado, on January 22, 1941.[561] Barbara reached age 55 and died in Bellevue, King Co., Washington, on November 29, 1996.[560, 562]

Ronald H. Gage married **Shirley Unknown** after 1996.

87. Robert R.[10] **Gage** (*Gwynn Ballard*[9], *Mamie Edna*[8] *Pegan, Pliny Moses Crume*[7], *Emmanuel*[6], *John*[5], *Robert A.*[4], *Andrew*[3], *Andrew*[2] *Pagan, James*[1]) was born on June 16, 1943, in St. Helens, Columbia Co., Oregon.[456, 457] He was the son of Gwynn Ballard Gage (60) and Inez Beatrice Lindseth. Robert R. died in Woodburn, Marion Co., Oregon, on December 20, 2005, at age 62.[456, 457] He was buried in Skyline Memorial Gardens, Portland, Multnomah Co., Oregon.[457, 563]

He married **Lynnda M. Unknown**. They divorced. They had two sons.

88. Daughter[10] **LeBlond** (*Frances Genevieve*[9] *Michael, Allie Belle*[8] *Cissel, Florence Genevieve*[7] *Pegan, Emmanuel*[6], *John*[5], *Robert A.*[4], *Andrew*[3], *Andrew*[2] *Pagan, James*[1]) was born on May 21, 1954, in Wichita, Sedgwick Co., Kansas. She is the daughter of Jack Donald LeBlond and Francis Genevieve Michael (61).

Daughter LeBlond married **James P. Knapp** on July 28, 1973, in Sedgwick Co., Kansas?[564] They had two children. James P. Knapp was born in Wichita, Sedgewick Co., Kansas?, on February 13, 1950.[135] He reached age 52 and died in Wichita, Sedgwick Co., Kansas, on August 17, 2002.[135, 563, 565] James P. was buried in Calvary Cemetery, Wichita, Sedgwick Co., Kansas.[563]

James P. Knapp was a quality specialist at the Boeing Aircraft Corporation in Wichita, Kansas.[564]

89. William Lawrence[10] **Aldrich II** (*Kathryn Louise*[9] *Mason, Laurence Victor*[8], *Charles Edwin*[7], *Mary Elizabeth*[6] *Pegan, John*[5], *Robert A.*[4], *Andrew*[3], *Andrew*[2] *Pagan, James*[1]) was born on February 10, 1928, in Marion, Marion Twp., Marion Co., Ohio.[135, 466, 467] He was the son of William Pascale Aldrich and Kathryn Louise Mason (62). William Lawrence died in Bradenton, Manatee Co., Florida, on June 7, 2005, at age 77.[135, 466, 467] He was buried in Palmetto Cemetery, Palmetto, Manatee Co., Florida.[466,467]

William Lawrence married **Jean McLean Perry** in 1951.[566] They had three children. Jean McLean Perry was born on July 4, 1933.

90. Dorothy Ann[10] **Mason** (*Donald Earl*[9], *Laurence Victor*[8], *Charles Edwin*[7], *Mary Elizabeth*[6] *Pegan, John*[5], *Robert A.*[4], *Andrew*[3], *Andrew*[2] *Pagan, James*[1]) was born on April 25, 1930, in Alliance, Lexington Twp., Stark Co., Ohio.[473] She was the daughter of Donald Earl Mason (63) and Doris Martha Aldrich. Dorothy Ann died in Alliance, Lexington Twp., Stark Co., Ohio, on April 25, 1930.[473] She was buried in Alliance City Cemetery, Alliance, Lexington Twp., Stark Co., Ohio.[473, 567]

91. Michael Leslie[10] **Ewing** (*Mary Jane*[9] *Mason, Paul Edwin*[8], *Charles Edwin*[7], *Mary Elizabeth*[6] *Pegan, John*[5], *Robert A.*[4], *Andrew*[3], *Andrew*[2] *Pagan, James*[1]) was born on February 5, 1949, in Bellefontaine,

Lake Twp., Logan Co., Ohio.[480] He was the son of Thomas J. Ewing and Mary Jane Mason (64). Michael Leslie died in Bellefontaine, Lake Twp., Logan Co., Ohio, on February 6, 1949.[480] He was buried in Blue Jacket Cemetery, Bellefontaine, Lake Twp., Logan Co., Ohio.[480]

92. **Daughter**[10] **Young** (*Oliver Gordon*[9], *Harold Mason*[8], *Alta Dell*[7] *Mason, Mary Elizabeth*[6] *Pegan, John*[5], *Robert A.*[4], *Andrew*[3], *Andrew*[2] *Pagan, James*[1]) was born in Chaing Mai, Thailand. She is the daughter of Oliver Gordon Young (67) and Margueriete Francia Karoleski.

She married **Mr. Howell**. They had three children.

Daughter Young and Mr. Howell had three children, including:

+ 106 f   III. **Rachel Lee**[11] **Howell** was born in Las Cruces, Dona Ana Co., New Mexico, on December 18, 1986.[135, 568] She died in College Park, Prince George's Co., Maryland, on April 29, 2013.[135, 567]

93. **Kathleen Helen**[10] **Suter** (*Helen Elizabeth*[9] *Young, Harold Mason*[8], *Alta Dell*[7] *Mason, Mary Elizabeth*[6] *Pegan, John*[5], *Robert A.*[4], *Andrew*[3], *Andrew*[2] *Pagan, James*[1]) was born on November 2, 1954, in Oxnard, Ventura Co., California.[135, 495, 496] She was the daughter of James Jacob Suter and Helen Elizabeth Young (68). She was also known as **Kate**. Kathleen Helen died in Sacramento, Sacramento Co., California, on May 22, 2011, at age 56.[135, 496] She was buried in Calvary Catholic Cemetery and Mausoleum, Sacramento, Sacramento Co., California.[496, 569]

Kathleen Helen married **Mr. Wade** on September 5, 1981, in Ventura Co., California.[570] They divorced. They had two children.

Kathleen Helen Suter Wade married **Michael Joseph Morrison** after 1990. Michael Joseph Morrison was born in Clinton, Worcester Co., Massachusetts, on August 27, 1952.[571] Michael Joseph reached age 63 and died in Sacramento, Sacramento Co., California, on December 19, 2015.[570]

94. **Michael James**[10] **Suter** (*Helen Elizabeth*[9] *Young, Harold Mason*[8], *Alta Dell*[7] *Mason, Mary Elizabeth*[6] *Pegan, John*[5], *Robert A.*[4], *Andrew*[3], *Andrew*[2] *Pagan, James*[1]) was born on August 27, 1956, in Oxnard, Ventura Co., California.[497, 498] He was the son of James Jacob Suter and Helen Elizabeth Young (68). Michael James lived in 2012 in Hollywood, Broward Co., Florida. He died in Coral Gables, Dade Co., Florida, on August 14, 2012, at age 55.[498]

Michael James Suter married and had two children.

95. **Daughter**[10] **Young** (*William Marcus*[9], *Harold Mason*[8], *Alta Dell*[7] *Mason, Mary Elizabeth*[6] *Pegan, John*[5], *Robert A.*[4], *Andrew*[3], *Andrew*[2] *Pagan, James*[1]) was born in 1978. She was the daughter of William Marcus Young II (69) and Thai Woman Two. Daughter was born in Thailand in 1968.[501] She died in Thailand in 1983 at age five.[501]

96. **Catherine Louise**[10] **Mantle** (*John Gregory*[9], *Mildred Elizabeth*[8] *Mason, John Pegan*[7], *Mary Elizabeth*[6] *Pegan, John*[5], *Robert A.*[4], *Andrew*[3], *Andrew*[2] *Pagan, James*[1]) was born on April 1, 1948, in Lafayette, Fairfield Twp., Tippecanoe Co., Indiana.[135, 511, 512, 513] She was the daughter of John Gregory Mantle (73) and Kay Joanne Storm. Catherine Louise lived in 1995 in Bakersfield, Kern Co., California. She died in West Linn, Clackamas Co., Oregon, on October 6, 2000, at age 52.[135, 511, 512, 513]

Catherine Louise married **Mr. Wilkin** on September 6, 1969, in Ventura Co., California.[572] They divorced. They have two children.

Catherine Louise Mantle Wilkin married **Mr. Neve** before 1995.[512]

97. **Sandra Kay**[10] **Mantle** (*John Gregory*[9], *Mildred Elizabeth*[8] *Mason, John Pegan*[7], *Mary Elizabeth*[6] *Pegan, John*[5], *Robert A.*[4], *Andrew*[3], *Andrew*[2] *Pagan, James*[1]) was born on December 13, 1953, in Livermore, Alameda Co., California.[514, 515] She was the daughter of John Gregory Mantle (73) and Kay Joanne Storm. Sandra Kay died in Grants Pass, Josephine Co., Oregon, on November 21, 1995, at age 41.[514, 515]

Sandra Kay married **Mr. Feraci** on May 24, 1975, in Ventura Co., California.[573] They divorced.

Sandra Kay Mantle Feraci married **Mr. Geiger** on January 6, 1979, in Ventura Co., California.[574] They divorced. They had one daughter.

98. **Richard Dawson**[10] **Park** (*Norma Louise*[9] *Mantle, Mildred Elizabeth*[8] *Mason, John Pegan*[7]*, Mary Elizabeth*[6] *Pegan, John*[5]*, Robert A.*[4]*, Andrew*[3]*, Andrew*[2] *Pagan, James*[1]) was born on June 25, 1949, in Golden, Jefferson Co., Colorado.[519] He was also known as **Dick**. He was the son of William Gray Park and Norma Louise Mantle (74). He also resided in 2015 in Elk City, Idaho Co., Idaho. Richard Dawson died in a hospital in Boise, Ada Co., Idaho, on July 31, 2015, at age 66.[519] He was cremated and his ashes scattered on Elk Mountain near his home.[519]

Richard Dawson married **Miss Sibley** on December 30, 1978, in Ada Co., Idaho.[514] They divorced. They had four children.

Richard Dawson Park had a relationship with **Unknown Carpentier?** They had one son.

Richard Dawson Park and Miss Sibley had four children, including:

+ 107 f IV. **Robyn Kathleen Sara**[11] **Park** was born in Springfield, Springfield Twp., Clark Co., Ohio, on December 19, 1988.[135, 575] She died in Urbana, Urbana Twp., Champaign Co., Ohio or Adams Co., Ohio, on December 21, 2007.[135, 574]

99. **Patricia Louise**[10] **Park** (*Norma Louise*[9] *Mantle, Mildred Elizabeth*[8] *Mason, John Pegan*[7]*, Mary Elizabeth*[6] *Pegan, John*[5]*, Robert A.*[4]*, Andrew*[3]*, Andrew*[2] *Pagan, James*[1]) was born on October 31, 1951, in Fort Sill, Lawton, Commanche Co., Oklahoma.[135, 520] She was the daughter of William Gray Park and Norma Louise Mantle (74). Patricia Louise lived before 1989 in Freehold Twp., Monmouth Co., New Jersey. She also resided between 1989 and 1999 in Howell Twp., Monmouth Co., New Jersey. Patricia Louise died in a hospital in Neptune, Neptune Twp., Monmouth Co., New Jersey, on June 15, 1999, at age 47.[135, 520]

She married **Mr. Reilly**. They had two children.

100. **Mark Lane**[10] **Vongundy** (*Margaret Jean*[9] *Mantle, Mildred Elizabeth*[8] *Mason, John Pegan*[7]*, Mary Elizabeth*[6] *Pegan, John*[5]*, Robert A.*[4]*, Andrew*[3]*, Andrew*[2] *Pagan, James*[1]) was born on October 29, 1950, in Denver, Denver Co., Colorado.[135, 529] He was the son of Joe L. Vongundy and Margaret Jean Mantle (75). Mark Lane lived in 1990 in Englewood, Arapahoe Co., Colorado. He died in Albuquerque, Bernalillo Co., New Mexico, on July 5, 1995, at age 44.[135, 529] He was cremated.[529]

He married and had one daughter.

101. **Wendy Renee (Jenich)**[10] **Secrest** (*Wayne Donovan*[9]*, Cathern*[8] *Albershardt, Elgie Elenor*[7] *Pegan, James Milton*[6]*, John*[5]*, Robert A.*[4]*, Andrew*[3]*, Andrew*[2] *Pagan, James*[1]) was born on March 28, 1967, in Ypsilanti, Washtenaw, Michigan[226, 543] She was the daughter of Wayne Donovan Secrest (82) and his wife. She died in Stone Mountain, De Kalb Co., Georgia, on May 11, 1986, at age 19.[544] Wendy Renee (Jenich) was buried in Floral Hills Memory Gardens Cemetery, Tucker, DeKalb Co., Georgia.[543, 576] Adopted by her stepfather Wayne Donovan Secrest.[226]

Never married.

102. **Dale Allen**[10] **Marotte** (*Gail Elizabeth*[9] *Pegan, Donald Abbott*[8]*, Edward Ephraim*[7]*, John Andrew*[6]*, John*[5]*, Robert A.*[4]*, Andrew*[3]*, Andrew*[2] *Pagan, James*[1]) was born on January 10, 1960, in San Diego, San Diego Co., California.[547,548] He was the son of Jack Lee Marotte and Gail Elizabeth Pegan (83). Dale Allen died in San Diego, San Diego Co., California, on September 13, 1977, at age 17.[548, 549] He was cremated.[548]

103. **Phillip Gregory**[10] **Costain** (*Gail Elizabeth*[9] *Pegan, Donald Abbott*[8]*, Edward Ephraim*[7]*, John Andrew*[6]*, John*[5]*, Robert A.*[4]*, Andrew*[3]*, Andrew*[2] *Pagan, James*[1]) was born on April 28, 1961, in San Diego, San Diego Co., California.[549] He was the son of Ralph Phillip Costain and Gail Elizabeth Pegan (83). Phillip Gregory died in Boynton Beach, Palm Beach Co., Florida, on September 2, 2015, at age 54.[550] He was cremated.[100, 577]

Childless.

Phillip Gregory Costain married and divorced twice.

104. **Stephen Blaine**[10] **Murdoch** (*Roberta Jean*[9] *Pegan, Donald Abbott*[8]*, Edward Ephraim*[7]*, John Andrew*[6]*, John*[5]*, Robert A.*[4]*, Andrew*[3]*, Andrew*[2] *Pagan, James*[1]) was born on May 19, 1960, in San Diego, San Diego Co., California.[135, 554] He was the son of William Alexander Murdoch and Roberta Jean Pegan (84). Stephen Blaine lived in 1993 in Lakeside, San Diego Co., California. He died in Golden Valley, Mohave Co., Arizona, on March 11, 2000, at age 39.[135, 555] He was cremated.[100, 578]

He married, but divorced. He and his wife had one son.

Stephen Blaine Murdoch was killed by his girlfriend's brother, John Lewis Cagle, on March 11, 2000 in Golden Valley, Mohave Co., Arizona. In September of that year, Cagle was sentenced to a term in the Lewis Bachman Arizona State Prison.[555]

105. **Donna Ruth**[10] **Murdoch** (*Roberta Jean*[9] *Pegan, Donald Abbott*[8]*, Edward Ephraim*[7]*, John Andrew*[6]*, John*[5]*, Robert A.*[4]*, Andrew*[3]*, Andrew*[2] *Pagan, James*[1]) was born on August 19, 1961, in San Diego, San Diego Co., California.[556] She was the daughter of William Alexander Murdoch and Roberta Jean Pegan (84). Donna Ruth died in San Diego, San Diego Co., California, on August 19, 1961.[557] She was buried in Fort Rosencrans National Military Cemetery, San Diego, San Diego Co., California.[579, 580] Infant Donna Ruth Murdoch is buried in Rosencrans National Military Cemetery in San Diego, San Diego Co., California. Her father, William Murdoch, was in the Navy at the time of her stillbirth.

11th Generation

106. Rachel Lee[11] Howell (*Julie[10] Young, Oliver Gordon[9], Harold Mason[8], Alta Dell[7] Mason, Mary Elizabeth[6] Pegan, John[5], Robert A.[4], Andrew[3], Andrew[2] Pagan, James[1]*) was born on December 18, 1986, in Las Cruces, Dona Ana Co., New Mexico.[135, 567] She was the daughter of Mr. Howell and Daughter Young (92). Rachel Lee lived in Las Cruces, Dona Ana Co., New Mexico. She died in College Park, Prince George's Co., Maryland, on April 29, 2013, at age 26.[135, 567] She was cremated, and her ashes taken to her family's cabin Gustavas, Alaska, or buried in Gustavas Cemetery, Gustavas, Hoonah-Angoon, Alaska.[567, 581]

Never married.

107. Robyn Kathleen Sara[11] Park (*Richard Dawson[10], Norma Louise[9] Mantle, Mildred Elizabeth[8] Mason, John Pegan[7], Mary Elizabeth[6] Pegan, John[5], Robert A.[4], Andrew[3], Andrew[2] Pagan, James[1]*) was born on December 19, 1988, in Springfield, Springfield Twp., Clark Co., Ohio.[135, 574] She was the daughter of Richard Dawson Park (98) and Miss Sibley. Robyn Kathleen Sara lived in 2007 in Urbana, Urbana Twp., Champaign Co., Illinois. She died in Urbana, Urbana Twp., Champaign Co., Ohio or Adams Co., Ohio, on December 21, 2007, at age 19.[135, 574] She was cremated.[582]

Never married.

Endnotes

1. Family Data: Robert and Christina "Engle" Pegan family bible, American Bible Society, Brattleboro(ugh), Vermont: Holbrook & Fessenden, 1828. In possession of the author, Ann Miller Carr.

2. Ohio, County Death Records, 1840-2001, FamilySearch.org, John Pegan, Logan County, Ohio Death Records, Vol. 1, pg. 122.

3. Find A Grave—Greenwood Cemetery, DeGraff, Pleasant Twp., Logan Co., Ohio, Findagrave.com, John Pegan, Find A Grave Memorial #18416902.

4. "James R. Pagin", *History of Porter County, Indiana: A Narrative History of its Progress, its People and Principal Interests.* Chicago: Lewis Publishing Co.; 1912, pg. 692. Genealogy Center, Allen County Public Library, 900 Library Plaza, Fort Wayne, IN.

5. Gilbert, Audrey, *Twin Valley Tidbits, 1888-1897, Vol. 3.* New Alexandria, Ohio: A. Gilbert; 1999, pg. 72. Lynchbury Public Library, 120 Main Street, Lynchburg, OH.

6. Ohio, County Marriages, 1789-2013, FamilySearch.org, John Pegan and Rebecca Shearer, Montgomery County, Ohio Marriage Records, Vol. B1, pg. 40.

7. Family Data: Johan Valentine and Catherine Wolford Shearer family bible records. Privately held.

8. Lewis Pegan by his Next Best Friend John Jacob Pegan vs. David Winters, Montgomery County, Ohio Common Pleas Court Records, September Term 1839, Book N, pg. 515. Montgomery County, Ohio Records Center and Archives, 117 South Main St., 6th Floor, Dayton, OH.

9. "All Ohio, Tax Lists, 1800-1850", Ancestry.com, entry for John J. or John Jacob Pagan, Knox Twp., Columbiana Co., Ohio, 1829-1833.

10. Miami County, Ohio Marriage Records, Miami County, Ohio Probate Court, 201 West Main Street, Troy, Ohio, John Pegan and Phebe Moore, Miami County, Ohio Marriage Records, Vol. F, pg. 120.

11. Phoebe Moore Pagan/Pegan tombstone, Greenwood Cemetery, Pleasant Twp., Logan Co., Ohio.

12. New Jersey Death Certificate, New Jersey Department of Health, Office of Vital Statistics and Registry, 140 East Front Street, Trenton, NJ, Phoebe Pegan, death cert. #J491.

13. Find A Grave—Greenwood Cemetery, DeGraff, Pleasant Twp., Logan Co., Ohio, Findagrave.com, Phoebe Moore Pegan, Find A Grave Memorial #18416891.

14. John Pegan will, Logan County Will Book B, page 443, Logan County, Ohio Probate Court, 140 North Main Street, Bellefontaine, OH.

15. Obituary of Mrs. Phebe Moore Pegan (Indianapolis, Indiana, Indianapolis Star, 25 Jun 1911). Indiana State Library, 315 West Ohio Street, Indianapolis, IN.

16. "Death of Aged Lady On Her Birthday (Bellefontaine, Ohio, Bellefontaine Examiner, 24 Jun 1911). Logan County, Ohio Public Libraries, Knowlton Library, 220 North Main Street, Bellefontaine, OH.

17. Obituary of Dr. Emmanuel Pegan (Rochester, Indiana, Rochester Chronicle, 22 Jun 1865), Fulton County Public Library, 320 West 7th Street, Rochester, IN.

18. Headstones Provided For Deceased Union Civil War Veterans, 1861-1904, Ancestry.com, David S. Pegan, Greenwood Cemetery, Hamilton, Butler Co., Ohio.

19. Obituary of Mary Elizabeth Mason (DeGraff, Ohio, DeGraff (OH) Journal, 16 Oct 1896), Ohio History Center Archives and Library, Ohio History Center, 800 East 17th Avenue, Columbus, OH.

20. Find A Grave—Greenwood Cemetery, DeGraff, Pleasant Twp., Logan Co., Ohio, Findagrave.com, Mary E. Mason, Find A Grave Memorial #18379962.

21. Ohio, County Death Records, 1840-2001, FamilySearch.org, Mary E. Mason, Logan Co., Ohio Death Record Vol. 2, pg. 202.

22. Obituary of Joshua B. Baughman (Bellefontaine, Ohio, Bellefontaine Daily Examiner, 06 Oct 1921), Logan County Libraries, Knowlton Library, 220 North Main Street, Bellefontaine, OH.

23. Civil War Pension Application, James Pegan, invalid, #413745; widow Catherine Pegan, #600509 (Washington, DC), NARA—National Archives and Records Administration, 8601 Adelphi Road, College Park, MD.

24. California Death Certificate, California Health and Strategic Planning, Vital Records, M.S. 5103, P.O. Box 997410, Sacramento, CA, Margaret Miller, death cert. #29-051897.

25. California Death Index, 1905-1940, FamilySearch.org, Margaret Miller, Index Book A., pg. 7421, California Death Record Book 1929, cert. #51897.

26. Ohio Death Certificate, Ohio Department of Health, Center for Vital and Health Statistics, 246 North High Street, Columbus, OH, Martha Ann Strayer, cert. #44739.

27. Marion County, Indiana Death Certificate, John A. Pegan, cert. #17725-1981. However, a non-family member, a nurse at the "city hospital" was the informant, and she gave the wrong birth year for him. He was born in Dec 1849, according to the 1900 census, and his age in all the other censuses, except for 1850, is consistent with a Dec 1849 birth. In 1850, he is listed as age two.

28 Obituary of John Andrew Pegan (II) (Indianapolis, Indiana, Indianapolis Star, 13 May 1918), Indiana State Library, 315 West Ohio Street, Indianapolis, IN.

29 California, Death Index, 1940-1997, Ancestry.com, Laura L. Hill. Ancestry.com.

30 Find A Grave—Greenwood Cemetery, DeGraff, Pleasant Twp., Logan Co., Ohio, Findagrave.com, Elsey Pegan, Find A Grave Memorial #18416896.

31 Wendell C. and Jean C. Tombaugh, Cemeteries of Miami County, Indiana, Vol. 2, Richland, Jefferson and Miami Townships. Self-publilshed (Rochester, Indiana: Tombaugh House), 1988), Old Cemetery at Mexico, entry for "Pecan(?)", Emmanuel, 1st Surgeon, 133? 155th? Regt. Ind. Inf., "Died at Camden, Delaware". Fulton County Library, 320 West 7th Street, Rochester, IN; Online database: http://www.fulco.lib.in.us/genealogy-files/cemeteries/Miami%20County/richland_jefferson_erie.htm

32 Miami County, Indiana Marriage Records, Miami County, Indiana Clerk of Court, Miami County Courthouse, 25 North Broadway, Peru, IN, Emmanuel Pegan and Sarah Strouse, Miami County, Indiana Marriage Records, Book C-2, pg. 257.

33 Indiana, Marriages 1811-2007, FamilySearch.org, Emmanuel Pegan and Sarah Strouse, Miami County, Indiana Marriage Records, Vol. C- 2, pg. 257.

34 Harper County Genealogical Society, Forest Park Cemetery Records (Harper City, Kansas), Sarah Shields, Harper County, Genealogical Society Library, Harper City Public Library, 1002 Oak Street, Harper, KS.

35 Find A Grave—Forest Park Cemetery, Anthony, Anthony Twp., Harper Co., Kansas, Sarah Shields, Find A Grave.com, Find A Grave Memorial #3240910.

36 *A History of Miami County, Indiana: A Narrative of Its Historical Progress, Its People, and Its Principal Interest, Vol. I*, ed. by Arthur L. Bodurtha. Chicago & New York: The Lewis Publishing Co., 1914, pg. 525.

37 Indiana, Marriages 1811-2007, FamilySearch.org, R.M. Shields and Sarah Pegan, Miami County, Indiana Marriage Records, Vol. B, pg. 312.

38 Miami County, Indiana Death Registrations, Robert M. Shields, Vol. C-6. Pg. 4. Miami County, Indiana Clerk of Court, Miami County Courthouse, 25 North Broadway, Peru, IN.

39 "Very Sudden Death" (Peru, Indiana, Peru Republican, 27 Mar 1903), Peru Public Library, 102 East Main Street, Peru, IN.

40 Olinger Crown Hill Cemetery Records, Pliny C. Pegan, burial #39715; Olinger Crown Hill Cemetery & Arboretum, 7777 West 29th Avenue, Wheat Ridge, CO.

41 Obituary of Mrs. Florence Cissel (Anthony, Kansas, Anthony Republican, 18 Apr 1929), Anthony Library, 624 East Main Street, Anthony, Kansas.

42 Harper Co., Kansas Genealogical Society, Forest Park Cemetery Records (Harper City, Kansas), Florence Genevieve Cissel, Harper County, Kansas Genealogical Society Library, Harper City Public Library, 1002 Oak Street, Harper, KS.

43 U.S., Civil War Soldier Records and Profiles, 1861-1865, Ancestry.com, David S. Pegan.

44 "The 35th Ohio Volunteer Infantry", Butler County Civil War 150, Online website. https://sites.google.com/site/butlercountycw150/bc-civil-war-history/cyclopaedia/the-35th-ohio-volunteer-infantry-1

45 Ohio, County Marriages, 1789-2013, FamilySearch.org, Samuel Mason and Mary E. Pegan, Logan County, Ohio Marriage Records, Vol. C, pg. 15.

46 Indiana Death Certificate (Indianapolis, Indiana, State of Indiana), Indiana State Department of Health, 2 North Meridian Street, Indianapolis, IN, S.M. Mason, Marion County, Indiana, death cert. #164 4479.

47 Indiana, Death Certificates, 1899-2011, Ancestry.com, S.M. Mason, Indianapolis, Marion Co., Indiana 14 Jun 1906.

48 Find A Grave—Greenwood Cemetery, DeGraff, Pleasant Twp., Logan Co., Ohio, Findagrave.com, Samuel M. Mason, Find A Grave Memorial #18379972.

49 "Death in Indianapolis" (Bellefontaine Ohio, Bellefontaine Examiner, 15 Jun 1906), Logan County Libraries, Knowlton Library, 220 North Main Street, Bellefontaine, OH.

50 Indiana Death Certificate (Indianapolis, Indiana, State of Indiana), Indiana State Department of Health, 2 North Meridian Street, Indianapolis, IN, Ida Mason, death cert. #23078.

51 Find A Grave—Miami Cemetery, Rush Creek Twp., Logan Co., Ohio, Findagrave.com, Ada Mason, Find A Grave Memorial #30943703.

52 Ohio Death Certificate, Ohio Department of Health, Center for Vital and Health Statistics, 246 North High Street, Columbus, OH, Charles Edwin Mason, #17262.

53 Marion County, Indiana Death Certificate, Katherine Mason, Death Record Vol. 32, pg. 215, cert. #2153.

54 U.S. Passport Applications 1795-1925, Ancestry.com, Alta Dell Mason Young, passport #4177, application 25 Sep 1919.

55 Reports of Deaths of American Citizens Abroad, Ancestry.com, Mrs. Alta Dell Young, died October 28, 1921, Rangoon, Burma, buried American Baptist Cemetery, Rangoon, Burma; reported by American Consular Service in Rangoon, Burma on November 11, 1921; Misc. Record Book, pg. 137.

56 Young, Harold Mason, compiled and ed. by Debbie Young Chase, *To The Mountain Tops: A Sojourn Among The Lahu of Asia*. Bloomington, Indiana: XLIBRIS; 2013, pg. 405. Copy owned by author Ann Miller Carr.

57 Ohio, County Births, 1841-2003 (County Courthouses), FamilySearch.org, Cora Mason, Logan Co., Ohio Birth Record, Vol. 1, pg. 152.

58 Indiana, Death Certificates, 1899-2011, Ancestry.com, Miss Cora Mason, cert. #8845.

59 Obituary of Cora Mason (Indianapolis, Indiana, Indianapolis Star, 28 Mar 1949), Indianapolis Public Library, 40 East St. Clair Street, Indianapolis, IN.

60 Ohio Marriages, 1800-1958, FamilySearch.org, Lawrence V. Mason and May Evans, Logan County, Ohio Marriage Records, Vol. J, pg. 112, lic. #232.

61 Ohio, County Births, 1841-2003 (County Courthouses), FamilySearch.org, John Pegan Mason, Logan Co., Ohio Birth Record Vol. 1, pg. 186.

62 Indiana, Death Certificates, 1899-2001, Ancestry.com, John Mason, death cert. #19388.

63 Marion County, Indiana Death Certificate, M. Elizabeth Mason, cert. #2303.

64 Find A Grave—Fairview Cemetery, Quincy, Miami Twp., Logan Co., Ohio, Findagrave.com, Catherine Baughman, Find A Grave Memorial #17816224.

65 Logan County, Ohio Marriage Records, Logan County Probate Court, 140 West Main Street, Bellefontaine, OH, Joshua B. Baughman and Catherine Pegan, Logan County, Ohio Marriage Records, Book C, pg. 65.

66 Ohio Death Certificate, Ohio Department of Health, Center for Vital and Health Statistics, 246 North High Street, Columbus, OH, Joshua B. Baughman, cert. #57858.

67 Ohio, Deaths. 1908-1932, 1938-2007, Ancestry.com, Joshua B. Baughman.

68 Find A Grave—Greenwood Cemetery, DeGraff, Pleasant Twp., Logan Co., Ohio, Findagrave.com, Joshua Baughman, Find A Grave Memoria l#180857278.

69 Find A Grave—Greenwood Cemetery, DeGraff, Pleasant Twp., Logan Co., Ohio, Findagrave.com, "Johney" Baughman, d. 07 Sep 1863 at age 5 yr., 3mo., 2 da. Buried in Greenwood Cemetery, DeGraff, Pleasant Twp., Logan Co., Ohio.

70 Ohio Death Certificate, Ohio Department of Health, Center for Vital and Health Statistics, 246 North High Street, Columbus, OH, Otto G. Baughman, #24230.

71 Find A Grave—Greenwood Cemetery, DeGraff, Pleasant Twp., Logan Co., Ohio, Findagrave.com, James Pegan, Find A Grave Memorial #18416900.

72 U.S. City Directories, 1822-1895, Ancestry.com. Indianapolis, Indiana, 1867, entry for Pegan, James M.

73 Indiana, Marriage Collection, 1800-1941, Ancestry.com, James M. Pegan and Kate Hendrickson, Marion County, Indiana Marriage Records, Book 10, pg. 93.

74 Ohio Death Certificate, Ohio Department of Health, Center for Vital and Health Statistics, 246 North High Street, Columbus, OH, Volume #4928, Certificate #1439.

75 Find A Grave—Greenwood Cemetery, DeGraff, Pleasant Twp., Logan Co., Ohio, Findagrave.com, Catherine H. Pegan, Find A Grave Memorial #18416893.

76 U.S. City Directories, 1822-1895, Ancestry.com. Indianapolis, Indiana, 1895, entry for Pegan, Catherine (wid. James M.).

77 Ohio Death Certificate, Ohio Department of Health, Center for Vital and Health Statistics, 246 North High Street, Columbus, OH, Orpha Estella Pegan, #71086.

78 Ohio, County Death Records, 1840-2001, FamilySearch.org, Infant Pegan, Logan Co. Death Records, Vol. 1, pg. 50.

79 Ohio, County Births, 1841-2003 (County Courthouses), FamilySearch.org, Gertrude Pegan, Logan County, Ohio Birth Record Vol. 1, pg. 156.

80 Find A Grave—Greenwood Cemetery, DeGraff, Pleasant Twp., Logan Co., Ohio, Findagrave.com, Gertrude Russell, Find A Grave Memorial #18525400.

81 Obituary of Gertrude Russell (Ann Arbor, Michigan, Ann Arbor News, 13 Apr 1959), Ann Arbor District Library, Main Branch—Ann Arbor, 343 South Fifth Avenue, Ann Arbor, MI.

82 Ohio Death Certificate, Ohio Department of Health, Center for Vital and Health Statistics, 246 North High Street, Columbus, OH, Arthur Pegan, #13763.

83 Ohio, County Births, 1841-2003 (County Courthouses), FamilySearch.org, Arthur and Elgie (Elzie) Pegan, twins, Logan County Birth Record Vol. 1, pg. 254.

84 Crown Hill Cemetery Records, Elgie Albershardt, Crown Hill Cemetery, 700 West 38th Street, Indianapolis, IN.

85 Indiana, Death Certificates, 1899-2011, Ancestry.com, "Elenor Elgie Albershardt", death cert. #60-028067. Incorrect indexing, certificate clearly says Elgie Elenor Albershardt.

86 Obituary of Elgie Albershardt (Indianapolis, Indiana, Indianapolis Star, 26 Jul 1960), Indianapolis Public Library, 40 East St. Clair Street, Indianapolis, IN.

87 Angeles Abbey Memorial Park Mausoleum Records, Margaret Miller, Angeles Abbey Memorial Park Mausoleum, 1515 East Compton Boulevard, Compton, California.

88 Ohio, County Marriages, 1789-2013, FamilySearch.org, Adam Brunner and Margaret Pegan, Logan County, Ohio Marriage Records, Book C, pg. 314, lic. #924.

89 Civil War Draft Registrations, Ancestry.com, Adam Brunner in Miami Twp., Logan Co., Ohio.

90 Find A Grave—Greenwood Cemetery, DeGraff, Pleasant Twp., Logan Co., Ohio, Findagrave.com, Adam Bruner, Find A Grave Memorial #13815107.

91 Ohio, County Marriages, 1789-2013, FamilySearch.org, William C. Miller and Margaret Bruner, Hardin County, Ohio Marriage Records, Vol. 5, pg. 48.

92 Ohio Death Certificate, Ohio Department of Health, Center for Vital and Health Statistics, 246 North High Street, Columbus, OH, William C. Miller, cert. #21360.

93 Find A Grave—Old Veterans Home Cemetery, Perkins Twp., Erie Co., Ohio, Findagrave.com, Sgt. William C. Miller, Find A Grave Memorial #50686971.

94 Ohio, County Marriages, 1789-2013, FamilySearch.org, Gustavus A. Reiling and Marcia Bruner, Lucas County, Ohio Marriage Records, Book 20, pg. 22, #13227.

95 California Death Index, 1905-1940, FamilySearch.org, Marcia Reiling, Index Book B., pg. 5713, California Death Record Book 1931, cert. #21599.

96 Ohio, County Births, 1841-2003 (County Courthouses), FamilySearch.org, Willetta Miller, Logan Co., Ohio Birth Record Vol. 1, pg. 250.

97 California Death Index, 1905-1940, FamilySearch.org, Willetta Sawyer, Index Book B, pg. 6101, California Death Record Book 1935, cert. #70604.

98 California Death Certificate, California Health and Strategic Planning, Vital Records, M.S. 5103, P.O. Box 997410, Sacramento, CA, Willette Sawyer, death cert. #35-070604.

99 California, Death Index, 1940-1997, Ancestry.com, Fred P. Miller, Fa: Miller, Mo: Pegan.

100 Family data: Research by Tamara Brush, Tamara Brush, Albuquerque, New Mexico.

101 California Death Certificate, California Health and Strategic Planning, Vital Records, M.S. 5103, P.O. Box 997410, Sacramento, CA, Fred P. Miller, death cert. #003316.

102 Ohio, County Births, 1841-2003 (County Courthouses), FamilySearch.org, "Blanch" Miller, Logan Co., Ohio Birth Record Vol. 2, pg. 4.

103 California Death Certificate, California Health and Strategic Planning, Vital Records, M.S. 5103, P.O. Box 997410, Sacramento, CA, Blanche H. Humason, death cert. #44-041775.

104 California Death Index, 1905-1940, FamilySearch.org, Blanche Humason.

105 Find A Grave—Greenwood Cemetery, DeGraff, Pleasant Twp., Logan Co., Ohio, Findagrave.com, Martha Strayer, Find A Grave Memorial #18680168.

106 Ohio, County Marriages, 1789-2013, FamilySearch.org, James M. Strayer and Martha A. Pegan, Lucas County, Marriage Records, Book G, pg. 433.

107 Ohio Death Certificate, Ohio Department of Health, Center for Vital and Health Statistics, 246 North High Street, Columbus, OH, James M. Strayer, #55399.

108 Find A Grave—Greenwood Cemetery, DeGraff, Pleasant Twp., Logan Co., Ohio, Findagrave.com, James M. Strayer, Find A Grave Memorial #18680141.

109 Find A Grave—Greenwood Cemetery, DeGraff, Pleasant Twp., Logan Co., Ohio, Findagrave.com, John Andrew Pegan, Jr., Find A Grave Memorial #143057912.

110 Ohio, County Marriages, 1789-2013, FamilySearch.org, John A. Pegan and "Annie B." Armstrong, Logan County, Ohio Marriage Records, Vol. E, pg. 546.

111 Ohio Death Certificate, Ohio Department of Health, Center for Vital and Health Statistics, 246 North High Street, Columbus, OH, Anna Pegan, #2258.

112 Find A Grave—Eastlawn Cemetery, Columbus, Franklin Co., Ohio, Findagrave.com, Anna B. Pegan, Find A Grave Memorial #47629366.

113 Ohio Death Certificate, Ohio Department of Health, Center for Vital and Health Statistics, 246 North High Street, Columbus, OH, Edward E. PeGan, #9130.

114 Ohio, County Births, 1841-2003 (County Courthouses), FamilySearch.org, Anna M. Pegan, Logan Co., Ohio Birth Record Vol. 3, pg. 180.

115 Ohio, County Death Records, 1840-2001, FamilySearch.org, "Lena" M. Pegan, Logan Co., Ohio Death Record, Vol. 1, pg. 326.

116 Find A Grave—Hollywood Forever Cemetery, Hollywood, Los Angeles Co., California, Findagrave.com, Laura L. Hill, Find A Grave Memorial #6567865.

117 Ohio, County Marriages, 1789-2013, FamilySearch.org, Edward Hill Jr. and Laura L. Pegan, Logan County, Ohio Marriage Records, Book E, pg. 263.

118 California Death Certificate, California Health and Strategic Planning, Vital Records, M.S. 5103, P.O. Box 997410, Sacramento, CA, Edward H. Hill, death cert. #37753.

119 Historical Newspapers, Birth, Marriage and Death Announcements—1851-2003, Ancestry.com, ("Vital Statistics", "Edward Hill", Los Angeles, California, Los Angeles Times, 29 Jul 1931).

120 California Death Index, 1905-1940, FamilySearch.org, Edward H. Hill, Index Book B, pg. 3095, California Death Book 1931, cert. #37753.

121 Find A Grave—Hollywood Forever Cemetery, Hollywood, Los Angeles Co., California, Findagrave.com, Edward H. Hill, Find A Grave Memorial #6567863.

122 U.S., WWI Draft Registration Cards, 1917-1918, Ancestry.com, Fred Rowland Hill, Philadelphia, Pennsylvania.

123 Ohio, County Births, 1841-2003 (County Courthouses), FamilySearch.org, Fred Roland Hill, Logan Co., Ohio Birth Record Vol. 1, pg. 330.

124 Clerk of the Orphans Court, Court Division, Court of Common Pleas, Philadelphia County, Pennsylvania, City Hall Room 415, Philadelphia, PA.

125 California, Death Index, 1940-1997, Ancestry.com, Fred Roland Hill.

126 Find A Grave—Crown Hill Cemetery, Wheat Ridge, Jefferson Co., Colorado, Findagrave.com, "Pleney" C. Pegan, Find A Grave Memorial #50072755.

127 U.S. School Catalogs, 1765-1935, Ancestry.com. Kansas State Agricultural College, Gatesburg, Barton, Kansas, 1877, Crume Pegan.

128 Barton County, Kansas Marriage Records, Barton County, Kansas Recorder's Office, 1400 Main St, #205, Courthouse, Great Bend, KS Pliny M. Crume and Francina Gwinn, Barton County, Kansas Marriage Records, Vol. A, pg. 142.

129 "Mother of Manual High Librarian Dies" (Denver, Colorado, Rocky Mountain News, 30 Jul 1931). Denver Public Library, 10 West Fourteenth Avenue Parkway, Denver, CO.

130 Find A Grave—Crown Hill Cemetery, Wheat Ridge, Jefferson Co., Colorado, Findagrave.com, Francina Pegan, Find A Grave Memorial #50072794.

131 U.S., Selected Federal Census Non-Population Schedules, 1850-1880, Ancestry.com, Schedule: Agriculture; Liberty, Barton, Kansas, entry for P. Crume Pegan, pg. 2.

132 "Easter 1882 market by city's first fatal shooting" (Garden City, Kansas, Garden City Telegram, 29 Jun 1979), Finney County Library, 605 East Walnut Street, Garden City, KS.

133 Colorado State Census, Ancestry.com, The National Archives at Washington, D.C.; Washington, D.C.; NAI Title: *Schedules of the Special Census of 1885*; NAI Number: *2791166*; Record Group Title: *Records of the Bureau of the Census, 1790 - 2007*; Record Group Number: *29*; Series Title: *Colorado State Census, 1885*; Series Number: *M158*; NARA Roll Number: *7, pg. 10*.

134 Kansas State Census Collection, 1855-1925, Ancestry.com, Kansas State Historical Society; Topeka, Kansas; 1895 Kansas Territory Census; Roll: v115_8; Line: 3, entry for "Sina" Pegan.

135 Social Security Death Index, Ancestry.com.

136 Phone interview with Edward Daniel Gage, Salem, OR, Ann Miller Carr, author, 02 Apr 2015.

137 Olinger Crown Hill Cemetery Records, Patience Pegan Crane, burial #42071; Olinger Crown Hill Cemetery & Arboretum, 7777 West 29th Avenue, Wheat Ridge, CO.

138 Find A Grave—Forest Park Cemetery, Anthony, Anthony Twp., Harper Co., Kansas, Findagrave.com, Florence G. Cissel, Find A Grave Memorial #32409074.

139 Sands, Dick, "At Home and Abroad" (Rochester, Indiana, Rochester Sentinel, 05 Aug 1876), Fulton County Library, 320 West 7th Street, Rochester, IN.

140 Miami County, Indiana Marriage Records, Miami County, Indiana Clerk of Court, Miami County Courthouse, 25 North Broadway, Peru, IN, Mervin O. Cissel and Jennie F. Pegan, Miami County, Indiana Marriage Records, Book C-6, pg. 26.

141 Indiana, Marriages 1811-2007, FamilySearch.org, Mervin O. Cissel and Jennie F. Pegan, Miami County, Indiana Marriage Records, Book C-6, pg. 26.

142 Harper County Genealogical Society, Forest Park Cemetery Records (Harper City, Kansas), Mervin O. Cissel; Harper County, Genealogical Society Library, Harper City Public Library, 1002 Oak Street, Harper, KS.

143 Obituary of M.O. Cissel (Anthony, Kansas, Anthony Republican, 01 Jun 1922), Anthony Library, 624 East Main Street, Anthony, KS.

144 Find A Grave—Forest Park Cemetery, Anthony, Anthony Twp., Harper Co., Kansas, Findagrave.com, Mervin O. Cissel, Find A Grave Memorial #32409052.

145 Kansas State Census Collection, 1855-1925, Ancestry.com, Kansas State Historical Society, Topeka, Kansas: 1895 Kansas Territory Census; Roll: v115_154; Line: 8, entry for M.O. Cissel.

146 Blackmar, Frank Wilson, *Kansas: A cyclopedia of state history, embracing events, institutions, industries, counties, cities, towns, prominent people, etc., Vol. III, Pt. 2*. Chicago: Standard Publishing Company; 1912, pg. 1461-1462. Genealogy Center, Allen County Public Library, 900 Library Plaza, Fort Wayne, IN.

147 Obituary of Mrs. B.F. Michael (Anthony, Kansas, Anthony Republican, 06 Nov 1939), Anthony Library, 624 East Main Street, Anthony, KS.

148 Harper County Genealogical Society, Forest Park Cemetery Records (Harper City, Kansas), Allie Belle Cissel Michael, Harper County Genealogical Society Library, Harper City Public Library, 1002 Oak Street, Harper, KS.

149 Harper County Genealogical Society, Forest Park Cemetery Records (Harper City, Kansas), Bennie F. Cissel, Harper County, Genealogical Society Library, Harper City Public Library, 1002 Oak Street, Harper, KS.

150 Find A Grave—Old Mission Cemetery, Wichita, Sedgwick Co., Kansas, Findagrave.com, Charles M. Cissel, Find A Grave Memorial #43462233.

151 U.S., WWI Draft Registration Cards, 1917-1918, Ancestry.com, Charles Mervin Cissel.

152 Find A Grave—Greenwood Cemetery, DeGraff, Pleasant Twp., Logan Co., Ohio, Findagrave.com, Ida May Mason, Find A Grave Memorial #18379952.

153 Obituary of John Pegan Mason (Indianapolis, Indiana, Indianapolis Star, 04 Jun 1924), Indiana State Library, 315 West Ohio Street, Indianapolis, IN.

154 Obituary of Ida M. Mason (Indianapolis, Indiana, Indianapolis News, 18 Aug 1927), Indiana State Library, 315 West Ohio Street, Indianapolis, IN.

155 Find A Grave—Bellefontaine City Cemetery, Bellefontaine, Lake Twp., Logan Co., Ohio, Findagrave.

com, Charles E. Mason, Find A Grave Memorial #21839927.

156 Ohio Death Certificate, Ohio Department of Health, Center for Vital and Health Statistics, 246 North High Street, Columbus, OH, Mary E. Mason, death cert. #64340.

157 Find A Grave—Bellefontaine City Cemetery, Bellefontaine, Lake Twp., Logan Co., Ohio, Findagrave.com, Mary E. Mason, Find A Grave Memorial #21839939.

158 "Mrs. Charles E. Mason Dies While Seated In Chair" (Bellefontaine, Ohio, Bellefontaine Examiner, 12 Nov 1927), Logan County Libraries, Knowlton Library, 220 North Main Street, Bellefontaine, OH.

159 Ohio, County Marriages, 1789-2013, FamilySearch.org, C. Edwin Mason and Mary Jane Saum, Logan County, Ohio Marriage Records, Vol. O, pg. 282, lic. #9072.

160 Ohio Death Certificate, Ohio Department of Health, Center for Vital and Health Statistics, 246 North High Street, Columbus, OH, Mary J. Mason, #51203.

161 U.S., WW II Draft Registration Cards, 1942, Ancestry.com, Laurence Victor Mason, Alliance, Ohio.

162 Obituary of Laurence V. Mason (Bradenton, Florida, Bradenton Herald, 28 Oct 1954), Manatee County Public Library-Central Branch, 1301 Barcarotta Boulevard West, Bradenton, FL.

163 Ohio, County Marriages, 1789-2013, FamilySearch.org, Elsworth Charles Voorhees and Laura Marguerite Mason, Marion County, Ohio Marriage Records, Vol. 18, pg. 279, lic. #557.

164 Obituary of Marguerite Mason Voorhees (Bellefontaine, Ohio, Bellefontaine Examiner, 01 Mar 1948), Logan County Libraries, Knowlton Library, 220 North Main Street, Bellefontaine, OH.

165 Obituary of Charles E. Mason, (Bellefontaine, Ohio, Bellefontaine Examiner, 04 Mar 1950), Logan County Libraries, Knowlton Library, 220 North Main Street, Bellefontaine, OH. Mentions his daughter Laura Mason Voorhees' death in Orlando, Florida on February 29, 1948.

166 Obituary of Mrs. M.L. Voorhees (Orlando, Florida, Orlando Morning Sentinel, 03 Mar 1948), State Library and Archives of Florida, R.A. Gray Building, 500 South Bronaugh Street, Tallahassee, FL, A Division of the Florida Dept. of State—Division of Library and Information Services, R.A. Gray Building, 500 South Bronough St., Tallahassee, Florida 32399-0250.

167 U.S., WWI Draft Registration Cards, 1917-1918, Ancestry.com, Ancestry.com, Paul E. Mason, Akron, Ohio.

168 California, Death Index, 1940-1997, Ancestry.com, Paul E. Mason.

169 Obituary of Paul Mason (Bellefontaine, Ohio, Bellefontaine Examiner, 03 Jan 1955), Logan County Libraries, Knowlton Library, 220 North Main Street, Bellefontaine, OH.

170 Find A Grave—Greenwood Cemetery, DeGraff, Pleasant Twp., Logan Co., Ohio, Findagrave.com, Kate Mason, Find A Grave Memorial #18379958.

171 "Kate Mason, Teacher, Dies" (Indianapolis, Indiana, Indianapolis Star, 16 Dec 1929), Indiana State Library, 315 West Ohio Street, Indianapolis, IN.

172 Montgomery, Helen Barrett, *Helping Hand,* Woman's Baptist Foreign Missionary Society, Boston, Massachusetts, October 1900, pg. 12-13.

173 Baptist Missionary Magazine (Boston, Massachusetts, American Baptist Foreign Missionary Society, March 1901), Marriage announcement for William M. Young and Alta Mason, Vol. LXXXI, No. 3, pg. 111.

174 Young, Harold Mason, *To The Mountain Tops: A Sojourn Among The Lahu of Asia*, pg. 469.

175 U.S., Passport Application, 1795-1925, Ancestry.com, William M. Young, passport issued 23 Oct 1923.

176 California Death Index, 1905-1940, FamilySearch.org, Wililam M. Young, death cert. #22447, index pg. 7656.

177 Phone interview with Oliver Gordon Young, San Luis Obispo, CA, Ann Miller Carr, author, 01 Aug 2012.

178 Young, Harold Mason, *To The Mountain Tops: A Sojourn Among The Lahu of Asia*, pg. 407, 472-473.

179 Tulare Cemetery Records, William Marcus Young, Tulare Cemetery, 900 East Kern Avenue, Tulare, CA.

180 Find A Grave—Tulare Cemetery, Tulare, Tulare Co., California, Findagrave.com, William Marcus Young, Find A Grave Memorial #181351360.

181 Young, Harold Mason, *To The Mountain Tops: A Sojourn Among The Lahu of Asia*, pg. 471.

182 "The Grand Old Man of Chaing Mai: The Life of Harold Young", by David Lawitts *Citylife Magazine*, Chaing Mai, Thailand, issue 4, April 2015.

183 Young, Harold Mason, *To The Mountain Tops: A Sojourn Among The Lahu of Asia*, pg. 470.

184 Lloyd G. James, "Death Notice—Rev. Harold Mason Young", (King of Prussia, Pennsylvania, International Ministries-American Baptist Churches USA, 26 Feb 1975), American Baptist Historical Society, 3001 Mercer University Drive, Atlanta, GA, Interoffice communication letter.

185 Young, Harold Mason, *To The Mountain Tops: A Sojourn Among The Lahu of Asia.*, pg. 474.

186 California, Death Index, 1940-1997, Ancestry.com, Marcus Vincent Young.

187 Young, Harold Mason, compiled and ed. by Debbie Young Chase, *Burma Headhunters*. Bloomington, Indiana: XLIBRIS, 2015, pg. 163. Library of Congress, 101 Independence Ave. SE, Washington, DC.

188 Young, Harold Mason, *Burma Headhunters*, pg. 81.

189 Young, Harold Mason, *Burma Headhunters*, pg. 81-82.

190 Find A Grave—Miami Cemetery, Rush Creek Twp., Logan Co., Ohio, Findagrave.com, Samuel Mason, Find A Grave Memorial #30943706.

191 Find A Grave—Greenwood Cemetery, DeGraff, Pleasant Twp., Logan Co., Ohio, Findagrave.com, Cora Mason, Find A Grave Memorial #18379949.

192 Find A Grave—Greenwood Cemetery, DeGraff, Pleasant Twp., Logan Co., Ohio, Findagrave.com, John P. Mason, Find A Grave Memorial #18379957.

193 Ohio, County Marriages, 1789-2013, FamilySearch.org, John P. Mason and Anna Slusser, Logan County, Ohio Marriage Records, Vol 1, pg. 119, lic. #237.

194 Indiana, Death Certificates, 1899-2011, Ancestry.com, Anna Louisa Mason, death cert. #38070.

195 "Mrs. Mantle's Mother Dies" (Vincennes, Indiana, Vincennes Sun-Commercial, 26 Dec 1940), Knox County Public Library, 502 North Seventh Street, Vincennes, IN.

196 Find A Grave—Greenwood Cemetery, DeGraff, Pleasant Twp., Logan Co., Ohio, Findagrave.com, Anna L. Mason, Find A Grave Memorial #150697760.

197 California, Death Index, 1940-1997, Ancestry.com, Mildred Elizabeth Mantle.

198 U.S. Passport Applications 1795-1925, Ancestry.com, Mildred Elizabeth Mason, #16493, dated 18 May 1920.

199 Indiana, Marriage Collection, 1800-1941, Ancestry.com, Lance A. Mantle and Mildred Elizabeth Mason, Marion County, Indiana Marriage Records, Book 110, pg. 561.

200 Florida Death Index 1877-1998, Ancestry.com, Alice Mason Honeycutt, death cert. #69718.

201 Florida Memorial Gardens Cemetery Records, Florida Memorial Gardens Cemetery, 5950 South U.S. Highway 1, Rockledge, FL, Alice I. Mason.

202 Find A Grave—Florida Memorial Gardens Cemetery, Findagrave.com, Alice I. Honeycutt, Find A Grave Memorial #161930588.

203 Find A Grave—Greenwood Cemetery, DeGraff, Pleasant Twp., Logan Co., Ohio, Findagrave.com, Minne E. Mason, Find A Grave Memorial #18379965.

204 Find A Grave—Greenwood Cemetery, DeGraff, Pleasant Twp., Logan Co., Ohio, Findagrave.com, Otto G. Baughman, Find A Grave Memorial #97820432.

205 Ohio Death Certificate, Ohio Department of Health, Center for Vital and Health Statistics, 246 North High Street, Columbus, OH, Tina Dreher, #45961.

206 Find A Grave—Greenwood Cemetery, DeGraff, Pleasant Twp., Logan Co., Ohio, Findagrave.com, Tina D. Stehler Dreher, Find A Grave Memorial #18186073.

207 Ohio, County Marriages, 1789-2013, FamilySearch.com, Emery Dreher and Tina D. Baughman, Marion County, Ohio Marriage Records, Vol. 22, pg. 313, lic. #1813.

208 "New Book of Short Stories" (Indianapolis, Indiana, Indianapolis Star, 01 Dec 1904), Indiana State Library, 315 West Ohio Street, Indianapolis, IN.

209 Virginia, Death Records, 1912-2014, Ancestry.com, Orpha M. Conklin, death cert. #9298.

210 "Ohio Accidents Fatal to 16 Over Week-End" (Coshocton, Ohio, Coshocton Tribune, 11 Dec 1939) Ohio Historical Society Archives/Library, Ohio History Center, 800 East 17th Avenue, Columbus, OH.

211 Ohio, County Marriages, 1789-2013, FamilySearch.org, Otto H. Russell and Gertrude Pegan, Logan County, Ohio Marriage Records, Vol. G, pg. 438.

212 Ohio Death Certificate, Ohio Department of Health, Center for Vital and Health Statistics, 246 North High Street, Columbus, OH, Otto H. Russell #77717.

213 Find A Grave—Greenwood Cemetery, DeGraff, Pleasant Twp., Logan Co., Ohio, Findagrave.com, Otto H. Russell, Find A Grave Memorial #18525409.

214 Ohio, County Births, 1841-2003 (County Courthouses), FamilySearch.org, Pauline Russell, Logan Co., Ohio Birth Record Vol. 4, pg. 177.

215 Obituary of Pauline R. Brown (Sarasota, Florida, Sarasota Herald Tribune, 30 Jun 1999) Selby Library, 1331 First Street, Sarasota, FL.

216 "Dr. Arthur Pegan…" (Bellefontaine Ohio, Bellefontaine Examiner, 26 Apr 1904), Logan County Libraries, Knowlton Library, 220 North Main Street, Bellefontaine, OH.

217 U.S. Patent and Trademark Office Patents, 1790-1909, Ancestry.com, Arthur C. Pegan, Patent #840,800.

218 U.S., WWI Draft Registration Cards, 1917-1918, Ancestry.com, Arthur Pegan, Indianapolis, Indiana.

219 "Toilet Water Blamed" (Indianapolis, Indiana, Indianapolis Star, 05 May 1920), Indiana State Library, 315 West Ohio Street, Indianapolis, IN.

220 Find A Grave—Crown Hill Cemetery, Indianapolis, Center Twp., Marion Co., Indiana, Findagrave.com, Elgie Albershardt, Find A Grave Memorial #16380334.

221 Marion County, Indiana Marriage Records, Marion County, Indiana County Clerk, City-County Building, W-122, 200 East Washington Street, Indianapolis, IN, August H. Albershardt and Elgie Pegan, Marion County, Indiana Marriage Records, Book 43, pg. 291.

222 Indiana, Marriage Index, 1800-1941, Ancestry.com, August H. Albershardt.

223 Indiana, Death Certificates, 1899-2011, Ancestry.com, "Augest A. Albergheni" (incorrect indexing), death cert. #61-009547. Certificate clearly says August H. Albershardt.

224 Obituary of Dr. A.H. Albershardt (Indianapolis, Indiana, Indianapolis Star, 13 Mar 1961), Indianapolis Public Library, 40 East St. Clair Street, Indianapolis, IN.

225 Find A Grave—Crown Hill Cemetery, Indianapolis, Center Twp., Marion Co., Indiana, Findagrave.com, Dr. August H. Albershardt, Find A Grave Memorial #16380319.

226 Phone interviews with Donald M. Albershardt, Indianapolis, IN, Ann Miller Carr, author, November 2011.

227 Indiana, Death Certificates, 1899-2011, Ancestry.com, "Millon Jams Albershardt", death cert. #20284.

228 Crown Hill Cemetery Records, Milton J. Albershardt, Crown Hill Cemetery, 700 West 38th Street, Indianapolis, IN.

229 Obituary of Cathern Ann Albershardt (Atlanta, Georgia, Atlanta Constitution, 08 Jul 1997), Stone Mountain-Sue Kellogg Library, DeKalb County Public Library System, 952 Leon Street, Stone Mountain, GA.

230 Indiana, Birth Certificates, 1907-1940, Ancestry.com, Catherine Albershardt, birth cert. #30438.

231 Georgia Deaths, 1919-1998, Ancestry.com, Cathern Secrest, death cert. ##029647.

232 Indiana, Death Certificates, 1899-2011, Ancestry.com, Arlton H. Albershardt, death cert. #87-034449

233 Indiana, Birth Certificates, 1907-1940, Ancestry.com, Arlton Henry Albershardt, birth cert. #32564

234 Oaklawn Memorial Gardens Cemetery Records, Arlton H. Albershardt, Oaklawn Memorial Gardens, 9700 Allisonville Road, Fishers, IN.

235 Obituary of Arlton Albershardt (Indianapolis, Indiana, Indianapolis Star, 22 Sep 1987), Indiana State Library, 315 West Ohio Street, Indianapolis, IN.

236 Find A Grave—Oaklawn Memorial Gardens, Fishers, Delaware Twp., Hamilton Co., Indiana, Findagrave.com, Arlton H. Albershardt, Find A Grave Memorial # 129403194.

237 Angeles Abbey Memorial Park Mausoleum Records, Marcia Reiling, Angeles Abbey Memorial Park Mausoleum, 1515 East Compton Boulevard, Compton, CA, Niche: E-53 Columbarium: West Buildilng.

238 Find A Grave—Angeles Abbey Memorial Park Cemetery, Compton, Los Angeles Co., California, Findagrave.com, Marcia Reiling, Find A Grave Memorial #181631540.

239 California Death Certificate, California Health and Strategic Planning, Vital Records, M.S. 5103, P.O. Box 997410, Sacramento, CA, Gustave Reiling, death cert. #D44-091610.

240 California, Death Index, 1940-1997, Ancestry.com, Gustave Adolph Reiling.

241 Find A Grave—Angeles Abbey Memorial Park Cemetery, Compton, Los Angeles Co., California, Findagrave.com, Gustave Reiling, Find A Grave Memorial #181631582.

242 Angeles Abbey Memorial Park Mausoleum Records, Gustave A. Reiling, Angeles Abbey Memorial Park Mausoleum, 1515 East Compton Boulevard, Compton, California.

243 U.S. City Directories, 1822-1995, Ancestry.com, Toledo, Ohio, pg. 1039, entry for Reiling, Gustave A.

244 U.S. City Directories, 1822-1995, Ancestry.com, Redondo Beach, California, pg. 63 entry for Reiling, Gustave A.

245 California, Voter Registrations, 1900-1968, Ancestry.com, G. Adolph Reiling.

246 Angeles Abbey Memorial Park Mausoleum Records, Willette Sawyer, Angeles Abbey Memorial Park Mausoleum, 1515 East Compton Boulevard, Compton, California.

247 Michigan, Marriages, 1868-1925, FamilySearch.org, Perry E. Sawyer and "Willett" Miller, Hilldale County, Michigan Marriage Records, Vol. 2, pg. 199, #5183.

248 U.S., WWI Draft Registration Cards, 1917-1918, Ancestry.com, Perry Elsworth Sawyer.

249 California, Death Index, 1940-1997, Ancestry.com, Perry E. Sawyer.

250 Find A Grave—Forest Lawn Memorial Park Cemetery, Glendale, Los Angeles Co., California, Findagrave.com, Perry E. Sawyer, Find A Grave Memorial #8756035.

251 Ohio, County Marriages, 1789-2013, FamilySearch.org, Charles M. Humason and Blanche Miller, Lucas County, Ohio Marriage Records, Book 6, pg. 171, cert. #512.

252 U.S., WWI Draft Registration Cards, 1917-1918, Ancestry.com, Charles Humason in Woodlawn Twp., Beaver Co., Pennsylvania.

253 Pennsylvania County Marriages, 1885-1950, FamilySearch.org, Beaver Co., Pennsylvania marriage license #16241, Charles M. Humason-Hazel Hendricks, 01 Apr 1916.

254 Pennsylvania Death Certificates, Pennsylvania Department of Health, Division of Vital Records, Health and Welfare Building, 8th Floor West, 625 Forster Street, Harrisburg, PA, Charles M. Humason, death cert. #32253 county #4.

255 Obituary of Charles Humason (Woodlawn, Pennsylvania, Woodlawn Gazette, 14 Mar 1924), Beaver County Genealogy & History Center, 1301 Seventh Avenue, Beaver Falls, PA.

256 U.S. City Directories, 1822-1995, Ancestry.com, Toledo, Ohio, pg. 755, entry for Humason, Blanche H.

257 U.S., WWI Draft Registration Cards, 1917-1918, Ancestry.com, Edward Ephraim Pegan, Springfield, Ohio.

258 Find A Grave—Findagrave.com, Edward Ephraim Pegan, Find A Grave Memorial #143047425.

259 Illinois-Cook County Marriages, 1871-1920, FamilySearch.org, Edward E. Pegan and Maude L. Abbott, Cook Co., Illinois Marriage Records, lic. #459929.

260 Illinois Marriages, 1815-1935, FamilySearch.org, Edward E. Pegan and Maude Abbott.

261 California, Death Index, 1940-1997, Ancestry.com, Maud L. Pegan. Ancestry.com.

262 U.S., Social Security Applications and Claims Index, 1936-2007, Ancestry.com, Maud Lillian Abbott PeGan.

263 U.S., Social Security Applications and Claims Index, 1936-2007, Ancestry.com, Maud Lillian Abbott PeGan.

264 Find A Grave—Mt. Hope Cemetery, San Diego, San Diego Co., California, Findagrave.com, Maude Abbott Pegan, Find A Grave Memorial#143049434.

265 U.S. City Directories, 1822-1995, Ancestry.com, Indianapolis, Indiana, 1913-1914, pg. 1340; 1918-1919, pg. 1003, entry for Pegan, Edward E.

266 U.S. City Directories, 1822-1995, Ancestry.com, San Diego, Californai, 1947, pg. 868; entry for Pegan, Donald, with Maud erroneously listed as spouse; 1965, pg. 611, entry for PeGan, Mrs. Maud L.

267 California, Death Index, 1940-1997, Ancestry.com, Donald Abbott Pegan. Ancestry.com.

268 Find A Grave—Hollywood Forever Cemetery, Hollywood, Los Angeles Co., California, Findagrave.com, Fred R. Hill, Find A Grave Memorial #6567871.

269 New York Marriages 1686-1980, FamilySearch.org, Fred Roland Hill and Eugenia Adelaide Edwards.

270 New York New York City Marriage Records, 1829-1940, FamilySearch.org, Fred Roland Hill and Eugenia Adelaide Edwards.

271 Newspapers and Periodicals, Ancestry.com, "Divorces Wife Who Forged His Name" (Trenton, New Jersey, Trenton Evening Times, 26 Jul 1909).

272 Los Angeles County, California Marriage Records, California Health and Strategic Planning, Vital Records, M.S. 5103, P.O. Box 997410, Sacramento, CA, Fred R. Hill and Helen Gibson, Book 1332, Pg. 74, cert. #21332.

273 California Divorce Index, 1940-1997, Ancestry.com, Helen Hilma Bye Baker.

274 Find A Grave—Forest Lawn Memorial Park Cemetery Hollywood Hills, Los Angeles, Los Angeles Co., California, Findagrave.com, Helen B. Bye Baker, Find A Grave Memorial #85846791.

275 Colorado Statewide Marriage Index, 1853-2006, FamilySearch.org, Edward B. Gage and Mamie E. Pegan, Denver County, Colorado Marriage Records, Colorado marriage lic. #32667.

276 Cook County, Illinois, Birth Certificates Index, 1871-1922, Ancestry.com, Edward B. Gage.

277 Obituary of Edward B. Gage (Chicago, Illinois, Chicago Tribune, 20 Jan 1959), Chicago Public Library, 400 South State Street, Chicago, IL.

278 U.S. Passport Applications 1795-1925, Ancestry.com, Edward B. Gage, #26023, 1916 to Canada.

279 Death notice, Mamie P. Gage (Denver, Colorado, Denver Post, 14 Jul 1968), Denver Public Library, 10 West Fourteenth Avenue Parkway, Denver, CO.

280 Cook County, Illinois, Birth Certificates Index, 1871-1922, Ancestry.com, Henry Crume Gage.

281 U.S. WWII Draft Cards Young Men, 1940-1947, Ancestry.com, Henry C. Gage, Denver, Denver Co., Colorado.

282 U.S., Department of Veterans Affairs BIRLS Death File, 1850-2010, Henry Gage.

283 Find A Grave—Skyline Memorial Gardens, Portland, Multnomah Co., Oregon, Findagrave.com, Gwynn B. Gage, Find A Grave Memorial #53553029.

284 Oregon, Death Index, 1898-2008, Ancestry.com, Gwynn B. Gage.

285 Find A Grave—Crown Hill Cemetery, Wheat Ridge, Jefferson Co., Colorado, Findagrave.com, Patience Pegan Crane, Find A Grave Memorial #50072773.

286 Obituary of Patience Crane (Denver, Colorado, Denver Post, 11 Sep 1949), Denver Public Library, 10 West Fourteenth Avenue Parkway, Denver, CO.

287 Cutter, Charles Ammi, Library Journal, Vol. 31, Boston: R.R. Bowker & Co., 1906, pg. 276.

288 "Drexel Institute Library School Association Alumni Notes", *Library Journal, Vol. 40*.

289 *American Library Annual, 1915-1916,* New York: Bowker & Co., 1916, pg. 444.

290 *Bulletin of the American Library Association, Vol. XXII, No. 4, November 1918,* Chicago: American Library Association, pg. 472.

291 Denver County, Colorado Marriage Records, Office of the Clerk and Recorder/Public Trustee, Wellington E. Webb Municipal Building, 201 West Colfax Avenue, Department 101, Denver, CO, Ross Crane and Patience Pegan, Denver County, Colorado Marriage Records, Book 31, pg. 314, #54025.

292 Charles Edgar Rosecrans, professional name Ross Crane, passport application #26035, special series #3715, Chicago, Illinois, 01 Aug 1924; granted 03 Sep 1924. National Archives and Records Administration (NARA), Washington, DC.

293 U.S., Social Security Applications and Claims Index, 1936-2007, Ancestry.com, Ross Crane.

294 Pine Lake Cemetery Records, Ross Crane, Pine Lake Cemetery, 1367 Pine Lake Road, LaPorte, IN.

295 "Cartoonist Crane in Lyceum Work" (Lompoc, California, Lompoc Journal, 26 Oct 1912, pg. 4) California Digital Newspaper Collection, Online database, https://cdnc.ucr.edu/cgi-bin/cdnc?a=d&d=LJ19121026.2.21&e=———en—20—1—txt-txIN————1

296 "Ross Crane", *The Luyceumite and Talent, The Committeeman's Year Book For 1913, Lyceum Magazine,* International Lyceum Association. Chicago: The Century Lyceum Bureau, 1912, pg. 84.

297 Tapia, John E., Circuit Chautauqua: From Rural Education to Popular Entertainment in Early Twentieth

298 Crane, Ross, *The Ross Crane Book of Home Furnishing and Decoration; a Practical, Authoritative and Sympathetic Guide for the Amateur Home Decorator*. Chicago: Frederick J. Drake & Company; 1925 and 1933. Funderburg Library, Manchester University, 604 East College Avenue, North Manchester, IN.

Century America, Jefferson, North Carolina, McFarland & Co., 1997, pg. 87.

299 Crane, Ross, *Interior Decoration: A Comprehensive Study Course for Furniture Men*. Chicago: Seng Company; 1928. The University of Chicago Library, 1100 East 57th Street, Chicago, IL.

300 Crane, Ross, *The Ross Crane Guide and Stylist*. Chicago: Charles E. Rosecrans; 1929. Chicago History Museum, Research Center, 1601 Clark Street, Chicago, IL.

301 Crane, Ross, *The Joy of Color*. Cleveland, Ohio: The Sherwin Williams Company; 1932. The University of Chicago Library, 1100 East 57th Street, Chicago, IL.

302 Crane, Ross, *Learn Interior Decoration by Looking*. Gainesville, Florida: General Division of the University of Florida; 1940. Theodore M. Hesburg Library, 221 Hesburg Library, University of Notre Dame, Notre Dame, IN.

303 Find A Grave—Forest Park Cemetery, Anthony, Anthony Twp., Harper Co., Kansas, Findagrave.com, Allie Belle Cissel Michael, Find A Grave Memorial #89249168.

304 Cowley County, Marriage Records, Cowley County, Kansas Clerk's Office, Cowley County South Annex, 321 East 10th Avenue, Winfield, KS, Bennett F. Michael and Allie B. Cissel, Cowley County, Kansas Marriage Records, Vol, M, pg. 476.

305 U.S., WWI Draft Registration Cards, 1917-1918, Ancestry.com, Bennett Franklin Michael, Wichita, Kansas.

306 "Dr. B.F. Michael, Organizer of Shrine Band, Dies at 90" (Wichita, Kansas, Wichita Eagle, 26 Mar 1996). Midwest Historical & Genealogical Society, 1203 North Main Street, Wichita, KS.

307 Find A Grave—Forest Park Cemetery, Anthony, Anthony Twp., Harper Co., Kansas, Findagrave.com, Bennett Franklin Michael, Find A Grave Memorial #89248866.

308 Find A Grave—Wichita Cemetery & Mausoleum, Wichita, Sedgwick Co., Kansas, Findagrave.com, Genevieve LeBlond, Find A Grave Memorial #45547799.

309 U.S., Social Security Applications and Claims Index, 1936-2007, Ancestry.com, Frances Genevieve Michael Leblond.

310 Obituary of Genevieve LeBlond (Wichita, Kansas, Wichita Eagle, 30 Mar 1996). Midwest Historical & Genealogical Society, 1203 North Main Street, Wichita, KS.

311 Obituary of Benjamin Franklin Cissel (Anthony, Kansas, Anthony Republican, 03 Jul 1913), Anthony Library, 624 East Main Street, Anthony, KS.

312 Find A Grave—Forest Park Cemetery, Anthony, Anthony Twp., Harper Co., Kansas, Findagrave.com, Bennie F. Cissel, Find A Grave Memorial #32409129.

313 Iowa, County Marriages, 1838-1934, FamilySearch.org, Charles M. Cissel and Louise Krouscup, Polk County, Iowa Marriage Records, pg. 57.

314 Caldwell County, Missouri, Marriage Records, Caldwell County, Missouri Recorder of Deeds, Caldwell County Courthouse, 49 East Main Street, Kingston, MO, Charles M. Cissel and Lottie H. Levitt, Caldwell County, Missouri Marriage Records, Vol. J, pg. 233.

315 Find A Grave—Old Mission Cemetery, Wichita, Sedgwick Co., Kansas, Findagrave.com, Lottie H. Cissel, Find A Grave Memorial #43462234.

316 Obituary of Lottie Hertha Cissel (Wichita, Kansas, Wichita Eagle, 25 Apr 1962) Midwest Historical & Genealogical Society, 1203 North Main Street, Wichita, KS.

317 "Services Planned for Lottie Cissel" (Wichita, Kansas, Wichita Eagle, 25 Apr 1962) Midwest Historical & Genealogical Society, 1203 North Main Street, Wichita, KS.

318 Missouri Marriage Records, 1805-2002, Ancestry.com, Walter J. Levitt and Lottie Irvine.

319 Tombstone Inscriptions in Cemeteries of Manatee County, Florida 1850-1980, 2nd edition (Bradenton, Florida, Manasota Genealogical Society (now Manatee Genealogical Society), 1982), Laurence V. Mason, pg. 258. Manasota (now Manatee) Genealogical Society, P.O. Box 1194, Bradenton, FL.

320 Find A Grave—Manasota Memorial Park Cemetery, Bradenton, Manatee Co., Florida, Findagrave.com, Laurence V. Mason, Find A Grave Memorial #126148123.

321 Obituary of Anna Mae Mason (Bradenton, Florida, Bradenton Herald, 24 Nov 1952), Manatee County Public Library-Central Branch, 1301 Barcarrota Boulevard West, Bradenton, FL.

322 Find A Grave—Manasota Memorial Park Cemetery, Bradenton, Manatee Co., Florida, Findagrave.com, Anna Mae Mason, Find A Grave Memorial #126148133.

323 WWI Draft Registration Cards, 1917-1918, Ancestry.com, Laurence Victor Mason, Stark County, Ohio.

324 Ohio, County Births, 1841-2003 (County Courthouses), FamilySearch.org, Catherine L. Mason, Logan Co., Ohio Birth Records, Vol. 4, pg. 128.

325 Florida Death Index 1877-1998, Ancestry.com, Kathryn Aldrich.

326 Ohio, County Births, 1841-2003 (County Courthouses), FamilySearch.org, Donald Earl Mason, Logan Co., Ohio Birth Records, Vol. 6, pg. 33.

327 Obituary of Donald Earl Mason (Bradenton, Florida, Bradenton Herald, 27 Aug 1994), Manasota (now Manatee) Historical Society, Genealogical Society, P.O. Box 1194, Bradenton, FL.

328 Find A Grave—Lone Oak Cemetery, Leesburg, Lake Co., Florida, Findagrave.com, Marguerite Voorhees, Find A Grave Memorial #30954625.

329 Florida Death Certificate, Florida Department of Health-State Office of Vital Statistics, 1217 North Pearl Street, Jacksonville, FL, Elsworth Charles Voorhees, death cert. #67-009478.

330 Find A Grave—Lone Oak Cemetery, Leesburg, Lake Co., Florida, Findagrave.com, Elsworth Charles Voorhees, Find A Grave Memorial #30954621.

331 Florida Marriage Collection, 1822-1875 and 1927-2001, Ancestry.com, Elsworth Charles Vorhees and Anna Bowen, Lake County, Florida Marriage Records, Vol. 1237, cert. #18754.

332 Find A Grave—Bellefontaine City Cemetery, Bellefontaine, Lake Twp., Logan Co., Ohio, Findagrave.com, Paul E. Mason, Find A Grave Memorial #21839943.

333 Ohio, County Marriages, 1789-2013, FamilySearch.org, Paul E. Mason and Frances L. Moore, Cuyahoga County, Ohio Marriage Records, Vol. 116, pg. 273, lic. #146363.

334 Ohio, Deaths, 1908-1932, 1938-2007, Ancestry.com, Frances L. Mason, death cert. #011471.

335 Obituary of Frances Louise Mason (Bellefontaine, Ohio, Bellefontaine Examiner, 28 Feb 1971), Logan County Libraries, Knowlton Library, 220 North Main Street, Bellefontaine, OH.

336 Find A Grave—Bellefontaine City Cemetery, Bellefontaine, Lake Twp., Logan Co., Ohio, Findagrave.com, Frances L. Mason, Find A Grave Memorial #21839933.

337 Ohio, Birth Index, 1908-1964, Ancestry.com, Mary J. Mason, state file #1922009090.

338 Ohio, Deaths, 1908-1932, 1938-2007, Ancestry.com, Mary J. Ewing, death cert. #086382.

339 Ohio, Birth Index, 1908-1964, Ancestry.com, Robert E. Mason, state file #1924026715.

340 U.S., Department of Veterans Affairs BIRLS Death File, 1850-2010, Ancestry.com, Robert Mason.

341 Ohio, Deaths, 1908-1932, 1938-2007, Ancestry.com, Robert E. Mason, death cert. #000533.

342 Ohio, Birth Index, 1908-1964, Ancestry.com, Charles S. Mason, state file #1926097127.

343 Family records: Email correspondence with Jerrick Young, Ann Miller Carr, author, 7-10 Aug 2014.

344 Young, Harold Mason, *To The Mountain Tops: A Sojourn Among The Lahu of Asia*, pg. 472.

345 California Birth Index, 1905-1995, Ancestry.com, Ruth S. Pinkerton, Los Angeles Co., California.

346 Obituary of Ruth S. Young (Ventura, California, Ventura Star Free Press, 08 Dec 1981), California State Library, California History Room, 900 N Street, Sacramento, CA.

347 California Death Certificate, California Health and Strategic Planning, Vital Records, M.S. 5103, P.O. Box 997410, Sacramento, CA, Ruth Saada Young, death cert. #81-171897; local cert. #2634.

348 California Death Index, 1940-1997, Ancestry.com, Ruth Saada Young.

349 Death Notice of Mrs. Harold M. (Ruth Saada Pinkerton) Young, 08 Dec 1981, Interoffice Communication, International Ministries, American Baptist Churches, 588 North Gulph Road, King of Prussia, PA.

350 Young, Harold Mason, *To The Mountain Tops: A Sojourn Among The Lahu of Asia*, pg. 472-3.

351 Young, Harold Mason, compiled and ed. by Debbie Young Chase, *Burma Headhunters*. Bloomington, Indiana: XLIBRIS, 2015, pg. 93-4, 161. Library of Congress, 101 Independence Ave. SE, Washington, DC.

352 "History of Chaing Mai Zoo", Chaing Mai Zoo Official Website, http://www.chiangmai.zoothailand.org/en/ewt_news.php?nid=183

353 Young, Harold Mason, *To The Mountain Tops: A Sojourn Among The Lahu of Asia*.

354 Young, Harold Mason, *Burma Headhunters*.

355 Seattle Passenger and Crew Lists, 1882-1957, Ancestry.com, Oliver Young, on the ship "President Grant" 24 Jan 1934 to Seattle.

356 Young, Gordon, *Journey from Banna, An Autobiography*. Bloomington, Indiana: Xlibris, 2011, pg. 315. Copy owned by author Ann Miller Carr.

357 Obituary of Oliver Gordon Young (San Luis Obispo, California, San Luis Obispo Tribune, 10 Aug 2016), San Luis Obispo Public Library, 995 Palm Street, San Luis Obispo, CA.

358 U.S. Consular Reports of Births, 1910-1949, Ancestry.com, Helen Elizabeth Young, born Kengtung, Burma.

359 California Birth Index, 1905-1995, Ancestry.com, William Marcus Young.

360 Fawthrup, Tom, "William Young Obituary, CIA agent in American's 'secret war' in Laos", (New York, The Guardian, U.S. edition, 04 May 2011), The Guardian, U.S. Main Office, 315 West 36th Street, New York, NY.

361 "CIA Suicide After A Life of God and Guns", 06 Apr 2011, Scoop Independent News, Website; and "Special Forces Obituaries: William Young", (The Telegraph, London, England, 18 May 2011; online); and Fuller, Tom, "William Young, 76, Leader In U.S. Secret War in Laos" (New York, New York, The New York Times, 0)3 Apr 2011); A Voice for the Laotian Who do not have Voice, Website: https://khampoua.wordpress.com/tag/william-young/; captured 14 Dec 2017.

362 Montecito Memorial Park Cemetery Records, Marcus V. Young, Montecito Memorial Park Cemetery, 3520 East Washington Street, Colton, CA.

363 Find A Grave—Montecito Memorial Park Cemetery, Colton, San Bernardino Co., California, Findagrave.com, Marcus V. Young, Find A Grave Memorial #171240289.

364 Young, Harold Mason compiled and ed. by Debbie Young Chase, *Burma Headhunters* (Bloomington, Indiana, XLIBRIS, 09 Jan 2015), pg. 160. Library of Congress, 101 Independence Ave. SE, Washington, DC.

365 California, Death Index, 1940-1997, Ancestry.com, Vera G. Young.

366 Obituary of Vera Young (Redlands, California, Redlands Daily Facts, 19 Mar 1973), California State Library, California History Room, 900 N Street, Sacramento, CA.

367 Find A Grave—Montecito Memorial Park Cemetery, Colton, San Bernardino Co., California, Findagrave.com, Vera Young, Find A Grave-Memorial #171240164.

368 Montecito Memorial Park Cemetery Records, Vera Young, Montecito Memorial Park Cemetery, 3520 East Washington Street, Colton, CA.

369 Gibson, Richard Michael, The Secret Army: Chaing Kai-shek and the Drug Warlords of the Golden Triangle. Singapore: John Wiley & Sons (Asia) Pte. Ltd., 2011.

370 Young, Marcus Vincent and Sara Yaw Su, *Hpuk lai singang si siyeh pa hkrao: The New Testament in Wa*. Rangoon: The American Baptist Mission Press, 1938, reprint 1950. Newberry Library, 60 West Walton Street, Chicago, IL.

371 New York Passenger Lists, 1820-1957, Ancestry.com, Vera Young, on the ship *Brazil*, on 13 Jul 1942 to New York.

372 California, Death Index, 1940-1997, Ancestry.com, Lael Marcus Young.

373 New York Passenger Lists, 1820-1957, Ancestry.com, Lael Young, on the ship *Brazil*, on 13 Jul 1942 to New York.

374 U.S., Social Security Applications and Claims Index, 1936-2007, Ancestry.com, Lael Marcus Young.

375 Obituary of Lael M. Young (San Bernardino, California, San Bernardino Sun, 29 May 1996). California State Library, California History Room, 900 N Street, Sacramento, CA

376 New York Passenger Lists, 1820-1957, Ancestry.com, Phillip Young, on the ship *Brazil*, 13 Jul 1942 to New York.

377 New York Passenger Lists, 1820-1957, Ancestry.com, (Daughter) Young, on the ship *Brazil*, 13 Jul 1942 to New York.

378 U.S., WWI Draft Registration Cards, 1917-1918, Ancestry.com, Lance Alfred Mantle.

379 California Death Certificate, California Health and Strategic Planning, Vital Records, M.S. 5103, P.O. Box 997410, Sacramento, CA, Lance Alfred Mantle, death cert. #39163000661.

380 California, Death Index, 1940-1997, Ancestry.com, Lance Alfred Mantle.

381 U.S. Passport Applications, 1795, 1925, Ancestry.com, Lance A. Mantle, applied on 14 May 1920.

382 U.S., WWII Draft Registration Cards, 1942, Ancestry.com, Lance Alfred Mantle.

383 England & Wales, Civil Registration Birth Index, 1837-1915, Ancestry.com, Launcelot Alfred Mantle, 1895, (July-Aug-Sep), Barton Registration District, Gloucestershire, Vol. 6A, pg. 167.

384 New York Passenger Lists, 1820-1957, Ancestry.com, Launcelot A. Mantle, arrived 24 Sep 1913 on the ship, *Oceanic*.

385 All U.S., Army Transport Service, Passenger Lists, 1910-1939, Ancestry.com, Lance A. Mantle, 1918 departing from Hoboken, New Jersey.

386 Phone interview with Peg Mantle, near Lansing, MI, Ann Miller Carr, author, 09 February 2012.

387 U.S. Consular Registrations, 1916-1925, Ancestry.com, Lance A. Mantle, Box 95, #37164.

388 U.S. City Directories, 1822-1995, Ancestry.com, Grand Rapids, Michigan, 1928, pg. 606, entry for Mantle, Lance.

389 U.S. City Directories, 1822-1995, Ancestry.com, Dallas, Texas, 1931, pg. 1257, entry for Mantle, Lance. A.; 1932, pg. 1073, entry for Mantle, Lance A.

390 U.S. City Directories, 1822-1995, Ancestry.com, Atlanta, Georgia, 1933, pg. 690, entry for Mantle, Lance. A.

391 U.S. City Directories, 1822-1995, Ancestry.com, Indianapolis, Indiana, 1935, pg. 808, entry for Mantle, Lance. A.

392 U.S. City Directories, 1822-1995, Ancestry.com, Indianapolis, Indiana, 1936, pg. 1009, entry for Mantle, Lance. A.

393 U.S. City Directories, 1822-1995, Ancestry.com, Denver, Colorado, 1945, pg. 861 entry for Mantle, Capt. Lance. A.

394 U.S. City Directories, 1822-1995, Ancestry.com, LaJolla, California, 1955, pg. 105 entry for Mantle, Lance. A.

395 California, Marriage Index, 1949-1959, Lance A. Mantle and Ella M. Wait Parente, San Diego County Marriage Records, state file #95724.

396 U.S. City Directories, 1822-1995, Ancestry.com, San Diego, California, 1961, pg.925, entry for Parente, Ella M. (wid. Earl).

397 U.S. City Directories, 1822-1995, Ancestry.com, Denver, Colorado, 1964, pg. 769 and 1965, pg. 732 entry for Mantle, Lance. A., a writer for a church extension service; 1966, pg. 799 and 1967, pg. 808, entry for Mantle, Lance A., a printer.

398 U.S., Social Security Applications and Claims Index, 1936-2007, John Gregory Mantle.

399 U.S. Department of Veterans Affairs BIRLS Death File, 1850-2010, John Mantle.

400 Indiana, Birth Certificates, 1907-1940, John Gregory Mantle, birth cert. #56519.

401 California, Death Index, 1940-1997, John Gregory Mantle.

402 Norma Mantle (Park) Birth Certificate, Nebraska Department of Health and Human Services, Vital Records, 1033 O Street, Suite 130, Lincoln, NE, birth cert. #M534-10025.

403 U.S., Social Security Applications and Claims Index, 1936-2007, Norma Louise Mantle Park.

404 U.S. Department of Veterans Affairs BIRLS Death File, 1850-2010, Norma Park.

405 Indiana, Marriage Collection, 1800-1941, Ancestry.com, Horace R. Honeycutt and Alice I. Mason, Marion County, Indiana Marriage Records, Vol.130, pg. 86, #9257.

406 Marion County, Indiana Marriage Records, Marion County, Indiana County Clerk, City-County Building, W-122, 200 East Washington Street, Indianapolis, IN, Horace R. Russell and Alice I. Mason, Marion County, Indiana Marriage Records, Vol.130, pg. 86, #9257.

407 Marriage License of Horace R. Honeycutt and Alice June Mason, Marion County, Indiana County Clerk, City-County Building, W-122, 200 East Washington Street, Indianapolis, IN, Horace R. Honeycutt and Alice June Mason, Marriage Book 30, pg. 86, #9257.

408 Florida Death Certificate, Florida Department of Health-State Office of Vital Statistics, 1217 North Pearl Street, Jacksonville, FL, Horace Russell Honeycutt, death cert.#59-4559.

409 Florida Death Index 1877-1998, Ancestry.com, Horace Russell Honeycutt, death cert. #4559.

410 Florida Memorial Gardens Cemetery Records, Florida Memorial Gardens Cemetery, 5950 South U.S. Highway 1, Rockledge, FL, Horace R. Honeycutt.

411 Find A Grave—Florida Memorial Gardens Cemetery, Findagrave.com, Horace R. Honeycutt, Find A Grave Memorial #161930585.

412 U.S. City Directories, 1822-1995, Ancestry.com, Evansville, Indiana, 1944, pg. 325, entry for Honeycutt, Horace R.

413 Florida, State Census, 1867-1945, Ancestry.com, 1945, entry for Horace Honeycutt, Jacksonville, Duval Co., Florida, S1371, Roll 15, pg. 84.

414 U.S. City Directories, 1822-1995, Ancestry.com, Jacksonville, Florida, 1946, pg. 450, entry for Honeycutt, Horace R.

415 Obituary of H.R. Honeycutt (Melbourne, Florida, Melbourne Times, 13 Feb 1959), State Library and Archives of Florida, R.A. Gray Building, 500 South Bronaugh Street, Tallahassee, FL.

416 Indiana, Birth Certificates, 1907-1940, Robert Lee Honeycutt, birth cert. #26675.

417 Florida Death Certificate, Florida Department of Health-State Office of Vital Statistics, 1217 North Pearl Street, Jacksonville, FL, Robert Lee Honeycutt, state file no. 66-052247.

418 Obituary of Robert Lee Honeycutt, (Gainesville, Florida, Gainesville Sun, 28 Nov 1966) Alachua County District Library, 401 East University Avenue, Gainesville, FL.

419 Indiana, Birth Certificates, 1907-1940, Donald James Honeycutt, birth cert. #28442.

420 Find A Grave—Greenwood Cemetery, DeGraff, Pleasant Twp., Logan Co., Ohio, Findagrave.com, Pauline R. Brown, Find A Grave Memorial #115275099.

421 Ohio, County Marriages, 1789-2013, FamilySearch.org, Donald O. Brown and Pauline E. Russell, Logan County, Ohio Marriage Records, Vol. O, pg. 404, cert. #9318.

422 Florida Death Index 1877-1998, Ancestry.com, Donald Otho Brown.

423 Find A Grave—Greenwood Cemetery, DeGraff, Pleasant Twp., Logan Co., Ohio, Findagrave.com, Donald O. Brown, Find A Grave Memorial #115275080.

424 Ohio Death Certificate, Ohio Department of Health, Center for Vital and Health Statistics, 246 North High Street, Columbus, OH, Otto H. Russell, death cert. #77717.

425 U.S. City Directories, 1822-1995, Ancestry.com, Ann Arbor, Michigan, 1938, pg. 113, entry for Brown, Donald O.

426 U.S. City Directories, 1822-1995, Ancestry.com, Ann Arbor, Michigan, 1951, pg. 38, entry for Brown, Donald O.

427 Phone interview with one of the sons of Donald O. and Pauline Russell Brown, FL, Ann Miller Carr, author, 16 Jun 2010. He wishes to remain anonymous.

428 Find A Grave—Crown Hill Cemetery, Indianapolis, Center Twp., Marion Co., Indiana, Findagrave.com, Milton James Albershardt, Find A Grave Memorial #16381035.

429 Web: Marion County, Indiana, Marriage Index, 1925-2012, Ancestry.com, Milton J. Albershardt and Francis Keaton, Marion County, Indiana Marriage Records, Book 135, pg. 34.

430 Obituary of Frances Poisel (Indianapolis, Indiana, Indianapolis Star, 22 Oct 2002), Indianapolis Public Library, 40 East St. Clair Street, Indianapolis, IN.

431 Find A Grave—Washington Park East Cemetery, Warren Twp., Marion Co., Indiana, Findagrave.com, Frances Poisel, Find A Grave Memorial#129057684.

432 Obituary of Norman R. Albershardt (Indianapolis, Indiana, Indianapolis Star, 03 Mar 2013), Indianapolis Public Library, 40 East St. Clair Street, Indianapolis, IN.

433 Find A Grave—Floral Hills Memory Gardens, Tucker, DeKalb Co., Georgia, Findagrave.com, Cathern Albershardt Secrest, Find A Grave Memorial #121879758.

434 Web: Marion County, Indiana, Marriage Index, 1925-2012, Ancestry.com, Wayne D. Secrest and Cathern Albershardt, Marion County, Indiana Marriage Records, Book 146, pg. 389.

435 Indiana Births, 1880-1920, Ancestry.com, Wayne D. Secrest, Hendricks Co. Births, Book 11, pg. 47.

436 Georgia Deaths, 1919-1998, Ancestry.com, Wayne Secrest, death cert. ##018123.

437 Obituary of Wayne D. Secrest (Atlanta, Georgia, Atlanta Constitution, 29 May 1984), Stone Mountain-Sue Kellogg Library, DeKalb County Public Library System, 952 Leon Street, Stone Mountain, GA, Sec. C., pg. 7.

438 Find A Grave—Floral Hills Memory Gardens, Tucker, DeKalb Co., Georgia, Findagrave.com, Wayne D. Secrest, Find A Grave Memorial #170939361.

439 Obituary of W. Donovan Secrest (Athens, Georgia, Athens Daily News, 24 Apr 2001), Athens-Clarke County Library, 2025 Baxter Street, Athens, GA.

440 Web: Marion County, Indiana, Marriage Index, 1925-2012, Ancestry.com, Arlton H. Albershardt and Verna M. Hynes, Marion County Marriage Records, Book 146, pg. 578.

441 Indiana Death Certificate (Indianapolis, Indiana, State of Indiana), Indiana State Department of Health, 2 North Meridian Street, Indianapolis, IN, Verna Albershardt, Indianapolis, Marion Co., Indiana, death cert. #11891.

442 Find A Grave—Crown Hill Cemetery, Indianapolis, Center Twp., Marion Co., Indiana, Findagrave.com, Verna Albershardt, Find A Grave Memorial #16381046.

443 Web: Marion County, Indiana, Marriage Index, 1925-2012, Ancestry.com, Arlton H. Albershardt and Mary Helen McAllister, Marion County Marriage Records, Book 155, pg. 429.

444 Find A Grave—Oaklawn Memorial Gardens, Fishers, Delaware Twp., Hamilton Co., Indiana, Findagrave.com, Helen Mary McAllister Albershardt, Find A Grave Memorial #66116803.

445 Find A Grave—Findagrave.com, Donald Abbott Pegan, Find A Grave Memorial #143045225.

446 California, Death Index, 1940-1997, Ancestry.com, Elizabeth B. Pegan.

447 Find A Grave—Findagrave.com, Elizabeth Bertha "Betty" Steinbrenner Pegan, Find A Grave Memorial #143045337.

448 U.S., Social Security Applications and Claims Index, 1936-2007, Ancestry.com, Roberta Jean Pegan Murdoch.

449 Find A Grave—Findagrave.com, Roberta Jean "Berta" Pegan Murdoch, Find A Grave Memorial #143045606.

450 Colorado Marriages Index, 1858-1939, Denver Public Library, 10 West Fourteenth Avenue Parkway, Denver, CO. Henry C. Gage and Floretta Gentry, Douglas County, Colorado Marriage Records, lic. 2659; Online database: https://history.denverlibrary.org/sites/history/files/COMARR.pdf.

451 U.S., Social Security Applications and Claims Index, 1936-2007, Ancestry.com, Floretta Gentry Gage King.

452 Obituary of Inez Beatrice Olson (Portland, Oregon, The Oregonian, 19 Apr 1996), Oregon Historical Society, 1200 SW Park Avenue, Portland, OR, The Oregonian (Portland, OR), pg. B9.

453 Find A Grave—Skyline Memorial Gardens, Portland, Multnomah Co., Oregon, Findagrave.com, Inez Beatrice Lindseth Gage Olson, Find A Grave Memorial #53553028.

454 U.S., Social Security Applications and Claims Index, 1936-2007, Ancestry.com, Inez Lindseth Gage Olson.

455 Washington Marriage Records, 1865-2004, Ancestry.com, Glen H. Olson and Inez Gage, Clark County Marriage Records, cert. #swclkmcaa27172.

456 Obituary of Robert R. Gage (Portland, Oregon, The Oregonian, 23 Dec 2005), Oregon Historical Society, 1200 SW Park Avenue, Portland, OR, The Oregonian (Portland, OR), pg. C9.

457 Find A Grave—Skyline Memorial Gardens, Portland, Multnomah Co., Oregon, Findagrave.com, Robert R. Gage, Find A Grave Memorial #46926913.

458 Sedgwick County, Kansas Marriage Records, Sedgwick County Clerk's Office, Sedgwick County Courthouse, 525 North Main Street, Wichita, KS, Jack D. LeBlond and Genevieve Michael, Sedgwick County, Kansas Marriager Records, Book PP, pg. 681.

459 Find A Grave—Wichita Park Cemetery & Mausoleum, Wichita, Sedgewick Co., Kansas, Findagrave.com, Jack Donald LeBlond, Find A Grave Memorial #45547802.

460 "Jack LeBlond, Golf Devotee" (Wichita, Kansas, Wichita Eagle, 14 Oct 1980). Midwest Historical & Genealogical Society, 1203 North Main Street, Wichita, KS.

461 Find A Grave—Manasota Memorial Park Cemetery, Bradenton, Manatee Co., Florida, Findagrave.com, Kathryn M. Aldrich, Find A Grave Memorial #118692854.

462 Florida Marriages, 18737-1974, FamilySearch.org, William P. Aldrich and Kathryn Mason, Manatee County, Florida (https://familysearch.org/ark:/61903/1:1:FW75-6ZC: 12 December 2014), William P. Aldrich and Kathryn Mason, 05 Sep 1925; citing Bradentown, Manatee, Florida;.

463 Florida Death Index 1877-1998, Ancestry.com, William Pascale Aldrich.

464 Obituary of William P. Aldrich (Bradenton, Florida, Bradenton Herald, 20 Feb 1986), Manatee County Public Library-Central Branch, 1301 Barcarrota Boulevard West, Bradenton, FL.

465 Find A Grave—Manasota Memorial Park Cemetery, Bradenton, Manatee Co., Florida, Findagrave.com, William P. Aldrich, Find A Grave Memorial #118692840.

466 Find A Grave—Palmetto Cemetery, Palmetto, Manatee Co., Florida, Findagrave.com, William L. Aldrich, Find A Grave Memorial #59277315.

467 Florida Marriages, 1837-1974, FamilySearch.org, William P. Aldrich and Kathryn Mason, Manatee County, Florida Marriage Records.

468 Manasota Memorial Park Cemetery Records, Donald E. Mason, Manasota Memorial Park Cemetery, 1221 53rd Avenue East, Bradenton, FL.

469 Find A Grave—Manasota Memorial Park Cemetery, Bradenton, Manatee Co., Florida, Findagrave.com, Donald E. Mason, Find A Grave Memorial #118422278.

470 Obituary of Doris Martha Mason (Bradenton, Florida, Bradenton Herald, 07 Jan 1992), Manatee County Public Library-Central Branch, 1301 Barcarrota Boulevard West, Bradenton, FL.

471 Manasota Memorial Park Cemetery Records, Doris M. Mason, Manasota Memorial Park Cemetery, 1221 53rd Avenue East, Bradenton, FL.

472 Find A Grave—Manasota Memorial Park Cemetery, Bradenton, Manatee Co., Florida, Findagrave.com, Doris Mason, Find A Grave Memorial #118422266.

473 Ohio Deaths, 1908-1953, FamilySearch.org, Dorothy Ann Mason, death cert. #26481.

474 Find A Grave—Huntsville Cemetery, McArthur Twp., Logan Co., Ohio, Findagrave.com, Mary J. Ewing, Find A Grave Memorial #19886676.

475 Michigan, Marriage Records, 1867-1952, Ancestry.com, Thomas J. Ewing and Mary Jane Mason, Monroe County, Michigan Marriage Records, county file #508; state file #58 10754.

476 Ohio Death Certificate, Ohio Department of Health, Center for Vital and Health Statistics, 246 North High Street, Columbus, OH, Thomas Ewing, death cert. #34538.

477 U.S. Veterans' Gravesites, ca. 1775-2006, Ancestry.com, Thomas Ewing, buried Huntsville Cemetery, Logan Co., Ohio.

478 Obituary of Thomas J. Ewing, (Bellefontaine, Ohio, Bellefontaine Examiner, 08 Apr 2005), Logan County Libraries, Knowlton Library, 220 North Main Street, Bellefontaine, OH.

479 Find A Grave—Huntsville Cemetery, McArthur Twp., Logan Co., Ohio, Findagrave.com, Thomas J. Ewing, Find A Grave Memorial #19886679.

480 Ohio Deaths, 1908-1953, FamilySearch.org, Michael Leslie Ewing, death cert. #10196.

481 U.S. Veterans' Gravesites, ca. 1775-2006, Ancestry.com, Robert E. Mason.

482 Obituary of Robert E. Mason (Bellefontaine, Ohio, Bellefontaine Examiner, 06 Sep 2005), Logan County Libraries, Knowlton Library, 220 North Main Street, Bellefontaine, OH.

483 Ohio, County Marriages, 1789-2013, FamilySearch.org, Robert Edwin Mason and Nancy Elisabeth Tarr, Allen County, Ohio Marriage Records, Vol. A, pg. 11, cert. #67793.

484 California, Divorce Index, 1966-1984, Ancestry.com, Robert E. Mason and Nancy E. Tarr, Eldorado County, California.

485 Ohio, Birth Index, 1908-1964, Ancestry.com, Nancy E. Tarr, state file #1928024165.

486 Ohio, County Marriages, 1789-2013, FamilySearch.org, Charles Stephen Mason and Mary Catherine Vanica, Logan County, Ohio Marriage Records, Vol. S, pg. 243, cert. #58898.

487 Ohio, Birth Index, 1908-1964, Ancestry.com, Mary C. Vanica, state file #1930092391.

488 California, Marriage Index, 1949-1959, Ancestry.com, Oliver G. Young and Peggy Karoleski, Los Angelles County, California Marriage Records, Book 3435, pg. 222, lic. #6863.

489 Obituary of Peggy Francia Young (San Luis Obispo, California, San Luis Obispo County Telegram-Tribune, 11 Mar 2010), San Luis Obispo Public Library, 995 Palm Street, San Luis Obispo, CA.

490 Find A Grave—Los Osos Memorial Park Cemetery, Los Osos, San Luis Obispo Co., California, Findagrave.com, Peggy F. Young, Find A Grave Memorial #130725149.

491 Young, Gordon, *The Hill Tribes of Northern Thailand*. Bangkok: Siam Society; 1962. William S. Carlson Library, University of Toledo, 2801 West Bancroft Street, Toledo, OH.

492 Young, Gordon, *Journey from Banna, An Autobiography*, pg. 193.

493 California, Marriage Index, 1949-1959, Ancestry.com, James J. Suter and Helen E. Young, Ventura County, California Marriage Records, California state lic. #37142.

494 Obituary of James J. Suter (San Francisco, California, San Francisco Chronicle, 17 May 2007). San Francisco Public Library, Main Brancy, 100 Larkin Street, San Francisco, CA.

495 California Birth Index, 1905-1995, Ancestry.com, Kathleen Helen Suter.

496 Obituary of Kathleen Wade Morrison (Sacramento, California, Sacramento Bee, 31 May 2011). Sacramento Public Library, Central Library, 828 I Street, Sacramento, CA.

497 California Birth Index, 1905-1995, Ancestry.com, Michael J. Suter.

498 Obituary of Michael J. Suter, 17 Aug 2012, Fred Hunter's Hollywood Memorial Gardens Cemetery, Crematory and

498 Community Center, 6301 Taft Street, Hollywood, FL. Online database: https://www.fredhunters.com/obituary/93999/Michael-Suter/

499 Fawthrup, Tom, "William Young Obituary, CIA agent in America's 'secret war' in Laos", (London, England, The Guardian, 04 May 2011). https://www.theguardian.com/world/2011/may/04/william-young-obituary

500 Loxton, Edward, "CIA Hitman Bill Young Found Dead in Chaing Mai", Constantine Report, 04 Apr 2011, Online, http://www.constantinereport.com/cia-hitman-bill-young-found-dead-in-chiang-mai/; captured 15 Dec 2017.

501 Email correspondence with Kwaw Kway San, Chaing Mai Zoo, Chaing Mai, Thailand, Ann Miller Carr, author, 13 Aug 2014.

502 Find A Grave—Montecito Memorial Park Cemetery, Colton, San Bernardino Co., California, Findagrave.com, Lael M. Young, Find A Grave Memorial #171240344.

503 Montecito Memorial Park Cemetery Records, Lael M. Young, Montecito Memorial Park Cemetery, 3520 East Washington Street, Colton, CA.

504 "UR Graduates Six With High Honors" (San Bernardino, California, San Bernardino Sun, 14 Jun 1957). California Digital Newspaper Collection, Center for Bibliographic Studies and Research, University of California-Riverside; Online database: https://cdnc.ucr.edu/cgi-bin/cdnc?a=p&p=home&e=———-en—20—1—txt-txIN————1

505 "Stanford Confers Ph.D.in Math on Lael Young" (Redlands, California, Redlands Daily Facts, 23 Jun 1961). California State Library, California History Room, 900 N Street, Sacramento, CA.

506 Young, Philip G., M.D., *Thyroid, Guardian of Health*. Bloomington, Indiana: Trafford Publishing, 2002.

507 California Birth Index, 1905-1995, Ancestry.com, Fred Allen Widlund.

508 Obituary of Fred Widlund (Baker City, Oregon, Baker City Herald, 27 Jun 2012), Baker County Library, 2400 Resort Street, Baker City, OR.

509 Obituary of John G. Mantle (Thousand Oaks, California, Thousand Oaks News Chronicle, 17 Dec 1988), Grant R. Brimhall Library, 1401 East Janss Road, Thousand Oaks, CA.

510 Obituary of Kay Mantle (Ventura, California, Ventura County Star, 02 Jan 2016) Avenue Library, 606 North Ventura Avenue, Ventura, CA.

511 Obituary of Catherine (Mantle) Neve (Portland, Oregon, The Oregonian, October 9, 2000). Multnomah County Central Library, 801 SW 10th Avenue, Portland, OR.

512 U.S., Social Security Applications and Claims Index, 1936-2007, Ancestry.com, Catherine Mantle Wilken Neve.

513 Oregon, Death Index, 1898-2008, Ancestry.com, Catherine Mantle Neve, death cert. #00-22580.

514 Oregon, Death Index, 1898-2008, Ancestry.com, Sandra Kay Geiger, death cert. #95-25870.

515 Obituary of Sandra Kay Geiger (Grants Pass, Oregon, Grants Pass Daily Journal, November 30, 1995), Jackson County Genealogical Library, Rogue River Genealogical Society and Jackson County Library, 3505 South Pacific Highway, Medford, OR.

516 Find A Grave—Arlington National Cemetery, Arlington, Virginia, Findagrave.com, Norma Louise Park, Find A Grave Memorial #49347077.

517 Obituary of William Gray Park (Harrisonburg, Virginia, Harrisonburg Daily News Journal, 01 Dec 2012), Massanutten Regional Library, 174 South Main Street, Harrisonburg, VA.

518 Find A Grave—Arlington National Cemetery, Arlington, Virginia, Findagrave.com, William Gray Park, Find A Grave Memorial #101546706.

519 Obituary of Richard 'Dick' Park (Mountain Home, Idaho, Mountain Home News, 26 Aug 2015), Mountain Home Public Library, Central Library, 790 North 10th Street East, Mountain Home, ID.

520 Obituary of Patricia L. Reilly (Asbury Park, New Jersey, Asbury Park Press, 28 Jun 2008), Austin Public Library-Central Library, 500 First Avenue, Asbury Park, NJ.

521 U.S. Public Records Index, 1950-1993, Vol. 1, Ancestry.com, Joe L. Vongundy.

522 Death Notice of Joe L. Vongundy (Tuscon, Arizona, Arizona Daily Star, 13 Jan 1015), Pima County Public Library, 101 North Stone Avenue, Tucson, AZ.

523 Death notice of M.R. "Jack" Hodges, (Austin, Texas, American-Statesman, 26 Feb 1999), Asbury Park Library, 710 West Cesar Chavez Street, Austin, TX.

524 California, Marriage Index, 1960-1985, Ancestry.com, Carl L. Ingraham and Margaret L. Mantle.

525 California Birth Index, 1905-1995, Ancestry.com, Carl L. Ingraham.

526 Virginia, Birth Records, 1864-2014, Ancestry.com, Kenwood Moore Jackson.

527 U.S., Social Security Applications and Claims Index, 1936-2007, Ancestry.com, Kenwood Moore Jackson.

528 Find A Grave—Cathedral Church of Saint John Columbarium, Albuquerque, Bernalillo Co., New Mexico, Findagrave.com, LTC. Kenwood M. Jackson, Find A Grave Memorial #116682387.

529 Obituary of Mark Lane Vongundy (Denver, Colorado, Rocky Mountain News, 03 Aug 1995), Denver Public Library, 10 West Fourteenth Avenue Parkway, Denver, CO.

530 Find A Grave—Forest Meadows Memorial Park East Cemetery (formerly Hillcrest Cemetery), Gainesville,

Alachua Co., Florida, Findagrave.com, Robert L. Honeycutt, Find A Grave Memorial #182371068.

531 Florida Marriage Collection, 1822-1875 and 1927-2001, Ancestry.com, Robert L. Honeycutt and Joan Kartzmark, Alachua County, Florida Marriage Records, Vol. CC, pg. 385, lic. #322.

532 Alachua County Marriage Records, Alachua County Clerk of the Court, 201 East University Avenue, Gainesville, FL, Robert L. Honeycutt and Joan Kartzmark, Alachua County, Florida Marriage Records, Vol. CC, pg. 385, cert. #322.

533 U.S. City Directories, 1822-1895, Ancestry.com. Orlando, Florida, 1957, pg. 338, entry for Honeycutt, Robert L.

534 Web: Marion County, Indiana, Marriage Index, 1925-2012, Ancestry.com, Donald M. Albershardt and Nancy Rogers, Marion County, Indiana Marriage Records, Book 200, pg 435.

535 Oaklawn Memorial Gardens Cemetery Records, Norman Ray Albershardt, Oaklawn Memorial Gardens, 9700 Allisonville Road, Fishers, IN.

536 Florida Marriage Collection, 1822-1875 and 1927-2001, Ancestry.com, Norman Ray Albershardt and Lila Jean Ziglar, Pinellas County, Florida Marriage Records, Florida Dept. of Health Marriage Vol. 2024, cert. #2217.

537 Florida Marriage Collection, 1822-1875 and 1927-2001, Ancestry.com, Norman Ray Albershardt and Carollee Angela Potts, Hillsborough County, Florida Marriage Records, Florida Dept. of Health Marriage Vol. 3201, cert. #052535.

538 Florida, Divorce Index, 1927-2001, Ancestry.com, Norman R. Albershardt and Carollee A. Albershardt.

539 Indiana, Marriage Certificates, 1917-2005, Ancestry.com, Norman Albershardt and Alta Leech, Bartholomew County, Indiana Marriage Records, cert. #80-047420.

540 Obituary of Alta J. Albershardt (Hampton-Gentry Funeral Home, 01 May 2011), Hampton Gentry Funeral Home, 106 Shaw Gentry Funeral Home, 106 Shaw Street, Plainfield, IN, http://www.hamptongentry.com/home/index.cfm/obituaries/view/fh_id/10395/id/1147534

541 Oaklawn Memorial Gardens Cemetery Records, Alta J. Albershardt, Oaklawn Memorial Gardens, 9700 Allisonville Road, Fishers, IN.

542 Find A Grave—Floral Hills Memory Gardens, Tucker, DeKalb Co., Georgia, Findagrave.com, Wayne Donovan Secrest, Find A Grave Memorial #180860959.

543 Find A Grave—Floral Hills Memory Gardens, Tucker, DeKalb Co., Georgia, Findagrave.com, Wendy Secrest, Find A Grave Memorial #170939472.

544 Georgia Deaths, 1919-1998, Ancestry.com, Wendy Secrest, death cert. #015984.

545 California, Marriage Index, 1949-1959, Ancestry.com, Jackie. Marotte and Gail E. Pegan, San Diego County, California Marriage Records, California state file #69026.

546 California, Marriage Index, 1960-1985, Ancestry.com, Ralph P. Costain and Gail Pegan, San Diego County, California Marriage Records, California state file #22029.

547 California Birth Index, 1905-1995, Ancestry.com, Dale A. Marotte.

548 Find A Grave—Findagrave.com, Dale Allan Costain (sic), Find A Grave Memorial #143046437.

549 California, Death Index, 1940-1997, Ancestry.com, Dale A. Marotte.

550 California Birth Index, 1905-1995, Ancestry.com, Philip G. Costain.

551 Find A Grave—Findagrave.com, Philip Gregory Costain, Find A Grave Memorial #152836427.

552 California, Marriage Index, 1949-1959, Ancestry.com, William A. Murdoch and Roberta J. Pegan, San Diego County, California Marriage Records, California state lic. #16724.

553 California Birth Index, 1905-1995, Ancestry.com, William Alexander Murdoch.

554 Find A Grave—Findagrave.com, William Alexander "Bill" Murdoch, Find A Grave Memorial #143045767.

555 California Birth Index, 1905-1995, Ancestry.com, Stephen B. Murdoch.

556 "Apparent homicide reported in valley" (Kingman, Arizona, Kingman Daily Miner, March 12, 2000), Mohave County District Library, 3269 North Burbank Street, Kingman, Arizona.

557 California Birth Index, 1905-1995, Ancestry.com, Donna Ruth Murdoch.

558 California, Death Index, 1940-1997, Ancestry.com, Donna Ruth Murdoch, d/o William Alexander Murdoch.

559 Denver Marriages, 1940-1974, Denver Public Library, 10 West Fourteenth Avenue Parkway, Denver, CO, George Rollert Jr. and Henrietta Gage, Denver County, Colorado Marriage Records, lic. #97870; Online database: https://history.denverlibrary.org/sites/history/files/Denver_Marr_Appl_1940_1974.pdf.

560 Denver Marriages, 1940-1974, Denver Public Library, 10 West Fourteenth Avenue Parkway, Denver, CO, Ronald Gage and Barbara Downs, Denver County, Colorado Marriage Records, lic. #133834; Online database: https://history.denverlibrary.org/sites/history/files/Denver_Marr_Appl_1940_1974.pdf.

561 State of Washington, Washington Death Certificate (Olympia, Washington, Washington State Department of Health), Washington State Department of Health, Center for Health Statistics, Town Center 1, 101 Israel Road SE, Tumwater, WA, Barbara Downs Gage, death cert. #6 36090, local file #11426.

562 Washington, Death Index, 1940-2014, Ancestry.com, Barbara D. Gage, death cert. #036090.

563 Obituary of Robert R. Gage (Woodburn, Oregon, The Independent, 24 Dec 2005), Oregon Historical Society, 1200 SW Park Avenue, Portland, OR.

564 Find A Grave—Calvary Cemetery, Wichita, Sedgwick Co., Kansas, Findagrave.com, James Knapp, Find A Grave Memorial #18228163.

565 Obituary of Jim Knapp (Wichita, Kansas, Wichita Eagle, 19 Aug 2002). Midwest Historical & Genealogical Society, 1203 North Main Street, Wichita, KS.

566 Florida Marriage Indexes, 1822-1875, 1927-2001, Ancestry.com, William L. Aldrich and Jean Perry, Manatee County, Florida, Florida Marriage Records, Vol. 1340, cert. #19889.

567 Find A Grave—Alliance City Cemetery, Alliance, Lexington Twp., Stark Co., Ohio, Findagrave.com, Dorothy Ann Mason, Find A Grave Memorial #137896110.

568 Obituary of Rachel Lee Howell (Las Cruces, New Mexico, Las Cruces Times, 08 and 09 May 2013). Thomas Branigan Memorial Library, 200 East Picacho Avenue, Las Cruces, NM.

569 Find A Grave—Calvary Catholic Cemetery and Mausoleum, Sacramento, Sacremento Co., California, Findagrave.com, Kathleen Suter Wade Morrison, Find A Grave Memorial #70652195.

570 California, Marriage Index, 1960-1985, Ancestry.com, Dennis L. Wade and Kathleen H. Suter.

571 Obituary of Michael Joseph Morrison, North Sacramento Funeral Home, 725 El Camino Avenue, Sacramento, CA; Online database: http://www.northsacfuneral.com/notices/Michael-Morrison

572 California, Marriage Index, 1960-1985, Ancestry.com, (Mr.) Wilkin and Catherine Mantle, Ventura County, California Marriage Records, California state cert #1921-120587.

573 California, Marriage Index, 1960-1985, Ancestry.com, (Mr.) Faraci and Sandra K. Mantle, Ventura County, California Marriage Records, California state file #53293.

574 Calfornia, Marriage Index, 1960-1985, Ancestry.com, Richard R. Geiger and Sandra K. Mantle, Ventura County, California Marriage Records, California state file #7369.

575 Ohio, Deaths, 1908-1932, 1938-2007, Ancestry.com, Robyn K. Park, death cert. #100427.

576 Obituary of Wendy Secrest (Atlanta, Georgia, Atlanta Constitution, 12 May 1986), Stone Mountain-Sue Kellogg Library, DeKalb County Public Library System, 952 Leon Street, Stone Mountain, GA.

577 Find A Grave—Findagrave.com, Phillip Gregory Costain, Find A Grave Memorial #152386427.

578 Find A Grave—Findagrave.com, Stephen Blaine "Steve" Murdoch, Find A Grave Memorial #143045845.

579 U.S. Veterans' Gravesites, ca. 1775-2006, Ancestry.com, Donna Ruth Murdoch.

580 Find A Grave—Fort Rosecrans National Military Cemetery, San Diego, San Diego Co., California, Findagrave.com, Donna Ruth Murdoch, Find A Grave Memorial #3420583.

581 Find A Grave—Gustavas Cemetery, Gustavas, Hoonah-Angoon, Alaska, Findagrave.com, Rachel Lee Howell, Find A Grave Memorial #151130077.

582 Obituary of Robyn Kathleen Sara Park (Urbana, Ohio, Urbana Daily Citizen, 29 Dec 2007), Champaign County Library, Main Branch, 1060 Scioto Street, Urbana, OH.

[A] "Captured" and "Robbers Roost" (Fort Wayne, Indiana, Fort Wayne Weekly Gazette, 28 Mar 1895), Genealogy Center, Allen County Public Library, 900 Library Plaza, Fort Wayne, IN.

[B] "Reiling Was In St. Louis" (Fort Wayne, Indiana, Fort Wayne News, 18 Apr 1895), Genealogy Center, Allen County Public Library, 900 Library Plaza, Fort Wayne, IN.

[C] "Headhunters Annoy Japs" (Reno Gazette-Journal, Reno, Nevada, 30 Mar 1944), Newspapers.com, online: https://wwwnewspapers.com/image/149831296/

[D] Obituary of M. Vincent Young, Missionary (San Bernardino County Sun, San Bernardino, California, 04 Dec 1990), San Bernardino County Historical Archives, 1808 Commercenter West, Suite B, San Bernardino, CA.

Henry Pegan

1. **Henry⁵ Pegan** (*Robert A.⁴, Andrew³, Andrew² Pagan, James¹*) was born on April 7, 1812, in Strabane Twp., Washington Co., Pennsylvania.[1] He was the son of Robert A. Pegan and Christina or Christiana Ingle. Henry died in Dodson Twp., Highland Co., Ohio, on March 29, 1880, at age 67.[2, 3] He was buried in Lynchburg Masonic Cemetery, Lynchburg, Dodson Twp., Highland Co., Ohio.[4]

Henry Pegan left Highland County, Ohio for Montgomery County, Ohio with his parents, Robert and Christina Ingle Pegan about 1826. But by 1833, Henry returned to his home area, perhaps residing with his eldest brother Andrew in Green Twp., Clinton Co., Ohio. By 1836, Henry was living in Martinsville, Clark Twp., Clinton Co., Ohio, according to Ohio tax lists.[A] Later that decade, both would move a short distance to Dodson Twp., Highland Co., Ohio.

By 1839, Henry Pegan seems to have moved very close to the original Pegan homesites near Webertown, Dodson Twp., Highland Co., Ohio. He married Harriet Stroup, daughter of a popular hat maker in the area. Several of Henry and Harriet Stroup Pegan's descendants married Stroup cousins.

Henry married **Harriet Stroup** on February 23, 1834, in Highland Co., Ohio.[1, 5] They had eight children. Harriet Stroup was born in New Market Twp., Highland Co., Ohio, on June 16, 1813.[6] Harriet reached age 83 and died in Dodson Twp., Highland Co., Ohio, on January 28, 1897.[6, 7] She was buried in Lynchburg Masonic Cemetery, Lynchburg, Dodson Twp., Highland Co., Ohio.[7] She was the daughter of Michael Stroup and Mary Ann Walker.

In the 1840 census, Henry Pegan is enumerated in Dodson Twp., Highland Co., Ohio with one son under five years old, two daughters under five, one male age 20-30, and a female also 23-30 *(Census Place: Highland, Ohio; Roll: 403; Page: 102)*. Nearby are brothers Andrew and Elsey; the latter had also returned to Highland County.

Henry Pegan is again found in Dodson Twp., Highland Co., Ohio in 1850 *(Census Place: Dodson, Highland, Ohio; Roll: M432_694; Page: 277; Image: 464)*; the actual census form says "Henry Pajan". In the household are Henry, 38, a farmer; Harriet, 37, Elvira, 15 Granville, 12, "Thos. J.", nine, Elma, seven, Eliza J., five, and Pleasant, two. All but Henry were Ohio-born. This time, Henry is a carpenter; he probably learned that trade by working with his brother Andrew. Living with them is a lodger, John Hunt.

In the 1860 census, Henry, age 48, born Pennsylvania, is still living in Dodson Twp., Highland Co., Ohio with wife Harriet, son Granville, 20, Thomas, 19, Elma or Emma, 17, Eliza, 14, Pleasant, 11, Michael, nine, and William, six *(Census Place: Dodson, Highland, Ohio; Roll: M653_986; Page: 72; Image: 145)*. Everyone except Henry was born in Ohio.

Henry Pegan served in the Union Army's 17th Ohio regiment in the Civil War; his widow, Harriet Stroup Pegan, files for a widow's pension in 1891. The U.S. Pension Office initially misspelled Henry's surname as "Paden".[8]

Henry Pegan is enumerated as "Henry Pagin" in Lynchburg, Dodson Twp., Highland Co., Ohio in 1870 *(Census Place: Lynchburgh (sic), Highland, Ohio; Roll: M593_1222; Page: 56; Image: 113)*. In the home are Henry, age 58, a cabinet maker born in Pennsylvania; Harriet, 56, born Ohio; and children Eliza, 26, and William, 15, who was working at carpentry; both children were born in Ohio. Also in the home is a Tilla Brower, age 13, born Ohio a school pupil; her relationship to the Pegans is unknown.

In the 1880 census, Harriet Stroup Pegan, widowed, is living with her son-in-law and daughter, Joseph and Elma Eleanor Pegan Schwartz, in Dodson Twp., Highland Co., Ohio *(Census Place: Dodson, Highland, Ohio; Roll: 1032; Page: 287A; Enumeration District: 41; Image: 0577)*. Harriet Stroup Pegan, age 67, a widow, enumerated as "mother-in-law", is listed as born in Ohio as were her parents (Incorrect—her parents were born in Pennsylvania). Joseph Swartz, age 37, a farmer, was born in Ohio with his parents born in Prussia; his wife, Elma Pegan Schwartz, also 37, says she and her parents were born in Ohio (Incorrect—her father was born in Pennsylvania). Children in the home include Mary H. Schwartz, 10, and Charles W. Schwartz, three, both born in Ohio. Also in the household is Harriet's son and Elma's brother, Michael Pegan, 25, single, born Ohio as were his parents (again, incorrect), who lists no occupation. (Michael suffered from epilepsy.)

According to *The County of Highland: A History of Highland County, Ohio, from its Earliest Days…Vol. 2*, Henry Pegan built a new pulpit for the Methodist Church in 1854, and was paid for his work with a quilt made by the women church members.[A]

Henry and Harriet Stroup Pegan are buried in the Masonic Cemetery, Lynchburg, Dodson Twp., Highland Co., Ohio. Buried next to them is Henry's brother Harrison Pegan Sr.

Children of Henry Pegan and Harriet Stroup:

+ 2 f I. **Elvira⁶ Pegan** was born in Green Twp. or Martinsville, Clark Twp., Clinton Co., Ohio, on August 11, 1835.[9] She died in Lynchburg, Dodson Twp., Highland Co., Ohio, on March 12, 1918.[9]

+ 3 m II. **Granville⁶ Pegan** was born in Martinsville, Clark Twp., Clinton Co., Ohio, on December 16, 1837.[10] He died in Dodson Twp., Highland Co., Ohio, on October 25, 1909.[10, 11]

+ 4 m III. **Thomas Jefferson⁶ Pegan** was born in Dodson Twp., Highland Co., Ohio, on December 2, 1839.[12] He was also known as **Jefferson or Jeff**. Thomas Jefferson died in Hamer Twp., Highland Co., Ohio, on February 9, 1900.[12, 13]

+ 5 f IV. **Elma Eleanor⁶ Pegan** was born in Dodson Twp., Highland Co., Ohio, on December 24, 1842.[14] She died in Lynchburg, Dodson Twp., Highland Co., Ohio, on October 25, 1914.[14]

+ 6 f V. **Eliza Jane⁶ Pegan** was born in Dodson Twp., Highland Co., Ohio, on October 17, 1845.[15] She was also known as **Jennie**. Eliza Jane died in Lynchburg, Dodson Twp., Highland Co., Ohio, on July 24, 1883.[16]

+ 7 m VI. **Pleasant⁶ Pegan** was born in Dodson Twp., Highland Co., Ohio, on April 26, 1848.[17] He died in Highland Co., Ohio, on March 22, 1870.[18]

+ 8 m VII. **Michael Stroup⁶ Pegan** was born in Dodson Twp., Highland Co., Ohio, on October 3, 1851.[19] He died in Dodson Twp., Highland Co., Ohio, on March 16, 1888.[19]

+ 9 m VIII. **William Henry⁶ Pegan** was born in Dodson Twp., Highland Co., Ohio, on November 2, 1854.[20] He died in Clark Twp., Clinton Co., Ohio, on August 26, 1939.[20]

6th Generation

2. Elvira[6] **Pegan** (*Henry*[5], *Robert A.*[4], *Andrew*[3], *Andrew*[2] *Pagan, James*[1]) was born in Green Twp. or Martinsville, Clark Twp., Clinton Co., Ohio, on August 11, 1835.[9] She was the daughter of Henry Pegan (1) and Harriet Stroup. Elvira died in Lynchburg, Dodson Twp., Highland Co., Ohio, on March 12, 1918, at age 82.[9] She was buried in Stroup Cemetery, Dodson Twp., Highland Co., Ohio.[9, 21, 22]

Elvira Stroup Pegan fell down "a short flight of stairs" on March 12, 1918 and died, according to her death certificate.

Elvira married **Levi Stroup** on April 8, 1855, in Highland Co., Ohio.[23] They had eight children. Levi Stroup was born in Dodsonville, Dodson Twp., Highland Co., Ohio, on October 1, 1832.[24] Levi reached age 80 and died in Salem Twp., Highland Co., Ohio, on May 26, 1913. He was buried in Stroup Cemetery, Dodson Twp., Highland Co., Ohio.[24, 25] He was the son of James Stroup and Harriet Strain.

Levi and Elvira Pegan Stroup were second cousins. Levi's paternal grandfather Anthony Stroup and Elvira's father Michael Stroup were both children of Adam Michael and Mary Unknown Stroup.

Levi and Elvira Pegan Stroup are enumerated in Dodson Twp., Highland Co., Ohio in 1860 (*Census Place: Dodson, Highland, Ohio; Roll: M653_986; Page: 72; Image: 149*). In the household are Levi Stroup, 25, a farmer; Elvira Pegan Stroup, 24, and daughters Josephine, four, and Hattie, two. All and their parents were born in Ohio.

In 1870, Levi and Elvira Pegan Stroup are found in Salem Twp., Highland Co., Ohio (*Census Place: Salem, Highland, Ohio; Roll: M593_1222; Page: 320A&B; Image: 644*). Levi Stroup, age 37, is a farmer. His wife, Elvira Pegan Stroup is 34. Children in the home are: Josephine, 14, Mary, nine, 'Arabella', six, John, four, and "Jane", two. All in the home were born in Ohio.

Levi and Elvira Pegan Stroup are still living in Salem Twp., Highland Co., Ohio in 1880 (*Census Place: Salem, Highland, Ohio; Roll: 1033; Page: 502C; Enumeration District: 53; Image: 0384*). In the home are Levi Stroup, age 47, a farmer; his wife Elvira Pegan Stroup, 44, and children Laura B., 16, John H., 13, Elma, 11, and Margaret, six. All were born in Ohio, as were their parents (Incorrect—Elvira's father, Henry Pegan, was born in Pennsylvania).

In 1900, Levi and Elvira Pegan Stroup are again Salem Twp., Highland Co., Ohio (*Census Place: Salem, Highland, Ohio; Roll: T623_1286; Page: 8B; Enumeration District: 128*). Levi Stroup, age 67, born Oct 1832, says he is still a farmer. Elvira Pegan Stroup, 64, was born in Aug 1835. The couple says they have been married 35 years and that Elvira has borne eight children, five still living. Both say they and their parents were born in Ohio (again, wrong, Elvira's father was born in Pennsylvania).

Levi and Elvira Pegan Stroup continue to reside in Salem Twp., Highland Co., Ohio in 1910 (*Census Place: Salem, Highland, Ohio; Roll: T624_1197; Page: 4A; Enumeration District: 0133; Image: 1030*). Levi Stroup is age 77 and a farmer. Elvira R. Pegan Stroup is 74. Levi and Elvira say they have been married 54 years and Elvira has borne eight children, with five still surviving. Once again, they say they and their parents were born in Ohio.

Children of Elvira Pegan and Levi Stroup:

+ 10 f I. **Josephine**[7] **Stroup** was born in Dodson Twp., Highland Co., Ohio, on April 24, 1856.[26] She died in Lynchburg, Dodson Twp., Highland Co., Ohio, on June 21, 1941.[26]

+ 11 f II. **Hattie Ann**[7] **Stroup** was born in Dodson Twp., Highland Co., Ohio, in 1858.[27] She died in Dodson Twp., Highland Co., Ohio, in 1861.[27]

+ 12 f III. **Mary E.**[7] **Stroup** was born in Dodson Twp., Highland Co., Ohio, on March 19, 1861.[28] She died in

Owensville, Stone Lick Twp., Clermont Co., Ohio, on November 15, 1943.[28]

+ 13 f IV. **Laura Arabella**[7] **Stroup** was born in Dodson Twp., Highland Co., Ohio, on October 27, 1863.[29, 30, 31] She died in Lynchburg, Dodson Twp., Highland Co., Ohio, on December 7, 1967.[29, 30, 32]

+ 14 m V. **John Henry**[7] **Stroup** was born in Dodson Twp., Highland Co., Ohio, on February 15, 1866.[33] He died in Dodsonville, Dodson Twp., Highland Co., Ohio, on June 3, 1946.[33]

+ 15 f VI. **Elma Jane**[7] **Stroup** was born in Salem Twp., Highland Co., Ohio, on April 4, 1868.[34] She died in Wilmington, Union Twp., Clinton Co., Ohio, on February 4, 1936.[34]

+ 16 m VII. **James Pegan**[7] **Stroup** was born in Salem Twp., Highland Co., Ohio, in 1871.[35] He died in Salem Twp., Highland Co., Ohio, in 1873.[35]

+ 17 f VIII. **Margaret**[7] **Stroup** was born in Salem Twp., Highland Co., Ohio, on March 14, 1874.[36] She died in Salem Twp., Highland Co., Ohio, on August 12, 1899.[37]

3. **Granville**[6] **Pegan** (*Henry*[5], *Robert A.*[4], *Andrew*[3], *Andrew*[2] *Pagan*, *James*[1]) was born on December 16, 1837, in Martinsville, Clark Twp., Clinton Co., Ohio.[10] He was the son of Henry Pegan (1) and Harriet Stroup. Granville died in Dodson Twp., Highland Co., Ohio, on October 25, 1909, at age 71.[10, 11] He was buried in Troutwine Cemetery, Dodson Twp., Highland Co., Ohio and Clark Twp., Clinton Co., Ohio.[10, 38, 39]

Granville married **Sarah A. Chaney** on June 11, 1863, in Brown Co., Ohio.[40] They had three children. Sarah A. Chaney was born in Dodson Twp., Highland Co., Ohio, on March 22, 1843.[41] Sarah A. reached age 86 and died in Webertown, Dodson Twp., Highland Co., Ohio, on June 10, 1929.[41] She was buried in Troutwine Cemetery, Dodson Twp., Highland Co., Ohio and Clark Twp., Clinton Co., Ohio.[41, 42, 43]

Granville Pegan is enumerated in Dodson Twp., Highland Co., Ohio in 1870 *(Census Place: Dodson, Highland, Ohio; Roll: M593_1222; Page: 348; Image: 698)*. In the home are Granville Pegan, 31, a farmer; Sarah Cheney Pegan, 26, and sons Adolphus, six, and Henry, two. All were born in Ohio.

In 1880, Granville Pegan is again Dodson Twp., Highland Co., Ohio *(Census Place: Dodson, Highland, Ohio; Roll: 1032; Page: 285B; Enumeration District: 041; Image: 0574)*. Granville Pegan is age 42, a farmer born in Ohio, with his father born in Pennsylvania and his mother in Ohio. Sarah Cheney Pegan, listed as "Sallie A.", 37, says she and her parents were born in Ohio. Living with them are their three children: Adolphus, 16, whose occupation is "works on farm", Henry, 11, and "Frances D.", six. All the children were born in Ohio.

Granville Pegan is listed as "Granville Peggan" in Dodson Twp., Highland Co., Ohio in 1900 *(Census Place: Dodson, Highland, Ohio; Roll: T623_1286; Page: 7A; Enumeration District: 107)*. The head of the household is Granville Pegan, age 62, born Dec 1837 in Ohio, with his father born in Pennsylvania and his mother in Ohio. His wife, Sarah Cheney Pegan, 57, born in March 1843, also says she and her mother were born in Ohio and her father in Pennsylvania. They state they have been married 37 years and Sarah has borne three children, all still alive. The only child still living with them is son Henry, 32, single, born May 1868 in Ohio, where his parents were also born. Both Granville and Henry list their occupation as farmer. Nearby is son Adolphus Pegan and his family.

In 1910, the widowed Sarah A. Cheney Pegan is found in Dodson Twp., Highland Co., Ohio *(Census Place: Dodson, Highland, Ohio; Roll: T624_1197; Page: 1A; Enumeration District: 0114; Image: 537)*. The head of the household is Sarah A. Cheney Pegan, 67, who lists her occupation as farmer. Sarah says she bore three children, two of them still alive. Living with her are her two unmarried siblings, sister

Della E. Chaney, 73 and brother Charles C. Cheney, 64. All say they were born in Ohio, their father in Pennsylvania, and their mother in Ohio.

In 1920, Sarah A. Cheney is residing with her widower son Henry L. Pegan and his children in Dodson Twp., Highland Co., Ohio *(Census Place: Dodson, Highland, Ohio; Roll: T625_1399; Page: 8B; Enumeration District: 83; Image: 96).* Sarah A. Cheney Pegan is age 75, a widow, born in Ohio, with her father born in Pennsylvania and her mother in Ohio. Henry L. Pegan, listed as Henry L. Pagan, is the head of the household. Henry Pegan, 51 and a widower, is a farmer born in Ohio, as were his parents. Henry's three children are also with them: Courtland A., 15, a farm laborer working on the family farm; Clarence C., 13, and Frances E., eight. All the children were born in Ohio.

Children of Granville Pegan and Sarah A. Chaney:

+ 18   m   I.   **Adolphus Vonesse**[7] **Pegan** was born in Dodson Twp., Highland Co., Ohio, on May 8, 1864.[44] He was also known as **Dolph**. Adolphus Vonesse died in Dodson Twp., Highland Co., Ohio, on November 22, 1910.[44, 45]

+ 19   m   II. **Henry Levy**[7] **Pegan** was born in Dodson Twp., Highland Co., Ohio, on May 12, 1868.[46, 47] He died in Dodson Twp., Highland Co., Ohio, on June 8, 1954.[48, 49]

+ 20   f   III. **Della Frances**[7] **Pegan** was born in Dodson Twp., Highland Co., Ohio, on October 2, 1873.[50] She was also known as **Frankie**. Della Frances died in Littleton, Dodson Twp., Highland Co., Ohio, on January 9, 1902.[51]

4. Thomas Jefferson[6] **Pegan** (*Henry*[5]*, Robert A.*[4]*, Andrew*[3]*, Andrew*[2] *Pagan, James*[1]) was born on December 2, 1839, in Dodson Twp., Highland Co., Ohio.[12] He was also known as **Jefferson or Jeff**. He was the son of Henry Pegan (1) and Harriet Stroup. He died in Hamer Twp., Highland Co., Ohio, on February 9, 1900, at age 60.[12, 13] Thomas Jefferson was buried in Stroup Cemetery, Dodson Twp., Highland Co., Ohio.[12, 52, 53]

Thomas Jefferson married **Eliza Bernard** on September 6, 1862, in Brown Co., Ohio.[54] They had one son. Eliza Bernard was born in Brown Co., Ohio?, on June 14, 1844.[55] Eliza reached age 20 and died in Jefferson Twp., Clinton Co., Ohio, on July 21, 1864.[55] She was buried in New Vienna Cemetery, Green Twp., Clinton Co., Ohio.[55] Eliza died in July 1864 most likely in childbirth.

Thomas Jefferson Pegan married **Mary Ann Bennington** on October 15, 1865, in Highland Co., Ohio.[56] They had six children. Mary Ann Bennington was born in White Oak Twp., Highland Co., Ohio, on April 17, 1845.[57] She was also known as **Mollie**. She reached age 72 and died in Milford Twp., Butler Co., Ohio, on July 8, 1917.[57, 58] Mary Ann was buried in Stroup Cemetery, Dodson Twp., Highland Co., Ohio.[57, 59]

Thomas J. Pegan married Mary Bennington after serving in the Civil War as a private in Company C, 48 Ohio Infantry and 48th Ohio Cavalry. They lived for a time in St. Martin, Perry Twp., Brown Co., Ohio, as their eldest child, daughter Laura Pegan Daggy Smith, was born there.

Thomas Jefferson Pegan, named as "Jefferson Pagan", is found in the 1870 census in Dodson Twp., Highland Co., Ohio *(Census Place: Dodson, Highland, Ohio; Roll: M593_1222; Page: 72; Image: 145).* In the home are Thomas "Jefferson" Pegan, age 31, a farmer; his wife, Mary Bennington Pegan, 23; and daughters "Luora" (Laura), four, and Anna, one. All were born in Ohio.

In 1880, Thomas Jefferson Pegan is found in Hamer Twp., Highland Co., Ohio *(Census Place: Hamer, Highland, Ohio; Roll: 1033; Page: 325A; Enumeration District: 043; Image: 0030).* He is erroneously enumerated as "Jefferson Dugan" (or "Bugan"). Thomas Jefferson Pegan is age 40, a farmer. With him is his wife, Mary Ann Bennington, again listed as Mary, 30, and daughters Laura ("Lora"), 13, Anna, 10, and Frances, listed as male with the name of "Frankie", six months. All in the home were born in Ohio, as were their parents.

According to an 1891 mention in the *Hillsboro (Oh) News-Herald*, "Jeff" Pegan had returned to Hamer Twp., Highland Co., Ohio after a couple of years in southeastern Hamilton Co., Ohio, first in Newtown and then in Linwood.

For some reason, Thomas Jefferson Pegan's will (1900) is filed in Hamilton County, Ohio, even though he died in Hamer Twp., Highland Co., Ohio. He did live in 1889 in Newtown, Hamilton Co., Ohio and in 1890 in Linwood, Hamilton Co., Ohio. But he was residing in 1891 in Hamer Twp., Highland Co., Ohio.[60]

Mary Ann Bennington Pegan, a widow, is enumerated in Hamer Twp., Highland Co., Ohio in 1900 *(Census Place: Hamer, Highland, Ohio; Roll: T623_1286; Page: 4B; Enumeration District: 111)*. "Mary A." Bennington Pegan is 54, born Apr 1846 in Ohio. Mary Ann Bennington Pegan, who lists no occupation, says she has born six children, with four still alive. The only child with her in the home is son Charles, listed as "Charley", age 15, born Apr 1885 in Ohio. Both say their parents were also born in Ohio.

In 1910, Mary Ann Bennington Pegan is living with her son-in-law and daughter, Lewis and Anna Pegan Surber, in White Oak Twp., Highland Co., Ohio *(Census Place: White Oak, Highland, Ohio; Roll: T624_1197; Page: 12-8A; Enumeration District: 0136; Image: 1096)*. Mary Ann Bennington Pegan is age 64 and says she bore six children, with four still alive. Lewis A. Surber is 41 and a farmer; Anna Pegan Surber is 40. Lewis and Anna say they have been married 20 years and Anna has born one child, still living. This is son Earl Surber, 17, listed as a farm laborer on the family farm. All were born in Ohio, as were their parents.

By the time she died, Mary Ann Bennington Pegan was residing with her son-in-law and daughter, Thomas L. Hamer and Laura Pegan Daggy in Milford Twp., Butler Co., Ohio. Thomas Daggy was the informant on her death certificate and lists Mary Ann's mother's maiden name as Mary McQuitty or McQuilty. However, Mary Ann Bennington Pegan was the daughter of Alexander and Lucinda Unknown Bennington of White Oak Twp., Highland Co., Ohio.

Son of Thomas Jefferson Pegan and Eliza Bernard:

+ 21 m I. **Henry J.**[7] **Pegan** was born in Jefferson Twp., Clinton Co., Ohio, on February 21, 1864.[61] He died in Jefferson Twp., Clinton Co., Ohio, on August 8, 1864.[61]

Children of Thomas Jefferson Pegan and Mary Ann Bennington:

+ 22 f I. **Laura**[7] **Pegan** was born in St. Martin, Perry Twp., Brown Co., Ohio, on August 24, 1866.[62, 63, 64] She died in Hamer Twp., Highland Co., Ohio, on January 24, 1923.[62, 64]

+ 23 f II. **Anna**[7] **Pegan** was born in Dodson Twp., Highland Co., Ohio, on October 20, 1869.[65] She died in White Oak Twp., Highland Co., Ohio, on January 28, 1955.[66]

+ 24 m III. **William Henry**[7] **Pegan** was born in Dodson Twp., Highland Co., Ohio, on January 15, 1874.[67] He died in Dodson Twp., Highland Co., Ohio, on July 15, 1874.[68]

+ 25 f IV. **Mattie**[7] **Pegan** was born in Dodson Twp., Highland Co., Ohio, on November 25, 1875.[69] She died in Dodson Twp., Highland Co., Ohio, on March 16, 1876.[70]

+ 26 f V. **Frances**[7] **Pegan** was born in Hamer Twp., Highland Co., Ohio, on November 12, 1879.[71, 72, 73] She was also known as **Frankie**. Frances died in Lynchburg, Dodson Twp., Highland Co., Ohio, on January 29, 1915.[73]

+ 27 m VI. **Charles**[7] **Pegan** was born in Hamer Twp., Highland Co., Ohio, on April 18, 1885.[74, 75] He died in Danville, Hamer Twp.,

Highland Co., Ohio, on February 6, 1960.[76, 77]

5. **Elma Eleanor**[6] **Pegan** (*Henry*[5], *Robert A.*[4], *Andrew*[3], *Andrew*[2] *Pagan*, *James*[1]) was born on December 24, 1842, in Dodson Twp., Highland Co., Ohio.[14] She was the daughter of Henry Pegan (1) and Harriet Stroup. Elma Eleanor died in Lynchburg, Dodson Twp., Highland Co., Ohio, on October 25, 1914, at age 71.[14] She was buried in Lynchburg Masonic Cemetery, Lynchburg, Dodson Twp., Highland Co., Ohio.[14, 78]

Elma Eleanor married **Joseph Schwartz or Swartz** on January 5, 1869, in Highland Co., Ohio.[79] They had four children. Joseph Schwartz or Swartz was born in Perry Twp., Brown Co., Ohio, on December 8, 1842.[80] Joseph Schwartz or reached age 49 and died in Lynchburg, Dodson Twp., Highland Co., Ohio, on August 23, 1892.[80, 81] He was buried in Lynchburg Masonic Cemetery, Lynchburg, Dodson Twp., Highland Co., Ohio.[73] He was the son of Andrew Schwartz and Veronika Unknown.

Joseph and Elma Pegan Schwartz are enumerated in 1870 in Lynchburg, Dodson Twp., Highland Co., Ohio *(Census Place: Lynchburgh, Highland, Ohio; Roll: M593_1222; Page: 57B; Image: 118)*. Joseph Schwartz, age 27, a shoemaker, says he was born in Ohio. His wife, Elma Pegan Schwartz, is 25, born Ohio. They have a daughter, Mary, who is three months old, listed as born in October in Ohio. Living with them are Joseph's brother Andrew Schwartz, 21, born in Ohio, also a shoemaker. (Later that year, Andrew Schwartz married Elma's sister Eliza Jane Pegan.) Also in the residence is a shoemaker's apprentice, Howard Thompson, 16.

In 1880, Joseph and Elma Eleanor Pegan Schwartz are found, in Dodson Twp., Highland Co., Ohio *(Census Place: Dodson, Highland, Ohio; Roll: 1032; Page: 287A; Enumeration District: 41; Image: 0577)*. Joseph Swartz, age 37, a farmer, who this time says he was born in Ohio with his parents born in Prussia; his wife, Elma Eleanor Pegan Swartz, also 37, says she and her parents were born in Ohio (again, incorrect). Children in the home include Mary H. Schwartz, 10, and "Charles W." Schwartz, three, both born in Ohio. Residing with them is Elma Eleanor's mother, Harriet Stroup Pegan, 67, a widow enumerated as "mother-in-law", Elma and her parents are listed as Ohio natives (but her parents were born in Pennsylvania). In addition, Harriet's son and Elma's brother, Michael Pegan, 25, is also in the household. Michael is single, born Ohio as were his parents (again, incorrect), who lists no occupation. (He had epilepsy.)

In 1900, widow Elma Pegan Schwartz is enumerated in Lynchburg, Dodson Twp., Highland Co., Ohio *(Census Place: Dodson, Highland, Ohio; Roll: T623_1286; Page: 9B; Enumeration District: 106)*. In the home are Elma Pegan Schwartz, age 57, born in Dec 1842 in Ohio, where her parents were born. Elma says her occupation is "land lady". She also states she bore four children, with two still alive in 1900. Both surviving children are living with her: "Hattie M.", 30, born Nov 1869; and Walter C., 23, born July 1876, a (wall)paper-hanger. Both children were born in Ohio.

Elma Pegan Schwartz is still residing in Lynchburg, Dodson Twp., Highland Co., Ohio in 1910 *(Census Place: Dodson, Highland, Ohio; Roll: T624_1197; Page: 8B; Enumeration District: 0115; Image: 572)*. In the home are Elma Pegan Schwartz, age 67, a widow, who says she has her "own income". Elma says she has borne three children with two still living. With her is son Walter C., age 33, a (house) painter. Both say they and their parents were Ohio natives.

A shoemaker, Joseph Schwartz also owned a meat store/butcher shop for a few years in the late 1880s and early 1890s, according to advertisements in the Highland County newspapers. His birth date is calculated from the information "Aged 49 Yrs 8mo 15ds" on his gravestone in Lynchburg Masonic Cemetery, Lynchburg, Dodson Twp., Highland Co., Ohio.

Elma Eleanor Pegan Schwartz's younger sister, Eliza Jane Pegan, married Andrew Schwartz, Joseph Schwartz' younger brother.

Children of Elma Eleanor Pegan and Joseph Schwartz or Swartz:

+ 28 f I. **Mary Hattie⁷ Schwartz** was born in Lynchburg, Dodson Twp., Highland Co., Ohio, on November 9, 1869.[82] She was also known as **Hattie**. Mary Hattie died in Clark Twp., Clinton Co., Ohio, on April 15, 1927.[82]

+ 29 m II. **William H.C.M.⁷ Schwartz** was born in Lynchburg, Dodson Twp., Highland Co., Ohio, on August 12, 1872.[83] He died in Lynchburg, Dodson Twp., Highland Co., Ohio, on August 16, 1873.[84]

+ 30 m III. **Walter Charles⁷ Schwartz** was born in Dodson Twp., Highland Co., Ohio, on July 27, 1876.[85, 86] He died in Lynchburg, Dodson Twp., Highland Co., Ohio, on November 27, 1942.[85]

+ 31   IV. **Child⁷ Schwartz** was born in Dodson Twp., Highland Co., Ohio, between 1869 and 1900. He or she died in Dodson Twp., Highland Co., Ohio, between 1869 and 1900.

6. **Eliza Jane⁶ Pegan** (*Henry⁵, Robert A.⁴, Andrew³, Andrew² Pagan, James¹*) was born on October 17, 1845, in Dodson Twp., Highland Co., Ohio.[15] She was also known as **Jennie**. She was the daughter of Henry Pegan (1) and Harriet Stroup. Eliza Jane died in Lynchburg, Dodson Twp., Highland Co., Ohio, on July 24, 1883, at age 37. She was buried in Lynchburg Masonic Cemetery, Lynchburg, Dodson Twp., Highland Co., Ohio.[15, 87]

Eliza Jane "Jennie" Pegan Schwartz' obituary states she died on which would be July 23, 1883.[87] But her tombstone in the Lynchburg Masonic Cemetery, Lynchburg, Dodson Twp., Highland Co, Ohio states she died on July 24, 1883 and was 37 years, none months and seven days old when she died. Her date of birth, calculated from this information, was October 17, 1845.[15]

Eliza Jane married **Andrew Schwartz II** on December 20, 1870, in Highland Co., Ohio.[88] They had one daughter. Andrew Schwartz II was born in Perry Twp., Brown Co., Ohio, between March 2, 1849 and July 30, 1849.[89] Andrew died in Lynchburg, Dodson Twp., Highland Co., Ohio, on March 2, 1894.[89] He was buried in Lynchburg Masonic Cemetery, Lynchburg, Dodson Twp., Highland Co., Ohio.[90] He was the son of Andrew Schwartz and Veronika Unknown.

In 1870, Andrew Schwartz II, age 21, single, a shoemaker, is living with his brother and sister-in-law, Joseph and Eleanor Stroup Schwartz, in Lynchburg, Dodson Twp., Highland Co., Ohio *(Census Place: Lynchburgh, Highland, Ohio; Roll: M593_1222; Page: 57B; Image: 118)*. Later that year, he married Eleanor's sister Eliza Jane Pegan.

Andrew and Eliza Jane Pegan Schwartz II are enumerated in Lynchburg, Dodson Twp., Highland Co., Ohio in 1880 *(Census Place: Lynchburg, Highland, Ohio; Roll: 1032; Page: 276C; Enumeration District: 041; Image: 0555)*. In the home are Andrew Schwartz II, age 31, a shoemaker, born Ohio with his parents born in Germany; his wife, Eliza J. Pegan Schwartz, 33, and their daughter Cora M., nine, both Ohio natives, as were their parents.

Andrew Schwartz II is still living in Highland Co., Ohio in 1889. His daughter Cora Schwartz either inherited money from his wife Eliza Jane Pegan Schwartz or from his own parents, as Andrew was appointed guardian of his daughter Cora Schwartz after Eliza's death in 1883. He reported to the Highland County court that his term of guardianship was completed in 1889 as Cora had reached age 18, the age of maturity for women. Andrew is not found in the census or mentioned in Highland county newspapers after this year.[91]

His Highland County death record states he died at age 54.[89] His parents, Andrew and Veronika Schwartz Sr. (also the parents of his brother Joseph who married Elma Pegan, this sister of Andrew's wife Eliza Jane Pegan Schwartz), were living in Perry Twp., Brown Co., Ohio in 1850 *(Census Place: Perry, Brown, Ohio; Roll: M432_662; Page: 299B; Image: 57)*. Andrew is enumerated as one year old in this census, which was taken July 30, 1850.

Daughter of Eliza Jane Pegan and Andrew Schwartz II:

+ 32 f I. **Cora May**[7] **Schwartz** was born in Lynchburg, Dodson Twp., Highland Co., Ohio, on May 22, 1871.[92] She died in Lafayette Twp., Coshocton Co., Ohio, on January 3, 1951.[92]

7. **Pleasant**[6] **Pegan** (*Henry*[5], *Robert A.*[4], *Andrew*[3], *Andrew*[2] *Pagan, James*[1]) was born on April 26, 1848, in Dodson Twp., Highland Co., Ohio.[17] He was the son of Henry Pegan (1) and Harriet Stroup. Pleasant died in Highland Co., Ohio, on March 22, 1870, at age 21.[18] He was buried in Lynchburg Masonic Cemetery, Lynchburg, Dodson Twp., Highland Co., Ohio.[17]

Never married.

Pleasant Pegan's gravestone in the Lynchburg Masonic Cemetery, Lynchburg, Dodson Twp., Highland Co., Ohio states he was age 21 years, 10 months and 24 days when he died. His birthdate, calculated from this information, was April 26, 1848.[17] He was undoubtedly named after his uncle Pleasant Pegan, Henry's younger brother, who died young.

8. **Michael Stroup**[6] **Pegan** (*Henry*[5], *Robert A.*[4], *Andrew*[3], *Andrew*[2] *Pagan, James*[1]) was born on October 3, 1851, in Dodson Twp., Highland Co., Ohio.[19] He was the son of Henry Pegan (1) and Harriet Stroup. Michael Stroup died in Dodson Twp., Highland Co., Ohio, on March 16, 1888, at age 36.[19] He was buried in Lynchburg Masonic Cemetery, Lynchburg, Dodson Twp., Highland Co., Ohio.[93]

Never married.

In 1870, there is a Michael Pegan, age 12, "insane", enumerated in the Southern Ohio Lunatic Asylum in Van Buren Twp., Montgomery Co., Ohio (*Census Place: Van Buren, Montgomery, Ohio; Roll: M593_1248; Page: 778B; Image: 781*). Michael was not insane—he was an epileptic, and many with that affliction were institutionalized in those days. His age, however, is incorrect; he was 16.

In 1880, Michael Pegan is living with his brother-in-law and sister, Joseph and Elma Eleanor Pegan Schwartz, in Dodson Twp., Highland Co., Ohio (*Census Place: Dodson, Highland, Ohio; Roll: 1032; Page: 287A; Enumeration District: 41; Image: 0577*). Michael Pegan, 25, single, born Ohio as were his parents (Incorrect—his father was born in Pennsylvania), lists no occupation. Joseph Swartz, age 37, a farmer, was born in Ohio with his parents born in Prussia; his wife, Elma Eleanor Pegan Swartz, also 37, says she and her parents were born in Ohio (Incorrect—her father was born in Pennsylvania). Children in the home include Mary H. Schwartz, 10, and "Charles W." Schwartz, three, both born in Ohio. Michael and Elma Eleanor's mother, Harriet Stroup Pegan, is also residing in the home. Harriet, age 67, a widow, enumerated as "mother-in-law", is listed as born in Ohio as were her parents (Incorrect—her parents were born in Pennsylvania).

9. **William Henry**[6] **Pegan** (*Henry*[5], *Robert A.*[4], *Andrew*[3], *Andrew*[2] *Pagan, James*[1]) was born on November 2, 1854, in Dodson Twp., Highland Co., Ohio.[19] He was the son of Henry Pegan (1) and Harriet Stroup. He died in Clark Twp., Clinton Co., Ohio, on August 26, 1939, at age 84.[20] William Henry was buried in Troutwine Cemetery, Dodson Twp., Highland Co., Ohio and Clark Twp., Clinton Co., Ohio.[20, 94, 95]

William Henry married **Margaret Louisa Jones** on September 29, 1878, in Clinton Co., Ohio.[96] They had four children. Margaret Louisa Jones was born in Clark Twp., Clinton Co., Ohio, on January 16, 1856.[97] Margaret Louisa reached age 70 and died in Lynchburg, Dodson Twp., Highland Co., Ohio, on September 11, 1926.[97] She was buried in Troutwine Cemetery, Dodson Twp., Highland Co., Ohio and Clark Twp., Clinton Co., Ohio.[97, 98]

William Henry Pegan is enumerated in 1880 in Clarke Twp., Clinton Co., Ohio (*Census Place: Clarke, Clinton, Ohio; Roll: 1001; Page: 39B; Enumeration District: 056; Image: 0080*). In the household are William H. Pegan, 25, a farmer; his wife Martha L. Jones Pegan, 24; and son Joseph, five months. Living with them is a farmhand, Harmon Larick, 23. All in the home were born in Ohio, as were their parents.

In 1900, William Henry Pegan is still living in Clark Twp., Clinton Co., Ohio (Census Place: Clark, Clinton, Ohio; Roll: T623_1248; Page: 8A; Enumeration District: 59). William Pegan, age 45, born Nov 1854, is a farmer. His wife, Margaret Louisa Jones Pegan is 44, was born Jan 1856. The couple says they have been married 21 years and Margaret has borne four children, three of them surviving. They are Frank, 17, born Jun 1882, a farmhand on the family farm; Ella, 14, born May 1886; and William O. (II), four, born Dec 1895. All were born in Ohio as were their parents, except for Margaret's father, who was born in Pennsylvania.

William H, Pegan continues to reside in Clark Twp., Clinton Co., Ohio in 1910 (Census Place: Clark, Clinton, Ohio; Roll: T624_1160; Page: 6B; Enumeration District: 0061; Image: 726). In the home are William H. Pegan, 55, a farmer, and his wife "Louisa" (Margaret Louisa Jones) Pegan, 54. They have been married 30 years and Margaret Louisa again states she has borne four children and three are still living. Children still with them are Ella, 23, and William II (William Otto), 14. Margaret says her father was born in Pennsylvania, but otherwise all and their parents were born in Ohio.

In 1920, William Henry Pegan ("W.H. Pegan") is again found in Clark Twp., Clinton Co., Ohio (Census Place: Clark, Clinton, Ohio; Roll: T625_1355; Page: 2B; Enumeration District: 113; Image: 676). William Henry Pegan is age 64 and still a farmer. Margaret Louisa Jones Pegan is listed as "Louie", and is 53 years old. Their daughter, Ella, 33 and single, in also living with them and lists no occupation. All of them were born in Ohio as were their parents, except for Margaret's father, who was born in Pennsylvania.

William H. Pegan, listed as "William H. Peagan", is once again enumerated in Clark Twp., Clinton Co., Ohio in 1930 (Census Place: Clark, Clinton, Ohio; Roll: 1761; Page: 9A; Enumeration District: 4; Image: 188.0). Household members are William H. Pegan, 75, a widower and a farmer; and his unmarried daughter Ella, 43. Both say they and their parents were born in Ohio.

Margaret Louisa Jones Pegan became seriously ill at a Jones family reunion at the home of a cousin Lynchburg, Dodson Twp., Highland Co., Ohio. Her condition caused her to remain at the cousin's home until she died two weeks later.[99]

Children of William Henry Pegan and Margaret Louisa Jones:

+ 33 m I. **Joseph T.[7] Pegan** was born in Clark Twp., Clinton Co., Ohio, on December 30, 1879.[100] He died in Clark Twp., Clinton Co., Ohio, on October 31, 1881.[101, 102]

+ 34 m II. **Frank Joseph[7] Pegan** was born in Clark Twp., Clinton Co., Ohio, on June 8, 1882.[31, 103, 104] He died in Waynesville, Wayne Twp., Warren Co., Ohio, on March 28, 1966.[103, 105]

+ 35 f III. **Ella Mae[7] Pegan** was born in Clark Twp., Clinton Co., Ohio, on May 25, 1886.[106, 107] She died in Wilmington, Union Twp., Clinton Co., Ohio, on October 25, 1948.[106]

+ 36 m IV. **William Otto[7] Pegan** was born in Clark Twp., Clinton Co., Ohio, on December 25, 1895.[31, 108, 109] He died in a facility in Sabina, Richland Twp., Clinton Co., Ohio, on October 28, 1985.[108, 110]

7th Generation

10. Josephine⁷ Stroup (*Elvira⁶ Pegan, Henry⁵, Robert A.⁴, Andrew³, Andrew² Pagan, James¹*) was born on April 24, 1856, in Dodson Twp., Highland Co., Ohio.[26] She was the daughter of Levi Stroup and Elvira Pegan (2). Josephine died in Lynchburg, Dodson Twp., Highland Co., Ohio, on June 21, 1941, at age 85.[26] She was buried in Stroup Cemetery, Dodson Twp., Highland Co., Ohio.[26, 111]

Josephine married **Henry A. Lemons** on September 25, 1875, in Highland Co., Ohio.[112] They had eight children. Henry A. Lemons was born in New Market Twp., Highland Co., Ohio, in 1847.[113] Henry A. reached age 51 and died in Salem Twp., Highland Co., Ohio, on February 5, 1898.[114] He was buried in Stroup Cemetery, Dodson Twp., Highland Co., Ohio.[112, 115]

The family surname is usually seen as "Lemons", but sometimes it is "Lemon". In this book, it will be "Lemons", unless otherwise quoted.

Although his entry in the Highland County death record book claims Henry Lemons died on March 5, 1898, his obituary appeared in the *Hillsboro (OH) News Herald* on February 10, 1898![113, 114] In the Lynchburg community column, written on February 7, the obituary says he died "last Saturday", which was February 5. The death record book is erroneous!

In 1880, Henry and Josephine Stroup Lemons are enumerated in Salem Twp., Highland Co., Ohio *(Census Place: Salem, Highland, Ohio; Roll: 1033; Page: 504C; Enumeration District: 53; Image: 0388)*. In the household are Henry Lemons, 28, a farmer and his wife, Josephine Stroup Lemons, 24. They have two children, Agnes ("Agnese"), three, and Grace, one. All in the home were born in Ohio, as were their parents.

Josephine Stroup Lemons is enumerated in 1900 in Lynchburg, Dodson Twp., Highland Co., Ohio *(Census Place: Dodson, Highland, Ohio; Roll: T623_1286; Page: 5B; Enumeration District: 106)*. Josephine Stroup Lemons is age 44, born Apr 1856, a dressmaker, who says she is a widow. Josephine says she has borne eight children, all still living. With her are children Grace, 21, born Jul 1878, a saleslady; James, 18, born Jul 1880; "Andy V.", 17, born Aug 1882; "De Witt", 15, born Dec 1884; Merrill, 13, born May 1886; Clarence O., nine, born Oct 1890; and Edgar R., seven, born May 1893. James, Andrew, and (Talmadge) DeWitt Lemons are working as day laborers. All in the home say they and their parents were Ohio-born.

By 1910, Josephine Stroup Lemons, listed as "Lamons", and some of her children have moved to Springfield, Springfield Twp., Clark Co., Ohio *(Census Place: Springfield Ward 3, Clark, Ohio; Roll: T624_1158; Page: 4A; Enumeration District: 0036; Image: 957)*. The head of the household, "Meril" Lemons, 23, single, is a bench hand at Harvester Works. The head of the household, Josephine Stroup Lemons, age 53, says she is a widow who bore eight children, all still alive. Merle's brothers in the household, all still unmarried, are Talmadge Lemons, 24, a chipper in a piano factory (probably a chipper at Piano Plate Company); and "Ottie" Lemons, 18, and Edgar Lemons, 17, who both say they are factory laborers. All say they and their parents were born in Ohio.

Josephine Stroup Lemons has relocated back to Lynchburg, Dodson Twp., Highland Co., Ohio by 1920 *(Census Place: Dodson, Highland, Ohio; Roll: T625_1399; Page: 2A; Enumeration District: 84; Image: 101)*. In the home are Josephine Stroup Lemons. 63, a widow, and her three unmarried sons: James, 36, "Meral", 28 and Edgar, 26. The three sons say they are general laborers. All in the home say they and their parents were Ohio natives.

In 1930, Josephine Stroup Lemons is listed as Josephine "Lemon" in Lynchburg, Dodson Twp., Highland Co., Ohio *(Census Place: Lynchburg, Highland, Ohio; Roll: 1823; Page: 5A; Enumeration District: 5; Image: 76.0)*. Josephine, listed as head of the household, is age 63. She says she was first married at age 20. Living with her are son James S. Lemons, 43, single, and a 10-year-old granddaughter, Josephine M. Lemons, the daughter of Clarence O. and Grace May Long Lemons. All in the home were born in Ohio, as were their parents. No one in the home lists any occupation.

Josephine Stroup Lemons still located in Lynchburg, Dodson Twp., Highland Co., Ohio in 1940 *(Census Place: Lynchburg, Highland, Ohio; Roll: T627_3085; Page: 1B; Enumeration District: 36-5)*. The home ison the south side of Main Street between High Street and the stock yards. Josephine Lemons, the head of the household, is age 83 and a widow. With her are unmarried sons James Lemons, 59, "Merl" Lemons, 53, and "Edgar" Lemons, 45. All were born in Ohio, and say they were living in the same house in 1935. Murrell ("Merl") and Edgar list their occupation as odd jobs; James has no occupation. The surname is spelled "Lemon".

Children of Josephine Stroup and Henry A. Lemons:

+ 37 f I. **Agnes**[8] **Lemons** was born in Salem Twp., Highland Co., Ohio, on June 23, 1876.[116] She died in a hospital in Columbus, Franklin Co., Ohio, on September 27, 1943.[116]

+ 38 f II. **Grace**[8] **Lemons** was born in Salem Twp., Highland Co., Ohio, on July 4, 1878.[117] She died in Lynchburg, Dodson Twp., Highland Co., Ohio, on October 19, 1959.[118]

+ 39 m III. **James Stroup**[8] **Lemons** was born in Salem Twp., Highland Co., Ohio, on July 3, 1880.[119] He died in Liberty Twp., Highland Co., Ohio, on January 2, 1948.[120]

+ 40 m IV. **Andrew Vance**[8] **Lemons** was born in Salem Twp., Highland Co., Ohio, on August 31, 1882.[121] He died in Bald Hill, Okmulgee Co., Oklahoma, on May 7, 1917.[122, 123, 124]

+ 41 m V. **Talmadge DeWitt**[8] **Lemons** was born in Salem Twp., Highland Co., Ohio, on December 30, 1885.[125] He was also known as **Tal** and **Spot**. Talmadge DeWitt died in Lynchburg, Dodson Twp., Highland Co., Ohio, on July 4, 1956.[126, 127]

+ 42 m VI. **Murrell or Merrill**[8] **Lemons** was born in Salem Twp., Highland Co., Ohio, on May 25, 1887.[128, 129, 130] He died in Springfield, Springfield Twp., Clark Co., Ohio, on July 11, 1953.[128]

+ 43 m VII. **Clarence Otto**[8] **Lemons** was born in Salem Twp., Highland Co., Ohio, on October 11, 1891.[131] He died in Hillsboro, Liberty Twp., Highland Co., Ohio, on October 22, 1944.[131]

+ 44 m VIII. **Edgar or Edward Roy**[8] **Lemons** was born in Salem Twp., Highland Co., Ohio, on May 24, 1893.[132] He was also known as **Eddie**. He died in Lynchburg, Dodson Twp., Highland Co., Ohio, on April 5, 1951.[132]

11. Hattie Ann[7] **Stroup** (*Elvira*[6] *Pegan, Henry*[5]*, Robert A.*[4]*, Andrew*[3]*, Andrew*[2] *Pagan, James*[1]) was born in 1858 in Dodson Twp., Highland Co., Ohio.[27] She was the daughter of Levi Stroup and Elvira Pegan (2). Hattie Ann died in Dodson Twp., Highland Co., Ohio, in 1861 at age three.[27] She was buried in Stroup Cemetery, Dodson Twp., Highland Co., Ohio.[27]

12. Mary E.[7] **Stroup** (*Elvira*[6] *Pegan, Henry*[5]*, Robert A.*[4]*, Andrew*[3]*, Andrew*[2] *Pagan, James*[1]) was born on March 19, 1861, in Dodson Twp., Highland Co., Ohio.[28] She was the daughter of Levi Stroup and Elvira Pegan (2). Mary E. died in Owensville, Stone Lick Twp., Clermont Co., Ohio, on November 15, 1943, at age 82.[28] She was buried in Stroup Cemetery, Dodson Twp., Highland Co., Ohio.[28, 133]

Mary E. married **Samuel Williams** on September 30, 1877, in Highland Co., Ohio.[134] They had eight children. Samuel Williams was born in Dodson Twp., Highland Co., Ohio, on October 18, 1854.[135] He reached age 85 and died in Dodsonville, Dodson Twp., Highland Co., Ohio, on December 3, 1939.[135] Samuel was buried in Stroup Cemetery, Dodson Twp., Highland Co., Ohio.[136]

Samuel and Mary Stroup Williams are enumerated in Dodson Twp., Highland Co., Ohio in 1880 *(Census Place: Dodson, Highland, Ohio; Roll: 1032; Page: 279B; Enumeration District: 41; Image: 0562)*. In the household are Samuel Williams, 25, a farmer; his wife, Mary Stroup Williams, 19, and daughter Cora M., one. All in the home were born in Ohio, as were their parents.

In 1900, Samuel and Mary Stroup Williams are found in Dodson Twp., Highland Co., Ohio *(Census Place: Dodson, Highland, Ohio; Roll: T623_1286; Page: 11A; Enumeration District: 106)*. Samuel Williams is age 45, born Oct 1854 in Ohio, but this time he says his father was born in Virginia and his mother in Germany. Samuel is a farmer. With him is wife Mary Stroup Williams, 39, born Mar 1861 in Ohio, where her parents were also born. They state they have been married 22 years and Mary has borne seven children, six of them still living. Children living in the home are Levi, 19, born May 1881, a farm laborer; Hattie E., 17, born May 1883; Stanley, 14, born Jan 1886; Josephus, 12, born Apr 1888; and Harley, three, born Nov 1896. All the children were born in Ohio. (Later that year, daughter Hattie Williams states on her marriage license that she was born on July 16, 1882.)

By 1910, Samuel and Mary Stroup Williams have removed to Clark Twp., Clinton Co., Ohio *(Census Place: Clark, Clinton, Ohio; Roll: T624_1160; Page: 9A; Enumeration District: 0061; Image: 731)*. In the home are Samuel Williams, 55, a farmer, born Ohio, with his father born in Scotland and his mother in Germany; and his wife, Mary Stroup Williams, 49, born Ohio as were her parents. Samuel and Mary say they are on their first marriage, have been married 33 years, and Mary has borne eight children, six still alive. The only child in the home is son Harley, age 14, born Ohio.

Samuel and Mary Stroup Williams are living in Salem Twp., Highland Co., Ohio in 1920 *(Census Place: Salem, Highland, Ohio; Roll: T625_1399; Page: 6B; Enumeration District: 102; Image: 548)*. Samuel Williams, age 65, is still a farmer who says he was born in Ohio. This time, however, he says his father was born in Ohio and his mother in Germany. Living with him are his wife, Mary Stroup Williams, 58, born Ohio as were her parents, and their son Harley, 23, single, born Ohio, a laborer.

In 1930, Samuel and Mary Stroup Williams are listed in Dodson Twp., Highland Co., Ohio *(Census Place: Dodson, Highland, Ohio; Roll: 1823; Page: 4A; Enumeration District: 6; Image: 90.0)*. Samuel Williams is 75 and is still a farmer. He says he and his father were born in Ohio and his mother in Germany. Mary Stroup Williams is age 69, born Ohio as were her parents. Samuel and Mary say they were first married at age 23 and 18 respectively. Son Harley N., who is listed as age 31 and unmarried, is still with them and is a farm laborer.

In 1940, Mary E. Stroup Williams, a widow, is enumerated in Lynchburg, Dodson Twp., Highland Co., Ohio *(Census Place: Lynchburg, Highland, Ohio; Roll: T627_3085; Page: 7B; Enumeration District: 36-5)*. She is living along in a home on "east short between Eastern Avenue and town's end" and lists no occupation. Mary E. Stroup Williams is 80 years old, born Ohio, and says she was living in Highland Co. in 1935.

The informant on Mary E. Stroup Williams' death certificate was her son-in-law, Allen Carroll. Allen states that he is living in Owensville, Stonelick Twp., Clermont Co., Ohio at the time. He also says that Mary died in Stonelick Twp., Clermont Co., Ohio on November 15, 1946, after living there for six weeks. Her regular residence was listed as Lynchburg, Dodson Twp., Highland Co., Ohio. Although the word "Owensville" is crossed out on the death certificate, it seems that Mary E. Stroup Williams was living with Allen and Cora May Williams Carroll at the time of her death.[28]

Children of Mary E. Stroup and Samuel Williams:

+ 45 f I. **Cora May**[8] **Williams** was born in Dodson Twp., Highland Co., Ohio, on May 16, 1879.[137] She died in Lynchburg, Dodson Twp., Highland Co., Ohio, on September 29, 1955.[138]

+ 46 m II. **Levi**[8] **Williams** was born in Dodson Twp., Highland Co., Ohio, on May 26, 1881.[139, 140] He was also known as **Lee**. Levi died in Lynchburg, Dodson Twp., Highland Co., Ohio, on December 1, 1947.[139]

+ 47 f III. **Hattie Ellen**[8] **Williams** was born in Dodson Twp., Highland Co., Ohio, on July 16, 1882.[141] She died in a hospital in Wilmington, Union Twp., Clinton Co., Ohio, on September 4, 1961.[142]

+ 48 m IV. **Stanley**[8] **Williams** was born in Salem Twp., Highland Co., Ohio, on January 31, 1886.[31, 143] He died in Hillsboro, Liberty Twp., Highland Co., Ohio, on September 2, 1972.[144]

+ 49 m V. **Josephus Everett**[8] **Williams** was born in Dodson Twp., Highland Co., Ohio, on April 25, 1888.[145] He was also known as **Joseph**. Josephus Everett died in Dodson Twp., Highland Co., Ohio, on June 17, 1923.[145]

+ 50 m VI. **Cary**[8] **Williams** was born in Salem Twp., Highland Co., Ohio, on February 25, 1890.[146] He died in Salem Twp., Highland Co., Ohio.[147]

+ 51 m VII. **Harley N.**[8] **Williams** was born in Dodson Twp., Highland Co., Ohio, on December 28, 1896.[31, 148] He died in Dodson Twp., Highland Co., Ohio, on July 26, 1963.[149]

+ 52 m VIII. **Infant Son**[8] **Williams** was born in Dodson Twp., Highland Co., Ohio, between 1900 and 1910. He died in Dodson Twp., Highland Co., Ohio, between 1900 and 1910.

13. **Laura Arabella**[7] **Stroup** (*Elvira*[6] *Pegan, Henry*[5], *Robert A.*[4], *Andrew*[3], *Andrew*[2] *Pagan, James*[1]) was born on October 27, 1863, in Dodson Twp., Highland Co., Ohio.[29, 30, 31] She was the daughter of Levi Stroup and Elvira Pegan (2). She was also known as **Laura Belle** or **Belle**. She died in Lynchburg, Dodson Twp., Highland Co., Ohio, on December 7, 1967, at age 104.[29, 30, 32] Laura Arabella was buried in Troutwine Cemetery, Dodson Twp., Highland Co., Ohio and Clark Twp., Clinton Co., Ohio.[29, 30]

Laura Arabella married **Joseph Henry Spilker** on August 9, 1887, in Highland Co., Ohio.[150] They had four children. Joseph Henry Spilker was born in Dodson Twp., Highland Co., Ohio, on April 5, 1860.[151, 152] Joseph Henry reached age 78 and died in Dodsonville, Dodson Twp., Highland Co., Ohio, on January 2, 1939.[151, 152, 153] He was buried in Troutwine Cemetery, Dodson Twp., Highland Co., Ohio and Clark Twp., Clinton Co., Ohio.[151, 152]

Although his tombstone says he was born on April 5, 1860, Joseph Henry Spilker's death certificate states he was born on April 5, 1861.[151, 152] Census records consistently support the 1860 date, including the 1860 census, where he is listed as two and one-half months old living with his parents Charles and Nancy Spilker in Dodson Twp., Highland Co., Ohio *(Census Place: Dodson, Highland, Ohio; Roll: M653_986; Page: 74; Image: 153)*. The death certificate also claims he was 78 years, eight months and 14 days old, which would make his birth date April 19, 1860. The death certificate seems to be wrong.

Joseph and "Laura Belle" Stroup Spilker are enumerated in Dodson Twp., Highland Co., Ohio in 1900 *(Census Place: Dodson, Highland, Ohio; Roll: T623_1286; Page: 5B; Enumeration District: 107)*. The head of the household is Joseph Spilker, age 40, a farmer, born Apr 1860 in Ohio, with his father born in Germany and his mother in Ohio. With him is his wife, Laura Arabella, "Laura Belle" Stroup, 36, born Oct 1863 Ohio, where her parents were born. The couple have been married 12 years and Laura has borne four children, all still alive. They are: Bessie B., 12, born Oct 1887; Earle E., 10, born March "1880" (here the enumerator erred and meant 1890); Ralph H., eight, born Feb 1892; and

Hazel, four, born Sep 1895. All the children were born in Ohio.

In 1910, Joseph H. and Laura Arabella "Laura Belle" Stroup Spilker are again living in Dodson Twp., Highland Co., Ohio *(Census Place: Dodson, Highland, Ohio; Roll: T624_1197; Page: 5A; Enumeration District: 0114; Image: 545)*. Joseph Spilker, age 50, is still a farmer born in Ohio, but this time he says his father was born in Germany and his mother in Pennsylvania. Laura Arabella Stroup Spilker is 46 and says she and her parents were Ohio natives. Joseph and Laura Belle say they have been married 23 years and Laura has borne four children, three of them surviving. Children living with them are: Earl E., 20, and Ralph H., 18, both farm laborers on the family farm; and Hazel F., 14. All the children were born in Ohio.

Joseph and Laura Arabella "Laura Belle" Stroup Spilker are still residing in Dodson Twp., Highland Co., Ohio in 1920 *(Census Place: Dodson, Highland, Ohio; Roll: T625_1399; Page: 2A; Enumeration District: 83; Image: 83)*. In the home are Joseph Spilker, age 59, a farmer who says he was born in Ohio, his father in Germany and his mother in Virginia; and Laura Arabella "Laura Belle" Stroup Spilker, 56, born Ohio as were her parents.

By 1930, Joseph and Laura Arabella "Laura Belle" Stroup Spilker have retired and moved to the village of Dodsonville, Dodson Twp., Highland Co., Ohio *(Census Place: Dodson, Highland, Ohio; Roll: 1823; Page: 7B; Enumeration District: 6; Image: 97.0)*. Joseph Spilker, listed as "Joe H. Spilker", is age 69, born Ohio, and states that his father was born in Germany and his mother in West Virginia. Laura Arabella "Laura Belle" Stroup Spilker, 66, states that she and her parents were born in Ohio. Joseph Spilker lists no occupation. The pair say they were first married at ages 27 and 24 respectively.

In 1940, the newly widowed Laura Arabella Stroup Spilker is enumerated in Dodsonville, Dodson Twp., Highland Co., *Ohio (Census Place: Dodson, Highland, Ohio; Roll: T627_3085; Page: 8A; Enumeration District: 36-6)*. "Belle" Spilker is 75 years old and listed as the head of the household. With her is her divorced son Ralph Spilker, 48. Neither lists an occupation. Both say they were Ohio natives and were living in the same house on U.S. Highway 50 (no numerical address) in 1935.

Laura Arabella "Belle" Stroup Spilker lived to be 104 years old, and, by newspaper accounts, was spry and mentally alert until her death—despite two broken hips sustained two years before she died. Even at her advanced age, she continued to enjoy quilting and sewing aprons.[29]

Children of Laura Arabella Stroup and Joseph Henry Spilker:

+ 53 f I. **Bessie B.**[8] **Spilker** was born in Salem Twp., Highland Co., Ohio, on November 19, 1887.[154, 155] She died in Dodson Twp., Highland Co., Ohio, on May 24, 1907.[156]

+ 54 m II. **Earl Everett**[8] **Spilker** was born in Dodson Twp., Highland Co., Ohio, on March 26, 1890.[157] He died in a hospital in Cincinnati, Hamilton Co., Ohio, on June 16, 1942.[157]

+ 55 m III. **Ralph Henry**[8] **Spilker** was born in Dodson Twp., Highland Co., Ohio, on February 8, 1892.[31] He died in a hospital in Cincinnati, Hamilton Co., Ohio, on December 21, 1966.[158]

+ 56 f IV. **Hazel A.**[8] **Spilker** was born in Dodson Twp., Highland Co., Ohio, on September 10, 1895.[159] She died in Clearwater, Pinellas Co., Florida, on January 12, 2000.[31, 160, 161]

14. John Henry[7] **Stroup** (*Elvira*[6] *Pegan, Henry*[5]*, Robert A.*[4]*, Andrew*[3]*, Andrew*[2] *Pagan, James*[1]) was born on February 15, 1866, in Dodson Twp., Highland Co., Ohio.[33] He was the son of Levi Stroup and Elvira Pegan (2). John Henry died in Dodsonville, Dodson Twp., Highland Co., Ohio, on June 3, 1946, at age 80.[33] He was buried in Stroup Cemetery, Dodson Twp., Highland Co., Ohio.[33, 162]

John Henry married **Catherine Olive Ballentine** on September 19, 1890, in Highland Co., Ohio.[163]

They had four children. Catherine Olive Ballentine was born in Washington Twp., Highland Co., Ohio, on May 24, 1868.[164] Catherine Olive reached age 91 and died in Spring Valley, Spring Valley Twp., Greene Co., Ohio, on April 20, 1960.[165] She was buried in Stroup Cemetery, Dodson Twp., Highland Co., Ohio.[166] She was the daughter of Robert Ballentine and Eliza Jane Stodgill.

John Henry Stroup is enumerated in Dodson Twp., Highland Co., Ohio in 1900 (*Census Place: Dodson, Highland, Ohio; Roll: T623_1286; Page: 3B; Enumeration District: 107*). In the household are John H. Stroup, age 34, a farmer, born Feb 1866 in Ohio, where his parents were born. With him are wife "Katherine" Ballentine Stroup, 32, born May 1868, in Ohio, the birth state of her parents. The couple says they have been married nine years and Katherine has borne four children, with two surviving. Children in the home are Vernice, six, born Apr 1894; and Clarence, one, born Jan 1899. Both children were born in Ohio.

In 1910, John Henry Stroup is found in Dodson Twp., Highland Co., Ohio (*Census Place: Dodson, Highland, Ohio; Roll: T624_1197; Page: 2B; Enumeration District: 0114; Image: 540*). In the household are John H. Stroup, 43, born Ohio as were his parents, a farmer; and his wife "Cathryn" Ballentine Stroup, 42, born Ohio, with her father "Scots-Irish" and her mother born in Ohio. They state they are on their first marriage, have been wed 18 years, and Catherine has borne four children, two of them still living. They are Vernice, 15, and Clarence H., 11, both born in Ohio.

By 1920, John H. Stroup has moved to Salem Twp., Highland Co., Ohio (*Census Place: Salem, Highland, Ohio; Roll: T625_1399; Page: 4A; Enumeration District: 102; Image: 543*). John H. Stroup is age 53, a farmer, born Ohio as were his parents. His wife Catherine O. Ballentine Stroup is 51, born Ohio, with her father born in Scotland and her mother in Ohio. Son Clarence H. Stroup is still residing with them; he is age 20, born Ohio, and lists his occupation as a laborer. Also living with them is a boarder, Ralph Vance, 19.

John Henry Stroup is still living in Salem Twp., Highland Co., Ohio in 1930 (*Census Place: Salem, Highland, Ohio; Roll: 1823; Page: 4A; Enumeration District: 23; Image: 502.0*). John H. Stroup, 64, was born in Ohio as were his parents. He says he is a farmer raising livestock. His wife is Catherine O. Ballentine Stroup, 63, who this time says she and her parents were born in Ohio. The pair say they were first married at ages 25 and 24 respectively.

In 1940, John Henry Stroup is again found in Salem Twp., Highland Co., Ohio (*Census Place: Salem, Highland, Ohio; Roll: T627_3085; Page: 6A; Enumeration District: 36-27*). In the home are John Stroup, age 74, who is still farming; and his wife, Catherine Ballentine Stroup, 72. Both say they were born in Ohio, and were living in the same house in 1935. There is no road or numerical address listed, but their home was near the settlement of Harwood, Salem Twp., Highland Co., Ohio.

John Henry and Catherine Ballentine Stroup had two children who died between 1890-1900. Although their names cannot be confirmed, there are two Stroups, who seem to be infant twins, buried in Stroup Cemetery who are most likely their children: Elton Stroup, who died September 17, 1892, and Edgar Stroup, who died September 20, 1892. There are no birth or death records for these two males in the Highland County vital records.

John Henry Stroup's wife Catherine Ballentine Stroup was a sister to Robert E. Ballentine II, who married John Henry's sister Elma Jane Stroup.

Children of John Henry Stroup and Catherine Olive Ballentine:

+ 57 m I. **Elton[8] Stroup?** was born in Dodson Twp., Highland Co., Ohio, about September 17, 1892. He died in Dodson Twp., Highland Co., Ohio, on September 17, 1892.[167]

+ 58 m II. **Edgar[8] Stroup?** was born in Dodson Twp., Highland Co., Ohio, about September 17, 1892. He died in Dodson Twp., Highland Co., Ohio, on September 20, 1892.[168]

+ 59 f III. **Vernice Catherine[8] Stroup** was born in Dodson Twp., Highland Co., Ohio, on April 20, 1894.[169, 170] She died in Hillsboro, Liberty Twp., Highland Co., Ohio, on July 5, 1971.[170, 171]

+ 60 m IV. **Clarence Harold**[8] **Stroup** was born in Dodson Twp., Highland Co., Ohio, on January 8, 1899.[31, 172, 173] He died in Xenia, Xenia Twp., Greene Co., Ohio, on January 20, 1980.[174, 175]

15. Elma Jane[7] **Stroup** (*Elvira*[6] *Pegan, Henry*[5]*, Robert A.*[4]*, Andrew*[3]*, Andrew*[2] *Pagan, James*[1]) was born on April 4, 1868, in Salem Twp., Highland Co., Ohio.[34] She was the daughter of Levi Stroup and Elvira Pegan (2). She died in Wilmington, Union Twp., Clinton Co., Ohio, on February 4, 1936, at age 67.[34] Elma Jane was buried in Blanchester IOOF Cemetery, Blanchester, Marion Twp., Clinton Co., Ohio.[34, 176]

Elma Jane married **Robert E. Ballentine II** on April 26, 1888, in Highland Co., Ohio.[177] They had two daughters. Robert E. Ballentine II was born in Washington Twp., Highland Co., Ohio, on December 29, 1863.[178] He was also known as **Robbie**. Robert E. reached age 65 and died in Goshen Twp., Clermont Co., Ohio, on October 6, 1929.[178] He was buried in Blanchester IOOF Cemetery, Blanchester, Marion Twp., Clinton Co., Ohio.[178, 179] He was the son of Robert Ballentine and Eliza Jane Stodgill.

Robert E. and Elma Jane Stroup Ballentine II are enumerated in 1900 in Dodson Twp., Highland Co., Ohio *(Census Place: Dodson, Highland, Ohio; Roll: T623_1286; Page: 11B; Enumeration District: 106)*. Robert E. Ballentine II is age 34, a farmer, born Dec 1865 in Ohio, with his father born in Scotland and his mother in Ohio. Elma J. Stroup Ballentine is 32, born April 1868 in Ohio, the birth state of her parents. The couple has been married 12 years and Elma has borne two children, both still alive. They are daughters Sadie D., eight, born Aug 1891; and Leatha M., nine months, born Oct 1899. Both the children were born in Ohio. Boarding in the home is Hoadley Runyon, 17, born Ohio, a farm laborer.

By 1910, Robert E. and Elma Jane Stroup Ballentine II have moved to Jefferson Twp., Clinton Co., Ohio *(Census Place: Jefferson, Clinton, Ohio; Roll: T624_1160; Page: 9B; Enumeration District: 0065; Image: 804)*. Robert E. Ballentine II, listed as "R.E. Ballentine", is age 44, a farmer, born Ohio, with his father born in Scotland and his mother in Virginia. Elma Jane Stroup Ballentine is 31, born Ohio as were her parents. Robert and Elma say they have been married 22 years and Elma has borne two children, both surviving. Their children Sadie D. Ballentine, age 18, and Leatha M., Ballentine, nine, are in the home.

In 1920, Robert E. and Elma Jane Stroup Ballentine II are residing in Dodson Twp., Highland Co., Ohio again *(Census Place: Dodson, Highland, Ohio; Roll: T625_1399; Page: 7B; Enumeration District: 84; Image: 112)*. In the household are Robert E. Ballentine II, 54, born Ohio, with his father born in Scotland and his mother in Ohio; and his wife Elma Jane Stroup Ballentine, 52, born Ohio as were her parents. Robert is still a farmer.

In 1930, widow Elma J. Stroup Ballentine is enumerated only as "Ballentine", in Goshen Twp., Clermont Co., Ohio *(Census Place: Goshen, Clermont, Ohio; Roll: 1757; Page: 13B; Enumeration District: 6; Image: 1007.0)*. Elma J. Stroup Ballentine is 60 years old and is living with her son-in-law and daughter, Silas and Sadie D. Ballentine Vance and their family. Silas Vance, age 43, is a farmer and his wife, Sadie D. Ballentine Vance is age 39. They were first wed at ages 28 and 20 respectively. Living with them are children Thelma, 16, Inez, 11, and Robert, seven. All and their parents were Ohio-born.

Elma Jane Stroup Ballentine's husband Robert Ballentine II was a brother to Catherine Ballentine Stroup, wife of Elma's brother John Henry Stroup.

Daughters of Elma Jane Stroup and Robert E. Ballentine II:

+ 61 f I. **Sadie D.**[8] **Ballentine** was born in Dodson Twp., Highland Co., Ohio, on August 5, 1891.[180] She died in a hospital in Dayton, Montgomery Co., Ohio, on October 1, 1951.[180]

+ 62 f II. **Letha May**[8] **Ballentine** was born in Dodson Twp., Highland Co., Ohio, on October 21, 1899.[31, 181] Letha May died in a hospital in Wilmington, Union Twp., Clinton Co., Ohio, on February 17, 1976.[182]

16. James Pegan[7] **Stroup** (*Elvira*[6] *Pegan, Henry*[5], *Robert A.*[4], *Andrew*[3], *Andrew*[2] *Pagan, James*[1]) was born in 1871 in Salem Twp., Highland Co., Ohio.[35] He was the son of Levi Stroup and Elvira Pegan (2). James Pegan died in Salem Twp., Highland Co., Ohio, in 1873 at age two.[35] He was buried in Stroup Cemetery, Dodson Twp., Highland Co., Ohio.[35]

17. Margaret[7] **Stroup** (*Elvira*[6] *Pegan, Henry*[5], *Robert A.*[4], *Andrew*[3], *Andrew*[2] *Pagan, James*[1]) was born on March 14, 1874, in Salem Twp., Highland Co., Ohio.[36] She was the daughter of Levi Stroup and Elvira Pegan (2). Margaret died in Salem Twp., Highland Co., Ohio, on August 12, 1899, at age 25.[37] She was buried in Stroup Cemetery, Dodson Twp., Highland Co., Ohio.[183, 184]

Never married.

18. Adolphus Vonesse[7] **Pegan** (*Granville*[6], *Henry*[5], *Robert A.*[4], *Andrew*[3], *Andrew*[2] *Pagan, James*[1]) was born on May 8, 1864, in Dodson Twp., Highland Co., Ohio.[44] He was also known as **Dolph**. He was the son of Granville Pegan (3) and Sarah A. Chaney. He died in Dodson Twp., Highland Co., Ohio, on November 22, 1910, at age 46.[44, 45] Adolphus Vonesse was buried in Troutwine Cemetery, Dodson Twp., Highland Co., Ohio.[44, 185, 186, 187]

Adolphus Vonesse married **Teresa Graham** on February 22, 1892, in Clinton Co., Ohio.[188] They had three sons. Teresa Graham was born in Jefferson Twp., Clinton Co., Ohio, on July 19, 1868.[189] Teresa lived in 1920 in Norwood, Mill Creek Twp., Hamilton Co., Ohio. She reached age 72 and died in Columbus, Franklin Co., Ohio, on November 18, 1940.[189] Teresa was buried in Troutwine Cemetery, Dodson Twp., Highland Co., Ohio and Clark Twp., Clinton Co., Ohio.[189, 190]

In 1900, Adolphus Vonesse Pegan is enumerated as "Adolphas Peggan" in Dodson Twp., Highland Co., Ohio *(Census Place: Dodson, Highland, Ohio; Roll: T623_1286; Page: 7A; Enumeration District: 107)*. Adolphus Pegan is age 36, a farmer, born May 1864 in Ohio, where his parents were born. Teresa Graham Pegan, listed as "Tereesa", is 29 and says she was born in Ohio and her parents in Ireland. The couple says they have been married eight years, and Teresa has borne two children, both living. They are sons "Freddie" (Frank), six, born Aug 1893; and Robert, four, born Nov 1895. Both the children were born in Ohio.

Adolphus Vonesse Pegan is listed as "Adolph V. Pegan" in Dodson Twp., Highland Co., Ohio *(Census Place: Dodson, Highland, Ohio; Roll: T624_1197; Page: 1B; Enumeration District: 0114; Image: 538)*. The head of the household is Adolphus Pegan, 45, a farmer born in Ohio as were his parents. Teresa Graham Pegan, this time listed as "Tresa", is 40, born Ohio with her parents born in Ireland. They are on their first marriage, have been married 18 years, and Teresa has borne four children, three of them surviving. Children include "Fred F.", 16, and Robert, 14, both listed as farm laborers on the home farm; and William H., six. All the children were born in Ohio.

Adolphus V. Pegan's was killed when the steam engine on his tractor exploded.[185] Adolphus' mother, Sarah A. Cheney Pegan, the informant on his death certificate. listed his occupation as "engineer".[44]

Widow Teresa Graham Pegan is found in Norwood, Hamilton Co., Ohio in 1920 *(Census Place: Norwood Ward 3, Mill Creek Twp., Hamilton, Ohio; Roll: T625_1395; Page: 9A; Enumeration District: 502; Image: 997)*. The head of the household is Teresa Graham Pegan, age 45, born in Ohio with her parents born in Ireland; she is a nurse working for a "private family". With her is her son William H. Pegan, 16, born Ohio as were his parents, who is a "chipper" at an electrical company. Living with them is a boarder, Fred Parr, age 23, born Ohio, who seems to be also working as a chipper at the same electrical company as William. Son Frank Frederick James Pegan and his family are also living in Norwood, Hamilton Co., Ohio.

Teresa Graham Pegan is not found in the 1930 census.

Teresa Graham Pegan was living with her son William H. Pegan and his family in Columbus, Franklin Co., Ohio when she died.[189]

Sons of Adolphus Vonesse Pegan and Teresa Graham:

+ 63 m I. **Frederick James Frank**[8] **Pegan** was born in Dodson Twp., Highland Co., Ohio, on October 9, 1893.[31, 191] He was also known as **Frank**. Frederick James Frank died in Cincinnati, Hamilton Co., Ohio, on November 19, 1972.[192]

+ 64 m II. **Robert**[8] **Pegan** was born in Dodson Twp., Highland Co., Ohio or Clinton Co., Ohio, on November 24, 1895.[193, 194] He died in Jefferson Twp., Clinton Co., Ohio, on July 14, 1913.[193, 195]

+ 65 m III. **William Henry**[8] **Pegan** was born in Dodson Twp., Highland Co., Ohio, on November 23, 1903.[196, 197] He died in a hospital in Richmond Heights, St. Louis Co., Missouri, on November 5, 1963.[197, 198]

19. Henry Levy[7] **Pegan** (*Granville*[6], *Henry*[5], *Robert A.*[4], *Andrew*[3], *Andrew*[2] *Pagan, James*[1]) was born on May 12, 1868, in Dodson Twp., Highland Co., Ohio.[46, 47] He was the son of Granville Pegan (3) and Sarah A. Chaney. Henry Levy died in Dodson Twp., Highland Co., Ohio, on June 8, 1954, at age 86.[48, 49] He was buried in Troutwine Cemetery, Dodson Twp., Highland Co., Ohio and Clark Twp., Clinton Co., Ohio.[48, 49]

Henry L. Pegan's birth record lists him as a male child with no name.[46]

In 1900 Henry L. Pegan, age 32 and single, is still living with his parents, Granville and Sarah Cheney Pegan, in Dodson Twp., Highland Co., Ohio (*Census Place: Dodson, Highland, Ohio; Roll: T623_1286; Page: 7A; Enumeration District: 107*). Henry, a farmer, says he and his parents were born in Ohio. The head of the household is Granville Pegan, age 62, a farmer, born Dec 1837 in Ohio, with his father born in Pennsylvania and his mother in Ohio. His wife, Sarah Cheney Pegan, 57, born in March 1843, also says she and her mother were born in Ohio and her father in Pennsylvania. The pair state they have been married 37 years and Sarah has borne three children, all still alive.

Henry Levy married **Elma Duvall Troutwine** on September 15, 1904, in Highland Co., Ohio.[199] They had three children. Elma Duvall Troutwine was born in Dodson Twp., Highland Co., Ohio, on November 6, 1882.[200] Elma Duvall reached age 32 and died in Dodson Twp., Highland Co., Ohio, on May 5, 1915.[200, 201] She was buried in Troutwine Cemetery, Dodson Twp., Highland Co., Ohio and Clark Twp., Clinton Co., Ohio.[200, 202]

Henry L. Pegan is enumerated in Dodson Twp., Highland Co., Ohio in 1910 (*Census Place: Dodson, Highland, Ohio; Roll: T624_1197; Page: 2A; Enumeration District: 0114; Image: 539*). Henry L. Pegan is age 41 and a farmer; his wife, Elma D. Troutwine Pegan, is 27. Henry and Elma are both on their first marriage, have been wed six years, and Elma has borne two children, both still living. They are sons Courtland H., five, and Clarence C., three. All in the home were born in Ohio, as were their parents.

Henry Pegan is listed as "Henry L. Pagan" in 1920 in Dodson Twp., Highland Co., Ohio (*Census Place: Dodson, Highland, Ohio; Roll: T625_1399; Page: 8B; Enumeration District: 83; Image: 96*). Henry L. Pegan is the head of the household. Henry L. Pegan, 51 and a widower, is a farmer born in Ohio, as were his parents. Henry's three children are also with them: Courtland A., 15, a farm laborer working on the family farm; Clarence C., 13, and Frances E., eight. All the children were Ohio natives. Also living in the home is Henry's mother, Sarah A. Cheney Pegan, 75, a widow, born in Ohio, with her father born in Pennsylvania and her mother in Ohio.

In 1930, Henry L. Pegan is still residing in Dodson Twp., Highland Co., Ohio *(Census Place: Dodson, Highland, Ohio; Roll: 1823; Page: 3B; Enumeration District: 6; Image: 89.0)*. In the household are Henry L. Pegan, age 61, a widower and a farmer who says his first marriage occurred when he was 35. Unmarried children still with him are son Clarence C., 23, a farm laborer on the family farm; and daughter Frances E. ("Francis"), 19. All in the home were born in Ohio, as were their parents.

Henry Pegan is living with his son Courtland H. Pegan in 1940 in Dodson Twp., Highland Co., Ohio *(Census Place: Dodson, Highland, Ohio; Roll: T627_3085; Page: 1A; Enumeration District: 36-6)*. Henry Pegan, age 73, is a widower who lists no occupation (retired?). The head of the household is Courtland H. Pegan, 35, a farmer. Also in the home are Courtland's wife, Stella Holladay Pegan, 33, and their children Elma, 13, Thelma, 12, Shirley, 10, Robert, six, and Russell, four. All in the home were born in Ohio, and say they were living in the same house at 113-A Setty Road in 1935 (except for Russell, who is too young).

Children of Henry Levy Pegan and Elma Duvall Troutwine:

+ 66 m I. **Courtland Homer**[8] **Pegan** was born in Dodson Twp., Highland Co., Ohio, on December 25, 1904.[31, 203] He died in Hillsboro, Liberty Twp., Highland Co., Ohio, on June 23, 1983.[204]

+ 67 m II. **Clarence Chilton**[8] **Pegan** was born in Dodson Twp., Highland Co., Ohio, on September 21, 1906.[31, 205] He was also known as **Bud**. Clarence Chilton died in St. Martin, Perry Twp., Brown Co., Ohio, on June 23, 1988.

+ 68 f III. **Frances Elizabeth**[8] **Pegan** was born in Dodson Twp., Highland Co., Ohio, on November 25, 1911.[31, 207, 208] She died in a facility in Pisgah, West Chester Twp., Butler Co., Ohio, on December 30, 1990.[31, 207, 208, 209]

20. **Della Frances**[7] **Pegan** (*Granville*[6], *Henry*[5], *Robert A.*[4], *Andrew*[3], *Andrew*[2] *Pagan*, *James*[1]) was born on October 2, 1873, in Dodson Twp., Highland Co., Ohio.[50] She was also known as **Frankie**. She was the daughter of Granville Pegan (3) and Sarah A. Chaney. Della Frances died in Littleton, Dodson Twp., Highland Co., Ohio, on January 9, 1902, age 28.[51] She was buried in Troutwine Cemetery, Dodson Twp., Highland Co., Ohio and Clark Twp., Clinton Co., Ohio.[210, 211]

Della Frances Pegan Thompson used her middle name, Frances, as her given name. Della Frances Pegan Thompson seems to have died of childbirth complications following the birth of her daughter Ruth Frances Thompson.

Della Frances married **William Robert Thompson** on July 20, 1898, in Highland Co., Ohio.[212] They had two daughters. William Robert Thompson was born in Dodson Twp., Highland Co., Ohio, on September 7, 1872.[213] He was also known as **Will**. He reached age 71 and died in Dodson Twp., Highland Co., Ohio, on October 8, 1943.[213, 214] William Robert was buried in Stroup Cemetery, Dodson Twp., Highland Co., Ohio.[213, 215]

William Robert and Della Frances Pegan Thompson are enumerated in Dodson Twp., Highland Co., Ohio in 1900 *(Census Place: Dodson, Highland, Ohio; Roll: T623_1286; Page: 2B; Enumeration District: 107)*. In the household are William Thompson, 27, born Sep 1872, a teacher; his wife, Della Frances Pegan Thompson, listed as "Francis", 26, born Oct 1873; and their daughter Mabel Letha, eight months, born Sep 1899. All were born in Ohio, as were their parents.

After Frances' death, William R. Thompson married Elizabeth Childers about 1908.[216]

In 1910, William Robert Thompson, 37, a teacher, and his second wife, Elizabeth Childers Thompson, 32, are living in Dodson Twp., Highland Co., Ohio *(Census Place: Dodson, Highland, Ohio; Roll: T624_1197; Page: 6A; Enumeration District: 0114; Image: 547)*. Children in the home are Mabel L.,

10, and Ruth F., eight, William's daughters by his first wife Della Frances Pegan; and Robert J., one year and six months, his son by Elizabeth Childers Thompson. All the children were born in Ohio. This time William Thompson is a farmer who says he and his parents were born in Ohio; Elizabeth Childers Thompson says she was born in Ohio and her parents in Kentucky.

Elizabeth Childers Thompson dies in 1919.[217]

In 1920, William Robert Thompson and his family are still in Dodson Twp., Highland Co., Ohio *(Census Place: Dodson, Highland, Ohio; Roll: T625_1399; Page: 6A; Enumeration District: 83; Image: 91)*. William Thompson, age 46, is a farmer. With him are dependent children Ruth, 18, by his late first wife Della Frances Pegan; and Robert, 11, and Genevieve, eight, his children by his second wife, Elizabeth Childers Thompson, who is also deceased. Also living in the home are his elder daughter by Della Frances Pegan, Mabel Leatha Thompson Stroup, 20, and her husband Galo Stroup, 22, a high school teacher. All were Ohio natives, as were their parents.

After his second wife died, William Robert Thompson took a third wife, Mrs. Leila Johnson Hixson.[218]

By 1930, William Robert Thompson is married to his third wife, Leila, and continues to live in Dodson Twp., Highland Co., Ohio *(Census Place: Dodson, Highland, Ohio; Roll: 1823; Page: 5A; Enumeration District: 6; Image: 92.0)*. William R. Thompson is age 57, a farmer who says he was first married at age 27. "Lelia" Johnson Hixson Thompson is 44 and states she was 20 when she was first wed. Also in the home are Genevieve Thompson, William's daughter, and Marianne Hixson, Leila's daughter, both 19. All were born in Ohio as were their parents.

William Robert Thompson is again residing in Dodson Twp., Highland Co., Ohio in 1940 *(Census Place: Dodson, Highland, Ohio; Roll: T627_3085; Page: 10B; Enumeration District: 36-6)*. William R. Thompson, age 67, is still a farmer; Leila Johnson Hixon Thompson is 54. Both are Ohio natives and say they were living in the same house on County Road 117-A in 1935.

Daughters of Della Frances Pegan and William Robert Thompson:

+ 69 f I. **Mabel Letha**[8] **Thompson** was born in Dodson Twp., Highland Co., Ohio, on September 14, 1899.[219] She died in Washington, District of Columbia, on September 5, 1950.[220]

+ 70 f II. **Ruth Frances**[8] **Thompson** was born in Dodson Twp., Highland Co., Ohio, on December 20, 1901.[31, 221] She died in St. Petersburg, Pinellas Co., Florida, on March 13, 1995.[31, 221]

21. Henry J.[7] **Pegan** (*Thomas Jefferson*[6], *Henry*[5], *Robert A.*[4], *Andrew*[3], *Andrew*[2] *Pagan, James*[1]) was born on February 21, 1864, in Jefferson Twp., Clinton Co., Ohio.[61] He was the son of Thomas Jefferson Pegan (4) and Eliza Bernard. Henry J. died in Jefferson Twp., Clinton Co., Ohio, on August 8, 1864.[61] He was buried in New Vienna Cemetery, Green Twp., Clinton Co., Ohio.[61]

22. Laura[7] **Pegan** (*Thomas Jefferson*[6], *Henry*[5], *Robert A.*[4], *Andrew*[3], *Andrew*[2] *Pagan, James*[1]) was born on August 24, 1866, in St. Martin, Perry Twp., Brown Co., Ohio.[62, 63, 64] She was the daughter of Thomas Jefferson Pegan (4) and Mary Ann Bennington. Laura lived in 1920 in Hamilton, Butler Co., Ohio. She died in Hamer Twp., Highland Co., Ohio, on January 24, 1923, at age 56.[62, 64] Laura was buried in Harwood Cemetery, Salem Twp., Highland Co., Ohio.[62, 222]

Laura married **Thomas Llewellyn Hamer Daggy** on July 5, 1883, in Highland Co., Ohio.[223] They had three children. Thomas Llewellyn Hamer Daggy was born in Salem Twp., Highland Co., Ohio, on April 10, 1861.[224] He reached age 57 and died in Hanover Twp., Butler Co., Ohio, on February 23, 1919.[224] Thomas Llewellyn Hamer was buried in Harwood Cemetery, Salem Twp., Highland Co., Ohio.[224, 225]

Thomas Llewellyn Hamer and Laura Pegan Daggy are enumerated in Salem Twp., Highland Co., Ohio in 1900 *(Census Place: Salem, Highland, Ohio; Roll:*

T623_1286; Page: 9A; Enumeration District: 128). Thomas L. H. Daggy, age 39, born Apr 1861, is a school teacher. His wife, Laura Pegan Daggy, is 33 years old, born Aug 1866. The couple says they have been married 17 years and Laura has borne three children, all still alive. They are daughters Lillie May, age 15, born Jul 1884; and "Luella", (Llewellyn), 12, born Jun 1887; and son Oliver, nine, born Aug 1890. All were born in Ohio as were their parents.

In 1910, Thomas L. Hamer and Laura Pegan Daggy have removed to Wayne Twp., Butler Co., Ohio (Census Place: Wayne, Butler, Ohio; Roll: T624_1155; Page: 11A; Enumeration District: 0044; Image: 1097). Thomas L. Hamer Daggy, listed as "Hainer" or "Haimer", is age 48 and a schoolteacher, while wife Laura ("Laurah") Pegan Daggy is 33. They say they are on their first marriage, have been married 26 years, and that Laura has borne three children, with two still living. The only child in the home is son Oliver, 19, listed as a farm laborer.

By July 1917, Thomas L. Hamer and Laura Pegan Daggy had moved to Milford Twp., Butler Co., Ohio, per the death certificate of Laura's mother, Mary Ann Bennington Pegan, who was living with them at the time of her death. After this, they relocated to Hanover Township in Butler County, where Thomas L.H. Daggy died in February 1919.[57, 224]

Widow Laura Pegan Daggy is enumerated as "Laura Daggie" in Hamilton, Butler Co., Ohio in 1920 (Census Place: Hamilton Ward 4, Butler, Ohio; Roll: T625_1351; Page: 5B; Enumeration District: 31; Image: 988). Laura Pegan Daggy, age 53, is a housekeeper in the home of Dennis Connolly, age 57, who lists himself as married and has two sons, but his wife is not in the household. Laura says she and her parents were born in Ohio.

Laura Pegan Daggy married **John Fred Smith** on December 11, 1920, in Butler Co., Ohio.[226] John Fred Smith was born in Salem Twp., Highland Co., Ohio, on October 12, 1856.[226, 227] John Fred reached age 89 and died in Hamer Twp., Highland Co., Ohio, on July 19, 1946.[227] He was buried in Barker Cemetery, Pricetown, Salem Twp., Highland Co., Ohio.[228]

Children of Laura Pegan and Thomas Llewellyn Hamer Daggy:

+ 71 f I. **Lillie May**[8] **Daggy** was born in Salem Twp., Highland Co., Ohio, on July 25, 1884.[229, 230] She died in a hospital in Hamilton, Butler Co., Ohio, on February 21, 1948.[229]

+ 72 f II. **Llewellyn**[8] **Daggy** was born in Salem Twp., Highland Co., Ohio, on June 25, 1887.[231] She was also known as **Louie or Luella**. Llewellyn died in Salem Twp., Highland Co., Ohio, on June 9, 1906.[232]

+ 73 m III. **Oliver John**[8] **Daggy** was born in Salem Twp., Highland Co., Ohio, on August 31, 1890.[31, 233] He died in St. Petersburg, Pinellas Co., Florida, on July 13, 1972.[234]

23. Anna[7] **Pegan** (*Thomas Jefferson*[6], *Henry*[5], *Robert A.*[4], *Andrew*[3], *Andrew*[2] *Pagan, James*[1]) was born on October 20, 1869, in Dodson Twp., Highland Co., Ohio.[65] She was the daughter of Thomas Jefferson Pegan (4) and Mary Ann Bennington. She died in White Oak Twp., Highland Co., Ohio, on January 28, 1955, at age 85.[66] Anna was buried in Union Cemetery, Taylorsville, White Oak Twp., Highland Co., Ohio.[66, 235]

An alternate birthday for Anna is October 24, 1869, as her birth seems to be recorded twice in the Highland County birth records. Her nativity is stated once on page 70 as a female child born to Thomas J. Pegan and Mary Pegan on October 20, 1869, and once more on page 90 as a child of unknown gender to the same parents on October 24 of the same year. (For some reason, some births were re-recorded on other pages?) In the 1900 and 1910 censuses, Mary Bennington Pegan states she bore six children, four still alive, and those four and the two deceased can be accounted for. This may be a clerical error, and her birthday is most likely October 20.

Anna married **Lewis Allen Surber** on February 20, 1890, in Highland Co., Ohio.[236] They had two sons. Lewis Allen Surber was born in Highland Co., Ohio, on May 10, 1868.[237] Lewis Allen reached age 61 and died in White Oak Twp., Highland Co., Ohio, on April 24, 1930.[237] He was buried in Union Cemetery, Taylorsville, White Oak Twp., Highland Co., Ohio.[238]

Lewis Allen and Anna Pegan Surber are enumerated in White Oak Twp., Highland Co., Ohio in 1900 (*Census Place: White Oak, Highland, Ohio; Roll: T623_1286; Page: 1A; Enumeration District: 131*). Lewis A. Surber, age 32, born May 1868, is a farmer; his wife, Anna Pegan Surber, is 30, born Oct 1869. The pair say they have been married 10 years and Anna has borne one child who survives. This would be son Earl L., seven, born Dec. 1892. This is incorrect, as Highland County birth and death records record another son for this couple, Lawrence, who died as an infant. All in the home were born in Ohio, as were their parents.

In 1910, Lewis A. and Anna Pegan Surber are still living in White Oak Twp., Highland Co., Ohio (*Census Place: White Oak, Highland, Ohio; Roll: T624_1197; Page: 12-8A; Enumeration District: 0136; Image: 1096*). Lewis A. Surber is 41 and a farmer; Anna Pegan Surber is 40. The couple says they have been married 20 years and Anna has born one child, still living. (Again, this is incorrect.) Son Earl, 17, is listed as a farm laborer on the family farm. Also in the home is Anna's mother, Mary Ann Bennington Pegan, age 64 who says she bore six children, with four still alive. All were born in Ohio, as were their parents.

Lewis A. and Anna Pegan Surber are again found in White Oak Twp., Highland Co., Ohio (*Census Place: White Oak, Highland, Ohio; Roll: T625_1399; Page: 6A; Enumeration District: 105; Image: 591*). In the home are Lewis A. Surber, 51, a farmer and his wife Anna Pegan Surber, 50. Also listed in the household is a hired farmhand, John A. Stroup, 61. All were born in Ohio, as were their parents. Next door are son Earl L. Surber and his wife, Gaynelle Roberts Surber.

In 1930, Lewis Allen and Anna Pegan Surber are listed in White Oak Twp., Highland Co., Ohio (*Census Place: White Oak, Highland, Ohio; Roll: 1823; Page: 2A; Enumeration District: 27; Image: 544.0*). Lewis A. Surber, 61, a farmer, says he was first married at age 21. His wife, Anna Pegan Surber, 60, says she was first married at age 20. Lodging in the home is Lewis Roush, age 59, a farm laborer on their farm. Still living next door is son Earl L. Sauber and his family. The census was taken in April, but no day is listed. Lewis Allen Surber died on April 24, 1930, just a very short time after the census was taken.

In 1940, Anna Pegan Surber, a widow, is living by herself in White Oak Twp., Highland Co., Ohio (*Census Place: White Oak, Highland, Ohio; Roll: T627_3085; Page: 61B; Enumeration District: 36-31*). Anna Pegan Surber, age 70, born Ohio, lists no occupation. She says she was residing in the same house in 1935 (there is no road or numerical address listed).

Sons of Anna Pegan and Lewis Allen Surber:

+ 74 m I. **Lawrence W.⁸ Surber** was born in White Oak Twp., Highland Co., Ohio, on April 20, 1890.[239] He died in White Oak Twp., Highland Co., Ohio, on January 2, 1891.[240]

+ 75 m II. **Earl Lester⁸ Surber** was born in White Oak Twp., Highland Co., Ohio, on December 19, 1892.[241] He died in White Oak Twp., Highland Co., Ohio, on February 27, 1964.[242]

24. William Henry⁷ Pegan (*Thomas Jefferson⁶, Henry⁵, Robert A.⁴, Andrew³, Andrew² Pagan, James¹*) was born on January 15, 1874, in Dodson Twp., Highland Co., Ohio.[67] He was the son of Thomas Jefferson Pegan (4) and Mary Ann Bennington. William Henry died in Dodson Twp., Highland Co., Ohio, on July 15, 1874.[68] He was buried in Lynchburg Masonic Cemetery, Lynchburg, Dodson Twp., Highland Co., Ohio.[243]

25. Mattie⁷ Pegan (*Thomas Jefferson⁶, Henry⁵, Robert A.⁴, Andrew³, Andrew² Pagan, James¹*) was born on November 25, 1875, in Dodson Twp., Highland Co., Ohio.[69] She was the daughter of Thomas Jefferson Pegan (4) and Mary Ann Bennington. Mattie died in Dodson Twp., Highland Co., Ohio, on March 16, 1876.[70] She was buried in Lynchburg Masonic Cemetery, Lynchburg, Dodson Twp., Highland Co., Ohio.[244]

26. Frances[7] **Pegan** (*Thomas Jefferson*[6], *Henry*[5], *Robert A.*[4], *Andrew*[3], *Andrew*[2] *Pagan, James*[1]) was born on November 12, 1879, in Hamer Twp., Highland Co., Ohio.[71, 72] She was also known as **Frankie**. She was the daughter of Thomas Jefferson Pegan (4) and Mary Ann Bennington. Frances died in Lynchburg, Dodson Twp., Highland Co., Ohio, on January 29, 1915, at age 35.[73] She was buried in Stroup Cemetery, Dodson Twp., Highland Co., Ohio.[73, 245]

Childless.

Frances "Frankie" Pegan Carr's death certificate says her birthdate was November 12, 1879.[73] However, her Highland County, Ohio birth record says August 18, 1879, and she states the same date on her marriage license in 1900.[71, 72]

Frances Pegan married **Edward Everett Carr** on May 26, 1900, in Highland Co., Ohio.[71] Edward Everett Carr was born in White Oak Twp., Highland Co., Ohio, on February 20 or 22, 1879.[31, 71, 246, 247, 248] He was also known as **Everett**. He reached age 93 and died in Greenfield, Greenfield Twp., Highland Co., Ohio, on December 13, 1972.[31, 249] Edward Everett was buried in West Chapel Cemetery, Clark Twp., Clinton Co., Ohio.[250, 251]

Edward Everett Carr's name on his Highland County birth record is Edward "Evarts" Carr, and his birthdate is given as February 20, 1879.[246] But his birth record seems to be incorrect, as on other documents for him—his marriage license, his WWI and WWII draft cards, and his Social Security information among them—list his birthdate as February 22, 1879, Also, all those documents have his name as "Everett Edward Carr" [31, 71, 247, 248] His Ohio death record states "Edward E. Carr".[249]

Edward Everett and Frances "Frankie" Pegan Carr are enumerated in 1900 in White Oak Twp., Highland Co., Ohio *(Census Place: White Oak, Highland, Ohio; Roll: T623_1286; Page: 2A; Enumeration District: 131)*. They are living with Edward's parents, Byron and Elvira Carr. Edward E. Carr, age 21, born Feb 1879, is a farmer and Frances, listed as "Frankie", is 20, born Nov 1879. The couple are newlyweds, married less than a year with no children born to Frances. Edward's father Byron Carr, a farmer, is 58 and his wife Elvira is 50; they have been married 30 years and Elvira has borne four children, all surviving. One is son Alvin, 29, born Dec 1870, also living in the home, oddly listed as "at school". Byron Carr says his father was born in Delaware and his mother in Pennsylvania. Otherwise, the rest in the home were born in Ohio, as were their parents.

In 1910 Edward Everett and Frances Pegan Carr are listed in Hamer Twp., Highland Co., Ohio *(Census Place: Hamer, Highland, Ohio; Roll: T624_1197; Page: 2A; Enumeration District: 0119; Image: 654)*. In the household are Edward E. Carr, age 31, a farmer, and his wife, Frances Pegan Carr, 30. The couple says they have been married nine years and Frances has borne no children. Both say they and their parents were born in Ohio.

After Frances "Frankie" Pegan Carr dies, Edward Everett Carr marries twice more, first to Helen West and then to Mabel Cumberland.

Edward Everett Carr, enumerated as Everett Carr, is found in Clark Twp., Clinton Co., Ohio in 1920 *(Census Place: Clark, Clinton, Ohio; Roll: T625_1355; Page: 2B; Enumeration District: 113; Image: 676)*. He has remarried to Helen West. Edward Everett Carr is age 40 and is a farmer; Helen is 28. Both were born in Ohio, as were their parents.

In 1930, Edward Everett Carr is once again listed as Everett Carr and is still living in Clark Twp., Clinton Co., Ohio *(Census Place: Clark, Clinton, Ohio; Roll: 1761; Page: 5B; Enumeration District: 4; Image: 181.0)*. Edward Everett Carr is 51, a farmer, and says he was first married at age 39—perhaps he or Helen misunderstood the question and gave his age at his second marriage. Helen C. Carr is 38 and says she was first married at 26. Both they and their parents were born in Ohio. Wilbur Brown, 49, a lodger, is living with them.

"Everett" Carr continues to reside in Clark Twp., Clinton Co., Ohio in 1940 *(Census Place: Clark, Clinton, Ohio; Roll: m-t0627-03042; Page: 5B; Enumeration District: 14-5)*. "Everett" Carr, a farmer, is 61 years old and his wife Helen is 48. Both were born in Ohio and say they were living in the same place in 1935. They have a farm hand, Eddie Stapleton, 21, residing with them.

27. Charles[7] Pegan (*Thomas Jefferson[6], Henry[5], Robert A.[4], Andrew[3], Andrew[2] Pagan, James[1]*) was born on April 18, 1885, in Hamer Twp., Highland Co., Ohio.[74, 75] He was the son of Thomas Jefferson Pegan (4) and Mary Ann Bennington. He died in Danville, Hamer Twp., Highland Co., Ohio, on February 6, 1960, at age 74.[76, 77] Charles was buried in Union Cemetery, Taylorsville, White Oak Twp., Highland Co., Ohio.[252]

Charles married **Resa Jane Pulliam** on May 1, 1907, in Highland Co., Ohio.[253] They had two sons. Resa Jane Pulliam was born in Winkle, Hamer Twp., Highland Co., Ohio, on November 8, 1883.[254, 255] Resa Jane reached age 59 and died in Winkle, Hamer Twp., Highland Co., Ohio, on July 25, 1943.[255] She was buried in Union Cemetery, Taylorsville, White Oak Twp., Highland Co., Ohio.[255, 256, 257]

In 1910, Charles Pegan is enumerated in Hamer Twp., Highland Co., Ohio *(Census Place: Hamer, Highland, Ohio; Roll: T624_1197; Page: 4B; Enumeration District: 0119; Image: 659)*. Charles and his family are living with his in-laws, William S. and Leah Pulliam. Charles Pegan, age 25, is a farmer; his wife, Resa Pulliam Pegan, listed as "Rissa", is 26 years old. The couple says they have been married three years and Resa has borne two children, with one surviving. This would be son Hugh Doyle Pegan, age three. The head of the household, William S. Pulliam, is 58 years old and his wife Leah is 47, they have been married 27 years and Resa Pulliam Pegan is their only child. All were born in Ohio, as were their parents.

Charles Pegan is listed as "Chas. Pegan" in Hamer Twp., Highland Co., Ohio in *1920 (Census Place: Hamer, Highland, Ohio; Roll: T625_1399; Page: 1A; Enumeration District: 88; Image: 169)*. In the home are Charles Pegan, age 33, a farmer; his wife Resa ("Rissa") Pulliam Pegan, 36, and son Hugh, 12. All were born in Ohio, as were their parents.

In 1930, Charles Pegan is still residing in Hamer Twp., Highland Co., Ohio *(Census Place: Hamer, Highland, Ohio; Roll: 1823; Page: 6A; Enumeration District: 10; Image: 166.0)*. In the household are Charles Pegan, listed as "Charley", age 44 a farmer, and Resa Jane Pulliam Pegan, is 46. The couple state they were first married at ages 22 and 24 respectively. Living with them, but listed as a separate household, are son Hugh Pegan, 22, and his wife Lillian Blanche King Pegan, 21. Hugh is also listed as a farmer. The have been married about a year, as Hugh says he was first married at age 21 and Lillian says her first marriage occurred at age 20. All were born in Ohio, as were their parents.

Charles Pegan continues to live in Hamer Twp., Highland Co., Ohio in 1940 *(Census Place: Hamer, Highland, Ohio; Roll: T627_3085; Page: 2A; Enumeration District: 36-10)*. Charles Pegan, listed as Charles "Peggan", age 54, is still farming. Resa Pulliam Pegan is 56 years old. Living with them are their son Hugh and his family: Hugh Pegan, age 32, also a farmer, his wife, Lillian Blanche King Pegan, 30, and their son Lowell, six. All were born in Ohio. Charles Pegan says he was living in Hamer Twp. in 1935, while Resa, Hugh and his family say they were living in the same house on East Danville Road in 1935.

After Resa died, Charles Pegan married Mrs. **Elizabeth Hawk** Knauer on November 16, 1944, in Highland Co., Ohio.[258] Elizabeth Hawk was born in Hamer Twp., Highland Co., Ohio, on February 1, 1887.[31] She was also known as **Lizzie**. Elizabeth reached age 93 and died in Hillsboro, Liberty Twp., Highland Co., Ohio, on February 16, 1980.[31, 259] She was buried in Barker Cemetery, Pricetown, Salem Twp., Highland Co., Ohio.[260, 261]

Sons of Charles Pegan and Resa Jane Pulliam:

+ 76   m   I.   **Hugh Doyle[8] Pegan** was born in Hamer Twp., Highland Co., Ohio, on January 4, 1908.[31, 262] He died in East Danville, New Market Twp., Highland Co., Ohio, on April 4, 1984.[263, 264]

+ 77   m   II. **Harlen J. Pulliam[8] Pegan** was born in Hamer Twp., Highland Co., Ohio, on September 1, 1909.[265, 266, 267] He died in Hamer Twp., Highland Co., Ohio, on September 15, 1909.[267, 268]

28. Mary Hattie[7] Schwartz (*Elma Eleanor[6] Pegan, Henry[5], Robert A.[4], Andrew[3], Andrew[2] Pagan, James[1]*) was born on November 9, 1869, in Lynchburg, Dodson Twp., Highland Co., Ohio.[82] She was also known as **Hattie**. She was the daughter of Joseph Schwartz or Swartz and Elma Eleanor Pegan (5). Mary Hattie died in Clark Twp., Clinton Co., Ohio, on April 15, 1927, at age 57.[82] She was buried in Lynchburg Masonic Cemetery, Lynchburg, Dodson Twp., Highland Co., Ohio.[82, 269]

Childless.

Her given name was Mary Hattie, but she always used Hattie as her preferred given name. Hattie Shaper is the name on her death certificate.[82]

Mary Hattie married **Edward M. Shaper** on October 10, 1909, in Highland Co., Ohio.[270] Edward M. Shaper was born in Concord Twp., Highland Co., Ohio, on October 6, 1869.[270] He reached age 72 and died in Waynesville, Wayne Twp., Warren Co., Ohio, on March 9, 1942.[271] Edward M. was buried in Lynchburg Masonic Cemetery, Lynchburg, Dodson Twp., Highland Co., Ohio.[271, 272]

Edward and Mary Hattie "Hattie" Schwartz Shaper are enumerated in 1910 in Lynchburg, Dodson Twp., Highland Co., Ohio (*Census Place: Dodson, Highland, Ohio; Roll: T624_1197; Page: 7A; Enumeration District: 0115; Image: 569*). Edward Shaper (whose middle initial is listed as "E." in this census but is listed as "M." on his death certificate), is age 41 and a laborer in a distillery. His wife, "Hattie M." Schwartz Shaper, is 40. TThey have been married less than a year and Hattie has borne no children. Both say they and their parents were born in Ohio.

In 1920, Edward and Mary Hattie "Hattie" Schwartz Shaper are found in Clark Twp., Clinton Co., Ohio (*Census Place: Clark, Clinton, Ohio; Roll: T625_1355; Page: 2A; Enumeration District: 113; Image: 675*). Edward Shaper, age 51, is a farmer and Hattie M. Schwartz Shaper is 50. Both were born in Ohio, as were their parents. Neighbors are Hattie's cousins Frank J. Pegan and William Otto Pegan and their families.

Edward Shaper is listed as "Ed. M Shaper" in 1930 in Clark Twp., Highland Co., Ohio (*Census Place: Clark, Clinton, Ohio; Roll: 1761; Page: 7B; Enumeration District: 0004*). Edward Shaper, age 61, born Ohio, a widower and farmer, is the only one in the household.

In 1940, widower Edward Shaper is living with his nephew, Lee Terrell, and Lee's family in Waynesville, Wayne Twp., Warren Co., Ohio (*Census Place: Waynesville, Warren, Ohio; Roll: T627_3164; Page: 8A; Enumeration District: 83-34*). Edward Shaper is age 71, lists no occupation, and says he was living in Highland County, Ohio in 1935. The home is at 188 Main Street.

Although on his marriage license Edward M. Shaper says he was born in Batavia, Batavia Twp., Clermont Co., Ohio, his parents were living in Concord Twp., Highland Co., Ohio in 1870 (*Concord, Highland, Ohio; Roll: M593_1222; Page: 51A; entry for Edward Shaper, Samuel Shaper, head of household*). In addition, Highland County is cited as his birthplace on his death certificate.[270, 271]

29. William H.C.M.[7] Schwartz (*Elma Eleanor[6] Pegan, Henry[5], Robert A.[4], Andrew[3], Andrew[2] Pagan, James[1]*) was born on August 12, 1872, in Lynchburg, Dodson Twp., Highland Co., Ohio.[83] He was the son of Joseph Schwartz or Swartz and Elma Eleanor Pegan (5). William H.C.M. died in Lynchburg, Dodson Twp., Highland Co., Ohio, on August 16, 1873, at age one.[84] He was buried in Lynchburg Masonic Cemetery, Lynchburg, Dodson Twp., Highland Co., Ohio.[84]

30. Walter Charles[7] Schwartz (*Elma Eleanor[6] Pegan, Henry[5], Robert A.[4], Andrew[3], Andrew[2] Pagan, James[1]*) was born on July 27, 1876, in Dodson Twp., Highland Co., Ohio.[85,86] He was the son of Joseph Schwartz or Swartz and Elma Eleanor Pegan (5). He died in Lynchburg, Dodson Twp., Highland Co., Ohio, on November 27, 1942, at age 66.[85] Walter Charles was buried in Lynchburg Masonic Cemetery, Lynchburg, Dodson Twp., Highland Co., Ohio.[85, 273]

Childless.

Walter Charles married **Nora Jane Reeves** on August 30, 1914, in Highland Co., Ohio.[274] Nora Jane Reeves was born in Silvercreek Twp., Greene Co., Ohio?, on April 11, 1874.[275] Nora Jane reached age

82 and died in Lynchburg, Dodson Twp., Highland Co., Ohio, on January 7, 1957.[276] She was buried in Lynchburg Masonic Cemetery, Lynchburg, Dodson Twp., Highland Co., Ohio.[277]

Walter C. Schwartz is enumerated in Lynchburg, Dodson Twp., Highland Co., Ohio in 1920 (*Census Place: Dodson, Highland, Ohio; Roll: T625_1399; Page: 6A; Enumeration District: 84; Image: 109*). In the home are Walter C. Schwartz, 43, a proprietor of a meat shop, and his wife Nora Jane Reeves Schwartz, 45. Both were born in Ohio, as were their parents.

In 1930, Walter C. Schwartz is still residing in Lynchburg, Dodson Twp., Highland Co., Ohio (*Census Place: Lynchburg, Highland, Ohio; Roll: 1823; Page: 8A; Enumeration District: 5; Image: 82.0*). This time Walter C. Schwartz, 53, says he is a building decorator; his wife Nora J. Reeves Schwartz is 55. The couple says they were first married at ages 37 and 39 respectively, and that they and their parents were born in Ohio.

31. **Child**[7] **Schwartz** (*Elma Eleanor*[6] *Pegan, Henry*[5], *Robert A.*[4], *Andrew*[3], *Andrew*[2] *Pagan, James*[1]) was born between 1869 and 1900 in Dodson Twp., Highland Co., Ohio. He or she was a child of Joseph Schwartz or Swartz and Elma Eleanor Pegan (5). Child died in Dodson Twp., Highland Co., Ohio, between 1869 and 1900.

32. **Cora May**[7] **Schwartz** (*Eliza Jane*[6] *Pegan, Henry*[5], *Robert A.*[4], *Andrew*[3], *Andrew*[2] *Pagan, James*[1]) was born on May 22, 1871, in Lynchburg, Dodson Twp., Highland Co., Ohio.[92] She was the daughter of Andrew Schwartz II and Eliza Jane Pegan (6). Cora May died in Lafayette Twp., Coshocton Co., Ohio, on January 3, 1951, at age 79.[92] She was buried in Roscoe Cemetery, Roscoe, Jackson Twp., Coshocton Co., Ohio.[92, 278, 279]

Never married.

Cora May Schwartz is not found in the 1900 U.S. Census.

Cora May Schwartz leaves Highland County and removes to Roscoe, Jackson Twp., Coshocton Co., Ohio, where some of her Schwartz line cousins resided.

Cora Schwartz, 38, single, a factory worker, is living alone in Roscoe, Jackson Twp., Coshocton Co., Ohio in 1910 (*Census Place: Roscoe, Coshocton, Ohio; Roll: T624_1162; Page: 3B; Enumeration District: 0007; Image: 748*). She says she and her parents were born in Ohio.

In 1920, Cora M. Schwartz, listed as Cora Swartz, is still residing in Roscoe, Jackson Twp., Coshocton Co., Ohio (*Census Place: Jackson, Coshocton, Ohio; Roll: T625_1357; Page: 13B; Enumeration District: 26; Image: 749*). Cora Schwartz, 48, single, is a leather worker in an art works and says she and her parents were born in Ohio.

She is listed as "Corra M. Schwartz" in Roscoe, Jackson Twp., Coshocton Co., Ohio in 1930 (*Census Place: Jackson, Coshocton, Ohio; Roll: T625_1357; Page: 13B; Enumeration District: 26; Image: 749*). Cora is the only member of the household; she is 58 and a leather worker in a factory. Once again, she says she and her parents were born in Ohio.

Cora M. Schwartz is not found in the 1940 U.S. Census.

33. **Joseph T.**[7] **Pegan** (*William Henry*[6], *Henry*[5], *Robert A.*[4], *Andrew*[3], *Andrew*[2] *Pagan, James*[1]) was born on December 30, 1879, in Clark Twp., Clinton Co., Ohio.[100] He was the son of William Henry Pegan (9) and Margaret Louisa Jones. Joseph T. died in Clark Twp., Clinton Co., Ohio, on October 31, 1881, at age one.[101, 102] He was buried in Troutwine Cemetery, Dodson Twp., Highland Co., Ohio and Clark Twp., Clinton Co., Ohio.[101, 102]

For some odd reason, the mother listed on Joseph T. Pegan's birth record is a Claretta Smithson. This is a clerical error.[100]

34. **Frank Joseph**[7] **Pegan** (*William Henry*[6], *Henry*[5], *Robert A.*[4], *Andrew*[3], *Andrew*[2] *Pagan, James*[1]) was born on June 8, 1882, in Clark Twp., Clinton Co., Ohio.[103, 104] He was the son of William Henry Pegan (9) and Margaret Louisa Jones. Frank Joseph died in Waynesville, Wayne Twp., Warren Co., Ohio, on March 28, 1966, at age 83.[104, 105] He was buried in Martinsville IOOF Cemetery, Martinsville, Clark Twp., Clinton Co., Ohio.[280, 281]

Frank Joseph married **Nelle Irene West** on March 9, 1904, in Clinton Co., Ohio.[282] They divorced in Ohio between 1920 and 1930. They had five children. Nelle Irene West was born in New Vienna, Green Twp., Clinton Co., Ohio, on July 12, 1884.[31, 283, 284] She reached age 91 and died in Mishawaka, Penn Twp., St. Joseph Co., Indiana, on March 13, 1976.[283] Nelle Irene was buried in Martinsville IOOF Cemetery, Martinsville, Clark Twp., Clinton Co., Ohio.[285, 286]

For some reason, Nelle Irene West Pegan's Clinton County, Ohio marriage license states that she was age 20 on July 6, 1903, which means her birthday was July 6, 1883.[282] But her Clinton County, Ohio birth record, the Social Security Death Index and her obituary in the *South Bend (IN) Tribune* say Nellie Irene West Pegan was born in July 12, 1884, Social Security Death Index entry is under Nellie Pegan.[31, 283, 284]

In 1910, Frank J. Pegan is enumerated in Silver Creek Twp., Greene Co., Ohio *(Census Place: Silver Creek, Greene, Ohio; Roll: T624_1185; Page: 4B; Enumeration District: 0094; Image: 651)*. In the household are Frank Pegan, 27, a farmer; is wife Nelle I. West Pegan, 25. Frank and Nelle state they have been married six years and Nelle has borne one child, still living—daughter "Ferol L.", who is four years old. All in the home and their parents were born in Ohio.

In 1920, Frank Pegan, listed as Frank "Pagen", is found in Clark Twp., Clinton Co., Ohio *(Census Place: Clark, Clinton, Ohio; Roll: T625_1355; Page: 2A; Enumeration District: 113; Image: 675)*. Frank Pegan, 37, is a farmer. His wife, Nelle I. West Pegan, is 35. Living with them are children Ferrol, enumerated incorrectly as a son, age 14, Ruby, seven, and Harold, one. All and their parents were Ohio natives. Next door is Frank's younger brother William Otto and his family. Their first cousin Mary Hattie "Hattie" Schwartz Shaper, daughter of Joseph and Elma Pegan Schwartz, and her husband Edward Shaper are also neighbors.

In September 1926, Frank J. Pegan and his family were living in Lynchburg, Dodson Twp., Highland Co., Ohio. Frank was the informant on his mother Margaret Louisa Jone's death certificate, and he lists his residence as Lynchburg. As Margaret dies in Lynchburg, she may have been residing with Frank and his family when she died.[97]

Frank Pegan has relocated Dayton, Montgomery Co., Ohio in 1930 *(Census Place: Dayton, Montgomery, Ohio; Roll: 1852; Page: 9B; Enumeration District: 61; Image: 1142.0)*. The head of the household is Frank Pegan, a laborer working at "Elb Irrigation". Frank is 40 years old and his wife, Nelle I. West Pegan, is age 43. Both ages are incorrect, Children in the home include Harold W., 11, and Ruth, eight. All were born in Ohio as were their parents.

In 1940, Frank Pegan has returned to Clark Twp., Clinton Co., Ohio *(Census Place: Clark, Clinton, Ohio; Roll: T627_3042; Page: 8A; Enumeration District: 14-5)*. Frank Pegan, age 57 is a truck driver doing hauling. Nellie West Pegan is 55 years old. Children still in the home are Harold, 21, an interior decorator who does painting and wallpaper hanging; and Ruth, 18. All in the home were born in Ohio, and say they were living in Clark Twp., Clinton Co., Ohio in 1935. Their home is on Glady Road. Frank's brother William Otto Pegan and his family are neighbors.

Frank Pegan had returned to Lynchburg, Dodson Twp., Highland Co., Ohio when he registered for the WWII draft in 1942.[103]

Children of Frank Joseph Pegan and Nelle Irene West:

+ 78 f I. **Ferol Margaret[8] Pegan** was born in Clark Twp., Clinton Co., Ohio, on July 8, 1905.[31, 287, 288] She was also known as **Peggy**. Ferol Margaret died in a facility in Sabina, Richland Twp., Clinton Co., Ohio, on October 30, 1989.[31, 287]

+ 79 f II. **Ruby W.[8] Pegan** was born in Silver Creek Twp., Greene Co., Ohio, on June 8, 1912.[31, 289] She died in a hospital in Batavia, Batavia Twp., Clermont Co., Ohio, on July 31, 1984.[289, 290]

+ 80 m III. **Harold West[8] Pegan** was born in Clark Twp., Clinton Co., Ohio, on June 3, 1918.[31, 291] He died in a hospital in Wilmington, Union Twp., Clinton Co., Ohio, on November 16, 1995.[31, 291]

+ 81　f　IV.　**Ruth Marie⁸ Pegan** was born in Martinsville, Clark Twp., Clinton Co., Ohio, on June 16, 1921.[31, 292, 293, 294, 295] She died in South Bend, St. Joseph Co., Indiana, on August 22, 2004.[31, 292, 294, 295]

+ 82　f　V.　**Rita Glea⁸ Pegan** was born in Martinsville, Clark Twp., Clinton Co., Ohio, on June 16, 1921.[296] She died in Martinsville, Clark Twp., Clinton Co., Ohio, on June 16, 1921.[296]

35. Ella Mae⁷ Pegan (*William Henry⁶, Henry⁵, Robert A.⁴, Andrew³, Andrew² Pagan, James¹*) was born on May 25, 1886, in Clark Twp., Clinton Co., Ohio.[106, 107] She was the daughter of William Henry Pegan (9) and Margaret Louisa Jones. Ella Mae died in Wilmington, Union Twp., Clinton Co., Ohio, on October 25, 1948, at age 62.[106] She was buried in Troutwine Cemetery, Dodson Twp., Highland Co., Ohio and Clark Twp., Clinton Co., Ohio.[106, 297]

Never married.

In 1920, Ella and her parents William Henry and Louisa Jones Pegan are in Clark Twp., Clinton Co., Ohio *(Census Place: Clark, Clinton, Ohio; Roll: T625_1355; Page: 2B; Enumeration District: 113; Image: 676)* William Henry Pegan is age 64 and still a farmer. Margaret Louisa Jones Pegan, listed as "Louie", is 53 years old. Ella, 33 and single, in also living with them and lists no occupation. All of them were born in Ohio as were their parents, except for Margaret's father, who was born in Pennsylvania.

Ella Mae Pegan is residing with her widowed father William H. Pegan, listed as "William H. Peagan", in Clark Twp., Clinton Co., Ohio in 1930 *(Census Place: Clark, Clinton, Ohio; Roll: 1761; Page: 9A; Enumeration District: 4; Image: 188.0)* Household members are William H. Pegan, 75, a widower and a farmer; and his unmarried daughter Ella, 43. Both say they and their parents were Ohio natives.

Ella Pegan is not enumerated in the 1940 census. However, her obituary says she lived with her brother William Otto Pegan and his family.[298]

36. William Otto⁷ Pegan (*William Henry⁶, Henry⁵, Robert A.⁴, Andrew³, Andrew² Pagan, James¹*) was born on December 25, 1895, in Clark Twp., Clinton Co., Ohio.[31, 108, 109] He was the son of William Henry Pegan (9) and Margaret Louisa Jones. William Otto died in a facility in Sabina, Richland Twp., Clinton Co., Ohio, on October 28, 1985, at age 89.[108, 110] He was buried in New Lynchburg Masonic Cemetery/Lynchburg F & AM Cemetery, Lynchburg, Dodson Twp., Highland Co., Ohio.[110, 299]

William Otto Pegan's Clinton County, Ohio birth record lists name as Otto William.[109]

William Otto married **Rosella Stroup** on August 30, 1916, in Clinton Co., Ohio.[300] They had four children. Rosella Stroup was born in Dodson Twp., Highland Co., Ohio, on August 26, 1897.[301, 302] She was also known as **Rose**. Rosella reached age 68 and died in Wilmington, Union Twp., Clinton Co., Ohio, on August 27, 1965.[301, 303] She was buried in Lynchburg Masonic Cemetery, Lynchburg, Dodson Twp., Highland Co., Ohio.[301, 304] She was the daughter of Charles Turner Stroup and Mary Fox.

In 1920, William Otto Pegan II is enumerated as William O. "Pagen" in Clark Twp., Clinton Co., Ohio *(Census Place: Clark, Clinton, Ohio; Roll: T625_1355; Page: 2A; Enumeration District: 113; Image: 675)*. In the home are William O. Pegan, age 24, a farmer; his wife Rosella Stroup Pegan, also 22, and their children Paul, two years and nine months, and Mary, nine months. All and their parents were born in Ohio. Neighbors are William Otto's brother Frank and his family, and their first cousin Mary Hattie "Hattie" Schwartz Shaper, daughter of Joseph and Elma Pegan Schwartz, and her husband Edward Shaper.

William Otto Pegan II is listed as "William O. Pagan" in Clark Twp., Clinton Co., Ohio *(Census Place: Clark, Clinton, Ohio; Roll: 1761; Page: 8B; Enumeration District: 4; Image: 187.0)*. William O.

Pegan II is age 34, a farmer, who says he was first married at age 21. His wife, Rosella Stroup Pegan is 32 years old and says her first marriage occurred at 19. Children in the home include Paul, 13, Audrey, nine, and "D. Helen", seven. All were Ohio natives, as were their parents. Next door are William unmarried sister Ella and their father, William Henry Pegan.

In 1940, William Otto Pegan is still residing in Clark Twp., Clinton Co., Ohio *(Census Place: Clark, Clinton, Ohio; Roll: T627_3042; Page: 8A; Enumeration District: 14-5)*. In the household are William O. Pegan, age 44, a farmer; his wife, Rosella Stroup Pegan, 42, and children Paul, 22, also a farmer; Audrey, 19, and Helen, 17. All were born in Ohio, and say they were living in the same place in 1935. Their home is on Glady Road, and William Otto's brother Frank Joseph Pegan and his family are living nearby.

After Rosella's death, William Otto Pegan married **Elsie Lohr** on March 6, 1967, in Clinton Co., Ohio.[305] Elsie Lohr was born in Clermont Co., Ohio, on December 28, 1894.[31, 306] Elsie lived in 1985 in Wilmington, Union Twp., Clinton Co., Ohio. She reached age 91 and died in a facility in Blanchester, Marion Twp., Clinton Co., Ohio, on March 14, 1986.[307] Elsie was buried in Lynchburg Masonic Cemetery, Lynchburg, Dodson Twp., Highland Co., Ohio.[306]

Children of William Otto Pegan and Rosella Stroup:

+ 83 m I. **Paul Stroup**[8] **Pegan** was born in Clark Twp., Clinton Co., Ohio, on March 17, 1917.[31, 308] He died in Zephyrhills, Pasco Co., Florida, on January 28, 2007.[31, 308]

+ 84 f II. **Mary Louise**[8] **Pegan** was born in Clark Twp., Clinton Co., Ohio, on March 13, 1919.[309] She died in Clark Twp., Clinton Co., Ohio, on August 19, 1928.[309]

+ 85 f III. **Audrey Mae**[8] **Pegan** was born in Clark Twp., Clinton Co., Ohio, on November 16, 1920.[31, 310, 311] She died in a hospital in Dayton, Montgomery Co., Ohio, on April 6, 1997.[31, 310, 311]

+ 86 f IV. **Doris Helen**[8] **Pegan** was born in Clark Twp., Clinton Co., Ohio, on December 29, 1922.[312, 313] She was also known as **Helen**. Doris Helen died in Wilmington, Union Twp., Clinton Co., Ohio, on February 17, 2004.[312]

8th Generation

37. Agnes[8] **Lemons** (*Josephine*[7] *Stroup, Elvira*[6] *Pegan, Henry*[5]*, Robert A.*[4]*, Andrew*[3]*, Andrew*[2] *Pagan, James*[1]) was born on June 23, 1876, in Salem Twp., Highland Co., Ohio.[116] She was the daughter of Henry A. Lemons and Josephine Stroup (10). Agnes lived in 1943 in Lynchburg, Dodson Twp., Highland Co., Ohio. She died in a hospital in Columbus, Franklin Co., Ohio, on September 27, 1943, at age 67.[116] Agnes was buried in New Lynchburg Masonic Cemetery/Lynchburg F & AM Cemetery, Lynchburg, Dodson Twp., Highland Co., Ohio.[314, 315]

Agnes married **Charles Philhower** on September 27, 1899, in Highland Co., Ohio.[316] They had two sons. Charles Philhower was born in Clark Twp., Clinton Co., Ohio, on January 11, 1873.[316, 317, 318] He reached age 87 and died in Highland, Fairfield Twp., Highland Co., Ohio, on January 23, 1960.[319] Charles was buried in New Lynchburg Masonic Cemetery/Lynchburg F & AM Cemetery, Lynchburg, Dodson Twp., Highland Co., Ohio.[320, 321]

Although Charles Philhower Sr. says on several documents that he was born in Clinton County, Ohio; however, his birth is recorded in Highland County, where his parents were living in Dodson Township.[318]

In 1900, Charles and Agnes Lemons Philhower are enumerated in Lynchburg, Dodson Twp., Highland Co., Ohio (*Census Place: Dodson, Highland, Ohio; Roll: T623_1286; Page: 9B; Enumeration District: 106*). They are living with Charles' widowed mother, Lydia Philhower, who is listed as head of household. Charles Philhower is age 27, born Jan 1873, a drayman. Agnes Lemons Philhower is 23, born Jun 1876. The couple has been married less than a year. Lydia Philhower is 56. Also in the home is Lydia's son and Charles' brother Harley, age 29. All in the home say they and their parents are Ohio natives.

Charles and Agnes Lemons Philhower are found in Lynchburg, Dodson Twp., Highland Co., Ohio in 1910 (*Census Place: Dodson, Highland, Ohio; Roll: T624_1197; Page: 2A; Enumeration District: 0115; Image: 559*). In the household are Charles Philhower, age 37, a laborer in a distillery, and his wife Agnes Lemons Philhower, 34. The pair say they have been married 10 years and Agnes has borne two children, both still living. They are sons Charles R. II, nine, and Lee D., six. All in the home were born in Ohio, as were their parents.

In 1920, Charles and Agnes Lemons Philhower are still living in Lyynchburg, Dodson Twp., Highland Co., Ohio (*Census Place: Dodson, Highland, Ohio; Roll: T625_1399; Page: 4A; Enumeration District: 84; Image: 105*). Charles Philhower, age 46, is still a laborer in a distillery. Agnes Lemons Philhower is age 43. Their son Donald Lee, 16, is with them. Everyone in the household, and their parents, were born in Ohio.

Charles and Agnes Lemons Philhower continue to reside in Lynchburg, Dodson Twp., Highland Co., Ohio in 1930 (*Census Place: Lynchburg, Highland, Ohio; Roll: 1823; Page: 4A; Enumeration District: 5; Image: 74.0*). Charles Philhower, age 57, is now an "engineer" at a school, probably a maintenance worker. Agnes Lemons Philhower is age 53. The couple says they and their parents were born in Ohio. Charles and Agnes were first married at ages 26 and 22 respectively.

In 1940, Charles and Agnes Lemons Philhower are found again Lynchburg, Dodson Twp., Highland Co., Ohio (*Census Place: Lynchburg, Highland, Ohio; Roll: T627_3085; Page: 9B; Enumeration District: 36-5*). In the home are Charles Philhower, age 68, a janitor ("engineer") at a public school, and his wife, Agnes Lemons Philhower, who is 63 years old. Both say they were born in Ohio and were living in the same house, on the west side of Broadway between Railroad and South streets, in 1935.

Sons of Agnes Lemons and Charles Philhower:

+ 87 m I. **Charles Randolph**[9] **Philhower II** was born in Lynchburg, Dodson Twp., Highland Co., Ohio, on July 14, 1900.[31, 322] He was also known

+ 88 m II. **Lee Donald**[9] **Philhower** was born in Lynchburg, Dodson Twp., Highland Co., Ohio, on November 29, 1903.[323] He was also known as **Donald**. Lee Donald died in Hollywood, Broward Co., Florida, on May 21, 1990.[323]

as **Dolph**. Charles Randolph died in Hollywood, Broward Co., Florida, on April 3, 1974.[322]

38. **Grace**[8] **Lemons** (*Josephine*[7] *Stroup, Elvira*[6] *Pegan, Henry*[5]*, Robert A.*[4]*, Andrew*[3]*, Andrew*[2] *Pagan, James*[1]) was born on July 4, 1878, in Salem Twp., Highland Co., Ohio.[117] She was the daughter of Henry A. Lemons and Josephine Stroup (10). Grace died in Lynchburg, Dodson Twp., Highland Co., Ohio, on October 19, 1959, at age 81.[118] She was buried in Ferncliff Cemetery, Springfield, Springfield Twp., Clark Co., Ohio.[324, 325]

Grace married **Edward W. Boesenberg** about October 1900.[326] They had one daughter. Edward Boesenberg was born in Cincinnati, Hamilton Co., Ohio, on January 10, 1877.[327] Edward reached age 74 and died in Springfield, Springfield Twp., Clark Co., Ohio, on April 3, 1951.[327] He was buried in Ferncliff Cemetery, Springfield, Springfield Twp., Clark Co., Ohio.[327, 328]

In 1910, Edward W. and Grace Lemons Boesenberg are found in Lynchburg, Dodson Twp., Highland Co., Ohio (*Census Place: Dodson, Highland, Ohio; Roll: T624_1197; Page: 8B; Enumeration District: 0115; Image: 572*). In the household are Edward "Bosenberg", 33, a baker, born Ohio with his parents born in Germany; and wife Grace Lemons Boesenberg, 31, born Ohio as were her parents. The pair say they have been married nine years, and that Grace has borne one child, daughter Marcia L., five, born Ohio.

Edward and Grace Lemons Boesenberg are enumerated in Springfield, Springfield Twp., Clark Co., Ohio in 1920 (*Census Place: Springfield Ward 7, Clark, Ohio; Roll: T625_1354; Page: 7B; Enumeration District: 103; Image: 1049*). In the home are Edward Boesenberg, 42, a baker, born in Ohio with his parents born in Germany; and his wife, Grace Lemons Boesenberg, 41, born Ohio as were her parents. They have a daughter, "Martha" (Marcia), 15, born Ohio.

In 1930, Edward W. Boesenberg is listed as Ed W. Boesenberg in Springfield, Springfield Twp., Clark Co., Ohio (*Census Place: Springfield, Clark, Ohio; Roll: 1757; Page: 5A; Enumeration District: 54; Image: 521.0*). In the home are Edward W. Boesenberg, 53, a baker, born Ohio with his parents born in Germany; and his wife, Grace Lemons Boesenberg, 51, born Ohio as were her parents. The couple have been married 30 years, as they were first married at ages 23 and 21 respectively. Living with them are their son-in-law and daughter, Kenneth and Marcia Boesenberg Roush. Kenneth Roush, age 27, born Ohio, is a machinist/pattern worker. His wife, Marcia Boesenberg Roush is 25. Kenneth and Marcia say they were first married at ages 20 and 18 respectively and have been married seven years.

Edward W. and Grace Lemons Boesenberg are still residing in Springfield, Springfield Twp., Clark Co., Ohio (*Census Place: Springfield, Clark, Ohio; Roll: T627_3040; Page: 2A; Enumeration District: 12-72*). Edward W. Boesenberg, listed as Ed, is age 63, is a baker in a wholesale bakery. His wife, Grace Lemons Boesenberg, is 61 years old. Both say they were living in the same house at 320 Western Street in 1935. Living with them is Grace's brother, Clarence Lemons, 47, listed as married, who is a laborer doing street repairs. Clarence says he was living in Springfield in 1935. All in the home were born in Ohio.

Edward Boesenberg's obituary says he and Grace Lemons Boesenberg had celebrated their 50th wedding anniversary the previous October. But no marriage record has been found in Ohio or Indiana.[326]

According to her grandniece, Carolyn Luck Barker, Grace Lemons Boesenberg baked the best sugar cookies you've ever tasted.[329]

Daughter of Grace Lemons and Edward W. Boesenberg:

+ 89 f I. **Marcia Lucille**[9] **Boesenberg** was born in Lynchburg, Dodson Twp., Highland Co., Ohio, on June 1, 1904.[330] She died in Springfield,

Springfield Twp., Clark Co., Ohio, on January 25, 1932.[331]

39. James Stroup⁸ Lemons (*Josephine⁷ Stroup, Elvira⁶ Pegan, Henry⁵, Robert A.⁴, Andrew³, Andrew² Pagan, James¹*) was born on July 3, 1880, in Salem Twp., Highland Co., Ohio.[119] He was the son of Henry A. Lemons and Josephine Stroup (10). James Stroup died in Liberty Twp., Highland Co., Ohio, on January 2, 1948, at age 67.[120] He was buried in New Lynchburg Masonic Cemetery/Lynchburg F & AM Cemetery, Lynchburg, Dodson Twp., Highland Co., Ohio.[120, 332]

Never married.

James Lemons, single, is a hired man on the farm of F.J. Wiedeman in Clark Twp., Clinton Co., Ohio in 1910 (*Census Place: Clark, Clinton, Ohio; Roll: T624_1160; Page: 1B; Enumeration District: 0061; Image: 716*). James Lemons is age 28 (?) and says he and his parents were born in Ohio.

In 1920, James S. Lemons is residing with his mother, Josephine Stroup Lemons and two of his brothers in Lynchburg, Dodson Twp., Highland Co., Ohio (*Census Place: Dodson, Highland, Ohio; Roll: T625_1399; Page: 2A; Enumeration District: 84; Image: 101*). In the home are Josephine Stroup Lemons, 63, a widow, and her three unmarried sons: James, 36, "Meral", 28 and Edgar, 26. The three sons say they are general laborers and are unmarried. All in the home say they and their parents are Ohio natives.

In 1930, James S. Lemons ("Lemon"), age 43, single, is still living with his mother, Josephine Stroup Lemon (enumerated as Josephine Lemon) in Lynchburg, Dodson Twp., Highland Co., Ohio (*Census Place: Lynchburg, Highland, Ohio; Roll: 1823; Page: 5A; Enumeration District: 5; Image: 76.0*). Josephine, listed as head of the household, is age 63. She says she was first married at age 20. Also in the home is a 10-year-old granddaughter, Josephine M. Lemons, the daughter of Clarence O. and Grace Long Lemons. All in the home were born in Ohio, as were their parents. No one in the home lists an occupation.

James Lemons is again found in the home of his mother, Josephine Stroup Lemon, in 1940 in Lynchburg, Dodson Twp., Highland Co., Ohio (*Census Place: Lynchburg, Highland, Ohio; Roll: T627_3085; Page: 1B; Enumeration District: 36-5*). James Lemons, age 59 and single, lists no occupation. His mother, Josephine Stroup Lemons, the head of the household, is 83 years old. Also in the home are James' brothers Murrell, listed as "Merle", 53, and Edgar, 45, both also single, who list odd jobs as their occupations. All in the home were born in Ohio, and were living in the same house, on the south side of Main Street between High Street and the stock yards, in 1935.

James S. Lemons died at the Highland County Home in Liberty Twp., Highland Co., Ohio, but lived in Lynchburg nearly all his life. His birth record says James S. Lemons was born on July 2, 1880. However, his death record at the state of Ohio says he was born July 2, 1879. The former is correct.[119, 120]

40. Andrew Vance⁸ J. Lemons (*Josephine⁷ Stroup, Elvira⁶ Pegan, Henry⁵, Robert A.⁴, Andrew³, Andrew² Pagan, James¹*) was born on August 31, 1882, in Salem Twp., Highland Co., Ohio.[121] He was the son of Henry A. Lemons and Josephine Stroup (10). Andrew Vance died in Bald Hill, Okmulgee Co., Oklahoma, on May 7, 1917, at age 34.[122, 123, 124] He was buried in White Rose Cemetery, Bartlesville, Washington Co., Oklahoma.[333]

Childless.

Andrew Vance J. Lemons is not found in the 1910 census.

He used the middle initial "J." while in Oklahoma. He is listed in the 1914 Muscogee, Oklahoma and the 1915-1916 Bartlesville, Oklahoma city directory.[334, 335]

Andrew Vance married **Anna R. Darling** on November 30, 1913, in Washington Co., Oklahoma.[336] Anna R. Darling was born on October 1, 1889 in Savonburg, Allen Co., Kansas?[337] Anna R. died on October 3, 1937 in Springfield, Greene Co., Missouri.[337] She was buried in White Rose Cemetery, Bartlesville, Washington Co., Oklahoma.[338]

Andrew Lemons states on his marriage license application on November 29, 1913 in Washington Co., Oklahoma that his name is Andrew J. Lemons and he is 31 years old. He and Anna R. Darling were married the next day.[336]

Andrew Lemons died in an explosion while he and a co-worker were transporting 80 quarts of nitroglycerin a "nitro wagon" to the Bald Hills oil field near Okmulgee, Okmulgee Co., Oklahoma. His obituary in the *Bartlesville (OK) Morning Examiner* on May 10, 1917, which refers to him as "Andrew J. Lemon", states that he was 35 years old and his wife survived him. His funeral was at the home of his brother- and sister-in-law, Fallie Arnold and Phildelia Darling Quaid; Fallie A. Quaid was the Washington, Oklahoma County clerk.[123]

Andrew Lemons' gravestone in White Rose Cemetery, Bartlesville, Washington Co., Oklahoma bears the incorrect birthdate of August 11, 1882; Highland Co., Ohio birth records indicate he was born on August 31, 1882.[333]

Although there is no death certificate in Oklahoma to confirm that this Andrew Lemons was the son of Henry A. and Josephine Stroup Lemons, there are no other Andrew Lemons/Lemon born in 1882 in Ohio in any other U.S. census or other online records. There is one born in 1881 in North Carolina and one in 1883 in Georgia, but both are accounted for in the 1920 census. By process of elimination, it is very highly probable that the Andrew J. Lemons who died on May 7, 1918 in Okmulgee Co., Oklahoma is the same Andrew Lemons born on August 31, 1882 in Salem Twp., Highland Co., Ohio.

There are unsourced online family tree records that say Andrew V. Lemons died on 16 May 1916, but they do not say where or offer any sources to document this date.

Anna R. Darling Lemons remarried to Roy R. Myers on December 22, 1922 in Washington Co., Oklahoma.[339]

She died under the name "Anna R. Myers". On her death certificate, Roy R. Myers says Anna was born in "Sanberg", Kansas.[337] But there has never been a Kansas town by that name. As she and her parents, Charles and Rachel Darling, were living in Iola, Allen Co., Kansas in 1900 *(Census Place: Iola, Allen, Kansas; Page: 10; Enumeration District: 0011; Anna Darling; Charles Darling, head of household)*, Anna was probably born in the nearby town of Savonburg, Allen Co., Kansas, which was an unincorporated village at the time.

41. **Talmadge DeWitt[8] Lemons** (*Josephine[7] Stroup, Elvira[6] Pegan, Henry[5], Robert A.[4], Andrew[3], Andrew[2] Pagan, James[1]*) was born on December 30, 1885, in Salem Twp., Highland Co., Ohio.[125] He was also known as **Tal** and **Spot**. He was the son of Henry A. Lemons and Josephine Stroup (10). Talmadge DeWitt died in Lynchburg, Dodson Twp., Highland Co., Ohio, on July 4, 1956, at age 70.[126, 127] He was buried in Glen Haven Memorial Gardens, Donnelsville, Bethel Twp., Clark Co., Ohio.[127, 340]

Childless.

In 1910, Talmadge DeWitt Lemons, age 24, a chipper in a piano factory (probably Piano Plate Company) is living with his mother, Josephine Stroup Lemons and some of his brothers in Springfield, Springfield Twp., Clark Co., Ohio *(Census Place: Springfield Ward 3, Clark, Ohio; Roll: T624_1158; Page: 4A; Enumeration District: 0036; Image: 957)*. Josephine Stroup Lemons, age 53, a widow with no occupation, is the head of the household. She says she bore eight children, all still alive. Talmadge's brothers residing with them are "Meril", 23, a bench hand at Harvester Works; and "Ottie", 18, and Edgar, 17, who are factory laborers. The sons are unmarried. All say they and their parents were born Ohioans by birth.

Talmadge DeWitt married **Irene May Lane** on April 20, 1916, in Clark Co., Ohio.[125] Irene May Lane was born in Fairfield Twp., Madison Co., Ohio, on September 3, 1885.[341] She was also known as **Rena May**. Irene May reached age 65 and died in Springfield, Springfield Twp., Clark Co., Ohio, on January 15, 1951.[341] She was buried in Glen Haven Memorial Gardens Cemetery, Donnelsville, Bethel Twp., Clark Co., Ohio.[342, 343]

Talmadge DeWitt Lemons is enumerated in Springfield, Springfield Twp., Clark Co., Ohio in 1920 *(Census Place: Springfield Ward 2, Clark, Ohio;*

Roll: T625_1354; Page: 8B; Enumeration District: 59; Image: 313). In the household are "Talmage" Lemons, 35, a foreman at Piano Plate Company, his wife Irene Mae "Rena" Lane Farrand Lemons, also 35, and Irene/Rena's two children by her first marriage, Charles Ferrand. 15, and Lenora Ferrand, 13. All say they and their parents were Ohio natives.

In 1930, Talmadge D. Lemons is still in Springfield, Springfield Twp., Clark Co., Ohio *(Census Place: Springfield, Clark, Ohio; Roll: 1757; Page: 18A; Enumeration District: 32; Image: 270.0).* Talmadge D. Lemons, 45, continues his job as a foreman at Piano Plate Co. "Rena M." Lane Farrand Lemons is with him and she is 45 years old also. Both say they and their parents were born in Ohio. Talmadge D. Lemons and Irene Mae "Rena Lane Ferrand Lemons say their first marriages occurred at ages 32 and 16 respectively.

Talmadge and Irena "Rena" Lane Lemons continue to reside in Springfield, Springfield Twp., Clark Co., Ohio in 1940 *(Census Place: Springfield, Clark, Ohio; Roll: T627_3040; Page: 7B; Enumeration District: 12-57).* Talmadge Lemons, age 54, is a foreman in a chipping department. With him is wife Irena Lane Lemons, listed as Rena, also 54 years old. Both were born in Ohio. Talmadge and Irena say they were living in Springfield in 1935. A boarder is living with them: Leotta Gibbons, 54, born Illinois. The house is at 25 Clark Street.

According to his obituary in the *Hillsboro (OH) Press Gazette,* Talmadge Lemons was a noted baseball player in his youth.[127]

42. Murrell or Merrill Clarence[8] Lemons (*Josephine[7] Stroup, Elvira[6] Pegan, Henry[5], Robert A.[4], Andrew[3], Andrew[2] Pagan, James[1]*) was born on May 25, 1887, in Salem Twp., Highland Co., Ohio.[128, 129, 130] He was the son of Henry A. Lemons and Josephine Stroup (10). He died in Springfield, Springfield Twp., Clark Co., Ohio, on July 11, 1953, at age 66.[128] Murrell or Merrill Clarence was buried in New Lynchburg Masonic Cemetery/Lynchburg F & AM Cemetery, Lynchburg, Dodson Twp., Highland Co., Ohio.[128, 344]

His name is spelled many ways. The spelling on the entry in the Highland County, Ohio birth records is "Myrle Lemons".[130] But his Ohio death certificate spells his given name "Merrill". (His brother Talmadge Lemons was the informant on the death certificate.)[128] On the death certificate, "Merrill" is listed as a widower and an army veteran who was living on Western Avenue in Springfield, which was his brother Talmadge's address. His obituary in the *Springfield (OH) Daily News* says his name is "Merrill Lemon".[345]

On his 1911 marriage application, he spells his own name "Murrell".[129] He writes it as "Murrill" on his WWII draft registration.[346]

Officially, according to Highland County birth records, "Myrle" Lemons was born on May 25, 1887.[130] On his WWII draft registration, "Murrill" Lemons says he was born on May 25, 1888.[346] However, on "Merrill" Lemons' death certificate, his brother Talmadge says "Merrill" was born on May 25, 1886.[128]

In 1910, "Meril" Lemons, single, a 23-year-old bench hand at Harvester Works, is living with his mother Josephine Stroup Lemons and some of his brothers in Springfield, Springfield Twp., Clark Co., Ohio *(Census Place: Springfield Ward 3, Clark, Ohio; Roll: T624_1158; Page: 4A; Enumeration District: 0036; Image: 957).* The head of the household, Josephine Stroup Lemons, age 53, a widow with no occupation, is the head of the household. She says she bore eight children, all still alive. Murrell/Merrill's brothers residing with them are Talmadge, 24, a chipper in a piano factory; and "Ottie", 18, and Edgar, 17, who are factory laborers. The sons are unmarried. All in the home and their parents were Ohio natives.

Murrell or Merrill Clarence married **Nora L. Cooper** on March 28, 1911, in Highland Co., Ohio.[129] They divorced before 1920. Nora L. Cooper was born in Hillsboro, Liberty Twp., Highland Co., Ohio, on January 17, 1890.[129, 347] She reached age 37 and died in Dayton, Montgomery Co., Ohio, on November 12, 1937.[347] Nora L. Cooper Lemons Sheehan is buried in Calvary Cemetery, Dayton, Montgomery Co., Ohio.[347]

Nora's date of birth is different in several sources. On her marriage license to "Murrell" C. Lemons in 1911, Nora L. Cooper stated she was age 19 on January 17, 1911, giving her a birth date of January 17, 1892.[129] But her death certificate has her birthday as January 17, 1893 (her second husband, Eugene Sheehan, was the informant. Perhaps she told him this date so she was the same age as he, and not older).[347] Strangely, the Highland County birth records says otherwise. Her parents, John and Ella Overman Cooper, have a female child, unnamed, registered as born on July 31, 1899, in Hillsboro, Ohio, listed among the January 1900 births.[348] This may be an error in the birth records. Nora's age in the 1900 is 10 years old, and her parents say she was born in January 1890. They list another daughter, Edna, as born in December 1892 *(Census Place: Hillsboro, Highland, Ohio; Page: 22; Enumeration District: 0118; Nora Cooper; John Cooper, head of household)*. Nora is 20 years old in 1910 *(Census Place: Liberty, Highland, Ohio; Roll: T624_1197; Page: 6A; Enumeration District: 0124; Nora Cooper; John Cooper, head of household)*. Nora L. Cooper Lemons Sheehan was probably born on January 17, 1900.

Merrill Lemons is listed in the 1918 Springfield, Ohio city directory, with his wife Nora. He is a machinist.[349] But by 1920, Merrill and Nora are no longer married.

After the divorce, Nora L. Cooper Lemons married Eugene Sheehan. She lived in Dayton, Montgomery Co., Ohio, and died in the mental hospital there.[347]

Murrell Lemons is residing with his mother and two of his brothers in Lynchburg, Dodson Twp., Highland Co., Ohio by 1920 *(Census Place: Dodson, Highland, Ohio; Roll: T625_1399; Page: 2A; Enumeration District: 84; Image: 101)*. In the home are Josephine Stroup Lemons. 63, a widow, and her three unmarried sons: James Lemons 36, "Merl" Lemons, 28 and "Edgar" Lemons, 26. All three sons say they are general laborers and are unmarried. All in the home say they and their parents were Ohio natives.

In 1930, "Murrell" Lemons is incarcerated in the Ohio State Penitentiary, Columbus, Franklin Co., Ohio *(Census Place: Columbus, Franklin, Ohio; Roll: 1799; Page: 40B; Enumeration District: 0110)*. He is age 41, born Ohio as were his parents.

Merrill Lemons, listed as Merle, is again living with his mother in 1940 in Lynchburg, Dodson Twp., Highland Co., Ohio *(Census Place: Lynchburg, Highland, Ohio; Roll: T627_3085; Page: 1B; Enumeration District: 36-5)*. Merrill Lemons, age 53 and single, lists odd jobs as his occupation. His mother, Josephine Stroup Lemons, listed as the head of the household, is 83 years old. Also in the home are Merrill's brothers, James, 59 and Edgar, 45, both single. James lists no occupation, while Edgar also odd jobs as his work. All in the home were born in Ohio, and were living in the same house, on the south side of Main Street between High Street and the stock yards, in 1935.

By 1942, according to his WWII draft registration, "Murrell" Lemons says he is a resident of Lynchburg, Ohio and is unemployed. He lists his next of kin as his sister Grace Boesenburg of Springfield, Ohio, only he calls her "Grace Rosenburg".[346]

43. Clarence Otto[8] Lemons (*Josephine[7] Stroup, Elvira[6] Pegan, Henry[5], Robert A.[4], Andrew[3], Andrew[2] Pagan, James[1]*) was born on October 11, 1891, in Salem Twp., Highland Co., Ohio.[131] He was the son of Henry A. Lemons and Josephine Stroup (10). He was also known as **Bill**. Clarence Otto died in Hillsboro, Liberty Twp., Highland Co., Ohio, on October 22, 1944, at age 53.[131] Clarence Otto was buried in New Lynchburg Masonic Cemetery/Lynchburg F & AM Cemetery, Lynchburg, Dodson Twp., Highland Co., Ohio.[131]

Clarence Otto Lemons' birth date on his WWI and WWII draft registrations and his Social Security application ("Clarence Otto Lemon") is October 12, 1891.[350, 351, 352] But his Ohio death record and an online birth database, which states his name as Clarence Otis Lemmons, say it was Oct 11, 1891.[131, 353]

In 1910, Clarence Otto Lemons, listed as "Ottie", 18, single, a factory laborer, is living with his mother, Josephine Stroup Lemons and some of his brothers in Springfield, Springfield Twp., Clark Co., Ohio *(Census Place: Springfield Ward 3, Clark, Ohio; Roll: T624_1158; Page: 4A; Enumeration District: 0036; Image: 957)*. Josephine Stroup Lemons, age 53, says she is a widow who bore eight children, all still alive. She lists no occupation. Clarence Otto's brothers with them, who are also single, are Talmadge, 24, a chipper in a piano factory; "Meril", 23, a bench hand at Harvester Works; and Edgar, 17, who is also a factory laborer. Ohio was the birthplace of all in the home and their parents.

Clarence Otto married **Grace May Long** on December 14, 1915, in Warren Co., Ohio.[354] They divorced before 1944. They had three children. Grace May Long was born in Blanchester, Marion Twp., Clinton Co., Ohio, on August 1, 1895.[354, 355] Grace May reached age 26 and died in Springfield, Springfield Twp., Clark Co., Ohio, on February 3, 1922.[355] She was buried in Ferncliff Cemetery, Springfield, Springfield Twp., Clark Co., Ohio.[355, 356] She was the daughter of Benjamin Long and Minnie Brown.

On their 1915 marriage license, Clarence says he is a farmer living in Lynchburg, Dodson Twp., Highland Co., Ohio, while Grace lived in Kings Mills, Deerfield Twp. Warren Co., Ohio.[354]

On his 1917 WWI draft registration, Clarence Otto Lemons says he is a resident of Springfield, Ohio, and has a wife and child. He lists his occupation as an apprentice tinner.[350]

In 1920, Clarence Otto and Grace Mae Long Lemons and family are residing at the Salvation Army Hotel in Springfield, Springfield Twp., Clark Co., Ohio (*Census Place: Springfield Ward 4, Clark, Ohio; Roll: T625_1353; Page: 7B; Enumeration District: 75; Image: 991*). Clarence Otto Lemons, who is listed as age 26 (incorrect), says he is a chipper at Piano Plate Co. (where his brother, Talmadge, was a foreman). His wife, Grace Mae Long Lemons, is 24. They have two children, Robert H., two years and nine months, and a daughter Josephine M., five months. All of them say that they and their parents were born in Ohio.

Two years later, Clarence Otto Lemons' first wife, Grace May Long Lemons, dies. His sons, Robert H. Lemons (Long) and Clarence Lemons II, (Long) born 1921, are reared by their maternal grandparents, Benjamin and Minnie Brown Long in Springfield, Springfield Twp., Clark Co., Ohio. The boys assume the surname Long. Josephine Mae Lemons, Clarence Otto Lemons' daughter, lives with her paternal grandmother, Josephine Stroup Lemons, in Lynchburg, Dodson Twp., Highland Co., Ohio and continues to use the surname Lemons. (Josephine Mae Lemons later married Albert J. Luck II.)

Clarence Otto Lemons married Mrs. **Daisy Loretta Thorpe** Ferrand in about 1927. They were legally separated in Clark Co., Ohio, before 1940 and divorced shortly afterwards. Daisy Loretta Thorpe was born in Columbus, Franklin Co., Ohio, on December 20, 1887.[357] She was also known as **Daisy**. She reached age 70 and died in Springfield, Springfield Twp., Clark Co., Ohio, on April 30, 1958.[358]

om Clarence Lemons, Daisy Loretta Thorpe retook her first married surname, Ferrand. She died under the name Daisy L. Ferrand.[358]

In 1930, Clarence Lemons is enumerated as "Clarence Lammons" in Springfield, Springfield Twp., Clark Co., Ohio (*Census Place: Springfield, Clark, Ohio; Roll: 1756; Page: 8A; Enumeration District: 42; Image: 777.0*). In the household are Clarence, age 38, still a chipper at Piano Plate Company, born Ohio as were his parents. He says his first marriage occurred when he was 26. With him is a wife, "Loretta" Lemons, 42, who says she was first married at age 39, so she and Clarence have been married three years. Of course, this is incorrect, as she was married in 1906 in Columbus, Franklin Co., Ohio to Frank Ferrand.[357] Perhaps she misunderstood the question. Loretta D. says she was born in Ohio, and her parents in the United States. Also in the home, incorrectly listed as Clarence's son, is Harry Ferrand, age 19, Daisy Loretta's son by her first marriage.

Clarence Lemons is living with his brother-in-law and sister, Edward W. and Grace Lemons Boesenberg, in 1940 in Springfield, Springfield Twp., Clark Co., Ohio (*Census Place: Springfield, Clark, Ohio; Roll: T627_3040; Page: 2A; Enumeration District: 12-72*). Clarence Lemons, 47, listed as married and a laborer doing street repairs, says he was living in Springfield in 1935. The head of the household, Edward W. Boesenberg, listed as "Ed", is age 63, is a baker in a wholesale bakery. His wife, Grace Lemons Boesenberg, is 61 years old. Both say they were living in the same house at 320 Western in 1935. All in the home were born in Ohio.

On Clarence Otto Lemons' death certificate, his daughter, Josephine Lemons Luck, says her father, divorced from Daisy Lemons, had been working in the radio department at Patterson Field (now Wright Patterson Air Force Base), and had been a resident of Hillsboro, Liberty Twp., Hillsboro Co., Ohio for three years.[131]

His death certificate also says Clarence Otto Lemons was buried in "Lynchburg".[131] His obituary in the *Hillsboro (OH) Press-Gazette* in the "Lynchburg" local column says he was buried "in the local Masonic Cemetery".[359] There are two Masonic Cemeteries with Lynchburg, Ohio addresses. Indications are he was buried in the New Masonic Cemetery in the rear of the Lynchburg A&M Cemetery, where indigent burials were taken since the 1940s. His name, however, does not appear in either Masonic Cemetery records. The sexton for both cemeteries says this is not unusual, as records from the New Masonic Cemetery were lost early on and some burials are missing from the records.

Children of Clarence Otto Lemons and Grace May Long:

+ 90 m I. **Robert H.**[9] **Lemons (Long)** was born in Springfield, Springfield Twp., Clark Co., Ohio, on March 5, 1917.[360] He died in Gallipolis, Gallipolis Twp., Gallia Co., Ohio?, between 1930 and 1944.

+ 91 f II. **Josephine Mae**[9] **Lemons** was born in Springfield, Springfield Twp., Clark Co., Ohio, on July 12, 1919.[31, 361] She died in Sabina, Richland Twp., Clinton Co., Ohio, on October 10, 2008.[31, 361]

+ 92 m III. **Clarence Junior**[9] **Lemons II (Long)** was born in Springfield, Springfield Twp., Clark Co., Ohio, on August 26, 1921.[31, 362] He died in West Allis, Milwaukee Co., Wisconsin, on January 23, 2012.[31, 362]

44. **Edgar or Edward Roy**[8] **Lemon** (*Josephine*[7] *Stroup, Elvira*[6] *Pegan, Henry*[5]*, Robert A.*[4]*, Andrew*[3]*, Andrew*[2] *Pagan, James*[1]) was born on May 24, 1893, in Salem Twp., Highland Co., Ohio.[132] He was the son of Henry A. Lemons and Josephine Stroup (10). He was also known as **Eddie**. Edgar/Edward Roy died in Lynchburg, Dodson Twp., Highland Co., Ohio, on April 5, 1951, at age 57.[132] He was buried in New Lynchburg Masonic Cemetery/ Lynchburg F & AM Cemetery, Lynchburg, Dodson Twp., Highland Co., Ohio.[132, 363, 364]

Edgar/Edward Roy Lemons' real name seems to have been Edgar, as that is the way his mother lists him in two early censuses. But he may have changed it by common usage to Edward.

Edgar Lemons is residing with his mother, Josephine Stroup Lemons, and three of his brothers in Lynchburg, Dodson Twp., Highland Co., Ohio in 1910 (*Census Place: Springfield Ward 3, Clark, Ohio; Roll: T624_1158; Page: 4A; Enumeration District: 0036; Image: 957*). Edgar, 17, is a factory laborer. Josephine Stroup Lemons, a 53-year-old widow with no occupation, is the head of the household. She says she bore eight children, all still alive. Edgar's brothers Talmadge, 24, a chipper in a piano factory; "Meril", 23, a bench hand at Harvester Works; and "Ottie" 18, also a factory laborer, are also in the home. The sons are unmarried. All say they and their parents were born in Ohio.

In 1917 on his WWI draft registration, Edward/ Edgar Lemons uses the name Edward Roy Lemons, and says he is a resident of Lynchburg, Ohio.[365]

Edgar or Edward Lemons is residing with his mother, Josephine Stroup Lemons and two of his brothers in Lynchburg, Dodson Twp., Highland Co., Ohio in 1920 (*Census Place: Dodson, Highland, Ohio; Roll: T625_1399; Page: 2A; Enumeration District: 84; Image: 101*). In the home are Josephine Stroup Lemons. 63, a widow, and her three unmarried sons: James Lemons, 36, "Merl" Lemons, 28, and Edgar Lemons, 26. All three sons say they are general laborers and are unwed. All in the home say they and their parents were born in Ohio.

Edgar/Edward married Mrs. **Wilhelmina Jane Leaverton** Frazier on January 31, 1920, in Highland

Co., Ohio.[366] They were separated before 1930 and divorced before 1940. They had one daughter. Wilhelmina Jane Leaverton was born in Hillsboro, Liberty Twp., Highland Co., Ohio, on June 16, 1899.[366, 367, 368] Wilhelmina Jane reached age 63 and died in Weed, Siskiyou Co., California, on January 20, 1963.[367, 368, 369] She was buried in Winema Cemetery, Weed, Siskiyou Co., California.[368, 369]

Wilhemina Leverton was married to Floyd E. Frazier before marrying Eddie Roy Lemons.[370]

In 1920, Wilhelmina Leaverton Frazier Lemons is enumerated as Wilhelmina Leaverton in Dodson Twp., Highland Co., Ohio *(Census Place: Dodson, Highland, Ohio; Roll: T625_1399; Page: 1B; Enumeration District: 84; Image: 100)*. She is living with her mother, Lulu Leaverton. Wilhelmina, age 20, born Ohio as were her parents, has no occupation.

In 1930, Edward/Edgar Lemons is enumerated as "Eddie Lemon" in Lynchburg, Dodson Twp., Highland Co., Ohio *(Census Place: Lynchburg, Highland, Ohio; Roll: 1823; Page: 4B; Enumeration District: 5; Image: 75.0)*. "Eddie" is 36 and a barber. He is married, but his wife Wilhelmina is not living with him. He says his first marriage was at age 26, and that he and his parents were born in Ohio.

Edgar/Edward Lemons is again found in his mother Josephine Stroup Lemons' household in 1940 in Lynchburg, Dodson Twp., Highland Co., Ohio *(Census Place: Lynchburg, Highland, Ohio; Roll: T627_3085; Page: 1B; Enumeration District: 36-5)*. "Edward", age 45 and single, lists odd jobs as his occupation. His mother, Josephine Stroup Lemons, listed as the head of the household, is 83 years old. Also in the home are Edward/Edgar's brothers James Lemons, 59, and Murrell/Myrle Lemons listed as "Merle", 53, both also single. James Lemons lists no occupation, while Murrell/Myrle Lemons also lists odd jobs as his occupation. All in the home were born in Ohio, and were living in the same house, on the south side of Main Street between High Street and the stock yards, in 1935.

Edward/Edgar Roy Lemons married **Margaret Unknown** between 1940 and 1942.

On his WWII draft registration form, Edward/Edgar Lemons states his name as "Eddie R. Lemons". He is age 48, has a wife, Margaret, and says he is a day laborer in Lynchburg, Ohio.[371] However, his death certificate in 1951 reads "Eddie R. Lemon" and says he is divorced.[132]

An article in the *Hillsboro (OH) Press Gazette* in 1948 reports that "Eddie" Lemons was found "virtually stripped of all his clothes: and lying "in ice and water" and "in a state of collapse" on a Highland County rural road. He told police that several men had forced him into a car and dumped him there. He was discovered by another motorist who almost ran over him.[372]

In 1930, "Eddie's" estranged wife, Wilhelmina Leaverton Frazier Lemons is found in Penn Twp., Highland Co., Ohio *(Census Place: Penn, Highland, Ohio; Roll: 1823; Page: 8B; Enumeration District: 22; Image: 491.0)*. Wilhelmina, age 30, born Ohio as were her parents, says she is married but she is not living with her husband. She says she was first married at age 20. With her is daughter Margaret Lemons, age seven, born Ohio as were her parents. They are living with Wilhelmina's father, Lewis Leaverton, 69, a farm laborer.

Before 1940, Wilhelmina and her daughter Margaret removed California. Her obituary in the *Weed (CA) Press* in 1963 says Wilhelmina Leaverton Frazier Lemons relocated to California to join her mother, "the late Mrs. Moffett", in Yreka.[369]

Wilhelmina Leaverton Frazier Lemons is residing in Yreka Twp., Siskiyou Co., California in 1940 *(Census Place: Yreka City, Siskiyou, California; Roll: T627_346; Page: 61A; Enumeration District: 47-40)*. Wilhelmina J. Leaverton Frazier Lemons, age 40, divorced, says she is a housekeeper in a private home. Margaret L. Lemons is 17. Both say they were born in Ohio, and were living in Hillsboro, Liberty Twp., Highland Co., Ohio in 1935. Cecil Nelson, a 35-year-old Montana native, is also in the household and says he was living in Sacramento County, California in 1935. He is listed as a "hitchhiker" in relationship to the head of the household, Wilhelmina, but the word is crossed out. He says he is a laborer on a stock ranch. They seem to be living in a trailer court south of the town of Yreka.

Later, Wilhelmina moves to Weed, Siskiyou Co., California.

Daughter of Edgar/Edward Lemons and Wilhelmina Jane Leaverton:

+ 93 f I. **Margaret Lucille[9] Lemons** was born in Lynchburg, Dodson Twp., Highland Co., Ohio, on March 17, 1923.[31, 373] She died in Stockton, Stockton Twp., San Joaquin Co., California, on January 12, 2013.[31]

45. Cora May[8] Williams (*Mary E.[7] Stroup, Elvira[6] Pegan, Henry[5], Robert A.[4], Andrew[3], Andrew[2] Pagan, James[1]*) was born on May 16, 1879, in Dodson Twp., Highland Co., Ohio.[137] She was the daughter of Samuel Williams and Mary E. Stroup (12). Cora May died in Lynchburg, Dodson Twp., Highland Co., Ohio, on September 29, 1955, at age 76.[138] She was buried in Stroup Cemetery, Dodson Twp., Highland Co., Ohio.[138, 374]

Cora May married **Allen Carroll** on August 26, 1896, in Highland Co., Ohio.[375] They had four children. Allen Carroll was born in Salem Twp., Warren Co., Ohio, on December 9, 1874.[376] Allen lived in 1964 in Lynchburg, Dodson Twp., Highland Co., Ohio. He reached age 89 and died in a hospital in Hillsboro, Liberty Twp., Highland Co., Ohio, on September 13, 1964.[377] Allen was buried in Stroup Cemetery, Dodson Twp., Highland Co., Ohio.[378]

Allen and Cora May Williams are not found in the 1900 census.

Allen and Cora May Williams Carroll are located in Clark Twp., Clinton Co., Ohio in 1910 *(Census Place: Clark, Clinton, Ohio; Roll: T624_1160; Page: 2B; Enumeration District: 0061; Image: 718)*. In the home are Allen Carroll, 35, a farm laborer, and his wife Cora May Williams Carroll, 31. The couple says they have been married 13 years and Cora May has borne three children, with two surviving. The children are Mary, seven, and William M., 10 months. (The census taker seems to have erred, as William Morrell Carroll's death certificate says he was born on June 13, 1908.) All in household were born in Ohio, as were their parents.

In 1914, Allen and Cora May's daughter, Mary Elinora Carroll, dies. Her death certificate says her family was living in Fayetteville, Perry Twp., Brown Co., Ohio.

By 1920, Allen and Cora May Williams Carroll have removed to Washington Twp., Highland Co., Ohio *(Census Place: Washington, Highland, Ohio; Roll: T625_1399; Page: 1A; Enumeration District: 104)*. Household members are: Allen Carroll, 45, a farmer, wife Cora May Williams Carroll, 41, and son "Morrell", 10. All were born in Ohio, as were their parents.

Allen and Cora May Williams Carroll are listed in Norwood, Hamilton Co., Ohio in 1930 *(Census Place: Norwood, Hamilton, Ohio; Roll: 1817; Page: 10A; Enumeration District: 312; Image: 978.0)*. Allen Carroll, age 56, is now a factory laborer who says he was first married at age 23. Cora May Williams Carroll is 51 years old and says she her first marriage occurred at age 18. With them are children Morrell W., 20, also a factory laborer, and Delbert, eight. Living with them are two boarders who seem to be brothers, Floyd Jacobs, 32 and Samuel Jacobs, 20. All in the home were Ohio-born, as were their parents.

In 1940, Allen and Cora May Williams Carroll are enumerated in Owensville, Stone Lick Twp., Clermont Co., Ohio *(Census Place: Owensville, Clermont, Ohio; Roll: T627_3041; Page: 4A; Enumeration District: 13-20)*. Allen Carroll, age 65, lists no occupation and may be retired. His wife, Cora May Williams Carroll, is 62 years old. Both were born in Ohio, and say they were living in Highland Co., Ohio in 1935. Their home is on East Broadway, but there is no house address listed.

Children of Cora May Williams and Allen Carroll:

+ 94 f I. **Infant Daughter[9] Carroll** was born in Union Twp., Highland Co., Ohio?, about October 4, 1900. She died in Union Twp., Highland Co., Ohio?, on October 4, 1900.[379]

+	95	f	II.	**Mary Elinora⁹ Carroll** was born in Union Twp., Highland Co., Ohio, on May 10, 1902.[380, 381] She died in Fayetteville, Perry Twp., Brown Co., Ohio, on June 14, 1914.[381]
+	96	m	III.	**William Morell⁹ Carroll** was born in Clark Twp., Clinton Co., Ohio, on June 13, 1908.[382] William Morrell died in a hospital in Cincinnati, Hamilton Co., Ohio, on December 8, 1953.[382]
+	97	m	IV.	**Delbert A.⁹ Carroll** was born in Washington Twp., Highland Co., Ohio, on April 12, 1921.[31, 383, 384] He died in Hillsboro, Liberty Twp., Highland Co., Ohio, on February 20, 1991.[31, 383]

46. Levi⁸ Williams (*Mary E.⁷ Stroup, Elvira⁶ Pegan, Henry⁵, Robert A.⁴, Andrew³, Andrew² Pagan, James¹*) was born on May 26, 1881, in Dodson Twp., Highland Co., Ohio.[139, 140] He was also known as **Lee**. He was the son of Samuel Williams and Mary E. Stroup (12). Levi died in Lynchburg, Dodson Twp., Highland Co., Ohio, on December 1, 1947, at age 66.[139] He was buried in New Lynchburg Masonic Cemetery/Lynchburg F & AM Cemetery, Lynchburg, Dodson Twp., Highland Co., Ohio.[139, 385]

Levi Williams preferred his nickname, Lee, as his given name.

Levi married **Bertha Frances Fawley** on August 21, 1901, in Highland Co., Ohio.[386] They had one son. Bertha Frances Fawley was born in Hamer Twp., Highland Co., Ohio, on October 5, 1883.[386, 387] Bertha lived in 1957 in Lynchburg, Dodson Twp., Highland Co., Ohio. She reached age 73 and died in a hospital in Wilmington, Union Twp., Clinton Co., Ohio, on January 8, 1957.[388] Bertha was buried in New Lynchburg Masonic Cemetery/Lynchburg F & AM Cemetery, Lynchburg, Dodson Twp., Highland Co., Ohio.[389]

"Lee" Williams is enumerated in Dodson Twp., Highland Co., Ohio in 1910 *(Census Place: Dodson, Highland, Ohio; Roll: T624_1197; Page: 9B; Enumeration District: 0114; Image: 554)*. Lee Williams is age 28 and a farmer. His wife, Bertha Frances Fawley Williams is 26. The couple state they have been married eight years and Bertha has borne one child, still living. This would be son Carl D., age seven. All in the home were Ohio-born, as were their parents.

In 1920, Lee Williams is still living in Dodson Twp., Highland Co., Ohio *(Census Place: Dodson, Highland, Ohio; Roll: T625_1399; Page: 7B; Enumeration District: 83; Image: 94)*. In the home are Levi "Lee" Williams, 38, a farmer; his wife, Bertha F. Fawley Williams, 36, and their son Carl D., 17. All in the home were born in Ohio as were their parents.

Levi "Lee" Williams is found in Lynchburg, Dodson Twp., Highland Co., Ohio *(Census Place: Lynchburg, Highland, Ohio; Roll: 1823; Page: 2B; Enumeration District: 5; Image: 71.0)*. Lee Williams, 48, is a farm laborer who says he was first married at age 18. His wife, Bertha F. Fawley Williams is 45 and states her first marriage occurred at age 15. Both say they and their parents were born in Ohio.

In 1940, Levi Williams is residing in Allensburg, Liberty Twp., Highland Co., Ohio *(Census Place: Dodson, Highland, Ohio; Roll: T627_3085; Page: 6B; Enumeration District: 36-6)*. Levi Williams, age 58, is a proprietor of a grocery. His wife, Bertha Fawley Williams, is 56 years old. Both were born in Ohio, and say they were living in Lynchburg, Dodson Twp., Highland Co., Ohio in 1935. Their home is on U.S. 50, but no house number is listed on the census form.

Son of Levi Williams and Bertha Frances Fawley:

+	98	m	I.	**Carl Delbert⁹ Williams** was born in Dodson Twp., Highland Co., Ohio, on February 16, 1902.[31, 390, 391] He died in Dayton, Montgomery Co., Ohio, on September 29, 1991.[31, 391]

47. Hattie Ellen⁸ Williams (*Mary E.⁷ Stroup, Elvira⁶ Pegan, Henry⁵, Robert A.⁴, Andrew³, Andrew² Pagan, James¹*) was born on July 16, 1882, in Dodson Twp., Highland Co., Ohio.[141] She was the daughter of Samuel Williams and Mary E. Stroup (12). She resided in Lynchburg, Dodson Twp., Highland Co., Ohio in September 1961. Hattie Ellen died in a hospital in Wilmington, Union Twp., Clinton Co., Ohio, on September 4, 1961, at age 79.[142] She was buried in New Lynchburg Masonic Cemetery/Lynchburg F & AM Cemetery, Lynchburg, Dodson Twp., Highland Co., Ohio.[142, 392]

Hattie Ellen married **George Robert Wilkin** on December 22, 1900, in Highland Co., Ohio.[393] They had eight children. George Robert Wilkin was born in Hamer Twp., Highland Co., Ohio, on June 12, 1877.[31, 394, 395] George Robert reached age 97 and died in Greenfield, Madison Twp., Highland Co., Ohio, on December 31, 1974.[31, 396] He was buried in New Lynchburg Masonic Cemetery/Lynchburg F & AM Cemetery, Lynchburg, Dodson Twp., Highland Co., Ohio.[397]

George Robert and Hattie Williams Wilkin are enumerated in Dodson Twp., Highland Co., Ohio in 1910 (*Census Place: Dodson, Highland, Ohio; Roll: T624_1197; Page: 9A; Enumeration District: 0114; Image: 553*). In the home are George R. Wilkin, 32, a farmer, and Hattie E. Williams Wilkin, 26. They say they are on their first marriage, have been wed eight years, and Hattie has borne three children, all living. They are: Edgar F., seven, Everett R., five, and Marjorie M., two. Also residing with them is Hattie's brother, Joseph Williams, 20, a farm laborer. All were born in Ohio, as were their parents.

In 1920, George Robert and Hattie E. Williams Wilkin are still in Dodson Twp., Highland Co., Ohio (*Census Place: Dodson, Highland, Ohio; Roll: T625_1399; Page: 7A; Enumeration District: 83; Image: 93*). George R. Wilkin is age 42, a farmer; Hattie E. Williams Wilkin is 35. Their children are: Edgar, 17, and "Everet", 15, both listed as farm laborers; "Marjory", 12, "Evylon", eight, Lenora, five, and Georgiana, three. All in the home were born in Ohio, as were their parents. A neighbor is Hattie's brother Stanley Williams and his family.

George Robert and Hattie E. Williams Wilkin are found once again Dodson Twp., Highland Co., Ohio in 1930 (*Census Place: Dodson, Highland, Ohio; Roll: 1823; Page: 2B; Enumeration District: 6; Image: 87.0*). In the household are George R. Wilkin, 53, a farmer who says he was first married at age 23 and his wife Hattie Williams Wilkin, 45, who says she was 16 years old when she first wed. Living with them are children Lenora, 16, Georgiana, 13, Samuel, nine, and "Roy", seven. All and their parents were Ohio natives.

In 1940, George R. and Hattie E. Williams Wilkin continue to live in Dodson Twp., Highland Co., Ohio (*Census Place: Dodson, Highland, Ohio; Roll: T627_3085; Page: 3A; Enumeration District: 36-6.*). George R. Wilkin, age 62, is still a farmer. Hattie E. Williams Wilkin is 56 years old. With them are their two youngest children, Samuel, 19, and LeRoy, 17, both listed as farm laborers. All in the home were born in Ohio, and say they were living in the same house at 33-c Anderson Road in 1935.

Children of Hattie Ellen Williams and George Robert Wilkin:

+ 99 m I. **Edgar Franklin**[9] **Wilkin** was born in Hamer Twp., Highland Co., Ohio, on May 30, 1902.[31, 398, 399] He died in Hillsboro, Liberty Twp., Highland Co., Ohio, on May 28, 1996.[31, 398, 400]

+ 100 m II. **Everett Robert**[9] **Wilkin** was born in Union Twp., Highland Co., Ohio, on July 10, 1904.[31, 401, 402] He died in a hospital in Georgetown, Pleasant Twp., Brown Co., Ohio, on November 11, 1980.[402, 403]

+ 101 f III. **Marjorie Marie**[9] **Wilkin** was born in Dodson Twp., Highland Co., Ohio, on May 4, 1907.[404] She died in Lynchburg, Dodson Twp., Highland Co., Ohio, on October 8, 1963.[405]

+ 102 f IV. **Evelyn Lorie**[9] **Wilkin** was born in Dodson Twp., Highland Co., Ohio, on July 7, 1911.[406, 407] She died in Hillsboro, Liberty Twp., Highland Co., Ohio, on August 8, 2002.[406, 407]

+ 103 f V. **Lenora**[9] **Wilkin** was born in Dodson Twp., Highland Co., Ohio, on February 14, 1914.[408] She died in Dodson Twp., Highland Co., Ohio, on February 14, 1933.[408]

+ 104 f VI. **Georgeanna**[9] **Wilkin** was born in Dodson Twp., Highland Co., Ohio, on July 27, 1916.[409, 410, 411] She died in Waverly, Pee Pee Twp., Pike Co., Ohio, on March 26, 1998.[410, 411]

+ 105 m VII. **Samuel**[9] **Wilkin** was born in Dodson Twp., Highland Co., Ohio, on September 14, 1920.[31, 412, 413] He died in Hillsboro, Liberty Twp., Highland Co., Ohio, on June 19, 1994.[31, 412, 413]

+ 106 m VIII. **LeRoy Thomas**[9] **Wilkin** was born in Dodson Twp., Highland Co., Ohio, on January 3, 1923.[31, 414] He was also known as **Tom**. LeRoy Thomas died in Wilmington, Union Twp., Clinton Co., Ohio, on August 1, 2010.[31, 414]

48. Stanley[8] **Williams** (*Mary E.*[7] *Stroup, Elvira*[6] *Pegan, Henry*[5]*, Robert A.*[4]*, Andrew*[3]*, Andrew*[2] *Pagan, James*[1]) was born on January 31, 1886, in Salem Twp., Highland Co., Ohio.[31, 143] He was the son of Samuel Williams and Mary E. Stroup (12). Stanley resided in 1972 in Lynchburg, Dodson Twp., Highland Co., Ohio. He died in a hospital in Hillsboro, Liberty Twp., Highland Co., Ohio, on September 2, 1972, at age 86.[144] Stanley was buried in New Lynchburg Masonic Cemetery/Lynchburg F & AM Cemetery, Lynchburg, Dodson Twp., Highland Co., Ohio.[415]

Stanley married **Mary Achor** on December 25, 1909, in Highland Co., Ohio.[416] They had four sons. Mary Achor was born in Union Twp., Highland Co., Ohio, on September 1, 1888.[31, 417, 418, 419, 420] Mary reached age 78 and died in Hillsboro, Liberty Twp., Highland Co., Ohio, on September 21, 1966.[421] She was buried in New Lynchburg Masonic Cemetery/Lynchburg F & AM Cemetery, Lynchburg, Dodson Twp., Highland Co., Ohio.[422]

Mary Achor Williams' birthdate on her marriage license to Stanley Williams, September 6, 1888, is incorrect. Mary's and her twin brother Joseph's births are registered as September 1, 1888 in Union Twp., Highland County, Ohio, according to county records.[417] This date is confirmed by Joseph's Social Security information and his WWI and WWII draft registrations.[31, 418, 419, 420]

Stanley Williams is enumerated in Perry Twp., Brown Co., Ohio in 1910 *(Census Place: Perry, Brown, Ohio; Roll: T624_1157; Page: 3B; Enumeration District: 0013; Image: 845)*. Stanley Williams, age 23, is a farmer and his wife Mary Achor Williams is 21. The couple have been married one year and Mary has borne no children.

By 1920, Stanley and Mary Achor Williams have removed to Dodson Twp., Highland Co., Ohio *(Census Place: Dodson, Highland, Ohio; Roll: T625_1399; Page: 7A; Enumeration District: 83; Image: 93)*. In the home are Stanley Williams, age 33, a farmer; and his wife Mary Achor Williams, 31. They have three children: "daughter" Eugene (Eugenie?), nine, and sons Virgil, seven, and "Wodrow" (Woodrow), three years and three months. All were born in Ohio, as were their parents. The census taker erred, as "daughter" Eugene was a son. Hattie E. Williams Wilkin, Stanley's sister, and her family are neighbors.

Stanley Williams is found again Dodson Twp., Highland Co., Ohio in 1930 *(Census Place: Dodson, Highland, Ohio; Roll: 1823; Page: 1A; Enumeration District: 0006)*. In the household are Stanley Williams, 44, a farmer who says he was first married at age 23, His wife, Mary Achor Williams is 42 and says she was 21 when first married. Children living with them are "Vergil", 16, Woodrow, 14, and "Mitchel", five. All in the home and their parents were born in Ohio.

In 1940, Stanley Williams continues to reside in Dodson Twp., Highland Co., Ohio *(Census Place:*

Dodson, Highland, Ohio; Roll: T627_3085; Page: 2B; Enumeration District: 36-6). Stanley Williams, age 54, is still farming. Mary Achor Williams is 51 years old. With them is son (Stanley) Mitchell, 15. Also living in the home is Mary's mother, Martha Achor, 76, a widow. All were born in Ohio, and say they were living in the same house on 11-A Sharpsville Road in 1935.

Stanley Williams was the informant on his brother Levi "Lee" Williams' death certificate in 1947, and at that time Stanley was living in Lynchburg, Dodson Twp., Highland Co., Ohio.[139]

Sons of Stanley Williams and Mary Achor:

+ 107 m I. **Eugene**[9] **Williams** was born in Perry Twp., Brown Co., Ohio, on December 30, 1910.[423] He died in Dodson Twp., Highland Co., Ohio, on April 10, 1923.[423]

+ 108 m II. **Virgil**[9] **Williams** was born in Perry Twp., Brown Co., Ohio, on November 1, 1913.[31, 424] He died in a hospital in Kenwood, Hamilton Co., Ohio, on June 6, 2001. [31, 424]

+ 109 m III. **Woodrow Wilson**[9] **Williams** was born in Dodson Twp., Highland Co., Ohio, on December 16, 1916.[31] He died in a hospital in Wilmington, Union Twp., Clinton Co., Ohio, on May 1, 1972.[31, 425, 426]

+ 110 m IV. **Stanley Mitchell**[9] **Williams II** was born in Dodson Twp., Highland Co., Ohio, on February 2, 1925.[31, 427] He was also known as **Mitchell**. Stanley Mitchell died in a hospital in Dayton, Montgomery Co., Ohio, on August 20, 2007.[427, 428]

49. Josephus Everett[8] **Williams** (*Mary E.*[7] *Stroup, Elvira*[6] *Pegan, Henry*[5]*, Robert A.*[4]*, Andrew*[3]*, Andrew*[2] *Pagan, James*[1]) was born on April 25, 1888, in Dodson Twp., Highland Co., Ohio.[145] He was also known as **Joseph**. He was the son of Samuel Williams and Mary E. Stroup (12). Joseph Everett died in Dodson Twp., Highland Co., Ohio, on June 17, 1923, at age 35.[145] He was buried in Stroup Cemetery, Dodson Twp., Highland Co., Ohio.[145, 429]

Josephus Williams preferred to use Joseph as his given name.

Josephus Williams is enumerated as Joseph Williams in Dodson Twp., Highland Co., Ohio in 1910 *(Census Place: Dodson, Highland, Ohio; Roll: T624_1197; Page: 9A; Enumeration District: 0114; Image: 553).* Joseph is living with his brother-in-law and sister, George Robert and Hattie E. Williams Wilkins and their family. Joseph Williams, age 20, is a farm laborer. Others in the home include George R. Wilkin, 32, a farmer, and Hattie E. Williams Wilkin, 26. The couple says they are on their first marriage, have been wed eight years, and Hattie has borne three children, all living. They are: Edgar F., seven, Everett R., five, and Marjorie M., two. All in the home and their parents were born in Ohio.

Joseph Everett married **Anna Mary Tolle** on December 23, 1915, in Highland Co., Ohio.[430] They had two children. Anna Mary Tolle was born in Blue Creek, Jefferson Twp., Adams Co., Ohio, on October 12, 1893.[430] She was also known as **Mary**. She reached age 82 and died in Cincinnati, Hamilton Co., Ohio, on October 30, 1975.[431, 432] Anna Mary Tolle Williams Glenn was buried in Stroup Cemetery, Dodson Twp., Highland Co., Ohio.[433]

Anna Mary was living in Hillsboro, Liberty Twp., Highland Co., Ohio and working as a telephone operator when she married Joseph E. Williams.[430]

In 1920, Josephus Williams is listed as "Joe Williams" in Dodson Twp., Highland Co., Ohio, *(Census Place: Dodson, Highland, Ohio; Roll: T625_1399; Page: 2A; Enumeration District: 83; Image: 83).* In the household are "Joe" Williams, age 30, a farmer; his wife, Anna Mary Tolle Williams, 28, and their daughter Imogene, two years and eight months. All were Ohio-born, like their parents.

After her first husband Joseph Everett Williams, died, Anna Mary Tolle Williams married Herbert Glenn.[434]

In 1930, Herbert and Anna Mary Tolle Williams Glenn are enumerated in Lynchburg, Dodson Twp., Highland Co., Ohio *(Census Place: Lynchburg, Highland, Ohio; Roll: 1823; Page: 2B; Enumeration District: 5; Image: 71.0)*. Herbert Glenn, age 36, was born in Ohio, as were his parents. He is an Rural Free Delivery mail carrier who states his first marriage occurred at age 32. Anna Mary Tolle Williams Glenn, also 36 years old, was born in Ohio, as was her father; this time, she says her mother was born in West Virginia. She says her first marriage was at age 22. With them are Anna's two children by Josephus Everett Williams: Imogene Williams, 12, and Paul T., nine.

In 1940, Anna Mary Tolle Williams Glenn is found in Mount Orab, Green Twp., Brown Co., Ohio *(Census Place: Mount Orab, Brown, Ohio; Roll: T627_3031; Page: 3B; Enumeration District: 8-6)*. Anna Mary Tolle Williams Glenn, age 46, says she is a widow and is working as a telephone operator. Living with her is her son Paul T., 19, a clerk in a retail grocery store. Both say they were born in Ohio, and were living in Highland Co., Ohio in 1935. Their home is at 89 South High Street.

Children of Joseph Everett Williams and Anna Mary Tolle:

+ 111 f I. **Hazel Imogene[9] Williams** was born in Dodson Twp., Highland Co., Ohio, on November 9, 1917.[435] She was also known as **Imogene** or **Genie**. Hazel Imogene died in Cincinnati, Hamilton Co., Ohio, on May 22, 2006.[435, 436]

+ 112 m II. **Paul T.[9] Williams** was born in Dodson Twp., Highland Co., Ohio, on July 4, 1920.[437, 438] He died in Deer Park, Hamilton Co., Ohio, on November 18, 2013.[437, 438]

50. Cary[8] Williams (*Mary E.[7] Stroup, Elvira[6] Pegan, Henry[5], Robert A.[4], Andrew[3], Andrew[2] Pagan, James[1]*) was born on February 25, 1890, in Salem Twp., Highland Co., Ohio.[147] He was the son of Samuel Williams and Mary E. Stroup (12). Cary died in Salem Twp., Highland Co., Ohio, on March 25, 1890.[147] He was buried in Stroup Cemetery, Dodson Twp., Highland Co., Ohio.[439]

51. Harley N.[8] Williams (*Mary E.[7] Stroup, Elvira[6] Pegan, Henry[5], Robert A.[4], Andrew[3], Andrew[2] Pagan, James[1]*) was born on December 28, 1896, in Dodson Twp., Highland Co., Ohio.[31, 148] He was the son of Samuel Williams and Mary E. Stroup (12). Harley N. died in Dodson Twp., Highland Co., Ohio, on July 26, 1963, at age 66.[149] He was buried in Stroup Cemetery, Dodson Twp., Highland Co., Ohio.[440, 441]

In 1930, Harley N. Williams, age 31, single, a farm laborer, is living with his parents, Samuel and Mary Stroup Williams, in Dodson Twp., Highland Co., Ohio *(Census Place: Dodson, Highland, Ohio; Roll: 1823; Page: 4A; Enumeration District: 6; Image: 90.0)*. He and his parents were born in Ohio. Samuel Williams is 75 and is still a farmer. He says he and his father were born in Ohio and his mother in Germany. Mary Stroup Williams is age 69, born Ohio as were her parents. Samuel and Mary say they were first married at age 23 and 18 respectively.

Harley N. married **Mary Johanna Freeman** on January 17, 1931, in Brown Co., Ohio.[442] They had six children. Mary Johanna Freeman was born in Perry Twp., Brown Co., Ohio, on November 14, 1902.[29, 443] She was also known as **Mary Jo**. Mary Johanna reached age 86 and died in Hillsboro, Liberty Twp., Highland Co., Ohio, on June 17, 1989.[29, 444] She was buried in Stroup Cemetery, Dodson Twp., Highland Co., Ohio.[444, 445]

Although on her marriage license Mary Jo Freeman Williams says she was born in Blanchester, Marion Twp., Clinton Co., Ohio and was age 27 (birth year 1903) on November 14, 1930, Brown Co, Ohio birth records confirm that she was born on November 2, 1902 in Perry Twp., Brown Co., Ohio.[442, 443]

Harley N. Williams is enumerated in Dodson Twp., Highland Co., Ohio in 1940 *(Census Place: Dodson, Highland, Ohio; Roll: T627_3085; Page: 1A; Enumeration District: 36-6)*. In the household are Harley N. Williams, age 43, a farmer; his wife, Mary Jo Freeman Williams, 37, and children Clarence, seven, Mary Elizabeth, six, Glenn Lewis, five, Dale "Matthew", four, and James Richard, two. All were born in Ohio, and Harley and Mary Jo and the older children were Highland County, Ohio residents in 1935. Their home is at 113-A Spilker Road. Next door is cousin Earl Spilker and his family.

Children of Harley N. Williams and Mary Johanna Freeman:

+ 113 m I. **Clarence E.⁹ Williams** was born in Dodson Twp., Highland Co., Ohio, on June 13, 1932.[31, 446, 447] He died in Hillsboro, Liberty Twp., Highland Co., Ohio, on August 29, 1996.[31, 446]

+ 114 f II. **Mary Elizabeth⁹ Williams** was born in Hillsboro, Liberty Twp., Highland Co., Ohio, on September 29, 1933.

+ 115 m III. **Glen Louis⁹ Williams** was born in Lynchburg, Dodson Twp., Highland Co., Ohio, on February 1, 1935.[31, 448] He died in Ponce de Leon, Holmes Co., Florida, on July 13, 2011.[31, 448]

+ 116 m IV. **Dale Mathew⁹ Williams** was born in Hillsboro, Liberty Twp., Highland Co., Ohio, on March 29, 1936.[31, 449] He died in Pawnee, Pawnee Twp., Sangamon Co., Illinois, on January 5, 1991.[31, 449]

+ 117 m V. **Stephen Thomas⁹ Williams** was born in Hillsboro, Liberty Twp., Highland Co., Ohio, on August 25, 1938.[450] He died in Dodson Twp., Highland Co., Ohio, on September 21, 1938.[450]

+ 118 m VI. **James Richard⁹ Williams** was born in Hillsboro, Liberty Twp., Highland Co., Ohio, on August 25, 1938.

52. **Infant Son⁸ Williams** (*Mary E.⁷ Stroup, Elvira⁶ Pegan, Henry⁵, Robert A.⁴, Andrew³, Andrew² Pagan, James¹*) was born between 1900 and 1910 in Dodson Twp., Highland Co., Ohio. He was the son of Samuel Williams and Mary E. Stroup (12). Infant Son died in Dodson Twp., Highland Co., Ohio, between 1900 and 1910. He was buried in Stroup Cemetery, Dodson Twp., Highland Co., Ohio.[451]

This child's headstone reads "Infant Williams, "sons of Sam'l and Mary Williams" and has no dates. Why the headstone says "sons" and not just "son" is confusing. Mary Stroup Williams states on the 1900 that she has borne seven children with six still surviving and in the 1910 census that she bore eight children, with six still alive. As son Cary Williams died in 1890, this unnamed infant was a single birth who was born and died between 1900-1910.[147]

53. **Bessie B.⁸ Spilker** (*Laura Arabella⁷ Stroup, Elvira⁶ Pegan, Henry⁵, Robert A.⁴, Andrew³, Andrew² Pagan, James¹*) was born on November 19, 1887, in Salem Twp., Highland Co., Ohio.[154, 155] She was the daughter of Joseph Henry Spilker and Laura Arabella Stroup (13). Bessie B. died in Dodson Twp., Highland Co., Ohio, on May 24, 1907, at age 19.[156] She is buried in Mount Olive Cemetery, Union Twp., Highland County, Ohio.[452]

Childless.

Bessie Fox is listed as buried in two places. She has a stone in Troutwine Cemetery, where her parents are buried.[453] However, according to her death certificate and burial records of Clinton County, Ohio, she is buried in Mount Olive Cemetery in Union Twp., Highland Co., Ohio, where her husband Stanley Fox and most of his family members are buried.[156, 452] (Note: This cemetery, which is just over the county line from Clinton County, is included in the Clinton County burial records because it has a New Vienna, Ohio mailing address. New Vienna is in Clinton County.)

Bessie B. married **Stanley W. Fox** on June 13, 1906, in Highland Co., Ohio.[454] Stanley W. Fox was born in Richland Co., Illinois, on February 13, 1883.[455, 456] He reached age 58 and died in Green Twp., Clinton Co., Ohio, on October 10, 1941.[457] Stanley W. is buried in Mount Olive Cemetery, Union Twp., Highland County, Ohio.[457]

After his wife Bessie Spilker Fox's death, Stanley W. Fox lived with his parents and then alone until his death.

In 1910, Stanley W. Fox is living with his parents, David H. and Sarah E. Wright Fox, in Green Twp., Clinton Co., Ohio *(Census Place: Green, Clinton, Ohio; Roll: T624_1160; Page: 6A; Enumeration District: 0064; Image: 773)*. Stanley is age 27, born Illinois, with his parents born in Ohio, a widower, and lists no occupation. His father David says he is a trader in stock.

Stanley Fox is still residing with his parents in 1920 in Green Twp., Clinton Co., Ohio *(Census Place: Green, Clinton, Ohio; Roll: T625_1355; Page: 5B; Enumeration District: 116; Image: 726)*. Stanley, a widower, is 38 years old and a mechanic in a garage. His father in a livery man in a feed stable. For some odd reason, Stanley is listed as born in Ohio.

In 1930, Stanley W. Fox, a widower, age 47 born Illinois, is living alone in New Vienna, Green Twp., Clinton Co., Ohio *(Census Place: New Vienna, Clinton, Ohio; Roll: 1761; Page: 6B; Enumeration District: 5; Image: 205.0)*. He lists his occupation as "none". Co., Ohio.

Stanley W. worked as a school bus driver in 1941.[457]

Although his Ohio death certificate claims he was born in 1882, his WWI Draft Registration and his Social Security Application and Claims information, both of which he signed himself, says he was born in 1883.[455, 456, 457]

54. Earl Everett⁸ Spilker (*Laura Arabella⁷ Stroup, Elvira⁶ Pegan, Henry⁵, Robert A.⁴, Andrew³, Andrew² Pagan, James¹*) was born on March 26, 1890, in Dodson Twp., Highland Co., Ohio.[157] He was the son of Joseph Henry Spilker and Laura Arabella Stroup (13). He lived in June 1942 in Perry Twp., Brown Co., Ohio. He died in a hospital in Cincinnati, Hamilton Co., Ohio, on June 16, 1942, at age 52.[157] Earl Everett was buried in Troutwine Cemetery, Dodson Twp., Highland Co., Ohio and Clark Twp., Clinton Co., Ohio.[157, 458]

Earl Everett married **Merle May Roades** on June 17, 1915, in Highland Co., Ohio.[459] They had one daughter. Merle May Roades was born in Clay Twp., Highland Co., Ohio, on June 7, 1897.[460, 461] Merle May lived in 1959 in Hillsboro, Liberty Twp., Highland Co., Ohio. She reached age 62 and died in a hospital in Cincinnati, Hamilton Co., Ohio, on September 8, 1959.[460, 462] Merle May Rhodes Spilker Sallee was buried in Troutwine Cemetery (also known as Webertown Cemetery), Dodson Twp., Highland Co., Ohio and Clark Twp., Clinton Co., Ohio.[463]

Earl E. Spilker is found in Dodson Twp., Highland Co., Ohio in 1920 *(Census Place: Dodson, Highland, Ohio; Roll: T625_1399; Page: 5A; Enumeration District: 83; Image: 89)*. Earl E. Spilker is age 29, a farmer and his wife Merle M. Roades Spilker is 22. Both say they and their parents were Ohionatives.

In 1930, Earl E. Spilker is still listed in Dodson Twp., Highland Co., Ohio *(Census Place: Dodson, Highland, Ohio; Roll: 1823; Page: 6A; Enumeration District: 6; Image: 94.0)*. In the household are Earl Spilker, 40, a farmer; and his wife, Merle Roades Spilker, 32. They were first married at ages 25 and 18 respectively. Living with them is their daughter Charlotte J. ("Charlette"), nine. All in the home say they and their parents were born in Ohio.

Earl E. Spilker is again residing in Dodson Twp., Highland Co., Ohio in 1940 *(Census Place: Dodson, Highland, Ohio; Roll: T627_3085; Page: 1A; Enumeration District: 36-6)*. Earl Spilker, age 50, is still farming. With him are his wife, Merle Roades Spilker, 42, and their daughter Charlotte M., 19. All were born in Ohio and say they were living in the same house on 113-A Spilker Road in 1935. Next door is cousin Harley N. Williams and his family.

After Earl's death, Earl Everett Spilker, Merle M. Rhodes Spilker married John Bradley Sallee on December 30, 1946.[463, 464]

Daughter of Earl Everett Spilker and Merle May Roades:

+ 119 f I. **Charlotte Jean⁹ Spilker** was born in Dodsonville, Dodson Twp., Highland Co., Ohio, on October 14, 1920.[31, 465, 466] She died in

Clearwater, Pinellas Co., Florida, on November 6, 2004.[31, 465, 466]

55. Ralph Henry[8] Spilker (*Laura Arabella[7] Stroup, Elvira[6] Pegan, Henry[5], Robert A.[4], Andrew[3], Andrew[2] Pagan, James[1]*) was born on February 8, 1892, in Dodson Twp., Highland Co., Ohio.[31] He was the son of Joseph Henry Spilker and Laura Arabella Stroup (13). He resided in 1966 in Dodsonville, Dodson Twp., Highland Co., Ohio. Ralph Henry died in a hospital in Cincinnati, Hamilton Co., Ohio, on December 21, 1966, at age 74.[158] He was buried in Troutwine Cemetery, Dodson Twp., Highland Co., Ohio and Clark Twp., Clinton Co., Ohio.[467, 468]

Ralph Henry married **Isma Roush Faris** before 1917. They divorced. They had two children. Isma Faris was born in Dodson Twp., Highland Co., Ohio, on June 14, 1894.[31, 469] She reached age 86 and died in North College Hill, Springfield Twp., Hamilton Co., Ohio, on May 14, 1981.[470, 471] Isma R. was buried in Spring Grove Cemetery, Cincinnati, Hamilton Co., Ohio.[472]

In 1920, Ralph H. Spilker is enumerated in Liberty Twp., Highland Co., Ohio *(Census Place: Liberty, Highland, Ohio; Roll: T625_1399; Page: 4B; Enumeration District: 90; Image: 208)*. In the household are Ralph H. Spilker, 27, a farmer; Isma Faris Spilker, 26, and son Joseph, two years and eight months. All in the home were Ohio-born, as were their parents.

Ralph and Isma divorce between 1922-1930.

By 1930, Ralph Spilker is found in Cincinnati, Hamilton Co., Ohio *(Cincinnati, Hamilton, Ohio; Roll: 1806; Page: 19B; Enumeration District: 24; Image: 976.0)*. Ralph, who is listed as age 40, is now divorced and is a roomer in the home of James and Susie Lee. His occupation is denoted as a carpenter.

Ralph H. Spilker was the informant on his father Joseph H. Spilker's death certificate in 1939. At the time, Ralph was living in Fayetteville, Perry Twp., Brown Co., Ohio.[151]

Ralph Spilker is living with his newly widowed mother, Laura Arabella Stroup Spilker, in 1940 in Dodsonville, Dodson Twp., Highland Co., Ohio *(Census Place: Dodson, Highland, Ohio; Roll: T627_3085; Page: 8A; Enumeration District: 36-6)*. Ralph Spilker, 48, lists no occupation. Neither does the head of the household, "Belle" Spilker, 75. Both say they were born in Ohio and were living in Highland County, Ohio in 1935.

In 1930, Ralph's ex-wife Isma Roush Faris Spilker is enumerated in Cincinnati, Hamilton Co., Ohio *(Census Place: Cincinnati, Hamilton, Ohio; Roll: 1806; Page: 15A; Enumeration District: 416; Image: 1031.0)*. Isma R. Faris Spilker, age 35, divorced, lists no occupation. With her are her children Joseph B., 12, and Shirley, seven. All and their parents were born in Ohio.

Isma Faris Spilker is again found in Cincinnati, Hamilton Co., Ohio in Mt. Auburn Twp. in 1940 *(Census Place: Cincinnati, Hamilton, Ohio; Roll: T627_3192; Page: 62B; Enumeration District: 91-169A)*. In the home are Isma Faris Spilker, age 45, divorced, a saleslady; her daughter, Shirley Lois Gail Spilker, 18, and Isma's widowed mother, Bernadine Good, 65. All say they were born in Ohio and living in Cincinnati (Mt. Auburn Twp.) in 1935. However, Isma Faris Spilker's full name is Isma Roush Faris Spilker, and her mother was Electa Roush of Highland Co., Ohio. It is unknown if Electa Roush Faris and "Bernadine Good" are the same person.

Children of Ralph Henry Spilker and Isma Roush Faris Spilker:

+ 120 m I. **Joseph Benjamin[9] Spilker** was born in Fayetteville, Perry Twp., Brown Co., Ohio, on April 15, 1917.[472, 473] He died in Cincinnati, Hamilton Co., Ohio, on September 28, 1940.[472, 474]

+ 121 f II. **Shirley Lois Gail[9] Spilker** was born in Hillsboro, Liberty Twp., Highland Co., Ohio, on March 5, 1922.[31, 475, 476, 477] She died in

Greenhills, Hamilton Co., Ohio, on January 27, 2003.[31, 475, 477, 478]

56. Hazel A.[8] **Spilker** (*Laura Arabella*[7] *Stroup, Elvira*[6] *Pegan, Henry*[5]*, Robert A.*[4]*, Andrew*[3]*, Andrew*[2] *Pagan, James*[1]) was born on September 10, 1895, in Dodson Twp., Highland Co., Ohio.[159] She was the daughter of Joseph Henry Spilker and Laura Arabella Stroup (13). Hazel A. died in Clearwater, Pinellas Co., Florida, on January 12, 2000, at age 104.[31, 160, 161] She was buried in Troutwine Cemetery, Dodson Twp., Highland Co., Ohio and Clark Twp., Clinton Co., Ohio.[479]

Childless.

Hazel Spilker is listed as "Hazel Silker" in Dayton, Montgomery Co., Ohio in 1920 *(Census Place: Dayton Ward 11, Montgomery, Ohio; Roll: T625_1422; Page: 12A; Enumeration District: 201; Image: 540)*. Hazel, who says she is 22 (she is 25), born Ohio as were her parents, is a lodger in the home of Edward and Dora Wagner. She lists her occupation as saleslady in a department store.

Hazel A. married **Harold J. Cruger,** a clerk at Wilbur Wright airfield in Bath, Greene Co., Ohio, on November 21, 1921. Harold J. Cruger was born in Pulaski Twp., Jackson Co., Michigan, on April 21, 1898.[31, 480] Harold J. reached age 76 and died in Clearwater, Pinellas Co., Florida, on May 15, 1974.[31, 480] He was buried in Troutwine Cemetery, Dodson Twp., Highland Co., Ohio and Clark Twp., Clinton Co., Ohio.[481, 482]

Harold J. and Hazel Spilker Cruger are enumerated in Dayton, Montgomery Co., Ohio in 1930 *(Census Place: Dayton, Montgomery, Ohio; Roll: 1855; Page: 7A; Enumeration District: 130; Image: 778.0)*. Harold J. Cruger, age 30, is a supervisor in aeronautics who says he and his parents were born in Michigan. Hazel Spilker Cruger says she is also 30 years old (she is 34), and she and her parents were born in Ohio. Both say they were first married at age 23.

Harold J. and Hazel Spilker Cruger are not found in the 1940 census. They may have been moving to Florida at the time.

Hazel Spilker Cruger had matched her mother's age of 104 when she died.[161] Oddly, her date of birth in her social security records is September 10, 1898.[31, 160] But her birth record and census enumerations indicate she was born in 1895.[159]

57. Elton[8] **Stroup?** (*John Henry*[7] *Stroup, Elvira*[6] *Pegan, Henry*[5]*, Robert A.*[4]*, Andrew*[3]*, Andrew*[2] *Pagan, James*[1]) was born about September 17, 1892 in Dodson Twp., Highland Co., Ohio. He was the son of John Henry Stroup (14) and Catherine Olive Ballentine. Elton died in Dodson Twp., Highland Co., Ohio, on September 17, 1892.[167] He was buried in Stroup Cemetery, Dodson Twp., Highland Co., Ohio.[167]

58. Edgar[8] **Stroup?** (*John Henry*[7] *Stroup, Elvira*[6] *Pegan, Henry*[5]*, Robert A.*[4]*, Andrew*[3]*, Andrew*[2] *Pagan, James*[1]) was born about September 17, 1892 in Dodson Twp., Highland Co., Ohio. He was the son of John Henry Stroup (14) and Catherine Olive Ballentine. Edgar was born about September 17, 1892. Edgar died in Dodson Twp., Highland Co., Ohio, on September 20, 1892.[168] He was buried in Stroup Cemetery, Dodson Twp., Highland Co., Ohio.[168]

59. Vernice Catherine[8] **Stroup** (*John Henry*[7]*, Elvira*[6] *Pegan, Henry*[5]*, Robert A.*[4]*, Andrew*[3]*, Andrew*[2] *Pagan, James*[1]) was born on April 20, 1894, in Dodson Twp., Highland Co., Ohio.[169, 170] She was the daughter of John Henry Stroup (14) and Catherine Olive Ballentine. Vernice Catherine died in Hillsboro, Liberty Twp., Highland Co., Ohio, on July 5, 1971, at age 77.[170, 171] She was buried Barnes Cemetery, Fairview, New Market Twp., Highland Co., Ohio.[483]

For some reason, Vernice Stroup Ludwick does not have a death certificate which appears in any online Ohio death index. She does have an entry on the U.S. Social Security Applications and Claims Index, but her birthdate is given as October 20, 1894.[171] Highland County, Ohio birth records, her marriage license, and her obituary state her birth date as April 20, 1894.[169, 170, 484]

Vernice Catherine married **Claude Hogard Ludwick** on August 29, 1913, in Highland Co., Ohio.[484] They had five sons. Claude Hogard Ludwick was born in Hamer Twp., Highland Co., Ohio, on September 10, 1892.[485, 486] Claude

Hogard also resided in 1978 in Allensburg, Liberty Twp., Highland Co., Ohio. Claude Hogard reached age 85 and died in a facility in Hillsboro, Liberty Twp., Highland Co., Ohio, on February 16, 1978.[487] He was buried in Barnes Cemetery, Fairview, New Market Twp., Highland Co., Ohio.[488, 489]

In 1920, Claude H. and Vernice Stroup Ludwick are living with Claude's mother Martha Ludwick, who is listed as head of household, in Dodson Twp., Highland Co., Ohio *(Census Place: Dodson, Highland, Ohio; Roll: T625_1399; Page: 5A; Enumeration District: 83; Image: 89)*. Claude H. Ludwick is age 27, a farmer, born in Ohio as were his parents. Vernice Stroup Ludwick is 25, born Ohio as were her parents. They have three sons: Dwight H., five, Lloyd C., three years and one month, and Harold S., seven months, all born in Ohio. Claude's mother, Martha Ludwick, is 61, born Ohio, with her father born in Kentucky and her mother in Ohio.

Claude H. and Vernice Stroup Ludwick are still residing in Dodson Twp., Highland Co., Ohio in 1930 *(Census Place: Dodson, Highland, Ohio; Roll: 1823; Page: 1B; Enumeration District: 6; Image: 85.0)*. Claude is listed as head of household, but his mother Martha, now 72, is still living with them. Claude H. Ludwick is age 37, a farmer, who says he was first married at age 21. His wife, Vernice Stroup Ludwick, 35, says she was first married at 19. Children in the home are: Dwight H., 15, Lloyd C., 13, Harold, 11, "Evret", nine, and Lowell, seven. All were born in Ohio like their parents, except for Martha B. Ludwick's father, who was born in Kentucky.

In 1940, Claude and Vernice Stroup Ludwick continue to live in Dodson Twp., Highland Co., Ohio *(Census Place: Dodson, Highland, Ohio; Roll: T627_3085; Page: 5B; Enumeration District: 36-6)*. Claude H. Ludwick, age 48, is still a farmer. Vernice Stroup Ludwick is 46 years old. With them are sons Harold S., 20, Everett O., 18, both listed as farm laborers; and Lowell, 16. Claude's mother, Martha Ludwick, age 84 and widowed, is also in the home, which is on U.S. Highway 50. All were born in Ohio.

Sons of Vernice Catherine Stroup and Claude Hogard Ludwick:

+ 122 m I. **Dwight H.[9] Ludwick** was born in Dodson Twp., Highland Co., Ohio, on December 4, 1914.[31, 490] He was also known as **Doc**. Dwight H. died in Fort Lauderdale, Broward Co., Florida, on July 4, 1989.[31, 490]

+ 123 m II. **Lloyd Claude[9] Ludwick** was born in Dodson Twp., Highland Co., Ohio, on December 7, 1916.[31, 491] He died in Hillsboro, Liberty Twp., Highland Co., Ohio, on January 8, 2006.[31, 491]

+ 124 m III. **Harold Stroup[9] Ludwick** was born in Dodson Twp., Highland Co., Ohio, on May 30, 1919.[31, 492] He died in Hillsboro, Liberty Twp., Highland Co., Ohio, on August 24, 1996.[31, 492]

+ 125 m IV. **Everett O.[9] Ludwick** was born in Dodson Twp., Highland Co., Ohio, on August 21, 1921.[31, 493] He was also known as **Rosie**. Everett O. died in Dayton, Montgomery Co., Ohio, on January 20, 1987.[494, 495]

+ 126 m V. **Lowell Arthur[9] Ludwick** was born in Dodson Twp., Highland Co., Ohio, on August 6, 1923.[496, 497, 498] He died in a hospital in Wilmington, Union Twp., Clinton Co., Ohio, on November 13, 1961.[497, 498]

60. Clarence Harold[8] Stroup (*John Henry[7], Elvira[6] Pegan, Henry[5], Robert A.[4], Andrew[3], Andrew[2] Pagan, James[1]*) was born on January 8, 1899, in Dodson Twp., Highland Co., Ohio.[31, 172, 173] He was the son of John Henry Stroup (14) and Catherine Olive Ballentine. He died in Xenia, Xenia Twp., Greene Co., Ohio, on January 20, 1980.[174, 175] Clarence H. was buried in Stroup Cemetery, Dodson Twp., Highland Co., Ohio.[175, 499]

Clarence Harold Stroup is not found in the 1930 census.

Clarence Harold married **Electra Lucile Connor** before 1937. They had one son. Electra Lucile Connor was born in Westboro, Jefferson Twp., Clinton Co., Ohio, on February 24, 1901.[500, 501] She was also known as **Lucile**. Electra Lucile reached age 103 and died in Xenia, Xenia Twp., Greene Co., Ohio, on June 9, 2004.[500, 501] She was buried in Stroup Cemetery, Dodson Twp., Highland Co., Ohio.[502]

In 1940, Clarence Stroup, listed as "Stroub", is enumerated in Jefferson Twp., Clinton Co. Ohio *(Census Place: Jefferson, Clinton, Ohio; Roll: T627_3042; Page: 2A; Enumeration District: 14-9)*. In the household are Clarence Stroup, age 40, a farmer, his wife, Lucille Connor Stroup, 39, and their son, James Richard, two. All were born in Ohio. Clarence and Lucille say they were living in Chillicothe, Scioto Twp., Ross Co., Ohio in 1935. The house is on Township Road.

Clarence Stroup had moved to Springfield, Ohio by 1941. Later, he lived in Spring Valley, Spring Valley Twp., Greene Co., Ohio, where his wife retired from many years of teaching in 1968.[500] In Spring Valley, he worked at several hardware stores.[175]

Son of Clarence Harold. Stroup and Electra Lucile Connor:

+ 127 m I. **James Richard**[9] **Stroup** was born in Jefferson Twp., Clinton Co., Ohio, on October 17, 1937.[503] He died in a hospital in Dayton, Montgomery Co., Ohio, on March 8, 2014.[504]

61. Sadie D.[8] **Ballentine** (*Elma Jane*[7] *Stroup, Elvira*[6] *Pegan, Henry*[5]*, Robert A.*[4]*, Andrew*[3]*, Andrew*[2] *Pagan, James*[1]) was born on August 5, 1891, in Dodson Twp., Highland Co., Ohio.[180] She was the daughter of Robert E. Ballentine II and Elma Jane Stroup (15). Sadie D. lived in October 1951 in Wilmington, Union Twp., Clinton Co., Ohio. She died in a hospital in Dayton, Montgomery Co., Ohio, on October 1, 1951, at age 60.[180] Sadie D. was buried in Sugar Grove Cemetery, Wilmington, Union Twp., Clinton Co., Ohio.[180, 505]

Sadie D. married **Silas Laymon Vance** before 1913. They had three children. Silas Laymon Vance was born in Clark Twp., Clinton Co., Ohio, on January 22, 1888.[506, 507] He reached age 73 and died in Columbus, Franklin Co., Ohio, on April 29, 1961.[508] Silas Laymon was buried in Sugar Grove Cemetery, Wilmington, Union Twp., Clinton Co., Ohio.[509, 510]

At the time of his 1917 WWI draft registration, Silas Laymon Vance and his family were residents of Westboro, Jefferson Twp., Clinton Co., Ohio.[507]

Silas Laymon and Sadie D. Ballentine Vance are enumerated in Goshen Twp., Clermont Co., Ohio in 1920 *(Census Place: Goshen, Clermont, Ohio; Roll: T625_1355; Page: 10A; Enumeration District: 53; Image: 136)*. In the household are Silas Vance, age 31, a farmer; his wife Sadie D. Ballentine Vance, 28, and their daughter Thelma, six. All in the household, and their parents, were Ohio natives.

In 1930, Silas and Sadie D. Ballentine Vance are still in Goshen Twp., Clermont Co., Ohio *(Census Place: Goshen, Clermont, Ohio; Roll: 1757; Page: 13B; Enumeration District: 6; Image: 1007.0)*. Silas Vance, age 43, is a farmer and his wife, Sadie D. Ballentine Vance is age 39. The couple says they were first married at ages 28 and 20 respectively. Living with them are children Thelma, 16, Inez, 11 (Incorrect—she was nine), and Robert, seven. Also in the home is Sadie's mother, Elma J. Stroup Ballentine, listed just as "Ballentine", age 60, a widow. All were born in Ohio, as were their parents.

The Vance family moved from Wilmington, Ohio to Columbus, Ohio almost immediately after the death of their son, Robert in 1939.

Silas and Sadie Ballentine Vance are found in 1940 in Columbus, Franklin Co., Ohio *(Census Place: Columbus, Franklin, Ohio; Roll: T627_3248; Page: 4B; Enumeration District: 93-240)*. Silas Vance, age 52, is a buyer with the Farm Bureau (Co-op). His wife, Sadie Ballentine Vance, is 48 years old. With them is daughter Inez, 19. All were born in Ohio, and say they were living in Wilmington, Union Twp., Clinton Co., Ohio in 1935. Their home is at 1597 Neil Avenue.

After Sadie D. Ballentine Vance died, Silas Vance married Opal Unknown.

Children of Sadie D. Ballentine and Silas Laymon Vance:

+ 128 f I. **Thelma Lavonne⁹ Vance** was born in Clark Twp., Clinton Co., Ohio or Lynchburg, Dodson Twp., Highland Co., Ohio, on July 16, 1913.[31, 511, 512] She died in a hospital in Millersburg, Hardy Twp., Holmes Co., Ohio, on March 6, 1993.[511, 513]

+ 129 f II. **Inez⁹ Vance** was born in Goshen Twp., Clermont Co., Ohio, on April 1, 1921.[514, 515, 516] She died in a facility in Dayton, Montgomery Co., Ohio, on March 5, 1989.[514, 516]

+ 130 m III. **Robert N.⁹ Vance** was born in Goshen Twp., Clermont Co., Ohio, on October 17, 1922.[517] He died in Wilmington, Union Twp., Clinton Co., Ohio, on June 13, 1939.[517]

62. Letha May⁸ Ballentine (*Elma Jane⁷ Stroup, Elvira⁶ Pegan, Henry⁵, Robert A.⁴, Andrew³, Andrew² Pagan, James¹*) was born on October 21, 1899, in Dodson Twp., Highland Co., Ohio.[31, 181] She was also known as **Letha**. She was the daughter of Robert E. Ballentine II and Elma Jane Stroup (15). She lived in 1976 in Lebanon, Turtle Creek Twp., Warren Co., Ohio. She died in a hospital in Wilmington, Union Twp., Clinton Co., Ohio, on February 17, 1976, at age 76.[182] Letha May was buried in Deerfield Cemetery, South Lebanon, Union Twp., Warren Co., Ohio.[518]

Birth records and census data spell her name Leatha; her death certificate and tombstone read Letha.[181, 182, 518]

Letha May married **Ennis Edmond Hawthorne** before 1920. They divorced. They had one daughter. Ennis Edmond Hawthorne was born in Blanchester, Marion Twp., Clinton Co., Ohio, on January 18, 1892.[519, 520] He reached age 73 and died in Norwood, Mill Creek Twp., Hamilton Co., Ohio, on August 15, 1965.[521] Ennis Edmond was buried in Greenlawn Cemetery, Milford, Miami Twp., Clermont Co., Ohio.[522]

In 1920, Ennis and Letha Ballentine Hawthorne are enumerated in Goshen Twp., Clermont Co., Ohio (*Census Place: Goshen, Clermont, Ohio; Roll: T625_1355; Page: 11A; Enumeration District: 53; Image: 138*). Ennis Hawthorne, age 28, is a farmer. Letha Ballentine Hawthorne is 20 years old. Both were born in Ohio, as were their parents. Living with them is Ennis' partner in the farming venture, Clyde Collis, 23, born Ohio.

Ennis and Letha Ballentine Hawthorne are found in 1930 in Salem Twp., Warren Co., Ohio (*Census Place: Salem, Warren, Ohio; Roll: 1890; Page: 5B; Enumeration District: 18; Image: 940.0*). In the home are Ennis Hawthorne, age 38, a farmer; his wife, Leatha Ballentine Hawthorne, 29, and their daughter Betty, age nine. All and their parents were born in Ohio. Ennis and Leatha say they were first married at ages 24 and 16 respectively.

Ennis and Leatha Ballentine Hawthorne divorce after 1930.

Letha May Ballentine Hawthorne married **Charles Cleveland Henderson** after 1930. Charles Cleveland Henderson was born in Washington Twp., Brown Co., Ohio, on March 25, 1887.[523, 524] Charles Cleveland reached age 76 and died in Morrow, Salem Twp., Warren Co., Ohio, on April 25, 1964.[525, 526] He was buried in Deerfield Cemetery, South Lebanon, Union Twp., Warren Co., Ohio.[527]

Charles Cleveland and Leatha May Ballentine Henderson are enumerated in Union Twp. Warren Co., Ohio in 1940 (*Census Place: Union, Warren, Ohio; Roll: T627_3164; Page: 3A; Enumeration District: 83-31*). Charles C. Henderson, age 52, is a plasterer. "Letha" Ballentine Henderson is 39 and says she is a wallpaper hanger. Both say they were born in Ohio and were living in Warren Co., Ohio in 1935. Their home is in a rural area and no address or road is given.

Charles Cleveland Henderson states on his WWI draft registration that he was born on March 24,

1887 in Georgetown, Pleasant Twp., Brown Co., Ohio.[528] But he says March 24, 1888 in Brown Co., Ohio on his WWII draft registration.[529] On September 11, 1952, he petitions the Warren County, Ohio Probate Court to issue a delayed birth certificate, and gives March 25, 1887 as his correct date of birth and his birthplace as "near Sardinia", Brown Co., Ohio. His older half-brother, Thomas L. Henderson, is a witness who attests to Charles' birthdate and place.[523]

Daughter of Letha May Ballentine and Ennis Edmond Hawthorne:

+ 131 f I. **Betty Louise**[9] **Hawthorne** was born in Goshen Twp., Clermont Co., Ohio, on October 13, 1920.[530] She died in a hospital in Montgomery, Sycamore Twp., Hamilton Co., Ohio, on December 12, 1998.[530, 531]

63. Frederick James Frank[8] **Pegan** (*Adolphus Vonesse*[7], *Granville*[6], *Henry*[5], *Robert A.*[4], *Andrew*[3], *Andrew*[2] *Pagan, James*[1]) was born on October 9, 1893, in Dodson Twp., Highland Co., Ohio.[31, 191] He was also known as **Frank**. He was the son of Adolphus Vonesse Pegan (18) and Teresa Graham. He died in Cincinnati, Hamilton Co., Ohio, on November 19, 1972, at age 79.[192] Frederick James Frank was buried in Gate of Heaven Cemetery, Montgomery, Sycamore Twp., Hamilton Co., Ohio.[532]

Although his parents listed him as "Fred" on census forms, Frederick Pegan rarely used Frederick or Fred in his adult life. He was always known as Frank. In fact, some of his descendants were surprised when told by the author that his name was Frederick on his birth certificate.[191]

Frank Pegan is listed as Fred Pegan in the 1900 census (*Census Place: Dodson, Highland, Ohio; Roll: T623_1286; Page: 7A; Enumeration District: 107; Adolphus Pegan, head of household*). He lists his birth date as August 9, 1894 on his WWII draft registration card.[533] but his birth record, his WWI draft registration and his Social Security information say he was born on August 9, 1893.[31, 191, 534, 535]

Frederick James Frank married **Clara Elizabeth Fye** on May 10, 1916, in Hamilton Co., Ohio.[536] They had three children. Clara Elizabeth Fye was born in Cincinnati, Hamilton Co., Ohio, on February 26, 1895.[537] Clara Elizabeth reached age 78 and died in Cincinnati, Hamilton Co., Ohio, on March 7, 1973.[538] She was buried in Gate of Heaven Cemetery, Montgomery, Sycamore Twp., Hamilton Co., Ohio.[539]

Frank Frederick James Pegan is enumerated as Frank Pegan in Norwood, Mill Creek Twp., Hamilton Co., Ohio in 1920 (*Census Place: Norwood Ward 1, Hamilton, Ohio; Roll: T625_1395; Page: 7A; Enumeration District: 498; Image: 741*). "Frank Pegan" age 26, born Ohio, says his father was born in Ohio and his mother in Germany. He is a pressman at a printing company. The census taker must have been confused, as Teresa Graham Pegan was born in Ohio. Clara Fye Pegan, 24, also says she and her father were born in Ohio and her mother in Germany. Their children, Robert, 2, and Ruth, an infant, are with them in the home. His mother, Teresa Pegan, and younger brother William H. are also living in Norwood.

In 1930, Frederick "Frank" Pegan is still in Norwood, Mill Creek Twp., Hamilton Co., Ohio (*Census Place: Norwood, Hamilton, Ohio; Roll: 1818; Page: 13A; Enumeration District: 306; Image: 276.0*). In the home are (Frederick) Frank Pegan, 37, born Ohio as were his parents, a printer at a card company; Clara Fye Pegan, 36, born Ohio with her parents in Germany; and children Robert H., 12, Ruth, nine, and Mary, three years and six months. All the children were born in Ohio. Frank and Clara Fye Pegan say they were first married at ages 21 and 20 respectively, so they have been married 16 years.

Frederick "Frank" J. Pegan continues to live in Norwood, Mill Creek Twp., Hamilton Co., Ohio in 1940 (*Census Place: Norwood, Hamilton, Ohio; Roll: T627_3078; Page: 13B; Enumeration District: 31-78*). The family is living at 1846 Cleveland Street. "Frank J." Pegan, age 46, is a printer at a labels manufacturing plant. Clara Fye Pegan is 45 years old. Children in the home are Robert, 22, a clerk at a clothing manufacturer, Ruth, 20, a stenographer at a pillow manufacturer, and Mary C., 13.

All were born in Ohio and were living in the same house in 1935.

Mary Pegan Kissel, daughter of Frederick James Frank Pegan, says that her father witnessed his father Adolphus V. Pegan's horrific death. Also, Mary says her father told of going for walks through the fields to escape the screams of his younger brother Robert, who was dying of meningitis following a case of measles.[540]

Children of Frederick James Frank Pegan and Clara Elizabeth Fye:

+ 132 m I. **Robert Henry**[9] **Pegan** was born in Norwood, Mill Creek Twp., Hamilton Co., Ohio, on October 18, 1917.[31, 541, 542, 543] He died in Garden Grove, Orange Co., California, on June 13, 1990.[31, 541, 543]

+ 133 f II. **Ruth Mary**[9] **Pegan** was born in Norwood, Mill Creek Twp., Hamilton Co., Ohio, on October 26, 1919.[544, 545] She died in Cincinnati, Hamilton Co., Ohio, on November 19, 2005.[544, 545]

+ 134 f III. **Mary C.**[9] **Pegan** was born in Norwood, Mill Creek Twp., Hamilton Co., Ohio, on August 19, 1926.[546]

64. Robert[8] **Pegan** (*Adolphus Vonesse*[7], *Granville*[6], *Henry*[5], *Robert A.*[4], *Andrew*[3], *Andrew*[2] *Pagan, James*[1]) was born on November 24, 1895, in Dodson Twp., Highland Co., Ohio or Clinton Co., Ohio.[193,194] He was the son of Adolphus Vonesse Pegan (18) and Teresa Graham. He died in Jefferson Twp., Clinton Co., Ohio, on July 14, 1913, at age 17.[193, 195] Robert was buried in Troutwine Cemetery, Dodson Twp., Highland Co., Ohio and Clark Twp., Clinton Co., Ohio.[193]

65. William Henry[8] **Pegan** (*Adolphus Vonesse*[7], *Granville*[6], *Henry*[5], *Robert A.*[4], *Andrew*[3], *Andrew*[2] *Pagan, James*[1]) was born on November 23, 1903, in Dodson Twp., Highland Co., Ohio.[196,197] He was the son of Adolphus Vonesse Pegan (18) and Teresa Graham. William Henry was living in 1963 in Bel-Nor, St. Louis Co., Missouri. He died in a hospital in Richmond Heights, St. Louis Co., Missouri, on November 5, 1963, at age 59.[197, 198] William Henry was buried in Calvary Cemetery and Mausoleum, St. Louis, Missouri.[197, 198]

William Henry married **Marie E. Moeller** before 1927. They had one daughter. Marie E. Moeller was born in Dayton, Campbell Co., Kentucky, on December 4, 1903.[31, 547, 548] Marie E. reached age 85 and died in St. Louis, Missouri, on August 5, 1989.[31, 547, 548] She was buried in Calvary Cemetery and Mausoleum, St. Louis, Missouri.[547]

William H. Pegan is enumerated in Columbus, Franklin Co., Ohio in 1930 *(Census Place: Columbus, Franklin, Ohio; Roll: 1797; Page: 2A; Enumeration District: 229; Image: 1007.0)*. William H. Pegan, age 26, born in Ohio as were his parents, is the manager of a shoe company. With him is his wife, Marie E. Moeller Pegan, also 26, born Kentucky, with her father born in Ohio and her mother in Kentucky. The couple say they were both first married at age 19, so they have been married seven years. They have a daughter, E. Joan, age 2 years and 10 months, born Ohio. Also in the household is a servant, Flora Tigner, 15.

In 1940, William Henry Pegan is again found in Columbus, Franklin Co., Ohio *(Census Place: Columbus, Franklin, Ohio; Roll: T627_3246; Page: 63A; Enumeration District: 93-191)*. In the home are William Pegan, age 36, born Ohio, a manager of a (shoe) heel factory; his wife, Marie Moeller Pegan, also 36, born Kentucky; and daughter Betty Jo, 12, born Ohio. They were living in Columbus in 1935. Their home is at 742 Binns Boulevard. Also living in the house is Ruth Crane, 44, a servant.

According to his obituary in the *St. Louis (MO) Post-Dispatch*, William Henry Pegan was the general manager of the Mears division of the United Shoe Machinery Corporation in St. Louis.[549]

Daughter of William Henry Pegan and Marie E. Moeller:

+ 135 f I. **Elizabeth Joan**[9] **Pegan** was born in Columbus, Franklin Co., Ohio, on May 21, 1927.[31] She was also known as **Betty**. Elizabeth Joan died in St. Louis, Missouri, on October 24, 2010.[31, 550]

66. **Courtland Homer**[8] **Pegan** (*Henry Levy*[7], *Granville*[6], *Henry*[5], *Robert A.*[4], *Andrew*[3], *Andrew*[2] *Pagan, James*[1]) was born on December 25, 1904, in Dodson Twp., Highland Co., Ohio.[31, 203] He was the son of Henry Levy Pegan (19) and Elma Duvall Troutwine. He died in Hillsboro, Liberty Twp., Highland Co., Ohio, on June 23, 1983, at age 78.[204] Courtland Homer was buried in Troutwine Cemetery, Dodson Twp., Highland Co., Ohio.[551]

Courtland Homer married **Stella Madge Holladay** on November 28, 1925, in Highland Co., Ohio.[552] They had five children. Stella Madge Holladay was born in Wilmington, Union Twp., Clinton Co., Ohio, on August 14, 1906.[553, 554] Stella lived in September 1970 in Highland Co., Ohio. She reached age 64 and died in Fort Campbell, Calloway Co., Kentucky, on September 17, 1970.[555, 556] Stella was buried in Troutwine Cemetery, Dodson Twp., Highland Co., Ohio and Clark Twp., Clinton Co., Ohio.[556]

Although her birth record lists her surname as "Holiday", on her marriage license Stella writes her surname as "Holladay" and says she was born in Wilmington, Ohio on June 14, 1906.[552, 553] Her birthdate is incorrect, as her Clinton County birth record says she was born on August 14, 1906.[553]

Strangely, Stella Madge Holladay Pegan has a death certificate, listed only under her surname "Pegan" and issued in Ohio, which says she died "at home" in that state, but this is not correct.[557]

Courtland Homer Pegan is enumerated in Dodson Twp., Highland Co., Ohio in 1930 *(Census Place: Dodson, Highland, Ohio; Roll: 1823; Page: 4A; Enumeration District: 6; Image: 90.0).* Courtland H. Pegan is age 26, a farmer, says he was first married at age 20 His wife, Stella Holiday Pegan, 24, says she was 18 years old when she married. They have three daughters: Elma, four years and nine months, Thelma, three years and nine months, and Shirley, eight months. All in the home were born in Ohio, as were their parents.

In 1940, Courtland Pegan is still living in Dodson Twp., Highland Co., Ohio *(Census Place: Dodson, Highland, Ohio; Roll: T627_3085; Page: 1A; Enumeration District: 36-6).* In the household are Courtland H. Pegan, age 35, a farmer; his wife, Stella Holiday Pegan, 33, and their children Elma, 13, Thelma, 12, Shirley, 10, Robert, six, and Russell, four. Also in the home is Courtland's father, Henry Pegan, age 73, a widower with no occupation (probably retired). All in the home were born in Ohio, and say they were living in the same house at 113-A Setty Road in 1935 (except for Russell, was born after 1935).

Courtland Homer was living in 1948 in Washington Court House, Union Twp., Fayette Co., Ohio and in 1954 in Berrysville, Liberty Twp., Highland Co., Ohio.[558, 559]

In 1962, Courtland was living in New Market Twp. Highland Co. Ohio. On September 16 of that year, a 16-year-old arsonist torched Courtland's barn. The Highland County fire department responded, but the barn was already past saving. The fire department hosed water from a tanker truck onto a garage "filled with valuable tools and equipment" next to the barn and called for another tanker to help save that garage and the nearby Pegan house. But the second tanker was delayed because they had to stop and order an onlooker's car, which was blocking the road, to move. A third tanker ran into a ditch trying to circumvent another car, which was unattended and blocking another road leading to the Pegan property. The incident prompted an editorial in the *Highland County Press Gazette (Hillsboro, OH)* warning county residents to heed flashing lights, to stay away from emergency situations and not impede or interfere with first responders.[560]

His daughter Thelma Pegan Kelley Smith says Homer Pegan was very athletic and "could jump as high as he was" and "his muscles had muscles"![561]

Children of Courtland Homer Pegan and Stella Madge Holladay:

+ 136 f I. **Elma Mary**[9] **Pegan** was born in Dodson Twp., Highland Co., Ohio, on July 6, 1926.[31, 562, 563] She died in Lake Orion Heights, Oakland Co., Michigan, on August 21, 2013.[31, 563]

+ 137 f II. **Thelma**[9] **Pegan** was born in Dodson Twp., Highland Co., Ohio, on July 20, 1927.

+ 138 f III. **Shirley C.**[9] **Pegan** was born in Dodson Twp., Highland Co., Ohio, on March 8, 1930.[564, 565] She died in Searcy, White Co., Arkansas, on October 5, 2010.[31, 565]

+ 139 m IV. **Robert Ivan**[9] **Pegan** was born in Dodson Twp., Highland Co., Ohio, on August 13, 1933.[31, 566, 567] He died in Hillsboro, Liberty Twp., Highland Co., Ohio, on February 12, 1978.[567, 568]

+ 140 m V. **Russell William**[9] **Pegan** was born in Lynchburg, Dodson Twp., Highland Co., Ohio, on June 7, 1935.[31, 569] He died in a hospital in Buena Vista, Green Twp., Fayette Co., Ohio, on August 10, 2008.[31, 569]

67. **Clarence Chilton**[8] **Pegan** (*Henry Levy*[7], *Granville*[6], *Henry*[5], *Robert A.*[4], *Andrew*[3], *Andrew*[2] *Pagan, James*[1]) was born on September 21, 1906, in Dodson Twp., Highland Co., Ohio.[31, 205] He was also known as **Bud**. He was the son of Henry Levy Pegan (19) and and Elma Duvall Troutwine. Clarence Chilton died in St. Martin, Perry Twp., Brown County, Ohio, on June 23, 1988, at age 81.[206] He was buried in St. Martin Cemetery, St. Martin, Perry Twp., Brown Co., Ohio.[570]

Clarence Chilton "Bud" Pegan is age 23, single and living with his widower father Henry L. Pegan, age 61, and his unmarried sister Frances, 19, in Dodson Twp., Highland Co., Ohio in 1930 (*Census Place: Dodson, Highland, Ohio; Roll: 1823; Page: 3B; Enumeration District: 6; Image: 89.0*). Henry is listed as a farmer and Clarence as a farm laborer on the family farm. All were born in Ohio, as were their parents.

Clarence Chilton married **Grace Catherine Walsh** on August 20, 1931, in Brown Co., Ohio.[571] They had eight children. Grace Catherine Walsh was born in St. Martin, Perry Twp., Brown Co., Ohio, on November 30, 1912.[572, 573] Grace Catherine reached age 84 and died in Hillsboro, Liberty Twp., Highland Co., Ohio, on March 2, 1997.[572, 573] She was buried in St. Martin Cemetery, St. Martin, Perry Twp., Brown Co., Ohio.[573]

In 1940, Clarence Pegan is enumerated in Salem Twp., Highland Co., Ohio (*Census Place: Salem, Highland, Ohio; Roll: T627_3085; Page: 6A; Enumeration District: 36-27*). In the home are "Clawerence" Pegan, age 34, a farm laborer, his wife Grace Walsh Pegan, 27, and their children: Twins Richard and Rita, seven, Julia, five, and James, three. All were born in Ohio, and all but James are listed as residents of Brown County, Ohio in 1935. They are living in a rural area; no specific address is given.

Clarence Chilton Pegan and Grace Catherine Walsh had eight children, including:

+ 141 m I. **Richard Thomas**[9] **Pegan** was born in St. Martin, Perry Twp., Brown Co., Ohio, on November 17, 1932.[31, 574, 575] He died in a hospital in Wilmington, Union Twp., Clinton Co., Ohio, on December 7, 1986.[575, 576]

+ 142 f II. **Rita Gertrude**[9] **Pegan** was born in Brown Co., Ohio, on November 17, 1932.[577] She died in Cocoa, Brevard Co., Florida, on June 15, 2016.[578]

+ 143 f III. **Julia Evelyn**[9] **Pegan** was born in St. Martin, Perry Twp., Brown Co., Ohio, on October 26, 1934.[579, 580] She died in Hillsboro, Liberty Twp., Highland Co., Ohio, on March 23, 2000.[579, 580]

+ 144 m IV. **James Eugene**[9] **Pegan** was born in St. Martin, Perry Twp., Brown Co., Ohio, on June 20,

+ 145 m VII. **Lawrence Joseph⁹ Pegan** was born in St. Martin, Perry Twp. Brown Co., Ohio, on January 13, 1948.[583, 584] He was also known as **Larry**. Lawrence Joseph died in, a facility in Georgetown, Pleasant Twp., Brown Co., Ohio, on October 4, 2013.[583, 584]

+ 146 m VIII. **Clarence Edward⁹ Pegan II** was born in St. Martin, Perry Twp., Brown Co., Ohio, on July 15, 1950.[585, 586, 587] He was also known as **Eddie**. Clarence Edward died in a hospital in Batavia, Batavia Twp., Clermont Co., Ohio, on September 9, 2013.[586, 587]

68. Frances Elizabeth⁸ Pegan (*Henry Levy⁷, Granville⁶, Henry⁵, Robert A.⁴, Andrew³, Andrew² Pagan, James¹*) was born on November 25, 1911, in Dodson Twp., Highland Co., Ohio.[31, 207, 208, 209] She was the daughter of Henry Levy Pegan (19) and Elma Duvall Troutwine. She also resided in 1990 in Lynchburg, Dodson Twp., Highland Co., Ohio. Frances Elizabeth died in a facility in Pisgah, West Chester Twp., Butler Co., Ohio, on December 30, 1990, at age 79.[31, 207, 208, 209] She was buried in Troutwine Cemetery, Dodson Twp., Highland Co., Ohio and Clark Twp., Clinton Co., Ohio.[209]

Childless.

Frances Elizabeth married **Harley Stubbs** on November 25, 1933, in Highland Co., Ohio.[588] Harley Stubbs was born in Clark Twp., Clinton Co., Ohio, on August 3, 1903.[31, 589] Harley reached age 72 and died in Lynchburg, Dodson Twp., Highland Co., Ohio, on June 25, 1976.[590] He was buried in Troutwine Cemetery, Dodson Twp., Highland Co., Ohio and Clark Twp., Clinton Co., Ohio.[591]

In 1940, Harley and Frances Elizabeth Pegan Stubbs are enumerated in Lynchburg, Dodson Twp., Highland Co., Ohio *(Census Place: Lynchburg, Highland, Ohio; Roll: T627_3085; Page: 9A; Enumeration District: 36-5)*. Harley Stubbs, age 38, is a salesman and truck driver for Queen City Bottling. Frances Pegan Stubbs is 28 years old. Both were born in Ohio and say they were residents of Lynchburg in 1935. Their home is on Bobbitt Avenue between Main and Bridge.

Harley Stubbs later worked at Wright-Patterson Air Force Base in Dayton, Ohio.[591]

69. Mabel Letha⁸ Thompson (*Della Frances⁷ Pegan, Granville⁶, Henry⁵, Robert A.⁴, Andrew³, Andrew² Pagan, James¹*) was born on September 14, 1899, in Dodson Twp., Highland Co., Ohio.[219] She was the daughter of William Robert Thompson and Della Frances Pegan (20). Mabel Letha died in Washington, District of Columbia, on September 5, 1950, at age 50.[220] She was buried in Cedar Hill Cemetery, Suitland, Prince George's Co., Maryland.[220, 592]

Mabel Letha married **Galo S. Stroup** on November 26, 1919, in Highland Co., Ohio.[593] They had one son. Galo S. Stroup was born in Lynchburg, Dodson Twp., Highland Co., Ohio, on June 25, 1897.[31, 594] Galo S. reached age 71 and died in Washington, District of Columbia, on September 16, 1968.[31, 595] He was buried in Cedar Hill Cemetery, Suitland, Prince George's Co., Maryland.[595, 596] He was the son of Franklin Pierce Stroup and Barbara Allie Stultz.

In 1920, newlyweds Galo and Mabel Letha Thompson Stroup are living with Mabel's twice-widowed father, William Robert Thompson, in Dodson Twp., Highland Co., Ohio *(Census Place: Dodson, Highland, Ohio; Roll: T625_1399; Page: 6A; Enumeration District: 83; Image: 91)*. Galo Stroup, 22, is a high school teacher and Mabel Letha is age 20. William Robert Thompson, 46, is a farmer. William's other children are also in the home: Ruth, 18, his other daughter by his late first wife Della Frances Pegan; and his two children by his deceased second wife Elizabeth Childers Thompson: Robert, 11, and Genevieve, eight. All were born in Ohio, as were their parents.

By 1930, Galo and Mabel Letha Thompson Stroup have removed to Washington, DC *(Census Place: Washington, Washington, District of Columbia; Roll:*

294; Page: 16A; Enumeration District: 77; Image: 235.0). Galo S. Stroup, 32, is manager of a piano store, and Mabel Letha Thompson Stroup is age 30. The pair say they were first married at ages 23 and 21 respectively, but they seem to have been younger according to the previous census. With them is their son, "Edward T." (Thurl Esto Stroup), who is eight years old. All in the home, and their parents, were Ohio natives.

Galo and Mabel Thompson Stroup are not found in the 1940 census.

According to Mabel Thompson Stroup's obituary, Galo S. Stroup was a realtor in 1950.[220]

Son of Mabel Letha Thompson and Galo S. Stroup:

+ 147 m I. **Thurl Esto**[9] **Stroup** was born in Dodson Twp., Highland Co., Ohio, on June 13, 1921.[31, 595, 597, 598] He died in Washington, District of Columbia, on October 29, 1982.[31, 597, 598, 599]

70. **Ruth Frances**[8] **Thompson** (*Della Frances*[7] *Pegan, Granville*[6]*, Henry*[5]*, Robert A.*[4]*, Andrew*[3]*, Andrew*[2] *Pagan, James*[1]) was born on December 20, 1901, in Dodson Twp., Highland Co., Ohio.[31, 221] She was the daughter of William Robert Thompson and Della Frances Pegan (20). Ruth Frances died in St. Petersburg, Pinellas Co., Florida, on March 13, 1995, at age 93.[31, 221]

Never married.

In 1930, Ruth Thompson is enumerated in Williamson, Williamson Hollow Precinct, Mingo Co., West Virginia *(Census Place: Williamson, Mingo, West Virginia; Roll: 2547; Page: 17A; Enumeration District: 24; Image: 996.0).* Ruth Thompson, age 24 (she is really 29 years old), says she and her parents were born in Ohio and lists her occupation as assistant cashier in a furniture store. She is a lodger in a large boarding house run by Jacob and Mary Alpert.

Ruth F. Thompson is still a resident of Williamson, Williamson Hollow Precinct, Mingo Co., West Virginia in 1940 *(Census Place: Williamson, Mingo, West Virginia; Roll: T627_4431; Page: 13B; Enumeration District: 30-25).* Ruth Thompson, age 36 (she is 38), is a lodger in the home of Allen and Jennette R. Saretice at 32 Seventh Avenue. She is listed as born in West Virginia (Incorrect—she was born in Ohio), and is a bookkeeper in an automotive garage. Jennette R. Saretice at 32 Seventh Avenue She is listed as born in West Virginia (incorrect, she was born in Ohio), and is a bookkeeper in an automotive garage.

William Robert Thompson's obituary states his daughter Ruth F. Thompson was unmarried and living in Williamsburg, Virginia. But according to a follow-up funeral says Ruth was a resident of Williamson, Mingo Co., West Virginia.[214] The latter seems to be the correct place, as she was located there in the 1930 and 1940 censuses. Her sister Mabel L. Thompson Stroup's obituary mentions that Ruth's home in 1950 was Cincinnati, Hamilton Co., Ohio.[220]

71. **Lillie May**[8] **Daggy** (*Laura*[7] *Pegan, Thomas Jefferson*[6]*, Henry*[5]*, Robert A.*[4]*, Andrew*[3]*, Andrew*[2] *Pagan, James*[1]) was born on July 25, 1884, in Salem Twp., Highland Co., Ohio.[229, 230] She was the daughter of Thomas Llewellyn Hamer Daggy and Laura Pegan (22). She also resided in 1948 in Oxford, Oxford Twp., Butler Co., Ohio. Lillie May died in a hospital in Hamilton, Butler Co., Ohio, on February 21, 1948, at age 63.[229] She was buried in Oxford Cemetery, Oxford Twp., Butler Co., Ohio.[229, 600]

Lillie May married **Alexander C. DuVall** on December 12, 1903, in Highland Co., Ohio.[601] They had two children. Alexander C. DuVall was born in Pricetown, Salem Twp., Highland Co., Ohio, on June 19, 1869.[602] Alexander C. reached age 68 and died in Oxford Twp., Butler Co., Ohio, on January 30, 1938.[602] He was buried in Oxford Cemetery, Oxford Twp., Butler Co., Ohio.[602, 603]

The surname on most census forms is "Duvall", although the surname is usually seen as "DuVall".

Alexander C. and Lillie May Daggy DuVall are enumerated in Milford Twp., Butler Co., Ohio in 1910*(Census Place: Milford, Butler, Ohio; Roll: T624_1154; Page: 8A; Enumeration District: 0036; Image: 888).* Alexander C. Duvall, listed as "Alex C. Duvall", is age 41, a farmer, and his wife Lillie M.

Daggy "Duvall" is 26. The couple says they are on their first marriage, have been married seven years, and Lillie has borne one child who is still alive. This is daughter Gwendolyn, who is four years old. All in the home, and their parents, were Ohio-born.

In 1920, Alexander and Lillie May Daggy DuVall are found in Oxford Twp., Butler Co., Ohio *(Census Place: Oxford, Butler, Ohio; Roll: T625_1352; Page: 9B; Enumeration District: 70; Image: 1193)*. In the home are Alexander C. DuVall, age 51, a farmer; his wife, Lillie M. Daggy DuVall, 35; and children Gwendolyn, 13, and John L., six. All were born in Ohio, as were their parents.

Alexander C. and Lillie May Daggy DuVall are still residing in Oxford Twp., Butler Co., Ohio in 1930 *(Census Place: Oxford, Butler, Ohio; Roll: 1755; Page: 12A; Enumeration District: 46; Image: 391.0)*. Alexander "Duvall", age 60, is now a real estate salesman who says he was first wed at age 35. Lillie May Daggy "Duvall", 45, says she was first married at age 18. With them is son John L. age 17.

In 1940, Lilly Daggy DuVall is living with her son-in-law and daughter, Harry and Gwendolyn DuVall Kleinfelder, in Oxford Twp., Butler Co., Ohio *(Census Place: Oxford, Butler, Ohio; Roll: T627_3035; Page: 8B; Enumeration District: 9-81)*. Lillian Daggy DuVall, age 55, a widow, says she was living in the same house on Ruby Road in 1935. The head of the household, Harry Kleinfelder, age 34, is a farmer. Gwendolyn DuVall Kleinfelder is 33 years old. They have a daughter, "B. Joyce", who is four months old. All were born in Ohio. Harry and Gwendolyn DuVall Kleinfelder say they were living in Oxford in 1935.

Lillie May Daggy DuVall married **Hudson H. Wagonfield** on May 12, 1945, in Butler Co., Ohio.[604] Hudson H. Wagonfield was born in Milford Twp., Butler Co., Ohio, on August 21, 1871.[605] Hudson H. reached age 79 and died in Hamilton, Butler Co., Ohio, on July 1, 1951.[605, 606] He was buried in Darrtown Pioneer Cemetery, Milford Twp., Butler Co., Ohio.[605, 606, 607]

Children of Lillie May Daggy and Alexander C. DuVall:

+ 148 f I. **Gwendolyn**[9] **DuVall** was born in Milford Twp., Butler Co., Ohio, on June 2, 1906.[31, 608] She died in Riverside, Riverside Co., California, on December 29, 1979.[31, 608]

+ 149 m II. **John Llewellyn**[9] **DuVall** was born in Oxford Twp., Butler Co., Ohio, on March 10, 1913.[31, 609] He died in Elkhart, Elkhart Co., Indiana, on January 31, 1984.[31, 610]

72. Llewellyn[8] **Daggy** (*Laura*[7] *Pegan, Thomas Jefferson*[6]*, Henry*[5]*, Robert A.*[4]*, Andrew*[3]*, Andrew*[2] *Pagan, James*[1]) was born on June 25, 1887, in Salem Twp., Highland Co., Ohio.[231] She was also known as **Louie or Luella**. She was the daughter of Thomas Llewellyn Hamer Daggy and Laura Pegan (22). Llewellyn died in Salem Twp., Highland Co., Ohio, on June 9, 1906, at age 18.[232] She was buried in Barker Cemetery, Pricetown, Salem Twp., Highland Co., Ohio.[232]

Childless.

On her marriage license to William Kelly Roberts, Llewellyn "Louie" Daggy Roberts states she was born in Mt. Orab, Green Twp., Brown Co., Ohio.[611] But the Highland County, Ohio birth records say she was born in Salem Twp. in Highland Co., Ohio.[231]

Llewellyn married **William Kelly Roberts** on July 23, 1904, in Highland Co., Ohio.[611] William Kelly Roberts was born in Mowreystown, White Oak Twp., Highland Co., Ohio, on July 12, 1883.[612] William Kelly reached age 76 and died in Dayton, Montgomery Co., Ohio, on December 28, 1959.[613, 614] He was buried in Sugartree Ridge Cemetery, Concord Twp., Highland Co., Ohio.[615]

After his first wife, Llewellyn "Louie" Daggy Roberts died, William Kelley Roberts remarried to an Anna Lewis.[616] They had several children. He and his family lived in Concord Twp., Highland Co., Ohio for many years, but after his second wife's death William moved Dayton, Montgomery Co., Ohio and lived with a son and his family.[613]

73. Oliver John[8] **Daggy** (*Laura*[7] *Pegan, Thomas Jefferson*[6]*, Henry*[5]*, Robert A.*[4]*, Andrew*[3]*, Andrew*[2] *Pagan, James*[1]) was born on August 31, 1890, in

Salem Twp., Highland Co., Ohio.[31, 233] He was the son of Thomas Llewellyn Hamer Daggy and Laura Pegan (22). He died in St. Petersburg, Pinellas Co., Florida, on July 13, 1972, at age 81.[234]

Oliver John married **Mary Jane Brookfield** before 1917. They divorced about 1940. They had two children. Mary Jane Brookfield was born in Kokomo, Center Twp., Howard Co., Indiana, on May 10, 1898.[617, 618] Mary Jane reached age 69 and died in Hamilton, Butler Co., Ohio, on January 15, 1968.[618, 619] She was buried in Greenwood Cemetery, Hamilton, Butler Co., Ohio.[618, 620]

In 1920, Oliver John Daggy is enumerated in Hamilton, Butler Co., Ohio *(Census Place: Hamilton Ward 4, Butler, Ohio; Roll: T625_1351; Page: 1A; Enumeration District: 30; Image: 955)*. In the home are Oliver Daggy, age 29, a photographer at an art store, who was born in Ohio as were his parens. His wife, Mary Jane Brookfield Daggy, is 21, born Indiana as were her parents. They have two children: Joseph H., three years and five months old, and Betty J., one year and seven months. Both children were born in Ohio.

Oliver John Daggy is still residing in Hamilton, Butler Co., Ohio in 1930 *(Census Place: Hamilton, Butler, Ohio; Roll: 1753; Page: 22B; Enumeration District: 5; Image: 677.0)*. Oliver Daggy, age 39, is a photographer with a studio. He was born in Ohio, as were his parents. His wife, Mary Jane Brookfield Daggy, is 30, born in Indiana where her parents were born. She is a receptionist at her husband's photography studio. Living with them is their daughter, Betty J., 11, born Ohio.

Oliver J. Daggy is not found in the 1940 U.S. Census.

A photographer, Oliver John Daggy lived between 1910 and 1959 in Hamilton, Butler Co., Ohio, except for a short while around 1923 when he resided in Cincinnati, Hamilton Co., Ohio. Oliver John was living in 1945 in Hamilton, Butler Co., Ohio. He retired to Florida around 1959.

Oliver John Daggy's ex-wife, Mary Jane Brookfield Daggy is enumerated in Hamilton, Butler Co., Ohio in 1940 *(Census Place: Hamilton, Butler, Ohio; Roll: T627_3032; Page: 10A; Enumeration District: 9-16)*. In the household are Mary J. Brookfield Daggy, age 40, born Indiana, the proprietor of a photography studio; and her daughter, Betty, 21, single, born Ohio. a stenographer at a retail outlet. They are living at 111 ½ South 3rd Street. Mary Jo Brookfield Daggy lists herself as married, but she is not living with her husband, Oliver J. Daggy, who is not in the 1940 census.

om Oliver Daggy, Mary Jane Brookfield remarried to Roger Thornton Stubbs.[621] Mary Jane Brookfield Daggy Stubbs death certificate says she was born in 1903, but Indiana birth records indicate she was born on 10 May 1898 in Kokomo, Center Twp., Howard Co., Indiana.[617, 619]

Children of Oliver John Daggy and Mary Jane Brookfield:

+ 150 m I. **Joseph Hamer**^{9} **Daggy** was born in Hamilton, Butler Co., Ohio, on August 21, 1917.[622] He died in Hamilton, Butler Co., Ohio, on January 6, 1927.[622]

+ 151 f II. **Betty Jane**^{9} **Daggy** was born in Hamilton, Butler Co., Ohio, on May 11, 1918.[31, 623] She died in Hamilton, Butler Co., Ohio, on September 11, 2008.[31, 623]

74. Lawrence W.^{8} **Surber** (*Anna*^{7} *Pegan, Thomas Jefferson*^{6}*, Henry*^{5}*, Robert A.*^{4}*, Andrew*^{3}*, Andrew*^{2} *Pagan, James*^{1}) was born on April 20, 1890, in White Oak Twp., Highland Co., Ohio.[239] He was the son of Lewis Allen Surber and Anna Pegan (23). Lawrence W. died in White Oak Twp., Highland Co., Ohio, on January 2, 1891.[240] He was buried in Union Cemetery, Taylorsville, White Oak Twp., Highland Co., Ohio.[624]

Birth and death records in Highland County, Ohio confirm this child's name was Lawrence W. Surber.[239, 240]

75. Earl Lester^8 **Surber** (*Anna*^{7} *Pegan, Thomas Jefferson*^{6}*, Henry*^{5}*, Robert A.*^{4}*, Andrew*^{3}*, Andrew*^{2} *Pagan, James*^{1}) was born on December 19, 1892, in White Oak Twp., Highland Co., Ohio.[241] He was the son of Lewis Allen Surber and Anna Pegan (23). He died in White Oak Twp., Highland Co., Ohio, on February 27, 1964, at age 71.[242] Earl Lester was buried in Union Cemetery, Taylorsville, White Oak Twp., Highland Co., Ohio.[625, 626]

Earl Lester married **Ganelle Ruth Roberts** on December 19, 1912, in Highland Co., Ohio.[627] They had three children. Ganelle Ruth Roberts was born in Concord Twp., Highland Co., Ohio, on May 12, 1894.[31, 628] Ganelle Ruth lived in 1976 in White Oak Twp., Highland Co., Ohio. She reached age 81 and died in a hospital in Wilmington, Union Twp., Clinton Co., Ohio, on April 3, 1976.[31, 629] Ganelle Ruth was buried in Union Cemetery, Taylorsville, White Oak Twp., Highland Co., Ohio.[630, 631]

Earl L. Surber is enumerated in White Oak Twp., Highland Co., Ohio in 1920 (*Census Place: White Oak, Highland, Ohio; Roll: T625_1399; Page: 6A; Enumeration District: 105; Image: 591*). In the household are Earl L. Surber, 27, a farmer, and his wife, "Gaynelle" Roberts Surber, 25. Both were Ohio natives, as were their parents. Next door are Earl's parents, Lewis A. and Anna Pegan Surber.

In 1930, Earl L. Surber is still residing in White Oak Twp., Highland Co., Ohio (*Census Place: White Oak, Highland, Ohio; Roll: 1823; Page: 2A; Enumeration District: 27; Image: 544.0*). Earl L. Surber, age 37, a farmer, says he was first married at age 20. His wife, "Gaynelle" Roberts Surber is 35 and says she was first married at age 18. Children in the home are Maynard, nine, and Cedric, seven. All were born in Ohio, as were their parents.

Earl Surber is again found in White Oak Twp., Highland Co., Ohio in 1940 (*Census Place: White Oak, Highland, Ohio; Roll: T627_3085; Page: 4B; Enumeration District: 36-31*). Earl Surber, age 47, is still farming. With him are his wife, Ganelle Roberts Surber, 45, and their sons Maynard, 18, and Cedric, 17, who are both listed as helpers on the farm. All in the home were born in Ohio, and say they were living in the same house, near the intersection of Mowrystown and East Danville roads, in 1935.

Earl worked as a supervisor at the Highland County, Ohio Conservation District in 1943.[625]

Children of Earl Lester Surber and Ganelle Ruth Roberts:

+ 152 f I. **Mary Sarah**[9] **Surber** was born in White Oak Twp., Highland Co., Ohio, on September 14, 1918.[632] She died in White Oak Twp., Highland Co., Ohio, on September 15, 1918.[632]

+ 153 m II. **Maynard Raymond**[9] **Surber** was born in White Oak Twp., Highland Co., Ohio, on April 14, 1920.[633, 634] He died in White Oak Twp., Highland Co., Ohio, on July 26, 2012.[633]

+ 154 m III. **Cedric Lewis**[9] **Surber** was born in White Oak Twp., Highland Co., Ohio, on January 26, 1923.[31, 635, 636] He died in White Oak Twp., Highland Co., Ohio, on April 13, 2013.[31, 635]

76. Hugh Doyle[8] **Pegan** (*Charles*[7], *Thomas Jefferson*[6], *Henry*[5], *Robert A.*[4], *Andrew*[3], *Andrew*[2] *Pagan, James*[1]) was born on January 4, 1908, in Hamer Twp., Highland Co., Ohio.[31, 262] He was the son of Charles Pegan (27) and Resa Jane Pulliam. He died in East Danville, New Market Twp., Highland Co., Ohio, on April 4, 1984, at age 76.[263, 264] Hugh Doyle was buried in Hamer Township Cemetery, Hamer Twp., Highland Co., Ohio.[235, 637]

Hugh Doyle married **Lillian Blanche King** on December 22, 1928, in Highland Co., Ohio.[638] They had one son. Lillian Blanche King was born in Clay Twp., Highland Co., Ohio, on March 14, 1910.[31, 639, 640] Lillian Blanche reached age 91 and died in Hillsboro, Liberty Twp., Highland Co., Ohio, on August 27, 2001.[31, 639, 640] She was buried in Hamer Township Cemetery, Hamer Twp., Highland Co., Ohio.[640, 641]

In 1930, newlyweds Hugh and Lillian Blanche King Pegan are living with Hugh's parents, Charles and Resa Jane Pulliam Pegan, in Hamer Twp., Highland Co., Ohio (*Census Place: Hamer, Highland, Ohio; Roll: 1823; Page: 6A; Enumeration District: 10; Image: 166.0*). Hugh Pegan, 22 is a farmer and his wife Lillian Unknown Pegan is 21. The have been married about a year, as Hugh says he was first married at age 21 and Lillian says her first marriage occurred at age 20. All were born in Ohio, as were their parents. Charles Pegan Charles Pegan, listed as "Charley", age 44 a farmer, and Resa Jane Pulliam Pegan, is 46. Charles and Resa say they were first married at ages 22 and 24 respectively.

Hugh Doyle Pegan and his family continue to live with Hugh's parents, Charles and Resa Pulliam Pegan, in 1940 in Hamer Twp., Highland Co., Ohio *(Census Place: Hamer, Highland, Ohio; Roll: T627_3085; Page: 2A; Enumeration District: 36-10)*. The surname is listed as "Peggan". Hugh Pegan, age 32, is a farmer; his wife, Lillian King Pegan, is 30 years old. They have a son, Lowell, six. The head of the household is Charles Pegan, 54, also a farmer. Resa Pulliam Pegan is 56 years old. All were born in Ohio. Charles Pegan says he was living in Hamer Twp. in 1935, while Resa, Hugh and his family say they were living in the same house on East Danville Road in 1935.

Son of Hugh Doyle Pegan and Lillian Blanche King:

+ 155 m I. **Lowell R.⁹ Pegan** was born in East Danville, Hamer Twp., Highland Co., Ohio, on March 15, 1934.[31, 642, 643] He died in East Danville, Hamer Twp., Highland Co., Ohio, on July 12, 1975.[642, 644]

77. **Harlen J. Pulliam⁸ Pegan** (*Charles⁷, Thomas Jefferson⁶, Henry⁵, Robert A.⁴, Andrew³, Andrew² Pagan, James¹*) was born on September 1, 1909, in Hamer Twp., Highland Co., Ohio.[265, 266, 267] He was the son of Charles Pegan (27) and Resa Jane Pulliam. Harlen J. Pulliam died in Hamer Twp., Highland Co., Ohio, on September 15, 1909.[267, 268] He was buried in Union Cemetery, Taylorsville, White Oak Twp., Highland Co., Ohio.[645]

Harlen Pulliam Pegan is buried under the name "Harlie J." Pegan.[645]

78. **Ferol Margaret⁸ Pegan** (*Frank Joseph⁷, William Henry⁶, Henry⁵, Robert A.⁴, Andrew³, Andrew² Pagan, James¹*) was born on July 8, 1905, in Clark Twp., Clinton Co., Ohio.[31, 287, 288] She was also known as **Peggy**. She was the daughter of Frank Joseph Pegan (34) and Nelle Irene West. She resided in 1989 in Blanchester, Marion Twp., Clinton Co., Ohio. Ferol Ferol Margaret died in a facility in Sabina, Richland Twp., Clinton Co., Ohio, on October 30, 1989, at age 84.[31, 287] She was buried in Martinsville IOOF Cemetery, Martinsville, Clark Twp., Clinton Co., Ohio.[646, 647]

Childless.

Ferol Margaret Pegan always used "Peggy" as her preferred given name.

In 1920, Ferol is incorrectly enumerated as a son in her parents, Frank Joseph and Nelle Irene West Pegan's household.

Ferol Pegan (Kies) is not found in the 1930 census.

Ferol Margaret married **Alfred Allen Kies** before 1931. Alfred Allen Kies was born in Jackson Twp., Shelby Co., Ohio, on July 27, 1906.[31, 648] Alfred Allen reached age 52 and died in Tampa, Hillsborough Co., Florida, on February 14, 1959.[31, 648, 649] He was buried in New Loramie Valley Cemetery, Botkins, Dinsmore Twp., Shelby Co., Ohio.[648]

In 1940, Alfred and Ferol Pegan Kies were enumerated in Dayton, Montgomery Co., Ohio *(Census Place: Dayton, Montgomery, Ohio; Roll: T627_3252; Page: 6A; Enumeration District: 94-48)*. Alfred Kies, age 33, is a paint salesman. Ferol Pegan Kies is incorrectly listed as 34 years old (she is 27). They are living at 133 Norman Street, and say they were living in Dayton in 1935.

After her husband Alfred died, "Peggy" Pegan Kies moved from Tampa, Hillsborough Co., Florida to Mishawaka, St. Joseph Co., Indiana, (where her mother Nellie West Pegan and sister Ruth Pegan Holmes lived, according to her mother Nellie's obituary.[283] Later, she returned to her hometown of Blanchester, Marion Twp., Clinton Co., Ohio where her brother Harold West Pegan resided.

79. **Ruby W.⁸ Pegan** (*Frank Joseph⁷, William Henry⁶, Henry⁵, Robert A.⁴, Andrew³, Andrew² Pagan, James¹*) was born on June 8, 1912, in Silver Creek Twp., Greene Co., Ohio.[31, 289] She was the daughter of Frank Joseph Pegan (34) and Nelle Irene West. Ruby W. was living in 1984 in Wilmington, Union Twp., Clinton Co., Ohio. She died in a hospital in Batavia, Batavia Twp., Clermont Co., Ohio, on July

31, 1984, at age 72.[289, 290] Ruby W. was buried in Martinsville IOOF Cemetery, Martinsville, Clark Twp., Clinton Co., Ohio.[289, 650]

Childless.

Ruby Pegan is not found in the 1930 or 1940 U.S. Censuses. However, an article about her sister Ruth M. Pegan Holmes' wedding in July 1941 indicates that Ruby Pegan was single and living in Baltimore, Baltimore Co., Maryland.[651]

Ruby W. married **Robert D. Anderson** on May 20, 1945.[652] They divorced.

According to the divorce ledger in the Highland County court report in the *Hillsboro (OH) Press Gazette* on April 11, 1947, Ruby Anderson and Robert D. Anderson were married on May 20, 1945 and had no children. Ruby, who sued for the divorce, petitioned the court to restore to her maiden name of Ruby Pegan. The court granted the divorce and name restoration.[652]

Ruby W. Pegan (Anderson) married **Harold William Rammel** on May 31, 1947, in Highland Co., Ohio.[653, 654] They divorced before 1952. Harold William Rammel was born in Lynchburg, Dodson Twp., Highland Co., Ohio, on December 13, 1912.[31, 654, 655, 656, 657] He was also known as **Bill**. Harold William reached age 79 and died in Columbus, Franklin Co., Ohio, on February 7, 1992.[31, 655, 656, 657] He was buried in New Lynchburg Masonic Cemetery/Lynchburg F & AM Cemetery, Lynchburg, Dodson Twp., Highland Co., Ohio.[658]

Although his death record says he was born in Columbiana County, Ohio, on his Social Security information and his marriage application to Ruby Pegan (Anderson) Harold "Bill" Rammel says he was born in Lynchburg, Dodson Twp., Highland Co., Ohio.[654, 656, 657]

Another mention in the *Wilmington (OH) News Journal*, says that Ruby Pegan, who had once again retained her maiden name after her second divorce, was a resident of Dayton, Montgomery Co., Ohio.[659]

Ruby W. Pegan (Anderson Rammel) married **Arthur Edward Woodall** after 1975. They divorced. Arthur Edward Woodall was born in Dayton, Montgomery Co., Ohio, on June 23, 1918.[31, 660] He reached age 68 and died in Dayton, Montgomery Co., Ohio, on July 12, 1986.[31, 661] Arthur E. was buried in Calvary Cemetery, Dayton, Montgomery Co., Ohio.[660, 662, 663]

After her third divorce, Ruby continued to use her third married name, Woodall. She lived in Blanchester, Marion Twp., and then Wilmington, Union Twp., both in Clinton Co., Ohio, before entering the hospital in Batavia, Batavia Twp., Clermont Co., Ohio, where she died.

80. Harold West[8] PeGan (*Frank Joseph[7] Pegan, William Henry[6], Henry[5], Robert A.[4], Andrew[3], Andrew[2] Pagan, James[1]*) was born on June 3, 1918, in Clark Twp., Clinton Co., Ohio.[31, 291] He was the son of Frank Joseph Pegan (34) and Nelle Irene West. He lived in 1995 in Blanchester, Marion Twp., Clinton Co., Ohio. He died in a hospital in Wilmington, Union Twp., Clinton Co., Ohio, on November 16, 1995, at age 77.[31, 291] Harold West was buried in Martinsville IOOF Cemetery, Martinsville, Clark Twp., Clinton Co., Ohio.[664, 665]

Harold West married Mrs. **Velma Powell** Pointer on February 20, 1943, in Highland Co., Ohio.[666] They had three sons. Velma Powell was born in Greenfield, Madison Twp., Highland Co., Ohio, on March 15, 1924.[667] Velma lived in 1975 in Blanchester, Marion Twp., Clinton Co., Ohio. She reached age 51 and died in a hospital in Wilmington, Union Twp., Clinton Co., Ohio, on September 14, 1975.[668] She was cremated and her ashes buried in Martinsville IOOF Cemetery, Martinsville, Clark Twp., Clinton Co., Ohio.[669, 670]

Harold West PeGan married Mrs. **Hazel Gebhart** Howard on March 16, 1982, in Montgomery Co., Ohio.[671] They divorced. Hazel Gebhart was born in Washington Twp., Montgomery Co., Ohio or Cincinnati, Hamilton Co., Ohio, on May 9, 1913.[31, 672] She reached age 83 and died in Madeira, Sycamore Twp., Hamilton Co., Ohio, on August 18, 1996.[31, 673, 674] Hazel was buried in Woodland Cemetery and Arboretum, Dayton, Montgomery Co., Ohio.[674]

Hazel Gebhardt Howard Pegan's birth date is May 9, 1913 on her Social Security information and her Ohio state birth record.[31, 672] Her death certificate and gravestone have her date of birth as May 19, 1913.[673, 674]

Harold West Pegan owned a service/gas station.[664]

Harold West PeGan and Velma Powell had three sons, including:

+ 156 m I. **Allan Jay**[9] **Pegan** was born in Leesburg, Fairfield Twp., Highland Co., Ohio, on June 25, 1944.[31, 675, 676] He died in Cincinnati, Hamilton Co., Ohio, on October 18, 1998.[31, 675, 676]

+ 157 m III. **Powell**[9] **Pegan** was born in a hospital in Wilmington, Union Twp., Clinton Co., Ohio, on February 23, 1959.[677] He died in a hospital in Wilmington, Union Twp., Clinton Co., Ohio, on February 23, 1959.[677]

81. **Ruth Marie**[8] **Pegan** (*Frank Joseph*[7], *William Henry*[6], *Henry*[5], *Robert A.*[4], *Andrew*[3], *Andrew*[2] *Pagan, James*[1]) was born on June 16, 1921, in Martinsville, Clark Twp., Clinton Co., Ohio.[31, 292, 293, 294] She was the daughter of Frank Joseph Pegan (34) and Nelle Irene West. Ruth Marie lived in 1984 in Blanchester, Marion Twp., Clinton Co., Ohio. She died in South Bend, St. Joseph Co., Indiana, on August 22, 2004, at age 83.[31, 292, 294] Ruth Marie was buried in Martinsville IOOF Cemetery, Martinsville, Clark Twp., Clinton Co., Ohio.[678]

Ruth Marie married **Raymond Holmes** on July 2, 1941, in Highland Co., Ohio.[679] They had three daughters. Raymond Holmes was born in Hillsboro, Liberty Twp., Highland Co., Ohio, on February 21, 1919.[31, 680, 681] Raymond reached age 67 and died in South Bend, St. Joseph Co., Indiana, on April 20, 1986.[31, 680, 682] He was buried in Southlawn Cemetery, South Bend, St. Joseph Co., Indiana.[682, 683]

A carpenter, Raymond lived in 1956 in Hillsboro, Liberty Twp., Highland Co., Ohio.[683]

Ruth Marie Pegan and Raymond Holmes had three daughters, including:

+ 158 f III. **Daughter Holmes** was born in Dayton, Montgomery Co., Ohio.[684]

82. **Rita Glea**[8] **Pegan** (*Frank Joseph*[7], *William Henry*[6], *Henry*[5], *Robert A.*[4], *Andrew*[3], *Andrew*[2] *Pagan, James*[1]) was born on June 16, 1921, in Martinsville, Clark Twp., Clinton Co., Ohio.[296] She was the daughter of Frank Joseph Pegan (34) and Nelle Irene West. Rita Glea died in Martinsville, Clark Twp., Clinton Co., Ohio, on June 16, 1921.[296] She was buried in Martinsville IOOF Cemetery, Martinsville, Clark Twp., Clinton Co., Ohio.[296, 685]

Rita's death certificate does not reveal a name, she is only listed as "twin daughter" or "infant" in cemetery and other records. Her twin sister Ruth Marie Pegan Holmes' tombstone in Martinsville IOOF Cemetery, Martinsville, Clark Twp., Clinton Co., Ohio names her as "Rita G."[678]

83. **Paul Stroup**[8] **Pegan** (*William Otto*[7], *William Henry*[6], *Henry*[5], *Robert A.*[4], *Andrew*[3], *Andrew*[2] *Pagan, James*[1]) was born on Saturday, March 17, 1917, in Clark Twp., Clinton Co., Ohio.[31, 308] He was the son of William Otto Pegan (36) and Rosella Stroup. He died in Zephyrhills, Pasco Co., Florida, on January 28, 2007, at age 89.[31, 308] Paul Stroup was buried in New Lynchburg Masonic Cemetery/Lynchburg F & AM Cemetery, Lynchburg, Dodson Twp., Highland Co., Ohio.[308, 686]

Paul S. Pegan was injured in the spring of 1939 and spent time in a Cincinnati hospital when a tractor fell on him.[687]

Paul Stroup, a farmer, married **Louise Warnick** about 1940. They had two children. Louise Warnick was born on September 23, 1922.

Paul Stroup also resided in 1982 in Cleveland, Cuyahoga Co., Ohio.

When this writer was in Cleveland, Ohio, photographing the first Championship Auto Racing Team's Indy car race in 1983, she looked in the Cleveland phone book and found a "Paul Stroup Pegan" listed Although I hadn't started my genealogical research, I'd always been curious about the surname—and it was the first time I'd seen the name outside of my hometown, Huntington, Indiana's phone book, or Fort Wayne's or Indianapolis', where some of my extended family members lived. I phoned him and he was curious too. He invited me to his house, where I met his son and other family members. He told me they came from Highland County, Ohio and his father's name was William Otto Pegan. But, at the time, I didn't know my great-grandfather, Harrison James PeGan Jr., was raised in Highland County—and Paul didn't know any PeGans from Indiana. Paul wrote what he knew about his ancestors on a small scrap of paper. I told him I'd keep it and, if I ever found out if we were related, I'd let him know. I called him again the next year when I was in Cleveland for the race, but he wasn't home. The next year, his name wasn't in the phone book. I never knew what happened to him. He had moved to New Vienna, Green Twp., Clinton Co., Ohio, where he is living when his father William Otto Pegan dies, according to William Otto's obituary in 1985.[110]

I still have that scrap of paper Paul gave me.

Children of Paul Stroup Pegan and Louise Warnick had two children, including:

+ 159 f II. **Daughter**[9] **Pegan** was born in Hillsboro, Liberty Twp., Highland Co., Ohio.

84. Mary Louise[8] **Pegan** (*William Otto*[7], *William Henry*[6], *Henry*[5], *Robert A.*[4], *Andrew*[3], *Andrew*[2] *Pagan*, *James*[1]) was born on March 13, 1919, in Clark Twp., Clinton Co., Ohio.[309] She was the daughter of William Otto Pegan (36) and Rosella Stroup. Mary Louise died in Clark Twp., Clinton Co., Ohio, on August 19, 1928, at age nine.[309] She was buried in New Lynchburg Masonic Cemetery/Lynchburg F & AM Cemetery, Lynchburg, Dodson Twp., Highland Co., Ohio.[309, 688]

85. Audrey Mae[8] **Pegan** (*William Otto*[7], *William Henry*[6], *Henry*[5], *Robert A.*[4], *Andrew*[3], *Andrew*[2] *Pagan*, *James*[1]) was born on November 16, 1920, in Clark Twp., Clinton Co., Ohio.[31, 310, 311] She was the daughter of William Otto Pegan (36) and Rosella Stroup. Audrey Mae lived in 1997 in Wilmington, Union Twp., Clinton Co., Ohio. She died in a hospital in Dayton, Montgomery Co., Ohio, on April 6, 1997, at age 76.[31, 310, 311] Audrey Mae was buried in Clinton County Memory Gardens, Union Twp., Clinton Co., Ohio.[689, 690]

Audrey Mae married **George Elton West** on December 4, 1943.[689] They had two daughters. George Elton West was born in Lynchburg, Dodson Twp., Highland Co., Ohio, on August 19, 1918.[31, 691] George Elton reached age 90 and died in Wilmington, Union Twp., Clinton Co., Ohio, on December 21, 2008.[31, 691] He was buried in Clinton County Memory Gardens, Union Twp., Clinton Co., Ohio.[691, 692] He was the son of George West and Mae Stroup.

George Elton worked as a procurement officer at Wright Patterson Air Force Base, Dayton, Ohio.[691]

Audrey Mae Pegan and George Elton West had two daughters, including:

+ 160 f I. **Daughter**[9] **West** was born in Wilmington, Union Twp., Clinton Co., Ohio?

86. Doris Helen[8] **Pegan** (*William Otto*[7], *William Henry*[6], *Henry*[5], *Robert A.*[4], *Andrew*[3], *Andrew*[2] *Pagan*, *James*[1]) was born on December 29, 1922, in Clark Twp., Clinton Co., Ohio.[312, 313] She was also known as **Helen**. She was the daughter of William Otto Pegan (36) and Rosella Stroup. Doris Helen died in Wilmington, Union Twp., Clinton Co., Ohio, on February 17, 2004, at age 81.[312] She was buried in Barnes Cemetery, Fairview, New Market Twp., Highland Co., Ohio.[693, 694]

Doris Helen Pegan Ludwick favored "Helen" as her given name. She and her husband, Lowell Arthur Ludwick, were third cousins.

Doris Helen married **Lowell Arthur Ludwick** about 1943. They had one son. Lowell Arthur Ludwick was born in Dodson Twp., Highland Co., Ohio, on August 6, 1923.[496, 497] Lowell Arthur reached age 38 and died in a hospital in Wilmington, Union Twp., Clinton Co., Ohio, on November 13, 1961.[497, 498] He was buried in Barnes Cemetery,

Fairview, New Market Twp., Highland Co., Ohio.[497, 914]

Son of Doris Helen Pegan and Lowell Arthur Ludwick:

+ 161 m I. **Arthur Lowell**[9] **Ludwick** was born in Cincinnati, Hamilton Co., Ohio, on November 11, 1943.[695, 696] He was also known as **Artie**. Arthur Lowell died in Lynchburg, Dodson Twp., Highland Co., Ohio, on January 21, 2014.[696]

9th Generation

87. Charles Randolph[9] Philhower II (*Agnes[8] Lemons, Josephine[7] Stroup, Elvira[6] Pegan, Henry[5], Robert A.[4], Andrew[3], Andrew[2] Pagan, James[1]*) was born on July 14, 1900, in Lynchburg, Dodson Twp., Highland Co., Ohio.[31, 322] He was also known as **Dolph**. He was the son of Charles Philhower and Agnes Lemons (37). Charles Randolph died in Hollywood, Broward Co., Florida, on April 3, 1974, at age of 73.[322] He was buried in Hamer Township Cemetery, Hamer Twp., Highland Co., Ohio.[697]

Charles R. Philhower II is not found in the 1920 census.

Charles Randolph married **Ella Lorie Jones** before 1925. They had one son. Ella Lorie Jones was born in Salem Twp., Highland Co., Ohio, on September 20, 1898.[698] Ella Lorie reached age 88 and died in Hillsboro, Liberty Twp., Highland Co., Ohio, on January 25, 1987.[699] She was buried in Hamer Township Cemetery, Hamer Twp., Highland Co., Ohio.[700, 701]

In 1930, Charles R. Philhower II is enumerated in Washington Court House, Union Twp., Fayette Co., Ohio (*Census Place: Washington Court House, Fayette, Ohio; Roll: 1792; Page: 7A; Enumeration District: 15; Image: 404.0*). Charles R. Philhower II, 29, is a rate clerk for the Stearn Railroad. His wife, (Ella) Lorie Jones Philhower, is 30. The couple have been married eight years, as they were first married at ages 21 and 22 respectively. Both say they and their parents were born in Ohio.

Charles Randolph Philhower II is again residing in Washington Court House, Union Twp., Fayette Co., Ohio in 1940 (*Census Place: Washington Court House, Fayette, Ohio; Roll: T627_3067; Page: 9A; Enumeration District: 24-18*). In the household are Charles R. Philhower, age 39, the general manager of a stockyard and his wife, (Ella) Lorie Jones Philhower, 41. Both were born in Ohio, and say they were living in Washington Court House in 1935. Their home is at 628 South Main Street.

Son of Charles Randolph Philhower II and Ella Lorie Jones:

+ 162 m I. **J. Bruce[10] Philhower** was born in Hillsboro, Liberty Twp., Highland Co., Ohio, on January 17, 1925.[702] He died in Hillsboro, Liberty Twp., Highland Co., Ohio, on January 17, 1925.[703]

88. Lee Donald[9] Philhower (*Agnes[8] Lemons, Josephine[7] Stroup, Elvira[6] Pegan, Henry[5], Robert A.[4], Andrew[3], Andrew[2] Pagan, James[1]*) was born on November 29, 1903, in Lynchburg, Dodson Twp., Highland Co., Ohio.[323] He was also known as **Donald**. He was the son of Charles Philhower and Agnes Lemons (37). Lee Donald died in Hollywood, Broward Co., Florida, on May 21, 1990, at age 86.[323] He was buried in Greenfield Cemetery, Greenfield Twp., Highland Co., Ohio.[704, 705]

Childless.

Lee Donald married **Chloe Marie Coffman** on September 18, 1926, in Highland Co., Ohio.[706] Chloe Marie Coffman was born in Perry Twp., Fayette Co., Ohio, on October 24, 1905.[707, 708, 709] She reached age 90 and died in a facility in Upper Arlington, Franklin Co., Ohio, on March 29, 1996.[583, 584] Chloe Marie was buried in Greenfield Cemetery, Greenfield Twp., Highland Co., Ohio.[583, 710]

Lee Donald Philhower is enumerated as "Donald Philhower" in Greenfield, Madison Twp., Highland Co., Ohio in 1930 (*Census Place: Greenfield, Highland, Ohio; Roll: 1823; Page: 4B; Enumeration District: 16; Image: 345.0*). In the home are Donald Philhower, 26, a stenographer at a textile factory, and his wife, Cloe, 24. They have been married two years, as they say their first marriage occurred at ages 24 and 22 respectively. Both say they and their parents were born in Ohio.

In 1940, Lee Donald Philhower, listed as L. Donald, is still a resident of Greenfield, Madison Twp., Highland Co., Ohio (*Census Place: Greenfield, Highland, Ohio; Roll: T627_3085; Page: 1A; Enumeration District: 36-19*). Lee Donald Philhower, age 36, is a foreman at a saddlery company. With him is wife Chloe Coffman Philhower, 34, who is the secretary at the saddlery company. Both were born in Ohio and say they were living in the same house at 153 Jefferson Street in Greenfield in 1935.

89. **Marcia Lucille[9] Boesenberg** (*Grace[8] Lemons, Josephine[7] Stroup, Elvira[6] Pegan, Henry[5], Robert A.[4], Andrew[3], Andrew[2] Pagan, James[1]*) was born on June 1, 1904, in Lynchburg, Dodson Twp., Highland Co., Ohio.[330] She was the daughter of Edward Boesenberg and Grace Lemons (38). Marcia Lucille died in Springfield, Springfield Twp., Clark Co., Ohio, on January 25, 1932, at age 27.[331] She was buried in Ferncliff Cemetery, Springfield, Springfield Twp., Clark Co., Ohio.[331, 711]

For some reason, Edward and Grace Lemons Boesenberg didn't register their only child Marcia Lucille's birth for nearly a year. Although the birth record says she was born in Lynchburg Ohio, her birth is not registered in the Highland County records. Instead, Marcia's birth is recorded in Preble County, Ohio, in May 1905, as they were living in Camden, Sommers Twp., Preble Co. Ohio at the time.[330] On her marriage license, Marcia Boesenberg Roush correctly says she was born in Lynchburg, Dodson Twp., Highland Co., Ohio, but, oddly, her death certificate states her birthplace was Mechanicsburg, Goshen Twp., Champaign Co., Ohio.[331, 712]

Marcia Lucille married **Kenneth Edward H. Roush** on April 12, 1923, in Clark Co., Ohio.[712] They had one son. Kenneth Edward H. Roush was born in Springfield, Springfield Twp., Clark Co., Ohio, on March 16, 1903.[31] Kenneth Edward H. reached age 73 and died in Oakland, Alameda Co., California, on March 5, 1977.[31, 713] He was buried in Evergreen Cemetery, Oakland, Alameda Co., California.[714, 715]

In 1930, Kenneth and Marcia Boesenberg Roush are living with Marcia's parents, Edward and Grace Lemon Boesenberg, in Springfield, Springfield Twp., Clark Co., Ohio *(Census Place: Springfield, Clark, Ohio; Roll: 1757; Page: 5A; Enumeration District: 54; Image: 521.0)*. Kenneth Roush, age 27, born Ohio, is a machinist/pattern worker. His wife, Marcia Boesenberg Roush is 25. Kenneth and Marcia say they were first married at ages 20 and 18 respectively and have been married seven years. The head of the household is Edward W. Boesenberg, listed as Ed W. Boesenberg, age 53, a baker, born Ohio with his parents born in Germany. Edward's wife, Grace Lemons Boesenberg, 51, was born Ohio as were her parents. Edward and Grace have been married 30 years, as they were first married at ages 23 and 21 respectively.

After Marcia L. Boesenberg Roush died, Kenneth Roush married Lois Ridgely.[716]

Kenneth Roush, widower of Marcia Boesenberg, is still located in Springfield, Springfield Twp., Clark Co., Ohio in 1940 *(Census Place: Springfield, Clark, Ohio; Roll: T627_3040; Page: 16B; Enumeration District: 12-69)*. Kenneth Roush, age 37, is a toolmaker in the motor truck industry. His second wife, Lois, is 25. With them is Kenneth Roush Jr., the son of Kenneth and Marcia Boesenberg Roush, who is nine years old. Kenneth and Lois also have a son, George, age four. All were born in Ohio and say they were living in the same house at 1236 Pleasant Street in 1935.

According to his son, Kenneth E. Roush II's obituary, Kenneth Roush Sr. moved his family to Oakland, Alameda Co., California, when Kenneth Jr. was a boy, probably shortly after the 1940 census and before the start of WWII on December 7, 1941.[717]

Son of Marcia Lucille Boesenberg and Kenneth Edward H. Roush:

+ 163 m I. **Kenneth Edward[10] Roush II** was born in Springfield, Springfield Twp., Clark Co., Ohio, on August 5, 1931.[31, 717, 718] He died in Show Low, Navajo Co., Arizona, on October 1, 2007.[31, 717]

90. **Robert H.[9] Lemons (Long)** (*Clarence Otto[8] Lemons, Josephine[7] Stroup, Elvira[6] Pegan, Henry[5], Robert A.[4], Andrew[3], Andrew[2] Pagan, James[1]*) was born on March 5, 1917, in Springfield, Springfield Twp., Clark Co., Ohio.[360] He was the son of Clarence Otto Lemons (43) and Grace May Long. Robert H. Lemons (Long) lived in 1930 in Gallipolis, Gallipolis Twp., Gallia Co., Ohio. He died in Gallipolis, Gallipolis Twp., Gallia Co., Ohio?, between 1930 and 1944.

In 1930, Robert "Lemon", age 12, born Ohio as were his parents, is a patient at the Ohio Hospital for Epileptics in Gallipolis, Gallia Co., Ohio *(Census Place: Gallipolis, Gallia, Ohio; Roll: 1803; Page: 7B; Enumeration District: 9; Image: 547.0).*

He is not found in the 1940 census, nor is he mentioned in his father Clarence Otto Lemons obituary in 1944 as his two siblings are.[359]

After his mother, Grace May Long Lemons died, Robert Lemons (Long) and his brother Clarence Lemons II (Long) were reared by their maternal grandparents, Benjamin and Minnie Brown Long, in Springfield, Springfield Twp., Clark Co., Ohio. (Robert was later institutionalized in the Ohio Hospital for Epileptics in Gallipolis.) Meanwhile their sister, Josephine Mae Lemons (later Luck) was reared by their paternal grandmother, Josephine Stroup Lemon(s) in Lynchburg, Dodson Twp., Highland Co., Ohio. She retained the surname Lemons and had close contact with their father, Clarence Lemons while she was growing up. But Clarence "Bill" Lemons' sons Robert and Clarence had little contact with their father.[329]

Robert is said to have assumed the surname of Long, but his census record above indicates he was still known as "Robert Lemon" in 1930.

91. Josephine Mae[9] **Lemons** (*Clarence Otto*[8], *Josephine*[7] *Stroup, Elvira*[6] *Pegan, Henry*[5], *Robert A.*[4], *Andrew*[3], *Andrew*[2] *Pagan, James*[1]) was born on July 12, 1919, in Springfield, Springfield Twp., Clark Co., Ohio.[31, 361] She was the daughter of Clarence Otto Lemons (43) and Grace May Long. Josephine Mae died in Sabina, Richland Twp., Clinton Co., Ohio, on October 10, 2008, at age 89.[31, 361] She was buried in Troutwine Cemetery, Dodson Twp., Highland Co., Ohio and Clark Twp., Clinton Co., Ohio.[361, 719, 720]

After her mother, Grace May Long Lemons died, Josephine Mae Lemons Luck was raised by her paternal grandmother, Josephine Stroup Lemons in Lynchburg, Dodson Twp., Highland Co., Ohio. As her father Clarence "Bill" Lemons also lived with his mother Josephine Stroup Lemons for a long time, Josephine Mae Lemons Luck knew her father while she was growing up. Meanwhile, her maternal grandparents, Benjamin and Minnie Brown Long, reared her two brothers, Robert (Lemons) Long and Clarence (Lemons) Long, in Springfield, Springfield Twp., Clark Co., Ohio. Robert later was institutionalized in a hospital for epileptics in Gallipolis, Ohio. The boys, who assumed their maternal grandparents' surname, and had little contact with their father Clarence Lemons.[329]

Josephine Mae Lemons, age 10, is residing with her widowed paternal grandmother, Josephine Stroup Lemons, in Lynchburg, Dodson Twp., Highland Co., Ohio *(Census Place: Lynchburg, Highland, Ohio; Roll: 1823; Page: 5A; Enumeration District: 5; Image: 76.0).* Josephine Stroup Lemons, age 63, says she was married at age 20. Also in the home are Josephine Mae Lemon's uncle and Josephine Stroup Lemons' son, James S. Lemons, 43, single. All and their parents were Ohio natives. No one in the home lists an occupation.

Josephine Mae married **Albert J. Luck II** on September 7, 1938, in Maysville, Mason Co., Kentucky.[329] They had three children. Albert J. Luck II was born in Clark Twp., Clinton Co., Ohio, on June 15, 1920.[31, 721, 722] Albert J. lived in 1994 in Lynchburg, Dodson Twp., Highland Co., Ohio. He reached age 73 and died in a hospital in Wilmington, Union Twp., Clinton Co., Ohio, on January 20, 1994.[31, 722] Albert J. was buried in Troutwine Cemetery, Dodson Twp., Highland Co., Ohio and Clark Twp., Clinton Co., Ohio.[722, 723]

In 1940, Albert and Josephine Mae Lemons Luck are enumerated in Dodson Twp., Highland Co., Ohio *(Census Place: Dodson, Highland, Ohio; Roll: T627_3085; Page: 2A; Enumeration District: 36-6).* Albert Luck Jr., age 19, is doing research field work for the Works Progress Administration (WPA). He says he was living in Highland Co., Ohio in 1935. His wife, Josephine Mae Lemons Luck, is 20 years old and says she was residing in Lynchburg, Dodson Twp., Highland Co., Ohio in 1935. Their home is located at 40-a Anderson Road.

Albert Luck Jr. was mayor of Lynchburg, Ohio for 20 years. A paraplegic, he was wounded in the WWII's Battle of the Bulge.[722]

According to their daughter, Carolyn Barker, 18-year-old Albert J. and 19-year-old Josephine Lemons Barker eloped just after Albert J., graduated from high school. Since Kentucky marriage laws were more lenient than Ohio's, they drove across the bridge to that state and wed there. Their marriage was against the wishes of Josephine's grandmother, Josephine Stroup Lemons, who raised young Josephine, her namesake. Josephine Stroup Lemons thought her granddaughter was too young to marry, despite that she herself was married when she was about Josephine Lemons Luck's age.[329]

Josephine Mae Lemons and Albert J. Luck II had three children, including:

+ 164 m III. **Gary Lee[10] Luck** was born in Lynchburg, Dodson Twp., Highland Co., Ohio, on June 13, 1945.[724] He died in Lynchburg, Dodson Twp., Highland Co., Ohio, on October 4, 1945.[724]

92. Clarence Junior[9] Lemons II (Long) (*Clarence Otto[8] Lemons, Josephine[7] Stroup, Elvira[6] Pegan, Henry[5], Robert A.[4], Andrew[3], Andrew[2] Pagan, James[1]*) was born on August 26, 1921, in Springfield, Springfield Twp., Clark Co., Ohio.[31, 362] He was the son of Clarence Otto Lemons (43) and Grace May Long. Clarence Junior (Lemons) Long died in West Allis, Milwaukee Co., Wisconsin, on January 23, 2012, at age 90.[31, 362] He was buried in Highland Memorial Park Cemetery, New Berlin, Waukesha Co., Wisconsin.[725]

His birth name was probably Clarence Junior Lemons II. Clarence Lemons II (Long) was adopted by his maternal grandparents, Benjamin and Minnie Brown Long, after the death of his mother Grace May Long Lemons. He used the surname Long for the rest of his life. His brother, Robert Lemons (Long), also lived with their grandparents Long in Springfield, Springfield Twp., Clark Co., Ohio until he was institutionalized in the Ohio Hospital for Epileptics in Gallipolis, Gallipolis Twp., Gallia Co., Ohio. Meanwhile their sister, Josephine Mae Lemons (later Luck) was reared by their paternal grandmother, Josephine Stroup Lemons in Lynchburg, Dodson Twp., Highland Co., Ohio. While Josephine Mae Lemons (Luck) had contact with their father, Clarence "Bill" Lemons, who also lived with his mother Josephine Stroup Lemons for a long time, Robert and Clarence (Lemons) Long had little contact with their father.[329]

In 1930, Clarence Junior Lemons II (Long), listed as Clarence Long, is enumerated in the home of his grandparents, B.F. (Benjamin) and Minnie Brown Long, in Springfield, Springfield Twp., Clark Co., Ohio. (*Census Place: Springfield, Clark, Ohio; Roll: 1756; Page: 15A; Enumeration District: 46; Image: 928.0*). Clarence Lemons II (Long) is age eight. Benjamin Long, 61, is a plater in a casket factory and Minnie Brown Long is 52 years old. All in the home, and their parents, were born in Ohio. Benjamin and Minnie Brown Long were married at ages 29 and 20 respectively.

Clarence Lemons II (Long) is still living with his grandparents in Springfield, Springfield Twp., Clark Co., Ohio in 1940 (*Census Place: Springfield, Clark, Ohio; Roll: T627_3040; Page: 16A; Enumeration District: 12-57*). Clarence Lemon Long, age 18, is a "new worker" (WPA). The head of the household is Benjamin Long, 70, a casket finisher. His wife, Minnie Brown Long, is 68 years old. All were born in Ohio, and say they were living in Springfield in 1935. Their home is at 823 Linder Street.

After serving in WWII, Clarence Lemons II (Long) moves to West Allis, Milwaukee Co., Wisconsin, where he became a police officer.[362]

Clarence Junior married **Dorothy Virginia Cleppe** on December 21, 1945, in Milwaukee Co., Wisconsin.[726] They had two sons. Dorothy Virginia Cleppe was born in Wauwatosa, Milwaukee Co., Wisconsin, on April 4, 1918.[31, 727, 728] Dorothy Virginia reached age 87 and died in West Allis, Milwaukee Co., Wisconsin, on August 30, 2005.[31, 727, 728, 729] She was buried in Highland Memorial Park Cemetery, New Berlin, Waukesha Co., Wisconsin.[728]

According to her obituary, Dorothy Cleppe Long served in the Women's Army Corps during WWII and was awarded the Bronze Star for meritorious service.

She met Clarence "Bill" (Lemons) Long, who was in the U.S. Army, in Oran, Africa during the war.[729]

Clarence Lemons II (Long) and Dorothy Virginia Cleppe had two sons:

+ 165 m I. **Jeffrey Richard**[10] **Long** was born in Milwaukee, Milwaukee Co., Wisconsin, on November 18, 1946.[31, 730, 731] He died in Sparks, Washoe Co., Nevada, on August 11, 2004.[31, 730, 731]

+ 166 m II. **Son**[10] **Long** was born in West Allis, Milwaukee Co., Wisconsin.

93. **Margaret Lucille**[9] **Lemons** ((*Edgar/Edward Roy*[8] *Lemons, Josephine*[7] *Stroup, Elvira*[6] *Pegan, Henry*[5], *Robert A.*[4], *Andrew*[3], *Andrew*[2] *Pagan, James*[1]) was born on March 17, 1923, in Lynchburg, Dodson Twp., Highland Co., Ohio.[31, 373] She was the daughter of Edgar/Edward Roy Lemons (44) and Wilhelmina Jane Leaverton. Margaret Lucille died in Stockton, Stockton Twp., San Joaquin Co., California, on January 12, 2013, at age 89.[31] She was buried in Winema Cemetery, Weed, Siskiyou Co., California.[313]

Margaret Lucille married **John James Brown** before 1948. They divorced. They had one son. John Jacob Brown was born in Jellico, Campbell Co., Tennessee, on November 8, 1924.[732] He reached age 72 and died in Columbia, Tuolumne Co., California, on October 31, 1999.[31, 732]

John James and Margaret Lemons Brown were living in Edgewood, Siskiyou Co., California in 1948.[733]

John James Brown's Social Security Death Index entry has the wrong year (1923) for his birth. His birth year was 1924, which is on his Social Security application and confirmed by his 1940 census enumeration *(Place: Campbell, Tennessee; Roll: m-t0627-03876; Page: 16A; Enumeration District: 7-18; entry for John J. Brown, nephew; Ada Stanaburg, head of household.)*

94. **Infant Daughter**[9] **Carroll** (*Cora May*[8] *Williams, Mary E.*[7] *Stroup, Elvira*[6] *Pegan, Henry*[5], *Robert A.*[4], *Andrew*[3], *Andrew*[2] *Pagan, James*[1]) was born about October 4, 1900, in Union Twp., Highland Co., Ohio? She was the daughter of Allen Carroll and Cora May Williams (45). Infant Daughter died in Union Twp., Highland Co., Ohio?, on October 4, 1900.[379] She was buried in Stroup Cemetery, Dodson Twp., Highland Co., Ohio.[379]

This unnamed infant daughter's headstone says she died October 4, 1900.[379] She was probably stillborn or died shortly after her birth.

95. **Mary Elinora**[9] **Carroll** (*Cora May*[8] *Williams, Mary E.*[7] *Stroup, Elvira*[6] *Pegan, Henry*[5], *Robert A.*[4], *Andrew*[3], *Andrew*[2] *Pagan, James*[1]) was born on May 10, 1902, in Union Twp., Highland Co., Ohio.[380, 381] She was the daughter of Allen Carroll and Cora May Williams (45). Mary Elinora died in Fayetteville, Perry Twp., Brown Co., Ohio, on June 14, 1914, at age 12.[381] She was buried in Stroup Cemetery, Dodson Twp., Highland Co., Ohio.[381, 734]

96. **William Morrell**[9] **Carroll** (*Cora May*[8] *Williams, Mary E.*[7] *Stroup, Elvira*[6] *Pegan, Henry*[5], *Robert A.*[4], *Andrew*[3], *Andrew*[2] *Pagan, James*[1]) was born on June 13, 1908, in Clark Twp., Clinton Co., Ohio.[382] He was the son of Allen Carroll and Cora May Williams (45). William Morrell was living in 1953 in Montgomery, Sycamore Twp., Hamilton Co., Ohio. He died in a hospital in Cincinnati, Hamilton Co., Ohio, on December 8, 1953, at age 45.[382] William Morrell was buried in Rest Haven Memorial Park Cemetery, Evendale, Sycamore Twp., Hamilton Co., Ohio.[382, 735]

William Morrell married **Dora Elizabeth Jones** on December 19, 1930, in Hamilton Co., Ohio.[736] They had one son. Dora Elizabeth Jones was born in Fleming Co. Kentucky on November 1, 1906.[737] She lived in 1943 in Pleasant Ridge, Hamilton Twp., Hamilton Co., Ohio. Dora Elizabeth reached age 36 and died in a hospital in Cincinnati, Hamilton Co., Ohio, on April 22, 1943.[737] She was buried in Rest Haven Memorial Park Cemetery, Evendale, Sycamore Twp., Hamilton Co., Ohio.[737]

In 1940, William Morrell Carroll ("Carrol") is enumerated in Cincinnati, Hamilton Co., Ohio *(Census Place: Cincinnati, Hamilton, Ohio; Roll: T627_3195; Page: 11B; Enumeration District: 91-236)*. William Carroll, age 31, born Ohio, is a foreman at an auto company. His wife, Dora Elizabeth Jones Carroll, is 29 years old, born in Kentucky. Living with them is William's brother, Delbert Carroll, age 19, single, a pin boy in a bowling alley. All were living in the same house, at 2624 Lysle Street, in 1935.

Widower William Morrell Carroll married **Lillian Hutchason** after 1943. They had one son. Lillian Hutchason was born in Dayton, Campbell Co., Kentucky, on May 12, 1906.[738] Lillian lived in 1961 in Blue Ash, Hamilton Co., Ohio. She reached age 81 and died in a hospital in Montgomery, Sycamore Twp., Hamilton Co., Ohio, on July 1, 1987.[738] Lillian Hutchason Carroll Whitten was buried in Spring Grove Cemetery, Cincinnati, Hamilton Co., Ohio.[739]

After William Morrell Carroll's death, Lillian Hutchason married Robert Whitten.

William Morrell Carroll was a foreman at Continental Can Company, Cincinnati, Hamilton Co., Ohio when he died.

Son of William Morrell Carroll and Lillian Hutchason:

+ 167 m I. **Douglas M.**[10] **Carroll** was born in Cincinnati, Hamilton Co., Ohio, on July 19, 1940.[740]

97. **Delbert A.**[9] **Carroll** (*Cora May*[8] *Williams, Mary E.*[7] *Stroup, Elvira*[6] *Pegan, Henry*[5]*, Robert A.*[4]*, Andrew*[3]*, Andrew*[2] *Pagan, James*[1]) was born on April 12, 1921, in Washington Twp., Highland Co., Ohio.[31, 383, 384] He was the son of Allen Carroll and Cora May Williams (45). He died in Hillsboro, Liberty Twp., Highland Co., Ohio, on February 20, 1991, at age 69.[31, 383] Delbert A. was buried in New Lynchburg Masonic Cemetery/Lynchburg F & AM Cemetery, Lynchburg, Dodson Twp., Highland Co., Ohio.[741, 742]

In 1940, Delbert Carroll is living with his brother and sister-in-law, William Morrell and Dora Elizabeth Jones Carroll, in Cincinnati, Hamilton Co., Ohio (*Census Place: Cincinnati, Hamilton, Ohio; Roll: T627_3195; Page: 11B; Enumeration District: 91-236*). Delbert Carroll, age 19, single, born Ohio, is a pin boy in a bowling alley. William Carroll, age 31, born Ohio, is a foreman at an auto company. His wife, Dora Elizabeth Jones Carroll, is 29 years old, born in Kentucky. All were living in the same house, at 2624 Lysle Street, in 1935.

Delbert A. married **Mary Helen Unknown** in 1941. They divorced. They have one daughter.

Delbert A. resided in 1946 in Lynchburg, Dodson Twp., Highland Co., Ohio.[743]

Delbert A. Carroll married **Ruth Louise Maas** on November 11, 1950, in Clinton Co., Ohio.[744, 745] They had three children. Ruth Louise Maas was born in Perry Twp., Brown Co., Ohio, on February 8, 1933.[746]

98. **Carl Delbert**[9] **Williams** (*Levi*[8]*, Mary E.*[7] *Stroup, Elvira*[6] *Pegan, Henry*[5]*, Robert A.*[4]*, Andrew*[3]*, Andrew*[2] *Pagan, James*[1]) was born on February 16, 1902, in Dodson Twp., Highland Co., Ohio.[31, 390, 391] He was the son of Levi Williams (46) and Bertha Frances Fawley. He died in Dayton, Montgomery Co., Ohio, on September 29, 1991, at age 89.[31, 391] Carl D. was buried in New Lynchburg Masonic Cemetery/Lynchburg F & AM Cemetery, Lynchburg, Dodson Twp., Highland Co., Ohio.[747, 748]

Carl D. married **Madge Ruble** on August 15, 1923, in Highland Co., Ohio.[749] They had two children. Madge Ruble was born in Union Twp., Highland Co., Ohio, on July 18, 1904.[31, 750, 751] Madge reached age 68 and died in Dayton, Montgomery Co., Ohio, on September 8, 1972.[750] She was buried in New Lynchburg Masonic Cemetery/Lynchburg F & AM Cemetery, Lynchburg, Dodson Twp., Highland Co., Ohio.[752, 753]

Carl D. Williams is enumerated in Wilmington, Union Twp., Clinton Co., Ohio in 1930 (*Census Place: Wilmington, Clinton, Ohio; Roll: 1761; Page: 6B; Enumeration District: 17; Image: 435.0*). Carl D. Williams, 28, a meat cutter in a meat shop, who says he was first married at age 21. His wife, Madge Ruble Williams, is 25 and says she 19 years old at her first marriage. Living with them are their children: Dwan, age five, and Caroline, age two years and 10 months. All in the home were born in Ohio, as were their parents.

In 1940, Carl D. Williams is found in Dayton, Montgomery Co., Ohio (*Census Place: Dayton, Montgomery, Ohio; Roll: T627_3256; Page: 1A;*

Enumeration District: 94-167). In the household are Carl D. Williams, 38, a health inspector for the welfare department; his wife Madge Ruble Williams, 35, and their two children, Dwayne ("Dwan"), 15, and Carolyn, 12. All were born in Ohio and say they were living in Dayton in 1935. Their home address is 3620 Wayne Avenue.

After Madge died, Carl D. Williams married Mrs. **Emily F. Land** Setty on August 26, 1976, in Montgomery Co., Ohio.[754] Emily F. Land was born in Cynthiana, Harrison Co., Kentucky, on March 21, 1908.[31, 755] Emily F. reached age 89 and died in Trotwood, Trotwood Twp., Montgomery Co., Ohio, on December 7, 1997.[31, 755] She was buried in Shiloh Park Cemetery, Shiloh, Harrison Twp., Montgomery Co., Ohio.[756]

Children of Carl D. Williams and Madge Ruble:

+ 168 m I. **Dwan Ruble**[10] **Williams** was born in Lynchburg, Dodson Twp., Highland Co., Ohio, on February 27, 1925.[757] He was also known as **Bill**. Dwan Ruble died in Boise, Ada Co., Idaho, on April 12, 2014.[757]

+ 169 f II. **Carolyn**[10] **Williams** was born in Lynchburg, Dodson Twp., Highland Co., Ohio, on June 24, 1927.

99. Edgar Franklin[9] **Wilkin** (*Hattie Ellen*[8] *Williams, Mary E.*[7] *Stroup, Elvira*[6] *Pegan, Henry*[5]*, Robert A.*[4]*, Andrew*[3]*, Andrew*[2] *Pagan, James*[1]) was born on May 30, 1902, in Hamer Twp., Highland Co., Ohio.[31, 398, 399] He was the son of George Robert Wilkin and Hattie Ellen Williams (47). He died in Hillsboro, Liberty Twp., Highland Co., Ohio, on May 28, 1996, age 93.[31, 399, 400] Edgar Franklin was buried in New Lynchburg Masonic Cemetery/Lynchburg F & AM Cemetery, Lynchburg, Dodson Twp., Highland Co., Ohio.[758, 759]

Edgar Franklin married **Ethalyn Teboe** on October 12, 1921, in Highland Co., Ohio.[760] They had four children. Ethalyn Teboe was born in Dodson Twp., Highland Co., Ohio, on September 7, 1900.[31, 761, 762] Ethalyn reached age 93 and died in Hillsboro, Liberty Twp., Highland Co., Ohio, on April 19, 1994.[31, 761, 762] She was buried in New Lynchburg Masonic Cemetery/Lynchburg F & AM Cemetery, Lynchburg, Dodson Twp., Highland Co., Ohio.[762, 763]

In 1930, Edgar F. Wilkin is enumerated in Dodson Twp., Highland Co., Ohio *(Census Place: Dodson, Highland, Ohio; Roll: 1823; Page: 3A; Enumeration District: 6; Image: 88.0).* Edgar F. Wilkin is age 28 and a farmer who says his first marriage occurred at age 18. His wife, Ethalyn Teboe Wilkin is 29 and says she was age 19 when first wed. They have three children: "Maryana", eight, Charles, seven, and Delores, four years and eight months. All in the home were born in Ohio, as were their parents.

Edgar Franklin Wilkin is still living in Dodson Twp., Highland Co., Ohio in 1940 *(Census Place: Dodson, Highland, Ohio; Roll: T627_3085; Page: 9A; Enumeration District: 36-6).* In the household are Edgar F. Wilkin, age 37, a farmer; his wife, Ethalyn Teboe Wilkin, 39, and their children Marianna, 18, Charles, 16, Delores, 14, and Joan, six. Their home is on U.S. 50, but there is no house number.

Children of Edgar Franklin Wilkin and Ethalyn Teboe:

+ 170 f I. **Marianna**[10] **Wilkin** was born in Dodson Twp., Highland Co., Ohio, on March 8, 1922.

+ 171 m II. **Charles Edgar**[10] **Wilkin** was born in Dodson Twp., Highland Co., Ohio, on May 17, 1923.[31, 764] He died in Tempe, Maricopa Co., Arizona, on March 19, 1982.[764, 765]

+ 172 f III. **Deloris**[10] **Wilkin** was born in Dodson Twp., Highland Co., Ohio, on July 23, 1925.

+ 173 f IV. **Joan**[10] **Wilkin** was born in Dodson Twp., Highland Co., Ohio, on August 20, 1933.[766]

100. Everett Robert[9] **Wilkin** (*Hattie Ellen*[8] *Williams, Mary E.*[7] *Stroup, Elvira*[6] *Pegan, Henry*[5]*, Robert A.*[4]*, Andrew*[3]*, Andrew*[2] *Pagan, James*[1]) was born on July 10, 1904, in Union Twp., Highland Co.,

Ohio.[31, 401, 402] He was the son of George Robert Wilkin and Hattie Ellen Williams (47). Everett Robert was living in 1980 in Hillsboro, Liberty Twp., Highland Co., Ohio. He died in a hospital in Georgetown, Pleasant Twp., Brown Co., Ohio, on November 11, 1980, at age 76.[402, 403] Everett Robert was buried in New Lynchburg Masonic Cemetery/Lynchburg F & AM Cemetery, Lynchburg, Dodson Twp., Highland Co., Ohio.[767]

Childless.

Everett Robert married **Florence Leona Fox** on December 10, 1928, in Marion Co., Ohio.[768] Florence Leona Fox was born in New Market Twp., Highland Co., Ohio, on August 7, 1909.[31, 769] Florence Leona lived in 1998 in Dodsonville, Dodson Twp., Highland Co., Ohio. She reached age 89 and died in Hillsboro, Liberty Twp., Highland Co., Ohio, on September 6, 1998.[31, 769] Florence Leona was buried in New Lynchburg Masonic Cemetery/Lynchburg F & AM Cemetery, Lynchburg, Dodson Twp., Highland Co., Ohio.[770]

Everett Robert Wilkin is enumerated as "Evrett Wilkin" in Dodson Twp., Highland Co., Ohio in 1930 *(Census Place: Dodson, Highland, Ohio; Roll: 1823; Page: 2A; Enumeration District: 6; Image: 86.0).* Everett and his wife, Florence Fox Wilkin are living with Florence's parents, Jesse C. and Pearl Fox. Everett R. Wilkin, 24, says he was first married at age 23. Although one of the columns for occupation is blank, the second says "Fox Ranch". He probably was helping his father-in-law on his farm/ranch. His wife, Florence Fox Wilkin, is 20 years old and says she was first wed at 19. Both say they and their parents were born in Ohio. Jesse C. Fox is age 40 and a farmer and his wife Pearl is 42, both born in Ohio as were their parents.

In 1940, Everett Wilkin is still residing in Dodson Twp., Highland Co., Ohio *(Census Place: Dodson, Highland, Ohio; Roll: T627_3085; Page: 8B; Enumeration District: 36-6).* In the household are Everett Wilkin, age 35, a farmer, and his wife, Florence L. Fox Wilkin, 30. Both were born in Ohio and say they were living in the same house on U.S. Highway 50 in 1935.

101. Marjorie Marie⁹ Wilkin (*Hattie Ellen⁸ Williams, Mary E.⁷ Stroup, Elvira⁶ Pegan, Henry⁵, Robert A.⁴, Andrew³, Andrew² Pagan, James¹*) was born on May 4, 1907, in Dodson Twp., Highland Co., Ohio.[404] She was the daughter of George Robert Wilkin and Hattie Ellen Williams (47). Marjorie Marie died in Lynchburg, Dodson Twp., Highland Co., Ohio, on October 8, 1963, at age 56.[405] She was buried in New Lynchburg Masonic Cemetery/Lynchburg F & AM Cemetery, Lynchburg, Dodson Twp., Highland Co., Ohio.[771]

Marjorie Marie married **Everett Guy Hawk** on June 26, 1929, in Fayette Co., Ohio.[772] They divorced. They had three children. Everett Guy Hawk was born in Salem Twp., Highland Co., Ohio, on September 5, 1903.[773, 774, 775] He was living in 1965 in Lynchburg, Dodson Twp., Highland Co., Ohio. Everett Guy reached age 62 and died in a hospital in Wilmington, Union Twp., Clinton Co., Ohio, on December 14, 1965.[775, 776] He was buried in New Lynchburg Masonic Cemetery/Lynchburg F & AM Cemetery, Lynchburg, Dodson Twp., Highland Co., Ohio.[773, 775]

In 1930, Everett G. and Marjorie Marie Wilkin Hawk are enumerated in Salem Twp., Highland Co., Ohio *(Census Place: Salem, Highland, Ohio; Roll: 1823; Page: 4B; Enumeration District: 23; Image: 503.0).* Everett G. Hawk, age 26, a farmer, says he was first married at age 25. Marjorie Marie Wilkin Hawk, 23, says her first marriage occurred when she was 22. Both say they and their parents were born in Ohio.

In 1940, Everett G. and Marjorie Wilkin Hawk have moved to Jackson Twp. Clermont Co., Ohio *(Census Place: Jackson, Clermont, Ohio; Roll: T627_3041; Page: 9B; Enumeration District: 13-9).* The house is on State Route 131. In the household are Everett Hawk, age 35, a timekeeper at the Works Progress Administration (WPA); his wife, Marjorie Wilkin Hawk, 33, and their daughters Sonya, nine, and Carolyn, six. All were born in Ohio and say they were living in Highland County, Ohio in 1935.

Marjorie Marie Wilkin and Everett Guy Hawk had three children, including:

+ 174 f I. **Sonia M.**[10] **Hawk** was born in Salem Twp., Highland Co., Ohio, on February 26, 1931.[777]

+ 175 f II. **Carolyn M.**[10] **Hawk** was born in Salem Twp., Highland Co., Ohio, on August 4, 1933.[778]

102. Evelyn Lorie[9] **Wilkin** (*Hattie Ellen*[8] *Williams, Mary E.*[7] *Stroup, Elvira*[6] *Pegan, Henry*[5]*, Robert A.*[4]*, Andrew*[3]*, Andrew*[2] *Pagan, James*[1]) was born on July 7, 1911, in Dodson Twp., Highland Co., Ohio.[406, 407] She was the daughter of George Robert Wilkin and Hattie Ellen Williams (47). Evelyn Lorie died in Hillsboro, Liberty Twp., Highland Co., Ohio, on August 8, 2002, at age 91.[406, 407] She was buried in New Lynchburg Masonic Cemetery/Lynchburg F & AM Cemetery, Lynchburg, Dodson Twp., Highland Co., Ohio.[779, 780]

Evelyn Lorie married **William E. Campbell** about 1927. They had five children. William E. Campbell was born in Salem Twp., Highland Co., Ohio, on May 9, 1906.[31, 781] Clinton Co., Ohio. William E. was living in 1974 in Highland Co., Ohio. He reached age 68 and died in a hospital in Wilmington, Union Twp., Clinton Co., Ohio, on August 22, 1974.[31, 782] William E. was buried in New Lynchburg Masonic Cemetery/Lynchburg F & AM Cemetery, Lynchburg, Dodson Twp., Highland Co., Ohio.[783]

In 1930, William E. and Evelyn Lorie Wilkin Campbell are found in Perry Twp., Brown Co., Ohio (*Census Place: Perry, Brown, Ohio; Roll: 1753; Page: 5A; Enumeration District: 16; Image: 251.0*). They are living with William's parents, Charles and Anna L. Campbell. William E. Campbell is age 23, a laborer (odd jobs), who says he was first married at age 21. Evelyn L. Wilkin Campbell, 18, says her first marriage was at age 16. They have a daughter, Betty E., one year and nine months. Charles Campbell is 54, a farmer and his wife Anna is 56, married at ages 30 and 28 respectively. All in the home, and their parents, were born in Ohio.

William E. and Evelyn Wilkin Campbell have relocated to Clark Twp., Clinton Co., Ohio by 1940 (*Census Place: Clark, Clinton, Ohio; Roll: T627_3042; Page: 13A; Enumeration District: 14-5*). In the household are William E. Campbell, age 34, a farmer, Evelyn Wilkin Campbell, 29, and their children Elaine, 11, June, nine, and Donald, six. All were born in Ohio and state they were residing in Clark Twp., Clinton Co., Ohio in 1935. Their home is on the Lynchburg and Webertown Road, but there is no numerical address.

After William died, Evelyn Lorie Wilkin Campbell married **Howard Laverne Fissel** about September 15, 1976 in Highland Co., Ohio.[784] Howard Laverne Fissel was born in Jennings Twp., Van Wert Co., Ohio, on January 6, 1914.[31, 785, 786] Howard reached age 76 and died in Hillsboro, Liberty Twp., Highland Co., Ohio, on March 10, 1990.[785, 786] He was buried in Spencerville Cemetery, Spencerville, Spencer Twp., Allen Co., Ohio.[786, 787]

Evelyn Lorie Wilkin Campbell Fissel married **Herbert M. Turner** after 1990. Herbert M. Turner was born in Chicago, Cook Co., Illinois, on January 28, 1905.[788, 789] Herbert M. reached age 97 and died in Hillsboro, Liberty Twp., Highland Co., Ohio, on February 8, 2002.[787, 789] He was cremated.[789]

Evelyn Lorie Wilkin and William E. Campbell had five children, including:

+ 176 f I. **Betty Elaine**[10] **Campbell** was born in Perry Twp., Brown Co., Ohio, on July 30, 1928.[790] She is also known as **Elaine**.

+ 177 f II. **June Phyllis**[10] **Campbell** was born in Perry Twp., Brown Co., Ohio, on May 31, 1931.[791]

+ 178 m III. **Donald E.**[10] **Campbell** was born in Lynchburg, Dodson Twp., Highland Co., Ohio, on June 9, 1933.[792, 793, 794] He was also known as **Don E**. He died in a hospital in Hillsboro, Liberty Twp.,

Highland Co., Ohio, on June 7, 2013.[793, 794]

+ 179 m IV. **John Lee**[10] **Campbell** was born in Clark Twp., Clinton Co., Ohio, on December 31, 1940.

103. Lenora[9] **Wilkin** (*Hattie Ellen*[8] *Williams, Mary E.*[7] *Stroup, Elvira*[6] *Pegan, Henry*[5] *, Robert A.*[4]*, Andrew*[3]*, Andrew*[2] *Pagan, James*[1]) was born on February 14, 1914, in Dodson Twp., Highland Co., Ohio.[408] She was the daughter of George Robert Wilkin and Hattie Ellen Williams (47). Lenora died in Dodson Twp., Highland Co., Ohio, on February 14, 1933, at age 19.[408] She was buried in Troutwine Cemetery, Dodson Twp., Highland Co., Ohio and Clark Twp., Clinton Co., Ohio.[408, 795]

Lenora married **Wendell D. Barker** on February 17, 1932, in Highland Co., Ohio.[796] They had one son. Wendell D. Barker was born in Fayetteville, Perry Twp., Brown Co., Ohio, on February 2, 1911.[29, 797] Wendell D. reached age 68 and died in Harrison Twp., Hamilton Co., Ohio, on July 24, 1979.[797, 798] He was buried in Troutwine Cemetery, Dodson Twp., Highland Co., Ohio and Clark Twp., Clinton Co., Ohio.[797, 799]

Lenora Wilkin Barker died of childbirth complications.

After his first wife, Lenora Wilkin Barker, died, Wendell D. Barker married Mary S. Campbell and had a family.

Son of Lenora Wilkin and Wendell D. Barker:

+ 180 m I. **Jimmie Gaylord**[10] **Barker** was born in Dodson Twp., Highland Co., Ohio, on January 27, 1933.[800] He died in Dodson Twp., Highland Co., Ohio, on January 28, 1933.[800]

104. Georgeanna[9] **Wilkin** (*Hattie Ellen*[8] *Williams, Mary E.*[7] *Stroup, Elvira*[6] *Pegan, Henry*[5]*, Robert A.*[4]*, Andrew*[3]*, Andrew*[2] *Pagan, James*[1]) was born on July 27, 1916, in Dodson Twp., Highland Co., Ohio.[409, 410, 411] She was the daughter of George Robert Wilkin and Hattie Ellen Williams (47). Georgeanna died in Waverly, Pee Pee Twp., Pike Co., Ohio, on March 26, 1998, at age 81.[410, 411] She was buried in Evergreen Union Cemetery, Waverly, Pee Pee Twp., Pike Co., Ohio.[410, 801]

For some odd reason, Georgiana Wilkin Roush Ross Holderby's death certificate says she was born in Columbiana Co., Ohio. This is incorrect; she was born in Dodson Twp., Highland Co., Ohio.[411]

Georgeanna married **Marcus C. Roush** on December 5, 1936, in Highland Co., Ohio.[409] They divorced. They had two daughters. Marcus C. Roush was born in Hamer Twp., Highland Co., Ohio, on December 15, 1915.[31, 409, 802, 803] Marcus C. reached age 57 and died in Clark Twp., Clinton Co., Ohio, on November 16, 1973.[803, 804] He was buried in Hamer Township Cemetery, Hamer Twp., Highland Co., Ohio.[805, 806]

In 1940, Marcus and Georgiana Wilkin Roush are enumerated in Dodson Twp., Highland Co., Ohio *(Census Place: Dodson, Highland, Ohio; Roll: T627_3085; Page: 2A; Enumeration District: 36-6)*. Marcus Roush, age 24, is a farmer, and his wife, Georgiana Wilkin Roush, is 23 years old. Both were born in Ohio and say they were living in Dodson Twp. in 1935. Their home was at 120-A Lemon Road.

A "Personals" mention in the *Hillsboro (OH) Press Gazette* in July 1964 notes that Marcus and Georgeanna Wilkin Roush were residents of Chillicothe, Scioto Twp., Ross Co., Ohio.[807]

om Marcus C. Roush, Georgeanna Wilkin Roush married **Paul Graham Ross** on May 9, 1971. Paul Graham Ross was born in Green Twp., Ross Co., Ohio, on April 9, 1904.[31, 808] Paul Graham lived in 1974 in Kinnikinnick, Green Twp., Ross Co., Ohio. He reached age 69 and died in a hospital in Chillicothe, Scioto Twp., Ross Co., Ohio, on April 2, 1974.[31, 809, 810] Paul Graham was buried in Salem White Church Cemetery, Kingston, Green Twp., Ross Co., Ohio.[809, 811]

Georgeanna Wilkin Roush Ross married **Malcolm William Edgar Holderby** on April 9, 1978, in Pike Co., Ohio.[812] Malcolm William Edgar Holderby was born in Proctorville, Union Twp., Lawrence Co., Ohio, on April 2, 1913.[31, 813, 814] Malcolm William Edgar lived in 1979 in Piketon, Seal Twp., Pike Co., Ohio. He reached age 65 and died in a hospital in Chillicothe, Scioto Twp., Ross Co., Ohio, on March 2, 1979.[813, 815] Malcolm William Edgar was buried in Evergreen Cemetery, Waverly, Pee Pee Twp., Pike Co., Ohio.[813, 816]

Daughters of Georgeanna Wilkin and Marcus C. Roush:

+ 181 f I. **Barbara Ann**[10] **Roush** was born in Dodson Twp., Highland Co., Ohio, on November 4, 1940.

+ 182 f II. **Daughter**[10] **Roush** was born in Lynchburg, Dodson Twp., Highland Co., Ohio.

105. Samuel[9] **Wilkin** (*Hattie Ellen*[8] *Williams, Mary E.*[7] *Stroup, Elvira*[6] *Pegan, Henry*[5] *, Robert A.*[4] *, Andrew*[3] *, Andrew*[2] *Pagan, James*[1]) was born on September 14, 1920, in Dodson Twp., Highland Co., Ohio.[31, 412, 413] He was the son of George Robert Wilkin and Hattie Ellen Williams (47). Samuel died in Hillsboro, Liberty Twp., Highland Co., Ohio, on June 19, 1994, at age 73.[31, 412, 413] He was buried in New Lynchburg Masonic Cemetery/Lynchburg F & AM Cemetery, Lynchburg, Dodson Twp., Highland Co., Ohio.[817]

Although his obituary says Samuel Wilkin was buried in the Sugar Grove Cemetery in Wilmington, Clinton Co., Ohio, Find A Grave records and pictures show he is buried in the New Masonic F & AM Cemetery in Lynchburg, Dodson Twp., Highland Co., Ohio.[817, 818]

Samuel married **Frances Hartman** on December 24, 1944, in Cleveland, Cuyahoga Co., Ohio.[819] They divorced. They had three children. Frances Hartman was born in Kingman, Chester Twp., Clinton Co., Ohio, on February 27, 1922.

Samuel Wilkin married Mrs. **Lucille Unknown** Gilbert on February 28, 1984, in Collier Co., Florida.[820] They divorced. Lucille Unknown Gilbert was born in 1926.

106. LeRoy Thomas[9] **Wilkin** (*Hattie Ellen*[8] *Williams, Mary E.*[7] *Stroup, Elvira*[6] *Pegan, Henry*[5] *, Robert A.*[4] *, Andrew*[3] *, Andrew*[2] *Pagan, James*[1]) was born on January 3, 1923, in Dodson Twp., Highland Co., Ohio.[31, 414] He was also known as **Tom**. He was the son of George Robert Wilkin and Hattie Ellen Williams (47). He died in Wilmington, Union Twp., Clinton Co., Ohio, on August 1, 2010, at age 87.[31, 414] LeRoy Thomas was buried in New Lynchburg Masonic Cemetery/Lynchburg F & AM Cemetery, Lynchburg, Dodson Twp., Highland Co., Ohio.[821]

LeRoy Thomas married **Helen Briggs** on January 9, 1943, in Highland Co., Ohio.[822] They had three children. Helen Briggs was born in Dodson Twp., Highland Co., Ohio, on May 14, 1922.

Children of LeRoy Thomas Wilkin and Helen Briggs had three children, including:

+ 183 m I. **Son**[10] **Wilkin** was born in Highland or Clinton Co., Ohio.

+ 184 f II. **Infant Daughter**[10] **Wilkin** was born in Highland or Clinton Co., Ohio?. She died in Highland or Clinton Co., Ohio?, in 1948.

107. Eugene[9] **Williams** (*Stanley*[8] *, Mary E.*[7] *Stroup, Elvira*[6] *Pegan, Henry*[5] *, Robert A.*[4] *, Andrew*[3] *, Andrew*[2] *Pagan, James*[1]) was born on December 30, 1910, in Perry Twp., Brown Co., Ohio.[423] He was the son of Stanley Williams (48) and Mary Achor. Eugene died in Dodson Twp., Highland Co., Ohio, on April 10, 1923, at age 12.[423] He was buried in New Lynchburg Masonic Cemetery/Lynchburg F & AM Cemetery, Lynchburg, Dodson Twp., Highland Co., Ohio.[823]

108. Virgil[9] **Williams** (*Stanley*[8] *, Mary E.*[7] *Stroup, Elvira*[6] *Pegan, Henry*[5] *, Robert A.*[4] *, Andrew*[3] *, Andrew*[2] *Pagan, James*[1]) was born on November 1, 1913, in Perry Twp., Brown Co., Ohio.[31, 424] He was the son of Stanley Williams (48) and Mary Achor. Virgil resided in 2001 in Lynchburg, Dodson Twp., Highland Co., Ohio. He died in a hospital in Kenwood, Hamilton Co., Ohio, on June 6, 2001, at age 87.[31, 424] Virgil was buried in Martinsville

IOOF Cemetery, Martinsville, Clark Twp., Clinton Co., Ohio.[824, 825]

Virgil married **Anna Rhonemus** on November 1, 1939.[826] They had one daughter. Anna Rhonemus was born in Lynchburg, Dodson Twp., Highland Co., Ohio, on October 28, 1918.[827] Anna reached age 96 and died in a facility in Wilmington, Union Twp., Clinton Co., Ohio, on January 12, 2015.[827] She was buried in Martinsville IOOF Cemetery, Martinsville, Clark Twp., Clinton Co., Ohio.[827, 828]

In 1940, Virgil Williams is enumerated in Lynchburg, Dodson Twp., Highland Co., Ohio *(Census Place: Lynchburg, Highland, Ohio; Roll: T627_3085; Page: 10A; Enumeration District: 36-5)*. Virgil Williams, age 26, is a meat cutter who says he was living in Clermont County, Ohio in 1935. His wife, Anna Rhonemus Williams, who is 21 years old. says she was residing in Clinton County, Ohio in 1935. Both were born in Ohio. Their house seems to be on the corner of Washington and College streets.

109. Woodrow Wilson[9] Williams (*Stanley[8], Mary E.[7] Stroup, Elvira[6] Pegan, Henry[5], Robert A.[4], Andrew[3], Andrew[2] Pagan, James[1]*) was born on December 16, 1916, in Dodson Twp., Highland Co., Ohio.[31] He was the son of Stanley Williams (48) and Mary Achor. He resided in May 1972 in Lynchburg, Dodson Twp., Highland Co., Ohio. Woodrow Wilson died in a hospital in Wilmington, Union Twp., Clinton Co., Ohio, on May 1, 1972, at age 55..[31, 425, 426] He was buried in New Lynchburg Masonic Cemetery/Lynchburg F & AM Cemetery, Lynchburg, Dodson Twp., Highland Co., Ohio.[426, 829]

Woodrow Wilson married **Mabel Fern Snyder** about 1935. They had four children. Mabel Fern Snyder was born in Bethel, Tate Twp., Clermont Co., Ohio, on December 26, 1913.[31, 830, 831, 832] Mabel Fern reached age 91 and died in Hillsboro, Liberty Twp., Highland Co., Ohio, on June 29, 2005.[31, 830, 832] She was buried in New Lynchburg Masonic Cemetery/Lynchburg F & AM Cemetery, Lynchburg, Dodson Twp., Highland Co., Ohio.[833]

Woodrow Wilson Williams is enumerated as in Lynchburg, Dodson Twp., Highland Co., Ohio in 1940 *(Census Place: Lynchburg, Highland, Ohio; Roll: T627_3085; Page: 5B; Enumeration District: 36-5)*. The head of the household is Woodrow Williams, age 23, who is a proprietor of a "retail and wholesale meat market". With him are wife Mabel Snyder Williams, 26, and daughters Carol G., age four, Janet E., two, and Julia M., one. All are Ohio natives and are living at 137 Pearl Street. Woodrow and Mabel Snyder Williams say they were living in Lynchburg in 1935.

Woodrow Wilson Williams was a grocer in Lynchburg, Dodson Twp., Highland Co., Ohio.[426]

Children of Woodrow Wilson Williams and Mabel Fern Snyder:

+ 185 f   I.   **Carol Jean[10] Williams** was born in Lynchburg, Dodson Twp., Highland Co., Ohio, on December 21, 1935.[834]

+ 186 f   II. **Janet E.[10] Williams** was born in Lynchburg, Dodson Twp., Highland Co., Ohio, on July 14, 1937.[835]

+ 187 f   III. **Judith Mae[10] Williams** was born in Lynchburg, Dodson Twp., Highland Co., Ohio, on January 19, 1939.[836] She died in a hospital in Wilmington, Union Twp., Clinton Co., Ohio, on January 3, 2014.[836]

+ 188 m   IV. **James Douglas[10] Williams** was born in Lynchburg, Dodson Twp., Highland Co., Ohio, on March 12, 1943.[31, 837] He died in Dodson Twp., Highland Co., Ohio, on May 18, 1986.[837, 838]

110. Stanley Mitchell[9] Williams II (*Stanley[8], Mary E.[7] Stroup, Elvira[6] Pegan, Henry[5], Robert A.[4], Andrew[3], Andrew[2] Pagan, James[1]*) was born on February 2, 1925, in Dodson Twp., Highland Co., Ohio.[29, 427] He was also known as **Mitchell**. He was the son of Stanley Williams (48) and Mary Achor. Stanley Mitchell lived in 2007 in Belmont Co., Ohio.

Stanley Mitchell died in a hospital in Dayton, Montgomery Co., Ohio, on August 20, 2007, at age 82.[427, 428] He was cremated and his ashes buried in New Lynchburg Masonic Cemetery/Lynchburg F & AM Cemetery, Lynchburg, Dodson Twp., Highland Co., Ohio.[428, 839]

Stanley Mitchell may have married **Unknown Unknown** before 1947. They have one daughter.

Stanley Mitchell Williams II married **Wanda Beatrice Shumard** on June 17, 1948, in Highland Co., Ohio.[840, 841] They divorced. They had two daughters. Wanda Beatrice Shumard was born in Miami Twp., Clermont Co., Ohio, on February 12, 1930.[842]

Stanley Mitchell Williams II married **Marianna Williamson** about 1956.[843] They had no children. Marianna Williamson was born in Clark Twp., Clinton Co., Ohio, on July 13, 1926.[31, 843, 844] She reached age 80 and died in Lynchburg, Dodson Twp., Highland Co., Ohio, on March 14, 2007.[31, 843, 844] Marianna was buried in New Lynchburg Masonic Cemetery/Lynchburg F & AM Cemetery, Lynchburg, Dodson Twp., Highland Co., Ohio (Ashes).[843, 845]

111. **Hazel Imogene[9] Williams** (*Joseph Everett[8], Mary E.[7] Stroup, Elvira[6] Pegan, Henry[5], Robert A.[4], Andrew[3], Andrew[2] Pagan, James[1]*) was born on November 9, 1917, in Dodson Twp., Highland Co., Ohio.[435] She was also known as **Imogene** or **Genie**. She was the daughter of Joseph Everett Williams (49) and Anna Mary Tolle. Hazel Imogene died in Cincinnati, Hamilton Co., Ohio, on May 22, 2006, at age 88.[435, 436] She was buried in Laurel Cemetery, Madisonville, Hamilton Co., Ohio.[436, 846]

Childless.

Hazel Imogene married **Ralph E. Davidson** before 1939. Ralph E. Davidson was born in Cincinnati, Hamilton Co., Ohio, on October 22, 1916.[31] Ralph E. lived in 2012 in Cincinnati, Hamilton Co., Ohio. He reached age 96 and died in Cincinnati, Hamilton Co., Ohio, on January 27, 2013.[31, 847] Ralph E. was buried in Laurel IOOF Cemetery, Madisonville, Hamilton Co., Ohio.[848]

112. **Paul T.[9] Williams** (*Joseph Everett[8], Mary E.[7] Stroup, Elvira[6] Pegan, Henry[5], Robert A.[4], Andrew[3], Andrew[2] Pagan, James[1]*) was born on July 4, 1920, in Dodson Twp., Highland Co., Ohio.[437, 438] He was the son of Joseph Everett Williams (49) and Anna Mary Tolle. He died in Deer Park, Hamilton Co., Ohio, on November 18, 2013, at age 93.[437, 438] Paul T. was buried in Arlington Memorial Gardens Cemetery, Mount Healthy, Springfield Twp., Hamilton Co., Ohio.[438, 849]

Childless.

Paul T. married **Madeleine Baker** in 1946.[850] Madeline Baker was born in Pulaski Co., Kentucky, on June 9, 1924.[31, 851, 852] Madeline reached age 82 and died in a hospital in St. Mary's, St. Mary's Twp., Auglaize Co., Ohio, on March 1, 2007.[31, 852] She was buried in Arlington Memorial Gardens Cemetery, Mount Healthy, Springfield Twp., Hamilton Co., Ohio.[853]

113. **Clarence E.[9] Williams** (*Harley N.[8], Mary E.[7] Stroup, Elvira[6] Pegan, Henry[5], Robert A.[4], Andrew[3], Andrew[2] Pagan, James[1]*) was born on June 13, 1932, in Dodson Twp., Highland Co., Ohio.[31, 446, 447] He was the son of Harley N. Williams (51) and Mary Johanna Freeman. Clarence E. lived in 1989 in Lynchburg, Dodson Twp., Highland Co., Ohio. He died in Hillsboro, Liberty Twp., Highland Co., Ohio, on August 29, 1996, at age 64.[31, 446] Clarence E. was buried in Barnes Cemetery, Fairview, New Market Twp., Highland Co., Ohio.[854]

May have been childless.

Clarence E. married **Janice Aileen Cadwallader** on July 18, 1954.[854] Janice Aileen Cadwallader was born in Dodson Twp., Highland Co., Ohio, on November 10, 1935.[855]

114. **Mary Elizabeth[9] Williams** (*Harley N.[8], Mary E.[7] Stroup, Elvira[6] Pegan, Henry[5], Robert A.[4], Andrew[3], Andrew[2] Pagan, James[1]*) was born on September 29, 1933, in Hillsboro, Liberty Twp., Highland Co., Ohio. She is the daughter of Harley N. Williams (51) and Mary Johanna Freeman.

Mary Elizabeth married **Karl Bendict Kelley** about 1958. They divorced. They had two sons.

Karl Bendict Kelley was born in Norwood, Mill Creek Twp., Hamilton Co., Ohio, on January 5, 1922.[31, 856, 857] Karl Bendict lived in 1992 in Norwood, Mill Creek Twp., Hamilton Co., Ohio. He reached age 70 and died in a hospital in Cincinnati, Hamilton Co., Ohio, on March 16, 1992.[31, 857] Karl Bendict was buried in Rose Hill Cemetery, Mason, Deerfield Twp., Warren Co., Ohio.[858, 859]

Sons of Mary Elizabeth Williams and Karl Bendict Kelley had two children, including:

+ 189 m II. **David Lee**[10] **Kelley** was born in Norwood, Mill Creek Twp., Hamilton Co., Ohio, on January 29, 1963.[860] He died in a hospital in Cincinnati, Hamilton Co., Ohio, on June 17, 1967.[861]

115. Glen Louis[9] **Williams** (*Harley N.*[8], *Mary E.*[7] *Stroup, Elvira*[6] *Pegan, Henry*[5], *Robert A.*[4], *Andrew*[3], *Andrew*[2] *Pagan, James*[1]) was born on February 1, 1935, in Lynchburg, Dodson Twp., Highland Co., Ohio.[31, 448] He was the son of Harley N. Williams (51) and Mary Johanna Freeman. Glen Louis lived in 1989 in Niceville, Okaloosa Co., Florida. He died in Ponce de Leon, Holmes Co., Florida, on July 13, 2011, at age 76.[31, 448] Glen Louis was buried in Black Creek Memorial Cemetery, Freeport, Walton Co., Florida.[448, 862]

Glen Louis married **Betty Lou Bishop** before 1962. They had five children. Betty Lou Bishop was born in Freeport, Walton Co., Florida, on February 1, 1939.[31, 863] Betty Lou reached age 70 and died in Freeport, Walton Co., Florida, on August 24, 2009.[31, 863] She was buried in Black Creek Memorial Cemetery, Freeport, Walton Co., Florida.[863, 864]

Glen Louis Williams and Betty Lou Bishop had five children, including:

+ 190 f III. **Candus Gay**[10] **Williams** was born in Hillsboro, Liberty Twp., Highland Co., Ohio, on February 9, 1965.[865] She died in DeFuniak Springs, Walton Co., Florida, on January 26, 2012.[865]

+ 191 m V. **Vincent B.**[10] **Williams** was born in DeFuniak Springs, Walton Co., Florida, on December 19, 1975.[866] He died in DeFuniak Springs, Walton Co., Florida, on December 19, 1975.[866]

116. Dale Mathew[9] **Williams** (*Harley N.*[8], *Mary E.*[7] *Stroup, Elvira*[6] *Pegan, Henry*[5], *Robert A.*[4], *Andrew*[3], *Andrew*[2] *Pagan, James*[1]) was born on March 29, 1936, in Hillsboro, Liberty Twp., Highland Co., Ohio.[29, 449] He was the son of Harley N. Williams (51) and Mary Johanna Freeman. He died in Pawnee, Pawnee Twp., Sangamon Co., Illinois, on January 5, 1991, at age 54.[29, 449] Dale Mathew was buried in Barnes Cemetery, Fairview, New Market Twp., Highland Co., Ohio.[449, 867]

Dale Mathew married **Rita Ann Crone** on September 17, 1961.[449] They had two children. Rita Ann Crone was born in Sabina, Richland Twp., Clinton Co., Ohio, on September 20, 1943.[868] Rita Ann reached age 66 and died in Springfield, Springfield Twp., Sangamon Co., Illinois, on November 15, 2009.[868] She was buried in Barnes Cemetery, Fairview, New Market Twp., Highland Co., Ohio.[868, 869]

Starting in 1965, Dale Matthew Williams worked for the U.S. Agricultural Department, particularly as a food inspector and compliance officer for its consumer products division. In his career, he was based in various Ohio cities, including Canton, Massillon, Youngstown, Cortland, and Defiance before eventually moving to Pawnee, Pawnee Twp., Sangamon Co., Illinois.[449]

117. Stephen Thomas[9] **Williams** (*Harley N.*[8], *Mary E.*[7] *Stroup, Elvira*[6] *Pegan, Henry*[5], *Robert A.*[4], *Andrew*[3], *Andrew*[2] *Pagan, James*[1]) was born on August 25, 1938, in Hillsboro, Liberty Twp., Highland Co., Ohio.[450] He was the son of Harley N. Williams (51) and Mary Johanna Freeman. Stephen Thomas died in Dodson Twp., Highland Co., Ohio, on

September 21, 1938.[450] He was buried in Stroup Cemetery, Dodson Twp., Highland Co., Ohio.[450]

118. **James Richard**[9] **Williams** (*Harley N.*[8], *Mary E.*[7] *Stroup, Elvira*[6] *Pegan, Henry*[5], *Robert A.*[4], *Andrew*[3], *Andrew*[2] *Pagan, James*[1]) was born on August 25, 1938, in Hillsboro, Liberty Twp., Highland Co., Ohio. He is the son of Harley N. Williams (51) and Mary Johanna Freeman.

James Richard married **Dixie M. Koch**. Dixie M. Koch was born on December 14, 1940.

119. **Charlotte Jean**[9] **Spilker** (*Earl Everett*[8], *Laura Arabella*[7] *Stroup, Elvira*[6] *Pegan, Henry*[5], *Robert A.*[4], *Andrew*[3], *Andrew*[2] *Pagan, James*[1]) was born on October 14, 1920, in Dodsonville, Dodson Twp., Highland Co., Ohio.[31, 465, 466] She was the daughter of Earl Everett Spilker (54) and Merle M. Roades. Charlotte Jean died in Clearwater, Pinellas Co., Florida, on November 6, 2004, at age 84.[31, 465, 466] She was buried in Sylvan Abbey Memorial Park Cemetery, Clearwater, Pinellas Co., Florida.[465]

Charlotte Jean married **Bernard E. Simms** on June 9, 1943 in Marion Co., Indiana.[870] They had no children. Bernard was born on August 16, 1917 in Goshen, Goshen Twp., Clermont Co., Ohio.[871] He lived in 1946 in Reading, Hamilton Co., Ohio. Bernard died on January 19, 1946 in Goshen Twp., Clermont Co., Ohio.[871, 872] He was buried in Goshen Cemetery, Goshen Twp., Clermont Co., Ohio.[871, 872, 873]

Bernard E. Simms was a teacher in the West Chester Township., Butler County, Ohio school system.[871, 872]

Charlotte Jean Spilker Simms married **Robert R. Hern** on June 19, 1948, in Highland Co., Ohio.[874] They had three children. Robert R. Hern was born in Liberty Twp., Highland Co., Ohio, on October 21, 1917.[31, 875] Robert R. reached age 92 and died in Clearwater, Pinellas Co., Florida, on March 22, 2010.[31, 875] He was buried in Sylvan Abbey Memorial Park Cemetery, Clearwater, Pinellas Co., Florida.[875]

Robert R. Hern was the district manager for Columbus and Southern Electric Company and lived in Liberty Twp., Highland Co., Ohio until retiring to Florida. He was an avid golfer who birdied the 18th hole at the famed St. Andrews course in Scotland when he was 88 years old.[875]

120. **Joseph Benjamin**[9] **Spilker** (*Ralph Henry*[8], *Laura Arabella*[7] *Stroup, Elvira*[6] *Pegan, Henry*[5], *Robert A.*[4], *Andrew*[3], *Andrew*[2] *Pagan, James*[1]) was born on April 15, 1917, in Fayetteville, Perry Twp., Brown Co., Ohio.[472, 473] He was the son of Ralph Henry Spilker (55) and Isma Faris. He died in Cincinnati, Hamilton Co., Ohio, on September 28, 1940, at age 23.[472, 474] Joseph Benjamin was buried in Spring Grove Cemetery, Cincinnati, Hamilton Co., Ohio.[472, 876]

Joseph Benjamin married **Dorothy Elenor Ernst** before 1938.[384, 29] They had one son. Dorothy Ernst was born in Washington Twp., Clermont Co., Ohio, on April 4, 1919.[31, 877, 878, 879] Dorothy reached age 85 and died in Cambridge, Cambridge Twp., Guernsey Co., Ohio, on February 9, 2005.[31, 877, 878, 879] She was buried in Spring Grove Cemetery, Cincinnati, Hamilton Co., Ohio.[877, 880]

In 1940, Joseph Spilker is enumerated in Cincinnati, Hamilton Co., Ohio in Mt. Auburn Twp. *(Census Place: Cincinnati, Hamilton, Ohio; Roll: T627_3192; Page: 4A; Enumeration District: 91-169A).* In the household are Joseph Spilker, age 23, a clerk in an automobile factory, and his wife, Dorothy Ernst Spilker, 20. Both say they were born in Ohio and were living in Cincinnati in 1935. They are residing at 5 View Court.

After Joseph Benjamin Spilker's death, Dorothy Ernst Spilker married Russell Atkinson.[877]

Son of Joseph Benjamin Spilker and Dorothy Ernst:

+ 192 m I. **Joseph Todd**[10] **Spilker II** was born in Cincinnati, Hamilton Co., Ohio (Mt. Auburn Twp.), on March 18, 1939.[31, 881] He died in Cambridge, Cambridge Twp., Guernsey Co., Ohio, on December 13, 2009.[31, 881]

121. **Shirley Lois Gail**[9] **Spilker** (*Ralph Henry*[8], *Laura Arabella*[7] *Stroup, Elvira*[6] *Pegan, Henry*[5], *Robert A.*[4], *Andrew*[3], *Andrew*[2] *Pagan, James*[1]) was born on March 5, 1922, in Hillsboro, Liberty

Twp., Highland Co., Ohio.[31, 475, 476, 477] She was the daughter of Ralph Henry Spilker (55) and Isma Faris. Shirley Lois Gail died in Cincinnati, Hamilton Co., Ohio, on January 27, 2003, at age 80.[31, 475, 477, 478] She was buried in Spring Grove Cemetery, Cincinnati, Hamilton Co., Ohio.[882]

Shirley Lois Gail married **Russell Howard Rogers** before 1946. They had two children. Russell Howard Rogers was born in Cleves, Miami Twp., Hamilton Co., Ohio, on December 21, 1917.[31, 883, 884, 885] He was also known as **Spud**. Russell Howard reached age 71 and died in Cincinnati, Hamilton Co., Ohio, on January 29, 1989.[31, 883, 884, 885] He was buried in Spring Grove Cemetery, Cincinnati, Hamilton Co., Ohio.[886]

Shirley Lois Gail Spilker and Russell Howard Rogers had two children, including:

+ 193 f II. **Mary Ann**[10] **Rogers** was born in Cincinnati, Hamilton Co., Ohio, on May 5, 1953.[887] She died in a hospital in Montgomery, Sycamore Twp., Hamilton Co., Ohio, on May 19, 1984.[887, 888]

122. Dwight H.[9] **Ludwick** (*Vernice Catherine*[8] *Stroup, John Henry*[7]*, Elvira*[6] *Pegan, Henry*[5]*, Robert A.*[4]*, Andrew*[3]*, Andrew*[2] *Pagan, James*[1]) was born on December 4, 1914, in Dodson Twp., Highland Co., Ohio.[31, 490] He was also known as **Doc**. He was the son of Claude Hogard Ludwick and Vernice Catherine Stroup (59). Dwight H. lived in 1943 in Dayton, Montgomery Co., Ohio. He died in Fort Lauderdale, Broward Co., Florida, on July 4, 1989, at age 74.[31, 490] Dwight H. was buried in Barnes Cemetery, Fairview, New Market Twp., Highland Co., Ohio.[889]

Dwight H. married **Kathryn R. McCoffin** on May 9, 1936, in Highland Co., Ohio.[890] They had one son. Kathryn R. McCoffin was born in Rush Creek Twp., Highland Co., Ohio, on July 7, 1917.[31, 890, 891] She was also known as **Kay**. Kathryn R. reached age 89 and died in Fort Lauderdale, Broward Co., Florida, on May 23, 2007.[31, 892] She was buried in Barnes Cemetery, Fairview, New Market Twp., Highland Co., Ohio?

Dwight Ludwick is not found in the 1940 census. Dwight lived in Dayton, Montgomery Co., Ohio before moving to Fort Lauderdale, Broward Co., Florida in 1960. He worked for the Univis Lens Company.[893]

Son of Dwight H. Ludwick and Kathryn R. McCoffin:

+ 194 m I. **Roger Owen**[10] **Ludwick** was born in Dodson Twp., Highland Co., Ohio?, on January 27, 1937.[894] He died in Clayton, Randolph Twp., Montgomery Co., Ohio, on December 15, 2016.[895]

123. Lloyd Claude[9] **Ludwick** (*Vernice Catherine*[8] *Stroup, John Henry*[7]*, Elvira*[6] *Pegan, Henry*[5]*, Robert A.*[4]*, Andrew*[3]*, Andrew*[2] *Pagan, James*[1]) was born on December 7, 1916, in Dodson Twp., Highland Co., Ohio.[31, 491] He was the son of Claude Hogard Ludwick and Vernice Catherine Stroup (59). Lloyd Claude Ludwick lived in Allensburg, Liberty Twp., Highland Co., Ohio in 2006.[896] He died in a hospital in Hillsboro, Liberty Twp., Highland Co., Ohio, on January 8, 2006, at age 89.[31, 491] Lloyd Claude was buried in Barnes Cemetery, Fairview, New Market Twp., Highland Co., Ohio.[897]

Lloyd Claude married **Mildred Pauline Claibourne** on April 29, 1938, in Highland Co., Ohio.[898] They had three children. Mildred Pauline Claibourne was born in Allensburg, Liberty Twp., Highland Co., Ohio, on August 25, 1921.[899, 900] Mildred Pauline lived in 1966 in Hillsboro, Liberty Twp., Highland Co., Ohio. She reached age 74 and died in a hospital in Cincinnati, Hamilton Co., Ohio, on March 31, 1996.[898, 899] Mildred Pauline was buried in Barnes Cemetery, Fairview, New Market Twp., Highland Co., Ohio.[901]

In 1940, Lloyd Ludwick is enumerated in Allensburg, Liberty Twp., Highland Co., Ohio (*Census Place: Dodson, Highland, Ohio; Roll: T627_3085; Page: 6B; Enumeration District: 36-6*). Lloyd Ludwick, age 23, is an attendant in a filling station. With him is his wife, Mildred Claiborne Ludwick, 18. Both were born in Ohio. Lloyd says he was living elsewhere in Highland

County in 1935, but Mildred says she was living in Allensburg. Their home is on Ohio Route 135.

Later, Lloyd C. Ludwick was the manager of the Fairley Hardware Store in Hillsboro, Ohio. Although his obituary claims he was born in Allensburg, Liberty Twp., Highland Co., Ohio, his parents, Claude H. and Vernice Stroup Ludwick, were living in Dodson Twp., Highland Co., Ohio at the time of his birth.[896]

Children of Lloyd Claude Ludwick and Mildred Pauline Claibourne:

+ 195   I.   **Child**[10] **Ludwick** was born in Allensburg, Liberty Twp., Highland Co., Ohio, in 1940.[902] He or she died in Allensburg, Liberty Twp., Highland Co., Ohio, in 1940.[902]

+ 196 m II. **Son**[10] **Ludwick** was born in Allensburg, Liberty Twp., Highland Co., Ohio.

124. Harold Stroup[9] **Ludwick** (*Vernice Catherine*[8] *Stroup, John Henry*[7]*, Elvira*[6] *Pegan, Henry*[5]*, Robert A.*[4]*, Andrew*[3]*, Andrew*[2] *Pagan, James*[1]) was born on May 30, 1919, in Dodson Twp., Highland Co., Ohio.[31, 492] He was the son of Claude Hogard Ludwick and Vernice Catherine Stroup (59). Harold Stroup Ludwick lived in August 1996 in Hillsboro, Liberty Twp., Highland Co., Ohio. He died in a hospital in Cincinnati, Hamilton Co., Ohio on August 24, 1996, at age 77.[31, 492] Harold. S. was buried in Hillsboro Cemetery, Hillsboro, Liberty Twp., Highland Co., Ohio.[492]

Harold Stroup married **Ruby M. Carey** on April 26, 1947, in Highland Co., Ohio.[903] They had one son. Ruby M. Carey was born in Hillsboro, Liberty Twp., Highland Co., Ohio, on April 1, 1922.[31, 904, 905] Ruby M. lived in 1967 in Hillsboro, Liberty Twp., Highland Co., Ohio. She reached age 44 and died in a hospital in Dayton, Montgomery Co., Ohio, on February 7, 1967.[905, 906] Ruby M. was buried in Hillsboro Cemetery, Hillsboro, Liberty Twp., Highland Co., Ohio.[905]

Harold Stroup Ludwick married Mrs. **Janell Sebert** Gluckian on July 4, 1973.[492] Janell Sebert was born in Camden, Somers Twp., Preble Co., Ohio, on February 24, 1914.[907, 908] Janell lived in 2006 in Xenia, Xenia Twp., Greene Co., Ohio. She reached age 92 and died in a hospital in Dayton, Montgomery Co., Ohio, on September 24, 2006.[907, 908] Janell was buried in Fairmount Cemetery, Camden, Somers Twp., Preble Co., Ohio.[907, 909]

125. Everett O.[9] **Ludwick** (*Vernice Catherine*[8] *Stroup, John Henry*[7]*, Elvira*[6] *Pegan, Henry*[5]*, Robert A.*[4]*, Andrew*[3]*, Andrew*[2] *Pagan, James*[1]) was born on August 21, 1921, in Dodson Twp., Highland Co., Ohio.[31, 493] He was also known as **Rosie**. He was the son of Claude Hogard Ludwick and Vernice Catherine Stroup (59). Everett O. died in Dayton, Montgomery Co., Ohio, on January 20, 1987, at age 65.[494, 495] He was buried in New Lynchburg Masonic Cemetery/Lynchburg F & AM Cemetery, Lynchburg, Dodson Twp., Highland Co., Ohio.[495, 910]

He married **Hilda Mae Hawk**. They had four children. Hilda Mae Hawk was born in Dodsonville, Dodson Twp., Highland Co., Ohio, on April 9, 1928.[911, 912] Hilda Mae lived in 1999 in Johnstown, Monroe Twp., Licking Co., Ohio. She reached age 84 and died in Dayton, Montgomery Co., Ohio, on June 4, 2012.[911] Hilda Mae was buried in New Lynchburg Masonic Cemetery/Lynchburg F & AM Cemetery, Lynchburg, Dodson Twp., Highland Co., Ohio.[911, 913]

126. Lowell Arthur[9] **Ludwick** (*Vernice Catherine*[8] *Stroup, John Henry*[7]*, Elvira*[6] *Pegan, Henry*[5]*, Robert A.*[4]*, Andrew*[3]*, Andrew*[2] *Pagan, James*[1]) was born on August 6, 1923, in Dodson Twp., Highland Co., Ohio.[496, 497, 498] He was the son of Claude Hogard Ludwick and Vernice Catherine Stroup (59). Lowell Arthur lived in 1961 in Highland Co., Ohio. He died in a hospital in Wilmington, Union Twp., Clinton Co., Ohio, on November 13, 1961, at age 38.[497, 498] Lowell Arthur was buried in Barnes Cemetery, Fairview, New Market Twp., Highland Co., Ohio.[497, 914]

Lowell Arthur Ludwick and his wife, Doris Helen Pegan, were third cousins. Lowell A. Ludwick's obituary says he was born on August 2, 1922.

But his birth and death records say August 6, 1923.[496, 497, 498]

Lowell Arthur married **Doris Helen Pegan** on about 1943. They had one son. Doris Helen Pegan was born in Clark Twp., Clinton Co., Ohio, on December 29, 1922.[312, 313]. She was also known as **Helen.** Doris Helen reached age 81 and died in Wilmington, Union Twp., Clinton Co., Ohio, on February 17, 2004.[312] She was buried in Barnes Cemetery, Fairview, New Market Twp., Highland Co., Ohio.[693, 694] She was the daughter of William Otto Pegan (36) and Rosella Stroup.

Doris Helen Pegan Ludwick favored "Helen" as her given name.

Son of Lowell Arthur Ludwick and Doris Helen Pegan:

+ 161 m I. **Arthur Lowell**[10] **Ludwick** was born in Cincinnati, Hamilton Co., Ohio, on November 11, 1943.[695, 696] He was also known as **Artie**. Arthur Lowell died in Lynchburg, Dodson Twp., Highland Co., Ohio, on January 21, 2014.[696]

127. James Richard[9] **Stroup** (*Clarence Harold*[8], *John Henry*[7], *Elvira*[6] *Pegan, Henry*[5], *Robert A.*[4], *Andrew*[3], *Andrew*[2] *Pagan, James*[1]) was born on October 17, 1937, in Jefferson Twp., Clinton Co., Ohio.[503] He was the son of Clarence Harold Stroup (60) and Electra Lucile Connor. James Richard lived in 2014 in Xenia, Xenia Twp., Greene Co., Ohio. James Richard died in a hospital in Dayton, Montgomery Co., Ohio, on March 8, 2014, at age 76.[504] He was buried in Spring Valley Cemetery, Spring Valley, Spring Valley Twp., Greene Co., Ohio.[504, 915]

James Richard married **Wilma Ellen Boerner** on September 27, 1958, in Greene Co., Ohio.[916] They had three children. Wilma Ellen Boerner was born in Dayton, Montgomery Co., Ohio, on June 11, 1940.

128. Thelma Lavonne[9] **Vance** (*Sadie D.*[8] *Ballentine, Elma Jane*[7] *Stroup, Elvira*[6] *Pegan, Henry*[5], *Robert A.*[4], *Andrew*[3], *Andrew*[2] *Pagan, James*[1]) was born on July 16, 1913, in Clark Twp., Clinton Co., Ohio or Lynchburg, Dodson Twp., Highland Co., Ohio.[29, 511, 512] She was the daughter of Silas Laymon Vance and Sadie D. Ballentine (61). Thelma Lavonne died in a hospital in Millersburg, Hardy Twp., Holmes Co., Ohio, on March 6, 1993, at age 79.[511, 513] She was buried in Sugar Grove Cemetery, Wilmington, Union Twp., Clinton Co., Ohio.[513, 917]

Thelma's birthplace isn't certain. Her birth was not registered until Thelma applies for a delayed birth certificate in 1966 in Clinton County, Ohio. This implies she was born in Clark Twp., Clinton Co., Ohio, but she her obituary says she was born in Lynchburg, Dodson Twp., Highland Co., Ohio.[512, 513] Her onine death certificate entry says she is of Mexican descent and born in Columbiana County, Ohio. This is totally incorrect.[511]

Thelma L. married **George M. Fudge** on September 2, 1935.[513, 918] They had two children. George M. Fudge was born in Farmersville, Jackson Twp., Montgomery Co., Ohio, on March 11, 1908.[31, 919] He reached age 82 and died in Walnut Creek, Walnut Creek Twp., Holmes Co., Ohio, on September 3, 1990.[31, 918, 919] George M. was buried in Sugar Grove Cemetery, Wilmington, Union Twp., Clinton Co., Ohio.[920]

In 1940, George M. and Thelma Lavonne Vance Fudge are enumerated in Wilmington, Union Twp., Clinton Co., Ohio *(Census Place: Wilmington, Clinton, Ohio; Roll: T627_3042; Page: 5B; Enumeration District: 14-19)*. In the household are George M. Fudge, age 32, born Ohio, a salesman for the Stul Steel Co.; his wife, Thelma Vance Fudge, 26, also born Ohio; and their daughter, Jo Ann, born Wisconsin. Their house address is 424 Birdsall Street, and George and Thelma say they were living in Madison, Dane Co., Wisconsin 1935.

Thelma Lavonne Vance and George M. Fudge had two children, including:

+ 197 f I. **JoAnn**[10] **Fudge** was born in Madison, Dane Co., Wisconsin, on May 6, 1938.

129. Inez[9] **Vance** (*Sadie D.*[8] *Ballentine, Elma Jane*[7] *Stroup, Elvira*[6] *Pegan, Henry*[5], *Robert A.*[4], *Andrew*[3], *Andrew*[2] *Pagan, James*[1]) was born on

April 1, 1921, in Goshen Twp., Clermont Co., Ohio.[514, 515, 516] She was the daughter of Silas Laymon Vance and Sadie D. Ballentine (61). Inez lived in 1989 in Lebanon, Turtle Creek Twp., Warren Co., Ohio. She died in a facility in Dayton, Montgomery Co., Ohio, on March 5, 1989, at age 67.[514, 516] Inez was buried in Lebanon Cemetery, Lebanon, Turtle Creek Twp., Warren Co., Ohio.[921, 922]

Inez married **Bernard Joseph Bowman** before 1944. They had four children. Bernard Joseph Bowman was born in Washington Twp., Clinton Co., Ohio, on March 15, 1919.[31, 923, 924, 925] He reached age 73 and died in Lebanon, Turtle Creek Twp., Warren Co., Ohio, on April 29, 1992.[31, 923, 924, 925] Bernard Joseph was buried in Lebanon Cemetery, Lebanon, Turtle Creek Twp., Warren Co., Ohio.[926]

Dr. Bernard Joseph Bowman, D.V.M., was a veterinarian..

Children of Inez Vance and Bernard Joseph Bowman:

+ 198 f I. **Robyn V.**[10] **Bowman** was born in Columbus, Franklin Co., Ohio, on April 1, 1944.[927] She died in a hospital in Kettering, Kettering Twp., Montgomery Co., Ohio, on April 23, 1996.[927, 928] Robyn was buried in Lebanon Cemetery, Lebanon, Turtle Creek Twp., Warren Co., Ohio.[928, 1163]

+ 199 f II. **Rebecca Sue**[10] **Bowman** was born in Lebanon, Turtle Creek Twp., Warren Co., Ohio, on January 7, 1947.[929, 930] She died in Lebanon, Turtle Creek Twp., Warren Co., Ohio, on October 11, 1962.[929, 930]

+ 200 m III. **Bruce Steven**[10] **Bowman** was born in Lebanon, Turtle Creek Twp., Warren Co., Ohio, on August 21, 1948.[931, 932] He died in a hospital in Montgomery, Hamilton Co., Ohio, on December 31, 2000.[931, 932]

+ 201 m IV. **Nicholas Brian**[10] **Bowman** was born in Lebanon, Turtle Creek Twp., Warren Co., Ohio, on June 29, 1951.[31] He died in a hospital in Montgomery, Hamilton Co., Ohio, on January 31, 1983.[933]

130. Robert N.[9] **Vance** (*Sadie D.*[8] *Ballentine, Elma Jane*[7] *Stroup, Elvira*[6] *Pegan, Henry*[5]*, Robert A.*[4]*, Andrew*[3]*, Andrew*[2] *Pagan, James*[1]) was born on October 17, 1922, in Goshen Twp., Clermont Co., Ohio.[517] He was the son of Silas Laymon Vance and Sadie D. Ballentine (61). Robert N. died in Wilmington, Union Twp., Clinton Co., Ohio, on June 13, 1939, at age 16.[517] He was buried in Sugar Grove Cemetery, Wilmington, Union Twp., Clinton Co., Ohio.[517, 934]

Robert N. Vance, age 16, accidentally lit his clothing on fire with a match and died of severe burns.[935]

131. Betty Louise[9] **Hawthorne** (*Letha May*[8] *Ballentine, Elma Jane*[7] *Stroup, Elvira*[6] *Pegan, Henry*[5]*, Robert A.*[4]*, Andrew*[3]*, Andrew*[2] *Pagan, James*[1]) was born on October 13, 1920, in Goshen Twp., Clermont Co., Ohio.[530] She was the daughter of Ennis Edmond Hawthorne and Letha May Ballentine (62). Betty Louise lived in Blue Ash and Deer Park, Hamilton Co., Ohio. She died in a hospital in Montgomery, Sycamore Twp., Hamilton Co., Ohio, on December 12, 1998, at age 78.[530, 531] Betty Louise was buried in Rest Haven Memorial Park Cemetery, Evendale, Sycamore Twp., Hamilton Co., Ohio.[936]

Betty Louise Hawthorne Fisher's death certificate says she was born in Clinton County, but her parents were living in Goshen Twp., Clermont Co., Ohio at the time of her birth.[530]

Betty Louise married **Walter John Fisher** before 1936. They had four children. Walter John Fisher was born in Cincinnati, Hamilton Co., Ohio, on April 6, 1915.[31, 937] Walter John reached age 50 and died in Cincinnati, Hamilton Co., Ohio, on October 23, 1965.[937] He was buried in Rest Haven Memorial Park Cemetery, Evendale, Sycamore Twp., Hamilton Co., Ohio.[938]

Walter J. and Betty Louise Hawthorne Fisher are enumerated in 1940 in Cincinnati, Hamilton Co., Ohio *(Census Place: Cincinnati, Hamilton, Ohio; Roll: m-t0627-03187; Page: 15B; Enumeration District: 91-24)*. Walter J. Fisher, age 24, is a scraper hand at a machining tool company. Betty is 19, and they have a son, John R., three. All were born in Ohio, and Walter and Betty say they were living in Cincinnati in 1935. Their home address is 4317 Simpson Avenue.

Betty Louise Hawthorne and Walter John Fisher had four children, including:

+ 202 m I. **John Robert**[10] **Fisher** was born in Cincinnati, Hamilton Co., Ohio, on September 8, 1936.[31, 939, 940, 941] He died in Cape Coral, Lee Co., Florida, on May 5, 1981.[939, 941]

+ 203 f II. **Linda Sue**[10] **Fisher** was born in Cincinnati, Hamilton Co., Ohio, on May 2, 1946.[942, 943] She died in Fernandina Beach, Amelia Island, Nassau Co., Florida, on January 1, 2017.[943]

+ 204 f III. **Karen Jean**[10] **Fisher** was born in Cincinnati, Hamilton Co., Ohio, on May 3, 1956.[944] She died in Anderson Twp., Hamilton Co., Ohio, on November 1, 2014.[944]

132. Robert Henry[9] **Pegan** (*Frederick James Frank*[8], *Adolphus Vonesse*[7], *Granville*[6], *Henry*[5], *Robert A.*[4], *Andrew*[3], *Andrew*[2] *Pagan, James*[1]) was born on October 18, 1917, in Norwood, Mill Creek Twp., Hamilton Co., Ohio.[31, 541, 542, 543] He was the son of Frederick James Frank Pegan (63) and Clara Elizabeth Fye. He died in Garden Grove, Orange Co., California, on June 13, 1990, at age 72.[31, 541, 543] Robert Henry was buried in Holy Sepulchre Cemetery, Orange, Orange Co., California.[543]

Although the California Death Index has Robert Henry Pegan's birthdate as October 17, 1917, but his Ohio birth record and the Social Security Death Index say it was October 18, 1917.[31, 541, 542]

Robert Henry married **Delores Reising** about 1945. They had four children. Delores Reising was born in Newport, Campbell Co., Kentucky, on October 17, 1919.[945, 946] Delores reached age 49 and died in Garden Grove, Orange Co., California, on January 31, 1969.[945, 946] She was buried in Good Shepherd Cemetery, Huntington Beach, Orange Co., California.[946]

Robert Henry Pegan married Mrs. **Grace Ida Roeder** O'Brien on August 20, 1969, in Orange Co., California.[947] Grace Ida Roeder was born in Cincinnati, Hamilton Co., Ohio, on August 12, 1919.[31, 948] Grace Ida reached age 84 and died in Yorba Linda, Orange Co., California, on April 10, 2004.[31, 948, 949] She was buried in Gate of Heaven Cemetery, Montgomery, Sycamore Twp., Hamilton Co., Ohio.[950]

When he died, Robert Henry Pegan worked as a salesman for the Barbara Ann Baking Company.[951]

133. Ruth Mary[9] **Pegan** (*Frederick James Frank*[8], *Adolphus Vonesse*[7], *Granville*[6], *Henry*[5], *Robert A.*[4], *Andrew*[3], *Andrew*[2] *Pagan, James*[1]) was born on October 26, 1919, in Norwood, Mill Creek Twp., Hamilton Co., Ohio.[544, 545] She was the daughter of Frederick James Frank Pegan (63) and Clara Elizabeth Fye. Ruth Mary died in Cincinnati, Hamilton Co., Ohio, on November 19, 2005, at age 86.[544, 545] She was buried in Spring Grove Cemetery, Cincinnati, Hamilton Co., Ohio.[952]

She married **Louis Adolph Dennig** after 1940. They had three sons. Louis Adolph Dennig was born in Cincinnati, Hamilton Co., Ohio, on November 9, 1918.[31, 953, 954] Louis Adolph reached age 76 and died in Cincinnati, Hamilton Co., Ohio, on May 28, 1995.[31, 953, 954] He was buried in Spring Grove Cemetery, Cincinnati, Hamilton Co., Ohio.[955]

134. Mary C.[9] **Pegan** (*Frederick James Frank*[8], *Adolphus Vonesse*[7], *Granville*[6], *Henry*[5], *Robert A.*[4], *Andrew*[3], *Andrew*[2] *Pagan, James*[1]) was born on August 19, 1926, in Norwood, Mill Creek Twp., Hamilton Co., Ohio.[546] She is the daughter of Frederick James Frank Pegan (63) and Clara Elizabeth Fye.

Mary C. married **Raymond B. Kissel** on April 26, 1948, in Hamilton Co., Ohio.[540] They had three children. Raymond B. Kissel was born in Cincinnati, Hamilton Co., Ohio, on November 23, 1921.[956]

135. Elizabeth Joan[9] Pegan (*William Henry[8], Adolphus Vonesse[7], Granville[6], Henry[5], Robert A.[4], Andrew[3], Andrew[2] Pagan, James[1]*) was born on May 21, 1927, in Columbus, Franklin Co., Ohio.[31] She was also known as **Betty**. She was the daughter of William Henry Pegan (65) and Marie E. Moeller. Elizabeth Joan died in St. Louis, Missouri, on October 24, 2010, at age 83.[31, 550] She was buried in Bellarive Heritage Gardens Cemetery, Creve Coeur, St. Louis Co., Missouri.[550]

Elizabeth Joan married **William Wrenn Marlatt** on June 7, 1947, in St. Louis Co., Missouri.[957] They divorced. They had one daughter. William Wrenn Marlatt was born in St. Louis, Missouri, on January 21, 1925.[31, 958] He reached age 74 and died in Florissant, St. Louis Co., Missouri, on December 7, 1999.[31, 958] William Wrenn was buried in Memorial Park Cemetery, Jennings, St. Louis Co., Missouri.[959, 960]

Elizabeth Joan Pegan Marlatt married **Ramon Martin Fisher** after 1955. Ramon Martin Fisher was born in St. Louis, Missouri, on December 11, 1924.[31, 961] Ramon Martin lived in 1978 in Sullivan, Missouri. He reached age 78 and died in St. Louis, Missouri, on October 28, 2003.[31, 961]

Her Social Security Death Index listing under Betty J. Fisher, St. Louis, Missouri.[31]

136. Elma Mary[9] Pegan (*Courtland Homer[8], Henry Levy[7], Granville[6], Henry[5], Robert A.[4], Andrew[3], Andrew[2] Pagan, James[1]*) was born on July 6, 1926, in Dodson Twp., Highland Co., Ohio.[31, 562, 563] She was the daughter of Courtland Homer Pegan (66) and Stella Madge Holladay. Elma Mary lived in 2008 in Fairfield, Butler Co., Ohio. She died in Lake Orion Heights, Oakland Co., Michigan, on August 21, 2013, at age 87.[31, 563] Elma Mary was buried in Troutwine Cemetery, Dodson Twp., Highland Co., Ohio and Clark Twp., Clinton Co., Ohio.[563]

Elma Mary married **William Clark May** on September 13, 1947, in Fort Thomas, Campbell Co., Kentucky.[962] They divorced. They had two children. William Clark May was born in Fort Thomas, Campbell Co., Kentucky, on October 2, 1924.[31, 963] He was also known as **Bill**. He reached age 61 and died in Peach Grove, Pendleton Co., Kentucky, on October 25, 1985.[31, 964] William Clark was buried in Peach Grove Cemetery, Peach Grove, Pendleton Co., Kentucky.[964]

His Social Security Death Index entry is under Bill May.[31]

137. Thelma[9] Pegan (*Courtland Homer[8], Henry Levy[7], Granville[6], Henry[5], Robert A.[4], Andrew[3], Andrew[2] Pagan, James[1]*) was born on July 20, 1927, in Dodson Twp., Highland Co., Ohio. She is the daughter of Courtland Homer Pegan (66) and Stella Madge Holladay.

Thelma married **Malcom Loraine Kelley** on January 23, 1947, in White Co., Arkansas.[965] They divorced. They had four children. Malcom Loraine Kelley was born in Belfast, Liberty Twp., Highland Co., Ohio, on September 28, 1926.[31, 966] He reached age 78 and died in Lancaster, Fairfield Co., Ohio, on December 14, 2004.[31, 966] Malcom Loraine was buried in Prospect Cemetery, Berrysville, Marshall Twp., Highland Co., Ohio.[967, 968]

Thelma Pegan Kelley married **William Alpheus Smith** before 1977. They divorced. William Alpheus Smith was born in Washington Court House, Union Twp., Fayette Co., Ohio, on January 3, 1928.[31, 969, 970] He was also known as **Wild Turkey**. William Alpheus reached age 73 and died in Hemet, Riverside Co., California, on July 28, 2001.[31, 970] He was buried in Riverside National Cemetery, Riverside, Riverside Co., California.[971, 972]

Thelma Pegan and Malcom Loraine Kelley had four children, including:

+ 205 f IV. **Daughter[10] Kelley**.

138. Shirley C.[9] Pegan (*Courtland Homer[8], Henry Levy[7], Granville[6], Henry[5], Robert A.[4], Andrew[3], Andrew[2] Pagan, James[1]*) was born on March 8, 1930, in Dodson Twp., Highland Co., Ohio.[564,

565] She was the daughter of Courtland Homer Pegan (66) and Stella Madge Holladay. She died in Searcy, White Co., Arkansas, on October 5, 2010, at age 80.[31, 565] Shirley C. was buried in White County Memorial Gardens Cemetery, Searcy, White Co., Arkansas.[973]

Shirley C. married **Howard Glenn Boyd** in December 1952 in White Co., Arkansas.[564] They had three children. Howard Glenn Boyd was born in Wewoka, Seminole Co., Oklahoma, on November 5, 1930. He is also known as **Glenn**.

Howard and Shirley C. Pegan Boyd lived in 1953 in South Point, Lawrence Co., Ohio; in 1958 in Karlsruhe, Germany, in Mankato, Blue Earth Co., Minnesota in 1963; and in Thousand Oaks, Ventura Co., California in 1973 before returning to in 1981 in Searcy, White Co., Arkansas in 1981.[974]

139. **Robert Ivan[9] Pegan** (*Courtland Homer[8], Henry Levy[7], Granville[6], Henry[5], Robert A.[4], Andrew[3], Andrew[2] Pagan, James[1]*) was born on August 13, 1933, in Dodson Twp., Highland Co., Ohio.[31, 566, 567] He was the son of Courtland Homer Pegan (66) and Stella Madge Holladay. Robert Ivan lived in 1965 in New Vienna, Green Twp., Clinton Co., Ohio. He died in Hillsboro, Liberty Twp., Highland Co., Ohio, on February 12, 1978, at age 44.[567, 568] Robert Ivan was buried in Troutwine Cemetery, Dodson Twp., Highland Co., Ohio and Clark Twp., Clinton Co., Ohio.[567, 975]

Robert Ivan married **Charma Louise Dick** on June 18, 1953, in Highland Co., Ohio.[976] They divorced before 1967. They remarried on January 15, 1967 in Highland Co., Ohio.[977] They divorced again 1972. They had six children. Charma Louise Dick was born in Highland Co., Ohio, on September 8, 1935.[978, 979] Charma Louise reached age 60 and died in Hillsboro, Liberty Twp., Highland Co., Ohio, on August 10, 1996.[978,979] She was buried in Troutwine Cemetery, Dodson Twp., Highland Co., Ohio and Clark Twp., Clinton Co., Ohio.[979, 980]

According to the July 22, 1958 edition of the *Hillsboro (OH) Press-Gazette*, Robert Ivan Pegan, then a milkman and resident of Hillsboro, was charged with assault with attempt to rape of a Pike County, Ohio woman on his delivery route in that county. Robert I. Pegan was almost caught by the woman's son, who arrived home during the incident, but Robert fled. He was apprehended by police shortly thereafter.[981]

Robert Ivan Pegan married Mrs. **Audrey Gibson** Nichols on March 13, 1976, in Highland County, Ohio.[982, 983] They were legally separated before 1976. Audrey Gibson was born in Salyersville, Magoffin Co., Kentucky, on December 9, 1927.[31, 984, 985] She reached age 65 and died in Newark, Newark Twp., Licking Co., Ohio, on September 3, 1993.[984, 985]

Robert Ivan Pegan and Charma Louise Dick had six children, including:

+ 206 m I. **Son[10] Pegan** was born in Hillsboro, Liberty Twp., Highland Co., Ohio.

140. **Russell William[9] Pegan** (*Courtland Homer[8], Henry Levy[7], Granville[6], Henry[5], Robert A.[4], Andrew[3], Andrew[2] Pagan, James[1]*) was born on June 7, 1935, in Lynchburg, Dodson Twp., Highland Co., Ohio. [31,569] He was the son of Courtland Homer Pegan (66) and Stella Madge Holladay. Russell William lived in 2008 in Danville, Hamer Twp., Highland Co., Ohio. Russell William died in a hospital in Buena Vista, Green Twp., Fayette Co., Ohio, on August 10, 2008, at age 73.[31, 569] He was buried in Hamer Township Cemetery, Hamer Twp., Highland Co., Ohio.[569]

Russell William married **Patricia Joan Ernst** on March 5, 1958, in South Point, Lawrence Co., Ohio.[569, 986] They had four children. Patricia Joan Ernst was born in Marshall Twp., Highland Co., Ohio, on February 28, 1940.[987]

Although they obtained their marriage license in Highland Co., Russell William Pegan's obituary says he and Patricia Joan Ernst married in South Point, Lawrence Co., Ohio.[569]

Russell Pegan worked as a farmer and truck driver. He also served on the Board of Governors, Highland District Hospital, Hillsboro, Ohio and as a central committeeman for the Highland County Democratic Party.[569]

141. Richard Thomas⁹ Pegan (*Clarence Chilton⁸, Henry Levy⁷, Granville⁶, Henry⁵, Robert A.⁴, Andrew³, Andrew² Pagan, James¹*) was born on November 17, 1932, in St. Martin, Perry Twp., Brown Co., Ohio.[31,575,576] He was the son of Clarence Chilton Pegan (67) and Grace Catherine Walsh. Richard Thomas also resided in 1986 in Lynchburg, Dodson Twp., Highland Co., Ohio. He died in a hospital in Wilmington, Union Twp., Clinton Co., Ohio, on December 7, 1986, at age 54.[575, 576] Richard Thomas was buried in St. Martin Cemetery, St. Martin, Perry Twp., Brown Co., Ohio.[575]

Never married.

A twin to Rita, Richard Thomas Pegan was employed between 1954 and 1986 as a groundskeeper at St. Martin Ursuline Center in Brown Co., Ohio.[575]

142. Rita Gertrude⁹ Pegan (*Clarence Chilton⁸, Henry Levy⁷, Granville⁶, Henry⁵, Robert A.⁴, Andrew³, Andrew² Pagan, James¹*) was born on November 17, 1932, in St. Martin, Perry Twp., Brown Co., Ohio.[577] She was the daughter of Clarence Chilton Pegan (67) and Grace Catherine Walsh. She died in Cocoa, Brevard Co., Florida, on June 15, 2016, at age 83.[578]

She was a twin to Richard.

Rita Gertrude married **Gerald Mcdonald Poston** before 1955. They divorced. They had five children. Gerald Mcdonald Poston was born in Farmers, Rowan Co., Kentucky, on March 21, 1931.[31, 988, 989, 990, 991] He was also known as **Don**. Gerald Mcdonald reached age 55 and died in Cocoa, Brevard Co., Florida, on June 15, 1986.[31, 990, 991] He was buried in Brevard Memorial Park Cemetery, Cocoa. Brevard Co., Florida.[992]

Rita Gertrude Pegan and Gerald Mcdonald Poston had five children, including:

+ 207 f II. **Debra Sue¹⁰ Poston** was born in Blanchester, Marion Twp., Clinton Co., Ohio, on April 11, 1955.[31, 993] She died in Jacksonville, Duval Co., Florida, on May 14, 2013.[31, 993]

143. Julia Evelyn⁹ Pegan (*Clarence Chilton⁸, Henry Levy⁷, Granville⁶, Henry⁵, Robert A.⁴, Andrew³, Andrew² Pagan, James¹*) was born on October 26, 1934, in St. Martin, Perry Twp., Brown Co., Ohio.[579, 580] She was the daughter of Clarence Chilton Pegan (67) and Grace Catherine Walsh. Julia Evelyn died in Hillsboro, Liberty Twp., Highland Co., Ohio, on March 23, 2000, at age 65.[579, 580] She was buried in Troutwine Cemetery, Dodson Twp., Highland Co., Ohio and Clark Twp., Clinton Co., Ohio.[994]

Julia Evelyn married **Richard H. Macke II** on November 28, 1953, in Brown Co., Ohio.[995] They had four daughters. Richard H. Macke II was born in Cincinnati, Hamilton Co., Ohio, on September 22, 1921.[996, 997 998] Richard H. lived in 1974 in Lynchburg, Dodson Twp., Highland Co., Ohio. He reached age 53 and died in a hospital in Wilmington, Union Twp., Clinton Co., Ohio, on December 18, 1974.[997, 998] Richard H. was buried in Troutwine Cemetery, Dodson Twp., Highland Co., Ohio and Clark Twp., Clinton Co., Ohio.[997]

Social Security Death Index and his Social Security application gives Richard Macke's date of birth as September 21, 1922, but these conflict with his birth record in Hamilton Co., Ohio.[31, 996, 999]

Julia Evelyn Pegan and Richard H. Macke II had four children, including:

+ 208 f IV. **Daughter One¹⁰ Macke** was born in Wilmington, Union Twp., Clinton Co., Ohio.

+ 209 f III. **Patricia J.¹⁰ Macke** was born in Wilmington, Union Twp., Clinton Co., Ohio, on August 7, 1957.[31, 1000] She died in a hospital in Columbus, Franklin Co., Ohio, on February 27, 2008.[31, 1000]

+ 210 f   IV. **Daughter Two**[10] **Macke** was born in Wilmington, Union Twp., Clinton Co., Ohio.

144. James Eugene[9] **Pegan** (*Clarence Chilton*[8]*, Henry Levy*[7]*, Granville*[6]*, Henry*[5]*, Robert A.*[4]*, Andrew*[3]*, Andrew*[2] *Pagan, James*[1]) was born on June 20, 1937, in St. Martin, Perry Twp., Brown Co., Ohio.[581, 582] He was the son of Clarence Chilton Pegan (67) and Grace Catherine Walsh. James Eugene died in Wilmington, Union Twp., Clinton Co., Ohio, on July 31, 2005, at age 68.[581, 582] He was buried in St. Martin Cemetery, St. Martin, Perry Twp., Brown Co., Ohio.[1001]

James Eugene married **Delores Duarte** on April 20, 1957, in San Diego Co., California.[1002] They had three children. Delores Duarte was born in San Diego, San Diego Co., California, on March 16, 1935.[1003, 1004] Delores reached age 61 and died in Wilmington, Union Twp., Clinton Co., Ohio, on October 12, 1996.[1004, 1005] She was buried in St. Martin Cemetery, St. Martin, Perry Twp., Brown Co., Ohio.[1004]

James Eugene Pegan and Delores Duarte had three children, including:

+ 211 f   III. **Bernadette Marie**[10] **Pegan** Bernadette died before 2005.

145. Lawrence Joseph[9] **Pegan** (*Clarence Chilton*[8]*, Henry Levy*[7]*, Granville*[6]*, Henry*[5]*, Robert A.*[4]*, Andrew*[3]*, Andrew*[2] *Pagan, James*[1]) was born on January 13, 1948, in St. Martin, Perry Twp., Brown Co., Ohio.[583, 584] He was also known as **Larry**. He was the son of Clarence Chilton Pegan (67) and Grace Catherine Walsh. He lived before 2013 in Fayetteville, Perry Twp., Brown Co., Ohio. before relocating to Bethel, Tate Twp., Clermont Co., Ohio. Lawrence Joseph died in a facility in Georgetown, Pleasant Twp., Brown Co., Ohio, on October 4, 2013, at age 65.[583, 584] He was buried in St. Martin Cemetery, St. Martin, Perry Twp., Brown Co., Ohio.[583, 584]

Lawrence Joseph Pegan married and divorced. He had one daughter.

146. Clarence Edward[9] **Pegan II** (*Clarence Chilton*[8]*, Henry Levy*[7]*, Granville*[6]*, Henry*[5]*, Robert A.*[4]*, Andrew*[3]*, Andrew*[2] *Pagan, James*[1]) was born on July 15, 1950, in St. Martin, Perry Twp., Brown Co., Ohio.[585, 586, 587] He was also known as **Eddie**. He was the son of Clarence Chilton Pegan (67) and Grace Catherine Walsh. Clarence Edward lived in 2013 in St. Martin, Perry Twp., Brown Co., Ohio. Clarence Edward died in a hospital in Batavia, Batavia Twp., Clermont Co., Ohio, on September 9, 2013, at age 63.[586, 587] He was buried in St. Martin Cemetery, St. Martin, Perry Twp., Brown Co., Ohio.[586, 587]

A tool and die maker, Clarence Edward Pegan II married and had three children.

147. Thurl Esto[9] **Stroup** (*Mabel Letha*[8] *Thompson, Della Frances*[7] *Pegan, Granville*[6]*, Henry*[5]*, Robert A.*[4]*, Andrew*[3]*, Andrew*[2] *Pagan, James*[1]) was born on June 13, 1921, in Dodson Twp., Highland Co., Ohio.[31, 595, 597, 598] He was the son of Galo S. Stroup and Mabel Letha Thompson (69). Thurl Esto lived in 1945 in Tampa, Hillsborough Co., Florida. He died in Washington, District of Columbia, on October 29, 1982, at age 61.[31, 597, 598, 599]

Thurl E. Stroup's birthdate is mentioned in his father Galo S. Stroup's obituary, among other sources.[595]

Thurl Esto married **Martha Jean Blair** on November 26, 1944, in Washington, District of Columbia.[1006, 1007] They divorced. They had three children. Martha Jean Blair was born in Portsmouth, Scioto Co., Ohio, on June 3, 1923.[31] She lived in 1990 in Edgewater, Anne Arundel Co., Maryland. Martha Jean Blair Stroup Allder reached age 66 and died in a hospital in Annapolis, Anne Arundel Co., Maryland, on May 14, 1990.[1008] She was buried in Gate of Heaven Cemetery, Silver Spring, Montgomery Co., Maryland.[1009]

Thurl Esto Stroup married **Mary Unknown** after 1949. Mary Unknown was born on October 22, 1919.[31] She was also known as **Midge**. Mary reached age 54 and died in Maryland in March 1974.[31]

Martha Jean Blair Stroup married **Harry Clifford Allder** om Thurl Stroup.[1008]

148. Gwendolyn[9] **DuVall** (*Lillie May*[8] *Daggy, Laura*[7] *Pegan, Thomas Jefferson*[6]*, Henry*[5]*, Robert A.*[4]*, Andrew*[3]*, Andrew*[2] *Pagan, James*[1]) was born on June 2, 1906, in Milford Twp., Butler Co., Ohio.[31, 608] She was the daughter of Alexander C. DuVall and Lillie May Daggy (71). Gwendolyn died in Riverside, Riverside Co., California, on December 29, 1979, at age 73.[31, 608] She was buried in Oxford Cemetery, Oxford Twp., Butler Co., Ohio.[1010]

Gwendolyn married **Harry Wakefield Kleinfelder** on September 25, 1928, in Butler Co., Ohio.[1011] They had one daughter. Harry Wakefield Kleinfelder was born in Ross Twp., Butler Co., Ohio, on December 26, 1904.[1012, 1013] Harry Wakefield was living in 1961 in Oxford, Oxford Twp., Butler Co., Ohio. He reached age 56 and died in a hospital in Hamilton, Butler Co., Ohio, on April 17, 1961.[1012, 1014] Harry Wakefield was buried in Oxford Cemetery, Oxford Twp., Butler Co., Ohio.[1014]

Harry W. and Gwendolyn Duvall Kleinfelter are enumerated in Oxford Twp., Butler Co., Ohio in 1930 *(Census Place: Oxford, Butler, Ohio; Roll: 1755; Page: 9A; Enumeration District: 46; Image: 385.0)*. Harry W. Kleinfelter is age 25, a farmer; and his wife Gwendolyn Duvall Kleinfelter is 24. The couple has been married about a year, as they were first married at ages 24 and 23 respectively. Both were born in Ohio, as were their parents.

In 1940, Harry and Gwendolyn DuVall Kleinfelder, are found in Oxford Twp., Butler Co., Ohio *(Census Place: Oxford, Butler, Ohio; Roll: T627_3035; Page: 8B; Enumeration District: 9-81)*. The head of the household, Harry Kleinfelder, age 34, is a farmer. Gwendolyn DuVall Kleinfelder is 33 years old. They have a daughter, "B. Joyce", who is four months old. All were born in Ohio. Harry and Gwendolyn DuVall Kleinfelder say they were living in Oxford in 1935. Living with them is Gwendolyn's mother, Lillian Daggy DuVall, 55, a widow, who says she was living in the same house on Ruby Road in 1935.

According to his obituary, Harry W. Kleinfelder operated a dairy before becoming a real estate agent around 1941.[1014]

Daughter of Gwendolyn DuVall and Harry Wakefield Kleinfelder:

+ 212 f I. **Brenda Joyce**[10] **Kleinfelder** was born in Oxford Twp., Butler Co., Ohio, on December 13, 1939.[31, 1015, 1016] She died in a facility in Escondido, San Diego Co., California, on October 31, 2002.[31, 1015, 1016]

149. John Llewellyn[9] **DuVall** (*Lillie May*[8] *Daggy, Laura*[7] *Pegan, Thomas Jefferson*[6]*, Henry*[5]*, Robert A.*[4]*, Andrew*[3]*, Andrew*[2] *Pagan, James*[1]) was born on March 10, 1913, in Oxford Twp., Butler Co., Ohio.[31, 609] He was the son of Alexander C. DuVall and Lillie May Daggy (71).

John Llewellyn died in Elkhart, Elkhart Co., Indiana, on January 31, 1984, at age 70.[31, 610] He was buried in Rice Cemetery, Elkhart, Elkhart Co., Indiana.[610, 1017, 1018]

John Llewellyn married **Inez M. McFarland** on February 12, 1938, in Brooke Co., West Virginia.[1019] They had two sons. Inez M. McFarland was born in Saint Clairsville, Belmont Co., Ohio, on December 9, 1913.[31, 1020] reached age 74 and died in Elkhart, Elkhart Co., Indiana, on May 9, 1988.[31, 1020] Inez M. was buried in Rice Cemetery, Elkhart, Elkhart Co., Indiana.[1020, 1021, 1022]

John DuVall and his wife, Inez McFarland DuVall had two marriage ceremonies. The first was on February 12, 1938 in Brooke Co., West Virginia.[1019] The second was in Belmont Co., Ohio on May 27, 1939.[1023] There are returned marriage licenses in both counties. At the time, they were teachers in Brooke County, West Virginia.[1019]

John DuVall is enumerated in Pease Twp., Belmont Co., Ohio in 1940 *(Census Place: Pease, Belmont, Ohio; Roll: T627_3029; Page: 1B; Enumeration District: 7-37)*. John DuVall, age 27 is a teacher in a public school who says he was living in Oxford, Oxford Twp., Butler Co., Ohio in 1935. His wife,

Inez McFarland DuVall, 26, says she was residing in St. Clairsville, Belmont Co., Ohio in 1935. Both were born in Ohio and are living on Ferry View Road.

John L. Duvall was the informant on his mother's, Lillie May Daggy Duvall's, death certificate in February 1948. He lists his residence as Richmond, Indiana.[229]

John Llewellyn Duvall was the vocational director of the Elkhart Community Schools, Elkhart, Indiana from 1941-1951, when he retired.[1018] Inez McFarland DuVall also was a teacher in Ohio and Indiana.[1022]

John Llewellyn DuVall and Inez M. McFarland had two sons, including:

+ 213 m II. **Donald Harry**[10] **DuVall** was born in Richmond, Wayne Co., Indiana, on April 14, 1945.[31] He died in Huntington, Suffolk Co., (Long Island), New York, on February 22, 1974.[31, 1024]

150. Joseph Hamer[9] **Daggy** (*Oliver John*[8], *Laura*[7] *Pegan, Thomas Jefferson*[6], *Henry*[5], *Robert A.*[4], *Andrew*[3], *Andrew*[2] *Pagan, James*[1]) was born on August 21, 1917, in Hamilton, Butler Co., Ohio.[622] He was the son of Oliver John Daggy (73) and Mary Jane Brookfield. Joseph Hamer died in Hamilton, Butler Co., Ohio, on January 6, 1927, at age nine.[622] He was buried in Greenwood Cemetery, Hamilton, Butler Co., Ohio.[622, 1025]

151. Betty Jane[9] **Daggy** (*Oliver John*[8], *Laura*[7] *Pegan, Thomas Jefferson*[6], *Henry*[5], *Robert A.*[4], *Andrew*[3], *Andrew*[2] *Pagan, James*[1]) was born on May 11, 1918, in Hamilton, Butler Co., Ohio.[31, 623] She was the daughter of Oliver John Daggy (73) and Mary Jane Brookfield. Betty Jane died in Hamilton, Butler Co., Ohio, on September 11, 2008, at age 90.[31, 623] She was buried in Greenwood Cemetery, Hamilton, Butler Co., Ohio.[1026]

Betty Jane married **Neil E. Stitsinger** on September 18, 1943, in New Brunswick, Somerset Co., New Jersey.[1027] They had two sons. Neil E. Stitsinger was born in Hamilton, Butler Co., Ohio, on May 28, 1909.[31, 1028, 1029] Neil E. reached age 80 and died in Hamilton, Butler Co., Ohio, on June 21, 1989.[31, 1027, 1029] He was buried in Greenwood Cemetery, Hamilton, Butler Co., Ohio.[1027, 1030]

Neil E. worked as a director of purchasing for the Mosier Safe Company. in Hamilton, Butler Co., Ohio.[1027]

Betty J. Daggy Stitsinger married **Paul C. Reidinger** on June 6, 1992, in Butler Co., Ohio.[1031] Paul C. Reidinger was born in Hamilton, Butler Co., Ohio, on March 14, 1917.[31, 1032, 1033] Paul C. reached age 80 and died in Hamilton, Butler Co., Ohio, on July 8, 1997.[31, 1032, 1033] He was buried in Greenwood Cemetery, Hamilton, Butler Co., Ohio.[1034, 1035]

Paul C. Reidinger worked as a training supervisor for Florida Power and Light for 28 years. He and Betty Jane Daggy Stitsinger Reidinger lived in Miami, Dade Co., Florida, returning to Hamilton, Butler Co., Ohio after he retired.[1035]

Betty Jane Daggy Stitsinger Reidinger worked in her parent's photography studio for years, retouching negatives. Later, she worked for Ohio Casualty Insurance Company.[623]

152. Mary Sarah[9] **Surber** (*Earl Lester*[8], *Anna*[7] *Pegan, Thomas Jefferson*[6], *Henry*[5], *Robert A.*[4], *Andrew*[3], *Andrew*[2] *Pagan, James*[1]) was born on September 14, 1918, in White Oak Twp., Highland Co., Ohio.[632] She was the daughter of Earl Lester Surber (75) and Ganelle Ruth Roberts. Mary Sarah died in White Oak Twp., Highland Co., Ohio, on September 15, 1918.[632] She was buried in Union Cemetery, Taylorsville, White Oak Twp., Highland Co., Ohio.[632]

153. Maynard Raymond[9] **Surber** (*Earl Lester*[8], *Anna*[7] *Pegan, Thomas Jefferson*[6], *Henry*[5], *Robert A.*[4], *Andrew*[3], *Andrew*[2] *Pagan, James*[1]) was born on April 14, 1920, in White Oak Twp., Highland Co., Ohio.[633, 634] He was the son of Earl Lester Surber (75) and Ganelle Ruth Roberts. Maynard Raymond died in White Oak Twp., Highland Co., Ohio, on July 26, 2012, at age 92.[633] He was buried in Union Cemetery, Taylorsville, White Oak Twp., Highland Co., Ohio.[1036]

Maynard Raymond married **America Isabelle Donohoo** on September 17, 1943, in Geary Co.,

Kansas.[1037, 1038] They had two sons. America Isabelle Donohoo was born in White Oak Twp., Highland Co., Ohio, on April 4, 1919.[31, 1039,] She was also known as **Isabelle**. America Isabelle lived in 2001 in White Oak Twp., Highland Co., Ohio. She reached age 81 and died in a hospital in Hillsboro, Liberty Twp., Highland Co., Ohio, on February 1, 2001.[31, 1039] America Isabelle was buried in Union Cemetery, Taylorsville, White Oak Twp., Highland Co., Ohio.[1040, 1041]

Maynard and Isabelle Donohoo Surber married during WWII in Junction City, Geary Co., Kansas while Maynard was stationed at Fort Riley. They returned to Highland Co., Ohio after the war.[1037, 1038]

Maynard and his brother Cedric were partners in the prosperous family dairy farms and agricultural business for more than 50 years, and their farms were landmarks in White Oak Twp., Highland Co., Ohio.[633]

154. Cedric Lewis[9] **Surber** (*Earl Lester*[8], *Anna*[7] *Pegan*, *Thomas Jefferson*[6], *Henry*[5], *Robert A.*[4], *Andrew*[3], *Andrew*[2] *Pagan*, *James*[1]) was born on January 26, 1923, in White Oak Twp., Highland Co., Ohio.[31, 635, 636] He was the son of Earl Lester Surber (75) and Ganelle Ruth Roberts. Cedric Lewis lived in 2001 in Hillsboro, Liberty Twp., Highland Co., Ohio. He died in White Oak Twp., Highland Co., Ohio, on April 13, 2013, at age 90.[31, 635] Cedric Lewis was buried in Union Cemetery, Taylorsville, White Oak Twp., Highland Co., Ohio.[635, 1042]

Cedric Lewis married **Mary Ruth Newhouse** on October 17, 1942, in Highland Co., Ohio.[636] They had three sons. Mary Ruth Newhouse was born in Clay Twp., Scioto Co., Ohio, on November 17, 1923.[31, 636, 1043, 1044, 1045] She was also known as **Ruth**. Mary Ruth reached age 74 and died in White Oak Twp., Highland Co., Ohio, on October 1, 1998.[31, 1044, 1045] She was buried in Union Cemetery, Taylorsville, White Oak Twp., Highland Co., Ohio.[1046, 1047]

Cedric Surber and his brother Maynard were partners in the prosperous family dairy farms and agricultural business for more than 50 years. Cedric's farm was honored by the Columbus (OH) Dispatch newspaper as a "Blue Ribbon Farm" in 1966.[635, 1048]

Sons of Cedric Lewis Surber and Mary Ruth Newhouse:

+ 214 m I. **Son One**[10] **Surber** was born in White Oak Twp., Highland Co., Ohio.

+ 215 m II. **Son Two**[10] **Surber** was born in White Oak Twp., Highland Co., Ohio.

155. Lowell R.[9] **Pegan** (*Hugh Doyle*[8], *Charles*[7], *Thomas Jefferson*[6], *Henry*[5], *Robert A.*[4], *Andrew*[3], *Andrew*[2] *Pagan*, *James*[1]) was born on March 15, 1934, in East Danville, Hamer Twp., Highland Co., Ohio.[31, 642, 643] He was the son of Hugh Doyle Pegan (76) and Lillian Blanche King. Lowell R. died in East Danville, Hamer Twp., Highland Co., Ohio, on July 12, 1975, age 41.[642, 644] He was buried in Hamer Township Cemetery, Hamer Twp., Highland Co., Ohio.[642]

Lowell R. married **Loretta Stroop** on March 15, 1958, in Highland Co., Ohio.[1049] They had three children. Loretta Stroop was born in East Danville, Hamer Twp., Highland Co., Ohio, on February 5, 1935.[31, 1049, 1050] Loretta reached age 37 and died in East Danville, Hamer Twp., Highland Co., Ohio, on August 19, 1972.[1050, 1051] She was buried in Hamer Township Cemetery, Hamer Twp., Highland Co., Ohio.[1050] She was the daughter of Truman Stroop and Mary McAdams.

Lowell R. Pegan and Loretta Stroop had three children, including:

+ 216 f I. **Mary Jane**[10] **Pegan** was born in Wilmington, Union Twp., Clinton Co., Ohio, on February 22, 1959.[1052] She died in Wilmington, Union Twp., Clinton Co., Ohio, on February 22, 1959.[1052]

+ 217 f II. **Daughter**[10] **Pegan** was born in Wilmington, Union Twp., Clinton Co., Ohio.

156. Allan Jay[9] **Pegan** (*Harold West*[8] *PeGan*, *Frank Joseph*[7] *Pegan*, *William Henry*[6], *Henry*[5], *Robert A.*[4], *Andrew*[3], *Andrew*[2] *Pagan*, *James*[1]) was born on June

25, 1944, in Leesburg, Fairfield Twp., Highland Co., Ohio.[31, 675, 676] He was the son of Harold West PeGan (80) and Velma Powell. Allan Jay lived in 1987 in Clermont Co., Ohio. He also resided in 1995 in Elsmere, Kenton Co., Kentucky. Allan Jay died in Cincinnati, Hamilton Co., Ohio, on October 18, 1998, at age 54.[31, 675, 676] He was cremated and his cremains buried in Martinsville IOOF Cemetery, Martinsville, Clark Twp., Clinton Co., Ohio.[676]

Allan Jay's name in the online Ohio birth records is Lawrence.[1053] On his Social Security application, he says he was born in Martinsville, Clark Twp., Clinton Co., Ohio.[1054] However, his obituary states he was born in Leesburg, Fairfield Twp., Highland Co., Ohio, where his parents were living at the time of his birth.[676]

Allan Jay married **Unknown Unknown** before 1963. They divorced. They had no children.

Allan Jay Pegan married **Ms. Cook** on November 2, 1963, in Clinton Co., Ohio.[1055] They divorced. They had two children.

157. **Powell⁹ Pegan** (*Harold West⁸ PeGan, Frank Joseph⁷ Pegan, William Henry⁶, Henry⁵, Robert A.⁴, Andrew³, Andrew² Pagan, James¹*) was born on February 23, 1959, in a hospital in Wilmington, Union Twp., Clinton Co., Ohio.[677] He was the son of Harold West PeGan (80) and Velma Powell. Powell died in a hospital in Wilmington, Union Twp., Clinton Co., Ohio, on February 23, 1959.[677] He was buried in Martinsville IOOF Cemetery, Martinsville, Clark Twp., Clinton Co., Ohio?

158. **Daughter⁹ Holmes** (*Ruth Marie⁸ Pegan, Frank Joseph⁷, William Henry⁶, Henry⁵, Robert A.⁴, Andrew³, Andrew² Pagan, James¹*) was born in Dayton, Montgomery Co., Ohio. She is the daughter of Raymond Holmes and Ruth Marie Pegan (81).

Daughter Holmes married **Robert Eugene Sheler II** on October 28, 1978, in St. Joseph Co., Indiana.[684, 1056] They divorced. They had three children. Robert Eugene Sheler II was born on October 9, 1947.[1056] He died on June 23, 2014 in South Bend, St. Joseph Co., Indiana.[1057] He was cremated.[1057]

After divorcing Robert E. Sheller II, Daughter Holmes remarried.

Daughter Holmes and Robert Eugene Sheler II had three children, including:

+ 218 m I. **Shaun¹⁰ Scheler** was born in LaPorte, Center Twp., LaPorte Co., Indiana, on April 24, 1968.[1058, 1059] He died in South Bend, St. Joseph Co., Indiana, on January 2, 2017.[1058, 1059]

159. **Daughter⁹ Pegan** (*Paul Stroup⁸, William Otto⁷, William Henry⁶, Henry⁵, Robert A.⁴, Andrew³, Andrew² Pagan, James¹*) was born in Hillsboro, Liberty Twp., Highland Co., Ohio. She is the daughter of Paul Stroup Pegan (83) and Louise Warnick.

Daughter Pegan married **Mr. Terrell**. They divorced.

Daughter Pegan Terrell married **John Colin Ridgeway** after 1967. They had one son. John Colin Ridgeway was born in Stewart, Choctaw Co., Mississippi, on August 5, 1931.[31, 1060, 1061 1062] John Colin reached age 64 and died in Longwood, Seminole Co., Florida, on August 6, 1995.[31, 1060, 1061, 1062]

160. **Daughter⁹ West** (*Audrey Mae⁸ Pegan, William Otto⁷, William Henry⁶, Henry⁵, Robert A.⁴, Andrew³, Andrew² Pagan, James¹*) was born in Wilmington, Union Twp., Clinton Co., Ohio. She is the daughter of George Elton West and Audrey Mae Pegan (85).

She married **Mark David Greene**. They divorced. They had two children. Mark David Greene was born in Columbus, Franklin Co., Ohio, on December 10, 1946.[31, 1063] He lived in 1999 in Springfield, Springfield Twp., Clark Co., Ohio. Mark David reached age 52 and died in a hospital in Kettering, Kettering Twp., Montgomery Co., Ohio, on January 16, 1999.[31, 1064] He was buried in Glen Haven Memorial Gardens, Donnelsville, Bethel Twp., Clark Co., Ohio.[1064, 1065]

Daughter West and Mark David Greene had two children, including:

+ 219 f I. **Melanie C.¹⁰ Greene** was born in Columbus, Franklin Co., Ohio, on January 5, 1973.[31, 1066] She died in Centerville, Washington Twp., Montgomery Co., Ohio, on January 15, 2003.[31, 1066]

10th Generation

161. Arthur Lowell[10] **Ludwick** (*Lowell Arthur*[9], *Vernice Catherine*[8] *Stroup, John Henry*[7], *Elvira*[6] *Pegan, Henry*[5], *Robert A.*[4], *Andrew*[3], *Andrew*[2] *Pagan, James*[1]) was born on November 11, 1943, in Cincinnati, Hamilton Co., Ohio.[695,696] He was also known as **Artie**. He was the son of Lowell Arthur Ludwick (126) and Doris Helen Pegan (86). Arthur Lowell lived in 2004 in Hillsboro, Liberty Twp., Highland Co., Ohio. He died in Lynchburg, Dodson Twp., Highland Co., Ohio, on January 21, 2014, at age 70.[696] Arthur Lowell was buried in Barnes Cemetery, Fairview, New Market Twp., Highland Co., Ohio.[696, 1067]

Arthur Lowell "Artie" Ludwick's obituary claims that he was born on November 10, 1943, but his birth record states his birth date as November 11, 1943.[695, 696]

Arthur Lowell married **Ms. Baker** before 1965. They divorced in Highland Co., Ohio, in 1980. They had two children.

Arthur Lowell Ludwick married **Paulette Pendall** on April 7, 1984, in Highland Co., Ohio.[1068] Paulette Pendall was born in Wilmington, Union Twp., Clinton Co., Ohio, on April 28, 1947.[31, 1069, 1070] Paulette lived in 2002 in Lynchburg, Dodson Twp., Highland Co., Ohio. She reached age 54 and died in a hospital in Dayton, Montgomery Co., Ohio, on January 26, 2002.[31, 1069, 1070] Paulette was buried in Sugar Grove Cemetery, Wilmington, Union Twp., Clinton Co., Ohio.[1070, 1071]

162. J. Bruce[10] **Philhower** (*Charles Randolph*[9], *Agnes*[8] *Lemons, Josephine*[7] *Stroup, Elvira*[6] *Pegan, Henry*[5], *Robert A.*[4], *Andrew*[3], *Andrew*[2] *Pagan, James*[1]) was born on January 17, 1925, in Hillsboro, Liberty Twp., Highland Co., Ohio.[702] He was the son of Charles Randolph Philhower II (87) and Ella Lorie Jones. J. Bruce died in Hillsboro, Liberty Twp., Highland Co., Ohio, on January 17, 1925.[703] He was buried in Hamer Township Cemetery, Hamer Twp., Highland Co., Ohio.[703]

163. Kenneth Edward[10] **Roush II** (*Marcia Lucille*[9] *Boesenberg, Grace*[8] *Lemons, Josephine*[7] *Stroup, Elvira*[6] *Pegan, Henry*[5], *Robert A.*[4], *Andrew*[3], *Andrew*[2] *Pagan, James*[1]) was born on August 5, 1931, in Springfield, Springfield Twp., Clark Co., Ohio.[31, 717, 718] He was the son of Kenneth Edward H. Roush and Marcia Lucille Boesenberg (89). Kenneth Edward died in Show Low, Navajo Co., Arizona, on October 1, 2007, at age 76.[31, 717] He was buried in Show Low Cemetery, Show Low, Navajo Co., Arizona.[1072]

Kenneth Edward married Mrs. **Helen Patricia Eldred** Shipps on December 13, 1952, in Sonoma Co., California.[1073] They divorced. They had five sons. Helen Patricia was born in Oakland, Alameda Co., California, on August 4, 1932.[31, 1074, 1075, 1076] Helen Patricia Eldred Shipps Roush Webber reached age 69 and died in Colton, San Bernardino, California, on September 9, 2001.[31, 1075, 1076] She was cremated.[1076]

After her divorce from Kenneth E. Roush, Helen P. Eldred Shipps Roush married Mr. Webber.

Kenneth Edward Roush II married **Judith K. Unknown** after 1965.

Kenneth Edward Roush II lived in several California cities: Oakland, Alameda Co. (1943); San Francisco, San Francisco Co. (1961); San Bernardino, San Bernardino Co. (1972). After his California residencies, he lived in Lake Tahoe, Placer Co., Nevada, and Phoenix, Maricopa Co., Arizona, before removing to Show Low, Nevada Co., Arizona. Kenneth Edward worked as an Episcopal minister, family counselor, and chaplain to NASA's Apollo Space Program.

164. Gary Lee[10] **Luck** (*Josephine Mae*[9] *Lemons, Clarence Otto*[8], *Josephine*[7] *Stroup, Elvira*[6] *Pegan, Henry*[5], *Robert A.*[4], *Andrew*[3], *Andrew*[2] *Pagan, James*[1]) was born on June 13, 1945, in Lynchburg, Dodson Twp., Highland Co., Ohio.[724] He was the son of Albert J. Luck II and Josephine Mae Lemons (91). Gary Lee died in Lynchburg, Dodson Twp., Highland Co., Ohio, on October 4, 1945.[724] He was buried in Troutwine Cemetery, Dodson Twp., Highland Co., Ohio and Clark Twp., Clinton Co., Ohio.[724, 1077]

165. Jeffrey Richard[10] **Long** (*Clarence J.*[9] *[Lemons II] Long, Clarence Otto*[8] *Lemons, Josephine*[7] *Stroup, Elvira*[6] *Pegan, Henry*[5]*, Robert A.*[4]*, Andrew*[3]*, Andrew*[2] *Pagan, James*[1]) was born on November 18, 1946, in West Allis, Milwaukee Co., Wisconsin.[31, 730, 731] He was the son of Clarence Junior (Lemons II) Long (92) and Dorothy Virginia Cleppe. Jeffrey Richard died in Sparks, Washoe Co., Nevada, on August 11, 2004, at age 57.[31, 730, 731] He was buried in Highland Memorial Park Cemetery, New Berlin, Waukesha Co., Wisconsin.[1078]

Jeffrey Richard married **Unknown Unknown** in 1971 in Maricopa Co., Arizona.

Jeffrey Richard Long married Mrs. **Unknown Unknown Thompson** in 1990, in Washoe Co., Nevada. They had one daughter.

166. Son[10] **Long** (*Clarence J.*[9] *[Lemons II] Long, Clarence Otto*[8] *Lemons, Josephine*[7] *Stroup, Elvira*[6] *Pegan, Henry*[5]*, Robert A.*[4]*, Andrew*[3]*, Andrew*[2] *Pagan, James*[1]) was born on April 6, 1950, in West Allis, Milwaukee Co., Wisconsin. He was the son of Clarence Junior (Lemons II) Long (92) and Dorothy Virginia Cleppe.

Son Long married **Mary Jo Jankowski**. She was also known as **Jo**. They have two daughters. Mary Jo Jankowski was born in Waukesha, Waukesha Twp., Waukesha Co., Wisconsin?, on September 20, 1950.[31, 1079] Mary Jo reached age 59 and died in Waukesha, Waukesha Twp., Waukesha Co., Wisconsin, on August 14, 2010.[31, 1079] She was buried in Highland Memorial Park Cemetery, New Berlin, Waukesha Co., Wisconsin.[1079, 1080]

167. Douglas M.[10] **Carroll** (*William Morrell*[9]*, Cora May*[8] *Williams, Mary E.*[7] *Stroup, Elvira*[6] *Pegan, Henry*[5]*, Robert A.*[4]*, Andrew*[3]*, Andrew*[2] *Pagan, James*[1]) was born on July 19, 1940, in Cincinnati, Hamilton Co., Ohio.[740] He is the son of William Morrell Carroll (96) and Lillian Hutchason.

Douglas M. married **Naomi Kay Prince** on September 16, 1961, in Hamilton Co., Ohio.[1081] Naomi Kay Prince was born in Mt. Washington, Hamilton County, Ohio, on November 13, 1940.

168. Dwan Ruble[10] **Williams** (*Carl D.*[9]*, Levi*[8]*, Mary E.*[7] *Stroup, Elvira*[6] *Pegan, Henry*[5]*, Robert A.*[4]*, Andrew*[3]*, Andrew*[2] *Pagan, James*[1]) was born on February 27, 1925, in Lynchburg, Dodson Twp., Highland Co., Ohio.[757] He was also known as **Bill**. He was the son of Carl D. Williams (98) and Madge Ruble. He died in Boise, Ada Co., Idaho, on April 12, 2014, at age 89.[757] Dwan Ruble was buried in Idaho State Veteran's Cemetery, Boise, Ada Co., Idaho.[1082]

Dwan Ruble married **Marilyn Joan Parker** on August 21, 1954, in Ada Co., Idaho.[757, 1083] They had three children. Marilyn Joan Parker was born in Filer, Twin Falls Co., Idaho?, on February 4, 1933.

169. Carolyn[10] **Williams** (*Carl D.*[9]*, Levi*[8]*, Mary E.*[7] *Stroup, Elvira*[6] *Pegan, Henry*[5]*, Robert A.*[4]*, Andrew*[3]*, Andrew*[2] *Pagan, James*[1]) was born on June 24, 1927, in Lynchburg, Dodson Twp., Highland Co., Ohio. She is the daughter of Carl D. Williams (98) and Madge Ruble.

Carolyn married **Jacob E. Roush** before 1972. They had one daughter. Jacob E. Roush was born in Dayton, Montgomery Co., Ohio, on January 21, 1920.[31, 1084, 1085] Jacob E. reached age 52 and died in Dayton, Montgomery Co., Ohio, on October 13, 1972.[1085, 1086] He was cremated and his ashes buried in Dayton Memorial Park Cemetery, Dayton, Montgomery Co., Ohio.[1087, 1088]

Carolyn Williams Roush married **Richard F. Tanner** after 1972. Richard F. Tanner was born in Madison Twp., Montgomery Co., Ohio, on July 31, 1924.[1089] Richard F. reached age 92 and died in Dayton, Montgomery Co., Ohio, on January 12, 2017.[1090] He was cremated.[1090]

170. Marianna[10] **Wilkin** (*Edgar Franklin*[9]*, Hattie Ellen*[8] *Williams, Mary E.*[7] *Stroup, Elvira*[6] *Pegan, Henry*[5]*, Robert A.*[4]*, Andrew*[3]*, Andrew*[2] *Pagan, James*[1]) was born on March 8, 1922, in Dodson Twp., Highland Co., Ohio. She was the daughter of Edgar Franklin Wilkin (99) and Ethalyn Teboe.

Marianna married **A.J. Smith** in 1944. They divorced before 1955. They have one son. A.J. Smith was born in Ohio in 1920. He may be deceased.

Marianna Wilkin Smith married **Alex Lesko** in 1964 in Arizona? They divorced. They have one son. This may be the Aleck Lesko, born November 15, 1925 in Coalgood, Harlan Co., Kentucky. Aleck died in August 1981 in Buckeye, Maricopa Co., Arizona?

Son of Marianna Wilkin and A.J. Smith:

+ 220 m I. **Douglas Troy**[11] **Smith** was born in Cincinnati, Hamilton Co., Ohio, on August 20, 1949.[31, 1091] He died in Mesa, Maricopa Co., Arizona, on January 7, 1994.[31, 1091]

171. Charles Edgar[10] **Wilkin** (*Edgar Franklin*[9], *Hattie Ellen*[8] *Williams*, *Mary E.*[7] *Stroup*, *Elvira*[6] *Pegan*, *Henry*[5], *Robert A.*[4], *Andrew*[3], *Andrew*[2] *Pagan*, *James*[1]) was born on Thursday, May 17, 1923, in Dodson Twp., Highland Co., Ohio.[31,764] He was the son of Edgar Franklin Wilkin (99) and Ethalyn Teboe. Charles Edgar lived in 1967 in Phoenix, Maricopa Co., Arizona. He died in Phoenix, Maricopa Co., Arizona, on March 19, 1982, at the age of 58.[764, 765] Charles Edgar was buried in Green Acres Memorial Park Cemetery, Scottsdale, Maricopa Co., Arizona.[764]

Charles Edgar married **Eilene Snead** on Tuesday, September 22, 1942, in Highland Co., Ohio.[1092] They divorced. They had one son. Eilene Snead was born in Lynchburg, Dodson Twp., Highland Co., Ohio, on Saturday, January 3, 1925.[31, 1093, 1094, 1095] She reached age 58 and died in Fort Wayne, Allen Co., Indiana, on September 20, 1983.[1095] Eilene Snead Wilkin Ross Spicer Davis was buried in Prairie Grove Cemetery, Fort Wayne, Allen Co., Indiana.[1096]

Eilene Snead Wilkin married three more times om Charles Wilkin. Her second husband was John Everett Ross, whose first wife was Rosalie Bussey, another Pegan descendant (see Harrison James Pegan chapter, #93).

Charles Edgar Wilkin married **Doris Geraldine Mason** on Saturday, January 25, 1947, in Highland Co., Ohio. They divorced. They had two children. Doris Geraldine Mason was born in Dodsonville, Dodson Twp., Highland Co., Ohio, on Tuesday, November 5, 1929.[1097, 1098, 1099] Doris Geraldine Mason Wilkin Rhoades reached age 86 and died in Lynchburg, Dodson Twp., Highland Co., Ohio, on June 29, 2016.[1098, 1099] She was buried in New Lynchburg Masonic Cemetery/Lynchburg F & AM Cemetery, Lynchburg, Dodson Twp., Highland Co., Ohio.[1099]

After her divorce from Charles E. Wilkin, Doris G. Mason Wilkin married Melvin R. Rhoades.[1098]

Son of Charles Edgar Wilkin and Eilene Snead:

+ 221 m I. **Kenneth Michael**[11] **Wilkin** was born in Lynchburg, Dodson Twp., Highland Co., Ohio, on June 1, 1943.[31, 1100, 11011102, 1103] He died in Fort Wayne, Allen Co., Indiana, on July 28, 1989, at the age of 46.[31, 1101, 1102, 1103]

Children of Charles Edgar Wilkin and Doris Geraldine Mason:

+ 222 f I. **Daughter**[11] **Wilkin**.

+ 223 m II. **Son**[11] **Wilkin**.

172. Deloris[10] **Wilkin** (*Edgar Franklin*[9], *Hattie Ellen*[8] *Williams*, *Mary E.*[7] *Stroup*, *Elvira*[6] *Pegan*, *Henry*[5], *Robert A.*[4], *Andrew*[3], *Andrew*[2] *Pagan*, *James*[1]) was born on July 23, 1925, in Dodson Twp., Highland Co., Ohio. She is the daughter of Edgar Franklin Wilkin (99) and Ethalyn Teboe.

Deloris married **Floyd W. Roades** on October 9, 1943, in Highland Co., Ohio.[1104] They had three children. Floyd W. Roades was born in Clay Twp., Highland Co., Ohio, on November 15, 1925.

173. Joan[10] **Wilkin** (*Edgar Franklin*[9], *Hattie Ellen*[8] *Williams*, *Mary E.*[7] *Stroup*, *Elvira*[6] *Pegan*, *Henry*[5], *Robert A.*[4], *Andrew*[3], *Andrew*[2] *Pagan*, *James*[1]) was born on August 20, 1933, in Dodson Twp., Highland Co., Ohio.[766] She is the daughter of Edgar Franklin Wilkin (99) and Ethalyn Teboe.

Joan married **Howard Robert Manis** on June 27, 1953, in Highland Co., Ohio.[766] They had two children. Howard Robert Manis was born in Indianapolis, Marion Co., Indiana, on May 27,

1931.[31, 766, 1105] He resided in 1993 in Cincinnati, Hamilton Co., Ohio. Howard Robert reached age 75 and died in St. Petersburg, Pinellas Co., Florida, on September 9, 2006.[31, 1105] He was buried in Arlington Memorial Gardens Cemetery, Mount Healthy, Hamilton Co., Ohio.[1106]

Joan Wilkin and Howard Robert Manis had two children, including:

+ 224 f I. **Daughter**[11] **Manis**

174. Sonia M.[10] **Hawk** (*Marjorie Marie*[9] *Wilkin, Hattie Ellen*[8] *Williams, Mary E.*[7] *Stroup, Elvira*[6] *Pegan, Henry*[5]*, Robert A.*[4]*, Andrew*[3]*, Andrew*[2] *Pagan, James*[1]) was born on February 26, 1931, in Salem Twp., Highland Co., Ohio.[777] She is the daughter of Everett Guy Hawk and Marjorie Marie Wilkin (101).

Sonia M. married **Unknown Cole** before 1955. They have one daughter.

Sonia M. Hawk Cole married **James Harold Price II** on April 19, 1975, in Franklin Co., Ohio.[1107] James Harold Price II was born in Scioto Co., Ohio, on July 5, 1927.[31, 1108, 1109] James Harold reached age 66 and died in Columbus, Franklin Co., Ohio, on September 19, 1993.[31,1108 964] He was buried in Kingwood Memorial Park Cemetery, Liberty Twp., Delaware Co., Ohio.[1110]

Sonia Hawk Cole Price, a longtime home economics teacher, was appointed the Ohio Department of Education's assistant director of vocational education for vocational home economics in 1969. In 1982, she became the Division of Vocational Education's associate director. A year later, the American Vocational Education's Vocational Home Economics Division awarded Sonia Hawk Cole Price the Outstanding Service Award for her efforts and leadership in the organization. She was also honored by the Ohio Division of Vocational Education. Sonia Hawk Cole Price also has authored several books on home economics and the teaching of the subject.

175. Carolyn M.[10] **Hawk** (*Marjorie Marie*[9] *Wilkin, Hattie Ellen*[8] *Williams, Mary E.*[7] *Stroup, Elvira*[6] *Pegan, Henry*[5]*, Robert A.*[4]*, Andrew*[3]*, Andrew*[2] *Pagan, James*[1]) was born on August 4, 1933, in Salem Twp., Highland Co., Ohio.[778] She is the daughter of Everett Guy Hawk and Marjorie Marie Wilkin (101).

Carolyn M. married **James Randall Barker** in 1951. They divorced. They had two sons. James Randall Barker was born in Lynchburg, Dodson Twp., Highland Co., Ohio, on February 22, 1932.[31, 1111] He was also known as **Rannie**. James Randall reached age 76 and died in Hillsboro, Liberty Twp., Highland Co., Ohio, on April 8, 2008.[31, 1111] He was buried in Lynchburg Masonic Cemetery, Lynchburg, Dodson Twp., Highland Co., Ohio.[1112]

176. Betty Elaine[10] **Campbell** (*Evelyn Lorie*[9] *Wilkin, Hattie Ellen*[8] *Williams, Mary E.*[7] *Stroup, Elvira*[6] *Pegan, Henry*[5]*, Robert A.*[4]*, Andrew*[3]*, Andrew*[2] *Pagan, James*[1]) was born on July 30, 1928, in Perry Twp., Brown Co., Ohio.[790] She is also known as **Elaine**. She is the daughter of William E. Campbell and Evelyn Lorie Wilkin (102).

Betty Elaine married **Ralph Doyle Walker** on July 4, 1947.[1113] They divorced. They had four children. Ralph Doyle Walker was born in College Corner, Israel Twp., Preble Co., Ohio, on September 11, 1923.[31, 1113, 1114, 1115] He reached age 66 and died in a hospital in Cincinnati, Hamilton Co., Ohio, on July 21, 1990.[31, 1113, 1114] Ralph Doyle was buried in Resthaven Memorial Gardens Cemetery, Hillsboro, Liberty Twp., Highland Co., Ohio.[1113, 1116]

177. June Phyllis[10] **Campbell** (*Evelyn Lorie*[9] *Wilkin, Hattie Ellen*[8] *Williams, Mary E.*[7] *Stroup, Elvira*[6] *Pegan, Henry*[5]*, Robert A.*[4]*, Andrew*[3]*, Andrew*[2] *Pagan, James*[1]) was born on May 31, 1931, in Perry Twp., Brown Co., Ohio.[791] She is the daughter of William E. Campbell and Evelyn Lorie Wilkin (102).

June Phyllis married **William Earl Hostetler** on June 30, 1950, in Highland Co., Ohio.[1117, 1118] They had two daughters. William Earl Hostetler was born in Myers, Nicholas Co., Kentucky, on December 5, 1921.[31, 1117, 1118, 1119] William Earl lived in 1992 in Lynchburg, Dodson Twp., Highland Co., Ohio. He reached age 70 and died in a facility in Dayton, Montgomery Co., Ohio, on October 29, 1992.[31, 1117, 1119] William Earl was buried in New Lynchburg Masonic Cemetery/ Lynchburg F & AM Cemetery, Lynchburg, Dodson Twp., Highland Co., Ohio.[1117, 1120]

178. Donald E.[10] **Campbell** (*Evelyn Lorie*[9] *Wilkin, Hattie Ellen*[8] *Williams, Mary E.*[7] *Stroup, Elvira*[6] *Pegan, Henry*[5], *Robert A.*[4], *Andrew*[3], *Andrew*[2] *Pagan, James*[1]) was born on June 9, 1933, in Lynchburg, Dodson Twp., Highland Co., Ohio. [792, 793, 794] He was also known as **Don E.** He was the son of William E. Campbell and Evelyn Lorie Wilkin (102). Donald E. was living in 2013 in Leesburg, Fairfield Twp., Highland Co., Ohio. He died in a hospital in Hillsboro, Liberty Twp., Highland Co., Ohio, on June 7, 2013, at age 79.[793] Donald E. was buried in Hightop Cemetery, Samantha, Penn Twp., Highland Co., Ohio.[793, 794]

Donald E. married **Mary Lou Cowman** on March 10, 1952, in Highland Co., Ohio.[1121] They divorced. They had one son. Mary Lou Cowman was born in Paint Twp., Highland Co., Ohio, on October 1, 1935.[1122]

Donald E. Campbell married **Charlotte Ann Griffith** on March 30, 1963 in Highland Co., Ohio.[793] Charlotte Ann Griffith was born on May 20, 1932 in Springfield, Springfield Twp., Clark Co., Ohio or Leesburg, Fairfield Twp., Highland Co., Ohio.

179. John Lee[10] **Campbell** (*Evelyn Lorie*[9] *Wilkin, Hattie Ellen*[8] *Williams, Mary E.*[7] *Stroup, Elvira*[6] *Pegan, Henry*[5], *Robert A.*[4], *Andrew*[3], *Andrew*[2] *Pagan, James*[1]) was born on December 31, 1940, in Clark Twp., Clinton Co., Ohio. He is the son of William E. Campbell and Evelyn Lorie Wilkin (102).

He married **Linda Unknown**.

180. Jimmie Gaylord[10] **Barker** (*Lenora*[9] *Wilkin, Hattie Ellen*[8] *Williams, Mary E.*[7] *Stroup, Elvira*[6] *Pegan, Henry*[5], *Robert A.*[4], *Andrew*[3], *Andrew*[2] *Pagan, James*[1]) was born on January 27, 1933, in Dodson Twp., Highland Co., Ohio.[800] He was the son of Wendell D. Barker and Lenora Wilkin (103). Jimmie Gaylord died in Dodson Twp., Highland Co., Ohio, on January 28, 1933.[800] He was buried in Troutwine Cemetery, Dodson Twp., Highland Co., Ohio and Clark Twp., Clinton Co., Ohio.[800, 1123]

181. Barbara Ann[10] **Roush** (*Georgeanna*[9] *Wilkin, Hattie Ellen*[8] *Williams, Mary E.*[7] *Stroup, Elvira*[6] *Pegan, Henry*[5], *Robert A.*[4], *Andrew*[3], *Andrew*[2] *Pagan, James*[1]) was born on November 4, 1940, in Dodson Twp., Highland Co., Ohio. She is the daughter of Marcus C. Roush and Georgeanna Wilkin (104).

Barbara Ann married **Ray Howard Hamilton** on March 15, 1959, in Highland Co., Ohio. [1124] They divorced. They had two daughters. Ray Howard Hamilton was born in New Vienna, Green Twp., Clinton Co., Ohio, on November 11, 1941.[31, 1125] He reached age 41 and died in Winter Haven, Polk Co., Florida, on October 8, 1983.[1125] Ray Howard was buried in Lakeside Memorial Park Cemetery, Winter Haven, Polk Co., Florida.[1126]

Forty-three-year-old Ray Howard Hamilton was murdered by his stepson, Jeffrey Allan Dodd. Ray Hamilton and his wife, Judy, Jeffrey Dodd's mother, came home in the early hours of Saturday morning, 08 Oct 1983, after a night of drinking and began arguing. The argument escalated into a fight and Jeffrey Dodd and his brother, Mark Dodd, tried to stop it. Jeffrey Dodd picked up a baseball bat and hit Ray Hamilton several times in the head. Hamilton was dead on arrival at the Polk Co., Hospital. Jeffrey Dodd was indicted for second-degree murder.[1127]

Barbara Ann Roush Hamilton married **William Beam Storer II** on June 28, 1980, in Highland Co., Ohio.[1128] They divorced. William Beam Storer II was born in Hillsboro, Liberty Twp., Highland Co., Ohio, on January 13, 1941.[31, 1129] He lived in 2007 in Belmont, Goshen Twp., Belmont Co., Ohio. William Beam reached age 66 and died in a hospital in Columbus, Franklin Co., Ohio, on May 18, 2007.[31,1129] He was buried in Hillsboro Cemetery, Hillsboro, Liberty Twp., Highland Co., Ohio.[1130]

182. Daughter[10] **Roush** (*Georgeanna*[9] *Wilkin, Hattie Ellen*[8] *Williams, Mary E.*[7] *Stroup, Elvira*[6] *Pegan, Henry*[5]*, Robert A.*[4]*, Andrew*[3]*, Andrew*[2] *Pagan, James*[1]) was born in Lynchburg, Dodson Twp., Highland Co., Ohio. She was the daughter of Marcus C. Roush and Georgeanna Wilkin (104).

Daughter Roush married **Mr. Graves** about 1969. They divorced. They had one son.

Daughter Roush Graves married **Daniel Allen Hupp** on October 5, 1974 in Ross Co., Ohio.[1131] They had two children. Daniel Allen Hupp was born in Chillicothe, Scioto Twp., Ross Co., Ohio, on January 18, 1947.[1132] Daniel Allen reached age 65 and died in Waverly, Pee Pee Twp., Pike Co., Ohio, on January 12, 2013.[1132] He was buried in Floral Hills Memory Gardens Cemetery, Massieville, Huntington Twp., Ross Co., Ohio.[1132, 1133]

183. Son[10] **Wilkin** (*LeRoy Thomas*[9]*, Hattie Ellen*[8] *Williams, Mary E.*[7] *Stroup, Elvira*[6] *Pegan, Henry*[5]*, Robert A.*[4]*, Andrew*[3]*, Andrew*[2] *Pagan, James*[1]) was born on September 22, 1944, in Highland or Clinton Co., Ohio. He is the son of LeRoy Thomas Wilkin (106) and Helen Briggs.

Son Wilkin married **Sharon Kay Fender** on January 3, 1964, in Highland Co., Ohio.[1134] They had four children. Sharon Kay Fender was born in Clay Twp., Highland Co., Ohio, on November 14, 1944.[31, 1134, 1135] Sharon Kay reached age 54 and died in Lynchburg, Dodson Twp., Highland Co., Ohio, on May 7, 1999.[31, 1134, 1135] She was buried in New Lynchburg Masonic Cemetery/Lynchburg F & AM Cemetery, Lynchburg, Dodson Twp., Highland Co., Ohio.[1136]

Son Wilkin remarried.

184. Infant Daughter[10] **Wilkin** (*LeRoy Thomas*[9]*, Hattie Ellen*[8] *Williams, Mary E.*[7] *Stroup, Elvira*[6] *Pegan, Henry*[5]*, Robert A.*[4]*, Andrew*[3]*, Andrew*[2] *Pagan, James*[1]) was born in 1948 in Highland or Clinton Co., Ohio?[1137] She was the daughter of LeRoy Thomas Wilkin (106) and Helen Briggs. Infant Daughter died in Highland or Clinton Co., Ohio?, in 1948.[1137] She was buried in New Lynchburg Masonic Cemetery/Lynchburg F & AM Cemetery, Lynchburg, Dodson Twp., Highland Co., Ohio.[1137]

185. Carol Jean[10] **Williams** (*Woodrow Wilson*[9]*, Stanley*[8]*, Mary E.*[7] *Stroup, Elvira*[6] *Pegan, Henry*[5]*, Robert A.*[4]*, Andrew*[3]*, Andrew*[2] *Pagan, James*[1]) was born on December 21, 1935, in Lynchburg, Dodson Twp., Highland Co., Ohio.[834] She is the daughter of Woodrow Wilson Williams (109) and Mabel Fern Snyder.

Carol Jean married **Jack Lynn Griffith** on September 4, 1951, in Highland Co., Ohio.[1138] They divorced. They had three children. Jack Lynn Griffith was born in Union Twp., Highland Co., Ohio, on June 17, 1930.[31, 1139] He was also known as **Lynn**. He reached age 79 and died in Scottsbluff, Scotts Bluff Co., Nebraska, on March 27, 2010.[31, 1139] Jack Lynn was buried in Dayton National Cemetery, Dayton, Montgomery Co., Ohio.[1140]

Jack L. Griffith worked as a building contractor in Lynchburg, Dodson Twp., Highland Co., Ohio. He moved to Nebraska after 1992.

Carol Jean Williams Griffith married **Alfred Milton Woodmansee III** on August 12, 1967, in Highland Co., Ohio.[1141] They had one son. Alfred Milton Woodmansee III was born in Cincinnati, Hamilton Co., Ohio, on April 16, 1931.[31, 1141, 1142] Alfred Milton reached age 78 and died in Cambridge, Cambridge Twp., Guernsey Co., Ohio, on January 2, 2010.[31, 1141] He was buried in Greenlawn Cemetery, Milford, Miami Twp., Clermont Co., Ohio.[1143]

Alfred worked at a Ford Company plant and lived in Lynchburg, Dodson Twp., Highland Co., Ohio before moving to Cambridge, Ohio.

Carol Jean Williams and Jack Lynn Griffith had three children, including:

+ 225 m III. **Jack W. Griffith II** was born in Wilmington, Union Twp., Clinton Co., Ohio, on August 6, 1954.[31, 1144] He died in a facility in Madeira, Hamilton Co., Ohio, on December 9, 1992.[31, 1144]

186. Janet E.[10] **Williams** (*Woodrow Wilson*[9], *Stanley*[8], *Mary E.*[7] *Stroup, Elvira*[6] *Pegan, Henry*[5], *Robert A.*[4], *Andrew*[3], *Andrew*[2] *Pagan, James*[1]) was born on July 14, 1937, in Lynchburg, Dodson Twp., Highland Co., Ohio.[835] She is the daughter of Woodrow Wilson Williams (109) and Mabel Fern Snyder.

Janet E. married **Charles Winkle II** on May 28, 1954.[1145] They had three children. Charles Winkle II was born in Willettsville, Union Twp., Highland Co., Ohio, on December 20, 1932.[1145, 1146] He was also known as **Junior**. Charles reached age 81 and died in Lynchburg, Dodson Twp., Highland Co., Ohio, on October 17, 2014.[1145] He was buried in New Lynchburg Masonic Cemetery/Lynchburg F & AM Cemetery, Lynchburg, Dodson Twp., Highland Co., Ohio.[1147]

187. Judith Mae[10] **Williams** (*Woodrow Wilson*[9], *Stanley*[8], *Mary E.*[7] *Stroup, Elvira*[6] *Pegan, Henry*[5], *Robert A.*[4], *Andrew*[3], *Andrew*[2] *Pagan, James*[1]) was born on January 19, 1939, in Lynchburg, Dodson Twp., Highland Co., Ohio.[836] She was the daughter of Woodrow Wilson Williams (109) and Mabel Fern Snyder. She resided in 2014 in Lynchburg, Dodson Twp., Highland Co., Ohio. Judith Mae died in a hospital in Wilmington, Union Twp., Clinton Co., Ohio, on January 3, 2014, at age 74.[836]

Judith Mae married **Roger H. Turner** on February 27, 1960, in Highland Co., Ohio.[836] They had one daughter. Roger H. Turner was born on August 22, 1938.

188. James Douglas[10] **Williams** (*Woodrow Wilson*[9], *Stanley*[8], *Mary E.*[7] *Stroup, Elvira*[6] *Pegan, Henry*[5], *Robert A.*[4], *Andrew*[3], *Andrew*[2] *Pagan, James*[1]) was born on March 12, 1943, in Lynchburg, Dodson Twp., Highland Co., Ohio.[31, 837] He was the son of Woodrow Wilson Williams (109) and Mabel Fern Snyder. James Douglas died in Dodson Twp., Highland Co., Ohio, on May 18, 1986, at age 43.[837, 838] He was buried in St. Martin Cemetery, St. Martin, Perry Twp., Brown Co., Ohio.[837]

James Douglas married **Ms. Kay** on May 2, 1964.[837] They had five children.

189. David Lee[10] **Kelley** (*Mary Elizabeth*[9] *Williams, Harley N.*[8], *Mary E.*[7] *Stroup, Elvira*[6] *Pegan, Henry*[5], *Robert A.*[4], *Andrew*[3], *Andrew*[2] *Pagan, James*[1]) was born on January 29, 1963, in Norwood, Mill Creek Twp., Hamilton Co., Ohio.[860] He was the son of Karl Bendict Kelley and Mary Elizabeth Williams (114). David Lee lived in 1967 in Norwood, Mill Creek Twp., Hamilton Co., Ohio. He died in a hospital in Cincinnati, Hamilton Co., Ohio, on June 17, 1967, at age four.[861] David Lee was buried in Rest Haven Cemetery, Evendale, Sycamore Twp., Hamilton Co., Ohio.[1148]

190. Candus Gay[10] **Williams** (*Glen Louis*[9], *Harley N.*[8], *Mary E.*[7] *Stroup, Elvira*[6] *Pegan, Henry*[5], *Robert A.*[4], *Andrew*[3], *Andrew*[2] *Pagan, James*[1]) was born on February 9, 1965, in Hillsboro, Liberty Twp., Highland Co., Ohio.[865] She was the daughter of Glen Louis Williams (115) and Betty Lou Bishop. She died in DeFuniak Springs, Walton Co., Florida, on January 26, 2012, at age 46.[865] Candus Gay was buried in Black Creek Memorial Cemetery, Freeport, Walton Co., Florida.[865, 1149]

She married **Mr. Nash**. They had two daughters.

191. Vincent B.[10] **Williams** (*Glen Louis*[9], *Harley N.*[8], *Mary E.*[7] *Stroup, Elvira*[6] *Pegan, Henry*[5], *Robert A.*[4], *Andrew*[3], *Andrew*[2] *Pagan, James*[1]) was born on December 19, 1975, in DeFuniak Springs, Walton Co., Florida.[866] He was the son of Glen Louis Williams (115) and Betty Lou Bishop. Vincent B. died in DeFuniak Springs, Walton Co., Florida, on December 19, 1975.[866] He was buried in Black Creek Memorial Cemetery, Freeport, Walton Co., Florida.[866]

192. Joseph Todd[10] **Spilker II** (*Joseph Benjamin*[9], *Ralph Henry*[8], *Laura Arabella*[7] *Stroup, Elvira*[6] *Pegan, Henry*[5], *Robert A.*[4], *Andrew*[3], *Andrew*[2] *Pagan, James*[1]) was born on March 18, 1939, in Cincinnati, Hamilton Co., Ohio (Mt. Auburn Twp.).[31, 881] He was the son of Joseph Benjamin Spilker (120) and Dorothy Ernst. Joseph Todd died in Cambridge, Cambridge Twp., Guernsey Co., Ohio, on December 13, 2009, at age 70.[31, 881] He was buried in Guernsey County Memorial Gardens, Cambridge, Cambridge Twp., Guernsey Co., Ohio.[881, 1150]

He was a surveyor.[881]

Joseph Todd married **Shirley Edna Smith** on November 7, 1959.[1151, 1152] They had three children. Shirley Edna Smith was born in Union Twp., Ohio Co., Indiana on May 10, 1938.[1153] Shirley Edna reached age 75 and died in Pataskala, Licking Co., Ohio, on June 15, 2013.[1151] She was buried in Guernsey County Memorial Gardens, Cambridge, Cambridge Twp., Guernsey Co., Ohio.[1151]

Shirley Edna Smith Spilker's birth certificate says she was born in "Laughery", Union Twp., Ohio Co., Indiana. But the town of Laughery is in adjacent Ripley Co., Indiana. However, on her marriage license, Shirley states she was born in Ohio County, Indiana.[1152, 1153]

193. Mary Ann[10] **Rogers** (*Shirley Lois Gail*[9] *Spilker, Ralph Henry*[8], *Laura Arabella*[7] *Stroup, Elvira*[6] *Pegan, Henry*[5], *Robert A.*[4], *Andrew*[3], *Andrew*[2] *Pagan, James*[1]) was born on May 5, 1953, in Cincinnati, Hamilton Co., Ohio.[887] She was the daughter of Russell Howard Rogers and Shirley Lois Gail Spilker (121). Mary Ann lived in 1984 in Greenhills, Springfield Twp., Hamilton Co., Ohio. She died in a hospital in Montgomery, Sycamore Twp., Hamilton Co., Ohio, on May 19, 1984, at age 31.[887,888] Mary Ann was buried in Oak Hill Cemetery, Glendale, Springfield Twp., Hamilton Co., Ohio.[887]

Never married.

194. Roger Owen[10] **Ludwick** (*Dwight H.*[9], *Vernice Catherine*[8] *Stroup, John Henry*[7], *Elvira*[6] *Pegan, Henry*[5], *Robert A.*[4], *Andrew*[3], *Andrew*[2] *Pagan, James*[1]) was born on January 27, 1937, in Dodson Twp., Highland Co., Ohio?[894] He was the son of Dwight H. Ludwick (122) and Kathryn R. McCoffin. He died in Clayton, Randolph Twp., Montgomery Co., Ohio, on December 15, 2016, age 79.[895] Roger Owen was buried in Royal Oak Memorial Gardens Cemetery, Brookville, Clay Twp., Montgomery Co., Ohio.[1154]

Roger Owen married **Joy A. Mann** about 1960. They had two children. Joy A. Mann was born in Medina, Medina Twp., Medina Co., Ohio, on August 23, 1936.[31, 1155, 1156] Joy A. reached age 71 and died in Dayton, Montgomery Co., Ohio, on March 11, 2008.[31,1156] She was buried in Royal Oak Memorial Gardens Cemetery, Brookville, Clay Twp., Montgomery Co., Ohio.[1156, 1157]

Children of Roger Owen Ludwick and Joy A. Mann:

+ 226 f I. **Daughter**[11] **Ludwick** was born in Dayton, Montgomery Co., Ohio.

195. Child[10] **Ludwick** (*Lloyd Claude*[9], *Vernice Catherine*[8] *Stroup, John Henry*[7], *Elvira*[6] *Pegan, Henry*[5], *Robert A.*[4], *Andrew*[3], *Andrew*[2] *Pagan, James*[1]) was born in 1940 in Allensburg, Liberty Twp., Highland Co., Ohio.[902] He or she was a child of Lloyd Claude Ludwick (123) and Mildred Pauline Claibourne. Child died in Allensburg, Liberty Twp., Highland Co., Ohio, in 1940.[902] He or she was buried in Barnes Cemetery, Fairview, New Market Twp., Highland Co., Ohio.[902]

196. Son[10] **Ludwick** (*Lloyd Claude*[9], *Vernice Catherine*[8] *Stroup, John Henry*[7], *Elvira*[6] *Pegan, Henry*[5], *Robert A.*[4], *Andrew*[3], *Andrew*[2] *Pagan, James*[1]) was born in Allensburg, Liberty Twp., Highland Co., Ohio.[758] He is the son of Lloyd Claude Ludwick (123) and Mildred Pauline Claibourne.

Son Ludwick married **June Loretta Tatum**. They have two children. June Loretta Tatum was born in Prattville, Autauga Co., Alabama, on September 4, 1943.[1158, 1159] June Loretta reached age 71 and died in Montgomery, Montgomery Co., Alabama, on August 23, 2015.[1159] She was buried in Prattville Memorial Gardens, Prattville, Autauga Co., Alabama.[1160]

197. JoAnn[10] **Fudge** (*Thelma L.*[9] *Vance, Sadie D.*[8] *Ballentine, Elma Jane*[7] *Stroup, Elvira*[6] *Pegan, Henry*[5], *Robert A.*[4], *Andrew*[3], *Andrew*[2] *Pagan, James*[1]) was born on May 6, 1938, in Madison, Dane Co., Wisconsin. She is the daughter of George M. Fudge and Thelma L. Vance (128).

JoAnn married **Robert Jean Ramseyer** about 1960. They had two children. Robert Jean Ramseyer was born in Millersburg, Hardy Twp., Holmes Co., Ohio, on April 29, 1938.[1161]

JoAnn Fudge and Robert Jean Ramseyer had two children, including:

+ 227   I.   **Infant**[11] **Ramseyer** was born in Millersburg, Hardy Twp., Holmes Co., Ohio, on November 28, 1961.[1162] He or she died in Millersburg, Hardy Twp., Holmes Co., Ohio, on November 28, 1961.[1162]

198. Robyn V.[10] **Bowman** (*Inez*[9] *Vance, Sadie D.*[8] *Ballentine, Elma Jane*[7] *Stroup, Elvira*[6] *Pegan, Henry*[5]*, Robert A.*[4]*, Andrew*[3]*, Andrew*[2] *Pagan, James*[1]) was born on April 1, 1944, in Columbus, Franklin Co., Ohio.[927] She was the daughter of Bernard Joseph Bowman and Inez Vance (129). Robyn V. lived in 1996 in Oakwood, Kettering Twp., Montgomery Co., Ohio. Robyn V. died in a hospital in Kettering, Kettering Twp., Montgomery Co., Ohio, on April 23, 1996, at age 52.[927, 928] She was buried in Lebanon Cemetery, Lebanon, Turtle Creek Twp., Warren Co., Ohio.[928, 1163]

Robyn V. married **Daniel Tsaloff** before 1974. They had one daughter. Daniel Tsaloff was born in Akron, Summit Co., Ohio, on August 18, 1943.[31, 1164] Daniel reached age 32 and died in Akron, Summit Co., Ohio, on September 12, 1975.[1164, 1165,] He was buried in Rose Hill Burial Park, Akron, Summit Co., Ohio.[1164]

Robyn V. Bowman Tsaloff married **Thomas Ward Kemp** on January 4, 1980, in Montgomery Co., Ohio.[1166] Thomas Ward Kemp was born in Fort Wayne, Allen Co., Indiana, on March 5, 1936.[1167]

199. Rebecca Sue[10] **Bowman** (*Inez*[9] *Vance, Sadie D.*[8] *Ballentine, Elma Jane*[7] *Stroup, Elvira*[6] *Pegan, Henry*[5]*, Robert A.*[4]*, Andrew*[3]*, Andrew*[2] *Pagan, James*[1]) was born on January 7, 1947, in Lebanon, Turtle Creek Twp., Warren Co., Ohio.[929, 930] She was the daughter of Bernard Joseph Bowman and Inez Vance (129). Rebecca Sue died in Lebanon, Turtle Creek Twp., Warren Co., Ohio, on October 11, 1962, at age 15.[929, 930] She was buried in Lebanon Cemetery, Lebanon, Turtle Creek Twp., Warren Co., Ohio.[930]

200. Bruce Steven[10] **Bowman** (*Inez*[9] *Vance, Sadie D.*[8] *Ballentine, Elma Jane*[7] *Stroup, Elvira*[6] *Pegan, Henry*[5]*, Robert A.*[4]*, Andrew*[3]*, Andrew*[2] *Pagan, James*[1]) was born on August 21, 1948, in Lebanon, Turtle Creek Twp., Warren Co., Ohio.[931, 932] He was the son of Bernard Joseph Bowman and Inez Vance (129). Bruce Steven lived in 2000 in Mason, Deerfield Twp., Warren Co., Ohio. He died in a hospital in Montgomery, Hamilton Co., Ohio, on December 31, 2000, at age 52.[931, 932] Bruce Steven was buried in Lebanon Cemetery, Lebanon, Turtle Creek Twp., Warren Co., Ohio.[932, 1168]

Never married.

Bruce Steven Bowman was a longtime resident in a mental health facility in Mason, Deerfield Twp., Warren Co., Ohio, as was his brother Nicholas Brian Bowman.

201. Nicholas Brian[10] **Bowman** (*Inez*[9] *Vance, Sadie D.*[8] *Ballentine, Elma Jane*[7] *Stroup, Elvira*[6] *Pegan, Henry*[5]*, Robert A.*[4]*, Andrew*[3]*, Andrew*[2] *Pagan, James*[1]) was born on June 29, 1951, in Lebanon, Turtle Creek Twp., Warren Co., Ohio.[31] He was the son of Bernard Joseph Bowman and Inez Vance (129). Nicholas Brian lived in 1983 in Mason, Deerfield Twp., Warren Co., Ohio. He died in a hospital in Montgomery, Hamilton Co., Ohio, on January 31, 1983, at age 31.[933] Nicholas Brian was buried in Lebanon Cemetery, Lebanon, Turtle Creek Twp., Warren Co., Ohio.[1169]

Never married.

Nicholas Brain Bowman was a longtime resident in a mental health facility in Mason, Deerfield Twp., Warren Co., Ohio, as was his brother, Bruce Steven Bowman.

202. John Robert[10] **Fisher** (*Betty Louise*[9] *Hawthorne, Letha May*[8] *Ballentine, Elma Jane*[7] *Stroup, Elvira*[6] *Pegan, Henry*[5]*, Robert A.*[4]*, Andrew*[3]*, Andrew*[2] *Pagan, James*[1]) was born on September 8, 1936, in Cincinnati, Hamilton Co., Ohio.[31, 939, 940, 941] He was the son of Walter John Fisher and Betty Louise Hawthorne (131). John Robert died in Cape Coral, Lee Co., Florida, on May 5, 1981, at age 44.[939, 941]

He married **Barbara Unknown**. They had five children.

203. Linda Sue[10] Fisher (*Betty Louise[9] Hawthorne, Letha May[8] Ballentine, Elma Jane[7] Stroup, Elvira[6] Pegan, Henry[5], Robert A.[4], Andrew[3], Andrew[2] Pagan, James[1]*) was born on May 2, 1946, in Cincinnati, Hamilton Co., Ohio.[942, 943] She was the daughter of Walter John Fisher and Betty Louise Hawthorne (131). She died in Fernandina Beach, Amelia Island, Florida, on January 1, 2017 Nassau Co., Florida, at age 70.[943] She was buried in Rest Haven Memorial Park Cemetery, Evendale, Sycamore Twp., Hamilton Co., Ohio.[943]

Linda Sue married **Mr. Dingman** in 1966.[943] They had two children.

204. Karen Jean[10] Fisher (*Betty Louise[9] Hawthorne, Letha May[8] Ballentine, Elma Jane[7] Stroup, Elvira[6] Pegan, Henry[5], Robert A.[4], Andrew[3], Andrew[2] Pagan, James[1]*) was born on May 3, 1956, in Cincinnati, Hamilton Co., Ohio.[944] She was the daughter of Walter John Fisher and Betty Louise Hawthorne (131). Karen Jean died in Anderson Twp., Hamilton Co., Ohio, on November 1, 2014, at age 58.[944]

Karen Jean married **Mr. Blakely.** They divorced. They had once son.

Karen Jean Fisher Blakely married **Mr. Brooks**.

205. Daughter[10] Kelley (*Thelma[9] Pegan, Courtland Homer[8], Henry Levy[7], Granville[6], Henry[5], Robert A.[4], Andrew[3], Andrew[2] Pagan, James[1]*) is the daughter of Malcom Loraine Kelley and Thelma Pegan (137).

Daughter Kelley married **Phillip Peter Rossy**. They had three children. Phillip Peter Rossy was born in Mount Vernon, Skagit Co., Washington, on April 10, 1961.[31, 1170] Phillip Peter lived in 1989 in Jackson, Camden Co., New Jersey. He reached age 47 and died in Torrance, Los Angeles Co., California, on April 10, 2008.[31, 1170]

206. Son[10] Pegan (*Robert Ivan[9], Courtland Homer[8], Henry Levy[7], Granville[6], Henry[5], Robert A.[4], Andrew[3], Andrew[2] Pagan, James[1]*) was born in Hillsboro, Liberty Twp., Highland Co., Ohio.

He is the son of Robert Ivan Pegan (139) and Charma Louise Dick.

Son Pegan married, but later divorced. He and his wife had five children.

While his ex-wife's surname was still Pegan, she had a child, Minnie Pegan, with another man on April 6, 1983 in Newark, Licking Co., Ohio. Minnie died on June 10, 1983 in Newark, Licking Co., Ohio, when she was two months old.[1171] Minnie Pegan, who is not of the Pegan descent but bears the surname, is buried with her cousin, Natoshia Pegan, who is a granddaughter of Son Pegan's, in Carmel Cemetery, Carmel, Brushcreek Twp., Highland Co., Ohio.[1172]

Son Pegan and his wife had five children, including:

+ 228 f II. **Daughter[11] Pegan** was born in Hillsboro, Liberty Twp., Highland Co., Ohio.

+ 229 m III. **James R.[11] Pegan** was born in Hillsboro, Liberty Twp., Highland Co., Ohio, about August 14, 1976.[1173] He died in Hillsboro, Liberty Twp., Highland Co., Ohio, on November 21, 1976.[1173]

207. Debra Sue[10] Poston (*Rita Gertrude[9] Pegan, Clarence Chilton[8], Henry Levy[7], Granville[6], Henry[5], Robert A.[4], Andrew[3], Andrew[2] Pagan, James[1]*) was born on April 11, 1955, in Blanchester, Marion Twp., Clinton Co., Ohio.[31, 993] She was the daughter of Gerald Mcdonald Poston and Rita Gertrude Pegan (142). Debra Sue died in Jack\sonville, Duval Co., Florida, on May 14, 2013, at age 58.[31, 993] She was buried in Jacksonville National Cemetery, Jacksonville, Duval Co., Florida.[993]

Debra Sue Poston married **Unknown Scott**.

Debra Sue Poston Scott married **Mr. Durett** on November 6, 1987, in Duval Co., Florida.[1174]

208. Daughter One[10] Macke (*Julia Evelyn[9] Pegan, Clarence Chilton[8], Henry Levy[7], Granville[6], Henry[5], Robert A.[4], Andrew[3], Andrew[2] Pagan, James[1]*) was born in Wilmington, Union Twp., Clinton Co.,

Ohio. She is the daughter of Richard H. Macke II and Julia Evelyn Pegan (143).

Margaret L. married **James Rickey Haney** on February 23, 1985, in Hamilton Co., Ohio.[1175] James Rickey Haney was born in Cincinnati, Hamilton Co., Ohio, on November 23, 1947.[31, 1176, 1177] He was also known as **Rickey**. James Rickey reached age 56 and died in Cincinnati, Hamilton Co., Ohio, on May 26, 2004.[31, 1176, 1177] He was buried in Arlington Memorial Gardens Cemetery, Mount Healthy, Springfield Twp., Hamilton Co., Ohio.[1178]

209. **Patricia J.**[10] **Macke** (*Julia Evelyn*[9] *Pegan, Clarence Chilton*[8], *Henry Levy*[7], *Granville*[6], *Henry*[5], *Robert A.*[4], *Andrew*[3], *Andrew*[2] *Pagan, James*[1]) was born on August 7, 1957, in Wilmington, Union Twp., Clinton Co., Ohio.[31, 1000] She was the daughter of Richard H. Macke II and Julia Evelyn Pegan (143). Patricia J. lived in 2008 in Hillsboro, Liberty Twp., Highland Co., Ohio. Patricia J. died in a hospital in Columbus, Franklin Co., Ohio, on February 27, 2008, at age 50.[31, 1000] She was buried in Hopkins Family Cemetery, Kentucky.[1000]

Patricia J. married **Mr. Felts**. They had two children.

210. **Daughter Two**[10] **Macke** (*Julia Evelyn*[9] *Pegan, Clarence Chilton*[8], *Henry Levy*[7], *Granville*[6], *Henry*[5], *Robert A.*[4], *Andrew*[3], *Andrew*[2] *Pagan, James*[1]) was born in Wilmington, Union Twp., Clinton Co., Ohio. She is the daughter of Richard H. Macke II and Julia Evelyn Pegan (143).

Daughter Macke married **Mr. Herdman** They divorced. They had one daughter.

Daughter of Daughter Macke and Dennis G. Herdman:

+ 230 f I. **Jennifer Renee**[11] **Herdman** was born in Wilmington, Union Twp., Clinton Co., Ohio, on March 8, 1988.[1179, 1180] She died in a hospital in Cincinnati, Hamilton Co., Ohio, on May 15, 1990, at age two.[1179, 1180]

211. **Bernadette Marie**[10] **Pegan** (*James Eugene*[9], *Clarence Chilton*[8], *Henry Levy*[7], *Granville*[6], *Henry*[5], *Robert A.*[4], *Andrew*[3], *Andrew*[2] *Pagan, James*[1]). She was the daughter of James Eugene Pegan (144) and Delores Duarte. Bernadette died before 2005. She is mentioned in her father James' obituary as predeceasing him.[1181] No records can be found for her birth or death.

212. **Brenda Joyce**[10] **Kleinfelder** (*Gwendolyn*[9] *DuVall, Lillie May*[8] *Daggy, Laura*[7] *Pegan, Thomas Jefferson*[6], *Henry*[5], *Robert A.*[4], *Andrew*[3], *Andrew*[2] *Pagan, James*[1]) was born on December 13, 1939, in Oxford Twp., Butler Co., Ohio.[31, 1015, 1016] She was the daughter of Harry Wakefield Kleinfelder and Gwendolyn DuVall (148). She lived in Rancho Bernardo, San Diego Co., California. Brenda Joyce died in a facility in Escondido, San Diego Co., California, on October 31, 2002, at age 62.[31, 1015, 1016] She was cremated.[1016]

Brenda Joyce married **Carl C. Lynch** on April 14, 1962, in Kern Co., California.[1182] They divorced. They had three children. Carl C. Lynch was born in Euclid, Cuyahoga Co., Ohio, on October 16, 1937.

When they married in April 1962, Carl C. Lynch was a marketing rep for Campbell's Soup Co. and Brenda J. Kleinfelder was a teacher at Bakersfield High School in Bakersfield, California.

213. **Donald Harry**[10] **DuVall** (*John Llewellyn*[9], *Lillie May*[8] *Daggy, Laura*[7] *Pegan, Thomas Jefferson*[6], *Henry*[5], *Robert A.*[4], *Andrew*[3], *Andrew*[2] *Pagan, James*[1]) was born on April 14, 1945, in Richmond, Wayne Co., Indiana.[31] He was the son of John Llewellyn DuVall (149) and Inez M. McFarland. He died in Huntington, Long Island, Suffolk Co., New York, on February 22, 1974, at age 28.[31, 1024] Donald Harry was buried in Northport Rural Cemetery, Long Island, Suffolk Co., New York.[1024, 1183]

Donald Harry married **Ms. Freed** on February 10, 1964, in Elkhart Co., Indiana.[1184] They had two sons. She remarried after Donald DuVall's death.

Donald Harry worked as an artist, art teacher, sculptor, and director of advertising display for Klein Department Stores.

Donald Harry DuVall and Ms. Freed had two children, including:

+ 231 m II. **Infant Son**[11] **DuVall** was born in Huntington, Long Island, Suf

214. Son One[10] **Surber** (*Cedric Lewis*[9], *Earl Lester*[8], *Anna*[7] *Pegan, Thomas Jefferson*[6], *Henry*[5], *Robert A.*[4], *Andrew*[3], *Andrew*[2] *Pagan, James*[1]) was born in White Oak Twp., Highland Co., Ohio.[909] He is the son of Cedric Lewis Surber (154) and Mary Ruth Newhouse.

Son One married Mrs. **Kim Loreen Sussman** Porter before June 1970. They divorced. They have one son. Kim Loreen Sussman was born in Cincinnati, Hamilton Co., Ohio, on August 11, 1950.[29, 1186, 1187] She reached age 55 and died in Mt. Healthy, Hamilton Co., Ohio, on March 20, 2006.[29, 1186] She was cremated.[1186]

Son One married Mrs. **Martha Unknown** Weber on July 22, 1978, in Hamilton Co., Ohio.[1188] They divorced, remarried, then divorced again. Martha Unknown was born in 1937.

215. Son Two[10] **Surber** (*Cedric Lewis*[9], *Earl Lester*[8], *Anna*[7] *Pegan, Thomas Jefferson*[6], *Henry*[5], *Robert A.*[4], *Andrew*[3], *Andrew*[2] *Pagan, James*[1]) was born in White Oak Twp., Highland Co., Ohio. He is the son of Cedric Lewis Surber (154) and Mary Ruth Newhouse.

Son Surber married **Barbara Miller Gilby** on July 14, 1979, in Montgomery Co., Ohio.[1189] Barbara Miller Gilby was born in Dayton, Montgomery Co., Ohio, on July 2, 1942.[31, 1190, 1191] She lived in 2005 in Trotwood, Trotwood Twp., Montgomery Co., Ohio. Barbara Miller reached age 63 and died in Dayton, Montgomery Co., Ohio, on October 11, 2005.[31, 1190, 1191]

Barbara Miller Gilby Surber contracted polio while in college, which left confined to a wheelchair. She was a speech and hearing specialist.[1190]

216. Mary Jane[10] **Pegan** (*Lowell R.*[9], *Hugh Doyle*[8], *Charles*[7], *Thomas Jefferson*[6], *Henry*[5], *Robert A.*[4], *Andrew*[3], *Andrew*[2] *Pagan, James*[1]) was born on February 22, 1959, in Wilmington, Union Twp., Clinton Co., Ohio.[1052] She was the daughter of Lowell R. Pegan (155) and Loretta Stroop. Mary Jane died in Wilmington, Union Twp., Clinton Co., Ohio, on February 22, 1959.[1052] She was buried in Hamer Township Cemetery, Hamer Twp., Highland Co., Ohio.[1192]

217. Daughter[10] **Pegan** (*Lowell R.*[9], *Hugh Doyle*[8], *Charles*[7], *Thomas Jefferson*[6], *Henry*[5], *Robert A.*[4], *Andrew*[3], *Andrew*[2] *Pagan, James*[1]) was born in Wilmington, Union Twp., Clinton Co., Ohio. She is the daughter of Lowell R. Pegan (155) and Loretta Stroop. Joy A. lived in 1977 in Concord Twp., Highland Co., Ohio.

Daughter Pegan married **Mr. Richards**. They divorced. They have two children.

Daughter Pegan Richards married for a second time, but she divorced again.

Daughter Pegan and Mr. Richards had two children, including:

+ 232 f II. **Mary Beth**[11] **Richards** was born in Hillsboro, Liberty Twp., Highland Co., Ohio, on April 15, 1977.[1193] She died in Concord Twp., Highland Co., Ohio, on July 15, 1977.[1193, 1194]

218. Shaun[10] **Scheler** (*Jeanette E.*[9] *Holmes, Ruth Marie*[8] *Pegan, Frank Joseph*[7], *William Henry*[6], *Henry*[5], *Robert A.*[4], *Andrew*[3], *Andrew*[2] *Pagan, James*[1]) was born on April 24, 1968, in LaPorte, Center Twp., LaPorte Co., Indiana.[1058, 1059] He was the son of Robert Eugene Sheler II and Daughter Holmes (158). Shaun died in South Bend, St. Joseph Co., Indiana, on January 2, 2017, at age 48.[1058, 1059] He was buried in Little Pine Cemetery, Middlebury, Middlebury Twp., Elkhart Co., Indiana.[1058, 1059]

Never married.

219. Melanie C.[10] **Greene** (*Karen*[9] *West, Audrey Mae*[8] *Pegan, William Otto*[7], *William Henry*[6], *Henry*[5], *Robert A.*[4], *Andrew*[3], *Andrew*[2] *Pagan, James*[1]) was born on January 5, 1973, in Columbus, Franklin Co., Ohio.[31, 1066] She was the daughter of Mark David Greene and Daughter West (160). Melanie C. died in Centerville, Washington Twp., Montgomery Co., Ohio, on January 15,

2003, at age 30.[31, 1066] She was buried in Ferncliff Cemetery, Springfield, Springfield Twp., Clark Co., Ohio.[1195]

Melanie is buried under her maiden name.

She married **Rodney E. Harris**. They had one son. Rodney E. Harris was born in Springfield, Springfield Twp., Clark Co., Ohio, on April 22, 1970.[31, 1196] Rodney E. reached age 21 and died in Dayton, Montgomery Co., Ohio, on March 14, 1992.[31, 1196] He was buried in Ferncliff Cemetery, Springfield, Springfield Twp., Clark Co., Ohio.[1197]

11th Generation

220. Douglas Troy[11] **Smith** (*Marianna*[10] *Wilkin, Edgar Franklin*[9]*, Hattie Ellen*[8] *Williams, Mary E.*[7] *Stroup, Elvira*[6] *Pegan, Henry*[5]*, Robert A.*[4]*, Andrew*[3]*, Andrew*[2] *Pagan, James*[1]) was born on August 20, 1949, in Cincinnati, Hamilton Co., Ohio.[31, 1091] He was the son of A.J. Smith and Marianna Wilkin (170). He died in Mesa, Maricopa Co., Arizona, on January 7, 1994, at age 44.[31, 1091]

221. Kenneth Michael[11] **Wilkin** (*Charles Edgar*[10]*, Edgar Franklin*[9]*, Hattie Ellen*[8] *Williams, Mary E.*[7] *Stroup, Elvira*[6] *Pegan, Henry*[5]*, Robert A.*[4]*, Andrew*[3]*, Andrew*[2] *Pagan, James*[1]) was born on June 1, 1943, in Lynchburg, Dodson Twp., Highland Co., Ohio.[31, 1100, 1101, 1102, 1103] He was the son of Charles Edgar Wilkin (171) and Eilene Snead. Kenneth Michael died in Fort Wayne, Allen Co., Indiana, on July 28, 1989, at age 46.[31, 1101, 1102, 1103] He was buried in Covington Memorial Gardens Cemetery, Fort Wayne, Allen Co., Indiana.[1103]

Kenneth Michael Wilkin married and divorced.

222. Daughter[11] **Wilkin** (*Charles Edgar*[10]*, Edgar Franklin*[9]*, Hattie Ellen*[8] *Williams, Mary E.*[7] *Stroup, Elvira*[6] *Pegan, Henry*[5]*, Robert A.*[4]*, Andrew*[3]*, Andrew*[2] *Pagan, James*[1]) was born in 1948. She is the daughter of Charles Edgar Wilkin (171) and Doris Geraldine Mason.

She married **Unknown Stewart** before 1970.

Daughter Wilkin Stewart married **William Harlan Ursell II** in Highland Co., Ohio.[1198] They had two children. William Harlan Ursell II was born in Highland, Fairfield Twp., Highland Co., Ohio, on May 2, 1946.[31, 1199, 1200, 1201] He lived in 2010 in Highland, Fairfield Twp., Highland Co., Ohio. William Harlan II reached age 64 and died in a hospital in Wilmington, Union Twp., Clinton Co., Ohio, on August 1, 2010.[31, 1199, 1200, 1201] He was buried in New Lynchburg Masonic Cemetery/Lynchburg F & AM Cemetery, Lynchburg, Dodson Twp., Highland Co., Ohio.[1200, 1201]

223. Son[11] **Wilkin** (*Charles Edgar*[10]*, Edgar Franklin*[9]*, Hattie Ellen*[8] *Williams, Mary E.*[7] *Stroup, Elvira*[6] *Pegan, Henry*[5]*, Robert A.*[4]*, Andrew*[3]*, Andrew*[2] *Pagan, James*[1]). He is the son of Charles Edgar Wilkin (171) and Doris Geraldine Mason.

Son Wilkin married Mrs. **Diane Louise Barker** Evans. Diane Louise Barker was born in Wilmington, Union Twp., Clinton Co., Ohio, on January 9, 1964.[1202, 1203, 1204, 1205] Diane Louise reached age 31 and died in Highland, Fairfield Twp., Highland Co., Ohio, on September 21, 1995.[1203, 1204, 1205] She was buried in Saint Patricks Cemetery, Perry Twp., Fayetteville, Brown Co., Ohio.[1205, 1206]

224. Daughter[11] **Manis** (*Joan*[10] *Wilkin, Edgar Franklin*[9]*, Hattie Ellen*[8] *Williams, Mary E.*[7] *Stroup, Elvira*[6] *Pegan, Henry*[5]*, Robert A.*[4]*, Andrew*[3]*, Andrew*[2] *Pagan, James*[1]) was born in 1958. She is the daughter of Howard Robert Manis and Joan Wilkin (173).

Daughter Manis married **Douglas Dean Willmann** on Saturday, September 17, 1977, in Hamilton Co., Ohio.[1207] They have three children. Douglas Dean Willmann was born in Chicago, Cook Co., Illinois, on Wednesday, May 25, 1955.[31, 1208] Douglas Dean lived in 2010 in Lebanon, Turtle Creek Twp., Warren Co., Ohio. He reached 55 years of age and died on October 12, 2010.[31, 1208] He is buried in Arlington Memorial Gardens Cemetery, Mount Healthy, Hamilton Co., Ohio.[1209]

Children of Daughter Manis and Douglas Dean Willmann:

+ 233 m I. **David Michael**[12] **Willmann** was born in Cincinnati, Hamilton Co., Ohio, on March 25, 1978.[1210] He died in Montgomery, Hamilton Co., Ohio, on September 16, 1986, at the age of eight.[1210]

225. Jack W.[11] **Griffith II** (*Carol Jean*[10] *Williams, Woodrow Wilson*[9]*, Stanley*[8]*, Mary E.*[7] *Stroup, Elvira*[6] *Pegan, Henry*[5]*, Robert A.*[4]*, Andrew*[3]*, Andrew*[2] *Pagan, James*[1]) was born on August 6, 1954, in Wilmington, Union Twp., Clinton Co., Ohio.[31, 1144] He was the son of Jack Lynn Griffith and

Carol Jean Williams (185). Jack W. lived in 1980 in Kenwood, Hamilton Co., Ohio. He also resided between 1983 and 1992 in Fort Myers, Lee Co., Florida. Jack W. died in a facility in Madeira, Hamilton Co., Ohio, on December 9, 1992, at age 38.[31, 1144]

Never married.

226. Daughter[11] Ludwick (*Roger Owen[10], Dwight H.[9], Vernice Catherine[8] Stroup, John Henry[7], Elvira[6] Pegan, Henry[5], Robert A.[4], Andrew[3], Andrew[2] Pagan, James[1]*) was born in Dayton, Montgomery Co., Ohio. She is the daughter of Roger Owen Ludwick (194) and Joy A. Mann.

She married **Mr. Nussman**. They had six children.

Daughter Ludwick and Mr. Nussman had six children, including:

+ 234 m   I.   **Son[12] Nussman**.

227. Infant[11] Ramseyer (*JoAnn[10] Fudge, Thelma L.[9] Vance, Sadie D.[8] Ballentine, Elma Jane[7] Stroup, Elvira[6] Pegan, Henry[5], Robert A.[4], Andrew[3], Andrew[2] Pagan, James[1]*) was born on November 28, 1961, in Millersburg, Hardy Twp., Holmes Co., Ohio.[1162] He or she was a child of Robert Jean Ramseyer and JoAnn Fudge (197). Infant died in Millersburg, Hardy Twp., Holmes Co., Ohio, on November 28, 1961.[1162]

228. Daughter[11] Pegan (*Son[10], Robert Ivan[9], Courtland Homer[8], Henry Levy[7], Granville[6], Henry[5], Robert A.[4], Andrew[3], Andrew[2] Pagan, James[1]*) was born in Hillsboro, Liberty Twp., Highland Co., Ohio. She is the daughter of Son Pegan (206) and his wife.

Daughter Pegan had a relationship with **Mr. George**.

Daughter of Daughter Pegan and Mr. George:

+ 235 f   I.   **Natoshia Shyann Marie[12] Pegan** was born in Newark, Newark Twp., Licking Co., Ohio, on October 14, 1994.[1211] She died in Newark, Newark Twp., Licking Co., Ohio, on October 14, 1994.[1211]

229. James R.[11] Pegan (*Son[10], Robert Ivan[9], Courtland Homer[8], Henry Levy[7], Granville[6], Henry[5], Robert A.[4], Andrew[3], Andrew[2] Pagan, James[1]*) was born about August 14, 1976 in Hillsboro, Liberty Twp., Highland Co., Ohio.[1173] He was the son of Son Pegan (206) and his wife. James R. died in Hillsboro, Liberty Twp., Highland Co., Ohio, on November 21, 1976.[1173]

230. Jennifer Renee[11] Herdman (*Daughter[10] Macke, Julia Evelyn[9] Pegan, Clarence Chilton[8], Henry Levy[7], Granville[6], Henry[5], Robert A.[4], Andrew[3], Andrew[2] Pagan, James[1]*) was born on March 8, 1988, in Wilmington, Union Twp., Clinton Co., Ohio.[1179, 1180] She was the daughter of Mr. Herdman and Daughter Two Macke (210). Jennifer Renee lived in 1990 in Hillsboro, Liberty Twp., Highland Co., Ohio. She died in a hospital in Cincinnati, Hamilton Co., Ohio, on May 15, 1990, at age two.[1179, 1180] Jennifer Renee was buried in Troutwine Cemetery, Dodson Twp., Highland Co., Ohio and Clark Twp., Clinton Co., Ohio.[1180]

231. Infant Son[11] DuVall (*Donald Harry[10], John Llewellyn[9], Lillie May[8] Daggy, Laura[7] Pegan, Thomas Jefferson[6], Henry[5], Robert A.[4], Andrew[3], Andrew[2] Pagan, James[1]*) was born in 1968 in Huntington, Long Island, Suffolk Co., New York.[1185] He was the son of Donald Harry DuVall (213) and Ms. Freed. Infant Son died in Huntington, Long Island, Suffolk Co., New York, in 1968.[1185] He was buried in Northport Rural Cemetery, Long Island, Suffolk Co., New York.[1185]

232. Mary Beth[11] Richards (*Daughter[10] Pegan, Lowell R.[9], Hugh Doyle[8], Charles[7], Thomas Jefferson[6], Henry[5], Robert A.[4], Andrew[3], Andrew[2] Pagan, James[1]*) was born on April 15, 1977, in Hillsboro, Liberty Twp., Highland Co., Ohio.[1193] She was the daughter of Mr. Richards and Daughter Pegan (217). Mary Beth died in Concord Twp., Highland Co., Ohio, on July 15, 1977.[1193, 1194] She was buried in Hamer Township Cemetery, Hamer Twp., Highland Co., Ohio.[1193]

12th Generation

233. David Michael[12] **Willmann** (*Daughter*[11] *Manis, Joan*[10] *Wilkin, Edgar Franklin*[9]*, Hattie Ellen*[8] *Williams, Mary E.*[7] *Stroup, Elvira*[6] *Pegan, Henry*[5]*, Robert A.*[4]*, Andrew*[3]*, Andrew*[2] *Pagan, James*[1]) was born on Saturday, March 25, 1978, in Cincinnati, Hamilton Co., Ohio.[1210] He was the son of Douglas Dean Willmann and Daughter Manis (224). David Michael died in Montgomery, Hamilton Co., Ohio, on September 16, 1986, at age eight.[1210] He was buried in Arlington Memorial Gardens Cemetery, Mount Healthy, Hamilton Co., Ohio.[1212]

234. Son[12] **Nussman** (*Daughter*[11] *Ludwick, Roger Owen*[10]*, Dwight H.*[9]*, Vernice Catherine*[8] *Stroup, John Henry*[7]*, Elvira*[6] *Pegan, Henry*[5]*, Robert A.*[4]*, Andrew*[3]*, Andrew*[2] *Pagan, James*[1]) was born in 1981. He is the son of Mr. Nussman and Daughter Ludwick (226).

He married and had at least one son.

Son of Son Nussman and his wife:

+ 236 m I. **Brady Owen**[13] **Nussman** was born in Blountville, Sullivan Co., Tennessee, on July 16, 2007.[31, 1213] He died in Blountville, Sullivan Co., Tennessee, on May 13, 2012.[31, 1213, 1214]

235. Natoshia Shyann Marie[12] **Pegan** (*Daughter*[11]*, Son*[10]*, Robert Ivan*[9]*, Courtland Homer*[8]*, Henry Levy*[7]*, Granville*[6]*, Henry*[5]*, Robert A.*[4]*, Andrew*[3]*, Andrew*[2] *Pagan, James*[1]) was born on October 14, 1994, in Newark, Newark Twp., Licking Co., Ohio.[1211] She was the daughter of Unknown Unknown and Daughter Pegan (228). Natoshia Shyann Marie died in Newark, Newark Twp., Licking Co., Ohio, on October 14, 1994.[1211] She was buried in Carmel Cemetery, Carmel, Brushcreek Twp., Highland Co., Ohio.[1211, 1215]

13th Generation

236. Brady Owen[13] Nussman (*Son Nussman[12], Karen Sue[11] Ludwick, Roger Owen[10], Dwight H.[9], Vernice Catherine[8] Stroup, John Henry[7], Elvira[6] Pegan, Henry[5], Robert A.[4], Andrew[3], Andrew[2] Pagan, James[1]*) was born on July 16, 2007, in Blountville, Sullivan Co., Tennessee.[31,1213] He was the son of Son Nussman (562) and his wife. Brady Owen died in Blountville, Sullivan Co., Tennessee, on May 13, 2012, at age four.[31, 1213] He was buried in East Tennesee Cemetery, Blountville, Sullivan Co., Tennessee.[1213, 1214]

Endnotes

1. Family Data: Robert and Christina "Engle" Pegan family bible, American Bible Society, Brattleboro(ugh), Vermont: Holbrook & Fessenden, 1828. In possession of the author, Ann Miller Carr.

2. Henry Pagan/Pegan tombstone, Masonic Cemetery, Lynchburg, Dodson Twp., Highland Co., Ohio.

3. Ohio, County Death Records, 1840-2001, FamilySearch.org, Henry Pegan, Highland Co., Ohio Death Record, Vol. 1, pg. 156.

4. Find A Grave—Lynchburg Masonic Cemetery, Lynchburg, Dodson Twp., Highland Co., Ohio, Find A Grave.com, Henry Pegan, Find A Grave Memorial #93717200.

5. Ohio, County Marriages, 1789-2013, FamilySearch.org, Henry "Pagan" and Harriet Stroup, Highland County, Ohio Marriage Records, Vol. 2, pg. 436, lic. #2229.

6. Harriet Stroup Pagan/Pegan tombstone, Masonic Cemetery, Lynchburg, Dodson Twp., Highland Co., Ohio.

7. Find A Grave—Lynchburg Masonic Cemetery, Lynchburg, Dodson Twp., Highland Co., Ohio, Find A Grave.com, Harriet Pegan, Find A Grave Memorial #93956941.

8. U.S., Civil War Pension Index: General Index to Pension Files, 1864-1934, Ancestry.com, Henry Pegan, widow Harriet Pegan, August 21, 1890, application 481 827, certificate #378 484.

9. Ohio Death Certificate, Ohio Department of Health, Center for Vital and Health Statistics, 246 North High Street, Columbus, OH, Elvira Stroup, death cert. #17599.

10. Ohio Death Certificate, Ohio Department of Health, Center for Vital and Health Statistics, 246 North High Street, Columbus, OH, Granville Pegan, death cert. #51905.

11. Ohio, Deaths, 1908-1932, 1938-2007, Ancestry.com, Granville Pegan, Dodson Twp., Highland Co., Ohio (Letter P., pg. 979), Vol. 216, file #51, 905.

12. Find A Grave—Stroup Cemetery, Dodson Twp., Highland Co., Ohio, Find A Grave.com, Thomas J. Pegan, Find A Grave Memorial #133601521.

13. Highland County, Ohio Death Records, T.J. Pegan, Highland Co. Death Records, Vol. 2, pg. 402.

14. Ohio Death Certificate, Ohio Department of Health, Center for Vital and Health Statistics, 246 North High Street, Columbus, OH, Elma "Swartz", death cert. #55850.

15. Eliza J. Schwartz tombstone, Lynchburg Masonic Cemetery, Lynchburg, Dodson Twp., Highland Co., Ohio.

16. Find A Grave—Lynchburg Masonic Cemetery, Lynchburg, Dodson Twp., Highland Co., Ohio, Find A Grave.com, Eliza J. Pegan Schwartz, Find A Grave Memorial #93957191.

17. Find A Grave—Lynchburg Masonic Cemetery, Lynchburg, Dodson Twp., Highland Co., Ohio, Find A Grave.com, Pleasant Pegan, Find A Grave Memorial #93954835.

18. Ohio, County Death Records, 1840-2001, FamilySearch.org, Pleasant Pegan, Highland Co., Ohio Death Record, Vol. 1, pg. 20.

19. Ohio, County Death Records, 1840-2001, FamilySearch.org, Michael Pegan, Highland Co., Ohio Death Record, Vol. 1, pg. 316.

20. Ohio Death Certificate, Ohio Department of Health, Center for Vital and Health Statistics, 246 North High Street, Columbus, OH, William Henry Pegan, death cert. #46825.

21. Obituary of Elvira Stroup, Ohio History Center Archives and Library, Ohio History Center, 800 East 17th Avenue, Columbus, OH, Hillsboro (OH) Dispatch, pub. 19 Mar 1918.

22. Find A Grave—Stroup Cemetery, Dodson Twp., Highland Co., Ohio, Find A Grave.com, Elvira Pegan Stroup, Find A Grave Memorial #112182617.

23. Ohio, County Marriages, 1789-2013, FamilySearch.org, Levi Stroup and Elvira "Pagan", Highland County, Ohio Marriage Records, Marriages, Vol. 5, pg. 405, lic. #30.

24. Ohio Death Certificate, Ohio Department of Health, Center for Vital and Health Statistics, 246 North High Street, Columbus, OH, Levi Stroup, death cert. #28942.

25. Find A Grave—Stroup Cemetery, Dodson Twp., Highland Co., Ohio, Find A Grave.com, Levi Stroup, Find A Grave Memorial# 112182400.

26. Ohio Death Certificate, Ohio Department of Health, Center for Vital and Health Statistics, 246 North High Street, Columbus, OH, Josephine Lemons, death cert. #37282.

27. Find A Grave—Stroup Cemetery, Dodson Twp., Highland Co., Ohio, Find A Grave.com, Hattie Ann Stroup, Find A Grave Memorial #121527890.

28. Ohio Death Certificate, Ohio Department of Health, Center for Vital and Health Statistics, 246 North High Street, Columbus, OH, Mary E. Williams, death cert. #66748.

29. Obituary of Mrs. Belle Spilker (Hillsboro, Ohio, Press-Gazette, 08 Dec 1967), Highland County District Library, 10 Willettsville Pike, Hillsboro, OH.

30. Find A Grave—Troutwine Cemetery, Dodson Twp., Highland Co., Ohio, Find A Grave.com, Laura Belle Stroup Spilker, Find A Grave Memorial #68772719.

31. Social Security Death Index, Ancestry.com.

32. Ohio, Deaths, 1908-1932, 1938-2007, Ancestry.com, Laura Spilker, death cert. #93655.

33. Ohio Death Certificate, Ohio Department of Health, Center for Vital and Health Statistics, 246 North High Street, Columbus, OH, John Henry Stroup, death cert. #36941.

34. Ohio Death Certificate, Ohio Department of Health, Center for Vital and Health Statistics, 246 North High Street, Columbus, OH, Elma J. Balantine (Ballentine), #7958.

35 Find A Grave—Stroup Cemetery, Dodson Twp., Highland Co., Ohio, Find A Grave.com, James P. Stroup, Find A Grave Memorial #121527912.

36 Ohio, County Births, 1841-2003 (County Courthouses), FamilySearch.org, Margaret Stroup, Highland Co., Ohio Birth Record Vol. 1, pg. 208.

37 Ohio, County Death Records, 1840-2001, FamilySearch.org, Margaret H. Stroup, Highland Co., Ohio Death Record Vol. 2, pg. 474

38 The Genealogical Committee of The Clinton County Historical Society, Cemetery Records of Clinton Co., Ohio, 1798-1998, Troutwine Cemetery: Granville Pegan. Clinton County, Ohio Records Center and Archives, 111 South Nelson Avenue, Suite 3, Wilmington, OH.

39 Find A Grave—Troutwine Cemetery, Dodson Twp., Highland Co., Ohio, Find A Grave.com, Granville Pegan, Find A Grave Memorial #112435363.

40 Ohio, County Marriages, 1789-2013, FamilySearch.org, "Graville" Pegan and Sallie A. Cheney, Brown County, Ohio Marriage Records, Vol. 2, pg. 317, lic. #951.

41 Ohio Death Certificate, Ohio Department of Health, Center for Vital and Health Statistics, 246 North High Street, Columbus, OH, Sarah A. Pegan, death cert. #41760.

42 Find A Grave—Troutwine Cemetery, Dodson Twp., Highland Co., Ohio, Find A Grave.com, Sarah A. Pegan, Find A Grave Memorial #112435444.

43 The Genealogical Committee of The Clinton County Historical Society, Cemetery Records of Clinton Co., Ohio, 1798-1998, Troutwine Cemetery: Sarah Pegan. Clinton County, Ohio Records Center and Archives, 111 South Nelson Avenue, Suite 3, Wilmington, OH.

44 Ohio Death Certificate, Ohio Department of Health, Center for Vital and Health Statistics, 246 North High Street, Columbus, OH, Adolphus Vonesse Pegan, death cert. #61399.

45 Ohio, Deaths, 1908-1932, 1938-2007, Ancestry.com, Adolphus Vonesse Pegan, Dodson Twp., Highland Co., Ohio; Letter P., 1910, pg. 846; Ohio; Vol 514, File #61, 399.

46 Ohio, County Births, 1841-2003 (County Courthouses), FamilySearch.org, "Pegan" male child, fa: Granville Pegan, mo: Sarah Pegan, Highland Co., Ohio Birth Record Vol. 1, pg. 30.

47 U.S., Social Security Applications and Claims Index, 1936-2007, Ancestry.com, Henry Levy Pegan.

48 Obituary of Henry L. Pegan (Hillsboro, Ohio, Press-Gazette, 11 Jun 1954), Highland County District Library, 10 Willettsville Pike, Hillsboro, OH.

49 The Genealogical Committee of The Clinton County Historical Society, Cemetery Records of Clinton Co., Ohio, 1798-1998, Troutwine Cemetery: Henry L. Pegan. Clinton County, Ohio Records Center and Archives, 111 South Nelson Avenue, Suite 3, Wilmington, OH.

50 Ohio, County Births, 1841-2003 (County Courthouses), FamilySearch.org, Della F. Pegan, Highland Co., Ohio Birth Record Vol. 1, pg. 196.

51 Ohio, County Death Records, 1840-2001, FamilySearch.org, Frances D. Thompson, Highland Co., Death Record Vol. 2, pg. 490.

52 Obituary of "Jeff" Pegan (Hillsboro, OH, Hillsboro (OH) News Herald, 15 Feb 1900), Ohio History Center Archives and Library, Ohio History Center, 800 East 17th Avenue, Columbus, OH.

53 Find A Grave—Stroup Cemetery, Dodson Twp., Highland Co., Ohio, Find A Grave.com, Thomas J. Pegan, Find A Grave Memorial #133601521.

54 Ohio, County Marriages, 1789-2013, FamilySearch.org, Thomas J. Pegan and Eliza Bernard, Brown County, Ohio Marriage Records, Vol. 2, pg. 275, lic. #8, 807.

55 The Genealogical Committee of The Clinton County Historical Society, Cemetery Records of Clinton Co., Ohio, 1798-1978, New Vienna Cemetery: Eliza Pegan. Clinton County, Ohio Records Center and Archives, 111 South Nelson Avenue, Suite 3, Wilmington, OH.

56 Ohio, County Marriages, 1789-2013, FamilySearch.org, Thomas J. Pegan and Mary A. Bennington, Highland County, Ohio Marriage Records, Vol. 8, pg. 86, lic. #426.

57 Ohio Death Certificate, Ohio Department of Health, Center for Vital and Health Statistics, 246 North High Street, Columbus, OH, Mary A. Pegan, death cert. #49084.

58 Ohio, Deaths, 1908-1932, 1938-2007, Ancestry.com, Mary A. Pegan, death cert. #49084; Ohio State Death Index, pg. 6524.

59 Find A Grave—Stroup Cemetery, Dodson Twp., Highland Co., Ohio, Find A Grave.com, Mary A. Pegan, Find A Grave Memorial #133601537.

60 Ohio. Wills and Probate Records, 1786-1998, Ancestry.com, Hamilton County, Ohio Wills, Thomas J. Pegan, Vol. 77, pg. 140.

61 The Genealogical Committee of The Clinton County Historical Society, Cemetery Records of Clinton Co., Ohio, 1798-1978, New Vienna Cemetery: Henry J. Pegan. Clinton County, Ohio Records Center and Archives, 111 South Nelson Avenue, Suite 3, Wilmington, OH.

62 Ohio Death Certificate, Ohio Department of Health, Center for Vital and Health Statistics, 246 North High Street, Columbus, OH, Laura Smith, death cert. #3922.

63 Ohio, County Marriages, 1789-2013, FamilySearch.org, John F. Smith and Laura Daggy, Butler County, Ohio Marriage Records, Vol. 22, pg. 86, lic. #5125.

64 Obituary of Laura D. Smith (Hillsboro, Ohio, Highland County News Herald, 08 Feb 1923), Highland County District Library, 10 Willettsville Pike, Hillsboro, OH.

65 Ohio, County Births, 1841-2003 (County Courthouses), FamilySearch.org, "Pegan", female child, fa: Jefferson Pegan,

mo: Mary Pegan, Highland Co., Ohio Birth Record Vol. 1, pg. 70.

66 Obituary of Anna Surber, Highland County District Library, 10 Willettsville Pike, Hillsboro, OH, Hillsboro (OH) Press-Gazette, pub. 01 Feb 1955.

67 Ohio, County Births, 1841-2003 (County Courthouses), FamilySearch.org, Wm. Henry Pegan, Highland Co., Ohio Birth Record Vol. 1, pg. 198.

68 Ohio, County Death Records, 1840-2001, FamilySearch.org, Wm. H. Pegan, Highland Co., Ohio Death Record, Vol. 1, pg. 88.

69 Ohio, County Births, 1841-2003 (County Courthouses), FamilySearch.org, Mattie Pegan, Highland Co., Ohio Birth Record Vol. 1, pg. 260.

70 Ohio, County Death Records, 1840-2001, FamilySearch.org, Mattie Pegan, Highland Co., Ohio Death Record, Vol. 1, pg. 94.

71 Ohio, County Marriages, 1789-2013, FamilySearch.org, Everett Carr and Frankie Pegan, Highland County, Ohio Marriage Records, Vol. 14, pg. 190, lic. #5635.

72 Ohio, County Births, 1841-2003 (County Courthouses), FamilySearch.org, Frances Pegan, Highland Co., Births, Vol. 2, pg. 34.

73 Ohio Death Certificate, Ohio Department of Health, Center for Vital and Health Statistics, 246 North High Street, Columbus, OH, Frances Carr, death cert. #3099.

74 Ohio, County Births, 1841-2003 (County Courthouses), FamilySearch.org, "Pegan", fa: Thomas J. Pegan, mo: Mary Bennington (but Charles is listed as a female child—a mistake), Highland Co., Ohio Birth Record Vol. 2, pg. 262.

75 U.S., WWI Draft Registration Cards, 1917-1918, Ancestry.com, Charles P. Pegan, Winkle, Ohio.

76 Ohio, Deaths, 1908-1932, 1938-2007, Ancestry.com, Charles Pegan, death cert. #13260.

77 Obituary of Charles Pegan (Hillsboro, Ohio, Press-Gazette, 09 Feb 1960), Highland County District Library, 10 Willettsville Pike, Hillsboro, OH.

78 Find A Grave—Lynchburg Masonic Cemetery, Lynchburg, Dodson Twp., Highland Co., Ohio, Find A Grave.com, Elma Schwartz, Find A Grave Memorial #93716968.

79 Ohio, County Marriages, 1789-2013, FamilySearch.org, Joseph Schwartz and Elinor Pegan, Highland County, Ohio Marriage Records, Vol. 8, pg. 336, lic. #1223.

80 Find A Grave—Lynchburg Masonic Cemetery, Lynchburg, Dodson Twp., Highland Co., Ohio, Find A Grave.com, Joseph Schwartz, Find A Grave Memorial #93441073.

81 Obituary of Joseph "Swartz" (Hillsboro, Ohio, Hillsborough Weekly Gazette, 26 Aug 1892), Highland County District Library, 10 Willettsville Pike, Hillsboro, OH.

82 Ohio Death Certificate, Ohio Department of Health, Center for Vital and Health Statistics, 246 North High Street, Columbus, OH, Hattie Shaper, death cert. #20617.

83 Ohio, County Births, 1841-2003 (County Courthouses), FamilySearch.org, William H.C.M. Swarts" male, fa: Joseph Schwarts, mo: Elma Pegan, Highland Co., Ohio Birth Record Vol. 1, pg. 182.

84 Find A Grave—Lynchburg Masonic Cemetery, Lynchburg, Dodson Twp., Highland Co., Ohio, Find A Grave.com, William H.C.M. Schwartz, Find A Grave Memorial #93440749.

85 Ohio Death Certificate, Ohio Department of Health, Center for Vital and Health Statistics, 246 North High Street, Columbus, OH, Walter C. Schwartz, death cert. #69960.

86 Ohio, County Births, 1841-2003 (County Courthouses), FamilySearch.org, Charles Walter Schwartz, Highland Co., Ohio Birth Record, Vol. 1, pg. 300.

87 Obituary of "Jennie" Schwartz (Hillsboro, Ohio, Highland County News Herald, 28 Jul 1883), Highland County District Library, 10 Willettsville Pike, Hillsboro, OH.

88 Ohio, County Marriages, 1789-2013, FamilySearch.org, Andrew Schwartz and Eliza Jane Pegan, Highland County, Ohio Marriage Records, Vol. 8, pg. 469, lic. #1958.

89 Ohio, County Death Records, 1840-2001, FamilySearch.org, Andrew Schwartz, Highland Co., Ohio Death Records, Vol. 2, pg. 464.

90 Find A Grave—Lynchburg Masonic Cemetery, Lynchburg, Dodson Twp., Highland Co., Ohio, Find A Grave.com, Andrew Schwartz, Find A Grave Memorial #92628718.

91 "Probate Court" (Hillsboro, Ohio, The News-Herald, 28 Dec 1889), Chronicling America, The Library of Congress, Washington, DC; Online database: https://chroniclingamerica.loc.gov/

92 Ohio Death Certificate, Ohio Department of Health, Center for Vital and Health Statistics, 246 North High Street, Columbus, OH, Cora May Schwartz, death cert. #00736.

93 Find A Grave—Lynchburg Masonic Cemetery, Lynchburg, Dodson Twp., Highland Co., Ohio, Find A Grave.com, Michael Pegan, Find A Grave Memorial #93957042.

94 Obituary of William Pegan (Hillsboro, Ohio, Press-Gazette, 01 Sep 1939), Highland County District Library, 10 Willettsville Pike, Hillsboro, OH.

95 The Genealogical Committee of The Clinton County Historical Society, Cemetery Records of Clinton Co., Ohio, 1798-1998, Troutwine Cemetery: William H. Pegan. Clinton County, Ohio Records Center and Archives, 111 South Nelson Avenue, Suite 3, Wilmington, OH.

96 Ohio, County Marriages, 1789-2013, FamilySearch.org, William H. Pegan and Margaret L. Jones, Clinton County, Ohio Marriage Records, Vol. 5, pg. 21.

97 Ohio Death Certificate, Ohio Department of Health, Center for Vital and Health Statistics, 246 North High Street, Columbus, OH, Margaret Louise Pegan, death cert. #56564.

98 The Genealogical Committee of The Clinton County Historical Society, Cemetery Records of Clinton Co., Ohio, 1798-1998, Troutwine Cemetery: Margaret L. Pegan.

98 Clinton County, Ohio Records Center and Archives, 111 South Nelson Avenue, Suite 3, Wilmington, OH.

99 "Mrs. Pegan Dead" (Wilmington, Ohio, Wilmington News-Journal, 14 Sep 1926), Wilmington Public Library of Clinton County, 268 North South Street, Wilmington, OH.

100 Ohio, County Births, 1841-2003 (County Courthouses), FamilySearch.org, Joseph T. Pegan, Clinton Co., Birth Record Vol. 2, pg. 137.

101 Find A Grave—Troutwine Cemetery, Dodson Twp., Highland Co., Ohio, Find A Grave.com, Joseph T. Pegan, Find A Grave Memorial #128710736.

102 The Genealogical Committee of The Clinton County Historical Society, Cemetery Records of Clinton Co., Ohio, 1798-1998, Troutwine Cemetery:Pegan. Clinton County, Ohio Records Center and Archives, 111 South Nelson Avenue, Suite 3, Wilmington, OH.

103 U.S., WWII Draft Registration Cards, 1942, Ancestry.com, U974. Ancestry.com.

104 Obituary of Frank Pegan (Wilmington, Ohio, Wilmington News-Herald, 29 Mar 1966), Wilmington Public Library of Clinton County, 268 North South Street, Wilmington, OH.

105 Ohio, Deaths, 1908-1932, 1938-2007, Ancestry.com, Frank J. Pegan, death cert. #23802.

106 Ohio Death Certificate, Ohio Department of Health, Center for Vital and Health Statistics, 246 North High Street, Columbus, OH, Ella Mae Pegan, death cert. #59313.

107 Ohio, County Births, 1841-2003 (County Courthouses), FamilySearch.org, Ella Pegan, Clinton Co., Ohio Birth Record, Vol. 2, pg. 140.

108 Ohio, Deaths, 1908-1932, 1938-2007, Ancestry.com, William O. Pegan, #072830.

109 Ohio, County Births, 1841-2003 (County Courthouses), FamilySearch.org, "Otto W. Pegan", Clinton Co., Ohio Birth Record, Vol. 3, pg.150.

110 Obituary of William O. Pegan (Wilmington, Ohio, Wilmington News-Journal, 04 Nov 1985), The Clinton County History Center, 149 East Locust Street, Wilmington, OH.

111 Find A Grave—Stroup Cemetery, Dodson Twp., Highland Co., Ohio, Find A Grave.com, Josephine Pegan Lemons, Find A Grave Memorial #112183551.

112 Ohio, County Marriages, 1789-2013, FamilySearch.org, Henry "Lemon" and Josephine Stroup, Highland County, Ohio Marriage Records, Vol. 9, pg. 317, lic. #626.

113 Find A Grave—Stroup Cemetery, Dodson Twp., Highland Co., Ohio, Find A Grave.com, Henry Lemons, Find A Grave Memorial #112184226.

114 Highland County, Ohio Death Records, Henry A. Lemons, Vol. 2, p. 280. Highland County, Ohio Probate Court, Highland County Courthouse, 105 North High Street, Hillsboro, OH.

115 Obituary of Henry Lemon (Hillsboro, Ohio, Hillsboro News-Herald, 10 Feb 1898), Library of Congress, Washington, DC; Online database: Chronicling America, http://chroniclingamerica.loc.gov/

116 Ohio Death Certificate, Ohio Department of Health, Center for Vital and Health Statistics, 246 North High Street, Columbus, OH, Agnes Philhower, death cert. #61608.

117 Ferncliff Cemetery Records, Grace Boesenberg, Ferncliff Cemetery & Arboretum, 501 West McCreight Avenue, Springfield, OH.

118 Ohio, Deaths, 1908-1932, 1938-2007, Ancestry.com, Grace Boesenberg, death cert. #71618.

119 Ohio, County Births, 1841-2003 (County Courthouses), FamilySearch.org, James S. Lemons, Highland Co., Ohio Birth Record Vol. 2, pg. 68.

120 Ohio Death Certificate, Ohio Department of Health, Center for Vital and Health Statistics, 246 North High Street, Columbus, OH, James Lemons, death cert. #3793.

121 Ohio, County Births, 1841-2003 (County Courthouses), FamilySearch.org, Andrew "Lemon", Highland Co., Ohio Birth Record Vol. 2, pg. 220.

122 "Nitro Kills Two" (Okmulgee, Oklahoma, Okmulgee Cheiftain, 10 May 1917), Oklahoma Historical Society Research Center & Library, 800 Nazhir Zuhdi Avenue, Oklahoma City, OK.

123 "Mortuary: Andrew J. Lemon" (Bartlesville, Oklahoma, Bartlesville Morning Examiner, 9 and 10 May 1917), Oklahoma Historical Society Research Center & Library, 800 Nazhir Zuhdi Avenue, Oklahoma City, OK.

124 "Two Killed in Okmulgee Blast" (Tulsa, Oklahoma, Tulsa Daily World, 08 May 1917), Oklahoma Historical Society Research Center & Library, 800 Nazhir Zuhdi Avenue, Oklahoma City, OK.

125 Ohio, County Marriages, 1789-2013, FamilySearch.org, Talmadge D. Lemons and "Rena" May Lane, Clark County, Ohio Marriage Records, Vol. 26, pg. 511, lic. #10349.

126 Obituary of Talmadge DeWitt Lemons (Springfield, Ohio, Springfield Daily News, 06 Jul 1956), Clark County Public Library, 201 South Fountain Avenue, Springfield, OH.

127 Obituary of Talmadge D. Lemon [sic] (Hillsboro, Ohio, Press-Gazette, 06 Jul 1956), Highland County District Library, 10 Willettsville Pike, Hillsboro, OH.

128 Ohio Death Certificate, Ohio Department of Health, Center for Vital and Health Statistics, 246 North High Street, Columbus, OH, Merrill Clarence Lemons, death cert. #43316.

129 Ohio, County Marriages, 1789-2013, FamilySearch.org, Murrell Lemons and Nora Cooper, Highland County, Ohio Marriage Records, Vol. 16, pg 559, lic. #10400.

130 Ohio, County Births, 1841-2003 (County Courthouses), FamilySearch.org, "Myrle Lemon", Highland Co., Ohio Birth Record Vol. 3, pg. 258.

131 Ohio Death Certificate, Ohio Department of Health, Center for Vital and Health Statistics, 246 North High Street, Columbus, OH, Clarence Otto Lemons, death cert. #62723.

132 Ohio Death Certificate, Ohio Department of Health, Center for Vital and Health Statistics, 246 North High Street, Columbus, OH, Eddie R. Lemons, death cert. #24592.

133 Find A Grave—Stroup Cemetery, Dodson Twp., Highland Co., Ohio, Find A Grave.com, Mary E. Stroup Williams, Find A Grave Memorial #110191088.

134 Ohio, County Marriages, 1789-2013, FamilySearch.org, Sam'l Williams and Mary E. Stroup, Highland County, Ohio Marriage Records, Vol. 9, pg. 565, lic. #1121.

135 Ohio Death Certificate, Ohio Department of Health, Center for Vital and Health Statistics, 246 North High Street, Columbus, OH, Samuel Williams, death cert. #73394.

136 Find A Grave—Stroup Cemetery, Dodson Twp., Highland Co., Ohio, Find A Grave.com, Samuel Williams, Find A Grave Memorial #110192020.

137 Ohio, County Births, 1841-2003 (County Courthouses), FamilySearch.org, Cora May Williams, Highland Co., Ohio Birth Record Vol. 2, pg. 54.

138 Obituary of Mrs. Allen Carroll (Hillsboro, Ohio, Press-Gazette, 04 Oct 1955), Highland County District Library, 10 Willettsville Pike, Hillsboro, OH.

139 Ohio Death Certificate, Ohio Department of Health, Center for Vital and Health Statistics, 246 North High Street, Columbus, OH, Lee Williams, death cert. #77691.

140 U.S., WWI Draft Registration Cards, 1917-1918, Ancestry.com, "Lee" Williams, Highland Co., Ohio.

141 Ohio, County Births, 1841-2003 (County Courthouses), FamilySearch.org, Hattie Ellen Williams, Highland Co., Ohio Birth Records, Delayed births with index, 1944-1951, Vol. 5, Case #1257, Doc. 5, pg. 248.

142 Obituary Mrs. George Wilkin (Hillsboro, Ohio, Highland Press-Gazette, 05 Sep 1961), Highland County District Library, 10 Willettsville Pike, Hillsboro, OH.

143 Ohio, County Births, 1841-2003 (County Courthouses), FamilySearch.org, Stanley Williams, Highland Co., Ohio Birth Record Vol. 2, pg. 330.

144 Ohio, Deaths, 1908-1932, 1938-2007, Ancestry.com, Stanley Williams, death cert. #070555.

145 Ohio Death Certificate, Ohio Department of Health, Center for Vital and Health Statistics, 246 North High Street, Columbus, OH, Joseph Williams, death cert. #39109.

146 Highland County, Ohio Birth Records, Highland County, Ohio Probate Court, Highland County Courthouse, 105 North High Street, Hillsboro, OH, Highland Co. Birth Records, Vol. 3, pg. 502.

147 Ohio, County Death Records, 1840-2001, FamilySearch.org, Cary Williams, Highland County Death Records, Vol. 1-2, pg. 376.

148 Ohio, County Births, 1841-2003 (County Courthouses), FamilySearch.org, Harley "M." Williams, Highland Co., Ohio Birth Record Vol. 3, pg. 514.

149 Ohio, Deaths, 1908-1932, 1938-2007, Ancestry.com, Harley N. Williams, death cert. #54433.

150 Ohio, County Marriages, 1789-2013, FamilySearch.org, Joseph Spilker and Belle Stroup, Highland County, Ohio Marriage Records, Vol. 11, pg. 215, lic. #2129.

151 Ohio Death Certificate, Ohio Department of Health, Center for Vital and Health Statistics, 246 North High Street, Columbus, OH, Joseph H. Spilker, death cert. #3580.

152 Find A Grave—Troutwine Cemetery, Dodson Twp., Highland Co., Ohio, Find A Grave.com, Joseph Henry Spilker, Find A Grave Memorial #68772554.

153 Ohio, Deaths, 1908-1932, 1938-2007, Ancestry.com, Joseph H. Spilker, death cert. #3580.

154 Ohio, County Births, 1841-2003 (County Courthouses), FamilySearch.org, Bessie Spilker, Highland Co., Ohio Birth Record Vol. 3, pg. 410.

155 Ohio, Births and Christenings Index, 1800-1962, Ancestry.com, "Berrie" Spilker.

156 Ohio, County Death Records, 1840-2001, FamilySearch.org, Bessie B. Fox, Highland Co., Ohio Death Records, Book 2, pg. 142.

157 Ohio Death Certificate, Ohio Department of Health, Center for Vital and Health Statistics, 246 North High Street, Columbus, OH, Earl E. Spilker, death cert. #36347.

158 Ohio, Deaths, 1908-1932, 1938-2007, Ancestry.com, Ralph H. Spilker, death cert. #92923.

159 Ohio, County Births, 1841-2003 (County Courthouses), FamilySearch.org, Hazel F. Spilker, Highland Co., Ohio Birth Record Vol. 3, pg. 432.

160 U.S., Social Security Applications and Claims Index, 1936-2007, Ancestry.com, Hazel S. Cruger.

161 Obituary of Hazel Cruger (St. Petersburg, Florida, St. Petersburg Times, 14 Jan 2000. Largo Library, 201 Highland Avenue NE, Largo, FL.

162 Find A Grave—Stroup Cemetery, Dodson Twp., Highland Co., Ohio, Find A Grave.com, John Henry Stroup, Find A Grave Memorial #112183875.

163 Ohio, County Marriages, 1789-2013, FamilySearch.org, John H. Stroup and Catherine Ballentine, Highland County, Ohio Marriage Records, Vol. 11, pg. 559, lic. #18.

164 Obituary of Catherine Stroup (Hillsboro, Ohio, Press-Gazette, 22 May 1960), Highland County District Library, 10 Willettsville Pike, Hillsboro, OH.

165 Ohio, Deaths, 1908-1932, 1938-2007, Ancestry.com, Catherine Stroup, death certificate #20 Apr 1960 ("Catheri" Stroup).

166 Find A Grave—Stroup Cemetery, Dodson Twp., Highland Co., Ohio, Find A Grave.com, Catherine Olive Stroup, Find A Grave Memorial #112273326.

167 Find A Grave—Stroup Cemetery, Dodson Twp., Highland Co., Ohio, Find A Grave.com, Elton Stroup, Find A Grave Memorial #121528100.

168 Find A Grave—Stroup Cemetery, Dodson Twp., Highland Co., Ohio, Find A Grave.com, Edgar Stroup, Find A Grave Memorial #121528091.

169 Ohio, County Births, 1841-2003 (County Courthouses), FamilySearch.org, "Vernis" Stroup, Highland Co., Ohio Birth Record Vol.3, pg. 428.

170 Obituary of "Bernice" (Vernice) C. Ludwick, Ancestry.com, Highland County Press-Gazette, Hillsboro, OH, pub. 09 Jul 1971.

171 U.S., Social Security Applications and Claims Index, 1936-2007, Ancestry.com, Vernice Ludwick.

172 U.S., WWI Draft Registration Cards, 1917-1918, Ancestry.com, Clarence Harold Stroup, Highland Co., Ohio.

173 Ohio, County Births, 1841-2003 (County Courthouses), FamilySearch.org, Clarence Stroup, Highland Co., Ohio Birth Record Vol. 3, pg. 438.

174 Ohio, Deaths, 1908-1932, 1938-2007, Ancestry.com, Clarence Harold Stroup, death cert. #002616.

175 Obituary of Clarence H. Stroup (Xenia, Ohio, Xenia Gazette, 20 Jan 1980), Greene County Public Library-Xenia Community Library, Greene County Room, 76 East Market Street, Xenia, OH.

176 The Genealogical Committee of The Clinton County Historical Society, Cemetery Records of Clinton Co., Ohio, 1798-1998, Blanchester IOOF Cemetery: Elma J. Ballentine. Clinton County, Ohio Records Center and Archives, 111 South Nelson Avenue, Suite 3, Wilmington, OH.

177 Ohio, County Marriages, 1789-2013, FamilySearch.org, Robert E. Ballentine and Elma J. Stroup, Highland County, Ohio Marriage Records, Vol. 11, pg. 288, lic. #2346.

178 Ohio Death Certificate, Ohio Department of Health, Center for Vital and Health Statistics, 246 North High Street, Columbus, OH, Robert Ballentine ("Balentine"), death cert. #62555.

179 The Genealogical Committee of The Clinton County Historical Society, Cemetery Records of Clinton Co., Ohio, 1798-1998, Blanchester IOOF Cemetery: Robert E. Ballentine Jr. Clinton County, Ohio Records Center and Archives, 111 South Nelson Avenue, Suite 3, Wilmington, OH.

180 Ohio Death Certificate, Ohio Department of Health, Center for Vital and Health Statistics, 246 North High Street, Columbus, OH, Sadie Vance, death cert. #65014.

181 Ohio, County Births, 1841-2003 (County Courthouses), FamilySearch.org, Leatha May Ballentine, Highland Co., Ohio Birth Record Vol. 3, pg. 38.

182 Ohio, Deaths, 1908-1932, 1938-2007, Ancestry.com, Letha Henderson, death cert. #007477.

183 Obituary of Margaret "Maggie" Stroup, Highland County District Library, 10 Willettsville Pike, Hillsboro, OH, Hillsboro (OH) News-Herald, pub. 17 Aug 1899.

184 Find A Grave—Stroup Cemetery, Dodson Twp., Highland Co., Ohio, Find A Grave.com, Margaret Stroup, Find A Grave Memorial #112182648.

185 Obituary of Adolphus Pegan (Hillsboro, Ohio, Hillsboro News Herald, 24 Nov 1910), Highland County District Library, 10 Willettsville Pike, Hillsboro, OH.

186 Find A Grave—Troutwine Cemetery, Dodson Twp., Highland Co., Ohio, Find A Grave.com, Adolphus Vonesse Pegan, Find A Grave Memorial # 165269600.

187 The Genealogical Committee of The Clinton County Historical Society, Cemetery Records of Clinton Co., Ohio, 1798-1998, Troutwine Cemetery: Adolphus V. Pegan. Clinton County, Ohio Records Center and Archives, 111 South Nelson Avenue, Suite 3, Wilmington, OH.

188 Ohio, County Marriages, 1789-2013, FamilySearch.org, "A.B." Pegan and Teresa Graham, Clinton County, Ohio Marriage Records, Vol. 7, pg. 155. Oddly, there is no marriage return completed. The license has a notation of "Lynchburg".

189 Ohio Death Certificate, Ohio Department of Health, Center for Vital and Health Statistics, 246 North High Street, Columbus, OH, Teresa Pegan, death cert. #67432.

190 The Genealogical Committee of The Clinton County Historical Society, Cemetery Records of Clinton Co., Ohio, 1798-1998, Troutwine Cemetery: Teresa Pegan. Clinton County, Ohio Records Center and Archives, 111 South Nelson Avenue, Suite 3, Wilmington, OH.

191 Ohio, County Births, 1841-2003 (County Courthouses), FamilySearch.org, Frederick "Pagin", Highland Co., Ohio Birth Record Vol. 3, pg. 364.

192 Ohio, Deaths, 1908-1932, 1938-2007, Ancestry.com, Frank Pegan, death cert. #094902.

193 Ohio Death Certificate, Ohio Department of Health, Center for Vital and Health Statistics, 246 North High Street, Columbus, OH, Robert Pegan, death cert. #38177.

194 Ohio, County Births, 1841-2003 (County Courthouses), FamilySearch.org, Robert Pegan, Highland Co., Ohio Birth Record Vol. 3, pg. 366.

195 Ohio, Deaths, 1908-1932, 1938-2007, Ancestry.com, Robert Pegan, death cert. #38177; Ohio State Death Index pg. 6524.

196 Ohio, County Births, 1841-2003 (County Courthouses), FamilySearch.org, William H. Pegan, Highland Co., Ohio Birth Record Vol. 1, pg. 374.

197 Missouri Death Certificates, 1910-1966, Missouri Secretary of State, 600 West Main Street, Jefferson City, MO; Online database: http://s1.sos.mo.gov/records/archives/archivesmvc/deathcertificates, William H. Pegan, death cert. #63-046532.

198 Find A Grave—Calvary Cemetery and Mausoleum, St. Louis, Missouri, Find A Grave.com, William H. Pegan, Find A Grave Memorial #47414603.

199 Ohio, County Marriages, 1789-2013, FamilySearch.org, Henry L. Pegan and Elma Duvall Troutwine, Highland County, Ohio Marriage Records, Vol. 15, pg. 244. lic. #6856.

200 Ohio Death Certificate, Ohio Department of Health, Center for Vital and Health Statistics, 246 North High Street, Columbus, OH, Elma Duvall Pegan, death cert. #28874.

201 Ohio, Deaths, 1908-1932, 1938-2007, Ancestry.com, Elma D. Pegan, death cert. #28874, Ohio State Death Index pg. 6524.

202 The Genealogical Committee of The Clinton County Historical Society, Cemetery Records of Clinton Co., Ohio, 1798-1998, Troutwine Cemetery: Elma D. Pegan. Clinton County, Ohio Records Center and Archives, 111 South Nelson Avenue, Suite 3, Wilmington, OH.

203 Ohio, County Births, 1841-2003 (County Courthouses), FamilySearch.org, Courtland Pegan, Highland Co., Ohio Birth Record Vol. 3, pg. 374.

204 Ohio, Deaths, 1908-1932, 1938-2007, Ancestry.com, Courtland Pegan, death cert. #042030.

205 Ohio, County Births, 1841-2003 (County Courthouses), FamilySearch.org, Clarence Pegan, Highland Co., Ohio Birth Record Vol. 3, pg. 542.

206 Ohio, Deaths, 1908-1932, 1938-2007, Ancestry.com, Clarence Pegan, death cert. #041102.

207 Ohio, Deaths, 1908-1932, 1938-2007, Ancestry.com, Frances E. Stubbs, death cert. #096692.

208 U.S., Social Security Applications and Claims Index, 1936-2007, Frances E. Stubbs.

209 Obituary of Frances E. Stubbs (Wilmington, Ohio, Wilmington News-Journal, 07 Jan 1990), Wilmington Public Library of Clinton County, 268 North South Street, Wilmington, OH.

210 Obituary of Mrs. William Thompson, (Hillsboro, Ohio, Highland County News-Herald, 18 Jan 1902), Highland County District Library, 10 Willettsville Pike, Hillsboro, OH.

211 Find A Grave—Troutwine Cemetery, Dodson Twp., Highland Co., Ohio, Find A Grave.com, Frances B. Thompson, Find A Grave Memorial #112435737.

212 Ohio, County Marriages, 1789-2013, FamilySearch.org, Will R. Thompson and Frankie D. Pegan, Highland County, Ohio Marriage Records, Vol. 13. pg. 40. lic. #5115.

213 Ohio Death Certificate, Ohio Department of Health, Center for Vital and Health Statistics, 246 North High Street, Columbus, OH, William Robert Thompson, death cert. #81239.

214 Obituary of W.R. Thompson (Hillsboro, Ohio, Hillsboro Press Gazette, 29 Oct 1943), Highland County District Library, 10 Willettsville Pike, Hillsboro, OH.

215 Find A Grave—Stroup Cemetery, Dodson Twp., Highland Co., Ohio, Find A Grave.com, William Robert Thompson, Find A Grave Memorial #91145278.

216 Ohio, County Marriages, 1789-2013, FamilySearch.org, Raymond Augustus Corbet and Genevieve Childers Thompson, Highland County, Ohio Marriage Records, Vol. 20, pg. 537, lic. #15132. Genevieve's mother's maiden name was Elizabeth Childers.

217 Find A Grave—Stroup Cemetery, Dodson Twp., Highland Co., Ohio, Find A Grave.com, Elizabeth Childers Thompson, Find A Grave Memorial # 1334149648.

218 Delaware County, Ohio, Burial Index, 1784-2011, Leila Thompson, buried Martinsville, Ohio, father's name Francis Johnson.

219 Obituary of Mabel L. Stroup (Washington, D.C, Washington Post, 07 Sep 1950), Historical Newspapers, Birth Marriage & Death Announcements, 1851-2003, Ancestry.com.

220 Historical Newspapers, Birth, Marriage, & Death Announcements, 1851-2003, Ancestry.com. Obituary of Mabel L. Stroup (Washington, D.C., Washington Post, 07 Sep 1950).

221 Florida Death Index 1877-1998, Ancestry.com, Ruth F. Thompson.

222 Find A Grave—Harwood Cemetery, Salem Twp., Highland Co., Ohio, Find A Grave.com, Laura Pegan Daggy, Find A Grave Memorial #109713170.

223 Ohio, County Marriages, 1789-2013, FamilySearch.org, T.H.L. Daggy and Laura Pegan, Highland County, Ohio Marriage Records, Vol. 10, pg. 469, lic. #1133.

224 Ohio Death Certificate, Ohio Department of Health, Center for Vital and Health Statistics, 246 North High Street, Columbus, OH, Thomas L. Hamer Daggy, death cert. #8555.

225 Find A Grave—Harwood Cemetery, Salem Twp., Highland Co., Ohio, Find A Grave.com, Thomas L. Hamer Daggy, Find A Grave Memorial #109713152.

226 Ohio, County Marriages, 1789-2013, FamilySearch.org, John F. Smith and Laura Daggy, Butler County, Ohio Marriage Records, Vol. 22, pg. 86, lic. #5125.

227 Obituary of John F. Smith (Hillsboro, Ohio, Hillsboro Gazette, 30 Jul 1946, Highland County District Library, 10 Willettsville Pike, Hillsboro, OH.

228 Find A Grave—Barker Cemetery, Pricetown, Salem Twp., Highland Co., Ohio, Find A Grave.com, John F. Smith, Find A Grave Memorial #119445247.

229 Ohio Death Certificate, Ohio Department of Health, Center for Vital and Health Statistics, 246 North High Street, Columbus, OH, Lillian M. Wagonfield, death cert. #6899.

230 Ohio, County Births, 1841-2003 (County Courthouses), FamilySearch.org, Lilly May Daggy, Highland Co., Ohio Birth Record Vol. 2, pg. 158.

231 Ohio, County Births, 1841-2003 (County Courthouses), FamilySearch.org, Llewellyn Daggy, Highland Co., Ohio Birth Record Vol. 3, pg. 88.

232 Obituary of "Luella" Daggy Roberts (Hillsboro, Ohio, Hillsboro News Herald, 14 Jun 1906), Highland County District Library, 10 Willettsville Pike, Hillsboro, OH.

233 Ohio, County Births, 1841-2003 (County Courthouses), FamilySearch.org, Oliver Daggy, Highland Co, Ohio Births, Vol. #, pg. 90.

234 Florida Death Index 1877-1998, Ancestry.com, Oliver Daggy, death cert. #49722.

235 Find A Grave—Union Cemetery, Taylorsville, White Oak Twp., Highland Co., Ohio, Find A Grave.com, Anna Pegan Surber, Find A Grave Memorial #119132349.

236 Ohio, County Marriages, 1789-2013, FamilySearch.org, Lewis Surber and Anna Pegan, Highland County, Ohio Marriage Records, Vol. 11, pg. 437, lic. #2793.

237 Ohio Death Certificate, Ohio Department of Health, Center for Vital and Health Statistics, 246 North High Street, Columbus, OH, Lewis A. Surber, death cert. #24193.

238 Find A Grave—Union Cemetery, Taylorsville, White Oak Twp., Highland Co., Ohio, Find A Grave.com, Lewis A. Surber, Find A Grave Memorial #119132346.

239 Ohio, County Births, 1841-2003 (County Courthouses), FamilySearch.org, Lawrence W. Surber, Highland Co., Ohio Birth Record Vol. 3, pg. 418.

240 Ohio, County Death Records, 1840-2001, FamilySearch.org, (infant) Surber; fa: L.A. Surber, mo: Annie Pegan; Logan Co., Ohio Death Record, Vol. 1, pg. 344.

241 Ohio, County Births, 1841-2003 (County Courthouses), FamilySearch.org, Earl L. Surber, Highland Co., Ohio Birth Record Vol. 3, pg. 424.

242 Ohio, Deaths, 1908-1932, 1938-2007, Ancestry.com, Earl. L. Surber, death cert. #12148.

243 Find A Grave—Lynchburg Masonic Cemetery, Lynchburg, Dodson Twp., Highland Co., Ohio, Find A Grave.com, William Pegan, Find A Grave Memorial #93957293.

244 Find A Grave—Lynchburg Masonic Cemetery, Lynchburg, Dodson Twp., Highland Co., Ohio, Find A Grave.com, Mattie Pegan, Find A Grave Memorial #93957394.

245 Find A Grave—Lynchburg Masonic Cemetery, Lynchburg, Dodson Twp., Highland Co., Ohio, Find A Grave.com, Frances Pegan Carr, Find A Grave Memorial #39028271.

246 Ohio, County Births, 1841-2003 (County Courthouses), FamilySearch.org, Edward "Evarts" Carr, Highland Co., Ohio Birth Record Vol. 2, pg. 10.

247 U.S., WWI Draft Registration Cards, 1917-1918, Ancestry.com, Everett E. Carr, Lynchburg, Highland Co., Ohio.

248 U.S., WWII Draft Registration Cards, 1942, Ancestry.com, Everett E. Carr, Clark Twp., Clinton Co., Ohio.

249 Ohio, Deaths, 1908-1932, 1938-2007, Ancestry.com, Everett E. Carr, death cert. #095986.

250 Obituary of Everett Carr (Hillsboro, Ohio, Press-Gazette, 15 Dec 1976), Highland County District Library, 10 Willettsville Pike, Hillsboro, OH.

251 Find A Grave—West Chapel Cemetery, Clark Twp., Clinton Co., Ohio, Find A Grave.com, Everett E. Carr, Find A Grave Memorial #81714995.

252 Find A Grave—Union Cemetery, Taylorsville, White Oak Twp., Highland Co., Ohio, Find A Grave.com, Charles Pegan, Find A Grave Memorial #119092478.

253 Ohio, County Marriages, 1789-2013, FamilySearch.org, Charles Pegan and Resa Pulliam, Highland County, Ohio Marriage Records, Vol. 16, pg. 57, lic. #9394.

254 Ohio, County Births, 1841-2003 (County Courthouses), FamilySearch.org, Resa J. Pulliam, Highland Co., Ohio Birth Record Vol. 2, pg. 262.

255 Ohio Death Certificate, Ohio Department of Health, Center for Vital and Health Statistics, 246 North High Street, Columbus, OH, Resa Pegan, death cert. #47612.

256 Obituary of Mrs. Charles Pegan (Hillsboro, Ohio, Press-Gazette, 27 Jul 1943), Highland County District Library, 10 Willettsville Pike, Hillsboro, OH.

257 Find A Grave—Union Cemetery, Taylorsville, White Oak Twp., Highland Co., Ohio, Find A Grave.com, Resa Pegan, Find A Grave Memorial #119092491.

258 Ohio, County Marriages, 1789-2013, FamilySearch.org, Charles Pegan and Elizabeth Knauer, Highland County, Ohio Marriage Records, Vol. 22, pg. 337, #17066.

259 Ohio, Deaths, 1908-1932, 1938-2007, Ancestry.com, Elizabeth Pegan, death cert. #010727.

260 Obituary of Elizabeth (Hawk) Pegan (Hillsboro, Ohio, Press-Gazette, 18 Feb 1980), Highland County District Library, 10 Willettsville Pike, Hillsboro, OH.

261 Find A Grave—Barker Cemetery, Pricetown, Salem Twp., Highland Co., Ohio, Find A Grave.com, Lizzie Hawk Pegan, Find A Grave Memorial #43038227.

262 Ohio, County Births, 1841-2003 (County Courthouses), FamilySearch.org, Hugh Doyle Pegan, Highland Co., Ohio Birth Record Vol. 3, pg. 544.

263 Ohio, Deaths, 1908-1932, 1938-2007, Ancestry.com, Hugh Pegan, death cert. #028030.

264 Obituary of Hugh D. Pegan (Hillsboro, Ohio, Press-Gazette, 06 Apr 1984), Highland County District Library, 10 Willettsville Pike, Hillsboro, OH.

265 Birth Announcement of Harlen Pulliam Pegan (Hillsboro, Ohio, The News-Herald, 09 Sep 1909). Chronicling America, Library of Congress, Washington, DC; Online database: http://chroniclingamerica.loc.gov/.

266 Ohio, Birth Index, 1908-1964, Ancestry.com, "Marlin" Pegan, state file #1909072751.

267 Ohio Death Certificate, Ohio Department of Health, Center for Vital and Health Statistics, 246 North High Street, Columbus, OH, Harlen Pegan, death cert. #46748.

268 Ohio, Deaths, 1908-1932, 1938-2007, Ancestry.com, Harlen ("Harlin") Pulliam Pegan, (no certificate number), Hamer Twp., Highland Co., Ohio, 1915, Letter P., pg. 979; Vol. 195, File #46, 748.

269 Find A Grave—Lynchburg Masonic Cemetery, Lynchburg, Dodson Twp., Highland Co., Ohio, Find A Grave.com, Hattie Shaper, Find A Grave Memorial #93370263.

270 Ohio, County Marriages, 1789-2013, FamilySearch.org, Edward M. Shaper and "Hattie" Schwartz, Highland County, Ohio Marriage Records, Vol. 16, pg. 373, lic. #10027.

271 Ohio Death Certificate, Ohio Department of Health, Center for Vital and Health Statistics, 246 North High Street, Columbus, OH, Edward M. Shaper, death cert. #20397.

272 Find A Grave—Lynchburg Masonic Cemetery, Lynchburg, Dodson Twp., Highland Co., Ohio, Find A Grave.com, Edward M. Shaper, Find A Grave Memorial #137530577.

273 Find A Grave—Lynchburg Masonic Cemetery, Lynchburg, Dodson Twp., Highland Co., Ohio, Find A Grave.com, Walter C. Schwartz, Find A Grave Memorial #93425002.

274 Ohio, County Marriages, 1789-2013, FamilySearch.org, Walter C. Schwartz and Nora Reeves, Highland County, Ohio Marriage Records, Vol.17, pg. 382, lic. #11927.

275 Marriage License of Walter Schwartz and Nora Reeves, Highland County, Ohio Probate Court, Highland County Courthouse, 105 North High Street, Hillsboro, OH, Highland County, Ohio Marriages, Vol. 17, pg. 382, #11927.

276 Obituary of Nora Schwartz (Lynchburg, Ohio, Lynchburg News, 10 Jan 1957), Highland County District Library, 10 Willettsville Pike, Hillsboro, OH.

277 Find A Grave—Lynchburg Masonic Cemetery, Lynchburg, Dodson Twp., Highland Co., Ohio, Find A Grave.com, Nora Jean Reeves Schwartz, Find A Grave Memorial #93425026.

278 Obituary of Cora May Schwartz (Coshocton, Ohio, Coshocton Times, 03 Jan 1951), Coshocton Public Library, 655 Main Street, Coshocton, OH.

279 Find A Grave—Roscoe Cemetery, Roscoe, Jackson Twp., Coshocton Co., Ohio, Find A Grave.com, Cora May Schwartz, Find A Grave Memorial #179602172.

280 Find A Grave—Martinsville IOOF Cemetery, Martinsville, Clark Twp., Clinton Co., Ohio, Find A Grave.com, Frank Pegan, Find A Grave Memorial #105023586.

281 The Genealogical Committee of The Clinton County Historical Society, Cemetery Records of Clinton Co., Ohio, 1798-1998, Martinsville IOOF Cemetery: Frank J. Pegan. Clinton County, Ohio Records Center and Archives, 111 South Nelson Avenue, Suite 3, Wilmington, OH.

282 Ohio, County Marriages, 1789-2013, FamilySearch.org, Frank Pegan and Nellie Irene West, Clinton County, Ohio Marriage Records, Vol. 9, pg. 523, lic. #733.

283 Obituary of Nelle I. Pegan (South Bend, Indiana, South Bend Tribune [Mishawaka Edition], 13 Mar 1976), Mishawaka-Penn Harris Library, 209 Lincoln Way East, Mishawaka, IN.

284 Ohio, County Births, 1841-2003 (County Courthouses), FamilySearch.org, Nelle Irene West, Clinton Co., Ohio Birth Record, Vol. 2, pg. 106.

285 Find A Grave—Martinsville IOOF Cemetery, Martinsville, Clark Twp., Clinton Co., Ohio, Find A Grave.com, Nelle Irene West Pegan, Find A Grave Memorial #105023445.

286 The Genealogical Committee of The Clinton County Historical Society, Cemetery Records of Clinton Co., Ohio, 1798-1998, Martinsville IOOF Cemetery: Nellie I. Pegan. Clinton County, Ohio Records Center and Archives, 111 South Nelson Avenue, Suite 3, Wilmington, OH.

287 Ohio, Deaths, 1908-1932, 1938-2007, Ancestry.com, Ferrol Kies, death cert. #071106.

288 Ohio, County Births, 1841-2003 (County Courthouses), FamilySearch.org, Ferrol Pegan, Clinton Co., Ohio Birth Record Vol. 4, pg. 157.

289 Obituary of Ruby Woodall (Wilmington, Ohio, Wilmington News-Journal, 01 Aug 1984), Wilmington Public Library of Clinton County, 268 North South Street, Wilmington, OH.

290 Ohio, Deaths, 1908-1932, 1938-2007, Ancestry.com, Ruby Woodall, death cert. #056769.

291 Ohio, Deaths, 1908-1932, 1938-2007, Ancestry.com, Harold West Pegan, death cert. #085500.

292 Obituary of Ruth M. Holmes (South Bend, Indiana, South Bend Tribune, 24 Aug 2004), St. Joseph County Public Library, 304 South Main Street, South Bend, IN.

293 Ohio, Birth Index, 1908-1964, Ancestry.com, Ruth Pegan, state file #1921055580.

294 U.S., Social Security Applications and Claims Index, 1936-2007, Ancestry.com, Ruth Marie Pegan Holmes.

295 Indiana, Death Certificates, 1908-2011, Ancestry.com, Ruth M. Holmes, death cert. #026348.

296 Ohio Death Certificate, Ohio Department of Health, Center for Vital and Health Statistics, 246 North High Street, Columbus, OH, Unnamed Daughter Pegan, death cert. #31655.

297 The Genealogical Committee of The Clinton County Historical Society, Cemetery Records of Clinton Co., Ohio, 1798-1998, Troutwine Cemetery: Ella Mae Pegan. Clinton County, Ohio Records Center and Archives, 111 South Nelson Avenue, Suite 3, Wilmington, OH.

298 Obituary of Ella Pegan (Wilmington, Ohio, Wilmington News-Herald, 25 Oct 1948), Pegan family file, The Clinton County History Center, 149 East Locust Street, Wilmington, OH.

299 Find A Grave—New Lynchburg Masonic Cemetery/Lynchburg F & AM Cemetery, Lynchburg, Dodson Twp., Highland Co., Ohio, Find A Grave.com, William O. Pegan, Find A Grave Memorial #98709031.

300 Ohio, County Marriages, 1789-2013, FamilySearch.org, William O. Pegan and Rose E. Stroup, Clinton County, Ohio Marriage Records, Vol. 18, pg. 31, lic. #11746.

301 Obituary of Rose Pegan (Wilmington, Ohio, Wilmington News-Journal, 28 Aug 1965), Pegan family file, The Clinton County History Center, 149 East Locust Street, Wilmington, OH.

302 U.S., Social Security Applications and Claims Index, 1936-2007, Ancestry.com, Rose Pegan (Life Claim).

303 Ohio, Deaths, 1908-1932, 1938-2007, Ancestry.com, Rose E. Pegan, death cert. #57969.

304 Find A Grave—New Lynchburg Masonic Cemetery/Lynchburg F & AM Cemetery, Lynchburg, Dodson Twp., Highland Co., Ohio, Find A Grave.com, Rose Stroup Pegan, Find A Grave Memorial #98708945.

305 Clinton County, Ohio Marriage Records, Clinton County, Ohio Records Center and Archives, 111 South Nelson Avenue, Suite 3, Wilmington, OH, William O. Pegan and Elsie Wilson, Clinton County, Ohio Marriage Records, Vol. 20, pg. 93, #1385.

306 Obituary of Elsie Pegan (Wilmington, Ohio, Wilmington News-Journal, 17 Mar 1986), Pegan family file, The Clinton County History Center, 149 East Locust Street, Wilmington, OH.

307 Ohio, Deaths, 1908-1932, 1938-2007, Ancestry.com, Elsie Pegan, death cert. #016535.

308 Obituary of Paul S. Pegan (Wilmington, Ohio, Wilmington News-Journal, 30 Jan 2007), Pegan family file, The Clinton County History Center, 149 East Locust Street, Wilmington, OH.

309 Ohio Deaths, 1908-1953, FamilySearch.org, Mary Louise Pegan, death cert. #19-47217.

310 Ohio, Deaths, 1908-1932, 1938-2007, Ancestry.com, Audrey Mae West, death cert. #032445.

311 U.S., Social Security Applications and Claims Index, 1936-2007, Ancestry.com, Audrey Mae Pegan West.

312 Ohio, Deaths, 1908-1932, 1938-2007, Ancestry.com, Doris Helen Ludwick, death cert. #000049.

313 Ohio, Birth Index, 1908-1964, Ancestry.com, Helen Pegan, state file #1922066334.

314 Obituary of Agnes Philhower (Hillsboro, Ohio, Press-Gazette, 08 Oct 1943), Highland County District Library, 10 Willettsville Pike, Hillsboro, OH.

315 Find A Grave—New Lynchburg Masonic Cemetery/Lynchburg F & AM Cemetery, Lynchburg, Dodson Twp., Highland Co., Ohio, Find A Grave.com, Agnes Philhower, Find A Grave Memorial #99489717.

316 Ohio, County Marriages, 1789-2013, FamilySearch.org, Charles Philhower and Agnes Lemons, Highland County, Ohio Marriage Records, Vol. 14, pg. 80, lic. #5415.

317 U.S., WWI Draft Registration Cards, 1917-1918, Ancestry.com, Charles Philhower.

318 Ohio, County Births, 1841-2003 (County Courthouses), FamilySearch.org, Charles Philhower, Clinton Co., Ohio Birth Record Vol. 1, pg. 176.

319 Ohio, Deaths, 1908-1932, 1938-2007, Ancestry.com, Charles Philhower, death cert. #04709.

320 Obituary of Charles Philhower, Ancestry.com, Charles Philhower, Hillsboro (OH) Press-Gazette, pub. 26 Jan 1960.

321 Find A Grave—New Lynchburg Masonic Cemetery/Lynchburg F & AM Cemetery, Lynchburg, Dodson Twp., Highland Co., Ohio, Find A Grave.com, Charles Philhower, Find A Grave Memorial #99489779.

322 Florida Death Index 1877-1998, Ancestry.com, Charles R. Philhower, death cert. #23991.

323 Florida Death Index 1877-1998, Ancestry.com, L. Donald Philhower, death cert. #50271.

324 Find A Grave—Ferncliff Cemetery, Springfield, Springfield Twp., Clark Co., Ohio, Grace Boesenberg, Find A Grave Memorial #34939977.

325 Obituary of Grace Boesenberg (Springfield, Ohio, Springfield Daily News, 22 Oct 1959), Clark County Public Library, 201 South Fountain Avenue Springfield, OH.

326 Obituary of E.W. Boesenberg (Springfield, Ohio, Springfield Daily News, 04 Apr 1951), Clark County Public Library, 201 South Fountain Avenue Springfield, OH.

327 Ohio Death Certificate, Ohio Department of Health, Center for Vital and Health Statistics, 246 North High Street, Columbus, OH, Edward W. Boesenberg, death cert. #21213.

328 Find A Grave—Ferncliff Cemetery, Springfield, Springfield Twp., Clark Co., Ohio, Edward W. Boesenberg, Find A Grave Memorial #35221621.

329 Phone interview with Carolyn Luck Barker, Wilmington, OH, Ann Miller Carr, author, 13 Aug 2013.

330 Ohio, Births and Christenings Index, 1800-1962, Ancestry.com, Marcia Boesenberg, Preble Co. Births, Vol. 4, pg. May 1905. Although registered in Preble Co., nearly a year later, the record says Marcia Lucille Boesenburg was born in Highland Co. on June 1, 1904.

331 Ohio Death Certificate, Ohio Department of Health, Center for Vital and Health Statistics, 246 North High Street, Columbus, OH, Marcia Roush, death cert. #583.

332 New Lynchburg Masonic Cemetery Records, James S. Lemons, New Lynchburg Masonic Cemetery, State Route 134, Lynchburg, OH.

333 Find A Grave—White Rose Cemetery, Bartlesville, Washington Co., Oklahoma, Find A Grave.com, Andrew J. Lemon [sic], Find A Grave Memorial #98770095.

334 U.S. City Directories, 1822-1995, Ancestry.com, Muskogee, Oklahoma, 1914, pg. 162, entry for Lemons, Andrew J.

335 Bartlesville, Oklahoma city directory, 1915-1916, pg. 105, entry for Lemons, Andrew J. Local and Family History Department, Bartlesville Public Library, 600 South Johnstone Avenue, Bartlesville, OK.

336 Oklahoma, County Marriages, 1890-1995, FamilySearch.org, Andrew "J." Lemons and Anna R. Darling, Washington County, Oklahoma Marriage Records, Book 3, pg. 335.

337 Missouri Death Certificates, 1910-1966, Missouri Secretary of State, 600 West Main Street, Jefferson City, MO; Online database: http://s1.sos.mo.gov/records/archives/

archivesmvc/deathcertificates, Anna R. Myers, death cert. #37649.

338 Find A Grave—White Rose Cemetery, Bartlesville, Washington Co., Oklahoma, Find A Grave.com, Anna R. Myers, Find A Grave Memorial #161098102.

339 Oklahoma, County Marriages, 1890-1995, FamilySearch.org, Roy R. Myers and Mrs. Anna Lemons, Washington County, Oklahoma Marriage Records, Book 8, pg. 103.

340 Find A Grave—Glen Haven Memorial Gardens Cemetery, Donnelsville, Bethel Twp., Clark Co., Ohio, Talmadge "Tal" Lemons, Find A Grave Memorial #169013643.

341 Ohio Death Certificate, Ohio Department of Health, Center for Vital and Health Statistics, 246 North High Street, Columbus, OH, Rena Mae Lemons, death cert. #00591.

342 Obituary of Mrs. Rena Mae Lemons (Springfield, Ohio, Springfield Daily News, 16 Jan 1951), Clark County Public Library, 201 South Fountain Avenue, Springfield, OH.

343 Find A Grave—Glen Haven Memorial Gardens Cemetery, Donnelsville, Bethel Twp., Clark Co., Ohio, Rena Mae Lemons, Find A Grave Memorial #169010577.

344 New Lynchburg Masonic Cemetery Records, Merrill Lemons, New Lynchburg Masonic Cemetery, State Route 134, Lynchburg, OH.

345 Obituary of Merrill Lemon [sic] (Springfield, Ohio, Springfield Daily News, 12 Jul 1953), Clark County Public Library, 201 South Fountain Avenue, Springfield, OH.

346 U.S., WWII Draft Registration Cards, 1942, Ancestry.com, Murrill Clarence Lemons, Lynchburg, Highland County, Ohio.

347 Ohio Deaths, 1908-1953, FamilySearch.org, Nora Sheehan, death cert. #70973.

348 Ohio, County Births, 1841-2003 (County Courthouses), FamilySearch.org, Highland County, Ohio Birth Records, Vol. 3, pg. 82, Unnamed female child, 31 Jul 1899, fa.: John Cooper; mo.: Ellen Overman.

349 U.S. City Directories, 1822-1995, Ancestry.com, Springfield, Ohio, 1918, pg. 516, entry for Lemons, Murrell C.

350 U.S., WWI Draft Registration Cards, 1917-1918, Ancestry.com, Clarence Otto Lemons, Springfield, Ohio.

351 U.S., WWII Draft Registration Cards, 1942, Ancestry.com, Clarence Otto "Lemmons", Springfield, Clark County, Ohio.

352 U.S., Social Security Applications and Claims Index, 1936-2007, Ancestry.com, Clarence Otto "Lemon".

353 Ohio, Births and Christenings Index, 1774-1973, Ancestry.com, Clarence Otis Lemmons, Lynchburg, Highland Co., Ohio.

354 Ohio, County Marriages, 1789-2013, FamilySearch.org, Otto Lemons and Grace May Long, Vol. 9, pg. 197, cert. #7297.

355 Ohio Death Certificate, Ohio Department of Health, Center for Vital and Health Statistics, 246 North High Street, Columbus, OH, Grace May Lemons, death cert. #6991.

356 Find A Grave—Ferncliff Cemetery, Springfield, Springfield Twp., Clark Co., Ohio, Grace M. Lemons, Find A Grave Memorial #54892479.

357 Ohio, County Marriages, 1789-2013, FamilySearch.org, Frank Ferrand and Daisy L. Thorpe, married April 17, 1906, Vol. 41, pg. 231, cert. #13953.

358 Ohio, Deaths, 1908-1932, 1938-2007, Ancestry.com, Daisy L. Ferrand, death cert. #23908.

359 Obituary of Clarence Otto "Bill" Lemon {sic} (Hillsboro, Ohio, Press-Gazette, 27 Oct 1944), Highland County District Library, 10 Willettsville Pike, Hillsboro, OH.

360 Ohio, Birth Index, 1908-1964, Ancestry.com, Robert H. Long, state file # #1917019298.

361 Obituary of Josephine Luck (Hillsboro, Ohio, Highland County Times-Gazette, 13 Oct 2008), Highland County District Library, 10 Willettsville Pike, Hillsboro, OH.

362 Obituary of Clarence J. Long (Milwaukee, Wisconsin, Milwaukee Journal-Sentinel, 25 Jan 2012), Milwaukee Public Library, 814 West Wisconsin Avenue, Milwaukee, WI.

363 Find A Grave—New Lynchburg Masonic Cemetery/Lynchburg F & AM Cemetery, Lynchburg, Dodson Twp., Highland Co., Ohio, Find A Grave.com, Eddie R. Lemons, Find A Grave Memorial #97943862.

364 New Lynchburg Masonic Cemetery Records, Eddie R. Lemons, New Lynchburg Masonic Cemetery, State Route 134, Lynchburg, OH.

365 U.S., WWI Draft Registration Cards, 1917-1918, Ancestry.com, Edward Roy Lemons, Lynchburg, Highland County, Ohio.

366 Ohio, County Marriages, 1789-2013, FamilySearch.org, "Eddie R. Lemon" and Wilhelmina Frazier, Highland County, Ohio Marriage Records, Vol. 18, pg. 452, lic. #12655.

367 California, Death Index, 1940-1997, Ancestry.com, Wilhelmina J. Lemons.

368 Find A Grave—Winema Cemetery, Weed, Siskiyou Co., California, Find A Grave.com, Wilhelmina Jane Leaverton Lemons, Find A Grave Memorial #84841443.

369 Obituary of Wilhelmina Lemons (Weed, California, Weed Press, 24 Jan 1963), Genealogical Society of Siskiyou County, 912 South Main Street, Yreka, CA.

370 Ohio, County Marriages, 1789-2013, FamilySearch.org, Floyd Frazier and Wilhelmina Leaverton, Highland County, Ohio Marriage Records, Vol. 18, pg. 181, lic. #12035.

371 U.S., WWII Draft Registration Cards, 1942, Ancestry.com, Eddie R. Lemons, Lynchburg, Highland County, Ohio.

372 "Man Is Discovered Lying in Roadway" [sic] (Hillsboro, Ohio, Press-Gazette, 13 Jan 1948), Highland County District Library, 10 Willettsville Pike, Hillsboro, OH.

373 Find A Grave—Winema Cemetery, Weed, Siskiyou Co., California, Find A Grave.com, Margaret L. Lemons Brown, Find A Grave Memorial #147404700.

374 Find A Grave—Stroup Cemetery, Dodson Twp., Highland Co., Ohio, Find A Grave.com, Cora Carroll, Find A Grave Memorial #140074466.

375 Ohio, County Marriages, 1789-2013, FamilySearch.org, Allen Carroll and Cora Williams, Highland County, Ohio Marriage Records, Vol. 12, pg. 431, lic. #4542.

376 Ohio, County Births, 1841-2003 (County Courthouses), FamilySearch.org, Allen Carroll, Warren Co., Ohio Birth Records, Vol. 1, pg. 158.

377 Ohio, Deaths, 1908-1932, 1938-2007, Ancestry.com, Allen Carroll, death cert. #67758.

378 Find A Grave—Stroup Cemetery, Dodson Twp., Highland Co., Ohio, Find A Grave.com, Allen Carroll, Find A Grave Memorial #140074486.

379 Find A Grave—Stroup Cemetery, Dodson Twp., Highland Co., Ohio, Find A Grave.com, Infant Daughter Carroll, Find A Grave Memorial #140074417.

380 Ohio, County Births, 1841-2003 (County Courthouses), FamilySearch.org, Mary E. Carroll, Highland Co., Ohio Birth Record Vol. 3, pg. 86.

381 Ohio Death Certificate, Ohio Department of Health, Center for Vital and Health Statistics, 246 North High Street, Columbus, OH, Mary Elinora Carroll, death cert. #34570.

382 Ohio Death Certificate, Ohio Department of Health, Center for Vital and Health Statistics, 246 North High Street, Columbus, OH, William Morrell Carroll, death cert. #81042.

383 Ohio, Deaths, 1908-1932, 1938-2007, Ancestry.com, Delbert A. Carroll, death cert. #010564.

384 Ohio, Birth Index, 1908-1964, Ancestry.com, Delbert Carroll, state file #1921036433.

385 Find A Grave—New Lynchburg Masonic Cemetery/Lynchburg F & AM Cemetery, Lynchburg, Dodson Twp., Highland Co., Ohio, Find A Grave.com, Lee Williams, Find A Grave Memorial #97728317.

386 Ohio, County Marriages, 1789-2013, FamilySearch.org, Levi Williams and Bertha Fawley, Highland County, Ohio Marriage Records, Vol. 14, pg. 360, lic. #5975.

387 Ohio, County Births, 1841-2003 (County Courthouses), FamilySearch.org, Bertha Fawley, Highland Co., Ohio Birth Record Vol. 2, pg. 174.

388 Obituary of Bertha Williams (Hillsboro, Ohio, Press-Gazette, 11 Jan 1957), Highland County District Library, 10 Willettsville Pike, Hillsboro, OH.

389 Find A Grave—New Lynchburg Masonic Cemetery/Lynchburg F & AM Cemetery, Lynchburg, Dodson Twp., Highland Co., Ohio, Find A Grave.com, Bertha Williams, Find A Grave Memorial #97728381.

390 Ohio, County Births, 1841-2003 (County Courthouses), FamilySearch.org, Carl Delbert Williams, Highland Co., Ohio Birth Records, Delayed births with index, 1942-1944, Vol. 4, Case #104, Doc. 4, pg. 115.

391 Ohio, Deaths, 1908-1932, 1938-2007, Ancestry.com, Carl D. Williams, death cert. #076451.

392 Find A Grave—New Lynchburg Masonic Cemetery/Lynchburg F & AM Cemetery, Lynchburg, Dodson Twp., Highland Co., Ohio, Find A Grave.com, Hattie E. Williams Wilkin, Find A Grave Memorial #44743338.

393 Ohio, County Marriages, 1789-2013, FamilySearch.org, G.R. Wilkin and Hattie Williams, Highland County, Ohio Marriage Records, Vol. 14., pg. 282, lic. #5819.

394 U.S., WWII Draft Registration Cards, 1942, Ancestry.com, George R. Wilkin, Lynchburg, Dodson Twp., Highland Co., Ohio

395 U.S., Social Security Applications and Claims Index, 1936-2007, Ancestry.com, George Robert Wilkin.

396 Obituary of George Wilkin (Hillsboro, Ohio, Press-Gazette, 02 Jan 1975), Highland County District Library, 10 Willettsville Pike, Hillsboro, OH.

397 Find A Grave—New Lynchburg Masonic Cemetery/Lynchburg F & AM Cemetery, Lynchburg, Dodson Twp., Highland Co., Ohio, Find A Grave.com, George Robert Wilkin, Find A Grave Memorial #44743265.

398 U.S., Social Security Applications and Claims Index, 1936-2007, Ancestry.com, Edgar Franklin Wilkin.

399 Ohio, County Births, 1841-2003 (County Courthouses), FamilySearch.org, Edgar Franklin Wilkin, Highland Co., Ohio Birth Record Vol. 3, pg. 526.

400 Ohio, Deaths, 1908-1932, 1938-2007, Ancestry.com, Edgar F. Wilkin, death cert. #047371.

401 Ohio, County Births, 1841-2003 (County Courthouses), FamilySearch.org, Everett E. Wilkin, Highland Co., Ohio Birth Record Vol. 3, pg. 528.

402 Obituary of Everett R. Wilkin (Hillsboro, Ohio, Press-Gazette, 13 Nov 1980), Highland County District Library, 10 Willettsville Pike, Hillsboro, OH.

403 Ohio, Deaths, 1908-1932, 1938-2007, Ancestry.com, Everett R. Wilkin, death cert. #086667.

404 Ohio, County Births, 1841-2003 (County Courthouses), FamilySearch.org, Marjorie Marie Wilkin, Highland Co., Ohio Birth Record Vol. 3, pg. 532.

405 Ohio, Deaths, 1908-1932, 1938-2007, Ancestry.com, Marjorie Hawk, death cert. #76946.

406 Ohio, Deaths, 1908-1932, 1938-2007, Ancestry.com, Evelyn L. Turner, death cert. #074250.

407 U.S., Social Security Applications and Claims Index, 1936-2007, Ancestry.com, Evelyn Wilkin Campbell Turner Fissel.

408 Ohio Death Certificate, Ohio Department of Health, Center for Vital and Health Statistics, 246 North High Street, Columbus, OH, Lenora Barker, death cert. #10109.

409 Ohio, County Marriages, 1789-2013, FamilySearch.org, Marcus C. Roush and Georgianna Wilkin, Highland County, Ohio Marriage Records, Vol. 21, pg. 184, lic. #15575.

410 Obituary of Georgeanne Holderby (Chillicothe, Ohio, Chillicothe Gazette, March 27, 1998), Chillicothe & Ross County Library, 140 South Paint Street, Chillicothe, OH.

411 Ohio, Deaths, 1908-1932, 1938-2007, Ancestry.com, Georgeanna Holderby, death cert. #25162.

412 Ohio Death Certificate, Ohio Department of Health, Center for Vital and Health Statistics, 246 North High Street, Columbus, OH, Samuel Wilkin, death cert. #054916.

413 U.S., Social Security Applications and Claims Index, 1936-2007, Ancestry.com, Samuel Wilkin.

414 Obituary of LeRoy "Tom" Wilkin (Wilmington, Ohio, Wilmington News-Journal, 03 Aug 2010),), Wilmington Public Library of Clinton County, 268 North South Street, Wilmington, OH.

415 Find A Grave—New Lynchburg Masonic Cemetery/Lynchburg F & AM Cemetery, Lynchburg, Dodson Twp., Highland Co., Ohio, Find A Grave.com, Stanley Williams, Find A Grave Memorial #99603644.

416 Ohio, County Marriages, 1789-2013, FamilySearch.org, Stanley Williams and Mary Achor, Highland County, Ohio Marriage Records, Vol. 16, pg. 408, lic. #10097.

417 Ohio, County Births, 1841-2003 (County Courthouses), FamilySearch.org, Mary "Acher" and Joseph "Acher", fa: Lafayette "Acher", mo: Martha Fox, Highland Co., Ohio Birth Record Vol. 3, pg. 62.

418 Social Security Applications and Claims Index, 1936-2007, Ancestry.com, Joseph Achor.

419 U.S., WWI Draft Registration Cards, 1917-1918, Ancestry.com, Joseph Achor, mailing address New Vienna, Ohio.

420 U.S., WWII Draft Registration Cards, 1942, Ancestry.com, Joseph Achor, Union Twp., Highland Co., Ohio.

421 Ohio, Deaths, 1908-1932, 1938-2007, Ancestry.com, Mary Williams, death cert. #69724.

422 Find A Grave—New Lynchburg Masonic Cemetery/Lynchburg F & AM Cemetery, Lynchburg, Dodson Twp., Highland Co., Ohio, Find A Grave.com, Mary Williams, Find A Grave Memorial #99603583.

423 Ohio Death Certificate, Ohio Department of Health, Center for Vital and Health Statistics, 246 North High Street, Columbus, OH, Eugene Williams, death cert. #26945.

424 Ohio, Deaths, 1908-1932, 1938-2007, Ancestry.com, Virgil Williams, death cert. #055907.

425 Ohio, Deaths, 1908-1932, 1938-2007, Ancestry.com, Woodrow Williams, death cert. #033979.

426 Obituary of Woodrow Williams (Hillsboro, Ohio, Press-Gazette, 05 May 1972), Highland County District Library, 10 Willettsville Pike, Hillsboro, OH.

427 Ohio, Deaths, 1908-1932, 1938-2007, Ancestry.com, Stanley M. Williams, death cert. #066629.

428 Obituary of Stanley M. Williams (Hillsboro, Ohio, Press-Gazette, 23 Aug 2007), Highland County District Library, 10 Willettsville Pike, Hillsboro, OH.

429 Find A Grave—Stroup Cemetery, Dodson Twp., Highland Co., Ohio, Find A Grave.com, Joseph Williams, Find A Grave Memorial #133411215.

430 Ohio, County Marriages, 1789-2013, FamilySearch.org, Joseph Williams and Anna Tolle, Highland County, Ohio Marriage Records, Vol. 17, pg. 543, lic. #11616.

431 Ohio Death Index, 1908-1932, 1938-1944, and 1958-2007, FamilySearch.org, Anna M. Glenn, Vol. 22274, cert. #14122.

432 Ohio, Deaths, 1908-1932, 1938-2007, Ancestry.com, Anna Glenn, death cert. #081034.

433 Find A Grave—Stroup Cemetery, Dodson Twp., Highland Co., Ohio, Find A Grave.com, Anna M. Tolle Glenn, Find A Grave Memorial #133411238.

434 Obituary of Anna Glenn Williams (sic) (Cincinnati, Ohio, Cincinnati Enquirer, 01 Nov 1975), The Public Library of Cincinnati and Hamilton County, 800 Vine Street, Cincinnati, OH.

435 Ohio, Deaths, 1908-1932, 1938-2007, Ancestry.com, Hazel Imogene Davidson, #40190.

436 Obituary of H. Imogene Davidson (Cincinnati, Ohio, Cincinnati Enquirer, 24 May 2006), The Public Library of Cincinnati and Hamilton County, 800 Vine Street, Cincinnati, OH.

437 Obituary of Paul T. Williams (Cincinnati, Ohio, Cincinnati Enquirer, 19 Nov 2013), The Public Library of Cincinnati and Hamilton County, 800 Vine Street, Cincinnati, OH.

438 Thomas-Justin Memorial Funeral Home Records, Paul T. Williams, Thomas-Justin Memorial Funeral Home, 7500 Montgomery Road, Cincinnati, OH.

439 Find A Grave—Stroup Cemetery, Dodson Twp., Highland Co., Ohio, Find A Grave.com, Cary Williams, Find A Grave Memorial #140236166.

440 Obituary of Harley Williams (Hillsboro, Ohio, Press-Gazette, 02 Aug 1963), Highland County District Library, 10 Willettsville Pike, Hillsboro, OH, Hillsboro (OH)

441 Find A Grave—Stroup Cemetery, Dodson Twp., Highland Co., Ohio, Find A Grave.com, Harley N. Williams, Find A Grave Memorial #133566404.

442 Ohio, County Marriages, 1789-2013, FamilySearch.org, Harley Williams and Mary Freeman, Brown County, Ohio Marriage Records, Vol. 30, pg. 4, lic. #497.

443 Ohio, County Births, 1841-2003 (County Courthouses), FamilySearch.org, Brown County, Ohio Birth Records, Vol. 3, pg. 136.

444 Obituary of Mary Jo Williams (Hillsboro, Ohio, Press-Gazette, 20 Jun 1989), Highland County District Library, 10 Willettsville Pike, Hillsboro, OH.

445 Find A Grave—Stroup Cemetery, Dodson Twp., Highland Co., Ohio, Find A Grave.com, Mary J. Williams, Find A Grave Memorial #133566355.

446 Ohio, Deaths, 1908-1932, 1938-2007, Ancestry.com, Clarence Williams, death cert. #071660.

447 Ohio, Birth Index, 1908-1964, Ancestry.com, Clarence E. Williams, state file #1932056413.

448 Obituary of Glen Louis Williams (Fort Walton Beach, Florida, Northwest Florida Daily News, 15 Jul 2011), Okaloosa County Library, 185 Miracle Strip Parkway SE, Fort Walton Beach, FL.

449 Obituary of Dale Matthew Williams (Greenfield, Ohio, Greenfield Daily Times, 07 Jan 1991), Highland County District Library, 10 Willettsville Pike, Hillsboro, OH.

450 Ohio Death Certificate, Ohio Department of Health, Center for Vital and Health Statistics, 246 North High Street, Columbus, OH, Stephen Thomas Williams, death cert. #52628.

451 Find A Grave—Stroup Cemetery, Dodson Twp., Highland Co., Ohio, Find A Grave.com, Infant Williams, Find A Grave Memorial #140236188.

452 The Genealogical Committee of The Clinton County Historical Society, Cemetery Records of Clinton Co., Ohio, 1798-1998, Mt. Olive Cemetery: Bessie B. Fox. Clinton County, Ohio Records Center and Archives, 111 South Nelson Avenue, Suite 3, Wilmington, OH.

453 Find A Grave—Troutwine Cemetery, Dodson Twp., Highland Co., Ohio, Find A Grave.com, Bessie Fox, Find A Grave Memorial #112432225.

454 Ohio, County Marriages, 1789-2013, FamilySearch.org, Stanley W. Fox and Bessie B. Spilker, Highland County, Ohio Marriage Records, Vol. 15, pg. 386, lic. #4192.

455 U.S., WWI Draft Registration Cards, 1917-1918, Ancestry.com, Stanley W. Fox, Clinton Co., Ohio.

456 U.S., Social Security Applications and Claims Index, 1936-2007, Ancestry.com, Stanley W. Fox.

457 Ohio Death Certificate, Ohio Department of Health, Center for Vital and Health Statistics, 246 North High Street, Columbus, OH, Stanley W. Fox, death cert. #58876.

458 Find A Grave—Troutwine Cemetery, Dodson Twp., Highland Co., Ohio, Find A Grave.com, Earl Spilker, Find A Grave Memorial #107056075.

459 Ohio, County Marriages, 1789-2013, FamilySearch.org, Earl E. Spilker and Merle Roads, Highland County, Ohio Marriage Records, Vol. 17, pg. 483, lic. #11497.

460 U.S., Social Security Applications and Claims Index, 1936-2007, Ancestry.com, Merle R. Sallee.

461 Ohio, County Births, 1841-2003 (County Courthouses), FamilySearch.org, Merle May Roades, Highland Co., Ohio Birth Records, Delayed births with index, 1942, Vol. 3, Case #644, Doc. 3, pg. 160.

462 Ohio, Deaths, 1908-1932, 1938-2007, Ancestry.com, Merle R. Sallee, death cert. #63924.

463 Obituary of Mrs. John Sallee (Hillsboro, Ohio, Press-Gazette, 11 Sep 1959), Highland County District Library, 10 Willettsville Pike, Hillsboro, OH.

464 Ohio, County Marriages, 1789-2013, FamilySearch.org, John Bradley Sallee and Merle Spilker, Highland County, Ohio Marriage Records, Vol. 22, pg. 559, lic. #18403.

465 Obituary of Charlotte Hern (Hillsboro, Ohio, Times-Gazette, 11 Nov 2004), Highland County District Library, 10 Willettsville Pike, Hillsboro, OH.

466 U.S., Social Security Applications and Claims Index, 1936-2007, Ancestry.com, Charlotte Spilker Simms Hern.

467 Funeral Notice for Ralph Spilker (Hillsboro, Ohio, Press-Gazette, 27 Dec 1966), Highland County District Library, 10 Willettsville Pike, Hillsboro, OH.

468 Find A Grave—Troutwine Cemetery, Dodson Twp., Highland Co., Ohio, Find A Grave.com, Ralph H. Spilker, Find A Grave Memorial #112432302.

469 Ohio, County Births, 1841-2003 (County Courthouses), FamilySearch.org, Isma Faris, Highland Co., Ohio Birth Records, Vol. 3, pg. 134.

470 Ohio, Deaths, 1908-1932, 1938-2007, Ancestry.com, Isma Spilker, death cert. #035658.

471 Find A Grave—Spring Grove Cemetery, Cincinnati, Hamilton Co., Ohio, Find A Grave.com, Isma A. Faris Spilker, Find A Grave Memorial #79046065.

472 Ohio Death Certificate, Ohio Department of Health, Center for Vital and Health Statistics, 246 North High Street, Columbus, OH, Joseph Spilker, death cert. #55885.

473 Ohio, Birth Index, 1908-1964, Ancestry.com, Joseph Spilker, state file #1917033121.

474 Obituary of Joseph B. Spilker (Cincinnati, Ohio, Cincinnati Post, 30 Sep 1940), The Public Library of Cincinnati and Hamilton County, 800 Vine Street, Cincinnati, OH.

475 Ohio, Deaths, 1908-1932, 1938-2007, Ancestry.com, Shirley Rogers, death cert. #10938.

476 Ohio, Birth Index, 1908-1964, Ancestry.com, Shirley L. Spilker, state file #1922023952.

477 U.S., Social Security Applications and Claims Index, 1936-2007, Ancestry.com, Shirley Lois Spilker Rogers.

478 Obituary of Shirley L. Rogers (Cincinnati, Ohio, Cincinnati Post, 31 Jan 2003), The Public Library of Cincinnati and Hamilton County, 800 Vine Street, Cincinnati, OH.

479 Find A Grave—Troutwine Cemetery, Dodson Twp., Highland Co., Ohio, Find A Grave.com, Hazel A. Cruger, Find A Grave Memorial #150959867.

480 Florida Death Index 1877-1998, Ancestry.com, Harold J. Cruger.

481 Obituary of Harold J. Cruger (Kruger) (Hillsboro, Ohio, Hillsboro Press Gazette, 16 May 1974), Ohio History Center Archives and Library, Ohio History Center, 800 East 17th Avenue, Columbus, OH.

482 Find A Grave—Troutwine Cemetery, Dodson Twp., Highland Co., Ohio, Find A Grave.com, Harold J. Cruger, Find A Grave Memorial #150959843.

483 Find A Grave—Barnes Cemetery, Fairview, New Market Twp., Highland Co., Ohio, Find A Grave.com, Vernice Catherine Stroup Ludwick, Find A Grave Memorial #93776541.

484 Ohio, County Marriages, 1789-2013, FamilySearch.org, Claude H. Ludwick and "Verna" Stroup, Highland County, Ohio Marriage Records, Vol. 17, pg. 259, lic. #10956.

485 Ohio, County Births, 1841-2003 (County Courthouses), FamilySearch.org, Claud Hoggard Ludwick, Highland Co., Ohio Birth Record Vol. 3, pg. 262.

486 U.S., WWII Draft Registration Cards, 1942, Ancestry.com, Claude Ludwick, Dodson Twp., Highland Co., Ohio.

487 Ohio, Deaths, 1908-1932, 1938-2007, Ancestry.com, Claude H. Ludwick, death cert. #012631.

488 Obituary of Claude H. Ludwick (Hillsboro, Ohio, Press-Gazette, 17 Feb 1978) Highland County District Library, 10 Willettsville Pike, Hillsboro, OH.

489 Find A Grave—Barnes Cemetery, Fairview, New Market Twp., Highland Co., Ohio, Find A Grave.com, Claude Hogard Ludwick, Find A Grave Memorial #93776549.

490 Florida Death Index 1877-1998, Ancestry.com, Dwight H. Ludwick.

491 Ohio, Deaths, 1908-1932, 1938-2007, Ancestry.com, Lloyd Ludwick, death cert. #01945.

492 Obituary of Harold S. Ludwick (Hillsboro, Ohio, Press-Gazette, 27 Aug 1996), Highland County District Library, 10 Willettsville Pike, Hillsboro, OH.

493 Ohio, Birth Index, 1908-1964, Ancestry.com, "Evert" Ludwick, state file #1921087250.

494 Ohio, Deaths, 1908-1932, 1938-2007, Ancestry.com, Everett O. Ludwick, death cert. #005653.

495 Obituary of Everett "Rosie" Ludwick, (Hillsboro, Ohio, Hillsboro Press-Gazette, 21 Jun 1987), Highland County District Library, 10 Willettsville Pike, Hillsboro, OH.

496 Ohio, Birth Index, 1908-1964, Ancestry.com, Ludwick, 06 Aug 1922, Highland Co.

497 Obituary of Lowell A. Ludwick, Highland County District Library, 10 Willettsville Pike, Hillsboro, OH, Hillsboro (OH) Press-Gazette, 17 Nov 1961.

498 Ohio, Deaths, 1908-1932, 1938-2007, Ancestry.com, Lowell A. Ludwick, death cert. #76145.

499 Find A Grave—Stroup Cemetery, Dodson Twp., Highland Co., Ohio, Find A Grave.com, Clarence H. Stroup. Find A Grave Memorial #133402271.

500 Obituary of Lucile Stroup (Xenia, Ohio, Xenia Daily Gazette, 11 Jun 2004), Greene County Public Library-Xenia Community Library, Greene County Room, 76 East Market Street, Xenia, OH.

501 U.S., Social Security Applications and Claims Index, 1936-2007, Ancestry.com, Electra Lucile Connor Stroup.

502 Find A Grave—Stroup Cemetery, Dodson Twp., Highland Co., Ohio, Find A Grave.com, E. Lucile Connor Stroup, Find A Grave Memorial #133402254.

503 Ohio, Birth Index, 1908-1964, Ancestry.com, James Richard Stroup, state file #1937086745.

504 Obituary of James R. Stroup (Xenia, Ohio, Xenia Daily Gazette, 10 Mar 2014), Greene County Public Library-Xenia Community Library, Greene County Room, 76 East Market Street, Xenia, OH.

505 Find A Grave—Sugar Grove Cemetery, Wilmington, Union Twp., Clinton Co., Ohio, Find A Grave.com, Sadie Ballentine Vance, Find A Grave Memorial #130619839.

506 Ohio, County Births, 1841-2003 (County Courthouses), FamilySearch.org, Silas D. Vance, Clinton County, Ohio Birth Record Vol. 2, pg. 195.

507 U.S., WWI Draft Registration Cards, 1917-1918, Ancestry.com, Silas Laymon Vance, Westboro, Ohio.

508 Ohio, Deaths, 1908-1932, 1938-2007, Ancestry.com, Silas L. Vance, death cert. #25861.

509 Obituary of Silas Vance, (Hillsboro, Ohio, Press-Gazette, 02 May 1961), Highland County District Library, 10 Willettsville Pike, Hillsboro, OH.

510 Find A Grave—Sugar Grove Cemetery, Wilmington, Union Twp., Clinton Co., Ohio, Find A Grave.com, Silas Laymon Vance, Find A Grave Memorial #130619828.

511 Ohio, Deaths, 1908-1932, 1938-2007, Ancestry.com, Thelma L. Fudge, death cert. #019596.

512 Ohio, County Births, 1841-2003 (County Courthouses), FamilySearch.org, Thelma Lavonne Vance, Clinton Co., Ohio Birth Records, Delayed births with index, 1964-1967, Co. 35, pg. 178, #13978-A.

513 Obituary of Thelma Fudge (Wooster Daily Record, Wooster, Ohio), Wayne County Public Library (Ohio), 220 West Liberty Street, Wooster, OH.

514 Ohio, Deaths, 1908-1932, 1938-2007, Ancestry.com, Inez Bowman, death cert. #022340.

515 Ohio, Birth Index, 1908-1964, Ancestry.com, Inez Vance, state file #1921033200.

516 U.S., Social Security Application and Claims Index, 1936-2007, Ancestry.com, Inez Vance Bowman.

517 Ohio Death Certificate, Ohio Department of Health, Center for Vital and Health Statistics, 246 North High Street, Columbus, OH, Robert N. Vance, death cert. #40256.

518 Find A Grave—Deerfield Cemetery, South Lebanon, Union Twp., Warren Co., Ohio, Find A Grave.com, Letha M. Henderson, Find A Grave Memorial #16494245.

519 U.S., WWI Draft Registration Cards, 1917-1918, Ancestry.com, Ennis Edmond Hawthorne, Springfield, Springfield Twp., Clark Co., Ohio.

520 Ohio, County Births, 1841-2003 (County Courthouses), FamilySearch.org, Ennis E. Hawthorn (sic), Clinton County, Ohio Birth Record Vol. 3, pg. 73. Blanchester.

521 Ohio, Deaths, 1908-1932, 1938-2007, Ancestry.com, Ennis Hawthorne, death cert. #61251.

522 Find A Grave—Greenlawn Cemetery, Milford, Miami Twp., Clermont Co., Ohio, Find A Grave.com, Ennis E. Hawthorne, Find A Grave Memorial #141100351.

523 Ohio, County Births, 1841-2003 (County Courthouses), FamilySearch.org, Charles Cleveland Henderson, Warren Co., Ohio Birth Records, Delayed births with index, 1951-1952, Vol. 12, Case #1306. Born near Sardinia, Brown Co., Ohio.

524 U.S., Social Security Application and Claims Index, 1936-2007, Ancestry.com, Charles Cleveland Henderson.

525 Ohio, Deaths, 1908-1932, 1938-2007, Ancestry.com, Charles Henderson, death cert. #31509.

526 "Henderson Rites Held Tuesday" (Lebanon, Ohio, The Western Star, 20 Apr 1964), Warren County History Center Library, 105 South Broadway Street, Lebanon, OH.

527 Find A Grave—Deerfield Cemetery, South Lebanon, Union Twp., Warren Co., Ohio, Find A Grave.com, Charles C. Henderson, Find A Grave Memorial #16494243.

528 U.S., WWI Draft Registration Cards, 1917-1918, Ancestry.com, Charles Cleveland Henderson, Lebanon, Warren Co., Ohio.

529 U.S., WWII Draft Registration Cards, 1942, Ancestry.com, Charles Cleveland Henderson, Morrow, Warren Co., Ohio.

530 Ohio, Deaths, 1908-1932, 1938-2007, Ancestry.com, Betty Louise Fisher, death cert. #098013.

531 Obituary of Betty L. Fisher (Cincinnati, Ohio, Cincinnati Post, 14 Dec 1998), The Public Library of Cincinnati and Hamilton County, 800 Vine Street, Cincinnati, OH.

532 Find A Grave—Gate of Heaven Cemetery, Montgomery, Sycamore Twp., Hamilton Co., Ohio, Find A Grave.com, Frank Pegan, Find A Grave Memorial #86990109.

533 U.S., WWII Draft Registration Cards, 1942, Ancestry.com, Frank J. Pegan, Norwood, Ohio.

534 U.S., WWI Draft Registration Cards, 1917-1918, Ancestry.com, Frank James Pegan, Hamilton Co., Ohio.

535 U.S., Social Security Applications and Claims Index, 1936-2007, Ancestry.com, Frank J. Pegan.

536 Ohio, County Marriages, 1789-2013, FamilySearch.org, Frank J. Pegan and Clara Fye, Hamilton County, Ohio Marriage Records, Vol. 272, lic. #214 (no page indicated).

537 Ohio, County Births, 1841-2003 (County Courthouses), FamilySearch.org, "Lizzie" Fye, 26 Feb 1895, Hamilton County Births, Vol. 1, pg. 97.

538 Ohio, Deaths, 1908-1932, 1938-2007, Ancestry.com, Clara Pegan, death cert. #020214.

539 Find A Grave—Gate of Heaven Cemetery, Montgomery, Sycamore Twp., Hamilton Co., Ohio, Find A Grave.com, Clara E. Pegan, Find A Grave Memorial #86990108.

540 Phone interview with Mary Pegan Kissel, Montgomery, OH, Ann Miller Carr, author, 09 Feb 2012.

541 California, Death Index, 1940-1997, Ancestry.com, Robert Henry Pegan.

542 Ohio, Birth Index, 1908-1964, Ancestry.com, Robert Pegan, state file #1917097643.

543 California Death Certificate, California Health and Strategic Planning, Vital Records, M.S. 5103, P.O. Box 997410, Sacramento, CA, Robert H. Pegan, death cert. #90-092659.

544 Ohio, Deaths, 1908-1932, 1938-2007, Ancestry.com, Ruth Mary Dennig, death cert. #93374.

545 U.S., Social Security Applications and Claims Index, 1936-2007, Ancestry.com, Ruth Mary Pegan Dennig.

546 Ohio, Birth Index, 1908-1964, Ancestry.com, Mary C. "Pegon", state file #1926080988.

547 Find A Grave—Calvary Cemetery and Mausoleum, St. Louis, Missouri, Find A Grave.com, Marie E. Pegan, Find A Grave Memorial #47414602.

548 U.S., Social Security Applications and Claims Index, 1936-2007, Ancestry.com, Marie E. Pegan.

549 Obituary of William H. Pegan (St. Louis, Missouri, St. Louis Post-Dispatch, 08 Nov 1963), St. Louis County Public Library, 1640 South Lindbergh Boulevard, St. Louis, MO.

550 Obituary of Betty J. Fisher (St. Louis, Missouri, St. Louis Post-Dispatch, 27 Oct 2010), St. Louis County Public Library, 1640 South Lindbergh Boulevard, St. Louis, MO.

551 Obituary of Courtland H. Pegan (Hillsboro, Ohio, Press-Gazette, 27 Jun 1983), Highland County District Library, 10 Willettsville Pike, Hillsboro, OH.

552 Ohio, County Marriages, 1789-2013, FamilySearch.org, Courtland H. Pegan and Stella M. Holladay, Highland County, Ohio Marriage Records, Vol. 19, pg. 501, lic. #13906.

553 Ohio, County Births, 1841-2003 (County Courthouses), FamilySearch.org, Stella "Holiday", Clinton Co., Ohio Birth Record Vol. 4, pg. 82.

554 Ohio, Births and Christenings Index, 1800-1962, Ancestry.com, Stella "Holiday".

555 Kentucky Death Index, 1911-2000, Ancestry.com, Stella M. Pegan, death cert. #21252.

556 Obituary of Stella M. Pegan (Hillsboro, Ohio, Press-Gazette, 22 Sep 1970), Highland County District Library, 10 Willettsville Pike, Hillsboro, OH.

557 Ohio, Deaths, 1908-1932, 1938-2007, Ancestry.com, "Pegan", died September 17, 1970, death cert. #202688.

558 "…Dinner guests in the home of Mr. and Mrs. Monroe Hamilton on June 13 were Mr. and Mrs. Courtland Pegan of Washington Court House…" (Hillsboro, Ohio, Press-

Gazette, 25 Jun 1948), Highland County District Library, 10 Willettsville Pike, Hillsboro, OH.

559 Obituary of Henry L. Pegan (Hillsboro, Ohio, Press-Gazette, 11 Jun 1954), Highland County District Library, 10 Willettsville Pike, Hillsboro, OH.

560 "Stay Away From Fires" (Hillsboro, Ohio, Press-Gazette, 06 Oct 1972), Highland County District Library, 10 Willettsville Pike, Hillsboro, OH.

561 Phone interview with Thelma Smith, Hesperia, CA, Ann Miller Carr, author, 12 Mar 2011.

562 Ohio, Birth Index, 1908-1964, Ancestry.com, Elma Pegan, state file #1926064672.

563 Obituary of Elma Mary May (Modetz Funeral Homes, 22 Aug 2013), Modetz Funeral Home-Waterford, 5630 Pontiac Road, Waterford, MI, http://www.modetzfuneralhomes.com/obituaries/obituary-listings?obId=31353, Captured 10 Oct 2013.

564 Ohio, Birth Index, 1908-1964, Ancestry.com, Shirley Pegan, state file #1930022775.

565 Obituary of Shirley C. Boyd (Searcy, Arkansas, Powell Funeral Home online, 07 Oct 2010), Powell Funeral Home, 2602 West Beebe-Capps Expressway, Searcy, AR. http://www.powellfuneralhome.net/obituaries.aspx?turl=http://hosting-24809.tributes.com/obituary/show/shirley-c.-boyd-89563885

566 Ohio, Birth Index, 1908-1964, Ancestry.com, Robert "G." Pegan, fa. Courtland, state file #1933058307.

567 Obituary of Robert Ivan Pegan (Hillsboro, Ohio, Press-Gazette, 14 Feb 1978), Highland County District Library, 10 Willettsville Pike, Hillsboro, OH.

568 Ohio, Deaths, 1908-1932, 1938-2007, Ancestry.com, Robert I. Pegan, death cert. #012629.

569 Obituary of Russell W. Pegan (Hillsboro, Ohio, Press-Gazette, 11 Aug 2008), Highland County District Library, 10 Willettsville Pike, Hillsboro, OH.

570 Obituary of Clarence "Bud" Pegan (Wilmington, Ohio, Wilmington News-Journal, 24 Jun 1988), Pegan family file, The Clinton County History Center, 149 East Locust Street, Wilmington, OH.

571 Ohio, County Marriages, 1789-2013, FamilySearch.org, Clarence C. Pegan and Grace C. Walsh, Brown County, Ohio Marriage Records, Vol. 30, pg. 186, lic.#24720.

572 Ohio, Deaths, 1908-1932, 1938-2007, Ancestry.com, Grace C. Pegan, death cert. #021874.

573 Obituary of Grace Pegan (Wilmington, Ohio, Wilmington News-Journal, 04 Mar 1977), Pegan family file, The Clinton County History Center, 149 East Locust Street, Wilmington, OH.

574 Ohio, Birth Index, 1908-1964, Ancestry.com, Richard Pegan, state file #1932084507.

575 Obituary of Richard Pegan (Wilmington, Ohio, Wilmington News-Journal, 09 Dec 1986), Wilmington Public Library of Clinton County, 268 North South Street, Wilmington, OH.

576 Ohio, Deaths, 1908-1932, 1938-2007, Ancestry.com, Richard T. Pegan, death cert. #089839.

577 Ohio, Birth Index, 1908-1964, Ancestry.com, Rita G. Pegan, state file #1932084508.

578 Obituary of Rita G. Pegan Poston (Melbourne, FL, Florida Today, 18 Jun 2016), Catherine Schweinsburg Rood Central Library, Central Brevard Library and Reference Center, Documents and Genealogy Dept., 308 Forest Ave., Cocoa, FL.

579 Ohio, Deaths, 1908-1932, 1938-2007, Ancestry.com, Julia Evelyn Macke, death cert. #021729.

580 U.S., Social Security Applications and Claims Index, 1936-2007, Ancestry.com, Julia Evelyn Pegan Macke.

581 Ohio, Deaths, 1908-1932, 1938-2007, Ancestry.com, James Eugene Pegan, death cert. #64720.

582 U.S., Social Security Applications and Claims Index, 1936-2007, Ancestry.com, James Eugene Pegan.

583 Obituary of Lawrence Joseph Pegan (Lynchburg, Ohio, Turner Funeral Home online, 08 Oct 2013), Turner Funeral Homes, 201 North Broadway Street, Lynchburg, OH, http://www.turnerfuneralhomes.cc/memsol.cgi?user_id=1122988

584 Find A Grave—St. Martin Cemetery, St. Martin, Perry Twp., Brown Co., Ohio, Find A Grave.com, Lawrence Joseph "Larry" Pegan, Find A Grave Memorial #159375645.

585 Ohio, Birth Index, 1908-1964, Ancestry.com, Clarence E. Pegan, state file #1950102128.

586 Obituary of Clarence Edward Pegan II (Hillsboro, OH, The Highland County Times Gazette, 11 Sep 2013), Highland County District Library, 10 Willettsville Pike, Hillsboro, OH.

587 Find A Grave—St. Martin Cemetery, St. Martin, Perry Twp., Brown Co., Ohio, Find A Grave.com, Clarence Edward "Eddie" Pegan, Find A Grave Memorial #116869065.

588 Ohio, County Marriages, 1789-2013, FamilySearch.org, Harley Stubbs and Frances Pegan, Highland County, Ohio Marriage Records, Vol. 20, pg. 492, lic. #15044.

589 Ohio, County Births, 1841-2003 (County Courthouses), FamilySearch.org, Harley Stubbs, Clark Co., Ohio Birth Record Vol. 4, pg. 180.

590 Ohio, Deaths, 1908-1932, 1938-2007, Ancestry.com, Harley E. Stubbs, death cert. #044109.

591 Obituary of Harley Stubbs (Hillsboro, Ohio, Press-Gazette, 6 Jun 1976), Highland County District Library, 10 Willettsville Pike, Hillsboro, OH.

592 Find A Grave—Cedar Hill Cemetery, Suitland, Prince George's Co., Maryland, Find A Grave.com, Mabel Stoup, Find A Grave Memorial #181067042.

593 Ohio, County Marriages, 1789-2013, FamilySearch.org, Galo S. Stroup and Mabel L. Thompson, Highland County, Ohio Marriage Records, Vol. 18, pg. 422, lic. #12595.

594 Ohio, County Births, 1841-2003 (County Courthouses), FamilySearch.org, Galo Stroup, Highland Co., Ohio Birth Record Vol. 3, pg. 436.

595 Obituary of Galo S. Stroup (Hillsboro, Ohio, Press-Gazette, 01 Oct 1968), Highland County District Library, 10 Willettsville Pike, Hillsboro, OH.

596 Find A Grave—Cedar Hill Cemetery, Suitland, Prince George's Co., Maryland, Find A Grave.com, Galo Stroup, Find A Grave Memorial #181066935.

597 U.S., Social Security Applications and Claims Index, 1936-2007, Ancestry.com, Thurl Esto Stroup.

598 U.S., Department of Veterans Affairs BIRLS File, 1850-2010, Ancestry.com, Thurl Stroup.

599 Obituary of Thurl E.. Stroup (Washington, D.C, Washington Post, 01 Oct 1982), Historical Newspapers, Birth Marriage & Death Announcements, 1851-2003. Ancestry.com.

600 Find A Grave—Oxford Cemetery, Oxford, Butler Co., Ohio, Find A Grave.com, Lillie M. Duvall, Find A Grave Memorial #131611044.

601 Ohio, County Marriages, 1789-2013, FamilySearch.org, A.C. DuVall and Lillie Daggy, Highland County, Ohio Marriage Records, Vol. 15, pg. 130. lic. #6330.

602 Ohio Death Certificate, Ohio Department of Health, Center for Vital and Health Statistics, 246 North High Street, Columbus, OH, Alexander Duvall, death cert. #542.

603 Find A Grave—Oxford Cemetery, Oxford, Chester Co., Pennsylvania, Find A Grave.com, Alex C. Duvall, Find A Grave Memorial #131611156.

604 Butler County, Ohio Marriage Records, Butler County, Ohio Records Center and Archives, 123 North Third Street, Hamilton, OH, Hudson H. Wagonfield and Laura Duvall, Butler County, Ohio Marriage Records, Vol. 39, pg. 419.

605 Ohio Death Certificate, Ohio Department of Health, Center for Vital and Health Statistics, 246 North High Street, Columbus, OH, Hudson H. Wagonfield, death cert. #41644.

606 Obituary of Hudson Wagonfield (Hamilton, Ohio, Hamilton Journal, 02 Jul 1951), Ohio History Center Archives and Library, Ohio History Center, 800 East 17th Avenue, Columbus, OH.

607 Find A Grave—Darrtown Pioneer Cemetery, Darrtown, Milford Twp., Butler Co., Ohio, Find A Grave.com, Hudson H. Wagonfield, Find A Grave Memorial #40641243.

608 California, Death Index, 1940-1997, Ancestry.com, Gwendolyn Kleinfelter.

609 Ohio, Birth Index, 1908-1964, Ancestry.com, John "Luuoen" DuVall, state file #1913017472.

610 Indiana, Death Certificates, 1908-2011, Ancestry.com, John L. DuVall, death cert. #84-000673.

611 Ohio, County Marriages, 1789-2013, FamilySearch.org, Wm. Kelley Roberts and Louie Daggy, Highland County, Ohio Marriage Records, Vol. 15, pg. 223, lic. #6815.

612 U.S., WWII Draft Registration Cards, 1942, Ancestry.com, William "Kelley" Roberts, Brown Co., Ohio.

613 Obituary of William Kelly Roberts (Hillsboro, Ohio, Press-Gazette, 01 Jan 1960), Highland County District Library, 10 Willettsville Pike, Hillsboro, OH.

614 Ohio, Deaths, 1908-1932, 1938-2007, Ancestry.com, William K. Roberts, death cert. #88814.

615 Find A Grave—Sugartree Ridge Cemetery, Concord Twp., Highland Co., Ohio, Find A Grave.com, W. Kelly Roberts, Find A Grave Memorial #87989352.

616 Ohio, County Marriages, 1789-2013, FamilySearch.org, Wm. Kelley Roberts and Louie Daggy, Highland County, Ohio Marriage Records, Vol. 17, pg. 209, lic. #10556.

617 Indiana Births, 1880-1920, Ancestry.com, (Mary Jane Brookfield) Brookfield, female, b. 10 May 1898, Howard County, Indiana Birth Records Index A-K Inclusive, Volume CH-1, pg. 14 (Fa. Albert, Mo. Clara).

618 Greenwood Cemetery Records, Greenwood Cemetery Association, 1602 Greenwood Avenue, Hamilton, OH http://gwdbow.cemeterydata.com, Mary Jane Daggy Stubbs, Section W, Lot:240, Space:2.

619 Ohio, Deaths, 1908-1932, 1938-2007, Ancestry.com, Mary J. Stubbs, death cert. #000492.

620 Find A Grave—Greenwood Cemetery, Hamilton, Butler Co., Ohio, Find A Grave.com, Mary Jane Stubbs, Find A Grave Memorial #155791805.

621 Obituary of Mrs. Stubbs (Hamilton, Ohio, Hamilton Daily News, 16 Jan 1968), Hamilton Lane Library, 300 North Third Street, Hamilton, OH.

622 Ohio Death Certificate, Ohio Department of Health, Center for Vital and Health Statistics, 246 North High Street, Columbus, OH, Joseph Hamer Daggy, death cert. #401.

623 Obituary of Betty Jane Stitsinger Reidinger (Hamilton, Ohio, Hamilton Journal, 13 Sep 2008), Hamilton Lane Library, 300 North Third Street, Hamilton, OH.

624 Find A Grave—Union Cemetery, Taylorsville, White Oak Twp., Highland Co., Ohio, Find A Grave.com, Infant Son Surber, Find A Grave Memorial #103751453.

625 Obituary of Earl L. Surber (Hillsboro, Ohio, Highland County Press-Gazette, 03 Mar 1964), Highland County District Library, 10 Willettsville Pike, Hillsboro, OH.

626 Find A Grave—Union Cemetery, Taylorsville, White Oak Twp., Highland Co., Ohio, Find A Grave.com, Earl L. Surber, Find A Grave Memorial #132309727.

627 Ohio, County Marriages, 1789-2013, FamilySearch.org, Earl L. Surber and Ganella Roberts, Highland County, Ohio Marriage Records, Vol. 17, pg. 179, lic. #10799.

628 Ohio, County Births, 1841-2003 (County Courthouses), FamilySearch.org, Ganella Ruth Roberts, Highland Co., Ohio Birth Record Vol. 3, pg. 390.

629 Ohio, Deaths, 1908-1932, 1938-2007, Ancestry.com, Ganelle R. Surber, death cert. #025032.

630 Obituary of Ganelle Surber (Hillsboro, Ohio, Press-Gazette, 05 Apr 1976), Highland County District Library, 10 Willettsville Pike, Hillsboro, OH.

631 Find A Grave—Union Cemetery, Taylorsville, White Oak Twp., Highland Co., Ohio, Find A Grave.com, Ganelle Ruth Roberts Surber, Find A Grave Memorial #132310182.

632 Ohio Death Certificate, Ohio Department of Health, Center for Vital and Health Statistics, 246 North High Street, Columbus, OH, Mary Sarah Surber, death cert. #54529.

633 Obituary of Maynard R. Surber (Hillsboro, Ohio, The Highland County Times Index, 27 Jul 2012), Highland County District Library, 10 Willettsville Pike, Hillsboro, OH.

634 Ohio, Birth Index, 1908-1964, Ancestry.com, "Raynard" Surber, mo. maiden name Roberts, state file #1920034172.

635 Obituary of Cedric Surber (Hillsboro, Ohio, The Highland County Times-Herald, 23 Apr 2013), Highland County District Library, 10 Willettsville Pike, Hillsboro, OH.

636 Ohio, County Marriages, 1789-2013, FamilySearch.org, Cedric L. Surber and M. Ruth Newhouse, Highland County, Ohio Marriage Records, Vol. 22, pg. 170, lic. #16732.

637 Find A Grave—Hamer Township Cemetery, Hamer Twp., Highland Co., Ohio, Find A Grave.com, Hugh Pegan, Find A Grave Memorial #132658429.

638 Ohio, County Marriages, 1789-2013, FamilySearch.org, Hugh "E." Pegan and Lillian B. King, Highland County, Ohio Marriage Records, Vol. 20, pg. 180, lic. #14421.

639 Ohio, Deaths, 1908-1932, 1938-2007, Ancestry.com, Lillian Blanche Pegan, death cert. #073111.

640 Obituary of Lillian B. Pegan (Hillsboro, Ohio, Hillsboro Times-Gazette, 28 Aug 2001), Highland County District Library, 10 Willettsville Pike, Hillsboro, OH.

641 Find A Grave—Hamer Township Cemetery, Hamer Twp., Highland Co., Ohio, Find A Grave.com, Lillian Pegan, Find A Grave Memorial #132658466.

642 Obituary of Lowell R. Pegan (Hillsboro, Ohio, Press-Gazette, 14 Jul 1975), Highland County District Library, 10 Willettsville Pike, Hillsboro, OH.

643 Ohio, Birth Index, 1908-1964, Ancestry.com, Lowell "Pagan", state file #1934017833.

644 Ohio, Deaths, 1908-1932, 1938-2007, Ancestry.com, Lowell Pegan, death cert. #051325.

645 Find A Grave—Union Cemetery, Taylorsville, White Oak Twp., Highland Co., Ohio, Find A Grave.com, Harlie J. Pegan, Find A Grave Memorial #123901006.

646 Obituary of Peggy Kies (Wilmington, Ohio, Wilmington News Journal, 06 Nov 1989), Pegan family file, The Clinton County History Center, 149 East Locust Street, Wilmington, OH.

647 The Genealogical Committee of The Clinton County Historical Society, Cemetery Records of Clinton Co., Ohio, 1798-1998, Martinsville IOOF Cemetery: Margaret "Peggy" Kies. Clinton County, Ohio Records Center and Archives, 111 South Nelson Avenue, Suite 3, Wilmington, OH.

648 Find A Grave—New Loramie Valley Cemetery, Botkins, Dinsmore Twp., Shelby Co., Ohio, Find A Grave.com, Alfred A. Kies, Find A Grave Memorial #44791050.

649 Florida Death Index 1877-1998, Ancestry.com, Alfred A. Kies.

650 Find A Grave—Martinsville IOOF Cemetery, Martinsville, Clark Twp., Clinton Co., Ohio, Find A Grave.com, Ruby W. Woodall, Find A Grave Memorial #119318662.

651 "Mr and Mrs. Frank Pegan announce the marriage of their daughter Ruth…" (Wilmington, Ohio, Wilmington News Journal, 11 Jul 1941), Wilmington Public Library of Clinton County, 268 North South Street, Wilmington, OH.

652 "Court News" (Hillsboro, Ohio, Hillsboro Press Gazette, 11 Apr 1947), Highland County District Library, 10 Willettsville Pike, Hillsboro, Ohio.

653 Ohio, County Marriages, 1789-2013, FamilySearch.org, Harold W. "Rammell" and Ruby PeGan, Highland County, Ohio Marriage Records, Vol. 22, pg. 592, #18474.

654 Marriage License of Harold Rammel and Ruby Pegan (Anderson), Highland County, Ohio Probate Court, Highland County Courthouse, 105 North High Street, Hillsboro, OH, Highland County Marriage Book 22, pg. 592, #18474.

655 Obituary of Harold "Bill" Rammel (Greenfield, Ohio, Greenfield Daily Times, 10 Feb 1992), Highland County District Library, 10 Willettsville Pike, Hillsboro, OH.

656 Ohio, Deaths, 1908-1932, 1938-2007, Ancestry.com, Harold Rammel, death cert. #016853.

657 U.S., Social Security Applications and Claims Index, 1936-2007, Ancestry.com, Harold Rammel.

658 Find A Grave—New Lynchburg Masonic Cemetery/Lynchburg F & AM Cemetery, Lynchburg, Dodson Twp., Highland Co., Ohio, Find A Grave.com, Harold Rammel, Find A Grave Memorial #104366140.

659 "Blanchester" (Wilmington, Ohio, Wilmington News Journal, 04 Dec 1958), Wilmington Public Library of Clinton County, 268 North South Street, Wilmington, OH.

660 U.S., Social Security Applications and Claims Index, 1936-2007, Ancestry.com, Arthur Edward Woodall.

661 Ohio, Deaths, 1908-1932, 1938-2007, Ancestry.com, Arthur E. Woodall, death cert. #055069.

662 Obituary of Arthur E. Woodall Sr., (Dayton, Ohio, Dayton Daily Journal, 15 Jul 1986), Dayton Metro Library, 215 East Third Street. Dayton, OH.

663 Find A Grave—Calvary Cemetery, Dayton, Montgomery Co., Ohio, Find A Grave.com, Arthur E. Woodall, Sr., Find A Grave Memorial #134065174.

664 Obituary of Harold W. PeGan (Hillsboro, Ohio, Press-Gazette, 21 Nov 1995), Highland County District Library, 10 Willettsville Pike, Hillsboro, OH.

665 The Genealogical Committee of The Clinton County Historical Society, Cemetery Records of Clinton Co., Ohio, 1798-1998, Martinsville IOOF Cemetery: Harold West Pegan. Clinton County, Ohio Records Center and Archives, 111 South Nelson Avenue, Suite 3, Wilmington, OH.

666 Ohio, County Marriages, 1789-2013, FamilySearch.org, Harold PeGan and Velma Pointer, Highland County, Ohio Marriage Records, Vol. 22, pg. 197, #16787.

667 Ohio, Birth Index, 1908-1964, Ancestry.com, Velma L. Powell, state birth cert. #1924031695.

668 Ohio, Deaths, 1908-1932, 1938-2007, Ancestry.com, Velma Pegan, death cert. #063368.

669 Obituary of Velma PeGan (Hillsboro, Ohio, Press-Gazette, 16 Sep 1975), Highland County District Library, 10 Willettsville Pike, Hillsboro, OH.

670 The Genealogical Committee of The Clinton County Historical Society, Cemetery Records of Clinton Co., Ohio, 1798-1998, Martinsville IOOF Cemetery: Velma Pegan. Clinton County, Ohio Records Center and Archives, 111 South Nelson Avenue, Suite 3, Wilmington, OH.

671 Ohio Marriage Index, 1970-1972-2007, Ancestry.com, Harold W. Pegan and Hazel L. Howard, Montgomery County, Ohio Marriage Records, Ohio state Vol. 11117, lic. #13949.

672 Ohio, Birth Index, 1908-1964, Ancestry.com, Hazel Gebhart, state file #1913029172.

673 Ohio, Deaths, 1908-1932, 1938-2007, Ancestry.com, Hazel Howard Pegan, death cert. #062553.

674 Find A Grave—Woodland Cemetery and Arboretum, Dayton, Montgomery Co., Ohio, Find A Grave.com, Hazel Gephart Pegan, Find A Grave Memoria #108806576.

675 Ohio, Deaths, 1908-1932, 1938-2007, Ancestry.com, Allan J. Pegan, death cert. #088291.

676 Obituary of Allen J. PeGan Sr. (Hillsboro, Ohio, Highland County Times Gazette, 21 Oct 1998), Highland County District Library, 10 Willettsville Pike, Hillsboro, OH.

677 Obituary of Son Pegan, (Wilmington, Ohio, Wilmington News Journal, 25 Feb 1959), Pegan family file, The Clinton County History Center, 149 East Locust Street, Wilmington, OH.

678 Find A Grave—Martinsville IOOF Cemetery, Martinsville, Clark Twp., Clinton Co., Ohio, Find A Grave.com, Ruth M. Pegan Holmes, Find A Grave Memorial #119318497.

679 Ohio, County Marriages, 1789-2013, FamilySearch.org, Raymond Holmes and Ruth M. Pegan, Highland County, Ohio Marriage Records, Vol. 22, pg. 19, lic. #16432.

680 U.S., Department of Veterans Affairs BIRLS Death File, 1850-2010, Ancestry.com, Raymond Holmes.

681 Ohio, Birth Index, 1908-1964, Ancestry.com, Raymond Holmes, state file #1919011598.

682 Find A Grave—Southlawn Cemetery, South Bend, St. Joseph Co., Indiana, Find A Grave.com, Raymond Holmes, Find A Grave Memorial #95464909.

683 Obituary of Raymond Holmes (South Bend, Indiana, South Bend Tribune, 21 Apr 1986), St. Joseph County Public Library, 304 South Main Street, South Bend, IN.

684 Indiana, Marriage Certificates, 1917-2005, Ancestry.com, Robert E. Scheler II and (Daughter) Holmes, St. Joseph County, Indiana Marriage Records, Indiana state lic. #78-049835.

685 Find A Grave—Martinsville IOOF Cemetery, Martinsville, Clark Twp., Clinton Co., Ohio, Find A Grave.com, Infant Pegan, Find A Grave Memorial #105022591. On her twin sister Ruth M. Holmes' tombstone in Martinsville IOOF Cemetery, this girl is named as "Rita G."

686 Find A Grave—New Lynchburg Masonic Cemetery/Lynchburg F & AM Cemetery, Lynchburg, Dodson Twp., Highland Co., Ohio, Find A Grave.com, Paul S. Pegan, Find A Grave Memorial #98707483.

687 "Lynchburg" (Hillsboro, Ohio, Press-Gazette, 16 May 1939), Highland County District Library, 10 Willettsville Pike, Hillsboro, OH.

688 Find A Grave—New Lynchburg Masonic Cemetery/Lynchburg F & AM Cemetery, Lynchburg, Dodson Twp., Highland Co., Ohio, Find A Grave.com, Mary L. Pegan, Find A Grave Memorial #98709230.

689 Obituary of Audrey West (Wilmington, Ohio, Wilmington News Journal, 07 Apr 1997), The Clinton County History Center, 149 East Locust Street, Wilmington, OH.

690 Find A Grave—Clinton County Memory Gardens, Union Twp., Clinton Co., Ohio, Find A Grave.com, Audrey West, Find A Grave Memorial #181593884.

691 Obituary of George Elton West (Wilmington, Ohio, Wilmington News Journal, 23 Dec 2008), Wilmington Public Library of Clinton County, 268 North South Street, Wilmington, OH.

692 Find A Grave—Clinton County Memory Gardens, Union Twp., Clinton Co., Ohio, Find A Grave.com, George E. West, Find A Grave Memorial #181593816.

693 Obituary of Helen Ludwick, (Wilmington, Ohio, Wilmington News Journal, 19 Feb 2004), Pegan family file, The Clinton County History Center, 149 East Locust Street, Wilmington, OH.

694 Find A Grave—Barnes Cemetery, Fairview, New Market Twp., Highland Co., Ohio, Find A Grave.com, Helen Pegan Ludwick, Find A Grave Memorial #94474729.

695 Ohio, Birth Index, 1908-1964, Ancestry.com, Arthur Ludwick, state file #1943124419.

696 Obituary of Arthur Lowell Ludwick (Hillsboro, Ohio, Highland County Times-Gazette, 22 Jan 2014), Highland County District Library, 10 Willettsville Pike, Hillsboro, OH.

697 Find A Grave—Hamer Township Cemetery, Hamer Twp., Highland Co., Ohio, Find A Grave.com, Charles Randolph "Dolph" Philhower, Find A Grave Memorial #132582847.

698 Ohio, County Births, 1841-2003 (County Courthouses), FamilySearch.org, Ella Lorie Jones, Highland Co., Ohio Birth Records, Vol. 3, pg. 228.

699 Ohio, Deaths, 1908-1932, 1938-2007, Ancestry.com, Lorie E. Philhower, death cert. #019667.

700 Obituary of Lorie Philhower (Hillsboro, Ohio, Press Gazette, 27 Jan 1987) Highland County District Library, 10 Willettsville Pike, Hillsboro, OH.

701 Find A Grave—Hamer Township Cemetery, Hamer Twp., Highland Co., Ohio, Find A Grave.com, Ella Lorie Jones Philhower, Find A Grave Memorial #132582884.

702 Ohio, Birth Index, 1908-1964, Ancestry.com, J.B. Philhower, state file #1925004619.

703 Find A Grave—Hamer Township Cemetery, Hamer Twp., Highland Co., Ohio, Find A Grave.com, J. Bruce Philhower, Find A Grave Memorial #132597899.

704 Find A Grave—Greenfield Cemetery, Greenfield Twp., Highland Co., Ohio, Find A Grave.com, L. Donald Philhower, Find A Grave Memorial #99043156.

705 Obituary of L. Donald Philhower (Chillicothe, Ohio, Chillicothe Gazette, 22 May 1990), Chillicothe & Ross County Library, 140 South Paint Street, Chillicothe, OH.

706 Ohio, County Marriages, 1789-2013, FamilySearch.org, L. Donald Philhower and Chloe M. Coffman, Highland County, Ohio Marriage Records, Vol. 19, pg. 562, #14029.

707 Find A Grave—Greenfield Cemetery, Greenfield Twp., Highland Co., Ohio, Find A Grave.com, Chloe Marie Coffman Philhower, Find A Grave Memorial #99043361.

708 Ohio, Deaths, 1908-1932, 1938-2007, Ancestry.com, Chloe Philhower, death cert. #028796.

709 Ohio, Births and Christenings Index, 1800-1962, Ancestry.com, Chloe M. Coffman.

710 Obituary of Chloe C. Philhower (Columbus, Ohio, Columbus Dispatch, 01 Apr 1996), Columbus Metropolitan Library, 96 South Grant Avenue, Columbus, OH.

711 Find A Grave—Ferncliff Cemetery, Springfield, Springfield Twp., Clark Co., Ohio, Marcia L. Roush, Find A Grave Memorial #60770352.

712 Ohio, County Marriages, 1789-2013, FamilySearch.org, Kenneth Roush and Marcia Boesenberg, Clark County, Ohio Marriage Records, Vol. 31, pg. 8, lic. #15575.

713 California, Death Index, 1940-1997, Ancestry.com, Kenneth Roush.

714 Obituary of Kenneth H. Roush (Oakland, California, Oakland Tribune, 12 Mar 1977), Oakland Public Library, 125 14th Street, Oakland, CA.

715 Find A Grave—Evergreen Cemetery, Oakland, Alameda Co., California, Find A Grave.com, Kenneth E. Roush, Find A Grave Memorial #167170218.

716 California, Death Index, 1940-1997, Ancestry.com, Lois Ridgley Roush.

717 Obituary of Rev. Kenneth Edward Roush (Show Low, Arizona, White Mountain Independent, 01 Oct 2007), Owens Livingston Mortuary, 320 North 9th Street, Show Low, AZ; Online database: http://www.owenslivingstonmortuary.com/memsol.cgi?user_id=182690

718 Ohio, Birth Index, 1908-1964, Ancestry.com, Kenneth E. Roush, state file #1931063095.

719 Troutwine Cemetery, Dodson Twp., Highland Co., Ohio Records, Clinton Co. Records Center and Archives, 111 South Nelson Avenue, Suite 3, Wilmington, OH.

720 The Genealogical Committee of The Clinton County Historical Society, Cemetery Records of Clinton Co., Ohio, 1798-1998, Troutwine Cemetery: Josephine Luck. Clinton County, Ohio Records Center and Archives, 111 South Nelson Avenue, Suite 3, Wilmington, OH.

721 Ohio, Deaths, 1908-1932, 1938-2007, Ancestry.com, Albert J. Luck, death cert. #000858.

722 Obituary of Albert Luck (Wilmington, Ohio, Wilmington News Journal, 23 Jan 1994), Wilmington Public Library of Clinton County, 268 North South Street, Wilmington, OH.

723 Find A Grave—Troutwine Cemetery, Dodson Twp., Highland Co., Ohio, Find A Grave.com, Albert J. Luck, Find A Grave Memorial #30743516.

724 Ohio Deaths, 1908-1953, FamilySearch.org, Gary Lee Luck, death cert. #60313.

725 Find A Grave—Highland Memorial Park Cemetery, New Berlin, Waukesha Co., Wisconsin, Clarence L. Long, #160680443.

726 "Army Veterans Dorothy Cleppe and C.J. Long Wed Here Dec 21" (West Allis, Wisconsin, West Allis Star, 23 Dec 1945), Milwaukee Public Library, 814 West Wisconsin Avenue, Milwaukee, WI.

727 U.S., Social Security Applications and Claims Index, 1936-2007, Ancestry.com, Dorothy Virginia Cleppe Long.

728 Find A Grave—Highland Memorial Park Cemetery, New Berlin, Waukesha Co., Wisconsin, Dorothy Virginia Cleppe Long, #1606890466.

729 Obituary of Dorothy V. Long, (Milwaukee, Wisconsin, Milwaukee Journal, 04 Sep 2005), Milwaukee Public Library, 814 West Wisconsin Avenue, Milwaukee, WI.

730 U.S., Social Security Applications and Claims Index, 1936-2007, Ancestry.com, Dorothy Virginia Cleppe Long.

731 Nevada, Death Index, 1980-2012, Ancestry.com, Jeffrey Richard Long.

732 U.S., Social Security Applications and Claims Index, 1936-2007, Ancestry.com, John James Brown.

733 "A son was born at Siskiyou County General Hospital…" (Weed, California, Weed Press, 27 Feb 1948), The Genealogical Society of Siskiyou County, California Research Center, 912 South Main Street, Yreka, CA.

734 Find A Grave—Stroup Cemetery, Dodson Twp., Highland Co., Ohio, Find A Grave.com, Mary E. Carroll, Find A Grave Memorial #140074242.

735 Obituary of William Carroll (Cincinnati, Ohio, Cincinnati Post, 08 Dec 1953), The Public Library of Cincinnati and Hamilton County, 800 Vine Street, Cincinnati, OH.

736 Ohio, County Marriages, 1789-2013, FamilySearch.org, William M. Carroll and Dora E. Jones, Hamilton County, Ohio Marriage Records, Vol. 389, lic. #278.

737 Ohio Death Certificate, Ohio Department of Health, Center for Vital and Health Statistics, 246 North High Street, Columbus, OH, Dora Elizabeth Carroll, death cert. #24408.

738 Ohio, Deaths, 1908-1932, 1938-2007, Ancestry.com, Lillian M. Carroll, death cert. #051783.

739 Find A Grave—Spring Grove Cemetery, Cincinnati, Hamilton Co., Ohio, Find A Grave.com, Lillian Carroll, Find A Grave Memorial #78905366.

740 Ohio, Birth Index, 1908-1964, Ancestry.com, "Douglass" Carroll, state file #1940057731.

741 Obituary of Delbert A. Carroll (Hillsboro, Ohio, Hillsboro Press Gazette, 26 Feb 1991), Highland County District Library, 10 Willettsville Pike, Hillsboro, OH.

742 Find A Grave—New Lynchburg Masonic Cemetery/Lynchburg F & AM Cemetery, Lynchburg, Dodson Twp., Highland Co., Ohio, Find A Grave.com, Delbert A. Carroll, Find A Grave Memorial #103784319.

743 U.S. Public Records Index, 1950-1993, Vol. 1, Ancestry.com, Ancestry.com.

744 Ohio, County Marriage Records, 1774-1993, Ancestry.com, Delbert A. Carroll and Ruth L. Maas, Highland County, Ohio Marriage Records (married in Clinton County).

745 Ohio, County Marriages, 1789-2013, FamilySearch.org, Delbert A. Carroll and Ruth L. Maas, Highland Co., Ohio Marriage Records, Vol. 23, pg. 294, state file #70689 (married in Clinton Co., Ohio).

746 Ohio, Birth Index, 1908-1964, Ancestry.com, Ruth L. Maas, state file #1933015732.

747 Obituary of Carl D. Williams, Dayton Metro Library, 215 East Third Street. Dayton, OH, Dayton (OH) Daily News, pub. 30 Sep 1991.

748 Find A Grave—New Lynchburg Masonic Cemetery/Lynchburg F & AM Cemetery, Lynchburg, Dodson Twp., Highland Co., Ohio, Find A Grave.com, Carl D. Williams, Find A Grave Memorial #97788699.

749 Ohio, County Marriages, 1789-2013, FamilySearch.org, Carl D. Williams and Madge R. Ruble. Highland County, Ohio Marriage Records, Vol. 19, pg 287, lic.#13478.

750 Ohio, Deaths, 1908-1932, 1938-2007, Ancestry.com, Madge R. Williams, death cert. #072082.

751 Ohio, Births and Christenings Index, 1800-1962, Ancestry.com, Madge R. Ruble, Union Twp., Highland Co., Ohio.

752 Obituary of Madge R. Williams (Dayton, Ohio, Dayton Daily News, 11 Sep 1972), Dayton Metro Library, 215 East Third Street, Dayton, OH.

753 Find A Grave—New Lynchburg Masonic Cemetery/Lynchburg F & AM Cemetery, Lynchburg, Dodson Twp., Highland Co., Ohio, Find A Grave.com, Madge R. Williams, Find A Grave Memorial #97788664.

754 Ohio Marriage Index, 1970-1972-2007, Ancestry.com, Carl D. Williams and Emily F. Setty, Montgomery County, Ohio Marriage Records, Vol. 8738, lic. #67622.

755 Ohio, Deaths, 1908-1932, 1938-2007, Ancestry.com, Emily F. Williams, death cert. #100367.

756 Find A Grave—Shiloh Park Cemetery, Shiloh, Harrison Twp., Montgomery Co., Ohio, Find A Grave.com, Emily F. Williams, Find A Grave Memorial #140928732.

757 Obituary of Dwan Ruble "Bill" Williams (Boise, Idaho, Idaho Statesman, April 24, 2014), Boise Public Library, 715 South Capitol Avenue, Boise, ID.

758 Obituary of Edgar F. Wilkin (Hillsboro, Ohio, Press Gazette, 30 May 1996), Highland County District Library, 10 Willettsville Pike, Hillsboro, OH.

759 Find A Grave—New Lynchburg Masonic Cemetery/Lynchburg F & AM Cemetery, Lynchburg, Dodson Twp., Highland Co., Ohio, Find A Grave.com, Edgar F. Wilkin, Find A Grave Memorial #164456227.

760 Ohio, County Marriages, 1789-2013, FamilySearch.org, Edgar F. Wilkin and Ethalyn Teboe, Highland County, Ohio Marriage Records, Vol. 19, pg. 86, lic. #13075.

761 Ohio, Deaths, 1908-1932, 1938-2007, Ancestry.com, Ethalyn T. Wilkin, death cert. #030108.

762 Obituary of Ethalyn T. Wilkin (Hillsboro, Ohio, Press Gazette, 27 Apr 1994), Highland County District Library, 10 Willettsville Pike, Hillsboro, OH.

763 Find A Grave—New Lynchburg Masonic Cemetery/Lynchburg F & AM Cemetery, Lynchburg, Dodson Twp., Highland Co., Ohio, Find A Grave.com, Ethalyn T. Wilkin, Find A Grave Memorial #164456224.

764 Find A Grave—Green Acres Memorial Park Cemetery, Scottsdale, Maricopa Co., Arizona, Find A Grave.com, Charles E. Wilkin, Find A Grave Memorial #45393969.

765 Obituary of Charles Wilkin (Phoenix, Arizona, Arizona Republic, 21 Mar 1982), Arizona State Library, Archives and Public Records, Archives and Records Management Branch, 1901 West Madison Street, Phoenix, AZ.

766 Marriage License of Howard Manis and Joan Wilkin, Highland County, Ohio Probate Court, Highland County Courthouse, 105 North High Street, Hillsboro, OH, Howard R. Manis and Joan Wilkin, Highland County, Ohio Marriage Records, Vol. 23, pg. 546, lic. #19580.

767 Find A Grave—New Lynchburg Masonic Cemetery/Lynchburg F & AM Cemetery, Lynchburg, Dodson Twp., Highland Co., Ohio, Find A Grave.com, Everett R. Wilkin, Find A Grave Memorial #110192285.

768 Ohio, County Marriages, 1789-2013, FamilySearch.org, Everett R. Wilkin and Florence Fox, Marion County, Ohio Marriage Records, Vol. 21, pg. 530, lic. #1060.

769 Ohio, Deaths, 1908-1932, 1938-2007, Ancestry.com, Florence Leona Wilkin, death cert. #072703.

770 Find A Grave—New Lynchburg Masonic Cemetery/Lynchburg F & AM Cemetery, Lynchburg, Dodson Twp., Highland Co., Ohio, Find A Grave.com, Florence Fox Wilkin, Find A Grave Memorial #98904546.

771 Find A Grave—New Lynchburg Masonic Cemetery/Lynchburg F & AM Cemetery, Lynchburg, Dodson Twp., Highland Co., Ohio, Find A Grave.com, Marjorie Marie Wilkin Hawk, Find A Grave Memorial #44743786.

772 Marriage Announcement of Everett G. Hawk and Marjorie Wilkin (Washington Court House, Ohio, Washington Court House Herald, 26 Jun 1929), Carnegie Public Library, 127 South North Street, Washington Court House, OH.

773 Find A Grave—New Lynchburg Masonic Cemetery/Lynchburg F & AM Cemetery, Lynchburg, Dodson Twp., Highland Co., Ohio, Find A Grave.com, Everett Guy Hawk, Find A Grave Memorial #44743693.

774 Ohio, Births and Christenings Index, 1800-1962, Ancestry.com, "Esert" G. Hawck.

775 Obituary of Everett G. Hawk (Hillsboro, Ohio, Press-Gazette, 17 Dec 1965), Highland County District Library, 10 Willettsville Pike, Hillsboro, OH.

776 Ohio, Deaths, 1908-1932, 1938-2007, Ancestry.com, Everett G. Hawk, death cert. #89499.

777 Ohio, Birth Index, 1908-1964, Ancestry.com, Sonia M. Hawk, state file #1931016343.

778 Ohio, Birth Index, 1908-1964, Ancestry.com, Carolyn M. Hawk, state file #1933076554.

779 Obituary of Evelyn L. Turner (Hillsboro, Ohio, Hillsboro News Gazette, 09 Aug 2002), Highland County District Library, 10 Willettsville Pike, Hillsboro, OH.

780 Find A Grave—New Lynchburg Masonic Cemetery/Lynchburg F & AM Cemetery, Lynchburg, Dodson Twp., Highland Co., Ohio, Find A Grave.com, Evelyn Campbell, Find A Grave Memorial #101175184.

781 Ohio, County Births, 1841-2003 (County Courthouses), FamilySearch.org, Highland Co. Births, Vol. 3, pg. 356.

782 Ohio, Deaths, 1908-1932, 1938-2007, Ancestry.com, William E. Campbell, death cert. #057700.

783 Find A Grave—New Lynchburg Masonic Cemetery/Lynchburg F & AM Cemetery, Lynchburg, Dodson Twp., Highland Co., Ohio, Find A Grave.com, William E. Campbell, Find A Grave Memorial #101175196.

784 Marriage License Announcement of Howard L. Fissel and Evelyn L. Campbell (Hillsboro, Ohio, Press-Gazette, 15 Sep 1976), Highland County District Library, 10 Willettsville Pike, Hillsboro, OH.

785 Ohio, Deaths, 1908-1932, 1938-2007, Ancestry.com, Howard Fissel, death cert. #020543.

786 Obituary of Howard Fissell (Greenfield, Ohio, Greenfield Daily Times, 12 Mar 1990), Highland County District Library, 10 Willettsville Pike, Hillsboro, OH, Hillsboro (OH) Press Gazette, pub. 19 Jan 1973.

787 Find A Grave—Spencerville Cemetery, Spencerville, Spencer Twp., Allen Co., Ohio, Find A Grave.com, Howard Fissel, Find A Grave Memorial #70269825.

788 Ohio, Deaths, 1908-1932, 1938-2007, Ancestry.com, Herbert M. Turner, death cert. #011421.

789 Obituary of Herbert M. Turner (Hillsboro, Ohio, Highland County Times Gazette, 09 Feb 2002), Highland County District Library, 10 Willettsville Pike, Hillsboro, OH.

790 Ohio, Birth Index, 1908-1964, Ancestry.com, Betty E. Campbell, state file #1928078409.

791 Ohio, Birth Index, 1908-1964, Ancestry.com, June P. Campbell, state file #1931042477.

792 Ohio, Birth Index, 1908-1964, Ancestry.com, Donald E. Campbell, state file #1933046275.

793 Obituary of Don E. Campbell (Hillsboro, Ohio, Highland County Times-Gazette, 09 Jun 2013), Highland County District Library, 10 Willettsville Pike, Hillsboro, OH.

794 Find A Grave—Hightop Cemetery, Samantha, Penn Twp., Highland Co., Ohio, Find A Grave.com, Don E. Campbell, Find A Grave Memorial #112127933.

795 Find A Grave—Troutwine Cemetery, Dodson Twp., Highland Co., Ohio, Find A Grave.com, Lenora Wilkin Barker, Find A Grave Memorial #45082777.

796 Ohio, County Marriages, 1789-2013, FamilySearch.org, Wendell Barker and Lenora Wilkin, Highland County, Ohio Marriage Records, Vol. 20, pg. 389, lic. #14837.

797 The Genealogical Committee of The Clinton County Historical Society, Cemetery Records of Clinton Co., Ohio, 1798-1998, Troutwine Cemetery: Wendell D. Barker. Clinton County, Ohio Records Center and Archives, 111 South Nelson Avenue, Suite 3, Wilmington, OH.

798 Ohio, Deaths, 1908-1932, 1938-2007, Ancestry.com, Wendell D. Barker, death cert. #056287.

799 Find A Grave—Troutwine Cemetery, Dodson Twp., Highland Co., Ohio, Find A Grave.com, Wendell D. Barker, Find A Grave Memorial #45082883.

800 Ohio Death Certificate, Ohio Department of Health, Center for Vital and Health Statistics, 246 North High Street, Columbus, OH, Jimmie Gaylord Barker, death cert. #6863.

801 Find A Grave—Evergreen Cemetery, Waverly, Pee Pee Twp., Pike Co., Ohio, Find A Grave.com, Georgeanna Holderby, Find A Grave Memorial #187376184.

802 U.S., Social Security Applications and Claims Index, 1936-2007, Ancestry.com, Marcus C. Roush.

803 U.S., Department of Veterans Affairs BIRLS File, 1850-2010, Ancestry.com, Marcus Roush.

804 Ohio, Deaths, 1908-1932, 1938-2007, Ancestry.com, Marcus Roush, death cert. #083293.

805 Obituary of Marcus Roush (Hillsboro, Ohio, Press Gazette, 19 Jan 1973), Highland County District Library, 10 Willettsville Pike, Hillsboro, OH.

806 Find A Grave—Hamer Township Cemetery, Hamer Twp., Highland Co., Ohio, Find A Grave.com, Marcus C. Roush, Find A Grave Memorial #113928450.

807 "Personals…Mr. and Mrs. Marcus Roush…" (Hillsboro, Ohio, Press Gazette, 24 Jul 1964). Highland County District Library, 10 Willettsville Pike, Hillsboro, OH.

808 Ohio, County Births, 1841-2003 (County Courthouses), FamilySearch.org, Paul Graham Ross, Ross County, Ohio Births, Vol. 5 (no pg. #), 09 Apr 1905, Green Twp.

809 Ohio, Deaths, 1908-1932, 1938-2007, Ancestry.com, Marcus Roush, death cert. #030864.

810 Obituary of Paul Ross (Chillicothe, Ohio, Chillicothe Gazette, 04 Apr 1974), Chillicothe & Ross County Library, 140 South Paint Street, Chillicothe, OH.

811 Find A Grave—Salem White Church Cemetery, Kingston, Green Twp., Ross Co., Ohio, Find A Grave.com, Paul G. Ross, Find A Grave Memorial #181468262.

812 Ohio Marriage Index, 1970-1972-2007, Ancestry.com, Malcolm Holderby and Georgia Ross, Pike County, Ohio Marriage Records, Ohio state Vol. 9388, #19060.

813 Obituary of Malcolm Holderby (Chillicothe, Ohio, Chillicothe Gazette, 02 Mar 1979), Chillicothe & Ross County Library, 140 South Paint Street, Chillicothe, OH.

814 Ohio, Birth Index, 1908-1964, Ancestry.com, Malcolm William Holderby, Proctorville, Lawrence County, Ohio, delayed birth record registered by Malcolm Holderby on 07 Dec 1943 through the Lawrence County Court.

815 Ohio, Deaths, 1908-1932, 1938-2007, Ancestry.com, Malcolm Holderby, death cert. #020065.

816 Find A Grave—Evergreen Cemetery, Waverly, Pee Pee Twp., Pike Co., Ohio, Find A Grave.com, Malcolm Holderby, Find A Grave Memorial #181468167.

817 Find A Grave—New Lynchburg Masonic Cemetery/Lynchburg F & AM Cemetery, Lynchburg, Dodson Twp., Highland Co., Ohio, Find A Grave.com, Samuel Wilkin, Find A Grave Memorial #97788034.

818 Obituary of Samuel Wilkin (Hillsboro, Ohio, Hillsboro News Gazette, 21 Jun 1994), Highland County District Library, 10 Willettsville Pike, Hillsboro, OH.

819 Marriage Announcement of Samuel Wilkin and Frances Hartman (Hillsboro, Ohio, Press-Gazette, 12 Jan 1945), Highland County District Library, 10 Willettsville Pike, Hillsboro, OH.

820 Florida Marriage Collection, 1822-1875 and 1927-2001, Ancestry.com, Samuel Wilkin and Lucille Gilbert, Collier County, Florida Marriage Records, Florida state Vol. 5534, lic. #007569.

821 Find A Grave—New Lynchburg Masonic Cemetery/Lynchburg F & AM Cemetery, Lynchburg, Dodson Twp., Highland Co., Ohio, Find A Grave.com, LeRoy Wilkin, Find A Grave Memorial #97787886.

822 Ohio, County Marriages, 1789-2013, FamilySearch.org, Leroy Wilkin and Helen Briggs, Highland County, Ohio Marriage Records, Vol. 22, pg. 187, lic. #16766.

823 Find A Grave—New Lynchburg Masonic Cemetery/Lynchburg F & AM Cemetery, Lynchburg, Dodson Twp., Highland Co., Ohio, Find A Grave.com, Eugene Williams, Find A Grave Memorial #99603703.

824 Obituary of Virgil Williams (Hillsboro, Ohio, Hillsboro News Gazette, June 8, 2001), Highland County District Library, 10 Willettsville Pike, Hillsboro, OH, Hillsboro (OH) News-Gazette, pub. 08 Jun 2001.

825 Find A Grave—Martinsville IOOF Cemetery, Martinsville, Clark Twp., Clinton Co., Ohio, Find A Grave.com, Sgt. Virgil Williams, Find A Grave Memorial #121730874.

826 Obituary of Virgil Williams (Hillsboro, Ohio, Hillsboro News Gazette, June 8, 2001), Highland County District Library, 10 Willettsville Pike, Hillsboro, OH.

827 Obituary of Anna Williams (Hillsboro, Ohio, Highland County Times Gazette, 15 Jan 2015), Highland County District Library, 10 Willettsville Pike, Hillsboro, OH.

828 Find A Grave—Martinsville IOOF Cemetery, Martinsville, Clark Twp., Clinton Co., Ohio, Find A Grave.com, Anna Williams, Find A Grave Memorial #121731059.

829 Find A Grave—New Lynchburg Masonic Cemetery/Lynchburg F & AM Cemetery, Lynchburg, Dodson Twp., Highland Co., Ohio, Find A Grave.com, Woodrow Wilson Williams, Find A Grave Memorial #99603972.

830 Ohio, Deaths, 1908-1932, 1938-2007, Ancestry.com, Mabel Fern Williams, death cert. #55239.

831 Ohio, Birth Index, 1908-1964, Ancestry.com, Mabel Fern Snyder, state file #1914083694.

832 Obituary of Mabel F. Williams (Hillsboro, Ohio, Hillsboro News-Gazette, 01 Jul 2005), Highland County District Library, 10 Willettsville Pike, Hillsboro, OH.

833 Find A Grave—New Lynchburg Masonic Cemetery/Lynchburg F & AM Cemetery, Lynchburg, Dodson Twp., Highland Co., Ohio, Find A Grave.com, Mabel Fern Snyder Williams, Find A Grave Memorial #99603918.

834 Ohio, Birth Index, 1908-1964, Ancestry.com, Carol J. Williams, state file #1935094991.

835 Ohio, Birth Index, 1908-1964, Ancestry.com, Janet E. Williams, state file #1937053522.

836 Obituary of Judith Mae Turner (Hillsboro, Ohio, Highland County Press, 05 Jan 2014), Highland County District Library, 10 Willettsville Pike, Hillsboro, OH.

837 Obituary of James D. Williams (Highland County Press Gazette, 26 May 1986), Highland County District Library, 10 Willettsville Pike, Hillsboro, OH.

838 Ohio, Deaths, 1908-1932, 1938-2007, Ancestry.com, James Douglas Williams, death cert. #037213.

839 Find A Grave—New Lynchburg Masonic Cemetery/Lynchburg F & AM Cemetery, Lynchburg, Dodson Twp., Highland Co., Ohio, Find A Grave.com, Stanley Mitchell Williams, Find A Grave Memorial #99603773.

840 Highland County, Ohio Marriage Records, Highland County, Ohio Probate Court, Highland County Courthouse, 105 North High Street, Hillsboro, OH.

841 Ohio, County Marriages, 1789-2013, FamilySearch.org, Stanley M. Williams and Wanda B. Shumard, Highland County, Ohio Marriage Records, Vol. 23, pg. 74, lic. #18641.

842 Ohio, Birth Index, 1908-1964, Ancestry.com, Wanda B. Shumard, state file #1930016994.

843 Obituary of Marianna Williams (Hillsboro, Ohio, Press-Gazette, 19 Mar 2007), Highland County District Library, 10 Willettsville Pike, Hillsboro, OH.

844 Ohio, Deaths, 1908-1932, 1938-2007, Ancestry.com, Marianna Williams, death cert. #019069.

845 Find A Grave—New Lynchburg Masonic Cemetery/Lynchburg F & AM Cemetery, Lynchburg, Dodson Twp., Highland Co., Ohio, Find A Grave.com, Marianna Williams, Find A Grave Memorial #99603832.

846 Find A Grave—Laurel IOOF Cemetery, Madisonville, Hamilton Co., Ohio, Find A Grave.com, Hazel Imogene "Gene" Davidson, Find A Grave Memorial #150951547.

847 Obituary of Ralph E. Davidson (Cincinnati, Ohio, Cincinnati Enquirer, 30 Jan 2013), The Public Library of Cincinnati and Hamilton County, 800 Vine Street, Cincinnati, OH.

848 Find A Grave—Laurel IOOF Cemetery, Madisonville, Hamilton Co., Ohio, Find A Grave.com, Ralph E. Davidson, Find A Grave Memorial #104364186.

849 Find A Grave—Arlington Memorial Gardens Cemetery, Mount Healthy, Springfield Twp., Hamilton Co., Ohio, Find A Grave.com, Paul T. Williams, Find A Grave Memorial #170920717.

850 Obituary of Madeline Williams (Cincinnati, Ohio, Cincinnati Enquirer, 03 Mar 2007), The Public Library of Cincinnati- Hamilton County, 800 Vine Street, Cincinnati, OH.

851 Kentucky, Birth Index, 1911-1999, Ancestry.com, Madeleon Baker, Vol. 067, cert. #33167.

852 Ohio, Deaths, 1908-1932, 1938-2007, Ancestry.com, Madeline Williams, death cert. #019475.

853 Find A Grave—Arlington Memorial Gardens Cemetery, Mount Healthy, Springfield Twp., Hamilton Co., Ohio, Find A Grave.com, Madeleine Williams, Find A Grave Memorial #170920718.

854 Find A Grave—Barnes Cemetery, Fairview, New Market Twp., Highland Co., Ohio, Find A Grave.com, Clarence E. Williams, Find A Grave Memorial #98408544.

855 Ohio, Birth Index, 1908-1964, Ancestry.com, Janice A. Cadwallader, state file #1935085667.

856 Ohio, Birth Index, 1908-1964, Ancestry.com, Karl B. Kelley, state file #1922003438.

857 Ohio, Deaths, 1908-1932, 1938-2007, Ancestry.com, Karl B. Kelley, death cert. #018735.

858 Obituary of Karl B. Kelley (Cincinnati, Ohio, Cincinnati Enquirer, 17 Mar 1992), The Public Library of Cincinnati-Hamilton County, 800 Vine Street, Cincinnati, OH.

859 Rose Hill Cemetery Records, Karl B. Kelley, Rose Hill Cemetery, 171 South Mason-Montgomery Road, Mason, OH.

860 Ohio, Birth Index, 1908-1964, Ancestry.com, David L. Kelley, state file #1963007146.

861 Ohio, Deaths, 1908-1932, 1938-2007, Ancestry.com, David L. Kelley, death cert. #45119.

862 Find A Grave—Black Creek Memorial Cemetery, Freeport, Walton Co., Florida, Find A Grave.com, Glen Louis Williams, Find A Grave Memorial #131956810.

863 Obituary of Betty Lou Williams (Fort Walton Beach, Florida, Northwest Florida Daily News, 26 Aug 2009), Okaloosa County Library, 185 Miracle Strip Parkway SE, Fort Walton Beach, FL.

864 Find A Grave—Black Creek Memorial Cemetery, Freeport, Walton Co., Florida, Find A Grave.com, Betty Lou Bishop Williams, Find A Grave Memorial #41157784.

865 Obituary of Candus Gay Nash (Fort Walton Beach, Florida, Northwest Florida Daily News, 29 Jan 2012), Okaloosa County Library, 185 Miracle Strip Parkway SE, Fort Walton Beach, FL.

866 Find A Grave—Black Creek Memorial Cemetery, Freeport, Walton Co., Florida, Find A Grave.com, Vincent B. Williams, Find A Grave Memorial #33755938.

867 Find A Grave—Barnes Cemetery, Fairview, New Market Twp., Highland Co., Ohio, Find A Grave.com, Dale M. Williams, Find A Grave Memorial #98408641.

868 Obituary of Rita A. Williams (Springfield, IL, The, 17 Nov 2009), The Lincoln Library, The Public Library of Springfield, Illinois, 326 South 7th Street, Springfield, IL.

869 Find A Grave—Barnes Cemetery, Fairview, New Market Twp., Highland Co., Ohio, Find A Grave.com, Rita A. Williams, Find A Grave Memorial #44466425.

870 Web: Marion County, Indiana, Marriage Index, 1925-2012, Bernard Simms and Charlotte Spilker.

871 Ohio Death Certificate, Ohio Department of Health, Center for Vital and Health Statistics, 246 North High Street, Columbus, OH, Bernard E. Simms, death cert. #669.

872 "Simms Funeral Today" (Cincinnati, Ohio, Cincinnati Enquirer, 22 Jan 1946), The Public Library of Cincinnati-Hamilton County, 800 Vine Street, Cincinnati, OH.

873 Find A Grave—Goshen Cemetery, Goshen, Goshen Twp., Clermont Co., Ohio, Find A Grave.com, Bernard E. Simms, Find A Grave Memorial #132864204.

874 Ohio, County Marriages, 1789-2013, FamilySearch.org, Robert R. Hern and Charlotte J. Simms, Vol. 33, pg. 78, lic. #18649.

875 Obituary of Robert R. Hern (Hillsboro, Ohio, Hillsboro News Gazette, 25 Mar 2010), Highland County District Library, 10 Willettsville Pike, Hillsboro, OH.

876 Find A Grave—Spring Grove Cemetery, Cincinnati, Hamilton Co., Ohio, Find A Grave.com, Joseph Spilker, Find A Grave Memorial #79046066.

877 Obituary of Dorothy Spilker Russell (Cambridge, Ohio, The Daily Jeffersonian, 10 Feb 2005), Guernsey County Public Library, Crossroads Branch, 63500 Byesville Road, Cambridge, OH.

878 Ohio, Deaths, 1908-1932, 1938-2007, Ancestry.com, Dorothy Atkinson, death cert. #11278.

879 U.S., Social Security Applications and Claims Index, 1936-2007, Ancestry.com, Dorothy Ernst Spilker Atkinson.

880 Find A Grave—Spring Grove Cemetery, Cincinnati, Hamilton Co., Ohio, Find A Grave.com, Dorothy E. Atkinson, Find A Grave Memorial #78886026.

881 Obituary of Joseph T. Spilker (Cambridge, Ohio, The Daily Jeffersonian, 18 Dec 2009), Guernsey County Public Library, Crossroads Branch, 63500 Byesville Road, Cambridge, OH.

882 Find A Grave—Spring Grove Cemetery, Cincinnati, Hamilton Co., Ohio, Find A Grave.com, Shirley Lois Gail Spilker Rogers, Find A Grave Memorial #79026679.

883 Ohio, Deaths, 1908-1932, 1938-2007, Ancestry.com, Russell Howard Rogers, death cert. #010594.

884 U.S., Social Security Applications and Claims Index, 1936-2007, Ancestry.com, Roger Howard Rogers.

885 U.S., Department of Veterans Affairs BIRLS File, 1850-2010, Ancestry.com, Roger Rogers.

886 Find A Grave—Spring Grove Cemetery, Cincinnati, Hamilton Co., Ohio, Find A Grave.com, Russell H. Rogers, Find A Grave Memorial #79026670.

887 Web: Cincinnati, Ohio, Oak Hill Cemetery Index, 1910-2012, Ancestry.com, Mary A. Rogers.

888 Obituary of Mary Ann Rogers (Cincinnati, Ohio, Cincinnati Post, 21 May 1984), The Public Library of Cincinnati-Hamilton County, 800 Vine Street, Cincinnati, OH.

889 Find A Grave—Barnes Cemetery, Fairview, New Market Twp., Highland Co., Ohio, Find A Grave.com, Dwight H. Ludwick, Find A Grave Memorial #94474691.

890 Ohio, County Marriages, 1789-2013, FamilySearch.org, Dwight Ludwick and "Kathryn Mccoffin", Highland County, Ohio Marriage Records, Vol. 21, pg. 124, lic. #15454.

891 Ohio, Birth Index, 1908-1964, Ancestry.com, Kathryn McCoffin, state file #1917062685.

892 Obituary of Katherine "Kay" Ludwick (Fort Lauderdale), Florida, The Sun Sentinel, 25 May 2007, Broward County Library, Main Branch, 100 South Andrews, Fort Lauderdale, FL.

893 Obituary of Dwight H. Ludwick (Dayton, Ohio, Dayton Daily News, 13 Jul 1989), Dayton Metro Library, 215 East Third Street. Dayton, OH.

894 U.S. Public Records Index, 1950-1993, Vol. 1, Ancestry.com, Roger O. Ludwick, Dayton, Ohio.

895 Obituary of Roger Ludwick (Englewood, Ohio, Englewood Independent, 21 Dec 2016), Dayton Metro Library, 215 East Third Street. Dayton, OH.

896 Obituary of Lloyd C. Ludwick (Hillsboro, Ohio, Highland County Times, 09 Jan 2006), Highland County District Library, 10 Willettsville Pike, Hillsboro, OH.

897 Find A Grave—Barnes Cemetery, Fairview, New Market Twp., Highland Co., Ohio, Find A Grave.com, Lloyd C. Ludwick, Find A Grave Memorial #33760286.

898 Ohio, County Marriages, 1789-2013, FamilySearch.org, Lloyd Ludwick and Mildred Claibourne, Highland County, Ohio Marriage Records, Vol. 21, pg. 334, #15872.

899 Ohio, Deaths, 1908-1932, 1938-2007, Ancestry.com, Mildred Pauline Ludwick, death cert. #029418.

900 Obituary of Mildred P. Ludwick (Hillsboro, Ohio, Hillsboro Press Gazette, 02 Apr 1996), Highland County District Library, 10 Willettsville Pike, Hillsboro, OH.

901 Find A Grave—Barnes Cemetery, Fairview, New Market Twp., Highland Co., Ohio, Find A Grave.com, Mildred Pauline Claibourne Ludwick, Find A Grave Memorial #94475734.

902 Find A Grave—Barnes Cemetery, Fairview, New Market Twp., Highland Co., Ohio, Find A Grave.com, Infant Ludwick, Find A Grave Memorial #94475748.

903 Ohio, County Marriages, 1789-2013, FamilySearch.org, Harold S. Ludwick and Ruby M. Carey, Highland County, Ohio Marriage Records, Vol. 22, pg. 586, lic. #18462.

904 Marriage License of Harold Ludwick and Ruby M. Carey, Highland County, Ohio Probate Court, Highland County Courthouse, 105 North High Street, Hillsboro, OH, Highland County, Ohio Marriage Book 22, pg. 586, #18462.

905 Obituary of Mrs. Harold Ludwick (Hillsboro, Ohio, Hillsboro Press Gazette, 10 Feb 1967), Highland County District Library, 10 Willettsville Pike, Hillsboro, OH.

906 Ohio Death Certificate, Ohio Department of Health, Center for Vital and Health Statistics, 246 North High Street, Columbus, OH, Ruby C. Ludwick, death cert. #22453.

907 Obituary of Janell (Gluckian) Ludwick (Xenia, Ohio, Xenia Daily Gazette, 26 Sep 2006), Greene County Public Library-Xenia Community Library, Greene County Room, 76 East Market Street, Xenia, OH.

908 Ohio, Deaths, 1908-1932, 1938-2007, Ancestry.com, Janell Ludwick, death cert. #77538.

909 Find A Grave—Fairmount Cemetery, Camden, Somers Twp., Preble Co., Ohio, Find A Grave.com, Janell Sebert Ludwick, Find A Grave Memorial #23485587.

910 Find A Grave—New Lynchburg Masonic Cemetery/Lynchburg F & AM Cemetery, Lynchburg, Dodson Twp., Highland Co., Ohio, Find A Grave.com, Everett O. Ludwick, Find A Grave Memorial #101169465.

911 Obituary of Hilda Mae Hawk Ludwick (Dayton, Ohio, Dayton Daily News, 07 Jun 2012), Dayton Metro Library, 215 East Third Street, Dayton, OH.

912 Ohio, Birth Index, 1908-1964, Ancestry.com, Hilda M. Hawk, state file #1928033271.

913 Find A Grave—New Lynchburg Masonic Cemetery/Lynchburg F & AM Cemetery, Lynchburg, Dodson Twp., Highland Co., Ohio, Find A Grave.com, Hilda M. Ludwick, Find A Grave Memorial #101169457.

914 Find A Grave—Barnes Cemetery, Fairview, New Market Twp., Highland Co., Ohio, Find A Grave.com, Lowell A. Ludwick, Find A Grave Memorial #94474705.

915 Find A Grave—Spring Valley Cemetery, Spring Valley, Spring Valley Twp., Greene Co., Ohio, Find A Grave.com, James R. Stroup, Find A Grave Memorial #143535084.

916 Ohio, County Marriages, 1789-2013, FamilySearch.org, James Richard Stroup and Wilma Ellen Boerner, Greene County, Ohio Marriage Records, Vol. 26, pg. 251, lic. #6776.

917 The Genealogical Committee of The Clinton County Historical Society, Cemetery Records of Clinton Co., Ohio, 1798-1998, Sugar Grove Cemetery: Thelma L. Fudge. Clinton County, Ohio Records Center and Archives, 111 South Nelson Avenue, Suite 3, Wilmington, OH.

918 Obituary of George Fudge (Wooster, Ohio, Wooster Daily Record, 05 Sep 1990), Wayne County Public Library, 220 West Liberty Street, Wooster, OH.

919 Ohio, Deaths, 1908-1932, 1938-2007, Ancestry.com, George M. Fudge, death cert. #067945.

920 The Genealogical Committee of The Clinton County Historical Society, Cemetery Records of Clinton Co., Ohio, 1798-1998, Sugar Grove Cemetery: George M. Fudge. Clinton County, Ohio Records Center and Archives, 111 South Nelson Avenue, Suite 3, Wilmington, OH.

921 Warren County, Ohio Cemetery Records, Inez Bowman, Lebanon Cemetery, Warren County Genealogical Society Library, 406 Justice Drive, Lebanon, OH.

922 Find A Grave—Lebanon Cemetery, Lebanon, Turtle Creek Twp., Warren Co., Ohio, Find A Grave.com, Inez Vance Bowman, Find A Grave Memorial #42296132.

923 Ohio, Deaths, 1908-1932, 1938-2007, Ancestry.com, Bernard Joseph Bowman, death cert. #038869.

924 U.S., Social Security Applications and Claims Index, 1936-2007, Ancestry.com, Bernard Joseph Bowman.

925 U.S., Department of Veterans Affairs BIRLS File, 1850-2010, Ancestry.com, Bernard Bowman.

926 Find A Grave—Lebanon Cemetery, Lebanon, Turtle Creek Twp., Warren Co., Ohio, Find A Grave.com, Bernard Jean Bowman, Find A Grave Memorial #42296131.

927 Ohio, Deaths, 1908-1932, 1938-2007, Ancestry.com, Robyn Bowman Kemp, death cert. #032320.

928 Obituary of Robyn Bowman Kemp (Dayton, Ohio, Dayton Daily News, 26 Apr 1996), Dayton Metro Library, 215 East Third Street. Dayton, OH.

929 Ohio, Deaths, 1908-1932, 1938-2007, Ancestry.com, Rebecca S. Bowman, death cert. #78048.

930 Find A Grave—Lebanon Cemetery, Lebanon, Turtle Creek Twp., Warren Co., Ohio, Find A Grave.com, Rebecca Sue Bowman, Find A Grave Memorial #42296136.

931 Ohio, Deaths, 1908-1932, 1938-2007, Ancestry.com, Bruce S. Bowman, death cert. #106961.

932 Obituary of Bruce Bowman (Lebanon, Ohio, The Western Star, 03 Jan 2001), Warren County History Center Library, 105 South Broadway Street, Lebanon, OH.

933 Ohio, Deaths, 1908-1932, 1938-2007, Ancestry.com, Nicholas B. Bowman, death cert. #010586.

934 Find A Grave—Sugar Grove Cemetery, Wilmington, Union Twp., Clinton Co., Ohio, Find A Grave.com, Robert "Bobby" Vance, Find A Grave Memorial #130619857.

935 "'Bobby' Vance Badly Burned In Home Monday" (Wilmington, Ohio, Wilmington News Journal, Wilmington Public Library of Clinton County, 268 North South Street, Wilmington, OH.

936 Find A Grave—Rest Haven Memorial Park Cemetery, Evendale, Sycamore Twp., Hamilton Co., Ohio, Find A Grave.com, Betty Louise Hawthorne Fisher, Find A Grave Memorial #118058761.

937 Ohio, Deaths, 1908-1932, 1938-2007, Ancestry.com, Walter J. Fisher, death cert. #76591.

938 Find A Grave—Rest Haven Memorial Park Cemetery, Evendale, Sycamore Twp., Hamilton Co., Ohio, Find A Grave.com, Walter J. Fisher, Find A Grave Memorial #118815879.

939 Florida Death Index 1877-1998, Ancestry.com, John Robert Fisher.

940 Ohio, Birth Index, 1908-1964, Ancestry.com, John R. Fisher, state file #1936070505.

941 U.S., Social Security Applications and Claims Index, 1936-2007, Ancestry.com, John Robert Fisher.

942 U.S. Public Records Index, 1950-1993, Ancestry.com, Linda S. Dingman, Amelia City, FL.

943 Obituary of Linda Sue Dingman (Cincinnati, Ohio, Strawser Funeral Home, 05 Jan 2017), Strawser Funeral Home, 9503 Kenwood Road, Cincinnati, OH; Online database: http://www.strawserfuneralhome.com/obituary/4058847

944 Obituary of Karen Jean Brooks (Newtown, Ohio, Moore Family Funeral Home, 02 Jan 2014), Moore Family Funeral Home, 6708 Main Street, Cincinnati, Ohio (Newtown);

945 California, Death Index, 1940-1997, Ancestry.com, Delores C. Pegan.

946 California Death Certificate, California Health and Strategic Planning, Vital Records, M.S. 5103, P.O. Box 997410, Sacramento, CA, Delores Catherine Pegan, death cert. #69-006758.

947 California, Marriage Index, 1960-1985, Ancestry.com, Robert H. Pegan and Grace I. Reising, Orange County, California Marriage Records, California state Vol. 7045, lic. #101415.

948 U.S., Social Security Applications and Claims Index, 1936-2007, Ancestry.com, Grace Ida Roeder O'Brien Pegan.

949 Obituary of Grace O'Brien-Pegan (Santa Ana, California, The Orange County Register, 28 Apr 2004), Santa Ana Public Library, 26 Civic Center Plaza, Santa Ana, CA.

950 Find A Grave—Gate of Heaven Cemetery, Montgomery, Sycamore Twp., Hamilton Co., Ohio, Find A Grave.com, Grace Ida O'Brien-Pegan, Find A Grave Memorial #86989185.

951 Obituary of Robert H. Pegan (Santa Ana, California, The Orange County Register, 16 Jun 1990), Santa Ana Public Library, 26 Civic Center Plaza, Santa Ana, CA.

952 Find A Grave—Spring Grove Cemetery, Cincinnati, Hamilton Co., Ohio, Find A Grave.com, Ruth Mary Pegan Dennig, Find A Grave Memorial #78917597.

953 Ohio, Deaths, 1908-1932, 1938-2007, Ancestry.com, Louis Adolph Dennig, death cert. #046437.

954 U.S., Social Security Applications and Claims Index, 1936-2007, Ancestry.com, Louis Adolph Dennig.

955 Find A Grave—Spring Grove Cemetery, Cincinnati, Hamilton Co., Ohio, Find A Grave.com, Louis Adolph Dennig, Find A Grave Memorial #78917596.

956 Ohio, Birth Index, 1908-1964, Ancestry.com, Raymond B. Kissel, state file #1921114076.

957 Missouri Marriage Records, 1805-2002, Ancestry.com, William Wren Marlatt and Betty Joan Pegan, both of Normandy, Normandy Twp., St. Louis Co., Missouri.

958 U.S., Social Security Applications and Claims Index, 1936-2007, Ancestry.com, William Wrenn Marlatt.

959 Obituary of William W. Marlatt (St. Louis, Missouri, St. Louis Post-Dispatch, 10 Dec 1999), St. Louis County Public Library, 1640 South Lindbergh Boulevard, St. Louis, MO.

960 Find A Grave—Memorial Park Cemetery, Jennings, St. Louis Co., Missouri, Find A Grave.com, William W. Marlatt, Find A Grave Memorial #171716422.

961 U.S., Social Security Applications and Claims Index, 1936-2007, Ancestry.com, Ramon Martin Fisher.

962 Marriage Announcement—William C. May and Elma M. Pegan (Hillsboro, Ohio, Press-Gazette, 19 Dec 1947), Highland County District Library, 10 Willettsville Pike, Hillsboro, OH.

963 Kentucky, Birth Index, 1911-1999, Ancestry.com, William C. May, Campbell County, state birth vol. 104, cert# 51818.

964 Obituary of William C. May (Cincinnati, Ohio, Cincinnati Enquirer, 27 Oct 1985), The Public Library of Cincinnati-Hamilton County, 800 Vine Street, Cincinnati, OH.

965 Marriage Announcement of Malcom L. Kelley and Thelma Pegan (Hillsboro, Ohio, Highland County Press-Gazette, February 14, 1947), Highland County District Library, 10 Willettsville Pike Hillsboro, OH.

966 Ohio, Deaths, 1908-1932, 1938-2007, Ancestry.com, Malcom Loraine Kelley, death cert. #86633.

967 Obituary of Malcom L. Kelley (Hillsboro, Ohio, Highland County Times Gazette, 16 Nov 2004), Highland County District Library, 10 Willettsville Pike, Hillsboro, OH.

968 Find A Grave—Prospect Cemetery, Berrysville, Marshall Twp., Highland Co., Ohio, Find A Grave.com, Malcom L. Kelley, Find A Grave Memorial #128734486.

969 U.S., Social Security Applications and Claims Index, 1936-2007, Ancestry.com, William Alpheus Smith Sr.

970 Obituary of Bill Smith Sr., San Diego Public Library, 330 Park Boulevard, San Diego, CA, San Diego (CA) Union Tribune, 10 Aug 2001.

971 Find A Grave—Riverside National Cemetery, Riverside, Riverside Co., California, Find A Grave.com, William A. Smith, Find A Grave Memorial #72612400.

972 U.S. Veterans' Gravesites, ca. 1775-2006, Ancestry.com, William A. Smith, Riverside National Cemetery.

973 Find A Grave—White County Memorial Gardens Cemetery, Searcy, White Co., Arkansas, Find A Grave.com Shirley C. Boyd, Find A Grave Memorial #175790708.

974 Phone interview with Howard Glenn, Searcy, AR, Ann Miller Carr, author, 28 Jul 2014.

975 Find A Grave—Troutwine Cemetery, Dodson Twp., Highland Co., Ohio, Find A Grave.com, Robert I. Pegan, Find A Grave Memorial #137490993.

976 Ohio, County Marriages, 1789-2013, FamilySearch.org, Robert I. Pegan and Charma L. Dick, Highland County, Ohio Marriage Records, Vol. 23, pg. 547, lic. #1958.

977 Highland County, Ohio Marriage Records, Highland County, Ohio Probate Court, Highland County Courthouse, 105 North High Street, Hillsboro, OH, Robert I. Pegan and Charma Pegan, Vol. 26, pg. 303, lic. #22737.

978 Ohio, Deaths, 1908-1932, 1938-2007, Ancestry.com, Charma Louise Pegan, death cert. #062869.

979 Obituary of Charma L. Pegan, Highland County District Library, 10 Willettsville Pike, Hillsboro, OH, Hillsboro (OH) Press-Gazette, pub. 13 Aug 1996.

Online database: http://www.moorefamilyfuneralhomes.com/obituaries/Karen-Brooks/#!/Obituary

980   Find A Grave—Troutwine Cemetery, Dodson Twp., Highland Co., Ohio, Find A Grave.com, Charma L. Pegan, Find A Grave Memorial #137490934.

981   "Truck Driver Jailed In Attack Case" (Hillsboro, Ohio, Press Gazette, 22 Jul 1958), Highland County District Library, 10 Willettsville Pike, Hillsboro, OH.

982   Highland County, Ohio Marriage Records, Highland County, Ohio Probate Court, Highland County Courthouse, 105 North High Street, Hillsboro, OH, Robert I. Pegan and Audrey Nichols, Vol. 28, pg. 448, #12587.

983   Ohio Marriage Index, 1970-1972-2007, Ancestry.com, Robert I. Pegan and Audrey Nichols, Highland County, Ohio Marriage Records, Ohio state Vol. 8518, lic. #12587.

984   Ohio, Deaths, 1908-1932, 1938-2007, Ancestry.com, Audrey Pegan, death cert. #069430.

985   U.S., Social Security Applications and Claims Index, 1936-2007, Ancestry.com, Audrey Gibson Nichols Pegan.

986   Highland County, Ohio Marriage Records, Highland County, Ohio Probate Court, Highland County Courthouse, 105 North High Street, Hillsboro, OH, Russell W. Pegan and Patricia J. Ernst, Highland County, Ohio Marriage Records, Vol. 24, pg. 426, lic. #20542.

987   Ohio, Birth Index, 1908-1964, Ancestry.com, Patricia Joan Ernst, state file #1940011695.

988   Kentucky, Birth Index, 1911-1999, Ancestry.com, Gerald M. Poston, Rowan Co., Kentucky, Vol. 028, cert. #13632.

989   U.S., Social Security Applications and Claims Index, 1936-2007, Ancestry.com, "Mcdonald Gerald" Poston.

990   Florida Death Index 1877-1998, Ancestry.com, Gerald McDonald Poston, Brevard Co., Florida.

991   U.S., Department of Veterans Affairs BIRLS File, 1850-2010, Ancestry.com, Gerald Poston.

992   Find A Grave—Brevard Memorial Park Cemetery, Cocoa. Brevard Co., Florida, Find A Grave.com, Gerald McDonald Poston, Find A Grave Memorial #134217911.

993   Find A Grave—Jacksonville National Cemetery, Jacksonville, Duval Co., Florida, Find A Grave.com, Debra Sue Durett, Find A Grave Memorial #132369264.

994   Obituary of Julia E. Macke (Hillsboro, Ohio, Hillsboro Times Gazette, 25 Mar 2000), Highland County District Library, 10 Willettsville Pike, Hillsboro, OH.

995   Ohio, County Marriages, 1789-2013, FamilySearch.org, Richard H. Macke and Julia Pegan, Brown County Marriage Records, Vol. 36, pg. 256, lic. #51971.

996   Ohio, Birth Index, 1908-1964, Ancestry.com, Richard "M." Macke, Hamilton Co., state file #1921091819.

997   Obituary of Richard H. Macke (Hillsboro, Ohio, Press-Gazette, 20 Dec 1974), Highland County District Library, 10 Willettsville Pike, Hillsboro, OH.

998   U.S., Department of Veterans Affairs BIRLS File, 1850-2010, Ancestry.com, Richard Macke.

999   U.S., Social Security Applications and Claims Index, 1936-2007, Ancestry.com, Richard Macke.

1000   Obituary of Patty Felts (Hillsboro, Ohio, Hillsboro Times Gazette, 29 Feb 2008), Highland County District Library, 10 Willettsville Pike, Hillsboro, OH.

1001   Obituary of James Eugene Pegan (Wilmington, Ohio, Wilmington News-Journal, 02 Aug 2005), Wilmington Public Library of Clinton County, 268 North South Street, Wilmington, OH, Wilmington News-Journal, pub. 02 Aug 2005.

1002   California, Marriage Index, 1949-1959, Ancestry.com, James E. Pegan and Delores Duarte, San Diego County, California Marriage Records, California state lic. 23160.

1003   California Birth Index, 1905-1995, Ancestry.com, Delores Duarte.

1004   Obituary of Delores Pegan (Wilmington, Ohio, Wilmington News-Journal, 14 Oct 1996), Wilmington Public Library of Clinton County, 268 North South Street, Wilmington, OH.

1005   Ohio, Deaths, 1908-1932, 1938-2007, Ancestry.com, Delores Pegan, death cert. #078736.

1006   District of Columbia Marriages, 1811-1950, FamilySearch.org, Thurl Estes Stroup and Martha Jean Blair, marriage lic., pg. 149, #272649.

1007   District of Columbia, Marriage Records, 1810-1953, Ancestry.com, Thurl Esto Stroup and Martha Jean Blair.

1008   Obituary of Martha Stroup Allder (Washington, D.C., Washington Post, May 18, 1990), Microfilm. The Genealogy Center, Allen County Public Library, 900 Library Plaza, Fort Wayne, IN.

1009   Find A Grave—Gate of Heaven Cemetery, Silver Spring, Montgomery Co., Maryland, Find A Grave.com, Martha B. Allder, Find A Grave Memorial #149432683.

1010   Obituary of Mrs. Kleinfelder (Hamilton, Ohio, Hamilton Daily News, 01 Feb 1980), Hamilton Lane Library, 300 North Third Street, Hamilton, OH.

1011   Ohio, County Marriages, 1789-2013, FamilySearch.org, Harry Kleinfelder and Gwendolyn DuVall, Butler County, Ohio Marriage Records, Vol. 29, page 227, lic. #12341.

1012   Ohio, Deaths, 1908-1932, 1938-2007, Ancestry.com, Harry W. Kleinfelder, death cert. #23223.

1013   Ohio, County Births, 1841-2003 (County Courthouses), FamilySearch.org, Harry Wakefield Kleinfelder, Butler Co., Ohio Birth Records, Vol. 3, pg. 148.

1014   Obituary of H.W. Kleinfelder (Hamilton, Ohio, Hamilton Journal News, 19 Apr 1961), Hamilton Lane Library, 300 North Third Street, Hamilton, OH.

1015   U.S., Social Security Applications and Claims Index, 1936-2007, Ancestry.com, Brenda Joyce Kleinfelder Lynch.

1016   Obituary of Brenda J. Lynch (San Diego, California, San Diego Union-Tribune, 08 Nov 2002), San Diego Public Library, 330 Park Boulevard, San Diego, CA.

1017 Find A Grave—Rice Cemetery, Elkhart, Elkhart Co., Indiana, Find A Grave.com, John L. DuVall, Find A Grave Memorial #100743571.

1018 Obituary of John L. DuVall (Elkhart, Indiana, Elkhart Truth, 01 Feb 1984), Elkhart Public Library, 300 South 2nd Street, Elkhart, IN.

1019 West Virginia Marriages, 1853-1970, FamilySearch.org, John L. DuVall and Inez M. McFarland, Brooke County, West Virginia Marriage Records, Vol. 74, pg. 206.

1020 Indiana, Death Certificates, 1908-2011, Ancestry.com, Inez DuVall, death cert. #88-017202.

1021 Find A Grave—Rice Cemetery, Elkhart, Elkhart Co., Indiana, Find A Grave.com, Inez M. DuVall, Find A Grave Memorial #100743560.

1022 Obituary of Inez DuVall (Elkhart, Indiana, Elkhart Truth, 10 May 1988), Elkhart Public Library, 300 South 2nd Street, Elkhart, IN.

1023 Ohio, County Marriages, 1789-2013, FamilySearch.org, John L. DuVall and Inez Mcfarland, Belmont County, Ohio Marriage Records, Vol. 34, pg. 266, lic. #19837.

1024 Obituary of Don DuVall (Elkhart, Indiana, Elkhart Truth, 2 Feb 1974), Elkhart Public Library, 300 South 2nd Street, Elkhart, IN.

1025 Find A Grave—Greenwood Cemetery, Hamilton, Butler Co., Ohio, Find A Grave.com, Oliver Hamer Daggy, Find A Grave Memorial #98354779.

1026 Find A Grave—Greenwood Cemetery, Hamilton, Butler Co., Ohio, Find A Grave.com, Betty Daggy Reidinger, Find A Grave Memorial #160324434.

1027 Obituary of Neil E. Stitsinger (Hamilton, Ohio, Hamilton Journal, 23 Jun 1989), Hamilton Lane Library, 300 North Third Street, Hamilton, OH.

1028 Ohio, Birth Index, 1908-1964, Ancestry.com, Neil A. Stitsinger, state file #1909035252.

1029 Ohio, Deaths, 1908-1932, 1938-2007, Ancestry.com, Neil Stitsinger, death cert. #040086.

1030 Find A Grave—Greenwood Cemetery, Hamilton, Butler Co., Ohio, Find A Grave.com, Neil E. Stitsinger, Find A Grave Memorial #147899204.

1031 Ohio Marriage Index, 1970-1972-2007, Ancestry.com, Paul C. Reidinger and Betty Stitsinger, Butler County, Ohio Marriage Records, Ohio state Vol. 15384, lic. #27711.

1032 Ohio, Deaths, 1908-1932, 1938-2007, Ancestry.com, Paul Reidinger, death cert. #050970.

1033 U.S., Department of Veterans Affairs BIRLS File, 1850-2010, Ancestry.com, Paul Reidinger.

1034 Find A Grave—Greenwood Cemetery, Hamilton, Butler Co., Ohio, Find A Grave.com, Paul Reidinger, Find A Grave Memorial # 160324265.

1035 Obituary of Paul C. Reidinger (Hamilton, Ohio, Hamilton Journal, 09 Jul 1997), Hamilton Lane Library, 300 North Third Street, Hamilton, OH.

1036 Find A Grave—Union Cemetery, Taylorsville, White Oak Twp., Highland Co., Ohio, Find A Grave.com, Maynard Raymond Surber, Find A Grave Memorial #94244474.

1037 Marriage Announcement of Maynard Surber and Isabelle Donohoo (Hillsboro, Ohio, Highland County Press-Gazette, 01 Oct 1943), Highland County District Library, 10 Willettsville Pike, Hillsboro, OH.

1038 Geary County, Kansas Marriage Records, Geary County, Kansas Clerk's Office, 200 East 8th Street, Junction City, KS, Maynard R. Surber and Isabelle Donohoo, Geary County, Kansas Marriage Records, Book W, pg. 309.

1039 Ohio, Deaths, 1908-1932, 1938-2007, Ancestry.com, America Isabelle Surber, death cert. #011655.

1040 Obituary of America Isabelle Surber (Hillsboro, Ohio, Times Gazette, 02 Feb 2001), Highland County District Library, 10 Willettsville Pike, Hillsboro, OH.

1041 Find A Grave—Union Cemetery, Taylorsville, White Oak Twp., Highland Co., Ohio, Find A Grave.com, America Isabelle Donohoo Surber, Find A Grave Memorial #134063090.

1042 Find A Grave—Union Cemetery, Taylorsville, White Oak Twp., Highland Co., Ohio, Find A Grave.com, Cedric Lewis Surber, Find A Grave Memorial #109068892.

1043 Ohio, Birth Index, 1908-1964, Ancestry.com, "Yvonne" Newhouse, Scioto Co., fa: Ira, state file #1929057625.

1044 Ohio, Deaths, 1908-1932, 1938-2007, Ancestry.com, Mary Ruth Surber, death cert. #081138.

1045 U.S., Social Security Applications and Claims Index, 1936-2007, Ancestry.com, Mary Ruth Newhouse Surber.

1046 Obituary of Ruth Surber (Hillsboro, Ohio, Hillsboro Times Gazette, 02 Oct 1998), Highland County District Library, 10 Willettsville Pike, Hillsboro, OH.

1047 Find A Grave—Union Cemetery, Taylorsville, White Oak Twp., Highland Co., Ohio, Find A Grave.com, Mary Ruth Newhouse Surber, Find A Grave Memorial #187688805.

1048 "Surber Farm Recognized By Paper" (Hillsboro, Ohio, Press Gazette,16 Aug 1966), Highland County District Library, 10 Willettsville Pike, Hillsboro, OH.

1049 Highland County, Ohio Marriage Records, Highland County, Ohio Probate Court, Highland County Courthouse, 105 North High Street, Hillsboro, OH, Lowell R. Pegan and Loretta Stroop, Highland County, Ohio Marriage Records, Vol. 24, pg. 248, lic. #20547.

1050 Obituary of Loretta (Stroop/Stroup) Pegan (Hillsboro, Ohio, Press-Gazette, 22 Aug 1972), Highland County District Library, 10 Willettsville Pike, Hillsboro, OH.

1051 Ohio, Deaths, 1908-1932, 1938-2007, Ancestry.com, Loretta J. Pegan, death cert. #070585.

1052 Ohio, Birth Index, 1908-1964, Ancestry.com, Stillborn, state file #1959000536.

1053 Ohio, Birth Index, 1908-1964, Ancestry.com, "Lawrence Pegan", fa: Harold, state file #1941074365.

1054 U.S., Social Security Applications and Claims Index, 1936-2007, Ancestry.com, Allan Jay Pegan.

1055 Clinton County, Ohio Marriage Records, Clinton County, Ohio Records Center and Archives, 111 South Nelson Avenue, Suite 3, Wilmington, OH, Allan J. Pegan and (Ms.) Cook, Vol.19, pg. 243.

1056 St. Joseph County, Indiana Marriage Records, St. Joseph County Clerk, 101 South Main Street, South Bend, IN, Robert E. Scheler II and (Daughter) Holmes, Vol. 157, pg. 195, lic. #46994.

1057 Find A Grave—Fairview Cemetery, South Bend, St. Joseph Co., Indiana, Find A Grave.com, Robert E. Sheler II, Find A Grave Memorial #174806001.

1058 Obituary of Shaun Sheler (Palmer Funeral Homes-Guisinger Chapel, 04 Jan 2012) Palmer Funeral Homes-Guisinger Chapel, 3718 South Michigan Street, South Bend, IN; Online database: http://www.palmerfuneralhomes.com/notices/Shaun-Sheler

1059 Find A Grave—Little Pine Cemetery, Middlebury, Middlebury Twp., Elkhart Co., Indiana, Find A Grave.com, Shaun Sheler, Find A Grave Memorial #174806001.

1060 U.S., Department of Veterans Affairs BIRLS File, 1850-2010, Ancestry.com, John Ridgeway.

1061 U.S., Social Security Applications and Claims Index, 1936-2007, Ancestry.com, John Colin Ridgeway.

1062 Florida Death Index 1877-1998, Ancestry.com, John Colin Ridgeway.

1063 Ohio, Deaths, 1908-1932, 1938-2007, Ancestry.com, Mark D. Greene, death cert. #45506.

1064 Obituary of Mark D. Greene (Dayton, Ohio, Dayton Daily News, 19 Jan 1999), Dayton Metro Library, 215 East Third Street. Dayton, OH.

1065 Find A Grave—Glen Haven Memorial Gardens Cemetery, Donnelsville, Bethel Twp., Clark Co., Ohio, Find A Grave.com, Mark D. Greene, Find A Grave Memorial #123121198.

1066 Ohio, Deaths, 1908-1932, 1938-2007, Ancestry.com, Melanie C. Greene, death cert. #04627.

1067 Find A Grave—Barnes Cemetery, Fairview, New Market Twp., Highland Co., Ohio, Find A Grave.com, Arthur Lowell "Artie" Ludwick, Find A Grave Memorial #123852009.

1068 Ohio Marriage Index, 1970-1972-2007, Ancestry.com, Arthur L. Ludwick and "Paulett" Bohl, Highland County, Ohio Marriage Records, Ohio state Vol. 12022, lic. #17635.

1069 Ohio, Deaths, 1908-1932, 1938-2007, Ancestry.com, Paulette Pendall Ludwick, death cert. #012936.

1070 Obituary of Paulette Pendall Ludwick (Hillsboro, Ohio, Highland County Times Gazette, 28 Jan 2002), Highland County District Library, 10 Willettsville Pike, Hillsboro, OH.

1071 Find A Grave—Sugar Grove Cemetery, Wilmington, Union Twp., Clinton Co., Ohio, Find A Grave.com, Paulette Pendall Ludwick, Find A Grave Memorial #116241655.

1072 Find A Grave—Show Low Cemetery, Show Low, Navajo Co., Arizona, Find A Grave.com, Kenneth Roush, Find A Grave Memorial #26585915.

1073 California, Marriage Index, 1949-1959, Ancestry.com, Kenneth E. Roush and Helen P. Shipps, Sonoma County, California Marriage Records, California state file #76950.

1074 California Birth Index, 1905-1995, Ancestry.com, Helen Patricia Eldred.

1075 U.S., Social Security Applications and Claims Index, 1936-2007, Ancestry.com, Helen Patricia Eldred Shipps Roush Webber.

1076 California Death Certificate, California Health and Strategic Planning, Vital Records, M.S. 5103, P.O. Box 997410, Sacramento, CA, Helen Patricia Webber, death cert. #36008996.

1077 Find A Grave—Troutwine Cemetery, Dodson Twp., Highland Co., Ohio, Find A Grave.com, Gary Lee Luck, Find A Grave Memorial #128016347.

1078 Find A Grave—Highland Memorial Park Cemetery, New Berlin, Waukesha Co., Wisconsin, Jeffrey R. Long, #160680522.

1079 Find A Grave—Highland Memorial Park Cemetery, New Berlin, Waukesha Co., Wisconsin, Mary Jo Jankowski Long, #160680352.

1080 Obituary of Mary Jo Long (Milwaukee, Wisconsin, Milwaukee Journal-Sentinel, August 18, 2010), Milwaukee Public Library, 814 West Wisconsin Avenue, Milwaukee, WI.

1081 Engagement Announcement of Douglas M. Carroll and Naomi Kay Prince (Cincinnati, Ohio, Cincinnati Enquirer, 25 Jun 1961), The Public Library of Cincinnati and Hamilton County, 800 Vine Street, Cincinnati, OH.

1082 Find A Grave—Idaho State Veterans Cemetery, Boise, Ada Co., Idaho, Find A Grave.com, Dwan Ruble "Bill" Williams, Find A Grave Memorial #127995313.

1083 Idaho, Marriage Index, 1947-1961, FamilySearch.org, Dwan Ruble Williams and Marilyn Joan Parker, Ada County, Idaho Marriage Records, lic. #04586.

1084 U.S., Social Security Applications and Claims Index, 1936-2007, Ancestry.com, Jacob E. Roush.

1085 U.S., Department of Veterans Affairs BIRLS File, 1850-2010, Ancestry.com, Jacob Roush.

1086 Ohio, Deaths, 1908-1932, 1938-2007, Ancestry.com, Jacob E. Roush, death cert. #080708.

1087 Find A Grave—Dayton Memorial Park Cemetery, Dayton, Montgomery Co., Ohio, Find A Grave.com, Jacob E. Roush, Find A Grave Memorial #137415705.

1088 Obituary of Jacob "Jake" Roush (Dayton, Ohio, Dayton Daily News, 15 Oct 1972), Dayton Metro Library, 215 East Third Street. Dayton, OH.

1089 Ohio, Birth Index, 1908-1964, Ancestry.com, Richard Tanner, state file ##1924073552.

1090 Obituary of Richard F. Tanner (Dayton, Ohio, Dayton Daily News, 29 Jan 2017), Dayton Metro Library, 215 East Third Street. Dayton, OH.

1091 U.S., Social Security Applications and Claims Index, 1936-2007, Ancestry.com, Douglas Troy Smith.

1092 Ohio, County Marriages, 1789-2013, FamilySearch.org, Charles Wilkin and Eilene Snead, Vol. 22, pg. 165, lic. #16722.

1093 Ohio, Birth Index, 1908-1964, Ancestry.com, Eilene Snead, state file #925004547.

1094 U.S., Social Security Applications and Claims Index, 1936-2007, Ancestry.com, Eilene Snead Wilkin Ross Spicer Davis.

1095 Indiana, Death Certificates, 1908-2011, Ancestry.com, Eilene Davis, death cert. #83-051518.

1096 Find A Grave—Prairie Grove Cemetery, Fort Wayne, Allen Co., Indiana, Find A Grave.com, Eilene Snead Davis, Find A Grave Memorial #31216447.

1097 Ohio, Birth Index, 1908-1964, Ancestry.com, Patsy G. Mason, fa. Norman, state file #1929108170.

1098 Obituary of Doris Geraldine Rhoades (Hillsboro, Ohio, Times Gazette, 01 Jul 2016), Highland County District Library, 10 Willettsville Pike, Hillsboro, OH.

1099 Find A Grave—New Lynchburg Masonic Cemetery/Lynchburg F & AM Cemetery, Lynchburg, Dodson Twp., Highland Co., Ohio, Find A Grave.com, Doris Geraldine Mason Rhoades, Find A Grave Memorial #166244013.

1100 Ohio, Birth Index, 1908-1964, Ancestry.com, Kenneth Wilkin, state file #1946080487.

1101 U.S., Social Security Applications and Claims Index, 1936-2007, Ancestry.com, Kenneth Michael Wilkin.

1102 U.S., Department of Veterans Affairs BIRLS File, 1850-2010, Ancestry.com, Kenneth Wilkin.

1103 Indiana, Death Certificates, 1908-2011, Ancestry.com, Kenneth M. Wilkin, death cert. #89-031553.

1104 Ohio, County Marriages, 1789-2013, FamilySearch.org, Floyd W. Roades and "Delores" Wilkin, Highland County, Ohio Marriage Records, Vol. 22, pg. 252, lic. #16897.

1105 U.S., Social Security Applications and Claims Index, 1936-2007, Ancestry.com, Howard Robert Manis.

1106 Find A Grave—Arlington Memorial Gardens Cemetery, Mount Healthy, Springfield Twp., Hamilton Co., Ohio, Find A Grave.com, Howard R. Manis, Find A Grave Memorial #166824571.

1107 Ohio Marriage Index, 1970-1972-2007, Ancestry.com, James H. Price and Sonia M. Cole, Franklin County, Ohio Marriage Records, Ohio state Vol. 8112, cert. #18174.

1108 Ohio, Deaths, 1908-1932, 1938-2007, Ancestry.com, James Harold Price, death cert. #067807.

1109 Ohio, Birth Index, 1908-1964, Ancestry.com, James H. Price, state file #1927079625.

1110 Obituary of James H. Price (Columbus, OH, Columbus Dispatch, 21 Sep 1993), Ohio History Center Archives and Library, Ohio History Center, 800 East 17th Avenue, Columbus, OH.

1111 Obituary of James R. Barker (Hillsboro, Ohio, Highland County News-Gazette, April 10, 2008), Highland County District Library, 10 Willettsville Pike, Hillsboro, OH.

1112 Find A Grave—Lynchburg Masonic Cemetery, Lynchburg, Dodson Twp., Highland Co., Ohio, Find A Grave.com, James Randall Barker, Find A Grave Memorial #35009271.

1113 Obituary of Ralph D. Walker (Greenfield, Ohio, Greenfield Daily Times, 23 Jul 1990), Highland County District Library, 10 Willettsville Pike, Hillsboro, OH.

1114 Ohio, Deaths, 1908-1932, 1938-2007, Ancestry.com, Ralph Doyle Walker, death cert. #059635.

1115 Ohio, Birth Index, 1908-1964, Ancestry.com, Ralph Walker, state file #1923091874.

1116 Find A Grave—Resthaven Memorial Gardens Cemetery, Hillsboro, Liberty Twp., Highland Co., Ohio, Find A Grave.com, Ralph D. Walker, Find A Grave Memorial #113568458.

1117 Obituary of William E. Hostetler (Greenfield, Ohio, Greenfield Daily Times, 30 Oct 1992), Ohio History Center Archives and Library, Ohio History Center, 800 East 17th Avenue, Columbus, OH.

1118 Ohio, County Marriages, 1789-2013, FamilySearch.org, William E. Hostetler and June Phyllis Campbell, Highland County, Ohio Marriage Records, Vol. 23, pg. 249, lic. #33481.

1119 Ohio, Deaths, 1908-1932, 1938-2007, Ancestry.com, William E. Hostetler, death cert. #085026.

1120 Find A Grave—New Lynchburg Masonic Cemetery/Lynchburg F & AM Cemetery, Lynchburg, Dodson Twp., Highland Co., Ohio, Find A Grave.com, William E. Hostetler, Find A Grave Memorial #164455707.

1121 Ohio, County Marriages, 1789-2013, FamilySearch.org, Donald E. Campbell and Mary L. Cowman, Highland County, Ohio Marriage Records, Vol. 23, pg. 424, lic. #08216.

1122 Ohio, Birth Index, 1908-1964, Ancestry.com, Mary L. Cowman, state file #1935077624.

1123 Find A Grave—Troutwine Cemetery, Dodson Twp., Highland Co., Ohio, Find A Grave.com, Jimmie Gaylord Barker, Find A Grave Memorial #95591515.

1124 Marriage Announcement of Ray Howard Hamilton and Barbara Ann Roush (Hillsboro, Ohio, Hillsboro Press Gazette, 20 Mar 1959), Highland County District Library, 10 Willettsville Pike, Hillsboro, OH.

1125 Florida Death Index 1877-1998, Ancestry.com, Ray Howard Hamilton.

1126 Find A Grave—Lakeside Memorial Park Cemetery, Winter Haven, Polk Co., Florida, Find A Grave.com, Ray H. Hamilton, Find A Grave Memorial #138338180.

1127 "Haven man charged with beating step-father to death with bat" (Lakeland, Florida, Lakeland Ledger, 09 Oct 1983),

State Library and Archives of Florida, R.A. Gray Building, 500 North Bronaugh Street, Tallahassee, FL.

1128 Ohio Marriage Index, 1970-1972-2007, Ancestry.com, William B. Storer and Barbara A. Hamilton, Highland County, Ohio Marriage Records, Ohio state Vol. 37354, cert. #10337.

1129 Ohio, Deaths, 1908-1932, 1938-2007, Ancestry.com, William B. Storer Junior, death cert. #041928.

1130 Find A Grave—Hillsboro Cemetery, Hillsboro, Liberty Twp., Highland Co., Ohio, Find A Grave.com, William B. Storer, Jr., Find A Grave Memorial #121938452.

1131 Ohio Marriage Index, 1970-1972-2007, Ancestry.com, Daniel A. Hupp and Janet S. Graves, Ross County, Ohio Marriage Records, Ohio state Vol. 7930, lic. #82019.

1132 Obituary of Daniel A. Hupp (Chillicothe, OH, Chillicothe Gazette, January 15, 2013), Chillicothe & Ross County Library, 140 South Paint Street, Chillicothe, OH.

1133 Find A Grave—Floral Hills Memory Gardens Cemetery, Massieville, Huntington Twp., Ross Co., Ohio, Find A Grave.com, Daniel Allen Hupp, Find A Grave Memorial #103553764.

1134 Obituary of Sharon K. Wilkin (Hillsboro, Ohio, Highland County Times Gazette, 10 May 1999), Highland County District Library, 10 Willettsville Pike, Hillsboro, OH.

1135 Ohio, Deaths, 1908-1932, 1938-2007, Ancestry.com, Sharon Kay Wilkin, death cert. #041814.

1136 Find A Grave—New Lynchburg Masonic Cemetery/Lynchburg F & AM Cemetery, Lynchburg, Dodson Twp., Highland Co., Ohio, Find A Grave.com, Sharon Kay Fender Wilkin, Find A Grave Memorial #97784026.

1137 Find A Grave—New Lynchburg Masonic Cemetery/Lynchburg F & AM Cemetery, Lynchburg, Dodson Twp., Highland Co., Ohio, Find A Grave.com, Infant Daughter Wilkin, Find A Grave Memorial #97788115.

1138 Ohio, County Marriages, 1789-2013, FamilySearch.org, Lynn Griffith and Carol J. Williams, Highland County, Ohio Marriage Records, Vol. 23, pg. 376, Ohio state file #46424.

1139 U.S., Department of Veterans Affairs BIRLS File, 1850-2010, Ancestry.com, Jack Griffith.

1140 Find A Grave—Dayton National Cemetery, Dayton, Montgomery Co., Ohio, Find A Grave.com, Jack L. Griffith, Find A Grave Memorial #72682067.

1141 Obituary of Alfred Milton "Milt" Woodmansee III (Hillsboro, Ohio, Highland County Times Gazette, 06 Jan 2010), Highland County District Library, 10 Willettsville Pike, Hillsboro, OH.

1142 Ohio, Birth Index, 1908-1964, Ancestry.com, Alfred Woodmansee, state file #1931029637.

1143 Find A Grave—Greenlawn Cemetery, Milford, Miami Twp., Clermont Co., Ohio, Find A Grave.com, Alfred Milton "Milt" Woodmansee III, Find A Grave Memorial #122420915.

1144 Ohio, Deaths, 1908-1932, 1938-2007, Ancestry.com, Jack W. Griffith, death cert. #091705.

1145 Obituary of Charles Winkle (Hillsboro, Ohio, Highland County Times Gazette, 19 Oct 2014), Highland County District Library, 10 Willettsville Pike, Hillsboro, OH.

1146 Ohio, Birth Index, 1908-1964, Ancestry.com, Charles Winkle, state file #1932096136.

1147 Find A Grave—New Lynchburg Masonic Cemetery/Lynchburg F & AM Cemetery, Lynchburg, Dodson Twp., Highland Co., Ohio, Find A Grave.com, Charles Junior Winkle, Find A Grave Memorial #137388003.

1148 Find A Grave—Rest Haven Memorial Park Cemetery, Evendale, Sycamore Twp., Hamilton Co., Ohio, Find A Grave.com, David Lee Kelley, Find A Grave Memorial #171468698.

1149 Find A Grave—Black Creek Memorial Cemetery, Freeport, Walton Co., Florida, Find A Grave.com, Candus Gay Williams Nash, Find A Grave Memorial #110297266.

1150 Find A Grave—Guernsey County Memorial Gardens, Cambridge, Cambridge Twp., Guernsey Co., Ohio, Find A Grave.com, Joseph T. Spilker, Find A Grave Memorial #45724093.

1151 Obituary of Shirley Edna Spilker (Cambridge, Ohio, The Daily Jeffersonian, 18 Jun 2013), Guernsey County Public Library, Crossroads Branch, 63500 Byesville Road, Cambridge, OH.

1152 Indiana, Marriages, 1810-2001, FamilySearch.com, Joseph Todd Spilker and Shirley Edna Smith, Blackford County, Indiana Marriage Records, Vol. 9, pg. 90, lic. #34-59

1153 Indiana, Birth Certificates, 1907-1940, Ancestry.com, Shirley Edna Smith, birth cert. #22852.

1154 Find A Grave—Royal Oak Memorial Gardens Cemetery, Brookville, Clay Twp., Montgomery Co., Ohio, Find A Grave.com, Roger O. Ludwick, Find A Grave Memorial #174047153.

1155 Ohio, Birth Index, 1908-1964, Ancestry.com, Joy A. Mann, state file #1936062994.

1156 Obituary of Joy A. Ludwick (Dayton, Ohio, Dayton Daily News, 14 Mar 2008), (Dayton, Ohio, Dayton Daily Journal, 15 Jul 1986), Dayton Metro Library, 215 East Third Street. Dayton, OH.

1157 Find A Grave—Royal Oak Memorial Gardens Cemetery, Brookville, Clay Twp., Montgomery Co., Ohio, Find A Grave.com, Joy A. Ludwick, Find A Grave Memorial# 2526892.

1158 U.S. Public Records Index, 1950-1993, Vol. 1, Ancestry.com, June Ludwick, Montgomery, Alabama.

1159 Obituary of June Ludwick (Montgomery, Alabama, Montgomery Advertiser, 27 Aug 2015), Montgomery City-County Library, Governors Square, Montgomery, AL.

1160 Find A Grave—Memorial Gardens Cemetery, Prattville, Autauga Co., Alabama, Find A Grave.com, June Loretta Ludwick, Find A Grave Memorial #151515595.

1161 Ohio, County Births, 1841-2003 (County Courthouses), FamilySearch.org, Robert J. Ramseyer, Holmes Co. Births, Vol. 4, pg. 200.

1162 Ohio, Birth Index, 1908-1964, Ancestry.com, Stillborn infant Ramseyer, state file #1961002739.

1163 Find A Grave—Lebanon Cemetery, Lebanon, Turtle Creek Twp., Warren Co., Ohio, Find A Grave.com, Robyn Bowman Kemp, Find A Grave Memorial #42296133.

1164 Obituary of Daniel Tsaloff (Akron, Ohio, Akron Beacon Journal, 13 Sep 1975), Akron-Summit County Public Library, 60 South High Street Akron, OH.

1165 Ohio, Deaths, 1908-1932, 1938-2007, Ancestry.com, Daniel Tsaloff, death cert. #202170.

1166 Ohio Marriage Index, 1970-1972-2007, Ancestry.com, Thomas W. Kemp and Robyn V. Tsaloff, Montgomery County, Ohio Marriage Records, Ohio state Vol. #10198, lic. #2651.

1167 Indiana, Birth Certificates, 1907-1940, Ancestry.com, Thomas Ward Kemp, birth cert. #9139.

1168 Find A Grave—Lebanon Cemetery, Lebanon, Turtle Creek Twp., Warren Co., Ohio, Find A Grave.com, Bruce Steven Bowman, Find A Grave Memorial #42296134.

1169 Find A Grave—Lebanon Cemetery, Lebanon, Turtle Creek Twp., Warren Co., Ohio, Find A Grave.com, Nicholas Brian Bowman, Find A Grave Memorial #42296135.

1170 Obituary of Phillip Peter Rossy (Asbury Park, New Jersey, Asbury Park Press, 16 Apr 2008), Asbury Park Library, 500 First Avenue, Asbury Park, New Jersey.

1171 Ohio, Deaths, 1908-1932, 1938-2007, Ancestry.com, Minnie Pegan, death cert, #042369.

1172 Find A Grave—Carmel Cemetery, Carmel, Brushcreek Twp., Highland Co., Ohio, Find A Grave.com, Minnie Pegan, Find A Grave Memorial #90431183.

1173 Ohio, Deaths, 1908-1932, 1938-2007, Ancestry.com, James R. Pegan, death cert. #081430.

1174 Florida Marriage Indexes, 1822-1875, 1927-2001, Ancestry.com, (Mr.) Durett and Debbie Scott, Duval County, Florida Marriage Records, Florida state Vol. 6564, lic. #136373.

1175 Ohio Marriage Index, 1970-1972-2007, Ancestry.com, James R. Haney and "Margare" Macke, Hamilton County, Ohio Marriage Records, Ohio state Vol. 5288, lic. #12413.

1176 Ohio, Deaths, 1908-1932, 1938-2007, Ancestry.com, James Rickey Haney, death cert. #40729.

1177 U.S., Social Security Applications and Claims Index, 1936-2007, Ancestry.com, James Rickey Haney.

1178 Find A Grave—Arlington Memorial Gardens Cemetery, Mount Healthy, Springfield Twp., Hamilton Co., Ohio, Find A Grave.com, James Rickey Haney, Find A Grave Memorial #171245737.

1179 Ohio, Deaths, 1908-1932, 1938-2007, Ancestry.com, Jennifer R. Herdman, death cert. #036624.

1180 Obituary of Jennifer Renee Herdman (Hillsboro, Ohio, Hillsboro Press Gazette, 17 May 1990), Ohio History Center Archives and Library, Ohio History Center, 800 East 17th Avenue, Columbus, OH.

1181 Obituary of James Eugene Pegan (Wilmington, Ohio, Wilmington News Journal, 02 Aug 2005), Wilmington Public Library of Clinton County, 268 North South Street, Wilmington, OH..

1182 California, Marriage Index, 1960-1985, Ancestry.com, Carl Lynch and Brenda J. Kleinfelder, Kern County, California Marriage Records, California state lic. #24317.

1183 Find A Grave—Northport Rural Cemetery, Long Island, Suffolk Co., New York, Find A Grave.com, Donald H. Duvall, Find A Grave Memorial# 181069534.

1184 Indiana, Marriage Certificates, 1917-2005, Ancestry.com, Donald Harry Duvall and (Miss) Freed, Elkhart County, Indiana Marriage Records, Indiana state lic. #64-020750.

1185 Find A Grave—Northport Rural Cemetery, Long Island, Suffolk Co., New York, Find A Grave.com, Infant Boy DuVall, Find A Grave Memorial #98363874.

1186 Ohio, Deaths, 1908-1932, 1938-2007, Ancestry.com, Kim. L. Surber, death cert. #27794.

1187 U.S., Social Security Applications and Claims Index, 1936-2007, Ancestry.com, Kim Loreen Sussman.

1188 Ohio Marriage Index, 1970-1972-2007, Ancestry.com, Mr. Surber and Martha Weber, Hamilton County, Ohio Marriage Records, Ohio state Vol. 9491, lic. #44773.

1189 Ohio, County Marriages, 1789-2013, FamilySearch.org, Terry L. Surber and Barbara Kaufman, Montgomery County, Ohio Marriage Records, Ohio state Vol. 9947, lic. #48954.

1190 Obituary of Barbara M. Surber (Hillsboro, Ohio, Highland County Times Gazette, 13 Oct 2005), Highland County District Library, 10 Willettsville Pike, Hillsboro, OH.

1191 Ohio, Deaths, 1908-1932, 1938-2007, Ancestry.com, Barbara Miller Surber, death cert. #96889.

1192 Find A Grave—Hamer Township Cemetery, Hamer Twp., Highland Co., Ohio, Find A Grave.com, Mary Jane Pegan, Find A Grave Memorial #132601928.

1193 Find A Grave—Hamer Township Cemetery, Hamer Twp., Highland Co., Ohio, Find A Grave.com, Mary. B. Richards, Find A Grave Memorial #132601871.

1194 Ohio, Deaths, 1908-1932, 1938-2007, Ancestry.com, Mary Beth Richards, death cert. #051307.

1195 Find A Grave—Ferncliff Cemetery, Springfield, Springfield Twp., Clark Co., Ohio, Melanie C. Greene, Find A Grave Memorial #11054896.

1196 Ohio Death Index, 1908-1932, 1938-1944, and 1958-2007, FamilySearch.org, Rodney E. Harris, death cert. #021018.

1197 Find A Grave—Ferncliff Cemetery, Springfield, Springfield Twp., Clark Co., Ohio, Rodney E. Harris, Find A Grave Memorial #45028298.

1198 Ohio Marriage Index, 1970-1972-2007, Ancestry.com, William H. Ursell and (Mrs.) Stewart, Highland County, Ohio Marriage Records, state Vol. 6250, lic. #73965.

1199 Ohio, Birth Index, 1908-1964, Ancestry.com, William Ursell, state file #1946053283.

1200 Obituary of William Harlan Ursell (Hillsboro, Ohio, Hillsboro Times Gazette, 04 Aug 2010), Highland County District Library, 10 Willettsville Pike, Hillsboro, OH.

1201 Find A Grave—New Lynchburg Masonic Cemetery/Lynchburg F & AM Cemetery, Lynchburg, Dodson Twp., Highland Co., Ohio, Find A Grave.com, William Harlan Ursell, Find A Grave Memorial #57464355.

1202 Ohio, Birth Index, 1908-1964, Ancestry.com, Diane Barker, state file #1964001341.

1203 Ohio, Deaths, 1908-1932, 1938-2007, Ancestry.com, Diane Evans Wilkin, death cert. #080672.

1204 U.S., Social Security Applications and Claims Index, 1936-2007, Ancestry.com, Diane Louise Barker Evans Wilkin.

1205 Find A Grave— Saint Patrick Cemetery, Fayetteville, Perry Twp., Brown Co., Ohio, Find A Grave.com, Diane L. Barker Evans Wilkin, Find A Grave Memorial #138761762

1206 Obituary of Diane Wilkin (Hillsboro, Ohio, Press Gazette, 26 Sep 1995), Highland County District Library, 10 Willettsville Pike, Hillsboro, OH.

1207 Ohio Marriage Index, 1970-1972-2007, Ancestry.com, Douglas D. Willman and (Daughter) Manis, Hamilton County, Ohio Marriage Records, state Vol. 9141, lic. #66774.

1208 Obituary of Douglas Dean Willmann (Lebanon, Ohio, Oswald-Hoskins Funeral Home, 13 Oct 2010), Oswald-Hoskins Funeral Home, 329 East Mulberry Street, Lebanon, OH; Online database: http://www.hoskinsfh.com/obituary/887103

1209 Find A Grave—Arlington Memorial Gardens Cemetery, Mount Healthy, Springfield Twp., Hamilton Co., Ohio, Find A Grave.com, Douglas D Willmann, Find A Grave Memorial #166884578.

1210 Ohio, Death Records, 1908-1932, 1938-2007, Ancestry.com, David M. Willmann, death cert. #068838.

1211 Obituary of Natoshia Shyann Marie Pegan, Licking County Genealogical Society Library, 101 West Main Street, Newark, OH, Newark (OH) Advocate, pub. 17 Oct 1994.

1212 Find A Grave—Arlington Memorial Gardens Cemetery, Mount Healthy, Springfield Twp., Hamilton Co., Ohio, Find A Grave.com, David M Willmann, Find A Grave Memorial #166886451.

1213 Find A Grave—East Tennessee Cemetery, Blountville, Sullivan Co., Tennessee, Find A Grave.com, Brady Nussman, Find A Grave Memorial #110893090.

1214 Obituary of Brady Owen Nussman (Johnson City, Tennessee, Johnson City Press, 15 May 2012), Johnson City Public Library, 100 West Millard Street, Johnson City, TN.

1215 Find A Grave—Carmel Cemetery, Carmel, Brushcreek Twp., Highland Co., Ohio, Find A Grave.com, Natoshia Pegan, Find A Grave Memorial #90431184.

[A] Klise, Rev. J.W., *The County of Highland: A History of Highland County, Ohio, from its Earliest Days; With Special Chapters on the Bench and Bar, Medical Profession, Educational Development, Industry and Agriculture, and Biographical Sketches, Vol. 2*; ed. by A.E. Hough. Madison, Wisconsin: Northwestern Historical Association; 1902, pg. 154.

Harrison James Pegan

1. **Harrison James[5] Pegan** (*Robert A.[4], Andrew[3], Andrew[2] Pagan, James[1]*) was born on September 30, 1813, in Strabane Twp., Washington Co., Pennsylvania.[1, 2] He was the son of Robert A. Pegan and Christina or Christiana Ingle. He died in Lynchburg, Dodson Twp., Highland Co., Ohio, on April 27, 1854, at age 40.[≠] He was buried in Lynchburg Masonic Cemetery, Lynchburg, Dodson Twp., Highland Co., Ohio.[2]

Harrison Pegan was probably born in Strabane Twp., Washington Co., Pennsylvania, as his parents, Robert and Christine Ingle Pegan, were residing there in the 1810 U.S. Federal Census *(Census Place: Strabane, Washington, Pennsylvania; Roll 57; Page: 12;& nbsp; Image: 00017; entry for Pagan, Robert)* and Strabane Twp., Washington Co., Pennsylvania tax records indicate.[3] He moved with his parents to Ohio, who were in Union Twp., Highland County by 1820 *(Census Place: Union, Highland, Ohio; Roll M33_92; Page: 37; Image: 74; entry for Pagan, Robert)* and Montgomery County in 1830 *(Census Place: Wayne, Montgomery, Ohio, Roll: M19-136, Page 245; entry for Pagan, Robert)*.

His middle name, James, is documented on his daughter Margaret Pegan Roush Warren's 1909 death certificate, as her father is listed as "Jas. Pegan".[4]

Harrison James married **Sarah Ann Mentzer** on March 6, 1834, in Greene Co., Ohio.[1, 5] They had five children. Sarah Ann Mentzer was born in Mount Joy Twp., Lancaster Co., Pennsylvania, on June 28, 1817.[6] Sarah Ann reached age 50 and died in New Market Twp., Highland Co., Ohio, on January 15, 1868.[7, 8] She was buried in Strange Cemetery, Hamer Twp., Highland Co., Ohio.[≠]

Harrison and Sarah applied for their marriage license in Greene County, Ohio, where Sarah's parents, Andrew and Nancy Wallace Mentzer, were living, according to Greene County tax records.[9] They were married by Rev. David Winters of David's Church, a German Reformed Church, named for its noted famous minister. (This church is still in existence at 170 West David Road in Van Buren Township., Montgomery County, Ohio, which is now in the city of Dayton.) But this church has no record of the marriage or membership of either family. This is the same Rev. David Winters who was sued for slander by Harrison's brother William Louis/Lewis Pagan in 1839, as described in chapters for Robert Pegan and William Louis Pegan.[10]

Harrison Pegan Sr. was a carpenter, who, like his brothers John and Elsey, was probably trained by Joseph Pagan/Pagin, the master carpenter of the Preble and Montgomery counties, Ohio area.[11] Joseph Pagan/Pagin may have been a relative, but no blood relationship has been established. However, Joseph's daughter Drusilla did marry Harrison's brother William Louis, so it is obvious that the two families had a prior connection and knew each other.

In 1835, Harrison Sr. buys property in Rossville, Spring Creek Twp., Miami Co., Ohio across the river from Piqua. His brother John Pegan may have sold him the property and not recorded it, as a deed for Harrison buying this land cannot be found. However, an earlier deed for John buying the property is recorded, as is the deed for Harrison selling it to John Amarine, the husband of Catherine Shearer Amarine, the sister of John's first wife Rebecca Shearer.[12, 13]

In late 1836, Harrison and Sarah Mentzer Pegan removed to Enon, Mad River Twp., Clark Co., Ohio. Harrison may have secured employment at the large carriage works in that town.[14] In June 1840, he buys lot #12 in Enon.[15]

Harrison Pegan Sr. first appears as "Harrison Pagan" in the U.S. Census in 1840 in Enon, Mad River Twp., Clark Co., Ohio *(Census Place: Clark, Ohio; Roll: 383; Page: 74; Image 152)*. The household includes one male child under five (John Andrew), one female child under five (Martha), one male 20-30 (Harrison Sr.), one female 20-30 (Sarah Mentzer Pegan).

While he lived in Enon, Harrison Pegan Sr. was either elected or appointed as one of three school directors for District #8 in Mad River Township. He and the other school directors buy a parcel of land in Enon for a new school in July 1843.[16]

In 1846, Harrison sells his property in Enon, Mad River Twp., Clark Co., Ohio and moves back to Miami County, this time to the town of Piqua, Washington Twp., Miami Co., Ohio.[17] Between 1846-1847 he buys two outlots and a piece of another in Piqua.[18, 19] In Piqua he may have worked for a cabinetmaker and furniture manufacturer, Robert Muchmore. A "Mrs. Muchmore" (Eliza) lived on property just west of Harrison Sr.'s. Three years later, Harrison sells his two largest land parcels in Piqua, one to his brother John.[20, 21]

In 1850, 35-year-old Harrison Pegan, a carpenter, is living in Piqua, Washington Twp., Miami Co., Ohio *(Census Place: Washington, Miami, Ohio; Roll: M432_711; Page: 346; Image: 69)*. Also in the household are Sarah, age 34, John Andrew, 14, Martha, 11, William, 10, and Margaret, two. As the census was taken on August 2, 1850, but retroactive to June 1. Listed as residing with them is "Margaret Mitchell", 19, born Ohio. This was Margaret Mentzer Mitchell, Sarah' Mentzer Pegan's sister, who married John Mitchell on July 30, 1850, but for some reason was enumerated under her married name instead of her maiden name.[22] Living nearby, in the same township, are Harrison's brothers, Elsey and John Pegan and their families.

In December 1853, Harrison and Sarah Mentzer Pegan sell their last property in Miami County to a relative of their brother-in-law John Mitchell.[23] Harrison, who may have already been ill, may have wished to move back to Highland County, Ohio, where he'd spent his boyhood. Or, perhaps they moved because their eldest son John Andrew had died, as in that era (and now) families often change residences after the death of a child.

Harrison died intestate on April 27, 1854 in Lynchburg, Dodson Twp., Highland County of "dropsy of the chest" (edema caused by congestive heart failure), according to his obituary in the Highland Weekly News.[24] Harrison Pegan Sr. was one of the first people buried in the (Old) Masonic Cemetery on High Street in Lynchburg, Dodson Twp., Highland Co., Ohio. He shares a plot with his brother Henry, Henry's wife Harriet Stroup Pegan and Henry's sons Pleasant and Michael.[2]

Harrison's estate in Highland County is probated there starting in May 1854, although the probate packet is mistakenly dated as 1852. His widow, Sarah, declines to administer the estate and she asks that a Samuel Agnew, a Highland County resident of unknown relationship to the family, is appointed administrator by the court.[25] Samuel Agnew was also the guardian of Harrison's three surviving minor (and unmarried) children, William Louis, Margaret and Harrison Jr., until 1856, although the children remained with their mother Sarah.[26]

Who was Samuel Agnew? Little is known about him. Research showed he married but had no children. Was he a cousin from either the Ingle or Pegan families, or just a trusted friend? Could he be the son of Robert Pegan's missing sister? There is no documentation to prove this, as the name of Samuel's mother is unknown. But Samuel Agnew's family resided in Washington County, Pennsylvania at the same time Andrew Pegan Sr. and Robert Pegan lived. Samuel wasn't old enough (b. 1808-9) to have been the husband or son of one of Harrison's mother Christiana/Christina Ingle Pegan's sisters. Nor was he the husband of one of Sarah Mentzer Pegan's sisters. It does seem odd that this seemingly unrelated man was chosen to administer Harrison's estate, and not one of Harrison's brothers, Andrew or Henry, who were also Highland County residents. However, there is a possibility that Agnew was descended from Margaret Pagan Herron, Harrison's great-aunt and a sister to his paternal grandfather, Andrew Pegan II. Her line has not been traced.

The only child not mentioned in the guardianships is daughter Martha Jane. Three months after

Harrison Sr. dies, Martha Jane, age 14, marries her first cousin, Leonidas Alonzo Pegan, the 24-year-old son of Harrison's eldest sibling Andrew Pegan. Sarah Mentzer Pegan gives permission for her underage daughter's marriage.[27]

In 1855, Sarah Mentzer Pegan, along with two sisters, inherits the rights to bounty land in Garfield Co., Nebraska, awarded posthumously to their late brother Abraham, who fought in the Mexican War. She and her two sisters sell it to a James Mix.[28]

Sarah Mentzer remarries to widower John Tedrick on March 25, 1856.[29] On April 11, 1856, John Tedrick petitions the court to become guardian of the remaining minor Pegan children, William age 14 years, 10 months, Margaret, six, and Harrison Jr., five. Samuel Agnew was the witness to this petition, which was granted.[26]

In 1860, Sarah Mentzer Pegan Tedrick is enumerated as Sarah "Tedwell", living with second husband John "Tedwell" and daughter and son, Margaret Pagan and Harrison Pagan II in New Market Twp., Highland Co., Ohio *(Census Place: New Market, Highland, Ohio; Roll: M653_987; Page: 277/16; Image: 201)*. John is age 55, born in Virginia, Sarah is 42, born in Pennsylvania; Margaret and Harrison II, both born in Ohio, are ages 12 and nine respectively. Also in the household is a George Pugh, age 21, born Ohio, probably a hired hand for their farm. Oddly, son John Tedrick II (1859-1878), Sarah's son by her second husband, is not enumerated.

Sarah Mentzer Pegan Tedrick is buried alongside her second husband, John Tedrick, and sons John Tedrick Jr. and William Louis Pegan in Strange Cemetery, Hamer Twp., Highland Co., Ohio.[6] As of August 2006, the top of her headstone, with her name, is missing. One published account of burial records in Hamer Township, has her birthdate as June 21, 1817, according to her age in years, months and days on her gravestone.[7,8] But according to the baptismal records at Christ Evangelical Lutheran Church in Elizabethtown, Mount Joy Twp., Lancaster Co., Pennsylvania, she was born on June 28, 1817 and baptized on October 12 of that year.[6]

Children of Harrison James Pegan and Sarah Ann Mentzer:

+ 2 m I. **John Andrew**[6] **Pegan** was born in Rossville, Springcreek Twp., Miami Co., Ohio, in 1836. He died in Piqua, Washington Twp., Miami Co., Ohio?, between 1850 and April 27, 1854, probably in early 1853.

+ 3 f II. **Martha Jane**[6] **Pegan** was born in Piqua, Washington Twp., Miami Co., Ohio, on August 19, 1839.[30] She was also known as **Mattie or Jane**. Martha Jane died in Houston, Harris Co., Texas, on June 22, 1916.[30, 31]

+ 4 m III. **William Louis**[6] **Pegan** was born in Enon, Mad River Twp., Clark Co., Ohio, on May 27, 1841.[32, 33] He died in Union Twp., Highland Co., Ohio, on November 18, 1881.[32]

+ 5 f IV. **Margaret Mary**[6] **Pegan** was born in Piqua, Washington Twp., Miami Co., Ohio, on September 15, 1847.[4, 34] She was also known as **Maggie**. Margaret Mary died in Martinsville, Clark Twp., Clinton Co., Ohio, on March 29, 1909.[4, 34]

+ 6 m V. **Harrison James**[6] **PeGan II** was born in Piqua, Washington Twp., Miami Co., Ohio, on June 22, 1851.[35, 36, 37] He died in Washington Twp., Miami Co., Indiana, on July 7, 1936.[35, 36, 37]

6th Generation

2. **John Andrew**[6] **Pegan** (*Harrison James*[5], *Robert A.*[4], *Andrew*[3], *Andrew*[2] *Pagan, James*[1]) was born in 1836 in Rossville, Springcreek Twp., Miami Co., Ohio. He was the son of Harrison James Pegan (1) and Sarah Ann Mentzer. John Andrew died in Piqua, Washington Twp., Miami Co., Ohio?, between 1850 and April 27, 1854.

John Andrew was probably named for his two grandfathers: John Ingle Sr. and Andrew Pegan Jr.

In Harrison Pegan Sr.'s obituary in April 1854, it states that he has a widow and four children to mourn him.[24] As his four other children Martha Jane, William Louis, Margaret and Harrison Jr., are all known to be alive at the time of their father's death, this John Andrew Pegan seems to have died between when the 1850 census was taken and April 27, 1854. When Harrison Sr. died, John Andrew would still be under age 21, but is no mention of him Harrison Pegan Sr.'s probate or guardianship files.[25, 26] Most likely, he died while his family lived in Piqua, Washington Twp., Miami Co., Ohio, in 1853, and his death may have been the reason, or a reason, the family moved to Lynchburg, Ohio. He has no known gravesite.

3. **Martha Jane**[6] **Pegan** (*Harrison James*[5], *Robert A.*[4], *Andrew*[3], *Andrew*[2] *Pagan, James*[1]) was born on August 19, 1839, in Piqua, Washington Twp., Miami Co., Ohio.[30] She was also known as **Mattie or Jane**. She was the daughter of Harrison James Pegan (1) and Sarah Ann Mentzer. She died in Houston, Harris Co., Texas, on June 22, 1916, at age 76.[30, 31] Martha Jane was buried in Glenwood Cemetery, Houston, Harris Co., Texas.[30, 31, 38]

Martha Jane Pegan Pegan Brown often used her middle name, Jane, as her common name.

The only record of Martha Jane Pegan Pegan Brown's birthdate is on her tombstone in Glenwood Cemetery, Houston, Harris Co., Texas.[30]

Martha Jane Pegan married **Leonidas Alonzo Pegan** on July 25, 1854, in Clinton Co., Ohio.[27] They had two children. Leonidas Alonzo Pegan was born on December 9, 1829, in Dodson Twp., Highland Co., Ohio.[39] He was the son of Andrew Pegan and Mary Jane McKibben. Leonidas Alonzo died in Perry's Landing, Brazoria Co., Texas, on April 3, 1883, at age 53.[39, 40] He was buried in Gulf Prairie Cemetery (also Peach Point Cemetery), Jones Creek, Brazoria Co., Texas.[39]

The only record of Leonidas Pegan's birthdate is on his tombstone in Gulf Prairie (Peach Pont) Cemetery, Jones Creek, Brazoria Co., Texas.[39]

Leonidas and his wife Martha PeGan were first cousins. Harrison Pegan Sr., Martha's father, was a brother to Leonidas' father Andrew. Leonidas was 24 years old and Martha only 14 when they wed in July 1854, three months after Martha's father died. Permission for the union was given by Sarah Mentzer Pegan, Martha's mother.[27] Soon after their marriage, Leonidas and Martha Jane left the Highland/Clinton counties, Ohio area for Poweshiek County, Iowa.

Leonidas and Martha PeGan Pegan had no children listed in any census and, in the 1900 U.S. Census, Martha Jane Pegan Pegan Brown says she has borne no children *(Census Place: Justice Precinct 6, Brazoria, Texas; Roll: T623_1614; Page: 14A; Enumeration District: 7)*. But according to Martha Pegan Brown's 1905 Civil War widow's pension application through Leonidas's service, the couple had two children who died in infancy.[41] These infants probably were born and died while Leonidas and Martha were residing in Montezuma Twp., Poweshiek Co., Iowa.

Leonidas and Martha Jane Pegan Pegan are listed in the 1856 Iowa State Census in Jackson Twp., Poweshiek Co., Iowa *(Iowa State Census, Roll IA-64, p. 60, line 30)*. Leonidas is a carpenter and a member of the militia.[42]

Leonidas Pegan is enumerated in the 1860 Census in Montezuma Twp., Poweshiek Co., Iowa as a carpenter *(Montezuma, Poweshiek, Iowa; Roll: M653_339; Page: 575; Image: 137)*. In the household are Leonidas Pegan, age 30, a journeyman carpenter, and Martha Pegan, 21. Both were born in Ohio.

Living in Poweshiek County, Iowa at this same time is Joel Pagin, son of Joseph Pagan/Pagin, the master carpenter of western Ohio and then northern Indiana, who is believed to have trained Martha's father Harrison, and their uncles John and Elsey Pegan in the carpentry trade.[43, 44] He may have also trained Leonidas' father Andrew. A familial relationship between the Joseph Pagan/Pagin and this Pagan/Pegan line has not been determined. In addition, Joseph Pagan/Pagin's daughter Drusilla married Leonidas' and Martha's uncle, William Louis Pegan, another brother to Andrew, John, Harrison, and Elsey Pegan.

Leonidas served in the Civil War in Company B, 40th Iowa Infantry as a hospital steward and was discharged because of a disability. He had contracted lung disease while encamped in Kentucky. Leonidas filed for a Civil War pension on April 16, 1878 and Martha for a widow's Civil War widow's pension in 1905. Both were refused, as the U.S. government pension office contended that neither Leonidas' lung problems nor his death could be directly attributed to his war service. According to an 1884 letter in Leonidas' file, Martha Jane Pegan Brown writes that her late husband Leonidas was never the same man physically after his discharge from the army. His lung illness prevented him from resuming the carpenter's trade. In 1865, they moved from Montezuma Twp., Poweshiek Co., Iowa to Burlington, Burlington Twp., Des Moines Co., Iowa, where he "engaged in any light employment he could obtain".[45]

In 1870, Leonidas is enumerated as "L. Pegan" in the 6th Ward, Burlington, Burlington Twp., Des Moines Co., Iowa *(Census Place: Burlington Ward 6, Des Moines, Iowa; Roll: M593_388; Page: 418A; Image: 379)*. Leonidas, 40, is a railroad baggageman (railroad); Martha Jane, listed as "M.J." is 30 years old and both were born in Ohio. Leonidas' brother Samuel Pegan is living in Ward 3 in Burlington.

But, according to Martha's 1884 letter in his pension application file, Leonidas' frequent sickness prevented him from working and he lost his railroad job and others because of it. He traveled Minnesota and sometime in the 1870s for health reasons and found work found work as a liveryman. But the move did not improve his health, and he only stayed in Minnesota for a short time before returning to Burlington. His health improved somewhat after he relocated to Colorado in late 1878, but then an attack of lung inflammation weakened him further and he returned to Burlington in early 1879. Meanwhile, Martha stayed in Burlington during her husband's absences and tried to find occasional work herself.[45]

Leonidas and Martha Jane Pegan Pegan are still living in Burlington, Burlington Twp., Des Moines Co., Iowa in 1880 *(Census Place: Burlington, Des Moines, Iowa; Roll: 337; Page: 284C; Enumeration District: 116; Image: 0568)* in the 5th Ward. Leonidas, 51, is a painter and Martha Jane is age 40. There is no other information on the census entry.

Leonidas' death notice in the *Burlington (IA) Weekly Hawk Eye And Telegraph* on April 12, 1883 says Leonidas and Martha Jane Pegan Pegan removed to Perry's Landing, Texas in the spring of 1882 and Leonidas was working on a cattle ranch in Jones Creek, Brazoria Co., Texas, when he died.[40] The cattle ranch was owned by Col. Reuben R. Brown Sr.

At his gravesite in Gulf Prairie Cemetery, Jones Creek, Brazoria Co., Texas (a famous historic cemetery associated with "The Father of Texas" Stephen F. Austin and his family), there are two very elaborate tombstones for him, which is highly unusual. The cemetery director says there are two graves at the site, but both tombstones are for Leonidas. The cemetery director thinks that one gravestone was ordered but thought lost in shipment (by sea) and another was ordered before the first finally arrived. Both stones have two hands clasped together, meaning one spouse (Martha Jane) was saying goodbye to the other (Leonidas).[46]

Leonidas Pegan's brother Joseph named a son Leonidas, and Harrison and Angeline Stout PeGan Jr. probably named their son Leonidas after Harrison's brother-in-law/cousin.

Four months after Leonidas' death, Martha Jane Pegan married his employer ranch owner, Colonel **Reuben Robinson Brown,** on August 11, 1883, in Brazoria Co., Texas.[47] Reuben Robinson Brown was born in Green Co., Georgia, on February 3, 1808.[48, 49] Reuben R. reached age 86 and died in Quintana, Brazoria Co., Texas, on March 2, 1894.[48,49] He was buried in Gulf Prairie Cemetery (also Peach Point Cemetery), Jones Creek, Brazoria Co., Texas.[49, 50]

There seems to be some confusion as to whether Colonel Reuben R. Brown's middle name was Robinson or Rodolphus. His Find A Grave memorial says his middle name was Rodolphus, but other, more credible sources, including the Handbook of Texas, claims his middle name was Robinson.[48] He had a son named Reuben Robinson Brown Jr.

Reuben R. Brown was an early settler of and major landowner in Brazoria County, Texas, who later became a Colonel in the 15th Texas, Confederate Army in the Civil War. His first wife, Jane Milton Brown, was a niece of Stephen F. Austin, and the Brown family was closely associated with the Austins in Brazoria County. In addition, he was also a good friend of Sam Houston, the first and third president of the Republic of Texas and later, after Texas' statehood, a governor of the state.

Reuben R. Brown Sr., born on February 3, 1808 in Green Co., Georgia, left his home state for Texas in November 1835. He arrived at the Alamo in San Antonio, Bexar Co., Texas the day after Mexican General Martin Perfecto de Cos surrendered to Republic of Texas Col. Edward Burleson. Reuben Brown promptly joined the Texas army and served in the Matamoros campaign under Capt. B. L. Lawrence. The drive to capture Matamoros was abandoned in Jan 1836 at the urging of Sam Houston. Brown remained with the 150 remnants of the expedition force, led by Frank W. Johnson, the commander of the volunteer army in Texas, and another officer, James Grant.

Later, Brown stated he escaped the massacre of James Grant's forces at the Battle of Agua Dulce Creek on March 2, 1836. Brown's account said that during this battle, Grant took 15 men and raided Mexican General Jose de Urrea's horse herd, guarded by a Capt. Rodriguez. Grant assigned Brown to lead the raid, in which Rodriguez was allegedly captured. Gen. Urrea counterattacked and surrounded all but three of the Texans, Brown, Grant and Placido Benavides, who were riding at the head of the group. Grant dispatched Benavides to notify James Fannin's forces at Goliad, Texas. Then, at Brown's suggestion, they decided to return to the battle. Grant was killed, along with nearly all of the remnant troops. Brown's horse was shot. After he remounted he was lanced through the arm. According to Brown, he and a handful of others were taken prisoner by Urrea. Although lassoed and beaten severely, he was allowed to live because Urrea wanted to question him. Brown was sent to San Patricio, Urrea's headquarters, and Urrea told him he could go free if he wouldgo to Fannin and convince the latter to surrender. When Brown refused, Urrea marched him to a prison camp in Metamoros, where he labored for 11 months. He escaped from the camp with the help of a man employed by Brown's parents in Georgia to find him. He rejoined the Texas troops, but was released from duty.

After a short respite in North Carolina, Brown returned to Texas and bought land near the mouth of the Brazos River. By 1860, he had become one of the most prominent and successful men in Texas. His plantation, with 21 slaves, was worth more than $40, 000. When the Civil War broke out, he was commissioned as a lieutenant colonel in the Confederate Army's Texas 13th Infantry. Promoted to full colonel in November 1863, he organized and commanded the Texas 35th Cavalry.

In 1881, Col. Reuben R. Brown received a generous pension from the State of Texas for his military service in both wars. A year later, his first wife, Jane Milton Brown, whom he married in 1837, died. In 1883, Reuben married Martha Jane. According to Reuben Brown's obituary, Martha "made (Brown) a devoted and affectionate companion. She was an excellent nurse and contributed to his happiness of his last few years."[48, 49]

In 1900, Martha J. (Pegan Pegan) Brown, age 60, a widow, born in Sep 1839 in Ohio, is living in Justice Precinct 6 (Quintana), Brazoria Co., Texas *(Census Place: Justice Precinct 6, Brazoria,*

Texas; Roll: T623_1614; Page: 14A; Enumeration District: 7). She is boarding in the home of S.W. Jarvis, along with a couple of other lodgers and two servants. On the census form, Martha states has borne no children; she does not list a birthplace for her father, but says her mother was born in Pennsylvania.

Quintana was hard hit during the September 8, 1900 hurricane which virtually destroyed greater Galveston area. It is estimated that 6-8000 people lost their lives during this vicious storm (estimated to be at least a level 4 on the Saffir-Simpson Hurricane Wind Scale and some scientists believe a level 5), which left many places in Brazoria County in ruins. In fact, most families who survived in Quintana left afterwards and moved inland, and (especially after it was struck again by a hurricane in 1915) the town never recovered its population. The 1900 hurricane still stands as the worst natural disaster ever to hit the United States. Martha Jane Pegan Pegan Brown survived this calamity![51]

By early August 1905, Martha J. Pegan Pegan Brown was back living in Poweshiek County, Iowa, according to a Brazoria County deed where she sells property in Brazoria County.[52] That same month, Martha Jane Pegan Brown "then of Poweshiek County, Iowa and formerly of Brazoria County, Texas, executes another deed to sell more land in Brazoria County. But the sale does not conclude until July 21, 1906, after Martha has moved to either Wabash County or Grant County, Indiana.[53]

On November 4, 1905, when Martha J. Pegan Pegan Brown applied for a Civil War widow's pension, she was living in Wabash Co., Indiana. Her nephew, Alvah PeGan, son of Harrison James PeGan Jr., was the witness on her application. Undoubtedly, she was living with or near her brother Harrison at the time. In that pension application, she says she and Leonidas had two children who died in infancy. Her request was rejected on February 3, 1907, and the denial letter was sent to Angleton (Brazoria Co.) Texas—so she seemed to be living back in Texas then. The reason given for the pension denial was that Leonidas' cause of death,

a stroke, was not related to his war injury (lung disease). But was she turned down because her second husband, Reuben Robinson Brown, was a Confederate Army colonel?[41]

In 1908, a Brazoria County deed indicates that Martha J. Pegan Pegan Brown had removed back to Texas and was living in Houston, Harris Co., Texas.[54]

In 1910, Martha Jane Pegan Pegan Brown is found in Ward 4, Houston, Harris Co., Texas *(Census Place: Houston Ward 4, Harris, Texas; Roll: T624_1559; Page: 1A; Enumeration District: 0076)*. Martha Brown, age 50 (incorrect, she is 70), lists herself as a lodger, but she is the only one living at the address 615 Elgin Avenue. Perhaps it was a double residence and the other side, inhabited by John and Emma Whitted, faced the other street. Martha, a widow, states her occupation as "capitalist". She says she and her father were born in Ohio and her mother in Pennsylvania, and that she bore two children, with none surviving.

A year later, Martha Jane Pegan Brown sells more property in Brazoria County, Texas through the Wabash County, Indiana recorder's office, stating she is a resident of the latter county.[55] She may have lived in Lagro, Lagro Twp., Wabash Co., Indiana with or near her brother, Harrison James PeGan Jr. Perhaps she was a "snowbird" who lived in Houston, Texas during the winter and Wabash Co., Indiana in the summer. But it seems she moved back to Houston permanently before her death, maybe when Harrison Jr. left Lagro to reside in Huntington, Huntington Twp., Huntington Co., Indiana in 1913.

"Mattie Brown" is the name on her death certificate, which has little information.[25] Her Glenwood Cemetery burial record, will, and probate are under the name "Mrs. Reuben R. Brown".[25, 38, 39] However, one of the claimants on the probate, Ed S. Phleps, her stepson-in-law, is the informant on the death certificate, so there is little doubt that this is Martha Jane Pegan Pegan Brown.[31, 57] She was buried the same day she died in Glenwood Cemetery in Houston, in a plot owned by her stepson-in-law lawyer and his wife, Ed and Olive Brown Phelps.[38] Her stepchildren didn't ship her body back to Peach Point/Gulf Prairie Cemetery to be buried next to her first husband and first cousin, Leonidas Pegan (her second husband, Col. Reuben R. Brown, is also buried there).[39, 50]

Her lawyer/stepson-in-law, Ed S. Phelps, filed her probate two days after her death, claiming an estate worth $7000 in monies, possessions and properties. But it seems that her property, two lots in Quintana, Brazoria Co., Texas, were sold for the mysterious price of $25 each, instead of the thousands they were worth. The appraisal listed assets of only about $3000, while claims against the estate were more than $5000.[57] It is unknown if her legatees named in her will, her brother Harrison PeGan Jr., (bequeathed $500), her niece Sarah PeGan Pearson ($600), and nephews Jesse, Clanzie, Alvah/Alvin and Philip (each $600) received any money from her estate.[56]

Children of Martha Jane Pegan and Leonidas Alonzo Pegan:

+ 7   I.   **Child One**[7] **Pegan** was born in Montezuma Twp., Poweshiek Co., Iowa, between 1855 and 1862.[41] He or she died in Montezuma Twp., Poweshiek Co., Iowa, between 1855 and 1862.[41]

+ 8   II. **Child Two**[7] **Pegan** was born in Montezuma Twp., Poweshiek Co., Iowa, between 1855 and 1862.[41] He or she died in Montezuma Twp., Poweshiek Co., Iowa, between 1855 and 1862.[41]

4. **William Louis**[6] **Pegan** (*Harrison James*[5], *Robert A.*[4], *Andrew*[3], *Andrew*[2] *Pagan, James*[1]) was born on May 27, 1841, in Enon, Mad River Twp., Clark Co., Ohio.[32, 33] He was the son of Harrison James Pegan (1) and Sarah Ann Mentzer. He died in Union Twp., Highland Co., Ohio, on November 18, 1881, at age 40.[32] William Louis was buried in Strange Cemetery, Hamer Twp., Highland Co., Ohio.[33, 58]

Childless.

In 1860 William L. Pegan is found in Liberty Twp., Union Co., Indiana (*Census Place: Liberty, Union, Indiana; Roll: M653_301; Page: 301; Image: 301*). He is age 19, a printer, and living in a large boarding house run by Daniel and Margaret Gary.

William Louis Pegan, named for his paternal uncle who died in the California gold rush, had two terms of service during the Civil War, one was with Company L, 12th Ohio Infantry as a private and the other with 24th Independant Battery, Ohio Light Artillery with the same rank (no company given).[59]

William L. Pegan is not found in the 1870 census, but he probably was living in or close to Highland Co., Ohio.

William Louis married **Rachel R. Barnes** on March 30, 1872, in Highland Co., Ohio.[60] Rachel R. Barnes was born in Dodson Twp., Highland Co., Ohio, on January 31, 1844.[61] Rachel R. reached age 57 and died in Union Twp., Highland Co., Ohio, on March 21, 1901.[61] She was buried in Barnes Cemetery, Fairview, New Market Twp., Highland Co., Ohio.[61]

Her birth and death dates are only recorded on her gravestone in Barnes Cemetery, Fairview, New Market Twp., Highland Co., Ohio.[61]

William L. Pegan is enumerated as William L. Pagan in Union Twp., Highland Co., Ohio in 1880 (*Census Place: Union, Highland, Ohio; Roll: 1033; Page: 516C; Enumeration District: 54; Image: 0412*). The household consists of William L. Pegan, 38, a laborer, who says he and his parents were born in Ohio; and his wife Rachel Barnes Pegan, 36, born Ohio, with her father born in Ohio and her mother in Virginia.

Rachel R. Barnes Pegan is enumerated in Union Twp., Highland Co., Ohio in 1900 (*Census Place: Union, Highland, Ohio; Roll: 1286; Page: 8B; Enumeration District: 129*). Rachel, a widow and housekeeper, age 56, born Jan 1844 in Ohio, says her father was born in Ohio and her mother in Virginia. A neighbor is her nephew-in-law, John Alven Roush, son of Margaret Pegan Roush, William Louis Pegan's sister.

5. **Margaret Mary**[6] **Pegan** (*Harrison James*[5], *Robert A.*[4], *Andrew*[3], *Andrew*[2] *Pagan, James*[1]) was born on September 15, 1847, in Piqua, Washington Twp., Miami Co., Ohio.[4, 34] She was also known as **Maggie**. She was the daughter of Harrison James Pegan (1) and Sarah Ann Mentzer. Margaret Mary died in Martinsville, Clark Twp., Clinton Co., Ohio, on March 29, 1909, at age 61.[4, 34] She was buried in Strange Cemetery, Hamer Twp., Highland Co., Ohio.[62]

Margaret Pegan Roush Warren's name on her Ohio death certificate is "Maggie Warren". Her father is listed as "Jas. Pegan" (James Pegan).[4]

Margaret Mary married **Philip Roush** on March 16, 1864, in Highland Co., Ohio.[63] They had six children. Philip Roush was born in Hamer Twp., Highland Co., Ohio, in 1844. Philip reached age 57 and died in Union Twp., Highland Co., Ohio, on June 19, 1901.[64] He was buried in Strange Cemetery, Hamer Twp., Highland Co., Ohio.[65]

In 1870, Philip and Margaret Pegan Roush are in Hamer Twp., Highland Co., Ohio *(Census Place: Hamer, Highland, Ohio; Roll: M593_1222; Page: 110; Image: 220)*. In the home are Philip Roush, 25, a farmer; Margaret Pegan Roush, 21, and children Clara, three, and James, one. Living with them is Harrison James PeGan Jr., Margaret's 19-year-old brother who is a farm hand. All in the home were born in Ohio.

About January 1875, Philip, Margaret and their children, along with Margaret's brother Harrison PeGan Jr., moved to Grant County, Indiana, where some of Philip's Roush relatives lived. Their residence was very near that of George Stout, Angeline Stout's father. Angeline Stout married Harrison PeGan Jr. the next year.

Philip Roush is found in the 1880 U.S. Federal Census in Monroe Twp., Grant Co., Indiana *(Census Place: Monroe, Grant, Indiana; Roll: 280; Page: 541B; Enumeration District: 175; Image: 0083)*. Philip Roush is 34 and a farmer. With him are wife Margaret M. Pegan Roush, 30, and children Clara B., 13, John, 10, Albert, 7, and Eli, seven months. All in the home were born in Ohio, as were their parents, except for son Eli, who was born in Indiana.

Philip and Margaret Pegan Roush remained in Grant County, Indiana until about 1881, when they moved back to Highland County, Ohio. However, Margaret's brother, Harrison PeGan Jr., stayed in Grant County.

In 1887, Philip Roush moved his family to Ravenna, Garfield Co., Kansas, now a ghost town located in Garfield Twp., Finney Co., Kansas. TThe *Hillsboro News-Herald (Hillsboro, OH)* mentions that Philip Roush moved his family back to Highland County because he thought better of Ohio than he did of Kansas![66]

In 1900, Philip and Margaret Pegan Roush are in Highland Co., Ohio, this time in Union Township *(Census Place: Union, Highland, Ohio; Roll: T623_1286; Page: 9A; Enumeration District: 129)*. In the household are Philip, 54, born Oct 1845 in Ohio, is a builder. He says his parents were born in Ohio. Margaret Pegan Roush is 40, born Oct 1849 (incorrect). Margaret says she and her mother were born in Ohio, but she does not list a place of birth for her father. Philip and Margaret say they have been married 35 years and Margaret has borne six children, four still alive. Children in the home are sons Eli K., 20, born Nov 1879, and Ira C., 17, born March 1883, both carpenters and born in Ohio.

Evidently, Philip Roush was highly regarded by his brother-in-law, Harrison PeGan Jr., as Harrison and Angeline Stout PeGan name their youngest son Philip after him in November 1901, five months after Philip Roush dies. He was respected by others as well— Philip's obituary says he was the best carpenter in the area.[64]

On August 31, 1905, the *Hillsboro (OH) News-Herald* notes that Margaret Roush left town that week to travel to Fort Wayne, Indiana, as "she will spend the winter with her brother Mr. Pegan." (Ed. Note: Harrison Jr.)[67]

Margaret Mary Pegan Roush married **George Warren** on May 25, 1907, in Highland Co., Ohio.[68] George Warren was born in Cambridge, England, on February 23, 1851.[69] George reached age 87 and died in Blanchester, Marion Twp., Clinton Co., Ohio, on August 22, 1938.[70] He was buried in Stroup Cemetery, Dodson Twp., Highland Co., Ohio.[71]

George Warren immigrated about 1870 and worked as a farmer. George was widowed twice before he married Margaret Pegan Roush. After her death, he married for a fourth time and his last wife survived him.

Children of Margaret Mary Pegan and Philip Roush:

+ 9 f I. **Clara Belle**[7] **Roush** was born in Hamer Twp., Highland Co., Ohio, on April 26, 1866.[72] She died in New Market Twp., Highland Co., Ohio, on August 25, 1948.[72]

+ 10 m II. **James**[7] **Roush** was born in Hamer Twp., Highland Co., Ohio in 1868. He died in Hamer Twp., Highland Co., Ohio or Monroe Twp., Grant Co., Indiana, between 1870 and 1880.

+ 11 m III. **John Alven**[7] **Roush** was born in Hamer Twp., Highland Co., Ohio, on November 9, 1870.[73, 74] He died in Coldwater, Coldwater Twp., Branch Co., Michigan, on October 22, 1955.[73, 74]

+ 12 m IV. **Albert Leroy**[7] **Roush** was born in Hamer Twp., Highland Co., Ohio, on May 20, 1873.[75] He was also known as **Leroy** and **Roy**. Albert Leroy died in Fairview, Hamer Twp., Highland Co., Ohio, on April 27, 1895.[75, 76]

+ 13 m V. **Eli Kenneth**[7] **Roush** was born in Washington Twp., Blackford Co., Indiana, on November 17, 1878.[77] He was also known as **Teddy**. Eli Kenneth died in Martinsville, Clark Twp., Clinton Co., Ohio, on May 21, 1943.[77]

+ 14 m VI. **Cecil Ira**[7] **Roush** was born in Fairview, Hamer Twp., Highland Co., Ohio, on April 12, 1882.[78, 79, 80, 81] He died in a hospital in Dayton, Montgomery Co., Ohio, on January 1, 1956.[79, 82]

6. **Harrison James**[6] **PeGan II** (*Harrison James*[5] *Pegan, Robert A.*[4], *Andrew*[3], *Andrew*[2] *Pagan, James*[1]) was born on June 22, 1851, in Piqua, Washington Twp., Miami Co., Ohio.[35, 36, 37] He was the son of Harrison James Pegan (1) and Sarah Ann Mentzer. Harrison James PeGan Jr. died in Washington Twp., Miami Co., Indiana, on July 7, 1936, at age 85.[35, 36, 37] He was buried in Miami County Infirmary Cemetery, Washington Twp., Miami Co., Indiana.[83]

Harrison James PeGan II capitalized the "g" in his surname. No one knows why.

Harrison PeGan Jr. says on all documents that he was born in Highland County, Ohio.

Harrison PeGan Jr. says on all documents that he was born in Highland County, Ohio. Harrison Jr.'s children also indicate on marriage applications that their father was born in Highland County. Actually, Harrison Jr. was born in Piqua, Washington Twp., Miami Co., Ohio, as his parents were still living there in 1851. They moved to Lynchburg, Dodson Twp., Highland Co., Ohio, Harrison Pegan Sr.'s home county, in 1853.[19, 23] His father died when he was three and his mother when he was 16. After he was orphaned, he lived with his brother-in-law and sister, Philip and Margaret Mary Pegan Roush (later Warren).

Harrison PeGan II was born with his left leg four inches shorter than his right, and he had to wear corrective shoes for all of his life. He walked with a cane in his latter years and may have always done so.[83]

In the 1870 census, Harrison PeGan Jr., age 19, is living with his sister and brother-in-law, Philip and Margaret Pegan Roush, and their two children Clara and James in Hamer Twp., Highland Co., Ohio (*Census Place: Hamer, Highland, Ohio; Roll: M593_1222; Page: 110A; Image: 223*). He lists himself as a farmhand who has attended school within the past year. The census was taken on July

20, 1870, so Harrison had just turned 19 the prior month.

Harrison Pegan married **First Cousin?** between July 20, 1870 and June 29, 1871, according to his grandson Hugh Frederick "Fritz" PeGan and his granddaughter Mattie Leona "Toots" Pearson Hatfield. (Harrison also indicates on the the 1930 census form that is first marriage was at age 19.) This "First Cousin" died before 1875.[83, 84]

The identity of this "First Cousin" is not known. A marriage license for Harrison PeGan Jr. cannot be found in any Ohio county. Also, in the research done by this author, (including the family of Sarah Mentzer Pegan, not included in this book), all the first cousins by blood in the Pegan and Mentzer lines have been accounted for—and Harrison Jr. did not marry any of them. Perhaps it was a first cousin once removed. But, again, research for this book seems to indicate this wasn't the case—at least for Alexander Pagan, Robert's brother, or either of his known sisters, Elizabeth Jane Pegan Goudy or Mary Pegan VanAusdall. However, there is a missing sister of Robert's who has not been traced yet. Or was it a second cousin…maybe from Ingle line in Pennsylvania or elsewhere. This line is also elusive.

More likely, she may have been a "first cousin" from his stepfather John Tedrick's family in Kentucky or Virginia. Many in that area of Ohio went to Kentucky to marry, and the records in Kentucky are difficult to research and often not complete.

Now, Harrison PeGan Jr.'s sister, Martha, did marry her first cousin, Leonidas, son of Andrew and Martha Jane McKibbon Pegan. Did family members confuse this marriage with one by Harrison Jr.? But, again, Harrison Jr. states on the 1930 census form that he first wed when he was 19 years old.

Harrison Jr.'s first wife died before 1875, when he moved to Monroe Twp., Grant Co., Indiana with Philip and Margaret Pegan Roush. There he met the "girl next door", who lived right across the road, Angeline Stout.

Harrison James married **Angeline Stout** on June 22, 1876, in Grant Co., Indiana.[85] They had eight children. Angeline Stout was born in Monroe Twp., Grant Co., Indiana, on June 19, 1858.[86, 87] Angeline reached age 51 and died in Lagro Twp., Wabash Co., Indiana, on January 11, 1910.[86, 87] She was buried in Hopewell Cemetery, Lagro Twp., Wabash Co., Indiana, on January 13, 1910.[87, 88]

Angeline was six feet tall, unusual for a woman in that era. Her late father, George Stout Sr., was a wealthy and prominent Grant County citizen, according to this author's research. But Angeline probably had no suitors until Harrison PeGan Jr. moved in across the road. Because of his deformed leg and her height, Harrison Jr. and Angeline were probably considered undesirable marriage partners—but that may have been what made them so attracted to one another.

In the 1880 U.S. Federal Census, Washington Twp., Blackford Co., Indiana *(Census Place: Washington, Blackford, Indiana; Roll T9_266; Page: 375.3000)*. Harrison PeGan Jr., age 37 (wrong. it is 28), born Ohio, is enumerated with wife Angeline, 22, born Indiana and daughter Laura, one month, also born in Indiana. Harrison does not list birthplaces for his parents; Angeline says both of her parents were born in North Carolina. They are living close to Samuel and Lucy Ann Gray Stout Palmer, Angeline's stepfather and mother.

A short time later, Harrison and Angeline Stout PeGan Jr. lived on land owned by Stout family members in Monroe Township, Grant Co., Indiana. The property is a few miles west of the Palmer home in near Roll, Washington Twp., Blackford Co., Indiana, and just a mile or so north of the (unincorporated) village of Arcana, Monroe Twp., Grant Co., Indiana. This land had been owned by Angeline's father George Stout Sr., and is right by the oil and natural gas fields which were active at the time. Most of their children were born there, but Harrison didn't buy this property from then owner George H. Stout Jr., son of Angeline's father George Stout by his first marriage, until the summer of 1897.[89] According to their grandson, Hugh Frederick "Fritz" Pegan, Harrison and Angeline lived first in a log cabin, then they built a house which they heated with natural gas—long before it was possible on a mass scale. Fritz PeGan says that, somehow, the resourceful Harrison Jr. devised a way to pipe the natural gas directly out of the ground to a furnace he built in the house. (The log cabin remained on the property and seems to be the one which two of Harrison and Angeline's grandchildren, "Fritz" PeGan and Mattie Leona Pearson Hatfield, remember their Great-Grandmother Lucy Ann Gray Stout Palmer living in after her second husband Samuel Palmer died.)[83, 84]

Tragedy struck the PeGan family in 1898-1899. First, their eldest child, daughter Laura Pegan Keplinger, dies in June 1898 in childbirth with her first child.[83, 84] Then, the following January, their second-eldest, Sarah Celeste "Lesta" Pegan was brutally raped and impregnated by a jilted suitor, George Keplinger, the brother of Harley Keplinger, Laura's husband. George Keplinger had continued to stalk Sarah after she refused to marry him. Following the rape, George still pursued Sarah, insisting that now she had to marry him. But Sarah, of course, would have nothing to do with him. Three weeks after the assault, George Keplinger came to the Pegan house asked for Sarah. When she came to the door, George Keplinger took out a pistol and shot her in the side of her neck. He then pointed the gun to his own head and fired, but the bullet only pierced his hat. He fell over Sarah's body and lay there. Harrison Jr., hearing the shot, ran to them and helped Keplinger up. Keplinger than fled from the PeGan home. The police caught him hours later at his employer's house and jailed him.[83, 90, 91, 92, 93]

The incident, and George William Keplinger's subsequent hearing when he pleaded guilty, was news for months in Grant County, Indiana and in newspapers around Indiana and even in other states. Sarah lay near death for days. One newspaper printed an obituary days later; another newspaper said in an article months later that she had died.[90, 91, 92, 94, 95, 96]

She recovered, but the bullet could not be removed. She lived the rest of her life with the bullet still lodged in her neck. She did not attend George Keplinger's hearing. Her father, Harrison PeGan Jr., did, and told the court that, because of the rape, Sarah was pregnant. In September 1899, her son, Raymond PeGan, was born. Sarah's other children were never told anything about the rape—or that Raymond PeGan was their half-brother. They thought Ray was Sarah's brother. As he was born four years after Sarah's brother Leonidas and two years before her youngest brother Philip, nothing was ever said and they just assumed Ray was another brother. As for the bullet still in her neck, they were told it was a goiter.[83, 84, 97]

George Keplinger pleaded guilty and spent about two years in an Indiana prison before escaping. He changed his name and fled to Missouri. Later he moved to Springfield, Illinois, where he died under his assumed name, Roy Clarence Scott.[83, 91, 92, 93, 94, 98, 99, 100]

In 1900, Harrison James PeGan Jr. (enumerated as Peugan or Pan Gean) is enumerated in Monroe Twp., Grant Co., Indiana *(Census Place: Monroe, Grant, Indiana; Roll T623_373; Pages: 11B-12A; Enumeration District: 43)*. In the home are Harrison, age 48, born June 1851; he and his parents were born in Ohio. Wife Angeline Stout PeGan is 41, born June 1858, who says both of her parents were born in Virginia (Incorrect—they were born in North Carolina). The couple says they have been married 25 years, and Angeline has borne seven children, with five still living. Children in the home include Sarah, 17, born May 1883 (should be 1882); Alvin (Alvah), 15, born June 1884, Jesse, 12, born October 1887; Clanzie, 10, born August 1889 (this is wrong, Clanzie was born in 1888); "Leonidas", four, born October 1895. Also living in the home is grandson "Ray" PeGan, born September 1899. However, Ray's mother, Sarah Celeste PeGan, is listed as having borne no children. All the children and grandson Ray were born in Indiana.

In 1903, Harrison and Angeline Stout Pegan sold their property in Monroe Twp., Grant Co., Indiana and relocated to Lagro Township, Wabash Co., Indiana. They bought a small farm on Hopewell Road, north of the town of Lagro.[101, 102] This home was next door to land once owned by the famous Hoosier author Gene Stratton Porter's parents; it was still owned by Ms. Porter's brother.[83] Harrison and Angeline may have moved there to prevent their four-year-old grandson Raymond Pegan avoid embarrassment in the Monroe Township (and entire Grant County) school system, as the circumstances of his birth and his mother Sarah Celeste Pegan's assault were well known in the Arcana area and, for that matter, in all of Grant County. A portion of Harrison Jr.'s Grant County land, including the log cabin, was retained by Lucy Ann Stout Palmer, Angeline's mother.

After Angeline's death in January 1910, Harrison sold the Hopewell land, and bought a house in the town of Lagro Indiana. The home was on the southwest corner of Main and Spencer streets next to the Presbyterian Church.[103, 104] Harrison also owned a blacksmith and machine shop, located down the hill at the rear of the house on the northwest corner of Washington and Spencer streets.[105]

In the 1910 census, Harrison PeGan II, age 58, born Ohio is enumerated in Lagro, Lagro Twp., Wabash Co., Indiana *(Census Place: Lagro, Wabash, Indiana; Roll T624_386; Page: 3A; Enumeration District: 144; Image: 118)*. Living with him are son Clanzie, 21, and his wife, Josephine Schetzszle PeGan, also 21, and their two sons, Leo, born 1907 and Paul, born 1908. Also in the house are Harrison II's sons "Alva," 25, Jesse, 23, Leonidus, 16 and Philip, eight. Harrison says he is widowed and has his "own income" in the occupation category. Harrison, either playing a joke or irritated with the questions asked, says he was born in Ohio, but his father is "born in the United States" and his mother in "Scotland". Both Clanzie and Leonidus say they are laborers on the railroad. Alvah lists his occupation as carpenter and Jesse is a farmer; both are unmarried. All of Harrison's children say they were born in Indiana, with their father born in Ohio and their mother in Indiana. Josephine Schetzszle PeGan says she is an Indiana native, and her father was born in Ohio and her mother in New York.

The *Wabash (IN) Plain Dealer* newspaper noted in February 1912 that Harrison Pegan had established a skating rink at the Redman Hall.[106]

In 1912-1913, Harrison PeGan II was involved in two court cases in Wabash County, both of which involved a neighbor, Harry Wiley. Harrison Pegan II and another man, Oden Howell, were indicted by the State of Indiana for criminal trespass charges against Richard Malloy. Allegedly, the two defendants cut down a bush on Malloy's land on 17 Jul 1913. A jury found Harrison and Mr. Howell innocent.[107] Soon afterwards, Harry Wiley was charged with the same crime. At the same time, Harrison PeGan II brought Harry Miley into civil court for violating a business contract. In 1910, Harrison leased his successful blacksmith shop he owned in Lagro to Harry Miley. The business continued to prosper for a few months, but soon started to fail, causing Harrison into "insolvency". Harrison sued Wiley for $1500. The case was dismissed later with costs paid.[108]

These legal battles may have spurred Harrison PeGan II and his son Clanzie into moving closer to Clanzie's new job with the Erie Railroad in Huntington, Huntington Twp., Huntington Co., Indiana. (Perhaps his father's legal troubles prompted Clanzie to leave his job with the Interurban and apply for the better-paying job with the Erie.) In any case, Harrison sold the home and blacksmith shop in Lagro in 1913. His children Clanzie and Sarah and their spouses are also listed as grantors on the house deed.[109, 110]

On June 10, 1913, Harrison Jr. bought a house on Sutton Hill in Huntington Township, just south of the town of Huntington near the junction of State Roads 5 and 224.[111] Clanzie and his family lived there with Harrison, and so did Harrison's youngest son Philip. Clanzie's two youngest sons were born there.

In late June 1919, he had a big argument with his daughter-in-law, Josephine, who often was at odds with him. As related by Fritz PeGan, Harrison Jr. and grandson Paul, Clanzie's second eldest, were supposed to weed the large vegetable garden in the backyard. Harrison got upset with Paul's indolent attitude about this chore—and others—berated the boy. Hearing Harrison yelling at Paul, Josephine came out of the house and confronted her father-in-law, and the incident became "the straw that broke the camel's back". Within a week, Harrison sold the house, apparently without telling Clanzie and Josephine beforehand. The Clanzie PeGans had to find another place to live in a hurry. Clanzie and Josephine lived in a succession of rental homes in Huntington for years—Fritz PeGan, in his nineties, could recite all the addresses. Philip, Harrison Jr.'s youngest son, moved in with his brother Jesse and his family in Wabash, Noble Twp., Wabash Co., Indiana.[83, 112]

Harrison Jr. then moved in with his daughter Sarah PeGan Pearson's family. Ike and Sarah's daughter Leona Pearson Hatfield said her grandfather Harrison was very grateful to Ike and Sarah for taking him into their household. According to Leona, when Harrison lived with them he didn't talk or interact much. "He didn't do anything!" Leona says with a laugh, "Except rock in his rocking chair!"[84]

In the 1920 census, Harrison PeGan Jr., age 68, is listed as a boarder in the home of his son-in-law and daughter, Isaac and Sarah PeGan Pearson, in Jonesboro, Mill Twp., Grant Co., Indiana *(Census Place: Jonesboro, Grant, Indiana; Roll T625_434; Page: 11B; Enumeration District: 75; Image: 465)*. Harrison, enumerated as "PeGan Harrison", lists his occupation as a carpenter. Living in the home in addition to Harrison, are Isaac Pearson ("Iisac Peirson" on the census form), 55, a laborer at Indiana Rubber Works; Sarah PeGan Pearson, 37, and their children Leona, 16, Herbert, 12, Truman, eight, and "Coline O.", six; plus Isaac's daughter by his first marriage, Vera, 20. The house is on West 6th Street in Jonesboro.

But the harmony was short-lived. About 1925, Sarah accused her father Harrison Jr. of stealing money from them and told her father to leave. After that, Harrison lived with his son Jesse and his family near Macy, Allen Twp., Miami Co., Indiana. Harrison didn't get along there either. In 1928, Jesse put Harrison in the Miami County Infirmary (the county home for the indigent), Washington Township, Miami Co., Indiana. just south of Peru.[83]

In 1930, Harrison PeGan Jr. is listed in the Miami Co., Infirmary *(Census Place: Washington, Miami, Indiana; Roll 618; Page: 10A; Enumeration District: 28; Image: 567.0)*. He is 78 years old, widowed, and was born in Ohio as were his parents. Harrison Jr. states he was first married at age 19.

Some family members did come to visit Harrison Jr. while he was at the Miami County Infirmary. Philip Ellsworth Pegan II recalls that his father, Philip Garl Pegan, took his family to see Harrison Jr. sometime in the early 1930s.[113]

Harrison PeGan II died in July 1936. His obituary in the *Peru (IN) Tribune* mentions only his sons Jesse and Philip as relatives.[114] On his death certificate, it states that Harrison was removed to Hopewell Cemetery, where his wife Angeline Stout PeGan and sons Leonidus and Alvah/Alvin were interred, for burial.[35] Fritz PeGan, however, said Harrison Jr. was buried in a pauper's grave in the Miami County Infirmary Cemetery, because none of his children wanted to pay for transporting Harrison Jr.'s body from the infirmary to Hopewell Cemetery in Lagro Twp., Wabash Co., Indiana.[83] According to the Miami County Historical Museum archivist, this cemetery was plowed over in the 1950s-60s by a farmer who had purchased the land. The farmer was told by Miami County officials to respect the cemetery, but he ignored this order. He was never fined or otherwise punished for this.[115]

Fritz PeGan recalls that his grandfather Harrison PeGan was an adept whittler. He whittled whistles, small animals and other small toys for his grandchildren. This evidently did not impress some of them, however. Fritz remembers that his two elder brothers, Leo and Paul, used to climb on the Sutton Hill house roof and throw things, like small stones, at their grandfather, who was sitting on the porch below. Harrison would try to wheedle them into being nice to him by whittling them more toys, but Lee and Paul continued tormenting Harrison Jr. until the day Harrison left to live with Ike and Sarah PeGan Pearson.[83]

Children of Harrison James PeGan II and Angeline Stout:

+ 15 f I. **Laura A.⁷ PeGan** was born in Washington Twp., Blackford Co.,

Indiana, on April 23, 1880.[116, 117] She died in Salamonie Twp., Huntington Co., Indiana?, on June 28, 1898.[116, 117]

+ 16 f II. **Sarah Celeste⁷ PeGan** was born in Monroe Twp., Grant Co., Indiana, on June 2, 1882.[118] She was also known as **Lesta**. Sarah Celeste died in Marion, Center Twp., Grant Co., Indiana, on July 28, 1963.[118, 119]

+ 17 m III. **Alvah or Alvin LeRoy⁷ PeGan** was born in Monroe Twp., Grant Co., Indiana, on July 22, 1884.[120, 121, 122, 123] He was also known as **Alvin or LeRoy**. Alvah or Alvin LeRoy died in Wabash, Noble Twp., Wabash Co., Indiana, on May 5, 1936.[120, 122, 123]

+ 18 m IV. **Jesse Harrison⁷ Pegan** was born in Monroe Twp., Grant Co., Indiana, on October 14, 1886.[124, 125, 126] He died in Huntington, Huntington Twp., Huntington Co., Indiana, on November 17, 1946.[124, 125, 126]

+ 19 m V. **Clanzie Herold⁷ PeGan** was born in Monroe Twp., Grant Co., Indiana, on October 7, 1888.[127, 128, 129, 130, 131] He was also known as **C.H.** Clanzie Herold died in Huntington, Huntington Twp., Huntington Co., Indiana, on May 17, 1972.[127, 128, 129, 131]

+ 20 f VI. **Phoebe⁷ PeGan** was born in Monroe Twp., Grant Co., Indiana, on July 14, 1891.[116, 132] She died in Monroe Twp., Grant Co., Indiana, on July 14, 1891?[116, 132]

+ 21 m VII. **Leonidus Alonzo⁷ PeGan** was born in Monroe Twp., Grant Co., Indiana, on October 3, 1894.[133] He was also known as **Alonzo**. Leonidus Alonzo died in Lagro, Lagro Twp., Wabash Co., Indiana, on March 28, 1911.[133, 134]

+ 22 m VIII. **Philip Garl⁷ PeGan** was born in Monroe Twp., Grant Co., Indiana, on November 5, 1901.[128, 135] He died in Niles Twp., Berrien Co., Michigan, on November 17, 1982.[135]

7th Generation

7. **Child One**[7] Pegan (*Martha Jane*[6], *Harrison James*[5], *Robert A.*[4], *Andrew*[3], *Andrew*[2] *Pagan, James*[1]) was born between 1855 and 1862 in Montezuma Twp., Poweshiek Co., Iowa.[41] He or she was a child of Leonidas Alonzo Pegan and Martha Jane Pegan (3). Child One died in Montezuma Twp., Poweshiek Co., Iowa, between 1855 and 1862.[41]

8. **Child Two**[7] Pegan (*Martha Jane*[6], *Harrison James*[5], *Robert A.*[4], *Andrew*[3], *Andrew*[2] *Pagan, James*[1]) was born between 1855 and 1862 in Montezuma Twp., Poweshiek Co., Iowa.[41] He or she was a child of Leonidas Alonzo Pegan and Martha Jane Pegan (3). Child Two died in Montezuma Twp., Poweshiek Co., Iowa, between 1855 and 1862.[41]

9. **Clara Belle**[7] Roush (*Margaret Mary*[6] *Pegan, Harrison James*[5], *Robert A.*[4], *Andrew*[3], *Andrew*[2] *Pagan, James*[1]) was born on April 26, 1866, in Hamer Twp., Highland Co., Ohio.[72] She was the daughter of Philip Roush and Margaret Mary Pegan (5). She died in New Market Twp., Highland Co., Ohio, on August 25, 1948, at age 82.[72] Clara Belle was buried in Strange Cemetery, Hamer Twp., Highland Co., Ohio.[72]

Clara B. Roush married **William Constantine Farr** on May 13, 1881 in St. Joseph Co., Michigan.[136] They divorced. They had one daughter. William C. Farr was born in Farrville, Van Buren Twp., Grant Co., Indiana on August 21, 1861.[137, 138] He lived in Peru, Washington Twp., Miami Co., Indiana in 1906.[139] He reached age 65 and died on January 20, 1906 in a hospital in Danville, Danville Twp., Vermilion Co., Illinois.[137, 138] He is buried in Estates of Serenity Cemetery, Marion, Center Twp., Grant Co., Indiana.[137]

William C. Farr, a brakeman for the Wabash Railroad and based in Peru, Washington Twp., Miami Co., Indiana, fell beneath and was run over by his train near Tilton, Danville Twp., Vermilion Co., Illinois on January 6, 1906. His right arm and leg were amputated, but he succumbed to his injuries on January 20.[138, 139]

Clara Belle Roush Farr married **James Louis Hunter II** on June 27, 1887. They had two children. James Louis Hunter II was born in Fairview, Hamer Twp., Highland Co., Ohio, on August 22, 1864.[140] James Louis reached age 74 and died in New Market Twp., Highland Co., Ohio, on July 22, 1939.[140] He was buried in Strange Cemetery, Hamer Twp., Highland Co., Ohio.[140]

Although Hunter family records indicate that James and Clara Belle Roush Farr Hunter II were married on June 27, 1887 in Highland Co., Ohio, that county does not have a marriage record for them. There is no marriage record in Indiana or in online Ohio marriage indices for them. However, they may have married in adjacent Hamilton County, Ohio, as that county's marriage records are spotty and incomplete in that era, or in Kentucky.

James and Clara Belle Roush Farr Hunter II are enumerated in Dodson Twp., Highland Co., Ohio in 1900 *(Census Place: Dodson, Highland, Ohio; Roll: T623_1286; Page: 11B; Enumeration District: 106)*. James L. Hunter, 35, born Aug 1864 in Ohio, is a farmer. Clara Bell Roush Farr Hunter, born Apr 1866, is age 34. The couple say they have been married 12 years and The couple states they have been married 12 years and Clara Belle has born three children, two still living. In the home with them is son John C. Hunter, 10. All say they were born in Ohio, as were their parents. James' mother Mary Hunter is also living there.

In 1910, James and Clara Belle are living in New Market Twp., Highland Co., Ohio *(Census Place: New Market, Highland, Ohio; Roll: T624_1197; Page: 8A; Enumeration District: 0129; Image: 954)*. James L. Hunter, 45, is a farmer. Clara Belle Roush Farr Hunter is 44. This time Clara Belle says she bore two children, with one surviving (Incorrect—she had three children and two were still alive). Son John C., 20, is still living with them, and is listed as a farmhand. All in the home were born in Ohio, as were their parents. Also in the home is a 15-year-old ward, Bernice Webster, born Ohio, who is a housemaid.

James L. Hunter II is enumerated as J. Louis Hunter in 1920 in New Market Twp., Highland Co., Ohio *(Census Place: New Market, Highland, Ohio; Roll: T625_1399; Page: 5A; Enumeration District: 98; Image: 469)*. In the home are James Louis Hunter, 55, born Ohio, a farmer; and Clara Belle Roush Farr Hunter, 53. Their son John Clark Hunter and his family are also in the household. John C. Hunter, 29, lists his occupation as laborer on a home farm. Rosa Mae Wilkin Hunter, John C.'s wife, is listed as "Rosie M." She is also 29 years old. John and Rosa have a son, Clyde C., age five. All in the home and their parents were Ohio natives.

In 1930, James L. and Clara Belle Roush Farr Hunter II are again New Market Twp., Highland Co., Ohio *(Census Place: New Market, Highland, Ohio; Roll: 1823; Page: 6B; Enumeration District: 19; Image: 435.0)*. James L. Hunter, 65, is still a farmer, but this time he says he and his father were born in Ohio and his mother in Indiana. Clara Belle is 63, born Ohio as were her parents. The pair say they first married at ages 22 and 20 respectively. Living with them are son John C. Hunter, listed as J. Clark Hunter, 40, born Ohio, a farmhand; John's wife, Rosa Wilkin Hunter, also 40, born Ohio as were her parents, and their son Clyde C., 16, born in Ohio.

Clara Belle Roush Farr Hunter is enumerated in New Market Twp., Highland Co., Ohio in 1940, where she is living in the home of her son, John Clark Hunter. Clara Belle Roush Hunter, a widow, is 74 years old. The head of the household is John C. Hunter, age 50, a farmer. Also in the home is John's wife, Rosa Mae Wilkin Hunter, also 50 years old. All were born in Ohio and were living in the same house on Concord Pike in 1935. Next-door is Clyde Hunter, John and Rosa Mae Wilkin's son and Clara's grandson, and his family.

The relationship between Clara Belle Roush Farr Hunter and her daughter by her first husband William C. Farr, Bertha May Farr Roll Bartlemay Roll, was strained. Bertha never lived with her mother after Clara remarried to James Louis Hunter II. In 1900, Clara says she has borne three children, two surviving. Her daughter Bertha Olive is not in the household. In 1910, she says she has borne two children, with one still alive. Apparently, she only includes her children by her husband, James Louis Hunter II, in 1910.

Daughter of Clara Belle Roush and William C. Farr:

+ 23 f I. **Bertha Olive**[8] **Farr** was born in Union Twp., Highland Co., Ohio, on December 23, 1882.[141] She was also known as **Olive**. Bertha Olive died in Fort Lauderdale, Broward Co., Florida, on April 8, 1966.[142, 143]

Children of Clara Belle Roush and James Louis Hunter II:

+ 24 m I. **John Clark**[8] **Hunter** was born in Ward Twp., Hocking Co., Ohio, on December 24, 1890.[128, 144] He died in a hospital in Hillsboro, Liberty Twp., Highland Co., Ohio, on May 21, 1968.[128, 145]

+ 25 II. **Child**[8] **Hunter** was born in Highland Co. or Hocking Co., Ohio, between 1887 and 1900. He or she died in Highland Co. or Hocking Co., Ohio, before 1900.

10. James[7] **Roush** (*Margaret Mary*[6] *Pegan, Harrison James*[5]*, Robert A.*[4]*, Andrew*[3]*, Andrew*[2] *Pagan, James*[1]) was born in 1868 in Hamer Twp., Highland Co., Ohio. He was the son of Philip Roush and Margaret Mary Pegan (5). James died in Hamer Twp., Highland Co., Ohio or Monroe Twp., Grant Co., Indiana, between 1870 and 1880.

11. John Alven[7] **Roush** (*Margaret Mary*[6] *Pegan, Harrison James*[5]*, Robert A.*[4]*, Andrew*[3]*, Andrew*[2] *Pagan, James*[1]) was born on November 9, 1870, in Hamer Twp., Highland Co., Ohio.[73, 74] He was the son of Philip Roush and Margaret Mary Pegan (5). John Alven died in Coldwater, Coldwater Twp., Branch Co., Michigan, on October 22, 1955, at age 84.[73, 74] He was buried in Evergreen Cemetery, Girard Twp., Branch Co., Michigan.[74, 146]

John Alven Roush seems to have been born on November 9, 1870 in Hamer Twp., Highland Co., Ohio. There is a birth record on online for him, but it says James Roush. This is unlikely, as Philip and Margaret Pegan Roush already have a son named James, and, according to the 1900 census, Margaret indicates she bore only six children, with four still alive. Oddly, however, John Alven Roush birthdate on the 1900 census form is November 1871.

John Alven married **Harriet Boxell** on May 28, 1891, in Grant Co., Indiana.[147, 148] They had six children. Harriet Boxell was born in Monroe Twp., Grant Co., Indiana, on July 14, 1874.[149, 150] She was also known as **Hattie**. Harriet reached age 78 and died in Girard, Girard Twp., Branch Co., Michigan, on February 27, 1953.[149, 150] She was buried in Evergreen Cemetery, Girard Twp., Branch Co., Michigan.[150, 151]

John A. Roush is enumerated in Union Twp., Highland Co., Ohio in 1900 *(Census Place: Union, Highland, Ohio; Roll: T623_1286; Page: 8B; Enumeration District: 129)*. In the household are John A. Roush, 28, born Nov 1871 in Ohio, a carpenter and builder, born Ohio as were his parents; and his wife Harriet Boxell Roush, 24, born July 1875 in Indiana, with her parents born in Virginia. The couple says they have been married nine years and Harriet has borne three children, with two surviving. They are Nellie F., five, born Oct. 1894, and Delbert L., three, born Mar 1897. Both children were born in Ohio.

About 1901, the John A. Roush family removed to Blackford County, Indiana, adjacent to Monroe Twp., Grant Co., Indiana, where his uncle, Harrison PeGan Jr. resided. There are Roush relatives in the area as well.

In 1910, John Alven Roush is found in Washington Twp., Blackford Co., Indiana *(Census Place: Washington, Blackford, Indiana; Roll: T624_340; Page: 4B; Enumeration District: 0014; Image: 1399)*. John A. Roush is age 38, a farmer, born Ohio as were his parents. His wife, Harriet Boxell Roush, is 34. John and Harriet say they have been married 17 years and Harriet has borne five children with three still alive. They are Nellie F., 15, Delbert L., 14, both born in Ohio; and Joseph L., seven, born in Indiana.

By 1920, John A. Roush has removed to Three Rivers, Fabius Twp., St. Joseph Co., Michigan *(Census Place: Three Rivers Ward 3, St Joseph, Michigan; Roll: T625_796; Page: 11A; Enumeration District: 171; Image: 545)*. John A. Roush, 45, again a house carpenter, says he and his parents were born in Ohio. Harriet Boxell Roush, 42, again says she was born in Indiana and her parents in Virginia. With them are their children: "Fay", 24, a milliner in a hat shop; Delbert, 22, a house carpenter, and Joseph, 17, a core maker in an auto factory. (Nellie) Fay and Delbert were born in Ohio and Joseph was born in Indiana.

John A. Roush is still living in Three Rivers, Fabius Twp., St. Joseph Co., Michigan in 1930 *(Census Place: Three Rivers, St Joseph, Michigan; Roll: 1026; Page: 15A; Enumeration District: 27; Image: 385.0)*. In the home are John A. Roush, 59, a carpenter, born Ohio as were his parents; and his wife, Harriet Boxell Roush, 54, born Indiana with her parents born in Virginia. John says he first married at age 20 and Harriet states she was 15 years old when she first wed.

John Alven and Harriet E. Boxell Roush later move to Girard, Girard Twp., Branch Co., Michigan.

In 1940, John Alven Roush is found in Girard, Girard Twp., Branch Co., Michigan *(Census Place: Girard, Branch, Michigan; Roll: T627_1734; Page: 1A; Enumeration District: 12-16)*. John Roush, age 69, born Ohio, and his wife, Harriet ("Harriette") Boxell Roush is 65, born Indiana. John Alven lists no occupation. They are living in West Girard Village. Both say they were residing in Three Rivers, Lockport Twp., St. Joseph Co., Michigan in 1935.

Children of John Alven Roush and Harriet Boxell:

+ 26 f I. **Lulu Belle**[8] **Roush** was born in Union Twp., Highland Co., Ohio, about 1892. She died in Union Twp., Highland Co., Ohio, before 1900.

+ 27 f II. **Nellie Fay**[8] **Roush** was born in Union Twp., Highland Co., Ohio, on September 29, 1894.[152] She was also known as **Fay**. Nellie Fay died in Canada? between July 22, 1925 and May 19, 1939.

+ 28 m III. **Delbert Leroy**[8] **Roush** was born in Union Twp., Highland Co., Ohio, on March 14, 1897.[153, 154] He died in South Bend, St. Joseph Co., Indiana, on May 16, 1939.[155, 156]

+ 29 m IV. **Joseph Lewis**[8] **Roush** was born in Monroe Twp., Grant Co., Indiana, on March 17, 1903.[157, 158] He died in Coldwater, Coldwater Twp., Branch Co., Michigan, on January 5, 1959.[157, 159]

+ 30 m V. **Milford**[8] **Roush** was born in Union Twp., Highland Co., Ohio, on November 16, 1905.[160, 161] He died in Harrison Twp., Blackford Co., Indiana on October 4, 1908.[161]

+ 31 m VI. **Arlo**[8] **Roush** was born in Fabius Twp., St. Joseph Co., Michigan?, in 1918.[162] He died in Fabius Twp., St. Joseph Co., Michigan?, in 1918.[162]

12. Albert Leroy[7] **Roush** (*Margaret Mary*[6] *Pegan, Harrison James*[5]*, Robert A.*[4]*, Andrew*[3]*, Andrew*[2] *Pagan, James*[1]) was born on May 20, 1873, in Hamer Twp., Highland Co., Ohio.[75] He was also known as **Leroy** and **Roy**. He was the son of Philip Roush and Margaret Mary Pegan (5). He died in Fairview, Hamer Twp., Highland Co., Ohio, on April 27, 1895, at age 21.[75, 76] Albert Leroy was buried in Strange Cemetery, Hamer Twp., Highland Co., Ohio.[75, 163]

Albert Leroy married **Mima Helen Beard** on December 16, 1893, in Highland Co., Ohio.[164] They had one son. Mima Helen Beard was born in Liberty Twp., Highland Co., Ohio, on April 17, 1877.[165] Mima Helen reached age 64 and died in Springfield, Springfield Twp., Clark Co., Ohio, on November 19, 1941.[166] She was buried in Glen Haven Memorial Gardens Cemetery, Donnelsville, Bethel Twp., Clark Co., Ohio.[167]

Albert Leroy Roush, known as "Leroy" or "Roy", was a lawyer who first practiced in Muncie, Center Twp., Delaware Co., Indiana. He married Mima Beard in 1893 in Highland Co., and later that year they moved back to Lynchburg, Dodson Twp., Highland Co., Ohio.[75]

His obituary in the *Hillsboro (OH) News-Herald* on April 2, 1895 states he was born on May 20, 1875, but then says he was 21 years old. His year of birth seems to be 1873. His other obituary in the Hillsboro Gazette does not state a birthdate. He was killed in a hunting incident, when his rifle discharged while he was climbing a fence.[75]

In 1900, widow Mima Beard Roush, is not living in the same household as her son George Beard Roush. Mina Beard Roush is llisted as "Jemima Poush", a boarder with a group of factory workers in Greenfield Twp., Highland Co., Ohio *(Census Place: Greenfield, Highland, Ohio; Roll: 1286; Page: 5B; Enumeration District: 122)*. Mima Beard Roush, age 23, single, born Ohio (no listings for parental birthplaces), who works in a machine pad factory. Her son George Beard Roush was living with his maternal grandmother, Christina McCall Beard, in Union Twp., Highland Co., OH *(Census Place: Union, Highland, Ohio; Roll: 1286; Page: 2B; Enumeration District: 129)*. George, age five, was born in Ohio, like his parents, but the census taker errs and says he was born in July 1884 instead of 1894.

Mima Beard Roush married John William Thacker on February 23, 1904 in Highland Co., Ohio.[167] John William Thacker preferred to use the name William J. Thacker.

Mima Beard Roush Thacker is living with her second husband William Thacker in 1910 in Springfield, Springfield Twp., Clark Co., Ohio *(Census Place: Springfield Ward 1, Clark, Ohio; Roll: T624_1159; Page: 5A; Enumeration District: 0027; Image: 292)*. In the home are William Thacker, 32, a street car motorman; Mima Beard Roush Thacker, 33, and their two sons, Harold, five, and Wayne, three. William and Mima say they have been married six years and Mima has borne three children, all still alive. Her son by Albert Leroy Roush, George Roush, 16, born Ohio as were his parents, is also in the house. George lists his occupation as laborer.

In 1920, Mima Beard Roush Thacker is again found in Springfield, Springfield, Clark Co., Ohio (*Census Place: Springfield Ward 5, Clark, Ohio; Roll: T625_1354; Page: 8B; Enumeration District: 90; Image: 790*). She is 41 years old, born Ohio as were her parents, and lists her occupation as "running a cutting machine in a leather factory". She is with her second husband, William Thacker, 45, a tinner in a motor truck factory, and their sons Harold and Wayne, ages 15 and 12 respectively.

Mima Beard Roush Thacker and her husband William J. Thacker are still residingi Springfield, Springfield Twp., Clark Co., Ohio in 1930 (*Census Place: Springfield, Clark, Ohio; Roll: 1757; Page: 11B; Enumeration District: 31; Image: 213.0*). William Thacker, age 52, is a school custodian Mima is also listed as 52 years old and this time lists no occupation. Also in the home are William's mother, Margaret, 74, and a cousin of Williams, Gertrude Swain, 16. All and their parents were born in Ohio.

John William/William J. and Mima Beard Roush Thacker are not found in the 1940 census.

Although some undocumented sources and the 1900 census say her given name was Jemima, "Mima" is the name on her Ohio birth and death certificates.[166, 167]

Son of Albert Leroy Roush and Mima Helen Beard:

+ 32 m I. **George Beard**[8] **Roush** was born in Union Twp., Highland Co., Ohio, on July 5, 1894.[168, 169] He died in Ogden, Weber Co., Utah, on January 28, 1964.[170, 171]

13. Eli Kenneth[7] **Roush** (*Margaret Mary*[6] *Pegan, Harrison James*[5], *Robert A.*[4], *Andrew*[3], *Andrew*[2] *Pagan, James*[1]) was born on November 17, 1878, in Washington Twp., Blackford Co., Indiana.[77] He was also known as **Teddy**. He was the son of Philip Roush and Margaret Mary Pegan (5). He died in Martinsville, Clark Twp., Clinton Co., Ohio, on May 21, 1943, at age 64.[77] Eli Kenneth was buried in Martinsville IOOF Cemetery, Martinsville, Clark Twp., Clinton Co., Ohio.[77, 172, 173]

A newspaper account in the *Hillsboro (OH) News-Herald* on November 23, 1899 reports that Eli Roush fell from a hickory tree at his parent's farm and was so severely injured he was not expected to recover.[174]

He married **Margaret A. Bish** on October 30, 1901 in Brown Co., Ohio.[175] They had three children. Margaret A. Bish was born in Dodson Twp., Highland Co., Ohio, on February 23, 1887.[176] Margaret A. reached age 28 and died in Indianapolis, Marion Co., Indiana on December 10, 1915.[A] She was buried in Crown Hill Cemetery, Indianapolis, Marion Co., Indiana.[A, B, C]

Margaret Bish Roush states that her birth occurred on February 9, 1883 in Brown Co., Ohio on her Brown County, Ohio marriage license to Eli Roush.[175] But she also lists her parents as George and Lucinda Barnett Bish, which are the parents listed on her birth certificate on February 23, 1887 in Highland Co., Ohio.[176]

Eli K. and Margaret Bish Roush had three children, sons Harry and Theodore and daughter Lora Belle, and lived very near the Highland County-Clinton County, Ohio line. Her sons Harry and Theodore were removed from the home in February 1908 by Clinton County authorities and taken to the Clinton County Children's Home, according to that institution's records in the Clinton County Archives. But a few days later Clinton County realized that the Roush home was really in Highland County, Ohio, so the boys were transferred to the Highland County Children's Home Her daughter, Lora Belle Roush, is not mentioned in these Clinton County records.[177] Margaret Bish Roush is not found in this census.

On April 23, 1908, the *Clinton County (OH) Democrat* reported that a grand jury in Clinton Co., Ohio indicted Eli Kenneth Roush on a charge of assault and battery.[178] He plead not guilty on June 11 of that year, according to The Democrat on the same day of the plea.[179] But, as nothing further is published on this case, perhaps the charges were dropped.

The February 9, 1909 edition of the *Clinton County Democrat* mentioned that Eli Roush sued Maggie Roush for divorce that week.[180]

An article in the *Highland County News-Herald (Hillboro, OH)* on May 12, 1910, "Mrs. Maggie Roush and children were at the home of (Moses) Jackson Ludwick.[181] (Lucinda Barnette Bish Ludwick was Margaret Bish Roush's mother.) However, just a few days earlier at the time of the 1910 U.S. Federal Census, all three of Eli and Margaret "Maggie" Bish Roush's children were residents of the Highland County Children's Home *(Census Place: Liberty, Highland, Ohio; Roll: T624_1197; Page: 25B; Enumeration District: 0124; Image: 805).*

According to her great-granddaughter, Christine "Christy" Wallace Gall, her grandmother, Lora Belle Roush Bussey Brust, told her that Margaret "Maggie" Bish Roush left Highland County with her second husband-to-be, Michael Randolph Stroup for Oklahoma, leaving all three of her children behind.[182] They married in Kay County, Oklahoma on August 24, 1911.[183] Michael Randolph Stroup died between May 24-June 19, 1919 in Blackwell, Kay Co., Oklahoma.[184]

But Margaret divorced Stoup and seems to have returned to the Highland County, Ohio area. She married at least twice more, to a Mr. Johnson and finally to James Melvin Lafferty of Pricetown, Salem Twp., Highland Co., Ohio. But no marriage licenses/applications have been found for either marriage. After her fourth divorce, she removed to Indianapolis, Marion Co., Indiana, where her sister Luella lived. She died under the name Margaret Johnson Lafferty in 1915.

When Margaret's son Theodore "Teddy" Roush dies at the Boy's Industrial School, an Ohio reform school, near Lancaster, Fairfield Co., Ohio in March 1920, his death certificate states his mother was deceased.[185]

Eli Kenneth Roush married **Loretta Mae Barnes** on March 6, 1910, in Clinton Co., Ohio.[186] They had ten children. Loretta Mae Barnes was born in Midland, Jefferson Twp., Clark Co., Ohio, on March 21, 1893.[187, 188] She was also known as **Retta or Rettie**. Loretta Mae reached age 49 and died in Martinsville, Clark Twp., Clinton Co., Ohio, on March 29, 1942.[187] She was buried in Martinsville IOOF Cemetery, Martinsville, Clark Twp., Clinton Co., Ohio.[187, 189, 190]

Loretta Mae Barnes Roush always used "Retta" or "Rettie" as her preferred given name.

Loretta had a son, Earl Franzy Nicely, out of wedlock before she married Eli Roush Sr.[191] No marriage record can be found for Loretta Barnes and a Nicely. Her name was Barnes upon her marriage to Eli K. Roush, and she states on the 1910 census form that her marriage to Eli Roush was her first. Eli Kenneth Roush Sr. raised Earl as his own and may have adopted him. Earl Nicely was renamed Earl Roush.

Eli Roush is enumerated in Clark Twp., Clinton Co., Ohio in 1910 *(Census Place: Clark, Clinton, Ohio; Roll: T624_1160; Page: 3B; Enumeration District: 0060; Image: 700).* In the household are Eli K. Roush, 29, born Indiana with his parents born in Ohio, a house carpenter. His wife, Loretta M. Barnes (Nicely) Roush is 18, born Ohio, as were her parents. (She is incorrectly named as "Ella" on the census form.) Eli Roush says this is his second marriage and Ella says it is her first. The couple says they've been married less than a year, and that Ella has borne one child, who was still alive. This was Earl (Nicely) Roush, age two, who is living with them and still using the surname Nicely. The boy was born Ohio, as were his parents. Also in the home is a boarder, Clinton Botts.

In 1920, Eli K. Roush is found in Washington Twp., Clinton Co., Ohio *(Census Place: Washington, Clinton, Ohio; Roll: T625_1355; Page: 6A; Enumeration District: 131; Image: 1061).* In the home are Eli K. Roush, 39, born Indiana and his parents in Ohio, a carpenter; and his wife, "Rettie" Barnes Roush, 25, born Ohio as were her parents. Children with them include: Theodore, 14, "Cary C.", nine, "Fred S." (Samuel Frederick), seven, Leroy K., five, Eulass, four, Leota, two, and Effie, who is a newborn. All the children were born in Ohio.

Soon after the census, son Theodore "Teddy" Roush is sent to the Ohio Boys Industrial School, an Ohio state-run reform school in Hocking Twp., Fairfield Co., Ohio, where he died a month later.

Eli Kenneth Roush is still in Washington Twp., Clinton Co., Ohio in 1930 *(Census Place: Washington, Clinton, Ohio; Roll: 1761; Page: 1B; Enumeration District: 22; Image: 545.0)*. Eli K. Roush, age 50, was born in Indiana and his parents in Ohio. He lists his occupation as carpenter. Rettie Barnes Roush is 37, born Ohio as were her parents. Eli says he was first married at age 20, while Rettie says she was 17. Children in the home include "C. Cecil", 20, a carpenter; "F. Samuel", 17, who lists no occupation; Leroy K., 16, a carpenter; Eulass J., 14, "Beatrice L.", 13, Effie N., 10, Dorothy O., eight, Mary L., six, and Floyd R., three years and eight months. All the children were born in Ohio.

In 1940, Eli Kenneth Roush is residing in Martinsville, Clark Twp., Clinton Co., Ohio *(Census Place: Martinsville, Clinton, Ohio; Roll: T627_3042; Page: 1A; Enumeration District: 14-4)*. Eli Roush, age 50, is a carpenter born in Indiana. With him are wife Rettie Barnes Roush, 47, and children "Letha", 16, "Richard", 14, and Eli, listed as "Junior", four, all born in Ohio. All, except Eli Jr., say they were living in Martinsville in 1935. Their home is on U.S. 28.

(Note: Earl Franzy [Nicely] Roush, Eli Roush's allegedly adopted son, was born on August 25, 1907 in Midland City, Jefferson Twp., Clinton Co., Ohio, and died on April 7, 1978 in Martinsville, Clark Twp., Clinton Co., Ohio. He is buried in Martinsville IOOF Cemetery, Martinsville, Clark Twp., Clinton Co., Ohio. He married Edith Marie Clemmer on February 25, 1939. They had two sons. Edith Marie was born on March 13, 1920 in Kingman, Chester Twp., Clinton Co., Ohio. She died on August 26, 2014 in Blanchester, Marion Twp., Clinton Co., Ohio. Edith is buried in Martinsville IOOF Cemetery, Martinsville, Clark Twp., Clinton Co., Ohio.)

Children of Eli Kenneth Roush and Margaret A. Bish:

+ 33 m I. **Harry Emmett[8] Roush** was born in Union Twp., Highland Co., Ohio, on January 22, 1904.[192, 193] He died in a hospital in Cranston, Providence Co., Rhode Island, on November 18, 1971.[193, 194]

+ 34 m II. **Theodore[8] Roush** was born in Union Twp., Highland Co., Ohio, on July 4, 1905.[185] He died in Hocking Twp., Fairfield Co., Ohio, on March 26, 1920.[185]

+ 35 f III. **Lora Belle[8] Roush** was born in New Market Twp., Highland Co., Ohio, on November 2, 1906.[195] She was also known as **Lorie**. Lora Belle died in Bainbridge, Paxton Twp., Ross Co., Ohio, on February 27, 1981.[196, 197]

Children of Eli Kenneth Roush and Loretta Mae Barnes:

+ 36 m I. **Cecil Cary[8] Roush** was born in Martinsville, Clark Twp., Clinton Co., Ohio, on September 22, 1910.[198] He died in a hospital in Dayton, Montgomery Co., Ohio, on March 1, 1949.[198, 199]

+ 37 m II. **Samuel Frederick[8] Roush** was born in Martinsville, Clark Twp., Clinton Co., Ohio, on May 31, 1912.[128] He died in Martinsville, Clark Twp., Clinton Co., Ohio, on November 13, 1975.[128, 200]

+ 38 m III. **Leroy Kenneth[8] Roush** was born in Martinsville, Clark Twp., Clinton Co., Ohio, on February 9, 1914.[128, 201] He was also known as **Roy**. Leroy Kenneth died in Martinsville, Clark Twp., Clinton Co., Ohio, on December 23, 1974.[202]

+ 39 f IV. **Euless Josephine[8] Roush** was born in Martinsville, Clark Twp., Clinton Co., Ohio, on December 25, 1915.[203, 204] She died in Xenia, Xenia Twp., Greene Co., Ohio, on December 19, 1975.[204, 205]

+ 40 f V. **Leota Beatrice⁸ Roush** was born in Washington Twp., Clinton Co., Ohio, on March 21, 1917.[128, 206] She died in Washington Court House, Union Twp., Fayette Co., Ohio, on May 18, 1982.[206, 207]

+ 41 f VI. **Effie Nondis⁸ Roush** was born in Washington Twp., Clinton Co., Ohio, on April 30, 1919.[208, 209] She died in Wilmington, Union Twp., Clinton Co., Ohio, on March 9, 1976.[208, 210]

+ 42 f VII. **Dorothy Opal⁸ Roush** was born in Washington Twp., Clinton Co., Ohio, on November 19, 1921.[128, 211, 212] She died in Troy, Concord Twp., Miami Co., Ohio, on July 11, 2004.[128, 211, 212]

+ 43 f VIII. **Mary Leatha⁸ Roush** was born in Washington Twp., Clinton Co., Ohio, on February 2, 1924.[213] She died in Wilmington, Union Twp., Clinton Co., Ohio, on October 16, 1946.[213]

+ 44 m IX. **Floyd Richard⁸ Roush** was born in Washington Twp., Clinton Co. Ohio, on July 4, 1926.[128] He was also known as **Dick**. Floyd Rich, ard died in Wilmington, Union Twp., Clinton Co., Ohio, on April 10, 1969.[214]

+ 45 m X. **Eli Kenneth⁸ Roush II** was born in Washington Twp., Clinton Co., Ohio, on July 12, 1931.[128, 215, 216] He was also known as **Junior**. Eli Kenneth died in a hospital in Dayton, Montgomery Co., Ohio, on May 8, 2009.[128, 217]

14. Cecil Ira⁷ Roush (*Margaret Mary⁶ Pegan, Harrison James⁵, Robert A.⁴, Andrew³, Andrew² Pagan, James¹*) was born on April 12, 1882, in Fairview, Hamer Twp., Highland Co., Ohio.[78, 79, 80, 81] He was the son of Philip Roush and Margaret Mary Pegan (5). Cecil Ira resided in 1956 in Fairview, Hamer Twp., Highland Co., Ohio. He died in a hospital in Dayton, Montgomery Co., Ohio, on January 1, 1956, at age 73.[79, 82] Cecil Ira was buried in Stroup Cemetery, Dodson Twp., Highland Co., Ohio.[79, 218]

Cecil Ira Roush's name on his birth certificate is Ira Cecil Roush, but he never uses that name; he is found as Cecil Ira Roush in nearly all records. The birth certificate name order may be an error.[78]

In 1910, Cecil Ira Roush is age 27, single, and in the U.S. Army, stationed at Fort Screven, Militia District 5, Tybee Island, Chatham Co., Georgia near Savannah (*Census Place: Militia District 5, Chatham, Georgia; Roll: T624_178; Page: 12B; Enumeration District: 0079; Image: 953*). He says he and his parents were born in Ohio.

Cecil Ira married **Electa Gertrude Stroup** on June 13, 1913, in Highland Co., Ohio.[219] They had five sons. Electa Gertrude Stroup was born in Dodson Twp., Highland Co., Ohio, on December 19, 1887.[128, 220, 221] Electa Gertrude reached age 86 and died in Hialeah, Dade Co., Florida, on April 17, 1974.[128, 221] She was buried in Stroup Cemetery, Dodson Twp., Highland Co., Ohio.[222, 223] She was the daughter of Michael C. Stroup and Sarah Kelley.

By 1917, Cecil and Electa Roush were living in Francisville, Dennison Twp., Lawrence Co., Illinois, where he files his WWI draft registration in Francisville, Dennison Twp., Lawrence Co., Illinois. On this application, he says he is an oil laborer working for the Ohio Oil Company.[224] Their first two sons, Philip and Randall, were born while they were living in Lawrence Co., Illinois.

Cecil Ira and Electa Stroup Roush and family are not found in the 1920 census, but in 1922 they were living in Dodson Twp., Highland Co., Ohio, as triplet sons were born to them. One died in just a few hours, one lived five months, and one, Gale, lived until 1998.

In 1930, Cecil Ira Roush is living in Mount Healthy, Hamilton Co., Ohio, enumerated as "Cecil Roesch" (*Census Place: Mount Healthy, Springfield Twp., Hamilton, Ohio; Roll: 1819; Page: 2A; Enumeration*

District: 362; Image: 506.0). In the home are Cecil Roush, 37, a house carpenter, born Ohio as were his parents. His wife, Electa Stroup Roush, is 41 and lists an occupation as pocket maker. Both say they and their parents were born in Ohio, and that they were first married at ages 31 and 25 respectively. Children in the home are sons Philip, 13, Randall, 11, both born in Illinois, and Gale, seven, born in Ohio.

Cecil Ira Roush has relocated to Wilmington, Union Twp., Highland Co., Ohio by 1940 *(Census Place: Wilmington, Clinton, Ohio; Roll: T627_3042; Page: 12A; Enumeration District: 14-18)*. In the home are Ira Roush, age 58, a carpenter, Electa Stroup Roush, 52, a cook in a restaurant, and their son Gale, 17. All were born in Ohio and say they were living in Wilmington in 1935. They are living at 1050 Nelson Avenue. (This is the only record found of Cecil using "Ira" as his name.)

Sons of Cecil Ira Roush and Electa Gertrude Stroup:

+ 46 m I. **Philip Stroup**[8] **Roush** was born in Francisville, Dennison Twp., Lawrence Co., Illinois, on June 17, 1916.[128] He died in Hialeah, Dade Co., Florida, on June 12, 1980.[225]

+ 47 m II. **Randall Cecil**[8] **Roush** was born in Lawrenceville, Lawrence Twp., Lawrence Co., Illinois, on April 22, 1918.[128, 226] He died in Orange Park, Clay Co., Florida, on March 9, 2004.[128, 226]

+ 48 m III. **Gale E.**[8] **Roush** was born in Dodson Twp., Highland Co., Ohio, on October 5, 1922.[128, 227, 228] He died in a hospital in Tampa, Hillsborough Co., Florida, on August 29, 1998.[128, 227, 228]

+ 49 m IV. **Dale E.**[8] **Roush** was born in Dodson Twp., Highland Co., Ohio, on October 5, 1922.[229] He died in Dodson Twp., Highland Co., Ohio, on May 11, 1923.[229]

+ 50 m V. **Ray E.**[8] **Roush** was born in Dodson Twp., Highland Co., Ohio, on October 5, 1922.[230] He died in Dodson Twp., Highland Co., Ohio, on October 5, 1922.[230]

15. Laura A.[7] **PeGan** (*Harrison James*[6], *Harrison James*[5] *Pegan, Robert A.*[4]*, Andrew*[3]*, Andrew*[2] *Pagan, James*[1]) was born on April 23, 1880, in Washington Twp., Blackford Co., Indiana.[116, 117] She was the daughter of Harrison James PeGan II (6) and Angeline Stout. Laura A. died in Salamonie Twp., Huntington Co., Indiana?, on June 28, 1898, at age 18.[116, 117] She was buried in McKinney Lugar Creek Cemetery, Center Twp., Grant Co., Indiana.[117]

Laura A. married **Harley Paul Keplinger** on April 11, 1897, in Grant Co., Indiana.[231] They had one child. Harley Paul Keplinger was born in Benton Twp., Pike Co., Ohio, on October 30, 1874.[232, 233, 234] Harley Paul reached age 68 and died in Warren, Salamonie Twp., Huntington Co., Indiana, on June 12, 1943.[232, 234] He was buried in Woodlawn Cemetery, Warren, Salamonie Twp., Huntington Co., Indiana.[235]

The inscription on Laura's headstone reads "Wife of H.P. Keplinger, Aged 18 years, 1 month, 23 days". According to her nephew, Hugh Frederick "Fritz" PeGan and cousin, Mattie Leona Pearson Hatfield, Laura A. PeGan Keplinger died in childbirth with her first child; the baby died as well.[83, 84] They probably died in Salamonie Twp., Huntington Co., Indiana, where the Keplinger family lived and where her husband Harley lived for the rest of his life.

According to Hugh Frederick PeGan, Harley Keplinger was a "nice guy". He remarried after his first wife, Laura died; he had four children by his second wife, Anne Chopson Keplinger, Occasionally, he would see Laura's family, and they in turn would visit him and his family. The PeGans evidently bore no grudges against Harley for the behavior of his brother, George, who caused much trouble for the PeGan family. George Keplinger raped Sarah Celeste PeGan and was the father her son, Raymond. George also shot Sarah in the neck in 1899 and spent time in an Indiana state prison for the crime.[83]

Child of Laura A. PeGan and Harley Paul Keplinger:

+ 51   I.   **Child**[8] **Keplinger** was born in Salamonie Twp., Huntington Co., Indiana?, on June 28, 1898.[83] He or she died in Salamonie Twp., Huntington Co., Indiana?, on June 28, 1898.[83]

16. Sarah Celeste[7] **PeGan** (*Harrison James*[6], *Harrison James*[5] *Pegan*, *Robert A.*[4], *Andrew*[3], *Andrew*[2] *Pagan*, *James*[1]) was born on June 2, 1882, in Monroe Twp., Grant Co., Indiana.[118] She was also known as **Lesta**. She was the daughter of Harrison James PeGan II (6) and Angeline Stout. Sarah Celeste died in Marion, Center Twp., Grant Co., Indiana, on July 28, 1963, at age 81.[118, 119] She was buried in Farrville Cemetery, Van Buren Twp., Grant Co., Indiana.[236]

Sarah Celeste "Lesta" PeGan, at age 16, became involved in an incident that forever affected her life—a sensational crime that was heavily covered by the local and state newspapers from February through April 1899. Newpapers in other states also followed the case.[237]

As told by Fritz PeGan: In 1898, George William Keplinger, the brother of Harvey Keplinger, the widowed husband of her late older sister, Laura PeGan Keplinger, had started to court young Sarah. It wasn't long before Sarah decided she didn't want George's attentions. He was odd and controlling. She declined to see him. But George Keplinger continued to pursue, even stalk, Sarah. In early January 1899, when she was walking home from a neighbor's, George Keplinger came along in a buggy. He jumped down from the buggy, then overpowered and abducted her, taking her to a deserted barn. There he raped her. She told no one.

For several weeks, George kept after her, coming to the Pegan house and insisting that, because of the intimacy, she had to marry him. "Lesta" steadfastly refused.[83]

On January 31, 1899, according to the *Hartford City (IN) Telegram,* George Keplinger, a farm worker on the Joseph Maddox farm near Jadden, Indiana, went to the Pegan home and "called Lista (sic) to the door put his left arm around her and with the right drew a bulldog revolver from his pocket and sent a bullet through her head." The girl fell in the doorway. Keplinger then placed the gun to his own head and fired, but the bullet missed its mark and passed through his hat. He fell across the body of the girl and lay there until Mr. Pegan, hearing the shots, rushed out and helped him to his feet. He then went to the home of Mr. Maddox where he remained until he was placed under arrest."[91]

The attending doctor later said that Keplinger had placed the gun directly on her head, causing ssevere powder burns. In addition, the bullet pierced her directly under her right ear and traveled downward almost completely through her head, lodging in the left side of her neck.[238] The wound became inflamed and septic. She lost a large amount of blood and was temporarily paralyzed.[239] For more than a week, her life hung in the balance, but miraculously she began to recover. One newspaper, the *Upland (IN) Monitor,* even published her obituary in their February 1, 1899 edition, but retracted it on February 9, adding that "Lesta" had denied that the shooting was intended to be a "double suicide", which Keplinger claimed.[90, 95] The *Bloomfield (IN) News* also reported that she had died, although the paper called Sarah by her elder sister's name, Laura.[240] Even in late April, at after George Keplinger had been sentenced to the Indiana state prison in Jeffersonville, the *Jeffersonville (IN) News* said Sarah had died in the shooting.[94]

To complicate matters, the critically injured Sarah discovered a few weeks after the incident that she was pregnant.

The Grant County newspapers constantly reported on Keplinger's shockingly strange behavior while jailed. He blamed his actions on a dose of quinine, and claimed he bought the gun "to shoot a white dog".[90] According to the *Grant County News (Marion, IN):* "He expressed the wish for Miss PeGan's recovery and for his early release. Then, said he, 'would be a better boy'".[241] George wrote a letter to Sarah begging her forgiveness and repeating his offer of marriage, telling her to forget the whole incident. Several times in this letter, he told her the charges would be dropped if she declined to testify against him, saying that would be the best option for them![239]

When Sarah did not reply, Keplinger turned his romantic intentions to a former girlfriend, writing to her that he "had thought of her all along" while courting Sarah. He wrote poetry to his past amour, declaring, "My love for you will never fail, as soon as I get out of jail".[242]

George W. Keplinger admitted in the Grant County court during his hearing that he "was criminally intimate" with Sarah, as stated in the *Grant County News*. He pleaded guilty of assault and battery with intent to kill. Sarah was not in court, but her father Harrison stated that she was "in a family way". The judge sentenced to a term of two to 14 years at the Indiana Reformatory in Jeffersonville, Clark Co., Indiana.[92] Keplinger remained calm during his sentencing, he was "in the best of humor" and puffing on a cigar.[243] He was transported to Jeffersonville immediately because the authorities had discovered he and another prisoner were planning to break out of the Grant County jail. He arrived at the prison fashionably attired—"dressed like a dude" according to the *Jeffersonville News*.[94] He entered prison on April 25, 1899, but escaped on July 14, 1901.[97]

Sarah bore George Keplinger's illegitimate son, Raymond PeGan, on September 23, 1899.

Later, Sarah's awful ordeal was never been discussed by the family. Sarah's descendants believed the swelling in her neck was caused by a goiter. Moreover, Sarah's children and grandchildren were never told that Raymond PeGan was their half-brother. They believed him to be Sarah's younger brother. As he was born in 1899, This was a reasonable assumption on their part, as Raymond was about four years younger than Sarah's brother Leonidus and two years older than Sarah's youngest brother, Philip Garl PeGan. In an April 2002 interview with Mattie Leona Pearson Hatfield and Betty Eastes Cowgill Reese, the author obliquely referred to Ray as their half-brother. They "corrected" her and said that Ray was their "uncle".[84, 97]

Sarah Celeste married **Isaac James Pearson** on February 15, 1902, in Grant Co., Indiana.[244] They had four children. Isaac James Pearson was born in Amboy, Jackson Twp., Miami Co., Indiana, on June 7, 1864.[245, 246] He was also known as **Ike**. Isaac James reached age 72 and died in Jonesboro, Mill Twp., Grant Co., Indiana, on December 9, 1936.[246, 247] He was buried in Farrville Cemetery, Van Buren Twp., Grant Co., Indiana.[245]

Even when Sarah married her first husband Isaac Pearson in 1902, their wedding announcement in a newspaper mentioned her assault by George Keplinger, who was imprisoned..[248] (Ed. Note: George W. Keplinger was not in the penitentiary; he had escaped by then—a fact Indiana Reformatory staff never made public.)

When Sarah wed widower Ike, he had four children, Lessie May, 14, Alpheus, 11, Walker, nine, and Vera Marie, almost three, by his late first wife Emma Oden Pearson. But those Pearson children were raised by other relatives after Emma's death in 1900. At first, Isaac Pearson refused to raise his wife Sarah Celeste Pegan Pearson's son, two-year-old Raymond, whom Sarah bore after being raped by George Keplinger. Raymond spent his early years with his grandparents, Harrison and Angeline Stout PeGan Jr. But after Angeline Stout PeGan's death in 1910, Ray is resided with his mother and stepfather.[83]

Isaac "Ike" and Sarah C. PeGan Pearson are enumerated in the 1910 census in Mill Twp., Grant Co., Indiana *(Census Place: Mill, Grant, Indiana; Roll: T624_351; Page: 11A; Enumeration District: 0068; Image: 704)*. In the household are Isaac J. Pearson, age 44, born Indiana as were his parents, lists his occupation as laborer doing odd jobs; and Sarah C. Pegan, 27, born in Indiana, with her father born in Ohio and her mother in Indiana. The couple says they have been married eight years and Sarah has borne three children, all still living. Children with them include "Ray Pearson", (Incorrect—his surname was PeGan), 11, Leona, seven, and Herbert, two. All the children were born in Indiana.

Sarah's father Harrison PeGan Jr. moved into their home in early July 1919 after he sold his house on Sutton Hill in Huntington Twp., Huntington Co., Indiana, just south of Huntington town, where he'd lived with his son Clanzie, Clanzie's family, and his youngest son Philip. He'd had a disagreement with Clanzie's wife, Josephine, which broke up the household. (Philip left to live with older brother Jesse.)[83, 84]

In 1920, Isaac and Sarah PeGan Pearson are found in Jonesboro, Mll Twp., Grant Co., Indiana *(Census Place: Jonesboro, Grant, Indiana; Roll: T625_434; Page: 11B; Enumeration District: 75; Image: 465)*. Isaac, whose name is spelled "Iisac Pierson", is age 55 and a laborer at Indiana Rubber Works. Again, he says he and his parents were born in Indiana. Sarah Pegan Pearson is 37, born Indiana, with her father born in Ohio and her mother in Indiana. Children living with them are Leona, 16, Herbert, 12, Truman, eight, and "Colina", six. All the children were born in Indiana. Oddly, Colene is listed as being a laborer at the Indiana Rubber Works. Also in the home is Vera Pearson, 20, Isaac's daughter by his first wife, Emma Oden Pearson, who lists no occupation, but she was probably the one working at the Rubber Works and not (Opal) Colene, who is listed just above her. Also in the home is Sarah's father, Harrison PeGan Jr., who oddly is listed as a boarder. He is 68, a widower, and born in Ohio, as were his parents. Harrison says he is a house carpenter.

Around 1925, Sarah allegedly caught her father Harrison Jr. stealing money from her. She told him to leave. Harrison Jr. left and moved in with sons Jesse and his family, who were living in Macy, Allen Twp., Miami Co., Indiana.[83]

Isaac and Sarah Celeste Pegan Pearson are listed in Jonesboro, Mill Twp., Grant Co., Indiana in 1930 *(Census Place: Jonesboro, Grant, Indiana; Roll: 589; Page: 15A; Enumeration District: 31; Image: 888.0)*. Isaac Pearson, 65, says he is a mill man in a rubber factory. Sarah Pegan Pearson is 47. Isaac Pearson says he was first wed at age 21, and Sarah says she was first married at 18 (Incorrect—she was 19). Daughter "Coleen O.", 16, is still living with them. Also listed are sons Herbert, listed as "ab." (absent?), 21, a braiden man in a rubber factory, and Truman, 18, a grinder at a sash factory, listed as "pt. ab." The sons were in the home part time; they were also living and working in Winchester, Indiana.

Widow Sarah PeGan Pearson is enumerated in Jonesboro, Mill Twp., Grant Co., Indiana in 1940 *(Census Place: Jonesboro, Grant, Indiana; Roll: T627_1048; Page: 22B; Enumeration District: 27-36)*. Sarah Pegan Pearson, age 57, is listed as the head of the household. Living with her are her son-in-law, Joseph Eastes, 29, an operator in a glass factory, her daughter and Joseph's wife, "Coleen" Pearson Eastes, 26, an inspector at a glass factory. Joseph and Colene have two children, Betty, nine, and Joseph Jr., three. All in the home were born in Indiana. Everyone but Joseph Jr., who is too young, was residing in the same house in 1935, but no address is listed.

After Ike's death, Sarah Celeste PeGan Pearson married **Eli Franklin Hewitt** on August 22, 1942, at Howard Co., Indiana in Grant Co., Indiana.[249] Eli Franklin Hewitt was born in Georgetown Twp., Vermilion Co., Illinois, on January 21, 1863.[249, 250] He was also known as **Frank**. He reached age 83 and died in Gas City, Mill Twp., Grant Co., Indiana, on January 28, 1946.[251] Eli Franklin was buried in Mount Hope Cemetery, Covington, Kenton Co., Kentucky.[250, 252]

Sarah Celeste PeGan Pearson Hewitt married **Clarence Branson Horner** on December 28, 1948, in Randolph Co., Indiana.[253] Clarence Branson Horner was born in Greensfork Twp., Randolph Co., Indiana, on July 5, 1878.[254, 255] Clarence Branson lived in 1961 in Lynn, Washington Twp., Randolph Co., Indiana. Clarence Branson reached age 82 and died in a hospital in Winchester, White River Twp., Randolph Co., Indiana, on April 11, 1961.[256, 257] He was buried in Willow Grove Cemetery, Fountain City, New Garden Twp., Wayne Co., Indiana.[258]

Clarence Horner was a farmer, roofer, and tinner.[257]

Although her surname was Horner when she died, Sarah Celeste PeGan Pearson Hewitt Horner's gravestone reads, "Sarah C. Pearson".[236]

According to her daughter, Mattie Leona Pearson Hatfield, Sarah was an undemonstrative woman, strict but kind. She very religious—a devout Wesleyan(?) who wore plain clothing and no perfume, cosmetics or jewelry—not even a wedding ring. (As her husband, Isaac Pearson, was a lifelong Quaker, Sarah may have been actually been a Quaker, as this description sounds more like she was a Quaker rather than a Wesleyan.) Sarah lived for a while with her son-in-law and daughter, Joseph and Opal Colene Eastes. Joseph and Colene worked, and Sarah cared for their three children. Betty remembers her grandmother making her "go to church all the time". Leona, Betty and Marylou Eastes, wife of Joseph Eastes Jr., all agree that Sarah PeGan Pearson made the best pies in the world. Raspberry, rhubarb and gooseberry were her specialties. They also say that Ike Pearson would not allow his children or grandchildren to sit on his lap, and that he abhored shoes and went barefoot whenever he could.[84]

But what happened to George Keplinger, Sarah's rapist?

George William Keplinger/Roy Clarence Scott was born on January 24, 1878, in Benton Twp., Pike Co., Ohio.[98] Keplinger/Scott reached age 91 and died in Springfield, Springfield Twp., Sangamon Co., Illinois, on October 19, 1969.[99] He was buried in Oak Ridge Cemetery, Springfield, Springfield Twp., Sangamon Co., Illinois.[99] He was the son of Jonathan Keplinger and Phoebe Moodespaugh or Motherspaugh.

His parents, Jonathan and Phoebe Moodespaugh Keplinger, were living in Benton Twp., Pike Co., Ohio in the 1880 census *(Census Place: Benton, Pike, Ohio; Roll: 1058; Page: 19B; Enumeration District: 122)*, and that is where his brother, Harley Paul Keplinger, was born in 1874.[233, 234]

George W. Keplinger is an inmate in the Indiana Reformatory in Clarksville, Clark Co., Indiana in 1900 *(Census Place: Jeffersonville, Clark, Indiana; Roll: 362; Page: 6A; Enumeration District: 0007)*, but he escaped on July 14, 1901.[97]

After he broke out of prison, he seems to have fled to St. Charles, St. Charles Co., Missouri area where he changed his name to "Roy Clarence Scott". There are no more records for a George Keplinger, born January 14, 1878, in the censuses or anywhere else.

By 1906, George William Keplinger, alias Roy Clarence Scott, has fathered another illegitimate son, James Roy "Roy" Mattocks II, born September 22, 1906 in St. Charles, St. Charles Co., Missouri.[259] James Roy Mattocks II is acknowledged as Roy Clarence Scott's son in the latter's obituary.[260] He is also mentioned as a stepson in Mollie Lamparter Scott's obituary.[261] The identity of James Roy Mattocks II's mother is unknown, but she may have been a relative of either James Robert Mattocks Sr. or Cora Belle Snarr Mattocks, James Roy Mattocks II's adoptive parents. "Roy" is enumerated as "adopted son" with his adoptive parents James Robert and Cora Belle Snarr Mattocks in St. Charles, St. Charles Co., Missouri in 1910 *(Census Place: St Charles Ward 4, Saint Charles, Missouri; Roll: T624_808; Page: 14A; Enumeration District: 0170)*. On the census form, Cora Belle says she has been married to James Robert Mattocks Sr. for 11 years and has borne one child, who was deceased (they had a daughter, Vera, who died at age four in 1903).

"Roy C. Scott" marries Mollie Lamparter on September 14, 1909 in St. Charles, St. Charles Co., Missouri.[262] (Their eldest child, daughter Pauline Scott Clayburg Klespitz, was born in Missouri in 1908.[263]) By 1911, Roy Clarence Scott and his family moved to Springfield, Sangamon Co., Illinois, where their youngest child, son Clarence H. Scott, was born.

Roy C. Scott is not found in the 1910 census.

Roy Clarence Scott has no history—no census data, etc.— at all until he files a WWI draft registration on September 9, 1917. On that document, Roy, a gas pipe fitter for the Springfield Gas & Electric Company, states his birthdate as January 24, 1878.[98] This birthdate is George W. Keplinger's date of birth.

Roy Clarence Scott is not found in the 1920 census.

This Roy Clarence Scott, age 52, born Ohio, is living in Springfield, Sangamon Co., Illinois in 1930 *(Census Place: Springfield, Sangamon, Illinois; Roll: 559; Page: 20B; Enumeration District: 0049; Image: 957.0)*. Roy's occupation is "driver", and he seems to be a taxi driver. Also in the home are his wife, Mollie Lampeter Scott, 46, born Missouri, and their children and spouses: son Clarence H. Scott, 19, born Illinois, Clarence's wife, Frances Unknown Scott, 18, born Illinois; and daughter Pauline Scott Clayburg, 22, born Missouri and her husband Leonard Clayburg, 21, born Illinois. Roy C. Scott says first marriage was at age 22, and Mollie, born about 1884, says hers was at age 23.

In 1940, Roy Clarence Scott is still residing in Springfield, Sangamon Co., Illinois *(Census Place: Springfield, Sangamon, Illinois; Roll: T627_887; Page: 19A; Enumeration District: 84-100)*. This time, Roy Clarence Scott, age 62, says he was born in Indiana. He is a laborer for the Works Progress Administration (WPA). Also in the home is his wife Mollie, age 55, born Missouri, and a grandson.

On his 1942 WWII draft registration form, Roy Clarence Scott says again that he was born on January 24, 1878. He also states his birthplace as New Paris, Ohio, which is in Preble County.[264] There is no Preble County, Ohio birth record for a Roy Scott on that date, or any date for that matter. This same date of birth, with "Ohio" as a birthplace, is listed on Roy Clarence Scott's Illinois death certificate—but no parents' names are on that record.[99]

There is some indication from online sources, including those from one of his grandsons, that his real surname was George W. Keplinger. Again, this information is not documented, but the circumstantial evidence presented is difficult to ignore.

Son of Sarah Celeste PeGan and George William Keplinger (a.k.a. Roy Clarence Scott):

+ 52 m I. **Raymond Harrison**[8] **PeGan** was born in Monroe Twp., Grant Co., Indiana, on September 22, 1899.[128, 265] He died in Fort Wayne, Allen Co., Indiana, on May 7, 1980.[266, 267]

Children of Sarah Celeste PeGan and Isaac James Pearson:

+ 53 f I. **Mattie Leona**[8] **Pearson** was born in Mill Twp., Grant Co., Indiana, on April 9, 1903.[128, 268, 269] She was also known as **Toots**. Mattie Leona died in Greentown, Liberty Twp., Howard Co., Indiana, on December 3, 2005.[128, 269]

+ 54 m II. **Herbert Harrison**[8] **Pearson** was born in Mill Twp., Grant Co., Indiana, on May 2, 1908.[128, 270] He was also known as **Bill**. Herbert Harrison died in a hospital in Pendleton, Umatilla Co., Oregon, on August 8, 1973.[270, 271]

+ 55 m III. **Truman Vaughn**[8] **Pearson** was born in Mill Twp., Grant Co., Indiana, on September 18, 1911.[128, 272] He died in a hospital in Orange, Orange Co., California, on April 30, 1998.[128, 272]

+ 56 f IV. **Opal Colene**[8] **Pearson** was born in Mill Twp., Grant Co., Indiana, on November 21, 1913.[128, 273, 274] She died in a hospital in Muncie, Center Twp., Delaware Co., Indiana, on December 25, 2000.[128, 273, 274]

17. **Alvah or Alvin LeRoy**[7] **PeGan** (*Harrison James*[6], *Harrison James*[5] *Pegan, Robert A.*[4]*, Andrew*[3]*, Andrew*[2] *Pagan, James*[1]) was born on July 22, 1884, in Monroe Twp., Grant Co., Indiana.[120, 121, 122, 123] He was also known as **Alvin or LeRoy**. He was the son of Harrison James PeGan II (6) and Angeline Stout. Alvah or Alvin LeRoy died in Wabash, Noble Twp., Wabash Co., Indiana, on May 5, 1936, at age 51.[120, 122, 123] He was buried in Hopewell Cemetery, Lagro Twp., Wabash Co., Indiana.[120, 122, 123, 275]

Childless.

His given name was Alvah Leroy, but as an adult, he preferred Alvin as his given name; sometimes he used LeRoy.

In 1910, Alvah PeGan, listed as "Alva", is age 25, unmarried, and living with his widowed father Harrison Jr. and most of his siblings in Lagro, Lagro Twp., Wabash Co., Indiana *(Census Place: Lagro, Wabash, Indiana; Roll T624_386; Page: 3A; Enumeration District: 144; Image: 118)*. The head of the household is Harrison PeGan Jr., 58, born Ohio as were his parents, Harrison says he is widowed and has his "own income" in the occupation category. Besides Alvah, residing in the home are Alvah's brother Clanzie, 21, and his wife, Josephine Schetzszle PeGan, also 21, and their two sons, Leo, born 1907, and Paul, born 1908. Alvah's other brothers are also there: Jesse, 23, Leonidus, 16, and

Philip, eight. Either Harrison—or whoever in the house talked with the census taker— is playing a joke or irritated with the questions asked. Harrison Jr. is listed as born in Ohio, but his father is "born in the United States" and his mother in "Scotland." Clanzie and Leonidas say they are laborers on the railroad. Alvah lists his occupation as carpenter and Jesse is a farmer; both are single. All in the home, except Harrison, were born in Indiana. All the PeGan sons say their father was born in Ohio and their mother in Indiana. Josephine Schetzszle PeGan states she is an Indiana native, and her father was born in Ohio and her mother in New York.

Alvah or Alvin LeRoy married **Edythe G. Wildoner** on May 13, 1911, in Wabash Co., Indiana.[276, 277] They divorced. Edythe G. Wildoner was born in Lagro, Lagro Twp, Wabash Co., Indiana, on October 3, 1890.[278] Edythe G. also resided in 1979 in Frederic Twp., Crawford Co., Michigan. She reached age 94 and died in Grayling, Crawford Co., Michigan, on November 19, 1984.[279] Edythe G. was buried in Falls Memorial Gardens Cemetery, Wabash, Noble Twp., Wabash Co., Indiana.[280]

In 1920, "Alvin" PeGan and first wife Edythe Wildoner Pegan are found in Flint, Genesee Co., Michigan *(Census Place: Flint Ward 4, Genesee, Michigan; Roll: T625_765; Page: 17A; Enumeration District: 42; Image: 662)*. Alvah/Alvin, age 36, says he is a plumbing in a plumbing shop and that his father was born in Ohio and his mother in Indiana (correct). Edythe ("Edith"), 29, says she and her mother were born in Indiana while her father was born in Pennsylvania.

Alvah and Edythe Wildoner Pegan divorce in 1925.

After divorcing Alvah Pegan, Edythe Wildoner Pegan married William C. Brown and is found with him in 1930 in Lansing, Ingham Co., Michigan in 1930 *(Census Place: Lansing, Ingham, Michigan; Roll: 991; Page: 2A; Enumeration District: 26; Image: 750.0)*. Neither Edythe Wildoner Pegan Brown and William C. Brown are found in the 1940 census, and they may have been divorced by 1942. The Social Security Death Index says her last residence was Roscommon, Roscommon Co., Michigan.[128]. However, according to her obituary in the *Wabash (IN) Plain Dealer*, she had moved to Frederic Twp., Crawford Co., Michigan in 1979 after living in Lansing for most of her life and later died in Grayling, Crawford Co., Michigan.[279]

Alvah or Alvin LeRoy PeGan married Mrs. **Leatha Mae Morrow** Rodgers on May 31, 1928, in Wabash Co., Indiana.[281, 282] Leatha Mae Morrow was born in Marion, Center Twp., Grant Co., Indiana, on May 19, 1885.[128, 283, 284, 285] Leatha Mae reached age 91 and died in Huntington, Huntington Twp., Huntington Co., Indiana, on May 2, 1977.[284, 285] She was buried in Pilgrim's Rest Cemetery, Huntington, Huntington Twp., Huntington Co., Indiana.[286]

Leatha Mae Morrow was the half-sister of Nancy "Hazel" Long Knight Pegan, the first wife of Raymond Harrison Pegan, Alvah/Alvin Leroy Pegan's nephew.[83] Raymond and "Hazel" had married in 1921. In 1900, Leatha Morrow, age 13, is enumerated with her mother and stepfather and half-sister, Nancy "Hazel" Long, age 10, in Center Twp., Grant Co., Indiana *(Census Place: Center, Grant, Indiana; Roll: 373; Page: 6B; Enumeration District: 31)*. Her half-sister "Hazel" married Raymond Harrison Pegan, Leatha's second husband Alvah/Alvin Pegan's nephew, in 1921.

In 1915, Leatha Morrow married a musician, Joseph Rodgers, a New York, New York native. They moved to Detroit and Highland Park, Wayne Co., Michigan, where Joseph also worked for the Ford Motor Company. But they divorced on May 1, 1928. On May 31, 1928 Leatha Morrow Rodgers married Alvah/Alvin Pegan.[282]

Alvah or Alvin Leroy PeGan is enumerated as "Leroy" PeGan, age 45, born in Indiana, and, along with second wife Leatha Morrow Rodgers Pegan, 44, born Indiana, is living in Flint, Genesee Co., Michigan in 1930 *(Census Place: Flint, Genesee, Michigan; Roll: 987; Page: 14A; Enumeration District: 52; Image: 69.0)*. "Leroy", a plumber born in Indiana, says he was first married at age 28 and Leatha, born in Indiana as were her parents, says her first marriage was at age 24. Oddly, Alvah Leroy PeGan says his father was born in France and his mother in Pennsylvania. This is not true; perhaps Leatha talked with the census taker and simply didn't know this information. Also in the household is nephew Paul

PeGan, age 21, born in Indiana as were his parents, and a lodger, Chris Wagner, 24. Both Paul PeGan and Wagner are apprentice plumbers.

Alvah/Alvin and Leatha Morrow Rodgers Pegan lived in Flint, Genesee Co., Michigan for a few more years before moving back to Wabash, Noble Twp., Wabash Co., Indiana, where Alvah died in 1936. The following year, Leatha married her third husband, Charles F. Hegel, in Wabash Co., Indiana.[283]

Leatha Morrow Rogers Pegan Hegel and her third husband Charles Hegel are found in 1940 in Andrews, Jackson Twp., Huntington Co., Indiana *(Census Place: Andrews, Huntington, Indiana; Roll: T627_1055; Page: 3B; Enumeration District: 35-2)*. Charles Hegel, age 74, is a farmer born in Indiana who says he was living in the same house in 1935. Leatha Morrow Rogers Pegan Hegel, 64, was also born in Indiana, says she was a Wabash County, Indiana resident in 1935. Their home is at 68 West Jefferson Street.

Charles F. Hegel died in 1946. After that, Leatha Morrow Rodgers Pegan Hegel married for a fourth time to William V. Class in Huntington Co., Indiana.[287] Leatha Morrow Rodgers Pegan Hegel Class is buried with William Class in Pilgrims Rest Cemetery in that county.[286]

Although he was a plumber by trade, Alvah/Alvin PeGan was also an expert carpenter, according to his obituary.[120] Leona Pearson Hatfield, daughter of Sarah PeGan Pearson, says her Uncle Alvah visited every spring, and her mother always had a carpentry or plumbing job in the Pearson home for him to do when he came.[84] By all accounts, Alvah/Alvin was a congenial, helpful man. Alvah's grave is the only PeGan grave in Hopewell with a marker. It reads, "Daddy", which was his second wife Leatha Morrow Rodgers PeGan's pet name for him.[275]

18. **Jesse Harrison**[7] **Pegan** *(Harrison James*[6] *PeGan II, Harrison James*[5] *Pegan, Robert A.*[4]*, Andrew*[3]*, Andrew*[2] *Pagan, James*[1]*)* was born on October 14, 1886, in Monroe Twp., Grant Co., Indiana.[124, 125, 126] He was the son of Harrison James PeGan II (6) and Angeline Stout. He died in Huntington, Huntington Twp., Huntington Co., Indiana, on November 17, 1946, at age 60.[124, 125, 126] Jesse Harrison was buried in Pilgrims Rest Cemetery, Huntington, Huntington Twp., Huntington Co., Indiana.[288]

Jesse Pegan and his descendants have never used the capital "G" in their surname as his siblings and their descendants have.

Jesse Pegan, age 23 and a farmer, was unmarried and living with his siblings and widowed father Harrison PeGan Jr. in Lagro, Lagro Twp., Wabash Co., Indiana *(Census Place: Lagro, Wabash, Indiana; Roll T624_386; Page: 3A; Enumeration District: 144; Image: 118)*. Harrison Pegan, 58, listed as head of the household. Harrison says he is widowed and has his "own income" in the occupation category. Either Harrison—or whoever in the house talked with the census taker— is playing a joke or irritated with the questions asked. Harrison Jr. is listed as born in Ohio, but his father is "born in the United States" and his mother in "Scotland". Also living in the home are Jesse's brother Clanzie, 21, and his wife, Josephine Schetzszle PeGan, also 21, and their two sons, Leo, born 1907, and Paul, born 1908. Jesse's brothers "Alva", 25, Leonidus, 16, and Philip, eight, are also residents in the home. Both Clanzie and Leonidus say they are laborers on the railroad. Alvah lists his occupation as carpenter and Jesse is a farmer. All the PeGan sons say they are Indiana natives, with their father was born in Ohio and their mother in Indiana. Josephine Schetzszle PeGan states she was born in Indiana, her father in Ohio and her mother in New York.

Shortly after this census, Jesse moves out of the PeGan home and boards with a Mrs. Story in Macy, Miami Co., Indiana. In 1917, Jesse, Elva and son James attended Mrs. Story's funeral. according to the March 17, 1917 *Rochester (IN) Sentinel,* Jesse made his home with Mrs. Story "after his mother died". Jesse worked on the Story farm, perhaps even after his marriage to Elva.[289]

Jesse Harrison married **Elva Coe Keith** on May 24, 1911, in Wabash Co., Indiana.[290, 291] They had five children. Elva Coe Keith was born in Noble Twp., Wabash Co., Indiana, on October 19, 1889.[290, 292, 293] Elva Coe reached age 82 and died in Huntington, Huntington Twp., Huntington Co., Indiana, on June 14, 1972.[294, 292, 293] She was buried in Pilgrims Rest Cemetery, Huntington, Huntington Twp., Huntington Co., Indiana.[295]

On his WWI Draft Registration, Jesse H. Pegan incorrectly lists his birthdate as October 14, 1887.[296] In December of that year, 1917, Jesse and another Macy, Indiana resident captured a badger, rarely found in Indiana, "after 10 hours of hard digging".[297]

In the 1920 census, Jesse H. and Elva Keith Pegan are living in Wabash, Wabash Co., Indiana (*Census Place: Wabash Ward 1, Wabash, Indiana; Roll: T625_472; Page: 7B; Enumeration District: 189; Image: 870*). In the home are Jesse Pegan, age 33, a blacksmith, says he was born in Indiana and his parents in the United States. Elva Keith Pegan, 30, says she and her parents were born in Indiana. With them are their children: Cecil, seven, Pauline, six, James, four, and seven months, Fern, two years and nine months, and Florence, five months. Daughter Florence is listed as a male with the name of "Lawrence". Philip PeGan, age 18, Jesse's youngest brother, is residing with them. Philip also lists his occupation as a blacksmith. Also in the household is a Kenneth Palmer, age 18, a lodger.

By 1925, Jesse and Elva Keith Pegan were back in Macy, Allen Twp., Miami Co., Indiana, as his father Harrison PeGan Jr., went to live with him there after Harrison was asked to leave Isaac and Sarah PeGan Pearson's home, in Jonesboro, Mill Twp., Grant Co., Indiana. By 1928, By 1928, Harrison Jr. had overstayed his welcome at Jesse's house, and Jesse placed him in the Miami County Poor Farm and Infirmary in Washington Twp., Miami Co., Indiana south of the county seat, Peru.]

In 1930, Jesse and Elva Keith Pegan are residing in Noble Twp., Wabash Co., Indiana (*Census Place: Noble, Wabash, Indiana; Roll: 636; Page: 8B; Enumeration District: 13; Image: 922.0.*). Jesse Pegan, age 43, is now a farmer. Elva is 40 years old. Children living in the home are Cecil, 17, a farmhand; Pauline, 16, James, 14, Fern, 12, and Florence, 10. All in the home are listed as born in Indiana, as were their parents (Incorrect—Harrison PeGan II, Jesse's father, was born in Ohio).

But was Jesse really living with Elva and his children on April 23, 1930, when this census enumeration was taken? Or did Elva Keith Pegan just list him as doing so? There are two strange entries for a "John Pegan" and "John W. Pegan" in Miami Co., Indiana in the 1930 census. The "John Pegan" is a lodger in the home of Ernest Moon in Peru, Washington Twp., Miami Co., Indiana (*Census Place: Peru, Miami, Indiana; Roll: 618; Page: 7A; Enumeration District: 0017; Image: 676.0*) on April 7, 1930, retroactive to April 1. He says he is age 47, and that he and his parents were Indiana-born. He also states he is married, and his first marriage occurred at age 21. His occupation is "shopman for a circus". On April 9, 1930, a "John W." Pegan is found in the "circus home" in Butler Twp., Miami Co., Indiana (*Census Place: Butler, Miami, Indiana; Roll: 618; Page: 5A; Enumeration District: 0003; Image: 246.0*). "John W." Pegan is age 43, single, and a blacksmith with the Hegenback Circus. He says he and his father were born in Indiana and his mother in Ohio. It is highly likely that the two "John Pegans" were the same man: Jesse Harrison Pegan, who abandoned his family around that time. (Note: Peru, Indiana was the winter "home" for several famous circuses in that time period.)

According to Fritz PeGan, Jesse left Elva and his children, eventually moving to Milwaukee, Milwaukee Co., Wisconsin—for reasons unknown.[83] On her marriage application to Charles Oswalt in September 1935, Pauline Pegan Oswalt stated that her mother was living in Wabash, Indiana and her father in Wisconsin.[298] So, Jesse's family had some idea of his whereabouts. But he may not have stayed in Milwaukee continuously.

The *Edwardsville (IL) Intelligencer* reports on November 14, 1936, that a Jesse Pegan was indicted for larceny and burglary.[299]

Jesse Pegan is enumerated as "John Pegan" in Milwaukee, Milwaukee Co., Wisconsin 1940 (*Census Place: Milwaukee, Milwaukee, Wisconsin; Roll: T627_4543; Page: 7A; Enumeration District: 72-52*). "John" Pegan, age 54, is a "horseshoer" born in Indiana. He is listed as the head of household in what appears to be a boarding house at 135 East Highland Avenue, where he says he was living in 1935. There are eight other men living in the household.

Jesse H. Pegan again lists a wrong birthdate on his WWII draft registration; he states he was born on October 14, 1885.[300]

In 1940, Elva Keith Pegan is enumerated in Pleasant Twp., Wabash Co., Indiana *(Census Place: Pleasant, Wabash, Indiana; Roll: T627_1106; Page: 6A; Enumeration District: 85-24)*. The head of the household is Elva ("Elvie") Keith Pegan, age 50, who says she is a widow. With her are two of her children: James, 24, a farmer, and Florence, 20. All were born in Indiana, and say they were living in the same house on Peru Road in 1935.

Elva remained steadfast after Jesse abandoned his family. She raised the children without him. She took in laundry and sewing, even sewing wedding dresses, to support the family. Until about 1941, the family remained in Wabash, Noble Twp., Wabash Co., Indiana. Then Elva moved the family to Huntington, Huntington Co., Indiana, to be nearer to her brother-in-law Clanzie and his family. "Fritz" Pegan, Clanzie's son, noted that Clanzie was angry with Jesse for abandoning Elva. Fritz says his father helped Elva often with household repairs and other chores during Jesse's long absence and helped Jesse's family in many other ways.[83]

According to Fritz PeGan and some of Jesse's grandchildren, Jesse Pegan returned to his wife Elva and family in 1946, who were residing in Huntington, Huntington Twp., Huntington Co., Indiana, just weeks before he died of cancer.[83, 292, 301, 302] When Jesse returned, Elva took him back, but Clanzie never forgave him for what he did. Clanzie did not speak to Jesse—and he may have not spoken to Elva either after Jesse returned. He seemed to disapprove of Elva's decision to take Jesse back. The two brothers' families had an icy relationship from then on.[83]

After Jesse's death, their son Cecil and his children moved in with Elva until Cecil remarried in 1956. Betty Jean Pegan Corn, Cecil's eldest child, remembers the wonderful care her grandmother gave the family.[302]

By then, Elva's daughter Fern Pegan Zimpelman was a widow, and Fern bought a house and Elva moved in with her. They lived on the southeast corner of Jefferson Street and Etna Avenue in Huntington. Fern, a beautician, had a shop attached to the house. Until she died, Elva lived with Fern.[302]

Jesse is said to have been a "hard man". Jesse's granddaughter, Betty Jean Pegan Corn, daughter of Cecil Pegan, says her grandfather didn't like her for some reason. Once, shortly after he returned to Huntington sick with cancer, Pauline Pegan Oswalt caught Jesse trying to put out a cigarette on her niece Betty Jean's arm.[302] By contrast, her granddaughter Betty and all the living PeGan nieces and nephews interviewed in preparing this book—from Sarah's, Clanzie's and Philip's families—agreed that Elva was loving and giving. Phillip Elsworth PeGan and Darlene Kay PeGan Stanley, Philip's children, remembered fondly their visits to Huntington and staying with Aunt Elva and her brood. They say Elva was a very good cook![113, 303]

Children of Jesse Harrison Pegan and Elva Coe Keith:

+ 57 m I. **Cecil Keith**[8] **Pegan** was born in Wabash, Noble Twp., Wabash Co., Indiana, on June 18, 1912.[128, 304, 305, 306, 307] He died in Wabash, Noble Twp., Wabash Co., Indiana, on July 7, 1990.[128, 304, 306]

+ 58 f II. **Pauline Miriam**[8] **Pegan** was born in Roann, Paw Paw Twp., Wabash Co., Indiana, on December 17, 1913.[128, 298, 308, 309, 310] She died in Huntington, Huntington Twp., Huntington Co., Indiana, on February 26, 1998.[128, 309]

+ 59 m III. **James Meredith**[8] **Pegan** was born in Macy, Allen Twp., Miami Co., Indiana, on September 29, 1915.[128, 311, 312, 313] He died in a hospital in Marion, Center Twp., Grant Co., Indiana, on February 23, 1987.[128, 311, 312]

+ 60 f IV. **Fern Maxine**[8] **Pegan** was born in Macy, Allen Twp., Miami Co., Indiana, on September 3, 1917.[128, 314, 315, 316, 317, 318] She died in a hospital in Indianapolis, Marion Co., Indiana, on June 16, 1979.[128, 315, 316, 317]

+ 61   f   V.   **Florence Willodean⁸ Pegan** was born in Wabash, Noble Twp., Wabash Co., Indiana, on August 22, 1919.[319, 320, 321] She died in a hospital in Coldwater, Butler Twp., Mercer Co., Ohio, on October 30, 1992.[319, 320]

19. Clanzie Herold⁷ PeGan (*Harrison James⁶, Harrison James⁵ Pegan, Robert A.⁴, Andrew³, Andrew² Pagan, James¹*) was born on October 7, 1888, in Monroe Twp., Grant Co., Indiana.[127, 128, 129, 130, 131] He was also known as **C. H.** He was the son of Harrison James PeGan II (6) and Angeline Stout. Clanzie Herold died in Huntington, Huntington Twp., Huntington Co., Indiana, on May 17, 1972, at age 83.[127, 128, 129, 131] He was buried in Gardens of Memory Cemetery, Banquo, Wayne Twp., Huntington Co., Indiana near the Grant County line.[129, 322]

"Herold" was the original spelling of his middle name. But later Clanzie would use the more common spelling, "Harold".

Clanzie Herold married **Josephine Sophia Schetzszle** on March 3, 1908, in Wabash Co., Indiana.[130, 323] They had five children. Josephine Sophia Schetzszle was born in Lagro Twp., Wabash Co., Indiana, on February 19, 1889.[130, 323, 324, 325, 326] Josephine Sophia reached age 62 and died in Huntington, Huntington Twp., Huntington Co., Indiana, on March 27, 1951.[324, 325, 326] She was buried in St. Patrick's Cemetery, Lagro, Wabash Co., Indiana.[325, 326, 327]

Clanzie and Josephine, a telephone operator, married on March 3, 1908. Exactly four months later, their first child, Leo, was born.

In 1910, Clanzie and Josephine Schetzszle PeGan, both 21 years old, are living with Clanzie's father Harrison PeGan II, age 58, born Ohio, in Lagro, Lagro Twp., Wabash Co., Indiana (*Census Place: Lagro, Wabash, Indiana; Roll T624_386; Page: 3A; Enumeration District: 144; Image: 118*). Also in the home are Clanzie and Josephine's two sons, Leo, born 1907, and Paul, born 1908; and Harrison II's sons: "Alva", 25, Jesse, 23, Leonidus, 16, and Philip, eight. All but Harrison Jr. were Indiana natives. Harrison says he is widowed and has his "own income" in the occupation category. Both Clanzie and Leonidas say they are laborers on the railroad. Alva lists his occupation as carpenter and Jesse is a farmer; both are unmarried.

According to their son Hugh Frederick "Fritz" PeGan, Josephine had to do more than her share of work during this time. When Josephine married Clanzie and moved into Harrison PeGan Jr.'s household, Angeline Stout PeGan was already ill with chronic hepatitis. Young Josephine, who bore three children between 1907 and 1911, assumed responsibility for the household chores and cooking for the family. Josephine also cared for Angeline until she succumbed, and for her brother-in-law, Leonidus PeGan, who died of pneumonia in 1911.[83]

In June 1913, The PeGans—Clanzie and his family, his father Harrison Jr. and brother Philip—relocated to Huntington Twp., Huntington Co., Indiana when Clanzie got a job with the Erie-Lackawana Railroad. They lived with Clanzie's father Harrison Jr. in a house Harrison bought. The house was on Sutton Hill just south of Huntington near the intersection of Indiana state roads 5 and 224. This arrangement lasted until late June 1919. Harrison and Clanzie's eight-year-old son Paul were weeding their large vegetable garden, but Harrison become irate that Paul wasn't working as hard as his grandfather thought he should be. Harrison started berating the boy, angering Paul's mother, Josephine. Harrison and Josephine's relationship was always contentious, and a big argument ensued. On July 1, Harrison Jr. sold the house, leaving Clanzie and his family homeless for a time until they found a rental home. Harrison Jr. relocated to Jonesboro, Mill Twp., Grant Co., Indiana to live with his daughter Sarah Pearson and her family. Philip PeGan moved in with older brother Jesse and his family, then in Wabash, Noble Twp., Wabash Co., Indiana.[83]

Clanzie PeGan, enumerated as "Clanaie" or "Claudie Pegan, is found in the 1920 census in Huntington, Huntington Co., Indiana (*Census Place: Huntington Ward 5, Huntington, Indiana; Roll: T625_437; Page: 8A; Enumeration District: 118; Image: 341*). In the home are Clanzie, 31, born Indiana; the enumerator has his father born in Indiana and his mother in

Ohio—this is transposed. Wife Josephine Schetzszle PeGan, 30, says she was born in Indiana, her father in Ohio and her mother in New York State. Children in the home are Leo, 11, Paul, 10, Mary, eight, "Frederick", five, and Kenneth, three and one-half; all the children were born in Indiana. Clanzie says he is a railroad worker. The family may be living on Henry Street by then, but Hugh Frederick "Fritz" PeGan says that their first home after living on Sutton Hill was on Briant Street.[83]

In 1930, Clanzie PeGan, listed as "Clausie Pegan", is enumerated in Huntington, Huntington Co., Indiana *(Census Place: Huntington, Huntington, Indiana; Roll 593; Page: 5A; Enumeration District: 10; Image: 854.0)*. Clanzie and Josephine Schetzszle PeGan both say they are 41 years of age, were born in Indiana, and have been married 19 years. Clanzie and Josephine say their fathers were born in Ohio; Clanzie says his mother was born in Indiana, and Josephine says hers was born in New York. Children living with them are Leo, 21, Mary, 18, "Frederick", 15, and Kenneth, 13; all were born in Indiana. The family is living on Clark Street. Clanzie says he is a locomotive engineer, Leo says he is an electrician, and Mary says she is a bank stenographer. Son Paul, age 20, is not in their household; he is living in Flint, Michigan with his uncle and aunt, Alvah/Alvin LeRoy and Leatha Mae Morrow Rodgers PeGan.

After Harrison PeGan Jr. hastily sold Sutton Hill home in 1919, Clanzie and Josephine and their five children had rented a string of houses in Huntington: Briant Street, 635 Hasty, 706 Hasty, 1554 Walnut, 55 Madison, 706 Clark, 448 Mayne, and 1053 William as Fritz PeGan recalled. The latter house on Mayne Street belonged to Clanzie and Josephine's daughter Mary, who acquired it for investment purposes from her employer, Bucher's Savings and Loan, after a client defaulted. Mary was renting it to her long-time boyfriend, George Miller, who had tuberculosis, and his aunt and uncle, but she evicted them when Josephine and three of her brothers needed a place to live in 1938.[83]

Clanzie's and Josephine's marriage, by all accounts, it may have never been serene. Many PeGan relatives told this writer that Josephine was difficult to get along with. She and Harrison Jr., her father-in-law, were often at odds. Josephine did not like her one sister-in-law, Dorothy Vermilyer PeGan, Philip's wife and was very vocal to other PeGan family members about it. Josephine considered Philip, who was only six years old when she married Clanzie and moved in with his family, as almost one of her own. Josephine considered Dorothy unworthy of Philip, because of Dorothy's mother's notoriety in the Peru area and Dorothy's questionable paternity. This wasn't Dorothy's fault, of course, but that never mattered to Josephine.[83, 84, 303, 328]

Josephine was very fearful of many things, making life with her a challenge. One thing she was especially afraid of was storms. During bad thunderstorms, Josephine would drag a featherbed into the living room, put all of her children on it, light candles and pray.[83]

Josephine was a devout Catholic and very strict with her children. Both her sons Fritz and Kenneth recalled the worst spanking they ever got from their mother: It was the height of the Klu Klux Klan's activity in Indiana in the 1920s. The Klan would hold parades in towns across the state. One day they were to have one in Huntington. The PeGan boys found out about it and had heard from their friends who'd seen other Klan parades that these events were quite the spectacle. But their mother forbade them to go, as the Klan was very anti-Catholic. But the boys didn't listen and sneaked out anyway. Soon they were on one of the downtown street corners, cheering at the men in the flowing white sheets on the beautiful, prancing horses. Of course, one of their (Prostestant) neighbors spotted the boys and told Josephine. She did not spare the rod.[83, 328]

Unprompted and without hesitation, Mattie Leona Pearson Hatfield remarked that her Uncle Clanzie was "the most henpecked man I've ever seen". She said her Aunt Josephine could be a "nice lady" until she became angry, which was often. Then, Josephine had "a temper that wouldn't stop" and was "always after" Clanzie. Mattie Leona said that Clanzie never talked much because Josephine would frequently get mad at what he said.[84]

Clanzie, in turn, would do things on purpose to upset her. When her sons would fight over their checkers game, which was all the time, Josephine would, sooner or later, throw the checkerboard into the pot-bellied stove to stop the argument and declare that there would be no more checkerboards. But when Clanzie would arrive home after his Erie run, he'd bring another checkerboard. Also, Clanzie contributed to the marital discord by his frequent absences because of his work, his drinking, and his extramarital affairs.[83, 328]

About 1938, Josephine suspected that Clanzie may have been cheating on her yet again. She had son Paul drive her to Marion, Ohio (the destination of his Erie Railroad runs) where she caught Clanzie with another woman. Josephine separated from Clanzie and moved into the Mayne Street house along with Paul, Fritz and Kenny. But when Clanzie contracted a life-threatening case of encephalitis, she reunited with him and nursed him back to health.[83]

In 1940, Clanzie and Josephine Schetzszle PeGan are residing in Huntington, Huntington Twp., Huntington Co., Indiana *(Census Place: Huntington, Huntington, Indiana; Roll: T627_1055; Page: 10A; Enumeration District: 35-8)*. In the home are Clanzie PeGan, age 52, a railroad engineer; and Josephine Schetzszle Pegan, who is also listed as 52. With them are their children: Mary, 28, a stenographer; (Hugh) Frederick, 25, a mechanic at a garage; and Kenneth, 23, a substitute teacher in the public schools. All in the home were born in Indiana, and say they were living in Huntington in 1935. The house address is 448 Mayne Street.

Shortly after this census, Mary PeGan sold the Mayne Street home to her parents. In 1946, Clanzie and Josephine sold it. Mary, then married to Ted Welch and living in Wisconsin Dells, Wisconsin, negotiated an agreement where she and her father bought another house at 1129 William Street, and Mary traded one of her rental houses in as a down payment.[83]

As she grew older, Josephine became more and more unstable and contentious; her behavior was increasingly strange and unpredictable. Josephine was acting strangely. Fritz and his wife Rosie brought a framed picture of their (then) three children to her, and she threw it into the street, claiming she didn't need any pictures of any grandchildren. Her youngest daughter-in-law, Patricia Keefe PeGan, wife of Kenneth, recalled another odd occurrence with Josephine at Kenneth and Patricia's home on Lynwood Drive in Huntington. One day soon after their marriage in August 1947, Patricia walked out of her kitchen into the living room and found her mother-in-law standing there. Patricia never heard Josephine open the unlocked front door. Startled, Patricia was speechless. Josephine didn't say a word either. Patricia said they stared at each other for a few minutes, then Josephine turned around and left.[328]

Josephine may have been suffering from atherosclerosis. She died of a cerebral hemhorrage in March 1951.

By then, Clanzie and Josephine were separated again. Clanzie ostensibly was residing with his son Leo and family. But he had become involved with his eventual second wife, Loretta Kastner Sellers, and was actually living with her in her second-floor apartment at 21 ½ West Market Street in Huntington. Josephine Schetzszle PeGan's death certificate says she was living alone when she succumbed in March 1951.[325] Clanzie and Loretta married in June 1952. Perhaps upset with her father's remarriage, Patricia Keefe PeGan told a different version: Mary and Ted were to share the money from the house sale with Clanzie. Also, there was a life insurance policy on Josephine, and some of Josephine's brothers thought all the children should share the insurance payout with their father. Mary and Ted talked Clanzie into investing all the money into some sort of uranium prospecting deal, perhaps arranged by one of Josephine's brothers, who lived in South Dakota and worked in the uranium industry. But the investment failed, and the money was lost.[328]

After this financial fiasco, Mary had no further contact with her father and did not return for his funeral. She had no contact with anyone else in the family except Fritz for 25 years until 1977, when she and Ted moved back to Indiana and bought a house in Fort Wayne. Then she reconciled with her brothers Paul and Kenneth.[83]

Clanzie Herold PeGan married Mrs. **Loretta Anne Kastner** Sellers on June 12, 1952, in Grant Co., Indiana.[329] Loretta Anne Kastner was born in Huntington, Huntington Twp., Huntington Co., Indiana, on February 7, 1897.[128, 330] Loretta Anne lived in 1992 in North Manchester, Chester Twp.,

Wabash Co., Indiana. Loretta Anne reached age 95 and died in a facility in North Manchester, Chester Twp., Wabash Co., Indiana, on July 11, 1992.[128, 330] She was buried in Gardens of Memory Cemetery, Banquo, Wayne Twp., Huntington Co., Indiana on the Grant Co. line.[330, 331]

Clanzie and Loretta PeGan continued to reside in the West Market Street apartment until Clanzie died. They also owned a lake cottage on Loon Lake in Whitley County, Indiana for five years from 1956-1961. As turbulent as both their first marriages were, Clanzie and Loretta's marriage was calm and content. They lived out their lives seemingly in harmony. They are buried beside each other at Gardens of Memory Cemetery, on State Road 9 and 37 in Huntington County, just north of the Grant County line. Loretta is remembered as a very sweet woman who was always kind to Clanzie's sons and their children.

According to an Erie railroad history online source, "C.H. Pegan" started working for the Erie Railroad on March 26, 1913 and was promoted to engineer on January 24, 1923. He retired on January 8, 1960 after 46 years of service. He was employee #8076.[83, 332]

Children of Clanzie Herold PeGan and Josephine Sophia Schetzszle:

+ 62 m I.   **Leo Everett⁸ PeGan** was born in Lagro, Lagro Twp., Wabash Co., Indiana, on July 3, 1908.[128, 333, 334] He died in Columbus, Franklin Co., Ohio, on July 26, 1986.[333, 335]

+ 63 m II. **Paul Harold⁸ PeGan** was born in Lagro Twp., Wabash Co., Indiana on June 26, 1909.[128, 336] He died in Fort Wayne, Allen Co., Indiana, on August 25, 1981.[336, 337],

+ 64 f III. **Mary Angeline⁸ PeGan** was born in Lagro, Lagro Twp., Wabash Co., Indiana, on August 11, 1911.[128, 338] She died in a facility in Edgerton, Fulton Twp., Rock Co., Wisconsin, on November 11, 1993, at age 82.[339, D]

+ 65 m IV. **Hugh Frederick⁸ PeGan** was born in Huntington Twp., Huntington Co., Indiana, on October 19, 1914.[128, 340] He was also known as **Fritz**. Hugh Frederick died in Huntington, Huntington Twp., Huntington Co., Indiana, on February 23, 2008.[128, 340]

+ 66 m V.   **Kenneth Austin Joseph⁸ PeGan** was born in Huntington Twp., Huntington Co., Indiana, on November 11, 1916.[128, 341, 342, 343, 344] He died in a facility in Fort Wayne, Allen Co., Indiana, on July 9, 1985.[341, 342, 344]

20. Phoebe⁷ PeGan (*Harrison James⁶, Harrison James⁵ Pegan, Robert A.⁴, Andrew³, Andrew² Pagan, James¹*) was born on July 14, 1891, in Monroe Twp., Grant Co., Indiana.[116, 132] She was the daughter of Harrison James PeGan II (6) and Angeline Stout. Phoebe died in Monroe Twp., Grant Co., Indiana, on July 14, 1891?[116, 132] She was buried in McKinney Lugar Creek Cemetery, Center Twp., Grant Co., Indiana.[83]

There is a family gravemarker in the McKinney-Lugar Cemetery in Grant County, Indiana, with the name "Pegan". This usually indicates a family burial plot. (This cemetery is located east of Marion on the Monroe Pike in Section #12 of Center Township in Grant County.) In this plot is at least one grave, that of Laura PeGan Keplinger. But there is probably another, unmarked, grave. This grave may be for Harrison and Angeline Stout PeGan Jr.'s sixth child, a daughter, born July 14, 1891. This daughter was the only one of Harrison and Angeline's children to have a birth certificate. There is no name on the birth certificate. However, according to Hugh Frederick "Fritz" PeGan, says his grandparents named this girl Phoebe. There is no death certificate for her in Grant County, but a health department staff member told this author that is was common in those days for a physician to issue only one document—either a birth or death certificate—for a stillborn baby. Since this was the only one of Harrison and Angeline Stout PeGan Jr's children to have a birth certificate, with no name for the girl, it may indeed indicate she was stillborn. Fritz PeGan wasn't sure about a stillborn birth; however, he did think Phoebe died before she was three years old. Fritz said she is buried next to her sister Laura A. PeGan Keplinger in the PeGan family plot at McKinney-Lugar Creek Cemetery.[83]

21. **Leonidas Alonzo**[7] **PeGan** (*Harrison James*[6], *Harrison James*[5] *Pegan, Robert A.*[4], *Andrew*[3], *Andrew*[2] *Pagan, James*[1]) was born on October 3, 1894, in Monroe Twp., Grant Co., Indiana.[133] He was also known as **Alonzo**. He was the son of Harrison James PeGan II (6) and Angeline Stout. Leonidas Alonzo died in Lagro, Lagro Twp., Wabash Co., Indiana, on March 28, 1911, at age 16.[133, 134] He was buried in Hopewell Cemetery, Lagro Twp., Wabash Co., Indiana.[133, 134, 345]

There is no death record in Wabash County, Indiana for Leonidus PeGan. Although some family members thought he died of tuberculosis, his obituary says he succumbed to pneumonia after a three-day illness.[134]

Leonidus PeGan was named for his uncle, Leonidas PeGan, who married Harrison PeGan Jr.'s oldest sister, Martha. This Leonidas PeGan the elder was also his wife Martha's, and Harrison Jr.'s first cousin; he was the son of Andrew Pegan, a brother to Harrison Pegan Sr.

22. **Philip Garl**[7] **PeGan** (*Harrison James*[6], *Harrison James*[5] *Pegan, Robert A.*[4], *Andrew*[3], *Andrew*[2] *Pagan, James*[1]) was born on November 5, 1901, in Monroe Twp., Grant Co., Indiana.[128, 135] He was the son of Harrison James PeGan II (6) and Angeline Stout. He died in Niles Twp., Berrien Co., Michigan, on November 17, 1982, at age 81.[135] Philip Garl was buried in Chapel Hill Memorial Gardens, Osceola, Penn Twp., St. Joseph Co., Indiana.[346]

Philip PeGan is named for his uncle, Philip Roush, first husband of Margaret Pegan Roush (Warren), who died in March 1901, a few months before Philip Garl PeGan was born. Philip's mother Angeline Stout PeGan died when he was only six years old, and she was ill for several years before that. His Josephine Schetzszle PeGan, wife of Clanzie PeGan, became a surrogate mother for her little brother-in-law Philip. When Clanzie and Josephine and their children and his father, Harrison PeGan Jr., left Lagro, Lagro Township, Wabash Co., Indiana for Huntington Twp., Huntington Co., Indiana in 1913, Philip went with them. But after the argument that broke up this household in 1919, 17-year-old Philip moved in with his older brother Jesse, where he was Jesse's apprentice in his blacksmith shop.

In 1920, Philip PeGan, age 18, was living with his elder brother Jesse and Jesse's family in Wabash, Noble Twp., Wabash Co., Indiana (*Census Place: Wabash Ward 1, Wabash, Indiana; Roll: T625_472; Page: 7B; Enumeration District: 189; Image: 870*). Philip says he was born in Indiana, his parents in the United States, and lists his occupation as a blacksmith. Jesse Pegan, also a blacksmith, is says he was born in Indiana and his parents in the United States. Elva Keith Pegan, 30, says she and her parents were born in Indiana. With them are their children: Cecil, seven, Pauline, six, James, four and seven months, Fern, two years and nine months, and Florence, five months. Daughter Florence is listed as a male with the name of "Lawrence". Also in the household is a Kenneth Palmer, age 18, a lodger.

Philip Garl married **Dorothy Margaret Vermilyer (Fry)** on November 25, 1922, in Miami Co., Indiana.[347] They had nine children. Dorothy Margaret Vermilyer (Fry) was born in Loveland, Miami Twp., Clermont Co., Ohio, on May 2, 1905.[128, 348] She was also known as **Dorothy Mae**. Dorothy Margaret Vermilyer reached age 83 and died in Niles, Niles Twp., Berrien Co., Michigan, on August 1, 1988.[128, 348, 349] She was buried in Chapel Hill Memorial Gardens, Osceola, Penn Twp., St. Joseph Co., Indiana.[350]

Dorothy Vermilyer's mother, Ida Schuyler (maiden name) was allegedly married five times to men with surnames of (Fred) Vermilyer, Kearns, (Bert) Fry, Runkle and Wilch. Even some her descendants admit Ida led a "colorful" life, "ran around with circus people", and "had a reputation" in Miami County, Indiana. (Peru, Indiana, the county seat of Miami County, was the winter home of several famous circuses in first half of 20th century.)

Philip PeGan family members say Ida was married longest to Fred Vermilyer, whom they think was Dorothy's biological father. They say Dorothy thought he was, although sometimes she would say that Vermilyer legally adopted her.[303] However, Hugh Frederick "Fritz" PeGan, Philip's nephew, noted other PeGan relatives, particularly his own mother, Josephine Schetzszle PeGan, Dorothy's sister-in-law, weren't so sure. They thought Dorothy's father might have been Mr. Kearns.[83]

Dorothy used the surname "Vermilyer" on her marriage application and some of her children's birth certificates.[347, 351, 352] But on other children's birth certificates, her maiden surname is given as "Fry".[353, 354]

For six years after their late 1922 marriage, Philip and Dorothy lived in Denver, Jefferson Twp., Miami Co., Indiana, then in Akron, Henry Twp., Fulton Co., Indiana (1923) before relocating back to Denver. IIn 1929, around the time that Philip's brother Jesse sent their father Harrison PeGan Jr. to the Miami County (Indiana) Poor Farm and Infirmary, Paul and Dorothy Vermilyer(?) PeGan moved to Mishawaka, Penn Twp., St. Joseph Co., Indiana. Philip worked at the Studebaker Automotive plant in South Bend in the same county. Later, they removed permanently to Niles Twp., Berrien Co., Michigan, just across the Indiana-Michigan state line from South Bend.[83, 303]

In 1930, Philip PeGan is enumerated as "Phillip Pejaeu" in Mishawaka, Penn Twp., St. Joseph Co., Indiana *(Census Place: Mishawaka, St Joseph, Indiana; Roll: 628; Page: 3A; Enumeration District: 85; Image: 235.0)*. Philip Pegan is 28 and a machine operator at an automobile plant. He says he was born in Indiana and his parents in Ohio (Incorrect—Angeline Stout PeGan was born in Indiana). His wife Dorothy Vermilyer Pegan is 25 and says she and her mother were born in Ohio and her father in Indiana. The couple states their first marriage was at age 21 and 19 respectively. Children in the home are "Phillip", six, Raymond, five, "Donnabelle", 4 1/2, Richard, one year and 11 months, and "Carl", 10 months. All the children were born in Indiana.

Philip PeGan is found in Niles Twp., Berrien Co., Michigan in 1940 *(Census Place: Niles, Berrien, Michigan; Roll: T627_1733; Page: 6A; Enumeration District: 11-64)*. In the household are "Phillipe Pegan", age 38, born Indiana, who is a machine operator in an auto plant. His wife, Dorothy, 35, was born in Ohio. Children in the home include "Philip Jr"., 16, Raymond, 15, "Donnabelle", 13, Richard, 11, Karl, 10, Juanita, eight, and Darlene, two. All in the family (except Darlene, who was too young) say there were living in St. Joseph County, Indiana in 1935. They are residents of rural Niles Township, but there is no address or road listed.

Philip and his family would visit his sister-in-law Elva Keith Pegan, estranged wife of his brother Jesse, and her children in Wabash, Noble Twp., Wabash Co., Indiana, and later after Elva moved to in Huntington, Huntington Twp., Huntington Co., Indiana. But they rarely saw his other brother Clanzie and his family, who lived in Huntington. Clanzie's wife Josephine Schetzszle PeGan, who had been a surrogate mother to Philip from the time he was eight years old until he was nearly 18, thought Dorothy was unworthy of Philip because of Dorothy's mother's notoriety in the Peru, Indiana area and Dorothy's doubtful paternity. Philip and Dorothy's children Phillip Elsworth PeGan II and Darlene Kay PeGan Stanley do remember their Uncle Clanzie coming to Niles occasionally to go fishing, a PeGan family passion, with their father.[83, 113, 303]

Philip and Dorothy's family are still close-knit and hold family reunions ever year. They keep a comprehensive family record of all births, deaths and marriages in their line.

Children of Philip Garl PeGan and Dorothy Margaret Vermilyer (Fry):

+ 67 m I. **Phillip Elsworth[8] PeGan II** was born in Denver, Jefferson Twp., Miami Co., Indiana, on September 22, 1923.[351, 355, 356] He died in Niles, Niles Twp. Berrien Co., Michigan, on October 3, 2012.[349, 356]

+ 68   m   II.   **Raymond Leon**[8] **PeGan** was born in Akron, Henry Twp., Fulton Co., Indiana, on September 6, 1924.[128, 357, 358] He died in a hospital in South Bend, St Joseph Co., Indiana, on April 8, 1997.[128, 357]

+ 69   f   III. **Donna Belle**[8] **PeGan** was born in Denver, Jefferson Twp., Miami Co., Indiana, on February 23, 1926.[128, 359] She was also known as **Donnabelle**. Donna Belle died in a hospital in South Bend, St. Joseph Co., Indiana, on November 14, 1987.[349, 360]

+ 70   m   IV. **Richard Schuyler**[8] **PeGan** was born in Denver, Jefferson Twp., Miami Co., Indiana, on April 6, 1928.[128, 353, 361, 362] He was also known as **Dick**. Richard Schuyler died in Pulaski, Giles Co., Tennessee, on September 17, 2001.[361, 363, 364]

+ 71   m   V.   **Karl Nelson**[8] **PeGan** was born in Mishawaka, Penn Twp., St. Joseph Co., Indiana, on June 2, 1929.[354, 365] He died in Niles Twp., Berrien Co., Michigan, on December 28, 1952.[349, 365, 366]

+ 72   m   VI. **Robert Harrison**[8] **PeGan** was born in Mishawaka, Penn Twp., St. Joseph Co., Indiana, on June 8, 1930.[367, 368] He died in Mishawaka, Penn Twp., St. Joseph Co., Indiana, on March 29, 1931.[367, 368]

+ 73   f   VII. **Juanita Mae**[8] **PeGan** was born in Mishawaka, Penn Twp., St. Joseph Co., Indiana, on September 22, 1931.[352, 369] She died in Niles, Niles Twp. Berrien Co., Michigan, on July 30, 2015.[349, 369]

+ 74   f   VIII. **Darlene Kay**[8] **PeGan** was born in South Bend, St. Joseph Co., Indiana, on October 6, 1937.[370]

+ 75   m   IX. **Vern Leroy**[8] **PeGan** was born in Niles, Niles Twp., Berrien Co., Michigan, on May 20, 1940.[349]

8th Generation

23. Bertha Olive[8] Farr (*Clara Belle[7] Roush, Margaret Mary[6] Pegan, Harrison James[5], Robert A.[4], Andrew[3], Andrew[2] Pagan, James[1]*) was born on December 23, 1882, in Union Twp., Highland Co., Ohio.[141] She was also known as **Olive**. She was the daughter of William Constantine Farr and Clara Belle Roush (9). Bertha Olive died in Fort Lauderdale, Broward Co., Florida, on April 8, 1966, at age 83.[142, 143] She was buried in Fairview Cemetery, Bluffton, Wells Co., Indiana.[371]

On her Social Security application, Bertha Olive Roll says she was born December 24, 1885, but her birth is registered in Highland County, Ohio birth records as December 23, 1882.[141, 372]

Bertha's parents divorced when she was very young. After her mother's remarriage to John Lewis Hunter II in 1887, Bertha seems to have been reared by Roush relatives in Highland County, Ohio. When she was 18, she moved to the Grant/Blackford counties, Indiana, area, closer to other Roush family members and, perhaps, her father and his Farr relatives. Her relationship with her mother seems to have been strained; Bertha is mentioned in Clara Belle Roush Farr Hunter's obituary, but the residence given for her, "Indiana" is incorrect, as she was living in Florida by then.[373] Bertha also seems to have had little contact with her half-brother, John C. Hunter. Bertha's relationship to her father, William C. Farr, is unknown. She is not named in her father's obituary, only listed as "a daughter by a previous marriage".[138]

In 1900, Bertha Farr, age 17, was a servant in the home of George and Sarah Roush, relatives on her mother's side, in Hamer Twp., Highland Co., Ohio *(Census Place: Hamer, Highland, Ohio; Roll: 1286; Page: 2B; Enumeration District: 111)*.

Bertha Olive married **Marion William Roll** on November 29, 1902, in Blackford Co., Indiana.[374] They divorced. They remarried on November 15, 1957, in Broward Co., Florida.[375, 376] They had four children. Marion William Roll was born in Washington Twp., Blackford Co., Indiana, on August 9, 1878.[128, 377] He reached age 98 and died in Huntington, Huntington Twp., Huntington Co., Indiana, on September 22, 1976.[128, 378, 379] Marion William was buried in Fairview Cemetery, Bluffton, Wells Co., Indiana.[379]

Marion and Bertha Farr Roll are enumerated in 1910 in Washington Twp., Blackford Co., Indiana *(Census Place: Washington, Blackford, Indiana; Roll: T624_340; Page: 2B; Enumeration District: 0015; Image: 1411)*. Marion Roll, listed as "Marrion Roll", age 32, is a painter for a company. He says he and his parents were born in Indiana. His wife, Bertha Farr Roll, 26, also says she and her parents were born in Indiana (Incorrect—she and her mother were born in Ohio). The pair say they have been married eight years and Bertha has borne two children, both still alive. They are daughter Leota, six, and son Edmund, four, both born in Indiana.

Marion Roll worked for the Delta Electric Company in 1917, residing in Marion, Center Twp., Grant Co., Indiana.[377]

By 1920, Marion and Bertha Farr Roll are in Lancaster Twp., Wells Co., Indiana *(Census Place: Lancaster, Wells, Indiana; Roll: T625_475; Page: 6B; Enumeration District: 188; Image: 38)*. Marion Roll, age 41, lists his occupation as a medical salesman. Bertha Farr Roll, 37, says she and her father were born in Indiana and her mother in Ohio (Again, incorrect—Bertha and her mother were Ohio natives). With them are children Leota, 16, "Edman", 12, Thelma, eight, and Marian, one year and eleven months old. All the children were born in Indiana.

In February 1920, their eldest daughter, Leota, gives birth to a daughter, who is named Margaret L. Roll. Margaret is raised by her grandmother Bertha Olive.

Marion and Bertha Olive separate by 1930.

Bertha Olive Farr Roll is not found in the 1930 census; her children are scattered. But Bertha and her granddaughter Margaret were probably living in Bluffton, Wells Co., Indiana.

Marion William Roll is found in 1930 in Fort Lauderdale, Broward Co., Florida *(Census Place: Fort Lauderdale, Broward, Florida; Roll: 307; Page: 2B; Enumeration District: 7; Image: 719.0)*. Marion Roll, age 51, born Indiana as were his parents, is a salesman selling spices. He says his first marriage occurred when he was 25 years old. He is living with Camilla Butts, 36, born Minnesota with her parents born in Czechoslovakia; she states she first married at age 26. Both Marion Roll and Camilla Butts state they are married, but they were probably still married to their first spouses and not to each other. With them is Camilla's son, Charles Butts, who is four years and seven months old.

Marion and Bertha Olive Farr Roll divorce after 1930.

Bertha Olive Farr married **Arthur Clarence Bartlemay** on December 9, 1939, in Wells Co., Indiana.[380] They divorced. Arthur Clarence Bartlemay was born in Harrison Twp., Wells Co., Indiana, on March 17, 1878.[381, 382, 383] Arthur Clarence reached age 72 and died in Dayton, Montgomery Co., Ohio, on February 3, 1951.[383, 384] He was buried in Fairview Cemetery, Bluffton, Wells Co., Indiana.[384, 385]

In 1940, Arthur and Bertha Olive Farr Roll Bartlemay are in Bluffton, Wells Co., Indiana *(Census Place: Bluffton, Wells, Indiana; Roll: m-t0627-01110; Page: 12A; Enumeration District: 90-5A)*. Arthur Bartlemey, age 62, is a mill foreman in a piano factory. Bertha Olive Farr Roll Bartlemay, listed as "Olive", is 55 years old. Bertha Olive's granddaughter Margaret Roll, 20, is living with them and listed as a "stepdaughter". All were born in Indiana, and say they were living in the same house at 518 West Wiley in 1935.

Marion William Roll is enumerated in the 1945 Florida State Census, living alone in Fort Lauderdale, Broward Co., Florida. He says he is 67 years old, born Indiana, and is a salesman.[386]

Shortly thereafter, Marion William Roll and Bertha Olive Farr Roll Bartlemay reconciled and were living together in Fort Lauderdale. They remarried in 1957. After Bertha Olive's death, Marion moved back to Indiana and lived with his daughter Thelma in Huntington, Huntington Twp., Huntington Co., Indiana.

Children of Bertha Olive Farr and Marion William Roll:

+ 76 f I. **Leota Fatima[9] Roll** was born in Washington Twp., Blackford Co., Indiana, on July 2, 1903.[387, 388] She died in Bluffton, Wells Co., Indiana, on October 12, 1965.[387, 389]

+ 77 m II. **Edmund Warren[9] Roll** was born in Washington Twp., Blackford Co., Indiana, on April 25, 1907.[128, 390, 391] He died in Kokomo, Center Twp., Howard Co., Indiana, on February 11, 1974.[390, 391, 392]

+ 78 f III. **Thelma Lynn[9] Roll** was born in Washington Twp., Blackford Co., Indiana, on July 18, 1911.[128, 393, 394] She was also known as **Lynn**. Thelma Lynn died in Huntington, Huntington Twp., Huntington Co., Indiana, on August 31, 1999.[128, 395]

+ 79 f IV. **Marian Colleen[9] Roll** was born in Marion, Center Twp., Grant Co., Indiana, on February 12, 1918.[396, 397, 398] She died in Bluffton, Wells Co., Indiana, on February 23, 1964.[396, 399]

24. **John Clark[8] Hunter** (*Clara Belle[7] Roush, Margaret Mary[6] Pegan, Harrison James[5], Robert A.[4], Andrew[3], Andrew[2] Pagan, James[1]*) was born on December 24, 1890, in Ward Twp., Hocking Co., Ohio.[128, 144] He was the son of James Louis Hunter II and Clara Belle Roush (9). John Clark died in a hospital in Hillsboro, Liberty Twp., Highland Co., Ohio, on May 21, 1968, at age 77.[128, 145] He was buried in Mt. Zion Cemetery, Danville, New Market Twp., Highland Co., Ohio.[400, 401]

John Clark married **Rosa Mae Wilkin** on April 12, 1913, in Highland Co., Ohio.[402] They had one son. Rosa Mae Wilkin was born in New Market Twp., Highland Co., Ohio, on August 11, 1889.[128, 403] Rosa Mae reached age 86 and died in a hospital in

Hillsboro, Liberty Twp., Highland Co., Ohio, on August 13, 1975.[404] She was buried in Mt. Zion Cemetery, Danville, New Market Twp., Highland Co., Ohio.[405, 406]

John Clark Hunter, his wife Rosa Mae Wilkin Hunter, and their son Clyde C. are living with John Clark's parents, James L. and Clara Belle Roush Farr Hunter in New Market Twp., Highland Co., Ohio in 1920 *(Census Place: New Market, Highland, Ohio; Roll: T625_1399; Page: 5A; Enumeration District: 98; Image: 469)*. John C. Hunter, 29, lists his occupation as laborer on a home farm. Rosa Mae Wilkin Hunter, John C.'s wife, is listed as "Rosie M." and is also 29 years old. Their son, Clyde C., is age five. James Louis Hunter, 55, a farmer, is listed as head of the household; Clara Belle Roush Farr Hunter is age 53. All were born in Ohio, as were their parents.

In 1930, John Clark Hunter, listed as "J. Clark Hunter", and his family are again living with his parents, James L. and Clara Belle Roush Farr Hunter, in New Market Twp., Highland Co., Ohio *(Census Place: New Market, Highland, Ohio; Roll: 1823; Page: 6B; Enumeration District: 19; Image: 435.0)*. John Clark Hunter, age 40, lists his occupation as a farmhand. Rosa Mae Wilkin Hunter, is also 40 years old. They say they were both first married at age 23, and have a son, Clyde C., age 10. John Clark Hunter's father, James L. Hunter, 65, a farmer, is listed as the head of the household. His wife, Clara Belle Roush Farr Hunter, is 63. James and Clara Belle say they were first married at ages 22 and 20 respectively. This time, everyone says they and their parents were Ohio natives, except for James Hunter's mother, who is listed as born in Indiana.

John C. Hunter is enumerated in New Market Twp., Highland Co., Ohio in 1940 *(Census Place: New Market, Highland, Ohio; Roll: T627_3085; Page: 4A; Enumeration District: 36-23)*. In the household are John C. Hunter, a farmer, and his wife, Rosa Mae Wilkin Hunter, who are both 50 years old. Also in the home is John's widowed mother, Clara Belle Roush Hunter, age 74. All were born in Ohio and were living in the same house on Concord Pike in 1935. Next-door is Clyde Hunter, John and Rosa Mae Wilkin's son and his family.

Son of John Clark Hunter and Rosa Mae Wilkin:

+ 80 m I. **Clyde Cisco**[9] **Hunter** was born in New Market Twp., Highland Co., Ohio, on January 22, 1914.[128, 407] He died in Hillsboro, Liberty Twp., Highland Co., Ohio, on April 9, 1973.[407, 408]

25. Child[8] **Hunter** (*Clara Belle*[7] *Roush, Margaret Mary*[6] *Pegan, Harrison James*[5]*, Robert A.*[4]*, Andrew*[3]*, Andrew*[2] *Pagan, James*[1]) was born between 1887 and 1900 in Highland Co. or Hocking Co., Ohio. He or she was a child of James Louis Hunter II and Clara Belle Roush (9). Child died in Highland Co. or Hocking Co., Ohio, before 1900.

26. Lulu Belle[8] **Roush** (*John Alven*[7]*, Margaret Mary*[6] *Pegan, Harrison James*[5]*, Robert A.*[4]*, Andrew*[3]*, Andrew*[2] *Pagan, James*[1]) was born about 1892 in Union Twp., Highland Co., Ohio. She was the daughter of John Alven Roush (11) and Harriet Boxell. Lulu Belle died in Union Twp., Highland Co., Ohio, before 1900.

Lulu Belle Roush's birth is not registered in the Highland Co., Ohio birth records. She dies before the 1900 census. Online Roush family records say her name was Lulu Belle. Both her parents' obituaries say they were preceeded in death by two daughters. The only other known daughter was Nellie Fay.[74, 150]

27. Nellie Fay[8] **Roush** (*John Alven*[7]*, Margaret Mary*[6] *Pegan, Harrison James*[5]*, Robert A.*[4]*, Andrew*[3]*, Andrew*[2] *Pagan, James*[1]) was born on September 29, 1894, in Union Twp., Highland Co., Ohio.[152] She was also known as **Fay**. She was the daughter of John Alven Roush (11) and Harriet Boxell. Nellie Fay died in Canada? between July 22, 1925 and May 19, 1939.

Nellie Fay is a mystery.

Nellie Fay married **Leo Ray Baker** about 1910-1911. They divorced. They had one son. Leo Ray Baker was born in Monroe Twp., Grant Co., Indiana, on April 1, 1893.[128, E, F] He reached age

70 and died in a hospital in Prescott, Yavapai Co., Arizona, on March 27, 1964.[128, E, G] Leo Ray was buried in Grant Memorial Park Cemetery, Marion, Center Twp., Grant Co., Indiana.[E, G]

There is no marriage record found yet for Leo Ray Baker and Nellie Fay Roush. They may have married in Kentucky. The couple was divorced by 1917, as Leo Ray's WWI draft registration states he is a single father with one child.[F]

Leo Ray Baker married again and had a family. He lived most of his adult life in Grant County, Indiana before removing to Rochester, Rochester Twp., Fulton Co., Indiana in his later years to live with his son by his second marriage. Leo Ray died while wintering in Arizona.

Nellie Fay Roush Baker married **Frank Leslie Schoonmaker** on September 30, 1920, in St. Joseph Co., Michigan.[409]

They divorced. Frank Leslie Schoonmaker was born in Moore Park, Park Twp., St. Joseph Co., Michigan, on September 23, 1887.[128, 409, 410] He reached age 80 and died in Schoolcraft Twp., Kalamazoo Co., Michigan, in December 1967.[128]

Frank L. Schoonmaker, age 40, a retail grocery salesman, is found in the 1930 census in Park Twp., St. Joseph Co., Michigan *(Census Place: Park, St Joseph, Michigan; Page: 8B; Enumeration District: 0018)*. He has remarried. But he is divorced again and lodging in a home in Three Rivers, Lockport Twp., St. Joseph Co., Michigan in 1940 *((Census Place: Three Rivers, St Joseph, Michigan; Roll: m-t0627-01817; Page: 2B; Enumeration District: 75-29; Harry C. Hughes, head of household)*. Frank L. Schoonmaker, 50 years old, lists no occupation.

Nellie Fay Roush Schoonmaker married **Elbridge Thompson** on July 22, 1925, in St. Joseph Co., Michigan.[411] Elbridge Thompson was born in Indiana in 1887.[411]

Elbridge Thompson is enumerated in 1920 only as "Thompson" in Marion, Center Twp., Grant Co., Indiana *(Census Place: Marion Ward 2, Grant, Indiana; Roll: T625_434; Page: 9B; Enumeration District: 90)*. His occupation is listed as lumberman— the same occupation he lists on his marriage application in 1925 when he marries Nellie Fay. He states his residence on the marriage application as Ann Arbor, Michigan, and that he was the son of John Thompson and Rose M. Miley.[411] No marriage records are found for this couple, and no appropriate Rose M. Miley is found in any census.

"Elbridge" Thompson may have been using an alias and his parental information on his marriage application to Nellie Fay may have been fictitious.

What happened to Nellie Fay Roush Baker Schoonmaker Thompson after 1925 is unknown. According to John Alven and Harriet Boxell Roush's granddaughter-in-law, Viola "Jane" Brown Roush, who knew each of them for nearly a decade, John and Harriet never spoke of a daughter, and neither did any of their children, including her husband. The granddaughter-in-law was shocked and perplexed when she found out her late husband had an aunt. She believes that, if Nellie had children, the family would have known about them or at least mentioned them to her.[412] But, as this writer discovered later, Viola Jane was wrong.

The last known documentation of Nellie Fay Roush Baker Schoonmaker Thompson is her 1925 marriage to "Elbridge" Thompson. Both her parents' obituaries say that two daughters and two sons preceeded them in death.[74, 150] Also, she is not mentioned as a survivor in her brother Delbert Roush's obituary in 1939, although their brother Joseph is.[155] There are no records for her or even a Nellie or Fay born on that date in the Social Security records or any other online databases.

Son of Nellie Fay Roush and Leo Ray Baker:

+ 80A m I. **Milford Earnest**[9] **Baker** was born in Monroe Twp., Grant Co., Indiana, on November 4, 1911.[128, H, I] He was also known as **Fred**. He died on September 18, 1971, in St. Louis, Missouri.[128, I, J]

28. Delbert Leroy[8] **Roush** (*John Alven*[7], *Margaret Mary*[6] *Pegan, Harrison James*[5], *Robert A.*[4], *Andrew*[3], *Andrew*[2] *Pagan, James*[1]) was born on March 14, 1897, in Union Twp., Highland Co., Ohio.[153, 154] He was the son of John Alven

Roush (11) and Harriet Boxell. He died in South Bend, St. Joseph Co., Indiana, on May 16, 1939, at age 42.[155, 156] Delbert Leroy was buried in Evergreen Cemetery, Girard Twp., Branch Co., Michigan.[413, 414]

Delbert Leroy married **Zona B. Linn** on July 17, 1920, in St. Joseph Co., Michigan.[415] They divorced. They had no children. Zona B. Linn was born in Fairmount Twp., Martin Co., Minnesota, on April 28, 1902.[128, 416, 417] Zona B. reached age 90 and died in Marshall, Lyon Co., Minnesota, on June 30, 1992.[128, 415] She was buried in Saints Cyril and Methodius Catholic Cemetery, Taunton, Lyon Co., Minnesota.[418]

Zona may have been born in Webster Twp., Hamilton Co., Iowa.

Zona Linn (Roush) is living alone and has resumed using her maiden name in the 1930 census in Fairmont Twp., Martin Co., Minnesota *(Census Place: Fairmont, Martin, Minnesota; Roll: 1107; Page: 19B; Enumeration District: 8; Image: 152.0)*. She says she is divorced and is 25 years old (she is 28). She lists her occupation as a telephone operator at a gas engine company. Zona Linn (Roush) says she was born in Minnesota and her parents in the United States.

On July 3, 1933, Zona Linn Roush marries John Thomas Tomek II in Minneapolis, Hennepin Co., Minnesota and she is buried as Zona Tomek.[416, 417] They are not found in the 1940 U.S. Federal Census.

Delbert Leroy Roush married **Mary C. Murphy** in 1929. They divorced in South Bend, St. Joseph Co., Indiana, before 1939. They had one daughter. Mary C. Murphy was born in Melrose, Jackson Twp., Monroe Co., Iowa, on April 27, 1899.[128, 419, 420, 421] She reached age 89 and died in Chicago, Cook Co., Illinois, on January 27, 1989.[128, 420] Mary C. was buried in Mount Carmel Cemetery, Hillside, Cook Co., Illinois.[422]

In 1930, Delbert Leroy Roush is enumerated in Mishawaka, Penn Twp., St. Joseph Co., Indiana *(Census Place: Mishawaka, St Joseph, Indiana; Roll: 628; Page: 27A; Enumeration District: 81; Image: 111.0)*. Delbert L. Roush, age 31, born Ohio, with his father born in Ohio and his mother in Virginia, is a carpenter. He has a second wife, Mary C. Murphy Roush, 30, born Iowa, who says her father was born in Ohio and her mother in Iowa. Delbert states his first marriage was at age 25, while Mary C. Murphy Roush says her first marriage was at age 29.

Mary Murphy Roush and her daughter Jane are not found in the 1940 U.S. Federal Census.

Although Delbert Roush is listed on census forms as born in Indiana, and he says on his marriage application that he was born in Blackford County, Indiana. But, according to the Highland County, Ohio birth records and his WWI draft registration, he was born in Union Twp., Highland Co., Ohio. [153, 154] On his death certificate, the informant, his father John Alven Roush, gave an incorrect birthday for Delbert, March 15, 1895, which was only six months after Nellie Fay Roush, John's daughter and Delbert's sister, was born. John A. Roush also says Delbert's middle initial was "S" when it was "L." [156]

Daughter of Delbert Leroy Roush and Mary C. Murphy:

+ 81 f I. **Jane**[9] **Roush** was born in South Bend, St. Joseph Co., Indiana, on March 3, 1937.[419] She died in Chicago, Cook Co., Illinois, on December 7, 2004.[128]

29. Joseph Lewis[8] **Roush** (*John Alven*[7]*, Margaret Mary*[6] *Pegan, Harrison James*[5]*, Robert A.*[4]*, Andrew*[3]*, Andrew*[2] *Pagan, James*[1]) was born on March 17, 1903, in Monroe Twp., Grant Co., Indiana.[157, 158] He was the son of John Alven Roush (11) and Harriet Boxell. He died in Coldwater, Coldwater Twp., Branch Co., Michigan, on January 5, 1959, at age 55.[157, 159] Joseph Lewis was buried in Evergreen Cemetery, Girard Twp., Branch Co., Michigan.[157, 158]

Joseph Lewis married **Edith Ellen Gaut** on September 30, 1922, in St. Joseph Co., Michigan.[157, 423] They had three sons. Edith Ellen Gaut was born in Vermontville, Vermontville Twp., Eaton Co., Michigan, on September 17, 1903.[424] She reached age 55 and died in Coldwater, Coldwater Twp., Branch Co., Michigan, on October 22, 1958.[424, 425] Edith Ellen was buried in Evergreen Cemetery, Girard Twp., Branch Co., Michigan.[424, 426]

Joseph L. Roush is enumerated in Fabius Twp., St. Joseph Co., Michigan in 1930 *(Census Place: Fabius, St Joseph, Michigan; Roll: 1025; Page: 7B; Enumeration District: 7; Image: 1035.0)*. In the household are Joseph L. Roush, 27, a carpenter at a railway supplies company, born Indiana with his parents born in Ohio; and his wife, Edith Gaut Roush, 26, born Michigan as were her parents. The couple says they were both 19 years old when they first married. They have one child, John M., age two, born Michigan.

Joseph Roush is residing in Girard, Girard Twp., Branch Co., Michigan in 1940 *(Census Place: Girard, Branch, Michigan; Roll: T627_1734; Page: 2B; Enumeration District: 12-16)*. Joseph Roush, age 36, born Indiana, is a farmer. His wife, Edith Gaut Roush, is also 36 years old, born Michigan. They have three sons: John, 12, George, eight and Harley, five, all born in Michigan. Joseph says his family was living in St. Joseph Co., Michigan in 1935.

According to Viola "Jane" Roush, Joseph and Edith Gaut Roush both worked from 1941 until 1959 at the L.A. Darling Co., a plant in Coldwater, Coldwater Twp., Branch Co., Michigan which manufacturered department store mannequins. Joseph was a carpenter there, while Edith was a clerk.[412]

Joseph L. Roush's obituary mistakenly says his year of birth is 1900.[157]

Sons of Joseph Lewis Roush and Edith Ellen Gaut:

+ 82 m I. **John Milford⁹ Roush** was born in Fabius Twp., St. Joseph Co., Michigan, on September 20, 1927.[427, 428] He died in a hospital in Fort Wayne, Allen Co., Indiana, on November 18, 1988.[427, 428]

+ 83 m II. **George Lewis⁹ Roush** was born in Fabius Twp., St. Joseph Co., Michigan, on December 27, 1931.[128, 429, 430, 431, 432] He died in Salisbury, Rowan Co., North Carolina, on July 16, 1978.[429, 430, 431, 432, 433]

+ 84 m III. **Harley Leroy⁹ Roush** was born in Fabius Twp., St. Joseph Co., Michigan, on March 19, 1935.[434, 435] He died in Niles, Niles Twp. Berrien Co., Michigan, on December 11, 1968.[128, 434, 435]

30. Milford⁸ Roush (*John Alven⁷, Margaret Mary⁶ Pegan, Harrison James⁵, Robert A.⁴, Andrew³, Andrew² Pagan, James¹*) was born on November 16, 1905, in Union Twp., Highland Co., Ohio.[160, 161] He was the son of John Alven Roush (11) and Harriet Boxell. Milford died in Harrison Twp., Blackford Co., Indiana, on October 4, 1908, at age two.[161] He was buried in Dundee Cemetery (now Roll Cemetery), Washington Twp., Blackford Co., Indiana.[161]

31. Arlo⁸ Roush (*John Alven⁷, Margaret Mary⁶ Pegan, Harrison James⁵, Robert A.⁴, Andrew³, Andrew² Pagan, James¹*) was born in 1918 in Fabius Twp., St. Joseph Co., Michigan?[162] He was the son of John Alven Roush (11) and Harriet Boxell. Arlo died in Fabius Twp., St. Joseph Co., Michigan?, in 1918.[162]

There is a gravestone with the date 1918 for Arlo Roush in Evergreen Cemetery, Girard Twp., Branch Co., Michigan next to those of John Alven and Harriet Boxell Roush. But the cemetery records do not have an exact burial date for him. This could be a "memorial" grave with no burial, and Arlo could be buried somewhere else. Neither St. Joseph County, Michigan nor the State of Michigan Vital Records division has a record for his birth or death. Are John Alven and Harriet E. Boxell his parents? Both of their obituaries say they were preceded in death by two sons and two daughters.[74, 150] But Arlo would have been a third son. Was Milford or Arlo forgotten in their obituaries? Or was this grave a memorial, and "Arlo" was Milford's middle name and commonly used as his given name? Also, there is a chance that "Arlo" was an illegitimate son, who died in infancy, who was borne by their daughter, Nellie Fay, who would have been 15-16 years old in 1918.

32. George Beard⁸ Roush (*Albert Leroy⁷, Margaret Mary⁶ Pegan, Harrison James⁵, Robert A.⁴, Andrew³, Andrew² Pagan, James¹*) was born on July 5, 1894, in Union Twp., Highland Co., Ohio.[168, 169] He was the son of Albert Leroy Roush (12) and Mima Helen Beard. He died in Ogden, Weber Co., Utah, on January 28, 1964, at age 69.[170, 171] George Beard was buried in Ferncliff Cemetery, Springfield, Springfield Twp., Clark Co., Ohio.[170, 171, 436]

George Beard Roush's father, Albert Leroy Beard, died when George was only eight months old.

In 1900 George Beard Roush was living with his maternal grandmother, Christina McCall Beard, in Union Twp., Highland Co., OH *(Census Place: Union, Highland, Ohio; Roll: 1286; Page: 2B; Enumeration District: 129)*. George, age five, was born in Ohio, like his parents, but the census taker errs and says he was born in July 1884 instead of 1894. His mother, Mima Beard Roush, is not listed in the household. She is listed as "Jemima Poush, a boarder with a group of factory workers in Greenfield Twp., Highland Co., Ohio *(Census Place: Greenfield, Highland, Ohio; Roll: 1286; Page: 5B; Enumeration District: 122)*. Mima Beard Roush, age 23, single, born Ohio (no listings for parental birthplaces), who works in a machine pad factory.

In 1910, George Beard Roush is living with his stepfather and mother, William and Mima Beard Roush Thacker, in Springfield, Springfield Twp., Clark Co., Ohio *(Census Place: Springfield Ward 1, Clark, Ohio; Roll: T624_1159; Page: 5A; Enumeration District: 0027; Image: 292)*. George Roush, age 16, born Ohio, is a laborer. His stepfather, William Thacker, 32, is a street car motorman. George's mother, Mima Thacker, is 33 and his two stepbrothers, Harold, five, and Wayne, three. William and Mima say they have been married six years and Mima has borne three children, all still alive.

George Beard Roush was a typewriter clerk at International Harvester Company's Champion Works in Springfield, Springfield Twp., Clark Co., Ohio in 1917 when he registered for the WWI draft.[168]

George Beard married **Nellie M. Armstrong** on April 17, 1917, in Kenton Co., Kentucky.[437] They had four children. Nellie M. Armstrong was born in Springfield, Springfield Twp., Clark Co., Ohio, on August 17, 1899.[437, 438] Nellie M. reached age 59 and died in Ogden, Weber Co., Utah, on June 17, 1959.[438, 439, 440] She was buried in Ferncliff Cemetery, Springfield, Springfield Twp., Clark Co., Ohio.[438, 439, 440]

Although her year of birth on her Utah death certificate and her tombstone is 1900, she appears in the 1900 census with her parents in Springfield, Springfield Twp., Clark Co., Ohio where she is age nine months old, born Sep 1899 (she was born in August) *(Census Place: Springfield Ward 2, Clark, Ohio; Roll: 1246; Page: 10B; Enumeration District: 0022; entry for Nellie Armstrong, Andrew J. Armstrong, head of household)*. Her obituary in the *Sprngfield (OH) Daily News* has the correct year; it says she was born in August 1899.[438]

Oddly, on his marriage record in Covington, Kenton Co., Kentucky in 1917, George says he was born in Savannah, Georgia![437]

In 1920, George B. Roush is enumerated in Springfield, Clark Co., Ohio *(Census Place: Springfield Ward 5, Clark, Ohio; Roll: T625_1354; Page: 10A; Enumeration District: 88; Image: 751)*. In the household are George B. Roush, 24, a stenographer at a factory; his wife Nellie Armstrong Roush, 20, and their daughter Dorothy, age two years and two months. All in the home were born in Ohio, as were their parents.

George Beard Roush is listed as George Rausch in the 1930 census in Springfield, Springfield Twp., Clark Co., Ohio *(Census Place: Springfield, Clark, Ohio; Roll: 1756; Page: 7A; Enumeration District: 23; Image: 514.0)*. George Roush, 35, is a blueprint clerk at an agricultural implements factory. With him is wife Nellie Armstrong Roush, 29. The couple says they were first married at ages 19 and 15 respectively(?). This seems to be an error. Children in the home are Dorothy, 12, and George Jr., eight. All Ohio natives.

In 1940, George Beard Roush is still a resident of Springfield, Springfield Twp., Clark Co., Ohio *(Census Place: Springfield, Clark, Ohio; Roll: T627_3039; Page: 5A; Enumeration District: 12-48)*.

George Roush, age 45, is now a restaurant chef. His wife, Nellie Armstrong Roush is 39 years old. Children in the home are Dorothy, 22, George, 19, and William, four. All were born in Ohio and were residents of Springfield in 1935. Their home address is 40 1/2 East Cassilly Street.

In 1942, George B. Roush's WWII draft registration states he is living in Springfield, Springfield Twp., Clark Co., Ohio and working at Patterson Field Material Division in Dayton, Ohio for the U.S. Government.[441] He moved to Utah around 1951, where he worked at Hill Air Force Base, Ogden, Weber Co., Utah for 13 years until he died.[170]

Children of George Beard Roush and Nellie M. Armstrong:

+ 85 f I. **Dorothy H.⁹ Roush** was born in Springfield, Springfield Twp., Clark Co., Ohio, on October 27, 1917.[128, 442, 443] She died in Springfield, Springfield Twp., Clark Co., Ohio, on November 26, 1981.[443, 444]

+ 86 f II. **Merle Margaret⁹ Roush** was born in Springfield, Springfield Twp., Clark Co., Ohio, on June 10, 1920.[445] She was also known as **Margaret**. Merle Margaret died in Springfield, Springfield Twp., Clark Co., Ohio, on September 12, 1923.[445]

+ 87 m III. **George Beard⁹ Roush II** was born in Springfield, Springfield Twp., Clark Co., Ohio, on December 29, 1921.[128, 446, 447] He was also known as **Buck**. George Beard died in a hospital in Sebastopol, Sonoma Co., California, on March 3, 1974.[128, 446, 447]

+ 88 m IV. **William Leroy⁹ Roush** was born in Springfield, Springfield Twp., Clark Co., Ohio, on February 21, 1936.[128, 448, 449, 450] He died in a hospital in Chillicothe, Ross Co., Ohio, on September 23, 2000.[128, 448, 450]

33. Harry Emmett⁸ Roush (*Eli Kenneth⁷, Margaret Mary⁶ Pegan, Harrison James⁵, Robert A.⁴, Andrew³, Andrew² Pagan, James¹*) was born on January 22, 1904, in Union Twp., Highland Co., Ohio.[192, 193] He was the son of Eli Kenneth Roush (13) and Margaret A. Bish. He died in a hospital in Cranston, Providence Co., Rhode Island, on November 18, 1971, at age 67.[193, 194] Harry Emmett was buried in River Bend Cemetery, Westerly, Washington Co., Rhode Island.[193, 194, 451]

In February 1908, Harry Roush and his brother Theodore ("Teddy") are removed from their parents, Eli and Margaret Bish Roush, by the Clinton County sheriff's office and taken to the Clinton County Children's Home. The Clinton County Children's Home records indicate that a week later Harry and Teddy were sent to the Highland County Children's Home because their parents' home was really in that county. Their sister, Lora Belle, is not mentioned. She was 14 months old at the time.[177]

In 1910, Harry Roush, who is listed as age 15, and his siblings Theodore, seven, and "Laura", five are enumerated as "boarders" in the Highland County Children's Home in Hillsboro, Liberty Twp., Highland Co., Ohio *(Census Place: Liberty, Highland, Ohio; Roll: T624_1197; Page: 25B; Enumeration District: 0124; Image: 805)*. The children say they and their parents were born in Ohio. Actually, Harry Roush is seven years old, Theodore is four, and Lora is three.

According to Lora Belle Roush Bussey Brust's granddaughter, Christina "Christy" Wallace Gall, her grandmother told her that her great-grandmother, Margaret Bish Roush, left Highland County in 1911 for Oklahoma with her eventual second husband, Michael Randolph Stroup, abandoning her children.[182] Margaret and Michael R. Stoup married in Kay Co., Oklahoma in 1911.[183]

It is not known when Harry left the Highland County Children's Home. He is not found in the 1920 census.

By 1926, he'd joined the Navy-Coast Guard. His granddaughter, Vikki Sorel of Iowa, who has Harry's service records, says Harry had a "colorful" time in the military. He was court-martialed twice, once for being intoxicated and shooting another sailor.[K]

Harry Emmett Roush is enumerated as "Harry E. Rouch" in New London, New London Co., Connecticut in 1930 *(Census Place: New London, New London, Connecticut; Roll: 282; Page: 19A; Enumeration District: 77; Image: 296.0)*. Harry Rouch, age 26 and single, says he and his parents were born in Ohio. He is an engineer 2nd grade on the *USS Cumming*s in the U.S. Coast Guard, then a part of the U.S. Navy.

Harry Emmett married **Mary Agnes Ballato** about 1934 in New London Co., Connecticut? They had two children. Mary Agnes Ballato was born in Sicily on May 6, 1898.[452] Mary Agnes reached age 46 and died in Bradford, Washington Co., Rhode Island, on November 9, 1944.[452] She was buried in River Bend Cemetery, Westerly, Washington Co., Rhode Island.[452, 453]

According to their son, Harry E. Roush Jr., Mary Agnes Ballato Roush's family lived in the Stonington/Pawcutuck, New London Co., Connecticut area. Her father worked in nearby Westerly, Washington Co., Rhode Island. By 1934, the Navy transferred Harry to Houston, Harris Co., Texas, where their son Harry Jr. was born.[454]

Harry Jr. says Mary Agnes Bullato Roush was married to another man, a Navy commander, before she married Harry Roush. While she and Harry were in Houston, her jealous first husband saw to it that Harry, an enlisted man, was discharged from the Navy-Coast Guard.[454]

By January 1935, Harry was a commercial seaman.[455] On March 14, 1937, Harry "Raush", age 34, an American, was a crewman on the SS Nishmana, an American freighter, arriving from Bremen, Germany to the port of New Orleans.[456] After his stint as a on the freighter, Harry and Mary Alice Bullato Roush moved back to Rhode Island, near her family, and settled in Westerly, Washington Co., Rhode Island.[454]

In 1940, Harry E. Roush Sr. is listed as Harry E. Raush in Westerly, Washington Co., Rhode Island *(Census Place: Westerly, Washington, Rhode Island; Roll: T627_3772; Page: 12B; Enumeration District:* *5-31)*. Harry E. Roush Sr., age 37, born in Ohio, is an electrician in a clothing mill that does dyeing and finishing. His wife Mary Agnes Ballato Roush is 41, born in Italy, is not an American citizen and is listed as an "alien". They have a son, Harry E. Jr., four years old, born in Texas. Harry and Mary Alice Ballato Roush say they were living in Houston, Harris Co., Texas in 1935. Their home is at 58 Bowling Lane.

Harry Roush never had any contact with his father or his father's second family after he left for the Navy-Coast Guard.[454] Harry Roush is mentioned as Eli's son in Eli's obituary in 1943. According to the article, Harry was still in the Navy, but, since there was no contact between Harry and his family, the family didn't know he had been out of the Navy since 1935.[457] Harry is not mentioned in any of his half-siblings' obituaries. However, Harry and his full sister, Lora Belle Roush Bussey Brust, did exchange letters for years.[182]

After Mary Alice Bullato Roush died in 1944, Harry Sr. had a mental breakdown. Harry Jr., nine years old, and his sister and Peggy, three, were sent to a Children's Home in Rhode Island. Harry Jr. later escaped, lied about his age, and joined the Navy. Peggy was adopted out to a couple named White who were childless at the time. However, the Whites had a child of their own later, and apparently didn't want Peggy after that. They mistreated her.[454]

Harry Roush Sr. was hospitalized for years at the Rhode Island Medical Center (now the Eleanor Slater Hospital), the state psychiatric facility in Cranston, Rhode Island. He died there on November 18, 1971. Harry Jr., just out of the service, had reunited with his father just months before and was arranging with the Rhode Island Medical Center for Harry Sr. to live with him when Harry Sr. died. Later, Harry Jr. was able to locate his sister Peggy and reunite with her.[454]

Children of Harry Emmett Roush and Mary Agnes Ballato:

+ 89 m I. **Harry Emmett⁹ Roush II** was born in Houston, Harris Co., Texas, on April 4, 1935.[458]

+ 90 f II. **Margaret A.⁹ Roush** was born in Westerly, Washington Co., Rhode Island, on February 18, 1941.[454] She was also known as **Peggy** and **Margaret A. White**. She died in Ashaway, Washington Co., Rhode Island, on December 9, 2014.[454]

34. Theodore⁸ Roush (*Eli Kenneth⁷, Margaret Mary⁶ Pegan, Harrison James⁵, Robert A.⁴, Andrew³, Andrew² Pagan, James¹*) was born on July 4, 1905, in Union Twp., Highland Co., Ohio.[185] He was the son of Eli Kenneth Roush (13) and Margaret A. Bish. Theodore died in Hocking Twp., Fairfield Co., Ohio, on March 26, 1920, at age 14.[185] He was buried in Blanchester IOOF Cemetery, Blanchester, Marion Twp., Clinton Co., Ohio.[185]

In February 1908, Harry Roush and his brother Theodore ("Teddy") are removed from their parents, Eli and Margaret Bish Roush, by the Clinton County sheriff's office and taken to the Clinton County Children's Home. The Clinton County Children's Home records indicate that a week later Harry and Teddy were sent to the Highland County Children's Home because their parents' home was really in that county. Their sister, Lora Belle, is not mentioned. She was 14 months old at the time.[177]

In 1910, Theodore Roush, who is listed as age seven, and his siblings Harry, 15(?), and "Laura", five (?) are enumerated as "boarders" in the Highland County Children's Home in Hillsboro, Liberty Twp., Highland Co., Ohio *(Census Place: Liberty, Highland, Ohio; Roll: T624_1197; Page: 25B; Enumeration District: 0124; Image: 805)*. The children say they and their parents were born in Ohio. Actually, Harry Roush is seven years old, Theodore is four, and Lora is three.

According to Lora Belle Roush Bussey Brust's granddaughter, Christina "Christy" Wallace Gall, her grandmother told her that her great-grandmother, Margaret Bish Roush, left Highland County in 1911 for Oklahoma with her eventual second husband, Michael Randolph Stroup, abandoning her children.[182]

After the 1910 census, Theodore Roush lived for a time with his father, Eli, his stepmother and half-siblings. But he was again admitted to the Clinton County Children's Home on February 14, 1920. A week later, he was sent to the Boy's Industrial School, an Ohio state reform school, in Hocking Twp., Fairfield Co., Ohio because of misbehavior. The records from the school say his mother was deceased. He died of influenza there on March 26th.[459]

35. Lora Belle⁸ Roush (*Eli Kenneth⁷, Margaret Mary⁶ Pegan, Harrison James⁵, Robert A.⁴, Andrew³, Andrew² Pagan, James¹*) was born on November 2, 1906, in New Market Twp., Highland Co., Ohio.[195] She was also known as **Lorie**. She was the daughter of Eli Kenneth Roush (13) and Margaret A. Bish. Lora Belle died in Bainbridge, Paxton Twp., Ross Co., Ohio, on February 27, 1981, at age 74.[196, 197] She was buried in Stringtown Quaker Cemetery, Paint Twp., Highland Co., Ohio.[460]

Her birth date on the Social Security Death Index and in her obituary, November 12, 1907, is incorrect.[128, 196] Her birth entry in the Highland County, Ohio birth records says November 2, 1906.[195] Also, Lora's obituary and her Ohio death record states she died on February 27, 1981.[196, 197] However, her gravestone says February 26.[460]

Sometime between February 1908 and 1910 Lora Belle Roush seems to have been taken away from her parents, Eli Kenneth and Margaret A. Bish Roush Sr., and placed in the Highland County, Ohio Children's Home. Her older brothers, Harry Roush and his brother Theodore ("Teddy") were removed from their parents in February 1908 by the Clinton County sheriff's office and taken to the Clinton County Children's Home. The Clinton County Children's Home records indicate that a week later Harry and Teddy were sent to the Highland County Children's Home because their parents' home was really in that county. But Lora Belle, is not mentioned in any of these records; she was about 14 months old at the time.[177]

In 1910, "Laura" Roush, listed as age five, and her brothers Harry Roush, 15 (?), and Theodore, seven (?), are enumerated as "boarders" in the Highland Co., Ohio Children's Home in Hillsboro, Liberty Twp., Highland Co., Ohio *(Census Place: Liberty,*

Highland, Ohio; Roll: T624_1197; Page: 25B; Enumeration District: 0124; Image: 805). The children say they and their parents were born in Ohio. Actually, Harry Roush is seven years old, Theodore is four, and Lora Belle is three.

Lora Belle later told her granddaughter, Christina "Christy" Wallace Gall, that her mother Margaret Bish Roush, abandoned her children and left Highland County in 1911 for Oklahoma with her eventual second husband, Michael Randolph Stroup. Lora Belle left the Highland County Children's Home and was reared by "an aunt and uncle".[182]

Lora Belle married **Hubert Clarence Bussey** about 1923, as she states on her 1930 census form that she was married at age 17. They had six children. Hubert Clarence Bussey was born in Boston, Paint Twp., Highland Co., Ohio, on November 5, 1886.[461] Hubert Clarence reached age 81 and died in Hillsboro, Liberty Twp., Highland Co., Ohio, on October 16, 1968.[462] He was buried in Stringtown Quaker Cemetery, Paint Twp., Highland Co., Ohio.[463]

The Busseys probably wed in Kentucky where 17-year-old Lora could wed without anyone's permission.

Hubert C. Bussey in enumerated in Paint Twp., Highland Co., Ohio in 1930 *(Census Place: Paint, Highland, Ohio; Page: 1A; Enumeration District: 0021).* Hubert C., age 41, a farm laborer, says he and his father were born in Ohio and his mother in Virginia. His wife, "Lorabelle" Roush Bussey, 24, states she and her parents were Ohio natives. Hubert states he was 34 years old at the time of his first marriage; Lora Belle says she was 17. With them are son James D. Bussey, five, and daughters Mary E., four, and "Rosalie", two, all born in Ohio.

In 1940, Hubert C. Bussey still resides in Paint Twp., Highland Co., Ohio *(Census Place: Paint, Highland, Ohio; Roll: m-t0627-03085; Page: 8A; Enumeration District: 36-25).* Hubert C. Bussey, 53 years old, is a hired hand on a farm. Also in the home are his wife, Lora Bussey, age 34, and children James D., 15, Mary E., 14, Rosalee, 12, and Elizabeth, five. All were born in Ohio and say there were living in the same house on Township Road in 1935.

After Hubert's death, Lora Belle Roush Bussey married **Leander Brust** about 1970.[464] They divorced. Leander Brust was born in Beaver, Jackson Twp., Pike Co., Ohio, on May 2, 1904.[128, 465] He was also known as **Lee**. Leander lived in 1985 in Ross Co., Ohio. He reached age 81 and died in a hospital in Greenfield, Greenfield Twp., Highland Co., Ohio, on June 9, 1985.[465, 466]

Lora Belle Roush is not mentioned in her father Eli's obituary in 1943.[457] According to her granddaughter, Christina "Christy" Wallace Gall, her grandmother hated her father Eli Roush Sr. and would have nothing to do with him.[182] Nor is Lora mentioned in her brother Theodore's obituary or any of her half-siblings' obituaries. However, on her brother Theodore Roush's records at the Industrial Boys School, where he was admitted in 1920, it is noted that he has one brother and one sister.[459]

Children of Lora Belle Roush and Hubert Clarence Bussey:

+ 91 m I. **James Donovan^9 Bussey** was born in Boston, Paint Twp., Highland Co., Ohio, on June 2, 1924.[128, 467, 468, 469, 470] He was also known as **Don**. He died in Akron, Summit Co., Ohio, on September 4, 1997.[128, 468, 469]

+ 92 f II. **Mary Ellen^9 Bussey** was born in Boston, Paint Twp., Highland Co., Ohio, on January 10, 1926.[471, 472] She died in a hospital in Montgomery, Hamilton Co., Ohio, on March 13, 2006.[471, 472]

+ 93 f III. **Rosalee^9 Bussey** was born in Boston, Paint Twp., High land Co., Ohio, on March 15, 1928.[128, 473, 474, 475] She died in Wewahitchka, Gulf Co., Florida, on March 13, 1991.[128, 474, 475, 476]

+ 94 f IV. **Margaret E.^{9} Bussey** was born in Boston, Paint Twp., Highland Co., Ohio, on February 23,

1933.[477, 478] She died in Boston, Paint Twp., Highland Co., Ohio.[477]

+ 95 f V. **Elizabeth Joanna**[9] **Bussey** was born in Greenfield, Greenfield Twp., Highland Co., Ohio, on April 1, 1935.[479] She was also known as **Joanna**. Elizabeth Joanna died in a hospital in Hillsboro, Liberty Twp., Highland Co., Ohio, on May 10, 2013.[480]

+ 96 f VI. **Helen Luella**[9] **Bussey** was born in Boston, Paint Twp., Highland Co., Ohio, on June 26, 1940.[128, 481, 482, 483] She died near Bradford, Darke Co., Ohio, on September 19, 1994.[128, 482, 483]

36. Cecil Cary[8] **Roush** (*Eli Kenneth*[7], *Margaret Mary*[6] *Pegan*, *Harrison James*[5], *Robert A.*[4], *Andrew*[3], *Andrew*[2] *Pagan*, *James*[1]) was born on September 22, 1910, in Martinsville, Clark Twp., Clinton Co., Ohio.[198] He was the son of Eli Kenneth Roush (13) and Loretta Mae Barnes. He resided in 1949 in Clark Twp., Clinton Co., Ohio. He died in a hospital in Dayton, Montgomery Co., Ohio, on March 1, 1949, at age 38.[198, 199] Cecil Cary was buried in Martinsville IOOF Cemetery, Martinsville, Clark Twp., Clinton Co., Ohio.[484, 485]

Never married.

In 1940, Cecil Cary Roush is enumerated in Clark Twp., Clinton Co., Ohio *(Census Place: Clark, Clinton, Ohio; Roll: T627_3042; Page: 2B; Enumeration District: 14-5)*. Listed as the head of the household, Cecil Roush is age 29, single, and a farmer. Living with him is his brother Leroy, listed as Roy, 26, also single and a farmer. Both were born in Ohio and say they were living in Clark Twp., Clinton Co., Ohio in 1935. No road or other address is listed.

37. Samuel Frederick[8] **Roush** (*Eli Kenneth*[7], *Margaret Mary*[6] *Pegan*, *Harrison James*[5], *Robert A.*[4], *Andrew*[3], *Andrew*[2] *Pagan*, *James*[1]) was born on May 31, 1912, in Martinsville, Clark Twp., Clinton Co., Ohio.[128] He was the son of Eli Kenneth Roush (13) and Loretta Mae Barnes. Samuel Frederick died in Martinsville, Clark Twp., Clinton Co., Ohio, on November 13, 1975, at age 63.[128, 200] He was buried in Martinsville IOOF Cemetery, Martinsville, Clark Twp., Clinton Co., Ohio.[486, 487]

Samuel Frederick married **Margaret Helen McCandless** on July 23, 1937.[488] They had two children. Margaret Helen McCandless was born in Camp, Camp Creek Twp., Pike Co., Ohio, on April 5, 1920.[128, 489, 490] Margaret Helen reached age 84 and died in Wilmington, Union Twp., Clinton Co., Ohio, on May 5, 2004.[128, 489, 490] She was buried in Martinsville IOOF Cemetery, Martinsville, Clark Twp., Clinton Co., Ohio.[491, 492]

In 1940, Samuel Roush is found in Clark Twp., Clinton Co., Ohio *(Census Place: Clark, Clinton, Ohio; Roll: T627_3042; Page: 5A; Enumeration District: 14-5)*. Samuel Roush, age 27, is a farm hand. With him are wife Margaret McCandless Roush, 20, and their son Kenneth, three. All were born in Ohio. Samuel says he was living in Clark Twp., Clinton Co., Ohio in 1935, while Margaret states she was a resident of Wilmington, Union Twp., Clinton Co., Ohio then.

Margaret Helen McCandless Roush was the sister of Elmer Glenn "Glenn" McCandless, who married Effie Roush (McCandless), the sister of Margaret's husband Samuel Frederick Roush.

According to her obituary in the *Wilmington (OH) News Journal*, Margaret Helen McCandless Roush was born in Pike Co., Ohio.[491] However, her parents, Herschell and Anna Anderson McCandless, were living in Morgan Twp., Scioto Co., Ohio at the time of the 1920 U.S. Census in January of that year *(Census Place: Morgan, Scioto, Ohio; Roll: T625_1432; Page: 5A; Enumeration District: 133; Image: 956; entry for Margaret McCandless, Herschell McCandless, head of household)*.

Children of Samuel Frederick Roush and Margaret Helen McCandless:

+ 97 m I. **Kenneth W.**[9] **Roush** was born in Clark Twp., Clinton Co., Ohio, on March 5, 1937.[128, 493] He died in a hospital in Cincinnati, Hamilton Co., Ohio, on June 3, 1974.[493, 494]

+ 98 f II. **Daughter**[9] **Roush** was born in Clark Twp., Clinton Co., Ohio.

38. Leroy Kenneth[8] **Roush** (*Eli Kenneth*[7], *Margaret Mary*[6] *Pegan, Harrison James*[5], *Robert A.*[4], *Andrew*[3], *Andrew*[2] *Pagan, James*[1]) was born on February 9, 1914, in Martinsville, Clark Twp., Clinton Co., Ohio.[128, 201] He was also known as **Roy**. He was the son of Eli Kenneth Roush (13) and Loretta Mae Barnes.

He died in Martinsville, Clark Twp., Clinton Co., Ohio, on December 23, 1974, at age 60.[202] Leroy Kenneth was buried in Martinsville IOOF Cemetery, Martinsville, Clark Twp., Clinton Co., Ohio.[495, 496]

Never married.

In 1940, Leroy "Roy" Roush is enumerated in Clark Twp., Clinton Co., Ohio *(Census Place: Clark, Clinton, Ohio; Roll: T627_3042; Page: 2B; Enumeration District: 14-5)*. He is living with his older brother Cecil. "Roy" Roush, 26 and single, is a farmer. The head of the household, Cecil Roush is age 29, also single and a farmer. Both were born in Ohio and say they were living in Clark Twp., Clinton County, Ohio in 1935. No road or other address is listed.

His obituary states that Leroy "Roy" Roush spent more than 28 years in the U.S. Army and was an instructor at the United States Military Academy at West Point for many years. He saw action in three wars, WWII, Korea and Vietnam, and won the Bronze Star for valor and other military honors.[497]

His Social Security Death Index file is under Roy K. Roush.[128]

39. Euless Josephine[8] **Roush** (*Eli Kenneth*[7], *Margaret Mary*[6] *Pegan, Harrison James*[5], *Robert A.*[4], *Andrew*[3], *Andrew*[2] *Pagan, James*[1]) was born on December 25, 1915, in Martinsville, Clark Twp., Clinton Co., Ohio.[203, 204] She was the daughter of Eli Kenneth Roush (13) and Loretta Mae Barnes. Euless Josephine died in Xenia, Xenia Twp., Greene Co., Ohio, on December 19, 1975, at age 59.[204, 205] She was buried in Martinsville IOOF Cemetery, Martinsville, Clark Twp., Clinton Co., Ohio.[204, 498]

Euless Josephine married **Thomas William Walker** on August 21, 1937, in Adams Co., Ohio.[203, 204] They had three children. Thomas William Walker was born in Sterling Twp., Brown Co., Ohio, on February 1, 1906.[128, 499] Thomas William reached age 73 and died in Xenia Twp., Greene Co., Ohio, on September 28, 1979.[500] He was buried in Martinsville IOOF Cemetery, Martinsville, Clark Twp., Clinton Co., Ohio.[501, 502]

In 1940, Thomas and Eulass Roush Walker are enumerated in Jefferson Twp., Clinton Co., Ohio *(Census Place: Jefferson, Clinton, Ohio; Roll: T627_3042; Page: 7A; Enumeration District: 14-9)*. Thomas Walker, age 34, works in road construction for the Works Progress Administration (WPA). Eulass Roush Walker is 24 years old. Children in the home are Shirley, three, Thomas Jr., one and Charles, six months. All were born in Ohio, and Thomas and Eulass say they were Clinton County residents in 1935. Their home is on Hales Branch Road.

Children of Euless Josephine Roush and Thomas William Walker:

+ 99 f I. **Shirley J.**[9] **Walker** was born in Jefferson Twp., Clinton Co., Ohio, on July 2, 1936.

+ 100 m II. **Thomas William**[9] **Walker II** was born in Midland, Jefferson Twp., Clinton Co., Ohio, on July 5, 1938.[128, 503, 504] He died in New Smyrna Beach, Volusia Co., Florida, on September 25, 1986.[504]

+ 101 m III. **Charles Robert**[9] **Walker** was born in Midland, Jefferson Twp., Clinton Co., Ohio, on July 5, 1938.[128, 503, 504] He died in New Smyrna Beach, Volusia Co., Florida, on September 25, 1986.[504]

40. Leota Beatrice[8] **Roush** (*Eli Kenneth*[7], *Margaret Mary*[6] *Pegan, Harrison James*[5], *Robert A.*[4], *Andrew*[3],

Andrew² Pagan, James¹) was born on March 21, 1917, in Washington Twp., Clinton Co., Ohio.[128, 507] She was the daughter of Eli Kenneth Roush (13) and Loretta Mae Barnes. Leota Beatrice died in Washington Court House, Union Twp., Fayette Co., Ohio, on May 18, 1982, at age 65.[507, 508] She was buried in Martinsville IOOF Cemetery, Martinsville, Clark Twp., Clinton Co., Ohio.[507, 508]

Leota Beatrice married **Harold H. Davis** in 1934.[509] They had two sons. Harold H. Davis was born in Jefferson Twp., Fayette Co., Ohio, on April 8, 1904.[128, 509, 510] Harold H. lived in 1940 in Adams Twp., Clinton Co., Ohio. He reached age 87 and died in Washington Court House, Union Twp., Fayette Co., Ohio, on November 29, 1991.[128, 509, 510] Harold H. was buried in Martinsville IOOF Cemetery, Martinsville, Clark Twp., Clinton Co., Ohio.[511]

Harold A. and Leota Roush Davis are enumerated in 1940 in Adams Twp., Clinton Co., Ohio *(Census Place: Adams, Clinton, Ohio; Roll: T627_3042; Page: 7A; Enumeration District: 14-1)*. Harold Davis, age 36, is a farmer. Leota Roush Davis is 23 years old. Children in the home are Perry Adams Davis, four, and Larry, one. All were born in Ohio, and Harold, Leatha and Perry were residents of Adams Twp., Clinton Co., Ohio in 1935. Their home is on Lebanon Pike.

Sons of Leota Beatrice Roush and Harold H. Davis:

+ 102 m I. **Perry Adams⁹ Davis** was born in Adams Twp., Clinton Co., Ohio, on August 6, 1935.[512]

+ 103 m II. **Larry Eugene⁹ Davis** was born in Adams Twp., Clinton Co., Ohio, on March 30, 1939.[128, 513] He died in Washington Court House, Union Twp., Fayette Co., Ohio, on July 20, 1995.[128, 513]

41. Effie Nondis⁸ Roush (*Eli Kenneth⁷, Margaret Mary⁶ Pegan, Harrison James⁵, Robert A.⁴, Andrew³, Andrew² Pagan, James¹*) was born on April 30, 1919, in Washington Twp., Clinton Co., Ohio.[208, 209] She was the daughter of Eli Kenneth Roush (13) and Loretta Mae Barnes. Effie Nondis died in Wilmington, Union Twp., Clinton Co., Ohio, on March 9, 1976, at age 56.[208, 210] She was buried in Maple Grove Cemetery (formerly Port William Cemetery), Port William, Liberty Twp., Clinton Co., Ohio.[209, 514]

Effie Nondis married **Elmer Glenn McCandless** on July 28, 1938.[208, 515] They had four children. Elmer Glenn McCandless was born in Morgan Twp., Scioto Co., Ohio, on November 14, 1912.[515, 516, 517] He was also known as **Glenn**. Elmer Glenn reached age 81 and died in Wilmington, Union Twp., Clinton Co., Ohio, on March 10, 1994.[515, 516] He was buried in Maple Grove Cemetery (formerly Port William Cemetery), Port William, Liberty Twp., Clinton Co., Ohio.[518, 519] He was the son of Hershell McCandless and Anna Anderson.

In 1940, (Elmer) Glenn and Effie Roush McCandless are enumerated in Union Twp., Clinton Co., Ohio *(Census Place: Union, Clinton, Ohio; Roll: T627_3042; Page: 10B; Enumeration District: 14-21)*. Glenn McCandless, age 25, a farm laborer, Effie Roush McCandless, 21, and their son Robert, who is one year old. All were born in Ohio, and Glenn and Effie say they were living in Clinton Co., Ohio in 1935. There is no road or other address listed.

Elmer Glenn McCandless was the brother of Margaret Helen McCandless Roush, who married Effie Roush McCandless' brother, Samuel Frederick Roush. Although his Ohio death index record and obituary claim he was born in Pike Co., Ohio, Elmer Glenn McCandless' parents, Herschel and Anna Anderson McCandless, were residing in Morgan Twp., Scioto Co., Ohio in both the 1910 U.S. Census *(Census Place: Morgan, Scioto, Ohio; Roll: T624_1228; Page: 2A; Enumeration District: 0134)* and the 1920 U.S. Census *(Census Place: Morgan, Scioto, Ohio; Roll: T625_1432; Page: 5A; Enumeration District: 133; Image: 956)*. In addition, when Herschel McCandless registered for the WWI draft in 1918, he was living in "Sedan, Scioto Co., O".[515, 516, 520]

Children of Effie Nondis Roush and Elmer Glenn McCandless:

+ 104 m I. **Robert Eugene⁹ McCandless** was born in Union Twp., Clinton Co., Ohio, on April 16, 1939.[521] He died in Adams Twp., Clinton Co., Ohio, on September 9, 1961.[521, 522, 523]

+ 104 f II. **Mona J.⁹ McCandless** was born in Union Twp., Clinton Co., Ohio, on September 22, 1940.

+ 106 m III. **James Glenn⁹ McCandless** was born in Wilmington, Union Twp., Clinton Co., Ohio, on April 27, 1954.[524] He died in Wilmington, Union Twp., Clinton Co., Ohio, on November 11, 2014.[524]

+ 107 m IV. **Samuel F.⁹ McCandless** was born in Union Twp., Clinton Co., Ohio, on November 25, 1955.[525] He died in Burtonville, Union Twp., Clinton Co., Ohio, on May 30, 1976.[526]

42. Dorothy Opal⁸ Roush (*Eli Kenneth⁷, Margaret Mary⁶ Pegan, Harrison James⁵, Robert A.⁴, Andrew³, Andrew² Pagan, James¹*) was born on November 19, 1921, in Washington Twp., Clinton Co., Ohio.[128, 211, 212] She was the daughter of Eli Kenneth Roush (13) and Loretta Mae Barnes. Dorothy Opal died in Troy, Concord Twp., Miami Co., Ohio, on July 11, 2004, at age 82.[128, 211, 212] She was buried in Riverside Cemetery, Troy, Concord Twp., Miami Co., Ohio.[527]

Dorothy Opal married **Emmett Faye Seitz** before 1940. They had six children. Emmett Faye Seitz was born in Greenfield, Greenfield Twp., Highland Co., Ohio, on September 19, 1920.[128, 528, 529] He was also known as **Jack or Faye**. He was living in 1998 in Troy, Concord Twp., Miami Co., Ohio. He reached age 78 and died in a hospital in Dayton, Montgomery Co., Ohio, on December 16, 1998.[128, 528, 529] Emmett Faye was buried in Riverside Cemetery, Troy, Concord Twp., Miami Co., Ohio.[530, 531]

In 1940, Emmett Faye "Jack" and Dorothy O. Roush Seitz are enumerated in Wilmington, Union Twp., Clinton Co., Ohio (*Census Place: Wilmington, Clinton, Ohio; Roll: T627_3042; Page: 7A; Enumeration District: 14-18*). Emmett Seitz, age 19, is a clerk for a street project by the Works Progress Administration (WPA). He says he was a resident of Greenfield, Greenfield Twp., Highland Co., Ohio in 1935. Dorothy Roush Seitz, 18, says she was living in Martinsville, Clark Twp., Clinton Co., Ohio in 1935. They have a son, William, who is two months old. All were born in Ohio and were residing at 5 Sparta Avenue.

Dorothy Opal Roush and Emmett Faye Seitz had six children, including:

+ 108 m I. **William Lee⁹ Seitz** was born in Wilmington, Union Twp., Clinton Co., Ohio, on March 11, 1940.[128, 532, 533] He died in Troy, Concord Twp., Miami Co., Ohio, on August 9, 2011.[128, 532]

+ 109 m II. **Darrel Joe⁹ Seitz** was born in Waynesville, Wayne Twp., Warren Co., Ohio, on July 22, 1941.[534, 535] He died in Nichols, Horry Co., South Carolina, on March 15, 1963.[534, 535]

+ 110 m VI. **Emmett⁹ Seitz II**. Emmett died before 2004. Seems to have died in infancy.

43. Mary Leatha⁸ Roush (*Eli Kenneth⁷, Margaret Mary⁶ Pegan, Harrison James⁵, Robert A.⁴, Andrew³, Andrew² Pagan, James¹*) was born on February 2, 1924, in Washington Twp., Clinton Co., Ohio.[213] She was the daughter of Eli Kenneth Roush (13) and Loretta Mae Barnes. Mary Leatha died in Wilmington, Union Twp., Clinton Co., Ohio, on October 16, 1946, at age 22.[213] She was buried in Sugar Grove Cemetery, Wilmington, Union Twp., Clinton Co., Ohio.[213, 536, 537]

Mary Leatha married **Grant Pomerance Bogan** on December 11, 1942.[536] Grant Pomerance Bogan was born in Harveysburg, Massie Twp., Warren Co., Ohio, on October 21, 1922.[128, 538, 539] Grant Pomerance lived in 1975 in Land-O-Lakes, Pasco

Co., Florida. He reached age 52 and died in a hospital in Tampa, Hillsborough Co., Florida, on March 22, 1975.[538, 539] Grant Pomerance was buried in Blanchester IOOF Cemetery, Blanchester, Marion Twp., Clinton Co., Ohio.[538, 540]

After Mary Leatha's death, Grant Bogan remarried and had a family. His obituary in the *Wilmington (OH) News-Journal* says he died at St. Joseph Hospital in Land-O-Lakes, Pasco Co., Florida, but the Florida Death Index, taken from official records, says the death certificate was filed from Hillsborough Co., Florida (Tampa).[538, 539]

Grant Pomerance Bogan is also memorialized on his second wife's, Betty L. Shilts Bogan's, gravestone in the Florida National Cemetery in Bushnell, Sumter Co., Florida, but all indications are he is buried in the Blanchester IOOF Cemetery, Blanchester, Marion Twp., Clinton Co., Ohio.[538, 540, 541]

44. Floyd Richard[8] **Roush** (*Eli Kenneth*[7], *Margaret Mary*[6] *Pegan, Harrison James*[5], *Robert A.*[4], *Andrew*[3], *Andrew*[2] *Pagan, James*[1]) was born on July 4, 1926, in Washington Twp., Clinton Co., Ohio.[128] He was also known as **Dick**. He was the son of Eli Kenneth Roush (13) and Loretta Mae Barnes. Floyd Richard died in Wilmington, Union Twp., Clinton Co., Ohio, on April 10, 1969, at age 42.[214] He was buried in Martinsville IOOF Cemetery, Martinsville, Clark Twp., Clinton Co., Ohio.[542, 543]

Floyd Richard married **Jennie Gertrude Hall** on January 11, 1947.[544] They had two children. Jennie Gertrude Hall was born in Cincinnati, Hamilton Co., Ohio, on May 14, 1928.[128, 545] Jennie Gertrude reached age 69 and died in Springboro, Clearcreek Twp., Warren Co., Ohio, on November 19, 1997.[128, 545] She was buried in Martinsville IOOF Cemetery, Martinsville, Clark Twp., Clinton Co., Ohio.[546, 547]

His Social Security Death Index entry is under F.R. Roush.[128]

45. Eli Kenneth[8] **Roush II** (*Eli Kenneth*[7], *Margaret Mary*[6] *Pegan, Harrison James*[5], *Robert A.*[4], *Andrew*[3], *Andrew*[2] *Pagan, James*[1]) was born on July 12, 1931, in Washington Twp., Clinton Co., Ohio.[128, 215, 216] He was also known as **Junior**. He was the son of Eli Kenneth Roush (13) and Loretta Mae Barnes. Eli Kenneth lived in 2009 in Wilmington, Union Twp., Clinton Co., Ohio. He died in a hospital in Dayton, Montgomery Co., Ohio, on May 8, 2009, at age 77.[128, 217] Eli Kenneth was buried in Martinsville IOOF Cemetery, Martinsville, Clark Twp., Clinton Co., Ohio.[217, 548]

Eli Kenneth married **Erma Lou Zeller** on April 11, 1959, in Miami Co., Ohio.[1215] They divorced. They had two children. Erma Lou Zeller was born in Fairfield Twp., DeKalb Co., Indiana, on January 16, 1935.[215] She reached age 80 and died in Piqua, Washington Twp., Miami Co., Ohio, on April 12, 2015.[549, 550] Erma Lou was buried in Riverside Cemetery, Troy, Concord Twp., Miami Co., Ohio.[549]

Eli Kenneth Roush II married Mrs. **Patricia L. Hardwick** Davis on January 9, 1980, in Clinton Co., Ohio.[551] They had one son. Patricia L. Hardwick was born in Clinton Co., Ohio, on January 9, 1941.[552] Patricia L. age 57 and died in Lynchburg, Dodson Twp., Highland Co., Ohio, on May 5, 1998.[552] She was buried in Martinsville IOOF Cemetery, Martinsville, Clark Twp., Clinton Co., Ohio.[553]

46. Philip Stroup[8] **Roush** (*Cecil Ira*[7], *Margaret Mary*[6] *Pegan, Harrison James*[5], *Robert A.*[4], *Andrew*[3], *Andrew*[2] *Pagan, James*[1]) was born on June 17, 1916, in Francisville, Dennison Twp., Lawrence Co., Illinois.[128] He was the son of Cecil Ira Roush (14) and Electa Gertrude Stroup. Philip Stroup lived in 1942 in Clinton Co., Ohio.[554] He may have also resided in 1956 in Glendive, Dawson Co., Montana. Philip Stroup died in Hialeah, Dade Co., Florida, on June 12, 1980, at age 63.[225]

Philip Stroup married **Jeannie Hume Keith** on August 6, 1958, in Monroe Co., Florida.[555] They divorced in Dade Co., Florida, in June 1964. They had three sons. Jeannie Hume Keith was born in Quincy, Norfolk Co., Massachusetts, on September 13, 1922.[128, 556, 557, 558] She reached age 75 and died in Tampa, Hillsborough Co., Florida, on January 23, 1998.[128, 556, 557] She was cremated.[556]

Married Philip S. Roush as Jeannie Hume Richardson. om Philip S. Roush, Jeannie married five more times. She died under the name Jeannie H. Behar.

Philip Stroup Roush married **Maria Isabel Elena Rodriguez** before 1971. They had one son. Maria Isabel Elena Rodriguez was born in Florida? on June 20, 1940.[128] Maria Isabel Elena reached age 69 and died in Hialeah, Dade Co., Florida, on March 10, 2010.[128]

Philip Stroup Roush and Jeannie Hume Keith had three sons, including:

+ 111 m I. **Philip Stroup⁹ Roush II** was born in Key West, Monroe Co., Florida, on March 29, 1959.[128, 559] He died at sea, 25 miles offshore from Port Canaveral, Brevard Co., Florida, on July 29, 1987.[128, 560]

47. Randall Cecil⁸ Roush (*Cecil Ira⁷, Margaret Mary⁶ Pegan, Harrison James⁵, Robert A.⁴, Andrew³, Andrew² Pagan, James¹*) was born on April 22, 1918, in Lawrenceville, Lawrence Twp., Lawrence Co., Illinois.[128, 226] He was the son of Cecil Ira Roush (14) and Electa Gertrude Stroup. Randall Cecil died in Orange Park, Clay Co., Florida, on March 9, 2004, at age 85.[128, 226] He was buried in Magnolia Cemetery, Orange Park, Clay Co., Florida.[561, 562]

Randall Cecil married **Florence Kay Librcajt** on May 30, 1942, in Washington, District of Columbia.[563] They divorced. They had four children. Florence Kay Librcajt was born in Winner, Tripp Co., South Dakota, on March 13, 1921.[564, 565] She was also known as **Kay.** Florence Kay lived in Orange Park, Clay Co., Florida. She reached age 52 and died in a hospital in Jacksonville, Duval Co., Florida, on December 27, 1973.[564, 565] Florence Kay was buried in Magnolia Cemetery, Orange Park, Clay Co., Florida.[566]

On his Social Security application, Randall Cecil Roush says he was born in Lawrenceville, Lawrence Twp., Lawrence Co., Illinois.[226] His parents, Cecil Ira and Electa Gertrude Stroup Roush were living in St. Francisville, Dennison Twp., Lawrence Co., Illinois at the time.

Randall Cecil Roush married Mrs. **Barbara Jean Long** Brownell on June 25, 1977, in Clay Co., Florida.[567] Barbara J. Long was born in Chicago, Cook Co., Illinois, on September 2, 1929.[568]

A U.S. Navy officer who retired with the rank of Commander after 30 years, Randall C. Roush earned numerous medals for his military service.[569]

Randall Cecil Roush and Florence Kay Librcajt had four children, including:

+ 112 m I. **Michael David⁹ Roush** was born in Corpus Christi, Nueces Co., Texas, on July 26, 1946.[570] He was also known as **Mickey**. Michael David died in Orange Park, Clay Co., Florida, on June 22, 2000.[571]

+ 113 m III. **William Randall⁹ Roush** was born in Midwest City, Oklahoma Co., Oklahoma, on March 3, 1953.[128, 572] He died in Big Pine Key, Monroe Co., Florida, on August 18, 2006.[128, 572]

48. Gale E.⁸ Roush (*Cecil Ira⁷, Margaret Mary⁶ Pegan, Harrison James⁵, Robert A.⁴, Andrew³, Andrew² Pagan, James¹*) was born on October 5, 1922, in Dodson Twp., Highland Co., Ohio.[128, 227, 228] He was the son of Cecil Ira Roush (14) and Electa Gertrude Stroup. He resided in 1998 in Fort Myers, Lee Co., Florida. Gale E. died in a hospital in Tampa, Hillsborough Co., Florida, on August 29, 1998, at age 75.[128, 227, 228] He was cremated.[573]

Gale E. Roush was the only son in a set of triplet boys who born to Cecil Ira and Electa Roush who lived to adulthood.

Gale E. married **Bernice Gertrude Julien** in 1948. They had one son. Bernice Gertrude Julien was born in Salt Lake City, Salt Lake Co., Utah, on August 22, 1918.[574] Bernice Gertrude reached age 85 and died in Fort Myers, Lee Co., Florida, on April 6, 2004.[574] She was cremated.[575]

The April 12, 1958 edition of the Salt Lake City Tribune reported that six-year-old Lee Roush, son of Gale and Bernice Roush of Florida, became lost while visiting his maternal grandmother, Mrs.

Walter G. Julien, in that city and had to be tracked down by a bloodhound which had rescued quite a few lost children.[576]

Son of Gale E. Roush and Bernice Gertrude Julien:

+ 114 m I. **Lee E. Donald**[9] **Roush** was born in Miami, Dade Co., Florida?, on August 13, 1951.[128] He died in Cape Coral, Lee Co., Florida, on March 26, 2012.[128, 577]

49. Dale E.[8] **Roush** (*Cecil Ira*[7], *Margaret Mary*[6] *Pegan, Harrison James*[5], *Robert A.*[4], *Andrew*[3], *Andrew*[2] *Pagan, James*[1]) was born on October 5, 1922, in Dodson Twp., Highland Co., Ohio.[229] He was the son of Cecil Ira Roush (14) and Electa Gertrude Stroup. Dale E. died in Dodson Twp., Highland Co., Ohio, on May 11, 1923.[229] He was buried in Stroup Cemetery, Dodson Twp., Highland Co., Ohio.[229, 578]

Dale E. Roush, who lived five months, was one of a set of triplet boys born to Cecil Ira and Electra Roush.

50. Ray E.[8] **Roush** (*Cecil Ira*[7], *Margaret Mary*[6] *Pegan, Harrison James*[5], *Robert A.*[4], *Andrew*[3], *Andrew*[2] *Pagan, James*[1]) was born on October 5, 1922, in Dodson Twp., Highland Co., Ohio.[230] He was the son of Cecil Ira Roush (14) and Electa Gertrude Stroup. Ray E. died in Dodson Twp., Highland Co., Ohio, on October 5, 1922.[230] He was buried in Stroup Cemetery, Dodson Twp., Highland Co., Ohio.[230, 579]

Ray E. Roush, who died at birth was one of a set of triplet boys born to Cecil Ira and Electra Roush.

51. Child[8] **Keplinger** (*Laura A.*[7] *PeGan, Harrison James*[6], *Harrison James*[5] *Pegan, Robert A.*[4], *Andrew*[3], *Andrew*[2] *Pagan, James*[1]) was born on June 28, 1898, in Salamonie Twp., Huntington Co., Indiana?[83] He or she was a child of Harley Paul Keplinger and Laura A. PeGan (15). Child died in Salamonie Twp., Huntington Co., Indiana?, on June 28, 1898.[83] He or she was buried in McKinney Lugar Creek Cemetery, Center Twp., Grant Co., Indiana.[83]

52. Raymond Harrison[8] **PeGan** (*Sarah Celeste*[7], *Harrison James*[6], *Harrison James*[5] *Pegan, Robert A.*[4], *Andrew*[3], *Andrew*[2] *Pagan, James*[1]) was born on September 22, 1899, in Monroe Twp., Grant Co., Indiana.[128, 265] He was the son of George William Keplinger (a.k.a. Roy Clarence Scott) and Sarah Celeste PeGan (16). He died in Fort Wayne, Allen Co., Indiana, on May 7, 1980, at age 80.[266, 267] Raymond Harrison was buried in Greenlawn Memorial Park Cemetery, Fort Wayne, Allen Co., Indiana.[266, 267, 580]

Childless.

Raymond Harrison PeGan was the illegitimate son of Sarah PeGan by George William Keplinger, the brother of her brother-in-law, Harley Keplinger, husband of Laura PeGan.

George William Keplinger courted Sarah PeGan, but she quickly realized he was odd and controlling. She told him she no longer wanted to see him, but he stalked her. When she refused his advances, he abducted her one day and raped her in January 1899. Then George insisted that they marry, but Sarah steadfastly refused. When George Keplinger realilzed Sarah wasn't going to marry him, he shot her in the neck. She almost died. When George admitted that he was "criminally intimate" with Sarah and pleaded guilty to assault and battery with intent to kill, Harrison PeGan stated that his daughter "was in a family way" from the rape. Raymond Pegan was born in September 1899.[83, 91, 92]

Sarah PeGan and her son Raymond PeGan lived with Harrison and Angeline PeGan on their farm near Arcana, Monroe Twp., Grant Co., Indiana. However, when Sarah married Isaac Pearson in 1902, he refused to allow Raymond to live with them. Raymond remained with his Grandparents PeGan, moving with them to Lagro Twp., Wabash Co., Indiana in 1903. They may have moved across the county line so that, when Raymond entered school, he would not be ridiculed, as his mother's assault was well known and talked about in Grant County. Raymond PeGan lived with Harrison and Angeline until Angeline died in 1910. He then resided with his stepfather Isaac Pearson and his mother Sarah in Mill Twp., Grant Co., Indiana.[83]

Raymond PeGan is not found in the 1920 census. According to his cousin, H. Frederick "Fritz" PeGan, Ray was living in Wabash, Noble Twp., Wabash Co., Indiana and working for Hipskind Plumbing and Heating Company.[83]

Raymond Harrison married Mrs. **Nancy Hazel Long** Knight on July 25, 1921, in Wabash Co., Indiana.[581, 582] They divorced. Nancy Hazel Long was born in Wabash, Noble Twp., Wabash Co., Indiana, on February 21, 1890.[581, 582] She was also known as **Hazel**. Nancy Hazel reached age 73 and died in Huntington, Huntington Twp., Huntington Co., Indiana, on February 26, 1963.[583, 584] She was buried in Mount Etna Cemetery, Mount. Etna, Jefferson Twp., Huntington Co., Indiana.[585] She was the daughter of William Long and Mary Luella Eagy.

Nancy Hazel Long preferred her middle name, Hazel, as her given name.

In 1900, Nancy "Hazel" Long, age 10, is found with her family in Center Twp., Grant Co., Indiana; also in the home in Leatha Morrow, her 13-year-old half-sister, who in 1928 would marry Alvah/Alvin Leroy Pegan, Raymond Pegan's uncle (*Census Place: Center, Grant, Indiana; Roll: 373; Page: 6B; Enumeration District: 31; Hazel Long, William Long, head of household*).

Hazel Long's first marriage was to Chester Orville Knight on March 26, 1907 in Grant Co., Indiana.[586] They divorced.

Raymond PeGan worked for Hipskind Plumbing and Heating at their two locations in Wabash, Indiana and Fort Wayne. Soon he became involved in bootlegging in the 1920s with some of his coworkers, a scheme allegedly devised by his boss, Mr. Hipskind. Ray drove an Apperson Jackrabbit automobile, one of the most desirable autos of the era, and he had the seats, the undercarriage, and every available nook and cranny stuffed with liquor bottles. According to Hugh Frederick "Fritz" PeGan, son of Raymond's uncle Clanzie PeGan, the car was a flashy, marvelous machine which was much admired by Fritz and his brothers. Occasionally, Raymond would visit Huntington, Indiana and take his Uncle Clanzie PeGan's children for a ride in his Jackrabbit—to the envy of all the other kids in town. Raymond also was a hero to his younger PeGan cousins because he played baseball with the Boulder City Cubs, a Huntington baseball team.[83]

In 1928, Nancy "Hazel" Long Knight Pegan's half-sister, Leatha Morrow Rodgers, would become the second wife of Alvah/Alvin Leroy Pegan. Raymond H. Pegan's uncle.[83]

Raymond Harrison PeGan is enumerated as "Ray Pegan" in the 1930 census in Fort Wayne, Allen Co., Indiana (*Census Place: Fort Wayne, Allen, Indiana; Roll: 576; Page: 25A; Enumeration District: 33; Image: 218.0*). Ray Pegan, age 31, born Indiana with his parents born in the United States, is a truck driver for a plumber. His wife, Nancy Hazel Long Knight PeGan, listed as "N. Hazel", is 37 years old and says she and her parents were born in Indiana. The pair state they were both first married at age 21.

Fritz PeGan remembers that before Prohibition ended, Raymond PeGan told the Hipskind's he wanted to stop bootlegging, much to his boss' displeasure. They apparently fired him. Then the Hipskind's later accused Raymond PeGan of embezzling. He was arrested that year in Fort Wayne, Allen County, Indiana, but the charges were dropped. But the next year, the Hipskinds again pressed charges. In April 1935, Raymond PeGan pleaded guilty to a grand larceny charge in the Allen County Circuit Court in Fort Wayne, Indiana and sentenced to one to 10 years in the Indiana State Prison in Michigan City, LaPorte Co., Indiana. He was paroled on May 7, 1936 and discharged on June 3, 1937. On his Indiana State Prison intake record, he states his father was Harley Keplinger, his former uncle by marriage (the husband of the late Laura Pegan Keplinger, his mother's older sister).[83, 587]

Raymond PeGan was still married to Nancy "Hazel" Long Knight PeGan when he went to prison. But they divorced after his release.[83, 587]

(Nancy) Hazel Long Knight PeGan is enumerated in Fort Wayne, Allen Co., Indiana in 1940 (*Census Place: Fort Wayne, Allen, Indiana; Roll: T627_1117; Page: 61A; Enumeration District: 94-71*). Listed as Hazel PeGan, she is age 50, divorced, and works as a cook in a school. Living with her is 15-year-old

Lenabell Reason (later Van Ryn), a foster daughter. Both say they were born in Indiana and were living in Fort Wayne in 1935. Their house address is 1614 Lanternier Street.

In February 1944, (Nancy) Hazel Long Knight PeGan married for a third time to a widower, James Benson, in Huntington Co., Indiana..[588]

Raymond Harrison PeGan married Mrs. **Nettie E. Gobbell** Goodson on October 8, 1938, in Grant Co., Indiana.[589] They divorced. Nettie E. Gobble was born in Abingdon, Washington Co., Virginia, on August 10, 1889.[128, 589, 590] She reached age 79 and died in Fort Wayne, Allen Co., Indiana, on February 13, 1969.[128, 590, 591] Nettie E. was buried in Greenlawn Memorial Park Cemetery, Fort Wayne, Allen Co., Indiana.[590, 591, 592]

Nettie Gobbell Goodson, a divorcee with three children, married Raymond Harrison PeGan in October 1938. Raymond states on this marriage application that his father was "Harley PeGan". The marriage lasts only a few months before they divorce or have the marriage annulled. On their marriage license, Nettie Gobbell Goodson says she was born in Abingdon, Virginia (correct) on August 10, 1894 (Incorrect—her birthdate was August 10, 1889). She also says had been married once, and this marriage ended in death in 1918.[589] But on the 1920 census form, she says she is divorced *(Census Place: Fort Wayne Ward 2, Allen, Indiana; Roll: T625_421; Page: 8B; Enumeration District: 40; Image: 615)*.

In 1940, Nettie Gobbell Goodson (PeGan) resides in Fort Wayne, Allen Co., Indiana *(Census Place: Fort Wayne, Allen, Indiana; Roll: T627_1117; Page: 2A; Enumeration District: 94-90)*. Nettie Goodson, widow, age 50, is a cook. She says she and her parents were Virginia natives. Nettie is residing at 2728 Queen Street.

Nettie E. Gobbell Goodson PeGan restored her first married surname "Goodson" after her marriage to Raymond Pegan ended, and died under the name, "Nettie E. Goodson".[590]

Raymond Harrison PeGan married Mrs. **Bessie E. Powell** Whitridge Bailey on December 2, 1939, in Huntington Co., Indiana.[593] They divorced. Bessie E. Powell was born in Portland, Wayne Twp., Jay Co., Indiana, on July 1, 1887.[128, 594] She reached age 71 and died in Fort Wayne, Allen Co., Indiana, on March 14, 1971.[128, 594] Bessie E. was buried in Green Park Cemetery, Portland, Wayne Twp., Jay Co., Indiana.[594, 595]

According to her entry on findagrave.com, Bessie Powell married her first husband, Frederick Whitridge, in Indianapolis, Marion Co., Indiana. After Frederick Whitridge's death in 1914, she moved to Fort Wayne, Allen Co., Indiana, where she met and married Raymond PeGan.[596]

This is incorrect, as a marriage announcement in the *Portland (IN) Review* on June 28, 1915 announces Bessie's marriage to Clarence Bailey.[596] Clarence and Bessie are living in Portland, Indiana when Clarence registers for the WWI draft in 1917.[597] He says on his draft form that he is married with two children under age 12 (Mack Bailey and Jack Raymond/Raymond Jack Whitridge, born 1910, Bessie's son by her first husband Frederick Whitridge. Bessie and Clarence Bailey divorce before 1922. Also, the death record of her 15-month-old son, Mack Beverly Bailey, has her still married to Clarence Bailey and living in her hometown, Portland, Wayne Twp., Jay Co., Indiana in 1918.[598]

Born in 1887, Bessie shaves 12 years off her age when she marries Raymond H. PeGan. She states on her marriage application in December 1939 that she was born on July 1, 1899—probably to be "younger" than her husband.[593]

In 1940, Raymond PeGan, again listed as Ray, is still residing in Fort Wayne, Allen Co., Indiana *(Census Place: Fort Wayne, Allen, Indiana; Roll: T627_1117; Page: 7B; Enumeration District: 94-69)*. Ray PeGan, age 45, is a stockman at a plumbing shop. With him is his third wife, Bessie Powell Whitridge Bailey PeGan, 42. Both say they were born in Indiana, and living in Ft. Wayne in 1935. They are lodgers in the home of Chester and Nellie Gillam at 1154 Division Street.

Later, according to Fritz Pegan, Raymond PeGan became a maintenance worker at several apartment buildings in Fort Wayne.[83]

On his marriage application to "Hazel", Raymond PeGan says his father is "Isaac PeGan".[582] On the one to Nettie, he states his father as "Harley PeGan".[589] On his marriage application to Bessie, his father is "Raymond PeGan". Also, on his application to Bessie, he says his mother's maiden name was "Sarah Keplinger".[593] These are incorrect. It seems Raymond never knew who his father was, but apparently someone must have hinted that it was a Keplinger and the only one he knew was Harley, the widower of Laura PeGan Keplinger, his mother Sarah's sister. Harley, after Laura's death, remained a family friend to the PeGans. Moreover, Sarah's children, all four by her first husband, Isaac Pearson, never knew Raymond Harrison PeGan was their half-brother. They were either told, or assumed, that Raymond, who lived with Sarah and Ike for a while and always visited Sarah, was Sarah's much younger brother. This would seem possible to them, as Raymond was two years older than Sarah's youngest brother, Philip Garl PeGan. When this author obliquely referred to Raymond as their half-brother, Leona Pearson Hatfield and her niece, Betty Jean Eastes Cowgill Reese insisted he was their uncle, not their half-brother.[84, 97]

Raymond Harrison PeGan seems to have made an impression on more than one of his relatives. His young uncle, Philip PeGan, who was two years younger than Raymond and grew up with him in Harrison and Angeline Stout PeGan's home, named a son Raymond. Hugh Frederick "Fritz" PeGan also named a son after his cousin.

53. Mattie Leona[8] Pearson (*Sarah Celeste[7] PeGan, Harrison James[6], Harrison James[5] Pegan, Robert A.[4], Andrew[3], Andrew[2] Pagan, James[1]*) was born on April 9, 1903, in Mill Twp., Grant Co., Indiana.[128, 268, 269] She was also known as **Toots**. She was the daughter of Isaac James Pearson and Sarah Celeste PeGan (16). Mattie Leona died in Greentown, Liberty Twp., Howard Co., Indiana, on December 3, 2005, at age 102.[128, 269] She was buried in Greenlawn Cemetery, Greentown, Liberty Twp., Howard Co., Indiana.[269, 599]

Childless.

Mattie Leona married **Arlie Joseph Hatfield** on August 11, 1928, in Grant Co., Indiana.[600] Arlie Joseph Hatfield was born in Union Twp., Howard Co., Indiana, on June 2, 1886.[601, 602, 603, 604] He was also known as **Joe**. He reached age 69 and died in Jonesboro, Mill Twp., Grant Co., Indiana, on July 12, 1955.[603, 605] Arlie Joseph was buried in Greenlawn Cemetery, Greentown, Liberty Twp., Howard Co., Indiana.[603, 606]

In 1930, Arlie and Mattie Leona Pearson Hatfield are not found in the census.

Arlie J. and Leona Mattie Pearson Hatfield are found in Kokomo, Center Twp., Howard Co., Indiana in 1940 *(Census Place: Kokomo, Howard, Indiana; Roll: T627_1054; Page: 1B; Enumeration District: 34-22)*. In the household are Arlie J. Hatfield, age 53, a watchmaker, and his wife, Leona Pearson Hatfield, 36. Both were born in Indiana and were living at the same address, 320 East Carter Street, in 1935. They have four lodgers in their home, Thomas and Dorothy Rainey and their two children.

Arlie Joseph Hatfield's marriage to Leona was his second. He had two children by his first wife; one died in infancy. Arlie worked as an owner of a watch shop; watch maker between 1932 and 1946.[84]

54. Herbert Harrison[8] Pearson (*Sarah Celeste[7] PeGan, Harrison James[6], Harrison James[5] Pegan, Robert A.[4], Andrew[3], Andrew[2] Pagan, James[1]*) was born on May 2, 1908, in Mill Twp., Grant Co., Indiana.[128, 270] He was also known as **Bill**. He was the son of Isaac James Pearson and Sarah Celeste PeGan (16). Herbert Harrison died in a hospital in Pendleton, Umatilla Co., Oregon, on August 8, 1973, at age 65.[270, 271] He was buried in Evergreen Cemetery, Ontario, Malheur Co., Oregon.[607]

Herbert Harrison married **Bernice Ann Kucera** on July 23, 1932, in Grant Co., Indiana.[270, 608] They had one daughter. Bernice Ann Kucera was born in Tama, Tama Twp., Tama Co., Iowa, on December 1, 1907.[608, 609,] She reached age 58 and died in Ontario, Malheur Co., Oregon, on October 5, 1966.[609, 610] Bernice Ann was buried in Evergreen Cemetery, Ontario, Malheur Co., Oregon.[611]

In 1940, Herbert Pearson is enumerated in Marshalltown, Marshall Co., Iowa *(Census Place: Marshalltown, Marshall, Iowa; Roll: T627_1182; Page: 13B; Enumeration District: 64-28)*. In the household are Herbert Pearson, age 31, born Indiana, a foreman at a manufacturing plant, his wife, Bernice Kucera Pearson, also 31, and their daughter, Mary Ann, two, both born in Iowa. The two adults say they were living in the same place in 1935. Their home is at 506 West Nevada Street.

Herbert Harrison Pearson was living in Marshalltown, Marshall Twp., Marshall Co., Iowa by 1934. He and his family stayed in Marshalltown untili 1951, when they relocated to New Plymouth, Payette Co., Idaho By 1955 he was a sporting goods salesman in Ontario, Malheur Co., Oregon, where he and Bernice spent the remainder of their lives.[612]

Herbert H. Pearson, known as "Bill", was a skilled outdoorsman who excelled at hunting and fishing. He sold sporting goods for The Outdoorsman, a well-known sporting goods outfitter in Ontario, Oregon for many years. Towards the latter years of his life, he sold sporting goods for a firm in Portland, Oregon.[612]

Bernice Pearson "fudged" on her marriage application and said she was born on December 1, 1909 in Tama, Tama Co., Iowa, most likely to appear younger than her husband Herbert "Bill" Pearson, who was born on May 2, 1908. However, her obituary, supported by census records, indicate she was born on December 1, 1907. Bernice Ann was working as a photographer when she married.[608, 609]

Daughter of Herbert Harrison Pearson and Bernice Ann Kucera:

+ 115 f I. **Marianne**[9] **Pearson** was born in Marshalltown, Marshall Twp., Marshall Co., Iowa, on November 9, 1937.

55. Truman Vaughn[8] **Pearson** (*Sarah Celeste*[7] *PeGan, Harrison James*[6]*, Harrison James*[5] *Pegan, Robert A.*[4]*, Andrew*[3]*, Andrew*[2] *Pagan, James*[1]) was born on September 18, 1911, in Mill Twp., Grant Co., Indiana.[128, 272] He was the son of Isaac James Pearson and Sarah Celeste PeGan (16). Truman Vaughn was living in 1998 in Calimesa, Riverside Co., California. He died in a hospital in Orange, Orange Co., California, on April 30, 1998, at age 86.[128, 272] Truman Vaughn was buried in Fairhaven Cemetery, Santa Ana, Orange Co., California.[613]

Truman Vaughn married **Mattie Mae Oliver** on February 12, 1935, in Grant Co., Indiana.[L] They divorced but remarried later. Mattie Mae Oliver was born in Bluffton, Wells Co., Indiana, on January 14, 1916.[128, 614] She age 89 and died in Santa Ana, Orange Co., California, on September 2, 2005.[128, 615] Mattie Mae was buried in Fairhaven Cemetery, Santa Ana, Orange Co., California.[616]

In 1940, Truman Pearson is enumerated in Winchester, White River Twp., Randolph Co., Indiana (*Census Place: Winchester, Randolph, Indiana; Roll: T627_1089; Page: 2A; Enumeration District: 68-26*). Truman Pearson, age 28, is a mould maker in a mould making factory. With him is his wife, Mattie Oliver Pearson, age 24, and their daughter, Patricia Ann, two. All were born in Indiana, and the adults say they were living in Winchester in 1935. They are living at 321 West North Street.

By 1943, Truman Vaughn Pearson had joined his brother Herbert "Bill" Pearson in Marshalltown, Marshall Twp., Marshall Co., Iowa. Between 1948 and 1954, he and his family resided in Downey, Los Angeles Co., California. By 1963, he had moved to Whittier, Los Angeles Co., California. He removed to John Day, Grant Co., Oregon by 1990, but was back in California, in Calimesa, Riverside Co., California, by the time he died.[617]

Truman V. and Mattie May Oliver Pearson divorced in 1973 in Oregon but reconciled later.[617]

Daughters of Truman Vaughn Pearson and Mattie Mae Oliver:

+ 116 f I. **Patricia Ann**[9] **Pearson** was born in Winchester, White River Twp., Randolph Co., Indiana, on September 5, 1937.[617]

+ 117 f II. **Marjorie Jane**[9] **Pearson** was born in Winchester, White River Twp., Randolph Co., Indiana, on February 26, 1943.[128, 617, M] She was also known as **Jane**. Marjorie Jane died in Orange, Orange Co., California, on May 11, 2005.[128, 618]

56. Opal Colene[8] **Pearson** (*Sarah Celeste*[7] *PeGan, Harrison James*[6]*, Harrison James*[5] *Pegan, Robert A.*[4]*, Andrew*[3]*, Andrew*[2] *Pagan, James*[1]) was born on November 21, 1913, in Mill Twp., Grant Co., Indiana.[128, 273, 274] She was the daughter of Isaac James Pearson and Sarah Celeste PeGan (16). She lived in 2000 in Gas City, Mill Twp., Grant Co., Indiana. Opal Colene died in a hospital in Muncie, Center Twp., Delaware Co., Indiana, on December 25, 2000, at age 87.[128, 273, 274] She was buried in Riverside Cemetery, Gas City, Mill Twp. Grant Co., Indiana.[274, 619]

Opal Colene married **Joseph Gerald Eastes** in 1930. They had three children. Joseph Gerald Eastes was born in Fairmount, Fairmount Twp., Grant Co., Indiana, on March 17, 1911.[128, 620, 621, 622] He was living in 1988 in Jonesboro, Mill Twp., Grant Co., Indiana. Joseph Gerald reached age 76 and died in a hospital in Muncie, Center Twp., Delaware Co., Indiana, on February 4, 1988.[128, 620, 622] He was buried in Riverside Cemetery, Gas City, Mill Twp. Grant Co., Indiana.[622, 623]

In 1940, Joseph and (Opal) Colene Pearson Eastes are residing with her mother, Sarah PeGan Pearson (Hewitt Horner) in Jonesboro, Mill Twp., Grant Co., Indiana *(Census Place: Jonesboro, Grant, Indiana; Roll: T627_1048; Page: 22B; Enumeration District: 27-36)*. Joseph Eastes, age 29, is an operator in a glass factory, his wife (Opal) "Coleen" Pearson Eastes, 26, an inspector at a glass factory. Joseph and Colene have two children, Betty, nine, and Joseph Jr., three. Listed as head of the household is Sarah PeGan Pearson, 57, a widow. All were born in Indiana, and all but Joseph Jr., who is too young, were living in the same house in 1935, but no address is listed.

Social Security Death Index entry under Joe G. Eastes.[128]

Children of Opal Colene Pearson and Joseph Gerald Eastes:

+ 118 f I. **Betty Jean**[9] **Eastes** was born in Jonesboro, Mill Twp., Grant Co., Indiana, on October 1, 1930.[128, 624, 625, 626] She died in a hospital in Muncie, Center Twp., Delaware Co., Indiana, on July 10, 2006.[128, 624, 625, 626]

+ 119 m II. **Joseph Edward**[9] **Eastes II** was born in Marion, Center Twp., Grant Co., Indiana, on September 28, 1936.[128, 627, 628, 629, 630] He was also known as **Ed**. Joseph Edward died in a hospital in Muncie, Center Twp., Delaware Co., Indiana, on November 26, 1998.[128, 627, 628, 630]

+ 120 m III. **John Frederick**[9] **Eastes** was born in Jonesboro, Mill Twp., Grant Co., Indiana, on June 28, 1942.[128, 631] He died in a hospital in Lafayette, Lafayette Parish, Louisiana, on November 19, 2010.[128, 632, 633]

57. Cecil Keith[8] **Pegan** (*Jesse Harrison*[7]*, Harrison James*[6] *PeGan II, Harrison James*[5] *Pegan, Robert A.*[4]*, Andrew*[3]*, Andrew*[2] *Pagan, James*[1]) was born on June 18, 1912, in Wabash, Noble Twp., Wabash Co., Indiana.[128, 304, 305, 306, 307] He was the son of Jesse Harrison Pegan (18) and Elva Coe Keith. Cecil Keith died in Wabash, Noble Twp., Wabash Co., Indiana, on July 7, 1990, at age 78.[128, 304, 306] He was buried in Gardens of Memory Cemetery, Banquo, Wayne Twp., Huntington Co., Indiana on the Grant Co. line.[306, 634]

Cecil Keith married **Bessie Mae Shoemaker** on February 6, 1938, in Muncie, Center Twp., Delaware Co., Indiana.[305, 635] They divorced. They had three children. Bessie Mae Shoemaker was born in Eaton, Union Twp., Delaware Co., Indiana, on June 27, 1920.[128, 305, 636, 637] She lived in 1994 in Palm Desert, Riverside Co., California. Bessie Mae also resided in 1996 in Cleveland, Bradley Co., Tennessee. She reached age 82 and died in

South Bend, St. Joseph Co., Indiana, on March 4, 2003.[128, 636, 637] She was cremated.[637]

Cecil Keith lived in 1935 in Yorktown, Mt. Pleasant Twp., Delaware Co., Indiana.[635]

In 1940, Cecil Pegan is enumerated in Licking Twp., Blackford Co., Indiana (*Census Place: Licking, Blackford, Indiana; Roll: T627_1027; Page: 9A; Enumeration District: 5-11*). Cecil Pegan, age 27, a farm laborer, says he was living in Wabash Co., Indiana in 1935. His wife, Bessie Shoemaker Pegan, 19, says she was residing in Delaware Co., Indiana in 1935. Both were born in Indiana. They are living in a rural area, and no road or house address is listed.

Bessie May Shoemaker Pegan Young abandoned her husband Cecil Pegan and their children. She remarried to Fred Young.[637, 638] For a while, she had sporadic contact with her children from her marriage to Cecil PeGan but was completely estranged from them for at least 20 years prior to her death.[302] Oddly, the occupation listed on her death certificate was missionary.[637]

When Cecil and Bessie divorced, Cecil retained custody of their three children. Cecil and his children moved in with his mother, Elva Keith Pegan, in Huntington. They lived with Elva until Cecil married his second wife, Audra Connolly.[638]

Cecil Keith Pegan married Mrs. **Audra Luella Connolly** Ridgeway on January 26, 1956, in Bryan, Williams Co., Ohio.[639] Audra Luella Connolly was born in Jefferson Twp., Williams Co., Ohio, on November 4, 1910.[128, 640, 641] Audra Luella reached age 75 and died in Huntington, Huntington Twp., Huntington Co., Indiana, on December 29, 1985.[128, 640, 641] She was buried in Gardens of Memory Cemetery, Banquo, Wayne Twp., Huntington Co., Indiana on the Grant Co. line.[641, 642]

Cecil and Audra continued in Huntington, Indiana.

Cecil Keith Pegan married Mrs. **Doris Loretta Figert** England on November 25, 1989, in Wabash Co., Indiana.[643, 644] Doris Loretta Figert was born in Wabash, Noble Twp., Wabash Co., Indiana, on April 24, 1919.[128, 644, 645] Doris Loretta reached age 84 and died in Wabash, Noble Twp., Wabash Co., Indiana, on April 30, 2003.[128, 644, 645] She was buried in Memorial Lawns Cemetery, Wabash, Noble Twp., Wabash Co., Indiana.[645, 646]

Four years after Audra Connolly Pegan died, Cecil Pegan went to his high school reunion and was reunited with a high school sweetheart, Mrs. Doris Figert England, who was a widow. The couple married 53 years after their first date, according to an article in the *Logansport (IN) Pharos-Tribune* and other Indiana newspapers.[647] Sadly, the couple were only married about eight months when Cecil died.

Cecil Keith Pegan and Bessie Mae Shoemaker had three children, including:

+ 121 f   I.   **Betty Jean⁹ Pegan** was born in Hartford City, Licking Twp., Blackford Co., Indiana, on April 12, 1940.[648]

58. Pauline Miriam⁸ Pegan (*Jesse Harrison⁷, Harrison James⁶ PeGan II, Harrison James⁵ Pegan, Robert A.⁴, Andrew³, Andrew² Pagan, James¹*) was born on December 17, 1913, in Roann, Paw Paw Twp., Wabash Co., Indiana.[128, 298, 308, 309, 310] She was the daughter of Jesse Harrison Pegan (18) and Elva Coe Keith. Pauline Miriam died in Huntington, Huntington Twp., Huntington Co., Indiana, on February 26, 1998, at age 84.[128, 308, 309] She was buried in Gardens of Memory Cemetery, Banquo, Wayne Twp., Huntington Co., Indiana on the Grant Co. line.[649]

Pauline Miriam married **Charles Raymond Oswalt** on September 29, 1935, in Wabash Co., Indiana.[298, 650] They had two children. Charles Raymond Oswalt was born in Noble Twp., Wabash Co., Indiana, on September 15, 1911.[128, 298, 651, 652] Charles Raymond reached age 80 and died in Huntington, Huntington Twp., Huntington Co., Indiana, on November 3, 1991.[128, 651, 652] He was buried in Gardens of Memory Cemetery, Banquo, Wayne Twp., Huntington Co., Indiana on the Grant Co. line.[652, 653]

Charles and Pauline Pegan Oswalt are enumerated in Wabash, Noble Twp., Wabash Co., Indiana (*Census*

Place: Wabash, Wabash, Indiana; Roll: T627_1106; Page: 10B-11A; Enumeration District: 85-12). In the household are Charles Oswalt, age 28, a salesman in a retail store; his wife Pauline Pegan Oswalt, 26, and Pauline's sister Fern Pegan, 22. a clerk in a retail store. All were born in Indiana, and all say they were living in Wabash in 1935. The house address is 23 Hill Street.

Pauline Miriam Pegan and Charles Raymond Oswalt had two children, including:

+ 122 f I. **Judith Kay**[9] **Oswalt** was born in Wabash, Noble Twp., Wabash Co., Indiana, on April 6, 1940.[654]

59. James Meredith[8] **Pegan** (*Jesse Harrison*[7], *Harrison James*[6] *PeGan II, Harrison James*[5] *Pegan, Robert A.*[4], *Andrew*[3], *Andrew*[2] *Pagan, James*[1]) was born on September 29, 1915, in Macy, Allen Twp., Miami Co., Indiana.[128, 311, 312, 313] He was the son of Jesse Harrison Pegan (18) and Elva Coe Keith. He died in a hospital in Marion, Center Twp., Grant Co., Indiana, on February 23, 1987, at age 71.[128, 311, 312] James Meredith was buried in Mount Etna Cemetery, Mount. Etna, Jefferson Twp., Huntington Co., Indiana.[655]

James M. Pegan is living with his mother Elva and his younger sister Florence Pegan in Pleasant Twp., Wabash Co., Indiana in 1940 *(Census Place: Pleasant, Wabash, Indiana; Roll: T627_1106; Page: 6A; Enumeration District: 85-24).* James Pegan, age 24, is a farmer. Elva C. Keith Pegan, listed as the head of the household, is 50 years old and says she is a widow. Florence Pegan is age 20. All say they were born in Indiana and were living in the same house on Peru Road in 1935.

James Meredith married **Onhawanha Carver Ludwig** on June 29, 1946.[301] They divorced. They had three children. Onhawanha Carver Ludwig was born in Barrington, Camden Co., New Jersey, on January 6, 1922.[656, 657] She was also known as **Ann**. Onhawanha Carver lived in 2009 in Lebanon, Center Twp., Boone Co., Indiana. She also resided in 2014 in Ann Arbor, Ann Arbor Twp., Washtenaw Co., Michigan. Onhawanha Carver reached age 94 years of age and died in Lebanon, Center Twp., Boone Co., Indiana, on December 26, 2016.[657] She was buried in Mount Etna Cemetery, Mount. Etna, Jefferson Twp., Huntington Co., Indiana.[658]

After residing in Huntington, Indiana for most of his life, James M. Pegan lived with a daughter in Zionsville, Eagle Twp., Boone Co., Indiana before he died.

Onhawanha Carver Ludwig Pegan Deem was Native American. She and her husband served in WWII, James in the Marines and Onhawanha in the United States Naval Reserve (Women's Reserve) or WAVES. om James M. Pegan, Onhawanha "Ann" Carver Ludwig Pegan relocated to Whatcom County, Washington, to live with her son and his family. There she met and married Lester Theodore Deem on June 12, 1982 in Whatcom Co., Washington.[301, 659] After he died, she moved back to the Midwest and lived with each of her daughters before her death.

James Meredith Pegan and Onhawanha Carver Ludwig had three children, including:

+ 123 f II. **Daughter**[9] **Pegan** was born in Huntington, Huntington Twp., Huntington Co., Indiana.

60. Fern Maxine[8] **Pegan** (*Jesse Harrison*[7], *Harrison James*[6] *PeGan II, Harrison James*[5] *Pegan, Robert A.*[4], *Andrew*[3], *Andrew*[2] *Pagan, James*[1]) was born on September 3, 1917, in Macy, Allen Twp., Miami Co., Indiana.[128, 314, 315, 316, 317, 318] She was the daughter of Jesse Harrison Pegan (18) and Elva Coe Keith. Fern Maxine lived in 1977 in Zionsville, Eagle Twp., Boone Co., Indiana. Fern Maxine died in a hospital in Indianapolis, Marion Co., Indiana, on June 16, 1979, at age 61.[128, 315, 316, 317] She was buried in Fairview Cemetery, Servia, Chester Twp., Wabash Co., Indiana.[317, 660]

Childless.

In 1940, Fern Pegan, age 22 and single, is living with her brother-in-law and sister, Charles and Pauline Pegan Oswalt in Wabash, Noble Twp., Wabash Co., Indiana *(Census Place: Wabash, Wabash, Indiana; Roll: T627_1106; Page: 10B-11A; Enumeration*

District: 85-12). Fern Pegan is a clerk in a retail store. The head of the household, Charles Oswalt, age 28, is salesman in a retail store; his wife Pauline Pegan Oswalt, is 26 years old. All were born in Indiana, and all say they were living in Wabash in 1935. The house address is 23 Hill Street.

Fern Maxine married **Vilas Hugo Zimpelman** on June 30, 1941, in Paulding Co., Ohio.[314] Vilas Hugo Zimpelman was born in Chester Twp., Wabash Co., Indiana, on May 26, 1910.[314, 661, 662, 663] He reached age 47 and died in Huntington, Huntington Twp., Huntington Co., Indiana, on February 5, 1958.[661, 662, 663] Vilas Hugo was buried in Fairview Cemetery, Servia, Chester Twp., Wabash Co., Indiana.[662, 663]

A mechanic, Vilas Zimpelman had been suffering from cancer for about two years when, despondent, he took his own life.[302]

After the death of her husband, Fern, who had become a beautician, lived with her mother, Elva Keith PeGan in Huntington, Huntington Twp., Huntington Co., Indiana. After her mother died, Fern moved to Twenty-Nine Palms, San Bernardino Co., California for a few years, but got homesick and returned to Indiana. She lived in Zionsville, Boone Co., Indiana, near one of her nieces, until her death.[302]

61. Florence Willodean[8] **Pegan** (*Jesse Harrison*[7], *Harrison James*[6] *PeGan II, Harrison James*[5] *Pegan, Robert A.*[4], *Andrew*[3], *Andrew*[2] *Pagan, James*[1]) was born on August 22, 1919, in Wabash, Noble Twp., Wabash Co., Indiana.[319, 320, 321] She was the daughter of Jesse Harrison Pegan (18) and Elva Coe Keith. Florence Willodean lived in 1992 in Celina, Jefferson Twp., Mercer Co., Ohio. She died in a hospital in Coldwater, Butler Twp., Mercer Co., Ohio, on October 30, 1992, at age 73.[319, 320] Florence Willodean was buried in Mercer Memorial Gardens Cemetery, Celina, Jefferson Twp., Mercer Co., Ohio.[319, 664]

Florence Willodean married **John Junior Flowers II** on March 20, 1947, in Wells Co., Indiana.[321] They had seven children. John Junior Flowers II was born in Moorehead, Rowan Co., Kentucky, on April 30, 1924.[128, 665, 666, 667, 668] He was also known as **Posey** and **Junior**. He resided in Wabash, Liberty Twp., Mercer Co., Ohio before moving to Celina, Jefferson Twp., Mercer Co., Ohio. John Junior reached age 75 and died in a hospital in Coldwater, Butler Twp., Mercer Co., Ohio, on September 20, 1999.[128, 665, 666, 668] He was buried in Mercer Memorial Gardens Cemetery, Celina, Jefferson Twp., Mercer Co., Ohio.[665, 669]

According to her granddaughter, Florence Marie Flowers Koesters, Florence Willodean Pegan Flowers loved chickens and collected chicken and rooster salt and pepper shakers. She had two curio cabinets full of them.[292]

Florence Willodean Pegan and John Junior Flowers II had seven children, including:

+ 124 m I. **Allen Eugene**[9] **Flowers** was born in Bluffton, Wells Co., Indiana, on February 18, 1948.[128, 292, 670, 671, 672] He died in a hospital in Coldwater, Butler Twp., Mercer Co., Ohio, on January 9, 2005.[128, 292, 670, 671, 672]

+ 125 m III. **Son**[9] **Flowers** was born in Huntington, Huntington Twp., Huntington Co., Indiana.

+ 126 f IV. **Kathleen Joann**[9] **Flowers** was born in Wabash, Liberty Twp., Mercer Co., Ohio, on February 24, 1952.[292, 673] She was also known as **Kathy**. Kathleen Joann died in a hospital in Coldwater, Butler Twp., Mercer Co., Ohio, on April 25, 2013.[673]

+ 127 m VII. **Son Two**[9] **Flowers** was born in Coldwater, Butler Twp., Mercer Co., Ohio.

62. Leo Everett[8] **PeGan** (*Clanzie Herold*[7], *Harrison James*[6], *Harrison James*[5] *Pegan, Robert A.*[4], *Andrew*[3], *Andrew*[2] *Pagan, James*[1]) was born on July 3, 1908, in Lagro, Lagro Twp., Wabash Co., Indiana.[128, 333, 334] He was the son of Clanzie Herold PeGan (19) and

Josephine Sophia Schetzszle. He died in Columbus, Franklin Co., Ohio, on July 26, 1986, at age 78.[333, 335] Leo Everett was buried in Calvary Hill Cemetery, Dallas, Dallas Co., Texas.[333, 674]

Leo Everett PeGan's original given name was "Everett Harold" PeGan, the name which appears on his birth certificate. His name was changed shortly after his birth.[334]

Leo Everett married **Loretta Jennette Ryan** on May 7, 1935, in Huntington Co., Indiana.[675, 676] They had two children. Loretta Jennette Ryan was born in Huntington, Huntington Twp., Huntington Co., Indiana, on February 28, 1909.[128, 677, 678] Loretta Jennette reached age 77 and died in Dallas, Dallas Co., Texas, on May 21, 1986.[678, 679, 680] She was buried in Calvary Hill Cemetery, Dallas, Dallas Co., Texas.[678, 681]

Leo PeGan is found in the 1940 census in Huntington, Huntington Twp., Huntington Co., Indiana *(Census Place: Huntington, Huntington, Indiana; Roll: T627_1055; Page: 12B; Enumeration District: 35-8)*. "Lee E. Pegan", age 31, is an electrician ("electrical wiring—own business"). His wife, Loretta J. Ryan PeGan, is also 31 years old. They have a daughter, Maryln ("Maralyn") Ann, age two. All were born in Indiana, and Lee and Loretta say they were living in Huntington in 1935. They are residing at 546 Briant Street.

Leo PeGan was an electrician. Lee and his wife, Loretta, lived in an apartment on Jefferson Street in Huntington for many years. They had an interest in horses, particularly show horses, and belonged to the Huntington Saddle Club. One of their horses, "Liberace," became an Indiana and Midwest regional champion.

Later in life, Lee and Loretta managed a ranch owned by their daughter and husband, Dr. James and Marilyn PeGan Crossen, near San Antonio Texas. They later moved to Dallas, Dallas Co., Texas where Loretta died. About two months later, Leo PeGan died in Columbus, Franklin Co., Ohio, while he was visiting his son Thomas, a resident of Hilliard, a Columbus suburb.

Children of Leo Everett PeGan and Loretta Jennette Ryan:

+ 128 f I. **Maryln Ann⁹ PeGan** was born in Huntington, Huntington Twp., Huntington Co., Indiana, on March 12, 1937.[682]

+ 129 m II. **Thomas Joseph⁹ PeGan** was born in Huntington, Huntington Twp., Huntington Co., Indiana, on January 13, 1941.[128, 683] He died at Bison Ranch, Overgaard, Navajo Co., Arizona, on July 28, 2002.[128, 683, 684]

63. Paul Harold⁸ PeGan (*Clanzie Herold⁷, Harrison James⁶, Harrison James⁵ Pegan, Robert A.⁴, Andrew³, Andrew² Pagan, James¹*) was born on June 26, 1909, in Lagro Twp., Wabash Co., Indiana.[128, 336] He was the son of Clanzie Herold PeGan (19) and Josephine Sophia Schetzszle. He died in Fort Wayne, Allen Co., Indiana, on August 25, 1981, at age 72.[336, 337] Paul Harold was buried in Hoverstock Cemetery, Zanesville, Union Twp., Wells Co, Indiana.[336, 685]

In 1930, Paul PeGan was living with his uncle, Alva/Alvin PeGan and Alvin's wife Leatha Knight PeGan in Flint, Flint Twp., Genesee Co., Michigan *(Census Place: Flint, Genesee, Michigan; Roll: 987; Page: 14A; Enumeration District: 52; Image: 69.0)*. He listed his occupation as an apprentice plumber; his uncle was a plumber. But Paul did not continue to pursue this trade.

Paul Harold married **Delores Bernadette Feighner** on July 15, 1933, in Huntington Co., Indiana.[686, 687] They had one son. Delores Bernadette Feighner was born in Union Twp., Allen Co., Indiana, on October 19, 1911.[128, 688, 689] She was also known as **Dee**. Delores Bernadette reached age 92 and died in a facililty in Warsaw, Wayne Twp., Koscuisko Co., Indiana, on May 2, 2004.[128, 689] She was buried in Hoverstock Cemetery, Zanesville, Union Twp., Wells Co, Indiana.[689, 690]

After Paul and Delores married in 1933, they lived in Greenfield, Hancock County, Indiana before returning to Huntington, Indiana by 1935.[83]

Paul PeGan is enumerated in Huntington, Huntington Twp., Huntington Co., Indiana in 1940 (*Census Place: Huntington, Huntington, Indiana; Roll: T627_1055; Page: 10B; Enumeration District: 35-12*). In the home are Paul PeGan, age 30, a manager of an auto agency; his wife, Delores Feighner Pegan, 28, and their son Harold, who is one year old. Also in the household is Darrel Feighner, Delores' brother, age 22, a salesman at the auto agency. All were born in Indiana, and the three adults say they were living in Huntington in 1935. The family is living at 353 Frederick Street.

Later, Paul and his family lived in Waynedale, Fort Wayne, Allen Co., Indiana and he worked in a bowling alley.[83]

Son of Paul Harold PeGan and Delores Bernadette Feighner:

+ 130 m I. **Harold Leon**[9] **PeGan** was born in Huntington, Huntington Twp., Huntington Co., Indiana on January 27, 1939.[691]

64. Mary Angeline[8] **PeGan** (*Clanzie Herold*[7], *Harrison James*[6], *Harrison James*[5] *Pegan, Robert A.*[4], *Andrew*[3], *Andrew*[2] *Pagan, James*[1]) was born on August 11, 1911, in Lagro, Lagro Twp., Wabash Co., Indiana.[128, 338] She was the daughter of Clanzie Herold PeGan (19) and Josephine Sophia Schetzszle. She was also known as **Angie**. Mary Angeline died in a facility in Edgerton, Fulton Twp., Rock Co., Wisconsin, on November 11, 1993, at age 82.[339, D] She was buried in Hoverstock Cemetery, Zanesville, Union Twp., Wells Co, Indiana.[692, D]

Childless.

Mary Angeline married **Ted Deroy Welch** on May 29, 1940, in Huntington Co., Indiana.[693, 694] Ted Deroy Welch was born in Roanoke, Jackson Twp., Huntington Co., Indiana, on April 23, 1910.[128, 695] He reached age 79 and died in Fort Wayne, Allen Co., Indiana, on August 6, 1989.[128, 696, N] Ted Deroy Welch was buried in Hoverstock Cemetery, Zanesville, Union Twp., Wells Co, Indiana.[697, N]

Although Ted and Mary PeGan Welch had no children of their own, they had a foster son after they moved to Wisconsin. They remained close to him until the end of their lives.

Mary Angeline PeGan Welch was a woman ahead of her time. She was a savvy businesswoman who worked for a Huntington, Indiana bank. When the bank would repossess a house, Mary would sometimes invest in it for a rental property. She owned one on Mayne Street in Huntington where a boyfriend and some of his family members lived. But in 1939, when her parents separated and her mother and some of her brothers needed a place to live, Mary evicted the now ex-boyfriend and his family and moved her own family in. Eventually, her parents Clanzie and Josephine Schetzszle PeGan reconciled, and Mary sold the home to them.

In 1946, Clanzie and Josephine sold it. Mary, then married to Ted Welch and residing in Wisconsin Dells, Wisconsin, negotiated an agreement where she and her father bought another house at 1129 William Street, and Mary traded one of her rental houses in as a down payment.[83]

But her relationship with her father soured when her father separated from her mother and moved in with his paramour, Loretta Kastner Sellers, whom he later married. Mary's brother Hugh Frederick "Fritz" PeGan said that after their mother Josephine died in 1953, Mary claimed the William Street house was hers. She sold it and kept the money, incensing her father, Leo, Paul and Kenny.[83] Patricia Keefe PeGan, wife of Mary's brother Kenneth, told a different version: Mary and Ted were to share the money from the house sale with Clanzie. Also, there was a life insurance policy on Josephine, and some of Josephine's brothers thought all the children should share the insurance payout with their father. Mary and Ted talked Clanzie into investing all the money into some sort of uranium prospecting deal, perhaps arranged by one of Josephine's brothers, who lived in South Dakota and worked in the uranium industry. But the investment failed, and the money lost.[328]

In any case, this financial fiasco caused a family rift.. Mary had no further contact with her father and did not return for his funeral. She had no contact with anyone else in the family except Fritz for 25 years until 1977, when she and Ted moved back to Indiana and bought a house in New Haven, Allen Co., Indiana. Then she reconciled with her brothers Paul and Kenneth.[83]

Following Ted's death in 1989, Mary moved back to Wisconsin Dells. When her health started failing, she relocated to Janesville, Rock Co., Wisconsin and lived with her foster son and his family until she died.[83]

65. **Hugh Frederick⁸ PeGan** (*Clanzie Herold⁷, Harrison James⁶, Harrison James⁵ Pegan, Robert A.⁴, Andrew³, Andrew² Pagan, James¹*) was born on October 19, 1914, in Huntington Twp., Huntington Co., Indiana.[128, 340] He was also known as **Fritz**. He was the son of Clanzie Herold PeGan (19) and Josephine Sophia Schetzszle. Hugh Frederick died in Huntington, Huntington Twp., Huntington Co., Indiana, on February 23, 2008, at age 93.[128, 340] He was buried in Mount Calvary Cemetery, Huntington Twp., Huntington Co., Indiana.[698]

Hugh Frederick married **Rosemary Josephine Etter** on May 24, 1941, in Huntington Co., Indiana.[699, 700] They had eight children. Rosemary Josephine Etter was born in Indianapolis, Marion Co., Indiana, on May 22, 1918.[128, 701, 702] Rosemary Josephine reached age 79 and died in Huntington, Huntington Twp., Huntington Co., Indiana, on February 14, 1998.[128, 701] She was buried in Mount Calvary Cemetery, Huntington Twp., Huntington Co., Indiana.[703]

Hugh Frederick PeGan, always called "Fritz", was the maintenance engineer at St. Mary's School and Huntington Catholic High School for many years. He had an interest in antiques and did marvelous refinishing and restoration work on furniture. Fritz and Rosie were beloved by everyone. They were the "salt of the earth". Rosemary loved having company and talking to people. Her door was always open and her coffepot full. They were truly wonderful people.

Hugh Frederick "Fritz" PeGan and Rosemary Josephine Etter had eight children, including:

+ 131   f   III.   **Daughter⁹ Pegan** was born in Huntington, Huntington Twp., Huntington Co., Indiana.

+ 131A m   IV.   **John Frederick⁹ PeGan** was born in Huntington, Huntington Twp., Huntington Co., Indiana, on November 18, 1947.[704, 705] He died in a hospital in Cleveland, Cuyahoga Co., Ohio, on April 29, 2012.[705]

+ 132   m   V.   **Son⁹ PeGan** was born in Huntington, Huntington Twp., Huntington Co., Indiana.

66. **Kenneth Austin Joseph⁸ PeGan** (*Clanzie Herold⁷, Harrison James⁶, Harrison James⁵ Pegan, Robert A.⁴, Andrew³, Andrew² Pagan, James¹*) was born on November 11, 1916, in Huntington Twp., Huntington Co., Indiana.[128, 341, 342, 343, 344] He was the son of Clanzie Herold PeGan (19) and Josephine Sophia Schetzszle. He died in a facility in Fort Wayne, Allen Co., Indiana, on July 9, 1985, at age 68.[341, 342, 344] Kenneth Austin Joseph was buried in Mount Calvary Cemetery, Huntington Twp., Huntington Co., Indiana.[341, 342, 706]

Kenneth Austin Joseph despised his actual middle name, Austin, and always used his Roman Catholic confirmation name, Joseph, as his legal middle name.

Kenneth Austin Joseph married **Margaret June Kilty** on May 1, 1943, in Huntington Co., Indiana.[707, 708] They had no children. Margaret June Kilty was born in Bippus, Warren Twp., Huntington Co., Indiana, on June 28, 1918.[709, 710] She was also known as **June**. Margaret June reached age 25 and died in Fort Wayne, Allen Co., Indiana, on January 31, 1944.[709] She was buried in Mount Calvary Cemetery, Huntington Twp., Huntington Co., Indiana.[711]

Kenneth Austin Joseph PeGan married **Patricia Ann Keefe** on August 16, 1947, in Huntington Co., Indiana.[712, 713] They had five children. Patricia Ann Keefe was born in Huntington, Huntington Twp., Huntington Co., Indiana, on March 31, 1926.[714, 715, 716] Patricia Ann reached age 69 and died in Huntington, Huntington Twp., Huntington Co., Indiana, on January 10, 1996.[714, 715] She was buried in Mount Calvary Cemetery, Huntington Twp., Huntington Co., Indiana.[715, 717]

Kenneth Austin Joseph PeGan served as a captain the U.S. Army Air Corps during WWII. His main occupation was a teacher and the basketball and baseball coach at Huntington Catholic High School. He and his Huntington Catholic Ramblers won the Huntington sectional in the Indiana High School Athletic Association tournament in 1949.

67. Phillip Elsworth[8] **PeGan II** (*Philip Garl*[7], *Harrison James*[6], *Harrison James*[5] *Pegan*, *Robert A.*[4], *Andrew*[3], *Andrew*[2] *Pagan*, *James*[1]) was born on September 22, 1923, in Denver, Jefferson Twp., Miami Co., Indiana.[351, 355, 356] He was the son of Philip Garl PeGan (22) and Dorothy Margaret Vermilyer (Fry). Phillip Elsworth died in Niles, Niles Twp. Berrien Co., Michigan, on October 3, 2012, at age 89.[349, 356] He was buried in Chapel Hill Memorial Gardens, Osceola, Penn Twp., St. Joseph Co., Indiana.[718]

Phillip Elsworth married **Josephine Clara Lewis** on October 10, 1942, in Berrien Co., Michigan.[355] They had four children. Josephine Clara Lewis was born in South Bend, St. Joseph Co., Indiana, on July 24, 1923.[128, 719] Josephine Clara reached age 86 and died in Niles, Niles Twp., Berrien Co., Michigan, on October 2, 2009.[128, 719] She was buried in Chapel Hill Memorial Gardens, Osceola, Penn Twp., St. Joseph Co., Indiana.[720]

Phillip Ellsworth PeGan served in the U.S. Army in World War II as a cook; in 1942, he was sent to Camp Gordon, Georgia, then Germany, France and Belgium. He was discharged in 1945 with the rank of sargeant.[113]

Phillip Elsworth PeGan II and Josephine Clara Lewis had four children, including:

+ 133 m I. **Robert Phillip**[9] **PeGan** was born in Niles, Niles Twp., Berrien Co., Michigan, on September 24, 1943.[128, 721] He died in a hospital in Elkhart, Elkhart Co., Indiana, on October 14, 2010.[128, 721]

+ 134 m II. **Son**[9] **PeGan** was born in Niles, Niles Twp., Berrien Co., Michigan.

+ 135 f III. **Daughter**[9] **PeGan** was born in Niles, Niles Twp., Berrien Co., Michigan.

+ 136 m IV. **Son Two**[9] **PeGan** was born in Niles, Niles Twp., Berrien Co., Michigan..

68. Raymond Leon[8] **PeGan** (*Philip Garl*[7], *Harrison James*[6], *Harrison James*[5] *Pegan*, *Robert A.*[4], *Andrew*[3], *Andrew*[2] *Pagan*, *James*[1]) was born on September 6, 1924, in Akron, Henry Twp., Miami Co., Indiana.[128, 357, 358] He was the son of Philip Garl PeGan (22) and Dorothy Margaret Vermilyer (Fry).He lived in 1997 in Niles, Niles Twp., Berrien Co., Michigan. Raymond Leon died in a hospital in South Bend, St. Joseph Co., Indiana, on April 8, 1997, at age 72.[128, 357] He was buried in Sliverbrook Cemetery, Niles, Niles Twp., Berrien Co., Michigan.[722]

Raymond Leon married **Doris Irene Fitz** on September 7, 1946, in Williams Co., Ohio.[723] They had six children. Doris Irene Fitz was born in Mishawaka, Penn Twp., St. Joseph Co., Indiana, on November 16, 1928.[128, 349, 724] Doris Irene reached age 81 and died in Niles, Niles Twp., Berrien Co., Michigan, on June 26, 2010.[128, 724] She was buried in Smith's Chapel Cemetery, Milton Twp., Cass Co., Michigan.[725]

Raymond Leon PeGan married Mrs. **Margaret Josephine Pfefferle** Scarbury on July 14, 1972, in St. Joseph Co., Indiana.[726, 727] Margaret Josephine Pfefferle was born in Bremen, German Twp., Marshall Co., Indiana, on July 31, 1926.[728, 729] She was also known as **Marge**. Margaret Josephine reached 91 years of age and died in Niles, Niles Twp. Berrien Co., Michigan, on August 3, 2017.[728] She was buried in Silverbrook Cemetery, Niles, Niles Twp., Berrien Co., Michigan.[730]

Raymond Leon PeGan and Doris Irene Fitz had six children, including:

+ 137 m V. **John Allen**[9] **PeGan** was born in Niles, Niles Twp., Berrien Co., Michigan, on December 7, 1956.[349, 731, 732] He died in Niles, Niles Twp., Berrien Co., Michigan, on April 19, 1972.[349, 731, 732]

69. Donna Belle[8] **PeGan** (*Philip Garl*[7], *Harrison James*[6], *Harrison James*[5] *Pegan, Robert A.*[4], *Andrew*[3], *Andrew*[2] *Pagan, James*[1]) was born on February 23, 1926, in Denver, Jefferson Twp., Miami Co., Indiana.[128, 359] She was also known as **Donnabelle.** She was the daughter of Philip Garl PeGan (22) and Dorothy Margaret Vermilyer (Fry). Donna Belle lived in 1987 in Niles, Niles Twp. Berrien Co., Michigan. She died in a hospital in South Bend, St. Joseph Co., Indiana, on November 14, 1987, at age 61.[349, 360] Donna Belle was buried in Chapel Hill Memorial Gardens, Osceola, Penn Twp., St. Joseph Co., Indiana.[733]

Donna Belle married **George Richard Reed** on February 16, 1946, in Berrien Co., Michigan.[734] They had six children. George Richard Reed was born in Gary, Lake Co., Indiana, on July 9, 1922.[128, 349, 734] He was also known as **Dick**. George Richard reached age 75 and died in New Port Richey, Pasco Co., Florida, on August 1, 1997.[128, 349, 735] He was cremated.[735]

Donna Belle PeGan and George Richard Reed had six children, including:

+ 138 m IV. **Brian Lee**[9] **Reed** was born in Watervliet, Watervliet Charter Twp., Berrien Co., Michigan, on August 15, 1958.[128, 349, 736] He died in Watervliet, Watervliet Charter Twp., Berrien Co., Michigan, on March 25, 2011.[128, 349, 736]

70. Richard Schuyler[8] **PeGan** (*Philip Garl*[7], *Harrison James*[6], *Harrison James*[5] *Pegan, Robert A.*[4], *Andrew*[3], *Andrew*[2] *Pagan, James*[1]) was born on April 6, 1928, in Denver, Jefferson Twp., Miami Co., Indiana.[128, 353, 361, 362] He was also known as **Dick**. He was the son of Philip Garl PeGan (22) and Dorothy Margaret Vermilyer (Fry). Richard Schuyler died in Pulaski, Giles Co., Tennessee, on September 17, 2001, at age 73.[361, 363, 364] He was buried in Silverbrook Cemetery, Niles, Niles Twp., Berrien Co., Michigan.[363, 364]

Richard Schuyler married **Dorothy Arilla Young** on April 10, 1948, in Berrien Co., Michigan.[349, 364] They had five children. Dorothy Arilla Young was born in Howard Twp., Cass Co., Michigan?, on November 24, 1927.[737] Dorothy Arilla lived in 2012 in Niles, Niles Twp. Berrien Co., Michigan. She reached age 84 and died in a hospital in South Bend, St. Joseph Co., Indiana, on August 4, 2012.[737] Dorothy Arilla was buried in Silverbrook Cemetery, Niles, Niles Twp., Berrien Co., Michigan.[738]

Although her obituary verifies her date of birth, it states that she was born in Berrien Co., Michigan. Her parents were living in Howard Twp., Cass Co., Michigan in 1930. *(Census Place: Howard, Cass, Michigan; Page: 7A; Enumeration District: 0005; entry for "Dorotha" Young, Claud Young, head of household).*

Richard Schuyler PeGan and Dorothy Arilla Young had five children, including:

+ 139 f I. **Katherine Jean**[9] **PeGan** was born in Niles, Niles Twp., Berrien Co., Michigan, on August 9, 1949.[349, 739] She was also known as **Kay**. Katherine Jean died in Maury Co., Tennessee, on August 25, 2001.[349, 739]

+ 140 f II. **Sue Ann**[9] **PeGan** was born in Niles, Niles Twp., Berrien Co., Michigan, on November 21, 1950.[128, 349, 740, 741] She died in Niles, Niles Twp., Berrien Co., Michigan, on October 20, 1998.[349, 741, 742]

+ 141 m III. **Richard Allen**[9] **PeGan** was born in Niles, Niles Twp., Berrien Co., Michigan, on March 4, 1952.[128, 349, 743, 744] He died in Prospect, Giles Co., Tennessee, on March 8, 2002. [128, 349, 743, 744]

+ 142 f IV. **Claudine Louise⁹ PeGan** was born in Niles, Niles Twp., Berrien Co., Michigan, on September 1, 1955.[349, 745] She died in Niles, Niles Twp., Berrien Co., Michigan, on September 3, 1955.[349, 745]

71. Karl Nelson⁸ PeGan (*Philip Garl⁷, Harrison James⁶, Harrison James⁵ Pegan, Robert A.⁴, Andrew³, Andrew² Pagan, James¹*) was born on June 2, 1929, in Mishawaka, Penn Twp., St. Joseph Co., Indiana.[354, 365] He was the son of Philip Garl PeGan (22) and Dorothy Margaret Vermilyer (Fry). Karl Nelson died in Niles Twp., Berrien Co., Michigan, on December 28, 1952, at age 23.[349, 365, 366] He was buried in Chapel Hill Memorial Gardens, Osceola, Penn Twp., St. Joseph Co., Indiana.[746]

Karl Nelson married **Elodie Lucy Turenne** on January 6, 1951, in St. Joseph Co., Indiana.[349, 747] They had two sons. Elodie Lucy Turenne was born in Marquette, Marquette Twp., Marquette Co., Michigan, on November 15, 1933.[349, 748, 749] Elodie Lucy reached age 60 and died in Laurel, Laurel Twp., Franklin Co., Indiana, on January 26, 1994.[748, 749] She was buried in Laurel North Cemetery, Laurel, Laurel Twp., Franklin Co., Indiana.[748, 750]

Karl Nelson PeGan and two friends, one the brother of Josephine Clara Lewis PeGan, the wife of Karl's eldest brother Phillip Elsworth PeGan, were fishing the night of December 28, 1952 on the St. Joseph River when their boat overturned. They all drowned. His elder son Steven was only a year old, and his wife was seven months pregnant with their younger son, Nelson, when Karl died.[366]

After Karl PeGan died, Elodie married to Robert S. McCoy.[349] Following his death, she married Mr. Bailey.[751] They divorced. Her last husband was Roy Herman Hunter, whom she married in 1986.[752]

Sons of Karl Nelson PeGan and Elodie Lucy Turenne:

+ 143 m I. **Steven Karl⁹ PeGan** was born in Niles, Niles Twp., Berrien Co., Michigan, on December 13, 1951.[128, 349, 753, 754] He died in Indianapolis, Marion Co., Indiana, on April 6, 2004.[128, 754]

+ 144 m II. **Nelson Michael⁹ PeGan** was born in Niles, Niles Twp., Berrien Co., Michigan, on February 19, 1953.[128, 349, 755, 756] He died in a hospital in Connersville, Connersville Twp., Fayette Co., Indiana, on May 20, 1999.[128, 349, 755, 756]

72. Robert Harrison⁸ PeGan (*Philip Garl⁷, Harrison James⁶, Harrison James⁵ Pegan, Robert A.⁴, Andrew³, Andrew² Pagan, James¹*) was born on June 8, 1930, in Mishawaka, Penn Twp., St. Joseph Co., Indiana.[367, 368] He was the son of Philip Garl PeGan (22) and Dorothy Margaret Vermilyer (Fry). Robert Harrison died in Mishawaka, Penn Twp., St. Joseph Co., Indiana, on March 29, 1931.[367, 368] He was buried in Fairview Cemetery, Mishawaka, Penn Twp., St. Joseph Co., Indiana.[368, 757]

73. Juanita Mae⁸ PeGan (*Philip Garl⁷, Harrison James⁶, Harrison James⁵ Pegan, Robert A.⁴, Andrew³, Andrew² Pagan, James¹*) was born on September 22, 1931, in Mishawaka, Penn Twp., St. Joseph Co., Indiana.[352, 369] She was the daughter of Philip Garl PeGan (22) and Dorothy Margaret Vermilyer (Fry). Juanita Mae died in Niles, Niles Twp. Berrien Co., Michigan, on July 30, 2015, at age 83.[349, 369] She was buried in Rose Hill Cemetery, Berrien Springs, Okonoko Twp., Berrien Co., Michigan.[369]

Juanita Mae married **Eugene Lyle Abbott** on December 9, 1951, in St. Joseph Co., Indiana.[758] They had two children. Eugene Lyle Abbott was born in Paw Paw, Van Buren Co., Michigan, on July 11, 1925.[128, 349, 759, 760] Eugene Lyle Abbott reached age 65 and died a hospital in South Bend, St. Joseph Co., Indiana, on October 4, 1990.[128, 349, 759, 760] He was buried in Rose Hill Cemetery, Berrien Springs, Okonoko Twp., Berrien Co., Michigan.[761]

Juanita Mae PeGan and Eugene Lyle Abbott had two children, including:

+ 145 f I. **Constance Sue⁹ Abbott** was born in Niles, Niles Twp., Berrien Co.,

Michigan, on November 27, 1952.[349, 762] She was also known as **Connie**. Constance Sue died in Niles, Niles Twp. Berrien Co., Michigan, on July 8, 2017.[349, 762]

74. Darlene Kay[8] **PeGan** (*Philip Garl*[7]*, Harrison James*[6]*, Harrison James*[5] *Pegan, Robert A.*[4]*, Andrew*[3]*, Andrew*[2] *Pagan, James*[1]) was born on September 22, 1931, in Mishawaka, Penn Twp., St. Joseph Co., Indiana.[352, 369] She is the daughter of Philip Garl PeGan (22) and Dorothy Margaret Vermilyer (Fry).

Darlene Kay married **Buddy Lynn Stanley** on August 6, 1954, in St. Joseph Co., Indiana.[763] They had five children. Buddy Lynn Stanley was born in Marion, Crainville Twp., Williamson Co., Illinois, on November 29, 1933.[303]

75. Vern Leroy[8] **PeGan** (*Philip Garl*[7]*, Harrison James*[6]*, Harrison James*[5] *Pegan, Robert A.*[4]*, Andrew*[3]*, Andrew*[2] *Pagan, James*[1]) was born on May 20, 1940, in Niles, Niles Twp., Berrien Co., Michigan.[303] He is the son of Philip Garl PeGan (22) and Dorothy Margaret Vermilyer (Fry).

Vern Leroy married **Miss Heckelbower**. They divorced. They had two sons.

Vern Pegan married twice more.

Vern Leroy PeGan and Miss Heckelbower had two sons, includlling:

+ 146 m I. **Son**[9] **PeGan** was born in Niles, Niles Twp., Berrien Co., Michigan.

9th Generation

76. Leota Fatima⁹ Roll (*Bertha Olive⁸ Farr, Clara Belle⁷ Roush, Margaret Mary⁶ Pegan, Harrison James⁵, Robert A.⁴, Andrew³, Andrew² Pagan, James¹*) was born on July 2, 1903, in Washington Twp., Blackford Co., Indiana.[387, 388] She was the daughter of Marion William Roll and Bertha Olive Farr (23). Leota Fatima died in Bluffton, Wells Co., Indiana, on October 12, 1965, at age 62.[387, 389] She was buried in Fairview Cemetery, Bluffton, Wells Co., Indiana.[764]

Leota Fatima Roll Lydy's death certificate says she was born in 1904, but other sources and census information say 1903.[387, 388, 389] On her marriage license, Leota says she was born in 1902.[765]

Leota Roll had a relationship with **Unknown Unknown**. Their daughter Margaret, born in 1920, was raised by her grandmother, Bertha Olive Roll Bartleymay Roll, as her own daughter.[766]

Leota Fatima married **Charles Wesley Lydy** on September 11, 1920, in Wells Co., Indiana.[767] They divorced. They had seven children. Charles Wesley Lydy was born in Frankfort, Center Twp., Clinton Co., Indiana, on May 31, 1893.[128, 768, 769, 770] Charles Wesley was living in 1966 in Fort Wayne, Allen Co., Indiana. He reached age 75 and died in a hospital in Marion, Center Twp., Grant Co., Indiana, on December 26, 1968.[769, 770, 771] Charles Wesley was buried in Oak Lawn Cemetery, Ossian, Jefferson Twp., Wells Co., Indiana.[769, 770, 771]

Charles and Leota Roll Lydy are enumerated in Lancaster Twp., Wells Co., Indiana in 1930 (*Census Place: Lancaster, Wells, Indiana; Roll: 638; Page: 3A; Enumeration District: 14; Image: 805.0*). Charles Lydy, age 36, is a sander at a furniture factory who says he and his parents were born in Indiana. Leota F. Roll Lydy is 28 years old and says she and her father were born in Indiana and her mother in Ohio. The couple state they were first married at ages 27 and 17 respectively. Children in the home are: Agnes, eight, Wayne, seven, Robert, six, Dale, three years and eleven months, and "Freta", two years and three months. All the children were born in Indiana.

In 1940, Charles and Leota Roll Lydy are found in Poneto, Harrison Twp., Wells Co., Indiana (*Census Place: Poneto, Wells, Indiana; Roll: T627_1110; Page: 1B; Enumeration District: 90-19*). In the household are Charles Lydy, age 46, a truck driver for the Indiana State Highway Department; his wife, Leota Roll Lydy, 35, and their children "Louise", 18, who does housework in a private home; "Wayne", 17, an apprentice in a tin shop; Robert, 16, Dale, 14, "Freda", 12, and "Joan", nine. All were born in Indiana, and say they were living in Bluffton, Wells Co., Indiana in 1935. Their home is on Grape Street, but no house number is given.

After residing in Fort Wayne, Allen Co., Indiana for some years, Charles Lydy Sr. was a resident of the Veterans Hospital complex in Marion, Center Twp., Grant Co., Indiana from 1966 until he died.[770, 771]

Children of Leota Fatima Roll and Unknown Unknown:

+ 147 f I. **Margaret L.¹⁰ Roll** was born in Lancaster Twp., Wells Co., Indiana, on February 26, 1920.[128, 766] She died in Port Orange, Volusia Co., Florida, on August 30, 2008.[128, 772]

Children of Leota Fatima Roll and Charles Wesley Lydy:

+ 148 f I. **Agnes Louise¹⁰ Lydy** was born in Bluffton, Wells Co., Indiana, on January 3, 1922.[128, 773, 774, 775] She was also known as **Louise** and **Bonnie**. Agnes Louise died in Bluffton, Wells Co., Indiana, on April 1, 1995.[128, 773, 774]

+ 149 m II. **Charles Wayne¹⁰ Lydy II** was born in Lancaster Twp., Wells Co., Indiana, on February 27, 1923.[776, 777, 778] He was also known as **Wayne**. Charles Wayne died in Bluffton, Wells Co., Indiana, on March 8, 2016.[777]

+ 150 m III. **Robert Eugene¹⁰ Lydy** was born in Lancaster Twp., Wells Co., Indiana, on April 1, 1924.[779]

+ 151 m IV. **Dale Edmund or Edmond**[10] **Lydy** was born in Lancaster Twp., Wells Co., Indiana, on April 25, 1926.[128, 780, 781] He died in a hospital in Fort Wayne, Allen Co., Indiana, on February 2, 1998.[128, 780, 782]

+ 152 f V. **Freida Mae**[10] **Lydy** was born in Lancaster Twp., Wells Co., Indiana, on January 26, 1928.[783, 784]

+ 153 f VI. **Bonnie Ilene**[10] **Lydy** was born in Lancaster Twp., Wells Co., Indiana, on January 17, 1929.[785, 786] She died in Murray, Lancaster Twp., Wells Co., Indiana on June 3, 1929.[785, 787]

+ 154 f VII. **Olive Joan**[10] **Lydy** was born in Murray, Lancaster Twp., Wells Co., Indiana, on April 20, 1930.[128, 788, 789, 790] She was also known as Joan. Olive Joan died in Bluffton, Wells Co., Indiana, on December 1, 1998.[128, 788, 789]

77. Edmund Warren[9] **Roll** (*Bertha Olive*[8] *Farr, Clara Belle*[7] *Roush, Margaret Mary*[6] *Pegan, Harrison James*[5]*, Robert A.*[4]*, Andrew*[3]*, Andrew*[2] *Pagan, James*[1]) was born on April 25, 1907, in Washington Twp., Blackford Co., Indiana.[128, 390, 391] He was the son of Marion William Roll and Bertha Olive Farr (23). Edmund Warren died in Kokomo, Center Twp., Howard Co., Indiana, on February 11, 1974, at age 66.[390, 391, 392] He was buried in Sunset Memory Garden Cemetery. Kokomo, Center Twp., Howard Co., Indiana.[391, 392]

Edmund Warren married Mrs. **Edna Mae Andrews** Moffitt on September 1, 1925, in Marion Co., Indiana. They divorced. They had no children. Edna Mae Andrews was born in Indianapolis, Marion Co., Indiana on January 22, 1898.[793] Edna Mae reached age 65 and died in Indianapolis, Marion Co., Indiana on September 26, 1965.[793] She is buried in New Crown Cemetery, Indianapolis, Marion Co., Indiana.[763]

In 1930, Edmund W. Roll is enumerated in Indianapolis, Warren Twp., Marion Co., Indiana (*Census Place: Indianapolis, Marion, Indiana; Roll: 613; Page: 6B; Enumeration District: 391; Image: 74.0*). Edmund W. Roll, listed as age 27 (he is 23), says he and his father were born in Indiana and his mother in Ohio. He has a wife, Edna M. Moffit Roll, 31, born Indiana, with her father born in Indiana and her mother in Missouri. The couple says they were first wed at ages 21 and 20 respectively. Edmund's occupation is laborer in a garage.

om Edmund Roll, Edna Mae Andrews Moffitt Roll married William Bollinger and died under the name Edna Mae Bollinger.[763]

Edmund Warren Roll married Mrs. **Corenne M. Becker** Baker before 1938.[794] They divorced. They had no children. Corena M. Becker was born in Bingham Twp., Clinton Co., Michigan?, in 1904. She reached age 49 and died in Lansing, Ingham Co., Michigan?, in 1953. Corena M. was buried in Mount Rest Cemetery, St. Johns, Bingham Twp., Clinton Co., Michigan.[795]

Edmund Warren Roll is listed as "E.W." Roll in 1940 in Kokomo, Center Twp., Howard Co., Indiana (*Census Place: Kokomo, Howard, Indiana; Roll: T627_1053; Page: 10B; Enumeration District: 34-20A*). Edmund, age 33, born Indiana, is the manager at Goodyear Rubber. He is with a second wife, "Corinna", 36, born in Michigan. They state they were both living in Rushville, Rushville Twp., Rush Co., Indiana in 1935. Their home in at 1506 South Washington Street.

Edmund Warren Roll married **Myrtle Mildred Gustafson** on January 20, 1949, in New York, King's Co., New York.[796] They had one daughter. Myrtle Mildred Gustafson was born in Webster, Day Co., South Dakota, on February 14, 1907.[796, 797, 798, 799] Myrtle Mildred reached age 62 and died in Kokomo, Center Twp., Howard Co., Indiana, on April 19, 1969.[796, 797, 798] She was buried in Sunset Memory Garden Cemetery. Kokomo, Center Twp., Howard Co., Indiana.[797, 798]

Edmund Roll's obituary mentions only one child, daughter born to Myrtle Gustafson Roll, his third and last wife. Although Myrtle's obituary says she and Edmund were married on January 20, 1949 in New York City, a wedding article appeared in the *Kokomo (IN) Tribune* on January 19, 1949 that said the couple had been married on January 18, 1949. [796, 800]

Edmund's Social Security Death Index entry is under E. Roll. [128]

78. Thelma Lynn⁹ Roll (*Bertha Olive⁸ Farr, Clara Belle⁷ Roush, Margaret Mary⁶ Pegan, Harrison James⁵, Robert A.⁴, Andrew³, Andrew² Pagan, James¹*) was born on July 18, 1911, in Washington Twp., Blackford Co., Indiana. [128, 393, 394] She was also known as **Lynn**. She was the daughter of Marion William Roll and Bertha Olive Farr (23). Thelma Lynn died in Huntington, Huntington Twp., Huntington Co., Indiana, on August 31, 1999, at age 88. [128, 395] She was buried in Fairview Cemetery, Bluffton, Wells Co., Indiana. [801]

Childless.

In 1930, Thelma Roll is an inmate in the Indiana Girls School in Wayne Twp., Marion Co., Indiana (*Census Place: Wayne, Marion, Indiana; Roll: 617; Page: 3B; Enumeration District: 290; Image: 496.0*). Thelma is age 18, single, and says she and her father were born in Indiana and her mother in Ohio.

Thelma Lynn married **Unknown Long** before 1939. [393] They divorced.

Thelma Lynn Roll Long married **Melvin Charles Kennedy** on November 5, 1941, in Wells Co., Indiana. [393] Melvin Charles Kennedy was born in Huntington, Huntington Twp., Huntington Co., Indiana, on April 7, 1901. [128, 393, 802] He was also known as **Red**. He reached age 93 and died in Huntington, Huntington Twp., Huntington Co., Indiana, on March 30, 1995. [128, 802] Melvin Charles was buried in Fairview Cemetery, Bluffton, Wells Co., Indiana. [802, 803]

Melvin Kennedy worked as a projectionist at the Huntington Theater, Huntington, Indiana.

79. Marian Colleen⁹ Roll (*Bertha Olive⁸ Farr, Clara Belle⁷ Roush, Margaret Mary⁶ Pegan, Harrison James⁵, Robert A.⁴, Andrew³, Andrew² Pagan, James¹*) was born on February 12, 1918, in Marion, Center Twp., Grant Co., Indiana. [396, 397, 398] She was the daughter of Marion William Roll and Bertha Olive Farr (23). Marian Colleen died in Bluffton, Wells Co., Indiana, on February 23, 1964, at age 46. [396, 398] She was buried in Fairview Cemetery, Bluffton, Wells Co., Indiana. [804]

Her middle name is sometimes seen as Coleen.

In 1930, 12-year-old Marian C. Roll is listed as a boarder in the home of Sarah Patterson, 81, in Lancaster Twp., Wells Co., *Indiana (Census Place: Lancaster, Wells, Indiana; Roll: 638; Page: 10A; Enumeration District: 13; Image: 793.0)*. They are the only two people in the household. Marian is listed as born in Indiana, with her father also born in Indiana and her mother in Ohio.

Marian Colleen married **Earl Alfred Bender** on November 4, 1938, in Allen Co., Indiana. [396, 397] They had two daughters. Earl Alfred Bender was born in Craigville, Lancaster Twp., Wells Co., Indiana, on August 29, 1913. [397, 805, 806] Earl Alfred reached age 53 and died in Bluffton, Wells Co., Indiana, on September 28, 1966. [805, 806] He was buried in Fairview Cemetery, Bluffton, Wells Co., Indiana. [805, 806]

Earl Alfred Bender and Marion Colleen Roll obtained their marriage license in Wells County, Indiana, but married in Fort Wayne, Allen Co., Indiana. [396]

Earl and Marian C. Roll Bender are found in Bluffton, Wells Co., Indiana in 1940 (*Census Place: Bluffton, Wells, Indiana; Roll: T627_1110; Page: 13A; Enumeration District: 90-4*). Earl Bender, 26, is a laborer in a bakery. His wife, Marian C. Roll Bender is 22 years old. They have a one-month old daughter, Sharon. All were born in Indiana, and Earl and Marian say they were living in Bluffton in 1935. Their home address is 658 South Bond Street.

Daughters of Marian Colleen Roll and Earl Alfred Bender:

+ 155 f I. **Sharon Yvonne¹⁰ Bender** was born in Bluffton, Wells Co., Indiana, on February 4, 1940. [808, 809] She died in Bluffton, Wells Co., Indiana, on May 14, 2013. [808]

+ 156 f II. **Daughter**[10] **Bender** was born in Bluffton, Wells Co., Indiana.

80. Clyde Cisco[9] **Hunter** (*John Clark*[8], *Clara Belle*[7] *Roush, Margaret Mary*[6] *Pegan, Harrison James*[5], *Robert A.*[4], *Andrew*[3], *Andrew*[2] *Pagan, James*[1]) was born on January 22, 1914, in New Market Twp., Highland Co., Ohio.[128, 407] He was the son of John Clark Hunter (24) and Rosa Mae Wilkin. Clyde Cisco lived in 1965 in Cynthiana, Perry Twp., Pike Co., Ohio. He died in Hillsboro, Liberty Twp., Highland Co., Ohio, on April 9, 1973, at age 59.[407, 408] Clyde Cisco was buried in Hillsboro Cemetery, Hillsboro, Liberty Twp., Highland Co., Ohio.[810]

Clyde Cisco married **Lucille Mildred Whiting** before 1936. They divorced. They had eleven children. Lucille Mildred Whiting was born in Eagle Twp., Brown Co., Ohio, on February 22, 1920.[811, 812] She reached age 73 and died in a hospital in Cincinnati, Hamilton Co., Ohio, on June 27, 1993.[811, 812] Lucille Mildred was buried in New Market Baptist Church Cemetery, New Market Twp., Highland Co., Ohio.[813]

In 1940, Clyde Hunter is enumerated in New Market Twp., Highland Co., Ohio *(Census Place: New Market, Highland, Ohio; Roll: T627_3085; Page: 4A; Enumeration District: 36-23)*. Clyde C. Hunter, age 25, drives a milk truck. With him is his wife, Mildred L. Whiting Hunter, 20, and their two daughters, Mary L., four, and Betty M., two. All were born in Ohio. They are living on Concord Pike, and next door are Clyde's parents, John Clark and Rosa Mae Wilkin Hunter, and Clyde's grandmother, Clara Belle Roush Hunter, Clyde and Mildred say they were Highland County residents in 1935.

Clyde Cisco Hunter married **Mary Alice Dillon** about 1963 in Cynthiana, Pike Co., Ohio? Mary Alice Dillon was born in Hillsboro, Liberty Twp., Highland Co., Ohio, on April 6, 1935.[814, 815, 816] Mary Alice reached age 54 and died in Hillsboro, Liberty Twp., Highland Co., Ohio, on December 1, 1989.[816, 817] She was buried in Green Lawn Cemetery, Columbus, Franklin Co., Ohio.[818]

Clyde Cisco Hunter and Lucille Mildred Whiting had 11 children, including:

+ 157 f I. **Mary Louise**[10] **Hunter** was born in New Market Twp., Highland Co., Ohio, on April 4, 1936.

+ 158 f II. **Betty Mae**[10] **Hunter** was born in New Market Twp., Highland Co., Ohio, on June 13, 1938.

+ 159 f III. **Virginia Ruth**[10] **Hunter** was born in New Market Twp., Highland Co., Ohio, on October 10, 1940.

+ 160 m VIII. **Infant Son**[10] **Hunter** was born in Highland Co., Ohio, on July 7, 1951.[819] He died in Highland Co., Ohio, on July 7, 1951.[819]

80A. Milford Earnest[9] **Baker** *(Nellie Fay Roush*[8], *John Alven*[7], *Margaret Mary*[6] *Pegan, Harrison James*[5], *Robert A.*[4], *Andrew*[3], *Andrew*[2] *Pagan, James*[1]) was born on November 4, 1911, in Monroe Twp., Grant Co., Indiana.[128, H, I] He was also known as **Fred.** He was the son of Leo Ray Baker and Nellie Fay Roush (27). Milford Earnest died on September 18, 1971, in St. Louis, Missouri, at age 59.[128, I, J] Milford Earnest was buried in Mount Hope Cemetery, Lemay, St. Louis Co., Missouri.[I]

Milford Earnest Baker always used "Fred" as his given name as an adult. In his funeral home records, Social Security information, obituary and other documents his name is "Fred E. Baker".

Milford Earnest Baker married **Etta L. Uhls** on December 28, 1931, in Marion Co., Indiana.[O] They divorced. They had one son. Etta L. Uhls was born in Indianapolis, Marion Co., Indiana, on June 20, 1912.[128, P, Q] She reached age 83 and died in Indianapolis, Marion Co., Indiana, on August 23, 1995.[128, Q] Etta L. was buried in Floral Park Cemetery, Indianapolis, Marion Co., Indiana.[Q, R]

Etta married twice more and died as Etta L. Davidson.

Milford Earnest Baker married **Violet Elizabeth Linton** about 1935. They divorced. They had one daughter. Violet Elizabeth Baker was born in Gillespie, Gillespie Twp., Macoupin Co., Illinois(?) on March 6, 1919.[128, S] She reached age 62 and died in St. Louis, Missouri, on March 28, 1981.[128, S, T] Violet E. is buried in Lake Charles Park Cemetery, Bel-Nor, St. Louis Co., Missouri.[S, T]

Violet Elizabeth remarried and died as Violet E. McCain.

Son of Milford Earnest Baker and Etta L. Uhls:

+ 160A m I **Robert Bernard**[10] **Baker** was born in Indianapolis, Marion Co., Indiana, on May 6, 1934.[128, U, V] He died in Tucson, Pima Co., Arizona, on March 26, 1973.[128, V, W]

Daughter of Milford Earnest Baker and Violet Elizabeth Linton:

+ 160B f I **Violet Nordeica**[10] **Baker** was born in St. Louis, Missouri, on November 26, 1935.[X, Y] She died in Tampico, Cuidad Madero, Tamaulipas, Mexico, on June 28, 1960.[Y, Z, AA]

81. Jane[9] **Roush** (*Delbert Leroy*[8], *John Alven*[7], *Margaret Mary*[6] *Pegan, Harrison James*[5], *Robert A.*[4], *Andrew*[3], *Andrew*[2] *Pagan, James*[1]) was born on March 3, 1937, in South Bend, St. Joseph Co., Indiana.[419] She was the daughter of Delbert Leroy Roush (28) and Mary C. Murphy. Jane died in Chicago, Cook Co., Illinois, on December 7, 2004, at age 67.[128]

Jane married **Kenneth Roy Thomas** on November 29, 1959, in Cook Co., Illinois.[820] They had one son. Kenneth Roy Thomas was born in Chicago, Cook Co., Illinois, on August 5, 1930.[821, 822, 823] Kenneth Roy reached age 71 and died in Chicago, Cook Co., Illinois, on April 19, 2002.[128, 823]

82. John Milford[9] **Roush** (*Joseph Lewis*[8], *John Alven*[7], *Margaret Mary*[6] *Pegan, Harrison James*[5], *Robert A.*[4], *Andrew*[3], *Andrew*[2] *Pagan, James*[1]) was born on September 20, 1927, in Fabius Twp., St. Joseph Co., Michigan.[427, 428] He was the son of Joseph Lewis Roush (29) and Edith Ellen Gaut. John Milford lived in 1988 in Fremont, Fremont Twp., Steuben Co., Indiana. He died in a hospital in Fort Wayne, Allen Co., Indiana, on November 18, 1988, at age 61.[427, 428] John Milford was buried in Evergreen Cemetery, Girard Twp., Branch Co., Michigan.[427, 824]

John Milford married **Wanetta Merritt** on January 22, 1946, in Branch Co., Michigan.[825, 826] They divorced. Wanetta Merritt was born in Coldwater, Coldwater Twp., Branch Co., Michigan, on October 7, 1928.[128, 827] She reached age 86 and died in Angola, Pleasant Twp., Steuben Co., Indiana, on October 21, 2014.[128, 827] Wanetta was buried in Flint Cemetery, Angola, Pleasant Twp., Steuben Co., Indiana.[828]

She died under the name Wanetta Ruth Warring.

John Milford Roush was 19 years old and Wanetta Merritt only about 16 when they married. On the marriage license, John states he is age 22 and Wanetta says she is 19. This marriage may have been annulled. In any case, it was short-lived.

John Milford Roush married **Viola Jane Brown** on October 22, 1947, in Morrowville, Washington Co., Kansas.[412] They divorced. They had four children. Viola Jane Brown was born in Arborville, Arborville Twp., York Co., Nebraska, on June 8, 1926.[412, E] She was also known as **Jane**. Viola Jane reached age 91 and died on August 14, 2018 in Coldwater, Coldwater Twp., Branch Co., Michigan.[BB]

John Milford Roush married Mrs. **Marjorie Jean Brown** Wilber on February 14, 1986, in Steuben Co., Indiana.[427, 829] Marjorie Jean Brown was born in Kendallville, Wayne Twp., Noble Co., Indiana, on August 8, 1928.[830] She reached age 88 and died in Angola, Pleasant Twp., Steuben Co., Indiana, on December 28, 2016.[830] Marjorie Jean was buried in Lakeside Cemetery, Fremont, Fremont Twp., Steuben Co., Indiana.[830, 831]

John Milford Roush and Viola Jane Brown had four children, including:

+ 161 m II. **Robert Dean**[10] **Roush** was born in Lincoln, Lancaster Co., Nebraska, on June 29, 1949.[412, 832] He died in a hospital in Kalamazoo, Kalamazoo Twp., Kalamazoo Co., Michigan, on September 10, 2015.[832]

+ 162 m III. **Gary Wayne**[10] **Roush** was born in Lincoln, Lancaster Co., Nebraska, on March 17, 1951.[128, 412, 833] He died in Quincy, Quincy Twp., Branch Co., Michigan, on April 9, 2006.[128, 412, 833]

+ 163 f IV. **Vicky Lynn**[10] **Roush** was born in Coldwater, Coldwater Twp., Branch Co., Michigan, on March 17, 1952.[412, 834] She died in Coldwater, Coldwater Twp., Branch Co., Michigan, on March 24, 2015.[834]

83. George Lewis[9] **Roush** (*Joseph Lewis*[8], *John Alven*[7], *Margaret Mary*[6] *Pegan*, *Harrison James*[5], *Robert A.*[4], *Andrew*[3], *Andrew*[2] *Pagan*, *James*[1]) was born on December 27, 1931, in Fabius Twp., St. Joseph Co., Michigan.[128, 429, 430, 431, 432] He was the son of Joseph Lewis Roush (29) and Edith Ellen Gaut. George Lewis lived in 1978 in China Grove, Rowan Co., North Carolina. He died in a hospital in Salisbury, Rowan Co., North Carolina, on July 16, 1978, at age 46.[429, 430, 431, 432, 433] George Lewis was buried in Salisbury National Cemetery, Salisbury, Rowan Co., North Carolina.[433, 835]

George Lewis married **Miss Smith**. They divorced. They had one son.

George Lewis Roush married **Kathleen Elizabeth Foster** on December 28, 1974, in Rowan Co., North Carolina.[431] Kathleen Elizabeth Foster was born in Miami, Dade Co., Florida, on December 1, 1926.[836, 837, 838] Kathleen Elizabeth reached age 65 and died in Salisbury, Rowan Co., North Carolina, on February 2, 1992.[836, 837, 838] She was buried in Salisbury National Cemetery, Salisbury, Rowan Co., North Carolina.[836, 839]

Son of George Lewis Roush and Miss Smith:

+ 164 m I. **George**[10] **Roush II**. George died before 1978. He seems to have died in infancy.

84. Harley Leroy[9] **Roush** (*Joseph Lewis*[8], *John Alven*[7], *Margaret Mary*[6] *Pegan*, *Harrison James*[5], *Robert A.*[4], *Andrew*[3], *Andrew*[2] *Pagan*, *James*[1]) was born on March 19, 1935, in Fabius Twp., St. Joseph Co., Michigan.[434, 435] He was the son of Joseph Lewis Roush (29) and Edith Ellen Gaut. Harley Leroy died in Niles, Niles Twp. Berrien Co., Michigan, on December 11, 1968, at age 33.[128, 434, 435] He was buried in Bertrand Bible Church Cemetery/Truitts Chapel Cemetery, Niles, Niles Twp. Berrien Co., Michigan.[435, 840]

Harley Leroy married **Shelby Jean Shoup** before 1955. They divorced. They had three children. Shelby Jean Shoup was born in Coldwater, Coldwater Twp., Branch Co., Michigan, on September 7, 1940.[OO, PP] She was also known as **Jean.** She lived in Centerville, Leon Co., Texas in 2018. She reached age 78 and died in a hospital in College Station, Brazos Co., Texas, on November 4, 2018.[OO, PP] Shelby Jean was buried in Centerville Cemetery, Centerville, Leon Co., Texas.[OO, PP]

After divorcing Harley Roush, Shelby Jean Shoup Roush married Unknown Burk and died with that surname.

Shelby Jean Shoup Roush Burk lived in Houston, Harris Co., Texas before moving to Centerville, Texas.

Harley Leroy Roush married Mrs. **Helen Marie Reid** Steinbach on February 13, 1964, in Coconino Co., Arizona.[841] They had two children. Helen Marie Reid was born in Niles, Niles Twp. Berrien Co., Michigan, about March 1930.

Helen Marie Reid Steinbach Roush married Kenneth Dean Fisher after Harley Roush's death.

Harley L. Roush lived in Houston, Harris Co., Texas and Los Angeles, Los Angeles Co., California before returning to Niles, Niles Twp., Berrien Co., Michigan, where he died.

Harley Leroy Roush and Shelby Jean Shoup had three children, including:

+ 165 f I. **Daughter One**[10] **Roush** was born in Coldwater, Coldwater Twp., Branch Co., Michigan.

Harley Leroy Roush and Helen Marie Reid had two children, including:

+ 165A f I. **Daughter Two**[10] **Roush** was born in Orange Co., California.

85. Dorothy H.[9] **Roush** (*George Beard*[8], *Albert Leroy*[7], *Margaret Mary*[6] *Pegan, Harrison James*[5], *Robert A.*[4], *Andrew*[3], *Andrew*[2] *Pagan, James*[1]) was born on October 27, 1917, in Springfield, Springfield Twp., Clark Co., Ohio.[128, 442, 443] She was the daughter of George Beard Roush (32) and Nellie M. Armstrong. Dorothy H. died in Springfield, Springfield Twp., Clark Co., Ohio, on November 26, 1981, at age 64.[443, 444] She was buried in Ferncliff Cemetery, Springfield, Springfield Twp., Clark Co., Ohio.[443, 842]

Childless.

Dorothy H. married **Paul O. Koeb** on October 26, 1940, in Clark Co., Ohio.[843] Paul O. Koeb was born in Springfield, Springfield Twp., Clark Co., Ohio, on May 13, 1908.[69, 844] Paul O. reached age 74 and died in Springfield, Springfield Twp., Clark Co., Ohio, on October 15, 1982.[844, 845] He was buried in Ferncliff Cemetery, Springfield, Springfield Twp., Clark Co., Ohio.[844, 846]

86. Merle Margaret[9] **Roush** (*George Beard*[8], *Albert Leroy*[7], *Margaret Mary*[6] *Pegan, Harrison James*[5], *Robert A.*[4], *Andrew*[3], *Andrew*[2] *Pagan, James*[1]) was born on June 10, 1920, in Springfield, Springfield Twp., Clark Co., Ohio.[445] She was also known as **Margaret**. She was the daughter of George Beard Roush (32) and Nellie M. Armstrong. Merle Margaret died in Springfield, Springfield Twp., Clark Co., Ohio, on September 12, 1923, at age three.[445] She was buried in Ferncliff Cemetery, Springfield, Springfield Twp., Clark Co., Ohio.[445, 847]

Merle Margaret Roush died of burns from a stove fire.[445]

87. George Beard[9] **Roush II** (*George Beard*[8], *Albert Leroy*[7], *Margaret Mary*[6] *Pegan, Harrison James*[5], *Robert A.*[4], *Andrew*[3], *Andrew*[2] *Pagan, James*[1]) was born on December 29, 1921, in Springfield, Springfield Twp., Clark Co., Ohio.[128, 446, 447] He was also known as **Buck**. He was the son of George Beard Roush (32) and Nellie M. Armstrong. George Beard was living in 1974 in Guerneville, Sonoma Co., California. He died in a hospital in Sebastopol, Sonoma Co., California, on March 3, 1974, at age 52.[128, 446, 447] George Beard was buried in Santa Rosa Memorial Park, Santa Rosa, Sonoma Co., California.[446, 848]

George Beard married **Madge Elaine Guyer** in 1945 in Mare Island, Vallejo, Solano Co., California.[849] They had four children. Madge Elaine Guyer was born in Bremerton, Kitsap Co., Washington, on September 1, 1926.[128, 849, 850] She was also known as **Elaine**. Madge Elaine lived in 1974 in Guerneville, Sonoma Co., California. She reached age 82 and died in Healdsburg, Sonoma Co., California, on February 28, 2009.[128, 849, 850] She was cremated and her ashes spread in Santa Rosa Memorial Park Cemetery, Santa Rosa, Sonoma Co., California.[849]

Social Security Index entry is Madg Elaine Roush.[128]

George Beard Roush II and Madge Elaine Guyer had four children, including:

+ 166 m II. **Larry Eugene**[10] **Roush** was born in Hardin Co., Kentucky, on May 28, 1948.[128, 851] He died in Yuma, Yuma Co., Arizona, on July 11, 2011.[128]

88. William Leroy[9] **Roush** (*George Beard*[8], *Albert Leroy*[7], *Margaret Mary*[6] *Pegan, Harrison James*[5], *Robert A.*[4], *Andrew*[3], *Andrew*[2] *Pagan, James*[1]) was born on February 21, 1936, in Springfield, Springfield Twp., Clark Co., Ohio.[128, 448, 449, 450] He was the son of George Beard Roush (32) and Nellie M. Armstrong. William Leroy lived in 1984 in Springfield, Springfield Twp., Clark Co., Ohio. William Leroy died in a hospital in Chillicothe, Ross Co., Ohio, on September 23, 2000, at age 64.[128, 448, 450] He was buried in Dayton National Cemetery, Dayton, Montgomery Co., Ohio.[852, 853]

William Leroy married **Miss Olsen** about 1956. They divorced. They had two children.

William Leroy Roush married **Beatrice A. Shatto?** on July 21, 1973, in Clark Co., Ohio.[854] They divorced. Beatrice A. Shatto? was born about 1933.

William Leroy Roush and Miss Olsen had two children, including:

+ 167 m II. **William Leroy**[10] **Roush II** was born in Wichita, Sedgwick Co., Kansas, on October 17, 1960.[855, 856] He died in Murray, Salt Lake Co., Utah, on October 7, 1991.[855, 856]

89. Harry Emmett[9] **Roush II** (*Harry Emmett*[8], *Eli Kenneth*[7], *Margaret Mary*[6] *Pegan*, *Harrison James*[5], *Robert A.*[4], *Andrew*[3], *Andrew*[2] *Pagan*, *James*[1]) was born on April 4, 1935, in Houston, Harris Co., Texas.[458] He was the son of Harry Emmet Roush (33) and Mary Agnes Ballato.

Childless.

Harry Roush Jr. has lived in Westerly, Rhode Island, Monticello, New York and finally Tamaquah, Pennsylvania.

According to Harry Emmet Roush Jr., his father "fell apart" after his mother (Mary Agnes Bullato Roush) died in 1944 and struggled with alcoholism. The authorities stepped in and removed Harry Jr. and his sister Peggy from the home and placed them in the Washington Co., Rhode Island Children's Home. (This mirrored the life of his own father, Harry Sr., who, along with his two siblings, were place in the Highland Co., Ohio Children's Home in 1908).

Peggy was adopted out and may have even been sold by the Children's Home (as Bullato family members told her brother Harry), to a couple. Mr. and Mrs. White, who had no children. But then this couple had a child of their own, and then they mistreated Peggy.

Harry Jr. "escaped" from the Children's Home. He lied about his age (he was only 15) and joined the army. Harry Roush Jr. served in the Korean War and remained in the army for a while. After his Army discharge, he returned to Rhode Island and started working for the U.S. Postal Service, eventually transferring to Monticello, Town of Thompson, Sullivan Co., New York. Then, in the autumn of 1971, a Bullato relative told Harry Jr. that his father, Harry Roush Sr., was in a Rhode Island state institution. Harry Jr. visited his father, and they reunited. Harry Sr. asked his son if he could come live with him, and Harry Jr. agreed. Harry Jr., who was living in Monticello, New York then, returned home to make arrangements for his father to be moved to his home. Sadly, Harry Roush Sr. died just a few weeks later before he could make the move to New York.

After their father died, Harry Jr. sought for and found his sister Peggy, who had married Edward Sorrel and lived in Ashaway, Washington Co., Rhode Island.

Harry Emmett married **Sally Bachert** on June 6, 1982. Sally Bachert was born in Tamaquah, Schuylkill Co., Pennsylvania, on September 1, 1939.[454]

90. Margaret A.[9] **Roush** (*Harry Emmett*[8], *Eli Kenneth*[7], *Margaret Mary*[6] *Pegan*, *Harrison James*[5], *Robert A.*[4], *Andrew*[3], *Andrew*[2] *Pagan*, *James*[1]) was born on February 18, 1941, in Westerly, Washington Co., Rhode Island.[454] She was also known as **Peggy** and **Margaret A. White**. She was the daughter of Harry Emmett Roush (33) and Mary Agnes Ballato. Margaret A. died in Ashaway, Washington Co., Rhode Island, on December 9, 2014, at age 73.[454]

After her mother, Mary Alice Bullato Roush, died in 1944, Margaret A. "Peggy" Roush and her brother Harry Emmett Roush were either taken away from their father or sent by him to an orphanage/children's home. According to her brother Harry, Bullato relatives told him that his sister was adopted out, perhaps even sold to, a childless couple whose surname was White in 1946. Margaret A. "Peggy" Roush became Margaret A. "Peggy" White. The Whites later had a child of their own. When they did, it seemed they didn't want Peggy anymore and they mistreated her.[454]

Margaret A. married **Edward A. Sorel II** before 1961. They had four children. Edward A. Sorel II was born in Smithfield, Providence Co., Rhode Island, on February 15, 1939.[454]

Margaret A. (Roush) White and Edward A. Sorel II had four children, including:

- 168 f I. **Nancy M.**[10] **Sorel** was born in Providence, Providence Co., Rhode Island, on January 16, 1961.[857] She died in Providence, Providence Co., Rhode Island, on February 3, 2017.[857]

91. **James Donovan**[9] **Bussey** (*Lora Belle*[8] *Roush, Eli Kenneth*[7]*, Margaret Mary*[6] *Pegan, Harrison James*[5]*, Robert A.*[4]*, Andrew*[3]*, Andrew*[2] *Pagan, James*[1]) was born on June 2, 1924, in Boston, Paint Twp., Highland Co., Ohio.[128, 467, 468, 469, 470] He was also known **Don**. He was the son of Hubert Clarence Bussey and Lora Belle Roush (35). James Donovan died in Akron, Summit Co., Ohio, on September 4, 1997, at age 73.[128, 468, 469] He was buried in Hillside Memorial Park Cemetery, Akron, Summit Co., Ohio.[858]

James Donovan Bussey married **Winifred Louise Eiler** on October 5, 1950, in Summit Co., Ohio.[859] They divorced. They had one daughter. Winifred Louise Eiler was born in Harrison Twp., Koscuisko Co., Indiana, on April 6, 1931.[860]

James Donovan Bussey married **Unknown Unknown**. They divorced.

James Donovan Bussey married Mrs. **Barbara Ann Heintzelman** Kelly on February 22, 1964, in Summit Co., Ohio.[861] They divorced. Barbara Ann Heintzelman was born in Akron, Summit Co., Ohio, on June 20, 1928.[128, 862, 863, 864] She lived in 2003 in Cuyahoga Falls, Summit Co., Ohio. Barbara Ann reached age 75 and died in a hospital in Akron, Summit Co., Ohio, on August 17, 2003.[128, 863, 864] She was buried in Greenlawn Memorial Park Cemetery, Akron, Summit Co., Ohio.[865]

She died under the name Barbara A. Kelly.

James Donovan Bussey married **Mary Edythe Starcher** on July 2, 1966, in Summit Co., Ohio.[467] Mary Edythe Starcher was born in Akron, Summit Co., Ohio, on July 27, 1923.[467, 866, 867] Mary Edythe lived in 1999 in Barberton, Summit Co., Ohio. She reached age 76 and died in a hospital in Akron, Summit Co., Ohio, on October 20, 1999.[867] Mary Edythe was buried in Hillside Memorial Park Cemetery, Akron, Summit Co., Ohio.[868]

92. **Mary Ellen**[9] **Bussey** (*Lora Belle*[8] *Roush, Eli Kenneth*[7]*, Margaret Mary*[6] *Pegan, Harrison James*[5]*, Robert A.*[4]*, Andrew*[3]*, Andrew*[2] *Pagan, James*[1]) was born on January 10, 1926, in Boston, Paint Twp., Highland Co., Ohio.[471, 472] She was the daughter of Hubert Clarence Bussey and Lora Belle Roush (35). Mary Ellen died in a hospital in Montgomery, Hamilton Co., Ohio, on March 13, 2006, at age 80.[471, 472]

She married **Glenn A. Moore**. They had three children. Glenn A. Moore was born in Hillsboro, Liberty Twp., Highland Co., Ohio, on February 21, 1927.[869]

Mary Ellen Bussey and Glenn A. Moore had three children, including:

- 169 m III. **Son**[10] **Moore** was born in Hillsboro, Liberty Twp., Highland Co., Ohio.

93. **Rosalee**[9] **Bussey** (*Lora Belle*[8] *Roush, Eli Kenneth*[7]*, Margaret Mary*[6] *Pegan, Harrison James*[5]*, Robert A.*[4]*, Andrew*[3]*, Andrew*[2] *Pagan, James*[1]) was born on March 15, 1928, in Boston, Paint Twp., Highland Co., Ohio.[128, 473, 474, 475] She was the daughter of Hubert Clarence Bussey and Lora Belle Roush (35). Rosalee died in Wewahitchka, Gulf Co., Florida, on March 13, 1991, at age 62.[128, 474, 475, 476]

Childless.

Rosalee married **John Everett Ross** on July 3, 1944, in Highland Co., Ohio.[870] They divorced. John Everett Ross was born in Newport, Campbell Co., Kentucky, on May 23, 1926.[871, 872] John Everett lived in 1954 in Fort Wayne, Allen Co., Indiana. He also resided in 1955 in Defiance, Defiance Co., Ohio. John Everett reached age 29 and died in Charleroi, Washington Co., Pennsylvania, on December 28, 1955.[872] He was buried in Bethany Church Cemetery, Springdale, Mason Co., Kentucky.[873]

John E. Ross and Rosalie Bussey lied on their marriage application. He states he was 22 years old.

He was 18. Rosalie said she was 21 years old, born March 15, 1923. She was only 16.[870]

John Ross' second wife was Eileen Snead Wilkin, first wife of Charles Edgar Wilkin, another Pegan descendant (Henry Pegan chapter, #171).

A truck driver, John Everett Ross died of accidental carbon monoxide poisoning while on the road. He was sleeping in the cab with the motor running at a truck stop in Charleroi, Pennsylvania. He had just moved from Fort Wayne, Allen Co., Indiana to Defiance, Defiance Co., Ohio.[874]

Rosalee Bussey Ross married **Clarence Christopher Yarger** after 1955. They divorced. Clarence Christopher Yarger was born in Wilmington, Union Twp., Clinton Co., Ohio, on April 17, 1924.[875, 876] Clarence Christopher lived before 2003 in Hillsboro, Liberty Twp., Highland Co., Ohio. He reached age 79 and died in a facility in Georgetown, Pleasant Twp., Brown Co., Ohio, on December 21, 2003.[875, 876]

Rosalee Bussey Ross Yarger married **Mr. Getz** about 1981. They divorced.

Rosalee Bussey Ross Yarger Getz married **Mr. Jones** after 1981.

94. Margaret E.^{9} Bussey (*Lora Belle^8 Roush, Eli Kenneth^7, Margaret Mary^6 Pegan, Harrison James^5, Robert A.^{4}, Andrew^3, Andrew^2 Pagan, James^1*) was born on February 23, 1933, in Boston, Paint Twp., Highland Co., Ohio.[477, 478] She was the daughter of Hubert Clarence Bussey and Lora Belle Roush (35). Margaret E. died in Boston, Paint Twp., Highland Co., Ohio, on February 4, 1934.[477] She was buried in Stringtown Quaker Cemetery, Paint Twp., Highland Co., Ohio.[477]

95. Elizabeth Joanna^9 Bussey (*Lora Belle^8 Roush, Eli Kenneth^7, Margaret Mary^6 Pegan, Harrison James^5, Robert A.^{4}, Andrew^3, Andrew^2 Pagan, James^1*) was born on April 1, 1935, in Greenfield, Greenfield Twp., Highland Co., Ohio.[479] She was also known as **Joanna**. She was the daughter of Hubert Clarence Bussey and Lora Belle Roush (35). Elizabeth Joanna lived in 2013 in Winchester, Winchester Twp., Adams Co., Ohio. She died in a hospital in Hillsboro, Liberty Twp., Highland Co., Ohio, on May 10, 2013, at age 78.[480] Elizabeth Joanna was buried in Locust Grove Cemetery, Peebles, Meigs Twp., Adams Co., Ohio.[877]

Elizabeth Joanna married **Harold L. Wallace** on February 2, 1953, in Highland Co., Ohio.[878] They had six children. Harold L. Wallace was born in Locust Grove, Meigs Twp., Adams Co., Ohio, on January 23, 1923.[128, 879] Harold L. reached age 86 and died in Winchester, Meigs Twp., Adams Co., Ohio, on August 4, 2009.[128, 879] He was buried in Locust Grove Cemetery, Peebles, Meigs Twp., Adams Co., Ohio.[880]

Elizabeth Joanna Bussey and Harold L. Wallace had six children, including:

+ 170 m I. **Michael Ray^{10} Wallace** was born in Winchester, Meigs Twp., Adams Co., Ohio, on June 15, 1954.[182] He died in a hospital in Lima, Ottawa Twp., Allen Co., Ohio, on June 2, 2015.[182]

96. Helen Luella^9 Bussey (*Lora Belle^8 Roush, Eli Kenneth^7, Margaret Mary^6 Pegan, Harrison James^5, Robert A.^{4}, Andrew^3, Andrew^2 Pagan, James^1*) was born on June 26, 1940, in Boston, Paint Twp., Highland Co., Ohio.[69, 481, 482, 483] She was the daughter of Hubert Clarence Bussey and Lora Belle Roush (35). Helen Luella lived in 1968 in Dayton, Montgomery Co., Ohio. She died near Bradford, Darke Co., Ohio, on September 19, 1994, at age 54.[69, 482, 483] Helen Luella was buried in Greenville Union Cemetery, Greenville, Greenville Twp., Darke Co., Ohio.[881]

She is buried under the name Helen L. Bills.

Helen Luella married **Raymond Eugene Bills** about 1959. They divorced. They had six daughters. Raymond Eugene Bills was born in St. Martin, Perry Twp., Brown Co., Ohio, on September 27, 1939.[69, 882, 883] He reached age 63 and died in Washington Court House, Union Twp., Fayette Co., Ohio, on June 8, 2003.[69, 882, 883] He was buried in Washington Cemetery, Washington Court House, Union Twp., Fayette Co., Ohio.[884]

Helen Luella Bussey Bills married **Mr. Kinsey**. They divorced.

Helen Luella Bussey Bills Kinsey married **Mr. Hill**. They divorced.

Helen Luella Bussey and Raymond Eugene Bills had six daughters, including:

+ 171 f II. **Jeanne E.**[10] **Bills** was born in Hillsboro, Liberty Twp., Highland Co., Ohio, on September 18, 1960.[885, 886] She died in a hospital in Richmond, Wayne Co., Indiana, on November 10, 2013.[885, 886]

97. **Kenneth W.**[9] **Roush** (*Samuel Frederick*[8], *Eli Kenneth*[7], *Margaret Mary*[6] *Pegan, Harrison James*[5], *Robert A.*[4], *Andrew*[3], *Andrew*[2] *Pagan, James*[1]) was born on March 5, 1937, in Clark Twp., Clinton Co., Ohio.[69, 493] He was the son of Samuel Frederick Roush (37) and Margaret Helen McCandless. Kenneth W. lived in 1974 in Martinsville, Clark Twp., Clinton Co., Ohio. He died in a hospital in Cincinnati, Hamilton Co., Ohio, on June 3, 1974, at age 37.[493, 494] Kenneth W. was buried in Martinsville IOOF Cemetery, Martinsville, Clark Twp., Clinton Co., Ohio.[887, 888]

Never married.

98. **Daughter**[9] **Roush** (*Samuel Frederick*[8], *Eli Kenneth*[7], *Margaret Mary*[6] *Pegan, Harrison James*[5], *Robert A.*[4], *Andrew*[3], *Andrew*[2] *Pagan, James*[1]) was born on October 15, 1942, in Clark Twp., Clinton Co., Ohio. She is the daughter of Samuel Frederick Roush (37) and Margaret Helen McCandless.

She married **Mr. Shuttleworth**. They divorced. They had three children.

Daughter Roush and Mr. Shuttleworth had three children, including:

+ 172 m III. **Son**[10] **Shuttleworth** was born in Wilmington, Union Twp., Clinton Co., Ohio.

99. **Shirley J.**[9] **Walker** (*Euless Josephine*[8] *Roush, Eli Kenneth*[7], *Margaret Mary*[6] *Pegan, Harrison James*[5], *Robert A.*[4], *Andrew*[3], *Andrew*[2] *Pagan, James*[1]) was born on July 2, 1936, in Jefferson Twp., Clinton Co., Ohio. She was the daughter of Thomas William Walker and Euless Josephine Roush (39).

Shirley J. married **Mr. Johnson**. They divorced. They had one son

Shirley J. Walker Johnson married **Robert Lee Brammer** on August 22, 1999, in Greene Co., Ohio.[889] Robert Lee Brammer was born in Ironton, Upper Twp., Lawrence Co., Ohio on January 12, 1942.[890, 891] Robert Lee lived in Bowersville, Jefferson Twp., Greene Co., Ohio. He reached age 66 and died in a facility in Jamestown, Silvercreek Twp., Greene Co., Ohio, on February 10, 2008.[891] He was buried in Woodlawn Cemetery, Bowersville, Jefferson Twp., Greene Co., Ohio.[891]

100. **Thomas William**[9] **Walker II** (*Euless Josephine*[8] *Roush, Eli Kenneth*[7], *Margaret Mary*[6] *Pegan, Harrison James*[5], *Robert A.*[4], *Andrew*[3], *Andrew*[2] *Pagan, James*[1]) was born on July 5, 1938, in Midland, Jefferson Twp., Clinton Co., Ohio.[128, 503, 504] He was the son of Thomas William Walker and Euless Josephine Roush (39). Thomas William II died in New Smyrna Beach, Volusia Co., Florida, on September 25, 1986, at age 48.[504] He was cremated.[504]

Thomas Wiliam Walker II, a carpenter, married four times. He had two daughters by his first wife and two sons by his second.

101. **Charles Robert**[9] **Walker** (*Euless Josephine*[8] *Roush, Eli Kenneth*[7], *Margaret Mary*[6] *Pegan, Harrison James*[5], *Robert A.*[4], *Andrew*[3], *Andrew*[2] *Pagan, James*[1]) was born on October 27, 1939, in Midland, Jefferson Twp., Clinton Co., Ohio.[505] He was the son of Thomas William Walker and Euless Josephine Roush (39). Charles Robert lived in 1975 in Xenia, Xenia Twp., Greene Co., Ohio. He died in Xenia, Xenia Twp., Greene Co., Ohio, on July 17, 2014, at age 74.[506]

Charles Robert married **Charlotte Pauline Moor** about 1960. They divorced. They had four children. Charlotte Pauline Moor was born in Clarksville, Vernon Twp., Clinton Co., Ohio, on December 27, 1942.[892, 893] She lived in 1991 in Washington Court House, Union Twp., Fayette Co., Ohio. Charlotte Pauline reached age 48 and died in a hospital in Columbus, Franklin Co., Ohio, on January 5, 1991.[892, 893] She was buried in Highlawn Memorial Gardens Cemetery, Washington Court House, Union Twp., Fayette Co., Ohio.[894]

om Charles Robert Walker, Charlotte Pauline Moor Walker married Robert Haines and died under that surname.

102. Perry Adams⁹ Davis (*Leota Beatrice⁸ Roush, Eli Kenneth⁷, Margaret Mary⁶ Pegan, Harrison James⁵, Robert A.⁴, Andrew³, Andrew² Pagan, James¹*) was born on August 6, 1935, in Adams Twp., Clinton Co., Ohio.[512] He is the son of Harold H. Davis and Leota Beatrice Roush (40).

He married Mrs. **Jo Ann Unknown** Scott before 1967. They had one son. Jo Ann Unknown was born in 1937.

103. Larry Eugene⁹ Davis (*Leota Beatrice⁸ Roush, Eli Kenneth⁷, Margaret Mary⁶ Pegan, Harrison James⁵, Robert A.⁴, Andrew³, Andrew² Pagan, James¹*) was born on March 30, 1939, in Adams Twp., Clinton Co., Ohio.[128, 513] He was the son of Harold H. Davis and Leota Beatrice Roush (40). Larry Eugene died in Washington Court House, Union Twp., Fayette Co., Ohio, on July 20, 1995, at age 56.[128, 513] He was buried in Washington Cemetery, Washington Court House, Union Twp., Fayette Co., Ohio.[895, 896]

Larry Eugene married **Rebecca Ann Graves** on June 1, 1957.[897] They divorced. They had four children. Rebecca Ann Graves was born in Washington Court House, Union Twp., Fayette Co., Ohio, on May 6, 1941.[898, 899] She lived in 1968 in Washington Court House, Union Twp., Fayette Co., Ohio. Rebecca Ann reached age 26 and died in a hospital in Columbus, Franklin Co., Ohio, on May 3, 1968.[898] She was buried in Sugar Creek Baptist Church Cemetery, Union Twp., Fayette Co., Ohio.[899]

Larry Eugene Davis married Mrs. **Janet Faye Curtis?** Clickner on August 3, 1968.[900] They had three children.

104. Robert Eugene⁹ McCandless (*Effie Nondis⁸ Roush, Eli Kenneth⁷, Margaret Mary⁶ Pegan, Harrison James⁵, Robert A.⁴, Andrew³, Andrew² Pagan, James¹*) was born on April 16, 1939, in Union Twp., Clinton Co., Ohio.[521] He was the son of Elmer Glenn McCandless and Effie Nondis Roush (41). Robert Eugene died in Adams Twp., Clinton Co., Ohio, on September 9, 1961, at age 22.[521, 522, 523] He was buried in Maple Grove Cemetery (formerly Port William Cemetery), Port William, Liberty Twp., Clinton Co., Ohio.[901, 902]

Never married.

Robert McCandless died in an auto wreck about two miles west of Wilmington, Ohio.

105. Mona J.⁹ McCandless (*Effie Nondis⁸ Roush, Eli Kenneth⁷, Margaret Mary⁶ Pegan, Harrison James⁵, Robert A.⁴, Andrew³, Andrew² Pagan, James¹*) was born on September 22, 1940, in Union Twp., Clinton Co., Ohio. She was the daughter of Elmer Glenn McCandless and Effie Nondis Roush (41).

She married **David Thomas Weller**. They divorced. They had four sons. David Thomas Weller was born in Wilmington, Union Twp., Clinton Co., Ohio, on March 6, 1937.[903, 904, 905] He reached age 55 and died in Springfield, Springfield Twp., Clark Co., Ohio, on April 14, 1992.[903, 904]

106. James Glenn⁹ McCandless (*Effie Nondis⁸ Roush, Eli Kenneth⁷, Margaret Mary⁶ Pegan, Harrison James⁵, Robert A.⁴, Andrew³, Andrew² Pagan, James¹*) was born on April 27, 1954, in Wilmington, Union Twp., Clinton Co., Ohio.[524] He was the son of Elmer Glenn McCandless and Effie Nondis Roush (41). James Glenn died in Wilmington, Union Twp., Clinton Co., Ohio, on November 11, 2014, at age 60.[524]

Never married.

107. Samuel F.⁹ McCandless (*Effie Nondis⁸ Roush, Eli Kenneth⁷, Margaret Mary⁶ Pegan, Harrison James⁵, Robert A.⁴, Andrew³, Andrew² Pagan, James¹*) was born on November 25, 1955, in Union Twp., Clinton Co., Ohio.[525] He was the son of Elmer Glenn McCandless and Effie Nondis Roush (41). Samuel F. died in Burtonville, Union Twp., Clinton Co., Ohio, on May 30, 1976, at age 20.[526] He was buried in Maple Grove Cemetery (formerly Port William Cemetery), Port William, Liberty Twp., Clinton Co., Ohio.[906, 907, 908]

Never married.

Samuel McCandless drowned while swimming with friends in Cowan's Creek near Burtonville, Clinton Co., Ohio.

108. William Lee[9] Seitz (*Dorothy Opal[8] Roush, Eli Kenneth[7], Margaret Mary[6] Pegan, Harrison James[5], Robert A.[4], Andrew[3], Andrew[2] Pagan, James[1]*) was born on March 11, 1940, in Wilmington, Union Twp., Clinton Co., Ohio.[128, 532, 533] He was the son of Emmett Faye Seitz and Dorothy Opal Roush (42). William Lee died in Troy, Concord Twp., Miami Co., Ohio, on August 9, 2011, at age 71.[128, 532] William L. Seitz donated his body to medical science.[532]

William Lee married **Lorraine Nickels** on August 27, 1960, in Miami Co., Ohio.[533] They divorced. They had three children. Lorraine Nickels was born in West Liberty, Morgan Co., Kentucky, on October 7, 1940.[533]

William L. Seitz married **Miss Gilliand**. They divorced. They had two sons.

William L. Seitz married **Linda L. Bradley** on April 8, 1981, in Miami Co., Ohio.[909] They had one son. Linda L. Bradley was born in Troy, Concord Twp., Miami Co., Ohio, on February 25, 1945.[910, 911] Linda L. lived in 1994 in Troy, Concord Twp., Miami Co., Ohio. She reached age 49 and died in a hospital in Dayton, Montgomery Co., Ohio, on September 28, 1994.[910, 911] Linda L. was buried in Riverside Cemetery, Troy, Concord Twp., Miami Co., Ohio.[912]

William Lee Seitz and Lorraine Nickels had three children, including:

+ 173 f I. **Daughter[10] Seitz** was born in Troy, Concord Twp., Miami Co., Ohio, on February 20, 1961.

+ 174 m II. **William Jeffrey[10] Seitz II** was born in Troy, Concord Twp., Miami Co., Ohio, on June 12, 1962.[913] He died in Troy, Concord Twp., Miami Co., Ohio, on June 12, 1962.[913]

William Lee Seitz and Miss Gilliand had two sons, including:

+ 175 m I. **Jeffrey[10] Seitz** was born in Troy, Concord Twp., Miami Co., Ohio, between 1967 and 2011. He died between 1967 and August 2011.

109. Darrel Joe[9] Seitz (*Dorothy Opal[8] Roush, Eli Kenneth[7], Margaret Mary[6] Pegan, Harrison James[5], Robert A.[4], Andrew[3], Andrew[2] Pagan, James[1]*) was born on July 22, 1941, in Waynesville, Wayne Twp., Warren Co., Ohio.[534,535] He was the son of Emmett Faye Seitz and Dorothy Opal Roush (42). Darrel Joe lived in 1963 in Jacksonville, Onslow Co., North Carolina. He died in Nichols, Horry Co., South Carolina, on March 15, 1963, at age 21.[534, 535] Darrel Joe was buried in Riverside Cemetery, Troy, Concord Twp., Miami Co., Ohio.[534, 914]

Never married.

Darrel Joe Seitz was a U.S. Marine stationed at Camp Lejeune in Jacksonville, Onslow Co., North Carolina when he was killed in an automobile crash while on leave.

110. Emmett[9] Seitz II (*Dorothy Opal[8] Roush, Eli Kenneth[7], Margaret Mary[6] Pegan, Harrison James[5], Robert A.[4], Andrew[3], Andrew[2] Pagan, James[1]*). He was the son of Emmett Faye Seitz and Dorothy Opal Roush (42). Emmett died before 2004.

May have died at birth. No birth or death records found for him.

111. Philip Stroup[9] Roush II (*Philip Stroup[8], Cecil Ira[7], Margaret Mary[6] Pegan, Harrison James[5], Robert A.[4], Andrew[3], Andrew[2] Pagan, James[1]*) was born on March 29, 1959, in Key West, Monroe Co., Florida.[128,559] He was the son of Philip Stroup Roush (46) and Jeannie Hume Keith. Philip Stroup worked as a shrimp fisherman in 1987. He died 25 miles off the Port Canaveral coast of Florida on July 29, 1987.[128, 560] Philip Stroup Roush II was buried at sea.[560]

According to a May 1, 1988 article in the *Fort Lauderdale (FL) Sun Sentinel*, Philip S. Roush Jr., 28, a shrimp boat captain, was killed by two mutineers, Eugene Gossett Jr., 24, and William Leroy Rector, 21, on his four-man boat, *The Leslie Rae*, off the coast of Port Canaveral, Florida on 29 Jul 1987. Early that evening, one of the two men hit Philip Roush on the head with a hammer, killing him. The boat's first mate, Willie Charpentier Jr., 21, was also hit on the head with a weapon. Injured and bleeding, Charpentier escaped by jumping overboard. While he was in the water near the boat, he saw the two murderers throw Philip Roush Jr.'s body overboard.

Amazingly, Charpentier survived, alternately swimming towards shore and treading water, for more than 12 hours in shark-infested waters. Bleeding and exhausted, he was picked up the morning of July 30 by a U.S. Coast Guard rescue helicopter.

The Coast Guard had been notified by a couple in a motorized sailboat who had spotted Charpentier earlier while trying to get their broken motor restarted. But the broken motor left the couple stranded, and waves washed Charpentier away from them. But just minutes before the couple radioed the Coast Guard, the mutineers aboard the now-listing *The Leslie Rae* had sent out a distress signal to the Coast Guard, alleging that their captain and first mate had fallen overboard during the night while the rest of the crew was sleeping. This aroused suspicions immediately, as shrimpers work during the night and rest during the day. Also, the Coast Guard doubted their story that two such experienced fisherman, Roush, who started fishing on shrimp boats when he was 16 and became a captain a few years later, and Charpentier, who had worked on Roush's boat for 14 months, would both fall off a boat the same night.

The U.S. Coast Guard located *The Leslie Rae* and boarded her, arresting the two perpetrators. An 18-year-old woman, Maria Barnes, was also taken into custody. Barnes, whom Gossett, Rector and Charpentier smuggled onboard before the boat sailed, was allegedly a cook, but Charpentier later claimed in court that Roush was the cook and Barnes was there for salacious reasons.

The case was turned over to the FBI and Gossett and Rector were tried in federal court in Orlando, Florida, in the first civilian trial for mutiny in America in more than 40 years. They were charged with mutiny, first-degree murder, conspiracy to commit felony murder and assault with intent to murder. During the trial, Charpentier told the court that *The Leslie Rae* left Tampa, Florida on July 15, 1987, heading for the fertile shrimp grounds off Port Canaveral. He said Gossett and Rector were drifters whom Roush met at a Tampa bar where shrimp boat captains often pick up "greenhorns" for their crews. At first Gossett and Rector, who did not know each other before they came onboard *The Leslie Rae,* claimed they were willing to do the heavy work and lengthy hours shrimp fishing required. But within a short time, Charpentier said the two rookie fishermen balked at the labor and slacked off. In addition, the first mate testified that the two greenhorns started talking about killing the captain, stealing the boat and intimated that they would sail it to Rio De Janeiro. But Charpentier thought the men were joking.

Gossett said in court that Roush died when Rector shot him three times in the chest with a rifle., But Rector's account of the incident agreed with that of Charpentier's—that Roush died when Gossett smashed his head several times with a ball peen hammer. Charpentier elaborated, saying that he and Roush were mending nets around 8 p.m. when Gossett came up behind them. Gossett hit Roush first, then Charpentier, and both men fell to the deck. Then Charpentier saw Gossett hit Roush on the head twice more with the hammer. The first mate was able to rise up and reached for a knife he had been using on the nets when Rector slashed him in the forehead with the chisel end of a pry bar. Charpentier fell again but got up and dived off the boat.

Barnes, who was not prosecuted, testified that she was in the cabin watching television at the time of the mutiny and didn't hear anything. She said she found out that Roush had been murdered and Charpentier attacked when Gossett and Rector came below deck and bragged about it.

Gossett and Rector were found guilty on all counts on December 2, 1987. The following January 29, they were sentenced to two life sentences, plus 10 years, to be served consecutively. Both were incarcerated in federal prisons, Gossett in Memphis, Tennessee and Rector at Terre Haute, Indiana.

Philip Stroup Roush Jr.'s body was never found.[560]

Philip S. Roush II married **Miss Cook.** They were legally separated before July 1987. They have one daughter.[560]

112. **Michael David⁹ Roush** (*Randall Cecil⁸, Cecil Ira⁷, Margaret Mary⁶ Pegan, Harrison James⁵, Robert A.⁴, Andrew³, Andrew² Pagan, James¹*) was born on July 26, 1946, in Corpus Christi, Nueces Co., Texas.[570] He was also known as **Mickey.** He was the son of Randall Cecil Roush (47) and Florence Kay Librcajt. Michael David died in Orange Park, Clay Co., Florida, on June 22, 2000.[571]

113. **William Randall⁹ Roush** (*Randall Cecil⁸, Cecil Ira⁷, Margaret Mary⁶ Pegan, Harrison James⁵, Robert A.⁴, Andrew³, Andrew² Pagan, James¹*) was born on March 3, 1953, in Midwest City, Oklahoma Co., Oklahoma.[128, 572] He was the son of Randall Cecil Roush (47) and Florence Kay Librcajt. William Randall died in Big Pine Key, Monroe Co., Florida, on August 18, 2006, at age 53.[128+72]

William Randall Roush married.

114. **Lee E. Donald⁹ Roush** (*Gale E.⁸, Cecil Ira⁷, Margaret Mary⁶ Pegan, Harrison James⁵, Robert A.⁴, Andrew³, Andrew² Pagan, James¹*) was born on August 13, 1951, in Miami, Dade Co., Florida?[128] He was the son of Gale E. Roush (48) and Bernice Gertrude Julien. Lee E. Donald lived in 1998 in Cape Coral, Lee Co., Florida. He died in Cape Coral, Lee Co., Florida, on March 26, 2012.[128, 577] He was cremated.[577]

Lee E. Donald Roush married and had one daughter.

The April 12, 1958 edition of the *Salt Lake City Tribune* reported that six-year-old Lee Roush, son of Gale and Bernice Roush of Florida, became lost while visiting his maternal grandmother, Mrs. Walter G. Julien, in that city and had to be tracked down by a bloodhound which had rescued quite a few lost children.[576]

115. **Marianne⁹ Pearson** (*Herbert Harrison⁸, Sarah Celeste⁷ PeGan, Harrison James⁶, Harrison James⁵ Pegan, Robert A.⁴, Andrew³, Andrew² Pagan, James¹*) was born on November 9, 1937, in Marshalltown, Marshall Twp., Marshall Co., Iowa. She is the daughter of Herbert Harrison Pearson (53) and Bernice Ann Kucera.

She married **Robert Lee Neely.** They divorced. They had two children. Robert Lee Neely was born on July 27, 1936.

Marianne Pearson Neely married **Unknown Kmak.** They have one daughter.

116. **Patricia Ann⁹ Pearson** (*Truman Vaughn⁸, Sarah Celeste⁷ PeGan, Harrison James⁶, Harrison James⁵ Pegan, Robert A.⁴, Andrew³, Andrew² Pagan, James¹*) was born on September 5, 1937, in Winchester, White River Twp., Randolph Co., Indiana.[618] She is the daughter of Truman Vaughn Pearson (54) and Mattie Mae Oliver.

Patricia Ann married **Everett Ray Geis** on January 26, 1957, in Los Angeles Co., California.[915] They had two sons. Everett Ray Geis was born in Downey, Los Angeles Co., California, on July 31, 1936.[916] He is also known as **Ray.**

117. **Marjorie Jane⁹ Pearson** (*Truman Vaughn⁸, Sarah Celeste⁷ PeGan, Harrison James⁶, Harrison James⁵ Pegan, Robert A.⁴, Andrew³, Andrew² Pagan, James¹*) was born on February 26, 1943, in Marshalltown, Marshall Twp., Marshall Co., Iowa.[128, 617] She was also known as **Jane.** She was the daughter of Truman Vaughn Pearson (54) and Mattie Mae Oliver. Marjorie Jane died in Orange, Orange Co., California, on May 11, 2005, at age 62.[128, 618] She was buried in Fairhaven Cemetery, Santa Ana, Orange Co., California.[618, 917]

Although her given name was Marjorie, she always used Jane as her preferred name.

Marjorie Jane married **Vincent James Conti** on May 9, 1964, in Clark Co., Nevada.[918] They had two sons. Vincent James Conti was born in Cleveland, Cuyahoga Co., Ohio, on February 5, 1940.

118. **Betty Jean⁹ Eastes** (*Opal Colene⁸ Pearson, Sarah Celeste⁷ PeGan, Harrison James⁶, Harrison James⁵*

Pegan, Robert A.⁴, Andrew³, Andrew² Pagan, James¹) was born on October 1, 1930, in Jonesboro, Mill Twp., Grant Co., Indiana.[128, 624, 625, 626] She was the daughter of Joseph Gerald Eastes and Opal Colene Pearson (55). Betty Jean lived in 2006 in Gas City, Mill Twp., Grant Co., Indiana. She died in a hospital in Muncie, Center Twp., Delaware Co., Indiana, on July 10, 2006, at age 75.[128, 624, 625, 626] Betty Jean was buried in Riverside Cemetery, Gas City, Mill Twp. Grant Co., Indiana.[624, 626, 919]

Betty Jean married **Charles Edward Cowgill** on December 24, 1949, in Grant Co., Indiana.[920] They divorced. They had one son. Charles Edward Cowgill was born in Mill Twp., Grant Co., Indiana, on March 11, 1930.[128, 921] He reached age 49 and died in Marion, Center Twp., Grant Co., Indiana, on May 24, 1979.[128, 921, 922] Charles Edward was buried in Estates of Serenity, Marion, Center Twp., Grant Co., Indiana.[921, 923]

Betty Jean Eastes Cowgill married **Charles Norman Reese** on January 15, 1966, in Grant Co., Indiana.[924] They divorced in Grant Co., Indiana, before 1988. Charles Norman Reese was born in Michigan City, Michigan Twp., LaPorte Co., Indiana, on August 7, 1929.[128, 925, 926] He was also known as **Mickey**. Charles Norman lived in 1988 in Webster, Sumter Co., Florida. He reached age 70 and died in Webster, Sumter Co., Florida, on August 22, 1999.[128, 925 926] He was cremated and his ashes buried in Riverside Cemetery, Gas City, Mill Twp. Grant Co., Indiana.[925, 927]

Son of Betty Jean Eastes and Charles Edward Cowgill:

+ 176 m I. **Danny Edward¹⁰ Cowgill** was born in Marion, Center Twp., Grant Co., Indiana, on August 11, 1950.[128, 928, 929, 930] He was also known as **Pete**. Danny Edward died in a hospital in Muncie, Center Twp., Delaware Co., Indiana, on August 26, 1998.[128, 928, 929, 930]

119. Joseph Edward⁹ Eastes II (*Opal Colene⁸ Pearson, Sarah Celeste⁷ PeGan, Harrison James⁶, Harrison James⁵ Pegan, Robert A.⁴, Andrew³, Andrew² Pagan, James¹*) was born on September 28, 1936, in Marion, Center Twp., Grant Co., Indiana.[128, 627, 628, 629, 630] He was also known as Ed. He was the son of Joseph Gerald Eastes and Opal Colene Pearson (55). Joseph Edward lived in 1998 in Jonesboro, Mill Twp., Grant Co., Indiana. Joseph Edward died in a hospital in Muncie, Center Twp., Delaware Co., Indiana, on November 26, 1998, at age 62.[128, 627, 628, 630] He was buried in Riverside Cemetery, Gas City, Mill Twp. Grant Co., Indiana.[627, 931]

Social Security Death Index entry under Joe E. Eastes.[128]

Joseph Edward married **Marilyn Louise James (McDaniel)** on September 29, 1957, in Grant Co., Indiana.[932, 933] They divorced before 1983. They remarried on September 29, 1983 in Grant Co., Indiana.[934] They had five children. Marilyn Louise James (McDaniel) was born in Gas City, Mill Twp., Grant Co., Indiana, on March 1, 1938.[128, 932, 935, 936] She reached age 69 and died in Jonesboro, Mill Twp., Grant Co., Indiana, on April 9, 2007.[128, 932, 936] Marilyn Louise James (McDaniel) was buried in Riverside Cemetery, Gas City, Mill Twp. Grant Co., Indiana.[932, 936, 937]

Marilyn James (McDaniel) Eastes birth name was "Merilyn" Louise James, according to her birth certificate.[936] Her Social Security Application is under Mary Lou James, and her father is listed as Arland V. James and her mother as Bertha Riddle.[938] She married Joseph Edward Eastes under the name Marilyn L. James.[934] Her obituary says her maiden name was McDaniel and her parents as Wallace and Bertha Riddle McDaniel. She may have been adopted by her stepfather, Wallace McDaniel.[932]

Joseph Edward Eastes II and Marilyn Louise James McDaniel had five children, including:

+ 177 f I. **Daughter¹⁰ Eastes** was born in Jacksonville, Onslow Co., North Carolina.

+ 178 m II. **Son¹⁰ Eastes** was born in Jonesboro, Mill Twp., Grant Co., Indiana.

120. **John Frederick**[9] **Eastes** (*Opal Colene*[8] *Pearson, Sarah Celeste*[7] *PeGan, Harrison James*[6] *, Harrison James*[5] *Pegan, Robert A.*[4]*, Andrew*[3]*, Andrew*[2] *Pagan, James*[1]) was born on June 28, 1942, in Jonesboro, Mill Twp., Grant Co., Indiana.[128, 631] He was the son of Joseph Gerald Eastes and Opal Colene Pearson (55). He resided in 2010 in Youngsville, Lafayette Parish, Louisiana. John Frederick died in a hospital in Lafayette, Lafayette Parish, Louisiana, on November 19, 2010, at age 68.[128, 632, 633] He was buried in Washington County Memorial Gardens Cemetery, Johnson City, Washington Co., Tennessee.[633, 939]

John Frederick Easters was married three times and had two daughters by his first wife.

John Frederick Eastes spent 20 years in the Marine Corps as a helicopter pilot and mechanic, serving two tours of duty in Vietnam. He later was a mechanic and pilot for helicopter companies. In addition to Youngsville, Lafayette Parish, Louisiana, he and his family also lived in several cities in the U.S., including Virginia Beach, Virginia, Fort Worth, Tarrant Co., Texas, Wautauga, Tennessee as well as in St. Thomas, Virgin Islands.[632, 633]

121. **Betty Jean**[9] **Pegan** (*Cecil Keith*[8]*, Jesse Harrison*[7]*, Harrison James*[6] *PeGan II, Harrison James*[5] *Pegan, Robert A.*[4]*, Andrew*[3]*, Andrew*[2] *Pagan, James*[1]) was born on April 12, 1940, in Hartford City, Licking Twp., Blackford Co., Indiana.[648] She was the daughter of Cecil Keith Pegan (57) and Bessie Mae Shoemaker.

Betty Jean married **Ronald Lee Jarvis** on July 16, 1960.[940] They divorced before 1973. They had two children. Ronald Lee Jarvis was born in Kokomo, Center Twp., Howard Co., Indiana, on July 15, 1939.[941, 942] He reached age 52 and died in Jacksonville, Duval Co., Florida, on June 29, 1992.[941, 942] Ronald Lee was buried in Arlington Park Cemetery, Jacksonville, Duval Co., Florida.[943]

Betty Jean Pegan Jarvis married **Mr. Corn**.

Betty Jean Pegan and Ronald Lee Jarvis had two children, including:

+ 179 m II. **Daniel Lee**[10] **Jarvis** was born in Huntington, Huntington Twp., Huntington Co., Indiana, on July 1, 1962.[128, 944, 945] He died in Kokomo, Center Twp., Howard Co., Indiana, on February 17, 2004.[128, 944, 945]

122. **Judith Kay**[9] **Oswalt** (*Pauline Miriam*[8] *Pegan, Jesse Harrison*[7]*, Harrison James*[6] *PeGan II, Harrison James*[5] *Pegan, Robert A.*[4]*, Andrew*[3]*, Andrew*[2] *Pagan, James*[1]) was born on April 6, 1940, in Wabash, Noble Twp., Wabash Co., Indiana.[654] She was the daughter of Charles Raymond Oswalt and Pauline Miriam Pegan (58).

Judith Kay married **Thomas Richard Wilbur** on November 19, 1960, in Huntington Co., Indiana.[946] They had two daughters. Thomas Richard Wilbur was born in Huntington, Huntington Twp., Huntington Co., Indiana, on February 18, 1939.[947, 948] Thomas R. lived in Huntington, Huntington Twp., Huntington Co., Indiana. He reached age 78 and died in a facility in Markle, Rock Creek Twp., Huntington Co., Indiana, on March 14, 2017.[947] Thomas Richard was buried in Pilgrims Rest Cemetery, Huntington, Huntington Twp., Huntington Co., Indiana.[949]

123. **Daughter**[9] **Pegan** (*James Meredith*[8]*, Jesse Harrison*[7]*, Harrison James*[6] *PeGan II, Harrison James*[5] *Pegan, Robert A.*[4]*, Andrew*[3]*, Andrew*[2] *Pagan, James*[1]) was born in Huntington, Huntington Twp., Huntington Co., Indiana. She is the daughter of James Meredith Pegan (59) and Onhawanha Carver Ludwig.

Daughter Pegan married **James E. Dodson** on October 31, 1971 in Huntington Co., Indiana.[950] They have two daughters. James Dodson was born on August 7, 1943 in Rickman, Overton Co., Tennessee.[950] He died in Lebanon, Center Twp., Boone Co., Indiana on June 3, 2018.[950] James E. was buried in Dodson Chapel Cemetery, Rickman, Overton Co., Tennessee.[950]

Daughter Pegan and Mr. Dodson had two daughters, including:

+ 180 f   II.   **Daughter**[10] **Dodson**.

124. Allen Eugene[9] **Flowers** (*Florence Willodean*[8] *Pegan, Jesse Harrison*[7]*, Harrison James*[6] *PeGan II, Harrison James*[5] *Pegan, Robert A.*[4]*, Andrew*[3]*, Andrew*[2] *Pagan, James*[1]) was born on February 18, 1948, in Bluffton, Wells Co., Indiana.[128, 292, 670, 671, 672] He was the son of John Junior Flowers II and Florence Willodean Pegan (61). Allen Eugene lived in 2003 in Wabash, Liberty Twp., Mercer Co., Ohio. He died in a hospital in Coldwater, Butler Twp., Mercer Co., Ohio, on January 9, 2005, at age 56.[128, 292, 670, 671, 672] Allen Eugene was buried in St. Paul's Lutheran Cemetery, Wabash, Washington Twp., Mercer Co., Ohio.[670, 951]

Allen Eugene married **Connie Margaret Kramer** on July 25, 1970.[952] They had seven children. Connie Margaret was born on November 19, 1951 in Coldwater, Butler Twp., Mercer Co., Ohio.[952] She lived in Celina, Jefferson Twp., Mercer Co., Ohio. Connie M. died on December 3, 2017 in a hospital in Columbus, Franklin Co., Ohio.[952] She was buried in St. Paul's Lutheran Cemetery, Wabash, Washington Twp., Mercer Co.,Ohio.[952, 953]

Allen Eugene Flowers and Miss Kramer had seven children, including:

+ 181 m   III. **Robert Lee**[10] **Flowers** was born in Van Wert, Van Wert Co., Ohio, on July 28, 1973.[292, 954] He died in Wabash, Liberty Twp., Mercer Co., Ohio, on September 9, 1978.[292, 954, 955]

125. Son[9] **Flowers** (*Florence Willodean*[8] *Pegan, Jesse Harrison*[7]*, Harrison James*[6] *PeGan II, Harrison James*[5] *Pegan, Robert A.*[4]*, Andrew*[3]*, Andrew*[2] *Pagan, James*[1]) was born in Huntington, Huntington Twp., Huntington Co., Indiana. He is the son of John Junior Flowers II and Florence Willodean Pegan (61).

Son Flowers married **Diana L. Hisey** on December 14, 1968. They divorced. They have one daughter. Diana L. Hisey was born in Celina, Jefferson Twp., Mercer Co., Ohio, on July 17, 1951.[128, 956] She lived in 1986 in Celina, Jefferson Twp., Mercer Co., Ohio. Diana L. reached age 35 and died in a hospital in Columbus, Franklin Co., Ohio, on August 25, 1986.[956, 957] She was buried in Swamp College Cemetery, Celina, Jefferson Twp., Mercer Co., Ohio.[956, 958]

After the divorce, Diana L. Hisey Flowers married Mr. Hughes and died under that surname.

Son Flowers married again and has three sons.

126. Kathleen Joann[9] **Flowers** (*Florence Willodean*[8] *Pegan, Jesse Harrison*[7]*, Harrison James*[6] *PeGan II, Harrison James*[5] *Pegan, Robert A.*[4]*, Andrew*[3]*, Andrew*[2] *Pagan, James*[1]) was born on February 24, 1952, in Wabash, Liberty Twp., Mercer Co., Ohio.[292, 673] She was also known as **Kathy**. She was the daughter of John Junior Flowers II and Florence Willodean Pegan (61). Kathleen Joann lived in 2013 in Celina, Jefferson Twp., Mercer Co., Ohio. She died in a hospital in Coldwater, Butler Twp., Mercer Co., Ohio, on April 25, 2013, at age 61.[673] Kathleen Joann was buried in Swamp College Cemetery, Celina, Jefferson Twp., Mercer Co., Ohio.[673, 959]

Kathleen Joann married **Mr. Hone** and had two children.

127. Son Two[9] **Flowers** (*Florence Willodean*[8] *Pegan, Jesse Harrison*[7]*, Harrison James*[6] *PeGan II, Harrison James*[5] *Pegan, Robert A.*[4]*, Andrew*[3]*, Andrew*[2] *Pagan, James*[1]) was born in Coldwater, Butler Twp., Mercer Co., Ohio. He is the son of John Junior Flowers II and Florence Willodean Pegan (61).

Son Two Flowers married and divorced.

Son Two Flowers and his wife had two daughters, including:

+ 182 f   II.   **Brandy Lee**[10] **Flowers** was born in Lima, Ottawa Twp., Allen Co., Ohio, on July 26, 1978.[292, 960] She died in a facility in Mantua, Mantua Twp., Portage Co., Ohio, on February 5, 2009.[292, 960]

128. Maryln Ann⁹ PeGan (*Leo Everett⁸, Clanzie Herold⁷, Harrison James⁶, Harrison James⁵ Pegan, Robert A.⁴, Andrew³, Andrew² Pagan, James¹*) was born on March 12, 1937, in Huntington, Huntington Twp., Huntington Co., Indiana.[682] She is the daughter of Leo Everett PeGan (62) and Loretta Jennette Ryan.

Maryln Ann was the head surgical nurse, Long Hospital, Indiana University Medical Center, Indianapolis, Indiana in the late 1950s-early 1960s. She later earned a degree and certifications in psychology and, in addition to her private practice, taught at several colleges in Texas.

Maryln Ann married **Dr. James Brent Crossen** on August 13, 1960, in Marion Co., Indiana.[961] They divorced. They had eight children. Dr. James Brent Crossen was born in Indianapolis, Marion Co., Indiana, on October 10, 1939.[962, 963, 964] He lived in 1977 in San Antonio, Bexar Co., Texas. James Brent also resided in 1990 in Dallas, Dallas Co., Texas. James Brent reached age 72 and died in Irving, Dallas Co., Texas, on September 7, 2012.[963,964] He was buried in Dallas-Fort Worth National Cemetery, Dallas, Dallas Co., Texas.[964]

Dr. James B. Crossen was an orthodontist and oral surgeon in San Antonio and Dallas, Texas.

Maryln Ann PeGan and James Brent Crossen had eight children, including:

+ 183 f I. **Danette Lee¹⁰ Crossen** was born in Indianapolis, Marion Co., Indiana, on June 25, 1961.[128, 965, 966] She died in Dallas, Dallas Co., Texas, on August 6, 2000.[128, 965, 966]

129. Thomas Joseph⁹ PeGan (*Leo Everett⁸, Clanzie Herold⁷, Harrison James⁶, Harrison James⁵ Pegan, Robert A.⁴, Andrew³, Andrew² Pagan, James¹*) was born on January 13, 1941, in Huntington, Huntington Twp., Huntington Co., Indiana.[128, 683] He was the son of Leo Everett PeGan (62) and Loretta Jennette Ryan. Thomas Joseph lived in 1970 in Big Lake, Noble Co., Indiana. Thomas Joseph resided between 1986-1996 in Hilliard, Norwich Twp., Franklin Co., Ohio. Thomas Joseph died at Bison Ranch, Overgaard, Navajo Co., Arizona, on July 28, 2002, at age 61.[128, 683, 684]

A teamster and over-the road truck driver, Thomas Joseph PeGan was married twice and had two adopted children with his first wife, Candy, and two stepdaughters by his second.

Thomas Joseph married **Candace Nan Snyder** on April 29, 1967, in Huntington Co., Indiana.[967] They divorced. They had two children. Candace Nan Snyder was born in Bluffton, Wells Co., Indiana, on July 25, 1946.[968] She lived in 1964 in Markle, Union Twp., Wells Co., Indiana. Candace Nan also resided before 2017 in Fort Wayne, Allen Co., Indiana. She was living in May 2017 in Rocky Mount, Osage Twp., Morgan Co., Missouri. Candace Nan reached age 70 and died in a hospital in Columbia, Boone Co., Missouri, on May 29, 2017.[968] She was buried in Hoverstock Cemetery, Zanesville, Union Twp., Wells Co., Indiana.[968, 969]

After the divorces, Candace Nan Snyder PeGan married Mr. Zimmerman and died under that surname.

Thomas Joseph PeGan married **Miss McConnell**.

130. Harold Leon⁹ PeGan (*Paul Harold⁸, Clanzie Herold⁷, Harrison James⁶, Harrison James⁵ Pegan, Robert A.⁴, Andrew³, Andrew² Pagan, James¹*) was born on January 27, 1939, in Huntington, Huntington Twp., Huntington Co., Indiana.[691] He is the son of Paul Harold PeGan (63) and Delores Bernadette Feighner.

Harold Leon married **Miss Parrott.** They had two children.

Harold Leon PeGan and his Miss Parrott had two children, including:

+ 184 m I. **Brent Christopher¹⁰ PeGan** was born in Fort Wayne, Allen Co., Indiana, on April 12, 1966.[116, 970] He died in Warsaw, Wayne Twp., Koscuisko Co., Indiana, on July 15, 1990.[970, 971]

131. **Daughter**[9] **PeGan** (*Hugh Frederick*[8], *Clanzie Herold*[7], *Harrison James*[6], *Harrison James*[5] *Pegan, Robert A.*[4], *Andrew*[3], *Andrew*[2] *Pagan, James*[1]) was born in Huntington, Huntington Twp., Huntington Co., Indiana. She is the daughter of Hugh Frederick PeGan (65) and Rosemary Etter.

Daughter PeGan married **Carl Weber Jaeger** on August 21, 1964, in Huntington Co., Indiana.[CC] They had four children. Carl Weber Jaeger was born in Fort Wayne, Allen Co., Indiana on December 14, 1935[DD] He reached age 83 and died in Waukazoo Woods, Park Twp., Ottawa Co., Michigan, on December 1, 2019.[CC] Carl Weber was buried in Lakewood Cemetery, Holland, Ottawa Co., Michigan.[CC, EE]

131A. **John Fredrick**[9] **PeGan** (*Hugh Frederick*[8], *Clanzie Herold*[7], *Harrison James*[6], *Harrison James*[5] *Pegan, Robert A.*[4], *Andrew*[3], *Andrew*[2] *Pagan, James*[1]) was born on November 18, 1947, in Huntington, Huntington Twp., Huntington Co., Indiana.[704, 705] He was the son of Hugh Frederick PeGan (65) and Rosemary Josephine Etter. John Frederick lived in 2012 in Greendale, Lawrenceburg Twp., Dearborn Co., Indiana. He died in a hospital in Cleveland, Cuyahoga Co., Ohio, on April 29, 2012, at age 64.[705]

John Frederick PeGan married **Miss Mitchell**. They had two children. He worked as an antique dealer, specializing in antique and reproduction lighting fixtures.

132. **Son**[9] **PeGan** (*Hugh Frederick*[8], *Clanzie Herold*[7], *Harrison James*[6], *Harrison James*[5] *Pegan, Robert A.*[4], *Andrew*[3], *Andrew*[2] *Pagan, James*[1]) in Huntington, Huntington Twp., Huntington Co., Indiana. He is the son of Hugh Frederick PeGan (65) and Rosemary Josephine Etter.

Children of Son PeGan and his wife had four children, including:

+ 185 f II. **Daughter**[10] **PeGan** was born in Lafayette, Fairfield Twp., Tippecanoe Co., Indiana.

133. **Robert Phillip**[9] **PeGan** (*Phillip Elsworth*[8], *Philip Garl*[7], *Harrison James*[6], *Harrison James*[5] *Pegan, Robert A.*[4], *Andrew*[3], *Andrew*[2] *Pagan, James*[1]) was born on September 24, 1943, in Niles, Niles Twp., Berrien Co., Michigan.[128, 721] He was the son of Phillip Elsworth PeGan (67) and Josephine Clara Lewis. Robert Phillip lived in 2010 in Goshen, Elkhart Twp., Elkhart Co., Indiana. He died in a hospital in Elkhart, Elkhart Co., Indiana, on October 14, 2010, at age 67.[128, 721] Robert Phillip was buried in Mission Hills Memorial Chapel, Crematory & Gardens, North Niles, Howard Twp., Cass Co., Michigan.[721, 972]

Robert Phillip married **Miss McClish**. They had one daughter.

Robert Phillip PeGan married **Miss Webber**. They had two children.

Robert Phillip PeGan married Mrs. **Ozela Rose Morgan** Unger after 1978. They divorced. Ozela Rose Morgan was born in Niles, Niles Twp., Berrien Co., Michigan, on December 10, 1943.[349] She was also known as **Rose**. Ozela Rose reached age 71 and died in Cassopolis, LaGrange Twp., Cass Co., Michigan, on December 11, 2014.[973] She was buried in Mission Hills Memorial Chapel, Crematory & Gardens, North Niles, Howard Twp., Cass Co., Michigan.[974]

She died under the name Ozella Rose Morgan-Zorn.

Robert Phillip PeGan married and divorced for a fourth time before he died.

134. **Son**[9] **PeGan** (*Phillip Elsworth*[8], *Philip Garl*[7], *Harrison James*[6], *Harrison James*[5] *Pegan, Robert A.*[4], *Andrew*[3], *Andrew*[2] *Pagan, James*[1]) was born in Niles, Niles Twp., Berrien Co., Michigan. He is the son of Phillip Elsworth PeGan (67) and Josephine Clara Lewis.

Son PeGan married **Hazel Marie McGraw** on April 13, 1968, in Berrien Co., Michigan.[349] They divorced. They had three children. Hazel Marie McGraw was born in Greencastle, Greencastle Twp., Putnam Co., Indiana, on November 28, 1951.[128, 349, 975, 976, 977] She lived in 2006 in Niles, Niles Twp. Berrien Co., Michigan. Hazel Marie reached age 55 and died in a hospital in South

Bend, St. Joseph Co., Indiana, on December 1, 2006.[128, 975, 976, 977] She was cremated and her cremains buried in Mission Hills Memorial Chapel, Crematory & Gardens, North Niles, Howard Twp., Cass Co., Michigan.[975, 978]

After she and Son PeGan divorced, Hazel Marie McGraw PeGan married Mr. Richer and died under that surname.

Son PeGan has married twice more.

Children of Roger Lee PeGan and Hazel Marie McGraw:

+ 186 m I. **Son**[10] **PeGan** was born in South Bend, St. Joseph Co., Indiana.

135. Daughter[9] **PeGan** (*Phillip Elsworth*[8], *Philip Garl*[7], *Harrison James*[6], *Harrison James*[5] *Pegan*, *Robert A.*[4], *Andrew*[3], *Andrew*[2] *Pagan*, *James*[1]) was born on July 21, 1952, in Niles, Niles Twp., Berrien Co., Michigan.[252] She is the daughter of Phillip Elsworth PeGan (67) and Josephine Clara Lewis.

Daughter PeGan married **James Roger Bakeman** on August 18, 1973, in Berrien Co., Michigan.[349] They have two daughters. James Roger Bakeman was born in South Bend, St. Joseph Co., Indiana, on February 3, 1952.[128, 349, 979, 980] James Roger reached age 49 years and died in Ann Arbor, Ann Arbor Twp., Washtenaw Co., Michigan, on March 30, 2001.[128, 349, 979, 980] He was buried in Mission Hills Memorial Chapel, Crematory & Gardens, North Niles, Howard Twp., Cass Co., Michigan.[979, 981]

Daughter PeGan and James Roger Bakeman had two daughters, including:

+ 187 f II. **Rebecca Ann**[10] **Bakeman** was born in Niles, Niles Twp., Berrien Co., Michigan, on November 6, 1977.[349, 982] She died in Niles, Niles Twp., Berrien Co., Michigan, on January 16, 1978.[349, 982]

136. Son Two[9] **PeGan** (*Phillip Elsworth*[8], *Philip Garl*[7], *Harrison James*[6], *Harrison James*[5] *Pegan*, *Robert A.*[4], *Andrew*[3], *Andrew*[2] *Pagan*, *James*[1]) was born on August 25, 1954, in Niles, Niles Twp., Berrien Co., Michigan. He is the son of Phillip Elsworth PeGan (67) and Josephine Clara Lewis.

Son Two PeGan has married four times and had one son by his second wife:

Son of Son Two PeGan and Wife Two:

+ 188 m I. **Ronald Gene**[10] **PeGan** was born in South Bend, St. Joseph Co., Indiana, on November 2, 1979.[349, 983] He died in Goshen, Elkhart Twp., Elkhart Co., Indiana, on July 5, 2012.[349, 983]

137. John Allen[9] **PeGan** (*Raymond Leon*[8], *Philip Garl*[7], *Harrison James*[6], *Harrison James*[5] *Pegan*, *Robert A.*[4], *Andrew*[3], *Andrew*[2] *Pagan*, *James*[1]) was born on December 7, 1956, in Niles, Niles Twp., Berrien Co., Michigan.[349, 731, 732] He was the son of Raymond Leon PeGan (68) and Doris Irene Fitz. John Allen died in Niles, Niles Twp., Berrien Co., Michigan, on April 19, 1972, at age 15.[349, 731, 732] He was buried in Silverbrook Cemetery, Niles, Niles Twp., Berrien Co., Michigan.[731, 732]

John Allen PeGan died when he was hit by a car while riding his bicycle.

138. Brian Lee[9] **Reed** (*Donna Belle*[8] *PeGan*, *Philip Garl*[7], *Harrison James*[6], *Harrison James*[5] *Pegan*, *Robert A.*[4], *Andrew*[3], *Andrew*[2] *Pagan*, *James*[1]) was born on Friday, August 15, 1958, in Watervliet, Watervliet Charter Twp., Berrien Co., Michigan.[128, 349, 736] He was the son of George Richard Reed and Donna Belle PeGan (69). Brian Lee died in Watervliet, Watervliet Charter Twp., Berrien Co., Michigan, on March 25, 2011, at the age of 52.[128, 349, 736] He was buried in Chapel Hill Memorial Gardens, Osceola, Penn Twp., St. Joseph Co., Indiana.[736, 984]

Never married.

139. Katherine Jean[9] **PeGan** (*Richard Schuyler*[8], *Philip Garl*[7], *Harrison James*[6], *Harrison James*[5] *Pegan*, *Robert A.*[4], *Andrew*[3], *Andrew*[2] *Pagan*, *James*[1]) was born on August 9, 1949, in Niles, Niles Twp., Berrien Co., Michigan.[349, 739] She was also known as **Kay**. She was the daughter of Richard Schuyler PeGan (70) and Dorothy Arilla Young. Katherine

Jean died in Maury Co., Tennessee, on August 25, 2001, at age 52.[349, 739]

Katherine Jean married **Mr. Swoveland**. They had one daughter.

Katherine Jean PeGan Swoveland married **Mr. Sweeney**. They divorced. They had three children.

Katherine Jean PeGan Swoveland Sweeney married **Mr. Swanson** and died under that surname.

140. **Sue Ann⁹ PeGan** (*Richard Schuyler⁸, Philip Garl⁷, Harrison James⁶, Harrison James⁵ Pegan, Robert A.⁴, Andrew³, Andrew² Pagan, James¹*) was born on November 21, 1950, in Niles, Niles Twp., Berrien Co., Michigan.[128, 349, 740, 741] She was the daughter of Richard Schuyler PeGan (70) and Dorothy Arilla Young. Sue Ann died in Niles, Niles Twp., Berrien Co., Michigan, on October 20, 1998, at age 47.[349, 741, 742] She was buried in Silverbrook Cemetery, Niles, Niles Twp., Berrien Co., Michigan.[741, 742]

Sue Ann married **Robert Clarence Masterman II** on March 22, 1969, in St. Joseph Co., Indiana.[349, 985, 986] They divorced. They had two sons. Robert Clarence Masterman II was born in Niles, Niles Twp., Berrien Co., Michigan, on June 4, 1950.[987] He reached age 63 and died in Niles, Niles Twp. Berrien Co., Michigan, on April 21, 2014.[987]

Sue Ann PeGan Masterman married **Jerome Terrence McQuaid** on December 19, 1989, in Berrien Co., Michigan.[349] Jerome Terrence McQuaid was born in Kalamazoo, Kalamazoo Twp., Kalamazoo Co., Michigan, on August 21, 1930.[128, 349, 988] He was also known as **J.T.** Jerome Terrence reached age 75 and died in Niles, Niles Twp. Berrien Co., Michigan, on June 11, 2006.[128, 988] He was buried in Mission Hills Memorial Chapel, Crematory & Gardens, North Niles, Howard Twp., Cass Co., Michigan.[988, 989]

141. **Richard Allen⁹ PeGan** (*Richard Schuyler⁸, Philip Garl⁷, Harrison James⁶, Harrison James⁵ Pegan, Robert A.⁴, Andrew³, Andrew² Pagan, James¹*) was born on March 4, 1952, in Niles, Niles Twp., Berrien Co., Michigan.[128, 349, 743, 744] He was the son of Richard Schuyler PeGan (70) and Dorothy Arilla Young. Richard Allen died in Prospect, Giles Co., Tennessee, on March 8, 2002, at age 50.[128, 349, 743, 744]

Richard Allen PeGan married **Miss Wirick.** They had two children.

142. **Claudine Louise⁹ PeGan** (*Richard Schuyler⁸, Philip Garl⁷, Harrison James⁶, Harrison James⁵ Pegan, Robert A.⁴, Andrew³, Andrew² Pagan, James¹*) was born on September 1, 1955, in Niles, Niles Twp., Berrien Co., Michigan.[349, 745] She was the daughter of Richard Schuyler PeGan (70) and Dorothy Arilla Young. Claudine Louise died in Niles, Niles Twp., Berrien Co., Michigan, on September 3, 1955.[349, 745] She was buried in Silverbrook Cemetery, Niles, Niles Twp., Berrien Co., Michigan.[745, 990]

143. **Steven Karl⁹ PeGan** (*Karl Nelson⁸, Philip Garl⁷, Harrison James⁶, Harrison James⁵ Pegan, Robert A.⁴, Andrew³, Andrew² Pagan, James¹*) was born on December 13, 1951, in Niles, Niles Twp., Berrien Co., Michigan.[128, 349, 753, 754] He was the son of Karl Nelson PeGan (71) and Elodie Lucy Turenne. Steven Karl lived in 1999 in Arizona and later in Laurel, Laurel Twp., Franklin Co., Indiana. He died in Indianapolis, Marion Co., Indiana, on April 6, 2004, at age 52.[128, 754] He was cremated.[754]

Never married.

144. **Nelson Michael⁹ PeGan** (*Karl Nelson⁸, Philip Garl⁷, Harrison James⁶, Harrison James⁵ Pegan, Robert A.⁴, Andrew³, Andrew² Pagan, James¹*) was born on February 19, 1953, in Niles, Niles Twp., Berrien Co., Michigan.[128, 349, 755, 756] He was the son of Karl Nelson PeGan (71) and Elodie Lucy Turenne. Nelson Michael lived in 1999 in Rushville, Rushville Twp., Rush Co., Indiana. He died in a hospital in Connersville, Connersville Twp., Fayette Co., Indiana, on May 20, 1999, at age 46.[128, 349, 755, 756] He was cremated.[756]

After Karl PeGan died, Steven and Nelson PeGan were raised by their paternal grandparents, Philip and Dorothy Vermilyer in Niles, Niles Twp., Berrien Co., Michigan until their mother, Elodie Lucille Turenne PeGan remarried to Robert McCoy. Steven and Nelson then moved with their mother to Paoli, Orange Co., Indiana. Nelson Pegan lived in Indianapolis, Marion Co., Indiana for a while, where his brother Steven Karl Pegan was also living. Later, Nelson moved to Knoxville, Pendleton Co., Kentucky before returning to Indiana. He was a resident of Greenfield, Center Twp., Hancock Co., Indiana before relocating to Rushville.

Nelson Michael Pegan, a carpenter, requested cremation, with his ashes to be scattered in the St. Joseph River near Niles, Niles Twp., Berrien Co., Michigan, where his father drowned.[991]

Nelson Pegan married twice and had four children by his first wife.

Nelson Michael PeGan and his first wife had four children, including:

+ 189 f II. **Daughter**[10] **PeGan** was born in Knoxville, Pendleton Co., Kentucky.

+ 190 f III. **Donna Lynn**[10] **PeGan** was born in Greenfield, Center Twp., Hancock Co., Indiana, on November 10, 1975.[349, 992] She died in Greenfield, Center Twp., Hancock Co., Indiana, on November 12, 2015.[349, 992]

145. Constance Sue[9] **Abbott** (*Juanita Mae*[8] *PeGan, Philip Garl*[7]*, Harrison James*[6]*, Harrison James*[5] *Pegan, Robert A.*[4]*, Andrew*[3]*, Andrew*[2] *Pagan, James*[1]) was born on November 27, 1952, in Niles, Niles Twp., Berrien Co., Michigan.[349, 762] She was also known as **Connie**. She was the daughter of Eugene Lyle Abbott and Juanita Mae PeGan (73). Constance Sue died in Niles, Niles Twp. Berrien Co., Michigan, on July 8, 2017, at age 64.[349, 762] She was buried in Rose Hill Cemetery, Berrien Springs, Okonoko Twp., Berrien Co., Michigan.[762]

Constance Sue married **Mr. Hamilton** They divorced. They had one adopted daughter.

146. Son[9] **PeGan** (*Vern Leroy*[8]*, Philip Garl*[7]*, Harrison James*[6]*, Harrison James*[5] *Pegan, Robert A.*[4]*, Andrew*[3]*, Andrew*[2] *Pagan, James*[1]) was born in Niles, Niles Twp., Berrien Co., Michigan. He is the son of Vern Leroy PeGan (75) and Miss Heckelbower.

Son PeGan married and had one daughter.

Daughter of Son PeGan and his wife:

+ 191 f I. **Daughter**[10] **PeGan** was born in South Bend, St. Joseph Co., Indiana.

10th Generation

147. Margaret L.¹⁰ Roll (*Leota Fatima⁹ Lydy, Bertha Olive⁸ Farr, Clara Belle⁷ Roush, Margaret Mary⁶ Pegan, Harrison James⁵, Robert A.⁴, Andrew³, Andrew² Pagan, James¹*) was born on February 26, 1920, in Lancaster Twp., Wells Co., Indiana.[69, 766] She was the daughter of Unknown Unknown and Leota Fatima Roll (76). Margaret L. lived in 1999 in Lee Center, Oneida Co., New York. She died in Port Orange, Volusia Co., Florida, on August 30, 2008, at age 88.[128, 772] Margaret L. was buried in Fairview Cemetery, Bluffton, Wells Co., Indiana.[772, 993]

Margaret L. Roll was reared by her grandmother, Bertha Olive Farr Roll Bartlemay Roll. Margaret may have never known that her real mother was Bertha's daughter Leota. Marion and Bertha Farr Roll are listed as her parents on her marriage license to Clarence Thomas Christensen and in her obituary.[772, 994]

Margaret L. married **Unknown Unknown** before 1939. She states on her York County, Virginia marriage license to Clarence T. Christensen that she had a previous marriage. Margaret and her first husband had no children and divorced; she reassumed her maiden name.[994]

Margaret L. Roll (Unknown) married **Clarence Thomas Christensen** on January 18, 1946, in Williamsburg, Virginia.[994, 995] They had one son. Clarence Thomas Christensen was born in Hinsdale, Valley Co., Montana, on March 14, 1920.[128, 994, 995, 996, 997, 998] Clarence Thomas worked as a federal government employee. He reached age 70 and died in Stokes Corner, Oneida Co., New York, on August 21, 1990.[128, 995, 996, 998] Clarence Thomas was buried in Fairview Cemetery, Bluffton, Wells Co., Indiana.[995, 999]

In addition to Bluffton, Wells Co., Indiana, Clarence and Margaret Roll Christensen lived in many other places, including Baltimore, Fairfield Co., Ohio, Pataskala, Licking Co., Ohio, Granite City, Madison Co., Illinois, Fort Lauderdale, Broward Co., Florida and Stokes Corner, Oneida Co., New York. Clarence's obituary says he was born on March 17, 1920, which is incorrect.[995]

148. Agnes Louise¹⁰ Lydy (*Leota Fatima⁹ Roll, Bertha Olive⁸ Farr, Clara Belle⁷ Roush, Margaret Mary⁶ Pegan, Harrison James⁵, Robert A.⁴, Andrew³, Andrew² Pagan, James¹*) was born on January 3, 1922, in Lancaster Twp., Wells Co., Indiana.[128, 773, 774, 775] She was also known as **Louise** and **Bonnie**. She was the daughter of Charles Wesley Lydy and Leota Fatima Roll (76). Agnes Louise died in Bluffton, Wells Co., Indiana, on April 1, 1995, at age 73.[128, 773, 774] She was buried in Fairview Cemetery, Bluffton, Wells Co., Indiana.[773, 774, 1000]

Agnes Louise married **Dwight Raymond Lutz** on April 12, 1941, in Wells Co., Indiana.[1001] They had two sons. Dwight Raymond Lutz was born in Bluffton, Wells Co., Indiana, on May 14, 1919.[128, 1002] Dwight Raymond reached age 56 and died in Bluffton, Wells Co., Indiana, on April 14, 1976.[1002, 1003] He was buried in Fairview Cemetery, Bluffton, Wells Co., Indiana.[1002, 1003, 1004]

149. Charles Wayne¹⁰ Lydy II (*Leota Fatima⁹ Roll, Bertha Olive⁸ Farr, Clara Belle⁷ Roush, Margaret Mary⁶ Pegan, Harrison James⁵, Robert A.⁴, Andrew³, Andrew² Pagan, James¹*) was born on February 27, 1923, in Lancaster Twp., Wells Co., Indiana.[776, 777, 778] He was also known as **Wayne**. He is the son of Charles Wesley Lydy and Leota Fatima Roll (76). Charles Wayne lived in 1998 in Bluffton, Wells Co., Indiana. He died in Bluffton, Wells Co., Indiana, on March 8, 2016, at age 93.[777] Charles Wayne was buried in Fairview Cemetery, Bluffton, Wells Co., Indiana.[777, 1005]

Charles Wayne married **Dorothy Crickmore** on September 28, 1946, in Wells Co., Indiana.[1006] They had five daughters. Dorothy Crickmore was born in Flint, Flint Twp., Genesee Co., Michigan, on April 17, 1927.[1006]

Charles Wayne Lydy II and Dorothy Crickmore had five daughters, including:

+ 192 f I. **Daughter**[11] **One Lydy** was born in Bluffton, Wells Co., Indiana, on July 30, 1947.

+ 193 f III. **Cheryl A.**[11] **Lydy** was born in Bluffton, Wells Co., Indiana, on January 29, 1955.[1007] She died in Bluffton, Wells Co., Indiana, on June 2, 2017.[1007]

+ 194 f I. **Daughter Two**[11] **Lydy** was born in Bluffton, Wells Co., Indiana.

150. Robert Eugene[10] **Lydy** (*Leota Fatima*[9] *Roll, Bertha Olive*[8] *Farr, Clara Belle*[7] *Roush, Margaret Mary*[6] *Pegan, Harrison James*[5]*, Robert A.*[4]*, Andrew*[3]*, Andrew*[2] *Pagan, James*[1]) was born on April 1, 1924, in Lancaster Twp., Wells Co., Indiana.[779] He was the son of Charles Wesley Lydy and Leota Fatima Roll (76).

He married **Maria Guiseppina Agness Fulginiti**. They divorced. They had four children. Maria Guiseppina Agness Fulginiti was born in Italy on January 21, 1929.[128, 1008] She reached age 54 and died in Goleta, Santa Barbara Co., California, on September 13, 1983.[128, 1008] She was cremated and her ashed interred in Davis Memorial Park Cemetery, Las Vegas, Clark Co., Nevada.[1009]

Robert Eugene Lydy married **Barbara Unknown**.

151. Dale Edmund or Edmond[10] **Lydy** (*Leota Fatima*[9] *Roll, Bertha Olive*[8] *Farr, Clara Belle*[7] *Roush, Margaret Mary*[6] *Pegan, Harrison James*[5]*, Robert A.*[4]*, Andrew*[3]*, Andrew*[2] *Pagan, James*[1]) was born on April 25, 1926, in Lancaster Twp., Wells Co., Indiana.[128, 780, 781] He was the son of Charles Wesley Lydy and Leota Fatima Roll (76). He was living in 1998 in Geneva, Wabash Twp., Adams Co., Indiana. Dale Edmond died in a hospital in Fort Wayne, Allen Co., Indiana, on February 2, 1998, at age 71.[128, 780, 782] He was cremated and his ashes buried in Fairview Cemetery, Bluffton, Wells Co., Indiana.[782, 1010, 1011]

Dale Edmond married **Mattie Lou Cromer** on July 4, 1947, in Cumberland Co., Pennsylvania.[1012] They divorced. They had one daughter. Mattie Lou Cromer was born in Chandler, Etowah Co., Alabama, on July 15, 1929.[1012]

Dale Edmond Lydy married **Pearl Yates** between April 1958 and June 1958 in Liverpool, Lancashire, England.[1013] They divorced. They have one daughter.

Dale Edmond Lydy married **Valerie Ruby Mann** on March 11, 1967, in Miami Co., Indiana.[1014, 1015] They divorced. They had two children. Valerie Ruby Mann was born in Crosby, Merseyside, Lancashire, England, on February 24, 1936.[1015, 1016] She lived in 1987 in Murray, Lancaster Twp., Wells Co., Indiana. Valerie Ruby reached age 51 and died in Bluffton, Wells Co., Indiana, on August 8, 1987.[1016, 1017] She was cremated and her cremains buried in Fairview Cemetery, Bluffton, Wells Co., Indiana.[1016, 1017, 1018]

Dale Edmond Lydy and Valerie Ruby Mann obtained their marriage license in Wells Co., Indiana, but married in Bunker Hill, Pipe Creek Twp., Miami Co., Indiana.[1014]

Dale's middle name is Edmund on his birth certificate, but Edmond on other records.[128, 781, 1014] He retired from the U.S. Army after 24 years of service.[1011]

Daughter of Dale Edmond Lydy and Valerie Ruby Mann:

+ 195 f I. **Daughter One**[11] **Lydy** was born in England.

152. Freida Mae[10] **Lydy** (*Leota Fatima*[9] *Roll, Bertha Olive*[8] *Farr, Clara Belle*[7] *Roush, Margaret Mary*[6] *Pegan, Harrison James*[5]*, Robert A.*[4]*, Andrew*[3]*, Andrew*[2] *Pagan, James*[1]) was born on January 26, 1928, in Lancaster Twp., Wells Co., Indiana.[783, 784] She is the daughter of Charles Wesley Lydy and Leota Fatima Roll (76).

Freida Mae married **Forrest Edwin DeBolt** on October 11, 1946, in Allen Co., Indiana.[783] They had two daughters. Forrest Edwin DeBolt was born in Blue Creek Twp., Adams Co., Indiana, on July 10, 1923.[128, 1019, 1020, 1021] He was also known as **Frosty**. Forrest Edwin lived in 2008 in Bluffton,

Wells Co., Indiana. He reached age 84 and died in a hospital in Fort Wayne, Allen Co., Indiana, on April 24, 2008.[128, 1019, 1021] Forrest Edwin was buried in Fairview Cemetery, Bluffton, Wells Co., Indiana.[1019, 1021, 1022]

Freida Mae Lydy and Forrest Edwin DeBolt had two daughters, including:

+ 196 f   I.   **Daughter**[11] **DeBolt** was born in Huntington, Huntington Twp., Huntington Co., Indiana.

153. Bonnie Ilene[10] **Lydy** (*Leota Fatima*[9] *Roll, Bertha Olive*[8] *Farr, Clara Belle*[7] *Roush, Margaret Mary*[6] *Pegan, Harrison James*[5], *Robert A.*[4], *Andrew*[3], *Andrew*[2] *Pagan, James*[1]) was born on January 17, 1929, in Lancaster Twp., Wells Co., Indiana.[785, 786] She was the daughter of Charles Wesley Lydy and Leota Fatima Roll (76). Bonnie Ilene died in Murray, Harrison Twp., Wells Co., Indiana, on June 3, 1929.[785, 787] She was buried in Oak Lawn Cemetery, Ossian, Jefferson Twp., Wells Co., Indiana.[785, 1023]

154. Olive Joan[10] **Lydy** (*Leota Fatima*[9] *Roll, Bertha Olive*[8] *Farr, Clara Belle*[7] *Roush, Margaret Mary*[6] *Pegan, Harrison James*[5], *Robert A.*[4], *Andrew*[3], *Andrew*[2] *Pagan, James*[1]) was born on April 20, 1930, in Lancaster Twp., Wells Co., Indiana.[128, 788, 789, 790] She was also known as **Joan**. She was the daughter of Charles Wesley Lydy and Leota Fatima Roll (76). Olive Joan died in Bluffton, Wells Co., Indiana, on December 1, 1998, at age 68.[128, 788, 789] She was buried in Fairview Cemetery, Bluffton, Wells Co., Indiana.[788, 1024, 1025]

Olive Joan Lydy Schorey always used her middle name, Joan, as her preferred given name. Her birth certificate says she was born in "Murray, Harrison Twp.", but Murray is in Lancaster Twp., Wells Co., Indiana.[790]

Olive Joan married **Richard Kay Schorey** on August 19, 1950, in Wells Co., Indiana.[1026, 1027] They divorced. They had four sons. Richard Kay Schorey was born in Bluffton, Wells Co., Indiana, on June 29, 1932.[1027, 1028, 1029, 1030] He lived about 1980 in Auburn, Union Twp., DeKalb Co., Indiana. Richard Kay Schorey also resided in 2000 in Junction City, Union Co., Arkansas. He reached age 68 and died in a hospital in El Dorado, Union Co., Arkansas, on September 25, 2000.[1028, 1030] Richard Kay was buried in Woodlawn Cemetery, Auburn. Union Twp., DeKalb Co., Indiana.[1028, 1031]

Olive Joan Lydy and Richard Kay Schorey had four sons, including:

+ 197 m   I.   **Richard Kay**[11] **Schorey II** was born in Junction City, Union Co., Arkansas, on October 15, 1951.[128, 1032, 1033] He died in a hospital in El Dorado, Union Co., Arkansas, on July 7, 2000.[128, 1032, 1033]

155. Sharon Yvonne[10] **Bender** (*Marian Colleen*[9] *Roll, Bertha Olive*[8] *Farr, Clara Belle*[7] *Roush, Margaret Mary*[6] *Pegan, Harrison James*[5], *Robert A.*[4], *Andrew*[3], *Andrew*[2] *Pagan, James*[1]) was born on February 4, 1940, in Bluffton, Wells Co., Indiana.[808, 809] She was the daughter of Earl Alfred Bender and Marian Colleen Roll (79). She died in Bluffton, Wells Co., Indiana, on May 14, 2013, at age 73.[808]

Sharon Yvonne married **Jackie Franklin Lewis** on June 7, 1968, in Wells Co., Indiana.[1034] They divorced. They have one son. Jack F. Lewis was born in Rochester, Rochester Twp., Fulton Co., Indiana, on October 16, 1935.[1035, 1036] He was also known as **Jack**. He lived in Rochester, Rochester Twp., Fulton Co., Indiana. Jackie Franklin Lewis died on August 5, 2017 in a facility in Fort Wayne, Allen Co., Indiana.[1035, 1036] He was buried in Mount Hope Athens Cemetery, Athens, Henry Twp., Fulton Co., Indiana.[1035, 1036]

Sharon Yvonne Bender Lewis married **Perry J. Graham II** on October 18, 1996, in Wells Co., Indiana.[1037] Perry Graham II was born in Louisville, Winston Co., Mississippi, on August 28, 1932 or 1933.[1038, 1039, 1040] Perry lived in 2016 in Bluffton, Wells Co., Indiana. He reached age 83 and died in Fort Wayne, Allen Co., Indiana, on September 22, 2016.[1038, 1039] He was cremated.[1039] Perry J. Graham Jr.'s birthdate in his obituary and Find A Grave entry is August

28, 1933.[1038, 1039] But the online U.S. Public Records Index indicates he was born on August 28, 1932.[1040]

156. Daughter Two[10] **Bender** (*Marian Colleen*[9] *Roll, Bertha Olive*[8] *Farr, Clara Belle*[7] *Roush, Margaret Mary*[6] *Pegan, Harrison James*[5], *Robert A.*[4], *Andrew*[3], *Andrew*[2] *Pagan, James*[1]) was born in Bluffton, Wells Co., Indiana. She is the daughter of Earl Alfred Bender and Marian Colleen Roll (79).

Daughter Bender married **Richard Dean Gardenour II** on July 8, 1967, in Wells Co., Indiana.[1041] Richard Dean Gardenour II was born in Michigan or Bluffton, Wells Co., Indiana, on March 13, 1943.[1042] Richard Dean lived in 1968 in New Haven, Allen Co., Indiana. He reached age 24 and died in Garland, Dallas Co., Texas, on January 3, 1968.[1042, 1043, 1044, 1045] Richard Dean was buried in Fairview Cemetery, Bluffton, Wells Co., Indiana.[1043, 1046]

Richard Dean Gardenour, a truck driver from New Haven, Allen Co., Indiana, was shot at an apartment complex parking lot in Garland, Texas by an unknown assailant. He and a friend, Keith K. Schenkel from Bluffton Indiana, were in Garland to pick up a tanker truck and visit Gardenour's father, who lived in Garland, a Dallas suburb. In Garland for a night, they met a man and two women at a Dallas nightclub or bar and decided to drive to an apartment with them. There two other men joined them. Gardenour argued in the parking lot with one of the men, who shot him in the head. Panicked, Schenkel drove away, while the assailant riddled his car with bullets. After Schenkel escaped, he returned to the apartment parking lot to retrieve Gardenour's body, then drove to a service station to phone police. The shooter was never caught.[1043, 1044]

Richard Dean Gardenour's Texas death certificate states he was born in Michigan, but other sources say he was born in Bluffton, Wells Co., Indiana.[1042, 1043, 1044]

Daughter Bender Gardenour married **Gerald Ray Weaver** on July 24, 1969, in Wells Co., Indiana.[1047] They divorced. Gerald Ray Weaver was born in Muncie, Center Twp., Delaware Co., Indiana, on July 26, 1942.[1048, 1049] He was also known as **Jerry**. Gerald Ray reached age 64 and died in Bluffton, Wells Co., Indiana, on October 18, 2006.[1048, 1049] He was buried in Gearnand Cemetery, Reiffsburg, Harrison Twp., Wells Co., Indiana.[1048, 1050]

157. Mary Louise[10] **Hunter** (*Clyde Cisco*[9], *John Clark*[8], *Clara Belle*[7] *Roush, Margaret Mary*[6] *Pegan, Harrison James*[5], *Robert A.*[4], *Andrew*[3], *Andrew*[2] *Pagan, James*[1]) was born on April 4, 1936, in New Market Twp., Highland Co., Ohio. She is the daughter of Clyde Cisco Hunter (80) and Lucille Mildred Whiting.

Mary Louise married **Alfred R. Groves** on August 12, 1951, in Highland Co., Ohio.[1051] They divorced. They had two daughters. Alfred R. Groves was born in Otway, Brush Creek Twp., Scioto Co., Ohio, on November 22, 1932.[1051, 1052]

158. Betty Mae[10] **Hunter** (*Clyde Cisco*[9], *John Clark*[8], *Clara Belle*[7] *Roush, Margaret Mary*[6] *Pegan, Harrison James*[5], *Robert A.*[4], *Andrew*[3], *Andrew*[2] *Pagan, James*[1]) was born on June 13, 1938, in New Market Twp., Highland Co., Ohio. She is the daughter of Clyde Cisco Hunter (80) and Lucille Mildred Whiting.

Betty Mae married **Bill Smith** in January 1955 in Lynchburg, Dodson Twp., Highland Co., Ohio? They divorced.

Betty Mae Hunter Smith married **Richard K. Smith**.

159. Virginia Ruth[10] **Hunter** (*Clyde Cisco*[9], *John Clark*[8], *Clara Belle*[7] *Roush, Margaret Mary*[6] *Pegan, Harrison James*[5], *Robert A.*[4], *Andrew*[3], *Andrew*[2] *Pagan, James*[1]) was born on October 10, 1940, in New Market Twp., Highland Co., Ohio. She is the daughter of Clyde Cisco Hunter (80) and Lucille Mildred Whiting.

Virginia Ruth married **Richard Lee Kinnison** on August 22, 1962.[1053] They had two daughters. Richard Lee Kinnison was born in Paint Twp., Ross Co., Ohio, on May 5, 1941.[1053] Richard Lee reached age 72 and died in Hillsboro, Liberty Twp., Highland Co., Ohio, on March 1, 2014.[1053] He was buried in New Market Baptist Church Cemetery, New Market Twp., Highland Co., Ohio.[1053, 1054]

160. Infant Son[10] **Hunter** (*Clyde Cisco*[9], *John Clark*[8], *Clara Belle*[7] *Roush, Margaret Mary*[6] *Pegan, Harrison James*[5], *Robert A.*[4], *Andrew*[3], *Andrew*[2] *Pagan, James*[1]) was born on July 7, 1951, in Highland Co., Ohio.[819] He was the son of Clyde Cisco Hunter (80) and Lucille Mildred Whiting. Infant Son died in Highland Co., Ohio, on July 7, 1951.[819] He was buried in Mt. Zion Cemetery, Danville, New Market Twp., Highland Co., Ohio.[819]

160A. Robert Bernard[10] **Baker** (*Milford Earnest*[9] *Baker, Nellie Fay*[8] *Roush, John Alven*[7], *Margaret Mary*[6] *Pegan, Harrison James*[5], *Robert A.*[4], *Andrew*[3], *Andrew*[2] *Pagan, James*[1]) was born on May 6, 1934, in Indianapolis, Marion Co., Indiana.[128, U, V] He was the son of Milford Earnest Baker (80A) and Etta L. Uhls. Robert Bernard died in Tucson, Pima Co., Arizona, on March 26, 1973, at age 39.[128, V, W] He was buried in Evergreen Memorial Park Cemetery, Tucson, Pima Co., Arizona.[V, W]

Robert Bernard married **Shirley Ann Lang** on June 15, 1956, in Marion Co., Indiana.[FF] They divorced. They had two children. Shirley Ann Lang was born in Indianapolis, Marion Co., Indiana, on October 8, 1936.[GG, HH, II] She reached age 78 and died in Tucson, Pima Co., Arizona, on April 7, 2015.[HH, II] Shirley Ann was buried in Evergreen Memorial Cemetery, Tucson, Pima Co., Arizona.[HH, II]

She remarried and died as Shirley Guyton.

Robert Bernard Baker and Shirley Ann Lang had two children, including:

+ 197A m I **Robert Travis**[11] **Baker** was born in Indianapolis, Marion Co., Indiana? on November 15, 1959.[128, II] He died in Tucson, Pima Co., Arizona, on September 12, 2008.[II., JJ]

160B. Violet Nordeica[10] **(Baker) McCain** (*Milford Earnest*[9] *Baker, Nellie Fay*[8] *Roush, John Alven*[7], *Margaret Mary*[6] *Pegan, Harrison James*[5], *Robert A.*[4], *Andrew*[3], *Andrew*[2] *Pagan, James*[1]) was born in on November 26, 1935, in St. Louis, Missouri.[X, Y] She was the daughter of Milford Earnest Baker (80A) and Violet Elizabeth Linton. She lived in Chicago, Cook Co., Illinois in 1960. Violet Nordeica died in Tampico, Cuidad Madero, Tamaulipas, Mexico, on June 28, 1960, at age 23.[Y, Z, AA] She was buried in Lake Charles Park Cemetery, Bel-Nor, St. Louis Co., Missouri.[Y, AA]

Violet Nordeica used her stepfather's surname. It is unknown whether her stepfather, Merle Lyle McCain, formally adopted her. Violet N. was an unmarried teacher working in Chicago, Illinois when she was killed in an auto accident while vacationing in Mexico.

161. Robert Dean[10] **Roush** (*John Milford*[9], *Joseph Lewis*[8], *John Alven*[7], *Margaret Mary*[6] *Pegan, Harrison James*[5], *Robert A.*[4], *Andrew*[3], *Andrew*[2] *Pagan, James*[1]) was born on June 29, 1949, in Lincoln, Lancaster Co., Nebraska.[412, 832] He was the son of John Milford Roush (82) and Viola Jane Brown. Robert Dean lived in 2015 in Coldwater, Coldwater Twp., Branch Co., Michigan. He died in a hospital in Kalamazoo, Kalamazoo Twp., Kalamazoo Co., Michigan, on September 10, 2015, at age 66.[832] He was cremated.[832]

Robert Dean Roush married **Miss Badders.** They divorced. They had three children.

Robert Dean Roush married **Ms. Schroth.**

162. Gary Wayne[10] **Roush** (*John Milford*[9], *Joseph Lewis*[8], *John Alven*[7], *Margaret Mary*[6] *Pegan, Harrison James*[5], *Robert A.*[4], *Andrew*[3], *Andrew*[2] *Pagan, James*[1]) was born on March 17, 1951, in Lincoln, Lancaster Co., Nebraska.[128, 412, 833] He was the son of John Milford Roush (82) and Viola Jane Brown. Gary Wayne died in Quincy, Quincy Twp., Branch Co., Michigan, on April 9, 2006, at age 55.[128, 412, 833] He was buried in Evergreen Cemetery, Girard Twp., Branch Co., Michigan.[833, 1055]

Gary Wayne married **Miss Towne.** They divorced. They have one daughter.

Gary Wayne Roush married **Sandra Ellen Burritt.** They divorced. They had two children. Sandra Ellen Burritt was born in Albion, Albion Twp., Calhoun Co., Michigan, on September 18, 1950.[128, 1056] She lived in 2013 in Coldwater,

Coldwater Twp., Branch Co., Michigan. Sandra Ellen reached age 60 and died in Allen, Allen Twp., Hillsdale Co., Michigan, on June 14, 2011.[128, 1056] She was buried in Lakeview Cemetery, Quincy, Quincy Twp., Branch Co., Michigan.[1056]

163. **Vicky Lynn**[10] **Roush** (*John Milford*[9], *Joseph Lewis*[8], *John Alven*[7], *Margaret Mary*[6] *Pegan, Harrison James*[5], *Robert A.*[4], *Andrew*[3], *Andrew*[2] *Pagan, James*[1]) was born on March 17, 1952, in Coldwater, Coldwater Twp., Branch Co., Michigan.[412, 834] She was the daughter of John Milford Roush (82) and Viola Jane Brown. Vicky Lynn died in Coldwater, Coldwater Twp., Branch Co., Michigan, on March 24, 2015, at age 63.[834]

Vicky Lynn married **Mr. Brown** They divorced. They had one daughter.

164. **George**[10] **Roush II** (*George Lewis*[9], *Joseph Lewis*[8], *John Alven*[7], *Margaret Mary*[6] *Pegan, Harrison James*[5], *Robert A.*[4], *Andrew*[3], *Andrew*[2] *Pagan, James*[1]). He was the son of George Lewis Roush (83) and Donna Smith. George died before 1978.

He seems to have died young.

165. **Daughter One**[10] **Roush** (*Harley Leroy*[9], *Joseph Lewis*[8], *John Alven*[7], *Margaret Mary*[6] *Pegan, Harrison James*[5], *Robert A.*[4], *Andrew*[3], *Andrew*[2] *Pagan, James*[1]) was born in Coldwater, Coldwater Twp., Branch Co., Michigan. She is the daughter of Harley Leroy Roush (84) and Shelby Jean Shoup.

Daughter One Roush married **Mr. Reagan.** They had two daughters.

Daughter One Roush and Mr. Reagan had two daughters, including:

+ 197A f I. **Daughter**[11] **Reagan** was born in Houston, Harris Co., Texas?

165A. **Daughter Two**[10] **Roush** (*Harley Leroy*[9], *Joseph Lewis*[8], *John Alven*[7], *Margaret Mary*[6] *Pegan, Harrison James*[5], *Robert A.*[4], *Andrew*[3], *Andrew*[2] *Pagan, James*[1]) was born in Orange Co., California. She is the daughter of Harley Leroy Roush (84) and Helen Marie Reid.

She married **Joseph Vindiola.** They have two daughters. Joseph Vindiola was born in Fontana, San Bernardino Co., California, on June 22, 1964.[1057, 1058, 1059] He was also known as **Joey** and **Bear.** Joseph reached age 50 and died in Loma Linda, San Bernardino Co., California, on November 2, 2014.[1058, 1059] He was buried in Bellevue Memorial Park Cemetery, Ontario, San Bernardino Co., California.[1058]

166. **Larry Eugene**[10] **Roush** (*George Beard*[9], *George Beard*[8], *Albert Leroy*[7], *Margaret Mary*[6] *Pegan, Harrison James*[5], *Robert A.*[4], *Andrew*[3], *Andrew*[2] *Pagan, James*[1]) was born on May 28, 1948, in Hardin Co., Kentucky.[128, 851] He was the son of George Beard Roush II (87) and Madge Elaine Guyer. Larry Eugene lived in 1974 in Chattanooga, Hamilton Co., Tennessee. He died in Yuma, Yuma Co., Arizona, on July 11, 2011, at age 63.[128]

167. **William Leroy**[10] **Roush II** (*William Leroy*[9], *George Beard*[8], *Albert Leroy*[7], *Margaret Mary*[6] *Pegan, Harrison James*[5], *Robert A.*[4], *Andrew*[3], *Andrew*[2] *Pagan, James*[1]) was born on October 17, 1960, in Wichita, Sedgwick Co., Kansas.[855, 856] He was the son of William Leroy Roush (88) and Geraldine Kay Olsen. William Leroy died in Murray, Salt Lake Co., Utah, on October 7, 1991, at age 30.[855, 856] He was buried in Manti Cemetery, Manti, Sanpete Co., Utah.[856]

Never married.

168. **Nancy M.**[10] **Sorel** (*Margaret A.*[9] *Roush, Harry Emmett*[8], *Eli Kenneth*[7], *Margaret Mary*[6] *Pegan, Harrison James*[5], *Robert A.*[4], *Andrew*[3], *Andrew*[2] *Pagan, James*[1]) was born on Monday, January 16, 1961, in Providence, Providence Co., Rhode Island.[857] She was the daughter of Edward A. Sorel II and Margaret A. Roush (90). Nancy M. lived in 2017 in Ashaway, Washington Co., Rhode Island. She died in Providence, Providence Co., Rhode Island, on February 3, 2017, at the age of 56.[857]

She married **Mr. Martell.** They had two daughters.

169. **Son**[10] **Moore** (*Mary Ellen*[9] *Bussey, Lora Belle*[8] *Roush, Eli Kenneth*[7], *Margaret Mary*[6] *Pegan, Harrison James*[5], *Robert A.*[4], *Andrew*[3], *Andrew*[2] *Pagan, James*[1]). Son Moore was born in Hillsboro,

Liberty Twp., Highland Co., Ohio. He is the son of Glenn A. Moore and Mary Ellen Bussey (92).

Son Moore married **Betty Lee Rhoads** on March 12, 1976.[1060] They have one son. Betty Rhoads was born in Hillsboro, Liberty Twp., Highland Co., Ohio, on Monday, October 12, 1953.[1060, 1061] Betty reached 62 years of age and died in Hillsboro, Liberty Twp., Highland Co., Ohio, on October 6, 2016.[1060]

Son of Son Moore and his wife:

+ 198 m I. **Robert A.**[11] **Moore** was born in Hillsboro, Liberty Twp., Highland Co., Ohio on September 24, 1980.[1062] in Hillsboro, Liberty Twp., Highland Co., Ohio on September 24, 1980.[1062]

170. Michael Ray[10] **Wallace** (*Elizabeth Joanna*[9] *Bussey, Lora Belle*[8] *Roush, Eli Kenneth*[7]*, Margaret Mary*[6] *Pegan, Harrison James*[5]*, Robert A.*[4]*, Andrew*[3]*, Andrew*[2] *Pagan, James*[1]) was born on June 15, 1954, in Winchester, Meigs Twp., Adams Co., Ohio.[182] He was the son of Harold L. Wallace and Elizabeth Joanna Bussey (95). Michael Ray lived in Winchester, Meigs Twp., Adams Co., Ohio. He died in a hospital in Lima, Ottawa Twp., Allen Co., Ohio, on June 2, 2015, at age 60.[182] He was cremated.[182]

Michael Ray Wallace was married twice. He had four children by his first wife and one by his second. An online obituary confirms his birthdate and place, and where he died, but does not give a date of death.[1063]

171. Jeanne E.[10] **Bills** (*Helen Luella*[9] *Bussey, Lora Belle*[8] *Roush, Eli Kenneth*[7]*, Margaret Mary*[6] *Pegan, Harrison James*[5]*, Robert A.*[4]*, Andrew*[3]*, Andrew*[2] *Pagan, James*[1]) was born on September 18, 1960, in Hillsboro, Liberty Twp., Highland Co., Ohio.[885, 886] She was the daughter of Raymond Eugene Bills and Helen Luella Bussey (96). Jeanne E. lived in 2013 in Eaton, Washington Twp., Preble Co., Ohio. She died in a hospital in Richmond, Wayne Co., Indiana, on November 10, 2013, at age 53.[885, 886] Jeanne E. was buried in Green Mound Cemetery, New Madison, Harrison Twp., Darke Co., Ohio.[885, 886]

Jeanne E. Bills married **Mr. McCombs**. They had one son.

Jeanne E. Bills McCombs married **Mr. Swartz** and died under that surname.

172. Son[10] **Shuttleworth** (*Daughter*[9] *Roush, Samuel Frederick*[8]*, Eli Kenneth*[7]*, Margaret Mary*[6] *Pegan, Harrison James*[5]*, Robert A.*[4]*, Andrew*[3]*, Andrew*[2] *Pagan, James*[1]) was born on April 14, 1967, in Wilmington, Union Twp., Clinton Co., Ohio. He was the son of Thomas Shuttleworth and Carol Sue Roush (98).

Son Shuttleworth has married twice and had one son by his first wife.

Son of Son Shuttleworth and his first wife:

+ 199 m I. **Matthew Thomas**[11] **Shuttleworth** was born in Wilmington, Union Twp., Clinton Co., Ohio, on September 11, 1993.[1064] He died in Warren Co., Ohio, on January 14, 2012.[1064]

173. Daughter[10] **Seitz** (*William Lee*[9]*, Dorothy Opal*[8] *Roush, Eli Kenneth*[7]*, Margaret Mary*[6] *Pegan, Harrison James*[5]*, Robert A.*[4]*, Andrew*[3]*, Andrew*[2] *Pagan, James*[1]) was born on February 20, 1961, in Troy, Concord Twp., Miami Co., Ohio. She is the daughter of William Lee Seitz (108) and Lorraine Nickels.

Daughter Seitz married **Mr. Kinyoun**. They divorced. They had three children.

Daughter Seitz partnered with **Unknown Unknown**. They have one son.

Daughter Seitz and Mr. Kinyoun had three children, including:

+ 100 m I. **Jesse Lee**[11] **Kinyoun** was born in St. Petersburg, Pinellas Co., Florida, on May 24, 1989.[128, 1065] He died in St. Petersburg, Pinellas Co., Florida, on March 9, 2002.[128, 1065]

174. William Jeffrey¹⁰ Seitz II (*William Lee⁹, Dorothy Opal⁸ Roush, Eli Kenneth⁷, Margaret Mary⁶ Pegan, Harrison James⁵, Robert A.⁴, Andrew³, Andrew² Pagan, James¹*) was born on June 12, 1962, in Troy, Concord Twp., Miami Co., Ohio.[913] He was the son of William Lee Seitz (108) and Lorraine Nickels. William Jeffrey died in Troy, Concord Twp., Miami Co., Ohio, on June 12, 1962.[913] He was buried in Riverside Cemetery, Troy, Concord Twp., Miami Co., Ohio.[1066]

175. Jeffrey¹⁰ Seitz (*William Lee⁹, Dorothy Opal⁸ Roush, Eli Kenneth⁷, Margaret Mary⁶ Pegan, Harrison James⁵, Robert A.⁴, Andrew³, Andrew² Pagan, James¹*) was born between 1967 and 2011 in Troy, Concord Twp., Miami Co., Ohio. He was the son of William Lee Seitz (108) and Mary Jane Gilliand. Jeffrey died between 1967 and August 2011.

He probably died in infancy.

176. Danny Edward¹⁰ Cowgill (*Betty Jean⁹ Eastes, Opal Colene⁸ Pearson, Sarah Celeste⁷ PeGan, Harrison James⁶, Harrison James⁵ Pegan, Robert A.⁴, Andrew³, Andrew² Pagan, James¹*) was born on August 11, 1950, in Marion, Center Twp., Grant Co., Indiana.[128, 928, 929, 930] He was also known as **Pete**. He was the son of Charles Edward Cowgill and Betty Jean Eastes (118). Danny Edward lived in 1998 in Gas City, Mill Twp., Grant Co., Indiana. He died in a hospital in Muncie, Center Twp., Delaware Co., Indiana, on August 26, 1998, at age 48.[128, 928, 929, 930] Danny Edward was buried in Riverside Cemetery, Gas City, Mill Twp. Grant Co., Indiana.[928, 930, 1067, 1068]

Danny Edward married **Tonya May Carroll** in 1985.[1069] They had two sons. Tonya May Carroll was born in Marion, Center Twp., Grant Co., Indiana, on September 12, 1955.[1069] Tonya May lived in 2016 in Gas City, Mill Twp., Grant Co., Indiana. She reached age 61 and died in a hospital in Indianapolis, Marion Co., Indiana, on October 19, 2016.[1069] Tonya May was buried in Riverside Cemetery, Gas City, Mill Twp. Grant Co., Indiana.[1069, 1070]

177. Daughter¹⁰ Eastes (*Joseph Edward⁹, Opal Colene⁸ Pearson, Sarah Celeste⁷ PeGan, Harrison James⁶, Harrison James⁵ Pegan, Robert A.⁴, Andrew³, Andrew² Pagan, James¹*) was born in Jacksonville, Onslow Co., North Carolina. She is the daughter of Joseph Edward Eastes II (119) and Marilyn Louise James McDaniel.

Daughter Eastes married **Richard Lee Jones** on September 28, 1974, in Grant Co., Indiana.[1071, 1072] They divorced. They have two daughters. Richard Lee Jones was born in Marion, Center Twp., Grant Co., Indiana, on August 11, 1956.[1073] He reached age 58 and died in Marion, Center Twp., Grant Co., Indiana, on May 15, 2015.[1073] Richard Lee was buried in Marion National Cemetery, Marion, Grant Co., Indiana.[1073, 1074]

She married another **Mr. Jones?** They divorced. They have one son.

178. Son¹⁰ Eastes (*Joseph Edward⁹, Opal Colene⁸ Pearson, Sarah Celeste⁷ PeGan, Harrison James⁶, Harrison James⁵ Pegan, Robert A.⁴, Andrew³, Andrew² Pagan, James¹*) was born on April 24, 1960, in Jonesboro, Mill Twp., Grant Co., Indiana. He is the son of Joseph Edward Eastes II (119) and Marilyn Louise James McDaniel.

Son Eastes married and divorced twice, then married for a third time.

Son Eastes married **Toni Rae Jacks** on April 5, 2002, in Grant Co., Indiana.[1075, 1076] Toni Rae Jacks was born in Marion, Center Twp., Grant Co., Indiana, on April 5, 1960.[1077, 1078, 1079] Toni Rae reached age 43 and died in Gas City, Mill Twp., Grant Co., Indiana, on November 19, 2003.[1077, 1078, 1079] She was buried in Riverside Cemetery, Gas City, Mill Twp. Grant Co., Indiana.[1077, 1079, 1080]

179. Daniel Lee¹⁰ Jarvis (*Betty Jean⁹ Pegan, Cecil Keith⁸, Jesse Harrison⁷, Harrison James⁶ PeGan II, Harrison James⁵ Pegan, Robert A.⁴, Andrew³, Andrew² Pagan, James¹*) was born on July 1, 1962, in Huntington, Huntington Twp., Huntington Co., Indiana.[128, 945, 946] He was the son of Ronald Lee Jarvis and Betty Jean Pegan (121). Daniel Lee died in Kokomo, Center Twp., Howard Co., Indiana, on February 17, 2004, at age 41.[128, 945, 946] He was buried in Crown Point Cemetery, Kokomo, Center Twp., Howard Co., Indiana.[945, 946, 1081]

Daniel Lee Jarvis had two relationships, one marital. He was divorced. He had two children by his first relationship.

180. Daughter[10] **Dodson** (*Daughter*[9] *Pegan, James Meredith*[8]*, Jesse Harrison*[7]*, Harrison James*[6] *PeGan II, Harrison James*[5] *Pegan, Robert A.*[4]*, Andrew*[3]*, Andrew*[2] *Pagan, James*[1]). She is the daughter of Mr. Dodson and Daughter Pegan (124).

She may have married **Unknown Unknown.** They have one daughter.

Daughter of Daughter Dodson and Unknown Unknown:

+ 201 f I. **Destiny**[11] **Unknown**. Destiny died before December 2016.

181. Robert Lee[10] **Flowers** (*Allen Eugene*[9]*, Florence Willodean*[8] *Pegan, Jesse Harrison*[7]*, Harrison James*[6] *PeGan II, Harrison James*[5] *Pegan, Robert A.*[4]*, Andrew*[3]*, Andrew*[2] *Pagan, James*[1]) was born on July 28, 1973, in Van Wert, Van Wert Co., Ohio.[292, 954] He was the son of Allen Eugene Flowers (124) and Connie Margaret Kramer. Robert Lee died in Wabash, Liberty Twp., Mercer Co., Ohio, on September 9, 1978, at age five.[823, 954, 955] He was buried in St. Paul's Lutheran Cemetery, Wabash, Washington Twp., Mercer Co., Ohio.[1082]

Robert "Bobby" Flowers was struck by a car and killed.

182. Brandy Lee[10] **Flowers** (*Son Two Flowers*[9]*, Florence Willodean*[8] *Pegan, Jesse Harrison*[7]*, Harrison James*[6] *PeGan II, Harrison James*[5] *Pegan, Robert A.*[4]*, Andrew*[3]*, Andrew*[2] *Pagan, James*[1]) was born on July 26, 1978, in Lima, Ottawa Twp., Allen Co., Ohio.[292, 960] She was the daughter of Son Two Flowers (127) and his wife. Brandy Lee died in a facility in Mantua, Mantua Twp., Portage Co., Ohio, on February 5, 2009, at age 30.[292, 960] She was buried in Walnut Grove Cemetery, Delphos, Marion Twp., Allen Co., Ohio.[960, 1083]

Brandy Flowers lived at the Hattie Larlham Foundation, a facility for the developmentally challenged, in Mantua, Ohio.

183. Danette Lee[10] **Crossen** (*Maryln Ann*[9] *PeGan, Leo Everett*[8]*, Clanzie Herold*[7]*, Harrison James*[6]*, Harrison James*[5] *Pegan, Robert A.*[4]*, Andrew*[3]*, Andrew*[2] *Pagan, James*[1]) was born on June 25, 1961, in Indianapolis, Marion Co., Indiana.[128, 965, 966] She was the daughter of James Brent Crossen and Maryln Ann PeGan (128). Danette Lee died in Dallas, Dallas Co., Texas, on August 6, 2000, at age 39.[128, 965, 966] She was buried in Calvary Hill Cemetery, Dallas, Dallas Co., Texas.[1084]

Died under the name Danette Lee Crossen.

Danette L. Crosson Williams married **Mr. Winter.** They divorced. They had one son.

Danette Lee married **Mr. Williams.** They divorced. They had no children.

184. Brent Christopher[10] **PeGan** (*Harold Leon*[9]*, Paul Harold*[8]*, Clanzie Herold*[7]*, Harrison James*[6]*, Harrison James*[5] *Pegan, Robert A.*[4]*, Andrew*[3]*, Andrew*[2] *Pagan, James*[1]) was born on April 12, 1966, in Fort Wayne, Allen Co., Indiana.[116, 970] He was the son of Harold Leon PeGan (131) and Miss Parrot. Brent Christopher died in Warsaw, Wayne Twp., Koscuisko Co., Indiana, on July 15, 1990, at age 24.[970, 971] He was buried in Oakwood Cemetery, Warsaw, Wayne Twp., Koscuisko Co., Indiana.[971, 1085]

Never married.

Brent C. PeGan died in a car-train accident at a poorly-marked railroad crossing.

185. Daughter[10] **PeGan** (*Son*[9]*, Hugh Frederick*[8]*, Clanzie Herold*[7]*, Harrison James*[6]*, Harrison James*[5] *Pegan, Robert A.*[4]*, Andrew*[3]*, Andrew*[2] *Pagan, James*[1]) was born in Lafayette, Fairfield Twp., Tippecanoe Co., Indiana. She is the daughter of Son PeGan (132) and his wife.

Daugher PeGan married **Mr. Lundstrom**. They had four children.

Daughter PeGan and Mr. Lundstrom have four children, including:

+ 202 f III. **Runner Cosette**[11] **Lundstrom** was born in Cincinnati, Hamilton Co., Ohio, on July 11, 2015.[1086] She died in Cincinnati, Hamilton Co., Ohio, on July 15, 2015.[1086]

186. Son¹⁰ PeGan (*Son⁹, Phillip Elsworth⁸, Philip Garl⁷, Harrison James⁶, Harrison James⁵ Pegan, Robert A.⁴, Andrew³, Andrew² Pagan, James¹*) was born in South Bend, St. Joseph Co., Indiana. He is the son of Son PeGan (134) and Hazel Marie McGraw.

Son PeGan has been married twice. He has two children by his first wife and one by his second.

Son PeGan and his first wife had two children, including:

+ 203 f I. **Stephine Ann¹¹ PeGan** was born in Niles, Niles Twp., Berrien Co., Michigan, on July 31, 1991.[349, 1087] She died in Niles, Niles Twp., Berrien Co., Michigan, on July 31, 1991.[349, 1087]

187. Rebecca Ann¹⁰ Bakeman (*Daughter⁹ PeGan, Phillip Elsworth⁸, Philip Garl⁷, Harrison James⁶, Harrison James⁵ Pegan, Robert A.⁴, Andrew³, Andrew² Pagan, James¹*) was born on November 6, 1977, in Niles, Niles Twp., Berrien Co., Michigan.[884, 252] She was the daughter of Mr. Bakeman and Daughter PeGan (135). Rebecca Ann died in Niles, Niles Twp., Berrien Co., Michigan, on January 16, 1978.[884, 252] She was buried in Mission Hills Memorial Chapel, Crematory & Gardens, North Niles, Howard Twp., Cass Co., Michigan.[884, 1088]

188. Ronald Gene¹⁰ PeGan (*Son⁹, Phillip Elsworth⁸, Philip Garl⁷, Harrison James⁶, Harrison James⁵ Pegan, Robert A.⁴, Andrew³, Andrew² Pagan, James¹*) was born on November 2, 1979, in South Bend, St. Joseph Co., Indiana.[886, 252] He was the son of Son PeGan (136) and his second wife. Ronald Gene died in Goshen, Elkhart Twp., Elkhart Co., Indiana, on July 5, 2012, at age 32.[886, 252] He was buried in Grace Lawn Cemetery, Middlebury, Middlebury Twp., Elkhart Co., Indiana.[886, 1089]

Ronald Gene PeGan II married twice. He had three children by his first wife.

Ronald Gene died in a motorcycle accident.

189. Daughter¹⁰ PeGan (*Nelson Michael⁹, Karl Nelson⁸, Philip Garl⁷, Harrison James⁶, Harrison James⁵ Pegan, Robert A.⁴, Andrew³, Andrew² Pagan, James¹*) was born in Knoxville, Pendleton Co., Kentucky. She is the daughter of Nelson Michael PeGan (144) and Joyce Ann Perry.

Daughter PeGan married **Bobby Lee Poe** on March 14, 1992, in Hancock Co., Indiana.[1090] They divorced. They had three children. Bobby Lee Poe was born in Greenfield, Center Twp., Hancock Co., Indiana, on July 7, 1964.[128, 1091, 1092, 1093] He lived in Morristown, Hanover Twp., Shelby Co., Indiana. Bobby Lee reached age 43 and died in a hospital in Greenfield, Center Twp., Hancock Co., Indiana, on September 28, 2007.[128, 1091, 1092, 1093] He was cremated and his cremains buried in South Mound Cemetery, New Castle, Henry Co., Indiana?[1092, 1093]

Although his obituary says he was to be buried in South Mound Cemetery in New Castle, Indiana, his death certificate says he was cremated.

Daughter PeGan and Bobby Lee Poe had three children, including:

+ 204 f I. **Daughter¹¹ Poe**

190. Donna Lynn¹⁰ PeGan (*Nelson Michael⁹, Karl Nelson⁸, Philip Garl⁷, Harrison James⁶, Harrison James⁵ Pegan, Robert A.⁴, Andrew³, Andrew² Pagan, James¹*) was born on Monday, November 10, 1975, in Greenfield, Center Twp., Hancock Co., Indiana.[349, 992] She was the daughter of Nelson Michael PeGan (144) and Joyce Ann Perry. Donna Lynn died in Greenfield, Center Twp., Hancock Co., Indiana, on November 12, 2015. at the age of 40.[349, 992]

Donna Lynn married **Mr. Haste.** They had three children.

191. Daughter¹⁰ PeGan (*Son⁹, Vern Leroy⁸, Philip Garl⁷, Harrison James⁶, Harrison James⁵ Pegan, Robert A.⁴, Andrew³, Andrew² Pagan, James¹*) was born in South Bend, St. Joseph Co., Indiana. She is the daughter of Son PeGan (146) and his wife.

She had a relationship with **Mr. Thiry**. They had one son:

Son of Daughter PeGan and Mr. Thiry:

+ 205 m I. **Ashton James[11] PeGan-Thiry** was born in Escanaba, Bark River Twp., Delta Co., Michigan, on August 2, 2010.[349, 1094] He died in Escanaba, Bark River Twp., Delta Co., Michigan, on August 2, 2010.[349, 1094]

11th Generation

192. Daughter One[11] **Lydy** (*Charles Wayne II*[10], *Leota Fatima*[9] *Roll, Bertha Olive*[8] *Farr, Clara Belle*[7] *Roush, Margaret Mary*[6] *Pegan, Harrison James*[5], *Robert A.*[4], *Andrew*[3], *Andrew*[2] *Pagan, James*[1]) was born on July 30, 1947, in Bluffton, Wells Co., Indiana. She is the daughter of Charles Wayne Lydy II (149) and Dorothy Crickmore.

Daughter One Lydy has been married five times, including:

Daughter One Lydy married **Mr. Johnson**.

Daughter One Lydy married **Robert A. Barnes** on January 3, 1981, in Wells Co., Indiana.[1095] They divorced. Robert A. Barnes was born in Fort Wayne, Allen Co., Indiana, on December 22, 1944.[128, 1096, 1097] He lived in 2000 in Ossian, Jefferson Twp., Wells Co., Indiana. Robert A. reached age 55 and died in a hospital in Fort Wayne, Allen Co., Indiana, on March 11, 2000.[128, 1096, 1097] He was buried in Elm Grove Cemetery, Bluffton, Wells Co., Indiana.[1097, 1098]

Daughter of Daughter One Lydy and Mr. Johnson:

+ 206 f I. **Holly Marie**[12] **Johnson** was born in Bluffton, Wells Co., Indiana, on December 12, 1971.[1099, 1100] She died in Bluffton, Wells Co., Indiana, on December 12, 1971.[1099, 1100]

193. Cheryl A.[11] **Lydy** (*Charles Wayne II*[10], *Leota Fatima*[9] *Roll, Bertha Olive*[8] *Farr, Clara Belle*[7] *Roush, Margaret Mary*[6] *Pegan, Harrison James*[5], *Robert A.*[4], *Andrew*[3], *Andrew*[2] *Pagan, James*[1]) was born on January 29, 1955, in Bluffton, Wells Co., Indiana.[1007] She was the daughter of Charles Wayne Lydy II (149) and Dorothy Crickmore. Cheryl A. died in Bluffton, Wells Co., Indiana, on June 2, 2017, at age 62.[1007] She was buried in Fairview Cemetery, Bluffton, Wells Co., Indiana.[1007, 1101]

Cheryl A. married **Samuel Robert Ramsey** on November 2, 1974, in Dubois Co., Indiana.[1102] They divorced. They had three children. Samuel Robert Ramsey was born in Grove City, Pine Twp., Mercer Co., Pennsylvania, on April 22, 1949.[128, 1103] He reached age 61 and died in Pine Twp., Mercer Co., Pennsylvania, on June 27, 2010.[128, 1103] Samuel Robert was buried in Carpenter Cemetery, Springfield Twp., Mercer Co., Pennsylvania.[1103, 1104]

Cheryl A. Lydy married **Carl Duane Blumenhorst** on August 30, 1980, in Blackford Co., Indiana.[1105] Carl Duane Blumenhorst was born in Bluffton, Wells Co., Indiana, on October 11, 1945.[128, 1106, 1107] Carl Duane lived in 1982 in Bluffton, Wells Co., Indiana. He reached age 37 and died in a hospital in Fort Wayne, Allen Co., Indiana, on January 1, 1983.[128, 1107] Carl Duane was buried in Hillside Cemetery, Pennville, Penn Twp., Jay Co., Indiana.[1108]

Cheryl A. Lydy married **Delbert James Lee** on June 10, 1983, in Adams Co., Indiana.[1007, 1109] They had two sons. Delbert James Lee was born in Morgantown, Butler Co., Kentucky, on February 26, 1935.[128, 1110] Delbert James lived in 2010 in Bluffton, Wells Co., Indiana. He reached age 75 and died in a hospital in Fort Wayne, Allen Co., Indiana, on March 22, 2010.[128, 1110] Delbert James was buried in Fairview Cemetery, Bluffton, Wells Co., Indiana.[1111]

194. Daughter Two[11] **Lydy** (*Charles Wayne II*[10], *Leota Fatima*[9] *Roll, Bertha Olive*[8] *Farr, Clara Belle*[7] *Roush, Margaret Mary*[6] *Pegan, Harrison James*[5], *Robert A.*[4], *Andrew*[3], *Andrew*[2] *Pagan, James*[1]) was born in Bluffton, Wells Co., Indiana. She is the daughter of Charles Wayne Lydy II (149) and Dorothy Crickmore. Carla Waynett lived in 2013 in Bluffton, Wells Co., Indiana.

Daughter Two Lydy married **Mr. Welsh**. They divorced. They had two children. Daughter Two Lydy Welsh married again.

Daughter Two Lydy and Mr. Welsh had two children, including:

+ 207 m II. **Robert John**[12] **Welsh** was born in Bluffton, Wells Co., Indiana, on August 19, 1992.[1112] He died in Bluffton, Wells Co., Indiana, on August 19, 1992.[1112]

195. **Daughter**[11] **Lydy** (*Dale Edmond*[10], *Leota Fatima*[9] *Roll, Bertha Olive*[8] *Farr, Clara Belle*[7] *Roush, Margaret Mary*[6] *Pegan, Harrison James*[5], *Robert A.*[4], *Andrew*[3], *Andrew*[2] *Pagan, James*[1]) was born on June 14, 1964, in England. She is the daughter of Dale Edmond Lydy (151) and Valerie Ruby Mann.

Daughter Lydy married **Rockey L. Hunter** on June 12, 1987, in Van Wert Co., Ohio.[1113] They divorced. Rockey L. Hunter was born in Decatur, St. Mary's Twp., Adams Co., Indiana, on August 7, 1954.[128, 1114] He reached age 33 and died in Wlshire, Wilshire Twp., Van Wert Co., Ohio, on April 23, 1988.[1114, 1115] Rockey L. was buried in Mount Tabor Cemetery, Decatur, St. Mary's Twp., Adams Co., Indiana.[1114, 1116]

Daughter Lydy Hunter married again.

196. **Daughter**[11] **DeBolt** (*Freida Mae*[10] *Lydy, Leota Fatima*[9] *Roll, Bertha Olive*[8] *Farr, Clara Belle*[7] *Roush, Margaret Mary*[6] *Pegan, Harrison James*[5], *Robert A.*[4], *Andrew*[3], *Andrew*[2] *Pagan, James*[1]) was born on February 27, 1947, in Huntington, Huntington Twp., Huntington Co., Indiana.[933] She is the daughter of Forrest Edwin DeBolt and Freida Mae Lydy (152).

Daughter DeBolt married **Mr. Harrold**. They divorced. They had three children.

Daughter DeBolt has married three more times.

Daughter DeBolt and her first husband had three children, including:

+ 208 f III. **Kari Ann**[12] **Harrold** was born in Bluffton, Wells Co., Indiana, on November 9, 1972.[1117, 1118] She died in Bluffton, Wells Co., Indiana, on August 3, 1984.[1117, 1118]

197. **Richard Kay**[11] **Schorey II** (*Olive Joan*[10] *Lydy, Leota Fatima*[9] *Roll, Bertha Olive*[8] *Farr, Clara Belle*[7] *Roush, Margaret Mary*[6] *Pegan, Harrison James*[5], *Robert A.*[4], *Andrew*[3], *Andrew*[2] *Pagan, James*[1]) was born on October 15, 1951, in Junction City, Union Co., Arkansas.[128, 1032, 1033] He was the son of Richard Kay Schorey and Olive Joan Lydy (154). He died in a hospital in El Dorado, Union Co., Arkansas, on July 7, 2000, at age 48.[128, 1032, 1033] Richard Kay was buried in Fairview Cemetery, Bluffton, Wells Co., Indiana.[1032, 1119]

Richard Kay married **Ruth Elaine Baxter** on October 16, 1971, in Wells Co., Indiana.[1120] They had one daughter. Ruth Elaine Baxter was born in Georgetown, Pleasant Twp., Brown Co., Ohio, on June 19, 1953.[1121, 1122] She was also known as **Elaine**. Ruth Elaine lived in 1989 in Bluffton, Wells Co., Indiana. She reached age 36 and died in a hospital in Indianapolis, Center Twp., Marion Co., Indiana, on October 25, 1989.[1123, 1124] Ruth Elaine was buried in Fairview Cemetery, Bluffton, Wells Co., Indiana.[1123, 1124, 1125]

Ruth Elaine Baxter Schorey's obituary says she was born in Kokomo, Indiana.[1123] Her death certificate says Bluffton, Indiana.[1124] But she was born in Georgetown, Ohio, according to her birth record and Social Security information.[1121, 1122]

197A. **Robert Travis**[11] **Baker** (*Robert Bernard*[10], *Milford Earnest*[9] *Baker, Nellie Fay*[8] *Roush, John Alven*[7], *Margaret Mary*[6] *Pegan, Harrison James*[5], *Robert A.*[4], *Andrew*[3], *Andrew*[2] *Pagan, James*[1]) was born on November 15, 1959, in Indianapolis, Marion Co., Indiana?[128, JJ] He was the son of Robert Bernard Baker (160A) and Shirley Ann Lang. Robert T. died in Tucson, Pima Co., Arizona, on September 12, 2008, at age 48.[128, JJ, KK] He was buried in Evergreen Memorial Park Cemetery, Tucson, Pima Co., Arizona.[JJ, KK]

Seems to have never married.

197B. **Daughter**[11] **Reagan** (*Daughter One*[10] *Roush, Harley Leroy*[9], *Joseph Lewis*[8], *John Alven*[7], *Margaret Mary*[6] *Pegan, Harrison James*[5], *Robert A.*[4], *Andrew*[3], *Andrew*[2] *Pagan, James*[1]) was born in Houston, Harris Co., Texas? She is the daughter of Mr. Reagan and Daughter One Roush (165).

Daughter Reagan had a relationship with **Unknown Unknown.** They had one son.

Son of Daughter Reagan and Unknown Unknown:

+ 208A m I. **Zachary James**[12] **Reagan** was born in Sugarland, Fort Bend Co., Texas? on March 20, 1995.[QQ, RR] He died in Houston, Harris Co., Texas, on March 26, 1995.[QQ, SS]

198. **Robert A.**[11] **Moore** (*Son*[10] *Moore, Mary Ellen*[9] *Bussey, Lora Belle*[8] *Roush, Eli Kenneth*[7] *, Margaret Mary*[6] *Pegan, Harrison James*[5] *, Robert A.*[4] *, Andrew*[3] *, Andrew*[2] *Pagan, James*[1]). He was the son of Son Moore (169) and Betty Lee Rhoads. Robert A. Moore II was born on September 24, 1980 in Hillsboro, Liberty Twp., Highland Co., Ohio.[1062] He died on September 24, 1980 in Hillsboro, Liberty Twp., Highland Co. Ohio.[1062]

199. **Matthew Thomas**[11] **Shuttleworth** (*Son*[10] *Shuttleworth, Daughter*[9] *Roush, Samuel Frederick*[8] *, Eli Kenneth*[7] *, Margaret Mary*[6] *Pegan, Harrison James*[5] *, Robert A.*[4] *, Andrew*[3] *, Andrew*[2] *Pagan, James*[1]) was born on September 11, 1993, in Wilmington, Union Twp., Clinton Co., Ohio.[1064] He was the son of Son Shuttleworth II (172) and his wife. Matthew Thomas died in Warren Co., Ohio, on January 14, 2012, at age 18.[1064] He was buried in Clinton County Memory Gardens, Union Twp., Clinton Co., Ohio.[1064, 1126]

Matthew Thomas Shuttleworth and his longtime girlfriend, both high school seniors in Wilmington, Ohio died in a car accident in adjacent Warren Co., Ohio.[1064]

200. **Jesse Lee**[11] **Kinyoun** (*Daughter*[10] *Seitz, William Lee*[9] *, Dorothy Opal*[8] *Roush, Eli Kenneth*[7] *, Margaret Mary*[6] *Pegan, Harrison James*[5] *, Robert A.*[4] *, Andrew*[3] *, Andrew*[2] *Pagan, James*[1]) was born on May 24, 1989, in St. Petersburg, Pinellas Co., Florida.[128, 1065] He was the son of Mr. Kinyoun and Daughter Seitz (173). Jesse Lee died in St. Petersburg, Pinellas Co., Florida, on March 9, 2002, at age 12.[128, 1065] He was cremated.[1127]

201. **Destiny**[11] **Unknown** (*Daughter*[10] *Dodson, Daughter*[9] *Pegan, James Meredith*[8] *, Jesse Harrison*[7] *, Harrison James*[6] *PeGan II, Harrison James*[5] *Pegan, Robert A.*[4] *, Andrew*[3] *, Andrew*[2] *Pagan, James*[1]). She was the daughter of Unknown Unknown and Daughter Dodson (180).

202. **Runner Cosette**[11] **Lundstrom** (*Daughter*[10] *PeGan, Son*[9] *, Hugh Frederick*[8] *, Clanzie Herold*[7] *, Harrison James*[6] *, Harrison James*[5] *Pegan, Robert A.*[4] *, Andrew*[3] *, Andrew*[2] *Pagan, James*[1]) was born on July 11, 2015, in Cincinnati, Hamilton Co., Ohio.[1086] She was the daughter of Mr. Lundstrom and Daughter PeGan (185). Runner Cosette died in Cincinnati, Hamilton Co., Ohio, on July 15, 2015.[1086]

203. **Stephine Ann**[11] **PeGan** (*Son*[10] *, Son*[9] *, Phillip Elsworth*[8] *, Philip Garl*[7] *, Harrison James*[6] *, Harrison James*[5] *Pegan, Robert A.*[4] *, Andrew*[3] *, Andrew*[2] *Pagan, James*[1]) was born on July 31, 1991, in Niles, Niles Twp., Berrien Co., Michigan.[349, 1087] She was the daughter of Son PeGan II (186) and his first wife. Stephine Ann died in Niles, Niles Twp., Berrien Co., Michigan, on July 31, 1991.[349, 1087] She was buried in Mission Hills Memorial Chapel, Crematory & Gardens, North Niles, Howard Twp., Cass Co., Michigan.[1087, 1128]

204. **Daughter**[11] **Poe** (*Daughter*[10] *PeGan, Nelson Michael*[9] *, Karl Nelson*[8] *, Philip Garl*[7] *, Harrison James*[6] *, Harrison James*[5] *Pegan, Robert A.*[4] *, Andrew*[3] *, Andrew*[2] *Pagan, James*[1]) was born in 1993. She is the daughter of Bobby Lee Poe and Daughter PeGan (189).

She partnered with **Mr. Whitaker.** They have one son.

She partnered with **Unknown Unknown.** They have one son.

Son of Daughter Poe and Mr. Whitaker:

+ 209 m I. **Bentlee Andrew Poe**[12] **Whitaker** was born in Indianapolis, Marion Co., Indiana, on January 11, 2012.[1129] He died in Indianapolis, Marion Co., Indiana, on January 11, 2012.[1129]

205. Ashton James[11] PeGan-Thiry (*Daughter[10] PeGan, Perry LeRoy[9], Vern Leroy[8], Philip Garl[7], Harrison James[6], Harrison James[5] Pegan, Robert A.[4], Andrew[3], Andrew[2] Pagan, James[1]*) was born on August 2, 2010, in Escanaba, Bark River Twp., Delta Co., Michigan.[349, 1094] He was the son of Mr. Thiry and Daughter PeGan (191). Ashton James died in Escanaba, Bark River Twp., Delta Co., Michigan, on August 2, 2010.[349, 1094]

12th Generation

206. Holly Marie[12] Johnson (*Daughter[11] Lydy, Charles Wayne II[10], Leota Fatima[9] Roll, Bertha Olive[8] Farr, Clara Belle[7] Roush, Margaret Mary[6] Pegan, Harrison James[5], Robert A.[4], Andrew[3], Andrew[2] Pagan, James[1]*) was born on December 12, 1971, in Bluffton, Wells Co., Indiana.[1099, 1100] She was the daughter of Mr. Johnson and Daughter Lydy (192). Holly Marie died in Bluffton, Wells Co., Indiana, on December 12, 1971.[1099, 1100] She was buried in Oak Lawn Cemetery, Ossian, Jefferson Twp., Wells Co., Indiana.[1099, 1100, 1130]

207. Robert John[12] Welsh (*Daughter Two[11] Lydy, Charles Wayne II[10], Leota Fatima[9] Roll, Bertha Olive[8] Farr, Clara Belle[7] Roush, Margaret Mary[6] Pegan, Harrison James[5], Robert A.[4], Andrew[3], Andrew[2] Pagan, James[1]*) was born on August 19, 1992, in Bluffton, Wells Co., Indiana.[1112] He was the son of Mr. Welsh and Daughter Two Lydy (194). Robert John died in Bluffton, Wells Co., Indiana, on August 19, 1992.[1112] He was buried in Fairview Cemetery, Bluffton, Wells Co., Indiana.[1112]

208. Kari Ann[12] Harrold (*Daughter[11] DeBolt, Freida Mae[10] Lydy, Leota Fatima[9] Roll, Bertha Olive[8] Farr, Clara Belle[7] Roush, Margaret Mary[6] Pegan, Harrison James[5], Robert A.[4], Andrew[3], Andrew[2] Pagan, James[1]*) was born on November 9, 1972, in Bluffton, Wells Co., Indiana.[1117, 1118] She was the daughter of Mr. Harrold and Daughter DeBolt (196). Kari Ann lived in 1984 in Decatur, Root Twp., Adams Co., Indiana. She died in Bluffton, Wells Co., Indiana, on August 3, 1984, at age 11.[1117, 1118] Kari Ann was buried in Fairview Cemetery, Bluffton, Wells Co., Indiana.[1117, 1118, 1131]

208A. Zachary James[12] Reagan (*Daughter[11] Reagan, Daughter One[10] Roush, Harley Leroy[9], Joseph Lewis[8], John Alven[7], Margaret Mary[6] Pegan, Harrison James[5], Robert A.[4], Andrew[3], Andrew[2] Pagan, James[1]*) was born in Sugarland, Fort Bend Co., Texas? on March 20, 1995.[PP, QQ] He was the son of Unknown Unknown and Daughter Reagan (197A). He died in Houston, Harris Co., Texas, on March 26, 1995.[QQ, RR] Zachary James was buried in Memorial Oaks Cemetery in Houston, Harris Co., Texas.[QQ]

209. Bentlee Andrew Poe[12] Whitaker (*Breanna Lee[11] Poe, Christane Ann[10] PeGan, Nelson Michael[9], Karl Nelson[8], Philip Garl[7], Harrison James[6], Harrison James[5] Pegan, Robert A.[4], Andrew[3], Andrew[2] Pagan, James[1]*) was born on January 11, 2012, in Indianapolis, Marion Co., Indiana.[1129] He was the son of Mr. Whitaker and Daughter Poe (204). Bentlee Andrew Poe died in Indianapolis, Marion Co., Indiana, on January 11, 2012.[1129]

Endnotes

1. Family Data: Robert and Christina "Engle" Pegan family bible, American Bible Society, Brattleboro(ugh), Vermont: Holbrook & Fessenden, 1828. In possession of the author, Ann Miller Carr.

2. Find A Grave—Lynchburg Masonic Cemetery, Lynchburg, Dodson Twp., Highland Co., Ohio, Find A Grave.com, Harrison Pegan, Find A Grave Memorial #93957435.

3. Robert "Pagan" entry, Washington County, Pennsylvania. Tax Records. Somerset Township through 1821; Strabane Township through 1811; roll #29. Genealogy Center, Allen County Public Library, 900 Library Plaza Fort Wayne, IN.

4. Ohio Death Certificate, Ohio Department of Health, Center for Vital and Health Statistics, 246 North High Street, Columbus, OH, "Maggie" Warren, death cert. #11463.

5. Ohio, County Marriages, 1789-2013, FamilySearch.org, Harrison "Pagan" and Sarah Mentzer, Greene County, Ohio Marriage Records, Vol. A, pg. 259.

6. Frederick Sheeley Weiser, Mr. & Mrs. M. Luther Heisey, *Christ Evangelical Lutheran Church Records, Elizabethtown, Lancaster County, Pennsylvania, Parish Registers, 1770-1904*. Gettysburg, Pennsylvania: Lutheran Theological Seminary, A.R. Wentz Library, 1971; Baptismal records: Sarah Mentzer, pg. 67. Lancaster County Historical Society, 230 North President Avenue, Lancaster, PA.

7. Find A Grave—Strange Cemetery, Hamer Twp., Highland Co., Ohio, Find A Grave.com, Sarah Pegan Tedrick, Find A Grave Memorial #106445945.

8. McBride, David Newton and Jane N. McBride, *Cemetery Inscriptions of Highland County, Ohio*. Hillsboro, Ohio: Southern Ohio Genealogical Society, 2nd Edition, 1972, pg. 173. Southern Ohio Genealogical Society Library, Resource Center, Southern State Community College, Hillsboro Campus, 100 Hobart Drive, Hillsboro, OH.

9. Greene County, Ohio Tax Records, Bath Township, personal property tax records, 1834, entry for Andrew Mentzer. Greene County, Ohio Archives, 535 Ledbetter Road, Xenia, OH.

10. Lewis Pegan by his Next Friend John Jacob Pegan vs. David Winters, Montgomery County, Ohio Common Pleas Court Records, September Term 1839, Book N, pg. 515. Montgomery County, Ohio Records Center and Archives, 117 South Main Street, 6th Floor, Dayton, OH.

11. Gilbert, Audrey, *Twin Valley Tidbits, 1888-1897, Vol. 3*. New Alexandria, Ohio: A. Gilbert; 1999; pg. 72. Lynchburg Public Library, 120 Main Street, Lynchburg, OH.

12. Miami County, Ohio Deeds, Elijah Ross to John Pegan, Miami County, Ohio Deed Book 12: 36 (02 Jul 1834). Miami County Recorder's office, 201 Main Street, Troy, OH.

13. Miami County, Ohio Deeds, Harrison and Sarah Pegan to John Amarine, Miami County, Ohio Deed Book 14: 702 (13 Oct 1836). Miami County Recorder's office, 201 Main Street, Troy, OH.

14. Photo, "Old Buggy and Carriage Factory", 1869, Enon Community Historical Society, Mike Barry Research Center, 45 Indian Mound Drive, Enon, OH. According to the Historical Society, this firm, although its name is lost to history, was established in the 1830s.

15. Clark County, Ohio Deeds, Ezra and Ann Baker to Harrison Pegan, Clark County, Ohio Deed Book T: 76 (27 June 1840). Clark County Recorder's office, 31 North Limestone Street, Springfield, OH.

16. Clark County, Ohio Deeds, David and Rhoda Cross to School Directors of District #8, Mad River Township, Clark County, Ohio Deed Book U: 433-4 (14 Jul 1843). Clark County Recorder's office, 31 North Limestone Street, Springfield, OH.

17. Clark County, Ohio Deeds, Harrison and Sarah Pegan to William Patton, Clark County, Ohio Deed Book 27: 307-8 (05 Mar 1846). Clark County Recorder's office, 31 North Limestone Street, Springfield, OH.

18. Miami County, Ohio Deeds, William Bigger to Harrison Pegan, Miami County, Ohio Deed Book 23: 79 (26 Oct 1846). Miami County Recorder's office, 201 Main Street, Troy, OH.

19. Miami County, Ohio Deeds, John W. and Delia Gordon to Harrison Pegan, Miami County, Ohio Deed Book 26: 377 (20 Sep 1847). Miami County Recorder's office, 201 Main Street, Troy, OH.

20. Miami County Deeds, Harrison and Sarah Pegan to John Pegan, Miami County, Ohio Deed Book 24: 757 (03 Feb 1849). Miami County Recorder's office, 201 Main Street, Troy, OH.

21. Miami County, Ohio Deeds, Harrison and Sarah Pegan to Jacob D. Holtzerman et. al, Miami County, Ohio Deed Book 24: 759 (14 May 1849). Miami County Recorder's office, 201 Main Street, Troy, OH.

22. Ohio, County Marriages, 1789-2013, FamilySearch.org, John M. Mitchell and Margaret "Menser", Miami County, Ohio Marriage Records, Vol. F, pg. 350, lic. #144. Harrison Pegan vouched for his sister-in-law Margaret's age, as both her parents were deceased.

23. Miami County, Ohio Deeds, Harrison and Sarah Pegan to Joseph Mitchell, Miami County, Ohio Deed Book 29: 162 (22 Dec 1853). Miami County Recorder's office, 201 Main Street, Troy, OH.

24. "Died" (Hillsboro, Ohio, Highland Weekly News, 02 May 1854), Highland County District Library, 10 Willettsville Pike, Hillsboro, OH.

25. Highland County, Ohio, probate case files, estate #1913, Harrison Pegan ("1852" [1854]). Highland County, Ohio

26 McBride, David Newton and Jane M. McBride, *Wills, Probates, Guardianships and Adoptions, Highland County, Ohio, 1805-1880*, Ann Arbor, Michigan: Edwards Letter Shop; 1957, pg. 191. Highland County District Library, 10 Willettsville Pike, Hillsboro, OH.

27 Clinton County, Ohio Marriage Records, Leonidas "Pagan" and Martha J. "Pagan", Clinton County, Ohio Marriage Records, Vol. 1, pg. 105. Clinton County, Ohio Probate Court, 46 South South Street, Wilmington, OH.

28 Abraham Mentzer, Garfield County, Nebraska, Bounty Land Patent, no.37712, Bureau of Land Management, "Land Patent Search", digital images, General Land Office Records, https://glorecords.blm.gov/results/default.aspx?searchCriteria=type=patent|st=|cty=|ln=mentzer|fn=abraham|sp=true|sw=true|sadv=false. Abraham Mentzer was awarded this bounty land patent for his service in the Mexican War. But by the time the patent was issued, Abraham, unmarried, had died. His heirs, his surviving siblings, Sarah Mentzer Pegan, Rachel Mentzer Snyder ("Snider" on the document), and Margaret Mentzer Mitchell, inherited the patent. They sold the rights to an assignee, James Mix, whose name is also on the patent.

29 Clinton County, Ohio Marriage Records, John Tedrick and Sarah Pegan, Clinton County, Ohio Marriage Records, Vol. 1, pg. 189. Clinton County, Ohio Probate Court, 46 South South Street, Wilmington, OH.

30 Find A Grave—Glenwood Cemetery, Houston, Harris Co., Texas, Find A Grave.com, Martha Jane (Mrs. Reuben R.) "Mattie" Brown, Find A Grave Memorial #108603016.

31 Texas Death Certificate, Texas Department of State Health Services, Vital Statistics Unit, 1100 West 49th Street, Austin, TX, Mattie Brown, death cert. #14453.

32 Ohio, County Death Records, 1840-2001, FamilySearch.org, William L. Pegan, Highland Co., Ohio Death Record, Vol. 1, pg. 180.

33 Find A Grave—Strange Cemetery, Hamer Twp., Highland Co., Ohio, Find A Grave.com.

34 Ohio Deaths, 1908-1953, FamilySearch.org, "Maggie" Warren.

35 Miami County, Indiana Death Registrations, Harrison Pegan, Vol. 1936, pg. 102. Miami County Health Department, Courthouse, 35 Court Street, Peru, IN.

36 Indiana Death Certificate (Indianapolis, Indiana, State of Indiana), Indiana State Department of Health, 2 North Meridian Street, Indianapolis, IN, Harrison PeGan, death cert. #25093/364213.

37 Indiana, Death Certificates, 1899-2011, Ancestry.com, Harrison "Degan", Indiana death cert. #25093.

38 Glenwood Cemetery Records, Mrs. Reuben R. Brown, Glenwood Cemetery (Texas), 2525 Washington Avenue, Houston, TX, Buried in section H-3, lot #024 with a gravestone.

39 Find A Grave—Gulf Prairie Cemetery (also Peach Point Cemetery), Jones Creek, Brazoria Co., Texas, Find A Grave.com, Leonidas Pegan, Find A Grave Memorial #66561018.

40 Obituary of Leonidas ("L.") Pegan (Burlington, Iowa, Weekly Hawk Eye and Telegraph, 12 Apr 1883), Newspapers and Periodicals, Ancestry.com.

41 Martha J. Brown, denied U.S. Civil War Widow's Pension Application, #837545, NARA: Washington, DC.

42 Iowa State Census Collection, 1836-1925, Ancestry.com, 1865: Leonidas Pegan, Roll IA-64, pg. 60, line 30.

43 "James R. Pagin", *History of Porter County, Indiana: A Narrative History of its Progress, its People and Principal Interests*. Chicago: Lewis Publishing Co., 1912, pg. 692.

44 Gilbert, Audrey, *Twin Valley Tidbits, 1888-1897, Vol. 3*. Eaton, Ohio: self-published, 1999, pg. 72.

45 Leonidas Pegan, denied U.S. Civil War Pension Application, #252858, NARA: Washington, DC.

46 Email from the Gulf Prairie Cemetery Association, PO Box 98, Brazoria, TX to Ann Miller Carr, author, 22 Aug 2015.

47 Texas, County Marriage Index, 1837-1977, FamilySearch.org, Reuben R. Brown and Martha J. Pegan, Brazoria County Marriage Records; familysearch.org; (https://familysearch.org/ark:/61903/1:1:XLQ6-VHM: 22 December 2016).

48 The Handbook of Texas (Denton, Texas, Texas State Historical Association, 15 Feb 1999), Texas State Historical Association, Texas State Historical Association, 1155 Union Circle #311580, Denton, TX. Bibliography includes Bruce S. Allardice, Confederate Colonels: A Biographical Register (Columbia: University of Missouri Press, 2008). Harbert Davenport, Notes from an Unfinished Study of Fannin and His Men (MS, Harbert Davenport Collection, Texas State Library, Austin; Dolph Briscoe Center for American History, University of Texas at Austin). James M. Day, comp., Texas Almanac, 1857-1873: A Compendium of Texas History (Waco: Texian Press, 1967). Phineas Jenks Mahan, Reminiscences of the War for Texas Independence (Houston, 1872). James A. Mundie, Jr., with Bruce S. Allardice, Dean E. Letzring, and John H. Luckey, Texas Burial Sites of Civil War Notables: A Biographical and Pictorial Field Guide (Hillsboro, Texas: Hill College Press, 2002). William S. Speer and John H. Brown, eds., Encyclopedia of the New West (Marshall, Texas: United States Biographical Publishing, 1881; rpt., Easley, South Carolina: Southern Historical Press, 1978). Vertical Files, Dolph Briscoe Center for American History, University of Texas at Austin. Thomas W. Cutrer and Bruce Allardice.

49 Obituary of Colonel Reuben Brown (Velasco, Texas, Velasco Times, 09 Mar 1894), Brazoria County Historical Museum, 100 East Cedar Street, Angleton, TX.

50 Find A Grave—Gulf Prairie Cemetery (also Peach Point Cemetery), Jones Creek, Brazoria Co., Texas, Find A Grave.com, Maj. Reuben Rodolphus Brown, Find A Grave Memorial #13971209.

Probate Court, Courthouse, 105 North High Street, Ste. 1, Hillsboro, OH.

51 "The Galveston Hurricane of 1900", National Oceanic and Atmospheric Administration, U.S. Department of Commerce, NOAA, Silver Spring, MD; Website: https://oceanservice.noaa.gov/news/features/sep13/galveston.html

52 Brazoria County, Texas Deeds, Mrs. Reuben R. Brown to Sam Lazarus and the City of St. Louis, Missouri, Deed Book D. Vol. 66: 580 (14 Aug 1905). Brazoria County, Texas Clerk's Office, Real Property Records Office, East Annex, 1524 East Mulberry Street, Angleton, TX.

53 Brazoria County, Texas Deeds, Mrs. Reuben R. Brown to St. Louis and Brownsville Railway, Deed Book D. Vol. 71: 182 (21 Aug 1905). Brazoria County, Texas Clerk's Office, Real Property Records Office, East Annex, 1524 East Mulberry Street, Angleton, TX.

54 Brazoria County, Texas Deeds, Martha Jane Brown to J.A. Hollingsworth, Deed Book D. Vol. 82: 499 (23 Nov 1908). Brazoria County, Texas Clerk's Office, Real Property Records Office, East Annex, 1524 East Mulberry Street, Angleton, TX.

55 Brazoria County, Texas Deeds, Mrs. R.R. Brown to T.J. McMillan, Deed Book D. Vol. 102: 462 (12 Jan 1911). Brazoria County, Texas Clerk's Office, Real Property Records Office, East Annex, 1524 East Mulberry Street, Angleton, TX.

56 Brazoria County, Texas Deeds, Estate of R.R. Brown, Mrs. Reuben R. Brown, Will (14 Jan 1915). Brazoria County, Texas Clerk's Office, Real Property Records Office, East Annex, 1524 East Mulberry Street, Angleton, TX.

57 Harris County, Texas, probate case files, Mrs. Reuben R. Brown, probate, #007293 (filed 24 Jun 1916; closed 06 Sep 1916). Harris County Clerk, Probate Department, Civil Courthouse, 201 Caroline Street, Suite 100, Houston, TX.

58 McBride, David Newton and Jane N. McBride, *Cemetery Inscriptions of Highland County, Ohio*; Wm. L. Pegan, pg. 171.

59 All U.S. Civil War Soldiers, 1861-1865, Ancestry.com, William L. Pegan.

60 Ohio, County Marriages, 1789-2013, FamilySearch.org, William L. Pegan and Rachel Barnes, Highland County, Ohio Marriage Records, Vol. 8, pg. 553, lic. #2291.

61 Find A Grave—Barnes Cemetery, Fairview, New Market Twp., Highland Co., Ohio, Find A Grave.com, Rachel Pegan, Find A Grave Memorial #30726112.

62 Find A Grave—Strange Cemetery, Hamer Twp., Highland Co., Ohio, Find A Grave.com, Margaret Roush, Find A Grave Memorial #106445719.

63 Ohio, County Marriages, 1789-2013, FamilySearch.org, Philip Roush and Margaret "Pagan", Highland County, Ohio Marriage Records, Vol. 7, pg. 796, lic. #33.

64 Obituary of Philip Roush (Hillsboro, Ohio, Hillsboro News Herald, 27 Jun 1901), Highland County District Library, 10 Willettsville Pike, Hillsboro, OH.

65 Find A Grave—Strange Cemetery, Hamer Twp., Highland Co., Ohio, Find A Grave.com, Philip Roush, Find A Grave Memorial #106445717.

66 Personals, "Philip Roush…" (Hillsboro, Ohio, The Hillsboro News-Herald, 12 Jan 1888) Highland County District Library, 10 Willettsville Pike, Hillsboro, OH.

67 Personals, "Margaret Roush…" (Hillsboro, Ohio, The Hillsboro News-Herald, 31 Aug 1905) Highland County District Library, 10 Willettsville Pike, Hillsboro, OH.

68 Ohio, County Marriages, 1789-2013, FamilySearch.org, George Warren and Margaret M. Roush, Highland County, Ohio Marriage Records, Vol. 16, pg. 62, lic. #9264.

69 Ohio, County Marriages, 1789-2013, FamilySearch.org, George Warren and Mary A. Parker, Highland County, Ohio Marriage Records, Vol. 16, pg. 363.

70 Ohio Death Certificate, Ohio Department of Health, Center for Vital and Health Statistics, 246 North High Street, Columbus, OH, George Warren, death cert. #44569.

71 Obituary of George Warren (Wilmington, Ohio, Wilmington News-Journal, 23 Aug 1938), Wilmington Public Library of Clinton County, 268 North South Street, Wilmington, OH.

72 Ohio Death Certificate, Ohio Department of Health, Center for Vital and Health Statistics, 246 North High Street, Columbus, OH, Clara Belle Hunter, death cert. #55815.

73 Branch County, Michigan Death Records, Branch County, Michigan County Clerk's Office, Courthouse, 31 Division Street, Coldwater, MI, John Alven Roush, Volume E., pg. 156, #4360.

74 Obituary of John A. Roush (Coldwater, Michigan, Coldwater Daily Reporter, 22 Oct 1955), Branch County Library, Coldwater Branch, 10 East Chicago Street, Coldwater, MI.

75 Obituary of (Albert Leroy) Roy Roush (Hillsboro, Ohio, Hillsboro News Herald, 02 Apr 1895), Highland County District Library, 10 Willettsville Pike, Hillsboro, OH.

76 Obituary of Leroy Roush (Hillsboro, Ohio, Hillsborough Gazette, 03 May 1895), Highland County District Library, 10 Willettsville Pike, Hillsboro, OH.

77 Ohio Death Certificate, Ohio Department of Health, Center for Vital and Health Statistics, 246 North High Street, Columbus, OH, Eli K. Roush—#28999.

78 Ohio, County Births, 1841-2003 (County Courthouses), FamilySearch.org, Ira Roush, Highland County Birth Records, Vol. 2, pg. 270.

79 Obituary of Cecil Roush (Hillsboro, Ohio, Hillsboro Press Gazette, 03 Jan 1956), Highland County District Library, 10 Willettsville Pike, Hillsboro, OH.

80 U.S., WWI Draft Registration Cards, 1917-1918, Ancestry.com, Cecil Ira Roush, Lawrence Co., Illinois.

81 U.S., WWII Draft Registration Cards, 1942, Ancestry.com, Cecil Ira Roush, Clinton Co., Ohio.

82 U.S., Headstone Applications for Military Veterans, 1925-1963, Ancestry.com, Cecil Roush.

83 Interview with Hugh Frederick "Fritz" PeGan, Huntington, IN, Ann Miller Carr, author, 10 Jun 2001.

84 Interview with Mattie Leona Pearson Hatfield, Greentown, IN, Ann Miller Carr, author, 16 Apr 2002.

85 Grant County, Indiana Marriage Records, Grant County, Indiana Clerk's Office, County Complex, 401 South Adams Street, Marion, IN, Harrison PeGan and Angeline Stout, Grant County, Indiana Marriage Records, Vol. 5, pg. 424.

86 Wabash Co., Indiana Death Registration, Angeline Pegan, Book 1907-1918, pg. 21. Wabash County Health Department, 89 West Hill Street, #1, Wabash, IN.

87 Indiana Death Certificate (Indianapolis, Indiana, State of Indiana), Indiana State Department of Health, 2 North Meridian Street, Indianapolis, IN, Angeline PeGan, death cert. #747206364214.

88 Find A Grave—Hopewell Cemetery, Lagro Twp., Wabash Co., Indiana, Find A Grave.com, Angeline Stout PeGan, Find A Grave Memorial #36194793.

89 Grant County, Indiana Deeds, George H. Stout to Harrison PeGan (28 Aug 1897), Deed Book 80: 81). Grant County Recorder of Deeds, 401 South Adams Street, Marion, IN.

90 "Geo. Keplinger" and "Will Recover" (Upland, Indiana, Upland Monitor, 04 Feb 1899), Herman B Wells Library, Indiana University, 1320 East 10th Street, Bloomington, IN.

91 "Shot His Sweetheart" (Hartford City, Indiana, Hartford City Telegram, 01 Feb 1899), Indiana State Library, 315 West Ohio Street, Indianapolis, IN.

92 "Keplinger In Court" (Marion, Indiana, Grant County News, 03 Feb 1899), Marion Public Library-Central Library, 1963, 600 South Washington Street, Marion, IN.

93 "From The First Wanted To Plead Guilty" (Marion, Indiana, Grant County News, 24 Apr 1899), Marion Public Library-Central Library, 1963, 600 South Washington Street, Marion, IN.

94 "Like A Dude—He Was Dressed When Received At Reformatory" (Jeffersonville, Indiana, Jeffersonville News, 26 Apr 1899), Indiana State Library, 315 West Ohio Street, Indianapolis, IN.

95 "Shot" (Upland, Indiana, Upland Monitor, 01 Feb 1899), Herman B Wells Library, Indiana a, 1320 East 10th Street, Bloomington, IN.

96 "Indiana State News" (Ligonier, Indiana, Ligonier Leader, 02 Mar 1899), Indiana State Library, 315 West Ohio Street, Indianapolis, IN.

97 Interview with Betty Jean Eastes Cowgill Reese, Marion, IN and Greentown, IN, 16 April 2002.

98 Indiana State Reformatory Records, George W. Keplinger, prisoner #2591, April 1899, Indiana State Archives, Commission on Public Records, 6440 East 30th Street, Indianapolis, IN.

99 U.S., WWI Draft Registration Cards, 1917-1918, Ancestry.com, Roy Clarence Scott, Springfield, Illinois.

100 Illinois Death Certificate, Illinois Department of Health, Division of Vital Records, 605 West Jefferson Street, Springfield, IL; Roy C. Scott, death cert. #69-055476.

101 Grant County, Indiana Deeds, Harrison and Angeline Pegan to John and Dora Armstrong, (02 Sep 1903), Deed Book 132: 304. Grant County Recorder of Deeds, 401 South Adams Street, Marion, IN.

102 Wabash County, Indiana Deeds, Calvin and Mary Jones to Harrison and Angeline PeGan (07 Sep 1903). Deed Book. 83: 434. Wabash County Recorder's Office, 1 West Hill Street, Suite 105, Wabash, IN.

103 Wabash County, Indiana Deeds, Harrison PeGan to Daniel and Viola Pratt (05 Jul 1910). Deed Book 97:10. Wabash County Recorder's Office, 1 West Hill Street, Suite 105, Wabash, IN.

104 Wabash County, Indiana Deeds, Frederick and Fredericka Grossman to Harrison PeGan (06 Aug 1910). Deed Book 10: 68. Wabash County Recorder's Office, 1 West Hill Street, Suite 105, Wabash, IN.

105 Wabash County, Indiana Deeds, George and Ada Todd to Harrison PeGan (23 Jul 1910). Deed Book 10: 67. Wabash County Recorder's Office, 1 West Hill Street, Suite 105, Wabash, IN.

106 "City Notes" (Wabash, Indiana, Wabash Plain Dealer, 17 Feb 1912), Wabash Carnegie Public Library, 188 West Hill Street, Wabash, IN.

107 State of Indiana vs. Harrison PeGan and Oden Howell, Wabash County, Indiana, Box 417, Case 33, #2546, filed 27 Sep 1913. Wabash County Clerk's Office, 69 West Hill Street, Wabash, IN.

108 Harrison Pegan vs. Harry T. Wiley, filed 22 Nov 1912, dismissed 13 Jan 1913; Wabash County, Indiana, Box 403, Case 11, #10358. Wabash County Clerk's Office, 69 West Hill Street, Wabash, IN.

109 Wabash County, Indiana Deeds, Harrison PeGan, Clanzie H. and Josephine PeGan, and Sarah C. and Isaac Pearson to Eliza Marie Koehler (29 May 1913). Deed Book 102: 58. Wabash County Recorder's Office, 1 West Hill Street, Suite 105, Wabash, IN.

110 Wabash County, Indiana Deeds, Harrison PeGan to Ora E. Talbert and Dorsey Smith (22 Aug 1913). Deed Book 102: 390. Wabash County Recorder's Office, 1 West Hill Street, Suite 105, Wabash, IN.

111 Huntington County, Indiana Deeds, William H. and Maggie Koch to Harrison PeGan (10 Jun 1913). Deed Book 111: 564. Huntington County Recorder's Office, 201 North Jefferson Street, #101, Huntington, IN.

112 Huntington County, Indiana Deeds, Harrison PeGan to Charles and Roena Edgar (01 Jul 1919). Deed Book 135: 393. Huntington County Recorder's Office, 201 North Jefferson Street, #101, Huntington, IN.

113 Interview with Phillip Ellsworth PeGan II, Niles, MI, Ann Miller Carr, author, 16 Jun 2007.

114 Obituary of Harrison Pegan (Peru, Indiana, Peru Tribune, 07 Jul 1936), Indiana State Library, 315 West Ohio Street, Indianapolis, IN.

115 Phone interview with Beverly Parker, Archivist, Miami County Historical Society Museum, on 13 June 2018. Miami County Historical Society Museum, 51 North Broadway, Peru, IN.

116 Family Data: PeGan Family Records, compiled by Mary Angeline PeGan Welch in 1977 and given to her niece, author Ann Miller Carr.

117 Find A Grave—McKinney Lugar Creek Cemetery, Center Twp., Grant Co., Indiana, Find A Grave.com, Laura A. Keplinger, Find A Grave Memorial #20293577.

118 Indiana, Death Certificates, 1899-2011, Ancestry.com, Sarah P. Horner, Indiana death cert. #63-025402.

119 Grant County, Indiana Death Certificate, Sarah Horner, Death Book 18, pg. 38, death cert. #823065).

120 Obituary of Alvin L. Pegan (Wabash, Indiana, Wabash Daily Plain Dealer, 09 May 1936), Wabash Carnegie Public Library, 188 West Hill Street, Wabash, IN.

121 U.S., WWI Draft Registration Cards, 1917-1918, Ancestry.com, Alvin LeRoy PeGan, Flint, Michigan.

122 Indiana Death Certificate (Indianapolis, Indiana, State of Indiana), Indiana State Department of Health, 2 North Meridian Street, Indianapolis, IN, Alvin Leroy PeGan, death cert. #18826.

123 Indiana, Death Certificates, 1899-2011, Ancestry.com, Alvin LeRoy "Pe Gam", Indiana death cert. #18826.

124 U.S., Social Security Applications and Claims Index, 1936-2007, Ancestry.com, Jesse H. Pegan.

125 Obituary of Jesse H. Pegan (Huntington, Indiana, Huntington Herald Press, 18 Nov 1946), Huntington City-Township Library, Indiana Room, 255 West Park Drive, Huntington, IN.

126 Indiana, Death Certificates, 1899-2011, Ancestry.com, Jesse H. Pegan, Indiana death cert. #32966.

127 Huntington County, Indiana Death Records, Huntington County, Indiana Department of Health, 354 North Jefferson St., #201, Huntington, IN, Clanzie PeGan, Book 22, pg. 22.

128 Social Security Death Index, Ancestry.com.

129 Indiana Death Certificate (Indianapolis, Indiana, State of Indiana), Indiana State Department of Health, 2 North Meridian Street, Indianapolis, IN, Clanzie H. PeGan, death cert. #72-017823/362211.

130 Indiana, Marriages 1811-2007, FamilySearch.org, Clanzie H. PeGan and Josephine S. "Schetzszle", Wabash County, Indiana Marriage Records, Applications, Vol. 2A, pg. 161.

131 Indiana, Death Certificates, 1899-2011, Ancestry.com, "Clanzte" H. PeGan, Indiana death cert. #72-017823.

132 Grant County, Indiana Birth Record, Grant County Health Department, Grant County Complex, 401 South Adams Street, Marion, IN, Unnamed Female PeGan, Grant Co. Birth Records, Vol. CO3, #111.

133 Indiana Death Certificate (Indianapolis, Indiana, State of Indiana), Indiana State Department of Health, 2 North Meridian Street, Indianapolis, IN, Leonidas Pegan, death cert. #239.

134 Obituary of Leonidus Pegan (Wabash, Indiana, Wabash Daily Plain Dealer, 29 Mar 1911), Wabash Carnegie Public Library, 188 West Hill Street, Wabash, IN.

135 Michigan, Death Index, 1971-1996, Ancestry.com, Philip Garl Pegan.

136 Michigan, County Marriage Records, 1820-1940, FamilySearch.org, St. Joseph Co., Michigan Marriage Records, William C. Farr and Clara B. Roush, Vol. E., pg. 284, lic. #162.

137 Find A Grave—Estates of Serenity Cemetery, Marion, Center Twp., Grant Co., Indiana, Find A Grave.com, William Constantine Farr, Find A Grave Memorial #11447234.

138 Obituary of W.C. Farr (Peru, Indiana, Peru Republican, 02 Feb 1906); Newspaper Archive, Online database: newspaperarchive.com, https://access-newspaperarchive-com.sjcpl.idm.oclc.org/us/indiana/peru/peru-republican/1906/01-12?tag=william+farr&rtserp=tags/william-farr?pc=22673&psi=38&pci=7&ndt=ex&pd=12&py=1906&pm=1&search=ymd

139 "Loses Leg and Arm" (Peru, Indiana, Peru Republican, 12 Jan 1906); Newspaper Archive, Online database: newspaperarchive.com, https://access-newspaperarchive-com.sjcpl.idm.oclc.org/tags/farr?pc=22673&psi=38&pci=7&ndt=ex&pd=2&py=1906&pm=2&psb=relevance&search=ymd

140 Ohio Death Certificate, Ohio Department of Health, Center for Vital and Health Statistics, 246 North High Street, Columbus, OH, James L. Hunter, death cert. #43353.

141 Ohio, County Births, 1841-2003 (County Courthouses), FamilySearch.org, Bertha Farr, Highland County, Ohio Birth Records, Vol. 2, pg. 172.

142 Obituary of Mrs. Marian Roll, Wells County Public Library, 200 West Washington Street, Bluffton, IN, Bluffton (IN) News Banner, pub. 09 Apr 1966.

143 Florida Death Certificate, Florida Department of Health-State Office of Vital Statistics, 1217 North Pearl Street, Jacksonville, FL, Bertha Olive Roll, state file #66-018092.

144 Ohio, County Births, 1841-2003 (County Courthouses), FamilySearch.org, John C. Hunter, Hocking Co., Ohio Birth Records, Vol. 1, pg. 107.

145 Ohio, Death Records, 1908-1932, 1938-2007, Ancestry.com, John C. Hunter, death cert. #038417.

146 Find A Grave—Evergreen Cemetery, Girard Twp., Branch Co., Michigan, Find A Grave.com, John A. Roush, Find A Grave Memorial #112638979.

147 Indiana, Marriage Index, 1800-1941, Ancestry.com, John Roush and Harriet Boxell, Grant County, Indiana Marriage Records.

148 Grant County, Indiana Marriage Records, Grant County, Indiana Clerk's Office, County Complex, 401 South Adams Street, Marion, IN, John Roush and Harriet Boxell, Grant County, Indiana Marriage Records, Vol, 9, pg. 236.

149 Branch County, Michigan Death Records, Branch County, Michigan County Clerk's Office, Courthouse, 31 Division Street, Coldwater, MI, Harriet Ettie Roush, Vol. E, pg. 109, #3267.

150 Obituary of Harriet E. Roush (Coldwater, Michigan, Coldwater Daily Reporter, 28 Feb 1953), Branch County Library, Coldwater Branch, 10 East Chicago Street, Coldwater, MI.

151 Find A Grave—Evergreen Cemetery, Girard Twp., Branch Co., Michigan, Find A Grave.com, Harriet E. Roush, Find A Grave Memorial #112638949.

152 Ohio, County Births, 1841-2003 (County Courthouses), FamilySearch.org, Nellie F. Roush, Highland County Birth Records, Vol 3, pg. 390.

153 Ohio, County Births, 1841-2003 (County Courthouses), FamilySearch.org, Delbert Roush, Highland County Birth Records, Vol. 3, pg. 394.

154 U.S., WWI Draft Registration Cards, 1917-1918, Ancestry.com, Delbert L. Roush, Three Rivers, St. Joseph County, Michigan.

155 Obituary of Delbert L. Roush (South Bend, Indiana, South Bend Tribune, 17 May 1939), St. Joseph County Public Library, 304 South Main Street, South Bend, IN.

156 Indiana, Death Certificates, 1899-2011, Ancestry.com, Delbert S. Roush, death cert. #17414.

157 Obituary of Joseph L. Roush (Coldwater, Michigan, Coldwater Daily Reporter, 06 Jan 1959), Branch County Library, Coldwater Branch, 10 East Chicago Street, Coldwater, MI.

158 Find A Grave—Evergreen Cemetery, Girard Twp., Branch Co., Michigan, Find A Grave.com, Joseph L. Roush, Find A Grave Memorial #112638795.

159 Branch County, Michigan Death Records, Branch County, Michigan County Clerk's Office, Courthouse, 31 Division Street, Coldwater, MI, Joseph Lewis Roush, Vol. E, pg. 221, #5938.

160 Ohio, County Births, 1841-2003 (County Courthouses), FamilySearch.org, Milford Roush, Highland County Birth Records, Vol. 3, pg. 406.

161 Indiana, Death Certificates, 1899-2011, Ancestry.com, "Millford" Roush, Indiana death cert. #252.

162 Branch County, Michigan Genealogical Society, Branch County, Branch County, Michigan Cemetery Records: Girard Township: Evergreen Cemetery Records, Arlo Roush; Branch County Genealogical Society, compiled 1999. Branch County Library, Coldwater Branch, 10 East Chicago Street, Coldwater, MI.

163 Find A Grave—Strange Cemetery, Hamer Twp., Highland Co., Ohio, Find A Grave.com, Albert L. Roush, Find A Grave Memorial #181547346.

164 Ohio, County Marriages, 1789-2013, FamilySearch.org, LeRoy Roush and Mina Beard, Highland County, Ohio Marriage Records, Vol. 12, pg. 191, lic. #3831.

165 Ohio, County Births, 1841-2003 (County Courthouses), FamilySearch.org, "Mirna" or Mima Beard, Highland County Birth Records, Vol. 1, pg. 342, #585.

166 Ohio Death Certificate, Ohio Department of Health, Center for Vital and Health Statistics, 246 North High Street, Columbus, OH, Mima Helen Thacker, death cert. #65092.

167 Ohio, County Marriages, 1789-2013, FamilySearch.org, William J. Thacker and Mina Roush, Highland County, Ohio Marriage Records, Vol. 15, pg. 167, lic. #6704.

168 U.S., WWI Draft Registration Cards, 1917-1918, Ancestry.com, George B. Roush, Springfield, Clark Co., Ohio.

169 Ohio, County Births, 1841-2003 (County Courthouses), FamilySearch.org, George Roush, Highland County Birth Records, Vol. 3, pg. 390.

170 Obituary of George Roush (Springfield, Ohio, Springfield Daily News, 30 Jan 1964), Clark County Public Library, 201 South Fountain Avenue, Springfield, OH.

171 Utah Death Certificates, 1904-1964, FamilySearch.org, George B. Roush, death cert. #64-29-0413.

172 Find A Grave—Martinsville IOOF Cemetery, Martinsville, Clark Twp., Clinton Co., Ohio, Find A Grave.com, Eli K. Roush, Sr., Find A Grave Memorial #154575443.

173 The Genealogical Committee of the Clinton County Historical Society, Cemetery Records of Clinton Co., Ohio, 1798-1998: Martinsville IOOF Cemetery, Eli K. Roush Sr. Clinton County, Ohio Records Center and Archives, 111 South Nelson Avenue, Suite 3, Wilmington, OH.

174 "Falls From Tree" (Hillsboro, Ohio, Hillsboro News-Herald, 23 Nov 1899), Highland County District Library, 10 Willettsville Pike, Hillsboro, OH.

175 Ohio, County Marriages, 1789-2013, FamilySearch.org, Eli Roush and Margaret Bish, Brown County, Ohio Marriage Records, Vol. 20, pg. 337, lic. #19, 256.

176 Ohio, County Births, 1841-2003 (County Courthouses), FamilySearch.org, Margaret A. Bish, Highland County, Ohio Birth Records, Vol. 2, pg. 134.

177 Clinton County, Ohio Children's Home Records, Year: 1908, entries for Harry and Theodore Roush, Clinton County, Ohio Records Center and Archives, 111 South Nelson Avenue, Suite 3, Wilmington, OH.

178 "The grand jury" (Wilmington, Ohio, Clinton County Democrat, 23 Feb 1908), Clark County Public Library, 201 South Fountain Avenue, Springfield, OH.

179 "The grand jury" (Wilmington, Ohio, Clinton County Democrat, 11 Jun 1908), Clark County Public Library, 201 South Fountain Avenue, Springfield, OH.

180 "Court House News…Common Pleas Court…Eli Roush" (Wilmington, Ohio, Clinton County Democrat, 18 Feb 1909), Wilmington Public Library of Clinton County, 268 North South Street, Wilmington, OH.

181 "Russell" (Hillsboro, Ohio, Highland County News Herald, 12 May 1910), Highland County District Library, 10 Willettsville Pike, Hillsboro, OH.

182 Family Data: Phone interviews with and emails from Christine "Christy" Ann Wallace Gall, Columbus, OH, Ann Miller Carr, author, March 2018.

183 Oklahoma, County Marriages, 1890-1995, FamilySearch.org, Michael Randolph Stroup and Margaret Roush, Kay County, Oklahoma Marriage Records, pg. 186

184 Oklahoma, Wills and Probate Records, 1801-2008, Ancestry.com, Michael R. Stroup, Kay County, Oklahoma Packet 4025-A.

185 Ohio Death Certificate, Ohio Department of Health, Center for Vital and Health Statistics, 246 North High Street, Columbus, OH, Teddy Roush, death cert. #21412.

186 Clinton County, Ohio Marriage Records, Clinton County, Ohio Records Center and Archives, 111 South Nelson Avenue, Suite 3, Wilmington, OH, Eli Roush and Retta Barnes, Clinton County, Ohio Marriage Records, Vol. 11, pg. 39.

187 Ohio Death Certificate, Ohio Department of Health, Center for Vital and Health Statistics, 246 North High Street, Columbus, OH, Rettie Roush, death cert. # 14498.

188 Obituary of Mrs. Eli Roush, (Wilmington, Ohio, Wilmington News-Journal, 30 Mar 1942), Clark County Public Library, 201 South Fountain Avenue, Springfield, OH.

189 Find A Grave—Martinsville IOOF Cemetery, Martinsville, Clark Twp., Clinton Co., Ohio, Find A Grave.com, Loretta M. Barnes Roush, Find A Grave Memorial #154575528.

190 The Genealogical Committee of the Clinton County Historical Society, Cemetery Records of Clinton Co., Ohio, 1798-1998: Martinsville IOOF Cemetery: Loretta Mae Roush. Clinton County, Ohio Records Center and Archives, 111 South Nelson Avenue, Suite 3, Wilmington, OH.

191 Ohio, County Births, 1841-2003 (County Courthouses), FamilySearch.org, Earl "Niceley", Highland County Birth Records, Vol. 4, pg. 144.

192 Ohio, County Births, 1841-2003 (County Courthouses), FamilySearch.org, Harrie Roush, Highland County Birth Records, Vol. 3, pg. 404.

193 Rhode Island Death Certificate, Westerly Town Clerk, Westerly Town Hall, 45 Broad Street, Westerly, RI, Harry Emmett Roush, Rhode Island state file #138-71-008-014.

194 Obituary of Harry Emmett Roush Sr., Providence Public Library, 150 Empire Street, Providence, RI, Providence (RI) Journal, pub. 19 Nov 1971.

195 Ohio, County Births, 1841-2003 (County Courthouses), FamilySearch.org, Lorie Roush, Highland County Birth Records, Vol. 3, pg. 408.

196 Obituary of Lora Bussey Brust (Hillsboro, Ohio, Hillsboro Press-Gazette, 27 Feb 1981), Highland County District Library, 10 Willettsville Pike, Hillsboro, OH.

197 Ohio, Death Records, 1908-1932, 1938-2007, Ancestry.com, Lora B. Brust, death cert. #022383.

198 Ohio Death Certificate, Ohio Department of Health, Center for Vital and Health Statistics, 246 North High Street, Columbus, OH, Cecil Roush #18350.

199 Stroup Cemetery Burial Records, Highland County, Ohio: Cecil C. Roush, died Grandview Hospital, Dayton, Ohio. Clinton County, Ohio Records Center and Archives, 111 South Nelson Avenue, Suite 3, Wilmington, OH.

200 Ohio, Death Records, 1908-1932, 1938-2007, Ancestry.com, Samuel F. Roush, death cert. #086691.

201 Ohio, Birth Index, 1908-1964, Ancestry.com, Leroy Kenneth Roush, state file #1914008596.

202 Ohio, Death Records, 1908-1932, 1938-2007, Ancestry.com, Roy K. Roush, death cert. #089189.

203 Ohio, County Marriages, 1789-2013, FamilySearch.org, Thomas W. Walker and Euless Roush, Adams County, Ohio Marriage Records, Vol. 7, pg. 265, lic. #2690.

204 Obituary of Euless J. Walker (Xenia, Ohio, Xenia Daily Gazette, 20 Dec 1975), Greene County Public Library, Greene County Room Genealogy & Local History, 76 East Market Street, Xenia, OH.

205 Ohio, Death Records, 1908-1932, 1938-2007, Ancestry.com, Eulass J. Walker, death cert. #089420.

206 Obituary of Mrs. Leota Davis (Wilmington, Ohio, Wilmington News-Journal, 19 May 1982), Wilmington Public Library of Clinton County, 268 North South Street, Wilmington, OH.

207 Ohio, Death Records, 1908-1932, 1938-2007, Ancestry.com, Leota B. Davis, death cert. #032903.

208 Obituary of Mrs. Effie McCandless (Wilmington, Ohio, Wilmington News Journal, 10 Mar 1976.), Wilmington Public Library of Clinton County, 268 North South Street, Wilmington, OH.

209 The Genealogical Committee of the Clinton County Historical Society, Cemetery Records of Clinton Co., Ohio, 1798-1998: Maple Grove Cemetery/Port William Cemetery: Effie N. McCandless. Clinton County, Ohio Records Center and Archives, 111 South Nelson Avenue, Suite 3, Wilmington, OH.

210 Ohio, Death Records, 1908-1932, 1938-2007, Ancestry.com, Effie N. McCandless, death cert. #013983.

211 Ohio, Death Records, 1908-1932, 1938-2007, Ancestry.com, Dorothy O. Seitz, death cert. #000376.

212 Obituary of Dorthy O. (Roush) Seitz (Troy, Ohio, Troy Daily News, 13 Jul 2004), Troy-Miami Co. Public Library, 419 West Main Street, Troy, OH.

213 Ohio Death Certificate, Ohio Department of Health, Center for Vital and Health Statistics, 246 North High Street, Columbus, OH, Mary Leatha Roush Bogan, death cert. #58771.

214 Ohio, Death Records, 1908-1932, 1938-2007, Ancestry.com, Floyd R. Roush, death cert. #024720.

215 Ohio, County Marriages, 1789-2013, FamilySearch.org, Eli Kenneth Roush Jr. and Erma Lou Davis, Miami County, Ohio Marriage Records, Vol. 35, pg. 385, lic. #46587.

216 Ohio, Birth Index, 1908-1964, Ancestry.com, Eli K. Roush, state file #1931069824.

217 Obituary of Eli K. Roush Jr. (Wilmington, Ohio, Wilmington News Journal, 12 May 2009), Wilmington Public Library of Clinton County, 268 North South Street, Wilmington, OH.

218 Find A Grave—Stroup Cemetery, Dodson Twp., Highland Co., Ohio, Find A Grave.com, Cecil Roush, Find A Grave Memorial #133606359.

219 Ohio, County Marriages, 1789-2013, FamilySearch.org, Cecil Pegan and Electa Stroup, Highland County, Ohio Marriage Records, Vol.7, pg. 235, lic. #10908.

220 Ohio, County Births, 1841-2003 (County Courthouses), FamilySearch.org, "Lecta" Gertrude Stroup, Highland County Birth Records, Vol. 3, pg. 410.

221 Florida Death Index 1877-1998, Ancestry.com, Electa G. Roush.

222 Obituary of Electa Stroup Roush (Hillsboro, Ohio, Hillsboro Press Gazette, 18 Apr 1974), Highland County District Library, 10 Willettsville Pike, Hillsboro, OH.

223 Find A Grave—Stroup Cemetery, Dodson Twp., Highland Co., Ohio, Find A Grave.com, Electa Gertrude Stroup Roush, Find A Grave Memorial #154649436.

224 U.S., WWI Draft Registration Cards, 1917-1918, Ancestry.com, Cecil Ira Roush, Francesville, Lawrence Co., Illinois.

225 Florida Death Index 1877-1998, Ancestry.com, Philip S. Roush.

226 U.S., Social Security Applications and Claims Index, 1936-2007, Ancestry.com, Randall Cecil Roush.

227 U.S., Social Security Applications and Claims Index, 1936-2007, Ancestry.com, Gale E. Roush.

228 Florida Death Index 1877-1998, Ancestry.com, Gale Roush.

229 Ohio Death Certificate, Ohio Department of Health, Center for Vital and Health Statistics, 246 North High Street, Columbus, OH, Dale Roush, death cert. #33328.

230 Ohio Death Certificate, Ohio Department of Health, Center for Vital and Health Statistics, 246 North High Street, Columbus, OH, (Unnamed) Roush, death cert. #53725.

231 Grant County, Indiana Marriage Records, Grant County, Indiana Clerk's Office, County Complex, 401 South Adams Street, Marion, IN, Harley P. Keplinger and Laura Pegan, Grant County, Indiana Marriage Records, Vol. 11, pg. 358.

232 Obituary of Harley Keplinger (Huntington, Indiana, Huntington Herald Press, 13 Jun 1943), Huntington City-Township Library, Indiana Room, 255 West Park Drive, Huntington, IN.

233 U.S., WWI Draft Registration Cards, 1917-1918, Ancestry.com, Harley Paul Keplinger, Warren, Indiana.

234 Indiana, Death Certificates, 1899-2011, Ancestry.com, Harley Paul Keplinger, Indiana death cert. #18611.

235 Find A Grave—Woodlawn Cemetery, Warren, Salamonie Twp., Huntington Co., Indiana, Find A Grave.com, Harley P. Keplinger, Find A Grave Memorial #60945718.

236 Find A Grave—Farrville Cemetery, Van Buren Twp., Grant Co., Indiana, Find A Grave.com, Sarah C. Pearson, Find A Grave Memorial #24220910.

237 "Begs His Intended Victim For Mercy" (Washington, Iowa, Washington Evening Journal, 09 Feb 1899); Newspaper Archive, Online database: newspaperarchive.com, https://access-newspaperarchive-com.sjcpl.idm.oclc.org/us/iowa/washington/washington-evening-journal/1899/02-09/page-4/pegan?page=4&ndt=by&py=1899&pey=1900

238 "Geo. Keplinger Writes Letters" (Marion, Indiana, Grant County News, 03 Feb 1899), Marion Public Library-Central Library, 1963, 600 South Washington Street, Marion, IN.

239 "Father's Advice To Keplinger" (Marion, Indiana, Grant County News, 10 Feb 1899), Marion Public Library-Central Library, 1963, 600 South Washington Street, Marion, IN.

240 "Marion Murder: George Keplinger Kills Laura Pegan Because She Refused To Wed Him" (Bloomfield, Indiana, Bloomfield News, 03 Feb 1899); Newspaper Archive, Online database: newspaperarchive.com, https://access-newspaperarchive-com.sjcpl.idm.oclc.org/us/indiana/bloomfield/bloomfield-news/1899/02-03/page-8/keplinger?ndt=by&py=1899&pey=1899&pci=7.

241 "To Be A Better Boy" (Marion, Indiana, Grant County News, 07 Feb 1899), Marion Public Library-Central Library, 1963, 600 South Washington Street, Marion, IN.

242 "Keplinger's Capers" (Marion, Indiana, Grant County News, 17 Feb 1899), Marion Public Library-Central Library, 1963, 600 South Washington Street, Marion, IN.

243 "Goes To The Penitentiary" (Kokomo, Indiana, Kokomo Daily Tribune, reprinted from the Marion [IN] Leader, 25 Apr 1899); Newspaper Archive, Online database: newspaperarchive.com https://access-newspaperarchive-com.sjcpl.idm.oclc.org/tags/keplinger?page=2&pci=7&ndt=by&py=1899&pey=1899

244 Grant County, Indiana Marriage Records, Grant County, Indiana Clerk's Office, County Complex, 401 South Adams Street, Marion, IN, Isaac J. Pearson and Sarah C. Pegan, Grant County, Indiana Marriage Records, Vol.13, pg. 550.

245 Find A Grave—Farrville Cemetery, Van Buren Twp., Grant Co., Indiana, Find A Grave.com, Isaac J. Pearson, Find A Grave Memorial #24220901.

246 Indiana, Death Certificates, 1899-2011, Ancestry.com, Isaac J. "Peasson", Indiana death cert. #39659.

247 Obituary of Isaac Pearson (Amboy, Indiana, Amboy Independent, 18 Dec 1936), Indiana State Library, 315 West Ohio Street, Indianapolis, IN.

248 "Miss Pegan Is Married" (Marion, Indiana, Grant County News, 15 Feb 1902), Marion Public Library, 600 South Washington Street, Marion, IN.

249 Howard County, Indiana Marriage Records, Howard County, Indiana County Clerk, Howard County Courthouse, 104 North Buckeye Street, Room 114, Kokomo, IN, Franklin E. Hewitt and Sarah C. Pearson, Howard County, Indiana Marriage Records, Vol. 68, pg. 167.

250 Indiana, Death Certificates, 1899-2011, Ancestry.com, Frank E. Hewitt, Indiana death cert. #880.

251 Obituary of Frank E. Hewitt (Marion, Indiana, Marion Chronicle, 30 Jan 1946), Marion, Indiana Public Library, 600 South Washington Street, Marion, IN.

252 Find A Grave—Mount Hope Cemetery, Covington, Kenton Co., Kentucky, Find A Grave.com, Eli Franklin "Frank" Hewitt, Find A Grave Memorial #22190175.

253 Randolph County, Indiana Marriage Records, Randolph County Clerk, 113 East Washington Street, Winchester, IN; Clarence B. Horner and Sarah C. Hewitt, Randolph County, Indiana Marriage Records, Vol. 41, pg. 102.

254 U.S., WWI Draft Registration Cards, 1917-1918, Ancestry.com, Clarence Branson Horner.

255 Indiana, Death Certificates, 1899-2011, Ancestry.com, Clarence Branson Horner, Indiana death cert. #61-013834.

256 Willow Grove Cemetery Records, Fountain City, Indiana, Clarence B. Horner, Willow Grove Cemetery, Fountain City, New Garden Twp., Wayne Co., Indiana.

257 Obituary of Clarence B. Horner (Richmond, Indiana, Richmond Palladium-Item, 12 Apr 1961), Indiana State Library, 315 West Ohio Street, Indianapolis, IN.

258 Find A Grave—Willow Grove Cemetery, Fountain City, New Garden Twp., Wayne Co., Indiana, Find A Grave.com.

259 U.S., WWII Draft Registration Cards Young Men, 1940-1947, Ancestry.com, James Roy Mattucks, Pine Lawn, St. Louis Co., Missouri.

260 Obituary of Roy Scott (Springfield, Illinois, Illinois State Journal, 20 Oct 1969), Lincoln Library, 326 South 7th Street, Springfield, IL.

261 Obituary of Mollie M. Scott (Springfield, Illinois, Illinois State Journal, 10 Aug 1977), Lincoln Library, 326 South 7th Street, Springfield, IL.

262 Missouri, Marriage Records, 1805-2002, Ancestry.com, Roy C. Scott and Mollie Lamparter, St. Charles County, Missouri Marriage Records, pg. 224.

263 Find A Grave—Roselawn Memorial Park Cemetery, Springfield, Sangamon Co., Illinois, Find A Grave.com, Pauline L. Klespitz, Find A Grave Memorial #167870180.

264 U.S., WWII Draft Registration Cards, 1942, Ancestry.com, Roy Clarence Scott, Springfield, Illinois.

265 U.S., WWI Draft Registration Cards, 1917-1918, Ancestry.com, Raymond Pegan, Wabash, Indiana.

266 Obituary of Raymond Pegan (Fort Wayne, Indiana, Fort Wayne Journal Gazette, 09 May 1980), Genealogy Center, Allen County Public Library, 900 Library Plaza, Fort Wayne, IN.

267 Indiana, Death Certificates, 1899-2011, Ancestry.com, Raymond Pegan, Indiana death cert. #80015892.

268 Web: Grant County, Indiana, Marion Public Library Birth Index, 1882-1981, Ancestry.com.

269 Indiana, Death Certificates, 1899-2011, Ancestry.com, Mattie Leona Hatfield, Indiana death cert. #042041.

270 Obituary of Herbert Pearson (Ontario, Oregon, Argus Observer, 09 Aug 1973), Ontario Community Library, 388 S.W. 2nd Avenue, Ontario, OR.

271 Oregon, Death Index, 1898-2008, Ancestry.com, Herbert Pearson, Umatilla Co., death cert. #73-13754.

272 U.S., Social Security Applications and Claims Index, 1936-2007, Ancestry.com, Truman Vaughn Pearson.

273 Obituary of Opal Colene Eastes (Marion, Indiana, Marion Chronicle Tribune, 21 Dec 2000), Marion, Indiana Public Library, 600 South Washington Street, Marion, IN.

274 Indiana, Death Certificates, 1899-2011, Ancestry.com, Opal Colene Eastes, Indiana death cert. #041809.

275 Find A Grave—Hopewell Cemetery, Lagro Twp., Wabash Co., Indiana, Find A Grave.com, Alvin L. PeGan, Find A Grave Memorial #36194767.

276 Indiana, Marriages, 1811-2001, FamilySearch.org, Alvah L. Pegan and Edythe Wildoner, Wabash County, Indiana Marriage Records, Applications, Vol. 5, pg. 47.

277 Wabash County, Indiana Marriage Records, Wabash County, Indiana Clerk, Courthouse Annex, 69 West Hill Street, Wabash, IN, Alvah L. PeGan and Edythe G. Wildoner, Wabash County, Indiana Marriage Records, Vol. 16, pg. 442.

278 Indiana, Marriages, 1811-2001, FamilySearch.org, William C. Brown and Edythe Pegan.

279 Obituary of Edythe G. Brown (Wabash, Indiana, Wabash Plain Dealer, 20 Nov 1984), Wabash Carnegie Public Library, 188 West Hill Street, Wabash, IN.

280 Find A Grave—Falls Memorial Gardens Cemetery, Wabash, Noble Twp., Wabash Co., Indiana, Find A Grave.com, Edythe G. Wildoner Brown, Find A Grave Memorial #39891425.

281 Indiana, Marriages, 1811-2001, FamilySearch.org, Alvin Pegan and Leatha Mae Rodgers, Wabash County, Indiana Marriage Records, Applications, Vol. 15, pg. 563.

282 Wabash County, Indiana Marriage Records, Wabash County, Indiana Clerk, Courthouse Annex, 69 West Hill Street, Wabash, IN, Alvin PeGan and Leatha Mae Rodgers, Wabash County, Indiana Marriage Records, Vol.15, pg. 563.

283 Indiana, Marriages, 1811-2001, FamilySearch.org, Charles F. Hegel and Leatha May Pegan, Wabash Co., Indiana, 21 Jul 1937, Book 19, pg. 391.

284 Obituary of Leatha M. Morrow Class (Huntington, Indiana, Huntington Herald Press, 03 May 1977), Huntington City-

285 Indiana, Death Certificates, 1899-2011, Ancestry.com, Leatha Mae Class, Indiana death cert. #77-016220.

286 Find A Grave—Pilgrims Rest Cemetery, Huntington, Huntington Twp., Huntington Co., Indiana, Find A Grave.com, Leatha M. Class, Find A Grave Memorial #133246693.

287 Obituary of William V. Class (Huntington, Indiana, Huntington Herald Press, 20 Jul 1970), Huntington City-Township Library, Indiana Room, 255 West Park Drive, Huntington, IN.

288 Find A Grave—Pilgrims Rest Cemetery, Huntington, Huntington Twp., Huntington Co., Indiana, Find A Grave.com, Jesse H. Pegan, Find A Grave Memorial #133088711.

289 "Macy Items" (Rochester, Indiana, Rochester Sentinel, 22 Mar 1917), Indiana State Library, 315 West Ohio Street, Indianapolis, IN.

290 Wabash County, Indiana Marriage Records, Wabash County, Indiana Clerk, Courthouse Annex, 69 West Hill Street, Wabash, IN, Jesse H. Harrison and Elva C. Keith, Wabash County, Indiana Marriage Records, Vol. 16, pg. 447.

291 Indiana, Marriages 1811-2007, FamilySearch.org, Jesse H. Pegan and Elva C. Keith, Wabash County, Indiana Marriage Records, Applications, Vol. 5, pg. 55.

292 Family Data: Phone interviews with and emails from Florence Marie Koesters, Toledo, OH, Ann Miller Carr, author, 2007-2010.

293 Indiana, Death Certificates, 1899-2011, Ancestry.com, Elva Coe Pegan, Indiana death cert. #72-021765.

294 Obituary of Elva Keith Pegan (Huntington, Indiana, Huntington Herald Press, 14 Jun 1972), Huntington City-Township Library, Indiana Room, 255 West Park Drive, Huntington, IN.

295 Find A Grave—Pilgrims Rest Cemetery, Huntington, Huntington Twp., Huntington Co., Indiana, Find A Grave.com, Elva C. Pegan, Find A Grave Memorial #133088675.

296 U.S, WWI Draft Registration Cards, 1917-1918, Ancestry.com, Jesse H. Pegan, Miami County, Indiana.

297 "Macy Men Capture Badger" (Rochester, Indiana, Rochester Weekly Republican, 20 Dec 1917); Newspaper Archive, Online database: newspaperarchive.com, https://access-newspaperarchive-com.sjcpl.idm.oclc.org/us/indiana/rochester/rochester-weekly-republican/1917/12-20/page-6/jesse-pegan?pc=24867&psi=38&pci=7

298 Wabash County, Indiana Marriage Records, Wabash County, Indiana Clerk, Courthouse Annex, 69 West Hill Street, Wabash, IN, Charles R. Oswalt and Pauline M. Pegan, Wabash County, Indiana Marriage Records, Vol. 18, pg. 415.

299 "One Murder Trial Set For Next Week" (Edwardsville, Illinois, Edwardsville Intelligencer, 14 Nov 1936), Newspapers and Periodicals, Ancestry.com.

300 U.S, WWII Draft Registration Cards, 1942, Ancestry.com, Jesse H. Pegan, Milwaukee, Wisconsin.

301 Family Data: Emails from James Hastings, Ann Arbor, MI, Ann Miller Carr, author, 2000-2001.

302 Phone interviews and emails from Betty Jean Pegan Corn, Kokomo, IN, Ann Miller Carr, author, 2008-2018.

303 Interview with Darlene PeGan Stanley, and Connie Abbott Hamilton, Niles, MI, Ann Miller Carr, author, 16 Jul 2007.

304 Obituary of Cecil K. PeGan (Huntington, Indiana, Huntington Herald Press, 08 Jul 1990), Huntington City-Township Library, Indiana Room, 255 West Park Drive, Huntington, IN.

305 Delaware County, Indiana Marriage Records, Delaware County, Indiana County Clerk, Courthouse, 100 West Main Street Muncie, IN, Cecil K. Pegan and Bessie M. Shoemaker.

306 Indiana, Death Certificates, 1899-2011, Ancestry.com, Cecil K. Pegan, Indiana death cert. #90-028493.

307 Indiana, Birth Certificates, 1907-1940, Ancestry.com, Cecil Keith Pegan, Wabash County, Indiana Birth Records, birth cert. #48511.

308 U.S., Social Security Applications and Claims Index, 1936-2007, Ancestry.com, Pauline Miriam Pegan Oswalt.

309 Indiana, Death Certificates, 1899-2011, Ancestry.com, Pauline M. Oswalt, Indiana death cert. #004851.

310 Indiana, Birth Certificates, 1907-1940, Ancestry.com, "Pegan" (female), Wabash County, Indiana Birth Records, birth cert. #57689.

311 Obituary of James M. Pegan (Huntington, Indiana, Huntington Herald Press, 24 Feb 1987), Huntington City-Township Library, Indiana Room, 255 West Park Drive, Huntington, IN.

312 Indiana, Death Certificates, 1899-2011, Ancestry.com, James M. Pegan, Indiana death cert. #87-004800.

313 Indiana, Birth Certificates, 1907-1940, Ancestry.com, James Meredith Pegan, Miami County, Indiana Birth Records, birth cert. #41122.

314 Ohio, County Marriages, 1789-2013, FamilySearch.org, Vilas H. Zimpelman and Fern M. Pegan, Paulding County, Ohio Marriage Records, Vol. 12, pg. 156, lic. #6781.

315 U.S., Social Security Applications and Claims Index, 1936-2007, Ancestry.com, Fern Maxine Pegan Zimpelman.

316 Obituary of Fern M. Zimpelman (Huntington, Indiana, Huntington Herald Press, 18 Jun 1979), Huntington City-Township Library, Indiana Room, 255 West Park Drive, Huntington, IN.

317 Indiana, Death Certificates, 1899-2011, Ancestry.com, Fern M. Zimpelman, Indiana death cert. #79-121429.

318 Indiana, Birth Certificates, 1907-1940, Ancestry.com, Fern Maxine Pegan, Miami County, Indiana Birth Records, birth cert. #42606.

319 Obituary of Florence Flowers (Celina, Ohio, Celina Daily Standard, 30 Oct 1992), Mercer County Library, 303 North Main Street, Celina, OH.

320 Ohio, Death Records, 1908-1932, 1938-2007, Ancestry.com, Florence W. Flowers, death cert. #084885.

321 Indiana, Marriages 1811-2007, FamilySearch.org, John Flowers and Florence Willodean Pegan, Allen County, Indiana Marriage Records, Vol. 120, pg. 236.

322 Find A Grave—Gardens of Memory Cemetery, Banquo, Wayne Twp., Huntington Co., Indiana on the Grant Co. line, Find A Grave.com, Clanzie H. PeGan, Find A Grave Memorial #14362447.

323 Wabash County, Indiana Marriage Records, Wabash County, Indiana Clerk, Courthouse Annex, 69 West Hill Street, Wabash, IN, Clanzie H. PeGan and Josephine S. Schetzszle, Wabash County, Indiana Marriage Records, Vol.16, pg. 63.

324 Huntington County, Indiana Death Records, Huntington County, Indiana Department of Health, 354 North Jefferson St., #201, Huntington, IN, Josephine PeGan, Book 6, pg. 47.

325 Indiana Death Certificate (Indianapolis, Indiana, State of Indiana), Indiana State Department of Health, 2 North Meridian Street, Indianapolis, IN, Josephine S. PeGan, death cert. #A2934-7889/364212.

326 Indiana, Death Certificates, 1899-2011, Ancestry.com, Josephine S. PeGan, Indiana death cert. #7889.

327 Find A Grave—Saint Patrick Cemetery, Lagro, Lagro Twp., Wabash Co., Indiana, Find A Grave.com, Josephine S. PeGan, Find A Grave Memorial #73023726.

328 Patricia Keefe PeGan was the author's mother.

329 Grant County, Indiana Marriage Records, Grant County, Indiana Clerk's Office, County Complex, 401 South Adams Street, Marion, IN, Clanzie H. PeGan and Loretta Sellers, Grant County, Indiana Marriage Records, Vol. 54, pg. 580.

330 Indiana, Death Certificates, 1899-2011, Ancestry.com, Loretta A. PeGan, Indiana death cert. #92-028315.

331 Find A Grave—Gardens of Memory Cemetery, Banquo, Wayne Twp., Huntington Co., Indiana on the Grant Co. line, Find A Grave.com, Loretta A. PeGan, Find A Grave Memorial #14362430.

332 U.S., Railroad Retirement Pension Index, 1934-1987, Ancestry.com, "G." Pegan, #A810681.

333 Ohio Death Certificate, Ohio Department of Health, Center for Vital and Health Statistics, 246 North High Street, Columbus, OH, Leo E. Pegan, death cert. #052056.

334 Indiana, Birth Certificates, 1907-1940, Ancestry.com, "Everett Harold" PeGan, Wabash County, Indiana Birth Records, birth cert. #53308.

335 Ohio, Death Records, 1908-1932, 1938-2007, Ancestry.com, Leo Pegan, #052056.

336 Indiana, Death Certificates, 1899-2011, Ancestry.com, Paul H. PeGan, Indiana death cert. #81-030612.

337 Obituary of Paul H. PeGan (Fort Wayne, Indiana, Fort Wayne Journal Gazette, 26 Aug 1981), Genealogy Center, Allen County Public Library, 900 Library Plaza, Fort Wayne, IN.

338 Indiana, Birth Certificates, 1907-1940, Ancestry.com, Mary Angeline PeGan, Wabash County, Indiana Birth Records, birth cert. #55298.

339 Wisconsin Death Index- 1959-1997, Ancestry.com, Mary Angeline Welch, death cert. #031660.

340 Indiana, Death Certificates, 1899-2011, Ancestry.com, H. Frederick PeGan, Indiana death cert. #008157.

341 Allen County, Indiana Death Certificate, Fort Wayne-Allen County, Indiana Department of Health, 200 East Berry St., Suite 360, Fort Wayne, IN, Kenneth Joseph PeGan, death cert. #1985-1512.

342 Indiana, Death Certificates, 1899-2011, Ancestry.com, Kenneth Joseph PeGan, Indiana death cert. #023520.

343 Indiana, Birth Certificates, 1907-1940, Ancestry.com, Kenneth Austin Pegan, Huntington County, Indiana Birth Records, birth cert. #21836.

344 U.S., Department of Veterans Affairs BIRLS Death File, 1850-2010, Ancestry.com, Kenneth "Pegan".

345 Find A Grave—Hopewell Cemetery, Lagro Twp., Wabash Co., Indiana, Find A Grave.com, Leonidus Pegan, Find A Grave Memorial #36194824.

346 Find A Grave—Chapel Hill Memorial Gardens, Osceola, Penn Twp., St. Joseph Co., Indiana, Find A Grave.com, Philip G. PeGan, Find A Grave Memorial #103341665.

347 Indiana, Marriages 1811-2007, FamilySearch.org, Philip Garl PeGan and Dorothy Margaret Vermilyer, Miami County, Indiana Marriage Records, Vol. 26, pg. 561.

348 Obituary of Dorothy Mae Pegan (Niles, Michigan, Niles Star, 01 Aug 1988), Niles District Library, 620 East Main Street, Niles, MI.

349 Family Data: Philip Garl PeGan family, Philip Garl PeGan Family Reunion Book (Niles, Niles Twp., Berrien Co., Michigan,), Philip Garl PeGan family.

350 Find A Grave—Chapel Hill Memorial Gardens, Osceola, Penn Twp., St. Joseph Co., Indiana, Find A Grave.com, Dorothy Mae PeGan, Find A Grave Memorial #103341681.

351 Indiana, Birth Certificates, 1907-1940, Ancestry.com, Phillip Ellsworth PeGan, Miami County, Indiana Birth Records, birth cert. #49262.

352 Indiana, Birth Certificates, 1907-1940, Ancestry.com, Juanita Mae Pegan, St. Joseph County, Indiana Birth Records, birth cert. #41411.

353 Indiana, Birth Certificates, 1907-1940, Ancestry.com, Richard "Scyler" Pegan, Miami County, Indiana Birth Records, birth cert. #18505.

354 Indiana, Birth Certificates, 1907-1940, Ancestry.com, Karl Nelson Pegan, St. Joseph County, Indiana Birth Records, birth cert. #28140.

355 Michigan, Marriage Records, 1867-1952, Ancestry.com, Phillip "Blleworth" PeGan and Josephine Clara "Lowis", Berrien County, Michigan Marriage Records, Vol. 1942, lic. #802.

356 Obituary of Phillip E. PeGan (South Bend, Indiana, South Bend Tribune, 06 Oct 2012), St. Joseph County Public Library, 304 South Main Street, South Bend, IN.

357 Obituary of Raymond L. PeGan (Niles, Michigan, Niles Star, 10 Apr 1997), Niles District Library, 620 East Main Street, Niles, MI.

358 Indiana, Birth Certificates, 1907-1940, Ancestry.com, Raymond Leon PeGan, Fulton County, Indiana Birth Records, birth cert. #52695.

359 Indiana, Birth Certificates, 1907-1940, Ancestry.com, Donna Belle Pegan, Miami County, Indiana Birth Records, birth cert. #8929.

360 Obituary of Donna B. Reed (Niles, Michigan, Niles Daily Star, 16 Nov 1987), Niles District Library, 620 East Main Street, Niles, MI.

361 U.S., Social Security Applications and Claims Index, 1936-2007, Ancestry.com, Richard Schuyler Pegan.

362 Michigan, Marriage Records, 1867-1952, Ancestry.com, Richard S. Pegan and Dorothy A. Young, Berrien County, Michigan Marriage Records, Vol. 1948, lic. #230; Michigan state file #11-15468.

363 Find A Grave—Silverbrook Cemetery, Niles, Niles Twp., Berrien Co., Michigan, Find A Grave.com, Richard S. PeGan, Find A Grave Memorial #136190839.

364 Obituary of Richard S. PeGan (Niles, Michigan, Niles Daily Star, 20 Sep 2001), Niles District Library, 620 East Main Street, Niles, MI.

365 Michigan, Deaths and Burials Index, 1867-1995, Ancestry.com, Karl Nelson Pegan.

366 "Three Are Believed Drowned Saturday Night" (Niles, Michigan, Niles Star, 29 Dec 1952), Niles District Library, 620 East Main Street, Niles, MI.

367 Obituary of Robert Harrison Pegan (South Bend, Indiana, South Bend Tribune, 30 Mar 1931), St. Joseph County Public Library, 304 South Main Street, South Bend, IN.

368 Indiana Death Certificate (Indianapolis, Indiana, State of Indiana), Indiana State Department of Health, 2 North Meridian Street, Indianapolis, IN, Robert Harrison PeGan, death cert. #10257.

369 Obituary of Juanita M. Abbott (Niles, Michigan, Niles Daily Star, 03 Aug 2015), Niles District Library, 620 East Main Street, Niles, MI.

370 Indiana, Birth Certificates, 1907-1940, Ancestry.com, Darlene Kay Pegan, St. Joseph County, Indiana Birth Records, birth cert. #45079.

371 Find A Grave—Fairview Cemetery, Bluffton, Wells Co., Indiana, Find A Grave.com, Olive Roll, Find A Grave Memorial #68005180.

372 U.S., Social Security Applications and Claims Index, 1936-2007, Ancestry.com, Bertha Olive Roll.

373 Obituary of Clara Belle Hunter (Hillsboro, Ohio, Hillsboro Press-Gazette, 27 Aug 1948), Highland County District Library, 10 Willettsville Pike, Hillsboro, OH.

374 Indiana, Marriages 1811-2007, FamilySearch.org, Marion Roll and Bertha Farr, Blackford County, Indiana Marriage Records, Vol. F, pg. 102.

375 Florida Marriage License, Florida Department of Health-State Office of Vital Statistics, 1217 North Pearl Street, Jacksonville, FL, Marion Roll and Olive Roll, Broward County Marriage Records, lic. #26609.

376 Florida Marriage Collection, 1822-1875 and 1927-2001, Ancestry.com, Marion Roll and Olive Roll.

377 U.S., WWI Draft Registration Cards, 1917-1918, Ancestry.com, Marion Roll, Marion, Grant Co., Indiana.

378 Obituary of Marion Roll (Huntington, Indiana, Huntington Herald Press, 23 Sep 1976), Huntington City-Township Library, Indiana Room, 255 West Park Drive, Huntington, IN.

379 Find A Grave—Fairview Cemetery, Bluffton, Wells Co., Indiana, Find A Grave.com, Marion Roll, Find A Grave Memorial #68005120.

380 Indiana, Marriages 1811-2007, FamilySearch.org, Arthur C. Bartlemay and Bertha Olive Roll, Wells County, Indiana Marriage Records, Vol, K, pg. 187.

381 U.S., WWI Draft Registration Cards, 1917-1918, Ancestry.com, Arthur Clarence Bartlemay.

382 U.S., Social Security Applications and Claims Index, 1936-2007, Ancestry.com, Arthur Clarence Bartlemay.

383 Ohio Deaths, 1908-1953, FamilySearch.org, Arthur Bartlemay, Ohio death cert. #11411.

384 Obituary of Arthur Bartlemay (Bluffton, Indiana, Bluffton News Banner, 03 Feb 1951), Wells County Public Library, 200 West Washington Street, Bluffton, IN.

385 Find A Grave—Fairview Cemetery, Bluffton, Wells Co., Indiana, Find A Grave.com, Arthur C. Bartlemay, Find A Grave Memorial #57288546.

386 Florida State Census, 1945, Ancestry.com, Fort Lauderdale, Broward County, Precinct 6, pg. 24, entry for Marion Roll.

387 Obituary of Leota Lydy (Bluffton, Indiana, Bluffton News Banner, 12 Oct 1965), Wells County Public Library, 200 West Washington Street, Bluffton, IN.

388 Find A Grave—Fairview Cemetery, Bluffton, Wells Co., Indiana, Find A Grave.com, Leota F. Lydy, Find A Grave Memorial #67987376.

389 Indiana, Death Certificates, 1899-2011, Ancestry.com, Leota F. Lydy, Wells County, Indiana death cert. #65-038513.

390 Obituary of Edmund W. Roll (Kokomo, Indiana, Kokomo Tribune, 12 Feb 1974), Kokomo-Howard County Public Library, 220 North Union Street, Kokomo, IN.

391 Indiana, Death Certificates, 1899-2011, Ancestry.com, Edmund Warren "Boll", Indiana death cert. #74-004846.

392 Find A Grave—Sunset Memory Garden Cemetery, Kokomo, Center Twp., Howard Co., Indiana, Find A Grave.com, Edmund W. Roll, Find A Grave Memorial #103743819.

393 Indiana, Marriages 1811-2007, FamilySearch.org, Melvin C. Kennedy and Thelma Long, Wells County, Indiana Marriage Records, Vol. L, pg. 56.

394 Indiana, Birth Certificates, 1907-1940, Ancestry.com, Thelma Roll, Blackford County, Indiana Birth Records, Roll 02, Vol. 368-372. cert. #3289.

395 Indiana, Death Certificates, 1899-2011, Ancestry.com, Thelma Lynn Kennedy, Indiana death cert. #95-009806.

396 Obituary of Mrs. Earl Bender (Bluffton, Indiana, Bluffton News Banner, 24 Feb 1964), Wells County Public Library, 200 West Washington Street, Bluffton, IN.

397 Indiana, Marriages 1811-2007, FamilySearch.org, Earl A. Bender and Marian C. Roll, Wells Co., Indiana Marriage Records, Vol. 18. pg. 102.

398 Indiana, Birth Certificates, 1907-1940, Ancestry.com, Marian "Coleine" Roll, Grant County, Indiana Birth Records, #6701.

399 Indiana, Death Certificates, 1899-2011, Ancestry.com, Marian Bender, Indiana death cert. #64-007485.

400 Obituary of John C. Hunter (Hillsboro, Ohio, Highland County Press-Gazette, 22 May 1968), Highland County District Library, 10 Willettsville Pike, Hillsboro, OH.

401 Find A Grave—Mt. Zion Cemetery, Danville, New Market Twp., Highland Co., Ohio, Find A Grave.com, John Clark Hunter, Find A Grave Memorial #34840961.

402 Ohio, County Marriages, 1789-2013, FamilySearch.org, John C. Hunter and Rosa M. Wilkin, Highland County, Ohio Marriage Records, Vol.17, pg. 218, lic. #10875.

403 Ohio, County Births, 1841-2003 (County Courthouses), FamilySearch.org, Rosa Mae Wilkin, Highland County Birth Records, Vol. 3, pg. 500.

404 Ohio, Death Records, 1908-1932, 1938-2007, Ancestry.com, Rosa W. (Wilkin) Hunter, death cert. #059006.

405 Obituary of Rosa W. Hunter (Hillsboro, Ohio, Hillsboro Press-Gazette, 14 Aug 1975), Highland County District Library, 10 Willettsville Pike, Hillsboro, OH.

406 Find A Grave—Mt. Zion Cemetery, Danville, New Market Twp., Highland Co., Ohio, Find A Grave.com, Rosa Wilkin Hunter, Find A Grave Memorial #34840984.

407 Obituary of Clyde C. Hunter (Hillsboro, Ohio, Hillsboro Press-Gazette, 10 Apr 1973), Highland County District Library, 10 Willettsville Pike, Hillsboro, OH.

408 Ohio, Death Records, 1908-1932, 1938-2007, Ancestry.com, Clyde C. Hunter, death cert. #029102.

409 Michigan, Marriages, 1868-1925, FamilySearch.org, Frank Schoonmaker and Fay Roush, St. Joseph County, Michigan Marriage Records, Vol. H., pg. 186, lic. #8047.

410 U.S., WWI Draft Registration Cards, 1917-1918, Ancestry.com, Frank Leslie Schoonmaker, Three Rivers, St. Joseph County, Michigan.

411 Michigan, Marriages, 1868-1925, FamilySearch.org, Elbridge Thompson and Fay Roush, St. Joseph County, Michigan Marriage Records, Vol H., pg. 296, lic #9765.

412 Interview with Viola Jane Brown Roush, Coldwater, MI, Ann Miller Carr, author, 15 Aug 2012.

413 Find A Grave—Evergreen Cemetery, Girard Twp., Branch Co., Michigan, Find A Grave.com, Delbert L. Roush, Find A Grave Memorial #112638827.

414 Find A Grave—Evergreen Cemetery, Girard Twp., Branch Co., Michigan, Find A Grave.com, Delbert L. Roush, Find A Grave Memorial #112638827.

415 Branch County, Michigan Genealogical Society, Branch County, Branch County, Michigan Cemetery Records: Girard Township: Evergreen Cemetery Records, Delbert L. Roush; Branch County Genealogical Society, compiled 1999. Branch County Library, Coldwater Branch, 10 East Chicago Street, Coldwater, MI.

416 Minnesota Death Certificate, Minnesota Historical Society, 345 Kellogg Boulevard West, St. Paul, MN, Zona Tomek, death cert. #021104.

417 Obituary of Zona Tomek (Marshall, Minnesota, Marshall Independent, 02 Jul 1992), Marshall-Lyon County Library, 201 C Street, Marshall, MN.

418 Find A Grave—Saints Cyril and Methodius Catholic Cemetery, Taunton, Lyon Co., Minnesota, Find A Grave.com, Zona Tomek, Find A Grave Memorial #154289735.

419 Indiana, Birth Certificates, 1907-1940, Ancestry.com, Jane Roush, St. Joseph County, Indiana Birth Records, birth cert. #12378, fa. Delbert, mo. Mary Murphy, mo. born Melrose, Iowa.

420 Cook County, Illinois Death Index, 1908-1988, Ancestry.com, Mary Roush, death cert. #6001765.

421 Iowa, Births and Christenings Index, 1800-1999, Ancestry.com, Mary Murphy, born Jackson Twp., Iowa.

422 Find A Grave—Mount Carmel Cemetery, Hillside, Cook Co., Illinois, Find A Grave.com, Mary Roush, Find A Grave Memorial #174972021.

423 Michigan Marriages, 1822-1995, Familysearch.org. Joseph L. Roush and Edith Gout, St. Joseph County, Michigan Marriage Records, Vol. H, pg. 226, lic. #8674.

424 Obituary of Edith E. Roush (Coldwater, Michigan, Coldwater Daily Reporter, 23 Oct 1958), Branch County Library, Coldwater Branch, 10 East Chicago Street, Coldwater, MI.

425 Branch County, Michigan Death Records, Branch County, Michigan County Clerk's Office, Courthouse, 31 Division Street. Coldwater, MI, Edith Gaut Roush, Vol. E, pg. 215, #5817.

426 Find A Grave—Evergreen Cemetery, Girard Twp., Branch Co., Michigan, Find A Grave.com, Edith E. Roush, Find A Grave Memorial #112638761.

427 Obituary of John M. Roush (Coldwater, Michigan, Coldwater Daily Reporter, 21 Nov 1988), Branch County Library, Coldwater Branch, 10 East Chicago Street, Coldwater, MI.

428 Indiana, Death Certificates, 1899-2011, Ancestry.com, John M. Roush, Indiana death cert. #88-044442.

429 North Carolina Death Collection, 1908-2004, Ancestry.com, George Lewis Roush.

430 U.S., Department of Veterans Affairs BIRLS Death File, 1850-2010, Ancestry.com, George Roush.

431 Obituary of George Lewis Roush (Salisbury, North Carolina, Salisbury Evening Post, 17 Jul 1978), Rowan Public Library, 210 West Fisher Street, Salisbury, NC..

432 North Carolina, Death Indexes, 1908-2004, Ancestry.com, George Lewis Roush.

433 U.S. Veterans' Gravesites, ca. 1775-2006, Ancestry.com, George Lewis Roush.

434 Obituary of Harley Leroy Roush Sr. (Niles, Michigan, Niles Daily Star, 11 Dec 1968), Niles District Library, 620 East Main Street, Niles, MI.

435 Find A Grave—Bertrand Bible Church Cemetery/Truitts Chapel Cemetery, Niles, Niles Twp., Berrien Co., Michigan, Find A Grave.com, Harley Leroy Roush Sr., Find A Grave Memorial #138717598.

436 Find A Grave—Ferncliff Cemetery, Springfield, Springfield Twp., Clark Co., Ohio, George B. Roush, Find A Grave Memorial #60770390.

437 Kentucky, County Marriages, 1785-1979, FamilySearch.org, George B. Roush and Nellie Armstrong, Kenton County, Kentucky Marriage Records, pg. 461.

438 Obituary of Nellie Roush (Mrs. George Roush) (Springfield, Ohio, Springfield Daily News, 20 Jun 1959), Clark County Public Library, 201 South Fountain Avenue, Springfield, OH.

439 Utah Death Certificates, 1904-1964, FamilySearch.org, Nellie M. Roush, death cert. #59-29-0384.

440 Find A Grave—Ferncliff Cemetery, Springfield, Springfield Twp., Clark Co., Ohio, Nellie Roush, Find A Grave Memorial #60770256.

441 U.S., WWII Draft Registration Cards, 1942, Ancestry.com, George Beard Roush, Springfield, Ohio.

442 Ohio, Birth Index, 1908-1964, Ancestry.com, Dorothy H. Roush, state file #1917094475.

443 Obituary of Dorothy H. Koeb (Springfield, Ohio, Springfield Daily News, 27 Nov 1987), Clark County Public Library, 201 South Fountain Avenue, Springfield, OH.

444 Ohio, Death Records, 1908-1932, 1938-2007, Ancestry.com, Dorothy H. Koeb, death cert. #079039.

445 Ohio Death Certificate, Ohio Department of Health, Center for Vital and Health Statistics, 246 North High Street, Columbus, OH, Merle M. Roush, death cert. #52856.

446 Obituary of George B. Roush (Santa Rosa, California, Santa Rosa Press Democrat, 04 Mar 1974.), Sonoma County Library, 211 E Street, Santa Rosa, CA.

447 California, Death Index, 1940-1997, Ancestry.com, George B. Roush.

448 Ohio, Death Records, 1908-1932, 1938-2007, Ancestry.com, William Leroy Roush, death cert. #076555.

449 Ohio, Birth Index, 1908-1964, Ancestry.com, William L. Roush, state file #1936014292.

450 U.S., Department of Veterans Affairs BIRLS Death File, 1850-2010, Ancestry.com, William Roush.

451 River Bend Cemetery Records, Harry E. Roush, River Bend Cemetery, 117 Beach Street, Westerly, RI.

452 Rhode Island Death Certificate, Westerly Town Clerk, Westerly Town Hall, 45 Broad Street, Westerly, RI, Mary Agnes Roush, Westerly Town Death Records, death cert. #44-142.

453 River Bend Cemetery Records, Mary A. Roush, River Bend Cemetery, 117 Beach Street, Westerly, RI.

454 Phone interviews and emails from Harry E. Roush Jr., Tamaquah, PA, Ann Miller Carr, author, 20-23 Jul 2017.

455 U.S., Applications for Seaman's Protection Certificates, 1916-1940, Ancestry.com, Harry Emmett Roush, #2902H ("Emmett" is spelled "Eurnette" on the index).

456 New Orleans, Passenger Lists, 1813-1963, Ancestry.com, Harry "Raush".

457 Obituary of Eli K. Roush (Hillsboro, Ohio, Hillsboro Press-Gazette, 25 May 1943), Highland County District Library, 10 Willettsville Pike, Hillsboro, OH.

458 Texas, Birth Index, 1903-1997, Ancestry.com, Harry Emmet Roush, roll 1935_007.

459 Ohio Boy's Industrial School Records, 1920, Theodore Roush, #22 525. Ohio History Center, 800 East 17th Avenue, Columbus, OH.

460 Find A Grave—Stringtown Quaker Cemetery, Paint Twp., Highland Co., Ohio, Find A Grave.com, Lora B. Bussey, Find A Grave Memorial #136340478.

461 U.S., WWI Draft Registration Cards, 1917-1918, Ancestry.com, Hubert C. Bussey, Hillsboro Co., Ohio.

462 Ohio, Death Records, 1908-1932, 1938-2007, Ancestry.com, Hubert C. Bussey, death cert. #087642.

463 Find A Grave—Stringtown Quaker Cemetery, Paint Twp., Highland Co., Ohio, Find A Grave.com, Hubert C. Bussey, Find A Grave Memorial #136340460.

464 Ohio Divorce Abstracts, 1962-1963, 1967-1971, 1973-2007, Ancestry.com, Lee Brust and Lora B. Brust, Ross County, Ohio, 27 May 1977, married seven years.

465 Obituary of Lee Brust (Hillsboro, Ohio, Press Gazette, 11 Jun 1985), Highland County District Library, 10 Willettsville Pike, Hillsboro, OH.

466 Ohio, Death Records, 1908-1932, 1938-2007, Ancestry.com, Leander Brust, death cert. #044787.

467 Summit County, Ohio Marriage Records, 1840-1980, Ancestry.com, James Donovan Bussey and Mary Edythe Hallbrook, Vol.194, pg. 156, lic. #95,374.

468 Ohio, Death Records, 1908-1932, 1938-2007, Ancestry.com, James "Donavan" Bussey, death cert. #084115.

469 U.S., Social Security Applications and Claims Index, 1936-2007, Ancestry.com, James Donovan Bussey.

470 Ohio, Birth Index, 1908-1964, Ancestry.com, James "O." Bussey, state file #1924058323.

471 Ohio, Death Records, 1908-1932, 1938-2007, Ancestry.com, Mary E. Moore, death cert. #27824.

472 U.S., Social Security Applications and Claims Index, 1936-2007, Ancestry.com, Mary Ellen Bussey Moore.

473 Ohio, Birth Index, 1908-1964, Ancestry.com, Rosalie Bussey, state file #1928023387.

474 U.S., Social Security Applications and Claims Index, 1936-2007, Ancestry.com, Rosalee Bussey Ross Getz Jones Yarger.

475 Florida Death Index 1877-1998, Ancestry.com, Rosalee Jones.

476 Obituary of Rosalee Jones (Hillsboro, Ohio, Hillsboro Press Gazette, 19 Mar 1991), Highland County District Library, 10 Willettsville Pike, Hillsboro, OH.

477 Ohio Deaths, 1908-1953, FamilySearch.org, Margaret E. Bussey, death cert. #10430.

478 Ohio, Birth Index, 1908-1964, Ancestry.com, Margaret E. Bussey, state file #1933010901.

479 Ohio, Birth Index, 1908-1964, Ancestry.com, Elizabeth J. Bussey, state file #1935026806.

480 Obituary of Elizabeth Joanna Wallace (Hillsboro, Ohio, Highland County Times Gazette, 11 May 2013), Highland County District Library, 10 Willettsville Pike, Hillsboro, OH.

481 Ohio, Birth Index, 1908-1964, Ancestry.com, Bussey, state file #1940053288.

482 U.S., Social Security Applications and Claims Index, 1936-2007, Ancestry.com, Helen Luella Bussey Kinsey Bills.

483 Ohio, Death Records, 1908-1932, 1938-2007, Ancestry.com, Helen L. Bills, death cert. #069432.

484 Find A Grave—Martinsville IOOF Cemetery, Martinsville, Clark Twp., Clinton Co., Ohio, Find A Grave.com, Cecil Roush, Find A Grave Memorial #119354944.

485 The Genealogical Committee of the Clinton County Historical Society, Cemetery Records of Clinton Co., Ohio, 1798-1998: Martinsville IOOF Cemetery: Cecil C. Roush. Clinton County, Ohio Records Center and Archives, 111 South Nelson Avenue, Suite 3, Wilmington, OH.

486 Find A Grave—Martinsville IOOF Cemetery, Martinsville, Clark Twp., Clinton Co., Ohio, Find A Grave.com, Capt. Samuel Roush, Find A Grave Memorial #119355162.

487 The Genealogical Committee of the Clinton County Historical Society, Cemetery Records of Clinton Co., Ohio, 1798-1998: Martinsville IOOF Cemetery: Samuel F. Roush. Clinton County, Ohio Records Center and Archives, 111 South Nelson Avenue, Suite 3, Wilmington, OH.

488 Obituary of Samuel Roush (Wilmington, Ohio, Wilmington News Journal, 14 Nov 1975), The Clinton County History Center, 149 East Locust Street, Wilmington, OH.

489 Ohio, Death Records, 1908-1932, 1938-2007, Ancestry.com, Margaret Helen Roush, death cert. #34069.

490 U.S., Social Security Applicatons and Claims Index, 1936-2007, Ancestry.com, Margaret Helen Roush.

491 Obituary of Margaret Helen Roush (Wilmington, Ohio, Wilmington News Journal, 07 May 2004), The Clinton County History Center, 149 East Locust Street, Wilmington, OH.

492 Find A Grave—Martinsville IOOF Cemetery, Martinsville, Clark Twp., Clinton Co., Ohio, Find A Grave.com, Margaret H. Roush, Find A Grave Memorial #119355403.

493 Obituary of Kenneth W. Roush (Wilmington, Ohio, Wilmington News Journal, 04 Jun 1974), Wilmington Public Library of Clinton County, 268 North South Street, Wilmington, OH.

494 Ohio, Death Records, 1908-1932, 1938-2007, Ancestry.com, Kenneth W. Roush, death cert. #044885.

495 Find A Grave—Martinsville IOOF Cemetery, Martinsville, Clark Twp., Clinton Co., Ohio, Find A Grave.com, Roy K. Roush, Find A Grave Memorial #119352569.

496 The Genealogical Committee of the Clinton County Historical Society, Cemetery Records of Clinton Co., Ohio, 1798-1998: Martinsville IOOF Cemetery: Roy K. Roush. Clinton County, Ohio Records Center and Archives, 111 South Nelson Avenue, Suite 3, Wilmington, OH.

497 Obituary of Roy Roush (Wilmington, Ohio, Wilmington News Journal, 24 Dec 1974), Roush family file, The Clinton County History Center, 149 East Locust Street, Wilmington, OH.

498 Find A Grave—Martinsville IOOF Cemetery, Martinsville, Clark Twp., Clinton Co., Ohio, Find A Grave.com, Euless J. Walker, Find A Grave Memorial #28684336.

499 Ohio, County Births, 1841-2003 (County Courthouses), FamilySearch.org, Thomas Walker, Brown County Birth Records, Vol. 3, pg. 446.

500 Ohio, Death Records, 1908-1932, 1938-2007, Ancestry.com, Thomas W. Walker, death cert. #071157.

501 Find A Grave—Martinsville IOOF Cemetery, Martinsville, Clark Twp., Clinton Co., Ohio, Find A Grave.com, Thomas W. Walker, Sr., Find A Grave Memorial #28684311.

502 Obituary of Thomas Walker Sr. (Xenia, Ohio, Xenia Daily Gazette, 28 Sep 1979), Greene County Public Library, Greene County Room Genealogy & Local History, 76 East Market Street, Xenia, OH.

503 U.S., Social Security Applications and Claims Index, 1936-2007, Ancestry.com, Thomas William Walker Jr.

504 Florida Death Certificate, Florida Department of Health-State Office of Vital Statistics, 1217 North Pearl Street, Jacksonville, FL, Thomas William Walker, death cert. #86-093888.

505 Greene County, Ohio Marriage Records (Greene County, Ohio), Greene County Record Center and Archives, 535 Ledbetter Road, Xenia, OH, Charles Robert Walker and

505 Cynthia Lou Baxley, Greene County, Ohio Marriage Records, Vol. 37, pg. 57, lic. #19588.

506 Obituary of Charles Walker (Xenia, Ohio, Xenia Daily Gazette, 19 Jul 2014), Greene County Public Library, Greene County Room Genealogy & Local History, 76 East Market Street, Xenia, OH.

507 Obituary of Mrs. Leota Davis (Wilmington, Ohio, Wilmington News Journal, 19 May 1982), Wilmington Public Library of Clinton County, 268 North South Street, Wilmington, OH.

508 Find A Grave—Martinsville IOOF Cemetery, Martinsville, Clark Twp., Clinton Co., Ohio, Find A Grave.com, Leota Beatrice Davis, Find A Grave Memorial #119248896.

509 Obituary of Harold H. Davis (Washington Court House, Ohio, Washington Court House Record Herald, 02 Dec 1991), Carnegie Public Library, 127 South North Street, Washington Court House, OH.

510 Ohio, Death Records, 1908-1932, 1938-2007, Ancestry.com, Harold H. Davis, death cert. #081154.

511 Find A Grave—Martinsville IOOF Cemetery, Martinsville, Clark Twp., Clinton Co., Ohio, Find A Grave.com, Harold H. Davis, Find A Grave Memorial #119248931.

512 Ohio, Birth Index, 1908-1964, Ancestry.com, Perry Davis, state file #1935063985.

513 Ohio, Death Records, 1908-1932, 1938-2007, Ancestry.com, Larry Eugene Davis, death cert. #053661.

514 Find A Grave—Maple Grove Cemetery, Port William, Liberty Twp., Clinton Co., Ohio, Find A Grave.com, Effie N. McCandless, Find A Grave Memorial #134525301.

515 Obituary of Glen McCandless (Wilmington, Ohio, Wilmington News-Journal, 11 Mar 1994), Wilmington Public Library of Clinton County, 268 North South Street, Wilmington, OH.

516 Ohio, Death Records, 1908-1932, 1938-2007, Ancestry.com, Elmer Glenn McCandless, death cert. #026505.

517 Ohio, Birth Index, 1908-1964, Ancestry.com, Elmer McCandless, state file #1912073599.

518 Find A Grave—Maple Grove Cemetery, Port William, Liberty Twp., Clinton Co., Ohio, Find A Grave.com, Elmer G. McCandless, Find A Grave Memorial #134525302.

519 The Genealogical Committee of the Clinton County Historical Society, Cemetery Records of Clinton Co., Ohio, 1798-1998: Maple Grove Cemetery/Port William Cemetery: Elmer G. McCandless. Clinton County, Ohio Records Center and Archives, 111 South Nelson Avenue, Suite 3, Wilmington, OH.

520 U.S., WWI Draft Registration Cards, 1917-1918, Ancestry.com, Hershell McCandless, "Sedan, Scioto Co., O."

521 Obituary of Robert Eugene McCandless (Wilmington, Ohio, Wilmington News Journal, 11 Sep 1961), Wilmington Public Library of Clinton County, 268 North South Street, Wilmington, OH.

522 Ohio, Death Records, 1908-1932, 1938-2007, Ancestry.com, Robert E. McCandless, death cert. #61160.

523 "Port William Man is Killed in Automobile-Truck Crash" (Wilmington, Ohio, Wilmington News-Journal, 11 Sep 1961), Roush family file, The Clinton County History Center, 149 East Locust Street, Wilmington, OH.

524 Obituary of James Glenn McCandless (Wilmington, Ohio, L. Eugene Smith & Son Funeral Home, 11 Nov 2014), L. Eugene Smith & Son Funeral Home, 327 North South Street, Wilmington, OH; Online database: http://smithandsonfuneralhomes.com/obituaries/james-glenn-mccandless/

525 Obituary of Samuel McCandless (Wilmington, Ohio, Wilmington News Journal, 01 Jun 1976), Wilmington Public Library of Clinton County, 268 North South Street, Wilmington, OH.

526 Ohio, Death Records, 1908-1932, 1938-2007, Ancestry.com, Samuel F. McCandless, death cert. #040557.

527 Find A Grave—Riverside Cemetery, Troy, Concord Twp., Miami Co., Ohio, Find A Grave.com, Dorothy O. Roush Seitz, Find A Grave Memorial #23422283.

528 Ohio, Death Records, 1908-1932, 1938-2007, Ancestry.com, Emmett F. Seitz, death cert. #099909.

529 Obituary of Emmett F. Seitz (Piqua, Ohio, Piqua Daily Call, 16 Dec 1998), Ohio History Center Archives and Library, Ohio History Center, 800 East 17th Avenue, Columbus, OH.

530 U.S. Veterans' Gravesites, ca. 1775-2006, Ancestry.com, Emmett F. Seitz.

531 Find A Grave—Riverside Cemetery, Troy, Concord Twp., Miami Co., Ohio, Find A Grave.com, Emmett F. Seitz, Find A Grave Memorial #150707189.

532 Obituary of William Seitz Sr. (Troy, Ohio, Troy Daily News, 11 Aug 2011), Troy-Miami Co. Public Library, 419 West Main Street, Troy, OH.

533 Ohio, County Marriages, 1789-2013, FamilySearch.org, William L. Seitz and Lorraine Nickels Wilcox, Miami County, Ohio Marriage Records, Vol. 37, pg. 6, lic. #47406.

534 State of South Carolina, South Carolina Death Certificate (Columbia, South Carolina, Division of Vital Records, South Carolina State Board of Health), Division of Vital Records, South Carolina State Board of Health, 2600 Bull Street, Columbia, SC, Darrel Joe Seitz, state file #33-006450.

535 South Carolina, Death Records, 1821-1965, Ancestry.com, Darrel Joe Seitz, death cert. #006450.

536 Obituary of Mary Bogan (Wilmington, Ohio, Wilmington News Journal, 16 Oct 1946), Wilmington Public Library of Clinton County, 268 North South Street, Wilmington, OH.

537 Find A Grave—Sugar Grove Cemetery, Wilmington, Union Twp., Clinton Co., Ohio, Find A Grave.com, Mary Leatha Roush Bogan, Find A Grave Memorial #139793961.

538 Obituary of Grant Bogan (Wilmington, Ohio, Wilmington News Herald, 24 Mar 1975), Wilmington Public Library of Clinton County, 268 North South Street, Wilmington, OH.

539 Florida Death Index 1877-1998, Ancestry.com, Grant P. Bogan.

540 Find A Grave—Blanchester IOOF Cemetery, Blanchester, Marion Twp., Clinton Co., Ohio, Find A Grave.com, Grant Pomerance Bogan, Find A Grave Memorial #91854378.

541 Find A Grave—Florida National Cemetery, Bushnell, Sumter Co., Ohio, Find A Grave.com, Betty L. Shilts Bogan, Find A Grave Memorial #49685814.

542 Find A Grave—Martinsville IOOF Cemetery, Martinsville, Clark Twp., Clinton Co., Ohio, Find A Grave.com, PFC. Floyd R. Roush, Find A Grave Memorial #119353117.

543 The Genealogical Committee of the Clinton County Historical Society, Cemetery Records of Clinton Co., Ohio, 1798-1998: Martinsville IOOF Cemetery: Floyd R. Roush. Clinton County, Ohio Records Center and Archives, 111 South Nelson Avenue, Suite 3, Wilmington, OH.

544 Obituary of Floyd Richard Roush (Wilmington, Ohio, Wilmington News Journal, 11 Apr 1969), Wilmington Public Library of Clinton County, 268 North South Street, Wilmington, OH.

545 Ohio, Death Records, 1908-1932, 1938-2007, Ancestry.com, Jennie Gertrude Roush, death cert. #093021.

546 Find A Grave—Martinsville IOOF Cemetery, Martinsville, Clark Twp., Clinton Co., Ohio, Find A Grave.com, Jennie Roush, Find A Grave Memorial #119354430.

547 The Genealogical Committee of the Clinton County Historical Society, Cemetery Records of Clinton Co., Ohio, 1798-1998: Martinsville IOOF Cemetery: Jennie G. Roush. Clinton County, Ohio Records Center and Archives, 111 South Nelson Avenue, Suite 3, Wilmington, OH.

548 Find A Grave—Martinsville IOOF Cemetery, Martinsville, Clark Twp., Clinton Co., Ohio, Find A Grave.com, Eli K. Roush Jr., Find A Grave Memorial #119352494.

549 Find A Grave—Riverside Cemetery, Troy, Concord Twp., Miami Co., Ohio, Find A Grave.com, Erma Lou Roush, Find A Grave Memorial #149265889.

550 Obituary of Erma Lou Roush (Dayton, Ohio, Dayton Daily News, 15 Apr 2015), Dayton Metro Library, 215 East Third Street. Dayton, OH.

551 Ohio Marriage Abstracts, 1970-1972-2007, Ancestry.com, Eli K. Roush and Patricia L. Davis, Clinton County, Ohio Marriage Records, Ohio state Vol. 10189, lic. #437.

552 Ohio, Death Records, 1908-1932, 1938-2007, Ancestry.com, Patricia L. Roush, death cert. #039452.

553 Find A Grave—Martinsville IOOF Cemetery, Martinsville, Clark Twp., Clinton Co., Ohio, Find A Grave.com, Patricia L. Roush, Find A Grave Memorial #119352475.

554 U.S., WWII Draft Registration Cards, 1942, Ancestry.com, Philip S. Roush, Clinton Co., Ohio.

555 Florida Marriage Collection, 1822-1875 and 1927-2001, Ancestry.com, Philip S. Roush and Jeannie Hume Richardson, Monroe County, Florida Marriage Records, Florida state Vol. 1753, lic. #21441.

556 Find A Grave—Global, Find A Grave Index for Non-Burials, Burials at Sea, and Other Select Burial Locations, 1300-Current, Find A Grave.com, Jeannie Hume Keith Behar, Find A Grave Memorial #54395476.

557 Florida Death Index 1877-1998, Ancestry.com, Jeannie H. Behar.

558 U.S., Social Security Applications and Claims Index, 1936-2007, Ancestry.com, Jeannie Hume Keith Hill Richardson Roush Behar.

559 U.S., Social Security Applications and Claims Index, 1936-2007, Ancestry.com, Philip Stroup Roush.

560 "Mutiny on The Leslie Rae" (Fort Lauderdale, Florida, South Florida Sun-Sentinel, 01 May 1988), Broward County Library, Main Branch, 100 South Andrews, Fort Lauderdale, FL.

561 U.S. Veterans' Gravesites, ca. 1775-2006, Ancestry.com, Randall C. Roush.

562 Find A Grave—Magnolia Cemetery, Orange Park, Clay Co., Florida, Find A Grave.com, Randall C. Roush, Find A Grave Memorial #88296686.

563 District of Columbia Marriages, 1811-1950, FamilySearch.org, Randall C. Roush and Florence Libercajt.

564 Florida Death Index 1877-1998, Ancestry.com, Florence Kay Roush.

565 Obituary of Mrs. Florence Kay Roush (Jacksonville, Florida, Florida Times-Union, 28 Dec 1973), State Library and Archives of Florida, R.A. Gray Building, 500 South Bronaugh Street, Tallahassee, FL.

566 Find A Grave—Magnolia Cemetery, Orange Park, Clay Co., Florida, Find A Grave.com, Florence Kay Roush, Find A Grave Memorial #88108831.

567 Florida Marriage Collection, 1822-1875 and 1927-2001, Ancestry.com, Randall Cecil Roush and Barbara Jean Brownell, Clay County, Florida Marriage Records, Florida state Vol. 4089, lic. #034122.

568 Cook County, Illinois Birth Index, 1916-1935, Ancestry.com, Barbara Long.

569 Obituary of Randall C. Roush. (Jacksonville, Florida, The Times-Union, 14 Mar 2004), Jacksonville Public Library, 303 North Laura Street, Jacksonville, FL.

570 Texas Birth Index, 1903-1997, Ancestry.com, Michael David Roush, Nuences County, Texas Birth Records, Roll #1946_0010, pg. 2587.

571 Obituary of Michael David Roush (Jacksonville, Florida, Florida Times-Union, 25 Jun 2000), State Library and Archives of Florida, R.A. Gray Building, 500 South Bronaugh Street, Tallahassee, FL.

572 U.S., Social Security Applications and Claims Index, 1936-2007, Ancestry.com, William Randall Roush.

573 Obituary of Gale E. Roush (Fort Myers, Florida, Fort Myers News Press, 04 Sep 1998), State Library and Archives of Florida, R.A. Gray Building, 500 South Bronaugh Street, Tallahassee, FL.

574 U.S., Social Security Applications and Claims Index, 1936-2007, Ancestry.com, Bernice G. Julien Holt Roush.

575 Obituary of Bernice G. Roush (Fort Myers, Florida, Fort Myers News Press, 06 Apr 2004), State Library and Archives of Florida, R.A. Gray Building, 500 South Bronaugh Street, Tallahassee, FL.

576 "Sun Holds Losing Influence on Ill-Navigated Moppets" (Salt Lake City, Salt Lake City Tribune 12 Apr 1958); Newspaper Archive, Online database: newspaperarchive.com, https://access-newspaperarchive-com.sjcpl.idm.oclc.org/us/utah/salt-lake-city/salt-lake-tribune/1958/04-12/page-9/roush?ndt=ex&pd=12&py=1958&pm=4&search=ymd

577 Obituary of Lee Roush (Fort Myers, Florida, The News-Press, 28 Mar 2012), State Library and Archives of Florida, R.A. Gray Building, 500 South Bronaugh Street, Tallahassee, FL.

578 Find A Grave—Stroup Cemetery, Dodson Twp., Highland Co., Ohio, Find A Grave.com, Dale E. Roush, Find A Grave Memorial #133564937.

579 Find A Grave—Stroup Cemetery, Dodson Twp., Highland Co., Ohio, Find A Grave.com, Ray E. Roush, Find A Grave Memorial #133564914.

580 Find A Grave—Greenlawn Memorial Park Cemetery, Fort Wayne, Allen Co., Indiana, Find A Grave.com, Raymond PeGan, Find A Grave Memorial #59759553.

581 Wabash County, Indiana Marriage Records, Wabash County, Indiana Clerk, Courthouse Annex, 69 West Hill Street, Wabash, IN, Raymond Pegan and Hazel Long Knight, Wabash County, Indiana Marriage Records, Vol. 13, pg. 280.

582 Indiana, Marriages, 1811-2001, FamilySearch.org, Raymond Pegan and Hazel Long Knight, Wabash County, Indiana Marriage Records, Vol. 13, pg. 280.

583 Indiana, Death Certificates, 1899-2011, Ancestry.com, Nancy Hazel Benson, Indiana death cert. #63-004956.

584 Obituary of Nancy Hazel Benson (Huntington, Indiana, Huntington Herald Press, 27 Feb 1963), Huntington City-Township Library, Indiana Room, 255 West Park Drive, Huntington, IN.

585 Find A Grave—Mtount Etna Cemetery, Mount Etna, Jefferson Twp., Huntington Co., Indiana, Find A Grave.com, N. Hazel Benson, Find A Grave Memorial #12253440.

586 Grant County, Indiana Marriage Records, Grant County, Indiana Clerk's Office, County Complex, 401 South Adams Street, Marion, IN, Chester O. Knight and Hazel Long, Grant County Indiana Marriage Records, Vol. 16, pg. 448.

587 Raymond Pegan, inmate #17499, Indiana State Prison (Michigan City) Records, 20 May 1935, Indiana State Archives. Commission on Public Records. 6440 East 30th Street, Indianapolis, IN.

588 Indiana, Marriages 1811-2007, FamilySearch.org, James Benson and Nancy Hazel Pegan, Allen County, Indiana Marriage Records, Vol. 107, pg. 467.

589 Grant County, Indiana Marriage Records, Grant County, Indiana Clerk's Office, County Complex, 401 South Adams Street, Marion, IN, Raymond PeGan and Nettie E. Goodson, Grant County, Indiana Marriage Records, Vol. 39, pg. 234, lic. #150.

590 Indiana, Death Certificates, 1899-2011, Ancestry.com, Nettie E. Goodson, Indiana death cert. #69-004350.

591 Obituary of Nettie E. Goodson (Fort Wayne, Indiana, Fort Wayne Journal Gazette, 14 Feb 1969), Genealogy Center, Allen County Public Library, 900 Library Plaza, Fort Wayne, IN.

592 Find A Grave—Greenlawn Memorial Park Cemetery, Fort Wayne, Allen Co., Indiana, Find A Grave.com, Nettie E. Goodson, Find A Grave Memorial #106278959.

593 Indiana, Marriages 1811-2007, FamilySearch.org, Raymond H. Pegan and Bessie Powell, Huntington County, Indiana Marriage Records, Vol. 32, pg. 135.

594 Indiana, Death Certificates, 1899-2011, Ancestry.com, Bessie E. PeGan, Indiana death cert. #71-011719.

595 Find A Grave—Green Park Cemetery, Portland, Wayne Twp., Jay Co., Indiana, Find A Grave.com, Bessie Powell Whitridge Pegan, Find A Grave Memorial# 74169836.

596 Marriage announcement of Clarence Bailey and Bessie Whitridge (Portland, Indiana, Portland Review, 28 Jun 1915), Indiana State Library, 315 West Ohio Street, Indianapolis, IN.

597 U.S., WWI Draft Registration Cards, 1917-1918, Ancestry.com, Clarence Bailey, Portland, Indiana.

598 Indiana, Death Certificates, 1899-2011, Ancestry.com, Mack Beverly Bailey, Indiana death cert. #1230.

599 Find A Grave—Greenlawn Cemetery, Greentown, Liberty Twp., Howard Co., Indiana, Find A Grave.com, Mattie Hatfield, Find A Grave Memorial #46191500.

600 Grant County, Indiana Marriage Records, Grant County, Indiana Clerk's Office, County Complex, 401 South Adams Street, Marion, IN, Arlie J. Hatfield and Leona M. Pearson, Grant County, Indiana Marriage Records, Vol. 30, pg. 86.

601 U.S., WWI Draft Registration Cards, 1917-1918, Ancestry.com, Arlie Hatfield, Winchester, Indiana.

602 U.S., Social Security Applications and Claims Index, 1936-2007, Ancestry.com, Arlie Joseph Hatfield, Life Claim.

603 Indiana, Death Certificates, 1899-2011, Ancestry.com, Arlie Joseph Hatfield, Indiana death cert. #21316.

604 U.S., WWII Draft Registration Cards, 1942, Ancestry.com, Arlie Joseph Hatfield.

605 Obituary of Arlie J. Hatfield (Kokomo, Indiana, Kokomo Tribune, 13 Jul 1955), Kokomo-Howard County Public Library, 220 North Union Street, Kokomo, IN.

606 Find A Grave—Greenlawn Cemetery, Greentown, Liberty Twp., Howard Co., Indiana, Find A Grave.com, Arlie Hatfield, Find A Grave Memorial #46191498.

607 Find A Grave—Evergreen Cemetery, Ontario, Malheur Co., Oregon, Find A Grave.com, H.H. Pearson, Find A Grave Memorial #28449471.

608 Grant County, Indiana Marriage Records, Grant County, Indiana Clerk's Office, County Complex, 401 South Adams Street, Marion, IN, Herbert H. Pearson and Bernice Ann Kucera. Grant County, Indiana Marriage Records, Vol. 33, pg. 219. lic. #18234.

609 Obituary of Bernice Pearson (Ontario, Oregon, Argus-Observer, 10 Oct 1966), Ontario Community Library, 388 S.W. 2nd Avenue, Ontario, OR.

610 Oregon, Death Index, 1898-2008, Ancestry.com, Bernice A. Pearson, death cert. #14857.

611 Find A Grave—Evergreen Cemetery, Ontario, Malheur Co., Oregon, Find A Grave.com, Bernice Pearson, Find A Grave Memorial #28449459.

612 Phone interview with Marianne Pearson Neely, Vancouver, WA, Ann Miller Carr, author, 16 Sep 2014.

613 Find A Grave—Fairhaven Cemetery, Santa Ana, Orange Co., California, Find A Grave.com, Truman V. Pearson, Find A Grave Memorial #59261648.

614 Social Security Application (SS-5), Social Security Administration, OEO FOIA Workgroup, 300 N. Greene Street, Baltimore, MD, Mattie Oliver Pearson.

615 Obituary of Mattie Mae Pearson (Santa Ana, California, The Orange County Register, 11 Sep 2005), Huntington Beach Central Library, 711 Talbert Avenue, Huntington Beach, CA.

616 Find A Grave—Fairhaven Cemetery, Santa Ana, Orange Co., California, Find A Grave.com, Mattie Mae Pearson, Find A Grave Memorial #155106801.

617 Phone interview with Patricia Pearson Geis, Tribuco Canyon, CA, Ann Miller Carr, author, 22 Apr 2016.

618 Obituary of Jane Conti (Santa Ana, California, Orange County Register, 13 May 2005), Santa Ana Public Library, 26 Civic Center Plaza, Santa Ana, CA.

619 Find A Grave—Riverside Cemetery, Gas City, Mill Twp., Grant Co., Indiana, Find A Grave.com, Opal Colene Pearson Eastes, Find A Grave Memorial #79537254.

620 Obituary of Joseph G. Eastes (Marion, Indiana, Marion Chronicle Tribune, 05 Feb 1988), Marion, Indiana Public Library, 600 South Washington Street, Marion, IN.

621 Web: Grant County, Indiana, Marion Public Library Birth Index, 1882-1981, Ancestry.com, Joseph Gerald Eastes.

622 Indiana, Death Certificates, 1899-2011, Ancestry.com, Joseph G. Eastes, Indiana death cert. #88-004622.

623 Find A Grave—Riverside Cemetery, Gas City, Mill Twp., Grant Co., Indiana, Find A Grave.com, Joseph Gerald Eastes, Find A Grave Memorial #79537226.

624 Obituary of Betty J. Eastes (Marion, Indiana, Marion Chronicle Tribune, 13 Jul 2006), Marion, Indiana Public Library, 600 South Washington Street, Marion, IN.

625 U.S., Social Security Applications and Claims Index, 1936-2007, Ancestry.com, Betty Jean Eastes Cowgill Reese.

626 Indiana, Death Certificates, 1899-2011, Ancestry.com, Betty J. Reese, Indiana death cert. #023765.

627 Obituary of Joseph E. Eastes (Marion, Indiana, Marion Chronicle Tribune, 28 Nov 1998), Marion, Indiana Public Library, 600 South Washington Street, Marion, IN.

628 U.S., Social Security Applications and Claims Index, 1936-2007, Ancestry.com, Joe Eddie Eastes.

629 Web: Grant County, Indiana, Marion Public Library Birth Index, 1882-1981, Ancestry.com, Joseph Edward Eastes.

630 Indiana, Death Certificates, 1899-2011, Ancestry.com, Joseph E. Eastes, Indiana death cert. #040355.

631 Web: Grant County, Indiana, Marion Public Library Birth Index, 1882-1981, Ancestry.com, John Frederick Eastes.

632 Obituary of John F. Eastes (delayed) (Lafayette, Louisiana, Lafayette Advertiser, 16 Jan 2011), Lafayette Public Library—Main Library, 301 West Congress Street, Lafayette, LA.

633 Obtuary of John F. Eastes (Johnson City, Tennessee, Johnson City Press, 23 Nov 2010), Johnson City Public Library, 100 West Millard Street, Johnson City, TN.

634 Find A Grave—Gardens of Memory Cemetery, Banquo, Wayne Twp., Huntington Co., Indiana on the Grant Co. line, Find A Grave.com, Cecil K. Pegan, Find A Grave Memorial #10710925.

635 Indiana, Marriages 1811-2007, FamilySearch.org, Cecil Keith Pegan and Bessie Mae Shoemaker, Delaware County, Indiana Marriage Records, Vol. 49, pg. 319.

636 U.S., Social Security Applications and Claims Index, 1936-2007, Ancestry.com, Bessie Shoemaker Pegan.

637 Indiana, Death Certificates, 1899-2011, Ancestry.com, Bessie M. Young, Indiana death cert. #009943.

638 Phone interview with Lois M. Kunz, Keokuk, Iowa, informant on Bessie Shoemaker Young's death certificate, Ann Miller Carr, author, 02 Apr 2019.

639 Williams County, Ohio Marriage Records, Williams County, Ohio Records Center, 107 West Butler Street, Bryan, OH, Cecil K. Pegan and Audra L. Ridgeway, Williams County, Ohio Marriage Records, Vol. 31, pg. 119.

640 Obituary of Audra L. Pegan (Huntington, Indiana, Huntington Herald Press, 30 Dec 1985), Huntington City-Township Library, Indiana Room, 255 West Park Drive, Huntington, IN.

641 Indiana, Death Certificates, 1899-2011, Ancestry.com, Audra L. Pegan, Indiana death cert. #85-044311.

642 Find A Grave—Gardens of Memory Cemetery, Banquo, Wayne Twp., Huntington Co., Indiana on the Grant Co. line, Find A Grave.com, Audra L. Connolly Pegan, Find A Grave Memorial #10710929.

643 Huntington County, Indiana Marriage Records, Huntington County, Indiana Clerk's Office, Courthouse, 201 North Jef-

643 ...ferson Street, Huntington, IN, Cecil K. Pegan and Doris L. England, Huntington Co., Indiana Marriage Records, Vol. 61, pg. 62.

644 Obituary of Doris L. Figert-Pegan (Wabash, Indiana, Wabash Plain Dealer, 02 May 2003), Wabash Carnegie Public Library, 188 West Hill Street, Wabash, IN.

645 Indiana, Death Certificates, 1899-2011, Ancestry.com, Doris Loretta England-Pegan, Indiana death cert. #016129.

646 Find A Grave—Memorial Lawns Cemetery, Wabash, Noble Twp., Wabash Co., Indiana, Find A Grave.com, Doris Loretta Figert England Pegan, Find A Grave Memorial #7794927.

647 "Waiting Game" (Logansport, Indiana, Logansport Pharos-Tribune, 26 Nov 1989; reprinted from the Wabash {IN} Plain Dealer); Newspaper Archive, Online database: newspaperarchive.com; https://access-newspaper-archive-com.sjcpl.idm.oclc.org/us/indiana/logansport/logansport-pharos-tribune/1989/11-26/page-12/cecil-pegan?psi=38&pci=7

648 Indiana, Birth Certificates, 1907-1940, Ancestry.com, Betty Jean Pegan, Blackford County, Indiana Birth Records, birth cert. #15274.

649 Find A Grave—Gardens of Memory Cemetery, Banquo, Wayne Twp., Huntington Co., Indiana on the Grant Co. line, Find A Grave.com, Pauline M. Oswalt, Find A Grave Memorial #11215613.

650 Indiana, Marriages 1811-2007, FamilySearch.org, Charles R. Oswalt and Pauline M. Pegan, Wabash County, Indiana Marriage Records, Vol. 18, pg. 435.

651 Obituary of Charles R. Oswalt (Huntington, Indiana, Huntington Herald Press, 04 Nov 1991), Huntington City-Township Library, Indiana Room, 255 West Park Drive, Huntington, IN.

652 Indiana, Death Certificates, 1899-2011, Ancestry.com, Charles R. Oswalt, Indiana death cert. #91-045638.

653 Find A Grave—Gardens of Memory Cemetery, Banquo, Wayne Twp., Huntington Co., Indiana on the Grant Co. line, Find A Grave.com, Charles R. Oswalt, Find A Grave Memorial #11215610.

654 Indiana, Birth Certificates, 1907-1940, Ancestry.com, Judith Kay Oswalt, Wabash County, Indiana Birth Records, birth cert. #19069.

655 Find A Grave—Mtount Etna Cemetery, Mount Etna, Jefferson Twp., Huntington Co., Indiana, Find A Grave.com, James M. Pegan, Find A Grave Memorial #54909303.

656 Washington, Marriage Records, 1865-2004, Ancestry.com, Lester T. Deem and Onhawanha Pegan, Whatcom County, Washington Marriage Records, Vol. 82A, pg. 480, #.50853, ref. #nwwctmcv82_480.

657 Obituary of Onhawanha Carver Deem (Huntington, Indiana, Huntington County TAB, 05 Jan 2017), Huntington County TAB, 1670 Etna Avenue, Huntington, IN, http://www.huntingtoncountytab.com/obituary/41946/onhawanha-c-deem.

658 Find A Grave—Mount Etna Cemetery, Mount Etna, Jefferson Twp., Huntington Co., Indiana, Find A Grave.com, Onhawanha Carter Ludwig Pegan Deem, Find A Grave Memorial #177703279.

659 Washington, Marriage Records, 1865-2004, Ancestry.com, Lester T. Deem and Onhawanha Pegan, Whatcom County, Washington Marriage Records, Vol. 82A, pg. 480, #.50853, ref. #nwwctmcv82_480.

660 Find A Grave—Fairview Cemetery, Servia, Chester Twp., Wabash Co., Indiana, Find A Grave.com, Fern Pegan Zimpelman, Find A Grave Memorial #32449552.

661 Obituary of Vilas Zimpelman (Huntington, Indiana, Huntington Herald Press, 06 and 07 Feb 1958), Huntington City-Township Library, Indiana Room, 255 West Park Drive, Huntington, IN.

662 Find A Grave—Fairview Cemetery, Servia, Chester Twp., Wabash Co., Indiana, Find A Grave.com, Vilas Hugo Zimpelman, Find A Grave Memorial #32449631.

663 Indiana, Death Certificates, 1899-2011, Ancestry.com, Vilas Hugo Zimpelman, Indiana death cert. #58-004841.

664 Find A Grave—Mercer Memorial Gardens Cemetery, Celina, Jefferson Twp., Mercer Co., Ohio, Find A Grave.com, Florence W. Pegan Flowers, Find A Grave Memorial #79524770.

665 Obituary of John Flowers (Celina, Ohio, Celina Daily Standard, 21 Sep 1999), Mercer County Library, 303 North Main Street, Celina, OH.

666 Ohio, Death Records, 1908-1932, 1938-2007, Ancestry.com, John Flowers, death cert. #076721.

667 Kentucky, Birth Index, 1911-1999, Ancestry.com, John Flowers, Rowan Co., Kentucky.

668 U.S., Social Security Applications and Claims Index, 1936-2007, Ancestry.com, John Junior Flowers.

669 Find A Grave—Mercer Memorial Gardens Cemetery, Celina, Jefferson Twp., Mercer Co., Ohio, Find A Grave.com, John Flowers, Jr., Find A Grave Memorial #79524772.

670 Obituary of Allen Flowers (Celina, Ohio, Celina Daily Standard, 11 Jan 2005), Mercer County Library, 303 North Main Street, Celina, OH.

671 Ohio, Death Records, 1908-1932, 1938-2007, Ancestry.com, Allen E. Flowers, death cert. #01342.

672 U.S., Social Security Applications and Claims Index, 1936-2007, Ancestry.com, Allen Eugene Flowers.

673 Obituary of Kathleen Joann Hone (Celina, Ohio, Ceilna Daily Standard, 26 Apr 2013), Mercer County Library, 303 North Main Street, Celina, OH.

674 Find A Grave—Calvary Hill Cemetery and Mausoleum, Dallas Co., Texas, Find A Grave.com, Leo E. PeGan, Find A Grave Memorial #171714959.

675 Huntington County, Indiana Marriage Records, Huntington County, Indiana Clerk's Office, Courthouse, 201 North Jefferson Street, Huntington, IN, Leo E. PeGan and Loretta J. Ryan, Huntington County, Indiana Marriage Records, Vol. 29, pg. 426.

676 Indiana, Marriages 1811-2007, FamilySearch.org, Leo E. PeGan and Loretta J. Ryan, Huntington County, Indiana Marriage Records, Vol. 26, pg. 426.

677 Indiana Births, 1880-1920, Ancestry.com, Loretta Ryan, Huntington Co. Birth Records, Vol. H-14, pg. 76.

678 Texas Death Certificate, Texas Department of State Health Services, Vital Statistics Unit, 1100 West 49th Street, Austin, TX, Loretta Pegan, death cert. #50018.

679 Texas, Deaths, 1890-1976, FamilySearch.org, Loretta Pegan.

680 Texas Death Index, 1903-2000, Ancestry.com, Loretta Pegan.

681 Find A Grave—Calvary Hill Cemetery and Mausoleum, Dallas Co., Texas, Find A Grave.com, Loretta J. Ryan PeGan, Find A Grave Memorial #171715142.

682 Indiana, Birth Certificates, 1907-1940, Ancestry.com, Maryln Ann PeGan, Huntington County, Indiana Birth Records, birth cert. #10223.

683 U.S., Social Security Applications and Claims Index, 1936-2007, Ancestry.com, Thomas Joseph PeGan.

684 Obituary of Thomas Joseph (Tom) PeGan (Fort Wayne, Indiana, News-Sentinel, 24 Aug 2002), Huntington City-Township Library, Indiana Room, 255 West Park Drive, Huntington, IN.

685 Find A Grave—Hoverstock Cemetery, Zanesville, Union Twp., Wells Co., Indiana, Find A Grave.com, Paul H. PeGan, Find A Grave Memorial #60559355.

686 Huntington County, Indiana Marriage Records, Huntington County, Indiana Clerk's Office, Courthouse, 201 North Jefferson Street, Huntington, IN, Paul H. PeGan and Delores B. Feighner, Huntington County, Indiana Marriage Records, Vol. 28, pg. 572.

687 Indiana, Marriages 1811-2007, FamilySearch.org, Paul H. PeGan and Delores B. Feighner, Huntington County, Indiana Marriage Records, Vol. 28, pg. 572.

688 Indiana, Birth Certificates, 1907-1940, Ancestry.com, Delores Bernadette Feighner, Allen County, Indiana Birth Records, birth cert. #2047.

689 Indiana, Death Certificates, 1899-2011, Ancestry.com, Delores B. PeGan, Indiana death cert. #016898.

690 Find A Grave—Hoverstock Cemetery, Zanesville, Union Twp., Wells Co., Indiana, Find A Grave.com, Delores B. PeGan, Find A Grave Memorial #60559202.

691 Indiana, Birth Certificates, 1907-1940, Ancestry.com, Harold Leon Pe Gan, Huntington County, Indiana Birth Records, birth cert. #1357.

692 Find A Grave—Hoverstock Cemetery, Zanesville, Union Twp., Wells Co., Indiana, Find A Grave.com, Mary P. Welch, Find A Grave Memorial #60568886.

693 Huntington County, Indiana Marriage Records, Huntington County, Indiana Clerk's Office, Courthouse, 201 North Jefferson Street, Huntington, IN, Ted D. Welch and Mary A. PeGan, Huntington County, Indiana Marriage Records, Vol. 32, pg. 304.

694 Indiana, Marriages 1811-2007, FamilySearch.org, Ted D. Welch and Mary A. PeGan, Huntington County, Indiana Marriage Records, Vol. 31, pg. 304.

695 Indiana, Birth Certificates, 1907-1940, Ancestry.com, Ted Deroy Welch, Huntington County, Indiana Birth Records, birth cert. #18912.

696 Indiana, Death Certificates, 1899-2011, Ancestry.com, Ted D. Welch, Indiana death cert. #89-031616.

697 Find A Grave—Hoverstock Cemetery, Zanesville, Union Twp., Wells Co., Indiana, Find A Grave.com, Ted D. Welch, Find A Grave Memorial #60568896.

698 Find A Grave—Mount Calvary Cemetery, Huntington, Huntington Twp., Huntington Co., Indiana, Find A Grave.com, H. Frederick PeGan, Find A Grave Memorial #24933107.

699 Huntington County, Indiana Marriage Records, Huntington County, Indiana Clerk's Office, Courthouse, 201 North Jefferson Street, Huntington, IN, H. Frederick PeGan and Rosemary J. Etter, Huntington County, Indiana Marriage Records, Vol. 33, pg. 12.

700 Indiana, Marriages 1811-2007, FamilySearch.org, H. Frederick PeGan and Rosemary Etter, Huntington County, Indiana Marriage Records, Vol. 33, pg. 12.

701 Indiana, Death Certificates, 1899-2011, Ancestry.com, Rosemary Josephine PeGan, Indiana death cert. #007148.

702 U.S., Social Security Applications and Claims Index, 1936-2007, Ancestry.com, Rosemary Josephine Etter PeGan.

703 Find A Grave—Mount Calvary Cemetery, Huntington, Huntington Twp., Huntington Co., Indiana, Find A Grave.com, Rosemary J. Etter PeGan, Find A Grave Memorial #13833657.

704 Marion County, Indiana Marriage Records, Marion County, Indiana County Clerk, City-County Building, W-122, 200 East Washington Street, Indianapolis, IN, John Frederick PeGan and Nicki Mitchell, Marriage Book 269, pg. 462.

705 Obituary of John F. PeGan (Huntington, Indiana, Huntington Herald Press, 01 May 2012), Huntington City-Township Library, Indiana Room, 255 West Park Drive, Huntington, IN.

706 Find A Grave—Mount Calvary Cemetery, Huntington, Huntington Twp., Huntington Co., Indiana, Find A Grave.com, Kenneth Joseph PeGan, Find A Grave Memorial #68607012.

707 Huntington County, Indiana Marriage Records, Huntington County, Indiana Clerk's Office, Courthouse, 201 North Jefferson Street, Huntington, IN, Kenneth J. Pegan and Margaret J. Kilty, Huntington County, Indiana Marriage Records, Vol. 34, pg. 61.

708 Indiana, Marriages 1811-2007, FamilySearch.org, Kenneth Joseph PeGan and Margaret June Kilty, Huntington County, Indiana Marriage Records, Vol. 34, pg. 61.

709 Allen County, Indiana Death Certificate, Fort Wayne-Allen County, Indiana Department of Health, 200 East Berry St.,

Suite 360, Fort Wayne, IN, Margaret June Pegan, death cert. #44-169.

710   Huntington County, Indiana Birth Records, Huntington County, Indiana Department of Health, 354 North Jefferson St., #201, Huntington, IN, Margaret June Kilty, Huntington Co. Births, Vol. H-17, pg. 35.

711   Find A Grave—Mount Calvary Cemetery, Huntington, Huntington Twp., Huntington Co., Indiana, Find A Grave.com, M. June Kilty PeGan, Find A Grave Memorial #71428750.

712   Huntington County, Indiana Marriage Records, Huntington County, Indiana Clerk's Office, Courthouse, 201 North Jefferson Street, Huntington, IN, Kenneth Joseph PeGan and Patricia Ann Keefe, Huntington County, Indiana Marriage Records, Vol. 36, pg. 417.

713   Indiana, Marriages 1811-2007, FamilySearch.org, Kenneth Joseph PeGan and Patricia Ann Keefe, Huntington County, Indiana Marriage Records, Vol. 36, pg. 417.

714   Huntington County, Indiana Death Records, Huntington County, Indiana Department of Health, 354 North Jefferson St., #201, Huntington, IN, Patricia PeGan, Book 28, pg. 2.

715   Indiana Death Certificate (Indianapolis, Indiana, State of Indiana), Indiana State Department of Health, 2 North Meridian Street, Indianapolis, IN, Patricia Ann PeGan, death cert. #96-001196/364201.

716   Indiana, Birth Certificates, 1907-1940, Ancestry.com, Patricia Ann Keefe, Huntington County, Indiana Birth Records, birth cert. #12548.

717   Find A Grave—Mount Calvary Cemetery, Huntington, Huntington Twp., Huntington Co., Indiana, Find A Grave.com, Patricia Ann PeGan, Find A Grave Memorial #68607037.

718   Find A Grave—Chapel Hill Memorial Gardens, Osceola, Penn Twp., St. Joseph Co., Indiana, Find A Grave.com, Phillip E. PeGan, Find A Grave Memorial #98346579.

719   Obituary of Josephine Clara PeGan (Niles, Michigan, Niles Daily Star, 04 Oct 2009), Niles District Library, 620 East Main Street, Niles, MI.

720   Find A Grave—Chapel Hill Memorial Gardens, Osceola, Penn Twp., St. Joseph Co., Indiana, Find A Grave.com, Josephine Clara Lewis PeGan, Find A Grave Memorial #42681671.

721   Obituary of Robert "Bob" Pegan (Goshen, Indiana, Goshen News, 15 Oct 2010), Goshen Public Library-Central Library, 601 South 5th Street, Goshen, IN.

722   Find A Grave—Silverbrook Cemetery, Niles, Niles Twp., Berrien Co., Michigan, Find A Grave.com, Raymond L. Pegan, Find A Grave Memorial #59306631.

723   Williams County, Ohio Marriage Records, Williams County, Ohio Records Center, 107 West Butler Street, Bryan, OH, Raymond L. Pegan and Doris I. Fitz, Williams County, Ohio Marriage Records, Ohio state Vol. 25, pg. 490.

724   Obituary of Doris I. Howard (Niles, Michigan, Niles Star, 27 Jun 2010), Niles District Library, 620 East Main Street, Niles, MI.

725   Find A Grave—Smith's Chapel Cemetery, Milton Twp., Cass Co., Michigan, Find A) Grave.com, Dorothy I. Fitz Howard, Find A Grave Memorial #54373994.

726   South Bend Genealogical Society, Marriage Record Index List (Mishawaka, Indiana, South Bend Genealogical Society, Mishawaka-Penn Harris Library, 209 Lincoln Way East, Mishawaka, IN; Raymond Leon Pegan and Margaret J. Scarbury, St. Joseph County, Indiana Marriage Records, Vol. 117, lic. #31187; Online database: https://www.sbags.org/marriagesrch.php

727   Indiana Marriages, 1958-2015, Indianapolis, Indiana, Indiana State Library Genealogy, 315 West Ohio Street, Indianapolis, IN; Raymond L. PeGan and Margaret J. Scarbury, St. Joseph County, Indiana Marriage Records; Online database, https://www.statelib.lib.in.us/INMarriages93to02/in_marriages_search.asp

728   Obituary of Margaret J. PeGan (South Bend, Indiana, South Bend Tribune, 05 Aug 2017) St. Joseph County Public Library-Main Library, 304 South Main Street, South Bend, IN.

729   Indiana, Birth Certificates, 1907-1940, Ancestry.com, Margaret Josephine Pfefferle, Marshall County, Indiana Birth Records, birth cert. #35652.

730   Find A Grave—Silverbrook Cemetery, Niles, Niles Twp., Berrien Co., Michigan, Find A Grave.com, Margaret J. PeGan, Find A Grave Memorial #182071962.

731   Obituary of John A. Pegan (Niles, Michigan, Niles Daily Star, 20 Apr 1972), Niles District Library, 620 East Main Street, Niles, MI.

732   Find A Grave—Silverbrook Cemetery, Niles, Niles Twp., Berrien Co., Michigan, Find A Grave.com, John A. Pegan, Find A Grave Memorial #59306624.

733   Find A Grave—Chapel Hill Memorial Gardens, Osceola, Penn Twp., St. Joseph Co., Indiana, Find A Grave.com, Donna B. Reed, Find A Grave Memorial #103341504.

734   Michigan, Marriage Records, 1867-1952, Ancestry.com, G. Richard Reed and Donna Bell PeGan, Berrien County, Michigan Marriage Records, Vol. 1946, lic. #172; Michigan state file #11-12307.

735   Obituary of George R. "Dick" Reed (St. Petersburg, Florida, St. Petersburg Times, 05 Aug 1997), Largo Library, 201 Highland Avenue NE, Largo, FL.

736   Obituary of Brian Lee Reed (South Bend, Indiana, South Bend Tribune, 28 Mar 2011), South Bend-St. Joseph County Public Library, 304 South Main Street, South Bend, IN.

737   Obituary of Dorothy Arilla PeGan (South Bend, Indiana, South Bend Tribune, 08 Aug 2012), St. Joseph County Public Library, 304 South Main Street, South Bend, IN.

738 Find A Grave—Silverbrook Cemetery, Niles, Niles Twp., Berrien Co., Michigan, Find A Grave.com, Dorothy A. PeGan, Find A Grave Memorial #136190864.

739 Obituary of Katherine Jean Swanson (Pulaski, Tennessee, Pulaski Citizen, 28 Aug 2001), Giles County Historical Society, 122 South Second Street, Pulaski, TN.

740 U.S., Social Security Applications and Claims Index, 1936-2007, Ancestry.com, Sue Ann PeGan Masterman McQuaid.

741 Obituary of Sue Ann McQuaid (Niles, Michigan, Niles Daily Star, 28 Aug 2001), Niles District Library, 620 East Main Street, Niles, MI.

742 Find A Grave—Silverbrook Cemetery, Niles, Niles Twp., Berrien Co., Michigan, Find A Grave.com, Sue Ann McQuaid, Find A Grave Memorial #99405212.

743 Obituary of Richard Allen Pegan (Pulaski, Tennessee, Pulaski Citizen, 12 Mar 2002), Giles County Historical Society, 122 South Second Street, Pulaski, TN.

744 U.S., Social Security Applications and Claims Index, 1936-2007, Ancestry.com, Richard Allen Pegan.

745 Obituary of Claudine Louise PeGan (Niles, Michigan, Niles Daily Star, 07 Sep 1955), Niles District Library, 620 East Main Street, Niles, MI.

746 Find A Grave—Chapel Hill Memorial Gardens, Osceola, Penn Twp., St. Joseph Co., Indiana, Find A Grave.com, Karl N. Pegan, Find A Grave Memorial #103341645.

747 South Bend Genealogical Society Marriage Record Index List, Mishawaka, Indiana, South Bend Genealogical Society, Mishawaka-Penn Harris Library, 209 Lincoln Way East, Mishawaka, IN; Karl Pegan and Elodie Turenne, St. Joseph County, Indiana Marriage Records, App. Vol. 179, pg. 330; Online database: https://www.sbags.org/marriagesrch.php

748 Obituary of Elodie Hunter (Connersville, Indiana, Connersville News Examiner, 27 Jan 1994), Fayette County Library, 828 North Grand Avenue, Connersville, IN.

749 Indiana, Death Certificates, 1899-2011, Ancestry.com, Elodie L. Hunter, Indiana death cert. #94-009738.

750 Find A Grave—Laurel North Cemetery, Laurel, Laurel Twp., Franklin Co., Indiana, Find A Grave.com, Elodie L. Hunter, Find A Grave Memorial #182220742.

751 Indiana, Marriage Certificates, Marriages, 1917-2005, Ancestry.com, (Mr.) Bailey and Elodie Lucille McCoy, Marion County, Indiana Marriage Records, lic. #81-015522.

752 Indiana Marriages, 1958-2015, Indianapolis, Indiana, Indiana State Library, Genealogy, 315 West Ohio Street, Indianapolis, IN; Roy H. Hunter and Elodie L. Bailey, Franklin County, Indiana Marriage Records; Online database: https://www.statelib.lib.in.us/INMarriages93to02/in_marriages_search.asp

753 U.S., Social Security Applications and Claims Index, 1936-2007, Ancestry.com, Steven Karl Pegan.

754 Indiana, Death Certificates, 1899-2011, Ancestry.com, Steven Karl PeGan, Indiana death cert. #102573.

755 U.S., Social Security Applications and Claims Index, 1936-2007, Ancestry.com, Nelson Michael Pegan.

756 Indiana, Death Certificates, 1899-2011, Ancestry.com, Nelson Michael PeGan, Indiana death cert. #103808.

757 Find A Grave—Fairview Cemetery, Mishawaka, Penn Twp., St. Joseph Co., Indiana, Find A Grave.com, Robert PeGan, Find A Grave Memorial #182225698.

758 South Bend Genealogical Society Marriage Record Index List, Mishawaka, Indiana, South Bend Genealogical Society, Mishawaka-Penn Harris Library, 209 Lincoln Way East, Mishawaka, IN; Eugene L. Abbott and Juanita Pegan, St. Joseph County, Indiana Marriage Records, Book 185, pg. 196; Online database: https://www.sbags.org/marriagesrch.php

759 U.S., Social Security Applications and Claims Index, 1936-2007, Ancestry.com, Eugene Lyle Abbott.

760 Obituary of Eugene Abbott (Niles, Michigan, Niles Daily Star, 06 Oct 1990), Niles District Library, 620 East Main Street, Niles, MI.

761 Find A Grave—Rose Hill Cemetery, Berrien Springs, Oronoko Twp., Berrien Co., Michigan, Find A Grave.com, Eugene L. Abbott, Find A Grave Memorial #126786005.

762 Obituary of Constance Sue Hamilton (Buchanan, Michigan, Hoven Funeral Home, no date) Hoven Funeral Home, 414 East Front Street, Buchanan, MI. Online database: http://www.hovenfunerals.com/fh/print.cfm?type=obituary&o_id=4300132&fh_id=13894

763 South Bend Genealogical Society Marriage Record Index List, Mishawaka, Indiana, South Bend Genealogical Society, Mishawaka-Penn Harris Library, 209 Lincoln Way East, Mishawaka, IN; Buddy Lynn Stanley and Darlene Kay Pegan, St. Joseph County, Indiana Marriage Records, App. Vol. 201, pg. 77; Online database: https://www.sbags.org/marriagesrch.php

764 Find A Grave—Fairview Cemetery, Bluffton, Wells Co., Indiana, Find A Grave.com, Leota F. Lydy, Find A Grave Memorial #67987376.

765 Indiana, Marriages 1811-2007, Applications, FamilySearch.org, Leota F. Roll, Wells County, Indiana Marriage Records, Vol. 12, pg. 283.

766 Indiana, Birth Certificates, 1907-1940, Ancestry.com, Unnamed Roll, female child, Wells County, Indiana, birth cert. #22148; fa.: Unknown, Mo.: Leota Roll.

767 Indiana, Marriages 1811-2007, FamilySearch.org, Charles W. Lydy and Leota F. Roll, Wells County, Indiana Marriage Records, Vol. 13, pg. 209.

768 U.S., WWI Draft Registration Cards, 1917-1918, Ancestry.com, Charles W. Lydy, Bluffton, Wells Co., Indiana.

769 Find A Grave—Oak Lawn Cemetery, Ossian, Jefferson Twp., Wells Co., Indiana, Find A Grave.com, Charles W. Lydy, Find A Grave Memorial #53696988.

770 Indiana, Death Certificates, 1899-2011, Ancestry.com, Charles W. Lydy, Indiana death cert. #68-044907.

771 Obituary of Charles Lydy Sr. (Bluffton, Indiana, Bluffton News Banner, 26 Dec 1968.), Wells County Public Library, 200 West Washington Street, Bluffton, IN, Bluffton (IN) News Banner, pub.

772 Obituary of Margaret Christensen (Bluffton, Indiana, Bluffton News Banner, 07 Nov 2000), Wells County Public Library, 200 West Washington Street, Bluffton, IN.

773 Obituary of A. Louise Lutz (Bluffton, Indiana, Bluffton News Banner, 04 Apr 1995), Wells County Public Library, 200 West Washington Street, Bluffton, IN.

774 Indiana, Death Certificates, 1899-2011, Ancestry.com, Agnes Louise Lydy, Indiana death cert. #95-017271.

775 Indiana, Birth Certificates, 1907-1940, Ancestry.com, Agnes Louise Lydy, Wells County, Indiana Birth Records, cert. #5547. (Mistakenly indexed on Ancestry as "Azues", but document clearly says Agnes.)

776 Wells County, Indiana Marriages, Wells County Clerk, 102 West Market Street, Suite 201, Bluffton, IN, Charles Wayne Lydy and Dorothy Crickmore, Marriage Book 20, pg. 259.

777 Obituary of Charles Wayne Lydy (Bluffton, Indiana, Goodwin- Cale & Harnish Memorial Chapel, 09 Mar 2016), Online database: http://www.thegmcfamily.com/memsol.cgi?user_id=1758119

778 Indiana, Birth Certificates, 1907-1940, Ancestry.com, Charles Wayne Lydy, Wells County, Indiana Birth Records, cert. #10896.

779 Indiana, Birth Certificates, 1907-1940, Ancestry.com, Robert Eugene Lydy, Wells County, Indiana Birth Records, cert. #23157.

780 U.S., Department of Veterans Affairs BIRLS Death File, 1850-2010, Ancestry.com, Dale Lydy.

781 Indiana, Birth Certificates, 1907-1940, Ancestry.com, Dale Edmund Lydy, Wells County, Indiana Birth Records, birth cert. #21300.

782 Indiana, Death Certificates, 1899-2011, Ancestry.com, Dale E. Lydy, Indiana death cert. #003524.

783 Indiana, Marriages 1811-2007, FamilySearch.org, Forrest Edwin Debolt and Freida Mae Lydy, Allen County, Indiana Marriage Records, Application, Vol. 118, pg. 225.

784 Indiana, Birth Certificates, 1907-1940, Ancestry.com, Freida Mae Lydy, Wells County, Indiana, cert. #4916.

785 Records of Oak Lawn Cemetery, Ossian, Jefferson Twp., Wells Co., Indiana, Bonnie Ilene Lydy, Oak Lawn Cemetery Association, 701 South Jefferson Street, Ossian, IN.

786 Indiana, Birth Certificates, 1907-1940, Ancestry.com, Bonnie Ilene Lydy, Wells County, Indiana, cert. #4516.

787 Indiana, Death Certificates, 1899-2011, Ancestry.com, Bonnie "Irene" Lydy, Indiana death cert. #22050.

788 Indiana, Death Certificates, 1899-2011, Ancestry.com, O. Joan Schorey, Indiana death cert. #043672.

789 U.S., Social Security Applications and Claims Index, 1936-2007, Ancestry.com, Olive Joan Lydy Schorey.

790 Indiana, Birth Certificates, 1907-1940, Ancestry.com, Olive Joan Lydy, Wells County, Indiana Birth Records, birth cert. #19465. Mistakenly indexed as "Alive Joan Sydy".

791 Web: Marion County, Indiana, Marriage Index, 1925-2012, Ancestry.com, Edmund Roll and Edna Moffitt, Marion County Marriage Records, Vol. 126, pg. 108.

792 Indiana, Marriage Index, 1800-1941, Ancestry.com, "Edward" Roll and Edna Moffitt, Marion County, Indiana Marriage Records.

793 Indiana Death Certificates, 1899-2010, Ancestry.com, Edna Mae Bollinger, Indiana death cert. #65-033641.

794 Web: Marion County, Indiana, Marriage Index, 1925-2012, Ancestry.com, Edmund Roll and Mary Curry, Marion County, Indiana Marriage Records, Vol. 152, pg. 85.

795 Find A Grave—Mount Rest Cemetery, St. Johns, Bingham Twp., Clinton Co., Michigan, Find A Grave.com, Corenne M. Roll, Find A Grave Memorial # #19205142.

796 Obituary of Myrtle Roll (Kokomo, Indiana, Kokomo Tribune, 20 Apr 1969), Kokomo-Howard County Public Library, 220 North Union Street, Kokomo, IN.

797 Find A Grave—Sunset Memory Garden Cemetery, Kokomo, Center Twp., Howard Co., Indiana, Find A Grave.com, Myrtle M. Roll, Find A Grave Memorial #103743855.

798 Indiana, Death Certificates, 1899-2011, Ancestry.com, Myrtle N. Roll, Indiana death cert. #69-013333.

799 U.S., Social Security Applications and Claims Index, 1936-2007, Ancestry.com, Myrtle Mildred Gustafson (Roll).

800 "Miss Myrtle M. Gustofson and Edmund W. Roll Are Married" (Kokomo, Indiana, Kokomo Tribune, 19 Jan 1949); Newspaper Archive, Online database: newspaperarchive.com; https://access-newspaperarchive-com.sjcpl.idm.oclc.org/us/indiana/kokomo/kokomo-tribune/1949/01-19/page-6/myrtle-roll?pc=15127&psi=38&pci=7&pt=8149&ndt=by&py=1940&pey=1949&ndt=ex&py=1949&search=y

801 Find A Grave—Fairview Cemetery, Bluffton, Wells Co., Indiana, Find A Grave.com, T. Lynn Roll Kennedy, Find A Grave Memorial #67987635.

802 Indiana, Death Certificates, 1899-2011, Ancestry.com, Melvin Charles Kennedy, Indiana death cert. #95-009806.

803 Find A Grave—Fairview Cemetery, Bluffton, Wells Co., Indiana, Find A Grave.com, M.C. Kennedy, Find A Grave Memorial #67987520.

804 Find A Grave—Fairview Cemetery, Bluffton, Wells Co., Indiana, Find A Grave.com, Marian C. Roll Bender, Find A Grave Memorial #65039521.

805 Obituary of Earl Bender, Wells County Public Library, 200 West Washington Street, Bluffton, IN, Bluffton (IN) News Banner, pub. 29 Sep 1966.

806 Indiana, Death Certificates, 1899-2011, Ancestry.com, Earl A. Bender, Indiana death cert. #66-035293. Mistakenly indexed under Earl A. "Mender".

807 Find A Grave—Fairview Cemetery, Bluffton, Wells Co., Indiana, Find A Grave.com, Earl Alfred Bender, Find A Grave Memorial #65039505.

808 Obituary of Sharon Y. Lewis Graham (Bluffton, Indiana, Goodwin—Cale & Harnish Memorial Chapel, 15 May 2013); Online database: http://www.thegmcfamily.com/memsol.cgi?user_id=986917

809 Indiana, Birth Certificates, 1907-1940, Ancestry.com, Sharon Yvonne Bender, Wells County, Indiana Birth Records, cert. #9567.

810 Obituary of Clyde C. Hunter (Hillsboro, Ohio, Highland County Press Gazette, 10 Apr 1973), Highland County District Library, 10 Willettsville Pike, Hillsboro, OH.

811 Ohio, Death Records, 1908-1932, 1938-2007, Ancestry.com, Lucille M. Hunter, death cert. #052605.

812 Obituary of Lucille M. Hunter (Hillsboro, Ohio, Hillsboro Press-Gazette, 29 Jan 1993), Highland County District Library, 10 Willettsville Pike, Hillsboro, OH.

813 Find A Grave—New Market Baptist Church Cemetery, New Market Twp., Highland Co., Ohio, Find A Grave.com, Lucille M. Hunter, Find A Grave Memorial #117341275.

814 Ohio, Birth Index, 1908-1964, Ancestry.com, Mary A. Dillon, state file #1935026813.

815 U.S., Social Security Applications and Claims Index, 1936-2007, Ancestry.com, Mary Alice Dillon Hunter.

816 Obituary of Mary Alice Hunter (Hillsboro, Ohio, Hillsboro Press-Gazette, 05 Dec 1989), Highland County District Library, 10 Willettsville Pike, Hillsboro, OH.

817 Ohio, Death Records, 1908-1932, 1938-2007, Ancestry.com, Mary Alice Hunter, death cert. #091526.

818 Find A Grave—Green Lawn Cemetery, Columbus, Franklin Co., Ohio, Find A Grave.com.

819 Find A Grave—Mt. Zion Cemetery, Danville, New Market Twp., Highland Co., Ohio, Find A Grave.com, Infant Son Hunter, Find A Grave Memorial #112714087.

820 Cook County, Illinois Clerk's Office Records, Cook County Clerk's Office—Bureau of Vital Records, 50 West Washington Street, East Concourse Level-25, Chicago, IL, Kenneth Thomas and Jane Roush, Cook County, Illinois Marriage Records, lic. #255038.

821 Cook County, Illinois Birth Index, 1916-1935, Ancestry.com, Kenneth R. Thomas, birth record #6034349.

822 Cook County, Illinois Clerk's Office Records, Cook County Clerk's Office—Bureau of Vital Records, 50 West Washington Street, East Concourse Level-25, Chicago, IL, Kenneth R. Thomas, birth record #6034349.

823 U.S., Social Security Applications and Claims Index, 1936-2007, Ancestry.com, Kenneth Roy Thomas.

824 Find A Grave—Evergreen Cemetery, Girard Twp., Branch Co., Michigan, Find A Grave.com, John M. Roush, Find A Grave Memorial #112638857.

825 Branch County, Michigan Marriage Records (Coldwater, Michigan), Branch County, Michigan County Clerk's Office, Courthouse, 31 Division Street. Coldwater, MI, John Milford Roush and Wanetta Merritt, Branch County, Michigan Marriage Records, Vol. I, pg. 171, lic. #13731.

826 Michigan, Marriage Records, 1867-1952, Ancestry.com, John Milford Roush and Wanetta Merritt, Branch County, Michigan Marriage Records, lic. #13731, Michigan state lic. #12 3524.

827 Obituary of Wanetta Warring (Angola, Indiana, Angola Herald Republican, 25 Oct 2014), Carnegie Public Library of Steuben County, 322 South Wayne Street, Angola, IN.

828 Find A Grave—Flint Cemetery, Angola, Pleasant Twp., Steuben Co., Indiana, Find A Grave.com, Wanetta Ruth Merritt Warring, Find A Grave Memorial #137638677.

829 Indiana, Marriage Certificates, 1917-2005, Ancestry.com, John M. Roush and Marjorie J. Wilber, Steuben County, Indiana Marriage Records, Vol. 256, pg. 33, lic. #86-003433.

830 Obituary of Marjorie Jean Brown Wilber Roush (Angola, Indiana, Weicht Funeral Home, 30 Dec 2016), Weicht Funeral Home, 207 North West Street, Angola, IN; Online database: http://www.weichtfh.com/obits/obituary.php?id=685967

831 Find A Grave—Lakeside Lakeside Cemetery, Fremont, Fremont Twp., Steuben Co., Indiana, Find A Grave.com, Marjorie Jean Brown Wilbur Roush, Find A Grave Memorial #174686990.

832 Obituary of Robert "Bob" Dean Roush (Coldwater, Michigan, Coldwater Daily Reporter, 15 Sep 2015), Branch County Library, Coldwater Branch, 10 East Chicago Street, Coldwater, MI.

833 Obituary of Gary Wayne Roush (Coldwater, Michigan, Coldwater Daily Reporter, 10 Apr 2006), Branch County Library, Coldwater Branch, 10 East Chicago Street, Coldwater, MI.

834 Obituary of Vicky L. Brown (Coldwater, Michigan, Coldwater Reporter, 27 Mar 2015), Branch County Library, Coldwater Branch, 10 East Chicago Street, Coldwater, MI.

835 Find A Grave—Salisbury National Cemetery, Salisbury, Rowan Co., North Carolina, Find A Grave.com, George L. Roush, Find A Grave Memorial #3265830.

836 Obituary of Kathleen F. Roush (Salisbury, North Carolina, Salisbury Post, 03 Feb 1992), Rowan Public Library, 210 West Fisher Street, Salisbury, NC.

837 North Carolina, Death Indexes, 1908-2004, Ancestry.com, Kathleen Elizabeth Roush.

838 U.S., Social Security Applications and Claims Index, 1936-2007, Ancestry.com, Kathleen Elizabeth Foster Bost Sellers Harwood Roush.

839 Find A Grave—Salisbury National Cemetery, Salisbury, Rowan Co., North Carolina, Find A Grave.com, Kathleen Foster Roush, Find A Grave Memorial #3265831.

840 Cemeteries of Berrien County, Michigan-Niles Township, Niles District Library, 620 East Main Street, Niles, MI, pg. 28, pub. 2012, Berrien County Genealogical Society, P.O. Box 8808, Benton Harbor, Michigan, 49203.

841 Arizona, County Marriage Records, 1865-1972, Ancestry.com, Harley LeRoy Roush and Helen Marie Steinbach, Coconino County, Arizona Marriage Records, Vol. 18, pg. 40.

842 Find A Grave—Ferncliff Cemetery, Springfield, Springfield Twp., Clark Co., Ohio, Dorothy H. Koeb, Find A Grave Memorial #51194762.

843 Ohio, County Marriages, 1789-2013, FamilySearch.org, Paul O. Koeb and Dorothy Roush, Clark County, Ohio Marriage Records, Vol. 37, pg. 613, lic. #24485.

844 Obituary of Paul O. Koeb (Springfield, Ohio, Springfield Daily News, 16 Oct 1982), Clark County Public Library, 201 South Fountain Avenue, Springfield, OH.

845 Ohio, Death Records, 1908-1932, 1938-2007, Ancestry.com, Paul Koeb, death cert. #068951.

846 Find A Grave—Ferncliff Cemetery, Springfield, Springfield Twp., Clark Co., Ohio, Paul O. Koeb, Find A Grave Memorial #51194701.

847 Find A Grave—Ferncliff Cemetery, Springfield, Springfield Twp., Clark Co., Ohio, "Margaret" Roush, Find A Grave Memorial #60741207.

848 Find A Grave—Santa Rosa Memorial Park Cemetery, Santa Rosa, Sonoma Co., California, Find A Grave.com, George B. Roush, Jr., Find A Grave Memorial #141384532.

849 Obituary of M. Elaine Roush (Petaluma, California, Petaluma Press Democrat, 03 Mar 2009), Ancestry.com.

850 California Death Certificate, California Health and Strategic Planning, Vital Records, M.S. 5103, P.O. Box 997410, Sacramento, CA, Madge Roush, death cert. #3052009034019.

851 Kentucky, Birth Index, 1911-1999, Ancestry.com, Larry E. Roush, Hardin County, Kentucky Birth Records, Vol. 058, cert. #28689.

852 U.S. Veterans' Gravesites, ca. 1775-2006, Ancestry.com, William L. Roush, Section 29 Site 1204.

853 Find A Grave—Dayton National Cemetery, Dayton, Montgomery Co., Ohio, Find A Grave.com, William Leroy Roush, Find A Grave Memorial #72092435.

854 Ohio Marriage Abstracts, 1970-1972-2007, Ancestry.com, William L. Roush and Beatrice A. Shatto, Clark County, Ohio Marriage Records, Ohio state Vol. 7335, lic. #40047.

855 Obituary of William L. Roush Jr. (Salt Lake City, Utah, Deseret News, 13 Oct 1991), Salt Lake City Public Library,210 East 400 South, Salt Lake City, UT.

856 Find A Grave—Manti Cemetery, Manti, Sanpete Co., Utah, Find A Grave.com, William LeRoy "Billy" Roush, Find A Grave Memorial #51757768.

857 Obituary of Nancy M. (Sorel) Martel (Westerly, Rhode Island, Westerly Sun, 09 Feb 2017), Westerly Library, 44 Broad Street, Westerly, RI.

858 Find A Grave—Hillside Memorial Park Cemetery, Akron, Summit Co., Ohio, Find A Grave.com, James D. Bussey, Find A Grave Memorial #165903912.

859 Summit County, Ohio Marriage Records, 1840-1980, Ancestry.com, James Donovan Bussey and Winifred Louise Eiler, Vol. 132, pg. 118, lic. #29,794.

860 Indiana, Birth Certificates, 1907-1940, Ancestry.com, Winifred Louise Eiler, birth certificate #15793.

861 Summit County, Ohio Marriage Records, 1840-1980, Ancestry.com, James Donovan Bussey and Barbara Ann Kelly, Vol. 184, pg. 583, lic. #76,636.

862 Ohio, Birth Index, 1908-1964, Ancestry.com, Barbara A. Heintzelman, state file #1928056288.

863 U.S., Social Security Applications and Claims Index, 1936-2007, Ancestry.com, Barbara Ann Heintzelman Kelly Bussey.

864 Ohio, Death Records, 1908-1932, 1938-2007, Ancestry.com, Barbara A. Kelly, death cert. #68189.

865 Find A Grave—Greenlawn Memorial Park Cemetery, Akron, Summit Co., Ohio, Find A Grave.com, Barbara A. Kelly, Find A Grave Memorial #131490283.

866 U.S., Social Security Applications and Claims Index, 1936-2007, Ancestry.com, Mary Edythe Starcher Hallbrook Bussey.

867 Ohio, Death Records, 1908-1932, 1938-2007, Ancestry.com, Mary Edythe Bussey, death cert. #085879.

868 Find A Grave—Hillside Memorial Park Cemetery, Akron, Summit Co., Ohio, Find A Grave.com, Mary E. Bussey, Find A Grave Memorial #165903938.

869 Ohio, Birth Index, 1908-1964, Ancestry.com, Glenn Moore, state file #1927018111.

870 Ohio, County Marriages, 1789-2013, FamilySearch.org, John E. Ross and Rosalee Bussey, Highland County, Ohio Marriage Records, Vol. 22, pg. 310, Lic, #17103.

871 Kentucky, Birth Index, 1911-1999, Ancestry.com, Johnie E. Ross, Campbell Co., Vol. 044, Year 1926, cert. #21591.

872 Pennsylvania, Death Certificates, 1906-1966, Ancestry.com, John E. Ross, death cert. #112325.

873 Find A Grave—Bethany Church Cemetery, Springdale, Mason Co., Kentucky, Find A Grave.com, John E. Ross, Find A Grave Memorial #147320038.

874 Obituary of John E. Ross (Fort Wayne, Indiana, Fort Wayne Journal Gazette, 29 Dec 1955) Genealogy Center, Allen County Library, 900 Library Plaza, Fort Wayne, IN.

875 U.S., Social Security Applications and Claims Index, 1936-2007, Ancestry.com, Clarence Christopher Yarger.

876 Ohio, Death Records, 1908-1932, 1938-2007, Ancestry.com, Clarence Christopher Yarger, death cert. #105870.

877 Find A Grave—Locust Grove Cemetery, Peebles, Meigs Twp., Adams Co., Ohio, Find A Grave.com, Elizabeth Joanna Peebles, Find A Grave Memorial #110308146.

878 Ohio, County Marriages, 1789-2013, FamilySearch.org, Harold L. Wallace and E. Joanna Bussey, Highland County, Ohio Marriage Records.

879 Obituary of Harold L. Wallace (Hillsboro, Ohio, Highland County Times Gazette, 06 Aug 2009), Highland County District Library, 10 Willettsville Pike, Hillsboro, OH.

880 Find A Grave—Locust Grove Cemetery, Peebles, Meigs Twp., Adams Co., Ohio, Find A Grave.com, Harold L. Wallace, Find A Grave Memorial #40441860.

881 Find A Grave—Greenville Union Cemetery, Greenville, Greenville Twp., Darke Co., Ohio, Find A Grave.com, Raymond Eugene Bills, Find A Grave Memorial #183755503.

882 U.S., Social Security Applications and Claims Index, 1936-2007, Ancestry.com, Raymond Eugene Bills.

883 Ohio, Death Records, 1908-1932, 1938-2007, Ancestry.com, Raymond Eugene Bills, death cert. #45161.

884 Find A Grave—Washington Cemetery, Washington Court House, Union Twp., Fayette Co., Ohio, Find A Grave.com, Helen L. Bills, Find A Grave Memorial #139795442.

885 Find A Grave—Green Mound Cemetery, New Madison, Harrison Twp., Darke Co., Ohio, Find A Grave.com, Jeanne E. Bills Swartz, Find A Grave Memorial #120155635.

886 Obituary of Jeanne E. Swartz (Greenville, Ohio, Daily Advocate, 11 Nov 2013), Greenville Public Library, 520 Sycamore Street, Greenville, OH.

887 Find A Grave—Martinsville IOOF Cemetery, Martinsville, Clark Twp., Clinton Co., Ohio, Find A Grave.com, Kenneth W. Roush, Find A Grave Memorial #119355460.

888 The Genealogical Committee of the Clinton County Historical Society, Cemetery Records of Clinton Co., Ohio, 1798-1998: Martinsville IOOF Cemetery: Kenneth W. Roush. Clinton County, Ohio Records Center and Archives, 111 South Nelson Avenue, Suite 3, Wilmington, OH.

889 Ohio Marriage Abstracts, 1970-1972-2007, Ancestry.com, Robert L. Brammer and Shirley J. Johnson, Greene County, Ohio Marriage Records, Ohio state Vol. 18328, lic. #48295.

890 Ohio, Birth Index, 1908-1964, Ancestry.com, Robert Lee Brammer, state file #1942009874.

891 Obituary of Robert "Bob" Brammer (Xenia, Ohio, Gazette News Current, 12 Feb 2008), Greene County Public Library-Xenia Community Library, Greene County Room, 6 East Market Street, Xenia, OH., Xenia, OH.

892 Ohio, Death Records, 1908-1932, 1938-2007, Ancestry.com, Charlotte Pauline Haines, death cert. #017009.

893 Obituary of Charlotte P. Haines (Xenia, Ohio, Xenia Daily Gazette, 08 Jan 1991), Greene County Public Library-Xenia Community Library, Greene County Room, 6 East Market Street, Xenia, OH., Xenia, OH.

894 Find A Grave—Highlawn Memorial Gardens Cemetery, Washington Court House, Union Twp., Fayette Co., Ohio, Find A Grave.com.

895 Obituary of Larry E. Davis (Washington Court House, Ohio, Washington Court House Record Herald, 21 Jul 1995), Carnegie Public Library, 127 South North Street, Washington Court House, OH.

896 Find A Grave—Washington Cemetery, Washington Court House, Union Twp., Fayette Co., Ohio, Find A Grave.com, Larry Davis, Find A Grave Memorial #168588879.

897 "Divorce Actions" (Washington Court House, Ohio, Washington Court House Record, 02 Jul 1965), Carnegie Public Library, 127 South North Street, Washington Court House, Ohio.

898 Ohio, Death Records, 1908-1932, 1938-2007, Ancestry.com, Rebecca A. Davis, death cert. #036758.

899 Find A Grave—Sugar Creek Baptist Church Cemetery, Union Twp., Fayette Co., Ohio, Find A Grave.com, Rebecca Ann Graves Davis, Find A Grave Memorial #34654574.

900 "Clickner-Davis Vows Read" (Washington Court House, Ohio, Washington Court House Records, 09 Aug 1968), Carnegie Public Library, 127 South North Street, Washington Court House, OH.

901 Find A Grave—Maple Grove Cemetery, Port William, Liberty Twp., Clinton Co., Ohio, Find A Grave.com, Robert E. McCandless, Find A Grave Memorial #154611851.

902 The Genealogical Committee of the Clinton County Historical Society, Cemetery Records of Clinton Co., Ohio, 1798-1998: Maple Grove Cemetery/Port William Cemetery: Robert Eugene McCandless. Clinton County, Ohio Records Center and Archives, 111 South Nelson Avenue, Suite 3, Wilmington, OH.

903 U.S., Social Security Applications and Claims Index, 1936-2007, Ancestry.com, David Thomas Weller.

904 Ohio, Death Records, 1908-1932, 1938-2007, Ancestry.com, David T. Weller, death cert. #023943.

905 Ohio, Birth Index, 1908-1964, Ancestry.com, David T. Weller, state file #1937016480.

906 Obituary of Samuel McCandless (Wilmington, Ohio, Wilmington News Journal, 01 Jun 1976), Wilmington Public Library of Clinton County, 268 North South Street, Wilmington, OH, "Local a drowns in Cowan Creek" on pg. 1.

907 Find A Grave—Maple Grove Cemetery, Port William, Liberty Twp., Clinton Co., Ohio, Find A Grave.com, Samuel F. McCandless, Find A Grave Memorial #154612103.

908 The Genealogical Committee of the Clinton County Historical Society, Cemetery Records of Clinton Co., Ohio, 1798-1998: Maple Grove Cemetery/Port William Cemetery: Samuel F. McCandless. Clinton County, Ohio Records Center and Archives, 111 South Nelson Avenue, Suite 3, Wilmington, OH.

909 Ohio Marriage Abstracts, 1970-1972-2007, Ancestry.com, William L. Seitz and Linda Baker, Miami County, Ohio Marriage Records, Ohio state Vol. 10701. lic. #19338.

910 U.S., Social Security Applications and Claims Index, 1936-2007, Ancestry.com, Linda Bradley Baker Seitz.

911 Ohio, Death Records, 1908-1932, 1938-2007, Ancestry.com, Linda L. Seitz, death cert. #080733.

912 Find A Grave—Riverside Cemetery, Troy, Concord Twp., Miami Co., Ohio, Find A Grave.com, Linda L. Bradley Seitz, Find A Grave Memorial #73235138.

913 Ohio, Death Records, 1908-1932, 1938-2007, Ancestry.com, William J. Seitz, death cert. #46298.

914 Find A Grave—Riverside Cemetery, Troy, Concord Twp., Miami Co., Ohio, Find A Grave.com, Darrell J. Seitz, Find A Grave Memorial #150707213.

915 California, Marriage Index, 1949-1959, Ancestry.com, Everett R. Geis and Patricia A. Pearson, Los Angeles County, California Marriage Records, California state file #1504.

916 California Birth Index, 1905-1995, Ancestry.com, Everett Ray Geis.

917 Find A Grave—Fairhaven Cemetery, Santa Ana, Orange Co., California, Find A Grave.com, Marjorie Jane Pearson Conti, Find A Grave Memorial #155107004.

918 Nevada, Marriage Index, 1956-2005, Ancestry.com, Vincent J. Conti and Marjorie Jane Pearson, Clark County, Nevada Marriage Records, Book 108, lic. #291015.

919 Find A Grave—Riverside Cemetery, Gas City, Mill Twp., Grant Co., Indiana, Find A Grave.com, Betty Jean Eastes Reese, Find A Grave Memorial #79536965.

920 Indiana: Marion Public Library Marriage Index, 1831-2008, Ancestry.com, Charles Cowgill and Betty Eastes, Grant County, Indiana Marriage Records.

921 Indiana, Death Certificates, 1899-2011, Ancestry.com, Charles Edward Cowgill, Indiana death cert. #79-016170.

922 Obituary of Charles Cowgill (Marion, Indiana, Marion Chronicle Tribune, 25 May 1979), Marion, Indiana Public Library, 600 South Washington Street, Marion, IN.

923 Find A Grave—Estates of Serenity, Marion, Center Twp., Grant Co., Indiana, Find A Grave.com, Charles Edward Cowgill, Find A Grave Memorial #83860787.

924 Indiana: Marion Public Library Marriage Index, 1831-2008, Ancestry.com, Charles Norman Reese and Betty Jean Cowgill.

925 Obituary of Charles Norman Reese Sr. (Marion, Indiana, Marion Chronicle Tribune, 27 Aug 1999), Marion, Indiana Public Library, 600 South Washington Street, Marion, IN.

926 U.S., Social Security Applications and Claims Index, 1936-2007, Ancestry.com, Charles Norman Reese.

927 Find A Grave—Riverside Cemetery, Gas City, Mill Twp., Grant Co., Indiana, Find A Grave.com, Charles Norman Reese, Find A Grave Memorial #104995095.

928 Obituary of Danny E. Cowgill (Marion, Indiana, Marion Chronicle Tribune, 28 Aug 1998), Marion, Indiana Public Library, 600 South Washington Street, Marion, IN.

929 U.S., Social Security Applications and Claims Index, 1936-2007, Ancestry.com, Danny Edward Cowgill.

930 Indiana, Death Certificates, 1899-2011, Ancestry.com, Danny Edward Cowgill, Indiana death cert. #026299.

931 Find A Grave—Riverside Cemetery, Gas City, Mill Twp., Grant Co., Indiana, Find A Grave.com, Joseph Edward Eastes, Find A Grave Memorial #41314259.

932 Obituary of Marilyn L. Eastes (Marion, Indiana, Marion Chronicle Tribune, 12 Apr 2007), Marion, Indiana Public Library, 600 South Washington Street, Marion, IN.

933 Indiana: Marion Public Library Marriage Index, 1831-2008, Ancestry.com, Joseph Edward Eastes and Marilyn Louise James, Grant County Marriage Records, Vol. 59, pg. 54.

934 Indiana, Marriage Certificates, 1917-2005, Ancestry.com, Joseph Edward Eastes and Marilyn Louise Eastes, Grant County Marriage Records, Vol. 97, pg. 332, lic. #83-052124.

935 Indiana, Death Certificates, 1899-2011, Ancestry.com, Marilyn L. Eastes, Indiana death cert. #015094.

936 Indiana, Birth Certificates, 1907-1940, Ancestry.com, "Merilyn" Louise James, Grant County, Indiana Birth Records, birth cert. #10749.

937 Find A Grave—Riverside Cemetery, Gas City, Mill Twp., Grant Co., Indiana, Find A Grave.com, Marilyn L. McDaniel Eastes, Find A Grave Memorial #18879395.

938 U.S., Social Security Applications and Claims Index, 1936-2007, Ancestry.com, Mary Lou James.

939 Find A Grave—Washington County Memorial Gardens Cemetery, Johnson City, Washington Co., Tennessee, Find A Grave.com, John F. Eastes, Find A Grave Memorial #62034116.

940 Indiana Marriages, 1958-2015, Indiana State Library, Genealogy, 315 West Ohio Street, Indianapolis, IN, Ronald L. Jarvis and Betty J. Pegan, Huntington County, Indiana Marriage Records; Online database: https://www.statelib.lib.in.us/INMarriages93to02/in_marriages_search.asp

941 Florida Death Index 1877-1998, Ancestry.com, Ronald L. Jarvis.

942 Obituary of Ronald L. Jarvis (Jacksonville, Florida, Florida Times-Union, 01 Jul 1992), Jacksonville Public Library, 303 North Laura Street, Jacksonville, FL.

943 Find A Grave—Arlington Park Cemetery, Jacksonville, Duval Co., Florida, Find A Grave.com, Ronald L. Jarvis, Find A Grave Memorial #28660931.

944 Obituary of Daniel Lee Jarvis (Kokomo, Indiana, Kokomo Tribune, 18 Feb 2004), Kokomo-Howard County Public Library, 220 North Union Street, Kokomo, IN.

945 Indiana, Death Certificates, 1899-2011, Ancestry.com, Daniel Lee Jarvis, Indiana death cert. #003405.

946 Indiana Marriages, 1958-2015, Indianapolis, Indiana, Indiana State Library, Genealogy, 315 West Ohio Street, Indianapolis, IN, Thomas R. "Wulbur" and Judith K. Oswalt, Huntington County, Indiana Marriage Records; Online database, https://www.statelib.lib.in.us/INMarriages93to02/in_marriages_search.asp

947 Obituary of Thomas R. Wilbur (Huntington, Indiana, Huntington County TAB, 15 Mar 2017), Huntington County

TAB, 1670 Etna Avenue, Huntington, IN, http://www.huntingtoncountytab.com/obituary/42889/thomas-r-wilbur.

948 Indiana, Birth Certificates, 1907-1940, Ancestry.com, Thomas Richard Wilbur, Huntington County, Indiana Birth Records, birth cert. #6266.

949 Find A Grave—Pilgrims Rest Cemetery, Huntington, Huntington Twp., Huntington Co., Indiana, Find A Grave.com, Thomas R. Wilbur, Find A Grave Memorial #177381014.

950 Obituary of James E. "Jim" Dodson (Livingston, Tennessee, Speck Funeral Home, no date) Speck Funeral Home, 300 North Church Street, Livingston, TN; Online database: https://www.speckfuneral.com/obituary/261575/James-E-Dodson/

951 Find A Grave—St. Paul's Lutheran Cemetery, Celina, Jefferson Twp., Mercer Co., Ohio, Allen E. Flowers, Find A Grave Memorial #10467539.

952 Obituary of Connie M. Kramer Flowers-Seals (Celina, Ohio, The Daily Standard, 05 Dec 2017), Mercer County Library, 303 North Main Street, Celina, OH.

953 Find A Grave—St. Paul's Lutheran Cemetery, Celina, Jefferson Twp., Mercer Co., Ohio, Allen E. Flowers, Find A Grave Memorial #10467539.

954 Obituary of Robert "Bobby" Flowers (Celina, Ohio, Celina Daily Standard, 11 Sep 1978), Mercer County Library, 303 North Main Street, Celina, OH.

955 Ohio, Death Records, 1908-1932, 1938-2007, Ancestry.com, Robert L. Flowers, death cert. #068169.

956 Obituary of Diana Hughes (Lima, Ohio, Lima News, 26 Aug 1986), Ohio History Center Archives and Library, Ohio History Center, 800 East 17th Avenue, Columbus, OH.

957 Ohio, Death Records, 1908-1932, 1938-2007, Ancestry.com, Diana Hughes, death cert. #067287.

958 Find A Grave—Swamp College Cemetery, Celina, Jefferson Twp., Mercer Co., Ohio, Find A Grave.com, Diana L. Hisey Hughes, Find A Grave Memorial #30786352.

959 Find A Grave—Swamp College Cemetery, Celina, Jefferson Twp., Mercer Co., Ohio, Find A Grave.com, Kathleen Joann "Kathy" Flowers Hone, Find A Grave Memorial #109550580.

960 Obituary of Brandy Flowers (Celina, Ohio, Celina Daily Standard, 07 Feb 2009), Mercer County Library, 303 North Main Street, Celina, OH.

961 Marion County, Indiana Marriage Records, Marion County, Indiana County Clerk, City-County Building, W-122, 200 East Washington Street, Indianapolis, IN, James Brent Crosson and Maryln Ann PeGan, Marion County, Indiana Marriage Records, Vol. 218, pg. 248.

962 Indiana, Birth Certificates, 1907-1940, Ancestry.com, James Brent Crossen, Marion County, Indiana Birth Records, birth cert. #47157.

963 Obituary of Dr. James "Jim" Crossen (Dallas, Texas, Dallas Morning News, 13 Sep 2012), Dallas Public Library, 1515 Young Street, Dallas, TX.

964 Find A Grave—Dallas-Fort Worth National Cemetery, Dallas, Dallas Co., Texas, Find A Grave.com, James B. Crossen, Find A Grave Memorial #107491225.

965 Texas Death Index, 1903-2000, Ancestry.com, Danette Lee Crossen, deaths for 2000, pg. 551.

966 U.S., Social Security Applications and Claims Index, 1936-2007, Ancestry.com, Danette Lee Crossen.

967 Indiana, Marriage Certificates, 1917-2005, Ancestry.com, Thomas Joseph PeGan and Candace Nan Snyder, Huntington County, Indiana Marriage Records, Vol. 47, pg. 264, lic. #67-013430.

968 Obituary of Candace N. Zimmerman (Huntington, Indiana, Huntington Tab, 07 Jun 2017), Huntington City-Township Library, Indiana Room, 255 West Park Drive, Huntington, IN.

969 Find A Grave—Hoverstock Cemetery, Zanesville, Union Twp., Wells Co., Indiana, Find A Grave.com, Candace N. Zimmerman, Find A Grave Memorial #180129881.

970 Indiana, Death Certificates, 1899-2011, Ancestry.com, Brent C. PeGan, Indiana death cert. #90-025813.

971 Obituary of Brett Pegan (Fort Wayne, Indiana, Fort Wayne News Sentinel, 17 Jul 1990), Genealogy Center, Allen County Public Library, 900 Library Plaza, Fort Wayne, IN.

972 Find A Grave—Mission Hills Memorial Chapel, Crematory & Gardens, North Niles, Howard Twp., Cass Co., Michigan, Find A Grave.com, Robert Phillip PeGan, Find A Grave Memorial #63495145.

973 Obituary of Ozella Rose Morgan-Zorn (South Bend, Indiana, South Bend Tribune, 15 Dec 2014), South Bend-St. Joseph County Public Library, 304 South Main Street, South Bend, IN.

974 Find A Grave—Mission Hills Memorial Chapel, Crematory & Gardens, North Niles, Howard Twp., Cass Co., Michigan, Find A Grave.com, Ozella Rose Morgan-Zorn, Find A Grave Memorial #140144990.

975 Obituary of Hazel Marie Richer (Niles, Michigan, Niles Star, 05 Dec 2006), Niles District Library, 620 East Main Street, Niles, MI.

976 U.S., Social Security Applications and Claims Index, 1936-2007, Ancestry.com, Helen Marie McGraw Pegan Richer.

977 Indiana, Death Certificates, 1899-2011, Ancestry.com, Hazel Marie Richer, Indiana death cert. #043501.

978 Find A Grave—Mission Hills Memorial Chapel, Crematory & Gardens, North Niles, Howard Twp., Cass Co., Michigan, Find A Grave.com, Hazel M. Richer, Find A Grave Memorial #182189808.

979 Obituary of James Roger Bakeman (Niles, Michigan, Niles Star, 31 Mar 2001), Niles District Library, 620 East Main Street, Niles, MI.

980 U.S., Social Security Applications and Claims Index, 1936-2007, Ancestry.com, James Roger Bakeman.

981 Find A Grave—Mission Hills Memorial Chapel, Crematory & Gardens, North Niles, Howard Twp., Cass Co., Michigan,

981 Find A Grave.com, James R. Bakeman, Find A Grave Memorial #182190206.

982 Obituary of Rebecca A. Bakeman (Niles, Michigan, Niles Star, 17 Jan 1978), Niles District Library, 620 East Main Street, Niles, MI.

983 Obituary of Ronald Gene PeGan II (Goshen, Indiana, Goshen News, 07 Jul 2012), Goshen Public Library-Central Library, 601 South 5th Street, Goshen, IN.

984 Find-A-Grave—Chapel Hill Memorial Gardens, Osceola, Penn Twp., St. Joseph Co., Indiana, Find-A-Grave.com, Brian Lee Reed, Find A Grave Memorial #67477625.

985 South Bend Genealogical Society Marriage Record Index List, Mishawaka, Indiana, South Bend Genealogical Society, Mishawaka-Penn Harris Library, 209 Lincoln Way East, Mishawaka, IN; Robert Clarence Masterman Jr. and Sue Ann Pegan, St. Joseph County, Indiana Marriage Records, Vol. 82, lic. #22423; Online database: https://www.sbags.org/marriagesrch.php

986 Indiana Marriages, 1958-2015, Indiana State Library, Genealogy, 315 West Ohio Street, Indianapolis, IN, "Rbrt" C. Masterman Jr. and Sue A. Pegan, St. Joseph County, Indiana Marriage Records; Online database: https://www.statelib.lib.in.us/INMarriages93to02/in_marriages_search.asp

987 Obituary of Robert C. Masterman Jr. (Niles, Michigan, Niles Star, 28 Apr 2014), Niles District Library, 620 East Main Street, Niles, MI.

988 Obituary of Jerome T. McQuaid (South Bend, Indiana, South Bend Tribune, 13 Jun 2006), St. Joseph County Public Library, 304 South Main Street, South Bend, IN.

989 Find A Grave—Mission Hills Memorial Chapel, Crematory & Gardens, North Niles, Howard Twp., Cass Co., Michigan, Find A Grave.com, Jerome T. McQuaid, Find A Grave Memorial #182216385.

990 Find A Grave—Silverbrook Cemetery, Niles, Niles Twp., Berrien Co., Michigan, Find A Grave.com, Claudine L. PeGan, Find A Grave Memorial #59306609.

991 Phone interview with the son of Nelson Michael PeGan, Brownsburg, IN, 06 Feb 2015.

992 Obituary of Donna Lynn Haste (PeGan) (Greenfield, Indiana, Greenfield Daily Reporter, 12 Nov 2015), Hancock County Public Library, 900 West McKenzie Road, Greenfield, IN.

993 Find A Grave—Fairview Cemetery, Bluffton, Wells Co., Indiana, Find A Grave.com, Margaret Roll Christensen, Find A Grave Memorial #68075223.

994 Virginia, Marriage Records, 1936-2014, Ancestry.com, Clarence T. Christensen and Margaret Roll, York County, Virginia Marriage Records, lic. #3646.

995 Obituary of Clarence T. Christensen (Bluffton, Indiana, Bluffton News Banner, 22 Aug 1990), Wells County Public Library, 200 West Washington Street, Bluffton, IN.

996 U.S., Social Security Applications and Claims Index, 1936-2007, Ancestry.com, Clarence Thomas Christensen.

997 Montana, Birth Index, 1870-1986, Ancestry.com, Clarence Thomas Christensen, Valley County Birth Records, birth cert. VAL 244.

998 U.S., Department of Veterans Affairs BIRLS Death File, 1850-2010, Ancestry.com, Clarence Christensen.

999 Find A Grave—Fairview Cemetery, Bluffton, Wells Co., Indiana, Find A Grave.com, Clarence T. Christensen, Find A Grave Memorial #21180842.

1000 Find A Grave—Fairview Cemetery, Bluffton, Wells Co., Indiana, Find A Grave.com, A. Louise Lutz, Find A Grave Memorial #68074482.

1001 Indiana, Marriages 1811-2007, FamilySearch.org, Dwight R. Lutz and Louise Lydy, Wells County, Indiana Marriage Records, Vol. 19. pg. 37.

1002 Indiana, Death Certificates, 1899-2011, Ancestry.com, Dwight R. Lutz, Indiana death cert. #76-015488.

1003 Obituary of Dwight Lutz Sr. (Bluffton, Indiana, Bluffton News Banner, 15 Apr 1976), Wells County Public Library, 200 West Washington Street, Bluffton, IN.

1004 Find A Grave—Fairview Cemetery, Bluffton, Wells Co., Indiana, Find A Grave.com, Dwight R. Lutz Sr., Find A Grave Memorial #68074387.

1005 Find A Grave—Fairview Cemetery, Bluffton, Wells Co., Indiana, Find A Grave.com, Charles "Wayne" Lydy, Find-A-Grave Memorial #68094806.

1006 Indiana, Marriages 1811-2007, FamilySearch.org, Charles Wayne Lydy and Dorothy Mae Crickmore, Wells County, Indiana Marriage Records, Application, Vol. M, pg. 43.

1007 Obituary of Cheryl A. Lee (Bluffton, Indiana, Goodwin-Cale & Harnish Memorial Chapel, 03 Jun 2017); Online database: http://www.thegmcfamily.com/m/?p=memorial&id=1970783.

1008 California, Death Index, 1940-1997, Ancestry.com, Maria Lydy.

1009 Find A Grave—Davis Memorial Park Cemetery, Las Vegas, Clark Co., Nevada, Find A Grave.com, Maria Lydy, Find A Grave Memorial #117599372.

1010 Find A Grave—Fairview Cemetery, Bluffton, Wells Co., Indiana, Find A Grave.com, Dale E. Lydy, Find A Grave Memorial #21181104.

1011 Obituary of Dale Lydy (Bluffton, Indiana, Bluffton News Banner, 04 Feb 1998), Wells County Public Library, 200 West Washington Street, Bluffton, IN.

1012 Virginia, Divorce Records, 1918-2014, Ancestry.com, Dale E. Lydy and Mattie L. Lydy, state file #1957-6290.

1013 England & Wales, Civil Registration Marriage Index, 1916-2005, Ancestry.com, Dale E. Lydy and (Pearl) Yates, Liverpool, Vol. !0d, pg. 549.

1014 Indiana, Marriage Certificates, 1917-2005, Ancestry.com, Dale Edmond Lydy and Valerie Ruby Mann, Wells County, Indiana Marriage Records, Vol. 26, pg. 363, lic. #67-008574.

1015 Wells County, Indiana Marriages, Wells County, Indiana Clerk's Office, 102 West Market Street, Suite 201, Bluffton, IN, Dale E. Lydy and Valerie R. Mann, Wells County, Indiana Marriage Records, Vol. 26, pg. 263.

1016 Obituary of Valerie R. Lydy (Bluffton, Indiana, Bluffton News Banner, 10 Aug 1987), Wells County Public Library, 200 West Washington Street, Bluffton, IN.

1017 Indiana, Death Certificates, 1899-2011, Ancestry.com, Valerie R. Lydy, Indiana death cert. #87-031488.

1018 Find A Grave—Fairview Cemetery, Bluffton, Wells Co., Indiana, Find A Grave.com, Valerie Lydy, Find A Grave Memorial #71026920.

1019 Indiana, Death Certificates, 1899-2011, Ancestry.com, Forrest E. DeBolt, Indiana death cert. #040403.

1020 Indiana, Birth Certificates, 1907-1940, Ancestry.com, Forrest Edwin Debolt, Adams County, Indiana Birth Records, birth cert. #33709.

1021 Obituary of Forrest E. DeBolt (Bluffton, Indiana, Bluffton News Banner, 26 Apr 2008), Wells County Public Library, 200 West Washington Street, Bluffton, IN.

1022 Find A Grave—Fairview Cemetery, Bluffton, Wells Co., Indiana, Find A Grave.com, Forrest E. DeBolt, Find A Grave Memorial #68074959.

1023 Find A Grave—Oak Lawn Cemetery, Ossian, Jefferson Twp., Wells Co., Indiana, Find A Grave.com, Bonnie I. Lydy, Find A Grave Memorial #53696962.

1024 Obituary of O. Joan Schorey (Bluffton, Indiana, Bluffton News Banner, 02 Dec 1998), Wells County Public Library, 200 West Washington Street, Bluffton, IN.

1025 Find A Grave—Fairview Cemetery, Bluffton, Wells Co., Indiana, Find A Grave.com, O. Joan Schorey, Find A Grave Memorial #21180894.

1026 Indiana, Marriages 1811-2007, FamilySearch.org, Richard Schorey and Joan Lydy, Wells County, IndIana Marriage Records, Application, Vol. 21, pg. 437.

1027 Wells County, Indiana Marriages, Wells County, Indiana Clerk's Office, 102 West Market Street, Suite 201, Bluffton, IN, Richard K. Schorey and Joan Lydy, Marriage Book 21, pg. 437.

1028 Obituary of Richard K. Schorey Sr. (Bluffton, Indiana, Bluffton News Banner, 28 Sep 2000), Wells County Public Library, 200 West Washington Street, Bluffton, IN.

1029 Indiana, Birth Certificates, 1907-1940, Ancestry.com, Richard Kay Schorey, Wells County, Indiana Birth Records, birth cert. #25532.

1030 U.S., Social Security Applications and Claims Index, 1936-2007, Ancestry.com, Richard Kaye Schorey.

1031 Find A Grave—Woodlawn Cemetery, Auburn, Union Twp., DeKalb Co., Indiana, Find A Grave.com, Richard K. Schorey, Find A Grave Memorial #145269501.

1032 Obituary of Richard K. Schorey Jr. (Bluffton, Indiana, Bluffton News Banner, 07 Jul 2000), Wells County Public Library, 200 West Washington Street, Bluffton, IN.

1033 U.S., Social Security Applications and Claims Index, 1936-2007, Ancestry.com, Richard Kaye Schorey.

1034 Indiana Marriages, 1958-2015, Indiana State Library, Genealogy, 315 West Ohio Street, Indianapolis, IN; Jack F. Lewis and Sharon Y. Bender, Wells County, Indiana Marriage Records; Online database: https://www.statelib.lib.in.us/INMarriages93to02/in_marriages_search.asp

1035 Obituary of Jack F. Lewis (Rochester, Indiana, Rochester Sentinel, 09 Aug 2017) Fulton County Library, 320 West 7th Street, Rochester, IN.

1036 Find A Grave—Mount Hope Athens Cemetery, Athens, Henry Twp., Fulton Co., Indiana, Find A Grave.com, Jackie Franklin "Jack" Lewis, Find A Grave Memorial #182272130.

1037 Indiana, Marriage Certificates, 1917-2005, Ancestry.com, Perry Graham Jr, and Sharon Yvonne Lewis, Wells County, Indiana Marriage Records, Vol. 38, pg. 135, lic. #045043.

1038 Obituary of Perry Graham (Bluffton, Indiana, Goodwin—Cale & Harnish Memorial Chapel, Memorial Networks); Online database: http://www.thegmcfamily.com/memsol.cgi?user_id=185

1039 Find A Grave, Perry Graham, cremated, Find A Grave Memorial #170426597.

1040 U.S., Public Records Index, 1950-1993, Volume 1, Ancestry.com, Perry J. Graham, Bluffton, Indiana.

1041 Indiana Marriages, 1958-2015 Indiana State Library, Genealogy, 315 West Ohio Street, Indianapolis, IN; Richard Gardenour and (Daughter) Bender, Wells County, Indiana Marriage Records; Online database: https://www.statelib.lib.in.us/INMarriages93to02/in_marriages_search.asp

1042 Texas, Death Certificates, 1903-1982, Ancestry.com, Richard Dean Gardenour, death cert. #057-01-3, 01790.

1043 "New Haven Man, 24, Killed By Gunman In Scuffle In Dallas" (Fort Wayne, Indiana, Fort Wayne Journal-Gazette, 04 Jan 1968), Genealogy Center, Allen County Public Library, 900 Library Plaza, Fort Wayne, IN.

1044 "Resident's son slain Dallas" (Garland, Texas, Garland Daily News, 04 Jan 1968); NewspaperArchive, Online database: https://access-newspaperarchive-com.sjcpl.idm.oclc.org/us/texas/garland/garland-daily-news/1968/01-04?tag=gardenour&rtserp=tags/gardenour?ndt=ex&pd=4&py=1968&pm=1&search=ymd

1045 "Hoosier Killed" (Tipton, Indiana, Tipton Tribune, 05 Jan 1968); NewspaperArchive, Online database: https://access-newspaperarchive-com.sjcpl.idm.oclc.org/us/indiana/tipton/tipton-daily-tribune/1968/01-05/page-2?tag=gardenour&rtserp=tags/gardenour?pc=29267&psi=38&pci=7d

1046 Find A Grave—Fairview Cemetery, Bluffton, Wells Co., Indiana, Find A Grave.com, Richard Dean Gardenour, Find A Grave Memorial #68075378.

1047 (Indiana) Marriages, 1958-2015, Indiana State Library, Genealogy, 315 West Ohio Street, Indianapolis, IN; Gerald R. Weaver and Michele Gardenour, Wells County, Indiana

Marriage Records; Online database: https://www.statelib.lib.in.us/INMarriages93to02/in_marriages_search.asp

1048 Indiana, Death Certificates, 1899-2011, Ancestry.com, Jerry R. Weaver, Indiana death cert. #037242.

1049 U.S., Social Security Applications and Claims Index, 1936-2007, Ancestry.com, Jerry Ray Weaver.

1050 Find A Grave—Gearnand Cemetery, Reiffsburg, Harrison Twp., Wells Co., Indiana, Find A Grave.com, Gerald Ray "Jerry" Weaver, Find A Grave Memorial #62807727.

1051 Ohio, County Marriages, 1789-2013, FamilySearch.org, Alfred Groves and Mary Hunter, Highland County, Ohio Marriage Records, Vol. 23, pg. 67, lic. #40176.

1052 Ohio, Birth Index, 1908-1964, Ancestry.com, "Alford" Groves, state file #1932092314.

1053 Obituary of Richard Lee Kinnison (Hillsboro, Ohio, Highland County Press, 03 Mar 2014), Highland County District Library, 10 Willettsville Pike, Hillsboro, OH.

1054 Find A Grave—New Market Baptist Church Cemetery, New Market Twp., Highland Co., Ohio, Find A Grave.com, Richard Lee Kinnison, Find A Grave Memorial #125825834.

1055 Find A Grave—Evergreen Cemetery, Girard Twp., Branch Co., Michigan, Find A Grave.com, Gary W. Roush, Find A Grave Memorial #107530974.

1056 Obituary of Sandra Ellen (Burritt) Roush (Coldwater, Michigan, Coldwater Daily Reporter, 16 Jun 2011), Branch County Library, Coldwater Branch, 10 East Chicago Street, Coldwater, MI.

1057 California Birth Index, 1905-1995, Ancestry.com, Joseph Vindiola.

1058 Find A Grave—Bellevue Memorial Park Cemetery, Ontario, San Bernardino Co., California, Find A Grave.com, Joseph Vindiola, Find A Grave Memorial #151243792.

1059 Obituary of Joseph "Joey Bear" Vindiola (Ontario, California, Draper Mortuary, no date) Draper Mortuary, *11 North Mountain Avenue, Ontario, CA; Online database: https://www.dignitymemorial.com/obituaries/ontario-ca/joey-vindiola-6183876

1060 Obituary of Betty Lee Moore (Hillsboro, Ohio, Hillsboro Press-Gazette, 11 Oct 2016), Highland County District Library, 10 Willettsville Pike, Hillsboro, OH.

1061 Ohio, Birth Index, 1908-1964, Ancestry.com, Bette Lee Rhoads, state file #1953162154.

1062 Ohio, Death Records, 1908-1932, 1938-2007, Ancestry.com, Robert A. Moore, death cert. #066981.

1063 Obituary of Michael Wallace (Lima, Ohio, Chamberlain-Huckriede Funeral Home, 04 Jun 2015) Chamberlain-Huckriede Funeral Home, 920 North Cable Road, Lima OH; Online database: https://www.chamberlainhuckeriede.com/notices/Michael-Wallace

1064 Obituary of Matthew Thomas Shuttleworth (Wilmington, Ohio, Wilmington News Journal, 16 Jan 2012) Wilmington Public Library of Clinton County, 268 North South Street, Wilmington, OH.

1065 Obituary of Jessie Lee Kinyoun (St. Petersburg, Florida, St. Petersburg Times, 11 Mar 2002), Largo Library, 201 Highland Avenue NE, Largo, FL.

1066 Find A Grave—Riverside Cemetery, Troy, Concord Twp., Miami Co., Ohio, Find A Grave.com, William Jeffrey Seitz, Find A Grave Memorial #151480555.

1067 U.S. Veterans' Gravesites, ca. 1775-2006, Ancestry.com, Danny E. Cowgill.

1068 Find A Grave—Riverside Cemetery, Gas City, Mill Twp., Grant Co., Indiana, Find A Grave.com, Danny Edward Cowgill, Find A Grave Memorial #51752028.

1069 Obituary of Tonya Cowgill (Gas City, Indiana, Needham-Storey-Wampner Funeral Home, 20 Oct 2016), Needham-Storey-Wampner Funeral Home, 400 East Main Street, Gas City, IN. https://nswcares.com/tribute/details/5744/Tonya-Cowgill/obituary.html.

1070 Find A Grave—Riverside Cemetery, Gas City, Mill Twp., Grant Co., Indiana, Find A Grave.com, Tonya May Carroll Cowgill, Find A Grave Memorial #171561887.

1071 Indiana: Marion Public Library Marriage Index, 1831-2008, Ancestry.com, Richard Lee Jones and (Daughter) Eastes.

1072 Indiana, Marriage Certificates, 1917-2005, Ancestry.com, Richard L. Jones and (Daughter) Eastes, Grant County Marriage Records, Vol. 83, pg. 341, lic. #74-049014.

1073 Obituary of Richard L. "Rick" Jones Sr. (Marion, Indiana, Owen-Weilert-Duncan Funeral Home, May 21, 2015), Owen-Weilert-Duncan Funeral Home, 2722 South Washington Street, Marion, IN; Online database: http://www.owenweilertduncan.com/site/richard-l-rick-jones-august-11-1956-may-15-2015/

1074 Find A Grave—Marion National Cemetery, Marion, Center Twp., Grant Co., Indiana, Find A Grave.com, Pvt. Richard Lee "Rick" Jones Sr., Find A Grave Memorial #146531128.

1075 Indiana: Marion Public Library Marriage Index, 1831-2008, Ancestry.com, Joseph Mitchell Eastes and Toni Rae Coffey.

1076 Indiana, Marriage Certificates, 1917-2005, Ancestry.com, Joseph Mitchell Eastes and Toni Rae Coffey, Grant County, Indiana Marriage Records, Vol. 118, pg. 453, lic. #007840.

1077 Obituary of Toni R. Eastes (Marion, Indiana, Marion Chronicle Tribune, 22 Nov 2003), Marion, Indiana Public Library, 600 South Washington Street, Marion, IN, Marion (IN) Chronicle, pub. 22 Nov 2003.

1078 U.S., Social Security Applications and Claims Index, 1936-2007, Ancestry.com, Toni Rae Jacks Collins Coffey Bannister. Although the record does not reflect it, she died as Toni Rae Eastes.

1079 Indiana, Death Certificates, 1899-2011, Ancestry.com, Toni R. Eastes, Indiana death cert. #038234.

1080 Find A Grave—Riverside Cemetery, Gas City, Mill Twp., Grant Co., Indiana, Find A Grave.com, Toni R. Eastes, Find A Grave Memorial #10071931.

1081 Find A Grave—Crown Point Cemetery, Kokomo, Center Twp., Howard Co., Indiana, Find A Grave.com, Daniel Lee Jarvis, Find A Grave Memorial #45508976.

1082 Find A Grave—St. Paul's Lutheran Cemetery, Celina, Jefferson Twp., Mercer Co., Ohio, Robert L. Flowers, Find A Grave Memorial #29723109.

1083 Find A Grave—Walnut Grove Cemetery, Delphos, Marion Twp., Allen Co., Ohio, Find A Grave.com, Brandy Lee Flowers, Find A Grave Memorial #33608298.

1084 Find A Grave—Calvary Hill Cemetery and Mausoleum, Dallas Co., Texas, Find A Grave.com, Danette Lee Crossen, Find A Grave Memorial #172809821.

1085 Find A Grave—Oakwood Cemetery, Warsaw, Wayne Twp., Koscuisko Co., Indiana, Find A Grave.com, Brent C. PeGan, Find A Grave Memorial #142089045.

1086 Yusko, Nora R., "Today" and "A Concurrence of Miracles". iwillcarryyou, *A Journal of Unconditional Love*. The Angel Days. WordPress.com. 12 Jul 2015 and 15 Jul 2015. https://noraroseyusko.com/2015/07/12/today-3/ and https://noraroseyusko.com/2015/07/15/a-concurrence-of-miracles/

1087 Obituary of Stephine PeGan (Niles, Michigan, Niles Star, 02 Aug 1991), Niles District Library, 620 East Main Street, Niles, MI.

1088 Find A Grave—Mission Hills Memorial Chapel, Crematory & Gardens, North Niles, Howard Twp., Cass Co., Michigan, Find A Grave.com, Rebecca Bakeman, Find A Grave Memorial #182190281.

1089 Find A Grave—Grace Lawn Cemetery, Middlebury, Middlebury Twp., Elkhart Co., Indiana, Find A Grave.com, Ronald G. "Ronnie" PeGan II, Find A Grave Memorial #134709226.

1090 Indiana, Marriage Certificates, 1917-2005, Ancestry.com, Bobby Lee Poe and (Daughter) PeGan, Henry County, Indiana Marriage Records, Vol. 76, pg. 572, lic. #92-005718.

1091 U.S., Social Security Applications and Claims Index, 1936-2007, Ancestry.com, Bobby Lee Poe.

1092 Obituary of Bobby Poe (Greenfield, Indiana, Greenfield Daily Reporter, 01 Oct 2007), Hancock County Public Library, 900 West McKenzie Road, Greenfield, IN.

1093 Indiana, Death Certificates, 1899-2011, Ancestry.com, Bobby L. Poe, Indiana death cert. #037588.

1094 Obituary of Ashton James PeGan-Thiry (Stephenson, Michigan, Menominee County Journal, 12 Aug 2010), Menominee County Library, S319 Railroad Street, Stephenson, MI.

1095 Indiana, Marriage Certificates, 1917-2005, Ancestry.com, Robert A. Barnes and Myra Mae Johnson, Wells County, Indiana Marriage Records, Vol. 32, pg. 108, lic. 81-001897.

1096 U.S., Social Security Applications and Claims Index, 1936-2007, Ancestry.com, Robert A. Barnes.

1097 Indiana, Death Certificates, 1899-2011, Ancestry.com, Robert A. Barnes, Indiana death cert. #007904.

1098 Find A Grave—Elm Grove Cemetery, Bluffton, Wells Co., Indiana, Find A Grave.com, Robert A. Barnes, Find A Grave Memorial #43608705.

1099 Obituary of Holly Marie Johnson (Bluffton, Indiana, Bluffton News Banner, 13 Dec 1971), Wells County Public Library, 200 West Washington Street, Bluffton, IN.

1100 Indiana, Death Certificates, 1899-2011, Ancestry.com, Holly Marie Johnson, Indiana death cert. #71-047993.

1101 Find A Grave—Fairview Cemetery, Bluffton, Wells Co., Indiana, Find A Grave.com, Cheryl A. Lydy Lee, Find A Grave Memorial #179958248.

1102 Indiana Marriages, 1958-2015, Indiana State Library Genealogy 315 West Ohio Street, Indianapolis, IN; Samuel Ramsey and Cheryl A. Lydy, Dubois County, Indiana Marriage Records; Online database: https://www.statelib.lib.in.us/INMarriages93to02/in_marriages_search.asp

1103 Obituary of Samuel Robert Ramsey (Grove City, Pennsylvania, Allied News, 07 Jul 2010), Mercer Area Library, Grove City Community Library, 125 West Main Street, Grove City, PA.

1104 Find A Grave—Carpenter Cemetery, Springfield Twp., Mercer Co., Pennsylvania, Samuel R. Ramsey, Find A Grave Memorial #135338351.

1105 Indiana, Marriage Certificates, 1917-2005, Ancestry.com, Carl Duane Blumenhorst and Cheryl A. Ramsey, Blackford County, Indiana Marriage Records, lic. #80-042694.

1106 Indiana, Marriage Certificates, 1917-2005, Ancestry.com, Robbie Blumenhorst and Jennifer Hunt, Blackford County, Indiana Marriage Records, lic. #92-045005; Robbie Blumenhorst states his father, Carl D. Blumenhorst, was born in Bluffton, Indiana.

1107 Indiana, Death Certificates, 1899-2011, Ancestry.com, Carl Duane Blumenhorst, Indiana death cert. #83-000016.

1108 Find A Grave—Hillside Cemetery, Pennville, Penn Twp., Jay Co., Indiana, Find A Grave.com, Carl Duane Blumenhorst, Find A Grave Memorial #100447651.

1109 Indiana, Marriage Certificates, 1917-2005, Ancestry.com, Delbert J. Lee and Cheryl A. Blumenhorst, Adams County, Indiana Marriage Records, lic. #83-016524.

1110 Obituary of Delbert J. Lee (Bluffton, Indiana, Goodwin-Cale & Harnish Memorial Chapel, 24 Mar 2010); Online database: http://www.thegmcfamily.com/m/?p=memorial&id=185276.

1111 Find A Grave—Fairview Cemetery, Bluffton, Wells Co., Indiana, Find A Grave.com, Delbert J. Lee, Find A Grave Memorial #76279660.

1112 Find-A-Grave—Fairview Cemetery, Bluffton, Wells Co., Indiana, Find-A-Grave.com, Robert John Welsh, Find A Grave Memorial #71902587.

1113 Ohio Marriage Abstracts, 1970-1972-2007, Ancestry.com, Rocky L. Hunter and Joanne Lydy, Van Wert County, Ohio Marriage Records, Ohio state Vol. 13382, lic. #38013.

1114 Obituary of Rockey L. Hunter (Bluffton, Indiana, Bluffton News Banner, 28 Apr 1988), Wells County Public Library, 200 West Washington Street, Bluffton, IN.

1115 Ohio, Death Records, 1908-1932, 1938-2007, Ancestry.com, Rockey L. Hunter, death cert. #032167.

1116 Find A Grave—Mount Tabor Cemetery, Decatur, St. Mary's Twp., Adams Co., Indiana, Find A Grave.com, Rocky L. Hunter, Find A Grave Memorial #61000255.

1117 Indiana, Death Certificates, 1899-2011, Ancestry.com, Kari Ann Harrold, Indiana death cert. #84-030873.

1118 "Kari Harrold, 11, Dies from Bluffton River Rd. Smashup" (Bluffton, Indiana, Bluffton News Banner, 03 Aug 1984), Wells County Public Library, 200 West Washington Street, Bluffton, IN.

1119 Find A Grave—Fairview Cemetery, Bluffton, Wells Co., Indiana, Find A Grave.com, Richard K. "Rick" Schorey Jr., Find A Grave Memorial #68076368.

1120 Indiana, Marriage Certificates, 1917-2005, Ancestry.com, Richard Kay Schorey Jr. and Ruth Elaine Baxter, Wells County, Indiana Marriage Records, Vol. 28, pg. 138, lic. #71-050929.

1121 U.S., Social Security Applications and Claims Index, 1936-2007, Ancestry.com, Ruth Elaine Baxter (Schorey).

1122 Ohio, Birth Index, 1908-1964, Ancestry.com, Ruth E. Baxter, cert. #1953094190.

1123 Obituary of R. Elaine Schorey (Bluffton, Indiana, Bluffton News Banner, 27 Oct 1989), Wells County Public Library, 200 West Washington Street, Bluffton, IN.

1124 Indiana, Death Certificates, 1899-2011, Ancestry.com, "Elaine R." Schorey, Indiana death cert. #89-041807.

1125 Find A Grave—Fairview Cemetery, Bluffton, Wells Co., Indiana, Find A Grave.com, R. Elaine Baxter Schorey, Find A Grave Memorial #68076479.

1126 Find A Grave—Clinton County Memory Gardens, Union Twp., Clinton Co., Ohio, Find A Grave.com, Matthew Thomas "Mat" Shuttleworth, Find A Grave Memorial #83511726.

1127 Find A Grave—Jesse Lee Kinyoun, Find A Grave.com, Find A Grave Memorial #12742082.

1128 Find A Grave—Mission Hills Memorial Chapel, Crematory & Gardens, North Niles, Howard Twp., Cass Co., Michigan, Find A Grave.com, Stephine PeGan, Find A Grave Memorial #182189500.

1129 Obituary of Bentlee Andrew Poe Whitaker (Indianapolis, Indiana, G.H. Hermann Funeral Home, 12 Jan 2012), G.H. Hermann Funeral Home, 5141 Madison Avenue, Indianapolis, IN; Online database: http://www.ghherrmann.com/obituaries/Bentlee-Andrew-Poe-Whitaker?obId=2696442#/obituaryInfo

1130 Find A Grave—Oak Lawn Cemetery, Ossian, Jefferson Twp., Wells Co., Indiana, Find A Grave.com, Holly Marie Johnson, Find A Grave Memorial #53651538.

1131 Find A Grave—Fairview Cemetery, Bluffton, Wells Co., Indiana, Find A Grave.com, Kari Ann Harrold, Find A Grave Memorial #21180532.

[A] Indiana, Death Certificates, 1899-2011, Ancestry.com, Margaret Johnson Lafferty, Indiana death cert. #3 (no other numbers on the certificate).

[B] Crown Hill Cemetery Records, Margaret Johnson Lafferty, Crown Hill Cemetery, 700 West 38th Street, Indianapolis, IN.

[C] Find A Grave—Crown Hill Cemetery, Indianapolis, Marion Co., Indiana, Find A Grave.com, Margaret Johnson Lafferty, Find A Grave Memorial #5956107.

[D] Emails from Vikki Sorel, Ankenny, Iowa, Ann Miller Carr, author, Dec 2018.

[E] Obituary of Viola Jane Roush (Coldwater, Michigan, Coldwater Daily Reporter, 17 Aug 2018), Branch County Library, Coldwater Branch, 10 East Chicago Street, Coldwater, MI.

[D] Obituary of Mary P. Welch (Fort Wayne, Indiana, Fort Wayne Journal Gazette, 12 Nov 1993) Genealogy Center, Allen County Public Library, Allen County Public Library, 900 Library Plaza, Fort Wayne, IN.

[E] Obituary of Leo R. Baker (South Bend, Indiana, South Bend Tribune, 02 Apr 1964) South Bend-St. Joseph Co. Library, 304 South Main St., South Bend, IN.

[F] U.S., WWI Draft Registration Cards, 1917-1918, Ancestry.com, Leo Ray Baker, Van Buren, Indiana.

[G] Find A Grave—Grant Memorial Park Cemetery, Marion, Center Twp., Grant Co., Indiana. Find A Grave.com, Leo R. Baker, Find A Grave Memorial #8547387.

[H] Indiana Birth Certificates, 1907-1940, Ancestry.com, Milford Earnest Baker, Grant County, Indiana Birth Records, birth cert. #15815.

[I] McLaughlin Funeral Home Records, Fred E. Baker, McLaughlin Funeral Home, 2301 Lafayette Avenue, St Louis, MO.

[J] Obituary of Fred E. Baker (St. Louis, Missouri, St. Louis Post Dispatch, 23 Sep 1971), St. Louis County Library, 1640 South Lindbergh Road, St. Louis, MO.

[K] Emails from Vikki Sorel, Ankenny, Iowa, Ann Miller Carr, author, Dec 2018.

[L] Indiana, Marriages 1811-2007, FamilySearch.org, Truman Pearson and Mattie Oliver, Howard County, Indiana Marriage Records, Vol. 35, pg. 302-3.

[M] Birth Announcement of Daughter Pearson (Muncie Star Press, Muncie, Indiana, 01 Mar 1943), Muncie Public Library, Maring-Hunt Branch, 2005 South High Street, Muncie, IN.

[N] Obituary of Ted D. Welch (Fort Wayne, Indiana, Fort Wayne News Sentinel, 07 Aug 1989) Genealogy Center, Allen County Public Library, Allen County Public Library, 900 Library Plaza, Fort Wayne, IN.

[O] Web: Marion County, Indiana, Marriage Index, 1925- 2012, Ancestry.com, Milford Baker and Etta L. Uhls.

[P] Kentucky, Birth Index, 1911-1999, Ancestry.com, Etta L. Uhls, Simpson Co., Kentucky, Vol. 17, cert. #8199.

[Q] Indiana, Death Certificates, 1908-2011, Ancestry.com, Etta L. Davidson, death cert. #95-036550.

[R] Find A Grave—Floral Park Cemetery, Indianapolis, Marion Co, Indiana. Find A Grave.com, Etta L. Davidson, Find A Grave Memorial #128663055.

[S] Find A Grave—Lake Charles Park Cemetery, Bel-Nor, St. Louis Co., Missouri. Find A Grave.com, Violet E. McCain, Find A Grave Memorial #168832892.

[T] Obituary of Violet E. McCain (St. Louis, Missouri, St. Louis Post Dispatch, 29 Mar 1981), St. Louis County Library, 1640 South Lindbergh Road, St. Louis, MO.

[U] Indiana Birth Certificates, 1907-1940, Ancestry.com, Robert Bernard Baker, Marion County, Indiana Birth Records, birth cert. #18381.

[V] Find A Grave—Evergreen Memorial Park Cemetery, Tucson, Pima Co., Arizona. Find A Grave.com, Robert B. Baker, Find A Grave Memorial #128663055.

[W] Obituary of Robert B. Baker (Tucson, Arizona, Arizona Daily Star, 28 Mar 1973), Pima County Library, Joel D. Valdez Main Library, 101 North Stone Avenue, Tucson, AZ.

[X] Railroad Retirement Board Benefits Application, Fred E. Baker, St. Louis, Missouri, August 7, 1938, #493761, PS 381; Beneficiary Violet Nordeica Baker, daughter, born November 25, 1936. National Archives and Records Administration, National Archives-Atlanta, 5780 Jonesboro Road, Morrow, GA.

[Y] Find A Grave—Find A Grave.com, Lake Charles Park Cemetery, Bel-Nor, St. Louis Co., Missouri. Violet Nordeica McCain, Find A Grave Memorial #168841652.

[Z] Reports of Deaths of American Citizens Abroad, Ancestry.com, Violet Nordica McCain, died June 28, 1960; reported by the American Consulate, Tampico, Mexico, July 8, 1960; #212.113; 7-860.

[AA] Obituary of Violet Nordeica McCain (St. Louis, Missouri, St. Louis Globe Democrat, 02 Jul 1960), St. Louis County Library, 1640 South Lindbergh Road, St. Louis, MO.

[BB] Obituary of Viola Jane Roush (Coldwater, Michigan, Coldwater Daily Reporter, 17 Aug 2018), Branch County Library, Coldwater Branch, 10 East Chicago Street, Coldwater, MI.

[CC] Obituary Carl Weber Jaeger (Fort Wayne, Indiana, Fort Wayne Journal Gazette, 05 Dec 2019) Genealogy Center, Allen County Public Library, Allen County Public Library, 900 Library Plaza, Fort Wayne, IN.

[DD] Indiana Birth Certificates, 1907-1940, Ancestry.com, Carl Weber Jaeger, Allen County, Indiana Birth Records, birth cert. #48517.

[EE] Find A Grave—Lakewood Cemetery, Holland, Holland Twp., Ottawa Co., Michigan. Find A Grave.com, Carl W. Jaeger, Find A Grave Memorial #205236755.

[FF] Web: Marion County, Indiana, Marriage Index, 1925- 2012, Ancestry.com, Robert B. Baker and Shirley A. Lang

[GG] Indiana Birth Certificates, 1907-1940, Ancestry.com, Shirley Ann Lang, Marion County, Indiana Birth Records, birth cert. #4653.

[HH] Find A Grave—Evergreen Memorial Park Cemetery, Tucson, Pima Co., Arizona. Find A Grave.com, Shirley Guyton, Find A Grave Memorial #144731238.

[II] Obituary of Shirley Guyton (Tucson, Arizona, Arizona Daily Star, 09 Apr 2015), Pima County Library, Joel D. Valdez Main Library, 101 North Stone Avenue, Tucson, AZ.

[JJ] Find A Grave—Evergreen Memorial Park Cemetery, Tucson, Pima Co., Arizona. Find A Grave.com, Robert T. Baker, Find A Grave Memorial #68973017.

[KK] Obituary of Robert T. Baker (Tucson, Arizona, Arizona Daily Star, 15 Sep 2008), Pima County Library, Joel D. Valdez Main Library, 101 North Stone Avenue, Tucson, AZ.

[LL] Illinois, Cook County Birth Certificates, Donald Fred Bonacker, Maywood, birth cert. #84, FamilySearch.org.

[MM] Obituary of Donald F. Bonacker, Hurson Funeral Home, 4001 Roosevelt Road, Hillside, IL; www.hursen.com/obituary/donald-bonacker.

[NN] Find A Grave—Arlington Cemetery, Elmhurst, DuPage Co., Illinois. Find A Grave.com, Donald F. Bonacker, Find A Grave Memorial #197331795.

[OO] Obituary of Shelby Jean Burk (Coldwater, Michigan, The Daily Reporter, 07 Nov 2018), Branch County Library, Coldwater Branch, 10 East Chicago Street, Coldwater, MI.

[PP] Find A Grave—Centerville Cemetery, Centerville, Leon Co., Texas. Find A Grave.com, Jean Shoup Burk, Find A Grave Memorial #194531121.

[QQ] Texas Birth Index, 1903-1997, Ancestry.com, Zachary James Reagan.

[RR] Find A Grave—Memorial Oaks Cemetery, Houston, Harris Co., Texas. Find A Grave.com, Zachary James Reagan, Find A Grave Memorial #16213075.

[SS] Texas Death Index, 1903-2000, Ancestry.com, Zachary James Reagan.

Mary Ann Pegan

1. **Mary Ann**[5] **Pegan** (*Robert A.*[4], *Andrew*[3], *Andrew*[2] *Pagan, James*[1]) was born on November 7, 1815, in Gallia Co., Ohio or Fairview, Union Twp., Highland Co., Ohio?[1] She was the daughter of Robert A. Pegan and Christina or Christiana Ingle. Mary Ann died in Bloomfield Twp., Logan Co., Ohio, on May 2, 1896, at age 80.[2] She was buried in Rea Cemetery, Bloomfield Twp., Logan Co., Ohio.[3]

Mary Ann married **Abraham Coover** on February 10, 1836, in Miami Co., Ohio.[1, 4] They had two children. Abraham Coover was born in Upper Dickinson Twp., Cumberland Co., Pennsylvania, on August 30, 1813.[5] Abraham reached age 37 and died in Upper Dickinson Twp., Cumberland Co., Pennsylvania, on May 10, 1851.[5] He was buried in Huntsdale Church of the Brethren/Dunkard Cemetery, Upper Dickinson Twp., Cumberland Co., Pennsylvania.[5]

Interestingly, the Robert and Christina "Engle" Pegan family bible has the marriage of Abraham Coover and Mary Pegan occurring on February 10, 1836, officiated by Rev. "Baritt".[1] However, the civil marriage records in Miami County, Ohio has them wed on January 10, 1836 by Rev. Barrett, who entered the marriage on March 15, 1836.[4] It is not clear which date is correct, but, given that it was recorded in March, it is probably the one in the bible is correct and the minister wrote the wrong date in the civil marriage registry.

Abraham and Mary Ann Pegan Coover are enumerated in Miami Twp., Logan Co., Ohio in 1840 (*Census Place: Miami, Logan, Ohio; Roll: 409; Page: 34; Image: 76*). There is a one in col. 5 and a one in col. 18. This would be one male (Abraham) and one female (Mary Ann) both age 20-30.

By 1849, however, Mary Ann's mother, Christina/Christiana Ingle Pegan is residing with the Abraham Coovers, despite seemingly still owning her house.[6] Abraham Coover says on a deed that Christina Pegan has built "a tenement" (perhaps an addition) to his house and the two agree that she can stay there permanently unless he sells the property. If he sells the house, he has to give her $50.[7] Abraham Coover does sell the house less than six months later, on February 28, 1850.[8] Then he and Mary Ann move to his former home, Upper Dickinson Twp., Cumberland Co., Pennsylvania, where many of his relatives still resided.

In 1850, Abraham and Mary Ann Pegan Coover are found in Upper Dickenson Twp., Cumberland Co., Pennsylvania (*Census Place: Upper Dickinson, Cumberland, Pennsylvania; Roll: M432_772; Page: 113B; Image: 233*). In the household are Abraham Coover, age 39, born Pennsylvania, and Mary Ann Pegan Coover, 39, William Coover, nine and Christiana Coover, six, all born in Ohio. No occupation is listed for Abraham, but he was known to be a farmer. As he died the next year, perhaps he was ill.

After Abraham Coover, died in May 1851, Mary Ann Pegan Coover and her two children returned to Logan Co., Ohio.

Mary Ann Pegan married **John Wagoner** on February 24, 1852, in Logan Co., Ohio.[9] They had no children. John Wagoner was born in Fairfield Co., Ohio?, in 1818.[10] He reached age 68 and died in Bloomfield Twp., Logan Co., Ohio, on March 3, 1886.[10, 11] John was buried in Rea Cemetery, Bloomfield Twp., Logan Co., Ohio.[11]

Upon her marriage to John Wagoner, Mary Ann became a stepmother to John Waggoner's daughter by his first marriage (Lydia Wagoner, later wife of John Henry Nothstine).

John's surname is sometimes seen as "Waggoner".

In 1860, John and Mary Ann Pegan Coover Wagoner are found in Bloomfield Twp., Logan Co., Ohio (*Census Place: Bloomfield, Logan, Ohio; Roll: M653_1000; Page: 114; Image: 231*). In the household are John Wagoner, age 35, a farmer, and his wife, Mary Ann Pegan Coover Wagoner. 30. For some reason, their ages are incorrect. With them are John's daughter by his first wife Margaret Slough, Lydia Wagoner, age 12, and "Christiana Wagoner", 14, who is actually Chrystiana Coover. All were born in Ohio.

In 1870, John and Mary Ann Pegan Coover Wagoner are again found in Bloomfield Twp., Logan Co., Ohio *(Census Place: Bloomfield, Logan, Ohio; Roll: M593_1234; Page: 8A; Image: 24)*. The only ones in the home are John Wagoner, 51, farmer, and Mary Ann Pegan Coover Wagoner, age 55. Both were born in Ohio.

John and Mary Ann Pegan Coover "Waggoner" are still living in Bloomfield Twp., Logan Co., Ohio in 1880 *(Census Place: Bloomfield, Logan, Ohio; Roll: 1041; Page: 8D; Enumeration District: 111; Image: 0019)*. John "Waggoner" is age 63 who is now a justice of the peace, says he was born in Ohio and his parents were born in Pennsylvania. Mary Ann Pegan Coover "Waggoner" is age 66, also born in Ohio with her parents born in Pennsylvania.

John and Mary Ann Pegan Coover Wagoner are buried in Rea Cemetery in that same township, along with Mary Ann's son-in-law and daughter, Andrew J. and Chrystiana Coover Smith and some of their children.

According to information on the Rea Cemetery site on Find A Grave, Mary Ann Pegan Coover Wagoner was born in Auglaize County, Ohio, but this is highly doubtful.[3] According to the terms of the Treaty of Greenville in 1795, the area that was eventually to become Auglaize Co. belonged to Native Americans. Settlement by others wasn't allowed until the Treaty of Maumee Rapids in 1817.[12] Some of Mary Ann Pegan Coover Waggoner's descendants say she was born in Gallia County, Ohio, where her great-uncle, John Pagan, son of Andrew Pagan/Pegan Sr., resided.

Children of Mary Ann Pegan and Abraham Coover:

+ 2 m I. **William**[6] **Coover** was born in Logansville, Pleasant Twp., Logan Co., Ohio, on September 4, 1841.[13] He died in Jefferson Twp., Logan Co., Ohio, on March 8, 1875.[13, 14]

+ 3 f II. **Chrystiana**[6] **Coover** was born in Logansville, Pleasant Twp., Logan Co., Ohio, on September 25, 1846.[15] She died in Bloomfield Twp., Logan Co., Ohio, on September 11, 1919.[15]

6th Generation

2. William[6] Coover (*Mary Ann[5] Pegan, Robert A.[4], Andrew[3], Andrew[2] Pagan, James[1]*) was born on September 4, 1841, in Logansville, Pleasant Twp., Logan Co., Ohio.[13] He was the son of Abraham Coover and Mary Ann Pegan (1). William died in Jefferson Twp., Logan Co., Ohio, on March 8, 1875, at age 33.[13, 14] He was buried in Goshen-Quaker Cemetery, Jefferson Twp., Logan Co., Ohio.[13]

William Coover is enumerated in Jefferson Twp., Logan Co., Ohio in 1860 *(Census Place: Jefferson, Logan, Ohio; Roll: M653_1000; Page: 140; Image: 283)*. William Coover, age 18, is living and working on a farm owned by Simon and Margaret Elliott. He is listed as born in Pennsylvania, but this is wrong—he was born in Ohio.

William Coover fought in the Civil War, in Company E, 82nd Ohio Infantry and was seriously wounded at Antietam.[14] He received a Civil War invalid's pension, filed for on October 4, 1864, and, after his death, his widow Elizabeth Watkins Coover files for a pension as well on May 1, 1875.[16]

William married **Elizabeth Watkins** on November 29, 1864, in Logan Co., Ohio.[17] They had two children. Elizabeth Watkins was born in Jefferson Twp., Logan Co., Ohio, on June 8, 1843.[18] She reached age 85 and died in Zanesfield, Jefferson Twp., Logan Co., Ohio, on September 29, 1928.[18] Elizabeth was buried in Goshen-Quaker Cemetery, Jefferson Twp., Logan Co., Ohio.[18, 19]

William Coover is found in 1870 in Valley Brook Twp., Osage Co., Kansas *(Census Place: Valley Brook, Osage, Kansas; Roll: M593_440; Page: 317B; Image: 638)*. William Coover, age 28, is a carpenter; his wife, "Emma B." (Elizabeth Watkins Coover) is 26. They have two children, "Matthias" (actually Melvin), five, and "Mary J." (Mary Iva), two. All were born in Ohio. Some names are incorrect, probably because the census taker did not talk to the Coovers themselves but asked a neighbor for the information (a practice sometimes done in that era).

William Coover survived the Civil War with a "minnie ball" or rifle bullet in his lung. But, eventually complications from his wound caused his death.[14]

Melvin Lester Coover, the "Matthias" in this census, says on the 1900 census form that he was born in Kansas. One of his daughters also consistently gives her father Melvin's birthplace as Kansas. But he was born in Ohio, as was his sister Mary Iva.

Elizabeth Watkins Coover is enumerated in the 1880 census in Jefferson Twp., Logan Co., Ohio *(Census Place: Jefferson, Logan, Ohio; Roll: 1041; Page: 42C; Enumeration District: 114; Image: 0086)*. Elizabeth Watkins Coover is listed as the head of household; she is age 37 and a widow. With her are children Melvin, listed as "Melville", 14, and Mary, 11. They were all born in Ohio, as were their parents. Living with them is Elizabeth's widowed mother, Hannah Watkins, 67, who says she was born in Ohio and her parents in North Carolina.

In May 1895, Elizabeth Watkins Coover married Oliver Fawcett, the father of her son-in-law, Elba Jonathan Fawcett. But her second marriage is short-lived, as Oliver dies that October.[20] Elizabeth remarries for a third time to George Pellett, a widower, in Oct 1897.[21]

In 1900, George and Elizabeth Watkins Coover Fawcett Pellett are found in Monroe Twp., Logan Co., Ohio *(Census Place: Monroe, Logan, Ohio; Roll: 1294; Page: 9B; Enumeration District: 118)*. In the home are George Pellett, age 73, born Aug 1826 in Ohio, a farmer who says he was born in Ohio, his father in Pennsylvania and his mother in New Jersey. Elizabeth B. Watkins Coover Fawcett Pellett, 56, says she was born in Jun 1843 in Ohio, where her parents were born. The couple states they have been married two years, and that Elizabeth has borne two children, both still living.

Elizabeth Watkins Coover Fawcett Pellett, age 66, is residing in Zanesfield, Jefferson Twp., Logan Co., Ohio in 1910 on Main Street *(Census Place: Jefferson, Logan, Ohio; Roll: T624_1204; Page: 3A; Enumeration District: 0124; Image: 680)*. She is a widow, who says she has her own income and that she and her parents were Ohio natives. She also states she bore two children, both still alive. Her daughter, Mary Iva Coover Fawcett and her family are living close by.

In 1920, Elizabeth Watkins Coover Fawcett Pellett is still living in Zanesfield, Jefferson Twp., Logan Co., Ohio (*Census Place: Jefferson, Logan, Ohio; Roll: T625_1405; Page: 2B; Enumeration District: 185; Image: 79*). Elizabeth is age 76, born Ohio like her parents. She lists no occupation. Elba J. and Mary Iva Coover Fawcett are still neighbors.

Children of William Coover and Elizabeth Watkins:

+ 4   m   I.   **Melvin Lester**[7] **Coover** was born in Jefferson Twp., Logan Co., Ohio, on September 23, 1866.[22] He died in Lancaster, Fairfield Co., Ohio, on August 13, 1953.[22]

+ 5   f   II. **Mary Iva**[7] **Coover** was born in Jefferson Twp., Logan Co., Ohio, on August 7, 1868.[23] She died in a facility in Bellefontaine, Lake Twp., Logan Co., Ohio, on December 23, 1964.[23]

3. **Chrystiana**[6] **Coover** (*Mary Ann*[5] *Pegan, Robert A.*[4]*, Andrew*[3]*, Andrew*[2] *Pagan, James*[1]) was born on September 25, 1846, in Logansville, Pleasant Twp., Logan Co., Ohio.[15] She was the daughter of Abraham Coover and Mary Ann Pegan (1). Chrystiana died in Bloomfield Twp., Logan Co., Ohio, on September 11, 1919, at age 72.[15] She was buried in Rea Cemetery, Bloomfield Twp., Logan Co., Ohio.[15, 24]

Chrystiana Coover Smith's given name is seen as Chrystiana, Chrystianna, Christiana, Christian, Christina, etc. The spelling on her Logan County, Ohio death certificate is Christina.[15] On her tombstone in Rea Cemetery, Bloomfield Twp., Logan Co., Ohio, it is Chrystiann.[24] In census records, her first name varies. The correct spelling is unknown, but some of her descendants say it was Chrystiana.

Chrystiana married **Andrew Jackson Smith** on October 19, 1863, in Logan Co., Ohio.[25] They had eleven children. Andrew Jackson Smith was born in Bloom Twp., Fairfield Co., Ohio, on September 28, 1841.[26] Andrew Jackson reached age 77 and died in Bloomfield Twp., Logan Co., Ohio, on July 6, 1919.[26] He was buried in Rea Cemetery, Bloomfield Twp., Logan Co., Ohio.[26, 27]

Andrew J. and Chrystiana Coover Smith are enumerated in 1870 in Bloomfield Twp., Logan Co., Ohio (*Census Place: Bloomfield, Logan, Ohio; Roll: M593_1234; Page: 8A; Image: 24*). Andrew J. Smith, listed as "A.J.", age 28, is a farmer. Chrystiana Coover Smith, listed as "Christin", is 23 years old. Their children are Mary E., five, Henry, three, and Elva A., one. All were born in Ohio.

In 1880, Andrew J. and Chrystiana Coover Smith continue to reside in Bloomfield Twp., Logan Co., Ohio (*Census Place: Bloomfield, Logan, Ohio; Roll: 1041; Page: 8C; Enumeration District: 111; Image: 0018*). In the household are Andrew J. Smith, age 38, a farmer, and his wife Chrystiann Coover Smith, 34. Children in the home are: Mary E., 15, Henry S., 13, "Bertie I." (Elva Alberta), 12, Ora B., seven, John A., five, and Roy T., three months. All and their parents were born in Ohio except for Chrystiann's father, who was born in Pennsylvania.

In 1900, Andrew Jackson and Chrystiana Coover Smith are living in Bloomfield Twp., Logan Co., Ohio (*Census Place: Bloomfield, Logan, Ohio; Roll: 1294; Page: 7A; Enumeration District: 105*). Andrew, age 58, a farmer, and Chrystiana, 53, say they have been married 36 years, although Logan County marriage records indicate they were married in 1862.[25] Christiana says she has borne 11 children, seven still living. With them are sons Roy and Hoadley Monroe Smith, ages 20 and 16 respectively. Except for Chrystiann's father, a Pennsylvania native, everyone in the home states they and their parents were Ohio natives.

Andrew and Chrystiana Coover Smith are still in Bloomfield Twp. Logan Co., Ohio in 1910 (*Census Place: Bloomfield, Logan, Ohio; Roll: T624_1204; Page: 3A; Enumeration District: 0120; Image: 606*). Andrew J. is age 68 and "Christian" is 64. Andrew says he and his parents were born in Ohio while Christina says she and her mother were born in Ohio and her father in Pennsylvania. The only child still at home is son Hoadley, age 26, born Ohio, as were his parents. However, this time Christiana says she has borne 11 children, but only six are still alive.

Although his son Hoadley M. Smith, the informant on Andrew Jackson Smith's death certificate, says his father was born in Pennsylvania, census records and other documentation indicate that Andrew was born in Bloom Twp., Fairfield Co., Ohio.[28, 29]

Andrew Jackson Smith is profiled in *The Historical Review of Logan County, Ohio* (etc.), by Gen. Robert P. Kennedy, and he and Chrystiana in the biography of their son, Hoadley M., in the "Logan County-Biographical" section of John Calvin Hover and Joseph Daniel Barnes' *Memoirs of the Miami Valley, Vol. III*.[28, 29]

Children of Chrystiana Coover and Andrew Jackson Smith:

+ 6   f   I.   **Mary Elizabeth**[7] **Smith** was born in Bloomfield Twp., Logan Co., Ohio, on November 14, 1864.[30] She died in DeGraff, Miami Twp., Logan Co., Ohio, on December 15, 1931.[30]

+ 7   m   II.   **Henry Sylvester**[7] **Smith** was born in Bloomfield Twp., Logan Co., Ohio, on September 9, 1866.[31, 32] He died in DeGraff, Miami Twp., Logan Co., Ohio, on April 3, 1951.[31, 32]

+ 8   f   III.   **Elva Alberta**[7] **Smith** was born in Bloomfield Twp., Logan Co., Ohio, on March 12, 1868.[33] She was also known as **Alberta or Bertie**. Elva Alberta died in Walker Twp., Huntingdon Co., Pennsylvania, on January 4, 1955.[33, 34.]

+ 9   m   IV.   **William C.**[7] **Smith** was born in Bloomfield Twp., Logan Co., Ohio, on January 7, 1871.[35] He died in Bloomfield Twp., Logan Co., Ohio, on February 8, 1871.[35]

+ 10   f   V.   **Ora Belle**[7] **Smith** was born in Bloomfield Twp., Logan Co., Ohio, on November 8, 1872.[36, 37] She died in Kenton, Pleasant Twp., Hardin Co., Ohio, on December 12, 1962.[38]

+ 11   m   VI.   **John Andrew**[7] **Smith** was born in Bloomfield Twp., Logan Co., Ohio, on May 29, 1875.[39] He died in Mandan, Almont Twp., Morton Co., North Dakota, on July 14, 1908.[39, 40]

+ 12   f   VII.   **Eliza E.**[7] **Smith** was born in Bloomfield Twp., Logan Co., Ohio, on October 6, 1877.[41] She died in Bloomfield Twp., Logan Co., Ohio, on June 7, 1878.[41]

+ 13   m   VIII.   **Roy Thurman**[7] **Smith** was born in Bloomfield Twp., Logan Co., Ohio, on March 29, 1880.[42, 43, 137, 138] He died in Bloomfield Twp., Logan Co., Ohio, on July 25, 1952, at age 72.[43, 139]

+ 14   m   IX.   **Hoadley Monroe**[7] **Smith** was born in Bloomfield Twp., Logan Co., Ohio, on September 12, 1883.[44, 150] He died in DeGraff, Miami Twp., Logan Co., Ohio, on April 19, 1926.[44, 151]

+ 15   X.   **Child One**[7] **Smith** was born in Bloomfield Twp., Logan Co., Ohio, between 1864 and 1900. He or she died in Bloomfield Twp., Logan Co., Ohio, between 1864 and 1900.

+ 16   XI.   **Child Two**[7] **Smith** was born in Bloomfield Twp., Logan Co., Ohio, between 1864 and 1900. He or she died in Bloomfield Twp., Logan Co., Ohio, between 1864 and 1900.

7th Generation

4. Melvin Lester[7] Coover (*William[6], Mary Ann[5] Pegan, Robert A.[4], Andrew[3], Andrew[2] Pagan, James[1]*) was born on September 23, 1866, in Jefferson Twp., Logan Co., Ohio.[22] He was the son of William Coover (2) and Elizabeth Watkins. He died in Lancaster, Fairfield Co., Ohio, on August 13, 1953, at age 86.[22] Melvin Lester was buried in Thurston Primitive Baptist Cemetery, Thurston, Walnut Twp., Fairfield Co., Ohio.[22, 45]

Melvin Lester Coover was born in near Zanesfield, Jefferson Twp., Logan Co., Ohio.[22] But when he was very young, his parents, William and Elizabeth Watkins Coover, moved to Kansas for a few years before returning to Logan County. Melvin may have been under the mistaken impression that he was born in Kansas. This is reflected in some of his census forms, and in those of some of his children.

Melvin Lester married **Dora Corbet** on November 25, 1886, in Champaign Co., Ohio.[46, 47] They divorced. They had three children. Dora Corbet was born in Allen Center, Allen Twp., Union Co., Ohio, on September 30, 1863.[47] She reached age 80 and died in Monroe Twp., Logan Co., Ohio, on March 18, 1944.[47] Dora was buried in Spain Cemetery (now Maple Grove Cemetery), North Lewisburg, Rush Twp., Champaign Co., Ohio.[47, 48]

Melvin Lester Coover married **Odella May Shaw** on April 12, 1896, in Athens Co., Ohio.[49] They had six children. Odella May Shaw was born in Union Twp., Cabell Co., West Virginia, on May 30, 1874.[50, 51, 52] She was also known as **Della**. Odella May reached age 36 and died in St. Cloud, Osceola Co., Florida, on September 1, 1910.[53, 54] She was buried in West Union Street Cemetery, Athens, Athens Twp., Athens Co., Ohio.[55]

Like her husband, Melvin Lester Coover, who thought he was born in Kansas, Odella "Della" May Shaw Coover thought she was a Meigs County, Ohio native. But her birth record is found in Cabell County, West Virginia.[51, 52] She, her parents George and Margaret "Victoria" Shaw and the rest of her family are found in nearby Wagonner, Mason Co., West Virginia in the 1880 census *(Census Place: Waggoner, Mason, West Virginia; Roll: 1408; Page: 401D; Enumeration District: 101; Della Shaw, George Shaw, head of household)*.

In 1900, Melvin Lester Coover is enumerated in Jacksonville, Trimble Twp., Athens Co., Ohio *(Census Place: Trimble, Athens, Ohio; Roll: 1239; Page: 8A; Enumeration District: 14)*. In the household are Melvin L. Coover, 27, a butcher, who says he was born in Sep 1872 in Kansas, but no birthplaces are given for his parents. The census taker may have received this erroneous information on Melvin's birthdate and place from his second wife, Odella "Della" Shaw Coover, who is with Melvin the home. Della Shaw Coover says she is 26, born May 1874 in Ohio, with her father born in Ohio and her mother in Virginia. Melvin and Della Shaw Coover have been married four years, and Della has borne three children, all still living. They are Sylvia, three, born Jan 1897; Hazel, one, born Jun 1898; and Helen, two months, born Mar 1900. All the children were born in Ohio.

In 1910, Melvin L. Coover is living in Precinct 4, Osceola Co., Florida *(Census Place: Precinct 4, Osceola, Florida; Roll: T624_166; Page: 3B; Enumeration District: 0120; Image: 330)*. Melvin L. Coover, 43, is now a house carpenter. He and his parents are listed as born in Kansas. Again, this could be incorrect information given by Della Shaw Coover, who may not have known the correct information. Melvin's second wife, "Della", is 35, and this time she says she and her parents were born in Ohio. The couple says they have been married 13 years and Della has borne six children, all surviving. With them are their children: Sylvia, 13, Hazel, 11, Helen, 10, Arthur, seven, Edna, five, and Elma, two. All the children were Ohio natives.

Della Shaw Coover's death date of September 1, 1910 is found in her father's, George Augustus Shaw's, obituary in the *Athens (OH) Messenger* on October 18, 1923.[53] Della Shaw Coover's descendants say she died in St. Cloud, Osceola Co., Florida, where her widower, Melvin Lester Coover, and her children are enumerated in the 1910 census. The family is said to have moved there in an effort to improve Della's failing health.[56] However, the State of Florida has no death certificate on file for her.[57] A descendant says she was buried in West Union Cemetery, Athens, Athens Co., Ohio, but there is no confirmation, as the cemetery's records do not date back to that era.[56]

After Della Shaw Coover died, Melvin L. Coover and his children returned to Ohio, and the family was separated. The children were given to various Shaw relatives. On June 11, 1911, Melvin and Della Shaw Coover's daughter Hazel Coover died at the home of a maternal uncle and aunt in Jacksonville, Trimble Twp., Athens Co., Ohio, according to her death certificate.[68]

In 1920, Melvin L. Coover, listed as M.L. Coover, is enumerated in Lancaster, Fairfield Co., Ohio *(Census Place: Lancaster Ward 4, Fairfield, Ohio; Roll: T625_1378; Page: 7A; Enumeration District: 23; Image: 573)*. He is a boarder in a large boarding house. Melvin Lester Coover says he is 53 years old, a widower, a butcher in a packing plant, and that he was born in Ohio, as were his parents. Arthur Francis Coover, Melvin's only living son, is also boarding in the same house. Arthur Coover, 17, single, a machinist in a foundry, says he and his parents were Ohio natives.

Melvin Lester Coover is not found in the 1930 census.

Melvin Coover is still residing in Lancaster, Fairfield Co., Ohio in 1940 *(Census Place: Lancaster, Fairfield, Ohio; Roll: T627_3066; Page: 61A; Enumeration District: 23-26)*. He is a lodger in the home of John and Leona Primmer. Melvin Coover, age 73, single, born Ohio, says he was living in Lancaster, Fairfield Co., Ohio in 1935. Melvin lists no occupation.

As for Dora Corbet Coover, Melvin's first wife, she is enumerated in Wayne Twp., Champaign Co., Ohio in 1900 *(Census Place: Wayne, Champaign, Ohio; Roll: 1245; Page: 5A; Enumeration District: 22)*. She and her two daughters are living in the home of Dora's uncle, Marion Corbet. Dora Corbet Coover, age 36, born Sep 1863, is divorced. She says she bore three children, two still alive. With her are Elta M. Coover, 12, born Sep 1887, and Doris E. Coover, eight, born Mar 1892. Dora and her daughters were born in Ohio, as were their parents. The head of the household, Marion Corbet, 52, a farmer, and his wife, Rebecca Corbet, also 52, were both Ohio natives.

Dora Corbet Coover is found in Urbana, Urbana Twp., Champaign Co., Ohio in 1910 *(Census Place: Urbana Ward 3, Champaign, Ohio; Roll: T624_1159; Page: 9B; Enumeration District: 0020; Image: 1077)*. She and her daughter Doris are residing with Dora's brother-in-law and sister, Christopher and Ella Corbet Foster and their family. Dora Corbet Coover, age 45, a seamstress and dressmaker, again says she is a widow (incorrect) who bore three children, with two of them still alive. With her is daughter Doris, 18, who also is indicated as having three children with two still living, but this is an error. Christopher C. Foster, a carpenter and Ella Corbet Foster are both 41 years old. All in the home and their parents were born in Ohio.

In 1920, Dora Corbet Coover is listed as "Cora I. Coover" in Woodstock, Rush Twp., Champaign Co., Ohio *(Census Place: Rush, Champaign, Ohio; Roll: T625_1353; Page: 3B; Enumeration District: 13; Image: 250)*. Dora Corbet Coover, the head of the household, says she is 56 years old, born Ohio, and married (?); she lists no occupation. Living with her is her daughter, Doris Coover, 27, single, a high school teacher. Both say they and their parents were born in Ohio. Lodging with them is a boarder, Lo Nard (Leonard?) Sessions, 16, born Iowa.

Dora Corbet Coover does not appear in the 1930 U.S. Census.

Dora Corbet Coover is doubly enumerated in the 1940 census. On April 12, 1940, Dora is residing with her son-in-law and daughter, Chlor and Doris Coover Pickering, in Sidney, Clinton Twp., Shelby Co., Ohio *(Census Place: Sidney, Shelby, Ohio; Roll: T627_3146; Page: 9A; Enumeration District: 75-7)*. Dora, age 76, born Ohio, says she is a widow. The head of the household, Chlor Pickering, age 47, is an insurance agent. Doris Coover Pickering is 48 years old. Oren and Doris Coover Pickering have a daughter, Aileen, 15. All say they were born in Ohio and were living in Urbana, Urbana Twp., Champaign Co., Ohio in 1935. The house address is 508 South West Avenue.

On April 18, 1940, she is found in Urbana, Urbana Twp., Champaign Co., Ohio *(Census Place: Urbana, Champaign, Ohio; Roll: T627_3037; Page: 11A; Enumeration District: 11-21)*. Dora, age 75, is living alone at 212 Reynolds Street; she says she is a widow, with no occupation, who was living in Urbana in 1935.

Dora Corbet Coover is listed as a widow living in Urbana, Ohio on her death certificate, but her ex-husband, Melvin Lester Coover, was still alive.[47]

Children of Melvin Lester Coover and Dora Corbet:

+ 17 f I. **Elta Modena**[8] **Coover** was born in Jefferson Twp., Logan Co., Ohio, on September 24, 1887.[58, 59] She died in McArthur Twp., Logan Co., Ohio, on September 23, 1956.[59, 60]

+ 18 m II. **Eslie or Elsey**[8] **Coover** was born in Jefferson Twp., Logan Co., Ohio, on October 20, 1889.[61] He died in Harrison Twp., Logan Co., Ohio, on November 18, 1891.[61]

+ 19 f III. **Doris E.**[8] **Coover** was born in Harrison Twp., Logan Co., Ohio, on March 4, 1892.[62] She died in Sidney, Clinton Twp., Shelby Co., Ohio, on April 10, 1983.[63]

Children of Melvin Lester Coover and Odella May Shaw:

+ 20 f I. **Sylvia**[8] **Coover** was born in Jacksonville, Trimble Twp., Athens Co., Ohio, on January 22, 1897.[64, 65] She died in Lancaster, Fairfield Co., Ohio, on December 10, 1985.[66]

+ 21 f II. **Hazel**[8] **Coover** was born in Jacksonville, Trimble Twp., Athens Co., Ohio, on June 22, 1898.[67, 68] She died in Jacksonville, Trimble Twp., Athens Co., Ohio, on July 20, 1911.[68]

+ 22 f III. **Helen Claire**[8] **Coover** was born in Jacksonville, Trimble Twp., Athens Co., Ohio, on March 14, 1900.[69,70] She died in Lancaster, Fairfield Co., Ohio, on September 29, 1992.[70, 71, 72]

+ 23 m IV. **Arthur Francis**[8] **Coover** was born in Jacksonville, Trimble Twp., Athens Co., Ohio, on March 14, 1900.[69, 70] She died in Lancaster, Fairfield Co., Ohio, on September 29, 1992.[70, 74, 75]

+ 24 f V. **Edna Victoria**[8] **Coover** was born in Jacksonville, Trimble Twp., Athens Co., Ohio, on March 7, 1905.[76] She died in Lancaster, Fairfield Co., Ohio, on March 25, 1932.[76]

+ 25 f VI. **Alma Pearle**[8] **Coover** was born in Jacksonville, Trimble Twp., Athens Co., Ohio, on September 26, 1907.[77] She died in Lancaster, Fairfield Co., Ohio, on September 9, 1995.[78]

5. **Mary Iva**[7] **Coover** (*William*[6], *Mary Ann*[5] *Pegan, Robert A.*[4], *Andrew*[3], *Andrew*[2] *Pagan, James*[1]) was born on August 7, 1868, in Jefferson Twp., Logan Co., Ohio.[23] She was the daughter of William Coover (2) and Elizabeth Watkins. Mary Iva died in a facility in Bellefontaine, Lake Twp., Logan Co., Ohio, on December 23, 1964, at age 96.[23] She was buried in Zanesfield Cemetery, Zanesfield, Jefferson Twp., Logan Co., Ohio.[79]

Mary Iva married **Elba Jonathan Fawcett** on November 1, 1888, in Logan Co., Ohio.[80] They had one son. Elba Jonathan Fawcett was born in Zanesfield, Jefferson Twp., Logan Co., Ohio, on March 8, 1866.[81] Elba Jonathan reached age 64 and died in Zanesfield, Jefferson Twp., Logan Co., Ohio, on October 17, 1930.[81] He was buried in Zanesfield Cemetery, Zanesfield, Jefferson Twp., Logan Co., Ohio.[81, 82] He was the son of Oliver Fawcett and Lucretta Thomas.

Elba J. and Mary Iva Coover Fawcett are enumerated in 1900 in Zanesfield, Jefferson Twp., Logan

Co., Ohio *(Census Place: Jefferson, Logan, Ohio; Roll: 1294; Page: 12B; Enumeration District: 108)*. Elba Fawcett's given name is written through and hard to read on the census form. Elba J. Fawcett is age 34, born Mar 1866, and was Ohio-born like his mother; his father's birthplace is not listed. He is a farmer. Mary Iva Coover Fawcett, listed as "Iva", is 31 and born in Ohio, as were her parents. The pair say they have been married 12 years and Mary Iva has borne one child, still living. This is son Alvin Fawcett, 11, born Sep 1888 in Ohio.

In 1910, Elba J. and Mary Iva Coover Fawcett are again living in Zanesfield, Jefferson Twp., Logan Co., Ohio *(Census Place: Jefferson, Logan, Ohio; Roll: T624_1204; Page: 3A; Enumeration District: 0124; Image: 680)*. Elba J. Fawcett, age 43, a farm laborer, says he was born in Ohio, like his mother, and his father was born in Virginia. His wife, Mary I. Coover Fawcett, 41, says she and her parents were Ohio natives. The couple have been married 21 years and Mary Iva has borne one child, who survives. With them is son Alvin, 20, born Ohio, who lists his occupation as baseball player. The family is living on Main Street, and Mary Iva's mother, Elizabeth Watkins Coover Fawcett Pellett, is living nearby.

Elba J. and Mary Iva Coover Fawcett continue to live in Zanesfield, Jefferson Twp., Logan Co., Ohio in 1920 *(Census Place: Jefferson, Logan, Ohio; Roll: T625_1405; Page: 2B; Enumeration District: 185; Image: 79)*. In the household are Elba J. Fawcett, age 53, born Ohio, with his father born in Virginia and his mother in Ohio; he is a farm laborer. Mary Iva Coover Fawcett, 51, says she was born in Ohio, as were her parents.

In 1930, Elba Jonathan and Mary Iva Coover Fawcett still reside in Zanesfield, Jefferson Twp., Logan Co., Ohio *(Census Place: Jefferson, Logan, Ohio; Roll: 1829; Page: 2A; Enumeration District: 12; Image: 995.0)*. Elba, enumerated as "Elbie", is age 64, who says he and his mother were born in Ohio and his father in Virginia. He lists no occupation. Mary Iva Coover Fawcett, 61, says she and her parents were born in Ohio. Elba says he was 21 years old at the time of his first marriage, and Mary Iva says she was 20. Living with them is Elba's first cousin Elijah Robert Fawcett, 59, a truck driver, who says he was born in Ohio, his father in Virginia and his mother in Ohio. He is single.

After her first husband, Elba Jonathan Fawcett, died, Mary Iva Coover Fawcett married Elba's cousin Elijah, who'd been residing in the home since at least 1930. Mary Iva Coover married **Elijah Robert Fawcett** on November 17, 1936.[83] Elijah Robert Fawcett was born in Walnut Grove, Pleasant Twp., Hardin Co., Ohio, on April 6, 1875.[84, 85] He also resided in 1951 in Zanesfield, Jefferson Twp., Logan Co., Ohio. Elijah Robert reached age 76 and died in a hospital in Bellefontaine, Lake Twp., Logan Co., Ohio, on June 11, 1951.[84] He was buried in Zanesfield Cemetery, Zanesfield, Jefferson Twp., Logan Co., Ohio.[84, 86]

Elijah and Mary Iva Coover Fawcett are enumerated in Zanesfield, Jefferson Twp., Logan Co., Ohio in 1940 *(Census Place: Zanesfield, Logan, Ohio; Roll: T627_3100; Page: 1B; Enumeration District: 46-16)*. They are living on the west side of Main Street. Elijah ("Elija") Fawcett, age 65, is a paperhanger and painter. Mary Iva Coover Fawcett is 71 years old. Both were born in Ohio, and say they were living in the same house in 1935.

Mary Iva's obituary in the *Bellefontaine (OH) Examiner* on December 24, 1964 says that Mary "Iva" Coover Fawcett was a Kansas native, but her death certificate, census data, and other documentation say she was born in Ohio, specifically Jefferson Twp., Logan Co., Ohio. Her obituary also gives an incorrect marriage date for her second marriage.[83, 23]

Oddly, her name is on two gravestones in Zanesville Cemetery, Zanesfield, Jefferson Twp., Logan Co., Ohio—one name is on a stone with her first husband, Elba Fawcett, and one is on a stone with Elijah Fawcett, her second husband.[82, 86]

Son of Mary Iva Coover and Elba Jonathan Fawcett:

+ 26 m I. **Alvin Coover⁸ Fawcett** was born in Zanesfield, Jefferson Twp., Logan Co., Ohio, on September 28,

1889.[87, 88] He died in a facility in Findlay, Liberty Twp., Hancock Co., Ohio, on June 21, 1982.[89]

6. **Mary Elizabeth**[7] **Smith** (*Chrystiana*[6] *Coover, Mary Ann*[5] *Pegan, Robert A.*[4]*, Andrew*[3]*, Andrew*[2] *Pagan, James*[1]) was born on November 14, 1864, in Bloomfield Twp., Logan Co., Ohio.[30] She was the daughter of Andrew Jackson Smith and Chrystiana Coover (3). She died in DeGraff, Miami Twp., Logan Co., Ohio, on December 15, 1931, at age 67.[30] Mary Elizabeth was buried in Rea Cemetery, Bloomfield Twp., Logan Co., Ohio.[30, 90]

Mary Elizabeth married **John W. Melvin** on December 21, 1882, in Logan Co., Ohio.[91] They had two children. John W. Melvin was born in Bloomfield Twp., Logan Co., Ohio, on May 15, 1843.[92] John W. reached age 67 and died in Bloomfield Twp., Logan Co., Ohio, on March 19, 1911.[92] He was buried in Rea Cemetery, Bloomfield Twp., Logan Co., Ohio.[92, 93]

John and Mary Elizabeth Smith Melvin are enumerated in Bloomfield Twp., Logan Co., Ohio in 1900 (*Census Place: Bloomfield, Logan, Ohio; Roll: T623_1294; Page: 7B; Enumeration District: 105*). In the home are John W. Melvin, age 57, a farmer, born Ohio with his parents born in Virginia; his wife Mary Elizabeth Smith Melvin, 35, born Ohio as were her parents; and children Otto J., 16, and Dessie L., 15, both born in Ohio. Also living with them is John's widowed sister Lydia Ruddell, 67 and John's nephew Ira Melvin, 16. John W. and Mary E. Smith Melvin say they have been married 18 years and Mary Elizabeth has borne two children, both alive.

In 1910, John W. and Mary Elizabeth Smith Melvin are still living in Bloomfield Twp., Logan Co., Ohio (*Census Place: Bloomfield, Logan, Ohio; Roll: T624_1204; Page: 1A; Enumeration District: 0120; Image: 602*). John W., age 66, a farmer, was born in Ohio but this time he says his parents were born in West Virginia. Mary Elizabeth Smith Melvin, age 45, was born in Ohio as were her parents. The couple states they have been married 27 years and Mary Elizabeth has borne two children, both of whom are still alive and in the home: Otto, 26, and Dessie, 25, both unmarried and born in Ohio.

The widowed Mary Elizabeth Smith Melvin is living in Bloomfield Twp., Logan Co., Ohio in 1920 (*Census Place: Bloomfield, Logan, Ohio; Roll: T625_1405; Page: 1A; Enumeration District: 181; Image: 6*). She is age 55 and says she is a farm manager. With her are her two children, Otto, 36, a farmer, and Dessie Leola, 34, both still single. All were Ohio natives, as were their parents.

In 1930, Mary Elizabeth Smith Melvin, widow, and her unmarried daughter Dessie are living in DeGraff Twp. Logan Co., Ohio (*Census Place: De Graff, Logan, Ohio; Roll: 1830; Page: 8A; Enumeration District: 19; Image: 41.0*). Mary Elizabeth Smith Melvin is age 65 and Dessie is 44 years old; neither lists an occupation. Both were born in Ohio as were their parents.

Children of Mary Elizabeth Smith and John W. Melvin:

+ 27 m I. **Otto J.**[8] **Melvin** was born in Bloomfield Twp., Logan Co., Ohio, on January 21, 1884.[94, 95] He died in Bellefontaine, Lake Twp., Logan Co., Ohio, on October 27, 1944.[94]

+ 28 f II. **Dessie Leola**[8] **Melvin** was born in Bloomfield Twp., Logan Co., Ohio, on March 7, 1885.[96, 97] She died in DeGraff, Miami Twp., Logan Co., Ohio, on January 31, 1959.[98]

7. **Henry Sylvester**[7] **Smith** (*Chrystiana*[6] *Coover, Mary Ann*[5] *Pegan, Robert A.*[4]*, Andrew*[3]*, Andrew*[2] *Pagan, James*[1]) was born on September 9, 1866, in Bloomfield Twp., Logan Co., Ohio.[31, 32] He was the son of Andrew Jackson Smith and Chrystiana Coover (3). Henry Sylvester died in DeGraff, Miami Twp., Logan Co., Ohio, on April 3, 1951, at age 84.[31, 32] He was buried in Greenwood Cemetery, DeGraff, Pleasant Twp., Logan Co., Ohio.[31, 32, 99]

Henry Sylvester married **Altia I. Mohr** on October 23, 1895, in Logan Co., Ohio.[100] They had one son. Altia I. Mohr was born in Union Twp., Logan Co., Ohio, on November 6, 1872.[101] Altia I. reached age

54 and died in Bloomfield Twp., Logan Co., Ohio, on June 28, 1927.[101] She was buried in Greenwood Cemetery, DeGraff, Pleasant Twp., Logan Co., Ohio.[101, 102]

In 1900, Henry Sylvester Smith is enumerated in Bloomfield Twp., Logan Co., Ohio *(Census Place: Bloomfield, Logan, Ohio; Roll: T623_1294; Page: 4B; Enumeration District: 105)*. Henry, age 33, is a farmer and wife Altia Mohr Smith is 27. Henry and Alta say they have been married four years and Alta has borne one child, still alive. Son Frederick, age three, is with them. All were born in Ohio as were their parents.

Henry Sylvester Smith is listed as "Sylvester Smith" in 1910 in Bloomfield Twp., Logan Co., Ohio *(Census Place: Bloomfield, Logan, Ohio; Roll: T624_1204; Page: 3A; Enumeration District: 0120; Image: 606)*. In the household are Henry Sylvester, 43, a farmer, wife Altia Mohr Smith, 37, and son Frederick, 13. Henry and Altia say they have been married 14 years and that Frederick is Altia's only child. Also living with them is Ora Hanks, a hired hand, age 29. All were Ohio natives, as were their parents. Henry's parents, Andrew J. and "Christian" (Chrystiana) Coover Smith are neighbors.

In 1920, Henry Sylvester Smith is again located in Bloomfield Twp., Logan Co., Ohio *(Census Place: Bloomfield, Logan, Ohio; Roll: T625_1405; Page: 1A; Enumeration District: 181; Image: 6)*. Henry Sylvester Smith is age 53 and a farmer, and wife Altia Mohr Smith is 47. Residing with them are son Frederick Smith, 23, a farm laborer, and his wife Lylah Rostofer Smith, 20. All were born in Ohio, as were their parents.

In 1930, the widower Henry Sylvester Smith continues to live with his son Fred J. Smith and his family in Bloomfield Twp., Logan Co., Ohio *(Census Place: Bloomfield, Logan, Ohio; Roll: 1829; Page: 4A; Enumeration District: 1; Image: 731.0)*. This time, Frederick is listed as head of household. Henry, age 63, is listed with no occupation. Fred J. Smith, age 33, is a farmer; his wife Lylah Rostofer Smith is 30, and their son Richard is nine years old. All were born in Ohio as were their parents.

In 1940, Henry Sylvester Smith, enumerated as "H.S. Smith", is residing alone in Washington Twp., Logan County, Ohio *(Census Place: Washington, Logan, Ohio; Roll: T627_3100; Page: 4B; Enumeration District: 46-40)*. Henry S. Smith is age 73, born Ohio, a widower and retired farmer, who says he was living in Logan Co., Ohio in 1935. He is living on a county road near Ohio State Road 269.

Son of Henry Sylvester Smith and Altia I. Mohr:

+ 29 m I. **Fredrick J.⁸ Smith** was born in Bloomfield Twp., Logan Co., Ohio, on November 21, 1896.[103, 104, 105, 106, 107] He died in Bellefontaine, Lake Twp., Logan Co., Ohio, on August 28, 1957.[103, 108, 109]

8. **Elva Alberta⁷ Smith** (*Chrystiana⁶ Coover, Mary Ann⁵ Pegan, Robert A.⁴, Andrew³, Andrew² Pagan, James¹*) was born on March 12, 1868, in Bloomfield Twp., Logan Co., Ohio.[33] She was also known as **Alberta or Bertie**. She was the daughter of Andrew Jackson Smith and Chrystiana Coover (3). Elva Alberta died in Walker Twp., Huntingdon Co., Pennsylvania, on January 4, 1955, at age 86.[33, 34] She was buried in Riverview Cemetery, Huntingdon, Huntingdon Twp., Huntingdon Co., Pennsylvania.[33, 110]

Elva Alberta married **Henry Bayer** on February 13, 1898, in Logan Co., Ohio.[111] They had two children. Henry Bayer was born in Antrim Twp., Franklin Co., Pennsylvania, on January 13, 1857.[112] He was also known as **Harry**. Henry reached age 75 and died in Walker Twp., Huntingdon Co., Pennsylvania, on May 22, 1932.[112, 113] He was buried in Plum Cemetery, Washington Twp., Logan Co., Ohio.[112, 114]

Henry Bayer's Pennsylvania death certificate is under the name "Harry Bayer".[113]

In 1900, Henry and Elva Smith Bayer are living in Sidney, Clinton Twp., Shelby Co., Ohio *(Census Place: Sidney, Clinton, Shelby, Ohio; Roll: 1321; Page: 11B; Enumeration District: 92)*. Henry Bayer, age 42, born Jun 1858, says he and his parents were born in Pennsylvania. He is the proprietor of a creamery. Elva Alberta Smith Bayer, 32, born Mar 1858, says she and her parents were born in Ohio. The couple states they have been married three years and Elva Alberta has borne no children.

In 1910, Henry and Elva Alberta Smith Bayer are found in Oneida Twp., Huntingdon Co., Pennsylvania *(Census Place: Oneida, Huntingdon, Pennsylvania; Roll: T624_1349; Page: 7A; Enumeration District: 0075; Image: 826)*. In the home are Henry Bayer, age 53, born Pennsylvania with his father born in Maryland and his mother in Pennsylvania; he is a farmer. Elva Alberta Alberta Smith Bayer, 42, is listed as "Alberta E.", and the census form erroneously says she and her father were born in Pennsylvania and her mother in Ohio (all were born in Ohio). Henry Bayer says he is on his second marriage, the marriage is Elva Alberta's first. The couple say they have been married 13 years and Elva Alberta has borne two children, one of them still living. This is son Franklin S., age six, born Pennsylvania, with his father born in Pennsylvania and his mother in Ohio (which contradicts the information given for Elva Alberta, who was definitely his mother).

Henry and Elva Alberta Smith Bayer are still residing in Oneida Twp., Huntingdon Co., Pennsylvania in 1920 *(Census Place: Oneida, Huntingdon, Pennsylvania; Roll: T625_1564; Page: 5B; Enumeration District: 71; Image: 503)*. Henry Bayer, age 62, born Pennsylvania, with his father born in Maryland and his mother born in Pennsylvania, is still farming. Elva Alberta Smith Bayer, again listed as Alberta, is 51, and says she and her parents were born in Ohio (correct). With them is son Franklin S., 16, born Pennsylvania like his father; his mother was born in Ohio.

In 1930, Henry and Elva Alberta Smith Bayer have moved to Walker Twp., Huntingdon Co., Pennsylvania *(Census Place: Walker, Huntingdon, Pennsylvania; Roll: 2045; Page: 1A; Enumeration District: 52; Image: 237.0)*. Henry Bayer, listed as "Harry", is age 72, born Pennsylvania with his father born in Maryland and his mother in Pennsylvania. Henry has retired from farming, as he lists no occupation. This time, Elva Alberta Smith Bayer is enumerated as Elva; she is 62 and was born in Ohio, as were her parents. Henry says he was first wed at age 32 and Elva says she was 28 at the time of her first marriage. Son Franklin S. Bayer, age 26 and single, says he and his father were born in Pennsylvania and his mother in Ohio. He is a caretaker at a country club.

Widow Elva Alberta Smith Bayer is not found in the 1940 census.

An article in the *Huntingdon (PA) Daily News* on March 13, 1953 says that Elva Bayer of rural Huntingdon celebrated her 84th birthday the previous day. The report mentions that Elva, who is residing in the home of her son Franklin Bayer, is bedfast and blind but in good spirits despite her health.[115]

The Plum Cemetery in Logan County, Ohio, where Henry Bayer is buried, was formerly known as Lewiston Cemetery. Oddly, Henry, a Pennsylvania native, was buried in Elva's home county, where it seems she intended to be buried as her name is on Henry's gravestone, along with that of his first wife, Almeda J. (Mohr). But Elva is buried in Huntingdon, Pennsylvania.[110, 114]

Children of Elva Alberta Smith and Henry Bayer:

+ 30 m I. **Franklin S.**[8] **Bayer** was born in Sidney, Clinton Twp., Shelby Co., Ohio, on May 12, 1903.[70, 116] He died in a hospital in Huntingdon, Huntingdon Co., Pennsylvania, on September 25, 1991.[70, 116]

+ 31 II. **Child**[8] **Bayer** was born in Sidney, Clinton Twp., Shelby Co., Ohio, between 1900 and 1910. He or she died in Sidney, Clinton Twp., Shelby Co., Ohio, before 1910.

9. **William C.**[7] **Smith** (*Chrystiana*[6] *Coover, Mary Ann*[5] *Pegan, Robert A.*[4]*, Andrew*[3]*, Andrew*[2] *Pagan, James*[1]) was born on January 7, 1871, in Bloomfield Twp., Logan Co., Ohio.[35] He was the son of Andrew Jackson Smith and Chrystiana Coover (3). William C. died in Bloomfield Twp., Logan Co., Ohio, on February 8, 1871.[35] He was buried in Rea Cemetery, Bloomfield Twp., Logan Co., Ohio.[35]

10. **Ora Belle**[7] **Smith** (*Chrystiana*[6] *Coover, Mary Ann*[5] *Pegan, Robert A.*[4]*, Andrew*[3]*, Andrew*[2] *Pagan, James*[1])

was born on November 8, 1872, in Bloomfield Twp., Logan Co., Ohio.[36, 37] She was the daughter of Andrew Jackson Smith and Chrystiana Coover (3). Ora Belle died in Kenton, Pleasant Twp., Hardin Co., Ohio, on December 12, 1962, at age 90.[38] She was buried in Greenwood Cemetery, DeGraff, Pleasant Twp., Logan Co., Ohio.[117]

Ora Belle married **Ellando Shawver** on January 15, 1891, in Logan Co., Ohio.[118] They had two children. Ellando Shawver was born in Harrison Twp., Logan Co., Ohio, on January 29, 1866.[119] He was also known as **Landy**. Ellando reached age 71 and died in Bellefontaine, Lake Twp., Logan Co., Ohio, on May 3, 1937.[119] He was buried in Greenwood Cemetery, DeGraff, Pleasant Twp., Logan Co., Ohio.[119, 120]

In 1900, Ellando S. and Ora B. Smith Shawver are enumerated in Pleasant Twp., Logan Co., Ohio (*Census Place: Pleasant, Logan, Ohio; Roll: 1294; Page: 2B; Enumeration District: 120*), In the home are Ellando Shawver, age 34, born Jan 1866, a farmer; and his wife, Ora Smith Shawer, 27, born Nov 1872. The pair say they have been married nine years and Ora has borne two children, both of whom survive. They are daughter Glady, eight, born Oct 1891, and son Jay, six, born Mar 1894. All and their parents were born in Ohio.

Ellando and Ora B. Smith Shawver have moved to Miami Twp., Logan Co., Ohio in 1910 (*Census Place: Miami, Logan, Ohio; Roll: T624_1204; Page: 9B; Enumeration District: 0138; Image: 999*). Ellando Shawver is age 43 and now a merchant. His wife, Ora B. Smith Shawver, is 37. They have been wed 20 years and Ora has borne two children, both still alive. Their children Glady, 18, and Jay, 16, are residing in the home. All and their parents were Ohio natives.

In 1920, Ellando S. Shawver is listed as "S." Shawver and Ora B. Smith Shawver is "Ona" in Bellefontaine, Lake Twp., Logan Co., Ohio (*Census Place: Bellefontaine Ward 2, Logan, Ohio; Roll: T625_1405; Page: 2A; Enumeration District: 190; Image: 188*). Ellando S. Shawver, age 53, is now a real estate agent; his wife Ora B. Smith Shawver is 47. Both were born in Ohio, like their parents.

In 1930, Ellando and Ora B. Smith Shawver are found in Bellefontaine, Lake Twp., Logan Co., Ohio (*Census Place: Bellefontaine, Logan, Ohio; Roll: 1829; Page: 3B; Enumeration District: 6; Image: 824.0*). Ellando Shawver is age 64 and Ora B. Smith Shawver is 57. Both were born in Ohio, as were their parents. Neither lists an occupation. Ellando says he was 25 when first married and Ora says she was 18.

Widow Ora B. Smith Shawver is not found in the 1940 census.

Children of Ora Belle Smith and Ellando Shawver:

+ 32 f I. **Glady Fern**[8] **Shawver** was born in Washington Twp., Logan Co., Ohio, on October 25, 1891.[121, 122] She died in Quincy, Miami Twp., Logan Co., Ohio, on June 18, 1933.[122]

+ 33 m II. **Jay**[8] **Shawver** was born in DeGraff, Pleasant Twp., Logan Co., Ohio, on March 3, 1894.[123, 124, 125] He died in Kenton, Pleasant Twp., Hardin Co., Ohio, on December 16, 1959.[126]

11. John Andrew[7] **Smith** (*Chrystiana*[6] *Coover, Mary Ann*[5] *Pegan, Robert A.*[4], *Andrew*[3], *Andrew*[2] *Pagan, James*[1]) was born on May 29, 1875, in Bloomfield Twp., Logan Co., Ohio.[39] He was the son of Andrew Jackson Smith and Chrystiana Coover (3). John Andrew died in Mandan, Almont Twp., Morton Co., North Dakota, on July 14, 1908, at age 33.[39, 40] He was buried in Rea Cemetery, Bloomfield Twp., Logan Co., Ohio.[39, 127]

John Andrew married **Cora C. Hanks** on February 1, 1898, in Logan Co., Ohio.[128] They had two children. Cora C. Hanks was born in Washington Twp., Logan Co., Ohio, on September 16, 1878.[40] Cora C. reached age 82 and died in Jackson Center, Jackson Twp., Shelby Co., Ohio, on February 17, 1961.[40, 129] She was buried in Rea Cemetery, Bloomfield Twp., Logan Co., Ohio.[40, 130]

John Andrew Smith is enumerated in Bloomfield Twp., Logan Co., Ohio in 1900 (*Census Place: Bloomfield, Logan, Ohio; Roll: T623_1294; Page:*

4B; *Enumeration District: 105*). In the household are John Smith, age 25, born May 1875, a farmer; and wife Cora Hanks Smith, 21, born Sep 1878. They say have been married two years and Cora has borne one child, son Harold, born May 1899, who is one year old. All were born in Ohio, as were their parents.

John Andrew Smith died in Mandan, Almont Twp., Morton Co., North Dakota, but his death certificate states that his usual residence was Bellefontaine, Ohio and that he'd only been in Mandan a few months. The informant on the death certificate was John's younger brother Hoadley Smith.[39]

Like many men in this era, John Andrew Smith was probably establishing a farm in a new place, his was Mandan, South Dakota, and intended to bring Cora and his children there after their new farm was ready.

Cora C. Smith is enumerated in 1910 in Bloomfield Twp., Logan Co., Ohio *(Census Place: Bloomfield, Logan, Ohio; Roll: T624_1204; Page: 3A; Enumeration District: 0120; Image: 606)*. The head of the household, Cora C. Smith, age 31, a widow, says she and her parents were born in Ohio. She lists no occupation, and says she has borne two children, both still alive. With her are her children, Harold D., 10, and Evelyn F., four, both born in Ohio, as were their parents. Also in the home is Cora's grandmother, Catherine Hanks, 72, born Ohio. Nearby are Cora's late husband John A. Smith's parents, Andrew Jackson and Chrystiana Coover Smith, and their youngest son Hoadley.

In 1920, widow Cora C. Smith is again found in Bloomfield Twp., Logan Co., Ohio *(Census Place: Bloomfield, Logan, Ohio; Roll: T625_1405; Page: 3A; Enumeration District: 181; Image: 10)*. Cora Smith, age 41, is keeping house for her unmarried brother Ona Hanks, 39, a farm laborer, who is listed as the head of the household. Cora's daughter Evelyn F. Smith, 13, is mistakenly listed as "daughter" instead of niece to the head of the household, her uncle Ona. All in the home were born in Ohio, as were their parents.

Cora C. Smith is still residing with her brother Ona in 1930 in Bloomfield Twp., Logan Co., Ohio *(Census Place: Bloomfield, Logan, Ohio; Roll: 1829; Page: 5A; Enumeration District: 1; Image: 733.0)*. Cora C. Smith is age 52 and widowed. Her brother Ona L. Hanks, 48, single, is a laborer doing odd jobs. Both say they and their parents were born in Ohio.

In 1940, Cora C. Smith continues to live in Bloomfield Twp., Logan Co., Ohio with her unmarried brother Ona Lee Hanks, again listed as the household head *(Census Place: Bloomfield, Logan, Ohio; Roll: T627_3100; Page: 2B; Enumeration District: 46-1)*. In the home are Cora Smith, age 62, a widow; Ora Lee Hanks, 59, single, a farm laborer, and Cora's grandson Don Rogers, 16, who is a "laborer tending to lawns". All were born in Ohio, and say they were living in the same house on Trout and Smith Road in 1935.

Children of John Andrew Smith and Cora C. Hanks:

+ 34 m I. **Harold D.⁸ Smith** was born in Bellefontaine, Lake Twp., Logan Co., Ohio, on May 26, 1899.[+31] He died in Bellefontaine, Lake Twp., Logan Co., Ohio, on April 19, 1984.[132, 133]

+ 35 f II. **Evelyn Fern⁸ Smith** was born in Bloomfield Twp., Logan Co., Ohio, on March 11, 1906.[70, 134] She died in a facility in Troy, Concord Twp., Miami Co., Ohio, on December 2, 1984.[135]

12. Eliza E.⁷ Smith (*Chrystiana⁶ Coover, Mary Ann⁵ Pegan, Robert A.⁴, Andrew³, Andrew² Pagan, James¹*) was born on October 6, 1877, in Bloomfield Twp., Logan Co., Ohio.[41] She was the daughter of Andrew Jackson Smith and Chrystiana Coover (3). Eliza E. died in Bloomfield Twp., Logan Co., Ohio, on June 7, 1878.[41] She was buried in Rea Cemetery, Bloomfield Twp., Logan Co., Ohio.[136]

13. Roy Thurman⁷ Smith (*Chrystiana⁶ Coover, Mary Ann⁵ Pegan, Robert A.⁴, Andrew³, Andrew² Pagan, James¹*) was born on March 29, 1880, in Bloomfield Twp., Logan Co., Ohio.[42, 43, 137] He was the son of Andrew Jackson Smith and Chrystiana Coover (3). He died in Bloomfield Twp., Logan Co., Ohio, on

July 25, 1952, at age 72.[43, 138] Roy Thurman was buried in Greenwood Cemetery, DeGraff, Pleasant Twp., Logan Co., Ohio.[43, 139]

Roy Thurman married **Mary Jane Poole** on November 6, 1902, in Logan Co., Ohio.[42] They had three children. Mary Jane Poole was born in Miami Twp., Logan Co., Ohio, on March 20, 1883.[42, 140] She reached age 76 and died in Miami Twp., Logan Co., Ohio, on February 29, 1960.[138] Mary Jane was buried in Greenwood Cemetery, DeGraff, Pleasant Twp., Logan Co., Ohio.[138, 141]

In 1910, Roy T. Smith is residing in Miami Twp., Logan Co., Ohio *(Census Place: Miami, Logan, Ohio; Roll: T624_1204; Page: 12A; Enumeration District: 0138; Image: 1004)*. Roy T. Smith, 30, is a farmer. With him is wife Mary J. Poole Smith, 27. The couple says they are on their first marriage and have been married seven years, and Mary Jane has borne two children, both still alive. They are Paul D., five, and B. "Lucile", two. All were born in Ohio, as were their parents, except for Mary Jane's mother, who was born in New Jersey.

Roy Thurman Smith is again residing in Miami Twp., Logan Co., Ohio in 1920 *(Census Place: Miami, Logan, Ohio; Roll: T625_1405; Page: 1B; Enumeration District: 198; Image: 386)*. In the household are Roy T. Smith, 39, a farmer; Mary J. Poole Smith, 36, and children Paul D., 15, Lucille B., 12, and Stanley, four years and eight months. This time, all say they and their parents were born in Ohio.

In 1930, Roy T. Smith is again found in Miami Twp., Logan Co., Ohio *(Census Place: Miami, Logan, Ohio; Roll: 1830; Page: 5A; Enumeration District: 21; Image: 65.0)*. In the home are Roy T. Smith, age 50, a farmer born in Ohio as were his parents. With him is wife Mary Jane Poole Smith, 47, born Ohio, who says her father was born in Ohio and her mother in New Jersey. Roy says he was first married at age 22 and Mary Jane says she was 19 when she was first wed. With them are sons Paul D., 25, a farm laborer, and Stanley, 14, both born in Ohio.

Roy T. Smith is still living in Miami Twp., Logan Co., Ohio in 1940 *(Census Place: Miami, Logan, Ohio; Roll: T627_3100; Page: 3A; Enumeration District: 46-26)*. The head of the household is Roy T. Smith, age 60, is now the postmaster at the DeGraff post office. With him are wife Mary J. Poole Smith, 57, who operates a dairy, and son Stanley Smith, 25, single, a salesman at the dairy. All were born in Ohio, and say they were living in the same house in 1935. Residing with them is Katherine Strasser, 43, single, a housekeeper born in Ohio. No address for the home is listed.

Children of Roy Thurman Smith and Mary Jane Poole:

+ 36 m I.   **Paul D.⁸ Smith** was born in DeGraff, Miami Twp., Logan Co., Ohio, on August 29, 1904.[70, 142] He died in DeGraff, Miami Twp., Logan Co., Ohio, on September 3, 1978.[70, 143]

+ 37 f II. **Bertha Lucile⁸ Smith** was born in DeGraff, Miami Twp., Logan Co., Ohio, on September 5, 1907.[70, 144, 145, 146] She was also known as **Lucille**. Bertha Lucile died in Bellefontaine, Lake Twp., Logan Co., Ohio, on June 27, 1993.[70, 145, 146]

+ 38 m III. **Stanley Andrew⁸ Smith** was born in DeGraff, Miami Twp., Logan Co., Ohio, on April 4, 1915.[70, 147, 148, 149] He died in DeGraff, Miami Twp., Logan Co., Ohio, on May 21, 1995.[70, 147, 148, 149]

14. Hoadley Monroe⁷ Smith (*Chrystiana⁶ Coover, Mary Ann⁵ Pegan, Robert A.⁴, Andrew³, Andrew² Pagan, James¹*) was born on September 12, 1883, in Bloomfield Twp., Logan Co., Ohio.[44, 150] He was the son of Andrew Jackson Smith and Chrystiana Coover (3). He died in DeGraff, Miami Twp., Logan Co., Ohio, on April 19, 1926, at age 42.[44, 151] Hoadley Monroe was buried in Greenwood Cemetery, DeGraff, Pleasant Twp., Logan Co., Ohio.[44, 152]

Hoadley Monroe married **Dolly Herring** on March 8, 1914, in Shelby Co., Ohio.[153] They had one son. Dolly Herring was born in Salem Twp., Shelby Co., Ohio, on August 16, 1884.[70, 154, 155] Dolly reached age 95 and died in a facility in Lima, Ottawa Twp., Allen Co., Ohio, on March 13, 1980.[154, 155] She was buried in Greenwood Cemetery, DeGraff, Pleasant Twp., Logan Co., Ohio.[155, 156]

Hoadley Smith is enumerated in Bloomfield Twp., Logan Co., Ohio in 1920 *(Census Place: Bloomfield, Logan, Ohio; Roll: T625_1405; Page: 1B; Enumeration District: 181; Image: 7)*. In the home are Hoadley Smith, age 35, a farmer; his wife Dolly Herring Smith, age 34, and son Thurman H., two. All and their parents were born in Ohio.

Widow Dolly Herring Smith is found in DeGraff, Miami Twp., Logan Co., Ohio *(Census Place: De Graff, Logan, Ohio; Roll: 1830; Page: 2B; Enumeration District: 0019; Image: 30.0)*. Dolly Herring Smith, age 45, is a cook for a private family. With her is son Thurman H. Smith, 13. Both were Ohio natives, as were their parents.

Dolly Herring Smith is enumerated in the 1940 census in DeGraff, Miami Twp., Logan Co., Ohio *(Census Place: De Graff, Logan, Ohio; Roll: T627_3100; Page: 4B; Enumeration District: 46-24)*. Dolly Herring Smith, age 54, a widow, born Ohio, is listed as the head of the household. Her son Thurman Smith, 23, single, a restaurant waiter, is living with her. Both say they were residing in the same house in 1935, but no address is on the census form.

Son of Hoadley Monroe Smith and Dolly Herring:

+ 39 m I. **Thurman Herring**[8] **Smith** was born in Bloomfield Twp., Logan Co., Ohio, on February 10, 1917.[70, 157] He died in Lima, Ottawa Twp., Allen Co., Ohio, on March 15, 1980.[158, 159]

15. **Child One**[7] **Smith** (*Chrystiana*[6] *Coover, Mary Ann*[5] *Pegan, Robert A.*[4], *Andrew*[3], *Andrew*[2] *Pagan, James*[1]) was born between 1864 and 1900 in Bloomfield Twp., Logan Co., Ohio. He or she was a child of Andrew Jackson Smith and Chrystiana Coover (3). Child One died in Bloomfield Twp., Logan Co., Ohio, between 1864 and 1900. He or she was buried in Rea Cemetery, Bloomfield Twp., Logan Co., Ohio.

16. **Child Two**[7] **Smith** (*Chrystiana*[6] *Coover, Mary Ann*[5] *Pegan, Robert A.*[4], *Andrew*[3], *Andrew*[2] *Pagan, James*[1]) was born between 1864 and 1900 in Bloomfield Twp., Logan Co., Ohio. He or she was a child of Andrew Jackson Smith and Chrystiana Coover (3). Child Two died in Bloomfield Twp., Logan Co., Ohio, between 1864 and 1900. He or she was buried in Rea Cemetery, Bloomfield Twp., Logan Co., Ohio.

8th Generation

17. Elta Modena⁸ Coover (*Melvin Lester⁷, William⁶, Mary Ann⁵ Pegan, Robert A.⁴, Andrew³, Andrew² Pagan, James¹*) was born on September 24, 1887, in Jefferson Twp., Logan Co., Ohio.[58, 59] She was the daughter of Melvin Lester Coover (4) and Dora Corbet. Elta Modena died in McArthur Twp., Logan Co., Ohio, on September 23, 1956, at age 68.[59, 60] She was buried in Zanesfield Cemetery, Zanesfield, Jefferson Twp., Logan Co., Ohio.[59, 160]

Elta Modena married **Walter Warren Stanley** on October 21, 1909, in Logan Co., Ohio.[161] They had three sons. Walter Warren Stanley was born in Monroe Twp., Logan Co., Ohio, on July 21, 1885.[162, 163] Walter Warren resided in 1965 in Logan County, Ohio.[164] Walter Warren reached age 80 and died in a hospital in Lima, Ottawa Twp., Allen Co., Ohio, on November 30, 1965.[164] He was buried in Zanesfield Cemetery, Zanesfield, Jefferson Twp., Logan Co., Ohio.[165]

In 1910, Walter and Elta Coover Stanley are enumerated in Monroe Twp., Logan Co., Ohio *(Census Place: Monroe, Logan, Ohio; Roll: T624_1204; Page: 10B; Enumeration District: 0139; Image: 1029)*. Walter Stanley, age 25, is a farmer who says he and his parents were born in Ohio. Elta Coover Stanley, listed as "Etta", 21, says she was born in Ohio and her parents in the U.S. The couple states they are on their first marriage, have been wed six years, and Elta has borne no children.

Walter and Elta Coover Stanley are again living in Monroe Twp., Logan Co., Ohio in 1920 *(Census Place: Monroe, Logan, Ohio; Roll: T625_1405; Page: 11A; Enumeration District: 200; Image: 447)*. In the household are Walter Stanley, age 34, a farmer; his wife, Elta M. Coover Stanley, 32, and their son "Marvin", six. All and their parents were born in Ohio.

In 1930, Walter and Elta Coover Stanley are found in Miami Twp., Logan Co., Ohio *(Census Place: Miami, Logan, Ohio; Roll: 1830; Page: 1A; Enumeration District: 21; Image: 57.0)*. Walter W. Stanley, 43, is a farmer. His wife, Elta Coover Stanley is 41 years old. Walter and Elta say they were first married at ages 24 and 22 respectively. With them are their sons "Marvin", 16, and "J. Darrell", nine. All say they and their parents were Ohio natives.

Walter and Elta Coover Stanley are residing in McArthur Twp., Logan Co., Ohio in 1940 *(Census Place: McArthur, Logan, Ohio; Roll: T627_3100; Page: 4A; Enumeration District: 46-23)*. The family farm is on North U.S. 68. In the home are Walter Stanley, 54, who is still a farmer. His wife, Elta Coover Stanley is 52 years old. They now have three sons: Marvin, 26, single, a farm laborer; "Darrell", 19, a clerk in a general store, and Wendell, six. All were born in Ohio, and say they were living in Logan County, Ohio in 1935. Also living with them is Walter Stanley's sister, Gertrude Stanley Green.

Sons of Elta Modena Coover and Walter Warren Stanley:

+ 40 m I. **Halsey Marvin⁹ Stanley** was born in Monroe Twp., Logan Co., Ohio, on May 8, 1913.[70, 166] He was also known as **Marvin** and **H. Marvin Stanley**. Halsey Marvin died in West Liberty, Liberty Twp., Logan Co., Ohio, on February 24, 2009.[70, 166]

+ 41 m II. **James Darrell⁹ Stanley** was born in Monroe Twp., Logan Co., Ohio, on July 1, 1920.[70, 167, 168] He died in Huntington, Huntington Twp., Huntington Co., Indiana, on May 29, 1990.[70, 167, 168]

+ 42 m III. **Wendell Wayne⁹ Stanley** was born in Miami Twp., Logan Co., Ohio, on August 13, 1933.[70, 169] He died in Columbus, Franklin Co., Ohio, on April 17, 2007.[70, 169]

18. Eslie or Elsey⁸ Coover (*Melvin Lester⁷, William⁶, Mary Ann⁵ Pegan, Robert A.⁴, Andrew³, Andrew² Pagan, James¹*) was born on October 20, 1889, in Jefferson Twp., Logan Co., Ohio.[61] He was the son of Melvin Lester Coover (4) and Dora Corbet. Eslie or Elsey died in Harrison Twp.,

Logan Co., Ohio, on November 18, 1891, at age two.[61] He was buried in Goshen-Quaker Cemetery, Jefferson Twp., Logan Co., Ohio.[61]

Elsey or Esley Coover is buried next to his paternal grandfather William Coover in Goshen-Quaker Cemetery, Jefferson Twp., Logan Co., Ohio. His gravestone reads: "Eslie (sic) Coover, son of M.L. and Dora, died Nov 18, 1891, age two years, 29 days".[61] As "Elsey" is a first name for other Pegan male descendants, it is quite possible that the gravestone is inscribed incorrectly and his name was Elsey.

19. **Doris E.⁸ Coover** (*Melvin Lester⁷, William⁶, Mary Ann⁵ Pegan, Robert A.⁴, Andrew³, Andrew² Pagan, James¹*) was born on March 4, 1892, in Harrison Twp., Logan Co., Ohio.[62] She was the daughter of Melvin Lester Coover (4) and Dora Corbet. Doris E. died in Sidney, Clinton Twp., Shelby Co., Ohio, on April 10, 1983, at age 91.[63] She was buried in Cedar Point Cemetery, Pasco, Perry Twp., Shelby Co., Ohio.[170]

Doris E. married **Chlor Washington Pickering** on June 24, 1921, in Champaign Co., Ohio.[171] They had one daughter. Chlor Washington Pickering was born in Rosewood, Adams Twp., Champaign Co., Ohio, on January 19, 1893.[171, 172] Chlor Washington reached age 67 and died in Sidney, Clinton Twp., Shelby Co., Ohio, on December 8, 1960.[173] He was buried in Cedar Point Cemetery, Pasco, Perry Twp., Shelby Co., Ohio.[174]

Chlor and Doris Coover Pickering are enumerated in St. Paris, Johnson Twp., Champaign Co., Ohio in 1930 *(Census Place: Saint Paris, Champaign, Ohio; Roll: 1755; Page: 1B; Enumeration District: 10; Image: 710.0)*. Chlor W. Pickering, age 37, owns an auto dealership, and says he was born in Ohio, his father in Virginia and his mother in Ohio. Doris Coover Picker is 38 years old, born Ohio, as were her parents. Chlor and Doris say they were first wed at ages 27 and 28 respectively. With them is daughter Aileen, age five, born Ohio.

In 1940, Chlor and Doris Coover Pickering are found in Sidney, Clinton Twp., Shelby Co., Ohio *(Census Place: Sidney, Shelby, Ohio; Roll: T627_3146; Page: 9A; Enumeration District: 75-7)*. The head of the household, Chlor Pickering, age 47, is an insurance agent. Doris Coover Pickering is 48 years old. Also in the home is their daughter Aileen, 15. Living with them is Doris' mother, Dora Corbet Coover, age 76, who says she is a widow. All say they were born in Ohio and were living in Urbana, Urbana Twp., Champaign Co., Ohio in 1935. The house address is 508 South West Avenue.

Daughter of Doris E. Coover and Chlor Washington Pickering:

+ 43 f I. **Aileen⁹ Pickering** was born in St. Paris, Johnson Twp., Champaign Co., Ohio, on May 31, 1924.[70, 175] She died in Sierra Vista, Cochise Co., Arizona, on November 26, 2006.[70, 175]

20. **Sylvia⁸ Coover** (*Melvin Lester⁷, William⁶, Mary Ann⁵ Pegan, Robert A.⁴, Andrew³, Andrew² Pagan, James¹*) was born on January 22, 1897, in Jacksonville, Trimble Twp., Athens Co., Ohio.[64, 65] She was the daughter of Melvin Lester Coover (4) and Odella May Shaw. Sylvia died in Lancaster, Fairfield Co., Ohio, on December 10, 1985, at age 88.[66] She was buried in New School Baptist Cemetery, Thurston, Walnut Twp., Fairfield Co., Ohio.[176, 177]

Sylvia married **Homer Elsworth Lawyer** on December 24, 1914, in Fairfield Co., Ohio.[178] They had five children. Homer Elsworth Lawyer was born in Dumontville, Greenfield Twp., Lancaster Co., Ohio, on January 2, 1894.[70, 179] Homer Elsworth reached age 76 and died in Thurston, Walnut Twp., Lancaster Co., Ohio, on July 22, 1970.[180] He was buried in New School Baptist Cemetery, Thurston, Walnut Twp., Fairfield Co., Ohio.[181, 182]

Homer and Sylvia Coover Lawyer are enumerated in Thurston, Walnut Twp., Lancaster Co., Ohio in 1920 *(Census Place: Walnut, Fairfield, Ohio; Roll: T625_1378; Page: 4B; Enumeration District: 34; Image: 1094)*. In the household are Homer Lawyer, age 25, a house painter; his wife, Sylvia Coover Lawyer, 23, and sons Arthur, four, and Nelson, two years and seven months. All in the home, and their parents, were Ohio natives.

In 1930, Homer and Sylvia Coover Lawyer are still residing in Thurston, Walnut Twp., Fairfield Co., Ohio *(Census Place: Walnut, Fairfield, Ohio; Roll: 1792; Page: 2A; Enumeration District: 37; Image: 100.0)*. Homer Lawyer, age 36, is a house painter. With him is wife Sylvia Coover Lawyer, who is 33 years old. Homer says his first marriage occurred at age 21, and Sylvia says hers was at age 18. Children in the home are: Arthur W., 14, William N., 12, Vivian J., eight, Melvin, six, and "Danny", two. All in the home were born in Ohio, like their parents.

In 1940, Homer and Sylvia Coover Lawyer are again found in Thurston, Walnut Twp., Fairfield Co., Ohio *(Census Place: Thurston, Fairfield, Ohio; Roll: T627_3066; Page: 4A; Enumeration District: 23-44)*. In the home are Homer Lawyer, age 46, a house painter; Sylvia Coover Lawyer, 43, and children Vivian, 18, Melvin, 16, and "Danny", 12. All were born in Ohio and living in the same house, at 78 East Main Street, in 1935.

Children of Sylvia Coover and Homer Elsworth Lawyer:

+ 44   m   I.   **Arthur Wilson**[9] **Lawyer** was born in Thurston, Walnut Twp., Lancaster Co., Ohio, on November 1, 1915.[70] He died in a hospital in Lancaster, Fairfield Co., Ohio, on June 16, 1981.[183]

+ 45   m   II. **William Nelson**[9] **Lawyer** was born in Thurston, Walnut Twp., Lancaster Co., Ohio, on May 5, 1917.[184, 185, 186] He was also known as **Dynamite**. William Nelson died in Lancaster, Fairfield Co., Ohio, on January 5, 1996.[184, 185, 186]

+ 46   f   III. **Vivian June**[9] **Lawyer** was born in Thurston, Walnut Twp., Lancaster Co., Ohio, on June 11, on June 11, 1921.[70, 187, 188] Vivian June died in Baltimore, Liberty Twp., Fairfield Co., Ohio on February 9, 1997.[187, 188, 189]

+ 47   m   IV. **Melvin Raymond**[9] **Lawyer** was born in Thurston, Walnut Twp., Lancaster Co., Ohio, on October 16, 1923.[70, 190] He died in Wildwood, Sumter Co., Florida, on December 13, 1998.[70, 190, 191]

+ 48   m   V.   **Daniel B.**[9] **Lawyer** was born in Thurston, Walnut Twp., Lancaster Co., Ohio, on October 17, 1927.[70, 192] He was also known as **Popeye**. Daniel B. died in Lancaster, Fairfield Co., Ohio, on July 12, 2008.[70, 192]

21. **Hazel**[8] **Coover** (*Melvin Lester*[7], *William*[6], *Mary Ann*[5] *Pegan*, *Robert A.*[4], *Andrew*[3], *Andrew*[2] *Pagan*, *James*[1]) was born on June 22, 1898, in Jacksonville, Trimble Twp., Athens Co., Ohio.[67, 68] She was the daughter of Melvin Lester Coover (4) and Odella May Shaw. Hazel died in Jacksonville, Trimble Twp., Athens Co., Ohio, on July 20, 1911, at age 13.[68] She was buried in Nye Cemetery, Chauncey, Dover Twp., Athens Co., Ohio.[68, 193]

Hazel Coover's Ohio death certificate says she was buried in Chauncey, Ohio. The only cemetery in Chauncey, Dover Twp., Athens Co., Ohio is the Nye Cemetery. The Nye Cemetery is mentioned specifically in Hazel Coover's obituary.[193]

22. **Helen Claire**[8] **Coover** (*Melvin Lester*[7], *William*[6], *Mary Ann*[5] *Pegan*, *Robert A.*[4], *Andrew*[3], *Andrew*[2] *Pagan*, *James*[1]) was born on March 14, 1900, in Jacksonville, Trimble Twp., Athens Co., Ohio.[69, 70] She was the daughter of Melvin Lester Coover (4) and Odella May Shaw. She died in Lancaster, Fairfield Co., Ohio, on September 29, 1992, at age 92.[70, 71, 72] Helen Claire was buried in Floral Hills Memory Gardens, Lancaster, Fairfield Co., Ohio.[72, 194]

Helen Claire married **Robert Cyril Finley** on January 27, 1917, in Fairfield Co., Ohio.[195] They divorced between 1930 and 1940. They had four children. Robert Cyril Finley was born in Redmon, Buck Twp., Edgar Co., Illinois, on August 26, 1889.[70, 196] Robert Cyril reached age 73 and died in Lancaster, Fairfield Co., Ohio, on January 18,

1963.[70, 197] He was buried in Forest Rose Cemetery, Lancaster, Fairfield Co., Ohio.[198]

In 1900, Robert Finley, born in Illinois, was living with his parents in Perry Twp., Hocking Co., Ohio *(Census Place: Perry, Hocking, Ohio; Roll: 1287; Page: 11B; Enumeration District: 0033, Robert "S." Finley under entry for Jefferson Finley, head of household)*. On his WWI draft registration, he says he was born in "Redmond", Illinois (Redmon) and was living in Lancaster, Ohio.[199] He has a wife and one child. However, on his WWII draft registration, Robert Finley, still living in Fairfield County, Ohio, correctly states his birthplace as Redmon, Illinois.[196]

In 1920, Robert and Helen Coover Finley are enumerated in Liberty Twp., Fairfield Co., Ohio *(Census Place: Liberty, Fairfield, Ohio; Roll: T625_1378; Page: 3A; Enumeration District: 24; Image: 861)*. Robert Finley, 30, born Illinois, with his father born in Ohio and his mother in Illinois, is a laborer in a box factory. His wife, Helen Coover Finley, is 19, born Ohio, with her father born in Kansas (Incorrect—he was an Ohio native) and her mother in Ohio. They have two children, Loretta, two years and eight months, and Raymond, eleven months, both born in Ohio. The children's ages are incorrect; they are switched, and Raymond is the elder child.

Robert and Helen Finley separated sometime after 1922. In early January 1929, Robert C. Finley was indicted on a charge of non-support of his family by a Fairfield County, Ohio grand jury, according to a front-page report in the *Lancaster (OH) Daily Gazette* on January 10, 1929.[200]

In 1930, Robert Finley is an inmate at the London Prison Farm in Union Twp., Madison Co., Ohio *(Census Place: Union, Madison, Ohio; Roll: 1847; Page: 7A; Enumeration District: 28; Image: 437.0)*, Robert is age 41, born Illinois, who says his parents were both born in Ohio.

Robert Finley is not found in the 1940 census.

In 1930, Helen Claire Coover Finley is enumerated in Lancaster, Fairfield Co., Ohio *(Census Place: Lancaster, Fairfield, Ohio; Roll: 1791; Page: 17B; Enumeration District: 20; Image: 945.0)*. Helen C. Coover Finley, age 30, says she is still married, but her husband Robert Finley is not in the home. (He is imprisoned in London Prison Farm in Union Twp., Madison Co., Ohio). Helen says she was born in Ohio, with her father born in Missouri (erroneous, he was born in Ohio) and her mother in Ohio, and gives her occupation as saddler in a shoe factory. She also says she was first married at age 16. With her are children Raymond, 13, Loretta M., 11, whose ages are corrected from the 1920 census; Esther M., eight, and Albert E., seven. All the children were born in Ohio, with their father born in Illinois and their mother in Ohio.

Helen Coover Finley is still residing in Lancaster, Fairfield Co., Ohio in 1940 *(Census Place: Lancaster, Fairfield, Ohio; Roll: T627_3066; Page: 6A; Enumeration District: 23-23)*. The house address is 614 East Main Street. Helen Coover Finley, listed as the head of the household, is age 40 and a decorator in a glass factory; she is hand-painting glasses and dinnerware. Living with her are her son Albert, 17, married daughter Esther Finley Crist, 19, a cashier at a theatre; and Esther's husband William Crist, also 19, who is a mechanic in a garage. All in the home were born in Ohio, and say they were living in Lancaster in 1935.

Children of Helen Claire Coover and Robert Cyril Finley:

+ 49 m I. **Raymond Lester**[9] **Finley** was born in Liberty Twp., Fairfield Co., Ohio, on April 27, 1917.[201, 202, 203, 204, 205] He died in Lancaster, Fairfield Co., Ohio, on May 13, 1998.[201, 202, 203, 205]

+ 50 f II. **Loretta May**[9] **Finley** was born in New Lexington, Pike Twp., Perry Co., Ohio, on January 30, 1919.[70, 206, 207, 208] She died in Columbus, Franklin Co., Ohio, on July 11, 1992.[206, 209]

+ 51 f III. **Esther Marie**[9] **Finley** was born in Liberty Twp., Fairfield Co., Ohio, on April 8, 1921.[70, 210, 211, 212] She died in Lancaster, Fairfield Co., Ohio, on October 31, 1991.[70, 210, 211]

+ 52 m IV. **Albert Earl**[9] **Finley** was born in Blacklick, Jefferson Twp., Franklin Co., Ohio, on November 16, 1922.[70, 213, 214] He died in Columbus, Franklin Co., Ohio, on October 2, 1993.[70, 213, 214]

23. Arthur Francis[8] **Coover** (*Melvin Lester*[7], *William*[6], *Mary Ann*[5] *Pegan, Robert A.*[4], *Andrew*[3], *Andrew*[2] *Pagan, James*[1]) was born on December 16, 1902, in Jacksonville, Trimble Twp., Athens Co., Ohio.[70, 73, 74] He was the son of Melvin Lester Coover (4) and Odella May Shaw. Arthur Francis died in Lancaster, Fairfield Co., Ohio, on May 21, 1994, at age 91.[70, 74, 75] He was buried in Forest Lawn Memorial Gardens Cemetery, Columbus, Franklin Co., Ohio.[215]

Childless.

Arthur Coover is enumerated in 1920 in Lancaster, Fairfield Co., Ohio (*Census Place: Lancaster Ward 4, Fairfield, Ohio; Roll: T625_1378; Page: 7A; Enumeration District: 23; Image: 573*). Arthur Coover, age 17, is a boarder in a large boarding house along with his father Melvin Lester Coover ("M.L. Coover"). Arthur Coover says he and his parents were born in Ohio, and he lists his occupation as a machinist in a foundry. Melvin Lester Coover says he is 53 years old, a widower, a butcher in a packing plant, and that he was born in Ohio, as were his parents.

In 1930, Arthur Coover is found in Dearborn, Wayne Co., Michigan (*Census Place: Dearborn, Wayne, Michigan; Roll: 1031; Page: 10B; Enumeration District: 897; Image: 176.0*). Arthur Coover, age 27 and single, is a machine operator in an auto factory. He says he and his parents were born in Ohio.

Arthur Francis married **Loretta Gray Faires** on September 28, 1932, in Fairfield Co., Ohio.[216] Loretta Gray Faires was born in Logan Co., Ohio, on March 16, 1905.[70, 216] Loretta Gray reached age 78 and died in Lancaster, Fairfield Co., Ohio, on October 16, 1983.[217] She was buried in Forest Lawn Memorial Gardens Cemetery, Columbus, Franklin Co., Ohio.[218]

Arthur Coover is residing in Basil, Liberty Twp., Fairfield Co., Ohio in 1940 (*Census Place: Basil, Fairfield, Ohio; Roll: T627_3066; Page: 1B; Enumeration District: 23-29*). In the home are Arthur Coover, age 37, a machinist in a paper mill, and his wife, Loretta Faires Coover, 34. Both were born in Ohio, and say they were living in Fairfield County, Ohio in 1935. Their home is at 18 Washington Street.

Arthur Coover and his wife Loretta Faires Coover may have been cousins. In 1920, Arthur's youngest sister, Alma Pearle Coover, is living with a William Faires in Zanesville, Muskingum Co., Ohio, and is listed as his niece (*Census Place: Zanesville Ward 5, Muskingum, Ohio; Roll: T625_1425; Page: 7B; Enumeration District: 141; Image: 1063, entry for William Faires*).

24. Edna Victoria[8] **Coover** (*Melvin Lester*[7], *William*[6], *Mary Ann*[5] *Pegan, Robert A.*[4], *Andrew*[3], *Andrew*[2] *Pagan, James*[1]) was born on March 7, 1905, in Jacksonville, Trimble Twp., Athens Co., Ohio.[76] She was the daughter of Melvin Lester Coover (4) and Odella May Shaw. Edna Victoria died in Lancaster, Fairfield Co., Ohio, on March 25, 1932, at age 27.[76] She was buried in Saint Mary Cemetery, Lancaster, Fairfield Co., Ohio.[76, 219]

In 1920, Edna Coover, age 15, is a servant in the home of Clerel and Nellie Muck in Lancaster, Fairfield Co., Ohio (*Census Place: Lancaster Ward 1, Fairfield, Ohio; Roll: T625_1378; Page: 6A; Enumeration District: 16; Image: 363, entry for Clerel Muck*). Edna says she and her parents were born in Ohio. The next year, she marries Arthur J. Noble.

Edna Victoria married **Arthur John Noble II** on April 2, 1921, in Fairfield Co., Ohio.[220] They had one daughter. Arthur John Noble II was born in Charleroi, Washington Co., Pennsylvania, on September 17, 1903.[70] Arthur John reached age 65 and died in Lancaster, Fairfield Co., Ohio, on October 27, 1968.[221] He was buried in Saint Mary Cemetery, Lancaster, Fairfield Co., Ohio.[222, 223]

Arthur J. and Edna Coover Noble are enumerated in Lancaster, Fairfield Co., Ohio in 1930 (*Census*

Place: Lancaster, Fairfield, Ohio; Roll: 1791; Page: 7B; Enumeration District: 17; Image: 806.0). In the household are Arthur J. Noble, age 26, says he and his parents were born in Pennsylvania. He lists his occupation as tacker in a shoe factory. His wife, Edna V. Coover Noble, is 25 years old and born in Ohio, as were her parents. Arthur Noble says he was 17 years old at the time of his first marriage, and Edna V. Coover Noble says she was 16. With them is their daughter, Ruth, who is eight years old and born in Ohio.

In 1940, widower Arthur J. Noble is living with his widowed mother Barbara Noble in Lancaster, Fairfield Co., Ohio *(Census Place: Lancaster, Fairfield, Ohio; Roll: T627_3066; Page: 20A; Enumeration District: 23-25).* Arthur J. Noble, age 35, works in a shoe factory and was born in Pennsylvania. His mother, Barbara, 69, was born in Pennsylvania. Both say they were living in Lancaster in 1935.

After 1940, Arthur J. Noble married Mrs. Frances Kane.

Arthur John Noble's obituary states he was survived by his daughter Ruth (Noble) Grimsley and one grandson.[222] However, this may have been a step-grandson from his second marriage.

Daughter of Edna Victoria Coover and Arthur John Noble II:

+ 53 f I. **Ruth L.⁹ Noble** was born in Lancaster, Fairfield Co., Ohio, on February 18, 1922.[70, 224, 225] She died in a hospital in Sycamore, Sycamore Twp., DeKalb Co., Illinois, on May 1, 1980.[225, 226]

25. Alma Pearle⁸ Coover *(Melvin Lester⁷, William⁶, Mary Ann⁵ Pegan, Robert A.⁴, Andrew³, Andrew² Pagan, James¹)* was born on September 26, 1907, in Jacksonville, Trimble Twp., Athens Co., Ohio.[77] She was the daughter of Melvin Lester Coover (4) and Odella May Shaw.

She died in Lancaster, Fairfield Co., Ohio, on September 9, 1995, at age 87.[78] Alma Pearle was buried in Forest Lawn Memorial Gardens Cemetery, Columbus, Franklin Co., Ohio.[227, 228]

Childless.

Alma Pearle Coover is enumerated as "Elma Coover" in the home of William and Harriette Faires in Zanesville, Muskingum County, Ohio *(Census Place: Zanesville Ward 5, Muskingum, Ohio; Roll: T625_1425; Page: 7B; Enumeration District: 141; Image: 1063).* Alma Coover, age 12, born Ohio, is listed as a niece to the head of the household. William Faires, 46, born Ohio, his wife Harriette, 45, a West Virginia native, and their daughter "Zelma", 15, born Ohio, are the other members of the household. These Faires may be related to Alma's future sister-in-law, Loretta Faires Coover, who married Alma's brother Arthur Francis Coover.

Alma Pearle married **Alton Herbert Lewis** on March 15, 1928, in Franklin Co., Ohio.[77] They divorced between 1930 and 1940. Alton Herbert Lewis was born in Falls Twp., Muskingum Co., Ohio, on November 23, 1895.[229, 230] He reached age 78 and died in Dresden, Muskingham Co., Ohio, on April 27, 1974.[231, 232] Alton Herbert was buried in Williams Cemetery, Zanesville, Muskingum Co., Ohio.[232]

Alton Herbert Lewis used several birth dates. According to the Muskingum County, Ohio birth records, "Anton" Herbert Lewis was born on November 23, 1895 in Falls Twp., Muskingum Co., Ohio to John M. Lewis and Jessie Williams (Lewis).[229, 230] But Alton Herbert Lewis uses another birth date, August 27, 1895, on his WWI draft registration card and his marriage license to Alma Pearle Coover in Franklin County, Ohio in 1928.[77] On his WWI draft registration, Alton H. Lewis states he was born in Zanesville, Muskingum Co., Ohio, but on his marriage license to Alma he says he was born in Detroit, Wayne Co., Michigan and named his parents as John Lewis and Jessie Williams.[77, 233] The August 27 birth date is also in his obituary.[232] To further confuse matters, his birthdate on the Social Security Death Index, which was on his Social Security application, is February 7, 1895.[70] In the 1900 census, his parents John and Jessie Williams Lewis list his birth month and year as Aug 1895 *(Census Place: Falls, Muskingum, Ohio; Roll: 1310; Page: 11B; Enumeration District:*

0046, entry for Alton Lewis, John Williams, head of household).

When Alton Herbert Lewis and Alma Pearle Coover married in 1928, he was a bookkeeper and she a beautician.[77]

Alton H. and Alma Coover Lewis are enumerated in Zanesville, Muskingum Co., Ohio in 1930 *(Census Place: Zanesville, Muskingum, Ohio; Roll: 1859; Page: 15A; Enumeration District: 54; Image: 555.0).* Alton H. Lewis, age 34, is a barber, born in Ohio like his parents. Alma P. Coover Lewis is 22 years old and says she and her mother were born in Ohio and her father in Kansas. The couple says they were first married at ages 32 and 20 respectively.

Alton H. Lewis is living alone in 1940 at 1623 Dearborn Street in Zanesville, Muskingham Co., Ohio *(Census Place: Zanesville, Muskingum, Ohio; Roll: T627_3123; Page: 12A; Enumeration District: 60-64).* Alton H. Lewis, age 44, born Ohio, lists no occupation, and says he was living in Zanesville in 1935. He says he is married, but his wife Alma Pearl Coover Lewis is not living in the home.

In 1940, Alma Pearle Coover Lewis is found in Zanesville, Muskingham Co., Ohio *(Census Place: Zanesville, Muskingum, Ohio; Roll: T627_3123; Page: 9A; Enumeration District: 60-40).* She is a roomer in the home of Earnest and Beulah Sode at 63 South Street. Alma Pearl Coover Lewis, age 32, born Ohio, is a waitress who says she was living in Zanesville in 1935. The census taker indicates she is married, but the "m" is crossed out. She may have been separated, but not yet divorced.

Alma Pearle Coover Lewis married **Unknown Coons** after 1940.[234]

Alma Pearle Coover Lewis Coons married **Unknown Ogle** before 1971.[234]

Alma Pearle Coover Lewis Coons Ogle married **Frank Bingham Hansen** on August 22, 1990, in Fairfield Co., Ohio.[235] Frank Bingham Hansen was born in Laramie, Albany Co., Wyoming, on December 5, 1919.[236, 237] Frank Bingham reached age 78 and died in Eaton, Washington Twp., Preble Co., Ohio, on April 29, 1998.[203, 204] He was buried in Dayton National Cemetery, Dayton, Montgomery Co., Ohio.[238]

Alma is buried under the name Alma P. Ogle, but her obituary names her as Alma P. Hansen.[227, 228]

26. **Alvin Coover[8] Fawcett** (*Mary Iva[7] Coover, William[6], Mary Ann[5] Pegan, Robert A.[4], Andrew[3], Andrew[2] Pagan, James[1]*) was born on September 28, 1889, in Zanesfield, Jefferson Twp., Logan Co., Ohio.[87, 88] He was the son of Elba Jonathan Fawcett and Mary Iva Coover (5). Alvin Coover died in a facility in Findlay, Hancock Co., Ohio, on June 21, 1982, at age 92.[89] He was buried in Memory Gardens Cemetery, Arcadia, Washington Twp., Hancock Co., Ohio.[239]

In 1910, 20-year-old Alvin Fawcett, living with his parents Elba J. and Mary Iva Coover Fawcett in Zanesfield, Jefferson Twp., Logan Co., Ohio, lists his occupation as baseball player *(Census Place: Jefferson, Logan, Ohio; Roll: T624_1204; Page: 3A; Enumeration District: 0124; Image: 680).*

Alvin Coover married **Anna Idell Creviston** on August 1, 1913, in Logan Co., Ohio.[88] They had one son. Anna Idell Creviston was born in Bellefontaine, Lake Twp., Logan Co., Ohio, on May 14, 1894.[240] She was also known as **Anne**. Anna Idell reached age 78 and died in Fostoria, Seneca Co., Ohio, on May 13, 1973.[241] She was buried in Memory Gardens Cemetery, Arcadia, Washington Twp., Hancock Co., Ohio.[240]

When he is married in 1913, Alvin Fawcett lists his occupation as "collector" and his bride, Anna Idell Creviston, says she is a clerk.[88]

In 1920, Alvin Coover Fawcett is found in Bellefontaine, Lake Twp., Logan Co., Ohio *(Bellefontaine Ward 4, Logan, Ohio; Roll: T625_1405; Page: 8A; Enumeration District: 194; Image: 315).* Alvin C. Fawcett, age 29 is a machinist; his wife Anna Creviston Fawcett is 25 and their son Robert is five. Living with them are Anna's parents, John T. and Margaret Creviston, both 67 years old. All in the home were born in Ohio, as were their parents.

Alvin C. Fawcett is enumerated in Lima, Ottawa Twp., Allen Co., Ohio in 1930 *(Census Place: Lima, Allen, Ohio; Roll: 1747; Page: 17A; Enumeration*

District: 24; Image: 65.0;). In the household are Alvin C. Fawcett, age 40, a railroad fireman, and his wife, Anna Creviston Fawcett, 35, a saleslady in a retail dry goods store. Alvin states he was 22 years old when he first married and Anna says she was 17. They have one child, Robert, 15. Also in the home is Anna's divorced brother, Haskell Creviston, 31, a salesman at the gas company (utility). All and their parents were born in Ohio.

In 1940, Alvin C. Fawcett is residing in Fostoria, Louden Twp., Seneca Co., Ohio *(Census Place: Fostoria, Hancock, Ohio; Roll: T627_3081; Page: 8B; Enumeration District: 32-45).* They are living at 565 West Fremont Street. Alvin Fawcett, age 50, is an engineer on a steam locomotive (railroad). "Ann" Fawcett, is 45 years old. Both say they were born in Ohio, and were living in Lima, Ottawa Twp., Allen Co., Ohio in 1935.

Son of Alvin Coover Fawcett and Anna Idell Creviston:

+ 54 m I. **Robert Alvin**[9] **Fawcett** was born in Bellefontaine, Lake Twp., Logan Co., Ohio, on July 20, 1914.[70, 242, 243, 244] He died in a hospital in Lima, Ottawa Twp., Allen Co., Ohio, on November 26, 1994.[70, 242, 243, 244]

27. Otto J.[8] **Melvin** (*Mary Elizabeth*[7] *Smith, Chrystiana*[6] *Coover, Mary Ann*[5] *Pegan, Robert A.*[4]*, Andrew*[3]*, Andrew*[2] *Pagan, James*[1]) was born on January 21, 1884, in Bloomfield Twp., Logan Co., Ohio.[94, 95] He was the son of John W. Melvin and Mary Elizabeth Smith (6). He died in Bellefontaine, Lake Twp., Logan Co., Ohio, on October 27, 1944, at age 60.[94] Otto J. was buried in Greenwood Cemetery, DeGraff, Pleasant Twp., Logan Co., Ohio.[94]

Childless.

Otto J. Melvin is unmarried in 1920 and living with his sister Dessie, age 34, also unmarried; and widowed mother, Mary Elizabeth Smith Melvin, in Bloomfield Twp., Logan Co., Ohio *(Census Place: Bloomfield, Logan, Ohio; Roll: T625_1405; Page: 1A; Enumeration District: 181; Image: 6).* Otto J. Melvin, age 36, is a farmer, while his mother Mary Elizabeth Smith Melvin, 55, is the farm manager. All in the home are Ohio natives, as were their parents.

Otto J. married Mrs. **Katharyn Ann Ward** McCalla on November 15, 1923, in Logan Co., Ohio.[245] Katharyn Ann Ward was born in Quincy, Miami Twp., Logan Co., Ohio, on August 27, 1890.[246] She reached age 46 and died in Lewiston, Bloomfield Twp., Logan Co., Ohio, on September 5, 1936.[246] Katharyn Ann was buried in Greenwood Cemetery, DeGraff, Pleasant Twp., Logan Co., Ohio.[246, 247]

When she married Otto J. Melvin 1923, Katharyn Ann Ward McCalla was working as a nurse.[245]

In 1930, Otto J. Melvin is enumerated in Bloomfield Twp., Logan Co., Ohio *(Census Place: Bloomfield, Logan, Ohio; Roll: 1829; Page: 3B; Enumeration District: 1; Image: 730.0).* Otto J., 46, is a farmer and wife Katharyn is 39. Otto and Katharyn say they were ages 39 and 33 respectively when they first married, but this is a misunderstanding on their part. Katharyn Ann Ward McCalla Melvin was 33 when she married Otto; she had been married before. Both they and their parents were born in Ohio.

Otto J. Melvin, now a widower, is still a resident of Bloomfield Twp., Logan Co., Ohio in 1940 *(Census Place: Bloomfield, Logan, Ohio; Roll: T627_3100; Page: 4A; Enumeration District: 46-1).* Otto, age 56, is still farming. Once again, his unmarried sister Dessie, 55, is residing with him. Both say they are Ohio natives and were living in the same house on Mt. Cully Road, near the intersection of Boundry Road, in 1935.

28. Dessie Leola[8] **Melvin** (*Mary Elizabeth*[7] *Smith, Chrystiana*[6] *Coover, Mary Ann*[5] *Pegan, Robert A.*[4]*, Andrew*[3]*, Andrew*[2] *Pagan, James*[1]) was born on March 7, 1885, in Bloomfield Twp., Logan Co., Ohio.[96, 97] She was the daughter of John W. Melvin and Mary Elizabeth Smith (6). She died in DeGraff, Miami Twp., Logan Co., Ohio, on January 31, 1959, at age 73.[98] Dessie Leola was buried in Rea Cemetery, Bloomfield Twp., Logan Co., Ohio.[248]

Never married.

In 1920, Dessie Leola Melvin, age 34, single, is living with her brother Otto, 36, a farmer, also unmarried, and widowed mother, Mary E. Smith Melvin, 55, the farm manager, in Bloomfield Twp., Logan Co., Ohio *(Census Place: Bloomfield, Logan, Ohio; Roll: T625_1405; Page: 1A; Enumeration District: 181; Image: 6)*. All were born in Ohio as were their parents.

In 1930, Mary E. Smith Melvin, 65, a widow, and her unmarried daughter Dessie Melvin, 44, are living in DeGraff Twp. Logan Co., Ohio *(Census Place: De Graff, Logan, Ohio; Roll: 1830; Page: 8A; Enumeration District: 19; Image: 41.0)*. Neither lists an occupation, and both were Ohio natives, as were their parents.

Dessie Melvin, age 55, is once again residing with her widower brother Otto in Bloomfield Twp., Logan Co., Ohio *(Census Place: Bloomfield, Logan, Ohio; Roll: T627_3100; Page: 4A; Enumeration District: 46-1)*. The head of the household, Otto Melvin, 56, is still farming. Both say they were born in Ohio and living in the same house on Mt. Cully Road, near the intersection of Boundry Road, in 1935.

29. Fredrick J.[8] Smith *(Henry Sylvester[7], Chrystiana[6] Coover, Mary Ann[5] Pegan, Robert A.[4], Andrew[3], Andrew[2] Pagan, James[1])* was born on November 21, 1896, in Bloomfield Twp., Logan Co., Ohio.[103, 104, 105, 106, 107] He was the son of Henry Sylvester Smith (7) and Altia I. Mohr. He was also known as **Fred J.** He died in Bellefontaine, Lake Twp., Logan Co., Ohio, on August 28, 1957, at age 60.[108, 109] Fredrick J. was buried in Greenwood Cemetery, DeGraff, Pleasant Twp., Logan Co., Ohio.[249]

Fredrick J. married **Lylah Rostofer** on December 24, 1919, in Logan Co., Ohio.[103] They had three children. Lylah Rostofer was born in Pleasant Twp., Hardin Co., Ohio, on July 5, 1899.[103, 250] Lylah reached age 83 and died in Bellefontaine, Lake Twp., Logan Co., Ohio, on January 28, 1983.[250, 251] She was buried in Greenwood Cemetery, DeGraff, Pleasant Twp., Logan Co., Ohio.[250, 252]

In 1920, Frederick and Lylah Rostofer Smith are living with Frederick's parents, Henry Sylvester and Alta Mohr Smith, in Bloomfield Twp., Logan Co., Ohio *(Census Place: Bloomfield, Logan, Ohio; Roll: T625_1405; Page: 1A; Enumeration District: 181; Image: 6)*. Frederick Smith, a farm laborer, is 23 years old and Lylah Rostofer Smith is 20. Henry Sylvester Smith, who owns the farm, is 53 and Alta is 47. All were born in Ohio as were their parents.

In 1930, Frederick J. Smith, listed as "Fred J. Smith", is enumerated in Bloomfield Twp., Logan Co., Ohio *(Census Place: Bloomfield, Logan, Ohio; Roll: 1829; Page: 4A; Enumeration District: 1; Image: 731.0)*. Although his father is living with him and they seem to be living on the same land, Fred J. is listed in listed as head of household. Fred J., age 33 is a farmer, wife Lylah Rostofer Smith is 30, and son Richard is nine years old. Henry, age 63, a widower, is listed with no occupation. All were born in Ohio as were their parents.

Frederick J. Smith, again enumerated as "Fred J. Smith", is still residing in Bloomfield Twp., Logan Co., Ohio in 1940 *(Census Place: Bloomfield, Logan, Ohio; Roll: T627_3100; Page: 5B; Enumeration District: 46-1)*. In the home are Fred J. Smith, age 43, a farmer ("owner operator"); his wife, Lylah Rostofer Smith, 40, and children Richard, 19, Christine, nine, and Mary Alice, five. Son Richard Smith is listed as "assistant operator" of the farm. All were born in Ohio, and say they were living in the same house, which is on Boundary Road, in 1935.

Children of Fredrick J. Smith and Lylah Rostofer:

+ 55 m I. **Richard Emerson[9] Smith** was born in Bloomfield Twp., Logan Co., Ohio, on March 10, 1921.[70, 253, 254] He died in Bellefontaine, Lake Twp., Logan Co., Ohio, on July 26, 1971.[254, 255]

+ 56 f II. **Christine LaVon[9] Smith** was born in Bloomfield Twp., Logan Co., Ohio, on May 23, 1930.[256, 257] She died in Bellefontaine, Lake Twp., Logan Co., Ohio, on May 6, 2016.[257]

+ 57 f III. **Mary Alice[9] Smith** was born in Bloomfield Twp., Logan Co.,

Ohio, on July 11, 1934.[70, 258 259] She died in West Liberty, Liberty Twp., Logan Co., Ohio, on October 19, 2008.[70, 259]

30. Franklin S.[8] Bayer (*Elva Alberta[7] Smith, Chrystiana[6] Coover, Mary Ann[5] Pegan, Robert A.[4], Andrew[3], Andrew[2] Pagan, James[1]*) was born on May 12, 1903, in Sidney, Clinton Twp., Shelby Co., Ohio.[70,116] He was the son of Henry Bayer and Elva Alberta Smith (8). He lived in Mapleton, Union Twp., Huntingdon Co., Pennsylvania in 1991. He died in a hospital in Huntingdon, Huntingdon Co., Pennsylvania, on September 25, 1991, at age 88.[70, 116] Franklin S. was buried in Riverview Cemetery, Huntingdon, Huntingdon Twp., Huntingdon Co., Pennsylvania.[116, 260]

Franklin S. married **Mary Katherine Kephart** on December 6, 1933, in Huntingdon Co., Pennsylvania.[116, 261] They had two daughters. Mary Katherine Kephart was born in Smithfield Twp., Huntingdon Co., Pennsylvania, on June 14, 1912.[70, 261] Mary Katherine reached age 84 and died in Mapleton, Union Twp., Huntingdon Co., Pennsylvania, on February 24, 1997.[70, 261] She was buried in Riverview Cemetery, Huntingdon, Huntingdon Twp., Huntingdon Co., Pennsylvania.[261, 262]

Franklin Bayer is enumerated as "Frank Boyers" in 1940 in Walker Twp., Huntingdon Co., Pennsylvania (*Census Place: Walker, Huntingdon, Pennsylvania; Roll: T627_3515; Page: 1A; Enumeration District: 31-59*). In the household are Franklin Bayer, age 36, a greenskeeper at a golf links (course); his wife, Mary K, 28, and their daughter Helen, six. All are listed as born in Pennsylvania (Incorrect—Frank was born in Ohio). They say they were living in the same home in 1935, but no road or address is given on the page.

Daughters of Franklin S. Bayer and Mary Katherine Kephart:

+ 58   f   I.   **Helen Kathleen[9] Bayer** was born in Walker Twp., Huntingdon Co., Pennsylvania, on February 18, 1935.[70, 263, 264] She died in Huntingdon, Huntingdon Twp., Huntingdon Co., Pennsylvania, on September 3, 1978.[70, 263]

+ 59   f   II. **Mary Lou[9] Bayer** was born in Walker Twp., Huntingdon Co., Pennsylvania, on August 26, 1944.[70, 265] She died in Mapleton, Union Twp., Huntingdon Co., Pennsylvania, on September 10, 2009.[70, 265]

31. Child[8] Bayer (*Elva Alberta[7] Smith, Chrystiana[6] Coover, Mary Ann[5] Pegan, Robert A.[4], Andrew[3], Andrew[2] Pagan, James[1]*) was born between 1900 and 1910 in Sidney, Clinton Twp., Shelby Co., Ohio. He or she was a child of Henry Bayer and Elva Alberta Smith (8). Child died in Sidney, Clinton Twp., Shelby Co., Ohio, before 1910.

32. Glady Fern[8] Shawver (*Ora Belle[7] Smith, Chrystiana[6] Coover, Mary Ann[5] Pegan, Robert A.[4], Andrew[3], Andrew[2] Pagan, James[1]*) was born on October 25, 1891, in Washington Twp., Logan Co., Ohio.[121, 122] She was the daughter of Ellando Shawver and Ora Belle Smith (10). She died in Quincy, Miami Twp., Logan Co., Ohio, on June 18, 1933, at age 41.[122] Glady Fern was buried in Greenwood Cemetery, DeGraff, Pleasant Twp., Logan Co., Ohio.[122, 266]

Childless.

Glady Fern married **Ray Heath Allinger** on October 20, 1914, in Logan Co., Ohio.[103] Ray Heath Allinger was born in Quincy, Miami Twp., Logan Co., Ohio, on April 19, 1892.[70, 121, 267, 268] Ray Heath reached age 69 and died in Quincy, Miami Twp., Logan Co., Ohio, on February 28, 1962.[269, 270] He was buried in Fairview Cemetery, Quincy, Miami Twp., Logan Co., Ohio.[271]

Ray and Glady Shawver Allinger are enumerated in 1920 in Quincy, Miami Twp., Logan Co., Ohio (*Census Place: Miami, Logan, Ohio; Roll: T625_1405; Page: 8B; Enumeration District: 199; Image: 426*). Ray Allinger, age 28, is a miller and

Glady ("Glady"), also 28, is a music teacher. They and their parents were born in Ohio.

In 1930, Ray H. and Glady Shawver Allinger are again found in Quincy, Miami Twp., Logan Co., Ohio (*Census Place: Quincy, Logan, Ohio; Roll: 1830; Page: 3B; Enumeration District: 20; Image: 52.0*), Ray, age 37, is still a miller in a flour mill and Glady is 38. She lists no occupation. Both say they were first married at age 22. They and their parents were born in Ohio.

After his first wife, Glady Shawver Allinger, dies, Ray Allinger remarries to Melba E. McDonald and has a family.[270]

33. **Jay**[8] **Shawver** (*Ora Belle*[7] *Smith, Chrystiana*[6] *Coover, Mary Ann*[5] *Pegan, Robert A.*[4]*, Andrew*[3]*, Andrew*[2] *Pagan, James*[1]) was born on March 3, 1894, in DeGraff, Pleasant Twp., Logan Co., Ohio.[123, 124, 125] He was the son of Ellando Shawver and Ora Belle Smith (10). Jay died in Kenton, Pleasant Twp., Hardin Co., Ohio, on December 16, 1959, at age 65.[126] He was buried in Greenwood Cemetery, DeGraff, Pleasant Twp., Logan Co., Ohio.[272]

Jay married **Grace Maud Rairdon** on August 7, 1915, in Logan Co., Ohio.[123] They had two children. Grace Maud Rairdon was born in Pleasant Twp., Logan Co., Ohio, on July 28, 1893.[70, 123, 273] Grace Maud reached age 89 and died in Upper Arlington, Franklin Co., Ohio, on April 28, 1983.[274, 275] She was buried in Greenwood Cemetery, DeGraff, Pleasant Twp., Logan Co., Ohio.[275, 276]

In 1920, Jay Shawver is enumerated in Lakewood, Rockport Twp., Cuyahoga Co., Ohio (*Census Place: Lakewood Ward 4, Cuyahoga, Ohio; Roll: T625_1376; Page: 5B; Enumeration District: 587; Image: 50*). The head of the household, Jay Shawver, is 25 and a salesman of steel tools. With him is wife Grace Rairdon Shawver, 26, and infant daughter Betty Lois. All and their parents were Ohio natives.

Jay Shawver is found in Kenton, Pleasant Twp., Hardin Co., Ohio in 1930 (*Census Place: Kenton, Hardin, Ohio; Roll: 1821; Page: 7B; Enumeration District: 5; Image: 91.0*). Jay Shawver, age 35, lists his occupation as manager of an electrical store. His wife, Grace Rairdon Shawver, is 36. Jay's first marriage occurred when he was 21 years old; Grace was 22. Children in the home are Betty Lois, 10, and Kenneth, six. All and their parents were born in Ohio.

In 1940, Jay Shawver is still a resident of Kenton, Pleasant Twp., Hardon Co., Ohio (*Census Place: Kenton, Hardin, Ohio; Roll: T627_3082; Page: 16B; Enumeration District: 33-4*). In the household are Jay Shawver, age 46, the owner of a plumbing and electrical store, and his wife, Grace Rairdon Shawver, also 46. Their children, Betty, 20, and Kenneth, 16, are also in the home. All were born in Ohio, and all were living in the same house, 326 Henry Street, in 1935.

Children of Jay Shawver and Grace Maud Rairdon:

+ 60 f I. **Betty Lois**[9] **Shawver** was born in Lakewood, Rockport Twp., Cuyahoga Co., Ohio, on June 10, 1919.[277] She died in Austin, Travis Co., Texas, on February 25, 2016.[278]

+ 61 m II. **Kenneth Rairdon**[9] **Shawver** was born in Bellefontaine, Lake Twp., Logan Co., Ohio, on June 16, 1923.[70, 279, 280, 281] He died in Nashau, Hillsborough Co., New Hampshire, on February 18, 1988.[70, 280, 281]

34. **Harold D.**[8] **Smith** (*John Andrew*[7]*, Chrystiana*[6] *Coover, Mary Ann*[5] *Pegan, Robert A.*[4]*, Andrew*[3]*, Andrew*[2] *Pagan, James*[1]) was born on May 26, 1899, in Bellefontaine, Lake Twp., Logan Co., Ohio.[70, 131] He was the son of John Andrew Smith (11) and Cora C. Hanks. Harold D. died in Bellefontaine, Lake Twp., Logan Co., Ohio, on April 19, 1984, at age 84.[132, 133] He was buried in Glen Cemetery, Port Jefferson, Salem Twp., Shelby Co., Ohio.[133, 282]

Childless.

Harold D. Smith is enumerated in Lima, Ottawa Twp., Allen Co., Ohio in 1920 (*Census Place: Lima Ward 1, Allen, Ohio; Roll: T625_1345; Page: 10A; Enumeration District: 16; Image: 48*). Harold D.

Smith, age 20, born Ohio as were his parents, is the assistant boys secretary for the YMCA.

Harold D. married **Emma C. Pulfer** on April 24, 1923, in Shelby Co., Ohio.[283] Emma C. Pulfer was born in Jackson Twp., Shelby Co., Ohio, on December 6, 1904.[70, 284] She reached age 68 and died in Jackson Center, Jackson Twp., Shelby Co., Ohio, on December 17, 1972.[284, 285] Emma C. was buried in Glen Cemetery, Port Jefferson, Salem Twp., Shelby Co., Ohio.[284, 286]

In 1930, Harold D. Smith is found in Jackson Center, Jackson Twp., Shelby Co., Ohio *(Census Place: Jackson, Shelby, Ohio; Roll: 1873; Page: 1A; Enumeration District: 13; Image: 882.0)*. Harold D. Smith, age 30, a cashier at a bank, says he was first married at age 23. His wife, Emma Pulfer Smith is 25 years old, and says she was first wed at age 18. Both say they and their parents were Ohio natives.

Harold D. Smith is still residing in Jackson Center, Jackson Twp., Shelby Co., Ohio in 1940 *(Census Place: Jackson Center, Shelby, Ohio; Roll: T627_3146; Page: 5A; Enumeration District: 75-17)*. In the home are Harold D. Smith, 40, a teller at the First National Bank. Emma Pulfer Smith, 34, is an operator at the telephone company. Both were born in Ohio, and say they were living in the same home on Davis Street in 1935, but no numerical address is listed.

After his first wife, Emma, died, Harold D. Smith married Mrs. **Grace L. Wright** Ward on August 2, 1975, in Logan Co., Ohio.[133, 287] Grace L. Wright was born in Bloomfield Twp., Logan Co., Ohio, on November 22, 1903.[70, 288] Grace L. lived in 1998 in Jackson Center, Jackson Twp., Shelby Co., Ohio. She reached age 94 and died in a facility in Bellefontaine, Lake Twp., Logan Co., Ohio, on January 20, 1998.[288, 289] Grace L. was buried in Glen Cemetery, Port Jefferson, Salem Twp., Shelby Co., Ohio.[289, 290]

35. Evelyn Fern[8] **Smith** (*John Andrew*[7], *Chrystiana*[6] *Coover, Mary Ann*[5] *Pegan, Robert A.*[4], *Andrew*[3], *Andrew*[2] *Pagan, James*[1]) was born on March 11, 1906, in Bloomfield Twp., Logan Co., Ohio.[134, 70] She was the daughter of John Andrew Smith (11) and Cora C. Hanks. She was living in 1984 in New Carlisle, Bethel Twp., Clark Co., Ohio. Evelyn Fern died in a facility in Troy, Concord Twp., Miami Co., Ohio, on December 2, 1984, at age 78.[135] She was buried in Medway Cemetery, Medway, Bethel Twp., Clark Co., Ohio.[291]

Evelyn Fern married **Clifford LeRoy Rogers** on February 4, 1922, in Logan Co., Ohio.[292] They divorced between 1930 and 1940. They had three children. Clifford LeRoy Rogers was born in Lewistown, Washington Twp., Logan Co., Ohio, on June 4, 1903.[293, 294] Clifford LeRoy lived in 1958 in Prospect Twp., Marion Co., Ohio. He reached age 55 and died in a hospital in Columbus, Franklin Co., Ohio, on August 27, 1958.[295] Clifford LeRoy was buried in Marion Cemetery, Marion, Marion Twp., Marion County, Ohio.[294, 296]

Clifford and Evelyn F. Smith Rogers are enumerated in 1930 in Arlington, Madison Twp., Hancock Co., Ohio *(Census Place: Arlington, Hancock, Ohio; Roll: 1820; Page: 3B; Enumeration District: 25; Image: 437.0)*. Clifford Rogers, age 25, is an automobile salesman. Evelyn Fern Smith Rogers is 23 years old. The pair state they were first wed at ages 18 and 16 respectively. They have three children: Smith D., seven, Don E., six, and Dorothy, five.

In 1940, Evelyn Fern Smith Rogers is living in Sidney, Turtle Creek Twp., Shelby Co., Ohio *(Census Place: Sidney, Shelby, Ohio; Roll: T627_3146; Page: 14B; Enumeration District: 75-6)*. Evelyn Smith Rogers, age 34, born Ohio, is a housekeeper for widower Glenn Knupp and his children. With her is her daughter, Dorothy Rogers, age 15, also born in Ohio. They say they were living in the same house at 711 Oak Street with the Knupps in 1935. The head of the household, Glenn Knupp, 41, born Illinois, is an assembler at a machine tool company. His children are Patricia, 13 and Thomas, six, both born in Ohio. Evelyn's elder son, Smith David, is with his father (see below), while her son Don is living with his grandmother, Cora Hanks Smith in 1940 *(Census Place: Bloomfield, Logan, Ohio; Roll: T627_3100; Page: 2B; Enumeration District: 46-1)*.

Evelyn Smith Rogers never remarried.

In 1940, Evelyn's ex-husband, Clifford Rogers, is found in Marion, Marion Twp., Marion Co., Ohio *(Census Place: Marion, Marion, Ohio; Roll: T627_3110; Page: 10A; Enumeration District: 51-11)*. Clifford Rogers, age 35, is a traveling blockman for a farm machinery company. He has a second wife, Rosie, 34. With him is Smith Rogers, his son by Evelyn Fern Smith Rogers, who is 17 years old. All were born in Ohio, and say they were living in Findlay, Findlay Twp., Hancock Co., Ohio in 1935. Their home is at 626 North Main Street. Clifford Rogers would marry for a third time in 1941 to a Cleora Lucille Brown.[294]

Children of Evelyn Fern Smith and Clifford LeRoy Rogers:

+ 62   m   I.   **Smith David**[9] **Rogers** was born in Lewistown, Washington Twp., Logan Co., Ohio, on May 12, 1922.[70, 297, 298] He was also known as **David**. Smith David died in a facility in Columbus, Franklin Co., Ohio, on May 5, 1988.[70, 297, 298, 299]

+ 63   m   II. **Don Elwood**[9] **Rogers** was born in Lewistown, Washington Twp., Logan Co., Ohio, on August 9, 1923.[70, 300] Don Elwood died in Mililani, Honolulu, Oahu, Hawaii, on February 15, 1986.[70, 300, 301]

+ 64   f   III. **Dorothy Evelyn**[9] **Rogers** was born in Lewistown, Washington Twp., Logan Co., Ohio, on September 11, 1924.[70, 302, 303] She died in Atlanta, DeKalb Co., Georgia, on January 22, 2003.[70, 302, 303]

36. Paul D.[8] **Smith** (*Roy Thurman*[7], *Chrystiana*[6] *Coover, Mary Ann*[5] *Pegan, Robert A.*[4], *Andrew*[3], *Andrew*[2] *Pagan, James*[1]) was born on August 29, 1904, in DeGraff, Miami Twp., Logan Co., Ohio.[70, 142] He was the son of Roy Thurman Smith (13) and Mary Jane Poole. He died in DeGraff, Miami Twp., Logan Co., Ohio, on September 3, 1978, at age 74.[70, 143] Paul D. was buried in Greenwood Cemetery, DeGraff, Pleasant Twp., Logan Co., Ohio.[142, 304] Childless, but may have legally adopted his stepdaughter, Twila Jean Eiler Smith.

In 1930, Paul D. Smith age 25 and unmarried, was living with his parents, Roy T. and Mary Jane Pool Smith in DeGraff, Miami Twp., Logan Co., Ohio *(Census Place: Miami, Logan, Ohio; Roll: 1830; Page: 5A; Enumeration District: 21; Image: 65.0)*. He says he was born in Ohio and lists his occupation as farm laborer.

Paul D. married Mrs. **Ruth Amelia Pence** Eiler on June 16, 1935, in Logan Co., Ohio.[305] Ruth Amelia Pence was born in Buckland, Logan Twp., Auglaize Co., Ohio, on August 10, 1902.[306, 307] Ruth Amelia reached age 60 and died in a hospital in Columbus, Franklin Co., Ohio, on February 28, 1963.[307, 308] She was buried in Greenwood Cemetery, DeGraff, Pleasant Twp., Logan Co., Ohio.[308, 309]

Paul D. Smith is enumerated in DeGraff, Miami Twp., Logan Co., Ohio in 1940 *(Census Place: De Graff, Logan, Ohio; Roll: T627_3100; Page: 10A; Enumeration District: 46-24)*. Paul D. Smith, age 35, is a laborer at a dairy (his mother operates the dairy and his brother Stanley is a salesman there). With him is wife Ruth Eiler Smith, who is 36 years old. A child is with them, Twila ("Iwilda") Smith, age 11, who is listed as a daughter (but, by birth, she is Ruth's daughter by her first husband, William Clifford Eiler). All were born in Ohio. All say they were residing elsewhere in 1935, but exactly where is not given. Vertress Napier, 28, single, born Ohio, a waitress, is a boarder in the home.

Like his father, Roy T. Smith, Paul D. Smith became postmaster at DeGraff, Ohio.[142]

37. Bertha Lucile[8] **Smith** (*Roy Thurman*[7], *Chrystiana*[6] *Coover, Mary Ann*[5] *Pegan, Robert A.*[4], *Andrew*[3], *Andrew*[2] *Pagan, James*[1]) was born on September 5, 1907, in DeGraff, Miami Twp., Logan Co., Ohio.[70, 144, 145, 146] She was also known as **Lucile**. She was the daughter of Roy Thurman Smith (13) and Mary Jane Poole. Bertha Lucile worked as a bookkeeper in 1928.[144] She died in Bellefontaine, Lake Twp., Logan Co., Ohio, on June 27, 1993, at age 85.[70, 145, 146] Bertha Lucile was buried in Greenwood Cemetery, DeGraff, Pleasant Twp., Logan Co., Ohio.[310, 311]

Childless.

Bertha Lucile Smith never used her real given name and always went by "Lucile".

Bertha Lucile married **Cline M. Jenkins** on December 24, 1928, in Logan Co., Ohio.[144] Cline M. Jenkins was born in Champaign Co., Ohio, on July 2, 1898.[70, 144, 312] Cline M. reached age 79 and died in Bellefontaine, Lake Twp., Logan Co., Ohio, on July 11, 1977.[70, 313] He was buried in Greenwood Cemetery, DeGraff, Pleasant Twp., Logan Co., Ohio.[314]

Cline and Lucille Smith Jenkins are enumerated in Johnson Twp., Champaign Co., Ohio in 1930 *(Census Place: Johnson, Champaign, Ohio; Roll: 1755; Page: 7A; Enumeration District: 11; Image: 765.0)*. "Kline" Jenkins is age 32, and is a laborer (most likely on his father's farm); and his wife, "Lucille" Smith Jenkins, is age 22. They are living with Cline's father, Willis Jenkins, age 70, a widower, who owns the farm. Cline and Lucille say they were first married at ages 31 and 21 respectively.

In 1940, Cline and Lucille Smith Jenkins are found in Bloomfield Twp., Logan Co., Ohio *(Census Place: Bloomfield, Logan, Ohio; Roll: T627_3100; Page: 3B; Enumeration District: 46-1)*. In the household are Cline Jenkins, age 41, a tenant farmer, and his wife Lucille Smith Jenkins, 31. Both were born in Ohio, and both say they were living in Shelby County, Ohio in 1935. They were living near the intersection of Bloom Center and DeGraff Road.

38. Stanley Andrew[8] **Smith** (*Roy Thurman*[7], *Chrystiana*[6] *Coover, Mary Ann*[5] *Pegan, Robert A.*[4], *Andrew*[3], *Andrew*[2] *Pagan, James*[1]) was born on April 4, 1915, in DeGraff, Miami Twp., Logan Co., Ohio.[70, 147, 148, 149] He died in DeGraff, Miami Twp., Logan Co., Ohio, on May 21, 1995, at age 80.[70, 147, 148, 149] Stanley Andrew was buried in Glen Cemetery, Port Jefferson, Salem Twp., Shelby Co., Ohio.[148, 315]

Childless.

Stanley A. Smith is living with his parents, Roy T. and Mary Jane Poole Smith, in DeGraff, Miami Twp., Logan Co., Ohio in 1940 *(Census Place: Miami, Logan, Ohio; Roll: T627_3100; Page: 3A; Enumeration District: 46-26)*. Stanley Smith is age 25, single, and a salesman at the dairy his mother operates. The head of the household is Roy T. Smith, age 60, the postmaster at the DeGraff post office. Mary J. Poole Smith, 57, operates a dairy. All were born in Ohio, and say they were living in the same house in 1935. Residing with them is Katherine Strasser, 43, single, a housekeeper born in Ohio.

Stanley Andrew married **Esther Louise Herring** on April 5, 1942, in Shelby Co., Ohio.[316] Esther Louise Herring was born in Salem Twp., Shelby Co., Ohio, on May 25, 1920.[70, 317, 318] Esther Louise lived in 2002 in DeGraff, Miami Twp., Logan Co., Ohio. She reached age 82 and died in a hospital in Lima, Ottawa Twp., Allen Co., Ohio, on September 25, 2002.[70, 317, 318] Esther Louise was buried in Glen Cemetery, Port Jefferson, Salem Twp., Shelby Co., Ohio.[318, 319]

39. Thurman Herring[8] **Smith** (*Hoadley Monroe*[7], *Chrystiana*[6] *Coover, Mary Ann*[5] *Pegan, Robert A.*[4], *Andrew*[3], *Andrew*[2] *Pagan, James*[1]) was born on February 10, 1917, in Bloomfield Twp., Logan Co., Ohio.[70,157] He was the son of Hoadley Monroe Smith (14) and Dolly Herring. Thurman Herring died in Lima, Ottawa Twp., Allen Co., Ohio, on March 15, 1980, at age 63.[158, 159] He was buried in Shawnee Cemetery, Fort Shawnee, Shawnee Twp., Allen Co., Ohio.[159, 320]

Childless.

Thurman Herring Smith, age 23, single and a restaurant waiter, is living with his widowed mother, Dolly Herring Smith, in 1940 in DeGraff, Miami Twp., Logan Co., Ohio *(Census Place: De Graff, Logan, Ohio; Roll: T627_3100; Page: 4B; Enumeration District: 46-24)*. Dolly Herring Smith, listed as the head of the household, is 54. Both were Ohio natives.

Thurman Herring married **Margaret R. Shambaugh** on June 18, 1942.[321] Margaret R. Shambaugh was born in Marathon, Jackson Twp., Clermont Co., Ohio, on December 24, 1915.[70, 321] She reached age 59 and died in Lima, Ottawa Twp., Allen Co., Ohio, on February 13, 1975.[322] Margaret R. was buried in Shawnee Cemetery, Fort Shawnee, Shawnee Twp., Allen Co., Ohio.[321, 323]

Margaret R. Shambaugh Smith worked as a language teacher.[321] Thurman Herring Smith and his wife Margaret later relocated to Lima, Ottawa Twp., Allen Co., Ohio, where he was the manager of Crouse Lumber, an Allen County commissioner, and the Allen County administrator of federal revenue sharing funds.[159]

Thurman H. Smith died just two days after his mother, Dolly Herring Smith, died.

9th Generation

40. Halsey Marvin[9] **Stanley** (*Elta Modena*[8] *Coover, Melvin Lester*[7]*, William*[6]*, Mary Ann*[5] *Pegan, Robert A.*[4]*, Andrew*[3]*, Andrew*[2] *Pagan, James*[1]) was born on May 8, 1913, in Monroe Twp., Logan Co., Ohio.[70,166] He was also known as **Marvin** and **H. Marvin Stanley**. He was the son of Walter Warren Stanley and Elta Modena Coover (17). He died in West Liberty, Liberty Twp., Logan Co., Ohio, on February 24, 2009, at age 95.[70,166] Halsey Marvin was buried in Fairview Cemetery, West Liberty, Liberty Twp., Logan County, Ohio.[324]

Halsey Marvin Stanley preferred his middle name, Marvin, as his given name.

Halsey Marvin married **Myrna Anne Miller** on July 20, 1941, in Logan Co., Ohio.[above] They had two children. Myrna Anne Miller was born in Salem Twp., Champaign Co., Ohio, on January 19, 1919.[325] She resided in 2016 in West Liberty, Liberty Twp., Logan Co., Ohio. Myrna Anne died on November 5, 2016 in a facility in Wooster, Wooster Twp., Wayne Co., Ohio.[325] She was buried in Fairview Cemetery, West Liberty, Liberty Twp., Logan County, Ohio.[326]

41. James Darrell[9] **Stanley** (*Elta Modena*[8] *Coover, Melvin Lester*[7]*, William*[6]*, Mary Ann*[5] *Pegan, Robert A.*[4]*, Andrew*[3]*, Andrew*[2] *Pagan, James*[1]) was born on July 1, 1920, in Monroe Twp., Logan Co., Ohio.[70, 167, 168] He was the son of Walter Warren Stanley and Elta Modena Coover (17). James Darrell died in Huntington Twp., Huntington Co., Indiana, on May 29, 1990, at age 69.[70, 167, 168] He was buried in Markle Cemetery, Markle, Rock Creek Twp., Huntington Co., Indiana.[167, 168, 327, 328]

James Darrell married **Anna Jane Lenwell** on December 21, 1941, in Huntington Co., Indiana.[167, 329] They had five children. Anna Jane Lenwell was born in Salinas, Monterey Co., California, on April 4, 1922.[70, 329] Anna Jane reached age 89 and died in Huntington, Huntington Twp., Huntington Co., Indiana, on July 3, 2011.[70, 329] She was buried in Markle Cemetery, Markle, Rock Creek Twp., Huntington Co., Indiana.[329, 330]

James Darrell Stanley and Anna Jane Lenwell had five children, including:

+ 67 m I. **Jerry Alan**[10] **(Rosebrook) Stanley** was born in Wheeling, Ohio Co., West Virginia, on July 10, 1946.[70, 331, 332] He was adopted about 1946. Jerry Alan died in a hospital in Fort Wayne, Allen Co., Indiana, on February 24, 2010, at age 63.[70, 331, 332]

+ 68 f II. **Barbara Catherine**[10] **Stanley** was born in Huntington, Huntington Twp., Huntington Co., Indiana, on March 24, 1949.[333] She died in a facility in Fort Wayne, Allen Co., Indiana, on December 12, 2015.[333]

+ 69 m III. **Walter David**[10] **Stanley** was born in Huntington, Huntington Twp., Huntington Co., Indiana, on October 26, 1957.[334, 335] He died in Huntington, Huntington Twp., Huntington Co., Indiana, on October 26, 1957.[334, 335]

42. Wendell Wayne[9] **Stanley** (*Elta Modena*[8] *Coover, Melvin Lester*[7]*, William*[6]*, Mary Ann*[5] *Pegan, Robert A.*[4]*, Andrew*[3]*, Andrew*[2] *Pagan, James*[1]) was born on August 13, 1933, in Miami Twp., Logan Co., Ohio.[70, 169] He was the son of Walter Warren Stanley and Elta Modena Coover (17). Wendell Wayne lived in 2007 in Ashtabula County, Ohio. He died in Colulmbus, Franklin Co., Ohio, on April 17, 2007, at age 73.[70, 169] Wendell Wayne was buried in Zanesfield Cemetery, Zanesfield, Jefferson Twp., Logan Co., Ohio.[336]

Never married.

43. Aileen[9] **Pickering** (*Doris E.*[8] *Coover, Melvin Lester*[7]*, William*[6]*, Mary Ann*[5] *Pegan, Robert A.*[4]*, Andrew*[3]*, Andrew*[2] *Pagan, James*[1]) was born on May 31, 1924, in St. Paris, Johnson Twp., Champaign Co., Ohio.[70, 175] She was the daughter of Chlor Washington Pickering and Doris E. Coover (19). Aileen died in Sierra Vista, Cochise Co., Arizona, on

November 26, 2006, at age 82.[70, 175] She was buried in Southern Arizona Veterans Memorial Cemetery, Sierra Vista, Cochise Co., Arizona.[337]

Aileen married **Wilford Wayne Frazier** before 1947. They had two sons. Wilford Wayne Frazier was born in Santee, Knox Co., Nebraska, on March 7, 1923.[70, 338, 339] He was also known as **Uncle Doc**. He reached age 86 and died in Sierra Vista, Cochise Co., Arizona, on May 5, 2009.[70, 338] Wilford Wayne was buried in Southern Arizona Veterans Memorial Cemetery, Sierra Vista, Cochise Co., Arizona.[340]

Wilford Wayne and Aileen Pickering Frazier met at Earlham College in Richmond, Wayne Co., Indiana during the early 1940s. He was Native American, mixed Apaalooske (Crow) and Mdwakaton Santee (Lakota). After his WWII service in the Marine Corps, Wilford intended to become a dentist, but got recalled for the Korean War before he could finish his education. After this war, he was approached by the Bureau of Indian Affairs to join the Public Health Department Division of Indian Health, to train other Native American administrators for the department. He worked on reservations in Michigan and near Portland, Oregon before a transfer to Billings, Montana in 1959. In 1970, Wilford and his family moved to Albuquerque, New Mexico, where he eventually becoming deputy director of the Albuquerque Area Indian Health Service. After his retirement, he and Aileen moved to Sierra Vista, Cochise Co., Arizona.[339] Aileen Pickering Frazier was an expert bead worker and Wilford an artist. Together, they operated Frazier Beadwork, traveling all over the U.S. and the world selling her jewelry and his artwork.[175, 339]

44. **Arthur Wilson**[9] **Lawyer** (*Sylvia*[8] *Coover, Melvin Lester*[7]*, William*[6]*, Mary Ann*[5] *Pegan, Robert A.*[4]*, Andrew*[3]*, Andrew*[2] *Pagan, James*[1]) was born on November 1, 1915, in Thurston, Walnut Twp., Lancaster Co., Ohio.[70, 341] He was the son of Homer Elsworth Lawyer and Sylvia Coover (20). Arthur Wilson also resided in 1981 in Baltimore, Liberty Twp., Fairfield Co., Ohio. He died in a hospital in Lancaster, Fairfield Co., Ohio, on June 16, 1981, at age 65.[183] Arthur Wilson was buried in Thurston Primitive Baptist Cemetery, Thurston, Walnut Twp., Fairfield Co., Ohio.[342, 343]

Arthur Wilson Lawyer was engaged to Mrs. Beulah (Eckard) Miller, and they obtained a marriage license in Franklin County, Ohio on May 11, 1936. But they never married.[341]

Arthur Wilson married **Virginia Katherine Sallaz** on February 21, 1937, in Fairfield Co., Ohio.[344] They divorced. They had three children. Virginia Katherine Sallaz was born in Ripley, Jackson Co., West Virginia, on August 25, 1912.[345, 346] She lived in 1983 in Lancaster, Fairfield Co., Ohio. Virginia Katherine reached age 70 and died in a hospital in Columbus, Franklin Co., Ohio, on January 22, 1983.[347, 348] She was buried in Basil Memorial Cemetery, Baltimore, Liberty Twp., Fairfield Co., Ohio.[349]

Arthur Lawyer is enumerated in Thurston, Walnut Twp., Fairfield Co., Ohio in 1940 *(Census Place: Thurston, Fairfield, Ohio; Roll: T627_3066; Page: 2A; Enumeration District: 23-44)*. In the household are Arthur Lawyer, age 24, a house painter, and his wife Virginia Slatz Lawyer, 27. Both say they were born in Ohio and were living in the same house, 31 Forest Street, in 1935.

Virginia Katherine Sallaz's birth seems to be recorded incorrectly in the Jackson County, West Virginia birth records a few days after she was born. Her birth, which was not the first birth to her parents, is first recorded for July 25, 1912 in Crooked Fork, Jackson Co., West Virginia, by a physician, B.E. Harrison. Her father, Vincent Sallaz, later came to the Jackson County Clerk's office to amend the record and says Virginia Katherine was born August 25, 1912 in Ripley, Jackson Co., West Virginia.[345] The date of her birth on her tombstone is July 25, 1914, but this is incorrect.[349] Her Ohio death record also states she was born in 1914.[347]

Children of Arthur Wilson Lawyer and Virginia Katherine Sallaz:

+ 70 m I. **Larry Eugene**[10] **Lawyer** was born in Fairfield Co., Ohio, on April 4, 1940.[70, 350, 351] He died in Lancaster, Fairfield Co., Ohio, on July 29, 2009.[70, 352]

+ 71   f   II.   **Daughter**[10] **Lawyer** was born in Fairfield Co., Ohio.

+ 72   m   III. **Bobby Wilson**[10] **Lawyer** was born in Lancaster, Fairfield Co., Ohio, on December 22, 1945.[70] He died in Lancaster, Fairfield Co., Ohio, on April 12, 1987.[353]

45. William Nelson[9] **Lawyer** (*Sylvia*[8] *Coover, Melvin Lester*[7]*, William*[6]*, Mary Ann*[5] *Pegan, Robert A.*[4]*, Andrew*[3]*, Andrew*[2] *Pagan, James*[1]) was born on May 5, 1917, in Thurston, Walnut Twp., Lancaster Co., Ohio.[184, 185, 186] He was also known as **Nelson** or **Dynamite**. He was the son of Homer Elsworth Lawyer and Sylvia Coover (20). He died in Lancaster, Fairfield Co., Ohio, on January 5, 1996, at age 78.[184, 185, 186] William Nelson was buried in Thurston Primitive Baptist Cemetery, Thurston, Walnut Twp., Fairfield Co., Ohio.[185]

William Nelson married **Betty Esther McCray** on July 18, 1936, in Fairfield Co., Ohio.[354] They divorced. They had no children. Betty Esther McCray was born in Catlettsburg, Boyd Co., Kentucky, on February 28, 1915.[70, 355, 356] She reached age 83 and died in Columbus, Franklin Co., Ohio, on September 16, 1998.[70, 355] Betty Esther was buried in Maple Grove Cemetery, Baltimore, Liberty Twp., Fairfield Co., Ohio.[357] She died with the name Betty E. Ferguson.

On April 24, 1940, William N. Lawyer is residing at 407 Union Street in Lancaster, Fairfield Co., Ohio *(Census Place: Lancaster, Fairfield, Ohio; Roll: T627_3065; Page: 20A; Enumeration District: 23-17)*. In the household is William N. Lawyer, age 22, a house painter, who says he was living in Thurston, Ohio in 1935. With him is a wife, Betty McCray Lawyer, 25, who says she was living in Lancaster in 1935. Both say they were born in Ohio.

William Nelson Lawyer, enumerated as Nelson Lawyer, age 22, born Ohio, married, was incarcerated in the Fairfield County, Ohio jail on April 10, 1940 in the same census. This time he says he was living in Lancaster in 1935 *(Census Place: Lancaster, Fairfield, Ohio; Roll: T627_3066; Page: 5B; Enumeration District: 23-25)*.

William Nelson Lawyer married **Mary Evelyn Hooker** Hiller on January 16, 1951, in Fairfield Co., Ohio.[358, 359] They divorced before 1957. They had one daughter. Mary Evelyn Hooker was born in Lancaster, Fairfield Co., Ohio, on April 20, 1914.[360, 361] She reached age 76 and died in Lancaster, Fairfield Co., Ohio, on July 17, 1990.[70, 361] Mary Evelyn was buried in Floral Hills Memory Gardens, Lancaster, Fairfield Co., Ohio.[362] She died under the name Mary E. Silcott.

William Nelson Lawyer married Mrs. **Donna Wilder?** Merkel on July 14, 1957, in Fairfield Co., Ohio.[363] They divorced before 1961. Donna Wilder? was born in Columbus, Franklin Co., Ohio, on April 1, 1917.[363] She died before 1996.

William Nelson Lawyer married Mrs. **Martha Magdalene Windle** Lane on February 3, 1961, in Fairfield Co., Ohio.[364] They divorced. They had two sons. Martha Magdalene Windle was born in Nelsonville, York Twp., Athens Co., Ohio, on March 12, 1933.[70, 365] She lived in 1976 in Reynoldsburg, Franklin Co., Ohio. Martha Magdalene reached age 43 and died in a hospital in Columbus, Franklin Co., Ohio, on November 1, 1976.[366] She was buried in Maple Grove Cemetery, Baltimore, Liberty Twp., Fairfield Co., Ohio.[368]

After she and William divorced, Martha Magdalene Windle Lane Lawyer married again and died under the name Martha Tackett.[365, 366]

46. Vivian June[9] **Lawyer** (*Sylvia*[8] *Coover, Melvin Lester*[7]*, William*[6]*, Mary Ann*[5] *Pegan, Robert A.*[4]*, Andrew*[3]*, Andrew*[2] *Pagan, James*[1]) was born on June 11, 1921, in Thurston, Walnut Twp., Lancaster Co., Ohio.[70, 187, 188] She was the daughter of Homer Elsworth Lawyer and Sylvia Coover (20). Vivian June died in Baltimore, Liberty Twp., Fairfield Co., Ohio, on February 9, 1997, at age 75.[187, 188, 189] She was buried in Maple Grove Cemetery, Baltimore, Liberty Twp., Fairfield Co., Ohio.[368]

Vivian June married **Raymond Doyle Armstrong** on March 27, 1941, in Fairfield Co., Ohio.[369] They had four children. Raymond Doyle Armstrong was born in Lancaster, Fairfield Co., Ohio, on April 27, 1915.[70, 370] Raymond Doyle lived in 1993 in Baltimore, Liberty Twp., Fairfield Co., Ohio.

He reached age 78 and died in a hospital in Lancaster, Fairfield Co., Ohio, on June 27, 1993.[70, 370, 371] Raymond Doyle was buried in Maple Grove Cemetery, Baltimore, Liberty Twp., Fairfield County, Ohio..[372]

Vivian June Lawyer and Raymond Doyle Armstrong had four children, including:

+ 73   f   I.   **Daughter**[10] **Armstrong** was born in Lancaster, Fairfield Co., Ohio.

+ 74   f   IV. **Susan Jayne**[10] **Armstrong** was born in Lancaster, Fairfield Co., Ohio, on September 2, 1957.[70, 373] She died in Wilmington, Union Twp., Clinton Co., Ohio, on March 31, 2007.[70, 374, 375]

47. Melvin Raymond[9] **Lawyer** (*Sylvia*[8] *Coover, Melvin Lester*[7]*, William*[6]*, Mary Ann*[5] *Pegan, Robert A.*[4]*, Andrew*[3]*, Andrew*[2] *Pagan, James*[1]) was born on October 16, 1923, in Thurston, Walnut Twp., Lancaster Co., Ohio.[70, 190] He was the son of Homer Elsworth Lawyer and Sylvia Coover (20). Melvin R. died in Wildwood, Sumter Co., Florida, on December 13, 1998, at age 75.[70, 190 191] He was buried in Floral Hills Memory Gardens, Lancaster, Fairfield Co., Ohio.[376, 377]

Melvin R. married **Nita Lois Botts** on December 22, 1946, in Fairfield Co., Ohio.[378] They had two sons. Nita Lois Botts was born in Cerro Gordo, Cerro Gordo Twp., Piatt Co., Illinois, on May 5, 1923.

48. Daniel B.[9] **Lawyer** (*Sylvia*[8] *Coover, Melvin Lester*[7]*, William*[6]*, Mary Ann*[5] *Pegan, Robert A.*[4]*, Andrew*[3]*, Andrew*[2] *Pagan, James*[1]) was born on October 17, 1927, in Thurston, Walnut Twp., Lancaster Co., Ohio.[70, 192] He was also known as **Popeye**. He was the son of Homer Elsworth Lawyer and Sylvia Coover (20). Daniel B. died in Lancaster, Fairfield Co., Ohio, on July 12, 2008, at age 80.[70, 192] He was buried in New School Baptist Cemetery, Thurston, Walnut Twp., Fairfield Co., Ohio.[192]

Never married.

49. Raymond Lester[9] **Finley** (*Helen Claire*[8] *Coover, Melvin Lester*[7]*, William*[6]*, Mary Ann*[5] *Pegan, Robert A.*[4]*, Andrew*[3]*, Andrew*[2] *Pagan, James*[1]) was born on April 27, 1917, in Liberty Twp., Fairfield Co., Ohio.[201, 202, 203, 204, 205] He was the son of Robert Cyril Finley and Helen Claire Coover (22). He died in Lancaster, Fairfield Co., Ohio, on May 13, 1998, at age 81.[201, 202, 203, 205] Raymond Lester was buried in Vega Cemetery, Bloomfield Twp., Jackson Co., Ohio.[203, 379]

Childless.

Raymond Lester married **Edith Marcella Julian** before 1940. They divorced. Edith Marcella Julian was born in Lancaster, Fairfield Co., Ohio, on April 29, 1916.[70, 380, 381] She was also known as **Marcella**. Edith Marcella reached age 87 and died as Marcella Julian Steiner in Oakdale, Washington Co., Minnesota, on January 7, 2004.[70,380] She was cremated and her cremains were buried in Graceland Memorial Park Cemetery and Mausoleum, Grand Rapids, Grand Rapids Twp., Kent Co., Michigan.[380, 382]

Raymond Finley is enumerated in 1940 in Lancaster, Fairfield Co., Ohio *(Census Place: Lancaster, Fairfield, Ohio; Roll: T627_3066; Page: 65A; Enumeration District: 23-24)*. Raymond Finley, age 23, born Ohio, is a boarder in the home of Esther Brocker at 354 East Chestnut Street. He lists his occupation as an office clerk at an electric company, and that he was living in Lancaster in 1935. He says he is married, but his wife is not in the household.

Raymond Lester Finley was U.S. Army major in WWII. After the war he was an accountant and realtor.[203]

Raymond Lester Finley married Mrs. **Susie Emo Gene Hawker** Jones on June 14, 1947, in Fairfield Co., Ohio.[383] Susie Emo Gene Hawker was born in Jackson, Lick Twp., Jackson Co., Ohio, on August 20, 1913.[384] She was also known as **Jean** or **EmoGene**. Susie Emo Gene reached age 102 and died in Lancaster, Fairfield Co., Ohio, on October 13, 2015.[384] She was buried in Vega Cemetery, Bloomfield Twp., Jackson Co., Ohio.[385]

50. Loretta May[9] **Finley** (*Helen Claire*[8] *Coover, Melvin Lester*[7]*, William*[6]*, Mary Ann*[5] *Pegan, Robert A.*[4]*, Andrew*[3]*, Andrew*[2] *Pagan, James*[1]) was born on January 30, 1919, in New Lexington, Pike Twp., Perry Co., Ohio.[70, 206, 207, 208] She was the daughter of Robert Cyril Finley and Helen Claire Coover

(22). Loretta May died in Columbus, Franklin Co., Ohio, on July 11, 1992, at age 73.[206, 209] She was buried in Floral Hills Memory Gardens, Lancaster, Fairfield Co., Ohio.[386]

Loretta May married **James Wilbert Rushia** before 1940. They had two sons. James Wilbert Rushia was born in Lancaster, Fairfield Co., Ohio, on December 12, 1910.[70] James Wilbert reached age 75 and died in Columbus, Franklin Co., Ohio, on August 21, 1986.[387] He was buried in Floral Hills Memory Gardens, Lancaster, Fairfield Co., Ohio.[388]

James W. and Loretta Finley Rushia are enumerated in 1940 in Columbus, Franklin, Ohio *(Census Place: Columbus, Franklin, Ohio; Roll: T627_3250; Page: 61A; Enumeration District: 93-286)*. In the household are James W. Rushia, 29, a furrier at a fur company, and his wife Loretta, 21, an accountant. Both were born in Ohio and say they were living in Columbus, Ohio in 1935. Living with them is James' brother Raymond Rushia, 33, born Ohio, divorced, a shoe salesman.

Loretta May Finley and James Wilbert Rushia had two sons, including:

+ 75   m   II.   **Rickey Lee**[10] **Rushia** was born in Lancaster, Fairfield Co., Ohio, on August 11, 1952.[70, 389, 390, 391] He died in Columbus, Franklin Co., Ohio, on December 17, 1995.[70, 389, 390]

51. Esther Marie[9] **Finley** (*Helen Claire*[8] *Coover, Melvin Lester*[7]*, William*[6]*, Mary Ann*[5] *Pegan, Robert A.*[4]*, Andrew*[3]*, Andrew*[2] *Pagan, James*[1]) was born on April 8, 1921, in Liberty Twp., Fairfield Co., Ohio.[70, 210, 211, 212] She was the daughter of Robert Cyril Finley and Helen Claire Coover (22). She died in Lancaster, Fairfield Co., Ohio, on October 31, 1991, at age 70.[70, 210, 211] Esther Marie was buried in Floral Hills Memory Gardens, Lancaster, Fairfield Co., Ohio.[392]

Esther Marie married **William D. Crist** on May 13, 1939 in Fairfield Co., Ohio.[393] They divorced. They had no children. William D. Crist was born in Lancaster, Fairfield Co., Ohio, on September 27, 1919.[394] William D. reached age 93 and died in Lancaster, Fairfield Co., Ohio, on December 11, 2012.[395]

William and Esther Finley Crist, both age 19 and born in Ohio, are enumerated in the home of Esther's mother, Helen Coover Finley, in 1940 *(Census Place: Lancaster, Fairfield, Ohio; Roll: T627_3066; Page: 6A; Enumeration District: 23-23)*. William lists his occupation as a mechanic in a garage, and Esther says she is a cashier at a theater. Helen Coover Finley, listed as the head of the household, is 40 years old, born Ohio, who is a decorator at a glass factory. Also in the home, at 614 East Main Street, is Helen's son and Esther's brother, Albert Finley, 17. All state they were residents of Lancaster, Fairfield Co., Ohio in 1935.

Esther Marie Finley Crist married **Myrell Franklin Wyrick** about 1941. They had two children. Myrell Franklin Wyrick was born in Junction City, Jackson Twp., Perry Co., Ohio, on January 29, 1917.[70, 396] He was also known as **Mutt**. Myrell Franklin reached age 44 and died in Lancaster, Fairfield Co., Ohio, on January 22, 1962.[397, 398] He was buried in Floral Hills Memory Gardens, Lancaster, Fairfield Co., Ohio.[399]

Esther Marie Finley and Myrell Franklin Wyrick had two children, including:

+ 76   m   I.   **Ronald Franklin**[10] **Wyrick** was born in Lancaster, Fairfield Co., Ohio, on December 5, 1941.[400] He died in Alexandria, Fairfax Co., Virginia, on March 17, 2012.[401]

52. Albert Earl[9] **Finley** (*Helen Claire*[8] *Coover, Melvin Lester*[7]*, William*[6]*, Mary Ann*[5] *Pegan, Robert A.*[4]*, Andrew*[3]*, Andrew*[2] *Pagan, James*[1]) was born on November 16, 1922, in Blacklick, Jefferson Twp., Franklin Co., Ohio.[70, 213, 214] He was the son of Robert Cyril Finley and Helen Claire Coover (22). Albert Earl died in Columbus, Franklin Co., Ohio, on October 2, 1993, at age 70.[70, 213, 214] He was buried in Mifflin Cemetery, Gahanna, Mifflin Twp., Franklin Co., Ohio.[402]

Albert Earl married **Fairy Faye Milligan** about 1946. They had three children. Fairy Faye Milligan was born in Oakland, Amanda Twp., Fairfield Co., Ohio, on November 23, 1918.[70, 403] Fairy Faye reached age 78 and died in Columbus, Franklin Co., Ohio, on October 1, 1997.[70, 403] She was buried in Mifflin Cemetery, Gahanna, Mifflin Twp., Franklin Co., Ohio.[404]

Children of Albert Earl Finley and Fairy Faye Milligan:

+ 77 f   I.   **Daughter One**[10] **Finley** was born in Columbus, Franklin Co., Ohio.

+ 78 m II.   **David Allen**[10] **Finley** was born in Columbus, Franklin Co., Ohio, on August 27, 1949.[70, 405] He died in Columbus, Franklin Co., Ohio, on June 24, 2005.[70, 405]

+ 79 f III. **Daughter Two**[10] **Finley** was born in Columbus, Franklin Co., Ohio.

53. Ruth L.[9] **Noble** (*Edna Victoria*[8] *Coover, Melvin Lester*[7]*, William*[6]*, Mary Ann*[5] *Pegan, Robert A.*[4]*, Andrew*[3]*, Andrew*[2] *Pagan, James*[1]) was born on February 18, 1922, in Lancaster, Fairfield Co., Ohio.[70,224,225] She was the daughter of Arthur John Noble II and Edna Victoria Coover (24). Ruth L. lived in 1968 in Marengo, Marengo Twp., McHenry Co., Illinois. She also resided in 1980 in Kirkland, Franklin Twp., DeKalb Co., Illinois. Ruth L. died in a hospital in Sycamore, Sycamore Twp., DeKalb Co., Illinois, on May 1, 1980, at age 58 and was cremated.[225, 226].

Childless?

Ruth L. Noble married **Unknown Unknown** before 1940. They divorced in March 1951.[406]

Ruth L. Noble Unknown married **Unknown Baron** about March 1951. They divorced that June.[406]

Ruth L. Noble Unknown Baron married **Clayton Morris Kendall** on December 8, 1951, in Franklin Co., Ohio.[407] They divorced in September 1952?[406] Clayton Morris Kendall was born in Glouster, Trimble Twp., Athens Co., Ohio, on August 28, 1910.[70, 407, 408] Clayton Morris reached age 80 and died in Hernando, Citrus Co., Florida, on January 4, 1991.[70, 409]

Ruth L. Noble Unknown Baron Kendall married **Albert Guyer** on August 15, 1953 in Wayne Co., Indiana.[406] Albert Guyer was born on September 5, 1907 in Columbus, Franklin Co., Ohio.[70, 406] He may have died in Columbus, Franklin Co. Ohio, on July 3, 1967.[410]

Albert Guyer states on his marriage application to Ruth that he was born on September 5, 1910, the son of George and Helen Warner Guyer.[406] But Social Security information and his death certificate say that the George F. Guyer who died on July 3, 1967 in Columbus, Ohio was born on September 5, 1907.[70, 410] Also, information on his alleged parents, George and Helen Warner Guyer cannot be found.

Ruth L. Noble Unknown Baron Kendall Guyer married **Melvin Walter Grimsley** after 1953. Melvin Walter Grimsley was born in Sweetwater, Ramsey Co., North Dakota, on July 21, 1923.[70, 411, 412] Melvin Walter was living before 2004 in Devils Lake, Ramsey Co., North Dakota. He reached age 80 and died in a facility in Bemidji, Beltrami Co., Minnesota, on April 17, 2004.[70, 411] Melvin Walter was buried in Grand Army of the Republic Cemetery, Devils Lake, Ramsey Co., North Dakota.[411, 413]

After his wife Ruth Noble Grimsley died, Melvin W. Grimsley removed from Kirkland, Franklin Twp., DeKalb Co., Illinois to his hometown of Devils Lake, Ramsey Co., North Dakota and resided there for some years. He died in a care facility in Bemidji, Beltrami Co., Minnesota.[411]

Ruth L. Noble was married at least five times. Ruth states on her Wayne County, Indiana marriage license to Albert Guyer in 1953 that she had been married and divorced three times. The first divorce was in March 1951, the second, from Unknown Baron, in June 1951, and the third in September 1951. However, as her third marriage to Clayton Kendall wasn't until December 1951, she may have meant the divorce was in September 1952.[406]

Ruth L. Noble Unknown Baron Kendall Guyer Grimsley may have had one child. If so, her child was born between 1953 and 1968, as she states on her Indiana marriage license application to George Guyer in 1953 that she has no children.[406] Her alleged child, of unknown gender, is listed as a "grandchild" in her father's. Arthur Noble's, 1968 obituary.[222] However, if she did have a child, he or she died before Ruth did in 1980, as no children are mentioned in her obituary.[225] The child was not by her last husband, Melvin W. Grimsley, as no child was mentioned in his obituary either.[411] This "grandchild" may have been a step-grandchild from Arthur Noble's second marriage.

54. **Robert Alvin**[9] **Fawcett** (*Alvin Coover*[8], *Mary Iva*[7] *Coover*, *William*[6], *Mary Ann*[5] *Pegan*, *Robert A.*[4], *Andrew*[3], *Andrew*[2] *Pagan*, *James*[1]) was born on July 20, 1914, in Bellefontaine, Lake Twp., Logan Co., Ohio.[70, 242, 243, 244] He was the son of Alvin Coover Fawcett (26) and Anna Idell Creviston. Robert Alvin lived in 1994 in Ottawa, Ottawa Twp., Putnam Co., Ohio. He died in a hospital in Lima, Ottawa Twp., Allen Co., Ohio, on November 26, 1994, at age 80.[70, 242, 243, 244] Robert Alvin was buried in SS. Peter and Paul Church Cemetery, Ottawa, Ottawa Twp., Putnam Co., Ohio.[242, 414]

Robert Alvin married **Mary Rose Leahey** on November 12, 1937.[242] They had four children. Mary Rose Leahey was born in Dayton, Montgomery Co., Ohio, on May 14, 1915.[70, 415] Mary Rose lived in 1984 in Ottawa, Ottawa Twp., Putnam Co., Ohio. She reached age 69 and died in a facility in Glandorf, Ottawa Twp., Putnam Co., Ohio, on October 26, 1984.[415, 416] Mary Rose was buried in SS. Peter and Paul Church Cemetery, Ottawa, Ottawa Twp., Putnam Co., Ohio.[415, 417]

Robert A. Fawcett is not found in the 1940 U.S. census.

Robert Alvin Fawcett and Mary Rose Leahey had four children, including:

+ 80   m   I.   **Son**[10] **Fawcett** was born in Ottawa, Ottawa Twp., Putnam Co., Ohio.

+ 81   f   II.   **Gail Anne**[10] **Finley** was born in Ottawa, Ottawa Twp., Putnam Co., Ohio, on September 7, 1943.[70, 418] She was also known as **Sissy**. Gail Anne died in Centerville, Washington Twp., Montgomery Co., Ohio, on May 16, 2008.[70, 419]

55. **Richard Emerson**[9] **Smith** (*Fredrick J.*[8], *Henry Sylvester*[7], *Chrystiana*[6] *Coover*, *Mary Ann*[5] *Pegan*, *Robert A.*[4], *Andrew*[3], *Andrew*[2] *Pagan*, *James*[1]) was born on March 10, 1921, in Bloomfield Twp., Logan Co., Ohio.[70, 253, 254] He was the son of Fredrick J. Smith (29) and Lylah Rostofer. He died in Bellefontaine, Lake Twp., Logan Co., Ohio, on July 26, 1971, at age 50.[254, 255] Richard Emerson was buried in Greenwood Cemetery, DeGraff, Pleasant Twp., Logan Co., Ohio.[254]

Never married.

Richard E. Smith, a staff sergeant in the U.S. Air Force, was based at Nellis Air Base, Clark Co., Nevada for many years. He served in WWII and the Korean and Vietnam wars.[254]

56. **Christine LaVon**[9] **Smith** (*Fredrick J.*[8], *Henry Sylvester*[7], *Chrystiana*[6] *Coover*, *Mary Ann*[5] *Pegan*, *Robert A.*[4], *Andrew*[3], *Andrew*[2] *Pagan*, *James*[1]) was born on May 23, 1930, in Bloomfield Twp., Logan Co., Ohio.[256, 257] She was the daughter of Fredrick J. Smith (29) and Lylah Rostofer. Christine LaVon died in Bellefontaine, Lake Twp., Logan Co., Ohio, on May 6, 2016, at age 85.[257] She was buried in Highland Memorial Cemetery, West Liberty, Liberty Twp., Logan Co., Ohio.[420]

Christine LaVon married **Isaac Wilcox II** on November 16, 1947, in New Hampshire.[421] They had three children. Isaac Wilcox II was born in McDonald Twp., Hardin Co., Ohio, on May 23, 1927.[70, 421] He reached age 53 and died in Bellefontaine, Lake Twp., Logan Co., Ohio, on January 11, 1981.[70, 422] Isaac was buried in Highland Memorial Cemetery, West Liberty, Liberty Twp., Logan Co., Ohio.[423]

Children of Christine LaVon Smith and Isaac Wilcox II:

+ 99   f   III.   **Daughter**[10] **Wilcox**

57. **Mary Alice**[9] **Smith** (*Fredrick J.*[8], *Henry Sylvester*[7], *Chrystiana*[6] *Coover*, *Mary Ann*[5] *Pegan*, *Robert A.*[4], *Andrew*[3], *Andrew*[2] *Pagan*, *James*[1]) was born on July 11, 1934, in Bloomfield Twp., Logan Co., Ohio.[70, 258, 259] She was the daughter of Fredrick J. Smith (29) and Lylah Rostofer. Mary Alice lived in 1983 in Naples, Collier Co., Florida. She died in West Liberty, Liberty Twp., Logan Co., Ohio, on October 19, 2008, at age 74.[70, 259] Mary Alice

was buried in Highland Memorial Cemetery, West Liberty, Liberty Twp., Logan Co., Ohio.[259, 424]

Mary Alice married **Richard Max Slonecker** on March 22, 1953, in San Diego Co., California.[259] They had two daughters. Richard Max Slonecker was born in Union Twp., Logan Co., Ohio, on October 4, 1931.[70, 425, 426] Richard Max reached age 70 and died in Bellefontaine, Lake Twp., Logan Co., Ohio, on December 5, 2001.[70, 425] He was buried in Highland Memorial Cemetery, West Liberty, Liberty Twp., Logan Co., Ohio.[427, 428]

According to Mary Alice Smith Slonecker's obituary, Max and Mary Alice Smith Slonecker were married at Camp Pendleton, Oceanside, San Diego Co., California. They lived in Naples, Collier Co., Florida from 1973-1993.[259]

Mary Alice Smith and Richard Max Slonecker had two daughers, including:

+ 83 f I. **Sharon Lee**[10] **Slonecker** was born in Columbus, Franklin Co., Ohio, on January 8, 1953.[70, 429, 430] She died in Naples, Collier Co., Florida, on February 5, 1990.[70, 429, 430]

58. Helen Kathleen[9] **Bayer** (*Franklin S.*[8], *Elva Alberta*[7] *Smith, Chrystiana*[6] *Coover, Mary Ann*[5] *Pegan, Robert A.*[4], *Andrew*[3], *Andrew*[2] *Pagan, James*[1]) was born on February 18, 1935, in Walker Twp., Huntingdon Co., Pennsylvania.[70, 263, 264] She was the daughter of Franklin S. Bayer (30) and Mary Katherine Kephart. Helen Kathleen died in Huntingdon, Huntingdon Twp., Huntingdon Co., Pennsylvania, on September 3, 1978, at age 43.[70, 263] She was buried in Riverview Cemetery, Huntingdon, Huntingdon Twp., Huntingdon Co., Pennsylvania.[263, 431]

Helen Kathleen married **Alfred Cozard Huhn II** before 1954. They had two sons. Alfred Cozard Huhn II was born in Huntingdon, Huntingdon Twp., Huntingdon Co., Pennsylvania, on December 29, 1924.[70, 432, 433] Alfred Cozard reached age 82 and died in Sebastian, Indiana River Co., Florida, on April 22, 2007.[70, 432, 434]

After Helen Kathleen Bayer Huhn died, Alfred Cozard married again.

Helen Kathleen Bayer and Alfred Cozard Huhn II had two sons, including:

+ 84 m I. **Max Robert**[10] **Huhn** was born in Mapleton, Union Twp., Huntingdon Co., Pennsylvania, on April 11, 1954.[435, 436] He died in a hospital in Woodstock, Shenandoah Co., Virginia, on September 13, 1985.[435, 436]

59. Mary Lou[9] **Bayer** (*Franklin S.*[8], *Elva Alberta*[7] *Smith, Chrystiana*[6] *Coover, Mary Ann*[5] *Pegan, Robert A.*[4], *Andrew*[3], *Andrew*[2] *Pagan, James*[1]) was born on August 26, 1944, in Walker Twp., Huntingdon Co., Pennsylvania.[70, 265] She was the daughter of Franklin S. Bayer (30) and Mary Katherine Kephart. Mary Lou died in Mapleton, Union Twp., Huntingdon Co., Pennsylvania, on September 10, 2009, at age 65.[70, 265]

Mary Lou married **Mr. Anderson** on June 6, 1964, in Huntingdon Co., Pennsylvania.[265] They had two children.

60. Betty Lois[9] **Shawver** (*Jay*[8], *Ora Belle*[7] *Smith, Chrystiana*[6] *Coover, Mary Ann*[5] *Pegan, Robert A.*[4], *Andrew*[3], *Andrew*[2] *Pagan, James*[1]) was born on June 10, 1919, in Lakewood, Rockport Twp., Cuyahoga Co., Ohio.[277] She was the daughter of Jay Shawver (33) and Grace Maud Rairdon. Betty Lois lived in 1959 in Munich, Germany. She also resided in 2012 in Columbus, Franklin Co., Ohio. Betty Lois died in Austin, Travis Co., Texas, on February 25, 2016, at age 96.[278]

Betty Lois married **Louis Emory** on October 3, 1942, in Marion Co., Indiana.[437] They had three children. Louis Emory was born in Ohio on July 22, 1917.[70, 438] He reached age 63 and died in Upper Arlington, Franklin Co., Ohio, on May 9, 1981.[439] Louis was buried in Arlington National Cemetery, Arlington, Virginia.[440]

U.S. Army Colonel Dr. Louis Emory, D.D.S., a dentist, served at several U.S. bases and in Germany and Japan. After he retired from the Air Force, he joined the faculty at the Ohio State University School of Dentistry.[278, 441]

Children of Betty Lois Shawver and Louis Emory had three children, including:

+ 85 m III. **Louis Dale**[10] **Emory II** was born in Tokyo, Japan, on December 2, 1949.[70, 442, 443, 444] He died in Columbus, Franklin Co., Ohio, on September 30, 1992.[70, 442, 444]

61. Kenneth Rairdan[9] **Shawver** (*Jay*[8], *Ora Belle*[7] *Smith, Chrystiana*[6] *Coover, Mary Ann*[5] *Pegan, Robert A.*[4], *Andrew*[3], *Andrew*[2] *Pagan, James*[1]) was born on June 16, 1923, in Bellefontaine, Lake Twp., Logan Co., Ohio.[70, 279, 280, 281] He was the son of Jay Shawver (33) and Grace Maud Rairdon. Kenneth Rairdan died in Nashau, Hillsborough Co., New Hampshire, on February 18, 1988, at age 64.[70, 280, 281] He was buried in Greenwood Cemetery, DeGraff, Pleasant Twp., Logan Co., Ohio.[445, 446]

Kenneth Rairdan married **Catherine Marie Nourse** on June 8, 1947, in Hardin Co., Ohio.[447, 448] They divorced. They had no children. Catherine Marie Nourse was born in Kenton, Pleasant Twp., Hardin Co., Ohio, on January 5, 1924.[448, 449] She reached age 93 and died in Austin, Travis Co., Texas, on December 14, 2017.[A]

Catherine Marie Nourse married twice more and died as Catherine M. Russell.

Kenneth Rairdan Shawver married **Rosemary Bushong** on January 16, 1957, in Hardin Co., Ohio.[450] They had four children. Rosemary Bushong was born in Kenton, Pleasant Twp., Hardin Co., Ohio, on February 1, 1936.[450, 451]

62. Smith David[9] **Rogers** (*Evelyn Fern*[8] *Smith, John Andrew*[7], *Chrystiana*[6] *Coover, Mary Ann*[5] *Pegan, Robert A.*[4], *Andrew*[3], *Andrew*[2] *Pagan, James*[1]) was born on May 12, 1922, in Lewistown, Washington Twp., Logan Co., Ohio.[58, 297, 298] He was also known as **David**. He was the son of Clifford LeRoy Rogers and Evelyn Fern Smith (35). He resided in 1988 in Marion, Marion Twp., Marion Co., Ohio. Smith David Rogers died in a facility in Columbus, Franklin Co., Ohio, on May 5, 1988, at age 65.[58, 297, 298, 299] He was buried in New Caledonia Cemetery, Caledonia, Claridon Twp., Marion Co., Ohio.[297, 452]

Smith David married **Rose Etta White** on February 28, 1942, in Morrow Co., Ohio.[297] They had one son. Rose Etta White was born in Marion, Marion Twp., Marion Co., Ohio?, on September 30, 1923.[70, 453] Rose Etta reached age 79 and died in Marion, Marion Twp., Marion Co., Ohio, on September 7, 2003.[70, 454] She was buried in New Caledonia Cemetery, Caledonia, Claridon Twp., Marion Co., Ohio.[454, 455]

63. Don Elwood[9] **Rogers** (*Evelyn Fern*[8] *Smith, John Andrew*[7], *Chrystiana*[6] *Coover, Mary Ann*[5] *Pegan, Robert A.*[4], *Andrew*[3], *Andrew*[2] *Pagan, James*[1]) was born on August 9, 1923, in Lewistown, Washington Twp., Logan Co., Ohio.[70, 300] He was the son of Clifford LeRoy Rogers and Evelyn Fern Smith (35). Don Elwood lived in Tokyo, Japan in 1961. He died in Mililani, Honolulu, Oahu, Hawaii, on February 15, 1986, at age 62.[70, 300, 301] He was cremated and his ashes buried in National Memorial Cemetery of the Pacific, Honolulu, Oahu Island, Hawaii.[456, 457]

Donald Elwood married **Jean Uno** about 1951. They had one daughter. Jean Uno was born in Hiroshima Ke, Japan, on March 30, 1925.[70, 458] Jean reached age 73 and died in San Francisco, San Francisco Co., California, on February 4, 1999.[70, 458] She was buried in National Memorial Cemetery of the Pacific, Honolulu, Oahu Island, Hawaii.[459]

64. Dorothy Evelyn[9] **Rogers** (*Evelyn Fern*[8] *Smith, John Andrew*[7], *Chrystiana*[6] *Coover, Mary Ann*[5] *Pegan, Robert A.*[4], *Andrew*[3], *Andrew*[2] *Pagan, James*[1]) was born on September 11, 1924, in Lewistown, Washington Twp., Logan Co., Ohio.[70, 302, 303] She was the daughter of Clifford LeRoy Rogers and Evelyn Fern Smith (35). Dorothy Evelyn lived in 1961 in Medway, Bethel Twp., Clark Co., Ohio. She also resided in 2003 in Peachtree City, Fulton Co., Georgia. Dorothy Evelyn died in Atlanta, DeKalb Co., Georgia, on January 22, 2003, at age 78.[70, 302, 303] She was cremated and her cremains buried in Medway Cemetery, Medway, Bethel Twp., Clark Co., Ohio.[460]

Dorothy Evelyn married **Raymond Maxwell Poland** on November 1, 1945.[302] They had two children. Raymond Maxwell Poland was born in Keyser, Mineral Co., West Virginia, on August 23,

1924.[70, 461] Raymond Maxwell reached age 75 and died in Peachtree City, Fulton Co., Georgia, on September 5, 1999.[70, 462] He was buried in Medway Cemetery, Medway, Bethel Twp., Clark Co., Ohio.[463] Raymond Maxwell Poland worked as a broadcast television engineer.[462]

10th Generation

67. Jerry Alan¹⁰ (Rosebrook) Stanley (*James Darrell⁹, Elta Modena⁸ Coover, Melvin Lester⁷, William⁶, Mary Ann⁵ Pegan, Robert A.⁴, Andrew³, Andrew² Pagan, James¹*) was born on July 10, 1946, in Wheeling, Ohio Co., West Virginia.[70, 331, 332] He was the son of James Darrell Stanley (41) and Anna Jane Lenwell. Jerry Alan (Rosebrook) was adopted about 1946. He lived in 2010 in Huntington, Huntington Twp., Huntington Co., Indiana. Jerry Alan died in a hospital in Fort Wayne, Allen Co., Indiana, on February 24, 2010, at age 63.[70, 331, 332]] He was buried in Marion National Cemetery, Marion, Grant Co., Indiana.[331, 464]

Jerry Alan married **Terry Lynn McGinniss** on April 28, 1979, in Huntington Co., Indiana.[331, 465] They had four children. Terry Lynn McGinniss was born in Huntington, Huntington Twp., Huntington Co., Indiana, on August 7, 1957.[466] Terry Lynn reached age 55 and died in Huntington, Huntington Twp., Huntington Co., Indiana, on March 4, 2013.[466] She was buried in Marion National Cemetery, Marion, Grant Co., Indiana.[467]

Jerry Alan Stanley was adopted. His birth father is named as John Rosebrook on Jerry's marriage license and death certificate, but his mother is "unknown".[332, 465] His father is listed in his obituary and a birth brother, Bill Rosebrook of Elk City, Oklahoma is mentioned also.[331]

68. Barbara Catherine¹⁰ Stanley (*James Darrell⁹, Elta Modena⁸ Coover, Melvin Lester⁷, William⁶, Mary Ann⁵ Pegan, Robert A.⁴, Andrew³, Andrew² Pagan, James¹*) was born on March 24, 1949, in Huntington, Huntington Twp., Huntington Co., Indiana.[333] She was the daughter of James Darrell Stanley (41) and Anna Jane Lenwell. Barbara Catherine lived in 2015 in Huntington, Huntington Twp., Huntington Co., Indiana. She died in a facility in Fort Wayne, Allen Co., Indiana, on December 12, 2015, at age 66.[333]

Barbara Catherine married **Mr. Meier.** They divorced. They had two children.

69. Walter David¹⁰ Stanley (*James Darrell⁹, Elta Modena⁸ Coover, Melvin Lester⁷, William⁶, Mary Ann⁵ Pegan, Robert A.⁴, Andrew³, Andrew² Pagan, James¹*) was born on October 26, 1957, in Huntington, Huntington Twp., Huntington Co., Indiana.[334, 335] He was the son of James Darrell Stanley (41) and Anna Jane Lenwell. Walter David died in Huntington, Huntington Twp., Huntington Co., Indiana, on October 26, 1957.[334, 335] He was buried in Pilgrims Rest Cemetery, Huntington, Huntington Twp., Huntington Co., Indiana.[334, 468]

70. Larry Eugene¹⁰ Lawyer (*Arthur Wilson⁹, Sylvia⁸ Coover, Melvin Lester⁷, William⁶, Mary Ann⁵ Pegan, Robert A.⁴, Andrew³, Andrew² Pagan, James¹*) was born on April 4, 1940, in Baltimore, Liberty Twp., Fairfield Co., Ohio.[70, 350, 351, 352] He was the son of Arthur Wilson Lawyer (44) and Virginia Katherine Sallaz. Larry Eugene lived in 1981 in Lancaster, Fairfield Co., Ohio. He died in Lancaster, Fairfield Co., Ohio, on July 29, 2009, at age 69.[70, 352] He was cremated.

Larry Eugene married **Miss Casteen** in 1964. They divorced. They had three children.

Larry Eugene Lawyer married **Della Catherine Penrod** on April 26, 1976, in Fairfield Co., Ohio.[469] Della Catherine Penrod was born in Perry Co., Ohio?, on April 10, 1950.[470, 471] She was also known as **Cathy**. Della Catherine reached age 62 and died in Columbus, Franklin Co., Ohio, on March 19, 2013.[470]

71. Daughter¹⁰ Lawyer (*Arthur Wilson⁹, Sylvia⁸ Coover, Melvin Lester⁷, William⁶, Mary Ann⁵ Pegan, Robert A.⁴, Andrew³, Andrew² Pagan, James¹*) was born on February 24, 1942, in Fairfield Co., Ohio.[303] She was the daughter of Arthur Wilson Lawyer (44) and Virginia Katherine Sallaz.

She married **Wesley Lydell Thomas** before 1963. They had two sons. Wesley Lydell Thomas was born in Birmingham, Jefferson Co., Alabama, on October 10, 1937.[70, 472, 473] He was also known as **Dell**. Wesley Lydell reached age 69 and died in a hospital in Columbus, Franklin Co., Ohio, on September 4, 2007.[70, 472, 473] He was buried in Basil Memorial Cemetery, Baltimore, Liberty Twp., Fairfield Co., Ohio.[472]

72. Bobby Wilson[10] Lawyer (*Arthur Wilson[9], Sylvia[8] Coover, Melvin Lester[7], William[6], Mary Ann[5] Pegan, Robert A.[4], Andrew[3], Andrew[2] Pagan, James[1]*) was born on December 22, 1945, in Lancaster, Fairfield Co., Ohio.[70] He was the son of Arthur Wilson Lawyer (44) and Virginia Katherine Sallaz. Bobby Wilson lived in 1981 in Lancaster, Fairfield Co., Ohio. He died in Lancaster, Fairfield Co., Ohio, on April 12, 1987, at age 41.[353] Bobby Wilson was buried in Basil Memorial Cemetery, Baltimore, Liberty Twp., Fairfield Co., Ohio.[474]

Bobby Wilson married **Miss Blauser.** They divorced. They had two children.

Bobby Wilson Lawyer married **Charlotte A. Conrad** Rager on May 22, 1972, in Fairfield Co., Ohio.[475] They divorced. Charlotte A. Conrad was born in Logan, Falls Twp., Hocking Co., Ohio, on April 17, 1937.[475] She reached age 72 and died in Logan, Falls Twp., Hocking Co., Ohio, on September 17, 2009.[475] Charlotte A. was buried in Carbon Hill Cemetery, Carbon Hill, Ward Twp., Hocking Co., Ohio.[476]

Bobby Wilson Lawyer married **Ms. Thrush** on July 31, 1982, in Fairfield Co., Ohio.[477] They divorced.

73. Daughter[10] Armstrong (*Vivian June[9] Lawyer, Sylvia[8] Coover, Melvin Lester[7], William[6], Mary Ann[5] Pegan, Robert A.[4], Andrew[3], Andrew[2] Pagan, James[1]*) was born in Lancaster, Fairfield Co., Ohio. She was the daughter of Raymond Doyle Armstrong and Vivian June Lawyer (46).

Daughter Armstrong married **Mr. Logue.** They had two children.

Daughter Armstrong and Mr. Logue had two children, including:

+ 86 f I. **Tracy Ann[11] Logue** was born in Lancaster, Fairfield Co., Ohio, on March 24, 1962.[70, 478, 479] She died in a hospital in Columbus, Franklin Co., Ohio, on June 24, 1987. [70, 480]

74. Susan Jayne[10] Armstrong (*Vivian June[9] Lawyer, Sylvia[8] Coover, Melvin Lester[7], William[6], Mary Ann[5] Pegan, Robert A.[4], Andrew[3], Andrew[2] Pagan, James[1]*) was born on September 2, 1957, in Lancaster, Fairfield Co., Ohio.[70, 373] She was the daughter of Raymond Doyle Armstrong and Vivian June Lawyer (46). Susan Jayne lived in 1997 in Ashland, Boyd Co., Kentucky. She also resided in 2007 in Greenup Co., Kentucky. Susan Jayne died in Wilmington, Union Twp., Clinton Co., Ohio, on March 31, 2007, at age 49.[70, 374, 375] She was buried as Susan J. Tomko in Golden Oaks Memorial Gardens Cemetery, Ashland, Boyd Co., Kentucky.[481]

Susan Jayne Armstrong married **Mr. Evans.** They divorced.

Susan Jayne Armstrong Evans married **Mr. Howard.** They divorced.

Susan Jayne Armstrong Evans Howard married **Mr. Tomko.**

75. Rickey Lee[10] Rushia (*Loretta May[9] Finley, Helen Claire[8] Coover, Melvin Lester[7], William[6], Mary Ann[5] Pegan, Robert A.[4], Andrew[3], Andrew[2] Pagan, James[1]*) was born on August 11, 1952, in Lancaster, Fairfield Co., Ohio.[70, 389, 390, 391] He was the son of James Wilbert Rushia and Loretta May Finley (50). Rickey Lee died in Columbus, Franklin Co., Ohio, on December 17, 1995, at age 43.[70, 389, 390] He was buried in Floral Hills Memory Gardens, Lancaster, Fairfield Co., Ohio.[482]

His name on his birth and death certificates is "Rickey Lee Rushia".[390, 391] His Social Security information is under "Rick L. Rushia".[70, 389]

Rickey Lee married **Miss Miller.** They divorced They have one daughter.

76. Ronald Franklin[10] Wyrick (*Esther Marie[9] Finley, Helen Claire[8] Coover, Melvin Lester[7], William[6], Mary Ann[5] Pegan, Robert A.[4], Andrew[3], Andrew[2] Pagan, James[1]*) was born on December 5, 1941, in Lancaster, Fairfield Co., Ohio.[400] He was the son of Myrell Franklin Wyrick and Esther Marie Finley (51). Ronald Franklin died in Alexandria, Fairfax Co., Virginia, on March 17, 2012, at age 70.[401] He was buried in Floral Hills Memory Gardens, Lancaster, Fairfield Co., Ohio.[400]

Never married.

77. Daughter One[10] Finley (*Albert Earl[9], Helen Claire[8] Coover, Melvin Lester[7], William[6], Mary Ann[5] Pegan,*

Robert A.⁴, Andrew³, Andrew² Pagan, James¹) was born in Columbus, Franklin Co., Ohio. She was the daughter of Albert Earl Finley (52) and Fairy Faye Milligan.

She married **David Dixon**. They divorced. They had three children. David Dixon was born in Columbus, Franklin Co., Ohio, on May 27, 1945.[70, 483, 484] He reached age 64 and died in Columbus, Franklin Co., Ohio, on January 2, 2010.[70, 485] David was buried in St. Joseph Cemetery, Lockbourne, Hamilton Twp., Franklin Co., Ohio.[451]

Daughter One Finley and David Dixon had three children, including:

+ 87 m I. **William Wesley**¹¹ **Dixon** was born in Columbus, Franklin Co., Ohio, on April 12, 1966.[70, 486] He died in Palo Alto, Santa Clara Co., California, on April 6, 2004.[70, 486]

78. David Allen¹⁰ **Finley** (*Albert Earl⁹, Helen Claire⁸ Coover, Melvin Lester⁷, William⁶, Mary Ann⁵ Pegan, Robert A.⁴, Andrew³, Andrew² Pagan, James¹*) was born on August 27, 1949, in Columbus, Franklin Co., Ohio.[70, 405] e was the son of Albert Earl Finley (52) and Fairy Faye Milligan. David Allen died in Columbus, Franklin Co., Ohio, on June 24, 2005, at age 55.[70, 405] He was buried in Mifflin Cemetery, Gahanna, Mifflin Twp., Franklin Co., Ohio.[487]

Never married.

79. Daughter Two¹⁰ **Finley** (*Albert Earl⁹, Helen Claire⁸ Coover, Melvin Lester⁷, William⁶, Mary Ann⁵ Pegan, Robert A.⁴, Andrew³, Andrew² Pagan, James¹*) was born in Columbus, Franklin Co., Ohio. She was the daughter of Albert Earl Finley (52) and Fairy Faye Milligan. Barbara Jean lived in Oveido, Seminole Co., Florida.

Daughter Finley married **Mr. Bartow**. They divorced. They have three daughters.

Daughter Finley Bartow married **Bert Kerr Waits II** on September 19, 1987, in Franklin Co., Ohio.[488] Bert Kerr Waits II was born in New Orleans, Jefferson Parish, Louisiana, on December 21, 1940.[489] He was also known as **Hank**. Bert Kerr reached age 73 and died in a hospital in Orlando, Orange Co., Florida, on July 27, 2014.[489] He was buried in Mifflin Cemetery, Gahanna, Mifflin Twp., Franklin Co., Ohio.[490]

Bert Kerr "Hank" Waits was a professor of mathematics from 1961-1991 at The Ohio State University, where he earned his BS, MS and Ph.D., and one of the preeminent mathematicians in the U.S. He served on the board of directors of the National Council of Teachers of Mathematics (NCTM), co-authoring the initial NCTM's Standards for Curriculum and Evaluation of School Mathematics in 1989, and was a member of the Advanced Placement Calculus Committee. A retired consultant for Texas Instruments' Education Technology Division he co-founded the Teachers Teaching with Technology program. In addition, Bert Waits wrote mathematics textbooks for Prentice Hall, Holt McDougal, and Addison Wesley publishing firms, and scores of articles for national and international mathematics and mathematics education journals. He also lectured on mathematics extensively around the world. Bert, along with a colleague, won the prestigious lifetime achievement award (Glenn Gilbert Award) of the National Council of Supervisors of Mathematics posthumously in 2015, and the Ohio Council of Teachers of Mathematics Christopherson-Fawcett Award for high achievement in mathematics education. The OCTM has since created an award in Bert Waits honor, given to a mathematics teacher for "positively influencing mathematics education"

One of Bert's hobbies was genealogical and historical researching. He was active in the Ohio Genealogical Society (OGS) and contributed a number of articles to OGS publications. In particular, he co-wrote, with his wife, a biography and full Civil War service history of Mrs. Wait's ancestor, William Coover, and his military unit: "Private William Coover, 82nd OVI: Chancellorsville and Gettysburg", which appeared in the Ohio Genealogical Society Quarterly, Vol. 52, No. 2, 2013.[489, 491, 492]

80. Son¹⁰ **Fawcett** (*Robert Alvin⁹, Alvin Coover⁸, Mary Iva⁷ Coover, William⁶, Mary Ann⁵ Pegan, Robert A.⁴, Andrew³, Andrew² Pagan, James¹*) was born in Ottawa, Ottawa Twp., Putnam Co., Ohio. He was the son of Robert Alvin Fawcett (54) and Mary Rose Leahey.

Son Fawcett married **Miss Menz.**

Son Fawcett and Miss Menz had three children, including:

+ 88   m   II.   **Brian J.**[11] **Fawcett** was born in Cincinnati, Hamilton Co., Ohio, on April 17, 1969.[493, 494] He was also known as **Beau**. Brian J. died in a hospital in Ottawa, Ottawa Twp., Putnam Co., Ohio, on October 26, 1986.[493, 494, 495]

81. **Gail Anne**[10] **Fawcett** (*Robert Alvin*[9], *Alvin Coover*[8], *Mary Iva*[7] *Coover*, *William*[6], *Mary Ann*[5] *Pegan*, *Robert A.*[4], *Andrew*[3], *Andrew*[2] *Pagan*, *James*[1]) was born on September 7, 1943, in Ottawa, Ottawa Twp., Putnam Co., Ohio.[70, 371] She was also known as **Sissy**. She was the daughter of Robert Alvin Fawcett (54) and Mary Rose Leahey. Gail Anne lived in 1994 in Dayton, Montgomery Co., Ohio. She died in Centerville, Washington Twp., Montgomery Co., Ohio, on May 16, 2008, at age 64.[70] Gail Anne was buried in SS. Peter and Paul Church Cemetery, Ottawa, Ottawa Twp., Putnam Co., Ohio.[496]

Gail Anne married **Mr. Imm.** They divorced. They had two sons.

Gail Anne Fawcett is buried under her maiden name.

Sons of Gail Anne Fawcett and James Michael Imm:

+ 89   m   I.   **Scott Allen**[11] **Imm** was born in Lima, Ottawa Twp., Allen Co., Ohio, on June 12, 1962.[497, 498] He died in near Cairo, Allen Co., Ohio, on April 11, 1965.[498, 499, 500]

+ 90   m   II.   **Andrew James**[11] **Imm** was born in Lima, Ottawa Twp., Allen Co., Ohio, on November 23, 1964.[498, 501] He died in near Cairo, Allen Co., Ohio, on April 11, 1965.[498, 500, 502]

82. **Daughter**[10] **Wilcox** (*Christine LaVon*[9] *Smith*, *Fredrick J.*[8], *Henry Sylvester*[7], *Chrystiana*[6] *Coover*, *Mary Ann*[5] *Pegan*, *Robert A.*[4], *Andrew*[3], *Andrew*[2] *Pagan*, *James*[1]) was born in 1953. She is the daughter of Isaac Wilcox II and Christine LaVon Smith (56).

Daughter Wilcox married **Mr. Cox.** They divorced. They had at least one son. Daughter Wilcox married again.

Son of Daughter Wilcox and Mr. Cox:

+ 91   m   I.   **Son**[11] **Cox** was born in 1969.

83. **Sharon Lee**[10] **Slonecker** (*Mary Alice*[9] *Smith*, *Fredrick J.*[8], *Henry Sylvester*[7], *Chrystiana*[6] *Coover*, *Mary Ann*[5] *Pegan*, *Robert A.*[4], *Andrew*[3], *Andrew*[2] *Pagan*, *James*[1]) was born on January 8, 1953, in Columbus, Franklin Co., Ohio.[70, 429, 430] She was the daughter of Richard Max Slonecker and Mary Alice Smith (57). Sharon Lee died in Naples, Collier Co., Florida, on February 5, 1990, at age 37.[70, 429, 430] She was buried in Naples Memorial Gardens Cemetery, North Naples, Collier Co., Florida.[430, 503]

Sharon Lee married **Mr. Bellamy.** They had one son.

Her Social Security Death Index entry is under "S.L. Bellamy".[70]

84. **Max Robert**[10] **Huhn** (*Helen Kathleen*[9] *Bayer*, *Franklin S.*[8], *Elva Alberta*[7] *Smith*, *Chrystiana*[6] *Coover*, *Mary Ann*[5] *Pegan*, *Robert A.*[4], *Andrew*[3], *Andrew*[2] *Pagan*, *James*[1]) was born on April 11, 1954, in Mapleton, Union Twp., Huntingdon Co., Pennsylvania.[435, 436] He was the son of Alfred Cozard Huhn II and Helen Kathleen Bayer (58). He lived in Star Tannery, Frederick Co., Virginia. Max Robert died in a hospital in Woodstock, Shenandoah Co., Virginia, on September 13, 1985, at age 31.[435, 436] He was buried in Riverview Cemetery, Huntingdon, Huntingdon Twp., Huntingdon Co., Pennsylvania.[435, 436, 504]

Max Robert Huhn, a carpenter, was married when he died in a car accident.

85. **Louis Dale**[10] **Emory II** (*Betty Lois*[9] *Shawver*, *Jay*[8], *Ora Belle*[7] *Smith*, *Chrystiana*[6] *Coover*, *Mary Ann*[5] *Pegan*, *Robert A.*[4], *Andrew*[3], *Andrew*[2] *Pagan*,

James¹) was born on December 2, 1949, in Tokyo, Japan.[70, 442, 443, 444] He was the son of Louis Emory and Betty Lois Shawver (60). Louis Dale lived in 1981 in Colorado Springs, El Paso Co., Colorado. He also resided in 1992 in Upper Arlington, Franklin Co., Ohio. Louis Dale died in Columbus, Franklin Co., Ohio, on September 30, 1992, at age 42.[70, 442, 444] He was buried in Greenwood Cemetery, DeGraff, Pleasant Twp., Logan Co., Ohio.[505]

Never married.

11th Generation

86. Tracy Ann[11] **Logue** (*Daughter*[10] *Armstrong, Vivian June*[9] *Lawyer, Sylvia*[8] *Coover, Melvin Lester*[7]*, William*[6]*, Mary Ann*[5] *Pegan, Robert A.*[4]*, Andrew*[3]*, Andrew*[2] *Pagan, James*[1]) was born on March 24, 1962, in Lancaster, Fairfield Co., Ohio.[70, 478, 479] She was the daughter of Mr. Logue and Daughter Armstrong (73). Tracy Ann lived in 1987 in Lancaster, Fairfield Co., Ohio. She died in a hospital in Columbus, Franklin Co., Ohio, on June 24, 1987, at age 25.[70, 480] Tracy Ann was buried in Carroll Cemetery, Carroll, Greenfield Twp., Fairfield Co., Ohio.[506]

Tracy Ann married **Mr. Huffman**. They divorced. They had three children.

87. William Wesley[11] **Dixon** (*S*[10] *Finley, Albert Earl*[9]*, Helen Claire*[8] *Coover, Melvin Lester*[7]*, William*[6]*, Mary Ann*[5] *Pegan, Robert A.*[4]*, Andrew*[3]*, Andrew*[2] *Pagan, James*[1]) was born on April 12, 1966, in Columbus, Franklin Co., Ohio.[70, 486] He was the son of David Dixon and Daughter Finley (77). William Wesley died in Palo Alto, Santa Clara Co., California, on April 6, 2004, at age 37.[70, 486] He was cremated and his ashes scattered at sea.[507]

William Wesley Dixon was married when he died.

88. Brian J.[11] **Fawcett** (*Son*[10]*, Robert Alvin*[9]*, Alvin Coover*[8]*, Mary Iva*[7] *Coover, William*[6]*, Mary Ann*[5] *Pegan, Robert A.*[4]*, Andrew*[3]*, Andrew*[2] *Pagan, James*[1]) was born on April 17, 1969, in Cincinnati, Hamilton Co., Ohio.[493, 494] He was also known as **Beau**. He was the son of Son Fawcett II (90) and his wife. Brian J. died in a hospital in Ottawa, Ottawa Twp., Putnam Co., Ohio, on October 26, 1986, at age 17.[493, 494, 495] He was buried in Saints Peter and Paul Cemetery, Ottawa, Ottawa Twp., Putnam Co., Ohio.[493, 494, 508]

89. Scott Allen[11] **Imm** (*Gail Anne*[10] *Fawcett, Robert Alvin*[9]*, Alvin Coover*[8]*, Mary Iva*[7] *Coover, William*[6]*, Mary Ann*[5] *Pegan, Robert A.*[4]*, Andrew*[3]*, Andrew*[2] *Pagan, James*[1]) was born on June 12, 1962, in Lima, Ottawa Twp., Allen Co., Ohio.[497, 498] He was the son of Mr. Imm and Gail Anne Fawcett (81). Scott Allen died in near Cairo, Allen Co., Ohio, on April 11, 1965, at age two.[498, 499, 500] He was buried in Saints Peter and Paul Cemetery, Ottawa, Ottawa Twp., Putnam Co., Ohio.[509]

Scott Allen Imm and his brother, Andrew James Imm, were victims of the infamous Palm Sunday tornado on April 11, 1965, which caused much damage and death throughout Indiana and Ohio. The Imm brothers drowned when the tornado swept them out of their parent's car.

90. Andrew James[11] **Imm** (*Gail Anne*[10] *Fawcett, Robert Alvin*[9]*, Alvin Coover*[8]*, Mary Iva*[7] *Coover, William*[6]*, Mary Ann*[5] *Pegan, Robert A.*[4]*, Andrew*[3]*, Andrew*[2] *Pagan, James*[1]) was born on November 23, 1964, in Lima, Ottawa Twp., Allen Co., Ohio.[498, 501] He was the son of Mr. Imm and Gail Anne Fawcett (81). Andrew James died in near Cairo, Allen Co., Ohio, on April 11, 1965.[498, 500, 502] He was buried in Saints Peter and Paul Cemetery, Ottawa, Ottawa Twp., Putnam Co., Ohio.[510]

Andrew James Imm and his brother, Scott Allen Imm, were victims of the infamous Palm Sunday tornado on April 11, 1965, which caused much damage and death throughout Indiana and Ohio. The Imm brothers drowned when the tornado swept them out of their parent's car.

91. Son[11] **Cox** (*Daughter*[10] *Wilcox, Christine LaVon*[9] *Smith, Fredrick J.*[8]*, Henry Sylvester*[7]*, Chrystiana*[6] *Coover, Mary Ann*[5] *Pegan, Robert A.*[4]*, Andrew*[3]*, Andrew*[2] *Pagan, James*[1]) is the son of Mr. Cox and Daughter Wilcox (82).

Son Cox married, then divorced.

Son Cox and his wife had two children, including:

+ 92 m II. **Steven James**[12] **Cox** was born in Marion, Marion Twp., Marion Co., Ohio, on March 24, 1989.[511, 512] He died in Richwood, Claibourne Twp., Union Co., Ohio, on June 6, 1989.[511, 512]

12th Generation

92. Steven James[12] **Cox** (*Son Cox*[11], *Daughter*[10] *Wilcox, Christine LaVon*[9] *Smith, Fredrick J.*[8]*, Henry Sylvester*[7]*, Chrystiana*[6] *Coover, Mary Ann*[5] *Pegan, Robert A.*[4]*, Andrew*[3]*, Andrew*[2] *Pagan, James*[1]) was born on March 24, 1989, in Marion, Marion Twp., Marion Co., Ohio.[511, 512] He was the son of Son Cox (92) and his wife. Steven James died in Richwood, Claibourne Twp., Union Co., Ohio, on June 6, 1989.[511, 512] He was buried in Claibourne Township Cemetery, Claibourne Township, Union Co., Ohio.[512, 513]

Endnotes

1. Family Data: Robert and Christina "Engle" Pegan family bible, American Bible Society. Brattleboro(ugh), Vermont: Holbrook & Fessenden; 1828. In possession of the author, Ann Miller Carr.

2. Ohio, County Death Records, 1840-2001, FamilySearch.org, Mary A. "Wagener", Logan County, Ohio Death Record, Vol. 2, pg. 416.

3. Find A Grave—Rea Cemetery, Bloomfield Twp., Logan Co., Ohio, Find A Grave.com, Mary A. Wagoner, Find A Grave Memorial #20326312.

4. Ohio, County Marriages, 1789-2013, FamilySearch.org, Abraham Coover and Mary Pegan, Miami County, Marriage Records, Vol. E., pg. 70, lic. #147. The record says they were married on 10 Jan 1835.

5. Find A Grave—Huntsdale Church of the Brethren/Dunkard Cemetery, Upper Dickinson Twp., Cumberland Co., Pennsylvania, Find A Grave.com, Abraham Coover, Find A Grave Memorial #77063183.

6. Logan County, Ohio Deeds, James Madison Vial to Christina Pegan, Logan County, Ohio Deed Book Q: 258 (17 Apr1846). Logan County, Ohio Recorder's Office, 100 South Mad River Street, #101, Bellefontaine, OH.

7. Logan County, Ohio Deeds, Abraham Coover to Christina Pegan, Agreement, Logan County, Ohio Deed Book T: 334 (31 Jan 1849). Logan County, Ohio Recorder's Office, 100 South Mad River Street, #101, Bellefontaine, OH.

8. Logan County, Ohio Deeds, Abraham Coover to Dennis Warner, Logan County, Ohio Deed Book U: 130 (08 Feb 1850). Logan County, Ohio Recorder's Office, 100 South Mad River Street, #101, Bellefontaine, OH.

9. Ohio, County Marriages, 1789-2013, FamilySearch.org, John "Wagginer" and Mary Coover, Logan County, Ohio Marriage Records, Vol. B, pg. 194.

10. Ohio, County Death Records, 1840-2001, FamilySearch.org, John Wagoner, Logan County, Ohio Death Record, Vol. 1, pg. 332.

11. Find A Grave—Rea Cemetery, Bloomfield Twp., Logan Co., Ohio, Find A Grave.com, John Wagoner, Find A Grave Memorial #20326308.

12. Hurt, R. Douglas, *The Ohio Frontier: Crucible of the Old Northwest*. Bloomington, Indiana: Indiana University Press; 1996. Genealogy Center, Allen County Public Library, 900 Library Plaza, Fort Wayne, IN.

13. Find A Grave—Goshen Quaker Cemetery, Jefferson Twp., Logan Co., Ohio, Find A Grave.com, William Coover, d. 08 Mar 1875, 33 yr, 6 mo, 4 d, Find A Grave Memorial #26907818.

14. Obituary of William Coover (Zanesfield, Ohio, The Mad River Blade, 18 Mar 1875), Logan County, Ohio Genealogical Library, 513 East Columbus Avenue, Bellefontaine, OH.

15. Ohio Death Certificate, Ohio Department of Health, Center for Vital and Health Statistics, 246 North High Street, Columbus, OH, Christiana Smith, death cert. #60800.

16. William Coover, Civil War Pension Application (1864), NARA—National Archives and Records Administration, 8601 Adelphi Road, College Park, MD, Application #92980; Elizabeth Coover, widow's pension application (1874) #220.814.

17. Ohio, County Marriages, 1789-2013, FamilySearch.org, William Coover and Elizabeth Watkins, Logan County, Ohio Marriage Records, Vol. C, pg. 376, lic. #123 (William Coover is incorrectly indexed as "William Cowin" on FamilySearch Ohio, County Marriages website as of 24 Aug 2015).

18. Ohio Death Certificate, Ohio Department of Health, Center for Vital and Health Statistics, 246 North High Street, Columbus, OH, Elizabeth Pellett, death cert. #55856.

19. Find A Grave—Goshen Quaker Cemetery, Jefferson Twp., Logan Co., Ohio, Find A Grave.com, Elizabeth B. Watkins Fawcett Pellett, Find A Grave Memoria l#127098275.

20. Ohio, County Marriages, 1789-2013, FamilySearch.org, Oliver Fawcett and Elizabeth Coover, Logan County, Ohio Marriage Records, Vol. H, pg. 20.

21. Ohio, County Marriages, 1789-2013, FamilySearch.org, George Pellett and Elizabeth B. Fawcett, Logan County, Ohio Marriage Records, Vol. H, pg. 220.

22. Ohio Death Certificate, Ohio Department of Health, Center for Vital and Health Statistics, 246 North High Street, Columbus, OH, Melvin L. Coover, death cert. #52332.

23. Ohio, Death Records, 1908-1932, 1938-2007, Ancestry.com, Iva Fawcett, death cert. #92236.

24. Find A Grave—Rea Cemetery, Bloomfield Twp., Logan Co., Ohio, Find A Grave.com, Christiann Coover Smith, Find A Grave Memorial #20308905.

25. Ohio, County Marriages, 1789-2013, FamilySearch.org, Andrew J. Smith and Christy Ann Coover, Logan County, Ohio Marriage Records, Vol. C, pg. 339, lic. #112.

26. Ohio Death Certificate, Ohio Department of Health, Center for Vital and Health Statistics, 246 North High Street, Columbus, OH, Andrew Jackson Smith, death cert. #46162.

27. Find A Grave—Rea Cemetery, Bloomfield Twp., Logan Co., Ohio, Find A Grave.com, Andrew Jackson Smith, Find A Grave Memorial #20308904.

28. Kennedy, Gen. Robert P., *The Historical Review of Logan County, Ohio, Together with Biographical Sketches of Many of its Leading and Prominent Citizens and Illustrious Dead. Illustrated*. Chicago: The S.J. Clarke Publishing Company; 1903, pg. 348-9. Ohio History Center Library, 800 East 17th Avenue, Columbus, OH.

29. Hover, John Calvin and Joseph Daniel Barnes, *Memoirs of the Miami Valley, Vol. III*. Chicago: The Robert O. Law Company, 1920, pg. 507-8. Indiana Historical Society Library, Eugene

and Marilyn Glick Indiana History Center, 450 West Ohio Street, Indianapolis, IN.

30 Ohio Death Certificate, Ohio Department of Health, Center for Vital and Health Statistics, 246 North High Street, Columbus, OH, Mary Elizabeth Melvin, death cert. #72913.

31 Ohio Death Certificate, Ohio Department of Health, Center for Vital and Health Statistics, 246 North High Street, Columbus, OH, Henry S. Smith, death cert. #32158.

32 Obituary of Henry S. Smith, (Bellefontaine, Ohio, Bellefontaine Examiner, pub. 04 Apr 1957) Logan County Libraries, Knowlton Library, 220 Main Street, Bellefontaine, OH.

33 Pennsylvania Death Certificates, Pennsylvania Department of Health, Division of Vital Records, Health and Welfare Building, 8th Floor West, 625 Forster Street, Harrisburg, PA, Elva A. Bayer, Book D55, pg. 31, death cert. #4261.

34 Huntingdon County, Pennsylvania Historical Society, Huntingdon County, Pennsylvania Historical Society, 106 4th Street, Huntingdon, PA.

35 Find A Grave—Rea Cemetery, Bloomfield Twp., Logan Co., Ohio, Find A Grave.com, Infant son, Find A Grave Memorial #20314238.

36 Obituary of Ora Shawver, (Bellefontaine, Ohio, Bellefontaine Examiner, 12 Dec 1962) Logan County Libraries, Knowlton Library, 220 Main Street, Bellefontaine, OH.

37 Ohio, County Births, 1841-2003 (County Courthouses), FamilySearch.org, Logan Co. Birth Records, Vol. 1, pg. 192.

38 Ohio, Death Records, 1908-1932, 1938-2007, Ancestry.com, Ora B. Shawver, death cert. #90385.

39 North Dakota Death Certificate, State of North Dakota, Bureau of Health Statistics, Division of Vital Records, 600 East Boulevard Avenue, Department 301, Bismarck, ND, John Andrew Smith, death cert. #1531, registered #378, no. 1334.

40 Obituary of Mrs. John Smith ((Bellefontaine, Ohio, Bellefontaine Examiner, 18 Feb 1961) Logan County Libraries, Knowlton Library, 220 Main Street, Bellefontaine, OH. Mrs. John Smith's (Cora's) obituary mentions her husband John Andrew Smith's date of death.

41 Logan County, Ohio Death Records, FamilySearch.org, Eliza Smith, Death Record Vol. 1, pg. 210.

42 Ohio, County Marriages, 1789-2013, FamilySearch.org, Roy Thurman Smith and Mary Jane "Pool", Logan County, Ohio Marriage Records, Vol. I, pg. 497, lic. #994.

43 Ohio Death Certificate, Ohio Department of Health, Center for Vital and Health Statistics, 246 North High Street, Columbus, OH, Roy T. Smith, death cert. #52320.

44 Ohio Death Certificate, Ohio Department of Health, Center for Vital and Health Statistics, 246 North High Street, Columbus, OH, Hoadley Monroe Smith, death cert. #23334.

45 Find A Grave—Thurston Primitive Baptist Cemetery, Thurston, Walnut Twp., Lancaster Co., Ohio, Find A Grave.com, Melvin L. Coover, Find A Grave Memorial #69494127.

46 Ohio, County Marriages, 1789-2013, FamilySearch.org, Melvin L. Coover and Dora Corbet, Champaign County, Ohio Marriage Records, Vol. J, pg. 154, lic. #27.

47 Ohio Death Certificate, Ohio Department of Health, Center for Vital and Health Statistics, 246 North High Street, Columbus, OH, Dora Coover, death cert. #18948.

48 Find A Grave—Maple Grove Cemetery, North Lewisburg, Rush Twp., Champaign Co., Ohio, Find A Grave.com, Dora Corbet Coover, Find A Grave Memorial #44703338.

49 Ohio, County Marriages, 1789-2013, FamilySearch.org, Melvin L. Coover and Della Shaw, Athens County, Ohio Marriage Records, Vol. 9, pg. 446 (Melvin L. Coover is incorrectly indexed as Melvin L. "Coovis" on the FamilySearch Ohio, County Marriages website).

50 West Virginia, Births Index, 1853-1969, Ancestry.com, Odella Shaw.

51 State of West Virginia Division of Culture and History, West Virginia Vital Records Research, Birth Records (West Virginia Archives & Records), West Virginia State Archives, West Virginia Archives & History Center Library, The Culture Center, 1900 Kanawha Boulevard E, Charleston, WV, Cabell Co. Births, Vol. 1, pg. 50; Online database: http://www.wvculture.org/vrr/va_viewaspx?Id=1472822&Type=BirthImage 4014156_00058.

52 West Virginia Births, 1853-1930, FamilySearch.org, Odella Shaw, Cabell Co. Births, Vol. 1, pg. 50.

53 Obituary of George Augustus Shaw (Athens, Ohio, Athens Messenger, 18 Oct 1923), Ohio History Center Archives and Library, Ohio History Center, 800 East 17th Avenue, Columbus, OH.

54 Find A Grave—West Union Cemetery, Athens, Athens Twp., Athens Co., Ohio, Find A Grave.com, Obituary of George Augustus Shaw, found on George A. Shaw, Find A Grave Memorial #81650121.

55 Find A Grave—West Union Cemetery, Athens, Athens Twp., Athens Co., Ohio, Find A Grave.com, Della May Shaw Coover, Find A Grave Memorial #98503188.

56 Phone interview with Bert. K. and Mrs. Waits, Orlando, FL, Ann Miller Carr, author, 15 Sep 2015.

57 Letter from the Bureau of Vital Statistics, State of Florida, to the author, Ann Miller Carr, March 13, 2015.

58 Ohio, County Births, 1841-2003 (County Courthouses), FamilySearch.org, Elta W. Coover, Logan Co., Ohio Birth Records, Vol. 2, pg. 254. (She is incorrectly indexed as "Ella W. on FamilySearch Ohio, County Births index).

59 Obituary of "Alta" C. Stanley (Urbana, Ohio, Urbana Daily Citizen, 24 Sep 1956), Champaign County Library, Main Branch, 1060 Scioto Street, Urbana, OH, (Given name misspelled; it was Elta).

60 Ohio, Death Records, 1908-1932, 1938-2007, Ancestry.com, "Elza" F. Stanley, death incorrectly listed as Columbiana Co., Ohio.

61 Find A Grave—Goshen Quaker Cemetery, Jefferson Twp., Logan Co., Ohio, Find A Grave.com, "Eslie" Coover, 2 yrs 29 da, Find A Grave Memorial #26907812.

62 Ohio, County Births, 1841-2003 (County Courthouses), FamilySearch.org, Doris Coover, Logan Co., Ohio Birth Records, Vol. 2, pg. 366.

63 Ohio, Death Records, 1908-1932, 1938-2007, Ancestry.com, Doris E. Pickering, death cert. #028989.

64 Ohio, Births and Christenings Index, 1800-1962, Ancestry.com, Sylvia Coover.

65 Ohio, County Births, 1841-2003 (County Courthouses), FamilySearch.org, Sylvia Coover, Allen Co., Ohio Birth Records, Vol. 3, pg. 32.

66 Ohio, Death Records, 1908-1932, 1938-2007, Ancestry.com, Sylvia Lawyer, death cert. #090891.

67 Ohio, County Births, 1841-2003 (County Courthouses), FamilySearch.org, "Hasel" Coover, Allen Co., Birth Records, Vol. 4, pg. 25.

68 Ohio Death Certificate, Ohio Department of Health, Center for Vital and Health Statistics, 246 North High Street, Columbus, OH, Hazel Coover, death cert. #36563.

69 Ohio, County Births, 1841-2003 (County Courthouses), FamilySearch.org, Helen Coover, Allen Co. Birth Records, Vol. 4, pg. 26.

70 Social Security Death Index, Ancestry.com.

71 Ohio, Death Records, 1908-1932, 1938-2007, Ancestry.com, Helen Finley, death cert. #065547.

72 Obituary of Helen Finley (Lancaster, Ohio, Lancaster Eagle-Gazette, 30 Sep 1992), Fairfield County Chapter of the Ohio Genealogical Society Library, 503 Lenwood Drive, Lancaster, OH.

73 Ohio, County Births, 1841-2003 (County Courthouses), FamilySearch.org, Arthur "Cover", Allen Co., Ohio Birth Records, Vol. 4, pg. 31; fa. Mel Coover, mo. Della Shaw.

74 U.S., Social Security Applications and Claims Index, 1936-2007, Ancestry.com, Arthur F. Coover.

75 Ohio, Death Records, 1908-1932, 1938-2007, Ancestry.com, Arthur Francis Coover, death cert. #036659.

76 Ohio Death Certificate, Ohio Department of Health, Center for Vital and Health Statistics, 246 North High Street, Columbus, OH, Edna V. Noble, death cert. #15504.

77 Ohio, County Marriages, 1789-2013, FamilySearch.org, Alton H. Lewis and Alma P. Coover, Franklin Co., Ohio Marriage Vol.100, pg. 127, lic. #83658.

78 Ohio, Death Records, 1908-1932, 1938-2007, Ancestry.com, Alma Pearle Hanson, death cert. #070093.

79 Find A Grave—Zanesfield Cemetery, Zanesfield, Jefferson Twp., Logan Co., Ohio, Find A Grave.com, Iva M. Fawcett, Find A Grave Memorial #27175504.

80 Ohio, County Marriages, 1789-2013, FamilySearch.org, Elba J. Fawcett and Mary I. Coover, Logan County, Ohio Marriage Records, Vol. G, pg. 105.

81 Ohio Death Certificate, Ohio Department of Health, Center for Vital and Health Statistics, 246 North High Street, Columbus, OH, "Elva" J. Fawcett, death cert. #60852.

82 Find A Grave—Zanesfield Cemetery, Zanesfield, Jefferson Twp., Logan Co., Ohio, Find A Grave.com, Elba Jonathan Fawcett, Find A Grave Memorial #27161769.

83 Obituary of Mrs. E.J. Fawcett (Mary Iva Fawcett) (Bellefontaine, Ohio, Bellefontaine Examiner, 24 Dec 1964), Logan County Libraries, Knowlton Library, 220 North Main Street, Bellefontaine, OH.

84 Ohio Death Certificate, Ohio Department of Health, Center for Vital and Health Statistics, 246 North High Street, Columbus, OH, Elijah R. Fawcett, death cert. #38749.

85 Ohio, County Births, 1841-2003 (County Courthouses), FamilySearch.org, Logan County Birth Record Vol. 1, pg. 274.

86 Find A Grave—Zanesfield Cemetery, Zanesfield, Jefferson Twp., Logan Co., Ohio, Find A Grave.com, Elijah R. Fawcett, Find A Grave Memorial #27161778.

87 U.S., WWI Draft Registration Cards, 1917-1918, Ancestry.com, Alvin Coover Fawcett, Bellefontaine, Ohio.

88 Ohio, County Marriages, 1789-2013, FamilySearch.org, Alvin C. Fawcet and Anna Idell Creviston, Logan County, Ohio Marriage Records, Vol. L, pg. 331, lic. #656.

89 Ohio, Death Records, 1908-1932, 1938-2007, Ancestry.com, Alvin C. Fawcett, death cert. #049414.

90 Find A Grave—Rea Cemetery, Bloomfield Twp., Logan Co., Ohio, Find A Grave.com, Mary E. Smith Melvin, Find A Grave Memorial #17564355.

91 Ohio, County Marriages, 1789-2013, FamilySearch.org, John W. Melvin and Mary E. Smith, Logan County, Ohio Marriage Records, Vol. F, pg. 217.

92 Ohio Death Certificate, Ohio Department of Health, Center for Vital and Health Statistics, 246 North High Street, Columbus, OH, John W. Melvin, death cert. #18830.

93 Find A Grave—Rea Cemetery, Bloomfield Twp., Logan Co., Ohio, Find A Grave.com, John W. Melvin, Find A Grave Memorial #17564332.

94 Ohio Death Certificate, Ohio Department of Health, Center for Vital and Health Statistics, 246 North High Street, Columbus, OH, Otto J. Melvin, #63059.

95 U.S., WWII Draft Registration Cards, 1942, Ancestry.com, Otto J. Melvin, Logan County, Ohio.

96 Ohio, Births and Christenings Index, 1800-1962, Ancestry.com, ("Bessie") Dessie L. Melvin, Logan Co., Ohio Birth Record, Vol. 2, pg. 176.

97 Ohio, County Births, 1841-2003 (County Courthouses), FamilySearch.org, "Bessie" L. Melvin, Vol. 2, pg. 176.

98 Ohio, Death Records, 1908-1932, 1938-2007, Ancestry.com, Dessie L. Melvin, death cert. #04631.

99 Find A Grave—Greenwood Cemetery, DeGraff, Pleasant Twp., Logan Co., Ohio, Find A Grave.com, Henry S. Smith, Find A Grave Memorial #18560731.

100 Ohio, County Marriages, 1789-2013, FamilySearch.org, "Sylvester" Smith and "Alta" Mohr, Logan County, Ohio Marriage Records, Vol. H, pg. 58.

101 Ohio Death Certificate, Ohio Department of Health, Center for Vital and Health Statistics, 246 North High Street, Columbus, OH, Altia I. Smith, death cert. #36074.

102 Find A Grave—Greenwood Cemetery, DeGraff, Pleasant Twp., Logan Co., Ohio, Find A Grave.com, Altia I. Smith, Find A Grave Memorial #18560672.

103 Ohio, County Marriages, 1789-2013, FamilySearch.org, Fred J. Smith and Lilah Rostofer, Logan County, Ohio Marriage Records, Vol. M, pg. 514, lic. #2191.

104 Obituary of Fred J. Smith, (Bellefontaine, Ohio, Bellefontaine Examiner, 30 Aug 1957) Logan County Libraries, Knowlton Library, 220 Main Street, Bellefontaine, OH.

105 Ohio, County Births, 1841-2003 (County Courthouses), FamilySearch.org, Fredrick Smith, Births Vol. 3, pg. 147.

106 U.S., Social Security Applications and Claims Index, 1936-2007, Fred J. Smith

107 U.S., WWI Draft Registration Cards, 1917-1918, Ancestry.com, Frederick J. Smith, Logan County, Ohio.

108 Ohio, Death Records, 1908-1932, 1938-2007, Ancestry.com, Fred J. Smith, "Lawrence" Co., Ohio. (incorrect)

109 Ohio, Ohio, Wills and Probate Records, 1786-1998, Ancestry.com, Fred J. Smith, Logan Co., Ohio.

110 Find A Grave—Riverview Cemetery, Huntingdon, Huntingdon Twp., Huntingdon Co., Pennsylvania, Find A Grave.com, Elva A. Bayer, Find A Grave Memorial #97007594.

111 Ohio, County Marriages, 1789-2013, FamilySearch.org, Henry Bayer and Alberta Smith, Logan County, Ohio Marriage Records, Vol. H, pg. 251.

112 Obituary of Henry Bayer (Huntingdon, Pennsylvania, Huntingdon Daily News, 23 May 1932), Huntingdon County, Pennsylvania Historical Society, 106 4th Street, Huntingdon, PA.

113 Pennsylvania Death Certificates, Pennsylvania Department of Health, Division of Vital Records, Health and Welfare Building, 8th Floor West, 625 Forster Street, Harrisburg, PA, Harry Bayer, Book D32, pg. 31, death cert. #49220.

114 Find A Grave—Plum Cemetery, Washington Twp., Logan Co., Ohio, Find A Grave.com, Henry Bayer, Find A Grave Memorial #19338698.

115 "Happy Birthday" (Huntingdon, Pennsylvania, The Daily News, 13 Mar 1953); Newspapers.com, Online database: https://www.newspapers.com/newspage/12785147/

116 Obituary of Franklin S. Bayer (Huntingdon, Pennsylvania, Huntingdon Daily News, 27 Sep 1991), Huntingdon County, Pennsylvania Historical Society, 106 4th Street, Huntingdon, PA.

117 Find A Grave—Greenwood Cemetery, DeGraff, Pleasant Twp., Logan Co., Ohio, Find A Grave.com, Ora B. Shawver, Find A Grave Memorial #18550747.

118 Ohio, County Marriages, 1789-2013, FamilySearch.org, Ellando Shawver and Ora B. Smith, Logan County, Ohio Marriage Records, Vol. G, pg. 281.

119 Ohio Death Certificate, Ohio Department of Health, Center for Vital and Health Statistics, 246 North High Street, Columbus, OH, Ellendoe Shawver, death cert. #33388.

120 Find A Grave—Greenwood Cemetery, DeGraff, Pleasant Twp., Logan Co., Ohio, Find A Grave.com, Ellando S. Shawver, Find A Grave Memorial #18550718.

121 Ohio, County Marriages, 1789-2013, FamilySearch.org, Ray Heath Allinger and Glady Fern Shawver, Logan County, Ohio Marriage Records, Vol. L, pg. 482, lic. #956.

122 Ohio Death Certificate, Ohio Department of Health, Center for Vital and Health Statistics, 246 North High Street, Columbus, OH, Glady Fern Allinger, death cert. #37553.

123 Ohio, County Marriages, 1789-2013, FamilySearch.org, Jay Shawver and Grace Rairdon, Logan County, Ohio Marriage Records, Vol. M, pg. 1, lic. #1148.

124 U.S., Social Security Applications and Claims Index, 1936-2007, Ancestry.com, Jay Shawver.

125 U.S., WWI Draft Registration Cards, 1917-1918, Ancestry.com, Jay Shawver, Bellefontaine, Ohio.

126 Ohio, Death Records, 1908-1932, 1938-2007, Ancestry.com, Jay Shawver, death cert. #86756.

127 Find A Grave—Rea Cemetery, Bloomfield Twp., Logan Co., Ohio, Find A Grave.com, John A. Smith, Find A Grave Memorial #20314185.

128 Ohio, County Marriages, 1789-2013, FamilySearch.org, John A. Smith and Cora Hanks, Logan County, Ohio Marriage Records, Vol. H, pg. 250.

129 Ohio Death Index, 1908-1932, 1938-1944, and 1958-2007, FamilySearch.org, Cora C. Smith, Vol. #16443, death cert. #14122.

130 Find A Grave—Rea Cemetery, Bloomfield Twp., Logan Co., Ohio, Find A Grave.com, Cora C. Smith, Find A Grave Memorial #20308909.

131 Ohio, County Births, 1841-2003 (County Courthouses), FamilySearch.org, Harold D. Smith, Logan County Birth Records, Vol. 3, pg. 152.

132 Ohio, Death Records, 1908-1932, 1938-2007, Ancestry.com, Harold D. Smith, death cert. #028537.

133 Obituary of Harold D. Smith (Bellefontaine, Ohio, Bellefontaine Examiner, April 20, 1984), Logan County Libraries, Knowlton Library, 220 North Main Street, Bellefontaine, OH.

134 Ohio, County Births, 1841-2003 (County Courthouses), FamilySearch.org, Evelyn Fern Smith, Logan Co., Ohio Birth Records, Vol. 4, pg. 189.

135 Ohio, Death Records, 1908-1932, 1938-2007, Ancestry.com, Evelyn Rogers, death cert. #092769.

136 Find A Grave—Rea Cemetery, Bloomfield Twp., Logan Co., Ohio, Find A Grave.com, Eliza E. Smith, Find A Grave Memorial #20308917.

137 U.S., WWI Draft Registration Cards, 1917-1918, Ancestry.com, Roy Thurman Smith, Logan Co., Ohio.

138 "Roy T. Smith Dies" (Bellefontaine, Ohio, Bellefontaine Examiner, 25 Jul 1952) Logan County Libraries, Knowlton Library, 220 North Main Street, Bellefontaine, OH.

139 Find A Grave—Greenwood Cemetery, DeGraff, Pleasant Twp., Logan Co., Ohio, Find A Grave.com, Roy T. Smith, Find A Grave Memorial #18576408.

140 Obituary of Mary Jane Smith (Mrs. Roy T. Smith), (Bellefontaine, Ohio, Bellefontaine Examiner, 29 Feb 1960) Logan County Libraries, Knowlton Library, 220 North Main Street, Bellefontaine, OH.

141 Find A Grave—Greenwood Cemetery, DeGraff, Pleasant Twp., Logan Co., Ohio, Find A Grave.com, Mary J. Smith, Find A Grave Memorial #18576363.

142 Obituary of Paul D. Smith (Bellefontaine, Ohio, Bellefontaine Examiner, 04 Sep 1978), Logan County Libraries, Knowlton Library, 220 North Main Street, Bellefontaine, OH.

143 Ohio, Death Records, 1908-1932, 1938-2007, Ancestry.com, Paul D. Smith, death cert. #067156.

144 Ohio, County Marriages, 1789-2013, FamilySearch.org, Cline Jenkins and "Lucille" Smith, Logan County, Ohio Marriage Records, Vol O, pg. 290, lic.#9087.

145 Ohio, Death Records, 1908-1932, 1938-2007, Ancestry.com, Bertha Lucile Jenkins, death cert. #045691.

146 U.S., Social Security Applications and Claims Index, 1936-2007, Ancestry.com, Bertha Lucile Smith Jenkins.

147 Ohio, Death Records, 1908-1932, 1938-2007, Ancestry.com, Stanley A. Smith, death cert. #039572.

148 Obituary of Stanley Andrew Smith (Bellefontaine, Ohio, Bellefontaine Examiner, 22 May 1995), Logan County Libraries, Knowlton Library, 220 North Main Street, Bellefontaine, OH.

149 U.S., Social Security Applications and Claims Index, 1936-2007, Ancestry.com, Stanley Andrew Smith.

150 U.S., WWI Draft Registration Cards, 1917-1918, Ancestry.com, "Hoadly" Monroe Smith, Logan Co., Ohio.

151 "Hoadley Smith Dies" (Bellefontaine, Ohio, Bellefontaine Examiner, 19 Apr 1926), Logan County Libraries, Knowlton Library, 220 North Main Street, Bellefontaine, OH.

152 Find A Grave—Greenwood Cemetery, DeGraff, Pleasant Twp., Logan Co., Ohio, Find A Grave.com, Hoadley M. Smith, Find A Grave Memorial #18576258.

153 Shelby County, Ohio Marriage Records, Shelby County, Ohio Probate Court, 100 East Court Street, Sidney, OH, Hoadley M. Smith and Dolly Herring, Shelby County, Ohio Marriage Records, Vol. 11, pg. 389.

154 Ohio, Death Records, 1908-1932, 1938-2007, Ancestry.com, Dolly Smith, death cert. #014724.

155 Obituary of Dolly Smith (Bellefontaine, Ohio, Bellefontaine Examiner, 13 Mar 1980), Logan County Libraries, Knowlton Library, 220 North Main Street, Bellefontaine, OH.

156 Find A Grave—Greenwood Cemetery, DeGraff, Pleasant Twp., Logan Co., Ohio, Find A Grave.com, Dolly Herring Smith, Find A Grave Memorial #18560696.

157 U.S., Social Security Applications and Claims Index, 1936-2007, Ancestry.com, Thurman Herring Smith.

158 Ohio, Death Records, 1908-1932, 1938-2007, Ancestry.com, Thurman H. Smith, death cert. #014670.

159 Obituary of Thurman H. Smith (Bellefontaine, Ohio, Bellefontaine Examiner, 17 Mar 1980), Logan County Libraries, Knowlton Library, 220 North Main Street, Bellefontaine, OH.

160 Find A Grave—Zanesfield Cemetery, Zanesfield, Jefferson Twp., Logan Co., Ohio, Find A Grave.com, Elta M. Coover Stanley, Find A Grave Memorial #27308413.

161 Ohio, County Marriages, 1789-2013, FamilySearch.org, Walter Warren Stanley and Elta Modena Coover, Logan County, Ohio Marriage Records, Vol. O, pg. 104, lic. #207.

162 U.S., WWI Draft Registration Cards, 1917-1918, Ancestry.com, Walter Warren Stanley, Zanesfield, Jefferson Twp., Logan Co., Ohio.

163 Ohio, County Births, 1841-2003 (County Courthouses), FamilySearch.org, W.W. Stanley, Logan Co., Ohio Birth Record, Vol. 2, pg. 214.

164 Ohio, Death Records, 1908-1932, 1938-2007, Ancestry.com, Walter W. Stanley, death cert. #80545.

165 Find A Grave—Zanesfield Cemetery, Zanesfield, Jefferson Twp., Logan Co., Ohio, Find A Grave.com, Walter W. Stanley, Find A Grave Memorial #27308438.

166 Obituary of H. Marvin Stanley (Bellefontaine, Ohio, Bellefontaine Examiner, 22 Feb 2009), Logan County Libraries, Knowlton Library, 220 North Main Street, Bellefontaine, OH.

167 Obituary of James D. Stanley Sr. (Huntington, Huntington Twp., Huntington Co., Indiana, Huntington Herald-Press, 30 May 1990), Huntington City-Township Library, Indiana Room, 255 West Park Drive, Huntington, IN.

168 Indiana, Death Certificates, 1899-2011, Ancestry.com, James Darrell Stanley Sr., death cert. #90-017381.

169 Ohio, Death Records, 1908-1932, 1938-2007, Ancestry.com, Wendell W. Stanley, death cert. #030688.

170 Find A Grave—Cedar Point Cemetery, Pasco, Perry Twp., Shelby Co., Ohio, Find A Grave.com, Doris E. Pickering, Find A Grave Memorial #53138302.

171 Ohio, County Marriages, 1789-2013, FamilySearch.org, Chlor W. Pickering and Doris E. Coover, Champaign County, Ohio Marriage Records, Vol. Q, pg. 38, lic. #73.

172 U.S., WWII Draft Registration Cards, 1942, Ancestry.com, Chlor Washington Pickering, Sidney, Shelby Co., Ohio.

173 Ohio, Death Records, 1908-1932, 1938-2007, Ancestry.com, Chlor W. Pickering, death cert. #91549.

174 Find A Grave—Cedar Point Cemetery, Pasco, Perry Twp., Shelby Co., Ohio, Find A Grave.com, Chlor W. Pickering, Find A Grave Memorial #19729341.

175 Obituary of Aileen "Pick" P. Frazier (Billings, Montana, Billings Gazette, 30 Nov 2006), Billings Public Library, 510 North Broadway, Billings, MT.

176 Obituary of Sylvia Lawyer (Lancaster, Ohio, Lancaster Eagle-Gazette, 11 Dec 1985), Fairfield County Chapter of the Ohio Genealogical Society Library, 503 Lenwood Drive, Lancaster, OH.

177 Find A Grave—New School Baptist Cemetery, Thurston, Walnut Twp., Fairfield Co., Ohio, Find A Grave.com, Sylvia Coover Lawyer, Find A Grave Memorial #75568496.

178 Fairfield County, Ohio Marriage Records, Fairfield County Probate Court, 224 East Main Street, #303, Lancaster, OH; Homer E. Lawyer and Sylvia Coover, Fairfield County, Ohio Marriage Records, Vol. 12, pg. 228, lic. #445.

179 U.S., WWII Draft Registration Cards, 1942, Ancestry.com, Homer Elsworth Lawyer, Fairfield Co., Ohio.

180 Ohio, Death Records, 1908-1932, 1938-2007, Ancestry.com, Homer E. Lawyer, death cert. #051305.

181 Obituary of Homer E. Lawyer (Lancaster, Ohio, Lancaster Eagle-Gazette, 27 Jul 1970), Fairfield County Genealogical Society Library, 503 Lenwood Drive, Lancaster, OH.

182 Find A Grave—New School Baptist Cemetery, Thurston, Walnut Twp., Fairfield Co., Ohio, Find A Grave.com, Homer Lawyer, Find A Grave Memorial #75568503.

183 Ohio, Death Records, 1908-1932, 1938-2007, Ancestry.com, Arthur W. Lawyer, death cert. #041783.

184 Ohio, Death Records, 1908-1932, 1938-2007, Ancestry.com, William N. Lawyer, death cert. #002230.

185 Obituary of William Lawyer (Lancaster, Ohio, Lancaster Eagle-Gazette, 06 Jan 1996), Fairfield County Genealogical Society Library, 503 Lenwood Drive, Lancaster, OH.

186 U.S., Social Security Applications and Claims Index, 1936-2007, Ancestry.com, William Nelson Lawyer.

187 Ohio, Death Records, 1908-1932, 1938-2007, Ancestry.com, Vivian June Armstrong, death cert. #010798.

188 U.S., Social Security Applications and Claims Index, 1936-2007, Ancestry.com, Vivian June Lawyer Armstrong.

189 Obituary of Vivian Armstrong (Lancaster, Ohio, Lancaster Eagle-Gazette, 11 Feb 1997), Fairfield County Chapter of the Ohio Genealogical Society Library, 503 Lenwood Drive, Lancaster, OH.

190 U.S., Social Security Applications and Claims Index, 1936-2007, Ancestry.com, Melvin Raymond Lawyer.

191 Obituary of Melvin Lawyer (Lancaster, Ohio, Lancaster Eagle-Gazette, 18 Dec 1998), Fairfield County Chapter of the Ohio Genealogical Society Library, 503 Lenwood Drive, Lancaster, OH.

192 Obituary of Danny Lawyer (Lancaster, Ohio, Lancaster Eagle-Gazette, 19 Jul 2008), Fairfield County Chapter of the Ohio Genealogical Society Library, 503 Lenwood Drive, Lancaster, OH.

193 Obituary of Hazel Coover (Athens, Ohio, Athens Daily Messenger, 21 Jul 1911), Ohio History Center Archives and Library, Ohio History Center, 800 East 17th Avenue, Columbus, OH.

194 Find A Grave—Floral Hills Memory Gardens Cemetery, Lancaster, Fairfield Co., Ohio, Find A Grave.com, Helen Coover Finley, Find A Grave Memorial #98223298.

195 Fairfield County, Ohio Marriage Records, Fairfield County Probate Court, 224 East Main Street, #303 Lancaster, OH; Robert C. Finley and Helen C. Coover, Fairfield County, Ohio Marriage Records, Vol. 12, pg. 548, lic. #1097.

196 U.S., WWII Draft Registration Cards, 1942, Ancestry.com, Robert Cyril Finley, Lancaster, Ohio.

197 Ohio, Death Records, 1908-1932, 1938-2007, Ancestry.com, Robert "S." Finley, death cert. #02588.

198 Find A Grave—Forest Rose Cemetery, Lancaster, Fairfield Co., Ohio, Find A Grave.com, Robert C. Finley, Find A Grave Memorial #19271449.

199 U.S., WWI Draft Registration Cards, 1917-1918, Ancestry.com, Robert Cyril Finley, Lancaster, Ohio.

200 "Only 2 Names Made Public With Report" (Lancaster, Ohio, Lancaster Daily Gazette, 10 Jan 1929); Newspaper Archive, Online database: https://access.newspaperarchive.com/us/ohio/lancaster/lancaster-daily-gazette/1929/01-10?tag=Robert+Finley&rtserp=tags/?pc=15734&psi=73&pci=7&pf=robert&pl=finley

201 Ohio, Death Records, 1908-1932, 1938-2007, Ancestry.com, Raymond Lester Finley, death cert. #037595.

202 U.S. Veterans' Gravesites, ca. 1775-2006, Ancestry.com, Maj. Raymond L. Finley.

203 Obituary of Ray Finley (Lancaster, Ohio, Lancaster Eagle-Gazette, 15 May 1998), Fairfield County Chapter of the Ohio Genealogical Society Library, 503 Lenwood Drive, Lancaster, OH.

204 Ohio, Birth Index, 1908-1964, Ancestry.com, Raymond Finley, state file #1917031685.

205 U.S., Social Security Applications and Claims Index, 1936-2007, Ancestry.com, Melvin Raymond Lawyer.

206 Ohio, Death Records, 1908-1932, 1938-2007, Ancestry.com, Loretta Rushia, death cert. #049755.

207 Ohio, Birth Index, 1908-1964, Ancestry.com, Loretta M. Finley, state file #1919005111.

208 U.S., Social Security Applications and Claims Index, 1936-2007, Ancestry.com, Loretta May Finley Rushia.

209 Obituary of Loretta Rushia (Lancaster, Ohio, Lancaster Eagle-Gazette, 13 Jul 1992), Fairfield County Chapter of the Ohio Genealogical Society Library, 503 Lenwood Drive, Lancaster, OH.

210 Ohio, Death Records, 1908-1932, 1938-2007, Ancestry.com, Esther Marie Wyrick, death cert. #073561.

211 U.S., Social Security Applications and Claims Index, 1936-2007, Ancestry.com, Esther Mae Finley Crist Wyrick.

212 Ohio, Birth Index, 1908-1964, Ancestry.com, Esther M. Finley, state file #1921036779.

213 Ohio, Death Records, 1908-1932, 1938-2007, Ancestry.com, Albert Earl Finley, death cert. #075741.

214 U.S., Social Security Applications and Claims Index, 1936-2007, Ancestry.com, Albert Earl Finley.

215 Obituary of Arthur Coover (Lancaster, Ohio, Lancaster Eagle-Gazette, 23 May 1994), Fairfield County Chapter of the Ohio Genealogical Society Library, 503 Lenwood Drive, Lancaster, OH.

216 Fairfield County, Ohio Marriage Records, Fairfield County Probate Court, 224 East Main Street, #303, Lancaster, OH; Arthur F. Coover and Loretta G. Faires, Fairfield County, Ohio Marriage Records, Vol. 110, pg. 593, lic. #96589.

217 Ohio, Death Records, 1908-1932, 1938-2007, Ancestry.com, Loretta Coover, death cert. #073870.

218 Obituary of Loretta Coover (Lancaster, Ohio, Lancaster Eagle-Gazette, 17 Oct 1983), Fairfield County Chapter of the Ohio Genealogical Society Library, 503 Lenwood Drive, Lancaster, OH.

219 Find A Grave—St. Mary Cemetery, Lancaster, Fairfield Co., Ohio, Find A Grave.com, Edna V. Noble, Find A Grave Memorial #111064846.

220 Fairfield County, Ohio Marriage Records, Fairfield County Probate Court, 224 East Main Street, #303, Lancaster, OH; Arthur J. Noble and Edna V. Coover, Fairfield County, Ohio Marriage Records, Vol.14, pg. 24, lic. #47.

221 Ohio, Death Records, 1908-1932, 1938-2007, Ancestry.com, Arthur J. Noble, death cert. #077549.

222 Obituary of Arthur J. Noble (Lancaster, Ohio, Lancaster Eagle, 28 Oct 1968), Fairfield County District Library, Main Branch, 219 North Broad Street, Lancaster, OH.

223 Find A Grave—St. Mary Cemetery, Lancaster, Fairfield Co., Ohio, Find A Grave.com, Arthur J. Noble, Find A Grave Memorial #111064778.

224 Ohio, Birth Index, 1908-1964, Ancestry.com, Ruth Noble, state file #1922012294.

225 Obituary of Ruth L. Grimsley (DeKalb, Illinois, DeKalb Daily Chronicle, 02 May 1980), Sycamore Public Library, Joiner History Room, 103 East State Street, Sycamore, IL.

226 DeKalb County, Illinois Deaths, 1843-1992, Ancestry.com, Ruth L. Grimsley.

227 Obituary of Alma Hansen (Lancaster, Ohio, Lancaster Eagle-Gazette, 13 Sep 1995), Fairfield County Chapter of the Ohio Genealogical Society Library, 503 Lenwood Drive, Lancaster, OH.

228 Find A Grave—Forest Lawn Memorial Gardens Cemetery, Columbus, Franklin Co., Ohio, Find A Grave.com, Alma P. Ogle, Find A Grave Memorial #153271188.

229 Ohio, Births and Christenings Index, 1800-1962, Ancestry.com, "Anton" Herbert Lewis; fa. John Lewis, mo. Jessie Williams.

230 Ohio, County Births, 1841-2003 (County Courthouses), FamilySearch.org, Muskingum County, Ohio Births, Vol. 4, pg. 137.

231 Ohio, Death Records, 1908-1932, 1938-2007, Ancestry.com, Alton H. Lewis, death cert. #030548.

232 Obituary of Alton H. Lewis Sr. (Zanesville, Ohio, Zanesville Times Recorder, 28 Apr 1974), Ohio History Center Archives and Library, Ohio History Center, 800 East 17th Avenue, Columbus, OH.

233 U.S., WWI Draft Registration Cards, 1917-1918, Ancestry.com, Alton H. Lewis, Zanesville, Muskingham Co., Ohio.

234 U.S., Social Security Applications and Claims Index, 1936-2007, Ancestry.com, Alma Coover Coons Ogle Hanson.

235 Ohio Marriage Index, 1970-1972-2007, Ancestry.com, Frank B. Hansen and Alma P. Ogle, Fairfield County, Ohio Marriage Records, Ohio state Vol. 14653, lic. #49500.

236 Ohio, Death Records, 1908-1932, 1938-2007, Ancestry.com, Frank B. Hansen, death cert. #042121.

237 Obituary of Frank B. Hansen (Eaton, Ohio, Eaton Register, 01 May 1998), Ohio History Center Archives and Library, Ohio History Center, 800 East 17th Avenue, Columbus, OH.

238 Find A Grave—Dayton National Cemetery, Dayton, Montgomery Co., Ohio, Find A Grave.com, Frank B. Hansen, Find A Grave Memorial #749500.

239 Obituary of Alvin C. Fawcett (Fostoria, Ohio, Fostoria Review Times, 22 Jul 1982), Kaubisch Memorial Public Library, 205 Perry Street, Fostoria, OH.

240 Obituary of Mrs. Anne Fawcett (Fostoria, Ohio, Fostoria Review Times, 14 May 1973), Kaubisch Memorial Public Library, 205 Perry Street, Fostoria, OH.

241 Ohio, Death Records, 1908-1932, 1938-2007, Ancestry.com, Anne Fawcett, death cert. #040179.

242 Obituary of Robert A. Fawcett, (Bellefontaine, Ohio, Bellefontaine Examiner, 28 Nov 1994), Logan County Libraries, Knowlton Library, 220 North Main Street, Bellefontaine, OH.

243 Ohio, Death Records, 1908-1932, 1938-2007, Ancestry.com, Robert A. Fawcett, death cert. #082934.

244 U.S., Social Security Applications and Claims Index, 1936-2007, Ancestry.com, Robert A. Fawcett.

245 Ohio, County Marriages, 1789-2013, FamilySearch.org, Otto J. Melvin and Kathryn Ann McCalla, Logan County, Ohio Marriage Records, Vol. N, pg. 376, lic. #3610.

246 Ohio Death Certificate, Ohio Department of Health, Center for Vital and Health Statistics, 246 North High Street, Columbus, OH, Katharyn Melvin, #60460.

247 Find A Grave—Greenwood Cemetery, DeGraff, Pleasant Twp., Logan Co., Ohio, Find A Grave.com, Katharyn A. Melvin, Find A Grave Memorial #17563077.

248 Find A Grave—Rea Cemetery, Bloomfield Twp., Logan Co., Ohio, Find A Grave.com, Dessie Melvin, Find A Grave Memorial #17564364.

249 Find A Grave—Greenwood Cemetery, DeGraff, Pleasant Twp., Logan Co., Ohio, Find A Grave.com, Mary E. Pegan, Find A Grave Memorial #18379962.

250 Obituary of Lylah Smith (Bellefontaine, Ohio, Bellefontaine, Examiner, 28 Jan 1983) Logan County Libraries, Knowlton Library, 220 North Main Street, Bellefontaine, OH.

251 Ohio, Death Records, 1908-1932, 1938-2007, Ancestry.com, Lylah Smith, death cert. #004232.

252 Find A Grave—Greenwood Cemetery, DeGraff, Pleasant Twp., Logan Co., Ohio, Find A Grave.com, Lylah Smith, Find A Grave Memorial #18576330.

253 Ohio, Birth Index, 1908-1964, Ancestry.com, Richard E. Smith, state file #1921118214.

254 Obituary of Richard E. Smith (Bellefontaine, Ohio, Bellefontaine Examiner, 27 Jul 1971), Logan County Libraries, Knowlton Library, 220 North Main Street, Bellefontaine, OH.

255 Ohio, Death Records, 1908-1932, 1938-2007, Ancestry.com, Richard E. Smith, death cert. #05944.

256 Ohio, Birth Index, 1908-1964, Ancestry.com, "Christi" L. Smith, state file #1930042536.

257 Obituary of Christine Wilcox (Bellefontaine, Ohio, Bellefontaine Examiner, 07 May 2016), Logan County Libraries, Knowlton Library, 220 North Main Street, Bellefontaine, OH.

258 Ohio, Birth Index, 1908-1964, Ancestry.com, Mary A. Smith, fa. Fred, state file #1934087690.

259 Obituary of Mary Alice Slonecker (Bellefontaine, Ohio, Bellefontaine Examiner, 21 Oct 2008), Logan County Libraries, Knowlton Library, 220 North Main Street, Bellefontaine, OH.

260 Find A Grave—Riverview Cemetery, Huntingdon, Huntingdon Twp., Huntingdon Co., Pennsylvania, Find A Grave.com, Franklin S. Bayer, Find A Grave Memorial #97007595.

261 Obituary of Mary K. Bayer (Huntingdon, Pennsylvania, Huntingdon Daily News, 26 Feb 1997), Huntingdon County, Pennsylvania Historical Society, 106 4th Street, Huntingdon, PA.

262 Find A Grave—Riverview Cemetery, Huntingdon, Huntingdon Twp., Huntingdon Co., Pennsylvania, Find A Grave.com, Mary K. Bayer, Find A Grave Memorial #97007596.

263 Obituary of Helen K. Huhn, (Huntingdon, Pennsylvania, Huntingdon News, 04 Sep 1978), Huntingdon County, Pennsylvania Historical Society, 106 4th Street, Huntingdon, PA.

264 U.S., Social Security Applications and Claims Index, 1936-2007, Ancestry.com, Helen Kathleen Bayer Huhn.

265 Obituary of Mary Lou (Bayer) Anderson (Huntingdon, Pennsylvania, Huntingdon News, 11 Sep 2009), Huntingdon County, Pennsylvania Historical Society, 106 4th Street, Huntingdon, PA.

266 Find A Grave—Greenwood Cemetery, DeGraff, Pleasant Twp., Logan Co., Ohio, Find A Grave.com, Glady Shawver Allinger, Find A Grave Memorial #18028567.

267 Ohio, County Births, 1841-2003 (County Courthouses), FamilySearch.org, "Roy" H. Allinger, Logan Co. Births, Vol. 2, pg. 386.

268 U.S., WWI Draft Registration Cards, 1917-1918, Ancestry.com, Ray Heath Allinger, Logan Co., Ohio.

269 Ohio, Death Records, 1908-1932, 1938-2007, Ancestry.com, Ray H. Allinger, death cert. #12827.

270 Obituary of Ray Heath Allinger (Bellefontaine, Ohio, Bellefontaine Examiner, 01 Mar 1962), Logan County Libraries, Knowlton Library, 220 North Main Street, Bellefontaine, OH.

271 Find A Grave—Fairview Cemetery, Quincy, Miami Twp., Logan Co., Ohio, Find A Grave.com, Ray H. Allinger, Find A Grave Memorial #17811086.

272 Find A Grave—Greenwood Cemetery, DeGraff, Pleasant Twp., Logan Co., Ohio, Find A Grave.com, Jay Shawver, Find A Grave Memorial #18550729.

273 Ohio, County Births, 1841-2003 (County Courthouses), FamilySearch.org, Grace Maud Rairdon, Logan Co. Births, Vol. 3, pg. 133.

274 Ohio, Death Records, 1908-1932, 1938-2007, Ancestry.com, Grace Shawver, death cert. #025659.

275 Obituary of Grace Shawver (Bellefontaine, Ohio, Bellefontaine Examiner, 29 Apr 1983), Logan County Libraries, Knowlton Library, 220 North Main Street, Bellefontaine, OH.

276 Find A Grave—Greenwood Cemetery, DeGraff, Pleasant Twp., Logan Co., Ohio, Find A Grave.com, Grace Shawver, Find A Grave Memorial #18550722.

277 Ohio, Birth Index, 1908-1964, Ancestry.com, Shawver, state file #1919110731, father, Jay.

278 Obituary of Betty Shawver Emory (Columbus, Ohio, Columbus Dispatch, 06 Mar 2016), Columbus Metropolitan Library, 96 South Grant Avenue, Columbus, OH.

279 Ohio, County Births, 1841-2003 (County Courthouses), FamilySearch.org, Kenneth Rairdan Shawver, Logan Co. Births Vol, 3, pg. 531.

280 U.S., Social Security Applications and Claims Index, 1936-2007, Ancestry.com, Kenneth Rairdon Shawver.

281 Obituary of Kenneth R. Shawver (Nashua, New Hampshire, Nashua Telegraph, 19 Feb 1988), Newspaper Archive; Online database: https//access.newspaperarchive.com/us/new-hampshire/nashua/nashua-telegraph/1988/02-19/page-21?tag=Shawver&rtserp=tags/?pc=19811&psi=64&pci=7&pl=shawver

282 Find A Grave—Glen Cemetery, Port Jefferson, Salem Twp., Shelby Co., Ohio, Find A Grave.com, Harold D. Smith, Find A Grave Memorial #95050722.

283 Shelby County, Ohio Marriage Records, Shelby County, Ohio Probate Court, 100 East Court Street, Sidney, OH, Harold D. Smith and Emma C. Pulfer, Shelby County, Ohio Marriage Records, Vol. 13, pg. 336.

284 Obituary of Emma C. Smith (Mrs. Harold D. Smith) (Bellefontaine, Ohio, Bellefontaine Examiner, 18 Dec 1972), Logan County Libraries, Knowlton Library, 220 North Main Street, Bellefontaine, OH.

285 Ohio, Death Records, 1908-1932, 1938-2007, Ancestry.com, Emma Smith, death cert. #099011.

286 Find A Grave—Glen Cemetery, Port Jefferson, Salem Twp., Shelby Co., Ohio, Find A Grave.com, Emma C. Smith, Find A Grave Memorial #74007282.

287 Ohio Marriage Index, 1970-1972-2007, Ancestry.com, Harold D. Smith and Grace L. Ward, Logan County, Ohio Marriage Records, Ohio state Vol. 8268, lic. #57003.

288 Ohio Death Index, 1908-1932, 1938-1944, and 1958-2007, FamilySearch.org, Grace L. Smith, death cert. #004863.

289 Obituary of Grace L. Ward Smith (Bellefontaine, Ohio, Bellefontaine Examiner, 21 Jan 1998), Logan County Libraries, Knowlton Library, 220 North Main Street, Bellefontaine, OH.

290 Find A Grave—Glen Cemetery, Port Jefferson, Salem Twp., Shelby Co., Ohio, Find A Grave.com, Grace L. Wright Ward, Find A Grave Memorial #137760564.

291 Find A Grave—Medford Cemetery, Medway, Bethel Twp., Clark Co., Ohio, Find A Grave.com, Evelyn Fern Rogers, Find A Grave Memorial #112539162.

292 Ohio, County Marriages, 1789-2013, FamilySearch.org, Clifford L. Rogers and Evelyn F. Smith, Logan County, Ohio Marriage Records, Vol. N, pg.185, lic. #3286.

293 Ohio, County Births, 1841-2003 (County Courthouses), FamilySearch.org, Logan Co., Ohio Birth Register 1003-1908, Vol. 4, pg. 174.

294 Obituary of Clifford LeRoy Rogers (Marion, OH, Marion Star, 28 Aug 1958), Ohio History Center Archives and Library, Ohio History Center, 800 East 17th Avenue, Columbus, OH.

295 Ohio Death Index, 1908-1932, 1938-1944, and 1958-2007, FamilySearch.org, "Cliffor L. Rogers", Vol. #15498, death cert. #56045.

296 Find A Grave—Marion Cemetery, Marion, Marion Twp., Marion Co., Ohio, Find A Grave.com, Clifford LeRoy Rogers, Find A Grave Memorial #144030414.

297 Obituary of David Rogers (Marion, OH, Marion Star, 06 May 1988), Ohio History Center Archives and Library, Ohio History Center, 800 East 17th Avenue, Columbus, OH.

298 U.S., Social Security Applications and Claims Index, 1936-2007, Ancestry.com, David Smith Rogers.

299 Ohio Death Index, 1908-1932, 1938-1944, and 1958-2007, FamilySearch.org, S.D. Rogers, Vol.#27294, death cert. #035414.

300 U.S., Department of Veterans Affairs BIRLS File, 1850-2010, Ancestry.com, Don Rogers.

301 Obituary of Don Elwood Rogers (Honolulu, Hawaii, Honolulu Advertiser, 19 Feb 1986), Hawaii State Library, 478 South King Street, Honolulu, HI.

302 Obituary of Dorothy Evelyn Poland (Dayton, Ohio, Dayton Daily News, 25 Jan 2003), Dayton Metro Library, 215 East Third Street. Dayton, OH.

303 U.S., Social Security Applications and Claims Index, 1936-2007, Ancestry.com, Dorothy Evelyn Rogers Poland.

304 Find A Grave—Greenwood Cemetery, DeGraff, Pleasant Twp., Logan Co., Ohio, Find A Grave.com, Paul D. Smith, Find A Grave Memorial #18576371.

305 Ohio, County Marriages, 1789-2013, FamilySearch.org, Paul D. Smith and Ruth Eiler, Logan County, Ohio Marriage Records, Vol. P, pg. 311, lic. #10167.

306 Ohio, County Births, 1841-2003 (County Courthouses), FamilySearch.org, Ruth Amelia Pence, Van Wert Co., Ohio birth records, Vol. 4, pg.372, line 17 (born Buckland, Auglaize Co.).

307 Ohio, Death Records, 1908-1932, 1938-2007, Ancestry.com, Ruth E. Smith, death cert. #11228.

308 Obituary of Ruth E. Smith, Logan County Libraries, Knowlton Library, 220 North Main Street, Bellefontaine, OH, Ruth E. Smith, Bellefontaine (OH) Examiner, pub. 01 Mar 1963, pg. 7, col. 1.

309 Find A Grave—Greenwood Cemetery, DeGraff, Pleasant Twp., Logan Co., Ohio, Find A Grave.com, Ruth Ellen Pence Smith, Find A Grave Memorial #18576421.

310 Obituary of Bertha Lucile Jenkins (Bellefontaine, Ohio, Bellefontaine Examiner, 28 June 1993), Logan County Libraries, Knowlton Library, 220 North Main Street, Bellefontaine, OH.

311 Find A Grave—Greenwood Cemetery, DeGraff, Pleasant Twp., Logan Co., Ohio, Find A Grave.com, Lucile S. Jenkins, Find A Grave Memorial #18307876.

312 Obituary of Cline Jenkins (Bellefontaine, Ohio, Bellefontaine Examiner, 07 Dec 1977), Logan County Libraries, Knowlton Library, 220 North Main Street, Bellefontaine, OH.

313 Ohio, Death Records, 1908-1932, 1938-2007, Ancestry.com, Cline Jenkins, death cert. #051669.

314 Find A Grave—Greenwood Cemetery, DeGraff, Pleasant Twp., Logan Co., Ohio, Find A Grave.com, Cline M. Jenkins, Find A Grave Memorial #18307845.

315 Find A Grave—Glen Cemetery, Port Jefferson, Salem Twp., Shelby Co., Ohio, Find A Grave.com, Stanley A. Smith, Find A Grave Memorial #151367943.

316 Shelby County, Ohio Marriage Records, Shelby County, Ohio Probate Court, 100 East Court Street, Sidney, OH, Stanley A. Smith and Esther L. Herring, Shelby County, Ohio Marriage Records, Vol.17, pg. 70.

317 Ohio, Death Records, 1908-1932, 1938-2007, Ancestry.com, Esther Louise Smith, death cert. #070689.

318 Obituary of Esther Louise Smith, Logan County Libraries, Knowlton Library, 220 North Main Street, Bellefontaine, OH, Bellefontaine (OH) Examiner, 27 Sep 2002.

319 Find A Grave—Glen Cemetery, Port Jefferson, Salem Twp., Shelby Co., Ohio, Find A Grave.com, Esther Herring Smith, Find A Grave Memorial #151367972.

320 Find A Grave—Shawnee Cemetery, Fort Shawnee, Shawnee Twp., Allen Co., Ohio, Find A Grave.com, Thurman H. Smith, Find A Grave Memorial #41557778.

321 Obituary of Mrs. Margaret R. Smith (Bellefontaine, Ohio, Bellefontaine Examiner, 13 Feb 1975), Logan County Librar-

ies, Knowlton Library, 220 North Main Street, Bellefontaine, OH.

322 Ohio, Death Records, 1908-1932, 1938-2007, Ancestry.com, Margaret R. Smith, death cert. #006381.

323 Find A Grave—Shawnee Cemetery, Fort Shawnee, Shawnee Twp., Allen Co., Ohio, Find A Grave.com, Margaret R. Smith, Find A Grave Memorial #41557833.

324 Find A Grave—Fairview Cemetery, West Liberty, Liberty Twp., Logan Co., Ohio, Find A Grave.com, H. Marvin Stanley, Find A Grave Memorial #46210901.

325 Obituary of Myrna Stanley (Logan County, Ohio, Weekly Currents, 08 Nov 2016); Legacy.com, Online database: http://www.legacy.com/obituaries/weeklycurrents/obituary.aspx?page=lifestory&pid=182407098

326 Find A Grave—Fairview Cemetery, West Liberty, Liberty Twp., Logan Co., Ohio, Find A Grave.com, Myrna Anne Miller Stanley, Find A Grave Memorial #172471869.

327 Obituary of James Darrell Stanley (Bellefontaine, Ohio, Bellefontaine Examiner, 30 May 1990), Logan County Libraries, Knowlton Library, 220 North Main Street, Bellefontaine, OH.

328 Find A Grave—Markle Cemetery, Markle, Rock Creek Twp., Huntington Co., Indiana, Find A Grave.com, James D. Stanley, Find A Grave Memorial #151167001.

329 Obituary of Anna Jane Stanley (Huntington, Huntington Twp., Huntington Co., Indiana, Huntington Herald-Press, 05 Jul 2011), Huntington City-Township Library, Indiana Room, 255 West Park Drive, Huntington, IN, Huntington Herald-Press, pub. 05 Jul 2011.

330 Find A Grave—Markle Cemetery, Markle, Rock Creek Twp., Huntington Co., Indiana, Find A Grave.com, Anna Jane Lenwell Stanley, Find A Grave Memorial #72990017.

331 Obituary of Jerry A. Stanley (Huntington, Indiana, Huntington Herald Press, 01 Mar 2010), Huntington City-Township Library, Indiana Room, 255 West Park Drive, Huntington, IN.

332 Indiana, Death Certificates, 1899-2011, Ancestry.com, Jerry Alan Stanley, death cert. #010338.

333 Obituary of Barbara C. Meier (Huntington, Indiana, Huntington Herald Press, 15 Dec 2015), Huntington City-Township Library, Indiana Room, 255 West Park Drive, Huntington, IN.

334 Obituary of Walter Stanley (Huntington, Huntington Twp., Huntington Co., Indiana, Huntington Herald-Press, 27 Oct 1957), Huntington City-Township Library, Indiana Room, 255 West Park Drive, Huntington, IN.

335 Indiana, Death Certificates, 1899-2011, Ancestry.com, Walter David Stanley, death cert. #032663.

336 Find A Grave—Zanesfield Cemetery, Zanesfield, Jefferson Twp., Logan Co., Ohio, Find A Grave.com, Wendell Wayne Stanley, Find A Grave Memorial #62128886.

337 Find A Grave—Southern Arizona Veterans Memorial Cemetery, Sierra Vista, Cochise Co., Arizona, Find A Grave.com, Aileen P. Pickering, Find A Grave Memorial #54378340.

338 U.S., Department of Veterans Affairs BIRLS File, 1850-2010, Ancestry.com, Wilford Frazier.

339 Obituary of Wilford Wayne Frazier (Billings, Montana, Billings Gazette, 10 May 2009), Billings Public Library, 510 North Broadway, Billings, MT.

340 Find A Grave—Southern Arizona Veterans Memorial Cemetery, Sierra Vista, Cochise Co., Arizona, Find A Grave.com, Wilford W. Frazier, Find A Grave Memorial #54378339.

341 Ohio, County Marriages, 1789-2013, FamilySearch.org, Arthur Lawyer and Mrs. Beulah (Eckard) Miller, Logan County, Ohio Marriage Records, Vol. 118, pg. 286, lic. #5571.

342 Obituary of Arthur W. Lawyer (Lancaster, Ohio, Lancaster Eagle-Gazette, 17 Jul 1981), Fairfield County Chapter of the Ohio Genealogical Society Library, 503 Lenwood Drive, Lancaster, OH.

343 Find A Grave—Thurston Primitive Baptist Cemetery, Thurston, Walnut Twp., Lancaster Co., Ohio, Find A Grave.com, Arthur Wilson Lawyer, Find A Grave Memorial #70342376.

344 Fairfield County, Ohio Marriage Records, Fairfield County Probate Court, 224 East Main Street, #303, Lancaster, OH; Arthur Wilson Lawyer and Virginia Katherine Sallaz, Fairfield County, Ohio Marriage Records, Vol. 18, pg. 13, lic. #25.

345 State of West Virginia Division of Culture and History, West Virginia Vital Records Research, Birth Records (West Virginia Archives & Records), West Virginia State Archives, West Virginia Archives & History Center Library, The Culture Center, 1900 Kanawha Boulevard E, Charleston, WV, Virginia Sallaz. Register of Births, Jackson County, W. Va.; Sa-Sl, pg. 15; Online database: http://www.wvculture.org/vrr/va_view.aspx?Id=1837080&Type=Birth.

346 West Virginia, Births Index, 1853-1969, Ancestry.com, Virginia K. Sallaz.

347 Ohio, Death Records, 1908-1932, 1938-2007, Ancestry.com, "Virgini" Householder, death cert. #002661.

348 Obituary of Virginia Householder (Lancaster, Ohio, Lancaster Eagle-Gazette, 24 Jan 1983), Fairfield County District Library, Main Branch, 219 North Broad Street, Lancaster, OH.

349 Find A Grave—Basil Memorial Cemetery, Baltimore, Liberty Twp., Fairfield Co., Ohio, Find A Grave.com, Virginia K. Sallee Lawyer Householder, Find A Grave Memorial #40626553.

350 Ohio, Birth Index, 1908-1964, Ancestry.com, Larry Eugene Lawyer, state file #1940028538.

351 North Carolina, Marriage Records, 1741-2011, Larry E. Lawyer and (Given Name) Casteen, Sampson Co., North Carolina Marriage Records, lic. #53898.

352 Obituary of Larry E. Lawyer (Lancaster, Ohio, Lancaster Eagle-Gazette, 06 Aug 2009), Fairfield County District Library, Main Branch, 219 North Broad Street, Lancaster, OH.

353 Ohio, Death Records, 1908-1932, 1938-2007, Ancestry.com, Bobby W. Lawyer, death cert. #026593.

354 Fairfield County, Ohio Marriage Records, Fairfield County Probate Court, 224 East Main Street, #303, Lancaster, OH;

William N. Lawyer and Betty McCray, Fairfield County, Ohio Marriage Records, Vol. 17, pg. 497, lic. #993.

355 Ohio, Death Records, 1908-1932, 1938-2007, Ancestry.com, Betty E. Ferguson, death cert. #071289.

356 U.S., Social Security Applications and Claims Index, 1936-2007, Ancestry.com, Betty E. McCray Lawyer Eliott Ferguson.

357 Find A Grave—Maple Grove Cemetery, Baltimore, Liberty Twp., Fairfield Co., Ohio, Find A Grave.com, Betty E. Ferguson, Find A Grave Memorial #77639755.

358 Fairfield County, Ohio Marriage Records, Fairfield County Probate Court, 224 East Main Street, #303, Lancaster, OH; William N. Lawyer and Mary Hiller, Fairfield County, Ohio Marriage Records, Vol. 23, pg. 59, lic. #117.

359 Ohio, County Marriages, 1789-2013, FamilySearch.org, William Nelson Lawyer and Mary Evelyn Hiller, Fairfield County, Ohio Marriage Records, Vol. 23, pg. 59, state lic. #26212.

360 U.S., Social Security Applications and Claims Index, 1936-2007, Ancestry.com, Mary Evelyn Hooker Silcott.

361 Ohio, Death Records, 1908-1932, 1938-2007, Ancestry.com, Mary Evelyn Silcott, death cert. #050584.

362 Find A Grave—Floral Hills Memory Gardens Cemetery, Lancaster, Fairfield Co., Ohio, Find A Grave.com, Mary E. Silcott, Find A Grave Memorial #76338609.

363 Fairfield County, Ohio Marriage Records, Fairfield County Probate Court, 224 East Main Street, #303, Lancaster, OH; William N. Lawyer and Donna Merkel, Fairfield County, Ohio Marriage Records, Vol. 25, pg. 408, lic. #816.

364 Fairfield County, Ohio Marriage Records, Fairfield County Probate Court, 224 East Main Street, #303, Lancaster, OH; William N. Lawyer and Martha Lane, Fairfield County, Ohio Marriage Records, Vol. 26, pg. 625, lic. #1250.

365 U.S., Social Security Applications and Claims Index, 1936-2007, Ancestry.com, Martha Tindle Lane Lawyer Tackett.

366 Ohio, Death Records, 1908-1932, 1938-2007, Ancestry.com, Martha M. Tackett, death cert. #079730.

367 Find A Grave—Green Lawn Cemetery, Columbus, Franklin Co., Ohio, Find A Grave.com, Martha M. Tackett, Find A Grave Memorial #21199885.

368 Find A Grave—Maple Grove Cemetery, Baltimore, Liberty Twp., Fairfield Co., Ohio, Find A Grave.com, Vivian June Lawyer Armstrong, Find A Grave Memorial #79824047.

369 Fairfield County, Ohio Marriage Records, Fairfield County Probate Court, 224 East Main Street, #303, Lancaster, OH; Raymond D. Armstrong and Vivian J. Lawyer, Fairfield County, Ohio Marriage Records, Vol. 19, pg. 311, lic. #621.

370 Ohio, Death Records, 1908-1932, 1938-2007, Ancestry.com, Raymond Doyle Armstrong, death cert. #043251.

371 Obituary of Raymond Armstrong (Lancaster, Ohio, Lancaster Eagle-Gazette, 28 Jun 1993), Fairfield County Chapter of the Ohio Genealogical Society Library, 503 Lenwood Drive, Lancaster, OH.

372 Find A Grave—Maple Grove Cemetery, Baltimore, Liberty Twp., Fairfield Co., Ohio, Find A Grave.com, Raymond Doyle Armstrong, Find A Grave Memorial #79823986.

373 Ohio, Birth Index, 1908-1964, Ancestry.com, Susan J. Armstrong, state file #1957162435.

374 Ohio Death Index, 1908-1932, 1938-1944, and 1958-2007, FamilySearch.org, Susan J. Tomko, death cert. #029541.

375 Ohio, Death Records, 1908-1932, 1938-2007, Ancestry.com, Susan J. Tomko, death cert. #45629.

376 U.S. Veterans' Gravesites, ca. 1775-2006, Ancestry.com, Melvin R. Lawyer.

377 Find A Grave—Floral Hills Memory Gardens Cemetery, Lancaster, Fairfield Co., Ohio, Find A Grave.com, Melvin R. Lawyer, Find A Grave Memorial #35372733.

378 Fairfield County, Ohio Marriage Records, Fairfield County Probate Court, 224 East Main St., #303, Lancaster, Ohio, Melvin R. Lawyer and Nita L. Botts, Fairfield County, Ohio Marriage Records, Vol. 21. pg. 348, lic. #695.

379 Find A Grave—Vega Cemetery, Bloomfield Twp., Jackson Co., Ohio, Find A Grave.com, Maj. Raymond L. Finley, Find A Grave Memorial #72664108.

380 Obituary of Marcella Julian Steiner (St. Paul, Minnesota, Pioneer Press, 11 Jan 2004), George Latimer Central Library, 90 West 4th Street, St. Paul, MN.

381 Ohio, Birth Index, 1908-1964, Ancestry.com, "Eojth" M. Julian, 29 Apr 1916, fa. Ray. Given name is incorrectly spelled in index.

382 Find A Grave—Graceland Memorial Park Cemetery and Mausoleum, Grand Rapids, Grand Rapids Twp., Kent Co., Michigan, Find A Grave.com, Marcella Steiner, Find A Grave Memorial #49947227.

383 Fairfield County, Ohio Marriage Records, Fairfield County Probate Court, 224 East Main St., #303, Lancaster, Ohio, Raymond L. Finley and EmoGene Jones, Fairfield County, Ohio Marriage Records, Vol. 21, pg. 443, lic. #886.

384 Obituary of Emo Gene "Jean" Hawker Finley (Lancaster, Ohio, Lancaster Eagle Gazette, 14 Oct 2015), Fairfield County District Library, Main Branch, 219 North Broad Street, Lancaster, OH.

385 Find A Grave—Vega Cemetery, Bloomfield Twp., Jackson Co., Ohio, Find A Grave.com, Emo Gene "Jean" Hawker Finley, Find A Grave Memorial #153654095.

386 Find A Grave—Floral Hills Memory Gardens Cemetery, Lancaster, Fairfield Co., Ohio, Find A Grave.com, Loretta M. Rushia, Find A Grave Memorial #79571789.

387 Ohio, Death Records, 1908-1932, 1938-2007, Ancestry.com, James W. Rushia, death cert. #059727.

388 Find A Grave—Floral Hills Memory Gardens Cemetery, Lancaster, Fairfield Co., Ohio, Find A Grave.com, James W. Rushia, Find A Grave Memorial #35067211.

389 U.S., Social Security Applications and Claims Index, 1936-2007, Ancestry.com, Rick Lee Rushia.

390 Ohio, Death Records, 1908-1932, 1938-2007, Ancestry.com, Rickey Lee Rushia, death cert. #097091.

391 Ohio, Birth Index, 1908-1964, Ancestry.com, Rickey L. Rushia, state file #1952118479.

392 Find A Grave—Floral Hills Memory Gardens Cemetery, Lancaster, Fairfield Co., Ohio, Find A Grave.com, Esther M. Wyrick, Find A Grave Memorial #35336089.

393 Fairfield County, Ohio Marriage Records, Fairfield County Probate Court, 224 East Main Street, #303, Lancaster, Oh; William D. Crist and Esther M. Finley, Fairfield County, Ohio Marriage Records, Vol. 18, pg. 451, lic. #902.

394 Ohio, Birth Index, 1908-1964, Ancestry.com, William D. Crist, state file #1919473576.

395 Obituary of William D. Crist (Lancaster, Ohio, Lancaster Eagle-Gazette, 14 Dec 2012), Fairfield County District Library, Main Branch, 219 North Broad Street, Lancaster, OH.

396 Ohio, Births and Christenings Index, 1800-1962, Ancestry.com, Myrell Franklin Wyrick.

397 Ohio, Death Records, 1908-1932, 1938-2007, Ancestry.com, Myrell F. Wyrick, death cert. #02520.

398 "Say Man Dies of Injury in Fall at Anchor Hocking" (Lancaster, Ohio, Lancaster Eagle-Gazette, 23 Jan 1963), Fairfield County District Library, Main Branch, 219 North Broad Street, Lancaster, OH.

399 Find A Grave—Floral Hills Memory Gardens Cemetery, Lancaster, Fairfield Co., Ohio, Find A Grave.com, Myrell F. Wyrick, Find A Grave Memorial #35336039.

400 Find A Grave—Floral Hills Memory Gardens Cemetery, Lancaster, Fairfield Co., Ohio, Find A Grave.com, Ronald F. Wyrick, Find A Grave Memorial #87088974.

401 Virginia, Death Records, 1912-2014, Ancestry.com, Ronald Franklin Wyrick.

402 Find A Grave—Mifflin Cemetery, Gahanna, Mifflin Twp., Franklin Co., Ohio, Find A Grave.com, Albert Earl "Al" Finley, Find A Grave Memorial #117059870.

403 Ohio, Death Records, 1908-1932, 1938-2007, Ancestry.com, Fairy Faye Finley, death cert. #079291.

404 Find A Grave—Mifflin Cemetery, Gahanna, Mifflin Twp., Franklin Co., Ohio, Find A Grave.com, F. Faye Milligan Finley, Find A Grave Memorial #117060751.

405 Ohio, Death Records, 1908-1932, 1938-2007, Ancestry.com, David Allen Finley, death cert. #51468.

406 Indiana, Marriage Certificates, 1810-2001, Ancestry.com, Albert Guyer and Ruth Kendall, Wayne Co., Indiana, Vol. 202, pg. 569, lic. #7711.

407 Ohio, County Marriages, 1789-2013, FamilySearch.org, Clayton M. Kendall and Ruth L. Baron, Franklin County, Ohio Marriage Records, Vol. 174, pg. 157, Ohio state lic. #61911.

408 Ohio, Birth Index, 1908-1964, Ancestry.com, Clayton M. Kendall.

409 Florida Death Index 1877-1998, Ancestry.com, Clayton Morris Kendall.

410 Ohio, Death Records, 1908-1932, 1938-2007, Ancestry.com, Albert F. Guyer, death cert. #52052.

411 Obituary of Melvin W. Grimsley (Devils Lake, North Dakota, Devils Lake Journal, 28 Apr 2004), Lake Region Public Library, 423 7th Street NE, Devils Lake, ND.

412 U.S., Social Security Applications and Claims Index, 1936-2007, Ancestry.com, Melvin Walter Grimsley.

413 Find A Grave—Grand Army of the Republic Cemetery, Devils Lake, Ramsey Co., North Dakota, Find A Grave.com, Melvin Grimsley, Find A Grave Memorial #123512410.

414 Find A Grave—SS. Peter And Paul Cemetery, Ottawa, Ottawa Twp., Putnam Co., Ohio, Find A Grave.com, Robert A. Fawcett, Find A Grave Memorial #140248612.

415 Obituary of Mary Rose Fawcett (Lima, Ohio, Lima News, 28 Oct 1994), Lima Public Library, 650 West Market Street, Lima, OH.

416 Ohio, Death Records, 1908-1932, 1938-2007, Ancestry.com, Mary R. Fawcett, death cert. #077316.

417 Find A Grave—SS. Peter And Paul Cemetery, Ottawa, Ottawa Twp., Putnam Co., Ohio, Find A Grave.com, Mary Rose Leahey Fawcett, Find A Grave Memorial #140248623.

418 Ohio, Birth Index, 1908-1964, Ancestry.com, Gail Ann Fawcett, state file #1946104364.

419 Obituary of Gail Anne Fawcett (Dayton, Ohio, Dayton Daily News, 18 May 2008), Dayton Metro Library, 6215 East Third Street, Dayton, OH.

420 Find A Grave—Highland Memorial Cemetery, West Liberty, Liberty Twp., Logan Co., Ohio, Find A Grave.com, Christine LaVon Smith Wilcox, Find A Grave Memorial #20184124.

421 Obituary of Isaac Wilcox Jr. (Bellefontaine, Ohio, Bellefontaine Examiner, 12 Jan 1981), Logan County Libraries, Knowlton Library, 220 North Main Street, Bellefontaine, OH.

422 Ohio, Death Records, 1908-1932, 1938-2007, Ancestry.com, Isaac Wilcox, death cert. #004467.

423 Find A Grave—Highland Memorial Cemetery, West Liberty, Liberty Twp., Logan Co., Ohio, Find A Grave.com, Isaac Wilcox, Jr., Find A Grave Memorial #20184131.

424 Find A Grave—Highland Memorial Cemetery, West Liberty, Liberty Twp., Logan Co., Ohio, Mary Alice Smith Slonecker, Find A Grave Memorial #20165287.

425 Ohio, Death Records, 1908-1932, 1938-2007, Ancestry.com, Richard M. Slonecker, deat cert. #102037.

426 Ohio, Birth Index, 1908-1964, Ancestry.com, Richard M. Slonecker, state file #1931084454.

427 U.S. Veterans' Gravesites, ca. 1775-2006, Ancestry.com, Richard "Max" Slonecker.

428 Find A Grave—Highland Memorial Cemetery, West Liberty, Liberty Twp., Logan Co., Ohio, Find A Grave.com, Richard Max Slonecker, Find A Grave Memorial #82185203.

429 Florida Death Index 1877-1998, Ancestry.com, Sharon L. Bellamy.

430 Obituary of Sharon L. Bellamy (Bellefontaine, Ohio, Bellefontaine Examiner, 16 Feb 1990), Logan County Libraries, Knowlton Library, 220 North Main Street, Bellefontaine, OH.

431 Find A Grave—Riverview Cemetery, Huntingdon, Huntingdon Twp., Huntingdon Co., Pennsylvania, Find A Grave.com, Helen Bayer Huhn, Find A Grave Memorial #97007642.

432 U.S., Social Security Applications and Claims Index, 1936-2007, Ancestry.com, Alfred Cozard Huhn Jr.

433 U.S. WWII Draft Cards Young Men, 1940-1947, Alfred Cozard Huhn.

434 Obituary of Alfred Huhn Jr. (Sebastian, Florida, Sebastian Sun, 27 Apr 2007), North Indiana River County Library, 1001 Sebastian Boulevard, Sebastian, FL.

435 Obituary of Max Huhn, Huntingdon County, Pennsylvania Historical Society, 106 4th Street, Huntingdon, PA, Huntington (PA) News, pub. 16 Sep 1985.

436 Virginia Death Certificate, Commonwealth of Virginia State Board of Health, Vital Records/Health Statistics, 2001 Maywill Street, Richmond, VA, Max Robert Huhn, death cert. #85-032883.

437 Web: Marion County, Indiana, Marriage Index, 1925-2012, Ancestry.com, Louis Emory and Betty "Shawner".

438 U.S., Select Military Registers, 1862-1985, Ancestry.com, Louis Emory; U.S. Army Registers 1948, 1951, 1953, 1956, 1961.

439 Ohio, Death Records, 1908-1932, 1938-2007, Ancestry.com, Louis Emory, death cert. #034856.

440 Find A Grave—Arlington National Cemetery, Arlington, Virginia, Find A Grave.com, Colonel Louis Emory, Find A Grave Memorial #34237257.

441 Obituary of Dr. Louis Emory (Columbus, Ohio, Columbus Dispatch, 11 May 1981), Columbus Metropolitan Library, 96 South Grant Avenue, Columbus, OH.

442 Ohio, Death Records, 1908-1932, 1938-2007, Ancestry.com, Louis D. Emory, death cert. #073738.

443 California, Passengers and Crew List, 1882-1959, Ancestry.com, Louis D. Emory, passenger on the USNS General Daniel I Sultan, embarked Yokohama, Japan 10 May 1950, arrived San Francisco, California on 19 May 1950, born Tokyo, Japan.

444 U.S., Social Security Applications and Claims Index, 1936-2007, Ancestry.com, Louis Dale Emory.

445 Find A Grave—Greenwood Cemetery, DeGraff, Pleasant Twp., Logan Co., Ohio, Find A Grave.com, Kenneth R. Shawver, Find A Grave Memorial #18550733.

446 Obituary of Kenneth R. Shawver (Bellefontaine, Ohio, Bellefontaine Examiner, 22 Feb 1988), Logan County Libraries, Knowlton Library, 220 North Main Street, Bellefontaine, OH.

447 "Kenton Marriage Licenses Issued" (Marion, Ohio, Marion Star, 27 May 1947), Marion Public Library, 445 East Church Street, Marion, OH, Kenneth Shawver, Columbus, student and Catherine Nourse, Kenton.

448 Hardin County, Ohio Marriage Records (Kenton, Ohio), Hardin County, Ohio Probate Court, Hardin County Clerk of Courts, One Courthouse Square, Kenton, OH, Kenneth R. Shawver and Catherine Nourse, Hardin County, Ohio Marriage Records, Vol. 26, pg. 307.

449 Ohio, Birth Index, 1908-1964, Ancestry.com, Catherine Nourse, state file #1924009512.

450 Hardin County, Ohio Marriage Records, Hardin County, Ohio Probate Court, Hardin County Clerk of Courts, One Courthouse Square, Kenton, OH, Kenneth Shawver and Rosemary Bushong, Hardin County, Ohio Marriage Records, Vol. 30, pg. 530, lic. #26130.

451 Ohio, Birth Index, 1908-1964, Ancestry.com, Rosemary Bushong, state file #1936104899.

452 Find A Grave—New Caledonia Cemetery, Caledonia, Claridon Twp., Marion Co., Ohio, Find A Grave.com, Smith David Rogers, Find A Grave Memorial #120016870.

453 Ohio, Death Records, 1908-1932, 1938-2007, Ancestry.com, Rose E. Rogers, death cert. #69874.

454 Obituary of Rose Etta Rogers (Marion, Ohio, Marion Star, 09 Sep 2003), Marion, Ohio Public Library, 445 East Church Street, Marion, OH.

455 Find A Grave—New Caledonia Cemetery, Caledonia, Claridon Twp., Marion Co., Ohio, Find A Grave.com, Rose Etta White Rogers, Find A Grave Memorial #120016787.

456 U.S. Veterans' Gravesites, ca. 1775-2006, Ancestry.com, Don E. Smith.

457 Find A Grave—National Memorial Cemetery of the Pacific, Honolulu, Oahu Island, Hawaii, Find A Grave.com, Don E. Rogers, Find A Grave Memorial #1131957.

458 U.S., Social Security Applications and Claims Index, 1936-2007, Ancestry.com, Jean Uno Rogers.

459 Find A Grave—National Memorial Cemetery of the Pacific, Honolulu, Oahu Island, Hawaii, Find A Grave.com, Jean U. Rogers, Find A Grave Memorial #1132296.

460 Find A Grave—Medford Cemetery, Medway, Bethel Twp., Clark Co., Ohio, Find A Grave.com, Dorothy E. Poland, Find A Grave Memorial #135288020.

461 West Virginia, Births Index, 1853-1969, Ancestry.com, Raymond Maxwell Poland.

462 Obituary of Raymond Maxwell Poland (Dayton, Ohio, Dayton Daily News, 09 Sep 1999), Dayton Metro Library, 215 East Third Street, Dayton, OH.

463 Find A Grave—Medford Cemetery, Medway, Bethel Twp., Clark Co., Ohio, Find A Grave.com, Raymond M. Poland, Find A Grave Memorial #122601661.

464 Find A Grave—Marion National Cemetery, Marion, Center Twp., Grant Co., Indiana, Find A Grave.com, Jerry Alan Stanley, Find A Grave Memorial #64920780.

465 Indiana, Marriage Certificates, 1917-2005, Ancestry.com, Jerry A. Stanley and "Jerry" Lynn McGinniss, Huntington County, Indiana Marriage Records, Indiana state lic. #79-013716 (document clearly says "Terry" but the record is indexed incorrectly).

466 Obituary of Terry L. Stanley (Huntington, Indiana, Huntington TAB (online), 06 Mar 2013), http://www.huntingtoncountytab.com/obituary/20993/terry-l-stanley, Captured 24 Aug 2015.

467 Find A Grave—Marion National Cemetery, Marion, Center Twp., Grant Co., Indiana, Find A Grave.com, Terry L. McGinniss Stanley, Find A Grave Memorial #107333529.

468 Find A Grave—Pilgrims Rest Cemetery, Huntington, Huntington Twp., Huntington Co., Indiana, Find A Grave.com, Walter David Stanley, Find A Grave Memorial #117399644.

469 Ohio Marriage Index, 1970-1972-2007, Ancestry.com, Larry E. Lawyer and Della C. King, Fairfield County, Ohio Marriage Records, Ohio state Vol. 8536, lic. #17131.

470 Obituary of Della C. Lawyer (Columbus, Ohio, Columbus Dispatch, 21 Mar 2013), Columbus Metropolitan Library, 96 South Grant Avenue, Columbus, OH.

471 Ohio, Birth Index, 1908-1964, Ancestry.com, Della C. Penrod, state file #1950052529.

472 Find A Grave—Basil Memorial Cemetery, Baltimore, Liberty Twp., Fairfield Co., Ohio, Find A Grave.com, Wesley Lydell "Dell" Thomas, Find A Grave Memorial #21419352.

473 Ohio, Death Records, 1908-1932, 1938-2007, Ancestry.com, Wesley L. Thomas, death cert. #071421.

474 Obituary of Bobby W. Lawyer (Lancaster, Ohio, Lancaster Eagle Gazette, April 14, 1987), Fairfield County District Library, Main Branch, 219 North Broad Street, Lancaster, OH.

475 Ohio Marriage Index, 1970-1972-2007, Ancestry.com, Bobby W. Lawyer and Charlotte A. Rager, Fairfield County, Ohio Marriage Records, Ohio state Vol. 6890, lic. #31271.

476 Find A Grave—Carbon Hill Cemetery, Carbon Hill, Ward Twp., Hocking Co., Ohio, Find A Grave.com, Charlotte A. Conrad Lawyer, Find A Grave Memoria #42180431.

477 Ohio Marriage Index, 1970-1972-2007, Ancestry.com, Bobby W. Lawyer and Nellie M. Smith, Fairfield County, Ohio Marriage Records, Ohio state Vol. 11296, lic. #58674.

478 Ohio, Birth Index, 1908-1964, Ancestry.com, Tracy A. Logue, state file #1962036762.

479 "Births…LOGUE, Mr. & Mrs. James B. Logue II, 2040 N. Columbus, daughter March 24, Lancaster-Fairfield Hospital…(Lancaster, Ohio, Lancaster Eagle Gazette, 24 Mar 1962), Fairfield County District Library, Main Branch 219 North Broad Street, Lancaster, OH.

480 Ohio, Death Records, 1908-1932, 1938-2007, Ancestry.com, Tracy A. Huffman, death cert. #050386.

481 Find A Grave—Golden Oaks Memorial Gardens Cemetery, Ashland, Boyd Co., Kentucky, Find A Grave.com, Susan Jayne Tomko, Find A Grave Memorial #82256064.

482 Find A Grave—Floral Hills Memory Gardens Cemetery, Lancaster, Fairfield Co., Ohio, Find A Grave.com, Rick L. Rushia, Find A Grave Memorial #35067224.

483 Ohio, Birth Index, 1908-1964, Ancestry.com, David Dixon, state file #1945044219.

484 Find A Grave—St. Joseph Cemetery, Lockbourne, Hamilton Twp., Franklin Co., Ohio, Find A Grave.com, David Dixon, Find A Grave Memorial #46376833.

485 Obituary of David Dixon (Columbus, Ohio, Columbus Dispatch, 06 Jan 2010), Columbus Metropolitan Library, 96 South Grant Avenue, Columbus, OH.

486 U.S., Social Security Applications and Claims Index, 1936-2007, Ancestry.com, William Wesley Dixon.

487 Find A Grave—Mifflin Cemetery, Gahanna, Mifflin Twp., Franklin Co., Ohio, Find A Grave.com, David Alan Finley, Find A Grave Memorial #117061486.

488 Ohio Marriage Index, 1970-1972-2007, Ancestry.com, Bert K. Waits and Barbara J. Bartow, Franklin County, Ohio Marriage Records, Ohio state Vol. 13475, lic. #61393.

489 Obituary of Bert Kerr Waits II (Columbus, Ohio, Colulmbus Dispatch, 21 Sep 2014), Columbus Metropolitan Library, 96 South Grant Avenue, Columbus, OH.

490 Find A Grave—Mifflin Cemetery, Gahanna, Mifflin Twp., Franklin Co., Ohio, Find A Grave.com, Bert Kerr Waits II, Find A Grave Memorial #133708466.

491 "Bert Waits, 1940-2014", Mathematical Association of America website, http://sections.maa.org/ohio/waits.pdf

492 "Joan Leitzel Awarded OCTM 2015 Bert Waits Award", Ohio Council of Teachers of Mathematics website, online, https://math.osu.edu/news/joan-leitzel-awarded-octm-2015-bert-waits-award

493 Ohio Death Certificate, Ohio Department of Health, Center for Vital and Health Statistics, 246 North High Street, Columbus, OH, Brian Fawcett, death cert. #6900/1988-125. Obtained from Putnam County District Library, 136 Putnam Parkway, Ottawa, OH.

494 Obituary of Brian Fawcett (Ottawa, Ohio, Putnam Sentinel, 29 Oct 1988), Putnam County District Library, 136 Putnam Parkway, Ottawa, OH.

495 Ohio, Death Records, 1908-1932, 1938-2007, Ancestry.com, Brian Fawcett, death cert. #079409.

496 Find A Grave—SS. Peter And Paul Cemetery, Ottawa, Ottawa Twp., Putnam Co., Ohio, Find A Grave.com, Gail Anne Fawcett, Find A Grave Memorial #138616720.

497 Ohio, Birth Index, 1908-1964, Ancestry.com, Scott A. Imm, state file #1962084563.

498 Obituary of Andrew James Imm and Scott Allen Imm (Lima, Ohio, Lima News, 13 Apr 1965), Lima Public Library, 650 West Market Street, Lima, OH.

499 Ohio, Death Records, 1908-1932, 1938-2007, Ancestry.com, Scott A. Imm, death cert. #25157.

500 "14 Stricken Palm Sunday in Hospitals" (Lima, Ohio, Lima News, 22 Apr 1965), Lima Public Library, 650 West Market Street, Lima, Ohio.

501 Ohio, Birth Index, 1908-1964, Ancestry.com, Andrew J. Imm, state file #1964172483.

502 Ohio, Death Records, 1908-1932, 1938-2007, Ancestry.com, Andrew J. Imm, death cert. #25156.

503 Find A Grave—Naples Memorial Gardens Cemetery, North Naples, Collier Co., Florida, Find A Grave.com, Shari L. Slonecker Bellamy, Find A Grave Memorial #16232233.

504 Find A Grave—Riverview Cemetery, Huntingdon, Huntingdon Twp., Huntingdon Co., Pennsylvania, Find A Grave.com, Max Robert Huhn, Find A Grave Memorial #97007643.

505 Find A Grave—Greenwood Cemetery, DeGraff, Pleasant Twp., Logan Co., Ohio, Find A Grave.com, Louis D. Emory, Find A Grave Memorial#18250376.

506 Find A Grave—Carroll Cemetery, Carroll, Greenfield Twp., Fairfield Co., Ohio, Find A Grave.com, Tracy Ann (Logue) Huffman, Find A Grave Memorial #38192088.

507 Find A Grave—William Wesley "Bill" Dixon, Find A Grave Memorial #120379111.

508 Find A Grave—Saints Peter and Paul Cemetery, Ottawa, Ottawa Twp., Putnam Co., Ohio, Find A Grave.com, Brian J. "Beau" Fawcett, Find A Grave Memorial #116512038.

509 Find A Grave—Saints Peter and Paul Cemetery, Ottawa, Ottawa Twp., Putnam Co., Ohio, Find A Grave.com, Scott Allen Imm, Find A Grave Memorial #138616887.

510 Find A Grave—Saints Peter and Paul Cemetery, Ottawa, Ottawa Twp., Putnam Co., Ohio, Find A Grave.com, Andrew J. Imm, Find A Grave Memorial #138616919.

511 Ohio, Death Records, 1908-1932, 1938-2007, Ancestry.com, Steven James Cox, death cert. #078490.

512 Obituary of Steven James Cox (Bellefontaine, Ohio, Bellefontaine Examiner, June 9, 1989), Ohio History Center Archives and Library, Ohio History Center, 800 East 17th Avenue, Columbus, OH.

513 Find A Grave—Claibourne Township Cemetery, Claibourne Township, Union Co., Ohio, Find A Grave.com.

[A] Obituary of Catherine M. Russell (Austin, Texas, Austin American-Statesman, 17 Dec 2017), Austin Public Library-Central Library, 710 Cesar Chavez Street, Austin, TX.

Elsey Pegan

1. **Elsey**[5] **Pegan** (*Robert A.*[4]*, Andrew*[3]*, Andrew*[2] *Pagan, James*[1]) was born on April 27, 1818, in Fairview, Union Twp., Highland Co., Ohio.[1] He was the son of Robert A. Pegan and Christina or Christiana Ingle. He died in DeGraff, Miami Twp., Logan Co., Ohio, on June 13, 1857, at age 39.[2, 3] Elsey was buried in Greenwood Cemetery, Pleasant Twp., Logan Co., Ohio.[4]

Elsey Pegan's given name could have been a family surname, perhaps a maiden name of a grandmother from the Pegan or Ingle line. It was common in that era to pass down a maiden name from a female line as a given name to a son. The name Elsey/Elzey is not found as a given name in any other Pagan/Pegan line except for Robert Pagan/Pegan's, including those of any other descendants of Andrew and Mary Unknown Pagan/Pegan, Elsey's paternal grandparents.

It is not known how Elsey Pegan met his wife, Mary Moore Pegan. Elsey was born and spent the first eight or nine years in Highland County, Ohio before his parents, Robert and Christiana/Christina Ingle Pegan moved the family in 1826 to Wayne Twp., Montgomery Co., Ohio. Elsey seems to have been trained in carpentry in Montgomery and Miami counties, Ohio, like his brothers John, Harrison and possibly Andrew, by the master carpenter, Joseph Pagin, who may have been related.[5, 6]

But by 1840, he is back in Highland County, Ohio, near his brothers Andrew and Henry, the latter of whom, because of his age, also must have moved with the family to Montgomery County and returned later to Highland County. Perhaps Henry and Elsey went back together in the mid-to-late 1830s.

Elsey married **Mary Moore** on June 18, 1840, in Clermont Co., Ohio.[7] They had seven children. Mary Moore was born in Clermont Co., Ohio?, in about 1817-1818. Mary reached approximately age 71 and died in DeGraff, Miami Twp., Logan Co., Ohio, on February 8, 1889.[8] She was buried in Greenwood Cemetery, DeGraff, Pleasant Twp., Logan Co., Ohio.[8]

Strangely, Elsey's marriage is the only one of Robert and Christina's children's marriages not recorded in their family bible.[1]

Newlywed Elsey "Pagan" is enumerated in the 1840 Census, Highland Co., Ohio with his wife, Mary *(Census Place: Highland, Ohio; Roll: 403; Page: 102)*. There is a one in col. 5 and a one in col. 18 (one male age 20-29 and one female 20-29). Living nearby are brothers Andrew and Henry Pegan.

In 1845, Elsey and Mary Moore Pegan and family removed to Piqua, Washington Twp., Miami Co., Ohio, where his brothers John and Harrison were living, and Elsey bought property, Lot 12, in that town.[9]

Elsey Pegan is found in the 1850 census in Piqua, Washington Twp., Miami Co., Ohio *(Census Place: Washington, Miami, Ohio; Roll: M432_711; Page: 378; Image: 132)*. In the home are Elsey and his wife Mary Moore Pegan, both age 32 and born in Ohio; and children: son Francis and his twin sister Josephine, age nine; Sarah Jane, seven, and Phebe Ann, four. All the children were born in Ohio. Elsey's brothers John and Harrison Pegan are neighbors.

Elsey's date of death is also not recorded in the Robert and Christina Pegan family bible, even though Elsey died in 1857 and his mother in 1858. His obituary says that Elsey died three days after falling off a church building while working in DeGraff, Ohio.[3]

Mary Moore Pegan, widowed, is enumerated in the 1860 census in DeGraff Twp., Logan Co., Ohio Mary Pegan, age 62, is living with her widowed daughter Laura Oder and granddaughter Anna Oder in the 1880 Census, DeGraff Twp., Logan Co., Ohio *(Census Place: De Graff, Logan, Ohio; Roll: M653_1000; Page: 87; Image: 174)*. In the home are Mary, 42, and daughters Josephine, 19, "Phoebe",

15, and "Sarah", five. This is a mistake on the census taker's part, as the youngest child was named Laura, not Sarah. For some reason, Sarah, who was 15, is not listed, but she was probably living there and somehow the census taker just erred.

Mary Moore "Pagan" is listed as the head of the household in DeGraff Twp., Logan Co., Ohio in the 1870 U.S. Census *(Census Place: De Graff, Logan, Ohio; Roll: M593_1234; Page: 167; Image: 334)*. In the home are Mary, age 55 (Incorrect—she is about 52) and her youngest (Laura) Olive, 15. George and Josephine Pegan Lane and daughter "Maud" are living with them, as are William and Phebe Pegan Wolfe and their family. George Lane is age 37, and works in a harness shop; Josephine Pegan Lane is 29 and their daughter Maude is three. William Wolfe, 24, is a farmer; Phoebe Pegan Wolfe is 23, and their children are Bertha, four and Effie Bell, two. All in the home were born in Ohio.

In 1880, Mary Moore Pegan is still residing in De Graff, Miami Twp., Logan Co., Ohio *(Census Place: De Graff, Logan, Ohio; Roll: 1041; Page: 146B; Enumeration District: 119; Image: 0295)*. In the home are Mary Moore Pegan, 62, a widow, born Ohio with her parents born in Virginia; Mary's daughter Laura Pegan Oder, 25, born Ohio like her parents, also a widow; and Laura's daughter Anna, six, born Ohio as were her parents. Next door is Sarah Pegan Greenawalt, Mary's daughter and also a widow, and her children.

Mary Moore Pegan may have been related to Phoebe Moore Pegan, second wife of John Pegan, brother of Elsey. Mary Moore Pegan and Phoebe Moore Pegan may have been related to David Greenawalt, husband of Elsey and Mary Moore Pegan's daughter Sarah Jane Pegan Greenawalt. David Greenawalt was born and died in Sewickley Twp., Westmoreland Co., Pennsylvania, and the Greenawalt families were neighbors of Moore families.

According to her gravestone in Greenwood Cemetery, DeGraff, Miami Twp., Logan Co., Ohio, Mary Moore Pegan was 69 years old when she died on February 8, 1889. This is incorrect. Although Mary Moore Pegan's exact date of birth is unknown, all census records indicate she was born abt. 1818, so she was probably closer to 71 years old at the time of her death.[8]

Children of Elsey Pegan and Mary Moore:

+ 2 m I. **Francis Marion**[6] **Pegan** was born in Washington Twp., Miami Co., Ohio, on April 12, 1841.[10] He was also known as **Frank**. Francis Marion died in DeGraff, Miami Twp., Logan Co., Ohio, on December 17, 1920.[10]

+ 3 f II. **Josephine Margaret**[6] **Pegan** was born in Washington Twp., Miami Co., Ohio, on April 12, 1841.[11] She was also known as **Josie**. Josephine Margaret died in Toledo, Lucas Co., Ohio, on August 6, 1914.[11]

+ 4 f III. **Sarah Jane**[6] **Pegan** was born in Washington Twp., Miami Co., Ohio, on August 2, 1843.[12, 13] She died in Alexandria, Monroe Twp., Madison Co., Indiana, on June 30, 1922.[12, 13, 14]

+ 5 f IV. **Phebe Ann**[6] **Pegan** was born in Washington Twp., Miami Co., Ohio, on August 5, 1847.[15] She died in Washington Twp., Logan Co., Ohio, on March 26, 1888.[15, 16]

+ 6 m V. **Elsey**[6] **Pegan II** was born in Washington Twp., Miami Co., Ohio, in July 1849.[17] He died in Washington Twp., Miami Co., Ohio, in July 1849.[17]

+ 7 m VI. **James**[6] **Pegan?** was born in Miami or Logan Co., Ohio, between 1851 and 1855. He died in DeGraff, Miami Twp., Logan Co., Ohio, before June 13, 1857.

+ 8 f VII. **Laura Belle Olive**[6] **Pegan** was born in DeGraff, Miami Twp., Logan Co., Ohio, on January 2, 1855.[18] She died in Toledo, Lucas Co., Ohio, on March 16, 1931.[18]

6th Generation

2. Francis Marion⁶ Pegan (*Elsey⁵, Robert A.⁴, Andrew³, Andrew² Pagan, James¹*) was born on April 12, 1841, in Washington Twp., Miami Co., Ohio.[10] He was also known as **Frank**. He was the son of Elsey Pegan (1) and Mary Moore. Francis Marion died in DeGraff, Miami Twp., Logan Co., Ohio, on December 17, 1920, at age 79.[10] He was buried in Greenwood Cemetery, DeGraff, Pleasant Twp., Logan Co., Ohio.[10, 19]

Childless.

Francis Marion married **Rebecca Jane Vankirk** on September 28, 1865, in Logan Co., Ohio.[20, 21] Rebecca Jane Vankirk was born in West Pennsboro Twp., Cumberland Co., Pennsylvania, on January 19, 1839.[21, 22] She was also known as **Jenny**. Rebecca Jane reached age 77 and died in DeGraff, Miami Twp., Logan Co., Ohio, on May 20, 1916.[21] She was buried in Greenwood Cemetery, DeGraff, Pleasant Twp., Logan Co., Ohio.[21, 22]

Francis Pegan and wife Rebecca are found in DeGraff, Miami Twp., Logan Co., Ohio in 1870 *(Census Place: DeGraff, Logan, Ohio; Roll: M593_1234; Page: 171; Image: 343.)* The household consists of Francis Pegan, age 29, born Ohio, a painter; and his wife Rebecca Jane Vankirk Pegan, 31, born Pennsylvania.

In 1880, Francis Marion Pegan is enumerated as "Frank" M. Pegan in DeGraff, Miami Twp., Logan Co., Ohio *(Census Place: De Graff, Logan, Ohio; Roll: 1041; Page: 148A; Enumeration District: 119; Image: 0298)*. In the household are Francis "Frank" Pegan, age 39, born Ohio as were his parents, a carpenter; and his wife Rebecca J. Vankirk Pegan, 40, born Pennsylvania as were her parents.

In 1900, Francis M. Pegan is again found in DeGraff, Miami Twp., Logan Co., Ohio *(Census Place: Miami, Logan, Ohio; Roll: T623_1294; Page: 10B; Enumeration District: 117)*. Francis Pegan is age 59, born Apr 1841, born in Ohio as were his parents, a carpenter; Rebecca Jane Vankirk Pegan is 61, born Jun 1839 in Pennsylvania, where her parents were also born. The couple says they have been married 34 years and Rebecca bore no children.

Francis M. Pegan is again listed as "Frank" M. Pegan in 1910 in DeGraff, Miami Twp., Logan Co., Ohio *(Census Place: Miami, Logan, Ohio; Roll: T624_1204; Page: 5B; Enumeration District: 0138; Image: 991)*. Francis Pegan is 69 years old, born Ohio as were his parents, and lists no occupation. Rebecca Jane Vankirk Pegan is 71, born Pennsylvania as were her parents. They have been married 45 years (the columns for children borne and surviving are blank).

In 1920, Francis Pegan is still living in DeGraff, Miami Twp., Logan Co., Ohio *(Census Place: Miami, Logan, Ohio; Roll: T625_1405; Page: 6A; Enumeration District: 198; Image: 395)*. Francis, a widower, is age 78. Living with him is his sister, "Lora" (Laura) Pegan Oder Walker, 64, a widow. Neither lists and occupation, and both were Ohio natives.

3. Josephine Margaret⁶ Pegan (*Elsey⁵, Robert A.⁴, Andrew³, Andrew² Pagan, James¹*) was born on April 12, 1841, in Washington Twp., Miami Co., Ohio.[11] She was also known as **Josephine**. She was the daughter of Elsey Pegan (1) and Mary Moore. She died in Toledo, Lucas Co., Ohio, on August 6, 1914, at age 73.[11] Josephine Margaret was buried in Greenwood Cemetery, DeGraff, Pleasant Twp., Logan Co., Ohio.[11, 23]

Josephine Margaret married **George Maley Lane** on May 10, 1863, in Logan Co., Ohio.[24, 25] They divorced before 1880. They had one daughter. George Maley Lane was born in Jefferson Twp., Logan Co., Ohio or Virginia, on February 7, 1833? He reached age 49 and died in DeGraff, Miami Twp., Logan Co., Ohio, on April 7, 1882.[26, 27] George Maley Lane was buried in Greenwood Cemetery, DeGraff, Pleasant Twp., Logan Co., Ohio.[26]

George Lane is listed as age 29 and born in Virginia on his Civil War draft registration in June 1863.[28] But on all other records he is listed as born in Ohio. A birth date of October 30, 1833, although not documented or sourced, is found in online databases However, his Logan County death record says he was 39 years and two months old when he died on April 7, 1882, which would mean a birth date of

February 7, 1843.[27] This seems to be an error. As he was the only George Lane known to be living in the DeGraff, Ohio area, he was probably 49 years old when he died, and a likely birth date is February 7, 1833.

George and Josephine Margaret Pegan Lane are enumerated in the 1870 census in De Graff, Miami Twp., Logan Co., Ohio (*Census Place: De Graff, Logan, Ohio; Roll: M593_1234; Page: 167A; Image: 342*). The Lanes are living with Josephine's widowed mother, Mary Moore Pegan, and Josephine's sister Phebe Pegan Wolfe and her family are also in the home. George Lane is age 37 and works in a harness shop; Josephine Pegan Lane is 29 and their daughter "Maud" is three. Listed as head of the household is Mary Moore Pegan, 55, who has her youngest child, (Laura) Olive Pegan, 15, enumerated on the census form on the line just below her mother. The Laws are listed below Laura, and below them are the Wolfes. William Wolfe, 24, is a farmer; "Phoebe" Pegan Wolfe is 23, and their children are Bertha, four and Effie Bell, two. All in the home were born in Ohio.

Josephine Margaret Pegan Lane married **Alexander Noble** on September 30, 1875, in Greene Co., Ohio.[29] They had one son. Alexander Noble was born in Clark Twp., Clinton Co., Ohio or Dodson Twp., Highland Co., Ohio, on November 9, 1833.[30] Alexander reached age 54 and died in Springfield, Springfield Twp., Clark Co., Ohio, on January 13, 1888.[31] He was buried in Lynchburg Masonic Cemetery, Lynchburg, Dodson Twp., Highland Co., Ohio.[31]

Alexander Noble, a widower with a married daughter and three sons, lived in Union Twp., Highland Co., Ohio prior to his marriage to Josephine Pegan Lane (*Census Place: Union, Highland, Ohio, Roll: M653_986; Page: 177, entry for Alexander Noble; Census Place: Union, Highland, Ohio; Roll: M593_1222; Page: 337B, entry for Alexander Noble*).

Josephine may have met him while visiting her Pegan relatives, her uncle Henry Pegan and his family, in Highland County. Alex still owned property there at least until 1887; his daughter and her family may have resided there.[32] But after they married, Alex and Josephine and their blended family were residents of Cedarville, Greene Co., Ohio and Springfield, Springfield Twp., Clark Co., Ohio.

Alexander and Josephine Pegan Lane Noble are enumerated in Cedarville Twp., Greene Co., Ohio in 1880 (*Census Place: Cedarville, Greene, Ohio; Roll: 1019; Page: 241C; Enumeration District: 080; Image: 0390*). Alexander Noble, listed as "Alex Noble", is age 46 and a blacksmith. Josephine Pegan Lane Noble is 37 years old. Living with them is Maude Lane, listed as "Maud" Noble, Josephine's daughter by her first husband George Lane. Other children in the home are Alexander's sons by his first marriage: John, 18, Albert, 15, and Charles, 12. All in the home, and their parents, were Ohio natives.

Alexander Noble's obituary in the *Hillsboro (OH) News Herald* says he died in Springfield, Springfield Twp., Clark Co., Ohio.[31]

After Alexander Noble's death in 1888, Josephine Margaret Pegan Lane Noble files for a Civil War widow's pension and is listed as his widow on the 1890 Veterans Schedule as a resident of Springfield, Springfield Twp., Clark Co., Ohio.[33]

Josephine Margaret Pegan Lane Noble is found in 1900 in Miami Twp., Logan Co., Ohio (*Census Place: Miami, Logan, Ohio; Roll: T623_1294; Page: 9B; Enumeration District: 117*). Josephine Margaret Pegan Lane Noble is age 59, born April 1841, and a widow who says she has borne two children, both living. With her is her son Frank Noble, 19, born October 1880, a day laborer. Also living in the home are Josephine's sister, Laura Pegan Oder Walker, 45, born Jun 1855, also a widow; and Laura's daughter Lona Oder, 26, born May 1874. Laura Pegan Oder Walker says she has borne two children, but Lona is the only one living. Lona dies later that year.

In 1910, Josephine Margaret Pegan Lane Noble is enumerated in Toledo, Lucas Co., Ohio (*Census Place: Toledo Ward 5, Lucas, Ohio; Roll: T624_1208; Page: 2B; Enumeration District: 0069; Image: 413*). Josephine Margaret Pegan Noble is age 68, and a widow who states she has her own income--she may have been renting out rooms. Josephine says she has borne two children, both still alive. Her children Maude, 32, and "Frank", 26, are still living with her.

Frank has no occupation and Maude is a tailoress. All were born in Ohio, as were their parents. They have several lodgers are residing with them.

Daughter of Josephine Margaret Pegan and George Maley Lane:

+ 9 f I. **Maude[7] Lane** was born in DeGraff, Miami Twp., Logan Co., Ohio, on August 11, 1866.[34] She died in a hospital in Bellefontaine, Lake Twp., Logan Co., Ohio, on October 20, 1955.[34]

Son of Josephine Margaret Pegan and Alexander Noble:

+ 10 m I. **Francis Edwin[7] Noble** was born in Cedarville, Cedarville Twp., Greene Co., Ohio, on October 9, 1880.[35, 36] He was also known as **Frank**. Francis Edwin died in DeGraff, Miami Twp., Logan Co., Ohio, on June 9, 1947.[35]

4. **Sarah Jane[6] Pegan** (*Elsey[5], Robert A.[4], Andrew[3], Andrew[2] Pagan, James[1]*) was born on August 2, 1843, in Washington Twp., Miami Co., Ohio.[12, 13] She was the daughter of Elsey Pegan (1) and Mary Moore. Sarah Jane died in Alexandria, Monroe Twp., Madison Co., Indiana, on June 30, 1922, at age 78.[12, 13, 14] She was buried in IOOF Cemetery, Summitville, Union Twp., Madison Co., Indiana.[12, 13, 14]

Sarah Jane married **Daniel Parker Greenawalt** on June 13, 1867, in Logan Co., Ohio.[37] They had three children. Daniel Parker Greenawalt was born in Sewickley Twp., Westmoreland Co., Pennsylvania, on August 21, 1845? Daniel Parker reached age 30 and died in Pittsburgh, Allegheny Co., Pennsylvania, between February 3-16, 1876 (February 13, 1876?).[38] He was buried in Funk Cemetery, Hutchinson, Sewickley Twp., Westmoreland Co., Pennsylvania.[39]

Daniel P. Greenawalt's exact birth and death dates, found online, are undocumented and are perhaps from unpublished Greenawalt family bible or other family records. There are no discernable dates on his tombstone in Funk Cemetery, Hutchinson, Sewickley Twp., Westmoreland Co., Pennsylvania. However, his will was written on February 3, 1876 in Pittsburgh, Allegheny Co., Pennsylvania and proved on February 17 of that year.[38]

Daniel's family, the Greenawalts, have a long history in Westmoreland County, and even today are famous for their farms specializing in egg production. His family was also said to have started a Brethren Church[40] The Greenawalts may have been related to the Moores, Sarah Jane Pegan's mother's line. There was a T. Moore and a "Thes. Moore" (may have been the same person) who was a neighbor to Greenawalt families in Sewickley Twp., Westmoreland Co., Pennsylvania.

As a young man, Daniel Parker Greenawalt moved to DeGraff, Logan Co., Ohio and met Sarah Jane Pegan there. After their marriage in Logan County in 1867, the couple moved back to Pennsylvania after their first child, Ola, was born. They resided first in Sewickley Twp., Westmoreland Co. and then in Pittsburgh.

Daniel Greenawalt is enumerated in Sewickley Twp., Westmoreland Co., Pennsylvania in 1870 (*Census Place: Sewickley, Westmoreland, Pennsylvania; Roll: M593_1466; Page: 610B; Image: 422*). In the household are Daniel Greenawalt, 26, a farm laborer, born Pennsylvania; his wife, Sarah Pegan Greenawalt, also 26, born Ohio; and their daughter "Olie" (Ola), two, born Pennsylvania. Also in the home is Sarah J. Bucker, age 13, born Pennsylvania, who may have been a servant.

After her husband's death, Sarah J. Pegan Greenawalt moved back to the DeGraff, Miami Twp., Logan Co., Ohio, where she gave birth to their son Richard Pegan Greenawalt there in December of that year.

In 1880, Sarah Pegan Greenawalt is a widow living with her three children in De Graff, Miami Twp., Logan Co., Ohio (*Census Place: De Graff, Logan, Ohio; Roll: 1041; Page: 146B; Enumeration District: 119; Image: 0295*). In the home are Sarah Pegan Greenawalt, 37, born Ohio as were her parents; and daughters "Olla", 12 and "Clyde", eight, and son Richard P., four. Olla and Clyda were born in Ohio, with their father born in Pennsylvania and their mother in Ohio. Oddly, Richard is listed as born in Pennsylvania, but his birth record is in Logan County, Ohio; Richard's parents' birthplaces match those given for his sisters. Sarah Pegan Greenawalt is living next door to her mother Mary Moore Pegan, her sister Laura Pegan Oder, both also widows, and Laura's daughter Anna.

Around 1890, Sarah J. Pegan Greenawalt and her daughter Clyda may have followed Sarah's son-in-law and daughter Charles S. and Ola Greenawalt Shultz and their son Ralph to Greencastle, Greencastle Twp., Putnam Co., Indiana. If not then, they did remove to Summitville, Van Buren Twp., Madison Co., Indiana after Charles S. and Ola Greenawalt Shultz and their family, which now included daughter Armintha, moved there between 1891 and 1900.

In 1900, Sarah J. Pegan Greenawalt is living in Summitville, Van Buren Twp., Madison Co., Indiana *(Census Place: Van Buren, Madison, Indiana; Roll: T623_386; Page: 2B; Enumeration District: 116)*. Sarah, age 54, born Aug 1845, a widow, is listed as head of household; she says she and parents were born in Ohio. Sarah Pegan Greenawalt lists no occupation, and states she has borne three children with two of them still alive. Living with her is her daughter, "Clyde" Greenawalt Humrickhouse, born Apr 1874, who says she and her father were born in Pennsylvania and her mother in Ohio. Clyda says she is has been married six years and has borne two children, both living. Clyda's two daughters, Vera, age five, born Jul 1894, and Ella, one, born Nov 1898, are also living in the home and were born in Indiana. But Clyda's husband Edgar Clyde Humrickhouse is not living in the home.

By 1910, Sarah Pegan Greenawalt (enumerated as Greenwald) is found in Alexandria, Monroe Twp., Madison Co., Indiana *(Census Place: Alexandria Ward 3, Madison, Indiana; Roll: T624_364; Page: 6A; Enumeration District: 0113; Image: 1196)*. Sarah Pegan Greenawalt, listed as age 62 (incorrect), states that she was born in Ohio, her father in the United States and her mother in Ohio. Once more, Sarah is enumerated as having borne three children, with two still surviving; she has no occupation. Her daughter Clyda Greenawalt Humrickhouse, 36, is still in residence with her, along with Clyda's daughters Vera and Ella, ages 14 and 11 respectively. Clyda Greenawalt Humrickhouse says she is still married and has been so for 16 years. Clyda also states she has borne two children, and both are alive. But her husband Edgar "Clyde" Humrickhouse is still not living with them. Clyda (spelled "Clyea" on the form), like her mother Sarah, lists no occupation, and says she and her father were born in Pennsylvania and her mother in Ohio. Both Vera and Ella were born in Indiana, their father in West Virginia and their mother in Pennsylvania.

In 1920, Sarah Jane Pegan Greenawalt, age 76, is still in Alexandria, Monroe Twp., Madison Co., Indiana *(Census Place: Alexandria Ward 3, Madison, Indiana; Roll: T625_449; Page: 2A; Enumeration District: 126; Image: 745)*. Her daughter Ola Greenawalt Shultz, 51, is also in the home; both women are widows. Sarah Jane Pegan Greenawalt says she and her parents were born in Ohio, while Ola Greenawalt Schultz says she and her mother were born in Ohio and her father in Pennsylvania. Neither woman is employed.

Sarah Jane Pegan Greenawalt's surname is spelled Greenwalt on her death certificate and in her obituary, and her husband's name is listed as "James", which is wrong. The informant was her grandson Ralph "Schultz".[12, 14]

Children of Sarah Jane Pegan and Daniel Parker Greenawalt:

+ 11 f I. **Ola**[7] **Greenawalt** was born in DeGraff, Miami Twp., Logan Co., Ohio, on March 17, 1868.[41, 42] She was also known as **Olie**. She died in Alexandria, Monroe Twp., Madison Co., Indiana, on August 9, 1923.[41, 42, 43]

+ 12 f II. **Clyda Estella**[7] **Greenawalt** was born in Pittsburgh, Allegheny Co., Pennsylvania, on April 30, 1872.[44, 45] She was also known as **Clyde**. She died in Anderson, Anderson Twp., Madison Co., Indiana, on November 18, 1935.[44, 45, 46]

+ 13 m III. **Richard Pegan[7] Greenawalt** was born in DeGraff, Miami Twp., Logan Co., Ohio, on December 15, 1876.[47, 48] He died in DeGraff, Miami Twp., Logan Co., Ohio, in February 1881.[49]

5. **Phebe Ann[6] Pegan** (*Elsey[5], Robert A.[4], Andrew[3], Andrew[2] Pagan, James[1]*) was born on August 5, 1847, in Washington Twp., Miami Co., Ohio.[15] She was the daughter of Elsey Pegan (1) and Mary Moore. Phebe Ann died in Washington Twp., Logan Co., Ohio, on March 26, 1888, at age 40.[15, 16] She was buried in Greenwood Cemetery, DeGraff, Pleasant Twp., Logan Co., Ohio.[15]

Phebe Ann Pegan Wolfe's tombstone in Greenwood Cemetery, Miami Twp., Logan Co., Ohio states incorrectly that she was 41 years., 7 months and 21 days old.[15]

Phebe Ann married **William Parsons Wolfe** on September 9, 1865, in Logan Co., Ohio.[50] They had five children. William Parsons Wolfe was born in DeGraff, Miami Twp., Logan Co., Ohio, on July 13, 1845.[51] He reached age 65 and died in Sidney, Clinton Twp., Shelby Co., Ohio, on November 25, 1910.[51] William Parsons was buried in Greenwood Cemetery, DeGraff, Pleasant Twp., Logan Co., Ohio.[51, 52]

William and Phoebe Ann Pegan Wolfe are listed in the home of Phebe's mother, Mary Moore Pegan in 1870 in De Graff, Miami Twp., Logan Co., Ohio (*Census Place: De Graff, Logan, Ohio; Roll: M593_1234; Page: 167A; Image: 342*). Phebe's sister Josephine Pegan Law and her family are also living there. William Wolfe, 24, is a farmer; Phebe Pegan Wolfe is 23, and their children are Bertha, four and Effie Bell, two. George Lane is age 37, and works in a harness shop; Josephine Pegan Lane is 29 and their daughter "Maud" is three. Listed as head of the household is Mary Moore Pegan, 55, who has her youngest child, Laura Olive Pegan, 15, listed beneath her. All in the home were born in Ohio. Mary lists her assets as $1500. The Lanes are listed below Laura, and below them are the Wolfes.

William and Phebe Ann Pegan Wolfe are enumerated in 1880 in DeGraff, Miami Twp., Logan Co., Ohio (*Census Place: De Graff, Logan, Ohio; Roll: 1041; Page 142A; Enumeration District: 119*). In the home are William, 34, a farmer, born Ohio, with his father born in Ohio and his mother in Virginia. Phoebe is 35, and she says she and her parents were born in Ohio. Children with them are Bertha, 13, Effie, 11, Frank, nine and "Roe William," six.

After Phebe's death, William P. Wolfe remarries to Mrs. Anna Hickey Johnston.[53]

In 1900, William Parsons Wolfe is living in Clinton Twp., Shelby Co., Ohio (*Census Place: Clinton, Shelby, Ohio; Roll: 1321; Page: 11B; Enumeration District: 91*). William Wolfe, age 54, born Jul 1845, is a farmer. He says he and his father were born in Ohio and his mother was a Virginia native. He says he has been married six years to his second wife, Anna Hickey Johnston Wolfe. Also in the home are three of Anna's children by her first husband, William Johnston.

William Parsons Wolfe is again residing in Clinton Twp., Shelby Co., Ohio in 1910 (*Census Place: Clinton, Shelby, Ohio; Roll: T624_1230; Page: 6B; Enumeration District: 0126; Image: 18*). In the household are William "Wolf," age 64, a farmer born in Ohio, with his father born in Ohio and his mother in Virginia; and his second wife Anna Hickey Johnston Wolfe, also 64, born Ohio, as were her parents. William and Anna say they have been married 17 years.

Children of Phebe Ann Pegan and William Parsons Wolfe:

+ 14 f I. **Bertha[7] Wolfe** was born in DeGraff, Miami Twp., Logan Co., Ohio, on August 31, 1866.[54] She died in a hospital in Toledo, Lucas Co., Ohio, on October 9, 1943.[54]

+ 15 f II. **Effie Belle[7] Wolfe** was born in DeGraff, Miami Twp., Logan Co., Ohio, on June 22, 1868.[55] She died in Akron, Summit Co., Ohio, on February 8, 1951.[55]

+ 16 m III. **Frank L.⁷ Wolfe** was born in DeGraff, Miami Twp., Logan Co., Ohio, on June 23, 1871.[56, 57] He died in Rexburg, Madison Co., Idaho, on February 2, 1920.[57, 58]

+ 17 m IV. **William Roe⁷ Wolfe** was born in Washington Twp., Logan Co., Ohio, on January 20, 1875.[59, 60, 61] He died in Robbinsdale, Becker Twp., Hennepin Co., Minnesota, on June 1, 1958.[59, 62]

+ 18 m V. **Guy Ernest⁷ Wolfe** was born in DeGraff, Miami Twp., Logan Co., Ohio, on December 10, 1880.[63] He died in a hospital in Minneapolis, Hennepin Co., Minnesota, on April 26, 1946.[63, 64]

6. **Elsey⁶ Pegan II** (*Elsey⁵, Robert A.⁴, Andrew³, Andrew² Pagan, James¹*) was born in July 1849 in Washington Twp., Miami Co., Ohio.[17] He was the son of Elsey Pegan (1) and Mary Moore. Elsey died in Washington Twp., Miami Co., Ohio, in July 1849.[17]

Elsey Pegan's birth and death are recorded in the 1850 U.S. Mortality Index for Washington Twp., Miami Co., Ohio and he is listed as one week old when he died. But only the month of July is given, no exact days.[17] His burial place is undocumented, but he is probably buried in Greenwood Cemetery, DeGraff, Pleasant Twp., Logan Co., Ohio.

7. **James⁶ Pegan?** (*Elsey⁵, Robert A.⁴, Andrew³, Andrew² Pagan, James¹*) was born between 1851 and 1855 in Miami or Logan Co., Ohio. He was the son of Elsey Pegan (1) and Mary Moore. James died in DeGraff, Miami Twp., Logan Co., Ohio, before June 13, 1857. He was probably buried in Greenwood Cemetery, DeGraff, Pleasant Twp., Logan Co., Ohio. There are no citations for this child, but he is noted in some Pegan family records. However, he may not have existed.

8. **Laura Belle Olive⁶ Pegan** (*Elsey⁵, Robert A.⁴, Andrew³, Andrew² Pagan, James¹*) was born on January 2, 1855, in DeGraff, Miami Twp., Logan Co., Ohio.[18] She was the daughter of Elsey Pegan (1) and Mary Moore. Laura Belle Olive died in Toledo, Lucas Co., Ohio, on March 16, 1931, at age 76.[18] She was buried in Greenwood Cemetery, DeGraff, Pleasant Twp., Logan Co., Ohio.[18, 65]

Laura Belle Olive married **Walter Alonzo Oder** on March 27, 1872, in Logan Co., Ohio.[66] They had one daughter. Walter Alonzo Oder was born in Eden Twp., Seneca Co., Ohio, about April 1849. Walter Alonzo reached age 24 and died in DeGraff, Miami Twp., Logan Co., Ohio, on March 17, 1874.[67] Walter Alonzo Oder is probably buried in Greenwood Cemetery, DeGraff, Pleasant Twp., Logan Co., Ohio.

A few days after Walter Oder died, Lona gave birth to their only child, daughter Lona.

In 1880, the widowed Laura Olive Pegan Oder and daughter Lona (listed as Anna) are enumerated with Laura's widowed mother, Mary Pegan, in De Graff, Miami Twp., Logan Co., Ohio (*Census Place: De Graff, Logan, Ohio; Roll: 1041; Page: 146B; Enumeration District: 119; Image: 0295*). Laura Pegan Oder, age 25, a widow, and her daughter "Anna", six, say they were born in Ohio like their parents. The head of the household is Mary Moore Pegan, 62, a widow, born Ohio with her parents born in Virginia; Next door is Sarah Pegan Greenawalt, Mary's daughter, also a widow.

Laura Belle Olive Pegan married **John S. Walker** on May 6, 1882, in Logan Co., Ohio.[68] They separated before 1900. They had one child. John S. Walker was born in Ohio before 1861. He died after 1931?

Very little is known about John S. Walker. Even his middle initial is in doubt, it may have been "L." According to the 1898 Indianapolis City Directory, Laura Pegan Oder Walker was listed as "Walker, Laura (wid John)".[69] But Laura's death certificate indicates she was still married to John S. Walker at the time of her death.[18] The informant was her niece, Maude Lane. Was this an error? Even Laura Pegan Oder Walker's obituary names her as Laura Oder.[70]

According to Lona Oder's obituary in the *DeGraff (OH) Journal* on June 22, 1900, Laura Pegan Oder Walker and daughter Lona lived in Missouri from sometime in the early 1880s until the later in that decade. The obituary does not mention John S. Walker, but he, Laura and Lona probably moved to Missouri together.

As mentioned above, Laura Pegan Oder Walker and Lona Oder removed to Indianapolis about 1897, as they are not found in city directories prior to 1898. Laura Pegan Oder Walker and Lona Oder were residents of Indianapolis until a week before Lona died, when Laura moved Lona, suffering from tuberculosis, back to DeGraff, Miami Twp., Logan Co., Ohio. They were living with Laura's widowed sister, Josephine Pegan Lane Noble, when Lona expired on June 14, 1900.

However, even though the cutoff date for the census was June 1, in the 1900 census, Laura Olive Pegan Oder Walker and daughter Lona Oder are said to already be living with Laura's sister Margaret Josephine Pegan Noble in Miami Twp., Logan Co., Ohio *(Census Place: Miami, Logan, Ohio; Roll: T623_1294; Page: 9B; Enumeration District: 117)*. Laura Pegan Oder Walker, age 45, has been widowed for the second time. Laura says she has borne two children but only one, daughter Lona, was still alive. Lona is 26 years old, born May 1874, with no occupation. Listed as head of the household, Josephine Margaret Pegan Lane Noble is age 59, born April 1841, and a widow who says she has borne two children, both living. Also in the home is Josephine's son Frank Noble, born October 1880, a day laborer. All and their parents were born in Ohio.

In 1910, Laura Olive Pegan Oder Walker is listed as "Laura Oder" in Bellefontaine, Lake Twp., Logan Co., Ohio *(Census Place: Bellefontaine Ward 3, Logan, Ohio; Roll: T624_1204; Page: 3A; Enumeration District: 0130; Image: 802)*. Laura Olive Pegan Oder Walker is age 55, a widow, and is the housekeeper in the home of a minister, G.L. Kalb, age 80. Laura says she and her parents were born in Ohio.

Laura Olive Pegan Oder Walker is residing with her widower brother, Francis Marion Pegan, in 1920 in DeGraff, Miami Twp., Logan Co., Ohio *(Census Place: Miami, Logan, Ohio; Roll: T625_1405; Page: 6A; Enumeration District: 198; Image: 395)*. Francis, a widower, is age 78. "Lora" Pegan Oder Walker is 64 and a widow. Neither lists and occupation, and both were born in Ohio, as were their parents. Laura Pegan Oder Walker signs her name as "Mrs. Laura Oder" when she is the informant on her brother, Francis Marion Pegan's, death certificate in December 1920.

In 1930, Laura Pegan Oder Walker is living with her niece and nephew, Maude Lane and Francis Noble, in Toledo, Lucas Co., Ohio *(Census Place: Toledo, Lucas, Ohio; Roll: 4639655; Page: 5A; Image: 1166.0)*. Laura Pegan Oder Walker, enumerated as Laura Walker, is age 75, and a widow with no occupation. Maude Lane, who is listed as "Maude Noble Lane", is the head of the household. Maude is single, age 64, and a tailoress in a tailor shop. Francis E. Noble, 49, listed as a half-brother to the head of the household, is single and a laborer at an auto company. All were born in Ohio, as were their parents.

Daughter of Laura Belle Olive Pegan and Walter Alonzo Oder:

+ 19   f   I.   **Lona**[7] **Oder** was born in DeGraff, Miami Twp., Logan Co., Ohio, in May 1874.[71, 72] She died in DeGraff, Miami Twp., Logan Co., Ohio, on June 14, 1900.[73]

Child of Laura Belle Olive Pegan and John S. Walker:

+ 20   I.   **Child**[7] **Walker** was born between 1882 and 1897 in Missouri? He or she died between 1882 and 1897 in Missouri?

7th Generation

9. Maude[7] **Lane** (*Josephine Margaret*[6] *Pegan, Elsey*[5]*, Robert A.*[4]*, Andrew*[3]*, Andrew*[2] *Pagan, James*[1]) was born on August 11, 1866, in DeGraff, Miami Twp., Logan Co., Ohio.[34] She was the daughter of George Maley Lane and Josephine Margaret Pegan (3). She died in a hospital in Bellefontaine, Lake Twp., Logan Co., Ohio, on October 20, 1955, at age 89.[34] Maude was buried in Greenwood Cemetery, DeGraff, Pleasant Twp., Logan Co., Ohio.[74]

Never married.

In 1900, Maude ("Maud") Lane is enumerated in Indianapolis, Center Twp., Marion Co., Indiana (*Census Place: Indianapolis, Marion, Indiana; Roll: T623; Page: 7A; Enumeration District: 99*). Maude, single, says she is age 30, a tailoress, born Aug 1869 in Ohio, where her parents were also born. (She seems to have shaved a few years off her age, as other records have her born in 1867.) Maude may have followed her cousins Catherine "Kate" Hendrickson Pegan, widow of James Milton Pegan, and Kate's children to Indianapolis. Also, Maude's Mason cousins, children of Samuel and Mary E. Pegan Mason, had also relocated from Logan County, Ohio to Indianapolis. In 1897, Maude's aunt and cousin, Laura Pegan Oder Walker and her daughter Lona Oder, came from Missouri to live in Indianapolis, but removed to their birthplace, DeGraff, Ohio, in June 1900, just before Lona died.

In 1910, Maude Lane, listed as "Maud Noble", 32, single, a tailoress, was living with her mother Josephine Pegan Lane Noble and her unmarried brother Frank Noble in Toledo, Lucas Co., Ohio (*Census Place: Toledo Ward 5, Lucas, Ohio; Roll: T624_1208; Page: 2B; Enumeration District: 0069; Image: 413*).

Maude Lane is not found in the 1920 census. Neither is her half-brother Francis E. Noble.

In 1930, Maude Lane is living with her half-brother, Francis Noble, and their aunt, Laura Pegan Oder Walker, in Toledo, Lucas Co., Ohio (*Census Place: Toledo, Lucas, Ohio; Roll: 4639655; Page: 5A; Image: 1166.0*). Maude Lane, enumerated as "Maude Noble Lane", is enumerated as the head of the household. Maude is single, age 64, and a tailoress in a tailor shop. Francis E. Noble, 49, listed as a half-brother to the head of the household, is single and a laborer at an auto company. Laura Pegan Oder Walker, age 75, is a widow. All were born in Ohio, as were their parents.

Maude Lane is still residing with her half-brother, Francis Noble, in 1940, but now they live in DeGraff, Miami Twp., Logan Co., Ohio (*Census Place: De Graff, Logan, Ohio; Roll: T627_3100; Page: 9B; Enumeration District: 46-24*). Maud Lane, single, is 73 years old is once again the head of the household, Francis Noble, 59, is also unmarried. Both were born in Ohio and list no occupation. Maude and Francis state they were living in the same house in 1935, but no street address is listed.

10. Francis Edwin[7] **Noble** (*Josephine Margaret*[6] *Pegan, Elsey*[5]*, Robert A.*[4]*, Andrew*[3]*, Andrew*[2] *Pagan, James*[1]) was born on October 9, 1880, in Cedarville, Cedarville Twp., Greene Co., Ohio.[35, 36] He was also known as **Frank**. He was the son of Alexander Noble and Josephine Margaret Pegan (3). He died in DeGraff, Miami Twp., Logan Co., Ohio, on June 9, 1947, at age 66.[35] Francis Edwin was buried in Greenwood Cemetery, DeGraff, Pleasant Twp., Logan Co., Ohio.[35]

Never married.

In 1910, Frank Noble, single, was living with his mother, Josephine Pegan Lane Noble and his unmarried sister Maude Lane in Toledo, Lucas Co., Ohio (*Census Place: Toledo Ward 5, Lucas, Ohio; Roll: T624_1208; Page: 2B; Enumeration District: 0069; Image: 413*). He lists no occupation.

Francis E. Noble is not found in the 1920 census. Neither is his half-sister Maude Lane.

In 1930, Francis Noble is living with his half-sister, Maude Lane, and their aunt, Laura Pegan Oder Walker, in Toledo, Lucas Co., Ohio (*Census Place: Toledo, Lucas, Ohio; Roll: 4639655; Page: 5A; Image: 1166.0*). Francis E. Noble, 49, listed as a half-brother to the head of the household, is single and a laborer at an auto company. Maude Lane, enumerated as "Maude Noble Lane", is the head of the household. Maude is single, age 64, and a tailoress in a tailor shop. Laura Pegan Oder Walker, age 75, is a widow. All were born in Ohio, as were their parents.

Francis Noble is found in 1940 in DeGraff, Miami Twp., Logan Co., Ohio *(Census Place: De Graff, Logan, Ohio; Roll: T627_3100; Page: 9B; Enumeration District: 46-24)*. Listed as the head of the household, Francis Noble, is age 59. Still residing with him is his half-sister, Maude Lane, who is 73 years old. Both were born in Ohio and are still unmarried; neither lists an occupation. Francis "Frank" Noble and Maude Lane state they were living in the same house in 1935, but no street address is given.

11. **Ola**[7] **Greenawalt** (*Sarah Jane*[6] *Pegan, Elsey*[5]*, Robert A.*[4]*, Andrew*[3]*, Andrew*[2] *Pagan, James*[1]) was born on March 17, 1868, in DeGraff, Miami Twp., Logan Co., Ohio.[41,42] She was the daughter of Daniel Parker Greenawalt and Sarah Jane Pegan (4). She was also known as **Olie**. Ola died in Alexandria, Monroe Twp., Madison Co., Indiana, on August 9, 1923, at age 55.[41, 42, 43] She was buried in IOOF Cemetery, Alexandria, Monroe Twp., Madison Co., Indiana.[41, 42, 43]

Ola married **Charles S. Shultz** on January 19, 1888, in Logan Co., Ohio.[75] They divorced. They had two children. Charles S. Shultz was born in Lewistown, Washington Twp., Logan Co., Ohio, on February 12, 1864.[76, 77] Charles S. reached age 52 and died in Alexandria, Monroe Twp., Madison Co., Indiana, on September 26, 1916.[76, 77, 78] He was buried in IOOF Cemetery, Summitville, Union Twp., Madison Co., Indiana.[76, 77, 78]

After their marriage in Logan County, Ohio in 1888, Charles and Ola Greenawalt Shultz lived near DeGraff, Miami Twp., Logan Co., Ohio. They removed before March 1891 to Greencastle, Greencastle Twp., Putnam Co., Indiana, where their daughter Armintha was born, according to Armintha's marriage license and death certificate.[86, 87]

Finally, they settled in Madison County, Indiana, first in Summitville, Van Buren Township., and then in Alexandria, Monroe Township.

In 1900, Charles and Ola Greenawalt Shultz are living in Summitville, Van Buren Twp., Madison Co., Indiana *(Census Place: Van Buren, Madison, Indiana; Roll: T623_386; Page: 1B; Enumeration District: 116)*. Charles Schutz, 36, born February 1864, says he was born in Ohio, his father in Pennsylvania and his mother in Virginia. He is a barber. HIs wife, Ola Greenawalt Shultz, 32, born March 1868, says she and her mother were born in Ohio and her father in Pennsylvania. The couple states they have been married 13 years and Ola has borne two children, both still alive. They are son Ralph, 11, born Aug 1888 in Ohio, and daughter Armintha, nine, born March 1891 in Indiana.

Charles S. Shultz and Ola Greenawalt Shultz divorce between 1900 and 1910. Charles S. Shultz does not appear in the 1910 U.S. Federal Census.

Ola (enumerated as "Ober") Greenawalt Shultz is living in Alexandria, Monroe Twp., Madison Co., Indiana in 1910 *(Census Place: Alexandria Ward 3, Madison, Indiana; Roll: T624_364; Page: 3A; Enumeration District: 0113; Image: 1190)*. Ola Greenawalt Shultz is age 42, born Ohio like her mother, with her father born in Pennsylvania. Ola says she has borne two children, both still living. Her two children are residing with her. Son Ralph, 21, born Ohio, is a barber. Although she was listed as born in Indiana in the 1900 census, daughter Armintha, listed as "Nettie", is now said to be born in Ohio. Both children say their parents were Ohio natives. Ola is listed as a widow, but her husband Charles, was still alive (he died in 1916).

In 1920, Ola Greenawalt Shultz, age 51, is living with her mother, Sarah Pegan Greenawalt, 76, in Alexandria, Monroe Twp., Madison Co., Indiana *(Census Place: Alexandria Ward 3, Madison, Indiana; Roll: T625_449; Page: 2A; Enumeration District: 126; Image: 745)*. Both women are widows. Sarah Jane Pegan Greenawalt says she and her parents were born in Ohio, while Ola Greenawalt Schultz says she and her mother were born in Ohio and her father in Pennsylvania. Neither woman lists an occupation.

Children of Ola Greenawalt and Charles S. Shultz:

+ 21 m I. **Ralph Richard**[8] **Shultz** was born in DeGraff, Miami Twp., Logan Co., Ohio, on August 9, 1888.[79, 80, 81, 82] He died in a hospital in Anderson, Anderson Twp., Madison Co., Indiana, on May 31, 1971.[80, 83, 84]

+ 22 f II. **Armintha**[8] **Shultz** was born in Greencastle, Greencastle Twp., Putnam Co., Indiana, on March 9, 1891.[85, 86] She was also known as **Nettie**. Armintha died in a hospital in Muncie, Center Twp., Delaware Co., Indiana, on July 1, 1924.[86, 87, 88, 89]

12. **Clyda Estella**[7] **Greenawalt** (*Sarah Jane*[6] *Pegan, Elsey*[5]*, Robert A.*[4]*, Andrew*[3]*, Andrew*[2] *Pagan, James*[1]) was born on April 30, 1872, in Pittsburgh, Allegheny Co., Pennsylvania.[44, 45] She was the daughter of Daniel Parker Greenawalt and Sarah Jane Pegan (4). She was also known as **Clyde**. Clyda Estella died in Anderson, Anderson Twp., Madison Co., Indiana, on November 18, 1935, at age 63.[44, 45, 46] She was buried in Maplewood Cemetery, Anderson, Anderson Twp., Madison Co., Indiana.[44, 45]

Clyda Estella married **Edgar Clyde Humerickhouse** on April 18, 1894, in Madison Co., Indiana.[90] They were separated before 1900. They had two daughters. Edgar Clyde Humerickhouse was born in Martinsburg, Berkeley Co., West Virginia, on November 18, 1867.[91, 92] Edgar Clyde reached age 43 and died in Bridgeport, Bellaire Twp., Belmont Co., Ohio, on April 20, 1911.[91, 93] He was buried in Linwood Cemetery, Blaine, Pease Twp., Belmont Co., Ohio.[91, 94]

Surrname is also seen as Humrickhouse.

Edgar Clyde Humerickhouse was said to have been a "dandy" who met his future wife Clyda Greenawalt while he was playing piano in a tavern or restaurant in Anderson, Indiana.[A] They married and had two daughters, but the marriage did not last. Edgar Clyde and Clyde Greenawalt Humerickhouse separated before 1900, but never divorced. Edgar Clyde Humrickhouse returned to his parent's home in Bridgeport, Bellaire Twp., Belmont Co., Ohio (where they had moved from West Virginia), where he died in 1911. He came from a family of glass-blowers, and that was his occupation at the time of his death.[91] Although Edgar Clyde Humerickhouse's birth date is stated as December 18, 1867 on his Ohio death certificate and on his tombstone, his West Virginia birth record indicates he was born on November 18, 1867 in Martinsburg, Berkeley Co., West Virginia.[92] His death certificate does state his birthplace, however.[91]

In 1900, Clyda Estella Greenawalt Humerickhouse and her two daughters are found in the U.S. Federal Census living with her mother, Sarah Jane Pegan Greenawalt. in Summitville, Van Buren Twp., Madison Co., Indiana (*Census Place: Van Buren, Madison, Indiana; Roll: T623_386; Page: 2B; Enumeration District: 116*). Clyda Greenawalt Humerickhouse, born Apr 1874, says she and her father were born in Pennsylvania and her mother in Ohio. Clyda says she has been married six years and has borne two children, both living. Clyda Greenawalt Humerickhouse's two daughters, Vera, age five, born Jul 1894, and Ella, one, born Nov 1898, are also living in the home and were born in Indiana, their father in West Virginia and their mother in Pennsylvania. But Clyda's husband Edgar "Clyde" Humerickhouse is not living in the home. Sarah Pegan Greenawalt, age 54, born Aug 1845, a widow, is listed as head of household. Sarah says she and parents were born in Ohio. Sarah Pegan Greenawalt lists no occupation, and states she has borne three children with two of them still alive.

Clyda Greenawalt Humerickhouse is still residing with her mother, Sarah Pegan Greenawalt, in 1910, but this time they are living in Alexandria, Monroe Twp., Madison Co., Indiana (*Census Place: Alexandria Ward 3, Madison, Indiana; Roll: T624_364; Page: 6A; Enumeration District: 0113; Image: 1196*). Clyda (spelled "Clyea") Greenawalt Humerickhouse, 36, states she is married, and has been so for 16 years, and has borne two children, both yet alive. Clyda says she was born in Pennsylvania, like her father, and her mother was born in Ohio. Once again, her husband, Edgar "Clyde" Humerickhouse, is not in the household. Clyda Greenawalt Humerickhouse's two daughters, Vera, 14, and Ella, 11, both born in Indiana, with their father born in West Virginia and their mother in Pennsylvania, are also in the household with their mother and grandmother. The head of the household, Sarah Pegan Greenawalt, listed as age 62 (incorrect), states that she was born in Ohio, her father in the United States and her mother in Ohio. Once more, Sarah is enumerated as having borne three children, with two still surviving. Neither Sarah nor Clyda lists an occupation.

In 1920, Clyda Estella Greenawalt Humerickhouse and her daughters Vera and Ella are living on their own in Anderson, Madison Co., Indiana *(Census Place: Anderson Ward 3, Madison, Indiana; Roll: T625_448; Page: 10B; Enumeration District: 108; Image: 1024)*. This time, Clyda Greenawalt Humerickhouse, age 46, says she is a widow who was born in Pennsylvania, like her father, and her mother was born in Ohio. Clyda lists no occupation. Vera Humerickhouse, is 24 and single. Ella, 21, who still has the surname Humerickhouse, is listed as divorced. Both Vera and Ella say they were born in Indiana, their father in West Virginia and their mother in Pennsylvania; both are telephone operators.. (Note: the census taker may have erred; Vera, who married Bert Hardy in 1915, was the one who was divorced, not her sister Ella).

Clyda Greenawalt Humerickhouse is residing with her son-in-law and daughter, Warren and Ella Humrickhouse Brane, and their family in 1930 in Anderson, Anderson Twp., Madison Co., Indiana *(Census Place: Anderson, Madison, Indiana; Roll: 605; Page: 2A; Image: 37.0)*. Clyda Estella Greenawalt Humerickhouse, age 57, a widow, says she was born in Pennsylvania, as was her father, and her mother was born in Ohio. She does not list an age of first marriage. Warren G. Brane, 29, born Indiana as were his parents, is a production manager at a container factory. His wife, Ella Humrickhouse Brane, 30, says she was born in Indiana, her father in West Virginia and her mother in Pennsylvania. Both say they were first married at age 22. Warren and Ella Humerickhouse Brane have two children, Constance, seven, and Richard L., two and one-half years old, both born in Indiana.

Daughters of Clyda Estella Greenawalt and Edgar Clyde Humerickhouse:

+ 23 f I. **Vera B.[8] Humerickhouse** was born in Summitville, Van Buren Twp., Madison Co., Indiana, on July 25, 1895.[80, 95, 96] She died in a facility in Elwood, Pipe Creek Twp., Madison Co., Indiana, on September 29, 1972.[80, 96, 97]

+ 24 f II. **Ella May[8] Humerickhouse** was born in Summitville, Van Buren Twp., Madison Co., Indiana, on November 24, 1898.[80, 98, 99, 100] She died in Chesterfield, Union Twp., Madison Co., Indiana, on December 11, 1970.[80, 100]

13. **Richard Pegan[7] Greenawalt** (*Sarah Jane[6] Pegan, Elsey[5], Robert A.[4], Andrew[3], Andrew[2] Pagan, James[1]*) was born on December 15, 1876, in DeGraff, Miami Twp., Logan Co., Ohio.[47, 48] He was the son of Daniel Parker Greenawalt and Sarah Jane Pegan (4). Richard Pegan died in DeGraff, Miami Twp., Logan Co., Ohio, in February 1881 at age four.[49]

Richard P. Greenawalt's death record ("R.P. Greenawalt") does not document an exact date of death, only that he died in February 1881.[49] Although his grave does not have a tombstone and Greenwood Cemetery records for that era do not exist, he is most likely buried in Greenwood Cemetery, DeGraff, Pleasant Twp., Logan Co., Ohio.

14. **Bertha[7] Wolfe** (*Phebe Ann[6] Pegan, Elsey[5], Robert A.[4], Andrew[3], Andrew[2] Pagan, James[1]*) was born on August 31, 1866, in DeGraff, Miami Twp., Logan Co., Ohio.[54] She was the daughter of William Parsons Wolfe and Phebe Ann Pegan (5). Bertha died in a hospital in Toledo, Lucas Co., Ohio, on October 9, 1943, at age 77.[54] She was buried in Greenwood Cemetery, DeGraff, Pleasant Twp., Logan Co., Ohio.[54, 101]

Bertha married **Eugene Webster Loffer** on September 22, 1886, in Logan Co., Ohio.[102] They divorced before 1910. They had three children.

Eugene Webster Loffer was born in Bloomfield Twp., Logan Co., Ohio, on March 17, 1863.[103] Eugene Webster reached age 77 and died in Myrtle Creek, North Myrtle Creek Precinct, Douglas Co., Oregon, on November 28, 1940.[104] He was buried in Roseburg IOOF Cemetery, Roseburg, Douglas Co., Oregon.[105]

In 1900 Eugene W. and Bertha Wolfe Loffer are enumerated in DeGraff, Miami Twp., Logan Co., Ohio *(Census Place: Miami, Logan, Ohio; Roll: T623_1294; Page: 3A; Enumeration District: 117)*. In the home are Eugene, age 37, a laborer and wife Bertha, 33. They state they and their parents were born in Ohio. The couple also says they have been married 12 years, and Bertha has born three children, all still alive. The children are Bertha P., 12, Lola E., 11, and Harold J., two. All the children were born in Ohio.

Bertha Wolfe Loffer and her husband, Eugene Loffer, were separated by 1910, but it is unclear whether they ever legally divorced. Bertha is listed as a widow on her death certificate. Eugene, however, married his second wife, Mrs. Anna Graham Hawkins, in Washington in 1923 before Bertha died.[106]

In 1910, Bertha Wolfe Loffer is enumerated in Springfield, Clark Co., Ohio as a lodger, along with others, in the home of a Martha Witbeck *(Census Place: Springfield Ward 1, Clark, Ohio; Roll: T624_1159; Page: 1A; Enumeration District: 0020; Image: 110)*. Bertha Loffer, age 43, says she and her parents were Ohio natives. Her marital status and information on children birthed and surviving are not given. Bertha is listed as a servant in the household, and correspondingly says her occupation is a domestic laborer. None of the children, not even young Harold, is found with her. (Harold is living with his brother-in-law and sister, Wallace and Lola Loffer Shaffer, in Tiffen, Seneca Co., Ohio *[Census Place: Tiffin Ward 4, Seneca, Ohio; Roll: T624_1229; Page: 3A; Enumeration District: 0151; Image: 306]*.)

In 1920, Bertha Wolfe Loffer, age 53, who says she is a widow, and son Harold, age 22, are living in Ward 22, Cleveland, Cuyahoga Co., Ohio *(Census Place: Cleveland Ward 22, Cuyahoga, Ohio; Roll: T625_1371; Page: 5B; Enumeration District: 432; Image: 956)*. Harold Loffer, single, says he is an automotive toolmaker. Also in the household, listed as a "partner", is Pearl Peck, age 36, born Michigan, and a man who seems to be Pearl's husband, Hiram Peck, 50, a church caretaker, and their child, four-year-old Eloise Peck. However, neither Bertha Wolfe Loffer or Pearl Peck have occupations.

In 1930, Bertha Wolfe Loffer, who says she is 55, is found in Sandusky, Erie Co., Ohio as a servant in the home of George Boehmer *(Census Place: Sandusky, Erie, Ohio; Roll: 1790; Page: 3B; Enumeration District: 15; Image: 685.0)*. Her son Harold Loffer and his family were also living in Sandusky.

Bertha Wolfe Loffer is still a resident of Sandusky, Erie Co., Ohio in 1940 *(Census Place: Sandusky, Erie, Ohio; Roll: T627_3063; Page: 14A; Enumeration District: 22-23B)*. She is a lodger, along with others, in the home of 70-year-old Jenny Peck, who may be a relative of Hiram and Pearl Peck, the "partner" listed in 1920. Bertha Wolfe Loffer, age 73, born Ohio, has no occupation, and says she was living in Sandusky in 1935. The house address is 1528 Columbus Street.

Bertha Wolfe Loffer, a widow, died in Toledo State Hospital in Toledo, Lucas Co., Ohio, after a three-week stay, according to her death certificate. A "V.V. Newby" from Toledo State Hospital was listed as the informant.[54] Her obituary in the *Bellefontaine (OH) Examiner* names her as "Mrs. E.W. Loffer", and states she was living with her daughter, Mrs. Wallace Shaffer, in Sandusky, Erie Co., Ohio before her admittance to the hospital.[107]

In 1910, Bertha's ex-husband Eugene Loffer is living alone in Ward 8, Cleveland, Cuyahoga Co., Ohio *(Census Place: Cleveland Ward 8, Cuyahoga, Ohio; Roll: T624_1168; Page: 18B; Enumeration District: 0093; Image: 450)*. He is age 47, a livestock salesman, who says he is still married.

Eugene Loffer lists himself as a widower in 1920, but his wife Bertha was alive. At the time, he is living with his brother Jesse Loffer and Jesse's family in Stillwater County, Montana. He is a laborer, age 56 *(Census Place: School District 34, Stillwater, Montana; Roll: T625_977; Page: 6A; Enumeration District: 128; Image: 364)*.

As mentioned, Eugene marries again 1923, but his second wife, Anna Graham Hawkins Loffer, dies in 1929.[106 108]

In 1930, Eugene Loffer is found in Myrtle Creek, Myrtle Creek, Douglas Co., Oregon *(Census Place: Myrtle Creek, Douglas, Oregon; Roll: 1943; Page: 1B; Enumeration District: 44; Image: 408.0)*. Eugene is age 57, a widower, and says he has no occupation. He is boarding in the home of Isaac Weaver and other boarders in the home are working for the state highway department.

Eugene Loffer is still residing in Myrtle Creek, North Myrtle Precinct, Douglas Co., Oregon in 1940 *(Census Place: Myrtle Creek, Douglas, Oregon; Roll: T627_3360; Page: 1A; Enumeration District: 10-44)*. Eugene Loffer, age 77, born Ohio, says he is a widower. He lists no occupation and says he was living in Myrtle Creek in 1935. His house is on 2nd Street, but there is no numerical address listed.

Children of Bertha Wolfe and Eugene Webster Loffer:

+ 25 f I. **Bertha Pearl**[8] **Loffer** was born in DeGraff, Miami Twp., Logan Co., Ohio, on July 23, 1887.[80, 109] She died in Urbana Twp., Champaign Co., Ohio, on September 9, 1974.[110, 111]

+ 26 f II. **Lola E.**[8] **Loffer** was born in DeGraff, Miami Twp., Logan Co., Ohio, on September 15, 1888.[80, 112] She died in Fremont, Sandusky Co., Ohio, on October 20, 1984.[113, 114]

+ 27 m III. **Harold J.**[8] **Loffer** was born in DeGraff, Miami Twp., Logan Co., Ohio, on July 16, 1897.[80, 115, 116] He died in a hospital in Cleveland, Cuyahoga Co., Ohio, on January 1, 1965.[117, 118]

15. Effie Belle[7] **Wolfe** (*Phebe Ann*[6] *Pegan, Elsey*[5]*, Robert A.*[4]*, Andrew*[3]*, Andrew*[2] *Pagan, James*[1]) was born on June 22, 1868, in DeGraff, Miami Twp., Logan Co., Ohio.[55] She was the daughter of William Parsons Wolfe and Phebe Ann Pegan (5). She died in Akron, Summit Co., Ohio, on February 8, 1951, at age 82.[55] Effie Belle was buried in Fountain/Fostoria Cemetery, Fostoria, Washington Twp., Hancock Co., Ohio.[55, 119]

Effie Belle married **Isaiah Luther Shaw** on June 16, 1892, in Seneca Co., Ohio? They had three children. Isaiah Luther Shaw was born in DeGraff, Miami Twp., Logan Co., Ohio, on April 25, 1857.[120] Isaiah Luther reached age 68 and died in Bowling Green, Plain Twp., Wood Co., Ohio, on December 6, 1925.[120, 121] He was buried in Fountain/Fostoria Cemetery, Fostoria, Washington Twp., Hancock Co., Ohio.[122]

In 1900, Isaiah and Effie Belle Wolfe Shaw are enumerated in Quincy, Miami Twp., Logan Co., Ohio *(Census Place: Miami, Logan, Ohio; Roll: T623_1294; Page: 6A; Enumeration District: 116)*. In the household are "Isaac" L. Shaw, 43, born Ohio with his father born in West Virginia and his mother in Pennsylvania, a dry goods salesman; "Effa B." Wolfe Shaw, 32, and sons Herbert, seven, and William R., one. Effie her sons, and their parents are Ohio natives. Isaiah Luther and Effie Belle Wolfe Shaw say they have been married nine years and Effie Belle has born two children, both surviving.

Isaiah and Effie Wolfe Shaw are living in Liberty Twp., Seneca Ohio, in 1910 *(Census Place: Liberty, Seneca, Ohio; Roll: T624_1229; Page: 9B; Enumeration District: 0164; Image: 818)*. In the home are Isaiah, 51, a dealer in a grain elevator; Effie B., 41, sons Herbert, 17, and "Russell", 11, and daughter Edith, nine. Effie says she has borne three children, all living. All were Ohio-born, as were their parents.

In 1920, Isaiah, again listed as "Isaac", and Effie Bell Wolfe Shaw are found in Fostoria, Jackson Twp., Seneca Co., Ohio *(Census Place: Fostoria Ward 1, Seneca, Ohio; Roll: T625_1432; Page: 8A; Enumeration District: 124; Image: 230)*. Isaiah, age 61, born Ohio, is the manager of a grain elevator. This time, he says his father was born in Ohio and his mother in Pennsylvania. With him are wife Effie, 51, born Ohio as were her parents; son William Russell, again enumerated as "Russell", 21, a bank clerk; and daughter Edith, 18. Both children were born in Ohio.

According to his death certificate, Isaiah Luther and Effie Belle Wolfe Shaw were living in Bowling Green, Plain Twp., Wood Co., Ohio, where Isaiah was a grain merchant, when he died.[120]

In 1930, Effie Belle Wolfe Shaw is living with her son-in-law and daughter, Charles and Laura Edith Snyder, and their daughter Patricia Ann in Bowling Green, Plain Twp., Wood Co., Ohio *(Census Place: Bowling Green, Wood, Ohio; Roll: 1888; Page: 14A; Enumeration District: 9; Image: 880.0).* Effie Belle Wolfe Shaw is age 60, born Ohio as were her parents. Charles Snyder, 28, is a sales manager at an automobile dealership; his wife L. Edith Shaw Snyder is 29, and Patricia Ann Snyder is five years old. All were born in Ohio, as were their parents.

Effie Belle Wolfe Shaw is still residing with her son-in-law and daughter, Charles and Laura Edith Snyder, in 1940 but now the family is living in Lima, Ottawa Twp., Allen Co., Ohio *(Census Place: Lima, Allen, Ohio; Roll: T627_3021; Page: 4B; Enumeration District: 2-40).* Effie Belle Wolfe Shaw is age 71 and a widow. The head of the household, Charles Snyder, 37, is an agent for an oil refining company. "Edith L." Shaw Snyder is 39 years old, and daughter Patricia Ann is now 15. All were born in Ohio, and say they were living in Lima in 1935. Their home is at 214 South Metcalf Street.

Her sister Bertha Wolfe Loffer's obituary mentions that Effie Belle Wolfe Shaw was then residing in Cuyahoga Falls, Summit Co., Ohio.[107] Effie Belle Wolfe Shaw was residing with her son-in-law and daughter, Charles and Laura Edith Shaw Snyder, in Akron, Summit Co., Ohio when she died.[123]

Children of Effie Belle Wolfe and Isaiah Luther Shaw:

+ 28 m I. **Frank Herbert**[8] **Shaw** was born in Quincy, Miami Twp., Logan Co., Ohio, on October 18, 1892.[124, 125, 126, 127] He died in Phoenix, Maricopa Co., Arizona, on November 28, 1961.[126, 127, 128]

+ 29 m II. **William Russell**[8] **Shaw** was born in Quincy, Miami Twp., Logan Co., Ohio, on September 19, 1898.[129] He was also known as **Russell**. William Russell died in New Rochester, Freedom Twp., Wood Co., Ohio, on August 27, 1963.[130, 131]

+ 30 f III. **Edith Laura**[8] **Shaw** was born in Quincy, Miami Twp., Logan Co., Ohio, on February 1, 1901.[132, 133] She died in Madisonville, Hopkins Co., Kentucky, on February 27, 1994.[80, 134]

16. Frank L.[7] **Wolfe** (*Phebe Ann*[6] *Pegan, Elsey*[5]*, Robert A.*[4]*, Andrew*[3]*, Andrew*[2] *Pagan, James*[1]) was born on June 23, 1871, in DeGraff, Miami Twp., Logan Co., Ohio.[56, 57] He was the son of William Parsons Wolfe and Phebe Ann Pegan (5). He died in Rexburg, Madison Co., Idaho, on February 2, 1920, at age 48.[57, 58] Frank L. was buried in Horton Cemetery, Horton, Brown Co., Kansas.[57, 58]

In 1900, Frank Wolfe is enumerated in DeGraff, Miami Twp., Logan Co., Ohio *(Census Place: Miami, Logan, Ohio; Roll: T623_1294; Page: 6B; Enumeration District: 117).* He is age 28, single, and a traveling salesman who says he and his parents were born in Ohio. He is a boarder in the home of Margaret Keyser.

Frank L. married **Etta L. Wilder,** a girl from Willis, Mission Twp., Brown Co., Kansas, on January 5, 1903, in Leavenworth Co., Kansas.[135] They had one son. Etta Wilder was born in Sterling Twp., Blue Earth Co., Minnesota, on October 26, 1875.[136] Etta L. Wilder Wolfe Ferguson reached age 60 and died in Paris, Bear Lake Co., Idaho, on January 19, 1936.[136] She was buried in Paris Cemetery, Paris, Bear Lake Co., Idaho.[136]

According to the 1900 census, Etta L. Wilder, the daughter of Julius and Margaret (actually Mary Etta) Wilder, was born in Feb 1876 in Minnesota; the family was living in Mission Twp., Brown Co., Kansas in 1900 *(Census Place: Mission, Brown, Kansas; Roll: T623; Page: 11A; Enumeration District: 29; Etta L. Wilder, Julius Wilder, head of household).*

In 1910, Frank Wolfe, listed as Frank Wolf, is found in Stella, West Muddy Twp., Richardson Co., Nebraska *(Census Place: West Muddy, Richardson,*

Nebraska; Roll: T624_854; Page: 3A; Enumeration District: 0164; Image: 60). Frank Wolfe is age 38, married, and a general merchant and says he and his parents were born in Ohio. With him is wife Etta Wilder Wolf, 32, born Minnesota with her parents born in New York. They say they are on their first marriage and have been wed seven years, with Etta bearing one child who is still living. This is son Hubert, age five, born Nebraska.

By 1917, the Wolfes have removed to Rexburg, Madison Co., Idaho.[137]

Frank L. Wolfe (again as "Wolf") is found in Rexburg, Madison Co., Idaho in 1920 *(Census Place: Rexburg, Madison, Idaho; Roll: T625_293; Page: 15B; Enumeration District: 198; Image: 509).* In the household is Frank L., 46, born Ohio as were his parents, a dry goods salesman; wife Etta Wilder Wolfe, 44, born Minnesota with her parents born in New York; son Hibbert, 14, born Nebraska, and Etta's mother, "Maryette" Wilder, age 83, born New York.

Frank Wolfe's obituary in the *Hiawatha (KS) Daily World* says he died in a hospital in Rexburg, Idaho. The death notice mentions that his widow, Etta Wilder Wolfe was "a Willis girl" before she married. The obituary notes that his body was being shipped to Horton, Kansas for burial.[58]

In 1930, Etta Wilder Wolfe, age 45. born Minnesota, a widow, is still living in Rexburg, Madison Co., Idaho *(Census Place: Rexburg, Madison, Idaho; Roll: 400; Page: 8B; Enumeration District: 13; Image: 1074.0).* Etta, listed as "Wolf", is a proprieter of a ladies wear store. She says her parents were both born in New York. Her mother, Mary E. Wilder, age 93, is living with her, and says she and her parents were born in New York. Her son, Hubert Wolfe, is not found in this census.

Etta L. Wilder Wolfe remarried to a druggist, Samuel Steward Ferguson, on November 28, 1935 in Weber Co., Utah.[138] Etta and Samuel moved to Paris, Bear Lake Co., Idaho, where she died in 1936. On her death certificate, it says she was to be buried in Horton Cemetery, Horton, Brown Co., Kansas where her first husband Frank L. Wolfe is buried. However, written above this is "Paris, Idaho" and the Paris Cemetery, Paris, Idaho records do have her buried there.[136]

Son of Frank L. Wolfe and Etta Wilder:

+ 31 m I. **Hubert Wilder⁸ Wolfe** was born in Stella, West Muddy Twp., Richardson Co., Nebraska, on June 6, 1905.[80, 139, 140] He died in Lady Lake, Lake Co., Florida, on January 31, 1989.[80, 139, 140]

17. William Roe⁷ Wolfe (*Phebe Ann⁶ Pegan, Elsey⁵, Robert A.⁴, Andrew³, Andrew² Pagan, James¹*) was born on January 20, 1875, in Washington Twp., Logan Co., Ohio.[59, 60, 61] He was the son of William Parsons Wolfe and Phebe Ann Pegan (5). He died in Robbinsdale, Becker Twp., Hennepin Co., Minnesota, on June 1, 1958, at age 83.[59, 62] William Roe was buried in Mound Cemetery, Brooklyn Center, Hennepin Co., Minnesota.[141]

Never married.

William Roe Wolfe and his brother, Guy Earnest Wolfe are found in Indianapolis, Center Twp., Marion Co., Ohio in 1900 *(Census Place: Center, Marion, Indiana; Roll: T623; Page: 2A; Enumeration District: 141).* They are roomers in the home of Harrison and Mary Perry. William, enumerated as "W.R. Wolf", is age 25, born in Jan 1875, and he is employed as a cook. Guy E. Wolf, is 19, born Dec 1880, is a grocery clerk. His surname is also listed as "Wolf". Both men are single and say they and their parents were Ohio natives.

In 1910, William R. Wolfe is living in East Hood River Twp., Hood River Co., Oregon *(Census Place: East Hood River, Hood River, Oregon; Roll: T624_1278; Page: 4B; Enumeration District: 0084; Image: 514).* He is age 35, single, and a hired man/farm laborer on a fruit farm belonging to a William Dickerson.

William Roe Wolfe, still single, is doubly enumerated in two different wards in Pocatello, Bannock Co., Idaho in 1920 *(Pocatello Ward 3, Bannock, Idaho; Roll: T625_288; Page: 8B; Enumeration District: 50; Image: 461; and Pocatello Ward 5, Bannock, Idaho; Roll: T625_288; Page: 19A; Enumeration District:*

47; Image: 346). In both boarding houses, he is listed as age 45, single, a lodger, and working as a carpenter on the steam railroad. In Ward 3, he is listed as "William R. Wolfe" and says he and his parents as born in Ohio. In Ward 5, he is named as "William Roe Wolfe", born in Ohio, with both parents born in the United States.

William Roe Wolfe does not appear in the 1930 census.

In 1940, William Roe Wolfe is residing in the home of his brother Guy Ernest Wolfe in Robbinsdale, Hennepin Co., Minnesota *(Census Place: Robbinsdale, Hennepin, Minnesota; Roll: T627_1926; Page: 8B; Enumeration District: 27-53).* William Wolfe, age 65, born Ohio, lists no occupation. The head of the household, Guy E. Wolfe, 59, also born Ohio, is a barber. Guy's wife, Lillian, 54 years old, was born in Minnesota. Guy and Lillian have two children still at home, both born in Minnesota: Margaret, 20, a bookkeeper in a loan office, and Warren, 17. All say they were living in the same house at 4038 Unity Street in 1935.

William Roe Wolfe's Minnesota death certificate says mother's maiden name was "Morgan".[59]

18. Guy Ernest⁷ Wolfe *(Phebe Ann⁶ Pegan, Elsey⁵, Robert A.⁴, Andrew³, Andrew² Pagan, James¹)* was born on December 10, 1880, in DeGraff, Miami Twp., Logan Co., Ohio.[63] He was the son of William Parsons Wolfe and Phebe Ann Pegan (5). He was living in 1946 in Robbinsdale, Becker Twp., Hennepin Co., Minnesota. Guy Ernest died in a hospital in Minneapolis, Hennepin Co., Minnesota, on April 26, 1946, at age 65.[63, 64] He was buried in Crystal Lake Cemetery, Minneapolis, Hennepin Co., Minnesota.[63, 128]

Guy Ernest Wolfe had a relationship with **Effa May Young**. They had one son. Effa May Young was born in Miami Twp., Logan Co., Ohio? on November 20, 1883.[80] Effa May Young Booze reached age 92 and died in Fremont, Sandusky Co., Ohio, on October 26, 1976.[142]

Guy Earnest Wolfe is listed as the father of a male child, born January 27, 1900, in Quincy, Miami Twp., Logan Co., Ohio. The mother's name was Effa ("Effie") Young. When their son was born, Guy was 18 years old and Effa 16, and Guy may have already removed to Indianapolis, Marion Co., Indiana. Effa would marry Everett Edward Booze, on June 19, 1901 in Logan County, Ohio. On their marriage license Effa says she has never been married.[143] The male child would be named Kenneth Vernon Booze, and was raised in the Booze household. In 1943, Kenneth Wolfe, who had used the surname Booze all of his life, would petition the Logan County, Ohio probate court to change the name of his father on his birth certificate from Guy Wolfe to Everett Booze. Kenneth Booze's two paternal uncles signed affadavits to support this petition, and a judge granted the request and changed the name.[144]

Oddly, Guy Earnest and his wife, Lillian Lundeen Wolfe would name their first child Kenneth Wolfe.

Guy Earnest Wolfe and his brother William Roe Wolfe are found in Indianapolis, Center Twp., Marion Co., Ohio in 1900 *(Census Place: Center, Marion, Indiana; Roll: T623; Page: 2A; Enumeration District: 141).* They are roomers in the home of Harrison and Mary Perry. Guy E. "Wolf", states he is 19 years of age, was born Dec 1880, his occupation is grocery clerk. William, age 25, born in Jan 1875, says he is a cook. He is enumerated as "W.R. Wolf". Both men are single say they and their parents were born in Ohio.

According to the 1905 Minnesota state census on June 13, 1905, Guy E. Wolfe was single and living on 10th Street North in Minneapolis, Hennepin Co., Minnesota *(Minnesota Historical Society. Minnesota State Population Census Schedules, 1865-1905. St. Paul, Minnesota: Minnesota Historical Society, 1977, Roll MNSC_122).* Although the census taker's writing seems to say he is a baker, he was probably a barber.

Guy Ernest married **Lillian Adelia Lundeen** on May 22, 1907, in Hennepin Co., Minnesota.[145] They had three children. Lillian Adelia Lundeen was born in Minneapolis, Hennepin Co., Minnesota, on October 8, 1885.[146] Lillian Adelia reached age 73 and died in Robbinsdale, Becker Twp., Hennepin Co., Minnesota, on December 26, 1958.[146] She was buried in Lakewood Cemetery, Minneapolis, Hennepin Co., Minnesota.[147, 148]

Guy Wolfe is listed in Ward 3, Minneapolis, Hennepin Co., Minnesota in 1910 *(Census Place: Minneapolis Ward 3, Hennepin, Minnesota; Roll: T624_701; Page: 11B; Enumeration District: 0054; Image: 219)*. In the home are Guy, age 29, was born in Ohio as were his parents; wife Lillian, 24, was born in Minnesota with her parents born in Sweden; and son Kenneth, two, was born Minnesota. The pair say they are on their first marriage, have been married three years and Lillian has born one child, still alive. Guy lists his occupation as barber.

In 1920, Guy E. Wolfe is enumerated in Minnetonka, Hennepin Co., Minnesota *(Census Place: Minnetonka, Hennepin, Minnesota; Roll: T625_839; Page: 4A; Enumeration District: 264; Image: 948)*. Guy. E., age 39, a traveling salesman selling barbershop supplies, says he was born in Ohio, as was his father. He says, erroneously, that his mother was born in Virginia. With him are his wife, Lillian "D.", 34, born in Minnesota with her parents born in Sweden; son Kenneth, 11, and newborn daughter Margaret. The children were both born in Minnesota.

Guy Ernest Wolfe is has moved to Robbinsdale, Hennepin Co., Minnesota by 1930 *(Census Place: Robbinsdale, Hennepin, Minnesota; Roll: 1101; Page: 9B; Enumeration District: 307; Image: 402.0)*. In the household are Guy Ernest, 49, born Ohio as were his parents, a barbershop supplies salesman; Guy's wife Lillian A., 44, a Minnesota native whose parents were born in Sweden; and their children Kenneth, 22, Margaret, 10, and Warren, seven. All the children were Minnesota natives.

In 1940, Guy Ernest Wolfe is still a resident of Robbinsdale, Hennepin Co., Minnesota *(Census Place: Robbinsdale, Hennepin, Minnesota; Roll: T627_1926; Page: 8B; Enumeration District: 27-53)*. The head of the household, Guy E. Wolfe, 59, born Ohio, is a barber. His wife, Lillian, is 54 years old and born in Minnesota. Two of their children are still at home, both born in Minnesota: Margaret, 20, a bookkeeper in a loan office; and Warren, 17. All say they were living in the same house at 4038 Unity Street in 1935. Guy's brother, William Wolfe, age 65, also born Ohio, is also in the home. He lists no occupation.

Son of Guy Ernest Wolfe and Effa May Young:

+ 32　m　I.　**Kenneth Vernon[8] (Wolfe) Booze** was born in Quincy, Miami Twp., Logan Co., Ohio, on January 27, 1900.[144, 149] He died in San Antonio, Bexar Co., Texas, on August 8, 1970.[80, 150, 151]

Children of Guy Ernest Wolfe and Lillian Adelia Lundeen:

+ 33　m　I.　**Kenneth William[8] Wolfe** was born in Minneapolis, Hennepin Co., Minnesota, on March 27, 1908.[80, 152, 153] He died in Louis Park, Hennepin Co., Minnesota, on January 11, 1981.[152]

+ 34　f　II.　**Margaret Carolyn Wolfe** was born in Minnetonka, Hennepin Co., Minnesota, on August 24, 1919.[154] She died in Brooklyn Park, Hennepin Co., Minnesota, on August 19, 2015.[155]

+ 35　m　III.　**Warren Charles Wolfe** was born in Minnetonka, Hennepin Co., Minnesota, on September 14, 1922.[80, 156] He died in Plymouth, Hennepin Co., Minnesota, on November 10, 2003.[80, 157]

19. Lona[7] Oder (*Laura Belle Olive[6] Pegan, Elsey[5], Robert A.[4], Andrew[3], Andrew[2] Pagan, James[1]*) was born in May 1874 in DeGraff, Miami Twp., Logan Co., Ohio.[71, 72] She was the daughter of Walter Alonzo Oder and Laura Belle Olive Pegan (8). Lona died in DeGraff, Miami Twp., Logan Co., Ohio, on June 14, 1900, at age 26.[73] She was buried in Greenwood Cemetery, DeGraff, Pleasant Twp., Logan Co., Ohio.[72]

Never married.

In 1900, Lona Oder is said to be living with her aunt Margaret Josephine Pegan Noble in Miami Twp., Logan Co., Ohio *(Census Place: Miami, Logan, Ohio; Roll: T623_1294; Page: 9B; Enumeration District: 117)*. Lona Oder is 26 years old, born May 1874, who has no occupation. (Two weeks after the census date, Lona Oder died.) Listed as head of the household is Josephine Margaret Pegan Lane Noble, age 59, born April 1841, a widow who says she has borne two children, both living. Also in the home is Josephine's son Frank Noble, born October 1880, a day laborer. Lona's mother, Laura Pegan Oder Walker, age 45, who says she is a widow, is also living there. Laura says she has borne two children but only one, daughter Lona, was still alive. All and their parents were Ohio natives. According to her obituary, Lona and her mother Laura were residents of Indianapolis, Marion Co., Indiana until early June 1900, when Laura took Lona, suffering from tuberculosis, back to their original home, DeGraff, Miami Twp., Logan Co., Ohio.[73] Her inclusion in her aunt's home in the 1900 census was a mistake. The cutoff date for residing in a household that year was June 1st, and the census was taken June 12th.

20. Child[7] Walker (*Laura Belle Olive[6] Pegan, Elsey[5], Robert A.[4], Andrew[3], Andrew[2] Pagan, James[1]*) was born between 1882 and 1897 in Missouri? He or she was a child of John S. Walker and Laura Belle Olive Pegan (8). Child Walker died between 1882 and 1897 in Missouri?

8th Generation

21. Ralph Richard[8] Shultz (*Ola[7] Greenawalt, Sarah Jane[6] Pegan, Elsey[5], Robert A.[4], Andrew[3], Andrew[2] Pagan, James[1]*) was born on August 9, 1888, in DeGraff, Miami Twp., Logan Co., Ohio.[79, 80, 81, 82] He was the son of Charles S. Shultz and Ola Greenawalt (11). He was living in May 1971 in Alexandria, Monroe Twp., Madison Co., Indiana. Ralph Richard died in a hospital in Anderson, Anderson Twp., Madison Co., Indiana, on May 31, 1971, at age 82.[80, 83, 84] He was buried in IOOF Cemetery, Alexandria, Monroe Twp., Madison Co., Indiana.[83, 84, 158]

Childless, but Ralph Richard and Mary Connolly Smith Shultz adopted Ralph's niece, Armintha Almack, after Ralph's sister, Armintha Shultz Almack, died.

Ralph Shultz is living in with his mother Ola Greenawalt Shultz and his sister Armintha Shultz in 1910 in Alexandria, Monroe Twp., Madison Co., Indiana in 1910 (*Census Place: Alexandria Ward 3, Madison, Indiana; Roll: T624_364; Page: 3A; Enumeration District: 0113; Image: 1190*). Ralph Shultz is age 21, single, born in Ohio, and a barber by trade. Ola (enumerated as "Ober") Greenawalt Shultz Greenawalt Shultz, 42, born Ohio like her mother, with her father born in Pennsylvania. Ola says she has borne two children, both still living. Although she was listed as born in Indiana in the 1900 census, Armintha, listed as "Nettie", is now said to be born in Ohio. Both children say their parents were Ohio natives. Ola states she is a widow, but her husband Charles, who does not appear in this census, was still alive (he died in 1916).

Ralph Richard married **Mary Sue Connolly** on August 28, 1919, in Lucas Co., Ohio.[82, 83, 159] Mary Sue Connolly was born in New Albany, New Albany Twp., Floyd Co., Indiana, on September 20, 1885.[80, 82] She was also known as **Mamie**. Mary Sue lived in June 1971 in Alexandria, Monroe Twp., Madison Co., Indiana. She reached age 85 and died in a hospital in Anderson, Anderson Twp., Madison Co., Indiana, on June 15, 1971.[80, 159, 160] Mary Sue was buried in IOOF Cemetery, Alexandria, Monroe Twp., Madison Co., Indiana.[159, 160, 161]

Ralph R. and Mary S. Connolly Shultz are not found in the 1920 census.

In 1930, Ralph Richard Shultz is enumerated in Alexandria, Monroe Twp., Madison Co., Indiana (*Census Place: Alexandria, Madison, Indiana; Roll: 605, Page: 3D, Image: 908.0*). Ralph R. Shultz, 41, a barber, says he and his father were born in Ohio and his mother in Pennsylvania (Incorrect—she was born in Ohio). His wife, Mary Connolly Shultz, 44, says she and her mother were born in Indiana and her father in Ohio. Ralph and Mary say they were first married at ages 31 and 34 respectively. Living with them and listed as a niece is five-year-old Armintha "Almeck", five, born Indiana like her parents, who is the daughter of his late sister Armintha "Nettie" Schultz Almack and her husband Earl Almack Sr.

Ralph Shultz is again located in Alexandria, Monroe Twp., Madison Co., Indiana in 1940 (*Census Place: Alexandria, Madison, Indiana; Roll: T627_1073; Page: 6A; Enumeration District: 48-54*). In the home at 1024 North Harrison Street are Ralph Shultz, 50, born Ohio, a barber who owns his own barber shop and his wife, Mary Connolly Shultz, 54, born Indiana. With them is Ralph's orphaned niece, Armintha Almack, 15 years old, born Indiana, whom they have adopted; she is listed as Armintha Shultz, daughter.

Ralph Shultz's birthdate on his Indiana death certificate and in his obituary is August 9, 1887, which is incorrect.[83, 84] The informant was his adopted daughter, Armintha (Almack) Shultz Smith. On his WWII draft registration, his birthplace is listed as "Depraph, Ohio," (DeGraff). However, his date of birth, given as August 9, 1889, is also wrong.[81]

Ralph and his father, Charles Shultz, operated a barber shop in Alexandria, Monroe Twp., Madison Co., Indiana. Ralph continued the business after the death of his father, and Ralph's obituary states he'd been a barber in Alexandria for more than 30 years.[83]

Ralph and Mary Connolly Shultz may have legally adopted Armintha Almack, as Ralph's and Mary's obituaries list her as a daughter.[83, 159] In addition,

Armintha Almack (Shultz) Smith's obituary in the *Anderson (IN) Daily Bulletin* on March 30, 1994 has her maiden name as Shultz. Her death notice also says that Ralph and Mary Connolly Shultz were her parents, although it also lists Earl Almack Jr., her father's son by his second wife, as a brother.[162] But on her marriage license Armintha Almack (Shultz) Smith's states her maiden name as Almack.[163]

22. **Armintha**[8] **Shultz** (*Ola*[7] *Greenawalt, Sarah Jane*[6] *Pegan, Elsey*[5]*, Robert A.*[4]*, Andrew*[3]*, Andrew*[2] *Pagan, James*[1]) was born on March 9, 1891, in Greencastle, Greencastle Twp., Putnam Co., Indiana.[85, 86] She was also known as **Nettie**. She was the daughter of Charles S. Shultz and Ola Greenawalt (11). Armintha lived in 1924 in Alexandria, Monroe Twp., Madison Co., Indiana. She died in a hospital in Muncie, Center Twp., Delaware Co., Indiana, on July 1, 1924, at age 33.[86, 87, 88, 89] Armintha was buried in Vinson Memorial Park Cemetery, Summitville, Van Buren Twp., Madison Co., Indiana.[88]

There is some confusion regarding Armintha "Nettie" Shultz Almack's birthplace. On the 1900 census form, her parents, Charles and Ola Greenawalt Shultz, say that Armintha was born in Indiana. But in the 1910 census, widowed Ola says her only child Armintha Shultz was born in Ohio. However, on her marriage license and her death certificate, Armintha's birthplace is cited as Greencastle, Greencastle Twp., Putnam Co., Indiana.[85, 86]

Armintha married **Earl Jesse Almack** on September 15, 1919, in Madison Co., Indiana.[164] They had one daughter. Earl Jesse Almack was born in Vernon, Vernon Twp., Jennings Co., Indiana, on November 5, 1889.[165, 166, 167] Earl Jesse reached age 43 and died in Anderson, Anderson Twp., Madison Co., Indiana, on May 3, 1933.[166, 167, 168, 169] He was buried in IOOF Cemetery, Alexandria, Monroe Twp., Madison Co., Indiana.[166, 167, 168]

Earl Josse and Armintha Shultz Almack are enumerated in 1920 in Alexandria, Monroe Twp., Madison Co., Indiana *(Census Place: Alexandria Ward 3, Madison, Indiana; Roll: T625_449; Page: 2B; Enumeration District: 126; Image: 746)*. In the household are Earl Almack, age 30, a photographer, born Indiana, as were his parents; and his wife Armintha ("Arminth") Shultz Almack, 28, says her father was born in New Jersey and her mother in New York(?). This is erroneous, as her parents were both born in Ohio. Perhaps Earl Almack gave this information to the census taker.

Armintha "Nettie" Shultz Almack died of complications following a caesarian section for the birth of her daughter Armintha in 1924.[86] After her death, Earl Almack leaves his infant daughter with his late wife's brother and his wife, Ralph R. and Mary Sue Connolly Shultz, and moves to the Meridian, Mississippi area, where he marries again to Mary Imelda Smith, a Meridian, Mississippi native.[170] They had one son, Earl Almack Jr.

In 1930, Earl Josse Almack Sr., age 40, is in again found in Alexandria, Monroe Twp., Madison Co., Indiana *(Census Place: Alexandria, Madison, Indiana; Roll: 605; Page: 3A; Image: 907.0)*. He has a second wife, Mary Watson Smith Almack, 32, born Mississippi. They have a son, Earl Almack Jr., age 2 years and 5 months, also born in Mississippi, with his father born in Indiana and his mother in Mississippi. Earl Almack and his wife Mary both say their first marriage occurred at age 29.

Earl's daughter by his first wife, five-year-old Armintha Shultz Almack, is living with her childless maternal uncle and aunt, Ralph and Mary Connolly Shultz, in 1930 *(Census Place: Alexandria, Madison, Indiana; Roll: 605; Page: 3B; Image: 908.0)*. After Earl Almack Sr.'s death in 1933, Ralph and Mary Connolly Shultz either legally or informally adopted their orphaned niece Armintha, who took the surname of Shultz.

Daughter of Armintha Shultz and Earl Jesse Almack:

+ 36 f I. **Armintha Euphema Almack**[9] **(Shultz)** was born in Muncie, Center Twp., Delaware Co., Indiana, on July 1, 1924.[80, 162, 163, 171, 172] She died in a hospital in Indianapolis, Marion Co., Indiana, on March 28, 1994.[80, 162, 171, 172]

23. **Vera B.**[8] **Humerickhouse** (*Clyda Estella*[7] *Greenawalt, Sarah Jane*[6] *Pegan, Elsey*[5]*, Robert A.*[4]*, Andrew*[3]*, Andrew*[2] *Pagan, James*[1]) was born on July 25, 1895, in Summitville, Van Buren Twp., Madison Co.,

Indiana.[80, 95, 96] She was the daughter of Edgar Clyde Humerickhouse and Clyda Estella Greenawalt (12). She was living in 1969 in Anderson, Anderson Twp., Madison Co., Indiana. Vera B. lived in 1970 in Elwood, Pipe Creek Twp., Madison Co., Indiana.[173] She died in a facility in Elwood, Pipe Creek Twp., Madison Co., Indiana, on September 29, 1972, at age 77.[80, 96, 97] Vera B. was buried in East Maplewood Cemetery, Anderson, Anderson Twp., Madison Co., Indiana.[96, 97, 174, 175]

Vera B. married **Bert Lawrence Hardy** on May 1, 1915, in Madison Co., Indiana.[176] They divorced. They had no children. Bert Lawrence Hardy was born in Anderson, Anderson Twp., Madison Co., Indiana, on May 22, 1890.[80, 177, 178] Bert Lawrence reached age 78 and died in Anderson, Anderson Twp., Madison Co., Indiana, on May 7, 1969.[80, 178, 179] He was buried in Anderson Memorial Park Cemetery, Anderson, Anderson Twp., Madison Co., Indiana.[178, 179]

Vera Humrickhouse Hardy is living with her mother, Clyde Greenawalt Humrickhouse, in Anderson, Anderson Twp., Madison Co., Indiana in 1920 (*Census Place: Anderson Ward 3, Madison, Indiana; Roll: T625_448; Page: 10B; Enumeration District: 108; Image: 1024*). Vera, who has re-assumed her maiden name Humerickhouse, is age 24 and single. This time, Clyda Greenawalt Humerickhouse, 46, says she is a widow who was born in Pennsylvania, like her father, and her mother was born in Ohio. Clyda lists no occupation. Both Vera and Ella say they were born in Indiana, their father in West Virginia and their mother in Pennsylvania; they are telephone operators. Ella Humerickhouse, 21, is listed as divorced! (Note: the census taker erred; Vera, who married Bert Hardy in 1915, was the one who was divorced, not her sister Ella).

Vera B. Humerickhouse Hardy married **Claude Almond McHarry** on September 17, 1921, in Madison Co., Indiana.[95] He was also known as **Almond** when he was young. They had three children. Claude Almond McHarry was born in White Cloud, Harrison Twp., Harrison Co., Indiana, on September 15, 1895.[95, 180, 181, 182] He reached age 43 and died in Anderson, Anderson Twp., Madison Co., Indiana, on March 29, 1939.[180, 181, 182] Claude Almond was buried in East Maplewood Cemetery, Anderson, Anderson Twp., Madison Co., Indiana.[182, 183]

Although his Social Security Claims documentation has the name Claud Almond McHarry, his given name is spelled Claude in censuses and other references.

In 1900, listed as Almond McHarry, he is age seven, born Indiana in Sep 1895, and living with his parents in Butler, Vermilion Co., Illinois (*Census Place: Butler, Vermilion, Illinois; Roll: 348; Page: 7B; Enumeration District: 0057, entry for William Mcharry*); in 1910, he and parents and siblings are in Paxton, Paxton Twp., Ford Co., Illinois (*Census Place: Paxton Ward 2, Ford, Illinois; Roll: T624_235; Page: 3B; Enumeration District: 0010*).

In 1920, Claude A. McHarry, age 25, an Indiana native like his parents, is living in San Francisco, San Francisco Co., California in the home of his then mother-in-law, Lillian Doyal, and is married to Mary Doyle McHarry, who is five years his senior. He is a machinist at the S.P. Company. (*Census Place: San Francisco Assembly District 23, San Francisco, California; Roll: T625_136; Page: 7A; Enumeration District: 140*).

Claude and Vera Humerickhouse Hardy McHarry are enumerated in Anderson, Anderson Twp., Madison Co., Indiana in 1930 (*Census Place: Anderson, Madison, Indiana; Roll: 605; Page: 10A; Image: 21.0*). In the home are Claude A. McHarry, 34, born Indiana, with his parents born in the United States; he is an engineer in a slaughterhouse. Vera B. Humerickhouse Hardy McHarry, lists her age as 33 (she is 35). She says she was born in Indiana, her father in Virginia (Incorrect—he was born in West Virginia), and her mother in Pennsylvania. They have three children: Jack, seven, "Billy", five, and Donna, one year and two months, all born in Indiana.

In 1940, widow Vera Humrickhouse Hardy McHarry is enumerated in Chesterfield, Union Twp., Madison Co., Indiana (*Census Place: Chesterfield, Madison, Indiana; Roll: T627_1074; Page: 6A; Enumeration District: 48-76*). In the home at 128 Sycamore Street are Vera Humrickhouse Hardy McHarry, age

43, and children Jack Edgar, 17, Billie Clyde, 15, and Donna May, 11. Vera lists no occupation. Jack Edgar McHarry is listed as a "new worker" (WPA). All in the home were born in Indiana, and say they were living in Anderson, Anderson Twp., Madison Co., Indiana in 1935.

Vera Humrickhouse Hardy McHarry's Social Security Death Index entry and her marriage license to Claude McHarry have her birthdate as July 25, 1895.[80, 95] Her death certificate does not state her date of birth.[96] But according to the 1900 census, she was born in Jul 1894 *(Census Place: Van Buren, Madison, Indiana; Roll: T623_386; Page: 2B; Enumeration District: 116, entry for Vera Humrickhouse, Sarah J. Greenawalt, head of household)*, and other censuses before her second marriage confirm this year of birth. Vera may have shaved a year off her age to be younger than Claude McHarry.

Children of Vera B. Humerickhouse and Claude Almond McHarry:

+ 37 m I. **Jack Edgar**[9] **McHarry** was born in Anderson, Anderson Twp., Madison Co., Indiana, on September 7, 1922.[184, 185] Jack Edgar died in Indianapolis, Marion Co., Indiana, on April 10, 1942.[184, 185, 186]

+ 38 m II. **Bill Clyde**[9] **McHarry** was born in Anderson, Anderson Twp., Madison Co., Indiana, on March 31, 1925.[80, 187, 188, 189] He died in Anderson, Anderson Twp., Madison Co., Indiana, on February 8, 1999.[80, 187, 188, 189]

+ 39 f III. **Donna May**[9] **McHarry** was born in Anderson, Anderson Twp., Madison Co., Indiana, on February 6, 1929.[190, 191] She died in Lafayette, Fairfield Twp., Tippecanoe Co., Indiana, on March 19, 1984.[191, 192, 193]

24. Ella May[8] **Humerickhouse** (*Clyda Estella*[7] *Greenawalt, Sarah Jane*[6] *Pegan, Elsey*[5]*, Robert A.*[4]*, Andrew*[3]*, Andrew*[2] *Pagan, James*[1]) was born on November 24, 1898, in Summitville, Van Buren Twp., Madison Co., Indiana.[80, 98, 99, 100] She was the daughter of Edgar Clyde Humerickhouse and Clyda Estella Greenawalt (12). Ella May died in Chesterfield, Union Twp., Madison Co., Indiana, on December 11, 1970, at age 72.[80, 100] She was buried in Bronnenberg Cemetery, Chesterfield, Union Twp., Madison Co., Indiana.[100, 173, 194]

Ella May married **Warren Grover Brane** on December 26, 1921, in Madison Co., Indiana.[195] They divorced in 1930. They had two children. Warren Grover Brane was born in LaFontaine, Liberty Twp., Wabash Co., Indiana, on May 21, 1900.[80, 98, 196] Warren Grover lived in 1971 in Los Altos, Santa Clara Co., California. He reached age 71 and died in a hospital in Mountain View, Santa Clara Co., California, on October 28, 1971.[80, 197, 198] Warren Grover was buried in Alta Mesa Memorial Park Cemetery, Palo Alto, Santa Clara Co., California.[198]

Warren G. and Ella Humerickhouse Brane are enumerated in Anderson, Anderson Twp., Madison Co., Indiana in 1930 *(Census Place: Anderson, Madison, Indiana; Roll: 605; Page: 2A; Image: 37.0)*. Warren G. Brane, 29, born Indiana as were his parents, is a production manager at a container factory. His wife, Ella Humerickhouse Brane, 30, says she was born in Indiana, her father in West Virginia and her mother in Pennsylvania. The couple both say they were first married at age 22. Warren and Ella Humerickhouse Brane have two children, Constance, seven, and Richard L., two and one-half, both born in Indiana. Living with them is Ella Humrickhouse Brane's mother, Clyde Greenawalt Humrickhouse, 57, a widow, who says she and her father were born in Pennsylvania and her mother in Ohio.

om her first husband, Ella May Humerickhouse Brane married **Robert Matthew Vasbinder** on July 10, 1931, in Madison Co., Indiana.[99] Robert Matthew Vasbinder was born in Union Twp., Madison Co., Indiana, on July 8, 1888.[80, 199, 200] He reached age 82 and died in Chesterfield, Union Twp., Madison Co., Indiana, on September 4, 1970.[80, 200, 201] Robert Matthew was buried in Bronnenberg Cemetery, Chesterfield, Union Twp., Madison Co., Indiana.[200, 201, 202]

In 1940, Robert and Ella Humerickhouse Brane Vasbinder are enumerated in Chesterfield, Union Twp., Madison Co., Indiana *(Census Place: Chesterfield, Madison, Indiana; Roll: T627_1074; Page: 4B; Enumeration District: 48-76)*. Robert Vasbinder, age 51, is a supervising clerk for the Works Progress Administration (WPA). Ella Humrickhouse Brane Vasbinder is 39 years old. With them are Ella's children by her first marriage: Connie Brane, 17, and Richard Brane, 15. All were born in Indiana and say they were living in Chesterfield in 1935. Also in the household is Robert Vasbinder's widowed cousin, Edith Runyon, 43.

Robert Vasbinder's WWII draft registration in 1942 indicates he and Ella had relocated to Angola, Pleasant Twp., Steuben Co., Indiana.[203] Later, Robert and Ella moved back to Chesterfield, Union Twp., Madison Co., Indiana.

In 1940, Ella's ex-husband Warren G. Brane is found in Chicago, Cook Co., Illinois *(Census Place: Chicago, Cook, Illinois; Roll: T627_948; Page: 10A; Enumeration District: 103-886)*. He is listed as Warren G. "Brene," and is living with his second wife, Josephine Deveikis Brane, and their son John Brane in her the home of Josephine's father and stepmother Joseph and Delphia "Deverkis". Warren Brane is age 45, a laborer in a factory (the census taker's handwriting is difficult to read). He is erroneously enumerated as born in Illinois. Josephine Deveikis Brane is 33 and John Brane is six years old; both were born in Illinois. The head of the household is Joseph Deveikis, 68, who lists no occupation. His wife, Delphia Deveikis, is 65. Both Delveikis' were natives of Lithuaunia. All were living in the same house at 7133 South Washtenaw Street in 1935.

Warren Grover Brane's birthdate is incorrectly listed as May 20, 1900 on his death certificate.[198]

According to her granddaughter, Penelope "Penny" Nichols Hughes of South Bend, Indiana, Ella Humerickhouse Brane was clairvoyant. Her psychic powers and fortune-telling abilities were well known and sought after by the Madison Co., Indiana law enforcement, teachers, and many others. A couple of examples from Ella's home life, as told by Penny:

Ella's daughter and Penny's mother, Constance "Connie" Brane Nichols (Schrock) was worried about her first husband, Harvey "Nick" Nichols during WWII. His letters had come regularly, but had stopped. Ella told Connie, "Let's see what the (tarot) cards say. Ella did a reading and laughed out loud. "He's fine," she declared, "but he's shacked up with an Italian woman with red hair."

Connie wouldn't believe her. After he came home from the war, Harvey "Nick" Nichols did confess to his wife Connie that while in Italy he lived with a red-haired woman, and she had borne his child.

Years later, Ella phoned Connie one day and said, "Are you OK?" Connie replied that she was and asked her mother why. Ella told Connie that she'd had a dream, and that Connie had injured her foot badly. Connie laughed it off. That very night, she got up out of bed to get a drink of water. When she opened the refrigerator, a big can of fruit juice fell on her foot, breaking several bones. Connie Brane Nichols Schrock had several foot surgeries, but her foot was never the same.

When Ella died, Connie was holding her hand. Ella looked at her and said, "Now the power passes to you." Apparently, Ella may have inherited these psychic powers from her own mother, Clyde Greenawalt Humerickhouse.[40]

Children of Ella May Humerickhouse and Warren Grover Brane:

+ 40 f I. **Constance[9] Brane** was born in Anderson, Anderson Twp., Madison Co., Indiana, on November 18, 1922.[80, 204, 205] She died in South Bend, St. Joseph Co., Indiana, on June 25, 2008.[80, 204, 205]

+ 41 m II. **Richard Lee[9] Brane** was born in Anderson, Anderson Twp., Madison Co., Indiana, on October 10, 1927.[206, 207] He died in Chesterfield, Union Twp., Madison Co., Indiana, on September 19, 1981.[207, 208, 209, 210]

25. Bertha Pearl⁸ Loffer (*Bertha⁷ Wolfe, Phebe Ann⁶ Pegan, Elsey⁵, Robert A.⁴, Andrew³, Andrew² Pagan, James¹*) was born on July 23, 1887, in DeGraff, Miami Twp., Logan Co., Ohio.[80, 109] She was the daughter of Eugene Webster Loffer and Bertha Wolfe (14). Bertha Pearl died in Urbana Twp., Champaign Co., Ohio, on September 9, 1974, age 87.[110, 111] She was buried in Spring Hills Presbyterian Church Cemetery, Springhills, Harrison Twp., Champaign Co., Ohio.[211]

Bertha Pearl married **Harley Milton Terrell** on December 22, 1904, in Logan Co., Ohio.[109] They had six children. Harley Milton Terrell was born in Harrison Twp., Champaign Co., Ohio, on October 5, 1884.[109, 212] Harley Milton also resided in 1946 in Springhills, Harrison Twp., Champaign Co., Ohio. Harley Milton reached age 61 and died in a hospital in Bellefontaine, Lake Twp., Logan Co., Ohio, on January 3, 1946.[212] He was buried in Spring Hills Presbyterian Church Cemetery, Springhills, Harrison Twp., Champaign Co., Ohio.[212, 213]

Harley Milton Terrell may, or may not, have been married to a Bertha C. Robinson before he married Bertha Pearl Loffer. Harley Milton Terrell and Bertha C. Robinson had a daughter, Opal Lucille Terrell, who was born in 1903 and died in 1908.[214, 215] She is buried in the Oak Dale Cemetery in Urbana, Ohio.[215]

In 1910, Harley and Bertha Pearl Loffer Terrell (spelled on the census form as "Terrel") are enumerated in Harrison Twp., Champaign Co., Ohio *(Census Place: Harrison, Champaign, Ohio; Roll: T624_1159; Page: 4B; Enumeration District: 0005; Image: 729)*. The head of the household, Harley Terrell, is age 25, born Ohio as were his parents, is a farmer. With him is wife Bertha Loffer Terrell, 22, who also says she and her parents were born in Ohio. Bertha Pearl says she has born two children, both of whom are still alive. They are Thelma, four, and Virgil, two. Also living with them are Harley's parents, Jeptha Terrell, 62, and Fidelia Terrell, 48.

Harley Terrell is listed as "Harley Terell" in 1920 in Harrison Twp., Champaign Co., Ohio *(Census Place: Harrison, Champaign, Ohio; Roll: T625_1353; Page: 3B; Enumeration District: 5; Image: 75)*. In the house are Harley, age 35, a farmer; Bertha Pearl Loffer Terrell (listed as Pearl) is 32; and children Thelma, 14, Virgil, 12, Damon, nine, Gaylord ("Gailord") five, and Garnet ("Garnett"), two. All in the home were Ohio natives, as were their parents.

In 1930, Harley and Bertha Pearl Loffer Terrell ("Terrel") are again found in Harrison Twp., Champaign Co., Ohio *(Census Place: Harrison, Champaign, Ohio; Roll: 1755; Page: 3A; Enumeration District: 6; Image: 687.0)*. Harley, age 45, is a farmer and Bertha P. is 42. The couple says they were first wed at ages 21 and 18 respectively. Children in the home are: Virgil, 23, Damon, 19, Gaylord, 14, and Garnet, 12. All in the home and their parents were Ohio-born. For some reason, their youngest child, Harold, who would have been an infant, is not listed.

Harley and Bertha Loffer Terrell are still residing in Harrison Twp., Champaign Co., Ohio in 1940 *(Census Place: Harrison, Champaign, Ohio; Roll: T627_3037; Page: 4B; Enumeration District: 11-6)*. In the household are Harley Terrell, age 55, who is still farming, and his wife, Bertha Loffer Terrell, 52. Both were born in Ohio, and say they were living in the same house in 1935, but no road or numerical address is listed.

Children of Bertha Pearl Loffer and Harley Milton Terrell:

+ 42 f I. **Thelma Marie⁹ Terrell** was born in Springhills, Harrison Twp., Champaign Co., Ohio, on June 28, 1905.[80, 216, 217] She died in a facility in Urbana, Urbana Twp., Champaign Co., Ohio, on July 27, 1986.[218]

+ 43 m II. **Virgil Milton⁹ Terrell** was born in Harrison Twp., Champaign Co., Ohio, on July 28, 1907.[219] He died in a hospital in Bellefontaine, Lake Twp., Logan Co., Ohio, on December 27, 1974.[220, 221] -

+ 44 m III. **Damon Eugene⁹ Terrell** was born in Harrison Twp., Champaign Co., Ohio, on July 17, 1910.[80, 222] He died in a facility in Urbana, Urbana Twp., Champaign Co., Ohio, on November 24, 1983.[223, 224]

+ 45 m IV. **Gaylord Philip**[9] **Terrell** was born in Harrison Twp., Champaign Co., Ohio, on December 4, 1914.[80, 225] He was also known as **Pip**. Gaylord Philip died in Urbana Twp., Champaign Co., Ohio, on July 22, 1984.[80, 225]

+ 46 f V. **Garnet Lucille**[9] **Terrell** was born in Harrison Twp., Champaign Co., Ohio, on May 18, 1917.[80, 226, 227] She died in Urbana, Urbana Twp., Champaign Co., Ohio, on September 1, 1993.[80, 226, 227]

+ 47 m VI. **Harold Reginold**[9] **Terrell** was born in Harrison Twp., Champaign Co., Ohio, on September 11, 1919.[228] He died in Harrison Twp., Champaign Co., Ohio, on July 28, 1929.[228]

26. Lola[8] **Loffer** (*Bertha*[7] *Wolfe, Phebe Ann*[6] *Pegan, Elsey*[5]*, Robert A.*[4]*, Andrew*[3]*, Andrew*[2] *Pagan, James*[1]) was born on September 15, 1888, in DeGraff, Miami Twp., Logan Co., Ohio.[80, 112] She was the daughter of Eugene Webster Loffer and Bertha Wolfe (14). Lola died in Fremont, Sandusky Co., Ohio, on October 20, 1984, age 96.[113, 114] She was buried in Meadow Green/Restlawn Memorial Park Cemetery, Huron Twp., Erie Co., Ohio.[114, 229]

Lola married **Welcome Wallace Shaffer** on February 25, 1908, in Cuyahoga Co., Ohio.[230] They had one daughter. Welcome Wallace Shaffer was born in Flat Rock, Thompson Twp., Seneca Co., Ohio, on March 5, 1884.[230, 231 232] He reached age 76 and died in Sandusky, Erie Co., Ohio, on November 28, 1960.[233, 234] Welcome Wallace was buried in Meadow Green/Restlawn Memorial Park Cemetery, Huron Twp., Erie Co., Ohio.[233, 235]

Welcome Wallace Shaffer almost always used his middle name, Wallace, as his given name. However, on his WWI draft registration card, he states his name as Welcome Wallace Shaffer.[231] His name on his WWII draft registration is "Wallace Welcome Shaffer".[236] On his marriage license and Social Security application, he uses Wallace W. Shaffer, and Wallace is the name seen on all his census forms.[230, 232]

In 1910, Welcome Wallace and Lola E. Loffer Shaffer are enumerated in Tiffin, Clinton Twp., Seneca Co., Ohio *(Census Place: Tiffin Ward 4, Seneca, Ohio; Roll: T624_1229; Page: 3A; Enumeration District: 0151; Image: 306)*. In the home are Wallace Shaffer, age 26, born Ohio, with his father born in Pennsylvania and his mother in Ohio, a salesman in a shoe store; and wife Lola Loffer Shaffer, 21, born Ohio, with her father born in Missouri (Incorrect—he was born in Ohio) and her mother in Ohio. The couple says they have been married two years and Lola has borne one child, daughter "Laverne", who is one month old. Living with them is Lola's brother Harold J. Loffer, age 13, born Ohio, who also says his father was born in Missouri (wrong) and his mother in Ohio.

Although they are not found in the 1920 census, Welcome Wallace and Lola E. Loffer Shaffer may have been living in Sandusky, Portland Twp., Erie Co., Ohio, as that is the residence Welcome Wallace Shaffer lists on his WWI draft application in 1917.[231]

In 1930, Welcome Wallace and Lola Loffer Shaffer are found in Ward 4, Lima, Ottawa ("Ottowa") Twp., Allen Co., Ohio *(Census Place: Lima, Allen, Ohio; Roll: 1747; Page: 1A; Enumeration District: 28; Image: 201.0)*. "Wallace" Shaffer, age 45, is the proprietor of a cigar store. Wife Lola Loffer Shaffer is 41. Daughter Elizabeth Laverne, listed as "Betty E.", is age 20.

Welcome Wallace and Lola E. Loffer Shaffer have moved back to Sandusky, Portland Twp., Erie Co., Ohio by 1940 *(Census Place: Sandusky, Erie, Ohio; Roll: T627_3063; Page: 10B; Enumeration District: 22-22)*. In the household are "Wallace" Shaffer, age 56, the proprietor of a cigar store; Lola Loffer Shaffer, 51, and daughter Elizabeth, 30. All were born in Ohio and say they were residing in the same house at 1107 Hancock Street in 1935. There are also two lodgers with them, Paul Frost, 29, and Nick Bosco, 27.

Daughter of Lola E. Loffer and Welcome Wallace Shaffer:

+ 48 f I. **Elizabeth Laverne Ellen⁹ Shaffer** was born in Cleveland, Cuyahoga Co., Ohio, on March 6, 1910.[80, 237, 238] She was also known as **Betty**. Elizabeth Laverne Ellen died in Fremont, Sandusky Co., Ohio, on November 27, 1995, at age 85.[237, 238]

27. Harold J.⁸ Loffer (*Bertha⁷ Wolfe, Phebe Ann⁶ Pegan, Elsey⁵, Robert A.⁴, Andrew³, Andrew² Pagan, James¹*) was born on July 16, 1897, in DeGraff, Miami Twp., Logan Co., Ohio.[80, 115, 116] He was the son of Eugene Webster Loffer and Bertha Wolfe (14). Harold J. was living in 1965 in Sandusky, Erie Co., Ohio. Harold J. died in a hospital in Cleveland, Cuyahoga Co., Ohio, on January 1, 1965, at age 67.[117, 118] He was buried in Oakland Cemetery, Sandusky, Erie Co., Ohio.[239]

Harold Loffer, age 13, is living with his brother-in-law and sister, (Welcome) Wallace and Lola Loffer Shaffer and their one-month-old daughter, (Elizabeth) Laverne in Tiffen, Clinton Twp., Seneca Co., Ohio in 1910 *(Census Place: Tiffin Ward 4, Seneca, Ohio; Roll: T624_1229; Page: 3A; Enumeration District: 0151; Image: 306)*.

In 1920, Harold J. Loffer, 22, born Ohio, is living with his mother, Bertha Wolfe Loffer, age 53, who says she is a widow, in Ward 22, Cleveland, Cuyahoga Co., Ohio *(Census Place: Cleveland Ward 22, Cuyahoga, Ohio; Roll: T625_1371; Page: 5B; Enumeration District: 432; Image: 956)*. Harold Loffer, single, says he is an automotive toolmaker. Also in the household, listed as a "partner," is Pearl Peck, age 36, born Michigan, and a man who seems to be Pearl's husband, Hiram Peck, 50, a church caretaker, and their child, four-year-old Eloise Peck. However, neither Bertha Wolfe Loffer or Pearl Peck have occupations.

Harold J. married **Wilma O. Walborn** on February 6, 1922, in Erie Co., Ohio.[240] They had three children. Wilma O. Walborn was born in Huron, Huron Twp., Erie Co., Ohio, on February 4, 1906.[80, 241] Wilma O. reached age 102 and died in Sandusky, Erie Co., Ohio, on April 3, 2008.[80, 241] She was buried in Oakland Cemetery, Sandusky, Erie Co., Ohio.[241, 242]

In 1930, Harold J. Loffer is enumerated in Sandusky, Erie Co., Ohio *(Census Place: Sandusky, Erie, Ohio; Roll: 1790; Page: 9A; Enumeration District: 14; Image: 644.0)*. Harold, age 31, born Ohio as were his parents, is a machinist in an iron foundry. His wife, Wilma Walborn Loffer, 24, says she was born Ohio, her father in Michigan and her mother in Germany. The couple have been married eight years, as Harold says he was first married at age 24 and Wilma at 16. Children in the home are William, eight, Lola, five, and "Dona", three months; all were born in Ohio.

Harold J. Loffer is still a resident of Sandusky, Erie Co., Ohio in 1940 *(Census Place: Sandusky, Erie, Ohio; Roll: T627_3064; Page: 2A; Enumeration District: 22-28)*. In the household are Harold Loffer, age 42, who is now a machinist at a steel company; Wilma Walborn Loffer, 34, and their children William, 17, "Peggy," 15, and Donna Jean, 10. All were born in Ohio and say they were living in their home at 1014 Carr Street in 1935.

Children of Harold J. Loffer and Wilma O. Walborn:

+ 49 m I. **William Eugene⁹ Loffer** was born in Sandusky, Erie Co., Ohio, on April 8, 1922.[80, 243, 244] He died in Temple Terrace, Hillsborough Co., Florida, on February 18, 2011.[80, 244]

+ 50 f II. **Lola Margaret⁹ Loffer** was born in Sandusky, Erie Co., Ohio, on March 27, 1925.[245] She is also known as **Peggy**.

+ 51 f III. **Donna Jean⁹ Loffer** was born in Sandusky, Erie Co., Ohio, on December 15, 1929.[80, 246, 247] She died in Sandusky, Erie Co., Ohio, on May 31, 2002, at age 72.[80, 246, 247]

28. Frank Herbert[8] **Shaw** (*Effie Belle*[7] *Wolfe, Phebe Ann*[6] *Pegan, Elsey*[5]*, Robert A.*[4]*, Andrew*[3]*, Andrew*[2] *Pagan, James*[1]) was born on October 18, 1892, in Quincy, Miami Twp., Logan Co., Ohio.[124, 125, 126, 127] He was the son of Isaiah Luther Shaw and Effie Belle Wolfe (15). He died in Phoenix, Maricopa Co., Arizona, on November 28, 1961, at age 69.[126, 127, 128] Frank Herbert was buried in Greenwood Memory Lawn Cemetery, Phoenix, Maricopa Co., Arizona.[126, 127]

Frank Herbert married **Marguerite Crocker** on June 6, 1919, in Seneca Co., Ohio.[248] They had two children. Marguerite Crocker was born in Fostoria, Seneca Co., Ohio, on July 11, 1897.[80, 249, 250] Marguerite reached age 81 and died in Scottsdale, Maricopa Co., Arizona, on May 9, 1979.[73, 250] She was buried in Greenwood Memory Lawn Cemetery, Phoenix, Maricopa Co., Arizona.[250]

In 1920, Frank Herbert Shaw and wife Marguerite L. Crocker Shaw are found in Ward 2, Bowling Green, Plain Twp., Wood Co., Ohio *(Census Place: Bowling Green Ward 2, Wood, Ohio; Roll: T625_1448; Page: 7A; Enumeration District: 147; Image: 1030)*. Frank H., 27, is a dealer at a grain elevator and Marguerite is age 22. They and their parents were born in Ohio. Frank Herbert Shaw is probably working in the same grain elevator as his father Isaiah L. Shaw.

Frank Herbert Shaw is enumerated in Fostoria, Seneca Co., Ohio in 1930 *(Census Place: Fostoria, Seneca, Ohio; Roll: 1869; Page: 3B; Image: 154.0)*. The head of the household is Frank H. Shaw, age 38, who is the manager of a grain elevator; and his wife, Marguerite Crocker Shaw, listed as "Margret", 33. They say were first married at age 24 and 21 respectively. They have a daughter, Winifred, age nine. Living with them is Marguerite's father, John R. Crocker, age 61. All and their parents were born in Ohio.

In 1940, Frank Shaw and his family living with Marguerite Crocker Shaw's father, John Crocker, in Fostoria, Jackson Twp., Seneca Co., Ohio *(Census Place: Fostoria, Seneca, Ohio; Roll: T627_3144; Page: 17B; Enumeration District: 74-15)*. Frank Shaw, listed as "F.H. Shaw", age 47, works as a grain dealer at a grain elevator. His wife, Marguerite Crocker Shaw, is 42 years old. They have two children, "Jane", 19, listed as absent (she only lives there part-time), and John, four. Designated as the head of the household is John Crocker, 71, a widower, who lists no occupation. All in the home were Ohio natives, and say they were residents in the same house at 135 East South Street in 1935.

After 1940, Frank Herbert Shaw and family relocated to Phoenix, Maricopa Co., Arizona.

Children of Frank Herbert Shaw and Marguerite Crocker:

+ 52 f I. **Winifred Jane**[9] **Shaw** was born in Bowling Green, Wood Co., Ohio, on April 25, 1920.[80, 251] She died in Tempe, Maricopa Co., Arizona, on March 12, 2006.[80, 251]

+ 53 m II. **John Crocker**[9] **Shaw** was born in Fostoria, Seneca Co., Ohio, on October 10, 1935.[80, 252, 253] He died in Phoenix, Maricopa Co., Arizona, on January 18, 2004.[80, 253]

29. William Russell[8] **Shaw** (*Effie Belle*[7] *Wolfe, Phebe Ann*[6] *Pegan, Elsey*[5]*, Robert A.*[4]*, Andrew*[3]*, Andrew*[2] *Pagan, James*[1]) was born on September 19, 1898, in Quincy, Miami Twp., Logan Co., Ohio.[129] He was also known as **Russell**. He was the son of Isaiah Luther Shaw and Effie Belle Wolfe (15). William Russell died in New Rochester, Freedom Twp., Wood Co., Ohio, on August 27, 1963, at age 64.[130, 131] He was buried in Fountain/Fostoria Cemetery, Fostoria, Washington Twp., Hancock Co., Ohio.[254]

William Russell Shaw used his middle name, Russell, as his preferred name.

William Russell married **Catherine Marguerite Murphy** before 1928. They had five children. Catherine Marguerite Murphy was born in Liberty Twp., Logan Co., Ohio, on February 21, 1902.[255] Catherine Marguerite reached age 61 and died in New Rochester, Freedom Twp., Wood Co., Ohio, on August 27, 1963.[130, 256] She was buried in Fountain/Fostoria Cemetery, Fostoria, Washington Twp., Hancock Co., Ohio.[257]

William Russell Shaw, enumerated as "Russell" Shaw, is found in Fostoria, Seneca Co., Ohio in 1930 *(Census Place: Fostoria, Seneca, Ohio; Roll: 1869; Page: 7B; Enumeration District: 21; Image: 16.0)*. (William) Russell, 31, is a grain dealer. With him are wife Catherine Murphy Shaw, 28, and son William II, age one year and three months. All were born in Ohio, as were their parents. (William) Russell Shaw and Catherine Murphy Shaw say they were first married at ages 29 and 21 respectively.

In 1940, William Russell Shaw is found in Cygnet, Bloom Twp., Wood Co., Ohio *(Census Place: Cygnet, Wood, Ohio; Roll: T627_3170; Page: 8B; Enumeration District: 87-3)*. William Shaw, age 41, is a grain dealer who owns his own business. His wife, Catherine Murphy Shaw, is 33. They have four children: William II, 11, Robert, eight, Nancy June, two, and Carl Luther, who has an "x" by his name and whose age, four months, is crossed out. All in the home were born in Ohio, and say they were living in the same house in 1935, but there is no street or address listed.

William Russell and Catherine Marguerite Murphy Shaw were killed in an auto accident.

Children of William Russell Shaw and Catherine Marguerite Murphy:

+ 54 m I. **William**[9] **Shaw II** was born in Fostoria, Seneca Co., Ohio, on May 31, 1928.[258]

+ 55 m II. **Blair**[9] **Shaw** was born in Fostoria, Seneca Co., Ohio, on March 1, 1930.[259] He died in Fostoria, Seneca Co., Ohio, on March 1, 1930.[259]

+ 56 m III. **Robert Leonard**[9] **Shaw** was born in Fostoria, Seneca Co., Ohio, on July 6, 1931.[260, 261] He died in San Rafael, Marin Co., California, on March 9, 1955.[260]

+ 57 f IV. **Nancy June**[9] **Shaw** was born in Cygnet, Bloom Twp., Wood Co., Ohio, on July 31, 1937.

+ 58 m V. **Carl Luther**[9] **Shaw** was born in Cygnet, Bloom Twp., Wood Co., Ohio, on November 23, 1939.[80, 262, 263] He died in Fostoria, Seneca Co., Ohio, on August 19, 2005.[80, 262]

30. Edith Laura[8] **Shaw** (*Effie Belle*[7] *Wolfe, Phebe Ann*[6] *Pegan, Elsey*[5]*, Robert A.*[4]*, Andrew*[3]*, Andrew*[2] *Pagan, James*[1]) was born on February 1, 1901, in Quincy, Miami Twp., Logan Co., Ohio.[132, 133] She was the daughter of Isaiah Luther Shaw and Effie Belle Wolfe (15). She died in Madisonville, Hopkins Co., Kentucky, on February 27, 1994, at age 93.[80, 134] Edith Laura was buried in Serenity Gardens Memorial Park Cemetery, Largo, Pinellas Co., Florida.[134, 264]

Edith Laura married **Charles Henry Snyder** on June 14, 1923, in Wood Co., Ohio.[132] They had one daughter. Charles Henry Snyder was born in Bowling Green, Wood Co., Ohio, on September 17, 1902.[80, 132, 265] Charles Henry reached age 90 and died in Largo, Pinellas Co., Florida, on December 2, 1992.[80, 265] He was buried in Serenity Gardens Memorial Park Cemetery, Largo, Pinellas Co., Florida.[266]

In 1930, Charles H. and L. Edith Shaw Snyder are enumerated in Bowling Green, Center Twp., Wood Co., Ohio *(Census Place: Bowling Green, Wood, Ohio; Roll: 1888; Page: 14A; Enumeration District: 9; Image: 880.0)*. In the home are Charles, age 28, a sales manager at an automobile dealership; wife L. Edith, 29, daughter Patricia Ann, five, and L. Edith's mother, Effie Belle Wolfe Shaw, 60, a widow. All were born in Ohio, as were their parents. Charles Snyder says he was first married at age 21 and L. Edith Shaw Snyder was 22, so they have been married about seven years.

Charles and Edith Shaw Snyder are found in Lima, Ottawa Twp., Allen Co., Ohio in 1940 *(Census Place: Lima, Allen, Ohio; Roll: T627_3021; Page: 4B; Enumeration District: 2-40)*. The head of the household, Charles Snyder, 37, is an agent for an oil refining company. "Edith L." Shaw Snyder is 39 years old, and daughter Patricia Ann is now 15. Still with them is Edith's mother, Effie Belle Wolfe Shaw, age 71 and a widow. All were born in Ohio, and say they were living in Lima in 1935. Their home is at 214 South Metcalf Street.

Charles Snyder was the informant on his mother-in-law's, Effie Belle Wolfe Shaw's, death certificate in 1951, when he, Edith and Patricia were residing in Akron, Summit Co., Ohio.[55]

Daughter of Edith Laura Shaw and Charles Henry Snyder:

+ 59 f I. **Patricia Ann**[9] **Snyder** was born in Bowling Green, Center Twp., Wood Co., Ohio, on July 21, 1925.[80, 267] She died in a hospital in Owensboro, Daviess Co., Kentucky, on January 18, 2004, at age 78.[80, 267]

31. Hubert Wilder[8] **Wolfe** (*Frank L.*[7], *Phebe Ann*[6] *Pegan, Elsey*[5], *Robert A.*[4], *Andrew*[3], *Andrew*[2] *Pagan, James*[1]) was born on June 6, 1905, in Stella, West Muddy Twp., Richardson Co., Nebraska.[80, 139, 140] He was the son of Frank L. Wolfe (16) and Etta Wilder. He died in Lady Lake, Lake Co., Florida, on January 31, 1989, at age 83.[80, 139, 140]

Hubert Wilder Wolfe is not found in the 1930 census, but, according to his obituary, he had just arrived in Chicago and was working for Walgreens, Inc. as a candy buyer in 1930.[140]

Hubert Wilder married **Ruth Victoria Sebastian** in 1931 in Illinois? They had one daughter. Ruth Victoria Sebastian was born in Minneapolis, Hennepin Co., Minnesota, on July 1, 1906.[80, 268] Ruth Victoria reached age 90 and died in Rockport, Essex Co., Massachusetts, on April 11, 1997.[80, 269] She was buried in Haverhill, Massachusetts.[270]

Hubert Wolfe is enumerated in 1940 in Chicago, Cook Co., Illinois *(Census Place: Chicago, Cook, Illinois; Roll: T627_1023; Page: 9A; Enumeration District: 103-3254)*. Hubert Wolfe, age 34, born Nebraska, lists his occupation as a candy merchandiser for retail drug outlets. His wife, Ruth, 33, was born in Minnesota. They have a daughter, Diane, six, born Illinois. Their home address is 6326 Talman Avenue, and all say they were living in Chicago in 1935.

His obituary says Hubert Wilder worked as a candy buyer for Walgreens Drug Company between 1930 and 1955 in Chicago, before becoming a sales manager at Paul F. Beich Candy Company in Bloomington, Normal Twp., Champaign Co., Illinois between 1955 and 1970. After that, Hubert Wilder was the national sales manager at DeMet Candy Corporation from 1970-1972. in Stamford, Fairfield Co., Connecticut. In 1972 he retired to Lady Lake, Lake Co., Florida.[140]

Daughter of Hubert Wilder Wolfe and Ruth Victoria Sebastian:

+ 60 f I. **Diane R.**[9] **Wolfe** was born in Chicago, Cook Co., Illinois, on February 6, 1934.[271]

32. Kenneth Vernon[8] **Wolfe (Booze)** (*Guy Ernest*[7] *Wolfe, Phebe Ann*[6] *Pegan, Elsey*[5], *Robert A.*[4], *Andrew*[3], *Andrew*[2] *Pagan, James*[1]) was born on January 27, 1900, in Quincy, Miami Twp., Logan Co., Ohio.[144, 149] He was the son of Guy Ernest Wolfe (18) and Effa May Young. He died in San Antonio, Bexar Co., Texas, on August 8, 1970, at age 70.[80, 150, 151] Kenneth Vernon (Wolfe) was buried in Forest Lawn Memorial Gardens Cemetery, Columbus, Franklin Co., Ohio.[272]

According to his original birth record in Logan County, Ohio, Kenneth Vernon (Wolfe) Booze is registered as a male child, born January 27, 1900 to Guy Wolfe and Effa Young. According to census and other records, Guy was age 18 and Effa 16 years old when their son was born. Guy and Effa never married; Effa Young later wed Everett Edward Booze. On July 10, 1943, Kenneth Vernon (Wolfe) Booze petitions the Logan County Probate Court to change his birth certificate and name Everett Edward Booze as his father. (Kenneth had been using the surname Booze all his life.) Two of Kenneth's uncles, W.W. Booze and J.G. Booze, signed supporting affidavits for this request on July 19th and 20th respectively. On July 20th, the Judge A. T. Bray granted his request and amended the birth certificate.[144]

It is not clear whether Everett Edward Booze ever officially adopted Kenneth Wolfe, but Kenneth Wolfe always used the surname Booze.

Kenneth Vernon (Wolfe) Booze, age 10, born Ohio, is found with Everett Edward and Effa Young Booze, his erstwhile father and birth mother, in Green Creek Twp., Sandusky Co., Ohio in 1910 *(Census Place: Green Creek, Sandusky, Ohio; Roll: T624_1227; Page: 4A; Enumeration District: 0119; Image: 652)*. His stepfather, Everett Booze, age 32, a foreman on a railroad section gang, says he was born in Ohio and his parents in Pennsylvania. "Effie" Young Booze is 26, born Ohio as were her parents. They state they have been married 10 years and Effa has borne six children, four still living. In addition to Kenneth, children in the home are son Marion, six, Edna, four, and Clarence, one year and three months. All these children were also born in Ohio.

Kenneth Vernon (Wolfe) Booze married **Iva Elizabeth Hufford** on June 29, 1918, in Monroe Co., Michigan.[273] They divorced. They had two children. Iva Elizabeth Hufford was born in Sandusky Twp., Sandusky Co., Ohio, on March 1, 1898.[80, 274] Iva Elizabeth reached age 83 and died in Sandusky, Erie Co., Ohio, on March 9, 1981.[275] She was buried in Oakwood Cemetery, Fremont, Sandusky Co., Ohio.[276]

Kenneth is married by the time he registers for the WWI draft in Fremont, Sandusky Co., Ohio. On that document, he says he is a die maker.[277]

In 1920, Kenneth Vernon (Wolfe) Booze is found in Fremont, Sandusky Co., Ohio *(Census Place: Fremont Ward 1, Sandusky, Ohio; Roll: T625_1429; Page: 13B; Enumeration District: 71; Image: 57)*. In the household are Kenneth ("Kenith") Booze, 21, a teamster in a flour mill, Iva Hufford Booze, who says she is 21, and daughter Doris ("Doras"), one. All and their parents were born in Ohio.

Kenneth Vernon (Wolfe) Booze is enumerated in 1930 in Lima, Ottawa Twp., Allen Co., Ohio *(Census Place: Lima, Allen, Ohio; Roll: 1746; Page: 28A; Enumeration District: 0020; Image: 1009.0)*. In the home are Kenneth Vernon Booze, age 30, a manufacturer of auto accessories. With him is wife Iva Huffer Booze, who says she is also 30 (?), and children Doris, 11, and Kenneth E., five. All in the home were born in Ohio as were their parents. Both Kenneth Vernon (Wolfe) Booze and Iva Huffer Booze say their first marriage occurred at age 19.

Kenneth Vernon married Mrs. **Virginia Pearl Kirtley** McCarthy. Virginia Pearl Kirtley before 1940. Virginia Pearl was born in Hardy Twp., Holmes Co., Ohio, on July 15, 1908. She was also known as **Pearl**. They had no children. Virginia Pearl reached age 60 and died in San Antonio, Bexar Co., Texas, on March 20, 1969.[278] She was buried in Forest Lawn Memorial Gardens Cemetery, Columbus, Franklin Co., Ohio.[279]

In the 1940 U.S. Census, Kenneth V. and V. Pearl Booze are doubly enumerated. The first enumeration, on April 8, is in Travis Co., Texas *(Census Place: Travis, Texas; Roll: m-t0627-04151; Page: 81A; Enumeration District: 227-84)*. The only two people in the household are Kenneth V. Booze, age 40, a wholesale drapery salesman, and V. Peral Booze, 35. Both were born in Ohio and say they were residents of Sandusky, Ohio in 1935. No street address is on the census form.

Then on April 16, 1940, Kenneth Vernon (Wolfe) Booze is a resident of Fremont, Sandusky Co., Ohio *(Census Place: Fremont, Sandusky, Ohio; Roll: T627_3139; Page: 10B; Enumeration District: 72-15)*. Kenneth Booze, who says he is age 44, lists his occupation as a drapery salesman ("salesman, drapes"). He is married to his second wife, (Virginia) Pearl Kirtley McCarthy Booze, 42 (Incorrect—she is 32). There are three children in the home, Doris Booze, 21, an office attendant; and Pearl's two children, June and Robert McCarthy, ages 15 and 14 respectively. All in the home were born in Ohio. Kenneth and Doris Booze say they were living in Sandusky County, in 1935, while "Pearl" and her children were in "Mt. Vernon, Ohio" then. Their house address is 1123 1/2 Croghau Street.

Kenneth Vernon (Wolfe) Booze is living in San Antonio, Bexar Co., Texas, in 1951, according to that city's directory.[280]

In 1940, Iva Huffer Booze is enumerated in Sandusky, Erie Co., Ohio *(Census Place: Sandusky, Erie, Ohio; Roll: T627_3063; Page: 61B; Enumeration District:*

22-19). Iva Huffer Booze, age 38, divorced, is a factory worker at a paper box factory. With her is her son, Kenneth Booze II, who is 15 years old. Both were born in Ohio, and say they were living in Fremont, Sandusky Co., Ohio in 1935. They are residing at 416 Clarkson Street.

Iva Huffer Booze remarries to Webster E. Werner on January 22, 1944 in Erie Co., Ohio. Ohio.[281] Kenneth Vernon (Wolfe) Booze's son Kenneth II, by his first wife Iva Huffer Booze Werner, later assumes the surname Werner. It is unknown if Kenneth Booze II/Kenneth Werner was legally adopted by his stepfather, Webster Werner.

Children of Kenneth Vernon (Wolfe) Booze and Iva Elizabeth Hufford:

+ 61 f I. **Doris Jeannette[9] Booze** was born in Fremont, Sandusky Co., Ohio, on January 2, 1919.[80, 282, 283, 284] She was also known as **Dodie**. Doris Jeannette died in Sun City, Maricopa Co., Arizona, on November 17, 1997.[80, 283]

+ 62 m II. **Kenneth E.[9] Booze (Werner)** was born in Fremont, Sandusky Co., Ohio, on March 10, 1925.[80, 285] He died in Phoenix, Maricopa Co., Arizona, on January 3, 2001.[80, 285]

33. **Kenneth William[8] Wolfe** (*Guy Ernest[7], Phebe Ann[6] Pegan, Elsey[5], Robert A.[4], Andrew[3], Andrew[2] Pagan, James[1]*) was born on March 27, 1908, in Minneapolis, Hennepin Co., Minnesota.[152, 153] He was the son of Guy Ernest Wolfe (18) and Lillian Adelia Lundeen. He died in Louis Park, Hennepin Co., Minnesota, on January 11, 1981, at age 72.[152]

Kenneth William married **Mary Alice Light** on April 19, 1930, in Hennepin Co., Minnesota.[286] They had two children. Mary Alice Light was born in Watertown, Carver Co., Minnesota, on November 18, 1909.[287, 288] Mary Alice reached age 78 and died in Minneapolis, Hennepin Co., Minnesota, on February 5, 1988.[287]

In 1940, Kenneth Wolfe is enumerated in Minneapolis, Hennepin Co., Minnesota (*Census Place: Minneapolis, Hennepin, Minnesota; Roll: T627_1977; Page: 7B; Enumeration District: 89-61*). Kenneth Wolfe, age 32, is a magazine salesman for a magazine distributor. With him are his wife, (Mary) Alice Light Wolfe, 30, and their children, Robert, nine, and Sharon, five. All were born in Minnesota and were residents of Hennepin County in 1935. The family is living at 2615 Oak Park Avenue.

Kenneth William Wolfe was a Minnesota state senator, according to his obituary.[289]

Children of Kenneth William Wolfe and Mary Alice Light:

+ 63 m I. **Robert Roe[9] Wolfe** was born in Minneapolis, Hennepin Co., Minnesota, on March 18, 1931.[290]

+ 64 f II. **Sharon Kay[9] Wolfe** was born in Minneapolis, Hennepin Co., Minnesota, on April 15, 1935.[291]

34. **Margaret Carolyn[8] Wolfe** (*Guy Ernest[7], Phebe Ann[6] Pegan, Elsey[5], Robert A.[4], Andrew[3], Andrew[2] Pagan, James[1]*) was born on August 24, 1919, in Minnetonka, Hennepin Co., Minnesota.[154] She was the daughter of Guy Ernest Wolfe (18) and Lillian Adelia Lundeen. Margaret Carolyn died in Brooklyn Park, Hennepin Co., Minnesota, on August 19, 2015, at age 95.[155] She was cremated and her cremains interred at Fort Snelling National Cemetery, Minneapolis, Hennepin Co., Minnesota.[292]

Margaret Carolyn married **Darwin Dean Rounds** on December 10, 1942, in Manhattan, Riley Co., Kansas. They had four children. Darwin Dean Rounds was born in Polk Twp., DeKalb Co., Missouri, on August 25, 1919.[80, 293,] He was also known as **Dixie**. Darwin Dean reached age 74 and died in Minneapolis, Hennepin Co., Minnesota, on June 25, 1994.[80, 293] He was buried in Fort Snelling National Cemetery, Minneapolis, Hennepin Co., Minnesota.[294, 295]

35. **Warren Charles[8] Wolfe** (*Guy Ernest[7], Phebe Ann[6] Pegan, Elsey[5], Robert A.[4], Andrew[3], Andrew[2] Pagan, James[1]*) was born on September 14, 1922, in Minnetonka, Hennepin Co., Minnesota.[80, 156] He was the son of Guy Ernest Wolfe (18) and Lillian

Adelia Lundeen. Warren Charles died in Plymouth, Hennepin Co., Minnesota, on November 10, 2003, at age 81.[80, 157]

Warren Charles married **Vallie Faye Lavinghouze** on April 2, 1950, in Hennepin Co., Minnesota.[296] They had three children. Vallie Faye Lavinghouze was born in Mobile, Mobile Co., Alabama, on July 16, 1929.[297]

9th Generation

36. Armintha Euphema Almack[9] **(Shultz)** (*Armintha*[8] *Shultz, Ola*[7] *Greenawalt, Sarah Jane*[6] *Pegan, Elsey*[5]*, Robert A.*[4]*, Andrew*[3]*, Andrew*[2] *Pagan, James*[1]) was born on July 1, 1924, in Muncie, Center Twp., Delaware Co., Indiana.[80, 162, 163, 171, 172] She was the daughter of Earl Jesse Almack and Armintha Shultz (22). Armintha Euphema Almack lived in March 1994 in Anderson, Anderson Twp., Madison Co., Indiana. Armintha Euphema Almack died in a hospital in Indianapolis, Marion Co., Indiana, on March 28, 1994, at age 69.[80, 162, 171, 172] She was buried in Anderson Memorial Park Cemetery, Anderson, Anderson Twp., Madison Co., Indiana. [162, 172, 298]

Armintha E. Almack was orphaned by age eight, as her mother Armintha "Nettie" Shultz Almack died in childbirth with her and her father Earl Almack Sr. died in 1933.[86, 167] After her mother died, her father, Earl Almack Sr., gave her to her her maternal Uncle Ralph and Aunt Mary Connolly Shultz to raise. After Earl Almack died, Ralph and Mary Connolly Shultz "adopted" her, and Armintha began to use the surname Shultz. Both Ralph and Mary's obituaries list her as a daughter.[83, 159] Also, Armintha Almack Smith's obituary lists her maiden name as Shultz and names Ralph and Mary as her parents, even though Earl Almack Jr. is listed as her brother.[162] But it seems that Armintha Almack Smith was never *formally* adopted by Ralph R. and Mary Connolly Shultz. On her marriage license to Alva J. Smith, she uses the name Armintha Almack.[163] Her Social Security application also has her name as Armintha Euphema Almack (Smith).[171]

In 1930, five-year-old Armintha "Almeck" was living with her childless maternal uncle and aunt, Ralph Richard and Mary Sue Connolly Shultz's home, in Alexandria, Monroe Twp., Madison Co., Indiana (*Census Place: Alexandria, Madison, Indiana; Roll: 605; Page: 3B; Image: 908.0*). She is listed as a niece to the head of the household (her uncle Ralph) and she and her parents were born in Indiana. Armintha is again with Ralph and Mary Shultz in Alexandria, Monroe Twp., Madison Co., Indiana in 1940 (*Census Place: Alexandria, Madison, Indiana; Roll: T627_1073; Page: 6A; Enumeration District: 48-54*). This time, however, Armintha E. Almack is enumerated as Armintha Shultz, and she is listed as a daughter to the head of household.

Armintha Euphema Almack married **Alva Jack Smith** on August 18, 1946, in Madison Co., Indiana.[163] They had three children. Alva Jack Smith was born in Columbus, Columbus Twp., Bartholomew Co., Indiana, on January 10, 1924.[80, 163, 299, 300] Alva Jack reached age 58 and died in a hospital in Indianapolis, Center Twp., Marion Co., Indiana, on November 14, 1982.[80, 299, 300] He was buried in Anderson Memorial Park Cemetery, Anderson Twp., Madison Co., Indiana.[299, 300, 301]

Armintha was employed as the secretary for the mayor of Anderson, Indiana; she was also a cosmotologist and beautician.[162] Alva Jack worked as a firefighter, Anderson, Indiana Fire Department.[282]

Armintha Euphema Almack (Shultz) and Alva Jack Smith had three children, including:

+ 73 f   II. **Patricia Ann**[10] **Smith** was born in Anderson, Anderson Twp., Madison Co., Indiana, on February 21, 1950.[302, 303, 304, 305] She died in Anderson, Anderson Twp., Madison Co., Indiana, on December 22, 1954.[302, 303, 305]

37. Jack Edgar[9] **McHarry** (*Vera B.*[8] *Humerickhouse, Clyda Estella*[7] *Greenawalt, Sarah Jane*[6] *Pegan, Elsey*[5]*, Robert A.*[4]*, Andrew*[3]*, Andrew*[2] *Pagan, James*[1]) was born on September 7, 1922, in Anderson, Anderson Twp., Madison Co., Indiana.[184, 185] He was the son of Claude Almond McHarry and Vera B. Humerickhouse (23). Jack Edgar lived in 1942 in Chesterfield, Union Twp., Madison Co., Indiana. He died in Indianapolis, Marion Co., Indiana, on April 10, 1942, at age 19.[184, 185, 186] Jack Edgar was buried in East Maplewood Cemetery, Anderson, Anderson Twp., Madison Co., Indiana.[184, 185, 186, 306]

According to his obituary, 19-year-old Jack Edgar McHarry had gone to Indianapolis from his home in Chesterfield to enlist in the Navy for WWII when he was hit by a car. He sustained a fractured skull and a broken leg, dying two days later in Robert Long Hospital, Indiana University Medical Center, Indianapolis. The accident happened at night during a heavy rainstorm, and the driver, who was not charged, said McHarry came out between two parked cars and he did not see him in time.[186]

38. **Bill Clyde⁹ McHarry** (*Vera B.⁸ Humerickhouse, Clyda Estella⁷ Greenawalt, Sarah Jane⁶ Pegan, Elsey⁵, Robert A.⁴, Andrew³, Andrew² Pagan, James¹*) was born on March 31, 1925, in Anderson, Anderson Twp., Madison Co., Indiana.[80, 187, 188, 189] He was the son of Claude Almond McHarry and Vera B. Humerickhouse (23). He died in Anderson, Anderson Twp., Madison Co., Indiana, on February 8, 1999, at age 73.[80, 187, 188, 189] Bill Clyde was buried in East Maplewood Cemetery, Anderson, Anderson Twp., Madison Co., Indiana.[188, 189, 307]

Bill Clyde married Mrs. **Ruth Mary Cowles** Skinner on November 2, 1946, in Delaware Co., Indiana.[308] They divorced. They had no children. Ruth Cowles was born in Edmonson Co., Kentucky, on August 22, 1919.[309]

Bill Clyde McHarry married **Mary Winifred Shelburn** on October 29, 1949, in Delaware Co., Indiana.[310] They had two daughters. Mary Winifred Shelburn was born in Anderson, Anderson Twp., Madison Co., Indiana, on March 23, 1928.[80, 311, 312] Mary Winifred reached age 67 and died in Anderson, Anderson Twp., Madison Co., Indiana, on July 30, 1995.[80, 311, 312] She was buried in East Maplewood Cemetery, Anderson, Anderson Twp., Madison Co., Indiana.[312, 313, 314]

39. **Donna May⁹ McHarry** (*Vera B.⁸ Humerickhouse, Clyda Estella⁷ Greenawalt, Sarah Jane⁶ Pegan, Elsey⁵, Robert A.⁴, Andrew³, Andrew² Pagan, James¹*) was born on February 6, 1929, in Anderson, Anderson Twp., Madison Co., Indiana.[190, 191] She was the daughter of Claude Almond McHarry and Vera B. Humerickhouse (23). Donna May died in Lafayette, Fairfield Twp., Tippecanoe Co., Indiana, on March 19, 1984, at age 55.[191, 192, 193] She was buried in East Maplewood Cemetery, Anderson, Anderson Twp., Madison Co., Indiana.[191, 192]

Childless.

Donna May married **Unknown Williams** between 1959 and 1963. They divorced.

40. **Constance⁹ Brane** (*Ella May⁸ Humerickhouse, Clyda Estella⁷ Greenawalt, Sarah Jane⁶ Pegan, Elsey⁵, Robert A.⁴, Andrew³, Andrew² Pagan, James¹*) was born on November 18, 1922, in Anderson, Anderson Twp., Madison Co., Indiana.[80, 204, 205] She was the daughter of Warren Grover Brane and Ella May Humerickhouse (24). Constance died in South Bend, St. Joseph Co., Indiana, on June 25, 2008, at age 85.[80, 204, 205] She was cremated.[191] Constance was cremated and her ashes buried in Crystal Cathedral Cemetery, Garden Grove, Orange Co., California.[205, 315]

Constance married **Horace Davis Nichols** on February 7, 1942, in Madison Co., Indiana.[316] They divorced. They had three children. Horace Davis Nichols was born in Union Twp., Madison Co., Indiana, on August 09, 1921.[80, 317, 318, 319 320] He was also known as **Nick**. He lived in 1990 in Victorville, San Bernardino Co., California. Horace Davis reached age 68 and died in San Diego, San Diego Co., California, on August 6, 1990.[318, 319, 320, 321] He was cremated and his ashes scattered in the Pacific Ocean, but he has a memorial stone in Fort Rosencrans National Military Cemetery, San Diego, San Diego Co., California.[321, 322, 323]

Horace Davis "Nick" and Constance Brane Nichols, and two of their children left Anderson, Anderson Twp., Madison Co., Indiana in 1963 and moved to San Diego. Diego, San Diego Co., California.[322] By 1972, they were living in San Jose, Santa Clara Co., California.

After divorcing Horace Nichols, Constance Brane Nichols married **David Ervin Schrock** on February 19, 1966, in Santa Clara Co., California.[324] They divorced. David Ervin Schrock was born in Topeka, Eden Twp., LaGrange Co., Indiana, on December 22, 1924.[80, 325, 326, 327] He reached age 70 and died in Fallon, Churchill Co., Nevada, on September 20, 1995.[80, 325] David Ervin was buried in Hawpatch

Cemetery, Topeka, Eden Twp., LaGrange Co., Indiana.[328]

41. Richard Lee⁹ Brane (*Ella May⁸ Humerickhouse, Clyda Estella⁷ Greenawalt, Sarah Jane⁶ Pegan, Elsey⁵, Robert A.⁴, Andrew³, Andrew² Pagan, James¹*) was born on October 10, 1927, in Anderson, Anderson Twp., Madison Co., Indiana.[206, 207, 209, 210] He was the son of Warren Grover Brane and Ella May Humerickhouse (24). Richard Lee died in Chesterfield, Union Twp., Madison Co., Indiana, on September 19, 1981, at age 53.[207, 208, 209, 210] He was cremated and his ashes buried in Bronnenberg Cemetery, Chesterfield, Union Twp., Madison Co., Indiana.[210]

Never married.

Although his death certificates and gravestone state he was born on October 12, 1927, Richard Lee Brane's birth record in Madison Co., Indiana says his birth date was October 10, 1927.[206, 207, 209, 210] He was a bookkeeper.[208]

42. Thelma Marie⁹ Terrell (*Bertha Pearl⁸ Loffer, Bertha⁷ Wolfe, Phebe Ann⁶ Pegan, Elsey⁵, Robert A.⁴, Andrew³, Andrew² Pagan, James¹*) was born on June 28, 1905, in Springhills, Harrison Twp., Champaign Co., Ohio.[80, 216, 217] She was the daughter of Harley Milton Terrell and Bertha Pearl Loffer (25). Thelma Marie lived in Mechanicsburg, Goshen Twp., Champaign Co., Ohio in 1986. She died in a facility in Urbana, Urbana Twp., Champaign Co., Ohio, on July 27, 1986, at age 81.[218] Thelma Marie was buried in Maple Grove Cemetery, Mechanicsburg, Goshen Twp., Champaign Co., Ohio.[329, 330]

Thelma Marie married **Harry Fulwider Mohr** on June 6, 1925, in Champaign Co., Ohio.[331] They had two sons. Harry Fulwider Mohr was born in Springhills, Harrison Twp., Champaign Co., Ohio, on January 27, 1904.[216, 332] Harry Fulwider reached age 56 and died in Mechanicsburg, Goshen Twp., Champaign Co., Ohio, on September 2, 1960.[333] He was buried in Maple Grove Cemetery, Mechanicsburg, Goshen Twp., Champaign Co., Ohio.[334, 335]

In 1930, Harry F. Mohr, enumerated as Harry Moore, is found in Mechanicsburg, Goshen Twp., Champaign Co., Ohio (*Census Place: Mechanicsburg, Champaign, Ohio; Roll: 1755; Page: 13A; Enumeration District: 3; Image: 655.0*). Harry F. Mohr, age 26, is the manager of a gasoline station. His wife, Thelma Terrell Mohr is 24 years old. Harry says he was 21 years old when he first married, and Thelma states she was 20. They have a son, Richard E., one year and 10 months old. All and their parents were born in Ohio.

Harry F. and Thelma Terrell Mohr are still residing in Mechanicsburg, Goshen Twp., Champaign Co., Ohio in 1940 (*Census Place: Mechanicsburg, Champaign, Ohio; Roll: T627_3037; Page: 9B; Enumeration District: 11-3*). In the home are Harry F. Mohr, age 35, who is now the postmaster of the town; Thelma Terrell Mohr, 34, and sons "Dick," 11, and James, six. All were born in Ohio and say there were living in the same house at 29 West Sandusky Street. in 1935.

At the time of their marriage in 1925, Harry F. Mohr says on the marriage license that he is a teacher.[216]

Sons of Thelma Marie Terrell and Harry Fulwider Mohr:

+ 80 m I. **Richard Eugene¹⁰ Mohr** was born in Mechanicsburg, Goshen Twp., Champaign Co., Ohio, on May 22, 1928.[80, 336] He died in a hospital in Urbana, Urbana Twp., Champaign Co., Ohio, on September 25, 1983, at age 55.[336, 337]

+ 81 m II. **Harry James¹⁰ Mohr II** was born in Mechanicsburg, Champaign Co., Ohio, on May 8, 1933.[338] He is also known as **James**.

43. Virgil Milton⁹ Terrell (*Bertha Pearl⁸ Loffer, Bertha⁷ Wolfe, Phebe Ann⁶ Pegan, Elsey⁵, Robert A.⁴, Andrew³, Andrew² Pagan, James¹*) was born on July 28, 1907, in Harrison Twp., Champaign Co., Ohio.[219] He was the son of Harley Milton Terrell and Bertha Pearl Loffer (25). He was living in 1974 in Springhills, Harrison Twp., Champaign Co., Ohio. Virgil Milton died in a hospital in Bellefontaine, Lake Twp., Logan Co., Ohio, on December 27, 1974, at age 67.[220, 221] He was buried in Spring Hills Presbyterian Church Cemetery, Springhills, Harrison Twp., Champaign Co., Ohio.[339]

Virgil Milton married **Ruth Elene Anderson** on November 8, 1933, in Wayne Co., Indiana.[221, 340, 341] They had one daughter. Ruth Elene Anderson was born in Terre Haute, Harrison Twp., Vigo Co., Indiana, on September 8, 1908.[342] Ruth Elene reached age 32 and died in a hospital in Bellefontaine, Lake Twp., Logan Co., Ohio, on January 19, 1941.[342] She was buried in Spring Hills Presbyterian Church Cemetery, Springhills, Harrison Twp., Champaign Co., Ohio.[342, 343]

When she married Virgil Terrell in 1933, Ruth Elene lived in Reelsville, Washington Twp., Putnam Co., Indiana.[341]

In 1940, Virgil Terrell is enumerated in Springhills, Harrison Twp., Champaign Co., Ohio *(Census Place: Springhills, Champaign, Ohio; Roll: T627_3037; Page: 2A; Enumeration District: 11-5)*. Virgil Terrell, age 32, is a farmer who was born in Ohio. His wife, Ruth Anderson Terrell is 31 years old and born in Indiana. They have a daughter, Marilyn ("Marlyn"), age two, born Ohio. Virgil and Ruth say they were both living in Springhills in 1935.

Widower Virgil Milton Terrell married Mrs. **Georgia Mae Jones** Howell on December 29, 1956, in Wayne Co., Indiana.[344] They divorced. Georgia Mae Jones was born in Logansville, Pleasant Twp., Logan Co., Ohio, on May 25, 1903.[80, 344] She died on October 30, 1978 in a hospital in Marion, Center Twp., Grant Co., Indiana.[345] Georgia May was buried in Park Cemetery, Fairmount, Fairmount Twp., Grant Co., Indiana.[345, 346]

She was married to Virgil Terrell as Georgia Mae Jones. After she and Virgil divorced, she restored her first married name and as Georgia Mae Howell.

Daughter of Virgil Milton Terrell and Ruth Elene Anderson:

+ 82 f I. **Marilyn Kay**[10] **Terrell** was born in Springhills, Harrison Twp., Champaign Co., Ohio, on May 4, 1937.[347]

44. Damon Eugene[9] **Terrell** (*Bertha Pearl*[8] *Loffer, Bertha*[7] *Wolfe, Phebe Ann*[6] *Pegan, Elsey*[5]*, Robert A.*[4]*, Andrew*[3]*, Andrew*[2] *Pagan, James*[1]) was born on July 17, 1910, in Harrison Twp., Champaign Co., Ohio.[80, 222] He was the son of Harley Milton Terrell and Bertha Pearl Loffer (25). He was living in 1983 in Conover, Brown Twp., Miami Co., Ohio. DDamon Eugene died in a facility in Urbana, Urbana Twp., Champaign Co., Ohio, on November 24, 1983, at age 73.[223, 224] He was buried in Rosedale Cemetery, Conover, Brown Twp., Miami Co., Ohio.[224, 348]

Damon Eugene married **Mary Virginia Bailar** on January 28, 1934, in Champaign Co., Ohio.[349] They had four children. Mary Virginia Bailar was born in Adams Twp., Champaign Co., Ohio, on May 30, 1914.[80, 350] Mary Virginia reached age 81 and died in Urbana, Urbana Twp., Champaign Co., Ohio, on July 31, 1995.[350, 351] She was buried in Rosedale Cemetery, Conover, Brown Twp., Miami Co., Ohio.[351, 352]

In 1940, Damon Terrell is enumerated in Rosewood, Adams Twp., Champaign Co., Ohio *(Census Place: Adams, Champaign, Ohio; Roll: T627_3037; Page: 12B; Enumeration District: 11-1)*. Damon Terrell, age 29, is a carpenter. His wife, Mary Virginia Bailor Terrell is 25 years old. They have two daughters, Barbara Lee, five, and Beverly Sue, two. All in the home were born in Ohio. Damon and Mary Virginia Bailor Terrell say they were living in Clark County, Ohio in 1935.

Children of Damon Eugene Terrell and Mary Virginia Bailar:

+ 83 f I. **Barbara Lee**[10] **Terrell** was born in Rosewood, Adams Twp., Champaign Co., Ohio, on March 3, 1935.[353]

+ 84 f II. **Beverly Sue**[10] **Terrell** was born in Rosewood, Adams Twp., Champaign Co., Ohio, on May 13, 1937.[354] She is also known as **Sue**.

+ 85 f III. **Daughter**[10] **Terrell** was born in Rosewood, Adams Twp., Champaign Co., Ohio.

+	86	m IV.	**Thomas Eugene**[10] **Terrell** was born in Bellefontaine, Lake Twp., Logan Co., Ohio, on February 21, 1947.[355] He died in a hospital in Urbana, Urbana Twp., Champaign Co., Ohio, on November 17, 2016, at age 69.[356]

45. Gaylord Philip[9] **Terrell** (*Bertha Pearl*[8] *Loffer, Bertha*[7] *Wolfe, Phebe Ann*[6] *Pegan, Elsey*[5]*, Robert A.*[4]*, Andrew*[3]*, Andrew*[2] *Pagan, James*[1]) was born on December 4, 1914, in Harrison Twp., Champaign Co.,Ohio.[80, 225] He was also known as **Pip**. He was the son of Harley Milton Terrell and Bertha Pearl Loffer (25). Gaylord P. died in Urbana, Urbana Twp., Champaign Co., Ohio, on July 22, 1984, at age 69.[80, 225, 357] He was buried in Terre Haute Cemetery, Mad River Twp., Champaign Co., Ohio.[358]

Gaylord P. married **Betty M. Evilsizor** on June 12, 1937? They had four children. Betty M. Evilsizor was born in Jackson Twp., Champaign Co., Ohio, on February 22, 1920.[80, 359, 360] Betty M. reached age 84 and died in Urbana, Urbana Twp., Champaign Co., Illinois, on November 27, 2004.[80, 359, 360] She was buried in Terre Haute Cemetery, Mad River Twp., Champaign Co., Ohio.[361]

In 1940, Gaylord P. Terrell is enumerated in Rosewood, Adams Twp., Champaign Co., Ohio *(Census Place: Adams, Champaign, Ohio; Roll: T627_3037; Page: 12B; Enumeration District: 11-1)*. In the household are Gaylord P. Terrell, age 25, a truck driver for Clark feed mill; his wife, Betty Evilsizor Terrell, 20, and their daughter Nancy Ann, two. All were born in Ohio, and Gaylord and Betty say they were residents of Champaign Co., Ohio in 1935. There is no street or numerical address listed.

Gaylord Philip Terrell and Betty M. Evilsizor had four children, including:

+	87	f I.	**Nancy Ann**[10] **Terrell** was born in Rosewood, Adams Twp., Champaign Co., Ohio, on December 22, 1937.[362]

46. Garnet Lucille[9] **Terrell** (*Bertha Pearl*[8] *Loffer, Bertha*[7] *Wolfe, Phebe Ann*[6] *Pegan, Elsey*[5]*, Robert A.*[4]*, Andrew*[3]*, Andrew*[2] *Pagan, James*[1]) was born on May 18, 1917, in Harrison Twp., Champaign Co., Ohio.[80, 226, 227] She was the daughter of Harley Milton Terrell and Bertha Pearl Loffer (25). Garnet Lucille died in Urbana, Urbana Twp., Champaign Co., Ohio, on September 1, 1993, at age 76.[80, 226, 227] She was buried in Spring Grove Cemetery, Saint Paris, Johnson Twp., Champaign Co., Ohio.[363]

Childless.

Garnet Lucille married **Garner Smith Calland** on June 12, 1937, in Maysville, Mason Co., Kentucky.[364] Garner Smith Calland was born in Adams Twp., Champaign Co., Ohio, on May 5, 1911.[80, 365] Garner Smith reached age 75 and died in DeGraff, Miami Twp., Logan Co., Ohio, on November 12, 1986.[365, 366] He was buried in Spring Grove Cemetery, Saint Paris, Johnson Twp., Champaign Co., Ohio.[367]

In 1940, Garner and Garnet Calland are enumerated in Adams Twp., Champaign Co., Ohio *(Census Place: Adams, Champaign, Ohio; Roll: T627_3037; Page: 3A; Enumeration District: 11-1)*. In the household are Garner Calland, age 28, a farmer, and his wife Garnet Terrell Calland, 22. Both were born in Ohio and say they were living in Champaign County in 1935. Although their home is in Champaign County, it is very near DeGraff, Miami Twp., Logan Co., Ohio, as their address is at the intersection of Saint Paris R-1 and RFD #2 DeGraff.

47. Harold Reginold[9] **Terrell** (*Bertha Pearl*[8] *Loffer, Bertha*[7] *Wolfe, Phebe Ann*[6] *Pegan, Elsey*[5]*, Robert A.*[4]*, Andrew*[3]*, Andrew*[2] *Pagan, James*[1]) was born on September 11, 1919, in Harrison Twp., Champaign Co., Ohio.[228] He was the son of Harley Milton Terrell and Bertha Pearl Loffer (25). Harold Reginold died in Harrison Twp., Champaign Co., Ohio, on July 28, 1929, at age nine.[228] He was buried in Spring Hills Presbyterian Church Cemetery, Springhills, Harrison Twp., Champaign Co., Ohio.[228, 368]

48. Elizabeth Laverne Ellen[9] **Shaffer** (*Lola*[8] *Loffer, Bertha*[7] *Wolfe, Phebe Ann*[6] *Pegan, Elsey*[5]*, Robert A.*[4]*, Andrew*[3]*, Andrew*[2] *Pagan, James*[1]) was born on March 6, 1910, in Cleveland, Cuyahoga Co.,

Ohio.[80, 237, 238] She was also known as **Betty**. She was the daughter of Welcome Wallace Shaffer and Lola Loffer (26). Elizabeth Laverne Ellen died in Fremont, Sandusky Co., Ohio, on November 27, 1995, at age 85.[237, 238] She was buried in Oakwood Cemetery, Fremont, Sandusky Co., Ohio.[238, 369]

Childless.

Elizabeth Laverne Ellen married **Lawrence Shafer Sentman** on November 9, 1963, in Steuben Co., Indiana.[238, 370] Lawrence Shafer Sentman was born in Mohall, Renville Co., North Dakota, on October 19, 1908.[371, 372] Lawrence Shafer reached age 86 and died in Fremont, Sandusky Co., Ohio, on March 30, 1995.[371, 372] He was buried in Oakwood Cemetery, Fremont, Sandusky Co., Ohio.[372, 373]

49. William Eugene⁹ Loffer (*Harold J.⁸, Bertha⁷ Wolfe, Phebe Ann⁶ Pegan, Elsey⁵, Robert A.⁴, Andrew³, Andrew² Pagan, James¹*) was born on April 8, 1922, in Sandusky, Erie Co., Ohio.[80, 243, 244] He was the son of Harold J. Loffer (27) and Wilma O. Walborn. William Eugene lived in 1995 in Niles, Niles Twp., Trumbull Co., Ohio. He died in Temple Terrace, Hillsborough Co., Florida, on February 18, 2011, at age 88.[80, 244] William Eugene was buried in McMillen Cemetery, Huron, Huron Twp., Erie Co., Ohio.[374]

Widower William Eugene Loffer married **Elizabeth Catherine A. Christy** on September 5, 1942, in Fulton Co., Ohio.[375] They had two children. Elizabeth Catherine A. Christy was born in West Frankfort, Frankfort Twp., Franklin Co., Illinois, on November 27, 1919.[375, 376, 377] She was also known as **Betty**. Elizabeth Catherine A. lived in 1995 in Niles, Niles Twp., Trumbull Co., Ohio. She reached age 75 and died in a hospital in Warren, Trumbull Co., Ohio, on June 12, 1995.[376, 377] Elizabeth Catherine A. was buried in McMillen Cemetery, Huron, Huron Twp., Erie Co., Ohio.[378]

Elizabeth A. Christy Loffer was named "Cathrin" in the 1920 census, the daughter of Louis and Helen Hovenac Christy who were living in Frankfort Twp., Franklin Co., Illinois (*Census Place: Frankfort, Franklin, Illinois; Roll: T625_365; Page: 16B; Enumeration District: 38*). By 1930, her mother Helen was remarried to Andrew Poskanek and she and her children were living with Andrew in Loraine, Loraine Co., Ohio (*Census Place: Lorain, Lorain, Ohio; Roll: 1830; Page: 21B; Enumeration District: 0024*). This time "Catherine" was listed as "Betty." Her mother's name and her sibling Ethel, found in both entries, confirm that this is the correct Betty Christy. Her obituary further confirms her birthdate and place.[377]

Widower William Eugene Loffer married **Carolyn Allen** on March 24, 1996, in Hillsborough Co., Florida.[379] Carolyn Allen was born in Westerville, Blendon Twp., Franklin Co., Ohio, on October 29, 1922.[380] Carolyn reached age 91 and died in Tampa, Hillsborough Co., Florida, on July 4, 2014.[380]

50. Lola Margaret⁹ Loffer (*Harold J.⁸, Bertha⁷ Wolfe, Phebe Ann⁶ Pegan, Elsey⁵, Robert A.⁴, Andrew³, Andrew² Pagan, James¹*) was born on March 27, 1925, in Sandusky, Erie Co., Ohio.[245] She was also known as **Peggy**. She is the daughter of Harold J. Loffer (27) and Wilma O. Walborn.

Lola Margaret married **Werner Clarence Marquart** on November 14, 1945, in Erie Co., Ohio.[245] They had two sons. Werner Clarence Marquart was born in Sandusky, Erie Co., Ohio, on March 4, 1925.[80, 381, 382] He was also known as **Bud**. Werner Clarence reached age 80 and died in Sandusky, Erie Co., Ohio, on October 3, 2005.[80, 382] He was buried in Oakland Cemetery, Sandusky, Erie Co., Ohio.[383, 384]

51. Donna Jean⁹ Loffer (*Harold J.⁸, Bertha⁷ Wolfe, Phebe Ann⁶ Pegan, Elsey⁵, Robert A.⁴, Andrew³, Andrew² Pagan, James¹*) was born on December 15, 1929, in Sandusky, Erie Co., Ohio.[80, 246, 247] She was the daughter of Harold J. Loffer (27) and Wilma O. Walborn. Donna Jean died in Sandusky, Erie Co., Ohio, on May 31, 2002, at age 72.[80, 246, 247] She was buried in Oakland Cemetery, Sandusky, Erie Co., Ohio.[246, 385]

Donna Jean married **Thomas LaRose** on February 8, 1954, in Erie Co., Ohio.[386] They had two daughters. Thomas LaRose was born in Sandusky, Erie Co., Ohio, on February 23, 1930.

52. Winifred Jane⁹ Shaw (*Frank Herbert⁸, Effie Belle⁷ Wolfe, Phebe Ann⁶ Pegan, Elsey⁵, Robert A.⁴, Andrew³, Andrew² Pagan, James¹*) was born on April 25, 1920, in Bowling Green, Wood Co., Ohio.[80, 251] She was the daughter of Frank Herbert Shaw (28) and Marguerite Crocker. Winifred Jane died in Tempe, Maricopa Co., Arizona, on March 12, 2006, at age 85.[80, 251] She was buried in Resthaven Park East Cemetery, Phoenix, Maricopa Co., Arizona.[387]

Winifred Jane Shaw Puse preferred to use her middle name, Jane, as her given name. Her Social Security Death Index listing is under "W. J. Puse".[80]

Winifred Jane married **Ervin Charles Puse** before 1945. They had two daughters. Ervin Charles Puse was born in Millbury, Lake Twp., Wood Co., Ohio, on August 19, 1915.[80, 388] He was also known as **Ernie**. Ervin Charles reached age 86 and died in Tempe, Maricopa Co., Arizona, on November 23, 2001.[80, 388] He was buried in Resthaven Park East Cemetery, Phoenix, Maricopa Co., Arizona.[389]

53. **John Crocker**[9] **Shaw** (*Frank Herbert*[8], *Effie Belle*[7] *Wolfe, Phebe Ann*[6] *Pegan, Elsey*[5], *Robert A.*[4], *Andrew*[3], *Andrew*[2] *Pagan, James*[1]) was born on October 10, 1935, in Fostoria, Seneca Co., Ohio.[80, 252, 253] He was the son of Frank Herbert Shaw (28) and Marguerite Crocker. John Crocker died in Phoenix, Maricopa Co., Arizona, on January 18, 2004, at age 68.[80, 253]

John Crocker married **Kay Marie Denison** about November 15, 1959 in Maricopa Co., Arizona.[390] Kay Marie Denison was born in Bayfield, La Plata Co., Colorado, on October 10, 1938.

54. **William**[9] **Shaw II** (*William Russell*[8], *Effie Belle*[7] *Wolfe, Phebe Ann*[6] *Pegan, Elsey*[5], *Robert A.*[4], *Andrew*[3], *Andrew*[2] *Pagan, James*[1]) was born on May 31, 1928, in Fostoria, Seneca Co., Ohio.[258] He is the son of William Russell Shaw (29) and Catherine Marguerite Murphy.

55. **Blair**[9] **Shaw** (*William Russell*[8], *Effie Belle*[7] *Wolfe, Phebe Ann*[6] *Pegan, Elsey*[5], *Robert A.*[4], *Andrew*[3], *Andrew*[2] *Pagan, James*[1]) was born on March 1, 1930, in Fostoria, Seneca Co., Ohio.[259, 241] He was the son of William Russell Shaw (29) and Catherine Marguerite Murphy. Blair died in Fostoria, Seneca Co., Ohio, on March 1, 1930.[259] Fountain/Fostoria Cemetery, Fostoria, Washington Twp., Hancock Co., Ohio.[391]

56. **Robert Leonard**[9] **Shaw** (*William Russell*[8], *Effie Belle*[7] *Wolfe, Phebe Ann*[6] *Pegan, Elsey*[5], *Robert A.*[4], *Andrew*[3], *Andrew*[2] *Pagan, James*[1]) was born on July 6, 1931, in Fostoria, Seneca Co., Ohio.[260, 261] He was the son of William Russell Shaw (29) and Catherine Marguerite Murphy. Robert Leonard died in San Rafael, Marin Co., California, on March 9, 1955, at age 23.[260] He was buried in Fountain/Fostoria Cemetery, Fostoria, Washington Twp., Hancock Co., Ohio.[392]

Never married.

Robert L. Shaw was one of eight persons who died in a rooming house fire in San Rafael, California. He was attending college at the time.[393]

57. **Nancy June**[9] **Shaw** (*William Russell*[8], *Effie Belle*[7] *Wolfe, Phebe Ann*[6] *Pegan, Elsey*[5], *Robert A.*[4], *Andrew*[3], *Andrew*[2] *Pagan, James*[1]) was born on July 31, 1937, in Cygnet, Bloom Twp., Wood Co., Ohio. She is the daughter of William Russell Shaw (29) and Catherine Marguerite Murphy.

Nancy June married **Alan Eugene Felix** between 1955 and 1963. They divorced. They had two children. Alan Eugene Felix was born in Toledo, Lucas Co., Ohio, on July 31, 1938.

Nancy June Shaw married **Frank Patrick Rowbottom** on April 17, 1982, in Orange Co., California.[394] They divorced.

58. **Carl Luther**[9] **Shaw** (*William Russell*[8], *Effie Belle*[7] *Wolfe, Phebe Ann*[6] *Pegan, Elsey*[5], *Robert A.*[4], *Andrew*[3], *Andrew*[2] *Pagan, James*[1]) was born on November 23, 1939, in Cygnet, Bloom Twp., Wood Co., Ohio.[80, 262, 263] He was the son of William Russell Shaw (29) and Catherine Marguerite Murphy. Carl Luther died in Fostoria, Seneca Co., Ohio, on August 19, 2005, at age 65.[80, 262]

Carl Luther married **Ms. Barkley**. They divorced. They had four children.

Carl Luther Shaw married Mrs. **Beulah Mae Tracy** Shultz on June 11, 1970, in Seneca Co., Ohio.[263] They divorced. They had no children. Beulah Mae Tracy was born in Baltimore, Baltimore Co., Maryland, on April 2, 1943.[80, 263] She lived about 1993 in Tampa, Hillsborough Co., Florida. Beulah Mae Tracy Shultz Shaw reached age 66 and died in Fostoria, Seneca Co., Ohio, on October 29, 2009.[80]

Carl Luther Shaw married for a third time. He and his third wife had one daughter.

59. **Patricia Ann**[9] **Snyder** (*Edith Laura*[8] *Shaw, Effie Belle*[7] *Wolfe, Phebe Ann*[6] *Pegan, Elsey*[5], *Robert A.*[4], *Andrew*[3], *Andrew*[2] *Pagan, James*[1]) was born on July 21, 1925, in Bowling Green, Center Twp., Wood Co., Ohio.[80, 267] She was the daughter of Charles Henry Snyder and Edith Laura Shaw (30). Patricia Ann lived in 2004 in Madisonville, Hopkins Co., Kentucky. She died in a hospital in Owensboro, Daviess Co., Kentucky, on January 18, 2004, at age 78.[80, 267] She was cremated.[267]

Patricia Ann married **Kermit Eugene Reed** before 1950. They had one son. Kermit Eugene Reed was born in Paulding, Latty Twp., Paulding Co., Ohio, on July 1, 1925.[80, 395] He was also known as **Kert**. Kermit Eugene reached age 85 and died in Madisonville, Hopkins Co., Kentucky, on March 22, 2011.[80, 395] He was cremated.[395]

60. **Diane R.**[9] **Wolfe** (*Hubert Wilder*[8], *Frank L.*[7], *Phebe Ann*[6] *Pegan, Elsey*[5], *Robert A.*[4], *Andrew*[3], *Andrew*[2] *Pagan, James*[1]) was born on February 6, 1934, in Chicago, Cook Co., Illinois.[271] She is the daughter of Hubert Wilder Wolfe (31) and Ruth Victoria Sebastian.

She married **Frederick Penn Westman II**. They divorced. They had three children. Frederick Penn Westman II was born in Milton, Norfolk Co., Massachusetts, on February 24, 1931.

61. **Doris Jeannette**[9] **Booze** (*Kenneth Vernon (Wolfe)*[8], *Guy Ernest*[7] *Wolfe, Phebe Ann*[6] *Pegan, Elsey*[5], *Robert A.*[4], *Andrew*[3], *Andrew*[2] *Pagan, James*[1]) was born on January 2, 1919, in Fremont, Sandusky Co., Ohio.[80, 282, 283, 284] She was also known as **Dodie**. She was the daughter of Kenneth Vernon (Wolfe) Booze (35) and Iva Elizabeth Hufford.

Doris Jeannette also resided in 1970 in Huntington Beach, Orange Co., California. She was living in 1973 in Sun City, Maricopa Co., Arizona. Doris Jeannette lived in 1981 in Huntington Beach, Orange Co., California. She died in Sun City, Maricopa Co., Arizona, on November 17, 1997, at age 78.[80, 283]

Doris Booze, age 21, is living with her father and stepmother, Kenneth and (Virginia) Pearl Kirtley McCarthy Booze, in 1940 in Fremont, Sandusky Co., Ohio *(Census Place: Fremont, Sandusky, Ohio; Roll: T627_3139; Page: 10B; Enumeration District: 72-15)*. Doris lists her occupation as office attendant. The head of the household, Kenneth Booze, says he is 44(?), and a drapery salesman ("salesman, drapes"). (Virginia) Pearl Kirtley McCarthy Booze is 42 years old. Also in the home are "Pearl's" two children, June and Robert McCarthy, ages 15 and 14 respectively. All were born in Ohio. Kenneth and Doris Booze say they were living in Sandusky County in 1935, while "Pearl" and her children were in "Mt. Vernon, Ohio" then. Their house address is 1123 1/2 Croghau Street.

Doris Jeannette married **Robert Staples Prario** in 1943 in Marshfield, Plymouth Co., Massachusetts.[396] They divorced. They had four children. Robert Staples Prario was born in Lexington, Middlesex Co., Massachusetts, on September 15, 1917.[80, 397, 398] He reached age 86 and died in Alpine, San Diego Co., California, on December 8, 2003.[80, 399] Robert Staples was buried in Fort Rosencrans National Military Cemetery, San Diego, San Diego Co., California.[399, 400]

Dr. Robert Staples Prario, D.D.S. was a dentist.

Doris Jeannette Booze Prario married **William Russell Cummings** on August 3, 1963, in San Diego, San Diego Co., California.[401] They divorced. William Russell Cummings was born in Baden, Beaver Co., Pennsylvania, on May 2, 1924.[402]

Doris J. "Dodie" Booze Prario Cummings was an aviatrix and a member of the Ninety-Nines ("99'ers"), an association for women airplane pilots established in 1929. She flew cross-country in the "Powder Puff Derby" twice after WWII.[283]

Doris Jeannette Booze and Robert Staples Prario had four children, including:

+ 125 f II. **Infant Daughter**[10] **Prario** was born in San Diego, San Diego Co., California, on March 27, 1949.[403] She died in San Diego, San Diego Co., California, on March 27, 1949.[404]

62. Kenneth E.[9] Booze (Werner) (*Kenneth Vernon (Wolfe)[8] Booze, Guy Ernest[7] Wolfe, Phebe Ann[6] Pegan, Elsey[5], Robert A.[4], Andrew[3], Andrew[2] Pagan, James[1]*) was born on March 10, 1925, in Fremont, Sandusky Co., Ohio.[80, 285] He was the son of Kenneth Vernon (Wolfe) Booze (35) and Iva Elizabeth Hufford. Kenneth E. Booze died in Phoenix, Maricopa Co., Arizona, on January 3, 2001, at age 75.[80, 285] He was buried in National Memorial Cemetery of Arizona, Phoenix, Maricopa Co., Arizona.[405, 406]

Kenneth E. Booze married **Rita Marie Russo** on September 10, 1950, in Erie Co., Ohio.[407] They divorced. They had three children. Rita Marie Russo was born in Sandusky, Erie Co., Ohio, on June 7, 1928.[408, 409] Rita Marie reached age 62 and died in Sandusky, Erie Co., Ohio, on November 7, 1990.[410] She was buried in Calvary Cemetery, Sandusky, Erie Co., Ohio.[411]

Kenneth Eugene (Booze) Werner was the son of Kenneth V. Booze and his first wife, Iva Huffer Booze (later Werner). According to a legal notice in the July 6, 1946 edition of the Sandusky Register (Sandusky, OH), Kenneth Eugene Booze, then 21 years old, was to petition the Erie County, Ohio Probate Court on August 12, 1946 to change his name to Kenneth Eugene Werner.[412] But it is not known if he was ever legally adopted by his stepfather, Webster Werner, Iva's second husband.[413] Kenneth E. Booze lived in Tennessee in the 1970s and in Pittsford and Rochester, Monroe Co., New York in the 1980s. He removed to Cortland, Cortland Co., New York in the 1990s before retiring to Phoenix.

63. Robert Roe[9] Wolfe (*Kenneth William[8], Guy Ernest[7], Phebe Ann[6] Pegan, Elsey[5], Robert A.[4], Andrew[3], Andrew[2] Pagan, James[1]*) was born on March 18, 1931, in Minneapolis, Hennepin Co., Minnesota.[290] He is the son of Kenneth William Wolfe (33) and Mary Alice Light.

Robert Roe married Mrs. **Betty Lou Stephan** Autry on July 16, 1955, in Hennepin Co., Minnesota.[414] They divorced. They had two children. Betty Lou Stephan was born in Winona Co., Minnesota, on February 25, 1936.[415]

Robert Roe Wolfe married **Sharon Katherine Goggin** on April 9, 1966, in Hennepin Co., Minnesota.[416, 417] They had one daughter. Sharon Katherine Goggin was born in St. Louis Park, Hennepin Co., Minnesota, on April 23, 1944.[418] Sharon Katherine reached age 65 and died in St. Louis Park, Hennepin Co., Minnesota, on December 21, 2009.[80]

64. Sharon Kay[9] Wolfe (*Kenneth William[8], Guy Ernest[7], Phebe Ann[6] Pegan, Elsey[5], Robert A.[4], Andrew[3], Andrew[2] Pagan, James[1]*) was born on April 15, 1935, in Minneapolis, Hennepin Co., Minnesota.[291] She is the daughter of Kenneth William Wolfe (33) and Mary Alice Light.

Sharon Kay married **Robert George Ondich** on July 1, 1956, in Hennepin Co., Minnesota.[419, 420] They had two children. Robert George Ondich was born in Minneapolis, Hennepin Co., Minnesota, on April 10, 1935.[421]

10th Generation

73. Patricia Ann[10] **Smith** (*Armintha Euphema Almack*[9] *(Shultz), Armintha*[8] *Shultz, Ola*[7] *Greenawalt, Sarah Jane*[6] *Pegan, Elsey*[5]*, Robert A.*[4]*, Andrew*[3]*, Andrew*[2] *Pagan, James*[1]) was born on February 21, 1950, in Anderson, Anderson Twp., Madison Co., Indiana.[302, 303, 304, 305] She was the daughter of Alva Jack Smith and Armintha Euphema Almack (Shultz) (36). Patricia Ann died in Anderson, Anderson Twp., Madison Co., Indiana, on December 22, 1954, at age four.[302, 303, 305] She was buried in Anderson Memorial Park Cemetery, Anderson, Anderson Twp., Madison Co., Indiana.[302, 303, 305, 422]

80. Richard Eugene[10] **Mohr** (*Thelma Marie*[9] *Terrell, Bertha Pearl*[8] *Loffer, Bertha*[7] *Wolfe, Phebe Ann*[6] *Pegan, Elsey*[5]*, Robert A.*[4]*, Andrew*[3]*, Andrew*[2] *Pagan, James*[1]) was born on May 22, 1928, in Mechanicsburg, Goshen Twp., Champaign Co., Ohio.[80, 336] He was the son of Harry Fulwider Mohr and Thelma Marie Terrell (42). Richard Eugene died in a hospital in Urbana, Urbana Twp., Champaign Co., Ohio, on September 25, 1983, at age 55.[336, 337] He was buried in Maple Grove Cemetery, Mechanicsburg, Goshen Twp., Champaign Co., Ohio.[336, 423]

Richard Eugene married **Louise Irma Pitzer** on June 15, 1952, in Champaign Co., Ohio.[424] They had four children. Louise Irma Pitzer was born in Mechanicsburg, Goshen Twp., Champaign Co., Ohio, on May 27, 1927.[425]

Richard Eugene Mohr and Louise Irma Pitzer had four children, including:

+ 140 f I. **Diane Louise**[11] **Mohr** was born in Urbana, Urbana Twp., Champaign Co., Ohio, on July 20, 1956.[426] She died in a hospital in Columbus, Franklin Co., Ohio, on March 2, 2012, at age 55.[426]

81. Harry James[10] **Mohr II** (*Thelma Marie*[9] *Terrell, Bertha Pearl*[8] *Loffer, Bertha*[7] *Wolfe, Phebe Ann*[6] *Pegan, Elsey*[5]*, Robert A.*[4]*, Andrew*[3]*, Andrew*[2] *Pagan, James*[1]) was born on May 8, 1933, in Mechanicsburg, Goshen Twp., Champaign Co., Ohio.[338] He is also known as **James**. He is the son of Harry Fulwider Mohr and Thelma Marie Terrell (42). Harry James lived in Milford Center, Union Co., Ohio.

Harry James married **Marlene E. Thiergartner** about 1956. They had two sons. Marlene E. Thiergartner was born in Union Twp., Union Co., Ohio, on June 15, 1934.

82. Marilyn Kay[10] **Terrell** (*Virgil Milton*[9]*, Bertha Pearl*[8] *Loffer, Bertha*[7] *Wolfe, Phebe Ann*[6] *Pegan, Elsey*[5]*, Robert A.*[4]*, Andrew*[3]*, Andrew*[2] *Pagan, James*[1]) was born on May 4, 1937, in Springhills, Harrison Twp., Champaign Co., Ohio.[347] She is the daughter of Virgil Milton Terrell (43) and Ruth Elene Anderson.

Marilyn Kay Terrell married **Alfred Lee Jones** on July 31, 1954, in Union Co., Indiana.[427] They had three children. Alfred Lee Jones was born in DeGraff, Miami Twp., Logan Co., Ohio, on May 21, 1934.[80, 427, 428, 429] He was also known as **Lee**. He reached age 59 and died in a hospital in Columbus, Franklin Co., Ohio, on October 20, 1993.[80, 429] Alfred Lee was buried in Greenwood Cemetery, DeGraff, Pleasant Twp., Logan Co., Ohio.[430]

Marilyn Kay Terrell Jones married **John R. Watt** on August 14, 1999, in Logan Co., Ohio.[431] John R. Watt was born in Charleston, Kanawha Co., West Virginia, on May 22, 1939.[80] John R. reached age 73 and died in Leesburg, Lake Co., Florida, on April 17, 2013.[80, 432] He was buried in Highland Cemetery, West Liberty, Liberty Twp., Logan Co., Ohio.[433]

83. Barbara Lee[10] **Terrell** (*Damon Eugene*[9]*, Bertha Pearl*[8] *Loffer, Bertha*[7] *Wolfe, Phebe Ann*[6] *Pegan, Elsey*[5]*, Robert A.*[4]*, Andrew*[3]*, Andrew*[2] *Pagan, James*[1]) was born on March 3, 1935, in Rosewood, Adams Twp., Champaign Co., Ohio.[353] She is the daughter of Damon Eugene Terrell (44) and Mary Virginia Bailar.

Barbara Lee married **James Edward Oelker** on March 17, 1956, in Champaign Co., Ohio.[434] They had three children. James Edward Oelker was born in Urbana, Urbana Twp., Champaign Co., Ohio, on August 10, 1931.

Barbara Lee Terrell and James Edward Oelker had two children, including:

+ 151 f   II. **Jill Elaine**[11] **Oelker** was born in Urbana, Urbana Twp., Champaign Co., Ohio, on November 1, 1959.[80, 435, 436, 437] She died in Urbana, Urbana Twp., Champaign Co., Ohio, on July 9, 1996.[80, 436, 437]

84. **Beverly Sue**[10] **Terrell** (*Damon Eugene*[9], *Bertha Pearl*[8] *Loffer, Bertha*[7] *Wolfe, Phebe Ann*[6] *Pegan, Elsey*[5], *Robert A.*[4], *Andrew*[3], *Andrew*[2] *Pagan, James*[1]) was born on May 13, 1937, in Rosewood, Adams Twp., Champaign Co., Ohio.[354] She is also known as **Sue**. She is the daughter of Damon Eugene Terrell (44) and Mary Virginia Bailar.

Beverly Sue married **William Iverson Marsalis** on October 24, 1958, in Champaign Co., Ohio.[438] They had two children. William Iverson Marsalis was born in Findlay, Findlay Twp., Hancock Co., Ohio, on November 21, 1935.[80, 439, 440] He was also known as **Tim**. William Iverson reached age 50 and died in Urbana, Urbana Twp., Champaign Co., Ohio, on April 26, 1986.[441, 442] He was buried in Oak Dale Cemetery, Urbana, Urbana Twp., Champaign Co., Ohio.[443]

Beverly Sue Terrell Marsalis married **Glenn Lawrence Stewart.**

85. **Daughter**[10] **Terrell** (*Damon Eugene*[9], *Bertha Pearl*[8] *Loffer, Bertha*[7] *Wolfe, Phebe Ann*[6] *Pegan, Elsey*[5], *Robert A.*[4], *Andrew*[3], *Andrew*[2] *Pagan, James*[1]) was born in Rosewood, Adams Twp., Champaign Co., Ohio. She is the daughter of Damon Eugene Terrell (44) and Mary Virginia Bailar.

Daughter Terrell married **Mr. Gunsaulies**. They divorced. They had one son.

Daughter Terrell Gunsaulies married **Douglas Edwin Murphy** on July 13, 1985, in Champaign Co., Ohio.[444] They divorced. Douglas Edwin Murphy was born in Springfield, Springfield Twp., Clark Co., Ohio, on September 22, 1942.[80, 445, 446] He reached age 59 and died in Bradenton, Manatee Co., Florida, on December 8, 2001.[80, 446] Douglas Edwin was buried in Pleasant Hill Cemetery, Moorefield Twp., Clark Co., Ohio.[447, 448]

86. **Thomas Eugene**[10] **Terrell** (*Damon Eugene*[9], *Bertha Pearl*[8] *Loffer, Bertha*[7] *Wolfe, Phebe Ann*[6] *Pegan, Elsey*[5], *Robert A.*[4], *Andrew*[3], *Andrew*[2] *Pagan, James*[1]) was born on February 21, 1947, in Bellefontaine, Lake Twp., Logan Co., Ohio.[355] He was the son of Damon Eugene Terrell (44) and Mary Virginia Bailar. Thomas Eugene died in a hospital in Urbana, Urbana Twp., Champaign Co., Ohio, on November 17, 2016, at age 69.[356] He was buried in Oak Dale Cemetery, Urbana, Urbana Twp., Champaign Co., Ohio.[449]

Thomas Eugene Terrell married **Ms. Woods.** They divorced. They had three children.

Thomas Eugene married **Ms. Hall.** They divorced. They had two children.

He lived in Conover, Brown Twp., Miami Co., Ohio; Fishers, Hamilton Co., Indiana; and Apache Junction, Pinal Co., Arizona before returning to Urbana, Urbana Twp., Champaign Co., Ohio.[356]

87. **Nancy Ann**[10] **Terrell** (*Gaylord Philip*[9], *Bertha Pearl*[8] *Loffer, Bertha*[7] *Wolfe, Phebe Ann*[6] *Pegan, Elsey*[5], *Robert A.*[4], *Andrew*[3], *Andrew*[2] *Pagan, James*[1]) was born on December 22, 1937, in Rosewood, Adams Twp., Champaign Co., Ohio.[362] She was the daughter of Gaylord Philip Terrell (45) and Betty M. Evilsizor.

Nancy Ann married **Robert Wayne Trimble** on February 10, 1956, in Champaign Co., Ohio.[450] They divorced. They had one son. Robert Wayne Trimble was born in Paintsville, Johnson Co., Kentucky, on June 15, 1937.

125. **Infant Daughter**[10] **Prario** (*Doris Jeannette*[9] *Booze, Kenneth Vernon (Wolfe)*[8], *Guy Ernest*[7] *Wolfe, Phebe Ann*[6] *Pegan, Elsey*[5], *Robert A.*[4], *Andrew*[3], *Andrew*[2] *Pagan, James*[1]) was born on March 27, 1949, in San Diego, San Diego Co., California.[403] She was the daughter of Robert Staples Prario and Doris Jeannette Booze (61). Infant Daughter Prario died in San Diego, San Diego Co., California, on March 27, 1949.[404]

11th Generation

140. Diane Louise[11] Mohr (*Richard Eugene[10], Thelma Marie[9] Terrell, Bertha Pearl[8] Loffer, Bertha[7] Wolfe, Phebe Ann[6] Pegan, Elsey[5], Robert A.[4], Andrew[3], Andrew[2] Pagan, James[1]*) was born on July 20, 1956, in Urbana, Urbana Twp., Champaign Co., Ohio.[426] She was the daughter of Richard Eugene Mohr (80) and Louise Irma Pitzer. Diane Louise lived in 1983 in Columbus, Franklin Co., Ohio. She died in a hospital in Columbus, Franklin Co., Ohio, on March 2, 2012, at age 55.[426] Diane Louise was buried in Maple Grove Cemetery, Mechanicsburg, Goshen Twp., Champaign Co., Ohio.[426, 451]

Never married.

151. Jill Elaine[11] Oelker (*Barbara Lee[10] Terrell, Damon Eugene[9], Bertha Pearl[8] Loffer, Bertha[7] Wolfe, Phebe Ann[6] Pegan, Elsey[5], Robert A.[4], Andrew[3], Andrew[2] Pagan, James[1]*) was born on November 1, 1959, in Urbana, Urbana Twp., Champaign Co., Ohio.[80, 435, 436, 437] She was the daughter of James Edward Oelker and Barbara Lee Terrell (83). Jill Elaine lived in 1996 in Spartanburg, Spartenburg Co., South Carolina. She died in Urbana, Urbana Twp., Champaign Co., Ohio, on July 9, 1996, at age 36.[80, 436, 437] Jill Elaine was buried in Kings Creek Baptist Church Cemetery, Kings Creek, Salem Twp., Champaign Co., Ohio.[452]

Never married.

Endnotes

1. Family Data: Robert and Christina "Engle" Pegan family bible, American Bible Society, Brattleboro(ugh), Vermont: Holbrook & Fessenden, 1828. In possession of the author, Ann Miller Carr.

2. Elsey Pagan/Pegan tombstone, Greenwood Cemetery, Pleasant Twp., Logan Co., Ohio.

3. Obituary of Elsey Pegan (Bellefontaine, Ohio, Bellefontaine Republican, 26 Jun 1857), Logan County, Ohio Genealogical Library, 513 East Columbus Avenue, Bellefontaine, OH.

4. Find A Grave—Greenwood Cemetery, DeGraff, Pleasant Twp., Logan Co., Ohio, Find A Grave.com, Elsey Pegan, Find A Grave Memorial #18416894.

5. "James R. Pagin," *History of Porter County, Indiana: A Narrative History of its Progress, its People and Principal Interests.* Chicago: Lewis Publishing Co.; 1912, pg. 692. Genealogy Center, Allen County Library, 900 Library Plaza, Fort Wayne, IN.

6. Gilbert, Audrey, *Twin Valley Tidbits, 1888-1897, Vol. 3.* New Alexandria, Ohio: A. Gilbert; 1999, pg. 72. Lynchburg Public Library, 102 Main Street, Lynchburg, OH.

7. Ohio, County Marriages, 1789-2013, FamilySearch.org, "Eliza" Pegan and Mary Moore, Clermont County, Ohio Marriage Records, Vol. 3, pg. 30.

8. Find A Grave—Greenwood Cemetery, DeGraff, Pleasant Twp., Logan Co., Ohio, Find A Grave.com, Mary Pegan, Find A Grave Memorial #18416905.

9. Miami County, Ohio Deeds, James and Minerva McKinney to "Elzy" Pegan (30 Apr 1845), Deed Book, 22: 263. Miami County Recorder's Office, 201 West Main Street, Troy, OH.

10. Ohio Death Certificate, Ohio Department of Health, Center for Vital and Health Statistics, 246 North High Street, Columbus, OH, Francis Pegan, #76665.

11. Ohio Death Certificate, Ohio Department of Health, Center for Vital and Health Statistics, 246 North High Street, Columbus, OH, Josephine Noble, death cert. #45889.

12. Madison County, Indiana Death Certificate, Madison County, Indiana Health Department, 206 East 9th Street, Anderson, IN, Sarah J. "Greenwalt", Madison County Deaths, Book 2CH8, pg. 82.

13. Indiana, Death Certificates, 1899-2011, Ancestry.com, Sarah Jane Greenwalt, death cert. #18752.

14. Obituary of Sarah J. "Greenwalt" (Anderson, Indiana, Anderson Daily Bulletin, 01 Jul 1922), Indiana Room, Anderson Public Library, 111 East 12th Street, Anderson, IN.

15. Find A Grave—Greenwood Cemetery, DeGraff, Pleasant Twp., Logan Co., Ohio, Find A Grave.com, Phebe A. Wolfe, Find A Grave Memorial #18884299.

16. Ohio, County Death Records, 1840-2001, FamilySearch.org, Phebe Wolfe, Logan County Deaths, Vol. 2, pg. 410.

17. U.S. Federal Census Mortality Schedules, 1850-1885, Ancestry.com, "Elsy" Pegan, Washington Twp., Miami Co., Ohio, ID #197_258006.

18. Ohio Death Certificate, Ohio Department of Health, Center for Vital and Health Statistics, 246 North High Street, Columbus, OH, Laura Bell Walker, death cert. #18431.

19. Obituary of Frank Pegan (Bellefontaine, Ohio, Bellefontaine Examiner, 21 Dec 1920) Logan County Libraries, Knowlton Library, 220 North Main Street, Bellefontaine, OH.

20. Logan County, Ohio Marriage Records, Logan County Probate Court, Logan County Courthouse, 140 West Main Street, Bellefontaine, OH, Francis M. Pegan and Rebecca J. Vankirk, Logan County, Ohio Marriage Records, Vol. C, pg. 410.

21. Ohio Death Certificate, Ohio Department of Health, Center for Vital and Health Statistics, 246 North High Street, Columbus, OH, Rebecca J. Pegan, #32717.

22. Obituary of Mrs. F.M. Pegan (DeGraff, Ohio, DeGraff Journal, 26 May 1916) Ohio History Center Archives and Library, Ohio History Center, 800 East 17th Avenue, Columbus, OH.

23. Obituary of Mrs. Josie Noble (Bellefontaine, Ohio, Bellefontaine Examiner, 10 Aug 1914), Logan Co., Ohio Public Libraries, Knowlton Library, 220 North Main Street, Bellefontaine, OH.

24. Ohio Marriages, 1800-1958, FamilySearch.org, George "W. Lain" and Josephine "Pegrain", Logan County, Ohio Marriage Records, Vol. C., pg. 315, lic. #930.

25. Logan County, Ohio Marriage Records, Logan County Probate Court, Logan County Courthouse, 140 West Main Street, Bellefontaine, OH, George "W. Lain" and Josephine Pegan, Logan County, Ohio Marriage Records, Vol. C., pg. 315, lic. #930.

26. Find A Grave—Greenwood Cemetery, DeGraff, Pleasant Twp., Logan Co., Ohio, Find A Grave.com, Gertrude Russell, Find A Grave Memorial #18525400.

27. Ohio, County Death Records, 1840-2001, FamilySearch.org, George "W." Lane, Logan Co., Deaths, Vol. 1, pg. 100.

28. U.S. Civil War Draft Registration Records, 1863-1865, Ancestry.com, George Lane, Pleasant Twp., Logan Co., Ohio.

29. Ohio, County Marriages, 1789-2013, FamilySearch.org, Alexander Noble and "Josephene" Lane, Greene County, Ohio Marriage Records, Vol. 6, pg. 144.

30. U.S. Civil War Pension, Widow's Pension, Josephine Noble, Application #433.856, Certificate #354.717, National Archives and Records Administration (NARA), Washington, DC.

31. Obituary of Alex Noble (Hillsboro, OH, Hillsboro News Herald, 19 Jan 1888), Ohio History Center Archives and Library, Ohio History Center, 800 East 17th Avenue, Columbus, OH.

32 U.S., Indexed County Land Ownership Maps, 1860-1919, Ancestry.com, A. Noble, Union Twp., Highland Co., Ohio.

33 1890 Veterans Schedule, Josephine Noble, Springfield, Clark, Ohio; Roll: 63; Page: 4; Enumeration District: 63. Ancestry.com, The National Archives at Washington, D.C.; Washington, D.C.; Special Schedules of the Eleventh Census (1890) Enumerating Union Veterans and Widows of Union Veterans of the Civil War; Series Number: *M123*; Record Group Title: Records of the Department of Veterans Affairs; Record Group Number: 15.

34 Obituary of Maude Lane (Bellefontaine, Ohio, Bellefontaine Examiner, 20 Oct 1955), Logan County, Ohio Genealogical Library, 513 East Columbus Avenue, Bellefontaine, OH.

35 Ohio Death Certificate, Ohio Department of Health, Center for Vital and Health Statistics, 246 North High Street, Columbus, OH, Francis E. Noble, #39104.

36 U.S., WWI Draft Registration Cards, 1917-1918, Ancestry.com, Francis Edwin Noble, Toledo, Ohio.

37 Ohio, County Marriages, 1789-2013, FamilySearch.org, Daniel Greenawalt and Sallie Pegan, Logan County, Ohio Marriage Records, Vol. D, pg. 15, lic. #74.

38 Obituary of Mrs. Josie Noble (Bellefontaine, Ohio, Bellefontaine Examiner, 10 Aug 1914), Logan County Libraries, Knowlton Library, 220 North Main Street, Bellefontaine, OH.

39 Find A Grave—Funk Cemetery, Hutchinson, Sewickley Twp., Westmoreland Co., Pennsylvania, Find A Grave.com, D. P. Greenawalt, Find A Grave Memorial #91285902.

40 Interview with Penny Brane Nichols, South Bend, IN, Ann Miller Carr, author, 22 Jul 2011.

41 Madison County, Indiana Death Certificate, Madison County, Indiana Health Department, 206 East 9th Street, Anderson, IN, Ola Shultz, d. 09 Aug 1923, Madison County Deaths, Book 2CH8, pg. 4.

42 Indiana, Death Certificates, 1899-2011, Ancestry.com, Ola Shultz, death cert. #27064.

43 Obituary of Ola Shultz (Anderson, Indiana, Anderson Daily Bulletin, 11 Aug 1923), Anderson Public Library, Anderson Public Library, Indiana Room, 111 East 12th Street, Anderson, Indiana.

44 Madison County, Indiana Death Certificate, Madison County, Indiana Health Department, 206 East 9th Street, Anderson, IN, Clyda Humrickhouse, d. 18 Nov 1935, Madison County Deaths, Book Ch-18, pg. 48.

45 Indiana, Death Certificates, 1899-2011, Ancestry.com, Mrs. Clida (Clyda) Humerickhouse, death cert. #34003.

46 Obituary of Clyda Humerickhouse (Anderson, Indiana, Anderson Daily Bulletin, 19 Nov 1935), Anderson Public Library, Anderson Public Library, Indiana Room, 111 East 12th Street, Anderson, Indiana.

47 Ohio, Births and Christenings Index, 1800-1962, Ancestry.com, Richard P. "Greenewalt".

48 Ohio, County Births, 1841-2003 (County Courthouses), FamilySearch.org, Richard P. Greenewalt, Logan Co., Ohio Birth Record Vol. 1, pg. 314.

49 Ohio, County Death Records, 1840-2001, FamilySearch.org, R.P. Greenawalt, age four, Logan Co., Ohio Death Record, Vol. 1, p. 232 (no exact date, just month and year available).

50 Ohio, County Marriages, 1789-2013, FamilySearch.org, William "Wolfe" and Phebe "Pegram", Logan County, Ohio Marriage Records, Vol. C, pg. 419, lic. #153.

51 Ohio Death Certificate, Ohio Department of Health, Center for Vital and Health Statistics, 246 North High Street, Columbus, OH, William Wolfe, death cert. #63281.

52 Find A Grave—Greenwood Cemetery, DeGraff, Pleasant Twp., Logan Co., Ohio, Find A Grave.com, William P. Wolfe, Find A Grave Memorial #151558061.

53 Ohio, County Marriages, 1789-2013, FamilySearch.org, "William Wolfe and Anna Johnston, Shelby County, Ohio Marriage Records, Vol. 8, pg. 183.

54 Ohio Death Certificate, Ohio Department of Health, Center for Vital and Health Statistics, 246 North High Street, Columbus, OH, Bertha Wolfe Loffer, death cert. #63309.

55 Ohio Death Certificate, Ohio Department of Health, Center for Vital and Health Statistics, 246 North High Street, Columbus, OH, Effie Belle Shaw, death cert. #12484.

56 Ohio, County Births, 1841-2003 (County Courthouses), FamilySearch.org, Frank Wolfe, Logan Co., Ohio Birth Records Vol. 1, pg. 164.

57 Framm Funeral Home Records, Frank Wolfe, Rexburg, Madison Co., Idaho, Framm Funeral Home, 51 North 1st East Rexburg, ID.

58 Obituary of Frank Wolf (sic) (Hiawatha, Kansas, Hiawatha Daily World, 03 Feb 1920), Brown County Genealogical Society, 116 South 7th Street, Hiawatha, KS.

59 Minnesota Death Certificates, Minnesota Death Index, 1908-2002 (Minnesota Historical Society), Ancestry.com, William Roe Wolfe, death cert. 1958-#023252.

60 U.S., WWI Draft Registration Cards, 1917-1918, Ancestry.com, William Roe Wolfe, Pocatello, Bannock Co., Idaho.

61 Ohio, Births and Christenings Index, 1800-1962, Ancestry.com, William Roe Wolfe, Washington Twp., Logan Co., Ohio.

62 Minnesota Historical Society Death Certificates Index (online) (St. Paul, Minnesota, Minnesota Historical Society), William Roe Wolfe, cert.ID #1958-MN-023252 http://people.mnhs.org/dci/Search.cfm.

63 Minnesota Death Certificate, Minnesota Historical Society, 345 Kellogg Boulevard West, St. Paul, MN, Guy Wolfe, death cert. #1946—20021.

64 Minnesota Death Certificates, Minnesota Death Index, 1908-2002, (Minnesota Historical Society), Ancestry.com, Guy Wolfe, death cert. 1946-#020021.

65 Find A Grave—Greenwood Cemetery, DeGraff, Pleasant Twp., Logan Co., Ohio, Find A Grave.com, Laura Oder, Find A Grave Memorial #18416585.

66 Ohio, County Marriages, 1789-2013, FamilySearch.org, Walter A. Oder and Laura Pegan, Logan County, Ohio Marriage Records, Vol. D, pg. 224, lic. #31.

67 Obituary of "Alonzo" Oder (Zanesfield, Ohio, Mad River Blade, 20 Mar 1874), Logan County, Ohio Genealogical Library, 513 East Columbus Avenue, Bellefontaine, OH.

68 Ohio, County Marriages, 1789-2013, FamilySearch.org, John L. Walker and Mrs. Laura "Odor", Logan County, Ohio Marriage Records, Vol. F, pg. 165.

69 U.S. City Directories, 1822-1995, Ancestry.com, Indianapolis, Indiana, 1898, pg. 914, entry for Walker, Laura.

70 Obituary of Mrs. Laura Oder (Bellefontaine, Ohio, Bellefontaine Examiner, 18 Mar 1931). Logan County, Ohio Genealogical Library, 513 East Columbus Avenue, Bellefontaine, OH.

71 1900 United States Federal Census, Ancestry.com, Year: 1900, Census Place: Census Place: Miami, Logan, Ohio; Roll: T623_1294; Page: 9B; Enumeration District: 117, entry for Oder, "Oona"; Noble, Josephine, head of household.

72 Find A Grave—Greenwood Cemetery, DeGraff, Pleasant Twp., Logan Co., Ohio, Find A Grave.com, Lona Oder, Find A Grave Memorial #18416586.

73 Obituary of Onna (Lona) Oder (DeGraff, Ohio, DeGraff Journal, 15 Jun 1900 and 22 Jun 1900), Ohio History Center Archives and Library, Ohio History Center, 800 East 17th Avenue, Columbus, OH.

74 Obituary of Maude Lane (Bellefontaine, Ohio, Bellefontaine Examiner, 20 Oct 1955), Logan County, Ohio Genealogical Library, 513 East Columbus Avenue, Bellefontaine, OH.

75 Ohio, County Marriages, 1789-2013, FamilySearch.org, C.S. Shultz and Ola Greenawalt, Logan County, Ohio Marriage Records, Vol. G, pg. 45.

76 Obituary of Charles Shultz (Alexandria, Indiana, Alexandria Times, 26 Sep 1916), Indiana State Library, 315 West Ohio Street, Indianapolis, IN.

77 Indiana, Death Certificates, 1899-2011, Ancestry.com, Charles S. Shultz, death cert. #229.

78 Madison County, Indiana Death Certificate, Madison County, Indiana Health Department, 206 East 9th Street, Anderson, IN, Charles S. Shultz, Madison County Deaths, Book 2CH-8, pg. 49.

79 U.S., WWI Draft Registration Cards, 1917-1918, Ancestry.com, Ralph R. Shultz, Alexandria, Indiana.

80 Social Security Death Index, Ancestry.com.

81 U.S., WWII Draft Registration Cards, 1942, Ancestry.com, Ralph Richard Shultz, Alexandria, Indiana.

82 Ohio, County Marriages, 1789-2013, FamilySearch.org, Ralph R. Shultz and Mayme S. Connolly, Lucas County, Ohio Marriage Records, Vol. 37, pg. 457, lic. #34253.

83 Obituary of Ralph Shultz (Anderson, Indiana, Anderson Daily Bulletin, 31 May 1971), Indiana Room, Anderson Public Library, 111 East 12th Street, Anderson, IN.

84 Indiana, Death Certificates, 1899-2011, Ancestry.com, Ralph Richard Shultz, death cert. #71-018072.

85 Madison County, Indiana Marriage Records, Madison County Clerk's Office, County Government Office, 16 East 9th Street, Anderson, IN, Earl Jesse Almack and Armintha Shultz, Book 33, pg. 280.

86 Indiana, Death Certificates, 1899-2011, Ancestry.com, Armintha Almack, death cert. #21357.

87 Delaware County, Indiana Death Certificate, Delaware County Department of Health, Bureau of Vital Statistics Delaware County Building,100 Main Street, Room 207, Muncie, IN, Armintha Almack, death cert. #1924-0003.

88 Find A Grave—Vinson Memorial Park Cemetery, Summitville, Van Buren Twp., Madison Co., Indiana, Find A Grave.com, Armintha Almack, Find A Grave Memorial #57747228.

89 Obituary of Armintha Almack (Muncie, Indiana, Muncie Evening Press, 02 Jul 1924), Indiana State Library, 315 West Ohio Street, Indianapolis, IN.

90 Madison County, Indiana Marriage Records, Madison County Clerk of Court, County Government Office, 16 East 9th Street, Anderson, IN, Edgar C. "Humrickhouse" and Clyda E. Greenawalt, Madison County, Indiana Marriage Records, Vol. C5, pg. 126.

91 Ohio Death Certificate, Ohio Department of Health, Center for Vital and Health Statistics, 246 North High Street, Columbus, OH, Edgar Clyde "Humrickhouse", death cert. #19212.

92 West Virginia, Births Index, 1853-1969, Ancestry.com, Edgar "Humrickhouse".

93 Ohio, Deaths, 1908-1932, 1938-2007, Ancestry.com, Edgar Clyde "Humrickhouse", death cert. #19212.

94 Find A Grave—Linwood Cemetery, Blaine, Pease Twp., Belmont Co., Ohio, Find A Grave.com, Edgar Clyde Humrickhouse, Find A Grave Memorial #87264288.

95 Marriage License of Claude McHarry and Vera "Hardee", Madison County Clerk of Court, County Government Office, 16 East 9th Street, Anderson, IN, Book 36, pg. 180.

96 Madison County, Indiana Death Certificate, Madison County, Indiana Health Department, 206 East 9th Street, Anderson, IN, Vera McHarry, Madison County Deaths, Book H=42, LN C233, pg. 359.

97 Indiana, Death Certificates, 1899-2011, Ancestry.com, Vera McHarry, death cert. #72-038155.

98 Marriage License of Warren G. Brane and Ella Humerickhouse, Madison County Clerk of Court, County Government Office, 16 East 9th Street, Anderson, IN, Vol. 36, pg. 376.

99 Marriage License of Robert M. Vasbinder and Ella Brane, Madison County Clerk's Office, County Government Office, 16 East 9th Street, Anderson, IN, Vol. 50, pg. 356.

100 Indiana, Death Certificates, 1899-2011, Ancestry.com, Ella May Vasbinder, death cert. #70-045586.

101 Find A Grave—Greenwood Cemetery, DeGraff, Pleasant Twp., Logan Co., Ohio, Find A Grave.com, Bertha Loffer, Find A Grave Memorial #151559057.

102 Ohio, County Marriages, 1789-2013, FamilySearch.org, Eugene Loffer and Bertha "Wolf", Logan County, Ohio Marriage Records, Vol. F, pg. 502.

103 Obituary of Eugene W. Loffer (Roseburg, Oregon, Roseburg News Review, 30 Nov 1940), University of Oregon Library, Knight Library, 1501 Kincaid Street, Eugene, OR.

104 Oregon, Death Index, 1898-2008, Ancestry.com, Eugene W. Loffer, Douglas County, death cert. #240.

105 Find A Grave—Roseburg IOOF Cemetery, Roseburg, Douglas Co., Oregon, Find A Grave.com, Eugene Webster Loffer, Find A Grave Memorial #112699618.

106 Washington, Marriage Records, 1854-2013, Ancestry.com, Eugene Webster Loffer and Annie Graham Hawkins, Thurston County, Washington Marriage Records, pg. 617, lic. #6702.

107 Obituary of Mrs. E.W. Loffer (Bellefontaine, Ohio, Bellefontaine, Examiner, 14 Jan 1943), Logan County Libraries, Knowlton Library, 220 North Main Street, Bellefontaine, OH.

108 Oregon, Death Index, 1898-2008, Ancestry.com, Anna Loffer, Douglas County, death cert. #171.

109 Ohio, County Marriages, 1789-2013, FamilySearch.org, Harley M. Terrell and Pearl Loffer, Logan County, Ohio Marriage Records, Vol. J, pg. 236, lic. #478.

110 Ohio, Deaths, 1908-1932, 1938-2007, Ancestry.com, Bertha Terrell, death cert. #065034.

111 Obituary of Bertha Terrell (Urbana, Ohio, Urbana Daily Citizen, 10 Sep 1974), Champaign County Library, Main Branch, 1060 Scioto Street, Urbana, OH.

112 Ohio, County Births, 1841-2003 (County Courthouses), FamilySearch.org, "Lala" Loffer, Logan Co. Births, Vol. 1, pg. 292.

113 Ohio, Deaths, 1908-1932, 1938-2007, Ancestry.com, Lola Shaffer, death cert. #077601.

114 Obituary of Lola Shaffer (Fremont, Ohio, Fremont News Messenger, 22 Oct 1984), Rutherford B. Hayes Presidential Center Library, Spiegel Grove, Fremont, OH.

115 Ohio, County Births, 1841-2003 (County Courthouses), FamilySearch.org, Harold J. Loffer, Logan County Births Vol. 3, pg. 91.

116 U.S., WWI Draft Registration Cards, 1917-1918, Ancestry.com, Harold J. Loffer, Sandusky, Erie Co., Ohio.

117 Ohio, Deaths, 1908-1932, 1938-2007, Ancestry.com, Harold J. Loffer, death cert. #00953.

118 Obituary of Harold J. Loffer (Fremont, Ohio, Fremont News Messenger, 04 Jan 1965), Rutherford B. Hayes Presidential Center Library, Spiegel Grove, Fremont, OH.

119 Find A Grave—Fountain Cemetery, Fostoria, Washington Twp., Hancock Co., Ohio, Find A Grave.com, Effie Belle Wolfe Shaw, Find A Grave Memorial #50380236.

120 Ohio Death Certificate, Ohio Department of Health, Center for Vital and Health Statistics, 246 North High Street, Columbus, OH, "Isiah"L. Shaw, death cert. #73053.

121 Obituary of I.L. Shaw (Fostoria, Ohio, Fostoria Daily Review Times, 07 Dec 1925), Kaubisch Memorial Public Library, 205 Perry Street, Fostoria, OH.

122 Find A Grave—Fountain Cemetery, Fostoria, Washington Twp., Hancock Co., Ohio, Find A Grave.com, Isaiah L. Shaw, Find A Grave Memorial #50380239.

123 Obituary of Mrs. Effie Shaw (Fostoria, Ohio, Fostoria Review Times, 12 Feb 1951), Kaubisch Memorial Public Library, 205 Perry Street, Fostoria, OH.

124 Ohio, County Births, 1841-2003 (County Courthouses), FamilySearch.org, Frank H. Shaw, Logan Co. Births, Vol. 2, pg. 406.

125 U.S., WWI Draft Registration Cards, 1917-1918, Ancestry.com, Frank Herbert Shaw, Seneca Co., Ohio.

126 Find A Grave—Greenwood Memory Lawn Cemetery, Phoenix, Mariicopa Co., Arizona, Find A Grave.com, Sgt. Frank Herbert Shaw, Find A Grave Memorial #76737891.

127 U.S., Headstone Applications for Military Veterans, 1925-1963, Ancestry.com, Frank Herbert Shaw.

128 Obituary of Frank H. Shaw (Fostoria. Ohio, Fostoria Review Times, 29 Nov 1961), Kaubisch Memorial Public Library, 205 Perry Street, Fostoria, OH.

129 U.S., WWI Draft Registration Cards, 1917-1918, Ancestry.com, William Russell Shaw.

130 "Trailer Smashes Car in Wayne County...Overturning Vehicle Hits Car At Curve" (Fostoria, Ohio, Fostoria Review Times, 28 Aug 1963), Kaubisch Memorial Public Library, 205 Perry Street, Fostoria, OH.

131 Ohio, Deaths, 1908-1932, 1938-2007, Ancestry.com, William R. Shaw, death cert. #65150.

132 Ohio, County Marriages, 1789-2013, FamilySearch.org, Charles H. Snyder and Edith Shaw, Wood County, Ohio Marriage Records, Vol. 19, pg. 537, lic. #24622.

133 Ohio, County Births, 1841-2003 (County Courthouses), FamilySearch.org, Edith Shaw, Logan Co. Birth Records, Vol. 3, pg. 154.

134 Obituary of Edith Snyder (Madisonville, Kentucky, Madisonville Messenger, 01 Mar 1994), Hopkins County, Kentucky Genealogical Society Library, 14 Court Street, Madisonville, KY.

135 Leavenworth County, Kansas Marriage Records, 1900-1920, Ancestry.com, Frank L. Wolfe and Etta Wilder, Leavenworth County Marriage Records, Book K, pg. 640.

136 Idaho Death Certificate, Idaho Department of Health and Welfare, Bureau of Vital Records and Health Statistics, 450 West State Street, Boise, ID, Etta Wilder Ferguson, death cert. #96886.

137 U.S., WWI Draft Registration Cards, 1917-1918, Ancestry.com, Frank Wolfe, Rexburg, Idaho.

138 Utah, Select County Marriages, 1887-1937, Ancestry.com, Weber County, Samuel S. Ferguson and Mary Etta Wolfe (sic)

139 Florida Death Index 1877-1998, Ancestry.com, Hubert Wilder Wolfe.

140 Obituary of Hubert Wilder Wolfe (Bloomington, Illinois, Bloomington Pantagraph, 05 Feb 1989), Bloomington Public Library, 205 East Olive Street. Bloomington, IL.

141 Find A Grave—Mound Cemetery, Brooklyn Center, Hennepin Co., Minnesota, Find A. Grave.com, William R. Wolfe, Find A Grave Memorial #103069771.

142 Ohio, Deaths, 1908-1932, 1938-2007, Ancestry.com, Effie Booze, death cert. #076327.

143 Ohio, County Marriages, 1789-2013, FamilySearch.org, Everett E. Booze and Effa M. Young, Logan County, Ohio Marriage Records, Vol. 1, pg. 390, lic. #618.

144 Logan County, Ohio Probate Court, Record of Registrations of Births, Kenneth Booze, Vol. 7, pg. 956. Logan County Courthouse, 140 West Main Street, Bellefontaine, OH.

145 Minnesota Official Marriage Systems-MOMS, Minnesota Association of County Officers, Minnesota Association of County Officers, 1000 Westgate Drive, Suite 252, St. Paul, MN, "Gary" E. Wolfe and Lillian A. Lundeen, Hennepin County, Minnesota Marriage Records, lic. #01210388; Online database: https://www.moms.mn.gov/Search

146 Minnesota Death Certificate, Minnesota Historical Society, 345 Kellogg Boulevard West, St. Paul, MN, Lillian Wolfe, death certificate #1958-MN-027051.

147 Find A Grave—Lakewood Cemetery, Minneapolis, Hennepin Co., Minnesota, Find A Grave.com, Lillian Adelia Wolfe, Find A Grave Memorial #125593614.

148 Obituary of Lillian Wolfe (Minneapolis, Minnesota, Minneapolis Morning Tribune, 8 Dec 1958), Hennepin County Library-Minneapolis Central Branch, 300 Nicolette Mall, Minneapolis, MN.

149 Ohio, County Births, 1841-2003 (County Courthouses), FamilySearch.org, Wolfe, male child, fa: Guy Wolfe, Mo: Effie Young, Logan Co., Ohio Birth Record Vol. 3, pg. 179.

150 "Residents Brother Died in San Antonio" (Fremont, Ohio, Fremont Messenger, 11 Aug 1970), Rutherford B. Hayes Presidential Center Library, Spiegel Grove, Fremont, OH.

151 Texas, Death Certificates, 1903-1982, Ancestry.com, Kenneth V. Booze, state file #53756.

152 Minnesota Death Certificates, Minnesota Death Index, 1908-2002 (345 W. Kellogg Blvd, St. Paul, MN 55102, Minnesota Historical Society), Ancestry.com, Kenneth William Wolfe, death cert. 1981- #000728.

153 Minnesota Birth Certificates, Minnesota Birth Index, 1900-1934 (345 W. Kellogg Blvd, St. Paul, MN 55102, Minnesota Historical Society), Ancestry.com, "Babe" Wolfe, birth cert. #1908-39718.

154 Minnesota Birth Certificates, Minnesota Birth Index, 1900-1934 (345 W. Kellogg Blvd, St. Paul, MN 55102, Minnesota Historical Society), Ancestry.com, Margaret Carolyn Wolfe, birth cert. #1919-43139.

155 Obituary of Margaret Carolyn (Wolfe) Rounds (Minneapolis, MN, Minneapolis Tribune-Star, 22 Aug 2015), Hennepin County Library-Minneapolis Central Branch, 300 Nicolet Mall, Minneapolis, MN.

156 Minnesota Birth Certificates, Minnesota Birth Index, 1900-1934 (Minnesota Historical Society), Ancestry.com, Warren Charles Wolfe, birth cert. #1922-47944.

157 Obituary of Warren Charles Wolfe, (Minneapolis, MN, Minneapolis Tribune-Star, 12 Nov 2003), Hennepin County Library-Minneapolis Central Branch, 300 Nicolet Mall, Minneapolis, MN.

158 Find A Grave—IOOF Cemetery, Alexandria, Monroe Twp., Madison Co., Indiana, Find A Grave.com, Ralph R. Shultz, Find A Grave Memorial #111307064.

159 Obituary of Mary Shultz (Anderson, Indiana, Anderson Daily Bulletin, 15 Jun 1971), Anderson Public Library, Anderson Public Library, Indiana Room, Anderson Public Library, 111 East 12th Street, Anderson, IN.

160 Indiana, Death Certificates, 1899-2011, Ancestry.com, Mary Sue Shultz, death certificate #71-021961.

161 Find A Grave—IOOF Cemetery, Alexandria, Monroe Twp., Madison Co., Indiana, Find A Grave.com, Mary S. Shultz, Find A Grave Memorial #111307090.

162 Obituary of Armintha E. Smith, (Anderson, Indiana, Anderson Herald-Bulletin, 30 Mar 1994), Indiana Room, Anderson Public Library, 111 East 12th Street, Anderson, IN.

163 Madison County, Indiana Marriage Records, Madison County Clerk of Court, County Government Office, 16 East 9th Street, Anderson, IN, Alva J. Smith and Armintha Almack, Madison County, Indiana Marriage Records, Book 75, pg. 391.

164 Madison County, Indiana Marriage Records, Madison County Clerk of Court, County Government Office, 16 East 9th Street, Anderson, IN, Earl J. Almack and Armintha Shultz, Madison County, Indiana Marriage Records, Vol. 33, pg. 280.

165 U.S., WWI Draft Registration Cards, 1917-1918, Ancestry.com, Earl J. Almack, New Castle, Indiana.

166 Madison County, Indiana Death Certificate, Madison County, Indiana Health Department, 206 East 9th Street, Anderson, IN, Earl Jesse Almack, Madison County Deaths, Book CH-17, LN 169, pg. 39.

167 Indiana, Death Certificates, 1899-2011, Ancestry.com, Earl J. Almack, death cert. #14959.

168 Obituary of Earl Almack Sr. (Anderson, Indiana, Anderson Daily Bulletin, 03 May 1933), Anderson Public Library, Anderson Public Library, Indiana Room, Anderson Public Library, 111 East 12th Street, Anderson, IN.

169 Find A Grave—IOOF Cemetery, Alexandria, Monroe Twp., Madison Co., Indiana, Find A Grave.com, Earl J. Almack, Find A Grave Memorial #72698069.

170 Indiana, Death Certificates, 1899-2011, Ancestry.com, Mary Imelda Almack, death cert. #94-019781.

171 U.S., Social Security Applications and Claims Index, 1936-2007, Ancestry.com, Armintha Euphema Almack Smith.

172 Indiana, Death Certificates, 1899-2011, Ancestry.com, Armintha E. Smith, death cert. #94-015602.

173 Obituary of Ella Vasbinder (Anderson, Indiana, Anderson Herald, 13 Dec 1970), Anderson Public Library, Anderson Public Library, Indiana Room, Anderson Public Library, 111 East 12th Street, Anderson, IN.

174 Obituary of Vera B. McHarry (Anderson, Indiana, Anderson Herald, 30 Sep 1972), Anderson Public Library, Anderson Public Library, Indiana Room, Anderson Public Library, 111 East 12th Street, Anderson, IN.

175 Find A Grave—Maplewood Cemetery, Anderson, Madison Co., Indiana, Find A Grave.com, Vera B. McHarry, Find A Grave Memorial #151510471.

176 Madison County, Indiana Marriage Records, Madison County Clerk of Court, County Government Office, 16 East 9th Street, Anderson, IN, Bert L. Hardy and Vera Humrickhouse, Madison County, Indiana Marriage Records, Vol. 28, pg. 100.

177 U.S., WWI Draft Registration Cards, 1917-1918, Ancestry.com, Bert Lawrence Hardy, #13-2-1-2A.

178 Indiana, Death Certificates, 1899-2011, Ancestry.com, Bert L. Hardy, death cert. #69-018222.

179 Obituary of Bert Hardy (Anderson, Indiana, Anderson Daily Bulletin, 08 May 1969), Indiana Room, Anderson Public Library, 111 East 12th Street, Anderson, IN.

180 Obituary of Claude McHarry (Anderson, Indiana, Anderson Daily Bulletin, 30 Mar 1939), Indiana Room, Anderson Public Library, 111 East 12th Street, Anderson, IN.

181 U.S., Social Security Applications and Claims Index, 1936-2007, Ancestry.com, Claud Almond McHarry.

182 Indiana, Death Certificates, 1899-2011, Ancestry.com, Claud A. McHarry, death cert. #9093.

183 Find A Grave—Maplewood Cemetery, Anderson, Madison Co., Indiana, Find A Grave.com, Claude A. McHarry, Find A Grave Memorial #106218684.

184 Marion County, Indiana Death Certificate, Marion County Health Department, Vital Records, Hasbrook Building, first floor, 3838 North Rural Street, Indianapolis, IN, Marion County, Jack Edgar McHarry, Death Record Vol. 43, pg. 160, cert. #1605.

185 Indiana, Death Certificates, 1899-2011, Ancestry.com, Jack Edgar McHarry, death cert. #11896.

186 "Chesterfield Youth Hit By Auto Expires" (Anderson, Indiana, Anderson Herald Bulletin, 10 Apr 1942), Anderson Public Library, Anderson Public Library, Indiana Room, Anderson Public Library, 111 East 12th Street, Anderson, IN.

187 U.S., Social Security Applications and Claims Index, 1936-2007, Ancestry.com, Bill Clyde McHarry.

188 Obituary of Bill C. McHarry (Anderson, Indiana, Anderson Herald-Bulletin, 10 Feb 1999), Anderson Public Library, Anderson Public Library, Indiana Room, Anderson Public Library, 111 East 12th Street, Anderson, IN.

189 Indiana, Death Certificates, 1899-2011, Ancestry.com, Bill C. McHarry, death cert. #006548.

190 Madison County, Indiana Birth Records, Madison County, Indiana Health Department, 206 East 9th Street, Anderson, IN, Donna May McHarry, Madison County Births, Vol. CH-11, pg. 94.

191 Indiana, Death Certificates, 1899-2011, Ancestry.com, Donna Williams, death cert. #84-011036.

192 Obituary of Donna M. Williams (Anderson, Indiana, Anderson Daily Bulletin, 19 Mar 1984), Anderson Public Library, Anderson Public Library, Indiana Room, Anderson Public Library, 111 East 12th Street, Anderson, IN.

193 Tippecanoe County, Indiana Death Records (Lafayette, Indiana, Tippecanoe Co., Indiana), Tippecanoe County Health Department, Vital Records Staff, 629 North 6th Street, Lafayette, IN, Donna M. Williams, Tippecanoe Co. Deaths, Vol. 84, pg. 229.

194 Find A Grave—Bronnenberg Cemetery, Chesterfield, Union Twp., Madison Co., Indiana, Find A Grave.com, Ella M. Vasbinder, Find A Grave Memorial #20764537.

195 Madison County, Indiana Marriage Records, Madison County Clerk of Court, County Government Office, 16 East 9th Street, Anderson, IN, Warren G. Brane and Ella M. Humerickhouse, Madison County, Indiana Marriage Records, Vol. 36, pg. 376.

196 U.S., WWI Draft Registration Cards, 1917-1918, Ancestry.com, Warren Grover Brane.

197 California, Death Index, 1940-1997, Ancestry.com, Warren G. Brane.

198 California Death Certificate, California Health and Strategic Planning, Vital Records, M.S. 5103, P.O. Box 997410, Sacramento, CA, Warren Grover Brane, death cert. #71-137488.

199 U.S., WWII Draft Registration Cards, 1942, Ancestry.com, Walter E. Vasbinder.

200 Indiana, Death Certificates, 1899-2011, Ancestry.com, Robert M. Vasbinder, death cert, #70-033554.

201 Obituary of Robert Mathew Vasbinder, (Anderson, Indiana, Anderson Herald, 06 Sep 1970), Indiana Room, Anderson Public Library, 111 East 12th Street, Anderson, IN.

202 Find A Grave—Bronnenberg Cemetery, Chesterfield, Union Twp., Madison Co., Indiana, Find A Grave.com, Robert M. Vasbinder, Find A Grave Memorial #20764574.

203 U.S., WWII Draft Registration Cards, 1942, Ancestry.com, Robert Mathew Vasbinder.

204 Obituary of Constance Schrock (South Bend, Indiana, South Bend Tribune, 27 Jun 2008), St. Joseph County Public Library, 304 South Main Street, South Bend, IN.

205 Indiana, Death Certificates, 1899-2011, Ancestry.com, Constance Nichols Schrock, death cert. #023488.

206 Madison County, Indiana Birth Records, Madison County, Indiana Health Department, 206 East 9th Street, Anderson, IN, Richard Lee Brane, Madison County Births, Vol. CH-11, pg. 3.

207 Indiana, Death Certificates, 1899-2011, Ancestry.com, Richard Lee Brane, death cert. #81-032571.

208 Obituary of Richard Brane, (Anderson, Indiana, Anderson Daily Bulletin, 23 Sep 1981), Indiana Room, Anderson Public Library, 111 East 12th Street, Anderson, IN.

209 Madison County, Indiana Death Certificate, Madison County, Indiana Health Department, 206 East 9th Street, Anderson, IN, Richard Lee Brane, Madison County Deaths, Book H-46, LN 0772, pg. 366.

210 Find A Grave—Bronnenberg Cemetery, Chesterfield, Union Twp., Madison Co., Indiana, Find A Grave.com, Richard Lee Brane, Find A Grave Memorial #79525546.

211 Find A Grave—Spring Hills Presbyterian Church Cemetery, Springhills, Harrison Twp., Champaign Co., Ohio, Find A Grave.com, Bertha P. Terrell, Find A Grave Memorial #11600157.

212 Ohio Death Certificate, Ohio Department of Health, Center for Vital and Health Statistics, 246 North High Street, Columbus, OH, Harley M. Terrell, death cert. #4208.

213 Find A Grave—Spring Hills Presbyterian Church Cemetery, Springhills, Harrison Twp., Champaign Co., Ohio, Find A Grave.com, Harley M. Terrell, Find A Grave Memorial #11600156.

214 Ohio, County Births, 1841-2003 (County Courthouses), FamilySearch.org, Thelma M. Terrell, Champaign County Births, Vol. 2, pg. 540.

215 Find A Grave—Spring Hills Presbyterian Church Cemetery, Springhills, Harrison Twp., Champaign Co., Ohio, Find A Grave.com, Opal Lucille Terrell, Find A Grave Memorial #38942393.

216 Marriage License of Harry F. Mohr and Thelma M. Terrell, FamilySearch.org, Champaign County Marriage Book Q, pg. 468, #925.

217 Ohio, County Births, 1841-2003 (County Courthouses), FamilySearch.org, Thelma M. Terrell, Champaign County Births, Vol. 3, pg. 10.

218 Ohio, Deaths, 1908-1932, 1938-2007, Ancestry.com, Thelma Mohr, death cert. #049599.

219 Ohio, County Births, 1841-2003 (County Courthouses), FamilySearch.org, Virgil Milton Terrell, Champaign County Births, Vol. 3, pg. 28, #1277.

220 Ohio, Deaths, 1908-1932, 1938-2007, Ancestry.com, Virgil M. Terrell, death cert. #092707.

221 Obituary of Virgil M. Terrell (Urbana, Ohio, Urbana Daily Citizen, 27 Dec 1974), Champaign County Library, Main Branch, 1060 Scioto Street, Urbana, OH.

222 Ohio, County Births, 1841-2003 (County Courthouses), FamilySearch.org, Damon Terrell, Champaign County Births, Journal Registration and Corrections, pg. 69, Case #18.

223 Ohio, Deaths, 1908-1932, 1938-2007, Ancestry.com, Damon Terrell, death cert. #079776.

224 Obituary of Damon E. Terrell (Urbana, Ohio, Urbana Daily Citizen, 25 Nov 1983), Champaign County Library, Main Branch, 1060 Scioto Street, Urbana, OH.

225 Ohio, Deaths, 1908-1932, 1938-2007, Ancestry.com, Gaylord P. Terrell, death cert. #048650.

226 Ohio, Deaths, 1908-1932, 1938-2007, Ancestry.com, Garnet Terrell Calland, death cert. #065470.

227 U.S., Social Security Applications and Claims Index, 1936-2007, Ancestry.com, Garnet Lucille Terrell Calland.

228 Ohio Death Certificate, Ohio Department of Health, Center for Vital and Health Statistics, 246 North High Street, Columbus, OH, Harold Reginold Terrell, death cert. #44940.

229 Find A Grave—Meadow Green/Restlawn Memorial Park Cemetery, Huron Twp., Erie Co., Ohio, Find A Grave.com, Lola Shaffer, Find A Grave Memorial #151681268.

230 Ohio, County Marriages, 1789-2013, FamilySearch.org, Wallace W. Shaffer and Lola E. Loffer, Cuyahoga County, Ohio Marriage Records, Vol. 69, pg. 343, lic. #56369.

231 U.S., WWI Draft Registration Cards, 1917-1918, Ancestry.com, Welcome Wallace Shaffer, Erie, Ohio.

232 U.S., Social Security Applications and Claims Index, 1936-2007, Ancestry.com, Wallace W. Shaffer.

233 Obituary of Wallace W. Shaffer (Tiffin, Ohio, Tiffin Advertiser Tribune, 30 Nov 1960), Tiffin-Seneca Public Library, 77 Jefferson Street, Tiffin, OH.

234 Ohio, Deaths, 1908-1932, 1938-2007, Ancestry.com, William W. Shaffer, death cert. #78509.

235 Find A Grave—Meadow Green/Restlawn Memorial Park Cemetery, Huron Twp., Erie Co., Ohio, Find A Grave.com, Wallace Shaffer, Find A Grave Memorial #151681371.

236 U.S., WWII Draft Registration Cards, 1942, Ancestry.com, Wallace Welcome Shaffer, Sandusky, Ohio.

237 Ohio, Deaths, 1908-1932, 1938-2007, Ancestry.com, Elizabeth Sentman, death cert. #092266.

238 Obituary of Elizabeth Sentman (Fremont, Ohio, Fremont News Messenger, 28 Nov 1995), Rutherford B. Hayes Presidential Center Library, Speigel Grove, Fremont, OH.

239 Find A Grave—Oakland Cemetery, Sandusky, Erie Co., Ohio, Find A Grave.com, Harold J. Loffer, Find A Grave Memorial #151682682.

240 Ohio, County Marriages, 1789-2013, FamilySearch.org, Harold J. Loffer and Wilma O. Walborn, Erie County, Ohio Marriage Records, Vol. 16, pg. 460, lic. #461.

241 Obituary of Wilma O. (Walborn) Loffer (Sandusky, Ohio, Sandusky Daily Register, 08 Apr 2008), Rutherford B. Hayes Presidential Center Library, Spiegel Grove, Fremont, OH.

242 Find A Grave—Oakland Cemetery, Sandusky, Erie Co., Ohio, Find A Grave.com, Wilma O. Loffer, Find A Grave Memorial #97088420.

243 Ohio, Birth Index, 1908-1964, Ancestry.com, William E. Loffer, state file #1922031970.

244 Obituary of William Eugene Loffer (Tampa, Florida, Tampa Tribune, 20 Feb 2011), State Library and Archives of Florida, R.A. Gray Building, 500 South Bronaugh Street, Tallahassee, FL.

245 Marriage License of Werner Marquart and Lola M. Loffer, Erie County, Ohio Probate Court, 323 Columbus Avenue, Sandusky, OH, Vol. 22, pg. 356.

246 Obituary of Donna J. (Loffer) LaRose (Sandusky, Ohio, Sandusky Register, 02 Jun 2002), Sandusky Library, Archives Research Center & Genealogy, 114 West Adams Street, Sandusky, OH.

247 U.S., Social Security Applications and Claims Index, 1936-2007, Ancestry.com, Donna Jean Loffer Larose.

248 Ohio, County Marriages, 1789-2013, FamilySearch.org, Frank Herbert Shaw and Marguerite L. Crocker, Seneca County, Ohio Marriage Records, Vol. 17, pg. 457, lic. #6595.

249 Ohio, County Births, 1841-2003 (County Courthouses), FamilySearch.org, "Margarette" Crocker, Seneca County Births, Vol. 4, pg. 32.

250 Find A Grave—Greenwood Memory Lawn Cemetery, Phoenix, Mariicopa Co., Arizona, Find A Grave.com, Marguerite C. Shaw, Find A Grave Memorial #76737927.

251 U.S., Social Security Applications and Claims Index, 1936-2007, Ancestry.com, Winifred Jane Shaw Puse.

252 Ohio, Birth Index, 1908-1964, Ancestry.com, John C. Shaw, state file #1935079541.

253 U.S., Social Security Applications and Claims Index, 1936-2007, Ancestry.com, John Crocker Shaw.

254 Find A Grave—Fountain Cemetery, Fostoria, Washington Twp., Hancock Co., Ohio, Find A Grave.com, William Russell Shaw, Find A Grave Memorial #50380248.

255 Ohio, County Births, 1841-2003 (County Courthouses), FamilySearch.org, Catherine Murphy, Logan County Births, Vol. 3, pg. 302.

256 Ohio, Deaths, 1908-1932, 1938-2007, Ancestry.com, "Catheri" M. Shaw, death cert. #65149.

257 Find A Grave—Fountain Cemetery, Fostoria, Washington Twp., Hancock Co., Ohio, Find A Grave.com, Catherine M. Shaw, Find A Grave Memorial #50380234.

258 Ohio, Birth Index, 1908-1964, Ancestry.com, Shaw, fa. Russell, state file #1928057748.

259 Ohio, Deaths, 1908-1932, 1938-2007, Ancestry.com, Stillborn male Shaw, death cert. #01043.

260 California, Death Index, 1940-1997, Ancestry.com, Robert Leonard Shaw.

261 Ohio, Birth Index, 1908-1964, Ancestry.com, Robert L. Shaw, state file #1931059155.

262 Ohio, Deaths, 1908-1932, 1938-2007, Ancestry.com, Carl Luther Shaw, death cert. #69548.

263 Seneca, Ohio County Marriage Records (Tiffin, Ohio,), Seneca County, Ohio Probate Court, 108 Jefferson Street, Tiffin, OH, Carl Luther Shaw and Beulah Mae Shultz, Seneca County, Ohio Marriage Records, lic. #25658.

264 Find A Grave—Serenity Gardens Memorial Park Cemetery, Largo, Pinellas Co., Florida, Find A Grave.com, Edith L. Shaw, Find A Grave Memorial #152091252.

265 Florida Death Index 1877-1998, Ancestry.com, Charles H. Snyder.

266 Find A Grave—Serenity Gardens Memorial Park Cemetery, Largo, Pinellas Co., Florida, Find A Grave.com, Charles H. Snyder, Find A Grave Memorial #117095727.

267 Obituary of Patricia Ann Reed (Madisonville, Kentucky, Madisonville Messenger, 20 Jan 2004), Hopkins County, Kentucky Genealogy Society Library, 14 Court Street, Madisonville, KY.

268 Minnesota, Births and Christenings Index, 1840-1980, Ancestry.com, Ruth Sebastian.

269 Massachusetts Death Index, 1970-2003, Ancestry.com, Ruth V. Wolfe, death cert. #027377.

270 Town of Rockport, Death Records, Rockport, Massachusetts Town Clerk, 34 Broadway, Rockport, MA, Ruth V. Wolfe, death cert #027377.

271 Cook County, Illinois Birth Index, 1916-1935, Ancestry.com, Diane Wolfe, birth cert. ##6004414.

272 Find A Grave—Forest Lawn Memorial Gardens Cemetery, Columbus, Franklin Co., Ohio, Find A Grave.com, Kenneth V. Booze, Find A Grave Memorial #52923111.

273 Michigan, Marriage Records, 1867-1952, Ancestry.com, Kenneth Booze and Iva Hufford, Monroe County, Michigan Marriage Records, Vol. 4, pg. 96, lic. #533.

274 Ohio, Births and Christenings Index, 1800-1962, Ancestry.com, Iva E. Hufford.

275 Ohio, Deaths, 1908-1932, 1938-2007, Ancestry.com, Iva E. Werner, death cert. #026165.

276 Obituary of Iva Werner (Sandusky, Ohio, Sandusky Register, 11 May 1981), Ohio History Center Archives and Library, Ohio History Center, 800 East 17th Avenue, Columbus, OH.

277 U.S., WWI Draft Registration Cards, 1917-1918, Ancestry.com, Kenneth Vernon Booze, Sandusky, Ohio.

278 Texas Death Index, 1903-2000, Ancestry.com, Virginia P. Booze.

279 Find A Grave—Forest Lawn Memorial Gardens Cemetery, Columbus, Franklin Co., Ohio, Find A Grave.com, Virginia P. Booze, Find A Grave Memorial #52923120.

280 U.S. City Directories, 1822-1895, Ancestry.com, San Antonio, Texas, 1951, pg. 154, entry for Kenneth V. Booze.

281 County Marriage Records, FamilySearch.com, Webster E. Werner and Iva E. Hufford Booze, Erie County, Ohio Marriage Records, Vol. 12, pg. 70, lic. #11220.

282 Ohio, Birth Index, 1908-1964, Ancestry.com, Doris J. Booze, state cert. #1919005396.

283 Obituary of Doris Booze Cummings (Fremont, Ohio, Fremont Messenger, 21 Nov 1997), Rutherford B. Hayes Presidential Center Library, Spiegel Grove, Fremont, OH.

284 U.S., Social Security Applications and Claims Index, 1936-2007, Ancestry.com, Doris Jeannette Booze.

285 U.S., Social Security Applications and Claims Index, 1936-2007, Ancestry.com, Kenneth E. Booze Werner.

286 Minnesota Official Marriage Systems-MOMS, Minnesota Association of County Officers, Minnesota Association of County Officers, 1000 Westgate Drive, Suite 252, St. Paul, MN, Kenneth William "Wolfo" and Mary A. Light, Hennepin County, Minnesota Marriage Records, lic. #03400430; Online database: https://www.moms.mn.gov/Search

287 Minnesota Death Certificates, Minnesota Death Index, 1908-2002 (Minnesota Historical Society), Ancestry.com, Mary Alice Wolfe, death cert. 1988-#009889.

288 Minnesota Birth Certificates, Minnesota Birth Index, 1900-1934 (345 W. Kellogg Blvd, St. Paul, MN 55102, Minnesota Historical Society), Ancestry.com, Mary Allice (sic) Light, birth cert. #1909-04033.

289 Obituary of Kenneth W. Wolfe (Minneapolis, Minnesota, Minneapolis Tribune, 12 Jan 1981), Minneapolis Central Library, Niclolett Mall, Minneapolis, MN.

290 Minnesota Birth Certificates, Minnesota Birth Index, 1900-1934 (Minnesota Historical Society), Ancestry.com, Robert Roe Wolfe, birth cert. #1931-35006.

291 Minnesota Birth Index, 1935-2002 (P.O. Box 64975, St. Paul, MN 55164-0975, Minnesota Department of Health), Ancestry.com, Sharon Kaye Wolfe, birth cert. #1935-MN-004331.

292 Find A Grave—Fort Snelling National Cemetery, Minneapolis, Hennepin Co., Minnesota, Find A Grave.com, Margaret Carolyn Rounds, Find A Grave Memorial #155466134.

293 Minnesota Death Certificate, Minnesota Historical Society, 345 Kellogg Boulevard West, St. Paul, MN, Darwin Dean Rounds, death cert. #1994-016139.

294 Find A Grave—Fort Snelling National Cemetery, Minneapolis, Hennepin Co., Minnesota, Find A Grave.com, Darwin Dean Rounds, Find A Grave Memorial #1139024.

295 U.S. Veterans' Gravesites, ca. 1775-2006, Ancestry.com, Darwin Dean Rounds.

296 Minnesota Official Marriage Systems-MOMS, Minnesota Association of County Officers, Minnesota Association of County Officers, 1000 Westgate Drive, Suite 252, St. Paul, MN, Warren Charles Wolfe and Vallie Fay Lavinghouze, Hennepin County, Minnesota Marriage Records, lic. #05710304; Online database: https://www.moms.mn.gov/Search

297 Minnesota Birth Index, 1935-2002 (Minnesota Department of Health), Ancestry.com, Kenneth Charles Wolfe, birth cert. #1953-MN-001562.

298 Find A Grave—Anderson Memorial Cemetery, Anderson, Madison Co., Indiana, Find A Grave.com, Armintha E. Smith, Find A Grave Memorial #108702957.

299 Obituary of Alva J. Smith (Anderson, Indiana, Anderson Herald-Bulletin, 15 Nov 1982), Indiana Room, Anderson Public Library, 111 East 12th Street, Anderson, IN.

300 Indiana, Death Certificates, 1899-2011, Ancestry.com, Alva Jack Smith, death cert. #82-040790.

301 Find A Grave—Anderson Memorial Cemetery, Anderson, Madison Co., Indiana, Find A Grave.com, Alva Jack Smith, Find A Grave Memorial #151512161.

302 Obituary of Patricia Smith (Anderson, Indiana, Anderson Daily Bulletin, 22 Dec 1954), Indiana Room, Anderson Public Library, 111 East 12th Street, Anderson, IN.

303 Madison County, Indiana Death Certificate, Madison County, Indiana Health Department, 206 East 9th Street, Anderson, IN, Patricia Smith, Madison County Deaths, Book CH-28, LN 0579, pg. 22.

304 Madison County, Indiana Birth Records, Madison County, Indiana Health Department, 206 East 9th Street, Anderson, IN, Patricia Ann Smith, Madison County Births, Vol. CH-28, pg. 95.

305 Indiana, Death Certificates, 1899-2011, Ancestry.com, Patricia Ann Smith, death cert. #37738.

306 Find A Grave—Maplewood Cemetery, Anderson, Madison Co., Indiana, Find A Grave.com, Jack E. McHarry, Find A Grave Memorial #106218697.

307 Find A Grave—Maplewood Cemetery, Anderson, Madison Co., Indiana, Find A Grave.com, Bill C. McHarry, Find A Grave Memorial #106218658.

308 Indiana, Marriages 1811-2007, FamilySearch.org, Bill C. McHarry and Ruth Skinner, Delaware County, Indiana Marriage Records, Vol. 62, pg. 212, lic. #774789.

309 Kentucky Birth Index, 1911-1999, Ancestry.com, Ruth Cowles, state Vol. 79, cert. #39297.

310 Indiana, Marriages 1811-2007, FamilySearch.org, Bill C. McHarry and Mary Shelburn, Delaware County, Indiana Marriage Records, Vol. 68, pg. 102, lic. #210316.

311 U.S., Social Security Applications and Claims Index, 1936-2007, Ancestry.com, Mary Winifred Shelburn McHarry.

312 Indiana, Death Certificates, 1899-2011, Ancestry.com, Mary W. McHarry, death cert. #95-028121.

313 Find A Grave—Maplewood Cemetery, Anderson, Madison Co., Indiana, Find A Grave.com, Mary Winifred Shelburn McHarry, Find A Grave Memorial #106218716.

314 Obituary of Mary McHarry (Anderson, Indiana, Anderson Herald-Bulletin, 31 Jul 1995), Indiana Room, Anderson Public Library, 111 East 12th Street, Anderson, IN.

315 Find A Grave—Crystal Cathedral Memorial Gardens Cemetery, Garden Grove, Orange Co., California, Find A Grave.com, Constance Schrock, Find A Grave Memorial #27910149.

316 Madison County, Indiana Marriage Records, Madison County Clerk of Court, County Government Office, 16 East 9th Street, Anderson, IN, Horace D. Nichols and Constance Brane, Madison County, Indiana Marriage Records, Vol. 61, pg. 450.

317 Indiana, Birth Certificates, 1907-1940, Ancestry.com, "Horrace" David Nichols, cert. #44177.

318 U.S., Social Security Applications and Claims Index, 1936-2007, Ancestry.com, Horace Davis Nichols.

319 U.S., Department of Veterans Affairs BIRLS Death File, 1850-2010, Horace Nichols.

320 California, Death Index, 1940-1997, Ancestry.com, Horace Davis Nichols.

321 U.S. Veterans' Gravesites, ca. 1775-2006, Ancestry.com, Horace Davis Nichols.

322 Obituary of Horace Nichols (Anderson, Indiana, Anderson Herald Bulletin, 08 Aug 1990), Indiana Room, Anderson Public Library, 111 East 12th Street, Anderson, IN.

323 Find A Grave—Fort Rosecrans National Military Cemetery, San Diego, San Diego Co., California, Find A Grave.com, Horace D. Nichols, Find A Grave Memorial #3421474.

324 California, Marriage Index, 1960-1985, Ancestry.com, David E. Schrock and Constance Nichols, Santa Clara County, California Marriage Records, California state lic. #751-18124.

325 Nevada, Death Index, 1980-2012, Ancestry.com, David E. Schrock.

326 Indiana, Birth Certificates, 1907-1940, Ancestry.com, David Schrock, birth cert. #70393.

327 U.S., Social Security Applications and Claims Index, 1936-2007, Ancestry.com, David E. Schrock.

328 Find A Grave—Hawpatch Cemetery, Topeka, Eden Twp., LaGrange Co., Indiana, Find A Grave.com, David E. Schrock, Find A Grave Memorial #171998164.

329 Obituary of Thelma Mohr (Urbana, Ohio, Urbana Daily Citizen, 29 Jul 1986), Champaign County Library, Main Branch, 1060 Scioto Street, Urbana, OH.

330 Find A Grave—Maple Grove Cemetery, Mechanicsburg, Goshen Twp., Champaign Co., Ohio, Find A Grave.com, Thelma M. Mohr, Find A Grave Memorial #104033003.

331 Ohio, County Marriages, 1789-2013, FamilySearch.org, Harry F. "Mohe" and Thelma M. Terrell, Champaign County, Ohio Marriage Records, Vol. Q, pg. 468, lic. #925.

332 Ohio, County Births, 1841-2003 (County Courthouses), FamilySearch.org, Harry Fulwider Mohr, Champaign County Births, Vol. 2, pg. 356.

333 Ohio, Deaths, 1908-1932, 1938-2007, Ancestry.com, Harry F. Mohr, death cert. #62141.

334 Obituary of Harry F. Mohr (Urbana, Ohio, Urbana Daily Citizen, 03 Sep 1960), Champaign County Library, Main Branch, 1060 Scioto Street, Urbana, OH.

335 Find A Grave—Maple Grove Cemetery, Mechanicsburg, Goshen Twp., Champaign Co., Ohio, Find A Grave.com, Harry F. Mohr, Find A Grave Memorial #104032953.

336 Obituary of Richard E. Mohr (Urbana, Ohio, Urbana Daily Citizen, 26 Sep 1983), Champaign County Library, Main Branch, 1060 Scioto Street, Urbana, OH.

337 Ohio, Deaths, 1908-1932, 1938-2007, Ancestry.com, Richard E. Mohr, death cert. #064147.

338 Ohio, Birth Index, 1908-1964, Ancestry.com, state file #1933031962.

339 Find A Grave—Spring Hills Presbyterian Church Cemetery, Springhills, Harrison Twp., Champaign Co., Ohio, Find A Grave.com, Virgil M. Terrell, Find A Grave Memorial #49864983.

340 Obituary of Mrs. Virgil Terrell (Bellefontaine, Ohio, Bellefontaine Examiner, 20 Jan 1941), Logan County Libraries, Knowlton Library, 220 Main Street, Bellefontaine, OH.

341 Indiana, Marriages 1811-2007, FamilySearch.org, Virgil Terrell and Ruth Anderson, Wayne County, Indiana Marriage Application Records, Vol. 51, pg. 14.

342 Ohio Death Certificate, Ohio Department of Health, Center for Vital and Health Statistics, 246 North High Street, Columbus, OH, Ruth Terrell, death cert. #4418.

343 Find A Grave—Spring Hills Presbyterian Church Cemetery, Springhills, Harrison Twp., Champaign Co., Ohio, Find A Grave.com, Ruth E. Terrell, Find A Grave Memorial #11600164.

344 Indiana, Marriages 1811-2007, FamilySearch.org, Virgil M. Terrell and Georgia M. Jones, Wayne County, Indiana Marriage Application Records, Vol. 231, pg. 65.

345 Indiana, Death Certificates, 1899-2010, Ancestry.com, Georgia May Howell, death cert. #78-035401.

346 Find A Grave—Park Cemetery, Fairmount, Fairmount Twp., Grant Co., Indiana, Find A Grave.com, Georgia May Howell, Find A Grave Memorial #96725890.

347 Ohio, Birth Index, 1908-1964, Ancestry.com, Marilyn K. Terrell, state file ##1937033263.

348 Find A Grave—Rosedale Cemetery, Conover, Brown Twp., Miami Co., Ohio, Find A Grave.com, Damon Eugene Terrell, Find A Grave Memorial #114732457.

349 Ohio, County Marriages, 1789-2013, FamilySearch.org, Damon Terrell and Mary Virginia Bailor, Champaign County, Ohio Marriage Records, Vol. R, pg. 542, lic. #1078.

350 Ohio, Deaths, 1908-1932, 1938-2007, Ancestry.com, Mary Virginia Terrell, death cert. #050981.

351 Obituary of Mary Terrell (Urbana, Ohio, Urbana Daily Citizen, 01 Aug 1995), Champaign County Library, Main Branch, 1060 Scioto Street, Urbana, OH.

352 Find A Grave—Rosedale Cemetery, Conover, Brown Twp., Miami Co., Ohio, Find A Grave.com, Mary Virginia Bailar Terrell, Find A Grave Memorial #114732391.

353 Ohio, Birth Index, 1908-1964, Ancestry.com, Barbara L. Terrell, state file #1935029779.

354 Ohio, Birth Index, 1908-1964, Ancestry.com, "Beverley S" Terrell, state file #1937039643.

355 Ohio, Birth Index, 1908-1964, Ancestry.com, Thomas E. Terrell, state file #1947022558.

356 Obituary of Thomas Terrell (Urbana, Ohio, Urbana Daily Citizen, 22 Nov 2016), Champaign County Library, Main Branch, 1060 Scioto Street, Urbana, OH.

357 Obituary of Gaylord P. Terrell (Urbana, Ohio, Urbana Daily Citizen, 23 Jul 1984), Champaign County Library, Main Branch, 1060 Scioto Street, Urbana, OH.

358 Find A Grave—Terre Haute Cemetery, Mad River Twp., Champaign Co., Ohio, Find A Grave.com, Gaylord P. Terrell, Find A Grave Memorial #11586313.

359 Ohio, Deaths, 1908-1932, 1938-2007, Ancestry.com, Betty Terrell, death cert. #92147.

360 U.S., Social Security Applications and Claims Index, 1936-2007, Ancestry.com, Betty M. Evilsizor Terrell.

361 Find A Grave—Terre Haute Cemetery, Mad River Twp., Champaign Co., Ohio, Find A Grave.com, Betty M. Terrell, Find A Grave Memorial #11586314.

362 Ohio, Birth Index, 1908-1964, Ancestry.com, state file #1937105256.

363 Find A Grave—Spring Grove Cemetery, St. Paris, Johnson Twp., Champaign Co., Ohio, Find A Grave.com, Garnet Terrell Calland, Find A Grave Memorial #66568984.

364 Obituary of Garnet Calland (Urbana, Ohio, Urbana Daily Citizen, 01 Sep 1993), Champaign County Library, Main Branch, 1060 Scioto Street, Urbana, OH.

365 Obituary of Garner Smith Calland (Urbana, Ohio, Urbana Daily Citizen, 13 Nov 1986), Champaign County Library, Main Branch, 1060 Scioto Street, Urbana, OH.

366 Ohio, Deaths, 1908-1932, 1938-2007, Ancestry.com, Garner S. Calland, death cert. #081647.

367 Find A Grave—Spring Grove Cemetery, St. Paris, Johnson Twp., Champaign Co., Ohio, Find A Grave.com, Garner Smith Calland, Find A Grave Memorial #66568924.

368 Find A Grave—Spring Hills Presbyterian Church Cemetery, Springhills, Harrison Twp., Champaign Co., Ohio, Find A Grave.com, Harold R. Terrell, Find A Grave Memorial #11600160.

369 Find A Grave—Oakwood Cemetery, Fremont, Sandusky Co., Ohio, Find A Grave.com, Elizabeth Ellen Shaffer Sentman, Find A Grave Memorial #129960314.

370 Indiana Marriages, 1958-2015 (Indianapolis, Indiana, Indiana State Library, Genealogy, Indiana State Library, Indiana Marriages Certificates, 1917-2005, Ancestry.com, Lawrence S. Sentman and "Ellen Elizabeth" Shaffer, Steuben County, Indiana Marriage Records, Vol. 239, pg. 585, lic. #63-113115.

371 Ohio, Deaths, 1908-1932, 1938-2007, Ancestry.com, Lawrence S. Sentman, death cert. #022802.

372 Obituary of Lawrence Sentman (Fremont, Ohio, Fremont News Messenger, 01 Apr 1995), Rutherford B. Hayes Presidential Center Library, Spiegel Grove, Fremont, OH.

373 Find A Grave—Oakwood Cemetery, Fremont, Sandusky Co., Ohio, Find A Grave.com, Lawrence Shafer Sentman, Find A Grave Memorial# 129959972.

374 Find A Grave—McMillen Cemetery, Huron, Huron Twp., Erie Co., Ohio, Find A Grave.com, William E. Loffer, Find A Grave Memorial #61722045.

375 Ohio, County Marriages, 1789-2013, FamilySearch.org, William E. Loffer and Elizabeth Christy, Fulton County, Ohio Marriage Records, Vol. 19, pg. 193, lic. #11821.

376 Ohio, Deaths, 1908-1932, 1938-2007, Ancestry.com, Elizabeth A. Loffer, death cert. #049911.

377 Obituary of Elizabeth A. Loffer (Lorain, Ohio, Morning Journal, 15 Dec 1995), Ohio History Center Archives and Library, Ohio History Center, 800 East 17th Avenue, Columbus, OH.

378 Find A Grave—McMillen Cemetery, Huron, Huron Twp., Erie Co., Ohio, Find A Grave.com, Elizabeth A. Loffer, Find A Grave Memorial #61721998.

379 Florida Marriage Collection, 1822-1875 and 1927-2001, Ancestry.com, William Eugene Loffer and Carolyn Allen Salzer, Hillsborough County, Florida.

380 Obituary of Carolyn Allen Walker Salzer (Tampa, Florida, Tampa Times (online), 06 Jul 2014), http://www.legacy.com/obituaries/tbo/obituary.aspx?pid=171628699.

381 Ohio, Birth Index, 1908-1964, Ancestry.com, Werner Marquart, state file #1925022956.

382 Ohio, Deaths, 1908-1932, 1938-2007, Ancestry.com, Werner Marquart, death cert. #79948.

383 U.S. Veterans' Gravesites, ca. 1775-2006, Ancestry.com, Werner Marquart.

384 Find A Grave—Oakland Cemetery, Sandusky, Erie Co., Ohio, Find A Grave.com, Werner C. Marquart, Find A Grave Memorial #151683905.

385 Find A Grave—Oakland Cemetery, Sandusky, Erie Co., Ohio, Find A Grave.com, Donna J. Larose, Find A Grave Memorial #151684060.

386 Erie County, Ohio Marriage Records, Erie County, Ohio Probate Court, 323 Columbus Avenue, Sandusky, OH, Thomas LaRose and Donna Jean Loffer, Erie County, Ohio Marriage Records, Vol, 26, pg. 349.

387 Find A Grave—Resthaven Park East Cemetery, Phoenix, Maricopa Co., Arizona, Find A Grave.com, W. Jane Puse, Find A Grave Memorial #70766757.

388 U.S., Social Security Applications and Claims Index, 1936-2007, Ancestry.com, Ervin Charles Puse.

389 Find A Grave—Resthaven Park East Cemetery, Phoenix, Maricopa Co., Arizona, Find A Grave.com, Ervin C. Puse, Find A Grave Memorial #70766745.

390 Arizona, County Marriage Records, 1865-1972, Ancestry.com, John Crocker Shaw and Kay Marie Denison, Maricopa

County, Arizona Marriage Records, Book 493, pg. 101, Marriage Affadavits 1959.

391 Find A Grave—Fountain Cemetery, Fostoria, Washington Twp., Hancock Co., Ohio, Find A Grave.com, Blair Shaw, Find A Grave Memorial #151851007.

392 Find A Grave—Fountain Cemetery, Fostoria, Washington Twp., Hancock Co., Ohio, Find A Grave.com, Robert Leonard Shaw, Find A Grave Memorial #50380246.

393 "Dies in Blaze Of San Rafael Rooming House" (Fostoria, Ohio, Fostoria Review Times, 17 Mar 1955), Kaubisch Memorial Public Library, 205 Perry Street, Fostoria, OH.

394 California, Marriage Index, 1960-1985, Ancestry.com, Francis P. Rowbottom and Nancy J. Felix, Orange Co., state file #30320.

395 Obituary of Kermit E. "Kert' Reed (Madisonville, Kentucky, Madisonville Messenger, 23 Mar 2011), Hopkins County, Kentucky Genealogical Society Library, 14 Court Street, Madisonville, KY.

396 Massachusetts, Marriage Index, 1901-1955 and 1966-1970, Ancestry.com, Robert Staples Prario and Doris Jeannette Booze, 1943, Marshfield, Plymouth County, Massachusetts Marriage Records, Vol. 58, pg. 257, ref. #F63.M36 v.136 and F63.M36 v.128.

397 Massachusetts Birth Index, 1901-1960 and 1967-1970, Ancestry.com, Robert Staples Prario, vol. 641, pg. 638 (index vol 101) #F63.M362 v.101.

398 U.S., Social Security Applications and Claims Index, 1936-2007, Ancestry.com, Robert Staples Prario.

399 U.S. Veterans' Gravesites, ca. 1775-2006, Ancestry.com, Robert Staples Prario.

400 Find A Grave—Fort Rosecrans National Military Cemetery, San Diego, San Diego Co., California, Find A Grave.com, Robert S. Prario, Find A Grave Memorial #72469075.

401 California, Marriage Index, 1960-1985, William R. Cummings and Doris J. Booze Prario, San Diego County, California Marriage Records, California state lic. #76349.

402 Pennsylvania, Veterans Compensation Applications, WWII, 1950, Ancestry.com, William Russell Cummings, batch #64723.

403 California Birth Index, 1905-1995, Ancestry.com, Infant daughter Prario.

404 California, Death Index, 1940-1997, Ancestry.com, Infant daughter Prario.

405 U.S. Veterans' Gravesites, ca. 1775-2006, Ancestry.com, Ken E. Werner.

406 Find A Grave—National Memorial Cemetery of Arizona, Phoenix, Maricopa Co., Arizona, Find A Grave.com, Ken E. Werner, Find A Grave Memorial #15812967.

407 Erie County, Ohio Marriage Records, Erie County, Ohio Probate Court, 323 Columbus Avenue, Sandusky, OH, Kenneth Eugene Werner and Rita Marie Russo, Vol. 24, pg. 284, lic. #48163.

408 Ohio, Birth Index, 1908-1964, Ancestry.com, Rita M. Russo, state file #1928051777.

409 U.S., Social Security Applications and Claims Index, 1936-2007, Ancestry.com, Rita Marie Russo Werner.

410 Ohio, Deaths, 1908-1932, 1938-2007, Ancestry.com, Rita M. Werner, death cert. #082431.

411 Obituary of Rita M. Werner (Lorain, Ohio, Lorain Journal, 08 Nov 1990), Ohio History Center Archives and Library, Ohio History Center, 800 East 17th Avenue, Columbus, OH.

412 Legal Notices (Classifieds), Kenneth E. Booze (Sandusky, Ohio, Sandusky Register, 06 Jul 1946), Ohio History Center Archives and Library, Ohio History Center, 800 East 17th Avenue, Columbus, OH.

413 Ohio, County Marriages, 1789-2013, FamilySearch.org, Webster E. Werner and Iva E. Huffer Booze, Erie County, Ohio Marriage Records, Vol. 12, pg. 70, lic. # 11.220.

414 Minnesota Official Marriage Systems-MOMS, Minnesota Association of County Officers, Minnesota Association of County Officers, 1000 Westgate Drive, Suite 252, St. Paul, MN, Robert Roe Wolfe and Betty Lou Autry, Hennepin County, Minnesota Marriage Records, lic. #06430272; Online database: https://www.moms.mn.gov/Search

415 Minnesota Birth Index, 1935-2002, Ancestry.com, Betty Lou Stephen, birth cert. #1936-MN-031932.

416 Minnesota Marriage Collection, 1958-2001, Ancestry.com, Robert R. Wolfe and Sharon K. Goggin, Hennepin County, Minnesota.

417 Minnesota Official Marriage Systems-MOMS, Minnesota Association of County Officers, Minnesota Association of County Officers, 1000 Westgate Drive, Suite 252, St. Paul, MN, Robert Roe Wolfe and Sharon Katherine Goggin, Hennepin County, Minnesota Marriage Records, lic. #07850104; Online database: https://www.moms.mn.gov/Search

418 Minnesota Birth Index, 1935-2002 (P.O. Box 64975, St. Paul, MN 55164-0975, Minnesota Department of Health), Ancestry.com, Sharon Catherine Goggin, birth cert. #1944-MN-033318.

419 Minnesota Marriage Collection, 1958-2001, Ancestry.com, Robert G. Ondich and Sharon K. Wolfe, Hennepin County, Minnesota.

420 Minnesota Official Marriage Systems-MOMS, Minnesota Association of County Officers, Minnesota Association of County Officers, 1000 Westgate Drive, Suite 252, St. Paul, MN, Robert George Ondich and Sharon Kay Wolfe, Hennepin County, Minnesota Marriage Records, lic. #06540274; Online database: https://www.moms.mn.gov/Search

421 Minnesota Birth Index, 1935-2002, Ancestry.com, Robert George Ondrich, birth cert. #1935-MN-008720.

422 Find A Grave—Anderson Memorial Cemetery, Anderson, Madison Co., Indiana, Find A Grave.com, Patricia Ann Smith, Find A Grave Memorial #151512293.

423 Find A Grave—Maple Grove Cemetery, Mechanicsburg, Goshen Twp., Champaign Co., Ohio, Find A Grave.com, Richard E. Mohr, Find A Grave Memorial #104033176.

424 Ohio, County Marriages, 1789-2013, FamilySearch.org, Richard E. Mohr and "Irma Louise" Pitzer, Champaign County, Ohio Marriage Records, Vol. V, pg. 134, lic. #268.

425 Ohio, Birth Index, 1908-1964, Ancestry.com, Louise I. Pitzer, state file #1927040837.

426 Obituary of Diane Louise Mohr (Columbus, Ohio, Columbus Dispatch, March 4, 2012), Columbus Metropolitan Library, 96 South Grant Avenue, Columbus, OH.

427 Obituary of Alfred Lee Jones (Bellefontaine, Ohio, Bellefontaine Examiner, 21 Oct 1993), Ohio History Center Archives and Library, Ohio History Center, 800 East 17th Avenue, Columbus, OH.

428 Ohio, Birth Index, 1908-1964, Ancestry.com, Alfred Lee Jones, state file #1934037208.

429 Ohio, Deaths, 1908-1932, 1938-2007, Ancestry.com, Alfred Lee Jones, death cert. #084131.

430 Find A Grave—Greenwood Cemetery, DeGraff, Pleasant Twp., Logan Co., Ohio, Find A Grave.com, Alfred Lee Jones, Find A Grave Memorial #18308063.

431 Ohio Marriage Index, 1970-1972-2007, Ancestry.com, John R. Watt and Marilyn K. Jones, Logan County, Ohio Marriage Records, Ohio state Vol. 18333, lic. #59654.

432 Obituary of John R. Watt (Bellefontaine, Ohio, Bellefontaine Examiner, 22 Apr 2013), Logan County Libraries, Knowlton Library, 220 North Main Street, Bellefontaine, OH.

433 Find A Grave—Highland Memorial Cemetery, West Liberty, Liberty Twp., Logan Co., Ohio, Find A Grave.com, John R. Watt, Find A Grave Memorial #20176690.

434 Ohio, County Marriages, 1789-2013, FamilySearch.org, James Edward Oelker and Barbara Lee Terrell, Champaign County, Ohio Marriage Records, Vol. V, pg. 384, lic. #766.

435 Ohio, Birth Index, 1908-1964, Ancestry.com, Jill E. Oelker, state file #1959191362.

436 Ohio, Deaths, 1908-1932, 1938-2007, Ancestry.com, Jill Elaine Oelker, death cert. #051817.

437 U.S., Social Security Applications and Claims Index, 1936-2007, Ancestry.com, Jill Elaine Oelker.

438 Ohio, County Marriages, 1789-2013, FamilySearch.org, William I. "Mausalis" and Beverly Sue Terrell, Champaign County, Ohio Marriage Records, Vol. V, pg. 594, lic. #2086.

439 Ohio, Birth Index, 1908-1964, Ancestry.com, state file #1935085605.

440 U.S., Social Security Applications and Claims Index, 1936-2007, Ancestry.com, William Iverson Marsalis.

441 Ohio, Deaths, 1908-1932, 1938-2007, Ancestry.com, William I. Marsalis, death cert. # #025179.

442 Obituary of William I. Marsalis (Urbana, Ohio, Urbana Daily Citizen, 28 Apr 1986), Champaign County Library, Main Branch, 1060 Scioto Street, Urbana, OH.

443 Find A Grave—Oak Dale Cemetery, Urbana, Urbana Twp., Champaign Co., Ohio, Find A Grave.com, William I. Marsalis, Find A Grave Memorial #120601415.

444 Ohio Marriage Index, 1970-1972-2007, Ancestry.com, Douglas E. Murphy and Janet Gunsaulies, Champaign County, Ohio Marriage Records, Ohio state Vol. 12553, lic. #40285.

445 Ohio, Birth Index, 1908-1964, Ancestry.com, Douglas Edwin Murphy, state file #1942090521.

446 Obituary of Douglas E. Murphy (Urbana, Ohio, Urbana Daily Citizen, 14 Dec 2001), Champaign County Library, Main Branch, 1060 Scioto Street, Urbana, OH.

447 Find A Grave—Pleasant Hill Cemetery, Moorefield Twp., Clark Co., Ohio, Find A Grave.com.

448 U.S. Veterans' Gravesites, ca. 1775-2006, Ancestry.com, Douglas Edwin Murphy.

449 Find A Grave—Oak Dale Cemetery, Urbana, Urbana Twp., Champaign Co., Ohio, Find A Grave.com, Thomas E. Terrell, Find A Grave Memorial #173041726.

450 Ohio, County Marriages, 1789-2013, FamilySearch.org, Robert Trimble and Nancy Terrell, Champaign County, Ohio Marriage Records, Vol. V, pg. 377, lic. #753.

451 Find A Grave—Maple Grove Cemetery, Mechanicsburg, Goshen Twp., Champaign Co., Ohio, Find A Grave.com, Diane Louise Mohr, Find A Grave Memorial #86341411.

452 Find A Grave—Kings Creek Baptist Church Cemetery, Kings Creek, Salem Twp., Champaign Co., Ohio, Find A Grave.com, Jill Elaine Oelker, Find A Grave Memorial #128101494.

[A] Phone interview with John W. Brane, Santa Clara, CA, author Ann Miller Carr, 15 Aug 2011. John Brane was a half-brother to Constance Brane Nichols Schrock and Richard Lee Brane.

William Louis/Lewis Pegan

1. **William Louis or Lewis[5] Pegan** (*Robert A.[4], Andrew[3], Andrew[2] Pagan, James[1]*) was born on June 7, 1820, in Fairview, Union Twp., Highland Co., Ohio.[1] He was the son of Robert A. Pegan and Christina or Christiana Ingle. William Louis or Lewis lived before 1845 in Koscuisko Co., Indiana. He also resided in 1846 in LaPorte Co., Indiana. William Louis or Lewis died in Marysville, Marysville Twp., Sutter Co., California, on November 8, 1849, at age 29.[1] He was buried in Marysville, Marysville Twp., Sutter Co., California.[1]

William Louis/Lewis Pegan was undoubtedly the "Lewis Pegan" who sued Rev. David Winters for slander and defamation of character in Montgomery Co., Ohio on September 24, 1839, claiming damages of $1000. Lewis Pegan said Winters slandered him by saying that Lewis committed sodomy with a man, allegedly a minister and teacher, who, in Dayton, Ohio, called himself Francis Frederick Langhoff. Lewis Pegan was a pupil of Langhoff's and was living in his house. Rev. Winters, a well-known and respected German Reformed Church "circuit rider" minister in Montgomery and Greene counties, Ohio, was highly respected and popular. He helped found two German Reformed Churches in the Xenia, Greene Co., Ohio area before becoming the minister of the First Reformed Church in Xenia. Later, he established David's Church in Kettering, Montgomery Co., Ohio, which still is active. Rev. Winters knew the Pegan family, earlier he had solemnized the marriages of several of Robert and Christiana/Christina Ingle Pegan's children and their spouses.

The court document language is stilted and hard to decipher, and some of the evidence is in German.

As he was a minor (under age 21), William "Lewis" was represented in court by John Jacob Pegan, who may have been his elder brother. However, William Louis/Lewis' brother John never used a middle initial on any documentation, and his middle name is unknown.

But "John Jacob Pegan" was more likely a cousin—there is a John J. Pegan is Knox Twp., Columbiana Co., Ohio from 1829-1833 who is later found in Wheeling, (West) Virginia, in 1840. He seems to be the grandson of James Pagan II, a brother to William L.'s great-grandfather. (See Vol. 2 for more information.) Was he a lawyer?

Also, we are sure that this "Lewis Pegan" was William Louis/Lewis, the son of Robert Pegan/Pagan. Although Joseph Pagan/Pagin, the master carpenter of the Preble and Montgomery counties, Ohio area and LaPorte County, Indiana, had a son named Lewis, there are several reasons why Joseph's son is not the right "Lewis Pegan" of the trial. Joseph's son Lewis never used the surname "Pegan", only "Pagan" or "Pagin". Also, according to the Joseph Pagan/Pagin family bible records, Joseph's son Lewis Pagan/Pagin, was born on August 24, 1818, and therefore would have been an adult, 21 years old, when the trial started. Moreover, by the time of the alleged incident and subsequent lawsuit, Joseph Pagan/Pagin and his family, including his son Lewis, had been residents of LaPorte County, Indiana for several years.

Lastly, Robert Pegan/Pagan, William Louis/Lewis Pegan's father was found in the 1830 census in Montgomery County Ohio. As Robert died in 1834, it is reasonable that his widow, Christina, who inherited no property and had no income except for what her grown sons could give her, would seek out help from her church—perhaps from Rev. Winters—for her younger sons like William Louis/Lewis, and that is how he came to live with the imposter minister Francis Langhoff.

The case was heard in Montgomery County Court of Common Pleas in Dayton, Ohio, on September

24, 1839, before Judge William L. Helfenstein. The attorneys for the plaintiffs, Lewis Pegan and his representative John Jacob Pegan, were "Crane and Henderson".

The Pegans testified that Rev. David Winters told a church congregation that Rev. David Winters told a church congregation in Lancaster, Ohio on July 1, 1839 that Langhoff had committed sodomy with a boy who was living with him in Dayton. In addition, on July 3, the Pegans claimed Rev. Winters repeated this same accusation in Dayton to another man, Simon Snyder, but this time naming Lewis Pegan as the boy Langhoff was involved with.

The Pegans testified that Winters assumed there was a carnal relationship between Langhoff and Lewis Pegan because of a letter, in German, from a Wheeling, West Virginia church Winters received on May 29, 1839. The Wheeling church wrote that Langhoff, under another, unspecified name, had been their minister prior to his move to Dayton. But the Wheeling church discovered that Langhoff had falsified his clerical credentials and had never been ordained. The letter from the Wheeling church went on to say that Langhoff "had attached a certain party to himself" and "his immoral sinful course of life came more and more into light". The Wheeling church had also found out that Langhoff, under yet another alias, had also been a clergyman in Pittsburgh, Pennsylvania before he was in Wheeling and had committed the same act.

Lewis Pegan, through John Jacob Pegan, told the court that, although he was still living in Langhoff's house, had always been "a good citizen of this State and as such hath always conducted and until the speaking of the false and defamatory words heriein (sic) after mentioned hath not been suspected of that horrid and detestable crime not fit to be named among Christians called sodomy". The Pegans said that Rev. Winters intended to "injure the said Lewis Pegan in his good name and reputation".

Rev. Winters, through his lawyers "Odlin and Schenk", disputed that he ever told anyone that Lewis Pegan had committed sodomy. In response to the first charge, telling the Lancaster, Ohio congregation, Winters told the court he was not guilty of "the said supposed grievances laid to his charge in manner and form". As to the to second count against him, recounting his accusation to Simon Snyder, he contested that "the matters therein contained are not sufficient in law to maintain the action".

The case ended shortly thereafter, although no date is given, when the Pegans discontinued their suit. The court assessed the Pegans $9.53 and Rev. Winters $3.53 in court costs.[103]

William Louis or Lewis married **Drusilla F. Pagin or Pagan** on January 7, 1845, in LaPorte, Center Twp., LaPorte Co., Indiana.[1] They had three daughters. Drusilla F. Pagin or Pagan was born in Gratis Twp., Preble Co., Ohio, on February 20, 1825.[2, 3] Drusilla F. Pagan/Pagin reached age 78 and died in East End, Westmoreland Co., Virginia, on March 28, 1903.[3, 4] She was buried in Oakwood Cemetery, Falls Church, Fairfax Co., Virginia.[2]

Drusilla F. Pagin Pegan's exact dates of birth and death are from a Pagan/Pagin family bible record.[3] Her gravestone in the Oakwood Cemetery in Falls Church, Virginia does say her birth year was 1825.[2] However, Drusilla's obituary in the *LaPorte (IN) Herald-Argus* on April 10, 1903 says she was 79 years old.[4] She has no death certificate, as the Commonwealth of Virginia and its counties and independent cities did not keep death records until 1912.

William and Drusilla may have been cousins. The family of Drusilla F. Pagin Pegan's parents, Joseph and Susanna Foshier Pagan/Pagin, is well-documented. Joseph grew up in Bedford County, Virginia, but later removed to Gratis Twp., Preble Co., Ohio.[5, 6] Joseph's surname is first seen as Pagan in Bedford Co., but by the time he removed to LaPorte Co., Indiana, the surname was also spelled Pagin. However, the exact kinship, if there is one, has not been documented or proven.

Joseph Pagan/Pagin was considered the most skilled carpenter in western Ohio and is mentioned as such in several history books of the area, including Audrey Gilbert's *Twin Valley Tidbits*.[5, 6] He undoubtedly trained William Louis Pegan's three carpenter brothers—John, Harrison Sr., and Elsey—which is likely how William Louis/Lewis Pegan met Drusilla Pagan/Pagin. It is also very possible that Joseph's ancestors were cousins and known to James Pegan Sr. and his sons who emigrated to Martic Twp., Lancaster Co., Pennsylvania. Did Robert Pagan/Pegan leave Highland County, Ohio and move to Montgomery County, Ohio, so his sons could be trained in carpentry and work for a cousin, Joseph Pagan/Pagin? It is interesting to note, however, that William Louis Pegan did not chose carpentry as an occupation—he chose farming, but he seemed to struggle.

The Joseph Pagan/Pagin family relocated to LaPorte Co., Indiana by 1832.[6] William Louis/Lewis Pegan removed to Indiana by 1843, when he bought land in Koscuisko Co., Indiana. But he sold this land a year later and bought land in LaPorte Co., Indiana, where his future in-laws had settled.[7]

In 1849, William Lewis Pegan went to northern California to seek his fortune during the California gold rush, either as a prospector or as a storekeeper/ vendor to the "'49'ers". When he left LaPorte County, Indiana for northern California, his brother- and sister-in-law, John and Charlotte Redmond Pagan/Pagin, went with him.[8] It is also possible that William Louis/Lewis Pegan's nephew, James Robert Pegan, son of his brother Andrew who lived in Highland County, Ohio, accompanied his uncle to California.

When he left to go West, William Louis/Lewis Pegan left behind his wife Drusilla and three daughters. William Louis wrote to Drusilla before he died in California. This letter also mentions Drusilla's brother and his wife, John and Charlotte Redmond Pagin. In the missive, William Louis apologizes to Drusilla for not doing well financially and laments his failings as a farmer. This letter was passed down from Drusilla to her granddaughter, Drusilla Davis Henoch, then from Drusilla to her daughter, Maybelle Henoch Costa. One of Maybelle's sons now possesses the letter.[8]

According to the Robert and Christina "Engle" Pegan bible, William Louis Pagan died of pleurisy after a sickness of only one day in Marysville, Yuba Co., California. The bible also states that he was buried in Marysville.[1] However, his probate is found in LaPorte Co., Indiana.[7, 9]

In 1850, the widow Drusilla Pegan and her daughters are living with her parents, Joseph and Susannah Foshier Pagin, in Springfield Twp., LaPorte Co., Indiana *(Census Place: Springfield, La Porte, Indiana; Roll: M432_157; Page: 205B; Image: 415)*. Drusilla is age 25, born Ohio; Orpha is five and the twins Henrietta and Marietta are two years old. All the children were born in Indiana.

Drusilla Pegan is enumerated twice in the 1860 census. Drusilla and her daughters are again included in her widower father Joseph Pagin's household in Springfield Twp., LaPorte Co., Indiana *(Census Place: Springfield, La Porte, Indiana; Roll: M653_275; Page: 166; Image: 166)*. Drusilla is 31(?) years old and born in Ohio; her daughters Orpha (listed as "Orpheus"), 12(?), and Henrietta, 10, but no Marietta. As Marietta was a twin to Henrietta, she was most likely the "Margaret, age 8" living in the home and the census taker made a mistake. Drusilla/Druzilla is also listed as "Eliza" Pagan in the 1860 census in LaPorte, Center Twp., LaPorte Co., Indiana *(Census Place: La Porte, La Porte, Indiana; Roll: M653_275; Page: 63; Image: 63)*. "Eliza Pagan", age 40, was born in Ohio. Her three daughters, Orpha, 15 (?), and twins Marietta and Henrietta, 10, were born in Indiana. Although she lists no occupation, Drusilla owns land, which was probably her husband William Louis', as she lists her property worth $200.

Drusilla Pagin Pegan and her daughters are not found in the 1870 or 1880 censuses. However, her twin daughters, Henrietta and Marietta, both marry in 1871 in Berrien and Cass counties, Michigan, respectively. Both state on their marriage licenses that they are residents of LaPorte, LaPorte Co., Indiana.

In 1900, Drusilla "Druzilla" Pagan/Pagin Pegan is living with her only surviving child, Orpha Marie Pegan Andrews/Andrus Conklin, in Brooklyn, Kings Co., New York *(Census Place: Brooklyn Ward 9, Kings, New York; Roll: T623_1048; Page: 3A; Enumeration District: 116)*. She says she is 75 years old and a widow who has born four children—but only one is still living. After the 1900 census, Isaac and Orpha Pegan Andrews/Andrus Conklin and Drusilla Pegan relocated to Falls Church, Virginia. (Falls Church is an independent city.)

Daughters of William Louis or Lewis Pegan and Drusilla F. Pagin or Pagan:

+ 2 f I. **Orpha Marie**[6] **Pegan** was born in Springfield Twp., LaPorte Co., Indiana, on February 18, 1846.[10] She died in Providence Twp., Fairfax Co., Virginia, on April 8, 1918.[10]

+ 3 f II. **Henrietta G.**[6] **Pegan** was born in Springfield Twp., LaPorte Co., Indiana, on October 22, 1848.[3] She was also known as **Etta or Ettie**. Henrietta G. died in Sidney, Port Orchard Twp., Kitsap Co., Washington, on December 31, 1888.[11, 12]

+ 4 f III. **Marietta Marilla**[6] **Pegan** was born in Springfield Twp., LaPorte Co., Indiana, on October 22, 1848.[3] She was also known as **May**. Marietta Marilla died in Jacksonville, Duvall Co., Florida, on March 13, 1882.[13, 14]

6th Generation

2. **Orpha Marie[6] Pegan** (*William Louis or Lewis[5], Robert A.[4], Andrew[3], Andrew[2] Pagan, James[1]*) was born on February 18, 1846, in Springfield Twp., LaPorte Co., Indiana.[10] She was the daughter of William Louis or Lewis Pegan (1) and Drusilla F. Pagin or Pagan. Orpha Marie died in Providence Twp., Fairfax Co., Virginia, on April 8, 1918, at age 72.[10] She was buried in Oakwood Cemetery, Falls Church, Fairfax Co., Virginia.[10, 15]

Orpha's life took her to many places—she was born in LaPorte, Springfield Twp., LaPorte Co., Indiana and moved to Adel Twp., Dallas Co., Iowa with her first husband Joseph Andrews/Andrus. She is not found in the 1880 census, but then she reappears in Brooklyn, Kings Co., New York with her second husband, Isaac Conklin, and her mother Drusilla Pagan Pegan. From there, all three move to Providence, Fairfax Co., Virginia.

Orpha Marie married **Joseph Andrews** on March 1, 1865, in LaPorte Co., Indiana.[16] They divorced. They had one son. Joseph Andrews was born in Kankakee Twp., LaPorte Co., Indiana about 1844. He died after 1910.

Joseph and Orpha Pegan Andrews are enumerated in Adel Twp., Dallas Co., Iowa in 1870 *(Census Place: Adel, Dallas, Iowa; Roll: M593_385; Page: 506A; Image: 282)*. In the household are Joseph Andrews, age 26, a farmer; his wife Orpha Pegan Andrews, 24; and their son, Milton, age three. All were born in Indiana. Milton dies before 1880, as he is not found in any more U.S. Federal Census records, and his mother Orpha says she has borne one child who is not surviving in both the 1900 and 1910 censuses.

Joseph Andrews is found in Adel Twp., Dallas Co., Iowa in 1880 *(Census Place: Adel, Dallas, Iowa; Roll: 335; Page: 253A; Enumeration District: 051; Image: 0510)*. Joseph Andrews, age 36, born Indiana with his parents born in Ohio, is a boarder in the home of Andrew and Mary Cornieliuson. His occupation is also listed as "boarder". Joseph's parents, Hiram and Rebecca Andrews, are also in Adel Twp., Dallas Co., Iowa.

In 1900, Joseph Andrews is living in Fall River Twp., Shasta Co., California *(Census Place: Fall River, Shasta, California; Roll: 112; Page: 7A; Enumeration District: 116)*. Joseph says he is a widower, age 56, born Apr 1844 in Indiana, with his father born in Pennsylvania and his mother in New Jersey. He is a boarder in the home of 79-year-old Rebecca Estep, and lists his occupation as day laborer.

Joseph Andrews is enumerated in 1910 in Justice Precinct 1, Lynn Co., Texas *(Census Place: Justice Precinct 1, Lynn, Texas; Roll: T624_1574; Page: 4A; Enumeration District: 0156; Image: 815)*. Joseph Andrews is age 66, born Indiana, with his father born in Pennsylvania and his mother in New Jersey; he again says he is a widower. Joseph is a boarder in the home of a young married couple, Hall and Ethel Robinson, but lists no occupation.

When and where Joseph Andrews died is unknown.

Orpha Marie Pegan Andrews married **Isaac Albert Conklin** about 1880. Isaac Albert Conklin was born in Hackensack, Bergen Co., New Jersey, on November 19, 1843.[17] He reached age 74 and died in Providence Twp., Fairfax Co., Virginia, on February 15, 1918.[17] Isaac Albert was buried in Oakwood Cemetery, Falls Church, Fairfax Co., Virginia.[18]

Isaac Conklin was born in New Jersey, but grew up and lived as a young adult in New York City, as he is found in the 1870 U.S. Federal census there with his parents Albert and Christiana Conklin 1870 *(Census Place: New York Ward 9 District 16, New York, New York; Roll: M593_983; Page: 524B)*. How Isaac and Orpha met, and when and where they married, is not known.

In 1900, Isaac and Orpha Pegan Andrews Conklin and Orpha's mother Drusilla Pagan Pegan are living in Brooklyn, Kings Co., New York *(Census Place: Brooklyn Ward 9, Kings, New York; Roll: T623_1048; Page: 3A; Enumeration District: 116)*. The head of the household is Isaac Conklin, 56, born Nov 1843 in New York with his parents born in New Jersey; he lists his occupation as gold refiner. With him are his wife, Orpha Pegan Conklin, 54, born Indiana in Jan 1846 with her parents born in Ohio; and Orpha's mother, Drusilla Pagin Pegan, 75, born Feb 1825, with her father born in Illinois and her mother in Virginia. Isaac and Orpha Pegan Andrews Conklin have been married 20 years. Orpha says she bore one child, who is no longer living. Drusilla Pagan Pegan says she bore four children, only one of whom, Orpha, is still alive. Also in the home is a 63-year-old servant, Francisco Banning, born in Holland.

After the 1900 census, the Conklins and Drusilla Pagan/Pagin Pegan remove to Fairfax Co., Virginia, where Drusilla dies.

Isaac A. and Orpha M. Pegan Andrews/Andrus Conklin are found in Providence Twp. (Precinct), Fairfax Co., Virginia in 1910 *(Census Place: Providence, Fairfax, Virginia; Roll: T624_1628; Page: 13B; Enumeration District: 0036; Image: 370)*. Isaac, age 66, is a horticulturalist; Orpha is 64. The couple says they are still on their first marriage and have been married 45 years. This is incorrect, as Orpha was married before. Perhaps she was confused, and gave the date (1865) of her first marriage. Once again, Orpha says she bore one child who is no longer alive. This time, Isaac says he and his parents are New Jersey natives. Orpha repeats that she was born in Indiana and her parents in Ohio.

Orpha M. Pegan Andrews Conklin died just two months after her second husband Isaac Albert Conklin. The informant on her death certificate was her first cousin once removed, Orpha Estella "Stella" Pegan, the daughter of James Pegan and granddaughter of John Pegan Orpha's uncle. "Stella" Pegan's residence at the time, 1918, is given as Falls Church, Virginia. Oddly, however, Orpha Estella "Stella" Pegan failed to enter the parental information on her elder Orpha's death certificate.[10]

Son of Orpha Marie Pegan and Joseph Andrews:

+ 5 m I. **Milton**[7] **Andrews** was born in LaPorte Co., Indiana, in 1866. He died in Adel Twp., Dallas Co., Iowa?, before 1880.

3. **Henrietta G.**[6] **Pegan** (*William Louis or Lewis*[5], *Robert A.*[4], *Andrew*[3], *Andrew*[2] *Pagan, James*[1]) was born on October 22, 1848, in Springfield Twp., LaPorte Co., Indiana.[3] She was also known as **Etta or Ettie**. She was the daughter of William Louis/Lewis Pegan (1) and Drusilla F. Pagin or Pagan. She died in Sidney (now Port Orchard), Port Orchard Twp., Kitsap Co., Washington, on December 31, 1888, at age 40.[11, 12] Henrietta G. is said to be buried on their property "on a bold bluff overlooking bright Orchard Bay", near what is now Port Orchard Twp., Kitsap Co., Washington.[12]

Henrietta G. married **Irwin James Hatch** on August 11, 1871, in Berrien Co., Michigan.[19] They were divorced after 1880. They had two sons. Irwin James Hatch was born in Niles, Niles Twp., Berrien Co., Michigan, on December 20, 1844.[20] Irwin James reached age 74 and died in Cleon Twp., Manistee Co., Michigan, on September 21, 1919.[20] He was buried in Cleon Township Cemetery, Copemish, Cleon Twp., Manistee Co., Michigan.[20, 21]

Irwin James and Henrietta "Etta" Pegan Hatch state they are living in Wayne Twp., Cass Co., Michigan when they witness the marriage of William Davis and Henrietta's twin sister Marietta "May" Pegan (Davis) in November 1871.[22]

Irwin and Henrietta Pegan Hatch are enumerated in 1880 in Chase, Chase Twp., Lake Co., Michigan *(Census Place: Chase, Lake, Michigan; Roll: 589; Page: 79C; Enumeration District: 155; Image: 0162)*. Irwin Hatch, 29, born in Michigan with his parents born in New York ("York State"), is a farmer. Wife Henrietta Pegan Hatch, listed as "Ettie", is 29 and a dressmaker; she was born in Indiana with her parents born in Ohio. They have two sons, "Glen", age seven, and "Clay", six, both born in Michigan.

The Hatches divorced shortly after the 1880 census. After the divorce, Henrietta Pegan Hatch and her two sons removed to Toledo, Lucas Co., Ohio, where she lived with her twin sister, Marietta Marilla Pegan Davis, and her family.[23] After her own son, William G. Hatch, and her sister Marietta both died in 1882, Henrietta and her remaining son Henry Clay Hatch moved back to LaPorte, LaPorte Co., Indiana to be near their Pagin relatives.

By 1900, Irwin Hatch has been remarried for 10 years to Clara Sears, and they have two sons. They are living in Cleon Twp., Manistee Co., Michigan

[Census Place: Cleon, Manistee, Michigan; Roll: 727; Page: 7B; Enumeration District: 0029]. Irwin and his second wife are still in Cleon in 1910 *[Cleon, Manistee, Michigan; Roll: T624_661; Page: 7A, Enumeration District: 0033]* and have three sons and a daughter.

Henrietta G. Pegan Hatch married **Ira Charles Rockwell** on July 10, 1888, in St. Joseph Co., Indiana.[24]

Ira Charles Rockwell was born in Odessa, Tioga Co., New York or the Town of Catherine, Tioga Co. (now Schuyler Co.), New York, on December 29, 1826.[25, 26] Ira Charles reached age 72 and died in Sidney (now Port Orchard), Port Orchard Twp., Kitsap Co., Washington, on January 3, 1899.[26, 27, 28] He was probably buried in Colby Cemetery, Port Orchard Twp., Kitsap Co., Washington.[29]

Ira Charles Rockwell's birth and death dates are recorded in a non-published bible, in possession of a Rockwell family member in Watkins Glen New York, who sent the information to this author. According to a short biography in *Barton's Legislative Handbook and Manual of the State of Washington*, Ira Charles Rockwell was born in Odessa, Tioga Co., New York[25]. But, most likely, he was born in the Town of Catherine in Tioga County, where his parents were living at that time. The Town of Catherine eventually became a part of Schuyler County when it was formed.

Ira C. Rockwell was living in LaPorte, Springfield Twp., LaPorte Co., Indiana in 1850 *(Census Place: La Porte, La Porte, Indiana; Roll: M432_157; Page: 265A; Image: 534)*. His age is listed as 31, born New York, but he would have been 26 years old. Ira returned to New York, to Tompkins County, and married. He came back to the LaPorte-St. Joseph counties, Indiana area in 1888, three years after his first wife, Lorinda Hopper, died. He was a lumber merchant, perhaps on his way to Washington State, when he stopped at his old home in LaPorte and met the divorcee Henrietta G. Pegan Hatch.

Immediately after their 1888 marriage, Ira and Henrietta Pegan Hatch Rockwell and Henrietta's son, Henry Clay Hatch, moved to Sidney (now Port Orchard), Port Orchard Twp., Kitsap Co., Washington. Her obituary in the *Ithaca (NY) Daily Journal* (many of her husband's relatives lived in Ithaca), says Ira and Henrietta, along with young Henry Clay Hatch, traveled to the Pacific Northwest on a wedding trip and stopped in Sidney. Henrietta, in particular, was smitten by the town, and the Rockwells decided to settle there.[12]

They had only lived in Sidney six months when tragedy struck the family. According to a January 4, 1899 article in the *Washington Standard (Olympia, WA)*, "Etta" gave her son "Clay" permission to go duck hunting. Unbeknownst to Henry, the gun was already loaded. While he was removing the gun from the cabinet in the kitchen, the weapon accidentally fired. The bullet pierced through a wall partition and hit his mother Etta in the chest while she was sitting in the living room. Etta died within minutes.[11]

Her *Ithaca Daily Journal* obituary mentions that Henrietta was buried "on a bold bluff overlooking bright Port Orchard Bay" on the Rockwell family property. Henrietta had told a friend just two weeks before her death that, in case she would die, she wanted to be buried there.[12]

Shortly thereafter, Henry Clay Hatch was formally adopted by his stepfather, Ira C. Rockwell.[30] Henry was known as Henry Clay Rockwell for the rest of his life. Ira raised Henry and sent him to college at the University of Washington.

In 1889, Ira C. Rockwell and the stepson he adopted, Henry Clay Hatch Rockwell, are found in Sidney Precinct, Kitsap Co., Washington *(Washington State and Territorial Censuses, 1857-1892, Roll V228_9, pg. 164)*. Henry Clay Hatch Rockwell, listed as Henry Rockwell, is age 14, born Michigan, and is a laborer. Ira C. Rockwell, listed as I.C. Rockwell, is 62, a farmer, born New York.[31]

Ira C. Rockwell was mayor of Sidney, Kitsap Co., Washington in 1890, and was also president of the board of trade in Sidney.[29] Starting in August 1896, Ira was the Clerk of the Superior Court in Kitsap Co.[29] He also served as a Washington state representative in 1891.[25]

Ira is either buried alongside his wife Henrietta Pegan Hatch Rockwell on the Rockwell property or, more likely, in Colby Cemetery, Port Orchard Twp., Kitsap Co., Washington, according to the Kitsap County Historical Society.[29] The cemetery dates to 1887 and was the only cemetery in the area at that time. But there are no cemetery records for Colby Cemetery in that era.[29]

Sons of Henrietta G. Pegan and Irwin James Hatch:

+ 6 m I. **William Glen**[7] **Hatch** was born in Wayne Twp., Cass Co., Michigan, on July 5, 1872.[3, 18] He died in Toledo, Lucas Co., Ohio, on July 12, 1882.[3, 18]

+ 7 m II. **Henry Clay**[7] **Hatch (Rockwell)** was born in Wayne Twp., Cass Co., Michigan, on May 22, 1874.[32, 33, 34, 35, 36] He was adopted by his stepfather, Ira Charles Rockwell, in Sidney (now Port Orchard), Port Orchard Twp., Kitsap Co., Washington, in 1889.[30] Henry Clay died in a facility in Brentwood, Town of Islip, Suffolk Co., New York, on February 24, 1950.[35, 36, 37]

4. **Marietta Marilla**[6] **Pegan** (*William Louis or Lewis*[5], *Robert A.*[4], *Andrew*[3], *Andrew*[2] *Pagan, James*[1]) was born on October 22, 1848, in Springfield Twp., LaPorte Co., Indiana.[3] She was also known as **May**. She was the daughter of William Louis or Lewis Pegan (1) and Drusilla F. Pagin or Pagan. Marietta Marilla died in Jacksonville, Duvall Co., Florida, on March 13, 1882, at age 33.[13, 14] She was buried in Woodlawn Cemetery, Toledo, Lucas Co., Ohio.[14]

Marietta Marilla married **William Milford Davis** on November 9, 1871, in Cass Co., Michigan.[22] They had four children. William Milford Davis was born in Niles, Niles Twp., Berrien Co., Michigan, on March 28, 1849.[38, 39] He was also known as **Will**. William Milford reached age 56 and died in Cincinnati, Hamilton Co., Ohio, on March 24, 1906.[38, 39] He was buried in Woodlawn Cemetery, Toledo, Lucas Co., Ohio.[38, 40, 41, 42]

William was the son of Moses and Sarah Lewis Davis, who were wealthy and prominent Roman Catholics in Niles, Niles Twp., Berrien Co., Michigan. Moses Davis, a pump company owner and first cousin to Confederate President Jefferson Davis, is credited for draining much of the lower Michigan area from Detroit to Chicago for the railroad companies. William's brother was Martin Simeon Davis, a noted trader of furs and hats, who was married to a doctor's daughter from Goshen, Indiana. Martin Simeon Davis devised the Mackinaw straw hat, which he manufactured in Toledo, Lucas Co., Ohio.

In November 1871, William Milford Davis states on his Cass County, Michigan marriage application that his current residence was Goshen, Elkhart Co., Indiana. Marietta Marilla "May" Pegan said she was living in LaPorte, LaPorte Co., Indiana.[22]

William M. and Marietta Marilla "May" Pegan Davis are enumerated in 1880 in Toledo, Lucas Co., Ohio *(Census Place: Toledo, Lucas, Ohio; Roll: 1043; Page: 122A; Enumeration District: 33; Image: 0139)*. In the home are William M. Davis, age 31, born Michigan, with his father born in Ohio and his mother in Virginia, an auctioneer; and "May" Davis, 31, born Indiana, who says her father was born in Ohio and her mother in Indiana. Children with them are Drusilla, seven, born Michigan, and Louis B., five, Mabel, four, and Sarah, two, all born in Ohio. There are six boarders and a servant in the home as well.

In March 1881, William Milford and Marietta "May" Davis moved to Jacksonville, Duvall Co., Florida for Marietta's health, but she died just a few days later. Her obituary in the *LaPorte (IN) Herald Chronicle* on April 13, 1882 says her remains were taken to Toledo, Lucas Co., Ohio for burial.[13] Toledo's Woodlawn Cemetery records has her buried under the name, "Mrs. Wm. Davis". However, unlike her husband William Milford Davis and daughters Mabel and Sarah Elizabeth "Bessie" Davis, Woodlawn Cemetery does not have a burial card for her. Her death date and burial, however, are noted on the cemetery's plot card for the family.[14]

After his wife Marietta's death, William Milford Davis moved his family back to Niles, Niles Twp., Berrien Co., Michigan. He educated his daughters at St. Mary's at Notre Dame in adjacent South Bend, St. Joseph Co., Indiana. The Davis family lived in Niles until after the death of William's mother, Sarah Lewis Davis, in January 1893.[102]

William M. Davis is not found in the 1900 U.S. Federal Census.

William Milford Davis married his second wife, Nora (Barber) Connavello, on December 17, 1905 in Montgomery Co., Ohio.[39] They'd been residing in Cincinnati, Ohio, only a short time before William's death; he is not listed in the 1904-1906 Cincinnati city directories.

Children of Marietta Marilla Pegan and William Milford Davis:

+ 8 f I. **Drusilla Madeline**[7] **Davis** was born in Niles, Niles Twp., Berrien Co., Michigan, on October 13, 1872.[45, 46, 47, 74] She died in Los Angeles, Los Angeles Co., California, on September 27, 1954.[47, 48, 74]

+ 9 m II. **Lewis B.**[7] **Davis** was born in Toledo, Lucas Co., Ohio, on June 26, 1874.[49, 50] He died in St. Louis, St. Louis Co., Missouri, on May 11, 1921, at age 46.[50, 51]

+ 10 f III. **Mabel**[7] **Davis** was born in Toledo, Lucas Co., Ohio, on February 26, 1876.[52] She died in Washington, District of Columbia, on April 25, 1894.[53, 54]

+ 11 f IV. **Sarah Elizabeth**[7] **Davis** was born in Toledo, Lucas Co., Ohio, on July 15, 1877.[55] She was also known as **Bessie**. Sarah Elizabeth died in South Bend, St. Joseph Co., Indiana, on April 2, 1893.[56, 57, 58]

7th Generation

5. **Milton**[7] **Andrews** (*Orpha Marie*[6] *Pegan, William Louis or Lewis*[5]*, Robert A.*[4]*, Andrew*[3]*, Andrew*[2] *Pagan, James*[1]) was born about 1866 in LaPorte Co., Indiana. He was the son of Joseph Andrews and Orpha Marie Pegan (2). Milton died in Adel Twp., Dallas Co., Iowa?, before 1880.

6. **William Glen**[7] **Hatch** (*Henrietta G.*[6] *Pegan, William Louis or Lewis*[5]*, Robert A.*[4]*, Andrew*[3]*, Andrew*[2] *Pagan, James*[1]) was born on July 5, 1872, in Wayne Twp., Cass Co., Michigan.[3, 18] He was the son of Irwin James Hatch and Henrietta G. Pegan (3). William Glen died in Toledo, Lucas Co., Ohio, on July 12, 1882, at age 10.[3, 18] He was buried in Woodlawn Cemetery, Toledo, Lucas Co., Ohio.[18] William Glen Hatch exact date of birth is found in privately-held Pagin family bible records. He is buried in Woodlawn Cemetery in Toledo, Lucas Co., Ohio, with his maternal aunt Marietta Pegan Davis, his mother Henrietta Pegan Hatch Rockwell's twin sister, Marietta's husband William Milford Davis, and their daughters Mabel and Sarah Elizabeth "Bessie" Davis.

7. **Henry Clay**[7] **Hatch (Rockwell)** (*Henrietta G.*[6] *Pegan, William Louis or Lewis*[5]*, Robert A.*[4]*, Andrew*[3]*, Andrew*[2] *Pagan, James*[1]) was born on May 22, 1874, in Wayne Twp., Cass Co., Michigan.[32, 33, 34, 35, 36] He was the son of Irwin James Hatch and Henrietta G. Pegan (3). He was adopted by his stepfather, Ira Charles Rockwell, in Sidney (now Port Orchard), Port Orchard Twp., Kitsap Co., Washington, in 1889.[30] He was also known as H. Clay Rockwell. Henry Clay died in a facility in Brentwood, Town of Islip, Suffolk Co., New York, on February 24, 1950.[35, 36, 37] He was buried in Green-Wood Cemetery, Brooklyn, Kings Co., New York, on May 5, 1950.[35, 37]

Childless.

Henry Clay Hatch Rockwell accidentally killed his mother, Henrietta "Etta" Pegan Hatch Rockwell. According to an article in the Washington Standard (Olympia, Washington) on January 4, 1889, Henrietta "Etta" had given Henry permission to go hunting. He was loading the gun in the kitchen, but he didn't know the weapon was already loaded. The gun accidentally discharged. The bullet pierced through a wall partition and hit Etta in the chest while she was sitting in their living room. She died within a few minutes.[11]

Shortly thereafter, Henry Clay Hatch was formally adopted by his stepfather, Ira C. Rockwell.[30] Henry Clay abandoned his use of his birth name of Hatch and went by the name" Henry Clay Rockwell" for the rest of his life. In adulthood, he often went by "H. Clay Rockwell".

In 1889, Henry Clay Hatch Rockwell is enumerated with his stepfather, his mother's, Henrietta G. Pegan Hatch Rockwell's, second husband, Ira C. Rockwell, in Sidney Precinct, Kitsap Co., Washington *(Washington State and Territorial Censuses, 1857-1892, Roll V228_9, pg. 164)*. Henry Clay is age 14, born Michigan, and is a laborer. Ira C. Rockwell, listed as I.C. Rockwell, is 62, a farmer, born New York.[31]

Henry Clay Hatch Rockwell is listed in the 1893 Seattle, Washington city directory as a student at the University of Washington.[A]

Henry Clay (Hatch) Rockwell is not found in the 1900 census.

Henry Clay (Hatch) Rockwell married Mrs. **Henrietta Breakey** Duke on October 10, 1904 in New York Co., New York.[59] Henrietta Breakey was born in New York, New York Co., New York, on April 21, 1854.[60] Henrietta reached age 75 and died in Brooklyn, Kings Co., New York, on April 21, 1929.[60, 61] She was buried in Green-Wood Cemetery, Brooklyn, Kings Co., New York.[60, 61]

Henrietta Breakey Duke Rockwell's death certificate and burial information indicate she died on her 75th birthday. She was 20 years older than her husband Henry C. Rockwell, and, coincidentally, had the same given name as his mother. Henrietta Breakey Duke had two grown children from her first marriage when she wed Henry.

Sometime between 1893-1910, but probably before 1900, Henry Clay (Hatch) Rockwell became a disciple and protege of "Reverend" Charles Taze

Russell, a self-proclaimed minister and founder of the religious movement, the Zion's Watch Tower Tract Society, later the International Bible Students Association (IBSA), and its publishing arm, the Watch Tower Bible and Tract Society. This religious organization eventually became the Jehovah's Witnesses.[62] Henry would become an influential member of this international religious movement.

The ISBA, founded in the 1870s in Pittsburgh, Pennsylvania, discounted many beliefs held by mainstream Christian organizations, such as the concept of the Trinity and the existence of an afterlife. Russell, who had never attended ministerial school, been ordained, or granted a minister's license, had published thousands of treatises, pamphlets and sermons, many of which were syndicated columns in newspapers. Russell's movement had spread worldwide and had many thousands of followers by 1908. That year, he moved his organization to Brooklyn, New York.[62]

By 1910 in Brooklyn, Henry Clay (Hatch) Rockwell was the vice president of the International Bible Students Association.[62] He was a noted evangelist for the new religion, and, as a part of the organization's "People's Pulpit Association", gave many speeches, particularly on the east coast, about the IBSA.[62, 63, 64] He was also active in Russell's publishing company, and was on the editorial staff for *The Watch Tower*, Russell's main publication.[65, 66] In addition, he authored the "Bible Question Box", a "question and answer" column printed in many newspapers across the country.[67] Henry C. Rockwell is listed on the 24-member "Board of Elders", appointed by Charles Taze Russell, and the seven-member Board of Directors for the Watch Tower Bible and Tract Society (later shortened to The Watch Tower Society) after Russell's death in 1916.[66, 68]

In 1910, Henry Clay (Hatch) Rockwell is enumerated in Brooklyn, Kings Co., Washington *(Census Place: Brooklyn Ward 1, Kings, New York; Roll: T624_955; Page: 19A; Enumeration District: 0003; Image: 124)*. Henry Clay (Hatch) Rockwell, listed as H. Clay Rockwell, is age 35, born Michigan, with his father born in Michigan and his mother in Indiana. He lists his occupation as minister in a bible society. He has a wife, Henrietta Breakey Duke Rockwell, 58, born New York, with her parents born in Ireland. The couple say they have been married four years. They have been married four years. Henry Clay says this is his first marriage, while Henrietta says it is her second. She says she has borne five children (by her first husband Mr. Duke), with two still living. They are residents in a large boarding house or building with other members of their bible society (The International Student Bible Association).

After Russell expired in 1916, the board of directors Russell chose was able to guide the Watch Tower Bible and Tract Society for only a year when Joseph Franklin Rutherford, the Society's legal counsel and the director his peers elected president, started to become more autocratic. A power struggle ensued and a schism in the movement developed. Rockwell, who had already left the board, joined a group opposing Rutherford and his faction. Rockwell and the other members of the opposition group maintained that Rutherford and his followers were totally going against Russell's teachings. At a conclave in November 1917, the two opposing sides stood in an election for a new board of directors of the IBSA and the WTS. According to the November 15, 1917 issue of *The Watch Tower*, H. Clay Rockwell was nominated by his own opposition group as the prospective secretary/treasurer of the board of directors. But Rutherford's faction wrested control, and Rockwell and others long active in the movement were forced out of any significant roles within the organization.[62, 66, 68, 69]

Rutherford and his followers retained the names of the Watch Tower Bible and Tract Society and the International Bible Students Association (IBSA), but in 1931 Rutherford renamed these groups "The Jehovah's Witnesses". Those, like Rockwell, who rejected Rutherford and wished to adhere to Russell's simpler organizational form (where all chapters of the Watch Tower Bible and Tract Society and IBSA were independent, self-governed units loosely guided by Russell or, after his death, the board he chose) became The Pastoral Bible Institute/The Associated Bible Students (PBI). They formed separate, self-governing chapters or "ecclesias" in a number of cities. Their members were called "pilgrims". H. Clay Rockwell helped organize the Brooklyn ecclesia, which initially had about 140 members and lasted until 1960. But the Pastoral Bible Institute overall membership has waned. Some members/ ecclesias re-associated with The Jehovah's Witnesses over the decades since the 1917 schism. Few PBI ecclesias still exist, most notably in St. Louis, Missouri, Batavia, Illinois and Bremerton, Washington, where the organization is now based.[62]

Henry Clay (Hatch) Rockwell is still living in Brooklyn, Kings Co., New York in 1920 *(Census Place: Brooklyn Assembly District 1, Kings, New York; Roll: T625_1143; Page: 3A; Enumeration District: 1; Image: 603)*. Henry Clay (Hatch) Rockwell is age 46, born in Michigan with his parents born in New York (Incorrect—His mother was born in Indiana and his birth father in Michigan. However, his stepfather who adopted him was born in New York). Henry is still a minister in a bible society. His wife, Henrietta, is 68, born New York with her parents born in Ireland. There is a boarder in the household, Grace Alexander, age 30, born New York. a clerk.

In April 1924, Henry Clay (Hatch) Rockwell wrote a letter to *Popular Mechanics* magazine, in response to that publication's request for readers to tell them what they had constructed after reading the magazine's articles. H. Clay Rockwell from Ulster Park, Ulster Co., New York, said as "the general all-around mechanic associated with a summer resort hotel", he'd built "several rustic summer houses...a Japanese pavilion (on a recreation dock on the resort's lake)...a swimming pool...an ornamental pagoda...swings, furniture and arbors".[70]

Henrietta Breakey Duke Rockwell died in 1929.

Henry Clay Hatch Rockwell married **Pauline Hermane Stutz** in 1930 in Paterson, Passaic Co., New Jersey.[24, 22] Pauline Hermane Stutz was born in Switzerland on October 11, 1885.[71] Pauline Hermane reached age 44 and died in Paterson, Passaic Co., New Jersey, on July 21, 1930.[71, 72] She was buried in Green-Wood Cemetery, Brooklyn, Kings Co., New York.[71, 72]

In 1930, Henry Clay (Hatch) Rockwell is living in Paterson, Passaic Co., New Jersey *(Census Place: Paterson, Passaic, New Jersey; Roll: 1381; Page: 15A; Enumeration District: 78; Image: 347.0)*. Henry Clay (Hatch) Rockwell is age 55, and this time he states that he and his parents were born in Michigan. (Incorrect—his mother was born in Indiana). He lists his occupation as truck driver for a wholesale linoleum company. His wife, listed as "Hermine", age 45, states she was born Switzerland, her father in Switzerland, and her mother in Germany. The pair say they were first married at age 55 and 45 respectively, so they have just married. But this is incorrect, as Henry was married previously when he was about 31 years old.

Pauline "Hermane" Stutz Rockwell died in July 1930.

By 1940, Henry Clay (Hatch) Rockwell has moved back to Brooklyn Kings Co., New York *(Census Place: New York, Kings, New York; Roll: T627_2576; Page: 4A; Enumeration District: 24-1154)*. (Note: The enumeration says New York, but the census page has New York City crossed out and Brooklyn written above it.) Henry C. Rockwell, age 66 and single, born Michigan, lists no occupation and is a lodger in the home of Joseph and Margaret Matthews at 303 Vanderbilt Avenue. He says he was living in Brooklyn in 1935.

Despite his visibility in his long association with Rev. Russell and the International Bible Students Association and The Watch Tower Bible and Tract Society, Henry C. (Hatch) Rockwell died in obscurity at Pilgrim State Mental Hospital in Brentwood, Suffolk Co., New York on February 24, 1950. According to his death certificate, however, he was still a minister. He was cremated and his ashes remained at Fresh Pond Crematory, Middle Village, Queens, Queens Co., New York.[36] More than two months later his ashes were removed and buried in the Rockwell-Breakey family plot at Green-Wood Cemetery, Brooklyn, Kings Co., New York, according that cemetery's records.[35, 37]

Henry Clay (Hatch) Rockwell was also a bodybuilder, and a proponent of one system of bodybuilding and lifting weights. He appeared in a brochure for this system in 1914 when he was 39 years old.[73]

8. **Drusilla Madeline⁷ Davis** (*Marietta Marilla⁶ Pegan, William Louis or Lewis⁵, Robert A.⁴, Andrew³,*

*Andrew*² *Pagan, James*¹) was born on October 13, 1872, in Niles, Niles Twp., Berrien Co., Michigan.[45, 46, 47, 74] She was the daughter of William Milford Davis and Marietta Marilla Pegan (4). She was also known as **Drusilla May** and **Drusie**. Drusilla Madeline died in Los Angeles, Los Angeles Co., California, on September 27, 1954, at age 81.[47, 48] She was buried in Calvary Cemetery, Los Angeles, Los Angeles Co., California.[47, 75]

Although her real middle name was "Madeline", as she states on her Social Security application, Drusilla usually used "May" as her middle name.[74]

According to her living granddaughter-in-law, Drusilla Davis Henoch was a savvy businesswoman—far ahead of the times for women in that era. She was an independent woman, highly educated and dedicated to her career in apartment management and ownership.[8]

After the death of her mother, Marietta Pegan Davis, her father, William Milford Davis, sent all his daughters to boarding school at St. Mary's-Notre Dame, which, at that time, also operated an educational institution for younger girls in addition to the well-known women's college. Drusilla graduated from St. Mary's-Notre Dame College and found a job in Washington, D.C.

Both Mabel and Sarah Elizabeth "Bessie" Davis died while they were students at St. Mary's-Notre Dame boarding school. Mabel expired in Washington, D.C. while visiting, or being cared for during an illness by, Drusilla; Bessie succumbed at the school.[54, 56, 57]

Following her own father's example, Drusilla sent her own daughter and only child, Maybelle Henoch, to board at convent schools to be educated. Later, Maybelle would attend college at her mother's alma mater, St. Mary's-Notre Dame in South Bend, St. Joseph Co., Indiana, near the extended Pagin and Henoch families in adjacent LaPorte County, Indiana.[8]

Drusilla Madeline married **Milton Henoch** on January 20, 1895, in Washington, District of Columbia.[76] They divorced. They had one daughter. Milton Henoch was born in Aurora, Aurora Twp., Kane Co., Illinois, on July 13, 1864.[77] Milton reached age 64 and died in San Diego, San Diego Co., California, on October 21, 1928.[77, 78] He was first buried in Greenwood Mausoleum, San Diego, San Diego Co., California.[77] However, he seems to have been disinterred and reburied in the Henoch family plot in B'Nae Zion Jewish Cemetery, LaPorte, Center Twp., LaPorte Co., Indiana, after October 24, 1928.[79]

At the time of the marriage, Milton says he was a resident of LaPorte, LaPorte Co., Indiana, while Drusilla says she was a resident of Washington, D.C.[76]

Drusilla Madeline Davis Henoch's marriage was a shock to her Catholic family and friends, as Milton was of the Jewish faith. Drucilla was a friend of Mr. James F. Edwards, a professor at the University of Notre Dame, and Edward's sister Elizabeth Edwards Nestor of Detroit. Letters from and about Drusilla ("Drusie") to Mr. Edwards are found in the Archives of the University of Notre Dame, including one after her marriage:

> 1895
> (Nester), Eliz(abeth): (Detroit), Michigan) to (James F. Edwards: Notre Dame, Indiana)
>
> The telegram that she enclosed will surprise Edwards. Drusie (Mrs. Milton Henoch) was married last Sunday; her husband is a Jew. She asks Edwards how Prof. (Newton A.) Preston is getting along. They were talking about their delightful visit to Notre Dame. *(XI-1-m - A.L.S. - 4pp. - 16to. - {2})*[80]
>
> 1895
> (Nester), Eliz(abeth): (Detroit, Michigan) to (James F. Edwards: Notre Dame, Indiana)
>
> She writes to tell Edwards how much she appreciated his letter…She has not heard from Drusie (Mrs. Milton Henoch) since her marriage…*(XI-1-m - A.L.S. - 4pp. - 16to. - {1})*[80]
>
> 1896
> (Nester), Eliz(abeth): (Detroit, Michigan) to J(ames) F. E(dwards): (Notre Dame, Indiana)
>
> …If Edwards wishes to see her he had better come before…June, for she sails for Paris the latter part of June. She asks for Fannie Gregori's address. Edwards should tell her

all about Drusie (Mrs. Milton Henoch).
(XI-1-n - A.L.S. - 8pp. - 16to - {1})[80]

1896 Mar. 31
(Henoch, Mrs. Milt) Drusie: La Porte, Ind(iana) to (James F. Edwards: Notre Dame, Indiana)

She regretted that she could not get back to say goodbye to Edwards but her plans conflicted with Mr. Henoch's. But Edwards can run down and spend a Sunday with them. They will be in La Porte all summer.
(XI-1-n - A.L.S. - 4pp. - 12mo. - {1})[80]

1896 May 1
(Nester) Elisa(beth)to (James F. Edwards: Notre Dame, Indiana)

She writes only to say that she will be at Notre Dame sometime next week. Drusie wrote a very friendly note.
(XI-1-n - A.L.S. – 1p. - 12mo. - {1})[80]

1896 May 22
(Nester) Eliza(beth): (Chicago, Illinois?) to (James F. Edwards: Notre Dame, Indiana)

Edwards got her in a fine scrape by giving them hope of expecting him that Friday afternoon. However she had a lovely visit with Drusie (Henoch), and also with Milton (Henoch)...(XI-1-n - A.L.S. - 3pp. - 12mo. - {1})[80]

1899
(Nester), Elizabeth: (Chicago, Illinois) to Brother: (Notre Dame, Indiana)

She gives many thanks for sending her Drusie's letter...(XI-2-b - A.L.S. - 4pp. - 12mo. - {2})[80]

Drusilla Davis Henoch and her first husband, Milton Henoch, are enumerated in the Bronx, New York Co., New York in 1900 *(Census Place: Bronx, New York, New York; Roll: T623; Page: 13A; Enumeration District: 1042)*. The head of the household is Milton Henoch, age 36, born Jul 1863 in Illinois, with his parents born in Germany. Milton lists his occupation as a materials inspector for a railroad. With him is his wife, Drusilla Pegan Henoch, 27, born Oct 1872 in Michigan, with her father born in Michigan and her mother in Indiana. Milton and Drusilla say they have been married six years, and Drusilla has borne one child who is still alive. Their daughter "Mabel M.", is eight months old, born Sep 1899 in New York. Living with them is a servant, Annie Saterling, 19, born Aug 1880 in New York.

Milton Henoch was a well-known expert in electrical appliances who worked for Westinghouse and later General Electric. He was sent by these companies to conventions and meetings to promote the use of electrical appliances in the home. He also toured the country giving demonstrations and talks to the public on electrical appliances. Milton would even give these demonstrations on ships and would work as a chef on many ocean liners in conjunction with promoting the appliances. He applied for two patents, one on November 17, 1903 for a bicycle support and another on January 5, 1921 for an apartment-size electrical stove, both while living in LaPorte, Indiana.[81]

After their divorce, Milton Henoch is not found in the 1910 U.S. Federal Census.

Drusilla Davis Henoch is enumerated in San Gabriel Twp., Los Angeles Co., California in 1910 *(Census Place: San Gabriel, Los Angeles, California; Roll: T624_87; Page: 11A; Enumeration District: 0352; Image: 120)*. Drusilla, age 36, says she and her parents were born in Michigan (Incorrect—her father was born in Michigan, and she and her mother were born in Indiana); she lists no occupation. Drusilla says she has borne one child, who survives. With her is her daughter, Maybelle Madeline Henoch, listed as "May", born New York with her father born in Indiana (Incorrect—he was born in Illinois) and her mother in Michigan. Residing in the home is a boarder, William G. Baker, 27, born Pennsylvania. Drusilla claims she is a widow; but her ex-husband, Milton Henoch, is alive, though he does not appear in this census.

According to an article in the *Appleton (WI) Post Crescent* newspaper on May 31, 1915, Drusilla's ex-husband Milton Henoch survived the infamous sinking of the ship *Lusitania* on May 7, 1915, in an incident which spurred U.S. involvement in WWI. Milton was returning from a business lecture in England and was listed as "chief cook" on the boat when it was torpedoed by a German submarine. Of the 1,960 known passengers onboard the *Lusitania*, only 767 survived initially and four of those later succumbed to their injuries.[82]

Drusilla Madeline Davis Henoch Ball's first husband Milton Henoch and their daughter Maybelle Madeline Henoch are enumerated in LaPorte, Center Twp., LaPorte Co., Indiana in 1920 *(Census Place: La Porte Ward 3, La Porte, Indiana; Roll: T625_447; Page: 2B; Enumeration District: 121; Image: 217)*. Milton Henoch, age 54, born Illinois with his parents born in Germany, is a "range expert" at Westinghouse (manufacturing plant). Milton's second wife, Katherine Regan Henoch, is 43, who says she and her mother were born in Pennsylvania and her father in Ireland. "Maybell M." Henoch is 20, and says she was born in New York, her father in Illinois and her mother in Michigan.

Milton Henoch died in 1928.

Drusilla Davis Henoch is listed in the 1918 Los Angeles, Los Angeles Co., California city directory, residing at 230 S. Flower Street. (She continues to be listed at this address in the 1937 and 1938 Los Angeles city directories).[83]

Drusilla Madeline Davis Henoch married **Frederick Haley Ball** on December 1, 1919, in Los Angeles Co., California.[84] Frederick Haley Ball was born in Bear Creek Twp., Montgomery Co., Missouri?, in Jan 1881.

Frederick Haley Ball's date of birth is not known. But census data indicate his birth year was 1881. On his marriage application to Drusilla, Frederick H. Ball says his parents were Alexander Green Ball and Theodosia Payne.[83]

Fred Haley Ball, age 19, born Missouri, is found living alone in Bear Creek Twp., Montgomery Co., Missouri in 1900 *(Census Place: Bear Creek, Montgomery, Missouri; Roll: 876; Page: 11A; Enumeration District: 59)*. He says he was born in Jan(?) 1881, and his father was born in Ohio and his mother in Missouri. But on the 1920 census he lists other data.

His marriage with Drusilla Davis Henoch seems troubled, and by the 1920 census they are separated.

In 1920, Fred H. Ball is living alone in Los Angeles, Los Angeles Co., California *(Census Place: Los Angeles Assembly District 64, Los Angeles, California; Roll: T625_108; Page: 13B; Enumeration District: 205; Image: 30)*. Fred is age 39, married, born Missouri like his father, with his mother born in Kentucky. He is a clerk for an oil company.

In 1920, Drusilla Davis Henoch Ball. enumerated as Drusilla Ball, is found in Los Angeles, Los Angeles Co., California *(Census Place: Los Angeles Assembly District 64, Los Angeles, California; Roll: T625_108; Page: 14A; Enumeration District: 205; Image: 31)*. Drusilla, age 46, born Michigan with her parents born in Ohio, is an "innkeeper at an apartment building". She says she is still married, but her husband, Fred Ball, is not in the home. Living with her are two women listed as "helpers", sisters Bessie, 21, and Nellie Young, 22, both born in Indiana.

In 1922, Drusilla Davis Henoch Ball, who lives in Los Angeles, applies for a passport to travel to Europe—Britain, France, Belgium, Holland, Switzerland, Germany, and Austria. Drusilla writes her name, "Drusilla Henoch-Ball". She says she is traveling with her "future" husband Frederick H. Ball, a Missouri native living in California, However, there is no passport application for Frederick H. Ball. Perhaps they were trying to reconcile? On her passport application, she says she was born on October 13, 1872 in Niles, Michigan.[45]

By 1930, the attempted reconciliation failed and Drusilla has resumed the use of her first married name, Drusilla Henoch. In 1930, Drusilla Davis Henoch is found in Los Angeles, Los Angeles Co., California *(Census Place: Los Angeles, Los Angeles, California; Roll: 148; Page: 34A; Image: 379.0)*. Drusilla Davis Henoch, age 57, single, says she and her father were born in Michigan and her mother in Indiana. She lists her occupation as manager of a rooming house, and she has four young men boarding in her home on South Flower Street.

Frederick H. Ball is not found in the 1930 or 1940 censuses. If he traveled with Drusilla to Europe in 1922, he may have stayed there.

After they divorce, Drusilla retains her first married name, Henoch.

In 1940, Drusilla Davis Henoch (Ball) is found in Los Angeles, Los Angeles Co., California (*Census Place: Los Angeles, Los Angeles, California; Roll: T627_378; Page: 62A; Enumeration District: 60-732*). She is enumerated as "Dressilla Henock". Drusilla Davis Henoch is age 68, born Michigan, an apartment complex owner, says she was living in the same house at 238 South Flower Street in 1935.

Daughter of Drusilla Madeline Davis and Milton Henoch:

+ 12 f I. **Maybelle Madeline⁸ Henoch** was born in Bronx, New York Co., New York, on September 27, 1899.[85, 86] She died in Long Beach, Los Angeles Co., California, on July 5, 1963.[86, 87]

9. Lewis B.⁷ Davis (*Marietta Marilla⁶ Pegan, William Louis or Lewis⁵, Robert A.⁴, Andrew³, Andrew² Pagan, James¹*) was born on June 26, 1874, in Toledo, Lucas Co., Ohio.[49, 50] He was the son of William Milford Davis and Marietta Marilla Pegan (4). Lewis B. died in St. Louis, Missouri, on May 11, 1921, at age 46.[50, 51] He was cremated and his ashes buried in Valhalla Cemetery, Bel-Nor, St. Louis Co., Missouri.[50, B]

Childless.

His name on his birth record is Louis B. Davis[49], but he used the spelling Lewis B. Davis. Also, his birth is documented in Lucas County, Ohio birth records as June 26, 1874, but on the 1900 census form Lewis B. Davis says he was born in Jun 1875. On his death certificate, his widow, Harriet "Hattie" Ohrendorf Davis gives his birthdate as June 26, 1875. For some reason, either Lewis himself or Hattie may have thought Lewis wasn't certain of his birth date. She says his occupation was "merchant of grocery supplies". She lists his father as "Unknown Davis" and his mother as "Unknown Pegan".[50]

Lewis B. Davis is found in Joplin, Joplin Twp., Jasper Co., Missouri in 1900 (*Joplin Ward 4, Jasper, Missouri; Roll: 865; Page: 29A; Enumeration District: 39*). Lewis Davis, age 25, born "Jan" (actually Jun) 1875 in Ohio, with parents born in Ohio, is living with several "partners" and working as a day laborer.

Lewis B. married **Harriett A. Ohrndorf** on August 15, 1906, in St. Louis, Missouri.[88] Harriett A. Ohrndorf was born in St. Louis, Missouri, on May 4, 1884.[97, C] She was also known as Hattie. Harriett A. reached age 91 and died in St. Louis, Missouri, on April 13, 1976.[97, C, D] She was cremated and her cremains buried in Valhalla Cemetery, Bel-Nor, St. Louis Co., Missouri.[C]

After Lewis B. Davis' death, Harriet "Hattie" Ohrndorf Davis married Dr. Eugene L. Broeker and died as Harriet A. Broeker.

In 1910, Lewis B. Davis has removed to St. Louis, Missouri (*Census Place: St Louis Ward 13, Saint Louis City, Missouri; Roll: T624_817; Page: 10B; Enumeration District: 0210; Image: 311*). Lewis B. Davis, age 36, a paving contractor, says he was born in Ohio, with his father born in Michigan and his mother in Ohio (Incorrect—she was born in Indiana). His wife, "Hattie" Ohrndorf Davis, 25, born Missouri with her parents both born in Germany. The couple says they have been married three years and Hattie has borne no children. Living with them is Harriet's mother, Martha Unknown "Orendorf", 50, born in Germany.

Lewis B. Davis is still residing in St. Louis, Missouri in 1920 (*Census Place: St Louis Ward 13, St Louis [Independent City], Missouri; Roll: T625_951; Page: 12B; Enumeration District: 264; Image: 138*). Lewis B. Davis is age 44, proprietor of a commissary, born Ohio with his parents born in the the U.S. His wife "Harriet A." is 35, and a Missouri native; she states her parents were born in Germany.

10. Mabel⁷ Davis (*Marietta Marilla⁶ Pegan, William Louis or Lewis⁵, Robert A.⁴, Andrew³, Andrew² Pagan, James¹*) was born on February 26, 1876, in Toledo, Lucas Co., Ohio.[52] She was the daughter of William Milford Davis and Marietta Marilla Pegan (4). Mabel died in Washington, District of Columbia, on April 25, 1894, at age 18.[53, 54] She was buried in Woodlawn Cemetery, Toledo, Lucas Co., Ohio.[54]

Mabel Davis is mistakenly registered as a male child in the Lucas County, Ohio birth records. But the father is listed as a "Wm. Davis" and the date matches with the 1880 census record.[52]

Her death mention in the *Niles (MI) Republican* on April 27, 1893 notes that "Marabell" Davis had been a student at St. Mary's-Notre Dame, but had withdrawn from school before the (January) semester because of illness.[54] Her burial record at Woodlawn Cemetery, which has her buried as "Marabell" Davis, states she died in Washington, District of Columbia, where her sister Drusilla was living.[54] But her school records at St. Mary's-Notre Dame boarding school, in South Bend, St. Joseph Co., Indiana, clearly register her as "Mabel Davis".[57] Her death mention in the Niles newspaper also says her given name was Mabel.[53]

11. Sarah Elizabeth[7] **Davis** (*Marietta Marilla*[6] *Pegan, William Louis or Lewis*[5], *Robert A.*[4], *Andrew*[3], *Andrew*[2] *Pagan, James*[1]) was born on July 15, 1877, in Toledo, Lucas Co., Ohio.[55] She was also known as **Bessie**. She was the daughter of William Milford Davis and Marietta Marilla Pegan (4). Sarah Elizabeth died in South Bend, St. Joseph Co., Indiana, on April 2, 1893, at age 15.[56, 57, 58] She was buried in Woodlawn Cemetery, Toledo, Lucas Co., Ohio.[58]

Sarah Elizabeth "Bessie" Davis died while she was a student at St. Mary's-Notre Dame boarding school for girls. Her obituary in the *St. Mary's Chimes* monthly newsletter, she died of peritonitis on Easter Sunday, and her body was transported to Toledo, Ohio for burial.[57] Her burial record at Toledo's Woodlawn Cemetery names her as "Bessie Davis".[58]

8th Generation

12. Maybelle Madeline[8] Henoch (*Drusilla Madeline[7] Davis, Marietta Marilla[6] Pegan, William Louis or Lewis[5], Robert[4], Andrew[3], Andrew[2] Pagan, James[1]*) was born on September 27, 1899, in Bronx, New York Co., New York.[85, 86] She was the daughter of Milton Henoch and Drusilla Madeline Davis (8). Maybelle Madeline died in Long Beach, Los Angeles Co., California, on July 5, 1963, at age 63.[86, 87] She was buried in Forest Lawn Memorial Park Cemetery, Glendale, Los Angeles Co., California.[87]

Her middle name is sometimes seen as Madelina.

Maybelle Madeline Henoch is enumerated with her father and stepmother, Milton and Catherine Regan Henoch, in LaPorte, Center Twp., LaPorte Co., Indiana in 1920 *(Census Place: La Porte Ward 3, La Porte, Indiana; Roll: T625_447; Page: 2B; Enumeration District: 121; Image: 217)*. Milton Henoch, age 54, born Illinois with his parents born in Germany, is a "range expert" at Westinghouse (manufacturing plant). Katherine Regan Henoch is 43 and says she and her mother were born in Pennsylvania and her father in Ireland. "Maybell M." Henoch (Costa) is 20, and says she was born in New York, her father in Illinois and her mother in Michigan.

According to her daughter-in-law, Maybelle Madeline Henoch was educated in Roman Catholic convent schools and was a graduate of St. Mary's-Notre Dame in South Bend, St. Joseph Co., Indiana, just as her mother, Drusilla Madeline Davis Henoch (Ball) was. Her schooling allowed her to be near her LaPorte, LaPorte Co., Indiana extended family. Maybelle was working in Chicago when she met her husband, Frank John Costa, M.D., who was in medical school at the time.[8]

She married Dr. **Frank John Costa** before 1924. They divorced. They had three children. Dr. Frank John Costa was born in Alessandria, Agrigento, Sicily, Italy, on January 10, 1897.[89, 90] He was living in 1963 in Hesperia, San Bernardino Co., California.[91] Frank John reached age 66 and died in a hospital in Los Angeles, Los Angeles Co., California, on March 29, 1963.[91, 92] He was buried in Green Hills Memorial Park Cemetery, Rancho Palos Verdes, Los Angeles Co., California.[92, 93]

According to his daughter-in-law, Frank John Costa was born in Sicily and came to America with his parents and siblings in 1908. The Costa family settled in Tampa, Hillsborough Co., Florida. Frank, the youngest child in the family, was chosen to be the only one given a college education, and the entire family pitched in money to send him through college and medical school—on the stipulation that he return to Tampa to practice.[8] Frank John Costa is a student in Chicago, Cook Co., California in 1917 when he registers for the WWI draft. He lists his birthdate as January 10, 1897, and he states he was born in Italy—even though on later census forms he claims he is a Florida native.[89]

He met his wife Maybelle Henoch Costa in Chicago, where they were both working. After Frank completed medical school, he, Maybelle and their first child Celeste, who was born in Chicago, moved to Tampa. The family lived in Tampa until about 1939, when Frank took his family to San Pedro, Los Angeles Co., California.[8]

On May 8, 1942, after the start of WWII, Dr. Frank John Costa applies for U.S. citizenship while living in San Pedro, Los Angeles Co., California. On the form, he states his original name was Francesco Costa.[90]

Dr. Frank and Maybelle Henoch Costa are enumerated in Tampa, Hillsborough Co., Florida in 1930 *(Census Place: Tampa, Hillsborough, Florida; Roll: 319; Page: 5A; Enumeration District: 38; Image: 261.0)*. Frank Costa, age 32, born Florida (incorrect) with his parents born in Italy, is a physician and surgeon. Wife Maybelle Henoch Costa, age 32, says she and her mother were born in New York while her father was born in Michigan. (Incorrect—her mother was born in Michigan and her father in Illinois). Children in the home are daughter Celeste, age six, born Illinois, and son Frank, age three years and six months, born Florida.

In 1935, Dr. Frank and Maybelle Henoch Costa are still living in Tampa, Hillsborough Co., Florida, according to the 1935 Florida State Census.[94] In the home are Frank Costa, age 38, born Florida (Again, wrong—he was born in Sicily); his wife Maybelle, 35, born New York; and children Celeste, 11, born in Illinois; and Franklin, eight, and Arthur, three, both born in Florida.

In 1940, Dr. Frank and Maybelle Henoch Costa are found in Los Angeles, Los Angeles Co., California *(Census Place: Los Angeles, Los Angeles, California; Roll: T627_432; Page: 7A; Enumeration District: 60-1283)*. Their house at 1192 Eighteenth Street must have been very near San Pedro, because "San Pedro" is written at the top on the census form but crossed out. Dr. Frank Costa, age 43, a physician and surgeon, says he was born in Florida (incorrect). Maybelle Henoch Costa, 40, says she was born in New York. Their daughter, Celeste, 16, is listed as born in Illinois, and their sons Frank, 14, and Arthur, eight, were both born in Florida. The family says they were living in Tampa, Hillsborough Co., Florida in 1935.

Dr. Frank Costa and his family are listed in the San Pedro and Wilmington, California city directory in 1940.[95]

After the divorce, Mrs. Maybelle Costa resided in Long Beach, Los Angeles Co., California according to the Long Beach city directories from 1948-61.[96] Dr. Frank Costa was living in Hesperia, San Bernardino Co., California at the time of his death, which occurred in a Los Angeles hospital.[92]

Children of Maybelle Madeline Henoch and Frank John Costa:

+ 13 f I. **Celeste Josephine[9] Costa** was born in Evanston, Cook Co., Illinois(?) on January 1, 1924.[8] She died in Santa Roseville, Placer Co., California on November 29, 2016.[8]

+ 14 m II. **Frank Milton[9] Costa II** was born in Tampa, Hillsborough Co., Florida, on December 27, 1926.[97] He died in North Hollywood, Los Angeles Co., California, on October 26, 2009.[97]

+ 15 m III. **Arthur Louis[9] Costa** was born in Tampa, Hillsborough Co., Florida, on November 30, 1931.

9th Generation

13. Celeste Josephine[9] Costa (*Maybelle Madeline[8] Henoch, Drusilla Madeline[7] Davis, Marietta Marilla[6] Pegan, William Louis or Lewis[5], Robert A.[4], Andrew[3], Andrew[2] Pagan, James[1]*) was born in Evanston, Cook Co., Illinois(?) on January 1, 1924.[8] She was the daughter of Frank John Costa and Maybelle Madeline Henoch (12). She died in Santa Roseville, Placer Co., California on November 29, 2016.[8]

Childless.

Celeste J. married **Warren Fred Flanagan** before 1952 in Los Angeles Co., California. Warren Fred Flanagan was born in Boston, Suffolk Co., Massachusetts, on October 13, 1920.[97, 98] He reached age 81 and died in Torrance, Los Angeles Co., California, on November 8, 2001.[97, 98]

Warren F. Flanagan is listed in the 1952 and 1956 San Pedro and Wilmington, California city directories.[99] By 1959, he had moved to Torrance, California.[100] According to his niece-in-law and his obituary, Warren F. Flanagan was a high school coach in the Los Angeles area, and over his career he coached football, basketball, baseball and other sports.[8, 98]

14. Frank Milton[9] Costa II (*Maybelle Madeline[8] Henoch, Drusilla Madeline[7] Davis, Marietta Marilla[6] Pegan, William Louis or Lewis[5], Robert A.[4], Andrew[3], Andrew[2] Pagan, James[1]*) was born on December 27, 1926, in Tampa, Hillsborough Co., Florida.[97] He was the son of Frank John Costa and Maybelle Madeline Henoch (12). Frank Milton died in North Hollywood, Los Angeles Co., California, on October 26, 2009, at age 82.[97] He was buried in Calvary Cemetery, Los Angeles, Los Angeles Co., California.[101]

Never married.

Frank Milton Costa II lived with his mother Maybelle Henoch Costa for many years. He worked at CBS Radio in Los Angeles.[8]

15. Arthur Louis[9] Costa (*Maybelle Madeline[8] Henoch, Drusilla Madeline[7] Davis, Marietta Marilla[6] Pegan, William Louis or Lewis[5], Robert A.[4], Andrew[3], Andrew[2] Pagan, James[1]*) was born on November 30, 1931, in Tampa, Hillsborough Co., Florida. He is the son of Frank John Costa and Maybelle Madeline Henoch (12).

Arthur is the co-founder of the Institute for Habits of Mind, Westport, Connecticut, and also worked as a Director of Educational Programs at the National Aeronautics and Space Administration (NASA).[8]

Arthur Louis married **Nancy Butler** in June 1953 in Los Angeles Co., California. They have two daughters. Nancy Butler was born in Long Beach, Los Angeles Co., California?, on December 27, 1931.

Endnotes

1. Family Data: Robert and Christina "Engle" Pegan family bible, American Bible Society, Brattleboro(ugh), Vermont: Holbrook & Fessenden, 1828. In possession of the author, Ann Miller Carr.

2. Find A Grave—Oakwood Cemetery, Falls Church, Fairfax Co., Virginia, Find A Grave.com, Drusilla F. Pegan, Find A Grave Memorial #200092502.

3. Family Data: Pagin family bible records, privately held.

4. Obituary of Drusilla Pegan (LaPorte, Indiana, LaPorte Herald-Argus, 10 Apr 1903), LaPorte County Historical Society, 2405 Indiana Avenue, #1, LaPorte, IN.

5. "James R. Pagin", *History of Porter County, Indiana: A Narrative History of its Progress, its People and Principal Interests.* Chicago: Lewis Publishing Co.; 1912, pg. 692. Genealogy Center, Allen County Public Library, 900 Library Plaza, Fort Wayne, IN.

6. Gilbert, Audrey, *Twin Valley Tidbits, 1888-1897, Vol. 3*. New Alexandria, Ohio: A. Gilbert; 1999, pg. 72. Lynchburg Public Library, 120 Main Street, Lynchburg, OH.

7. Guardianship Record, Orpha, Henrietta and "Martha" (Marietta) Pegan, LaPorte County, Indiana, Common Pleas Court Record Book C, pg. 511. Clerk of Circuit Court, 813 Lincolnway, Suite 105, LaPorte, IN.

8. Phone interview with and emails from the son and daughter-in-law of Maybelle Madeline Henoch Costa, Ann Miller Carr, author, 2011-2018.

9. LaPorte County, Indiana Probate Records, LaPorte County Clerk of Court, 813 Lincolnway, Suite 105, LaPorte, IN. William L. Pegan, Probate Order Book B, pg. 707.

10. Virginia Death Certificate, Commonwealth of Virginia State Board of Health, Vital Records/Health Statistics 2001 Maywill Street, Richmond, VA 23230 (P.O. Box 1000, Richmond, VA), Orpha M. Conklin, death cert. #9298.

11. "Mrs. Ira P. Rockwell…" (Olympia, Washington, Washington Standard, 04 Jan 1889), Chronicling America: Historic American Newspapers Library of Congress, 101 Independence Avenue, Washington, DC; Online database: https://chroniclingamerica.loc.gov/lccn/sn84022770/1889-01-04/ed-1/seq-2/

12. "The Shooting Of Mrs. Rockwell" (Ithaca, New York, Ithaca Journal, 15 Jan 1889), Tompkins County Public Library, 101 East Green Street, Ithaca, NY.

13. Obituary of "May" Davis (LaPorte, Indiana, LaPorte Herald-Chronicle, 13 Apr 1882), LaPorte County Library, Main Library, 904 Indiana Avenue, La Porte, IN.

14. Woodlawn Cemetery Records, Mrs. Wm. Davis, Woodlawn Cemetery, 1502 West Central Ave., Toledo, OH.

15. Find A Grave—Oakwood Cemetery, Falls Church, Fairfax Co., Virginia, Find A Grave.com, Orpha M. Conklin, Find A Grave Memorial #20081492.

16. LaPorte County, Indiana Marriage Records, LaPorte County Clerk of the Circuit Court, 813 Lincolnway, Suite 105, LaPorte, IN, Joseph Andrews and Orpha Pegan, Vol. E, pg. 547.

17. Virginia Death Certificate, Commonwealth of Virginia State Board of Health, Vital Records/Health Statistics 2001 Maywill Street, Richmond, VA (P.O. Box 1000, Richmond, VA), "Isacc" Albert Conklin, death cert. #3324.

18. Find A Grave—Oakwood Cemetery, Falls Church, Fairfax Co., Virginia, Find A Grave.com, Isaac A. Conklin, Find A Grave Memorial #20106864.

19. Michigan, Marriage Records, 1868-1925, FamilySearch.org, Erwin (Irwin) Hatch and Etta G. Pegan, Berrien County Marriage Records, Vol. 1, pg. 78.

20. State of Michigan, Michigan Death Certificates, 1897-1920 (Lansing, Michigan, Michigan History Foundation, Michigan Historical Commission), Michigan Historical Museum, 702 West Kalamazoo St., Lansing, MI. I. J. Hatch, 1-48, registered #7, Cleon Twp., Manistee Co., 07 Oct 1919; http://seekingmichigan.org/discover-collection?collection=p129401coll7

21. Find A Grave—Cleon Township Cemetery, Copemish, Cleon Twp., Manistee Co., Michigan, Find A Grave.com, I.J. Hatch, Find A Grave Memorial #11826849.

22. Michigan, Marriages, 1868-1925, FamilySearch.org, William M. Davis and May Pegan, Cass County, Michigan Marriages, Vol 1, pg. 146.

23. Woodlawn Cemetery Records, Wm. G. Hatch, Woodlawn Cemetery, 1502 West Central Ave., Toledo, OH.

24. St. Joseph County, Indiana Marriage Records, St. Joseph County Clerk, 101 South Main Street, South Bend, IN 46601, Ira Rockwell and Etta Hatch, Marriage Book 11, pg. 179.

25. Barton, Clarence M., *Barton's Legislative Hand-book and Manual of the State of Washington*, Olympia, Wash.: Thomas Henderson Boyd, publisher, State Printing and Publishing Co.; 1891, pg. 333. Princeton University Library, 1 Washington Road, Princeton, NJ.

26. Family Data: Rockwell family bible, privately held in Watkins Glen, New York by a Rockwell descendant who wishes to remain anonymous; information sent to author Ann Miller Carr.

27. "I. Rockwell, a prominent citizen of Sidney…" (Shelton, Washington, Mason County Journal, 13 Jan 1899), Chronicling America: Historic American Newspapers, Library of Congress, 101 Independence Avenue, Washington, DC; Online database: https://chroniclingamerica.loc.gov/lccn/sn88085081/1899-01-13/ed-1/seq-3/

28. Obituary of Ira Rockwell (Ithaca, New York, Ithaca Journal, 12 Jan 1899), Tompkins County Public Library, 101 East Green Street, Ithaca, NY.

29 Research on Ira Rockwell, Bonnie Chrey, researcher, Kitsap County Historical Society & Museum, 280 Fourth Street, Bremerton, WA 98337. Information sent to the author in April 2013.

30 "Frontier Justice", Washington State Digital Archives, Secretary of State, Olympia, Washington. Kitsap County Frontier Justice, Kitsap County Probate Court, Ira C. Rockwell and Henry C. Hatch, Guardianship, 1889, case ##KSP-134. Online database: https://www.digitalarchives.wa.gov/Record/View/FE77EB2C73D5755B7D5096D39899BC8A

31 Washington State and Territorial Censuses, 1857-1892, Ancestry.com, I.C. Rockwell.

32 Michigan, Births and Christenings Index, 1867-1911, Ancestry.com, Henry Clay Hatch.

33 Michigan Births, 1867-1902, FamilySearch.org, Henry Clay Hatch, State of Michigan, Cass County Birth Records, Vol. 2, pg. 331, #802.

34 U.S., WWI Draft Registration Cards, 1917-1918, Ancestry.com, Henry Clay Rockwell, Brooklyn, Kings Co., New York.

35 Green-Wood Cemetery Records, Henry C. Rockwell, Green-Wood Cemetery, Administrative Offices, 500 25th Street, Brooklyn, NY.

36 New York Death Certificate, State of New York Department of Health, Vital Records Section, Genealogy Unit, P.O. Box 2602, Albany, NY (800 North Pearl Street, Menands, NY), Henry C. Rockwell, death cert. #11651.

37 Find A Grave—Green-Wood Cemetery, Brooklyn, Kings Co., New York, Henry C. Rockwell, Find A Grave.com, Find A Grave Memorial #58362586.

38 Cincinnati Birth and Death Records, 1904-1907, University of Cincinnati Archives, University of Cincinnati Library Archives and Rare Books, 8th Floor Blegen Library, P.O. Box 210113, 2602 McMicken Circle, Cincinnati, OH 45221-0113, William Milford Davis, death cert. #777.

39 Ohio, County Marriages, 1789-2013, FamilySearch.org, William M. Davis and Nora Connavello, Montgomery County Marriage Records, Vol. 38, pg. 77, lic. #25019.

40 Woodlawn Cemetery Records, William M. Davis, Woodlawn Cemetery, 1502 West Central Avenue, Toledo, OH.

41 Find A Grave—Woodlawn Cemetery, Toledo, Lucas Co., Ohio, William M. Davis, Find A Grave.com, Find A Grave Memorial #181628489.

42 Ohio, County Death Records, 1840-2001, FamilySearch.org, William M. Davis, Transportation of Corpse record, transit permit #141, for William M. Davis, age 56 years, 11 months, 24 days, born Niles, Michigan, fa: Moses Davis, mo: Sarah Lewis, to be sent by rail to Toledo, Ohio for burial in Woodlawn Cemetery.

45 U.S. Passport Applications 1795-1925, Ancestry.com, Drusilla Henoch-Ball, application #116974, dated 02 Feb 1922.

46 Michigan Births, 1867-1902, FamilySearch.org, "Drugie" Davis, Berrien County Birth Records, Vol. 2, pg. 211.

47 California Death Certificate, California Health and Strategic Planning, Vital Records, M.S. 5103 P.O. Box 997410, Sacramento, CA, Drusilla May Henoch, death cert. #54-075731.

48 California, Death Index, 1940-1997, Ancestry.com, Drusilla May Henoch.

49 Ohio, County Births, 1841-2003 (County Courthouses), FamilySearch.org, "Louis" B. Davis, Lucas Co., Ohio Birth Record Vol. 1, pg. 182-183.

50 Missouri Death Certificates, 1910-1964, Missouri Secretary of State, 600 West Main Street, Jefferson City, MO; Lewis B. Davis, death cert. #13402. Online database: http://s1.sos.mo.gov/records/archives/archivesmvc/deathcertificates.

51 Obituary of Lewis B. Davis (St. Louis, Missouri, St. Louis Post-Dispatch, 12 May 1921, pg. 31), St. Louis Co., Missouri Public Library, 1640 South Lindbergh Blvd., St. Louis, MO.

52 Ohio, County Births, 1841-2003 (County Courthouses), FamilySearch.org, "Davis" fa: Wm. Davis, Lucas Co. Birth Record Vol. 2, pg. 81.

53 Obituary of Mabel Davis (Niles, Michigan, Niles Republican, 27 Apr 1893), Niles District Library, 620 East Main Street, Niles, MI.

54 Woodlawn Cemetery Records, "Marabel" Davis, Woodlawn Cemetery, 1502 West Central Ave., Toledo, OH.

55 Ohio, County Births, 1841-2003 (County Courthouses), FamilySearch.org, Sarah Davis, Lucas Co., Ohio Birth Record Vol. 2, pg. 158-159.

56 Obituary of Bessie Davis (South Bend, Indiana, South Bend Daily Tribune, 03 Apr 1893), St. Joseph County Public Library, 304 South Main Street, South Bend, IN.

57 Obituary of Bessie Davis (Notre Dame, Indiana, St. Mary's Chimes, monthly newsletter, May 1893), St. Mary's College -Notre Dame Records, St. Mary's College Archives, 105 Madeleva Hall, Cushwa-Leighton Library, St. Mary's College, Notre Dame, IN.

58 Woodlawn Cemetery Records, Bessie Davis, Woodlawn Cemetery, 1502 West Central Avenue, Toledo, OH.

59 New York, New York, Marriage Certificate Index 1866-1937, Ancestry.com, Henry C. Rockwell and Henrietta Duke, lic. #20434.

60 New York City Death Index, New York Public Library, 476 Fifth Avenue, South Court Mezzanine, New York, NY 10018, Henrietta Rockwell, death cert. #10100, Kings Co., NY.

61 Green-Wood Cemetery Records, Henrietta Rockwell, Green-Wood Cemetery, Administrative Offices, 500 25th Street, Brooklyn, NY.

62 Wills, Tony, *A People For His Name: The History of the Jehovah's Witnesses and An Evaluation*, Second Ed., 2006, Morrisville, NC: Lulu Enterprises, Inc. (First edition published in 1967 under the pseudonym Timothy White, New York: Vantage Press.) Kansas City Public Library, Central Library, 14 West 10th Street, Kansas City, MO.

63 "Sermon by H.C. Rockwell" (Washington, D.C., The Washington Herald, 07 Nov 1910), Chronicling America: Historic American Newspapers, Library of Congress, 101 Independence Avenue SE, Washington, DC; Online database: https://chroniclingamerica.loc.gov/lccn/sn83045433/1910-11-07/ed-1/seq-2/

64 "What Are We Here For" (Washington, D.C., The Washington Herald, 02 May 1914), Chronicling America: Historic American Newspapers, Library of Congress, 101 Independence Avenue SE, Washington, DC; Online database: https://chroniclingamerica.loc.gov/lccn/sn83045433/1914-05-02/ed-1/seq-8/#date1=1789&index=4&rows=20&searchType=advanced&language=&sequence=0&words=People+Peoples+Pulpit+Rockwell+ROCKWELL&proxdistance=5&date2=1943&ortext=&proxtext=%22rockwell%22+%2B+%22people%27s+pulpit%22&phrasetext=&andtext=&dateFilterType=yearRange&page=1

65 Chryssides, George D., Jehovah's Witnesses: Continuity and Change. New York: Ashgate Publishing, 2016, no page numbers.

66 Van Amburgh, W.E., The Way to Paradise. New York: The Watch Tower Bible and Tract Society, 1924, pg. 22-23. Reprinted by Morrisville, NC: Lulu Enterprises, Inc., 2007, pg. 22-23.

67 "Bible Question Box" (Norwich, Connecticut, Norwich Bulletin, 25 Sep 1911), Chronicling America: Historic American Newspapers, Library of Congress, 101 Independence Avenue SE, Washington, DC; Online database: https://chroniclingamerica.loc.gov/lccn/sn82014086/1911-09-25/ed-1/seq-4/#date1=1900&index=10&rows=20&searchType=advanced&language=&sequence=0&words=C+H+ROCKWELL&proxdistance=5&date2=1920&ortext=&proxtext=&phrasetext=H.C.+Rockwell&andtext=&dateFilterType=yearRange&page=1

68 Goodrich, Roy D., Demonism and the Watch Tower & other writings. Morrisville, NC: Lulu Enterprises, Inc., 2010, pg. 169.

69 "Prefatory" in "Facts For Shareholders", The Watch Tower, The Watch Tower Bible and Tract Society, Brooklyn, NY, 15 Nov 1917, pg. 3.

70 "Letters to the Editor", *Popular Mechanics,* Chicago, Illinois, Vol. 41, No. 4, Apr 1924, p. 650.

71 New Jersey Death Certificate, New Jersey Department of Health, Office of Vital Statistics and Registry, P.O. Box 370, Trenton, New Jersey 08625-0370, "Hermane" Rockwell, death cert. #1007-1013.

72 Green-Wood Cemetery Records, "Hermane" Rockwell, Green-Wood Cemetery, Administrative Offices, 500 25th Street, Brooklyn, NY.

73 "Rockwell, H. Clay", The Outley R. Coulter Sport Photography Collection, Box 16, Folder 242. H.J. Lutcher Stark Center for Physical Culture and Sports, Gate 16; North End Zone Suite 5.700m D.K.R. Texas Memorial Stadium, 403 East 23rd Street, The University of Texas, Austin, TX.

74 U.S. Social Security Applications and Claims Index, 1936-2007, Ancestry.com, Drusilla Madeline Henoch.

75 Find A Grave—Calvary Cemetery, Los Angeles, Los Angeles Co., California, Drusilla M. Henoch, Find A Grave Memorial #181628911.

76 District of Columbia Marriages, 1811-1950, FamilySearch.org, Milton Henoch and Drusilla Davis, Vol. 36, pg. 196, #20541.

77 California Death Certificate, California Health and Strategic Planning, Vital Records, M.S. 5103, P.O. Box 997410, Sacramento, CA 95899-7410, Milton Henoch, death cert. #28-052628.

78 California Death Index, 1940-1997, Ancestry.com, Milton Henoch.

79 Find A Grave—B'Nae Zion Jewish Cemetery, LaPorte Co., Indiana, Find A Grave.com, Milton Henoch, Find A Grave Memorial #18549945.

80 "Letters of James F. Edwards", Archives of the University of Notre Dame, Theodore M. Hesburgh Library, 607 Hesburgh Library, Notre Dame, IN.

81 "U.S. Patent and Trademark Office Patents, 1790-1909", Ancestry.com, entry for Milton Henoch (1903 and 1921). 82 Newspapers and Periodicals, Ancestry.com ("Demonstrator Was Cook Aboard the Lusitania", Appleton, Wisconsin, Appleton Post Crescent, 31 May 1915)

82 "Demonstrator Was Cook Aboard the Lusitania" (Appleton, Wisconsin, Appleton Post Crescent, 31 May 1915), Newspapers and Periodicals, Ancestry.com.

83 U.S. City Directories, 1822-1995", Ancestry.com (Los Angeles, California City Directory, 1918 (pg. 977), 1937 (pg. 905), 1938 (pg. 943) entries for Drusilla M. Henoch.

84 California, County Marriages, 1850-1952, FamilySearch.org, Fred Haley Ball and Drusilla Henoch, 1919 Book, pg. 351.

85 New York City, Births, 1891-1902, Ancestry.com, "Mabel" Henoch, birth cert. #18156.

86 California, Death Index, 1940-1997, Ancestry.com, Maybelle Costa.

87 Find A Grave—Forest Lawn Memorial Park Cemetery, Glendale, Los Angeles Co., California, Find A Grave.com, Maybelle Madeline Costa, Find A Grave Memorial #85371343.

88 City of St. Louis Marriage Records, St. Louis Co., Missouri Public Library, 1640 South Lindbergh Boulevard, St. Louis, MO. Lewis "O." Davis and Harriet A. "Orhndrof", Marriage lic. #128705.

89 U.S., WWI Draft Registration Cards, 1917-1918, Ancestry.com, Frank J. Costa, Chicago, Cook Co., Illinois.

90 U.S. Naturalization Record Indexes, 1791-1992, Ancestry.com, Frank John Costa, application #5501246, petition #9557665 b. abt. 1898 in Italy, applied for citizenship on 08 May 1942 in San Pedro, Los Angeles Co., California.

91 California, Death Index, 1940-1997, Ancestry.com, Frank J. Costa.

92 California Death Certificate, California Health and Strategic Planning, Vital Records, M.S. 5103, P.O. Box 997410, Sacramento, CA 95899-7410, Frank John Costa, death cert. #63-040923.

93 Find A Grave—Green Hills Memorial Park Cemetery, Rancho Palos Verdes, Los Angeles Co., California, Find A Grave.com, Frank John Costa, M.D., Find A Grave Memorial #71298591.

94 Ancestry.com. Florida, State Census, 1867-1945, Frank J. Costa [Microfilm series S 5, 30 reels; Record Group 001021; State Library and Archives of Florida, R.A. Gray Building, 500 South Bronough Street, Tallahassee, FL.

95 U.S. City Directories, Ancestry.com, San Pedro and Wilmington, California City Directory 1940, pg. 644, entry for Costa, (Dr.) Frank J.

96 U.S. City Directories, Ancestry.com, Long Beach, California City Directories 1955 and 1960, entry for Costa, Maybelle.

97 Social Security Death Index, Ancestry.com.

98 Obituary of Warren Fred Flanagan (Los Angeles, California, Los Angeles Times, 21 Nov 2001), Southern California Genealogical Society and Family Research Library, 417 Irving Drive, Burbank, CA.

99 U.S. City Directories, Ancestry.com, San Pedro and Wilmington, California City Directory 1952 (pg. 80) and 1956 (pg. 134), entry for Flanagan, Warren F.

100 U.S. City Directories, Ancestry.com, Torrance, California City Directory 1959, pg. 65, entry for Flanagan, Warren F.

101 Find A Grave—Calvary Cemetery, Los Angeles, Los Angeles Co., California, Find A Grave.com, Frank M. Costa, Find A Grave Memorial #180404690.

102 Obituary of Mrs. Moses Davis (Niles, Michigan, Niles Sun, 01 Feb 1893), Niles District Library, 620 East Main Street, Niles, MI.

103 Lewis Pegan by his Next Friend John Jacob Pegan vs. David Winters, Montgomery County, Ohio Common Pleas Court Records, September Term 1839, Book N, pg. 515. Montgomery County, Ohio Records Center and Archives, 117 South Main Street, 6th Floor, Dayton, OH.

A. U.S. City Directories, Ancestry.com, Polk's City Directory, Seattle, Washington, 1893, pg. 779, entry for Rockwell, H. Clay.

B. Find A Grave—Valhalla Cemetery, Bel-Nor, St. Louis Co., Missouri, Find A Grave.com, Lewis B. Davis, Find A Grave Memorial #168759306.

C. Find A Grave—Valhalla Cemetery, Bel-Nor, St. Louis Co., Missouri, Find A Grave.com, Harriett A. Davis-Broeker, Find A Grave Memorial #168759389.

D. Obituary of Harriett A. Broeker (St. Louis, Missouri, St. Louis Post Dispatch, 18 Apr 1976), St. Louis County Public Library, 1640 South Lindbergh Boulevard, St. Louis, MO.

Isaiah Ira Pegan

1. **Isaiah Ira[5] Pegan** (*Robert A.[4], Andrew[3], Andrew[2] Pagan, James[1]*) was born on May 19, 1829, in Wayne Twp., Montgomery Co., Ohio or Toronto, Ontario, Canada.[1, 2, 3] He was also known as **Ira**. He was the son of Robert A. Pegan and Christina or Christiana Ingle. He died in Shelbyville, Shelby Twp., Shelby Co., Illinois, on February 1, 1911, at age 81.[2, 4, 5] Isaiah Ira was buried in Glenwood Cemetery, Shelbyville, Shelby Twp., Shelby Co., Illinois.[6, 7]

Isaiah Pegan's middle name was most likely Ira, as he is also known by that name on at least one census form and in other references.

Isaiah Pegan says consistently in censuses that he was born in Ohio. Ohio is also listed as his birthplace on his death certificate in Shelby Co., Illinois. Most likely, he was born in Montgomery County, Ohio, as his father Robert is enumerated there in the 1830 census. However, on his civil war pension application, Isaiah says he was born in Toronto, Canada! This claim is repeated on his second wife Jennie's widow's pension application.[3]

Isaiah may have been a resident of Platteville, Wisconsin Territory, in 1845. In January 1846, two editions of a Platteville, Wisconsin newspaper, *The Independent American and General Advertiser*, mention that "I.C." Pegan has a letter for him at the post office.[8]

Isaiah Pegan is found in Kenosha, Kenosha Co., Wisconsin 1850 *(Census Place: Kenosha Ward 1, Kenosha, Wisconsin; Roll: M432_1000; Page: 234; Image: 456)*. He is living in what seems to be a boarding house owned by an O.H. Waldo a 40-year-old man born in Massachusetts. Isaiah says he is a tailor born in Ohio.

He returned to Ohio by 1851.

Isaiah Ira married **Jeannette Rose Whitney** on October 12, 1851, in Montgomery Co., Ohio.[1, 9] They had no children. Jeannette Rose Whitney was born in New York about 1831. Jeannette Rose died in Montgomery Co. or Butler Co., Ohio, before 1860?

Jeanette Rose Whitney, age 18, was living with her parents, Thomas and Mary, and her siblings in Spring Creek Twp., Miami Co., Ohio in 1850 *(Census Place: Spring Creek, Miami, Ohio; Roll: M432_711; Page: 315A; Image: 11)*. She was born in New York about 1831-2. Jeanette Rose Whitney Pegan probably dies before the 1860 census. She may have died in Montgomery County, Ohio or Butler Co., Ohio.

In 1860, Isaiah Pegan, a tailor and "single", is residing in a boarding house owned by H.S. Cone in Oxford, Oxford Twp., Butler Co., Ohio *(Census Place: Oxford, Butler, Ohio; Roll: M653_940; Page: 110; Image: 222)*. He is enumerated as "I." Pegan.

Isaiah Pegan was a private in the Company D, Regiment 24 in the Michigan Infantry during the Civil War. The Michigan 24th was organized at Detroit, Wayne Co., Michigan on August 31, 1862, and was one of the most distinguished regiments in the Civil War. Along with 2nd, 6th, and 7th Wisconsin and the 19th Indiana, they formed the famed "Black Hat Battalion", the only western brigade of the Army of the Potomac and comprised of units from the east. This battalion was nicknamed "The Iron Brigade" because of their bravery and refusal to bend in enemy fire. The 24th Michigan began with 463 men, and fought in some of the deadliest battles in the war, including Chambersburg and Fredericksburg in Virginia. The 24th Michigan was the most devastated of any unit in the war, losing half their men before Gettysburg, where they incurred an additional 71% casualties.

Apparently, Isaiah was one of the less than 120 men in the unit at war's end. But he didn't see action in any of these battles. He didn't join the unit until March 15, 1865, when the war was all but over. The Confederate Army, led by General Robert E. Lee, surrendered at Appomattox, Virginia three weeks after he enlisted.

Isaiah Pegan only participated in the unit's two final assignments. While the other companies in the Iron Brigade were at Appomattox to witness Lee's surrender, the 24th Michigan were ordered to a garrison in Illinois in March 1865, which is probably where Isaiah joined them. Their last official duty was as the honor guard escorting slain President Abraham Lincoln's body on the funeral train to his Springfield, Illinois gravesite. Even though he only served two-and-one-half months until the 24th Michigan was mustered out on June 30, 1865, as he states in his pension application, Isaiah applied for, and received, a pension for his Civil War service in 1907. His second wife Jennie Tipton Pegan also was granted a widow's pension after Isaiah's death.[3, 10, 11, 12]

According to his Civil War pension application, Isaiah returned to Detroit after he was discharged, but moved to LaPorte, Center Twp., LaPorte Co., Indiana the next year. There he met Jennie Almeda Tipton.

Isaiah Ira Pegan married **Jennie Almeda Tipton** on February 7, 1867, in Kalamazoo Co., Michigan.[3] They had two children. Jennie Almeda Tipton was born in Brown Twp., Delaware Co., Ohio, on June 14, 1846.[3, 13] She was also known as **Jane or Jennie**. Jennie Almeda lived in 1920 in Chicago, Cook Co., Illinois. She reached age 82 and died in Minneapolis, Hennepin Co., Minnesota, on March 27, 1929.[13] Jennie Almeda was buried in Glenwood Cemetery, Shelbyville, Shelby Twp., Shelby Co., Illinois.[13, 14, 15]

Her given name may have been Jane, but her death record and all census data have her as Jennie.

There is no civil marriage record found for Isaiah and Jennie. This fact is noted in their civil war pension papers. As Jennie mentions in her widow's pension application, the State of Michigan did not mandate civil records on marriages until 1867, and adherence to the new rule was spotty at first. There is no marriage record found in Kalamazoo County, Michigan for their marriage. Also in her pension papers, Jennie states that the minister who performed the ceremony, Rev. Brooks, gave them a marriage certificate, but it had been lost. A good portion of the pension application are affidavits from Jennie's neighbors in Shelbyville, Illinois and her some of her siblings that she was indeed married to Isaiah from 1867 until he died. In her pension file statements, Jennie also states that, although Isaiah was the youngest of a very large family, she and Isaiah had not heard from any of his siblings for more than 25 years and she presumed them all dead (Ed. note: She was correct).[3] According to his obituary in the *Decatur (IL) Daily Review* on February 2, 1911, Isaiah "Ira" Pegan married Jane "Jenny" Tipton "of Delaware Co., Ohio" "two years after he was honorably discharged" after serving in the Civil War.[2]

However, Isaiah Pegan is recorded as living in Kalamazoo, Kalamazoo Twp., Kalamazoo Co., Michigan in 1867, as his name is found in the Kalamazoo city directory for that year.[16] Isaiah and Jennie lived in Kalamazoo only for two weeks before relocating to nearby Battle Creek, Pennfield Twp., Calhoun Co., Michigan, according to the Civil War pension papers.[3]

Isaiah Pegan is listed as "Isaih Pegan" in 1870 in Battle Creek, Calhoun Co., Michigan *(Census Place: Battle Creek Ward 1, Calhoun, Michigan; Roll: M593_666; Page: 420; Image: 168)*. In the home are Isaiah, 40, born Ohio; "Jam" (Jane), 24, born Ohio and son Frankie, two, born Michigan. Living with them is a George Watts, a tanner, age 40 and born in England.

After the 1870 census, Isaiah and Jennie A. Tipton Pegan and their two children became residents of Toledo, Lucas Co., Ohio for about four years, as stated in the pension file.[3]

In the pension application, Isaiah's employer for more than 30 years in Shelbyville, Illinois, B.P. Dearing, the owner of a tailoring shop, says that the Pegans moved to Shelbyville, Shelby Twp., Shelby Co., Illinois in 1875.[3]

In 1880, Isaiah and Jennie Pegan, are found in Shelbyville, Shelbyville Twp., Shelby Co., Illinois *(Census Place: Shelbyville, Shelby, Illinois; Roll: T9_251; Page: 277.2000; Enumeration District: 200; Image: 0557)*. In the home are Isaiah Pegan, age 51, a tailor; Jennie Tipton Pegan, age 34, and their daughter Ina, age six. All are listed as born in Ohio. Also in the home is Rebecca Goddard, age 69, born Pennsylvania and listed as "mother". However, this woman is Jane "Jenny" Tipton Pegan's mother. Isaiah says his father was born in Virginia and his mother in Pennsylvania. (Incorrect—Robert Pegan was born in Pennsylvania). Jane "Jenny" Tipton Pegan says her father was born in Maryland and her mother in Pennsylvania. The family is living on South First Street.

Isaiah and Jennie Tipton Pegan are again residing in Shelbyville, Shelbyville Twp., Shelby Co., Illinois in 1900 *(Census Place: Shelbyville, Shelby, Illinois; Roll: 345; Page: 9A; Enumeration District: 0124)*. Isaiah is enumerated as "Ira Pogan". In the home are Isaiah Ira Pegan, age 71, born May 1829; his wife "Janette" (Jennie) Tipton Pegan, age 53, born June 1846; and their daughter Ina, age 26, born May 1874. All were born in Ohio. Isaiah says his father was born in Virginia and his mother in Pennsylvania. (Incorrect—his father was also a Pennsylvania native). Jennie Tipton Pegan says her father was born in Virginia and her mother in Pennsylvania. The couple says they have been married 34 years and Jennie has borne two children, with one still alive. This would be daughter Ina M., 26, born May 1874 in Ohio, a music teacher, who is in the home with her parents. Isaiah's occupation is listed as a "Taylor".

In 1910, Isaiah and Jennie Tipton Pegan are still living in Shelbyville, Shelbyville Twp., Shelby Co., Illinois in 1910 *(Census Place: Shelbyville Ward 1, Shelby, Illinois; Roll: T624_326; Page: 14B; Enumeration District: 0175)*. Isaiah (spelled Isaih) Pegan, age 80, is now the Shelbyville postmaster. He says he was born in Ohio and his parents in Pennsylvania. Jennie Tipton Pegan, age 63, says she is an Ohio native and her parents, like her husband's, were born in Pennsylvania. They state they have been wed 43 years and this is the first marriage for both. (Incorrect—this is Isaiah Pegan's second marriage.) Jennie again says she bore two children and one is surviving. Unmarried daughter Ina, age 35, born Ohio, is still residing with them and is a music teacher.

Jennie Tipton Pegan and her unmarried daughter Ina moved to Chicago, Cook Co., Illinois by 1916, documented in her widow's pension file.[3] Although they are not found in the 1920 census, Jennie and Ina May were still living in Chicago, as mentioned in a brief wedding article in the *Findlay Enterprise (Shelbyville, IL)* in September of that year announcing Ina and Thad's marriage in July.[22]

Jennie Tipton Pegan was living with her son-in-law and daughter, Thad and Ina May Pegan Martin, in Minneapolis, Hennepin Co., Minnesota when she died on March 27, 1929.[13] Jennie is buried next to Isaiah and young son Franklin Glenwood Cemetery in Shelbyville, Shelby Twp., Shelby Co., Illinois.

Isaiah and Jennie claim on their Civil War pension applications that their marriage was a first for both. This, on Isaiah's part, was not true. Was he also lying about his place of birth on his pension application? Was Jennie also lying? Or was she just repeating what her husband had always told her—that he had never been married before?[3]

Why Isaiah Pegan denied his first marriage—to his second wife Jennie Tipton Pegan and her family and in his Civil War pension application—is unknown. This first marriage is documented by a civil marriage record in Montgomery County, Ohio, and by an entry in Robert and Christina Pegan's bible.[1, 9] Also, he declares himself "single and not a widower or divorced in the 1860 census. Was the marriage annulled? The fate of his first wife, Jeannette Rose Whitney Pegan, is also a mystery. She is not found in any U.S. Federal Censuses other than 1850, There is no death record for her, as, if she died before 1860, her death would pre-date civil death registrations. (Ohio first registered deaths on the county level in some counties in the 1860s). Her parents are also not found in any other censuses.

Children of Isaiah Ira Pegan and Jennie Almeda Tipton:

+ 2 m I. **Franklin⁶ Pegan** was born in Battle Creek, Pennfield Twp., Calhoun Co., Michigan, in 1868.[17] He died in Shelbyville, Shelby Twp., Shelby Co., Illinois, about 1879.[18]

+ 3 f II. **Ina May⁶ Pegan** was born in Toledo, Lucas Co., Ohio, on May 15, 1874.[19, 20] She died in Minneapolis, Hennepin Co., Minnesota, on January 6, 1956.[19, 20]

6th Generation

2. **Franklin**[6] **Pegan** (*Isaiah Ira*[5], *Robert A.*[4], *Andrew*[3], *Andrew*[2] *Pagan, James*[1]) was born in 1868 in Battle Creek, Pennfield Twp., Calhoun Co., Michigan.[17] He was the son of Isaiah Ira Pegan (1) and Jennie Almeda Tipton. Franklin died in Shelbyville, Shelby Twp., Shelby Co., Illinois, about 1879 at age 11.[18] He was buried in Glenwood Cemetery, Shelbyville, Shelby Twp., Shelby Co., Illinois.[18]

3. **Ina May**[6] **Pegan** (*Isaiah Ira*[5], *Robert A.*[4], *Andrew*[3], *Andrew*[2] *Pagan, James*[1]) was born on May 15, 1874, in Toledo, Lucas Co., Ohio.[19, 20] She was the daughter of Isaiah Ira Pegan (1) and Jennie Almeda Tipton. Ina May died in Minneapolis, Hennepin Co., Minnesota, on January 6, 1956, at age 81.[19, 20] She was buried in Lakewood Cemetery, Minneapolis, Hennepin Co., Minnesota.[19, 21]

Childless.

Ina May Pegan, single, is residing with her parents, Isaiah and Jennie A. Tipton Pegan in 1900 in Shelbyville, Shelby Twp., Shelby Co., Illinois (*Census Place: Shelbyville, Shelby, Illinois; Roll: 345; Page: 9A; Enumeration District: 0124*). Ina, age 26, a music teacher, was born in Ohio like her parents. Isaiah is enumerated as "Ira Pogan", and is the head of the household. Isaiah, age 71, born May 1829; is a "Taylor". Born in Ohio, he says his father was born in Pennsylvania and his mother in Vermont (incorrect; she was also born in Pennsylvania). "Janette" (Jennie) Tipton Pegan, age 53, born June 1846 in Ohio; says her father was born in Virginia and her mother in Pennsylvania. Isaiah and Jennie have been married 34 years and Jennie has borne two children, with one, Ina, still alive.

In 1910, Ina May Pegan is still living with parents Isaiah and Jennie Shelbyville, Shelbyville Twp., Shelby Co., Illinois (*Census Place: Shelbyville Ward 1, Shelby, Illinois; Roll: T624_326; Page: 14B; Enumeration District: 0175*). Ina, 35, continues to teach music. Isaiah (spelled Isaih) Pegan, age 80, is now the postmaster. He says he was born in Ohio and his parents in Pennsylvania. Jennie Tipton Pegan, age 63, says she is an Ohio native and her parents, like her husband's, were born in Pennsylvania. Isaiah and Jennie Tipton Pegan say they have been married 43 years and this is the first marriage for both. (Incorrect: This is Isaiah Pegan's second marriage.) Jennie again says she bore two children and one is surviving. Isaiah Pegan says he is the postmaster now.

After her father Isaiah Pegan died in 1911, Ina May Pegan and her mother Jennie moved to Chicago, Cook Co., Illinois by 1916, documented in Jennie's widow's pension file.[3] Although they are not found in the 1920 census, Jennie and Ina May were still living in Chicago, as mentioned in a brief wedding article in the *Findlay Enterprise (Shelbyville, IL)* in September of that year announcing Ina and Thad's marriage in July.[22]

Ina May married **Thaddeus Orlando or Orrie Martin** on July 18, 1920, in Berlin, Berlin Twp., Green Lake Co., Wisconsin.[22, 23] Thaddeus Orlando or Orrie Martin was born in Shelbyville, Shelby Twp., Shelby Co., Illinois? on December 1, 1872.[24, 25] He was also known as **Thad O**. He reached age 86 and died in Minneapolis, Hennepin Co., Minnesota, on August 30, 1959.[25] Thaddeus Orlando or Orrie Martin was cremated and his ashes scattered in Lakewood Cemetery, Minneapolis, Hennepin Co., Minnesota.[26]

Thaddeus O. Martin's middle name was either Orlando, which appears on his death record and his 1880 census enumeration (*Census Place: Shelbyville, Shelby, Illinois; Roll: 251; Page: 272C; Enumeration District: 200*, entry for "Orlando" Martin, nephew, "Horris" Martin, head of household) or Orrie, which is stated on his WWI draft registration and noted in his wedding announcement to Ina. According to that wedding announcement he was "raised in the home of M/M Horace Martin of Shelbyville (Illinois)".[22, 24, 25]

Ina married Thad, a childhood friend, after his first wife, Elizabeth Belle Ford died, leaving him with three motherless children: Roland, Ward and Margaret.[27, 28] Thad had been a resident of Minneapolis, Minnesota since before the 1900 census (*Census Place: Minneapolis Ward 8, Hennepin,*

Minnesota; Roll: 769; Page: 3A; Enumeration District: 0092, entry for Thad O. Martin). After her marriage, Ina's mother, Jennie A. Tipton Pegan, moved from Chicago to live with Thad and Ina in Minneapolis, Hennepin Co., Minnesota.

Thaddeus O. and Ina M. Pegan Martin are enumerated in Minneapolis, Hennepin Co., Minnesota in 1930 *(Census Place: Minneapolis, Hennepin, Minnesota; Roll: 1099; Page: 9B; Enumeration District: 237; Image: 246.0).* Their ages are incorrect, as Thad is listed as age 50 and Ina as 45. Also, the census taker says that Thad was first married at age 25 (correct) but Ina was first wed at age 20 (incorrect). Both say they were born in Illinois. Thad says he is an agent for a transport company. Also in the home is Thad's daughter by his first marriage, Margaret, age 23, born Minnesota.

In 1940, "Thad O." Martin and Ina are still residing in Minneapolis, Hennepin Co., Minnesota *(Census Place: Minneapolis, Hennepin, Minnesota; Roll: T627_1980; Page: 9B; Enumeration District: 89-146).* Their house address is 3553 Portland Avenue, which was their same address in 1935. Thad Martin, age 67, born Illinois, lists no occupation and may be retired. Ina Pegan Martin is 65 and says she is an Ohio native.

According to the Shelby Co., Illinois Historical and Genealogical Society, Ina May Pegan Martin was very skilled at painting china and was known in the city for her china art. Some society members own china painted by Ina.[29]

Endnotes

1. Family Data: Robert and Christina "Engle" Pegan family bible, American Bible Society, Brattleboro(ugh), Vermont: Holbrook & Fessenden, 1828. In possession of the author, Ann Miller Carr.

2. Obituary of Isaiah "Ira" Pegan (Decatur, Illinois, The Daily Review, 02 Feb 1911), Decatur Public Library, 130 North Franklin Street, Decatur, IL.

3. Isaiah Pegan, Civil War Pension Application (1904), NARA—National Archives and Records Administration, 8601 Adelphi Road, College Park, MD, Application #7322096, 1904; Jennie A. Pegan, widow's pension application (1911) #928323.

4. Illinois Statewide Death Index, Pre-1916, Isaiah Pegan, Illinois State Archives, Margaret Cross Norton Building, Capitol Complex, Springfield, IL; Online database: http://www.ilsos.gov/isavital/deathSearch.do

5. Shelby County, Illinois Death Records, Shelby County Clerk of Court, Shelby County Courthouse, 301 East Main Street, Shelbyville, IL, Vol. 5, pg. 110, Isaiah Pegan.

6. Find A Grave—Glenwood Cemetery, Shelbyville, Shelby Twp., Shelby Co., Illinois, Find A Grave.com, Isaiah Pegan, Find A Grave Memorial #84740920.

7. Glenwood Cemetery Records, Isaiah Pegan, Glenwood Cemetery, 306 North 6th Street, Shelbyville, IL.

8. "Letters Remaining at the Post Office at Platteville W.T." (Platteville, Wisconsin, Independent American and General Advertiser, 09 Jan 1946 and 15 Jan 1846); Newspaper Archive, Online database: https://access.newspaperarchive.com/us/wisconsin/platteville/independent-american-and-general-advertiser/1846/01-16/page-3?tag=Pegan&rtserp=tags/?pc=23085&psi=103&pci=7&pl=pegan

9. Ohio, County Marriages, 1789-2013, FamilySearch.org, Isaiah Pegan and Jeanette Rose Whitney, Montgomery Co., Ohio Marriage Records, Vol. 3, pg. 455.

10. Roscoe, Andrew, "The History of the Michigan 24th Infantry", All Michigan Civil War Website, http://www.allmichigancivilwar.com/Regiments/24MIInfantry/24thMIInfantry.html

11. "No Man Can Take These Colors and Live", Civil War Trust, Website, https://www.civilwar.org/learn/articles/no-man-can-take-those-colors-and-live, accessed June 11, 2017.

12. "Less is More", Civil War Trust, https://www.civilwar.org/learn/articles/less-is-more, accessed June 11, 2017.

13. Minnesota Death Certificate, Minnesota Historical Society, 345 Kellogg Boulevard West, St. Paul, MN, Jennie A. Pegan, death cert. #18061.

14. Find A Grave—Glenwood Cemetery, Shelbyville, Shelby Twp., Shelby Co., Illinois, Find A Grave.com, Jennie Tipton Pegan, Find A Grave Memorial #84740795.

15. Glenwood Cemetery Records, Jennie A. Pegan, Glenwood Cemetery, 306 North 6th Street, Shelbyville, IL.

16. U.S., City Directories, 1822-1995, Ancestry.com, Kalamazoo, Michigan, 1867, Thomas' Kalamazoo Directory and Business Advertiser, pg. 155, entry for Pegan, I.

17. 1870 United States Federal Census, Ancestry.com, (Census Place: Battle Creek Ward 1, Calhoun, Michigan; Roll: M593_666; Page: 420; Image: 168).

18. Glenwood Cemetery Records, Child Pegan, about age 10, Glenwood Cemetery, 306 North 6th Street, Shelbyville, IL.

19. Minnesota Death Certificate, Minnesota Historical Society, 345 Kellogg Boulevard West, St. Paul, MN, Ina May Martin, death cert. #19498.

20. Minnesota Death Certificates, Minnesota Death Index, 1908-2002 (345 W. Kellogg Blvd, St. Paul, MN 55102, Minnesota Historical Society), Ancestry.com, Ina May Martin, death cert. 1956-#019498.

21. Find A Grave—Lakewood Cemetery, Minneapolis, Hennepin Co., Minnesota, Find A Grave.com, Ina May Martin, Find A Grave Memorial #72197006.

22. Loise Riley Cruitt, *Births, Marriages and Obituaries, 1897-1930, From the Pages of the Findlay Enterprise*. Shelbyville, Illinois: Shelby County Historical Society; 1987; Marriages, pg. 73, Miss Ina May Pegan and Thad Orrie Martin, September 30, 1920. The Genealogy Center, Allen County Public Library, 900 Library Plaza, Fort Wayne, IN.

23. Green Lake County, Wisconsin Marriage Records, Green Lake, Wisconsin County Register of Deeds, Vital Records, 571 County Rd. A, Green Lake, WI, Thaddeus Martin and Ina May Pegan, Green County Marriages, Vol. 3, pg. 137.

24. U.S., WWI Draft Registration Cards, 1917-1918, Ancestry.com, Thaddeus Orrie Martin, Minneapolis, Minnesota.

25. Minnesota Death Certificates, Minnesota Death Index, 1908-2002 (Minnesota Historical Society), Ancestry.com, Thaddeus Orlando Martin, death cert. #1959-025379.

26. Find A Grave—Lakewood Cemetery, Minneapolis, Hennepin Co., Minnesota, Find A Grave.com, Thaddeus O. Martin, Find A Grave Memorial #135466903.

27. Obituary of Ina Martin (Minneapolis, Minnesota, Minneapolis Sunday Tribune, 08 Jan 1956). Hennepin County Library, Minneapolis Central Branch, 300 Nicollet Mall, Minneapolis, MN.

28. Obituary of Thaddeus O. Martin (Minneapolis, Minnesota, Minneapolis Morning Tribune, 02 Sep 1959). Hennepin County Library, Minneapolis Central Branch, 300 Nicollet Mall, Minneapolis, MN.

29. Phone interview with the Shelby County, Illinois Genealogical and Historical Society, 151 South Washington Street, Shelbyville, IL, Ann Miller Carr, author, 23 Feb 2016.

Addendum

To All Pegan descendants:

1. I apologize to those living Pegan family members who expected to see their name in this book. Present-day lineage books do not include the full names or birthdates of living people born after the 1940 census, the latest one released by the U.S. Census Bureau. In the past, publishing information on living family members wasn't much of a problem. Times have changed. Privacy, on the internet and otherwise, is a deep concern of genealogists and family historians, and genealogical societies urge family historians, when publishing, not to include full information on living descendants, especially children. I have tried to adhere to this custom to respect the privacy of living descendants. Also, legal experts recommend that, if an author does want to include the names of the living, the author should obtain permission from every living person—or, in the case of minors, their parents—which is extremely difficult and time-consuming.

   However, if a living Pegan descendant, born after 1940, had the misfortune of losing a spouse, child, grandchild, or great-grandchild to death, he or she is listed in this book as "Son" or "Daughter". So are the pertinent living descendants and most spouses, the latter by surname, until the deceased person is named. I only wish to honor these deceased family members by including them.

2. More than a few Pegan descendants have asked me if there are any genetic conditions or other diseases "running in the family". I didn't intend to say anything at first, but I've reconsidered. The evidence found on death certificates, in newspaper accounts, etc. is just too compelling. Moreover, some descendants have urged me to issue a warning about this "family condition". So here it is: There is a strong predisposition to alcoholism and other substance abuse throughout the Pegan line. There are too many instances to ignore. Heart disease is also somewhat prevalent.

3. I have collected obituaries for the vast majority of Pegans descended from Robert and Christina Ingle Pegan. They are scanned and in PDF form.

4. I am bequeathing all my genealogical information on the Pegans, including Robert and Christina's family bible and all the obituaries, to the Allen County Library, 900 Library Plaza, Fort Wayne, Indiana.

   I hope those who read this book enjoy it as much as I did while researching and writing it.

   Yours sincerely,

   Ann (PeGan) Miller Carr
   indyphotog@hotmail.com

Appendix

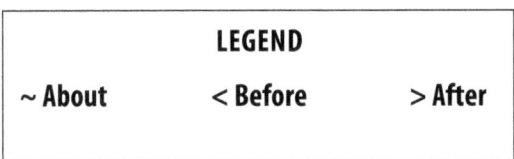

Descendant Chart for James Pagan I

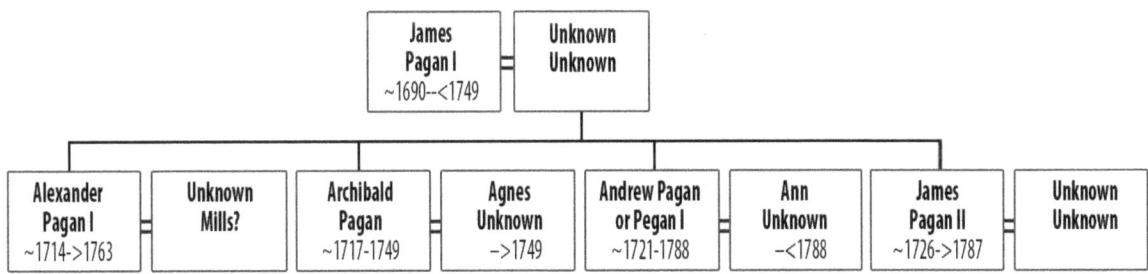

Descendant Chart for Andrew Pagan or Pegan I

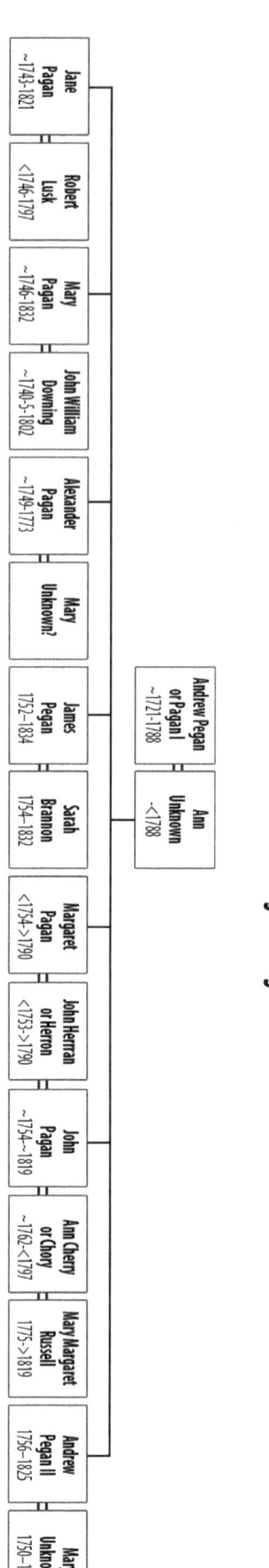

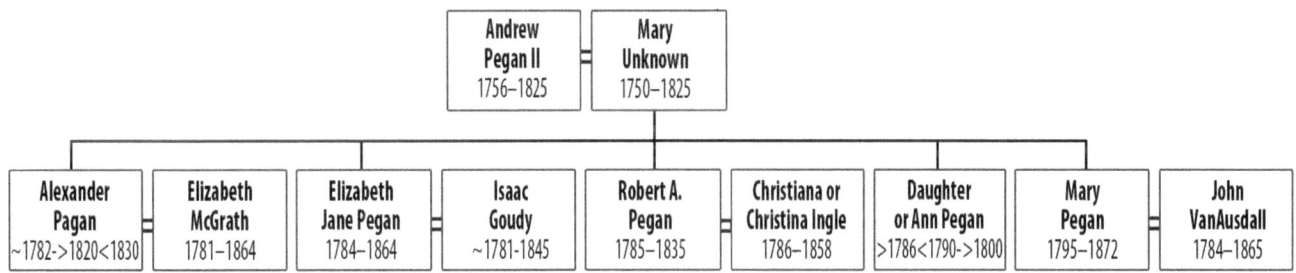

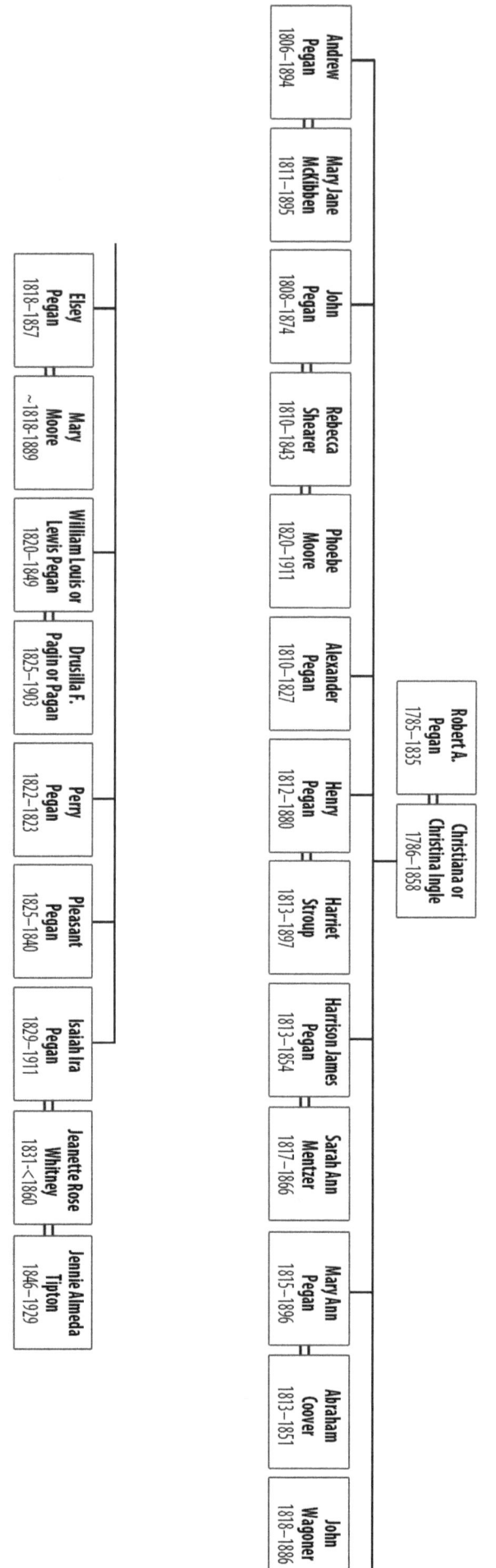

James Pagan/Pegan I selected as a juror for a 741 Lancaster County, Pennsylvania Court Case. This is the first evidence of our Pegan line in America.

COURT HELD 4 AUGUST 1741

"Before Thomas Edwards Esqr and his Associates Justices".

Sheriff: Robert Buchanen Esqr.

Persons sworn on the Grand Inquest: Gabriel Davies, William Caldwell, James Stewart, Charles Vance, John Morgan, James McAffarson, Mathew Atkinson, Andrew Middleton, James McConnel, David Shields, David Mitchel, Chales [sic] Caldwell, John Dickson, Hugh Long, Samuel McCullough.

Recognizances Ret to this present Sessions

Henry Mosselman that Abraham Mier shall be of good behavior to ffelix Landus and appear at ye next Court. Cont.

John Atcheson to appear and prosecute William Bailey and Charles King for felony.

Mathew Atchison to appear and give evidence against said King.

William Steel: for commiting fornication with Elizabeth Miller. Says he is not guilty. Prosecutor: John Kinsey, Esqr.

Jury: Daniel McConnel, Andrew Allison, James Buchanen, James Rutherford, Theophelus Simonton, Andrew Hamilton, James McClelin, Samuel Leard, William McCloghlin, James Pegan, Samuel Dickson, and David Logan find him not guilty. Discharged on paying fees.

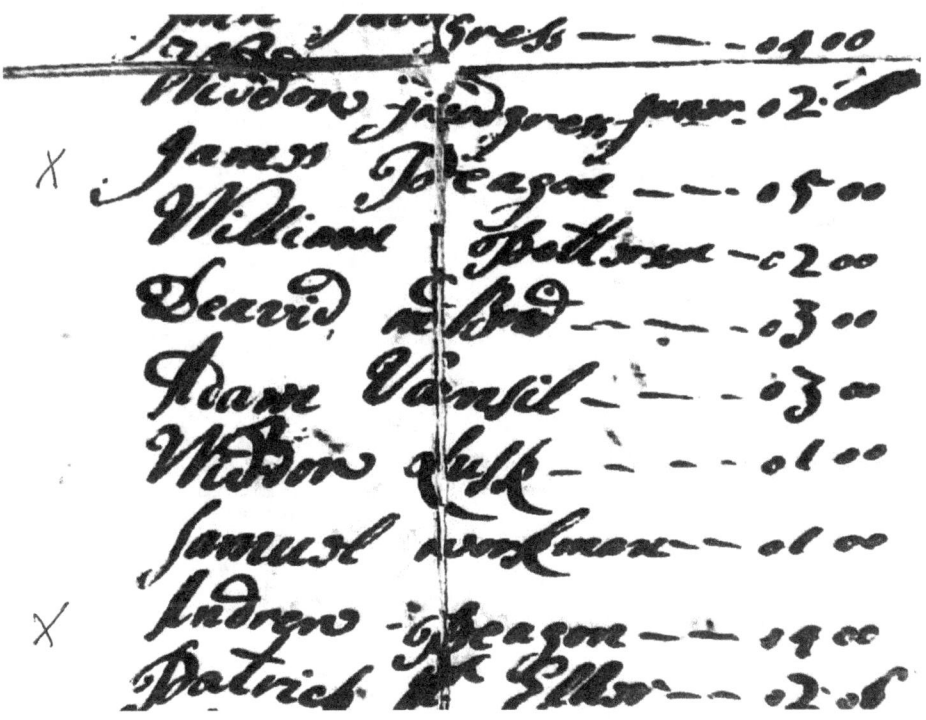

Andrew Pegan/Pagan I and his younger brother James Pagan II in the 1751 Martic Township, Lancaster County, Pennsylvania Tax List, the first extent for that county.

Pegans in Martic Township, Lancaster County, Pennsylvania, who signed "Memorials Against Calling a Convention" in 1779. Included are James Pegan II (Sr.), and his sons John, James III and Archibald; and Andrew Pegan I and his sons James and Andrew II (Andy). James Pegan, the miller, the son of Archibald Pagan, brother to Andrew I and James II, seems not to have signed it. Also signing was James Heron (Herran), husband of Margaret Pegan, daughter of Andrew I.

Memorials Against Calling a Convention, 1779

```
Martick's Township.
To the Honorable the Bepresentatives of the Freemen of the Slate
of Pennsylvania in this Memorial Humbly Skeweth :

That your memorialist are of opinion that frequent changes
in Government have a tendency to weaken it and to create di-
visions and contests among the people, & ought, as much as
possible, to be avoided.

Therefore, your taking up and passing a late resolve for tak-
ing ye sense of the people upon certain matters in the Consti-
tution of this Commonwealth before the people had sufficient
experience of it, has a tendency to produce the above men-
tioned bad effects, especially as said resolve appears to have
been grounded merely upon supposed inconveniences in the
present Constitution and form of Government, suggested by
Divers petitions to former assemblies of this Commonwealth,
and adopted without any call, of the community, without any
representation from the executive Branch specifying the in-
competency of the present Constitution for the purposes of
Good Government, without any concurrence of that honorable
Body that we know of, or any opposition or embarrassment in
the way obstructing the execution of your Laws that we have
heard of. We cannot help, therefore, being of opinion that
in passing the resolve in Question, especially in the manner
and circumstances above mentioned, you have exceeded the
powers Delegated to you, and treated that constitution, of
which you were the appointed Guardians, with Great neglect.

That, however, your memorialists, if just and weighty rea-
sons would be assigned, might not be against caUing a con-
vention, yet we cannot look upon the manner in which you
have appointed the votes to be taken to be fare and unexcep-
tionable ; the question is perplexed by your doubling it, and.
```

```
however, they, who arc for a convention, may vote on both
sides, we cannot see the propriety or consistency of voting
against one, and at the same time electing the members who
are to compose it.

There are Great Numbers of your constituents who have
taken a solemn oath to preserve the present Commonwealth,
who are apprehensive will not think themselves justifiable in
putting it into the hands of a Convention in any other way
than by the Constitution itself is directed, and who, we are
persuaded, cannot bring themselves to a compliance with the
resolve in question in its proposed mode of execution.

For these causes and before you put the good people of this
state to the great trouble and expense of a new convention,
your Memorialists presume that you will take the first opper-
tunity of revising your late resolve, and that your wisdom and
goodness and your regard to the peace & Tranquility of this
state will induce you either to drop it entirely, or to adopt it
and carry it into execution in a manner not liable to any great
and just exceptions.
```

JOHN BRANNON,
JAMES DUNCAN,
JOHN PAGAN,

JAMES WHARRY,
JOHN McCALSTER,
JOHN BARR,
SAMUEL DICKSON,
JAMES PEGAN,
JOHN BOYD,
THOS. BOYD,
JAS. MOORE,
SAMUEL McCOLLOUCH,
DAVID McCOLLOUGH,
ROBERT McCOLLOUGH,
PATRICK CAMPBELL,
JAMES MITCHEL,
VALENTINE GARTER,
JAMES ALEXANDER,
WILLIAM CLARK,
JOHN HART,
SAMUEL WILSON, Sen.,
JOHN McCREARY,
HUGH BIGHAM,

ARCHIBALD PEGAN,
JAMES PAGAN,
ANDY PEGAN,
ANDREW PEGAN,
JOHN BROWN,
JAMES BROWN,
JAMES PEGAN, Sen.,
JAMES HERON,
ADAM MOORE,
JAMES MOORE,
WILLIAM MOORE,
SAMUEL SIMPSON,
DAVID GIBSON,
PETER SIMPSON,
SAMUEL SIMPSON,
JAMES SAVAGE,
JOSEPH McCOLLAGH,
WILLIAM KENNEDY,
JAMES CALLAHAN,

Andrew Pegan II listed among the deserters from the Pennsylvania/Virginia navy ship Montgomery, June 25, 1776, *Philadelphia Gazette*?

TWENTY DOLLARS REWARD,

RUN AWAY from the Province Ship (called the Montgomery) lying in the river Delaware, opposite the Fort Island: Five Marines, belonging to William Brown's Company, viz. PETER ABLE, about 26 years of age, 5 feet 9 or 10 inches high, fair curly hair, large white eye brows, very light eyes, was born in Conogocheague, Cumberland county, speaks broken Dutch: had on when he went away, a new oznabrig shirt and trowsers.

WILLIAM TINLY, born in England, about 15 years of age, 5 feet 6 inches high, fresh complexion, curly hair, formerly lived in or near Leesbury, Virginia, but enlisted in Lancaster.

EDWARD THOMAS, born in England, about 26 years of age, 5 feet 6 inches high, red hair and much freckled, formerly lived in or near Harford, Maryland.

ANDREW PEGAN, country born, about 19 years of age, 5 feet 8 or 9 inches high, straight and well made, a weaver by trade, supposed to have gone to his father's in Martick township, Lancaster county.

JOSEPH KENNIER, born in Ireland, about 5 feet 8 inches high, 24 years of age, well made, wears his hair tied; will, it is supposed, go towards Harford in Maryland, where he formerly lived.

Whoever takes up said Deserters and brings them on board said ship, or confines them in jail, shall have the above reward, or FOUR DOLLARS for each, paid by
B W.   WILLIAM BROWN

Will of Andrew Pegan I, written September 9, 1788, proved January 13, 1789, Lancaster County, Pennsylvania.

Andrew Pegan II's first Revolutionary War pension application, April 1818, Brooke County, (West) Virginia.

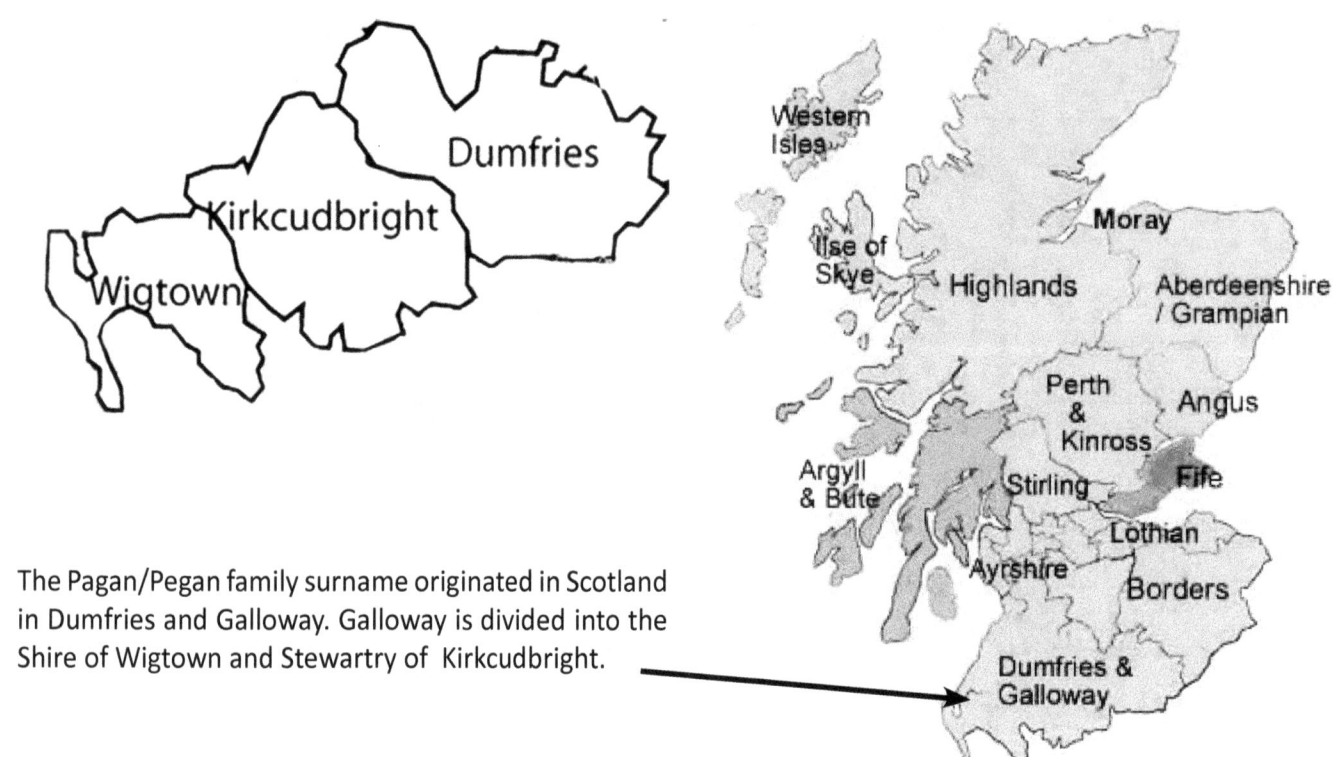

The Pagan/Pegan family surname originated in Scotland in Dumfries and Galloway. Galloway is divided into the Shire of Wigtown and Stewartry of Kirkcudbright.

SCOTLAND

The Pagans/Pegans left Scotland and immigrated to Ulster (Northern Ireland) before coming to America.

IRELAND

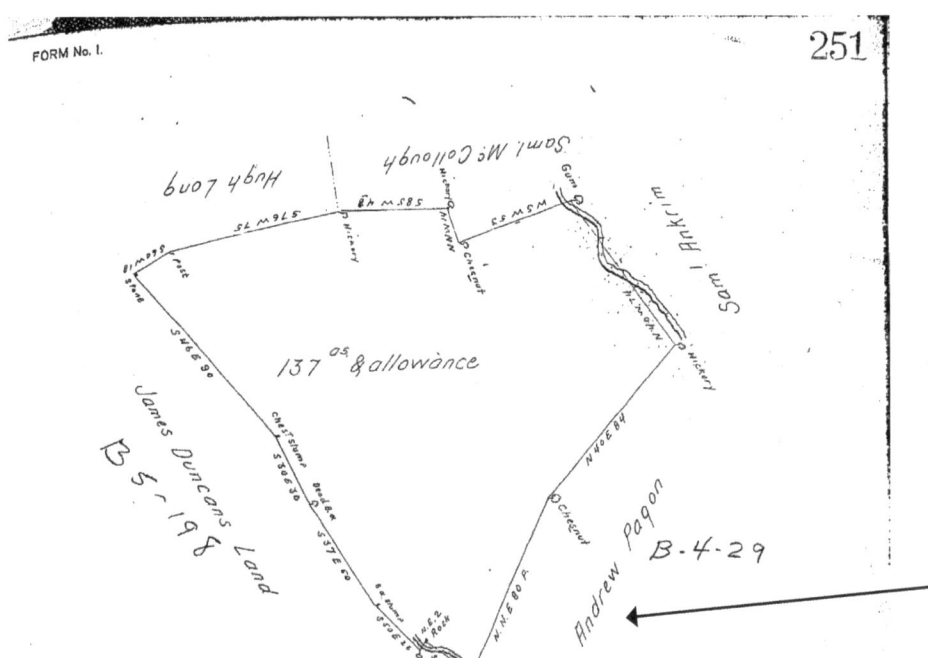

Andrew Pegan I squatted on land in Martic Township, Lancaster County, Pennsylvania. Even though he never legally owned the land, his name appears on others' surveys, like this one in 1769.

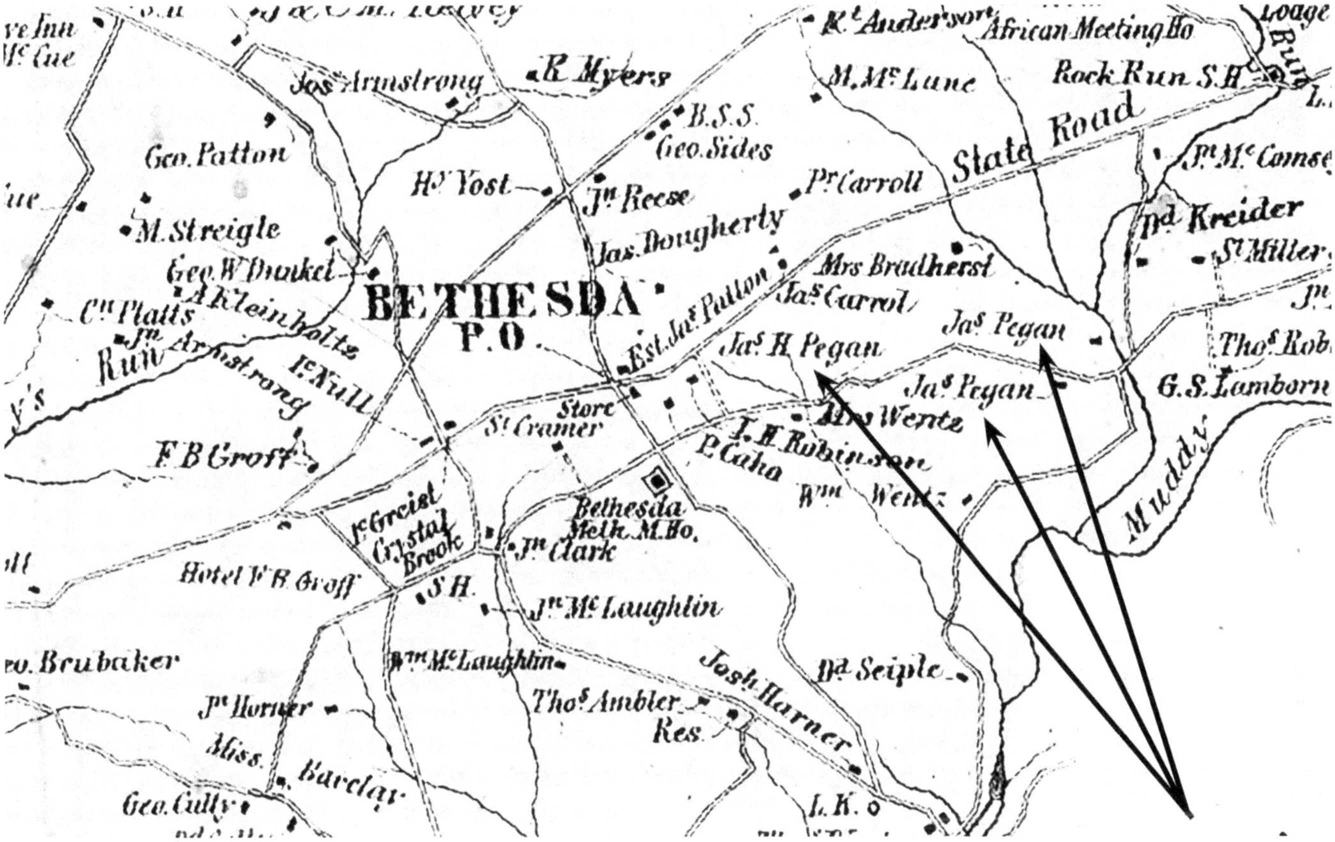

Andrew Pagan/Pegan I's son James Pegan inherited this land in Martic Township, Lancaster County, Pennsylvania from his father. James did apply for a patent to finally legally own the property, which he called "Pegan's Fancy". This map, from 1864, shows the land, which is now underwater in the Muddy Run Recreation Reservoir in Lancaster County, Pennsylvania. The two James Pegans listed on the map are James Pegan, are James Henry Pegan, a grandson of the James who obtained the patent, and James Pegan Jr., the son of the original patent holder and an uncle to James Henry Pegan.

Lancaster County, Pennsylvania

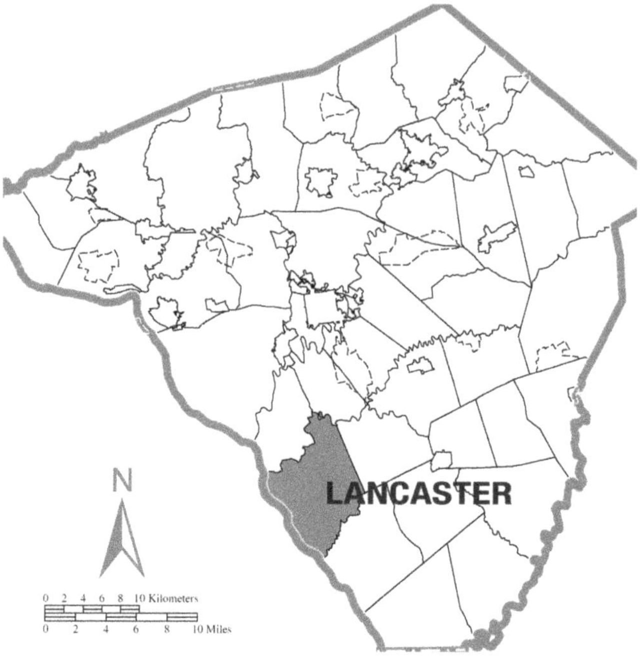

Martic Township in Lancaster County, Pennsylvania

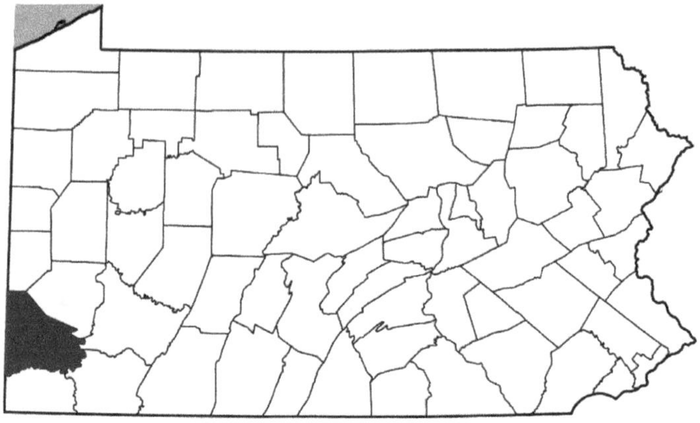

Washington County, Pennsylvania

Around 1790, Andrew Pegan II and his sister, Margaret Pegan Herran, were residents of Strabane Township, Washington County, Pennsylvania. Later, as this modern-day map shows this township was split into two, Northern and Southern Strabane.

Brooke County, Virginia (now West Virginia)

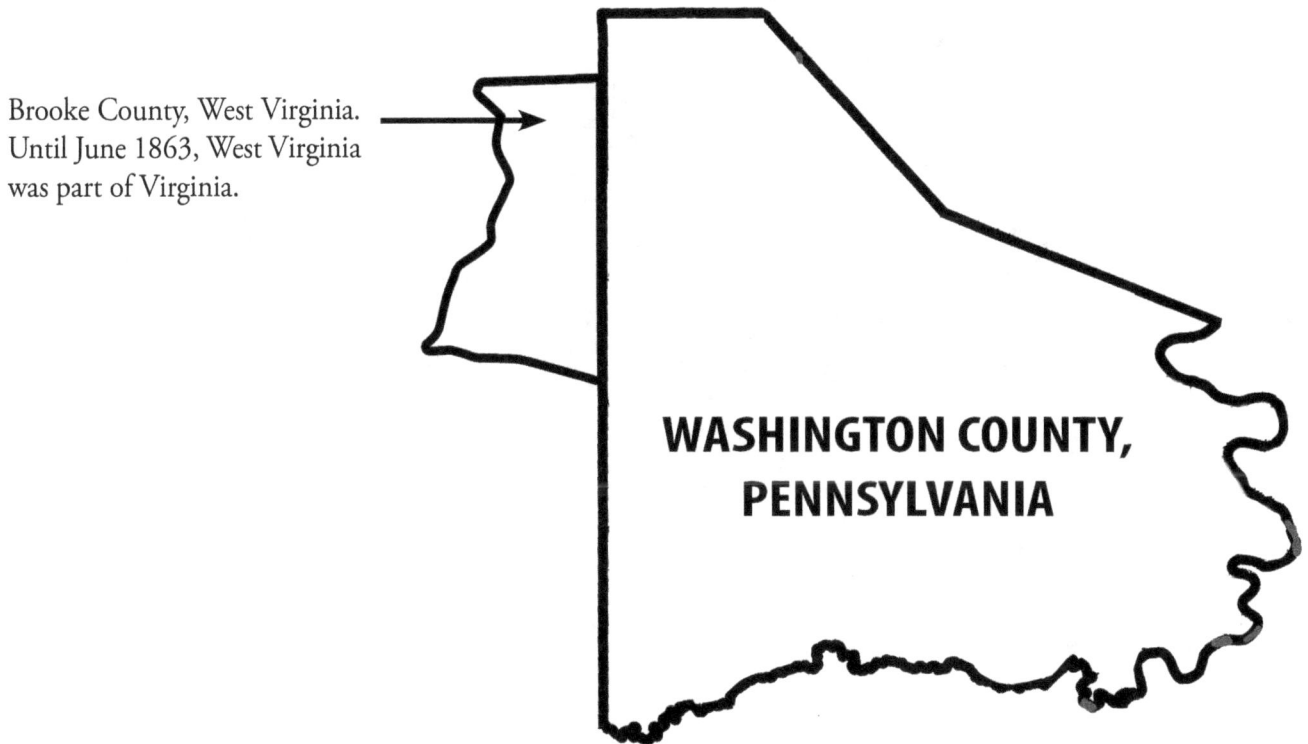

Brooke County, West Virinia. Until June 1863, West Virginia was part of Virginia.

WASHINGTON COUNTY, PENNSYLVANIA

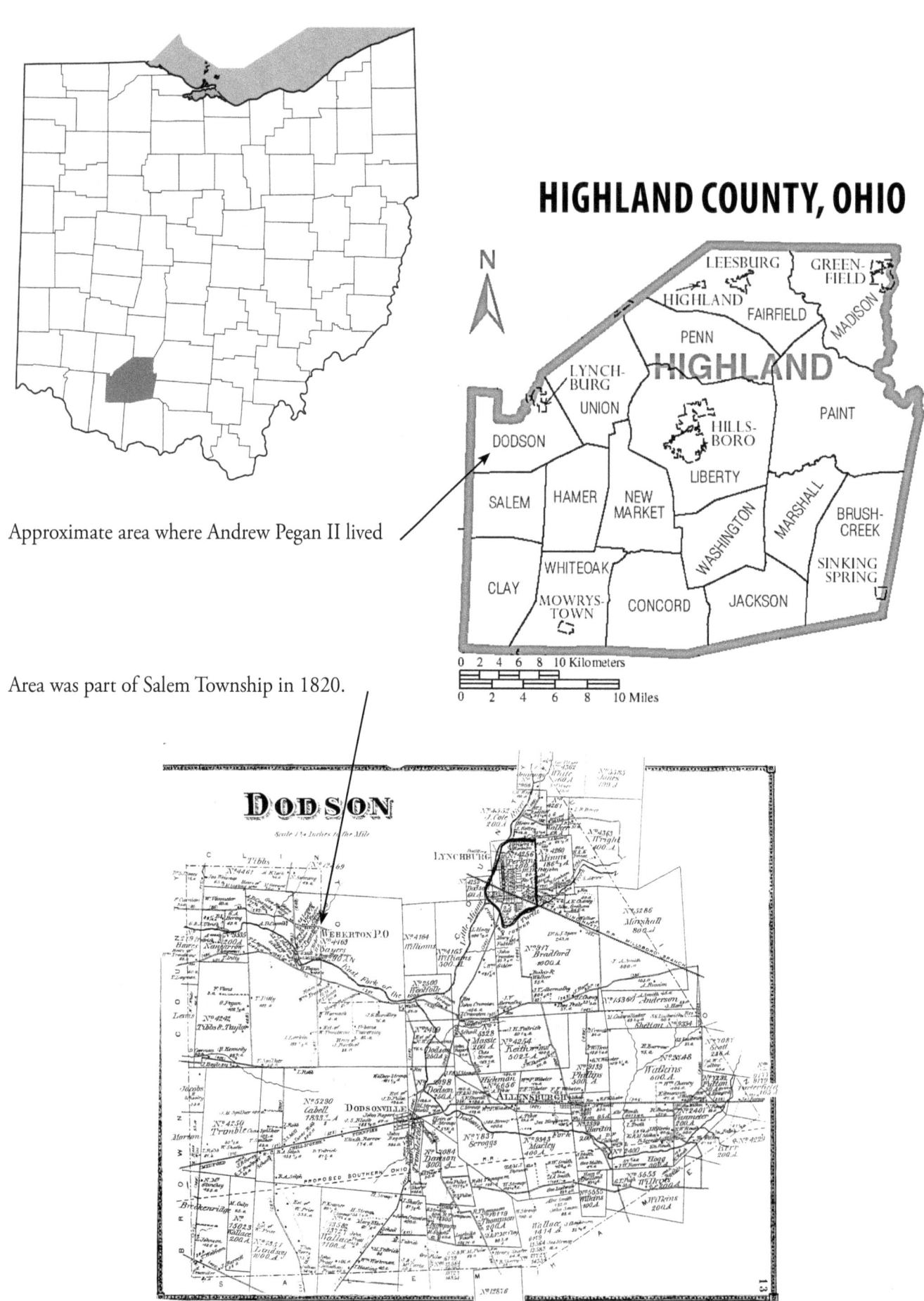

Approximate area where Andrew Pegan II lived

Area was part of Salem Township in 1820.

Robert and Christina Ingle Pegan Family Bible

THE
HOLY BIBLE,

CONTAINING THE

OLD AND NEW TESTAMENTS:

TRANSLATED OUT OF THE ORIGINAL TONGUES;

AND WITH THE FORMER

TRANSLATIONS DILIGENTLY COMPARED AND REVISED.

WITH

CANNE'S MARGINAL REFERENCES.

TOGETHER WITH THE

APOCRYPHA AND CONCORDANCE.

TO WHICH ARE ADDED,

AN INDEX,
A TABLE OF TEXTS,

AND WHAT HAS NEVER BEFORE BEEN ADDED,

AN ACCOUNT OF

THE LIVES AND MARTYRDOM OF THE APOSTLES AND EVANGELISTS.

WITH PLATES.

THE TEXT CORRECTED ACCORDING TO THE STANDARD

OF THE

AMERICAN BIBLE SOCIETY.

STEREOTYPED BY JAMES CONNER, NEW-YORK.

Brattleborough, Vt.

PRINTED AND PUBLISHED BY HOLBROOK AND FESSENDEN.

1828.

Robert and Christina Ingle Pegan bible pages outlining the family.

MARRIAGES.

Robert Pegan & Christina Ingle was Married In January the 16th Anno Domini 1806 on Thursday By Mr Andrew Swenengen. Washington County, Penn.

Andrew Pegan & Jane McKibben was Married in December the 21st Anno Domini 1828 on Sunday By Mr John Hambrick. Clinton Co. Ohio

John Pegan our 2nd Son & Rebecca Shearer was Married June the 3d Anno Domini 1830 On Thursday By the Revd David Winters. Montgomery County Ohio

Henry Pegan Son to Robert & Teney Pegan Married Harriet Stroup in January the 23d Anno Domini 1834 On Thursday By Mr John Hamricks

Harrison Pegan Son to Robert & Teney Pegan Married to Sarah Mincer in March the 6th Anno Domini 1834 On Thursday By Rev. David Winters Ohio

Mary Pegan Daughter to Robert & Teney Pegan Maried to Abraham Corver in february 10 A D 1836 on Sun Day the Reverent Barret

Isaac Pegan Son to Robert & Teney Pegan married Jannett R Whitmer October 12th A.D. 1851 on Sunday

William L. Pegan son of Robert & Christina Pegan married to Drusilla F. Sayers in LaPorte Indiana Jany. 7th 1848.

FAMILY RECORD.

BIRTHS.

Robert Pegan Son to Andrew & Mary Pegan was Born May the 14th Domini 1785 on Saturday

Christina Pegan alis Engle was Born March the 26th Domini 1786

Andrew Pegan Son to Robert & Tincy Pegan was Born November 22nd Domini 1806 on Saturday   Penn

John Pegan was Born September the 14th Domini 1808 on Wednesday   Penn

Alexander Pegan was Born May the 5th on Wednesday 1810   Penn

Henry Pegan was born April the 7th Domini 1812 on Tuesday
                                   Penn

DEATHS.

Perry Pegan Son to Robert & Tincy Pegan Died in October the 25th Domini 1823 Aged 18 mo & 12 days

Mary Pegan departed this life in September the 13th Domini 1825 on Tuesday aged 74 yrs

Andrew Pegan departed this life in September the 16th D. 1825 on Friday aged 68 years

Alexander Pegan Son to Robert & Tincy departed this life in December the 16th D. 1827 on Sunday aged 17 years 7 months 17 days

Robert Pegan Son to Andrew & Mary Pegan departed this life in September the 12nd D. 1735 on Sunday aged 50 years 3 months and 29 days

Christina Pegan wife of Robert Pegan departed this Life the 16th of January 1858 Aged 71 yrs 9 mo 20 days

FAMILY RECORD.

BIRTHS.

Harrison Pegan Was born September The 29th Domini 1813 On Wednesday, Penn

Mary Ann Pegan Was Born November The 7th D. 1815 On Tuesday, State of Ohio

Elsey Pegan Was Born April The 27th on Monday 1818 Ohio

William L. Pegan Was Born June The 7th D. 1820 On Wednesday

Perry Pegan Was Born Aprile The 6th on Saturday 1822

Pleasent Pegan Was Born February 25th D. 1825 On Friday

Isaiah Pegan Was Born May The 19th Domini 1829 on Tuesday

~~Emmett Pegan Son to John~~ ~~& Betsey was born the 22d of~~ ~~April 1831 on Friday~~

DEATHS.

Pleasant Pegan Son of Robert Pegan and Christenna Pegan Departed This life fra jurre the 13 on Satureday aged 15 years 2 month and 13 Days

Harrison Pegan son of Christenna and Robert Pegan Departed This life April The 27th 1852

William L. Pegan died in Marysville California of pleurisy after less than 24 hours sickness. Nov. 8th 1849 and was buried there.

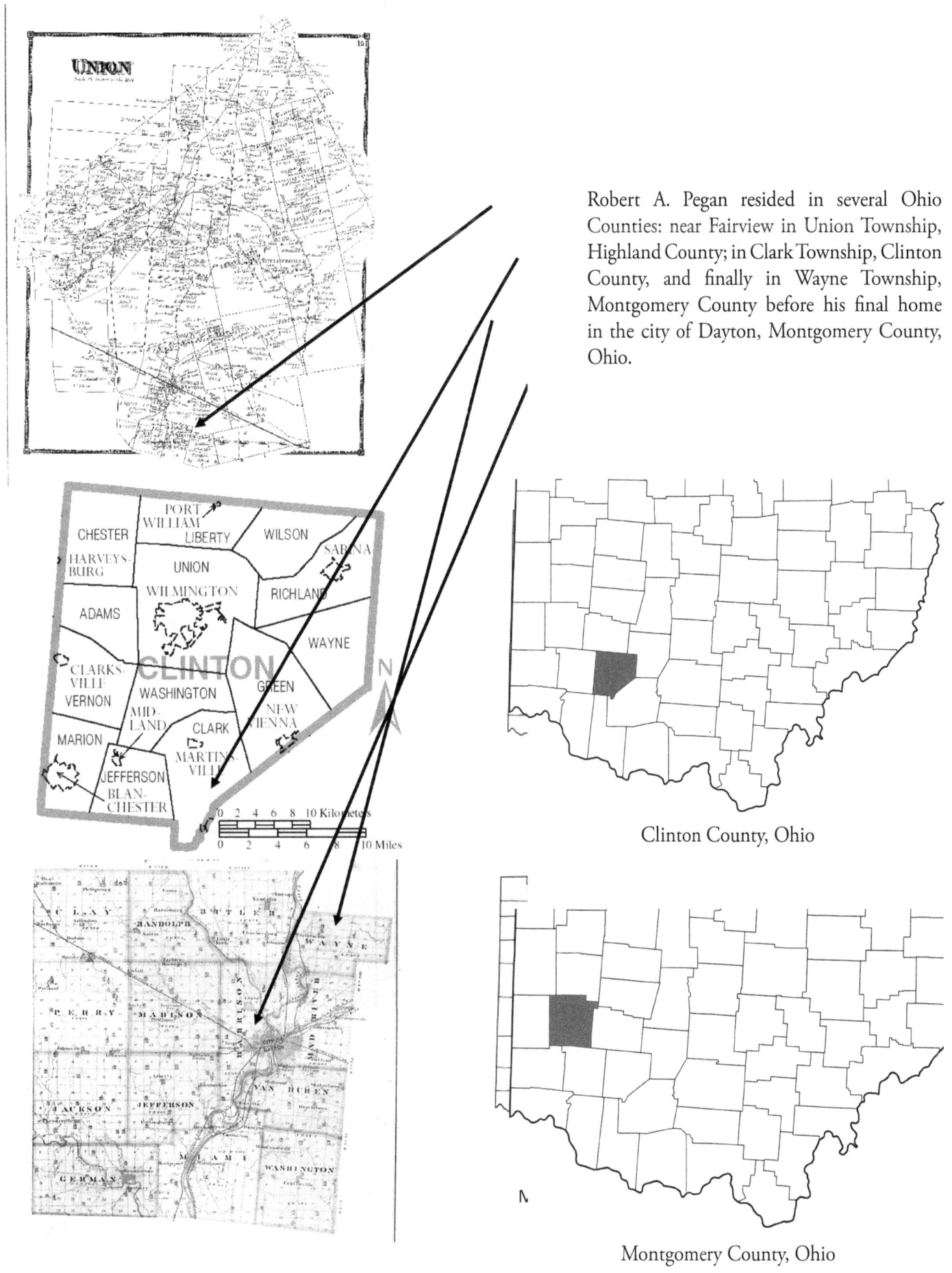

Robert A. Pegan resided in several Ohio Counties: near Fairview in Union Township, Highland County; in Clark Township, Clinton County, and finally in Wayne Township, Montgomery County before his final home in the city of Dayton, Montgomery County, Ohio.

Clinton County, Ohio

Montgomery County, Ohio

Robert Pegan (Pagan) in the 1810 tax list, Strabane Twp., Washington County, Pennsylvania

Robert Pegan (Pagan) in the 1834 personal tax list, Dayton, Montgomery County, Ohio

A few years after her husband Robert's death, Christina Ingle Pegan purchases a house in in Logansville, Pleasant Township, Logan County, Ohio in 1837.

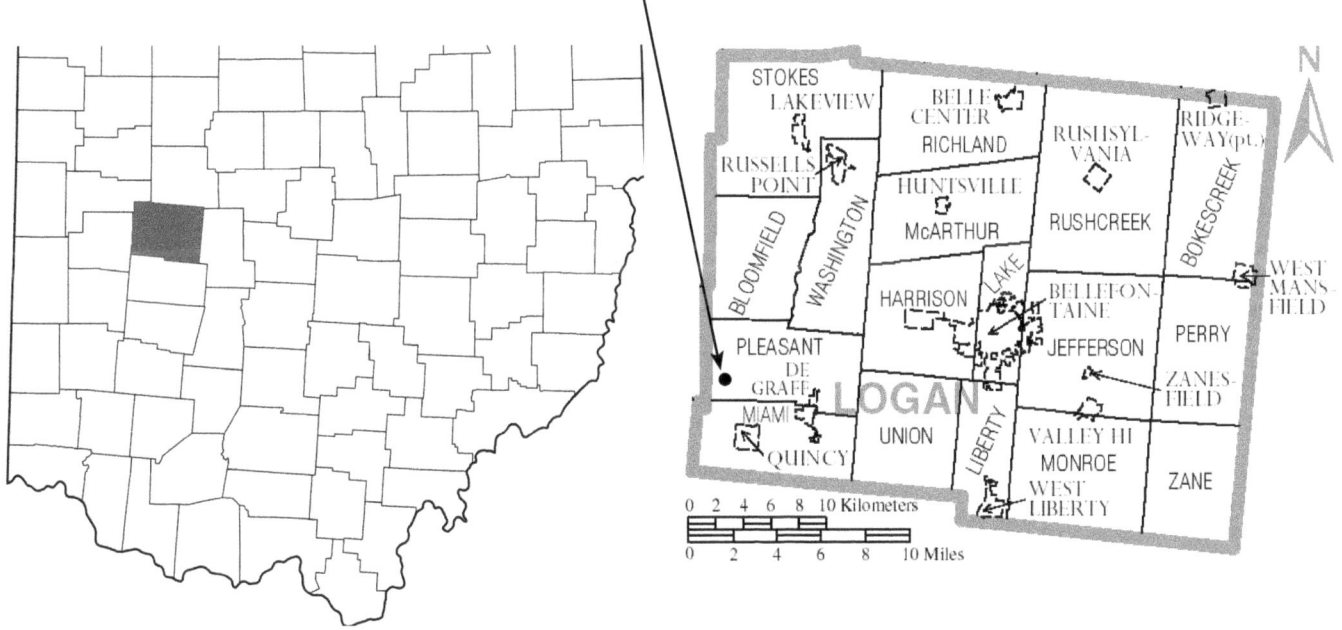

Christina Ingle Pegan on 1838 tax list, Logansville, Pleasant Township, Logan County, Ohio

Index

Abbott, Constance Sue (Hamilton)—462, 486
Abbott, Eugene Lyle—462
Abbott, Maud Lillian—190
Achor, Mary—287
Albershardt, Arlton Henry—185, 209
Albershardt, August H.—184
Albershardt, Cathern (Secrest)—185, 208
Albershardt, Donald Milton—208, 219
Albershardt, Milton James—185, 207
Albershardt, Norman Ray—208, 219
Aldrich, Doris Martha—213
Aldrich, William Lawrence II—212, 221
Aldrich, William Pascale—212
Allen, Carolyn—642
Allinger, Ray Heath—564
Almack (Shultz), Armintha Euphema (Smith)—624, 637
Almack, Earl Jesse—624
Anderson, Mr.—577
Anderson, Robert D—307
Anderson, Ruth Elene—640
Andrews, Edna Mae—465
Andrews, Joseph—666
Andrews, Milton—667, 671
Armstrong, Anna Belle—165
Armstrong, Daughter (Logue)—573, 581
Armstrong, Nellie M.—437
Armstrong, Raymond Doyle—572
Armstrong, Susan Jayne (Evans Howard Tomko)—573, 581
Assister, Willie—79
Bach, Donald Wallace—121
Bachert, Sally—471
Badders, Miss—491
Bader, John Henry—81
Bailor, Mary Virginia—640

Bakeman, James Roger—484
Bakeman, Rebecca Ann—484, 496
Baker, Leo Ray—433
Baker, Madeleine—323
Baker, Milford Earnest—434, 467
Baker, Ms.—339
Baker, Robert Bernard—468, 491
Baker, Robert Travis—491, 499
Baker, Violet Nordeica—468, 491
Bakulich, Frank Vincent—116
Baldwin, Robert Newell—59
Ball, Frederick Haley—676
Ballard, Iva Jane—103
Ballato, Mary Agnes—439
Ballentine, Catherine Olive—259
Ballentine, Letha May (Hawthorne Henderson)—262, 296
Ballentine, Robert E. II—261
Ballentine, Sadie D. (Vance)—261, 295
Barker, Diane Louise—352
Barker, Frances—112
Barker, James Randall—342
Barker, Jimmie Gaylord—320, 343
Barker, Wendell D.—320
Barkley, Ms.—643
Barnes, Loretta Mae—411
Barnes, Rachel R.—398
Barnes, Robert A.--498
Baron, Unknown—575
Bartlemay, Arthur Clarence—432
Bartow, Mr.—582
Bass, Dempsey Summers—47
Baughman, John B.—160, 180
Baughman, Joshua B.—159
Baughman, Otto G.—160, 180
Baxter, Ruth Elaine—499
Bayer, Child—550, 564
Bayer, Franklin S.—550, 564
Bayer, Helen Kathleen (Huhn)—564, 577

Bayer, Henry—549
Bayer, Mary Lou (Anderson)—564, 577
Beard, Mima Helen—409
Becker, Corenne M.—465
Bellamy, Mr.—583
Bender, Daughter (Gardenour Weaver)—467, 490
Bender, Earl Alfred—466
Bender, Sharon Kay (Lewis Graham)—466, 489
Bennington, Mary Ann—249
Bernard, Eliza—249
Berry, Thelma Rita Illene (Leitschuh)—86
Bills, Jeanne E. (McCombs Swartz)—474, 493
Bills, Raymond Eugene—473
Bish, Margaret A.—410
Bishop, Betty Lou—324
Blair, Martha Jean—334
Blakely, Mr.—348
Blauser, Miss—581
Bliss?, Jackie—78
Blumenauer, Juanita Malissa—97
Blumenhorst, Carl Duane—498
Boerner, Wilma Jean—328
Boesenberg, Edward W.—276
Boesenberg, Marcia Lucille (Roush)—276, 312
Bogan, Grant Pomerance—445
Bogardus, Unknown—101
Boggs, Francis Llewellyn—92
Boggs, John Francis—93, 112
Boggs, Katherine Anne (Davie Strep)—92, 112
Boggs, Lorraine Cornelius—92
Boggs, Mary Lee (Landerholm)—93, 113
Bologna, Leonardo—116
Bonacker, Donald Fred—106, 121

Bonacker, Fred John—106
Booze (Werner), Kenneth E.—635, 645
Booze, Doris Jeanette (Prario Cummings)—635, 644
Botts, Nita Lois—573
Bowman, Bernard Joseph—329
Bowman, Bruce Steven—329, 347
Bowman, Nicholas Brian—329, 347
Bowman, Rebecca Sue—329, 347
Bowman, Robyn V. (Tsaloff Kemp)—329, 347
Boxell, Harriet—408
Boyd, Howard Glen—332
Bradley, Linda L.—476
Brammer, Robert Lee—474
Brane, Constance (Nichols Schrock)—627, 638
Brane, Richard Lee—627, 639
Brane, Warren Grover—626
Brannon, Sarah—9
Breakey, Henrietta—671
Briggs, Helen—321
Brockman, Harry Gus—83
Brockman, Martha Lee (Krueger)—84, 107
Brockman, Raymond Harry—84, 108
Brockman, Son—108, 122
Bronson, Florida Arnetta—218
Brookfield, Mary Jane—304
Brooks, Mr.—348
Brown—Pauline Theresa (Buchanan Fabian Slusarz)—82, 107
Brown, Donald Otho—207
Brown, Ellie Faye—105
Brown, James II—82, 106
Brown, James Russell—207, 219
Brown, James—82
Brown, John James—315
Brown, Marjorie Jean—468
Brown, Mr.—492
Brown, Robert Rodney—207, 219
Brown, Violet Jane—468
Brown, Walter David—82, 107
Bruner, Child—163, 185
Bruner, Marcia Pet (Reiling)—164, 185

Brunner or Bruner, Adam Addison—162
Brust, Leander—441
Buchanan, Unknown—107
Budek, Peggy—121
Burritt, Sandra Ellen—491
Bushong, Rosemary—578
Bussey, Elizabeth Joanna (Wallace)—442, 473
Bussey, Helen Luella (Bills Kinsey Hill)—442, 473
Bussey, Hubert Clarence—441
Bussey, James Donovan—441, 472
Bussey, Margaret—441, 473
Bussey, Mary Ellen (Moore)—441, 472
Bussey, Rosalee (Ross Yarger Getz Jones)—441, 472
Butcher, Unknown—120
Butler, Nancy—681
Bye, Helen Helma—192
Cadwallader, Janice Aileen—323
Calland, Garner Smith—641
Camp, Ernest Franklin—70
Camp, Richard Ernie—71, 96
Campbell, Betty Elaine (Walker)—319, 342
Campbell, Donald E.—319, 343
Campbell, John Lee—320, 343
Campbell, June Phyllis (Hostetler)—319, 342
Campbell, William E.—319
Cappelina, Unknown—119
Carey, Ruby M.—327
Carlisle, Sarah—56
Carpentier, Unknown—223
Carr, Edward Everett—268
Carroll, Allen—284
Carroll, Delbert A.—285, 316
Carroll, Douglas M.—316, 340
Carroll, Infant Daughter—284, 315
Carroll, Mary Elinora—285, 315
Carroll, Tonya May—494
Carroll, Wendell Eugene—114
Carroll, William Morell—285, 315
Casteen, Miss—580
Cauldwell III, William A.—114

Chaney, Aubrey Bailey—110
Chaney, Sarah A.—248
Child One Pegan—398, 406
Child Two Pegan—398, 406
Chorry or Cherry, Ann—9
Christensen, Clarence Thomas—487
Christy, Elizabeth Catherine A.—642
Cissel, Allie Belle (Michael)—173, 196
Cissel, Benjamin Franklin—173, 197
Cissel, Charles Mervin—173, 198
Cissel, Melvin Osborne—172
Claibourne, Mildred Pauline—326
Clayton, Laura M.—79
Cleppe, Dorothy Virginia—314
Coates, Queen Isabella—39
Coffman, Chloe Marie—311
Cole, Unknown—342
Conklin, Isaac Albert—666
Connolly, Audra Luella—454
Connolly, Mary Sue—623
Connor, Electra Lucille—295
Conrad, Charlotte A.—581
Conti, Vincent James—478
Cook, Ms.—338
Coons, Unknown—561
Cooper, Nora I.—279
Coover, Abraham—539
Coover, Alma Pearle (Lewis Coons Ogle Hansen)—546, 560
Coover, Arthur Francis—546, 559
Coover, Chrystiana (Smith)—540, 542
Coover, Doris E. (Pickering)—546, 556
Coover, Edna Victoria (Noble)—546, 559
Coover, Elsey—546, 555
Coover, Elta Modena (Stanley)—546, 555
Coover, Hazel—546, 557
Coover, Helen Claire (Finley)—546, 557
Coover, Mary Iva (Fawcett Fawcett)—542, 546
Coover, Melvin Lester—542, 544
Coover, Sylvia (Lawyer)—546, 557
Coover, William—540, 541

Corbet, Dora--544
Corn, Mr.—480
Costa, Arthur Louis—680, 681
Costa, Celeste Josephine (Flanagan)—680, 681
Costa, Frank John—679
Costa, Frank Milton II—680, 681
Costain, Phillip Gregory—220, 223
Costain, Ralph Philip—220
Cowgill, Charles Edward--479
Cowgill, Danny Edward—479 ,494
Cowles, Ruth Mary—638
Cowman, Mary Lou—343
Cox, Mr.—583
Cox, Son—583, 585
Cox, Steven James—585, 586
Creviston, Anna Idell—561
Crickmore, Dorothy—487
Crist, William D.—574
Crocker, Marguerite—631
Cromer, Mattie Lou—488
Crone, Rita Ann—324
Crossen, Danette Lee (Winter Williams)—482, 495
Crossen, James Brent--482
Crosson, Alma?—60, 86
Crosson, Archibald—53, 58
Crosson, Frances Maurene (Eudailey)—60, 87
Cruger, Harold J.—293
Cummings, William Russell—644
Currin, Earl Carlyle—109
Currin, Infant Son—109, 122
Curry, Mary Elizabeth—33
Curtis?, Janet Faye—475
Daggy, Betty Jane (Stitsinger Reidinger)—304, 336
Daggy, Joseph Hamer—304, 336
Daggy, Lillie May (DuVall Wagonfield)—266, 302
Daggy, Llewellyn—266, 303
Daggy, Oliver John—266, 303
Daggy, Thomas Llewellyn Hamer—265
Dailey, Emily Star—216
Darling, Anna R.—277

Davidson, Ralph E.—323
Davie, Thomas W.—112
Davis, Drusilla Madeline (Henoch Ball)—670, 673
Davis, Harold H.—444
Davis, Larry Eugene—444, 475
Davis, Lewis B.—670, 677
Davis, Mabel—670, 677
Davis, Perry Adams—444, 475
Davis, Sarah Elizabeth—670, 678
Davis, William Milford—669
DeBolt, Daughter (Harrold)—489, 499
DeBolt, Forrest Edwin—488
Denison, Kay Marie—643
Dennig, Louis Adolf—330
Devlin, Ray Matthew—119
DiBello, Joseph James—111
Dick, Charma Louise—332
Dillon, Mary Alice—467
Dillon, Norma Eleanor—117
DiMichele, Minerva—107
Dingman, Mr.—348
Dixon, David—582
Dixon, Mae Missouri—61
Dixon, William Wesley—582, 585
Dodson, Daughter—481, 495
Dodson, James E.—480
Donohoo, America Isabelle—336
Donovan, Gloria Louise—113
Downing, John—9
Downs, Barbara—221
Duarte, Delores—334
Duncan, Margaret N.—40
Durett, Mr.—348
DuVall, Alexander C.—302
DuVall, Donald Harry—336, 349
DuVall, Gwendolyn (Kleinfelder)—303, 335
DuVall, Infant Son—350, 353
DuVall, John Llewellyn—303, 335
Eastes, Betty Jean (Cowgill Reese)—453, 478
Eastes, Daughter (Jones)—479, 494
Eastes, John Frederick—453, 480
Eastes, Joseph Edward II—453, 479

Eastes, Joseph Gerald—453
Eastes, Son—479, 494
Edwards, Eugenia Adelaide—191
Eiler, Winifred Louise—472
Eldred, Helen Patricia—339
Emory, Louis Dale II—578, 583
Emory, Louis—577
Erickson, Mr.—120
Ernst, Dorothy Elenor—325
Ernst, Patricia Joan—332
Etter, Rosemary Josephine—459
Eudailey, Edith Virginia (Chaney Tomlinson)—88, 110
Eudailey, Frances Lucille (Currin)—88, 109
Eudailey, Richard Louis—88, 109
Eudailey, Sam Mason—87
Eudailey, Samuel Purnell—88, 109
Evans, Anna Mae—199
Evans, Mr.—581
Evilsizor, Betty M.—641
Ewing, Arthur Jerome—79
Ewing, Arthur Warren—81, 103
Ewing, Charlene Effie Lilliebelle (Heathco)—81, 105
Ewing, Charles—105, 121
Ewing, Claribel (Williams)—81, 104
Ewing, Claud Richard—80
Ewing, Daughter (Bach)—105, 121
Ewing, Daughter (Moore)—104, 120
Ewing, Gladys Wynne (Fischer)—81, 102
Ewing, Infant Son—103, 119
Ewing, Janet Carolyn (Butcher)—104, 120
Ewing, Lawrence Howard II—103, 119
Ewing, Lawrence Howard—81, 103
Ewing, Marvin Kenneth—105, 120
Ewing, Michael Leslie—213, 221
Ewing, Son—104, 120
Ewing, Thomas Butler—81, 105
Ewing, Thomas J.—213
Fabian, Bradley Fred—107, 121
Fabian, Frank J.—107
Fabian, James W.—107, 121

Faires, Loretta Gray—559
Faris, Isma Roush—292
Farr, Bertha Olive (Roll Bartlemay Roll)—407, 431
Farr, William Constantine—406
Farrington, Jessie—44
Farwell, William Raymond—118
Fawcett, Alvin Coover—547, 561
Fawcett, Brian J.—583, 585
Fawcett, Elba Jonathan—546
Fawcett, Elijah Robert—547
Fawcett, Gail Anne (Imm)—576, 583
Fawcett, Robert Alvin—562, 576
Fawcett, Son—576, 582
Fawley, Bertha Frances—285
Feighner, Delores Bernadette—457
Felix, Alan Eugene—643
Felts, Mr.—349
Fender, Sharon Kay—344
Feraci, Mr.—222
Figert, Doris Loretta—454
Finley, Albert Earl—559, 574
Finley, Daughter One (Dixon)—575, 581
Finley, Daughter Two (Bartow Waits)—575, 582
Finley, David Alan—575, 582
Finley, Esther Marie (Crist Wyrick)—558, 574
Finley, Loretta May (Rushia)—558, 573
Finley, Raymond Lester—558, 573
Finley, Robert Cyril—557
First Cousin?—401
Fischer, BillyJo—103, 119
Fischer, Charles—103, 119
Fischer, Daughter (Devlin)—103, 119
Fischer, Harm Meint—102
Fischer, Jay Jackson—103, 119
Fischer, Marie Wynne (Morris Cappelina Keller)—103, 119
Fisher, John Robert—330, 347
Fisher, Linda Sue (Dingman)—330, 348
Fisher, Ramon Martin—331
Fisher, Walter John—329

Fisher. Karen Jean (Blakely Brooks)—330, 348
Fissel, Howard Laverne—319
Fitz, Doris Irene—460
Flanagan, Warren Fred—681
Flowers, Allen Eugene—456, 481
Flowers, Brandy Lee—481, 495
Flowers, John Junior—456
Flowers, Kathleen Joann (Hone)—456, 481
Flowers, Robert Lee—481, 495
Flowers, Son Two—456, 481
Flowers, Son—456, 481
Foster, Kathleen Elizabeth—469
Fox, Florence Leona—318
Fox, Stanley W.—290
Frazier, Wilford Wayne—571
Freed, Ms.—349
Freeman, Mary Johanna—289
Fudge, George M.—328
Fudge, JoAnne (Ramseyer)—328, 346
Fulginiti, Maria Guiseppina Agness—488
Fye, Clara Elizabeth—297
Gage, Edward Ballard—193
Gage, Gwynn Ballard—194, 211
Gage, Henrietta June (Rollert)—211, 221
Gage, Henry Crume—194, 211
Gage, Robert R.—211, 221
Gage, Ronald H.—211, 221
Gaines, Fred Dee—98
Gallagher, LaVerne Marie or Marie LaVerne—117
Gardenour, Richard Dean II—490
Gaut, Edith Ellen—435
Gebhart, Hazel—307
Geiger, Mr.—223
Geis, Everett Ray—478
Gentry, Floretta May—211
George, Mr.—353
Gerald Mcdonald Poston—333
Getz, Mr.—473
Gibbs, Vera—203
Gibson, Audrey—332
Gilby, Barbara Miller—350

Gilliand, Miss—476
Gobbell, Nettie E.--450
Goeway, Minerva Alida—49
Goggin, Sharon Kay—645
Gough, Dempsey Rachel—77, 102
Gough, Miles Prudie—76
Gowdy, Isaac—15
Graboff, Abner—114
Graham, Perry II—489
Graham, Teresa—262
Graves, Mr.—344
Graves, Rebecca Ann—475
Green, Albert Lawrence II—86, 109
Green, Albert Lawrence—85
Green, Daughter (Kirby Olbekson)—109, 122
Greenawalt, Clyda Estella—608, 614
Greenawalt, Daniel Parker—607
Greenawalt, Ola (Schultz)—608, 613
Greenawalt, Richard Pegan—609, 615
Greene, Mark David—338
Greene, Melanie (Harris)—338, 350
Gregor, Anne Sewall (Cauldwell Graboff Kaelber)—95, 114
Gregor, Daughter—67, 94
Gregor, David Gilbert II—95, 113
Gregor, David Gilbert—67, 94
Gregor, Gilbert David—66
Gregor, Mary Margaret (Pirnie Sexsmith)—67, 95
Griffith, Charlotte Ann—343
Griffith, Hattie Ann—37
Griffith, Jack Lynn—344
Griffith, Jack W. II—344, 352
Grimsley, Melvin Walter--575
Groves, Alfred R.—490
Gruett, Charles Peter—115
Guilbault, Beatrice Florence—79
Gunsaulies, Mr.—647
Gustafson, Myrtle Mildred—465
Guyer, Albert—575
Guyer, Madge Elaine—470
Gwinn, Francina Caroline—168
Hall, Jennie Gertrude--446
Hall, Ms.—647
Hamilton, Mr.—486

Hamilton, Ray Howard—343
Haney, James Rickey—349
Hanks, Cora C.—551
Hansen, Frank Bingham—561
Hardwick, Patricia L.—446
Hardy, Bert Lawrence—625
Harris, Rodney E.—351
Harrold, Kari Ann—499, 502
Harrold, Mr.—499
Hartman, Frances—321
Haste, Mr.—496
Hatch (Rockwell), Henry Clay—669, 671
Hatch, Irwin James—667
Hatch, William Glen—669, 671
Hatfield, Arlie Joseph—451
Hawk, Carolyn (Barker)—319, 342
Hawk, Everett Guy—318
Hawk, Hilda Mae—327
Hawk, Sonia (Cole Price)—319, 342
Hawker, Susie Emo Gene—573
Hawthorne, Betty Louise (Fisher)—297, 329
Hawthorne, Ennis Edmond—296
Heathco, Deryl Richard—106
Heckelbower, Miss—463
Heintzelman, Barbara—472
Henderson, Charles Cleveland—296
Hendrickson, Catherine—160
Henoch, Maybelle Madeline (Costa)—677, 679
Henoch, Milton—674
Herdman, Jennifer Renee—349, 353
Herdman, Mr.—349
Heritage, Karen Kay—121
Hern, Robert R.—325
Herran or Herron, John—9
Herring, Dolly—554
Herring, Esther Louise—568
Hewitt, Eli Franklin--417
Higgens, Emma Lou—54
Hill, Fred Roland—167, 191
Hill, Mr.—474
Hill. Edward Henry II—166
Hisey, Diana L.—481
Hodges, Meredith Ray—218

Holderby, Malcolm William Edgar—320
Holladay, Stella Madge—299
Holmes, Daughter (Sheller)—308, 338
Holmes, Raymond—308
Hone, Mr.—481
Honeycutt, Donald James—207, 219
Honeycutt, Horace Russell—206
Honeycutt, Robert Lee—206, 218
Hooker, Mary Evelyn—572
Horner, Clarence Branson—417
Hostetler, William Earl—342
Howard, Mr.—581
Howell, Alta J.—219
Howell, Mr.—222
Howell, Rachel Lee—222, 225
Huffman, Mr.—585
Hufford, Iva Elizabeth—634
Huhn, Alfred Cozard—577
Huhn, Max Robert—577, 583
Humason, Charles Martin—188
Humerickhouse, Edgar Clyde—614
Humerickhouse, Ella May (Brane Vasbinder)—615, 626
Humerickhouse, Vera B. (Hardy McHarry)—615, 624
Hunter, Betty Mae (Smith Smith)—467, 490
Hunter, Child—407, 433
Hunter, Clyde Cisco—433, 467
Hunter, Infant Son—467, 491
Hunter, James Louis II—406
Hunter, John Clark—407, 432
Hunter, Mary Louise (Groves)—467, 490
Hunter, Rockey L.—499
Hunter, Virginia Ruth (Kinnison)—467, 490
Hupp, Daniel Allen—344
Hutchason, Lillian—316
Hynes, Verna Mae—209
Imm, Andrew James—583, 585
Imm, Mr.—583
Imm, Scott Alan—583, 585
Ingle, Christina or Christiana—15, 19
Ingraham, Carl Lee—218

Irvine, Lottie Hertha—198
Jacks, Toni Rae—494
Jackson, Kenwood Moore—218
Jacobs (Cochran), Lois Lorraine (Bonacker)—82, 106
Jacobs, James Walter—81
Jacobs, Ms.—113
Jaeger, Carl Weber—483
James (McDaniel), Marilyn Louise—479
Jankowski, Mary Jo—340
Jarvis, Daniel Lee—480, 494
Jarvis, Ronald Lee—480
Jeans, Dulcinea Nannie Vaughn—41
Jenkins, Cline M.—568
Johnson, Holly Marie—498, 502
Johnson, Kenneth Whitford—91
Johnson, Mr.—474
Johnson, Mr.—498
Johnson, Ms.—121
Johnston, Flora—43
Jones, Alfred Lee—646
Jones, Dora Elizabeth—315
Jones, Ella Lorie—311
Jones, Georgia Mae—640
Jones, Margaret Louisa—253
Jones, Mr.—473
Jones, Richard Lee—494
Jones?, Mr.—494
Julian, Edith Marcella—573
Julien, Bernice Gertrude—447
Kaelber, Edward Graham—114
Kapp, Unknown—111
Karoleski, Margueriete Francia—214
Kartzmark, Joan—219
Kastner, Loretta Ann—426
Kay, Ms.—345
Keaton, Frances L.—208
Keefe, Patricia Ann—459
Keith, Elva Coe—421
Keith, Jeannie Hume—446
Keller, Charles—119
Kelley, Alice Lucille (Green)—57, 85
Kelley, Daughter (Rossy)—331, 348
Kelley, David Lee—324, 345
Kelley, Fannie Anna (Shaw)—36, 61

Kelley, Harrison—36, 56
Kelley, John A. II—36, 55
Kelley, John A.—35
Kelley, John Carlisle—58, 86
Kelley, Joshua—36, 60
Kelley, Karl Bendict—323
Kelley, Laura Belle (Crosson Baldwin Unknown)—36, 53, 58
Kelley, Lewis Albert—36, 56
Kelley, Lorenzo—35, 55
Kelley, Malcom Lorraine—331
Kelley, Mary Etta—57, 84
Kelso, Eleanor Lois (Theriault Kapp Seed DiBello)—91, 111
Kelso, Emma May—62
Kelso, George Lewis—91, 111
Kelso, Joseph Sinclair—91, 112
Kelso, Son—112, 122
Kelso, Thomas Lewis—122, 124
Kelso, Tony Son—112, 122
Kemp, Thomas Ward—347
Kendall, Clayton Morris—575
Kennedy, Melvin Charles—466
Kephart, Mary Katherine—564
Keplinger, Child—415, 448
Keplinger, George W., Roy Clarence Scott—415, 418
Keplinger, Harley Paul—414
Kies, Alfred Allen—306
Kilty, Margaret June—459
King, Lillian Blanche—305
Kinnison, Richard Lee—490
Kinsey, Mr.—474
Kinyoun, Jesse Lee—493, 500
Kinyoun, Mr.—493
Kirby, Mr.—122
Kirtley, Virginia Pearl—634
Kissel, Raymond B.—331
Kleinfelder, Brenda Joyce (Lynch)—335, 349
Kleinfelder, Harry Wakefield—335
Kmak, Unknown—478
Knapp, James P.—221
Knowles, Lilly Belle—49
Koch, Dixie M.—325
Koeb, Paul L.—470

Kondos, Emily—116, 122
Kondos, James Gary—116
Kondos, Stephen Mark—116, 123
Kondos, Thomas George—116, 123
Kramer, Connie Margaret—481
Krouscup, Louise—198
Krueger, Robert George—108
Krueger, William Robert—108, 122
Kucera, Bernice Ann—451
Lachmeyer, Phyllis Jean—118
Land, Emily F.—317
Landerholm, Merle Edwin—113
Lane, George Maley—605
Lane, Irene May—278
Lane, Maude—607, 612
Lang, Shirley Ann—491
LaRose, Thomas—642
Lavinghouze, Vallie Faye—636
Lawyer, Arthur Wilson—557, 571
Lawyer, Bobby Wilson—572, 581
Lawyer, Daniel B.—557, 573
Lawyer, Daughter (Thomas)—572, 580
Lawyer, Homer Elsworth—556
Lawyer, Larry Eugene—571, 580
Lawyer, Melvin Raymond—557, 573
Lawyer, Vivian June (Armstrong)—557, 572
Lawyer, William Nelson—557, 572
Leahey, Mary Rose—576
Leake, Mason Avery—115
Leaverton, Wilhelmina Jane—282
LeBlond, Daughter (Knapp)—212, 221
LeBlond, Jack Donald—212
Lee, Delbert James—498
Lemons (Long), Clarence Junior II—282, 314
Lemons (Long), Robert H.—282, 312
Lemons, Agnes (Philhower)—256, 275
Lemons, Andrew Vance—256, 277
Lemons, Clarence Otto—256, 280
Lemons, Edgar or Edward Roy—256, 282
Lemons, Grace (Boesenberg)—256, 276

Lemons, Henry A.—255
Lemons, James Stroup—256, 277
Lemons, Joseph Mae (Luck)—282, 313
Lemons, Margaret Lucille (Brown)—284, 315
Lemons, Murrell or Merrill—256, 279
Lemons, Talmadge DeWitt—256, 278
Lenwell, Anna Jane—570
Lesko, Alan—341
Lewis, Alton Herbert—560
Lewis, Jackie Franklin—489
Lewis, Josephine Clara—460
Librcajt, Florence Kay—447
Liggett, Mary Ann—36
Light, Mary Alice—635
Lindseth, Inez Beatrice—211
Linn, Zona B.—435
Linton, Violet Elizabeth—467
Loffer, Bertha Pearl (Terrell)—617, 628
Loffer, Donna Jean (LaRose)—630, 642
Loffer, Eugene Webster—615
Loffer, Harold J.—617, 630
Loffer, Lola E. (Shaffer)—617, 629
Loffer, Lola Margaret (Marquart)—630, 642
Loffer, William Eugene—630, 642
Logue, Mr.—581
Logue, Tracy Ann (Huffman)—581, 585
Lohr, Elsie—274
Long, Barbara Jean—447
Long, Gayle Aileen—104
Long, Grace May—281
Long, Jeffrey Richard—315, 340
Long, Nancy Hazel—449
Long, Son—315, 340
Long, Unknown—466
Lucas, Clifford Young—83
Lucas, Jean (Rush)—83, 107
Luck, Albert J. II—313
Luck, Gary Lee—314, 339
Ludwick, Arthur Lowell—310, 328, 339
Ludwick, Child—327, 346

Ludwick, Claud Hogard—293
Ludwick, Daughter (Nussman)—346, 353
Ludwick, Dwight H.—294, 326
Ludwick, Everett O.—294, 327
Ludwick, Harold Stroup—294, 327
Ludwick, Lloyd Claude—294, 326
Ludwick, Lowell Arthur—294, 309, 327
Ludwick, Roger Owen—326, 346
Ludwick, Son—327, 346
Ludwig, Onhawanha Carver—455
Lundeen, Lillian Adelia—620
Lundstrom, Mr.—495
Lundstrom, Runner Cossette—495, 500
Lusk, Robert—9
Lusk, Robert—9
Lutz, Dwight Raymond—487
Lydy, Agnes Louise (Lutz)—464, 487
Lydy, Bonnie Ilene—465, 489
Lydy, Charles Wayne—464, 487
Lydy, Charles Wesley—464
Lydy, Cheryl A. (Ramsey Blumenhorst Lee)—488, 498
Lydy, Dale E.—465, 488
Lydy, Daughter (Hunter Smitley)—488, 499
Lydy, Daughter One (Johnson, Barnes,)—488, 498
Lydy, Daughter Two (Welsh)—488, 498
Lydy, Freida Mae (DeBolt) –465, 488
Lydy, Olive Joan (Schorey)—465, 489
Lydy, Robert Eugene—464, 488
Lynch, Carl C.—349
Lynch, W. Kathryn—79
Maas, Ruth Louise—316
Macke, Daughter One (Haney)—333, 348
Macke, Daughter Two (Herdman)—334, 349
Macke, Patricia J. (Felts)—333, 349
Macke, Richard H. II—333
MacQueen, Leslie E.—117
MacQueen, Sharon (Rainey)—117, 123

Main, Vinnie Mary—74
Maletzki, Elizabeth Marie—93
Manis, Daughter (Willman)—342, 352
Manis, Howard Robert—341
Mann, Joy A.—346
Mann, Valerie Ruby—488
Mantle, Catherine Louise (Wilkin Neve)—217, 222
Mantle, John Gregory—205, 217
Mantle, Launcelot Alfred—204
Mantle, Margaret Jean (Vongundy Hodges Ingraham Jackson—206, 218
Mantle, Norma Louise (Park)—205, 217
Mantle, Sandra Kay (Feraci Geiger)—217, 222
Marlatt, William Wren—331
Marotte, Dale Allen—220, 223
Marotte, Jack Lee—220
Marquart, Werner Clarence—642
Marsalis, William Iverson—647
Martell, Mr.—492
Martin, Kate or Katherine—63
Martin, Lorraine Ruth (Lucas)—53, 82
Martin, Major Oury—51
Martin, Thaddeus O.—690
Mason, Ada—158, 173
Mason, Alice Irene (Honeycutt)—179, 206
Mason, Alta Dell (Young)—159, 175
Mason, Charles Edwin—158, 173
Mason, Charles Stephen—201, 214
Mason, Child One—175, 201
Mason, Child Two—175, 201
Mason, Clarence Edwin—177, 204
Mason, Cora—159, 177
Mason, Donald Earl—199, 213
Mason, Doris Geraldine—341
Mason, Dorothy Ann—213, 221
Mason, Ida May—158, 173
Mason, John Pegan—159, 178
Mason, Katherine, 158, 175
Mason, Kathryn Louise (Aldrich)—199, 212

Mason, Laura Marguerite—174, 200
Mason, Laurence Victor—174, 199
Mason, Marcus Vincent—177, 203
Mason, Mary Jane (Ewing)—201, 213
Mason, Mildred Elizabeth (Mantle)—179, 204
Mason, Minnie or Mary Elizabeth—159, 179
Mason, Paul Edwin—175, 200
Mason, Robert Edwin—201, 213
Mason, Samuel III—159, 177
Mason, Samuel M.—158
Masterman, Robert Clarence II—485
Mathis, Anna May—103
May, William Clark—331
McAllister, Helen Mary—209
McCandless, Elmer Glen—444
McCandless, James Glenn—445, 475
McCandless, Margaret Helen—442
McCandless, Mona J. (Weller)—445, 475
McCandless, Robert Eugene—445, 475
McCandless, Samuel F.—445, 475
McCann, Ada Frances (MacQueen)—101, 117
McCann, David Donald—101, 118
McCann, Herbert Eugene II—101, 116
McCann, Herbert Eugene—100
McCann, Infant Son—101, 118
McCann, Michael Kevin—117, 123
McCann, Shirley Theresa (Pratto Farwell)—101, 117
McCoffin, Kathryn R.—326
McCombs, Mr.—493
McConnell, Miss—482
McCray, Betty Esther—572
McFarland, Inez M.—335
McGinnis, Terry Lynn—580
McGrath?, Elizabeth—14
McGraw, Hazel Marie—483
McHarry, Bill Clyde—626, 638
McHarry, Claude Almond—625
McHarry, Donna May (Williams)—626, 638
McHarry, Jack Edgar—626, 637

McKay, Robert Hamilton—114
McKibben, Mary Jane—27
McLaughlin, Eleanor Margaret (Nittler)—90, 110
McLaughlin, William Francis—88
McLish, Miss—483
McQuaid, Jerome Terrence—485
Meier, Mr.—580
Meloan, Julia—72
Melvin, Dessie Leola—548, 562
Melvin, John W.—548
Melvin, Otto J.—548, 562
Mentzer, Sarah Ann—391
Menz, Miss—583
Merritt, Waneta—468
Michael, Bennett Franklin—196
Michael, Frances Genevieve (LeBlond)—197, 211
Miller, Blanche H. (Humason)—164, 188
Miller, Child—164, 189
Miller, Fred Pegan—164, 188
Miller, Miss—581
Miller, Myrna Ann—570
Miller, Shirley Jean—120
Miller, Willette (Sawyer)—164, 187
Miller, William C.—162
Milligan, Fairy Faye—574
Mills, John Charles—113
Minor, Mary Bragg—73
Mitchell, Miss—483
Mohr, Altia I.—548
Mohr, Diane Louise—646, 648
Mohr, Harry Fulwider—639
Mohr, Harry James II—638, 646
Mohr, Richard Eugene—639, 646
Moor, Charlotte Pauline—474
Moore, Frances Louise—200
Moore, Glenn A.—472
Moore, Mary—603
Moore, Phoebe or Phebe—153
Moore, Richard G.—120
Moore, Robert A.—493, 500
Moore, Son—472, 492
Morgan, Ozella Rose—483
Morris III, Jack—119

Morrison, Michael Joseph—222
Morrow, Leatha May—420
Murdoch, Donna Ruth—220, 224
Murdoch, Steven Blaine—220, 224
Murdoch, William Alexander—220
Murphy, Catherine Marguerite—631
Murphy, Douglas Edward—647
Murphy, Mary C.—435
Myers?, Joan Marie—107
Nash, Mr.—345
Neely, Robert Lee—478
Neill, Jean L.—214
Neve, Mr.—222
Newhouse, Mary Ruth—337
Nicely, (Roush) Earl Franzy—412
Nichols, Horace Davis—638
Nickels, Lorraine—476
Nittler, Rudolph John—110
Noble, Alexander—606
Noble, Arthur John II—559
Noble, Francis Edwin—607, 612
Noble, Ruth L. (Unknown Baron Kendall Guyer Grimsley)—560, 575
Nourse, Catherine Marie—578
Nussman, Brady Owen—354, 355
Nussman, Mr.—353
Nussman, Son—353, 354
O'Brien, Grace—78
Oder, Lona—611, 621
Oder, Walter Alonzo—610
Oelker, James Edward—646
Oelker, Jill Elaine—647, 648
Ogle, Unknown—561
Ohrndorf, Harriett A.—677
Olbekson, Harold Lawrence—122
Oliver, Mattie Mae—452
Olsen, Miss—470
Ondich, Robert George—645
Oswalt, Charles Raymond—454
Oswalt, Judith Kay (Wilbur)—455, 480
Owens, Harold Munger—67
Pagan or Pagin, Drusilla F.—663
Pagan, Alexander I—2
Pagan, Alexander—14

Pagan, Alexander—9
Pagan, Andrew II—9, 11
Pagan, Archibald I—2
Pagan, James II—2
Pagan, Jane (Lusk)—9
Pagan, John—9
Pagan, Margaret (Herran)—9
Pagan, Mary (Downing)—9
Paganetti, Angelo Anthony—69
Park, Patricia Louise (Reillly)—218, 223
Park, Richard Dawson—218, 223
Park, Robyn Kathleen Sara—223, 225
Park, William Gray—218
Parker, Marilyn Joan—340
Parrott, Miss—482
Pearson, Herbert Harrison—419, 451
Pearson, Isaac James—416
Pearson, Marianne (Neely Kmak)—452, 478
Pearson, Marjorie Jane (Conti)—452, 478
Pearson, Mattie Leona (Hatfield)—419, 451
Pearson, Opal Colene (Eastes)—419, 453
Pearson, Patricia Ann (Geis)—452, 478
Pearson, Truman Vaughn—419, 452
Pegan (Kelso) Lewis Sinclair—64, 90
Pegan or Pagan—Andrew I—2, 5
Pegan or Pagan, James I the Immigrant—1
PeGan-Thiry, Ashton James—497, 501
Pegan, Adolphus Vonesse—249, 262
Pegan, Alexander Campbell—34, 47
Pegan, Alexander—23
Pegan, Allan Jay—308, 337
Pegan, Alta Lee (Jacobs Bader Brown)—51, 81
PeGan, Alvah or Alvin—405, 419
Pegan, Andrew M.—42, 71
Pegan, Andrew, Son of Robert—23, 27
Pegan, Anna (Surber)—250, 266
Pegan, Anna Marie (Unknown Mills)—94, 113
Pegan, Anna or Lena M.—166, 191

Pegan, Arthur—162, 182
Pegan, Audrey Mae (West)—274, 309
Pegan, Bernadette Marie—334, 349
Pegan, Betty Jean (Jarvis Corn)—454, 480
PeGan, Brent Christopher—482, 495
Pegan, Carrie Etta (VanBlarcum Stevenson)—40, 68
Pegan, Catherine (Baughman)—155, 159
Pegan, Cecil Keith—423, 453
Pegan, Charles H.—34, 49
Pegan, Charles—250, 269
Pegan, Child One—32, 47, 398, 406
Pegan, Child Two—33, 47, 398, 406
Pegan, Child—34, 55
PeGan, Clanzie Herold—405, 424
Pegan, Clarence Chilton—264, 300
Pegan, Clarence Edward—301, 334
PeGan, Claudine Louise—462, 485
Pegan, Courtland Homer—264, 299
PeGan, Darlene Kay (Stanley)—430, 463
PeGan, Daughter (Bakeman)—460, 484
PeGan, Daughter (Jaeger)—459, 483
PeGan, Daughter (Lundstrom)—483, 495
PeGan, Daughter (Poe)—486, 496
Pegan, Daughter (Richards)—337, 350
Pegan, Daughter (Ridgeway Terrell)—309, 338
Pegan, Daughter (Talbott Dodson)—455, 480
Pegan, Daughter One—15
Pegan, Daughter—162, 181
Pegan, Daughter—348, 353
PeGan, Daughter—486, 496
Pegan, David Shearer—155, 157
Pegan, Della Frances (Thompson)—249, 264
Pegan, Donald Abbott—191, 209
PeGan, Donna Belle (Reed)—430, 461
PeGan, Donna Lynn (Haste)—486, 496
Pegan, Doris Helen (Ludwick)—274, 309, 328

Pegan, Dorothy Geneva (Reher Gaines)—74, 98
Pegan, Edward Ephraim—166, 189
Pegan, Edwin—34, 54
Pegan, Eleanor Margaret (McLaughlin, Ridge)—64, 88
Pegan, Elgie Elenor (Albershardt)—162, 184
Pegan, Eliza Jane (Schwartz)—246, 252
Pegan, Elizabeth Jane (Gowdy)—15
Pegan, Elizabeth Jane (Gregor)—38, 65
Pegan, Elizabeth Joan (Marlatt Fisher)—298, 331
Pegan, Ella Mae—254, 273
Pegan, Elma Eleanor (Schwartz)—246, 251
Pegan, Elma Mary (May)—299, 331
Pegan, Elsey II—604, 610
Pegan, Elsey—155, 167
Pegan, Elsey—24, 603
Pegan, Elvira (Stroup)—246, 247
Pegan, Emmanuel—155, 156
Pegan, Erman Henry—74, 99
Pegan, Fern Maxine (Zimpelman)—423, 455
Pegan, Ferol Margaret (Kies)—272, 306
Pegan, Flora Josephine (McCann Bogardus Shields)—74, 100
Pegan, Flora—42, 71
Pegan, Florence Genevieve (Cissel)—157, 171
Pegan, Florence Willodean (Flowers)—424, 456
Pegan, Frances (Carr)—250, 268
Pegan, Frances Elizabeth (Stubbs)—264, 301
Pegan, Francis Marion—604, 605
Pegan, Frank Joseph—254, 271
Pegan, Franklin Andrew—40, 69
Pegan, Franklin—689, 690
Pegan, Frederick James Frank—263, 297
Pegan, Gail Elizabeth (Marotte Costain)—210, 220
Pegan, Gertrude P. (Russell)—162, 181

Pegan, Grace (Boggs)—65, 92
Pegan, Grace May (Ewing Ewing)—51, 79
Pegan, Granville—246, 248
Pegan, Harlan J. Pulliam—269, 306
PeGan, Harold Leon—458, 482
Pegan, Harold West—272, 307
Pegan, Harrison James I—23, 391
Pegan, Harrison James II—393, 400
Pegan, Harry Clark—43, 73
Pegan, Henrietta G. (Hatch Rockwell)—665, 667
Pegan, Henry J.—250, 265
Pegan, Henry Levy—249, 263
Pegan, Henry—23, 245
Pegan, Hugh Doyle—269, 305
PeGan, Hugh Frederick—427, 459
Pegan, Ina May (Martin)—689, 690
Pegan, Inez Mae (Owens)—38, 67
Pegan, Isaiah Ira—24, 686
Pegan, Jacquelin K. (Risler Bologna)—100, 116
Pegan, James Andrew—72, 96
Pegan, James Eugene—300, 334
Pegan, James Kenneth—100, 116
Pegan, James Meredith—423, 455
Pegan, James Milton—155, 160
Pegan, James R.—348, 353
Pegan, James Robert—29, 38
Pegan, James—604, 610
Pegan, James—9
Pegan, Jane Temple—73, 97
Pegan, Jesse Harrison—405, 421
Pegan, Joan Kathryn (Bakulich)—100, 116
PeGan, John Allen—461, 484
Pegan, John Andrew II—155, 165
Pegan, John Andrew—393, 394
Pegan, John Edward II—94, 113
Pegan, John Edwin—65, 93
PeGan, John Frederick—459, 483
Pegan, John Robert—73, 97
Pegan, John S.—29, 40
Pegan, John, Son of Robert—23, 153
Pegan, Joseph T.—254, 271
Pegan, Joseph—28, 33

Pegan, Josephine (Martin Reed)—34, 51

Pegan, Josephine Margaret (Lane Noble)—604, 605

PeGan, Juanita Mae (Abbott)—430, 462

PeGan, Julia Evelyn (Macke)—300, 333

PeGan, Karl Nelson—430, 462

PeGan, Katherine Jean (Swoveland Sweeney Swanson)—461, 484

PeGan, Kenneth Austin Joseph—427, 459

Pegan, Laura (Daggy Smith)—250, 265

PeGan, Laura A.—404, 414

Pegan, Laura Belle Olive (Oder Walker)—604, 610

Pegan, Laura Louise (Hill)—155, 166

Pegan, Lawrence Joseph—301, 334

PeGan, Leo Everett—427, 456

Pegan, Leonidas Alonzo—28, 30, 394

Pegan, Leonidas Alonzo—34, 47

PeGan, Leonidus Alonzo—405, 428

Pegan, Leonora or Nora Lee (Reneau, Crosson)—34, 53, 59

Pegan, Leslie Meloan—98, 115

Pegan, Lowell R.—306, 337

Pegan, Luther Carlisle—49, 78

Pegan, Mamie Edna—171, 193

Pegan, Margaret (Brunner Miller)—155, 162

Pegan, Margaret Mary (Roush Warren)—393, 399

Pegan, Marietta Marilla (Davis)—665, 669

Pegan, Martha Ann (Strayer)—155, 164

Pegan, Martha Jane (Pegan)—30, 393, 394

Pegan, Mary (VanAusdall)—15

PeGan, Mary Angeline (Welch)—427, 458

Pegan, Mary Ann (Coover Wagoner)—24, 539

Pegan, Mary C. (Kissel)—298, 330

Pegan, Mary Elizabeth (Johnson Boggs)—65, 91

Pegan, Mary Elizabeth (Mason)—155, 157

Pegan, Mary Jane (Kelley)—28, 34

Pegan, Mary Jane—337, 350

Pegan, Mary Louise—274, 309

PeGan, Maryln Ann (Crossen)—457, 482

Pegan, Mattie—250, 267

Pegan, Michael Stroup—246, 253

Pegan, Morrow Walton—42, 72

Pegan, Natoshia Shyann Marie—353, 354

PeGan, Nelson Michael—462, 485

Pegan, Orpha Estella—161, 180

Pegan, Orpha Marie (Andrews Conklin)—665, 666

Pegan, Otho M.—49, 77

Pegan, Paul Harold—427, 457

Pegan, Paul Stroup—274, 308

Pegan, Pauline Meriam (Oswalt)—423, 454

Pegan, Perry—24

PeGan, Philip Garl—405, 428

PeGan, Phillip Elsworth II—429, 460

PeGan, Phoebe Ann (Wolfe)—604, 609

PeGan, Phoebe—405, 427

Pegan, Pleasant—24

Pegan, Pleasant—246, 253

Pegan, Pliny Moses Crume—157, 168

Pegan, Powell—308, 338

PeGan, Raymond Harrison—419, 448

PeGan, Raymond Leon—430, 460

Pegan, Richard Allen—461, 485

PeGan, Richard Schuyler—430, 461

Pegan, Richard Thomas—300, 333

Pegan, Rita Gertrude (Poston)—300, 333

Pegan, Rita Glea—273, 308

Pegan, Robert A.—15, 19

Pegan, Robert Andrew—29, 44

Pegan, Robert Donald—46, 75

Pegan, Robert Edwin—94, 113

Pegan, Robert Harrison—430, 462

Pegan, Robert Henry—298, 330

Pegan, Robert Ivan—300, 332

PeGan, Robert Phillip—460, 483

Pegan, Robert—263. 298

Pegan, Roberta Jean (Murdoch)—210, 220

PeGan, Ronald Gene—484, 496

Pegan, Ruby Patience—171, 194

Pegan, Ruby W. (Anderson Rammel Woodall)—272, 306

Pegan, Ruby Zetta (Paganetti)—40, 69

Pegan, Russell William—300, 332

Pegan, Ruth Marie (Holmes)—273, 308

Pegan, Ruth Mary (Dennig)—298, 330

Pegan, Samuel Alexander—29, 42

PeGan, Sarah Celeste (Pearson Hewitt Horner)—405, 415

Pegan, Sarah Jane (Greenawalt)—604, 607

Pegan, Shirley C. (Boyd)—300, 331

Pegan, Sinclair Edwin—38, 62

Pegan, Son —332, 348

PeGan, Son Two—460, 484

PeGan, Son—459, 483

PeGan, Son—460, 483

PeGan, Son—463, 486

PeGan, Son—484, 496

Pegan, Stella Frances (Gough)—49, 76

PeGan, Stephine Ann—496, 500

PeGan, Steven Karl—462, 485

PeGan, Sue Ann (Masterman McQuaid)—461, 485

PeGan, Thelma (Kelley Smith)—300, 331

Pegan, Thomas Jefferson—246, 249

PeGan, Thomas Joseph—457, 482

PeGan, Vern Leroy—430, 463

Pegan, William Henry—246, 253

Pegan, William Henry—250, 267

Pegan, William Henry—263, 298

Pegan, William Henry—28, 36

Pegan, William Louis or Lewis—24, 662

Pegan, William Louis—393, 398

Pegan, William Otto—254, 273

Pegan, Zoa Faretta (Camp)—40, 70

Pence, Ruth Amelia—567

Pendall, Paulette—339

Penrod, Della Catherine—580
Perry, Jean McLean—221
Pfefferle, Margaret Josephine—460
Philhower, Charles Randolph II—275, 311
Philhower, Charles—275
Philhower, J. Bruce—311, 339
Philhower, Lee Donald—276, 311
Pickerell, Mary Ellen—174
Pickering, Aileen (Frazier)—556, 570
Pickering, Chlor Washington—556
Pinkerton, Ruth Saada—201
Pirnie, Elisabeth (McKay Carroll Gruet)—96, 114
Pirnie, Roderick II—96, 114
Pirnie, Roderick—95
Pitzer, Irma Louise—646
Poe, Bobby Lee—496
Poe, Daughter—496, 500
Poland, Raymond Maxwell—578
Poole, Mary Jane—553
Poston, Debra Sue (Scott Durett)—333, 348
Potts, Carolee Angela—219
Powell, Bessie E.—450
Powell, Velma—307
Prario, Infant Daughter—643, 647
Prario, Robert Staples—644
Pratto, Albert Dominic—118
Pratto, Jeanine Marie—118, 123
Pratto, Patrick Dominic—118, 123
Price, James Harold—342
Prince, Naomi Kay—340
Procise, Mabel Lucy—109
Pulliam, Resa Jane—269
Pulver, Emma C.—566
Puse, Ervin Charles—643
Rainey, Thomas Benjamin—123
Rairdon, Grace Maud—565
Rammel, Harold William—307
Ramsey, Samuel Robert—498
Ramsmeyer, Infant—347, 353
Ramsmeyer, Robert Jean—346
Reagan, Daughter—492, 499
Reagan, Mr.—492
Reagan, Zachary James—500, 502

Reed, Angus Frederick--52
Reed, Brian Lee—461, 484
Reed, Edna Earl—109
Reed, George Richard—461
Reed, Kermit Eugene—644
Reese, Charles Norman—479
Reeves, Nora Jane—270
Reher, Rosena Cecilia (Leake Kondos)—99, 115
Reher, Stephen Albert Paul—98
Reid, Helen Marie—469
Reidinger, Paul C.—336
Reiling, Gustave Adolph—186
Reilly, Mr.—223
Reising, Doris—330
Reneau—Samuel Houston—53
Reneau, Hazel (Brockman)—54, 83
Rhoads, Betty Lee—493
Rhonemus, Anna—322
Richards, Mary Beth—350, 353
Richards, Mr.—350
Ridge, Victor Emmanuel—89
Ridgeway, John Colin—338
Risler, Leonard Robert—116
Roades, Floyd W.—341
Roades, Merle May—291
Robb, Oretta I.—78
Roberts, Ganelle Ruth—305
Roberts, William Kelly—303
Rockwell, Ira Charles—668
Rodriguez, Maria Isabelle Elena—447
Roeder, Grace Ida—330
Rogers, Clifford Leroy—566
Rogers, Don Elwood—567, 578
Rogers, Dorothy Evelyn (Poland)—567, 578
Rogers, Mary Ann—326, 346
Rogers, Nancy—219
Rogers, Russell Howard—326
Rogers, Smith David—567, 578
Roll, Edmund Warren—432, 465
Roll, Leota Fatima (Lydy)—432, 464
Roll, Margaret L. (Unknown Christensen)—464, 487
Roll, Marian Colleen (Bender)—432, 466

Roll, Marion William--431
Roll, Thelma Lynn (Kennedy)—432, 466
Rollert, George E. II—221
Rosencrans, Charles Edgar (Ross Crane)—195
Ross, John Everett—472
Ross, Paul Graham—320
Rossy, Phillip Peter—348
Rostofer, Lylah—563
Rounds, Darwin Dean—635
Roush (White), Margaret (Sorel II)—440, 471
Roush, Albert Leroy—400, 409
Roush, Arlo—409, 436
Roush, Barbara Ann (Hamilton Storer II)—321, 343
Roush, Cecil Cary—412, 442
Roush, Cecil Ira—410, 413
Roush, Clara Belle (Farr Hunter II)—400, 406
Roush, Dale E.—414, 448
Roush, Daughter (Graves Hupp)—321, 344
Roush, Daughter (Shuttleworth)—443, 474
Roush, Daughter One (Reagan)—469, 492
Roush, Daughter Two (Vindiola)—470, 492
Roush, Delbert Leroy—409, 434
Roush, Dorothy H. (Koeb)—438, 470
Roush, Dorothy Opal (Seitz)—413, 445
Roush, Effie Nondis (McCandless)—413, 444
Roush, Eli Kenneth II—413, 446
Roush, Eli Kenneth—400, 410
Roush, Euless Josephine (Walker)—412, 443
Roush, Floyd Richard—413, 446
Roush, Gale E.—414, 447
Roush, Gary Wayne—469, 491
Roush, George Beard II—438, 470
Roush, George Beard—410, 437
Roush, George II—469, 492
Roush, George Lewis—436, 469

Roush, Harley Leroy—436, 469
Roush, Harry Emmett II—439, 471
Roush, Harry Emmett—412, 438
Roush, Jacob E.—340
Roush, James—400, 407
Roush, Jane (Thomas)—435, 468
Roush, John Alven—400, 407
Roush, John Milford—436, 468
Roush, Joseph Lewis—409, 435
Roush, Kenneth Edward H.—312
Roush, Kenneth Edward II—312, 339
Roush, Kenneth W.—442, 474
Roush, Larry Eugene—470, 492
Roush, Lee E. Donald—448, 478
Roush, Leota Beatrice (Davis)—413, 443
Roush, Leroy Kenneth—412, 443
Roush, Lora Belle (Bussey Brust)—412, 440
Roush, Lulu Belle—408, 433
Roush, Marcus—320
Roush, Mary Leatha (Bogan)—413, 445
Roush, Merle Margaret—438, 470
Roush, Michael David—447, 478
Roush, Milford—409, 436
Roush, Nellie Fay (Baker Schoonmaker Thompson)—408, 433
Roush, Philip Stroup II—447, 476
Roush, Philip Stroup—414, 446
Roush, Philip—399
Roush, Randall Cecil—414, 447
Roush, Ray E.—414, 448
Roush, Robert Dean—468, 491
Roush, Samuel Frederick—412, 442
Roush, Theodore—412, 440
Roush, Vicky Lynn (Brown)—469, 492
Roush, William Leroy II—471, 492
Roush, William Leroy—438, 470
Roush, William Randall—447, 478
Rowbottom, Frank Patrick—643
Ruble, Madge—316
Rush, George Farrell—107
Rushia, James Wilbert—574
Rushia, Rickey Lee—574, 581

Russell, Mary Margaret—9
Russell, Otto H.—181
Russell, Pauline Elizabeth (Brown)—182, 206
Russo, Rita Marie—645
Ryan, Loretta Jennette—457
Sallaz, Virginia Katherine—571
Sample, Opal E.—97
Sawyer, Perry Elsworth—187
Schetzszle, Josephine Sophia—424
Schoonmaker, Frank Leslie—434
Schorey, Richard Kay II—489, 499
Schorey, Richard Kay—489
Schrock, David Ervin—638
Schroth, Ms.—491
Schultz, Armintha (Almack)—614, 624
Schultz, Ralph Richard—614, 623
Schwartz, Andrew II—252
Schwartz, Child—252, 271
Schwartz, Cora May—253, 271
Schwartz, Joseph—251
Schwartz, Marcella B.—108
Schwartz, Mary Hattie—252, 270
Schwartz, Walter Charles—252, 270
Schwartz, William H.C.M.—252, 270
Scott, Unknown—348
Sebastian, Ruth Victoria—633
Secrest (Jenich), Wendy Renee—220, 223
Secrest, Wayne D.—208
Secrest, Wayne Donovan II—208, 219
Seed, Walter C.—111
Seitz, Darrel Joe—445, 476
Seitz, Daughter (Kinyoun)—476, 493
Seitz, Emmett Fay—445
Seitz, Emmett II—445, 476
Seitz, Jeffrey—476, 494
Seitz, William Jeffrey II—476, 494
Seitz, William Lee—445, 476
Sentman, Lawrence Shafer—642
Sexsmith, James Raymond—96
Shaffer, Elizabeth Laverne Ellen (Sentman)—630, 641
Shaffer, Welcome Wallace—629
Shambaugh, Margaret R.—568

Shaper, Edward M.—270
Shatto?, Beatrice A.—470
Shaw, Blair—632, 643
Shaw, Carl Luther—632, 643
Shaw, Edith Laura (Snyder)—618, 632
Shaw, Frank Herbert—618, 631
Shaw, George Henry—61
Shaw, Isaiah Luther—617
Shaw, John Crocker—631, 643
Shaw, Nancy June (Felix Rowbottom)—632, 643
Shaw, Odella May—544
Shaw, Robert Leonard—632, 643
Shaw, William Russell II—632, 643
Shaw, William Russell—618, 631
Shaw, Winifred Jane (Puse)—631, 642
Shawver, Betty Lois (Emory)—565, 577
Shawver, Ellando—551
Shawver, Glady Fern (Allinger)—551, 564
Shawver, Jay—551, 565
Shawver, Kenneth Rairdon—565, 578
Shearer, Rebecca—153
Shelburn, Mary Winifred—638
Sheler, Robert Eugene II—338
Sheler, Shaun—338, 350
Shields, William B.—101
Shoemaker, Bessie Mae—453
Shoup, Shelby Jean—469
Shultz, Charles—613
Shumard, Wanda Beatrice—323
Shuttleworth, Matthew Thomas—493, 500
Shuttleworth, Mr.—474
Shuttleworth, Son—474, 493
Sibley, Miss—223
Simms, Bernard E.—325
Slagle, Ruby C.—77
Slonecker, Richard Max—577
Slonecker, Sharon Lee (Bellamy)—577, 583
Slusarz, Walter?—107
Slusser, Anna Louise-178
Smith, A.J.—340
Smith, Alva Jack—637

Smith, Andrew Jackson—542
Smith, Bertha Lucile (Jenkins)—553, 567
Smith, Bill—490
Smith, Child One—543, 554
Smith, Child Two—543, 554
Smith, Christine LaVon (Wilcox)—563, 576
Smith, Douglas Troy—341, 352
Smith, Eliza E.—543, 552
Smith, Elva Alberta (Bayer)—543, 549
Smith, Evelyn Fern (Rogers)—552, 566
Smith, Frederick J.—549, 563
Smith, Harold D.—552, 565
Smith, Henry Sylvester—543, 548
Smith, Hoadley Monroe—543, 553
Smith, John Andrew—543, 551
Smith, Mary Alice (Slonecker)—563, 576
Smith, Mary Elizabeth (Melvin)—543, 548
Smith, Miss—469
Smith, Ora Belle (Shawver)—543, 550
Smith, Patricia Ann—637, 646
Smith, Paul D.—553, 567
Smith, Richard Emerson—563, 576
Smith, Richard K.—490
Smith, Roy Thurman—543, 552
Smith, Shirley Edna—346
Smith, Stanley Andrew—553, 568
Smith, Thurman Herring—554, 568
Smith, William Alpheus—331
Smith, William C.—543, 550
Snead, Eilene—341
Snellstrom, Ethel—79
Snyder, Candace Nan—482
Snyder, Charles Henry—632
Snyder, Juanita C.—121
Snyder, Mabel Fern—322
Snyder, Patricia Ann (Reed)—633, 644
Sorel, Edward A. II—471
Sorel, Nancy A. (Martell)—472, 492
Spilker, Bessie B. (Fox)—259, 290
Spilker, Charlotte Jean (Hern)—291, 325

Spilker, Earl Everett—259, 291
Spilker, Hazel (Cruger)—259, 293
Spilker, Joseph Benjamin—292, 325
Spilker, Joseph Henry—258
Spilker, Joseph Todd—325, 345
Spilker, Ralph Henry—259, 292
Spilker, Shirley Lois Gail (Rogers)—292, 325
Stahler, Tina D.—180
Stanley, Barbara Catherine (Meier)—570, 580
Stanley, Buddy Lynn—463
Stanley, Halsey Marvin—555, 570
Stanley, James Darrell—555, 570
Stanley, Jerry Alan (Rosebrook)—570, 580
Stanley, Walter David—570, 580
Stanley, Walter Warren—555
Stanley, Wendell Wayne—555, 570
Starcher, Mary Edythe—472
Stebbins, Elizabeth Quincy—94
Steinbrenner, Elizabeth Bertha—209
Stephan, Betty Lou—645
Stevenson, Daniel McKenzie—69
Stewart, Glenn Lawrence—647
Stewart, Unknown—352
Stickney, Barbara Ann—109
Stitsinger, Neil E.—336
Storer, William Beam II—343
Storm, Kay Joanne—217
Stoup, Rosella—273
Stout, Angeline—401
Strayer, James Monroe—164
Strep, Richard Edward—112
Stroop, Loretta—337
Stroup, Clarence Harold—261, 294
Stroup, Edgar?—260, 293
Stroup, Electra Gertrude—413
Stroup, Elma Jane (Ballentine)—248, 261
Stroup, Elton?—260, 293
Stroup, Galo S.—301
Stroup, Harriet—245
Stroup, Hattie Ann—247, 256
Stroup, James Pegan—248, 262
Stroup, James Richard—295, 328

Stroup, John Henry—248, 259
Stroup, Josephine (Lemon/s)—247, 255
Stroup, Laura Arabella (Spilker)—248, 258
Stroup, Levi—247
Stroup, Margaret—248, 262
Stroup, Mary E. (Williams)—247, 256
Stroup, Thurl Esto—302, 334
Stroup, Vernice Catherine—260, 293
Strouse, Sarah—156
Stubbs, Harley—301
Stults, Helen Pauline—75
Stutz, Pauline Hermane—673
Surber, Cedric Lewis—305, 337
Surber, Earl Lester—267, 304
Surber, Lawrence W.—267, 304
Surber, Lewis Allen—266
Surber, Mary Sarah—305, 336
Surber, Maynard Raymond—305, 336
Surber, Son One—337, 350
Surber, Son Two—337, 350
Sussman, Kim Loreen—350
Suter, James Jacob—214
Suter, Kathleen Helen—215, 222
Suter, Michael James—215, 222
Swanson, Mr.—485
Swartz, Mr.—493
Sweeney, Mr.—485
Swoveland, Mr.—485
Tanner, Richard F.—340
Tarr, Nancy Elizabeth—214
Tatum, June Loretta—346
Taylor, Mary Jane—174
Teboe, Ethalyn—317
Terrell, Barbara Lee (Oelker)—640, 646
Terrell, Beverly Sue (Marsalis Stewart)—640, 647
Terrell, Damon Eugene—628, 640
Terrell, Daughter (Gunsaulies Murphy)—640, 647
Terrell, Garnet Lucille (Calland)—629, 641
Terrell, Gaylord Philip—629, 641
Terrell, Harley Milton—628

Terrell, Harold Reginold—629, 641
Terrell, Marilyn Kay (Jones Watt)—640, 646
Terrell, Nancy Ann (Trimble)—641, 647
Terrell, Thelma Marie (Mohr)—628, 639
Terrell, Thomas Eugene—641, 647
Terrell, Virgil Milton—628, 639
Thai Woman One—216
Thai Woman Two—216
Theriault, Unknown—111
Thiergartner, Marlene E.—646
Thiry, Mr.—496
Thomas, Kenneth Roy—468
Thomas, Wesley Lydell—580
Thompson, Elbridge--434
Thompson, Mabel Letha (Stroup)—265, 301
Thompson, Mrs. Unknown—340
Thompson, Ruth Frances—265, 302
Thompson, William Robert—264
Thornton, Helen Kathryn—99
Thorpe, Daisy Loretta—281
Thrush, Ms.—581
Tipton, Jennie Almeda—687
Tolle, Anna Mary—288
Tomko, Mr.—581
Tomlinson, Claude Lee—110
Tomlinson, Robert Victor—110, 122
Towne, Miss—491
Tracy, Beulah Mae—643
Trimble, Robert Wayne—647
Tripplett, Cora A.—90
Troutwine, Elma Duvall—263
Tsaloff, Daniel—347
Turenne, Elodie Lucy—462
Turner, Herbert M.—319
Turner, Roger H.—345
Udy, Ruth—217
Uhls, Etta L.—467
Unknown, Alice—78
Unknown, Ann?—5
Unknown, Barbara—348
Unknown, Barbara—488
Unknown, Catherine Adeline—191

Unknown, Catherine—39
Unknown, Cheryl L.—123
Unknown, Destiny—495, 500
Unknown, Dorothy Inez—94
Unknown, Evelyn—78
Unknown, Jessie (Taylor)—43
Unknown, Jo Ann—475
Unknown, Judith Kay—339
Unknown, Karen J.—122
Unknown, Laura—48
Unknown, Linda—343
Unknown, Lois M.—219
Unknown, Lucille—321
Unknown, Lynnda M.—221
Unknown, Margaret—283
Unknown, Martha—350
Unknown, Mary Helen—316
Unknown, Mary—334
Unknown, Mary—9, 11
Unknown, Shirley—221
Unknown, Unknown—113
Unknown, Unknown—323
Unknown, Unknown—338
Unknown, Unknown—340
Unknown, Unknown—464
Unknown, Unknown—472
Unknown, Unknown—487
Unknown, Unknown—493
Unknown, Unknown—495
Unknown, Unknown—500
Unknown, Unknown—500
Unknown, Unknown—575
Unknown, Unknown—59
Unknown, Virginia Marie—113
Uno, Jean—578
Ursell, William Harlan II—352
VanAusdall, John—15
VanBlarcum, Augustus Saxton—68
Vance, Inez (Bowman)—296, 328
Vance, Robert N.—296, 329
Vance, Silas Laymon—295
Vance, Thelma Lavonne (Fudge)—296, 328
Vanica, Nancy Catherine—214
Vankirk, Rebecca Jane—605
Vasbinder, Robert Matthew—626

Vermilyer or Fry, Dorothy Margaret—428
Via, Frances—110
Vindiola, Joseph—492
Vongundy, Joe L.—218
Vongundy, Mark Lane—218, 223
Voorhees, Elsworth Charles—200
Wade. Mr.—222
Wagoner, John—539
Wagonfield, Hudson H.—303
Waits, Bert Kerr—582
Walborn, Wilma O.—630
Walker, Charles Robert—443, 474
Walker, Child—611, 622
Walker, John S.—610
Walker, Ralph Doyle—342
Walker, Shirley J. (Johnson Brammer)—443, 474
Walker, Thomas William II—443, 474
Walker, Thomas William—443
Wallace, Harold. L.—473
Wallace, Michael Ray—473, 493
Walsh, Grace Catherine—300
Ward, Katharyn Ann—562
Warnick, Louise—308
Warren, George—399
Wasson (Klahn), Janice Orilla—112
Watkins, Elizabeth—541
Watt, John R.—646
Weaver, Gerald Ray—490
Webber, Miss—483
Welch, Ted Deroy—458
Weller, Thomas David—475
Welsh, Mr.—498
Welsh, Robert John—499, 502
West, Daughter (Greene)—309, 338
West, Nelle Irene—272
West. George Elton—309
Westaway, Alta Grace—105
Westman, Frederick Penn II—644
Whitaker, Bentlee Andrew Poe—500, 502
Whitaker, Mr.—500
White, Rose Etta—578
Whiting, Lucille Mildred—467
Whitney, Jeanette Rose—686

Widlund, Fred Allen—217
Wilbur, Thomas Richard—480
Wilcox, Daughter (Cox)—576, 583
Wilcox, Isaac II—576
Wilder, Etta L.—618
Wilder?, Donna—572
Wildoner, Edythe G.—420
Wilkin, Charles Edgar—317, 341
Wilkin, Daughter (Stewart Ursell II)—341, 352
Wilkin, Deloris (Roades)—317, 341
Wilkin, Edgar Franklin—286, 317
Wilkin, Evelyn Lorie (Campbell Fissel Turner)—286, 319
Wilkin, Everett Robert—286, 317
Wilkin, George Robert—286
Wilkin, Georgeanna (Roush Ross Holderby)—287, 320
Wilkin, Infant Daughter—321, 344
Wilkin, Joan (Manis)—317, 341
Wilkin, Kevin Michael—341, 352
Wilkin, Lenora (Barker)—287, 320
Wilkin, Leroy Thomas—287, 321
Wilkin, Marianna (Smith Lesko)—317, 340
Wilkin, Marjorie Marie (Hawk)—286, 318
Wilkin, Mr.—222
Wilkin, Rosa Mae—432
Wilkin, Samuel—287, 321
Wilkin, Son—321, 344
Wilkin, Son—341, 352
Williams, Candus Gay (Nash)—324, 345
Williams, Carl Delbert—285, 316
Williams, Carol Jean (Griffith Woodmansee)—322, 344
Williams, Carolyn (Tanner)—317, 340
Williams, Cary—258, 289
Williams, Clarence E.—290, 323
Williams, Cora May (Carroll)—257, 284
Williams, Dale Mathew—290, 324
Williams, Dolores M. (Erickson)—105, 120
Williams, Dwan Ruble—317, 340
Williams, Eugene—288, 321
Williams, Glen Louis—290, 324
Williams, Harley N.—258, 289
Williams, Hattie Ellen (Wilkin)—258, 285
Williams, Hazel Imogene (Davidson)—289, 323
Williams, Infant Son—258, 290
Williams, James Douglas—322, 345
Williams, James Richard—290, 325
Williams, Janet E. (Winkle)—322, 345
Williams, Josephus Everett—258, 288
Williams, Judith Mae (Turner)—322, 345
Williams, Levi—258, 285
Williams, Mary Elizabeth (Kelley)—290, 323
Williams, Mr.—495
Williams, Ona S.—50
Williams, Paul T.—289, 323
Williams, Richard Emil—105, 120
Williams, Robert Karl—104, 120
Williams, Roy Emil—104
Williams, Samuel—256
Williams, Stanley Mitchell II—288, 322
Williams, Stanley—258, 287
Williams, Stephen Thomas—290, 324
Williams, Unknown—638
Williams, Vincent B.—324, 345
Williams, Virgil—288, 321
Williams, Woodrow Wilson—288, 322
Williamson, Marianna—323
Willman, David Michael—352, 354
Willman, Douglas Dean—352
Windle, Martha Magdalene—572
Winkle, Charles II—345
Winter, Mr.—495
Wirick, Miss—485
Wolfe (Booze), Kenneth Vernon—621, 633
Wolfe, Bertha (Loffer)—609, 615
Wolfe, Diana R. (Westman)—633, 644
Wolfe, Effie Belle (Shaw)—609, 617
Wolfe, Frank L.—610, 618
Wolfe, Guy Ernest—610, 620
Wolfe, Hubert Wilder—619, 633
Wolfe, Kenneth William—621, 635
Wolfe, Margaret Carolyn (Rounds)—621, 635
Wolfe, Robert Roe—635, 645
Wolfe, Sharon Kay (Ondich)—635, 645
Wolfe, Warren Charles—621, 635
Wolfe, William Parsons—609
Wolfe, William Roe—610, 619
Woodall, Arthur Edward—307
Woodmansee, Alfred Milton III—344
Woods, Ms.—647
Wright, Grace L.—566
Wyrick, Myrell Franklin—574
Wyrick, Ronald Franklin—574, 581
Yarger, Clarence Christopher—473
Yates, Pearl—488
Young, Daughter (Howell)—214, 222
Young, Daughter (Widlund)—204, 217
Young, Daughter—216, 222
Young, Dorothy Arilla—461
Young, Effa May—620
Young, Ella M.—71
Young, Harold Mason—177, 201
Young, Helen Elizabeth (Suter)—203, 214
Young, Kathleen Mary—122
Young, Lael Marcus—204, 216
Young, Oliver Gordon—203, 214
Young, Philip Gibbs—204, 216
Young, William Marcus II—203, 215
Young, William Marcus—176
Yung, Sang Soon—112
Zeller, Erma Lou—446
Ziglar?, Lila Jean—219
Zimpleman, Vilas Hugo—456

Graphics Sources

Page

701 *Lancaster County., Pennsylvania, Quarter Sessions Abstracts (1729-1742), Book 1*, ed. by Gary T. Hawbaker. Hershey, Pennsylvania: Gary T Hawbaker; 1986, pg. 104. Originals at the Lancaster County, Pennsylvania Archives, 230 North President Avenue, Lancaster, PA. Greene County Room, Greene County Public Library-Xenia

Pagan/Pegan entries, Lancaster County, Pennsylvania Tax Lists, 1751-1800, Microfilm, Roll #23, Genealogy Center, Allen County Public Library, Fort Wayne, IN.

702-3 "Memorials Against Calling a Convention, 1779", *Pennsylvania Archive Series: Series 2, Vol. III*; ed. by Samuel Hazard, et. al. Harrisburg, Pennsylvania: C.M. Busch; 1875, pg. 359. Family History Library, 35 North West Temple, Salt Lake City, UT.

703 Article from a Philadelphia, Pennsylvania newspaper (the *Pennsylvania Gazette*?) in late June or early July 1776. Given to the author, Ann Miller Carr, by Vikki Sorel, Ankenny, IA, 04 Apr 2019.

704 Andrew Pegan will (1787), Lancaster County, Pennsylvania Will Book F: Vol. 1: 84-86. Lancaster County, Pennsylvania Archives, 150 North Queen Street, Lancaster, PA.

705 Andrew Pegan, Revolutionary War Pension Application, National Archives, Virginia, Series M805, Roll 642, Image 432, Penn. Sea Service S40249. National Archives, Washington, DC.

Letter, along with warrant survey documents and maps, from Aaron McWilliams, research historian at the Pennsylvania State Archives, Harrisburg, Pennsylvania, to author Ann Miller Carr on July 24, 2015.

Bridgens, H.F., Bridgen's Atlas of Lancaster County, Pennsylvania From actual surveys by H.F. Bridgens. Martic Township map. Lancaster, Penn, D.F. Bare, 1864, pg. 43.

707 Map of Pennsylvania highlighting Lancaster County.svg Wikipedia.org from Wikimedia Commons.org. David Benbennick, Feb. 2006. The maps use data from http://www.nationalatlas.gov/", specifically http://edcftp.cr.usgs.gov/pub/data/nationalatlas/countyp020.tar.gz The maps also use state outline data from http://edcftp.cr.usgs.gov/pub/data/nationalatlas/statesp020.tar.gz

Highlighted Lancaster County Map of Martic Township.png Wikipedia.org from Wikimedia Commons.org. Created by Derek Ramsey, 23:38 5 Oct 2006, from U.S. Census Bureau maps from U.S. Census Bureau website http://www2.census.gov

Permission is granted to copy, distribute and/or modify this document under the terms of the Creative Commons CCO license

Map of Pennsylvania highlighting Washington County.svg. Wikipedia.org from Wikimedia Commons.org. Created by David Benbennick, 12 Feb. 2006. The maps use data from http://www.nationalatlas.gov/", specifically http://edcftp.cr.usgs.gov/pub/data/nationalatlas/countyp020.tar.gz The maps also use state outline data from http://edcftp.cr.usgs.gov/pub/data/nationalatlas/statesp020.tar.gz

Permission is granted to copy, distribute and/or modify this document under the terms of the Creative Commons CCO license

Map of Washington County.png Wikipedia.org from Wikimedia Commons.org Created by Derek Ramsey, 00:55 11 Oct 2006, from Source: U.S. Census Bureau maps from U.S. Census Bureau website http://www2.census.gov/geo/maps/general_ref/cousub_outline/cen2k_pgsz/pa_cosub.pdf pa

Permission is granted to copy, distribute and/or modify this document under the terms of the Creative Commons CCO license

708 Map of West Virginia highlighting Brooke County.svg. Wikipedia.org from Wikimedia Commons.org. Created by David Benbennick, 16:23 12 Feb. 2006. The maps use data from http://www.nationalatlas.gov/", specifically http://edcftp.cr.usgs.gov/pub/data/nationalatlas/countyp020.tar.gz The maps also use state outline data from http://edcftp.cr.usgs.gov/pub/data/nationalatlas/statesp020.tar.gz Permission is granted to copy, distribute and/or modify this document under the terms of the Creative Commons CCO license

Map of Brooke County, West Virginia and Washington County, Pennsylvania. Traced from a larger and more detailed map of counties, the API Programs Map of the Rand Corporation, by Ann Miller Carr on 10 Apr 2020. (https://www.rand.org/pubs/tools/TL254/reach-of-api-programs.html)

709 Map of Ohio highlighting Highland County.png Wikipedia.org from Wikimedia Commons.org. Created by David Benbennick, 16:08 12 Feb. 2006. The maps use data from http://www.nationalatlas.gov/", specifically http://edcftp.cr.usgs.gov/pub/data/nationalatlas/countyp020.tar.gz The maps also use state outline data from http://edcftp.cr.usgs.gov/pub/data/nationalatlas/statesp020.tar.gz

Permission is granted to copy, distribute and/or modify this document under the terms of the Creative Commons CCO license

Map of Highland County, Ohio, United States with township and municipal boundaries.png. Wikipedia.org from Wikimedia Commons.org. Created by Paul E. Giroux, Jul 2006 from Source: U.S. Census Bureau maps from U.S. Census Bureau website, http://www2.census.gov/geo/maps/general_ref/cousub_outline/cen2k_pgsz/oh_cosub.pdf

Permission is granted to copy, distribute and/or modify this document under the terms of the Creative Commons CCO license

Lake, D.J., C.E., *Atlas of Highland County, Ohio,* Dodson Township. Philadelphia: C.O. Titus, 1871, pg. 13.

710-13   Robert and Christina "Engle" Pegan family bible, family pages, American Bible Society, Brattleboro(ugh), Vermont: Holbrook & Fessenden, 1828. In possession of the author, Ann Miller Carr.

714   Lake, D.J., C.E., *Atlas of Highland County, Ohio,* Union Township. Philadelphia: C.O. Titus, 1871, pg. 15.

Map of Clinton CountyOhio With Municipal and Township Labels.png. Wikipedia.org from Wikimedia Commons.org. Created by Paul E. Giroux, Jul 2006 from Source: U.S. Census Bureau maps from U.S. Census Bureau website, http://www2.census.gov/geo/maps/general_ref/cousub_outline/cen2k_pgsz/oh_cosub.pdf

Permission is granted to copy, distribute and/or modify this document under the terms of the Creative Commons CCO license

Map of Ohio highlighting Clinton County.png Wikipedia.org from Wikimedia Commons.org. Created by David Benbennick, 16:07 12 Feb. 2006. The maps use data from http://www.nationalatlas.gov/", specifically http://edcftp.cr.usgs.gov/pub/data/nationalatlas/countyp020.tar.gz The maps also use state outline data from http://edcftp.cr.usgs.gov/pub/data/nationalatlas/statesp020.tar.gz Permission is granted to copy, distribute and/or modify this document under the terms of the Creative Commons CCO license

Everts, L.H., New Historical Atlas of Montgomery County, Ohio, Illustrated. Philadelphia: Hunter Press, 1875, pg. 16.

Map of Ohio highlighting Montgomery County.png Wikipedia.org from Wikimedia Commons.org. Created by David Benbennick, 16:10 12 Feb. 2006. The maps use data from http://www.nationalatlas.gov/", specifically http://edcftp.cr.usgs.gov/pub/data/nationalatlas/countyp020.tar.gz The maps also use state outline data from http://edcftp.cr.usgs.gov/pub/data/nationalatlas/statesp020.tar.gz

Permission is granted to copy, distribute and/or modify this document under the terms of the Creative Commons CCO license

715   Robert "Pagan" entry, 1810-11, Washington County, Pennsylvania. Tax Records. Somerset Township through 1821; Strabane Township through 1811. Washington County, roll #29. Genealogy Center, Allen County Public Library, 900 Library Plaza, Fort Wayne, IN.

Ohio, Tax Records, 1800-1850, FamilySearch.com, Robert Pagan, Wayne Twp., Montgomery Co., Ohio, 1830-1833; City of Dayton, Montgomery Co. Ohio in 1834 (Andrew"Pagun").

716   Map of Ohio highlighting Montgomery County.png Wikipedia.org from Wikimedia Commons.org. Created by David Benbennick, 16:09 12 Feb. 2006. The maps use data from http://www.nationalatlas.gov/", specifically http://edcftp.cr.usgs.gov/pub/data/nationalatlas/countyp020.tar.gz The maps also use state outline data from http://edcftp.cr.usgs.gov/pub/data/nationalatlas/statesp020.tar.gz

Permission is granted to copy, distribute and/or modify this document under the terms of the Creative Commons CCO license

Map of Logan County, Ohio, United States with township and municipal boundaries.png. Wikipedia.org from Wikimedia Commons.org. Created by Paul E. Giroux, 28:38 26 Jun 2006 from Source: U.S. Census Bureau maps from U.S. Census Bureau website, http://www2.census.gov/geo/maps/general_ref/cousub_outline/cen2k_pgsz/oh_cosub.pdf

Permission is granted to copy, distribute and/or modify this document under the terms of the Creative Commons CCO license

Ohio, Tax Records, 1800-1850, FamilySearch.com, "Christina Pagan", Logansville, Pleasant Township, Logan County, Ohio, 1838.

www.ingramcontent.com/pod-product-compliance
Lightning Source LLC
LaVergne TN
LVHW082010090526
838202LV00006B/275